BEST BOOKS FOR PUBLIC LIBRARIES

BEST BOOKS FOR PUBLIC LIBRARIES™

THE 10,000 TOP FICTION AND NONFICTION TITLES

STEVEN AROZENA

EDITOR

R. R. BOWKER®

A Reed Reference Publishing Company
New Providence, New Jersey

Published by R. R. Bowker,
A Reed Reference Publishing Company
Copyright © 1992 by Reed Publishing (USA) Inc.
All rights reserved
Printed and bound in the United States of America

Library of Congress Cataloging-in-Publication Data

Arozena, Steven.
Best books for public libraries : the 10,000 top fiction &
nonfiction titles / Steven Arozena.
p. cm.
Includes bibliographical references and index.
ISBN 0-8352-3073-2
1. Public libraries—United States—Book lists. 2. Bibliography—
Best books—English imprints. I. Title.
Z1035.A72 1992
025.2′1874—dc20   92-18410
                                                          CIP

ISBN 0 - 8352 - 3073 - 2

9 780835 230735

CONTENTS

PREFACE

This first edition of *Best Books for Public Libraries* is designed to give librarians a current, single-volume guide to the top critically acclaimed books suitable for general readers (patrons who possess a layperson's knowledge of a wide variety of subjects). Providing one comprehensive but concise source of some of the best titles available, *Best Books for Public Libraries* will eliminate time-consuming research through vast numbers of book review indexes and book review journals. Librarians who want to expand their collections in particular subject areas will find the latest titles as well as classics from the recent past. In addition, librarians faced with budget concerns can tell at a glance which are the best titles in a certain subject area and how much they will cost.

Arrangement and Title Selection

This volume contains entries for over 6,000 nonfiction titles and over 4,000 fiction works published from 1965 through early 1992. Nonfiction titles in Part 1 are arranged alphabetically by author within the Dewey Decimal Classification system. Fiction titles in Part 2 are arranged alphabetically by author within 15 broad genres. All titles included received positive book reviews from two or three of the 15 commonly consulted book review sources (see "Book Review Sources," below). Titles that received starred ("books of particular merit") reviews from *Booklist* dating from 1980, *Library Journal* starred reviews ("books of outstanding quality, significance or popular appeal") dating to their inception in 1983, and titles from the *New York Times Book Review*'s annual "Notable Books of the Year" list beginning in 1965 are all found here. In addition, titles that received major awards (see "Awards" list, below) or appeared on the year-end "best" lists of *Library Journal, Booklist, Publishers Weekly, Time*, or the *New York Times Book Review* are included, and this is noted within each entry.

Not surprisingly, the largest nonfiction categories are the 300s (Social Sciences), the 700s (The Arts), and the 900s (Geography and History), this emphasis reflecting the holdings and demands of most public libraries.

Works of a scholarly nature, reference titles, and children's books have been excluded from this volume. Those seeking titles to enlarge their reference collections are encouraged to consult *General Reference Books for Adults* (Marion Sader, ed., R. R. Bowker, 1988), *Topical Reference Books* (Marion Sader, ed., R. R. Bowker, 1991), or *Guide to Reference*

Books (Eugene P. Sheehy, ed., American Library Association, 10th edition, 1986).

Fiction titles have been divided into 15 genres roughly based on the 1990 American Library Association publication "Guidelines on Subject Access to Individual Works of Fiction, Drama, Etc.," produced by a subcommittee of the Cataloging and Classification Section. Definitions of these genres follow.

Following the main body of text are three indexes. The Author Index cites authors, titles, and entry numbers (joint authors are listed separately). The Title Index gives the text's entry number. Finally, the extensive Subject Index offers easy access by topic to the more than 10,000 entries.

Fiction Genres

BIOGRAPHICAL FICTION denotes fictional accounts of real lives, and includes autobiographical works. A representative title is *Confessions of Nat Turner* by William Styron, a fictional account of the life of a leader of the slave revolution during the 1830s.

DETECTIVE AND MYSTERY FICTION also includes crime fiction. Representative authors in this genre include Robert Barnard, Sue Grafton, Tony Hillerman, Ed McBain, and Ruth Rendell.

FABLES includes works of fiction designed as allegorical tales. Representative titles include Sean O'Faolain's *And Again?* and Nancy Willard's *Things Invisible to See.*

FANTASTIC FICTION includes fantasies, apocalyptic tales, alternative histories, and time travel. Representative authors include R. A. MacAvoy, Anne McCaffrey, and Kim Stanley Robinson.

GENERAL FICTION includes all works of fiction that do not clearly fit into one of the other 14 categories. Larry McMurtry's *Texasville,* Sue Miller's *Family Pictures,* and Margaret Atwood's *Life Before Man* are representative titles of this category.

HISTORICAL FICTION includes novels set prior to the outbreak of the Second World War. Representative titles include Jean Auel's *Clan of the Cave Bear* (set during prehistoric times) and Gabriel Garcia Marquez's *The General in His Labyrinth* (a fictionalized account of the life of the South American liberator Simon Bolivar).

HUMOROUS FICTION includes works of fiction whose primary motive is satire or humor. Representative titles include Thomas Berger's *Who Is Teddy Villanova?* (a spoof of detective stories) and Roy Blount, Jr.'s *First Hubby.*

LOVE STORIES includes romance and gothic novels. Representative titles include John Nichols's *Sterile Cuckoo* and Gabriel Garcia Marquez's *Love in the Time of Cholera.*

OCCULT FICTION includes works concerning the supernatural, ghosts, and horror tales. Authors representative of this genre are Clive Barker and Stephen King. Anne Rice's Chronicles of the Vampires series falls into this category.

SCIENCE FICTION includes works based on imagined developments in science and technology. Representative authors include Isaac Asimov, William Gibson, and Frank Herbert.

SHORT STORIES includes collections of short stories or collections in which the predominant form is the short story. These can be by one or several authors.

SPORTS STORIES includes works whose primary focus is on athletic events and competitions. Representative titles include Frederick Exley's *A Fan's Notes* and Robert Coover's *Universal Baseball Association Inc., J. Henry Waugh, Prop.*

SPY STORIES includes works regarding spies or acts of espionage. Representative writers of this genre include Len Deighton and John Le Carre. William F. Buckley Jr.'s Blackford Oakes series can be found in this category.

WAR STORIES includes works set during—or with primary emphasis on— a war or events surrounding wartime. This genre also includes works of fiction dealing with the Holocaust. Titles representative of this genre include Elie Wiesel's *Gates of the Forest* and William Wharton's *Birdy*.

WESTERN STORIES includes novels set during the nineteenth-century American West. Titles representative of this genre include *Deadwood* by Pete Dexter and *Mamaw* by Susan M. Dodd.

Entry Format

Each numbered entry may contain some or all of the following information:

(1) Author or editor; (2) Title: subtitle; (3) Publisher; (4) Date of publication; (5) Price; (6) ISBN; (7) Publisher of paper edition (if there is no publisher listed, it is the same as the hardbound edition); (8) Price of paper edition; (9) ISBN of paper edition; (10) Review citations (at least two, and whenever possible, three); (11) List of awards received (or inclusion on "best books" lists); (12) Annotation (contains a brief description of the work. Some entries are supplemented with direct quotations from cited reviews); (13) Dewey Decimal number (for nonfiction).

Dewey Decimal numbers and subject headings used throughout this book are based on *Dewey Decimal Classification*, twentieth edition, and were derived from CIP sources, OCLC cataloging, or book review media (generally *Booklist*). Biographical works may be found under disciplines of the subject, as is current practice in the Dewey system. (Readers will find the Subject Index helpful in accessing these entries.) A wide range of variance in Dewey numbers is possible among individual libraries, but OCLC has been used whenever possible to obtain the most universal classification.

Publishing information and prices have been verified using *Books in Print* 1990–1991 edition, and whenever possible 1991–1992, *Forthcoming Books*, or, for the most recent titles, book review media.

Research Sources

The collections of the following Arizona public libraries were consulted during the course of this book: Sedona Public Library (29,000 volumes); Flagstaff Public Library (160,000 volumes); Scottsdale Public Library (360,000 volumes); and Phoenix Library (nearly 2 million volumes). The author also drew heavily on his personal experiences working at the public libraries of Carpinteria, Goleta, Santa Barbara, and Pasadena (all located in Southern California). Much of the actual research for this volume was conducted at the Cline Library of Northern Arizona University in Flagstaff.

Book Review Sources

The review citations listed in the entries will give librarians sources for more detailed information about each of the books listed. The sources and their abbreviations are:

Atl	*Atlantic*
BL	*Booklist*
Choice	*Choice*
CSM	*Christian Science Monitor*
LJ	*Library Journal*
Natl Rev	*National Review*
New Rep	*New Republic*
NYRB	*New York Review of Books*
NYTBR	*New York Times Book Review*
New Yorker	*New Yorker*
Newsweek	*Newsweek*
PW	*Publishers Weekly*
Sat Rev	*Saturday Review*
Time	*Time*
TLS	*Times Literary Supplement*

Awards

Award-winning titles are indicated in the entries by the following abbreviations:

ALA	American Library Association annual notable books list
Edgar	Mystery Writers of America Edgar Allen Poe Award for best mystery novel
Hugo	World Science Fiction Society's Science Fiction Achievement Award for best science fiction novel
NBA	National Book Award
Nebula	Science Fiction Writers of America's Award for best science fiction novel
PP:field	Pulitzer Prize: Autobiography/Biography; Drama; Fiction; General nonfiction; History; Poetry

Acknowledgments

I would like to extend special thanks to Marion Sader, Group Publisher, R. R. Bowker, who helped to define the concept of this book; Laura Mosberg Cohen, Production Editor, whose painstaking care and infinite patience have resulted in the fine editorial work on these pages, and the rest of the R. R. Bowker staff for their assistance and hard work on this project. I would also like to thank Jean Collins, Brian Forney, and Tom Carpenter of the Cline Library at Northern Arizona University for their generous help on this book, and, most of all my wife, Mary Schimmoller, for her love, support, and understanding.

PART ONE

NONFICTION

000   GENERALITIES

001   Knowledge

Scholarship and learning

1 Adler, Mortimer J. *Guidebook to Learning: For the Lifelong Pursuit of Wisdom.* 1986, Macmillan $13.95 (0-02-500340-2). A guide to self-teaching and learning by the author of *How to Read a Book.* (Rev: BL 3/1/86; LJ 3/1/86; PW 1/17/86)   **[001.2]**

Research

2 Regis, Edward. *Who Got Einstein's Office? Eccentricity and Genius at the Institute for Advanced Study.* 1987, Addison Wesley $17.95 (0-201-12065-8). A study of the history and personalities of the Institute for Advanced Study; an organization devoted to theoretical science and located in Princeton, New Jersey. (Rev: Choice 1/88; LJ 9/15/87; NYTBR 9/27/87)   **[001.4]**

Controversial knowledge

3 Bauer, Henry H. *Enigma of Loch Ness: Making Sense of a Mystery.* 1986, Univ. of Illinois Pr. $22.95 (0-252-01284-4); paper $9.95 (0-252-06031-8). An account of the sightings of the legendary Loch Ness monster and one of the efforts made to determine its existence. (Rev: Atl 2/87; BL 10/1/86)   **[001.9]**

4 Blum, Howard. *Out There: The Government's Secret Quest for Extraterrestrials.* 1990, Simon & Schuster $19.95 (0-671-66260-0); Pocket paper $5.99 (0-671-66261-9). A history of the United States government's secret investigations of UFOs from World War II to the 1980s. (Rev: NYTBR 9/9/90; PW 7/13/90)   **[001.9]**

5 Vallee, Jacques. *Confrontations: A Scientist's Search for Alien Contact.* 1990, Ballantine $19.95 (0-345-36453-8); paper $4.95 (0-345-36501-1). An analysis of the author's interviews with over 100 persons who claim they have seen or contacted UFOs or their inhabitants. (Rev: BL 4/15/90; LJ 3/1/90)   **[001.9]**

6 Walters, Ed, and Frances Walters. *UFO-Proof Positive: The Gulf Breeze Sightings.* 1989, Morrow $19.95 (0-688-09087-7); Avon paper $5.95 (0-380-70870-1). An account of the authors' Florida UFO sightings illustrated with color photographs they took of the objects. (Rev: BL 1/1/90; LJ 3/1/90)   **[001.9]**

003   Systems

7 Gleick, James. *Chaos: Making a New Science.* 1988, Penguin paper $11.95 (0-14-009250-1). A presentation of the science of chaos which attempts to explain unpredictable natural behaviors and properties. "Gleick makes the challenging accessible, and makes it exciting, too."—LJ (Rev: BL 10/1/87; LJ 8/87; NYTBR 10/25/87. Awards: LJ, 1987; NYTBR, 1987)   **[003]**

8 Hofstadter, Douglas R. *Metamagical Themas: Questing for the Essence of Mind and Pattern.* 1986, Bantam paper $14.95 (0-553-34279-7). Essays examining aspects of the workings of the human brain by the author of *Godel, Escher, Bach: An Eternal Golden Braid.* (Rev: BL 6/1/85; LJ 5/15/85; PW 3/29/85)   **[003]**

Theory of communication and control

9 Campbell, Jeremy. *Grammatical Man: Information, Entropy, Language and Life.* 1983, Simon & Schuster paper $10.95 (0-671-44062-4). How the scientific fields of linguistics, thermodynamics, and biology can be linked together through the new field of study named information theory. "There is an excitement in this book that is almost touchable."—BL (Rev: BL 9/1/82; Choice 12/82; LJ 8/82. Awards: ALA, 1982)   **[003.5]**

10 Johnson, George. *Machinery of the Mind: Inside the New Science of Artificial Intelligence.* 1986, Random $19.95 (0-8129-1229-2); Microsoft paper $9.95 (1-55615-010-5). An investigation into science's attempts to create a thinking machine. (Rev: Choice 3/87; LJ 10/1/86; NYTBR 10/5/86. Awards: LJ, 1986)   **[003.5]**

11 Waldrop, M. Mitchell. *Man-Made Minds: The Promise of Artificial Intelligence.* 1987, Walker $22.95 (0-8027-0899-4); paper $14.95 (0-8027-7297-8). A study of the history and future of man's attempts to create artificial intelligence. (Rev: BL 2/15/87; LJ 3/15/87; NYTBR 10/4/87)   **[003.5]**

004 Data processing; Computer science

12 Bove, Tony, and Cheryl Rhodes. *Well-Connected Macintosh: An Overview of Desktop Communications.* 1987, Harcourt $19.95 (0-15-195610-3); paper $11.95 (0-15-695666-7). An introduction to inter-terminal communications and resource sharing through the Macintosh computer. (Rev: BL 3/1/88; LJ 3/15/88)   **[004]**

13 McCorduck, Pamela. *Universal Machine: Confessions of a Technological Optimist.* 1985, McGraw-Hill $16.95 (0-07-044882-5). A study of long-range effects the computer will have upon American society, culture, and work. (Rev: Choice 2/86; LJ 10/15/85; PW 8/16/85)   **[004]**

14 Pagnoni, Mario. *Computers and Small Fries.* 1987, Avery paper $7.95 (0-89529-350-1). An introduction to computer applications and software programs for two- to seven-year-olds. (Rev: BL 3/1/87; LJ 5/15/87)   **[004]**

15 Shurkin, Joel N. *Engines of the Mind: A History of the Computer.* 1985, Pocket paper $4.95 (0-671-60036-2). A popular history of the computer and computing machines from the Neolithic Age to the twentieth century. (Rev: BL 2/15/84; Choice 7–8/84; LJ 2/1/84)   **[004]**

16 Turkle, Sherry. *Second Self: Computers and the Human Spirit.* 1985, Simon & Schuster paper $10.95 (0-671-60602-6). An examination of the socio-logical and psychological impact of computers and their technology upon society. "An invaluable addition to the computer-science collection."—BL (Rev: BL 4/15/84; CSM 10/1/84; LJ 6/15/84) **[004]**

General works on specific types of computers

17 Karin, Sidney, and Norris P. Smith. *Supercomputer Era.* 1987, Harcourt $19.95 (0-15-186787-9). A study of the development of supercomputers and their applications. (Rev: BL 9/1/87; LJ 7/87)   **[004.1]**

Digital microcomputers

18 Rothman, David H. *Complete Laptop Computer Guide: How to Choose and Get the Most Out of Your Portable PC or MAC.* 1990, St. Martin's paper $14.95 (0-312-05062-3). A guide to the selection and purchase of the best laptop computer to fill your personal needs. "An absolute necessity for anyone who is even remotely considering buying a laptop."—BL (Rev: BL 11/1/90; LJ 11/15/90)   **[004.16]**

005 Computer programming, programs, data

Data security

19 Fites, Philip, Peter Johnston, and Martin Kratz. *Computer Virus Crisis.* 1988, Van Nostrand Reinhold paper $24.95 (0-442-28532-9). An examination of the problem of computer viruses primarily concerned with their effects upon microcomputers. (Rev: Choice 7–8/89; LJ 3/1/89)   **[005.8]**

006 Special computer methods

Artificial intelligence

20 Moravec, Hans. *Mind Children: The Future of Robot and Human Intelligence.* 1988, Harvard Univ. Pr. $18.95 (0-674-57616-0); paper $8.95 (0-674-57618-7). A study of the future of robotics and artificial intelligence and its impact upon human society and culture. (Rev: NYRB 2/1/90; NYTBR 1/1/89; New Yorker 1/9/89)   **[006.3]**

21 Penrose, Roger. *Emperor's New Mind: Concerning Computers, Minds and the Laws of Physics.* 1989, Oxford Univ. Pr. $24.95 (0-19-851973-7); Viking paper $12.95 (0-14-104534-6). A study of modern physics, artificial intelligence, and current theories regarding the essence of thought and consciousness. (Rev: LJ 3/1/90; NYTBR 11/19/89; TLS 9/29/89)   **[006.3]**

020 LIBRARY AND INFORMATION SCIENCE

028 Reading, use of other information media

22 Kaestle, Carl F. *Literacy in the United States: Readers and Reading Since 1880.* 1991, Yale Univ. Pr. $35.00 (0-300-02249-3). A historical overview and analysis of literacy and reading in the United States from the late nineteenth century to the present. (Rev: Choice 12/91; LJ 5/1/91)   **[028]**

Reviews

23 Henderson, Bill, ed. *Rotten Reviews: A Literary Companion.* 1986, Pushcart Pr. $12.50 (0-916366-40-5); Penguin paper $4.95 (0-14-010195-0). Excerpts from 175 reviews critical of notable writers or their works. (Rev: BL 12/1/86; CSM 12/5/86; PW 10/31/86)   **[028.1]**

24 Updike, John. *Hugging the Shore: Essays and Criticism.* 1983, Knopf $19.95 (0-394-53179-5); Random paper $14.95 (0-394-72497-6). A collection of a decade of Updike's essays and criticisms. "Updike at his best."—Choice (Rev: BL 9/1/83; Choice 2/84; LJ 9/15/83. Awards: ALA, 1983; NYTBR, 1983) **[028.1]**

Reading and use of other information by children and young adults

25 Copperman, Paul. *Taking Books to Heart: How to Develop a Love of Reading in Your Child—For Parents of Children 2 to 9.* 1986, Addison Wesley paper $9.95 (0-201-05717-4). A guide for parents on ways to promote reading and reading enjoyment for their young children. (Rev: BL 10/1/86; CSM 11/7/86; LJ 10/1/86)   **[028.5]**

26 Sendak, Maurice. *Caldecott & Co: Notes on Books and Pictures.* 1988, Farrar $18.95 (0-374-22598-2); paper $8.95 (0-374-52218-9). Commentaries on children's literature by the noted writer and illustrator. (Rev: LJ 12/88; NYTBR 1/29/89; TLS 4/7/89)   **[028.5]**

27   Van Doren, Charles. *Joys of Reading: 210 Favorite Books, Plays, Poems, Essays, Etc.; What's in Them, Why Read Them.* 1985, Crown $19.95 (0-517-55580-8). A guide to the reading of classic literature with essays regarding the significance of works selected, biographical profiles of their authors, and background on the thought and social climate of the era in which they were written. (Rev: CSM 7/18/86; LJ 11/15/85)   **[028.5]**

030   GENERAL ENCYCLOPEDIC WORKS

031   American

Books of miscellaneous facts

28   Feldman, David. *Imponderables: The Solution to the Mysteries of Everyday Life.* 1986, Morrow $15.75 (0-688-05913-9). Solutions to common puzzlements encountered in daily living. (Rev: NYTBR 9/6/87; PW 2/28/87)   **[031.02]**

050   GENERAL SERIALS AND THEIR INDEXES

051   American

29   Draper, Robert. *Rolling Stone Magazine: The Uncensored History.* 1990, Doubleday $19.95 (0-385-26060-1). A history of the development of *Rolling Stone* magazine from its beginnings as an alternative rock music journal to its current mainstream popularity. "A significant sociocultural document."—BL (Rev: BL 5/1/90; LJ 4/1/90; NYTBR 6/17/90)   **[051]**

30   Tebbel, John, and Mary Ellen Waller-Zuckerman. *Magazine in America, 1740–1990.* 1991, Oxford Univ. Pr. $35.00 (0-19-505127-0). An illustrated history of the development of the American magazine over its first 250 years. (Rev: BL 6/15/91; LJ 6/15/91; PW 4/26/91)   **[051]**

060   GENERAL ORGANIZATIONS AND MUSEOLOGY

069   Museology (Museum science)

31   Park, Edwards. *Treasures of the Smithsonian.* 1983, Smithsonian Inst. $60.00 (0-89599-012-1). An illustrated survey of the holdings of the Smithsonian Institution with over 400 color plates. "An absolutely wonderful book . . . a treasure."—BL (Rev: BL 3/15/84; Choice 6/84; NYTBR 12/4/83)   **[069]**

32   Preston, Douglas J. *Dinosaurs in the Attic: The Behind-the-Scenes Story of the American Museum of Natural History.* 1986, St. Martin's $18.95 (0-312-21098-1); Ballantine paper $4.50 (0-345-34732-3). An account of the history and operations of New York's American Museum of Natural History. (Rev: LJ 10/15/86; PW 10/17/86)   **[069]**

070   NEWS MEDIA, JOURNALISM, PUBLISHING

33   Edwards, Julia. *Women of the World: The Great Foreign Correspondents.* 1988, Houghton $17.95 (0-395-44486-1); Ivy Books paper $3.95 (0-8041-0491-3). Stories of female foreign correspondents from 1846 to the present including Margaret Bourke-White, Marguerite Higgins, and Martha Gellhorn. (Rev: LJ 8/88; NYTBR 8/7/88; PW 5/20/88)   **[070]**

34   Stephens, Mitchell. *A History of News: From Oral Culture to the Information Age.* 1988, Viking $24.95 (0-670-81378-8); Penguin paper $9.95 (0-14-009490-3). The history of the gathering and dissemination of news from 3000 B.C. to the present. (Rev: Choice 4/89; LJ 10/15/88; PW 7/8/88)   **[070]**

Documentary media, news media

35   Halberstam, David. *Powers That Be.* 1986, Dell paper $6.95 (0-440-36997-5). A study of the American media and its impact on U.S. politics and culture as seen through the histories of CBS, *Time*, the *Los Angeles Times*, the *New York Times*, and the *Washington Post*. (Rev: LJ 4/15/79; NYTBR 4/22/79; Newsweek 4/30/79)   **[070.1]**

36   Joyce, Edward M. *Prime Times, Bad Times: A Personal Drama of Network TV.* 1988, Doubleday $19.95 (0-385-23923-8); paper $9.95 (0-385-26102-0). Memoirs of the former president of "CBS News" regarding his 30 years with the network. (Rev: Atl 5/88; LJ 7/88; PW 4/15/88)   **[070.1]**

37   MacNeil, Robert. *Wordstruck: A Memoir.* 1989, Viking $18.95 (0-670-81871-2); Penguin paper $8.95 (0-14-010401-1). Memoirs of the writer and newscaster regarding his lifelong love of the English language. (Rev: LJ 3/15/89; NYTBR 3/26/89; PW 1/6/89)   **[070.1]**

38   Parenti, Michael J. *Inventing Reality: Politics and the Mass Media.* 1985, St. Martin's $16.95 (0-312-43473-1). An analysis of the media and how its selective coverage of world political events distorts American perceptions. (Rev: Choice 4/86; LJ 1/86; PW 12/13/85)   **[070.1]**

Television

39   Trotta, Liz. *Fighting for Air: In the Trenches with Television.* 1991, Simon & Schuster $19.95 (0-671-67529-X). Memoirs of a female news correspondent who reported for NBC-TV and CBS-TV from Vietnam, Iran, Israel, and Northern Ireland. "A deft writer who pulls no punches."—CSM (Rev: BL 4/15/91; CSM 6/13/91; PW 4/26/91)   **[070.195]**

Journalism

40   Bassow, William. *Moscow Correspondents: John Reed to Nicholas Daniloff.* 1988, Morrow $18.95 (0-688-04392-5); Paragon House paper $12.95 (1-55778-227-X). Profiles of notable American journalists who have reported from the Soviet Union since the Russian Revolution. (Rev: BL 1/15/88; LJ 2/1/88; NYTBR 3/27/88)   **[070.4]**

41   Berkow, Ira. *Red: A Biography of Red Smith.*
**1986, Random $17.95 (0-8129-1203-9); McGraw-Hill
paper $4.95 (0-07-004852-5).** A portrait of the Pulit-
zer Prize-winning American sports columnist who
wrote for the *New York Herald Tribune* and later for
the *New York Times*. (Rev: BL 6/1/86; CSM 7/16/86; LJ 6/
15/86)   **[070.4]**

42   Caputo, Philip. *Means of Escape.* **1991, Har-
perCollins $25.00 (0-06-018312-8).** Memoirs of the
Pulitzer Prize-winning journalist and author of *A
Rumor of War*. (Rev: BL 9/1/91; LJ 10/1/91)   **[070.4]**

43   Cowley, Malcolm. *Dream of the Golden Mountains: Remembering the 1930s.* **1981, Penguin
paper $8.95 (0-14-005919-9).** Memoirs of the literary
world of the 1930s by the American critic and
former editor for the *New Republic*. (Rev: LJ 3/1/80;
New Rep 3/15/80; Sat Rev 3/1/80)   **[070.4]**

44   Davis, Linda H. *Onward and Upward: A Biography of Katherine S. White.* **1989, Fromm International paper $11.95 (0-88064-109-6).** A biography of
the former *New Yorker* editor, writer, and wife of
E. B. White. (Rev: CSM 7/1/87; LJ 7/87; New Yorker 8/10/
87)   **[070.4]**

45   Goulden, Joseph C. *Fit to Print: A. M. Rosenthal
and His Times.* **1988, Carol Publg. Group $21.95 (0-
8184-0474-4).** A biography of the former executive
editor of the *New York Times* based on 300 interviews with current and former employees of the
newspaper. (Rev: BL 11/1/88; LJ 10/15/88; PW 8/19/88)
                                                                                   [070.4]

46   Knightley, Phillip. *The First Casualty: From the
Crimea to Vietnam; the War Correspondent as
Hero, Propagandist, and Myth Maker.* **1976, Harcourt paper $16.95 (0-15-631130-5).** A critical look at
U.S. and British war reporting in the nineteenth
and twentieth centuries. "Exciting reading . . .
engrossing."—LJ (Rev: BL 11/15/75; Choice 2/76; LJ 10/
15/75. Awards: ALA, 1975)   **[070.4]**

47   McFadden, Cyra. *Rain or Shine: A Family
Memoir.* **1986, Knopf $16.95 (0-394-51937-X); Ran-
dom paper $4.95 (0-394-74879-4).** Memoirs of the
author's relationship with her father, a touring
rodeo announcer, and her mother, a trick rider.
"The considerable power of this book and of these
lives are burned permanently into the reader's
memory."—Thomas McGuane, NYTBR (Rev: LJ 4/1/
86; NYTBR 4/13/86; Time 3/24/86. Awards: ALA, 1986)
                                                                                   [070.4]

48   Matthews, T. S. *Jacks or Better.* **1986, Macmillan paper $8.95 (0-689-70705-3).** Memoirs of the
author's experiences and friendships among a
group during the 1920s that included Robert
Graves and Laura Riding. (Rev: LJ 10/1/77; NYTBR
10/23/77; PW 8/29/77)   **[070.4]**

49   Pfaff, Daniel W. *Joseph Pulitzer II and the Post-
Dispatch: A Newspaperman's Life.* **1991, Penn
State Univ. Pr. $29.95 (0-271-00748-6).** A biography
of the son of newspaper magnate Joseph Pulitzer
analyzes his years as head of the *St. Louis Post-
Dispatch*. "An outstanding biography."—PW (Rev:
BL 9/15/91; PW 8/2/91)   **[070.4]**

50   Pope, Edwin. *Edwin Pope Collection.* **1988,
Taylor $14.95 (0-87833-609-5).** Twenty years of sports
reporting collected from the Florida-based writer's
columns. (Rev: BL 5/1/88; LJ 6/1/88; PW 4/8/88)   **[070.4]**

51   Rollyson, Carl. *Nothing Ever Happens to the
Brave: The Story of Martha Gellhorn.* **1990, St.
Martin's $24.95 (0-312-05125-5).** A biography of the
American journalist, writer, and third wife of
Ernest Hemingway. (Rev: BL 12/1/90; PW 10/26/90)
                                                                                   [070.4]

52   Taylor, S. J. *Stalin's Apologist: Walter Duranty.*
1990, Oxford Univ. Pr. $24.95 (0-19-505700-7). An
account of the reporting of the *New York Times*
journalist who served as Moscow correspondent
for 20 years during the reign of Stalin. (Rev: Natl
Rev 3/19/90; NYTBR 6/24/90)   **[070.4]**

53   Whittemore, Hank. *CNN: The Inside Story.*
1990, Little, Brown $19.95 (0-316-93761-4). A history
of the founding and evolution of the 24-hour Cable
News Network. "Crucial reading for students of
media history."—PW (Rev: LJ 5/15/90; PW 4/27/90)
                                                                                   [070.4]

Editing

54   Stegner, Wallace. *Uneasy Chair: A Biography of
Bernard De Voto.* **1989, Gibbs Smith paper $12.95
(0-87905-299-6).** A biography of the American historian, editor, conservationist, and spokesman for
social reform. "An exceptional personal and intellectual biography."—BL (Rev: BL 5/1/74; Choice 9/74;
Time 2/11/74)   **[070.41]**

Features and special topics

55   Malcolm, Janet. *Journalist and the Murderer.*
**1990, Knopf $18.95 (0-394-58312-4); Random paper
$10.95 (0-679-73183-0).** A study of the libel case that
arose from journalist Joe McGinniss's depiction of
Jeffrey MacDonald in the book *Fatal Vision*. (Rev:
BL 2/1/90; LJ 2/15/90. Awards: BL, 1990)   **[070.44]**

Pictorial journalism

56   Nachtwey, James. *Deeds of War: Photographs
1981 to 1988.* **1989, Thames & Hudson $35.00 (0-
500-54152-3).** A collection of the author's photographs documenting the wars of the 1980s with an
introduction by Robert Stone. (Rev: BL 11/1/89; LJ
12/89; NYTBR 11/5/89)   **[070.49]**

Publishing

57   Byron, Christopher. *Fanciest Dive: What Happened When the Giant Media Empire of Time-Life
Leapt Without Looking into the Age of High-Tech.*
1986, Norton $16.95 (0-393-02661-7). An account of
the financial failure of Time-Life's magazine *TV-
Cable Week* as told by a former editor. "A thoroughly enjoyable and salient addition to the
literature of business."—BL (Rev: BL 2/15/86; LJ 2/15/
86; PW 1/10/86)   **[070.5]**

58   Cerf, Bennett. *At Random: The Reminiscences
of Bennett Cerf.* **1977, Random $16.95 (0-394-47877-
0).** Memoirs of the founder of Random House

culled from recordings of him from the Columbia Oral History program. (Rev: BL 6/15/77; LJ 7/77; New Rep 9/10/77)   **[070.5]**

59 Coser, Lewis A. *Books: The Culture and Commerce of Publishing.* **1985, Univ. of Chicago Pr. paper $16.95 (0-226-11593-3).** An inside look at the world of publishing and the major publishing houses. (Rev: CSM 2/12/82; LJ 1/1/82; Sat Rev 1/82)   **[070.5]**

60 Fitch, Noel Riley. *Sylvia Beach and the Lost Generation: A History of Literary Paris in the 20's and 30's.* **1983, Norton $25.00 (0-393-01713-3).** A biography of the woman who owned and operated the Paris bookshop Shakespeare & Company, a noted literary hangout between the wars. "A rich, delightful, compulsively readable book."—PW (Rev: BL 6/15/83; LJ 8/83; PW 4/22/83)   **[070.5]**

61 Hearst, William Randolph, and Jack Casserly. *The Hearsts: Father and Son.* **1991, Roberts Rinehart $29.95 (1-879373-04-1).** Memoirs of the American newspaper heir's career and his relationship with his father. (Rev: BL 9/1/91; PW 6/28/91)   **[070.5]**

62 Martin, Ralph G. *Henry and Clare: An Intimate Portrait of the Luces.* **1991, Putnam $24.95 (0-399-13652-5).** Biography of the Time, Inc., founder Henry Luce and his politician/diplomat wife Clare Boothe Luce. (Rev: BL 9/15/91; LJ 9/15/91; PW 6/21/91)   **[070.5]**

63 Robinson, Judith. *The Hearsts: An American Dynasty.* **1991, Univ. of Delaware Pr. $49.50 (0-87413-383-1).** A collective biography of the American publishing family. (Rev: BL 9/1/91; Choice 12/91; NYTBR 9/22/91)   **[070.5]**

Journalism and publishing—Persons

64 Baker, Russell. *Good Times.* **1989, Morrow $19.95 (0-688-06170-2).** The sequel to Baker's award-winning *Growing Up*, these memoirs deal with his career in journalism from the 1930s to the late 1960s. (Rev: BL 4/15/89; LJ 5/1/89; NYTBR 5/28/89)   **[070.92]**

65 Barnes, Kathleen. *Trial by Fire: A Woman Correspondent's Journey to the Frontline.* **1990, Thunder's Mouth $19.95 (1-56025-004-6).** Memoirs of the author's experiences as an ABC news correspondent in the Philippines during the latter half of the 1980s. (Rev: BL 10/15/90; LJ 11/1/90; PW 9/28/90)   **[070.92]**

66 Binyan, Liu. *Higher Kind of Loyalty: A Memoir by China's Foremost Journalist.* **1990, Pantheon $22.95 (0-394-57471-0).** An autobiography of a Chinese journalist who was forced into exile for his criticism of official government policies. (Rev: CSM 6/14/90; LJ 6/1/90; NYTBR 5/27/90)   **[070.92]**

67 Chace, James. *What We Had: A Memoir.* **1990, Simon & Schuster $17.95 (0-671-69478-2).** Memoirs of the journalist's childhood in Fall River, Massachusetts, during the depression and years of World

War II. (Rev: NYTBR 6/17/90; PW 4/13/90; TLS 12/28/90)   **[070.92]**

68 Davis, Paxton. *Being a Boy.* **1988, Blair $16.95 (0-89587-065-7).** Memoirs of growing up during the Great Depression in Winston-Salem, North Carolina. (Rev: LJ 8/88; PW 6/24/88)   **[070.92]**

69 Donaldson, Sam. *Hold On, Mr. President!* **1987, Random $17.95 (0-394-55393-4); Fawcett paper $4.95 (0-449-21520-2).** Memoirs of the ABC news journalist known for his coverage of the White House. (Rev: LJ 3/1/87; New Rep 4/13/87; Time 3/16/87)   **[070.92]**

70 Ellerbee, Linda. *And So It Goes: Adventures in Television.* **1986, Putnam $18.95 (0-399-13047-0); Berkley paper $4.50 (0-425-10237-8).** Memoirs of the journalist's career in television broadcasting with reflections on being a woman in the business. (Rev: BL 3/15/86; LJ 5/1/86; Time 7/7/86)   **[070.92]**

71 Ellerbee, Linda. *Move On: Adventures in the Real World.* **1991, Putnam $21.95 (0-399-13623-1).** The second volume of memoirs by the broadcast journalist recalling her recent career and personal life. (Rev: BL 3/1/91; LJ 4/1/91; PW 3/22/91)   **[070.92]**

72 Judis, John B. *William F. Buckley, Jr.: Patron Saint of the Conservatives.* **1988, Simon & Schuster $22.95 (0-671-45494-3); paper $10.95 (0-671-69593-2).** A biography of the writer, political commentator, and founder-editor of the *New Republic*. "Impeccable . . . a book everyone interested in Buckley will find both useful and compelling."—BL (Rev: BL 5/1/88; LJ 6/1/88; New Rep 5/30/88) **[070.92]**

73 Kahn, E. J., Jr. *About the New Yorker and Me: A Sentimental Journey.* **1988, Penguin paper $9.95 (0-14-011428-9).** Reflections on the writer's 40-year career at *The New Yorker*. (Rev: Atl 5/79; BL 5/15/79; PW 2/5/79)   **[070.92]**

74 Kurth, Peter. *American Cassandra: The Life of Dorothy Thompson.* **1990, Little, Brown $24.95 (0-316-50723-7).** A biography of the American journalist and wife of writer Sinclair Lewis. (Rev: LJ 4/15/90; NYTBR 7/29/90; New Yorker 9/17/90)   **[070.92]**

75 Muggeridge, Malcolm. *Chronicles of Wasted Time: The Infernal Grove.* **1989, Regnery paper $12.95 (0-89526-762-4).** This second volume of the English editor and journalist's autobiography covers the 1930s and his experiences as an espionage agent during World War II. (Rev: BL 9/1/74; Time 8/5/74; TLS 9/28/73)   **[070.92]**

76 Parker, Peter. *Ackerley: The Life of J. R. Ackerley.* **1989, Farrar $25.00 (0-374-10050-0).** A biography of the English journalist and writer. (Rev: BL 9/1/89; New Rep 12/18/89; NYRB 1/1/90. Awards: BL, 1989)   **[070.92]**

77 Patner, Andrew. *I. F. Stone: A Portrait.* **1988, Pantheon $15.95 (0-394-55808-1); Doubleday paper $9.95 (0-385-41382-3).** A profile of the life and opinions of the American journalist. "A short book as rich as shelves of American history tomes . . . enough to renew your faith in democracy, in humanity."—BL (Rev: BL 2/15/88; LJ 3/1/88; PW 12/18/87)   **[070.92]**

78 Peters, Charles. *Tilting at Windmills.* **1988, Addison Wesley $18.95 (0-201-05657-7); paper $12.95 (0-201-52415-5).** An autobiography of the writer and editor of the *Washington Monthly.* "A compelling account of a quietly inspiring life."—LJ (Rev: CSM 9/1/88; LJ 7/88; NYTBR 7/3/88)   **[070.92]**

79 Reston, James. *Deadline.* **1991, Random $25.00 (0-394-58558-5).** Memoirs of the American journalist and syndicated columnist. (Rev: BL 8/91; NYTBR 10/22/91)   **[070.92]**

80 Root, Waverley Lewis. *Paris Edition: The Autobiography of Waverley Root, 1927–1934.* **Ed. by Samuel Abt. 1987, North Point $16.95 (0-86547-276-9); paper $9.95 (0-86547-388-9).** Memoirs of the American journalist's years in Paris as a correspondent for the *Chicago Tribune.* (Rev: LJ 6/15/87; Natl Rev 12/4/87; New Rep 9/28/87)   **[070.92]**

81 Rosenstone, Robert A. *Romantic Revolutionary: A Biography of John Reed.* **1990, Harvard Univ. Pr. paper $12.95 (0-674-77938-X).** A biography of the journalist and author of *Ten Days That Shook the World* and *Insurgent Mexico,* from his youth in Portland, Oregon, to his death in Moscow in 1920. (Rev: LJ 9/15/75; Natl Rev 12/19/75; New Rep 9/20/75)   **[070.92]**

82 Rowan, Carl. *Breaking Barriers: A Memoir.* **1991, Little, Brown $22.95 (0-316-73977-3).** Memoirs of the American journalist and diplomat under the Kennedy and Johnson administrations. (Rev: LJ 11/1/90; NYTBR 1/20/91; PW 11/9/90)   **[070.92]**

83 Salisbury, Harrison E. *A Journey for Our Times.* **1984, Carroll & Graf paper $10.95 (0-88184-037-8).** The first volume of the reporter's memoirs regarding his beginnings in journalism, his experiences covering World War II, and his years living and working in the Soviet Union. (Rev: CSM 5/11/83; LJ 5/1/83; NYTBR 5/15/83)   **[070.92]**

84 Salisbury, Harrison E. *A Time of Change: A Reporter's Tale of Our Time.* **1988, Harper & Row $19.95 (0-06-039083-2); paper $10.95 (0-06-091568-4).** Second volume of the author's autobiography covering his years at the *New York Times* from 1954 to 1988 and his experiences reporting on the civil rights movement, the Vietnam War, and in China. (Rev: BL 1/1/88; LJ 3/1/88; NYTBR 3/20/88)   **[070.92]**

85 Sanders, Marlene, and Marcia Rock. *Waiting for Prime Time: The Women of Television News.* **1988, Univ. of Illinois Pr. $19.95 (0-252-01435-9); Harper & Row paper $8.95 (0-06-097294-7).** Memoirs of a female news broadcaster presenting her personal experiences in the business along with a history of women in television journalism. (Rev: BL 9/15/88; NYTBR 1/22/89)   **[070.92]**

86 Shirer, William L. *The Nightmare Years, 1930–1940: Twentieth Century Journey—A Memoir of a Life and the Times, Volume 2.* **1984, Little, Brown $24.95 (0-316-78703-5); Bantam paper $14.95 (0-553-34179-0).** Second volume of Shirer's memoirs as a

journalist in Asia and Nazi Germany. "A combination of history and adventure story . . . more history than readers of his other books really need . . . enough adventure . . . to make it well worth reading."—John Chancellor, NYTBR (Rev: LJ 5/1/84; NYTBR 5/27/84; New Yorker 7/2/84. Awards: ALA, 1984)   **[070.92]**

87 Shirer, William L. *20th Century Journey: A Memoir of a Life and the Times—The Start, 1904–1930.* **1990, Little, Brown $24.95 (0-316-78713-2); Bantam paper $12.95 (0-553-34204-5).** The first volume of Shirer's memoirs covers his life from birth to his appointment as *Chicago Tribune* bureau chief in Vienna. (Rev: LJ 8/76; NYTBR 10/10/76; Sat Rev 8/21/76)   **[070.92]**

88 Sokolov, Raymond. *Wayward Reporter: The Life of A. J. Liebling.* **1984, Creative Arts paper $10.95 (0-916870-63-4).** A biography of the American journalist and sportswriter. (Rev: BL 10/15/80; LJ 10/15/80; PW 9/5/80)   **[070.92]**

89 Sperber, Ann M. *Murrow: His Life and Times.* **1986, Freundlich $25.00 (0-88191-008-2); Bantam paper $12.95 (0-553-34384-X).** The life of the CBS broadcast journalist Edward R. Murrow. "An absorbing, exhaustively researched, and powerful biography."—LJ (Rev: CSM 6/5/86; LJ 7/86; NYTBR 7/6/86. Awards: ALA, 1986; PW, 1986)   **[070.92]**

90 Steel, Ronald. *Walter Lippmann and the American Century.* **1981, Random paper $15.95 (0-394-74731-3).** A biography of the great journalist and political columnist. (Rev: CSM 9/8/80; LJ 9/1/80; NYTBR 10/9/80. Awards: ALA, 1980; NBA, 1982; Time, 1980; Time, the 1980s)   **[070.92]**

91 Wallace, Mike, and Gary P. Gates. *Close Encounters: Mike Wallace's Own Story.* **1985, Berkley paper $4.95 (0-425-08269-5).** An autobiography of the television journalist known for his investigative reporting for CBS's "60 Minutes." (Rev: BL 8/84; LJ 9/1/84; NYTBR 9/30/84)   **[070.92]**

92 White, Theodore H. *In Search of History: A Personal Adventure.* **1986, Warner paper $7.95 (0-446-37559-4).** Autobiography of the journalist and historian best known for his accounts of pre- and post-revolutionary China, and for his coverage of American political campaigns. "The reporter's analysis of his life reads as astutely and eloquently as his noted political writings."—BL (Rev: BL 9/1/78; NYTBR 8/6/78; Sat Rev 9/2/78. Awards: ALA, 1978; Time, 1978)   **[070.92]**

93 Woods, Donald. *Asking for Trouble.* **1988, Peter Smith $18.00 (0-8446-6324-7).** A white South African newspaper editor's story of his anti-apartheid stand, his harassment by the government, and his eventual flight from the country with his family. (Rev: BL 6/15/81; Newsweek 8/31/81; PW 7/3/81. Awards: ALA, 1981)   **[070.92]**

071 Journalism in North America

94 Broder, David. *Behind the Front Page: A Candid Look at How the News Is Made.* **1987, Simon & Schuster $18.95 (0-671-44943-5); paper $9.95 (0-671-**

65721-6). The *Washington Post* journalist examines the methodology and influence of modern political reporting. "As an exploration of political journalism, this book is nearly perfect."—BL (REV: BL 4/15/87; CSM 6/9/87; PW 3/6/87)   **[071]**

95   Cose, Ellis. *Press: Inside America's Great Newspaper Empires.* **1989, Morrow $22.95 (0-688-07403-3).** An examination of the United States' most powerful newspapers including the *New York Times, Washington Post, Los Angeles Times,* and the Gannett and Knight-Ridder chains. (REV: BL 3/15/89; LJ 6/1/89; NYTBR 4/9/89)   **[071]**

96   Isaacs, Norman E. *Untended Gate: The Mismanaged Press.* **1986, Columbia Univ. Pr. $22.50 (0-231-05876-4); paper $25.00 (0-231-05877-2).** Essays concerning questionably ethical reporting by the press during the 1980s. "An astute volume that is bound to be highly regarded by anyone interested in the performance of the press."—BL (REV: BL 3/15/86; CSM 2/6/86; LJ 2/1/86)   **[071]**

97   Kluger, Richard. *The Paper: The Life and Death of the New York Herald Tribune.* **1989, Random paper $16.95 (0-394-75565-0).** An exhaustive history of New York's "other paper," the *Herald Tribune,* from its inception in 1835 to its demise in 1966, by one of its former editors. (REV: Choice 4/87; PW 9/5/87; Time 10/27/86. AWARDS: Time, 1986)   **[071]**

98   Scharff, Edward E. *Worldly Power: The Making of the Wall Street Journal.* **1985, Beaufort Books $18.95 (0-8253-0359-1); paper $9.95 (0-317-56711-X).** A history of the financial daily newspaper from its founding in 1882 to the present. (REV: BL 5/1/86; CSM 7/24/86; LJ 4/15/86)   **[071]**

99   Talese, Gay. *The Kingdom and the Power.* **1986, Dell paper $6.95 (0-440-34525-1).** An inside look at the history, personalities, and influence of the *New York Times.* "Seldom has anyone been so successful in making a newspaper come alive as a human institution."—NYTBR (REV: CSM 7/3/69; NYTBR 6/8/69; Sat Rev 6/14/69. AWARDS: ALA, 1969)   **[071]**

080   GENERAL COLLECTIONS

100   Naipaul, V. S. *Return of Eva Peron with the Killings in Trinidad.* **1981, Random paper $5.95 (0-394-74675-9).** A collection of four essays by the Trinidad-born author regarding his native country, Argentinian politics, his travels in Zaire, and the writings of Joseph Conrad. (REV: CSM 3/10/80; LJ 3/1/80; New Rep 4/12/80)   **[080]**

081   American

101   Ascher, Barbara Lazear. *Playing after Dark.* **1987, Harper & Row paper $6.95 (0-06-09112-6).** A collection of personal and literary essays that formerly appeared in the *New York Times* and various magazines. (REV: BL 7/86; CSM 8/20/86; LJ 8/86)   **[081]**

102   Epstein, Joseph. *A Line Out for a Walk: Familiar Essays.* **1991, Norton $21.95 (0-393-02955-7).** The editor of *The American Scholar* presents his third collection of familiar essays. (REV: BL 2/15/91; NYTBR 3/31/91; PW 2/15/91)   **[081]**

103   Epstein, Joseph. *Partial Payments: Essays Arising from the Pleasures of Reading.* **1989, Norton $18.95 (0-393-02631-0); paper $12.95 (0-393-30716-6).** Literary essays regarding the works of writers from Barbara Pym to V. S. Naipaul by the editor of *American Scholar* magazine. (REV: LJ 12/88; Natl Rev 4/21/89; TLS 10/13/89)   **[081]**

104   Fussell, Paul. *Boy Scout Handbook and Other Observations.* **1982, Oxford Univ. Pr. $22.95 (0-19-503102-4); paper $8.95 (0-19-503579-8).** A collection of essays by the author of *Wartime* and *The Great War and Modern Memory.* (REV: CSM 9/10/82; LJ 8/82; NYTBR 8/29/82)   **[081]**

105   Fussell, Paul. *Thank God for the Atom Bomb: And Other Essays.* **1990, Ballantine paper $4.95 (0-345-36135-0).** A collection of 14 essays on various subjects by the author of *Class* and *Wartime.* (REV: LJ 6/15/88; Natl Rev 9/2/88; Time 6/27/88)   **[081]**

106   Hart, Jeffrey. *Acts of Recovery: Essays on Culture and Politics.* **1989, Univ. Pr. of New England $19.95 (0-87451-504-1).** Collected essays on topics of culture, politics, literature, and religion by a Dartmouth English professor. "A stimulating and refreshingly affirmative intellectual tour-de-force."—BL (REV: BL 11/15/89; LJ 11/15/89; Natl Rev 2/5/90. AWARDS: BL, 1989)   **[081]**

107   Kelly, Mary Olsen, ed. *Fireside Treasury of Light.* **1990, Simon & Schuster paper $10.95 (0-671-68505-8).** Selected writings on aspects of the New Age movement and its philosophies including selections by Baba Ram Dass, Robert Pirsig, and M. Scott Peck. (REV: BL 11/1/90; LJ 10/1/90)   **[081]**

108   Kenner, Hugh. *Mazes: Sixty-Four Essays.* **1989, North Point $22.95 (0-86547-341-2).** A collection of essays by the literary critic covering topics from writing to mathematics. (REV: LJ 6/1/89; Natl Rev 9/29/89; NYTBR 7/9/89)   **[081]**

109   Kimber, Robert. *Upcountry.* **1991, Lyons & Burford $18.95 (1-55821-121-7).** A collection of essays portraying life on the author's Maine farm. (REV: BL 10/15/91; PW 8/2/91)   **[081]**

110   McPhee, John. *Giving Good Weight.* **1979, Farrar $9.95 (0-374-16306-5); paper $8.95 (0-374-51600-6).** Five pieces from the author of *Basin and Range* on subjects ranging from canoeing to pinball. (REV: BL 1/1/80; LJ 12/1/79; NYTBR 11/18/79) **[081]**

111   Thomas, Lewis. *Late Night Thoughts on Listening to Mahler's Ninth.* **1983, Viking $12.95 (0-670-703990-7); Bantam paper $8.95 (0-553-34533-8).** A collection of essays regarding the relationship of modern science to modern society by the author of *The Youngest Science.* (REV: Choice 3/84; LJ 10/15/83; Time 10/24/83)   **[081]**

082   In English

112   Enright, D. J., ed. *Oxford Book of Death.* **1987, Oxford Univ. Pr. paper $8.95 (0-19-282013-3).** An anthology of prose and poetry writings about death and its meaning. (Rev: LJ 6/1/83; NYTBR 6/19/83; TLS 5/6/83)   **[082]**

113   **Munro, Eleanor, ed.** *Wedding Readings: Centuries of Writing and Rituals on Love and Marriage.* **1989, Viking $17.95 (0-670-81088-6).** Collected wedding readings from many cultures and religions compiled by the noted author and art critic. (Rev: BL 5/1/89; LJ 5/15/89)   **[082]**

085   In Italian, Romanian, Rhaeto-Romanic

In Italian

114   **Eco, Umberto.** *Travels in Hyperreality: Essays.* **1986, Harcourt $15.95 (0-15-191079-0).** Collected essays by the Italian author of *The Name of the Rose* and *Foucault's Pendulum.* (Rev: Atl 6/86; NYTBR 7/27/87; New Yorker 8/18/86)   **[085.1]**

115   **Ginzburg, Natalia.** *Little Virtues.* **1986, Seaver Books $13.95 (0-8050-0077-1); Arcade paper $7.95 (1-55970-028-9).** A collection of autobiographical and philosophical essays by the Italian writer. (Rev: LJ 9/15/85; NYRB 11/7/85; NYTBR 10/13/85)   **[085.1]**

PHILOSOPHY AND PSYCHOLOGY

100 PHILOSOPHY AND PSYCHOLOGY

116 **Danto, Arthur C.** *Connections to the World: The Basic Concepts of Philosophy.* 1989, Harper & Row **$22.95 (0-06-015960-X)**; paper **$8.95 (0-06-091641-9)**. A survey of the central ideas and problems of contemporary philosophy. "An excellent introduction to philosophy for the general reader."—LJ (Rev: LJ 3/15/89; NYTBR 5/14/89; PW 1/13/89) **[100]**

110 METAPHYSICS

111 Ontology

117 **Nozick, Robert.** *Examined Life: Philosophical Meditations.* 1989, Simon & Schuster **$21.95 (0-671-47218-6)**; paper **$10.95 (0-671-72501-7)**. Philosophical discussions of current topics and concerns by the author of *Anarchy, State and Utopia.* "This strikingly original book will arouse much discussion."—LJ (Rev: LJ 12/89; NYTBR 10/29/89; PW 10/13/89) **[111]**

118 **O'Flaherty, Wendy Doniger.** *Dreams, Illusions and Other Realities.* 1984, Univ. of Chicago Pr. **$25.00 (0-226-61854-4)**. An examination of the relationship between dreams and reality in Western and Eastern philosophies. (Rev: Choice 11/84; LJ 8/84; NYTBR 11/18/84) **[111]**

113 Cosmology (Philosophy of nature)

119 **Morowitz, Harold J.** *Cosmic Joy and Local Pain: Musings of a Mystic Scientist.* 1987, Ox Bow **$18.95 (0-684-18443-5)**. A philosophical view of man, earth, and its place in the universe as seen by a biophysicist. (Rev: LJ 4/15/87; PW 3/6/87) **[113]**

120 **Sheldrake, Rupert.** *Rebirth of Nature: The Greening of Science and God.* 1991, Bantam **$21.95 (0-553-07105-X)**. A study of the current philosophical and scientific views of nature, the universe, and God. "A thoughtful and stimulating contribution to the ongoing discourse."—CSM (Rev: BL 12/15/90; CSM 1/30/91; PW 11/9/90) **[113]**

115 Time

121 **Flood, Raymond, and Michael Lockwood, eds.** *Nature of Time.* 1987, Basil Blackwell **$29.95 (0-631-14807-8)**; paper **$11.95 (0-631-16578-9)**. Eight essays regarding current philosophic and scientific concepts of time. "Clever, erudite, enjoyable, even mind-expanding."—LJ (Rev: Choice 10/87; LJ 6/1/87) **[115]**

122 **Morris, Richard.** *Time's Arrows: Scientific Attitudes Toward Time.* 1986, Simon & Schuster paper **$8.95 (0-671-61766-4)**. An analysis of the history of scientific ideas regarding the nature of time from Babylonian times to the present. (Rev: Choice 6/85; LJ 3/15/85; NYTBR 4/21/85) **[115]**

123 **Szamosi, Geza.** *Twin Dimensions: The Invention of Time and Space.* 1986, McGraw-Hill **$15.95 (0-07-062646-4)**. A study of the concepts of time and space and their influence upon various facets of human thought and culture. "Fascinating . . . enlightening and entertaining."—BL (Rev: BL 7/86; Choice 4/87; LJ 8/86) **[115]**

120 EPISTEMOLOGY, CAUSATION, HUMANKIND

126 The self

124 **Dennett, Daniel C.** *Consciousness Explained.* 1991, Little, Brown **$27.95 (0-316-18065-3)**. A study of the essence and meaning of human consciousness. (Rev: BL 10/1/91; PW 8/16/91. Awards: NYTBR, 1991) **[126]**

125 **Hofstadter, Douglas R., and Daniel C. Dennett.** *Mind's I: Fantasies and Reflections of Self and Soul.* 1982, Bantam paper **$13.95 (0-553-34343-2)**. A synthesis of contemporary philosophy exploring the essence of the human mind. (Rev: LJ 11/1/81; NYTBR 12/13/81; PW 9/24/82) **[126]**

128 Humankind

126 **Aries, Philippe.** *Hour of Our Death.* 1982, Random paper **$13.95 (0-394-75156-6)**. An exploration of the history of attitudes toward death in Western culture from the Middle Ages to the present. "A stunning achievement of historical synthesis . . . fascinating reading."—BL (Rev: BL 12/1/80; Choice 5/81; Time 3/9/81. Awards: Time, 1981) **[128]**

127 Barrett, William E. *Death of the Soul: From Descartes to the Computer.* **1987, Doubleday paper $8.95 (0-385-17327-X).** A history of the rise of science and its dehumanizing influences upon philosophy from the seventeenth century to the present. (Rev: Choice 10/86; LJ 4/15/86; NYTBR 9/7/86) **[128]**

128 Canetti, Elias. *Human Province.* **1986, Farrar paper $9.95 (0-374-51890-4).** Collected philosophical writings by the Nobel Prize winner. (Rev: LJ 10/15/78; NYTBR 4/29/79; Sat Rev 12/78) **[128]**

129 Fadiman, Clifton, ed. *Living Philosophies: The Reflections of Some Eminent Men and Women of Our Time.* **1990, Doubleday $22.50 (0-385-24880-6).** An anthology of philosophical thought from 35 contemporary writers including Alistair Cooke, Elie Wiesel, and William F. Buckley, Jr. (Rev: BL 9/15/90; LJ 10/1/90; PW 7/27/90) **[128]**

130 Gervais, Karen Grandstand. *Redefining Death.* **1987, Yale Univ. Pr. $27.50 (0-300-03616-7); paper $10.95 (0-300-04197-7).** A discussion of the biological and philosophical meaning of death. "The most important work yet written on what 'death' means."—LJ (Rev: Choice 5/87; LJ 1/87) **[128]**

131 Singer, Irving. *Nature of Love, Vol. 3: The Modern World.* **1987, Univ. of Chicago Pr. $24.95 (0-226-76098-7).** The third and final volume in the author's trilogy, regarding the history of love, covers the philosophical and literary concepts of love in the late nineteenth and twentieth centuries. "In scope and attention to detail, the entire work will not soon be equalled."—LJ (Rev: CSM 3/16/88; LJ 11/15/87; NYTBR 12/27/87) **[128]**

132 Wright, Sam. *Koviashuvik: A Time and Place of Joy.* **1989, Sierra Club $17.95 (0-87156-688-5).** Life one hundred miles north of the Arctic Circle described by a biologist who made his home there for two decades. "The best book written about Alaska this decade, possibly this half-century."—BL (Rev: BL 3/15/89; LJ 3/15/89; PW 2/17/89) **[128]**

130 PARANORMAL PHENOMENA

133 Parapsychology and occultism

133 Frazier, Kendrick, ed. *Hundredth Monkey and Other Paradigms of the Paranormal.* **1991, Prometheus paper $17.95 (0-87975-655-1).** A collection of 44 essays from the *Skeptical Inquirer* magazine by scientists considering the unexplained and paranormal. (Rev: BL 6/15/91; LJ 7/91) **[133]**

134 Gardner, Martin. *New Age: Notes of a Fringe-Watcher.* **1988, Prometheus $19.95 (0-87975-432-X).** Essays on the New Age movement by the *Skeptical Inquirer* columnist. (Rev: BL 4/1/88; NYTBR 3/27/88; TLS 7/29/88) **[133]**

135 Zukav, Gary. *Seat of the Soul.* **1989, Simon & Schuster $17.95 (0-671-25383-2).** An examination of the existence and purpose of the human soul as discussed by the author of *The Dancing Wu Li Masters.* (Rev: BL 2/15/89; LJ 3/1/89; PW 1/13/89) **[133]**

Demonology and witchcraft

136 Adler, Margot. *Drawing Down the Moon: Witches, Druids, Goddess-Worshippers and Other Pagans in America Today.* **1987, Beacon paper $15.95 (0-8070-3253-0).** An examination of goddess worship and witchcraft as practiced in contemporary American society. (Rev: Choice 7–8/80; LJ 11/1/79; NYTBR 1/20/80) **[133.4]**

Magic and witchcraft

137 Siegel, Lee. *Net of Magic: Wonders and Deceptions in India.* **1991, Univ. of Chicago Pr. $60.00 (0-226-75686-6); paper $19.95 (0-226-75687-4).** The author recalls his experiences observing the magicians, street performers, and holy men of India. (Rev: BL 6/15/91; LJ 6/15/91) **[133.43]**

Astrology

138 Tester, S. J. *A History of Western Astrology.* **1987, Boydell & Brewer $48.00 (0-85115-446-8); Ballantine paper $9.95 (0-345-35870-8).** A history of astrology from prehistoric times to the eighteenth century. "Not only the only book of its kind, it's a very good book."—CSM (Rev: Choice 5/88; CSM 7/7/88; NYTBR 1/31/88) **[133.5]**

Psychic phenomena

139 Fairley, John, and Simon Welfare. *Arthur C. Clarke's World of Strange Powers.* **1985, Putnam $19.95 (0-399-13066-7).** An illustrated survey of parapsychological phenomena based on a British television series hosted by the eminent science fiction writer. (Rev: LJ 8/85; PW 6/28/85) **[133.8]**

Spiritualism

140 Cott, Jonathan, and Hanny El Zeini. *Search for Omm Sety: A Story of Eternal Love.* **1987, Doubleday $17.95 (0-385-23746-4); Warner paper $9.95 (0-446-39040-2).** A study of the life of a British woman who claimed to have memories of a past life in ancient Egypt and applied her internal knowledge to make archaelogical discoveries in the present-day land of the pharoahs. (Rev: BL 3/15/87; NYTBR 7/26/87) **[133.9]**

141 Cranston, Sylvia, and Carey Williams, eds. *Reincarnation: A New Horizon in Science, Religion and Society.* **1984, Crown $16.95 (0-517-55496-8).** An anthology containing selections from past and present, and Eastern and Western works regarding reincarnation. (Rev: BL 12/15/84; LJ 2/15/85) **[133.9]**

142 Wilson, Ian. *After Death Experience: The Physics of the Non-Physical.* **1989, Morrow $16.95 (0-688-08000-6); paper $8.95 (0-688-09419-8).** A study of "after-death" accounts from ancient times to the

present. (Rev: LJ 2/1/89; NYTBR 4/9/89; PW 12/6/88)
[133.9]

143 Zaleski, Carol. *Otherworld Journeys: Accounts of Near-Death Experiences in Medieval and Modern Times.* 1988, Oxford Univ. Pr. paper $8.95 (0-19-515665-5). A comparative study of the accounts of individuals who experienced near-death situations during the Middle Ages and the twentieth century. (Rev: Choice 10/87; LJ 3/15/87; NYTBR 6/14/87) **[133.9]**

140 SPECIFIC PHILOSOPHICAL SCHOOLS

149 Other philosophical systems

Realism, neorealism, critical realism

144 Lehman, David. *Signs of the Times: Deconstruction and the Fall of Paul de Man.* 1991, Poseidon $19.95 (0-671-68239-3). A look at the career of Yale deconstructivist philosopher Paul de Man and the posthumous discovery that he supported Nazi activities in World War II Belgium. (Rev: LJ 3/1/91; Natl Rev 3/18/91; NYTBR 2/27/91) **[149.2]**

150 PSYCHOLOGY

145 Asbell, Bernard, and Karen Wynn. *What They Know about You.* 1991, Random $20.00 (0-394-55791-3). A selection of findings about human psychology and behavior taken from over 30,000 studies. "An irresistible reflection of our private and public selves."—BL (Rev: BL 5/1/91; PW 3/29/91) **[150]**

146 Donohue, Phil. *Human Animal.* 1986, Simon & Schuster paper $10.95 (0-671-63035-0). The television talk-show host studies human activities, actions, and behaviors with help from prominent sociologists, psychologists, and anthropologists. (Rev: LJ 9/1/85; PW 7/5/85) **[150]**

147 Skinner, B. F. *Beyond Freedom and Dignity.* 1971, Knopf $25.00 (0-394-42555-3); Bantam paper $4.95 (0-553-25404-9). The behavioral scientist's plea for a simplification of societal values, and the uses of scientific study and societal control to create a better society. (Rev: BL 11/1/71; Choice 4/72; LJ 8/71. Awards: ALA, 1971; Time, 1971) **[150]**

148 Skinner, B. F. *Particulars of My Life.* 1985, New York Univ. Pr. paper $13.50 (0-8147-7843-7). The first volume of the memoirs of the behaviorist regarding his childhood, adolescence, and undergraduate studies. (Rev: LJ 4/15/76; NYTBR 4/11/76; Newsweek 4/11/76) **[150]**

Philosophy and theory—Systems, schools, viewpoints

149 Bettelheim, Bruno. *Freud and Man's Soul.* 1983, Random paper $7.95 (0-394-71036-3). The author of *The Empty Fortress* argues that many of Freud's fundamental ideas have been misinterpreted due to imprecise early translations of his work

from German to English. (Rev: BL 12/15/82; LJ 12/15/82; PW 11/26/82) **[150.19]**

150 Bettelheim, Bruno. *Freud's Vienna and Other Essays.* 1989, Knopf $22.95 (0-394-57209-2); Random paper $12.95 (0-679-73188-1). A collection of 18 essays by the noted child psychologist regarding Freud and his theories, children, and various aspects of the Holocaust. (Rev: LJ 1/90; NYTBR 1/21/90; Time 1/8/90) **[150.19]**

151 Bruner, Jerome Seymour. *Actual Minds, Possible Worlds.* 1986, Harvard Univ. Pr. $16.95 (0-674-00365-9); paper $8.95 (0-674-00366-7). Essays examining the relationship between human language and thought and how the two influence perception. (Rev: Choice 9/86; LJ 7/86; NYTBR 3/23/86) **[150.19]**

152 Coles, Robert. *Erik H. Erikson: The Growth of His Work.* 1987, Da Capo paper $12.95 (0-306-80291-0). An analysis of the life, work, and writings of the noted psychoanalyst. "A brilliant achievement."—Choice (Rev: Choice 4/71; LJ 1/1/71; NYTBR 11/22/70) **[150.19]**

153 Gay, Peter. *Freud: A Life for Our Time.* 1988, Norton $30.00 (0-393-02517-9); Doubleday paper $14.95 (0-385-26256-6). "Beautifully written . . . essential for *all* reader levels with an interest in Freud."—Choice (Rev: Choice 11/88; NYTBR 3/24/88; Newsweek 5/2/88. Awards: BL, the 1980s; LJ, 1988) **[150.19]**

154 Gay, Peter. *A Godless Jew: Freud, Atheism and the Making of Psychoanalysis.* 1987, Yale Univ. Pr. $20.00 (0-300-04008-3); paper $9.95 (0-300-04608-1). A study of the philosophical, historical, and intellectual roots of psychoanalysis. (Rev: Choice 2/88; NYRB 8/18/88; PW 8/21/87) **[150.19]**

155 Grosskurth, Phyllis. *Melanie Klein: Her World and Her Work.* 1986, Knopf $25.00 (0-394-51342-8); paper $12.50 (0-674-56470-7). A biography of the pioneer of psychoanalysis for children. (Rev: BL 5/1/86; LJ 3/15/86; NYTBR 5/18/86) **[150.19]**

156 Hillman, James. *A Blue Fire: Selected Writings.* Ed. by Thomas Moore. 1989, Harper & Row $22.50 (0-06-016132-9). A selection of writings from books and articles by the influential revisionist Jungian psychoanalyst. (Rev: BL 9/15/89; LJ 10/1/89; NYTBR 3/11/90) **[150.19]**

157 Krull, Marianne. *Freud and His Father.* 1986, Norton $18.95 (0-393-01854-7). An examination of the influence of Freud's father and their relationship upon the thought of the pioneer of psychoanalysis. (Rev: BL 2/15/86; Choice 3/87; LJ 3/1/86) **[150.19]**

158 Quinn, Susan. *A Mind of Her Own: The Life of Karen Horney.* 1988, Addison Wesley $14.95 (0-201-15573-7). A biography of the psychoanalyst who challenged many of Freud's ideas regarding the psychology of women. (Rev: LJ 10/15/87; NYRB 11/5/87; NYTBR 11/29/87. Awards: LJ, 1987) **[150.19]**

159 Roazen, Paul. *Freud and His Followers.* 1985, New York Univ. Pr. paper $17.50 (0-8147-7394-X). A study of Freud and his legacy based on interviews with 70 people who knew him. (Rev: LJ 9/15/75; New Rep 3/1/75; Sat Rev 1/25/75)   **[150.19]**

160   Sagan, Eli. *Freud, Women and Morality: The Psychology of Good and Evil.* **1988, Basic Books $19.95 (0-465-02570-6).** A reassessment of Freud's three components of the mind (id, ego, superego) and their relationship to morality. "A profound book, one that may well be among the most important issued in this decade."—BL (Rev: BL 4/1/88; LJ 4/1/88; NYTBR 5/1/88)   **[150.19]**

161   Sayers, Janet. *Mothers of Psychoanalysis: Helene Deutsch, Karen Horney, Anna Freud, Melanie Klein.* **1991, Norton $24.95 (0-393-03041-5).** A study of the lives and work of four European-born psychoanalysts who fled the continent during the 1930s to practice their craft in Great Britain and the United States. "A useful, deeply intelligent book."—BL (Rev: BL 10/1/91; NYTBR 9/29/91; TLS 3/1/91)   **[150.19]**

162   Symington, Neville. *Analytic Experience.* **1986, St. Martin's $29.95 (0-312-03288-9).** A series of essays regarding the theory and nature of psychoanalysis and its development since Freud. (Rev: BL 10/1/86; LJ 11/15/86; TLS 10/31/86)   **[150.19]**

Persons

163   Hoffman, Edward. *The Right to Be Human: A Biography of Abraham Maslow.* **1988, J. P. Tarcher $19.95 (0-87477-461-6); paper $12.95 (0-87477-508-6).** A biography of the psychologist who helped popularize self-realization techniques. "Will be of interest to the many people touched by his humanistic vision of personal growth."—PW (Rev: BL 5/1/88; LJ 6/1/88; PW 4/1/88)   **[150.92]**

164   Leary, Timothy. *Flashbacks: A Personal and Cultural History of an Era.* **1990, J. P. Tarcher paper $14.95 (0-87477-497-7).** Memoirs of the controversial psychologist who promoted the use of psychoactive drugs during the 1960s. (Rev: LJ 7/83; NYTBR 7/5/83; Newsweek 7/11/83)   **[150.92]**

165   Young-Bruehl, Elizabeth. *Anna Freud: A Biography.* **1988, Summit $24.95 (0-671-61696-X); paper $12.95 (0-671-68751-4).** An authorized biography of Freud's daughter and a noted psychoanalyst in her own right based on her private papers. (Rev: LJ 10/1/86; NYTBR 10/16/88; PW 8/12/88. Awards: PW, 1988)   **[150.92]**

152   Perception, movement, emotions, drives

166   Dienstfrey, Harris. *Where the Mind Meets the Body.* **1991, HarperCollins $19.95 (0-06-016570-7).** A study surveying the relationship between the mind and health of the human body. (Rev: BL 2/15/91; LJ 3/15/91)   **[152]**

167   Franklin, Jon. *Molecules of the Mind: The Brave New Science of Molecular Psychology.* **1988, Dell paper $8.95 (0-440-50005-2).** A study of the biological basis for human behavior. "Unsurpassed in its clarity and depth of insight, this thoroughly

engrossing account delights as it instructs."—BL (Rev: BL 1/15/87; LJ 2/15/87; NYTBR 2/8/87)   **[152]**

168   Harrington, Anne. *Medicine, Mind, and the Double Brain: A Study in 19th Century Thought.* **1987, Princeton Univ. Pr. $39.95 (0-691-08465-3); paper $12.95 (0-691-02422-7).** A study of nineteenth-century theories on the structure and processes of the human brain. (Rev: Choice 5/88; LJ 11/1/87; NYTBR 10/11/87)   **[152]**

169   Hooper, Judith, and Dick Teresi. *Three-Pound Universe.* **1987, Dell paper $12.95 (0-440-58507-4).** A survey of neuroscience and neurology for the general reader. "One of the best books of its kind."—PW (Rev: BL 2/15/86; NYTBR 3/23/86; PW 1/17/86)   **[152]**

170   Restak, Richard M. *Mind.* **1988, Bantam $29.95 (0-553-05314-0).** An introduction to the mental processes of human beings by the author of *The Brain.* (Rev: BL 10/1/88; LJ 11/1/88; NYTBR 1/1/89)   **[152]**

Emotions and feelings

171   Barker, Robert. *Green-Eyed Marriage: Surviving Jealous Relationships.* **1987, Free Pr. $24.95 (0-02-901791-2).** A study of jealousy in marriages with tips on how to help your relationship survive a jealous spouse. (Rev: Choice 2/88; LJ 11/15/87) **[152.4]**

172   Gaylin, Willard. *Rage Within: Anger in Modern Life.* **1989, Penguin paper $7.95 (0-14-012003-3).** A psychiatrist's study of the physiological and psychological causes and functions of anger in human beings. (Rev: BL 10/15/84; LJ 11/15/84; NYTBR 2/10/85)   **[152.4]**

173   Gaylin, Willard. *Rediscovering Love.* **1986, Viking $15.95 (0-670-81120-3); Penguin paper $4.50 (0-14-010431-3).** A psychologist's look at the essence of love. (Rev: BL 9/15/86; Choice 2/87; PW 7/18/86)   **[152.4]**

174   Hindy, Carl, and J. Conrad Schwarz. *If This Is Love, Why Do I Feel So Insecure?* **1989, Atlantic Monthly $18.95 (0-87113-310-5); Fawcett paper $4.95 (0-449-21859-7).** An analysis of what makes love relationships unstable or unfulfilling based on over 1,750 interviews with people who were asked about problems in their love lives. (Rev: BL 3/15/89; LJ 4/1/89; PW 2/24/89)   **[152.4]**

175   Tavris, Carol. *Anger: The Misunderstood Emotion.* **1989, Simon & Schuster paper $9.95 (0-671-67523-0).** An examination of the roots, expression, and social and personal effects of anger. (Rev: BL 2/1/83; Choice 7–8/83; LJ 1/1/83)   **[152.4]**

153   Mental processes and intelligence

176   Campbell, Jeremy. *Improbable Machine: What the New Upheaval in Artificial Intelligence Research Reveals about How the Mind Really Works.* **1989, Simon & Schuster $19.95 (0-671-67511-9).** An analysis of how recent research into artificial intelligence can help us understand the workings of the human brain. (Rev: BL 10/1/89; LJ 10/1/89; NYTBR 12/24/89)   **[153]**

177   Corbalis, Michael C. *Lopsided Ape: Evolution of the Generative Mind.* **1991, Oxford Univ. Pr. $24.95 (0-19-506675-8).** A study of the evolution of human thought and language written by a New Zealand psychology professor. (Rev: BL 7/91; LJ 6/1/91)   **[153]**

178   Goleman, Daniel. *Vital Lies, Simple Truths: The Psychology of Self-Deception and Shared Illusions.* **1986, Simon & Schuster paper $9.95 (0-671-62815-1).** An explanation of the reasons for psychological denial and deception, from the personal level to the national. (Rev: Choice 10/85; LJ 6/1/85; NYTBR 6/16/85)   **[153]**

179   Minsky, Marvin Lee. *Society of Mind.* **1988, Simon & Schuster paper $12.95 (0-671-65713-5).** An analysis of the processes of human thought and their relationship to artificial intelligence. "A fun and informative journey through the workings of the mind."—BL (Rev: BL 1/15/87; NYRB 6/11/87; NYTBR 2/22/87)   **[153]**

180   Morris, Desmond. *Manwatching: A Field Guide to Human Behavior.* **1979, Abrams paper $19.95 (0-8109-2184-7).** A look at human body language by the author of *The Naked Ape.* "Sparkles with Morris's insights and illumes the reader with a deeper appreciation and understanding of human nature."—Choice (Rev: BL 1/1/78; Choice 3/78; LJ 1/1/78)   **[153]**

181   Ornstein, Robert. *Evolution of Consciousness—Of Darwin, Freud and Cranial Fire: The Origins of the Way We Think.* **1991, Prentice Hall $25.00 (0-13-587569-2).** An analysis of the modern human psyche and the evolution of modern human thought by the author of *The Psychology of Consciousness.* (Rev: BL 11/15/91; PW 9/13/91. Awards: BC, 1991)   **[153]**

182   Sagan, Carl. *The Dragons of Eden: Speculations on the Evolution of Human Intelligence.* **1977, Random $10.95 (0-394-41045-9); Ballantine paper $4.95 (0-345-34629-7).** The history and development of the human brain as explained by the author of *Cosmos.* (Rev: Atl 8/77; Choice 12/77; Newsweek 6/27/77. Awards: ALA, 1977; PP:NF, 1978)   **[153]**

183   Schank, Roger C. *Tell Me a Story: A New Look at Real and Artificial Memory.* **1991, Scribner $19.95 (0-684-19049-4).** A comparative study of memory and intelligence in humans and computers. (Rev: NYTBR 1/13/91; PW 11/23/90)   **[153]**

Memory and learning

184   Johnson, George. *In the Palaces of Memory: How We Build the Worlds Inside Our Heads.* **1991, Knopf $22.95 (0-394-58348-5).** A study of the scientific and psychological theories on the creation, storage, and retrieval processes of the human memory. (Rev: BL 2/15/91; LJ 2/1/91; NYTBR 2/27/91)   **[153.1]**

185   Luria, A. R. *Mind of a Mnemonist: A Little Book about a Vast Memory.* **1987, Harvard Univ. Pr. paper $7.95 (0-674-57622-5).** An analysis of the author's patient whose prodigious memory inter-

fered with his ability to think logically and live a normal life. (Rev: BL 9/1/68; NYRB 5/9/68; New Yorker 4/27/68)   **[153.1]**

186   Moss, Robert A., and Helen Duff Dunlap. *Why Johnny Can't Concentrate: Coping with Attention Deficit Problems.* **1990, Bantam $9.95 (0-553-34968-6).** A guide to the diagnosis and treatment of Attention Deficit disorder and other related child behavioral problems. (Rev: BL 11/1/90; LJ 11/1/90)   **[153.1]**

Imagination and imagery

187   Gardner, Howard. *Art, Mind and Brain: A Cognitive Approach to Creativity.* **1982, Basic Books paper $15.95 (0-465-00445-8).** A study of musical and artistic creativity and the human brain based on research with children and developmentally disabled adults. (Rev: BL 2/1/83; LJ 12/15/82; NYTBR 2/6/83)   **[153.3]**

188   Grudin, Robert. *Grace and Great Things: Creativity and Innovation.* **1990, Ticknor & Fields $20.95 (0-89919-940-2).** A study of the psychological processes behind creativity. (Rev: BL 4/15/90; LJ 5/15/90; PW 3/30/90)   **[153.3]**

Communication

189   Ekman, Paul. *Telling Lies: Clues to Deceit in the Marketplace, Politics, and Marriage.* **1986, Berkley paper $3.95 (0-425-09298-4).** A study of nonverbal communication and how it can be used to determine the veracity or falsehood of a person's statements. (Rev: Choice 6/85; LJ 2/1/85; NYTBR 3/31/85)   **[153.6]**

Perceptual processes

190   Gifford, Don. *Farther Shore: A Natural History of Perception, 1789–1984.* **1990, Atlantic Monthly $19.95 (0-87113-335-0).** A study of the ways human perceptions of space and time have been changed by technological and social changes during the past two centuries. "Redefines the way we look at the world."—PW (Rev: BL 2/15/90; LJ 12/89; PW 12/8/89)   **[153.7]**

Intelligence and aptitudes

191   Gould, Stephen Jay. *The Mismeasure of Man.* **1981, Norton $17.95 (0-393-01489-4).** The history of the measuring of intelligence by "science" and how the misuse of "facts" has led to racist conclusions. "An outstanding book written for an understanding readership."—LJ (Rev: Choice 4/82; CSM 3/12/82; LJ 10/15/81. Awards: ALA, 1981)   **[153.9]**

192   Sternberg, Robert J. *Triarchic Mind: A New Theory of Human Intelligence.* **1988, Viking $19.95 (0-70-80364-2); Penguin paper $9.95 (0-14-009210-2).** The author argues for new standards and methods for testing human intelligence to include measurements of creativity and wisdom. (Rev: BL 8/88; Choice 2/89; NYTBR 9/25/88)   **[153.9]**

154 Subconscious and altered states

Sleep phenomena

193 Hobson, J. Allan. *Dreaming Brain*. 1989, Basic Books paper $10.95 (0-465-01702-9). The author presents his theories on the meaning and processes of dreaming. (Rev: Choice 9/88; PW 3/11/88)   **[154.6]**

155 Differential and developmental psychology

194 Kotre, John, and Elizabeth Hall. *Seasons of Life: Our Dramatic Journey from Birth to Death*. 1990, Little, Brown $24.95 (0-316-50252-9). A guide to the mental and physiological development of humans from birth to death. (Rev: BL 9/1/90; LJ 10/1/90; PW 8/24/90)   **[155]**

Individual psychology

195 Csikzentmihaly, Mihaly. *Flow: The Psychology of Optimal Experience*. 1990, Harper & Row $18.95 (0-06-016253-8); HarperCollins paper $9.95 (0-06-092043-2). A study of the optimal achievable physical and mental state and how to obtain it. (Rev: BL 3/1/90; LJ 3/15/90; NYTBR 3/18/90)   **[155.2]**

196 Hunt, Morton. *Compassionate Beast: The Scientific Inquiry into Human Altruism*. 1990, Morrow $18.95 (0-688-07577-0); Doubleday paper $11.00 (0-385-41859-0). A scientific study of the impulses, rewards, and societal need for human altruistic activity. (Rev: LJ 3/1/90; NYTBR 4/8/90; PW 3/9/90)   **[155.2]**

197 Konner, Melvin. *Why the Reckless Survive: And Other Secrets of Human Nature*. 1990, Viking $18.95 (0-670-82936-6). A study of the connection between genetics and human behavior by the author of *Becoming a Doctor*. (Rev: BL 7/90; NYTBR 7/29/90)   **[155.2]**

198 Lasch, Christopher. *The Minimal Self: Psychic Survival in Troubled Times*. 1984, Norton $16.95 (0-393-01922-5). Lasch's book on the retreat of self as a psychic defense mechanism due to overwhelming feelings of potential disaster in modern society. (Rev: BL 10/1/84; LJ 10/1/84; Newsweek 11/5/84. Awards: LJ, 1984)   **[155.2]**

199 Seligman, Martin E. *Learned Optimism: The Skill to Conquer Life's Obstacles, Large and Small*. 1991, Knopf $19.95 (0-394-57915-1). A guide to the development of a positive mental attitude toward life. (Rev: BL 1/15/91; LJ 1/91; PW 12/7/90)   **[155.2]**

Sex psychology and psychology of the sexes

200 Friday, Nancy. *Jealousy*. (0-553-26265-7); Bantam paper $5.95. A study of jealousy and its effects upon personal relationships by the author of *My Secret Garden*. (Rev: BL 8/85; LJ 10/1/85; NYTBR 10/6/85)   **[155.3]**

201 Gilmore, David D. *Manhood in the Making: Cultural Concepts of Masculinity*. 1990, Yale Univ. Pr. $22.50 (0-300-04646-4). An examination of the roles of males and concepts of masculinity in human society. (Rev: LJ 4/15/90; NYTBR 4/15/90; TLS 6/1/90)   **[155.3]**

202 Levinson, Daniel. *Seasons of a Man's Life*. 1978, Knopf $24.95 (0-394-40694-X); Ballantine paper $10.95 (0-345-33901-0). Levinson's study of adult development was the inspiration and partial basis for Gail Sheehy's *Passages*. (Rev: BL 4/1/78; LJ 4/1/78; Sat Rev 4/1/78)   **[155.3]**

Child psychology

203 Bettelheim, Bruno. *The Empty Fortress: Infantile Autism and the Birth of the Self*. 1972, Free Pr. $17.95 (0-02-903130-3); paper $10.95 (0-02-903140-0). Bettelheim describes his two decades of work with autistic children, and includes three extended case studies. (Rev: NYRB 5/4/67; NYTBR 2/26/67; New Yorker 5/18/68. Awards: NYTBR, 1967)   **[155.4]**

204 Carlsson-Paige, Nancy, and Diane E. Levin. *Who's Calling the Shots: How to Respond Effectively to Children's Fascination with War Play and War Toys*. 1990, New Society $39.95 (0-86571-164-X); paper $12.95 (0-86571-165-8). A study of methods to combat the damaging psychological effects of war toys on children. (Rev: BL 4/15/90; LJ 9/1/90; Time 3/26/90)   **[155.4]**

205 Coles, Robert. *Moral Life of Children*. 1986, Atlantic Monthly $19.95 (0-87113-034-3); Houghton paper $10.95 (0-395-43153-0). A study of the moral state of children based on interviews with young people from many nations by the child psychiatrist. (Rev: BL 1/15/86; LJ 2/15/86; NYTBR 1/19/86)   **[155.4]**

206 Coles, Robert. *Political Life of Children*. 1986, Atlantic Monthly $19.95 (0-87113-035-1); Houghton paper $11.95 (0-395-43152-2). A study of children's concepts of politics based on interviews with the youth of the United States, Brazil, Canada, South Africa, Ireland, Nicaragua, and Poland. (Rev: BL 1/15/86; LJ 2/15/86; NYTBR 1/19/86)   **[155.4]**

207 Gardner, Howard. *Artful Scribbles: The Significance of Children's Drawings*. 1982, Basic Books paper $15.95 (0-465-00455-5). An analysis of children's art work and its significance by the psychologist and author of *The Shattered Mind*. (Rev: LJ 4/15/80; NYTBR 4/6/80; Sat Rev 5/80)   **[155.4]**

208 Greenspan, Stanley I., and Nancy Thorndike Greenspan. *First Feelings: Milestones in the Emotional Development of Your Baby and Child*. 1989, Penguin paper $7.95 (0-14-011988-4). An outline of identifiable stages of emotional development in the newborn and young child. "A must for the child-rearing shelf."—PW (Rev: BL 2/15/85; LJ 4/15/85; PW 2/15/85)   **[155.4]**

209 Healy, Jane M. *Endangered Minds: Why Our Children Don't Think*. 1990, Simon & Schuster $22.95 (0-671-67349-1). A critical analysis of contemporary teaching methods and their effectiveness on children. (Rev: BL 10/15/90; LJ 10/15/90; PW 8/24/90)   **[155.4]**

210 Kagan, Jerome. *The Nature of the Child.* **1986, Basic Books paper $12.95 (0-465-04851-X).** Kagan refutes some popularly held theories of child development. "A scholarly landmark by Harvard's renowned developmental psychologist."—LJ (Rev: BL 9/1/84; LJ 9/15/84; PW 7/20/84. Awards: LJ, 1984) **[155.4]**

211 Lane, Harlan. *Wild Boy of Aveyron.* **1976, Harvard Univ. Pr. $25.50 (0-674-95282-0); paper $10.95 (0-674-95300-2).** The story of the "feral boy" found living in the forests of Southern France in 1797. "A fascinating discussion of the nature of humanity."—BL (Rev: BL 2/1/76; LJ 2/1/76; NYTBR 5/17/76) **[155.4]**

212 McCoy, Kathleen. *Solo Parenting: Your Essential Guide.* **1988, NAL paper $4.50 (0-451-15137-2).** A child-raising manual for single parents with advice from others who have reared children on their own. (Rev: BL 12/15/87; LJ 2/15/87) **[155.4]**

213 Maurer, Daphne, and Charles Maurer. *World of the Newborn.* **1989, Basic Books paper $11.95 (0-465-09229-2).** A study of the mental and physical perceptions of newborn infants. (Rev: BL 2/15/88; Choice 10/88; NYTBR 3/27/88) **[155.4]**

214 Miller, Alice. *Untouched Key: Tracing Childhood Trauma in Creativity and Destructiveness.* **1990, Doubleday $17.95 (0-385-26763-0).** A study of the effects of childhood abuse upon creativity. (Rev: BL 3/1/90; PW 3/9/90) **[155.4]**

215 Restak, Richard M. *Infant Mind.* **1986, Doubleday $18.95 (0-385-19531-1).** The author of *The Brain* focuses on the mental development of the infant prior to and following birth. (Rev: BL 10/1/86; LJ 11/15/86) **[155.4]**

216 Roiphe, Herman, and Anne Roiphe. *Your Child's Mind: The Complete Guide to Infant and Child Emotional Well-Being.* **1986, St. Martin's paper $10.95 (0-312-89784-7).** A guide to the mental and emotional stages of development of children from birth to age ten. (Rev: BL 5/17/85; LJ 6/1/85) **[155.4]**

217 Segal, Marilyn, and Dan Adcock. *Your Child at Play: Three to Five Years.* **1986, Newmarket $16.95 (0-937858-72-2); paper $9.95 (0-937858-73-0).** An introduction to the creative and imaginative world of the three- to five-year-old. (Rev: LJ 2/1/87; PW 12/19/86) **[155.4]**

218 Ulene, Art, and Steven Shelov. *Bringing Out the Best in Your Baby: Introducing Discovery Play.* **1987, Macmillan $14.95 (0-02-620880-6); paper $3.95 (0-02-078110-5).** A recounting of current theories of infant development with recommended methods for activities, and exercises to increase your baby's awareness and well-being. (Rev: BL 12/15/86; LJ 1/87; PW 12/5/86) **[155.4]**

219 Youngs, Bettie B. *Stress in Children: How to Avoid, Overcome and Benefit from It.* **1986, Avon paper $3.95 (0-380-70161-8).** A study of the symptoms and effects of stress on children with suggested treatments and preventative measures. (Rev: BL 7/85; LJ 7/85; PW 7/5/85) **[155.4]**

Psychology of young adults

220 Ames, Louise Bates. *Your Ten-to-Fourteen-Year-Old.* **1989, Doubleday paper $8.95 (0-385-29699-1).** A revised update of the author's 1956 *Youth: The Years from Ten to Sixteen* discussing issues in the development and parenting of adolescents. (Rev: BL 3/1/88; LJ 2/1/88) **[155.5]**

221 Hendin, Herbert. *Age of Sensation.* **1975, Norton $19.95 (0-393-01122-4).** Based on over 400 interviews with college students, the psychologist argues that youth in today's society are drawn toward instant gratification at the cost of intimacy and emotional stability. (Rev: BL 12/15/75; LJ 9/15/75; PW 8/11/75) **[155.5]**

Psychology of adults

222 Brandes, Stanley H. *Forty: The Age and the Symbol.* **1985, Univ. of Tennessee Pr. $19.95 (0-87049-463-5); paper $8.95 (0-87049-516-X).** A look at the social and anthropological significance of the age 40 and the "mid-life crisis." (Rev: Choice 12/85; LJ 7/85; NYTBR 9/8/85) **[155.6]**

223 Chernin, Kim. *Hungry Self: Women, Eating and Identity.* **1986, Harper & Row paper $8.95 (0-06-097026-X).** A study of the relationships between food, eating, self-image, and identity for women in contemporary American society. (Rev: BL 6/15/85; LJ 6/15/85; NYTBR 7/21/85) **[155.6]**

224 Eichenbaum, Luise, and Susie Orbach. *Between Women: Love, Envy, and Competition in Women's Friendships.* **1988, Viking $17.95 (0-670-81141-6); paper $7.95 (0-14-008980-2).** A study of the dynamics and current trends in women's friendships in modern American society. (Rev: BL 12/15/87; LJ 12/87; NYTBR 1/24/88) **[155.6]**

225 Freudenberger, Herbert J., and Gail North. *Women's Burnout.* **1986, Penguin paper $8.95 (0-14-009414-8).** A guide to the diagnosis, treatment, and prevention of burnout in women. (Rev: BL 8/85; LJ 9/1/85; PW 7/26/85) **[155.6]**

226 Friedman, Sonya, and Gary Kettelhack. *On a Clear Day You Can See Yourself: Turning the Life You Have into the Life You Want.* **1991, Little, Brown $18.95 (0-316-29385-7).** A guide by the popular television psychologist to methods women can use to gain control over their lives. (Rev: BL 11/15/90; LJ 11/1/90; PW 11/30/90) **[155.6]**

227 Gould, Jean. *Spirals: A Woman's Journey Through Family Life.* **1988, Random $18.95 (0-394-55705-0); Penguin paper $8.95 (0-14-012089-0).** Memoirs of the author's life and her relationship with members of her family. (Rev: BL 4/15/88; LJ 4/1/88; NYTBR 7/17/88) **[155.6]**

228 Hancock, Emily. *Girl Within: Recapture the Childhood Self, the Key to Female Identity.* **1989, Dutton $17.95 (0-525-24774-2).** A treatise urging women to recover their childhood self as a role model and basis for strength. (Rev: BL 10/1/89; LJ 11/1/89; PW 9/15/89)   **[155.6]**

229   Llewelyn, Sue, and Kate Osborne. *Women's Lives.* **1990, Routledge $45.00 (0-415-01701-7); paper $12.95 (0-415-01702-5).** Two English psychologists' views of the particular pressures and situations facing women in contemporary society. (Rev: LJ 9/1/90; PW 7/27/90)   **[155.6]**

230   Miller, Jean Baker. *Toward a New Psychology of Women.* **1986, Beacon paper $8.95 (0-8070-2902-2).** A revised edition of the 1976 work that called for a reevaluation of the study of women's psychological and emotional states. (Rev: BL 4/1/87; Choice 7–8/87; NYTBR 5/3/87)   **[155.6]**

231   Scarf, Maggie. *Unfinished Business: Pressure Points in the Lives of Women.* **1980, Doubleday $14.95 (0-385-12248-9).** A study of key emotional crises in women's lives based on ten case studies. (Rev: BL 7/15/80; Choice 12/80; NYTBR 8/24/80)   **[155.6]**

Environmental psychology

232   Bettelheim, Bruno. *Surviving and Other Essays.* **1980, Random paper $9.95 (0-394-74264-8).** Essays regarding the Holocaust and its psychological effects upon its survivors. (Rev: BL 5/15/79; LJ 5/1/79; NYRB 4/19/79)   **[155.9]**

233   Caine, Lynn. *Widow.* **1987, Bantam paper $3.95 (0-553-26422-2).** A woman tells of her husband's death from cancer and her readjustment to life as a widow. "Direct, passionate and unerring in its determination to tell the truth."—Newsweek (Rev: LJ 4/15/74; NYTBR 6/9/74; Newsweek 6/10/74)   **[155.9]**

234   Des Pres, Terrence. *Survivor: An Anatomy of Life in the Death Camps.* **1976, Oxford Univ. Pr. paper $8.95 (0-19-502703-5).** Using over seventy personal accounts, Des Pres explores the psychological aspects of survival in Hitler's and Stalin's concentration camps. "A provocative and exciting book, superbly written."—LJ (Rev: BL 6/1/76; LJ 9/15/76; NYTBR 3/14/76. Awards: ALA, 1976)   **[155.9]**

235   Lifton, Robert Jay. *Broken Connection: On Death and the Continuity of Life.* **1983, Basic Books paper $14.95 (0-465-00776-7).** A study of the psychological denial of death and its impact upon human life. "Lifton's magnum opus, a work of profound psychological penetration."—PW (Rev: LJ 9/1/79; NYTBR 11/4/79; PW 8/27/79)   **[155.9]**

236   Lifton, Robert Jay. *Death in Life: Survivors of Hiroshima.* **1982, Basic Books paper $12.95 (0-465-01582-4).** The psychological and sociological effects of the atomic bomb based on interviews with survivors. (Rev: LJ 1/15/68; New Yorker 8/3/68; Newsweek 2/19/68. Awards: ALA, 1968; NBA, 1969)   **[155.9]**

237   Storr, Anthony. *Solitude: A Return to the Self.* **1988, Free Pr. $17.95 (0-02-931620-0); Ballantine paper $8.95 (0-345-35847-3).** Storr argues that solitude can be an effective way to personal peace and self-discovery, and uses historical examples to make his case. (Rev: BL 6/15/88; LJ 8/88; NYTBR 10/2/88)   **[155.9]**

158   Applied psychology

Personal improvement and analysis

238   Beal, Edward W., and Gloria Hochman. *Adult Children of Divorce.* **1991, Delacorte $18.95 (0-385-29924-9).** A study of the life-long effects of divorce upon the children of broken families with suggestions on ways to escape the cycle and achieve successful interpersonal relationships. (Rev: BL 3/1/91; LJ 2/15/91)   **[158.1]**

239   Carter, Jimmy, and Rosalynn Carter. *Everything to Gain: Making the Best of the Rest of Your Life.* **1988, Thorndike Pr. $17.95 (0-89621-124-X); Fawcett paper $4.95 (0-449-14538-7).** The former president and first lady provide advice and personal reflections on the art of living and enjoying life. (Rev: BL 4/15/87; NYTBR 5/31/87; Time 6/15/87)   **[158.1]**

240   Forward, Susan, and Craig Buck. *Obsessive Love: When Passion Holds You Prisoner.* **1991, Bantam $21.50 (0-553-07385-0).** Forward, a bestselling psychotherapist, examines obsession and dominance in personal relationships. (Rev: BL 5/15/91; LJ 4/15/91)   **[158.1]**

241   Goliszek, Andrew. *Breaking the Stress Habit: A Modern Guide to One Minute Stress Management.* **1987, Carolina Pr. $16.95 (0-9616475-2-3).** A study of the physical and mental effects of stress with recommended exercises, and relaxation methods for the reduction of tension. (Rev: Choice 6/88; LJ 2/15/88)   **[158.1]**

242   Kinder, Melvin. *Going Nowhere Fast: Stepping Off Life's Treadmills and Finding Peace of Mind.* **1990, Prentice Hall $19.95 (0-13-358995-1).** A psychologist's self-help guide for individuals who are unsatisfied by material pleasures and business success. (Rev: BL 8/90; LJ 9/15/90; PW 8/10/90)   **[158.1]**

Leadership

243   Bennis, Warren. *On Becoming a Leader.* **1989, Addison Wesley $19.95 (0-201-08059-1); paper $8.95 (0-201-55087-3).** Profiles of 30 leaders and the techniques they have used to provide leadership by the author of *Leaders: The Strategies of Taking Charge.* (Rev: BL 9/1/89; LJ 8/89; PW 8/11/89)   **[158.4]**

Cooperation and negotiation

244   Woolf, Bob. *Friendly Persuasion: My Life as a Negotiator.* **1990, Putnam $21.95 (0-399-13352-9).** A contract lawyer's guide to successful negotiation techniques laced with anecdotes concerning his famous clients. (Rev: LJ 9/15/90; PW 8/10/90)   **[158.5]**

170   ETHICS (MORAL PHILOSOPHY)

245   Fletcher, Joseph. *Situation Ethics: The New Morality.* **1966, Westminster paper $9.95 (0-664-24691-5).** An examination of the "new Protestant ethics" of situationalism. (Rev: LJ 4/15/66; New Rep 9/3/66; PW 2/28/66. Awards: ALA, 1966)   **[170]**

246 Jonas, Hans. *Imperative of Responsibility: In Search of an Ethics for the Technological Age.* 1985, Univ. of Chicago Pr. $25.00 (0-226-40596-6); paper $10.95 (0-226-40597-4). A look at the long-term ethical problems caused by environmental changes due to modern-day technology. (REV: Choice 10/84; CSM 12/7/84; LJ 6/1/84)   **[170]**

247 Williams, Bernard. *Ethics and the Limits of Philosophy.* 1985, Harvard Univ. Pr. $18.50 (0-674-26857-1); paper $8.95 (0-674-26858-X). A study of philosophical works examining ethics and ethical behavior. (REV: LJ 6/15/85; NYTBR 7/14/85; New Yorker 10/14/85)   **[170]**

171 Systems and doctrines

Based on biology, genetics, evolution, education, social factors

248 Rachels, James. *Created from Animals: The Moral Implications of Darwinism.* 1990, Oxford Univ. Pr. $19.95 (0-19-217775-3); paper $9.95 (0-19-286129-8). An exploration of the philosophical implications of Darwin's theories regarding man's role on earth and place in nature. (REV: BL 5/15/90; NYTBR 7/29/90)   **[171.7]**

Based on altruism

249 Kohn, Alfie. *Brighter Side of Human Nature: Altruism and Empathy in Everyday Life.* 1990, Basic Books $19.95 (0-465-00757-0). An examination of the good in human nature. (REV: LJ 4/15/90; PW 3/23/90)   **[171.8]**

172 Political ethics

250 Erikson, Erik H. *Gandhi's Truth: On the Origins of Militant Nonviolence.* 1970, Norton paper $5.95 (0-393-00741-3). An assessment of Gandhi's philosophy and role in history by a noted psychoanalyst. (REV: LJ 9/1/69; New Rep 10/18/69; Newsweek 8/18/69. AWARDS: ALA, 1969; NBA, 1970; NYTBR, 1969; PP:NF, 1970)   **[172]**

251 Hampshire, Stuart. *Innocence and Experience.* 1989, Harvard Univ. Pr. $20.00 (0-674-45448-0). A philosophical work examining the development and essence of ethical behavior and judgment in man. (REV: Choice 2/90; LJ 9/1/89; NYRB 3/1/90) **[172]**

252 Mojtabai, A. G. *Blessed Assurance: At Home with the Bomb in Amarillo, Texas.* 1988, Univ. of New Mexico Pr. paper $10.95 (0-8263-1057-5). A look at the nuclear bomb assembly industry of Amarillo, Texas, and its effect on the attitudes of those who live and work there. (REV: BL 7/86; CSM 6/27/86; NYTBR 6/8/86)   **[172]**

253 Nye, Joseph S., Jr. *Nuclear Ethics.* 1986, Free Pr. $14.95 (0-02-922460-8); paper $8.95 (0-02-923091-8). A philosophical study of contemporary nuclear strategy. (REV: CSM 7/24/86; LJ 5/1/86; NYTBR 4/27/86)   **[172]**

174 Economic and professional ethics

254 Lyon, Jeff. *Playing God in the Nursery.* 1986, Norton paper $9.95 (0-393-30309-8). An examination

of the ethical treatment of the severely handicapped newborn. (REV: Choice 6/85; LJ 3/1/85; NYTBR 3/31/85)   **[174]**

255 Nelkin, Dorothy, and Laurence Tancredi. *Dangerous Dossiers: The Social Power of Biological Information.* 1989, Basic Books $18.95 (0-465-01573-5). The social implications of increasingly predictive health technologies, and how biological information can be used and abused by the state and businesses. "An important and provocative contribution to current thought."—Choice (REV: Choice 3/90; LJ 9/1/89)   **[174]**

256 Proctor, Robert. *Racial Hygiene: Medicine Under the Nazis.* 1988, Harvard Univ. Pr. $34.95 (0-674-74580-9). A study of medical practice and philosophy under the Third Reich. (REV: Choice 2/89; LJ 8/88; NYTBR 8/21/88)   **[174]**

257 Yolen, Edward. *Gene Business: Who Should Control Biotechnology?* 1986, Oxford Univ. Pr. paper $7.95 (0-19-504042-2). An examination of the social and ethical issues raised by recent breakthroughs in biotechnology. (REV: BL 5/15/84; Choice 9/84; NYTBR 7/15/84)   **[174]**

Medical professions

258 Macklin, Ruth. *Mortal Choices: Ethical Dilemmas in Modern Medicine.* 1988, Houghton $19.95 (0-317-58080-9); paper $12.95 (0-395-46847-7). A study of ethical problems brought about by recent developments in medical technology. (REV: Choice 12/87; LJ 5/15/87; NYTBR 8/2/87)   **[174.2]**

259 Suzuki, David, and Peter Knudtson. *Genethics: The Clash Between the New Genetics and Human Values.* 1989, Harvard Univ. Pr. $25.00 (0-674-34565-7); paper $12.95 (0-674-34566-5). An examination of potential ethical problems arising from the practice of genetic engineering. "This book deserves wide attention for its timely warning of problems now on the cultural horizon."—BL (REV: BL 1/1/89; LJ 1/89; TLS 12/15/89)   **[174.2]**

260 Tisdale, Sallie. *Sorcerer's Apprentice: Tales of a Modern Hospital.* 1986, McGraw-Hill $15.95 (0-07-064784-4); Henry Holt paper $9.95 (0-8050-0578-1). A nurse focuses on modern medical treatments and technologies in the areas of neonatal, kidney dialysis, and burn units, and the lack of human compassion these advances have caused in the modern hospital environment. (REV: BL 4/1/86; LJ 4/15/86; PW 3/14/86)   **[174.2]**

Trade, manufacture, finance (Business ethics)

261 Baida, Peter. *Poor Richard's Legacy: American Business Values from Benjamin Franklin to Donald Trump.* 1990, Morrow $22.95 (0-688-07729-3). Biographical essays examining the lives and values of American business leaders over four centuries. (REV: BL 7/90; LJ 5/15/90; NYTBR 7/8/90) **[174.4]**

176 Ethics of sex and reproduction

262 Bonnickson, Andrea. *In Vitro Fertilization: Building Policy from Laboratories to Legisla-*

tures. 1989, Columbia Univ. Pr. $27.50 (0-231-06904-9). An overview of the medical, legal, social, and ethical questions surrounding in-vitro fertilization. (REV: Choice 9/89; LJ 7/89)   **[176]**

179 Other ethical norms

263 Adams, Carol J. *Sexual Politics of Meat: A Feminist-Vegetarian Critical Theory.* 1990, Continuum $22.95 (0-8264-0455-3); paper $12.95 (0-8264-0513-4). A study of the historical and philosophical connections between vegetarianism and feminism. "A major contribution to the debate on animal rights."—PW (REV: Choice 2/91; LJ 1/90; PW 12/1/89)   **[179]**

264 Alvarez, A. *Savage God: A Study of Suicide.* 1990, Norton paper $8.95 (0-393-30657-7). Alvarez recounts his own suicide attempt, examines the suicide of his friend Sylvia Plath, and looks at the philosophy of suicide throughout history. "A moving, poetically intuitive and extremely personal study."—PW (REV: LJ 4/1/72; Newsweek 4/24/72; PW 2/14/72. AWARDS: ALA, 1972)   **[179]**

265 Fox, Michael Allen. *Case for Animal Experimentation: An Evolutionary and Ethical Perspective.* 1985, Univ. of California Pr. $27.50 (0-520-05501-2); paper $9.95 (0-520-06023-7). An ethical study in support of animal experimentation. (REV: Choice 6/86; LJ 5/15/86; NYTBR 3/30/86)   **[179]**

266 Fox, Michael W. *Inhumane Society: The American Way of Exploiting Animals.* 1990, St. Martin's $18.95 (0-312-04274-4). A veterinarian's view of current animal rights debate. (REV: BL 10/1/90; LJ 8/90; PW 7/27/90)   **[179]**

267 Francke, Linda Bird. *Ambivalence of Abortion.* 1978, Random $10.00 (0-394-41080-7). Based on interviews with members of both sexes, the author records the emotional and psychological effects of abortion on the family and individual. "A balanced, sensitive, valuable book."—PW (REV: BL 6/1/78; LJ 3/1/78; PW 1/23/78)   **[179]**

268 Fraser, Laura. *Animal Rights Handbook: Everyday Ways to Save Animal Lives.* 1990, Living Planet Pr. paper $4.95 (0-9626072-0-7). An overview of ways to alter life-style to help save or improve the lives of our animals. (REV: BL 10/1/90; LJ 10/15/90)   **[179]**

269 Malcolm, Andrew H. *Someday.* 1991, Knopf $22.00 (0-394-58782-0). The journalist examines euthanasia-related issues in light of his mother's terminal illness. (REV: BL 3/15/91; NYTBR 3/24/91; PW 1/25/91)   **[179]**

270 Nash, Roderick Frazier. *Rights of Nature: A History of Environmental Ethics.* 1989, Univ. of Wisconsin Pr. $27.50 (0-299-11840-1); paper $12.95 (0-299-11844-4). A history of the changing attitudes of man toward the environment chronicled by the author of *Wilderness and the American Mind.* (REV: Choice 7–8/89; LJ 12/88; PW 10/28/88)   **[179]**

271 Regan, Tom. *Case for Animal Rights.* 1983, Univ. of California Pr. $29.95 (0-520-04904-7); paper $11.95 (0-520-05460-1). A philosophical defense of the rights of animals in support of vegetarianism. "No sensible person should venture into the issue without consulting it."—LJ (REV: Choice 3/84; LJ 10/1/83)   **[179]**

272 Rolston, Holmes, III. *Environmental Ethics: Duties and Values to the Natural World.* 1987, Temple Univ. Pr. $39.95 (0-87722-501-X); paper $16.95 (0-87722-628-8). A philosophical work regarding ethical problems in man's relationship to other animals and the earth. (REV: Choice 6/88; CSM 8/16/88; LJ 2/15/88)   **[179]**

273 Wennberg, Robert. *Terminal Choices: Euthanasia, Suicide and the Right to Die.* 1990, Eerdmans paper $13.95 (0-8028-0454-3). A Presbyterian minister examines ethical issues regarding suicide and euthanasia. "A delight to read despite its somber themes."—LJ (REV: BL 9/15/89; LJ 11/15/89)   **[179]**

180 ANCIENT, MEDIEVAL, ORIENTAL PHILOSOPHY

183 Sophistic and Socratic philosophies

Socratic philosophy

274 Stone, I. F. *Trial of Socrates.* 1988, Little, Brown $18.95 (0-316-81758-9); Doubleday paper $9.95 (0-385-26032-6). The political journalist looks at the thought and personality of the Greek philosopher, and the issues behind his trial and fatal sentencing. (REV: BL 2/1/88; LJ 12/87; Time 1/25/88. AWARDS: LJ, 1988)   **[183.2]**

275 Vlastos, Gregory. *Socrates: Ironist and Moral Philosopher.* 1991, Cornell Univ. Pr. $57.50 (0-8014-2551-4); paper $16.95 (0-8014-9787-6). A study of the life and thought of the ancient Greek philosopher. "All libraries with a serious interest in Socrates and Plato should acquire this volume."—Choice (REV: Choice 11/91; LJ 4/1/91)   **[183.2]**

190 MODERN WESTERN PHILOSOPHY

276 Gay, Peter. *The Enlightenment: An Interpretation.* 1977, Norton paper $27.90 (0-393-00870-3). A history of the thought of the eighteenth century. "An absolute necessity for all persons interested in the field."—Choice (REV: Choice 10/67; NYTBR 1/1/67; Sat Rev 11/26/66. AWARDS: NBA, 1967)   **[190]**

Historic and geographical treatment

277 Hamlyn, D. W. *History of Western Philosophy.* 1989, Penguin paper $6.95 (0-14-022863-2). A survey of Western philosophy from ancient times to the twentieth century. "For its compactness, philosophical acumen, fairness and clarity of prose, this book will be a welcome, even necessary resource in all libraries."—Choice (REV: Choice 12/87; LJ 7/87; TLS 4/10/87)   **[190.9]**

191 United States and Canada

278 Capra, Fritjof. *Uncommon Wisdom: Conversations with Remarkable People.* **1989, Bantam paper $10.95 (0-553-34610-5).** Profiles of R. D. Laing, Werner Heisenberg, and Gregory Bateson are included in this collection of interviews with the author of *The Tao of Physics.* (REV: Choice 6/88; LJ 2/15/88; PW 12/4/87) **[191]**

279 Hook, Sidney. *Convictions.* **1990, Prometheus $24.95 (0-87975-473-7).** A posthumously published collection of essays by the American philosopher and political thinker. "One of the most intelligent and articulate defenders of democracy since Madison."—NYTBR (REV: LJ 7/90; New Rep 12/3/90; NYTBR 8/26/90) **[191]**

280 Hook, Sidney. *Out of Step: An Unquiet Life in the 20th Century.* **1988, Carroll & Graf paper $14.95 (0-88184-399-7).** An autobiography of the leftist political philosopher regarding the intellectual life of the twentieth century and personalities he has known including Russell, Sartre, and Einstein. (REV: Choice 7–8/87; CSM 4/23/87; LJ 2/15/87) **[191]**

281 Nozick, Robert. *Philosophical Explanations.* **1981, Harvard Univ. Pr. $33.00 (0-674-66448-5); paper $12.50 (0-674-66479-5).** "A strikingly original and imaginative attempt by a first-rate philosopher to deal with the classic problems of philosophy in a new way and by so doing to make philosophy once again more relevant to the concerns of laymen."—NYTBR (REV: Choice 1/82; LJ 11/1/81; NYTBR 9/20/81. AWARDS: NYTBR, 1981) **[191]**

192 British Isles

282 Berlin, Isaiah. *Crooked Timber of Humanity: Chapters in the History of Ideas.* **1991, Knopf $22.00 (0-679-40131-8).** Essays collected over three decades from the pen of the British political philosopher. (REV: BL 3/1/91; NYTBR 3/24/91; PW 1/25/91) **[192]**

283 Clark, Ronald W. *Life of Bertrand Russell.* **1990, DaCapo $17.95 (0-306-80397-6).** A biography of the mathematician, author, and philosopher. "There were many Bertrand Russells and Clark, writing with an easy simplicity occasionally heightened by wit, does justice to all of them."—PW (REV: Choice 9/76; LJ 11/1/75; PW 11/24/75) **[192]**

284 Russell, Bertrand. *Autobiography of Bertrand Russell.* **1967, Unwin Hyman $29.95 (0-04-921003-3); paper $16.95 (0-04-921022-X).** An autobiography of the English philosopher and mathematician. (REV: NYRB 4/20/67; NYTBR 4/16/67; Newsweek 4/17/67. AWARDS: ALA, 1967; NYTBR, 1967) **[192]**

193 Germany and Austria

285 Monk, Ray. *Ludwig Wittgenstein: The Duty of Genius.* **1990, Free Pr. $29.95 (0-02-9216670-2).** A study of the life and writings of the twentieth-century Austrian philosopher. "I loved this book . . . it reveals the work in the man and the man in the work."—CSM (REV: CSM 12/12/90; LJ 10/15/90; NYTBR 12/30/90) **[193]**

286 Nehamas, Alexander. *Nietzsche: Life as Literature.* **1985, Harvard Univ. Pr. $22.50 (0-674-62435-1); paper $9.95 (0-674-62426-2).** A study of the life and thought of German philosopher Friedrich Nietzche. (REV: Choice 2/86; LJ 12/85; NYTBR 1/15/86) **[193]**

287 Safranski, Rudiger. *Schopenhauer and the Wild Years of Philosophy.* **1990, Harvard Univ. Pr. $30.00 (0-674-79275-0).** A biography of the nineteenth-century German philosopher and author of *The World As Will and Representation.* "The most complete and detailed account."—Choice (REV: Choice 10/90; LJ 3/15/90) **[193]**

194 France

288 Coles, Robert. *Simone Weil: A Modern Pilgrimage.* **1987, Addison Wesley $17.95 (0-201-02205-2).** A biography of the French philosopher. (REV: Choice 11/87; NYTBR 9/6/87; PW 5/15/87) **[194]**

289 Wilson, Arthur M. *Diderot.* **1972, Oxford Univ. Pr. $45.00 (0-19-501506-1).** "*Diderot* is worthy of the man."—New Rep (REV: LJ 8/72; New Rep 9/30/72; New Yorker 7/29/72. AWARDS: NBA, 1973) **[194]**

200 RELIGION

290 Coles, Robert. *Harvard Diary: Reflections on the Sacred and the Secular.* 1988, Crossroad $16.95 (0-8245-0885-8); paper $10.95 (0-8245-1034-8). Selected essays by the Harvard child psychiatrist and author. (Rev: BL 9/1/88; LJ 9/15/88; PW 7/15/88) **[200]**

291 Young, Dudley. *Origins of the Sacred: The Ecstasies of Love and War.* 1991, St. Martin's $24.95 (0-312-06432-2). An English professor examines the connections between love, war, and religion from prehistoric times to the present. (Rev: BL 10/15/91; PW 8/30/91) **[200]**

United States

292 Ahlstrom, Sydney E. *Religious History of the American People.* 1972, Yale Univ. Pr. $60.00 (0-300-01475-9); paper $24.95 (0-300-01762-6). Survey of the roots and history of religion as practiced in the United States. "No single work has incorporated such a broad analysis of the nation's religious history . . . a *must*."—Choice (Rev: Choice 5/73; LJ 11/1/72; NYTBR 10/29/72) **[200.973]**

293 Berman, Phillip L. *Search for Meaning: Americans Talk about What They Believe and Why.* 1990, Ballantine $19.95 (0-345-33171-0). Results of the author's survey of Americans regarding their religious and spiritual beliefs and their reasons for them. (Rev: BL 8/90; LJ 9/1/90) **[200.973]**

210 NATURAL THEOLOGY

211 Concepts of God

Atheism

294 Turner, James. *Without God, Without Creed: The Origins of Unbelief in America.* 1986, Johns Hopkins paper $14.95 (0-8018-3407-4). An analysis of the rise and development of agnosticism and atheism in the United States. "Will surely be a standard reference in the study of the history of ideas."—BL (Rev: BL 5/1/85; Choice 7–8/85; LJ 4/15/85) **[211.8]**

220 BIBLE

Interpretation and criticism

295 Alter, Robert, and Frank Kermode, eds. *Literary Guide to the Bible.* 1987, Harvard Univ. Pr. $29.95 (0-674-87530-3); Belknap Pr. paper $14.95 (0-674-87531-1). A series of essays studying the Bible as literature. (Rev: BL 9/15/87; CSM 10/21/87; NYTBR 12/20/87) **[220.6]**

296 Frye, Northrop. *Great Code: The Bible and Literature.* 1983, Harcourt paper $8.95 (0-15-636480-8). A study of the Bible as literature by the critic noted for his work on Shakespeare. (Rev: LJ 6/1/82; New Rep 6/9/82; New Yorker 5/31/82) **[220.6]**

297 Frye, Northrop. *Words With Power: Being a Second Study of "The Bible and Literature."* 1990, Harcourt $24.95 (0-15-198462-X). An interpretative look at biblical themes and influences in modern Western literature. (Rev: BL 10/15/90; LJ 11/15/90; PW 10/5/90) **[220.6]**

298 Greeley, Andrew M., and Jacob Neusner. *Bible and Us: A Priest and a Rabbi Read Scripture Together.* 1990, Warner $24.95 (0-446-51522-1). Discussions of the Bible from Jewish and Christian perspectives as seen by a priest and a rabbi. (Rev: BL 8/90; NYTBR 9/2/90; Newsweek 7/30/90) **[220.6]**

221 Old Testament

Interpretation and criticism

299 Friedman, Richard Elliott. *Who Wrote the Bible?* 1987, Summit $18.95 (0-671-63161-6); Harper & Row paper $8.95 (0-06-097214-9). A study of the origins of the first five books of the Bible. (Rev: LJ 6/15/87; NYTBR 8/9/87) **[221.6]**

300 Rosenberg, David, ed. *Congregation: Contemporary Writers Read the Jewish Bible.* 1987, Harcourt $29.95 (0-15-146350-6); paper $14.95 (0-15-622040-7). A collection of essays regarding the Jewish Bible by such authors as Cynthia Ozick, Elie Wiesel, and I. B. Singer. (Rev: NYTBR 12/20/87; Newsweek 1/18/88; TLS 6/17/88) **[221.6]**

222   Historical books of Old Testament

301 **Bloom, Harold.** *Book of J.* 1990, Grove-Weidenfeld $19.95 (0-8021-1050-9). A study of the identity of the author of the first five books of the Bible. "Prolific and gifted though he [Bloom] has always been, this is his best book."—Frank Kermode, NYTBR (Rev: BL 1/15/91; LJ 10/15/90; NYTBR 9/23/90. Awards: BL, 1990)   **[222]**

302 **Walzer, Michael.** *Exodus and Revolution.* 1986, Basic Books paper $9.95 (0-465-02163-8). Walzer cites the biblical story of Exodus as an inspiration for revolutions and popular movements throughout history. "This book captures Walzer at his formidable best: learned, humane, lively."—Newsweek (Rev: LJ 4/15/85; NYTBR 1/20/85; Newsweek 4/15/85. Awards: LJ, 1985)   **[222]**

230   CHRISTIAN THEOLOGY

Persons

303 **Fox, Richard Wightman.** *Reinhold Niebuhr: A Biography.* 1985, Pantheon $19.95 (0-394-51659-1). A biography of the American theologian. "Definitive . . . sympathetic yet critical."—BL (Rev: BL 1/1/86; CSM 4/4/86; New Rep 3/31/86)   **[230.092]**

304 **Tillich, Paul.** *Future of Religions.* 1976, Greenwood Pr. $35.00 (0-8371-8861-X). Essays by and about the theologian collected in a posthumous tribute. "Exceedingly relevant to an understanding of religion today."—Choice (Rev: BL 7/15/66; Choice 11/66; LJ 5/15/66. Awards: ALA, 1966)   **[230.092]**

231   God

Relation to the world

305 **Strahler, Arthur Newell.** *Science and Earth History: The Evolution-Creation Controversy.* 1988, Prometheus $39.95 (0-87975-414-1). An analysis of the ongoing debate between evolutionists and creationists regarding the theories of evolution and creation and public school education. (Rev: Choice 4/88; LJ 12/87)   **[231.7]**

232   Jesus Christ and his family

306 **Mitchell, Stephen.** *Gospel According to Jesus: A New Translation and Guide to His Essential Teachings for Believers and Unbelievers.* 1991, HarperCollins $21.95 (0-06-016641-X). A study of the teachings of Jesus including comparisons of his philosophy with other major religions. (Rev: BL 11/15/91; LJ 10/1/91)   **[232]**

Family and life of Jesus

307 **Dimont, Max I.** *Appointment in Jerusalem: A Search for the Historical Jesus.* 1991, St. Martin's $17.95 (0-312-06291-5). A portrait of the life and times of Jesus by the author of *Jesus, God, and History.* (Rev: BL 11/15/91; LJ 9/15/91)   **[232.9]**

308 **Pelikan, Jaroslav.** *Jesus through the Centuries: His Place in the History of Culture.* 1987, Harper & Row paper $9.95 (0-06-097080-4). A history of the portrayals and depictions of Jesus Christ from the first to the twentieth centuries. (Rev: Choice 2/86; CSM 10/16/85; LJ 10/1/85)   **[232.9]**

309 **Zimdars-Swartz, Sandra L.** *Encountering Mary: From La Salette to Medjugorje.* 1991, Princeton Univ. Pr. $24.95 (0-691-07371-6). A University of Kansas professor analyzes the history of seven Marian sightings during the nineteenth and twentieth centuries. (Rev: BL 9/1/91; NYTBR 8/11/91) **[232.9]**

235   Spiritual beings

Beatification and canonization

310 **Woodward, Kenneth.** *Making Saints: How the Catholic Church Determines Who Becomes a Saint, Who Doesn't, and Why.* 1990, Simon & Schuster $24.95 (0-671-64246-4). A study of the process of canonization within the Roman Catholic church. "Easily the most comprehensive, critical and up-to-date look at saint making so far written."—Peter Hebblethwaite, NYTBR (Rev: BL 10/15/90; LJ 11/15/90; NYTBR 11/4/90)   **[235.24]**

240   CHRISTIAN MORAL AND DEVOTIONAL THEOLOGY

241   Moral theology

Specific moral issues

311 **Pagels, Elaine.** *Adam, Eve and the Serpent.* 1988, Random $17.95 (0-394-52140-4); paper $8.95 (0-679-72232-7). A historical analysis of Christian sexual attitudes as reflected in the Book of Genesis and the first four centuries after Christ. "An important contribution to religion, politics and women's studies collections."—BL (Rev: BL 6/1/88; CSM 9/14/88; NYTBR 8/21/88. Awards: ALA, 1988; BL, the 1980s)   **[241.66]**

312 **Ranke-Heinemann, Uta.** *Eunuchs for the Kingdom of Heaven: Women, Sexuality and the Catholic Church.* 1991, Doubleday $19.95 (0-385-26527-1). A study of the contemporary Roman Catholic view of women and sexuality as written by a German scholar and ousted theologian. (Rev: BL 11/15/90; LJ 12/90; PW 10/19/90)   **[241.66]**

242   Devotional literature

313 **Dillard, Annie.** *Holy the Farm.* 1988, Harper & Row paper $7.95 (0-06-091543-9). The author of *Pilgrim at Tinker Creek* presents a meditation on the nature of God. "A movingly beautiful book."—PW (Rev: LJ 11/1/77; NYTBR 9/25/77; PW 8/1/77)   **[242]**

314 **Wangerin, Walter, Jr.** *Manger Is Empty: Stories in Time.* 1989, Harper & Row $14.95 (0-06-069269-3). A collection of inspirational stories on the theme of the birth of Christ by the author of *Miz Lil and the Chronicles of Grace.* (Rev: BL 12/15/89; LJ 11/1/89)   **[242]**

248 Christian experience, practice, life

315 Vanauken, Sheldon. *A Severe Mercy: C.S. Lewis and a Pagan Love Invaded by Christ, Told by One of the Lovers.* 1980, Harper & Row $14.45 (0-06-060882-X); paper $6.95 (0-06-068824-6). A story of a married couple, and their conversion to Christianity. (Rev: LJ 2/15/78; Natl Rev 8/4/78. Awards: NBA, 1980)   **[248]**

Religious experience

316 Gilman, Richard. *Faith, Sex, Mystery: A Memoir.* 1988, Penguin paper $7.95 (0-14-010587-8). An account of the author's conversion from Judaism to Roman Catholicism and how he left the church eight years later. (Rev: LJ 5/1/87; NYTBR 1/18/87)   **[248.2]**

Christian life and practice

317 McNeill, Donald P. *Compassion: A Reflection on the Christian Life.* 1983, Doubleday paper $6.95 (0-385-18957-5). A reflection on the meaning and practice of compassion in living a Christian life. "May become a classic of our time."—BL (Rev: BL 2/15/82; LJ 1/15/82)   **[248.4]**

250 CHRISTIAN ORDERS AND LOCAL CHURCH

255 Religious congregations and orders

Trappists

318 Bianco, Frank. *Voices of Silence: Lives of the Trappists Today.* 1991, Paragon House $18.95 (1-55778-305-5). The author recounts his experiences with Trappist monks at French and American abbeys. "Seekers of all faiths will be intrigued by and gain respect for the contemplative life as portrayed in these pages."—PW (Rev: LJ 5/15/91; PW; 4/26/91)   **[255.12]**

Jesuits (Society of Jesus)

319 Barthel, Manfred. *Jesuits: Legend and Truth of the Society of Jesus—Yesterday, Today, Tomorrow.* 1987, Morrow paper $8.70 (0-688-06970-3). A history of the Roman Catholic order founded by St. Ignatius Loyola. (Rev: BL 5/15/84; NYTBR 7/22/84; PW 5/4/84)   **[255.53]**

Congregations and orders of women

320 Curb, Rosemary, and Nancy Manahan, eds. *Lesbian Nuns: Breaking Silence.* 1985, Naiad Pr. $16.95 (0-930044-63-0); paper $9.95 (0-930044-62-2). An examination of the lives and attitudes of 50 lesbian nuns as told in their own words. (Rev: BL 5/15/85; LJ 6/1/85; PW 4/5/85)   **[255.9]**

260 CHRISTIAN SOCIAL THEOLOGY

261 Social theology

321 Wood, Forrest G. *Arrogance of Faith: Christianity and Race in America from the Colonial Era to the Twentieth Century.* 1990, Knopf $29.95 (0-394-57993-3). A study of the influence of Christianity upon the shaping of American attitudes toward race and racism. (Rev: LJ 3/15/90; PW 3/16/90)   **[261]**

Christianity and secular disciplines

322 Davies, Paul. *God and the New Physics.* 1984, Simon & Schuster paper $9.95 (0-671-52806-8). The impact of recent discoveries in theoretical physics on issues of religion and metaphysics. "Highly recommended to anyone who has ever pondered over the meaning of existence."—LJ (Rev: Choice 1/84; LJ 11/15/83; NYTBR 11/20/83)   **[261.5]**

323 Redondi, Pietro. *Galileo: Heretic.* 1990, Princeton Univ. Pr. $35.00 (0-691-08451-3); paper $9.95 (0-691-02426-X). An investigation into the events leading up to the heresy trial of the seventeenth-century Italian scientist. "No one interested in the origins of modern science or the history of the Catholic Church can ignore this volume."—BL (Rev: BL 9/15/87; NYRB 10/8/87; NYTBR 11/15/87)   **[261.5]**

Christianity and political affairs

324 Lernoux, Peggy. *People of God: The Struggle for World Catholicism.* 1989, Viking $19.95 (0-670-81529-2); Penguin paper $9.95 (0-14-009816-X). A study of the internal and external problems facing the contemporary Roman Catholic church. (Rev: BL 2/1/89; LJ 4/1/89; PW 2/17/89)   **[261.7]**

325 Silk, Mark. *Spiritual Politics: Religion and America Since World War II.* 1989, Simon & Schuster paper $8.95 (0-671-67563-X). An appraisal of trends and developments in religion in America since 1945. (Rev: BL 4/1/88; NYTBR 4/3/88; PW 3/4/88)   **[261.7]**

Christianity and socioeconomic problems

326 Lernoux, Peggy. *Cry of the People: The Struggle for Human Rights in Latin America; the Catholic Church in Conflict with U.S. Policy.* 1982, Penguin paper $9.95 (0-14-006047-2). An examination of the conflicts between policies of the Roman Catholic church and the United States-supported governments in Latin America. (Rev: BL 7/15/80; LJ 5/1/80; NYTBR 7/27/80)   **[261.8]**

262 Ecclesiology

327 Reese, Thomas J. *Archbishop: Inside the Power of the American Catholic Church.* 1989, Harper & Row $17.95 (0-06-066836-9). A Jesuit priest's introduction to the political structure of the Roman Catholic church in the United States. (Rev: LJ 6/15/89; NYTBR 5/28/89)   **[262]**

Popes and patriarchs

328 De Rosa, Peter. *Vicars of Christ: The Dark Side of the Papacy.* 1988, Crown $18.95 (0-517-57027-0). A survey history of the papacy focusing on its negative aspects and the current ethical dilemmas facing the Roman Catholic church. (Rev: BL 1/1/89; LJ 11/15/88)   **[262.13]**

Local clergy

329 Rice, David. *Shattered Vows: Priests Who Leave.* 1990, Morrow $18.45 (0-688-07805-2). A former priest analyzes the reasons behind the continuing exodus from the Roman Catholic clergy. (REV: BL 11/15/90; LJ 11/11/90; PW 10/5/90) **[262.14]**

266 Missions

330 Lewis, Norman. *Missionaries: God Against the Indians.* 1990, Penguin paper $8.95 (0-14-013175-2). A critical examination of the deeds and influence of missionaries upon the native peoples of South America and the Pacific. (REV: LJ 10/15/88; NYTBR 12/25/88; TLS 7/1/88) **[266]**

331 Pettifer, Julian, and Richard Bradley. *Missionaries.* 1991, Parkwest $33.95 (0-563-20702-7). An overview of the history and present state of missionary activities, written as a companion to the PBS television series. (REV: BL 10/1/91; LJ 9/15/91) **[266]**

332 Service, Grace. *Golden Inches: The China Memoir of Grace Service.* Ed. by John S. Service. 1989, Univ. of California Pr. $19.95 (0-520-06656-1). Memoirs of an American missionary in China from 1905 to 1935 edited for publication by the author's eldest son. (REV: BL 9/15/89; LJ 9/15/89; NYTBR 11/5/89) **[266]**

Jesuits (Society of Jesus)

333 Spence, Jonathan. *Memory Palace of Matteo Ricci.* 1984, Viking $19.95 (0-670-46830-4); Penguin paper $8.95 (0-14-008098-8). Biography of Matteo Ricci, the first Jesuit missionary in China. "An illuminating journey through an intriguing mind and a fascinating era."—BL (REV: Choice 6/85; New Rep 6/10/85; NYTBR 11/24/84. AWARDS: ALA, 1984; LJ, 1984; NYTBR, 1984) **[266.2]**

267 Associations for religious work

334 Coles, Robert. *Dorothy Day: A Radical Devotion.* 1987, Addison Wesley $17.95 (0-201-02829-8). A biography of the American Catholic writer and social activist. (REV: BL 6/1/87; Choice 11/87; NYTBR 9/6/87) **[267]**

335 Miller, William D. *Dorothy Day: A Biography.* 1984, Harper & Row paper $10.95 (0-06-065749-9). A biography examining the public and private life of the founder of the Catholic worker movement. (REV: BL 6/1/82; LJ 7/82; NYTBR 6/13/82) **[267]**

269 Spiritual renewal

336 Balmer, Randall H. *Mine Eyes Have Seen the Glory: A Journey into the Evangelical Subculture in America.* 1990, Oxford Univ. Pr. paper $8.95 (0-19-506653-7). An examination of the history, theology, and present state of evangelical religions in the United States. (REV: Choice 12/89; LJ 7/89; PW 5/26/89) **[269]**

337 Sims, Patsy. *Can Somebody Shout Amen? Inside the Tents and Tabernacles of American Revivalists.* 1988, St. Martin's $15.95 (0-312-01397-3). A study of American revivalist religion and evangelism as practiced in the Deep South. (REV: BL 5/1/88; LJ 5/15/88; NYTBR 8/14/88) **[269]**

270 CHRISTIAN CHURCH HISTORY

338 McManners, John, ed. *Oxford Illustrated History of Christianity.* 1990, Oxford Univ. Pr. $39.95 (0-19-822928-3). An illustrated international history of the spread and development of Christianity from the times of Jesus to the twentieth century. (REV: BL 9/15/90; LJ 9/1/90; PW 9/14/90) **[270]**

Apostolic period to 325

339 Lane Fox, Robin. *Pagans and Christians.* 1987, Knopf $45.00 (0-394-55495-7); Harper & Row paper $16.95 (0-06-062852-9). An account of the rise of Christianity and its relationship to paganism from the time of Christ to the rise of Constantine. (REV: BL 12/15/86; NYTBR 2/1/87; TLS 2/20/87) **[270.1]**

340 Wilken, Robert L. *Christians as the Romans Saw Them.* 1984, Yale Univ. Pr. $24.00 (0-300-03066-5); paper $10.95 (0-300-03637-2). Accounts of the early Christians taken from Roman writings. "A very readable synthesis of current scholarship."—LJ (REV: Atl 3/84; LJ 2/15/84; NYTBR 2/26/84) **[270.1]**

Period of Reformation and Counter-Reformation, 1517–1648

341 Spitz, Lewis W. *Protestant Reformation: 1517 to 1559; the Rise of Modern Europe.* 1986, Harper & Row paper $9.95 (0-06-132069-2). A study of the history and significance of the sixteenth-century Protestant Reformation. (REV: BL 5/1/84; Choice 6/85; NYTBR 2/24/85) **[270.6]**

271 Religious orders in church history

342 Mott, Michael. *Seven Mountains of Thomas Merton.* 1986, Houghton paper $12.95 (0-395-40451-7). A biography of the French-born Catholic convert, writer, and Trappist monk. "Mott's life is the most complete to date . . . an indispensable work."—Choice (REV: BL 1/1/85; Choice 4/85; LJ 12/84) **[271]**

343 Pennington, M. Basil. *Thomas Merton, Brother Monk: The Search for True Freedom.* 1987, Harper & Row $15.95 (0-06-066497-5); paper $8.95 (0-06-066504-1). A biography of the Catholic convert who became a Trappist monk and authored *The Seven Storey Mountain.* "This profound and revealing study may be the best book so far on the real Merton."—LJ (REV: BL 8/87; LJ 7/87; PW 7/10/87) **[271]**

Franciscans (Gray Friars)

344 Green, Julien. *God's Fool: The Life of Francis of Assisi.* 1985, Harper & Row $16.45 (0-06-063462-6); paper $7.95 (0-06-063464-2). An interpretation of the life of St. Francis of Assisi by the French

novelist. (Rᴇᴠ: BL 9/1/85; LJ 9/15/85; NYTBR 9/29/85)
[271.3]

Other Roman Catholic orders of women

345 **Ferraro, Barbara, and Patricia Hussey.** *No Turning Back: Two Nuns' Battle with the Vatican Over Women's Right to Choose.* **1990, Poseidon $19.95 (0-671-64406-8).** Personal accounts by two nuns who publicly asked the Roman Catholic church to reconsider its stand on abortion. (Rᴇᴠ: BL 10/1/90; LJ 10/1/90; NYTBR 9/23/90)
[271.97]

273   Heresies in Church history

346 **Pagels, Elaine.** *Gnostic Gospels.* **1979, Random $14.95 (0-394-50278-7); paper $5.95 (0-394-74043-2).** A look at Gnostic texts predating the New Testament, which were rediscovered in this century. (Rᴇᴠ: Atl 2/80; CSM 12/3/79; NYTBR 1/20/80. Aᴡᴀʀᴅs: NBA, 1980)
[273]

277   Christian Church in North America

347 **Bryan, Michael.** *Chapter and Verse: A Skeptic Revisits Christianity.* **1991, Random $20.00 (0-394-57509-1).** An agnostic journalist recounts his experiences attending an evangelical Texas bible college. (Rᴇᴠ: BL 5/15/91; LJ 6/1/91; PW 5/3/91)
[277. 3]

United States

348 **Lincoln, C. Eric, and Lawrence H. Mamiya.** *Black Church in the African-American Experience.* **1990, Duke Univ. Pr. $47.50 (0-8223-1097-0); paper $18.95 (0-8223-1073-2).** A study of the historical and present-day role of religion and the church in the lives of African Americans. (Rᴇᴠ: BL 1/15/91; LJ 1/91; NYTBR 12/23/90)
[277.3]

349 **Marty, Martin E.** *Pilgrims in Their Own Land: Five Hundred Years of Religion in America.* **1984, Little, Brown $25.00 (0-316-54867-7); Penguin paper $9.95 (0-14-008268-9).** A social history of religion in the United States focusing on many of the prominent individuals. "The most engaging one-volume history of American religion."—NYTBR (Rᴇᴠ: Choice 10/84; LJ 5/15/84; NYTBR 6/17/84. Aᴡᴀʀᴅs: LJ, 1984)
[277.3]

350 **Ruthven, Malise.** *Divine Supermarket: Travels in Search of the Soul of America.* **1990, Morrow $18.95 (0-87795-955-2).** An analysis of American religions and religious practices by a British journalist. (Rᴇᴠ: LJ 2/1/90; TLS 10/6/89)
[277.3]

280   CHRISTIAN DENOMINATIONS AND SECTS

282   Roman Catholic Church

351 **Spence, Jonathan.** *Question of Hu.* **1988, Knopf $18.95 (0-394-57190-8); Random paper $8.95 (0-679-72580-6).** A portrait of the life and times of John Hu, a Chinese convert to Roman Catholicism who was confined to an asylum following strange behavior during his voyage from China to France

in 1722. (Rᴇᴠ: BL 10/1/88; NYTBR 12/18/88; New Yorker 4/3/89)
[282]

Persons

352 **Berrigan, Daniel.** *To Dwell in Peace.* **1988, Harper & Row $19.95 (0-06-250057-0).** An autobiography of the Jesuit priest best known for his anti-Vietnam War activities and social welfare causes. (Rᴇᴠ: LJ 1/88; PW 11/20/87. Aᴡᴀʀᴅs: PW, 1987) **[282.092]**

353 **Glynn, Paul.** *Song for Nagasaki.* **1990, Eerdmans paper $11.95 (0-8028-0476-4).** A biography of a Japanese Christian activist who was living in Nagasaki when the atomic bomb was dropped. (Rᴇᴠ: BL 6/15/90; LJ 7/90)
[282.092]

354 **Hebblethwaite, Peter.** *Pope John XXIII: Shepherd of the Modern World.* **1987, Doubleday paper $10.95 (0-385-25337-2).** A biography of the pope who called Vatican Council II, which led to a restructuring and reassessment of the modern Roman Catholic church. (Rᴇᴠ: BL 6/15/85; Choice 9/85; NYTBR 3/24/85)
[282.092]

355 **Horgan, Paul.** *Lamy of Santa Fe: His Life and Times.* **1975, Farrar paper $12.95 (0-374-51588-3).** A biography of the French Roman Catholic missionary who was the basis for Willa Cather's *Death Comes for the Archbishop.* "A major addition to the history of the Southwest."—LJ (Rᴇᴠ: Atl 10/75; LJ 2/15/76; Time 11/10/75. Aᴡᴀʀᴅs: ALA, 1975; PP:History, 1976)
[282.092]

356 **Occhiogrosso, Peter.** *Once a Catholic: Prominent Catholics and Ex-Catholics Discuss the Church's Influence on Their Lives and Work.* **1987, Houghton $18.95 (0-395-42111-X); Ballantine paper $4.95 (0-345-35670-5).** Collected interviews with practicing and non-practicing Catholics regarding their feelings about the church and its teachings. (Rᴇᴠ: Choice 1/88; LJ 10/15/87; NYTBR 10/11/87)
[282.092]

United States

357 **Cateura, Linda Brandi.** *Catholics U.S.A.: Makers of a Modern Church.* **1989, Morrow $19.95 (0-688-07911-3).** Portraits of the lives and careers of 24 influential American Catholics. (Rᴇᴠ: LJ 11/1/89; PW 9/29/89)
[282.73]

358 **Dolan, Jay P.** *American Catholic Experience: A History from Colonial Times to the Present.* **1987, Doubleday paper $12.95 (0-385-15207-8).** A history of Roman Catholicism in the United States from the colonial era to the 1980s. (Rᴇᴠ: BL 12/1/85; Choice 3/86; LJ 10/15/85)
[282.73]

359 **Greeley, Andrew M.** *Catholic Myth.* **1990, Macmillan $21.95 (0-684-19184-9).** A portrait of the lives and beliefs of Roman Catholics in the United States today. (Rᴇᴠ: BL 3/15/90; LJ 2/15/90; PW 1/5/90)
[282.73]

360 **Hennessey, James J.** *American Catholics: A History of the Roman Catholic Community in the United States.* **1981, Oxford Univ. Pr. $29.95 (0-19-502946-1); paper $12.95 (0-19-503268-3).** A history of

Roman Catholicism in America and its relationship with the Papacy. (REV: BL 11/1/81; NYTBR 11/29/81; PW 12/4/81)   **[282.73]**

284   Protestants of Continental origin

Calvinistic and Reformed churches of European origin

361   **Bouwsma, William J. *John Calvin: A 16th-Century Portrait*. 1987, Oxford Univ. Pr. $24.95 (0-19-504394-4); paper $9.95 (0-19-505951-4).** A portrait of the life, thought, and influence of the sixteenth-century Reformation theologian. (REV: CSM 1/6/88; LJ 10/1/87; NYTBR 1/10/88)   **[284.2]**

285   Presbyterian, Reformed, Congregational

Presbyterian churches of United States origin

362   **Buechner, Frederick. *Now and Then*. 1983, Harper & Row $13.95 (0-06-061161-8).** A second volume of memoirs by the Presbyterian minister and novelist. (REV: BL 1/15/83; LJ 2/1/83; PW 11/19/82)   **[285.1]**

363   **Buechner, Frederick. *Sacred Journey*. 1982, Harper & Row $13.95 (0-06-061158-8).** Memoirs of the Presbyterian minister and novelist describing his personal spiritual growth. "A treasure for all library collections."—BL (REV: BL 6/15/82; LJ 3/15/82; NYTBR 4/11/82)   **[285.1]**

Congregationalism

364   **Silverman, Kenneth. *The Life and Times of Cotton Mather*. 1985, Columbia Univ. Pr. paper $20.00 (0-231-06125-0).** A portrait of the colonial American clergyman. (REV: BL 1/1/84; LJ 1/84; PW 1/27/84. AWARDS: PP:Biography, 1985)   **[285.8]**

289   Other denominations and sects

Latter-Day Saints (Mormons)

365   **Arrington, Leonard J. *Brigham Young: American Moses*. 1985, Knopf $24.95 (0-394-51022-4); Univ. of Illinois Pr. paper $14.95 (0-252-01296-8).** The life of the man who led the Mormons from Illinois to establish their church in Utah. "Likely to become one of the definitive works on the Mormon Church."—BL (REV: BL 4/15/85; LJ 3/15/85; NYTBR 4/15/85)   **[289.3]**

366   **Bushman, Richard L. *Joseph Smith and the Beginnings of Mormonism*. 1984, Univ. of Illinois Pr. $17.95 (0-252-01143-0); paper $8.95 (0-252-06012-1).** A study of the origins of the Mormon church and of its founder, Joseph Smith. (REV: Choice 7–8/85; LJ 10/15/84; NYTBR 7/21/85)   **[289.3]**

367   **Shipps, Jan. *Mormonism: The Story of a New Religious Tradition*. 1987, Univ. of Illinois Pr. paper $9.95 (0-252-01417-0).** The history of the origin and development of the Church of Jesus Christ of Latter-Day Saints. "Superbly researched and well written . . . a landmark study."—LJ (REV: Choice 10/85; LJ 3/1/85; NYTBR 7/21/85)   **[289.3]**

Mennonite churches

368   **Hostetler, John A. *Hutterite Society*. 1974, Johns Hopkins $45.00 (0-8018-1584-3).** The history, culture, and social structure of the Hutterites, a Mennonite sect of the United States and Canada. "A most welcome, essential, and readable addition to the fields of history, anthropology and sociology . . . a definitive work."—Choice (REV: BL 12/15/74; Choice 6/75; LJ 4/1/75)   **[289.7]**

290   OTHER AND COMPARATIVE RELIGIONS

291   Comparative religion

369   **Marty, Martin E. *Modern American Religion, Vol. 1: The Irony of It All, 1893–1919*. 1986, Univ. of Chicago Pr. $24.95 (0-226-50893-5).** The first of four volumes analyzing changing patterns in twentieth-century American religion. (REV: BL 10/15/86; Choice 4/87; LJ 10/15/86)   **[291]**

370   **Munro, Eleanor. *On Glory Roads: A Pilgrim's Book about Pilgrimages*. 1988, Thames & Hudson paper $10.95 (0-500-27500-9).** An examination of the tradition of pilgrimages as practiced in the world's great religions based on the author's travels to holy sites in India, Israel, Spain, and Indonesia. (REV: BL 4/15/87; CSM 8/26/87; LJ 5/15/87)   **[291]**

Miscellany

371   **Andrews, Lynn V. *Woman of Wyrrd: The Arousal of the Inner Fire*. 1990, HarperCollins $17.95 (0-06-250066-X); paper $9.95 (0-06-097410-9).** The author discusses her past life as a young woman in medieval England and the teachings of an older friend from that era. (REV: BL 9/1/90; LJ 9/15/90; PW 9/14/90)   **[291.02]**

372   **Eliade, Mircea. *Journey East, Journey West, 1907–1937: Autobiography, Vol. 1*. 1990, Univ. of Chicago Pr. paper $15.95 (0-226-20407-3).** The first volume of the autobiography of the Rumanian writer known for his contributions to the study of religion and myth. (REV: NYTBR 11/22/81; Time 10/26/81; TLS 4/2/82)   **[291.02]**

Historical treatment

373   **Campbell, Joseph. *Way of the Animal Powers*. 1988, Harper & Row paper $49.90 (0-06-096348-4).** A two-volume analysis of myths regarding animals from prehistoric times to the present. (REV: LJ 1/84; Natl Rev 7/13/84; NYTBR 12/18/83)   **[291.09]**

374   **Gimbutas, Marija. *Language of the Goddess: Unearthing the Hidden Symbols of Western Civilization*. 1989, Harper & Row $49.95 (0-06-250356-1).** The author presents her theories regarding the existence of a European neolithic goddess religion that allegedly flourished four thousand years before Christ. "This will surely be a classic in its field."—BL (REV: BL 10/1/89; LJ 12/89)   **[291.09]**

United States

375 Goldman, Ari. *Search for God at Harvard.* **1991, Times Books $20.00 (0-8129-1653-0).** An account of the author's year studying comparative religion at Harvard Divinity School. (REV: BL 3/15/91; LJ 4/1/91; PW 3/8/91. AWARDS: LJ, 1991)   **[291.0973]**

376 Jorstad, Erling. *Holding Fast/Pressing On: Religion in America in the 1980's.* **1990, Greenwood Pr. $45.00 (0-313-26599-2); paper $14.95 (0-275-93607-4).** A survey of American religious trends and developments of the 1980s. (REV: Choice 2/91; LJ 8/90)   **[291.0973]**

Mythology and mythological foundations

377 Campbell, Joseph. *Hero's Journey: Joseph Campbell on His Life and Work.* **Ed. by Phil Cousineau. 1990, Harper & Row $24.95 (0-06-250102-X).** A biography of the twentieth-century mythologist and author of *The Masks of God* and *Myths, Dreams, and Religion* compiled from his writings. (REV: Choice 10/90; LJ 5/15/90; PW 4/13/90)   **[291.13]**

378 Larsen, Stephen, and Robin Larsen. *A Fire in the Mind: The Life of Joseph Campbell.* **1991, Doubleday $25.00 (0-385-26635-9).** The authorized biography of the mythologist, written with access to his private papers and journals. (REV: BL 10/15/91; LJ 11/15/91. AWARDS: BL, 1991)   **[291.13]**

Doctrines

379 Gadon, Elinor. *Once and Future Goddess: A Symbol of Our Time.* **1989, Harper & Row $34.95 (0-06-250346-4); paper $22.50 (0-06-250354-5).** The history of the symbolic representation of goddesses in art from ancient times to the twentieth century. (REV: BL 10/1/89; Choice 6/90; LJ 11/1/89)   **[291.2]**

380 Galland, China. *Longing for Darkness: Tara and the Black Madonna.* **1990, Viking $21.95 (0-670-82818-1).** An examination by a former Catholic of depictions of sacred female figures by the world's religions. "An impressive, moving document of the spirit."—BL (REV: BL 9/1/90; LJ 9/1/90; PW 7/20/90)   **[291.2]**

381 Highwater, Jamake. *Myth and Sexuality.* **1990, NAL $18.95 (0-453-00708-2).** The social history of the West exploring the relationship between myths, religion, and human sexuality. "Beautifully written, provocative and highly recommended."—LJ (REV: BL 11/15/89; LJ 11/15/89; PW 12/22/89)   **[291.2]**

382 Phillips, John A. *Eve: The History of an Idea.* **1985, Harper & Row paper $7.95 (0-06-250670-6).** A tracing of the changing concepts regarding the first woman and her role in the development of attitudes toward women in general. (REV: Choice 12/84; LJ 5/1/84; NYTBR 7/15/84)   **[291.2]**

Religious experience, life, practice

383 Appleton, George, ed. *Oxford Book of Prayer.* **1989, Oxford Univ. Pr. paper $8.95 (0-19-282108-3).** Selections of prayers from Christianity and other religions. (REV: BL 1/1/86; CSM 7/31/85; LJ 7/85) **[291.4]**

384 Carroll, David. *Spiritual Parenting.* **1990, Paragon House paper $12.95 (1-55778-112-5).** A primer directed at parents who wish to raise their children with concepts of spirituality without following the tenets of a particular organized religion. (REV: BL 6/15/90; LJ 6/1/90)   **[291.4]**

385 Coles, Robert. *Spiritual Life of Children.* **1990, Houghton $22.95 (0-395-55999-5).** A multicultural study of the development of spiritual and religious concepts among children. (REV: CSM 2/12/91; LJ 11/1/90; PW 10/26/90. AWARDS: PW, 1990)   **[291.4]**

386 Harvey, Andrew. *Hidden Journey: A Spiritual Awakening.* **1991, Henry Holt $22.50 (0-8050-1454-3).** The author of *A Journey to Ladakh* chronicles his further spiritual adventures in India. "Will touch skeptics as well as seekers."—PW (REV: BL 4/15/91; LJ 3/15/91; PW 2/15/91)   **[291.4]**

294 Religions of Indic origin

Buddhism

387 Dalai Lama. *Freedom in Exile: The Autobiography of the Dalai Lama.* **1990, HarperCollins $22.95 (0-06-039116-2).** An autobiography of the exiled Tibetan religious leader and winner of the 1989 Nobel Peace Prize. (REV: BL 9/1/90; LJ 9/15/90; NYTBR 9/30/90. AWARDS: BL, 1990)   **[294.3]**

388 Foster, Barbara M. *Forbidden Journey: The Life of Alexandra David-Neal.* **1987, Harper & Row $21.95 (0-06-250345-6); paper $12.95 (0-06-250357-X).** A biography of the French woman who introduced many Buddhist writings to the West following her visit to Lhasa. (REV: LJ 9/15/87; NYTBR 1/10/88; PW 7/31/87)   **[294.3]**

389 Matthiessen, Peter. *Nine-Headed Dragon River: Zen Journals, 1969–1982.* **1987, Shambhala $16.95 (0-394-55251-2); paper $12.50 (0-87773-401-1).** Journals of the author of *Killing Mister Watson* detailing his experiences with Zen Buddhism. (REV: BL 3/15/86; LJ 3/15/86; PW 3/14/86)   **[294.3]**

390 Piburn, Sidney D. *Dalai Lama.* **1990, Snow Lion paper $4.95 (0-937938-91-2).** Collected writings by and about Tibet's exiled religious leader. (REV: BL 5/1/90; LJ 6/1/90)   **[294.3]**

391 Powell, Andrew, and Graham Harrison. *Living Buddhism.* **1989, Crown $24.95 (0-517-57266-4).** An illustrated introduction to various schools of Buddhist thought and religion for the general reader. (REV: BL 8/89; LJ 8/89)   **[294.3]**

392 Shin, Nan. *Diary of a Zen Nun.* **1986, Dutton $15.95 (0-525-24408-5); paper $10.95 (0-525-48372-1).** A guide to the art of Zen living and thinking. (REV: BL 5/1/86; LJ 6/1/86; PW 4/11/86)   **[294.3]**

393 Watts, Alan. *In My Own Way: An Autobiography, 1915–1965.* **1973, Random paper $6.95 (0-394-71951-4).** Watts tells the story of his youth in England, his conversion to Buddhism, and his role

as a popularizer of Eastern philosophy in the West. "A thoroughly entertaining book."—PW (REV: LJ 1/1/73; NYTBR 11/12/72; PW 9/4/72) **[294.3]**

Hinduism—Vishnuism

394 **Hubner, John, and Lindsey Gruson.** *Monkey on a Stick: Murder, Madness and the Hare Krishnas.* **1988, Harcourt $19.95 (0-15-162086-5); NAL paper $4.95 (0-451-40187-5).** An exposé of the Hare Krishna sect and their colony in West Virginia where crimes and rape, child sexual abuse, and murder took place. (REV: NYTBR 11/20/88; PW 9/30/88) **[294.5512]**

296 Judaism

395 **Fackenheim, Emil L.** *What Is Judaism? An Interpretation for the Present Age.* **1988, Macmillan paper $9.95 (0-02-032191-0).** An introduction to contemporary Judaism and its significance in the modern world. (REV: BL 10/15/87; LJ 10/1/87) **[296]**

Women

396 **Ochs, Vanessa L.** *Words on Fire: One Woman's Journey into the Sacred.* **1990, Harcourt $22.95 (0-15-198380-1).** Observations on Judaism and its relationship to feminism based on the author's research of religious texts in Israel. (REV: LJ 6/15/90; PW 4/13/90) **[296.082]**

Persons

397 **Liebman, Charles S., and Steven M. Cohen.** *Two Worlds of Judaism: The Israeli and American Experiences.* **1990, Yale Univ. Pr. $25.00 (0-300-04726-6).** A comparative study of contemporary Judaism in the United States and Israel. (REV: LJ 6/1/90; PW 4/27/90) **[296.092]**

Sources

398 **Frankel, Ellen.** *Classic Tales: Four Thousand Years of Jewish Lore.* **1989, Aronson $40.00 (0-87668-904-7).** A collection of 300 Jewish folktales and stories from around the world and from over four millenium. (REV: BL 11/1/89; LJ 6/15/89) **[296.1]**

Doctrinal, moral, social theology

399 **Wolpe, David J.** *Healer of Shattered Hearts: A Jewish View of God.* **1990, Henry Holt $18.95 (0-8050-1211-7).** A rabbi's presentation of the Jewish conception of God and His relationship to man based on the Bible and the scholarship of Judaism. (REV: BL 5/15/90; LJ 4/1/90; PW 2/2/90. AWARDS: BL, 1990) **[296.3]**

Leaders, organization, religious education

400 **Kamin, Ben.** *Stones in the Soul: One Day in the Life of an American Rabbi.* **1990, Hafner $18.95 (0-02-560655-7).** Reflections by a Cleveland rabbi on an average day of work. (REV: BL 9/15/90; LJ 8/90; PW 7/6/90) **[296.6]**

Religious experience, life, practice

401 **Kaplan, Aryeh.** *Jewish Meditation: A Practical Guide.* **1985, Schocken paper $9.95 (0-8052-0781-3).** A step-by-step guide to the techniques of Jewish meditation as presented by an Orthodox Rabbi. (REV: BL 8/85; LJ 9/15/85) **[296.7]**

402 **Lester, Julius.** *Lovesong: Becoming a Jew.* **1988, Henry Holt $17.95 (0-8050-0588-9).** A black journalist's account of his search for spiritual fulfillment and his eventual conversion to Judaism. "A touching and challenging story."—BL (REV: BL 12/1/87; LJ 12/87; NYTBR 1/31/88. AWARDS: ALA, 1988; LJ, 1988) **[296.7]**

403 **Soloveitchik, Joseph B.** *Halakhic Man.* **1984, JPS Phila $12.95 (0-8276-0222-7).** The first English translation of a work in defense of Jewish rationalist philosophy written by a rabbi in 1944. "Magisterial . . . a major statement of traditional Jewish thought."—LJ (REV: Choice 6/84; LJ 7/29/83; PW 7/27/83) **[296.7]**

Sects and movements

404 **Scholem, Gershom.** *From Berlin to Jerusalem: Memories of My Youth.* **1988, Schocken paper $9.95 (0-8052-0871-2).** Memoirs by the Hebrew scholar regarding his childhood in Berlin, his conversion to Zionism, and his emigration to Palestine in 1923. (REV: BL 12/1/80; NYRB 12/18/80; PW 7/18/80) **[296.8]**

405 **Wiesel, Elie.** *Souls on Fire: Portraits and Legends of Hasidic Masters.* **1982, Summit paper $9.95 (0-671-44171-X).** An overview of Hasidic life and customs, based on the tales of Wiesel's grandfather. "Should be read . . . by every sensitive and thinking human being."—NYTBR (REV: LJ 3/1/72; NYTBR 3/5/72; Newsweek 2/28/72) **[296.8]**

297 Islam and religions originating in it

406 **Naipaul, V. S.** *Among the Believers: An Islamic Journey.* **1982, Random paper $9.95 (0-394-71195-5).** A study of contemporary Islamic religion and culture by the author of *Guerrillas* and *A House for Mr. Biswas.* (REV: BL 7/15/81; CSM 10/14/81; New Rep 11/4/81) **[297]**

407 **Ruthven, Malise.** *Islam in the World.* **1984, Oxford Univ. Pr. paper $10.95 (0-19-520-454-9).** An overview of the rise, development, and spread of Islam from the times of Mohammed to the twentieth century. (REV: Choice 5/85; LJ 2/1/85; TLS 9/7/84) **[297]**

Islamic doctrinal theory

408 **Esposito, John L.** *Islam: The Straight Path.* **1988, Oxford Univ. Pr. $29.95 (0-19-504398-7); paper $10.95 (0-19-504399-5).** An introduction to the history and thought of Islam. (REV: BL 9/15/88; Choice 4/89; LJ 9/15/88) **[297.2]**

Muhammed the Prophet

409 **Rodinson, Maxime.** *Mohammed.* **1980, Pantheon paper $7.96 (0-394-73822-5).** The life and thought of the founder of Islam, including an analysis of the Koran and how Islam spread through the Arab world soon after his death. (REV: LJ 11/15/71; NYTBR 11/7/71; New Yorker 5/20/72) **[297.63]**

Shiites

410 Ajami, Fouad. *Vanished Imam: Musa al Sadr and the Shia of Lebanon.* **1986, Cornell Univ. Pr. $21.50 (0-8104-1910-7); paper $8.95 (0-8014-9416-8).** The life of the Lebanese religious leader who disappeared following a trip to Libya in 1979. "May give Americans a deeper understanding of Lebanon and the Middle East than any other book."—NYTBR (REV: LJ 7/86; New Rep 5/12/86; NYTBR 5/25/86. AWARDS: NYTBR, 1986) **[297.82]**

299 Other religions

411 Tedlock, Dennis, ed. *Popol Vuh: The Definitive Edition of the Mayan Book of the Dawn of Life and the Glorious Gods and Kings.* **1986, Simon & Schuster paper $10.95 (0-671-61771-0).** A modern translation of a sixteenth-century Mayan holy book dealing with the story of creation and the history of the Mayan people. (REV: Choice 11/85; LJ 6/15/85; TLS 4/18/85. AWARDS: LJ, 1985) **[299]**

412 Tedlock, Dennis, and Barbara Tedlock, eds. *Teachings from the American Earth: Indian Religion and Philosophy.* **1976, Liveright paper $8.95 (0-87140-097-9).** A collection of 15 essays by scholars and Native Americans regarding their religion and philosophy. "One of the best compilations on Native American religion available."—Choice (REV: Choice 12/75; LJ 4/15/75) **[299]**

413 Watts, Jill. *God, Harlem U.S.A.: The Father Divine Story.* **1991, Univ. of California Pr. $30.00 (0-520-07455-6).** A biography of the early twentieth-century African-American religious and social leader who found the peace mission movement. (REV: BL 2/1/92; PW 12/13/91) **[299]**

Other religions of South American native origin

414 Bierhorst, John. *Mythology of South America.* **1988, Morrow $15.95 (0-688-06722-0).** An overview of the mythology and folklore of South America. (REV: BL 9/15/88; NYTBR 10/2/88) **[299.8]**

415 Villoldo, Alberto, and Erik Jendresen. *Four Winds: A Shaman's Odyssey into the Amazon.* **1990, Harper & Row $18.95 (0-06-250911-X).** An account of the authors' experiences among shaman native doctors in Peru. (REV: BL 8/90; Choice 12/90; NYTBR 9/9/90) **[299.8]**

Scientology

416 Miller, Russell. *Bare-Faced Messiah: A Biography of L. Ron Hubbard.* **1988, Henry Holt $19.95 (0-8050-0654-0).** A biography of the science fiction writer who founded the Church of Scientology and spread the religious cult throughout the world. (REV: BL 8/88; LJ 8/88; TLS 1/8/88) **[299.936]**

300 SOCIAL SCIENCES

417 Schelling, Thomas C. *Choice and Consequence*. 1984, Harvard Univ. Pr. $23.95 (0-674-12770-6); paper $9.95 (0-674-12771-4). Essays exploring human nature and behavior. "There is no way the panorama of insights in this book can be summarized adequately in a brief review."—NYTBR (Rev: New Rep. 8/27/84; NYTBR 7/1/84) **[300]**

Persons

418 Harrington, Michael. *Long-Distance Runner: An Autobiography*. 1988, Henry Holt $19.95 (0-8050-0790-3). Memoirs of life in the 1970s and 1980s by the American socialist writer and critic. (Rev: LJ 8/88; NYRB 3/16/89; NYTBR 7/24/88) **[300.92]**

301 Sociology and anthropology

Sociology of small groups

419 Berkhofer, Robert F., Jr. *White Man's Indian: Images of the American Indian from Columbus to the Present*. 1979, Random paper $8.76 (0-394-72794-0). How the white American concept and imagery of Native Americans has historically had little basis in reality. (Rev: Choice 9/78; LJ 3/15/78; NYTBR 3/26/78) **[301.15]**

420 Burns, James MacGregor. *Leadership*. 1979, Harper & Row paper $12.95 (0-06-131975-9). A study of leadership and traits of great leaders as seen by the American historian. (Rev: Atl 3/79; LJ 7/78; New Rep 12/23/78) **[301.15]**

421 Wolfe, Tom. *Radical Chic and Mau-Mauing the Flak Catchers*. 1987, Farrar $16.95 (0-374-24600-9); paper $5.95 (0-374-52072-0). Two extended satirical essays in one volume: the first recounts a fundraiser for the Black Panther Party held at the home of Leonard Bernstein; the second, the competition for grant money by black activist groups in the Bay Area. (Rev: Natl Rev 1/26/71; New Rep 12/19/70; Time 12/21/70. Awards: Time, 1970) **[301.15]**

Arts and society

422 Bell, Daniel. *Coming of Post-Industrial Society: A Venture in Social Forecasting*. 1976, Basic Books paper $15.95 (0-465-09713-8). How our society is changing from one based on industry to one founded in specialized theoretical knowledge. "A book that could affect thinking for years to come."—CSM (Rev: Choice 12/73; CSM 7/5/73; LJ 7/73. Awards: ALA, 1973) **[301.2]**

423 Hall, Edward T. *Beyond Culture: Into the Cultural Unconscious*. 1977, Doubleday paper $7.95 (0-385-12474-0). How cultural differences in communication and forming concepts limit our ability to understand each other. "His wide-ranging survey . . . should reward careful readers with new ways of thinking about themselves and others."—PW (Rev: BL 2/1/76; LJ 3/15/76; PW 11/10/75. Awards: ALA, 1976) **[301.2]**

424 Harris, Marvin. *Cannibals and Kings: The Origins of Cultures*. 1978, Random paper $8.95 (0-394-72700-2). An analysis of the development, rise, and decline of human societies from prehistory to the present. "An absolutely fascinating book . . . highly recommended both for its popular interest and its scholarship."—Choice (Rev: Choice 3/78; LJ 9/1/77; PW 8/29/77. Awards: ALA, 1977) **[301.2]**

425 Mead, Margaret. *Blackberry Winter: My Earlier Years*. 1972, Peter Smith $24.50 (0-317-60065-6). Memoirs of the anthropologist regarding her first 38 years of life. (Rev: LJ 10/15/72; NYTBR 11/12/72; Sat Rev 11/25/72) **[301.2]**

426 Patai, Raphael. *Arab Mind*. 1976, Macmillan paper $9.95 (0-684-14547-2). A study of the history and culture of Arab society. "A valuable and welcome contribution to the understanding of the people of the Middle East."—Choice (Rev: BL 12/15/73; Choice 1/74; New Yorker 9/10/73. Awards: ALA, 1973) **[301.2]**

427 Wolfe, Tom. *Electric Kool-Aid Acid Test*. 1987, Farrar $22.50 (0-374-14704-3); Bantam paper $5.95 (0-553-26491-5). A look at Ken Kesey and his "Merry Pranksters" during the height of the psychedelic era in the San Francisco Bay Area. "An American classic."—Newsweek (Rev: LJ 8/68; Natl Rev 8/27/68; Newsweek 8/26/68. Awards: ALA, 1968) **[301.2]**

31

Sociology of large groups

428 Coles, Robert. *South Goes North.* **1973, Little, Brown paper $19.95 (0-316-15177-7).** Volume 3 of Coles's Children of Crisis series examines the lives of those who moved to the North from the South in search of employment and a better life. (Rev: Choice 11/72; NYRB 3/9/72; Sat Rev 4/8/72. Awards: ALA, 1972; PP:NF, 1973) **[301.3]**

429 Hall, Edward T. *Hidden Dimension.* **1969, Doubleday paper $5.95 (0-385-08476-5).** The relationship of space, especially living space, to human behaviors and perceptions. (Rev: BL 5/1/66; LJ 2/1/66. Awards: ALA, 1966) **[301.3]**

430 Ward, Barbara, and Rene Dubos. *Only One Earth: The Care and Maintenance of a Small Planet.* **1972, Norton $13.95 (0-393-06391-7); paper $5.95 (0-393-30129-X).** Report on global ecology commissioned by the United Nations Conference on Human Environment. "PW has seen many books on . . . global environmental concerns . . . but few have even approached the stylistic quality, balance, and scientific accuracy that this book has achieved."—PW (Rev: BL 7/15/72; LJ 8/72; PW 5/22/72. Awards: ALA, 1972) **[301.3]**

431 Wuthnow, Robert. *Acts of Compassion: Caring for Others and Helping Ourselves.* **1991, Princeton Univ. Pr. $24.95 (0-691-07390-2).** A study of the role and practice of compassion and altruism in contemporary American society. (Rev: BL 10/15/91; LJ 10/1/91) **[301.3]**

Sociology and gender

432 Coles, Robert, and Jane Hallowell Coles. *Women of Crisis: Lives of Struggle and Hope.* **1990, Addison Wesley paper $9.95 (0-201-16808-X).** The life stories and attitudes of five economically struggling American women of differing social backgrounds. (Rev: Choice 11/78; CSM 8/14/78; LJ 6/15/78) **[301.41]**

433 Daly, Mary. *Beyond God the Father: Toward a Philosophy of Women's Liberation.* **1985, Beacon paper $10.95 (0-8070-1503-2).** A feminist reevaluation of traditional patriarchal concepts of God written by the author of *Pure Lust.* (Rev: Choice 3/74; LJ 11/15/73; PW 10/1/73) **[301.41]**

434 Mailer, Norman. *Prisoner of Sex.* **1985, Donald I. Fine paper $8.95 (0-917657-59-4).** Mailer's rebuttal to Kate Millett's *Sexual Politics* is an attack on the ideas and ideals of the Women's Liberation Movement. (Rev: Atl 7/71; LJ 6/1/71; PW 4/19/71) **[301.41]**

435 Millett, Kate. *Sexual Politics.* **1990, Simon & Schuster paper $10.95 (0-671-70740-X).** An examination of the political relations between the sexes during the past century and a half. "An impressive, serious and important work . . . so intellectually rigorous and so theoretically pioneering . . . that it is essential for every library."—LJ (Rev: LJ 8/70; New Rep 8/1/70; NYTBR 9/6/70. Awards: ALA, 1970; NYTBR, 1970) **[301.41]**

436 Pinzer, Maimie. *Maimie Papers.* **Ed. by Ruth Rosen and Sue Davidson. 1977, Feminist Pr. paper $10.95 (0-912670-48-7).** Collected letters written between a former prostitute and her philanthropist benefactor between 1910–1922. (Rev: Atl 2/78; LJ 3/15/78; New Yorker 12/26/77) **[301.41]**

437 Pomeroy, Sarah B. *Goddesses, Whores, Wives and Slaves: Women in Classical Antiquity.* **1975, Schocken paper $11.95 (0-8052-0530-6).** A study of the social roles of women in ancient Greece and Rome. (Rev: LJ 5/15/75; NYTBR 9/7/75; TLS 9/26/75) **[301.41]**

438 Tripp, C. A. *Homosexual Matrix.* **1987, NAL paper $10.95 (0-452-00847-6).** A study of the historical and sociological impact of homosexuality. "One of the most fascinating studies of sexual behavior that has come along . . . it may well turn out to be one of the most influential."—PW (Rev: BL 12/15/75; Newsweek 10/20/75; PW 9/15/75) **[301.41]**

The family

439 Kitzinger, Sheila. *Women as Mothers: How They See Themselves in Different Cultures.* **1980, Random paper $5.95 (0-394-74079-3).** A cross-cultural study of motherhood by a British anthropologist who specializes in the field. (Rev: BL 11/1/79; Choice 2/80; PW 8/20/79) **[301.42]**

440 Lasch, Christopher. *Haven in a Heartless World: The Family Besieged.* **1979, Basic Books paper $11.95 (0-465-02884-5).** An analysis of the deterioration of American family life in the twentieth century by the noted social critic. (Rev: Choice 4/78; LJ 1/15/78; NYTBR 1/15/78) **[301.42]**

441 Moore, Katharine. *Victorian Wives.* **1987, Schocken paper $5.95 (0-8052-8245-9).** A comparative study of the roles and lives of American and English wives in the late nineteenth century. (Rev: BL 11/15/74; LJ 8/74) **[301.42]**

442 Rich, Adrienne. *Of Woman Born: Motherhood as Experience and Institution.* **1986, Norton $17.95 (0-393-02379-6); paper $8.95 (0-393-30386-1).** A look at the institution of motherhood and its social ramifications throughout history, with personal reflections on Rich's own experiences and feelings as a mother. (Rev: LJ 10/15/76; NYTBR 10/10/76; PW 8/23/76) **[301.42]**

443 Thompson, Thomas. *Richie: The Ultimate Tragedy Between One Decent Man and the Son He Loved.* **1989, NAL paper $3.95 (0-451-16129-7).** The story of how a middle-class father came to kill his drug-addicted son. "Somewhat of a classic of its time . . . ranks with such books as *In Cold Blood.*"—Choice (Rev: Choice 10/73; LJ 5/1/73; Newsweek 6/4/73) **[301.42]**

Aging and the aged

444 Butler, Robert N. *Why Survive: Being Old in America.* **1985, Harper & Row paper $10.95 (0-06-131997-X).** The aged, medicine, and society in modern America. (Rev: Choice 10/75; LJ 5/15/75; PW 3/31/75. Awards: PP:NF, 1976) **[301.43]**

445   Coles, Robert. *Privileged Ones: The Well-Off and Rich in America.* **1980, Little, Brown $24.95 (0-316-15150-5).** The fifth and final volume of the *Children of Crisis* series explores the lives and attitudes of the offspring of the American upper class. (Rev: BL 2/15/78; LJ 3/1/78; NYTBR 1/22/78) **[301.43]**

446   Gould, Roger L. *Transformations: Growth and Change in Adult Life.* **1979, Simon & Schuster paper $12.95 (0-671-25066-3).** Predictable changes and crises experienced by adults with particular attention paid to the "mid-life crisis." (Rev: LJ 6/1/78; PW 5/22/78; Time 8/14/78) **[301.43]**

447   Sheehy, Gail. *Passages: Predictable Crises of Adult Life.* **1984, Bantam paper $5.95 (0-553-27106-7).** Based on 115 interviews, the author gives a lifeline for the stages of an adult's life, and points in a person's life where one can expect changes or high stress. "An intelligent and informative treatment that is near universal in its appeal."—LJ (Rev: BL 7/15/76; LJ 5/15/76; NYTBR 5/30/76. Awards: ALA, 1976) **[301.43]**

Social groups and customs

448   Davis, David B. *The Problem of Slavery in the Age of Revolution, 1770–1823.* **1975, Cornell Univ. Pr. paper $14.95 (0-8014-9156-8).** The sequel to the Pulitzer Prize-winning *Problem of Slavery in Western Culture.* (Rev: Choice 4/75; NYTBR 2/9/75; TLS 9/5/75. Awards: NBA, 1976; NYTBR, 1975) **[301.44]**

449   Girouard, Mark. *Life in the English Country House: A Social and Architectural History.* **1978, Yale Univ. Pr. $45.00 (0-300-02273-5); Penguin paper $12.95 (0-14-005406-5).** A social and architectural history of the English country home from the Middle Ages to the twentieth century. (Rev: CSM 11/13/78; LJ 10/1/78; NYRB 10/26/78) **[301.44]**

450   Lemasters, E. E. *Blue-Collar Aristocrats: Life Styles at a Working-Class Tavern.* **1975, Univ. of Wisconsin Pr. $25.00 (0-299-06550-2); paper $10.95 (0-299-06554-5).** The results of a five-year study of the attitudes of people who frequented a Madison, Wisconsin, bar and their feelings regarding work, marriage, sex, race, and religion. (Rev: Choice 9/75; LJ 5/15/75; NYTBR 5/18/75) **[301.44]**

Ethnic groups

451   Berlin, Ira. *Slaves Without Masters: The Free Negro in the Antebellum South.* **1981, Oxford Univ. Pr. paper $10.95 (0-19-502905-4).** Life of the free blacks in the pre-emancipation South, and an examination of race relations of the era. "It can be read with ease and pleasure by the general public while providing specialists with all the footnotes they could ask for."—Eugene D. Genovese, New Rep (Rev: LJ 1/15/75; New Rep 2/1/75; NYTBR 2/9/75. Awards: ALA, 1975) **[301.45]**

452   Clark, Kenneth B. *Dark Ghetto: Dilemmas of Social Power.* **1989, Univ. Pr. of New England $14.95 (0-8195-6226-2).** The psychology of the black ghetto as seen by the founder of HARYOU (Harlem Youth Opportunities Unlimited). "The richness of

the materials and the clarity and sincerity of the writing are admirable."—Choice (Rev: Choice 12/65; LJ 5/1/65; NYTBR 6/20/65. Awards: ALA, 1965) **[301.45]**

453   Coles, Robert. *Children of Crisis: A Study of Courage and Fear.* **1977, Little, Brown paper $19.95 (0-316-15176-9).** A look at the people and personalities involved in and affected by school desegregation in the South in the late 1950s and early 1960s, written by a child psychiatrist and participant in the civil rights movement. (Rev: NYTBR 6/25/67; Newsweek 6/12/67; Time 11/29/67. Awards: ALA, 1967; NYTBR, 1967) **[301.45]**

454   Genovese, Eugene D. *Roll, Jordan, Roll: The World the Slaves Made.* **1976, Random paper $16.95 (0-394-71652-3).** A look at the culture that developed among African-American slaves. "The most profound, learned and detailed analysis of slavery to appear since World War II."—NYTBR (Rev: LJ 9/1/74; New Rep 11/9/74; NYTBR 9/25/74. Awards: ALA, 1974; NYTBR, 1974) **[301.45]**

455   Grier, William H., and Price M. Cobbs. *Black Rage.* **1980, Basic Books paper $11.95 (0-465-00703-1).** Analysis by two black psychologists of the psychological effects of racism, and economic separatism on African Americans. "A very fine book, eloquent, moving, closely reasoned, and written from clinical experience."—PW (Rev: LJ 8/68; PW 6/10/68; Time 7/26/68. Awards: ALA, 1968) **[301.45]**

456   Gutman, Herbert. *Black Family in Slavery and Freedom, 1750–1925.* **1977, Random paper $16.95 (0-394-72451-8).** Based on slave narratives, manuscripts, and personal testimonies, Gutman traces the tradition of the black family throughout American history. "One of the most important books published in the field of race relations in the last ten years."—Choice (Rev: Choice 3/77; LJ 12/1/76; New Rep 12/4/76. Awards: ALA, 1976) **[301.45]**

457   Howe, Irving. *World of Our Fathers.* **1989, Harcourt $34.95 (0-15-146353-0); Schocken paper $14.95 (0-8052-0928-X).** The story of the Eastern European Jews who immigrated to New York. (Rev: Atl 4/76; LJ 2/1/76; Newsweek 2/2/76. Awards: ALA, 1976; NBA, 1977; NYTBR, 1976; Time, 1976) **[301.45]**

458   Malcolm X, and Alex Haley. *Autobiography of Malcolm X.* **1987, Ballantine paper $5.95 (0-345-35068-5).** The rise of Malcolm X from petty criminal, to spokesman for the Nation of Islam and his conversion to Islam. "Here we may read . . . the agony of an entire people in their search for identification."—I. F. Stone, NYRB (Rev: Atl 12/65; NYRB 11/11/65; Newsweek 11/15/65. Awards: NYTBR, 1965) **[301.45]**

459   Rogler, Lloyd H. *Migrant in the City: The Life of a Puerto Rican Action Group.* **1984, Waterfront paper $9.95 (0-943862-16-7).** A study of the organization and accomplishments of a nonpartisan group designed to assist Spanish-speaking immigrants in their adjustment to life in the United States. (Rev: Choice 11/72; LJ 12/15/72; PW 5/15/72) **[301.45]**

460 Thomas, Piri. *Down These Mean Streets.* 1991, Random paper $10.95 (0-679-73238-1). Autobiography of a young man of Puerto Rican descent growing up in New York during the 1930s in a world of drugs, gangs, and street crime. (REV: LJ 4/15/67; Newsweek 5/29/67; PW 3/13/67. AWARDS: ALA, 1967) **[301.45]**

461 Wallace, Michele. *Black Macho and the Myth of the Superwoman.* 1990, Routledge paper $15.95 (0-86091-518-2). A study of the myths surrounding African-American men and women and how these myths are perpetuated in American society. (REV: BL 5/1/79; LJ 3/1/79; Newsweek 2/5/79) **[301.45]**

462 Woods, Donald. *Biko.* 1983, Peter Smith $15.25 (0-8446-6037-X). A biography of Stephen Biko, a South African black activist, who was killed while being interrogated by the government's Security Police. (REV: LJ 5/15/78; NYRB 6/15/78; NYTBR 4/30/78) **[301.45]**

302 Social interaction

463 Epstein, Joseph. *Ambition: The Secret Passion.* 1989, I. R. Dee paper $8.95 (0-929587-18-9). Ruminations on ambition and its past and present role in American society by the editor of the *American Scholar.* (REV: BL 2/15/81; NYTBR 1/18/81; Sat Rev 1/81) **[302]**

Communication

464 Bagdikian, Ben H. *Media Monopoly.* 1990, Beacon Pr. paper $12.95 (0-8070-6159-X). An account of the growing concentration of the power of the media and of the impact of advertising upon American society. (REV: BL 6/1/83; CSM 8/10/83; PW 4/8/83) **[302.2]**

465 Brand, Stewart. *Media Lab: Inventing the Future at MIT.* 1987, Viking $20.00 (0-670-81442-3); Penguin paper $12.00 (0-14-009701-5). A look into the research facilities at MIT laboratories. (REV: BL 7/87; CSM 9/29/87; NYTBR 9/27/87) **[302.2]**

466 Gumpert, Gary. *Talking Tombstones and Other Tales of the Media Age.* 1988, Oxford Univ. Pr. paper $7.95 (0-19-505651-5). An inside look at the technological tools of the modern media and their influence on contemporary society. (REV: BL 2/1/87; LJ 4/1/87; NYTBR 3/8/87) **[302.2]**

467 King, Stephen. *Danse Macabre.* 1985, Berkley paper $5.50 (0-425-10433-8). A history of horror literature and entertainment from the 1950s to the 1980s by the author of *Christine* and *It.* (REV: BL 1/15/81; LJ 4/1/81; NYTBR 5/10/81) **[302.2]**

468 Marchand, Philip. *Marshall McLuhan: The Medium and the Messenger.* 1989, Ticknor & Fields $19.95 (0-89919-485-0). A biography of the Canadian social critic best known for his book *The Medium Is the Message.* (REV: BL 5/1/89; LJ 3/15/89; PW 1/27/89) **[302.2]**

469 Meyerowitz, Joshua. *No Sense of Place: The Impact of Electronic Media on Social Behavior.* 1985, Oxford Univ. Pr. $24.95 (0-19-503474-0); paper $9.95 (0-19-504231-X). An analysis of the ways television influences social and personal behavior in American society. (REV: BL 2/15/85; Choice 11/85) **[302.2]**

470 Miller, Mark Crispin. *Boxed In: The Culture of TV.* 1988, Northwestern $39.95 (0-8101-0791-0); paper $14.95 (0-8101-0792-9). A series of essays criticizing the effects of television on American life and culture. (REV: Atl 9/88; NYTBR 9/25/88; PW 7/29/88. AWARDS: PW, 1988) **[302.2]**

471 Oberg, James E. *Uncovering Soviet Disasters: Exploring the Limits of Glasnost.* 1988, Random $19.95 (0-394-56095-7). A revealing overview of recent Soviet disasters discussing the government's reluctance to reveal the details of such events to the world community. (REV: Choice 7–8/88; LJ 3/15/88; NYTBR 2/28/88) **[302.2]**

472 Postman, Neil. *Amusing Ourselves to Death: Public Discourse in the Age of Show Business.* 1986, Penguin paper $7.95 (0-14-009438-5). An account of America's intellectual deadening by constant exposure to television. (REV: BL 10/1/85; Choice 3/86; NYTBR 11/24/85) **[302.2]**

Social interaction within groups

473 Campbell, Anne. *Girls in the Gang: A Report from New York City.* 1984, Basil Blackwell $29.95 (0-631-13374-7); paper $12.95 (0-631-14926-0). A study of Latin female gangs in New York as portrayed through the stories of three young women. (REV: NYTBR 12/9/84; TLS 12/14/84) **[302.3]**

474 Deikman, Arthur J. *Wrong Way Home: Uncovering the Patterns of Cult Behavior in American Society.* 1991, Beacon $19.95 (0-8070-2914-9). A psychiatrist's look at the appeal of cults and cult leaders in contemporary American society. (REV: BL 12/15/90; LJ 12/90; PW 11/9/90) **[302.3]**

475 Pogrebin, Letty C. *Among Friends: Who We Like, Why We Like Them, and What We Do with Them.* 1986, McGraw-Hill $19.95 (0-07-050404-0). A study of the development, evolution, and need for human friendship. (REV: BL 10/1/86; NYTBR 12/14/86; PW 10/31/86) **[302.3]**

Social interaction between people

476 Bateson, Mary Catherine. *Composing a Life.* 1989, Atlantic Monthly $18.95 (0-87113-334-2); NAL paper $8.95 (0-452-26505-3). Portrayals of the lives of five women by the author of *With a Daughter's Eye.* (REV: BL 9/1/89; NYTBR 11/26/89) **[302.4]**

477 Silk, Leonard, and Mark Silk. *American Establishment.* 1984, Avon paper $3.95 (0-380-56556-0). An examination of the key institutions of American society that make up the "Establishment," and how they inordinately influence the American centers of power and thought. (REV: Choice 12/80; CSM 10/15/80; LJ 10/15/80. AWARDS: ALA, 1980) **[302.4]**

303 Social processes

Coordination and control

478 Galbraith, John Kenneth. *Anatomy of Power.* **1983, Houghton $15.95 (0-395-34400-X).** An analysis of the nature and use of public and private power by the liberal economist. (REV: BL 10/1/83; New Rep 12/31/83; NYTBR 10/9/83) **[303.3]**

479 Iacocca, Lee, and Sonny Kleinfield. *Talking Straight.* **1988, Bantam $21.95 (0-553-05270-5).** The outspoken CEO of Chrysler offers his opinions on business, the state of the world, America, and American life in this sequel to *Iacocca: An Autobiography.* (REV: BL 7/88; LJ 9/1/88; Time 6/13/88) **[303.3]**

480 Koppes, Clayton R., and Gregory D. Black. *Hollywood Goes to War: How Politics, Profits and Propaganda Shaped World War II Movies.* **1987, Free Pr. $22.50 (0-317-56421-8); Univ. of California Pr. paper $12.95 (0-520-07161-1).** A look at the U.S. government influence in the production of Hollywood motion pictures during World War II. (REV: Choice 12/87; LJ 8/87; NYTBR 8/23/87) **[303.3]**

481 Sowell, Thomas. *A Conflict of Visions: Ideological Origins of Political Struggles.* **1987, Morrow $15.95 (0-688-06912-6); paper $9.95 (0-688-07951-2).** A study of contemporary Western social thought tracing its development and practical applications over the past three centuries. (REV: CSM 2/4/87; LJ 1/87; NYTBR 1/25/87) **[303.3]**

Leadership

482 Bethel, Sheila Murray. *Making a Difference: Twelve Qualities That Make You a Leader.* **1990, Putnam $18.95 (0-399-13467-0); Berkley paper $7.95 (0-425-12309-X).** A study of key personality traits that are essential to effective leadership. (REV: BL 1/1/90; LJ 1/90) **[303.34]**

483 Cleveland, Harlan. *Knowledge Executive: Leadership in an Information Society.* **1989, Dutton paper $10.95 (0-525-48434-5).** A guide to methods of effective management in an increasingly complex information-based business environment. (REV: BL 7/85; Choice 3/86; LJ 8/85) **[303.34]**

Social change

484 Forester, Tom. *High-Tech Society: The Story of the Information Technology Revolution.* **1989, MIT Pr. $24.95 (0-262-06107-4); paper $9.95 (0-262-56044-5).** A study of the effects of modern technology on the contemporary workplace. (REV: Choice 1/88; LJ 7/87) **[303.4]**

485 Hoffman, Abbie. *Best of Abbie Hoffman.* **1989, Four Walls Eight Windows $21.95 (0-941423-27-1); paper $14.95 (0-941423-42-5).** Selections from *Revolution for the Hell of It, Woodstock Nation, Steal This Book,* and other writings of the late American political activist. (REV: LJ 2/15/90; NYTBR 3/11/90) **[303.4]**

486 Lappe, Marc. *Broken Code: The Exploitation of DNA.* **1985, Sierra Club $17.95 (0-87156-835-7).** A study of the ethical, social, and legal issues brought about by developments in the field of biotechnology. (REV: Choice 11/85; LJ 8/85; PW 6/14/85) **[303.4]**

487 Lewis, Bernard. *Muslim Discovery of Europe.* **1982, Norton $19.95 (0-393-01529-7).** An examination of Muslim contacts and perceptions of Europe and European culture to the beginning of the nineteenth century. (REV: LJ 9/1/82; New Rep 8/16/82; NYRB 11/4/82) **[303.4]**

488 Pagels, Heinz R. *Dreams of Reason: The Computer and the Rise of the Sciences of Complexity.* **1988, Simon & Schuster $18.95 (0-671-62708-2); Bantam paper $9.95 (0-553-34710-1).** A study of computers and their applications in contemporary science. (REV: Choice 11/88; LJ 7/88; NYTBR 8/14/88) **[303.4]**

489 Roszak, Theodore. *Cult of Information: The Folklore of Computers and the True Art of Thinking.* **1987, Pantheon paper $9.95 (0-394-75175-2).** Roszak's humanistic attack on the pervasiveness of computers in our society. (REV: BL 3/15/86; Choice 9/86; PW 3/7/86. AWARDS: ALA, 1986) **[303.4]**

490 Shils, Edward. *Tradition.* **1981, Univ. of Chicago Pr. $25.00 (0-226-75325-5).** A study of the role tradition plays in human societies. (REV: Choice 1/82; LJ 5/15/81; NYTBR 2/14/82) **[303.4]**

Growth and development

491 Lasch, Christopher. *True and Only Heaven: Progress and Its Critics.* **1991, Norton $25.00 (0-393-02916-6).** The author of *The Culture of Narcissism* examines the future direction of the American economy and its potential effects upon American society. (REV: BL 1/15/91; LJ 12/90; NYTBR 1/27/91) **[303.44]**

Causes of changes

492 Bonner, Arthur. *Averting the Apocalypse: Social Movements in India Today.* **1990, Duke Univ. Pr. $52.50 (0-8223-1029-5); paper $17.95 (0-8223-1048-1).** A study of movements seeking social changes in modern India. (REV: BL 5/15/90; Choice 11/90; NYTBR 10/21/90) **[303.48]**

493 Hardison, O. B., Jr. *Disappearing Through the Skylight: Culture and Technology in the 20th Century.* **1989, Viking $22.95 (0-670-82505-0).** The effects rapid changes in technology have had upon twentieth-century culture and human awareness. "A far-ranging exploration of our time."—BL (REV: BL 11/15/89; LJ 10/15/89; NYTBR 12/31/89) **[303.48]**

494 Postman, Neil. *Technopoly.* **1992, Knopf $21.00 (0-394-58272-1).** A critical analysis of America's drift toward a machine-controlled society written by the author of *Conscientious Objections.* (REV: BL 12/1/91; PW 12/13/91) **[303.48]**

Social forecasts

495 Dublin, Max. *Futurehype: The Tyranny of Prophecy.* **1991, Dutton $19.95 (0-525-24968-0).** A critical study of man's recent attempts to predict future events and trends. (REV: BL 2/15/91; PW 2/1/91) **[303.49]**

496   Halberstam, David. *Next Century.* 1991, Morrow $16.95 (0-688-10391-X). The author of *The Best and the Brightest* provides his analysis and predictions of the economic and political future of the world and the United States. (REV: BL 12/15/90; NYTBR 2/17/91; PW 12/21/90) **[303.49]**

497   Toffler, Alvin. *Powershift: Knowledge, Wealth and Violence at the Edge of the 21st Century.* 1990, Bantam $22.95 (0-553-05776-6). The author of *Future Shock* examines the information age and the future of business and society in the next century. (REV: LJ 11/1/90; NYTBR 11/4/90; PW 8/31/90) **[303.49]**

498   Wagar, W. William. *A Short History of the Future.* 1989, Univ. of Chicago Pr. $24.95 (0-226-89601-6). A speculative history of the future as told in the guise of a historian in the year 2200. "Thought-provoking, disturbing and immensely worthwhile."—PW (REV: LJ 11/1/89; PW 10/13/89) **[303.49]**

Conflict

499   Billington, James H. *Fire in the Minds of Men: Origins of the Revolutionary Faith.* 1983, Basic Books paper $16.95 (0-465-02407-6). A survey of revolutionary thoughts and writings and their influence in Europe from the French to the Russian Revolutions. (REV: BL 9/1/80; LJ 8/80; NYTBR 9/14/80) **[303.6]**

500   Elshtain, Jean Bethke. *Women and War.* 1987, Basic Books $18.95 (0-465-09214-4). A feminist analysis of the roles women have played and should play in past and future wars. (REV: Choice 10/87; LJ 4/15/87) **[303.6]**

501   Ford, Franklin L. *Political Murder: From Tyrannicide to Terrorism.* 1985, Harvard Univ. Pr. $32.50 (0-674-68635-7); paper $9.95 (0-674-68636-5). The use of assassination to evoke political change from ancient times to the twentieth century. (REV: Choice 2/86; LJ 1/86; NYTBR 11/13/85) **[303.6]**

502   Holmes, Richard. *Acts of War: The Behavior of Men in Battle.* 1986, Free Pr. $24.95 (0-02-915020-5); paper $12.95 (0-02-914851-0). A study of the behavior of soldiers in battle conditions based on firsthand historical accounts and interviews with veterans. "An outstanding contribution to military literature."—BL (REV: BL 5/15/86; CSM 5/6/86; LJ 2/1/86) **[303.6]**

503   Long, David E. *Anatomy of Terrorism.* 1990, Free Pr. $22.95 (0-02-919345-1). A study of terrorist psychology, the history of terrorism, and a compendium of the world's known terrorist groups by a former State Department expert on the subject. (REV: BL 8/90; Choice 2/91; LJ 7/90) **[303.6]**

504   May, Rollo. *Power and Innocence: A Search for the Sources of Violence.* 1972, Norton $14.95 (0-393-01065-1). An analysis of the relationship between the feeling of helplessness and its release

through violence. "His jargon-free inquiry is an exploration of the human need for dignity, significance and self-assertion."—PW (REV: BL 1/15/73; LJ 12/1/72; Time 1/1/73. AWARDS: Time, 1972) **[303.6]**

505   Melman, Yossi. *Master Terrorist: The True Story Behind Abu Nidal.* 1986, Adama $16.95 (0-915361-52-3); Avon paper $3.95 (0-380-70428-5). A profile of the Palestinian terrorist and his followers. (REV: BL 11/1/86; NYTBR 9/14/86) **[303.6]**

506   Morgan, Robin. *Demon Lover: On the Sexuality of Terrorism.* 1989, Norton $18.95 (0-393-03642-6); paper $9.95 (0-393-30677-1). A feminist treatise examining the roots and causes of terrorism. (REV: BL 2/1/89; CSM 6/7/89; NYTBR 4/30/89) **[303.6]**

304   Factors affecting social behavior

Human ecology

507   Berry, Wendell. *What Are People For?* 1990, North Point $19.95 (0-86547-420-6); paper $9.95 (0-86547-437-0). Essays on the role of humans on earth and their relationship to the planet and each other. (REV: BL 4/1/90; LJ 4/1/90; NYTBR 4/15/90) **[304.2]**

508   Commoner, Barry. *Making Peace with the Planet.* 1990, Pantheon $19.95 (0-394-56598-3). A guide to environmentally sound action by the scientist and social commentator. (REV: BL 5/1/90; LJ 4/15/90; NYTBR 4/22/90. AWARDS: BL, 1990) **[304.2]**

509   Dubos, Rene. *Wooing of Earth.* 1980, Macmillan paper $8.95 (0-684-16951-7). The biologist and writer examines mankind's role on earth and his relationship to other living things. (REV: CSM 6/9/80; NYTBR 6/1/80; Time 6/9/80) **[304.2]**

510   Eckholm, Eric P. *Down to Earth: Environment and Human Needs.* 1983, Norton paper $7.95 (0-393-30040-4). "An important assessment of where we stand today in the struggle for environmental and economic improvement on the planet."—PW (REV: BL 3/15/83; LJ 6/1/82; PW 4/23/82. AWARDS: ALA, 1982) **[304.2]**

511   Hiss, Tony. *Experience of Place.* 1990, Knopf $19.95 (0-394-56849-4). A study of how landscapes and environments influence the human body and psyche. (REV: BL 7/90; Newsweek 9/10/90; PW 6/15/90. AWARDS: BL, 1990; PW, 1990) **[304.2]**

512   McKibben, Bill. *End of Nature.* 1989, Random $19.95 (0-394-57601-2); Doubleday paper $9.95 (0-385-41604-0). The author maintains that the future of nature has been irrevocably changed by man. "This elegantly written near-elegy of nature will be a touchstone for any future discussion on the fate of the earth."—LJ (REV: BL 9/15/89; CSM 10/10/89; LJ 10/1/89. AWARDS: LJ, 1989) **[304.2]**

513   McPhee, John. *Control of Nature.* 1989, Farrar $17.95 (0-374-12890-1). Three essays providing examples of nature rebelling against man's attempts to control and exploit it for economic profit. (REV: BL 3/1/89; Natl Rev 6/2/89; NYTBR 8/6/89) **[304.2]**

514 Pyne, Stephen J. *Burning Bush: A Fire History of Australia.* **1991, Henry Holt $27.50 (0-8050-1472-1).** A history of fire on the continent of Australia and its effects upon its ecology and human inhabitants. (Rev: BL 1/15/91; LJ 3/1/91; NYTBR 3/10/91)   **[304.2]**

515 Pyne, Stephen J. *Fire in America: A Cultural History of Wildland and Rural Fire.* **1982, Princeton Univ. Pr. $60.00 (0-691-08300-2).** A history of the causes and effects of wildfires in America from prehistoric times to the present and of the methods used to combat them. (Rev: Choice 11/82; LJ 9/15/82; NYTBR 8/15/82)   **[304.2]**

516 Weiner, Jonathan. *Next 100 Years: Shaping the Fate of Our Living Earth.* **1990, Bantam $19.95 (0-553-05744-8).** An overview of the delicate ecological balance of life on earth with grim predictions for the following century if current trends are not reversed. (Rev: LJ 2/1/90; New Rep 4/30/90; NYTBR 3/4/90)   **[304.2]**

Genetic factors

517 Degler, Carl N. *In Search of Human Nature: The Decline and Revival of Darwinism in American Social Thought.* **1991, Oxford Univ. Pr. $24.95 (0-19-506380-5).** A study of current social theories of genetic and biological determinism and the legacy of Darwin and social Darwinist thought. (Rev: LJ 6/1/91; NYTBR 3/17/91; PW 3/8/91)   **[304.5]**

518 Kevles, Daniel J. *In the Name of Eugenics: Genetics and the Uses of Human Heredity.* **1985, Knopf $22.95 (0-394-50702-9); Univ. of California Pr. paper $10.95 (0-520-05763-5).** A study of the history of the "science" of eugenics from the racist gene theories of the nineteenth century to present-day genetic engineering. (Rev: Choice 10/85; LJ 5/15/85; NYTBR 6/9/85)   **[304.5]**

519 Kitcher, Philip. *Vaulting Ambition: Sociobiology and the Quest for Human Nature.* **1985, MIT Pr. $30.00 (0-262-11109-8).** A study of current evolutionary and sociobiological theories regarding the essence of human nature. (Rev: LJ 3/1/86; NYTBR 10/6/85; TLS 1/3/86)   **[304.5]**

Population

520 Easterlin, Richard. *Birth and Fortune: The Impact of Numbers on Personal Welfare.* **1987, Univ. of Chicago Pr. paper $12.95 (0-226-18032-8).** A study of demographics and their effects upon the individual in American society. (Rev: LJ 10/15/80; New Rep 10/4/80; NYTBR 11/9/80)   **[304.6]**

521 Thornton, Russell. *American Indian Holocaust and Survival: A Population History since 1492.* **1987, Univ. of Oklahoma Pr. $29.95 (0-8061-2074-6).** A history of the rise and fall of native populations in the Americas following European colonization. (Rev: Choice 6/88; LJ 12/87)   **[304.6]**

522 Wattenberg, Ben W. *First Universal Nation: Leading Indicators and Ideas about the Surge of America in the 1990's.* **1990, Free Pr. $22.95 (0-02-934001-2).** A study of the demographic trends of the

United States and their meaning for the future of America. "A clear vision of an America that is robust, growing, and dynamic."—CSM (Rev: BL 12/1/90; CSM 1/31/91; LJ 12/90)   **[304.6]**

Movement of people

523 Bailyn, Bernard. *Voyagers to the West: A Passage in the Peopling of America on the Eve of the Revolution.* **1986, Knopf $35.00 (0-394-51569-2); Random paper $14.95 (0-394-75778-5).** The story of immigration to the colonies in the 1760s and 1770s. (Rev: Choice 4/87; LJ 11/1/86; New Yorker 2/23/87. Awards: LJ, 1986; PP:History, 1987)   **[304.8]**

524 Gregory, James N. *American Exodus: The Dust Bowl Migration and Okie Culture in California.* **1989, Oxford Univ. Pr. $24.95 (0-19-504423-1).** An account of the migration of midwest farmers to California during the Great Depression and their impact upon California's economy and culture. (Rev: BL 9/15/89; LJ 9/15/89)   **[304.8]**

525 Kramer, Jane. *Unsettling Europe.* **1990, Penguin paper $8.95 (0-14-012898-0).** A look at the lives of four European families, three of them in exile, who are isolated from their communities. "No-nonsense journalism at its best . . . by a writer who combines the skills of a social historian with those of a novelist."—Newsweek (Rev: BL 7/15/80; NYTBR 5/18/80; Newsweek 6/9/80. Awards: ALA, 1980)   **[304.8]**

526 Portes, Alejandro, and Ruben G. Rumbaut. *Immigrant America: A Portrait.* **1990, Univ. of California Pr. $35.00 (0-520-06894-7); paper $9.95 (0-520-07038-0).** A comparative study between contemporary American immigrants and those who came to the United States at the turn of the century. (Rev: BL 5/1/90; LJ 5/1/90)   **[304.8]**

305 Social groups

527 Klein, Joe. *Payback: Five Marines after Vietnam.* **1984, Knopf $17.95 (0-394-52369-5); Ballantine paper $3.95 (0-345-32506-0).** A study of the lives of five Marines after returning to their Midwestern homes following service in Vietnam. (Rev: CSM 5/16/85; LJ 9/15/84; Newsweek 11/12/84)   **[305]**

Age groups

528 Sheehy, Gail. *Pathfinders.* **1982, Bantam paper $5.50 (0-553-25601-7).** The author of *Passages* examines the lives and careers of people who successfully changed the directions of their lives. (Rev: BL 9/1/81; PW 8/28/81; Sat Rev 10/81)   **[305.2]**

Young people

529 Anson, Robert Sam. *Best Intentions: The Education and Killing of Edmund Perry.* **1988, Random paper $7.95 (0-394-75707-6).** An account of the life of a Harlem teenager who was killed by a policeman during an alleged mugging incident two weeks after he had graduated with honors from Phillips Exeter Academy. (Rev: BL 4/15/87; LJ 6/1/87; Time 8/17/87)   **[305.23]**

530 Blume, Judy. *Letters to Judy: What Your Kids Wish They Could Tell You.* 1986, Putnam $17.95 (0-399-13129-9); Pocket paper $4.50 (0-671-62696-5). Collected letters written to the children's author concerning common problems of childhood and adolescence. (Rev: LJ 6/15/86; NYTBR 6/8/86; TLS 11/28/86) **[305.23]**

531 Chin, Ann-Ping. *Children of China: Voices from Recent Years.* 1988, Knopf $22.95 (0-394-57116-9); Cornell Univ. Pr. paper $10.95 (0-8014-9683-7). The feelings, ideas, and lives of Chinese children are presented in this book based on 130 interviews conducted in the early 1980s with youth between the ages of 6 and 19. (Rev: CSM 10/25/88; LJ 9/15/88; NYTBR 1/15/89) **[305.23]**

532 Ianni, Francis A. *Search for Structure: A Report on American Youth Today.* 1989, Free Pr. $22.50 (0-02-915360-3). A study of the attitudes and aspirations of American adolescents based on a decade of research carried out by the director of the Institute of Social Analysis at Columbia University. (Rev: BL 3/15/89; LJ 2/15/89; PW 1/20/89) **[305.23]**

533 Kotlowitz, Alex. *There Are No Children Here: The Story of Two Boys Growing Up in the Other America.* 1991, Doubleday $21.95 (0-385-26526-3). An account of two brothers, ages ten and seven, and their lives in a Chicago housing project. (Rev: BL 1/15/91; LJ 4/1/91; PW 2/15/91. Awards: ALA, 1992; BL, 1991; LJ, 1991) **[305.23]**

534 Lefkowitz, Bernard. *Tough Change: Growing Up on Your Own in America.* 1987, Free Pr. $19.95 (0-02-918490-8). A portrait of adolescent street life in America based on interviews with 280 runaways and abandoned children. (Rev: Choice 6/87; LJ 1/87; NYTBR 6/5/88) **[305.23]**

535 McBride, Angela B. *Secret of a Good Life with Your Teenager: Thriving in the Second Decade of Parenthood.* 1987, Random $16.95 (0-8129-1642-5); Fisher Books paper $9.95 (1-55561-023-4). A guide to successfully parenting your teenage child by a psychology professor and mother. (Rev: LJ 8/87; PW 6/5/87) **[305.23]**

536 Nasaw, David. *Children of the City: At Work and at Play.* 1986, Oxford Univ. Pr. paper $9.95 (0-19-504015-5). A re-creation of the lives of turn-of-the-century urban American immigrant children. "A fascinating and useful piece of social history."—LJ (Rev: LJ 3/15/85; PW 2/1/85) **[305.23]**

537 Nazario, Thomas A. *In Defense of Children: Understanding the Rights, Needs and Interests of the Child.* 1988, Macmillan $27.50 (0-684-18606-3). A resource guide for the protection of the rights of children. (Rev: LJ 11/15/88; PW 10/21/88) **[305.23]**

538 Powell-Hopson, Darlene, and Derek Hopson. *Different and Wonderful: Raising Black Children in a Race-Conscious Society.* 1990, Prentice Hall $19.45 (0-13-211509-3). A guide to childrearing focusing on the special needs and societal pressures facing African-American youngsters. (Rev: BL 12/1/90; LJ 11/15/90) **[305.23]**

539 Winn, Marie. *Children Without Childhood: Growing Up Too Fast in a World of Sex and Drugs.* 1983, Pantheon $13.95 (0-394-51136-0); Penguin paper $7.95 (0-14-007105-9). A look at the problems of today's youth with suggestions for improvement. "She has asked all of the right questions, and has come up with a lot of the right answers."—Natl Rev (Rev: CSM 6/24/83; LJ 5/15/83; Natl Rev 12/23/83. Awards: BL, the 1980s) **[305.23]**

Adults

540 Merser, Cheryl. *"Grown-Ups": A Generation in Search of Adulthood.* 1988, NAL paper $8.95 (0-452-26265-1). A look at the developmental stages in the lives of baby-boomers. "A thoughtful, poignant, questioning book."—PW (Rev: LJ 10/1/87; NYTBR 10/18/87; PW 8/21/87) **[305.24]**

Late adulthood

541 Dychtwald, Ken, and Joe Flower. *Age Wave: The Challenges and Opportunities of an Aging America.* 1989, J. P. Tarcher $19.95 (0-87477-441-1); Bantam paper $11.95 (0-553-34806-X). A gerontologist's assessment of the problems and benefits of the steadily increasing number of elderly Americans. (Rev: BL 11/15/88; LJ 3/15/89; PW 11/18/88) **[305.26]**

542 Kaufman, Sharon R. *Ageless Self: Sources of Meaning in Late Life.* 1986, Univ. of Wisconsin Pr. $22.50 (0-299-10860-0); NAL paper $8.95 (0-452-00888-3). Interviews with 60 persons, aged 60 to 90, form the basis for this work concerning the opinions of the aged regarding aging. (Rev: Choice 4/87; LJ 2/15/87; NYTBR 2/15/87) **[305.26]**

543 Le Shan, Eda. *Oh, to Be Fifty Again! On Being Too Old for a Mid-Life Crisis.* 1988, Pocket paper $3.95 (0-671-64668-0). A guide for the aging to living a full and active life. (Rev: BL 9/15/86; LJ 9/15/86; PW 7/25/86) **[305.26]**

Men and women

544 French, Marilyn. *Beyond Power: On Women, Men and Morals.* 1986, Ballantine paper $11.95 (0-345-33405-1). An examination of sex roles and the relationship between the sexes by the author of *The Women's Room.* (Rev: LJ 6/1/85; PW 5/3/85; TLS 1/24/86) **[305.3]**

545 Lopate, Phillip. *Bachelorhood: Tales of the Metropolis.* 1989, Poseidon paper $8.95 (0-671-67681-4). Essays and poems regarding the bachelor life by the author of *The Rug Merchant.* (Rev: BL 10/15/81; LJ 10/1/81; NYTBR 10/11/81) **[305.3]**

Men

546 Bly, Robert. *Iron John: A Book about Men.* 1990, Addison Wesley $18.95 (0-201-51720-5). The American poet analyzes the contemporary male psyche and the concept of masculinity. "A refreshing, daring, and truly liberating study."—BL (Rev: BL 10/15/90; LJ 11/15/90; PW 10/12/90. Awards: BL, 1990) **[305.31]**

Social role and status of men

547 Astrachan, Anthony. *How Men Feel: Their Response to Women's Demands for Equality and Power.* 1988, Doubleday paper $12.95 (0-385-23334-5). An analysis of men's feelings regarding the women's movement and feminist philosophy based on over 400 interviews conducted over a 20-year period. (Rev: BL 8/86; LJ 8/86; NYTBR 8/10/86) **[305.32]**

548 Ehrenreich, Barbara. *Hearts of Men: American Dreams and the Flight from Commitment.* 1984, Doubleday paper $7.95 (0-385-17615-5). The decline of the male work and family ethic in the years 1950–1980, and its effects on women and the family. "A pleasure to read, entertaining and imaginative."—NYTBR (Rev: LJ 7/83; NYTBR 6/5/83; PW 4/8/83) **[305.32]**

549 Keen, Sam. *Fire in the Belly: On Being a Man.* 1991, Bantam $19.95 (0-553-07188-2). A former *Psychology Today* editor examines the definition of maleness and the role of the man in contemporary society. "Men—and women—will be enriched by the uncommon insights in Keen's speculative primer."—PW (Rev: BL 3/1/91; LJ 2/1/91; PW 1/11/91) **[305.32]**

550 Raphael, Ray. *Men from the Boys: Rites of Passage in Male America.* 1988, Univ. of Nebraska Pr. $19.95 (0-8032-3888-6); paper $8.95 (0-8032-8937-5). A study of the ways males in American society make the transition from boyhood to adulthood. (Rev: BL 10/15/88; NYTBR 3/12/89) **[305.32]**

Specific types of men

551 Duberman, Martin. *Cures: A Gay Man's Odyssey.* 1991, Dutton $19.95 (0-525-24955-9). Memoirs of the author's coming to terms with his homosexuality. (Rev: LJ 2/15/91; NYTBR 4/21/91; PW 2/15/91) **[305.38]**

552 Hippler, Mike. *So Little Time: Essays on Gay Life.* 1990, Celestial Arts paper $11.95 (0-89097-609-6). A collection of 50 essays on aspects of gay life in today's United States. (Rev: BL 10/1/90; PW 10/12/90. Awards: BL, 1990) **[305.38]**

Women

553 Anderson, Bonnie S., and Judith P. Zinsser. *A History of Their Own: Women in Europe from Prehistory to the Present, Vol. I.* 1988, Harper & Row $27.50 (0-06-015850-6); paper $14.95 (0-06-091452-1). This first volume surveys the historical contributions of European women from prehistoric times to 1600. (Rev: Choice 3/89; NYTBR 8/14/88; PW 3/25/88) **[305.4]**

554 Anderson, Bonnie S., and Judith P. Zinsser. *A History of Their Own: Women in Europe from Prehistory to the Present, Vol. II.* 1988, Harper & Row $29.95 (0-06-015899-9); paper $12.95 (0-06-091563-3). The second volume surveys the history of women in Europe from 1600 to the present. "Combining superb scholarship and sheer readabil-

ity . . . reading this book is an education."—PW (Rev: Choice 3/89; NYTBR 12/18/88; PW 8/12/88) **[305.4]**

555 Berg, Barbara. *Crisis of the Working Mother: Resolving the Conflict Between Family and Work.* 1987, Summit paper $7.95 (0-671-64165-4). Reflections on the challenge of being a working mother in contemporary American society. (Rev: BL 8/86; LJ 4/15/86; NYTBR 5/11/86) **[305.4]**

556 Bleier, Ruth. *Science and Gender: A Critique of Biology and Its Theories on Women.* 1984, Pergamon paper $17.95 (0-08-030971-2). A study of the biological differences between the sexes and how scientists have manipulated facts to the detriment of women throughout history. (Rev: Choice 10/84; LJ 3/1/85; NYTBR 8/12/84) **[305.4]**

557 Brownmiller, Susan. *Femininity.* 1985, Fawcett paper $8.95 (0-449-90142-4). A study of the real and socially constructed differences between the sexes by the author of *Against Our Will.* (Rev: Choice 5/84; NYTBR 1/15/84; PW 11/25/83) **[305.4]**

558 Bumiller, Elizabeth. *May You Be the Mother of a Hundred Sons: A Journey Among the Women of India.* 1990, Random $19.95 (0-394-56391-3). A study of the role of women in contemporary Indian society based upon the author's travels and interviews. (Rev: BL 4/15/90; LJ 5/1/90; NYTBR 6/24/90) **[305.4]**

559 Conway, Jill Ker. *Road from Coorain: An Autobiography.* 1989, Knopf $19.95 (0-394-57456-7); Random paper $8.95 (0-679-72436-2). A memoir of the author's childhood in Australia on her parent's sheep ranch and the tragic effects of an extended drought on her family. (Rev: BL 5/1/89; CSM 7/26/89; NYTBR 5/7/89. Awards: ALA, 1989) **[305.4]**

560 Crosby, Faye J. *Juggling: The Unexpected Advantages of Balancing Career and Home for Women and Their Families.* 1991, Free Pr. $19.95 (0-02-906705-7). A Smith College psychology professor's analysis of current gender roles and women who balance their career and family life. (Rev: LJ 10/1/91; PW 9/6/91) **[305.4]**

561 Daly, Mary. *Pure Lust: Elemental Feminist Philosophy.* 1984, Beacon paper $13.95 (0-8070-1505-9). A feminist philosophical tract by the author of *Gyn/Ecology.* "An important, poetic, and profound book."—BL (Rev: BL 3/1/84; Choice 10/84; NYTBR 7/22/84) **[305.4]**

562 Daly, Mary. *Webster's First New Intergalactic Wickedary of the English Language.* Ed. by Jane Caputi. 1987, Beacon paper $14.95 (0-8070-6733-4). A study of sexism in the English language in the form of a feminist dictionary created by the author of *Gyn/Ecology.* (Rev: BL 10/1/87; NYTBR 1/17/88; TLS 6/3/88) **[305.4]**

563 Davis, Angela Y. *Women, Culture and Politics.* 1989, Random $17.95 (0-394-56976-8); paper $9.95 (0-679-72487-7). A collection of essays written by Davis in the 1980s concerning the plight of women, and the underclass in today's America. (Rev: LJ 2/1/89; NYTBR 3/26/89; PW 12/16/88) **[305.4]**

564   Doress, Paula Brown, and Diana L. Siegel. *Ourselves Growing Older: Women Aging with Knowledge and Power.* 1987, Simon & Schuster paper $15.95 (0-671-64424-6). An overview of the mental and physical health concerns of women in midlife by the authors of *Our Bodies, Ourselves.* "May well prove to be a landmark in consciousness-raising."—PW (REV: BL 11/15/87; LJ 11/1/87; PW 10/16/87. AWARDS: PW, 1987)   **[305.4]**

565   Evans, Sara M. *Born for Liberty: A History of Women in America.* 1989, Free Pr. $24.95 (0-02-902990-2). An illustrated social and political history of women in America focusing on events and trends of the twentieth century. (REV: BL 6/15/89; LJ 6/1/89; PW 4/28/89)   **[305.4]**

566   Fox-Genovese, Elizabeth. *Within the Plantation Household: Black and White Women of the Old South.* 1988, Univ. of North Carolina Pr. $34.95 (0-8078-1808-9); paper $12.95 (0-8078-4232-X). An analysis of black and white women and their relationship toward each other in antebellum Southern society. "An illuminating and solid book of social history."—BL (REV: BL 11/15/88; Choice 9/89; PW 11/4/88. AWARDS: PW, 1988)   **[305.4]**

567   Friedl, Erika. *Women of Deh Koh: Lives in an Iranian Village.* 1989, Smithsonian $24.95 (0-87474-400-8); paper $10.95 (0-87474-403-2). An anthropologist's study of the lives of women living in a small Iranian moutain village. (REV: LJ 5/1/89; NYTBR 5/14/89; PW 2/24/89)   **[305.4]**

568   Friedman, Sonya. *Smart Cookies Don't Crumble: A Modern Women's Guide to Living and Loving Her Own Life.* 1985, Putnam $15.95 (0-399-13040-3); Pocket paper $3.95 (0-317-61748-6). A guide to solving the problems of everyday life for women by the psychologist and talk-show host. (REV: LJ 6/1/85; PW 5/10/85)   **[305.4]**

569   Gentry, Diane Koos. *Enduring Women.* 1988, Texas A & M Univ. Pr. $29.95 (0-89096-362-2); paper $16.95 (0-89096-324-X). Profiles of ten American working women and their lives told through essays and photographs. (REV: LJ 2/1/88; NYTBR 4/17/88; PW 1/8/88)   **[305.4]**

570   Giddings, Paula. *When and Where I Enter: The Impact of Black Women on Race and Sex in America.* 1984, Morrow $17.95 (0-688-01943-9); Bantam paper $8.95 (0-553-34225-8). A history of African-American women and their impact on American society and attitudes from the seventeenth century to the present. (REV: Choice 11/84; LJ 5/1/84; NYTBR 7/8/84)   **[305.4]**

571   Greer, Germaine. *Madwoman's Underclothes: Essays and Occasional Writings.* 1987, Atlantic Monthly $17.95 (0-87113-160-9); paper $8.95 (0-87113-308-3). A collection of nonfiction writings by the author of *The Female Eunuch* spanning her career from the 1960s to the 1980s. (REV: BL 9/15/87; LJ 8/87; NYTBR 10/11/87)   **[305.4]**

572   Hite, Shere. *Women and Love: A Cultural Revolt in Progress.* 1987, Knopf $24.95 (0-394-53052-7); St. Martin's paper $5.95 (0-312-91378-8). An examination of women's feelings about their love relationships with men based on the answers of 4,500 questionnaires. (REV: BL 9/1/87; LJ 10/15/87; PW 9/25/87)   **[305.4]**

573   Inoue, Yasushi. *Chronicle of My Mother.* 1985, Kodansha paper $4.95 (0-87011-737-8). The Japanese novelist chronicles the deterioration and death of his mother in these memoirs. (REV: BL 6/15/83; NYTBR 6/26/83; TLS 2/17/84)   **[305.4]**

574   Jensen, Joan M. *Loosening the Bonds: Mid-Atlantic Farm Women, 1750–1850.* 1986, Yale Univ. Pr. $30.00 (0-300-03366-4); paper $12.95 (0-300-04265-5). A study of the changing social roles of American rural women in the late eighteenth and early nineteenth centuries. (REV: Choice 11/86; LJ 7/86)   **[305.4]**

575   Jones, Jacqueline. *Labor of Love, Labor of Sorrow: Black Women, Work and the Family from Slavery to the Present.* 1985, Basic Books $25.95 (0-465-03756-9); Random paper $12.95 (0-394-74536-1). A history of black working-class women and their role in the American job market. "A valuable contribution to scholarship about black women."—Toni Morrison, NYTBR (REV: Choice 9/85; LJ 3/1/85; NYTBR 4/14/85. AWARDS: LJ, 1985)   **[305.4]**

576   Lanker, Brian. *I Dream a World: Portraits of Black Women Who Have Changed America.* 1989, Stewart, Tabori & Chang $40.00 (1-55670-063-6); paper $24.95 (1-55670-092-X). Photographic portraits with accompanying essays regarding the achievements of 75 African-American women. (REV: LJ 5/1/89; NYTBR 5/7/89; PW 3/17/89)   **[305.4]**

577   Lennox, Joan, and Judith Hatch Shapiro. *Lifechanges: How Women Can Make Courageous Choices.* 1990, Crown $17.95 (0-517-57686-4). A guide to decision making for women facing major changes in their lives. (REV: BL 4/15/90; LJ 5/15/90; PW 4/20/90)   **[305.4]**

578   Lerner, Gerda. *Creation of Patriarchy.* 1986, Oxford Univ. Pr. $24.95 (0-19-503996-3). An account of the development of male methods to culturally subjugate women in ancient societies. (REV: BL 4/1/86; LJ 7/86; PW 3/21/86)   **[305.4]**

579   Mahmoody, Betty, and William Hoffer. *Not Without My Daughter.* 1988, St. Martin's paper $4.95 (0-312-91193-9). An account of the author's escape to Turkey with her four-year-old daughter following her Persian husband's insistence that the family remain in Iran. (REV: BL 9/1/87; LJ 11/1/87; NYTBR 12/27/87)   **[305.4]**

580   Margolis, Maxine L. *Mothers and Such: Views of American Women and Why They Changed.* 1984, Univ. of California Pr. $32.50 (0-520-04995-0); paper $10.95 (0-520-05596-9). The history of social and economic changes that affected the American idea of motherhood in the nineteenth and twentieth centuries. (REV: BL 9/15/84; LJ 5/15/84; NYTBR 9/16/84)   **[305.4]**

581   Miles, Rosalind. *Women's History of the World.* 1990, Harper & Row paper $8.95 (0-06-097317-X). A feminist history of women's contributions to civilization. "Eminently readable and full of fresh insights."—PW (Rᴇᴠ: BL 3/15/89; PW 1/27/89; TLS 6/3/88) **[305.4]**

582 Miller, Inette. *Burning Bridges: Diary of a Mid-Life Affair.* **1989, Bantam paper $4.50 (0-553-27976-9).** A chronicle of the author's affair that led to the dissolution of her marriage. (Rᴇᴠ: LJ 11/1/87; PW 8/21/87) **[305.4]**

583 Murray, Janet Horowitz. *Strong-Minded Women: And Other Lost Voices of 19th Century England.* **1982, Pantheon paper $11.95 (0-394-71044-4).** A collection of nineteenth century English writings on the role of women in society by such authors as Charlotte Brontë, John Stuart Mill, and Florence Nightingale. (Rᴇᴠ: Choice 9/82; LJ 4/1/82; NYTBR 5/16/82) **[305.4]**

584 Patai, Daphne, ed. *Brazilian Women Speak: Contemporary Life Stories.* **1988, Rutgers Univ. Pr. $37.00 (0-8135-1300-6); paper $13.95 (0-8135-1301-4).** An oral history based on interviews with twenty Brazilian women regarding their lives and opinions. "One of the best-written oral histories ever published."—BL (Rᴇᴠ: BL 9/1/88; CSM 11/17/88; PW 9/2/88) **[305.4]**

585 Russell, Diana E. H. *Lives of Courage: Women for a New South Africa.* **1989, Basic Books $22.95 (0-465-04139-6).** A collection of 24 oral histories of South African women concerning their lives under the apartheid system. (Rᴇᴠ: BL 9/1/89; NYTBR 12/17/89; PW 7/21/89) **[305.4]**

586 Seid, Roberta P. *Never Too Thin: A History of American Women's Obsession with Weight Loss.* **1988, Prentice Hall $16.45 (0-13-925116-2).** A history of the societal concepts of beauty that influence women's perceptions of their body and self focusing on twentieth-century America. (Rᴇᴠ: Choice 9/89; LJ 4/1/89) **[305.4]**

587 Smith-Rosenberg, Carroll. *Disorderly Conduct: Visions of Gender in Victorian America.* **1985, Knopf $19.95 (0-394-53545-6); Oxford Univ. Pr. paper $9.95 (0-19-504039-2).** A selection of essays examining changing women's roles during the nineteenth century in America. (Rᴇᴠ: BL 5/1/85; LJ 5/1/85; NYTBR 8/25/85) **[305.4]**

588 Stansell, Christine. *City of Women: Sex and Class in New York, 1789–1860.* **1986, Knopf $30.00 (0-394-51534-X); Univ. of Illinois Pr. paper $9.95 (0-252-01481-2).** A social history of pre-Civil War New York focusing on the changing roles of working women. "An immensely important book."—NYTBR (Rᴇᴠ: LJ 11/1/86; NYTBR 11/30/86; PW 9/19/86) **[305.4]**

589 Westkott, Marcia. *Feminist Legacy of Karen Horney.* **1986, Yale Univ. Pr. $25.00 (0-300-03706-6); paper $9.95 (0-300-04204-3).** An analysis of the life, work, and influence of the psychoanalyst who pioneered research in women's psychology. (Rᴇᴠ: Choice 2/87; LJ 10/15/86) **[305.4]**

Social role and status of women

590 Barry, Kathleen L. *Susan B. Anthony, a Biography: A Singular Feminist.* **1988, New York Univ. Pr. $30.00 (0-8147-1105-7).** A biography of the nineteenth-century crusader for women's rights. (Rᴇᴠ: BL 9/15/88; Choice 5/89; LJ 10/1/88) **[305.42]**

591 Bergmann, Barbara R. *Economic Emergence of Women.* **1988, Basic Books paper $10.95 (0-465-01797-5).** A historical study of the increasing economic influence of women in modern society. (Rᴇᴠ: Choice 2/87; LJ 2/1/87; NYTBR 10/26/86) **[305.42]**

592 Bok, Sissela. *Alva Myrdal: A Daughter's Memoir.* **1991, Addison Wesley $22.95 (0-201-57086-6).** A portrait of the Swedish Nobel Peace Prize winner by her daughter. "An inspiring and engaging account of one of the most remarkable women of the 20th century."—PW (Rᴇᴠ: LJ 6/1/91; PW 5/10/91. Aᴡᴀʀᴅs: LJ, 1991) **[305.42]**

593 Davis, Flora. *Moving the Mountain: The Women's Movement in America Since 1960.* **1991, Simon & Schuster $23.00 (0-671-60207-1).** An overview of the women's movement and its accomplishments from the early 1960s through the 1990s. "Should be a standard resource for years to come."—PW (Rᴇᴠ: LJ 11/1/91; PW 9/20/91) **[305.42]**

594 Dworkin, Andrea. *Letters from a War Zone: Writings, 1976–1989.* **1989, Dutton $18.95 (0-525-24824-2).** A collection of the author's speeches and essays concerning the pornography and the exploitation of women in our society. (Rᴇᴠ: LJ 9/15/89; NYTBR 10/29/89; TLS 6/3/88) **[305.42]**

595 Faludi, Susan. *Backlash: The Undeclared War Against American Women.* **1991, Crown $24.00 (0-517-57698-8).** A study revealing the 1980s to be an antifemale era in the United States. "Deserves the largest possible readership."—BL (Rᴇᴠ: BL 9/1/91; LJ 9/15/91; NYTBR 10/27/91. Aᴡᴀʀᴅs: ALA, 1992; BL, 1991; LJ, 1991) **[305.42]**

596 Forster, Margaret. *Significant Sisters: The Grassroots of Active Feminism, 1839–1939.* **1986, Oxford Univ. Pr. paper $9.95 (0-19-504014-7).** A study of the rise and development of feminism and feminist thought as reflected through the lives of eight women leaders of the nineteenth and twentieth centuries. (Rᴇᴠ: Choice 7–8/85; LJ 2/1/85; NYTBR 2/17/85) **[305.42]**

597 Fraser, Antonia. *Weaker Vessel: Woman's Lot in 17th Century England.* **1985, Random paper $9.95 (0-394-73251-0).** A look at the lives of about 100 women in seventeenth-century England. "A valuable and comprehensive distillation of the social history of a violent, changeable time."—Mary Lee Settle, NYTBR (Rᴇᴠ: CSM 10/5/84; NYTBR 11/18/84; Newsweek 9/10/84. Aᴡᴀʀᴅs: LJ, 1984) **[305.42]**

598 Friedan, Betty. *Second Stage.* **1981, Summit $14.95 (0-671-41034-2); paper $9.95 (0-671-63064-4).** An examination of the state of the women's movement twenty years after the author's groundbreaking *Feminine Mystique.* (Rᴇᴠ: BL 9/15/81; LJ 11/1/81; Sat Rev 10/81) **[305.42]**

599 Gordon, Suzanne. *Prisoners of Men's Dreams: Striking Out for a New Feminine Future.* **1991, Little, Brown $19.95 (0-316-32106-0).** An examination of the recent past and potential future of feminism and feminist goals in the United States. (REV: BL 12/1/90; LJ 12/90; PW 11/16/90)   **[305.42]**

600 Gray, Francine du Plessix. *Soviet Women: Walking the Tightrope.* **1990, Doubleday $19.95 (0-385-24757-5).** A study of Soviet women's lives and attitudes based on extensive interviews the author conducted in their country. "A terrific book, probably the most sensitive and intelligent written on the subject to date."—NYTBR (REV: LJ 2/15/90; Newsweek 3/26/90; NYTBR 3/11/90)   **[305.42]**

601 Harrison, Cynthia. *On Account of Sex: The Politics of Women's Issues, 1945–1968.* **1988, Univ. of California Pr. $25.00 (0-520-06121-7).** A study of legislative and political action on women's issues from the Truman to Johnson administrations. (REV: BL 6/15/88; Choice 9/88; LJ 7/88)   **[305.42]**

602 Hewlett, Sylvia Ann. *A Lesser Life: The Myth of Women's Liberation in America.* **1987, Warner paper $10.95 (0-446-38511-5).** A study of ways women are economically exploited or disadvantaged in contemporary American society. (REV: BL 12/1/85; CSM 5/18/87; PW 1/24/86)   **[305.42]**

603 Lebsock, Suzanne. *Free Women of Petersburg: Status and Culture in a Southern Town, 1784–1860.* **1984, Norton $24.95 (0-393-01738-9).** A study of the changing role of women in an antebellum Virginia community. (REV: BL 1/15/84; LJ 9/84; NYTBR 2/26/84)   **[305.42]**

604 Mansbridge, Jane. *Why We Lost the ERA.* **1986, Univ. of Chicago Pr. $35.00 (0-226-50357-7); $9.95 paper (0-226-50358-5).** An analysis of the defeat of the campaign to add an Equal Rights Amendment to the U.S. Constitution. (REV: Choice 2/87; LJ 12/86; NYTBR 10/19/86)   **[305.42]**

605 Pogrebin, Letty C. *Deborah, Golda, and Me: Being Female and Jewish in America.* **1991, Crown $22.00 (0-517-57517-5).** A collection of essays by an editor of *Ms.* magazine examining her life as a Jewish activist for women's issues. (REV: LJ 8/91; NYTBR 10/22/91; PW 8/2/91)   **[305.42]**

606 Rix, Sara E. *American Woman, 1990–91: A Status Report.* **1990, Norton $22.95 (0-393-02840-2); paper $10.95 (0-393-30686-0).** An examination of the current status of American women in society. (REV: LJ 10/1/90; PW 3/9/90)   **[305.42]**

607 Russett, Cynthia Eagle. *Sexual Science: The Victorian Construction of Womanhood.* **1989, Harvard Univ. Pr. $25.00 (0-674-80290-X).** An analysis of arguments used by nineteenth-century scientists to "prove" the inferiority of women to men. (REV: Choice 10/89; LJ 3/1/90; NYTBR 8/9/89)   **[305.42]**

608 Scott, Kesho Yvonne. *Habit of Surviving: Black Women's Strategies for Life.* **1991, Rutgers Univ. Pr. $19.95 (0-8135-1646-3).** Four biographies of African-American women discussing their lives

and philosophies for living. (REV: BL 6/15/91; LJ 5/1/91)   **[305.42]**

609 Sidel, Ruth. *On Her Own: Growing Up in the Shadow of the American Dream.* **1990, Viking $18.95 (0-670-83154-9).** Interviews with over 150 women form the basis for this analysis of the state of women in contemporary American society. "A powerful, important book."—BL (REV: BL 11/15/89; LJ 11/15/89; PW 11/24/89)   **[305.42]**

610 Steinem, Gloria. *Outrageous Acts and Everyday Rebellions.* **1984, NAL paper $7.95 (0-452-25579-1).** Collected essays, most of which appeared originally in *New York* and *Ms.* magazines, by a key leader of the women's movement. (REV: BL 7/83; CSM 10/5/83; LJ 8/83)   **[305.42]**

611 Wandersee, Winifred D. *On the Move: American Women in the 1970s.* **1988, G. K. Hall $19.95 (0-8057-9909-5); paper $9.95 (0-8057-9910-9).** The history of the status of women and the women's movement during the 1970s. (REV: BL 3/15/88; Choice 10/88; LJ 4/15/88)   **[305.42]**

612 Wolf, Naomi. *Beauty Myth: How Images of Beauty Are Used Against Women.* **1991, Morrow $21.95 (0-688-08510-5).** An analysis of society's concepts of female beauty and its harmful effects on women. (REV: BL 2/1/91; LJ 4/1/91; PW 3/1/91) **[305.42]**

Social classes

613 Baritz, Loren. *Good Life: The Meaning of Success for the American Middle Class.* **1988, Knopf $19.95 (0-394-54947-3); Harper & Row paper $9.95 (0-06-097275-0).** A history of the changing concepts of success within the American middle class. (REV: BL 1/15/89; NYTBR 4/16/89; PW 12/9/88)   **[305.5]**

614 Birmingham, Stephen. *America's Secret Aristocracy.* **1990, Berkley paper $4.95 (0-425-11912-2).** The history of America's most powerful families from the eighteenth century to the twentieth century. (REV: BL 9/1/87; LJ 9/15/87; PW 9/4/87) **[305.5]**

615 Ehrenreich, Barbara. *Fear of Falling: The Inner Life of the Middle Class.* **1989, Pantheon $18.95 (0-394-55692-5); Harper & Row paper $9.95 (0-06-097333-1).** A study of the development of American middle class social values from the 1950s to the 1980s. (REV: NYTBR 8/6/89; Newsweek 8/14/89; PW 6/2/89)   **[305.5]**

616 Fussell, Paul. *Class: A Guide Through the American Status System.* **1984, Ballantine paper $3.95 (0-345-31816-1).** A guide to the American class system and the identification of such identifying social indicators as speech, clothing, housing, ideas, and choice of recreational activities. (REV: Atl 10/83; LJ 10/15/83; NYTBR 11/13/83)   **[305.5]**

617 Graham, Maury, and Robert Hemming. *Tales of the Iron Road: My Life as King of the Hobos.* **1990, Paragon House $19.95 (1-55778-129-X).** An autobiography of a hobo recounting his experiences riding America's rails from 1931 to 1980. (REV: LJ 12/89; PW 11/17/89)   **[305.5]**

618 Harrington, Michael. *New American Poverty.* 1984, Henry Holt $17.95 (0-03-062157-7); **Penguin paper** $7.95 (0-14-008112-7). An examination of American poverty in the 1980s by the author of *The Other America.* (REV: Atl 10/84; LJ 8/84; NYTBR 8/26/84) **[305.5]**

619 Lapham, Lewis H. *Money and Class in America: Notes and Observations on the American Character.* 1987, Grove-Weidenfeld $18.95 (1-55584-109-0); **Ballantine paper** $4.95 (0-345-35871-6). A social history of money and its relationship to status and class in American society. (REV: NYTBR 2/14/88; Newsweek 2/29/88; Time 2/22/8) **[305.5]**

Religious groups

620 Fein, Leonard. *Where Are We? The Inner Life of America's Jews.* 1988, Harper & Row $19.95 (0-06-015872-7); **1989 paper** $8.95 (0-06-091564-1). A study of contemporary issues facing the American Jewish community by the editor of *Moment* magazine. (REV: BL 4/15/88; Choice 10/88; LJ 5/15/88) **[305.6]**

621 Gilbert, Martin. *Jews of Hope.* 1985, **Penguin paper** $7.95 (0-14-008510-6). Accounts of the lives of Jews who have been refused requests to emigrate from the Soviet Union. (REV: BL 1/15/85; LJ 1/85; PW 11/30/84) **[305.6]**

622 Harris, Lis. *Holy Days: The World of a Hasidic Family.* 1985, Summit $18.95 (0-671-46296-2); **Macmillan paper** $8.95 (0-02-020970-3). A writer for the *New Yorker* describes her experiences with members of a Brooklyn Hasidic Jewish family. "Like the best fiction, *Holy Days* reads smoothly, buoyed by strong characterizations and powerful themes."—BL (REV: BL 11/1/85; LJ 11/15/85; NYTBR 11/10/85) **[305.6]**

623 Hertzberg, Arthur. *Jews in America: Four Centuries of an Uneasy Encounter.* 1989, Simon & Schuster $22.95 (0-671-62709-0). The history of Jews in America since the seventeenth century, and the ongoing dilemma of how to assimilate into American society, yet retain traditional Jewish culture and values. (REV: BL 11/1/89; LJ 12/89; NYTBR 11/26/89) **[305.6]**

624 Karp, Abraham J. *Haven and Home: A History of the Jews in America.* 1985, Schocken $24.95 (0-8052-3920-0). A history of the American Jewish experience from the seventeenth century to the present. (REV: Choice 6/85; NYTBR 8/4/85; PW 4/12/85) **[305.6]**

625 Sanders, Ronald. *Shores of Refuge: A Hundred Years of Jewish Emigration.* 1988, Henry Holt $27.95 (0-8050-0563-3); **Schocken paper** $14.95 (0-8052-0916-6). A history of Jewish persecution and emigration from the assassination of the Russian Tsar Alexander II to the present. (REV: Choice 5/88; LJ 12/87; NYTBR 4/24/88) **[305.6]**

626 Silberman, Charles E. *A Certain People: American Jews and Their Lives Today.* 1985, Summit $19.95 (0-671-44761-0); **paper** $8.95 (0-671-62877-1). An optimistic study of the past, present, and future of the American Jewish community. (REV: BL 8/85; LJ 9/15/85; Time 8/26/85) **[305.6]**

Racial, ethnic, national groups

627 Ashmore, Harry S. *Hearts and Minds: A Personal Chronicle of Race in America.* 1988, Seven Locks Pr. **paper** $14.95 (0-932020-58-5). A history of racism in America from the 1930s to the 1980s as viewed by a Pulitzer Prize-winning journalist. (REV: BL 6/1/82; NYTBR 6/20/82; PW 3/26/82) **[305.8]**

628 Brookhiser, Richard. *Way of the WASP: How It Made America, and How It Can Save It, So to Speak.* 1991, Free Pr. $19.95 (0-02-904721-8). A celebration of WASP values and characteristics trumpeting them as central to America's past and future success. (REV: BL 11/15/90; NYTBR 1/20/91; PW 11/9/90) **[305.8]**

629 Chafets, Ze'ev. *Devil's Night and Other True Tales of Detroit.* 1990, Random $19.95 (0-394-58525-9). A relocated Israeli author's portrait of his former hometown. "An enormously unsettling read and a tragically accurate picture of a dying metropolis."—PW (REV: BL 9/15/90; LJ 10/15/90; PW 8/24/90) **[305.8]**

630 Chicago Tribune Staff. *American Millstone: An Examination of the Nation's Permanent Underclass.* 1986, Contemporary **paper** $8.95 (0-8092-4931-6). Collected articles by *Chicago Tribune* reporters portraying life in that city's ghettos. (REV: BL 12/1/86; LJ 12/86) **[305.8]**

631 Crouch, Stanley. *Notes of a Hanging Judge: Essays and Reviews, 1979–1988.* 1990, Oxford Univ. Pr. $22.95 (0-19-505591-8); **paper** $8.95 (0-19-506998-6). Selected essays originally published in the *New Republic* and *Village Voice* by the outspoken critic and observer of African-American life and culture. (REV: BL 2/1/90; LJ 2/15/90; NYTBR 3/11/90) **[305.8]**

632 Frederickson, George M. *White Supremacy: A Comparative Study in American and South African History.* 1981, Oxford Univ. Pr. $39.95 (0-19-502759-0); **paper** $10.95 (0-19-503042-7). A study of United States and South African history comparing the legacy of the white domination of racially mixed societies. (REV: New Rep 2/21/81; NYTBR 1/25/81; Newsweek 7/23/81) **[305.8]**

633 Hochschild, Adam. *Mirror at Midnight: A South African Journey.* 1990, Viking $19.95 (0-670-83539-0). An account of the Boers' settling of South Africa and the legacy and influence of those events in the present day. "One of the most illuminating books ever written on contemporary South Africa."—PW (REV: BL 11/15/90; LJ 10/15/90; PW 10/5/90) **[305.8]**

634 Langley, Lester D. *MexAmerica: Two Countries, One Future.* 1988, Crown $19.95 (0-517-56732-6). An examination of the economic and cultural interdependence of the United States and Mexico. (REV: LJ 7/88; NYTBR 4/24/88; PW 2/19/88) **[305.8]**

635 Lester, Julius. *Falling Pieces of the Broken Sky.* 1990, Arcade $19.95 (1-55970-059-9). A collection of 35 essays about race, writing, and other topics. (REV: LJ 10/1/90; PW 9/14/90) **[305.8]**

636 North, James. *Freedom Rising.* **1986, NAL paper $8.95 (0-452-25805-7).** An introduction to the history and culture of Southern Africa. "For the general reader there is no better source on South Africa than this compelling account."—BL (Rev: BL 2/1/85; LJ 5/1/85; NYTBR 7/14/85) **[305.8]**

637 Sleeper, Jim. *Closest of Strangers: Liberalism and the Politics of Race in New York.* **1990, Norton $21.95 (0-393-02902-6).** A historical study of African Americans and attitudes toward them in New York City politics. (Rev: BL 8/90; Choice 3/91; PW 7/13/90) **[305.8]**

638 Sowell, Thomas. *Economics of Politics and Race: An International Perspective.* **1983, Morrow $15.95 (0-688-01891-2).** An examination of the relationship between race, culture, and economic well-being examining the status of European, Chinese, and African immigrants. (Rev: BL 10/1/83; LJ 12/15/83; New Rep 11/21/83) **[305.8]**

639 Sway, Marlene. *Familiar Strangers: Gypsy Life in America.* **1990, Univ. of Illinois Pr. $19.95 (0-252-01512-6).** A look at the lives and culture of the one million gypsies that reside in the United States. (Rev: BL 7/88; Choice 12/88; LJ 7/88) **[305.8]**

640 Weyr, Thomas. *Hispanic U.S.A.: Assimilation or Separation?* **1988, Harper & Row $19.95 (0-06-039066-2).** An examination of the current state of Hispanic-American demographics, culture, and rates of assimilation into the American mainstream. (Rev: LJ 4/5/88; NYTBR 4/24/88; PW 2/12/88) **[305.8]**

Semites

641 Beckwith, Carol, Angela Fisher, and Graham Hancock. *African Ark: People and Ancient Cultures of Ethiopia and the Horn of Africa.* **1990, Abrams $65.00 (0-8109-1902-8).** A photographic tour and textual survey of the lands and peoples of Kenya, Somalia, and Ethiopia. (Rev: BL 10/1/90; LJ 9/15/90; PW 8/31/90) **[305.892]**

642 Lewis, Bernard. *Semites and Anti-Semites: An Inquiry into Conflict and Prejudice.* **1986, Norton $18.95 (0-393-02314-1).** A study of the historical roots and contemporary manifestations of anti-Semitism by the noted historian of the Muslim world. (Rev: BL 6/1/86; CSM 10/6/86; LJ 5/15/86) **[305.892]**

643 Patai, Raphael. *Seed of Abraham: Jews and Arabs in Conflict.* **1986, Univ. of Utah Pr. $29.95 (0-87480-251-2); Macmillan paper $11.95 (0-684-18752-3).** An examination of Jewish-Arab relations and attitudes toward each other through the centuries. (Rev: Choice 10/86; LJ 7/86; PW 4/25/86) **[305.892]**

Africans and people of African descent

644 Bell, Derrick. *And We Are Not Saved: The Elusive Quest for Racial Justice.* **1987, Basic Books $19.95 (0-465-00328-1); paper $11.95 (0-465-00329-X).** A history of the struggle for racial justice and equality for minorities in the United States. "A fascinating and provocative contribution to the continuing search for a more perfect union."—NYTBR (Rev: LJ 8/87; New Rep 11/16/87; NYTBR 10/11/87) **[305.896]**

645 Blauner, Bob. *Black Lives, White Lives: Three Decades of Race Relations in America.* **1989, Univ. of California Pr. $25.00 (0-520-06261-2).** A collection of interviews with black and white Americans regarding racial attitudes and race relations from the 1960s to the 1980s. (Rev: BL 5/1/89; LJ 3/15/89; NYTBR 7/9/89) **[305.896]**

646 Cruse, Harold. *Plural but Equal: Blacks and Minorities in America's Plural Society.* **1987, Morrow $22.95 (0-688-04486-7); paper $12.95 (0-688-08331-5).** An examination of the status of minorities in contemporary American society and how their interests can best be improved by social and political action. (Rev: LJ 5/1/87; Natl Rev 9/11/87; PW 4/10/87) **[305.896]**

647 Kaufman, Jonathan. *Broken Alliance: The Turbulent Times Between Blacks and Jews in America.* **1988, Macmillan $19.95 (0-684-18699-3); NAL paper $4.95 (0-451-62737-7).** A history of Black-Jewish relations in the United States since the seventeenth century focusing on reasons why their traditional alliance has become strained in recent years. (Rev: Choice 1/89; LJ 10/1/88; NYTBR 10/9/88) **[305.896]**

648 Lapping, Brian. *Apartheid: A History.* **1987, Braziller $19.95 (0-8076-1177-8).** An introductory history of the apartheid system in South Africa from the arrival of the Dutch in the seventeenth century to the present. (Rev: BL 6/1/87; Choice 10/87; LJ 4/15/87) **[305.896]**

649 Mathabane, Mark. *Kaffir Boy in America: An Encounter with Apartheid.* **1989, Macmillan $19.95 (0-684-19043-5); paper $8.95 (0-02-034530-5).** A critical study of American life, culture, and race relations by the relocated South African author of *Kaffir Boy.* (Rev: BL 5/1/89; LJ 6/1/89; NYTBR 8/13/89) **[305.896]**

650 Neuhaus, Richard John. *Dispensations: The Future of South Africa as South Africans See It.* **1986, Eerdmans $16.95 (0-8028-3627-5).** Collected interviews with South Africans of varying backgrounds regarding the future of their nation and its apartheid system. (Rev: BL 4/1/86; Choice 11/86; LJ 7/86) **[305.896]**

651 Rose, Willie Lee. *Slavery and Freedom.* **1982, Oxford Univ. Pr. paper $9.95 (0-19-503266-7).** Essays and reviews regarding aspects of the institution of slavery in the American South. (Rev: BL 12/1/81; LJ 1/1/82; NYTBR 1/24/82) **[305.896]**

652 Steele, Shelby. *Content of Our Character: A New Vision of Race in America.* **1990, St. Martin's $15.95 (0-312-05064-X).** An analysis of the psychology of race and race relations in the United States. (Rev: BL 9/1/90; LJ 8/90; New Rep 12/10/90) **[305.896]**

653 Stuckey, Sterling. *Slave Culture: Nationalist Theory and the Foundations of Black America.* **1988, Oxford Univ. Pr. paper $11.95 (0-19-505664-7).**

A study of the traditional African cultural institutions which flourished and evolved in North America. (Rev: Choice 10/87; LJ 4/1/87; New Rep 10/12/87)
[305.896]

654 Teague, Bob. *Flip Side of Soul: Letters to My Son.* 1989, Morrow $15.95 (0-688-08260-2). The African-American newscaster discusses the challenges of being black in a largely white dominated profession and offers suggestions on how best to meet those challenges. (Rev: LJ 2/1/89; PW 12/16/88)
[305.896]

655 Thompson, Leonard. *Political Mythology of Apartheid.* 1986, Yale Univ. Pr. $37.50 (0-300-03368-0); paper $11.95 (0-300-03512-8). A study of the philosophical basis for South Africa's apartheid system. (Rev: Choice 3/86; LJ 9/15/85; NYRB 9/26/85)
[305.896]

656 Williamson, Joel. *Crucible of Race: Black-White Relations in the American South Since Emancipation.* 1984, Oxford Univ. Pr. $35.00 (0-19-503382-5). A study of black-white relations in the American South from 1850 to 1915 and how they influenced future social trends. (Rev: CSM 9/10/84; LJ 10/15/84; New Rep 10/15/84)
[305.896]

657 Wilson, Francis. *South Africa: The Cordoned Heart.* Ed. by Omar Badsha. 1986, Norton $25.00 (0-393-02341-9); paper $14.95 (0-393-30335-7). A photographic essay by 20 South Africans documenting life under the apartheid system. (Rev: BL 5/15/86; CSM 9/5/86; LJ 5/15/86)
[305.896]

306 Culture and institutions

658 Alverson, Marianne. *Under African Sun.* 1989, Univ. of Chicago Pr. $19.95 (0-226-01623-4); paper $11.95 (0-226-01624-2). An American woman recounts her experiences living with an African tribe in Botswana. "A valuable as well as entertaining account of disappearing African society."—PW (Rev: Choice 9/87; LJ 4/1/87; PW 2/13/87)
[306]

659 Bateson, Mary Catherine. *With a Daughter's Eye: A Memoir of Margaret Mead and Gregory Bateson.* 1985, Pocket paper $4.95 (0-671-55424-7). A dual biography of the noted anthropologists by their daughter. "Not only a biography of Mead and Bateson but a warm story of growing up with two brilliant eccentrics and coming out of the experience a wise and strong person."—NYTBR (Rev: Choice 12/84; LJ 8/84; NYTBR 8/26/84. Awards: ALA, 1984; LJ, 1984; NYTBR, 1984)
[306]

660 Bellah, Robert N. *Habits of the Heart: Individualism and Commitment in American Life.* 1986, Harper & Row paper $9.95 (0-06-097027-8). Based on four detailed interview projects, this study of morals in America contrasts current observations with those of historical observers of American life beginning with Tocqueville. (Rev: New Rep 5/20/85; NYTBR 4/14/85; Newsweek 4/29/85)
[306]

661 Cheneviere, Alain. *Vanishing Tribes: Primitive Man on Earth.* 1987, Doubleday $35.00 (0-385-23897-5). An introduction to the cultures of 20 tribal

groups whose existence or way of life is threatened. (Rev: BL 12/1/87; LJ 9/15/87; NYTBR 2/28/88)
[306]

662 Collier, Peter, and David Horowitz. *Destructive Generation: Second Thoughts about the '60s.* 1989, Summit $21.95 (0-671-66752-1); paper $9.95 (0-671-70128-2). Two former activists who became right-wing conservatives reflect on the flaws of the political thought of the 1960s. (Rev: BL 2/1/89; LJ 3/15/89; Natl Rev 3/24/89)
[306]

663 Connolly, Bob, and Robin Anderson. *First Contact: New Guinea's Highlanders Encounter the Outside World.* 1988, Penguin paper $10.95 (0-14-007465-1). An account of a 1930 Australian expedition to New Guinea that encountered a tribe that was unexposed to outside influences. (Rev: Choice 11/87; LJ 7/87; NYTBR 8/2/87)
[306]

664 Cowan, Paul. *An Orphan in History: One Man's Triumphant Search for His Roots.* 1990, Doubleday paper $9.95 (0-385-41127-8). The story of the author's search for his lost Jewish past and his embracing of the religion of his ancestors. (Rev: LJ 10/1/82; NYTBR 10/10/82; PW 7/9/82)
[306]

665 Davis, David B. *Slavery and Human Progress.* 1986, Oxford Univ. Pr. paper $11.95 (0-19-503733-2). A historical analysis of how and why slavery develops and declines in societies. "A work of awesome intellectual depth and range . . . ranks among the most important studies of slavery."—LJ (Rev: Choice 1/85; LJ 10/1/84; TLS 2/1/85)
[306]

666 Freeman, Derek. *Margaret Mead and Samoa: The Making and Unmaking of an Anthropological Myth.* 1983, Harvard Univ. Pr. $25.00 (0-674-54830-2); Penguin paper $6.95 (0-14-022555-2). A critical appraisal of the anthropological studies conducted by Margaret Mead in Samoa during the 1920s and 1930s. (Rev: Choice 7–8/83; PW 3/4/83; Time 2/14/83)
[306]

667 Geertz, Clifford. *Local Knowledge: Further Essays in Interpretive Anthropology.* 1985, Basic Books paper $11.95 (0-465-04162-0). An anthropologist's essays on the study of human culture. (Rev: CSM 12/14/83; LJ 8/83; NYTBR 3/15/84)
[306]

668 Howard, Robert. *Brave New Workplace.* 1986, Penguin paper $8.95 (0-14-009434-2). An examination of the effects of high technology upon work and those who perform it. (Rev: Atl 5/86; LJ 1/86; NYTBR 12/22/85)
[306]

669 Kertzer, David I. *Ritual, Politics and Power.* 1988, Yale Univ. Pr. $25.00 (0-300-04007-5); paper $10.95 (0-300-04362-7). A study of political rituals and their importance in human societies. (Rev: Choice 11/88; LJ 3/15/88)
[306]

670 Koonz, Claudia. *Mothers in the Fatherland: Women, Family Life and Nazi Ideology, 1919–1945.* 1987, St. Martin's $25.00 (0-312-54933-4); paper $16.95 (0-312-02256-5). The role of women in the politics and society of Hitler's Germany. "A book of great historical and moral importance."—Robert Jay Lifton, NYTBR (Rev: LJ 11/1/86; NYRB 7/16/87; NYTBR 1/3/88. Awards: ALA, 1987)
[306]

671 Lesy, Michael. *Forbidden Zone.* **1987, Farrar $16.95 (0-374-15756-1); Doubleday paper $7.95 (0-385-26034-2).** Profiles of persons who work in occupations that deal with death on a daily basis. (REV: BL 5/1/87; LJ 5/1/87; PW 7/20/87)   **[306]**

672 Louv, Richard. *America II.* **1985, Penguin paper $7.95 (0-14-007560-7).** An examination of the social consequences of the American population shift towards the sunbelt cities of the South and West. (REV: BL 10/15/83; Choice 3/84; LJ 12/15/83) **[306]**

673 Marcus, Greil. *Lipstick Traces: A Secret History of the Twentieth Century.* **1989, Harvard Univ. Pr. $29.95 (0-674-53580-4); paper $14.95 (0-674-53581-2).** An attempt to place punk rock music into the tradition of nihilist and nonconformist movements throughout history. (REV: BL 3/1/89; NYTBR 4/9/89; PW 2/10/89)   **[306]**

674 Naisbitt, John, and Patricia Aburdene. *Megatrends 2000: Ten New Directions for the 1990's.* **1990, Morrow $21.95 (0-688-07224-0).** Key social and economic trends that will influence the economy and events of the 1990s are identified in this sequel to the authors' best-selling book *Megatrends.* (REV: BL 11/1/89; CSM 2/12/90; PW 11/1/89)   **[306]**

675 Nelson, Richard. *Island Within.* **1989, North Point Pr. $18.95 (0-86547-404-4).** The author recounts his experiences living in Alaska among the Kuyukon Indians. (REV: BL 9/15/89; CSM 1/30/90; LJ 10/1/89. AWARDS: BL, 1989)   **[306]**

676 Patterson, Orlando. *Slavery and Social Death: A Comparative Study.* **1982, Harvard Univ. Pr. $35.50 (0-674-81082-1); paper $12.95 (0-674-81083-X).** Slavery and its social effects in over 60 societies from ancient times to the twentieth century. (REV: Choice 2/83; LJ 11/15/82; TLS 9/9/83)   **[306]**

677 Sawyer, Robert. *Slavery in the 20th Century.* **1986, Routledge $39.95 (0-7102-0475-2).** A look at forms of slavery existing in the world today with case studies of victims of forced labor, apartheid, and prostitution among others. (REV: Choice 6/87; LJ 5/15/87)   **[306]**

678 Schickel, Richard. *Intimate Strangers: The Culture of Celebrity.* **1986, Fromm International paper $10.95 (0-88064-055-3).** A study of the American obsession with celebrity and its effects upon society and the famous. "Provocative, disturbing and often brilliant."—PW (REV: LJ 3/1/85; PW 1/25/85; Time 4/8/85)   **[306]**

679 Stevens, Jay. *Storming Heaven: LSD and the American Dream.* **1987, Atlantic Monthly $19.95 (0-87113-076-9); Harper & Row paper $9.95 (0-06-097172-X).** The history of the psychoreactive drug LSD and its influence upon the culture of the 1960s. (REV: LJ 10/15/87; NYTBR 9/6/87; Newsweek 8/24/87)   **[306]**

680 Wallechinsky, David. *Midterm Report: The Class of '65; Chronicles of an American Generation.* **1986, Viking $19.95 (0-670-80428-2).** A sequel to the author's *What Really Happened to the Class of 1965* continues to trace the lives of 28 former classmates through the decade of 1975–1985. (REV: BL 5/1/86; LJ 7/86; PW 6/20/86)   **[306]**

681 Walvin, James. *Victorian Values.* **1988, Univ. of Georgia Pr. $20.00 (0-8203-1012-3); paper $9.95 (0-8203-1013-1).** An examination of contemporary British society and its views and adaptations of the values of the Victorians. (REV: CSM 6/1/88; LJ 3/1/88)   **[306]**

682 Williamson, Judith. *Consuming Passions: Politics and Images of Popular Culture.* **1985, M. Boyars $19.95 (0-7145-2828-5); paper $12.95 (0-7145-2851-X).** Miscellaneous writings on popular culture and its symbolism in American culture. (REV: NYTBR 6/15/86; PW 2/14/86)   **[306]**

683 Willner, Ann Ruth. *Spellbinders: Charismatic Political Leadership.* **1984, Yale Univ. Pr. $27.50 (0-300-02809-1); paper $9.95 (0-300-03405-9).** A study of personal charisma and its effects upon political leadership and power in the twentieth century. (REV: Choice 6/84; LJ 3/15/84; NYTBR 3/4/84)   **[306]**

684 Wuthnow, Robert. *Restructuring of American Religion.* Ed. by John F. Wilson. **1988, Princeton Univ. Pr. $39.50 (0-691-07328-7).** An examination of social and political trends in American religion since World War II. (REV: Choice 10/88; LJ 6/1/88; TLS 6/9/89)   **[306]**

685 Zerubavel, Eviatar. *Seven Day Circle: The History and Meaning of the Week.* **1985, Free Pr. $19.95 (0-02-934680-0); Univ. of Chicago Pr. paper $9.95 (0-226-98165-7).** A study of the concept of the week and its influences upon human activities and perceptions of time. (REV: Choice 1/86; LJ 6/15/85; NYTBR 6/23/85)   **[306]**

Indigenous racial, ethnic, national groups

686 Read, Kenneth E. *Return to the High Valley: Coming Full Circle.* **1986, Univ. of California Pr. $25.00 (0-520-05664-7); paper $10.95 (0-520-06468-2).** A cultural anthropologist describes his return visit to the Gahaku tribe of New Guinea three decades after doing fieldwork study of the group. (REV: BL 4/15/86; Choice 9/86; LJ 4/15/86)   **[306.08]**

Persons

687 Christianson, Gale E. *Fox at the Wood's Edge: A Biography of Loren Eiseley.* **1990, Henry Holt $29.95 (0-8050-1187-0).** A biography of the American anthropologist and author of *Darwin's Century* and *The Unexpected Universe.* (REV: BL 8/90; LJ 8/90; NYTBR 8/19/90)   **[306.092]**

688 Howard, Jane. *Margaret Mead: A Life.* **1989, Fawcett paper $12.95 (0-449-90497-0).** A biography of the cultural anthropologist based on interviews with 300 friends and acquaintances. (REV: BL 6/15/84; Choice 1/85; PW 7/13/84)   **[306.092]**

689 Leakey, Mary D. *Disclosing the Past.* **1986, McGraw-Hill paper $9.95 (0-07-036837-6).** An autobiography of the archaeologist who, along with her husband Louis, made fossil finds critical to our current theories of evolution. (REV: LJ 10/1/84; NYTBR 11/4/84; Newsweek 10/29/84)   **[306.092]**

United States

690 Nisbet, Robert A. *Present Age: Progress and Anarchy in Modern America.* 1988, Harper & Row $17.95 (0-06-015902-2); paper $7.95 (0-06-091578-1). A study of the detrimental influence of eighteenth and nineteenth century thought upon contemporary American political philosophy. (Rev: BL 6/1/88; LJ 9/15/88) **[306.0973]**

691 Stern, Jane, and Michael Stern. *Encyclopedia of Bad Taste: A Celebration of American Pop Culture at Its Most Joyfully Outrageous.* 1990, HarperCollins $29.95 (0-06-016470-0); paper $15.95 (0-06-092121-8). An illustrated survey of bad taste in America featuring the histories of such items as lava lamps, Nehru jackets, Charo, and bell-bottoms. (Rev: BL 9/1/90; Time 12/17/90) **[306.0973]**

692 Weiss, Michael J. *Clustering of America.* 1988, Harper & Row $22.50 (0-06-015790-9); paper $10.95 (0-06-091599-4). A demographic study of the United States dividing the country into 40 zip code-defined subgroups for marketing purposes. (Rev: LJ 3/15/89; NYTBR 1/22/89) **[306.0973]**

Cultural institutions

693 Ewen, Stuart. *All Consuming Images: The Politics of Style in Contemporary Culture.* 1988, Basic Books $19.95 (0-465-00100-9). An illustrated survey of the role of style and image in contemporary popular culture. (Rev: BL 9/15/88; PW 9/2/88) **[306.4]**

694 Herzlich, Claudine, and Janine Pierret. *Illness and Self in Society.* 1987, Johns Hopkins $32.50 (0-8018-3228-4). A social history of the sick, and attitudes toward them from the Middle Ages to the twentieth century. (Rev: BL 10/15/87; LJ 11/1/87) **[306.4]**

695 Morris, David B. *Culture of Pain.* 1991, Univ. of California Pr. $29.95 (0-520-07266-9). A history of the concept of pain in various cultures and literatures. (Rev: BL 10/1/91; PW 8/9/91) **[306.4]**

696 Patterson, Orlando. *Freedom Volume One: Freedom in the Making of Western Culture.* 1991, Basic Books $29.95 (0-465-02535-8). This first of a projected two-volume work traces the Western concept and meaning of freedom during ancient times and the Middle Ages. (Rev: LJ 7/91; NYTBR 11/17/91. Awards: NBA, 1991) **[306.4]**

697 Schor, Juliet B. *Overworked American: The Unexpected Decline of Leisure.* 1992, Basic Books $21.00 (0-465-05433-1). An analysis of the American workweek comparing present to past and the United States to other nations. "A book with a challenging, provocative message."—BL (Rev: BL 12/15/91; LJ 1/92; PW 11/22/91) **[306.4]**

Language

698 Lakoff, Robin T. *Talking Power: The Politics of Language in Our Lives.* 1990, Basic Books $22.95 (0-465-08358-7). A study of the relationships between language, communication, and power. (Rev: BL 10/1/90; LJ 9/15/90) **[306.44]**

Science

699 Weissmann, Gerald. *Doctor with Two Heads: And Other Essays.* 1990, Knopf $19.95 (0-394-57833-3). Fourteen essays on subjects ranging from the writing style of Gertrude Stein to Lyme disease. (Rev: CSM 6/26/90; LJ 3/15/90; NYTBR 7/15/90) **[306.45]**

Art

700 Haraszti, Miklos. *Velvet Prison: Artists Under State Socialism.* 1987, Basic Books $14.95 (0-465-09800-2); Farrar paper $7.95 (0-374-52181-6). A study of the effects of government control in the socialist state upon artists and their creative efforts. (Rev: LJ 12/87; NYTBR 11/22/87; PW 9/4/87) **[306.47]**

Recreation

701 Boskin, Joseph. *Sambo: The Rise and Demise of an American Jester.* 1986, Oxford Univ. Pr. $22.95 (0-19-504074-0). A study of African-American stereotypes and their manifestations in nineteenth- and twentieth-century popular culture. (Rev: Choice 6/87; LJ 2/1/87; NYTBR 1/4/87) **[306.48]**

Religious institutions

702 Martin, David. *Tongues of Fire: The Explosion of Protestantism in Latin America.* 1990, Basil Blackwell $39.95 (0-631-17186-X). An examination of the recent spread of evangelical religions in the nations of Latin America. (Rev: LJ 6/1/90; Natl Rev. 12/31/90) **[306.6]**

Institutions pertaining to relations of the sexes

703 Ackerley, J. R. *My Father and Myself.* 1988, Pocket $7.95 (0-671-65675-9); Harcourt paper $3.95 (0-15-662325-0). Memoirs of the British journalist and author of *Hindoo Holiday.* "A classic of autobiographical literature."—NYTBR (Rev: LJ 5/1/69; New Rep 3/29/69; NYTBR 4/27/69) **[306.7]**

704 Braudy, Leo. *Frenzy of Renown: Fame and Its History.* 1986, Oxford Univ. Pr. $27.50 (0-19-504003-1). A history of the changing concept of fame in Western culture from Alexander the Great to the twentieth century. "A marvelously provocative study, chock full of characters."—NYTBR (Rev: Choice 1/87; LJ 10/15/86; NYTBR 9/7/86) **[306.7]**

705 Coles, Robert, and Geoffrey Stokes. *Sex and the American Teenager.* 1985, Harper & Row paper $5.95 (0-06-096002-7). A study of the sexual knowledge, attitudes, and practices of the American teenager based on interviews and questionnaires. (Rev: BL 4/15/85; LJ 5/1/85; PW 3/29/85) **[306.7]**

706 Dalby, Lisa C. *Geisha.* 1983, Univ. of California Pr. $37.00 (0-520-04742-7); Random paper $9.95 (0-394-72893-9). The role of the geisha in Japanese society, culture, and history as described by a Westerner who became one. "The first real look that the West has had into this closed world."—

NYTBR (Rev: LJ 11/1/83; NYTBR 2/5/84; Newsweek 1/16/84. Awards: ALA, 1984) **[306.7]**

707 Dash, Lem. *When Children Want Children: The Urban Crisis of Teenage Childbearing.* **1989, Morrow $18.95 (0-688-06957-6); Penguin paper $8.95 (0-14-011789-X).** A look at the social and psychological problems arising from teenage pregnancy and childbearing. (Rev: LJ 12/88; PW 11/18/88) **[306.7]**

708 D'Emilio, John, and Estelle Freedman. *Intimate Matters: A History of Sexuality in America.* **1988, Harper & Row $24.95 (0-06-015855-7); paper $9.95 (0-06-091550-1).** A history of sex and sexuality in American society from the Puritans to the present day. (Rev: BL 4/15/88; LJ 5/1/88; NYTBR 4/24/88) **[306.7]**

709 Dworkin, Andrea. *Intercourse.* **1987, Free Pr. $19.95 (0-02-907970-5); paper $9.95 (0-02-907971-3).** A feminist analysis of the submission of women forced upon them by their receiving role in sexual intercourse. (Rev: Choice 9/87; LJ 4/15/87; TLS 10/16/87) **[306.7]**

710 Ehrenreich, Barbara. *Re-Making Love: The Feminization of Sex.* **1986, Doubleday paper $15.95 (0-385-18498-0).** An account of the role women have played in America's reassessment of sexual attitudes and mores. (Rev: BL 9/1/86; LJ 9/1/86; NYTBR 9/14/86) **[306.7]**

711 Faderman, Lillian. *Surpassing the Love of Men: Love Between Women from the Renaissance to the Present.* **1981, Morrow paper $14.95 (0-688-00396-6).** An examination of female friendships and love from the sixteenth century to the present. (Rev: Atl 3/81; LJ 2/15/81; NYRB 5/28/81) **[306.7]**

712 Forward, Susan, and Joan Torres. *Men Who Hate Women and the Women Who Love Them.* **1987, Bantam paper $4.50 (0-553-26507-5).** The best-selling self-help guide for women involved in destructive personal relationships with misogynists. (Rev: BL 9/1/86; LJ 8/86; Newsweek 6/1/87) **[306.7]**

713 Gay, Peter. *Bourgeois Experience: Victoria to Freud; the Tender Passion, Vol. II.* **1986, Oxford Univ. Pr. $27.95 (0-19-503741-3); paper $10.95 (0-19-505183-1).** A study of love and romance among the nineteenth-century European middle-class. "A fine, highly readable work of intellectual history."—PW (Rev: LJ 2/15/86; NYTBR 3/16/86; PW 1/10/86) **[306.7]**

714 Gay, Peter. *Education of the Senses: Victoria to Freud.* **1984, Oxford Univ. Pr. $27.95 (0-19-503352-3); paper $11.95 (0-19-503728-6).** Volume 1 of Gay's projected five-volume Bourgeois Experience examining various aspects of Victorian culture; this volume looks at social views of sex and sexuality during the era. (Rev: LJ 12/1/83; NYRB 2/2/84; NYTBR 1/8/84. Awards: LJ, 1984; NYTBR, 1984) **[306.7]**

715 Gonzalez-Crussi, F. *On the Nature of Things Erotic.* **1988, Harcourt $16.95 (0-15-169966-6).** A collection of eight essays regarding human sexual-

ity by the Mexican author of *The Five Senses.* (Rev: BL 4/1/88; LJ 5/1/88; NYTBR 7/10/88) **[306.7]**

716 Kaplan, Louise J. *Female Perversions: The Temptations of Emma Bovary.* **1991, Doubleday $24.95 (0-385-26233-7).** A psychoanalytical study of sexual perversions in society and sexually related themes in Flaubert's *Madame Bovary.* (Rev: LJ 12/90; NYTBR 2/17/91; PW 11/30/90) **[306.7]**

717 Margulis, Lynn, and Dorion Sagan. *Mystery Dance: On the Evolution of Human Sexuality.* **1991, Summit $19.95 (0-671-63341-4).** A study of the development of human sexual adaptions from prehistory to the present. (Rev: LJ 7/91; PW 6/14/91) **[306.7]**

718 Masters, William H., Virginia E. Johnson, and Robert C. Kolodny. *Masters and Johnson on Sex and Human Loving.* **1988, Little, Brown paper $12.95 (0-316-50160-3).** A survey of sex, sexual behaviors, and current sexually related issues. "Likely to become the cornerstone of library sex-information collections."—BL (Rev: BL 2/15/86; LJ 4/1/86; PW 5/9/86) **[306.7]**

719 Mosse, George L. *Nationalism and Sexuality: Respectability and Abnormal Sexuality in Modern Europe.* **1985, Fertig $40.00 (0-86527-350-2); Univ. of Wisconsin Pr. paper $12.50 (0-299-11894-0).** An examination of abnormal sexuality and its relationship to the rise of fascism in Europe. "Cultural history at its best and most intriguing . . . a masterpiece."—BL (Rev: BL 2/15/85; Choice 2/86; LJ 4/15/85) **[306.7]**

720 Ransohoff, Rita M. *Venus after 40: Sexual Myths, Men's Fantasies and Truths about Middle-Aged Women.* **1990, New Horizon $11.95 (0-88882-064-8).** A psychotherapist's studies of the myths and realities of the sexuality of American women over the age of 40. (Rev: BL 9/1/87; LJ 11/1/87; PW 10/30/87) **[306.7]**

721 Rutter, Peter. *Sex in the Forbidden Zone.* **1989, J. P. Tarcher $17.95 (0-87477-486-1); Fawcett paper $5.99 (0-449-14727-4).** A psychiatrist presents the results of his research regarding sexual relations between male professionals and their female clients. (Rev: BL 9/15/89; LJ 10/1/89; PW 8/4/89) **[306.7]**

722 Sternberg, Robert J. *Triangle of Love: Intimacy, Passion and Commitment.* **1988, Basic Books $18.95 (0-465-08746-9).** A theory of heterosexual love presented by the Yale psychologist. "An illuminating book."—LJ (Rev: BL 9/15/88; LJ 10/15/88; PW 9/16/88) **[306.7]**

723 Stoltenberg, John. *Refusing to Be a Man: Essays on Sex and Justice.* **1989, Breitenbush Books $16.95 (0-932576-73-7); NAL paper $8.95 (0-452-01043-8).** A collection of essays concerning male sexual identity and its relationship to rape and war. "Some of the clearest, most compelling statements of feminist thought ever made."—BL (Rev: BL 4/1/89; Choice 12/89; LJ 5/1/89) **[306.7]**

724 Talese, Gay. *Thy Neighbor's Wife.* **1987, Dell paper $5.95 (0-440-38497-4).** A study of American sexual trends and mores by the author of *The Kingdom and the Power.* (Rev: LJ 6/15/80; NYTBR 5/4/80; PW 3/28/80)   **[306.7]**

Sexual orientation

725 Abbott, Sidney, and Barbara Love. *Sappho Was a Right-On Woman: A Liberated View of Lesbianism.* **1973, Scarborough paper $3.95 (0-8128-1590-4).** Two lesbian writers explore the historical and contemporary status of female love. (Rev: NYTBR 2/25/73; PW 5/29/72)   **[306.76]**

726 Berzon, Betty. *Permanent Partners: Building Gay and Lesbian Relationships That Last.* **1988, Dutton $18.95 (0-525-24698-3); NAL paper $9.95 (0-452-26308-5).** Practical suggestions on building long-lasting same-sex partnerships by a psychotherapist who specializes in counseling homosexual couples. (Rev: BL 11/1/88; LJ 11/15/88; PW 11/15/88)   **[306.76]**

727 Boswell, John. *Christianity, Social Tolerance and Homosexuality: Gay People in Western Europe from the Beginning of the Christian Era to the Fourteenth Century.* **1981, Univ. of Chicago Pr. paper $12.95 (0-226-06711-4).** A history and analysis of the attitudes toward homosexuality throughout early Western history. (Rev: Choice 11/80; LJ 6/1/80; NYTBR 8/10/80. Awards: NBA, 1981; NYTBR, 1980)   **[306.76]**

728 Curry, Hayden, and Denis Clifford. *Legal Guide for Lesbian and Gay Couples.* **1988, Nolo Pr. paper $17.95 (0-87337-077-5).** The fifth edition of a guide to the legal rights of homosexual couples. (Rev: BL 3/1/89; LJ 3/1/89)   **[306.76]**

729 Duberman, Martin, ed. *Hidden from History: Reclaiming the Gay and Lesbian Past.* **1989, NAL $24.95 (0-453-00689-2).** A collection of 30 essays by historians regarding the roles and influence of homosexuals throughout history. (Rev: LJ 9/1/89; PW 10/6/89)   **[306.76]**

730 Hippler, Mike. *Matlovich.* **1989, Alyson Pubs. $15.95 (1-55583-138-9); paper $8.95 (1-55583-129-X).** A biography of a gay Air Force sergeant who challenged the armed forces restrictions against homosexuals. (Rev: BL 6/15/89; LJ 6/1/89)   **[306.76]**

731 Isay, Richard A. *Being Homosexual: Gay Men and Their Development.* **1989, Farrar $14.95 (0-374-11012-3); Avon paper $7.95 (0-380-71022-6).** A psychiatrist outlines the developmental stages in the life of the homosexual male. "An important work, radically different in its assumptions and conclusions from many others on this topic."—LJ (Rev: BL 3/1/89; LJ 4/1/89; PW 2/17/89. Awards: BL, 1989)   **[306.76]**

732 Kirk, Marshall, and Hunter Madsen. *After the Ball: How America Will Conquer Its Fear and Hatred of Homosexuals in the '90s.* **1989, Doubleday $19.95 (0-385-23906-8); NAL paper $10.95 (0-452-26498-X).** The authors present their proposals on how gay men can gain acceptance in American society. "Well-argued . . . certainly the most sensi-

ble gay political book ever written."—BL (Rev: BL 6/15/89; Choice 11/89; PW 4/28/89)   **[306.76]**

733 Plant, Richard. *Pink Triangle: Nazi War Against Homosexuals.* **1986, Henry Holt $19.95 (0-8050-0059-3); paper $9.95 (0-8050-0600-1).** An analysis of the Nazi persecution of homosexuals by a refugee of Hitler's Germany. "A classic addition to gay studies, Holocaust studies and German history."—BL (Rev: BL 9/1/86; Choice 1/87; NYTBR 11/16/86)   **[306.76]**

734 White, Edmund. *States of Desire: Travels in Gay America.* **1983, Dutton paper $8.95 (0-525-48223-7).** The novelist examines the lifestyles of male homosexuals in the United States based on his travels in gay communities and interviews with gay individuals. (Rev: LJ 2/15/80; Newsweek 2/11/80; TLS 9/5/80)   **[306.76]**

735 Whitney, Catherine. *Uncommon Lives: Gay Men and Straight Women.* **1990, NAL $18.95 (0-453-00715-5); Dutton paper $8.95 (0-452-26590-8).** A study of alternative living arrangements among persons of varying sexual preferences in the United States. (Rev: LJ 2/1/90; PW 1/26/90)   **[306.76]**

Marriage and family

736 Bernstein, Anne C. *Yours, Mine and Ours: How Families Change When Remarried Parents Have a Child Together.* **1989, Macmillan $21.95 (0-684-18700-0); Norton paper $10.95 (0-393-30668-2).** A study of the dynamics of mixed-family households by a California-based family therapist. (Rev: LJ 2/15/89; PW 12/23/88)   **[306.8]**

737 Blumstein, Philip, and Pepper Schwartz. *American Couples: Money, Work, Sex.* **1985, Pocket paper $12.95 (0-671-52353-8).** A study of contemporary American lifestyles based on the responses from 6,000 questionaires. (Rev: Choice 4/84; LJ 10/15/83; NYTBR 10/23/83)   **[306.8]**

738 Cherlin, Andrew J., and Frank F. Furstenberg, Jr. *New American Grandparent: A Place in the Family, a Life Apart.* **1988, Basic Books paper $9.95 (0-465-04994-X).** Results of a study of over 500 American grandparents and their place in contemporary family structure. (Rev: Choice 12/86; LJ 8/86; NYTBR 9/21/86)   **[306.8]**

739 Chesler, Phyllis. *Sacred Bond: The Legacy of Baby M.* **1989, Random paper $7.95 (0-679-72226-2).** A study of the 1987 surrogate motherhood case and its bearing on child custody policy. (Rev: BL 5/15/88; LJ 8/88; NYTBR 6/26/88)   **[306.8]**

740 Cosby, Bill. *Fatherhood.* **1986, Doubleday $14.95 (0-385-23410-4); Berkley paper $6.95 (0-425-09772-2).** A humorous primer on the challenges and rewards of fathering as seen by the comedian and actor. (Rev: Atl 7/86; LJ 6/15/86; Newsweek 5/19/86)   **[306.8]**

741 Dally, Ann. *Inventing Motherhood: The Consequences of an Ideal.* **1987, Schocken $19.95 (0-8052-3830-1).** An overview of the changing perception of the meaning and role of motherhood in the ninteenth and twentieth centuries. (Rev: BL 3/1/83; LJ 4/15/83; NYTBR 7/24/83) **[306.8]**

742 Degler, Carl N. *At Odds: Women and the Family in America from the Revolution to the Present.* 1980, Oxford Univ. Pr. paper $13.95 (0-19-502934-8). A social history of women and their role in American society and within the family unit over the past two centuries. (Rev: BL 7/1/80; Choice 10/80; NYTBR 4/20/80) **[306.8]**

743 Dinesen, Isak. *On Modern Marriage: And Other Observations.* 1987, St. Martin's paper $7.95 (0-312-01074-5). A philosophical study of love and marriage by the author of *Out of Africa.* (Rev: LJ 11/15/86; NYTBR 12/21/86; Time 2/9/87) **[306.8]**

744 Gies, Frances, and Joseph Gies. *Marriage and the Family in the Middle Ages.* 1987, Harper & Row $22.50 (0-06-015791-7); paper $8.95 (0-06-091468-8). An examination of family and sex roles from late Roman times to the Medieval era. "Clear, readable, well organized . . . should be considered the current standard."—Choice (Rev: Choice 7–8/88; LJ 1/88) **[306.8]**

745 Hanawalt, Barbara A. *Ties That Bound: Peasant Families in Medieval England.* 1989, Oxford Univ. Pr. paper $8.95 (0-19-504564-5). A study of the family life of the medieval English peasant. (Rev: Choice 7–8/86; LJ 2/1/86; NYTBR 5/11/86) **[306.8]**

746 Hemphill, Paul. *Me and the Boy: The Journey of Discovery.* 1987, Ivy Books paper $3.95 (0-8041-0142-6). An account of a father's 500-mile hiking trek with his son and the effect the journey had upon their relationship. (Rev: BL 5/1/86; PW 3/14/86) **[306.8]**

747 Hochschild, Arlie, and Anne Machung. *Second Shift: Inside the Two-Job Marriage.* 1989, Viking $18.95 (0-670-82463-1). A study of two-career families in America, and how working parents pass their behavioral patterns and sex roles onto their children. (Rev: BL 6/15/89; NYTBR 6/25/89; Newsweek 7/31/89) **[306.8]**

748 Koch, Thomas. *Mirrored Lives: Aging Children and Elderly Parents.* 1990, Greenwood Pr. $19.95 (0-275-93671-6). A journalist's account of his father's declining health and of their family efforts to care for him. (Rev: LJ 11/15/90; PW 11/2/90) **[306.8]**

749 Mathabane, Mark, and Gail Mathabane. *Love in Black and White: The Triumph of Love Over Prejudice and Taboo.* 1991, HarperCollins $20.00 (0-06-016495-6). The author of *Kaffir Boy* and his wife discuss their interracial marriage. (Rev: BL 12/15/91; PW 12/6/91) **[306.8]**

750 Maynard, Joyce. *Domestic Affairs: Enduring the Pleasures of Motherhood and Family.* 1987, Random $17.95 (0-8129-1244-6); McGraw-Hill paper $7.95 (0-07-041092-5). A collection of the author's columns on mothering and motherhood. (Rev: BL 6/15/87; LJ 7/87; NYTBR 7/19/87) **[306.8]**

751 Mintz, Steven, and Susan Kellogg. *Domestic Revolutions: A Social History of American Family Life.* 1987, Free Press $22.50 (0-07-921290-1); paper $11.95 (0-02-921291-X). A history of American family structure from the Puritans to the present, exploring the diversity within American subcultures, and the changes caused by historical events and trends. (Rev: LJ 12/87; NYTBR 1/31/88; PW 11/13/87) **[306.8]**

752 Pogrebin, Letty C. *Family Politics: Love and Power on an Intimate Frontier.* 1983, McGraw-Hill $14.95 (0-07-050386-9). An examination of the power relationships and dynamics of the contemporary American family. (Rev: BL 9/1/83; LJ 11/15/83; NYTBR 12/18/83) **[306.8]**

753 Rothman, Barbara Katz. *Recreating Motherhood: Ideology and Technology in a Patriarchal Society.* 1989, Norton $18.95 (0-393-02645-0); paper $10.95 (0-393-30712-3). A study of surrogate motherhood and the mother-child relationship. "A powerful, compassionate analysis . . . an important, perhaps vital book."—BL (Rev: BL 1/1/89; LJ 1/89; NYTBR 4/16/89) **[306.8]**

754 Ruben, Harvey L. *Supermarriage: Overcoming the Predictable Crises of Married Life.* 1987, Bantam paper $4.50 (0-553-26135-5). A guide to the developmental stages and predictable crises in the relationships of married couples. (Rev: LJ 8/86; PW 5/2/86) **[306.8]**

755 Scarf, Maggie. *Intimate Partners: Patterns in Love and Marriage.* 1987, Random $18.95 (0-345-35070-7); Ballantine paper $5.95 (0-345-35070-7). A study of how marriages are formed and the dynamics between partners that make marriages flourish or collapse. (Rev: BL 1/1/87; LJ 2/15/87; PW 12/26/86) **[306.8]**

756 Shukert, Elfrieda, and Barbara Scibetta. *War Brides of World War II.* 1988, Presidio Pr. $18.95 (0-89141-309-X). An account of the lives of those women who married English-speaking soldiers, and later became citizens of their husband's countries, based on correspondence and interviews with over 2,000 war brides. (Rev: BL 2/1/88; LJ 1/88; TLS 9/2/88) **[306.8]**

757 Smith, Audrey D., and William J. Read. *Role-Sharing Marriage.* 1985, Columbia Univ. Pr. $25.00 (0-231-06110-2). An analysis of the dynamics of 64 marriages that share tasks and incomes. (Rev: Choice 4/86; LJ 11/15/85) **[306.8]**

758 Whitehead, Mary Beth, and Loretta Schwartz-Nobel. *A Mother's Story: The Truth about the Baby M Case.* 1989, St. Martin's $17.95 (0-312-02614-5). An autobiography of the surrogate mother who became embroiled in the "Baby M" trial for custody of her child. (Rev: LJ 2/15/89; NYTBR 3/12/89; PW 1/13/89) **[306.8]**

Marriage

759 Haskell, Molly. *Love and Other Infectious Diseases: A Memoir.* 1990, Morrow $18.95 (0-688-07006-X). Memoirs of the author's marriage to film critic Andrew Sarris and how his near-fatal illness affected their relationship. (Rev: LJ 3/15/90; NYTBR 4/8/90; Time 4/30/90) **[306.81]**

The family

760 Corea, Gena. *Mother Machine: From Artificial Insemination to Artificial Wombs.* **1986, Harper & Row paper $9.95 (0-06-091325-8).** A study of modern reproductive technologies and their physical and emotional effects upon women. (REV: BL 3/1/85; Choice 10/85; LJ 4/1/85)   **[306.85]**

Interfamily relationships

761 Brazelton, T. Berry, and Bertrand Cramer. *Earliest Relationship: Parents, Infants and the Drama of Early Attachment.* **1990, Delacorte $19.95 (0-201-10639-6).** A study of the formative early years of the parent-child relationship. (REV: BL 1/1/90; Choice 7–8/90; LJ 2/15/90)   **[306.87]**

762 Caron, Ann F. *"Don't Stop Loving Me": A Reassuring Guide for Mothers of Adolescent Daughters.* **1991, Henry Holt $19.95 (0-8050-1136-6).** A psychologist examines the development of adolescent females and the mother-daughter relationship. (REV: BL 12/15/90; PW 12/7/90)   **[306.87]**

763 Greer, Germaine. *Daddy, We Hardly Knew You.* **1990, Knopf $19.95 (0-394-58313-2); Fawcett paper $12.95 (0-449-90561-6).** Memoirs by the author of *The Female Eunuch* regarding her relationship with her father during her childhood in Australia. (REV: BL 12/1/89; NYTBR 1/28/90; New Yorker 4/16/90)   **[306.87]**

764 Sidransky, Ruth. *In Silence: Growing Up Hearing in a Deaf World.* **1990, St. Martin's $18.95 (0-312-04589-1).** Memoirs of a hearing daughter regarding her life with two deaf parents. "For the hearing, the book helps demystify the world of the deaf."— PW (REV: BL 10/1/90; LJ 10/15/90; PW 8/31/90) **[306.87]**

Alteration of family arrangements

765 Caine, Lynn. *Being a Widow.* **1988, Morrow $18.95 (0-87795-966-8); Penguin paper $7.95 (0-14-013025-X).** The author's sequel to her own *Widow* provides guidance and advice for women who have lost their spouses on how to rebuild their lives. (REV: BL 10/1/88; LJ 10/1/88)   **[306.88]**

766 Ginsburg, Genevieve Davis. *To Live Again: Rebuilding Your Life after You've Become a Widow.* **1987, J. P. Tarcher $14.95 (0-87477-426-8); Bantam paper $4.50 (0-553-27986-6).** A manual for methods of adjusting to the practical, psychological, and emotional problems of being widowed. (REV: BL 4/15/87; LJ 5/1/87)   **[306.88]**

767 Graham, Virginia. *Life after Harry: My Adventures in Widowhood.* **1989, Dell paper $7.95 (0-440-50183-0).** A manual on methods of adjusting to being a widow by the television performer and author or *There Goes What's Her Name.* (REV: BL 5/1/88; LJ 3/15/88; PW 3/18/88)   **[306.88]**

768 Robertson, John, and Betty Utterback. *Suddenly Single: Learning to Start Over; A Personal Guide.* **1986, Simon & Schuster $15.95 (0-671-54442-X).** A guide for persons who have recently lost a spouse to death or desertion. (REV: BL 5/15/86; LJ 6/1/86)   **[306.88]**

769 Rose, Xenia. *Widow's Journey: A Return to the Loving Self.* **1990, Seaver $19.95 (0-8050-1193-5).** The widow of a concert musician describes the healing process by which she recovered from the death of her husband. (REV: BL 9/15/90; LJ 10/1/90; PW 8/31/90)   **[306.88]**

Separation and divorce

770 Arendell, Terry. *Mothers and Divorce: Legal, Economic, and Social Dilemmas.* **1986, Univ. of California Pr. $25.00 (0-520-05708-2); paper $9.95 (0-520-06215-9).** A study of the economic and social effects of divorce on mothers. (REV: BL 9/1/86; LJ 10/1/86)   **[306.89]**

771 Belli, Melvin M., and Mel Krantzler. *Divorcing.* **1988, St. Martin's $22.95 (0-312-01760-X); paper $14.95 (0-312-03816-X).** A guide to the legal and emotional problems of divorce presented by the prominent attorney and a therapist. (REV: BL 6/15/88; LJ 8/88; PW 7/1/88)   **[306.89]**

772 Diamond, Susan Arnsberg. *Helping Children of Divorce: A Handbook for Parents and Teachers.* **1985, Schocken $11.95 (0-8052-3974-X); paper $6.95 (0-8052-0821-6).** A guidebook for parents and teachers to assisting and understanding common psychological and social problems of children adjusting to divorce. (REV: BL 5/15/85; LJ 6/1/85; PW 5/24/85)   **[306.89]**

773 Francke, Linda Bird. *Growing Up Divorced.* **1984, Fawcett paper $4.95 (0-449-20570-3).** An examination of the social and psychological effects of divorce on children based on 100 interviews with youth of divorced parents. (REV: BL 8/83; LJ 7/83; NYTBR 7/24/83)   **[306.89]**

774 Wallerstein, Judith, and Sandra Blakeslee. *Second Chances: Men, Women and Children a Decade after Divorce.* **1989, Ticknor & Fields $19.95 (0-89919-648-9).** The psychological and economic effects of divorce on 60 middle class American families as reported by a longtime counselor. (REV: BL 11/1/88; LJ 2/1/89; NYTBR 2/26/89)   **[306.89]**

307 Communities

775 Dore, Ronald Philip. *Shinohata: Portrait of a Japanese Village.* **1980, Pantheon paper $8.76 (0-394-73843-8).** A study of the social and industrial changes which took place in a small Japanese farming community during the twentieth century. (REV: BL 11/1/79; LJ 12/15/78; NYTBR 1/28/79)   **[307]**

776 Fitzgerald, Frances. *Cities on a Hill: A Journey Through Contemporary American Cultures.* **1986, Simon & Schuster $19.95 (0-671-55209-0); paper $9.95 (0-671-64561-7).** A study of four American social experiments: the predominantly gay Castro District in San Francisco; Sun City, Florida's haven for the aged; cult-leader Bhagwan Shree Rajneesh's Oregon community; and the community of Lynchburg, Virginia, which surrounds Jerry Falwell's Liberty College. (REV: BL 9/1/86; NYTBR 10/12/86; PW 8/15/86)   **[307]**

777 Frieden, Bernard J., and Lynne B. Sagalyn. *Downtown, Inc.: How America Rebuilds Cities.* **1989, MIT Pr. $24.95 (0-262-06128-7).** A look at recent efforts to rebuild projects designed to revitalize fading centers of American cities. (REV: LJ 11/1/89; NYTBR 6/17/90; PW 11/3/89)   **[307]**

778 Mangione, Jerre. *A Passion for Sicilians: The World Around Danilo Dolici.* **1985, Transaction paper $16.95 (0-88738-606-7).** A biography of a Sicilian social activist who fought for improvements in labor, education, and housing in his native land. (REV: LJ 2/1/69; NYTBR 11/17/68; PW 7/15/68)   **[307]**

779 Myrdal, Jan. *Report from a Chinese Village.* **1984, Pantheon paper $7.95 (0-394-72453-4).** An account of a month the Swedish anthropologist and his wife spent in China in 1962; complete with interviews they conducted about the daily life of the people. (REV: BL 7/15/65; Choice 10/65; NYTBR 6/13/65. AWARDS: ALA, 1965)   **[307]**

780 Oldenburg, Ray. *Great Good Place.* **1989, Paragon House $19.95 (1-55778-110-9); paper $14.95 (1-55778-458-2).** An examination of the role of social gathering places in human society. (REV: BL 10/1/89; NYTBR 12/24/89)   **[307]**

Planning and development

781 Robin, Peggy. *Saving the Neighborhood: You Can Fight Developers and Win!* **1990, Woodbine House paper $16.95 (0-933149-33-6).** A guide to community organization and action to fight real estate development projects. (REV: BL 12/15/89; LJ 1/90)   **[307.1]**

Structure

782 Anderson, Elijah. *Streetwise: Race, Class and Change in an Urban Community.* **1990, Univ. of Chicago Pr. $19.95 (0-226-01815-6).** A sociologist's study of life in a Philadelphia ghetto. "A powerful and intensely frightening picture of the inner city."—NYTBR (REV: BL 12/1/90; NYTBR 12/9/90; PW 9/28/90)   **[307.3]**

783 Sennett, Richard. *Conscience of the Eye: The Design and Social Life of Cities.* **1990, Knopf $24.45 (0-394-57104-5).** An analysis of life within the modern city focusing on the author's home, New York. (REV: BL 12/1/90; LJ 1/91; NYTBR 3/3/91) **[307.3]**

Specific kinds of communities

784 Bly, Carol. *Letters from the Country.* **1988, Harper & Row paper $6.95 (0-06-091467-X).** Essays portraying life and thought in a small farm town in Minnesota in the 1950s. "An absolute gem of modern rural Americana."—PW (REV: New Rep 6/20/81; Newsweek 6/15/81; PW 3/6/81)   **[307.7]**

785 Critchfield, Richard. *Villages.* **1983, Doubleday paper $10.95 (0-385-18375-5).** A study of village life and culture in many nations including Indonesia, Mexico, Bangladesh, and Egypt. (REV: BL 6/1/81; CSM 7/13/81; LJ 5/15/81)   **[307.7]**

786 Garreau, Joel. *Edge City: Life on the New Frontier.* **1991, Doubleday $22.50 (0-385-26249-3).** A demographic study of American cities that have developed around urban cores. "An eminently readable, thought-provoking, optimistic text."—PW (REV: BL 7/91; NYTBR 9/22/91; PW 7/12/91. AWARDS: BL, 1991)   **[307.7]**

787 Jackson, Kenneth T. *Crabgrass Frontier: The Suburbanization of America.* **1985, Oxford Univ. Pr. $24.95 (0-19-503610-7).** A history of the development and expansion of American suburbs from the nineteenth century to the present. (REV: Choice 1/86; LJ 9/1/85; NYTBR 4/27/86)   **[307.7]**

788 Jerome, John. *Stone Work: Reflections on Serious Play and Other Aspects of Country Life.* **1989, Viking $17.95 (0-670-90195-X); Penguin paper $8.95 (0-14-008881-4).** The author recounts his experiences living on a Massachusetts farm after fleeing New York City in search of solitude. (REV: BL 5/15/89; LJ 5/1/89; NYTBR 8/20/89)   **[307.7]**

789 Kostof, Spiro. *City Shaped: Urban Patterns and Meanings Through History.* **1991, Little, Brown $50.00 (0-8212-1867-0).** A history survey analyzing the organization and design of cities. "Will . . . fascinate non-professionals as much as it enlightens scholars."—BL (REV: BL 12/1/91; LJ 10/1/91. AWARDS: LJ, 1991)   **[307.7]**

790 Stilgoe, John R. *Borderland: Origins of the American Suburb, 1820–1939.* **1988, Yale Univ. Pr. $37.50 (0-300-04257-4); paper $18.95 (0-300-04866-1).** An illustrated history of the development of suburbs in the United States in the nineteenth and twentieth centuries. (REV: CSM 4/25/89; PW 11/4/88; TLS 7/7/89)   **[307.7]**

791 Wallace, Anthony F. *St. Clair: A Nineteenth Century Coal Town's Experience with a Disaster-Prone Industry.* **1987, Knopf $35.00 (0-394-52867-0); Cornell Univ. Pr. paper $12.95 (0-8014-9900-3).** A recreation of the life and social history of a Pennsylvania mining community. "An excellent industrial history with a vivid human component."—LJ (REV: Choice 3/88; LJ 8/87; NYTBR 10/18/87. AWARDS: LJ, 1987)   **[307.7]**

792 Whyte, William F. *City: Rediscovering the Center.* **1989, Doubleday $24.95 (0-385-05458-0); paper $14.95 (0-385-26209-4).** An illustrated analysis of city life and contemporary urban planning by the author of *The Organization Man.* (REV: BL 2/15/89; NYTBR 2/26/89; Time 2/27/89)   **[307.7]**

320 POLITICAL SCIENCE

793 McDonald, Forrest. *Novus Ordo Seclorum: The Intellectual Origins of the Constitution.* **1985, Univ. Pr. of Kansas $25.00 (0-7006-0284-4); paper $9.95 (0-7006-0311-5).** A study of the European intellectual roots and foundations of the U.S. Constitution. (REV: Choice 5/86; CSM 11/27/85; Natl Rev 4/11/86)   **[320]**

Philosophy and theory

794 Morgan, Edmund Sears. *Inventing the People: The Rise of Popular Sovereignty in England and America.* **1988, Norton $18.95 (0-393-02505-5); paper $8.95 (0-393-30623-2).** A look at the development and practice of popular sovereignty in seventeenth- and eighteenth-century English and American society. (REV: LJ 4/1/88; NYTBR 7/3/88; PW 2/26/88) **[320.01]**

Persons

795 De Grazia, Sebastian. *Machiavelli in Hell.* **1990, Princeton Univ. Pr. $49.50 (0-691-05538-6); paper $14.95 (0-691-00861-2).** A biography of the sixteenth-century Italian political theorist and historian. "Both monumental and intimate, provocative and winning."—CSM (REV: CSM 8/9/89; NYTBR 11/5/89; TLS 1/19/90. AWARDS: PP:Biography, 1990) **[320.092]**

796 Miller, James. *Rousseau: Dreamer of Democracy.* **1986, Yale Univ. Pr. $30.00 (0-300-03044-4); paper $11.95 (0-300-03518-7).** A study of the life, ideas, and influence of the eighteenth-century French writer and philosopher. (REV: Choice 12/84; NYTBR 9/16/84; PW 6/22/84) **[320.092]**

The state

797 Bickel, Alexander M. *Morality of Consent.* **1975, Yale Univ. Pr. $25.00 (0-300-01911-4); paper $8.95 (0-300-02119-4).** A work of political theory examining the implied will of the populace to be governed and its consequences. (REV: Choice 3/76; LJ 11/15/75; NYTBR 9/21/75. AWARDS: ALA, 1975) **[320.1]**

798 Nozick, Robert. *Anarchy, State & Utopia.* **1974, Basic Books paper $13.95 (0-465-09720-0).** "Nozick's powers of argument are profound and his insights are at times staggering in their brilliance."—New Rep (REV: Choice 3/75; New Rep 4/26/75; NYRB 3/6/75. AWARDS: NBA, 1975) **[320.1]**

Political ideologies

799 Ayer, Alfred J. *Thomas Paine.* **1989, Macmillan $19.95 (0-689-11996-8).** An examination of the life and thought of the political theorist and author of *Common Sense* and *Age of Reason.* (REV: Choice 6/89; LJ 4/1/89; NYRB 4/13/89) **[320.5]**

800 Blumenthal, Sidney. *Rise of the Counter-Establishment: From Conservative Ideology to Political Power.* **1988, Random $19.95 (0-8129-1205-5); Harper & Row paper $9.95 (0-06-097140-1).** A history of the rise of American conservatism from the 1950s to the present. (REV: LJ 11/15/86; New Rep 12/15/86; NYTBR 10/5/86) **[320.5]**

801 Craig, Gordon A. *Triumph of Liberalism: Zurich in the Golden Age, 1830–1869.* **1989, Macmillan $24.95 (0-684-19062-1); paper $10.95 (0-02-031140-0).** A social and cultural history of Zurich in the mid-nineteenth century. (REV: NYRB 10/26/89; NYTBR 6/8/89; PW 3/24/89) **[320.5]**

802 Dionne, E. J., Jr. *Why Americans Hate Politics.* **1991, Simon & Schuster $22.95 (0-671-68255-5).** A study of the reasons behind Americans' distrust of politics and government. (REV: LJ 4/15/91; New Rep 6/3/91; Time 5/20/91) **[320.5]**

803 Flacks, Richard. *Making History: The American Left and the American Mind.* **1990, Columbia Univ. Pr. $35.00 (0-231-04832-7); paper $13.00 (0-231-04833-5).** A survey of the history of American socialism in the nineteenth and twentieth centuries with suggestions on how the leftist tradition can be revitalized in years to come. (REV: Choice 9/89; LJ 6/15/88; NYTBR 8/28/88) **[320.5]**

804 Goldman, Peter. *Death and Life of Malcolm X.* **1979, Univ. of Illinois Pr. paper $11.95 (0-252-00774-3).** A biography of the former spokesman for the Nation of Islam concentrating on his later years, his death, and the legacy he left behind. "This book is a splendid companion to Malcolm's own passionately eloquent 'Autobiography,' and that is high praise indeed."—Newsweek (REV: Choice 5/73; New Yorker 1/13/73; Newsweek 1/8/73. AWARDS: ALA, 1973) **[320.5]**

805 Isserman, Maurice. *If I Had a Hammer: The Death of the Old Left and the Birth of the New Left.* **1989, Basic Books paper $8.95 (0-465-03195-1).** A study of the legacy of the American Communist party during the 1950s and 1960s. (REV: BL 9/1/87; LJ 10/1/87; NYRB 10/22/87) **[320.5]**

806 Lappe, Frances M. *Rediscovering America's Values.* **1989, Ballantine paper $22.50 (0-345-32040-9).** A dialogue between classic liberal thought and the author's perspective on issues facing the United States today. "Intellectually provocative and presented in a manner accessible to educated adults, this serious book demands serious readers."—LJ (REV: BL 3/15/89; LJ 3/1/89; PW 1/27/89. AWARDS: BL, 1989) **[320.5]**

807 Matusow, Allen J. *Unraveling of America: A History of Liberalism in the 1960's.* **1984, Harper & Row $22.95 (0-06-015224-9); paper $10.95 (0-06-132058-7).** Liberalism and liberal thought in American politics of the 1960s. "Should figure as a standard study . . . for some time to come."—LJ (REV: Atl 4/84; BL 2/1/84; LJ 12/1/83) **[320.5]**

808 Pangle, Thomas L. *Spirit of Modern Republicanism: The Moral Vision of the American Founders and the Philosophy of Locke.* **1988, Univ. of Chicago Pr. $22.50 (0-226-64550-1).** A study of the liberal philosophy of the American founding fathers and its relationship to the thought of John Locke. (REV: BL 7/88; Choice 12/88; CSM 12/21/88) **[320.5]**

Conservatism

809 Gottfried, Paul, and Thomas Fleming. *Conservative Movement.* **1988, G. K. Hall $18.95 (0-8057-9723-8); paper $10.95 (0-8057-9724-6).** A study of conservative political philosophy in the United States since World War II. (REV: Choice 10/88; LJ 1/88; Natl Rev 2/19/88) **[320.52]**

Nationalism

810 **Pawel, Ernst.** *Labyrinth of Exile: A Life of Theodore Herzl.* **1989, Farrar $30.00 (0-374-18256-6).** A biography of the founder of the Zionist movement. (Rev: BL 12/15/79; LJ 10/1/89; NYTBR 12/31/89) **[320.54]**

Racism

811 **Peace, Judy B.** *Boy Child Is Dying: A South African Experience.* **1986, Harper & Row $9.45 (0-06-066482-7).** Profiles of the lives of several people in South Africa suffering under the apartheid system. (Rev: BL 6/1/86; PW 6/20/86) **[320.56]**

Soviet Union

812 **Sakharov, Andrei D.** *My Country and the World.* **1975, Random paper $3.95 (0-394-72067-9).** Essays on international politics by the Soviet physicist and dissident. "The grand personal testimony of an outstanding humanist on the state of his country and the world."—Choice (Rev: Choice 6/76; NYTBR 11/9/75; PW 9/22/75) **[320.94]**

Asia

813 **Fitzgerald, Frances.** *Fire in the Lake: The Vietnamese and the Americans in Vietnam.* **1989, Random paper $9.95 (0-679-72394-3).** This author's first full-length work analyzes the conflicts between Vietnamese and American cultures and their effects upon the Vietnam War. "One of the best descriptions and analyses of Vietnam ever published."—LJ (Rev: CSM 8/23/72; LJ 6/15/72; NYTBR 8/27/72. Awards: ALA, 1972; NBA, 1972; PP:NF, 1973; Time, 1972) **[320.95]**

United States

814 **Buckley, William F., Jr.** *Right Reason: A Collection.* **1986, Little, Brown paper $10.95 (0-316-11444-8).** Selected nonfiction writings by the *National Review* editor on politics and culture during the late 1970s and 1980s. (Rev: BL 11/1/85; LJ 1/86; Natl Rev 1/31/86) **[320.973]**

815 **Garment, Suzanne.** *Scandal: The Culture of Mistrust in American Politics.* **1991, Times Books $23.00 (0-8129-1942-4).** A survey of recent political scandals in the United States and their effect on the American public's perception of its government. (Rev: BL 12/1/91; PW 8/16/91) **[320.973]**

816 **Goodwyn, Lawrence.** *Democratic Promise: The Populist Movement in America.* **1976, Oxford Univ. Pr. $29.95 (0-19-501996-2).** The rise and fall of populism in America in the late nineteenth century and its influence on politics in the twentieth century. (Rev: LJ 10/1/76; New Rep 2/12/77; NYRB 10/28/76) **[320.973]**

817 **Hofstadter, Richard.** *Paranoid Style in American Politics, and Other Essays.* **1979, Univ. of Chicago Pr. paper $5.95 (0-226-34817-2).** Seven essays examining the threads of extremism and conservatism in American politics by the Pulitzer

Prize-winning historian. (Rev: Choice 3/66; LJ 5/1/66; NYTBR 11/14/65. Awards: NYTBR, 1965) **[320.973]**

818 **Kissinger, Henry.** *Years of Upheaval.* **1982, Little, Brown $29.95 (0-316-28591-9).** Memoirs of Nixon's secretary of state covering January 1973 to August 1974. "The book reads like fiction but never lacks the depth and detail of a scholarly analysis . . . an engrossing piece of literature."—Choice (Rev: BL 4/15/82; Choice 11/82; NYTBR 4/19/82. Awards: NYTBR, 1982) **[320.973]**

819 **McPherson, Harry.** *A Political Education: A Washington Memoir.* **1988, Houghton paper $11.95 (0-395-48899-0).** The political education of a former assistant and counsel to Lyndon Johnson in the 1950s and 1960s. (Rev: CSM 6/21/72; New Yorker 7/8/72; PW 4/17/72) **[320.973]**

820 **O'Rourke, P. J.** *Parliament of Whores: A Lone Humorist Attempts to Explain the Entire U.S. Government.* **1991, Atlantic Monthly $19.95 (0-87113-455-1).** The conservative humorist and frequent *Rolling Stone* contributor explains the workings of the American government. (Rev: LJ 6/1/91; NYTBR 6/30/91; PW 4/19/91. Awards: BL, 1991) **[320.973]**

821 **Smith, Hedrick.** *Power Game: How Washington Really Works.* **1988, Random $24.95 (0-394-55447-7); Ballantine paper $5.95 (0-345-36015-X).** An inside look at the workings of Washington politics by the author of *The Russians.* (Rev: BL 2/15/88; CSM 3/4/88; NYTBR 3/27/88) **[320.973]**

Latin America

822 **Boeker, Paul, ed.** *Lost Illusions: Latin America's Struggle for Democracy, as Recounted by Its Leaders.* **1990, Wiener $24.95 (1-55876-023-7); paper $12.95 (1-55876-024-5).** A collection of 26 interviews with Latin American leaders reflecting on the future of their nations and of the region. (Rev: Choice 7–8/90; LJ 2/15/90; NYTBR 4/29/90) **[320.98]**

321 Systems of government and states

823 **Manuel, Frank E., and Fritzie P. Manuel.** *Utopian Thought in the Western World.* **1979, Harvard Univ. Pr. $41.00 (0-674-93185-8); paper $17.50 (0-674-93186-6).** A comprehensive review of Utopian thought in the West spanning over 2,500 years. "A magnificent achievement in the history of ideas."—Choice (Rev: Choice 4/80; NYTBR 10/21/79; New Rep 10/21/79. Awards: NBA, 1983) **[321]**

Democratic systems

824 **Barber, Benjamin R.** *Strong Democracy: Participatory Politics for a New Age.* **1984, Univ. of California Pr. paper $10.95 (0-520-05616-7).** A guide to reforms to increase political participation in democratic societies. (Rev: Choice 12/84; LJ 5/1/84) **[321.8]**

825 **Dahl, Robert A.** *Democracy and Its Critics.* **1990, Yale Univ. Pr. $29.95 (0-300-04409-7).** A study of the history and development of democracy since the early nineteenth century with an examination of its possible future. (REV: LJ 8/89; Natl Rev 3/5/90; NYTBR 11/12/89)   **[321.8]**

322 Relation of state to organized groups

826 Cornford, Daniel A. *Workers and Dissent in the Redwood Empire.* **1987, Temple Univ. Pr. $39.95 (0-87722-499-4).** The history of the lumber industry and the public reaction to it in the redwood region of Northern California. (REV: Choice 5/88; LJ 5/1/88)   **[322]**

827 Reich, Robert B. *Next American Frontier.* **1983, Random $16.95 (0-8129-1067-2); Penguin paper $7.95 (0-14-007040-0).** A proposal for better cooperation between American government and business to compete more effectively on the world market. (REV: LJ 7/83; New Yorker 6/20/83; PW 3/25/83)   **[322]**

828 Vogel, David. *Fluctuating Fortunes: The Political Power of Business in America.* **1989, Basic Books $20.95 (0-465-02470-X).** A study of the political influence of big business in contemporary America. (REV: Choice 10/89; LJ 3/1/89; NYTBR 4/9/89)   **[322]**

829 Wills, Garry. *Under God: Religion and American Politics.* **1990, Simon & Schuster $22.95 (0-671-65705-4).** A historical study of the relationship between religion and politics in the United States. (REV: BL 9/15/90; LJ 11/1/90; PW 9/14/90. AWARDS: ALA, 1990; BL, 1990)   **[322]**

Business and industry

830 Lodge, George C. *American Disease.* **1986, New York Univ. Pr. paper $16.50 (0-8147-5028-1).** An analysis of the decline of the American economy and ways to improve its standing through revisions of international trade policies. (REV: BL 3/15/84; LJ 3/1/84; PW 1/6/84)   **[322.3]**

Political action groups

831 Benson, Mary. *Nelson Mandela: The Man and His Movement.* **1986, Norton paper $8.95 (0-393-30322-5).** A biography of the African National Congress leader and crusader for equal rights in his native South Africa. (REV: Choice 10/86; LJ 3/15/86; NYTBR 4/27/86)   **[322.4]**

832 Corcoran, James. *Bitter Harvest: Gordon Kahl and the Rise of the Posse Comiatus in the Heartland.* **1990, Viking $18.95 (0-670-81561-6).** An account of a North Dakota man who became involved in a right-wing extremist organization and was killed in a shoot-out with federal agents in Arkansas in 1983. (REV: LJ 3/1/90; NYTBR 8/12/90; PW 3/9/90)   **[322.4]**

833 Downs, Donald Alexander. *Nazis in Skokie: Freedom, Community, and the First Amendment.* **1986, Univ. of Notre Dame Pr. paper $9.95 (0-268-01462-0).** A discussion of First Amendment questions raised by the marches of Nazi supporters in a predominately Jewish-American community. (REV: Choice 9/85; LJ 3/1/85; NYTBR 4/7/85)   **[322.4]**

834 Martinez, Thomas, and John Guinther. *Brotherhood of Murder.* **1988, McGraw-Hill $17.95 (0-07-040699-5); paper $4.95 (0-671-67858-2).** An account by a former member of the Neo-Nazi group, the Order, that tells of his assistance to the FBI that led to the indictment of other members on murder charges. (REV: BL 6/1/88; LJ 8/88; PW 2/12/88)   **[322.4]**

835 Sims, Patsy. *The Klan.* **1978, Scarborough $12.95 (0-8128-2268-4); paper $10.95 (0-8128-6096-9).** A study of the Ku Klux Klan during the 1970s based on research and interviews with Klan members. (REV: BL 11/15/78; Choice 6/79; PW 9/18/78) **[322.4]**

836 Wade, Wyn Craig. *Fiery Cross: The Ku Klux Klan in America.* **1988, Simon & Schuster paper $11.95 (0-671-65723-2).** The history of the white supremacist group from its beginnings in the mid-nineteenth century to the present. (REV: BL 3/15/87; LJ 3/1/87; NYTBR 4/26/87)   **[322.4]**

Revolutionary and subversive groups

837 Blee, Kathleen M. *Women of the Klan: Racism and Gender in the 1920s.* **1991, Univ. of California Pr. $25.00 (0-525-07263-4).** An examination of the role of women in the Ku Klux Klan during the 1910s and 1920s. "No future history of the Ku Klux Klan will be written without reference to this ground-breaking work."—PW (REV: LJ 7/91; PW 6/7/91)   **[322.42]**

838 Holland, Heidi. *Struggle: A History of the African National Congress.* **1990, Braziller $19.95 (0-8076-1238-3).** A history of the African National Congress since its founding in 1912. (REV: BL 2/15/90; LJ 2/15/90; PW 1/5/90)   **[322.42]**

839 Livingstone, Neil C., and Joseph D. Douglass. *Inside the PLO: Covert Units, Secret Funds and the War Against Israel and the United States.* **1990, Morrow $21.45 (0-688-09335-3).** A study of the origins and inside workings of the Palestine Liberation Organization. (REV: BL 1/1/90; LJ 2/1/90; PW 1/19/90)   **[322.42]**

Reform movements

840 Bobo, Kim. *Organizing for Social Change: A Manual for Activists in the 1990s.* **1991, Seven Locks Pr. paper $19.95 (0-932020-93-3).** A guide to organizing grassroots political movements in the 1990s. "Manuals don't come much better than this."—BL (REV: BL 5/15/91; LJ 5/15/91)   **[322.44]**

841 Bordin, Ruth B. *Frances Willard: A Biography.* **1986, Univ. of North Carolina Pr. $27.50 (0-8078-1697-3).** A biography of the nineteenth-century American temperance leader and social activist. (REV: Choice 2/87; LJ 11/15/86; NYTBR 12/14/86)**[322.44]**

323 Civil and political rights

842 Jackson, George L. *Blood in My Eye.* **1990, Black Classic paper $11.95 (0-933121-23-7).** A posthumously published collection of essays and letters by a black revolutionary who spent much of his adult life in prison. "Staggering in impact . . .

remorseless in its passionate criticism."—LJ (Rev: Choice 9/72; LJ 3/1/72; NYTBR 4/16/72)   **[323]**

843 Mailer, Norman. *Armies of the Night.* **1968, NAL paper $4.95 (0-451-14070-2).** Mailer recounts his experiences during the October 1967 march on the Pentagon. (Rev: New Rep 6/8/68; NYTBR 5/6/68; Sat Rev 5/4/68. Awards: ALA, 1968; NBA, 1969; NYTBR, 1968; PP:NF, 1969; Time, the 1960s)   **[323]**

Persons

844 Sachs, Albie. *Running to Maputo.* **1990, HarperCollins $19.95 (0-06-016468-9).** An account of the recovery of a South African political activist from a 1988 car bombing. (Rev: BL 9/1/90; LJ 8/90; PW 7/27/90)   **[323.092]**

845 Sterling, Dorothy. *Ahead of Her Time: Abby Kelley and the Politics of Antislavery.* **1991, Norton $22.95 (0-393-03026-1).** A biography of a nineteenth-century American Quaker abolitionist leader and campaigner for women's rights. (Rev: BL 11/1/91; PW 11/1/91)   **[323.092]**

846 Walker, Samuel E. *In Defense of American Liberties: A History of the ACLU.* **1990, Oxford Univ. Pr. $24.95 (0-19-504539-4).** The history of the American Civil Liberties Union and its role in defending the Bill of Rights from its founding in 1917 to the present. (Rev: BL 1/1/90; LJ 12/89; NYTBR 1/14/90)   **[323.092]**

Of nondenominate aggregates

847 Azbel, Mark Ya. *Refusenik: Trapped in the Soviet Union.* **1987, Paragon House paper $10.95 (0-913729-65-5).** Memoirs of a Jewish physicist and his efforts to emigrate from the Soviet Union. (Rev: BL 4/15/81; CSM 5/11/81; NYTBR 6/7/81)   **[323.1]**

848 Durham, Michael S., and Charles Moore. *Powerful Days: The Civil Rights Photography of Charles Moore.* **1991, Stewart, Tabori & Chang $35.00 (1-55670-171-3); paper $24.95 (1-55670-202-7).** A collection of photographs by the former Montgomery, Alabama, newspaper photographer documenting the civil rights movement of the 1950s and 1960s. (Rev: LJ 4/15/91; NYTBR 3/10/91)   **[323.1]**

849 Hampton, Henry, Steve Fayer, and Sarah Flynn. *Voices of Freedom: An Oral History of the Civil Rights Movement from the 1950s Through the 1980s.* **1990, Bantam $25.95 (0-553-05734-0); paper $15.95 (0-553-35232-6).** An oral history of 31 key events of the civil rights movement. (Rev: BL 12/15/89; LJ 2/15/90; PW 12/22/89)   **[323.1]**

850 Harding, Vincent. *There Is a River: The Black Struggle for Freedom in America.* **1981, Harcourt $19.95 (0-15-189342-X); Random paper $10.00 (0-394-71148-3).** The history of the African-American struggle for freedom and equality from the rise of slavery to the 1980s. (Rev: CSM 11/9/81; LJ 10/15/81; NYTBR 11/1/81)   **[323.1]**

851 King, Mary. *Freedom Song: A Personal Story of the 1960's Civil Rights Movement.* **1987, Morrow $22.95 (0-688-05772-1).** An account of the au-

thor's social activism in support of civil rights during the 1960s in the American South. (Rev: BL 6/1/87; LJ 7/87; NYTBR 8/30/87)   **[323.1]**

852 Powledge, Fred. *Free at Last?* **1991, Little, Brown $27.95 (0-316-71632-4).** An overview of the key events and figures of the American civil rights movement. (Rev: BL 12/1/90; LJ 1/15/91; NYTBR 3/10/91)   **[323.1]**

853 Prucha, Francis Paul. *Great Father: The United States Government and the American Indians.* **1984, Univ. of Nebraska Pr. $80.00 (0-8032-3668-9).** A history of the relationship between the federal government and Native Americans. "Truly the definitive work on the subject."—LJ (Rev: Choice 5/85; LJ 11/1/84)   **[323.1]**

854 Rogers, Mary Beth. *Cold Anger: A Story of Faith and Power Politics.* **1990, Univ. of North Texas Pr. paper $14.95 (0-929398-13-0).** A study of a Hispanic-American political organizer and his tactics to increase Latin political participation and influence. (Rev: BL 10/1/90; LJ 10/1/90)   **[323.1]**

Women

855 Pisan, Christine de. *Book of the City of Ladies.* **1982, Persea Books paper $11.95 (0-89255-066-X).** A translation of a fifteenth-century work by an Italian who was a member of the court of French King Charles V, regarding women and their role in history and society. (Rev: BL 5/1/82; NYTBR 7/25/82; PW 3/26/82)   **[323.34]**

Specific civil rights

856 Abernathy, Ralph D. *And the Walls Came Tumbling Down: An Autobiography.* **1989, Harper & Row $25.00 (0-06-016192-2); paper $12.95 (0-06-091986-8).** An autobiography of the former civil rights activist and close personal friend of Martin Luther King, Jr., and Jesse Jackson. "Inspirational and deeply moving."—PW (Rev: BL 9/15/89; NYTBR 10/29/89; PW 8/18/89)   **[323.4]**

857 Anderson, Jervis. *A. Philip Randolph: A Biographical Portrait.* **1986, Univ. of California Pr. paper $11.95 (0-520-05505-5).** A biography of the black labor organizer and key figure in the civil rights movement. "Thorough and well documented . . . a major contribution."—LJ (Rev: Choice 9/73; CSM 3/28/73; LJ 2/15/73)   **[323.4]**

858 Campbell, Will D. *Brother to a Dragonfly.* **1980, Continuum paper $12.95 (0-8264-0032-9).** An autobiography of a civil rights activist and minister intertwined with the story of his elder brother, a pharmacist who died of a drug overdose. "A masterpiece of Southern literature."—LJ (Rev: Choice 9/78; CSM 8/17/78; LJ 10/15/77)   **[323.4]**

859 Farmer, James. *Lay Bare the Heart: An Autobiography of the Civil Rights Movement.* **1986, NAL paper $8.95 (0-452-25803-0).** A founder of CORE recounts his life as an activist in the civil rights movement. (Rev: BL 3/1/85; LJ 3/1/85; NYTBR 3/24/85)   **[323.4]**

860 Korn, David A. *Human Rights in Iraq.* **1991, Yale Univ. Pr. $19.95 (0-300-04959-5).** A review of recent human rights abuses in Iraq documented by Human Rights Watch. (REV: LJ 11/1/90; NYRB 9/27/90; NYTBR 12/16/90) **[323.4]**

861 Oates, Stephen B. *Let the Trumpet Sound: The Life of Martin Luther King, Jr.* **1983, NAL paper $10.95 (0-452-25627-5).** The fourth and final volume of the author's quartet of key figures in the history of American civil rights that includes biographies of King, Nat Turner, Abraham Lincoln, and John Brown. (REV: CSM 8/13/82; LJ 7/82; NYTBR 9/12/82) **[323.4]**

862 O'Reilly, Kenneth. *Racial Matters: The FBI's Secret File on Black America, 1960–1972.* **1989, Free Pr. $24.95 (0-02-923681-9).** A history of the FBI's domestic spying campaign against civil rights activists in the 1960s and early 1970s. "A frightening book, recounting an outrageous era."—BL (REV: BL 5/1/89; LJ 6/15/89; NYTBR 7/19/89) **[323.4]**

863 Pfeffer, Paula F. *A. Philip Randolph, Pioneer of the Civil Rights Movement.* **1990, Louisiana State Univ. Pr. $29.95 (0-8071-1554-1).** A biography of the African-American labor leader who founded the Brotherhood of Sleeping Car Porters. (REV: Choice 9/90; LJ 5/15/90; NYTBR 9/23/90) **[323.4]**

864 Raines, Howell. *My Soul Is Rested: Movement Days in the Deep South Remembered.* **1983, Penguin paper $8.95 (0-14-006753-1).** An oral history of the civil rights movement based on interviews with over 100 participants from 1955 to 1968. (REV: BL 9/15/77; LJ 9/1/77; NYTBR 10/23/77) **[323.4]**

865 Sharansky, Natan. *Fear No Evil.* **1988, Random $19.95 (0-394-55878-2).** The story of the Soviet dissident's experience as a political prisoner of the KGB over a nearly ten-year period. (REV: CSM 7/1/88; LJ 7/88; NYTBR 6/5/88. AWARDS: ALA, 1988; LJ, 1988) **[323.4]**

866 Williams, Juan. *Eyes on the Prize: America's Civil Rights Years, 1954–1965.* **1987, Viking $24.95 (0-670-81412-1); Penguin paper $10.95 (0-14-009653-1).** A companion volume to the PBS television series tracing the history of the civil rights movement from the Brown v. Board of Education decision to the Voting Rights Act of 1965. (REV: BL 12/12/86; LJ 1/87; NYTBR 1/25/87) **[323.4]**

867 Witherspoon, William Roger. *Martin Luther King, Jr.: To the Mountaintop.* **1985, Doubleday $24.95 (0-385-19883-3).** An illustrated profile of the life of the American civil rights leader. (REV: BL 12/15/85; LJ 12/85; NYTBR 1/26/86) **[323.4]**

Freedom of action (Liberty)

868 Burnham, David. *Rise of the Computer State.* **1984, Random paper $6.95 (0-394-72375-9).** How the use of bureaucratic computers invades and threatens the privacy of individuals. "A fresh perspective on a much-discussed subject."—BL (REV: BL 6/1/83; LJ 9/1/83; NYTBR 8/21/83) **[323.44]**

869 Levy, Leonard W. *Emergence of a Free Press.* **1985, Oxford Univ. Pr. paper $9.95 (0-19-504902-0).** A history of the legal use and interpretation of the First Amendment to the Constitution. (REV: Choice 9/85; LJ 2/15/85; NYTBR 2/24/85) **[323.44]**

870 Miller, William Lee. *First Liberty: Religion and the American Republic.* **1986, Knopf $24.95 (0-394-53476-X); Paragon House paper $10.95 (1-55578-007-2).** A study of the relationship between religious freedom and the U.S. government in the developing years of the republic. (REV: BL 1/15/86; Natl Rev 2/28/86; NYTBR 1/26/86) **[323.44]**

871 Reston, James. *Artillery of the Press.* **1967, Books on Demand $32.00 (0-8357-9150-5).** An analysis of the relationship of the American press to the American government and its influence upon American foreign policy. (REV: Atl 4/67; LJ 3/1/67; PW 1/30/67. AWARDS: ALA, 1967) **[323.44]**

Limitation and suspension of civil rights

872 Schultz, Bud, and Ruth Schultz. *It Did Happen Here: Recollections of Political Repression in America.* **1989, Univ. of California Pr. $22.50 (0-520-06508-5); paper $12.95 (0-520-07197-2).** An oral history documenting incidents in the lives of 30 Americans where their Constitutional rights were violated due to their political beliefs. (REV: BL 5/15/89; LJ 5/1/89; NYTBR 8/6/89) **[323.49]**

324 The political process

873 Garrow, David J. *Protest at Selma: Martin Luther King, Jr. and the Voting Rights Act of 1965.* **1978, Yale Univ. Pr. $35.00 (0-300-02247-6); paper $13.95 (0-300-02498-3).** Garrow explores the relationship between the civil rights protests King led at Selma, and the passage of the Voting Rights Act of 1965. (REV: Choice 2/79; LJ 8/78; New Rep 11/4/78) **[324]**

874 Romney, Ronna, and Beppie Harrison. *Momentum: Women in American Politics Now.* **1988, Crown $18.95 (0-517-56890-X).** A study of the past, present, and future of women in American politics with profiles of prominent female leaders. (REV: BL 3/15/88; LJ 4/1/88; PW 2/5/88) **[324]**

Political parties in Germany

875 Morais, Fernando. *Olga.* **1990, Grove-Weidenfeld $21.95 (0-8021-1086-X).** A biography of a Brazilian Communist of German descent who was deported to Nazi Germany and perished in the concentration camps. (REV: BL 10/15/90; LJ 11/1/90; PW 9/28/90) **[324.243]**

Political parties in Israel

876 Friedman, Robert I. *False Prophet: Rabbi Meir Kahane—From FBI Informant to Knesset Member.* **1990, Chicago Review $19.95 (1-55652-078-6).** A biography of the founder of the Jewish Defense League and Israeli political figure who was assassinated in Brooklyn, New York, in 1990. (REV: BL 3/15/90; LJ 4/15/90; PW 2/9/90) **[324.25694]**

Auxiliary organizations

877 Gluck, Sherna Berger, ed. *From Parlor to Prison: Five American Suffragettes Talk about Their Lives.* 1976, Hippocrene Books $20.00 (0-374-93161-5); Monthly Review paper $12.00 (0-85345-676-3). Interviews with five former suffragettes regarding their lives and their efforts to win women the right to vote. "Oral history at its most vivid."—PW (Rev: BL 5/1/76; LJ 4/1/76; PW 3/8/76)   **[324.3]**

Nomination of candidates

878 Duncan, Dayton. *Grass Roots: One Year in the Life of the New Hampshire Primary.* 1991, Viking $22.95 (0-670-81851-8). A study of the lives and actions of several political volunteer campaigners prior to the 1988 New Hampshire primary. (Rev: BL 1/1/91; LJ 12/90; PW 12/14/90)   **[324.5]**

Election systems and procedures; Suffrage

879 Griffith, Elisabeth. *In Her Own Right: The Life of Elizabeth Cady Stanton.* 1985, Oxford Univ. Pr. paper $10.95 (0-19-503729-4). The life story of the women's rights activist and abolitionist. "A well-rounded biography that does full justice to this truly extraordinary woman."—NYTBR (Rev: Choice 1/85; LJ 8/1/84; NYTBR 10/21/84. Awards: NYTBR, 1984)   **[324.6]**

Conduct of election campaigns

880 Abramson, Jeffrey B. *Electronic Commonwealth: The Impact of New Media Technologies on Democratic Politics.* 1988, Basic Books $21.95 (0-465-01878-5). An investigation into the ways new technologies in the media affect politics and society in America. (Rev: BL 7/88; Choice 2/89; LJ 9/15/88)   **[324.7]**

United States

881 Blumenthal, Sidney. *Pledging Allegiance: The Last Campaign of the Cold War.* 1990, Harper & Row $22.95 (0-06-016189-2). An analysis of the 1988 U.S. presidential campaign by the author of *The Rise of the Counter-Establishment.* (Rev: BL 9/15/90; NYTBR 10/14/90; PW 9/7/90)   **[324.973]**

882 Boller, Paul F., Jr. *Presidential Campaigns.* 1984, Oxford Univ. Pr. $22.95 (0-19-503420-1). A survey of the campaigns for the U.S. presidency from the first election in 1789 to the 1980 Reagan-Carter race. (Rev: Choice 7–8/84; CSM 7/16/84; LJ 4/15/84)   **[324.973]**

883 Drew, Elizabeth. *Election Journal: The Political Events of 1987–1988.* 1989, Morrow $19.95 (0-688-08332-3). A collection of the author's journalistic columns from the *New Yorker* regarding the 1988 presidential campaign and election. (Rev: BL 2/15/89; LJ 4/15/89)   **[324.973]**

884 Edsall, Thomas Byrne, and Mary D. Edsall. *Chain Reaction: The Impact of Race, Rights, and Taxes on American Politics.* 1991, Norton $22.95 (0-393-02983-3). An analysis of recent politics and the impact of Republican administrations on American social policies. (Rev: NYTBR 10/20/91; PW 8/23/91)   **[324.973]**

885 Ehrenhalt, Alan. *United States of Ambition: Politicians, Power and the Pursuit of Office.* 1991, Times Books $23.00 (0-8129-1894-0). A study of the contemporary methods used by American politicians to win election. (Rev: BL 3/1/91; LJ 4/1/91)   **[324.973]**

886 Germond, Jack W., and Jules Witcover. *Whose Broad Stripes and Bright Stars? The Trivial Pursuit of the Presidency, 1988.* 1989, Warner $22.95 (0-446-51424-1). The authors' third in a series covering the events of presidential races exhaustively recounts the 1988 campaign. (Rev: BL 8/89; LJ 9/1/89; NYTBR 9/3/89)   **[324.973]**

887 Goldman, Peter, and Tom Mathews. *Quest for the Presidency, 1988.* 1989, Simon & Schuster $22.95 (0-671-69079-5); paper $9.95 (0-671-69080-9). A chronology and analysis of the 1988 presidential campaign and election as reported by two *Newsweek* editors and their journalistic team. (Rev: BL 10/15/89; LJ 11/1/89)   **[324.973]**

888 McCarthy, Eugene. *Up 'Til Now: A Memoir of the Decline of American Politics.* 1987, Harcourt $16.95 (0-15-193170-4). Memoirs and reflections of the former U.S. senator and Democratic presidential candidate. (Rev: BL 3/15/87; LJ 2/1/87; NYTBR 3/29/87)   **[324.973]**

889 Pomper, Gerald. *Election of 1988: Reports and Interpretations.* 1989, Chatham House Pubs. $25.00 (0-93450-77-2); paper $12.95 (0-934540-76-4). An account of the 1988 presidential campaign and election. "Indispensable reading for an informed electorate."—LJ (Rev: Choice 10/89; LJ 5/15/89)   **[324.973]**

890 Sheehy, Gail. *Character: America's Search for Leadership.* 1988, Morrow $17.95 (0-688-08072-3); Bantam paper $5.95 (0-553-27924-6). A study of the American system of choosing a president with profiles of leading recent candidates for the post. (Rev: BL 6/1/88; LJ 8/88; NYTBR 5/29/88)   **[324.973]**

891 Taylor, Paul. *See How They Run: Electing the President in an Age of Mediaocracy.* 1990, Knopf $22.95 (0-394-57059-6). A history and analysis of the 1988 American presidential campaign and election. (Rev: BL 9/15/90; NYTBR 9/30/90; PW 7/27/90)   **[324.973]**

892 Thompson, Hunter S. *Fear and Loathing on the Campaign Trail '72.* 1983, Warner paper $4.50 (0-446-31268-1). The *Rolling Stone* reporter's coverage of the 1972 presidential campaign. "It reeks with an understanding of American politics which should put most academics to shame."—Choice (Rev: Choice 12/73; LJ 6/1/72; Newsweek 5/21/73)   **[324.973]**

325 International migration and colonization

Immigration

893 Tifft, Wilton S. *Ellis Island.* 1990, Contemporary $35.00 (0-8092-4418-7). A photographic history of the American immigration processing station in New York harbor. (REV: BL 12/1/90; LJ 12/90)   **[325.1]**

Emigration from Soviet Union

894   **Gilbert, Martin.** *Shcharansky: A Hero of Our Time.* **1986, Viking $24.95 (0-317-46605-4).** A biography of the Soviet Jewish dissident who was released to the West in 1986. (REV: Choice 10/86; LJ 6/1/86; NYRB 9/25/86)   **[325.24]**

United States

895   **Morgan, Ted.** *On Becoming American.* **1988, Paragon paper $8.95 (1-55778-070-6).** The author's story of how and why he left France, changed his name, and became an American citizen. (REV: CSM 3/29/78; NYTBR 4/2/78; Sat Rev 2/1/78)   **[325.73]**

896   **Reimers, David M.** *Still the Golden Door: The Third World Comes to America.* **1985, Columbia Univ. Pr. $29.00 (0-231-05770-9).** A study of recent immigration to the United States focusing on the post-1965 period. (REV: Choice 2/86; LJ 9/1/85; PW 6/21/85)   **[325.73]**

897   **Santoli, Al.** *New Americans: An Oral History; Immigrants and Refugees in the U.S. Today.* **1988, Viking $19.95 (0-670-81583-7); Ballantine paper $10.95 (0-345-36455-4).** An oral history of 18 recent immigrants to the U.S. regarding their lives and their feelings toward America. (REV: BL 9/15/88; LJ 11/15/88; NYTBR 4/2/89)   **[325.73]**

326   Slavery and emancipation

898   **Brandt, Nat.** *Town That Started the Civil War.* **1990, Syracuse Univ. Pr. $29.95 (0-8156-0243-X).** An account of an 1858 Oberlin, Ohio, incident involving the fate of a runaway slave. "A work of first-rate scholarship as well as popular history at its most enjoyable."—PW (REV: LJ 4/1/90; NYTBR 5/20/90; PW 3/16/90)   **[326]**

899   **Davis, David B.** *The Problem of Slavery in Western Culture.* **1988, Oxford Univ. Pr. paper $13.95 (0-19-505639-6).** Traces the institution of slavery from ancient times to the 1770s. (REV: Atl 8/66; LJ 7/66. AWARDS: PP:NF, 1967)   **[326]**

900   **Fogel, Robert William.** *Without Consent or Contract: The Rise and Fall of American Slavery.* **1989, Norton $22.50 (0-393-01887-3).** An analysis of the social and economic basis of American slavery. "No student of slavery, America or the Atlantic world can ignore this book."—LJ (REV: LJ 10/15/89; New Rep 10/23/89; PW 8/25/89)   **[326]**

901   **Jones, Howard.** *Mutiny on the Amistad: The Saga of a Slave Revolt and Its Impact on American Abolition, Law and Diplomacy.* **1987, Oxford Univ. Pr. $22.95 (0-19-503828-2).** An account of the 1839 mutiny of slaves aboard a Spanish trading ship and how they were returned to Africa following the ship's seizure by the U.S. Navy. (REV: LJ 2/1/87; Natl Rev 7/3/87; PW 12/12/86)   **[326]**

902   **McLaurin, Melton A.** *Celia: A Slave.* **1991, Univ. of Georgia Pr. $19.95 (0-8203-1352-1).** A chronicle of the life of a slave sentenced to death for the killing of an abusive owner. "Reads like a fine novel."—PW (REV: BL 11/15/91; NYTBR 11/17/91; PW 10/11/91)   **[326]**

903   **Mellon, James, ed.** *Bullwhip Days: The Slaves Remember.* **1989, Grove-Weidenfeld $27.50 (1-55584-210-0); Avon paper $12.95 (0-380-70884-1).** Twenty-nine interviews and selected excerpts from 2,000 former slaves made by the WPA in the 1930s. (REV: NYTBR 1/8/89; Newsweek 1/23/89; PW 11/18/88)   **[326]**

327   International relations

904   **Gorbachev, Mikhail.** *Perestroika: New Thinking for Our Country and the World.* **1988, Harper & Row paper $9.95 (0-06-091528-5).** The former Soviet leader's presentation of his political philosophy and what it means for the future of the USSR and the world. (REV: BL 1/15/88; Choice 4/88; Natl Rev 2/19/88)   **[327]**

905   **Marchetti, Victor, and John D. Marks.** *CIA and the Cult of Intelligence.* **1989, Dell paper $4.95 (0-440-20336-8).** This history of the CIA's covert actions by a former agent was delayed in court and censored on grounds of national security. "Marchetti and Marks' account of CIA skulduggery is the most complete we have had to date, even in its sanitized form."—LJ (REV: CSM 6/26/74; LJ 8/74; Newsweek 7/1/74)   **[327]**

906   **Schaeffer, Robert.** *Warpaths: The Politics of Partition.* **1990, Hill & Wang $25.00 (0-8090-9663-3).** A study of the effects of political partition upon nations and peoples during the twentieth century. (REV: BL 1/15/90; PW 12/8/89)   **[327]**

General topics of international relations

907   **Bamford, James.** *Puzzle Palace: A Report on America's Most Secret Agency.* **1983, Penguin paper $10.95 (0-14-006748-5).** An account of the history and present day function of the little-known National Security Agency. (REV: Choice 1/83; CSM 11/5/82; NYTBR 9/19/82)   **[327.1]**

908   **Bundy, McGeorge.** *Danger and Survival: The Political History of the Nuclear Weapon.* **1988, Random $24.95 (0-394-52278-8); paper $12.95 (0-679-72568-7).** The former national security advisor traces the history of the events and issues where the discussion of the military use of nuclear weapons has arisen, from the development of the atomic bomb through the 1980s. (REV: BL 10/15/88; LJ 1/89; NYRB 2/2/89)   **[327.1]**

909   **Dallin, Alexander.** *Black Box: KAL 007 and the Superpowers.* **1985, Univ. of California Pr. $22.50 (0-520-05515-2); paper $8.95 (0-520-05516-0).** An analysis of the events leading up to, and the repercussions following, the downing of a Korean Air Lines plane by Soviet missiles. (REV: LJ 5/1/85; NYRB 4/25/85; NYTBR 4/21/85)   **[327.1]**

910   Dyson, Freeman J. *Weapons and Hope.* **1985, Harper & Row paper $7.95 (0-06-039039-5).** The British-born physicist's argument for the eventual abolition of nuclear weapons. "This fair-minded and hopeful analysis deserves wide and thoughtful readership."—LJ (REV: BL 1/1/84; LJ 2/15/84; Time 6/11/ 84. AWARDS: LJ, 1984)   **[327.1]**

911   Morris, Charles R. *Iron Destinies, Lost Opportunities: The Arms Race Between the U.S.A. and the U.S.S.R., 1945–1987.* **1989, Carroll & Graf paper $13.95 (0-88184-474-8).** The history and analysis of the military buildup and competition between the United States and the Soviet Union following World War II. (REV: BL 5/15/88; LJ 8/88; NYTBR 5/22/88)   **[327.1]**

912   Schmidt, Helmut. *A Grand Strategy for the West: The Anachronism of National Strategies in an Interdependent World.* **1985, Yale Univ. Pr. $20.00 (0-300-03535-7); paper $8.95 (0-300-04003-2).** The former West German chancellor presents his views on the future of international relations and political alliances. (REV: LJ 12/85; NYTBR 12/1/85; TLS 1/17/86)   **[327.1]**

913   Shevchenko, Arkady N. *Breaking with Moscow.* **1985, Knopf $18.95 (0-394-52055-6); Ballantine paper $4.95 (0-345-30088-2).** Memoirs of the Soviet U.N. diplomat who defected to the United States in 1978, the highest ranking Soviet official ever to do so. (REV: BL 3/15/85; Natl Rev 5/31/85; NYTBR 2/17/85)   **[327.1]**

914   Talbott, Strobe. *Deadly Gambits: The Reagan Administration and the Stalemate in Nuclear Arms Control.* **1984, Knopf $17.95 (0-394-53637-1).** An inside view of arms control negotiations during the first Reagan administration. "An account that historians will be using for years to come."— McGeorge Bundy, NYTBR (REV: CSM 11/9/84; LJ 11/ 15/84; NYTBR 10/7/84. AWARDS: ALA, 1984; NYTBR, 1984)   **[327.1]**

915   Talbott, Strobe. *Master of the Game: Paul Nitze and the Nuclear Peace.* **1988, Knopf $19.95 (0-394-56881-8); Random paper $10.95 (0-679-72165-7).** A biography of the American diplomat best known for his role in arms control negotiations and his formulation of defense policies during the Reagan administrations. (REV: BL 9/15/88; CSM 11/15/ 88; NYTBR 11/6/88)   **[327.1]**

916   Weart, Spencer. *Nuclear Fear: A History of Images.* **1988, Harvard Univ. Pr. $29.50 (0-674-62835-7).** A history of the depiction of nuclear weaponry in fact and fiction from prefission legends and stories to the present. (REV: CSM 6/3/88; LJ 5/1/88; NYTBR 5/1/88)   **[327.1]**

917   Woodward, Bob. *Veil: The Secret Wars of the CIA.* **1988, Pocket paper $4.95 (0-671-66159-0).** Woodward's controversial book on the CIA's covert actions during the Reagan era. His sources remain unnamed. (REV: BL 10/15/87; Choice 12/87; LJ 12/87. AWARDS: LJ, 1987)   **[327.1]**

Espionage and subversion

918   Agee, Philip. *On the Run.* **1987, Carol Publg. Group $19.95 (0-8184-0419-1).** Memoirs of the former CIA agent and author of *Inside the Company* regarding the intelligence activities and dealings with the CIA following his resignation. (REV: LJ 7/87; NYTBR 8/2/87; PW 5/29/87)   **[327.12]**

919   Andrew, Christopher. *Her Majesty's Secret Service: The Making of the British Intelligence Community.* **1986, Viking $25.00 (0-670-80941-1); Penguin paper $8.95 (0-14-009428-8).** A history of British intelligence operations in the twentieth century from its beginnings prior to the outbreak of World War I to the present. (REV: LJ 3/1/86; Newsweek 2/24/ 86; TLS 7/4/86)   **[327.12]**

920   Andrew, Christopher, and Oleg Gordievsky. *KGB: The Inside Story of Its Foreign Operations from Lenin to Gorbachev.* **1990, HarperCollins $29.95 (0-06-016605-3); paper $15.95 (0-06-092109-9).** A collaboration between an American historian and a former KGB officer tracing the history of Soviet foreign intelligence operations from the Russian Revolution to the 1980s. "The best look yet into one of history's largest black holes."—NYTBR (REV: BL 12/15/90; Choice 5/91; NYTBR 11/18/90)   **[327.12]**

921   Barron, John. *Breaking the Ring: The Bizarre Case of the Walker Family Spy Ring.* **1988, Avon paper $3.95 (0-380-70520-6).** An account of the FBI investigation into the doings of the Walker family spy ring, which supplied American secrets to the KGB. (REV: LJ 4/1/87; Natl Rev 7/31/87; NYTBR 6/7/87)   **[327.12]**

922   Blitzer, Wolf. *Territory of Lies: The Exclusive Story of Jonathan J. Pollard.* **1989, Harper & Row $22.50 (0-06-015972-3).** The story of a U.S. Naval intelligence officer and his wife who were convicted of spying for Israel. "A thoroughly provocative tale that needed to be told and was done so with a great deal of passion."—LJ (REV: LJ 6/1/89; New Rep 6/5/89; NYTBR 5/7/89)   **[327.12]**

923   Blum, Howard. *I Pledge Allegiance: The True Story of an American Spy Family.* **1987, Simon & Schuster $17.95 (0-317-63133-0); Pocket paper $4.95 (0-671-66717-3).** An account of three U.S. Navy men who were convicted of spying for the Soviet Union. "The most involving treatment of the case."—BL (REV: BL 10/15/87; LJ 11/1/87)   **[327.12]**

924   Cecil, Robert. *A Divided Life: A Biography of Donald MacLean.* **1989, Morrow $18.95 (0-688-08119-3).** A study of the life and career of MacLean, a British spy who served as a Russian double agent following World War II. (REV: BL 3/1/89; LJ 2/15/89; NYTBR 4/16/89)   **[327.12]**

925   Earley, Pete. *Family of Spies: Inside the John Walker Spy Ring.* **1989, Bantam paper $4.95 (0-553-28222-0).** An account of the U.S. Navy spy family who passed secrets to the KGB undetected for nearly two decades. "A classic of the genre."—PW (REV: LJ 11/15/88; NYTBR 1/8/89; PW 9/30/88)   **[327.12]**

926 Everett, Melissa. *Breaking Ranks.* 1988, New Society Pubs. $34.95 (0-86571-134-8); paper $12.95 (0-86571-135-6). Profiles of former cold war supporters who became disillusioned and have spoken out against U.S. government policies regarding foreign relations and nuclear strategy. (Rev: BL 2/15/89; LJ 2/1/89; PW 12/23/88) **[327.12]**

927 Kessler, Ronald. *Moscow Station: How the KGB Penetrated the American Embassy.* 1989, Macmillan $19.95 (0-684-18981-X); Pocket paper $4.95 (0-671-69338-7). An investigation into the KGB bugging of the American Embassy in Moscow. (Rev: BL 4/15/89; LJ 5/15/89; NYTBR 3/19/89) **[327.12]**

928 Knightley, Phillip. *Master Spy: The Story of Kim Philby.* 1989, Knopf $19.95 (0-394-57890-2); Random paper $9.95 (0-679-72688-8). A biography of the double agent who worked for British Intelligence while passing on information to the KGB. (Rev: BL 2/1/89; LJ 4/15/89; NYTBR 4/16/87) **[327.12]**

929 Knightley, Phillip. *Second Oldest Profession: Spies and Spying in the 20th Century.* 1988, Penguin paper $7.95 (0-15-631130-5). A history of British, American, and Soviet spying in the twentieth century. (Rev: Newsweek 1/12/87; Time 1/12/87; TLS 1/30/87) **[327.12]**

930 Lamphere, Robert, and Thomas Schactman. *FBI-KGB War: A Special Agent's Story.* 1986, Random $18.95 (0-394-54151-0); Berkley paper $4.50 (0-425-10338-2). An account of the FBI's breakup of a Soviet spy network in the 1950s by a former special agent. (Rev: LJ 6/1/86; New Rep 9/8/86; NYTBR 8/13/86) **[327.12]**

931 Laqueur, Walter. *World of Secrets: The Uses and Limits of Intelligence.* 1985, Basic Books $21.95 (0-465-09237-3). A study of the methods and uses of American and European intelligence since World War II. (Rev: BL 9/15/85; Choice 3/86; LJ 9/15/85) **[327.12]**

932 Lindsey, Robert. *Falcon and the Snowman: A True Story of Friendship and Espionage.* 1985, Pocket paper $4.50 (0-671-45160-X). An account of the spy scandal involving two young southern California men who sold satellite surveillance secrets to the Soviets. (Rev: BL 11/15/79; NYTBR 11/4/79; Newsweek 11/26/79) **[327.12]**

933 Mangold, Tom. *Cold Warrior: James Jesus Angleton; the CIA's Master Spy Hunter.* 1991, Simon & Schuster $24.95 (0-671-66273-2). A biography of the man who served as CIA chief of counterintelligence for three decades. "First-class . . . an intriguing account."—PW (Rev: LJ 7/91; NYTBR 6/30/91; PW 5/3/91) **[327.12]**

934 Miller, Nathan. *Spying for America: The Hidden History of U.S. Intelligence.* 1989, Paragon House $24.95 (1-55778-186-9). History of American intelligence gathering from the Revolutionary War to the Iran-Contra affair. (Rev: LJ 3/15/89; NYTBR 7/23/89; PW 2/17/89) **[327.12]**

935 Newton, Verne W. *Cambridge Spies: The Untold Story of MacLean, Philby and Burgess in America.* 1991, Madison Books $24.95 (0-8191-8059-9). A study of the espionage activities of spies stationed in the British embassy in Washington during the late 1940s. (Rev: NYTBR 6/30/91; PW 4/19/91) **[327.12]**

936 Penrose, Barrie, and Simon Freeman. *Conspiracy of Silence: The Secret Life of Anthony Blunt.* 1987, Farrar $22.95 (0-374-12885-5); Random paper $10.95 (0-679-72044-8). An examination of the career of the British art historian who was exposed as a Soviet spy. (Rev: CSM 8/7/87; PW 5/29/87; Time 8/10/87) **[327.12]**

937 Persico, Joseph E. *Casey: From the OSS to the CIA.* 1990, Viking $24.95 (0-670-82342-2); paper $14.95 (0-14-011314-2). A biography of William Casey tracing his career in intelligence from OSS European chief during World War II to head of the CIA under Reagan. (Rev: BL 9/15/90; LJ 10/1/90; NYTBR 10/7/90) **[327.12]**

938 Phillips, David Atlee. *Careers in Secret Operations: How to Be a Federal Intelligence Officer.* 1984, Univ. Publications of America $15.00 (0-89093-653-6). A career guide for those interested in intelligence work by a 25-year veteran of the CIA. **[327.12]**

939 Raviv, Dan, and Yossi Melman. *Every Spy a Prince: The Complete History of Israel's Intelligence Community.* 1990, Houghton $24.95 (0-395-47102-8). A history and analysis of the rise and fall of Israeli intelligence. (Rev: LJ 7/90; NYTBR 7/8/90; PW 6/8/90) **[327.12]**

940 Rodriguez, Felix I., and John Weisman. *Shadow Warrior: The CIA Hero of a Hundred Unknown Battles.* 1989, Simon & Schuster $19.95 (0-671-66721-1). Memoirs of a former CIA agent about his secret activities in Cuba, El Salvador, Bolivia, and Vietnam. (Rev: BL 10/1/89; LJ 10/15/89; NYTBR 11/5/89) **[327.12]**

941 Roosevelt, Archibald, Jr. *For Lust of Knowing: The Memoirs of an Intelligence Officer in the Middle East.* 1988, Little, Brown $24.95 (0-316-75600-8). The grandson of Theodore Roosevelt recounts his years serving as a CIA agent in the Arabic-speaking world. (Rev: BL 2/15/88; LJ 3/15/88; Natl Rev 7/8/88) **[327.12]**

942 Stockwell, John. *In Search of Enemies: A CIA Story.* 1984, Norton paper $9.95 (0-393-00926-2). A former CIA agent describes his experiences working for the agency in Angola during the mid-1970s. (Rev: Choice 12/78; LJ 7/78; NYTBR 7/16/78) **[327.12]**

943 West, Nigel. *Molehunt: Searching for Soviet Spies in MI5.* 1989, Morrow $19.95 (0-688-07653-X). An investigation of the infiltration of Soviet spies and double agents into Britain's top intelligence-gathering agency. (Rev: BL 3/1/89; LJ 3/15/89; TLS 5/22/87) **[327.12]**

944 Winks, Robin W. *Cloak and Gown: Scholars in the Secret War, 1939–1961.* 1987, Morrow $22.95 (0-688-07300-X); paper $14.95 (0-688-08665-9). A look at the relationship between academic institutions

and intelligence-gathering organizations in the United States from World War II to the beginning of the Kennedy administration. (REV: Choice 12/87; LJ 9/1/87; PW 6/26/87) **[327.12]**

945 Wise, David. *Spy Who Got Away: The Inside Story of Edward Lee Howard, the CIA Agent Who Betrayed His Country's Secrets and Escaped to Moscow.* **1988, Random $18.95 (0-394-56281-X); Avon paper $4.95 (0-380-70772-1).** An account of a CIA agent that passed information to the Soviets and then defected to the U.S.S.R. (REV: BL 9/15/88; LJ 9/1/88) **[327.12]**

946 Wright, Peter, and Paul Greengrass. *Spycatcher: The Candid Autobiography of a Senior Intelligence Officer.* **1988, G. K. Hall $21.95 (0-8161-4512-1); Dell paper $4.95 (0-440-20132-2).** An autobiography of a former British spy describing his 20 years of work in intelligence. (REV: BL 9/1/87; NYTBR 8/16/87; Time 8/10/87) **[327.12]**

Diplomacy

947 Hiss, Alger. *Recollections of a Life.* **1989, Arcade paper $9.95 (1-55970-024-6).** Memoirs of the American diplomat who was accused of pro-Communist activities in the early 1950s and convicted of perjury charges following his famous trial. (REV: BL 4/1/88; LJ 5/15/88; PW 4/8/88) **[327.2]**

948 Kennan, George F. *Sketches from a Life.* **1989, Pantheon $22.95 (0-394-57504-0); paper $12.95 (0-679-72877-5).** Selections from the American diplomat's journals from 1927 to the 1980s, covering his travels to such varied places as Moscow, Baghdad, Italy, and Mexico City. (REV: NYRB 8/17/89; NYTBR 5/7/89; PW 3/24/89. AWARDS: PW, 1989) **[327.2]**

949 Taft, John. *American Power: The Rise and Decline of U.S. Globalism, 1918–1988.* **1989, Harper & Row $22.50 (0-06-016133-7).** A study of America's declining global power as evidenced by its diplomatic history since World War I. (REV: BL 10/15/89; LJ 11/1/89; PW 8/18/89) **[327.2]**

950 Urquhart, Brian E. *A Life in Peace and War.* **1987, Harper & Row $25.00 (0-06-015840-9).** An autobiography of a former World War II British intelligence officer who served as undersecretary-general of the United Nations. (REV: Choice 1/88; LJ 9/1/87; NYRB 11/5/87) **[327.2]**

Soviet Union

951 Bialer, Seweryn. *Soviet Paradox: External Expansion, Internal Decline.* **1986, Knopf $22.95 (0-394-54095-6); Random paper $9.95 (0-394-75288-0).** A study of Soviet politics between the death of Leonid Brezhnev and the ascension of Mikhail Gorbachev. (REV: Choice 10/86; New Rep 8/25/86; NYTBR 7/27/86) **[327.47]**

952 Kennan, George F. *Nuclear Delusion: Soviet-American Relations in the Atomic Age.* **1983, Pantheon paper $8.95 (0-394-71318-4).** The American statesman traces the history of the arms race between the Soviet Union and the United States

from World War II to the 1980s. (REV: Atl 12/82; LJ 12/1/82; NYTBR 11/7/82) **[327.47]**

United States

953 Barnet, Richard J. *Rockets' Red Glare: When America Goes to War.* **1990, Simon & Schuster $24.95 (0-671-63376-7).** The history of American public opinion, nationalism, and its influence on diplomacy and war-making by the United States government. (REV: BL 12/1/89; LJ 3/1/90; NYTBR 2/4/90) **[327.73]**

954 Barnet, Richard J. *Roots of War: The Men and Institutions Behind U.S. Foreign Policy.* **1973, Penguin paper $7.95 (0-14-021698-7).** Examination of how American power is used throughout the world and how the decisions to use it are made. "An important contribution . . . to the appreciation of fundamental concepts underlying contemporary American foreign policy."—Choice (REV: Choice 11/72; LJ 5/1/72; PW 2/28/72) **[327.73]**

955 Beisner, Robert L. *Twelve Against Empire: The Anti-Imperialists, 1898–1900.* **1985, Univ. of Chicago Pr. paper $9.95 (0-226-04171-9).** Profiles of 12 Americans critical of U.S. colonialist actions at the turn of the century including Carl Schurz, Andrew Carnegie, and William James. (REV: BL 6/15/68; CSM 3/28/68; NYTBR 4/7/68) **[327.73]**

956 Bill, James A. *Eagle and the Lion: The Tragedy of American-Iranian Relations.* **1988, Yale Univ. Pr. $30.00 (0-300-04097-0); paper $13.95 (0-300-04412-7).** A history of relations between the United States and Iran in the nineteenth and twentieth centuries. "The book to buy for a definitive analysis of our Iranian adventure."—LJ (REV: Choice 7–8/88; LJ 4/1/88; NYTBR 5/8/88. AWARDS: LJ, 1988) **[327.73]**

957 Blitzer, Wolf. *Between Washington and Jerusalem: A Reporter's Notebook.* **1985, Oxford Univ. Pr. $21.95 (0-19-503708-1).** The CNN reporter and former Washington correspondent for the *Jerusalem Post* traces the history of American-Israeli relations. (REV: BL 9/15/85; LJ 9/1/85; NYTBR 3/9/86) **[327.73]**

958 Bonner, Raymond. *Waltzing with a Dictator: The Marcoses and the Making of American Policy.* **1987, Random $19.95 (0-8129-1326-4); paper $11.95 (0-394-75835-8).** A study of American policy toward the Philippine regime of Ferdinand Marcos. "This solidly researched journalistic account of the rise and fall of the Marcos dictatorship offers the clearest view to date of the U.S. role in these events."—LJ (REV: Choice 11/87; NYTBR 5/17/87; Newsweek 6/8/87. AWARDS: LJ, 1987) **[327.73]**

959 Brandon, Henry. *Special Relationships: A Foreign Correspondent's Memoirs from Roosevelt to Reagan.* **1988, Macmillan $25.95 (0-689-11588-1).** Reflections upon American politics and life by the Washington correspondent from the *London Times*. (REV: BL 1/1/89; LJ 1/89; NYTBR 2/12/89) **[327.73]**

960 Brzezinski, Zbigniew. *Power and Principle: Memoirs of the National Security Advisor, 1977–1981.* **1983, Farrar $22.00 (0-374-23663-1); paper**

$11.95 (0-374-51877-7). Memoirs of Carter's national security advisor. "A valuable and articulate interpretation of foreign policy during the Carter Administration."—BL (Rev: BL 3/15/83; LJ 4/15/83; NYTBR 4/17/83) **[327.73]**

961 **Cockburn, Leslie.** *Out of Control.* 1987, Atlantic Monthly $18.95 (0-87113-169-2). A study of the covert arms and drug trade used to create funding for the rebel forces in Nicaragua during the Reagan years. (Rev: Choice 7–8/88; LJ 2/1/88; NYTBR 1/3/88) **[327.73]**

962 **Cook, Blanche W.** *Declassified Eisenhower: A Divided Legacy of Peace and Political Warfare.* 1984, Penguin paper $8.95 (0-14-007061-3). A study of the underside of the Eisenhower administration focusing on covert foreign political activities. (Rev: Choice 11/81; LJ 6/15/81; PW 5/8/81) **[327.73]**

963 **Dallek, Robert.** *American Style of Foreign Policy: Cultural Politics and Foreign Affairs.* 1983, Knopf $19.95 (0-394-51360-6); Oxford Univ. Pr. paper $8.95 (0-19-506205-1). A look at how U.S. foreign policy is often overly influenced by domestic situations, and executed in an effort to draw attention away from domestic problems. (Rev: CSM 11/22/83; LJ 3/15/83; New Rep 6/20/83) **[327.73]**

964 **Dickey, Christopher.** *With the Contras: A Reporter in the Wilds of Nicaragua.* 1987, Simon & Schuster paper $6.95 (0-671-63313-9). An account of the year the author spent with the Nicaraguan revolutionary forces covering the war for the *Washington Post.* (Rev: BL 2/15/86; LJ 3/1/86; NYTBR 1/21/86) **[327.73]**

965 **Dimbleby, David, and David Reynolds.** *An Ocean Apart: The Relationship Between Britain and America in the 20th Century.* 1988, Random $24.95 (0-394-56968-7); paper $9.95 (0-679-72190-8). The history of the changing relationship between Great Britain and the United States in the twentieth century. (Rev: BL 6/15/88; LJ 7/88; TLS 8/5/88) **[327.73]**

966 **Draper, Theodore.** *A Present of Things Past: Selected Essays.* 1990, Hill & Wang $22.95 (0-8090-7874-0). A collection of ten essays analyzing aspects of post-World War II American foreign policy. (Rev: NYRB 3/15/90; NYTBR 1/28/90; PW 12/1/89) **[327.73]**

967 **Fulbright, J. William, and Seth P. Tillman.** *Price of Empire.* 1989, Pantheon $17.95 (0-394-57224-6). An analysis of the current state of America, and its foreign policy, by the former senator from Arkansas. (Rev: BL 2/15/89; LJ 2/1/89; NYTBR 2/19/89) **[327.73]**

968 **Gaddis, John Lewis.** *Long Peace: Inquiries into the History of the Cold War.* 1989, Oxford Univ. Pr. paper $8.95 (0-19-504335-9). Essays analyzing United States and Soviet relations during the cold war years. (Rev: BL 8/87; LJ 10/15/87; NYTBR 11/15/87) **[327.73]**

969 **Gaddis, John Lewis.** *Strategies of Containment: A Critical Appraisal of Postwar American National Security Policy.* 1982, Oxford Univ. Pr.

paper $10.95 (0-19-503097-4). An account of American post-World War II relations with the Soviet Union. "The most balanced and clear-eyed account to date of the Cold War."—LJ (Rev: LJ 1/1/82; NYTBR 1/17/82; TLS 3/5/82) **[327.73]**

970 **Grose, Peter.** *Israel in the Mind of America.* 1983, Random $17.95 (0-394-51658-3); Schocken paper $9.95 (0-8052-0767-8). A history of American influence on the creation and support of the state of Israel. (Rev: LJ 11/15/83; New Rep 12/31/83; NYTBR 12/25/83) **[327.73]**

971 **Gutman, Roy.** *Banana Diplomacy: The Making of the American Foreign Policy in Nicaragua, 1981–1987.* 1988, Simon & Schuster $19.95 (0-671-60626-3); paper $9.95 (0-671-68294-6). An indictment of the Reagan administration's destructive policies toward the newly formed Sandinista government of Nicaragua. (Rev: BL 9/1/88; CSM 10/31/88; NYTBR 8/7/88) **[327.73]**

972 **Hamilton, John Maxwell.** *Entangling Alliances: How the Third World Shapes Our Lives.* 1990, Seven Locks Pr. $24.95 (0-932020-82-8); paper $12.95 (0-932020-83-6). A study of the increasingly interdependent relationship between the United States and Third World nations. (Rev: Atl 7/90; BL 3/1/90; LJ 3/1/90) **[327.73]**

973 **Hersh, Seymour.** *Price of Power: Kissinger in the Nixon White House.* 1984, Summit paper $9.95 (0-671-50688-9). Kissinger's years as National Security Advisor (1969–1973) are analyzed in this work based on over 1,000 interviews with American and Vietnamese government officials. "A powerful indictment of a foreign policy leadership that backfired to produce a complex of domestic crimes and cover-ups."—LJ (Rev: CSM 6/24/83; LJ 8/83; NYTBR 7/3/83. Awards: ALA, 1983; NYTBR, 1983) **[327.73]**

974 **Holland, Jack.** *American Connection: U.S. Guns, Money, and Influence in Northern Ireland.* 1987, Viking $19.95 (0-670-80894-6); Penguin paper $7.95 (0-14-008495-9). A study of the Irish-American community's monetary and gun-running support of the efforts to reunite Ireland. (Rev: BL 3/1/87; LJ 2/1/87; NYTBR 3/22/87) **[327.73]**

975 **Hyland, William G.** *Mortal Rivals: Superpower Relations from Nixon to Reagan.* 1987, Random $19.95 (0-394-55768-9); paper $8.95 (0-671-66871-4). Memoirs of a former CIA and National Security Agency member regarding U.S. and Soviet relations from the Nixon to Reagan administrations. (Rev: LJ 6/15/87; New Rep 7/27/87; NYTBR 7/5/87) **[327.73]**

976 **Kennan, George F.** *Memoirs: 1950–1963.* 1983, Pantheon paper $10.95 (0-394-71624-8). The second and concluding volume of the memoirs of the career diplomat and former U.S. ambassador to the Soviet Union. "A work of personal reflection which can be read with pleasure and profit by the general reader and specialist alike."—Choice (Rev: Choice 4/73; LJ 8/72; NYTBR 10/8/72. Awards: ALA, 1972) **[327.73]**

977 **Kissinger, Henry.** *White House Years.* **1979, Little, Brown $29.95 (0-316-49661-8).** The first volume of Kissinger's memoirs covering his years as Nixon's national security advisor. (Rev: LJ 12/1/79; New Rep 12/15/79; NYTBR 11/11/79. Awards: NBA, 1980; NYTBR, 1979)   **[327.73]**

978 **Kwitny, Jonathan.** *Endless Enemies: America's Worldwide War Against Its Own Best Interests.* **1984, Congdon & Weed $19.95 (0-312-92178-0); Penguin paper $9.95 (0-14-008093-7).** A study of America's failed foreign policy toward the Third World in recent years. "This book should be required reading for government officials and American taxpayers."—BL (Rev: BL 6/15/84; LJ 6/15/84; NYTBR 7/29/84)   **[327.73]**

979 **LaFeber, Walter.** *Inevitable Revolutions: The United States in Central America.* **1984, Norton paper $7.95 (0-393-30212-1).** A study of the United States' policies over the past 150 years in Central America and their effects upon the region's current instability. (Rev: Choice 2/84; LJ 12/1/83; NYTBR 11/16/83)   **[327.73]**

980 **Lake, Anthony.** *Somoza Falling: A Case Study in the Making of U.S. Foreign Policy.* **1989, Houghton $18.95 (0-395-41983-2); Univ. of Massachusetts Pr. paper $11.95 (0-87023-733-0).** A former Carter administration diplomat recounts the collapse of the Somoza government in Nicaragua, and the rise of the Sandinistas to power. (Rev: LJ 3/1/89; NYTBR 4/2/89; Newsweek 3/13/89)   **[327.73]**

981 **Langguth, A. J.** *Hidden Terrors.* **1979, Pantheon paper $7.95 (0-394-73802-0).** An exposé of CIA activities in Latin America during the 1960s and 1970s. (Rev: Choice 10/78; LJ 5/1/78; NYTBR 6/25/78)   **[327.73]**

982 **McNamara, Robert S.** *Out of the Cold: New Thinking for American Foreign and Defense Policy for the 20th Century.* **1989, Simon & Schuster $18.95 (0-671-68983-5); paper $8.95 (0-671-72515-7).** A study of the past and future of American international defense policies as seen by the former secretary of defense. (Rev: BL 9/15/89; LJ 9/15/89; NYTBR 10/8/89)   **[327.73]**

983 **McNeil, Frank.** *War and Peace in Central America: Reality and Illusion.* **1988, Macmillan $19.95 (0-684-18917-8).** The former U.S. ambassador to Costa Rica charges that the Reagan administration sought to undermine fledgling democracies in Latin America. (Rev: LJ 12/88; NYTBR 1/29/89; PW 12/2/88)   **[327.73]**

984 **Moynihan, Daniel Patrick.** *On the Law of Nations.* **1990, Harvard Univ. Pr. $22.50 (0-674-63575-2).** The New York senator's analysis of the applications of international law. "Intelligent and timely."—New Yorker (Rev: LJ 6/15/90; NYTBR 8/26/90; New Yorker 12/10/90)   **[327.73]**

985 **Musicant, Ivan.** *Banana Wars.* **1990, Macmillan $24.95 (0-02-0588210-4).** An examination of the United States' twentieth-century military interventions in Latin America. (Rev: BL 6/15/90; LJ 6/15/90; PW 6/22/90)   **[327.73]**

986 **Nitze, Paul, Steven L. Rearden, and Ann M. Smith.** *From Hiroshima to Glasnost: A Memoir of Five Perilous Decades.* **1989, Grove-Weidenfeld $25.00 (1-55584-110-4).** Memoirs of the American statesman and advisor known for his key roles in arms control discussions. (Rev: LJ 9/1/89; NYTBR 10/15/89; PW 8/4/89)   **[327.73]**

987 **Nixon, Richard M.** *1999: The Global Challenges We Face in the Next Decade.* **1988, Simon & Schuster $19.95 (0-671-62712-0); paper $10.95 (0-671-70626-8).** The former president's views on the role of the United States in international affairs during the next decade and into the next century. (Rev: BL 4/15/88; LJ 6/1/88; NYTBR 4/17/88)   **[327.73]**

988 **Nixon, Richard M.** *Seize the Moment: America's Challenge in a One-Superpower World.* **1992, Simon & Schuster $23.00 (0-671-74343-0).** An analysis of the United States' role in the world following the restructuring of Eastern Europe and the Soviet Union. (Rev: BL 12/15/91; LJ 1/92; NYTBR 1/19/92)   **[327.73]**

989 **Pfaff, William.** *Barbarian Sentiments: Nationalism and Ideology in the Modern Age.* **1989, Hill & Wang $19.95 (0-8090-6665-3).** The author presents a synthesis of the world's present and future political struggles, and predicts international trends into the twenty-first century. (Rev: BL 4/1/89; LJ 5/15/89; NYTBR 5/28/89)   **[327.73]**

990 **Powers, Thomas.** *Man Who Kept the Secrets: Richard Helms and the CIA.* **1979, Knopf $22.50 (0-394-50678-2).** A look inside the American intelligence community as reflected in the life of the former head of the CIA. "One of the best spy stories in a long time, all the better for being nonfiction."—NYTBR (Rev: NYTBR 10/14/79; Newsweek 10/22/79; Time 11/12/79. Awards: NYTBR, 1979) **[327.73]**

991 **Quandt, William B.** *Camp David: Peacemaking and Politics.* **1986, Brookings $32.95 (0-8157-7290-4); paper $12.95 (0-8157-7289-0).** Memoirs of the diplomat regarding the Camp David meetings between Begin, Sadat, and Carter. (Rev: Choice 7–8/86; LJ 3/1/86; New Rep 9/1/86)   **[327.73]**

992 **Roosevelt, Selwa.** *Keeper of the Gate: An Intimate View of American Diplomacy.* **1990, Simon & Schuster $21.95 (0-671-69207-0).** Memoirs of the Reagan administration chief of protocol's years of diplomatic service. (Rev: BL 10/15/90; LJ 10/15/90; NYTBR 11/4/90)   **[327.73]**

993 **Rubin, Barry M.** *Secrets of State: The State Department and the Struggle Over U.S. Foreign Policy.* **1987, Oxford Univ. Pr. paper $9.95 (0-19-505010-X).** A former State Department foreign relations expert analyzes the formation and enactment of international policies from the Roosevelt administration through Reagan's first term. (Rev: BL 5/1/85; Choice 11/85; LJ 8/85)   **[327.73]**

994 **Smith, Geoffrey.** *Reagan and Thatcher.* **1991, Norton $22.95 (0-393-02948-4).** A study of the relationship between the former American president and former British prime minister and their nations during the 1980s. (REV: BL 2/15/91; NYTBR 4/14/91; PW 1/25/91) **[327.73]**

995 Thomson, James C., Jr., Peter W. Stanley, and John Curtis Perry. *Sentimental Imperialists: The American Experience in East Asia.* 1982, Harper & Row paper $9.95 (0-06-131998-8). A survey of the history and legacy of United States involvement in East Asia over the past two centuries. (REV: LJ 6/1/81; New Rep 9/16/81; NYTBR 9/13/81) **[327.73]**

996 Tuchman, Barbara W. *Stilwell and the American Experience in China, 1911–1945.* 1971, Macmillan $21.95 (0-02-620290-5); Bantam paper $6.95 (0-553-25798-6). A biography of General Joseph W. Stilwell analyzing America's role in China before and during World War II. (REV: LJ 1/15/71; Natl Rev 4/20/71; NYTBR 2/7/71. AWARDS: ALA, 1971; PP:NF, 1972; Time, 1971) **[327.73]**

997 Yergin, Daniel. *Shattered Peace: The Origins of the Cold War and the National Security State.* 1990, Penguin paper $10.95 (0-14-012177-3). An analysis of how the United States became involved in the Cold War. "A book of great importance . . . must reading for all seriously interested in the subject."—Choice (REV: Choice 10/77; LJ 4/15/77; NYTBR 6/12/77) **[327.73]**

328 The legislative process

United States

998 Abourezk, James G. *Advise and Dissent: Memoirs of South Dakota, Southern Lebanon and the U.S. Senate.* 1989, Chicago Review $18.95 (1-55652-066-2). Political memoirs of the former senator from South Dakota. "Political apologia of the first order."—BL (REV: BL 11/1/89; LJ 11/1/89) **[328.73]**

999 Barry, John M. *Ambition and the Power: Jim Wright and the Will of the House.* 1989, Viking $22.95 (0-670-81924-7). The rise and fall of the political career of Jim Wright, former Speaker of the House. (REV: BL 9/15/89; Natl Rev 12/31/89; NYTBR 11/19/89) **[328.73]**

1000 Bisnow, Mark. *In the Shadow of the Dome: Chronicles of a Capitol Hill Aide.* 1990, Morrow $18.45 (0-688-08719-1). Memoirs of the author's decade as a congressional research aide. (REV: BL 6/1/90; LJ 7/90; PW 4/27/90) **[328.73]**

1001 O'Neill, Thomas P., and Michael Novak. *Man of the House: The Life and Political Memoirs of Speaker Tip O'Neill.* 1988, St. Martin's paper $4.95 (0-312-91191-2). Recollections of the former Speaker of the House. "Captures the inside feel of the political rough and tumble."—Time (REV: BL 8/87; NYTBR 9/6/87; Time 9/14/87. AWARDS: LJ, 1987) **[328.73]**

1002 Reedy, George E. *U.S. Senate: Paralysis or a Search for Consensus?* 1986, Crown $16.95 (0-517-56239-1); NAL paper $4.95 (0-451-62608-7). A study of the inner workings and politics of the U.S. Senate from the 1950s to the mid-1980s. (REV: BL 10/15/86; Choice 2/87; LJ 11/1/86) **[328.73]**

Pacific Coast states

1003 Hayden, Tom. *Reunion: A Memoir.* 1989, Macmillan $12.95 (0-02-033105-3). Memoirs of the author's activities as a radical and political activist, and of his relationship with former wife Jane Fonda. "One of the best books to date on the 1960s."—BL (REV: BL 4/15/88; CSM 6/3/88; LJ 6/15/88) **[328.79]**

330 ECONOMICS

1004 Blinder, Alan S. *Hard Heads, Soft Hearts: Tough-Minded Economics for a Just Society.* 1987, Addison Wesley $17.95 (0-201-11504-2). An examination of the American economy of the 1980s by a Princeton University economist. "Elegantly written and crisply reasoned . . . a book to treasure."—Robert Lekachman, NYTBR (REV: Choice 5/88; LJ 12/87; NYTBR 10/25/87) **[330]**

History

1005 Galbraith, John Kenneth. *Economics in Perspective: A Critical History.* 1987, Houghton $19.95 (0-395-35572-9). The history of economic thought from the ancient Greeks to the modern day. "One of the best overviews of the evolution of economic ideas available to general audiences."—Choice (REV: BL 9/1/87; Choice 4/88; LJ 10/15/87. AWARDS: LJ, 1987) **[330.09]**

Persons

1006 Galbraith, John Kenneth. *A Life in Our Times: Memoirs.* 1981, Houghton $16.95 (0-395-31135-7). An autobiography detailing the public life of the Canadian-born economist. (REV: BL 3/1/81; New Rep 5/23/81; NYTBR 5/3/81) **[330.092]**

1007 Simon, Herbert A. *Models of My Life.* 1991, Basic Books $26.95 (0-465-04640-1). An autobiography of the Nobel Prize–winning scientist and economist noted for his role in the development of artificial intelligence. (REV: BL 3/1/91; NYTBR 3/17/91; PW 1/25/91) **[330.092]**

Systems and theories

1008 Allen, Michael Patrick. *Founding Fortunes: A New Anatomy of the Corporate-Rich Families in America.* 1989, Dutton paper $12.95 (0-525-48484-1). A profile of 160 of America's richest families who built their fortunes through big business. (REV: LJ 12/87; PW 11/13/87) **[330.1]**

1009 Daly, Herman E., and John B. Cobb, Jr. *For the Common Good: Redirecting the Economy Toward Community, the Environment and a Sustainable Future.* 1989, Beacon $24.95 (0-8070-4702-3); paper $14.95 (0-8070-4703-1). The authors make a plea for international environment-conscious economic development. (REV: Choice 5/90; LJ 1/90; PW 12/1/89) **[330.1]**

1010 Sampson, Anthony. *Midas Touch: Understanding the Dynamic New Global Money Soci-*

eties Around Us. 1990, NAL $19.95 (0-525-24891-9). A study of international finance and financial trends of the 1980s and 1990s. (Rev: BL 5/1/90; LJ 4/15/90; PW 6/22/90) **[330.1]**

Systems

1011 Berger, Peter L. *Capitalist Revolution: Fifty Propositions about Prosperity, Equality and Liberty.* 1986, Basic Books $17.95 (0-465-00867-4); paper $10.95 (0-465-00868-2). A treatise comparing relative merits of the socialist and capitalist systems. (Rev: BL 9/1/86; Choice 2/87; Natl Rev 9/12/86) **[330.12]**

1012 Heilbroner, Robert L. *Nature and Logic of Capitalism.* 1986, Norton paper $7.95 (0-393-95529-X). A study of the thoretical and practical aspects of capitalism and its relationship to other social systems. (Rev: Choice 2/86; LJ 10/15/85; New Rep 10/28/85) **[330.12]**

Keynesianism

1013 Hession, Charles H. *John Maynard Keynes: A Personal Biography of the Man Who Revolutionized Capitalism and the Way We Live.* 1984, Macmillan $22.07 (0-02-551310-9). A psychological biography of the English economist based on his private papers. (Rev: BL 4/15/84; LJ 4/1/84; NYRB 7/19/84) **[330.156]**

Economic situation and conditions

1014 Galbraith, John Kenneth. *New Industrial State.* 1985, Houghton $19.95 (0-395-38991-7). Currently in its fourth revised edition, Galbraith's work looks at the great American corporations and their influence on the nation's economy, government, and public policy. (Rev: Choice 12/67; LJ 5/1/67; NYTBR 6/25/67. Awards: ALA, 1967; NYTBR, 1967) **[330.9]**

1015 Jacobs, Jane. *Cities and the Wealth of Nations: Principles of Economic Life.* 1985, Random paper $5.95 (0-394-72911-0). Jacobs, author of the 1961 *Death and Life of Great American Cities*, argues that cities are the source of economic vitality and stability, not nations, whose economic policies often restrict the growth of cities. (Rev: BL 5/15/84; NYTBR 5/27/84; PW 3/30/84. Awards: ALA, 1984) **[330.9]**

1016 Reich, Robert B. *Work of Nations: Preparing Ourselves for 21st-Century Capitalism.* 1991, Knopf $24.00 (0-394-58352-3). A study of the present and future state of the world economy with suggested plans for the United States to compete successfully in the twenty-first-century international marketplace. (Rev: BL 1/15/91; LJ 3/15/91; PW 1/18/91) **[330.9]**

1017 Rosenberg, Nathan, and L. E. Birdzell, Jr. *How the West Grew Rich: The Economic Transformation of the Industrial World.* 1987, Basic Books paper $12.95 (0-465-03109-9). A history of the Western world's dominance of the modern international economy. "A superbly rendered . . . volume

that is highly recommended."—BL (Rev: BL 2/1/86; Choice 9/86; NYTBR 2/9/86) **[330.9]**

Economic geography—Japan

1018 Emmott, Bill. *Sun Also Sets: The Limits to Japan's Economic Power.* 1989, Random $19.95 (0-8129-1816-9). The former Tokyo bureau chief for the *Economist* argues that Japan has overextended itself economically, and that their dominant position in the world economy is imperiled. (Rev: BL 10/15/89; LJ 10/15/89; NYTBR 10/29/89) **[330.95]**

Economic geography—United States

1019 Bensman, David, and Roberta Lynch. *Rusted Dreams: Hard Times in a South Chicago Steel Community.* 1987, McGraw-Hill $17.95 (0-07-004781-2); Univ. of California Pr. paper $8.95 (0-520-06302-3). An examination of the social and economic effects of the closing of two Chicago steel plants in the early 1980s. "Masterfully presented and argued, this is brilliant social criticism."—BL (Rev: BL 3/1/87; Choice 6/87; LJ 2/1/87) **[330.973]**

1020 Bruchey, Stuart. *Enterprise: The Dynamic Economy of a Free People.* 1990, Harvard Univ. Pr. $49.50 (0-674-25745-6). A study of the development of capitalism and the free enterprise system from fourteenth-century Italy to its present form. (Rev: Choice 10/90; LJ 1/90; NYTBR 4/29/90) **[330.973]**

1021 Kiplinger, Austin, and Knight Kiplinger. *America in the Global Nineties: The Shape of the Future.* 1989, Kiplinger Washington Editions $12.95 (0-938721-07-0); Kampmann paper $9.95 (1-55704-049-4). A prediction of America's economic trends in the near future with hints on successful investing techniques to capitalize on them. (Rev: BL 8/89; LJ 8/89; PW 7/14/89) **[330.973]**

1022 Malabre, Alfred L., Jr. *Beyond Our Means: How Reckless Borrowing Now Threatens to Overwhelm Us.* 1988, Random paper $6.95 (0-394-75816-1). An analysis of the precarious state of the current American economy which the author believes is heading for collapse in the near future. (Rev: BL 3/15/87; NYTBR 4/12/87; PW 2/6/87) **[330.973]**

1023 Malabre, Alfred L., Jr. *Understanding the New Economy.* 1988, Dow Jones-Irwin $21.95 (1-55623-117-2). The *Wall Street Journal's* economic news editor presents an overview of the U.S. economy of the late 1980s and its probable future. (Rev: NYTBR 10/23/88; PW 9/30/88) **[330.973]**

1024 Mattera, Philip. *Prosperity Lost.* 1990, Addison Wesley $19.18 (0-201-19897-5). An analysis of the effects of economic policies in the 1980s upon the distribution of wealth in the United States. (Rev: BL 8/90; LJ 8/90; PW 7/13/90) **[330.973]**

1025 Nash, Gerald D. *American West Transformed: The Impact of the Second World War.* 1985, Indiana Univ. Pr. $35.00 (0-253-30649-3); Univ. of Nebraska Pr. paper $12.50 (0-8032-8360-1). A study of the significance of the economic and social changes that took place in the American West due

to World War II. (Rev: Choice 10/85; LJ 5/15/85)
[330.973]

1026 Smith, Adam. *Roaring '80's.* **1988, Summit $18.95 (0-671-44788-2); Penguin paper $8.95 (0-14-012811-5).** A look at the economic and social climate of the 1980s by the American economist. (Rev: BL 11/1/88; NYTBR 11/27/88)
[330.973]

1027 Stein, Herbert. *Washington Bedtime Stories: The Politics of Money and Jobs.* **1986, Free Pr. $19.95 (0-02-930870-4).** Collected writings regarding the relationship between economics and government in the United States since the 1930s. (Rev: CSM 3/18/87; LJ 10/15/86; PW 10/17/86)
[330.973]

1028 Thurow, Lester C. *Zero-Sum Society: Distribution and the Possibilities for Economic Change.* **1981, Penguin paper $8.95 (0-14-005807-9).** A study of the present and future of capitalism and the capitalist system in the United States as seen by the noted economist. (Rev: LJ 8/80; New Rep 4/12/80; NYTBR 6/8/80)
[330.973]

1029 Wright, Gavin. *Old South, New South: Revolutions in the Southern Economy Since the Civil War.* **1987, Basic Books paper $9.95 (0-465-05194-4).** A study of the economic history and development of the American South following the Civil War. (Rev: Choice 9/86; LJ 3/15/86; NYRB 5/8/86)
[330.973]

331 Labor economics

Labor market

1030 Terkel, Studs. *Working: People Talk about What They Do All Day and How They Feel about What They Do.* **1985, Ballantine paper $5.95 (0-345-32569-9).** Terkel's interviews with 134 people about their occupations. "A remarkable achievement. It contributes to the understanding of scholar or layman concerned with work and those who do it, and, happily, is readable by anyone with these concerns."—Choice (Rev: Choice 7–8/74; NYTBR 3/24/74; Newsweek 4/1/74. Awards: ALA, 1974)
[331.12]

Women workers

1031 Gluck, Sherna Berger. *Rosie the Riveter Revisited: Women, the War and Social Change.* **1987, G. K. Hall $19.95 (0-8057-9022-5); NAL paper $8.95 (0-452-00911-1).** Oral histories of ten women who worked in West Coast aviation factories during World War II. (Rev: BL 5/1/87; LJ 5/15/87; NYTBR 6/14/87)
[331.4]

1032 Neville, Kathleen. *Corporate Attractions: The New Rules for Men and Women on the Job.* **1989, Acropolis $19.95 (0-87491-952-5); paper $12.95 (0-87491-953-3).** A guide to identifying and combatting sexual harassment in the workplace. (Rev: BL 2/15/90; LJ 3/1/90; PW 3/23/90)
[331.4]

1033 Niemann, Linda. *Boomer: Railroad Memoirs.* **1990, Univ. of California Pr. $25.00 (0-520-06844-0).** Memoirs of a former Southern Pacific railroad brakeperson regarding her decade on the rails. (Rev: BL 3/1/90; LJ 2/1/90; PW 1/5/90)
[331.4]

1034 Schroedel, Jean Reith. *Alone in a Crowd: Women in the Trades Tell Their Stories.* **1985, Temple Univ. Pr. $32.95 (0-87722-378-5); paper $14.95 (0-87722-397-1).** Collected interviews with 25 women working in traditionally male-dominated blue-collar jobs. (Rev: BL 8/85; LJ 8/85; NYTBR 8/4/85)
[331.4]

Special categories of workers other than by age or sex

1035 Carter, Stephen L. *Reflections of an Affirmative Action Baby.* **1991, Basic Books $22.95 (0-465-06871-5).** A study of affirmative action policies and their ramifications written by an African-American Yale law professor based on his personal experiences. (Rev: LJ 9/15/91; NYTBR 9/1/91; PW 7/5/91)
[331.5]

1036 Coles, Robert. *Migrants, Sharecroppers, Mountaineers.* **1973, Little, Brown paper $19.95 (0-316-15176-9).** Volume 2 of the author's Children of Crisis series focuses on the lives of farm workers and manual laborers in the South and in the Appalachians. (Rev: Choice 11/72; LJ 1/1/72; NYTBR 2/13/72. Awards: ALA, 1972; PP:NF, 1973; Time, 1972)
[331.5]

1037 Sowell, Thomas. *Preferential Policies: An International Perspective.* **1990, Morrow $17.95 (0-688-08599-7).** A cross-cultural examination of the history of preferential policies for minorities. "An essential addition to any public-affairs collection."—BL (Rev: BL 4/1/90; LJ 6/15/90; PW 4/27/90)
[331.5]

1038 Wilkinson, Alec. *Big Sugar: Seasons in the Cane Fields of Florida.* **1989, Knopf $18.95 (0-394-57312-9); paper $9.95 (0-679-73187-3).** A study of life in the sugarcane fields of Florida, revealing the exploitation of West Indian workers there. "Wilkinson epitomizes the best in investigative journalism."—BL (Rev: BL 9/15/89; LJ 9/1/89; NYTBR 9/17/89)
[331.5]

Immigrants and aliens from Mexico

1039 Conover, Ted. *Coyotes: A Journey Through the Secret World of America's Illegal Aliens.* **1987, Random paper $9.95 (0-394-75518-9).** The author recounts his experiences crossing the border between the United States and Mexico posing as an illegal alien. (Rev: LJ 9/15/87; NYTBR 9/13/87; PW 7/31/87)
[331.6272]

Labor by industry and occupation

1040 Reynolds, Patrick, and Tom Shachtman. *Gilded Leaf: Triumph, Tragedy and Tobacco.* **1989, Little, Brown $19.95 (0-316-74121-3).** A biography of the R. J. Reynolds family and its tobacco fortune. "A lurid, well-written book with timeless lessons in between the lines."—LJ (Rev: BL 4/1/89; LJ 4/1/89; NYTBR 8/20/89)
[331.7]

1041 Sculley, John, and John A. Byre. *Odyssey: Pepsi to Apple . . . a Journey of a Marketing Impresario.* **1988, Harper & Row paper $10.95 (0-06-091527-7).** Memoirs of a marketing expert's careers at PepsiCo and Apple Computer. (REV: BL 9/15/87; LJ 12/87; NYTBR 10/25/87)   **[331.7]**

Labor unions

1042   **Bird, Stewart.** *Solidarity Forever: An Oral History of the I. W. W.* **1985, Lake View Pr. $25.00 (0-941702-11-1); paper $9.95 (0-941702-12-X).** An oral history of the Industrial Workers of the World labor union. (REV: BL 9/1/85; LJ 8/85; Choice 1/86)   **[331.88]**

1043   **Brill, Steven.** *Teamsters.* **1979, Pocket paper $2.75 (0-671-82905-X).** An exposé of crime and corruption within the International Brotherhood of Teamsters, including speculations on the fate of former leader Jimmy Hoffa. (REV: Choice 1/79; LJ 12/1/78; Newsweek 10/2/78)   **[331.88]**

1044   **Dickmeyer, Elisabeth Reuther.** *Reuther: A Daughter Strikes.* **1989, Health ProInk $21.95 (0-933803-11-7); paper $14.95 (0-933803-10-9).** A biography of the former United Auto Workers president by his daughter. (REV: BL 2/15/89; LJ 2/15/89; PW 1/20/89)   **[331.88]**

1045   **Dubofsky, Melvyn.** *Big Bill Haywood.* **1987, St. Martin's $19.95 (0-312-01272-1).** A biography of the American labor leader who founded the International Workers of the World in 1905. (REV: BL 12/15/87; LJ 12/1/87; PW 11/6/87)   **[331.88]**

1046   **Fraser, Steven.** *Labor Will Rule: Sidney Hillman and the Rise of American Labor.* **1991, Free Pr. $29.95 (0-02-910630-3).** A biography of the politically influential American labor leader. "A superb, vibrant biography."—PW (REV: LJ 6/1/91; PW 4/12/91)   **[331.88]**

1047   **Geoghegan, Thomas.** *Which Side Are You On? Trying to Be for Labor When It's Flat on Its Back.* **1991, Farrar $19.95 (0-374-28919-0).** A Chicago labor lawyer's look at the history and present state of unions in the United States. (REV: BL 7/91; LJ 6/15/91; NYTBR 8/5/91)   **[331.88]**

1048   **Jones, G. C.** *Growing Up Hard in Harlan County.* **1985, Univ. Pr. of Kentucky $19.00 (0-8131-1521-3).** Memoirs of life in a poor Appalachian region noted for its violent labor disputes between coal mine owners and the United Mine Workers. "Unforgettable Americana."—PW (REV: BL 4/15/86; LJ 1/85; PW 11/23/84. AWARDS: ALA, 1985)   **[331.88]**

1049   **Neff, James.** *Mobbed Up: Jackie Presser's High-Wire Life in the Teamsters, the Mafia, and the FBI.* **1989, Atlantic Monthly $22.95 (0-87113-344-X).** A profile of the former Teamster head and his union's ties with organized crime and the U.S. government. (REV: BL 11/1/89; NYTBR 12/10/89)   **[331.88]**

332   Financial economics

Personal finance

1050   **Card, Emily.** *Ms. Money Book: Strategies for Prospering in the Coming Decade.* **1990, Dutton $19.95 (0-525-24669-X).** A financial guide for women

in the 1990s. (REV: BL 1/15/90; LJ 1/90; PW 1/26/90)   **[332.024]**

1051   **Lee, Barbara, and Paula M. Siegel.** *Take Control of Your Money: A Life Guide to Financial Freedom.* **1986, Random $16.95 (0-394-54392-0).** A guide to practical personal money management. (REV: BL 9/15/86; LJ 9/15/86)   **[332.024]**

1052   **Lewin, Elizabeth.** *Financial Fitness for New Families.* **1989, Facts on File paper $12.95 (0-8160-1980-0).** A primer to the basics of investing and money management for new couples. (REV: BL 10/15/89; LJ 9/15/89)   **[332.024]**

1053   **Porter, Sylvia.** *Sylvia Porter's Your Finances in the 1990s.* **1990, Prentice Hall $22.95 (0-13-879776-5).** A guide to personal financial planning in the economic climate of the 1990s. (REV: BL 10/1/90; LJ 10/1/90)   **[332.024]**

1054   **Sloane, Leonard.** *New York Times Book of Personal Finance.* **1985, Random paper $9.95 (0-8129-1160-1).** An introduction to the basic skills and concepts of personal money management. (REV: BL 2/15/85; LJ 2/15/85; PW 1/25/85)   **[332.024]**

Dictionaries

1055   **Lee, Susan.** *Susan Lee's ABZ's of Money and Finance: From Annuities to Zero Coupon Bonds.* **1988, Poseidon $16.95 (0-671-55712-2); Pocket paper $7.95 (0-671-67440-4).** A *Forbes* editor's guide to financial terminology for the layperson. (REV: BL 6/15/88; LJ 8/88; NYTBR 7/24/88)   **[332.03]**

Persons

1056   **Klein, Maury.** *Life and Legend of Jay Gould.* **1986, Johns Hopkins $38.95 (0-8018-2880-5).** A biography of the nineteenth-century American entrepreneur and railroad magnate. (REV: LJ 4/15/86; NYRB 5/29/86; NYTBR 6/29/86)   **[332.092]**

1057   **Lenzner, Robert.** *Great Getty: The Life and Loves of J. Paul Getty.* **1986, Crown $18.95 (0-517-56222-7); NAL paper $4.95 (0-451-14699-9).** A biography of the Oklahoma oil tycoon who made his first million dollars by the age of 23. (REV: NYTBR 3/30/86; PW 1/24/86; Time 3/17/86)   **[332.092]**

Persons—Collective treatment

1058   **Collier, Peter, and David Horowitz.** *Rockefellers: An American Dynasty.* **1989, Summit paper $14.95 (0-671-67445-5).** The history of the Rockefeller clan is traced through four generations, based on the author's access to family records. (REV: LJ 4/1/76; NYTBR 3/28/76; Newsweek 4/5/76)   **[332.0922]**

1059   **Packard, Vance.** *Ultra Rich: How Much Is Too Much?* **1989, Little, Brown $22.95 (0-316-68752-9).** Interviews and profiles of 30 ultra-rich Americans regarding their lives and attitudes. (REV: BL 12/15/88; LJ 2/15/89; NYTBR 2/19/89)   **[332.0922]**

Banks and banking

1060   **Chernow, Ron.** *House of Morgan: An American Banking Dynasty and the Rise of the Modern*

Financial World. **1990, Atlantic Monthly $24.95 (0-87113-338-5); Simon & Schuster paper $14.95 (0-671-73400-8).** A family history of the Morgan financial dynasty and its effects on the banking world. (Rev: Atl 4/90; BL 1/1/90; LJ 2/1/90. Awards: BL, 1990; LJ, 1990; NBA, 1990) **[332.1]**

1061 Cohen, Benjamin J. *In Whose Interest? International Banking and American Foreign Policy.* **1986, Yale Univ. Pr. $30.00 (0-300-03614-0); paper $13.95 (0-300-04025-1).** A study of international finance and American banking's loans to foreign nations. (Rev: Choice 4/87; New Rep 12/8/86; NYTBR 12/21/86) **[332.1]**

1062 Greider, William. *Secrets of the Temple: How the Federal Reserve Runs the Country.* **1989, Simon & Schuster paper $12.95 (0-671-67556-7).** A look at the history and inner workings of the Federal Reserve System and how national monetary decisions are made. (Rev: BL 12/15/87; Choice 6/88; LJ 12/87) **[332.1]**

1063 Mrkvicka, Edward F., Jr. *The Bank Book.* **1991, HarperCollins paper $10.00 (0-06-273052-5).** A former bank CEO discusses the many ways that banks financially manipulate consumers to their advantage. (Rev: BL 6/1/89; LJ 5/1/89) **[332.1]**

1064 Sampson, Anthony. *Money Lenders: The People and Politics of International Banking.* **1988, Peter Smith $16.75 (0-8446-6302-6); Penguin paper $9.95 (0-14-006485-0).** A study of international bankers and banking including profiles of the International Monetary Fund and the World Bank. (Rev: Choice 5/82; LJ 2/1/82; Sat Rev 1/82) **[332.1]**

1065 Singer, Mark. *Funny Money.* **1985, Knopf $19.95 (0-394-53236-8).** An account of the collapse of the Penn Square Bank, an Oklahoma firm whose reckless oil investments nearly led to the fall of several other lending institutions. "Business reportage at its provocative best."—BL (Rev: BL 5/15/85; LJ 6/1/85; NYTBR 6/23/85) **[332.1]**

1066 Sprague, Irvine H. *Bailout: An Insider's Account of Bank Failures and Rescues.* **1986, Basic Books $17.95 (0-465-00577-2).** A former FDIC director reflects on bank failures and rescues during the 1970s and 1980s (Rev: Choice 1/87; LJ 9/1/86; NYTBR 10/26/86) **[332.1]**

Commercial banks

1067 Zweig, Philip L. *Belly Up: The Collapse of the Penn Square Bank.* **1985, Crown $18.95 (0-517-55708-8).** An examination of the events surrounding the financial collapse of the Oklahoma City–based Penn Square Bank. (Rev: BL 8/85; NYTBR 10/20/85; PW 8/2/85) **[332.12]**

Savings and loan associations

1068 Adams, James Ring. *Big Fix: The Inside Story of the Great American S & L Crisis.* **1990, Wiley $19.95 (0-471-51535-3).** A study of the background and future ramifications of the collapses and bailouts of American savings and loans during the 1980s. (Rev: BL 10/15/89; LJ 1/90; NYTBR 12/17/89) **[332.32]**

1069 Lowy, Martin. *High Rollers: Inside the Savings and Loan Debacle.* **1991, Greenwood Pr. $24.95 (0-275-93980-X).** A chronicle and analysis of the savings and loan scandals of the 1980s and 1990s. (Rev: BL 9/1/91; NYTBR 9/8/91) **[332.32]**

1070 Mayer, Martin. *Greatest-Ever Bank Robbery: The Collapse of the Savings and Loan Industry.* **1990, Macmillan $22.50 (0-684-19152-0).** An analysis of the greed and corruption behind the savings and loan scandal. (Rev: BL 9/1/90; LJ 10/1/90; PW 9/12/90) **[332.32]**

1071 Pizzo, Stephen, Mary Fricker, and Paulo Muolo. *Inside Job: The Looting of America's Savings and Loans.* **1989, McGraw-Hill $19.95 (0-07-050230-7).** An exposé of how America's savings and loans were plundered by organized crime figures and their associates following the deregulation of the industry in 1982. (Rev: LJ 9/15/89; NYTBR 10/29/89; PW 9/8/89. Awards: BL, 1989) **[332.32]**

1072 Robinson, Michael A. *Overdrawn: The Collapse of American Savings.* **1990, Dutton $19.95 (0-525-24903-6).** An account of the financial collapse and bailout of the California-based savings and loan. (Rev: BL 10/15/90; LJ 10/15/90; PW 10/19/90) **[332.32]**

Money

1073 Smith, Adam. *Paper Money.* **1981, Summit $13.95 (0-671-44825-0).** The noted popular economist traces the use of paper money in commerce, the history of inflation, and the role of the dollar on the international market. "*Paper Money* will inform the layman and fascinate the expert."—Choice (Rev: BL 2/1/81; Choice 7–8/81; Time 2/23/81. Awards: ALA, 1981) **[332.4]**

Investment and investments

1074 Ady, Ronald W. *Investment Evaluator: How to Size Up Your Investments at a Glance.* **1984, Prentice Hall $22.50 (0-13-503673-9); paper $9.95 (0-317-07154-8).** A handbook for the private investor covering stocks, bonds, futures, collectibles, and other potential investments. "This guide cannot fail to be useful to any would-be investor."—BL (Rev: BL 10/15/84; LJ 9/15/84) **[332.6]**

1075 Carrington, Tim. *Year They Sold Wall Street.* **1987, Penguin paper $6.95 (0-14-009794-5).** An account of the buyout of several large Wall Street brokerage companies by big business in 1984. (Rev: BL 1/15/86; LJ 1/86; NYTBR 12/8/85) **[332.6]**

1076 Frantz, Douglas, and Catherine Collins. *Selling Out.* **1989, Contemporary $19.95 (0-8092-4518-3).** An analysis of increasing Japanese investments in the United States and their impact on the future of the American economy. (Rev: BL 5/1/89; LJ 5/1/89) **[332.6]**

1077　Gardiner, Robert K. *Dean Witter Guide to Personal Investing.* 1989, NAL paper $3.95 (0-451-15918-7). A guide to personal investing for financial security. (Rev: BL 2/15/88; LJ 4/1/88)　　　**[332.6]**

1078　Lowry, Ritchie P. *Good Money: A Guide to Profitable Social Investing in the '90's.* 1991, Norton $19.95 (0-393-02966-2). A guide to socially responsible investing for the 1990s. (Rev: BL 6/1/91; LJ 5/1/91)　　　**[332.6]**

1079　Morris, Charles R. *Coming Global Boom.* 1990, Bantam $19.95 (0-553-05898-3); paper $12.95 (0-553-35311-X). The author's prediction for an international economic boom with suggestions on how best to capitalize on upcoming trends. (Rev: BL 6/1/90; 5/1/90; NYTBR 6/24/90)　　　**[332.6]**

1080　Sterngold, James. *Burning Down the House.* 1990, Summit $19.95 (0-671-70901-1). A story of the events leading to the collapse of the E. F. Hutton brokerage firm in the late 1980s. (Rev: BL 10/1/90; NYTBR 10/21/90; Newsweek 11/19/90)　　　**[332.6]**

1081　Stevens, Mark. *Sudden Death: The Rise and Fall of E. F. Hutton.* 1989, NAL $19.95 (0-453-00673-6); paper $9.95 (0-452-26438-3). How internal feuding and financial mismanagement led to the collapse of the brokerage firm E. F. Hutton, and its eventual buyout by Shearson Lehman. (Rev: LJ 6/15/89; Newsweek 8/28/89; PW 6/9/89)　　　**[332.6]**

1082　Stewart, James B. *Den of Thieves.* 1991, Simon & Schuster $25.00 (0-671-63802-5). A survey of the careers of four Wall Street traders who brought about the financial collapse of the Drexel Burnham investment firm. "An absolutely splendid book and a tremendously important book, as good a book on Wall Street as I have ever read."—NYTBR (Rev: BL 9/15/91; LJ 10/1/91; NYTBR 10/13/91. Awards: Time, 1991)　　　**[332.6]**

1083　Tolchin, Martin, and Susan Tolchin. *Buying into America: How Foreign Money Is Changing the Face of Our Nation.* 1988, Random $19.95 (0-8129-1667-0); Berkley paper $4.95 (0-425-11610-7). An investigation into how the increasing foreign investments in the United States affect our economy and our world standing. (Rev: BL 1/15/88; LJ 2/1/88; NYTBR 2/21/88. Awards: LJ, 1988)　　　**[332.6]**

1084　Train, John. *New Money Masters: Winning Investment Strategies of Soros-Lynch-Steinhardt-Rogers-Neff-Waryer-Michaelis-Carret.* 1989, Harper & Row $22.50 (0-06-015966-9); paper $10.95 (0-06-092005-X). How eight top investors made their fortunes through their personal skills and insights. (Rev: BL 10/1/89; NYTBR 11/29/89; PW 9/29/89)　　　**[332.6]**

Brokerage firms

1085　Lewis, Michael. *Liar's Poker: Rising Through the Wreckage on Wall Street.* 1989, Norton $18.95 (0-393-02750-3); Penguin paper $8.95 (0-14-014345-9). Recollections of the author's three years at the Salomon Brothers investment banking firm. (Rev: BL 11/1/89; LJ 9/1/89; NYTBR 10/29/89)　　　**[332.62]**

Forms of investment

1086　Allen, Robert G. *Nothing Down: Dynamic New High-Profit, Low-Risk Strategies for Building Real Estate Wealth in the 90s.* 1990, Simon & Schuster $21.95 (0-671-72558-0). An updated and revised edition of the best-selling book for real estate entrepreneurs. (Rev: BL 11/1/90; LJ 11/1/90)　　　**[332.63]**

1087　Bruck, Connie. *Predator's Ball: How the Junk Bond Machine Staked the Corporate Raiders.* 1988, Simon & Schuster $19.95 (0-671-61780-X); Penguin paper $8.95 (0-14-012090-4). The rise and fall of the Drexel Burnham Lambert investment firm due to its junk-bond financing practices under Michael Milken. (Rev: LJ 1/89; NYRB 11/24/88. Awards: LJ, 1988)　　　**[332.63]**

1088　Janik, Carolyn. *Money-Making Real Estate: Your Personal Guide to Successful Investing.* 1988, Viking $18.95 (0-670-81137-8); Penguin paper $9.95 (0-14-008974-8). A guide to successful investing in real estate for the private citizen. "Few investment guides are as clear and well organized as this one."—PW (Rev: BL 1/15/88; LJ 3/1/88; PW 2/12/88)　　　**[332.63]**

1089　Keyes, Thomas R. *Global Investor: How to Buy Stocks Around the World.* 1989, Longman Financial Services $29.95 (0-88462-914-7). A guide to investing in foreign stocks presenting information about markets in 45 countries. (Rev: BL 11/15/89; LJ 12/89)　　　**[332.63]**

1090　McLean, Andrew James. *Home Equity Kit.* 1989, Wiley $27.95 (0-471-50641-9); paper $12.95 (0-471-50642-7). A guide to high-yield real estate investments for future financial security. (Rev: BL 10/1/89; LJ 9/15/89)　　　**[332.63]**

1091　Mayer, Martin. *Markets: Who Plays, Who Risks, Who Gains, Who Loses.* 1988, Norton $18.95 (0-393-02602-7); paper $8.95 (0-393-30652-6). The ins and outs of stock, bond, and commodity trading by the author of *The Bankers.* (Rev: BL 7/88; Time 7/25/88; PW 6/17/88)　　　**[332.63]**

1092　Wayner, Stephen A. *Buying Right: Getting Started in Real Estate Investment.* 1987, Franklin Watts $17.95 (0-531-15524-2); NAL paper $4.95 (0-451-16581-0). A primer to real estate investment for the individual purchasing a single-family dwelling. (Rev: BL 4/1/87; LJ 4/15/87)　　　**[332.63]**

Exchange of securities and commodities

1093　Gordon, John Steele. *Scarlet Woman of Wall Street: Jay Gould, Jim Fisk, Cornelius Vanderbilt, and Erie Railway Wars and the Birth of Wall Street.* 1988, Grove-Weidenfeld $22.95 (1-55584-212-7); paper $11.95 (1-55584-428-6). A look at the nineteenth-century financial battles for the control of the Erie Railroad. (Rev: BL 7/88; Choice 12/88; LJ 8/88)　　　**[332.64]**

1094　Gunther, Max. *Zurich Axioms: Investment Secrets of the Swiss Bankers.* 1989, NAL paper $4.50 (0-451-15839-3). Twelve rules of investment for

budding financiers. (Rev: PW 2/8/85; TLS 12/27/85)
[332.64]

Investment banks and banking

1095 **Auletta, Ken.** *Greed and Glory on Wall Street: The Fall of the House of Lehman.* **1985, Random $19.95 (0-394-54410-2); Warner paper $9.95 (0-446-38406-2).** An account of the takeover of the investment banking firm of Lehman Brothers Kuhn Loeb by Shearson/American Express. (Rev: BL 2/15/86; LJ 2/15/86; PW 12/20/85)   **[332.66]**

333   Land economics

1096 **Berry, Wendell.** *Home Economics: Fourteen Essays.* **1987, North Point $20.00 (0-86547-274-2); paper $9.95 (0-86547-275-0).** Fourteen essays regarding farming, agriculture, and the natural order of economics. (Rev: BL 6/15/87; LJ 5/15/87; NYTBR 9/27/87)   **[333]**

Public ownership and control of land and other natural resources

1097 **Shanks, Bernard.** *This Land Is Your Land: The Struggle to Save America's Public Lands.* **1984, Sierra Club $19.95 (0-87156-822-5).** A study of the government agencies that dictate public land use policies in the United States. (Rev: Choice 3/85; LJ 1/85; NYTBR 5/5/85)   **[333.1]**

Transfer of possession and right to use

1098 **Bloch, H. I., and Grace Lichtenstein.** *Inside Real Estate: The Complete Guide to Buying and Selling Your Home, Co-op or Condominium.* **1989, Grove-Weidenfeld paper $9.95 (1-55584-320-4).** A collection of 360 questions and answers concerning the buying and selling of properties. "An essential title for the real estate collection."—LJ (Rev: BL 5/1/87; LJ 6/15/87)   **[333.33]**

1099 **Moss, Michael.** *Palace Coup: The Inside Story of Hotel Magnates Harry and Leona Helmsley.* **1989, Doubleday $18.95 (0-385-24973-X).** A dual biography of the controversial hotel and real estate magnates. (Rev: BL 3/1/89; LJ 4/1/89; NYTBR 4/9/89)   **[333.33]**

1100 **Percelay, Bruce A., and Peter Arnold.** *Packaging Your Home for Profit: How to Sell Your House or Condo for More Money in Less Time.* **1986, Little, Brown paper $12.95 (0-316-69896-2).** Suggested marketing techniques to expedite home sales for the best price. (Rev: BL 12/1/85; LJ 1/86)   **[333.33]**

1101 **Trump, Donald J., and Tony Schwartz.** *Trump: The Art of the Deal.* **1987, Random $19.95 (0-394-55528-7); Warner paper $5.95 (0-446-35325-6).** The New York financier recounts the background of his most successful real estate deals. (Rev: BL 12/1/87; New Rep 2/1/88; NYTBR 12/20/87)   **[333.33]**

Natural resources and energy

1102 **LaBastille, Anne.** *Beyond Black Bear Lake: Life at the Edge of the Wilderness.* **1987, Norton**

$15.95 (0-393-02388-5); paper $7.95 (0-393-30539-2). An account of the author's life in the Adirondack wilderness. (Rev: BL 12/15/86; LJ 12/86; PW 12/5/86)
[333.7]

1103 **McPhee, John.** *Encounters with the Archdruid.* **1971, Farrar $16.95 (0-374-14822-8); paper $7.95 (0-374-51431-3).** A look at the activities of David Brower, conservationist and founder of the Sierra Club. "A masterful job of reportage, one of the most engrossing and objective books we have yet encountered on the conflict between conservationists and their inevitable adversaries."—PW (Rev: BL 10/1/71; CSM 9/30/71; PW 6/7/71. Awards: ALA, 1971)   **[333.7]**

1104 **Porritt, Jonathon.** *Save the Earth.* **1991, Turner $29.50 (1-878685-05-8).** Collected essays by environmental experts on the current state of the earth's ecology with suggestions on how to contribute to the planet's well-being. (Rev: BL 10/1/91; PW 8/30/91)   **[333.7]**

Conservation and protection

1105 **Turner, Frederick W.** *Rediscovering America: John Muir in His Time and Ours.* **1987, Sierra Club paper $10.95 (0-87156-704-0).** An account of the life, work, and influence of the Scottish-born naturalist. (Rev: Choice 2/86; LJ 9/15/85; NYTBR 11/3/85)   **[333.72]**

Subsurface resources

1106 **Holing, Dwight.** *Coastal Alert: Ecosystems, Energy and Offshore Oil Drilling.* **1990, Island Pr. paper $10.95 (1-55963-050-7).** An overview of the processes, politics, and environmental consequences of offshore oil drilling in the United States. (Rev: BL 10/15/90; LJ 10/15/90)   **[333.8]**

Water

1107 **Crawford, Stanley.** *Mayordomo: Chronicle of an Acequia in Northern New Mexico.* **1989, Doubleday paper $8.95 (0-385-26254-X).** The author describes his experiences serving as community overseer of the lone irrigation ditch in a New Mexican farming town. (Rev: BL 6/15/88; LJ 10/1/88; PW 6/24/88)   **[333.91]**

1108 **Gottlieb, Robert.** *A Life of Its Own: The Politics and Power of Water.* **1988, Harcourt $20.95 (0-15-195190-X).** The author, a member of the Metropolitan Water District of Southern California, examines the relationship between public and private water concerns. (Rev: LJ 10/15/88; Natl Rev 10/28/88; PW 9/9/88)   **[333.91]**

1109 **Reisner, Marc.** *Cadillac Desert: The American West and Its Disappearing Water.* **1987, Penguin paper $10.95 (0-14-010432-1).** How the limited water resources of the West are manipulated by the government, for present profit, at the cost of the future of the region. "His well-written book should appeal to a much wider audience than its title might suggest."—Choice (Rev: Choice 12/86; LJ 8/86; NYTBR 9/14/86. Awards: LJ, 1986; PW, 1986)   **[333.91]**

1110 Worster, David. *Rivers of Empire: Water, Aridity, and the Growth of the American West.* 1987, Pantheon paper $12.95 (0-394-75161-2). An examination of the role of water and its distribution to the development and future of the American West. (Rev: Choice 5/86; LJ 2/1/86; NYTBR 2/23/86) **[333.91]**

Biological resources

1111 Allen, Thomas B. *Guardian of the Wild.* 1988, Indiana Univ. Pr. $25.00 (0-253-32605-2). The history of the role of the National Wildlife Federation in American conservation efforts since its founding in 1936. (Rev: BL 11/15/87; LJ 12/87) **[333.95]**

1112 Bellamy, David J. *Bellamy's New World: A Botanical History of America.* 1985, Parkwest $24.95 (0-88186-025-5). An overview of the development and changes of the vegetation of North America from prehistoric times to the present. (Rev: BL 8/85; LJ 8/85; PW 6/14/85) **[333.95]**

1113 Chase, Alston. *Playing God in Yellowstone: The Destruction of America's First National Park.* 1987, Harcourt paper $13.95 (0-15-672036-1). A critical account of U.S. government policies as practiced in Yellowstone National Park. "A challenging, compellingly readable account."—LJ (Rev: LJ 4/15/86; Natl Rev 9/26/86; PW 2/28/86) **[333.95]**

1114 Cowell, Adrian. *Decade of Destruction: The Crusade to Save the Amazon Rain Forest.* 1990, Seaver $19.95 (0-8050-1494-2). A British filmmaker's appraisal of current efforts to save the Amazon rain forest. (Rev: BL 9/15/90; LJ 9/15/90. Awards: LJ, 1990) **[333.95]**

1115 Di Silvestro, Robert. *Endangered Kingdom: The Struggle to Save America's Wildlife.* 1989, Wiley $19.95 (0-471-60600-6). A history of the decline of wildlife in America due to human impact, focuses on presently endangered species. (Rev: Choice 11/89; LJ 5/15/89; PW 4/28/89) **[333.95]**

1116 Fox, Stephen. *American Conservation Movement: John Muir and His Legacy.* 1986, Univ. of Wisconsin Pr. paper $14.95 (0-299-10634-9). A study of the life and legacy of the American naturalist. (Rev: Choice 7/13/81; LJ 6/1/81; NYTBR 6/21/81) **[333.95]**

1117 McNeely, Jeffrey A., and Paul Spencer Wachtel. *Soul of the Tiger: Searching for Nature's Answers in Southeast Asia.* 1990, Paragon House paper $12.95 (1-55778-280-6). A study of the relationship between man and nature in Southeast Asia written by two former Peace Corps members who lived there. (Rev: LJ 6/1/88; NYTBR 9/11/88; PW 4/22/88) **[333.95]**

1118 Revkin, Andrew. *Burning Season: The Murder of Chico Mendes and the Fight for the Amazon Rain Forest.* 1990, Houghton $19.95 (0-395-52394-X). A study of the life and death of the Brazilian union leader and environmental activist. (Rev: BL 7/90; LJ 6/1/90; NYTBR 8/19/90) **[333.95]**

1119 Shoumatoff, Alex. *World Is Burning: Murder in the Rain Forest.* 1990, Little, Brown $19.95 (0-316-78739-6). A study of the life, death, and legacy of Chico Mendes and his efforts to stop the destruction of the Amazon rain forest. (Rev: BL 7/90; LJ 8/90; NYTBR 8/19/90) **[333.95]**

1120 Wallace, David Rains. *Life in the Balance.* 1987, Harcourt $29.95 (0-15-151561-1). A study of 11 animal species threatened by man's encroachment upon their natural habitat. (Rev: BL 9/15/87; LJ 9/1/87; NYTBR 5/8/88) **[333.95]**

335 Socialism and related systems

1121 Harrington, Michael. *Socialism: Past and Future.* 1989, Arcade $19.95 (1-55970-000-9); NAL paper $9.95 (0-452-26504-5). A survey of the past, present, and future of world socialism by the author of *Toward a Democratic Left.* (Rev: LJ 6/1/89; NYTBR 7/16/89; PW 5/19/89) **[335]**

1122 Howe, Irving. *Socialism and America.* 1985, Harcourt $17.95 (0-15-183575-6); paper $5.95 (0-15-683520-7). A history of socialism and socialist thought in the United States by the author of *World of Our Fathers.* (Rev: LJ 11/15/85; New Rep 11/25/85; NYTBR 10/20/85) **[335]**

1123 O'Neill, William L., ed. *Echoes of Revolt: The Masses, 1911–1917.* 1989, I. R. Dee paper $18.95 (0-929587-15-4). An anthology of writings from the leftist magazine published during the 1910s. (Rev: LJ 2/1/67; NYTBR 12/11/66; Newsweek 11/28/86) **[335]**

Systems of French origin

1124 Beecher, Jonathan. *Charles Fourier: The Visionary and His World.* 1987, Univ. of California Pr. $55.00 (0-520-05600-0). A portrait of the life and thought of the nineteenth-century French social theorist. "Sure to become the standard on Fourier's life and writings."—LJ (Rev: Choice 9/87; LJ 5/15/87; NYTBR 5/17/87) **[335.2]**

Marxian systems

1125 Cameron, Kenneth Neill. *Marxism: The Science of Society.* 1984, Greenwood Pr. $34.95 (0-89789-051-5); paper $16.95 (0-89789-086-8). An introduction to Marxist thought and political theory. "Excellent for public libraries."—LJ (Rev: Choice 9/85; LJ 2/1/85) **[335.4]**

1126 Heilbroner, Robert L. *Marxism: For and Against.* 1980, Norton $9.95 (0-393-01307-3); paper $6.95 (0-393-95166-9). An assessment of the positive and negative aspects of Marxism in theory and practice. (Rev: BL 4/15/80; LJ 2/1/80; NYTBR 4/13/80) **[335.4]**

1127 Sowell, Thomas. *Marxism: Philosophy and Economics.* 1985, Morrow $15.95 (0-688-02963-9); paper $8.95 (0-688-06426-4). An interpretation of the thought and ideas of Karl Marx by the conservative economist. "There are many books on Marx, but this is one of the best."—LJ (Rev: LJ 3/1/85; Natl Rev 5/3/85; NYTBR 3/31/85) **[335.4]**

Communism

1128 Bernstein, Carl. *Loyalties: A Son's Memoir.* 1990, Simon & Schuster paper $8.95 (0-671-69598-3). Memoirs of the reporter's youth examining the lives of his parents who were active in leftist political causes. (Rev: New Rep 3/27/89; NYTBR 3/5/89; Time 3/20/89) **[335.43]**

1129 Brzezinski, Zbigniew. *Grand Failure: The Birth and Death of Communism in the 20th Century.* 1989, Macmillan $19.95 (0-684-19034-6); paper $9.95 (0-02-030730-6). An analysis of the past, present, and future of Communism by the former National Security Council director. (Rev: BL 3/1/89; NYTBR 3/26/89; PW 2/3/89) **[335.43]**

1130 Ettinger, Elzbieta. *Rosa Luxemburg: A Life.* 1987, Beacon $24.95 (0-8070-7006-8). A biography of the German socialist writer and Communist party leader. (Rev: LJ 12/86; NYRB 3/26/87; NYTBR 6/14/87) **[335.43]**

1131 Wren, Christopher Sale. *End of the Line: The Failure of Communism in the Soviet Union and China.* 1990, Simon & Schuster $22.95 (0-671-63864-5). A study of the decline of communism in the Soviet Union and the People's Republic of China over the past decade. (Rev: BL 8/90; LJ 6/15/90; NYTBR 8/5/90) **[335.43]**

Anarchism

1132 Duberman, Martin. *Mother Earth: An Epic Drama of Emma Goldman's Life.* 1991, St. Martin's $15.95 (0-312-05954-X). A play tracing the life and career of the American anarchist and social activist. (Rev: BL 6/1/91; LJ 6/15/91) **[335.83]**

1133 Falk, Candace A. *Love, Anarchy and Emma Goldman: A Biography.* 1990, Rutgers Univ. Pr. $45.00 (0-8135-1512-2); paper $14.95 (0-8135-1513-0). A personal biography of the American anarchist and social activist based on her private papers and letters. (Rev: BL 9/1/84; LJ 9/15/84; NYTBR 11/4/84) **[335.83]**

336 Public finance

Public borrowing, debt, expenditure

1134 Friedman, Benjamin M. *Day of Reckoning: The Consequences of American Economic Policy in the 1980s.* 1988, Random $19.95 (0-394-56553-3); paper $9.95 (0-679-72569-5). A survey of the state of the American economy warning that our standard of living and international influence will decline if we continue our overspending, and maintain our current status as a debtor nation. (Rev: Choice 3/89; LJ 11/15/88; NYTBR 10/23/88) **[336.3]**

1135 Malkin, Lawrence. *National Debt: How America Crashed into a Black Hole and How It Can Climb Out.* 1988, NAL paper $4.95 (0-451-62668-0). An examination of the history of the American national debt and its dramatic increase during the Reagan years. (Rev: BL 4/15/87; NYTBR 5/3/87; PW 3/13/87) **[336.3]**

New York

1136 Shefter, Martin. *Political Crisis-Fiscal Crisis: The Collapse and Revival of New York City.* 1987, Basic Books paper $9.95 (0-465-05876-0). An analysis of the fiscal collapse and recovery of New York City during the mid-1970s. (Rev: Choice 12/85; LJ 9/15/85; NYTBR 10/27/85) **[336.74]**

Soviet Union

1137 Shelton, Judy. *Coming Soviet Crash: Gorbachev's Desperate Search for Credit in the Western Financial Market.* 1989, Free Pr. $22.50 (0-02-928581-X); paper $9.95 (0-02-928582-8). An analysis of the current state of the Soviet economy, and its need for foreign capital to prevent its collapse. (Rev: Choice 5/89; CSM 2/9/89; NYTBR 2/5/89) **[336.94]**

337 International economics

1138 Choate, Pat. *Agents of Influence: How Japan's Lobbyists Manipulate America's Political and Economic System.* 1990, Knopf $22.95 (0-394-57901-1); Simon & Schuster paper $11.00 (0-671-74339-2). TRW policy analyst Choate traces recent Japanese contributions and lobbying tactics in the United States. (Rev: BL 12/1/90; New Rep 2/11/91; NYRB 11/8/90) **[337]**

Foreign economic policies—South Africa

1139 Hanlon, Joseph. *Beggar Your Neighbors: Apartheid Power in Southern Africa.* 1986, Indiana Univ. Pr. $35.00 (0-253-33131-5); paper $12.95 (0-253-20452-6). An analysis of South Africa's efforts to destabilize its neighboring nations to maintain its dominance in the region. (Rev: Choice 3/87; LJ 10/15/86; TLS 1/16/87) **[337.68]**

Foreign economic policies—North America

1140 Weintraub, Sidney. *A Marriage of Convenience: Relations Between Mexico and the United States.* 1990, Oxford Univ. Pr. $24.95 (0-19-506125-X). An analysis of the current relationship between the United States and Mexico focusing on political and economic problems as seen by a former State Department expert. (Rev: LJ 11/15/89; PW 11/24/89) **[337.7]**

338 Production

1141 Kiam, Victor. *Going for It! How to Succeed as an Entrepreneur.* 1987, NAL paper $4.95 (0-451-14851-7). A guide to successful entrepreneurship by the owner of Remington. (Rev: LJ 4/15/86; NYTBR 6/8/86) **[338]**

1142 Manning, Richard. *Last Stand: Logging, Journalism, and the Case for Humility.* 1991, Peregrine Smith $19.95 (0-87905-389-5). A Montana journalist examines the practices of logging companies in the American West during the 1980s. "Should be required reading for anyone interested in the truth about corporate logging."—NYTBR (Rev: LJ 10/1/91; NYTBR 11/10/91) **[338]**

1143 Meyer, Michael R. *Alexander Complex: Six Businessmen and the Empires They Built.* **1989, Random $19.95 (0-8129-1662-X).** A study of six successful businessmen and the personality traits that helped catapult them to success. (Rev: BL 9/1/89; LJ 8/89)　　　　　　　　　　**[338]**

Production efficiency

1144 Zuboff, Shoshana. *In the Age of the Smart Machine: The Future of Work and Power.* **1988, Basic Books $19.95 (0-465-03212-5).** A survey of the ways new technologies and computerization are transforming the workplace. (Rev: CSM 7/14/88; LJ 6/15/88; NYTBR 4/24/88)　　　　**[338.06]**

Persons—Collective treatment

1145 Davis, John H. *The Guggenheims: An American Epic (1848–1948).* **1989, Shapolsky $19.95 (0-944007-07-4).** The history of the Guggenheim family and how its fortune was built. "A dynamic . . . family dynasty and an engaging, informative book."—LJ (Rev: BL 3/1/78; LJ 3/1/78; New Rep 3/4/78. Awards: ALA, 1978)　　**[338.0922]**

Japan

1146 Tatsuno, Sheridan M. *Created in Japan: From Imitators to World-Class Innovators.* **1989, Harper $24.95 (0-88730-373-0); paper $12.95 (0-88730-492-3).** A look at the creative process and innovations developed in Japan. (Rev: BL 1/15/90; LJ 1/90)　　　　　　　　　**[338.0951]**

United States

1147 Dertouzos, Michael L., Richard K. Lester, and Robert M. Solow. *Made in America: Regaining the Productive Edge.* **1989, MIT Press $17.95 (0-262-04100-6); Harper & Row paper $10.95 (0-06-097340-4).** A presentation of the results of an MIT study analyzing American industrial performance compared to that of Europe and Japan. (Rev: Choice 12/89; LJ 6/15/89; NYTBR 7/23/89)　　**[338.0973]**

Agriculture

1148 Lappe, Frances M., and Joseph Collins. *Food First: Beyond the Myth of Scarcity.* **1981, Ballantine paper $4.95 (0-345-29818-7).** An examination of the politics and profit making behind world hunger and food shortages. (Rev: LJ 6/15/77; NYTBR 7/17/77; PW 5/9/77)　　　　　　　　　**[338.1]**

Extraction of minerals

1149 Petzinger, Thomas, Jr. *Oil and Honor: The Texaco-Pennzoil Wars.* **1989, Berkley paper $4.95 (0-425-11172-5).** An examination of the legal battle for the acquisition rights to Getty Oil between Pennzoil and Texaco in 1984. (Rev: BL 5/15/87; LJ 6/15/87; NYTBR 6/21/87)　　　　　**[338.2]**

1150 Yergin, Daniel. *Prize: The Epic Quest for Oil, Money and Power.* **1990, Simon & Schuster $24.95 (0-671-50248-4).** A history of petroleum and its effects upon the world economy and political relations. (Rev: BL 12/1/90; NYTBR 12/9/90; Time 12/31/

90. Awards: BL, 1991; LJ, 1991; PP:NF, 1992; Time, 1990)　　　　　　　　　　　　　**[338.2]**

Products of fishing, whaling, hunting, trapping

1151 Matthiessen, Peter. *Men's Lives: Surfmen and Baymen of the South Fork.* **1986, Random $29.95 (0-394-55280-6); paper $7.95 (0-394-75560-X).** The decline of the fishing industry of Long Island due to the area's development for resort housing. "Filled with salty detail and deep affection, his account gives a clear understanding of the forces involved in their struggle."—LJ (Rev: Atl 9/86; LJ 5/1/86; Newsweek 8/11/86. Awards: ALA, 1986; LJ, 1986)　　　　　　　　　　　　　**[338.372]**

Secondary industry and services

1152 Biddle, Wayne. *Barons of the Sky: From Early Flight to Strategic Warfare.* **1991, Simon & Schuster $22.95 (0-671-66726-2).** A history of the development of the American aerospace industry from its beginnings through the late 1940s. (Rev: BL 7/91; LJ 6/1/91; NYTBR 7/21/91)　　　**[338.4]**

1153 Califano, Joseph A., Jr. *America's Health Care Revolution: Who Lives? Who Dies? Who Pays?* **1986, Random $17.95 (0-394-54291-6); Simon & Schuster paper $9.95 (0-671-68371-3).** An assessment of America's health care system by the former secretary of housing, education, and welfare. "A timely and vital contribution to an important national concern."—BL (Rev: BL 6/15/86; Choice 7–8/86; LJ 3/15/86)　　　　　　　　　**[338.4]**

1154 Dannen, Fredrick. *Hit Men: Power Brokers and Fast Money Inside the Music Business.* **1990, Random $19.95 (0-8129-1658-1).** An inside look at promoters and big business in the world of popular music. "Will intrigue and appall readers with its disclosures."—PW (Rev: Choice 11/90; NYTBR 8/12/90; PW 6/22/90)　　　　　　　　　**[338.4]**

1155 Halberstam, David. *The Reckoning.* **1987, Avon paper $5.95 (0-380-70447-1).** The history of postwar economic competition between Japan and the U.S. as reflected in the Ford and Nissan companies. "The most ambitious literary undertaking of the year . . . an impressive achievement."—John Kenneth Galbraith, NYTBR (Rev: Choice 1/87; LJ 12/86; NYTBR 10/26/86. Awards: LJ, 1986; PW, 1986)　　　　　　**[338.4]**

1156 Hamper, Ben. *Rivethead: Tales from the Assembly Line.* **1991, Warner $19.95 (0-446-51501-9).** Memoirs of the author's decade of work on a General Motors automobile assembly line. (Rev: LJ 7/91; NYTBR 8/18/91)　　　　　　　**[338.4]**

1157 Kenney, Martin. *Biotechnology: The University-Industrial Complex.* **1986, Yale Univ. Pr. $25.00 (0-300-03392-3).** A study of the ties between universities and corporations in the area of biological research. (Rev: Choice 2/87; LJ 8/86; NYTBR 2/15/87)　　　　　　　　**[338.4]**

1158 McDougall, Walter A. *Heavens and the Earth: A Political History of the Space Age.* **1986, Basic Books paper $13.95 (0-465-02888-8).** "Destined to become the standard history of the origins of the Space Age."—Choice (REV: Choice 9/85; CSM 7/5/85; NYTBR 4/7/85. AWARDS: PP:History, 1986) **[338.4]**

1159 O'Brien, Richard. *Story of American Toys: From the Puritans to the Present.* 1990, Abbeville $49.95 (0-89659-921-3). An illustrated history of American toys and their development over the past three centuries. (REV: LJ 10/1/90; PW 5/4/90; Time 12/17/90) **[338.4]**

1160 Preston, Richard. *American Steel: Hot Metal Men and the Resurrection of the Rust Belt.* 1991, Prentice Hall $19.95 (0-13-029604-X). A study of an Indiana steel company that built a German-designed factory in 1987. "An absorbing, informative, moving reading experience."—PW (REV: LJ 4/15/91; PW 2/22/91) **[338.4]**

1161 Reutter, Mark. *Sparrows Point: Making Steel—The Rise and Ruin of American Industrial Might.* 1988, Summit $24.95 (0-671-55335-6); paper $14.95 (0-671-68752-2). A study of the rise and fall of American steel over the past century as reflected through the history of a Bethlehem steel plant. (REV: BL 11/15/88; LJ 11/15/88; PW 10/21/88) **[338.4]**

1162 Rogers, Everett M., and Judith K. Larsen. *Silicon Valley Fever: Growth of High-Technology Culture.* 1986, Basic Books paper $9.95 (0-465-07822-2). A sociological and technological history of the center of the Bay Area's computer industry. (REV: BL 3/15/84; LJ 2/15/84; PW 2/3/84) **[338.4]**

1163 Sobel, Robert. *IBM vs. Japan: The Struggle for the Future.* 1985, Scarborough $18.95 (0-8128-3071-7). A study of the rivalry between IBM and Japanese-owned firms for dominance in the data processing world. (REV: LJ 2/1/86; PW 12/6/85) **[338.4]**

1164 Sperber, Murray. *College Sports Inc.: The Athletic Department vs. the University.* 1990, Seaver $19.95 (0-8050-1445-4). A study of contemporary university athletic programs and their relationship to the goals of higher learning and academic excellence. (REV: BL 9/15/90; LJ 8/90; PW 8/3/90. AWARDS: BL, 1990) **[338.4]**

1165 Teitelman, Robert. *Gene Dreams: Wall Street, Academia and the Rise of Biotechnology.* 1989, Basic Books $19.95 (0-465-02659-1). An analysis of the early days of the biotechnology industry, and how investors sank money into projects and companies that had no real promise of success. (REV: BL 9/1/89; LJ 8/89; PW 7/14/89) **[338.4]**

1166 Tiffany, Paul A. *Decline of American Steel: How Management, Labor, and Government Went Wrong.* 1988, Oxford Univ. Pr. $24.95 (0-19-504382-0). A look at how changing economic trends led to the decline of the U.S. steel industry. (REV: Choice 9/88; LJ 4/15/88) **[338.4]**

1167 Womack, James. *Machine That Changed the World.* 1990, Rawson $22.50 (0-89256-350-8). A study of current automobile production methods developed in Japan and their applications to other manufacturing jobs. (REV: CSM 11/28/90; LJ 10/1/90; NYTBR 10/28/90) **[338.4]**

General production economics

1168 Frumkin, Norman. *Tracking America's Economy.* 1987, ME Sharpe $39.95 (0-87332-437-4); paper $14.95 (0-87332-438-2). A guide to the statistical indicators of America's economy for the layman. (REV: Choice 7-8/88; LJ 3/1/88) **[338.5]**

1169 Garraty, John Arthur. *Great Depression: An Inquiry into the Causes, Course, and Consequences of the Worldwide Depression of the 1930s as Seen by Contemporaries and in the Light of History.* 1986, Harcourt $17.95 (0-15-504385-5); Doubleday paper $9.95 (0-385-24085-6). A survey of the worldwide effects and ramifications of the economic depression of the 1930s. (REV: LJ 9/1/86; NYTBR 10/26/86; PW 8/29/86) **[338.5]**

Organization of production

1170 Bluestone, Barry, and Bennet Harrison. *Deindustrialization of America: Plant Closings, Community Abandonment and the Dismantling of Basic Industry.* 1984, Basic Books paper $12.95 (0-465-01592-1). The authors argue that changes in the world economic structure and improvement in worldwide telecommunications have led American industry to move to foreign countries and withdraw capital from the United States. (REV: BL 11/1/82; LJ 12/1/82; NYTBR 12/12/82) **[338.6]**

Business enterprises and their structure

1171 Butcher, Lee. *Accidental Millionaire: The Rise and Fall of Steve Jobs at Apple Computer.* 1987, Paragon House $19.95 (0-913729-79-5); paper $9.95 (1-55778-143-5). The history of the founding and rise of Apple Computer and the circumstances that led co-founder Steven Jobs to leave the company. (REV: BL 9/1/87; LJ 9/15/87; NYTBR 10/25/87) **[338.7]**

1172 Drosnin, Michael. *Citizen Hughes.* 1985, Bantam paper $4.50 (0-553-25453-7). A biography of the American entrepreneur Howard Hughes based on his private papers. (REV: BL 3/1/85; LJ 4/1/85; NYTBR 2/17/85) **[338.7]**

1173 Greenberg, Jonathan D. *Staking a Claim: Jake Simmons and the Making of an African-American Oil Dynasty.* 1990, Macmillan $19.95 (0-689-11791-4). A biography of the African-American petroleum magnate and civil rights activist. (REV: BL 12/15/89; CSM 4/4/90; LJ 12/89) **[338.7]**

1174 Harevan, Tamara K., and Randolph Langenbach. *Amoskaeg: Life and Work in an American Factory-City.* 1980, Pantheon paper $11.95 (0-394-73855-1). An illustrated oral history of the lives of people in a New Hampshire textile-producing city. (REV: Atl 1/79; Choice 3/79; LJ 10/1/78) **[338.7]**

1175 Holland, Max. *When the Machine Stopped: A Cautionary Tale from Industrial America.* 1990, Harvard Business $24.95 (0-87584-208-9); paper $14.95 (0-87584-244-5). A history of the Burgmaster Corporation examining why the machine tool company declined prior to its 1986 dissolution. (Rev: BL 3/15/89; Choice 10/89; LJ 4/1/89)   **[338.7]**

1176 Kusumoto, Sam, and Edmund P. Murray. *My Bridge to America: Discovering the New World for Minolta.* 1989, Dutton $19.95 (0-525-24787-4). A biography of the President of Minolta tracing the company's rise to capture a large share of the world's camera market. "A moving personal and cultural document . . . highly recommended."—LJ (Rev: BL 1/15/90; LJ 11/15/89)   **[338.7]**

1177 Lacey, Robert. *Ford: The Men and the Machine.* 1986, Little, Brown $24.95 (0-316-51166-8); Ballantine paper $5.95 (0-345-34312-3). A history of the Ford family and the Ford Motor Company. (Rev: BL 7/86; LJ 9/1/86; NYTBR 7/13/86)   **[338.7]**

1178 Love, John F. *McDonald's: Behind the Arches.* 1986, Bantam $21.95 (0-553-05127-X). A study of the history and organizational techniques of the international fast-food chain. (Rev: BL 9/1/86; LJ 10/1/86; NYTBR 10/26/86)   **[338.7]**

1179 Mintz, Morton. *At Any Cost: Corporate Greed, Women and the Dalkon Shield.* 1985, Pantheon $8.95 (0-394-54846-9). The story of the A. H. Robins Company's Dalkon Shield I.U.D., its lack of proper testing, and its marketing to American women with tragic results. "A fascinating and well-researched book that takes a hard look at white-collar crime."—BL (Rev: LJ 11/1/85; NYRB 4/10/86; NYTBR 1/12/86. Awards: LJ, 1985)   **[338.7]**

1180 Monaghan, Thomas, and Robert Anderson. *Pizza Tiger.* 1986, Random $17.95 (0-394-55359-4). Memoirs of the founder and owner of Domino's Pizza regarding his life and business success. (Rev: BL 11/15/86; LJ 12/86; PW 10/24/86)   **[338.7]**

1181 Nader, Ralph, and William Taylor. *Big Boys: Styles of Corporate Powers.* 1986, Pantheon $22.95 (0-394-53338-0); paper $8.95 (0-394-72111-X). Profiles of nine CEO's analyzing their personalities and how they reflect the business styles of their corporations. (Rev: BL 5/1/86; Choice 9/86; NYTBR 6/22/86)   **[338.7]**

1182 Pallister, David. *South Africa, Inc.: The Oppenheimer Empire.* 1988, Yale Univ. Pr. $27.50 (0-300-04251-5). A study of the workings of South Africa's largest multinational corporation and its relationship to the apartheid system. (Rev: BL 9/1/88; LJ 12/88)   **[338.7]**

1183 Pickens, T. Boone. *Boone.* 1987, Houghton $18.95 (0-395-41433-4). An autobiography of the Texas oil magnate who developed Mesa Petroleum into a powerful independent company. (Rev: BL 4/1/87; LJ 4/15/87; PW 2/13/87)   **[338.7]**

1184 Rose, Frank. *West of Eden: The End of Innocence at Apple Computer.* 1989, Viking $19.95 (0-670-81278-1); Penguin paper $8.95 (0-14-009372-9). The history of Apple Computer's beginnings, development, and the eventual shake-up that led to the ouster of its two founders. (Rev: BL 2/15/89; LJ 4/1/89; NYTBR 5/7/89)   **[338.7]**

1185 Segal, Harvey H. *Corporate Makeover: The Reshaping of the American Economy.* 1989, Viking $19.95 (0-670-82099-7). The author argues that recent corporate trends toward mergers, buyouts, and takeovers have made American companies better able to compete in the international market. (Rev: BL 8/89; LJ 9/1/89; PW 7/14/89)   **[338.7]**

1186 Strohmeyer, John. *Crisis in Bethlehem: Big Steel's Struggle to Survive.* 1987, Penguin paper $7.95 (0-14-010370-8). A former Bethlehem, Pennsylvania, newspaper editor presents a study of the rise and decline of Bethlehem Steel and America's steel industry from the 1950s to the 1980s. (Rev: BL 10/15/86; LJ 11/1/86; NYTBR 10/26/86)   **[338.7]**

1187 Wang, An, and Eugene Linden. *Lessons: An Autobiography.* 1986, Addison Wesley $17.95 (0-201-09400-2). Memoirs of the founder of Wang Laboratories discussing his life and business success. (Rev: BL 10/15/86; Choice 1/87; LJ 10/1/86)   **[338.7]**

1188 Weaver, Paul H. *Suicidal Corporation: How Big Business Has Failed America.* 1988, Simon & Schuster $18.95 (0-317-67757-8); paper $9.95 (0-671-67559-1). The author relates his perceptions of the problems of big business in America based on his experiences with Ford Motor Company. (Rev: BL 3/1/88; LJ 3/1/88; Natl Rev 4/15/88)   **[338.7]**

Partnerships

1189 Ouchi, William G. *M-Form Society: How American Teamwork Can Recapture the Competitive Edge.* 1986, Avon paper $4.95 (0-380-69914-1). An examination of the relationship between government and industry in the United States and how it can be restructured to revitalize the American economy. (Rev: BL 5/1/84; Choice 9/84; LJ 5/1/84)   **[338.73]**

Corporations

1190 Heller, Robert. *Decision Makers.* 1989, Dutton $22.50 (0-525-24798-X). A comparison between decision-makers and decision making in Eastern and Western companies. "A lively and incisive overview of worldwide economics."—PW (Rev: BL 9/1/89; LJ 9/1/89; PW 8/11/89)   **[338.74]**

Combinations

1191 Brooks, John. *Takeover Game: The Men, the Moves, and the Wall Street Money Behind Today's Great Merger Wars.* 1988, Dutton paper $9.95 (0-525-48440-X). A history of investment banking and financial practices used by bankers to create mergers and business takeovers. (Rev: BL 9/15/87; LJ 9/15/87; PW 8/21/87)   **[338.8]**

1192 Burrough, Bryan, and John Helyar. *Barbarians at the Gate: The Fall of RJR Nabisco.* 1990, Harper & Row $22.50 (0-06-016172-8); paper $10.95 (0-06-092038-6). An account of the 1988 corporate fight to buy and control RJR Nabisco. (Rev: BL 12/1/89; LJ 1/90; Newsweek 1/15/90)   **[338.8]**

1193 Commons, Dorman L. *Tender Offer: The Sneak Attack in Corporate Warfare.* 1985, Univ. of

California Pr. $22.50 (0-520-05583-7); Penguin paper $6.95 (0-14-009406-7). An analysis of the managerial strategies behind the takeover of the Natomas Company by Diamond Shamrock in the early 1980s. (Rev: BL 9/15/85; LJ 12/85; NYTBR 10/20/85)
[338.8]

1194 Gelsanliter, David. *Jump Start: Japan Comes to the Heartland.* **1990, Farrar $19.95 (0-374-13827-3).** An account of the introduction of Japanese-owned automobile factories into the United States over the past decade. (Rev: BL 7/90; LJ 6/15/90; NYTBR 8/12/90)
[338.8]

1195 McCartney, Laton. *Friends in High Places: The Bechtel Story.* **1989, Ballantine paper $8.95 (0-345-36044-3).** A history of the Bechtel Group and its influence upon U.S. domestic and foreign policies. (Rev: BL 3/1/88; LJ 5/1/88; PW 1/29/88)
[338.8]

1196 Mann, Jim. *Beijing Jeep: The Short, Unhappy Romance of American Business in China.* **1990, Simon & Schuster paper $12.95 (0-671-72504-1).** A study of AMC's failed attempts to produce Jeeps in China. (Rev: CSM 3/1/90; LJ 11/15/89; NYTBR 11/19/90)
[338.8]

1197 Sampson, Anthony. *Sovereign State of ITT.* **1980, Scarborough paper $7.95 (0-404-20226-8).** The history of the multinational corporation International Telephone and Telegraph. "An arresting picture . . . as readable as an Ian Fleming thriller."—BL (Rev: BL 10/1/73; CSM 8/1/73; Time 8/6/73. Awards: Time, 1973)
[338.8]

1198 Taylor, John. *Storming the Magic Kingdom: Wall Street, the Raiders and the Battle for Disney.* **1987, Knopf $18.95 (0-394-54640-7); Ballantine paper $9.95 (0-345-34507-9).** An examination of the financial battle for Disney in the mid-1980s. (Rev: LJ 6/1/87; NYTBR 5/10/87; PW 3/6/87)
[338.8]

Economic development and growth

1199 Bailey, George. *Galileo's Children: Scientific Discovery vs. the Power of the State.* **1990, Arcade $24.95 (1-55970-078-5).** A study of the relationship between scientists and the state in the twentieth century focusing on the career of Soviet physicist Andrei Sakharov. (Rev: BL 2/15/90; Natl Rev 9/3/90; PW 3/2/90. Awards: BL, 1990)
[338.9]

1200 Harding, Harry. *China's Second Revolution: Reform after Mao.* **1987, Brookings $32.95 (0-8157-3462-X); paper $12.95 (0-8157-3461-1).** An assessment of Chinese culture and reform under the rule of Deng Xiaoping. (Rev: Choice 5/88; LJ 1/88; New Rep 4/18/88)
[338.9]

1201 McCraw, Thomas K. *Prophets of Revolution: Charles Francis Adams, Louis D. Brandeis, James M. Landis, Alfred E. Kahn.* **1984, Harvard Univ. Pr. $23.95 (0-674-71607-8); paper $9.95 (0-674-71608-6).** "This book ought to be in every public library."—Choice (Rev: Choice 12/84; LJ 10/1/84; NYTBR 10/21/84. Awards: PP:History, 1985)
[338.9]

1202 Stein, Herbert. *Presidential Economics: The Making of Economic Policy from Roosevelt to*

Reagan and Beyond. **1988, American Enterprise Institute paper $13.75 (0-8447-3656-2).** A study of the formulation and enactment of American economic policies from the 1930s to the 1980s. (Rev: Choice 5/84; LJ 4/1/84; NYTBR 2/12/84)
[338.9]

International development and growth

1203 Lappe, Frances M. *Betraying the National Interest.* **1987, Grove-Weidenfeld $18.95 (0-8021-0012-0); paper $8.95 (0-8021-3027-5).** A critical look at how U.S. foreign aid is used and distributed once it reaches its destination. (Rev: BL 1/15/88; LJ 1/88)
[338.91]

Economic development and growth—Africa

1204 Klitgaard, Robert E. *Tropical Gangsters: Development and Decadence in Deepest Africa.* **1990, Basic Books $22.95 (0-465-08758-2).** Memoirs of the author's three years working for the World Bank in an attempt to improve the economy of Equatorial Guinea. (Rev: NYTBR 9/9/90; PW 7/20/90. Awards: NYTBR, 1990)
[338.96]

Economic development and growth—United States

1205 Edsall, Thomas Byrne. *New Politics of Inequality.* **1985, Norton paper $6.95 (0-393-30250-4).** A study of the recent dominance of conservative ideas and power in American politics and the decline of the liberal sector of the Democratic party and its ideals and programs. (Rev: LJ 6/15/84; New Rep 10/29/84; NYTBR 7/1/84)
[338.973]

1206 Harrington, Michael. *Next Left: The History of a Future.* **1987, Henry Holt $17.95 (0-8050-0104-2); paper $8.95 (0-8050-0792-X).** A survey of the history of the American Left since 1929 analyzing the future of the left wing in American political thought and influence. (Rev: Choice 11/87; LJ 1/87; NYTBR 3/1/87)
[338.973]

1207 Janeway, Eliot. *Economics of Chaos: On Revitalizing the American Economy.* **1989, Dutton $22.50 (0-525-24711-4); paper $12.95 (0-525-48545-7).** The financial newsletter editor presents his ideas on methods of stimulating the U.S. economy. (Rev: BL 1/1/89; PW 1/6/89)
[338.973]

1208 Kuttner, Robert. *End of Laissez-Faire: National Purpose and the Global Economy after the Cold War.* **1991, Knopf $22.95 (0-394-57995-X).** A study of current international economics and the future of free trade. (Rev: BL 1/15/91; LJ 2/15/91; PW 12/21/90)
[338.973]

1209 Reich, Robert B. *Resurgent Liberal: And Other Unfashionable Prophecies.* **1989, Random $19.95 (0-8129-1833-9); paper $12.95 (0-679-73152-0).** Essays regarding the American economic, political, and cultural climate of the 1980s. (Rev: BL 9/1/89; LJ 8/89; PW 8/4/89)
[338.973]

1210 Stockman, David. *Triumph of Politics: Why the Reagan Revolution Failed.* **1986, Harper & Row $21.95 (0-06-015560-4); Avon paper $4.95 (0-380-70311-4).** A study of the economic policies of the early Reagan years by the former director of the Office of Management and Budget. (Rev: BL 5/1/86; LJ 7/86; NYTBR 5/11/86) **[338.973]**

1211 Thurow, Lester C. *Dangerous Currents: The State of Economics.* **1984, Random paper $7.95 (0-394-72368-6).** A study of the international economy and the current state of economic theory. (Rev: Atl 6/83; New Rep 6/6/83; NYTBR 6/5/83) **[338.973]**

1212 Thurow, Lester C. *Zero-Sum Solution: Building a World-Class American Economy.* **1986, Simon & Schuster paper $9.95 (0-671-62814-3).** An examination of the decline of the dominance of the United States in the world economy with proposals on how best to regain it. (Rev: BL 10/15/85; Choice 2/86; LJ 12/85) **[338.973]**

339 Macroeconomics and related topics

Distribution of income and wealth

1213 Phillips, Kevin. *Politics of Rich and Poor: Wealth and the American Electorate in the Reagan Aftermath.* **1990, Random $19.95 (0-394-55954-1).** An analysis of economic practices under the Reagan administration and how the gap between rich and poor was accentuated under his command. (Rev: LJ 5/15/90; New Rep 7/30/90; NYRB 7/19/90. Awards: BL, 1990; Time, 1990) **[339.2]**

National product, wealth, income accounts and accounting

1214 Waring, Marilyn. *If Women Counted: A New Feminist Economics.* **1989, Harper & Row $18.95 (0-06-250933-0); paper $12.95 (0-06-250940-3).** A feminist view of world economic sexual discrimination, how "women's work" is often discounted in economic statistics, and ways these distorted facts are used to affect public policy to the detriment of women. (Rev: BL 2/15/89; LJ 4/1/89) **[339.3]**

340 LAW

1215 Dworkin, Ronald M. *Law's Empire.* **1986, Harvard Univ. Pr. $25.00 (0-674-51835-7); paper $11.95 (0-674-51836-5).** An overview of the professor's legal philosophy and theory of law and its applications. (Rev: LJ 5/1/86; NYTBR 5/25/86; TLS 8/22/86) **[340]**

1216 Dworkin, Ronald M. *A Matter of Principle.* **1985, Harvard Univ. Pr. $28.00 (0-674-55460-4); paper $12.50 (0674-55461-2).** Studies of controversial issues facing the legal community from pornography and its relation to First Amendment rights to quotas. (Rev: Choice 10/85; NYTBR 6/9/85; PW 4/12/85) **[340]**

1217 Morello, Karen Berger. *Invisible Bar: The Woman Lawyer in America, 1638 to the Present.* **1986, Random $19.95 (0-394-52964-2).** A history of female lawyers in the United States from the seventeenth century to the present. (Rev: Choice 3/87; LJ 11/1/86; NYTBR 11/9/86) **[340]**

Organizations and management

1218 Eisler, Kim Isaac. *Shark Tank.* **1990, St. Martin's $18.95 (0-312-03830-5).** An account of the 1986 financial collapse of the Finley, Kumble, America's second largest law firm. (Rev: BL 2/1/90; LJ 2/15/90; PW 1/19/90) **[340.06]**

1219 Kumble, Steven J., and Kevin J. Lahart. *Conduct Unbecoming: The Rise and Ruin of Finley, Kumble.* **1990, Carroll & Graf $19.95 (0-88184-625-2).** An account of the history and eventual financial collapse of the Finley, Kumble law firm by one of its founders. "A devastatingly candid confession and exposé."—PW (Rev: BL 11/15/90; LJ 11/1/90) **[340.06]**

Education

1220 Turow, Scott. *One L: An Inside Account of Life in the First Year at Harvard Law School.* **1988, Farrar $19.95 (0-374-22647-4); Warner paper $4.95 (0-446-35170-9).** The author of *Presumed Innocent* recounts his experience during his first year as a student at Harvard Law School. (Rev: BL 9/1/77; LJ 9/1/77; NYTBR 9/25/77) **[340.07]**

Persons

1221 Chestnut, J. L., Jr., and Julia Cass. *Black in Selma: The Uncommon Life of J. L. Chestnut, Jr.* **1990, Farrar $22.95 (0-374-11404-8).** An autobiography of an African-American lawyer in Selma, Alabama, describing his experiences during the civil rights movement. "A major contribution to our understanding of recent U.S. history."—LJ (Rev: BL 6/1/90; LJ 7/90; PW 6/15/90) **[340.092]**

1222 Cohn, Roy, and Sidney Zion. *Autobiography of Roy Cohn.* **1988, St. Martin's paper $4.95 (0-312-91402-4).** An autobiography of the government lawyer rewritten by Zion after Cohn's death. "Appealingly honest without being exploitative."—BL (Rev: BL 4/1/88; LJ 4/15/88; Time 4/4/88) **[340.092]**

1223 Thomas, Evan. *The Man to See: Edward Bennett Williams.* **1991, Simon & Schuster $27.50 (0-671-68934-7).** A biography of the lawyer, political figure, and sports executive. (Rev: Newsweek 11/25/91; PW 9/13/91) **[340.092]**

Philosophy and theory of law

1224 Rawls, John. *A Theory of Justice.* **1971, Harvard Univ. Pr. $28.00 (0-674-88010-2); paper $11.95 (0-674-88014-5).** An updated look at the social contract and its proposed modern societal applications. "The most substantial and interesting contribution to moral philosophy since the war."—NYRB (Rev: LJ 4/1/72; NYRB 2/24/72; NYTBR 7/16/72. Awards: NYTBR, 1972) **[340.11]**

341 International law

Law of war

1225 Brackman, Arnold C. *Other Nuremberg: The Untold Story of the Tokyo War Crimes Trials.* **1987, Morrow $19.95 (0-688-04783-1); paper $9.95 (0-**

688-07957-1). A study of the Tokyo War Crimes Trials following World War II by a United Press correspondent who covered them. (REV: BL 2/15/87; Choice 6/87; LJ 2/15/87) **[341.6]**

International cooperation

1226 Cook, Don. *Forging the Alliance: NATO, 1945–1950.* **1989, Morrow $22.95 (1-557-10043-8); paper $9.95 (0-688-10000-7).** Traces the history of the establishment and early years of the North Atlantic Treaty Organization following World War II. "No one who wants to understand American foreign policy today should miss it."—NYTBR (REV: Choice 10/89; LJ 6/1/89; NYTBR 5/21/89) **[341.7]**

1227 Robinson, Jeffrey. *Yamani: The Inside Story of the Man Who Ran OPEC.* **1989, Atlantic Monthly $19.95 (0-87113-323-7).** A biography of the oil magnate who was in charge of Saudi Arabian petroleum policies from 1962 to 1986. (REV: BL 5/15/89; PW 4/14/89) **[341.7]**

International criminal law

1228 Kuper, Leo. *Prevention of Genocide.* **1986, Yale Univ. Pr. $30.00 (0-300-03418-0).** An examination of the United Nations efforts to prevent genocidal acts since World War II. (REV: Choice 2/86; CSM 8/1/86; LJ 3/1/86) **[341.77]**

342 Constitutional and administrative law

1229 Friendly, Fred W. *Minnesota Rag: The Dramatic Story of the Landmark Supreme Court Case That Gave New Meaning to Freedom of the Press.* **1982, Random paper $7.95 (0-394-71241-2).** A study of a landmark Supreme Court case that ruled against prior restraint of the publication of newspaper articles. (REV: Choice 11/81; LJ 5/15/81; PW 4/24/81) **[342]**

Jurisdiction of governmental units over persons

1230 Marwick, Christine M. *Your Right to Government Information.* **1985, Southern Illinois Univ. Pr. paper $4.95 (0-8093-9960-1).** An ACLU primer on methods of obtaining information from the U.S. government. (REV: BL 2/15/85; LJ 2/15/85) **[342.08]**

South Africa

1231 Carlson, Joel. *No Neutral Ground.* **1974, Charles River $4.95 (0-7043-3158-6).** A white lawyer describes his experiences fighting for racial justice for black Africans in South Africa, and his eventual forced extradition to the United States. "This remarkable and fascinating book must be read by everyone."—LJ (REV: Atl 4/73; Choice 9/73; LJ 3/15/73. AWARDS: ALA, 1973) **[342.68]**

United States

1232 Bernstein, Richard B., and Kym S. Rice. *Are We to Be a Nation? The Making of the Constitution.* **1987, Harvard Univ. Pr. paper $14.95 (0-674-04476-2).** A study of the years between the Declaration of Independence and the ratification of the

U.S. Constitution. (REV: Choice 9/87; LJ 3/1/87; NYTBR 5/3/87) **[342.73]**

1233 Collier, Christopher, and James Lincoln Collier. *Decision in Philadelphia: The Constitutional Convention, 1787.* **1987, Ballantine paper $4.95 (0-345-34652-1).** An account of the 1787 convention called to create and write the U.S. Constitution. "The best popular history . . . available."—LJ (REV: LJ 5/1/86; NYTBR 3/2/86) **[342.73]**

1234 Garbus, Martin. *Traitors and Heroes: A Lawyer's Memoir.* **1987, Macmillan $19.95 (0-689-11888-0); Carroll & Graf paper $10.95 (0-88184-540-X).** Memoirs of the human rights activist and lawyer regarding cases he has worked on in Chile, South Africa, and the United States. (REV: BL 7/87; LJ 9/1/87; NYTBR 8/30/87) **[342.73]**

1235 Irons, Peter. *Courage of Their Convictions: Sixteen Americans Who Fought Their Way to the Supreme Court.* **1988, Free Pr. $22.95 (0-02-915670-X); Penguin paper $8.95 (0-14-012810-7).** An account of 16 Americans who took civil rights cases to the Supreme Court between 1940 and 1986. (REV: Choice 4/89; CSM 11/21/88; LJ 2/1/89) **[342.73]**

1236 Irons, Peter. *Justice at War: The Inside Story of the Japanese American Internment.* **1983, Oxford Univ. Pr. $24.95 (0-19-503273-X); $11.95 paper (0-19-503497-X).** An examination of the legal cases brought before the U.S. Supreme Court upholding the constitutionality of the internment of Japanese Americans during the Second World War. (REV: Choice 1/84; LJ 10/1/83; Newsweek 10/24/83) **[342.73]**

1237 Kaminer, Wendy. *Fearful Freedom: Women's Flight from Equality.* **1990, Addison Wesley $18.95 (0-201-09234-4).** An examination of the definition of gender equality in legal and social terms. (REV: LJ 4/15/90; NYTBR 5/27/90; PW 3/30/90) **[342.73]**

1238 Kammen, Michael. *A Machine That Would Go of Itself: The Constitution in American Culture.* **1986, Knopf $35.00 (0-394-52905-7).** The history of the American public's perception of the U.S. Constitution. "This wide-ranging account, which breaks new ground yet is suitable for general readers, should be in most libraries."—LJ (REV: Choice 2/87; LJ 10/1/86; NYTBR 9/14/86. AWARDS: LJ, 1986; NYTBR, 1986) **[342.73]**

1239 Levy, Leonard W. *Original Intent and the Framer's Constitution.* **1988, Macmillan $19.95 (0-02-918791-5).** The history of judicial interpretation of the constitution, and the role that the founding fathers' intentions have played in justices' decision-making. (REV: Choice 5/89; LJ 10/1/88; NYTBR 11/6/88. AWARDS: NYTBR, 1988) **[342.73]**

1240 Lewis, Anthony. *Make No Law: The Sullivan Case and the First Amendment.* **1991, Random $25.00 (0-394-58774-X).** A study of the 1964 landmark First Amendment Supreme Court case of *New York Times* vs. Sullivan. (REV: Choice 12/91; CSM 10/1/91; NYTBR 9/1/91) **[342.73]**

1241 Peters, Williams. *A More Perfect Union: The Men and Events That Made the Constitution.*

1987, **Crown $22.50** (0-517-56450-5). A study of the personalities and events leading up to the creation of the U.S. Constitution. "Captures both the humanity and the significance of the Constitutional conclave."—BL (Rev: BL 1/1/87; LJ 3/15/87; NYTBR 3/15/87) **[342.73]**

1242 **Polenberg, Richard.** *Fighting Faiths: The Abrams Case, the Supreme Court and Free Speech.* 1987, **Viking $24.95** (0-670-81373-7); **Penguin paper $9.95** (0-14-011736-9). A study of the issues surrounding a 1919 case of five Russian immigrants who were deported for espousing anarchy. (Rev: Choice 3/88; LJ 11/15/87; NYTBR 1/17/88) **[342.73]**

343   Military, tax, trade, industrial law

United States

1243 **Birnbaum, Jeffrey H., and Alan S. Murray.** *Showdown at Gucci Gulch: Lawmakers, Lobbyists and the Unlikely Triumph of Tax Reform.* 1987, **Random $18.95** (0-394-56024-8); **paper $9.95** (0-394-75811-0). A story of the lobbyists and politicians who helped pass the 1986 act reforming tax legislation. (Rev: BL 5/15/87; NYTBR 7/5/87; PW 5/15/87) **[343.73]**

1244 **Block, Julian.** *Julian Block's Year-Round Tax Strategies for the $40,000 Plus Household.* 1990, **Prima paper $12.95** (1-55958-048-8). A guide to tax information for those individuals in the upper tax brackets. (Rev: BL 10/15/89; LJ 12/89) **[343.73]**

1245 **Headley, Lake, and William Hoffman.** *Court-Martial of Clayton Lonetree.* 1989, **Henry Holt $19.95** (0-8050-0893-4). An analysis of Lonetree's court-martial trial on charges of leaking confidential documents to the Soviets while working at the American embassy in Moscow. (Rev: BL 8/89; LJ 9/1/89) **[343.73]**

1246 **Larsen, David C.** *You Can't Take It with You: A Step-by-Step Personalized Approach to Your Will to Avoid Probate and Taxes.* 1988, **Random paper $9.95** (0-394-75543-X). An introduction to will writing and estate planning for financial security. (Rev: BL 3/1/88; LJ 3/1/88) **[343.73]**

344   Social, labor, welfare and related law

United States

1247 **De Grazia, Edward.** *Girls Lean Back Everywhere: The Law of Obscenity and the Assault on Genius.* 1992, **Random $30.00** (0-394-57611-X). A history of censorship and the struggle to define what constitutes obscenity. "Required reading for all librarians and everyone interested in intellectual freedom issues."—LJ (Rev: BL 12/1/91; LJ 2/1/92) **[344.73]**

1248 **Kluger, Richard.** *Simple Justice: The History of Brown v. Board of Education and Black America's Struggle for Equality.* 1975, **Knopf $35.00** (0-394-47289-6); **Random paper $18.95** (0-394-72255-8). Legislative history of the case that overturned the concept of "separate but equal" in the

American education system. "By itself, very possibly the best book we have on race relations in the U.S. up to the 1950s . . . and the Supreme Court at work and in conflict under Chief Justice Earl Warren."—Choice (Rev: Choice 6/76; CSM 2/4/76; Time 2/9/76. Awards: Time, 1976) **[344.73]**

1249 **Mohr, James C.** *Abortion in America: The Origins and Evolution of National Policy, 1800–1900.* 1978, **Oxford Univ. Pr. paper $9.95** (0-19-502616-0). An examination of the history and changing social attitudes toward abortion in nineteenth-century America. (Rev: BL 5/1/78; Choice 6/78; Natl Rev 7/7/78) **[344.73]**

1250 **Sapinsky, Barbara.** *Private War of Mrs. Packard.* 1991, **Paragon House $19.95** (1-55778-330-6). The story of a nineteenth-century Massachusetts woman who was institutionalized by her pastor husband after publicly questioning his beliefs. (Rev: BL 6/15/91; LJ 6/1/91; NYTBR 8/25/91) **[344.73]**

345   Criminal law

1251 **Caplan, Lincoln.** *Insanity Defense and the Trial of John W. Hinckley, Jr.* 1984, **Godine $13.95** (0-87923-533-0); **Dell paper $3.95** (0-440-34644-4). A study of the use of the insanity defense in the American court system in the nineteenth and twentieth centuries culminating in the trial of the man who attempted to assassinate Ronald Reagan. (Rev: LJ 8/84; New Rep 12/31/84; NYTBR 11/4/84) **[345]**

France

1252 **Davis, Natalie Zemon.** *Return of Martin Guerre.* 1983, **Harvard Univ. Pr. $19.95** (0-674-76690-3). The story of the disappearance of Martin Guerre, a sixteenth-century French peasant, his imposter, and the trial that took place upon the real Guerre's return. (Rev: LJ 9/1/83; NYRB 12/22/83; NYTBR 10/2/83) **[345.44]**

United States

1253 **Adams, Randall, William Hoffer, and Marilyn Mona Hoffer.** *Adams v. Texas.* 1991, **St. Martin's $19.95** (0-312-05811-X). An account of an Ohio man wrongfully accused of the murder of a Texas policeman and the 12 years he spent in jail before his retrial and release. (Rev: LJ 6/15/91; NYTBR 7/21/91) **[345.73]**

1254 **Adler, Renata.** *Reckless Disregard: Westmoreland v. CBS et al; Sharon v. Time.* 1988, **Random paper $6.95** (0-394-75525-1). A study of the libel suits brought by military figures Westmoreland and Sharon against media powers CBS and Time and the trials that followed in 1984 and 1985. (Rev: BL 12/1/86; LJ 2/1/87; Natl Rev 4/10/87) **[345.73]**

1255 **Coll, Steve, and David Vise.** *Eagle on the Street: Based on the Pulitzer Prize-Winning Account of the SEC's Battle with Wall Street.* 1991, **Scribner $24.95** (0-684-19314-0). A historical analysis of the internal working of the Securities and Exchange Commission and its relationship with Wall Street traders during the 1980s. "A spellbinding account."—NYTBR (Rev: BL 10/1/91; NYTBR 11/3/91. Awards: BL, 1991) **[345.73]**

1256 Dershowitz, Alan M. *Best Defense*. 1983, Random paper $7.95 (0-394-71380-X). Reflections upon the practice of law and the American legal system by the Harvard Law School professor and attorney. (Rev: BL 6/1/82; NYRB 6/24/82; PW 4/9/82) **[345.73]**

1257 Dershowitz, Alan M. *Reversal of Fortune: Inside the Von Bulow Case*. 1986, Random $19.95 (0-394-53903-6); paper $4.95 (0-671-70724-8). An inside account of the second trial of Claus Von Bulow as related by his defense attorney. (Rev: BL 2/15/86; LJ 4/1/86; New Rep 6/16/86) **[345.73]**

1258 Farber, Stephen. *Outrageous Conduct: Art, Ego and the Twilight Zone Case*. 1988, Morrow $18.95 (0-87795-948-X); Ivy Books paper $4.95 (0-8041-0478-6). A study of the manslaughter case arising from the death of three actors during the filming of *Twilight Zone: The Movie*. (Rev: BL 5/1/88; LJ 9/1/88; NYTBR 9/25/88) **[345.73]**

1259 Faux, Marian. *Roe vs. Wade: The Story of the Landmark Supreme Court Decision That Made Abortion Legal*. 1988, Macmillan $22.50 (0-02-537151-7); NAL paper $4.95 (0-451-62719-9). A study of the events that led to the controversial 1973 Supreme Court ruling that legalized abortion in the United States. (Rev: Choice 12/88; LJ 6/1/88; NYTBR 6/26/88) **[345.73]**

1260 Fletcher, George P. *A Crime of Self-Defense: Bernhard Goetz and the Law on Trial*. 1988, Free Pr. $19.95 (0-02-910311-8). An examination of the facts and issues raised by the trial and acquittal of Bernhard Goetz. "A fascinating book—disturbing and edifying."—BL (Rev: Choice 12/88; CSM 7/14/77; LJ 7/88) **[345.73]**

1261 Forer, Lois G. *A Chilling Effect: The Growing Threat of Libel and Invasion of Privacy Actions to the First Amendment*. 1987, Norton $18.95 (0-393-02396-6); paper $9.95 (0-393-30566-X). A judge's view of prominent libel cases and their potential threat to erode First Amendment rights. (Rev: BL 5/1/87; LJ 6/1/87; NYTBR 6/14/87) **[345.73]**

1262 Gaylin, Willard. *Killing of Bonnie Garland: A Question of Justice*. 1983, Penguin paper $8.95 (0-14-006727-2). A study of the murder of a Yale co-ed by her boyfriend and his use of the insanity defense during his trial to receive a lesser sentence for his crime. (Rev: BL 6/1/82; PW 4/9/82; Time 6/21/82) **[345.73]**

1263 Hans, Valerie P., and Neil Vidmar. *Judging the Jury*. 1986, Plenum $19.95 (0-306-42255-7). A historical and contemporary study of the development and function of the American jury system. (Rev: Choice 9/86; LJ 6/1/86; PW 4/11/86) **[345.73]**

1264 Kunen, James S. *How Can You Defend Those People? The Making of a Criminal Lawyer*. 1985, McGraw-Hill paper $7.95 (0-07-035631-9). Memoirs of a former Washington D.C. public defender concerning the theory and practice of his occupa-

tion. (Rev: LJ 3/1/84; NYTBR 11/20/83; PW 9/16/83) **[345.73]**

1265 Loftus, Elizabeth, and Katherine Ketcham. *Witness for the Defense*. 1991, St. Martin's $19.95 (0-312-05537-4). A study of human memory and its role and accuracy in the American judicial process. (Rev: LJ 3/15/91; PW 2/8/91) **[345.73]**

1266 Rubin, Ellis, and Dary Matera. *Get Me Ellis Rubin! The Life, Times and Cases of a Maverick Lawyer*. 1989, St. Martin's $19.95 (0-312-03352-4). The Miami trial attorney recounts a dozen of his most challenging cases. "An absorbing read, sure to intrigue all courtroom aficionados."—LJ (Rev: BL 11/1/89; LJ 10/1/89; PW 10/20/89) **[345.73]**

1267 Smolla, Rodney A. *Jerry Falwell v. Larry Flynt: The First Amendment on Trial*. 1988, St. Martin's $18.95 (0-312-02225-5); Univ. of Illinois Pr. paper $12.95 (0-252-06151-9). An examination of the case in which Reverend Falwell sued the publisher of *Hustler* magazine for an allegedly libelous parody that appeared in the publication. (Rev: BL 11/15/89; LJ 12/88; NYTBR 3/5/89) **[345.73]**

1268 Stewart, James B. *Prosecutors: Inside the Offices of the Government's Most Powerful Lawyers*. 1988, Simon & Schuster paper $8.95 (0-671-68835-8). Studies of six white-collar criminal cases and the federal lawyers who prosecuted them. (Rev: BL 9/15/87; LJ 9/15/87; NYTBR 9/27/87) **[345.73]**

Northeastern United States

1269 Heilbroner, David. *Rough Justice: Days and Nights of a Young D.A.* 1990, Pantheon $19.95 (0-394-58191-1). Accounts of the author's experiences as a New York district attorney. (Rev: LJ 7/90; NYTBR 9/30/90; Newsweek 8/27/90) **[345.74]**

1270 Trilling, Diana. *Mrs. Harris: The Death of the Scarsdale Diet Doctor*. 1981, Harcourt $14.95 (0-15-176902-8); Penguin paper $4.95 (0-14-006363-3). The murder of Dr. Herman Tarnower by his mistress and the account of her subsequent trial and conviction. "A work of social criticism that reads like a novel . . . the best nonfiction trade book of the year."—Time (Rev: LJ 11/15/81; New Rep 11/4/81; Time 10/19/81. Awards: Time, 1981) **[345.74]**

346 Private law

1271 Fehrenbacher, Don E. *Dred Scott Case: Its Significance in American Law and Politics*. 1978, Oxford Univ. Pr. $39.95 (0-19-502403-6). "By far the best book ever written on the celebrated case."—Choice (Rev: Choice 3/79; LJ 10/1/78; Natl Rev 3/2/79. Awards: PP:History, 1979) **[346]**

Persons and domestic relations

1272 Bernard, Mitchell. *Rights of Single People*. 1985, Southern Illinois Univ. Pr. paper $4.95 (0-8093-9956-3). An ACLU primer on the legal rights of single people in the United States. (Rev: BL 2/1/85; LJ 2/15/85) **[346.01]**

1273 Chesler, Phyllis. *Mothers on Trial: The Battle for Children and Custody.* 1985, McGraw-Hill $22.95 (0-07-010701-7). A critical account of current child custody and protection laws that treat mothers unfairly. (Rev: LJ 1/86; PW 11/29/85)   **[346.01]**

1274 Shalev, Carmel. *Birth Power: The Case for Surrogacy.* 1989, Yale Univ. Pr. $19.95 (0-300-04216-7). A feminist argument for the legalization of surrogate motherhood. "This book cannot and should not be ignored."—Choice (Rev: BL 11/15/89; Choice 3/90; NYTBR 12/17/89)   **[346.01]**

Wills (Testate succession)

1275 Clifford, Denis. *Nolo's Simple Will Book.* Ed. by Stephen Elias. 1989, Nolo Pr. paper $17.95 (0-87337-123-2). A do-it-yourself guide to will preparation without an attorney. (Rev: BL 10/15/86; LJ 11/1/86)   **[346.054]**

Administration of estates

1276 Goldsmith, Barbara. *Johnson vs. Johnson.* 1987, Knopf $18.95 (0-394-56043-4); Dell paper $4.95 (0-440-20041-5). A history of the family that founded the American pharmaceutical company and of the legal struggle that ensued when the terms of the will of the heir to the fortune were announced. (Rev: BL 2/15/87; LJ 5/1/87; Time 4/13/87)   **[346.056]**

United States

1277 Esperti, Robert A., and Renno L. Peterson. *Loving Trust: The Right Way to Provide for Yourself and Guarantee the Future of Your Loved Ones.* 1988, Viking $22.50 (0-670-81881-X). A guide to the preparation and execution of a loving trust for the financial security of the trustee and his or her family. (Rev: BL 5/1/88; LJ 6/15/88; PW 3/18/88)   **[346.73]**

1278 Forer, Lois G. *Unequal Protection: Women, Children, and the Elderly in Court.* 1991, Norton $22.95 (0-393-02949-2). A survey of the ways the American judicial system discriminates against gender and age. (Rev: BL 3/1/91; LJ 3/1/91; PW 2/1/91)   **[346.73]**

1279 Herman, Stephen P. *Parent vs. Parent: How You and Your Child Can Survive the Custody Battle.* 1990, Pantheon $20.95 (0-394-57173-8). A child psychiatrist discusses custody suits and their effects on family members. (Rev: BL 10/1/90; LJ 10/1/90)   **[346.73]**

1280 National Parks and Conservation Association Staff. *Our Common Lands: Defending the National Parks.* Ed. by David J. Simon. 1988, Island Pr. $45.00 (0-933280-58-0); paper $24.95 (0-933280-57-2). A collection of 18 essays by legal experts regarding legislation designed to protect the environment. (Rev: Choice 5/89; LJ 11/15/88)   **[346.73]**

1281 Sitarz, Daniel. *Divorce Yourself: The No-Fault, No-Lawyer Divorce Handbook.* 1990, Nova paper $24.95 (0-935755-05-5). A do-it-yourself divorce guide covering the laws and legal forms of all 50 states. (Rev: BL 8/90; LJ 6/15/90)   **[346.73]**

1282 Smolla, Rodney A. *Suing the Press: Libel and the Media.* 1986, Oxford Univ. Pr. $21.95 (0-19-503901-7); $9.95 paper (0-19-505192-0). A study of recent libel and slander cases testing the protection offered by the First Amendment. (Rev: Choice 10/86; LJ 6/15/86; NYTBR 6/8/86)   **[346.73]**

1283 Weitzman, Lenore J. *Divorce Revolution: The Unexpected Social and Economic Consequences for Women and Children in America.* 1985, Free Pr. $24.95 (0-02-934710-6); paper $14.95 (0-02-934711-4). A study of the legal and social ramifications of changing divorce laws upon American women and children. (Rev: Choice 2/86; LJ 10/1/85; NYTBR 10/13/85)   **[346.73]**

1284 Woodhouse, Violet. *Divorce and Money: Everything You Need to Know about Dividing Property.* 1992, Nolo Pr. paper $19.95 (0-87337-143-7). A guide to solving financial problems associated with divorce. (Rev: BL 1/15/91; LJ 1/92)   **[346.73]**

347   Civil procedure and courts

United States

1285 Bork, Robert H. *Tempting of America: The Political Seduction of the Law.* 1989, Free Pr. $22.50 (0-02-903761-1). The judge's analysis and commentary regarding the events that led to his rejection as Reagan's nominee to the Supreme Court. "A lucid, elegant, provocative work of legal scholarship . . . accessible to the general reader."—NYTBR (Rev: LJ 11/1/89; Natl Rev 12/22/89; NYTBR 11/19/89)   **[347.73]**

1286 Bronner, Ethan. *Battle for Justice: The Bork Defeat and the End of the Reagan Era.* 1989, Norton $22.50 (0-393-02690-6); Doubleday paper $12.95 (0-385-41549-4). An account of Reagan's nomination of Judge Robert Bork to the Supreme Court and his rejection by Congress following a national grassroots anti-Bork campaign. (Rev: BL 9/1/89; LJ 9/1/89; NYTBR 9/10/89)   **[347.73]**

1287 Caplan, Lincoln. *Tenth Justice: The Solicitor General and the Rule of Law.* 1987, Knopf $19.95 (0-394-55523-6); Random paper $9.95 (0-394-75955-9). An examination of the role of the solicitor general in representing the U.S. government before the Supreme Court. (Rev: Choice 3/88; LJ 11/15/87; NYTBR 10/25/87)   **[347.73]**

1288 Cox, Archibald. *Court and the Constitution.* 1989, State Mutual $80.00; Houghton paper $8.95 (0-395-48071-X). The former Watergate Special Prosecutor presents a historical survey of the Supreme Court's interpretation of the United States Constitution. (Rev: Choice 11/87; LJ 8/87; Natl Rev 8/28/87. Awards: LJ, 1987)   **[347.73]**

1289 Dunne, Gerald T. *Hugo Black and the Judicial Revolution.* 1977, Irvington $36.50 (0-8290-0344-4). An examination of Black's career in the Supreme Court. "Dunne's masterful achievement will properly be regarded as *the* public biography."—LJ (Rev: LJ 2/15/77; PW 1/17/77; Sat Rev 3/5/77)   **[347.73]**

1290 Fried, Charles. *Order and Law: Arguing the Reagan Revolution.* **1991, Simon & Schuster $19.95 (0-671-72575-0).** Memoirs of Reagan's solicitor general regarding his years representing the executive branch before the U.S. Supreme Court. (Rev: BL 4/15/91; LJ 4/15/91; NYTBR 5/19/91) **[347.73]**

1291 Grodin, Joseph R. *In Pursuit of Justice: Reflections of a State Supreme Justice.* **1989, Univ. of California Pr. $20.00 (0-520-06654-5).** A view of judges and the current judiciary system by a former member of the California Supreme Court. (Rev: Choice 12/89; LJ 6/1/89) **[347.73]**

1292 Murphy, Bruce Allen. *Brandeis-Frankfurter Connection: The Secret Political Activities of Two Supreme Court Justices.* **1982, Oxford Univ. Pr. $27.95 (0-19-503122-9).** An investigation into questionable political dealings by U.S. Supreme Court Justices Felix Frankfurter and Louis Brandeis. (Rev: BL 6/1/82; Choice 9/82; Time 3/8/82) **[347.73]**

1293 Murphy, Bruce Allen. *Fortas: The Rise and Ruin of a Supreme Court Justice.* **1988, Morrow $25.00 (0-688-05357-2).** An examination of the factors that led Fortas to resign his post as Supreme Court Justice following confirmation hearings that would have raised him to the position of Chief Justice. (Rev: BL 7/88; Choice 12/88; LJ 7/88) **[347.73]**

1294 Neely, Richard. *How Courts Govern America.* **1981, Yale Univ. Pr. paper $11.95 (0-300-02980-2).** A justice of the West Virginia Supreme Court presents his views on the political function of the judiciary and its relationship to the legislative branch of government. (Rev: Choice 12/81; Natl Rev 10/30/81; NYRB 11/19/81. Awards: ALA, 1981) **[347.73]**

1295 O'Brien, David M. *Storm Center: The Supreme Court in American Politics.* **1990, Norton paper $10.95 (0-393-02230-3).** A look at the day-to-day workings of the Supreme Court and its historical role in the U.S. political system. (Rev: Choice 10/86; LJ 7/86; NYTBR 7/27/86) **[347.73]**

1296 Rehnquist, William. *Supreme Court: The Way It Was, the Way It Is.* **1987, Morrow $18.95 (0-688-05714-4).** The Chief Justice of the U.S. Supreme Court provides an insider's look into its past and present role in our government. (Rev: BL 9/15/87; NYTBR 9/20/87; PW 7/31/87) **[347.73]**

1297 Satter, Robert. *Doing Justice: A Trial Judge at Work.* **1990, Simon & Schuster $19.95 (0-671-69152-X); paper $9.95 (0-671-73295-1).** A Connecticut judge recounts memorable cases from his 15 years on the bench. (Rev: Atl 3/90; BL 2/1/90; NYTBR 3/18/90) **[347.73]**

1298 Schwartz, Bernard. *Super Chief: Earl Warren and His Supreme Court.* **1983, NYU Pr. $50.00 (0-8147-7825-9); paper $25.00 (0-8147-7826-7).** A biography of the former chief justice of the Supreme Court investigating both the man and the influence of the Warren Court during and after his tenure. (Rev: Choice 11/83; LJ 4/15/83; TLS 10/28/83) **[347.73]**

1299 Schwartz, Herman, ed. *Burger Years: Rights and Wrongs in the Supreme Court, 1969–1986.*

1987, Viking $22.95 (0-670-81270-6). Selected essays on the legacy of Warren Burger's years as chief justice of the Supreme Court. (Rev: Choice 7–8/87; LJ 3/1/87; NYTBR 6/21/87) **[347.73]**

1300 Simon, James F. *Antagonists: Hugo Black, Felix Frankfurter and Civil Liberties in Modern America.* **1989, Simon & Schuster $19.95 (0-671-47797-8).** A study of the relationship of Supreme Court Justices Felix Frankfurter and Hugo Black and how they shaped the course of American law over the nearly two-and-a-half decades they served together on the court. (Rev: BL 10/1/89; Natl Rev 12/31/89; NYTBR 10/15/89. Awards: BL, 1989) **[347.73]**

1301 Spence, Gerry. *With Justice for None: Destroying an American Myth.* **1989, Random $19.95 (0-8129-1696-4); Penguin paper $9.95 (0-14-013325-9).** The Wyoming attorney examines the deficiencies of justice in the American legal system. (Rev: Atl 6/89; BL 3/1/89; LJ 4/1/89) **[347.73]**

1302 Warner, Ralph. *Everybody's Guide to Small Claims Court.* **1990, Nolo Pr. paper $14.95 (0-87337-120-8).** A guide to the function and legal proceedings of small claims courts. (Rev: BL 4/15/90; LJ 11/1/90) **[347.73]**

1303 Wishman, Seymour. *Anatomy of a Jury: The System on Trial.* **1987, Penguin paper $6.95 (0-14-009851-8).** A study of the processes of an American jury trial as illustrated in a hypothetical case. (Rev: BL 6/15/86; LJ 6/1/86; PW 5/2/86) **[347.73]**

1304 Woodward, Bob, and Scott Armstrong. *Brethren: Inside the Supreme Court.* **1981, Avon paper $5.95 (0-380-52183-0).** A study of the inner workings and personalities on the United States Supreme Court in the early 1970s. (Rev: NYRB 2/7/80; NYTBR 1/20/80; Sat Rev 3/1/80) **[347.73]**

349   Law of specific jurisdictions and areas

United States

1305 Belli, Melvin M., and Allen P. Wilkinson. *Everybody's Guide to the Law.* **1986, Harcourt $19.95 (0-15-142166-8); Harper & Row paper $11.95 (0-06-097121-5).** A layperson's guide to everyday law by the outspoken San Francisco-based attorney. (Rev: BL 11/15/86; LJ 12/86) **[349.73]**

1306 Harnett, Bertram. *Put the Law on Your Side: Strategies for Winning the Legal Game.* **1986, Harper & Row paper $6.95 (0-06-097056-1).** A layperson's guide to the law, legal rights, and legal strategies for frequently encountered problems. (Rev: BL 6/1/85; LJ 5/15/85; PW 5/24/85) **[349.73]**

1307 Jenkins, John A. *Litigators: The Powerful World of America's High-Stakes Trial Lawyers.* **1989, Doubleday $19.95 (0-385-24408-8).** Profiles of six plaintiff trial lawyers who regularly handle million-dollar-plus cases. (Rev: LJ 4/1/89; PW 1/13/89) **[349.73]**

1308 Von Hoffman, Nicholas. *Citizen Cohn: The Life and Times of Roy Cohn.* **1988, Doubleday $19.95 (0-385-23690-5); Bantam paper $5.50 (0-553-**

27893-2). A biography of the American lawyer known for his role in the anti-Communist fervor of the early 1950s as counsel to Senator Joe McCarthy. (Rᴇᴠ: BL 4/1/88; LJ 6/1/88; Time 4/4/88) **[349.73]**

350 PUBLIC ADMINISTRATION

1309 Neustadt, Richard E., and Ernest R. May. *Thinking in Time: The Uses of History for Decision Makers.* 1988, Free Pr. $19.95 (0-02-922790-9); paper $9.95 (0-02-922791-7). Case studies of recent political situations that could have had better results if the active participants had applied the lessons of history. (Rᴇᴠ: Atl 7/86; LJ 3/1/86; New Rep 7/7/86) **[350]**

351 Of central governments

Malfunctioning of administration

1310 Woodward, Bob, and Carl Bernstein. *All the President's Men.* 1987, Simon & Schuster paper $8.95 (0-671-64644-3). The reporters that broke the Watergate scandal for the *Washington Post* tell their story. "A first-rate, firsthand description of big-time journalism."—Choice (Rᴇᴠ: Choice 9/74; LJ 5/15/74; NYTBR 6/9/74) **[351.9]**

353 Of U.S. federal and state governments

1311 Bell, Terrel Howard. *Thirteenth Man: A Reagan Cabinet Memoir.* 1988, Free Pr. $27.95 (0-02-902351-3). Memoirs of a former secretary of education regarding his service under the Reagan administration. (Rᴇᴠ: BL 2/1/88; LJ 2/15/88; NYTBR 3/20/88) **[353]**

1312 Burnham, David. *A Law Unto Itself: Power, Politics and the IRS.* 1990, Random $22.50 (0-394-56097-3); paper $12.95 (0-679-73283-7). A history and analysis of the U.S. Internal Revenue Service and the federal tax system. (Rᴇᴠ: LJ 3/1/90; NYTBR 2/11/90; Time 2/5/90. Awᴀʀᴅs: LJ, 1990) **[353]**

1313 Fisher, Louis. *Presidential Spending Power.* 1975, Princeton Univ. Pr. $44.00 (0-691-07575-1). A historical examination of how the executive branch obtains, manipulates, and uses its funding. (Rᴇᴠ: Choice 1/76; LJ 11/15/75; NYTBR 11/16/75) **[353]**

1314 Gentry, Curt. *J. Edgar Hoover: The Man and the Secrets.* 1991, Norton $29.95 (0-393-02404-0). A biography of the controversial FBI director who reigned over the agency for five decades. (Rᴇᴠ: BL 6/1/91; LJ 8/91; NYTBR 9/15/91) **[353]**

1315 Powers, Richard Gid. *Secrecy and Power: The Life of J. Edgar Hoover.* 1988, Free Pr. $27.95 (0-02-925060-9). A biography of the former head of the Federal Bureau of Investigation by the author of *G-Men: Hoover's FBI in American Popular Culture.* (Rᴇᴠ: CSM 3/6/87; LJ 2/1/87; PW 12/26/87. Awᴀʀᴅs: PW, 1987) **[353]**

1316 Theoharis, Athan G., ed. *From the Secret Files of J. Edgar Hoover.* 1991, I. R. Dee $26.50 (0-929587-67-7). Selected writings from the former FBI director spanning over five decades of his rule from files obtained under the Freedom of Information Act. (Rᴇᴠ: BL 7/91; NYTBR 9/15/91; PW 7/25/91) **[353]**

1317 Theoharis, Athan G., and John S. Cox. *The Boss: J. Edgar Hoover and the Great American Inquisition.* 1988, Temple Univ. Pr. $27.95 (0-87222-532-X); Bantam paper $5.95 (0-533-28539-4). An analysis of the life of J. Edgar Hoover and FBI practices under his command. "They have set a standard no single book on the subject is likely to match."—Choice (Rᴇᴠ: Choice 3/89; LJ 6/1/88; NYTBR 9/11/88) **[353]**

1318 Wilson, James Q. *Bureaucracy: What Government Agencies Do and Why They Do It.* 1989, Basic Books $24.95 (0-465-00784-8); paper $12.95 (0-465-00785-6). A study of the operation and purpose of selected U.S. government agencies. (Rᴇᴠ: BL 11/1/89; Choice 4/90; CSM 11/28/89) **[353]**

The Presidency

1319 Schlesinger, Arthur M., Jr. *Imperial Presidency.* 1989, Houghton paper $12.95 (0-395-51561-0). History of the conflict in power between the executive and legislative branches of the American government concentrating on the abuses of power by the Nixon administration. "Few books in recent times have presented so informed yet balanced a study of the growth of presidential power at the expense of the democratic safeguards built into the Constitution by the Founding Fathers."—PW (Rᴇᴠ: Choice 4/74; PW 10/8/74; Time 11/26/73. Awᴀʀᴅs: ALA, 1973; Time, 1973) **[353.03]**

1320 Tebbel, John, and Sarah M. Watts. *Press and the Presidency: From George Washington to Ronald Reagan.* 1985, Oxford Univ. Pr. $29.95 (0-19-503628-X). A history of the relationship between the American press and the presidents of the United States. (Rᴇᴠ: Choice 4/86; LJ 9/1/85; NYTBR 10/13/85) **[353.03]**

Administration of public finances

1321 Heymann, Philip B. *Politics of Public Management.* 1988, Yale Univ. Pr. paper $9.95 (0-300-04291-4). A guide to the art of public administration and management. (Rᴇᴠ: Choice 11/88; LJ 3/15/88) **[353.07]**

Department of State

1322 Clubb, O. Edmund. *Witness and I.* 1975, Columbia Univ. Pr. $30.00 (0-231-03859-3). Clubb recounts his 24 years in the U.S. Foreign Service and his dismissal for his China reportage during the McCarthy era. (Rᴇᴠ: Choice 6/75; LJ 6/1/75; NYTBR 2/23/75) **[353.1]**

State governments

1323 Osborne, David. *Laboratories of Democracy.* 1990, Harvard Business $24.95 (0-87584-192-9); paper $14.95 (0-87584-233-X). Case studies of successful and innovative state governments during the mid-1980s. (Rᴇᴠ: LJ 8/88; NYTBR 9/18/88; PW 5/13/88) **[353.9]**

354 Of specific central governments

Soviet Union

1324 **Deriabian, Peter, and T. H. Bagley.** *KGB: Masters of the Soviet Union.* **1990, Hippocrene $21.95 (0-87052-804-1).** A history of the KGB and its operations by a former member who served in the organization during the 1940s and 1950s. (REV: BL 1/15/90; PW 12/15/89)   **[354.47]**

Japan

1325 **Packard, Jerrold M.** *Sons of Heaven: A Portrait of the Japanese Monarchy.* **1988, Macmillan $25.00 (0-684-18633-0); paper $12.95 (0-02-023281-0).** A history of the Japanese monarchy from its inception through Emperor Hirohito. (REV: BL 11/15/87; LJ 11/15/87; PW 10/30/87. AWARDS: PW, 1987)   **[354.52]**

355 Military science

1326 **Atkinson, Rick.** *Long Grey Line.* **1989, Houghton $24.95 (0-395-48008-6).** The careers of the West Point class of 1966 following their graduation from the Academy. "A sensitive, stunningly eloquent book."—BL (REV: BL 8/89; LJ 9/15/89; PW 8/11/89)**[355]**

1327 **Barkalow, Carol.** *In the Men's House.* **1990, Poseidon $19.45 (0-671-67312-2).** An account of army training and life by a member of the first class at West Point to have female graduates. (REV: BL 11/15/90; LJ 11/1/90; NYTBR 11/4/90)   **[355]**

1328 **Blumenson, Martin.** *Patton: The Man Behind the Legend, 1885–1945.* **1987, Morrow $17.95 (0-688-06082-X).** A biography of the American general known for his military conquests in North Africa, Sicily, France, and Germany during World War II. (REV: Natl Rev 4/25/86; NYTBR 12/29/85; PW 10/4/85)   **[355]**

1329 **Bruce-Briggs, B.** *Shield of Faith: A Chronicle of Strategic Defense from Zeppelins to Star Wars.* **1988, Simon & Schuster $22.95 (0-671-61086-4); paper $10.95 (0-671-69594-0).** A history of the strategy and implementation of air defense systems in the United States. (REV: BL 11/15/88; Choice 3/89; PW 10/7/88)   **[355]**

1330 **Calleo, David P.** *Beyond American Hegemony: The Future of the Western Alliance.* **1987, Basic Books $20.95 (0-465-00655-8).** A call for the restructuring of NATO due to recent economic and political changes. "A book that every serious student of contemporary international affairs should read."—Paul Kennedy, NYTBR (REV: LJ 10/15/87; NYTBR 11/1/87)   **[355]**

1331 **Cockburn, Andrew.** *Threat: Inside the Soviet Military Machine.* **1984, Random paper $6.95 (0-394-72379-1).** A detailed examination of the Soviet military force and its capabilities; the author concludes that its threat has been exaggerated by the American government for its own purposes. (REV: Atl 5/83; NYTBR 6/26/83; Newsweek 5/16/83) **[355]**

1332 **Cohen, Roger, and Claudio Gatti.** *In the Eye of the Storm: The Life of General H. Norman Schwarzkopf.* **1991, Farrar $19.95 (0-374-17708-2).** A biography of the military commander of Operation Desert Storm. (REV: BL 9/15/91; NYTBR 8/25/91) **[355]**

1333 **Davis, Benjamin O., Jr.** *Benjamin O. Davis, Jr., American.* **1991, Smithsonian $19.95 (0-87474-742-2).** An autobiography of the Air Force general who became the first African American to graduate from West Point. (REV: BL 2/1/91; LJ 3/1/91; PW 1/4/91)   **[355]**

1334 **Ellis, Joseph, and Robert Moore.** *School for Soldiers: An Inquiry into West Point.* **1974, Oxford Univ. Pr. $21.95 (0-19-501843-5); paper $5.95 (0-19-502022-7).** Two former West Point instructors discuss the education methods used at the school to train future military leaders. (REV: Choice 2/75; NYTBR 10/27/75; PW 9/9/74)   **[355]**

1335 **Fallows, James.** *National Defense.* **1981, Random $12.95 (0-394-51824-1); paper $6.95 (0-394-75306-2).** A critical look at America's national defense system focusing on strategy, personnel, and spending. (REV: LJ 6/1/81; NYTBR 6/28/81; Sat Rev 6/81. AWARDS: ALA, 1981; NBA, 1983)   **[355]**

1336 **Farwell, Byron.** *Eminent Victorian Soldiers: Seekers of Glory.* **1988, Norton paper $7.95 (0-393-30533-3).** Profiles of eight Victorian military leaders of the British Empire. (REV: BL 5/1/85; Natl Rev 3/28/86; NYTBR 6/16/85)   **[355]**

1337 **Hadley, Arthur Twining.** *Straw Giant: America's Armed Forces.* **1986, Random $19.95 (0-394-55181-8); Avon paper $10.95 (0-380-70391-2).** An analysis of the decline of America's military strength following World War II. (REV: Choice 11/86; NYTBR 7/13/86; Newsweek 7/21/86)   **[355]**

1338 **Herken, Gregg.** *Counsels of War.* **$10.95, Oxford Univ. Pr. paper 1987 (0-19-504986-1).** A history of the nuclear era from the viewpoint of those scientists and politicians who directed nuclear development and strategy. (REV: BL 2/15/85; Choice 7–8/85; New Rep 4/22/85)   **[355]**

1339 **Kahn, Herman.** *Thinking About the Unthinkable in the 1980s.* **1985, Simon & Schuster $8.95 (0-671-47544-4).** An analysis of nuclear weaponry and its military and strategic applications by the author of *On Thermonuclear War.* (REV: BL 6/1/84; Choice 2/85; PW 6/1/84)   **[355]**

1340 **Keegan, John, and Richard Holmes.** *Soldiers: A History of Men in Battle.* **1986, Viking $22.95 (0-670-80969-1).** A historical survey of the combat experience of soldiers. (REV: LJ 2/1/86; NYTBR 3/23/86; PW 1/31/86)   **[355]**

1341 **Lee, David D.** *Sergeant York: An American Hero.* **1985, Univ. Pr. of Kentucky $18.00 (0-8131-1517-5).** A biography of the legendary Tennessee soldier who distinguished himself by his heroic actions against German troops in the Argonne Forest. "A highlight of American World War I literature."—LJ (REV: BL 6/15/85; Choice 9/85; LJ 1/85)   **[355]**

1342 Luttwak, Edward N. *Pentagon and the Art of War: The Question of Military Reform.* 1986, Simon & Schuster paper $8.95 (0-671-61770-2). A study of the lack of direction and mismanagement within the U.S. military establishment. (Rev: BL 2/15/85; New Rep 3/4/85; Newsweek 4/1/85)   **[355]**

1343 Miller, Merle. *Ike the Soldier: As They Knew Him.* 1988, Putnam paper $13.95 (0-399-51483-X). A study of the life of Eisenhower from his birth through his decision to run for the presidency. Based on interviews and his unpublished papers. (Rev: BL 10/15/87; NYTBR 12/20/87; PW 10/2/87)   **[355]**

1344 Mueller, John. *Retreat from Doomsday: The Obsolescence of Major War.* 1989, Basic Books $20.95 (0-465-06939-8); paper $11.95 (0-465-06940-1). An analysis of modern warfare maintaining that its costliness and abhorrent nature has helped keep the world free from major war since 1945. (Rev: LJ 4/15/89; NYTBR 4/30/89)   **[355]**

1345 Nalty, Bernard C. *Strength for the Fight: A History of Black Americans in the Military.* 1986, Free Pr. $22.50 (0-02-922410-1); paper $12.95 (0-02-922411-X). A survey of the contributions of African Americans to the American military from colonial times to the present. (Rev: BL 5/15/86; LJ 5/15/86; NYTBR 6/22/86)   **[355]**

1346 Newhouse, John. *War and Peace in the Nuclear Age.* 1989, Knopf $22.95 (0-394-56217-8); Random paper $16.95 (0-679-72645-4). A review of the events and strategies of the nuclear era and the effects the bomb has had on international foreign relations. (Rev: BL 11/15/88; LJ 1/89; NYTBR 1/22/89)   **[355]**

1347 Nolan, Janne E. *Guardians of the Arsenal: The Politics of Nuclear Strategy.* 1989, Basic Books $21.95 (0-465-09802-9). An analysis of American nuclear strategy from Truman to Reagan. "An excellent review."—BL (Rev: BL 9/15/89; LJ 9/15/89; PW 9/15/89)   **[355]**

1348 Paret, Peter, and Gordon A. Craig, eds. *Makers of Modern Strategy from Machiavelli to the Nuclear Age.* 1985, Princeton Univ. Pr. $59.00 (0-691-05448-7); paper $14.95 (0-691-02764-1). Collected essays regarding the history of military strategy from the sixteenth century to the twentieth. (Rev: Choice 9/86; LJ 5/1/86; NYTBR 4/13/86)   **[355]**

1349 Scheer, Robert. *With Enough Shovels: Reagan, Bush and Nuclear War.* 1983, Random paper $4.95 (0-394-72203-5). An examination of the nuclear strategy of the Reagan administration revealing a plan for a winnable nuclear war with the Soviet Union. (Rev: LJ 12/15/82; NYTBR 11/28/82; Newsweek 2/7/83)   **[355]**

1350 Schell, Jonathan. *Fate of the Earth.* 1982, Knopf $19.95 (0-394-52559-0); Avon paper $4.95 (0-380-61325-5). A description of the horrors of nuclear war, and an argument for the elimination of nuclear weaponry. "A work of enormous force . . . an event of profound historical moment."—NYTBR (Rev: BL 4/15/82; NYTBR 4/11/82; New Rep 4/28/82. Awards: ALA, 1982; NYTBR, 1982)   **[355]**

1351 Seabury, Paul, and Angelo Codevilla. *War: Ends and Means.* 1989, Basic Books $19.95 (0-465-09067-2); paper $11.95 (0-465-09068-0). An analysis of the causes of war and its role in human history and society. (Rev: LJ 6/1/89; Natl Rev 7/14/89; NYRB 8/17/89)   **[355]**

1352 Smith, Jean Edward. *Lucius D. Clay: An American Life.* 1990, Henry Holt $35.00 (0-8050-0999-X). A biography of the American general noted for his direction of the 1947–1948 Berlin Airlift. (Rev: BL 9/1/90; LJ 8/90; NYTBR 7/29/90)   **[355]**

1353 Smith, William Jay. *Army Brat.* 1980, Persea Books $15.95 (0-89255-047-3). Memoirs of the author's childhood spent on an army base in Missouri where his father served as a corporal. (Rev: NYRB 11/20/88; NYTBR 11/16/80; PW 8/29/80)   **[355]**

1354 Smythe, Donald. *Pershing: General of the Armies.* 1986, Indiana Univ. Pr. $35.00 (0-253-34381-X). A biography of the Spanish-American War veteran who became military commander of the United States' forces in World War I. (Rev: BL 4/15/86; LJ 4/1/86; NYTBR 9/28/86)   **[355]**

1355 York, Herbert F. *Advisors: Oppenheimer, Teller and the Superbomb.* 1989, Stanford Univ. Pr. $32.50 (0-8047-1713-3); paper $8.95 (0-8047-1714-1). An analysis of the decision to develop the hydrogen bomb by a physicist who participated in the debate. (Rev: Choice 4/76; LJ 4/15/76; NYTBR 3/28/76)   **[355]**

War and warfare

1356 Lifton, Robert Jay, and Eric Markusen. *Genocidal Mentality: Nazi Holocaust and Nuclear Threat.* 1990, Basic Books $22.95 (0-465-02662-1). An examination of the psychological and moral ramifications of mankind's potential annihilation from nuclear war. (Rev: BL 4/1/90; LJ 4/15/90; NYTBR 5/27/90)   **[355.02]**

1357 Paulson, Dennis, ed. *Voices of Survival in the Nuclear Age.* 1988, Borgo Pr. $22.95 (0-8095-4024-X). Essays by 125 people on the threat of nuclear annihilation and its effects on their lives. (Rev: BL 10/15/86; LJ 10/1/86; PW 8/29/86)   **[355.02]**

Military resources

1358 Gioglio, Gerald R. *Days of Decision: An Oral History of Conscientious Objectors in the Military during the Vietnam War.* 1989, Broken Rifle Pr. paper $14.95 (0-9620024-0-2). An oral history of 22 conscientious objectors who served in the military in non-battle capacities during the Vietnam War. "A powerful document of resistance . . . major anti-war literature."—BL (Rev: BL 3/1/89; Choice 10/89. Awards: BL, 1989)   **[355.2]**

Human resources

1359 Saywell, Shelley. *Women in War: First-Hand Accounts.* 1987, Penguin paper $6.95 (0-14-007623-9). Profiles of 22 women who served in combat situations in the world's wars since 1945. (Rev: BL 10/15/85; LJ 12/85; PW 11/8/85)   **[355.22]**

Organization and personnel of military forces

1360   Black, Ian, and Benny Morris. *Israel's Secret Wars: The Untold History of Israel's Intelligence Services.* **1991, Grove-Weidenfeld $24.95 (0-8021-1159-9).** A history of the triumphs and failures of Israeli intelligence from the founding of the nation to the present. (REV: LJ 6/1/91; NYTBR 6/30/91; PW 4/26/91)   **[355.3]**

1361   Chace, James, and Caleb Carr. *America Invulnerable: The Quest for Absolute Security from 1812 to Star Wars.* **1988, Summit $19.95 (0-671-61778-8); paper $12.95 (0-671-68876-6).** An overview of American foreign policy and national defense strategies from the War of 1812 to the Reagan administration's Strategic Defense Initiative. (REV: BL 3/15/88; LJ 3/15/88; PW 2/5/88)   **[355.3]**

1362   Keegan, John. *Mask of Command.* **1987, Viking $18.95 (0-670-45988-7); Penguin paper (0-14-011406-8).** A study of four different types of military leadership exemplified by Grant, Hitler, Wellington, and Alexander the Great. (REV: Atl 1/88; BL 10/15/87; Newsweek 12/14/87)   **[355.3]**

1363   McPhee, John. *La Place de la Concorde Suisse.* **1984, Farrar $12.95 (0-374-18241-8); paper $6.95 (0-374-51932-3).** An analysis of the national defense system and civilian army of Switzerland. (REV: CSM 5/18/84; LJ 4/15/84; NYTBR 5/6/84)   **[355.3]**

1364   Manchester, William. *American Caesar: Douglas MacArthur, 1880–1964.* **1978, Little, Brown $29.95 (0-316-54498-1); Dell paper $12.95 (0-440-30424-5).** A biography of the outstanding general of World Wars I and II, and the Korean War. "Manchester's book is gracefully written, impeccably researched and scrupulous in every way."— Newsweek (REV: Choice 2/79; New Rep 9/30/78; Newsweek 9/11/78. AWARDS: ALA, 1978; Time, 1978)   **[355.3]**

1365   Porch, Douglas. *French Foreign Legion.* **1991, HarperCollins $40.00 (0-06-016652-5).** A history of the French elite combat force. "Captures the romance, mystery and drama of the Legion as well as the iron at its core."—PW (REV: LJ 6/1/91; NYTBR 7/14/91; PW 5/24/91)   **[355.3]**

1366   Suvorov, Viktor. *Inside the Aquarium: The Making of a Top Soviet Spy.* **1987, Berkley paper $3.95 (0425-09474-X).** Memoirs of a former Soviet military intelligence agent who defected to England. (REV: LJ 4/15/86; NYTBR 5/11/86; TLS 8/30/85)   **[355.3]**

Military operations

1367   Allen, Thomas B. *War Games.* **McGraw-Hill; Berkley paper $4.95 (0-425-11647-6).** A study of the tradition and present state of the military's simulated war games by the author of *Rickover.* (REV: Choice 10/87; CSM 12/16/87; LJ 7/87)   **[355.4]**

1368   Connell, Evan S. *Son of the Morning Star: Custer and the Little Bighorn.* **1984, North Point $20.00 (0-86547-160-6); Harper & Row paper $10.95 (0-06-097003-0).** Connell's story of the how and why of the Battle of the Little Bighorn. It was labelled

"a new American classic."—Kenneth Turan, Time. (REV: Atl 10/84; LJ 9/1/84; NYTBR 1/20/85. AWARDS: ALA, 1984; Time, 1984; Time, the 1980s)   **[355.4]**

Nuclear operations

1369   McNamara, Robert S. *Blundering into Disaster: Surviving the First Century of the Nuclear Age.* **1987, Pantheon $14.95 (0-394-55850-2); paper $5.95 (0-394-74987-1).** An analysis of nuclear strategy and its dangerous fallacies by the former U.S. secretary of defense. (REV: CSM 11/25/86; LJ 11/1/86; NYTBR 11/16/86)   **[355.43]**

Technical analyses of military events

1370   Ground Zero Staff. *Nuclear War: What's in It for You?* **1986, Pocket paper $4.50 (0-671-63753-3).** A primer on nuclear weaponry and its effects by a nonpartisan group dedicated to educating laypersons. (REV: BL 6/15/82; LJ 5/15/82; PW 3/12/82)   **[355.48]**

Military administration

1371   Weiner, Tim. *Blank Check: The Pentagon's Black Budget.* **1990, Warner $21.45 (0-446-51452-7).** A study of the Pentagon's unaccounted for appropriations for secret projects. (REV: BL 9/1/90; LJ 8/90; NYTBR 9/16/90)   **[355.6]**

358   Other specialized forces and services

1372   Lakoff, Sanford, and Herbert F. York. *A Shield in Space: Technology, Politics and the Strategic Defense Initiative.* **1989, Univ. of California Pr. $35.00 (0-520-06650-2).** A critical evaluation of the Strategic Defense Initiative arguing against its feasibility. (REV: Choice 5/90; LJ 12/89; New Rep 1/29/90)   **[358]**

Air forces and warfare

1373   Kotz, Nick. *Wild Blue Yonder: Money, Politics and the B-1 Bomber.* **1988, Pantheon $19.95 (0-394-55700-X); Princeton Univ. Pr. paper $9.95 (0-691-02306-9).** A study of the 30 years of debate over the design and construction of the B-1 bomber, and of the political and economic factors behind U.S. military decision-making. (REV: Choice 6/88; LJ 5/1/88; NYTBR 3/6/88)   **[358.4]**

1374   Samson, Jack. *Chennault.* **(0-385-23171-7); Doubleday paper $19.95.** A biography of the U.S. Air Force general known for his command of the Flying Tigers during World War II. (REV: BL 10/1/87; LJ 11/15/87; NYTBR 11/29/87)   **[358.4]**

1375   Sherry, Michael S. *Rise of American Air Power: The Creation of Armageddon.* **1987, Yale Univ. Pr. $29.95 (0-300-03600-0); paper $14.95 (0-300-04414-3).** A history of the development of American military air power. "Massive and magisterial . . . a seminal volume on the subject."—BL (REV: BL 4/1/87; Choice 10/87; LJ 5/1/87)   **[358.4]**

Space forces and warfare

1376   Burrows, William E. *Deep Black: Space Espionage and National Security.* **1987, Random $22.50**

(0-394-54124-3); Berkley paper $4.95 (0-425-10879-1). An examination of the evolution of America's space information gathering systems. "Wonderfully readable."—CSM (Rev: BL 1/1/87; CSM 8/7/87; NYTBR 2/15/87)   **[358.8]**

359   Sea (Naval) forces and warfare

1377   **Hagan, Kenneth J. *This People's Navy: The Making of American Sea Power.* 1990, Free Pr. $27.95 (0-02-913470-6).** An overview of the political, technological, and strategic development of the United States Navy. (Rev: BL 11/15/90; NYTBR 1/27/91; PW 11/2/90)   **[359]**

1378   **Keegan, John. *Price of Admiralty: The Evolution of Naval Warfare.* 1989, Viking $21.95 (0-670-81416-4); Penguin paper $9.95 (0-14-009650-7).** The British military historian's accounts of four key naval war engagements from the Battle of Trafalgar to the Second World War. (Rev: Atl 4/89; LJ 2/1/89; Newsweek 4/3/89)   **[359]**

1379   **Lehman, John F. *Command of the Seas: A Personal Story.* 1989, Macmillan $21.95 (0-684-18995-X).** A study of American naval policies and strategies by Reagan's former secretary of the navy. (Rev: CSM 1/9/89; LJ 4/1/89; NYTBR 2/19/89) **[359]**

1380   **Maloney, Linda M. *Captain from Connecticut: The Life and Naval Times of Isaac Hull.* 1986, Northeastern Univ. Pr. $47.50 (0-930350-90-1).** A biography of the American naval officer who commanded the USS *Constitution* during the War of 1812. (Rev: Choice 12/86; LJ 9/15/86)   **[359]**

1381   **Polmar, Thomas, and Thomas P. Allen. *Rickover: Controversy and Genius.* 1982, Nautical and Aviation $15.95.** A biography of the admiral who was largely responsible for the development of America's nuclear submarine fleet. (Rev: BL 12/15/81; LJ 1/15/82; NYRB 4/1/82)   **[359]**

1382   **Potter, E. B. *Admiral Arleigh Burke: A Biography.* 1990, Random $24.95 (0-394-58424-4).** A biography of the American World War II Pacific naval commander who became chief of naval operations in 1955. (Rev: BL 4/1/90; LJ 3/15/90; PW 2/23/90)   **[359]**

Organization and personnel of naval forces

1383   **Pocock, Tom. *Horatio Nelson.* 1988, Knopf $22.95 (0-394-57056-1).** A biography of the English admiral best known for his defeat of the French and Spanish fleets at the Battle of Trafalgar in 1806. (Rev: BL 4/15/88; LJ 4/15/88; TLS 12/25/87) **[359.3]**

1384   **Wilson, George C. *Supercarrier: An Inside Account of Life on the World's Most Powerful Ship, the U.S.S. John F. Kennedy.* 1986, Macmillan $19.95 (0-02-630120-2); Berkley paper $3.95 (0-425-10926-7).** A journalist's account of his seven months aboard an American aircraft carrier. (Rev: BL 8/86; LJ 8/86; PW 6/27/86)   **[359.3]**

Naval operations

1385   **Beach, Edward L. *United States Navy: A 200 Year History.* 1990, Houghton paper $12.95 (0-395-**

55996-0). A history of the American Navy by the author of *Run Silent, Run Deep.* "With this . . . book he takes his place among the great names of American historical writing."—CSM (Rev: BL 2/15/86; CSM 6/19/86; PW 4/11/86)   **[359.4]**

Specialized combat forces

1386   **Bradlee, Ben, Jr. *Guts and Glory: The Oliver North Story.* 1988, Donald I. Fine $21.95 (1-55611-053-7).** A biography of the Marine Lieutenant Colonel examining his role in the Iran-Contra scandal. (Rev: BL 6/1/88; LJ 8/88; NYTBR 7/3/88)   **[359.9]**

1387   **Parry, Francis Fox. *Three-War Marine: Pacific-Korea-Vietnam.* 1987, Pacifica Pr. $22.95 (0-935553-02-9); Jove paper $3.95 (0-515-09872-8).** An autobiography of a U.S. Marine who served in the Pacific Theater during World War II and saw action in both Korea and Vietnam. "A perceptive self-portrait of the best sort of soldier."—BL (Rev: BL 9/1/87; PW 8/17/87)   **[359.9]**

360   SOCIAL SERVICES: ASSOCIATIONS

361   General social problems and welfare

1388   **Ignatieff, Michael. *Needs of Strangers.* $6.95, Penguin paper 1986 (0-14-008681-1).** An examination of human needs and societal obligations to meet them. "A delightful book that treats its subject with wit and learning."—LJ (Rev: BL 2/1/85; LJ 2/1/85; New Rep 5/13/85)   **[361]**

1389   **Kotz, Nick, and Mary L. Kotz. *A Passion for Equality: George Wiley and the Movement.* 1977, Norton $8.95 (0-393-07517-6).** A biography of the civil rights leader who was formerly involved with the Congress of Racial Equality and then founded the National Welfare Rights Organization. (Rev: CSM 1/18/78; NYTBR 9/4/77; PW 6/27/77)   **[361]**

Social action

1390   **Hollender, Jeffrey A. *How to Make the World a Better Place: A Beginner's Guide to Doing Good.* 1990, Morrow $19.95 (0-688-09577-1); paper $9.95 (0-688-08479-6).** A guide to practical environmental and social activism. (Rev: BL 11/1/89; LJ 1/90) **[361.2]**

1391   **Horwitt, Sanford D. *Let Them Call Me Rebel: Saul Alinsky—His Life and Legacy.* 1989, Knopf $29.95 (0-394-57243-2).** A biography of the political activist and organizer who devoted his life to fighting social injustices. (Rev: BL 10/1/89; LJ 12/89; NYTBR 11/12/89)   **[361.2]**

Social work

1392   **Berkowitz, Bill. *Local Heroes.* 1987, Lexington Books paper $8.95 (0-669-15830-5).** Profiles of 20 individuals who engineered positive changes in their communities. (Rev: Choice 3/88; LJ 10/1/87; PW 10/16/87)   **[361.3]**

Government action

1393 Buckley, William F., Jr. *Gratitude: Reflections on What We Owe to Our Country.* **1990, Random $16.95 (0-394-57674-8).** The *National Review* editor presents his views regarding compulsory nonmilitary national service for young Americans. (Rev: BL 9/1/90; Natl Rev 11/19/90; NYTBR 10/28/90) **[361.6]**

1394 Ellwood, David T. *Poor Support: Poverty in the American Family.* **1988, Basic Books $19.95 (0-465-05996-1).** A critical look at the welfare state in America and how we provide assistance to our nation's impoverished. (Rev: Choice 11/88; LJ 6/15/88; NYTBR 7/31/88) **[361.6]**

1395 Glazer, Nathan. *Limits of Social Policy.* **1988, Harvard Univ. Pr. $22.50 (0-674-53443-3); paper $10.95 (0-674-53444-1).** An analysis of the American government's involvement in social welfare over the past three decades. (Rev: Choice 2/89; LJ 10/15/88; NYTBR 11/6/88) **[361.6]**

1396 Katz, Michael B. *In the Shadow of the Poorhouse: A Social History of Welfare in America.* **1988, Basic Books paper $12.95 (0-465-03226-5).** A historical survey of American governmental efforts to deal with its impoverished citizens. (Rev: BL 9/15/86; LJ 8/86; NYTBR 11/2/86) **[361.6]**

1397 Salins, Peter, ed. *New York Unbound: The City and the Politics of the Future.* **1988, Basil Blackwell $19.95 (1-55786-008-4).** An examination of the present and future economics and politics of New York City by a dozen researchers and city officials. (Rev: LJ 2/1/89; TLS 4/7/89) **[361.6]**

1398 Schorr, Lisbeth, and Daniel Schorr. *Within Our Reach: Breaking the Cycle of Disadvantage and Despair.* **1988, Doubleday $19.95 (0-385-24243-3); paper $9.95 (0-385-24244-1).** A call for increased funding for social service programs for poor young Americans that will allow them to rise out of poverty and become functional members of society. (Rev: LJ 6/15/88; NYTBR 7/17/88; PW 3/11/88) **[361.6]**

Private action

1399 Guerrier, Edith. *An Independent Woman: The Autobiography of Edith Guerrier.* **Ed. by Molly Matson. 1992, Univ. of Massachusetts Pr. $27.50 (0-87023-756-X).** An autobiography of a Boston librarian and social activist who devoted her life to helping the working-class women of New England. (Rev: BL 12/15/91; LJ 1/92; PW 11/29/91) **[361.7]**

1400 Nielsen, Waldemar A. *Golden Donors: A New Anatomy of the Great Foundations.* **1989, Dutton paper $12.95 (0-525-48463-9).** A look at the inner workings and philanthropic activities of America's largest foundations. (Rev: CSM 2/22/86; LJ 12/85; NYTBR 12/29/85) **[361.7]**

1401 Pryor, Elizabeth B. *Clara Barton: Professional Angel.* **1987, Univ. of Pennsylvania Pr. paper $18.95 (0-8122-1273-8).** A biography of the Civil War nurse who founded the American Red Cross. (Rev: Choice 3/88; CSM 1/13/88; LJ 11/1/87) **[361.7]**

By individual philanthropists

1402 Odendahl, Teresa. *Charity Begins at Home: Generosity and Self-Interest Among the Philanthropic Elite.* **1990, Basic Books $22.95 (0-465-00962-X).** An anthropologist's study of reasons and motives behind charity gift giving in the United States. (Rev: Choice 9/90; LJ 3/1/90; PW 1/5/90) **[361.74]**

362 Social welfare problems and services

1403 Kozol, Jonathan. *Rachel and Her Children: Homeless Families in America.* **1988, Crown $17.95 (0-517-56730-X); Fawcett paper $8.95 (0-449-90339-7).** The plight of the homeless in America as told through the stories of several families living in New York welfare hotels and shelters. (Rev: BL 1/1/88; LJ 3/15/88; NYTBR 1/31/88. Awards: LJ, 1988) **[362]**

Physical illness

1404 Bogdanich, Walt. *Great White Lie: How America's Hospitals Betray Our Trust and Endanger Our Lives.* **1991, Simon & Schuster $23.00 (0-671-68452-3).** A scathing portrait of internal corruption and mismanagement within America's hospital system. (Rev: BL 11/1/91; LJ 11/15/91) **[362.1]**

1405 Cole, Harry A., and Martha M. Jablow. *One in a Million.* **1990, Little, Brown $18.95 (0-316-15117-3).** The author presents the story of his wife's coma and the ethical struggles his family underwent before her reawakening. (Rev: BL 2/15/90; LJ 1/90) **[362.1]**

1406 Cousins, Norman. *Healing Heart: Antidotes to Panic and Helplessness.* **1983, Norton $13.95 (0-393-01816-4); Avon paper $4.95 (0-380-69245-7).** An account of the author's recovery from a heart attack through a program of self-determination and regimentation with the assistance of physicians. (Rev: BL 9/1/83; LJ 10/1/83; TLS 3/30/84) **[362.1]**

1407 Cowen, David L., and William H. Helfand. *Pharmacy: An Illustrated History.* **1991, Mosby $75.00 (0-8109-1498-0).** An illustrated overview of the history of pharmacies and pharmacists from ancient times to the present. (Rev: BL 12/15/90; Choice 2/91) **[362.1]**

1408 Craig, Jean. *Between Hello and Goodbye: A Life-Affirming Story of Courage in the Face of Tragedy.* **1990, J. P. Tarcher $18.95 (0-87477-604-X).** Journals the author kept during her husband's two-year fight against cancer. "Rises above the cliches of the genre."—PW (Rev: BL 11/15/90; LJ 12/90; PW 11/16/90) **[362.1]**

1409 Doelp, Alan. *In the Blink of an Eye: Inside a Children's Trauma Center.* **1989, Prentice Hall $17.95 (0-13-131871-3); Fawcett paper $4.95 (0-449-21830-9).** A look inside the Children's Hospital National Medical Center in Washington, D.C. "An extraordinary book . . . utterly fascinating."—BL (Rev: BL 2/1/89; LJ 3/15/89; PW 1/6/89) **[362.1]**

1410 Doernberg, Myrna. *Stolen Mind: The Slow Disappearance of Ray Doernberg.* **1986, Algonquin $14.95 (0-912697-32-6).** An account of the author's husband's fight against a rare mental disorder known as Binswanger's disease. (Rev: BL 4/1/86; LJ 6/1/86; NYTBR 3/23/86) **[362.1]**

1411 Fishman, Steven. *A Bomb in the Brain: A Journalist's True Story of His Brain Disease and of the Surgery and Science That Saved Him.* **1988, Macmillan $19.95 (0-684-18706-X); Avon paper $8.95 (0-380-70898-1).** The author's account of his brain hemorrhage and the neurosurgery required to correct it. "A striking combination of personal memoir and medical history."—BL (Rev: LJ 11/1/88; NYTBR 11/27/88; PW 11/15/88. Awards: LJ, 1988) **[362.1]**

1412 Goshen-Gottstein, Esther. *Recalled to Life: The Story of a Coma.* **1990, Yale Univ. Pr. $25.00 (0-300-04473-9).** An account of the recovery of the author's husband from a four-month-long coma that followed heart surgery. (Rev: BL 8/90; LJ 9/15/90; PW 9/7/90) **[362.1]**

1413 Greene, A. C. *Taking Heart.* **1990, Simon & Schuster $18.95 (0-671-68392-6).** An account of the author's heart transplant at age 64. "A commonsensical low-key account that may help potential transplantees and their families."—BL (Rev: BL 6/1/90; NYTBR 7/8/90; Newsweek 8/6/90) **[362.1]**

1414 Holland, Gail Bernice. *For Sasha, with Love: An Alzheimer's Crusade—The Anne Bashkiroff Story.* **1985, Dembner Books $16.95 (0-934878-54-4); paper $9.95 (0-934878-84-6).** An account of the shattering effects of Alzheimer's disease on a family and marriage. (Rev: BL 5/1/85; LJ 5/15/85; PW 4/19/85) **[362.1]**

1415 Horowitz, Lawrence C. *Taking Charge of Your Medical Fate.* **1988, $18.95 (0-394-56336-0); Ballantine paper $4.95 (0-345-36318-3).** An account of the American health care system with advice for the individual on how to receive the best possible medical treatment. (Rev: BL 9/1/88; LJ 11/1/88; PW 7/29/88) **[362.1]**

1416 Inlander, Charles B. *Medicine on Trial: The Appalling Story of Ineptitude, Malfeasance, Neglect and Arrogance.* **1988, Prentice Hall $18.95 (0-13-573544-0); Pantheon paper $11.95 (0-679-72732-9).** An exposé revealing substandard health care practices in the United States. (Rev: LJ 5/1/88; NYTBR 3/27/88; PW 3/4/88) **[362.1]**

1417 Kahane, Deborah Hobler. *No Less a Woman: Ten Women Shatter the Myths about Breast Cancer.* **1990, Prentice Hall paper $18.95 (0-13-624073-9).** Case studies of the lives of ten women who survived breast cancer. (Rev: LJ 5/15/90; PW 5/4/90) **[362.1]**

1418 Lasker, Judith, and Susan Borg. *In Search of Parenthood: Coping with Infertility and High-Tech Conception.* **1987, Beacon $17.95 (0-8070-2706-5).** A look at the social, ethical, and psychological problems arising from scientific methods to assist conception. (Rev: BL 8/87; LJ 9/1/87) **[362.1]**

1419 Lerner, Max. *Wrestling with the Angel: A Memoir.* **1990, Norton $18.95 (0-393-02846-1).** An account of the author's fight against cancer and heart disease. (Rev: BL 6/1/90; LJ 7/90; NYTBR 7/8/90) **[362.1]**

1420 Levin, Rhoda F. *Heartmates: A Survival Guide for the Cardiac Spouse.* **1987, Prentice Hall paper $18.95 (0-13-385162-1).** A guidebook for spouses and families of those who have survived heart attacks or suffer from cardiovascular diseases. (Rev: BL 10/1/87; LJ 11/1/87) **[362.1]**

1421 Maier, Frank, and Ginny Maier. *Sweet Reprieve: One Couple's Journey to the Frontiers of Medicine.* **1991, Crown $20.00 (0-517-58161-2).** The former *Newsweek* bureau chief and his wife discuss their experiences with his liver transplant surgery. (Rev: BL 4/15/91; LJ 4/1/91; Newsweek 6/5/91) **[362.1]**

1422 Noll, Peter. *In the Face of Death.* **1990, Viking $19.95 (0-670-80703-6).** A chronicle of the author's nine months facing cancer without medical treatment. "A powerful book."—BL (Rev: BL 11/15/89; LJ 12/89; NYTBR 1/21/90) **[362.1]**

1423 Payer, Lynn. *Medicine and Culture: Varieties of Treatment in the United States, England, West Germany and France.* **1988, Henry Holt $18.95 (0-8050-0443-2); Penguin paper $8.95 (0-14-012404-7).** A comparative study of medical treatment and procedures in three Western European countries and the United States. (Rev: Choice 9/88; LJ 5/15/88; TLS 7/7/89) **[362.1]**

1424 Rollin, Betty. *Last Wish.* **1986, Warner paper $8.95 (0-446-37032-0).** The author discusses her mother's terminal illness and her role in allowing her to commit suicide. (Rev: LJ 12/85; NYTBR 9/8/85) **[362.1]**

1425 Schreiber, LeAnne. *Midstream: A Daughter's Memoir.* **1990, Viking $18.95 (0-670-82819-X); paper $8.95 (0-14-012187-0).** A journal tracing the history of the author's mother's fight against a fatal cancer. (Rev: BL 12/15/89; Newsweek 1/22/90; Time 1/22/90. Awards: BL, 1990) **[362.1]**

1426 Severo, Richard. *Lisa H: The True Story of an Extraordinary and Courageous Woman.* **1986, Penguin paper $6.95 (0-14-008645-5).** The profile of a woman suffering from neurofibromatosis (Elephant Man's disease) and of the operations she had to remove tumorous growths and save her life. (Rev: BL 2/1/85; NYTBR 2/10/85; Newsweek 3/18/85) **[362.1]**

1427 Stehli, Annabel. *Sound of a Miracle.* **1991, Doubleday $19.95 (0-385-41140-5).** A mother's account of her daughter's recovery from autism. (Rev: BL 1/1/91; LJ 1/91; PW 11/30/90) **[362.1]**

1428 Strong, Maggie. *Mainstay: For the Spouse of the Chronically Ill.* **1988, Little, Brown $17.95 (0-316-81923-9); Penguin paper $9.95 (0-14-011978-7).** A practical guide to the care of the chronically ill spouse. "Well written, moving and immensely helpful."—LJ (Rev: BL 4/1/88; LJ 3/15/88; PW 2/26/88) **[362.1]**

1429 Szasz, Suzy. *Living with It: Why You Don't Have to Be Healthy to Be Happy.* **1991, Prome-**

theus $22.95 (0-87975-659-4). A woman stricken with lupus gives suggestions on ways ailing people can lead productive and satisfying lives. (REV: BL 8/91; LJ 7/91)   **[362.1]**

1430 Williams, Terry Tempest. *Refuge: An Unnatural History of Family and Place.* **1991, Pantheon $21.00 (0-679-40516-X).** Memoirs of a naturalist intertwining her battle to save a Utah bird refuge with an account of her mother's simultaneous battle against cancer. (REV: BL 9/1/91; PW 8/30/91)
[362.1]

Services of hospitals and related institutions

1431 Anderson, Peggy. *Children's Hospital.* **1986, Bantam paper $4.50 (0-553-25539-8).** An examination of the daily lives of patients and staff at the Children's Hospital of Philadelphia based on five years of research by the author. (REV: BL 6/1/85; LJ 5/15/85; PW 4/5/85)   **[362.11]**

1432 Gutkind, Lee. *One Children's Place: A Profile of Pediatric Medicine.* **1990, Grove-Weidenfeld $18.95 (0-8021-1272-2).** A profile of the daily workings of a children's hospital in Pittsburgh. (REV: BL 7/90; LJ 6/1/90)   **[362.11]**

1433 Levenson, Dorothy. *Montefiore: The Hospital as Social Instrument.* **1984, Farrar $19.95 (0-374-21228-3).** A history of the South Bronx Montefiore Hospital and how it has affected the surrounding community. (REV: BL 6/15/84; Choice 11/84; LJ 6/15/84)   **[362.11]**

1434 Rosenberg, Charles E. *Care of Strangers: The Rise of America's Hospital System.* **1987, Basic Books $22.95 (0-465-00877-1).** A tracing of the development of the American hospital from the early nineteenth century to the present. "Undoubtedly the most important book ever written on the history of hospitals in the U.S."—Choice (REV: Choice 7–8/88; LJ 11/1/87; NYTBR 11/22/87)   **[362.11]**

1435 Stevens, Rosemary. *In Sickness and In Wealth: American Hospitals in the 20th Century.* **1989, Basic Books $24.95 (0-465-03223-0).** An analysis of the relationship between federal, state, and local governments, community organizations, and America's hospital system. (REV: BL 3/15/89; Choice 9/89; NYTBR 8/20/89)   **[362.11]**

1436 Taylor, Robert. *Saranac: America's Magic Mountain.* **1988, Paragon paper $9.95 (1-55578-069-2).** A history of the sanatorium for tuberculosis patients founded by Dr. Edward Trudeau and built on Saranac Lake in Upstate New York. (REV: Atl 6/86; LJ 5/15/86; NYTBR 4/6/86)   **[362.11]**

1437 Yalof, Ina. *Life and Death: The Story of a Hospital.* **1989, Random $18.95 (0-394-56215-1); Fawcett paper $4.95 (0-449-21836-8).** Collected interviews with over 70 employees at a large New York hospital depicting the daily activities of the institution. (REV: BL 1/15/89; LJ 2/1/89; NYTBR 2/12/89)   **[362.11]**

Services of extended care facilities

1438 Goldsmith, Seth B. *Choosing a Nursing Home.* **1990, Prentice Hall paper $6.95 (0-13-298779-1).** A guide to the evaluation and selection of nursing homes. (REV: BL 7/90; LJ 6/15/90)   **[362.16]**

1439 Matthews, Joseph L. *Elder Care: Choosing and Financing Long-Term Care.* **1990, Nolo Pr. paper $16.95 (0-87337-113-5).** A discussion of options open to those seeking long-term care and housing for the aging, ill person. (REV: BL 7/90; LJ 11/1/90)
[362.16]

Services to patients with specific conditions

1440 Corea, Gena. *Hidden Malpractice: How American Medicine Mistreats Women.* **1984, Harper & Row paper $9.95 (0-06-091215-4).** The author demonstrates ways American medicine has discriminated against and mistreated women. (REV: LJ 4/1/77; New Rep 5/28/77; NYTBR 8/28/77)   **[362.19]**

1441 Massie, Robert K., and Suzanne Massie. *Journey.* **1984, Ballantine paper $3.95 (0-345-31629-0).** The author of *Nicolas and Alexandra* and his wife jointly tell the story of raising their hemophiliac son from birth to age 18. (REV: NYTBR 5/11/75; Newsweek 5/26/75; Time 5/19/75)   **[362.19]**

1442 Schwerin, Doris. *Diary of a Pigeon Watcher.* **1987, Paragon House paper $8.95 (0-913729-63-9).** A diary of the author's five years spent recovering from cancer surgery with reflections and observations of pigeons viewed from her New York apartment. (REV: BL 5/15/76; NYTBR 5/23/76; PW 3/8/76)
[362.19]

Social services—AIDS

1443 Bartlett, John G., and Ann K. Finkbeiner. *Guide to Living with HIV Infection.* **1991, Johns Hopkins $38.95 (0-8018-4193-3); paper $15.95 (0-8018-4194-1).** An overview of the current state of knowledge about the HIV virus with suggestions on how best to live with AIDS. (REV: BL 7/91; LJ 7/91)
[362.196]

1444 Bayer, Ronald. *Private Acts, Social Consequences: AIDS and the Politics of Public Health.* **1988, Free Pr. $22.95 (0-02-901961-3).** A survey of the problems caused by AIDS to public health officials and legislators, and how those problems were handled. "A powerful book with an important and timely message."—Choice (REV: Choice 5/89; LJ 2/1/89; NYTBR 2/5/89)   **[362.196]**

1445 Callen, Michael. *Surviving AIDS.* **1990, Harper & Row $18.95 (0-06-016148-5).** A study of long-term survivors of AIDS. (REV: BL 10/1/90; NYTBR 12/9/90; PW 9/14/90)   **[362.196]**

1446 Cox, Elizabeth. *Thanksgiving: An AIDS Journal.* **1990, Harper & Row $18.95 (0-06-016230-9); HarperCollins paper (0-06-092041-6).** An account of the author's husband's fight against AIDS and how it changed their relationship. (REV: LJ 1/90; PW 12/8/89)   **[362.196]**

1447 Fumento, Michael. *Myth of Heterosexual AIDS.* 1990, Basic Books $22.95 (0-465-09803-7). The author dismisses concerns that AIDS poses a threat to the heterosexual community. "The best documented, most provocative and informative AIDS book since *And The Band Played On.*" Natl Rev (Rev: BL 12/15/89; Natl Rev 2/5/90; PW 11/17/89) **[362.196]**

1448 Glaser, Elizabeth, and Laura Palmer. *In the Absence of Angels: A Hollywood Family's Courageous Story.* 1991, Putnam $21.95 (0-399-13577-4). A mother's account of how she contracted AIDS from a blood transfusion and passed the virus on to her two children. (Rev: LJ 2/15/91; NYTBR 3/3/91; PW 12/21/90) **[362.196]**

1449 Kirp, David L. *Learning by Heart: AIDS and Schoolchildren in America's Communities.* 1989, Rutgers Univ. Pr. $30.00 (0-8135-1396-0); paper $14.95 (0-8135-1609-9). Case studies of seven schoolchildren infected with the AIDS virus and how their communities reacted after learning the information. (Rev: BL 5/15/89; LJ 5/1/89; NYTBR 6/4/89) **[362.196]**

1450 Lapierre, Dominique. *Beyond Love.* 1991, Warner $22.95 (0-446-51438-1). A history of the AIDS epidemic and the efforts of doctors, researchers, nurses, and patients to fight the disease. "Extraordinary, deeply moving."—PW (Rev: LJ 4/15/91; NYTBR 5/5/91; PW 2/1/91) **[362.196]**

1451 Monette, Paul. *Borrowed Time: An AIDS Memoir.* 1988, Harcourt $18.95 (0-15-113598-3); Avon paper $8.95 (0-380-70779-9). A memoir of the author's friend, Roger Horwitz, who contracted and died of AIDS. "Definitely the best-written AIDS memoir thus far."—BL (Rev: BL 6/1/88; LJ 8/88; NYTBR 9/11/88. Awards: LJ, 1988) **[362.196]**

1452 Nixon, Nicholas, and Bebe Nixon. *People with AIDS.* 1991, Godine $45.00 (0-87923-908-5); paper $25.00 (0-87923-908-0). Depictions of the lives of 15 AIDS victims in words and photographs. "Extraordinarily moving."—PW (Rev: BL 5/15/91; LJ 6/1/91; PW 4/26/91. Awards: LJ, 1991) **[362.196]**

1453 Rieder, Ines, and Patricia Ruppelt, eds. *AIDS: The Women.* 1988, Cleis Pr. $24.95 (0-939416-20-4); paper $9.95 (0-939416-21-2). Collected essays by women of many nations concerning the effects of AIDS upon their lives. (Rev: BL 1/15/89; LJ 2/1/89; PW 11/18/88) **[362.196]**

1454 Shilts, Randy. *And the Band Played On: Politics, People and the AIDS Crisis.* 1987, St. Martin's $24.95 (0-312-00994-X); Penguin paper $12.95 (0-14-011369-X). Shilts's history of the AIDS epidemic and its spread throughout the U.S. is highly critical of the government's handling of the crisis. (Rev: LJ 11/15/87; NYTBR 11/8/87; Newsweek 10/19/87. Awards: ALA, 1987; BL, the 1980s; LJ, 1987; PW, 1987) **[362.196]**

1455 Wachter, Robert M. *Fragile Coalition: Scientists, Activists, and AIDS.* 1991, St. Martin's $19.95 (0-312-05801-2). An account of the events that took place at the Sixth International Conference on

AIDS in San Francisco. "Surprisingly enthralling, often profoundly moving, this is an absolutely essential addition to AIDS literature."—BL (Rev: BL 5/1/91; LJ 4/15/91; PW 4/12/91) **[362.196]**

1456 White, Ryan, and Ann Marie Cunningham. *Ryan White: My Own Story.* 1991, Dial $16.95 (0-8037-0977-3). An autobiography of the Indiana hemophiliac teenager who contracted the AIDS virus via a blood transfusion and died at the age of 18. (Rev: BL 2/1/91; NYTBR 5/12/91; PW 4/19/91) **[362.196]**

1457 Whitmore, George. *Someone Was Here: Profiles in the AIDS Epidemic.* 1988, NAL $17.95 (0-453-00601-9); paper $8.95 (0-452-26237-2). Portraits of three AIDS victims and the people who care for them. "An inspiring work as worthy of respect as the remarkable individuals that it commemorates."—PW (Rev: BL 4/1/88; NYTBR 4/10/88; PW 2/26/88) **[362.196]**

Mental and emotional illnesses and disturbances

1458 Cocks, Geoffrey. *Psychotherapy in the Third Reich.* 1986, Oxford Univ. Pr. paper $10.95 (0-19-504227-1). A study of psychotherapy as practiced in Nazi Germany. (Rev: BL 2/1/85; Choice 5/85; NYTBR 1/27/85) **[362.2]**

1459 Hendin, Herbert. *Suicide in America.* 1982, Norton $16.95 (0-393-01517-3). A psychiatrist's study of the social factors influencing suicidal behavior in America. (Rev: BL 4/1/82; New Rep 8/30/82; NYTBR 6/20/82) **[362.2]**

1460 Marek, Elizabeth. *Children at Santa Clara.* 1987, Viking $16.95 (0-670-81509-8); Penguin paper $6.95 (0-14-011118-2). An account of the author's experiences working at an institution for emotionally disturbed children. (Rev: BL 3/15/87; LJ 4/1/87; NYTBR 4/5/87) **[362.2]**

1461 Porter, Roy. *A Social History of Madness: The World Through the Eyes of the Insane.* 1988, Grove-Weidenfeld $18.95 (1-55584-185-6); Dutton paper $8.95 (0-525-48514-7). Case studies of persons confined to mental institutions told in their own words. (Rev: NYTBR 11/5/89; PW 8/4/89) **[362.2]**

1462 Showalter, Elaine. *Female Malady: Women, Madness and English Culture, 1830–1980.* 1985, Pantheon $19.95 (0-394-52021-1); Penguin paper (0-14-010169-1). A study of the definition of mental illness in women in American and English culture during the nineteenth and twentieth centuries. (Rev: BL 1/1/86; Choice 5/86; LJ 1/86) **[362.2]**

1463 Torrey, E. Fuller. *Nowhere to Go: The Tragic Odyssey of the Homeless Mentally Ill.* 1988, Harper & Row $18.95 (0-06-015993-6); paper $8.95 (0-06-091597-8). An account of the mentally ill population among America's homeless. "No other book has dealt with this crisis so thoroughly."—PW (Rev: Choice 2/89; NYTBR 12/18/88; PW 7/14/89) **[362.2]**

Suicide

1464 Hammer, Signe. *By Her Own Hand: Memoirs of a Suicide's Daughter.* 1991, Soho Pr. $18.95 (0-

939149-49-4). The author reflects upon her mother's suicide and its effects upon her life and thinking. (Rev: BL 3/15/91; PW 4/5/91)   **[362.28]**

Substance abuse

1465   Black, Claudia. *Double Duty.* 1990, Ballantine **$25.00 (0-345-36152-0).** A guide to the family dynamics of the chemically dependent household with guidelines for recovery. (Rev: LJ 10/1/90; PW 8/24/90)   **[362.29]**

1466   Cahalan, Don. *Understanding America's Drinking Problem: How to Combat the Hazards of Alcohol.* **1987, Jossey-Bass $24.95 (1-55542-057-5).** An overview of problems associated with American alcohol abuse with suggested methods of combatting them. (Rev: BL 10/1/87; Choice 4/88; LJ 11/1/87)   **[362.29]**

1467   Cole, Lewis. *Never Too Young to Die: The Death of Len Bias.* **1989, Pantheon $18.95 (0-394-56440-5).** An examination of the cocaine-related death of University of Maryland basketball star, Len Bias, only days after his selection in the professional basketball draft by the Boston Celtics. (Rev: BL 10/15/89; LJ 11/1/89; PW 8/11/89)   **[362.29]**

1468   Dorris, Michael. *Broken Cord: A Family's Ongoing Struggle with Fetal Alcohol Syndrome.* **1989, Harper & Row $18.95 (0-06-016071-3); paper $8.95 (0-06-091682-6).** An investigation of the problem of Fetal Alcohol Syndrome, and a memoir of the author's own experiences with his afflicted adopted son. (Rev: BL 6/1/89; LJ 7/89; NYTBR 7/30/89. Awards: ALA, 1989; BL, 1989; LJ, 1989)   **[362.29]**

1469   Francis, Charlie, and Jeff Coplan. *Speed Trap.* **1990, St. Martin's $18.95 (0-312-04877-7).** The former track coach of Canadian sprinter Ben Johnson discusses the use of drugs and steroids by athletes. "Well worth a read."—PW (Rev: BL 1/15/91; LJ 1/91; PW 12/14/90)   **[362.29]**

1470   Goodwin, Donald W. *Alcohol and the Writer.* **1988, Andrews & McMeel $16.95 (0-8362-5925-4); Penguin paper $8.95 (0-14-012655-4).** A study of alcoholism and its effects on the creative writing process with case studies of eight notable writers with drinking problems. (Rev: BL 10/15/88; Choice 4/89; PW 10/14/88)   **[362.29]**

1471   Hoffman, Abbie, and Jonathan Silvers. *Steal This Urine Test: Fighting Drug Hysteria in America.* **1987, Penguin paper $6.95 (0-14-010400-3).** An examination of drug testing and its social and legal issues as seen by the former Yippie and author of *Steal This Book.* (Rev: BL 10/15/87; LJ 11/1/87; NYTBR 11/29/87)   **[362.29]**

1472   Huncke, Herbert. *Guilty of Everything: The Autobiography of Herbert Huncke.* **1990, Paragon House $19.95 (1-55778-044-7).** An autobiography of the Beat generation figure and writer. "An important literary and sociological document."—LJ (Rev: LJ 4/1/90; NYTBR 6/10/90)   **[362.29]**

1473   Musto, David. *American Disease: Origins of Narcotic Control.* **1988, Oxford Univ. Pr. paper $13.95 (0-19-505211-0).** The history of legislation and enforcement of narcotics laws in the United States. "Satisfies a long-standing need for a competent history of narcotic control."—Choice (Rev: Choice 2/74; NYTBR 4/29/73; TLS 7/20/73)   **[362.29]**

1474   Olson, Steve, and Dean R. Gerstein. *Alcohol in America: Taking Action to Prevent Abuse.* **1985, National Academy Pr. $9.95 (0-309-03449-3).** A guide to preventative action against alcohol-related problems. (Rev: BL 1/15/86; Choice 4/86; LJ 10/1/85) **[362.29]**

1475   Robertson, Nan. *Getting Better: Inside Alcoholics Anonymous.* **1988, Morrow $17.95 (0-688-06869-3); Fawcett paper $3.95 (0-449-21711-6).** An examination of the history, structure, and techniques used by the self-help group Alcoholics Anonymous. "Few readers will emerge with their preconceptions about this complicated organization—or about alcoholics themselves—intact."—NYTBR (Rev: LJ 5/1/88; NYTBR 5/1/88; PW 3/14/88)   **[362.29]**

1476   Strom-Paikin, Joyce E. *Medical Treason: Nurses on Drugs.* **1989, New Horizon $21.95 (0-88282-043-5).** An account of a former nurse regarding the drug abuse and trade she witnessed at the urban hospital where she worked. (Rev: BL 4/15/89; LJ 7/89; PW 3/3/89)   **[362.29]**

Mental retardation

1477   Bernstein, Jane. *Loving Rachel: A Family's Journey from Grief.* **1988, Little, Brown $17.95 (0-316-09204-5); NAL paper $4.50 (0-451-16099-1).** The author's account of her initial sadness and eventual acceptance and love of her brain-damaged blind daughter. "A story of courageous love that rises above misfortune . . . an inspiring tale."—NYTBR (Rev: BL 5/1/88; NYTBR 10/30/88; PW 4/22/88)   **[362.3]**

1478   Busselle, Rebecca. *An Exposure of the Heart.* **1989, Norton $18.95 (0-393-02547-0); Penguin paper $8.95 (0-14-012989-8).** A collection of text and photographs documenting the lives of several individuals within a New York State mental institution. (Rev: BL 2/1/89; LJ 4/1/89; NYTBR 5/12/89)   **[362.3]**

1479   Greenfeld, Josh. *A Child Called Noah: A Family Journey.* **1972, Holt $7.95 (0-03-091384-5); Harcourt paper $7.95 (0-15-616862-6).** A diary of the father of an autistic child. "Throughout the book, the honest feeling of human beings facing tragedy come through to make this a completely credible account."—LJ (Rev: LJ 6/1/72; PW 3/27/72; Time 5/29/72. Awards: Time, 1972)   **[362.3]**

1480   Greenfeld, Josh. *A Client Called Noah: A Family Journey Continued.* **1989, Harcourt paper $7.95 (0-15-618168-1).** This third volume of the author's journals regarding the care of his brain-damaged son covers Noah's first years of adolescence. (Rev: LJ 4/15/87; NYTBR 2/15/87; Time 2/9/87)   **[362.3]**

1481 Greenfeld, Josh. *A Place for Noah.* **1978, Holt $10.50 (0-03-089896-X); Harcourt paper $7.95 (0-15-672000-0).** The sequel to *A Child Called Noah,* this is the journal of the father of a brain-damaged child that covers his ages 5 to 11. "An account of Josh Greenfeld's trying and tender life . . . a record of his profound hurt and profound courage."—NYTBR (REV: BL 5/1/78; NYTBR 4/23/78; Time 4/10/78. AWARDS: Time, 1978)   **[362.3]**

1482 Unsworth, Tim. *Lambs of Libertyville: A Working Community of Retarded Adults.* **1990, Contemporary $17.95 (0-8092-4178-1).** A history of a progressive Illinois facility founded in 1962 to help the developmentally disabled. (REV: BL 11/1/90; PW 10/19/90)   **[362.3]**

Problems of and services to people with physical disabilities

1483 Browne, Susan E., ed. *With the Power of Each Breath: A Disabled Women's Anthology.* **1985, Cleis Pr. $24.95 (0-939416-09-3); paper $10.95 (0-939416-06-9).** An anthology of the writings of 54 disabled women. (REV: BL 7/85; LJ 8/85)   **[362.4]**

1484 Hoffa, Helynn, and Gary Morgan. *Yes You Can: A Helpbook for the Physically Disabled.* **1990, Pharos Books paper $12.95 (0-88687-480-7).** A guidebook for the physically disabled with information on services and organizations to help them live life to the fullest. "A truly invaluable book, for both its spirit and data."—BL (REV: BL 12/1/90; LJ 10/15/90)   **[362.4]**

1485 Sacks, Oliver. *A Leg to Stand On.* **1984, Summit $14.95 (0-671-46780-8); Harper & Row paper $9.95 (0-06-097082-0).** The author of *Awakenings* recounts his hiking accident in Norway and the surgery necessary to repair torn muscles in his leg. (REV: BL 9/15/84; NYRB 9/27/84; Newsweek 8/20/84)   **[362.4]**

Persons with impaired vision

1486 Clark, Eleanor. *Eyes, Etc.* **1979, Pocket paper $1.95 (0-671-82516-X).** Memoirs by the author of *Oysters of Locmariaquer* regarding her visual impairment due to retinal scarring. (REV: NYTBR 10/16/77; Newsweek 10/17/77; Sat Rev 10/29/77)   **[362.41]**

1487 De Montalembert, Hugues. *Eclipse: A Nightmare.* **1985, Viking $15.95 (0-670-44437-5).** An account of the author's recovery from a vicious mugging that robbed him of his sight. (REV: BL 10/1/85; LJ 10/15/85; PW 10/25/85)   **[362.41]**

1488 Mehta, Ved. *Ledge Between the Streams.* **1984, Norton $17.50 (0-393-08128-8).** The fourth volume of Mehta's autobiography covers his years as a teenager during India's struggle for independence. "I want to proclaim this autobiography as nothing less than a literary masterpiece."—R. K. Narayan, TLS (REV: BL 3/15/84; NYTBR 5/6/84; TLS 7/6/84. AWARDS: ALA, 1984)   **[362.41]**

1489 Mehta, Ved. *Stolen Light.* **1989, Norton $19.95 (0-393-02632-9); paper $9.95 (0-393-30673-9).** This sixth volume of the Indian writer's memoirs deals

with his education at Pomona College in California and his immersion into American culture. (REV: BL 3/1/89; LJ 3/15/89; TLS 5/12/89. AWARDS: BL, 1989)   **[362.41]**

1490 Mehta, Ved. *Vedi.* **$1987, Norton paper $7.95 (0-393-30417-5).** Childhood memoirs recounting the author's loss of sight and his enrollment in a school for the blind. (REV: LJ 8/82; NYRB 10/7/82; NYTBR 10/17/82)   **[362.41]**

Persons with impaired hearing

1491 Forecki, Marcia C. *Speak to Me.* **1989, Gallaudet paper $12.95 (0-930323-68-8).** A mother's account of her son's deafness and how she came to accept and cope with it. (REV: BL 7/85; LJ 6/1/85)   **[362.42]**

1492 Kisor, Henry. *What's That Pig Outdoors? A Memoir of Deafness.* **1990, Hill & Wang $18.95 (0-8090-9689-7).** The *Chicago Sun-Times* journalist and Northwestern University lecturer recounts his life's experiences as a deaf person. (REV: BL 3/15/90; LJ 4/15/90; NYTBR 6/3/90. AWARDS: BL, 1990)   **[362.42]**

1493 Lane, Harlan. *When the Mind Hears: A History of the Deaf.* **1984, Random $29.95 (0-394-50878-4); McKay paper $15.95 (0-679-72023-5).** The history of education for the deaf, and the controversy between the oral and sign schools. (REV: Choice 3/85; LJ 10/15/84; NYTBR 10/21/84. AWARDS: BL, the 1980s)   **[362.42]**

1494 Nieminen, Raija. *Voyage to the Island.* **1990, Gallaudet Univ. Pr. $15.95 (0-930323-62-9).** A memoir by a deaf Finnish woman who accepted a United Nations post on the Caribbean island of St. Lucia. (REV: BL 1/1/91; LJ 1/91)   **[362.42]**

1495 Rezen, Susan V., and Carl Hausman. *Coping with Hearing Loss: A Guide for Adults and Their Families.* **1985, Dembner Books paper $15.95 (0-93478-48-X).** A guide for adults to the treatment and commonly encountered emotional problems that may accompany the onset of hearing loss. (REV: BL 4/15/85; LJ 4/15/85; PW 3/1/85)   **[362.42]**

1496 Sacks, Oliver. *Seeing Voices: A Journey into the World of the Deaf.* **1989, Univ. of California Pr. $15.95 (0-520-06083-0); Harper & Row paper $8.95 (0-06-097347-1).** A study of the deaf and their acquisition and concept of language by the author of *Awakenings.* (REV: BL 10/15/89; NYTBR 10/8/89; Newsweek 10/2/89)   **[362.42]**

1497 Schaller, Susan. *A Man Without Words.* **1991, Summit $17.95 (0-671-70310-2).** An interpreter's account of a 27-year-old deaf man who had never been exposed to language. (REV: BL 12/1/90; LJ 1/91; NYTBR 2/3/91)   **[362.42]**

Problems of and services to the poor

1498 Coates, Robert C. *A Street Is Not a Home: Solving America's Homeless Dilemma.* **1990, Prometheus paper $14.95 (0-87975-621-7).** A California judge presents proposals to help solve the problem

of homelessness in America. (Rev: BL 1/15/91; LJ 1/91)
[362.5]

1499 Himmelfarb, Gertrude. *Idea of Poverty: England in the Early Industrial Age.* 1983, Knopf $25.00 (0-394-53062-4); Random paper $12.95 (0-394-72607-3). A social history of poverty and the poor in eighteenth and nineteenth-century England. (Rev: CSM 3/7/84; LJ 3/84; NYTBR 1/1/84)
[362.5]

1500 Hirsch, Kathleen. *Songs from the Alley.* 1989, Ticknor & Fields $22.95 (0-89919-488-5); Doubleday paper $10.95 (0-385-41277-0). An examination of the problem of homelessness, and the history of social welfare in America as exemplified by the lives of two Boston women. "A moving and timely social study."—BL (Rev: BL 4/1/89; LJ 4/15/89; PW 2/24/89. Awards: ALA, 1989; BL, 1989)
[362.5]

1501 Katz, Michael B. *Underserving Poor: From the War on Poverty to the War on Welfare.* 1990, Pantheon $22.95 (0-394-53457-3); paper $14.95 (0-679-72561-X). A study of U.S. government relief efforts for the poor from the Johnson administration to the present. (Rev: CSM 3/12/90; NYTBR 1/21/90; PW 12/15/89)
[362.5]

1502 Rossi, Peter H. *Down and Out in America: The Origins of Homelessness.* 1989, Univ. of Chicago Pr. $15.95 (0-226-72828-5). A historic and demographic analysis of homelessness in America. (Rev: Choice 5/90; LJ 11/1/90)
[362.5]

1503 Wilson, William Julius. *Truly Disadvantaged: The Inner City, the Underclass and Public Policy.* 1987, Univ. of Chicago Pr. $19.95 (0-226-90130-0). An examination of the reasons behind black urban poverty in America with suggestions on ways the cycle of poverty can be reversed. (Rev: Choice 3/88; LJ 10/1/87; NYTBR 10/25/87. Awards: LJ, 1987; NYTBR, 1987)
[362.5]

Problems of and services to persons in late adulthood

1504 Callahan, Daniel. *Setting Limits: Medical Goals in an Aging Society.* 1988, Simon & Schuster paper $9.95 (0-671-66831-5). An ethical and medical analysis weighing the quality of life for the aged versus the extension of life by technological means. (Rev: BL 11/15/87; Choice 1/88; NYTBR 9/27/87. Awards: BL, the 1980s)
[362.6]

Problems of and services to young people

1505 Besharov, Douglas J. *Recognizing Child Abuse: A Guide for the Concerned.* 1990, Free Pr. $24.95 (0-02-903081-1); paper $12.95 (0-02-903082-X). Besharov, former director of the National Center on Child Abuse and Neglect, presents a guide for the professional and layperson to determine whether a child is abused. (Rev: BL 6/1/90; NYTBR 9/9/90)
[362.7]

1506 Boswell, John. *Kindness of Strangers: The Abandonment of Children in Western Europe from Late Antiquity to the Renaissance.* 1989, Pantheon $24.95 (0-394-57240-8); Random paper $15.95 (0-679-72499-0). A study of the practice of child abandonment in Europe in the Middle Ages, and how most of the children were able to survive to maturity. (Rev: New Rep 2/27/89; NYTBR 3/19/89; New Yorker 2/6/89)
[362.7]

1507 Canape, Charlene. *Adoption: Parenthood without Pregnancy.* 1986, Holt $18.95 (0-03-001594-4); Avon paper $4.95 (0-380-70505-2). A practical guide for those considering adoption. (Rev: BL 5/15/86; LJ 6/1/86)
[362.7]

1508 Caplan, Lincoln. *Open Adoption.* 1990, Farrar $17.95 (0-374-10558-8). An examination of adoptions where birth and adoptive parents know each other. (Rev: LJ 5/15/90; NYTBR 7/8/90; PW 4/27/90)
[362.7]

1509 Crewdson, John. *By Silence Betrayed: The Sexual Abuse of Children in America.* 1988, Little, Brown $17.95 (0-316-16094-6); Harper & Row paper $8.95 (0-06-097203-3). An overview of the problem of sexual abuse of children in American society. Based on interviews with molesters and their victims. (Rev: BL 2/1/88; LJ 12/87; NYTBR 2/7/88)
[362.7]

1510 Crowley, Patricia. *Not My Child: A Mother Confronts Her Child's Sexual Abuse.* 1990, Doubleday $19.95 (0-385-26098-9); Avon paper $4.95 (0-380-71276-8). A mother whose child was the victim of sexual abuse at a New Jersey day care center discusses the effects on the child and her family. (Rev: BL 1/15/80; LJ 1/90)
[362.7]

1511 Dear, William C. *Dungeon Master: The Disappearance of James Dallas Egbert III.* 1985, Ballantine paper $3.95 (0-345-32695-4). A study of the case of a Michigan State student who disappeared from his dormitory room as told by the private investigator assigned to the case. "Surpasses even the best detective fiction."—BL (Rev: BL 10/1/84; LJ 9/15/84; NYTBR 12/23/84)
[362.7]

1512 Donofrio, Beverly. *Riding in Cars with Boys: Confessions of a Bad Girl Who Makes Good.* 1990, Morrow $16.45 (0-688-08337-4). Memoirs of teenage life in the 1960s. (Rev: BL 7/90; LJ 7/90; PW 6/22/90)
[362.7]

1513 Garbarino, James. *Psychologically Battered Child: Strategies for Identification, Assessment and Intervention.* 1986, Jossey-Bass $27.95 (1-55542-002-8). A study of the effects of psychological abuse on children and possible solutions to the problem. (Rev: BL 12/1/86; Choice 4/87)
[362.7]

1514 Jones, E. P. *Where Is Home? Living Through Foster Care.* 1989, Four Walls Eight Windows $17.95 (0-941423-34-4). A woman recalls her experiences growing up in a series of foster homes from age four to eighteen. (Rev: BL 6/1/90; NYTBR 9/9/90; PW 4/27/90)
[362.7]

1515 Kempe, Ruth, and C. Henry Kempe. *Common Secret: Sexual Abuse of Children and Adolescents.* 1984, W. H. Freeman paper $14.95 (0-7167-1625-9). An overview of the problem and treatment of sexual abuse of the young. "A comprehensive, factual, and caring book on a timely subject."—BL (Rev: BL 10/1/84; Choice 12/84)
[362.7]

1516   Kingsbury, Daniel F. *Everyday Guide to Opening and Operating a Child Care Center.* 1990, Vade Denver paper $14.95 (0-945847-03-3). An overview of procedures necessary to start and operate a day care center. (Rev: BL 2/1/90; LJ 12/89)   **[362.7]**

1517   Klagsbrun, Francine. *Too Young to Die: Youth and Suicide.* 1976, Houghton $14.95 (0-395-24752-7); Pocket paper $3.50 (0-671-60405-8). A study of the legal, ethical, and societal issues surrounding the problem of teen suicide. (Rev: NYTBR 2/6/77; PW 7/25/77)   **[362.7]**

1518   Leitch, David. *Family Secrets: A Writer's Search for His Parents and His Past.* 1986, Delacorte $17.95 (0-385-29457-3). An account of the author's search for his natural parents and their eventual reunion. (Rev: LJ 3/15/86; NYTBR 7/13/86; Time 4/28/86)   **[362.7]**

1519   Lindsay, Jeanne Warren. *Parents, Pregnant Teens and the Adoption Option: Help for Families.* 1988, Morning Glory $13.95 (0-930934-29-6); paper $8.95 (0-930934-28-8). Interviews with teenage mothers who gave up babies for adoption form the basis for this guide for those facing similar decisions. (Rev: BL 12/15/88; CSM 11/14/88; LJ 1/89) **[362.7]**

1520   Reaves, John, and James Austin. *How to Find Help for a Troubled Kid: A Parent's Guide to Programs and Services for Adolescents.* 1990, Henry Holt $19.95 (0-8050-0885-3); HarperCollins paper $9.95 (0-06-273058-4). A guide to the options facing parents of troubled teenagers. (Rev: BL 3/15/90; LJ 3/1/90; PW 2/16/90)   **[362.7]**

1521   Register, Cheri. *Are Those Kids Yours? American Families with Children Adopted from Other Countries.* 1990, Free Pr. $22.95 (0-02-925750-6). A study of American families who have adopted foreign-born children by a woman who has two Korean-born adopted daughters. (Rev: BL 12/1/90; LJ 12/90; PW 9/28/90)   **[362.7]**

1522   Rhodes, Richard. *A Hole in the World: An American Boyhood.* 1990, Simon & Schuster $19.95 (0-671-69066-3); paper $10.00 (0-671-74725-8). The author of *The Making of the Atomic Bomb* and *Farm* reflects on his abuse as a child and its effects on his life and development. (Rev: LJ 9/1/90; PW 7/27/90; Time 10/29/90. Awards: PW, 1990; Time, 1990) **[362.7]**

1523   Sanford, Linda Tschirhart. *Strong at the Broken Places: Overcoming the Trauma of Childhood Abuse.* 1990, Random $18.95 (0-394-56563-4). A self-help guide for adults who were abused as children. (Rev: BL 6/1/90; LJ 7/90; NYTBR 9/9/90)   **[362.7]**

1524   Sessions, Shelley, and Peter Meyer. *Dark Obsession: A True Story of Incest and Justice.* 1990, Putnam $19.95 (0-399-13497-2); Berkley paper $4.95 (0-425-12296-4). An account of a Texas case in which a woman successfully sued her stepfather for damages for her sexual abuse as a child. (Rev: LJ 12/89; NYTBR 2/25/90; PW 11/10/89)   **[362.7]**

1525   Simpson, Eileen. *Orphans: Real and Imaginary.* 1988, NAL paper $8.95 (0-452-26060-4). An interweaving of the author's experiences as an

orphan and of the history of orphans and orphanhood in society. "A moving memoir and a provocative cultural history, richly written and keenly felt."—BL (Rev: BL 8/87; NYTBR 7/19/87; PW 5/15/87)   **[362.7]**

1526   Stavsky, Lois, and I. E. Mozeson. *Place I Call Home: The Faces and Worlds of Homeless Teens.* 1990, Shapolsky $14.95 (0-944007-81-3). Profiles of the lives of 30 homeless American teenagers in photographs and their own words. (Rev: BL 11/15/90; LJ 12/90)   **[362.7]**

1527   Stephenson, Mary. *My Child Is a Mother.* 1991, Corona $17.95 (0-931722-87-X). An account of a mother's relationship with a teenage daughter who became pregnant and decided to put her baby up for adoption. (Rev: LJ 5/15/91; PW 1/11/91) **[362.7]**

1528   Tower, Cynthia Crosson. *Secret Scars: A Guide for Survivors of Child Sexual Abuse.* 1988, Viking $16.95 (0-670-82214-0); Penguin paper $7.95 (0-14-012229-X). A guide for recovery for adult survivors of child sexual abuse. (Rev: BL 7/88; LJ 7/88)   **[362.7]**

Problems of and services to other groups

1529   Auletta, Ken. *Underclass.* 1983, Random paper $6.95 (0-394-71388-5). A study of the very poor in America examining current and proposed solutions to aid them economically and socially. (Rev: BL 5/1/82; New Rep 6/9/82; PW 3/26/82)   **[362.8]**

1530   Gordon, Margaret T., and Stephanie Riger. *Female Fear.* 1988, Free Pr. $19.95 (0-02-912490-5). A study of women's fears and attitudes toward the threat of sexual assault and how it effects their day-to-day lives. (Rev: BL 2/1/89; LJ 2/1/89; NYTBR 5/7/89)   **[362.8]**

1531   Moynihan, Daniel Patrick. *Family and Nation: The Godkin Lectures.* 1986, Harcourt $12.95 (0-15-130143-3); paper $5.95 (0-15-630140-7). The New York senator's plea for reform of United States welfare policies. (Rev: LJ 4/1/86; New Rep 3/17/86; PW 1/3/86)   **[362.8]**

1532   Noble, Elizabeth. *Having Your Baby by Donor Insemination: A Complete Resource Guide.* 1988, Houghton $21.95 (0-395-36897-9); paper $12.95 (0-395-45395-X). An examination of the moral, legal, and practical issues regarding donor insemination for infertile couples. (Rev: LJ 2/15/88)   **[362.8]**

1533   Rapoport, Louis. *Redemption Song: The Story of Operation Moses.* 1986, Harcourt $18.95 (0-15-176120-5). An account of the Israeli evacuation and rescue of over 10,000 Ethiopian Jews from starvation and persecution in 1984 and 1985. (Rev: BL 5/15/86; LJ 5/15/86; PW 4/18/86)   **[362.8]**

Problems of and services to families

1534   Gelles, Richard J., and Murray A. Straus. *Intimate Violence: The Causes and Consequences of Abuse in the American Family.* 1989, Simon & Schuster paper $10.95 (0-671-68296-2). The results of the authors' 15 years of research regarding domes-

tic violence, its situations, its treatment, and its prevention. (Rev: BL 11/15/88; LJ 7/88; PW 6/10/88)
[362.82]

1535 Gordon, Linda. *Heroes of Their Own Lives: The Politics and History of Family Violence, Boston, 1880–1960.* 1988, Viking $24.95 (0-670-81909-3); Penguin paper $8.95 (0-14-010468-2). A study of domestic violence and its treatment based on the case records of three Boston child welfare agencies. (Rev: Choice 9/88; LJ 2/15/88; NYTBR 5/8/88)
[362.82]

1536 Statman, Jan Berliner. *Battered Woman's Survival Guide: Breaking the Cycle.* 1990, Taylor $18.95 (0-87833-718-0); paper $9.95 (0-87833-707-5). A guide to combating the abuse of women and getting help for abuse victims. (Rev: BL 4/1/90; LJ 7/90)
[362.82]

Problems of and services to women

1537 Maltz, Wendy. *Sexual Healing Journey: A Guide for Survivors of Sexual Abuse.* 1991, HarperCollins $19.95 (0-06-016661-4). A guide to the treatment for survivors of sexual abuse. "Can help victims . . . along the road to healing."—LJ (Rev: BL 5/15/91; LJ 7/91)
[362.83]

1538 NiCarthy, Ginny, and Sue Davidson. *You Can Be Free: An Easy-to-Read Handbook for Abused Women.* 1989, Seal Pr. paper $6.95 (0-931188-68-7). A guidebook for women who want to free themselves from abusive or destructive relationships. (Rev: BL 5/15/89; LJ 4/15/89)
[362.83]

1539 Sidel, Ruth. *Women and Children Last: The Plight of Poor Women in Affluent America.* 1987, Penguin paper $6.95 (0-14-010013-X). An examination of the feminization of poverty in America over the past two decades by the author of *On Her Own.* (Rev: Atl 4/86; LJ 3/1/86; NYTBR 4/27/86)
[362.83]

Victims of crimes

1540 Ledray, Linda E. *Recovering from Rape.* 1986, Holt $9.95 (0-03-064001-6). A guide to recovery for rape victims. (Rev: BL 3/1/86; LJ 3/1/86; PW 3/21/86)
[362.88]

1541 Persico, J. E., and George Sutherland. *Keeping Out of Crime's Way: The Practical Guide for People over 50.* 1987, American Assn. of Retired Persons paper $6.95 (0-673-24801-1). An AARP guide to avoiding crime for those over 50. "This book should be required reading for every senior citizen."—BL (Rev: BL 5/15/85; LJ 5/1/85)
[362.88]

1542 Saldana, Theresa. *Beyond Survival.* 1987, Bantam paper $4.50 (0-553-26517-2). The actress writes of her recovery from a vicious stabbing attack outside her Los Angeles home. (Rev: BL 11/15/86; PW 8/1/86)
[362.88]

1543 Stark, James, and Howard Goldstein. *Rights of Crime Victims.* 1985, Southern Illinois Univ. Pr. paper $4.95 (0-8093-9952-0). An ACLU handbook on the legal rights of crime victims. (Rev: BL 2/15/85; LJ 2/15/85)
[362.88]

1544 Warshaw, Robin. *I Never Called It Rape: The Ms. Report on Recognizing, Fighting, and Surviving Date and Acquaintance Rape.* 1988, Harper & Row $17.95 (0-06-055126-7); paper $7.95 (0-06-096276-3). A study of the widespread problem of date and acquaintance rape based on a nationwide survey of women on college campuses. "It should be a lifeline to help and understanding."—BL (Rev: BL 9/1/88; LJ 9/1/88; PW 7/1/88. Awards: LJ, 1988)
[362.88]

363   Other social problems and services

Public safety programs

1545 Adato, Michelle. *Safety Second: The NRC and America's Nuclear Power Plants.* Ed. by Union of Concerned Scientists Staff. 1987, Indiana Univ. Pr. $25.00 (0-253-35034-4). A critical scientific appraisal of the safety record of the Nuclear Regulatory Commission. (Rev: Choice 5/87; CSM 6/9/87; LJ 2/15/87)
[363.1]

1546 Ball, Howard. *Justice Downwind: America's Nuclear Testing Program in the 1950's.* 1986, Oxford Univ. Pr. $24.95 (0-19-503672-7); paper $8.95 (0-19-505357-5). A study of the health consequences of the testing of atomic bombs in Nevada during the 1950s. (Rev: BL 3/15/86; Choice 9/86; LJ 4/1/86)
[363.1]

1547 Cherniack, Martin. *Hawk's Nest Incident: America's Worst Industrial Disaster.* 1986, Yale Univ. Pr. $25.00 (0-300-03522-5); paper $10.95 (0-300-04485-2). An account of the deaths of over 700 workers from silicosis following a Union Carbide construction project during the 1930s. (Rev: Choice 2/87; LJ 11/1/86)
[363.1]

1548 Fradkin, Philip L. *Fallout: An American Nuclear Tragedy.* 1989, Univ. of Arizona Pr. $24.95 (0-8165-1086-5); paper $14.95 (0-8165-1143-8). A study of the victims of radioactive fallout from American nuclear testing during the 1950s and of the 1978 lawsuit filed on their behalf against the United States Department of Energy. (Rev: BL 2/1/89; NYTBR 4/9/89; PW 1/13/89)
[363.1]

1549 Gough, Michael. *Dioxin, Agent Orange: The Facts.* 1986, Plenum $19.95 (0-306-42247-6). A study of the effects of exposure to dioxin in humans. (Rev: Choice 9/86; LJ 5/1/86)
[363.1]

1550 Hoffer, William, and Marilyn Mona Hoffer. *Freefall.* 1989, St. Martin's $17.95 (0-312-02919-5). An account of an Air Canada jetliner that ran out of fuel and lost electrical power at 40,000 feet, but was able to land safely at a Canadian air force base. (Rev: BL 5/15/89; LJ 4/1/89)
[363.1]

1551 Lansky, Vicki. *Baby Proofing Basics: How to Keep Your Child Safe.* 1991, Book Peddlers paper $5.95 (0-916773-28-0). A guide to creating a safe home environment for babies and young children. (Rev: BL 6/1/91; LJ 5/15/91)
[363.1]

1552　Le Riche, W. Harding. *A Chemical Feast*. 1982, Facts on File $19.95 (0-87196-643-3). A survey of the history and present practices related to food additives. "Excellent reading for anyone interested in the truth about food."—BL (Rev: BL 3/15/83; LJ 12/15/82)　　　　**[363.1]**

1553　Lewis, H. W. *Technological Risk*. 1990, Norton $22.95 (0-393-02883-6). A study of human fears of current technology and the true risks associated with it. "A valuable, clearly written appraisal."—John Allen Paulos, NYTBR (Rev: LJ 9/15/90; NYTBR 11/25/90; PW 8/24/90)　　　　**[363.1]**

1554　Morehouse, Ward, and Ayun Subramaniam. *Bhopal Tragedy*. 1986, Learning Resources paper $13.50 (0-936876-47-6). An account of the 1984 Union Carbide chemical gas leak that killed, maimed, and blinded thousands of citizens in Bhopal, India, and the possible ramifications for the chemical industry. (Rev: BL 5/15/86; LJ 6/15/86)　　**[363.1]**

1555　Mott, Lawrie, and Karen Snyder. *Pesticide Alert: A Guide to Pesticides in Fruits and Vegetables*. 1988, Sierra Club $15.95 (0-87156-728-8); paper $6.95 (0-87156-726-1). A consumer guide to pesticides commonly used in produce and how to minimize health risks associated with pesticides in the diet. (Rev: BL 5/1/88; LJ 6/15/88)　　**[363.1]**

1556　Pellegrino, Charles. *Her Name, Titanic: The Real Story of the Sinking and Finding of the Unsinkable Ship*. 1988, McGraw-Hill $18.95 (0-07-049280-8); Avon paper $4.95 (0-380-70892-2). The author's account of the sinking of the *Titanic* and how the expedition he was a part of found its wreckage in 1987. (Rev: LJ 1/89; PW 10/28/88) **[363.1]**

1557　Weir, David. *Bhopal Syndrome: Pesticides, Environment and Health*. 1987, Sierra Club $17.95 (0-87156-718-0); paper $8.95 (0-87156-797-0). A study of the international chemical industry and its potentially dangerous facilities with a profile of the 1984 Union Carbide disaster in Bhopal, India. (Rev: BL 10/1/87; LJ 9/15/87; NYTBR 11/29/87)　**[363.1]**

1558　Wilcox, Fred A. *Waiting for an Army to Die: The Tragedy of Agent Orange*. 1989, Seven Locks Pr. paper $10.95 (0-932020-68-2). An examination of the medical effects caused by exposure to the defoliant Agent Orange, widely used during the Vietnam War. (Rev: BL 7/83; PW 5/13/83; Sat Rev 7–8/83. Awards: ALA, 1983)　　　**[363.1]**

Transportation services

1559　Emerson, Steven, and Brian Duffy. *Fall of Pan Am 103: Inside the Lockerbie Investigation*. 1990, Putnam $21.95 (0-399-13521-9). An investigative report of the 1988 bombing over Scotland that killed 270 people. "An important addition to all library collections."—LJ (Rev: LJ 5/1/90; NYTBR 4/29/90)　　　　　　　　　　**[363.12]**

Hazardous materials

1560　Becker, Robert O. *Cross Currents: The Promise of Electromedicine, the Perils of Electropollution*. 1990, J. P. Tarcher $19.95 (0-87477-536-1). An examination of the potential positive and negative health effects of electromagnetic energy. (Rev: Choice 6/90; LJ 12/89)　　**[363.17]**

1561　Center for Investigative Reporting, and Bill Moyers. *Global Dumping Ground*. 1990, Seven Locks Pr. paper $11.95 (0-932020-95-X). A study of the international trade in toxic waste and techniques used to dispose of it. (Rev: LJ 12/90; NYTBR 11/25/90)　　　　　　　　　**[363.17]**

Radioactive materials

1562　Medvedev, Grigori. *Truth about Chernobyl*. 1991, Basic Books $22.95 (0-465-08775-2). A former engineer at the Chernobyl nuclear power station recounts the events surrounding the 1986 disaster and its aftermath. "A slender classic."—NYTBR (Rev: LJ 2/1/91; NYTBR 4/7/91; PW 2/1/91. Awards: NYTBR, 1991)　　　　　　　**[363.1799]**

1563　Medvedev, Zhores A. *Legacy of Chernobyl*. 1990, Norton $24.95 (0-393-02802-X). An analysis of the 1986 Soviet nuclear reactor disaster and its legacy. "The most comprehensive and revealing account of Chernobyl to date."—PW (Rev: BL 5/15/90; LJ 6/15/90; PW 4/20/90)　　　**[363.1799]**

1564　Miller, Richard L. *Under the Cloud: The Decades of Nuclear Testing*. 1986, Free Pr. $24.95 (0-02-921620-6). A history of atomic testing in the Nevada desert and its effects upon the surrounding population and environment. (Rev: Choice 2/87; CSM 1/23/87; LJ 10/15/86)　　　**[363.1799]**

1565　Robinson, Marilynne. *Mother Country*. 1989, Farrar $16.95 (0-374-21361-5). An exposé of the British production and handling of radioactive materials by the author of *Housekeeping*. (Rev: BL 6/15/89; LJ 5/1/89; PW 5/5/89)　　**[363.1799]**

1566　Shcherbak, Iurii. *Chernobyl: A Documentary Story*. 1989, St. Martin's $29.95 (0-312-03097-5). Collected interviews with workers involved in the clean-up of the Chernobyl nuclear disaster. (Rev: Choice 1/90; LJ 7/89; PW 6/2/89)　　**[363.1799]**

Hazardous machinery

1567　Brodeur, Paul. *Currents of Death: Power Lines, Computer Terminals and the Attempt to Cover Up Their Threat to Your Health*. 1989, Simon & Schuster $19.95 (0-671-67845-0). A survey of the potentially detrimental health effects caused by exposure to power lines, computer terminals, and low-level microwave radiation. (Rev: BL 10/15/89; LJ 10/1/89; PW 8/18/89)　　**[363.18]**

Police services

1568　Bouza, Anthony V. *Police Mystique: An Insider's Look at Cops, Crime and the Criminal Justice System*. 1990, Plenum $23.50 (0-306-43464-4). A former police chief's view of the American criminal justice system. (Rev: BL 5/1/90; LJ 4/1/90; NYTBR 5/6/90)　　　　　**[363.2]**

1569　Daley, Robert. *Prince of the City: The True Story of a Cop Who Knew Too Much*. 1986,

Berkley paper $4.50 (0-425-09789-7). An account of an investigation into corruption within the New York Police Department as told through the story of Robert Leuci, a detective working undercover for the FBI. (Rev: BL 2/15/79; LJ 11/15/78; NYTBR 1/29/79)   **[363.2]**

1570 Fallis, Greg, and Ruth Greenberg. *How to Be Your Own Detective: How to Find Out Anything about Just about Anybody.* **1989, Evans paper $9.95 (0-87131-579-3).** A licensed private investigator details the tricks of his trade for the interested layperson. (Rev: BL 12/1/89; LJ 12/89; PW 12/8/89)   **[363.2]**

1571 Gelb, Barbara. *Varnished Brass: The Decade after Serpico.* **1983, Putnam $16.95 (0-399-12871-9).** An inside view of the inner workings of the New York Police Department in the late 1970s and early 1980s. (Rev: LJ 9/1/83; NYTBR 11/6/83; PW 9/9/83)   **[363.2]**

1572 Lewis, Alfred Allan, and Herbert Leon Mac-Donnell. *Evidence Never Lies: The Casebook of a Modern Sherlock Holmes.* **1989, Dell paper $4.95 (0-440-20342-2).** A criminologist presents his most notable cases and details the investigative procedures used to solve them. (Rev: BL 9/1/84; LJ 9/1/84; Natl Rev 5/17/85)   **[363.2]**

1573 McClure, James. *Cop World: Policing the Streets of San Diego.* **1984, Macmillan $12.95 (0-333-30688-0).** The author's observations and interviews with police officers form the basis for this portrayal of the operations of the San Diego Police Department. "Brings us remarkably close to daily police work."—PW (Rev: BL 2/15/85; PW 1/18/85)   **[363.2]**

1574 Mitgang, Herbert. *Dangerous Dossiers: Exposing the Secret War Against America's Greatest Authors.* **1988, Donald I. Fine $18.95 (0-317-65633-3); Ballantine paper $4.95 (0-345-35801-5).** An examination of the FBI files of surveillance kept on eminent American writers including Faulkner, Hemingway, Mailer, and Tennessee Williams. "An important, brave, chilling exposé."—PW (Rev: LJ 4/1/88; NYTBR 4/10/88; PW 2/26/88)   **[363.2]**

1575 Murano, Vincent, and William Hoffer. *Cop Hunter.* **1990, Simon & Schuster $19.95 (0-671-66958-3); Pocket paper $4.95 (0-671-66959-1).** An account of the author's ten years as an undercover cop fighting police corruption in the New York Police Department. (Rev: LJ 6/1/90; Newsweek 7/2/90; PW 5/25/90)   **[363.2]**

1576 Rachlin, Harvey. *Making of a Cop.* **1991, Pocket $19.95 (0-671-66525-1).** An account tracing the lives and careers of four New York police officers from the academy to the streets. "Very informative and engrossing."—LJ (Rev: LJ 2/1/91; PW 1/11/91)   **[363.2]**

1577 Roemer, William F., Jr. *Roemer: Man Against the Mob.* **1989, Donald I. Fine $18.95 (1-55611-146-0); Ivy Books paper $4.95 (0-8041-0718-1).** An autobiography of a former FBI agent describing his career combatting organized crime in Chicago. (Rev: BL 10/1/89; NYTBR 10/15/89; PW 9/8/89)   **[363.2]**

1578 Stalker, John. *Stalker Affair: The Shocking True Story of a Notorious Cover-Up in Northern Ireland.* **1988, Viking $19.95 (0-670-82262-0); Penguin paper $7.95 (0-14-011051-8).** A former Manchester constable reveals the results of his investigations into police violence against suspected IRA members in Northern Ireland. (Rev: CSM 5/23/88; LJ 6/15/88; NYTBR 6/18/88)   **[363.2]**

1579 Stroud, Carsten. *Close Pursuit: A Week in the Life of a NYPD Homicide Cop.* **1987, Bantam paper $4.50 (0-553-26645-4).** A look at the lives and methods of New York homicide detectives. "Graphic and gripping."—PW (Rev: BL 2/1/87; NYTBR 4/12/87; PW 1/16/87)   **[363.2]**

1580 Thompson, Josiah. *Reflections in a Private Eye.* **1988, Little, Brown $17.95 (0-316-84175-7); Fawcett paper $4.95 (0-449-021769-8).** Remembrances of a San Francisco private investigator regarding his experiences in a year on the job. (Rev: BL 6/1/88; CSM 6/15/88; Newsweek 6/13/88)   **[363.2]**

1581 Wambaugh, Joseph. *Lines and Shadows.* **1985, Bantam paper $4.50 (0-553-24607-0).** An account of a San Diego, California, police task force created to crack down on criminals preying on illegal aliens. "Police writing at its best."—LJ (Rev: LJ 4/1/84; NYTBR 2/5/84; PW 12/16/83)   **[363.2]**

1582 Wexler, Richard. *Wounded Innocents: The Real Victims of the War Against Child Abuse.* **1990, Prometheus Books $21.95 (0-87975-602-0).** A critical examination of the United States' system of child protection. (Rev: BL 10/1/90; LJ 12/90; PW 9/7/90)   **[363.2]**

Services of special kinds of security and law enforcement agencies

1583 Reisner, Marc. *Game Wars: The Undercover Pursuit of Wildlife Poachers.* **1991, Viking $19.95 (0-670-81486-5).** An examination of wildlife poachers and poaching in the United States and the government officials combatting the illicit practice. (Rev: BL 3/15/91; LJ 2/8/91)   **[363.28]**

Fire hazards

1584 Pyne, Stephen J. *Fire on the Rim: A Firefighter's Season at the Grand Canyon.* **1989, Grove-Weidenfeld $19.95 (1-55584-251-8); Ballantine paper $4.95 (0-345-36219-5).** Accounts of the author's years of firefighting on the North Rim of the Grand Canyon. (Rev: BL 3/1/89; LJ 4/15/89; NYTBR 5/14/89)   **[363.37]**

Controversies related to public morals and customs

1585 Demaris, Ovid. *Boardwalk Jungle.* **1987, Bantam paper $4.95 (0-553-26121-5).** A study of organized crime's ties to gambling in Atlantic City. (Rev: BL 4/15/86; LJ 6/1/86; PW 3/28/86)   **[363.4]**

1586 Griffin, Susan. *Pornography and Silence: Culture's Revenge Against Nature.* 1981, Harper & Row paper $9.95 (0-06-090915-3). An attack on pornography and its damaging personal and societal effects. "A disturbing, enlightening study that plumbs both the meaning and long-ranging effects of pornography."—BL (REV: BL 4/15/81; New Rep 6/29/81; NYTBR 7/12/81) **[363.4]**

1587 Gugliotta, Guy, and Jeff Leen. *Kings of Cocaine: Inside the Medellin Cartel, an Astonishing True Story of Murder, Money and International Corruption.* 1989, Simon & Schuster $19.95 (0-671-64957-4); Harper & Row paper $4.95 (0-06-100027-2). How a group of Colombian gangs parleyed its forces and cornered the world cocaine market in the 1980s. "The most gripping, complete account yet."—LJ (REV: LJ 5/1/89; New Rep 11/27/89; Newsweek 5/15/89) **[363.4]**

1588 Luker, Kristin. *Abortion and the Politics of Motherhood.* 1984, Univ. of California Pr. $27.50 (0-520-04314-6); paper $10.95 (0-520-05597-7). An examination of the social factors behind the abortion controversy. "One of the most objective recent books on this subject."—LJ (REV: LJ 4/15/84; New Rep 4/30/84; NYTBR 5/6/84. AWARDS: BL, the 1980s) **[363.4]**

1589 Marsh, Dave. *50 Ways to Fight Censorship: And Important Facts to Know about the Censors.* 1991, Thunder's Mouth paper $5.95 (1-56025-011-9). The rock music critic presents an examination of the current state of censorship in the United States with proposals on how to fight censors. "Essential for public libraries."—LJ (REV: BL 6/1/91; LJ 7/91; PW 4/26/91) **[363.4]**

1590 Mills, James. *Underground Empire: Where Crime and Governments Embrace.* 1986, Doubleday $22.95 (0-385-17535-3); Dell paper $5.95 (0-440-19026-4). A report on the international drug trade examining the role of world governments in its proliferation. (REV: CSM 5/29/86; LJ 6/1/86; NYTBR 6/29/86) **[363.4]**

1591 Prescott, Peter S. *Child Savers: Juvenile Justice Observed.* 1990, Random $3.98 (0-394-50235-3). An account of the workings of the juvenile justice system in New York City with suggested reforms by the *Newsweek* editor and reporter. (REV: BL 5/15/81; LJ 5/1/81; New Rep 8/15/81) **[363.4]**

1592 Shannon, Elaine. *Desperados: Latin Drug Lords, U.S. Lawmen and the War America Can't Win.* 1988, Viking $21.95 (0-670-81026-6); NAL paper $5.95 (0-451-82207-2). An account of the Drug Enforcement Agency's efforts in Latin America focusing on the kidnapping and murder of DEA Agent Kiki Camarena. (REV: LJ 11/15/88; NYRB 3/30/89; NYTBR 11/6/88) **[363.4]**

1593 Wennberg, Robert. *Life in the Balance: Exploring the Abortion Controversy.* 1985, Eerdmans paper $8.95 (0-8028-0061-0). An examination of the ethical issues involved in the debate surrounding abortion. (REV: BL 10/15/85; NYTBR 11/17/85; PW 12/20/85) **[363.4]**

Drug traffic

1594 Epstein, Edward Jay. *Agency of Fear: Opiates and Political Power in America.* 1990, Routledge $54.95 (0-8091-312-0); paper $17.95 (0-86091-529-8). How the Nixon administration set up a secret police force for domestic surveillance under the guise of drug enforcement. (REV: BL 5/1/77; LJ 3/15/77; NYTBR 5/4/77) **[363.45]**

1595 Goddard, Donald. *Undercover: The Secret Lives of a Federal Agent.* 1988, Random $19.95 (0-8129-1220-9); Dell paper $4.95 (0-440-20516-6). A former U.S. Treasury agent recounts his career fighting illicit drug traders during the 1960s and 1970s. (REV: BL 11/1/88; NYTBR 1/1/89) **[363.45]**

1596 Nicholl, Charles. *Fruit Palace.* 1987, St. Martin's paper $3.95 (0-312-90725-7). A look at Colombia's cocaine industry from the production of coca plants to the drug's refining and international distribution. (REV: LJ 4/15/86; NYTBR 7/6/86; TLS 9/13/85) **[363.45]**

1597 Poppa, Terrence E. *Druglord: The Life and Death of a Mexican Kingpin.* 1990, Pharos Books $18.95 (0-88687-561-7). A study of the life and methods of a Mexican drug smuggler who imported huge quantities of cocaine, heroin, and marijuana into the United States during the 1970s and 1980s. (REV: BL 3/15/90; LJ 3/15/90; PW 2/2/90) **[363.45]**

1598 Rice, Berkeley. *Trafficking: The Boom and Bust of the Air America Cocaine Ring.* 1990, Macmillan $19.95 (0-684-19024-9). An account of the Air America smuggling ring that illegally imported cocaine from Colombia to the United States over a four-year period. (REV: BL 12/15/89; LJ 1/90; NYTBR 1/7/90) **[363.45]**

1599 Smith, Rita Webb, and Tony Chapelle. *Woman Who Took Back Her Streets: One Woman Fights the Drug Wars and Rebuilds Her Community.* 1991, New Horizon $19.95 (0-88282-065-6). A story of a Harlem woman who organized her neighbors against drug trafficking on her block following the 1979 shooting of her son. (REV: LJ 2/1/91; PW 12/14/90) **[363.45]**

1600 Strong, Arturo Carrillo. *Corrido de Cocaine: Inside Stories of Hard Drugs, Big Money and Short Lives.* 1990, Harbinger $17.95 (0-943173-57-4). An account of the U.S.-Mexican illicit drug trade as related by a former Tucson, Arizona, narcotics officer. (REV: BL 4/15/90; LJ 4/1/90; PW 2/23/90) **[363.45]**

Abortion

1601 Bonavoglia, Angela, ed. *Choices We Made: 25 Women and Men Speak Out about Abortion.* 1991, Random $19.95 (0-394-58463-5). Twenty-five writers present personal experiences that have led them to a pro-choice stand on abortion. (REV: BL 1/15/91; LJ 12/90; PW 11/23/90) **[363.46]**

1602 Hertz, Sue. *Caught in the Crossfire: A Year on Abortion's Front Line.* 1991, Prentice Hall $20.00 (0-13-381914-0). An account of a year of protests by the Boston chapter of Operation Rescue against a Brookline, Massachusetts, abortion clinic. (REV: LJ 10/1/91; NYTBR 1/19/92)   **[363.46]**

1603   Tribe, Laurence H. *Abortion: The Clash of Absolutes.* 1990, Norton $19.95 (0-393-02845-3). An overview of the legal, social, and moral issues surrounding abortion in the United States today. (REV: BL 5/1/90; LJ 6/15/90; NYTBR 6/3/90)   **[363.46]**

1604   Whitney, Catherine. *Whose Life?* 1991, Morrow $20.00 (0-688-06922-0). A survey of the current ethical, social, and political issues surrounding abortion in the United States with coverage of recent state legislation and a survey of state-by-state laws concerning the subject. (REV: BL 7/91; PW 5/17/91)   **[363.46]**

Environmental problems and services

1605   Ashworth, William. *Late, Great Lakes: An Environmental History.* 1986, Knopf $24.95 (0-394-55151-6); Wayne State Univ. Pr. paper $14.95 (0-8143-1887-8). A history of man's environmental abuse of the Great Lakes region. "Should be required reading for anyone interested in the environment."—PW (REV: BL 5/15/86; LJ 5/15/86; PW 4/18/86)   **[363.7]**

1606   Berger, John J. *Restoring the Earth: How Americans Are Working to Renew Our Damaged Environment.* 1985, Knopf $18.95 (0-394-52372-5); Doubleday paper $9.95 (0-385-23931-9). Accounts of recent efforts by Americans to restore environmentally damaged sites. (REV: Choice 3/86; LJ 11/1/85; PW 10/18/85)   **[363.7]**

1607   Brown, Michael H. *Toxic Cloud: The Poisoning of America's Air.* 1988, Harper & Row paper $9.95 (0-06-091509-9). An account of polluted air and its effects in the United States by the author of *Laying Waste.* (REV: CSM 1/26/88; NYTBR 12/27/87; PW 9/18/87)   **[363.7]**

1608   Coffel, Steve. *But Not a Drop to Drink: The Life-Saving Guide to Good Water.* 1989, Rawson $19.95 (0-89256-328-1). A study of problems and solutions regarding water quality in contemporary America. "A sound treatment of a complex subject that has a bearing on all American lives."—BL (REV: BL 3/1/89; LJ 3/1/89; PW 2/17/89)   **[363.7]**

1609   Davidson, Art. *In the Wake of the Exxon Valdez: The Story of America's Most Devastating Oil Spill.* 1990, Sierra Club $19.95 (0-87156-614-1). A study of the background and environmental consequences of the 1989 Exxon Valdez oil spill in Alaska. (REV: BL 9/15/90; LJ 5/1/90; NYTBR 5/27/90)   **[363.7]**

1610   Elkington, John. *Green Consumer: A Guide for the Environmentally Aware.* 1990, Penguin paper $9.95 (0-14-778576-6). A guide to environmentally sound purchases for the American consumer. (REV: BL 4/15/90; LJ 3/1/90; TLS 11/18/88)   **[363.7]**

1611   Fisher, David E. *Fire and Ice: The Greenhouse Effect, Ozone Depletion and Nuclear Winter.* 1990, Harper & Row $19.95 (0-06-016214-7). An overview of three atmospheric problems of current concern threatening life on earth. (REV: LJ 2/15/90; Natl Rev 4/1/90; NYTBR 3/4/90)   **[363.7]**

1612   Foreman, Dave. *Confessions of an Eco-Warrior.* 1991, Crown $19.95 (0-517-581230-X). Memoirs of the founder and former head of the radical environmental organization EarthFirst! "Environmental philosophy at its best."—LJ (REV: BL 3/1/91; LJ 3/1/91; PW 1/25/91)   **[363.7]**

1613   Gould, Roy R. *Going Sour: Science and Politics of Acid Rain.* 1985, Birkhauser $14.95 (0-8176-3251-4). A look at the causes and effects of acid rain detailing political inaction regarding the problem. (REV: Choice 12/85; CSM 4/4/86; LJ 7/85)   **[363.7]**

1614   Hynes, H. Patricia. *Earthright.* 1990, Prima $24.95 (1-55958-028-3); paper $12.95 (1-55958-027-5). A guide to environmentally sound practices the average person can follow to help the earth's ecology. (REV: BL 3/15/90; LJ 6/1/90)   **[363.7]**

1615   Manes, Christopher. *Green Rage: Radical Environmentalism and the Unmaking of Civilization.* 1990, Little, Brown $17.95 (0-316-54513-9). An Earth First! member details the philosophy and goals of the radical environmentalist organization. (REV: BL 5/1/90; Choice 11/90; LJ 5/1/90)   **[363.7]**

1616   Ocko, Stephanie. *Environmental Vacations: Volunteer Projects to Save the Planet.* 1990, John Muir paper $15.95 (0-945465-78-5). A guide to environmentally beneficial volunteer projects around the world. (REV: BL 11/1/90; LJ 11/1/90)   **[363.7]**

1617   Roan, Sharon. *Ozone Crisis: The Fifteen Year Evolution of a Sudden Global Emergency.* 1989, Wiley $18.95 (0-471-61985-X); paper $9.95 (0-471-52823-4). An account of the destruction of the ozone layer, its detection, and the slow response of the world to the crisis. (REV: BL 7/89; Choice 12/89; LJ 7/89)   **[363.7]**

1618   Schneider, Stephen H. *Global Warming: Are We Entering the Greenhouse Century?* 1989, Sierra Club $18.95 (0-87156-693-1). A climatologist's assessment of the causes, effects, and consequences of man-made changes in the earth's atmosphere. (REV: BL 8/89; LJ 12/89; NYRB 12/21/89)   **[363.7]**

1619   Sierra Club Legal Defense Fund Staff. *Poisoned Well: New Strategies for Groundwater Protection.* Ed. by Eric P. Jorgensen. 1989, Island Pr. $31.95 (0-933280-56-4); paper $19.95 (0-933280-55-6). A citizen's guide to the protection of America's groundwater resources. "The best existing work for the general reader who is concerned with the pollution of groundwater sources."—Choice (REV: BL 10/1/89; Choice 6/90; LJ 9/15/89)   **[363.7]**

1620   Silver, Cheryl Simon, and Ruth DeFries. *One Earth, One Future: Our Changing Global Environment.* 1990, National Academy Pr. $14.95 (0-309-04141-4). An analysis of the human impact on the earth and its ecosystem. (REV: BL 9/15/90; LJ 9/15/90)   **[363.7]**

1621 Timberlake, Lloyd. *Africa in Crisis: The Causes, the Cures of Environmental Bankruptcy.* **1986, New Society $34.95 (0-86571-081-3); paper $12.95 (0-86571-082-1).** An examination of the causes and possible solutions to the famine threatening the African continent. (REV: BL 5/1/86; Choice 9/86; LJ 8/86)   **[363.7]**

1622 Young, Louise B. *Sowing the Wind: Reflections on the Earth's Atmosphere.* **1990, Prentice Hall $17.95 (0-13-083510-2).** A study of the earth's atmosphere and problems currently affecting it. "A valuable addition to the environmentalist shelf."—PW (REV: BL 7/90; LJ 8/90; PW 6/15/90)   **[363.7]**

Pollution

1623 Brower, Kenneth. *One Earth: Portrait of a Fragile Planet.* **1990, Collins SF $39.95 (0-00-215730-6); paper $24.95 (0-00-637660-6).** Photo essays by 80 photojournalists with commentary by Kenneth Brower regarding the worldwide state of the environment. (REV: BL 10/1/90; LJ 9/15/90; PW 9/7/90)   **[363.73]**

1624 Mitchell, George, and Jack Waugh. *World on Fire.* **1991, Scribner $22.50 (0-684-19231-4).** The Senate majority leader examines the present and future state of the earth's environment. "A highly readable, disturbing, yet ultimately hopeful book."—LJ (REV: BL 12/15/90; LJ 12/90; PW 11/16/90)   **[363.73]**

Food supply

1625 Hunger Project. *Ending Hunger: An Idea Whose Time Has Come.* **1985, Greenwood $38.95 (0-275-90118-1); paper $19.95 (0-275-91809-2).** An analysis of the problem of world hunger and proposed strategies to overcome it. (REV: BL 12/15/85; Choice 2/86; LJ 10/1/85)   **[363.8]**

1626 Physician Task Force on Hunger in America. *Hunger in America: The Growing Epidemic.* **1985, Univ. Pr. of New England $25.00 (0-8195-5150-3); paper $10.95 (0-8195-6158-4).** A report that places the blame for the rise in hunger and malnutrition in the United States on governmental policies. "Should be read not only by specialists in public health but by government officials and by the general public."—Choice (REV: BL 4/15/86; Choice 3/86; LJ 11/1/85. AWARDS: ALA, 1985)   **[363.8]**

1627 Rodale, Robert. *Save Three Lives: A Plan for Famine Protection.* **1991, Sierra Club $18.00 (0-87156-621-4).** The late publisher presents his plan to revolutionize and streamline agricultural production in the Third World to eliminate famine. (REV: BL 9/1/91; LJ 9/1/91; PW 9/13/91)   **[363.8]**

Sterilization

1628 Smith, J. David, and K. Ray Nelson. *Sterilization of Carrie Buck: Was She Feebleminded or Society's Pawn?* **1989, New Horizon $22.95 (0-88282-045-1).** An account of the forced sterilization of a teenage girl in 1927 that led to a Supreme Court ruling upholding the measure. (REV: BL 9/1/89; LJ 8/89)   **[363.97]**

364 Criminology

1629 Buchanan, Edna. *Corpse Had a Familiar Face: Covering Miami, America's Hottest Beat.* **1987, Random $17.95 (0-394-55794-8); Berkley paper $4.95 (1-55773-284-1).** An autobiography of the Miami-based Pulitzer Prize-winning crime reporter. (REV: BL 10/15/87; LJ 11/15/87; NYTBR 12/13/87)   **[364]**

Criminal offenses

1630 Anderson, David C. *Crimes of Justice: Improving the Police, the Courts, the Prisons.* **1988, $17.95 (0-8129-1607-7).** A history and analysis of the American criminal justice system with proposed reforms suggested by the *New York Times* journalist. (REV: BL 3/1/88; LJ 3/15/88; NYTBR 4/17/88)   **[364.1]**

1631 Barthel, Joan. *Love or Honor: The True Story of a Mafia Daughter and an Undercover Cop.* **1989, Morrow $17.95 (0-688-07485-5).** A story of an undercover police officer's experiences during his five-year infiltration of the mafia in New York. (REV: NYTBR 6/19/89; PW 3/24/89)   **[364.1]**

1632 Beresford, David. *Ten Men Dead: The Story of the 1981 Irish Hunger Strike.* **1989, Atlantic Monthly $18.95 (0-87113-269-9).** An analysis of the events surrounding the Irish hunger strike of 1981, in which ten men starved themselves to death in a Belfast prison, in protest of British policies toward Ireland. (REV: LJ 4/1/89; PW 1/6/89)   **[364.1]**

1633 Bing, Leon. *Do or Die.* **1991, HarperCollins $19.95 (0-06-016326-7).** This author's first book examines the gang lives of warring Bloods and Crips in south central Los Angeles. "Should be read by everyone professionally involved or personally concerned with the future of urban America."—PW (REV: BL 7/91; LJ 7/91; PW 7/5/91. AWARDS: BL, 1991)   **[364.1]**

1634 Blum, Howard. *Wanted: The Search for Nazis in America.* **1989, Simon & Schuster paper $8.95 (0-671-67607-5).** The author presents evidence that former Nazi war criminals are living in the United States but escape persecution due to government and public apathy. (REV: BL 2/15/77; LJ 1/1/77; NYTBR 1/16/77)   **[364.1]**

1635 Blumenthal, Ralph. *Last Days of the Sicilians: At War with the Mafia, the FBI Assault on the Pizza Connection.* **1988, Random $18.95 (0-8129-1594-1); Pocket paper $4.95 (0-671-68277-6).** A study of the FBI investigation and subsequent trial of the organized crime drug and money-laundering ring dubbed the Pizza Connection. (REV: NYTBR 9/11/88; TLS 12/16/88)   **[364.1]**

1636 Bonner, Elena. *Alone Together.* **1986, Knopf $17.95 (0-394-55835-9); Random paper $8.95 (0-394-75538-3).** Memoirs of the Soviet dissident and wife of Andrei Sakharov. (REV: BL 11/15/86; LJ 1/87; New Yorker 1/19/87)   **[364.1]**

1637 Bugliosi, Vincent T. *Drugs in America: The Case for Victory.* **1991, Knightsbridge $21.95 (1-56129-064-5).** The California trial lawyer and writer presents his plan to combat drug abuse on the national and international fronts. "A ringing call to action."—PW (Rev: LJ 8/91; PW 5/31/91) **[364.1]**

1638 Collin, Richard O., and Gordon Freedman. *Winter of Fire: The Abduction of General Dozier and the Downfall of the Red Brigades.* **1990, Dutton $19.95 (0-525-24880-3).** An account of the 1981 kidnapping of an American general in Italy at the hands of the leftist Red Brigade. (Rev: BL 6/15/90; LJ 5/15/90; PW 6/22/90) **[364.1]**

1639 Cox, Donald. *Mafia Wipeout: How the Feds Put Away an Entire Mob Family.* **1989, Shalpolsky $18.95 (0-944007-52-X).** An account of the 1988 investigation and persecution of 17 Philadelphia organized crime members. (Rev: BL 1/1/90; LJ 2/15/90) **[364.1]**

1640 Domanick, Joe. *Faking It in America: Barry Minkow and the Great ZZZZ Best Scam.* **1989, Contemporary $19.95 (0-8092-4497-7).** An account of the multimillion dollar Southern California investment fraud scam run through the ZZZZ Best carpet-cleaning company. (Rev: LJ 9/1/89; PW 9/15/89) **[364.1]**

1641 Eddy, Paul. *Cocaine Wars: Murder, Money, Corruption and the World's Most Valuable Commodity.* **1988, Norton $18.95 (0-393-02579-9); Bantam paper $4.95 (0-553-28171-2).** A look at the cocaine trade of a prominent crime cartel between its base in Colombia and Miami. (Rev: BL 5/15/88; LJ 7/88; NYTBR 8/21/88) **[364.1]**

1642 English, T. J. *Westies: Inside the Hell's Kitchen Irish Mob.* **1990, Putnam $19.95 (0-399-13540-5); St. Martin's paper $5.95 (0-312-92429-1).** An account of the Irish organized crime group that controlled New York's Hell's Kitchen from the mid-1960s through the mid-1980s. (Rev: BL 1/1/90; LJ 2/1/90; NYTBR 4/8/90) **[364.1]**

1643 Fox, Stephen. *Blood and Power: Organized Crime in 20th Century America.* **1989, Morrow $22.95 (0-688-04350-X); Penguin paper $10.95 (0-14-013438-7).** A history of organized crime in the United States from the era of Prohibition to the present. (Rev: BL 6/1/89; LJ 7/89; PW 5/26/89) **[364.1]**

1644 Frantz, Douglas. *Levine & Co: Wall Street's Insider Trading Scandal.* **1988, Avon paper $4.50 (0-380-70625-3).** A study of the financial career of Wall Street inside trader Dennis Levine and the events that led to his arrest by SEC officials in 1986. (Rev: BL 9/15/87; LJ 9/1/87; NYTBR 10/25/87) **[364.1]**

1645 Greene, A. C. *Santa Claus Bank Robbery.* **1986, Pacesetter Pr. paper $9.95 (0-87719-055-0).** The West Texas writer re-creates a bank robbery in 1922 in a small town in which one of the robbers wore a Santa Claus suit to avoid detection. (Rev: Atl 9/72; LJ 7/72; New Yorker 9/16/72) **[364.1]**

1646 Greene, Melissa Fay. *Praying for Sheetrock.* **1991, Addison Wesley $21.95 (0-201-55048-2).** A biography of a controversial Georgia county commissioner who initiated a program of local reform

but was convicted of drug conspiracy charges following a 1988 sting operation. (Rev: NYTBR 11/3/91; PW 8/16/91. Awards: ALA, 1992) **[364.1]**

1647 Greising, David, and Laurie Morse. *Brokers, Bagmen, and Moles: Fraud and Corruption in the Chicago Futures Market.* **1991, Wiley $24.95 (0-471-53057-3).** An exposé of corruption and practices of questionable ethics occurring within the Chicago futures market. (Rev: LJ 7/91; PW 5/17/91) **[364.1]**

1648 Hubbard, David G. *Winning Back the Sky: A Tactical Analysis of Terrorism.* **1986, Saybrook $14.95 (0-933071-04-3); paper $7.95 (0-933071-14-0).** A program for the prevention of hijacking incidents based on the author's study of past hijackings and their outcomes. (Rev: BL 1/1/86; LJ 1/86; PW 11/29/85) **[364.1]**

1649 Katz, Robert. *Naked by the Window: The Fatal Marriage of Carl Andre and Ana Mendieta.* **1990, Atlantic Monthly $19.95 (0-87113-354-7).** An account of the death of a New York artist and her husband's subsequent trial for her murder in which he was acquitted. (Rev: NYTBR 6/10/90; Newsweek 5/28/90; PW 3/30/90) **[364.1]**

1650 Kwitny, Jonathan. *Crimes of Patriots: A True Tale of Dope, Dirty Money, and the CIA.* **1988, Simon & Schuster paper $7.95 (0-671-66637-1).** A story of an Australian bank run by former U.S. military and intelligence corps members to facilitate the laundering of illicit drug and arms monies. (Rev: BL 9/1/87; CSM 9/18/87; NYTBR 9/6/87) **[364.1]**

1651 Lacey, Robert. *Little Man: Meyer Lansky and the Gangster's Life.* **1991, Little, Brown $24.95 (0-316-51168-4).** A biography of the Polish-born man who became an American casino owner and bootlegger. "A major contribution to the history of organized crime in the United States."—PW (Rev: BL 9/1/91; NYTBR 10/22/91; PW 8/16/91) **[364.1]**

1652 McClintick, David. *Indecent Exposure: A True Story of Hollywood and Wall Street.* **1983, Dell paper $5.95 (0-440-14007-2).** An inside story of the financial scandal that led to the resignation of David Begelman, former president of Columbia Pictures. (Rev: BL 9/1/82; LJ 8/82; NYTBR 8/22/82) **[364.1]**

1653 Malkin, Peter Z., and Harry Stein. *Eichmann in My Hands.* **1990, Warner $22.95 (0-446-51418-7).** Memoirs of the Israeli agent who captured Nazi war criminal Adolf Eichmann in Argentina in 1960. (Rev: BL 3/15/90; LJ 4/15/90; PW 3/30/90) **[364.1]**

1654 Mass, Peter. *Manhunt.* **1986, Random $17.95 (0-394-55293-8); Jove paper $3.95 (0-515-09014-X).** An account of the spy career of Edwin P. Wilson, a CIA agent who supplied Libya with arms and explosives in exchange for cash. (Rev: LJ 7/86; NYTBR 4/27/86; Time 7/7/86) **[364.1]**

1655 Meeropol, Robert, and Michael Meeropol. *We Are Your Sons: The Legacy of Ethel and Julius Rosenberg.* **1986, Univ. of Illinois Pr. $27.50 (0-252-01263-1).** The sons of the Rosenbergs, who were convicted and executed in 1953 of conspiracy to commit espionage, tell their memoirs of their parents, publish letters from them, and make a case for their innocence. (REV: NYTBR 5/25/75; PW 2/24/75; Time 5/5/75) **[364.1]**

1656 Mokhiber, Russell. *Corporate Crime and Violence: Big Business Power and the Abuse of the Public Trust.* **1988, Sierra Club $25.00 (0-87156-723-7); paper $12.95 (0-87156-608-7).** Thirty-six case studies of the abuse of power by American big businesses including the Three Mile Island, Love Canal, and Bhopal incidents. (REV: Choice 2/89; LJ 10/1/88; PW 5/13/88) **[364.1]**

1657 Pileggi, Nicholas. *Wise Guy: Life in a Mafia Family.* **1990, Pocket paper $4.95 (0-671-72322-7).** This autobiography by a former organized crime member was the basis for the Martin Scorcese film *Good Fellas.* (REV: NYTBR 1/26/86; Newsweek 2/10/86; Time 3/3/86) **[364.1]**

1658 Pistone, Joseph D., and Richard Woodley. *Donnie Brasco: My Undercover Life in the Mafia.* **1989, NAL paper $4.95 (0-451-15749-4).** An account of a former FBI undercover agent who infiltrated the Mafia and spent five years posing as a jewel thief. (REV: NYTBR 2/14/88; PW 11/18/88; Time 1/18/88) **[364.1]**

1659 Ritchie, Robert C. *Captain Kidd and the War Against the Pirates.* **1986, Harvard Univ. Pr. $22.50 (0-674-09501-4); paper $11.95 (0-674-09502-2).** A biography of William Kidd provides the setting for the historical analysis of pirates and piracy along the U.S. Atlantic Coast. (REV: Choice 3/87; LJ 11/1/86; NYRB 1/29/87) **[364.1]**

1660 Rubin, Lillian B. *Quiet Rage: Bernie Goetz in a Time of Madness.* **1988, Univ. of California Pr. paper $9.95 (0-520-06446-1).** A psychological profile of the man involved in the 1984 New York subway shooting case. (REV: BL 9/15/86; LJ 9/15/86; PW 8/22/86) **[364.1]**

1661 Sakharov, Andrei D. *Memoirs.* **1990, Knopf $29.95 (0-394-53740-8).** Memoirs of the Nobel Peace Prize–winning Soviet physicist. (REV: BL 4/15/90; LJ 6/1/90; Newsweek 7/9/90. AWARDS: LJ, 1990) **[364.1]**

1662 Sakharov, Andrei D. *Moscow and Beyond: 1986 to 1989.* **1991, Knopf $19.95 (0-394-58797-9).** The second and concluding volume of the memoirs of the Russian physicist tracing the last three years of his life following his release from forced exile in Gorky. (REV: BL 12/1/90; LJ 1/91; NYTBR 12/30/90) **[364.1]**

1663 Soares, John. *Loaded Dice: The True Story of a Casino Cheat.* **1987, Dell paper $3.95 (0-440-14858-8).** Memoirs of the author's career as a casino hustler in Las Vegas. "An unusually fascinating book that deserves a wide audience."—BL (REV: BL 9/1/85; NYTBR 9/22/85) **[364.1]**

1664 Sterling, Claire. *Octopus: The Long Reach of the Sicilian Mafia.* **1990, Norton $19.95 (0-393-02796-1).** A study of the role of the Sicilian mafia in the international heroin trade. (REV: LJ 1/90; NYTBR 1/28/90; TLS 2/23/90) **[364.1]**

1665 Stoll, Clifford. *Cuckoo's Egg: Inside the World of Computer Espionage.* **1989, Doubleday $19.95 (0-385-24946-2).** The author describes how he was able to track a spy, engaged in computer espionage against the United States, through his computer lab in Berkeley, California. (REV: CSM 10/13/89; LJ 9/15/89; NYTBR 11/26/89) **[364.1]**

1666 Taibbi, Mike, and Anna Sims-Phillips. *Unholy Alliances: Working the Tawana Brawley Story.* **1989, Harcourt $18.95 (0-15-188050-6).** The account of two television reporters who were assigned to cover the Tawana Brawley case and how the case became a media circus. (REV: CSM 6/26/89; LJ 5/15/89; NYTBR 6/4/89) **[364.1]**

1667 Talese, Gay. *Honor Thy Father.* **1986, Dell paper $4.95 (0-440-33468-3).** The history of the Mafia in the United States as told through a study of the Bonanno crime family. "Not fiction but raw undisguised and penetrating writing of the highest journalistic order."—PW (REV: Newsweek 10/4/71; PW 8/30/71; Time 10/4/71) **[364.1]**

1668 Traub, James. *Too Good to Be True: The Outlandish Story of Wedtech.* **1990, Doubleday $21.95 (0-385-26182-9).** An account of the circumstances surrounding the Wedtech financial scandal that involved a small New York company, inflated military contracts, and the Reagan administration. "A delightfully written book."—NYTBR (REV: LJ 7/90; NYTBR 7/29/90; New Yorker 10/1/90) **[364.1]**

1669 Weinstein, Allen. *Perjury: The Hiss-Chambers Case.* **1978, Knopf $39.95 (0-394-49546-2).** An examination of the 1949–1950 case in which Hiss was accused by Chambers of espionage and eventually convicted on charges of perjury. (REV: CSM 4/19/78; LJ 3/1/78; NYRB 4/20/78) **[364.1]**

1670 Wilkinson, Alec. *Moonshine: A Life in Pursuit of White Liquor.* **1985, Knopf $13.95 (0-394-54587-7); Penguin paper (0-14-008985-3).** A profile of a North Carolina Alcoholic Beverage Control officer detailing the author's observations while on patrol for illegal alcohol. (REV: LJ 8/85; NYTBR 10/13/85; Time 9/9/85) **[364.1]**

1671 Williams, Terry. *Cocaine Kids: The Inside Story of a Teenage Drug Ring.* **1989, Addison Wesley $16.95 (0-201-09360-X); paper $7.95 (0-201-57003-3).** A study of a group of teenage drug dealers in Spanish Harlem, and how the underground economy works, as told through the subjects' own words. (REV: BL 8/89; NYTBR 8/27/89; PW 6/9/89) **[364.1]**

Murder

1672 Alexander, Shana. *Nutcracker: Money, Madness, Murder.* **1986, Dell paper $3.95 (0-440-16512-1).** An account of the murder of a Salt Lake City millionaire plotted and carried out by members of his family. (REV: BL 6/15/85; LJ 7/85; NYTBR 6/16/85) **[364.152]**

1673 Begg, Paul. *Jack the Ripper: The Uncensored Facts.* **1990, Parkwest $19.95 (0-86051-528-1).** Collected evidence surrounding the infamous Whitechapel murders of 1888. (Rev: BL 1/1/90; LJ 12/89; PW 12/1/89)   **[364.152]**

1674 Borowitz, Albert J. *Thurtell-Hunt Murder Case: Dark Mirror to Regency England.* **1987, Louisiana State Univ. Pr.** $29.95 (0-8071-1371-9). A study of the events surrounding an 1823 London murder case in which three criminals conspired to kill a former accomplice and were captured shortly after the act by the local citizenry. (Rev: Atl 11/87; LJ 10/1/87)   **[364.152]**

1675 Bugliosi, Vincent T. *And the Sea Will Tell.* **1991, Norton** $22.95 (0-393-02919-0). An account of a 1974 murder case involving two couples on a South Pacific island. (Rev: BL 11/15/90; LJ 12/90)   **[364.152]**

1676 Burdick, Thomas, and Charlene Mitchell. *Blue Thunder: How the Mafia Owned and Finally Murdered Cigarette Boat King Donald Aronow.* **1990, Simon & Schuster** $22.95 (0-671-66321-6). An examination of the 1987 Miami murder of speedboat racer and builder Donald Aronow. (Rev: LJ 12/90; NYTBR 11/25/90)   **[364.152]**

1677 Cahill, Tim, and Russ Ewing. *Buried Dreams: Inside the Mind of a Serial Killer.* **1987, Bantam** $17.95 (0-553-05115-6); paper $4.95 (0-553-25836-2). A profile of the crimes and psychological makeup of Chicago-area serial killer John Wayne Gacy. (Rev: BL 12/15/85; LJ 2/1/86; NYTBR 3/30/86)   **[364.152]**

1678 Carpenter, Teresa. *Missing Beauty: A Story of Murder and Obsession.* **1988, Norton** $18.95 (0-393-02569-1); Zebra paper $4.95 (0-8217-2755-9). A true-crime story of the murder of a prostitute in Boston's Combat Zone. "Absorbing and unsettling . . . an outstanding piece of crime reportage."—BL (Rev: BL 6/15/88; LJ 10/1/88; NYTBR 6/26/88)   **[364.152]**

1679 Cauffiel, Lowell. *Masquerade: A True Story of Seduction, Compulsion and Murder.* **1988, Doubleday** $18.95 (0-385-23772-3); Zebra paper $4.95 (0-8217-2833-4). An account of the 1985 Detroit murder of a psychologist following his involvement with a young prostitute. (Rev: NYTBR 10/9/88; PW 7/1/88)   **[364.152]**

1680 Davies, Nick. *White Lies: Rape, Murder and Justice, Texas Style.* **1991, Pantheon** $22.95 (0-679-40167-9). An account of a 1980 Texas case in which an African-American janitor was convicted with circumstantial evidence of the murder of a high school girl, and served nine years on Death Row before his conviction was overturned in an appeals court. (Rev: LJ 3/1/91; NYTBR 3/24/91)   **[364.152]**

1681 DeSantis, John. *For the Color of His Skin: The Murder of Yusef Hawkins and the Trial of Bensonhurst.* **1991, Pharos Books** $18.95 (0-88687-621-4). An examination of the 1989 murder of a young African-American man by a group of white teenagers in Bensonhurst and the subsequent trial of eight of them for the crime. (Rev: BL 11/15/91; LJ 10/15/91; PW 9/27/91)   **[364.152]**

1682 Dillmann, John. *Blood Warning.* **1989, Putnam** $19.95 (0-399-13485-9). An account of two New Orleans murders and their solution by the police detective assigned to the case. (Rev: BL 8/89; LJ 9/1/89; PW 7/28/89)   **[364.152]**

1683 Egginton, Joyce. *From Cradle to Grave.* **1989, Morrow** $18.95 (0-688-07566-5); Jove paper $4.95 (0-515-10301-2). An account of Marybeth Tinning, a Schenectady, New York, mother who killed her nine children shortly after their births. (Rev: BL 3/1/89; LJ 3/1/89; PW 1/20/89)   **[364.152]**

1684 Elkind, Peter. *Death Shift: A Tale of Murder and Medicine.* **1989, Viking** $19.95 (0-670-81397-4); NAL paper $4.95 (0-451-40196-4). An account of a San Antonio nurse and her possible role in the mysterious deaths of up to 13 children under her care. "True-crime reporting at its most compelling."—BL (Rev: BL 7/89; LJ 6/1/89; PW 6/16/89)   **[364.152]**

1685 Fox, James. *White Mischief: The Murder of Lord Erroll.* **1988, Random paper** $4.95 (0-394-75687-8). The investigation of the murder, unsolved until the publication of this book, of the Earl of Erroll in Kenya in 1941. "Fox's gift for narrative immediately carries the reader into a long-gone, closed world of privilege and debauchery."—Time (Rev: BL 3/1/83; LJ 4/1/83; Time 4/4/83. Awards: Time, 1983)   **[364.152]**

1686 Frank, Gerold. *Boston Strangler.* **1986, NAL paper** $5.95 (0-451-16625-6). The story of ten murders which shook Boston in the early 1960s and the search for the killer. "A shocking, revealing version of as scary a true murder-story as ever hit American papers."—PW (Rev: LJ 11/15/66; NYTBR 10/23/66; PW 9/26/66. Awards: NYTBR, 1966)   **[364.152]**

1687 Ganey, Terry. *St. Joseph's Children: A True Story of Terror and Justice.* **1989, Carol Publg. Group** $17.95 (0-8184-0509-0). A true account of the murders of up to 16 children in St. Joseph, Missouri, and of the capture, trial, and conviction of a drifter for one of the crimes. (Rev: BL 11/1/89; LJ 10/1/89; PW 9/8/89)   **[364.152]**

1688 Hammer, Richard. *CBS Murders.* **1988, NAL paper** $4.50 (0-451-15544-0). An account of a 1982 murder case in which a woman and three CBS technicians were killed near the Manhattan waterfront. (Rev: BL 4/15/87; NYTBR 6/21/87; PW 5/1/87)   **[364.152]**

1689 Harris, Jean. *Stranger in Two Worlds.* **1987, Zebra paper** $4.50 (0-8217-2112-7). An autobiography of the woman currently serving time for the murder of Dr. Herman Tarnower. (Rev: BL 7/86; LJ 9/1/86; NYTBR 8/24/86)   **[364.152]**

1690 Headley, Lake, and William Hoffman. *Loud and Clear.* **1990, Henry Holt** $22.50 (0-8050-1138-2). An account of the car-bomb murder of an *Arizona Republic* newspaper reporter in 1976 and the subsequent trial and cover-up. (Rev: BL 9/1/90; LJ 8/90; PW 7/27/90)   **[364.152]**

1691 Horton, Sue. *Billionaire Boys Club: Rich Kids, Money and Murder.* 1989, St. Martin's $18.95 (0-312-02872-5); paper $4.95 (0-312-92232-9). An account of a Beverly Hills investment group whose financial troubles led four of its members to commit a kidnapping and murder. (Rev: BL 10/1/89; LJ 10/15/89; PW 9/29/89) **[364.152]**

1692 Humes, Edward. *Buried Secrets: A True Story of Serial Murder, Black Magic and Drug Running on the U.S. Border.* 1991, Dutton $19.95 (0-525-24946-X). A study of the Matamoros, Mexico, cult responsible for illicit drug smuggling and a series of ritual torture-murders. "One of the best true-crime tales in recent times."—PW (Rev: BL 1/15/91; LJ 12/90; PW 12/14/90) **[364.152]**

1693 Hynes, Charles Joseph, and Bob Drury. *Incident at Howard Beach: The Case for Murder.* 1990, Putnam $22.95 (0-399-13500-6). An account of the 1986 race-motivated murder of an African American in New York City and the trial that followed. (Rev: BL 1/1/90; LJ 3/1/90; PW 1/5/90) **[364.152]**

1694 James, P. D., and T. A. Critchley. *Maul and the Pear Tree: The Ratcliffe Highway Murders.* 1986, Mysterious $17.95 (0-89296-152-X). A true crime account of a nineteenth-century English murder case and its effects by the master mystery writer. (Rev: BL 2/1/86; CSM 9/2/86; NYTBR 4/6/86) **[364.152]**

1695 Johnson, Joyce. *What Lisa Knew: The Secrets of an American Family.* 1990, Putnam $19.95 (0-399-13474-3); Zebra paper $4.95 (0-8217-3387-7). An account of the Hedda Nussbaum-Joel Steinberg case of the child abuse manslaughter death of their adopted daughter. (Rev: BL 2/15/90; NYTBR 4/8/90; Newsweek 4/23/90) **[364.152]**

1696 Kaminsky, Alice. *Victim's Song.* 1985, Prometheus $22.95 (0-87975-292-0). An account of the murder of the author's son and the subsequent trial and sentencing of his killers. "A forceful, stinging indictment."—PW (Rev: BL 9/1/85; Natl Rev 3/28/86; PW 8/2/85) **[364.152]**

1697 Kaplan, Joel, et al. *Murder of Innocence: The Tragic Life and Final Rampage of Laurie Dunn.* 1990, Warner $19.95 (0-446-51572-8). The extremely troubled life of the woman who went on a shooting assault at an elementary school in Winnetka, Illinois, in 1988. (Rev: BL 8/90; LJ 8/90; PW 7/13/90) **[364.152]**

1698 Kates, Brian. *Murder of a Shopping Bag Lady.* 1985, Harcourt $15.95 (0-15-763540-4). An account of a *New York Daily News* reporter's investigation into the 1981 murder of a homeless woman. (Rev: BL 9/15/85; LJ 10/15/85; NYTBR 11/3/85) **[364.152]**

1699 Keyes, Daniel. *Unveiling Claudia: A True Story of Serial Murder.* 1986, Bantam $17.95 (0-553-05126-1); paper $4.50 (0-553-26502-4). An account of the role of a woman afflicted with multiple personalities in an Ohio serial murder case. "A masterfully told, absorbing story."—LJ (Rev: BL 5/1/86; LJ 7/86) **[364.152]**

1700 Kleinman, Dena. *A Deadly Silence: The Ordeal of Cheryl Pierson, a Case of Incest and Murder.* 1988, Atlantic Monthly $19.95 (0-87113-244-3); NAL paper $4.95 (0-451-16261-7). An examination of the trial of Cheryl Pierson, who hired a high school friend to kill her father because he had been sexually abusing her. "Investigative journalism at its best—fair and even-handed, written with compassion for human suffering."—PW (Rev: NYTBR 10/9/88; PW 8/12/88) **[364.152]**

1701 Kolarik, Gera-Lind, and Wayne Klatt. *Freed to Kill: The True Story of Larry Eyler.* 1990, Chicago Review $18.95 (1-55652-092-1). A study of an Indiana-Illinois serial killer who was released on a Fourth Amendment violation only to kill again. (Rev: BL 12/15/90; LJ 10/1/90; PW 8/17/90) **[364.152]**

1702 Lane, Mark. *Plausible Denial.* 1991, Thunder's Mouth $22.95 (1-56025-000-3). An analysis of the potential role of the CIA in the assassination of John F. Kennedy. "A highly stimulating, disturbing book."—PW (Rev: LJ 11/1/91; PW 9/6/91) **[364.152]**

1703 Levy, Steven. *Unicorn's Secret: Murder in the Age of Aquarius.* 1988, Prentice Hall $18.95 (0-13-937830-8); NAL paper $4.95 (0-451-40166-2). An account of a Philadelphia teacher and guru who murdered one of his students, fled, and is currently in hiding. (Rev: BL 10/15/88; LJ 11/15/88; NYTBR 10/9/88) **[364.152]**

1704 Lincoln, Victoria. *A Private Disgrace: Lizzie Borden by Daylight.* 1986, International Polygonics paper $5.95 (0-930330-35-8). An account of the 1893 Massachusetts trial of Lizzie Borden for the murder of her parents. "The best book, and the last word, on this legendary case."—New Yorker (Rev: BL 12/15/67; NYTBR 1/28/68; New Yorker 11/25/67) **[364.152]**

1705 Lindsey, Robert. *A Gathering of Saints: A True Story of Money, Murder, and Deceit.* 1988, Simon & Schuster $18.95 (0-671-65112-9); Dell paper $4.95 (0-440-20558-1). An examination of the bombing and forgery scandal that shook the Latter-day Saints church in 1985. (Rev: BL 9/15/88; NYTBR 10/9/88; TLS 6/9/89) **[364.152]**

1706 Maas, Peter. *In a Child's Name: The Legacy of a Mother's Murder.* 1990, Simon & Schuster $19.95 (0-671-69416-2). An account of an Indiana dentist who murdered his wife and the subsequent child custody fight between his family and hers for control of their son. (Rev: BL 10/15/90; LJ 11/15/90; PW 9/28/90) **[364.152]**

1707 McFarland, Gerald. *Counterfeit Man: The True Story of the Boorn-Colvin Murder Case.* 1991, Pantheon $22.95 (0-394-58009-5). A study of an early nineteenth-century Vermont murder mystery involving the seven-year disappearance and reappearance of a man and the trial of his two brothers-in-law for the crime. (Rev: LJ 12/90; NYTBR 1/6/91; PW 11/9/90) **[364.152]**

1708 McGinniss, Joe. *Blind Faith.* 1989, Putnam $21.95 (0-399-13352-6); NAL paper $5.95 (0-451-16806-

2). A true crime story of a man who had his wife murdered to collect insurance money, and how his three sons reacted when they found out the truth about their mother's death. (REV: BL 11/15/88; LJ 1/89; NYTBR 1/29/89) **[364.152]**

1709 McGinniss, Joe. *Fatal Vision.* **1983, Putnam $17.95 (0-399-12816-6).** An account of the murder trial of Dr. Jeffrey MacDonald, a former member of the Green Beret who was convicted of killing three members of his family. (REV: BL 8/83; NYTBR 9/25/83; Newsweek 9/12/83) **[364.152]**

1710 Malcolm, Andrew H. *Final Harvest.* **1987, NAL paper $4.95 (0-451-16455-5).** An account of the 1981 Minnesota murder of two bankers by an angered farmer who had had his land repossessed. (REV: LJ 5/1/86; NYTBR 4/20/86; PW 3/7/86) **[364.152]**

1711 Marton, Kati. *Polk Conspiracy: Murder and Cover-Up in the Case of CBS Correspondent George Polk.* **1990, Farrar $22.95 (0-374-13553-3).** A study of the murder of CBS news correspondent George Polk in Greece in 1948 and its aftermath. (REV: LJ 8/90; Newsweek 10/8/90; Time 10/8/90. AWARDS: Time, 1990) **[364.152]**

1712 Meyer, Peter. *Death of Innocence: A Case of Murder in Vermont.* **1985, Putnam $17.95 (0-399-13025-X); Berkley paper $3.95 (0-425-10172-X).** An examination of a Vermont murder case and trial involving the rape and murder of two young girls by teenage boys. (REV: BL 1/15/85; LJ 2/1/85; PW 2/15/85) **[364.152]**

1713 Naifeh, Steven, and Gregory W. Smith. *Mormon Murders: A True Story of Greed, Forgery, Deceit, and Death.* **1988, Grove-Weidenfeld $19.95 (1-55584-064-7); NAL paper $4.95 (0-451-40152-2).** An account of the 1985 Salt Lake City bombings by a document dealer and forger that scandalized the Church of Jesus Christ of Latter-day Saints. (REV: BL 6/15/88; LJ 8/88; PW 7/1/88) **[364.152]**

1714 North, Mark. *Act of Treason: The Role of J. Edgar Hoover in the Assassination of John F. Kennedy.* **1991, Carroll & Graf $25.95 (0-88184-747-X).** A Texas attorney's book speculating that the assassination of John F. Kennedy was carried out by members of the Louisiana mafia with the knowledge of the FBI director. (REV: LJ 11/1/91; PW 9/20/91) **[364.152]**

1715 O'Brien, Darcy. *Murder in Little Egypt.* **1989, Morrow $19.95 (0-688-07137-6); NAL paper $4.95 (0-451-40167-0).** The story of an Illinois doctor who murdered two of his sons in an attempt to collect insurance money. (REV: BL 2/1/89; LJ 2/1/89; NYTBR 3/12/89) **[364.152]**

1716 O'Brien, Darcy. *Two of a Kind: The Hillside Stranglers.* **1990, NAL paper $4.95 (0-451-16302-8).** An account of the serial killer team that terrorized Los Angeles in the fall of 1977. "Definitive . . . riveting . . . an outstanding true crime story."—PW (REV: BL 10/15/85; LJ 9/1/85; PW 8/23/85) **[364.152]**

1717 Olsen, Jack. *Give a Boy a Gun: The True Story of Law and Disorder in the American West.* **1986,**

Dell paper $3.95 (0-440-13168-5). An account of the 1981 murders of two Idaho game wardens by a modern-day outlaw. (REV: LJ 11/1/85; NYTBR 1/21/86; Newsweek 12/9/85) **[364.152]**

1718 Prendergast, Alan. *Poison Tree: A True Story of Family Terror.* **1987, Avon paper $4.95 (0-380-70346-7).** An account of the 1982 murder of a Wyoming father by his teenage son and daughter and the subsequent trial that freed them both. (REV: LJ 6/1/86; PW 5/2/86) **[364.152]**

1719 Provost, Gary. *Perfect Husband: The True Story of the Trusting Bride Who Discovered Her Husband was a Cold-Blooded Killer.* **1991, Pocket $20.00 (0-671-72493-2).** The story of a Florida woman who married a homicidal Greek immigrant who attempted to kill her. (REV: BL 12/1/91; PW 10/25/91) **[364.152]**

1720 Robins, Natalie S., and M. L. Aronson. *Savage Grace.* **1986, Dell paper $4.95 (0-440-17576-3).** A study of the murder of a socialite mother by her son in 1972. Based on interviews and letters from those involved in the case. (REV: BL 6/1/85; Newsweek 8/5/85; Time 8/12/85) **[364.152]**

1721 Siegel, Barry. *Death in White Bear Lake: The True Chronicle of an All-American Town.* **1990, Bantam $19.95 (0-553-05790-1).** A study of a child abuse murder case that was reopened 21 years after the crime. (REV: BL 5/15/90; LJ 6/15/90; NYTBR 7/29/90) **[364.152]**

1722 Simon, David. *Homicide: A Year on the Killing Streets.* **1991, Houghton $22.95 (0-395-48829-X).** A *Baltimore Sun* journalist recounts his year spent accompanying the Baltimore police homicide unit at work. (REV: LJ 6/1/91; PW 4/26/91) **[364.152]**

1723 Thernstrom, Melanie. *Dead Girl.* **1990, Pocket $19.95 (0-671-66332-1).** An account of a 1984 murder of an Oakland woman by her boyfriend, as written by a childhood friend. (REV: LJ 8/90; PW 8/10/90) **[364.152]**

1724 Thompson, Thomas. *Blood and Money.* **1989, Dell paper $5.95 (0-440-10679-6).** The story of the murder of a Houston socialite and the subsequent trial of her husband. "Spellbinding . . . a meticulous examination of a crime."—LJ (REV: LJ 10/15/76; NYTBR 10/3/76; PW 7/12/76) **[364.152]**

1725 Wambaugh, Joseph. *Blooding.* **1989, Morrow $18.95 (0-688-08617-9); Bantam paper $5.95 (0-553-28281-6).** An account of an English murder case that was solved through the first use of DNA "fingerprinting." (REV: BL 12/1/88; LJ 2/15/89; NYTBR 2/19/89) **[364.152]**

1726 Wambaugh, Joseph. *Echoes in the Darkness.* **1987, Morrow $18.95 (0-688-06889-8); Bantam paper $5.95 (0-553-26932-1).** An account of the 1979 murder of a Pennsylvania schoolteacher by her boyfriend for insurance purposes. (REV: BL 1/1/87; LJ 2/15/87; PW 1/9/87) **[364.152]**

1727 Wambaugh, Joseph. *Onion Field.* **1974, Dell paper $5.95 (0-440-17350-7).** An account of the murder of one policeman and the effects of the murder trial on his partner. "Wambaugh's spare, vivid documentary style draws the marrow out of police, court and psychiatric records while shaping a strong case for the reform of the American criminal justice system."—PW (Rᴇᴠ: LJ 9/1/73; NYTBR 9/2/73; PW 7/23/73)   **[364.152]**

1728 Whitfield, Stephen J. *Death in the Delta: The Story of Emmett Till*. 1988, Free Pr. $19.95 (0-02-935121-9). An investigation into the 1955 murder of a black teenager and the subsequent trial that acquitted the alleged killers. (Rᴇᴠ: Choice 5/89; LJ 11/15/88; PW 9/30/88)   **[364.152]**

1729 Wolfe, Linda. *Professor and the Prostitute: And Other True Tales of Murder and Madness*. 1986, Houghton $16.95 (0-395-40049-X); Ballantine paper $4.95 (0-345-34367-0). Case studies of unusual true murder cases. "Compelling reading for true crime buffs."—BL (Rᴇᴠ: BL 5/1/86; PW 4/11/86; Time 8/4/86)   **[364.152]**

1730 Wolfe, Linda. *Wasted: The Preppy Murder*. 1989, Simon & Schuster $19.95 (0-671-64184-0); Pocket paper $4.95 (0-671-70900-3). A true crime story of a girl murdered in Central Park by her boyfriend. Based on police and court records and 200 interviews with persons involved in the case. (Rᴇᴠ: BL 8/89; LJ 8/89; NYTBR 9/10/89)   **[364.152]**

Rape

1731 Brownmiller, Susan. *Against Our Will: Men, Women and Rape*. 1986, Bantam paper $5.95 (0-553-34516-8). Historical, cross-cultural, societal, and legal attitudes about rape. "Far more than a feminist polemic . . . it blends investigative and personal journalism into a demand for justice."—NYTBR (Rᴇᴠ: Choice 2/76; LJ 10/1/75; NYTBR 10/12/75. Awards: ALA, 1975; NYTBR, 1975)   **[364.153]**

1732 Olsen, Jack. *Doc: The Rape of the Town of Lovell*. 1989, Macmillan $19.95 (0-689-11959-3); Dell paper $5.95 (0-440-20668-5). An account of a physician in Lovell, Wyoming, who raped dozens of women over a period of 25 years while performing gynecological examinations. (Rᴇᴠ: BL 5/15/89; LJ 5/15/89; NYTBR 6/18/89)   **[364.153]**

1733 Olsen, Jack. *Predator: Rape, Madness and Injustice in Seattle*. 1991, Delacorte $19.95 (0-385-29935-4). A study of a serial rape case and of the man falsely accused of one of the crimes. "Arguably the best true-crime author around."—PW (Rᴇᴠ: BL 2/1/91; LJ 4/1/91; PW 2/15/91)   **[364.153]**

1734 Porter, Roy, and Sylvana Tomaselli, eds. *Rape*. 1986, Basil Blackwell $34.95 (0-631-13748-3); paper $14.95 (0-631-16906-7). Collected essays by scholars in various fields regarding rape. (Rᴇᴠ: Choice 4/87; NYTBR 1/4/87)   **[364.153]**

Business, financial, professional offenses

1735 Hafner, Katie, and John Markoff. *Cyberpunk: Outlaws and Hackers on the Computer Frontier*. 1991, Simon & Schuster $22.95 (0-671-68322-5).

Three case studies of computer hackers and their exploits. (Rᴇᴠ: BL 7/91; LJ 6/1/91; PW 5/10/91) **[364.168]**

Causes of crime and delinquency

1736 Wilson, James Q., and Richard J. Herrnstein. *Crime and Human Nature*. 1986, Simon & Schuster paper $13.95 (0-671-62810-0). A look at whether certain individuals are biologically predisposed towards criminal behavior. "A definitive work on a vitally important subject."—BL (Rᴇᴠ: BL 9/15/85; Choice 1/86; LJ 10/1/85)   **[364.2]**

Offenders

1737 Wideman, John Edgar. *Brothers and Keepers*. 1985, Penguin paper $7.95 (0-14-008267-0). Wideman's story of his life and that of his brother's, confined to life imprisonment for murder. "A superb book."—Choice (Rᴇᴠ: Choice 4/85; LJ 10/1/84; NYTBR 11/4/84. Awards: ALA, 1984; BL, the 1980s; NYTBR, 1984)   **[364.3]**

Penology

1738 Black, Charles L. *Capital Punishment: The Inevitability of Caprice and Mistake*. 1982, Norton paper $6.95 (0-393-95289-4). An argument against the death penalty focusing on its arbitrary enforcement and possibility for error in the judicial process. (Rᴇᴠ: Choice 5/75; LJ 12/15/74; New Yorker 12/30/74)   **[364.6]**

1739 Silberman, Charles E. *Criminal Violence, Criminal Justice: Criminals, Police, Courts and Prisons in America*. 1978, Random $15.00 (0-394-48036-5); paper $8.95 (0-394-74147-1). A critical look at the American criminal justice system. "By far the best single, comprehensive treatment . . . no library can afford to be without this volume."—Choice (Rᴇᴠ: Atl 12/78; Choice 3/79; NYTBR 11/26/78. Awards: ALA, 1978)   **[364.6]**

United States

1740 Currie, Elliot. *Confronting Crime: An American Challenge*. 1986, Pantheon $9.95 (0-394-53219-8); paper $12.95 (0-394-74636-8). A criminologist's view of the causes and solutions of the problem of violent crime in the United States. "A brilliantly daring if controversial study."—BL (Rᴇᴠ: Choice 3/86; LJ 10/15/85; New Rep 1/20/86)   **[364.973]**

365   Penal and related institutions

1741 Abbott, Jack Henry. *In the Belly of the Beast: Letters from Prison*. 1991, Random paper $9.95 (0-679-73237-3). Collected letters written to Norman Mailer concerning life in prison. Written by Abbott from his cell in a federal penitentiary. (Rᴇᴠ: Natl Rev 8/21/81; NYTBR 7/19/81; Time 7/20/81) **[365]**

1742 Breytenbach, Breyten. *True Confessions of an Albino Terrorist*. 1985, Farrar $18.95 (0-374-27935-7); McGraw-Hill paper $5.95 (0-07-007674-X). The diary of the South African novelist's experiences on trial and in prison after being convicted on charges of terrorism. "One more agonized cry by the writer against inhumanity and injustice . . .

painful but essential reading."—Choice (Rev: Choice 7–8/85; New Rep 3/11/85; NYTBR 2/10/85)   **[365]**

1743   Earley, Pete. *Hot House: Life Inside Leavenworth Prison.* 1992, Bantam $22.50 (0-553-07573-X). A journalist's account of life inside Leavenworth prison based on two years of observing and interviewing staff and prisoners there. (Rev: BL 1/15/92; PW 12/20/91)   **[365]**

1744   Foucault, Michael. *Discipline and Punish: The Birth of the Prison.* 1979, Random paper $10.95 (0-394-72767-3). A history of the modern penal institution and its relationship to other methods of social control. "Intelligently presented . . . it contains many profound insights."—Choice (Rev: Choice 5/78; CSM 3/15/78; NYTBR 2/19/78. Awards: NYTBR, 1978)   **[365]**

1745   Mitford, Jessica. *Kind and Usual Punishment: The Prison Business.* 1974, Random paper $8.76 (0-394-71093-2). An indictment of the American prison system. "Thrusts the reality of prison life in the United States into the open."—CSM (Rev: Choice 12/73; CSM 9/19/73; LJ 9/1/73. Awards: ALA, 1973)   **[365]**

1746   O'Malley, Padraig. *Biting at the Grave: The Irish Hunger Strikes and the Politics of Despair.* 1990, Beacon $22.95 (0-8070-0208-9). An account of the 1981 hunger strikes by imprisoned IRA members and of the political background that led to the starvation of ten prisoners. (Rev: Natl Rev 5/28/90; NYTBR 4/15/90; PW 3/2/90. Awards: NYTBR, 1990) **[365]**

1747   Solzhenitsyn, Aleksandr. *Gulag Archipelago.* 1974, Harper & Row paper $6.95 (0-06-080332-0). The daily life of political prisoners in Soviet forced-labor camps. "Relentless and harrowing . . . but impossible to put down . . . a work of enduring importance."—LJ (Rev: LJ 12/15/75; NYTBR 10/26/75; Newsweek 11/3/75. Awards: NYTBR, 1975)   **[365]**

1748   Solzhenitsyn, Aleksandr. *Gulag Archipelago Three: Katorga, Exile, Stalin Is No More.* 1979, Harper & Row paper $4.95 (0-06-080396-7). The third volme of the author's Soviet prison camp memoirs examines the special camps set up for political prisoners and discusses organized resistance and revolts within the camps. (Rev: CSM 6/14/78; LJ 4/15/78; NYTBR 6/18/78)   **[365]**

1749   Timerman, Jacobo. *Prisoner Without a Name, Cell Without a Number.* 1981, Knopf $12.50 (0-394-51448-3); paper $8.95 (0-679-72048-0). The horrifying first-person account of the seizure and torture of an Argentine journalist in Buenos Aires in the late 1970s. (Rev: LJ 5/15/81; NYTBR 5/10/81; Newsweek 5/18/81. Awards: ALA, 1981; BL, the 1980s; NYTBR, 1981)   **[365]**

1750   Valladares, Armando. *Against All Hope: The Prison Memoirs of Armando Valladares.* 1986, Knopf $18.95 (0-394-53425-5); Ballantine paper $4.95 (0-345-34403-0). Memoirs of the author's 20 years in Cuban prisons prior to his release due to international pressure. "A powerful testament to his ability to survive and a searing commentary on

the Castro regime as well."—LJ (Rev: LJ 5/1/86; New Rep 7/28/86; Time 6/30/86. Awards: LJ, 1986; Time, 1986)   **[365]**

Institutions for specific classes of inmates—For political prisoners and related classes of persons

1751   Marchenko, Anatoly. *To Live Like Everyone.* 1989, Henry Holt $19.95 (0-8050-0898-5). Memoirs of a Soviet dissident writer concerning his 20 years spent in prison camps within the Soviet Union. (Rev: BL 6/1/89; LJ 5/15/89; NYTBR 10/22/89)   **[365.4]**

Inmates

1752   Harris, Jean. *They Always Call Us Ladies: Stories from Prison.* 1990, Zebra paper $4.95 (0-8217-2986-1). History and present-day realities of life in the Bedford Hills Correctional Facility as described by the woman serving a sentence for the murder of Dr. Herman Tarnower. (Rev: BL 9/1/88; NYTBR 9/25/88; Newsweek 9/5/88)   **[365.6]**

368   Insurance

Conventional comprehensive sales groupings

1753   Taylor, Barbara J. *How to Get Your Money's Worth in Home and Auto Insurance.* 1990, McGraw-Hill $19.95 (0-07-063178-6); paper $12.95 (0-07-063179-4). A consumer guide to purchasing the best value insurance policies for your home and automobile. (Rev: BL 10/15/90; LJ 10/1/90)   **[368.09]**

United States

1754   Nader, Ralph, and Wesley J. Smith. *Winning the Insurance Game: The Complete Consumer's Guide to Saving Money.* 1990, Knightsbridge $24.95 (1-877961-17-5). A layman's guide to the evaluation and purchase of insurance. (Rev: LJ 9/1/90; PW 7/20/90)   **[368.973]**

369   Miscellaneous kinds of associations

Boy Scouts

1755   Jeal, Tim. *Boy-Man: The Life and Times of Baden-Powell.* 1990, Morrow $24.95 (0-688-04899-4). A biography of the British founder of the Boy Scouts by the author of *Livingstone.* (Rev: BL 3/15/90; NYTBR 4/1/90; TLS 10/13/89)   **[369.43]**

1756   Rosenthal, Michael. *Character Factory: Baden-Powell's Boy Scouts and the Imperatives of Empire.* 1986, Pantheon $22.95 (0-394-51169-7). A history of the Boy Scouts from their founding in 1908 through the 1980s exploring the background and philosophy of the institution and reflecting on the personality of its founder. (Rev: BL 4/15/86; Choice 10/86; LJ 5/1/86)   **[369.43]**

370   EDUCATION

1757   Kozol, Jonathan. *Illiterate America.* 1986, NAL paper $9.95 (0-452-26203-8). A look at the widespread problem of illiteracy in the United

States today. "Everyone who cares about the future of our country must read this book and think through what can be done to meet this national crisis."—Choice (REV: BL 2/15/85; Choice 6/85; LJ 3/1/85. AWARDS: LJ, 1985) **[370]**

1758 Ravitch, Diane. *Schools We Deserve: Reflections on the Educational Crisis of Our Time.* 1985, Basic Books $19.95 (0-465-07236-4). Essays on the current state of the American educational system. "Of interest to all citizens concerned about the institutions of learning in our culture."—PW (REV: LJ 5/1/85; NYTBR 6/2/85; PW 3/15/85) **[370]**

1759 Ravitch, Diane. *Troubled Crusade: American Education, 1945–1980.* 1985, Basic Books paper $14.95 (0-465-08757-4). The history of the developments and changes in American education since World War II. (REV: CSM 10/14/83; LJ 9/1/83; NYTBR 9/18/83) **[370]**

Philosophy, theories, general aspects

1760 Lickona, Thomas. *Educating for Character: How Our Schools Can Teach Respect and Responsibility.* 1991, Bantam $22.50 (0-553-07570-5). The author of *Raising Good Children* discusses the role of the school in teaching values and morality. (REV: BL 10/15/91; LJ 10/1/91) **[370.1]**

Education for specific objectives

1761 Gardner, Howard. *To Open Minds: Chinese Clues to the Dilemma of American Education.* 1989, Basic Books $21.95 (0-465-08630-6); paper $14.95 (0-465-08629-2). A comparative study of the educational methods and philosophies of the United States and the People's Republic of China. (REV: LJ 9/1/89; NYTBR 11/26/89; PW 7/7/89) **[370.11]**

Social aspects of education

1762 D'Souza, Dinesh. *Illiberal Education: The Politics of Race and Sex on Campus.* 1991, Free Pr. $19.95 (0-02-908100-9). A study of race and gender-related issues currently facing higher education in the United States. (REV: LJ 3/15/91; Natl Rev 4/15/91; PW 2/15/91) **[370.19]**

1763 Formisano, Ronald P. *Boston Against Busing: Race, Class, and Ethnicity in the 1960's and 1970's.* 1991, Univ. of North Carolina Pr. $34.95; paper $12.95 (0-8078-4292-5). A study of the Boston public school integration struggles of the 1960s and 1970s. (REV: BL 3/1/91; LJ 3/15/91; PW 1/25/91) **[370.19]**

1764 Haskins, James. *Diary of a Harlem Schoolteacher.* 1979, Scarborough paper $4.95 (0-8128-6043-8). A teacher's diary of his experience teaching a class of academically disadvantaged children during the 1967–1968 school year. "The saddest book on education I have ever read."—NYTBR (REV: CSM 3/12/70; LJ 2/15/70; NYTBR 2/8/70) **[370.19]**

1765 Hirsch, E. D., Jr. *Cultural Literacy: What Every American Needs to Know.* 1987, Houghton $18.95 (0-395-43095-X); Random paper $8.95 (0-394-75843-9). A presentation of the essential terms and phrases Americans need to know to be considered culturally literate and an advocacy for teaching these bits of knowledge in America's schools. (REV: Choice 7–8/87; NYTBR 4/26/87; New Yorker 6/1/87) **[370.19]**

1766 Kohl, Herbert. *36 Children.* 1988, NAL paper $7.95 (0-452-26155-4). Experiences of a sixth-grade Harlem schoolteacher who introduced an innovative curriculum into his classroom. "A testimony to what can be accomplished by a gifted teacher."—Choice (REV: Choice 9/68; LJ 9/1/67; New Rep 12/23/67. AWARDS: ALA, 1968) **[370.19]**

1767 Kozol, Jonathan. *Death at an Early Age: The Destruction of the Hearts and Minds of Negro Children in the Boston Public Schools.* 1985, NAL paper $8.95 (0-452-26292-5). Kozol's experiences as a fourth-grade teacher in an all black classroom in Boston during the 1960s. "Moving . . . well-written . . . a very important book."—PW (REV: BL 12/1/67; LJ 7/67; PW 9/4/67. AWARDS: ALA, 1967) **[370.19]**

1768 Maeroff, Gene I. *School-Smart Parent.* 1989, Random $19.95 (0-8129-1631-X); Henry Holt paper $12.95 (0-8050-1380-6). A guide for parents to help choose the best school for their children and to gauge what they should be learning. (REV: CSM 6/16/89; LJ 4/1/89; PW 3/10/89) **[370.19]**

1769 Orr, Eleanor Wilson. *Twice as Less: Black English and the Performance of Black Students in Mathematics and Science.* 1987, Norton $15.95 (0-393-02392-3). A study of the fundamental differences between black and standard English and how those differences account for difficulties African-American children often have in the comprehension of concepts relating to mathematics and science. "A landmark in its field."—Choice (REV: Choice 3/88; LJ 9/1/87; PW 6/26/87) **[370.19]**

Professional education of teachers

1770 Damerell, Reginald G. *Education's Smoking Gun: How Teachers' Colleges Have Destroyed Education in America.* 1985, Freundlich $17.95 (0-88191-025-2). A former faculty member of the University of Massachusetts School of Education presents an attack on teacher's education colleges and their methods. (REV: BL 8/85; LJ 8/85; PW 6/14/85) **[370.71]**

Persons

1771 Lifton, Betty Jean. *King of Children: A Portrait of Janusz Korczak.* 1988, Farrar $22.50 (0-374-18124-1); Schocken paper $14.95 (0-8052-0930-1). A biography of the Polish doctor and children's rights advocate who died in Treblinka in 1942. (REV: Choice 9/88; LJ 8/88; NYRB 9/29/88) **[370.92]**

United States

1772 Adler, Mortimer J. *Reforming Education: The Opening of the American Mind.* 1989, Macmillan $19.95 (0-02-500551-0). An anthology of Adler's writings concerning the American educational system collected from a 50-year period. (REV: LJ 4/15/89; PW 1/27/89) **[370.973]**

1773 Cetron, Marvin, and Margaret Gayle. *Educational Renaissance: Our Schools at the Turn of the 21st Century.* **1991, St. Martin's $19.95 (0-312-05422-X).** A study of successful education programs and effective teachers throughout the United States and how their methods can be applied to the future. (REV: BL 11/15/90; LJ 12/90; PW 11/30/90) **[370.973]**

1774 Honig, Bill. *Last Chance to Save Our Children: How You Can Help Save Our Schools.* **1987, Addison Wesley paper $8.95 (0-201-12648-6).** A survey of problems facing the public education system with suggestions for effective reforms as seen by the California state superintendent for public education. (REV: CSM 10/7/85; LJ 10/1/85; NYTBR 3/2/86) **[370.973]**

1775 Postman, Neil, and Charles Weingartner. *Teaching as a Subversive Activity.* **1987, Dell paper $4.95 (0-440-38485-0).** A critical analysis of American teaching methods and its educational system. (REV: LJ 5/15/69; NYTBR 5/11/69; Sat Rev 7/19/69) **[370.973]**

371 School management; Special education

1776 Fiske, Edward B. *Smart Schools, Smart Kids: Why Do Some Schools Work?* **1991, Simon & Schuster $22.95 (0-671-69063-9).** This study of American elementary and secondary education focuses on successful programs and is written by the former *New York Times* education correspondent. (REV: BL 9/1/91; LJ 8/91; NYTBR 9/15/91) **[371]**

Public schools and school systems

1777 Goodlad, John I. *A Place Called School: Prospects for the Future.* **1984, McGraw-Hill paper $12.00 (0-07-023627-5).** A study of the current American public education system with suggested reforms for its improvement. (REV: BL 9/15/83; Choice 1/84; LJ 10/15/83) **[371.01]**

Teaching and teaching personnel

1778 Johnson, Susan Moore. *Teachers at Work: Achieving Success in Our Schools.* **1990, Basic Books $19.95 (0-465-07228-3).** Over 100 interviews with public school teachers form the basis of this analysis and criticism of the American education system. (REV: Choice 1/91; LJ 5/1/90; NYTBR 7/1/90) **[371.1]**

1779 Kramer, Rita. *Ed School Follies: The Miseducation of America's Teachers.* **1991, Free Pr. $22.95 (0-02-917642-5).** A critical appraisal of America's education programs for teachers with recommendations for reform. (REV: LJ 9/1/91; PW 7/12/91) **[371.1]**

1780 Paton, Alan. *Toward the Mountain: An Autobiography.* **1988, Peter Smith $18.50 (0-8446-6322-0); Macmillan paper $9.95 (0-684-18892-9).** The first volume of memoirs of the South African writer and social reformer covering his life from birth to publication of *Cry, the Beloved Country.* (REV: CSM 10/15/80; LJ 9/15/80; New Rep 11/15/80) **[371.1]**

1781 Strane, Susan. *A Whole-Souled Woman: The Story of Penelope Crandall.* **1990, Norton $19.95 (0-393-02826-7).** A biography of a Connecticut school teacher who became the center of controversy in the 1830s when she allowed a black girl to attend classes at her school. (REV: LJ 4/1/90; NYTBR 4/29/90; PW 3/30/90) **[371.1]**

School administration and management

1782 Owen, David. *None of the Above: Behind the Myth of Scholastic Aptitude.* **1986, Houghton paper $7.95 (0-395-41500-4).** A critical look at the uses and accuracy of scholastic aptitude and other standardized education tests. (REV: BL 4/1/85; LJ 4/15/85; PW 3/1/85) **[371.2]**

Special education

1783 Coles, Gerald. *Learning Mystique: A Critical Look at "Learning Disabilities."* **1987, Pantheon $22.95 (0-394-54898-1); Fawcett paper $10.95 (0-449-90351-6).** An assessment of current theories regarding the origins and treatments of children with learning disabilities. (REV: BL 1/15/88; NYTBR 1/24/88; PW 11/20/87) **[371.9]**

1784 Lyman, Donald E. *Making the Words Stand Still: How to Rescue the Learning Disabled Child.* **1988, Houghton paper $8.95 (0-395-48681-5).** The author, the founder of a North Carolina school for learning disabled children, discusses teaching techniques and programs he has found successful. "Should be required reading for all parents and teachers of learning disabled children."—BL (REV: BL 2/15/86; LJ 2/1/86; PW 12/13/85) **[371.9]**

Students with physical handicaps

1785 Lash, Joseph P. *Helen and Teacher: The Story of Helen Keller and Anne Sullivan Macy.* **1980, Dell paper $6.95 (0-440-53506-3).** A dual biography of the blind writer and activist and the woman who taught her. "A master biographer ... a respectful celebration of two remarkable lives and a brilliant contribution to feminist studies."—CSM (REV: CSM 3/11/80; LJ 5/15/80; Newsweek 6/2/80. AWARDS: ALA, 1980) **[371.91]**

Emotionally disturbed students

1786 Hayden, Torey L. *Just Another Kid.* **$4.95, Avon paper 1989 (0-380-70564-8).** A memoir of the author's experiences during a year she spent teaching six children in a special education program. (REV: LJ 5/15/88; NYTBR 3/6/88) **[371.94]**

Students exceptional because of class distinction

1787 Kozol, Jonathan. *Savage Inequalities: Children in America's Schools.* **1991, Crown $20.00 (0-517-58221-X).** A portrait of the inferior conditions faced in public schools by the children of poor Americans, by the author of *Death at an Early Age.* (REV: BL 8/91; LJ 9/15/91; NYTBR 10/6/91. AWARDS: ALA, 1992; BL, 1991; PW, 1991) **[371.96]**

1788 Rose, Mike. *Lives on the Boundary: The Struggles and Achievements of America's Underprepared.* **1988, Free Pr. $27.95 (0-02-926821-4); Penguin paper $8.95 (0-14-012403-9).** An analysis, based on the author's personal experiences, of the problems facing ghetto children in the American educational system. (Rev: LJ 2/15/89; NYTBR 4/23/89; PW 12/16/88)   **[371.96]**

Students exceptional because of racial, ethnic, national origin

1789 Porter, Rosalie P. *Forked Tongue: The Politics of Bilingual Education.* **1990, Basic Books $19.95 (0-465-02487-4).** A study of the political and social history of bilingual education in the United States over the past two decades. (Rev: LJ 5/15/90; PW 3/9/90)   **[371.97]**

1790 Rodriguez, Richard. *Hunger of Memory: The Education of Richard Rodriguez.* **1983, Bantam paper $4.95 (0-553-27293-4).** This personal story of a Mexican American's education argues against bilingual education and affirmative action programs. (Rev: CSM 3/12/82; LJ 3/1/82; NYTBR 2/28/82. Awards: ALA, 1982; BL, the 1980s)   **[371.97]**

372 Elementary education

1791 Elkind, David. *Miseducation: Preschoolers at Risk.* **1987, Knopf $18.95 (0-394-55256-3); paper $10.95 (0-394-75634-7).** The author presents his opinion that formal instructional education of preschoolers causes the children more harm than good. (Rev: LJ 10/1/87; NYTBR 1/10/88; PW 8/17/87)   **[372]**

1792 Featherstone, Joseph. *Schools Where Children Learn.* **1971, Liveright paper $2.95 (0-87140-251-3).** An introduction to primary schools in the British educational system, and comparison of methods used in the United States. "The finest achievement of educational journalism over the past 10 years."—NYTBR (Rev: Choice 10/71; LJ 5/15/71; NYTBR 9/12/71)   **[372]**

1793 Holt, John. *How Children Fail.* **1988, Dell paper $9.95 (0-440-53837-8).** The journal of a mathematics teacher containing his observations on why children do poorly in school. "Every teacher who wants to get more real learning and less apparent learning will profit from this book."—Choice (Rev: Choice 4/65; NYRB 1/14/65; NYTBR 7/26/65. Awards: NYTBR, 1965)   **[372]**

1794 Holt, John. *How Children Learn.* **1983, Dell paper $8.95 (0-385-28425-X).** A Boston elementary schoolteacher's observations on the learning processes of the young. "Nearly meets the very high standards set by his brilliant and angry first book, *How Children Fail.* These two works . . . deserve to become classics."—New Rep (Rev: Choice 5/68; LJ 12/1/67; New Rep 3/2/68. Awards: ALA, 1968)   **[372]**

1795 Holt, John. *Learning All the Time.* **1989, Addison Wesley $15.95 (0-201-12095-X); paper $8.95 (0-201-55091-1).** A posthumously published collection of essays and writings by the elementary

education expert. (Rev: Choice 4/90; NYTBR 2/18/90; PW 9/29/89)   **[372]**

1796 Tobin, Joseph Jay. *Preschool in Three Cultures: Japan, China and the United States.* **1989, Yale Univ. Pr. $26.95 (0-300-04235-3).** Comparative analysis of preschool educational techniques in Japan, China, and the United States. (Rev: Choice 11/89; LJ 5/15/89; NYTBR 6/25/89)   **[372]**

Organization and management of elementary education

1797 Kidder, Tracy. *Among Schoolchildren.* **1989, Houghton $19.95 (0-395-47591-0); Avon paper $9.95 (0-380-71089-7).** A year in the life of an elementary schoolteacher and her class, as witnessed by the author. (Rev: LJ 8/89; New Rep 11/13/89; NYTBR 9/17/89. Awards: ALA, 1989; BL, 1989; BL, the 1980s)   **[372.1]**

1798 Paley, Vivian Gussin. *Boy Who Would Be a Helicopter.* **1990, Harvard Univ. Pr. $19.95 (0-674-08030-0).** A look at child development and the learning processes of the young. "Should be required reading for all working with children of any age."—Choice (Rev: Choice 10/90; LJ 2/15/90; NYTBR 4/29/90)   **[372.1]**

Reading

1799 Bettelheim, Bruno, and Karen Zelan. *On Learning to Read: The Child's Fascination with Meaning.* **1982, Random paper $9.95 (0-394-71194-7).** An analysis of methods of teaching reading in elementary schools based on the results of a four-year study. (Rev: BL 1/15/82; NYRB 4/1/82; PW 11/19/82)   **[372.4]**

Language and literature

1800 Lopate, Phillip. *Being with Children.* **1989, Poseidon paper $9.95 (0-671-67680-6).** The author's experiences teaching creative writing to elementary school children in New York City. (Rev: CSM 10/29/75; LJ 10/15/75; NYTBR 11/2/75)   **[372.6]**

373 Secondary education

Personal characteristics and qualifications of teachers

1801 Freedman, Samuel G. *Small Victories: The Real World of a Teacher, Her Students and Their High School.* **1990, Harper & Row $22.95 (0-06-016254-6).** An account of a year in the life of a Lower East Side, New York City, schoolteacher. "Unparalleled in its depiction of the human side to the current educational crisis."—LJ (Rev: BL 3/15/90; LJ 5/1/90; NYTBR 5/20/90. Awards: ALA, 1990; LJ, 1990)   **[373.11]**

The student

1802 Cary, Loraine. *Black Ice.* **1991, Knopf $19.95 (0-394-57465-6).** An account of an African-American girl's experiences attending an elite New Hampshire prep school. (Rev: BL 2/15/91; NYTBR 3/31/91; PW 2/1/91. Awards: ALA, 1992; BL, 1991)   **[373.18]**

Types and levels of secondary education

1803 **Cookson, Peter W., Jr., and Caroline Hodges Persell.** *Preparing for Power: America's Elite Boarding Schools.* **1987, Basic Books paper $10.95 (0-465-06269-5).** An examination of 57 American boarding schools and the methods they use to prepare future leaders. (REV: Choice 4/86; NYTBR 2/16/86; PW 9/27/85) **[373.2]**

South Africa

1804 **Finnegan, William.** *Crossing the Line: A Year in the Land of Apartheid.* **1987, Harper & Row paper $10.95 (0-06-091430-0).** An American teacher's experiences at a "coloured" school in Cape Town; during his term his students organized a school boycott, which spread throughout South Africa, and were violently suppressed by the government. (REV: LJ 9/15/86; NYRB 10/23/86; NYTBR 9/21/86. AWARDS: NYTBR, 1986) **[373.68]**

United States

1805 **Lightfoot, Sara Lawrence.** *Good High School: Portraits of Character and Culture.* **1985, Basic Books paper $13.95 (0-465-02696-6).** A study of six American public high schools noted for their academic and social excellence. (REV: Choice 3/84; LJ 10/15/83; NYTBR 3/25/84) **[373.73]**

376   Education of women

1806 **Horowitz, Helen Lefkowitz.** *Alma Mater: Design and Experience in the Women's Colleges from Their Nineteenth-Century Beginnings to the 1930's.* **1984, Knopf $25.00 (0-394-53439-5).** An illustrated study of the history and social life of the Seven Sister colleges from their foundings through the 1930s. (REV: LJ 8/84; NYTBR 10/28/84; PW 8/3/84) **[376]**

United States

1807 **Solomon, Barbara M.** *In the Company of Educated Women: A History of Women and Higher Education in America.* **1985, Yale Univ. Pr. $35.00 (0-300-03314-1); paper $13.95 (0-300-03639-5).** A history of the struggle for women in the U.S. to receive equal education and respect for their academic achievements. (REV: Choice 9/85; LJ 4/15/85; NYTBR 10/6/85) **[376.973]**

378   Higher education

1808 **Aisenberg, Nadya, and Mona Harrington.** *Women of Academe: Outsiders in the Sacred Grove.* **1988, Univ. of Massachusetts Pr. $30.00 (0-87023-606-7); paper $12.95 (0-87023-607-5).** Over 60 interviews form the basis of this work examining the role of women in the academic community, and their struggle for acceptance and recognition. (REV: Choice 1/89; LJ 4/15/88; NYTBR 7/24/88) **[378]**

1809 **Miller, James E.** *"Democracy Is in the Streets": From Port Huron to the Siege of Chicago.* **1988, Simon & Schuster paper $19.95 (0-671-66235-X).** A study of the "New Left" as reflected in the SDS (Students for a Democratic Society) and

the individuals of the movement. (REV: Choice 11/87; LJ 7/87; NYTBR 6/21/87. AWARDS: LJ, 1987) **[378]**

1810 **Tinto, Vincent.** *Leaving College: Rethinking the Causes and Cures of Student Attrition.* **1987, Univ. of Chicago Pr. $19.95 (0-226-80446-1).** An examination of the reasons students leave college without completing degrees. "An important contribution to the literature of higher education."—LJ (REV: Choice 9/87; LJ 2/15/87) **[378]**

Organization and management

1811 **Hesburgh, Theodore M., and Jerry Reedy.** *God, Country, Notre Dame: The Autobiography of Theodore M. Hesburgh.* **1990, Doubleday $21.95 (0-385-26680-4).** An autobiography of the social activist and president of the University of Notre Dame for over 35 years. (REV: BL 11/15/90; LJ 12/90; NYTBR 1/6/91) **[378.1]**

1812 **Lockerbie, D. Bruce, and Donald R. Fonseca.** *College: Getting in and Staying In.* **1990, Eerdmans paper $11.95 (0-8028-0424-1).** A guide to entering, surviving, and thriving in an academic setting. (REV: BL 9/15/90; LJ 9/15/90) **[378.1]**

1813 **Pope, Loren.** *Looking Beyond the Ivy League: Finding the College That's Right for You.* **1990, Penguin paper $7.95 (0-14-012209-5).** A guide for prospective college students to choosing the best school to fit their needs. (REV: BL 3/1/90; LJ 3/15/90) **[378.1]**

Europe

1814 **Brooke, Christopher, and Roger Highfield.** *Oxford and Cambridge.* **1988, Cambridge Univ. Pr. $52.50 (0-521-30139-4).** An illustrated history of the English universities of Oxford and Cambridge, with profiles of prominent individuals who contributed to the schools' development. (REV: LJ 7/88; NYTBR 8/7/88; TLS 11/25/88) **[378.4]**

Japan

1815 **Schoolland, Ken.** *Shogun's Ghost: The Dark Side of Japanese Education.* **1990, Greenwood Pr. paper $19.95 (0-89789-218-6).** A report on the Japanese education system by a teacher who spent five years employed in Japanese colleges. (REV: BL 11/15/90; LJ 11/1/90; PW 9/28/90) **[378.52]**

United States

1816 **Duberman, Martin.** *Black Mountain: An Exploration in Community.* **1988, Peter Smith $25.00 (0-8446-6338-7).** The history of Black Mountain College (1933–1956), an experimental art school and community devoted to the avant-garde. (REV: LJ 10/15/72; PW 9/18/72; Sat Rev 10/21/72) **[378.73]**

1817 **Giamatti, A. Bartlett.** *A Free and Ordered Space: The Real World of the University.* **1988, Norton $19.95 (0-393-02622-1); paper $9.95 (0-393-30671-2).** Essays exploring America's system of higher education by the former Yale University president. (REV: BL 11/15/88; LJ 1/89; PW 10/7/88) **[378.73]**

1818 Horowitz, Helen Lefkowitz. *Campus Life: Undergraduate Cultures from the End of the 18th Century to the Present*. 1987, Knopf $24.95 (0-394-54997-X); Univ. of Chicago Pr. paper $13.95 (0-226-35373-7). A survey of undergraduate classes, society, and customs from the 1700s to the present. (REV: BL 4/15/87; CSM 5/11/87; LJ 5/15/87)   **[378.73]**

1819 Rosovsky, Henry. *University: An Owner's Manual*. 1990, Norton $19.95 (0-393-02782-1). A study of the contemporary American university by a former Harvard dean and current faculty member. (REV: BL 2/1/90; Natl Rev 4/1/90; NYTBR 4/22/90)   **[378.73]**

1820 Sykes, Charles J. *ProfScam*. 1988, Regnery $18.95 (0-89526-559-1); St. Martin's paper $9.95 (0-312-03916-6). A critical view of the current state of higher education in the United States. (REV: BL 3/1/89; CSM 5/15/89; NYTBR 2/19/89)   **[378.73]**

Northeastern United States

1821 Toth, Susan Allen. *Ivy Days: Making My Way Out East*. 1985, Little, Brown paper $6.95 (0-316-85079-9). Remembrances of the author's relocation from an Iowa town to attend Smith College in Massachusetts during the 1950s. (REV: BL 5/15/84; LJ 5/15/84; NYTBR 6/17/84)   **[378.74]**

380 COMMERCE, COMMUNICATIONS, TRANSPORT

Commerce (Trade)

1822 Herbert, John. *Inside Christie's*. 1990, St. Martin's $24.95 (0-312-04609-X). A history of the development and workings of the English auction house by its former public relations director. (REV: BL 12/1/90; LJ 11/15/90; PW 10/19/90)   **[380.1]**

1823 Simpson, Colin. *Artful Partners: Bernard Berenson and Joseph Duveen*. 1987, Macmillan $22.50 (0-02-611330-9). An account of the licit and illicit art dealings carried out by the American art connoisseur Berenson and the English art dealer Duveen. (REV: BL 4/15/87; LJ 5/1/87; Time 4/6/87)**[380.1]**

381 Internal commerce (Domestic trade)

1824 Katz, Donald R. *Big Store: Inside the Crisis and Revolution at Sears*. 1987, Viking $22.95 (0-670-80512-2); Penguin paper $9.95 (0-14-011525-0). A history of Sears Roebuck and the changes the company made in order to better compete during the 1970s and 1980s. (REV: Atl 10/87; BL 9/15/87; NYTBR 10/25/87)   **[381]**

1825 Montgomery, M. R. *In Search of L. L. Bean*. 1987, NAL paper $4.50 (0-451-62583-8). A history of the founding, development, and operations of the Maine mail-order sporting goods and clothing outlet. (REV: Choice 6/85; CSM 12/26/86; LJ 12/84) **[381]**

Franchise businesses

1826 Perry, Robert L. *Fifty Best Low-Investment High-Profit Franchises*. 1990, Prentice Hall paper $12.95 (0-13-313529-2). A guide to best low-risk franchise investments for entrepreneurs. (REV: BL 6/15/90; LJ 6/1/90)   **[381.13]**

Consumer protection

1827 Eiler, Andrew. *Consumer Protection Manual*. 1983, Facts on File $35.00 (0-87196-310-8). A guide to the legal rights and potential recourses of consumers. (REV: BL 3/1/85; Choice 4/85; LJ 4/1/85)   **[381.34]**

1828 Portnoy, J. Elias, and Chris Stern. *Let the Seller Beware*. 1991, Macmillan paper $9.95 (0-02-036047-9). A guide to consumer activism to combat fraud and deception in the American marketplace. (REV: BL 12/15/90; LJ 12/90)   **[381.34]**

382 International commerce (Foreign trade)

1829 Morgan, Daniel. *Merchants of Grain*. 1980, Penguin paper $9.95 (0-14-005502-9). An investigation into the world's great grain distributors, and the hows and whys of international food shortages. (REV: BL 6/15/79; Choice 11/79; NYTBR 5/27/79. AWARDS: ALA, 1979)   **[382]**

384 Communication; Telecommunications

1830 Bart, Peter. *Fade Out: The Calamitous Final Days of MGM*. 1990, Morrow $19.95 (0-688-08460-5). A former MGM executive recalls his experiences with the motion picture studio during the mid-1980s. (REV: LJ 5/1/90; NYTBR 6/24/90)   **[384]**

1831 Gabler, Neal. *An Empire of Their Own: How the Jews Invented Hollywood*. 1988, Crown $24.95 (0-517-56808-X); Doubleday paper $12.95 (0-385-26557-3). A study of the founding and development of the American motion picture in Hollywood, and of the movie studios largely run and operated by Jewish immigrants. (REV: BL 9/1/88; LJ 11/1/88; NYTBR 10/27/88)   **[384]**

1832 Hamilton, Ian. *Writers in Hollywood, 1915–1951*. 1990, Harper & Row $25.00 (0-06-016231-7); Carroll & Graf paper $10.95 (0-88184-710-0). A history of writers in Hollywood from the early silent feature films to the collapse of the studio system. (REV: CSM 5/21/90; NYTBR 5/27/90; TLS 6/15/90)   **[384]**

1833 Moldea, Dan E. *Dark Victory: Ronald Reagan, MCA and the Mob*. 1986, Viking $18.95 (0-670-80903-9); paper $7.95 (0-14-010478-X). A study of Reagan's relationship with MCA, and MCA's dealings with organized crime figures, during his stint as president of the Screen Actors Guild in the 1950s. (REV: BL 10/15/86; LJ 10/1/86; NYRB 1/15/87)   **[384]**

Radiobroadcasting

1834 Lewis, Tom. *Empire of the Air: The Men Who Made Radio*. 1991, HarperCollins $25.00 (0-06-018215-6). The overview of the history and development of radio that accompanies a Ken Burns PBS documentary of the same name. (REV: BL 10/15/91; LJ 9/15/91)   **[384.54]**

1835   Paper, Lewis J. *Empire: William S. Paley and the Making of CBS.* **1988, St. Martin's paper $12.95 (0-312-02572-6).** A biography of the CBS chairman examining his role in the history of television broadcasting. "Deserves a high place among the essential books on TV."—PW (REV: BL 7/87; CSM 2/1/88; LJ 10/1/87)   **[384.54]**

1836   Smith, Sally Bedell. *In All His Glory: The Life of William S. Paley.* **1990, Simon & Schuster $29.95 (0-671-61735-4).** A biography of the founder and chairman of the board of the Columbia Broadcasting System. (REV: NYTBR 11/4/90; PW 1/4/91; Time 11/19/90. AWARDS: PW, 1990; Time, 1990)   **[384.54]**

Television

1837   Auletta, Ken. *Three Blind Mice: How the Networks Lost Their Way.* **1991, Random $25.00 (0-394-56358-1).** An account of the 1986 corporate takeovers of the three major television networks and the effects upon their operations and programming. (REV: BL 7/91; LJ 9/15/91; NYTBR 8/25/91)   **[384.55]**

1838   Barnouw, Erik. *Tube of Plenty: The Evolution of American Television.* **1990, Oxford Univ. Pr. $34.95 (0-19-506483-6); paper $14.95 (0-19-506-484-4).** This condensation of the author's three volume *History of Broadcasting* covers the history of television, tracing its roots from the discovery of radio. (REV: BL 1/1/76; NYTBR 11/30/75; TLS 6/25/76)   **[384.55]**

1839   Boyer, Peter J. *Who Killed CBS? How America's Number One News Network Went Down the Tubes.* **1988, Random $18.95 (0-394-56034-5); St. Martin's paper $5.95 (0-312-91531-4).** An analysis of how CBS News lost its number one rating in the 1980s, after dominating network news coverage since the inception of television. (REV: BL 3/15/88; NYTBR 5/1/88; PW 4/15/88)   **[384.55]**

1840   Friendly, Fred W. *Due to Circumstances Beyond Our Control.* **1968, Random paper $5.95 (0-394-70409-6).** Remembrances by the former president of CBS News concerning the history and role of television news, programming, and his personal relationship with Edward R. Murrow. "An engrossing personal memoir."—New Yorker (REV: LJ 3/15/67; NYRB 12/7/67; New Yorker 5/20/67. AWARDS: ALA, 1967)   **[384.55]**

1841   Gitlin, Todd. *Inside Prime Time.* **1985, Pantheon paper $11.95 (0-394-73787-3).** A behind-the-scenes account of network television production based on 200 interviews with people involved in the industry. (REV: BL 9/15/83; LJ 10/1/83; NYTBR 10/2/83)   **[384.55]**

1842   Montgomery, Kathryn C. *Target: Prime Time.* **1989, Oxford Univ. Pr. $25.00 (0-19-504964-0); paper $8.95 (0-19-506320-1).** The history of advocacy groups and their efforts to influence American television programming from 1951 to the present. (REV: BL 3/15/89; Choice 9/89; NYTBR 3/26/89)   **[384.55]**

1843   Williams, Huntington III. *Beyond Control: ABC and the Fate of the Networks.* **1989, Mac-**

millan **$19.95 (0-689-11818-X).** The history of the rise of ABC from bottom to top of the three networks and the development of problems that led to its buyout by Capital Cities in 1985. (REV: BL 9/15/89; LJ 10/1/89; PW 8/11/89)   **[384.55]**

Telephone

1844   Bruce, Robert V. *Bell: Alexander Graham Bell and the Conquest of Solitude.* **1990, Cornell Univ. Pr. $39.95 (0-8014-2419-4); paper $12.95 (0-8014-9691-8).** A biography of the inventor of the telephone and teacher of the deaf who immigrated from Scotland to the United States. "Sound, scholarly, thoroughly documented . . . should stand as the definitive biography for many years."—LJ (REV: BL 7/1/73; LJ 4/15/73; NYTBR 4/15/73. AWARDS: ALA, 1973)   **[384.6]**

1845   Schoenberg, Robert J. *Geneen.* **1986, Warner paper $9.95 (0-446-37008-8).** A biography of the executive who served as head of ITT from 1959 to 1977. (REV: BL 10/15/84; Choice 7–8/85; NYTBR 3/10/85)   **[384.6]**

1846   Tunstall, W. Brooke. *Disconnecting Parties: Managing the Bell System Break-up; An Inside View.* **1985, McGraw-Hill $17.95 (0-07-065434-4).** An AT&T corporate vice-president's inside story of the 1984 break-up of the world's largest corporation. (REV: LJ 4/1/85; NYTBR 2/24/85; PW 1/25/85)   **[384.6]**

Motion pictures

1847   Schatz, Thomas. *Genius of the System: Hollywood Filmmaking in the Studio Era, 1920–1955.* **1989, Pantheon $24.95 (0-679-72885-6); paper $14.95 (0-679-72885-6).** A study of three of the top Hollywood studios, MGM, Warner Brothers, and Universal, and how films were made under the studio system. (REV: BL 2/1/89; LJ 1/89; New Rep 2/27/89)   **[384.8]**

385   Railroad transportation

1848   Link, O. Winston, and Tim Hensley. *Steam, Steel and Stars: America's Last Steam Railroad.* **1987, Abrams $35.00 (0-8109-1645-2).** A photographic essay taken in the mid-1950s of the Norfolk and Western line, the last steam railroad to have run in the United States. (REV: BL 8/87; NYTBR 12/6/87; PW 5/1/87)   **[385]**

1849   Stilgoe, John R. *Metropolitan Corridor: Railroads and the American Scene.* **1983, Yale Univ. Pr. $40.00 (0-300-03042-8); paper $17.95 (0-300-03481-4).** A study of railroads and how they shaped America and its landscape. (REV: Choice 1/84; LJ 9/1/83; Newsweek 12/15/83)   **[385]**

387   Water, air, space transportation

Ocean (Marine) transportation

1850   Davis, L. J. *Onassis: Aristotle and Christina.* **1987, St. Martin's paper $4.50 (0-312-90289-1).** A portrait of the Greek shipping magnate and his family. (REV: BL 7/86; LJ 6/15/86; NYTBR 8/3/86)   **[387.5]**

1851 Evans, Peter. *Ari: The Life and Times of Aristotle Onassis.* 1988, Berkley paper $4.50 (1-55773-006-7). A biography of the Greek shipping magnate and financier who married Jacqueline Kennedy in 1968. (Rev: LJ 6/15/86; PW 5/2/86; TLS 9/19/86) **[387.5]**

Air transportation

1852 Serling, Robert J. *Eagle: The History of American Airlines.* 1985, St. Martin's $19.95 (0-312-22453-2). A history of American Airlines from its founding in the 1920s through the mid-1980s. (Rev: BL 12/15/85; LJ 12/85) **[387.7]**

Space transportation

1853 Matsunaga, Spark M. *Mars Project: Journeys beyond the Cold War.* 1986, Hill & Wang $17.95 (0-8090-6790-0). The former Hawaiian senator presents his proposal for a joint U.S.–Soviet mission to Mars at the beginning of the next century. (Rev: BL 5/1/86; LJ 5/1/86; NYTBR 9/28/86) **[387.8]**

388 Transportation; Ground transportation

Road and highways

1854 Hokanson, Drake. *Lincoln Highway: Main Street Across America.* 1988, Univ. of Iowa Pr. paper $19.95 (0-87745-261-X). An illustrated history of the Lincoln Highway, the nation's first transcontinental automobile roadway. "An affable classic of Americana."—BL (Rev: BL 9/1/88; CSM 7/6/88) **[388.1]**

1855 Patton, Phil. *Open Road: A Celebration of the American Highway.* 1987, Simon & Schuster paper $7.95 (0-317-59998-4). A history of the development of roadways in the United States and their impact on American life and culture. (Rev: BL 7/86; LJ 6/1/86; NYTBR 6/29/86) **[388.1]**

390 CUSTOMS, ETIQUETTE, FOLKLORE

1856 Aries, Philippe, ed. *A History of Private Life, Vol. 1: From Pagan Rome to Byzantium.* 1987, Harvard Univ. Pr. $35.00 (0-674-39975-7). A history of privacy and personal life in Ancient Rome and Byzantium. "It is unlikely that any other volume contains so much useful information about the social life of the period."—LJ (Rev: Atl 5/87; CSM 3/11/87; LJ 2/15/87) **[390]**

1857 Cohen, David, ed. *Circle of Life: Rituals from the Human Family Album.* 1991, HarperCollins $39.95 (0-06-250152-6). A collection of over 200 photographs documenting aspects of human rituals that includes essays and commentary by writers Peter Matthiessen and Gabriel García Marquez. (Rev: BL 10/15/91; CSM 12/19/91. Awards: BL, 1991) **[390]**

1858 Perrot, Michelle, ed. *History of Private Life, Vol. 4: From the Fires of Revolution to the Great War.* 1990, Harvard Univ. Pr. $39.95 (0-674-39978-1). A history of the domestic life of nineteenth-century France as seen by six scholars. (Rev: BL 2/15/90; LJ 2/1/90) **[390]**

391 Costume and personal appearance

1859 Garber, Marjorie. *Vested Interests: Cross-Dressing and Cultural Anxiety.* 1991, Routledge $35.00 (0-415-90072-7). A cross-cultural analysis of the role of cross-gender dressing throughout history. (Rev: LJ 11/1/91; NYTBR 12/15/91) **[391]**

1860 Hollander, Anne. *Seeing Through Clothes.* 1988, Penguin paper $14.95 (0-14-011084-4). A history of fashion and its social significance in Western society. (Rev: LJ 10/1/78; NYTBR 12/17/78; Newsweek 11/13/78) **[391]**

1861 Kidwell, Claudia B., and Valerie Steele. *Men and Women: Dressing the Part.* 1989, Smithsonian Inst. $40.00 (0-87474-550-0); paper $24.95 (0-87474-559-4). A history of fashion examining the difference in apparel between the sexes. (Rev: LJ 6/15/89; PW 4/28/89) **[391]**

1862 Milbank, Caroline Rennolds. *New York Fashion: The Evolution of American Style.* 1989, Abrams $49.50 (0-8109-1388-7). An illustrated history of the fashion design and trade industry in New York City from the nineteenth century to the present. (Rev: BL 12/15/89; Choice 6/90; LJ 1/90) **[391]**

1863 Mulvagh, Jane. *Vogue History of 20th Century Fashion.* 1989, Viking $50.00 (0-670-80172-0). An illustrated history of fashion from the early 1900s to 1986. (Rev: BL 6/15/89; Choice 9/89; LJ 4/1/89. Awards: BL, 1989) **[391]**

1864 Peacock, John. *Chronicle of Western Fashion: From Ancient Times to the Present Day.* 1991, Abrams $29.95 (0-8109-3953-3). An illustrated history of fashion from approximately 3000 B.C. to the present. (Rev: BL 6/1/91; Choice 10/91) **[391]**

Auxiliary garments and accessories

1865 McDowell, Colin. *Shoes: Fashion and Fantasy.* 1989, Rizzoli $50.00 (0-8478-1112-3). A history of shoes as fashion accessory from ancient times to the twentieth century. (Rev: LJ 5/15/90; NYTBR 12/3/89; Time 12/18/89) **[391.4]**

392 Customs of life cycle and domestic life

Customs relating to attainment of majority

1866 Diliberto, Gioia. *Debutante: The Story of Brenda Frazier.* 1987, Knopf $19.95 (0-394-53516-2); Pocket paper $4.95 (0-671-66022-5). A biography detailing the fall of a wealthy American debutante into a life filled with drugs, depression, and disease. (Rev: BL 5/1/87; PW 5/1/87; Time 6/8/87) **[392.15]**

393 Death customs

Cremation

1867 Tierney, Patrick. *Highest Altar: The Story of Human Sacrifice.* 1989, Viking $22.50 (0-670-82809-

2); **Penguin paper $11.95 (0-14-013974-5).** A report on the continued practice of ritual killings in the South American nations of Bolivia, Chile, and Peru. (Rev: NYTBR 1/7/90; PW 6/23/90) **[393.2]**

394 General customs

Eating, drinking, using drugs

1868 **Brennan, Jennifer.** *Curries and Bugles: A Memoir and Cookbook of the British Raj.* 1990, **HarperCollins $25.00 (0-06-016434-4).** Memoirs of the author regarding her life in India and the cuisine developed under two centuries of British influence. (Rev: BL 10/1/90; LJ 9/15/90; PW 7/20/90) **[394.1]**

1869 **Infante, G. Cabrera.** *Holy Smoke.* 1986, **Harper & Row $16.95 (0-06-015432-2); Faber paper $8.95 (0-571-14594-9).** The Cuban writer details the history of cigars and the customs surrounding cigar smoking. "A rich book written by an extraordinary linguist."—TLS (Rev: NYRB 5/8/86; PW 12/20/85; TLS 8/29/86) **[394.1]**

1870 **Simeti, Mary T.** *Pomp and Sustenance: Twenty-Five Centuries of Sicilian Food.* 1989, **Knopf $25.00 (0-394-56850-8).** A look at the history and culture of the food of Sicily, including historical and contemporary recipes. (Rev: BL 9/1/89; LJ 8/89; PW 8/18/89. Awards: PW, 1989) **[394.1]**

1871 **Williams, Susan.** *Savory Suppers and Fashionable Feasts: Dining in Victorian America.* 1985, **Strong Museum $17.95 (0-318-23129-8).** A look at the development of American customs regarding food and eating during the Victorian era. (Rev: BL 10/1/85; LJ 1/86; Natl Rev 2/14/86) **[394.1]**

395 Etiquette (Manners)

1872 **Baldridge, Letitia.** *Letitia Baldridge's Complete Guide to the New Manners for the '90's.* 1990, **Rawson $24.95 (0-89256-320-6).** A guide to contemporary etiquette by the author of *Complete Guide to Executive Manners.* (Rev: BL 11/15/89; LJ 1/90; PW 12/8/89) **[395]**

1873 **Bryan, Dawn.** *Art and Etiquette of Gift Giving.* 1987, **Bantam $18.95 (0-553-05223-3).** An international guide to proper gift giving etiquette in both business and personal situations. (Rev: BL 11/15/87; LJ 10/1/87; PW 10/30/87) **[395]**

1874 **Martin, Judith.** *Miss Manners' Guide to Rearing Perfect Children.* **Penguin paper $9.95 (0-14-008308-1).** Collections of her writings on etiquette dealing with children and child rearing. "Hilarious yet practical advice on how to teach behavior to youngsters in almost every imaginable situation."—PW (Rev: LJ 12/84; NYTBR 10/21/84; PW 8/31/84. Awards: LJ, 1984) **[395]**

1875 **Visser, Margaret.** *Rituals of Dinner.* 1991, **Grove-Weidenfeld $22.95 (0-8021-1116-5).** A cross-cultural study of eating habits and table manners by the author of *Much Depends on Dinner.* (Rev: BL 9/1/91; PW 5/17/91) **[395]**

Business and office etiquette

1876 **Baldridge, Letitia.** *Letitia Baldridge's Complete Guide to Executive Manners.* 1985, **Rawson $24.95 (0-89256-290-0).** A guide to proper etiquette for the business executive. "No business person should be without her well-mannered guidance."—PW (Rev: LJ 10/1/85; PW 9/13/85) **[395.52]**

398 Folklore

1877 **Barber, Paul.** *Vampires, Burial and Death: Folklore and Reality.* 1990, **Yale Univ. Pr. paper $9.95 (0-300-04859-9).** A study of vampires and vampirism in fact, folklore, and fiction. (Rev: Atl 10/88; BL 9/1/88; Choice 2/89) **[398]**

Folklore and folk literature

1878 **Abrahams, Roger D., ed.** *African Folktales: Traditional Stories of the Black World.* 1983, **Pantheon paper $12.95 (0-394-72117-9).** Collected folktales from the African continent south of the Sahara Desert. (Rev: BL 11/15/83; LJ 11/1/83; NYTBR 11/20/83) **[398.2]**

1879 **Abrahams, Roger D., ed.** *Afro-American Folktales: Stories from Black Traditions in the New World.* 1985, **Pantheon paper $12.95 (0-394-72885-8).** Over 100 folktales collected from persons of African descent from throughout the continents of North and South America. (Rev: Atl 5/85; Choice 8/85; LJ 2/15/85) **[398.2]**

1880 **Bettelheim, Bruno.** *Uses of Enchantment: The Meaning and Importance of Fairy Tales.* 1976, **Knopf $24.95 (0-394-48771-6); Random paper $10.95 (0-679-72393-5).** The effects of fairy tales on young people by the noted child psychologist. (Rev: LJ 6/1/76; New Rep 5/29/76; NYTBR 5/23/76. Awards: ALA, 1976; NYTBR, 1976) **[398.2]**

1881 **Bierhorst, John.** *Mythology of Mexico and Central America.* 1990, **Morrow $14.95 (0-688-06721-2).** An introduction to the myths of the indigenous peoples of Mexico and Central America. (Rev: BL 10/1/90; Choice 6/91; NYTBR 1/6/91) **[398.2]**

1882 **Brunvand, Jan H.** *Choking Doberman and Other "New" Urban Legends.* 1984, **Norton $13.95 (0-393-01844-X).** A collection of 40 tales of modern folklore by the author of *The Vanishing Hitchhiker.* (Rev: CSM 8/17/84; LJ 5/1/84; Time 7/23/84) **[398.2]**

1883 **Brunvand, Jan H.** *Mexican Pet: More "New" Urban Legends and Some Old Favorites.* 1988, **Norton paper $6.95 (0-393-30542-2).** A study of contemporary folklore and its role in popular culture by the author of *The Choking Doberman.* (Rev: Atl 10/86; LJ 6/15/86; NYTBR 7/6/86) **[398.2]**

1884 **Brunvand, Jan H.** *Vanishing Hitchhiker: American Urban Legends and Their Meanings.* 1989, **Norton $14.95 (0-393-01473-8); paper $7.95 (0-393-95169-3).** A collection of modern urban folktales with extensive bibliographies, a glossary of terms, and appendices on the study and collection of urban legends. (Rev: BL 10/1/81; Choice 5/82; TLS 8/13/82. Awards: BL, the 1980s) **[398.2]**

1885 **Calvino, Italo.** *Italian Folktales.* **1980, Harcourt $27.50 (0-15-145770-0); Pantheon paper $14.95 (0-394-74909-X).** A selection of folktales from the different regions of Italy, retold by one of the century's great storytellers. (REV: New Rep 9/27/80; NYTBR 10/12/80; Newsweek 11/17/80. AWARDS: ALA, 1980; BL, the 1980s; NYTBR, 1980) **[398.2]**

1886 **Dadie, Bernard Binlin.** *Black Cloth: A Collection of African Folk Tales.* **1987, Univ. of Massachusetts Pr. $9.95 (0-87023-557-5).** A collection of African folktales retold by a writer native to the Ivory Coast. (REV: BL 9/1/87; LJ 3/1/87; NYTBR 6/28/87) **[398.2]**

1887 **De Larrabeiti, Michael.** *Provencal Tales.* **1989, St. Martin's $17.95 (0-312-02968-3).** A collection of 13 French folktales retold by the author. (REV: BL 8/89; LJ 7/89; PW 6/16/89. AWARDS: BL, 1989) **[398.2]**

1888 **Erdoes, Richard, and Alfonso Ortiz, eds.** *American Indian Myths and Legends.* **1985, Pantheon paper $12.95 (0-394-74018-1).** A collection of 160 tales from 100 North American native tribes. (REV: BL 10/1/84; LJ 11/15/84; NYTBR 2/3/85) **[398.2]**

1889 **Glassie, Henry, ed.** *Irish Folktales.* **1987, Pantheon paper $12.95 (0-394-74637-6).** A collection of over 100 Irish folktales. (REV: BL 10/1/85; LJ 10/1/85; NYTBR 11/17/85) **[398.2]**

1890 **Goss, Linda, and Marian E. Barnes, eds.** *Talk That Talk: An Anthology of African-American Storytelling.* **1989, Simon & Schuster $24.95 (0-671-67167-7).** An anthology of African-American folktales from the last four centuries. (REV: BL 12/1/89; PW 1/21/90. AWARDS: PW, 1989) **[398.2]**

1891 **Sadeh, Pinhas.** *Jewish Folktales.* **1989, Doubleday $24.95 (0-385-19573-7); paper $12.95 (0-385-19574-5).** The author retells Jewish folktales collected from Eastern Europe, Asia, North Africa, and the Middle East. "Continually engaging."—PW (REV: BL 11/1/89; PW 10/6/89. AWARDS: PW, 1989) **[398.2]**

1892 **Tyler, Royall, ed.** *Japanese Tales.* **1989, Pantheon paper $12.95 (0-394-75656-8).** A collection of over 200 folktales from medieval Japan ranging from the twelfth to fourteenth centuries. (REV: BL 5/1/87; LJ 4/1/87; PW 3/20/87) **[398.2]**

1893 **Zipes, Jack David.** *Brothers Grimm: From Enchanted Forest to Modern World.* **1988, Routledge $29.50 (0-415-90081-6); paper $13.95 (0-415-90209-6).** An examination of the creation and significance of *Grimm's Fairy Tales.* (REV: Choice 6/89; LJ 9/15/88) **[398.2]**

Persons as subjects of folklore

1894 **Anderson, William.** *Green Man: The Archetype of Our Oneness with the Earth.* **1990, HarperCollins $27.95 (0-06-250077-5); paper $14.95 (0-06-250075-9).** A look at the symbolism of the green man found as a decorative figure on Gothic cathedrals. (REV: Atl 4/91; BL 1/15/91; NYTBR 7/21/91) **[398.352]**

LANGUAGE

400 LANGUAGE

401 Philosophy and theory

1895 Paz, Octavio. *Monkey Grammarian.* 1981, Seaver $14.95 (0-394-51807-1). A treatise on the writer's search for self-awareness by the Mexican Nobel laureate. (REV: LJ 9/15/81; NYTBR 12/27/81) **[401]**

410 LINGUISTICS

Persons

1896 Culler, Jonathan. *Roland Barthes.* 1983, Oxford Univ. Pr. $21.95 (0-19-520420-4); paper $7.95 (0-19-520421-2). A survey of the life and work of the French social critic, linguist, and writer. "A real gem . . . a first-rate introduction."—LJ (REV: Choice 11/83; LJ 7/83; TLS 7/15/83) **[410.92]**

411 Writing systems

1897 Logan, Robert K. *Alphabet Effect: The Impact of the Phonetic Alphabet on the Development of Western Civilization.* 1986, Morrow $16.95 (0-688-06389-6); St. Martin's paper $9.95 (0-312-00993-3). A study of the development of the phonetic alphabet and its influence upon Western thought and culture. (REV: BL 8/86; PW 7/4/86) **[411]**

413 Dictionaries

1898 Landau, Sidney I. *Dictionaries: The Art and Craft of Lexicography.* 1984, Macmillan $30.00 (0-684-18096-0); Cambridge Univ. Pr. paper $13.95 (0-521-36725-5). A history of English language dictionaries and their production from 1604 to the present. (REV: BL 12/1/84; Choice 1/85; LJ 8/84) **[413]**

420 ENGLISH AND OLD ENGLISH

1899 Bryson, Bill. *Mother Tongue: English and How It Got That Way.* 1990, Morrow $18.95 (0-688-07895-8). A history of the development of English from its beginnings to its current position as an international language. (REV: BL 6/1/90; NYTBR 8/5/90) **[420]**

1900 Burchfield, Robert W. *Unlocking the English Language.* 1991, Hill & Wang $18.95 (0-8090-9490-8). A study of recent changes in the English language and issues confronting lexicographers by the former editor of the *Oxford English Dictionary.* (REV: BL 4/15/91; PW 2/22/91) **[420]**

1901 Michaels, Leonard, and Christopher Ricks, eds. *State of the Language.* 1979, Univ. of California Pr. $35.00 (0-520-03763-4); paper $19.95 (0-520-04400-2). Fifty-six essays and seven poems regarding the current state of the English language and its regional forms and variations. (REV: BL 3/1/80; Choice 5/80; NYTBR 1/6/80) **[420]**

History

1902 Burchfield, Robert W. *English Language.* 1985, Oxford Univ. Pr. $19.95 (0-19-219173-X). A history of the English language by the chief editor of the *Oxford English Dictionary.* (REV: BL 2/1/85; CSM 3/27/85; LJ 5/15/85) **[420.9]**

1903 McCrum, Robert. *Story of English.* 1986, Viking $24.95 (0-670-80467-3); Penguin paper $14.95 (0-14-009435-0). An accompaniment to the PBS television series tracing the history and development of the English language. (REV: BL 7/86; LJ 8/86; TLS 9/26/86) **[420.9]**

422 Etymology of standard English

1904 Thomas, Lewis. *Et Cetera, Et Cetera: Notes of a Word-Watcher.* 1990, Little, Brown $17.95 (0-316-84099-8); Penguin paper $8.95 (0-14-015875-8). Collected essays on the English language written by the author of *Lives of a Cell.* (REV: BL 10/1/90; NYTBR 10/21/90; PW 8/31/90) **[422]**

1905 Williams, Raymond. *Keywords: A Vocabulary of Culture and Society.* 1976, Oxford Univ. Pr. paper $9.95 (0-19-520469-7). An exploration of the derivation and changing meanings of 100 English words and how their evolution reflects changes in society. "Precise and illuminating scholarship that is full of surprises."—PW (REV: LJ 4/15/76; PW 3/1/76; TLS 3/26/76) **[422]**

423   Dictionaries of standard English

Persons

1906   Murray, K. M. Elizabeth. *Caught in the Web of Words: James A. H. Murray and the Oxford English Dictionary*. 1977, Yale Univ. Pr. $40.00 (0-300-02131-3); Oxford Univ. Pr. paper $8.95 (0-19-281265-3). A biography of the author's grandfather, the first editor of the *Oxford English Dictionary*. "This life of both the dictionary and the man deserves to be in every sizeable library in the country."—Choice (Rev: Choice 3/78; LJ 11/15/77; NYTBR 10/30/77)   **[423.09]**

427   English language variations

1907   Dillard, J. L. *Black English: Its History and Usage in the United States*. 1973, Random paper $8.95 (0-394-71872-0). Dillard argues that the form of English spoken by African Americans has its own history and grammar and, as such, should be taught in American schools. "The most extensive research study on black dialect . . . no library, however small, should be without this book."—Choice (Rev: Choice 12/72; LJ 9/1/72; NYTBR 9/3/72)   **[427]**

United States

1908   Hendrickson, Robert. *American Talk: The Words and Ways of American Dialects*. 1987, Penguin paper $7.95 (0-14-009421-0). A study of the regional dialects of the United States and their development. (Rev: BL 9/15/86; LJ 10/1/86; PW 9/26/86)   **[427.973]**

428   Standard English usage

1909   Safire, William. *I Stand Corrected: More on Language*. 1984, Random $19.95 (0-8129-1097-4). Essays by the author of *What's the Good Word?* regarding the English language and its contemporary usage. (Rev: BL 4/1/85; CSM 12/31/84; LJ 6/1/84)   **[428]**

1910   Safire, William. *Language Maven Strikes Again*. 1990, Doubleday $22.95 (0-385-41299-1). The sixth collection of the author's columns regarding the English language and its contemporary usage. (Rev: BL 6/1/90; LJ 7/90; PW 5/25/90)   **[428]**

1911   Safire, William. *You Could Look It Up: More on Language*. 1988, Random $22.50 (0-8129-1324-8); Henry Holt paper $12.95 (0-8050-0975-2). A collection of the writer's musings on the English language taken from his column for the *New York Times*. (Rev: BL 6/1/88; LJ 6/15/88; PW 7/1/88)   **[428]**

430   GERMANIC (TEUTONIC) LANGUAGES

Yiddish

1912   Rosten, Leo. *Joys of Yiddish*. 1970, Pocket paper $4.95 (0-317-56876-0). An informal dictionary of Yiddish words and phrases, with jokes, folklore, explanations, and examples. (Rev: LJ 10/1/68; New Yorker 11/30/68; PW 8/19/68. Awards: ALA, 1968)   **[439.937]**

500 NATURAL SCIENCES AND MATHEMATICS

1913 Brockman, John, ed. *Doing Science: Reality Club 2.* 1990, Prentice Hall paper $10.95 (0-13-795097-7). A collection of essays discussing the scientific method and scientific thought. (Rev: BL 12/1/90; LJ 11/15/90; PW 11/2/90) **[500]**

1914 Flanagan, Dennis. *Flanagan's Version: A Spectator's Guide to Science on the Eve of the 21st Century.* 1988, Knopf $18.95 (0-394-55547-3); Random paper $8.95 (0-679-72156-8). An overview of the history and current state of the major fields of science. "A primer of science for the common reader that belongs in every public library."—BL (Rev: BL 4/15/88; LJ 4/15/88; NYTBR 5/29/88) **[500]**

1915 Flaste, Richard, ed. *New York Times Book of Science Literacy: What Everyone Needs to Know from Newton to Knuckleball.* 1991, Random $24.95 (0-685-34611-0). A collection, containing contributions by 21 different writers, of columns from the *New York Times* regarding science. (Rev: BL 1/15/91; LJ 2/15/91; NYTBR 2/24/91) **[500]**

1916 Flatow, Ira. *Rainbows, Curve Balls: And Other Wonders of the Natural World Explained.* 1988, Morrow $15.95 (0-688-06705-0); Harper & Row paper $7.95 (0-06-097237-8). Essays explaining the workings of nature and human technology. (Rev: BL 7/88; NYTBR 8/28/88; PW 5/27/88) **[500]**

1917 Gorman, James. *Man with No Endorphins: And Other Reflections on Science.* 1988, Viking $15.95 (0-670-81842-9); Penguin paper $6.95 (0-14-010359-7). A collection of the author's columns, originally published in *Discover* magazine, concerning the lighter side of science. "One of our funniest humorists."—BL (Rev: BL 4/15/88; LJ 3/1/88; NYTBR 3/27/88) **[500]**

1918 Gornick, Vivian. *Women in Science: Portraits from a World in Transition.* 1990, Simon & Schuster paper $8.95 (0-671-69592-4). An account of contemporary women scientists, their work, and their relationships with their male colleagues based on 100 confidential interviews. (Rev: LJ 7/83; NYTBR 10/2/83; PW 6/17/83) **[500]**

1919 Gould, Stephen Jay. *Flamingo's Smile: Reflections in Natural History.* 1985, Norton $17.95 (0-393-02228-5); paper $8.95 (0-393-30375-6). The fourth collection of the author's monthly essays for *Natural History Magazine* on science and evolution. (Rev: BL 8/85; LJ 9/15/85; Newsweek 10/28/85) **[500]**

1920 Hazen, Robert M., and James Trefil. *Science Matters: Achieving Scientific Literacy.* 1991, Doubleday $19.95 (0-385-24796-6). A survey of key concepts of modern science directed at the layperson. (Rev: BL 12/15/90; LJ 1/91; PW 12/14/90) **[500]**

1921 Lightman, Alan P. *A Modern Day Yankee in a Connecticut Court: And Other Essays on Science.* 1988, Penguin paper $6.95 (0-14-009476-8). A collection of science-related essays by an American physicist. (Rev: BL 10/15/86; LJ 11/15/86; PW 11/7/86) **[500]**

1922 Page, Jake. *Pastoral: A Natural History of Sorts.* 1985, Norton $13.95 (0-393-01903-9). Collected miscellaneous essays by the *Science* magazine contributor. "One of those special books that can be read and re-read with enjoyment."—PW (Rev: LJ 5/1/85; NYTBR 5/19/85; PW 1/25/85) **[500]**

1923 Perutz, Max. *Is Science Necessary? Essays on Science and Scientists.* 1989, Dutton $19.95 (0-525-24673-8); Oxford Univ. Pr. paper $9.95 (0-19-286118-2). Essays regarding science and its contributions to modern society. (Rev: BL 12/15/88; CSM 8/17/89; LJ 3/1/90) **[500]**

1924 Regis, Ed. *Great Mambo Chicken and the Transhuman Condition: Science Slightly Over the Edge.* 1990, Addison Wesley $18.95 (0-201-09258-1). The author of *Who Got Einstein's Office?* takes a look at offbeat scientific research. (Rev: BL 8/90; LJ 8/90; PW 8/17/90) **[500]**

1925 Rensberger, Bruce. *How the World Works: A Guide to Science's Greatest Discoveries.* 1986, Morrow $18.95 (0-688-05398-X); paper $7.95 (0-688-07293-3). A background of 24 of science's most important discoveries with profiles of the people and concepts behind the breakthroughs. (Rev: BL 3/15/86; Choice 6/86; PW 2/17/86) **[500]**

1926 Smith, James Allen. *Idea Brokers: Think Tanks and the Rise of the New Policy Elite.* **1991, Free Pr. $24.95 (0-02-929551-3).** A study of the recent history and influence of American policy research groups. (REV: BL 1/15/91; LJ 2/1/91; NYTBR 2/10/91) **[500]**

1927 Wolpert, Lewis, and Alison Richards, eds. *Passion for Science.* **1989, Oxford Univ. Pr. paper $8.95 (0-19-854212-7).** Thirteen scientists discuss their work and what they find appealing about it. (REV: LJ 3/1/89; PW 6/24/88) **[500]**

Men

1928 Christianson, Gale E. *In the Presence of the Creator: Isaac Newton and His Times.* **1984, Free Pr. $19.95 (0-02-905190-8).** A study of the life and times of the English scientist Isaac Newton. (REV: Choice 10/84; LJ 8/84; TLS 9/13/85) **[500.81]**

1929 Eiseley, Loren. *All the Strange Hours: Excavations of a Life.* **1983, Peter Smith $18.50 (0-8446-5978-9); Macmillan paper $8.95 (0-684-18907-0).** An autobiography of the science writer and essayist. "A beautiful, sensitive, and all too rare vision of what it meant to grow up sickly, be poor in the Depression, and struggle to find a professional base as an intellectual."—Choice (REV: Choice 6/76; CSM 12/11/75; LJ 10/15/75. AWARDS: ALA, 1975) **[500.81]**

Personal accounts

1930 Burroughs, John. *Deep Woods: A John Burroughs Reader.* **1990, Gibbs Smith paper $9.95 (0-87905-030-6).** Ten essays by the late nineteenth- and early twentieth-century naturalist. (REV: BL 9/15/90; LJ 7/90) **[500.9]**

1931 Dillard, Annie. *Pilgrim at Tinker Creek.* **1988, Harper & Row paper $8.95 (0-06-09545-5).** A look at the wonders of nature surrounding her home, Dillard's first work received widespread critical acclaim. (REV: LJ 5/1/74; NYTBR 3/24/74; Time 3/18/74. AWARDS: ALA, 1974; PP:NF, 1975) **[500.9]**

1932 Teale, Edwin W. *Wandering Through Winter.* **1990, St. Martin's paper $12.95 (0-312-04458-5).** One of four works Teale wrote on the natural history of the American seasons. (REV: Atl 12/65; CSM 10/2/65; LJ 10/1/65. AWARDS: ALA, 1965; PP:NF, 1966) **[500.9]**

501 Philosophy and theory

1933 Berlinski, David. *Black Mischief: Language, Life, Logic, Luck.* **1988, Harcourt paper $17.95 (0-15-613063-7).** A critical study of the methodologies of modern science. (REV: BL 2/1/86; LJ 2/15/86; PW 1/31/86) **[501]**

1934 Bronowski, Jacob. *Ascent of Man.* **1976, Little, Brown $35.00 (0-316-10930-4); paper $24.95 (0-316-10933-9).** The history of science and human intellect from prehistoric times to the present. "Bronowski's competence and authority are extraordinary . . . this book must be in every library: academic and public."—Choice (REV: Choice 7–8/74; CSM 6/25/74; LJ 6/15/74. AWARDS: ALA, 1974) **[501]**

1935 Casti, John. *Searching for Certainty: What Scientists Can Know about the Future.* **1991, Morrow $22.95 (0-688-08980-1).** An analysis of science's ability to predict future events. (REV: BL 2/15/91; LJ 1/91; NYTBR 3/24/91) **[501]**

1936 Dyson, Freeman J. *Infinite in All Directions: An Exploration of Science and Belief.* **1988, Harper & Row $19.95 (0-06-039081-6); paper $8.95 (0-06-091569-2).** A presentation of current scientific thought regarding the nature of the universe. (REV: Choice 11/88; NYTBR 7/24/88; Time 3/21/88) **[501]**

1937 Medawar, P. B. *Threat and the Glory: Reflections on Science and Scientists.* **1990, Harper-Collins $22.50 (0-06-039112-X).** Collected essays on science written over a period of 30 years by the Nobel laureate. (REV: BL 8/90; LJ 8/90; PW 7/13/90) **[501]**

1938 Medawar, Peter. *Limits of Science.* **1988, Oxford Univ. Pr. $8.95 (0-19-505212-9).** Reflections on science and its methods by a 1960 Nobel Prize winner in medicine. (REV: Choice 3/85; CSM 12/7/84; LJ 9/15/84) **[501]**

1939 Prigogine, Ilya, and Isabelle Stengers. *Order Out of Chaos: Man's New Dialogue with Nature.* **1984, Shambhala $18.95 (0-87773-302-3); Bantam paper $11.95 (0-553-34363-7).** The 1977 Nobel Laureate for Chemistry's reinterpretation of the laws of physics, and their interrelationship with other sciences and the humanities. (REV: Choice 1/85; LJ 3/1/84; PW 2/17/84. AWARDS: LJ, 1984) **[501]**

1940 Raymo, Chet. *Virgin and the Mousetrap: Essays in Search of the Soul of Science.* **1991, Viking $18.95 (0-670-83315-0).** A collection of 21 science-related essays by a Stonehill College physics professor. "Eminently readable and thoroughly enjoyable."—NYTBR (REV: BL 8/91; LJ 8/91; NYTBR 8/18/91) **[501]**

1941 Sagan, Carl. *Broca's Brain: Reflection on the Romance of Science.* **1979, Random $14.95 (0-394-50169-1); Ballantine paper $4.95 (0-345-33689-5).** A collection of essays regarding science and the human mind by the author of *Comet.* (REV: BL 9/1/79; Natl Rev 8/3/79; NYTBR 6/10/79) **[501]**

1942 Talbot, Michael. *Holographic Universe.* **1991, HarperCollins $19.95 (0-06-016381-X).** The author's refutation of current theories concerning the essence of the universe and the workings of the human brain. "Controversial but fascinating."—BL (REV: BL 3/15/91; LJ 4/15/91) **[501]**

1943 Wright, Robert. *Three Scientists and Their Gods: A Search for Meaning in an Age of Information.* **1988, Random $18.95 (0-8129-1328-0); Harper & Row paper $8.95 (0-06-097257-2).** A study of the lives and work of three scientists looking for unified systems in the fields of physics, biology, and economics. (REV: BL 5/1/88; LJ 8/88; NYTBR 8/7/88) **[501]**

502   Miscellany

1944   Morrison, Philip, and Phyllis Morrison. *Ring of Truth: An Inquiry into How We Know What We Know.* 1987, Random $24.95 (0-394-55663-1); paper $15.95 (0-679-72130-4). An illustrated survey of science, scientists, and the scientific method written to accompany the PBS television series. (REV: BL 10/1/87; LJ 12/87; NYTBR 1/31/88)   **[502]**

1945   Stone, Judith. *Light Elements: Essays in Science from Gravity to Levity.* 1991, Ballantine paper $8.00 (0-345-36608-5). Science-related essays penned by the *Discover* magazine columnist. "Makes science not only intelligible but entertaining as well."—PW (REV: BL 4/15/91; LJ 5/1/91; PW 4/5/91)   **[502]**

508   Natural history

1946   Attenborough, David. *First Eden: The Mediterranean World and Man.* 1987, Little, Brown $24.95 (0-316-05750-9). A survey of the natural history of the Mediterranean region and the impact of man upon it. (REV: BL 2/15/88; LJ 9/1/87; PW 7/24/87)   **[508]**

1947   Dillard, Annie. *Teaching a Stone to Talk: Expeditions and Encounters.* 1988, Harper & Row paper $8.95 (0-06-091541-2). Essays regarding the natural world by the author of *Pilgrim at Tinker Creek.* (REV: BL 7/82; CSM 11/5/82; PW 8/27/82)   **[508]**

1948   Finch, Robert, and John Elder, eds. *Norton Book of Nature Writing.* 1990, Norton $29.95 (0-393-02799-6). A collection of two centuries of American and British nature writing. (REV: LJ 3/1/90; PW 2/23/90)   **[508]**

1949   Gould, Stephen Jay. *Bully for Brontosaurus: Reflections in Natural History.* 1991, Norton $22.95 (0-393-02961-1). A collection of essays regarding aspects of natural history and evolution by the author of *Wonderful Life.* "His best yet."—BL (REV: BL 3/15/91; LJ 5/15/91; PW 3/22/91)   **[508]**

1950   Hubbell, Sue. *A Country Year: Living the Questions.* 1986, Random $17.95 (0-394-55146-X); Harper & Row paper $7.95 (0-06-097086-3). Essays regarding nature and the author's experiences living by herself on a farm in the Ozarks. "Her delightful, witty book will appeal to all those who are intrigued by the natural world."—LJ (REV: BL 4/15/86; LJ 4/1/86; NYTBR 4/13/86)   **[508]**

1951   Quammen, David. *Flight of the Iguana: A Sidelong Look at Science and Nature.* 1988, Delacorte $17.95 (0-385-29592-8); Doubleday paper $8.95 (0-385-26327-9). A collection of writings on natural history culled from the author's columns for *Outdoor Magazine.* (REV: BL 8/88; LJ 6/15/88; NYTBR 6/26/88)   **[508]**

1952   Quammen, David. *Natural Acts: A Sidelong View of Science and Nature.* 1986, Lyons & Burford $16.95 (0-8052-3967-7); Dell paper $6.95 (0-440-55696-1). Collected essays on natural history by the author of *Flight of the Iguana.* (REV: CSM 5/29/85; LJ 3/15/85; NYTBR 4/21/85)   **[508]**

Persons

1953   Mitchell, John Hanson. *Living at the End of Time.* 1990, Houghton $19.95 (0-395-44594-9). Ruminations on nature and the writings of Thoreau as written in journals at the author's retreat cabin. (REV: BL 5/1/90; LJ 6/1/90; NYTBR 5/13/90)   **[508.092]**

Soviet Union

1954   Medvedev, Zhores A. *Soviet Science.* 1978, Norton $15.95 (0-393-06435-2). A chronicle of Soviet scientific research since the Russian Revolution and the effect of state control upon its subjects. (REV: BL 7/15/78; LJ 5/1/78; NYTBR 5/28/78)   **[508.47]**

China

1955   Temple, Robert. *Genius of China: 3,000 Years of Discovery, Invention and Science.* 1987, Simon & Schuster $19.95 (0-671-62028-2); paper $14.95 (0-671-67407-2). An overview of the accomplishments of Chinese scientists and inventors throughout history. "An exhilarating celebration of historic achievements, the breadth of which will astonish the general reader."—PW (REV: BL 3/15/87; Choice 5/87; PW 11/28/86)   **[508.51]**

United States

1956   Leopold, Aldo. *Sand County Almanac: And Sketches Here and There.* 1987, Oxford Univ. Pr. $19.95 (0-19-505305-2); paper $8.95 (0-19-505928-X). A posthumous reprint of a collection of writings by an American conservationist regarding man's ethical responsibilities toward the Earth. (REV: LJ 3/1/88; NYTBR 2/28/88)   **[508.73]**

Northeastern United States

1957   Finch, Robert. *Outlands: Journeys to the Outer Edges of Cape Cod.* 1986, Godine $15.95 (0-87923-619-1); paper $9.95 (0-87923-742-2). Essays on the natural world of Cape Cod. (REV: BL 8/86; LJ 6/1/86; Time 11/3/86)   **[508.74]**

South Central United States

1958   Lockwood, C. C. *Gulf Coast: Where Land Meets Sea.* 1984, Louisiana State Univ. Pr. $34.95 (0-8071-1170-8). A photographic essay detailing the plant and animal life of America's Gulf of Mexico coastline. (REV: BL 9/1/84; PW 4/27/84. AWARDS: ALA, 1984)   **[508.76]**

Great Basin and Pacific slope region of the United States

1959   Aitchison, Stewart. *A Wilderness Called Grand Canyon.* 1991, Voyageur Pr. $27.95 (0-89658-149-7). An illustrated survey of the wildlife and natural history of Arizona's Grand Canyon. (REV: BL 6/1/91; LJ 4/1/91)   **[508.79]**

1960   Carson, Rob. *Mount St. Helens: The Eruption and Recovery of a Volcano.* 1990, Sasquatch Books $28.00 (0-912365-33-1); paper $19.95 (0-912365-32-3). An illustrated study of the eruption of Washington's Mount St. Helens and the aftereffects of the cataclysmic event. "A resplendent popular survey."—BL (REV: BL 6/15/90; LJ 9/1/90)   **[508.79]**

1961 DeSantis, Marie. *California Currents: An Exploration of the Ocean's Pleasures, Mysteries and Dilemmas.* 1985, Tioga $15.95 (0-89141-191-7). Forty-five essays regarding various aspects of the California coastline. (REV: BL 1/1/85; LJ 5/1/85; PW 4/26/85)   **[508.79]**

1962 Zwinger, Ann Haymond. *Mysterious Lands.* 1989, Dutton $22.50 (0-525-24546-4); NAL paper $10.95 (0-452-26513-4). An introduction to life in the deserts of the American Southwest. "Excellent nature writing for a general audience."—LJ (REV: BL 3/15/89; LJ 4/1/89; PW 2/10/89)   **[508.79]**

Alaska

1963 Murray, John A., ed. *Republic of Rivers: Three Centuries of Nature Writing from Alaska and the Yukon.* 1990, Oxford Univ. Pr. $19.95 (0-19-506102-0). Selected writings about the natural history of the Far North by authors ranging from John Muir to Thomas Merton. (REV: BL 9/1/90; CSM 9/11/90; LJ 9/15/90)   **[508.798]**

South America

1964 Steadman, David W., and Steven Zousmer. *Galapagos: Discovery on Darwin's Islands.* 1988, Smithsonian Inst. $24.95 (0-87474-882-8); paper $14.95 (0-87474-891-7). The author presents the results of his eight years' research concerning the wildlife of the Galapagos Islands. (REV: BL 7/88; Choice 9/88; LJ 5/15/88)   **[508.8]**

Brazil

1965 Cousteau, Jacques-Yves, and Mose Richards. *Jacques Cousteau's Amazon Journey.* 1984, Abrams $39.95 (0-8109-1813-7). Details of Cousteau and his crew's year-and-a-half study of the Amazon basin and its wildlife. (REV: BL 3/15/85; LJ 1/85; NYTBR 12/2/84)   **[508.81]**

New Zealand

1966 Lockley, Ronald, and Betty Brownlie. *Secrets of Natural New Zealand.* 1988, Viking $40.00 (0-670-81248-X). A survey of the unique natural history of the island nation of New Zealand. "A superb introduction to a strange and wonderful land."—PW (REV: LJ 4/1/88; PW 3/25/88)   **[508.93]**

Australia

1967 Vandenbeld, John. *Nature of Australia: A Portrait of the Island Continent.* 1988, Facts on File $29.95 (0-8160-2006-X). An examination of the natural history of the continent of Australia, its unique evolution, and the changes brought upon it by European colonization. (REV: BL 9/15/88; Choice 3/89; LJ 4/1/89)   **[508.94]**

The Arctic

1968 Bruemmer, Fred. *Arctic Animals: A Celebration of Survival.* 1987, Northword $29.95 (1-55971-

020-9); paper $19.95 (1-55971-021-7). A study of the environment and wildlife of the Arctic. "One of the best popular works on the Arctic . . . a work of unpretentious authority and beauty."—BL (REV: BL 9/1/87; PW 8/14/87)   **[508.98]**

1969 Lopez, Barry. *Arctic Dreams: Imagination and Desire in a Northern Landscape.* 1989, Bantam paper $9.95 (0-553-34664-4). A sweeping overview of the Arctic region: its history and exploration, its peoples, and its flora and fauna. (REV: Choice 5/86; LJ 3/1/86; NYTBR 2/16/86. AWARDS: ALA, 1986; LJ, 1986; NBA, 1986; NYTBR, 1986)   **[508.98]**

1970 Miles, Hugh, and Mike Salisbury. *Kingdom of the Ice Bear: A Portrait of the Arctic.* 1986, Univ. of Texas Pr. $19.95 (0-292-70393-7). Accounts of two BBC documentary filmmakers of their experiences in the Arctic. (REV: LJ 5/1/86; TLS 4/4/86)   **[508.98]**

509 Historical, areas, persons treatment

1971 Bruce, Robert V. *Launching of Modern American Science, 1846–1876.* 1987, Knopf $30.00 (0-317-59128-2); Cornell Univ. Pr. paper $12.95 (0-8014-9496-6). "A much-needed interpretive history of American science; highly recommended for public libraries."—LJ (REV: Choice 7–8/87; LJ 4/15/87; NYTBR 11/19/87. AWARDS: PP:History, 1988)   **[509]**

1972 Cohen, I. Bernard. *Revolution in Science.* 1985, Harvard Univ. Pr. $30.95 (0-674-76777-2); paper $14.95 (0-674-76778-0). Cohen explores how single momentous ideas have revolutionized science through the past three centuries, and how changes in thought in the social sciences have influenced ideas in the hard sciences. (REV: LJ 6/1/85; NYTBR 4/21/85; PW 3/29/85)   **[509]**

1973 Ferris, Timothy. *Coming of Age in the Milky Way.* 1988, Morrow $19.95 (0-688-05889-2); Doubleday paper $10.95 (0-385-26326-0). An overview of the history of man's struggle to understand the nature of the universe. "A glorious adventure for the reader."—NYTBR (REV: Choice 12/88; CSM 7/13/88; NYTBR 7/17/88. AWARDS: NYTBR, 1988)   **[509]**

1974 Ronan, Colin A. *Science: Its History and Development Among the World's Cultures.* 1983, Facts on File $29.95 (0-87196-745-6); paper $16.95 (0-8160-1165-6). A survey of the history and development of science from ancient civilizations to the twentieth century. (REV: BL 9/1/83; Choice 11/83; LJ 7/83)   **[509]**

1975 Stearns, Raymond P. *Science in the British Colonies of America.* 1970, Univ. of Illinois Pr. $34.95 (0-252-00120-6). "For a long time to come students of the history of science in America will have to read Stearns."—Choice (REV: Choice 6/71; LJ 5/1/71; TLS 1/7/72. AWARDS: NBA, 1971)   **[509]**

510 MATHEMATICS

1976 Guillen, Michael. *Bridges to Infinity.* 1984, Jeremy P. Tarcher $12.95 (0-87477-233-8). Essays on the history and concepts of mathematics for the layman. "A fine readable introduction to modern mathematics . . . will help reduce the reader's level of math anxiety."—LJ (REV: LJ 12/1/83; NYTBR 2/5/84; PW 10/28/83) **[510]**

1977 Hoffman, Paul. *Archimedes' Revenge: The Challenge of the Unknown.* **1988, Norton $17.95 (0-393-02522-5); Fawcett paper $4.95 (0-449-21750-7).** Essays about mathematical concepts and their relationship to human understanding of the universe. (REV: BL 7/88; Choice 11/88; LJ 9/1/88) **[510]**

1978 Paulos, John A. *Beyond Numeracy.* **1991, Knopf $21.50 (0-394-58640-9).** A collection of short essays on mathematics by the author of *Innumeracy.* (REV: BL 5/1/91; LJ 4/1/91; PW 3/8/91) **[510]**

1979 Paulos, John A. *Innumeracy: Mathematical Illiteracy and Its Consequences.* **1989, Hill & Wang $18.95 (0-8090-7447-8); Random paper $8.95 (0-679-72601-2).** An examination of how the general American lack of skill in the understanding of numbers affects our society. (REV: BL 11/1/88; CSM 2/14/89; NYTBR 1/15/89) **[510]**

1980 Peterson, Ivars. *Mathematical Tourist: Snapshots of Modern Mathematics.* **1989, W. H. Freeman paper $10.95 (0-7167-2064-7).** An introduction to modern mathematical concepts and their application to other sciences. (REV: CSM 10/8/88; NYTBR 10/16/88) **[510]**

Philosophy and theory

1981 Davis, Philip J., and Reuben Hersh. *Descartes' Dream: The World According to Mathematics.* **1986, Harcourt $24.95 (0-15-125260-2); Houghton paper $12.95 (0-395-43154-9).** Essays on the role of mathematics in the modern world by the authors of *The Mathematical Experience.* (REV: BL 10/15/86; LJ 10/15/86; TLS 2/13/87) **[510.1]**

1982 Davis, Philip J., and Reuben Hersh. *Mathematical Experience.* **1981, Birkhauser $29.95 (0-8176-3018-X).** This history of mathematics and mathematicians was called "truly an exceptional book" by *Library Journal.* (REV: Choice 9/81; LJ 5/1/81; NYRB 8/13/81. AWARDS: NBA, 1983) **[510.1]**

Education, research, related topics

1983 Kaye, Peggy. *Games for Math: Playful Ways to Teach Your Child Math.* **1988, Pantheon $17.95 (0-394-54281-9); paper $8.95 (0-394-75510-3).** Over 60 games designed to improve the math skills of children from kindergarten to third grade. (REV: BL 4/1/89; LJ 3/1/88) **[510.7]**

Persons

1984 Hodges, Andrew. *Alan Turing: The Enigma.* **1984, Simon & Schuster paper $10.95 (0-671-52809-2).** A biography of the British mathematician who helped break Nazi codes during the Second World War and whose research was instrumental in the development of computers. (REV: Choice 4/84; NYRB 1/19/84; NYTBR 11/13/83) **[510.92]**

1985 Hyman, Anthony. *Charles Babbage: Pioneer of the Modern Computer.* **1982, Princeton Univ. Pr.** $35.00 (0-691-08303-7); paper $14.50 (0-691-02377-8). A biography of the nineteenth-century British mathematician whose ideas foresaw the creation of the modern computer. "The best biography of him so far."—New Yorker (REV: Choice 11/82; NYTBR 11/14/82; New Yorker 8/23/82) **[510.92]**

1986 Kac, Mark. *Enigmas of Chance: An Autobiography.* **1985, Harper & Row $18.95 (0-06-015433-0); Univ. of California Pr. paper $9.95 (0-520-05986-7).** Memoirs of the Polish mathematician who emigrated to the United States prior to World War II. "A rare but enjoyable glimpse into the academic side of science."—BL (REV: BL 9/1/85; Choice 12/85; LJ 8/85) **[510.92]**

1987 Kanigel, Robert. *Man Who Knew Infinity: A Life of the Indian Genius, Ramanujan.* **1991, Scribner $24.95 (0-684-19259-4).** A biography of the twentieth-century Indian mathematician who died at the age of 32. (REV: BL 6/1/91; LJ 5/1/91; PW 3/15/91) **[510.92]**

1988 Stein, Dorothy. *Ada: A Life and Legacy.* **1985, MIT Pr. $27.50 (0-262-19242-X).** A biography of Ada Byron, the daughter of poet Lord Byron and a noted mathematician in her own right. (REV: LJ 2/1/86; NYTBR 12/29/85; TLS 3/7/86) **[510.92]**

513 Arithmetic

Numeration systems

1989 Ifrah, Georges. *From One to Zero: A Universal History of Numbers.* **1987, Penguin paper $14.95 (0-14-00919-0).** An overview of the history of numbers and numeration. "This engaging survey opens the mysteries of numbers to the general reader."—BL (REV: BL 7/85; Choice 2/86; LJ 7/85) **[513.5]**

520 ASTRONOMY AND ALLIED SCIENCES

1990 Asimov, Isaac. *Relativity of Wrong.* **1988, Doubleday $17.95 (0-385-24473-8); Windsor paper $3.95 (1-55817-169-X).** Collected essays regarding astronomy and chemistry by the prolific science and science fiction writer. (REV: BL 4/15/88; LJ 4/15/88) **[520]**

1991 Field, George B., and Eric J. Chaisson. *Invisible Universe: Probing the Frontiers of Astrophysics.* **1985, Birkhauser $29.95 (0-8176-3235-2).** A survey of the current state of our knowledge regarding the physical forces and properties of deep space. (REV: BL 2/1/85; Choice 4/85; LJ 2/1/85) **[520]**

1992 Jastrow, Robert. *God and the Astronomers.* **1978, Norton $9.95 (0-393-85000-5).** A study of the current theories concerning the creation of the universe and the conflicts between scientific and religious thought on the subject. (REV: BL 12/15/78; Natl Rev 11/24/78; PW 9/18/78) **[520]**

1993 Sagan, Carl. *Cosmos.* **1980, Random $34.95 (0-394-50294-9); paper $21.95 (0-394-71596-9).** An illustrated companion to the PBS series regarding the universe and man's relation to it. (REV: CSM 11/19/80; LJ 11/15/80; NYTBR 1/25/81) **[520]**

Historical treatment

1994   Hadingham, Evan. *Early Man and the Cosmos: Explorations in Astroarchaeology.* **1984, Walker $22.50 (0-8027-0745-9); Univ. of Oklahoma Pr. paper $14.95 (0-8061-1919-5).** A study of primitive and prehistoric man and his knowledge and perceptions of the universe. "A well-written book of wide, general interest."—Choice (REV: Choice 6/84; LJ 4/15/84; PW 12/16/84)   **[520.9]**

1995   Harrison, Edward. *Darkness at Night: A Riddle of the Universe.* **1987, Harvard Univ. Pr. $25.00 (0-674-19270-2); paper $12.95 (0-674-19271-0).** An examination of current scientific theories and explanations for the darkness of the universe. "For any reader . . . who wonders at the mystery of the dark night sky."—Timothy Ferris, NYTBR (REV: BL 10/1/87; Choice 2/88; NYTBR 9/27/87)   **[520.9]**

Persons

1996   Bedini, Silvio A. *Life of Benjamin Banneker.* **1984, Landmark Enterprises $24.00 (0-910845-20-4).** A biography of the eighteenth-century black astronomer, surveyor, and mathematician. "Valuable both as biography of an unusually brilliant man and a comprehensive profile of historical Maryland society."—BL (REV: BL 4/15/72; LJ 10/15/71; NYTBR 2/27/72)   **[520.92]**

1997   Shkolvsky, Iosif. *Five Billion Vodka Bottles to the Moon: Tales of a Soviet Scientist.* **1991, Norton $19.95 (0-393-02990-5).** A physicist's autobiography discussing science and life under Soviet rule from Stalin through the mid-1980s. (REV: BL 5/15/91; LJ 6/15/91; PW 4/12/91)   **[520.92]**

521   Celestial mechanics

1998   Kippenhahn, Rudolf. *One Hundred Billion Suns: The Birth, Life and Death of the Stars.* **1985, Basic Books paper $12.95 (0-465-05262-2).** An overview of the life cycle and nature of the stars. "Anyone who is curious about how stars are born, evolve, and die will be delighted with this book."—Choice (REV: Choice 10/83; LJ 6/1/83; NYTBR 8/21/83)   **[521]**

1999   Zee, A. *An Old Man's Toy: Gravity at Work and Play in Einstein's Universe.* **1988, Macmillan $22.50 (0-02-633440-2); paper $9.95 (0-02-040915-X).** The role of gravity in man's concept of the universe, and the history of his efforts to understand it. "Successfully renders complex concepts perfectly understandable."—LJ (REV: LJ 3/1/89; NYTBR 7/30/89; PW 1/20/89)   **[521]**

522   Techniques, equipment, materials

Observations

2000   Preston, Richard. *First Light: The Search for the Edge of the Universe.* **1987, Atlantic Monthly $18.95 (0-87113-200-1); NAL paper $8.95 (0-452-26170-8).** A portrait of the astronomical research carried out at California's Mt. Palomar observatory. (REV: CSM 4/8/88; LJ 12/87; NYTBR 5/15/88)   **[522.19]**

523   Specific celestial bodies and phenomena

2001   Harrington, Philip S. *Touring the Universe Through Binoculars: A Complete Astronomer's Guidebook.* **1990, Wiley $24.95 (0-471-51337-7).** A guide to the home viewing of astronomical phenomena using binoculars or a low-powered telescope. (REV: BL 11/1/90; LJ 11/1/90)   **[523]**

2002   Schaaf, Fred. *Starry Room: Naked-Eye Astronomy in the Intimate Universe.* **1988, Wiley $19.95 (0-471-62088-2); paper $12.95 (0-471-53025-5).** Tips on how to best appreciate astronomical phenomena with the naked eye in our modern society. (REV: LJ 12/88; PW 11/4/88)   **[523]**

The Universe

2003   Barrow, John D., and Joseph Silk. *Left Hand of Creation: The Origin and Evolution of the Expanding Universe.* **1986, Basic Books paper $7.95 (0-465-03897-2).** An account of the creation and evolution of the universe. "A reliable and tough-minded guide to the latest scientific ideas about genesis."—Timothy Ferris, NYTBR (REV: Choice 3/84; LJ 11/1/83; NYTBR 11/20/83)   **[523.1]**

2004   Bartusiak, Marcia. *Thursday's Universe: A Report from the Frontier on the Origin, Nature and Destiny of the Universe.* **1986, Random $19.95 (0-8129-1202-0); Microsoft paper $8.95 (1-55615-153-5).** A review of major recent cosmological theories for the general reader. "For a few years at least this will be a book that can render the arena of astrophysical research understandable to the public."—NYTBR (REV: LJ 9/15/86; NYTBR 12/21/86)   **[523.1]**

2005   Darling, David. *Deep Time: The Journey of a Single Subatomic Particle from the Moment of Creation to the Death of the Universe and Beyond.* **1989, Delacorte $16.95 (0-385-29757-2); paper $9.95 (0-385-30229-0).** A survey of modern astrophysics, the nature of time and matter, and speculation about the future of the universe as traced through the history of a single proton. (REV: BL 8/89; LJ 5/15/89)   **[523.1]**

2006   Durham, Frank, and Robert D. Purrington. *Frame of the Universe: A History of Physical Cosmology.* **1983, Columbia Univ. Pr. $29.50 (0-231-05392-4).** The history of theories of the development of the cosmos from the mythology of ancient cultures to the present. "A book of extraordinary virtue . . . a first-class history."—Choice (REV: Choice 10/83; LJ 5/1/83)   **[523.1]**

2007   Ferris, Timothy. *Galaxies.* **1981, Outlet $24.95 (0-517-63176-8); Stewart, Tabori & Chang paper $18.95 (0-941434-02-8).** An illustrated volume detailing the beauty of the universe containing nearly 150 photographs. "One of the handsomest books ever published on astronomy."—James Michener, NYTBR (REV: BL 11/15/80; LJ 11/1/80; NYTBR 1/25/81)   **[523.1]**

2008   Fritzsch, Harald. *Creation of Matter: The Universe from Beginning to End.* **1988, Basic Books paper $9.95 (0-465-01447-X).** An overview of current cosmological theories compiled by a German physicist. (Rev: BL 10/15/84; Choice 3/85; LJ 1/85) **[523.1]**

2009 Greenstein, George. *Frozen Star.* 1984, Freundlich $16.95 (0-88191-011-2). The history of research on black holes, pulsars, and other recently discovered astrological phenomena. "Greenstein excels at conveying the spirit of science, and his book is a joy to read."—LJ (Rev: LJ 3/15/84; New Yorker 9/17/84. Awards: LJ, 1984) **[523.1]**

2010 Greenstein, George. *Symbiotic Universe: An Unorthodox Look at the Origin of the Cosmos and the Development of Life.* 1988, Morrow $18.95 (0-688-07604-1). An intertwining of metaphysics and current scientific knowledge regarding the creation and development of intelligent life on earth. "A rare adventure for the mind . . . few books expand the mental horizons like this one."—BL (Rev: BL 2/15/88; LJ 2/15/88; PW 12/18/87) **[523.1]**

2011 Hawking, Stephen W. *Brief History of Time: From the Big Bang to Black Holes.* 1988, Bantam $18.95 (0-553-05340-X); paper $9.95 (0-553-34614-8). An overview of current theories concerning the nature of the universe, written for the layman, by the Cambridge University physicist. (Rev: LJ 4/15/88; NYTBR 4/3/88; PW 2/19/88. Awards: LJ, 1988; NYTBR, 1988; PW, 1988) **[523.1]**

2012 Lerner, Eric J. *Big Bang Never Happened: A Startling Refutation of the Dominant Theory of the Universe.* 1991, Times Books $21.95 (0-8129-1853-3). An examination of recent discoveries in astrophysics that contradict the generally accepted Big Bang theory. (Rev: LJ 4/1/91; NYRB 5/16/91; PW 1/25/91) **[523.1]**

2013 Overbye, Dennis. *Lonely Hearts of the Cosmos: The Scientific Quest for the Secret of the Universe.* 1991, HarperCollins $25.00 (0-06-015964-2). An overview of the contributions of recent cosmologists to our current understanding of the structure and essence of the universe. (Rev: BL 1/15/91; LJ 1/91; PW 11/9/90) **[523.1]**

2014 Pagels, Heinz R. *Perfect Symmetry: The Search for the Beginning of Time.* 1986, Bantam paper $4.95 (0-553-24000-5). The history of the universe as currently understood by theoretical physicists. "The educated layperson will come away much better informed."—LJ (Rev: LJ 7/85; NYTBR 9/22/85; PW 5/3/85. Awards: LJ, 1985) **[523.1]**

2015 Reeves, Hubert. *Atoms of Silence: An Exploration of Cosmic Evolution.* 1983, MIT Pr. $27.50 (0-262-18112-6). An overview of current theories regarding the initial formation of the universe and its subsequent development. (Rev: CSM 8/1/84; NYTBR 9/23/84; PW 6/1/84) **[523.1]**

2016 Trefil, James. *Dark Side of the Universe: Searching for the Outer Limits of the Cosmos.* 1988, Macmillan $17.95 (0-684-18795-7); Doubleday paper $9.95 (0-385-26212-4). An overview of current cosmological theories about the nature of the universe and what may lie beyond. "Fascinating

science reading served up by a modern master."—BL (Rev: BL 9/1/88; Choice 1/89; NYTBR 10/16/88) **[523.1]**

2017 Trefil, James. *Moment of Creation: Big Bang Physics from Before the First Millisecond to the Present Universe.* 1984, Macmillan paper $10.95 (0-02-096770-5). An account of the creation of the universe from its beginnings to the present. (Rev: Choice 1/84; LJ 10/1/83; NYTBR 9/25/83) **[523.1]**

2018 Tucker, Wallace, and Karen Tucker. *Dark Matter: Contemporary Science's Quest for the Mass Hidden in Our Universe.* 1988, Morrow $16.95 (0-688-06112-5). An examination of science's struggle to account for the mass of the universe. (Rev: Choice 10/88; LJ 6/1/88; NYTBR 6/26/88) **[523.1]**

Planets

2019 Burgess, Eric. *Venus: An Errant Twin.* 1985, Columbia Univ. Pr. $29.95 (0-231-05856-X). The history and results of space research conducted upon the planet Venus from 1961 to the present by the Soviet Union and the United States. (Rev: Choice 2/86; LJ 10/15/85) **[523.4]**

2020 Wilford, John Noble. *Mars Beckons: The Mysteries, the Challenges, the Expectations of Our Next Great Adventure in Space.* 1990, Knopf $24.95 (0-394-58359-0). The history of man's knowledge and legends about the Red Planet with speculations on future manned voyages, by the author of *The Riddle of the Dinosaur.* (Rev: BL 5/15/90; LJ 6/15/90; NYTBR 7/15/90. Awards: LJ, 1990) **[523.4]**

Meteoroids

2021 Dodd, Robert T. *Thunderstones and Shooting Stars: The Meaning of Meteorites.* 1988, Harvard Univ. Pr. paper $11.95 (0-674-89138-4). A study of meteorites and the information that can be obtained from them. (Rev: BL 11/1/86; Choice 1/87; LJ 9/15/86) **[523.51]**

Comets

2022 Sagan, Carl, and Ann Druyan. *Comet.* 1985, Random $27.50 (0-394-54908-2); Pocket paper $14.95 (0-671-61917-9). An overview regarding the nature of comets and current theories concerning them by the author of *Cosmos* and his wife. (Rev: Choice 4/86; LJ 11/15/85; NYTBR 12/29/85) **[523.6]**

2023 Yeomans, Donald K. *Comets: A Chronological History of Observation, Science, Myth and Folklore.* 1991, Wiley $35.00 (0-471-61011-9). A history of man's understanding of comets from ancient times to the 1986 arrival of Halley's. "Lively to look at as well as to read."—PW (Rev: BL 2/1/91; LJ 2/1/91; PW 1/11/91) **[523.6]**

Stars

2024 Asimov, Isaac. *Exploding Suns: The Secrets of the Supernovas.* 1986, NAL paper $4.50 (0-451-62481-5). A study of supernovas and their role in the universe by the prolific science/science fiction writer. (Rev: LJ 3/15/85; NYTBR 4/21/85; PW 3/29/85) **[523.8]**

2025 Cooke, Donald A. *Life and Death of Stars.* **1985, Crown $29.95 (0-517-55268-X).** An illustrated account of the life cycle of stars. (REV: BL 8/85; LJ 8/85) **[523.8]**

2026 Moore, Patrick. *Astronomer's Stars.* **1989, Norton $17.95 (0-393-02663-9).** A review of 16 stars and other astronomical phenomena touching on their locations and scientific significance. "For those who read this thoroughly engaging book, the night sky will never be the same."—PW (REV: BL 7/89; LJ 7/89; PW 6/16/89) **[523.8]**

2027 Sesti, Giuseppe Maria. *Glorious Constellations: History and Mythology.* **1991, Abrams $95.00 (0-8109-3355-1).** A study of the history of astronomy and the myths and thoughts about the constellations. (REV: BL 11/1/91; LJ 1/92) **[523.8]**

525 Earth (Astronomical geography)

2028 Kelley, Kevin W., ed. *Home Planet.* **1988, Addison Wesley $39.95 (0-201-15197-9).** One hundred fifty color photographs of Earth taken from space and combined with comments and essays by Soviet cosmonauts and American astronauts. (REV: BL 10/1/88; LJ 11/1/88; Newsweek 11/28/88. AWARDS: LJ, 1988) **[525]**

529 Chronology

2029 Aveni, Anthony. *Empires of Time: Calendars, Clocks, and Cultures.* **1989, Basic Books $24.95 (0-465-01950-1).** A study of methods of timekeeping and measurement from prehistoric times to the present. (REV: BL 10/1/89; LJ 9/15/89; PW 8/4/89) **[529]**

2030 Coveney, Peter, and Roger Highfield. *Arrow of Time: A Voyage Through Science to Solve Time's Greatest Mystery.* **1991, Fawcett $22.50 (0-449-90630-2).** An examination of current scientific thought regarding the nature of time. "The seeds of a profound scientific revolution lie within this book."—BL (REV: BL 6/1/91; PW 4/5/91) **[529]**

530 PHYSICS

2031 Davies, Paul. *Cosmic Blueprints: New Discoveries in Nature's Creative Ability to Order the Universe.* **1989, Simon & Schuster paper $9.95 (0-671-67561-3).** A study of order in the universe by the author of *God and the New Physics.* (REV: BL 3/1/88; LJ 3/1/88; PW 12/25/87) **[530]**

2032 Kevles, Daniel J. *Physicists: The History of a Scientific Community in Modern America.* **1987, Harvard Univ. Pr. paper $12.95 (0-674-66655-0).** A study of the development of a community of physicists in the United States and their contributions to American society and science since the Civil War. (REV: Choice 7–8/78; CSM 6/13/78; LJ 1/1/78) **[530]**

2033 Morris, Richard. *Edges of Science: Crossing the Boundary from Physics to Metaphysics.* **1990, Prentice Hall $18.45 (0-13-235029-7).** A study of the relationship between modern particle physics and cosmology. (REV: BL 9/15/90; LJ 9/1/90; NYTBR 10/21/90) **[530]**

2034 Pais, Abraham. *Inward Bound: Of Matter and Forces in the Physical World.* **1986, Oxford Univ. Pr. $39.95 (0-19-851971-0).** The history of particle physics from the discovery of X-rays to the present. "This monument to sound scholarship should become a major reference in this field."—LJ (REV: BL 4/1/86; Choice 11/86; LJ 6/1/86. AWARDS: LJ, 1986) **[530]**

2035 Trefil, James. *A Scientist at the Seashore.* **1987, Macmillan $8.95 (0-02-025920-4).** The author reveals and explains the common wonders that can be found at the seashore, in a work written with the layman in mind. (REV: BL 1/15/85; Choice 6/85; NYTBR 2/24/85) **[530]**

2036 Weisskopf, Victor. *Privilege of Being a Physicist.* **1988, W. H. Freeman $17.95 (0-7167-1982-7); paper $12.95 (0-7167-2106-6).** Essays discussing physics and human society. "A consistently interesting and informative look at the complex subject of high-energy physics."—BL (REV: BL 11/15/88; Choice 5/89; NYTBR 5/14/89) **[530]**

Persons

2037 Alvarez, Luis W. *Alvarez: The Adventures of a Physicist.* **1987, Basic Books $19.95 (0-465-00115-7).** An autobiography of the Nobel Prize–winning physicist. "A great scientific autobiography."—BL (REV: BL 4/15/87; LJ 4/1/87; NYTBR 6/7/87) **[530.092]**

2038 Bernstein, Jeremy. *Life It Brings: One Physicist's Beginnings.* **1987, Ticknor & Fields $16.95 (0-89919-470-2); Penguin paper $7.95 (0-14-010988-9).** Memoirs of the physicist's first three decades including remembrances of such acquaintances as J. Robert Oppenheimer and members of Duke Ellington's orchestra. (REV: BL 3/15/87; Choice 7–8/87; NYTBR 4/5/87) **[530.092]**

2039 Blumberg, Stanley A., and Louis G. Panos. *Edward Teller: Giant of the Golden Age of Physics.* **1990, Macmillan $24.95 (0-684-19042-7).** A biography of the nuclear physicist known as "The Father of the Hydrogen Bomb." (REV: Choice 6/90; LJ 1/90; PW 12/8/89) **[530.092]**

2040 Clark, Ronald W. *Einstein: The Life and Times.* **1979, Avon paper $5.95 (0-380-01159-X).** Explores the scientific, intellectual, and humanitarian aspects of the life of the physicist. "The finest biography of Einstein to date."—LJ (REV: CSM 8/19/71; LJ 10/15/71; Newsweek 8/9/71. AWARDS: ALA, 1971) **[530.092]**

2041 Einstein, Albert. *Albert Einstein: The Human Side.* Ed. by Helen Dukas and Banesh Hoffmann. **1979, Princeton Univ. Pr. paper $9.95 (0-691-02368-9).** Selections from the writings of Einstein compiled by his former secretary and a former collaborator. (REV: Choice 7/8/79; LJ 3/15/79) **[530.092]**

2042 Feynman, Richard P. *Surely You're Joking, Mr. Feynman! Adventures of a Curious Character.* **1984, Norton $18.95 (0-393-01921-7); Bantam paper $10.95 (0-553-34668-7).** An autobiography of the

Nobel Prize–winning physicist. "A vivid portrait of a lively, brilliant thinker who is intellectually and personally adventurous."—BL (REV: BL 11/15/84; LJ 3/15/85; NYTBR 1/27/85) **[530.092]**

2043 Feynman, Richard P., and Ralph Leighton. *What Do You Care What People Think? Further Adventures of a Curious Character.* 1988, Norton $17.95 (0-393-02659-0). Autobiographical writings by the Nobel Prize–winning physicist and professor. (REV: BL 10/15/88; LJ 11/15/88; NYTBR 11/13/88) **[530.092]**

2044 Orlov, Yuri. *Dangerous Thoughts.* 1991, Morrow $21.00 (0-688-10471-1). An autobiography of the Soviet physicist and human rights activist. (REV: BL 5/15/91; LJ 7/91; PW 4/12/91) **[530.092]**

2045 Pais, Abraham. *Subtle Is the Lord: The Science and Life of Albert Einstein.* 1982, Oxford Univ. Pr. $35.00 (0-19-853907-X). "Of all the biographies of Einstein, this, I think, is the one he himself would have liked the best."—Timothy Ferris, NYTBR (REV: Choice 12/82; CSM 10/8/82; NYTBR 11/28/82. AWARDS: ALA, 1982; NBA, 1983) **[530.092]**

2046 Rigden, John S. *Rabi: Scientist and Citizen.* 1989, Basic Books paper $9.95 (0-465-06793-X). A biography of the American physicist and Nobel Prize winner who pioneered research in the area of quantum mechanics. (REV: BL 4/15/87; LJ 4/1/87; PW 2/20/87) **[530.092]**

2047 Sayen, Jamie. *Einstein in America: The Scientist's Conscience in the Age of Hitler and Hiroshima.* 1985, Crown $17.95 (0-517-55604-9). A profile of the German physicist's years at Princeton University where he became increasingly outspoken on social causes. (REV: BL 6/1/85; LJ 7/85; NYTBR 8/18/85) **[530.092]**

2048 Weisskopf, Victor. *Joy of Insight: Passions of a Physicist.* 1991, Basic Books $26.95 (0-465-03678-3). An autobiography of the American physicist who played a crucial role in the development of the first atomic bomb. (REV: BL 3/1/91; LJ 4/1/91; NYTBR 3/24/91) **[530.092]**

2049 Williams, L. Pearce. *Michael Faraday: A Biography.* 1987, Da Capo paper $13.95 (0-306-80299-6). A biography of the nineteenth-century English chemist and physicist. (REV: BL 10/1/65; Time 7/23/65; TLS 8/12/65) **[530.092]**

Theories and mathematical physics

2050 Chaisson, Eric J. *Relatively Speaking: Relativity, Black Holes, and the Fate of the Universe.* 1990, Norton paper $9.95 (0-393-30675-5). An introduction to the theory of relativity and its implications directed toward the general reader. (REV: BL 9/15/88; Choice 1/89; LJ 11/1/88) **[530.1]**

2051 Davies, Paul. *Superforce: The Search for a Grand Unified Theory of Nature.* 1985, Simon & Schuster paper $8.95. An account of the efforts of modern physicists to establish a Grand Unified Theory of matter. (REV: LJ 11/15/84; NYTBR 12/23/84; TLS 6/21/85) **[530.1]**

2052 Gribbin, John. *In Search of Schrodinger's Cat: Quantum Physics and Reality.* 1984, Bantam paper $10.95 (0-553-34253-3). The history of the development of ideas leading to quantum mechanics and how new theories of physics have changed ideas of the fundamental nature of the universe. (REV: BL 8/84; LJ 7/84) **[530.1]**

2053 Morris, Richard. *Nature of Reality: The Universe after Einstein.* 1987, McGraw-Hill $17.95 (0-07-043278-3); Farrar paper $8.95 (0-374-52124-7). A discussion of current theories of subatomic particle physics. (REV: Choice 3/87; LJ 10/15/86; NYTBR 10/5/86) **[530.1]**

2054 Pagels, Heinz R. *Cosmic Code: Quantum Physics as the Language of Nature.* 1984, Bantam paper $5.95 (0-553-24625-9). An account of the scientists and discoveries that led to the revision of traditional physics in the nineteenth and twentieth centuries. (REV: LJ 2/15/82; New Rep 3/24/82; NYTBR 3/24/82) **[530.1]**

2055 Taubes, Gary. *Nobel Dreams: Power, Deceit, and the Ultimate Experiment.* 1987, Random $19.95 (0-394-54503-6); Microsoft paper $8.95 (1-55615-112-8). An inside look at the competition between nuclear physicists searching for a Grand Unified Theory of matter. (REV: LJ 3/1/87; NYTBR 1/25/87; PW 12/5/86) **[530.1]**

2056 Will, Clifford M. *Was Einstein Right? Putting General Relativity to the Test.* 1988, Basic Books paper $8.95 (0-465-09087-7). An account of the testing of Einstein's theory of relativity in the past two decades. (REV: NYRB 12/4/86; NYTBR 10/5/86) **[530.1]**

2057 Zee, A. *Fearful Symmetry: The Search for Beauty in Modern Physics.* 1988, Macmillan paper $9.95 (0-02-040911-7). A study of the symmetry and beauty of physics for nonscientists. "Eye-opening reading for those who know science only as a boring catalog of dry facts and sterile formulas."—BL (REV: BL 1/15/87; LJ 1/87; NYTBR 2/8/87) **[530.1]**

535 Light and paraphotic phenomena

2058 Bova, Ben. *Beauty of Light.* 1988, Wiley $24.95 (0-471-62580-9). An illustrated survey of the effects, physics, and scientific applications of light by the noted science fiction writer. (REV: BL 12/1/88; Choice 3/89; LJ 11/1/88) **[535]**

2059 Sobel, Michael I. *Light.* 1989, Univ. of Chicago Pr. $14.95 (0-226-76751-5). The history of the scientific study and applications of light. "An attractive, unpretentious and readable popular-level survey."—Choice (REV: Choice 1/88; LJ 1/88; NYTBR 9/27/87. AWARDS: LJ, 1987) **[535]**

537 Electricity and electronics

Electrodynamics (Electric currents) and thermoelectricity

2060 Schechter, Bruce. *Path of No Resistance: The Story of the Worldwide Race That Led to the Revolution in Superconductivity.* 1989, Simon &

Schuster $18.95 (0-671-65785-2); paper $8.95 (0-671-69599-1). A history and analysis of the search for superconductors, and its social and economic implications for the future. "An ideal primer on the subject."—BL (Rᴇᴠ: BL 4/15/89; LJ 3/1/90; NYTBR 4/9/89)   **[537.6]**

539 Modern physics

2061 Crease, Robert P., and Charles C. Mann. *Second Creation: Makers of the Revolution in 20th Century Physics.* **1987, Macmillan paper $11.95 (0-02-084550-2).** The development of physics in this century and the search by modern physicists for a Grand Unified Theory of matter. "Rarely has the frontier of science been so grippingly presented."—PW (Rᴇᴠ: Choice 10/86; LJ 6/1/86; PW 3/21/86. Aᴡᴀʀᴅs: PW, 1986)   **[539]**

Atomic and nuclear physics

2062 Bunch, Bryan H. *Reality's Mirror: Exploring the Mathematics of Symmetry.* **1989, Wiley $19.95 (0-471-50127-1).** A guide to symmetry in the arts, science, and nature. (Rᴇᴠ: Choice 1/90; LJ 3/1/90)   **[539.7]**

2063 Feynman, Richard P. *QED: The Strange Theory of Light and Matter.* **1985, Princeton Univ. Pr. $25.00 (0-691-08388-6); paper $8.95 (0-691-02417-0).** An explanation of the theory of quantum mechanics and its relation to light by the former California Institute of Technology professor. (Rᴇᴠ: Choice 5/86; CSM 3/11/86; LJ 12/85)   **[539.7]**

2064 Friedlander, Michael W. *Cosmic Rays.* **1989, Harvard Univ. Pr. $27.50 (0-674-17458-5); paper $10.95 (0-674-17459-3).** An overview of cosmic rays and their scientific applications written for the general reader. (Rᴇᴠ: BL 2/15/89; Choice 12/89; LJ 4/1/89)   **[539.7]**

2065 Glashow, Sheldon L., and Ben Bova. *Interactions: A Journey Through the Mind of a Particle Physicist and the Matter of This World.* **1989, Warner $12.95 (0-446-38946-3).** An autobiography of the physicist who was awarded the Nobel Prize in 1979 for his work in particle physics. (Rᴇᴠ: CSM 6/17/88; NYTBR 9/11/88; PW 4/8/88)   **[539.7]**

2066 Heisenberg, Werner. *Physics and Beyond: Encounters and Conversations.* **1971, Harper & Row paper $8.95 (0-06-131622-9).** In a work aimed at the general reader, the development of modern physics is discussed by the Nobel Prize-winning German physicist noted for his contributions to the study of quantum mechanics. (Rᴇᴠ: Choice 5/71; LJ 1/1/71; NYTBR 1/17/71)   **[539.7]**

2067 Keller, Alex. *Infancy of Atomic Physics: Hercules in His Cradle.* **1983, Oxford Univ. Pr. $29.95 (0-19-853904-5).** The history of the development of theories regarding the physics and internal structure of atoms in the nineteenth and early twentieth centuries. (Rᴇᴠ: Choice 7–8/84; LJ 6/1/83)   **[539.7]**

2068 Riordan, Michael. *Hunting of the Quark: A True Story of Modern Physics.* **1987, Simon & Schuster paper $9.95 (0-671-64884-5).** A study of recent research into subatomic particles and their properties. (Rᴇᴠ: CSM 6/17/88; LJ 1/88; NYTBR 9/27/87)   **[539.7]**

2069 Wilson, David. *Rutherford: Simple Genius.* **1983, MIT Pr. $40.00 (0-262-23115-8).** A biography of the British physicist known for his nuclear theory of the atom. "Excellent . . . this carefully documented book does full justice to a great man."—LJ (Rᴇᴠ: LJ 10/15/83; TLS 5/15/84)   **[539.7]**

540 CHEMISTRY AND ALLIED SCIENCES

Persons

2070 Pflaum, Rosalynd. *Grand Obsession: Madame Curie and Her World.* **1989, Doubleday $22.50 (0-385-26135-7).** A biography of the Polish-born physicist and chemist renowned for her research into radioactivity. (Rᴇᴠ: BL 11/15/89; LJ 10/15/89; NYTBR 1/7/90)   **[540.92]**

549 Mineralogy

Education, research, related topics

2071 Sofianides, Anna S., George E. Harlow, and Erica Van Pelt. *Gems and Crystals: From the American Museum of Natural History.* **1991, Simon & Schuster $40.00 (0-671-68704-2).** An illustrated survey of the precious stones and minerals collection housed at the American Museum of Natural History. "An excellent resource on a popular topic."—BL (Rᴇᴠ: BL 12/1/90; LJ 1/91)   **[549.07]**

550 EARTH SCIENCES

2072 Kurten, Bjorn. *How to Deep-Freeze a Mammoth.* **1986, Columbia Univ. Pr. $16.95 (0-231-05978-7).** Essays by the Swedish paleontologist on the life and culture of prehistoric times. (Rᴇᴠ: BL 6/15/86; Choice 12/86; LJ 8/86)   **[550]**

2073 McPhee, John. *Basin and Range.* **1981, Farrar $10.95 (0-374-10914-1); paper $7.95 (0-374-51873-4).** An introduction to geology and geologic time for the layperson by the author of *Oranges* and *Deltoid Pumpkin Seed.* (Rᴇᴠ: Atl 5/81; CSM 5/27/81; LJ 4/1/81)   **[550]**

551 Geology, hydrology, meteorology

2074 Cone, Joseph. *Fire Under the Sea: The Discovery of Hot Springs on the Ocean Floor and the Origin of Life.* **1991, Morrow $23.00 (0-688-09834-7).** An examination of the results of three decades of exploration of the world's seafloor vents and their biological and geological significance. (Rᴇᴠ: BL 7/91; LJ 7/91; PW 5/31/91. Aᴡᴀʀᴅs: BL, 1991)   **[551]**

Gross structure and properties of the earth

2075 Allegre, Claude. *Behavior of the Earth: Continental and Seafloor Mobility.* **1988, Harvard Univ. Pr. $35.00 (0-674-06457-7); paper $14.95 (0-674-06458-5).** An overview of current geological theories and research developments in the field from 1912 to the present. (REV: BL 3/1/88; Choice 12/88; LJ 2/15/88)

[551.1]

Hydrosphere; Oceanography

2076 Groves, Donald. *Oceans: A Book of Questions and Answers.* 1989, Wiley $12.95 (0-471-60712-6). An introduction to oceanography for the general reader presented in a question and answer format. (REV: BL 4/15/89; LJ 4/15/89)

[551.46]

Meteorology

2077 Cable, Mary. *Blizzard of '88.* 1988, Macmillan $19.95 (0-689-11591-1). An account of the blizzard of March 1888 that paralyzed the East Coast of the United States. (REV: Atl 4/88; BL 2/1/88; LJ 1/88)

[551.5]

2078 Trefil, James. *Meditations at Sunset: A Scientist Looks at the Sky.* 1987, Macmillan $16.95 (0-684-18787-6); paper $8.95 (0-02-025760-0). A University of Virginia physics professor discusses physical properties of the earth's atmosphere. (REV: BL 6/15/87; LJ 6/15/87; NYTBR 7/12/87)

[551.5]

Climatology and weather

2079 Schneider, Stephen H., and Randi Londer. *Coevolution of Climate and Life.* 1984, Sierra Club $25.00 (0-87156-693-1). An examination of the interrelationships between climate and lifeforms from prehistoric times to the present. (REV: Choice 9/84; LJ 5/15/84; NYTBR 8/19/84)

[551.6]

Historical geology

2080 Gould, Stephen Jay. *Time's Arrow, Time's Cycle: Myth and Metaphor in the Discovery of Geological Time.* 1987, Harvard Univ. Pr. $17.50 (0-674-89198-8); paper $8.95 (0-674-89199-6). A study of the different theories of geological time espoused by three of geology's founding fathers: Thomas Burnet, James Hutton, and Charles Lyell. (REV: LJ 3/15/87; NYRB 5/28/87; New Yorker 9/7/87)

[551.7]

557 Earth sciences of North America

2081 McPhee, John. *In Suspect Terrain.* 1983, Farrar $12.95 (0-374-17650-7); paper $7.95 (0-374-51794-0). A survey of the geological features and processes visible along Interstate 80 east of the Mississippi. "Puts a difficult and complex subject within the grasp of the lay reader."—PW (REV: LJ 4/1/83; PW 1/21/83; Time 1/31/83)

[557]

2082 Redfern, Ron. *Making of a Continent.* 1986, Random paper $19.95 (0-8129-1617-4). An overview of the geological history and development of North America. (REV: LJ 11/1/86; PW 8/8/86)

[557]

Western United States

2083 McPhee, John. *Rising from the Plains.* 1987, Farrar $15.95 (0-374-25082-0). McPhee examines the Rocky Mountains and their landforms with David Love, a prominent geologist of the region. (REV: CSM 11/5/86; LJ 10/1/86; NYTBR 11/23/86)

[557.8]

560 PALEONTOLOGY; PALEOZOOLOGY

2084 Cvancara, Alan M. *Sleuthing Fossils: The Art of Investigating Past Life.* 1990, Wiley $24.95 (0-471-51046-7); paper $12.95 (0-471-62077-7). An overview of paleontology and paleontological techniques for the nonscientist. (REV: BL 11/15/89; LJ 11/15/89)

[560]

2085 Eldredge, Niles. *Life Pulse: Episodes from the Story of the Fossil Record.* 1987, Facts on File $21.95 (0-8160-1151-6). A survey of what paleontologists have learned about past life on earth as revealed through the fossil record. (REV: BL 1/15/87; NYTBR 4/12/87; PW 12/12/86)

[560]

2086 Muller, Richard. *Nemesis—The Death Star: The Story of a Scientific Revolution.* 1988, Grove-Weidenfeld $17.95 (1-55584-173-2); paper $8.95 (1-55584-421-9). The University of California physicist presents his theory that a companion star, which distantly circles our sun, passes close enough to Earth to cause death and extinction approximately every 25 million years. (REV: Choice 10/88; LJ 5/1/88; PW 4/1/88)

[560]

2087 Raup, David M. *Nemesis Affair: A Story of the Death of Dinosaurs and the Ways of Science.* 1987, Norton paper $6.95 (0-393-30409-4). The author presents his theory that extinction of the dinosaurs was due to the passing of a "death star" close to the earth and traces the reaction of the scientific community to his theory. (REV: BL 6/15/86; Choice 10/86; LJ 8/86)

[560]

History

2088 Gould, Stephen Jay. *Wonderful Life: The Burgess Shale and the Nature of History.* 1989, Norton $19.95 (0-393-02705-8); paper $10.95 (0-393-30700-X). An investigation into the significance of the fossil record found in the Burgess Shale region of British Columbia. "Perhaps the finest of his many fine books."—BL (REV: Atl 11/89; BL 10/1/89; LJ 8/1/89. AWARDS: LJ, 1989)

[560.9]

567 Fossil cold-blooded vertebrates

Reptilia (Dinosaurs)

2089 Bakker, Robert T. *Dinosaur Heresies: New Theories Unlocking the Mystery of the Dinosaurs and Their Extinction.* 1986, Morrow $22.95 (0-688-04787-2); Zebra paper $11.95 (0-8217-2471-1). Bakker sets forth his theories about the disappearance of the dinosaurs. "Without question, this is the finest book currently available on dinosaurs."—Choice (REV: Choice 3/87; LJ 11/1/86; NYTBR 10/26/86. AWARDS: LJ, 1986)

[567.9]

2090 Dixon, Dougal. *New Dinosaurs: An Alternative Evolution.* 1989, Fawcett paper $14.95 (0-449-90442-3). A speculative look at how dinosaurs potentially would have evolved if they had survived the Great Extinction and what the resulting world would be like. (REV: BL 10/1/88; LJ 11/15/88; PW 8/26/88)

[567.9]

2091 **Horner, John R., and James Gorman.** *Digging Dinosaurs: The Search That Unravelled the Mystery of Baby Dinosaurs.* **1988, Workman $17.95 (0-89480-220-8); Harper & Row paper $8.95 (0-06-097314-5).** The discovery of the nesting ground of dinosaurs in Montana, and its impact on paleontology, is described in this book by the man who made the discovery. (Rev: BL 11/1/88; Choice 4/89; NYTBR 12/25/88. Awards: LJ, 1988)   **[567.9]**

2092 **Weishampel, David B., ed.** *Dinosauria.* **1990, Univ. of California Pr. $85.00 (0-520-06726-6).** Essays by 23 paleontologists reflecting the current state of man's knowledge about the dinosaurs. (Rev: Choice 3/91; LJ 3/15/91; NYRB 4/25/91)   **[567.9]**

2093 **Wilford, John Noble.** *Riddle of the Dinosaur.* **1985, Knopf $24.95 (0-394-52763-1); paper $8.95 (0-394-74392-X).** A wide-ranging overview of what and how we know about the dinosaurs, with a discussion of the various current theories as to their extinction. (Rev: Atl 2/86; Choice 5/86; NYTBR 1/12/86. Awards: BL, the 1980s)   **[567.9]**

569 Fossil mammalia

2094 **Johanson, Donald C., and Maitland A. Edey.** *Lucy: The Beginnings of Human Kind.* **1988, Warner paper $13.95 (0-446-38625-1).** The story of the noted paleoanthropologist's discovery of man's oldest known ancestor. (Rev: LJ 2/1/81; NYTBR 2/22/81; Time 3/16/81. Awards: ALA, 1981; NBA, 1982)   **[569]**

2095 **Simpson, George Gaylord.** *Discoverers of the Lost World: An Account of Some of Those Who Brought Back to Life South American Mammals Long Buried in the Abyss of Time.* **1984, Yale Univ. Pr. $32.50 (0-300-03188-2).** An overview of paleontological work and discoveries in South America. (Rev: BL 9/1/84; Choice 12/84; LJ 8/84)   **[569]**

570 LIFE SCIENCES

572 Human races

Races of Asia

2096 **Said, Edward W.** *After the Last Sky: Palestinian Lives.* **1986, Pantheon paper $17.95 (0-394-74469-1).** The lives of Palestinians in exile punctuated by striking photographs. "An extraordinary book."—NYTBR (Rev: LJ 12/86; NYTBR 11/9/86; TLS 6/12/87. Awards: LJ, 1986)   **[572.95]**

Races of Africa

2097 **Turnbull, Colin.** *Mountain People.* **1988, Peter Smith $16.75 (0-8446-6334-4); Simon & Schuster paper $10.95 (0-671-64098-4).** The story of the Ik, an African tribe forced to relocate from their ancestral home to an arid mountain region, and the subsequent degeneration of their culture. (Rev: LJ 8/72; New Rep 12/9/72; Sat Rev 10/14/72. Awards: ALA, 1972)   **[572.96]**

573 Physical anthropology

Evolution and genetics of humankind

2098 **Calvin, William H.** *Ascent of Mind: Ice Age Climate and the Evolution of Intelligence.* **1991, Bantam $21.95 (0-553-07084-3).** A study of the effects of earth's climatological changes upon the development of the brain of early hominids. (Rev: BL 1/1/91; LJ 11/15/90; PW 11/9/90)   **[573.2]**

2099 **Claiborne, Robert.** *God or Beast: Evolution and Human Nature.* **1974, Norton $7.95 (0-393-06399-2).** An appraisal of what we know about human nature from evolutionary evidence written as a rebuttal to popular books that the author claims lack scientific method. "A balanced picture of human evolution as it appears to serious investigators."—NYTBR (Rev: BL 2/1/75; Choice 12/74; NYTBR 9/22/74)   **[573.2]**

2100 **Johanson, Donald C., and James Shreeve.** *Lucy's Child: The Search for Our Origins.* **1989, Morrow $22.95 (0-688-06492-2); Avon paper $10.95 (0-380-71234-2).** The story of Johanson's recovery of a partial early hominid skeleton forms the basis for a presentation of the paleoanthropologist's views regarding human evolution. (Rev: Choice 3/90; LJ 9/1/89; NYTBR 11/12/89)   **[573.2]**

2101 **Leakey, Richard E., and Roger Lewin.** *Origins: What New Discoveries Reveal about the Emergence of Our Species and Its Possible Future.* **1982, Dutton paper $8.95 (0-525-48246-6).** Leakey synthesizes the discoveries of his parents and of himself into a comprehensive view of evolution. "Perhaps no other book has presented so graphic and informative a picture of our early ancestors."—PW (Rev: Choice 2/78; NYTBR 10/30/77; PW 9/5/77. Awards: ALA, 1977)   **[573.2]**

2102 **Lewin, Roger.** *Bones of Contention: Controversies in the Search for Human Origins.* **1988, Simon & Schuster paper $10.95 (0-671-66837-4).** The history of paleoanthropology examining key discoveries in the field and current theories of human evolution. (Rev: Atl 10/87; Choice 1/88; LJ 10/1/87)   **[573.2]**

2103 **Lewin, Roger.** *In the Age of Mankind: A Smithsonian Book of Human Evolution.* **1989, Smithsonian Inst. $37.50 (0-89599-027-9); paper $19.95 (0-89599-025-3).** An illustrated introduction to current theories of human evolution. "This should be a first recommendation when someone asks for an introduction to anthropology."—LJ (Rev: Choice 3/89; LJ 12/88)   **[573.2]**

2104 **McCrone, John.** *Ape That Spoke: Language and the Evolution of the Human Mind.* **1991, Morrow $19.45 (0-688-10326-X).** A study of the development of language in early man and its impact upon the evolution of the human brain. (Rev: BL 1/1/91; LJ 11/15/90; PW 10/23/90)   **[573.2]**

2105 **Willis, Delta.** *Hominid Gang: Behind the Scenes in the Search for Human Origins.* **1989, Viking $21.95 (0-670-82808-4).** An examination of the key contemporary figures in human evolutionary

study and thought, including profiles of the Leakeys, Donald Johanson, and Stephen Jay Gould. (REV: BL 9/15/89; LJ 9/1/89; NYTBR 11/12/89)
[573.2]

Prehistoric humankind

2106 Gowlett, John. *Ascent to Civilization: The Archaelogy of Early Man.* 1984, McGraw-Hill paper $19.95 (0-07-554724-4). An overview of prehistoric man as revealed through the archaelogical record. (REV: BL 3/15/84; LJ 3/1/84; NYTBR 5/13/84)
[573.3]

2107 Ross, Anne, and Don Robins. *Life and Death of a Druid Prince: The Story of Lindow Man, an Archaeological Sensation.* 1990, Simon & Schuster $19.95 (0-671-69536-3). An account of the discovery of a 2,000-plus-year-old corpse preserved in an English bog and its potential significance for the understanding of the human history of the region. (REV: BL 4/15/90; LJ 6/1/90; NYTBR 6/17/90)
[573.3]

2108 Spencer, Frank. *Piltdown: A Scientific Forgery.* 1990, Oxford Univ. Pr. $24.95 (0-19-858522-5). An account of the infamous twentieth-century British archaeological forgery. (REV: LJ 10/15/90; NYTBR 11/11/90; TLS 12/14/90)
[573.3]

574 Biology

2109 Attenborough, David. *Living Planet: A Portrait of the Earth.* 1985, Little, Brown $25.00 (0-316-05748-7); paper $17.95 (0-316-05749-5). This accompaniment to the PBS series is a study of how living creatures have adapted to their environmental surroundings. (REV: LJ 12/84; Newsweek 2/11/85; TLS 9/28/84)
[574]

2110 Durrell, Gerald, and Lee Durrell. *Amateur Naturalist: A Practical Guide to the Natural World.* 1983, Knopf $29.95 (0-394-53390-9). An introduction to the study of nature in a variety of natural habitats. "Of great value to any student of nature, of any age."—PW (REV: CSM 12/2/83; LJ 10/1/83; PW 9/30/83)
[574]

2111 Eiseley, Loren. *Unexpected Universe.* 1972, Harcourt paper $6.95 (0-15-692850-7). A series of essays on natural wonders and the relationship of man and science toward them. "Taken together, these introspective pieces comprise nothing less than a corrective statement on the modern view of the universe and the human priorities set within it."—Time (REV: Atl 11/69; LJ 9/1/69; Time 11/14/69. AWARDS: ALA, 1969)
[574]

2112 Gould, Stephen Jay. *Urchin in the Storm: Essays about Books and Ideas.* 1987, Norton $18.95 (0-393-02492-X). Collected book reviews by the author of *The Panda's Thumb.* (REV: BL 10/15/87; NYTBR 11/15/87; TLS 8/12/88)
[574]

2113 Heinrich, Bernd. *In a Patch of Fireweed.* 1984, Harvard Univ. Pr. $20.00 (0-674-44548-1). An autobiography that explores the author's lifelong fascination with nature and, most particularly, insects. "A science-oriented *Walden.*"—BL (REV: BL

4/15/84; CSM 8/24/84; LJ 4/15/84. AWARDS: ALA, 1984)
[574]

2114 Kaufman, Les, and Kenneth Mallory, eds. *The Last Extinction.* 1988, MIT Pr. paper $8.95 (0-262-61053-1). A study of contemporary issues surrounding extinction and today's endangered species. (REV: Choice 3/87; LJ 11/1/86; NYTBR 11/30/86)
[574]

2115 Morowitz, Harold J. *Mayonnaise and the Origin of Life: Thoughts of Mind and Molecules.* 1987, Berkley paper $3.95 (0-425-09566-5). Science essays by the physicist and author of *The Wine of Life.* (REV: BL 11/15/85; NYTBR 1/19/86; PW 10/11/85)
[574]

2116 Morowitz, Harold J. *Wine of Life: And Other Essays on Societies, Energy and Living Things.* 1979, Ox Bow $14.00 (0-312-88227-0). A collection of 50 essays on various aspects of science and philosophy written for both laymen and scientists by a Yale University biology professor. "Delightfully readable . . . scientific browsing at its best."—PW (REV: BL 2/15/80; LJ 12/15/79; PW 10/1/79. AWARDS: ALA, 1979)
[574]

2117 Thomas, Lewis. *Lives of a Cell: Notes of a Biology Watcher.* 1978, Penguin paper $5.95 (0-14-004743-3). A collection of essays on biology penned by the noted medical researcher and scholar. "Anticipates the kind of writing that will appear more and more frequently, as scientists take on the language of poetry in order to communicate human truths too mysterious for old-fashioned common sense."—Joyce Carol Oates, in NYTBR (REV: NYTBR 5/26/74; New Yorker 7/15/74; Time 7/22/74. AWARDS: ALA, 1974; NBA, 1975; Time, 1974; Time, the 1970s)
[574]

2118 Weissmann, Gerald. *Woods Hole Cantata: Essays on Science and Society.* 1986, Houghton paper $7.95 (0-395-42113-6). A series of essays by a physician and biologist on aspects of life, medicine, and ethics. "Full of literary imagination besides medical information, these are examples of popular and passionate scientific writing at its best."—BL (REV: BL 8/85; LJ 3/1/86; PW 8/2/85)
[574]

Philosophy and theory

2119 Skutch, Alexander F. *Life Ascending.* 1985, Univ. of Texas Pr. $22.50 (0-292-70374-0); paper $10.95 (0-292-74644-X). A study of human evolution and the development of man's attitudes toward his environment. (REV: BL 6/15/85; LJ 6/15/85)
[574.01]

History

2120 Mowat, Farley. *Sea of Slaughter.* 1986, Bantam paper $9.95 (0-553-34269-X). The Canadian naturalist examines the history of man's assault upon the wildlife of the northern Atlantic region. (REV: BL 4/15/85; LJ 4/15/85; NYTBR 4/7/85)
[574.09]

Persons

2121 Brooks, Paul. *House of Life: Rachel Carson at Work.* 1989, Houghton paper $9.95 (0-395-51742-7). A look at Carson's biology work for the U.S. Fish and Wildlife Service, and the writing of her anti-pesticide classic *Silent Spring*, as witnessed by her former editor. (REV: Choice 7–8/72; LJ 4/1/72; NYTBR 4/30/72. AWARDS: ALA, 1972)　　**[574.092]**

2122　Keller, Betty. *Black Wolf: The Life of Ernest Thompson Seton.* **1985, Salem $18.95 (0-88894-439-X).** A biography of the American naturalist and writer of animal stories for children. (REV: BL 3/15/85; Choice 4/85; LJ 5/1/85)　　**[574.092]**

2123　Levi-Montalcini, Rita. *In Praise of Imperfection: My Life and Work.* **1988, Basic Books $18.95 (0-465-03217-6).** An autobiography of the 1986 winner of the Nobel Prize for medicine. (REV: BL 3/15/88; NYTBR 5/1/88; PW 2/26/88)　　**[574.092]**

2124　Manning, Kenneth R. *Black Apollo of Science: The Life of Ernest Everett Just.* **1983, Oxford Univ. Pr. $35.00 (0-19-503299-3); paper $11.95 (0-19-503498-8).** A biography of the African-American zoologist and marine biologist known for his research at the Woods Hole Institute. (REV: LJ 12/1/83; NYRB 11/24/83; NYTBR 1/1/84)　　**[574.092]**

Physiology

2125　Campbell, Jeremy. *Winston Churchill's Afternoon Nap: A Wide-Awake Inquiry into the Human Nature of Time.* **1988, Simon & Schuster paper $9.95 (0-671-65717-8).** The author of *Grammatical Man* concerns himself in this volume with the nature of biological time and man's perceptions of it. (REV: LJ 5/1/87; NYTBR 3/8/87; PW 1/16/87)　　**[574.1]**

2126　Catton, Chris, and James Gray. *Sex in Nature.* **1985, Facts on File $22.95 (0-8160-1294-6).** An examination of the reproductive process in animals ranging from single-celled creatures to the primates. (REV: BL 2/15/86; LJ 3/1/86)　　**[574.1]**

2127　Forsyth, Adrian. *A Natural History of Sex: The Evolution of Sexual Behavior in Man and Other Living Things.* **1986, Macmillan $18.95 (0-684-18338-2).** A biologist's overview of sexual behavior in animals. (REV: BL 6/1/86; Choice 12/86; NYTBR 8/31/86)　　**[574.1]**

Biophysics and biochemistry

2128　Moss, Ralph W. *Free Radical: The Life of Albert Szent-Gyorgyi and the Battle over Vitamin C.* **1987, Paragon House $22.95 (0-913729-78-7).** A biography of the Hungarian scientist who spied for the Allies during World War II and won a Nobel Prize for his research regarding Vitamin C. (REV: BL 11/15/87; LJ 11/15/87; NYTBR 3/6/88)　　**[574.19]**

Ecology

2129　Alcock, John. *Sonoran Desert Summer.* **1990, Univ. of Arizona Pr. $19.95 (0-8165-1150-0).** A study of the life of the Sonoran Desert during the summer season. (REV: BL 3/1/90; LJ 3/15/90; NYTBR 4/8/90)　　**[574.5]**

2130　Caufield, Catherine. *In the Rainforest: Report from a Strange, Beautiful, Imperiled World.* **1984, Knopf $24.95 (0-394-52701-1); Univ. of Chicago Pr.** paper $11.95 (0-226-09786-2). A first-hand appraisal of the human impact upon and the human need for tropical rainforests. "This forthright account makes a valuable contribution to our understanding and awareness of ecological repercussions."—BL (REV: BL 12/1/84; CSM 3/5/85; NYTBR 3/24/85. AWARDS: ALA, 1985)　　**[574.5]**

2131　Dotto, Lydia. *Planet Earth in Jeopardy: Environmental Consequences of Nuclear War.* **1986, Wiley $19.95 (0-471-99636-2).** A study of the probable environmental effects of nuclear war. (REV: BL 4/15/86; Choice 9/86; LJ 5/15/86)　　**[574.5]**

2132　Ehrlich, Paul R. *The Cold and the Dark: The World after Nuclear War.* **1984, Norton $12.95 (0-393-01870-9).** The conclusions of a scientific conference on the potential consequences of nuclear war. "A remarkable testament to the power of free scientific inquiry."—NYTBR (REV: Choice 11/84; LJ 9/1/84; NYTBR 8/12/84. AWARDS: ALA, 1984)　　**[574.5]**

2133　Ehrlich, Paul R. *Machinery of Nature.* **1987, Simon & Schuster paper $10.95 (0-671-63312-0).** An introduction to ecology and its processes by the author of *The Population Bomb*. (REV: Choice 9/86; LJ 5/15/86; PW 2/7/86)　　**[574.5]**

2134　Eiseley, Loren. *Invisible Pyramid.* **1985, Macmillan paper $7.95 (0-684-12732-6).** The history of man's relationship with the earth and how he has abused its resources throughout time. "It communicates the awesome spectacle of our environmental crisis without a single shrill note."—NYTBR (REV: Atl 11/70; LJ 10/1/70; NYTBR 11/15/70)　　**[574.5]**

2135　Forsyth, Adrian, and Ken Miyata. *Tropical Nature: Life and Death in the Rain Forests of Central and South America.* **1987, Macmillan paper $8.95 (0-684-18710-8).** A look at the balance of nature within the rain forests of Costa Rica and Ecuador. "A pure celebration of the tropical rain forest and a plea for its preservation."—LJ (REV: BL 5/1/84; LJ 6/1/84; Newsweek 2/18/85. AWARDS: LJ, 1984)　　**[574.5]**

2136　Hecht, Susanna, and Alexander Cockburn. *Fate of the Forest: Developers, Destroyers and Defenders of the Amazon.* **1989, Routledge $24.95 (0-86091-261-2); HarperCollins paper $9.95 (0-06-097322-6).** An introduction to the ecology and recent history of the Amazon rain forest. (REV: BL 12/1/89; LJ 1/90; TLS 3/9/90)　　**[574.5]**

2137　Madson, John. *Up on the River: An Upper Mississippi Chronicle.* **1985, Schocken $17.95 (0-8052-3966-9); Penguin paper $7.95 (0-14-008746-X).** A portrait of the Upper Mississippi River and the wildlife that depends on it. (REV: BL 4/15/85; CSM 4/30/85; LJ 4/15/85)　　**[574.5]**

2138　Madson, John. *Where the Sky Began: Land of the Tallgrass Prairie.* **1985, Sierra paper $8.95 (0-87156-836-5).** A description of the American prairie: its history, life-forms, weather, and geology. "Delightful writing by an author sincerely devoted to his subject."—LJ (REV: BL 4/15/82; LJ 5/15/82; NYTBR 10/24/82. AWARDS: ALA, 1982)　　**[574.5]**

2139 Marchand, Peter J. *Life in the Cold: An Introduction to Winter Ecology.* **1987, Univ. Pr. of New England paper $9.95 (0-87451-417-7).** A study of winter animal and plant life and how living things adapt to conditions of extreme cold. (REV: Choice 3/88; LJ 11/15/87)   **[574.5]**

2140 Maser, Chris. *Forest Primeval: The Natural History of an Ancient Forest.* **1989, Sierra Club $25.00 (0-87156-683-4).** A history of a millenium of life in an Oregon forest. (REV: BL 9/15/90; Choice 4/90; LJ 3/1/90)   **[574.5]**

2141 Newman, Arnold. *Tropical Rainforest.* **1990, Facts on File $40.00 (0-8160-1944-4).** An introduction to the ecology of the world's rain forests and methods that can be adopted to help save them. (REV: BL 9/15/90; CSM 1/17/91; LJ 9/15/90. AWARDS: BL, 1990)   **[574.5]**

2142 Thompson, Gerald, and Jennifer Coldrey. *The Pond.* **1984, MIT Pr. $35.00 (0-262-20049-X).** An introduction to plant and animal pond life. "This brilliant achievement is a must for all libraries great and small."—BL (REV: BL 6/15/84; Choice 7–8/84; TLS 5/11/84)   **[574.5]**

2143 Wertheim, Anne. *Intertidal Wilderness.* **1985, Sierra Club $25.00 (0-87156-839-X); $14.95 paper (0-87156-831-4).** An illustrated introduction to the flora and fauna of Pacific Coast intertidal zones. (REV: BL 6/15/85; CSM 8/12/85; LJ 7/85)   **[574.5]**

Tissue, cellular, molecular biology

2144 Judson, Horace. *Eighth Day of Creation: Makers of the Revolution in Biology.* **1980, Simon & Schuster paper $15.95 (0-671-25410-3).** The history of the discovery of DNA and its essential amino acids, largely told in the words of the researchers who made the discoveries. (REV: LJ 1/15/79; New Rep 5/5/79; NYTBR 4/8/79. AWARDS: NYTBR, 1979)   **[574.8]**

2145 Sayre, Anne. *Rosalind Franklin and DNA.* **1978, Norton paper $7.95 (0-393-00868-1).** The role that Franklin played in the discovery of DNA is examined in a work designed to refute Watson's account set forth in *The Double Helix.* (REV: LJ 8/75; NYTBR 9/21/75; Newsweek 9/22/75)   **[574.8]**

2146 Watson, James D. *Double Helix: Being a Personal Account of the Discovery of the Structure of DNA.* **1968, Macmillan paper $6.95 (0-689-70602-2).** The discovery of DNA as described by the Nobel Prize Laureate. "As tense as suspense fiction, his gaily irreverent story of the search and of his fellow scientists is entrancing even to a reader unversed in science."—BL (REV: BL 6/1/68; Choice 5/68; NYTBR 2/25/68. AWARDS: ALA, 1968; NYTBR, 1968)   **[574.8]**

Cytology (Cell biology)

2147 Hall, Stephen S. *Invisible Frontiers: The Race to Synthesize a Human Gene.* **1988, Microsoft paper $8.95 (1-55615-172-1).** An account of a race between three teams of biologists to engineer an artificial gene capable of producing insulin. "Popular science written in the best adventure-story

tradition."—BL (REV: BL 8/87; LJ 9/1/87; NYTBR 9/27/87)   **[574.87]**

Geographical treatment of organisms

2148 Moorehead, Alan. *Darwin and the Beagle.* **1979, Penguin paper $14.95 (0-14-003327-0).** Darwin's five-year voyage on the *Beagle,* re-created by the use of his journals, letters, autobiography, and the ship's captain's accounts of the voyage. (REV: Choice 2/70; LJ 12/15/69; NYTBR 11/9/69. AWARDS: ALA, 1969)   **[574.9]**

2149 Ogburn, Charlton, Jr. *Winter Beach.* **1990, Morrow paper $12.95 (0-688-09418-X).** A natural history and travelogue based on a four-month winter camping trip on the Atlantic coast. "A thoughtful work . . . written by a man who thinks deeply and well and sees into the poetry of things."—Choice (REV: Choice 6/67; LJ 11/1/66; NYTBR 11/6/66. AWARDS: ALA, 1966)   **[574.9]**

2150 Terres, John K. *From Laurel Hill to Siler's Bog: The Walking Adventures of a Naturalist.* **1985, Algonquin $12.95 (0-912697-26-1).** Collected observations of natural history made on a North Carolina nature reserve by a former *Audubon* editor. (REV: BL 4/15/70; LJ 11/1/69; NYTBR 11/16/69)   **[574.9]**

Aquatic biology; Marine biology

2151 Rudloe, Jack. *Wilderness Coast: Adventures of a Gulf Coast Naturalist.* **1988, Dutton $22.50 (0-525-24607-X).** An account of the sea life of the coast surrounding the Gulf of Mexico by a marine biologist and researcher. (REV: LJ 3/1/88; NYTBR 5/1/88; PW 2/26/88)   **[574.92]**

Extraterrestrial worlds

2152 McDonough, Thomas. *Search for Extraterrestrial Intelligence: Listening for Life in the Cosmos.* **1988, Wiley $19.95 (0-471-84684-8); $14.95 paper (0-471-84683-X).** An overview of science's attempts to contact or receive signals from extraterrestrial life forms since the late 1950s. (REV: Choice 4/87; LJ 12/86; NYTBR 12/28/86)   **[574.99]**

575 Evolution and genetics

2153 Calvin, William H. *Cerebral Symphony: Seashore Reflections on the Structure of Consciousness.* **1990, Bantam $19.95 (0-553-05707-3).** An investigation into the processes of thought, perception, memory, and language; written by a neurobiologist for the lay reader. (REV: BL 12/15/89; LJ 11/15/89; PW 11/24/89)   **[575]**

2154 Clark, Ronald W. *Survival of Charles Darwin: A Biography of a Man and an Idea.* **1986, Avon paper $5.95 (0-380-69991-5).** A look at the life, thought, and legacy of the nineteenth-century scientist. "A superb, full-scale biography in the classical mode."—PW (REV: BL 1/1/85; LJ 1/85; PW 12/7/84)   **[575]**

2155 Dawkins, Richard. *Blind Watchmaker: Why the Evidence of Evolution Reveals a Universe

Without Design. **1986, Norton $18.95 (0-393-02216-1); paper $7.95 (0-393-30448-5).** A look at design flaws in nature and evolution. "Readers who are not outraged will be delighted."—NYTBR (Rev: LJ 2/1/87; NYTBR 12/14/86; PW 10/24/86)   **[575]**

2156   Dixon, Dougal. *After Man: A Zoology of the Future.* **1983, St. Martin's paper $10.95 (0-312-01162-8).** An illustrated speculation regarding possible life forms on earth in the distant future. (Rev: BL 10/15/81; LJ 10/15/81; PW 9/18/81)   **[575]**

2157   Edey, Maitland A., and Donald C. Johanson. *Blueprints: Solving the Mystery of Evolution.* **1989, Little, Brown $19.95 (0-316-21076-5); Penguin paper $9.95 (0-14-013265-1).** The history of evolutionary theory, based on the fossil record and genetics, by two of the world's most respected paleoanthropologists. (Rev: Choice 9/89; LJ 4/15/89; NYTBR 4/9/89)   **[575]**

2158   Eldredge, Niles. *Miner's Canary: A Paleontologist Unravels the Mysteries of Extinction.* **1991, Prentice Hall $20.00 (0-13-583659-X).** An analysis of the phenomenon of species extinction traced over the past 670 million years of life on earth. (Rev: BL 9/15/91; PW 8/23/91)   **[575]**

2159   Gould, Stephen Jay. *Hen's Teeth and Horse's Toes: Further Reflections in Natural History.* **1983, Norton $15.50 (0-393-01716-8).** A collection of essays regarding biology and evolutionary theory which originally appeared in the author's monthly columns for *Natural History* magazine. (Rev: BL 3/1/83; LJ 4/15/83; Newsweek 8/1/83)   **[575]**

2160   Gruber, Howard E. *Darwin on Man: A Psychological Study of Scientific Creativity.* **1981, Univ. of Chicago Pr. paper $7.95 (0-226-31007-8).** This study of Darwin and the genesis of his theories of evolution concerning man contains previously unpublished notebooks. "A startling and important record of the young scientist."—NYTBR (Rev: LJ 8/74; NYTBR 7/14/74; New Yorker 5/13/74. Awards: NYTBR, 1974)   **[575]**

2161   Margulis, Lynn, and Dorion Sagan. *Microcosmos: Four Billion Years of Microbial Evolution.* **1986, Summit $17.95 (0-671-44169-8).** A tracing of the evolution of life on earth from the earliest microbes to the development of hominids. (Rev: Atl 7/86; LJ 6/15/86; NYTBR 7/13/86)   **[575]**

Philosophy and theory

2162   Eldredge, Niles. *Time Frames: The Evolution of Punctuated Equilibria.* **1989, Princeton Univ. Pr. paper $8.95 (0-691-02435-9).** A presentation of the author's theory that evolution takes place during abrupt jumps following periods of stability rather than in a gradual manner over time. (Rev: Choice 10/85; LJ 5/1/85; NYTBR 4/21/85)   **[575.01]**

2163   Gould, Stephen Jay. *Ever Since Darwin: Reflections in Natural History.* **1977, Norton $19.95 (0-393-06425-5).** Collected essays on evolution, the development of evolutionary theory, and biology. "In lively prose, the author explains . . . difficult biological concepts . . . in easily understood and almost anecdotal style."—Choice (Rev: Choice 5/78; LJ 10/1/77; PW 8/23/77)   **[575.01]**

2164   Gould, Stephen Jay. *Panda's Thumb: More Reflections in Natural History.* **1980, Norton $15.95 (0-393-01380-4).** A series of essays concerning animal adaptations to their environment by the noted evolutionary scientist. (Rev: LJ 10/1/80; NYTBR 9/14/80; Newsweek 10/13/80. Awards: ALA, 1990; NBA, 1981)   **[575.01]**

2165   Lovelock, James. *Ages of Gaia: A Biography of Our Living Earth.* **1988, Norton $16.95 (0-393-02583-7); Bantam paper $10.95 (0-553-34816-7).** An examination of the interrelationship of all living things to the planet Earth. "He weaves an easily digested account of the systems and processes which make up and maintain our planetary environment into a religion for our times."—TLS (Rev: BL 10/1/88; Choice 9/89; TLS 6/16/89)   **[575.01]**

Genetics

2166   Dawkins, Richard. *Selfish Gene.* **1989, Oxford Univ. Pr. $22.95 (0-19-217773-7); paper $8.95 (0-19-286092-5).** The author argues that genes that benefit individual members of a species will be passed on to future generations, rather than those which may better the entire group. (Rev: Choice 5/77; LJ 12/1/76; Sat Rev 2/19/77)   **[575.1]**

2167   Jacob, Francois. *Statue Within: An Autobiography.* **1988, Basic Books $22.95 (0-465-08223-8).** An autobiography of the French 1965 Nobel Prize winner for Physiology and Medicine. "Sensitive and thoughtful . . . a beautiful example of science as process . . . enthusiastically recommended."—LJ (Rev: Choice 9/88; LJ 3/15/88; PW 1/29/88. Awards: LJ, 1988)   **[575.1]**

2168   Keller, Evelyn Fox, and W. H. Freeman. *A Feeling for the Organism: The Life and Work of Barbara McClintock.* **1983, W. H. Freeman $20.95 (0-7167-1433-7); paper $11.95 (0-7167-1504-X).** A biography of the Nobel Prize–winning scientist noted for her research into the properties of DNA. (Rev: Choice 7–8/84; LJ 6/1/83; PW 4/8/83)   **[575.1]**

577   General nature of life

2169   Jastrow, Robert. *Until the Sun Dies.* **1977, Norton $12.95 (0-393-06415-8); Warner paper $3.95 (0-446-32195-8).** A speculative look at the creation of matter and life on our planet, its evolutionary history, and the possibility that life may exist elsewhere in the universe. "A tour de force of lucid science writing."—PW (Rev: LJ 9/1/77; NYTBR 10/2/77; PW 4/18/77)   **[577]**

2170   Scott, Andrew. *Creation of Life: Past, Future, Alien.* **1986, Basil Blackwell $34.95 (0-631-14883-3); paper $12.95 (0-631-16336-0).** An introduction to current scientific theories explaining the creation and evolution of the first life forms on earth. (Rev: Choice 4/87; LJ 12/86)   **[577]**

580 BOTANICAL SCIENCES

581 Botany

2171 Bernhardt, Peter. *Wily Violets and Underground Orchids: Revelations of a Botanist.* 1989, Morrow $18.95 (0-688-08350-1). Writings by a botany professor regarding his experiences studying the plant life of Australia and the Americas. (REV: BL 5/15/89; CSM 8/7/89; NYTBR 7/9/89) **[581]**

2172 Wilkins, Malcolm B. *Plant Watching: How Plants Remember, Tell Time, Form Partnerships and More.* 1988, Facts on File $29.95 (0-8160-1736-0). An introduction to plants and plant life for the layperson. "An excellent, up-to-date background in basic botany."—LJ (REV: BL 4/1/89; LJ 11/1/88) **[581]**

Physiology of plants

2173 Prance, Ghillean T. *Leaves: The Formation, Characteristics and Uses of Leaves Found in All Parts of the World.* 1985, Crown $35.00 (0-517-55152-7). The function and uses of leaves from their anatomy to their uses in art. "Both informative and delightful reading . . . truly a book that should be included in every library."—Choice (REV: BL 4/15/85; Choice 7–8/85; LJ 5/1/85. AWARDS: LJ, 1985) **[581.1]**

Economic botany

2174 Hobhouse, Henry. *Seeds of Change: Five Plants That Transformed Mankind.* 1987, Harper & Row paper $11.95 (0-06-091440-8). A look at the historical ramifications of man's contact with cotton, quinine, sugar, potatoes, and tea. "This original book . . . deserves to become a classic."—PW (REV: Choice 3/87; LJ 11/15/86; PW 9/5/86) **[581.6]**

582 Spermatophyta (Seed-bearing plants)

Herbaceous flowering plants

2175 Anderson, Frank J. *A Treasury of Flowers.* 1990, Little, Brown $60.00 (0-8212-1758-5). Selected botanical illustrations from the eighteenth and nineteenth centuries from the holdings of the New York Botanical Garden. (REV: BL 9/1/90; NYTBR 12/2/90) **[582.13]**

2176 Johnson, Lady Bird, and Carlton B. Lees. *Wildflowers Across America.* 1988, Abbeville $39.95 (0-89659-770-9). The former first lady and Lees, a horticulturist, join forces in this tribute to the wildflowers of America. "A magnificent book . . . as refreshing and restorative as a stroll through a spring meadow."—PW (REV: BL 6/15/88; LJ 7/88; PW 4/22/88) **[582.13]**

2177 Stone, Doris M. *Lives of Plants: Exploring the Wonders of Biology.* 1983, Macmillan $15.95 (0-684-17907-5). An illustrated introduction to botany for the layperson and student. (REV: BL 8/83; Choice 11/83; LJ 6/15/83) **[582.13]**

2178 Thomas, Graham Stuart. *Complete Flower Paintings and Drawings of Graham Stuart Thomas.* 1987, Saga Pr. $45.00 (0-8109-1666-5). One

hundred seventy illustrations of flowers by the garden advisor to the British National Trust. "A book to be treasured by all who love gardening and painting."—NYTBR (REV: BL 11/1/87; NYTBR 12/6/87; PW 9/18/87. AWARDS: PW, 1987) **[582.13]**

585 Gymnospermae (Pinophyta)

2179 Pielou, E. C. *World of Northern Evergreens.* 1988, Cornell Univ. Pr. $36.50 (0-8014-2116-0); paper $12.95 (0-8014-9424-9). An introduction to the trees, flora, and fauna of the northern United States and Canada. "Guaranteed to enrich the reader's next forest visit."—LJ (REV: Choice 12/88; LJ 4/1/88) **[585]**

589 Thallobionta and Prokaryotae

Basidomycetes

2180 Friedman, Sara Ann. *Celebrating the Wild Mushroom: A Passionate Quest.* 1986, Lubrecht & Cramer $15.00 (0-396-08755-8). A guide to the identification and uses of wild mushrooms for the aspiring mycologist. (REV: BL 6/1/86; LJ 5/15/86; PW 5/23/86) **[589.22]**

590 ZOOLOGICAL SCIENCES

2181 Bruns, Bill. *A World of Animals: The San Diego Zoo and Wild Animal Park.* 1983, Abrams $39.95 (0-8109-1601-0). An illustrated history of the San Diego Zoo and Wild Animal Park providing insights into zoo management and philosophy. (REV: Choice 1/84; LJ 11/1/83; PW 9/23/83) **[590]**

Persons

2182 Bodry-Sanders, Penelope. *Carl Akeley: Africa's Collector, Africa's Savior.* 1991, Paragon House $19.95 (1-55778-243-1). A biography of the late nineteenth- early twentieth-century museum curator known for his work at the American Museum of Natural History and his African wildlife expeditions. (REV: LJ 5/1/91; PW 3/15/91) **[590.92]**

591 Zoology

2183 Ackerman, Diane. *Moon by Whale Light: And Other Adventures Among Bats, Penguins, Crocodilians and Whales.* 1991, Random $20.00 (0-394-58574-7). A collection of animal essays by the American poet and author of *A Natural History of the Senses.* "Popular natural-history writing at its most persuasive."—PW (REV: BL 10/1/91; LJ 10/15/91; PW 9/6/91. AWARDS: BL, 1991) **[591]**

2184 Bale, Peter. *Wildlife Through the Camera.* 1985, Parkwest $24.95 (0-88186-452-8). Three hundred photographs of animals in their native habitats. (REV: BL 7/85; LJ 6/15/85) **[591]**

2185 Elia, Irene. *Female Animal.* 1988, Henry Holt $21.95 (0-8050-0702-4); paper $12.95 (0-8050-1183-8). A study of the societal role of females throughout the animal kingdom by a British physical anthropologist. "Should stand as a model for scientific writing . . . as suspenseful and compelling as a well-paced novel."—BL (Rev: BL 6/1/88; LJ 6/1/88; NYTBR 11/20/88) **[591]**

2186 Lorenz, Konrad. *On Aggression.* **1974, Peter Smith $18.75 (0-8446-6213-5); Harcourt paper $9.95 (0-15-688741-0).** The behavioral scientist discusses the roots and causes of aggression in humans and other animals. (Rev: Choice 12/66; LJ 6/15/66; NYTBR, 6/19/66. Awards: ALA, 1966; NYTBR, 1966) **[591]**

Persons

2187 Goodall, Jane. *Through a Window: My Thirty Years with the Chimpanzees of Gombe.* **1990, Houghton $21.95 (0-395-50081-8).** The author recalls three decades of researching and observing chimpanzees in their native African habitats. (Rev: BL 8/90; LJ 9/15/90; PW 8/10/90. Awards: ALA, 1990) **[591.092]**

2188 Lorenz, Konrad, and Kurt Mundl. *On Life and Living.* **1990, St. Martin's $17.95 (0-312-03901-8).** Philosophical thoughts regarding human life and man's relationship to nature by the Austrian behaviorist. (Rev: LJ 3/15/90; PW 3/2/90) **[591.092]**

Physiology of animals

2189 Burton, Robert. *Eggs: Nature's Perfect Package.* **1987, Facts on File $24.95 (0-8160-1384-5).** An illustrated introduction to eggs and embryology covering species from throughout the animal kingdom. (Rev: BL 9/1/87; LJ 8/87; NYTBR 8/2/87) **[591.1]**

2190 Cooke, John. *Restless Kingdom: An Exploration of Animal Movement.* **1991, Facts on File $39.95 (0-8160-1205-9).** An illustrated study of animal movement written by a former American Museum of Natural History curator. (Rev: BL 2/1/91; LJ 2/15/91) **[591.1]**

2191 Sinclair, Sandra. *How Animals See: Other Visions of the World.* **1986, Facts on File $29.95 (0-87196-273-X).** A look at the eye structure and visual perceptions of other animals. (Rev: BL 7/85; LJ 6/15/85) **[591.1]**

Development and maturation of animals

2192 Ward, Peter Douglas. *On Methuselah's Trail: Living Fossils and the Great Extinctions.* **1991, W. H. Freeman $18.95 (0-7167-2203-8).** An analysis of animals that have adapted and survived earth's periodic changes of climate and extinctions. (Rev: BL 10/15/91; LJ 9/15/91) **[591.3]**

Ecology of animals

2193 Wilson, Edward O. *Sociobiology: The New Synthesis.* **1975, Harvard Univ. Pr. $40.50 (0-674-81621-8).** An examination of the biological reasons behind behavioral patterns. "This definitive book is certain to become a classic in its field."—LJ (Rev: Choice 11/75; LJ 10/1/75; NYTBR 7/27/75) **[591.5]**

Habits and behavior patterns

2194 Griffin, Donald R. *Animal Thinking.* **1985, Harvard Univ. Pr. paper $9.95 (0-674-03713-8).** A study of animal consciousness and its relationship

to animal behavior. (Rev: Choice 9/84; LJ 5/15/84; NYTBR 5/27/84) **[591.51]**

2195 Jordan, William. *Divorce among the Gulls: An Uncommon Look at Human Nature.* **1991, North Point Pr. $17.95 (0-86547-426-5).** Essays regarding animal behavior and the interrelationships between species. (Rev: BL 2/15/91; PW 1/25/91) **[591.51]**

2196 Morris, Desmond. *Animalwatching: A Field Guide to Animal Behavior.* **1990, Crown $35.00 (0-517-57859-X).** An illustrated introduction to animal behavior by the author of *Dogwatching.* (Rev: BL 2/1/91; NYTBR 12/2/90) **[591.51]**

Specific kinds of environments

2197 Kappel-Smith, Diana. *Night Life: Nature from Dusk to Dawn.* **1990, Little, Brown $19.95 (0-316-48300-1).** An overview of the activities of nocturnal animals. "A book to place beside Aldo Leopold's *Sand County Almanac.*"—CSM (Rev: CSM 2/20/90; LJ 11/1/89; PW 12/15/89) **[591.526]**

Rare and endangered animals

2198 Adams, Douglas, and Mark Cawardine. *Last Chance to See.* **1991, Crown $19.95 (0-517-57195-1).** An account of the authors' worldwide expeditions in search of endangered species in their native habitats. "An excellent choice for readers who enjoy natural history, travel and adventure."—PW (Rev: BL 12/1/90; LJ 1/91; PW 12/7/90) **[591.529]**

2199 Tongren, Sally. *To Keep Them Alive: Wild Animal Breeding.* **1985, Dembner Books $19.95 (0-934878-66-8).** An examination of the efforts to breed animals in captivity to prevent them from extinction in the wild. (Rev: BL 11/1/85; Choice 3/86; LJ 10/15/85) **[591.529]**

Reproductive and related adaptations

2200 Walters, Mark Jerome. *Dance of Life: Courtship in the Animal Kingdom.* **1988, Morrow $17.95 (0-87795-934-X); Doubleday paper $8.95 (0-385-26338-4).** An introduction to sexual behavior among the animals. (Rev: BL 1/1/88; LJ 12/87; NYTBR 3/27/88) **[591.56]**

Communication and production of sound

2201 Hearne, Vicki. *Adam's Task: Calling Animals by Name.* **1986, Knopf $17.95 (0-394-54214-2); Random paper $9.95 (0-394-75530-8).** A dog and horse trainer explores the dynamics of human-animal communications. (Rev: CSM 10/17/86; LJ 8/86; PW 7/11/86) **[591.59]**

Animals of Africa

2202 Iwago, Mitsuaki. *Serengeti: Natural Order on the African Plain.* **1987, Chronicle $22.95 (0-87701-441-8); paper $19.95 (0-87701-432-9).** Three hundred color photographs of the wildlife of Africa's Serengeti Plain. (Rev: CSM 7/24/87; LJ 11/1/87; NYTBR 8/9/87) **[591.96]**

595 Other invertebrates

Insects

2203 Berenbaum, May R. *Ninety-nine Gnats, Nits, and Nibblers.* 1990, Univ. of Illinois Pr. $29.95 (0-252-01571-1); paper $9.95 (0-252-06027-X). A collection of 99 essays about insects and insect life. (REV: Choice 10/89; LJ 4/15/89)   **[595.7]**

2204 Evans, Howard Ensign. *Pleasures of Entomology: Portraits of Insects and the People Who Study Them.* 1985, Smithsonian Inst. paper $14.95 (0-87474-421-0). Essays by a Colorado State University entomologist regarding insects and their study. "A book to curl up with and lovingly enjoy."—BL (REV: BL 8/85; Choice 7/85; LJ 3/1/86)   **[595.7]**

2205 Wilson, Edward O. *Insect Societies.* 1971, Harvard Univ. Pr. paper $20.00 (0-674-45495-2). A study of the group behavior of wasps, bees, ants, and termites. "It is fair to say that this work is the most masterful synthesis of knowledge of the social insects to appear in the last half-century."—LJ (REV: Choice 3/72; LJ 11/15/72; NYTBR 3/19/72)   **[595.7]**

Formicidea (Ants)

2206 Holldobler, Bert, and Edward O. Wilson. *The Ants.* 1990, Harvard Univ. Pr. $65.00 (0-674-04075-9). An illustrated account of the world's ants and their behaviors. (REV: LJ 3/1/91; NYTBR 7/29/90; TLS 8/24/90. AWARDS: PP:NF, 1991)   **[595.796]**

Apoidea (Bees)

2207 Heinrich, Bernd. *Bumblebee Economics.* 1979, Harvard Univ. Pr. $22.00 (0-674-08580-9); paper $10.95 (0-674-05881-7). An examination of bee life and behavior and how it affects the environment by the University of California entomologist. (REV: BL 12/15/79; Choice 3/80; NYTBR 9/2/79) **[595.799]**

597 Cold-blooded vertebrates; Fishes

2208 Thomson, Keith Stewart. *Living Fossil: The Story of the Coelacanth.* 1991, Norton $19.95 (0-393-02956-5). An overview of the biological significance of the fish thought to have been extinct prior to its rediscovery during the late 1930s. (REV: BL 4/15/91; LJ 5/15/91; PW 4/12/91)   **[597]**

598 Aves (Birds)

2209 Brooks, Bruce. *On the Wing.* 1989, Macmillan $40.00 (0-684-19119-9). This companion to the PBS series *Nature*, provides a survey of bird physiology, behavior, and the relationship between birds and man. "A thoughtful look at birds . . . recommended for lay readers and experts alike."—LJ (REV: BL 9/15/89; LJ 11/1/89)   **[598]**

Research

2210 Kastner, Joseph. *A World of Watchers: An Informal History of the American Passion for Birds.* 1986, Knopf $25.00 (0-394-52869-7); Sierra Club paper $10.95 (0-87156-784-9). An illustrated history of American bird watching with profiles of some of its key enthusiasts. (REV: Choice 5/87; LJ 11/15/86; PW 10/17/86)   **[598.072]**

2211 Sutton, George Miksch. *Birds Worth Watching.* 1986, Univ. of Oklahoma Pr. $19.95 (0-8061-1975-6). An ornithologist's guide to his favorite 60 American bird species. (REV: BL 6/1/86; LJ 7/86; PW 8/8/86)   **[598.072]**

Processes and parts

2212 Burton, Robert. *Bird Behavior.* 1985, Knopf $18.95 (0-394-53957-5). Ten chapters detailing various aspects of bird behavior. (REV: Choice 12/85; LJ 9/1/85; NYTBR 8/18/85)   **[598.2]**

Land birds

2213 Fisk, Emma J. *Parrot's Wood.* 1985, Norton $15.95 (0-393-01997-7). A journal of an ornithologist and her adventures studying exotic birds in Belize. (REV: BL 8/85; LJ 8/85; NYTBR 10/13/85)   **[598.2922]**

2214 Stap, Don. *A Parrot Without a Name: The Search for the Last Unknown Birds on Earth.* 1990, Knopf $19.95 (0-394-55596-1). An account of the author's experiences with a group of ornithological researchers in the jungles of Peru. (REV: CSM 7/17/90; LJ 5/1/90; NYRB 10/25/90)   **[598.2922]**

Water birds

2215 Harrison, Peter. *Seabirds: An Identification Guide.* 1983, Houghton $35.00 (0-395-33253-2). A guide to the sighting and identification of over 300 species of ocean birds. (REV: Choice 1/84; CSM 12/28/83; LJ 11/1/83)   **[598.2924]**

Anseriforms and other water birds

2216 Dunning, Joan. *Loon: Voice of the Wilderness.* 1985, Yankee Books $17.95 (0-89909-080-X). A profile of the loon illustrated with the author's watercolors and drawings. (REV: BL 4/1/86; CSM 4/4/86; NYTBR 6/2/85)   **[598.4]**

2217 Haley, Delphine, ed. *Seabirds of Eastern North Pacific and Arctic Waters.* 1984, Pacific Search $22.95 (0-914718-86-X). An illustrated natural history of the ocean birds of the North Pacific and Arctic. "Splendid . . . a standard-setting achievement."—BL (REV: BL 10/15/84; Choice 11/84; LJ 9/1/84)   **[598.4]**

2218 Lockley, Ronald M., and Eric Hosking. *Seabirds of the World.* 1984, Facts on File $24.95 (0-87196-249-7). An illustrated overview of 120 species of ocean birds. (REV: BL 1/15/84; LJ 1/84; PW 12/23/83)   **[598.4]**

2219 Taylor, Kip. *Loon.* 1989, K. Taylor $45.00 (0-9623422-0-3). A selection of the author's best photographs of loons taken over an 18-year period in the Adriondacks. "A remarkable achievment, a joy to behold."—LJ (REV: BL 2/1/90; LJ 12/89)   **[598.4]**

Sphenisciformes, Gaviiformes, Podicipediformes

2220　Gorman, James. *Total Penguin.* **1990, Prentice Hall $29.95 (0-13-925041-7).** An illustrated guide to the world's penguins with photographs by Frans Lanting. (Rev: BL 11/1/90; NYTBR 12/2/90)　**[598.44]**

2221　La Bastille, Anne. *Mama Poc: An Ecologist's Account of the Extinction of a Species.* **1990, Norton $19.95 (0-393-02830-5).** An account of the extinction of a bird species in Guatemala and of the author's 20-year effort to save it. (Rev: BL 6/1/90; LJ 6/15/90. Awards: BL, 1990)　**[598.44]**

Passeriformes, Coraciiformes, Apodiformes

2222　Heinrich, Bernd. *Ravens in Winter.* **1989, Summit $19.95 (0-671-67809-4).** The results of the author's scientific observations of raven behavior, carried out over four winters in Maine. "He demonstrates the difficulties, the tedium, and the excitement of real scientific research."—BL (Rev: Atl 10/89; BL 9/1/89; LJ 8/89)　**[598.8]**

Falconiformes, Strigiformes, Caprimulgiformes

2223　Houle, Marcy Cottrell. *Wings for My Flight: The Peregrine Falcons of Chimney Rock.* **1991, Addison Wesley $17.95 (0-201-57706-2).** An account of the author's studies of peregrine falcons and her conflicts with the U.S. Forest Service over the development of one of the few falcon nesting grounds. (Rev: LJ 5/15/91; PW 2/22/91)　**[598.9]**

599　Mammalia (Mammals)

2224　Moss, Cynthia. *Portraits in the Wild: Animal Behavior in East Africa.* **1982, Univ. of Chicago Pr. paper $14.95 (0-226-54233-5).** What scientific observation has told us about the behavioral patterns and social structure of the animals of East Africa. (Rev: BL 12/15/75; Choice 3/76; LJ 10/1/85)　**[599]**

2225　Schaller, George. *Serengeti Lion: A Study of Predator-Prey Relations.* **1976, Univ. of Chicago Pr. paper $24.95 (0-226-73640-7).** A groundbreaking study of lion behavior in their natural habitat. (Rev: Choice 3/73; LJ 11/15/72; Sat Rev 10/28/72. Awards: NBA, 1973)　**[599]**

Persons

2226　Van Lawick, Hugo. *Among Predators and Prey: A Photographer's Reflections on African Wildlife.* **1986, Sierra Club $35.00 (0-87156-774-1).** Collected wildlife photographs taken over the quarter century of the author's residence in Africa. (Rev: BL 9/15/86; LJ 11/5/86; PW 10/10/86)　**[599.092]**

Marine mammals

2227　Cousteau, Jacques Yves, and Yves Pacculet. *Jacques Cousteau: Whales.* **1988, Abrams $49.50 (0-8109-1046-2).** A natural history of whales and man's relationship to them. "This book should have a tremendous impact on public opinion for the conservation of the rapidly disappearing ma-

rine mammals."—Choice (Rev: Choice 2/89; LJ 12/88; NYTBR 12/11/88)　**[599.5]**

2228　Ellis, Richard A. *Men and Whales.* **1991, Knopf $40.00 (0-394-55839-1).** An illustrated history of human contacts with whales from ancient times to the twentieth century. (Rev: BL 10/15/91; LJ 10/15/91; PW 8/30/91. Awards: BL, 1991; LJ, 1991)　**[599.5]**

2229　Gormley, Gerard. *A Dolphin Summer.* **1985, Taplinger $14.95 (0-8008-2264-1).** A look at the year in the life of a young dolphin provides the basis for an overview of dolphins and other marine life. (Rev: BL 9/1/85; LJ 8/85; NYTBR 6/29/86)　**[599.5]**

2230　Scheffer, Victor. *Year of the Whale.* **1971, Macmillan paper $8.95 (0-684-71886-3).** A year in the life of a sperm whale, with accounts of man's relationship to and interactions with whales. "What 'Moby Dick' did not reveal, 'The Year of the Whale' does—and on terms that can stand the comparison."—Time (Rev: Choice 11/69; NYTBR 8/10/69; Time 8/15/69. Awards: ALA, 1969)　**[599.5]**

2231　Whitehead, Hal. *Voyage to the Whales.* **1990, Chelsea Green $22.50 (0-930031-25-3).** An account of the author's experiences with whales during three years of research in the Indian Ocean. (Rev: LJ 5/15/90; PW 2/16/90)　**[599.5]**

2232　Winn, Lois King, and Howard E. Winn. *Wings in the Sea: The Humpback Whale.* **1985, Univ. Pr. of New England $30.00 (0-87451-335-9); paper $10.95 (0-87451-336-7).** A husband and wife team present the results of their 15 years of researching the humpback whale. (Rev: BL 8/85; LJ 8/85)　**[599.5]**

Paenungulata

2233　Moss, Cynthia. *Elephant Memories: Thirteen Years in the Life of an Elephant Family.* **1988, Morrow $22.95 (0-688-05348-3); Fawcett paper $10.95 (0-449-90362-1).** A study of elephant behavior and social structure based on observations made by the author of a single family over the course of 13 years in a Kenyan National Park. (Rev: LJ 2/15/88; NYTBR 3/27/88; Newsweek 5/9/88)　**[599.6]**

2234　Orenstein, Ronald, ed. *Elephants: The Deciding Decade.* **1991, Sierra Club $35.00 (0-87156-565-X).** An account of the present state and possible future of elephants in the wild by the director of the International Wildlife Coalition. (Rev: LJ 11/15/91; PW 10/11/91)　**[599.6]**

Carnivora

2235　Berkeley, Ellen Perry. *Maverick Cats: Encounters with Feral Cats.* **1987, New England Pr. paper $7.95 (0-933050-45-3).** The lives and personalities of feral cats are examined based on the author's personal experiences and the studies of zoologists. (Rev: BL 11/15/82; LJ 11/1/82; PW 11/12/82)　**[599.74]**

2236　Feazel, Charles T. *Grizzly Years: Encounters with the Master of the Arctic Ice.* **1990, Henry Holt $19.95 (0-8050-1153-6).** An overview of the life and behavior of the polar bear in its native Arctic habitat. (REV: BL 10/1/90; LJ 9/1/90; PW 8/17/90) **[599.74]**

2237 Hyde, Dayton O. *Don Coyote: The Good and Bad Times of a Maligned American Original.* **1986, Morrow $16.95 (0-87795-783-5); Ballantine paper $3.95 (0-345-34704-8).** Hyde uses the example of the coyote, a traditional "enemy" of ranchers, to demonstrate that man would be better to coexist with nature than to battle it. (REV: BL 6/15/86; LJ 6/1/86; NYTBR 7/27/86. AWARDS: BL, the 1980s) **[599.74]**

2238 Jackman, Brian. *Marsh Lions: The Story of an African Pride.* **1983, Godine $24.95 (0-87923-473-3).** A stunningly illustrated account of four years following a pride of lions in Kenya. (REV: BL 9/15/83; Choice 1/84; LJ 10/15/83. AWARDS: BL, the 1980s) **[599.74]**

2239 McNamee, Thomas. *Grizzly Bear.* **1984, Knopf $24.95 (0-394-52998-7); McGraw-Hill paper $8.95 (0-07-045668-2).** A study of the life and behavior of a grizzly bear family as observed by the author in Yellowstone National Park. (REV: Choice 3/85; CSM 1/16/85; LJ 10/15/84) **[599.74]**

2240 Peacock, Doug. *Grizzly Years: In Search of the American Wilderness.* **1990, Henry Holt $19.95 (0-8050-0448-3).** The author recounts his experiences studying and photographing grizzly bears in their native habitats. (REV: BL 9/1/90; LJ 7/90; PW 6/29/90) **[599.74]**

2241 Peters, Roger. *Dance of the Wolves.* **1986, Ballantine paper $3.95 (0-345-32870-1).** The author's study of wolf behavior on Michigan's Upper Peninsula. (REV: BL 1/15/85; Choice 6/85; LJ 2/1/85) **[599.74]**

2242 Preiss, Byron, and Gao Xueyu, eds. *The Secret World of Pandas.* **1990, Abrams paper $24.95 (0-8109-2457-9).** A photographic study with accompanying text of the world's remaining pandas. (REV: BL 11/1/90; LJ 11/15/90; PW 10/12/90) **[599.74]**

2243 Schaller, George. *Golden Shadows, Flying Hooves.* **1989, Univ. of Chicago Pr. paper $16.95 (0-226-73650-4).** Schaller's personal and field observations of the behavior of large predatory animals made while living in Serengeti National Park. "The author's vibrant feeling for the natural world will delight readers who share this interest."—LJ (REV: BL 2/1/74; LJ 8/73; NYTBR 11/11/73. AWARDS: ALA, 1973) **[599.74]**

2244 Stirling, Ian, and Dan Guravich. *Polar Bears.* **1988, Univ. of Michigan Pr. $39.50 (0-472-10100-5).** An illustrated natural history of polar bears and their Arctic habitat. (REV: Choice 3/89; LJ 3/1/89) **[599.74]**

2245 Sunquist, Fiona, and Mel Sunquist. *Tiger Moon.* **1988, Univ. of Chicago Pr. $24.95 (0-226-78001-5).** An account of the authors' adventures studying the wildlife of Royal Chitwan National Park in Nepal for the Smithsonian Institution. (REV: BL 6/15/88; LJ 5/1/88; PW 4/29/88) **[599.74]**

Primates

2246 De Waal, Frans. *Peacemaking among Primates.* **1989, Harvard Univ. Pr. $29.95 (0-674-65920-1).** A study of conflict resolution among primates. (REV: BL 4/1/89; LJ 3/1/89; NYTBR 4/9/89. AWARDS: BL, 1989) **[599.8]**

2247 Hardy, Sarah B. *Woman That Never Evolved.* **1983, Harvard Univ. Pr. $21.00 (0-674-95540-4); paper $9.95 (0-674-95541-2).** A study and comparison between the social behavior of human and other female primates. (REV: Choice 2/82; LJ 11/15/81; NYTBR 11/15/81) **[599.8]**

2248 Peterson, Dale. *Deluge and the Ark: A Journey into Primate Worlds.* **1989, Houghton $24.95 (0-395-51039-2).** A survey of the habitats of the world's primates and how their existence is threatened by man. (REV: LJ 9/1/89; NYTBR 9/24/89; Newsweek 8/14/89) **[599.8]**

Cebidae (New World monkeys), Callithricadae, Cercopithecidae (Old World monkeys)

2249 Strum, Shirley C. *Almost Human: A Journey into the World of Baboons.* **1987, Random $22.50 (0-394-54724-1); Norton paper $12.95 (0-393-30708-5).** An account of the anthropologist's 15 years spent researching the behavior of baboons in Kenya. (REV: BL 11/15/87; LJ 10/15/87; NYTBR 1/10/88) **[599.82]**

Apes

2250 Fossey, Dian. *Gorillas in the Mist.* **1984, Houghton paper $11.95 (0-395-36638-0).** Fossey's account of 13 years in Africa studying the behaviors of mountain gorillas in their natural habitat. "A monument to scientific devotion."—NYTBR (REV: LJ 5/15/83; NYTBR 9/4/83; Newsweek 8/29/83. AWARDS: ALA, 1983) **[599.88]**

2251 Goodall, Jane. *Chimpanzees of Gombe: Patterns of Behavior.* **1986, Harvard Univ. Pr. $37.95 (0-674-11649-6).** The author presents the results of 25 years of research studying chimpanzee behavior in their natural habitat. "A landmark in ethology . . . as always, Goodall's deep commitment to her work shines through."—LJ (REV: Choice 12/86; LJ 8/86; NYTBR 8/24/86. AWARDS: LJ, 1986) **[599.88]**

2252 Goodall, Jane. *In the Shadow of Man.* **1983, Houghton paper $9.95 (0-395-33145-5).** Observations made over a ten-year period of chimpanzees in their natural habitat. "A milestone in the study of the chimpanzee."—LJ (REV: Choice 1/72; LJ 12/1/71; TLS 11/19/71. AWARDS: ALA, 1971) **[599.88]**

2253 Hayes, Harold T. P. *Dark Romance of Dian Fossey.* **1990, Simon & Schuster $21.95 (0-671-63339-2).** A biography of the primatologist who studied mountain gorillas in their native Africa prior to her 1985 murder. (REV: BL 5/1/90; LJ 6/15/90; Newsweek 6/25/90. AWARDS: BL, 1990) **[599.88]**

2254 Montgomery, Sy. *Walking with the Great Apes: Jane Goodall, Dian Fossey, Birute Galdikas.* **1991, Houghton $19.95 (0-395-51597-1).** A study of the lives and works of three key figures in the field of primatology. "Exciting . . . a splendid, well-written account."—BL (Rev: BL 3/15/91; LJ 2/1/91; PW 1/1/91)   **[599.88]**

2255 Mowat, Farley. *Woman in the Mists: The Story of Dian Fossey and the Mountain Gorillas of Africa.* **1988, Warner paper $10.95 (0-446-38720-7).** A biography of the American anthropologist based on her journals by the author of *Never Cry Wolf.* (Rev: LJ 10/15/87; NYTBR 10/25/87; Time 10/26/87)   **[599.88]**

2256 **Schwartz, Jeffrey H.** *Red Ape: Orangutans and Human Origins.* **1987, Houghton $18.95 (0-395-38017-0).** The author presents his theory that man's closest relative among the great apes is the orangutan. "A classic of evolutionary biology."—BL (Rev: BL 4/1/87; Choice 5/87; LJ 4/1/87)   **[599.88]**

TECHNOLOGY (APPLIED SCIENCES)

600 TECHNOLOGY (APPLIED SCIENCES)

2257 Brennan, Richard P. *Levitating Trains and Kamikaze Genes: Technical Literacy for the 1990's.* 1990, Wiley $18.95 (0-471-62295-8); Harper-Collins paper $8.95 (0-06-0097369-2). An overview of key contemporary technologies and their jargons. (REV: BL 3/1/90; LJ 2/1/90; NYTBR 4/8/90) **[600]**

2258 Macaulay, David. *The Way Things Work.* 1988, Houghton $29.95 (0-395-42857-2). Illustrated explanations of the way contemporary machines, both simple and complex, work. "Absolutely superb."—LJ (REV: BL 1/15/89; LJ 1/89; PW 1/6/89) **[600]**

602 Miscellany

Trademarks and service marks

2259 Morgan, Hal. *Symbols of America.* 1986, Viking $40.00 (0-670-80667-6); Penguin paper $14.95 (0-14-008077-5). Histories of notable American symbols and trademarks. (REV: CSM 5/9/86; LJ 2/1/86; NYTBR 2/9/86) **[602.75]**

608 Inventions and patents

2260 Clark, Ronald W. *Works of Man.* 1985, Viking $29.95 (0-670-80483-5). A history of man's technological achievements from ancient times to the twentieth century. "This wide-ranging, well-written, and amply illustrated history will appeal to a multitude of readers."—PW (REV: Choice 1/86; CSM 11/1/85; PW 8/9/85) **[608]**

2261 Diebold, John. *Innovators: The Discoveries, Inventions, and Breakthroughs of Our Time.* 1990, Dutton $19.95 (0-525-24830-7); paper $9.95 (0-452-26575-4). A study of recent American technological innovations and how they were made. (REV: LJ 2/1/90; NYTBR 2/4/90) **[608]**

609 Historical, areas, persons treatment

2262 Basalla, George. *Evolution of Technology.* 1989, Cambridge Univ. Pr. $32.50 (0-521-22855-7); paper $10.95 (0-521-29681-1). A history of the development of technology from the Stone Age to the present. "An absorbing and richly informative interweaving of conflicting theories with well-chosen examples to test the elements of truth in each."—NYRB (REV: Choice 9/89; NYRB 12/7/89; NYTBR 4/9/89) **[609]**

2263 Mumford, Lewis. *Myth of the Machine.* 1971, Harcourt paper $12.95 (0-15-662341-2). A two-volume set tracing the development and influence of technology from prehistory to the twentieth century. (REV: BL 4/1/67; Choice 10/67; NYTBR 4/30/67. AWARDS: ALA, 1967; NYTBR, 1967) **[609]**

2264 Vare, Elthie Ann, and Greg Ptacek. *Mothers of Invention: From the Bra to the Bomb, Forgotten Women and Their Unforgettable Ideas.* 1988, Morrow $17.95 (0-688-06464-7); paper $8.95 (0-688-08907-0). An introduction to twentieth-century women inventors and their inventions. (REV: LJ 12/87; NYTBR 2/14/88; PW 11/20/87) **[609]**

England and Wales

2265 Bracegirdle, Brian. *Archaeology of the Industrial Revolution.* 1973, Farleigh Dickinson $50.00 (0-8386-1424-8). A guide to methods and findings of archaelogical studies undertaken upon industrial ruins in Great Britain. "Both a valuable document for the historian and a superb introduction for the general reader."—LJ (REV: Choice 5/74; LJ 3/15/74; TLS 8/31/73. AWARDS: ALA, 1973) **[609.42]**

610 MEDICAL SCIENCES; MEDICINE

2266 Chopra, Deepak. *Return of the Rishi: A Doctor's Search for the Ultimate Healer.* 1989, Houghton $16.95 (0-395-45516-2); paper $7.95 (0-395-50077-X). The autobiography of an Indian-born American doctor that focuses on his personal rediscovery of the healing ways of ancient India. (REV: LJ 6/1/88; NYTBR 3/27/88) **[610]**

2267 Prevention Magazine Health Books Staff. *Doctor's Book of Home Remedies.* Ed. by Debora Tkac. 1990, Rodale Pr. $26.95 (0-87587-873 0). Over 2,000 home remedies to common ailments collected by the staff of *Prevention* magazine. (REV: BL 4/15/90; LJ 4/1/90) **[610]**

2268 Smolan, Rick. *Power to Heal: Ancient Arts and Modern Medicine.* 1990, Prentice Hall $40.00

(0-13-684549-5). Collected essays accompanied by photographs detailing health-care practices throughout the world. (Rev: BL 12/1/90; LJ 3/1/91; Newsweek 9/24/90) **[610]**

Miscellany

2269 Skrabanek, Peter, and James McCormick. *Follies and Fallacies in Medicine.* 1990, Prometheus $19.95 (0-87975-630-6). Two doctors' critical examination of the current state of medical thought and practice. (Rev: LJ 9/15/90; PW 9/28/90) **[610.2]**

Medical personnel

2270 Morantz, Regina Marshall. *In Her Own Words: Oral Histories of Women Physicians.* 1982, Greenwood Pr. $38.50 (0-313-22686-5); Yale Univ. Pr. paper $12.95 (0-300-03352-4). Nine female doctors describe their training and lives in a largely male-dominated profession. "An important contribution to medical history."—LJ (Rev: Choice 1/83; LJ 9/1/82) **[610.69]**

Education

2271 Hellerstein, David. *Battles of Life and Death.* 1986, Houghton $16.95 (0-395-40459-2); Warner paper $6.95 (0-446-38422-4). The author recounts his education and training en route to becoming a physician. (Rev: BL 3/15/86; LJ 5/1/86; NYTBR 3/23/86) **[610.7]**

2272 Klass, Perri. *A Not Entirely Benign Procedure: Four Years as a Medical Student.* 1987, Putnam $18.95 (0-399-13223-6); NAL paper $4.50 (0-451-15358-8). Essays tracing the author's education at Harvard Medical School. (Rev: BL 4/1/87; LJ 5/1/87; NYTBR 5/10/87) **[610.7]**

2273 Klitzman, Robert. *Year-Long Night: Tales of a Medical Internship.* 1989, Viking $17.95 (0-670-81777-5); Penguin paper $7.95 (0-14-010253-1). An account of the author's first year as a medical intern. (Rev: BL 2/1/89; LJ 2/1/89; PW 12/9/88) **[610.7]**

2274 Konner, Melvin. *Becoming a Doctor: A Journey of Initiation in Medical School.* 1987, Viking $19.95 (0-670-80554-8); Penguin paper $8.95 (0-14-011116-6). A critical view of the training and education of doctors by a candidate who returned to anthropology after medical school. (Rev: BL 7/87; LJ 9/1/87; NYTBR 7/26/87. Awards: LJ, 1987) **[610.7]**

2275 Ludmerer, Kenneth M. *Learning to Heal: The Development of American Medical Education.* 1988, Basic Books paper $12.95 (0-465-03881-6). A history of American medical education and its development. "Thoroughly researched, well-documented, and readable . . . may long serve as a definitive work."—BL (Rev: BL 11/1/85; Choice 3/86; LJ 11/15/85) **[610.7]**

2276 Marion, Robert. *Intern Blues: The Private Ordeals of Three Young Doctors.* 1989, Morrow $19.95 (0-688-06886-3); Fawcett paper $5.95 (0-449-21898-8). Profiles of the work and personal lives of three medical interns. "A thought-provoking study

of real human beings."—BL (Rev: BL 3/15/89; LJ 3/15/89; NYTBR 4/9/89) **[610.7]**

2277 Sacco, Joseph. *Morphine, Ice Cream, Tears: Tales of a City Hospital.* 1989, Morrow $17.95 (0-688-08466-4). Memoirs of the author's experiences serving as an intern at a New York City Hospital. (Rev: BL 9/15/89; LJ 9/1/89) **[610.7]**

Nursing

2278 Donahue, M. Patricia, and Patricia Russac. *Nursing, the Finest Art: An Illustrated History.* 1986, Abrams $39.95 (0-8109-1113-2). An illustrated history of nursing from 300 A.D. to the present. "It stands alone in its breadth of coverage and its dedication to eye-catching illustrations."—BL (Rev: BL 5/1/86; LJ 7/86; PW 2/21/86) **[610.73]**

2279 Kraegel, Janet, and Mary Kachoyeanos. *"Just a Nurse": The Hearts and Minds of Nurses, in Their Own Words.* 1989, Dutton $18.95 (0-525-24760-2). Collected accounts of nurses speaking about their profession. (Rev: BL 4/15/89; LJ 5/1/89; PW 4/14/89) **[610.73]**

Women

2280 Achterberg, Jeanne. *Woman as Healer.* 1990, Shambhala $19.95 (0-87773-444-5). An overview of the historical and present role of women in medicine and human healing. (Rev: BL 5/1/90; LJ 5/15/90) **[610.82]**

History

2281 Shorter, Edward. *Health Century.* 1987, Doubleday $21.95 (0-385-24236-0). An account of the medical accomplishments of the twentieth century. (Rev: BL 10/1/87; LJ 10/1/87) **[610.9]**

2282 Weissmann, Gerald. *They All Laughed at Christopher Columbus: Tales of Medicine and the Art of Discovery.* 1987, Random $17.95 (0-8129-1618-2). A collection of essays by a physician regarding the art of medicine and medical discovery. (Rev: BL 3/15/87; LJ 4/1/87; NYTBR 4/5/87) **[610.9]**

Persons

2283 Kean, B. H., and Tracy Dahlby. *M.D.* 1990, Ballantine $19.95 (0-345-35821-X). Memoirs of a physician whose career took him to the jungles of Central America, post-World War II Germany, and Manhattan. (Rev: BL 2/1/90; LJ 2/1/90; NYTBR 2/11/90) **[610.92]**

2284 Koop, C. Everett. *Koop: The Memoirs of the Former Surgeon General.* 1991, Random $22.50 (0-394-57626-8). Memoirs of Reagan's controversial activist surgeon general focusing on his beliefs and actions on AIDS, abortion, smoking, and the rights of the handicapped. (Rev: BL 9/1/91; LJ 9/15/91; NYTBR 9/8/91) **[610.92]**

2285 Nuland, Sherwin. *Doctors: The Biography of Medicine.* 1988, Knopf $29.95 (0-394-55130-3); Random paper $12.95 (0-679-72215-7). The collective biography of prominent individuals in the history of medicine from ancient times to the twentieth century. (Rev: BL 5/15/88; Choice 10/88; NYTBR 10/23/88) **[610.92]**

2286 Roueche, Berton. *Medical Detectives.* **1984, Pocket paper $4.95 (0-671-54449-7).** Twenty essays regarding medical discoveries and the people who made them. "As suspenseful and gripping as any imaginary mystery story."—PW (Rev: BL 9/15/80; LJ 10/1/80; PW 7/25/80) **[610.92]**

2287 Slocum, Milton Jonathan. *Manhattan Country Doctor.* **1988, Ballantine paper $7.95 (0-345-35659-4).** Memoirs of the author's medical practice in New York's Hell's Kitchen during the depression. (Rev: BL 10/15/86; PW 9/26/86) **[610.92]**

612 Human physiology

2288 Gazzaniga, Michael S. *Social Brain: Discovering the Networks of the Mind.* **1987, Basic Books paper $11.95 (0-465-07852-4).** A presentation of current theories concerning the organization and thought processes of the human mind. (Rev: BL 10/15/85; LJ 2/1/86; Natl Rev 4/25/86) **[612]**

2289 Goldberg, Jeff. *Anatomy of a Scientific Discovery.* **1989, Bantam paper $8.95 (0-553-34631-8).** An account of the efforts of Scottish and American scientists to isolate endorphins during the 1970s. (Rev: LJ 5/15/88; NYTBR 7/17/88; PW 3/25/88) **[612]**

2290 Hite, Shere. *Hite Report.* **1987, Dell paper $6.95 (0-440-13690-3).** A report on female sexuality based upon and largely consisting of the responses of nearly 2,000 American women to a series of questionnaires. (Rev: Choice 12/76; LJ 7/76; NYTBR 10/3/76) **[612]**

2291 Nilsson, Lennart. *Behold Man: A Photographic Journey of Discovery Inside the Body.* **1978, Little, Brown $29.95 (0-316-60751-7).** Enlarged photographs of the human interior by the Swedish medical photographer known for *A Child Is Born.* "The overwhelming impact of the work is to give us a new vision of ourselves, for as can plainly be seen, we are one of nature's greatest spectacles."—NYTBR (Rev: LJ 9/1/74; NYTBR 11/3/74; PW 6/3/74. Awards: ALA, 1974) **[612]**

2292 Rose, Steven. *Conscious Brain.* **1988, Paragon House paper $14.95 (1-55778-150-8).** A biologist's look at what we know about the human brain. "A model of just how good 'popular' science writing can be."—NYTBR (Rev: LJ 3/15/74; NYTBR 3/31/74; Time 12/31/74. Awards: Time, 1973) **[612]**

Pregnancy and childbirth

2293 Sorel, Nancy Caldwell. *Ever Since Eve: Personal Reflections on Childbirth.* **1984, Oxford Univ. Pr. paper $19.95 (0-19-503460-0).** Collected essays from Europeans and Americans on the experience of childbirth. (Rev: BL 5/15/84; LJ 5/1/84; NYTBR 7/22/84) **[612.63]**

Longevity factors

2294 Kahn, Carol. *Beyond the Helix: DNA and the Quest for Longevity.* **1985, Random $17.95 (0-8129-1153-9).** The history of DNA research investigating its relationship to the aging process. "Anyone interested in the processes of scientific discovery will find this book impossible to put down."—LJ (Rev: BL 10/15/85; LJ 11/1/85; NYTBR 12/1/85) **[612.68]**

Muscles

2295 Podell, Richard N. *Doctor, Why Am I So Tired? A Guide for Overcoming Chronic Fatigue.* **1988, Pharos Books $17.95 (0-88687-321-5); Fawcett paper $3.95 (0-449-14578-6).** A doctor's guide to fatigue and its treatment. (Rev: BL 3/15/88; LJ 6/15/88) **[612.74]**

Nervous functions; Sensory functions

2296 Ackerman, Diane. *A Natural History of the Senses.* **1990, Random $19.95 (0-394-57335-8).** A look at the function and folklore of the five human senses. (Rev: BL 5/1/90; LJ 5/1/90; NYTBR 7/29/90. Awards: ALA, 1990; BL, 1990) **[612.8]**

2297 Dotto, Lydia. *Asleep in the Fast Lane: The Impact of Sleep on Work.* **1990, Morrow $16.95 (0-688-09131-8).** A study of current theories of sleep and its effects upon the human brain and body. (Rev: LJ 8/90; PW 7/27/90) **[612.8]**

2298 Gonzalez-Crussi, F. *Five Senses.* **1989, Harcourt $17.95 (0-15-131398-9).** Essays combining a mixture of medical history, anecdotes, and personal experiences to explain our senses. "His richest book to date."—BL (Rev: BL 3/1/89; LJ 4/1/90; NYTBR 4/9/89. Awards: BL, 1989; BL, the 1980s) **[612.8]**

2299 Martin, Russell. *Matters Gray and White: A Neurologist, His Patients, and the Mysteries of the Brain.* **1988, Fawcett paper $4.95 (0-449-21606-3).** An account of a year in the life of a neurologist tracing his most notable patients and their case histories. (Rev: BL 10/15/86; LJ 11/1/86; NYTBR 4/26/87) **[612.8]**

2300 Smith, Jillyn. *Senses and Sensibilities.* **1989, Wiley $18.95 (0-471-50657-5); paper $9.95 (0-471-61839-X).** An introduction to the five senses of the human body. "Lively and entertaining."—LJ (Rev: BL 6/15/89; LJ 8/89) **[612.8]**

The brain

2301 Allman, William F. *Apprentices of Wonder: Reinventing the Mind.* **1989, Bantam $18.95 (0-553-05389-2); paper $10.95 (0-553-34946-5).** A comparative study of the workings of the human brain and the workings of the modern computer. (Rev: BL 9/15/89; LJ 3/1/90; PW 8/14/89) **[612.82]**

2302 Hutchison, Michael. *Megabrain.* **1986, Morrow $18.95 (0-688-04880-3).** A study of scientific efforts to create devices or substances that will increase brain functions. (Rev: BL 1/15/86; LJ 3/15/86; PW 1/3/86) **[612.82]**

2303 **Rosenfield, Israel.** *Invention of Memory: A New View of the Brain.* 1988, Basic Books **$18.95** (0-465-03592-2). An investigation of the essence and process of human memorization. (REV: LJ 3/1/89; NYTBR 10/22/89; PW 8/4/89) **[612.82]**

2304 **Smith, Anthony.** *The Mind.* 1986, Penguin paper **$6.95** (0-14-022596-X). A study of the evolution, development, and present state of the human brain by the author of *The Body.* (REV: BL 1/1/84; LJ 3/1/84; NYTBR 4/22/84) **[612.82]**

613 Promotion of health

2305 **Boston Women's Health Book Collective.** *New Our Bodies, Ourselves.* 1985, Simon & Schuster paper **$16.95** (0-671-46088-9). A guide to the social, political, medical, personal, and legal concerns of women. (REV: Choice 6/85; LJ 3/15/85; NYTBR 1/13/85) **[613]**

2306 **Butler, Kurt, and Lynn Rayner.** *Best Medicine: The Complete Health and Preventative Medicine Handbook.* 1985, Harper & Row **$32.45** (0-06-250123-2); paper **$16.95** (0-06-250124-0). A guide to the prevention of medical problems by an active program of exercise and nutrition. (REV: BL 8/85; LJ 9/1/85) **[613]**

2307 **Cooper, Robert K.** *Health and Fitness Excellence: The Scientific Action Plan for Integrated Total Achievement.* 1989, Houghton **$19.95** (0-395-47589-9); paper **$12.95** (0-395-54453-X). A guide to increasing self-awareness and integrating it with a health and fitness plan to achieve a total body healthiness. (REV: BL 2/1/89; LJ 11/1/89; PW 12/16/88) **[613]**

2308 **Hensel, Bruce.** *Smart Medicine: How to Get the Most Out of Your Checkup and Stay Healthy.* 1989, Putnam **$18.95** (0-399-13446-8); Berkley paper **$7.95** (0-425-12103-8). A guide for individuals to determine if and when they require medical care and how to choose a physician when it becomes necessary. (REV: BL 4/1/89; LJ 5/15/89) **[613]**

2309 **Rosenfeld, Isadore.** *Modern Prevention: The New Medicine.* 1987, Bantam paper **$10.95** (0-553-34460-9). A guide to preventative medicine for the layperson. (REV: BL 4/15/86; LJ 5/1/86) **[613]**

2310 **Roud, Paul C.** *Making Miracles: An Exploration into the Dynamics of Self-Healing.* 1989, Warner **$19.95** (0-446-51467-5). Eleven case studies of people who recovered from life-threatening illnesses. (REV: LJ 12/89; PW 12/1/89) **[613]**

2311 **Samuels, Mike, and Hal Zina Bennett.** *Well Body, Well Earth: The Sierra Club Environmental Health Sourcebook.* 1983, Sierra Club paper **$12.95** (0-87156-808-X). An illustrated health handbook detailing the interrelations between humans and the environment. (REV: Choice 3/84; LJ 12/15/83; PW 10/14/83) **[613]**

2312 **Taylor, Robert L.** *Health Fact, Health Fiction: Getting Through the Media Maze.* 1990, Taylor **$16.95** (0-87833-683-4). A study of the mass media's presentation and coverage of health and medical-related issues. (REV: BL 2/15/90; LJ 2/15/90) **[613]**

2313 **White, Evelyn S., ed.** *Black Women's Health Book: Speaking for Ourselves.* 1990, Seal Pr. paper **$14.95** (0-931188-86-5). Collected essays addressing the health concerns of African-American women. (REV: BL 5/1/90; LJ 4/15/90; NYTBR 8/5/90) **[613.04]**

Mature adults

2314 **Shaftoe, Marjorie, and Gerald L. Hunt.** *Body at 40.* 1988, Putnam paper **$10.95** (0-399-51378-7). A guide to common health problems and concerns of people in their forties. "An excellent addition to any health collection."—BL (REV: BL 1/15/88; LJ 4/1/88) **[613.0434]**

Dietetics

2315 **Brody, Jane.** *Jane Brody's Good Food Book: Living the High-Carbohydrate Way.* **$13.95**, Bantam paper 1987 (0-553-34618-0). Three hundred recipes emphasizing high carbohydrates, low fats and sugars, and a moderate intake of proteins for a healthy diet. (REV: BL 10/1/85; LJ 11/1/85; Newsweek 8/4/86) **[613.2]**

2316 **Carper, Jean.** *Jean Carper's Total Nutrition Guide: The Complete Official Report on Healthful Eating.* 1987, Bantam paper **$12.95** (0-553-34350-5). A guide to the healthful selection and preparation of food based on a decade of research by the U.S. Department of Agriculture. (REV: BL 3/1/87; LJ 3/15/87) **[613.2]**

2317 **Colvin, Robert H., and Susan C. Olson.** *Keeping It Off: Winning at Weight Loss.* 1985, KIO paper **$6.95** (0-9625628-0-7). A study of successful diets and dieting techniques for long-term results emphasizing the psychological factors involved in weight-loss programs. (REV: LJ 12/85; PW 9/20/85) **[613.2]**

2318 **Conners, C. Keith.** *Feeding the Brain: How Foods Affect Children.* 1989, Plenum **$23.95** (0-306-43306-0). A neuropsychiatrist's study of the biological effects of food upon children's behavior. (REV: BL 9/15/89; LJ 9/15/89) **[613.2]**

2319 **Long, Patricia.** *Nutritional Ages of Women: A Lifetime Guide to Eating Right for Health, Beauty and Well-Being.* 1987, Bantam paper **$4.50** (0-553-26472-9). Women's guide to lifetime nutritional needs and developmental stages of the female body. (REV: BL 5/15/86; LJ 5/1/86; PW 4/18/86) **[613.2]**

2320 **Manahan, William.** *Eat for Health: Fast and Simple Ways of Eliminating Diseases Without Medical Assistance.* Ed. by Suzanne Lipsett. 1988, H. J. Kramer paper **$10.95** (0-915811-11-1). A guide to adjusting one's diet to prevent or combat disease. "Essential reading and an outstanding selection."—LJ (REV: BL 10/1/88; LJ 2/1/89) **[613.2]**

2321 **Mayer, Jean, and Jeanne P. Goldberg.** *Dr. Jean Mayer's Diet and Nutrition Guide.* 1990, Pharos Books **$19.95** (0-88687-568-4). A guide to proper diet and nutrition with suggestions for treatment for diet-related health disorders. (REV: BL 4/1/90; LJ 4/15/90; PW 2/16/90) **[613.2]**

2322 Tracy, Lisa. *Gradual Vegetarian.* **1986, Dell paper $8.95 (0-440-53124-1).** A program designed to gradually eliminate meat consumption from the diet for health or ethical purposes. (REV: BL 4/1/85; LJ 4/1/85; PW 3/15/85) **[613.2]**

Weight-losing programs

2323 Cohen, Mindy, Louis Abramson, and Ruth Winter. *Thin Kids: The Proven, Healthy, Sensible Program for Children.* **1985, Beaufort Books paper $9.95 (0-8253-0277-3).** A program designed to restructure eating and exercise habits for children with weight problems. (REV: BL 7/85; LJ 7/85; PW 7/19/85) **[613.25]**

2324 Duff, Susan. *Post-Pregnancy Diet: How to Regain Your Figure after Your Baby Is Born.* **1989, NAL $17.95 (0-453-00595-0); paper $4.95 (0-451-16580-2).** Program designed by a nutritionist and diet columnist to help new mothers regain and retain their prepregnancy figure in a healthy manner. (REV: BL 3/1/89; LJ 4/1/89) **[613.25]**

2325 Ferguson, James M. *Habits Not Diets: The Secret to Lifetime Weight Control.* **1988, Bull Publg. paper $12.95 (0-915950-85-5).** A 21-week behavior modification program to promote a more healthy diet and exercise regimen to keep weight under control. (REV: BL 11/15/88; LJ 2/1/89) **[613.25]**

2326 Gilbert, Sara. *Psychology of Dieting.* **1989, Routledge paper $11.95 (0-415-02844-2).** A look at the psychological aspects of dieting and weight control. (REV: BL 3/1/89; LJ 4/1/89; PW 2/17/89) **[613.25]**

2327 Goor, Ron. *Choose to Lose Diet: A Food Lover's Guide to Permanent Weight Loss.* **1990, Houghton $17.95 (0-395-49336-6).** A high-carbohydrate, low-fat diet program designed for permanent weight reduction. (REV: LJ 2/1/90; PW 1/26/90) **[613.25]**

2328 Hamilton, Michael. *Duke University Medical Center Book of Diet and Fitness.* **1991, Ballantine $19.95 (0-449-90526-0).** A behavior modification program designed at Duke University to promote total fitness and weight reduction. (REV: BL 1/15/91; LJ 1/91) **[613.25]**

2329 Katahn, Martin. *Rotation Diet.* **1986, Norton $15.95 (0-317-64887-X); Bantam paper $4.95 (0-553-27667-0).** A clinically tested diet that rotates caloric consumption on a weekly basis and stresses daily exercise in tandem with the diet to lose weight. "A simple, sensible approach to controlling weight on a long-term basis."—PW (REV: BL 3/1/86; LJ 5/1/86; PW 4/18/86. AWARDS: PW, 1986) **[613.25]**

2330 Mirkin, Gabe. *Getting Thin: All about Fat—How You Get It, How You Lose It, How You Keep It Off for Good.* **1986, Little, Brown paper $9.95 (0-316-57439-2).** A 1,300-calorie-a-day diet with a prescribed regimen of exercise for permanent weight loss. (REV: BL 4/15/83; LJ 4/1/83; PW 2/18/83) **[613.25]**

Specific nutritive elements

2331 Fisher, Jeffrey A. *Chromium Program.* **1990, Harper & Row $18.95 (0-06-016368-2).** An overview of the beneficial health effects of chromium. (REV: BL 4/15/90; LJ 11/1/90) **[613.28]**

2332 Stare, Frederick. *Balanced Nutrition: Beyond the Cholesterol Scare.* **1989, Adams $22.95 (1-55850-920-8); paper $12.95 (1-55850-997-6).** A series of health experts present their views regarding the hazards of cholesterol while providing suggestions on proper nutrition and a healthy diet. (REV: BL 9/1/89; LJ 9/15/89; PW 8/18/89) **[613.28]**

Personal safety

2333 Garcia Marquez, Gabriel. *Story of a Shipwrecked Sailor.* **1986, Knopf $13.95 (0-394-54810-8).** An account of the sole survivor of a 1955 Colombian shipwreck. "A superb example of journalism by a professional of the art."—PW (REV: LJ 6/1/86; PW 3/21/86; Time 4/14/86) **[613.6]**

2334 Smith, Susan E. *Fear or Freedom: A Woman's Options in Social Survival and Physical Defense.* **1987, Mother Courage paper $11.95 (0-941300-03-X).** A guide to self-defense for women emphasizing preventative measures that can be taken to avoid physical or sexual assault. (REV: BL 4/1/87; LJ 3/1/87) **[613.6]**

Travel health

2335 Herrero, Stephen. *Bear Attacks: Their Causes and Avoidance.* **1988, Lyons & Burford $12.95 (0-941130-87-8); paper $9.95 (0-941130-82-7).** A study of dangers posed by grizzly and black bears to humans. "Anyone planning outdoor activity in bear country should read this book first."—LJ (REV: BL 5/15/85; LJ 4/1/85) **[613.68]**

Physical fitness

2336 Gardner, David C., and Grace J. Beatty. *Never Be Tired Again.* **1988, Rawson $19.95 (0-89256-337-0); Harper & Row paper $8.95 (0-06-097298-X).** A program for curing problems of fatigue using exercise, diet, and mental imagery. (REV: BL 11/15/88; LJ 2/1/89; PW 11/18/88) **[613.7]**

2337 Green, Harvey. *Fit for America: Health, Fitness, Sport and American Society.* **1986, Pantheon $12.50 (0-394-54621-0); Johns Hopkins paper $11.95 (0-8018-3642-5).** A history of the American quest for physical fitness and good health during the nineteenth and twentieth centuries. (REV: Choice 7–8/86; LJ 4/1/86; NYTBR 3/23/86) **[613.7]**

2338 Jerome, John. *Staying Supple.* **1987, Bantam paper $8.95 (0-553-34429-3).** A guide to stretching and its health benefits including sections on rolfing, massage, and chiropractics. (REV: BL 7/87; PW 7/17/87) **[613.7]**

2339 Lansbury, Angela, and Mimi Avins. *Angela Lansbury's Positive Moves: My Personal Plan for Fitness and Well-Being.* **1990, Delacorte $18.95 (0-385-30223-1).** A guide to a healthy life-style written by the theater, film, and television actress. (REV: LJ 10/1/90; PW 10/19/90. AWARDS: PW, 1990)   **[613.7]**

2340 **Yanker, Gary, and Kathy Burton.** *Walking Medicine.* 1990, McGraw-Hill $19.95 (0-07-072234-X). A walking program for health designed for persons at all stages of life. (REV: BL 6/1/90; LJ 6/1/90)
[613.7]

Exercise

2341 **Shangold, Mona, and Gabe Mirkin.** *Complete Sports Medicine Book for Women.* 1985, Simon & Schuster paper $9.95 (0-671-53062-3). A guidebook devoted to the special health concerns of the female athlete. (REV: BL 6/1/85; LJ 7/85; PW 4/19/85)
[613.71]

Relaxation, rest, sleep

2342 **Borbely, Alexander.** *Secrets of Sleep.* 1988, Basic Books paper $8.95 (0-465-07593-2). An overview of the process of sleep by a Swiss specialist in the field. "Excellent science writing by an innovative scientist."—LJ (REV: Choice 3/87; LJ 11/1/86)
[613.79]

2343 **Bourke, Dale H.** *Sleep Management Plan.* 1990, Harper $14.95 (0-06-250110-0). A guide to the dynamics of sleep and the treatment of common sleep disorders. (REV: LJ 12/90; PW 11/9/90)   **[613.79]**

Substance abuse (Drug abuse)

2344 **Lawson, John.** *Friends You Can Drop: Alcohol and Other Drugs.* 1986, Quinlan Pr. paper $10.95 (0-933341-10-5). A primer on the physical and psychological effects of drugs and alcohol. (REV: BL 10/15/86; PW 9/5/86)   **[613.8]**

Tobacco

2345 **Farquhar, John W., and Gene A. Spiller.** *Last Puff.* 1990, Norton $18.95 (0-393-02789-9). Thirty-two former smokers tell how they were able to quit the habit. (REV: BL 3/1/90; PW 2/16/90. AWARDS: PW, 1990)   **[613.85]**

Birth control (Contraception)

2346 **Baran, Annette, and Reuben Pannor.** *Lethal Secrets.* 1989, Warner $19.95 (0-446-71003-2). An examination of the techniques and problems associated with artificial insemination. (REV: BL 3/1/89; LJ 3/1/89)   **[613.94]**

Manuals of sex technique

2347 **Pearsall, Paul.** *Super Marital Sex: Loving for Life.* 1987, Doubleday $18.95 (0-385-24018-X); Ivy Books paper $4.95 (0-8041-0367-4). A therapist's guide to a happy and lifelong sex life for married couples. (REV: BL 9/15/87; LJ 9/15/87)   **[613.96]**

2348 **Reinisch, June M., and Ruth Beasley.** *Kinsey Institute New Report on Sex: What You Must Know to Be Sexually Literate.* 1990, St. Martin's $22.95 (0-88687-573-0). A guide to contemporary American sex and sexuality produced by the

Bloomington, Indiana, research center. "An immensely useful and informative compendium."—PW (REV: BL 8/90; LJ 10/1/90; PW 8/10/90)   **[613.96]**

614   Incidence and prevention of disease

Forensic medicine

2349 **Baden, Michael, and Judith A. Hennessee.** *Unnatural Death: Confessions of a Medical Examiner.* 1989, Random $17.95 (0-394-56982-2); Ivy Books paper $4.95 (0-8041-0599-5). Reflections of a forensic examiner regarding his profession and case studies of the deaths of John Kennedy, Marilyn Monroe, John Belushi, and others. (REV: Atl 7/89; LJ 5/15/89; NYTBR 6/25/89)   **[614.1]**

2350 **Joyce, Christopher, and Eric Stover.** *Witnesses from the Grave: The Stories Bones Tell.* 1991, Little, Brown $17.95 (0-316-47399-5). An introduction to the history, methods, and applications of forensic anthropology. (REV: BL 12/15/90; LJ 12/90; NYTBR 1/20/91)   **[614.1]**

2351 **Klawans, Harold L.** *Trials of an Expert Witness: Tales of Clinical Neurology and the Law.* 1991, Little, Brown $19.95 (0-316-49683-9). A study of the role of the medical expert in court testimony documented by 20 case studies. (REV: BL 2/1/91; LJ 3/15/91; PW 1/11/91)   **[614.1]**

Incidence of and public measure to prevent disease

2352 **Goodfield, June.** *Quest for the Killers.* 1987, Hill & Wang paper $9.95 (0-8090-1532-3). Case studies of steps taken to locate, isolate, and eradicate five deadly diseases. (REV: BL 9/15/85; Choice 1/86; LJ 8/85)   **[614.4]**

2353 **McNeill, William H.** *Plagues and People.* 1977, Doubleday paper $8.95 (0-385-12122-9). The impact of disease on human history and civilizations from the prehistoric era to the twentieth century. "An important, original and well-researched work."—LJ (REV: Atl 10/76; LJ 9/15/76; Time 11/22/76. AWARDS: ALA, 1976)   **[614.4]**

615   Pharmacology and therapeutics

2354 **Snyder, Solomon H.** *Brainstorming: The Science and Politics of Opiate Research.* 1989, Harvard Univ. Pr. $22.50 (0-674-08048-3). A study of the effects of opiates upon the human brain. (REV: Choice 3/90; LJ 8/89; NYTBR 10/22/89)   **[615]**

Organic drugs

2355 **Clark, Ronald W.** *Life of Ernst Chain: Penicillin and Beyond.* 1986, St. Martin's $25.00 (0-312-48419-4). A biography of the Nobel Prize–winning scientist who pioneered research in penicillin and the development of antibiotics. (REV: BL 4/15/86; LJ 4/15/86; PW 3/14/86)   **[615.3]**

Therapeutics

2356 **Graedon, Joe, and Teresa Graedon.** *Fifty Plus: The Graedon's People's Pharmacy for Older*

Adults. **1988, Bantam $24.95 (0-553-05245-4); paper $14.95 (0-553-34485-4).** A pharmaceutical guide for older adults and their common ailments. "A must for every consumer-health collection."—BL (Rev: BL 5/15/88; LJ 9/1/88; PW 5/20/88) **[615.5]**

2357 Siegel, Bernie S. *Love, Medicine and Miracles: Lessons Learned about Self-Healing from a Surgeon's Experience with Exceptional Patients.* **1990, Harper & Row paper $9.95 (0-06-091983-3).** A surgeon's examination of the relationship between positive mental attitudes and the human healing process. (Rev: BL 5/1/86; LJ 5/15/86; PW 3/28/86) **[615.5]**

2358 Siegel, Bernie S. *Peace, Love and Healing: The Bodymind and the Path to Self-Healing.* **1989, Harper & Row $18.95 (0-06-016077-2); paper $9.95 (0-06-091705-9).** A self-help guide for individuals and their families facing serious illness. (Rev: BL 4/15/89; LJ 9/15/89) **[615.5]**

2359 Weil, Andrew. *Health and Healing: Understanding Conventional and Alternative Medicine.* **1988, Houghton paper $8.95 (0-395-36200-8).** A study of the interrelationship between medicine, the psychological state, and healing. (Rev: Choice 5/84; LJ 11/15/83; PW 10/14/83) **[615.5]**

General therapeutic systems

2360 Chopra, Deepak. *Perfect Health: A Complete Mind/Body Guide.* **1990, Crown $19.95 (0-517-57195-1).** A guide to a program of mental and physical health based on Eastern concepts and practices. (Rev: LJ 6/1/90; PW 4/20/90) **[615.53]**

Drug therapy

2361 Bruning, Nancy. *Coping with Chemotherapy.* **1986, Ballantine paper $3.95 (0-345-33090-0).** A study of the medical, physical, and psychological effects of chemotherapy based on the experience of doctors and cancer patients undergoing the treatments. (Rev: BL 6/15/85; LJ 4/15/85; PW 2/8/85) **[615.58]**

Specific therapies and kinds of therapies

2362 Fuchs, Nan Kathryn. *Nutrition Detective: Treating Your Health Problems Through the Food You Eat.* **1985, J.P. Tarcher $16.95 (0-87477-363-6); paper $9.95 (0-87477-350-4).** Twenty-five dietary programs designed to improve or alleviate common health ailments. (Rev: BL 6/1/85; LJ 5/15/85) **[615.8]**

616 Diseases

2363 Chopra, Deepak. *Unconditional Life: Mastering the Forces That Shape Personal Reality.* **1991, Bantam $21.50 (0-553-07609-4).** An Indian doctor discusses the healing powers of the human mind and its effects upon perception and the body. (Rev: BL 9/1/91; LJ 10/1/91) **[616]**

2364 Ober, William B. *Bottom's Up! A Pathologist's Essays on Medicine and the Humanities.* **1987, Southern Illinois Univ. Pr. $19.95 (0-8093-1419-3); Harper & Row paper $8.95 (0-06-097188-6).** A selection of 14 essays by a New Jersey doctor on such varying topics as spanking, leprosy, and the

Katzenjammer Kids. (Rev: BL 10/1/87; NYTBR 11/29/87; TLS 6/3/88) **[616]**

2365 Rosenfeld, Isadore. *Symptoms.* **1989, Simon & Schuster $19.95 (0-671-66140-X); Bantam paper $12.95 (0-553-34902-3).** A physician's home health guide for laymen to various symptoms of illness and what they may mean. "A hypochondriac's delight . . . his book will save readers time, money and, best of all, anxiety."—PW (Rev: BL 4/1/89; LJ 11/1/89; PW 3/17/89) **[616]**

2366 Ziegler, Edward, and Lewis R. Goldfrank. *Emergency Doctor.* **1988, Ballantine paper $4.95 (0-345-35664-0).** An account of the goings-on inside the emergency room of New York's Bellevue Hospital as told by its head physician. (Rev: BL 10/1/87; LJ 9/15/87; NYTBR 9/6/87) **[616]**

Medical microbiology

2367 Gallo, Robert. *Virus Hunting: AIDS, Cancer, and the Human Retrovirus.* **1991, Basic Books $22.95 (0-465-09806-1).** An account of recent medical efforts to find the causes and cures of AIDS and cancer as written by a National Institutes of Health researcher. (Rev: BL 3/1/91; New Rep 4/22/91; NYTBR 3/24/91. Awards: LJ, 1991) **[616.01]**

2368 Radetsky, Peter. *Invisible Invaders: The Story of the Emerging Age of Viruses.* **1991, Little, Brown $19.95 (0-316-73216-8).** A study of the past, present, and future of viruses and their treatments. (Rev: BL 1/1/91; LJ 11/15/90; PW 11/9/90. Awards: ALA, 1992) **[616.01]**

First aid

2369 Auerbach, Paul S. *Medicine for the Outdoors: A Guide to Emergency Medical Procedures and First Aid.* **1986, Little, Brown $24.95 (0-316-05928-5); paper $12.95 (0-316-05929-3).** A first-aid manual covering the most common outdoors medical emergencies and their treatments. (Rev: BL 1/15/86; LJ 2/1/86) **[616.0252]**

Genetic diseases, pain

2370 Bishop, Jerry E., and Michael Waldholz. *Genome: The Story of the Most Astonishing Scientific Adventure of Our Time.* **1990, Simon & Schuster $21.45 (0-671-67094-8).** A study of the process and implications of the current scientific attempts to chart the functions of every human gene. (Rev: LJ 7/90; Natl Rev 8/6/90; NYTBR 8/12/90. Awards: ALA, 1990; LJ, 1990) **[616.04]**

2371 Milunsky, Aubrey. *Choices, Not Chances: Controlling Your Genetic Heritage.* **1989, Little, Brown $22.50 (0-316-57423-6).** A guide to hereditary diseases and options parents considering childbirth should take into account. (Rev: BL 2/1/89; LJ 2/15/89) **[616.04]**

2372 Sternbach, Richard A. *Mastering Pain: A Twelve-Step Program for Coping with Chronic Pain.* **1987, Putnam $18.95 (0-399-13237-6); Ballantine paper $3.95 (0-345-35428-1).** A program for living with chronic pain designed by the director of California's Scripps Clinic Pain Treatment Center. (Rev: BL 4/1/87; LJ 5/15/87) **[616.04]**

2373 Wingerson, Lois. *Mapping Our Genes: Genome Project and the Future of Medicine.* **1990, Dutton $19.95 (0-525-24877-3).** A study of gene-mapping and its implications for the future diagnosis and treatment of genetically transmitted diseases. (Rev: BL 6/1/90; LJ 6/1/90; NYTBR 9/2/90)   **[616.04]**

Pathology

2374 Dwyer, John M. *Body at War: The Miracle of the Immune System.* **1989, NAL $18.95 (0-453-00646-9); paper $4.95 (0-451-62812-8).** An introduction to the immune system of the human body for the layperson. "Dwyer's humane, authoritative, accessible work is a major accomplishment."—PW (Rev: LJ 2/1/89; PW 2/17/89)   **[616.07]**

2375 Gonzalez-Crussi, F. *Notes of an Anatomist.* **1985, Harcourt $12.95 (0-15-167285-7); paper $4.95 (0-15-667430-0).** Essays by a Chicago pathologist on his work and other subjects of life and death. (Rev: BL 5/15/85; NYTBR 7/7/85; PW 4/19/85)   **[616.07]**

2376 Medawar, Jean. *Very Dedicated Preference: Life with Peter Medawar.* **1990, Norton $19.95 (0-393-02820-8).** Remembrances of the late immunologist written by his widow. (Rev: BL 6/1/90; LJ 6/1/90; PW 5/4/90)   **[616.07]**

2377 Sobel, David S., and Tom Ferguson. *People's Book of Medical Tests.* **1985, Summit paper $14.95 (0-671-55377-1).** An overview of 200 medical tests and what they mean. "An important purchase for every public library."—BL (Rev: BL 10/1/85; LJ 9/1/85)   **[616.07]**

Psychosomatic medicine

2378 Baur, Susan. *Hypochondria: Woeful Imaginings.* **1988, Univ. of California Pr. $19.95 (0-520-06107-1); paper $9.95 (0-520-06751-7).** A study of the causes and treatments of hypochondria. (Rev: LJ 4/15/88; NYTBR 3/27/88; PW 3/18/88)   **[616.08]**

2379 Cousins, Norman. *Head First: The Biology of Hope and the Healing Power of the Human Spirit.* **1989, Dutton $19.95 (0-525-24805-6); paper $9.95 (0-14-013965-6).** The author of *Anatomy of an Illness* reveals the role positive mental outlooks play in the healing of the human body. "An important and necessary purchase for medical, academic and public libraries."—LJ (Rev: BL 9/1/89; LJ 10/1/89; PW 8/25/89)   **[616.08]**

Diseases of the cardiovascular system

2380 Gordon, Neil F., and Larry W. Gibbons. *Cooper Clinic Cardiac Rehabilitation Program: Featuring the Unique Heart Points System.* **1990, Simon & Schuster $22.45 (0-671-68260-1).** A guide to recovery from heart disease and surgery by staff members of the Dallas clinic. (Rev: BL 4/15/90; LJ 4/1/90)   **[616.1]**

2381 Horovitz, Emmanuel. *Cholesterol Control Made Easy: How to Lower Your Cholesterol for a Healthier Heart.* **1990, Health Trend $19.95 (0-9619329-4-5).** An examination of the relationship between cholesterol and heart disease with suggestions on how to reduce cholesterol for a healthier life. (Rev: BL 4/1/90; LJ 8/90)   **[616.1]**

2382 Kwiterovich, Peter O., Jr. *Beyond Cholesterol: The Johns Hopkins Complete Guide for Avoiding Heart Disease.* **1989, Johns Hopkins $18.95 (0-8018-3828-2).** Recent case studies and research form the basis for this layman's guide to avoiding heart disease. "One of the most thorough, intelligent works on its subject for a lay audience ... a must."—BL (Rev: BL 10/15/89; LJ 10/15/89; PW 9/22/89)   **[616.1]**

2383 Legato, Marianne J., and Carol Colman. *Female Heart.* **1991, Prentice Hall $19.95 (0-13-321811-2).** A cardiac researcher's analysis of the dangers of heart disease for women. (Rev: LJ 9/1/91; PW 7/25/91)   **[616.1]**

2384 Moore, Thomas J. *Heart Failure: A Critical Inquiry into the Revolution in Heart Care.* **1989, Random $19.95 (0-394-56958-X); Simon & Schuster paper $10.95 (0-671-72444-4).** A critical examination of current treatments of heart disease and of information disseminated to the general public by experts in the field. (Rev: BL 9/15/89; LJ 9/15/89)   **[616.1]**

2385 Pantano, James A. *Living with Angina: A Practical Guide to Dealing with Coronary Artery Disease and Your Doctor.* **1990, Harper & Row $17.95 (0-06-016240-6).** A cardiologist's guide to the control of the chest pain associated with heart disease. (Rev: BL 1/15/90; LJ 2/15/90; PW 1/26/90)   **[616.1]**

2386 Piscatella, Joseph. *Choices for a Healthy Heart.* **1987, Workman paper $15.95 (0-89480-138-4).** A guide to the prevention of heart disease through positive life-style changes. (Rev: BL 1/15/88; LJ 3/1/88)   **[616.1]**

2387 Rothfeder, Jeffrey. *Heart Rhythms: Breakthrough Treatments for Cardiac Arrhythmia—The Silent Killer of 400,000 Americans Each Year.* **1989, Little, Brown $17.95 (0-316-75785-3).** A program to detect and treat the problem of cardiac arrhythmia. "An excellent account of a lethal disease."—LJ (Rev: BL 12/15/88; LJ 2/1/89; PW 11/18/88)   **[616.1]**

2388 Sorrentino, Sandy, and Carl Hausman. *Coping with High Blood Pressure.* **1986, Dembner Books $16.95 (0-934878-76-5); $9.95 paper (0-942637-25-9).** A guide to controlling hypertension through diet, exercise, and stress management. (Rev: BL 10/1/86; LJ 10/15/86)   **[616.1]**

2389 Stone, John. *In the Country of Hearts: Journeys in the Art of Medicine.* **1990, Delacorte $17.95 (0-385-30169-3).** Memoirs of a Georgia cardiologist reviewing his quarter-century career in medicine. (Rev: BL 8/90; LJ 7/90; PW 7/6/90)   **[616.1]**

Bronchial asthma

2390 Stevens, Maryann. *Breathing Easy: A Parent's Guide to Dealing with Your Child's Asthma.* **1991,**

Prentice Hall paper $9.95 (0-13-083692-3). A guide-book for parents raising an asthmatic child that offers guidelines for preventing attacks as well as programs and organizations designed to help both family and child deal with the disorder. (REV: BL 2/1/91; LJ 2/15/91) **[616.238]**

2391 Weinstein, Allan M. *Asthma: A Complete Guide to Self-Management of Asthma and Allergies for Patients and Their Families.* 1987, McGraw-Hill $17.95 (0-07-069-058-8); Fawcett paper $4.95 (0-449-21562-8). A guide to the causes and treatment of asthma and allergies designed as a self-help guide for sufferers. (REV: BL 12/15/88; LJ 12/86) **[616.238]**

2392 Young, Stuart H., Susan A. Shulman, and Martin D. Shulman. *Asthma Handbook: A Complete Guide for Patients and Their Families.* 1989, Bantam paper $9.95 (0-553-34712-8). A manual focusing on asthma and its treatment. (REV: BL 1/1/85; LJ 2/1/85) **[616.238]**

Diseases of the lungs

2393 Haas, François, and Sheila Sperber Hass. *Chronic Bronchitis and Emphysema Handbook.* 1990, Wiley paper $12.95 (0-471-62263-X). A guide to the diagnosis, care, and treatment of two common respiratory ailments. (REV: BL 6/1/90; LJ 7/90) **[616.24]**

Diseases of the digestive system

2394 Carper, Steve. *No Milk Today: How to Live with Lactose Intolerance.* 1986, Simon & Schuster $15.95 (0-671-62020-7). A primer regarding lactose intolerance with suggested dietary regimens for those suffering from the lack of the enzyme necessary for the digestion of dairy products. (REV: BL 6/15/86; LJ 7/86) **[616.3]**

Diabetes mellitus

2395 Biermann, June, and Barbara Toohey. *Diabetic's Book: All Your Questions Answered.* 1990, J. P. Tarcher paper $10.95 (0-87477-552-3). An overview of the care and treatment of Type I and Type II diabetes. (REV: BL 2/1/90; LJ 3/1/90) **[616.462]**

2396 Edelwich, Jerry, and Archie Brodsky. *Diabetes: Caring for Your Emotions as Well as Your Health.* 1986, Addison Wesley $17.95 (0-201-10609-4); paper $16.95 (0-201-10608-6). A guide to the care of emotional problems that may accompany diabetes. (REV: BL 12/15/86; LJ 12/86) **[616.462]**

Diseases of the integument, hair, nails

2397 Siegel, Mary Ellen. *Safe in the Sun: Your Skin Survival Guide for the 1990s.* 1990, Walker $21.95 (0-8027-1100-6); paper $14.95 (0-8027-7290-0). A guide to the harmful effects of sun exposure to the human body with preventative measures to avoid possible risks. (REV: BL 5/15/90; LJ 5/1/90; PW 4/20/90) **[616.5]**

Shingles (Herpes zoster)

2398 Thomsen, Thomas Carl. *Shingles.* 1990, Cross River Pr. $17.95 (0-945288-01-8). An overview of the symptoms and treatment of shingles based on the author's experiences suffering from the illness. (REV: BL 4/15/90; LJ 11/1/90) **[616.522]**

Diseases of bladder and urethra

2399 Chalker, Rebecca, and Kristene F. Whitmore. *Overcoming Bladder Disorders.* 1990, Harper & Row $19.95 (0-06-016277-5); paper $9.95 (0-06-092083-1). Information on the care and treatment of bladder problems. (REV: BL 5/15/90; LJ 5/1/90) **[616.62]**

Cystitis

2400 Gillespie, Larrian. *You Don't Have to Live with Cystitis: A Woman Urologist Tells How to Avoid It—What to Do about It.* 1986, Rawson $19.95 (0-89256-302-8); Avon paper $7.95 (0-380-70486-2). A urologist's guide to the care and treatment of bladder inflammation. (REV: BL 10/15/86; LJ 12/86) **[616.623]**

Impotence and infertility

2401 Berger, Gary S. *Couple's Guide to Fertility: How New Medical Advances Can Help You Have a Baby.* 1989, Doubleday $22.95 (0-385-24546-7); paper $14.95 (0-385-26390-2). An overview of current reproductive techniques available to assist couples having fertility problems. (REV: BL 11/1/89; LJ 11/15/89) **[616.692]**

Diseases of the musculoskeletal system

2402 Heaney, Robert, and Janet Barger-Lux. *Calcium and Common Sense: How to Have Strong Bones All Your Life.* 1988, Doubleday paper $16.95. An examination of calcium and its role in human health. (REV: BL 3/15/88; LJ 6/15/88) **[616.7]**

Arthritis

2403 Arthritis Foundation. *Understanding Arthritis: What It Is, How It's Treated, How to Cope with It.* Ed. by Irving Kushner. 1985, Macmillan $18.95 (0-684-18199-1); paper $10.95 (0-684-18736-1). An overview of the diagnosis, care, and treatment of arthritis. (REV: BL 1/1/85; LJ 2/1/85) **[616.722]**

2404 Davidson, Paul. *Are You Sure It's Arthritis? A Guide to Soft-Tissue Rheumatism.* 1985, Macmillan $15.95 (0-02-529770-8); NAL paper $4.95 (0-451-15101-1). A guide to the diagnosis and treatment of soft-tissue rheumatism, whose symptoms are similar to those of arthritis but often easier to treat effectively. (REV: BL 11/15/85; LJ 11/15/85) **[616.722]**

2405 Gach, Michael Reed. *Arthritis Relief at Your Fingertips: The Complete Self-Care Guide to Easing Aches and Pains without Drugs.* 1989, Warner $19.95 (0-446-51474-8); paper $14.95 (0-446-39156-5). A presentation of acupressure techniques for the relief of pain as practiced at the author's acupressure institute in California. (REV: BL 2/1/89; LJ 2/15/89; PW 1/20/89)   **[616.722]**

2406   Kantrowitz, Fred G. *Taking Control of Arthritis: A Noted Doctor Tells You All You Need to Know to Triumph.* 1990, HarperCollins $19.95 (0-06-016136-1). A self-help guide to the diagnosis and treatment of the many forms of arthritis. (REV: BL 9/15/90; LJ 11/1/90)   **[616.722]**

Diseases of connective tissue

2407   Davidson, Paul. *Chronic Muscle Pain Syndrome: Understanding and Treating Fibrositis.* 1990, Random $17.95 (0-394-56860-5); Berkley paper $4.95 (0-425-12775-3). An overview of the symptoms and treatment of fibrositis, a stress-related muscular complaint. (REV: BL 1/15/90; LJ 11/1/90)   **[616.77]**

Diseases of the nervous system and mental disorders

2408   Bettelheim, Bruno. *Home for the Heart.* 1985, Univ. of Chicago Pr. paper $14.95 (0-226-04439-4). Bettelheim discusses his 30 years of work with mentally ill children, and lays forth his suggestions on how mental facilities should be designed and operated. (REV: LJ 2/1/74; Natl Rev 5/10/74; NYTBR 3/17/74)   **[616.8]**

2409   Cohen, Donna, and Carl Eisdorfer. *Loss of Self: A Family Resource for the Care of Alzheimer's Disease and Related Disorders.* 1986, Norton $19.95 (0-393-02263-3); NAL paper $9.95 (0-452-25946-0). A guide for families and friends to the care and treatment of Alzheimer's patients. (REV: Choice 7–8/86; LJ 3/1/86; NYTBR 3/23/86)   **[616.8]**

2410   Ferguson, Sarah A. *A Guard Within.* 1988, Pantheon paper $7.95 (0-394-75834-X). Journals and writings concerning the author's analyst and her struggle to continue living following his death. (REV: LJ 4/1/74; NYTBR 3/31/74; TLS 11/23/73)   **[616.8]**

2411   Gardner, Howard. *Shattered Mind: The Person after Brain Damage.* 1976, Random paper $7.95 (0-394-71946-8). A study of behavior and symptomatic problems prevalent in brain damaged individuals. "An unprecedented and impressive accomplishment in presenting in clear and understandable terms a field of tremendous complexity."—NYTBR (REV: LJ 5/1/75; NYTBR 3/2/75; PW 12/2/74. AWARDS: ALA, 1975)   **[616.8]**

2412   Heller, Joseph, and Speed Vogel. *No Laughing Matter.* 1986, Putnam $18.95 (0-399-13086-1); Avon paper $4.95 (0-380-70267-3). The American novelist recounts his affliction with Guillain-Barre syndrome and his eventual recovery from the disease. (REV: BL 12/15/85; LJ 5/1/86; NYTBR 2/16/86)   **[616.8]**

2413   Jonas, Gerald. *Stuttering: The Disorder of Many Theories.* 1977, Farrar paper $2.95 (0-374-51429-1). A look at the theories on why people stutter, a historical survey of treatment of the condition, and its psychological and social ramifications by a former sufferer. (REV: BL 12/1/77; Choice 3/78; LJ 10/1/77)   **[616.8]**

2414   Klawans, Harold L. *Newton's Madness: Further Tales of Clinical Neurology.* 1990, Harper & Row $17.95 (0-06-016256-2). Twenty-two case studies of neurological patients and their disorders related by a Rush University professor. (REV: Choice 10/90; NYTBR 4/8/90; PW 4/13/90)   **[616.8]**

2415   Klawans, Harold L. *Toscanini's Fumble: And Other Tales of Clinical Neurology.* 1989, Bantam paper $8.95 (0-553-34662-8). Case studies of brain disorders and their symptoms as described by a neurologist. "Lively reading . . . vivid and moving."—NYTBR (REV: BL 3/15/88; NYTBR 6/19/88; PW 4/1/88)   **[616.8]**

2416   McGoon, Dwight C. *Parkinson's Handbook.* 1990, Norton $18.95 (0-393-02880-1). An overview of Parkinson's disease written by a former surgeon now suffering from the ailment. (REV: BL 9/15/90; LJ 9/15/90)   **[616.8]**

2417   Mack, John E., and Holly Hickler. *Vivienne: The Life and Suicide of an Adolescent Girl.* 1982, NAL paper $4.95 (0-451-62664-8). An account of a teenager's life and suicide drawing heavily on the young woman's personal writings. (REV: BL 9/15/81; LJ 10/15/81; PW 9/11/81)   **[616.8]**

2418   Noonan, David. *Neuro: Life on the Front Lines of Brain Surgery and Neurological Medicine.* 1989, Simon & Schuster $18.95 (0-671-49392-2); Ivy Books paper $4.95 (0-8041-0598-7). An overview of our current understanding of the brain and nervous system and of the medical procedures performed upon it. (REV: BL 3/1/89; LJ 3/1/89; PW 1/20/89)   **[616.8]**

2419   Parker, Beulah. *A Mingled Yarn: Chronicle of a Troubled Family.* 1972, Yale Univ. Pr. $32.50 (0-300-01568-2); paper $13.95 (0-300-02292-1). A family genealogical history is traced in an effort to show how one of its members could have developed schizophrenia. (REV: Choice 10/73; LJ 11/15/72; NYTBR 10/8/72)   **[616.8]**

2420   Sacks, Oliver. *Man Who Mistook His Wife for a Hat and Other Clinical Tales.* 1990, Harper & Row paper $9.95 (0-06-097079-0). A neurologist's collection of unusual case histories of people with brain disorders. "He provides literary pleasure as well as keen scientific interest."—BL (REV: BL 2/1/86; LJ 2/15/86; NYTBR 3/2/86. AWARDS: NYTBR, 1986)**[616.8]**

Cerebrovascular diseases

2421   Lavin, John H. *Stroke: From Crisis to Victory—A Family Guide.* 1985, Watts $16.95 (0-531-09787-0). The case history of a stroke victim and his treatment forms the basis of an overview of the health problem and preventative measures to reduce the risk of becoming a victim. (REV: BL 4/1/85; LJ 3/15/85; PW 3/18/85)   **[616.81]**

Multiple sclerosis

2422   Mairs, Nancy. *Carnal Acts: Essays.* 1990, HarperCollins $19.95 (0-06-016494-8). Selected essays by an Arizona writer about the effect multiple sclerosis has had on her life. (Rev: BL 8/90; LJ 9/1/90; NYTBR 9/2/90)   **[616.834]**

2423 Rosner, Louis J., and Shelley Ross. *Multiple Sclerosis.* **1987, Prentice Hall paper $19.95 (0-13-604695-9).** An overview of the causes, symptoms, and treatments of multiple sclerosis. (Rev: BL 10/1/87; LJ 11/1/87; PW 9/18/87)   **[616.834]**

Poliomyelitis

2424 Smith, Jane S. *Patenting the Sun: Polio, the Salk Vaccine, and the Children of the Baby Boom.* **1990, Morrow $22.95 (0-688-09494-5).** A history of the disease of polymyelitis and the development of the vaccine that stopped it as a threat to human health. (Rev: LJ 4/15/90; NYTBR 5/6/90; New Yorker 6/18/90)   **[616.835]**

Manifestations of neurological diseases and mental disorders

2425 Hauri, Peter, and Shirley Linde. *No More Sleepless Nights: The Complete Program for Ending Insomnia.* **1990, Wiley $19.95 (0-471-40770-9).** A guide to the evaluation and treatment of sleep disorders. (Rev: BL 5/1/90; LJ 5/1/90; PW 4/20/90)   **[616.84]**

Miscellaneous diseases of the nervous system and mental disorders

2426 Dowling, Colette. *You Mean I Don't Have to Feel This Way? New Help for Depression, Anxiety and Addiction.* **1992, Scribner $19.95 (0-684-19257-8).** A self-help guide examining the results of recent studies into biochemistry and its effects on the brain and psychological states. (Rev: BL 12/15/91; LJ 1/92)   **[616.85]**

2427 Feiden, Karyn. *Hope and Help for Chronic Fatigue Syndrome: The Official Guide of the CPS/CFIDS Network.* **1990, Prentice Hall $17.95 (0-13-809708-9).** A study of the symptoms and treatment of chronic fatigue syndrome. (Rev: BL 1/15/90; LJ 1/90)   **[616.85]**

2428 Gabriel, Richard A. *No More Heroes: Madness and Psychiatry in War.* **1987, Hill & Wang $17.95 (0-8090-7389-7).** An analysis of the past and future effects of combat upon the mental condition of soldiers. (Rev: LJ 5/1/87; Natl Rev 4/10/87; PW 2/27/87)   **[616.85]**

2429 Henry, Jules. *Pathways to Madness.* **1973, Random paper $10.95 (0-394-71882-8).** An anthropologist's study of five families with one psychotic child in each, and the family dynamics within each of those families. (Rev: Choice 11/72; LJ 3/1/72; New Rep 3/4/72)   **[616.85]**

2430 Rapoport, Judith L. *Boy Who Couldn't Stop Washing: The Experience and Treatment of Obsessive-Compulsive Disorders.* **1989, Dutton $18.95 (0-525-24708-4); paper $5.99 (0-451-17202-7).** A child psychiatrist presents an overview of obsessive-compulsive disorders. "Excellent . . . highly readable and free of jargon."—PW (Rev: BL 1/15/89; NYTBR 2/26/89; PW 11/18/88)   **[616.85]**

Dual and multiple personalities

2431 Keyes, Daniel. *Minds of Billy Milligan.* **1982, Bantam paper $4.50 (0-553-26381-1).** An examination of the case of Billy Milligan who was cleared of rape charges due to his suffering from multiple personalities. (Rev: BL 10/15/81; LJ 10/1/81; NYTBR 11/15/81)   **[616.85236]**

2432 Sizemore, Chris Costner. *A Mind of My Own: The Woman Who Was Known as Eve Tells the Story of Her Triumph Over Multiple Personality Disorder.* **1989, Morrow $19.95 (0-688-08199-1).** An autobiography of the woman whose battles with multiple personality disorder became the basis for the popular film *The Three Faces of Eve*. (Rev: LJ 8/89; NYTBR 11/12/89; PW 7/21/89)   **[616.85236]**

Anorexia nervosa

2433 Brumberg, Joan. *Fasting Girls: The Emergence of Anorexia Nervosa as a Modern Disease.* **1988, Harvard Univ. Pr. $25.00 (0-674-29501-3); NAL paper $9.95 (0-452-26327-1).** A history of anorexia nervosa from its first identification in Victorian England to the present day examining the social and cultural reasons for the prevalence of the disease. (Rev: Atl 7/88; BL 3/15/88; LJ 3/15/88)   **[616.85262]**

2434 Orbach, Susie. *Hunger Strike: The Anorectic's Struggle as a Metaphor for Our Age.* **1988, Avon paper $4.50 (0-380-70393-9).** An analysis of the social causes of anorexia nervosa by the author of *Fat Is a Feminist Issue*. (Rev: BL 2/15/86; LJ 2/15/86; TLS 4/25/86)   **[616.85262]**

Depressive neuroses

2435 Styron, William. *Darkness Visible: A Memoir of Madness.* **1990, Random $15.95 (0-394-58888-6).** The American novelist discusses his bouts with depression and its effects upon his life. (Rev: BL 7/90; LJ 8/90; Time 9/3/90)   **[616.8527]**

Epilepsy

2436 Richard, Adrienne. *Epilepsy: A New Approach.* **1990, Prentice Hall paper $17.45 (0-13-551847-4).** An overview of the current knowledge and treatment of epilepsy. (Rev: BL 6/15/90; LJ 6/1/90)   **[616.853]**

Migraine

2437 Lance, James W. *Migraine and Other Headaches: A Renowned Physician's Guide to Diagnosis and Effective Treatment.* **1986, Macmillan paper $10.95 (0-684-18654-3).** A neurologist's guide to the diagnosis, care, and treatment of a variety of types of headaches. (Rev: BL 4/15/86; LJ 4/15/86)   **[616.857]**

Substance abuse

2438 Katz, Stan J., and Aimee E. Liu. *Codependency Conspiracy: What's Wrong with Recovery Programs, What's Right about Helping Yourself.* **1991, Warner $18.95 (0-446-51595-7).** A critical view of current codependency recovery programs. (REV: BL 2/15/91; LJ 3/1/91; PW 1/18/91) **[616.86]**

2439 Ketcham, Katherine, and Ginny L. Gustafson. *Living on the Edge: A Guide to Intervention for Families with Drug and Alcohol Problems.* 1989, Bantam paper $7.95 (0-553-34606-7). A guide to crisis intervention techniques for families who have members with advanced drug or alcohol problems. (REV: BL 3/1/89; LJ 3/15/89) **[616.86]**

2440 Siegel, Ronald K. *Intoxication: Life in Pursuit of Artificial Paradise.* 1989, Simon & Schuster $19.95 (0-525-24764-5); paper $9.95 (0-671-69192-9). The author presents his theory that the need for intoxication is a human drive comparable to that for sex, food, and water. (REV: BL 5/1/89; LJ 4/15/89) **[616.86]**

Alcohol

2441 Mueller, L. Ann, and Katherine Ketcham. *Recovering: How to Get and Stay Sober.* 1987, Bantam paper $9.95 (0-553-34303-3). A manual regarding the development, detection, and treatment of alcoholism. "An excellent guide to a pervasive problem."—BL (REV: BL 4/1/87; LJ 4/15/87) **[616.861]**

Cocaine

2442 Weiss, Roger D., and Steven M. Mirin. *Cocaine.* 1986, American Psychiatric $19.50 (0-88048-216-8); Ballantine paper $6.95 (0-345-35135-5). An overview of the effects and history of cocaine use. (REV: LJ 2/1/87; PW 12/4/87) **[616.8647]**

Tobacco

2443 Sussman, Les, and Sally Bordwell. *An Ex-Smoker's Survival Guide: Positive Steps to a Slim, Smoke-Free Life.* 1986, McGraw-Hill paper $12.95 (0-07-062344-9). A step-by-step guide to cutting down and quitting smoking. "Well-written and sensitive . . . destined to be a classic in its field."—BL (REV: BL 7/86; LJ 7/86) **[616.865]**

Mental disorders

2444 Baur, Susan. *Dinosaur Man: Tales of Madness and Enchantment from the Back Ward.* 1991, HarperCollins $19.95 (0-06-016538-3). A psychologist recounts her experiences treating people with schizophrenia. (REV: BL 6/1/91; LJ 6/15/91; PW 5/10/91) **[616.89]**

2445 Beisser, Arnold. *Flying Without Wings: Personal Reflections on Loss, Disability and Healing.* 1989, Doubleday $15.95 (0-385-24770-2); Bantam paper $7.95 (0-553-34868-X). Memoirs of a doctor who became paralyzed following the contraction of polio in 1950. (REV: LJ 2/1/89; PW 11/25/88) **[616.89]**

2446 Berger, Diane, and Lisa Berger. *We Heard the Angels of Madness: One Family's Struggle with Manic Depression.* 1990, Morrow $19.95 (0-688-09178-4). A mother and daughter discuss their family's experiences while dealing with the manic

depression of a loved one. (REV: BL 2/15/91; LJ 4/1/91; PW 2/8/91) **[616.89]**

2447 Borysenko, Jean. *Minding the Body, Mending the Mind.* 1987, Addison Wesley $14.95 (0-201-10707-4); Bantam paper $9.95 (0-553-34556-7). A biologist examines the relationship between psychological and physiological states of well-being. (REV: BL 5/15/87; LJ 8/87; PW 5/8/87) **[616.89]**

2448 Chesler, Phyllis. *Women and Madness.* 1989, Harcourt paper $9.95 (0-15-698295-1). How social demands restrict women's roles in our society, and how deviance from expected behavior by women is often categorized as madness. (REV: BL 2/1/73; LJ 10/15/72; NYTBR 12/31/72) **[616.89]**

2449 Dollinger, Malin. *Everyone's Guide to Cancer Therapy: How Cancer Is Diagnosed, Treated, and Managed on a Day-to-Day Basis.* 1991, Andrews & McMeel $29.95 (0-8362-2418-3); paper $19.95 (0-8362-2417-5). A layperson's guide to cancer and its treatments. "Stands out . . . as a uniquely comprehensive, thorough source of up-to-date information."—LJ (REV: BL 5/15/91; LJ 5/15/91; PW 4/26/91) **[616.89]**

2450 Ehrenberg, Otto, and Miriam Ehrenberg. *Psychotherapy Maze: A Consumer's Guide to Getting In and Out of Therapy.* 1986, Armson $17.95 (0-87668-959-4). A guide by two psychologists on what to expect when undergoing therapy and how to get the most out of it. "An unfailingly intelligent, accessible and practical user's guide."—BL (REV: BL 7/86; LJ 8/86) **[616.89]**

2451 Freeman, Lucy. *Beloved Prison: A Journey into the Unknown Self.* 1989, St. Martin's $18.95 (0-312-02866-0); paper $10.95 (0-312-04265-5). An account of the author's life and how Freudian therapy and analysis helped free her from her past. (REV: BL 4/1/89; LJ 4/15/89) **[616.89]**

2452 Goodwin, Donald W. *Anxiety.* 1986, Oxford Univ. Pr. $21.95 (0-19-503665-4). A study of current psychological theories regarding human anxieties and phobias. (REV: LJ 12/85; TLS 5/16/86) **[616.89]**

2453 Harris, Amy Bjork, and Thomas A. Harris. *Staying OK.* 1986, Avon paper $4.95 (0-380-70130-8). A sequel to the authors' *I'm OK-You're OK* regarding transactional analysis and its applications. (REV: BL 1/15/85; LJ 3/1/85; TLS 7/19/85) **[616.89]**

2454 Havens, Leston. *A Safe Place: Laying the Groundwork of Psychotherapy.* 1989, Harvard Univ. Pr. $22.50 (0-674-00085-4); Ballantine paper $8.95 (0-345-37060-0). A presentation of the concepts and theories underlying the practice of psychotherapy. (REV: Choice 2/90; LJ 9/15/89; PW 7/28/89) **[616.89]**

2455 Israeloff, Roberta. *In Confidence.* 1990, Houghton $18.95 (0-395-47101-X). An account of the author's four years of psychotherapy. (REV: BL 2/15/90; Choice 5/90; NYTBR 4/8/90) **[616.89]**

2456 Lightfoot, Sara Lawrence. *Balm in Gilead: Journey of a Healer.* 1988, Addison Wesley $18.95 (0-201-09312-X); paper $9.95 (0-201-51807-4). A biogra-

phy of the author's mother, Margaret Morgan Lawrence, a pioneer African-American psychoanalyst. (Rev: CSM 1/23/89; New Rep 3/27/89; NYTBR 1/1/89)
[616.89]

2457 Malcolm, Janet. *Psychoanalysis: The Impossible Profession.* 1982, Random paper $8.95 (0-394-71034-7). The process and profession of psychoanalysis with a discussion of the theories and research in the field since Freud. "A model of eloquent, intelligent, skeptical journalism."—BL (Rev: BL 9/1/81; Newsweek 9/21/81; Time 9/28/81. Awards: Time, 1981)
[616.89]

2458 Masson, Jeffrey Moussaieff. *Against Therapy: Emotional Tyranny and the Myth of Psychological Healing.* 1988, Macmillan $18.95 (0-689-11929-1). Controversial work by a nonpracticing psychoanalyst attempting to show the worthlessness of psychotherapy. (Rev: LJ 6/15/88; PW 5/27/88; Time 8/22/88)
[616.89]

2459 Masson, Jeffrey Moussaieff. *Final Analysis: The Making and Unmaking of a Psychoanalyst.* 1990, Addison Wesley $18.95 (0-201-52368-X). An autobiography of the outspoken critic of psychoanalysis recalling his training and practice in the field. (Rev: BL 10/15/90; LJ 10/15/90; NYTBR 10/21/90)
[616.89]

2460 Millett, Kate. *Looney-Bin Trip.* 1990, Simon & Schuster $19.45 (0-671-67930-9). The author of *Sexual Politics* recounts her struggles against mental illness over the past decade. (Rev: BL 3/1/90; LJ 4/15/90; NYTBR 6/3/90)
[616.89]

2461 Perry, Helen S. *Psychiatrist of America: The Life of Harry Stack Sullivan.* 1982, Harvard Univ. Pr. $25.00 (0-674-72076-8); paper $12.50 (0-674-72077-6). A biography of the American psychiatrist known for his research into the effects of interpersonal relationships on human development. "Exceeds all expectations . . . an invaluable addition."—LJ (Rev: LJ 4/15/82; NYTBR 3/7/82; PW 1/22/82)
[616.89]

2462 Roazen, Paul. *Helene Deutsch: A Psychoanalyst's Life.* 1985, Simon & Schuster $19.95 (0-671-25028-0). A study of the life and work of the Freudian feminist psychoanalyst. (Rev: Choice 10/85; LJ 5/15/85; NYTBR 5/26/85)
[616.89]

2463 Rodman, F. Robert. *Keeping Hope Alive: On Becoming a Psychotherapist.* 1987, Harper & Row paper $7.95 (0-06-091388-6). A personal account of the training and practice of a psychotherapist. (Rev: Choice 7–8/86; LJ 3/1/86; NYTBR 3/23/86) **[616.89]**

2464 Seager, Stephen B. *Psychward: A Year Behind Locked Doors.* 1991, Putnam $21.95 (0-399-13608-8). An account of the author's experiences during a year of psychiatric training at Los Angeles County General Hospital. (Rev: BL 4/15/91; LJ 3/15/91; PW 2/8/91)
[616.89]

2465 Valenstein, Eliot S. *Great and Desperate Cures: The Rise and Decline of Psychosurgery and Other Radical Treatments for Mental Illness.* 1987, Basic Books paper $10.95 (0-465-02711-3). A

history of the practice of lobotomy and other surgeries to treat mental illness. (Rev: LJ 4/15/86; NYTBR 4/6/86; PW 3/21/86)
[616.89]

2466 Vonnegut, Mark. *Eden Express.* 1988, Dell paper $4.95 (0-440-20205-1). Autobiographical work by the son of novelist Kurt Vonnegut, Jr., describing his personal bout with schizophrenia. "A painfully honest document of a life in transition."—Time (Rev: Atl 10/75; NYTBR 10/26/75; Time 10/6/75. Awards: ALA, 1975)
[616.89]

2467 Wallace, Marjorie. *Silent Twins.* 1987, Ballantine paper $3.95 (0-345-34802-8). A study of two identical twins who developed a secret language only comprehensible to themselves and eventually chose a life of crime before being committed to a mental institution. (Rev: BL 10/1/86; NYTBR 10/19/86; TLS 2/28/86)
[616.89]

2468 Yalom, Irvin D. *Love's Executioner and Other Tales of Psychotherapy.* 1989, Basic Books $19.95 (0-465-03298-2); Harper & Row paper $9.95 (0-06-097334-X). A collection of psychiatric case studies by a professor of psychiatry at the Stanford University School of Medicine. (Rev: BL 6/15/89; LJ 8/89; NYTBR 9/3/89)
[616.89]

Bacterial and viral diseases

2469 Benzaia, Diana. *Protect Yourself from Lyme Disease.* 1989, Dell paper $4.50 (0-440-20437-2). A primer to the avoidance, detection, and treatment of the disease spread by tick bites. (Rev: LJ 8/89; PW 6/16/89)
[616.92]

Venereal diseases and zoonoses

2470 Jones, James H. *Bad Blood: The Tuskegee Syphilis Experiment.* 1981, Free Pr. $14.95 (0-02-916670-5); paper $8.95 (0-02-916690-X). The story of an untreated syphilis experiment conducted on 400 unknowing black men by the Public Health Service with the cooperation of the Tuskegee Institute from 1932 to 1972. "One cannot read it without repeatedly experiencing rage, shock, disbelief and finally, an overwhelming sorrow."—NYTBR (Rev: LJ 4/1/81; NYTBR 6/21/81; Newsweek 7/20/81. Awards: NYTBR, 1981)
[616.95]

Diseases of the immune system

2471 Orenstein, Neil S., and Sarah L. Orenstein. *Food Allergies: How to Tell If You Have Them, What to Do about Them If You Do.* 1988, Putnam paper $9.95 (0-399-51383-3). An introduction to the detection, causes, and treatments of food allergies. (Rev: BL 11/15/87; LJ 2/1/88)
[616.97]

AIDS

2472 Callaway, C. Wayne, and Catherine Whitney. *Surviving with AIDS: A Comprehensive Program of Nutritional Co-Therapy.* 1991, Little, Brown $14.45 (0-316-12467-2). An endocrinologist's guide to nutritional therapy designed to maintain the strength and health of AIDS patients. (Rev: LJ 7/91; PW 7/25/91)
[616.979]

2473 Kubler-Ross, Elizabeth. *AIDS: The Ultimate Challenge.* 1989, Macmillan $4.95 (0-02-059001-6). Collected writings by the author of *On Death and Dying* regarding the AIDS epidemic and its impact upon society. (Rev: BL 11/15/87; Choice 5/88; LJ 3/1/88) **[616.979]**

2474 Langone, John. *AIDS: The Facts.* 1988, Little, Brown paper $8.95 (0-316-51412-8). An overview of what is currently known about the AIDS disease. (Rev: LJ 3/1/89; NYTBR 4/10/88) **[616.979]**

2475 Masters, William H. *Crisis: Heterosexual Behavior in the Age of AIDS.* 1988, Grove-Weidenfeld $15.95 (0-8021-1049-5). The author of *Human Sexual Response* warns of the coming spread of AIDS throughout the heterosexual community. "The most cogent and cautious AIDS polemic to date."—BL (Rev: BL 4/1/88; LJ 6/1/88; Natl Rev 5/27/88) **[616.979]**

Tumors and miscellaneous communicable diseases

2476 Angier, Natalie. *Natural Obsessions: The Search for the Oncogene.* 1988, Houghton $19.95 (0-395-45370-4). The day-to-day operations of two teams of cancer researchers at MIT and New York's Cold Spring Harbor Laboratory are analyzed. (Rev: BL 6/1/88; LJ 8/88; NYTBR 7/10/88) **[616.99]**

2477 Barrett, Marvin. *Spare Days.* 1988, Morrow $16.95 (1-55710-006-3). A journal of the author's year of suffering and recovery from cancer and heart disease. (Rev: BL 4/15/88; NYTBR 7/3/88; PW 5/6/88) **[616.99]**

2478 Holleb, Arthur I., ed. *American Cancer Society's Complete Book of Cancer: Prevention, Detection, Diagnosis, Treatment, Rehabilitation, Cure.* 1986, Doubleday paper $24.95 (0-385-17847-6). A guide to differing types of cancer and their treatments produced under the auspices of the American Cancer Society. (Rev: BL 6/1/86; LJ 7/86) **[616.99]**

2479 Lerner, Gerda. *A Death of One's Own.* 1985, Univ. of Wisconsin Pr. paper $7.95 (0-299-10444-3). An account of the illness and death of the author's husband from a brain tumor. (Rev: LJ 7/78; NYTBR 8/6/78) **[616.99]**

2480 Radner, Gilda. *It's Always Something.* 1989, Simon & Schuster $18.95 (0-671-63868-8); Avon paper $4.95 (0-380-71072-2). An account of the comedienne's bout with ovarian cancer. (Rev: BL 5/15/89; LJ 6/15/89; NYTBR 6/25/89) **[616.99]**

Lung cancer

2481 Meyer, John A. *Lung Cancer Chronicles.* 1990, Rutgers Univ. Pr. $35.00 (0-8135-1492-4); paper $10.95 (0-8135-1493-2). A look at the medical, sociological, and economic costs of lung cancer and its treatment, with case studies of several of its victims. "A well-written, comprehensive, and interesting presentation."—Choice (Rev: Choice 10/90; LJ 4/15/90) **[616.99424]**

Breast cancer

2482 Butler, Sandra, and Barbara Rosenblum. *Cancer in Two Voices.* 1991, Spinsters/Aunt Lute paper $12.95 (0-933216-84-X). A chronicle of the illness and death of a woman from breast cancer, as told through the ailing woman's journal and the words of her surviving lover. (Rev: LJ 10/1/91; PW 9/20/91) **[616.99449]**

2483 Murcia, Andy, and Bob Stewart. *Man to Man: When the Woman You Love Has Breast Cancer.* 1989, St. Martin's $16.95 (0-312-02605-6); paper $10.95 (0-312-04347-3). A support guide for men whose wives or girlfriends have breast cancer. (Rev: BL 2/15/89; LJ 3/1/89) **[616.99449]**

2484 Rollin, Betty. *First, You Cry.* 1986, NAL paper $3.50 (0-451-14427-9). The author's description of her bout with breast cancer, and the medical and psychological ramifications of her mastectomy. (Rev: LJ 9/15/76; NYTBR 9/26/76; PW 7/12/76) **[616.99449]**

Tuberculosis

2485 Caldwell, Mark. *Last Crusade: The War on Consumption, 1872–1954.* 1988, Macmillan $22.50 (0-689-11810-4). A history of tuberculosis and its treatment in America focusing upon the disease's effects on the medical community and the search for a cure. (Rev: BL 2/15/88; LJ 4/1/88; PW 12/25/87) **[616.995]**

617　Surgery and related medical specialties

2486 Luria, A. R. *Man with a Shattered World: The History of a Brain Wound.* 1987, Harvard Univ. Pr. paper $7.95 (0-674-54625-3). The Russian psychologist gives an account of a brain-wounded soldier's struggle to regain mental functions. (Rev: Choice 9/73; LJ 4/1/73; Time 1/29/73) **[617]**

2487 Selzer, Richard. *Mortal Lessons: Notes on the Art of Surgery.* 1987, Simon & Schuster paper $7.95 (0-671-64102-6). Autobiographical essays concerning the life of a surgeon, surgery, and the human body. "At his best, Selzer invites comparison with the invaluable Loren Eiseley."—Edward Hoagland, NYTBR (Rev: Choice 5/77; NYTBR 1/9/77; Newsweek 1/24/77. Awards: ALA, 1977) **[617]**

Persons

2488 Selzer, Richard. *Confessions of a Knife.* 1987, Morrow paper $6.95 (0-688-06491-4). Twenty-four essays by a surgeon regarding his craft. (Rev: BL 9/15/79; LJ 9/1/79; Newsweek 9/3/79) **[617.092]**

2489 Selzer, Richard. *Taking the World in for Repairs.* 1987, Penguin paper $7.95 (0-14-010305-8). A collection of a dozen essays regarding the art and practice of medicine by the author of *Mortal Lessons.* (Rev: BL 9/1/86; LJ 12/86; PW 7/25/86) **[617.092]**

Cardiovascular system

2490 Kra, Siegfried. *Coronary Bypass Surgery: Who Needs It?* 1987, Norton paper $7.95 (0-393-

30449-3). A discussion of the practice of coronary bypass surgery and possible alternatives to the procedure. (Rᴇᴠ: BL 1/15/86; LJ 2/1/86) **[617.41]**

Nervous system

2491 Rainer, J. Kenyon. *First Do No Harm: Reflections on Becoming a Brain Surgeon.* 1987, Random $17.95 (0-394-55669-0). Memoirs of a brain surgeon regarding his private life, training, and professional development. (Rᴇᴠ: BL 4/15/87; LJ 5/15/87; NYTBR 4/5/87) **[617.48]**

2492 Shelton, Mark. *Working in a Very Small Place: The Making of a Neurosurgeon.* 1989, Norton $19.95 (0-393-02681-7); **Random paper $9.95** (0-679-72815-5). A study of the work of Peter Janetta, a Pittsburgh neurosurgeon, who pioneered new techniques of brain surgery and overcame medical politics to gain acceptance of his procedures. (Rᴇᴠ: BL 6/1/89; LJ 6/1/89; PW 4/28/89) **[617.48]**

Back

2493 Bean, Constance A. *Better Back Book: Simple Exercises for the Prevention and Care of Back Pain.* 1989, Morrow $17.95 (0-688-07915-6); **Greenwillow paper $7.95** (0-688-10003-1). A discussion of the causes of back pain with suggested exercises for its prevention and control. (Rᴇᴠ: BL 3/15/89; LJ 4/1/89; PW 3/17/89) **[617.56]**

2494 White, Augustus A. *Your Aching Back: A Doctor's Guide to Relief.* 1990, Simon & Schuster $21.95 (0-671-68933-9); **paper $9.95** (0-671-71000-1). An orthopedist's guide to preventing and controlling back pain. (Rᴇᴠ: LJ 8/90; PW 7/20/90) **[617.56]**

Ophthalmology

2495 Kelman, Charles D. *Through My Eyes: The Story of a Surgeon Who Took on the Medical World and Won.* 1985, Crown $14.95 (0-517-55600-6). The story of an opthalmologist who pioneered an innovative approach to cataract surgery and was ostracized within the medical community. (Rᴇᴠ: BL 4/1/85; LJ 4/15/85; PW 1/25/85) **[617.7]**

Cosmetic and restorative plastic surgery, transplantation of tissue and organs, implantation of artificial organs

2496 Gutkind, Lee. *Many Sleepless Nights: The World of Organ Transplants.* 1988, Norton $18.95 (0-393-02520-9); **Univ. of Pittsburgh Pr. paper $12.95** (0-8229-5905-4). The world of organ transplantation and the patients, doctors, and assistants who make the procedure possible. "A fascinating look at the emotional and physical complexities of a harrowing process."—BL (Rᴇᴠ: BL 6/15/88; LJ 9/1/88; PW 5/13/88) **[617.95]**

618 Gynecology and other medical specialties

Gynecology

2497 Gillespie, Clark. *Hormones, Hot Flashes and Mood Swings: Living Through the Ups and Downs of Menopause.* 1989, Harper & Row $16.95 (0-06-055162-3); **paper $8.95** (0-06-096355-7). A gynecologist's introduction to menopause and its physical and psychological effects upon the female body. (Rᴇᴠ: BL 6/1/89; LJ 7/89; PW 6/16/89) **[618.1]**

2498 Goldfarb, Herbert A., and Judith Grief. *No-Hysterectomy Option: Your Body—Your Choice.* 1990, Wiley $24.95 (0-471-53232-0); **paper $12.95** (0-471-51615-5). A gynecologist's overview of the options of patients facing hysterectomies. (Rᴇᴠ: BL 11/15/90; LJ 11/1/90) **[618.1]**

2499 Perloe, Mark, and Linda G. Christie. *Miracle Babies and Other Happy Endings for Couples with Fertility Problems.* 1987, Penguin paper $7.95. A guide to the problems and solutions facing couples dealing with infertility. (Rᴇᴠ: BL 8/86; LJ 12/86) **[618.1]**

2500 Sher, Geoffrey, Virginia A. Marriage, and Jean Stoess. *In-Vitro Fertilization.* 1989, McGraw-Hill $18.95 (0-07-056761-1). An introduction to the processes and decisions facing couples who want children and are considering in-vitro fertilization. (Rᴇᴠ: BL 2/15/89; LJ 4/1/89) **[618.1]**

2501 Utian, Wulf H., and Ruth S. Jacobowitz. *Managing Your Menopause.* 1990, Prentice Hall paper $18.45 (0-13-582362-5). A guide to menopausal symptoms and treatments. (Rᴇᴠ: BL 6/15/90; LJ 7/90; PW 6/22/90) **[618.1]**

Diseases of the breast

2502 Gross, Amy, and Dee Ito. *Women Talk about Breast Surgery from Diagnosis to Recovery.* 1990, Crown $21.95 (0-517-56353-3). Collected interviews with women and physicians regarding the diagnosis and treatment of breast problems. (Rᴇᴠ: BL 6/1/90; LJ 6/1/90; PW 6/22/90. Awards: PW, 1990) **[618.19]**

2503 Halbert, David S. *Your Breast and You.* 1986, Askon $14.95 (0-931609-00-3). A guide to the preventative care of the female breast. (Rᴇᴠ: BL 12/15/85; LJ 1/86) **[618.19]**

2504 Love, Susan M., and Karen Lindsey. *Dr. Susan Love's Breast Book.* 1990, Addison Wesley $18.95 (0-201-09665-X). An overview of the female breast and its care. "This thoughtful, candid book is highly recommended for virtually all libraries."—BL (Rᴇᴠ: BL 6/1/90; LJ 11/1/90) **[618.19]**

Obstetrics

2505 De Lyser, Femmy. *Jane Fonda's New Pregnancy Workout and Total Birth Program.* 1989, Simon & Schuster $24.95 (0-671-66763-7). A guide to using exercise for a healthy pregnancy with advice on other concerns and decisions facing expectant mothers. (Rᴇᴠ: BL 10/1/89; LJ 10/1/89; PW 10/20/89) **[618.2]**

2506 Fay, Francesca C., and Kathy S. Smith. *Childbearing after 35: The Risks and the Rewards.* 1985, Balsam Pr. $24.95 (0-917439-08-2); **paper $12.95** (0-917439-05-8). A guide to pregnancy and childbirth for women from ages 35 to 39. (Rev: BL 9/1/85; LJ 10/1/85) **[618.2]**

2507 Kaiser, Grace H. *Dr. Frau.* **1986, Good Books $14.95 (0-934672-34-2); paper $8.95 (0-934672-71-7).** An account of the author's three decades as a physician serving Pennsylvania Mennonite and Amish communities. (Rev: BL 9/1/86; LJ 10/1/86) **[618.2]**

2508 Kitzinger, Sheila. *Birth over Thirty.* **1985, Penguin paper $6.95 (0-14-007610-7).** An overview of the physical and social issues facing women over 30 contemplating childbirth. (Rev: BL 2/1/85; PW 1/4/85) **[618.2]**

2509 Kitzinger, Sheila. *Complete Book of Pregnancy and Childbirth.* **1989, Knopf $18.95 (0-394-58011-7).** A study of life from conception to the first days following childbirth. "A very supportive, beautiful book and most certainly a classic-to-be."—BL (Rev: BL 2/15/81; LJ 3/1/81) **[618.2]**

2510 Kitzinger, Sheila. *Your Baby, Your Way: Making Pregnancy Decisions and Birth Plans.* **1987, Pantheon $19.95 (0-394-54573-7); paper $12.95 (0-394-75249-X).** An overview of the choices facing expectant mothers regarding their fetus and the birthing process. (Rev: BL 6/1/87; LJ 7/87) **[618.2]**

2511 Korte, Diana, and Roberta A. Scaer. *A Good Birth, a Safe Birth.* **1990, Bantam paper $4.95 (0-553-28612-9).** A survey of current practices and options for childbirth. (Rev: BL 3/15/84; LJ 4/1/84; PW 2/10/84) **[618.2]**

2512 Logan, Onnie Lee, and Katherine Clark. *Motherwit: An Alabama Midwife's Story.* **1989, Dutton $16.95 (0-525-24751-3).** Logan, a midwife for 40 years, recounts her experiences and knowledge in her own words as told to Katherine Clark. "Oral history doesn't come any better than this."—BL (Rev: BL 8/89; LJ 8/89; NYTBR 9/10/89) **[618.2]**

2513 Samuels, Mike, and Nancy Samuels. *Well-Pregnancy Book.* **1986, Summit paper $16.95 (0-671-46080-3).** An illustrated guide to good health during pregnancy for mother and fetus. (Rev: BL 10/1/85; LJ 2/15/86; PW 9/6/85) **[618.2]**

Multiple pregnancy and childbirth

2514 Alexander, Terry Pink. *Make Room for Twins.* **1987, Bantam paper $9.95 (0-553-34207-X).** A guide for parents to the care, rearing, and special considerations of multiple births. (Rev: BL 5/15/87; LJ 8/87) **[618.25]**

Diseases and other complications of pregnancy

2515 Abrams, Richard S. *Will It Hurt the Baby? The Safe Use of Medications during Pregnancy and Breastfeeding.* **1990, Addison Wesley paper $14.95 (0-201-51809-0).** A guide to the use and effects of medication on the fetus and the breastfeeding newborn. (Rev: BL 7/90; LJ 8/90) **[618.3]**

2516 Hales, Dianne, and Timothy R. B Johnson. *Intensive Caring: New Hope for High-Risk Preg-*

nancy. **1990, Crown paper $16.95 (0-517-57477-2).** A guide to avoiding problems associated with high-risk pregnancies. "A model self-help book on its subject."—BL (Rev: BL 4/1/90; LJ 3/1/90) **[618.3]**

2517 Huggins, Kathleen. *Nursing Mother's Companion.* **1986, Harvard Common paper $8.95 (0-916782-72-7).** A nurse's guide to breastfeeding techniques and solutions for common problems of nursing mothers. (Rev: LJ 3/1/86; PW 1/10/86) **[618.3]**

2518 Kolata, Gina. *Baby Doctors: Probing the Limits of Fetal Medicine.* **1990, Doubleday $18.95 (0-385-29938-9).** A study of current practices in fetal medicine and the ethical questions surrounding recent advances in technology. (Rev: BL 9/15/90; LJ 9/1/90; PW 8/10/90) **[618.3]**

2519 Rothman, Barbara Katz. *Tentative Pregnancy: Prenatal Diagnosis and the Future of Motherhood.* **1986, Viking $17.95 (0-670-80841-5); Penguin paper $9.95 (0-14-009486-5).** A look at the social and ethical ramifications of amniocentesis. (Rev: BL 12/15/85; LJ 5/15/86) **[618.3]**

2520 Scher, Jonathan, and Carol Dix. *Preventing Miscarriages: The Good News.* **1990, Harper & Row $18.95 (0-06-016137-X).** An overview of the common causes of miscarriages and measures that can be taken to prevent them. (Rev: BL 3/1/90; LJ 4/15/90) **[618.3]**

2521 Semchyshen, Stefan, and Carol Colman. *How to Prevent Miscarriage and Other Crises of Pregnancy.* **1989, Macmillan $17.95 (0-02-609661-7); paper $8.95 (0-02-036855-0).** A guide to problems surrounding pregnancy and procedures for their avoidance, detection, and treatment. (Rev: BL 5/1/89; LJ 6/1/89) **[618.3]**

Childbirth (Parturition); Labor

2522 Hill, Susan. *Family.* **1990, Viking $18.95 (0-670-82883-1).** An account of the author's daughter who was born prematurely and died at the age of five weeks. "A moving and deeply personal account."—BL (Rev: BL 1/1/90; LJ 11/15/90; PW 11/17/89) **[618.4]**

Complicated labor

2523 Robertson, Patricia Anne, and Peggy Henning Berlin. *Premature Labor Handbook: Successfully Sustaining Your High-Risk Pregnancy.* **1986, Doubleday paper $9.95 (0-385-19924-4).** An examination of the medical, physical, and social problems associated with premature births. (Rev: BL 1/15/86; LJ 4/15/86) **[618.5]**

Caesarean section

2524 Flamm, Bruce L. *Birth after Cesarean: The Medical Facts.* **1990, Prentice Hall paper $16.95 (0-13-080102-X).** An overview of current medical thought regarding natural childbirth following prior cesarean births. (Rev: BL 5/15/90; LJ 6/1/90) **[618.86]**

2525 Rosen, Mortimer, and Lillian Thomas. *Cesarean Myth: Choosing the Best Way to Have Your Baby.* **1989, Viking $18.95 (0-670-82340-6); Penguin paper $7.95 (0-14-011312-6).** An examination of the medical and ethical issues of Cesarean childbirth designed to give expectant mothers information to make informed choices. (Rev: BL 4/15/89; LJ 5/15/89; PW 5/12/89) **[618.86]**

Asepsis and antisepsis

2526 Bartocci, Barbara. *My Angry Son: Sometimes Love Is Not Enough.* **1985, Donald I. Fine $15.95 (0-917657-16-0).** A mother's account of raising an emotionally disturbed son prone to self-destructive violent acts. (Rev: BL 5/15/85; LJ 7/85; PW 4/12/85) **[618.89]**

Pediatrics

2527 Callahan, Mary. *Fighting for Tony.* **1987, Simon & Schuster paper $6.95 (0-671-63265-5).** A chronicle of a nurse's experiences raising a son who was diagnosed as autistic at the age of two. (Rev: BL 9/15/87; LJ 9/15/87; NYTBR 12/27/87) **[618.92]**

2528 Gershwin, M. Eric. *Conquering Your Child's Allergies.* **1989, Addison Wesley $18.95 (0-201-12967-1).** An overview of the causes and treatments of children's allergies. "An outstanding choice."—LJ (Rev: BL 6/1/89; LJ 7/89) **[618.92]**

2529 Jason, Janine, and Antonia Van Der Meer. *Parenting Your Premature Baby.* **1989, Henry Holt $19.95 (0-8050-0880-2); Doubleday paper $9.95 (0-385-29906-0).** An introduction to the special needs of premature babies as explained by a pediatrician. (Rev: BL 5/1/89; LJ 6/15/89) **[618.92]**

2530 Marion, Robert. *Boy Who Felt No Pain: Tales from the Pediatric Ward.* **1990, Addison Wesley $17.26 (0-201-55049-0).** Fourteen accounts of memorable patients and cases encountered during the career of a New York pediatrician. (Rev: BL 9/1/90; LJ 8/90; PW 7/20/90) **[618.92]**

2531 Terr, Lenore. *Too Scared to Cry: Psychic Trauma in Childhood.* **1990, Harper & Row $19.95 (0-06-016335-6).** A psychiatrist's study of the lifelong effects of childhood trauma. (Rev: BL 5/15/90; LJ 5/1/90; PW 3/30/90) **[618.92]**

Geriatrics

2532 Kra, Siegfried. *Aging Myths: Reversible Causes of Mind and Memory Loss.* **1986, McGraw-Hill $17.95 (0-07-035229-1).** An examination of curable causes of memory loss and brain impairment. (Rev: BL 12/15/85; LJ 3/1/86; NYTBR 3/23/86) **[618.97]**

619 Experimental medicine

Primates

2533 Altman, Lawrence K. *Who Goes First? The Story of Self-Experimentation in Medicine.* **1987, Random $24.95 (0-394-50382-1).** A history of medical experiments and research conducted by physicians upon themselves. "An important and thoroughly

enjoyable book."—NYTBR (Rev: BL 6/15/87; LJ 7/87; NYTBR 6/28/87) **[619.98]**

620 ENGINEERING AND ALLIED OPERATIONS

621 Applied physics

2534 Ney, David E. *Electrifying America: Social Meanings of a New Technology, 1880–1940.* **1991, MIT Pr. $29.95 (0-262-18048-9).** A social history examining the changes electricity brought to America in the late nineteenth and early twentieth centuries. (Rev: Choice 6/91; NYTBR 9/15/91) **[621]**

Electric, electronic, magnetic, communications, computer engineering, lighting

2535 Conot, Robert. *Thomas A. Edison: A Streak of Luck.* **1986, DaCapo paper $13.95 (0-306-80261-9).** A biography of the American inventor revealing his private life. "Conot has succeeded perhaps better than anyone else in stripping away the myths of Olympian genius to uncover the real Edison."—PW (Rev: Choice 7–8/79; LJ 2/1/79; PW 12/11/78. Awards: ALA, 1979) **[621.3]**

Electronics and communications engineering

2536 Bernstein, Jeremy. *Three Degrees Above Zero: Bell Labs in the Information Age.* **1984, Macmillan $19.95 (0-684-18170-3).** A profile of the research and development arm of the American Telephone and Telegraph Corporation. (Rev: Choice 1/85; CSM 10/23/84; LJ 9/15/84) **[621.38]**

Nuclear engineering

2537 McPhee, John. *Curve of Binding Energy: A Journey into the Awesome and Alarming World of Theodore Taylor.* **1974, Farrar $10.95 (0-374-13373-5); paper $8.95 (0-374-51598-0).** A profile of Taylor, a nuclear scientist conducting research at the Los Alamos Laboratories on methods of miniaturizing atomic weapons, and his concerns with nuclear proliferation. (Rev: BL 9/1/74; LJ 8/74; NYTBR 6/23/74) **[621.48]**

Turning tools

2538 Raffan, Richard. *Turning Wood with Richard Raffan.* **1985, Taunton paper $17.95 (0-918804-24-8).** An illustrated introduction to the art of wood turning. (Rev: BL 8/85; LJ 5/15/85) **[621.94]**

622 Mining and related operations

2539 Alvarez, A. *Offshore: A North Sea Journey.* **1986, Houghton $15.95 (0-395-39972-6).** Alvarez's first-hand account of life in the North Sea oil fields, and the methods used to find and extract the oil located there. (Rev: CSM 5/27/86; LJ 4/15/86; NYTBR 5/18/86. Awards: LJ, 1986) **[622]**

2540 Bass, Rick. *Oil Notes: A Narrative.* **1989, Houghton $16.95 (0-395-48675-0); $8.95 paper (0-395-53844-0).** A discussion of the petroleum industry by the noted short story writer. (REV: PW 5/26/89; Time 7/17/89; TLS 11/24/89)   **[622]**

Prospecting and exploring for treasure

2541 Ballard, Robert D., and Rick Archbold. *Discovery of the Titanic: Exploring the Greatest of All Lost Ships.* **1987, Warner $35.00 (0-446-51385-7); paper $17.95 (0-446-38912-9).** An account of the author's discovery of the remains of the *Titanic* during a 1985 expedition. (REV: BL 12/1/87; LJ 1/88; NYTBR 12/27/87)   **[622.19]**

623   Military and nautical engineering

Ordnance

2542 MacPherson, Malcolm C. *Time Bomb: Fermi, Heisenberg and the Race for the Atomic Bomb.* **1987, Berkley paper $3.95 (0-425-10423-0).** An account of the race between German and American scientists to develop the first atomic bomb. (REV: BL 6/15/86; LJ 5/15/86; PW 4/11/86)   **[623.4]**

2543 Paul, Jim. *Catapult: Harry and I Build a Siege Weapon.* **1991, Random $18.00 (0-394-58507-0).** An account of two friends' construction of a catapult with ruminations on the history of weaponry and its design. (REV: BL 5/1/91; LJ 5/1/91; PW 4/5/91) **[623.4]**

Vehicles

2544 Yeager, Chuck, and Leo Janos. *Yeager: An Autobiography.* **1986, Bantam $17.95 (0-553-05093-1); paper $5.95 (0-553-25674-2).** The legendary test pilot tells the story of his life. "A life story that leaves its own legacy of courage and daring—to men, women, and kids alike."—CSM (REV: BL 5/1/85; CSM 8/6/85; Time 7/29/85)   **[623.74]**

Nautical engineering and seamanship

2545 Nicolson, Ian. *Improve Your Own Boat: Projects and Tips for the Practical Boat Owner.* **1986, Norton $24.95 (0-393-03310-4).** A practical guide for boat owners wanting to upgrade their craft. (REV: BL 5/1/86; LJ 3/15/86)   **[623.8]**

2546 Rubin, Louis D., Jr. *Small Craft Advisory: A Book about the Building of a Boat.* **1991, Atlantic Monthly $21.95 (0-87113-508-6).** A Carolina writer describes his designing of a boat and its construction. (REV: NYTBR 12/1/91; PW 9/27/91)   **[623.8]**

Seamanship

2547 Beaglehole, J. C. *Life of Captain James Cook.* **1974, Stanford Univ. Pr. $45.00 (0-8047-00543-6).** The life of the great explorer and cartographer. "The powerful narrative never falters despite its great length . . . the definitive life of Cook."—LJ (REV: Choice 9/74; LJ 4/1/74; NYTBR 3/24/74)   **[623.88]**

624   Civil engineering

Bridges

2548 Billington, David P. *Tower and the Bridge: The New Art of Structural Engineering.* **1985,**

Princeton Univ. Pr. paper $13.95 (0-691-02393-X). An illustrated history of structural engineering and design. (REV: CSM 11/17/83; LJ 11/1/83; NYTBR 2/26/84)   **[624.2]**

2549 McCullough, David. *Great Bridge.* **1983, Simon & Schuster paper $14.95 (0-671-45711-X).** The story of the Roebling family, and the building of the Brooklyn Bridge. "The Brooklyn Bridge is probably the most famous bridge in the world: McCullough's book is worthy of its subject."—LJ (REV: Choice 5/73; LJ 10/15/72; NYTBR 10/15/72. AWARDS: ALA, 1972)   **[624.2]**

2550 Outerbridge, David, and Graeme Outerbridge. *Bridges.* **1989, Abrams $45.00 (0-8109-1239-2).** A history of bridges including their design and construction; containing 375 photographs of notable examples. (REV: BL 12/1/89; LJ 1/90; NYTBR 12/3/89. AWARDS: BL, 1989)   **[624.2]**

2551 Trachtenberg, Alan. *Brooklyn Bridge: Fact and Symbol.* **1979, Univ. of Chicago Pr. paper $9.95 (0-226-81115-8).** The history and symbolism of the Brooklyn Bridge. "Gives the meaning of this great bridge as has no other writer."—LJ (REV: BL 9/1/65; LJ 6/15/65; NYRB 7/15/65. AWARDS: NYTBR, 1965)   **[624.2]**

627   Hydraulic engineering

2552 Stevens, Joseph E. *Hoover Dam: An American Adventure.* **1988, Univ. of Oklahoma Pr. $26.95 (0-8061-2115-7); $12.95 paper (0-8061-2283-8).** An account of the construction of Hoover Dam from its initial conception to its completion in 1935. (REV: Choice 12/88; LJ 6/15/88; NYTBR 2/12/89)   **[627]**

628   Sanitary and municipal engineering

2553 Carr, Donald Eaton. *Death of the Sweet Waters.* **1966, Norton $6.95 (0-393-06354-2).** A historical and modern-day survey of the use and abuse of water; examining its supply, treatment, and pollution. "A vigorous, angry book."—PW (REV: BL 7/1/66; Choice 12/66; LJ 4/15/66. AWARDS: ALA, 1966)   **[628]**

629   Other branches of engineering

Aerospace engineering

2554 Bryan, C. D. B. *National Air and Space Museum.* **1988, Abrams $65.00 (0-8109-1380-1).** A profile of the collection of the Smithsonian's National Air and Space Museum in Washington, D.C. (REV: BL 12/15/88; LJ 2/15/89)   **[629.1]**

2555 McPhee, John. *Deltoid Pumpkin Seed.* **1973, Farrar $14.95 (0-374-13781-1); paper $8.95 (0-374-51635-9).** The secret design and development by a group of private investors of an "aereon," a type of flying machine without wings. (REV: LJ 10/1/73; New Rep 9/1/73; NYTBR 7/29/73)   **[629.1]**

Aeronautics

2556 Bernstein, Burton J. *Plane Crazy: A Celebration of Flying.* **1985, Houghton $16.95 (0-89919-390-**

0). Memoirs on the author's lifelong love of aviation. (REV: BL 9/1/85; LJ 9/1/85; NYTBR 3/9/86) **[629.13]**

2557   Ceruzzi, Paul. *Beyond the Limits: Flight Enters the Computer Age.* 1989, MIT Pr. $35.00 (0-262-03143-4); $17.50 paper (0-262-53082-1). A study of the influences of technology upon aviation and space flight. (REV: Choice 10/89; LJ 6/15/89) **[629.13]**

2558   Crouch, Tom D. *Bishop's Boys: A Life of Wilbur and Orville Wright.* 1989, Norton $22.50 (0-393-02660-4); paper $14.95 (0-393-30695-X). A biography of the brothers who pioneered manned flight. "A definitive, well researched version of an authentic American epic guaranteed to supersede all previous profiles."—BL (REV: BL 6/15/89; Choice 1/90; LJ 5/15/89) **[629.13]**

2559   Gillispie, Charles C. *Montgolfier Brothers and the Invention of Aviation, 1783–1784.* 1983, Princeton Univ. Pr. $39.00 (0-691-08321-5). A biography of the French brothers who invented the balloon and their impact upon future scientists and inventors. (REV: Choice 1/84; LJ 6/15/83; New Yorker 7/25/83) **[629.13]**

2560   Howard, Fred. *Wilbur and Orville: A Biography of the Wright Brothers.* 1987, Knopf $24.95 (0-394-54269-X); Ballantine paper $12.95 (0-345-35393-5). A dual biography of the brothers who pioneered man's first flight. "The definitive biography."—BL (REV: BL 6/1/87; Choice 11/87; LJ 8/87) **[629.13]**

2561   Lovell, Mary S. *Sound of Wings: The Biography of Amelia Earhart.* 1989, St. Martin's $22.95 (0-312-03431-8). A biography of the aviatrix who became the first woman to fly the Atlantic Ocean. "A realistic, full-bodied portrait . . . highly recommended to supersede previous treatments to Earhart's life."—BL (REV: BL 12/15/89; CSM 1/31/90; LJ 10/15/89) **[629.13]**

2562   Lovell, Mary S. *Straight on Till Morning: A Biography of Beryl Markham.* 1987, St. Martin's $16.95 (0-312-01096-6); paper $10.95 (0-312-01895-9). An exhaustive biography of the noted aviatrix called "a breathtaking chronicle" by *Booklist*. (REV: BL 9/1/87; LJ 9/15/87; NYTBR 8/23/87. AWARDS: BL, the 1980s) **[629.13]**

2563   Rich, Doris L. *Amelia Earhart: A Biography.* 1989, Smithsonian Inst. $19.95 (0-87474-836-4). A biography of the famed American flyer and crusader for equality for women. (REV: BL 11/1/89; LJ 10/15/89; NYTBR 11/26/89) **[629.13]**

2564   Yeager, Jeana, Dick Rutan, and Paul Patton. *Voyager.* 1987, Knopf $19.95 (0-394-55266-0). The story of the couple who in 1986 became the first persons to fly nonstop around the world without refueling. (REV: BL 10/15/87; LJ 12/87; NYTBR 12/27/87) **[629.13]**

Motor land vehicles

2565   Boyne, Walter J. *Power Behind the Wheel: Creativity and the Evolution of the Automobile.* 1988, Stewart, Tabori & Chang $40.00 (1-55670-042-3). An illustrated history of the automobile with over 200 photographs. (REV: BL 1/1/89; LJ 2/1/89; PW 9/2/88) **[629.2]**

2566   Hirsch, Jay. *Great American Dream Machine: Classic Cars of the 50s and 60s.* 1988, Random $19.95 (0-679-72160-6). An illustrated survey of the great American automobiles of the 1950s and 1960s. (REV: BL 12/15/85; LJ 2/1/86) **[629.2]**

2567   Taub, Eric. *Taurus: The Making of the Car That Saved Ford.* 1991, Dutton $21.95 (0-525-93372-7). The story of the design, construction, and marketing of the Ford Taurus. (REV: LJ 10/1/91; NYTBR 10/1/91) **[629.2]**

Manned space flight

2568   Aldrin, Buzz, and Malcolm McConnell. *Men from Earth: An Apollo Astronaut's Exciting Account of America's Space Program.* 1989, Bantam $19.95 (0-553-05374-4). An account of America's space program and rivalry with the Soviets in space by the former *Apollo* astronaut. (REV: BL 5/15/89; LJ 6/15/89; NYTBR 7/2/89) **[629.45]**

2569   Allen, Joseph P., and Russell Martin. *Entering Space: An Astronaut's Odyssey.* 1985, Stewart, Tabori & Chang paper $18.95 (0-941434-74-5). An illustrated overview of the procedures of manned space missions by a former space shuttle astronaut. (REV: Choice 5/85; LJ 2/1/85; PW 9/7/84) **[629.45]**

2570   Bond, Peter R. *Heroes in Space: From Gagarin to Challenger.* 1987, Basil Blackwell $29.95 (0-631-15349-7). A history of man's accomplishments in space from the late 1950s to the 1986 *Challenger* tragedy. (REV: BL 10/1/87; Choice 12/87; LJ 6/15/87) **[629.45]**

2571   Collins, Michael. *Carrying the Fire: An Astronaut's Journey.* 1989, Farrar $19.95 (0-374-11919-8); Bantam paper $4.95 (0-553-23948-1). The Apollo 11 astronaut who didn't walk on the moon tells about his career, training, and experiences on the mission. "No other person who has flown in space has captured the experience so vividly."—NYTBR (REV: Atl 9/74; NYTBR 8/11/74; PW 6/13/74) **[629.45]**

2572   Collins, Michael. *Liftoff: The Story of America's Adventure in Space.* 1989, Grove-Weidenfeld $25.00 (0-8021-1011-8); paper $10.95 (0-8021-3188-3). The history of the U.S. space program from Project Mercury to the space shuttle as presented by the former astronaut and author of *Carrying the Fire.* (REV: Choice 1/89; LJ 8/88; NYTBR 7/24/88) **[629.45]**

2573   Cooper, Henry S. F., Jr. *Before Lift-Off: The Making of a Space Shuttle Crew.* 1987, Johns Hopkins $22.50 (0-8018-3524-0). An account of the selection and training of a space shuttle crew prior to a 1984 mission. (REV: BL 10/15/87; LJ 10/15/87) **[629.45]**

2574   Lewis, Richard S. *Challenger: The Final Voyage.* 1988, Columbia Univ. Pr. $29.95 (0-231-06490-X). An examination of the fateful last voyage of the space shuttle *Challenger* with an analysis of the future of America's shuttle program. (REV: BL 5/15/88; LJ 4/1/88) **[629.45]**

2575 Murray, Charles, and Catherine Bly Cox. *Apollo: The Ten-Year Race to Put a Man on the Moon.* **1989, Simon & Schuster $24.95 (0-671-61101-1); paper $12.95 (0-671-70625-X).** The history of the Apollo space program and the NASA engineers who made its success possible. "A marvelous, deftly written book that captures the mood and spirit of the people who found a way to the moon."—NYTBR (Rev: CSM 7/20/89; LJ 6/15/89; NYTBR 7/16/89)   **[629.45]**

2576 Oberg, James E. *Red Star in Orbit.* **1981, Random $16.95 (0-394-51429-7).** The history of the development and accomplishments of the Russian space program from the late 1950s to the early 1980s. (Rev: BL 7/1/81; CSM 7/13/81; NYTBR 6/7/81)   **[629.45]**

2577 Wolfe, Tom. *Right Stuff.* **1983, Farrar $15.95 (0-374-25033-2); Bantam paper $4.95 (0-553-25596-7).** A history of the early space program from the test pilots of Edward's Air Force Base to the Mercury astronauts. "Tom Wolfe's most ambitious book, and his best."—Atl (Rev: Atl 10/79; NYTBR 9/23/79; Time 9/24/79. Awards: ALA, 1979; NBA, 1980; Time, the 1970s)   **[629.45]**

Automatic control engineering

2578 Fjermedal, Grant. *Tomorrow Makers: A Brave New World of Living-Brain Machines.* **1987, Macmillan $18.95 (0-02-538560-7); Microsoft paper $8.95 (1-55615-113-6).** The author visited experts throughout the country at its leading research institutions to compile this report on artificial intelligence and robotics. "A fascinating, non-technical account of the state of the art in machine intelligence."—LJ (Rev: LJ 2/1/87; NYTBR 4/10/88; PW 12/4/87. Awards: ALA, 1987)   **[629.8]**

630   AGRICULTURE

2579 Klinkenborg, Verlyn. *Making Hay.* **1986, Lyons & Burford $14.95 (0-941130-18-5); Random paper $5.95 (0-394-75599-5).** A survey of the processes involved in making hay. "A fascinating excursion into American farmland."—PW (Rev: NYTBR 10/12/86; PW 8/8/86)   **[630]**

2580 Westfall, Patricia Tichenor. *Real Farm: Encounters with Perception.* **1989, New Chapter Pr. $14.95 (0-942257-17-0); Avon paper $7.95 (0-380-71221-0).** Memoirs of a former college professor who bought and ran an Iowa farm along with her husband. (Rev: BL 6/1/89; NYTBR 10/8/89; PW 8/4/89)   **[630]**

Persons

2581 Kohn, Howard. *Last Farmer: An American Memoir.* **1988, Summit $18.95 (0-671-49803-7).** Memoirs about the author's father's life as a farmer in Germany and Michigan. (Rev: BL 9/15/88; CSM 1/18/89; NYTBR 11/6/88)   **[630.092]**

Philosophy and theory

2582 Johnson, Josephine. *Inland Island.* **1987, Ohio State Univ. Pr. paper $8.95 (0-8142-0450-3).** A journal recording the author's perceptions of nature in Ohio. (Rev: CSM 3/27/69; NYTBR 3/2/69; Sat Rev 2/15/69)   **[630.1]**

History

2583 Heilman, Grant. *Farm.* **1988, Abbeville $45.00 (0-89659-889-6).** An illustrated introduction to contemporary farm life and farm production. (Rev: BL 4/15/89; LJ 2/1/89)   **[630.9]**

2584 Rhodes, Richard. *Farm: A Year in the Life of an American Farmer.* **1989, Simon & Schuster $19.95 (0-671-63647-2); paper $10.95 (0-671-72507-6).** A chronicle of a year in the life of two Missouri farmers and their three children. "Rhodes does a masterful job of relating, for today's largely urban population, one farmer's story."—LJ (Rev: LJ 10/1/89; Natl Rev 12/8/89; Time 9/25/89. Awards: LJ, 1989)   **[630.9]**

2585 Silber, Terry. *A Small Farm in Maine.* **1989, Doubleday paper $6.95 (0-385-26055-5).** Memoirs of the author's life on a small farm with her husband following their relocation from Boston to Maine. (Rev: BL 4/1/88; LJ 5/1/88; PW 2/19/88)   **[630.9]**

632   Plant injuries, diseases, pests

Weeds

2586 Stein, Sara B. *My Weeds: A Gardener's Botany.* **1988, Harper & Row $19.95 (0-06-015882-4); paper $8.95 (0-06-091653-2).** Collected essays regarding the anatomy and botany of weeds and their place in nature and the garden. (Rev: BL 5/1/88; NYRB 9/29/88; NYTBR 12/4/88)   **[632.58]**

635   Garden crops (Horticulture)

2587 Bittman, Sam. *Seeds: The Ultimate Guide to Growing Vegetables, Herbs and Flowers.* **1989, Bantam $35.00 (0-553-05366-3).** An illustrated guide to beginning a garden using seeds. "A beautiful and informative book for all gardeners."—BL (Rev: BL 5/1/89; LJ 4/1/89; PW 3/17/89)   **[635]**

2588 Boisset, Caroline. *Town Gardens.* **1990, Little, Brown $40.00 (0-316-10109-5).** An illustrated guide to the design and construction of successful gardens in urban areas. (Rev: LJ 3/1/90; PW 3/23/90)**[635]**

2589 Creasy, Rosalind. *Cooking from the Garden.* **1988, Sierra Club $35.00 (0-87156-731-8).** A primer on the growing and cooking of fresh fruits, vegetables, and herbs with examples of different types of gardens from around the world. (Rev: BL 10/1/88; CSM 12/14/88; PW 9/16/88)   **[635]**

2590 Creasy, Rosalind. *Earthly Delights.* **1985, Sierra Club $19.95 (0-87156-841-1).** A survey of gardening styles and techniques focusing on the cultivation of native plants. (Rev: BL 10/1/85; LJ 9/15/85; PW 8/16/85)   **[635]**

2591 Damrosch, Barbara. *Garden Primer.* 1988, Workman $24.95 (0-89480-317-4); paper $16.95 (0-89480-316-6). A single-volume illustrated introduction to gardening containing detailed instructions for the cultivation of over 300 types of plants. (Rev: BL 11/15/88; CSM 4/7/89; LJ 2/15/89) **[635]**

2592 De Saulles, Denys. *Home Grown.* 1988, Houghton $29.95 (0-395-45686-X). A heavily illustrated guide to the planting, care, and harvesting of over 1,000 types of fruits and vegetables. (Rev: BL 4/1/88; LJ 5/1/88; NYTBR 12/4/88) **[635]**

2593 Jabs, Carolyn. *Heirloom Gardener.* 1984, Sierra Club $17.95 (0-87156-803-9); paper $9.95 (0-87156-809-8). A guide to the cultivation and preservation of genetically threatened varieties of fruits and vegetables. (Rev: BL 8/84; LJ 7/84; PW 4/20/84) **[635]**

2594 Jones, Pamela. *How Does Your Garden Grow? The Essential Home Garden Book.* 1989, Viking $19.95 (0-670-82636-7). An introduction to home gardening for beginners. (Rev: BL 3/1/89; LJ 3/1/89; PW 2/17/89) **[635]**

2595 Lawrence, Elizabeth. *Gardening for Love: The Market Bulletins.* 1987, Duke $24.95 (0-8223-0715-4); paper $10.95 (0-8223-0887-8). A collection of correspondence by the author with plant and seed dealers who advertised their products in state agriculture bulletins. (Rev: LJ 5/15/87; NYTBR 10/11/87) **[635]**

2596 Lawrence, Elizabeth. *Through the Garden Gate.* Ed. by Bill Neil. 1990, Univ. of North Carolina Pr. $19.95 (0-8078-1907-7). A collection of 144 gardening essays selected from the author's *Charlotte Observer* newspaper columns. (Rev: LJ 5/1/90; NYTBR 6/10/90; PW 4/20/90) **[635]**

2597 Leighton, Ann. *American Gardens in the 18th Century: For Use or for Delight.* 1986, Univ. of Massachusetts Pr. paper $16.95 (0-87023-531-1). This sequel to the author's *Early American Gardens* is an illustrated survey of gardens and their gardeners during the eighteenth century. (Rev: BL 10/1/76; LJ 10/1/76) **[635]**

2598 Leighton, Ann. *Early American Gardens: "For Meate or Medicine."* 1986, Univ. of Massachusetts Pr. paper $16.95 (0-87023-530-3). An introduction to the plants and gardening techniques used by early New England colonists. (Rev: LJ 7/69; NYTBR 3/8/70; New Yorker 3/28/70) **[635]**

2599 National Gardening Association. *Gardening: The Complete Guide to Growing America's Favorite Fruits and Vegetables.* 1986, Addison Wesley paper $19.95 (0-201-10855-0). An illustrated guide to the cultivation and harvest of 40 popular fruits and vegetables. (Rev: BL 3/1/86; LJ 3/1/86; PW 2/21/86)**[635]**

2600 Olwell, Carol. *Gardening from the Heart: Why Gardeners Garden.* 1990, Antelope Island Pr. $24.95 (0-917946-04-9); paper $18.50 (0-917946-05-7). An illustrated collection of interviews with over 21 Western gardeners regarding the pleasures of their pastime. (Rev: BL 6/1/90; LJ 7/90; NYTBR 6/10/90)**[635]**

2601 Paterson, Allen. *Herbs in the Garden.* 1985, Biblio $24.95 (0-460-04520-2). A guide to the cultivation of herbs and their uses. (Rev: LJ 10/1/85; TLS 7/26/85) **[635]**

2602 Perenyi, Eleanor. *Green Thoughts: A Writer in the Garden.* 1983, Random paper $8.95 (0-394-71714-7). Essays about the joys of gardening by the journalist and former editor of *Mademoiselle.* "A book to keep by the bedside to read when one is tired of the problems of the day."—NYTBR (Rev: New Rep 10/7/81; NYRB 11/5/81; NYTBR 10/11/81) **[635]**

2603 Phillips, Roger, and Nicky Fry. *Random House Book of Herbs.* 1990, Random paper $22.95 (0-679-73213-6). An illustrated guide to the cultivation and uses of over 400 herbs. (Rev: BL 12/15/90; LJ 1/91; NYTBR 12/2/90) **[635]**

2604 Sackville-West, Vita. *Illustrated Garden Book: A New Anthology.* 1986, Macmillan $22.50 (0-689-11844-9). An illustrated collection of the writer's gardening columns from the *London Observer.* (Rev: BL 10/1/86; PW 9/19/86) **[635]**

2605 Staw, Jane A., and Mary Swander. *Parsnips in the Snow: Talks with Midwestern Gardeners.* 1990, Univ. of Iowa Pr. $24.95 (0-87745-269-5); paper $12.50 (0-87745-279-2). Collected interviews with 12 gardeners regarding vegetable cultivation. (Rev: CSM 5/25/90; NYTBR 6/10/90; PW 1/26/90. Awards: PW, 1990) **[635]**

2606 Swain, Roger B. *Practical Gardener: A Guide to Breaking New Ground.* 1989, Little, Brown $18.95 (0-316-82472-0). Advice on growing edible and decorative plants in the garden by the science editor of *Horticulture* magazine. (Rev: LJ 4/1/89; NYTBR 6/11/89; PW 3/17/89) **[635]**

2607 Wolfe, Pamela. *Midwest Gardens.* 1992, Chicago Review $39.95 (1-55652-138-3). A botanist's illustrated guide to Midwestern gardens and gardening. (Rev: BL 12/15/91; LJ 1/92; PW 12/20/91) **[635]**

Flowers and ornamental plants

2608 Christopher, Thomas. *In Search of Lost Roses.* 1989, Summit $18.95 (0-671-66220-1). The author recounts his quests in America and Europe searching for increasingly rare original strains of roses. (Rev: BL 8/89; LJ 8/89; NYTBR 12/3/89) **[635.9]**

2609 Forsell, Mary. *Heirloom Herbs: Using Old-Fashioned Herbs in Gardens, Recipes, and Decorations.* 1990, Random $29.95 (0-394-58336-1). An overview of the culinary and decorative uses of herbs. (Rev: NYTBR 12/2/90; PW 1/25/91) **[635.9]**

2610 Halpin, Anne Moyer. *Year Round Flower Gardener.* 1989, Simon & Schuster paper $16.95 (0-671-67711-X). An illustrated primer on methods of maintaining flowers in your garden through all the seasons. (Rev: BL 3/15/89; LJ 4/1/89; PW 3/17/89)**[635.9]**

2611 Hobhouse, Penelope. *Color in Your Garden.* 1985, Little, Brown $40.00 (0-316-36748-6). An illustrated guide to the care and cultivation of plants that can add color to your garden in all seasons. (Rev: BL 10/1/85; CSM 4/10/85; LJ 11/1/85)   **[635.9]**

2612 Lacy, Allen. *Farther Afield: A Gardener's Excursions.* **1986, Farrar $17.95 (0-374-15355-8); paper $8.95 (0-374-52063-1).** Essays on botany and gardening. "All gardeners will find intriguing information here. Other readers . . . are sure to enjoy the finely crafted writing."—LJ (Rev: LJ 5/15/86; NYTBR 6/1/86; PW 3/14/86. Awards: PW, 1986)**[635.9]**

2613 Lacy, Allen. *Garden in Autumn.* **1990, Atlantic Monthly $29.95 (0-87113-347-4).** An introduction to growing plants that thrive in American gardens during the fall season. (Rev: NYTBR 12/2/90; PW 1/4/91. Awards: PW, 1990)   **[635.9]**

2614 Lima, Patrick. *Harrowsmith Perennial Garden: Flowers for Three Seasons.* **1987, Camden House paper $19.95 (0-920656-74-9).** A primer on the growth and upkeep of an organic perennial flower garden. (Rev: BL 2/15/88; LJ 3/1/88; PW 1/22/88) **[635.9]**

2615 McGourty, Frederick. *Perennial Gardener.* **1989, Houghton $24.95 (0-395-45373-9).** A discussion of methods and plants to use when designing and cultivating a year-round garden. (Rev: CSM 4/7/89; LJ 3/1/89; NYTBR 6/11/89)   **[635.9]**

2616 Martin, Tovah. *Once Upon a Windowsill: A History of Indoor Plants.* **1989, Timber $29.95 (0-88192-120-3).** A social history of the introduction of plants into homes during the nineteenth and twentieth centuries. "Avid gardeners and floral enthusiasts will particularly enjoy this."—Choice (Rev: BL 5/15/89; Choice 9/89; NYTBR 6/11/89)   **[635.9]**

2617 Mitchell, Henry. *Essential Gardener: Henry Mitchell on Gardening.* **1983, Farrar paper $8.95 (0-374-57165-7).** Reflections on the pleasures of gardening culled from the author's *Washington Post* columns. "The most soul-satisfying gardening book in years."—NYTBR (Rev: BL 1/1/82; LJ 10/1/81; NYTBR 3/28/82)   **[635.9]**

2618 Osler, Mirabel. *A Gentle Plea for Chaos: The Enchantment of Gardening.* **1990, Simon & Schuster $22.95 (0-671-69238-0).** The author's reflections on her garden and the joys of gardening. (Rev: BL 3/1/90; CSM 5/25/90; PW 1/26/90. Awards: BL, 1990)   **[635.9]**

2619 Pemberthy, Ian. *Building Your Garden.* **1989, Macmillan $17.95 (0-02-595491-1).** Suggested construction and masonry projects to enhance the beauty and enjoyment of outdoor gardens. (Rev: BL 7/89; LJ 6/15/89; PW 6/16/89)   **[635.9]**

2620 Phillips, Roger. *Shrubs.* **1989, Random paper $22.95 (0-679-72345-5).** A guide to the world's shrubs containing descriptions, photographs, and growing tips for more than 2,000 varieties. "This should become the definitive book on shrubs for American libraries."—LJ (Rev: BL 3/15/89; LJ 4/15/89)   **[635.9]**

2621 Rapp, Joel. *Mr. Mother Earth's Most Rewarding Houseplants.* **1989, Ballantine paper $8.95 (0-449-90355-9).** An introduction to the care and cultivation of over 100 plants for the home by the *Redbook*

gardening editor. (Rev: BL 3/1/89; LJ 4/1/89; PW 2/17/89)   **[635.9]**

2622 Rittershausen, Brian, and Wilma Rittershausen. *Orchid Growing Illustrated.* **1985, Sterling $24.95 (0-7137-1365-8).** An illustrated guide to orchid cultivation for the experienced gardener. (Rev: BL 10/1/85; LJ 10/1/85; PW 9/20/85)   **[635.9]**

2623 Taylor, Norman. *Taylor's Guide to Annuals.* **Ed. by Gordon P. De Wolf, Jr. 1986, Houghton paper $16.95 (0-395-40447-9).** A guide to the growing and care of annual plants. (Rev: BL 8/86; LJ 8/86)   **[635.9]**

2624 Taylor, Norman. *Taylor's Guide to Bulbs.* **Ed. by Gordon P. De Wolf, Jr. 1986, Houghton paper $16.95 (0-395-40449-5).** An illustrated guide to the gardening of bulbs. (Rev: BL 8/86; LJ 8/86)   **[635.9]**

2625 Taylor, Norman. *Taylor's Guide to Perennials.* **Ed. by Gordon P. De Wolf, Jr. 1986, Houghton paper $16.95 (0-395-40448-7).** A gardening guide to the care and raising of perennials. (Rev: BL 8/86; LJ 8/86)   **[635.9]**

2626 Taylor, Norman. *Taylor's Guide to Roses.* **Ed. by Gordon P. De Wolf, Jr. 1986, Houghton paper $16.95 (0-395-40450-9).** A guide to the care and propagation of roses. (Rev: BL 8/86; LJ 8/86)   **[635.9]**

2627 Verey, Rosemary. *Garden in Winter.* **1988, Bulfinch $40.00 (0-8212-1669-4).** An introduction to plants that may be cultivated or appreciated in the winter. "One of the most appealing books on gardening to appear in this decade."—NYTBR (Rev: LJ 3/1/89; NYTBR 12/4/88; PW 10/21/88)   **[635.9]**

2628 White, Katherine S. *Onward and Upward in the Garden.* **1979, Farrar paper $9.95 (0-374-51629-4).** Fourteen essays regarding the art and pleasures of gardening by the wife of E. B. White. (Rev: LJ 7/79; Newsweek 9/2/79; Time 9/17/79)   **[635.9]**

2629 Yang, Linda. *City Gardener's Handbook: From Balcony to Backyard.* **1990, Random $26.95 (0-394-58371-X).** A guide to successful gardening in urban environments. (Rev: BL 5/15/90; LJ 4/15/90; PW 4/20/90. Awards: PW, 1990)   **[635.9]**

General and taxonomic groupings

2630 Galle, Fred C. *Azaleas.* **1987, Timber $65.00 (0-88192-012-6).** A comprehensive guide to the care of azaleas covering over 6,000 varieties. "A boon for the weekend gardener and the botanical professional."—BL (Rev: BL 3/15/86; Choice 5/86)   **[635.93]**

636   Animal husbandry

Production and maintenance, animals for specific purposes, veterinary sciences

2631 Schell, Orville. *Modern Meat.* **1985, Random paper $5.95 (0-394-72919-6).** Examination of the use of drugs, hormones, and antibiotics in modern meat production. "Schell, in this report, has done a great service for the consumer."—PW (Rev: BL 4/1/84; LJ 4/1/84; PW 2/24/84. Awards: LJ, 1984) **[636.08]**

Horses

2632 Ashley, John Denny, and Billy Reed. *Thoroughbred: A Celebration of the Breed.* 1990, Simon & Schuster $50.00 (0-671-66440-9). A photographic study of the thoroughbred and the sport of horse racing. (Rev: BL 6/15/90; LJ 7/90; PW 4/20/90) **[636.1]**

2633 Dossenbach, Monique, and Hans D. Dossenbach. *Noble Horse.* 1985, G. K. Hall $83.00 (0-8161-8744-4). An illustrated natural history of the horse with over 3,000 drawings and photographs. "The ultimate in the literature of the horse."—PW (Rev: BL 11/15/85; LJ 11/1/85; PW 10/18/85) **[636.1]**

2634 Morris, Desmond. *Horsewatching.* 1989, Crown $12.95 (0-517-57267-2). An introduction to horses and horse behaviors by the author of *Catwatching* and *The Human Ape.* (Rev: BL 5/1/89; LJ 4/15/89; PW 3/31/89) **[636.1]**

2635 Schwartz, Jane. *Ruffian: Burning from the Start.* 1991, Ballantine $18.00 (0-345-36017-6). The life and career of the thoroughbred filly who had to be destroyed following a tragic accident in a 1975 match race. (Rev: BL 9/1/91; LJ 7/91) **[636.1]**

Dogs

2636 Fergus, Charles. *A Rough-Shooting Dog: Reflections from Thick and Uncivil Sorts of Places.* 1991, Lyons & Burford $18.95 (1-55821-128-4). The author recollects a Pennsylvania hunting season with his springer spaniel. (Rev: BL 8/91; LJ 8/91) **[636.7]**

2637 Fox, Michael W. *Superdog: Raising the Perfect Canine Companion.* 1990, Howell Bk. $17.95 (0-87605-741-5). A veterinarian's guide to effective dog rearing and training. (Rev: BL 7/90; LJ 6/1/90) **[636.7]**

2638 Hearne, Vicki. *Bandit: Dossier of a Dangerous Dog.* 1991, HarperCollins $21.95 (0-06-019005-1). An account of the social ramifications of a case in which a Connecticut dog is accused of a pair of vicious attacks upon a neighbor. "A deeply eccentric lesson in justice, linguistics, racism and teleology."—NYTBR (Rev: LJ 10/15/91; NYTBR 12/15/91) **[636.7]**

2639 Herriot, James. *James Herriot's Dog Stories.* 1986, St. Martin's $19.95 (0-312-43968-7); paper $4.95 (0-312-90143-7). Collected essays on canines by the author of *All Creatures Great and Small.* (Rev: BL 4/15/86; LJ 6/1/86; Time 7/7/86) **[636.7]**

2640 Lowell, Michele. *Your Purebred Puppy: A Buyer's Guide.* 1990, Henry Holt $22.50 (0-8050-1411-X). Descriptions of 176 dog breeds with suggestions on ways to choose the best breed and puppy for your personal needs. (Rev: BL 12/15/90; LJ 12/90) **[636.7]**

2641 Milani, Myrna M. *Invisible Leash: A Better Way to Communicate with Your Dog.* 1985, NAL

$14.95 (0-453-00500-4); paper $4.95 (0-451-16812-7). A guide to nonviolent dog training through positive reinforcement. (Rev: BL 11/1/85; LJ 11/15/85; PW 10/18/85) **[636.7]**

2642 Siegal, Mordecai, and Matthew Margolis. *When Good Dogs Do Bad Things.* 1986, Little, Brown $16.95 (0-316-79008-7). Training solutions to 20 of the most common canine behavioral problems. (Rev: LJ 9/15/86; PW 7/18/86) **[636.7]**

2643 Taylor, David. *Ultimate Dog Book.* 1990, Simon & Schuster $29.95 (0-671-70988-7). An illustrated guide to the selection, care, and training of over 100 breeds of dogs. (Rev: BL 9/15/90; LJ 11/15/90) **[636.7]**

Cats

2644 Caras, Roger. *A Cat Is Watching: A Look at the Way Cats See Us.* 1989, Simon & Schuster $17.95 (0-671-65708-9); paper $8.95 (0-671-72443-6). An exploration of the psychology and perception of cats and their relationship toward humans. (Rev: LJ 9/1/89; NYTBR 10/1/89; PW 7/21/89. Awards: PW, 1989) **[636.8]**

2645 Stephens, Gloria, and Tetsu Yamazaki. *Legacy of the Cat.* 1990, Chronicle $29.95 (0-87701-728-X); paper $14.95 (0-87701-695-X). An illustrated guide to cat breeds and their histories. (Rev: BL 12/15/90; PW 6/22/90. Awards: PW, 1990) **[636.8]**

2646 Taylor, David, and Daphne Negus. *Ultimate Cat Book.* 1989, L. J. Kaplan $29.95 (0-671-68649-6). A guide to domestic cats covering the care, description, and history of each breed. "Feline devotees will find this book . . . more than worthy of its title."—PW (Rev: LJ 12/89; PW 9/22/89. Awards: PW, 1989) **[636.8]**

637 Processing dairy and related products

2647 Pistorius, Alan. *Cutting Hill: A Chronicle of a Family Farm.* 1990, Knopf $20.95 (0-394-57439-7). An account of the events of one year on a Vermont dairy farm. "A roller-coaster ride from one crisis to the next."—Atl (Rev: Atl 8/90; LJ 6/15/90; PW 5/25/90) **[637]**

638 Insect culture

Bee keeping

2648 Hubbell, Sue. *A Book of Bees: And How to Keep Them.* 1988, Random $17.95 (0-394-55894-4); Ballantine paper $8.95 (0-345-34261-5). A look at the pleasures and chores of beekeeping as seen by a former librarian. "It is a wondrous subject, and Hubbell does it justice."—PW (Rev: BL 4/15/89; NYTBR 10/30/88; PW 7/15/88) **[638.1]**

2649 Vivian, John. *Keeping Bees.* 1986, Williamson paper $10.95 (0-913589-19-5). A professional beekeeper discusses the art of his trade. (Rev: BL 4/1/86; LJ 4/15/86) **[638.1]**

2650 Whynott, Douglas. *Following the Bloom: Across America with Migratory Beekeepers.* 1991, Stackpole $19.95 (0-8117-1944-8). A study of the lives and work of the approximately 1,000 migratory beekeepers in the United States. (Rev: BL 2/15/91; LJ 2/15/91; NYTBR 2/27/91) **[638.1]**

639 Hunting, fishing, conservation

2651 Clark, Eleanor. *Oysters of Locmariaquer.* **1978, Univ. of Chicago Pr. paper $3.95 (0-226-10763-9).** An extended essay on the oysters and oystermen of Brittany. (Rev: Atl 8/64; New Rep 8/8/64; Newsweek 7/13/64. Awards: NBA, 1965) **[639]**

2652 Iglauer, Edith. *Fishing with John.* **1988, Farrar $19.95 (0-374-15524-0).** A memoir of the author's husband and their experiences fishing along the northern Pacific Coast. (Rev: BL 7/88; LJ 10/15/88; NYTBR 9/15/88) **[639]**

2653 Warner, William W. *Beautiful Swimmers: Watermen, Crabs, and the Chesapeake Bay.* **1976, Little, Brown $22.50 (0-316-92326-5); Penguin paper $8.95 (0-14-017004-9).** A look at the people and wildlife of the Chesapeake Bay, the nation's largest estuary. (Rev: CSM 3/31/76; NYTBR 6/13/76; Time 3/29/76. Awards: ALA, 1976; PP:NF, 1976) **[639]**

2654 Warner, William W. *Distant Water: The Fate of the North Atlantic Fisherman.* **1984, Penguin paper $8.95 (0-14-006967-4).** A study of the lives and methods of the fishermen working on large fishing ships in the North Atlantic, based on the author's experiences living with crews from five different nations. (Rev: CSM 6/24/83; LJ 3/15/83; NYTBR 4/17/83. Awards: ALA, 1983) **[639]**

Conservation of biological resources

2655 Day, David. *Whale War.* **1987, Sierra Club $19.95 (0-87156-775-X); paper $9.95 (0-87156-778-4).** A study of the history of whaling and recent efforts to stop whale hunting and save the marine mammals. (Rev: LJ 10/1/87; TLS 1/15/88) **[639.9]**

2656 DeBlieu, Jan. *Meant to Be Wild: The Struggle to Save Endangered Species Through Captive Breeding.* **1991, Fulcrum $24.95 (1-55591-074-2).** An examination of the successes and failures of recent efforts to protect and breed endangered species. (Rev: LJ 10/1/91; PW 8/16/91) **[639.9]**

2657 Dunlap, Thomas R. *Saving America's Wildlife.* **1988, Princeton Univ. Pr. $24.95 (0-691-04750-2).** An examination of the changing attitudes of America toward its wildlife and measures that can be taken to preserve it. (Rev: LJ 10/1/88; PW 5/6/88) **[639.9]**

2658 Merilees, William J. *Attracting Backyard Wildlife: A Guide for Nature Lovers.* **1989, Voyageur Pr. paper $10.95 (0-89658-130-6).** A guide to attracting animals from moths to mammals to your backyard. (Rev: BL 5/15/89; LJ 11/1/89; PW 5/26/89) **[639.9]**

2659 Stretch, Mary Jane, and Phyllis Hobe. *The Swan in My Bathtub and Other Adventures in the Aark.* **1991, Dutton $19.95 (0-525-24999-0).** An account of the author's 15 years as an animal rehabilitator in Pennsylvania. (Rev: BL 6/1/91; LJ 6/15/91; PW 4/5/91) **[639.9]**

2660 Ure, Jim. *Hawks and Roses.* **1991, Gibbs Smith $19.95 (0-87905-373-9).** The author recalls his experiences with birds of prey at the injured bird rehabilitation center he and his family operate at their Utah home. (Rev: LJ 4/1/91; PW 3/15/91) **[639.9]**

Habitat improvement for animals

2661 Dennis, John V. *Wildlife Gardener.* **1985, Knopf $19.95 (0-394-53582-0).** A guide to gardening techniques designed to draw beneficial animal species into the garden. "A worthwhile addition to active gardening collections."—BL (Rev: BL 7/85; LJ 6/1/85; NYTBR 6/2/85) **[639.92]**

Reserves and refuge areas for animals

2662 Clark, Bill. *High Hills and Wild Goats: Life Among the Animals of the Hai-Bar Wildlife Refuge.* **1990, Little, Brown $19.95 (0-316-14600-5).** An introduction to the wildlife of the Hai-Bar Wildlife Refuge, located in Israel's Negev Desert, by a former curator of the park. (Rev: BL 11/15/89; LJ 11/1/89; PW 11/17/89) **[639.95]**

2663 Turner, Myles. *My Serengeti Years: The Memoirs of an African Game Warden.* **1988, Norton $17.95 (0-393-02576-4).** An autobiography of the man who served as game warden for Tanzania's Serengeti National Park for nearly 20 years. (Rev: BL 6/1/88; PW 4/1/88) **[639.95]**

640 HOME ECONOMICS AND FAMILY LIVING

2664 Christensen, Karen. *Home Ecology: Making Your Home a Better Place.* **1990, Fulcrum paper $15.95 (1-55591-062-9).** A guide to creating an environmentally sound living space. (Rev: CSM 12/20/90; LJ 9/1/90) **[640]**

2665 Cowan, Ruth Schwartz. *More Work for Mother: The Ironies of Household Technology from the Open Hearth to the Microwave.* **1985, Basic Books paper $11.95 (0-465-04732-7).** A study of the effects of technological improvements upon household tasks. (Rev: Choice 2/84; LJ 10/1/83) **[640]**

2666 Hunter, Linda Mason. *Healthy Home: An Attic to Basement Guide to Toxin-Free Living.* **1989, Rodale Pr. $21.95 (0-87857-813-7); Simon & Schuster paper $9.95 (0-671-70819-8).** A guide to freeing one's home from toxins and hazardous substances. (Rev: LJ 6/15/89; PW 4/21/89) **[640]**

641 Food and drink

2667 Hess, John L., and Karen Hess. *Taste of America.* **1989, Univ. of South Carolina Pr. $29.95 (0-87249-640-6); paper $12.95 (0-87249-641-4).** The former *New York Times* food editor and his wife decry the decline in quality of American food in this century. (Rev: BL 12/15/76; LJ 12/15/76; PW 10/24/77) **[641]**

Persons

2668 Fisher, M. F. K. *Long Ago in France: The Years in Dijon.* **1991, Prentice Hall $17.95 (0-13-**

929548-8). Memoirs of the food writer's years living in Dijon with her husband sampling the joys of the region's cooking. (Rev: BL 1/15/91; LJ 2/15/91; PW 1/4/91)   **[641.092]**

Applied nutrition

2669   Brody, Jane. *Jane Brody's Nutrition Book.* **1982, Bantam paper $12.95 (0-553-34421-8).** An introduction to nutrition and a healthy diet based on the results of a government study. (Rev: BL 5/15/81; NYTBR 8/30/81; PW 3/20/81)   **[641.1]**

2670   Griggs, Barbara. *Food Factor: Why We Are What We Eat.* **1987, Viking $19.95 (0-670-80201-8); Penguin paper $7.95 (0-14-007034-6).** A history of the science of nutrition and of man's understanding of the content of foods. (Rev: LJ 4/1/87; PW 1/23/87; TLS 12/26/86)   **[641.1]**

Wine

2671   Clarke, Oz. *Essential Wine Book: An Indispensable Guide to the Wines of the World.* **1989, Simon & Schuster paper $14.95 (0-671-67049-2).** A nation-by-nation guide to the wines of the world with photographs and maps detailing the key regions of wine production. (Rev: BL 1/15/86; LJ 1/86)   **[641.22]**

2672   Cox, Jeff. *From Vines to Wines: The Complete Guide to Growing Grapes and Making Your Own Wine.* **1989, Storey Communications paper $10.95 (0-88266-528-6).** A guide to home winemaking from grape cultivation to the storage and aging of the finished product. (Rev: BL 9/1/85; LJ 9/1/85; PW 8/16/85)   **[641.22]**

2673   Darlington, David. *Angels' Visits: An Inquiry into the Mystery of Zinfandel.* **1991, Henry Holt $19.95 (0-8050-1608-2).** The author's homage to his favorite wine and its history. (Rev: BL 2/15/91; PW 1/25/91)   **[641.22]**

2674   Maresca, Thomas E. *Mastering Wine: A Taste at a Time.* **1985, Bantam paper $9.95 (0-553-34202-9).** An introduction to the methods and pleasures of wine tasting. (Rev: BL 10/15/85; LJ 10/1/85; PW 9/20/85)   **[641.22]**

2675   Parker, Robert M., Jr. *Wines of the Rhone Valley and Provence: The Definitive Guide.* **1987, Simon & Schuster $22.95 (0-671-63379-1).** A handbook to the wines of France's Rhone Valley and Provence region by the editor of *The Wine Advocate.* (Rev: BL 11/1/87; LJ 1/88)   **[641.22]**

2676   Rothschild, Philippe de, and Joan Littlewood. *Baron Philippe: The Very Candid Autobiography of Baron Philippe de Rothschild.* **1984, Crown $16.95 (0-517-55557-3).** Memoirs of the French baron regarding his experiences during the Second World War and the development of his internationally renowned vineyards and winery. (Rev: Atl 3/85; BL 1/1/85; PW 1/4/85)   **[641.22]**

2677   Sutcliffe, Serena. *Champagne: The History and Character of the World's Most Celebrated Wine.* **1988, Simon & Schuster $29.95 (0-671-66672-**

X). An illustrated survey of the history of true champagne. (Rev: LJ 1/89; NYTBR 12/4/88)   **[641.22]**

2678   Zraly, Kevin. *Windows on the World Complete Wine Course.* **1990, Sterling $21.95 (0-8069-5795-6).** A guide to wine tasting and appreciation by the former sommelier for New York's Windows on the World restaurant. (Rev: BL 5/15/85; LJ 6/1/85; PW 4/19/85)   **[641.22]**

Brewed and malted beverages

2679   Jackson, Michael. *New World Guide to Beer.* **1990, Running Pr. $17.98 (0-89471-884-3).** A revised illustrated guide to beers of the world. "This exceptional guide is as rewarding to scan as to study."—PW (Rev: BL 1/15/89; LJ 2/15/89; PW 12/16/88)   **[641.23]**

Food

2680   Eckhardt, Linda West. *New West Coast Cuisine.* **1985, J. P. Tarcher $16.95 (0-87477-358-X); paper $10.95 (0-87477-359-8).** An introduction to innovative West Coast cuisine. "This delightfully written book will guide cooks from the garden (or store) to the table."—PW (Rev: BL 10/1/85; LJ 8/85; PW 8/16/85)   **[641.3]**

2681   Edelman, Edward, and Susan Grodnick. *Ideal Cheese Book.* **1986, Harper & Row $22.95 (0-06-055073-2).** A guide to the making, selection, and eating of the world's cheeses. (Rev: BL 11/1/86; LJ 11/1/86; PW 9/19/86)   **[641.3]**

2682   Lang, Jenifer Harvey. *Tastings: The Best from Ketchup to Caviar; 31 Pantry Basics and How They Rate with the Experts.* **1986, Crown paper $14.95 (0-517-56497-1).** Results of blind taste testings conducted to determine the best products in 31 different food categories. (Rev: BL 10/1/86; LJ 10/1/86; PW 11/21/86)   **[641.3]**

2683   Robertson, Laurel. *New Laurel's Kitchen: A Handbook for Vegetarian Cookery and Nutrition.* **1986, Ten Speed $24.95 (0-89915-167-8); paper $19.95 (0-89815-166-X).** A revised and updated version of the author's *Laurel's Kitchen,* a guide to vegetarian cooking and living on a meatless diet. (Rev: BL 12/15/86; LJ 12/86)   **[641.3]**

2684   Tannahill, Reay. *Food in History.* **1989, Crown $19.95 (0-517-57186-2).** The history of food and how food affected history. "A fascinating addition to any collection."—LJ (Rev: BL 11/15/73; LJ 8/73; Newsweek 8/6/73)   **[641.3]**

2685   Trillin, Calvin. *Third Helpings.* **1984, Penguin paper $5.95 (0-14-007314-0).** Trillin's third tome regarding his quests for good food in America. (Rev: CSM 6/8/83; LJ 4/1/83; NYTBR 4/17/83)   **[641.3]**

2686   Visser, Margaret. *Much Depends on Dinner: The Extraordinary History and Mythology, Allure and Obsessions, Perils and Taboos, of an Ordinary Meal.* **1987, Grove-Weidenfeld $19.95 (0-8021-0023-6).** An anthropological study of the cultural traditions behind the preparation and consumption of an ordinary American dinner. "An enlightening contribution to the study of food and culture."—BL (Rev: BL 1/15/88; LJ 1/88; PW 1/8/88. Awards: PW, 1987) **[641.3]**

Food preservation and storage

2687 Bailey, Janet. *Keeping Food Fresh: How to Choose and Store Everything You Eat.* 1989, Harper & Row paper $10.95 (0-06-097254-8). A survey of methods of food selection and preservation. (Rev: BL 7/85; LJ 9/1/85) **[641.4]**

Cookery

2688 Axcell, Claudia. *Simple Foods for the Pack: The Sierra Club Guide to Delicious Natural Foods for the Trail.* 1986, Sierra Club paper $8.95 (0-87156-757-1). A guide to recipes and food compatible with the backpacking experience. "Worth its weight both on the trail and off."—PW (Rev: LJ 4/15/86; PW 3/14/86) **[641.5]**

2689 Beck, Simone, and Suzy Patterson. *Food and Friends: A Memoir with Recipes.* 1991, Viking $25.00 (0-670-83934-5). Memoirs of the French chef's life and career laced with over 200 recipes. "An essential purchase."—LJ (Rev: BL 8/91; LJ 8/91) **[641.5]**

2690 Berkowitz, George, and Jane Doerfer. *Legal Seafoods Cookbook.* 1988, Doubleday paper $12.95 (0-385-23183-0). An introduction to the selection and preparation of seafood by the owner of Boston's Legal Sea Food restaurants. (Rev: BL 2/1/88; LJ 3/15/88) **[641.5]**

2691 Bertolli, Paul, and Alice Waters. *Chez Panisse Cooking: New Tastes and Techniques.* 1988, Random $24.95 (0-394-56970-9). An introduction to the styles of cooking developed and featured at Berkeley's Chez Panisse restaurant, by their long-time chef. (Rev: BL 7/88; LJ 8/88; PW 9/16/88) **[641.5]**

2692 Blanc, Georges. *Natural Cuisine of Georges Blanc.* 1987, Stewart, Tabori & Chang $50.00 (1-55670-008-3). An illustrated cookbook by the celebrated French chef on the art of cooking with fruits, vegetables, and seafood. (Rev: BL 12/15/87; NYTBR 12/6/87; PW 9/8/87. Awards: PW, 1987) **[641.5]**

2693 Bodger, Lorraine. *Christmas Kitchen.* 1989, Doubleday $19.95 (0-385-24742-7). Collected recipes, menus, and entertaining suggestions for the Christmas season. (Rev: BL 10/15/89; LJ 10/15/89) **[641.5]**

2694 Brody, Jane. *Jane Brody's Good Food Gourmet: Recipes and Menus for Delicious and Healthful Entertaining.* 1990, Norton $25.00 (0-393-02878-X). A selection of 500 low-fat, low-cholesterol recipes for healthful living. (Rev: BL 9/15/90; LJ 9/15/90; PW 8/24/90. Awards: BL, 1990; PW, 1990) **[641.5]**

2695 Brown, Edward Espe. *Tassajara Recipe Book: Favorites of the Guest Season.* 1985, Shambhala paper $8.95 (0-87773-308-2). A collection of over 200 vegetarian recipes by the author of the *Tassajara Bread Book.* (Rev: LJ 5/15/85; PW 5/7/85) **[641.5]**

2696 Bugialli, Giuliano. *Bugialli on Pasta.* 1988, Simon & Schuster $27.50 (0-671-62024-X). An introduction to the making and preparation of pasta by the Italian chef. (Rev: BL 11/1/88; LJ 11/15/88; NYTBR 12/4/88) **[641.5]**

2697 Burros, Marian. *Twenty Minute Menus.* 1989, Simon & Schuster $19.95 (0-671-62390-7). The *New York Times* food columnist's guide to the selection and preparation of quick meals for two or three people. (Rev: BL 3/15/89; NYTBR 6/11/89; PW 2/17/89) **[641.5]**

2698 Canzoneri, Robert. *Potboiler: An Amateur's Affair with La Cuisine.* 1989, North Point $17.95 (0-86547-360-9). The development of a self-taught cook from novice to gourmet status with recipes and anecdotes tracing his progression. (Rev: BL 9/1/89; LJ 7/89; PW 7/21/89. Awards: PW, 1989) **[641.5]**

2699 Chantiles, Vilma Liancouras. *International Diabetic Cookbook.* 1989, Harper & Row $19.95 (0-06-016057-8). Presentation of international recipes adapted to the special dietary needs of diabetics. (Rev: BL 1/15/89; LJ 3/15/89; PW 2/17/89) **[641.5]**

2700 Child, Julia. *Julia Child and More Company.* 1979, Knopf $17.95 (0-394-73806-3); paper $12.95 (0-394-73806-3). One of a series of chatty and charming cookbooks by America's most popular chef. (Rev: CSM 12/21/78; LJ 12/1/78; NYTBR 12/3/78. Awards: NBA, 1980) **[641.5]**

2701 Child, Julia. *Way to Cook.* 1989, Knopf $50.00 (0-394-53264-3). A guide to the art of cooking by the chef who helped popularize Gallic cuisine via her PBS series "The French Chef." "Julia's long-awaited masterwork . . . an essential purchase."—LJ (Rev: BL 1/15/90; LJ 8/89; NYTBR 12/3/89. Awards: BL, 1989; BL, the 1980s; LJ, 1989) **[641.5]**

2702 Colwin, Laurie. *Home Cooking: A Writer in the Kitchen.* 1988, Knopf $17.95 (0-394-55969-X); Bantam paper $10.95 (0-551-34807-8). A lighthearted cookbook/memoir of the American novelist and short story writer's experiences in the kitchen. (Rev: CSM 2/15/89; NYTBR 12/4/88) **[641.5]**

2703 Conason, Emil G., and Ella Metz. *Original Salt-Free Diet Cookbook.* 1986, Putnam paper $8.95 (0-399-51231-4). An updated revised edition of the 1949 cookbook with recipes for 60 complete salt-free meals. (Rev: BL 5/1/86; PW 6/20/86) **[641.5]**

2704 Cone, Marcia, and Thelma Snyder. *Mastering Microwave Cookery.* 1986, Simon & Schuster $24.95 (0-671-54162-5). A guide to recipes and effective techniques of cooking with a microwave oven. (Rev: BL 10/1/86; LJ 9/15/86; PW 8/15/86) **[641.5]**

2705 Cunningham, Marion. *Fannie Farmer Cookbook.* 1990, Knopf $24.95 (0-394-56788-9). Thirteenth revised edition of the American classic cookbook. "The best edition . . . since Fannie's 1896 original."—Newsweek (Rev: BL 8/90; LJ 8/24/90; Newsweek 11/19/90) **[641.5]**

2706 David, Elizabeth. *An Omelette and a Glass of Wine.* 1990, Penguin paper $8.95 (0-14-046846-3). A selection of essays by the British food critic. "David doesn't disappoint ... she teaches and entertains, offering precious gifts of recipes and insights along the way."—PW (REV: LJ 9/1/85; NYTBR 7/14/85; PW 6/21/85)   **[641.5]**

2707   Fisher, M. F. K. *Dubious Honors: A Book of Prefaces.* **1988, North Point paper $9.95 (0-86547-414-1).** A collection of 35 prefaces contributed to cookbooks by the food writer from 1937 to 1985. (REV: BL 4/1/88; LJ 4/15/88; NYTBR 6/5/88)   **[641.5]**

2708   Franey, Pierre. *New York Times More Sixty-Minute Gourmet.* **1981, Random $15.95 (0-8129-0982-8); Fawcett paper $8.95 (0-449-90194-7).** One hundred menus containing 300 recipes for quality food that is quick to prepare. (REV: BL 11/15/81; CSM 12/3/81; LJ 12/15/81)   **[641.5]**

2709   Franey, Pierre, and Bryan Miller. *Cuisine Rapide.* **1989, Random $22.50 (0-8129-1746-4).** A cookbook featuring quick gourmet meals designed by the *New York Times* food columnist to accompany a PBS series. (REV: BL 3/15/89; NYTBR 6/11/89; PW 3/17/89)   **[641.5]**

2710   Freiman, Jane. *Dinner Party: The New Entertaining; Over One Hundred Simple, Stylish Menus for the Way We Live and Eat Today.* **1989, Harper & Row $27.50 (0-06-016051-9).** Collected recipes, menus, and suggestions for entertaining for the modern dinner party. (REV: BL 12/15/89; LJ 12/89; PW 11/17/89)   **[641.5]**

2711   Fussell, Betty. *Betty Fussell's Home Plates: A Shopping, Cooking, Eating and Wine Guide for Everyday.* **1990, Dutton $12.95 (0-525-24861-7).** A collection of 90 recipes for everyday meals by the author of *I Hear America Cooking.* (REV: BL 6/15/90; NYTBR 6/10/90; PW 4/20/90)   **[641.5]**

2712   Giobbi, Edward. *Pleasures of the Good Earth.* **1991, Knopf $23.00 (0-394-56130-9).** A guide to the growing and preparation of foods and meats at home. Includes an introduction by Chez Panisse's Alice Waters. (REV: BL 6/15/91; NYTBR 6/9/91; PW 3/29/91)   **[641.5]**

2713   Goldberg, Betty S. *International Cooking for the Kosher Home.* **1987, Jonathan David $16.95 (0-8246-0323-0).** A collection of international recipes adapted for kitchens conforming to kosher dietary restrictions. (REV: LJ 3/15/88; PW 1/22/88)   **[641.5]**

2714   Gunst, Kathy. *Leftovers: 200 Recipes.* **1991, HarperCollins $25.00 (0-06-055296-4); paper $14.00 (0-06-096863-X).** A guide to the creative use of leftovers in cooking. (REV: LJ 12/90; PW 12/21/90)   **[641.5]**

2715   Hecht, Helen. *Simple Pleasures: Casual Cooking for All Occasions.* **1986, Macmillan $16.95 (0-689-11523-7).** Easy-to-prepare dishes for both small and large dining parties. (REV: BL 6/1/86; LJ 5/15/86; PW 5/16/86)   **[641.5]**

2716   Hewitt, Jean, and Marjorie Page-Blanchard. *Cooking for Two Today.* **1985, Little, Brown $14.95 (0-316-35979-3).** A selection of recipes for

quick, light meals for couples. (REV: BL 6/15/85; LJ 7/85; PW 6/21/85)   **[641.5]**

2717   Hodgson, Moira. *Good Food from a Small Kitchen.* **1989, Prentice Hall paper $10.95 (0-13-360306-7).** Over 240 recipes that can be prepared in a minimum of space with limited kitchen utensils and gadgetry. (REV: BL 4/19/85; LJ 5/15/85)   **[641.5]**

2718   Jones, Evan. *Epicurean Delight: The Life and Times of James Beard.* **1990, Random $24.95 (0-394-57415-X).** A biography of the American food critic and cookbook writer. (REV: BL 10/1/90; PW 8/24/90)   **[641.5]**

2719   Kafka, Barbara. *Microwave Gourmet.* **1987, Morrow $22.95 (0-688-06843-X).** Gourmet recipes designed to be prepared in the microwave. "Her thorough and creative approach is simply the best in the field ... a new standard."—LJ (REV: BL 9/15/87; LJ 9/15/87; PW 8/21/87)   **[641.5]**

2720   Kamman, Madeleine. *Madeleine Cooks.* **1986, Morrow $19.95 (0-688-06203-2).** Two hundred recipes derived from French traditions and adapted for the American kitchen. "A marvelous cookbook ... gracefully written."—PW (REV: BL 1/1/86; LJ 12/85; PW 11/15/85)   **[641.5]**

2721   Kennedy, Diana. *Nothing Fancy: Recipes and Recollections of Soul-Satisfying Food.* **1989, North Point paper $12.95 (0-86547-374-6).** A survey of "down-home" cooking by the author of *The Cuisines of Mexico.* "An exceptional treat from an exceptional cook and writer."—BL (REV: BL 9/15/84; LJ 10/15/84; PW 10/19/84)   **[641.5]**

2722   La Place, Viana, and Evan Kleiman. *Cucina Fresca.* **1987, Harper & Row paper $12.95 (0-06-096211-9).** A cookbook focusing on innovative Italian-inspired recipes that can be served cold or at room temperature for spring or summer enjoyment. (REV: BL 4/15/85; LJ 4/15/85; PW 4/19/85)   **[641.5]**

2723   Lemlin, Jeanne. *Vegetarian Pleasures: A Menu Cookbook.* **1986, Knopf paper $16.95 (0-394-74302-4).** Over 70 complete vegetarian meals selected from a variety of international cuisines are presented in this illustrated cookbook. (REV: BL 5/1/86; LJ 4/15/86; PW 4/18/86)   **[641.5]**

2724   Lindsay, Anne, and Diane J. Fink. *American Cancer Society Cookbook: A Menu for Good Health.* **1988, Hearst Books $17.95 (0-688-07484-7).** Two hundred recipes for low-fat, high-fiber dishes following American Cancer Society dietary guidelines. (REV: BL 3/1/88; LJ 3/15/88)   **[641.5]**

2725   Lloyd, Linda. *Ma Cuisine Cooking School Cookbook.* **1988, Random $19.95 (0-394-55289-X).** A collection of innovative recipes and menus from the Los Angeles cooking school cofounded by Wolfgang Puck. (REV: BL 4/1/88; LJ 4/15/88; NYTBR 6/5/88)   **[641.5]**

2726   McGee, Harold. *On Food and Cooking.* **1984, Macmillan $35.00 (0-684-18132-0); paper $16.95 (0-02-034621-2).** A study of the origins and scientific properties of food. (Rᴇᴠ: BL 10/1/84; Choice 4/85; NYTBR 1/13/85)   **[641.5]**

2727 Madison, Deborah. *Savory Way: High Spirited, Down-to-Earth Recipes from the Author.* **1990, Bantam $22.95 (0-553-05780-4).** A collection of innovative vegetable recipes from the coauthor of the *Greens Cook Book.* (Rᴇᴠ: LJ 5/15/90; PW 4/20/90. Aᴡᴀʀᴅs: PW, 1990)   **[641.5]**

2728 Marks, Copeland. *Exotic Kitchens of Indonesia: Recipes from the Outer Islands.* **1989, Evans $19.95 (0-87131-576-9).** A guide to the cuisine of the outer Indonesian islands adapted for American kitchens. (Rᴇᴠ: BL 1/1/90; LJ 11/15/89)   **[641.5]**

2729 Olney, Judith. *Judith Olney's Farm Market Book.* **1991, Doubleday $25.00 (0-385-41096-4).** A collection of 125 recipes and interviews culled from farmers' markets throughout the United States. "A tribute to the best in culinary writing."—BL (Rᴇᴠ: BL 6/1/91; NYTBR 6/9/91; PW 5/31/91)   **[641.5]**

2730 Pepin, Jacques. *Art of Cooking, Vol. 1.* **1987, Knopf $35.00 (0-394-54658-X).** Step-by-step cooking instructions presented by the French chef in both text and photographs. (Rᴇᴠ: BL 10/1/87; LJ 10/15/87; PW 10/16/87. Aᴡᴀʀᴅs: PW, 1987)   **[641.5]**

2731 Pepin, Jacques. *Art of Cooking, Vol. 2.* **1988, Knopf $39.95 (0-394-54659-8).** The second volume of the French chef's illustrated course to the techniques of cooking. "As impressive as the first . . . obviously, an essential purchase."—LJ (Rᴇᴠ: BL 7/88; LJ 6/15/88)   **[641.5]**

2732 Puck, Wolfgang. *Wolfgang Puck Cookbook.* **1986, Random $19.95 (0-394-53366-6).** A cookbook by the innovative chef of Los Angeles' Chinois on Main and Spago restaurants. (Rᴇᴠ: BL 11/1/86; LJ 11/15/86; PW 10/17/86)   **[641.5]**

2733 Puckett, Susan. *A Cook's Tour of Iowa.* **1988, Univ. of Iowa Pr. paper $10.95 (0-87745-289-X).** A cookbook combining recipes with oral histories of the regional dishes of Iowa. (Rᴇᴠ: LJ 5/15/88; NYTBR 6/5/88)   **[641.5]**

2734 Renggli, Seppi. *Four Seasons Spa Cuisine.* **1986, Simon & Schuster $17.95 (0-671-54440-3).** Fifty complete menus featuring low calorie, high nutrition recipes devised by the chef of New York's Four Seasons restaurant. (Rᴇᴠ: BL 4/15/86; LJ 4/15/86; PW 4/18/86)   **[641.5]**

2735 Roberts, Michael, and Janet Spiegel. *Fresh from the Freezer.* **1990, Morrow $19.95 (0-688-08543-1).** A guide to freezing techniques for food preservation and as the basis for innovative cookery. (Rᴇᴠ: BL 10/15/90; LJ 11/15/90; PW 10/19/90) **[641.5]**

2736 Rosso, Julee, and Sheila Lukins. *New Basics Cookbook.* **1989, Workman $29.95 (0-89480-392-1); paper $18.95 (0-89480-341-7).** A collection of more than 900 recipes by the former owners of the Silver Palate. "An essential purchase."—LJ (Rᴇᴠ: BL 3/1/90; LJ 12/89; PW 11/17/89)   **[641.5]**

2737 Rosso, Julee, and Sheila Lukins. *Silver Palate Good Times Cookbook.* **1985, Workman $22.50 (0-89480-832-X); paper $12.95 (0-89480-831-1).** A seasonally arranged guide to innovative cooking with over 450 recipes by the authors of the *Silver Palate Cookbook.* (Rᴇᴠ: BL 7/85; NYTBR 6/2/85)   **[641.5]**

2738 Sass, Lorna J., and Ann Bramson. *Cooking Under Pressure.* **1989, Hearst Books $18.95 (0-688-08814-7).** A guide to pressure cookery for the modern kitchen. "The perfect book for a generation that demands quality in its instant gratification."—BL (Rᴇᴠ: BL 11/1/89; LJ 11/15/89; PW 10/20/89)   **[641.5]**

2739 Schneider, Sally. *Art of Low Calorie Cooking.* **1990, Stewart, Tabori & Chang $35.00 (1-55670-157-8).** An illustrated guide to the preparation of 125 low-calorie recipes. "A must for solid cookery collections."—BL (Rᴇᴠ: BL 11/15/90; LJ 9/15/90; NYTBR 12/2/90)   **[641.5]**

2740 Shapiro, Laura. *Perfection Salad: Women and Cooking at the Turn of the Century.* **1986, Farrar $16.95 (0-374-23075-7); Henry Holt paper $8.95 (0-8050-0228-6).** An examination of the changes in American cuisine that took place at the end of the nineteenth century. (Rᴇᴠ: LJ 4/1/86; NYTBR 3/23/86; Newsweek 4/28/86)   **[641.5]**

2741 Sokolov, Raymond. *How to Cook: An Easy and Imaginative Guide for the Beginner.* **1986, Morrow $16.95 (0-688-04968-0).** An introduction to cooking techniques for the novice. (Rᴇᴠ: LJ 6/15/86; PW 5/16/86)   **[641.5]**

2742 Stern, Jane, and Michael Stern. *Square Meals: Taste Thrills of Only Yesterday—From Mom's Best Pot Roast and Tuna Noodle Casserole to the Perfect Tea Time Chocolate Bread.* **1984, Knopf $17.95 (0-394-53112-4); Andrews & McMeel paper $9.95 (0-8362-2126-5).** A study of middle-American food from the 1920s to the 1950s. (Rᴇᴠ: BL 8/84; LJ 8/84; NYTBR 12/2/84)   **[641.5]**

2743 Stone, Sally, and Martin Stone. *Essential Root Vegetable Cookbook: A Primer for Choosing and Serving Nature's Buried Treasures.* **1991, Crown $22.50 (0-517-57623-6).** A guide to the cultivation and preparation of 31 varieties of root vegetables. (Rᴇᴠ: NYTBR 6/9/91; PW 1/25/91)   **[641.5]**

2744 Thorne, John. *Simple Cooking.* **1987, Viking $20.00 (0-670-81212-9); Penguin paper $9.95 (0-14-011737-7).** Essays on food and cooking intertwined with recipes reprinted from the author's newsletter, *Simple Cooking.* "This book belongs as much to a literary collection as it does to cookery."—BL (Rᴇᴠ: BL 9/1/87; LJ 9/15/87; PW 9/18/87. Aᴡᴀʀᴅs: PW, 1987)   **[641.5]**

2745 Weaver, William W. *Christmas Cook: Three Centuries of American Yuletide Sweets.* **1990, HarperCollins $35.00 (0-06-055212-3); paper $18.95 (0-06-096552-5).** A history of American Christmas sweets and guide to their preparation. (Rᴇᴠ: BL 10/1/90; CSM 12/6/90; LJ 10/15/90)   **[641.5]**

2746 **Willan, Anne.** *La Varenne Pratique: The Complete Illustrated Guide to the Techniques, Ingredients and Tools of Classic Modern Cooking.* 1989, Crown $60.00 (0-517-57383-0). An illustrated step-by-step guide to modern French cooking by the founder of the La Varenne Paris cooking school. (REV: CSM 12/6/89; LJ 2/15/90; Time 8/20/90) **[641.5]**

2747 **Williams, Chuck.** *Williams-Sonoma Cookbook and Guide to Kitchenware.* 1986, Random $19.95 (0-394-54411-0). A cookbook and guide to cooking utensils and their uses by the head of the mail-order and retail chain. (REV: LJ 6/15/86; NYTBR 6/1/86; PW 3/14/86) **[641.5]**

2748 **Witty, Helen.** *Fancy Pantry.* 1986, Workman paper $11.95 (0-89480-037-X). A guide to the construction and stocking of a kitchen pantry for the active home chef. (REV: BL 6/15/86; LJ 5/15/86; PW 4/18/86) **[641.5]**

2749 **Worthington, Diane Rossen.** *Taste of Summer: Inspired Recipes for Casual Entertaining.* 1991, Bantam $19.95 (0-553-05273-X); paper $14.00 (0-553-34879-5). A collection of California-inspired summer recipes for indoor and outdoor preparation. (REV: BL 4/1/88; LJ 4/15/88; NYTBR 6/5/88) **[641.5]**

Breakfast

2750 **Kolpas, Norman.** *Breakfast and Brunch Book.* 1988, Price/Stern/Sloan $19.95 (0-89586-616-1). A guide to the history of the breakfast, with recipes and menus, for recommended morning meals. (REV: BL 3/15/88; LJ 4/15/88) **[641.52]**

For various specific times of year

2751 **Fussell, Betty.** *Food in Good Season: A Month-by-Month Harvest of Country Recipes for Cooks Everywhere.* 1988, Knopf $18.95 (0-394-57117-7). A guide to the best seasonal dishes including their history, and recipes for their preparation. (REV: BL 9/15/88; LJ 9/15/88) **[641.564]**

Ethnic cooking

2752 **Africa News Staff, and Tami Hultman.** *Africa News Cookbook.* 1986, Penguin paper $14.95 (0-14-046751-3). Recipes from over 40 African nations adapted to the modern American kitchen. (REV: CSM 7/3/86; LJ 9/15/85) **[641.59]**

2753 **Anderson, Jean.** *Food of Portugal.* 1986, Morrow $24.95 (0-688-04363-1). An introduction to Portuguese food and cooking. "The most definitive boon on Portuguese cuisine yet published."—BL (REV: BL 9/15/86; LJ 8/86; PW 7/18/86) **[641.59]**

2754 **Andrews, Colman.** *Catalan Cuisine: Europe's Last Great Culinary Secret.* 1988, Macmillan $24.95 (0-689-11781-7). An introduction to the cuisine of Northeast Spain. "A wonderfully intriguing and inspiring book."—BL (REV: BL 4/15/88; LJ 4/15/88; NYTBR 6/5/88) **[641.59]**

2755 **Bailey, Lee, and Pilgrimage Garden Club.** *Lee Bailey's Southern Food and Plantation Houses.* 1990, Crown $30.00 (0-517-57280-X). A collection of recipes from Natchez, Mississippi, with illustrations of the area's plantation homes. (REV: BL 9/1/90; NYTBR 6/10/90) **[641.59]**

2756 **Barr, Nancy Verde.** *We Called It Macaroni: An American Heritage of Southern Italian Cooking.* 1990, Knopf $23.00 (0-394-55798-0). A collection of 250 Italian-American recipes developed by Southern Italian immigrants and their offspring. "A delight for the mind as well as the palate."—BL (REV: BL 2/1/91; NYTBR 12/2/90; PW 10/19/90) **[641.59]**

2757 **Batmangli, Najmieh.** *Food of Life: A Book of Ancient Persian and Modern Iranian Cooking and Ceremonies.* 1990, Mage $32.95 (0-934211-27-2). An introduction to traditional and contemporary Persian cooking. (REV: BL 9/15/86; PW 7/18/86) **[641.59]**

2758 **Bayless, Rick, and Deann G. Bayless.** *Authentic Mexican: Regional Cooking from the Heart of Mexico.* 1987, Morrow $24.95 (0-688-04394-1). A guide to the regional cuisines of Mexico. "A definitive bible on the subject . . . a must purchase for any self-respecting cookery collection."—BL (REV: BL 4/15/87; LJ 12/86; NYTBR 5/31/87) **[641.59]**

2759 **Belk, Sarah.** *Around the Southern Table.* 1991, Simon & Schuster $24.95 (0-671-52833-5). A cookbook tracing the culinary history of the American South written by a *Bon Appetit* editor. (REV: BL 3/1/91; NYTBR 6/9/91; PW 2/22/91) **[641.59]**

2760 **Brack, Fred, and Tina Bell.** *Tastes of the Pacific Northwest: Traditional and Innovative Recipes from America's Newest Regional Cuisine.* 1988, Doubleday paper $16.95 (0-385-24387-1). An introduction to the regional cuisines and recipes of the Pacific Northwest. (REV: BL 6/15/88; LJ 6/15/88) **[641.59]**

2761 **Bugialli, Giuliano.** *Giuliano Bugialli's Foods of Italy.* 1984, Stewart, Tabori & Chang $50.00 (0-941434-52-4). A survey of the cuisines of Italy. "A jewel of a book."—LJ (REV: BL 1/15/85; LJ 12/84; NYTBR 12/2/84) **[641.59]**

2762 **Carpenter, Hugh, and Teri Sandison.** *Chopstix: Quick Cooking with Pacific Flavors.* 1990, Stewart, Tabori & Chang $29.95 (1-55670-133-0). Pacific-Asian recipes adapted for the American kitchen. (REV: BL 6/15/90; LJ 8/90) **[641.59]**

2763 **Casas, Penelope.** *Tapas: The Little Dishes of Spain.* 1985, Knopf $24.95 (0-394-54086-7); paper $16.95 (0-394-74235-4). A guide to the preparation and presentation of the famous Spanish hors d'oeuvres. (REV: BL 10/1/85; LJ 9/15/85; PW 9/20/85) **[641.59]**

2764 **Chirinian, Linda.** *Secrets of Cooking: Armenian, Lebanese, Persian.* 1986, Lionhart $24.95 (0-9617033-0-X). An illustrated guide to three cuisines of the Middle East. (REV: BL 12/15/86; PW 10/17/86) **[641.59]**

2765 **Claiborne, Craig.** *Craig Claiborne's Southern Cooking.* 1987, Random $19.95 (0-8129-1599-2). A presentation of American Southern cuisine by the

Mississippi-raised chef and author. (Rev: BL 7/87; LJ 8/87; NYTBR 12/6/87)   **[641.59]**

2766 Claiborne, Craig. *New York Times Cook Book: The Classic Gourmet Cookbook for the Home Kitchen with Hundreds of New Recipes.* 1990, Harper & Row $25.00 (0-06-016010-1). An updated and revised edition of the 1961 classic cookbook. (Rev: BL 4/1/90; LJ 4/15/90)   **[641.59]**

2767 Cost, Bruce. *Bruce Cost's Asian Ingredients: Buying and Cooking the Staple Foods of China, Japan and Southeast Asia.* 1988, Morrow $22.95 (0-688-05877-9). A guide to the acquisition, selection, and preparation of Asian food currently available in American markets. (Rev: BL 9/1/88; LJ 10/15/88; PW 9/16/88)   **[641.59]**

2768 Curnonsky, pseud. *Larousse Traditional French Cooking.* Ed. by Jeni Wright. 1989, Doubleday $45.00 (0-385-26532-8). A revised edition of the 1953 classic introduction to French cuisine containing over 1,200 recipes. (Rev: BL 9/1/89; LJ 9/15/89; NYTBR 12/3/89)   **[641.59]**

2769 Deighton, Len. *ABC of French Food.* 1990, Bantam $19.95 (0-553-05759-6). An introduction to the art of French cooking by the British spy novelist. (Rev: BL 6/15/90; LJ 3/15/90; PW 3/23/90)   **[641.59]**

2770 De Medici, Lorenza. *Heritage of Italian Cooking.* 1990, Random $40.00 (0-394-58876-2). An illustrated survey of Italian cooking with historical recipes compiled by the author of *The Renaissance of Italian Cooking.* (Rev: BL 12/1/90; NYTBR 12/2/90; PW 8/24/90)   **[641.59]**

2771 Dent, Huntley. *Feast of Santa Fe: Cooking of the American Southwest.* 1985, Simon & Schuster $19.95 (0-671-47686-6). An introduction to the history and preparation of New Mexican cuisine. (Rev: LJ 3/15/85; NYTBR 6/2/85; Time 11/25/85)   **[641.59]**

2772 Dille, Carolyn, and Susan Belsinger. *New Southwestern Cooking.* 1986, Macmillan $19.95 (0-07-531610-9). Creative interpretations of traditional Southwestern cooking. "A new, fresh, and immensely appealing way of looking at the traditional food of this region."—LJ (Rev: BL 6/15/86; LJ 6/15/86; PW 5/16/86. Awards: PW, 1986)   **[641.59]**

2773 Dupree, Nathalie. *New Southern Cooking.* 1986, Knopf $22.95 (0-394-55818-9). A companion volume to the author's PBS television series, exploring both traditional and nouvelle Southern cooking. (Rev: BL 12/15/86; LJ 12/86; PW 11/21/86. Awards: PW, 1986)   **[641.59]**

2774 Esposito, Mary Ann. *Ciao Italia: Traditional Italian Recipes from Family Kitchens.* 1991, Morrow $20.00 (0-688-10317-0). A companion volume to the author's PBS series on Italian cooking. (Rev: BL 9/1/91; PW 8/23/91)   **[641.59]**

2775 Fussell, Betty. *I Hear America Cooking.* 1986, Viking $24.95 (0-670-81241-2). A history of American regional cooking with recipes representative of different sections of the United States. "A major

contribution to American culinary history."—LJ (Rev: BL 9/1/86; LJ 11/15/86; Time 11/24/86)   **[641.59]**

2776 Giobbi, Edward, and Richard Wolff. *Eat Right, Eat Well: The Italian Way.* 1985, Knopf $24.95 (0-394-53071-3). A cookbook prepared by a chef and a cardiologist presenting healthful recipes in the Italian tradition. (Rev: LJ 4/15/85; NYTBR 6/2/85; PW 4/19/85)   **[641.59]**

2777 Goldstein, Joyce. *Mediterranean Kitchen.* 1989, Morrow $22.95 (0-688-07283-6). A collection of recipes and food lore from around the Mediterranean world. "Goldstein sets a literary and culinary scene . . . with great warmth and a true writer's sense of place."—BL (Rev: BL 11/15/89; CSM 12/6/89; LJ 11/15/89. Awards: BL, 1989)   **[641.59]**

2778 Greer, Anne Lindsay. *Foods of the Sun: Cooking of the West and Southwest.* 1988, Harper & Row $22.50 (0-06-181321-4). An introduction to contemporary cooking styles of the American West and Southwest. (Rev: BL 3/1/88; LJ 2/15/88; NYTBR 6/5/88)   **[641.59]**

2779 Harris, Jessica B. *Sky Juice and Flying Fish: Traditional Caribbean Cooking.* 1991, Simon & Schuster paper $12.95 (0-671-68165-6). An introduction to the cuisines of the Caribbean islands. (Rev: BL 1/15/91; LJ 12/90; PW 1/18/91)   **[641.59]**

2780 Hazan, Marcella. *Marcella's Italian Kitchen.* 1986, Knopf $27.50 (0-394-50892-0). A collection of 250 Italian recipes by the author of *The Classic Italian Cook Book.* "Her prose is vivid, enticing and imbued with pleasure and ease . . . the recipes are a personal and far-ranging collection."—PW (Rev: BL 9/1/86; LJ 9/15/86; PW 8/15/86. Awards: PW, 1986)   **[641.59]**

2781 Hom, Ken, and Harvey Steiman. *Chinese Technique.* 1984, Pocket paper $12.95 (0-671-25348-4). An illustrated introduction to Chinese cooking. "Well written, well organized and well illustrated."—BL (Rev: BL 1/1/82; CSM 12/3/81; LJ 10/15/81)   **[641.59]**

2782 Hom, Ken, and Leong Ka Tai. *Taste of China.* 1990, Simon & Schuster $29.95 (0-671-69221-6). An illustrated guide to the cuisines of China and their place in Chinese culture and history. (Rev: BL 10/15/90; LJ 11/15/90; PW 10/19/90)   **[641.59]**

2783 Jones, Judith, and Evan Jones. *L. L. Bean Book of New New England Cookery.* 1987, Random $27.95 (0-394-54456-0). A selection of over 800 traditional and innovative recipes collected from the New England states. (Rev: BL 10/1/87; LJ 9/15/87; PW 10/16/87)   **[641.59]**

2784 Kamman, Madeleine. *Madeleine Kamman's Savoie: The Land, People, and Food of the French Alps.* 1989, Macmillan $24.95 (0-689-11969-0). A cultural and culinary history of the Savoy region of the French Alps. (Rev: LJ 10/15/89; NYTBR 12/3/89)   **[641.59]**

2785 Kennedy, Diana. *Art of Mexican Cooking: Traditional Mexican Cooking for Aficionados.*

1989, Bantam $24.95 (0-553-05706-5). Traditional Mexican recipes collected from all over Mexico with tips on food selection and preparation. (REV: BL 10/1/89; LJ 8/89; PW 9/22/89. AWARDS: PW, 1989) **[641.59]**

2786 Killeen, Johanne, and George Germon. *Cucina Simpatica: Robust Trattoria Cooking.* **1991, HarperCollins $25.00** (0-06-016119-1). A collection of 135 recipes from the couple's Providence, Rhode Island, trattoria. (REV: BL 4/15/91; NYTBR 6/9/91; PW 3/29/91) **[641.59]**

2787 Lambert, Henry A. *Pasta and Cheese: The Cookbook.* **1986, Pocket paper $9.95** (0-671-62778-3). Recipes by the owner of New York's Pasta and Cheese gourmet take-out food stores. (REV: BL 4/15/85; LJ 3/15/85; PW 3/15/85) **[641.59]**

2788 Law, Ruth. *Southeast Asia Cookbook.* **1990, Donald I. Fine $24.95** (1-55611-214-9). A guide to the preparation of dishes from the cuisines of Southeast Asia. (REV: BL 11/15/90; LJ 8/90) **[641.59]**

2789 Lin, Florence. *Florence Lin's Complete Book of Chinese Noodles, Dumplings, and Breads.* **1986, Morrow $19.95** (0-688-03796-8). An illustrated step-by-step guide to the preparation of Chinese noodles, breads, and dumplings. (REV: BL 6/1/86; LJ 6/15/86; Time 11/24/86) **[641.59]**

2790 Luongo, Pino, Barbara Raines, and Angela Hederman. *A Tuscan in My Kitchen: Recipes and Tales from My Home.* **1988, Crown $24.95** (0-517-56916-7). Collected recipes and memoirs of Tuscany by the New York restaurant owner. (REV: CSM 2/15/89; LJ 2/15/89; PW 9/16/88) **[641.59]**

2791 Manjon, Maite. *Gastronomy of Spain and Portugal.* **1990, Prentice Hall paper $35.00** (0-13-347691-X). A Spanish-born writer's guided tour through the cuisines of the Iberian Peninsula. (REV: BL 9/15/90; PW 8/24/90) **[641.59]**

2792 Maresca, Thomas E., and Diane Darrow. *La Tavola Italiana.* **1988, Morrow $22.95** (0-688-06629-1). A regional guide to the cuisines of Italy with suggestions for wines to accompany them. (REV: BL 1/15/88; NYTBR 6/5/88; PW 1/22/88) **[641.59]**

2793 Nathan, Jean. *American Folklife Cookbook.* **1984, Schocken $18.95** (0-8052-3914-6). A selection of 150 recipes representing the best of American regional cuisine. (REV: LJ 10/15/84; NYTBR 12/2/84; Newsweek 12/17/84) **[641.59]**

2794 Neal, Bill. *Bill Neal's Southern Cooking.* **1989, Univ. of North Carolina Pr. $19.95** (0-8078-1859-3); **paper $12.95** (0-8078-4255-9). A collection of recipes from throughout the American South. "As simple and unpretentious as its title."—CSM (REV: BL 10/15/85; Choice 12/11/85; LJ 10/15/85) **[641.59]**

2795 Neal, Bill. *Biscuits, Spoonbread and Sweet Potato Pie.* **1990, Knopf $19.95** (0-394-55941-X). A celebration of Southern cooking with excerpts from historical recipes and cookbooks. (REV: BL 5/1/90; LJ 4/15/90; NYTBR 6/10/90) **[641.59]**

2796 Orsini, Joseph. *Father Orsini's Italian Kitchen.* **1991, St. Martin's $19.95** (0-312-06352-0). A retired priest's guide to the regional cuisines of Italy. (REV: BL 9/1/91; PW 8/23/91) **[641.59]**

2797 Patout, Alex. *Patout's Cajun Home Cooking.* **1986, Random $19.95** (0-394-54725-X). An introduction to Cajun cooking by the Lafayette, Louisiana, restaurateur. (REV: BL 10/1/86; LJ 10/15/86; PW 8/15/86) **[641.59]**

2798 Prudhomme, Paul. *Prudhomme Family Cookbook: Old Time Louisiana Recipes.* **1987, Morrow $19.95** (0-688-07549-5). Collected Cajun recipes from the members of the family of chef Paul Prudhomme. (REV: BL 10/15/87; LJ 10/15/87; PW 9/18/87) **[641.59]**

2799 Roden, Claudia. *Good Food of Italy: Region by Region.* **1990, Knopf $24.95** (0-394-58250-0). A regional guide to the cuisines of Italy. (REV: BL 11/15/90; LJ 10/15/90; PW 1/4/91. AWARDS: PW, 1990) **[641.59]**

2800 Rojas-Lombardi, Felipe. *Art of South American Cooking.* **1991, HarperCollins $25.00** (0-06-016425-5). A Peruvian-born chef's overview of the cuisines of South America, laced with memoirs of his life and career. (REV: BL 10/1/91; CSM 12/5/91; NYTBR 12/1/91. AWARDS: BL, 1991) **[641.59]**

2801 Salloum, Mary. *A Taste of Lebanon: Cooking Today the Lebanese Way.* **1989, Interlink $17.95** (0-940793-08-3). An introduction to traditional Lebanese cuisine containing over 200 recipes. (REV: BL 1/15/89; LJ 3/15/89; PW 1/20/89) **[641.59]**

2802 Scaravelli, Paola, and Jon Cohen. *Mediterranean Harvest.* **1988, Dutton paper $9.95** (0-525-48373-X). A guide to meatless cooking from the cuisines of countries bordering the Mediterranean Sea. (REV: BL 9/15/86; LJ 10/15/86; PW 9/19/86) **[641.59]**

2803 Sedlar, John. *Modern Southwest Cuisine.* **1986, Simon & Schuster $29.95** (0-671-61162-3). A presentation of innovative recipes inspired by the traditional cuisine of the American Southwest. "One of the most interesting of all those available on Southwest cooking."—CSM (REV: BL 12/1/86; CSM 12/3/86; PW 8/16/86) **[641.59]**

2804 Simonds, Nina. *Chinese Seasons.* **1986, Houghton $19.95** (0-395-36802-2). Traditional foods to accompany Chinese festivals throughout the year are presented, as well as Simonds's own French-influenced variants of Chinese dishes. (REV: BL 11/1/86; LJ 11/15/86; PW 9/19/86. AWARDS: PW, 1986) **[641.59]**

2805 Sinclair, Kevin. *China: The Beautiful Cookbook.* **1986, Collins SF $39.95** (0-002-15999-6). Over 250 recipes selected from a number of Chinese provinces illustrated with color photographs. "Almost too lovely for the kitchen . . . the recipes presented here are as striking as the photographs."—PW (REV: CSM 12/3/76; PW 7/18/86. AWARDS: PW, 1986) **[641.59]**

2806 Sokolov, Raymond. *Fading Feast: A Compendium of Disappearing American Regional Foods.*

1981, Farrar $17.95 (0-374-15213-6). A history of endangered American regional specialties with one hundred recipes for their preparation. (Rev: CSM 3/3/82; LJ 12/1/81; NYTBR 2/28/82) **[641.59]**

2807 Volokh, Anne. *Art of Russian Cuisine.* 1989, Macmillan $14.95 (0-02-038102-6). A guide to the preparation of traditional Russian food with over 500 recipes. "The indispensable guide to Russian cooking."—BL (Rev: BL 11/1/83; LJ 11/15/83; NYTBR 12/11/83) **[641.59]**

2808 Von Bremzen, Anya, and John Welchman. *Please to the Table: The Russian Cookbook.* 1990, Workman $27.95 (0-89480-845-1); paper $18.95 (0-89480-753-6). An illustrated introduction to the regional cuisines of the Soviet Union. (Rev: BL 1/15/91; LJ 12/90; PW 12/21/90) **[641.59]**

2809 Vongerichten, Jean-Georges. *Simple Cuisine: The Easy New Approach to Cooking from Jean-Georges.* 1990, Prentice Hall $29.95 (0-13-195059-2). A guide to health-conscious French cooking with over 200 recipes created by the author. (Rev: BL 11/1/90; LJ 10/15/90) **[641.59]**

2810 Von Welanetz, Diana, and Paul Von Welanetz. *Von Welanetz Guide to Ethnic Ingredients.* 1983, J. P. Tarcher $20.95 (0-87477-225-7); Warner paper $10.95 (0-446-38420-8). A guide to the purchase and preparation of 1,000 items used in ethnic cooking with a recommendation of cookbooks representative of international cuisines. (Rev: BL 3/15/83; LJ 2/1/83) **[641.59]

2811 Wells, Patricia. *Bistro Cooking.* 1989, Workman $22.95 (0-89480-622-X); paper $12.95 (0-89480-623-8). Two hundred recipes of classic French bistro cooking are included along with original recipes by the author. (Rev: LJ 12/89; PW 11/17/89. Awards: PW, 1989) **[641.59]

2812 Wells, Patricia. *Simply French: Patricia Wells Presents the Cuisine of Joel Robuchon.* 1991, Morrow $30.00 (0-688-06642-9). Over 100 modern French recipes representing the cuisine developed by the Parisian chef. (Rev: BL 11/1/91; LJ 9/15/91) **[641.59]**

2813 Wolfert, Paula. *Paula Wolfert's World of Food: A Collection of Recipes from Her Kitchen, Travels and Friends.* 1988, Harper & Row $25.00 (0-06-015955-3). A collection of recipes from the author's travels through Europe and North Africa adapted for the American cook. (Rev: BL 10/15/88; LJ 10/15/88; NYTBR 12/4/88) **[641.59]

2814 Yin-Fei Lo, Eileen. *Eileen Yin-Fei Lo's New Cantonese Cooking: Classic and Innovative Recipes from China's Haute Cuisine.* 1988, Viking $19.95 (0-670-81519-5). A survey of traditional and innovative Cantonese dishes, with a guide to the selection of ingredients, and tips on how to create menus for full meals. (Rev: BL 8/88; LJ 10/15/88) **[641.59]

Specific methods

2815 Andoh, Elizabeth. *An Ocean of Flavor: The Japanese Way with Fish and Seafood.* 1988, Morrow $20.75 (0-688-07061-2). An introduction to Japanese methods of seafood preparation adapted to the American kitchen. (Rev: BL 5/15/88; LJ 5/15/88) **[641.6]**

2816 Baggett, Nancy, and Martin Jacobs. *International Chocolate Cookbook.* 1991, Stewart, Tabori & Chang $40.00 (1-55670-178-0). An illustrated guide to cooking with chocolate. (Rev: BL 12/1/91; PW 11/22/91) **[641.6]

2817 Beck, Bruce. *Official Fulton Fish Market Cookbook.* 1989, Dutton $19.95 (0-525-24773-4). Collected fish and shellfish recipes from New York's most famous seafood market. (Rev: LJ 5/15/89; PW 5/26/89) **[641.6]

2818 Butel, Jane. *Hotter Than Hell: Hot and Spicy Dishes from Around the World.* 1987, Price/Stern/Sloan paper $9.95 (0-89586-542-4). A collection of American and international recipes for hot and spicy dishes and drinks. (Rev: BL 9/15/87; LJ 9/15/87) **[641.6]

2819 Davidson, Alan. *Seafood: A Connoisseur's Guide and Cookbook.* 1989, Simon & Schuster $29.95 (0-671-67011-5). An illustrated guide to the selection and preparation of seafood. (Rev: BL 10/15/89; NYTBR 12/3/89; PW 10/20/89) **[641.6]

2820 La Place, Viana. *Verdura: Vegetables Italian Style.* 1991, Morrow $22.95 (0-688-08764-7). Over 250 recipes and 50 menus for the preparation of Italian-style vegetables written and compiled by the author of *Cucina Fresca.* (Rev: BL 4/15/91; NYTBR 6/9/91; PW 4/26/91) **[641.6]

2821 Loomis, Susan Herrmann. *Great American Seafood Cookbook: From Sea to Shining Sea.* 1988, Workman $19.95 (0-89480-585-1); paper $12.95 (0-89480-578-9). A guide to the selection and preparation of native American seafood. (Rev: BL 10/1/88; LJ 10/15/88) **[641.6]

2822 Marshall, Lydie. *A Passion for Potatoes.* 1992, HarperCollins $28.00 (0-06-055323-5). More than 180 recipes using potatoes compiled by the owner of New York's La Brune Cocotte cooking school. (Rev: BL 1/1/92; PW 12/20/91) **[641.6]

2823 Schneider, Carol E. *Fresh: A Greenmarket Cookbook.* 1989, Random $19.95 (0-679-7602-0). A collection of fresh fruit and vegetable recipes strikingly illustrated and punctuated with food lore. "A godsend for home gardeners . . . or shoppers."—PW (Rev: BL 2/1/90; LJ 9/15/89; PW 8/18/89. Awards: PW, 1989) **[641.6]

2824 Schneider, Elizabeth. *Uncommon Fruits and Vegetables: A Common-Sense Guide from Arugula to Yucca; an Encyclopedic Cookbook of America's New Produce.* 1986, Harper & Row $25.95 (0-06-015420-9); paper $16.95 (0-06-091669-9). A survey of the history and preparation of over 90 exotic fruits and vegetables including more than 400 recipes. (Rev: LJ 5/15/86; Natl Rev 4/10/87; Time 11/24/86) **[641.6]

2825   Smith, Jeff. *Frugal Gourmet Cooks with Wine.* Ed. by Maria Guarnaschelli. 1986, Morrow $18.95 (0-688-05852-3); Avon paper $4.95 (0-380-70671-7). The uses of wine as an ingredient in, and as compliment to, foods. "An eminently practical and sumptuous compendium on the use of wine in the kitchen."—BL (REV: BL 9/15/86; LJ 10/15/86; PW 9/19/86. AWARDS: PW, 1986)   **[641.6]**

2826   Smoler, Roberta Wolfe. *Useful Pig: 150 Succulent Pork Recipes.* 1990, HarperCollins $22.95 (0-06-016197-3). An international cookbook and guide to the use of pork in cookery. (REV: BL 8/90; LJ 6/15/90)   **[641.6]**

2827   Spieler, Marlene. *Hot and Spicy: Unusual, Innovative Recipes from the World's Fiery Cuisines.* 1985, J. P. Tarcher $17.95 (0-87477-370-9); paper $10.95 (0-87477-371-7). A guide to the preparation of hot and spicy dishes from around the world. (REV: BL 10/15/85; LJ 10/15/85; PW 9/20/85)   **[641.6]**

2828   Zisman, Larry, and Honey Zisman. *Burger Book.* 1987, St. Martin's paper $7.95 (0-312-00084-7). An illustrated handbook to different methods of hamburger preparation, and construction from its simplest forms to gourmet varieties. (REV: BL 3/15/87; LJ 3/15/87)   **[641.6]**

Vegetarian cooking

2829   Araldo, Josephine, and Robert Reynolds. *From a Breton Garden: The Vegetable Cookery of Josephine Araldo.* 1990, Addison Wesley $18.95 (0-201-51759-0). Vegetable creations and memoirs from the French cook. (REV: BL 11/15/90; LJ 10/15/90; PW 10/19/90. AWARDS: PW, 1990)   **[641.65]**

2830   Ballantyne, Janet. *Garden Way's Joy of Gardening Cookbook.* 1984, Storey Communications $25.00 (0-88266-356-9); paper $17.95 (0-88266-355-0). A guide to the cultivation, preparation, and storage of fresh vegetables, containing over 300 recipes. (REV: BL 6/1/84; LJ 5/15/84; PW 4/20/84)   **[641.65]**

2831   Greene, Bert. *Greene on Greens.* 1989, Workman $22.95 (0-89480-610-6); paper $14.95 (0-89480-612-2). A cookbook containing over 500 recipes for 30 types of vegetables which provides tips on their selection and preparation. "An unabashed celebration of good eating."—PW (REV: BL 8/84; LJ 7/84; PW 6/15/84)   **[641.65]**

2832   Levy, Faye. *Fresh from France: Vegetable Creations.* 1987, Dutton $21.95 (0-525-24533-2); paper $9.95 (0-525-48506-6). An examination of French cooking techniques applied to vegetables. "This effective volume should not even pause at the coffee table but go directly to the kitchen."—NYTBR (REV: LJ 2/15/88; NYTBR 12/6/87; PW 1/8/88)   **[641.65]**

2833   Morash, Marian. *Victory Garden Cookbook.* 1982, Knopf $35.00 (0-394-50897-1); paper $24.95 (0-394-70780-X). An overview of the raising, care, and cooking of vegetables with over 600 recipes. (REV: BL 10/15/82; CSM 7/22/82; LJ 9/15/82)   **[641.65]**

Meat

2834   Aidells, Bruce, and Denis Kelly. *Hot Links and Country Flavors: Sausages in American Regional Cooking.* 1990, Knopf $19.95 (0-394-57430-3). A guide to the use of various types of sausages in American regional cuisines. "For the real sausage aficionado, this is the book."—Time (REV: BL 4/1/90; LJ 4/15/90; Time 8/20/90)   **[641.66]**

Specific cooking processes and techniques

2835   Cox, Beverly, and Joan Whitman. *Cooking Techniques: How to Do Anything a Recipe Tells You to Do.* 1984, Little, Brown paper $17.95 (0-316-93753-3). A step-by-step illustrated introduction to both simple and complex techniques of food preparation. (REV: Choice 6/82; CSM 12/24/81; LJ 1/15/82)   **[641.7]**

2836   Eckhardt, Linda West. *Barbecue: Indoors and Out.* Ed. by Janice Gallagher. 1987, J. P. Tarcher $18.95 (0-87447-428-4); paper $11.95 (0-87477-438-1). An introduction to the styles and techniques of American barbecue. (REV: BL 5/1/87; LJ 5/15/87; PW 4/17/87)   **[641.7]**

2837   Field, Carol. *Italian Baker.* 1985, Harper & Row $27.50 (0-06-181266-8). A presentation of regional baked goods with recipes designed for the modern American kitchen. (REV: BL 11/15/85; LJ 11/15/85; Time 11/25/85)   **[641.7]**

2838   Schlesinger, Chris, and John Willoughby. *Thrill of the Grill: Techniques, Recipes and Down Home Barbecue.* 1990, Morrow $22.95 (0-688-08832-5). Collected international dishes to be prepared on the grill. "Perfect summer food."—LJ (REV: LJ 6/15/90; NYTBR 6/10/90)   **[641.7]**

Baking and roasting

2839   Haedrich, Ken. *Country Baking: Simple Home Baking with Wholesome Grains and the Pick of the Harvest.* 1990, Bantam $24.95 (0-553-07048-7). An overview of baking preparations, techniques, and recipes from calzones to cookies. (REV: BL 9/15/90; PW 1/4/91. AWARDS: PW, 1990)   **[641.71]**

Cooking specific kinds of composite dishes

2840   Cunningham, Marion. *Fannie Farmer Baking Book.* 1984, Knopf $16.95 (0-394-53332-1). A comprehensive cookbook devoted to the art of baking with over 800 recipes. (REV: BL 10/1/84; LJ 11/15/84; Newsweek 12/17/84)   **[641.8]**

2841   Gubser, Mary. *Mary's Quick Breads, Soups and Stews.* 1990, Council Oak Books paper $16.95 (0-933031-33-5). A collection of recipes and recommended techniques for the successful preparation of breads, soups, and stews. (REV: LJ 2/15/91; PW 12/21/90)   **[641.8]**

2842   La Place, Viana, and Evan Kleiman. *Pasta Fresca: An Exuberant Collection of Fresh, Vivid and Uncomplicated Pasta Recipes from the Authors of Cucina Fresca.* 1988, Morrow $19.95 (0-688-07763-3). A selection of pasta recipes chosen by

La Place, a food writer, and Kleiman, a chef. (Rev: BL 11/1/88; LJ 11/15/88; PW 10/21/88) **[641.8]**

2843 Levy, Faye. *Faye Levy's Chocolate Sensations.* 1986, Price Story $25.00 (0-89586-411-8). One hundred fifty chocolate dessert recipes with step-by-step instructions and instructional photographs. (Rev: LJ 10/15/86; PW 9/19/86. Awards: PW, 1986) **[641.8]**

2844 Purdy, Susan. *A Piece of Cake.* 1989, Macmillan $24.95 (0-689-11766-3). An introduction to the techniques and processes involved in making a successful cake. (Rev: BL 8/89; LJ 8/89; PW 8/18/89) **[641.8]**

2845 Romer, Elizabeth. *Italian Pizza and Hearth Breads.* 1987, Crown $15.95 (0-517-56693-1). An introduction to the baking of Italian breads and the preparation of Italian-style pizzas. (Rev: LJ 2/15/88; PW 12/18/87) **[641.8]**

2846 Scott, Maria Luisa, and Jack Denton Scott. *New Complete Book of Pasta: An Italian Cookbook.* 1985, Morrow $24.95 (0-688-04312-7). An illustrated cookbook including nearly 400 pasta-based recipes. "As close to comprehensive as one could want."—PW (Rev: BL 11/15/85; LJ 11/15/85; PW 10/18/85) **[641.8]**

2847 Stewart, Martha. *Martha Stewart's Hors d'Oeuvres: The Creation and Presentation of Fabulous Finger Food.* 1984, Crown $19.95 (0-517-55455-0). A guide to the preparation and serving of elegant appetizers for large social gatherings. (Rev: BL 2/15/85; PW 11/16/84) **[641.8]**

Desserts

2848 Heatter, Maida. *Maida Heatter's Best Dessert Book Ever.* 1990, Random $24.95 (0-394-57832-5). Selected meal-stopping recipes by the author of *Great Chocolate Desserts.* "An essential purchase."—LJ (Rev: BL 8/90; LJ 8/90; PW 7/20/90) **[641.86]**

642 Meals and table service

2849 Stern, Jane, and Michael Stern. *Goodfood: The Adventurous Eater's Guide to Restaurants Serving America's Best Regional Specialties.* 1983, Knopf paper $8.95 (0-394-71392-3). An introduction to regional dishes of the United States with recommendations for the best restaurants to sample them in. (Rev: LJ 5/15/83; Newsweek 6/27/83) **[642]**

2850 Trillin, Calvin. *Travels with Alice.* 1989, Ticknor & Fields $18.95 (0-89919-910-0). A chronicle of travels with the Trillin family throughout Mexico, Europe, and the Caribbean in search of excitement and a good meal. (Rev: BL 9/1/89; CSM 10/12/89; LJ 9/15/89) **[642]**

Meals for social and public occasions

2851 Evans, Michelle. *Fearless Cooking for Crowds: Beautiful Food for Groups of Eight to Fifty.* 1986, Random $18.95 (0-8129-1209-8). A guide to the planning and preparation of meals for large groups with complete menus and recipes. (Rev: BL 6/15/86; PW 5/16/86) **[642.4]**

Table furnishings

2852 Hetzer, Linda. *Fancy Folds: Napkin Folding Step-by-Step.* 1980, Hearst Books $15.95 (0-87851-040-0). An introduction to the art of napkin folding from the simple to the complex. (Rev: BL 1/15/81; CSM 1/6/81) **[642.7]**

643 Housing and household equipment

Selecting, renting, buying houses

2853 Janik, Carolyn, and Ruth Rejnis. *All America's Real Estate Book: Everyone's Guide to Buying, Selling, Renting and Investing.* 1986, Penguin paper $14.95 (0-14-009416-4). An 800-page guide detailing the concepts and procedures of successful real estate transactions. (Rev: BL 4/15/85; LJ 4/15/85; PW 3/22/85) **[643.12]**

2854 Makower, Joel. *How to Buy a House and How to Sell a House.* 1990, Putnam paper $8.95 (0-399-51565-8). Step-by-step advice on the best methods of buying and selling homes. (Rev: BL 1/1/90; LJ 12/89) **[643.12]**

2855 Miller, Peter G. *Buy Your First Home Now: A Practical Guide to Better Deals, Cheaper Mortgages and Bigger Tax Breaks for the First-Time Home Buyer.* 1990, Harper & Row $17.95 (0-06-016233-3); paper $8.95 (0-06-092051-3). A guide to the contemporary real estate market for prospective first-time home buyers. (Rev: BL 2/1/90; LJ 2/1/90) **[643.12]**

2856 Vila, Bob, and Carl Oglesby. *Bob Vila's Guide to Buying Your Dream House.* 1990, Little, Brown paper $10.95 (0-316-90291-8). A guide by the former host of *This Old House* for first-time home buyers on finding the dwelling most suitable for your family and financial means. (Rev: BL 1/1/90; LJ 11/15/89) **[643.12]**

Household security

2857 Wacker, David Alan. *Complete Guide to Home Security: How to Protect Your Family and Home from Harm.* 1990, Betterway paper $14.95 (1-55870-163-X). A guide to security measures that can be taken to provide a safer home for you and your family. (Rev: BL 11/15/90; LJ 12/90) **[643.16]**

Renovation, improvement, remodeling

2858 Chrisman, Katherine. *Dreaming in the Dust: Restoring an Old House.* 1986, Houghton $16.95 (0-395-38168-1). A day-by-day account of the two years the author and her husband spent renovating a century-old home. (Rev: BL 7/86; LJ 3/1/86; NYTBR 4/13/86) **[643.7]**

2859 Conran, Terence. *New House Book.* 1989, Crown $19.95 (0-517-67905-1). An illustrated introduction to home design and interior decorating. (Rev: LJ 2/1/86; PW 9/20/85) **[643.7]**

2860 Evers, Christoper. *Old House Doctor.* 1988, Overlook $17.95 (0-87951-090-0); paper $9.95 (0-87951-239-3). An illustrated guide to rebuilding and repairing the aging dwelling. (Rev: BL 6/1/86; LJ 5/1/86; PW 3/14/86) **[643.7]**

2861 **Gray, Linda, and Jocasta Innes.** *Complete Book of Decorating Techniques.* 1987, Little, Brown $29.95 (0-316-32595-3). A survey of interior decorating techniques. "A source of endless inspiration."—LJ (Rev: BL 9/1/87; LJ 6/15/87) **[643.7]**

2862 **Litchfield, Michael W.** *Renovation: A Complete Guide.* 1991, Prentice Hall $29.95 (0-13-159336-6). A 600-page guide to home renovation. "Invaluable . . . an essential purchase for all home repair collections."—LJ (Rev: BL 10/15/82; LJ 10/15/82; PW 9/17/82) **[643.7]**

2863 **McCormick, Dale.** *Housemending: Home Repair for the Rest of Us.* 1987, Dutton $22.50 (0-525-24456-5); paper $14.95 (0-525-48258-X). A guide to home repairs and the proper use of tools for the amateur. (Rev: BL 9/1/87; LJ 10/1/87; PW 8/21/87) **[643.7]**

2864 **Owen, David.** *Walls Around Us: The Thinking Person's Guide to How a House Works.* 1992, Villard $21.00 (0-394-57824-4). A history and analysis of home construction written by a *New Yorker* staff member. "Unexpectedly enjoyable and thoroughly useful, this will tickle and inform all homeowners."—BL (Rev: BL 9/1/91; NYTBR 12/1/91; PW 9/27/91) **[643.7]**

2865 **Pearson, David.** *Natural House Book: Creating a Healthy, Harmonious and Ecologically Sound Home Environment.* 1989, Simon & Schuster paper $17.95 (0-671-66635-5). A guide to the design and construction of an ecologically sound and environmentally healthy home. (Rev: BL 10/15/89; LJ 11/15/89) **[643.7]**

2866 **Vila, Bob, and Norma Abram.** *This Old House Guide to Building and Remodeling Materials.* 1986, Little, Brown paper $19.95 (0-446-38246-9). A guide to the selection and use of home construction materials by the host of PBS' "This Old House" series. (Rev: BL 2/1/87; LJ 11/1/86; PW 10/17/86) **[643.7]**

645 **Household furnishings**

2867 **Musheno, Elizabeth.** *Fast and Easy Home Decorating: An A to Z Guide to Creating a Beautiful Home with a Minimum of Time and Money.* 1986, St. Martin's paper $11.95 (0-312-28469-1). A guide to quick methods of home improvement and decorating. (Rev: BL 8/86; LJ 9/15/86) **[645]**

646 **Sewing, clothing, personal living**

Sewing and related operations

2868 **Eaton, Jan.** *Encyclopedia of Sewing Techniques.* 1987, Barron $19.95 (0-8120-5815-1). A guide to the art and techniques of sewing by the author of *The Complete Stitch Encyclopedia.* "A must addition to craft shelves."—BL (Rev: BL 9/1/87; PW 3/20/87) **[646.2]**

Management of personal and family living

2869 **Betcher, William.** *Intimate Play: Creating Romance in Everyday Life.* 1987, Viking $16.95 (0-670-80657-9); NAL paper $4.95 (0-451-82183-1). A manual on how to increase trust and love within established relationships using creative play. (Rev: LJ 1/87; PW 12/26/86) **[646.7]**

2870 **Chase, Deborah.** *New Medically Based No-Nonsense Beauty Book.* 1989, Henry Holt $19.95 (0-8050-1043-2); Avon paper $8.95 (0-380-71203-2). An introduction to skin, facial, and body care using medically sound techniques and cosmetics. (Rev: BL 6/15/89; LJ 5/15/89) **[646.7]**

2871 **Fussell, Samuel Wilson.** *Muscle: Confessions of an Unlikely Bodybuilder.* 1991, Poseidon $18.95 (0-671-70195-9). Memoirs of the author's career as a bodybuilder providing an insider view of the controversial sport. (Rev: BL 1/15/91; PW 1/18/91) **[646.7]**

2872 **Jarvik, Lissy, and Gary Small.** *Parentcare: A Commonsense Guide for Grown-Up Children.* 1988, Crown $19.95 (0-517-56765-2); Bantam paper $10.95 (0-553-34823-8). A guide to the care of aging parents directed at their children. (Rev: LJ 3/1/88; PW 2/19/88) **[646.7]**

2873 **Powlis, La Verne.** *Beauty from the Inside Out: A Guide for Black Women.* 1988, Doubleday $19.95 (0-385-23631-X). A guide to personal health and beauty for the African-American woman. (Rev: LJ 2/1/88; PW 1/22/88) **[646.7]**

2874 **Roberts, Nancy.** *Breaking All the Rules: Feeling Good and Looking Great, No Matter What Your Size.* 1986, Viking $17.95 (0-670-80145-3); Penguin paper $9.95 (0-14-007463-5). Advice on beauty and fashion for the full-figured woman. (Rev: BL 12/1/85; LJ 1/86; PW 11/15/85) **[646.7]**

2875 **Weiner, Florence.** *No Apologies: A Survival Guide and Handbook for the Disabled Written by the Real Authorities.* 1986, St. Martin's paper $13.95 (0-312-57523-8). A guide to living with disabilities written by disabled persons and those who care for and live with them. (Rev: BL 7/86; LJ 9/15/86; PW 5/30/86) **[646.7]**

Family living

2876 **Canape, Charlene.** *Part-Time Solution: The New Strategy for Managing Your Career While Managing Motherhood.* 1990, Harper & Row $18.95 (0-06-016237-6); paper $8.95 (0-06-092040-8). A guide to part-time employment as a means of career development for women who have children. (Rev: BL 3/1/90; LJ 2/15/90) **[646.78]**

2877 **Klagsbrun, Francine.** *Married People: Staying Together in the Age of Divorce.* 1985, Bantam $16.95 (0-553-05080-X); paper $4.95 (0-553-27451-1). A look at the secrets of a successful, healthy, long-lasting marriage with firsthand accounts by long-term couples. (Rev: BL 5/15/85; LJ 8/85; PW 5/31/85) **[646.78]**

Guides for persons in late adulthood

2878 Kaplan, Lawrence J. *Retiring Right: Planning for Your Successful Retirement.* 1990, Avery paper $12.95 (0-89529-461-3). A guide to financial planning for future retirement. (Rev: BL 8/90; LJ 9/1/90) **[646.79]**

648 Housekeeping

Laundering and related operations

2879 Aslett, Don. *Stain Buster's Bible: The Complete Guide to Spot Removal.* 1990, NAL paper $8.95 (0-452-26385-9). An illustrated household guide to the treatment and removal of spots and stains. (Rev: BL 3/1/90; LJ 2/1/90; PW 4/20/90) **[648.1]**

Control and eradication of pests

2880 Lifton, Bernice. *Bugbusters: Poison Free Pest Control for House and Garden.* 1990, Avery paper $9.95 (0-89529-451-6). A guide to methods of natural pest control without using toxic substances. "A must in household information collections."—BL (Rev: BL 6/15/85; LJ 5/15/85; PW 5/17/85) **[648.7]**

649 Child rearing and home care of sick

2881 Lickona, Thomas. *Raising Good Children: Helping Your Child Through the Stages of Moral Development.* 1985, Bantam paper $4.95 (0-553-26385-4). A child-rearing guide by a psychologist tracing the stages of moral development in children. (Rev: LJ 9/15/83; PW 6/24/83) **[649]**

Child rearing

2882 American Academy of Pediatrics. *Caring for Your Baby and Young Child: Birth to Age Five.* Ed. by Steven P. Shelov. 1991, Bantam $32.50 (0-553-07186-6). A guide to the mental and physical development of children during the first five years of life. "The closest one can get to having a live-in pediatrician."—PW (Rev: LJ 4/1/91; PW 3/29/91) **[649.1]**

2883 Bettelheim, Bruno. *A Good Enough Parent: A Book on Child Rearing.* 1987, Knopf $18.95 (0-394-47148-2); Random paper $11.95 (0-394-75776-9). A guide to child rearing and the dynamics of the parent-child relationship by the noted child psychologist. (Rev: BL 5/15/87; LJ 6/15/87; PW 4/10/87) **[649.1]**

2884 Brazelton, T. Berry. *What Every Baby Knows.* 1987, Addison Wesley $14.95 (0-201-09262-X); Ballantine paper $8.95 (0-345-34455-3). A study of the knowledge and perceptions of infants by the Harvard Medical School pediatrics professor. (Rev: BL 10/1/87; LJ 11/1/87; PW 9/25/87) **[649.1]**

2885 Brazelton, T. Berry. *Working and Caring.* 1985, Addison Wesley $16.95 (0-201-10623-X). A guide for working mothers to help balance their careers with child nurturing. "A valuable book, made so by its realistic, intelligent approach."—PW (Rev: BL 10/1/85; LJ 11/1/85; PW 9/27/85) **[649.1]**

2886 Chess, Stella, and Alexander Thomas. *Know Your Child: An Authoritative Guide for Today's Parents.* 1989, Basic Books paper $12.95 (0-465-03731-3). A study of child development theories and the dynamics of the parent-child relationship. "A welcome addition to child-development collections."—BL (Rev: BL 4/15/87; LJ 4/15/87) **[649.1]**

2887 Finston, Peggy. *Parenting Plus: Raising Children with Special Health Needs.* 1990, Dutton $19.95 (0-525-24885-4). A guide to the parenting of children with health problems. (Rev: BL 6/15/90; LJ 6/15/90) **[649.1]**

2888 Lansky, Vicki. *Practical Parenting Tips for the School Age Years.* 1985, Bantam paper $5.95 (0-553-34187-1). A guide to raising children between the ages of six and twelve. (Rev: BL 1/25/85; LJ 3/15/85; PW 1/25/85) **[649.1]**

2889 Levant, Ronald, and John Kelly. *Between Father and Child: How to Become the Kind of Father You Want to Be.* 1989, Viking $18.95 (0-670-82805-X). A guide for fathers who want to increase communication and understanding with their children. (Rev: BL 5/1/89; LJ 5/15/89) **[649.1]**

2890 Mantle, Margaret. *Some Just Clap Their Hands: Raising a Handicapped Child.* 1985, Adams $16.95 (0-915361-24-8). Accounts by parents of handicapped children of their child rearing experiences. (Rev: BL 5/1/86; LJ 2/1/86) **[649.1]**

2891 Melina, Lois Ruskai. *Raising Adoptive Children: A Manual for Adoptive Parents.* 1986, Harper & Row $17.95 (0-06-055004-X); paper $9.95 (0-06-096039-6). A guidebook for the parents of adopted children covering issues related to adoption. (Rev: BL 7/86; LJ 6/15/86) **[649.1]**

2892 Miller, Alice. *For Your Own Good: Hidden Cruelty in Child-Rearing and the Roots of Violence.* 1983, Farrar $16.50 (0-374-15750-2); paper $8.95 (0-374-51859-9). A psychoanalyst's appraisal of the effects of psychological and physical abuse upon children and their manifestations in later negative behaviors. (Rev: BL 3/15/83; LJ 4/1/83; PW 2/18/83) **[649.1]**

2893 Miller, Joanne L., and Susan Weissman. *Parents' Guide to Day Care.* 1986, Bantam paper $8.95 (0-553-34295-9). A guide to choosing a day-care center that will fill the needs of your child. (Rev: BL 12/15/86; LJ 8/86) **[649.1]**

2894 Neifert, Marianne Egeland, Anne Price, and Nancy Dana. *Dr. Mom: A Guide to Baby and Child Care.* 1987, NAL paper $5.95 (0-451-16311-7). A pediatrician's guide to child-care and rearing. (Rev: BL 5/1/86; LJ 6/1/86) **[649.1]**

2895 Schaffer, Judith, and Christina Lindstrom. *How to Raise an Adopted Child: A Guide to Help Your Child Flourish from Infancy Through Adoles-*

cence. 1989, Crown $18.95 (0-517-57303-2). A guide for parents to raising adopted children by the cofounders of New York's Center for Adoptive Families. (REV: BL 7/89; LJ 8/89)   **[649.1]**

2896   Shiff, Eileen, ed. *Experts Advise Parents: A Guide to Raising Loving, Responsible Children.* 1987, Delacorte $19.95 (0-385-29522-7); paper $10.95 (0-385-29526-X). Twelve essays by experts in their fields regarding different aspects of child rearing. (REV: BL 6/15/87; LJ 5/15/87)   **[649.1]**

2897   Spock, Benjamin. *Dr. Spock on Parenting: Sensible Advice for Today.* 1988, Simon & Schuster $17.95 (0-671-63958-7); Pocket paper $4.95 (0-671-68386-1). The noted children's doctor offers his advice on child care and rearing for modern parents. (REV: BL 7/88; LJ 9/1/88)   **[649.1]**

2898   Taubman, Bruce. *Curing Infant Colic: The 7-Minute Program for Soothing the Fussy Baby.* 1990, Bantam paper $9.95 (0-553-34903-1). A guide to the diagnosis and cure of the infant with colic symptoms. (REV: BL 6/15/90; LJ 6/1/90)   **[649.1]**

2899   Theroux, Phyllis. *Night Lights: Bedtime Stories for Parents in the Dark.* 1987, Viking $14.95 (0-670-81111-4); Penguin paper $6.95 (0-14-008923-3). Essays on the trials of raising children. Based on the author's experiences with her children. (REV: BL 1/15/87; LJ 2/1/87; PW 12/19/86)   **[649.1]**

Children of specific age groups

2900   Dodson, Fitzhugh, and Ann Alexander. *Your Child: Pregnancy Through Preschool.* 1986, Simon & Schuster paper $14.95 (0-671-45894-9). A guide for parents to the rearing and health care of preschoolers. (REV: BL 9/15/86; Choice 1/87; LJ 11/1/86)   **[649.12]**

Feeding

2901   Kuntzleman, Charles. *Healthy Kids for Life.* 1988, Simon & Schuster $16.95 (0-671-60742-1); paper $8.95 (0-671-69586-X). A fitness and diet program designed to promote the health and well-being of school-age children. (REV: LJ 2/1/89; PW 11/18/88)   **[649.3]**

Breast feeding

2902   Dana, Nancy, and Anne Price. *Successful Breastfeeding: A Complete Step-by-Step Guide to Nursing Your Baby.* 1989, Meadowbrook paper $9.95 (0-671-68995-9). An overview of the benefits and techniques of breast feeding. "An excellent addition to any collection."—BL (REV: BL 1/1/86; LJ 1/86)   **[649.33]**

Exercise, gymnastics, sports

2903   Gerard, Patty Carmichael, and Marian Cohn. *Gerard Method: Teaching Your Child Basic Body Confidence.* 1988, Houghton paper $12.95 (0-395-47590-2). Nearly 100 exercises designed to increase the physical abilities and awareness of youngsters by a former gymnast and coach.   **[649.57]**

Reading and related activities

2904   Wiener, Harvey S. *Any Child Can Read Better: Developing Your Child's Reading Skills.* 1990, Bantam $9.95 (0-553-34773-X). A parental guide to developing critical reading skills as a supplement to those taught in schools. (REV: BL 9/15/90; LJ 10/1/90)   **[649.58]**

Home care of sick and infirm

2905   Baulch, Evelyn M. *Extended Health Care at Home.* 1989, Celestial Arts paper $9.95 (0-89087-539-1). A primer on health care at home for the seriously ill. (REV: BL 1/15/89; LJ 12/88)   **[649.8]**

2906   Hastings, Diana. *Complete Guide to Home Nursing.* 1986, Barron's $16.95 (0-8120-5754-6). A guide to home care and treatment of the sick and terminally ill person. (REV: BL 9/15/86; LJ 10/15/86)   **[649.8]**

2907   Portnow, Jay, and Martha Houtmann. *Home Care for the Elderly: A Complete Guide.* 1987, McGraw-Hill $16.95 (0-07-050582-9); Pocket paper $8.95 (0-671-66012-8). A guide to providing home care for the physically ill elderly person. (REV: BL 5/1/87; LJ 2/1/87)   **[649.8]**

650   MANAGEMENT AND AUXILIARY SERVICES

Education

2908   Ewing, David W. *Inside the Harvard Business School: Strategies and Lessons of America's Leading School of Business.* 1990, Random $19.95 (0-8129-1827-4). An inside look at the curriculum and operations of the Harvard Business School by a longtime faculty member. (REV: BL 7/90; LJ 7/90; PW 7/6/90)   **[650.07]**

2909   Kelly, Francis J., and Heather M. Kelly. *What They Really Teach You at the Harvard Business School.* 1986, Warner paper $9.95 (0-446-38317-1). An overview of the key points of the business curriculum taught at the Harvard Business School. (REV: BL 9/1/86; LJ 10/1/86)   **[650.07]**

Personal success in business

2910   Avis, Warren. *Take a Chance to Be First: Hands-On Advice from America's Number-One Entrepreneur.* 1988, McGraw-Hill paper $6.95 (0-07-002547-9). A guide to techniques of successful entrepreneurship by the founder of the Avis automobile rental company. (REV: BL 6/15/86; LJ 6/15/86; PW 5/9/86)   **[650.1]**

2911   DuBrin, Andrew J. *Winning Office Politics: DuBrin's New Guide for the 90's.* 1990, Prentice Hall paper $12.95 (0-13-964958-1). An updated guide to playing office politics for career advancement. (REV: BL 9/1/90; LJ 7/90)   **[650.1]**

2912   Kehrer, Daniel M. *Doing Business Boldly: The Art of Taking Intelligent Risks.* 1989, Random $19.95 (0-8129-1312-4); Simon & Schuster paper

$9.95 (0-671-70616-0). A study of successful creative ventures taken by American big business with advice for companies considering potentially risky measures. (Rev: BL 1/1/89; LJ 2/15/89; PW 12/16/88) **[650.1]**

2913 Kiam, Victor. *Live to Win: Achieving Success in Life and Business.* **1989, Harper & Row $18.95 (0-06-016261-9).** The Remington shaver magnate presents his advice for prospering in business and life. (Rev: BL 11/1/89; LJ 10/15/89) **[650.1]**

2914 Kushner, Malcolm L. *Light Touch: How to Use Humor for Business Success.* **1990, Simon & Schuster $18.95 (0-671-68625-9).** Tips on the effective use of humor in business situations. (Rev: BL 6/1/90; LJ 5/1/90) **[650.1]**

2915 McCormack, John, and David R. Legge. *Self-Made in America: Plain Talk for Plain People about Extraordinary Success.* **1991, Addison Wesley $19.95 (0-201-55099-7).** A guide to successful entrepreneurial techniques by the owner of a major haircutting chain. (Rev: BL 1/15/91; LJ 2/15/91; PW 12/7/90) **[650.1]**

2916 Mackay, Harvey. *Swim with the Sharks Without Being Eaten Alive: Outsell, Outmanage, Outmotivate and Outnegotiate Your Competition.* **1988, Morrow $17.95 (0-688-07473-1).** A guide to achieving success in the contemporary American business world. (Rev: BL 3/1/88; LJ 4/15/88) **[650.1]**

2917 Mackoff, Barbara. *What Mona Lisa Knew: A Woman's Guide to Getting Ahead in Business by Lightening Up.* **1990, Contemporary $16.95 (0-929923-20-0).** A guide for businesswomen on the tactful use of humor to gain respect and understanding. (Rev: BL 9/1/90; LJ 9/15/90) **[650.1]**

Success in obtaining jobs and promotions

2918 Brudney, Juliet, and Hilda Scott. *Forced Out: What Veteran Employees Can Do When Driven from Their Careers.* **1987, Simon & Schuster paper $7.95 (0-671-64411-4).** Interviews with and profiles of 100 men and women over 50 who were forced out of their careers. Contains suggestions for aging job seekers. (Rev: BL 12/1/87; LJ 11/1/87; NYTBR 10/25/87) **[650.14]**

2919 Chusmir, Leonard H. *Thank God It's Monday: The Guide to a Happier Job.* **1990, NAL paper $7.95 (0-452-26374-3).** A guide to increasing job satisfaction. (Rev: BL 3/15/90; LJ 1/90) **[650.14]**

2920 Hyatt, Carole. *Shifting Gears: How to Master Career Change and Find the Work That's Right for You.* **1990, Simon & Schuster $18.95 (0-671-67311-4).** A guide to handling the emotional and psychological pressures that may accompany a change in careers. (Rev: BL 12/1/90; LJ 10/15/90) **[650.14]**

658 General management

2921 Bursteiner, Irving. *Small Business Handbook.* **1989, Prentice Hall paper $17.95 (0-13-814344-7).** A guide for entrepreneurs to the start-up and operation of privately owned small businesses. (Rev: BL 12/1/88; LJ 2/15/89) **[658]**

2922 Drucker, Peter F. *Frontiers of Management: Where Tomorrow's Decisions Are Being Shaped Today.* **1987, Harper & Row paper $9.95 (0-06-097111-8).** Essays on management and organizational theory by the author of *The New Realities.* (Rev: BL 10/1/86; Choice 2/87; NYTBR 10/26/86) **[658]**

2923 Drucker, Peter F. *Managing in Turbulent Times.* **1980, Harper & Row $14.95 (0-06-011094-5); paper $8.95 (0-06-091208-1).** A guide to business survival techniques for managers that surveys potential crises and their solutions. (Rev: BL 5/15/80; LJ 4/15/80; PW 3/7/80) **[658]**

2924 Hickman, Craig R., and Michael A. Silva. *Future 500: Creating Tomorrow's Organizations Today.* **1987, NAL $19.95 (0-453-00544-6); paper $9.95 (0-452-26168-6).** A look at the future of management and the traits successful managers will need to possess. (Rev: BL 10/15/87; NYTBR 10/25/87) **[658]**

Management of enterprises

2925 Adler, Bill. *Bill Adler's Chance of a Lifetime.* **1985, Warner $15.00 (0-446-51327-X).** A guide to raising money and successfully marketing innovative business enterprises. (Rev: LJ 9/15/85; PW 6/21/85) **[658.02]**

2926 Parson, Mary Jean. *Managing the One-Person Business.* **1990, Putnam paper $10.95 (0-399-51613-1).** An introduction to the founding and operations of single-proprietor businesses. (Rev: BL 2/1/88; LJ 3/15/88) **[658.02]**

2927 Silver, A. David. *Your First Book of Wealth.* **1989, Career Pr. paper $10.95 (0-934829-47-0).** A primer to methods of investment and money making for the beginner. (Rev: BL 4/15/89; LJ 5/1/89) **[658.02]**

Management of specific forms

2928 Drucker, Peter F. *Managing the Nonprofit Organization: Principles and Practices.* **1990, HarperCollins $22.95 (0-06-016507-3).** Advice on successful managing techniques for nonprofit organizations. "Sensible, suggestive and stirring—a rare blend."—NYTBR (Rev: BL 10/15/90; LJ 10/15/90; NYTBR 10/28/90) **[658.04]**

2929 Geneen, Harold, and Alvin Moscow. *Managing.* **1985, Avon paper $4.95 (0-380-69986-9).** Advice on management techniques and corporate decision-making from the former president of IT&T. (Rev: BL 9/1/84; LJ 10/1/84; PW 9/28/84) **[658.04]**

2930 Holz, Herman. *Complete Work-at-Home Companion.* **1990, St. Martin's $15.95 (1-55958-010-0).** A guidebook to the planning and operations of home-based businesses. (Rev: BL 1/15/90; LJ 1/90) **[658.04]**

Organization and finance

2931 Abegglen, James C., and George Stalk, Jr. *Kaisha: The Japanese Corporation.* **1985, Basic**

Books $23.95 (0-465-03711-9); paper $15.95 (0-465-03712-7). An analysis of the business secrets of Japan's most successful corporations. (REV: Choice 5/86; LJ 12/85; NYTBR 10/20/85) **[658.1]**

2932 Williams, Robert. *World's Largest Market: A Business Guide to Europe, 1992.* 1990, AMACOM $29.95 (0-8144-5989-7). A guide to doing business in the new economically unified Europe. (REV: BL 11/1/90; LJ 9/1/90) **[658.1]**

Personnel management

2933 Aubrey, Charles A., and Patricia K. Felkins. *Team Work: Involving People in Quality and Productivity Improvement.* 1988, Quality paper $21.50 (0-527-91626-9). A guide for managers on methods to increase employee participation and involvement in the business environment. (REV: Choice 10/88; LJ 8/88) **[658.3]**

2934 Half, Robert. *Robert Half on Hiring.* 1985, Crown $15.95 (0-517-55436-4); NAL paper $9.95 (0-452-25811-1). A guidebook for managers on effective personnel selection. (REV: BL 1/1/85; LJ 4/15/85) **[658.3]**

2935 Josefowitz, Natasha. *You're the Boss: A Guide to Managing People with Understanding and Effectiveness.* 1985, Warner paper $8.95 (0-446-37744-9). A guide to management style emphasizing interpersonal communication with your employees. (REV: BL 4/1/85; PW 2/15/85) **[658.3]**

2936 Kanter, Rosabeth Moss. *Change Masters: Innovation for Productivity in the American Corporation.* 1985, Simon & Schuster paper $10.95 (0-671-52800-9). A presentation of suggested innovative and progressive methods to be used by American companies to better compete with overseas rivals. (REV: CSM 5/21/84; LJ 8/83; NYTBR 10/16/83) **[658.3]**

2937 Ouchi, William G. *Theory Z: How American Business Can Meet the Japanese Challenge.* 1982, Avon paper $4.95 (0-380-59451-X). A study of Japanese management techniques and their applications to American business. (REV: LJ 3/1/82; NYTBR 12/27/81; PW 12/11/81) **[658.3]**

2938 Werther, William B., Jr. *Dear Boss.* 1989, Simon & Schuster $14.95 (0-671-68381-0); paper $8.95 (0-671-72597-1). Collected notes and letters employees have written to managers regarding methods of improving business and management skills. (REV: BL 6/1/89; LJ 6/1/89) **[658.3]**

Executive management

2939 Ansoff, H. Igor. *New Corporate Strategy.* 1988, Wiley $24.95 (0-471-62950-2). Revised and expanded edition of the author's 1965 *Corporate Strategy* regarding management and decision-making techniques. (REV: Choice 12/88; LJ 3/15/89) **[658.4]**

2940 Asman, David, ed. *Wall Street Journal on Management: Adding Value Through Synergy.* 1990, Doubleday $19.95 (0-385-26492-5). A collection of essays regarding management techniques culled from the author's *Wall Street Journal* column. (REV: BL 3/1/90; LJ 3/15/90) **[658.4]**

2941 Cohen, William A. *Art of the Leader.* 1989, Prentice Hall $19.95 (0-13-046657-3). Descriptions of successful management and leadership techniques. "Destined to be a best seller and possibly a management classic."—LJ (REV: BL 11/1/89; LJ 11/1/89; PW 10/13/89) **[658.4]**

2942 Davis, George, and Glegg Watson. *Black Life in Corporate America: Swimming in the Mainstream.* 1985, Doubleday paper $7.95 (0-385-14702-3). A study of African Americans involved in corporate management. (REV: Choice 2/83; LJ 8/82; NYTBR 10/24/82) **[658.4]**

2943 Drucker, Peter F. *Innovation and Entrepreneurship: Practice and Principles.* 1985, Harper & Row $19.95 (0-06-015428-4); paper $10.95 (0-06-091360-6). Strategies and techniques on successful entreprenuership by the respected management expert. "A thoughtful analysis of what the future holds . . . and of the skills and policy changes needed to get there."—LJ (REV: BL 4/15/85; Choice 10/85; LJ 5/15/85. AWARDS: LJ, 1985) **[658.4]**

2944 Eigen, Barry. *How to Think Like a Boss and Get Ahead at Work.* 1990, Carol Publg. Group $16.95 (0-8184-0537-6). Guidelines on the effective use of office politics and psychology as seen by a former corporate head. (REV: BL 9/1/90; LJ 10/1/90) **[658.4]**

2945 Kotter, John P. *Leadership Factor.* 1988, Free Pr. $19.95 (0-02-918331-6). A study of leadership styles for mid- to lower-level management. "A first-rate management volume that is definitely a cut above the competition."—BL (REV: BL 12/15/87; Choice 5/88; LJ 1/88) **[658.4]**

2946 Loden, Marilyn. *Feminine Leadership: Or, How to Succeed in Business Without Being One of the Boys.* 1985, Random $16.95 (0-8129-1240-3). A guide to management style for businesswomen. (REV: BL 10/15/85; LJ 12/85; PW 10/25/85) **[658.4]**

2947 Maccoby, Michael. *Why Work: Motivating the New Generation.* 1988, Simon & Schuster $18.95 (0-671-47281-X); paper $9.95 (0-671-67560-5). A study of methods used to create motivation for individual workers within the contemporary corporate setting. (REV: BL 3/15/88; LJ 5/1/88; PW 2/5/88) **[658.4]**

2948 Manz, Charles, and Henry P. Simms. *Superleadership: Leading Others to Lead Themselves.* 1989, Prentice Hall paper $22.95 (0-13-876517-0). An introduction to leadership methods designed to bring out the best in yourself and your workers. "It should become a classic of the '90's."—LJ (REV: BL 6/1/89; LJ 5/15/89) **[658.4]**

2949 Peters, Tom. *Thriving on Chaos: Handbook for a Management Revolution.* 1987, Knopf $19.95 (0-394-56784-6); Harper & Row paper $12.95 (0-06-097184-3). A guide to business survival during turbulent economic conditions by the coauthor of *In Search of Excellence.* (REV: BL 9/1/87; LJ 10/15/87; PW 9/18/87) **[658.4]**

2950 Peters, Tom, and Nancy K. Austin. *A Passion for Excellence: The Leadership Difference.* **1989, Warner paper $12.95 (0-446-38639-1).** A study of quality leaders and leadership techniques. (Rev: BL 5/1/85; LJ 6/15/85; NYTBR 5/26/85)   **[658.4]**

2951 Ringer, Robert J. *Million Dollar Habits.* **1990, Wynwood Pr. $19.95 (0-922066-29-9); Fawcett paper $5.95 (0-449-21878-3).** The author of *Winning Through Intimidation* presents ten future growth areas that can be exploited for financial gain. (Rev: BL 4/1/90; LJ 4/15/90)   **[658.4]**

2952 Scollard, Jeanette Reddish. *Self-Employed Woman: How to Start Your Own Business and Gain Control of Your Life.* **1989, Simon & Schuster paper $7.95 (0-671-68407-8).** A woman's guide to starting a successful personally owned business. "An excellent starting point for male or female aspiring entrepreneurs."—LJ (Rev: BL 1/15/86; LJ 3/1/86)   **[658.4]**

2953 Tragoe, Benjamin B. *Vision in Action: Putting a Winning Strategy to Work.* **1989, Simon & Schuster $18.95 (0-671-68068-4).** Accounts from the managers of nearly 20 successful businesses regarding the formation and execution of management strategies. (Rev: BL 6/15/89; LJ 6/15/89)   **[658.4]**

Middle management

2954 Bennett, Amanda. *Death of the Organization Man.* **1990, Morrow $19.95 (0-87795-961-7).** A study of the changing roles and personalities of middle managers in corporate organizational structures. (Rev: BL 2/1/90; LJ 2/1/90; NYTBR 3/18/90)   **[658.43]**

Management of production

2955 Gabor, Andrea. *Man Who Discovered Quality.* **1990, Random $21.95 (0-8129-1774-X).** A biography of W. Edwards Deming, an American statistician who introduced the idea of quality control to Japan in 1950, which was later adopted by many American companies such as Ford, Xerox, and General Motors. "A must for all business collections."—LJ (Rev: BL 9/1/90; LJ 9/15/90; NYTBR 10/28/90. Awards: BL, 1990)   **[658.5]**

2956 Lynn, Gary S. *From Concept to Market.* **1989, Wiley $39.95 (0-471-50126-3); paper $17.95 (0-471-50125-5).** A guide to the design, patenting, and successful marketing of new products. (Rev: BL 10/1/89; LJ 1/90)   **[658.5]**

Marketing

2957 Goldzimer, Linda Silverman, and Gregory L. Beckmann. *I'm First.* **1989, Rawson $19.95 (0-89256-334-6); Berkley paper $9.95 (0-425-12561-0).** Recommendations for management techniques and business adjustments to capitalize and implement changes in a consumer-driven marketplace. (Rev: BL 3/15/89; LJ 4/1/89)   **[658.8]**

2958 Luxenberg, Stan. *Roadside Empires: How the Chains Franchised America.* **1985, Viking $17.95 (0-670-32658-5); Penguin paper $7.95 (0-14-007734-0).** A study of the development and proliferation of franchise businesses in the United States. (Rev: Choice 5/85; LJ 1/85; NYTBR 2/24/85)   **[658.8]**

2959 Webster, Bruce. *Insider's Guide to Franchising.* **1986, AMACOM $19.95 (0-8144-5660-X).** A guide to the purchase and operations of franchise businesses. (Rev: BL 5/15/86; LJ 5/15/86)   **[658.8]**

2960 Zemke, Ron, and Dick Schaaf. *Service Edge: Inside 101 Companies That Profit from Customer Care.* **1989, NAL $19.95 (0-453-00647-7); paper $10.95 (0-452-26493-6).** Profiles of the top service companies in a variety of business areas and methods they use to please their customers. (Rev: BL 1/15/89; LJ 3/1/89)   **[658.8]**

659 Advertising and public relations

Advertising

2961 Goodrum, Charles, and Helen Dalrymple. *Advertising in America.* **1990, Abrams $60.00 (0-8109-1187-6).** An illustrated history of advertising in America over the past two centuries. (Rev: BL 10/1/90; CSM 9/17/90; PW 9/7/90)   **[659.1]**

2962 Schudson, Michael. *Advertising, the Uneasy Persuasion: Its Dubious Impact on American Society.* **1986, Basic Books paper $11.95 (0-465-00079-7).** A study of advertising and its influence on American thought and values. "Splendid . . . thorough, thoughtful, well researched, and well documented."—LJ (Rev: Choice 4/85; LJ 1/85; NYTBR 12/23/84)   **[659.1]**

2963 Strasser, Susan. *Satisfaction Guaranteed: The Making of the American Mass Market.* **1989, Pantheon $24.95 (0-394-55292-X); paper $14.95 (0-679-72558-X).** A history of mass marketing and how it has influenced American buying trends. (Rev: BL 11/15/89; LJ 10/15/89; NYTBR 11/19/89)   **[659.1]**

Public relations

2964 Dilenschneider, Robert C. *Power and Influence: Mastering the Art of Persuasion.* **1990, Prentice Hall $19.95 (0-13-464041-1).** A guide to successful persuasive techniques for the business manager. (Rev: BL 5/15/90; LJ 4/15/90; PW 3/30/90)   **[659.2]**

670 MANUFACTURING

674 Lumber processing, wood products, cork

2965 Lewontin, Timothy. *Parsons' Mill.* **1989, Univ. Pr. of New England $15.95 (0-87451-479-7); NAL paper $8.95 (0-452-26420-0).** A look at the daily life and operations of a New England sawmill. "Immensely entertaining . . . a fine piece of Americana."—PW (Rev: LJ 4/1/89; NYTBR 9/24/89; PW 3/3/89)   **[674]**

680 MANUFACTURE FOR SPECIFIC USES

681 Precision instruments and other devices

2966 Bennett, J. A. *Divided Circle: A History of Instruments for Astronomy, Navigation and Surveying.* 1988, Salem $75.00 (0-7148-8038-8). An illustrated history of measuring instruments used in astronomy, navigation, and surveying. "The most comprehensive treatment of the subject available."—LJ (Rev: BL 4/1/88; Choice 6/88; LJ 5/1/88) **[681]**

Instruments for measuring time, counting and calculating machines and instruments

2967 Landes, David. *Revolution in Time: Clocks and the Making of the Modern World.* 1983, Harvard Univ. Pr. $27.50 (0-674-76800-0); paper $10.95 (0-674-76802-7). A history of mechanical timekeeping and its impact upon human society. "Will undoubtedly remain the standard for years to come."—LJ (Rev: LJ 12/15/87; NYRB 12/8/83; NYTBR 10/23/83) **[681.1]**

Printing, writing, duplicating machines and equipment

2968 Thomson, George L. *Rubber Stamps and How to Make Them.* 1982, Pantheon paper $5.95 (0-394-71124-6). An introduction to the design and construction of rubber stamps. (Rev: BL 10/1/82; LJ 9/15/82) **[681.6]**

684 Furnishings and home workshops

Woodworking

2969 Scott, Ernest. *Working in Wood: An Illustrated Manual for Tools, Methods, Materials, and Classic Constructions.* 1980, Putnam $25.00 (0-399-12550-7). An illustrated handbook of the tools and techniques of woodworking. "Sure to become a standard manual for woodworkers at all levels of proficiency."—BL (Rev: BL 2/1/81; LJ 3/15/81) **[684.08]**

690 BUILDINGS

2970 Kidder, Tracy. *House.* 1985, Houghton $17.95 (0-395-36317-9); Avon paper $4.50 (0-380-70176-6). The design and construction of a home, from conception to finished product. "Reads like an old-fashioned novel that proceeds calmly to a conclusion that gives the reader deep pleasure."—NYTBR (Rev: LJ 8/85; NYTBR 10/6/85; PW 8/9/85. Awards: ALA, 1985; LJ, 1985; NYTBR, 1985; PW, 1985) **[690]**

2971 Sabbagh, Karl. *Skyscraper: The Making of a Building.* 1990, Viking $22.95 (0-670-83229-4). A look at the construction of a New York skyscraper from conception to completion. (Rev: BL 2/15/90; LJ 3/15/90) **[690]**

Home construction

2972 Youssef, Wasfi. *Building Your Own Home: A Step-by-Step Guide.* 1988, Wiley $22.95 (0-471-63501-8). A guide to the design, financing, and construction of private homes. "An excellent overview of the essential issues in home building."—BL (Rev: BL 11/1/88; LJ 11/15/88) **[690.8]**

700 THE ARTS

2973 Berger, John. *Keeping a Rendezvous.* **1991, Pantheon $21.00 (0-679-40632-8).** Twenty-five essays by the art critic, philosopher, and novelist. (Rev: BL 11/1/91; NYTBR 1/5/92; PW 10/11/91) **[700]**

2974 Berger, John. *Sense of Sight.* **1986, Pantheon paper $10.95 (0-394-74206-0).** A collection of essays and poems by the artist, novelist, and art critic. "Intellectually, morally and literally challenging."—BL (Rev: BL 1/15/86; PW 11/29/85; Time 7/21/86. Awards: PW, 1986) **[700]**

2975 Gottner-Abendroth, Heide. *Dancing Goddess: Principles of a Matriarchal Aesthetic.* **1991, Beacon paper $15.95 (0-8070-6753-9).** A history of the depiction and symbolism of female goddesses in art from ancient times to the present. (Rev: BL 6/15/91; PW 6/28/91) **[700]**

2976 Jencks, Charles. *Post-Modernism: The New Classicism in Art and Architecture.* **1987, Rizzoli $75.00 (0-8478-0835-1).** An analysis of the major trends in art and architecture since 1970 by the prolific architectural historian. (Rev: Choice 3/88; LJ 1/88; NYTBR 12/6/87. Awards: LJ, 1987) **[700]**

2977 Kluver, Billy, and Julie Martin. *Kiki's Paris: Artists and Lovers, 1900 to 1930.* **1989, Abrams $39.95 (0-8109-1210-4).** A social history of the artists, their models, and friends of Paris in the first part of the twentieth century. "A must for art and cultural history collections."—BL (Rev: BL 6/15/89; LJ 6/15/89; NYTBR 6/11/89. Awards: ALA, 1989) **[700]**

2978 Montale, Eugenio. *Second Life of Art: Selected Essays.* **1982, Ecco Pr. $17.50 (0-912946-84-9).** Essays regarding twentieth-century art and culture by the Italian Nobel laureate and critic. (Rev: Choice 2/83; LJ 9/1/82; NYTBR 11/14/82) **[700]**

2979 Russell, John. *Reading Russell: Essays 1941–1988 on Ideas, Literature, Art, Theatre, Music, Places and Persons.* **1989, Abrams $29.95 (0-8109-1550-2).** More than 50 essays on a variety of topics spanning the writing career of art critic John Russell. (Rev: NYTBR 10/22/89; PW 7/14/89) **[700]**

2980 Torgovnick, Marianna. *Gone Primitive: Savage Intellects, Modern Lives.* **1990, Univ. of Chicago Pr. $24.95 (0-226-80831-9).** A study of modern Western concepts and depictions of "primitive" societies. (Rev: LJ 6/15/90; NYTBR 6/24/90; PW 5/15/90) **[700]**

2981 Updike, John. *Just Looking: Essays on Art.* **1989, Knopf $35.00 (0-394-57904-6).** Twenty-four pieces on art and artists by the author of *Rabbit Is Rich.* (Rev: BL 10/1/89; LJ 10/1/89; NYTBR 10/15/89) **[700]**

Management

2982 Hoover, Deborah A. *Supporting Yourself as an Artist: A Practical Guide.* **1989, Oxford Univ. Pr. $29.95 (0-19-505971-9); paper $9.95 (0-19-505972-7).** A financial guide for artists by a former employee of the National Endowment for the Arts. (Rev: BL 9/15/85; LJ 9/1/85) **[700.68]**

Museums, collections, exhibits

2983 Cantor, Jay E. *Winterthur.* **1985, Abrams $49.50 (0-8109-1785-8).** An illustrated overview of the holdings and gardens of the Wilmington, Delaware, museum. (Rev: BL 12/15/85; LJ 1/86; NYTBR 12/8/85) **[700.74]**

History

2984 Klein, Dan. *In the Deco Style.* **1986, Rizzoli $40.00 (0-8478-0633-2).** A survey of art deco decorative arts focusing on furniture, ceramics, and fashion. (Rev: BL 2/15/87; Choice 4/87; LJ 1/87) **[700.9]**

2985 Lippard, Lucy. *Overlay: Contemporary Art and the Art of Prehistory.* **1983, Pantheon paper $19.95 (0-394-71145-9).** An illustrated exploration of the connections between prehistoric art and the art of the twentieth century. (Rev: BL 4/15/83; Choice 9/83; LJ 7/83) **[700.9]**

Persons

2986 Bockris, Victor. *Life and Death of Andy Warhol.* **1989, Bantam $21.95 (0-553-05708-1); paper $14.95 (0-553-34929-5).** A biography of the American pop artist and filmmaker by a former colleague who worked with him at *Interview* magazine. (REV: BL 6/15/89; LJ 9/1/89; PW 7/28/89)   **[700.92]**

2987   Bourdon, David. *Warhol.* 1989, Abrams $49.50 (0-8109-1761-0). An illustrated biography of Andy Warhol, the late American pop artist. (REV: Choice 2/90; LJ 12/89; NYTBR 11/12/89)   **[700.92]**

2988   Colacello, Bob. *Holy Terror: Andy Warhol Close Up.* 1990, HarperCollins $22.95 (0-06-016419-0). A biography of the late pop artist by the former editor of Andy Warhol's *Interview* magazine. (REV: BL 6/1/90; LJ 8/90; NYTBR 8/26/90)   **[700.92]**

2989   Goldsmith, Barbara. *Little Gloria: Happy at Last.* 1982, Dell paper $4.95 (0-440-15120-1). An account of the celebrated 1934 child custody battle for ten-year-old Gloria Vanderbilt between her mother and aunt. (REV: NYTBR 6/22/80; PW 5/2/80; TLS 10/3/80)   **[700.92]**

2990   Kirstein, Lincoln. *By With To and From: A Lincoln Kirstein Reader.* Ed. by Nicholas Jenkins. 1991, Farrar $30.00 (0-374-18765-7). A collection of essays on art criticism by the New York City Ballet director. (REV: BL 6/1/91; PW 7/12/91)   **[700.92]**

2991   Kruger, Barbara, and Kate Linker. *Love for Sale: The Words and Pictures of Barbara Kruger.* 1990, Abrams $29.95 (0-8109-1219-8). A study of the work of the contemporary American artist known for her photomontages. (REV: BL 7/90; LJ 12/90; NYTBR 8/5/90)   **[700.92]**

2992   Rosenthal, Mark, and Richard Marshall. *Jonathan Borofsky.* 1984, Abrams $45.00 (0-8109-0740-2); Philadelphia Museum of Art paper $18.95 (0-87633-059-6). An exhibition catalog commemorating a retrospective of the contemporary artist's work containing 250 reproductions. "A masterpiece of contemporary art publishing."—BL (REV: BL 2/15/85; Choice 5/85; LJ 2/15/85)   **[700.92]**

2993   Ultra Violet. *Famous for Fifteen Minutes: My Years with Andy Warhol.* 1990, Avon paper $8.95 (0-380-70843-4). The inside story of Andy Warhol and his circle from the 1960s to his death in 1987. (REV: LJ 11/15/88; PW 9/23/88)   **[700.92]**

2994   Vanderbilt, Gloria. *Black Knight, White Knight.* 1987, Knopf $18.95 (0-394-54412-9). An autobiography of the American actress, artist, and writer focusing on her childhood and early adult years. (REV: LJ 5/15/87; NYTBR 5/31/87; Time 4/27/87)   **[700.92]**

2995   Vanderbilt, Gloria. *Once Upon a Time: A True Story.* 1985, Knopf $16.95 (0-394-54112-X); Fawcett paper $4.50 (0-449-12902-0). The author's view of the 1934 court battle for her custody involving her mother and aunt. (REV: CSM 5/2/85; LJ 5/1/85; Time 5/6/85)   **[700.92]**

2996   Warhol, Andy. *Andy Warhol Diaries.* Ed. by Pat Hackett. 1989, Warner $29.95 (0-446-51426-8). A collection of the pop artist's diaries from 1976 to 1987. (REV: BL 6/15/89; NYTBR 6/25/89; Newsweek 5/22/89)   **[700.92]**

704   Special topics

2997   Cancel, Luis R., ed. *Latin American Spirit: Art and Artists in the United States, 1920–1970.* 1988, Abrams $45.00 (0-8109-1271-6). A survey of twentieth-century Latin American art produced or displayed in the United States emphasizing its variety and influences upon other artists and art forms. (REV: Choice 2/89; CSM 12/7/88; LJ 12/88)   **[704]**

History and description with respect to racial, ethnic, national groups

2998   Honour, Hugh. *Image of the Black in Western Art.* 1989, Harvard Univ. Pr. $100.00 (0-939594-17-X). A history of the depiction of people of African descent in Western artworks from the eighteenth century to the present. "A visual feast combined with a compelling text . . . a book to pore over."—TLS (REV: LJ 4/1/89; NYTBR 4/2/89; TLS 9/15/89)   **[704.03]**

2999   McElroy, Guy C. *Facing History: The Black Image in American Art, 1710–1940.* 1991, Bedford Arts $24.95 (0-938491-39-3). An examination of the portrayal of African Americans in American art from the early 1700s to 1940. (REV: BL 4/1/90; Choice 6/90; LJ 4/15/90)   **[704.03]**

3000   Wardlaw, Alvia J. *Black Art: Ancestral Legacy; the African Impulse in African-American Art.* Ed. by Robert V. Rozelle. 1990, Abrams $45.00 (0-8109-3104-4). A study of the influence of African culture upon African-American artists. (REV: BL 4/1/90; LJ 6/15/90; PW 3/2/90)   **[704.03]**

Iconography

3001   Foister, Susan. *National Portrait Gallery Collection.* 1989, Cambridge Univ. Pr. $55.00 (0-521-37392-1). A survey of the collections of London's National Portrait Gallery. "Will fascinate anyone interested in art or history."—LJ (REV: BL 12/1/89; LJ 12/89)   **[704.9]**

3002   Lippard, Lucy. *A Different War: Vietnam in Art.* 1990, Real Comet paper $18.95 (0-941104-43-5). A study of the depiction of the Vietnam War in 99 artworks as perceived by the American art critic. (REV: BL 4/15/90; LJ 7/90; PW 3/9/90)   **[704.9]**

708   Galleries, museums, private collections

3003   Solomon, Holly, and Alexandra Anderson. *Living with Art.* 1988, Rizzoli $37.50 (0-8478-0960-9). Profiles of 22 private collections of art and their owners with advice on how to cultivate an art collection. (REV: LJ 1/89; PW 11/18/88)   **[708]**

In Northeastern United States

3004   Tomkins, Calvin. *Merchants and Masterpieces: The Story of the Metropolitan Museum of Art.* 1989, Henry Holt $24.95 (0-8050-1034-3). The history of the first century of the New York Metropolitan Museum of Art. "Sheer enjoyment, cover to cover."—PW (REV: LJ 4/15/70; NYTBR 4/12/70; PW 2/9/70)   **[708.14]**

709   Historical, areas, persons treatment

3005 Coe, Ralph T. *Lost and Found Traditions: Native American Art, 1965–1985.* Ed. by Irene Gordon. 1988, Univ. of Washington Pr. $24.95 (0-295-96699-8). A survey of Native American art produced from the mid-1960s to the mid-1980s. (Rev: BL 11/15/86; Choice 1/87; LJ 11/1/86)   **[709]**

3006 Coen, Ester. *Boccioni.* 1988, Abrams $65.00 (0-8109-0721-6). A survey of the life and works of the Italian futurist artist written to accompany a New York Metropolitan Museum of Art exhibition. (Rev: Choice 2/89; LJ 1/89; PW 11/4/88)   **[709]**

3007 Courtney-Clarke, Margaret. *Ndebele: The Art of an African Tribe.* 1986, Rizzoli $60.00 (0-8478-0685-5). An illustrated study of the arts and crafts of the Ndebele tribe of South Africa. (Rev: Choice 10/86; LJ 8/86; NYTBR 8/3/86)   **[709]**

3008 Gordon, Robert, and Andrew Forge. *Degas.* 1988, Abrams $75.00 (0-8109-1142-6). A study of the life and work of the French artist with over 300 illustrations. (Rev: Choice 1/89; LJ 11/15/88; PW 9/16/88)   **[709]**

3009 Levenson, Jay A., ed. *Circa 1492: Art in the Age of Exploration.* 1991, Yale Univ. Pr./National Gallery of Art $59.95 (0-300-05167-0). The exhibition catalog accompanying a National Gallery of Art show and presenting an overview of late fifteenth-century art. (Rev: BL 12/15/91; LJ 8/91. Awards: BL, 1991)   **[709]**

3010 Rosenblum, Robert, and H. W. Janson. *19th Century Art.* 1984, Abrams $49.50 (0-8109-1362-3). An illustrated survey of the painting and sculpture of the nineteenth century. (Rev: Choice 6/84; LJ 4/15/84; NYTBR 4/22/84)   **[709]**

Arts of nonliterate peoples and earliest times to 499

3011 Ruspoli, Mario. *Cave at Lascaux: The Final Photographs.* 1987, Abrams $49.50 (0-8109-1267-8). Photographs and narratives regarding the Lascaux cave, noted for its pictographs and paintings from Paleolithic times. "A splendid work of spiritual artistry."—LJ (Rev: Choice 7–8/87; LJ 6/15/87; NYTBR 5/31/87. Awards: LJ, 1987)   **[709.01]**

Art, 1900–1999

3012 Andrews, Wayne. *Surrealist Parade.* 1990, New Directions $22.95 (0-8112-1126-6); paper $11.95 (0-8112-1127-4). A study of twentieth-century surrealist art profiling the lives and works of such artists as Andre Breton, Salvador Dali, and Louis Aragon. (Rev: LJ 5/15/90; NYTBR 7/1/90; New Yorker 10/1/90)   **[709.04]**

3013 Ashton, Dore, ed. *Twentieth-Century Artists on Art.* 1986, Pantheon paper $14.95 (0-394-73489-0). Collected statements of over 200 twentieth-century artists regarding their work. (Rev: BL 2/1/86; Choice 9/86; PW 1/3/86)   **[709.04]**

3014 Barron, Stephanie. *"Degenerate Art": The Fate of the Avant-Garde in Nazi Germany.* 1991, Abrams $75.00 (0-8109-3653-4). This catalog that accompanied a traveling exhibition of a re-created 1937 German art show critical of trends in modern art was called "an essential work" by *Library Journal.* (Rev: BL 5/15/91; LJ 8/91; New Rep 5/6/91)   **[709.04]**

3015 Danto, Arthur C. *Encounters and Reflections: Art in the Historical Present.* 1990, Farrar $19.95 (0-374-14819-8). A collection of 40 essays of art criticism written from 1986 to 1990. (Rev: LJ 3/1/90; NYTBR 8/5/90)   **[709.04]**

3016 Elderfield, John. *Frankenthaler.* 1989, Abrams $150.00 (0-8109-0916-2). A study of the life and work of the American artist best known for her abstract expressionist works. (Rev: Choice 7–8/89; LJ 4/15/89; NYTBR 6/11/89. Awards: LJ, 1989)   **[709.04]**

3017 Ferrier, Jean-Louis. *Art of Our Century: The Chronicle of Western Art, 1900 to the Present.* 1989, Prentice Hall $60.00 (0-13-011644-0). A year-by-year chronicle of twentieth-century art containing close to 2,000 reproductions. "An invaluable resource for art collections of all sizes."—BL (Rev: BL 5/1/90; NYTBR 12/3/89)   **[709.04]**

3018 Green, Martin. *New York 1913: The Armory Show and the Paterson Strike Pageant.* 1988, Macmillan $24.95 (0-684-18993-3). A study of two key historical events which took place in New York in 1913: the Armory Show which introduced modern European art to America, and the Paterson textile strike which failed and was the beginning of the decline of the IWW union. (Rev: LJ 11/1/88; NYTBR 12/11/88; PW 10/7/88)   **[709.04]**

3019 Hughes, Robert. *Shock of the New: Art and the Century of Change.* 1990, Knopf paper $24.95 (0-679-72876-7). Overview of the art and architecture of the past century. "Easily the best book to date on 20th century art."—Sat Rev (Rev: LJ 2/15/81; NYTBR 2/15/81; Sat Rev 1/81. Awards: ALA, 1981)   **[709.04]**

3020 Hulten, Pontus. *Futurism and Futurisms.* 1986, Abbeville Pr. $85.00 (0-89659-675-3). A survey of the Italian-dominated art style of the early twentieth century known as futurism. (Rev: BL 12/1/86; Choice 2/87; PW 9/26/86)   **[709.04]**

3021 Knight, Christopher. *Art of the Sixties and Seventies: The Panza Collection.* 1988, Rizzoli $60.00 (0-8478-0916-1). A catalog of modern art works in the collection of Italian industrialist Count Giuseppe Panza including works by Segal, Rauschenberg, Johns, Rothko, and Oldenberg. (Rev: BL 7/88; LJ 8/88; PW 6/10/88)   **[709.04]**

3022 Kramer, Hilton. *Revenge of the Philistines: Art and Culture, 1972–1984.* 1984, Free Pr. $25.00 (0-02-918470-3). Selections of essays and art reviews by the former *New York Times* critic. (Rev: BL 11/15/85; LJ 2/15/85; NYTBR 11/17/85)   **[709.04]**

3023 Livingstone, Marco. *Pop Art: A Continuing History.* 1990, Abrams $49.50 (0-8109-3707-7). An illustrated history of pop art surveying the works of over 130 artists. "A readable, informative and visually attractive book."—Choice (Rev: BL 12/15/90; Choice 2/91; LJ 11/90) **[709.04]**

3024   Rosenberg, Harold. *Anxious Object: Art Today and Its Audience.* **1982, Univ. of Chicago Pr. paper $9.95 (0-226-72682-7).** Essays concerning postwar art by one of its most important critics. "A sample of this vigorous mind at its best."—Atl (Rev: Atl 2/65; NYRB 12/17/64; Newsweek 12/14/64. Awards: ALA, 1965) **[709.04]**

3025   Rosenberg, Harold. *Art on the Edge: Creators and Situations.* **1983, Univ. of Chicago Pr. paper $10.95 (0-226-72674-6).** A collection of essays by the art critic for the *New Yorker* on the state of modern art and its future. (Rev: BL 2/1/76; Choice 4/76; NYTBR 2/15/76) **[709.04]**

3026   Rosenberg, Harold. *De-Definition of Art: Action Art to Pop to Earthworks.* **1983, Univ. of Chicago Pr. paper $10.95 (0-226-72673-8).** A collection of 22 essays on various aspects of modern art. "Enjoyable to read, articulate and learned . . . the most fruitful of contemporary writers on modern art."—Choice (Rev: Choice 9/72; NYTBR 4/30/72; Newsweek 5/29/72) **[709.04]**

3027   Rubin, William, ed. *Primitivism in 20th Century Art: Affinity of the Tribal and the Modern.* **1984, Museum of Modern Art $100.00 (0-87070-518-0); paper $50.00 (0-87070-534-2).** A two-volume set tracing the influence of "primitive" and tribal art upon the art and artists of the twentieth century. (Rev: Choice 2/85; LJ 12/84; TLS 9/6/85) **[709.04]**

3028   Russell, John. *Meanings of Modern Art.* **1989, Harper & Row $50.00 (0-06-438496-9); paper $25.95 (0-06-430165-6).** A survey of twentieth-century art, its key movements and relation to society. "The most readable and literate work in the category of basic texts on modern art."—Choice (Rev: Choice 2/82; LJ 1/1/82; NYTBR 11/15/81) **[709.04]**

3029   Tomkins, Calvin. *Bride and the Bachelors: The Heretical Courtship in Modern Art.* **1976, Penguin paper $8.95 (0-14-004313-6).** Profiles of four twentieth-century artists: Marcel Duchamp, Jean Tinguely, Robert Rauschenberg, and John Cage. "Readable, factually accurate and provocative."—Choice (Rev: Atl 6/65; Choice 6/66. Awards: ALA, 1965) **[709.04]**

3030   Varnedoe, Kirk. *A Fine Disregard: What Makes Modern Art Modern.* **1990, Abrams $35.00 (0-8109-3106-0).** A study of the meaning of modern art and its development from the mid-nineteenth century to the present. (Rev: LJ 7/90; New Yorker 6/4/90; TLS 12/14/90) **[709.04]**

Artists not identified with a specific form

3031   Ashton, Dore. *Joseph Cornell Album.* **1989, Da Capo paper $22.95 (0-306-80372-0).** A tribute to the artist, best known for his assembled boxes, with examples of his work and writings. (Rev: Choice 4/75; LJ 1/15/75; NYTBR 12/29/74) **[709.2]**

3032   Bailly, Jean-Christophe. *Duchamp.* **1986, Universe paper $9.95 (0-87663-887-6).** A survey of the works of the French surrealist artist. "A very useful introduction to an important 20th century artist."—PW (Rev: LJ 9/1/86; PW 8/1/86) **[709.2]**

3033   Baldwin, Neil. *Man Ray: American Artist.* **1988, Crown $25.00 (0-517-56001-1).** The first full-length biography of the American painter, photographer, and filmmaker. "A model biography—judicious, compulsively readable . . . a remarkable feat of sleuthing."—PW (Rev: BL 12/1/88; LJ 10/1/88; PW 10/7/88. Awards: PW, 1988) **[709.2]**

3034   Bernier, Rosamond. *Matisse, Picasso, Miro as I Knew Them.* **1991, Knopf $50.00 (0-394-58670-0).** An art journalist's memoirs of her friendships with artists Matisse, Picasso, and Miro illustrated with 350 reproductions and photographs. (Rev: BL 10/1/91; LJ 9/1/91; PW 8/2/91) **[709.2]**

3035   Bramley, Serge. *Leonardo: Discovering the Life of Leonardo da Vinci.* **1991, HarperCollins $35.00 (0-06-016065-9).** A biography of the Italian Renaissance artist, philosopher, and scientist. (Rev: BL 11/15/91; LJ 9/15/91) **[709.2]**

3036   Duby, Georges. *Age of the Cathedrals: Art and Society, 980–1420.* **1983, Univ. of Chicago Pr. paper $11.95 (0-226-16770-4).** A survey of the social, political, and cultural history of Medieval Europe. (Rev: Choice 11/81; LJ 4/1/81; NYTBR 8/23/81) **[709.2]**

3037   Flam, Jack. *Matisse: The Man and His Art, 1869–1918.* **1986, Cornell Univ. Pr. $75.00 (0-8014-1840-2).** A biography of French artist Henri Matisse concentrating on his stylistic development and including nearly 500 illustrations. (Rev: Choice 4/87; LJ 9/1/86; TLS 3/27/87) **[709.2]**

3038   Gilot, Françoise. *Matisse and Picasso: A Friendship in Art.* **1990, Doubleday $30.00 (0-385-26044-X).** An account of the friendship and artistic relationship between the two great twentieth-century artists, told by Picasso's former lover. (Rev: BL 10/15/90; LJ 9/15/90; PW 10/12/90) **[709.2]**

3039   Goodrich, Lloyd. *Thomas Eakins.* **1988, Harvard Univ. Pr. $90.00 (0-674-88490-6).** A two-volume survey of the life and works of the American artist containing 275 illustrations. (Rev: Choice 3/83; LJ 2/1/83; NYTBR 1/2/83) **[709.2]**

3040   Greenfeld, Howard. *Devil and Mr. Barnes: Portrait of an American Art Collector.* **1987, Viking $19.95 (0-670-80650-1).** A study of the life and times of the American art connoisseur who founded the Barnes Foundation and amassed a significant art collection. (Rev: LJ 10/15/87; NYTBR 11/22/87; PW 10/9/87) **[709.2]**

3041   Grooms, Red. *Red Grooms: A Retrospective.* **1986, Abrams paper $29.95 (0-8109-2315-7).** A retrospective of the artist best known for his huge, colorful assemblages depicting urban life in America. (Rev: Choice 9/86; LJ 7/86; PW 2/21/86. Awards: ALA, 1986) **[709.2]**

3042 Gruen, John. *Keith Haring: The Authorized Biography.* 1991, Prentice Hall $35.00 (0-13-516113-4). A survey of the life and works of the Pennsylvania-born artist who became known for his graffiti art in New York during the 1970s and 1980s prior to his 1990 death from AIDS. (REV: BL 9/15/91; NYTBR 8/23/91; PW 8/23/91) **[709.2]**

3043 Hockney, David. *David Hockney: A Retrospective.* Ed. by R. B. Kitaj and Henry Geldzahler. 1988, Abrams $60.00 (0-8109-1167-1). A retrospective of the English artist's work in painting, collage, prints, and photography. (REV: BL 6/1/88; Choice 10/88; LJ 6/15/88) **[709.2]**

3044 Huffington, Arianna Stassinopoulous. *Picasso: Creator and Destroyer.* 1988, Simon & Schuster $22.95 (0-671-45446-3); Avon paper $4.95 (0-380-70755-1). A biography of the Spanish artist concentrating on his personal life. (REV: LJ 9/1/88; NYTBR 6/12/88; PW 4/29/88) **[709.2]**

3045 Hunter, Sam. *Larry Rivers.* 1990, Rizzoli $75.00 (0-8478-1094-1). An examination of the career of the American artist known for his abstract expressionist works that served as a precursor to the pop art of the 1960s. (REV: LJ 5/15/90; NYTBR 8/12/90; PW 3/16/90) **[709.2]**

3046 Kornbluth, Jesse. *Pre-Pop Warhol.* 1988, Random $29.95 (0-394-57015-4). An introduction to the early commercial art career of Andy Warhol. (REV: BL 1/1/89; LJ 1/89; NYTBR 11/20/88) **[709.2]**

3047 Liberman, Alexander. *Artist in His Studio: The Heroes of Modern Art.* 1988, Random $60.00 (0-394-56567-3). A presentation of the art, materials, and methods used by 30 twentieth-century artists who lived and worked in France. "An invaluable and insightful documentation of the giants of modern art."—BL (REV: BL 2/1/89; LJ 1/89) **[709.2]**

3048 McShine, Kynaston, ed. *Andy Warhol: A Retrospective.* 1989, Bulfinch $60.00 (0-87070-680-2). An exhibition catalog to accompany the retrospective of the pop artist's work at the Museum of Modern Art containing over 600 reproductions of his art and essays by and about the artist. (REV: Choice 7–8/89; LJ 5/15/89; PW 3/17/89) **[709.2]**

3049 Marquis, Alice Goldfarb. *Alfred H. Barr, Jr.: Missionary for the Modern.* 1989, Contemporary $21.95 (0-8092-4404-7). A biography of the Museum of Modern Art's first director, who held the position from 1929 to 1982 (REV: LJ 4/15/89; NYTBR 4/30/89; PW 2/24/89) **[709.2]**

3050 Munro, Eleanor. *Memoir of a Modernist's Daughter.* 1988, Viking $18.95 (0-670-81605-1); Penguin paper $7.95 (0-14-009944-1). Remembrances of the author's relationship with her father, a noted art critic whose profession she followed. (REV: BL 3/1/88; CSM 6/28/88; LJ 7/88) **[709.2]**

3051 Richardson, John. *A Life of Picasso: Volume One, 1881–1906.* 1991, Random $39.95 (0-394-53192-2). The first of a projected four-volume biography of the Spanish artist. "A very impressive and enormously important work."—LJ (REV: BL 1/15/91; LJ 2/1/91; NYTBR 3/3/91. AWARDS: LJ, 1991; NYTBR, 1991; PW, 1991; Time, 1991) **[709.2]**

3052 Rose, June. *Modigliani: The Pure Bohemian.* 1991, St. Martin's $22.95 (0-312-06416-0). A biography of the Italian sculptor and painter. "A grand portrait."—PW (REV: BL 11/15/91; PW 9/13/91) **[709.2]**

3053 Rouart, Denis. *Degas: In Search of His Technique.* 1988, Rizzoli paper $25.00 (0-8478-0949-8). A heavily illustrated analysis of the techniques used by the artist Edgar Degas. (REV: Atl 1/89; LJ 11/15/88; PW 9/16/88. AWARDS: PW, 1988) **[709.2]**

3054 Samuels, Ernest. *Bernard Berenson: The Making of a Connoisseur.* 1979, Harvard Univ. Pr. $30.50 (0-674-06775-4); paper $12.50 (0-674-06777-0). The first volume of the author's biography of the American art critic and collector. (REV: CSM 4/9/79; LJ 6/1/79; Natl Rev 6/8/79) **[709.2]**

3055 Samuels, Ernest, and Jane Samuels. *Bernard Berenson: The Making of a Legend.* 1987, Harvard Univ. Pr. $27.50 (0-674-06779-7). A biography of the later years of the American art critic and collector who spent most of his life in Italy. (REV: BL 4/15/87; LJ 4/1/87; Time 4/6/87) **[709.2]**

3056 Shapiro, Michael Edward, and Peter H. Hassrick. *Frederic Remington: The Masterworks.* 1988, Abrams $35.00 (0-8109-1595-2). Collected essays regarding the work of artist Frederic Remington with 180 reproductions of his art. "This is the Remington book to have above all others."—BL (REV: BL 6/15/88; Choice 9/88; LJ 6/15/88) **[709.2]**

3057 Stachelhaus, Heiner. *Joseph Beuys.* 1991, Abbeville $24.95 (1-55859-107-9). An illustrated biography surveying the life and works of the influential German artist. (REV: BL 3/1/91; Choice 9/91; PW 2/22/91) **[709.2]**

3058 Truitt, Anne. *Turn: The Journal of an Artist.* 1986, Viking $16.95 (0-670-81175-0); Penguin paper $6.95 (0-14-09249-8). This sequel to Truitt's *Daybook* is a highly personal account of the changes in the artist's life. "A reader feels privileged to be a part of this full, reasoned, creative life."—BL (REV: BL 11/15/86; LJ 10/15/86; PW 10/17/86. AWARDS: BL, the 1980s) **[709.2]**

3059 Waldman, Diane. *Willem De Kooning.* 1988, Abrams $39.95 (0-8109-1134-5). A survey of the work of the American Abstract Expressionist artist containing over 400 photographic reproductions. (REV: Choice 7–8/88; LJ 6/1/88; PW 2/19/88) **[709.2]**

Italian art

3060 Andres, Glenn M., John Hunisak, and Richard Turner. *Art of Florence.* 1989, Abbeville $385.00 (0-89659-402-5). A two-volume set containing reproductions of the art of Medieval and Renaissance Florence. "The next best thing to being there for student and traveler, lay reader and scholar alike."—LJ (REV: Choice 11/89; LJ 9/15/89; PW 7/28/89. AWARDS: LJ, 1989; PW, 1989) **[709.45]**

3061 **Huse, Norbert, and Wolfgang Wolters.** *Art of Renaissance Venice: Architecture, Sculpture, and Painting, 1460–1590.* 1990, Univ. of Chicago Pr. $57.95 (0-226-36107-1). A critical look at the art world of Venice during the Renaissance. (Rev: LJ 1/91; TLS 5/17/91)   **[709.45]**

3062 **Labella, Vincenzo.** *Season of Giants: Michelangelo, Leonardo, Raphael, 1492–1508.* 1990, Little, Brown $45.00 (0-316-85646-0). A study of the lives and careers of three great Italian Renaissance artists at the turn of the fifteenth century. (Rev: BL 12/1/90; LJ 9/15/90)   **[709.45]**

Soviet art

3063 **Razina, Tatyana.** *Folk Art in the Soviet Union.* 1990, Abrams $49.50 (0-8109-0944-8). An illustrated survey of Soviet folk art containing over 1,400 photographs. "This breathtaking album makes a vital contribution to our understanding of Soviet art and culture."—PW (Rev: BL 10/1/90; LJ 6/1/90; PW 7/13/90)   **[709.47]**

3064 **Solomon, Andrew.** *Irony Tower: Soviet Artists in a Time of Glasnost.* 1991, Knopf $25.00 (0-394-58513-5). An introduction to the lives and works of contemporary artists in Leningrad and Moscow. (Rev: BL 6/15/91; PW 5/3/91)   **[709.47]**

Japanese art

3065 **Smith, Lawrence.** *Japanese Art: Masterpieces in the British Museum.* 1990, Oxford Univ. Pr. $50.00 (0-19-520834-X). An illustrated survey of the holdings of Japanese art in the British Museum. "A comprehensive initiation to the study of Japanese art."—BL (Rev: BL 9/15/90; LJ 9/15/90)   **[709.52]**

Indian art

3066 **Sethi, Rajeev, ed.** *Aditi: The Living Arts of India.* 1985, Smithsonian Inst. $27.50 (0-87474-852-6); paper $19.95 (0-87474-853-4). An illustrated study of the impact of Indian arts and crafts on that nation's people and daily life. (Rev: Choice 2/86; LJ 8/85)   **[709.54]**

3067 **Welch, Stuart C.** *India: Art and Culture, 1300–1900.* 1985, Metropolitan Museum of Art $49.95 (0-87099-383-6); paper $35.00 (0-87099-384-4). A catalog to accompany a traveling exhibition of Indian art. "As grand, in its impact, as the exhibition of which it is the permanent record . . . beautifully produced."—Choice (Rev: BL 11/15/85; Choice 3/86; LJ 12/85. Awards: LJ, 1985)   **[709.54]**

Persian art

3068 **Ferrier, R. W.** *Arts of Persia.* 1989, Yale Univ. Pr. $60.00 (0-300-03987-5). An illustrated introduction to the arts of Persia from the sixth century B.C. to current Islamic traditions. (Rev: Choice 3/90; LJ 1/90)   **[709.55]**

Indonesian art

3069 **Jessup, Helen Ibbitson.** *Court Arts of Indonesia.* 1990, Abrams $65.00 (0-8109-3165-6). An illustrated survey of the artworks that surrounded the royal family of Indonesia. (Rev: BL 10/15/90; LJ 9/15/90. Awards: BL, 1990)   **[709.59]**

African art

3070 **Courtney-Clarke, Margaret.** *African Canvas: The Art of West African Women.* 1990, Rizzoli $60.00 (0-8478-1166-2). An illustrated survey of West African tribal women's art the author encountered on a three-year research trip. (Rev: CSM 8/16/90; LJ 9/15/90; NYTBR 9/2/90)   **[709.66]**

3071 **Vogel, Susan.** *Africa Explores: 20th Century African Art.* 1991, Te Neues $70.00 (3-7913-1143-3). A survey of twentieth-century art in Africa. (Rev: BL 11/1/91; LJ 10/1/91. Awards: LJ, 1991)   **[709.66]**

American art

3072 **Baker, Kenneth.** *Minimalism: Art of Circumstance.* 1989, Abbeville $39.95 (0-89659-887-X). Analysis of the 1960s art movement known as minimalism. "A short, informative, and beautiful overview."—BL (Rev: BL 5/1/89; Choice 9/89; LJ 5/1/89)   **[709.73]**

3073 **Berman, Avis.** *Rebels on Eighth Street: Juliana Force and the Whitney Museum of American Art.* 1990, Macmillan $29.95 (0-689-12086-9). A biography of the first director and cofounder of New York's Whitney Museum of American Art. (Rev: BL 1/15/90; LJ 12/89; NYTBR 4/15/90)   **[709.73]**

3074 **Davidson, Marshall B., and Elizabeth Stillinger.** *American Wing at the Metropolitan Museum of Art.* 1988, Crown $24.95 (0-517-64626-9). An illustrated survey of the holdings of the American wing of New York's Metropolitan Museum of Art. (Rev: BL 12/15/85; LJ 1/86; NYTBR 12/8/85)   **[709.73]**

3075 **Kloss, William.** *Treasures from the National Museum of American Art.* 1986, Smithsonian Inst. $39.95 (0-87474-594-2). Selected artworks from the collections of the Washington museum representing American art from the mid-1800s to the 1970s. (Rev: BL 6/1/86; Choice 9/86; LJ 4/1/86)   **[709.73]**

3076 **Munro, Eleanor.** *Originals: American Women Artists.* 1982, Simon & Schuster paper $17.95 (0-671-42812-8). A study of the lives and works of 30 prominent American women artists. (Rev: Atl 9/79; LJ 5/15/79; NYTBR 6/17/79)   **[709.73]**

3077 **Scully, Vincent.** *New World Visions of Household Gods and Sacred Places: American Art and the Metropolitan Museum, 1650–1914.* 1988, Bulfinch $35.00 (0-8212-1647-3). A companion to the PBS television series, this survey by the art historian covers American painting, sculpture, urban design, architecture, and decorative art. (Rev: BL 9/15/88; LJ 9/15/88; PW 7/15/88)   **[709.73]**

3078 **Vance, William.** *America's Rome.* 1989, Yale Univ. Pr. $60.00 (0-300-03670-1). A two-volume history of the influence of the city of Rome upon American thought and culture. (Rev: Choice 12/89; NYTBR 8/13/89; TLS 11/17/89)   **[709.73]**

Art of the Western United States

3079 **Axelrod, Alan.** *Art of the Golden West.* **1990, Abbeville $95.00 (1-55859-103-6).** An illustrated history of the art of the American West from the sixteenth through the nineteenth centuries containing over 400 reproductions. (REV: BL 1/1/91; Choice 3/91. AWARDS: BL, 1990)   **[709.78]**

3080 **Hassrick, Royal B.** *History of Western American Art.* **1987, Simon & Schuster $17.98 (0-671-08930-7).** Survey history of the art of the American West by the former Denver Art Museum curator. (REV: BL 10/15/87; LJ 11/1/87)   **[709.78]**

710   CIVIC AND LANDSCAPE ART

711   Area planning (Civic art)

3081 **McHarg, Ian.** *Design with Nature.* **1971, Natural History paper $15.95 (0-385-05509-9).** The use of natural environment in landscape design is explored. "A pleasure to read . . . it may well be one of the most important books of the century."—LJ (REV: Choice 11/69; CSM 11/27/70; LJ 10/1/69. AWARDS: ALA, 1969)   **[711]**

Local community (City) plans and planning

3082 **Huxtable, Ada Louise.** *Will They Ever Finish Bruckner Boulevard?* **1988, Univ. of California Pr. paper $10.95 (0-520-06205-1).** Essays by the architecture critic for the *New York Times* regarding the preservation of architectural treasures, criticizing the lack of planning in modern cities, and appraising the current state of architecture. "Splendidly witty and devastating."—PW (REV: LJ 10/15/70; NYTBR 7/12/70; PW 3/30/70. AWARDS: ALA, 1970) **[711.4]**

712   Landscape architecture

3083 **Creese, Walter L.** *Crowning of the American Landscape: Eight Great Spaces and Their Buildings.* **1985, Princeton Univ. Pr. $65.00 (0-691-04029-X).** Studies of eight American sites where architecture has enhanced or blended with the surrounding landscape. (REV: Choice 6/86; LJ 1/86)   **[712]**

3084 **Griswold, Mac, and Eleanor Weller.** *Golden Age of American Gardens: Proud Owners, Private Estates, 1890–1940.* **1991, Abrams $75.00 (0-8109-3358-6).** An illustrated history of prominent American gardens and their owners from 1890 to 1940. (REV: BL 10/15/91; NYTBR 12/1/91)   **[712]**

3085 **Hobhouse, Penelope.** *Garden Style.* **1988, Little, Brown $40.00 (0-316-36750-8).** An introduction to various styles of gardens and their designs. (REV: BL 9/1/88; LJ 9/15/88)   **[712]**

3086 **Lazzaro, Claudia.** *Italian Renaissance Garden: From the Conventions of Planting, Design and Ornament to the Grand Gardens of 16th-Century Italy.* **1990, Yale Univ. Pr. $55.00 (0-300-04765-7).** A study of the historical development of the design and landscaping of sixteenth-century Italian gardens. (REV: BL 8/90; LJ 10/15/90; PW 7/20/90)   **[712]**

3087 **Mosser, Monique, and Georges Teyssot, eds.** *Architecture of Western Gardens: A Design History from the Renaissance to the Present Day.* **1991, MIT Pr. $125.00 (0-262-13264-8).** An illustrated history of the design and construction of Western gardens from the sixteenth to the twentieth centuries. (REV: CSM 8/15/91; LJ 9/15/91)   **[712]**

3088 **Tankard, Judith B., and Michael Van Valkenburgh.** *Gertrude Jekyll: A Vision of Garden and Wood.* **1989, Saga Pr. $35.00 (0-8109-1158-2).** A photographic look at the private garden of the English landscape artist Gertrude Jekyll. "A gorgeous book, one that gardeners, architects, and nature buffs will cherish."—BL (REV: BL 5/1/89; PW 4/21/89; TLS 5/19/89. AWARDS: PW, 1989)   **[712]**

715   Woody plants

Trees

3089 **American Forestry Association Staff, and Gary Moll, eds.** *Shading Our Cities: A Resource Guide for Urban and Community Forests.* **1989, Island Pr. $34.95 (0-933280-96-3); paper $19.95 (0-933280-95-5).** A manual by the American Forestry Association detailing the importance of urban trees to making cities livable. (REV: BL 10/15/89; LJ 12/89)   **[715.2]**

716   Herbaceous plants

3090 **Brown, Emily.** *Landscaping with Perennials.* **1986, Timber $39.95 (0-88192-063-0).** A guide to 2,000 perennials and their use in the garden. "Brown's love of gardening shows through on every page."—BL (REV: BL 10/1/86; LJ 11/1/86; NYTBR 5/31/87)   **[716]**

720   ARCHITECTURE

3091 **Curtis, William J. R.** *Le Corbusier: Ideas and Forms.* **1986, Rizzoli $45.00 (0-8478-0726-6).** An overview of the architectural designs and completed projects of the French architect. (REV: LJ 3/15/87; NYRB 12/17/87; TLS 2/13/87)   **[720]**

Auxiliary techniques and procedures; apparatus, equipment, materials

3092 **Diamonstein, Barbara.** *Remaking America: New Uses, Old Places.* **1986, Crown $30.00 (0-517-56287-1).** A survey of architectural projects where buildings were converted or redesigned for uses other than their original purpose. (REV: Atl 1/87; LJ 2/1/87; NYTBR 12/7/86)   **[720.28]**

Tall buildings

3093 **Saliga, Pauline A., ed.** *Sky's the Limit: A Century of Chicago Skyscrapers.* **1990, Rizzoli $60.00 (0-8478-1179-4).** An architectural and historical study of over 110 of Chicago's tallest buildings. (REV: Choice 3/91; LJ 1/91)   **[720.483]**

History

3094 Kostof, Spiro. *History of Architecture: Settings and Rituals.* **1985, Oxford Univ. Pr. $60.00 (0-19-503472-4); paper $35.00 (0-19-503473-2).** A survey of the history of architecture, examining the aesthetic, technological, and social aspects of buildings. (Rev: BL 8/85; CSM 7/22/85; NYTBR 4/28/85) **[720.9]**

3095 Morris, Jan. *Architecture of the British Empire.* **1986, Vendome $35.00 (0-86565-062-4).** A study of the architectural designs and traditions of the British Empire. (Rev: LJ 9/15/86; PW 7/4/86) **[720.9]**

3096 Olsen, Donald J. *City as a Work of Art: London, Paris, Vienna.* **1986, Yale Univ. Pr. $45.00 (0-300-02870-9).** A study of urban planning and social life in nineteenth-century London, Paris, and Vienna. (Rev: CSM 11/26/87; LJ 7/86; PW 7/25/86) **[720.9]**

3097 Yarwood, Doreen. *Chronology of Western Architecture.* **1988, Facts on File $29.95 (0-8160-1861-8).** A survey of Western architecture from the Ancient Greeks to the mid-1980s. (Rev: BL 3/15/88; LJ 4/1/88) **[720.9]**

Persons

3098 Baker, Paul R. *Stanny: The Gilded Life of Stanford White.* **1989, Free Pr. $24.95 (0-02-901781-5).** A biography of the late nineteenth-, early twentieth-century American architect known for his designs of palatial homes. (Rev: Choice 3/90; LJ 10/15/89; PW 8/25/89) **[720.92]**

3099 Boutelle, Sara Holmes. *Julia Morgan, Architect.* **1988, Abbeville $55.00 (0-89659-792-X).** A study of the life and works of the California-based architect with over 360 illustrations. (Rev: Choice 1/89; LJ 10/1/88; NYTBR 12/4/88) **[720.92]**

3100 Brownlee, David B., and David G. De Long. *Louis I. Kahn: In the Realm of Architecture.* **1991, Museum of Contemporary Art/Rizzoli $60.00 (0-8478-1323-1); paper $40.00 (0-8478-1330-4).** An illustrated survey of the career of the American architect. (Rev: LJ 1/92; NYTBR 12/29/91) **[720.92]**

3101 Gill, Brendan. *A Life of Frank Lloyd Wright.* **1987, Putnam $24.95 (0-399-13232-5); Ballantine paper $12.95 (0-345-35698-5).** The life of the American architect by a writer who knew him in his later years. "Witty, irreverent, and refreshingly honest, this is essential reading for anyone interested in architecture."—LJ (Rev: BL 11/15/87; LJ 11/15/87; PW 10/23/87. Awards: PW, 1987) **[720.92]**

3102 Newhouse, Victoria. *Wallace K. Harrison, Architect.* **1989, Rizzoli $50.00 (0-8478-0644-8); paper $35.00 (0-8478-1071-2).** A study of the architectural career of the man who designed such projects as Rockefeller Center and the United Nations building. (Rev: Choice 12/89; LJ 9/15/89) **[720.92]**

3103 Pasternak, Alexander. *A Vanished Present: The Memoirs of Alexander Pasternak.* **1985, Harcourt $17.95 (0-15-193364-2); Cornell Univ. Pr. paper** $9.95 (0-8014-9576-8). Memoirs of the Russian architect and brother of writer Boris regarding the Pasternak family and life under the Soviet regime. (Rev: BL 6/1/85; CSM 4/19/85; Time 3/25/85) **[720.92]**

3104 Schulze, Franz. *Mies Van Der Rohe: A Critical Biography.* **1985, Univ. of Chicago Pr. $39.95 (0-226-74059-5).** An illustrated study of the life and works of the German-born architect known for his projects in Europe and North America. (Rev: Choice 4/86; CSM 2/10/86; LJ 2/15/86) **[720.92]**

3105 Tafel, Edgar. *Years with Frank Lloyd Wright: Apprentice to Genius.* **1979, Peter Smith $18.25 (0-8446-6181-3); Dover paper $9.95 (0-486-24801-1).** Memories of Wright by an architect who spent nine years studying with him at Taliesin, with a discussion of Wright buildings in the United States currently open to the public. (Rev: Choice 10/79; Natl Rev 8/31/79; Newsweek 8/20/79. Awards: ALA, 1979) **[720.92]**

3106 Twombly, Robert C. *Louis Sullivan: His Life and Work.* **1987, Univ. of Chicago Pr. paper $16.95 (0-226-82006-8).** A biography of the American architect. "Twombly has done a remarkable job of bringing Sullivan's complex personality and artistic genius to life."—LJ (Rev: BL 2/1/86; LJ 1/86; NYTBR 4/6/86) **[720.92]**

3107 Wiseman, Carter. *I. M. Pei: A Profile in American Architecture.* **1990, Abrams $49.50 (0-8109-3709-3).** An illustrated survey of the life and career of the Chinese-American architect. (Rev: BL 1/1/91; LJ 3/1/91) **[720.92]**

Scandinavia

3108 Gaynor, Elizabeth. *Scandinavia: Living Design.* **1987, Stewart, Tabori & Chang $50.00 (1-55670-009-1).** An illustrated overview of Scandinavian architecture and design by an editor of *European Travel and Life.* (Rev: BL 2/15/88; PW 8/21/87. Awards: PW, 1987) **[720.948]**

United States

3109 Kennedy, Roger G. *Architecture, Men, Women and Money in America, 1600–1860.* **1986, Random $35.00 (0-394-53579-0).** An illustrated social history of the great American mansions and plantations from the seventeenth century to the Civil War. (Rev: BL 5/1/86; LJ 3/1/86; PW 12/20/85) **[720.973]**

3110 Kostof, Spiro. *America by Design.* **1987, Oxford Univ. Pr. $24.95 (0-19-504283-2).** An illustrated history of American architecture and design, and its reflection of society from prehistoric times to the present. (Rev: BL 6/15/87; Choice 2/88; LJ 9/15/87) **[720.973]**

3111 Maddex, Diane, ed. *Built in the U.S.A: American Buildings from Airports to Zoos.* **1985, Preservation Pr. paper $8.95 (0-89133-118-2).** An illustrated look at the architectural design and development of specific types of buildings in the U.S. "A must for active architecture and tourism collections."—BL (Rev: BL 6/15/85; LJ 6/1/85) **[720.973]**

3112 Nabokov, Peter, and Robert Easton. *Native American Architecture.* **1988, Oxford Univ. Pr. $65.00 (0-19-503781-2).** An examination of the architectural traditions of Native American tribes dividing the continent into nine major regions. (REV: LJ 9/15/88; NYTBR 12/4/88) **[720.973]**

3113 Rifkind, Carole. *Field Guide to American Architecture.* **1985, Crown $12.98 (0-517-46005-X); NAL paper $15.95 (0-452-26269-0).** This survey provides visual and textual explanations of what make up the various styles of American architecture. "A most welcome addition to the literature of architecture . . . the book has no rival for the purpose of identifying styles of individual buildings."—BL (REV: BL 4/1/80; Choice 10/80; NYTBR 5/18/80) **[720.973]**

3114 Stern, Robert A. M. *New York 1930: Architecture and Urbanism Between Two World Wars.* **1987, Rizzoli $75.00 (0-8478-0618-9).** An illustrated architectural history of New York City in the 1930s. "Splendidly conceived, beautifully produced . . . provides enlightenment and joy."—Paul Goldberger, NYTBR (REV: Choice 7–8/87; LJ 7/87; NYTBR 5/31/87) **[720.973]**

724 Architecture from 1400

3115 Frampton, Kenneth, and Yukio Futagawa. *Modern Architecture: A Critical History.* **1985, Thames & Hudson paper $11.95 (0-500-20201-X).** An illustrated history of modern architecture from the mid-nineteenth century to the end of World War II. (REV: BL 3/15/84; Choice 5/84; LJ 3/1/84) **[724]**

3116 Hochman, Elaine. *Architects of Fortune: Mies Van der Rohe and the Third Reich.* **1989, Grove-Weidenfeld $22.50 (1-55584-182-1).** The career and life of the German architect Mies Van der Rohe in the 1930s prior to his emigration to the United States in 1937. (REV: LJ 3/1/89; New Rep 5/22/89; NYTBR 6/18/89) **[724]**

725 Public structures

3117 Diehl, Lorraine B. *Late Great Pennsylvania Station.* **1987, Greene paper $12.95 (0-8289-0603-3).** An illustrated history of the New York railroad terminal designed by McKim, Mead, & White which was demolished in 1964. "A vital addition to popular architecture collections."—BL (REV: Atl 12/85; BL 10/15/85; LJ 12/85) **[725]**

3118 Liebs, Chester H. *Main Street to Miracle Mile: American Roadside Architecture.* **1985, Bulfinch paper $19.95 (0-8212-1586-8).** An illustrated history of the development and spread of American commercial architecture. (REV: Choice 7–8/86; LJ 3/1/86; NYTBR 4/20/86) **[725]**

Office and communications buildings

3119 Goldberger, Paul. *Skyscraper.* **1983, Knopf paper $24.95 (0-394-71586-1).** A history and commentary on the skyscraper and its design by the *New York Times* architecture critic. (REV: BL 2/1/82; LJ 2/1/82; TLS 3/26/82) **[725.23]**

3120 Huxtable, Ada Louise. *Tall Building Artistically Reconsidered: The Search for a Skyscraper Style.* **1986, Pantheon $21.95 (0-394-53773-4); paper $12.95 (0-394-74154-4).** A critical history of the American skyscraper and its design. "Not to be missed by any library."—Choice (REV: Choice 9/85; CSM 4/16/85; LJ 6/15/85) **[725.23]**

Restaurant buildings

3121 Hess, Alan. *Googie: Fifties Coffee Shop Architecture.* **1986, Chronicle paper $14.95 (0-87701-334-9).** A study of the rise of fast food and coffee shop architecture following World War II and its influence on modern-day buildings. "Extensively researched and highly entertaining."—PW (REV: BL 5/15/86; PW 1/3/86; Time 6/2/86) **[725.71]**

3122 Langdon, Philip. *Orange Roofs, Golden Arches: The Architecture of American Chain Restaurants.* **1986, Knopf $30.00 (0-394-74129-3).** A chronological history of chain restaurants, their architecture, and their influence on American culture and society. (REV: BL 5/15/86; Choice 11/86; LJ 6/1/86) **[725.71]**

726 Buildings for religious purposes

3123 Norman, Edward. *House of God: Church Architecture, Style and History.* **1990, Thames & Hudson $60.00 (0-500-25108-8).** A survey of the history, development, and social impact of Christian church architecture and design. (REV: BL 12/15/90; LJ 11/15/90) **[726]**

Cathedrals

3124 Favier, Jean, and Jean Bernard. *World of Chartres.* **1990, Abrams $60.00 (0-8109-1796-3).** An illustrated architectural study of the fourteenth-century French cathedral. (REV: BL 5/1/90; LJ 4/1/90; NYTBR 12/2/90) **[726.6]**

727 Buildings for education and research

Art museum and gallery buildings

3125 Davis, Douglas. *Museum Transformed: Design and Culture in the Post-Pompidou Age.* **1990, Abbeville $55.00 (1-55859-064-1).** An illustrated survey of museum design and architecture since 1977. (REV: LJ 12/90; PW 8/17/90) **[727.7]**

728 Residential and related buildings

3126 Rybczynski, Witold. *Home: A Short History of an Idea.* **1986, Viking $16.95 (0-670-81147-5); Penguin paper $7.95 (0-14-010231-0).** A history of domestic life and the concept of privacy from the Middle Ages to the present. (REV: CSM 7/10/86; NYTBR 8/3/86; New Yorker 9/1/86) **[728]**

Specific kinds of conventional housing

3127 Kaufmann, Edgar, Jr. *Fallingwater: A Frank Lloyd Wright Country House.* **1986, Abbeville $55.00 (0-89659-662-1).** A photographic and textual essay regarding the Pennsylvania home Frank

Lloyd Wright designed for the author's father. (REV: BL 12/1/86; LJ 2/1/87; Newsweek 12/8/86)   **[728.3]**

3128   Rybczynski, Witold. *Most Beautiful House in the World.* **1989, Viking $18.95 (0-670-81961-6); Penguin paper $8.95 (0-14-101566-2).** Musings on architecture pervade the author's tale of how he designed and built his own home. "This delightful ramble through the creative process will beguile architecture buffs and general readers alike."—PW (REV: NYTBR 5/21/89; Newsweek 5/8/89; PW 3/3/89)   **[728.3]**

Separate houses

3129   Innes, Miranda. *Country Home Book: A Practical Guide to Restoring and Decorating in the Country Style.* **1990, Simon & Schuster $29.95 (0-671-68717-4).** A guide by the garden editor of *Country Living* to the decoration of a second home in the country. (REV: BL 9/1/90; LJ 2/15/90; PW 1/26/90)   **[728.37]**

3130   Stageberg, James, and Susan Allen Toth. *A House of One's Own: An Architect's Guide to Designing the House of Your Dreams.* **1991, Crown $20.00 (0-517-58214-7).** A guide to the design and construction of a home, written for laypeople by a practicing architect. (REV: BL 5/1/91; PW 5/31/91)   **[728.37]**

Large and elaborate private dwellings

3131   Aslet, Clive. *Last Country Houses.* **1982, Yale Univ. Pr. $40.00 (0-300-02904-7); paper $16.95 (0-300-03474-1).** An illustrated look at British country homes built between the end of the Victorian era and the beginning of World War II. (REV: BL 10/1/82; CSM 3/2/83; TLS 11/26/82)   **[728.8]**

3132   Cornforth, John. *Search for a Style: Country Life and Architecture, 1897–1935.* **1989, Norton $39.95 (0-393-02703-1).** The influence of the magazine *Country Life* on the architecture of the English country home. "Its evocation of a gracious, forever-lost era will appeal to any Anglophile."—PW (REV: LJ 10/1/89; PW 9/22/89. AWARDS: PW, 1989)   **[728.8]**

3133   Moss, Roger W. *American Country House.* **1990, Henry Holt $50.00 (0-8050-1248-6).** An architectural survey of notable American country homes and their owners from the eighteenth to the twentieth centuries. (REV: BL 1/1/91; LJ 11/15/90; PW 10/5/90)   **[728.8]**

729   Design and decoration

3134   Jensen, Robert, and Patricia Conway. *Ornamentalism: The New Decorativeness in Architecture and Design.* **1982, Crown $40.00 (0-517-54383-4).** A heavily illustrated examination of ornamentalism, a style of architecture and design that places heavy emphasis upon the use of ornaments and decorations. (REV: CSM 3/4/83; LJ 1/15/82; Newsweek 12/13/82. AWARDS: ALA, 1983)   **[729]**

730   PLASTIC ARTS; SCULPTURE

3135   Stewart, Hilary. *Totem Poles.* **1990, Univ. of Washington Pr. $29.95 (0-295-97052-9).** An illustrated survey of totem poles constructed by Native Americans of the Pacific Northwest and Alaska. (REV: BL 3/15/91; Choice 7–8/91)   **[730]**

Persons

3136   Grunfeld, Frederic V. *Rodin: A Biography.* **1987, Henry Holt $35.00 (0-8050-0279-0).** A survey of the life, works, and time of the French sculptor Auguste Rodin. (REV: LJ 10/1/87; NYTBR 12/13/87; TLS 4/8/88)   **[730.92]**

3137   Lord, James. *Giacometti: A Biography.* **1985, Farrar $35.00 (0-374-16198-4).** A revealing biography of the Swiss-born sculptor. "Moving and well-written . . . a major contribution."—LJ (REV: BL 11/15/85; Choice 2/86; LJ 9/15/85. AWARDS: LJ, 1985)   **[730.92]**

Africa

3138   Drewal, Henry, and John Pemberton, III. *Yoruba: Nine Centuries of African Art and Thought.* **1989, Abrams $65.00 (0-8109-1794-7).** A survey of the art and culture of the West African Yoruba tribe. (REV: BL 8/90; LJ 8/90; PW 4/13/90)   **[730.96]**

733   Greek, Etruscan, Roman sculpture

Greek (Hellenic) sculpture

3139   Stewart, Andrew. *Greek Sculpture: An Exploration.* **1990, Yale Univ. Pr. $95.00 (0-300-04072-5).** An illustrated survey of the sculpture of ancient Greece by a University of California–Berkeley art history professor. (REV: Choice 10/90; LJ 8/90; NYTBR 9/30/90)   **[733.32]**

735   Sculpture from 1400

1800–1899

3140   Janson, H. W. *19th Century Sculpture.* **1990, Group Three Pub. $49.50 (0-940913-69-0).** An illustrated survey of the major trends in sculpture during the 1800s. (REV: Choice 9/85; LJ 6/15/85; NYTBR 6/30/85)   **[735.22]**

738   Ceramic arts

United States

3141   Levin, Elaine. *History of American Ceramics: 1607 to the Present from Pipkins and Bean Pots to Contemporary Forms.* **1988, Abrams $65.00 (0-8109-1172-8).** An overview of four centuries of American ceramic work, and the artists that produced it, presented in one heavily illustrated volume. (REV: BL 12/15/88; Choice 3/89; LJ 12/88)   **[738.0973]**

739　Art metalwork

Work in precious metals

3142　Hill, Gerald, ed. *Faberge and the Russian Master Goldsmiths.* 1989, H. L. Levin $75.00 (0-88363-889-4). The works of Faberge and others who created art objects for the Russian czars are presented in this book containing 277 color plates. (Rev: BL 12/1/89; LJ 9/15/89; PW 10/6/89)　　**[739.2]**

Jewelry

3143　Cartlidge, Barbara. *Twentieth-Century Jewelry.* 1985, Abrams $60.00 (0-8109-1685-1). An illustrated survey of jewelry produced during the twentieth century. (Rev: BL 2/1/86; LJ 1/86; Time 12/16/85)　　**[739.27]**

3144　Snowman, A. Kenneth, ed. *Master Jewelers.* 1990, Abrams $49.50 (0-8109-3606-2). An illustrated study of the lives and works of 15 jewelers of the nineteenth and twentieth centuries. (Rev: Choice 12/90; LJ 10/15/90; PW 10/5/90)　　**[739.27]**

740　DRAWING AND DECORATIVE ARTS

741　Drawing and drawings

3145　Hirst, Michael. *Michelangelo: And His Drawings.* 1990, Yale Univ. Pr. $24.95 (0-300-04796-7). An illustrated study of the drawings, workbooks, and techniques of the Italian master. (Rev: LJ 2/15/89; NYTBR 12/4/88)　　**[741]**

Techniques, procedures, apparatus, equipment, materials

3146　Edwards, Betty. *Drawing on the Artist Within: An Inspirational and Practical Guide to Increasing Your Creative Powers.* 1987, Simon & Schuster paper $12.95 (0-671-63514-X). A sequel to the author's *Drawing on the Right Side of the Brain* discussing the relationship between brain function and creative activity. (Rev: BL 4/1/86; LJ 5/15/86)　　**[741.2]**

Cartoons, caricatures, comics

3147　Callahan, Bob, ed. *New Comics Anthology.* 1991, Macmillan paper $19.95 (0-02-009361-6). An anthology of alternative comic books printed during the 1980s compiled by a former *San Francisco Examiner* columnist. (Rev: BL 9/15/91; PW 9/13/91. Awards: BL, 1991)　　**[741.5]**

3148　Canemaker, John. *Felix: The Twisted Tale of the World's Most Famous Cat.* 1991, Pantheon $29.50 (0-679-40127-X). An illustrated history of the life of the comic strip cat who made his debut in the year 1919. (Rev: BL 4/1/91; NYTBR 3/31/91)　**[741.5]**

3149　Canemaker, John. *Winsor McCay: His Life and Art.* 1987, Abbeville $29.98 (0-89659-687-7). A biography of the American cartoonist and pioneer film animator known for his comic strip "Little Nemo." (Rev: BL 9/15/87; NYTBR 12/6/87; Newsweek 6/29/87)　　**[741.5]**

3150　Gonick, Larry. *Cartoon History of the Universe, Vols. 1–7: From the Big Bang to Alexander the Great.* 1990, Doubleday paper $14.95 (0-385-26520-4). A cartoon history of the development of life on earth. "It's hard to imagine how Gonick's achievement could be equaled, let alone bettered."—BL (Rev: BL 9/15/90; PW 7/27/90. Awards: PW, 1990)　　**[741.5]**

3151　Hernandez, Gilbert. *Reticent Heart.* 1988, Fantagraph Books paper $10.95 (0-930193-65-2). Cartoon stories tracing the adventures of two young men in a Latin American community named Palomar compiled from the magazine *Love and Rockets.* (Rev: BL 11/15/88; PW 8/5/88. Awards: PW, 1988)　　**[741.5]**

3152　Hernandez, Jaime. *Lost Women and Other Stories.* 1988, Fantagraph Books paper $10.95 (0-930193-66-0). Cartoon adventures of a group of Los Angeles mechanics and their friends. (Rev: BL 11/15/88; PW 8/5/88. Awards: PW, 1988)　　**[741.5]**

3153　Hirschfeld, Al. *Hirschfeld: Art and Recollections from Eight Decades.* 1991, Scribner $50.00 (0-684-19365-5). A collection of 200 drawings from over eight decades by the American cartoonist and caricaturist. (Rev: BL 10/15/91; NYTBR 12/1/91)**[741.5]**

3154　Katchor, Ben. *Cheap Novelties: The Pleasures of Urban Decay.* 1991, Penguin paper $12.95 (0-14-015997-5). A comic strip portrayal of the lives of American immigrant urban Jews during the Great Depression. (Rev: BL 12/15/91; PW 9/27/91)　　**[741.5]**

3155　Pekar, Harvey. *American Splendor: The Life and Times of Henry Pekar.* 1986, Doubleday paper $8.95 (0-385-23195-4). An anthology of work from the first decade of the comic strip/magazine *American Splendor.* (Rev: Atl 8/86; BL 4/15/86; NYTBR 5/11/86)　　**[741.5]**

3156　Reidelbach, Maria. *Completely Mad: A History of the Comic Book and Magazine.* 1991, Little, Brown $39.95 (0-316-73890-5). A history of the satirical magazine founded in 1956. (Rev: BL 10/15/91; PW 9/13/91)　　**[741.5]**

3157　Sennett, Ted. *Art of Hanna-Barbera: Fifty Years of Creativity.* 1989, Viking $50.00 (0-670-82978-1). An illustrated guide to the animation artwork produced by the team responsible for the Flintstones, the Jetsons, and Yogi Bear. (Rev: BL 11/15/89; LJ 1/90)　　**[741.5]**

3158　Spiegelman, Art, and Francoise Monly. *Read Yourself Raw.* 1987, Pantheon $14.95 (0-394-75551-0). Selections from the authors' first three comic-strip magazines. "Artistically the Cadillac of comic books . . . patently a fine art book, too."—BL (Rev: BL 12/15/87; Newsweek 1/18/88)　　**[741.5]**

3159　Thomas, Bob. *Disney's Art of Animation: From Mickey Mouse to Beauty and the Beast.* 1991, Hyperion $39.95 (1-56282-997-1). A revised and updated version of the author's classic *Art of*

Animation chronicling the history and development of the art at Walt Disney Studios. (Rev: BL 11/1/91; LJ 11/15/91) **[741.5]**

Animated cartoons

3160 Solomon, Charles. *Enchanted Drawings: The History of Animation.* 1989, Knopf $75.00 (0-394-54684-9). A history of animation from the seventeenth century to the present containing more than 500 illustrations detailing the processes behind the finished form. (Rev: BL 11/1/89; LJ 9/15/89; NYTBR 12/3/89) **[741.58]**

Graphic design, illustration, commercial art

3161 Armitage, Shelley. *John Held, Jr.: Illustrator of the Jazz Age.* 1987, Syracuse Univ. Pr. $37.50 (0-8156-0215-4); $24.95 paper (0-8156-0238-3). A biography of the American illustrator and novelist who gained fame for his drawings in Fitzgerald's *Tales of the Jazz Age.* (Rev: Choice 5/88; NYTBR 12/6/87; PW 11/20/87) **[741.6]**

Books and book jackets

3162 Kiefer, Anselm. *Books of Anselm Kiefer, 1969–1990.* 1991, Braziller $95.00 (0-8076-1261-5). An illustrated large-format study of books designed by the contemporary German artist. "An important book."—Choice (Rev: Choice 12/91; LJ 10/15/91) **[741.64]**

3163 Lanes, Selma G. *Art of Maurice Sendak.* 1980, Abrams $34.95 (0-8109-8063-0). An examination of the artwork of the children's author and illustrator. "A comprehensive and well written book . . . a masterwork in book production."—Choice (Rev: Choice 2/81; NYTBR 11/9/80; TLS 3/27/81. Awards: ALA, 1980) **[741.64]**

Advertisements and posters

3164 Weill, Alan. *Poster: A Worldwide Survey and History.* 1985, G. K. Hall $39.95 (0-8161-8746-0). An overview of the history and production methods of poster making. (Rev: Choice 2/86; CSM 12/12/85; LJ 8/85) **[741.67]**

Collections of drawings

3165 Tedeschi, Martha. *Great Drawings from the Art Institute of Chicago: The Harold Joachim Years.* 1985, Art Institute of Chicago $50.00 (0-933920-69-5); paper $29.95 (0-86559-065-6). Reproductions of over 100 drawings added to the collections of the Art Institute of Chicago under the curatorship of Harold Joachim. (Rev: BL 10/1/85; LJ 10/1/85; PW 8/9/85) **[741.9]**

745 Decorative arts

3166 Glassie, Henry. *Spirit of Folk Art: The Girard Collection at the Museum of International Folk Art.* 1989, Abrams $60.00 (0-8109-1522-7). A survey of folk art and its artists throughout the world as reflected through objects from the Girard Collection housed at the Museum of International Folk

Art in Santa Fe, New Mexico. (Rev: LJ 10/15/89; NYTBR 1/21/90; PW 7/21/89) **[745]**

3167 Sprigg, June. *Shaker Design.* 1986, Norton $40.00 (0-393-02338-9). The catalog that accompanied a 1986 Whitney Museum exhibition tracing the history of Shaker art and design from the eighteenth century to the contemporary era. (Rev: BL 9/1/86; Choice 12/86; LJ 9/1/86) **[745]**

Industry art and design

3168 Wilson, Richard Guy. *Machine Age in America, 1918–1941.* 1986, Abrams $39.95 (0-8109-1421-2). Examines the influences of technology on art and industrial design as an art form. "The illustrations alone would make this book most important for anyone interested in 20th century America. Add the lucid text, extensive notes, and brief bibliographies, and *The Machine Age* becomes, simply, indispensable."—Choice (Rev: Choice 12/86; LJ 12/86; NYTBR 12/7/86. Awards: LJ, 1986) **[745.2]**

Pure and applied design and decoration

3169 Collins, Michael, and Andreas Papadakis. *Post-Modern Design.* 1989, Rizzoli $65.00 (0-8478-1136-0). The British Museum curator presents an illustrated study of postmodern design and its influences from the past. (Rev: Choice 3/90; LJ 1/90; NYTBR 12/3/89) **[745.4]**

3170 Hine, Thomas. *Populuxe: The Look and Life of America in the '50s and '60s.* 1987, Knopf paper $24.95 (0-394-74014-9). A look at American popular culture in the 1950s and 1960s. "A splendid book."—NYTBR (Rev: BL 11/1/86; NYTBR 11/9/86; PW 10/3/86) **[745.4]**

3171 Mauries, Patrick. *Fornasetti: Designer of Dreams.* 1991, Little, Brown $85.00 (0-8212-1872-7). A survey of the life and career of the twentieth-century Italian designer. (Rev: BL 11/15/91; LJ 1/92; PW 10/18/91) **[745.4]**

1800–1899

3172 Hartigan, Lynda Roscoe. *Made with Passion: The Hemphill Folk Art Collection in the National Museum of American Art.* 1990, Smithsonian Inst. $50.00 (0-87474-293-5). An illustrated survey of the folk art collection housed in Washington's National Museum of American Art. (Rev: BL 10/1/90; LJ 9/15/90) **[745.444]**

Handicrafts—In paper

3173 Longenecker, Martha. *Paper Innovations: Objects of Cut, Folded or Molded Paper.* 1986, Univ. of Washington Pr. paper $24.95 (0-295-96387-5). A survey of the international art of paper making and constructions throughout history. (Rev: BL 10/15/86; LJ 10/1/86; PW 8/15/86) **[745.54]**

Making specific objects

3174 Kuiming, Ha, and Ha Yiqi. *Chinese Artistic Kites.* 1990, China Books paper $16.95 (0-8351-2279-

4). An introduction to the history and art of Chinese kite making. (Rev: BL 9/1/90; LJ 7/90) **[745.59]**

Floral arts

3175 **Cook, Hal.** *Arranging: The Basics of Contemporary Floral Design.* **1985, Morrow $19.95 (0-688-02572-2).** An illustrated step-by-step guide to contemporary floral arranging. (Rev: BL 9/1/85; LJ 8/85) **[745.92]**

746   Textile arts

Yarn preparation and weaving

3176 **Hecht, Ann.** *Art of the Loom: Weaving, Spinning, and Dyeing Across the World.* **1990, Rizzoli $35.00 (0-8478-1147-6).** An illustrated survey of international techniques of weaving. "Visually exceptional and informatively superb."—BL (Rev: BL 3/15/90; Choice 7–8/90; LJ 5/1/90. Awards: BL, 1990)**[746.1]**

Needle and handwork

3177 **Cooper, Patricia, and Norma B. Buferd.** *Quilters: Women and Domestic Art.* **1978, Doubleday $15.95 (0-385-12039-7).** A profile of American women quiltmakers and what quiltmaking means to them. "An illuminated introduction to pioneer life in the Southwestern states, carefully edited and tastefully illustrated."—LJ (Rev: BL 9/1/77; LJ 9/1/77; NYTBR 12/11/77. Awards: ALA, 1977) **[746.4]**

3178 **Wilson, Erica.** *Erica Wilson's Needlework to Wear.* **1982, Oxmoor House $19.95 (0-8487-0527-0).** Ideas and techniques for the making of needlework fashions including clothing, jewelry, and accessories. (Rev: BL 2/1/83; LJ 11/15/82) **[746.4]**

Knitting, crocheting, tatting

3179 **Fassett, Kaffe.** *Glorious Knits: Thirty Designs for Sweaters, Dresses, Vests and Shawls.* **1985, Crown $24.95 (0-517-55843-2).** Designs and instructions for knitting 30 varied items of clothing. (Rev: BL 12/15/85; LJ 1/86) **[746.43]**

3180 **MacDonald, Anne L.** *No Idle Hands: The Social History of American Knitting.* **1988, Ballantine $19.95 (0-345-33906-1); paper $12.95 (0-345-36253-5).** A social history of knitting in America from colonial times to the present. (Rev: BL 10/1/88; NYTBR 12/4/88) **[746.43]**

Patchwork and quilting

3181 **Better Homes and Gardens.** *Better Homes and Gardens American Patchwork and Quilting.* **1985, Better Homes and Gardens $24.95 (0-696-01015-1).** An illustrated survey of the history and techniques behind American quiltmaking. "One of the best all-around tributes to patchwork and quilting ever published."—BL (Rev: BL 11/1/85; PW 6/2/85) **[746.46]**

3182 **Duke, Dennis, and Deborah Harding.** *America's Glorious Quilts.* **1989, Crown $39.99 (0-517-68611-2).** An illustrated history of American quilts and quiltmaking with over 270 reproductions.

(Rev: BL 1/1/88; LJ 1/88; PW 10/16/87. Awards: PW, 1987) **[746.46]**

3183 **Fox, Sandi.** *Small Endearments: 19th Century Quilts for Children.* **1985, Macmillan $24.95 (0-684-18185-1).** Illustrated examples of children's quilts of the 1800s detailing their history and construction. "A poetic appreciation of the quilter's craft."—BL (Rev: BL 6/15/85; Choice 7–8/85; LJ 5/1/85) **[746.46]**

3184 **Walker, Michele.** *Complete Guide to Quiltmaking.* **1986, Knopf paper $18.95 (0-394-74372-5).** Photographic examples of fine quiltmaking with detailed diagrams and instructions. "The only problem it poses . . . is how to choose among the numerous, enticing patterns."—PW (Rev: BL 3/15/86; LJ 3/15/86; PW 3/14/86. Awards: PW, 1986) **[746.46]**

Costume

3185 **Boucher, Francois, and Yvonne Deslandres.** *20,000 Years of Fashion: The History of Costume and Personal Adornment.* **1987, Abrams $45.00 (0-8109-1693-2).** An illustrated history of Western costume from prehistoric times to the present. (Rev: BL 10/1/87; PW 8/21/87. Awards: PW, 1987) **[746.9]**

3186 **Cassini, Oleg.** *In My Own Fashion: An Autobiography.* **1990, Pocket paper $5.95 (0-671-70350-1).** An autobiography of the Russian-Italian fashion designer who settled in Hollywood and was a fixture in the city's social scene. (Rev: BL 8/87; NYTBR 9/6/87; Time 9/7/87) **[746.9]**

Bedclothing

3187 **Linsley, Leslie.** *Weekend Quilter.* **1986, St. Martin's $19.95 (0-312-86016-1).** An illustrated guide to simplified quilting techniques. (Rev: LJ 11/1/86; PW 5/16/86) **[746.97]**

3188 **Lipsett, Linda Otto.** *Remember Me: Women and Their Friendship Quilts.* **1985, Quilt Digest Pr. $29.95 (0-913327-04-2); paper $19.95 (0-913327-17-4).** Biographies of seven nineteenth-century quiltmakers with illustrations of their work. (Rev: BL 1/15/86; LJ 1/86) **[746.97]**

747   Interior decoration

3189 **Calloway, Stephen.** *Twentieth-Century Decoration.* **1988, Rizzoli $100.00 (0-8478-0886-6).** An overview of twentieth-century interior design and decoration containing 500 illustrations. (Rev: LJ 9/15/88; NYTBR 12/4/88) **[747]**

3190 **Conran, Terence.** *Terence Conran's Home Furnishings.* **1990, Crown paper $14.99 (0-517-01984-1).** An illustrated introduction to interior decoration by the author of *The Bed and Bath Book.* (Rev: BL 4/1/87; LJ 6/1/87; PW 2/20/87) **[747]**

3191 **Gilliatt, Mary.** *Complete Book of Home Design.* **1989, Little, Brown $29.95 (0-316-31406-4).** An illustrated guide to home design and interior decorating. (Rev: BL 1/15/85; LJ 1/85) **[747]**

3192   Gilliatt, Mary. *Setting Up Home.* 1986, Little, Brown paper **$16.95** (0-316-31383-1). A guide to inexpensive home decorating methods by the English interior designer. (Rev: BL 10/15/86; LJ 10/1/86)   **[747]**

3193   Pile, John F. *Interior Design.* 1988, Abrams **$49.50** (0-8109-1121-3); Prentice Hall paper **$38.95** (0-13-469248-9). An overview of current trends in interior design for both businesses and private residences. (Rev: BL 5/15/88; Choice 9/88; LJ 8/88) **[747]**

1800–1899

3194   Kemp, Jim. *Victorian Revival in Interior Design.* 1988, Simon & Schuster paper **$17.95** (0-671-66180-9). A guide to the use of late-nineteenth-century patterns and furnishings in contemporary design. (Rev: BL 12/15/85; LJ 1/86)   **[747.2048]**

England

3195   Parry, Linda. *William Morris Textiles.* 1983, Viking **$46.95** (0-670-77075-2). A look at the textile making and design of one of the most prominent artists of the Arts and Crafts Movement. (Rev: BL 5/15/83; Choice 7–8/83; LJ 3/1/83. Awards: ALA, 1983)   **[747.22]**

Decoration of specific rooms of residential buildings

3196   Torrice, Antonio F., and Ro Logrippo. *In My Room: Designing for and with Children.* 1989, Fawcett **$22.95** (0-449-90193-9). An illustrated guide to designing living and play spaces for children. (Rev: BL 11/1/89; LJ 11/15/89)   **[747.7]**

3197   Varney, Carleton. *Room-by-Room Decorating.* 1984, Fawcett paper **$9.95** (0-449-90114-9). A guide to determining proper styles and decorating schemes for specific rooms in the home. (Rev: BL 2/1/85; LJ 3/1/85; PW 1/18/85)   **[747.7]**

748   Glass

Glassware makers

3198   Dawes, Nicholas M. *Lalique Glass.* 1986, Crown **$27.50** (0-517-55835-1). An illustrated guide to the glass art objects designed by Lalique. (Rev: LJ 8/86; PW 4/25/86)   **[748.2092]**

749   Furniture and accessories

United States

3199   Gilborn, Craig. *Adirondack Furniture: And the Rustic Tradition.* 1987, Abrams **$60.00** (0-8109-1844-7). A study of the nineteenth- and twentieth-century rustic style of furniture design developed in the Adirondacks. "Splendidly illustrated, definitive and fascinating."—BL (Rev: BL 2/1/88; Choice 1/88; LJ 2/1/88)   **[749.2973]**

750   PAINTING AND PAINTINGS

3200   Kemp, Martin. *Science of Art: Optical Themes in Western Art from Brunelleschi to Seurat.* 1989, Yale Univ. Pr. **$60.00** (0-300-04337-6). An introduction to sight lights and visual perceptions in Western art from the late Renaissance to post-impressionism. "An achievement that probably no other living scholar could match."—TLS (Rev: Choice 6/90; LJ 5/1/90; TLS 8/31/90)   **[750]**

Museums, collections, exhibits

3201   Eisler, Colin. *Paintings in the Hermitage.* 1990, Stewart, Tabori & Chang **$95.00** (1-55670-159-4). A collection of 750 color reproductions representing masterworks housed at the St. Petersburg museum. "The book itself amounts to a work of art."—Time (Rev: LJ 9/15/90; NYTBR 12/2/90; Time 12/17/90)   **[750.74]**

3202   Stebbins, Theodore E., and Peter C. Sutton, eds. *Masterpiece Paintings from the Museum of Fine Arts, Boston.* 1987, Abrams **$39.95** (0-8109-1424-7). One hundred fifty reproductions of works with essays on their significance from the collection of the Museum of Fine Arts, Boston. (Rev: BL 4/15/87; LJ 6/15/87)   **[750.74]**

751   Techniques, equipment, forms

Watercolor painting

3203   Couch, Tony. *Watercolor: You Can Do It!* 1987, North Light Books **$26.95** (0-89134-188-9). A beginner's introduction to the tools and techniques of watercolor painting. (Rev: BL 6/15/87; LJ 6/1/87)   **[751.42]**

3204   Crespo, Michael. *Watercolor Day by Day.* 1987, Watson-Guptill **$27.50** (0-8230-5668-6). An introductory course in the art of watercolor painting based on the author's classes in the subject at Louisiana State University. (Rev: BL 5/15/87; LJ 6/1/87)   **[751.42]**

Oil painting

3205   Clark, Roberta Carter. *How to Paint Living Portraits.* 1990, North Light Books **$27.95** (0-89134-326-1). Tips for successful portrait painting and sketching. (Rev: BL 9/1/90; LJ 9/1/90)   **[751.45]**

Specific forms

3206   Beckham, Sue Bridwell. *Depression Post Office Murals and Southern Culture: A Gentle Reconstruction.* 1989, Louisiana State Univ. Pr. **$32.50** (0-8071-1447-2). A study of the Southern depression-era post office murals commissioned by the U.S. government and their reflection of the culture of the time. (Rev: Choice 1/90; LJ 7/89) **[751.7]**

3207   Robinson, David. *Soho Walls: Beyond Graffiti.* 1990, Thames & Hudson paper **$18.95** (0-500-27602-1). A study of the graffiti art of New York's Soho District with 85 photographic reproductions. (Rev: LJ 10/15/90; PW 7/27/90)   **[751.7]**

Murals and frescos

3208 Marling, Karal Ann. *Wall-to-Wall America: A Cultural History of Post Office Murals in the Great Depression.* 1982, Univ. of Minnesota Pr. $14.95 (0-8166-1116-5). A study of the 1,100 murals commissioned by the Treasury Department in the 1930s to adorn American post offices. (Rev: CSM 1/11/83; LJ 11/15/82; NYTBR 11/14/82) **[751.73]**

758 Other subjects

3209 Novak, Barbara. *Nature and Culture: American Landscape and Painting.* 1980, Oxford Univ. Pr. $45.00 (0-19-502606-3); paper $25.00 (0-19-502935-6). An analysis of the imagery used by nineteenth-century American landscape painters and the relationship between art and religion in that era. "Indispensable for comprehending 19th century thought as manifested in landscape painting."—Choice (Rev: Choice 10/80; LJ 7/80; NYTBR 4/27/80. Awards: NYTBR, 1980) **[758]**

Landscape painting

3210 Arthur, John. *Spirit of Place: Contemporary Landscape Painting and the American Tradition.* 1989, Little, Brown $50.00 (0-8212-1707-0). An illustrated overview of American landscape painting since the 1950s. "An irresistible asset for any public library's art department."—BL (Rev: BL 11/1/89; Choice 3/90; LJ 10/15/89) **[758.1]**

3211 Brettell, Richard R., ed. *A Day in the Country: Impressionism and the French Landscape.* 1984, Abrams $45.00 (0-8109-0827-1). An exhibition catalog surveying landscape paintings by French Impressionist painters containing 137 reproductions. (Rev: BL 11/1/84; LJ 11/15/84; PW 9/21/84) **[758.1]**

3212 Freeman, Judi, et al. *Fauve Landscape.* 1990, Abbeville $65.00 (1-55859-025-0); paper $35.00 (0-87587-151-8). A study of fauvist landscape paintings. (Rev: LJ 1/91; PW 9/28/90; Time 12/17/90) **[758.1]**

3213 Lurie, Patty. *A Guide to the Impressionist Landscape: Day-Trips from Paris to Sites of Nineteenth-Century Paintings.* 1990, Little, Brown paper $16.95 (0-8212-1796-8). An illustrated tome comparing the works of impressionist landscape painters to the sites that inspired them. (Rev: BL 11/15/90; LJ 11/15/90) **[758.1]**

759 Historical, areas, persons treatment

3214 Greer, Germaine. *Obstacle Race: The Fortunes of Women Painters and Their Work.* 1979, Farrar $25.00 (0-374-22412-9); paper $12.95 (0-374-51582-4). A study of women artists and their critical reception throughout history. (Rev: BL 12/15/79; NYTBR 10/28/79; Newsweek 11/12/79) **[759]**

Painting and paintings, 1800–1899

3215 Adams, Steven. *The Impressionists.* 1990, Running Pr. $35.00 (0-89471-868-1). An English art historian's illustrated survey of key Impressionist artists and their works. (Rev: BL 11/15/90; PW 7/20/90) **[759.05]**

3216 Broude, Norma, ed. *World Impressionism: The International Movement, 1860–1920.* 1990, Abrams $75.00 (0-8109-1774-2). A study of the spread and development of the Impressionist style of painting outside of France. (Rev: BL 11/15/90; LJ 11/15/90; PW 9/28/90) **[759.05]**

3217 Kelder, Diane. *Great Book of Post-Impressionism.* 1986, Abbeville $49.98 (0-89659-966-3). A survey of Post-Impressionist art from Monet to Chagall containing over 400 reproductions. (Rev: BL 12/15/86; Choice 12/86; LJ 11/1/86) **[759.05]**

3218 Rosenblum, Robert. *Modern Painting and the Northern Romantic Tradition: Friedrich to Rothko.* 1975, Harper & Row paper $17.95 (0-06-430057-9). A history of the nineteenth- and twentieth-century painting influenced and inspired by the Northern European blend of art and spiritualism. (Rev: Choice 1/76; LJ 10/1/75; NYTBR 10/19/75) **[759.05]**

3219 Rosenblum, Robert. *Paintings in the Musee d'Orsay.* 1989, Stewart, Tabori & Chang $95.00 (1-55670-099-7). A catalog of the holdings of the Paris museum, which opened in 1986 dedicated to nineteenth-century art and containing over 800 color plates. (Rev: LJ 10/1/89; PW 9/15/89. Awards: LJ, 1989) **[759.05]**

Painting and paintings, 1900–1999

3220 Wolfe, Tom. *Painted Word.* 1975, Farrar $18.95 (0-374-22878-7); Bantam paper $3.95 (0-553-27379-5). How modern art began as a form of rebellion and became as predictable as the art it originally railed against. (Rev: BL 7/15/75; LJ 6/1/75; Natl Rev 8/1/75) **[759.06]**

United States

3221 Beam, Philip C. *Winslow Homer in the 1890s: Prout's Neck Observed.* 1990, Hudson Hills $35.00 (1-55595-042-6). A study of Homer's life and artistic career following his relocation from New York City to the coast of Maine. (Rev: BL 10/15/90; LJ 11/1/90) **[759.13]**

3222 Broun, Elizabeth. *Albert Pinkham Ryder.* 1989, Smithsonian Inst. $55.00 (0-87474-328-1); paper $29.95 (0-87474-327-3). An illustrated study of the works and significance of American painter Albert Pinkham Ryder. (Rev: Choice 3/90; LJ 2/15/90; NYTBR 5/27/90) **[759.13]**

3223 Callaway, Nicholas. *Georgia O'Keeffe in the West.* 1989, Knopf $100.00 (0-394-57971-2). Nearly 100 plates reproducing the artist's landscapes of the American West. (Rev: BL 10/1/89; CSM 1/3/90; LJ 12/89) **[759.13]**

3224 Cikovsky, Nicolai, Jr. *Winslow Homer.* 1990, Abrams $39.95 (0-8109-1193-0). An illustrated survey of the works of the nineteenth-century American artist. "A highly intelligent, measured, and excellent introduction to Homer's art."—Choice (Rev: BL 7/90; Choice 9/90) **[759.13]**

3225   Cooper, Helen A. *Winslow Homer Watercolors.* 1986, Yale Univ. Pr. $50.00 (0-300-03695-7); paper $24.95 (0-300-03997-2). Over 200 illustrations highlight this survey of the watercolor paintings of Winslow Homer. (Rev: Atl 6/86; Choice 9/86; LJ 6/1/86. Awards: LJ, 1986) **[759.13]**

3226   Erffa, Helmut Von, and Allen Staley. *Paintings of Benjamin West.* 1986, Yale Univ. Pr. $90.00 (0-300-03355-9). A descriptive catalog of the paintings of the eighteenth-century American-born artist who became the president of England's Royal Academy. (Rev: Choice 9/86; LJ 5/15/86; NYTBR 6/1/86) **[759.13]**

3227   Gerdts, William H. *American Impressionism.* 1990, Abbeville $39.95 (0-89660-001-7). A survey of the lives and works of over 125 American Impressionist artists containing over 400 illustrations. "The nucleus for any library's collection on American Impressionists."—LJ (Rev: BL 12/1/84; Choice 1/85; LJ 11/15/84. Awards: LJ, 1984) **[759.13]**

3228   Gerdts, William H. *Art Across America: Two Centuries of Regional Painting.* 1990, Abbeville $495.00 (1-55859-033-1). A three-volume survey of American rural and regional painting from the eighteenth century to the twentieth. (Rev: BL 12/1/90; LJ 9/15/90; Newsweek 12/10/90. Awards: BL, 1990) **[759.13]**

3229   Goldwater, Marge, Roberta Smith, and Calvin Tomkins. *Jennifer Bartlett.* 1990, Abbeville $29.95 (1-55859-125-7). A study of the works of the contemporary American painter and multimedia artist. (Rev: Choice 12/85; LJ 8/85; PW 5/10/85) **[759.13]**

3230   Howat, John K. *Hudson River and Its Painters.* 1973, Apollo $25.00 (0-317-54888-3). A survey of the nineteenth-century American landscape painting school known as the Hudson River that included Cole, Bierstadt, Homer, Church, and Inness, among others. "A truly beautiful art book . . . the text . . . is clear, interesting, and just right in length."—PW (Rev: LJ 7/72; NYTBR 7/30/72; PW 5/8/72) **[759.13]**

3231   Hurlburt, Laurance P. *Mexican Muralists in the United States.* 1990, Univ. of New Mexico Pr. $45.00 (0-8263-1134-2); paper $24.95 (0-8263-1245-4). A study of the lives and artistic careers of Mexican artists Siquieros, Rivera, and Orozco in the United States. (Rev: Choice 4/90; LJ 2/1/90; NYTBR 1/7/90) **[759.13]**

3232   Mayer, Musa. *Night Studio: A Memoir of Philip Guston by His Daughter.* 1988, Knopf $30.00 (0-394-56377-8). Illustrated memoirs of the American abstract expressionist artist by his daughter. (Rev: Choice 2/89; NYTBR 12/18/88; Newsweek 9/26/88) **[759.13]**

3233   Meisel, Louis K. *Richard Estes: The Complete Paintings, 1966–1985.* 1986, Abrams $39.95 (0-8109-0881-6). Collected paintings by the New York–based photo-realist. (Rev: BL 12/15/86; LJ 12/86; PW 9/19/86) **[759.13]**

3234   Naifeh, Steven, and Gregory W. Smith. *Jackson Pollock: An American Saga.* 1989, Crown $29.95 (0-517-56084-4); HarperCollins paper $16.95 (0-06-097367-6). A portrait of the American abstract expressionist painter. "Richly satisfying . . . an intimate portrait."—PW (Rev: BL 12/1/89; LJ 9/1/89; PW 11/17/89. Awards: PP:Biography, 1991) **[759.13]**

3235   O'Keeffe, Georgia. *Georgia O'Keeffe: Art and Letters.* Ed. by Jack Cowart, Juan Hamilton and Sarah Greenough. 1987, Bulfinch $60.00 (0-8212-1686-4). A collection of reproductions of artistic works and letters by Georgia O'Keeffe. (Rev: Atl 1/88; LJ 3/15/88. Awards: LJ, 1987) **[759.13]**

3236   O'Keeffe, Georgia. *Georgia O'Keeffe: One Hundred Flowers.* 1989, Knopf paper $29.95 (0-679-72408-7). Reproductions of 100 of the artist's flower paintings executed in the 1920s and early 1930s. (Rev: NYTBR 12/13/87; PW 1/8/88; TLS 12/18/87) **[759.13]**

3237   Pollitzer, Anita. *A Woman on Paper: Georgia O'Keeffe, the Letters and Memoir of a Legendary Friendship.* 1988, Simon & Schuster paper $12.95 (0-671-66242-2). Memoirs of the author's relationship with artist Georgia O'Keeffe intertwined with their correspondence and reflections by others on her work and life. (Rev: BL 7/88; LJ 8/88; New Rep 1/30/89) **[759.13]**

3238   Robinson, Roxana. *Georgia O'Keeffe: A Life.* 1989, Harper & Row $25.00 (0-06-015965-0); paper $12.95 (0-06-092000-9). An authorized biography of the American artist focusing on her personal life and particularly on her relationships with men. "A resourceful, imaginatively rendered portrait of a dauntingly difficult subject."—PW (Rev: BL 9/15/89; PW 8/4/89; Time 11/20/89) **[759.13]**

3239   Scott, Gail R. *Marsden Hartley.* 1988, Abbeville $65.00 (0-89659-879-9). Survey of the life and works of the American painter known for his Expressionist landscapes and experiments with abstraction. (Rev: BL 12/1/88; LJ 9/15/88; PW 9/23/88) **[759.13]**

3240   Shapiro, Michael Edward. *George Caleb Bingham.* 1990, Abrams $37.50 (0-8109-3102-8). A survey of the life and art career of the nineteenth-century American painter. (Rev: BL 3/15/90; LJ 6/1/90; PW 3/9/90) **[759.13]**

3241   Weintraub, Stanley. *Whistler: A Biography.* 1988, Dutton paper $12.95 (0-525-48432-9). Biography of the American painter who lived most of his adult life in Europe. "This readable, lively book makes clear the debt that art lovers and painters owe to its troubled, troublesome hero."—New Yorker (Rev: NYTBR 3/3/74; New Yorker 2/18/74; Newsweek 1/28/74. Awards: ALA, 1974) **[759.13]**

British Isles

3242   Murphy, William M. *Prodigal Father: The Life of John Butler Yeats, 1839–1922.* 1978, Cornell Univ. Pr. $46.50 (0-8014-1047-9); paper $19.95 (0-8014-9179-7). A biography of the father of William Butler Yeats, who was a portrait painter and prominent figure in the artistic and literary circles of his day. (REV: Choice 11/78; LJ 4/15/78; NYTBR 7/9/78)   **[759.2]**

3243   Penny, Nicholas. *Reynolds.* **1986, Abrams $49.50 (0-8109-1565-0); Moyer Bell paper $24.95 (0-918825-23-7).** A survey of the art and life of eighteenth-century English portrait painter Sir Joshua Reynolds. (REV: Choice 12/86; LJ 11/15/86; PW 10/10/86)   **[759.2]**

3244   Spencer, Robin, ed. *Whistler: A Retrospective.* **1989, H. L. Levin $75.00 (0-88363-689-1).** This retrospective of the nineteenth-century artist contains over 200 reproductions of his works with essays by and about Whistler. (REV: BL 11/15/89; LJ 11/15/89; PW 10/13/89)   **[759.2]**

Poland

3245   Fluek, Toby Knobel. *Memories of My Life in a Polish Village, 1930–1949.* **1990, Random $19.95 (0-394-58617-4).** Memoirs of a Jewish woman's life in Poland during the 1930s and 1940s illustrated with her own artwork. (REV: BL 9/15/90; LJ 9/15/90; PW 9/14/90)   **[759.38]**

France

3246   Brettell, Richard R. *Pissarro and Pontoise: The Painter in a Landscape.* **1990, Yale Univ. Pr. $45.00 (0-300-04336-8).** A study of the work compiled by the French Impressionist artist Camille Pissarro while living in the city of Pontoise from 1866 to 1883. (REV: Choice 2/91; LJ 2/1/91; NYTBR 12/2/90)   **[759.4]**

3247   Herbert, Robert L. *Impressionism: Art, Leisure and Parisian Society.* **1988, Yale Univ. Pr. $60.00 (0-300-04262-0).** A study of the French Impressionist artists in relation to their environment and society. "A visual and intellectual feast."—PW (REV: LJ 10/15/88; NYTBR 11/13/88; PW 8/5/88. AWARDS: LJ, 1988)   **[759.4]**

3248   Higonnet, Anne. *Berthe Morisot: A Biography.* **1990, Harper & Row $25.00 (0-06-016232-5).** A biography of the nineteenth-century French Impressionist artist. (REV: LJ 6/1/90; NYTBR 6/3/90; PW 3/23/90)   **[759.4]**

3249   Hoog, Michael. *Paul Gauguin: Life and Work.* **1987, Rizzoli $85.00 (0-8478-0843-2).** A biography of the French post-Impressionist artist. "A visually stunning and scholarly reassessment of the artist's life and work."—BL (REV: BL 4/15/88; LJ 1/88; PW 12/4/87. AWARDS: LJ, 1988)   **[759.4]**

3250   House, John. *Monet: Nature into Art.* **1988, Yale Univ. Pr. $24.95 (0-300-04361-9).** A study of the artistic techniques of the French Impressionist painter. (REV: Choice 12/86; CSM 10/15/86; LJ 11/1/86)   **[759.4]**

3251   Lewis, Mary Tompkins. *Cezanne's Early Imagery.* **1989, Univ. of California Pr. $39.95 (0-520-06561-1).** A study of the first decade of painting of the French artist and its relationship to his later work. (REV: LJ 8/89; TLS 9/8/89)   **[759.4]**

3252   Merot, Alain. *Nicholas Poussin.* **1990, Abbeville $95.00 (1-55859-120-6).** An illustrated study of the life and career of the seventeenth-century French painter. (REV: BL 1/15/91; LJ 2/1/91; PW 12/7/90)   **[759.4]**

3253   Moffett, Charles S. *New Painting: Impressionism, 1874–1886.* **1986, Univ. of Washington Pr. $60.00 (0-295-96367-0); paper $29.95 (0-295-96883-4).** A study of Impressionist paintings exhibited in eight salon shows with reproductions of the works and comments from reviewers of the day. (REV: Choice 6/86; LJ 4/1/86; TLS 8/22/86)   **[759.4]**

3254   Palau i Fabre, Josep. *Picasso Cubism, 1907–1917.* **1990, Rizzoli $250.00 (0-8478-1238-3).** A study of the works of Picasso during his cubist era containing over 1,500 reproductions. "May well be the definitive resource on this artist and this era."—LJ (REV: LJ 2/1/91; NYTBR 12/2/90; PW 12/14/90)   **[759.4]**

3255   Picasso, Pablo. *Late Picasso: Paintings, Sculpture, Drawings, Prints 1953–1972.* **1989, Univ. of Washington Pr. $50.00 (0-295-96786-2); paper $29.95 (0-295-96785-4).** An examination of the artworks produced by the Spanish artist during the last 20 years of his lifetime. (REV: BL 1/15/89; Choice 8/89; LJ 3/1/89)   **[759.4]**

3256   Rewald, John. *Cezanne: A Biography.* **1986, Abrams $75.00 (0-8109-0775-5).** A biography of the nineteenth-century French painter with over 250 reproductions of his work. "Reveals Cezanne as he has never been revealed before."—LJ (REV: Choice 12/76; LJ 11/15/76; TLS 12/5/86. AWARDS: LJ, 1986)   **[759.4]**

3257   Rewald, John. *Seurat: A Biography.* **1990, Abrams $75.00 (0-8109-3814-6).** A revised and updated edition of the author's 1943 biography of the French post-Impressionist. "Essential for art collections."—LJ (REV: BL 12/15/90; LJ 1/91; NYTBR 12/2/90)   **[759.4]**

3258   Rubin, William, ed. *Cezanne: The Late Work.* **1977, Museum of Modern Art $45.00 (0-87070-278-5).** The last decade of Cezanne's work is presented with essays by art historians assessing his technique and influence. (REV: Choice 4/78; LJ 1/1/78; NYTBR 12/4/77)   **[759.4]**

3259   Rubin, William, ed. *Pablo Picasso: A Retrospective.* **1980, Museum of Modern Art $50.00 (0-87070-528-8).** This exhibition catalog for the Museum of Modern Art retrospective contains over 900 reproductions of Picasso's work. "An astonishing visual document."—LJ (REV: Choice 11/80; LJ 7/80; New Rep 6/14/80. AWARDS: ALA, 1980)   **[759.4]**

3260   Rubin, William. *Picasso and Braque: Pioneering Cubism.* **1989, Museum of Modern Art $70.00 (0-87070-675-6).** A study of the development of cubism and of the artistic and personal relationship between its two key figures. (REV: Choice 4/90; LJ 1/90; NYRB 5/31/90)   **[759.4]**

3261   Thomsen, Richard. *Camille Pissarro.* **1990, New Amsterdam $26.50 (0-941533-90-5).** An illustrated study of the life and work of the French Impressionist painter. (REV: BL 6/15/90; LJ 7/90) **[759.4]**

3262 Tucker, Paul H. *Monet in the '90's: The Series Paintings.* 1990, Yale Univ. Pr. $45.00 (0-300-04659-6); Museum of Fine Arts, Boston paper $24.95 (0-87846-313-5). A study of the series paintings Monet executed during the 1890s. "An important book for all collections."—LJ (REV: BL 2/15/90; LJ 4/15/90; NYRB 5/17/90. AWARDS: LJ, 1990) **[759.4]**

3263 Wadley, Nicholas. *Renoir: A Retrospective.* 1989, Crown $34.99 (0-517-68613-9). A retrospective of the work of the French artist containing 250 reproductions and excerpts from his writings. (REV: LJ 1/88; PW 10/31/87) **[759.4]**

Italy

3264 Goffen, Rona. *Giovanni Bellini.* 1989, Yale Univ. Pr. $60.00 (0-300-04334-1). A survey of the life and works of the Italian Renaissance artist. (REV: LJ 2/15/90; New Rep 3/12/90; NYTBR 3/4/90) **[759.5]**

3265 Januszczak, Waldemar. *Sayonara, Michelangelo: The Sistine Chapel Restored and Repackaged.* 1990, Addison Wesley $16.30 (0-201-52395-7). An analysis of Michelangelo's creation of the Sistine Chapel and of modern efforts to restore the artwork to its former glory. (REV: BL 10/1/90; PW 8/10/90) **[759.5]**

3266 Links, J. G., Katherine Baetjer, and Michael Levey, eds. *Canaletto.* 1989, Abrams $60.00 (0-8109-3155-9). A survey of the life and artworks of the eighteenth-century Venetian landscape painter. (REV: Choice 6/90; LJ 6/1/90; PW 1/19/90. AWARDS: PW, 1990) **[759.5]**

China

3267 Biadene, Susanna, ed. *Titian: Prince of Painters.* 1990, Prestel Art Books $70.00 (3-7913-1102-6). A survey of the life and work of the sixteenth-century Italian artist. "A most desirable acquisition for all libraries."—Choice (REV: Choice 3/91; LJ 1/91) **[759.51]**

Soviet Union

3268 Decter, Jacqueline. *Nicholas Roerich: The Life and Art of a Russian Master.* 1989, Inner Traditions $39.95 (0-89281-156-0). A biography of the Russian artist, diplomat, and philosopher. (REV: Choice 4/90; LJ 1/90) **[759.7]**

Netherlands

3269 Clark, Kenneth. *Introduction to Rembrandt.* 1978, Harper & Row paper $9.95 (0-06-430092-7). The British critic discusses the Dutch artist's life and works. "I can imagine no better introduction to the art of Rembrandt."—LJ (REV: BL 6/1/78; LJ 5/1/78; PW 1/16/78. AWARDS: ALA, 1978) **[759.942]**

3270 Hulsker, Jan. *Vincent and Theo Van Gogh: A Dual Biography.* 1990, Fuller Technical $39.00 (0-940537-05-2). A dual biography of Vincent Van Gogh and his brother Theo based on their correspondence. (REV: BL 6/1/90; Choice 9/90; LJ 7/90) **[759.942]**

3271 Sweetman, David. *Van Gogh.* 1990, Crown $30.00 (0-517-57406-3). A study of the life, times, and work of the Dutch post-Impressionist artist. (REV: BL 6/1/90; LJ 7/90; NYTBR 8/12/90) **[759.942]**

3272 Van Gogh, Vincent. *Vincent Van Gogh: Paintings and Drawings.* 1990, Rizzoli $90.00 (0-8478-1288-X). An illustrated overview of the works of Vincent Van Gogh containing over 500 reproductions. (REV: BL 10/15/90; CSM 12/7/90; LJ 9/15/90. AWARDS: LJ, 1990) **[759.942]**

Spain

3273 Brown, Jonathan. *Velazquez: Painter and Courier.* 1988, Yale Univ. Pr. $35.00 (0-300-03894-1). An examination of the life and work of the seventeenth-century Spanish artist. "By far the best book ever devoted to Velazquez."—NYTBR (REV: Choice 10/86; NYTBR 8/10/86; TLS 8/1/86. AWARDS: NYTBR, 1986) **[759.946]**

Mexico

3274 Herrera, Hayden. *Frida: A Biography of Frida Kahlo.* 1984, Harper & Row paper $15.95 (0-06-091127-1). A biography of the Mexican artist and wife of Diego Rivera. "Vivid and riveting . . . a particularly satisfying blend of history and intimacy."—BL (REV: BL 2/1/83; LJ 1/15/83; Time 3/28/83) **[759.972]**

3275 Herrera, Hayden. *Frida Kahlo: The Paintings.* 1991, HarperCollins $40.00 (0-06-016699-1). A collection of the paintings of the influential Mexican artist, which was compiled by her biographer. (REV: BL 10/15/91; LJ 9/15/91) **[759.972]**

3276 Zamora, Martha. *Frida Kahlo: The Brush of Anguish.* 1990, Chronicle $29.95 (0-87701-746-8). An illustrated biography of the Mexican artist and wife of Diego Rivera. (REV: BL 12/15/90; LJ 1/91; PW 8/31/90) **[759.972]**

760 GRAPHIC ARTS; PRINTMAKING AND PRINTS

3277 Corn, Wanda M. *Grant Wood: The Regionalist Vision.* 1985, Yale Univ. Pr. $40.00 (0-300-03103-3); paper $17.95 (0-300-03401-6). A retrospective of the life and work of American artist Grant Wood with over 200 reproductions. (REV: Choice 3/84; LJ 7/83; TLS 3/23/84) **[760]**

3278 Zurier, Rebecca. *Art for the Masses: A Radical Magazine and Its Graphics, 1911–1917.* 1988, Temple Univ. Pr. $34.95 (0-87722-670-9). Political art and cartoons collected from *The Masses*, a left-wing American magazine that listed as contributors Picasso, Carl Sandberg, Robert Henri, John Sloan, and others. (REV: BL 11/1/88; Choice 12/88; NYTBR 9/4/88) **[760]**

Persons

3279 Fine, Ruth E. *John Marin.* 1990, Abbeville $62.50 (1-55859-015-3). An exhibition catalog surveying the life and work of the American artist. (REV: BL 3/15/90; Choice 5/90; LJ 4/1/90) **[760.092]**

3280   Flavell, M. Kay. *George Grosz: A Biography.* **1988, Yale Univ. Pr. $45.00 (0-300-04145-4).** A study of the life and work of the German artist and political satirist who emigrated to the United States from his native land in 1933. (REV: BL 9/1/88; LJ 6/1/88; NYTBR 9/4/88)   **[760.092]**

3281   Hutchison, Jane C. *Albrecht Durer: A Biography.* **1990, Princeton Univ. Pr. $24.95 (0-691-03978-X).** A biography of the sixteenth-century German artist. "Informative and engrossing."—NYTBR (REV: LJ 10/1/90; NYTBR 11/18/90; PW 8/24/90) **[760.092]**

3282   Rand, Paul. *Paul Rand: A Designer's Art.* **1988, Yale Univ. Pr. $24.95 (0-300-04213-2).** Essays by the American graphic designer on his career and craft. (REV: Choice 2/86; CSM 12/23/85; LJ 2/15/86)   **[760.092]**

3283   Webb, Peter. *Portrait of David Hockney.* **1989, Dutton $35.00 (0-525-24826-9).** A biography of the contemporary British artist who lives in southern California and often draws inspiration from Los Angeles and its surroundings. (REV: LJ 10/1/89; PW 10/6/89)   **[760.092]**

769   Prints

Forms of posters

3284   Wrede, Stuart. *Modern Poster.* **1988, Bulfinch $50.00 (0-87070-570-9).** A survey of the art of postermaking in the nineteenth and twentieth centuries written to accompany a 1988 Museum of Modern Art exhibition. (REV: BL 11/15/88; Choice 1/89; LJ 12/88)   **[769.5]**

Postage stamps and related devices

3285   Krause, Barry. *Advanced Stamp Collecting: A Serious Collector's Guide to the Collection and Study of Postage Stamps and Related Materials.* **1990, Betterway paper $9.95 (1-55870-159-1).** A guide to stamp collecting and research for the dedicated philatelist. (REV: BL 11/15/90; LJ 11/15/90)   **[769.56]**

Printmakers

3286   Mathews, Nancy Mowll, and Barbara Stern Shapiro. *Mary Cassatt: The Color Prints.* **1989, Abrams $39.95 (0-8109-1049-7).** An examination of the print work of the American Impressionist artist Mary Cassatt. "This sumptuous work surely will remain the leading resource for decades to come."—LJ (REV: Choice 1/90; LJ 11/15/89)   **[769.92]**

770   PHOTOGRAPHY AND PHOTOGRAPHS

3287   Allard, William Albert, Erla Zwingle, and Russell Hart. *Photographic Essay: William Albert Allard.* **1989, Little, Brown $40.00 (0-8212-1674-0); paper $19.95 (0-8212-1735-6).** An examination of the work and techniques of the veteran *National Geographic* photographer. (REV: Choice 7–8/89; LJ 9/15/89)   **[770]**

3288   Sontag, Susan. *On Photography.* **1990, Doubleday paper $9.95 (0-385-26706-1).** An analysis of the medium of photography, its history, its role in shaping society's perception of itself, and its impact on our consciousness. "Not many photographs are worth a thousand of her words."—Time (REV: Choice 9/78; NYTBR 12/18/77; Time 12/26/77. AWARDS: NYTBR, 1977)   **[770]**

History

3289   Grundberg, Andy. *Crisis of the Real: Writings on Photography, 1974–1989.* **1990, Aperture $39.95 (0-89381-400-8); paper $16.95 (0-89381-401-6).** Collected essays by the *New York Times* photography critic. (REV: BL 7/90; LJ 8/90; PW 5/25/90)   **[770.9]**

3290   Rosenblum, Naomi. *A World History of Photography.* **1989, Abbeville $55.00 (1-55859-054-4).** A survey of the history of photography containing 800 reproductions and covering both its technical and artistic aspects. (REV: BL 2/1/85; LJ 2/1/85; NYTBR 12/2/84)   **[770.9]**

3291   Sandweiss, Martha A., ed. *Photography in Nineteenth-Century America.* **1991, Abrams $49.50 (0-8109-3659-3).** This illustrated study of the rise and development of photography in nineteenth-century America analyzes the art form's social impact. (REV: LJ 11/15/91; PW 9/13/91)   **[770.9]**

3292   Szarkowski, John. *Photography Until Now.* **1990, Museum of Modern Art $60.00 (0-87070-573-3).** A history of photography written by the MOMA curator and critic. "Essential for anyone with an interest in photography."—PW (REV: BL 5/15/90; LJ 5/1/90; PW 3/2/90. AWARDS: ALA, 1990)   **[770.9]**

3293   Trachtenberg, Alan. *Reading American Photographs: Images as History from Matthew Brady to Walker Evans.* **1989, Hill & Wang $25.00 (0-8090-8037-0).** A study of photography as art form, social commentary, and historical document from the Civil War to the Great Depression. (REV: LJ 7/89; NYTBR 8/20/89)   **[770.9]**

Persons

3294   Adams, Ansel. *Ansel Adams: An Autobiography.* **1985, Bulfinch $60.00 (0-8212-1596-5); Little, Brown paper $29.95 (0-8212-1787-9).** An autobiography of the American photographer, profusely illustrated with his work. "Wonderfully gratifying . . . an almost perfect mix of interacting text and images."—Choice (REV: Choice 3/86; LJ 10/15/85; Time 1/20/86. AWARDS: ALA, 1985; LJ, 1985)   **[770.92]**

3295   Adams, Ansel. *Examples: The Making of Forty Photographs.* **1983, Bulfinch $45.00 (0-8212-1551-5).** The noted photographer selects forty of his favorite pictures and describes their technical and aesthetic aspects. (REV: BL 1/15/84; CSM 3/9/84; LJ 2/15/84)   **[770.92]**

3296   Bosworth, Patricia. *Diane Arbus.* **1985, Avon paper $10.95 (0-380-69927-3).** An intimate unauthorized biography of the photographer best known for her revealing and disturbing portraiture. "The book merits high praise for touching the heart and extending our understanding of so popular an art."—LJ (Rᴇᴠ: BL 6/1/84; LJ 6/1/84; Time 6/4/84. Aᴡᴀʀᴅs: ALA, 1984) **[770.92]**

3297 **Galassi, Peter.** *Henri Cartier-Bresson: The Early Work.* **1987, Museum of Modern Art $35.00 (0-87070-261-0).** The French photographer's work in the early 1930s presented and analyzed in a catalog written to accompany the Museum of Modern Art exhibition. (Rᴇᴠ: BL 1/15/88; Choice 3/88; LJ 1/88) **[770.92]**

3298 **Goldberg, Vicki.** *Margaret Bourke-White: A Biography.* **1987, Addison Wesley paper $14.95 (0-201-09819-9).** A biography of the *Life* photojournalist noted for her work in World War II and during the partition of India. (Rᴇᴠ: BL 5/15/86; LJ 6/1/86; PW 5/2/86. Aᴡᴀʀᴅs: ALA, 1986) **[770.92]**

3299 **Hughes, Jim W.** *W. Eugene Smith, Shadow and Substance: The Life and Work of an American Photographer.* **1989, McGraw-Hill $29.95 (0-07-031123-4).** A study of the life and work of the American photographer known for his photo essays of World War II combat and the Minamata mercury poisoning tragedy. (Rᴇᴠ: Choice 3/90; LJ 11/15/89) **[770.92]**

3300 **Katz, D. Mark.** *Witness to an Era: The Life and Photographs of Alexander Gardner.* **1991, Viking $60.00 (0-670-082820-8).** An illustrated biography of the photojournalist who covered the Civil War and American expansion to the West. "A painstaking record of a most significant era in American history."—LJ (Rᴇᴠ: BL 4/15/91; Choice 6/91; LJ 4/15/91. Aᴡᴀʀᴅs: BL, 1991) **[770.92]**

3301 **Kertesz, Andre.** *Kertesz on Kertesz.* **1985, Abbeville $25.00 (0-89659-510-2).** A survey of the life and work of the Hungarian photographer. (Rᴇᴠ: BL 9/1/85; Choice 11/85; LJ 8/85) **[770.92]**

3302 **Lowe, Sue Davidson.** *Stieglitz: A Memoir/ Biography.* **1983, Farrar $25.50 (0-374-26990-4); paper $14.95 (0-374-51827-0).** A biography by his grandniece of the great photographer, art gallery owner, and husband of Georgia O'Keeffe. "An intimate but wide-ranging perspective on both the man and his achievements."—BL (Rᴇᴠ: LJ 1/1/83; Newsweek 3/14/83; Time 2/28/83. Aᴡᴀʀᴅs: Time, 1983) **[770.92]**

3303 **Mark, Mary Ellen.** *Photo Essay: Photographs by Mary Ellen Mark.* **1990, Smithsonian Inst. paper $15.95 (1-56098-003-6).** A collection of selected photo essays by the documentary photographer with commentaries on the technique and back-grounds of the subjects. (Rᴇᴠ: LJ 11/15/90; PW 9/14/90) **[770.92]**

3304 **Meltzer, Milton.** *Dorothea Lange: A Photographer's Life.* **1978, Farrar paper $9.95 (0-374-51910-2).** A biography of the photographer responsible for some of the most remembered images of the Dust Bowl and Great Depression. "This well-researched balanced account . . . belongs in most photography collections."—LJ (Rᴇᴠ: BL 9/15/78; LJ 8/78; NYTBR 8/6/78) **[770.92]**

3305 **Mydans, Carl.** *Carl Mydans: Photo-Journalist.* **1985, Abrams $39.95 (0-8109-1323-2).** A photographic survey of the career of the Time-Life photojournalist from the 1930s through the 1980s. (Rᴇᴠ: BL 12/1/85; Choice 2/86; LJ 2/15/86) **[770.92]**

3306 **Parks, Gordon.** *Choice of Weapons.* **1986, Minnesota Historical Society paper $8.95 (0-87351-202-2).** Memoirs of the *Life* photojournalist from his birth to entry in World War II, concentrating on his struggle for acceptance and against racism. (Rᴇᴠ: BL 3/15/66; Choice 7/66; Time 2/18/66. Aᴡᴀʀᴅs: ALA, 1966) **[770.92]**

3307 **Parks, Gordon.** *Voices in the Mirror: An Autobiography.* **1990, Doubleday $22.95 (0-385-26698-7).** An autobiography of the American photographer, writer, and filmmaker. (Rᴇᴠ: BL 11/1/90; NYTBR 12/9/90; PW 10/12/90. Aᴡᴀʀᴅs: BL, 1990) **[770.92]**

3308 **Penn, Irving.** *Passage: A Work Record.* **1991, Knopf $100.00 (0-679-40491-0).** A collection of over 450 photographs spanning the career of the American known for his fashion and portrait photography. (Rᴇᴠ: LJ 2/1/92; PW 9/13/91) **[770.92]**

3309 **Penrose, Anthony.** *Lives of Lee Miller.* **1989, Thames & Hudson paper $19.95 (0-500-27509-2).** A biography and photographic portrayal of the life of the model and photographer who worked with Man Ray, Edward Steichen, and Jean Cocteau. (Rᴇᴠ: BL 12/1/85; LJ 12/85; Newsweek 12/16/85) **[770.92]**

3310 **Stieglitz, Alfred.** *Alfred Stieglitz: Photographs and Writings.* **Ed. by Sarah Greenough and Juan Hamilton. 1982, Callaway Editions $75.00 (0-935112-09-X).** A collection of letters, articles, and photographs by the American photographer. "Gives the reader a sense of the man . . . and also the aesthetic climate of the time."—BL (Rᴇᴠ: BL 3/1/83; LJ 1/15/83; NYTBR 12/19/82) **[770.92]**

3311 **Vickers, Hugo.** *Cecil Beaton: A Biography.* **1987, Donald I. Fine paper $12.95 (1-55611-021-9).** A biography of the British fashion photographer and designer. (Rᴇᴠ: BL 11/15/86; LJ 9/15/86; NYTBR 6/15/86) **[770.92]**

3312 **Whelan, Richard.** *Robert Capa: A Biography.* **1985, Knopf $19.95 (0-394-52488-8).** An authorized biography of the great war photographer noted for his work in the Spanish Civil War and World War II prior to his death in Vietnam. (Rᴇᴠ: BL 11/1/85; Newsweek 10/21/85; PW 7/19/85. Aᴡᴀʀᴅs: ALA, 1985) **[770.92]**

771 Techniques, equipment, materials

3313 **Grundberg, Andy.** *Grundberg's Goof-Proof Photography Guide.* **1989, Simon & Schuster paper $8.95 (0-671-67291-6).** An introduction to photography for the beginner by the photographer and critic. (Rᴇᴠ: BL 12/15/89; LJ 10/15/89) **[771]**

778 Fields and kinds of photography

3314 **Rowell, Galen.** *Art of Adventure.* **1989, Collins SF $19.95 (0-00-215324-6).** A collection of over 120 photographs by Rowell of the world's mountains and the sportsmen who attempt to conquer the challenges afforded by them. (Rev: LJ 11/15/89; NYTBR 1/14/90; PW 9/8/89)   **[778]**

Close-up photography

3315   Shaw, John. *John Shaw's Closeups in Nature.* 1987, Watson-Guptill $27.50 (0-8174-4051-8). A guide to outdoor close-up photographic techniques for the serious photographer. (Rev: BL 11/15/87; PW 9/18/87. Awards: PW, 1987)   **[778.324]**

Aerial and space photography

3316   Ferris, Timothy. *Spaceshots: The Beauty of Nature Beyond Earth.* 1985, Pantheon $15.95 (0-394-53890-0). Photographs displaying the beauty of astronomical phenomena by the author of *Coming of Age in the Milky Way.* (Rev: BL 12/15/84; LJ 1/85; NYTBR 3/3/85)   **[778.35]**

Motion-picture photography (Cinematography) and editing

3317   Rawlence, Christopher. *Missing Reel: The Untold Story of the Lost Inventor of Motion Pictures.* 1990, Macmillan $19.95 (0-689-12068-0). A study of the life and mysterious disappearance of the French inventor who may have been the first to invent the motion picture. (Rev: BL 10/1/90; PW 9/28/90; TLS 6/1/90)   **[778.53]**

Photography under special conditions—Indoors and by artificial light

3318   Hunter, Fil, and Paul Fuqua. *Light: Science and Magic; an Introduction to Scientific Lighting.* 1989, Focal Pr. $34.95 (0-240-51796-2). A guide to the properties of light and its use in photography. (Rev: BL 12/15/89; LJ 1/90)   **[778.72]**

Photography of specific subjects

3319   Moeller, Susan D. *Shooting War: Photography and the American Experience of Combat.* 1989, Basic Books $25.95 (0-465-07777-3). A history of the use of photography to record American war experiences from the Civil War through the Vietnam conflict. (Rev: BL 3/1/89; Choice 9/89; LJ 3/1/89)   **[778.9]**

3320   Rokach, Allen, and Anne Millman. *Focus on Flowers: Discovering and Photographing Beauty in Gardens and Wild Places.* 1990, Abbeville $39.95 (1-55859-066-8). An illustrated guide to techniques of floral photography. "A very beautiful, even inspirational volume."—BL (Rev: BL 6/15/90; NYTBR 6/10/90; PW 4/20/90)   **[778.9]**

779   Photographs

3321   Arnold, Eve. *In China.* 1980, Knopf $50.00 (0-394-50901-3). A photographic essay of China and its peoples. "A superb portrait of modern China . . . a volume of stunning beauty and revelation."—BL (Rev: BL 1/1/80; Choice 2/81; LJ 11/15/80. Awards: ALA, 1980)   **[779]**

3322   Boyer, William Scott. *American Roads.* 1989, Little, Brown $50.00 (0-8212-1708-9). A photo essay of the roads of the United States with an introduction by William Least Heat Moon. (Rev: CSM 12/1/89; LJ 9/15/89)   **[779]**

3323   Bunnell, Peter C. *Minor White: The Eye That Sleeps.* 1989, Princeton Univ. Pr. $60.00 (0-943012-10-4); paper $25.00 (0-943012-09-0). A retrospective of the career of one of America's finest artistic photographers containing reproductions of nearly 300 of his works. (Rev: Choice 11/89; LJ 8/89. Awards: LJ, 1989)   **[779]**

3324   Capa, Cornell, and Richard Whelan. *Children of War, Children of Peace: Photographs by Robert Capa.* 1991, Little, Brown $50.00 (0-8212-1789-5). A collection of 130 portraits by Robert Capa of children in wartime selected by his brother. (Rev: LJ 10/1/91; NYTBR 9/1/91; PW 7/12/91)   **[779]**

3325   De Carava, Roy. *Roy de Carava: Photographs.* 1982, Friends of Photography $40.00 (0-933286-26-0). Eighty-two photographs by the African-American best known for his portrayals of life in Harlem. "This regal book is one of the great photographic testaments."—BL (Rev: BL 9/82; LJ 6/15/82)   **[779]**

3326   Greenough, Sarah, ed. *On the Art of Fixing a Shadow: One Hundred and Fifty Years of Photography.* 1989, National Gallery of Art $75.00 (0-8212-1757-7). A history of photography with over 400 reproductions. (Rev: Choice 10/89; CSM 8/21/89; LJ 8/89. Awards: BL, 1989)   **[779]**

3327   Livingston, Jane. *Odyssey: The Art of Photography at National Geographic.* 1988, Thomasson-Grant $65.00 (0-934738-45-9). A collection of nearly 300 pictures detailing the history of photography at the National Geographic Society. "A beautiful book that invites repeated examination."—LJ (Rev: BL 11/15/88; Choice 3/89; LJ, 12/88)   **[779]**

3328   Mark, Mary Ellen, and Marianne Fulton. *Mary Ellen Mark: 25 Years.* 1991, Little, Brown $60.00 (0-8212-1837-9). A survey of the works of a quarter-century by the photographer known for her portraits of homeless youths. (Rev: BL 9/15/91; LJ 10/15/91)   **[779]**

3329   Plachy, Sylvia. *Sylvia Plachy's Unguided Tour.* 1990, Aperture $39.95 (0-89381-393-1). A collection of 130 black-and-white photos taken by the *Village Voice* photographer. (Rev: BL 10/15/90; LJ 11/1/90; NYTBR 11/18/90)   **[779]**

3330   Sandweiss, Martha A. *Laura Gilpin: An Enduring Grace.* 1985, Amon Carter $75.00 (0-88360-077-3); paper $39.95 (0-88360-080-3). A biographical work with over 120 reproductions tracing the career of the southwestern photographer. (Rev: BL 8/86; Choice 9/86; LJ 5/15/86)   **[779]**

3331   Silverman, Ruth, ed. *Dog Observed: Photographs, 1844–1988.* 1988, Chronicle paper $16.95 (0-87701-499-X). Selected photographs of dogs taken over 140 years by notable photographers including works by Avedon, Capa, Genthe, and Wegman. (REV: CSM 9/14/84; LJ 9/15/84; NYTBR 9/30/84) **[779]**

3332 Szarkowski, John. *Looking at Photographs: One Hundred Pictures from the Collection of the Museum of Modern Art.* 1976, Bulfinch Pr. $40.00 (0-87070-514-8); paper $27.50 (0-87070-515-6). The MOMA curator of photography takes 100 examples from their collections and discusses the artistic and historical significance of each photograph. "A remarkable achievement . . . one of the best introductions to the world of photography that I have ever seen."—LJ (REV: LJ 12/15/73; NYTBR 10/7/73; New Yorker 11/5/73) **[779]**

3333 Weaver, Mike. *Art of Photography, 1839–1989.* 1989, Yale Univ. Pr. $55.00 (0-300-04457-7). Over 450 photographs tracing the history of photography. (REV: Choice 10/89; CSM 8/21/89; LJ 6/15/89) **[779]**

Collections

3334 Abell, Sam. *Stay This Moment: The Photographs of Sam Abell.* 1990, Thomasson-Grant $50.00 (0-934738-72-6). A retrospective catalog of the works of the *National Geographic* photographer. (REV: BL 2/15/91; LJ 2/15/91) **[779.09]**

3335 Coke, Van Deren, and Diana C. DuPont. *Photography: A Facet of Modernism; Photographs from the San Francisco Museum of Modern Art.* 1987, Hudson Hills $45.00 (0-933920-73-3); paper $25.00 (0-933920-74-1). A history of modern photography with essays and reproductions representing different movements within the art form. (REV: BL 4/15/87; LJ 4/1/87; PW 2/6/87) **[779.09]**

3336 Davidson, Bruce. *Subway.* 1986, Aperture $29.95 (0-89381-231-5). A photographic essay regarding the New York subway system. "A remarkable art book full of stunning images."—BL (REV: BL 12/1/86; LJ 2/1/87; NYTBR 2/1/87) **[779.09]**

3337 Frank, Robert. *Lines of My Hand.* 1989, Pantheon $50.00 (0-394-55255-5). A reissue of a collection of over 350 photographs by the photographer, originally published in a limited edition. (REV: LJ 9/15/89; NYTBR 12/3/89) **[779.09]**

3338 Mora, Gilles, and Walker Evans. *Walker Evans: Havana 1933.* 1989, Pantheon $35.00 (0-394-57493-1). A collection of 88 photographs by Walker Evans taken in Havana in 1933, including many published for the first time. (REV: LJ 9/15/89; NYTBR 12/3/89) **[779.09]**

3339 Salgado, Sebastiao. *Uncertain Grace.* 1990, Aperture $60.00 (0-89381-421-0). A collection of photographs by the Brazilian photographer documenting life in the contemporary Third World. (REV: BL 12/15/90; LJ 2/15/91; NYTBR 12/2/90) **[779.09]**

3340 Wenner, Jann, and Laurie Kratochvil, eds. *Rolling Stone: The Photographs.* 1989, Simon & Schuster $50.00 (0-671-68097-8). A selection of 150 photographs that originally appeared in *Rolling Stone* magazine between 1967 and 1989. (REV: BL 9/1/89; PW 8/18/89) **[779.09]**

Human portraits

3341 Bull, Clarence Sinclair, and Terence Pepper. *Man Who Shot Garbo: The Hollywood Photographs of Clarence Sinclair Bull.* 1989, Simon & Schuster $40.00 (0-671-69700-5). Nearly 200 reproductions of portraits taken by the former head of MGM's still photography department. (REV: BL 2/1/90; NYTBR 12/17/89) **[779.2]**

3342 Mapplethorpe, Robert. *Certain People.* 1985, Twelvetrees Pr. $50.00 (0-942642-14-7). Selected portraits by the late photographer with an introduction by Susan Sontag. "The best portrait photographer to emerge in the last 10 years."—NYTBR (REV: BL 11/1/85; LJ 11/15/85; NYTBR 12/8/85) **[779.2]**

3343 Newman, Arnold. *Arnold Newman: Five Decades.* 1986, Harcourt $49.95 (0-15-107900-5); paper $24.95 (0-15-607937-2). A survey of five decades of the work of American photographer Arnold Newman. (REV: BL 2/15/87; LJ 2/15/87) **[779.2]**

Portraits of men

3344 Mellon, James, ed. *Face of Lincoln.* 1980, Viking $100.00 (0-670-30433-6). Reproductions of the 120 known extant photographic portraits of Abraham Lincoln. "Achieves an excellence worthy of its subject."—NYRB (REV: BL 10/15/80; LJ 8/80; NYRB 8/14/80) **[779.23]**

Portraits of women

3345 Mapplethorpe, Robert. *Some Women.* 1989, Little, Brown $50.00 (0-8212-1716-X). A series of 85 female portraits taken by the late photographer including those of Patti Smith, Louise Nevelson, Yoko Ono, and Grace Jones. (REV: BL 11/1/89; LJ 11/15/89; NYTBR 12/3/89) **[779.24]**

Landscapes

3346 Nichols, John. *Sky's the Limit: A Defense of the Earth.* 1990, Norton $25.00 (0-393-02865-8); paper $14.95 (0-393-30717-4). A collection of landscape photographs of New Mexico scenes. (REV: CSM 12/20/90; LJ 8/90) **[779.36]**

3347 Porter, Eliot. *Eliot Porter's Southwest.* 1985, Henry Holt $37.95 (0-03-006013-3). Collected scenes of the American Southwest captured by the noted nature photographer. (REV: BL 12/1/85; LJ 1/86; Newsweek 12/16/85) **[779.36]**

Architectural subjects

3348 Kreitler, Peter G., ed. *Flatiron: A Photographic History of the World's First Steel Frame Skyscraper, 1901–1990.* 1991, American Institute of Architects Pr. $29.95 (1-55835-060-8). A photographic history of New York's 1903 Flatiron Building. (REV: LJ 2/15/91; NYTBR 4/14/91) **[779.44]**

3349 Saunders, William, and Ezra Stoller. *Modern Architecture: Photographs by Ezra Stoller, 1939–1989.* 1990, Abrams $35.00 (0-8109-3556-2). A collection of over 400 photographs of key twentieth-century works of architecture. (REV: BL 11/1/90; PW 10/12/90) **[779.44]**

Other specific subjects

3350 Smolan, Rick, and David Cohen. *A Day in the Life of Japan.* 1985, Collins SF $45.00 (0-00-217580-0). A photographic essay, by 100 of the world's most outstanding photojournalists, of Japan on June 7, 1985. (REV: CSM 12/20/85; LJ 2/1/86; Time 12/16/85) **[779.9]**

780 MUSIC

3351 Brendel, Alfred. *Music Sounded Out: Essays, Lectures, Interviews, Afterthoughts.* 1991, Farrar $25.00 (0-374-21651-7). Commentaries on music and the art of making music by the acclaimed pianist. (REV: BL 4/15/91; LJ 4/1/91; TLS 1/25/91) **[780]**

3352 Hemming, Roy. *Discovering Great Music: A New Listening Guide to the Top Classical Composers on CD's, LP's and Tapes.* 1990, Newmarket $21.95 (1-55704-027-3); paper $12.95 (1-55704-057-5). A guide for the beginning classical music aficionado on the best recordings available in different formats to introduce the listener to music of great composers. (REV: BL 11/15/88; CSM 12/13/88) **[780]**

3353 Rorem, Ned. *Settling the Score: Essays on Music.* 1988, Harcourt $27.95 (0-15-180895-3); Doubleday paper $10.95 (0-385-26213-2). A collection of the composer and music critic's essays from the past two decades. "The frankly opinionated best of all current popular writers on his subject."—BL (REV: BL 6/15/88; LJ 8/88) **[780]**

Education, research, related topics

3354 Kogan, Judith. *Nothing but the Best: The Struggle for Perfection at the Juilliard School.* 1987, Random $18.95 (0-394-55514-7); paper $10.95 (0-87910-122-9). An inside account of the Juilliard School of Music by a woman who studied harp there for a decade. (REV: BL 7/87; Choice 2/88; PW 2/20/87) **[780.7]**

History

3355 Treitler, Leo. *Music and the Historical Imagination.* 1989, Harvard Univ. Pr. $35.00 (0-674-59128-3); paper $14.95 (0-674-59129-1). Collected essays spanning over 20 years regarding music and its appreciation. (REV: Choice 9/89; LJ 3/1/89; TLS 9/29/89) **[780.9]**

ca. 1750–ca. 1825

3356 Rosen, Charles. *Classical Style: Haydn, Mozart, Beethoven.* 1972, Norton paper $12.95 (0-393-00653-0). The noted pianist examines the music of the classical era through the works of its three greatest composers. (REV: LJ 5/15/71; NYTBR 5/23/71; TLS 4/16/71. AWARDS: NBA, 1972) **[780.9033]**

Persons

3357 Cooper, Martin. *Beethoven: The Last Decade, 1817–1827.* 1985, Oxford Univ. Pr. paper $21.00 (0-19-315321-1). A study of the later life and works of the immortal German composer. (REV: BL 4/15/70; Choice 6/70; Sat Rev 1/31/70) **[780.92]**

3358 Copland, Aaron, and Vivian Perlis. *Copland: 1900–1942.* 1987, St. Martin's paper $12.95 (0-312-01149-0). The first volume of the American composer's autobiography. "It's difficult to imagine that this book could have been any better than it is . . . an essential purchase."—LJ (REV: BL 7/84; LJ 7/84; NYTBR 9/30/84. AWARDS: ALA, 1984) **[780.92]**

3359 Copland, Aaron, and Vivian Perlis. *Copland: Since 1943.* 1989, St. Martin's $29.95 (0-312-03313-3). The second volume of the memoirs of the American composer with commentaries on his life and work by Perlis, a professor at the Yale School of Music. (REV: BL 11/15/89; LJ 12/89; NYTBR 2/18/90) **[780.92]**

3360 Drew, David. *Kurt Weill: A Handbook.* 1987, Univ. of California Pr. $45.00 (0-520-05839-9). An introduction to the life and works of the German composer containing a complete bibliography of his compositions. (REV: Choice 2/88; LJ 1/88; TLS 3/25/88) **[780.92]**

3361 Hampl, Patricia. *Spillville: A Collaboration.* 1987, Milkweed Editions paper $9.95 (0-915943-17-4). A collection of pieces regarding the author's pilgrimage to the Iowa town of Spillville, where Dvorak spent a summer composing a century before. (REV: BL 9/1/87; Choice 1/88; NYTBR 7/26/87) **[780.92]**

3362 Hildesheimer, Wolfgang. *Mozart.* 1982, Farrar $30.00 (0-374-21483-2); Random paper $8.95 (0-394-71591-8). A study of the Austrian composer and his works drawing heavily upon Mozart's letters and personal writings. (REV: LJ 9/1/82; NYRB 11/18/82; NYTBR 10/31/82) **[780.92]**

3363 Hogwood, Christopher. *Handel.* 1988, Thames & Hudson paper $14.95 (0-500-27498-3). A biography of the German composer known to millions through his *Messiah.* "The clear biography of choice for anyone interested in one of the great figures of music."—NYTBR (REV: Choice 9/85; LJ 4/15/85; NYTBR 6/23/85. AWARDS: LJ, 1985) **[780.92]**

3364 Holomon, D. Kern. *Berlioz.* 1989, Harvard Univ. Pr. $30.00 (0-674-06778-9). An examination of the life and work of the nineteenth-century French romantic composer. (REV: CSM 1/5/90; LJ 10/15/89; New Rep 3/19/90) **[780.92]**

3365 Horowitz, Joseph. *Understanding Toscanini: How He Became an American Culture-God and Helped Create a New Audience for Old Music.* 1987, Knopf $30.00 (0-394-52918-0); Univ. of Minnesota Pr. paper $12.95 (0-8166-1678-7). A survey of the music of Toscanini and how the media and music critics influenced popular opinion in regards to him. (REV: Choice 6/87; Newsweek 3/2/87; PW 1/8/88. AWARDS: PW, 1987) **[780.92]**

3366 Jablonski, Edward. *Gershwin: A Biography.* **1987, Doubleday paper $21.95 (0-385-19431-5).** A portrait of the life and work of the American composer with a bibliography and discography of his compositions. (REV: BL 9/15/87; NYTBR 9/27/87; Time 9/21/87) **[780.92]**

3367 MacDonald, Ian. *New Shostakovich.* **1990, Northeastern Univ. Pr. $27.50 (1-55553-089-3).** A biography of the twentieth-century Soviet composer. "Full of revelations."—PW (REV: LJ 11/15/90; NYTBR 11/25/90; PW 10/12/90. AWARDS: PW, 1990) **[780.92]**

3368 MacDonald, Malcolm. *Brahms.* **1990, Schirmer $29.95 (0-02-871393-1).** A biography of the nineteenth-century German composer. (REV: Choice 12/90; LJ 10/15/90; TLS 3/16/90) **[780.92]**

3369 Peyser, Joan. *Bernstein: A Biography.* **1988, Ballantine paper $5.95 (0-345-35296-3).** A psychobiography of the American conductor and composer. "A fascinating and well-written account of one of the most important figures in twentieth-century international music."—Choice (REV: Choice 9/87; LJ 6/1/87; NYTBR 5/10/87) **[780.92]**

3370 Robinson, Harlow. *Sergei Prokofiev: A Biography.* **1987, Viking $29.95 (0-670-80419-3); Paragon House paper $12.95 (1-55778-009-9).** A portrait of the life and work of the Russian composer. "The best biography in English to date . . . the writing is . . . crisp, fast-paced and unencumbered by technical jargon."—LJ (REV: BL 2/15/87; LJ 12/86; PW 1/30/87) **[780.92]**

3371 Rosen, Charles. *Arnold Schoenberg.* **1981, Princeton Univ. Pr. paper $9.95 (0-691-02706-4).** An analysis of the music and musical innovations of one of the most important composers of the twentieth century. (REV: Choice 2/76; LJ 1/15/76; NYTBR 12/28/75) **[780.92]**

3372 Schonberg, Harold C. *Glorious Ones: Classical Music's Legendary Performers.* **1985, Random $24.95 (0-8129-1189-X).** The author of *The Great Pianists* and *The Great Conductors* turns his attention to the great performers of classical music from the eighteenth century to the present. "Good reading even for casual classical music fans."—BL (REV: BL 8/85; LJ 8/85; NYTBR 8/25/85) **[780.92]**

3373 Slonimsky, Nicholas. *Perfect Pitch: A Life Story.* **1988, Oxford Univ. Pr. $21.95 (0-19-315155-3).** Memoirs of the Polish musician and writer regarding his 93 years of life, and experiences with such fellow musical talents as Charles Ives, Igor Stravinsky, and Frank Zappa. (REV: CSM 3/23/88; LJ 3/15/88; NYTBR 3/13/88) **[780.92]**

3374 Solomon, Maynard. *Beethoven.* **1979, Schirmer paper $13.95 (0-02-872240-X).** An examination of Beethoven's personal life and ideals and how they influenced his music. "A definitive biography . . . that is also truly entertaining, absorbing reading."—BL (REV: BL 12/15/77; Choice 6/78; LJ 11/15/77) **[780.92]**

3375 Thomson, Virgil. *Virgil Thomson.* **1977, Da Capo paper $6.95 (0-306-80081-0).** Memoirs of the American composer and music critic. (REV: BL 11/1/66; CSM 10/27/66; NYTBR 10/9/66) **[780.92]**

3376 Walker, Alan. *Franz Liszt: Vol. 2, the Weimar Years, 1848–1861.* **1989, Knopf $39.95 (0-394-52541-8).** The second volume of Walker's biography of the musician and composer examines the years he lived in Weimar as court composer. (REV: BL 6/1/89; LJ 5/15/89; PW 4/21/89. AWARDS: PW, 1989) **[780.92]**

3377 Zaslaw, Neal, and William Cowdery, eds. *Compleat Mozart: A Guide to the Works of Wolfgang Amadeus Mozart.* **1991, Norton $29.95 (0-393-02886-0).** Essays by music experts analyzing the works of the composer Wolfgang A. Mozart. (REV: Choice 6/91; LJ 1/91) **[780.92]**

781   Basic principles and musical forms

Basic principles

3378 Wilson, Frank. *Tone Deaf and All Thumbs? An Invitation to Music Making.* **1986, Viking $15.95 (0-670-80842-3); Random paper $8.95 (0-394-75354-2).** A guide to the physical and mental processes of playing music. (REV: LJ 3/1/86; NYTBR 6/8/86; PW 2/7/86) **[781.1]**

Film music

3379 Palmer, Christopher. *Composer in Hollywood.* **1990, M. Boyars $35.00 (0-7145-2885-4).** A study of composers of music for Hollywood motion pictures and their works from 1935 to the early 1950s. (REV: BL 6/15/90; LJ 4/15/90; PW 3/30/90) **[781.542]**

Folk music

3380 Baez, Joan. *And a Voice to Sing With: A Memoir.* **1988, NAL paper $8.95 (0-452-26094-9).** An autobiography of the American folksinger and political activist. (REV: BL 6/15/87; NYTBR 6/21/87; Newsweek 7/20/87) **[781.62]**

3381 Collins, Judy. *Trust Your Heart: An Autobiography.* **1987, Houghton $18.95 (0-395-41285-4); Fawcett paper $4.95 (0-449-21662-4).** An autobiography of the American folksinger and songwriter. "One of the best written and wisest portraits of the 1960's music scene."—LJ (REV: BL 9/15/87; LJ 11/1/87; PW 10/23/87) **[781.62]**

3382 Klein, Joe. *Woody Guthrie: A Life.* **1986, Ballantine paper $4.95 (0-345-33519-8).** A biography of the American folksinger and songwriter. (REV: LJ 10/15/80; New Rep 10/18/80; Newsweek 11/10/80) **[781.62]**

Popular music

3383 Furia, Philip. *Poets of Tin Pan Alley: A History of America's Great Lyricists.* **1990, Oxford Univ. Pr. $22.95 (0-19-506408-9).** An overview of American songwriters and songwriting from 1900 to 1960. (REV: BL 10/15/90; Choice 2/91; PW 8/24/90) **[781.63]**

3384 Greenwood, Earl, and Kathleen Tracy. *Boy Who Would Be King: An Intimate Portrait of Elvis Presley.* 1990, Dutton $18.95 (0-525-24902-8). A portrait of the Tupelo-born entertainer by his cousin and former press agent. (REV: BL 9/1/90; LJ 8/90; NYTBR 9/23/90) **[781.63]**

3385 Lee, Peggy. *Miss Peggy Lee: An Autobiography.* 1988, Donald I. Fine $18.95 (1-55611-112-6). An autobiography of the jazz/popular singer discovered by Benny Goodman. (REV: BL 3/15/89; LJ 3/15/89; PW 1/16/89) **[781.63]**

3386 Lees, Gene. *Singers and the Song.* 1989, Oxford Univ. Pr. paper $8.95 (0-19-506087-3). A series of essays concerning the contribution of popular singers and songwriters to the music of the 1940s and 1950s. (REV: BL 10/15/87; LJ 10/15/87; NYTBR 11/15/87) **[781.63]**

3387 Makeba, Miriam, and James Hall. *Makeba: My Story.* 1988, NAL $18.95 (0-453-00561-6); paper $9.95 (0-452-26234-8). An autobiography of the South African singer who has been living in forced exile from her country since 1959. (REV: BL 1/15/88; LJ 2/15/88; NYTBR 1/31/88) **[781.63]**

3388 Rosenberg, Deena. *Fascinating Rhythm: The Collaboration of George and Ira Gershwin.* 1991, Dutton $24.95 (0-525-93356-5). Dual biographies of the songwriting team of George and Ira Gershwin. (REV: LJ 10/15/91; PW 11/15/91) **[781.63]**

3389 Torme, Mel. *It Wasn't All Velvet: An Autobiography.* 1988, Viking $18.95 (0-670-82289-2); Zebra paper $4.95 (0-8217-2862-8). An autobiography of the American popular singer reviewing his life and career in show business. (REV: BL 10/15/88; NYTBR 10/30/88; PW 9/19/88) **[781.63]**

Country music

3390 Milsap, Ronnie, and Tom Carter. *Almost Like a Song.* 1990, McGraw-Hill $19.95 (0-07-042374-1). An autobiography of the country-western singer and songwriter. (REV: BL 5/15/90; LJ 5/15/90; PW 5/4/90) **[781.642]**

3391 Morton, David C., and Charles K. Wolfe. *DeFord Bailey: A Black Star in Early Country Music.* 1991, Univ. of Tennessee Pr. $27.95 (0-87049-698-0). A biography of the legendary country music harmonica player who died in 1982. (REV: LJ 11/15/91; PW 10/18/91) **[781.642]**

Blues

3392 Barlow, William. *Looking Up at Down: The Emergence of Blues Culture.* 1989, Temple Univ. Pr. $29.95 (0-87722-583-4); paper $16.95 (0-87722-722-5). A history of the rise and development of African-American blues music in America from Reconstruction to the 1920s. (REV: BL 1/15/90; Choice 4/90; LJ 12/89) **[781.643]**

3393 George, Nelson. *Death of Rhythm and Blues.* 1988, Pantheon $18.95 (0-394-55238-5); Dutton paper $8.95 (0-525-48510-4). An examination of the assimilation of African-American music into white American culture. (REV: CSM 7/27/88; LJ 9/1/88; NYTBR 12/11/88) **[781.643]**

3394 Guralnick, Peter. *Searching for Robert Johnson.* 1989, Dutton $14.95 (0-525-24801-3). An extended essay analyzing the life and legacy of the Mississippi Delta blues musician who was a major influence on subsequent blues and rock music. (REV: BL 9/1/89; NYTBR 11/5/89; TLS 7/27/90) **[781.643]**

3395 Harrison, Daphne Duval. *Black Pearls: Blues Queens of the 1920s.* 1988, Rutgers Univ. Pr. $19.95 (0-8135-1279-4); paper $12.95 (0-8135-1280-8). A look at the lives and music of four American blues singers of the 1920s: Sippie Wallace, Victoria Spivey, Edith Wilson, and Alberta Hunter. (REV: Choice 11/88; LJ 4/1/88; TLS 11/11/88) **[781.643]**

3396 Palmer, Robert. *Deep Blues.* 1982, Penguin paper $7.95 (0-14-006223-8). A look at the development of American blues music and its key figures including portraits of Muddy Waters, Howlin' Wolf, Charlie Patton, and Sonny Boy Williamson. (REV: BL 5/1/81; LJ 5/15/81; PW 4/3/81) **[781.643]**

3397 Scott, Frank. *Down Home Guide to the Blues.* 1991, A Capella paper $14.95 (1-55652-130-8). Collected reviews and recording information on blues recordings from the 1920s to the present. (REV: BL 11/1/91; LJ 9/15/91) **[781.643]**

Soul

3398 Guralnick, Peter. *Sweet Soul Music: Rhythm and Blues and the Southern Dream of Freedom.* 1986, Harper & Row $32.95 (0-06-015514-0); paper $15.95 (0-06-096049-3). A history of American soul and rhythm and blues music from the 1950s to the present. (REV: Choice 10/86; LJ 6/1/86; Newsweek 8/4/86) **[781.644]**

3399 Hirshey, Gerri. *Nowhere to Run: The Story of Soul Music.* 1984, Random $17.95 (0-8129-1111-3); Penguin paper $6.95 (0-14-008149-6). A history of the development and popularization of American soul music from its Southern roots to the 1980s. (REV: LJ 6/1/85; Newsweek 9/3/84; TLS 12/7/84) **[781.644]**

3400 Shaw, Arnold. *Black Popular Music in America: From the Spirituals, Minstrels and Ragtime to Soul, Disco, and Hip-Hop.* 1986, Schirmer $19.95 (0-02-872310-4). The history of the development and influence of nineteenth- and twentieth-century African-American music. "A worthy, much needed well-documented history."—LJ (REV: Choice 10/86; LJ 3/15/86) **[781.644]**

3401 Wilson, Mary. *Dreamgirl: My Life as a Supreme.* 1987, St. Martin's paper $4.95 (0-312-90759-1). Memoirs of the former member of the Supremes regarding her years as a Motown singer and her relationship with Diana Ross. (REV: BL 9/15/86; NYTBR 10/26/86) **[781.644]**

Jazz music

3402 Abe, Keishi, ed. *Jazz Giants: A Visual Retrospective.* 1988, Watson-Guptill $60.00 (0-8230-7536-2). "The best and most satisfying book of jazz photographs ever published . . . there could be no better gift for a jazz fan."—NYTBR (Rev: LJ 10/15/88; NYTBR 12/18/88; Newsweek 12/5/88) **[781.65]**

3403 Balliett, Whitney. *American Musicians: Fifty-Six Portraits in Jazz.* 1986, Oxford Univ. Pr. $27.95 (0-19-503758-8). A collection of pieces on jazz musicians by the *New Yorker* critic. "His witty, effortlessly readable prose not only provides eloquent proof of any encyclopedic knowledge of jazz, but also brings his subjects to life with incredible ease."—BL (Rev: BL 12/15/86; LJ 12/86; NYTBR 12/21/86. Awards: LJ, 1986) **[781.65]**

3404 Basie, Count, and Albert Murray. *Good Morning Blues: The Autobiography of Count Basie.* 1985, Donald I. Fine paper $10.95 (0-917657-89-6). Memoirs of the jazz musician and band leader. "A valuable record of a personality and an age."—LJ (Rev: Choice 7–8/86; CSM 2/7/86; TLW 7/11/86) **[781.65]**

3405 Berry, Jason, Jonathan Foose, and Tad Jones. *Up from the Cradle of Jazz: New Orleans Music since World War II.* 1986, Univ. of Georgia Pr. paper $15.95 (0-8203-0854-4). A history of the jazz, rhythm and blues, and popular music of New Orleans since 1945. (Rev: Choice 4/87; LJ 9/15/86; NYTBR 12/14/86) **[781.65]**

3406 Collier, James Lincoln. *Duke Ellington.* 1987, Oxford Univ. Pr. $19.95 (0-19-503770-7). A biography of the American jazz composer, musician, and orchestra leader. "A valuable addition to the literature of jazz."—LJ (Rev: Choice 1/88; LJ 9/1/87; Newsweek 10/12/87) **[781.65]**

3407 Collier, James Lincoln. *Louis Armstrong: An American Genius.* 1983, Oxford Univ. Pr. $24.95 (0-19-503377-9); paper $9.95 (0-19-503727-8). "A long-overdue, first-rate biography of a major American artist that far surpasses anything else in print."—Choice (Rev: Choice 2/84; LJ 11/15/83; NYTBR 10/30/83. Awards: BL, the 1980s) **[781.65]**

3408 Dahl, Linda. *Stormy Weather: The Music and Lives of a Century of Jazzwomen.* 1989, Limelight paper $14.95 (0-87190-128-8). A survey of the contributions of women to jazz from the 1890s to the present. (Rev: BL 4/15/84; LJ 6/15/84; PW 3/9/84) **[781.65]**

3409 Dance, Stanley. *World of Count Basie.* 1985, Da Capo paper $10.95 (0-306-80245-7). An oral history of Count Basie and his orchestra based on interviews with former band members. "A must for jazz fans."—BL (Rev: BL 12/15/80; Choice 1/81; LJ 9/15/80) **[781.65]**

3410 Davis, Francis. *In the Moment: Jazz in the 1980s.* 1986, Oxford Univ. Pr. $24.95 (0-19-504090-2); paper $7.95 (0-19-505419-9). Collected essays by the music critic regarding the state of jazz in the 1980s. (Rev: Choice 3/87; NYTBR 1/4/87; TLS 9/18/87) **[781.65]**

3411 Davis, Francis. *Outcats: Jazz Composers, Instrumentalists, and Singers.* 1990, Oxford Univ. Pr. $22.95 (0-19-505587-X). Profiles of 37 jazz musi-

cians from the 1920s to the 1980s. (Rev: LJ 3/15/90; NYTBR 6/17/90; PW 4/6/90) **[781.65]**

3412 Friedwald, Will. *Jazz Singing: America's Great Voices from Bessie Smith to Bebop and Beyond.* 1990, Macmillan $24.95 (0-684-18522-9). A survey of blues and jazz vocalists from the 1920s to the present by the *Village Voice* music critic. (Rev: BL 6/15/90; PW 4/27/90) **[781.65]**

3413 Giddins, Gary. *Rhythm-a-Ning: Jazz Tradition and Innovation in the '80's.* 1986, Oxford Univ. Pr. paper $9.95 (0-19-504214-X). Sixty essays formerly published in the *Village Voice* regarding the state of jazz in the 1980s. "One of a handful of essential books on jazz."—NYTBR (Rev: Choice 9/85; CSM 10/2/85; NYTBR 4/7/85) **[781.65]**

3414 Giddins, Gary. *Riding on a Blue Note: Jazz and American Pop.* 1981, Oxford Univ. Pr. $24.95 (0-19-502835-X); paper $10.95 (0-19-503213-6). Profiles of jazz musicians by the author of *Celebrating Bird.* (Rev: BL 2/15/81; LJ 2/15/81; NYTBR 7/19/81) **[781.65]**

3415 Gitler, Ira. *Swing to Bop: An Oral History of the Transition in Jazz in the 1940s.* 1987, Oxford Univ. Pr. paper $10.95 (0-19-505070-3). An oral history detailing the change in jazz styles from the swing of the big bands of the 1930s to the bop of smaller groups in the 1940s. (Rev: Choice 2/86; CSM 1/17/86; NYTBR 12/22/85) **[781.65]**

3416 Herman, Woody, and Stuart Troop. *Woodchopper's Ball: The Autobiography of Woody Herman.* 1990, Dutton $18.95 (0-525-24853-6). An autobiography of the clarinetist and big band leader. (Rev: BL 3/1/90; LJ 2/15/90; PW 1/19/90) **[781.65]**

3417 Lees, Gene. *Meet Me at Jim and Andy's: Jazz Musicians and Their World.* 1988, Oxford Univ. Pr. $24.95 (0-19-504611-0). Profiles of jazz musicians and jazz music by the author of *Singers and the Song.* "Masterpieces . . . by the best jazz essayist there is."—BL (Rev: BL 9/15/88; Choice 5/89; LJ 10/15/88) **[781.65]**

3418 O'Day, Anita, and George Eells. *High Times, Hard Times.* 1989, Limelight paper $12.95 (0-87910-118-0). An autobiography of the jazz singer recounting her experiences as a member of the Gene Krupa and Stan Kenton bands and detailing her battle against heroin addiction. (Rev: BL 9/1/81; NYTBR 9/27/81; PW 7/10/81) **[781.65]**

3419 Pearson, Nathan W., Jr. *Goin' to Kansas City.* 1987, Univ. of Illinois Pr. $24.95 (0-252-01336-0). This study of Kansas City as a center for jazz innovations in the 1920s and 1930s includes profiles of some of the city's top musicians including Lester Young, Count Basie, and Charlie Parker. (Rev: Choice 6/88; LJ 2/1/88; PW 12/4/87) **[781.65]**

3420 Sales, Grover. *Jazz: America's Classical Music.* 1984, Prentice Hall paper $11.95 (0-13-509118-7). An introduction to the history and styles of jazz music. (Rev: BL 2/1/85; Choice 4/85) **[781.65]**

3421 Schuller, Gunther. *Early Jazz: Its Roots and Musical Development.* 1968, Oxford Univ. Pr.

$25.00 (0-19-500097-8). This first volume of the author's history of jazz covers its beginnings to the 1930s. (REV: BL 9/1/68; Choice 7/68; NYTBR 5/12/68) **[781.65]**

3422 Schuller, Gunther. *Musings: The Musical Worlds of Gunther Schuller.* 1986, Oxford Univ. Pr. $27.95 (0-19-503745-6); paper $11.95 (0-19-505921-2). Collected essays of the musician, music critic, and jazz historian. (REV: Choice 9/86; LJ 2/1/86; NYTBR 2/16/86) **[781.65]**

3423 Schuller, Gunther. *Swing Era: The Development of Jazz, 1930–1945.* 1989, Oxford Univ. Pr. $35.00 (0-19-504312-X). The second of three volumes tracing the history and development of jazz in the United States. "Provides unparalleled insights . . . an invaluable work for the serious jazz lover."—LJ (REV: LJ 1/89; NYRB 4/13/89; NYTBR 4/2/89. AWARDS: LJ, 1989) **[781.65]**

3424 Shaw, Arnold. *Jazz Age: Popular Music in the 1920s.* 1989, Oxford Univ. Pr. paper $9.95 (0-19-506082-2). A study of the evolution of jazz in America from 1917 to 1929 and the social factors that influenced its development. (REV: Choice 3/88; LJ 9/15/87; PW 7/24/87) **[781.65]**

3425 Smith, Michael P. *New Orleans Jazz Fest: A Pictorial History.* 1991, Pelican $21.95 (0-88289-810-8). A photographic history of the annual New Orleans Jazz and Heritage Festival covering the years 1970 to 1990. (REV: BL 6/15/91; LJ 6/15/91) **[781.65]**

3426 Spellman, A. B. *Four Lives in the BeBop Business.* 1985, Limelight paper $12.95 (0-87910-042-7). A study of jazz music and the jazz world based on interviews with Jackie McLean, Herbie Nichols, Ornette Coleman, and Cecil Taylor. (REV: BL 2/15/67; LJ 11/15/66; NYTBR 11/20/66) **[781.65]**

3427 Starr, S. Frederick. *Red and Hot: The Fate of Jazz in the Soviet Union.* 1983, Oxford Univ. Pr. $21.95 (0-19-503163-6); Limelight paper $9.95 (0-87910-026-5). A history of jazz music and its suppression in the Soviet Union since its introduction in 1922. (REV: Choice 10/83; NYTBR 4/17/83; TLS 8/12/83) **[781.65]**

3428 Torme, Mel. *Traps, the Boy Wonder: The Life of Buddy Rich.* 1991, Oxford Univ. Pr. $19.95 (0-19-507038-0). A biography of the legendary drummer written by the popular jazz singer. (REV: LJ 6/15/91; NYTBR 9/22/91; PW 7/12/91) **[781.65]**

3429 Williams, Martin. *Jazz Heritage.* 1985, Oxford Univ. Pr. $21.95 (0-19-503611-5). A collection of essays on jazz from its beginnings to the 1960s. "Indispensable in any collection of books on jazz."—BL (REV: BL 9/1/85; Choice 1/86; LJ 8/85) **[781.65]**

Rock music

3430 Bangs, Lester. *Psychotic Reactions and Carburetor Dung.* Ed. by Greil Marcus. 1987, Knopf $19.95 (0-394-53896-X); Random paper $15.00 (0-679-72045-6). An anthology of writings by the rock critic

who died in 1982 at the age of 34. (REV: BL 9/15/87; NYTBR 11/22/87; Newsweek 10/12/87) **[781.66]**

3431 Berry, Chuck. *Chuck Berry: The Autobiography.* 1987, Crown $17.95 (0-517-56666-4); Simon & Schuster paper $8.95 (0-671-67159-6). An autobiography of the influential rock and roll singer, songwriter, and guitarist. (REV: BL 9/15/87; LJ 11/1/87; NYTBR 10/18/87) **[781.66]**

3432 Brown, James, and Bruce Tucker. *James Brown: The Godfather of Soul.* 1988, Thunder's Mouth paper $13.95 (0-938410-97-0). An autobiography of the soul/funk singer known for such hits as "Super Bad," "Cold Sweat," and "Night Train." (REV: LJ 2/1/87; NYTBR 11/30/86) **[781.66]**

3433 Coleman, Ray. *Lennon.* 1986, McGraw-Hill paper $5.95 (0-07-011788-8). A detailed profile of the former Beatle examining his life and musical career. (REV: BL 3/15/85; Choice 9/85; LJ 6/1/85) **[781.66]**

3434 Coleman, Ray. *Man Who Made the Beatles: An Intimate Biography of Brian Epstein.* 1989, McGraw-Hill $19.95 (0-07-011789-6). A biography of the Beatles' former manager who died in 1967 in a drug-related accident. (REV: BL 6/15/89; LJ 7/89; NYTBR 9/3/89) **[781.66]**

3435 Crosby, David, and Carl Gottlieb. *Long Time Gone.* 1988, Doubleday $18.95 (0-385-24530-0); Dell paper $9.95 (0-440-50270-5). Rock music singer and songwriter David Crosby's autobiography tells the story of his rise to fame and his fight against drug addiction. (REV: BL 10/1/88; LJ 11/15/88; PW 10/21/88) **[781.66]**

3436 Davis, Stephen. *Bob Marley.* 1990, Schenkman Books $29.95 (0-87047-045-0); paper $15.95 (0-87047-044-2). A biography of the innovative Jamaican singer and songwriter who helped popularize reggae music worldwide as the leader of the Wailers. (REV: BL 1/15/85; NYTBR 3/31/85; PW 1/11/85) **[781.66]**

3437 Densmore, John. *Riders on the Storm: My Life with Jim Morrison.* 1990, Delacorte $19.95 (0-385-30033-6); Dell paper $10.00 (0-385-30447-1). Memoirs of the former Doors drummer's life with the rock music group and its singer Jim Morrison. "Well-written and touching."—NYTBR (REV: LJ 8/90; NYTBR 4/28/91; PW 7/27/90) **[781.66]**

3438 Dylan, Bob. *Lyrics: 1962 to 1985.* 1985, Knopf paper $21.95 (0-394-54278-9). Collected song lyrics and miscellaneous writings by the Minnesota-born folk-rock singer and songwriter. (REV: BL 11/1/85; LJ 11/1/85) **[781.66]**

3439 Eliot, Marc. *Rockonomics: The Money Behind the Music.* 1989, Watts $19.95 (0-531-15106-9). An account of the business and money-making aspects of the rock music world. "An excellently written book sure to interest music fans."—LJ (REV: BL 5/1/89; LJ 5/1/89) **[781.66]**

3440 Escott, Colin, and Martin Hawkins. *Good Rockin' Tonight: Sun Records and the Birth of Rock 'n' Roll.* 1991, St. Martin's $19.95 (0-312-

05439-4). A history of the Memphis record company that first recorded Carl Perkins, Jerry Lee Lewis, Johnny Cash, and Elvis Presley. (REV: BL 4/1/91; LJ 3/15/91; PW 2/22/91) **[781.66]**

3441 Flanagan, Bill. *Written in My Soul.* 1986, Contemporary $16.95 (0-8092-5153-1); paper $11.95 (0-8092-4650-3). Interviews with 28 rock music songwriters—including Bob Dylan, Mick Jagger, and Paul Simon—regarding the creative process and their work. (REV: BL 9/15/86; LJ 11/15/86; PW 8/22/86) **[781.66]**

3442 Frith, Simon. *Sound Effects: Youth, Leisure and the Politics of Rock 'n' Roll.* 1981, Pantheon paper $11.95 (0-394-74811-5). An examination of the cultural, social, and economic significance of rock music. (REV: Choice 6/82; Newsweek 1/18/82; NYTBR 2/7/82) **[781.66]**

3443 Geldof, Bob, and Paul Vallely. *Is That It?* 1988, Ballantine paper $5.95 (0-345-35197-5). An autobiography of the founder of the rock group Boomtown Rats and organizer of the 1985 Live Aid concert for famine relief. (REV: BL 3/15/87; LJ 5/1/87; TLS 8/8/86) **[781.66]**

3444 George, Nelson. *Where Did Our Love Go? The Rise and Fall of the Motown Sound.* 1985, St. Martin's $17.95 (0-312-86698-4); paper $9.95 (0-312-01109-1). A history of the business and music of Motown Records from its founding in 1959. (REV: CSM 2/26/86; LJ 1/86; NYTBR 3/30/86) **[781.66]**

3445 Giuliano, Geoffrey. *Dark Horse: The Private Life of George Harrison.* 1990, Dutton $18.95 (0-525-24854-4). A biography of the former Beatle and current film producer and member of the Traveling Wilburys. (REV: BL 4/1/90; LJ 5/1/90; PW 3/9/90) **[781.66]**

3446 Goldrosen, John, and John Beecher. *Remembering Buddy: The Definitive Biography of Buddy Holly.* 1987, Penguin paper $12.95 (0-14-010363-5). A biography of the early rock and roll star who died in a tragic plane crash in 1959. "One of the best rock biographies."—LJ (REV: BL 10/1/87; LJ 10/15/87; PW 7/31/87) **[781.66]**

3447 Heylin, Clinton. *Bob Dylan: Behind the Shades.* 1991, Summit $22.95 (0-671-73894-1). A biography of the singer/songwriter and composer of such songs as "Ballad of a Thin Man," "Idiot Wind," and "Lay Lady Lay." (REV: LJ 6/1/91; TLS 5/10/91) **[781.66]**

3448 Loder, Kurt. *Bat Chain Puller: Rock and Roll in the Age of Celebrity.* 1990, St. Martin's $19.95 (0-312-04588-3); paper $12.95 (0-312-06301-6). Essays on rock music and popular culture by the MTV newscaster. (REV: BL 11/15/90; PW 10/12/90) **[781.66]**

3449 Marcus, Greil. *Dead Elvis: A Chronicle of a Cultural Obsession.* 1991, Doubleday $25.00 (0-385-41718-7). A rock critic's analysis of the social phenomenon that developed surrounding the late singer and entertainer after his death. "Provocative reading, revealing much about the American people."—BL (REV: BL 10/1/91; PW 10/4/91) **[781.66]**

3450 Marcus, Greil. *Mystery Train: Images of America in Rock 'n' Roll Music.* 1990, Dutton paper $12.95 (0-525-48556-2). A critical examination of imagery and recurrent themes reflected in rock music by the author of *Lipstick Traces.* (REV: BL 10/15/75; LJ 4/1/75; PW 2/24/75) **[781.66]**

3451 Marsh, Dave. *Heart of Rock and Soul: The 1001 Greatest Singles Ever Made.* 1989, Dutton paper $14.95 (0-452-26305-0). Rock critic Dave Marsh selects and ranks his choices for the 1,001 best singles of the rock 'n' roll era. "Terrifically entertaining."—NYTBR (REV: BL 8/89; NYTBR 10/8/89) **[781.66]**

3452 Norman, Philip. *Shout! The Beatles in Their Generation.* 1983, Warner paper $4.95 (0-446-32255-5). A history and collective biography of the English musical group. "This lucid, forthright book bids fair to be the definitive Beatles biography."—PW (REV: BL 6/15/81; LJ 7/81; PW 2/13/81) **[781.66]**

3453 Pawlowski, Gareth L. *How They Became the Beatles: A Definitive History of the Early Years, 1960–1964.* 1989, Dutton $24.95 (0-525-24823-4); paper $12.95 (0-452-26506-1). An illustrated account of the evolution of the legendary rock band during its formative years. (REV: BL 3/1/90; LJ 4/15/90) **[781.66]**

3454 Riley, Tom. *Tell Me Why: A Beatles Commentary.* 1988, Knopf $19.95 (0-394-55061-7); Random paper $9.95 (0-679-72198-3). A song-by-song analysis of the Beatles' recorded music. "An essential work for all interested parties."—PW (REV: Choice 11/88; NYTBR 6/19/88; PW 3/18/88) **[781.66]**

3455 Robertson, John. *Art and Music of John Lennon.* 1991, Birch Lane Pr. $17.95 (1-55972-076-X). The life and artistic endeavors of the late Beatle. (REV: BL 3/15/91; Choice 12/91; LJ 2/15/91) **[781.66]**

3456 Shapiro, Harry, and Caesar Glebbeek. *Jimi Hendrix: Electric Gypsy.* 1991, St. Martin's $29.95 (0-312-05861-6). A biography of the legendary rock guitarist. "One of the year's best musical biographies and a mandatory purchase for all libraries."—LJ (REV: LJ 7/91; PW 5/17/91) **[781.66]**

3457 Shelton, Robert. *No Direction Home: The Life and Music of Bob Dylan.* 1987, Ballantine paper $5.95 (0-345-34721-8). A biography of the American folk-rock singer and songwriter. "First-rate biography and a marvelous re-creation of the music scene of the '60's."—PW (REV: BL 9/1/86; Choice 1/87; PW 8/1/86) **[781.66]**

3458 Turner, Tina, and Kurt Loder. *I, Tina: My Life Story.* 1987, Avon paper $4.50 (0-380-70097-2). An autobiography of the American popular singer. (REV: BL 9/1/86; LJ 11/1/86) **[781.66]**

3459 Ward, Ed, Geoffrey Stokes, and Ken Tucker. *Rock of Ages: The Rolling Stone History of Rock and Roll.* 1986, Summit paper $14.95 (0-671-63068-7). The history of the nearly 40 years of rock and roll music as seen by the writers of *Rolling Stone.* (REV: Choice 6/87; LJ 2/1/87; NYTBR 12/28/86) **[781.66]**

3460   Wenner, Jann. *Twenty Years of Rolling Stone: What a Long Strange Trip Its Been.* 1987, Friendly Pr. $24.95 (0-914919-10-5). An illustrated anthology of the best articles and photographs published in *Rolling Stone* magazine during its first 20 years as selected by its editor. (REV: BL 11/15/87; LJ 11/15/87; PW 10/16/87) **[781.66]**

3461   White, Charles. *Life and Times of Little Richard: The Quasar of Rock.* 1984, Crown $15.95 (0-517-55498-4). A biography of Richard Penniman who, as "Little Richard," recorded such rock and roll classics as "Lucille" and "Tutti Frutti." "The woolliest, funniest, funkiest rock memoir ever."—Time (REV: BL 12/1/84; PW 8/10/84; Time 9/10/84) **[781.66]**

3462   White, Timothy. *Rock Lives: Profiles and Interviews.* 1990, Henry Holt $24.95 (0-8050-1396-2). Biographical sketches and interviews with nearly 60 influential rock music figures. (REV: BL 10/1/90; LJ 10/1/90; PW 10/19/90. AWARDS: BL, 1990) **[781.66]**

3463   Wyman, Bill, and Ray Coleman. *Stone Alone: The Story of a Rock 'n' Roll Band.* 1990, Viking $22.95 (0-670-82894-7); NAL paper $6.99 (0-451-17055-5). The Rolling Stones' bassist recalls his life with the world's most infamous rock band. (REV: BL 10/15/80; LJ 11/15/90; NYTBR 11/18/90) **[781.66]**

782   Vocal music

Singers

3464   Carreras, Jose. *Singing from the Soul.* 1991, YCP $27.95 (1-87856-89-3). An autobiography of the Spanish opera singer describing his career in music and his bout with leukemia. (REV: BL 5/1/91; LJ 4/15/91) **[782.0092]**

3465   Goldman, Herbert G. *Jolson: The Legend Comes to Life.* 1988, Oxford Univ. Pr. $22.95 (0-19-505505-5). A biography of the Lithuanian-born singer and entertainer who starred in the *Jazz Singer,* the first motion picture with sound. (REV: BL 9/1/88; Choice 2/89; LJ 9/15/88) **[782.0092]**

3466   Thomas, Bob. *I Got Rhythm! The Ethel Merman Story.* 1985, Putnam $16.95 (0-399-13041-1). A biography of the American entertainer by a veteran Hollywood reporter and writer. (REV: BL 11/15/85; LJ 10/15/85; PW 10/18/85) **[782.0092]**

Dramatic vocal forms; operas

3467   Alpert, Hollis. *Life and Times of Porgy and Bess: The Story of an American Classic.* 1990, Knopf $35.00 (0-394-58339-6). A history of the musical play *Porgy and Bess* from its appearance as a 1925 novel to current stage productions. (REV: BL 1/15/91; NYTBR 11/18/90; New Yorker 12/24/90) **[782.1]**

3468   Bergreen, Laurence. *As Thousands Cheer: The Life of Irving Berlin.* 1990, Viking $24.95 (0-670-81874-7). A biography of the American songwriter known for such songs as "White Christmas"

and "God Bless America." "An essential work for all libraries."—Choice (REV: Choice 1/91; LJ 6/1/90; NYTBR 7/1/90) **[782.1]**

3469   Bing, Rudolf. *5000 Nights at the Opera.* 1982, Amereon $20.00 (0-8488-0430-9). Memoirs of the former manager of the New York Metropolitan Opera. "As absorbing, and sometimes as incredible, as the man himself."—Sat Rev (REV: BL 1/15/73; LJ 9/1/72; Sat Rev 11/4/72) **[782.1]**

3470   Clement, Catherine. *Opera, or the Undoing of Women.* 1988, Univ. of Minnesota Pr. $35.00 (0-8166-1653-1); paper $13.95 (0-8166-1655-8). A critical feminist appraisal of women's roles in opera. (REV: Choice 6/89; NYTBR 1/1/89; PW 9/9/88) **[782.1]**

3471   Conati, Marcello, ed. *Encounters with Verdi.* 1984, Cornell Univ. Pr. $31.50 (0-8014-1717-1); paper $12.95 (0-8014-9430-3). Fifty personal accounts of the Italian composer by his friends and acquaintances. (REV: Choice 12/84; LJ 7/84; NYTBR 6/17/84) **[782.1]**

3472   Conrad, Peter. *A Song of Love and Death: The Meaning of Opera.* 1988, Poseidon paper $9.95 (0-671-67263-0). A survey of great operas and their composers from the seventeenth century to the twentieth. "The most intellectually stimulating book on the subject in the past 30 years."—PW (REV: Choice 1/88; NYTBR 11/8/87; PW 7/17/87) **[782.1]**

3473   Donington, Robert. *Opera and Its Symbols: The Unity of Words, Music, and Staging.* 1991, Yale Univ. Pr. $29.95 (0-300-04713-4). A study of the symbolic meanings in operatic presentations. "The best essay on opera in print."—NYTBR (REV: LJ 12/90; NYTBR 1/13/91) **[782.1]**

3474   Fischer-Dieskau, Dietrich. *Reverberations: The Memoirs of Dietrich Fischer-Dieskau.* 1989, Fromm International $24.95 (0-88064-137-1). Memoirs of the German opera baritone including his childhood remembrances of the Nazi era. (REV: BL 7/89; Choice 3/90; LJ 9/1/89) **[782.1]**

3475   Mayer, Martin. *The Met: 100 Years of Grand Opera.* 1983, Simon & Schuster $35.00 (0-671-47087-6). A commemorative history of the New York Metropolitan Opera's one hundredth anniversary based on its archives and interviews with past and present notables. (REV: Choice 4/84; LJ 10/1/83; PW 9/9/83) **[782.1]**

3476   Rasponi, Lanfranco. *Last Prima Donnas.* 1985, Limelight paper $19.95 (0-87910-040-0). Interviews with and profiles of 56 female opera singers and their careers. (REV: BL 10/15/82; CSM 3/9/83; LJ 11/1/82) **[782.1]**

3477   Robinson, Paul. *Operas and Ideas: From Mozart to Strauss.* 1986, Cornell Univ. Pr. $10.95 (0-8014-9428-1). A history and analysis of the ideas and social mores reflected in the operas of the nineteenth century. "A valuable contribution."—NYTBR (REV: Choice 11/85; LJ 10/15/85; NYTBR 8/4/85) **[782.1]**

3478   Scott, Michael. *Great Caruso.* 1988, Knopf $24.95 (0-394-53681-9); Northeastern Univ. Pr. paper

$14.95 (1-55553-061-3). A study of the career of the legendary turn-of-the-century Italian opera singer. (Rev: Choice 1/89; LJ 9/15/88; New Rep 8/8/88) **[782.1]**

3479 Sills, Beverly, and Lawrence Linderman. *Beverly: An Autobiography.* 1988, Bantam paper $4.95 (0-553-26647-0). An autobiography of the American opera singer and opera house manager. "Her success story makes for fascinating reading that is both rewarding and inspiring."—LJ (Rev: BL 4/15/87; LJ 6/1/87; Time 5/18/87) **[782.1]**

3480 Vishnevskaya, Galina. *Galina: A Russian Story.* 1985, Harcourt paper $10.95 (0-15-634320-7). An autobiography of the exiled Soviet opera singer. "A tale of social horror and political intrigue—a poignant, daring, frightening, sometimes even humorous saga."—NYTBR (Rev: LJ 10/1/84; NYTBR 9/23/84; Time 10/29/84. Awards: LJ, 1984) **[782.1]**

Musical plays

3481 Adler, Richard, and Lee Davis. *You Gotta Have Heart: An Autobiography.* 1990, Donald I. Fine $19.95 (1-55611-201-7). An autobiography of the American popular music composer and songwriter known for his musicals *The Pajama Game* and *Damn Yankees.* (Rev: BL 8/90; LJ 1/90; PW 6/15/90) **[782.14]**

3482 Bordman, Gerald. *American Music Revue: From the Passing Show to Sugar Babies.* 1985, Oxford Univ. Pr. $24.95 (0-19-503630-1). A study of the development, rise, and decline of the American musical revue. (Rev: Choice 12/85; LJ 8/85; NYTBR 9/22/85) **[782.14]**

3483 Grote, David. *Staging the Musical: Planning, Rehearsing, and Marketing the Amateur Production.* 1986, Prentice Hall $16.95 (0-13-840190-X); paper $10.95 (0-13-840182-9). A guidebook to the production of amateur musicals. (Rev: BL 4/15/86; LJ 5/15/86) **[782.14]**

3484 Lerner, Alan Jay. *Musical Theatre: A Companion.* 1989, Da Capo paper $16.95 (0-306-80364-X). A history of musical theater in the United States and Great Britain from the nineteenth century to the 1980s by the famed lyricist. (Rev: BL 11/15/86; Choice 4/87; LJ 11/1/86) **[782.14]**

3485 Mordden, Ethan. *Broadway Babies: The People Who Made the American Musical.* 1983, Oxford Univ. Pr. $24.95 (0-19-503345-0). Profiles of key personalities who shaped the direction of the twentieth-century American musical. (Rev: Choice 2/84; LJ 10/15/83; NYTBR 2/26/84) **[782.14]**

3486 Walsh, Michael. *Andrew Lloyd Webber: His Life and Works.* 1989, Abrams $39.95 (0-8109-1275-9). An illustrated study of the life and works of the British musical composer. (Rev: BL 1/1/90; LJ 1/90; PW 11/3/89) **[782.14]**

3487 Zadan, Craig. *Sondheim and Co.* 1986, Harper & Row $27.95 (0-06-015649-X); paper $17.95 (0-06-091400-9). An account of the career of the American musical composer and songwriter. "An essential volume for any collection on the current American

musical theatre."—Choice (Rev: BL 12/1/86; Choice 3/87; LJ 12/86) **[782.14]**

Songs

3488 Ligget, Mark, and Cathy Ligget. *Complete Handbook to Songwriting: An Insider's Guide to Making It in the Music Industry.* 1985, NAL paper $9.95 (0-452-25687-9). A guide to the creative and business aspects of songwriting. "For budding songwriters . . . this is *the* book."—BL (Rev: BL 8/85; LJ 10/1/85) **[782.42]**

3489 Wenner, Hilda E., and Elizabeth Freilicher. *Here's to the Women: 100 Songs for and about American Women.* 1987, Syracuse Univ. Pr. $45.00 (0-8156-2400-X); paper $19.95 (0-8156-0209-X). An anthology of American folk songs by and about women including a discography and annotated bibliography on the subject. (Rev: BL 7/87; LJ 7/87) **[782.42]**

3490 Wilder, Alec. *American Popular Song: The Great Innovators, 1900–1950.* 1972, Oxford Univ. Pr. $39.95 (0-19-501445-6). A survey of over 700 popular songs with individual chapters devoted to the most important popular songwriters. "Richly entertaining . . . the definitive critical browse on the subject."—PW (Rev: Choice 11/72; Newsweek 7/31/72; PW 2/21/72) **[782.42]**

785 Chamber music

String ensembles

3491 Blum, David. *Art of Quartet Playing: The Guarneri Quartet in Conversation with David Blum.* 1987, Cornell Univ. Pr. paper $9.95 (0-8014-9456-7). An examination of the inner workings of a string quartet. "Arguably the best book on the subject and one of the most important books on music issued in recent years."—PW (Rev: BL 6/15/87; LJ 6/1/86; PW 4/25/86) **[785.7]**

786 Keyboard and other instruments

Piano music

3492 Dubal, David. *Reflections from the Keyboard: The World of the Concert Pianist.* 1986, Summit paper $12.95 (0-671-60594-1). Collected interviews with 30 concert pianists regarding their careers and music. (Rev: CSM 12/7/84; LJ 10/15/84; NYTBR 12/30/84) **[786.2]**

3493 Friedrich, Otto. *Glenn Gould: A Life and Variations.* 1989, Random $24.95 (0-394-56299-2); paper $14.95 (0-679-73207-1). A biography of the Canadian pianist known for his masterful interpretations of the works of Bach and Mozart. (Rev: BL 4/15/89; LJ 4/15/89; NYTBR 4/23/89) **[786.2]**

3494 Graffman, Gary. *I Really Should Be Practicing: Reflections on the Pleasures and Perils of Playing the Piano in Public.* 1982, Avon paper $4.95 (0-380-59873-6). An account of the life and career of a concert pianist. (Rev: CSM 6/10/81; LJ 2/15/81; NYTBR 4/26/81) **[786.2]**

3495 Reich, Nancy B. *Clara Schumann: The Artist and the Woman.* 1985, Cornell Univ. Pr. $32.50 (0-8014-1748-1); paper $9.95 (0-8014-9388-9). A biography of the German musician and wife of composer Robert Schumann. (Rev: Choice 9/85; NYTBR 8/11/85; TLS 11/22/85) **[786.2]**

787   Stringed instruments (Chordophones)

Violin music

3496 Dubinsky, Rostislav. *Stormy Applause: Making Music in a Worker's State.* 1989, Hill & Wang $19.95 (0-8090-8895-9). Memoirs of a Jewish musician in the Soviet Union who emigrated to the United States in the mid-1970s. "No other emigré memoir . . . so vividly captures what it is like to be a precariously successful Jew in the Soviet Union."—New Rep (Rev: LJ 6/1/89; New Rep 11/6/89; NYTBR 6/25/89) **[787.2]**

3497 Schwarz, Boris. *Great Masters of the Violin: From Corelli and Vivaldi to Stern, Zuckerman and Perlman.* 1985, Simon & Schuster paper $13.95 (0-671-60491-9). A guide to virtuoso violinists from the seventeenth to twentieth centuries by a Queens College professor of music. (Rev: Choice 4/84; LJ 12/1/83; Natl Rev 6/15/84) **[787.2]**

788   Wind instruments (Aerophones)

Recorder music

3498 Wollitz, Kenneth. *Recorder Book.* 1982, Knopf paper $12.95 (0-394-74999-5). A complete introduction to the recorder for the beginning student. "Very nearly the ideal one-volume book on the recorder."—BL (Rev: BL 1/15/82; LJ 1/15/82) **[788.56]**

Clarinet music

3499 Bigard, Barney. *With Louis and the Duke: The Autobiography of a Jazz Clarinetist.* Ed. by Barry Martyn. 1988, Oxford Univ. Pr. paper $8.95 (0-19-520637-1). Memoirs of a jazz clarinet player's experiences touring and working with Louis Armstrong and Duke Ellington. (Rev: NYTBR 4/27/86; TLS 4/11/86) **[788.62]**

Alto saxophone

3500 Giddins, Gary. *Celebrating Bird: The Triumph of Charlie Parker.* 1987, Morrow paper $12.95 (0-688-05951-1). A biography of the legendary alto saxophone player who revolutionized jazz in the 1940s. (Rev: BL 1/1/87; NYTBR 1/11/87) **[788.73]**

Tenor saxophone

3501 Porter, Lewis. *Lester Young.* 1985, G. K. Hall $20.95 (0-8057-9459-X); paper $10.95 (0-8057-9471-9). A profile of the life and career of the jazz tenor saxophonist nicknamed "The President" by Billie Holliday. "An absolute must for jazz collections."—BL (Rev: BL 9/1/85; Choice 2/86; LJ 8/85) **[788.74]**

Trumpet music

3502 Chambers, Jack. *Milestones: The Music and Times of Miles Davis.* 1989, Morrow paper $15.45 (0-688-09602-6). A study of the life and career of the innovative jazz musician and trumpeter responsible for such classic albums as "Kind of Blue" and "Bitches Brew." (Rev: LJ 2/1/86; NYTBR 11/3/85; TLS 4/11/86) **[788.92]**

3503 Davis, Miles, and Quincy Troupe. *Miles: An Autobiography.* 1989, Simon & Schuster $22.95 (0-671-63504-2); paper $12.95 (0-671-72582-3). An autobiography of the innovative jazz musician and composer. "An extraordinarily colorful narrative."—NYTBR (Rev: BL 9/1/89; LJ 10/1/89; NYTBR 10/15/89) **[788.92]**

790   RECREATIONAL AND PERFORMING ARTS

3504 Rybczynski, Witold. *Waiting for the Weekend.* 1991, Viking $18.95 (0-670-83001-1). The author of *Home* examines the societal aspects of the institution of the weekend. (Rev: BL 7/91; NYTBR 8/18/91) **[790]**

Performing arts in general

3505 Angelou, Maya. *Singin' and Swingin' and Gettin' Merry Like Christmas.* 1976, Random $19.95 (0-394-40545-5); Bantam paper $4.50 (0-553-25199-6). The third volume of the author's autobiography covering her early attempts to break into show business. (Rev: LJ 9/1/76; PW 8/9/76; Sat Rev 10/30/76) **[790.2]**

3506 Duberman, Martin. *Paul Robeson: A Biography.* 1989, Knopf $24.95 (0-394-52780-1); Ballantine paper $14.95 (0-345-36413-9). A portrait of the American entertainer and political activist. "A monumental biography . . . a powerful work."—LJ (Rev: LJ 1/89; NYTBR 2/12/89; Time 3/13/89. Awards: ALA, 1989; LJ, 1989) **[790.2]**

3507 Hart, Kitty Carlisle. *Kitty: An Autobiography.* 1988, Doubleday $18.95 (0-385-24425-8); St. Martin's paper $12.95 (0-312-03373-7). An autobiography of the entertainer, wife of playwright Moss Hart, and regular on television's "To Tell the Truth." (Rev: BL 10/1/88; NYTBR 10/9/88; PW 9/16/88) **[790.2]**

3508 Jay, Ricky. *Learned Pigs and Fireproof Women.* 1986, Random $29.95 (0-394-53750-5); Warner paper $12.95 (0-446-38590-5). Accounts of odd entertainers and entertainments throughout history from educated pigs to freak shows. (Rev: LJ 11/1/86; NYTBR 12/14/86; Time 2/9/87) **[790.2]**

791   Public performances

3509 Ely, Melvin Patrick. *Adventures of Amos 'n' Andy: A Social History of an American Phenomena.* 1991, Free Pr. $22.95 (0-02-909502-6). An analysis of the popular situation comedy that ran for three decades and the changing American public opinion of its portrayal of racial stereotypes. (Rev: CSM 7/17/91; NYTBR 7/17/91) **[791]**

3510   **Hemingway, Ernest.** *Dangerous Summer.* **1986, Macmillan $9.95 (0-684-18720-5).** Hemingway's account of the 1959 Spanish bullfighting season and of the rivalry between Dominguen and Ordonez, two of the country's top matadors. (Rev: BL 4/15/85; LJ 6/1/85; Natl Rev 7/12/85)   **[791]**

Circuses

3511   **Antekeier, Kristopher, and Greg Aunapu.** *Ringmaster: My Year on the Road with "The Greatest Show on Earth."* **1989, Dutton $19.95 (0-525-24757-2).** An account of the year the author spent as ringmaster for Ringling Brothers/Barnum and Bailey Circus as the result of a contest. "Anyone who enjoys circuses will savor this account."—PW (Rev: BL 11/1/89; LJ 10/15/89; PW 9/22/89. Awards: BL, 1989)   **[791.3]**

3512   **Culhane, John.** *American Circus: An Illustrated History.* **1989, Henry Holt $35.00 (0-8050-0424-6).** An illustrated history of the American circus from 1768 to the present day. (Rev: BL 4/15/90; LJ 2/15/90; NYTBR 4/22/90)   **[791.3]**

3513   **Gebel-Williams, Gunther, and Toni Reinhold.** *Untamed: The Autobiography of the Circus's Greatest Animal Trainer.* **1991, Morrow $19.95 (0-688-08645-4).** An autobiography of the legendary animal trainer known for his career with the Ringling Brothers/Barnum and Bailey Circus. (Rev: BL 2/1/91; LJ 2/1/91)   **[791.3]**

Motion pictures

3514   **Bacall, Lauren.** *Lauren Bacall by Myself.* **1978, Knopf $12.95 (0-394-41308-3); Ballantine paper $5.95 (0-345-33321-7).** Memoirs of the American motion picture and stage actress. "A remarkably generous and unpretentious book."—Newsweek (Rev: LJ 2/1/79; NYTBR 1/7/79; Newsweek 1/15/79; NBA, 1980)   **[791.43]**

3515   **Bach, Steven.** *Final Cut: Dreams and Disaster in the Making of Heaven's Gate.* **1986, NAL $8.95 (0-425-25845-9); paper $4.95 (0-451-40036-4).** An inside account of the making of the film *Heaven's Gate* whose high budget and commercial failure led to the demise of United Artists. "Exciting, fascinating reading."—LJ (Rev: BL 7/85; LJ 8/85; Time 8/5/85. Awards: LJ, 1985; Time, 1985)   **[791.43]**

3516   **Bell-Metereau, Rebecca.** *Hollywood Androgyny.* **1986, Columbia Univ. Pr. $32.00 (0-231-05834-9); paper $13.00 (0-231-05835-7).** A study of the switching of sex roles and cross-dressing in Hollywood motion pictures. "One of the best film books of recent years."—BL (Rev: BL 5/1/85; NYTBR 3/31/85; PW 2/1/85)   **[791.43]**

3517   **Belushi, Judith Jacklin.** *Samurai Widow.* **1990, Carroll & Graf $21.95 (0-88184-575-2).** Memoirs of John Belushi's wife recounting the comic actor and their relationship together. (Rev: BL 4/1/90; LJ 5/15/90)   **[791.43]**

3518   **Berg, A. Scott.** *Goldwyn: A Biography.* **1989, Knopf $24.95 (0-394-51059-3); Ballantine paper $12.95 (0-345-36582-8).** A biography of the motion picture mogul and producer. "Samuel Goldwyn performs a star turn in this inclusive, amusing and thoroughly engrossing account of his private life and career."—PW (Rev: LJ 3/1/89; NYTBR 3/26/89; PW 2/3/89. Awards: PW, 1989)   **[791.43]**

3519   **Bergen, Candice.** *Knock Wood.* **1985, Ballantine paper $4.95 (0-345-32137-5).** An autobiography of the actress currently starring in "Murphy Brown" and the daughter of ventriloquist/entertainer Edgar Bergen. (Rev: LJ 3/15/84; NYTBR 4/8/84; Time 4/16/84)   **[791.43]**

3520   **Bergman, Ingmar.** *Magic Lantern: An Autobiography.* **1988, Viking $19.95 (0-670-81911-5); Penguin paper $10.95 (0-14-010469-0).** Autobiography of the great Swedish director known for such films as *The Seventh Seal, Wild Strawberries,* and *The Virgin Spring.* "The book has all the quickness and assurance, the minute detail, and the fascination with character that make the director's films so remarkable."—BL (Rev: BL 9/15/88; NYTBR 9/18/88. Awards: New Rep 10/3/88; NYTBR, 1988)   **[791.43]**

3521   **Betrock, Alan.** *I Was a Teenage Juvenile Delinquent Rock 'n' Roll Horror Beach Party Movie Book.* **1986, St. Martin's paper $12.95 (0-312-40293-7).** An illustrated history of the teen exploitation film during the 1950s and 1960s. (Rev: BL 12/1/86; LJ 12/86)   **[791.43]**

3522   **Bjorkman, Stig, Torsten Manns, and Jonas Sima.** *Bergman on Bergman: Interviews with Ingmar Bergman.* **1975, Simon & Schuster paper $9.95 (0-671-22157-4).** Collected interviews with the Swedish filmmaker known for such motion pictures as *Cries and Whispers* and *Fanny and Alexander.* (Rev: BL 9/1/74; NYTBR 8/4/74; TLS 7/19/74)   **[791.43]**

3523   **Bosworth, Patricia.** *Montgomery Clift: A Biography.* **1990, Limelight paper $14.95 (0-87910-135-0).** The rise and fall of one of the top motion picture stars of the 1950s and 1960s. "An amazing excursion into a life."—NYTBR (Rev: LJ 3/1/78; NYTBR 3/5/78; Newsweek 2/27/78)   **[791.43]**

3524   **Bowser, Eileen.** *Transformation of Cinema, 1907–1915.* **1990, Macmillan $60.00 (0-684-18414-1).** This second volume in the History of American Cinema series traces the development of the art form and business during the years 1907 to 1915. (Rev: BL 3/1/91; Choice 6/91; NYTBR 9/1/91)   **[791.43]**

3525   **Brooks, Louise.** *Lulu in Hollywood.* **1989, Limelight paper $13.95 (0-87910-125-3).** Seven essays regarding Hollywood and the film business during the 1920s and 1930s by a former motion picture actress. (Rev: NYRB 10/21/82; NYTBR 5/30/82; New Yorker 8/16/82)   **[791.43]**

3526   **Brownlow, Kevin.** *Behind the Mask of Innocence: Sex, Violence, Prejudice, Crime; Films of Social Conscience.* **1990, Knopf $50.00 (0-394-57747-7).** A study of social commentary in early silent motion pictures. (Rev: BL 11/15/90; LJ 10/15/90; NYTBR 12/16/90)   **[791.43]**

3527 Bryson, John. *Private World of Katharine Hepburn.* 1990, Little, Brown $39.95 (0-316-11332-8). A collection of the author's photographs of Katharine Hepburn on and off the set. (Rev: BL 11/15/90; NYTBR 1/6/91)   **[791.43]**

3528 Buñuel, Luis. *My Last Sigh.* 1984, Random paper $8.95 (0-394-72051-8). An autobiography of the Spanish surrealist filmmaker known for his early collaborations with Salvador Dali, and for later films such as *Exterminating Angel, Discreet Charm of the Bourgeoisie,* and *Viridiana.* "Quite simply the loveliest testament ever left by a film director."—NYTBR (Rev: BL 9/1/83; NYTBR 11/13/83; Newsweek 11/7/83)   **[791.43]**

3529 Carney, Raymond. *American Vision.* 1986, Cambridge Univ. Pr. $29.95 (0-521-32619-2). An illustrated survey and analysis of the motion pictures of Italian-American director Frank Capra. (Rev: CSM 7/21/88; LJ 11/1/86)   **[791.43]**

3530 Corman, Roger, and Jim Jerome. *How I Made a Hundred Movies in Hollywood and Never Lost a Dime.* 1990, Random $18.95 (0-394-56974-1); Dell paper $12.00 (0-385-30489-7). An autobiography of the influential independent filmmaker tracing his life and career in film. "A significant contribution to the history of American movies."—PW (Rev: BL 4/15/90; LJ 5/1/90; PW 4/6/90)   **[791.43]**

3531 Dietrich, Marlene. *Marlene.* 1989, Grove-Weidenfeld $18.95 (0-8021-1117-3); Avon paper $4.95. An autobiography of the German motion picture actress and entertainer. (Rev: BL 3/1/89; NYTBR 5/28/89; PW 3/17/89)   **[791.43]**

3532 Douglas, Kirk. *Ragman's Son: An Autobiography.* 1988, Simon & Schuster $21.95 (0-671-63717-7); Pocket paper $5.50 (0-671-63718-5). An autobiography of the motion picture actor and star of such films as *Lust for Life* and *Paths of Glory.* (Rev: LJ 10/15/88; NYTBR 8/14/88; PW 6/3/88)   **[791.43]**

3533 Durgnat, Raymond, and Scott Simmon. *King Vidor, American.* 1988, Univ. of California Pr. $42.50 (0-520-05798-8); paper $13.95 (0-520-05815-1). A biography of the motion picture director known for such films as *The Crowd, The Fountainhead,* and *Duel in the Sun.* (Rev: LJ 8/88; PW 6/10/88)   **[791.43]**

3534 Ebert, Roger. *A Kiss Is Still a Kiss: Roger Ebert at the Movies.* 1984, Andrews & McMeel $8.95 (0-8362-7926-3). Collected interviews with motion picture figures and film criticism by the critic from the *Chicago Sun-Times.* (Rev: BL 11/1/84; PW 5/28/84)   **[791.43]**

3535 Edwards, Anne. *Early Reagan: The Rise to Power.* 1987, Morrow $21.95 (0-688-06050-1). A biography of the former president's early years covering his motion picture career up to his decision to run for governor of California in 1966. (Rev: BL 5/1/87; LJ 7/87; NYTBR 7/26/87)   **[791.43]**

3536 Eyman, Scott. *Mary Pickford: America's Sweetheart.* 1989, Donald I. Fine $19.95 (1-55611-147-9); paper $11.95 (1-55611-243-2). A biography of

the Canadian-born silent film star. (Rev: BL 1/15/90; LJ 2/1/90; PW 2/2/90)   **[791.43]**

3537 Furmanek, Bob, and Ron Palumbo. *Abbott and Costello in Hollywood.* 1991, Putnam paper $13.95 (0-399-51605-0). An illustrated history and analysis of the Bud Abbott and Lou Costello comedy team. (Rev: BL 4/15/91; LJ 5/1/91)   **[791.43]**

3538 Gallagher, Tag. *John Ford: The Man and His Work.* 1986, Univ. of California Pr. $37.50 (0-520-05097-5); paper $14.95 (0-520-06334-1). A study of the life and work of the Irish-American motion picture director known for such films as *She Wore a Yellow Ribbon* and *Stagecoach.* (Rev: Choice 11/86; LJ 4/1/86; NYTBR 9/14/86)   **[791.43]**

3539 Gifford, Barry. *Devil Thumbs a Ride: And Other Unforgettable Films.* 1988, Grove-Weidenfeld paper $6.95 (0-8021-3078-X). A collection of 90 essays regarding American film noir cinema. (Rev: BL 4/15/88; Choice 11/88)   **[791.43]**

3540 Grodin, Charles. *It Would Be So Nice If You Weren't Here: My Journey Through Show Business.* 1989, Morrow $18.95 (0-688-08873-2); Random paper $9.95 (0-679-73134-2). An autobiography of the motion picture actor and director telling the story of his career in show business and of the inner dealings that go on behind the scenes in Hollywood. (Rev: BL 8/89; LJ 8/89; PW 7/14/89)   **[791.43]**

3541 Harmetz, Aljean. *Making of the Wizard of Oz: Movie Magic and Studio Power in the Prime of MGM.* 1989, Delacorte $12.95 (0-385-29746-7). An account of the adaptation of the Frank Baum classic to the silver screen. (Rev: LJ 10/1/77; NYTBR 11/13/77; PW 9/5/77)   **[791.43]**

3542 Harrison, Rex. *A Damned Serious Business: My Life in Comedy.* 1991, Bantam $21.95 (0-553-07341-9). An autobiography of the English actor known for his roles in *Doctor Dolittle* and *My Fair Lady.* (Rev: LJ 12/90; NYTBR 1/6/91; PW 11/30/90)   **[791.43]**

3543 Hartley, Mariette, and Anne Commire. *Breaking the Silence.* 1990, Putnam $21.95 (0-399-13552-9). Memoirs of the American actress's childhood and tragic family life. "Rises well above other efforts of its kind."—PW (Rev: BL 10/1/90; LJ 10/1/90; PW 9/7/90)   **[791.43]**

3544 Harvey, James. *Romantic Comedy: In Hollywood, from Lubitsch to Sturges.* 1987, Knopf $35.00 (0-394-50339-2). A survey of romantic comedy genre motion pictures from 1929 to 1948 focusing on the careers and works of Ernst Lubitsch, Frank Capra, and Preston Sturges. "A genuine monument of film scholarship."—BL (Rev: BL 11/1/87; LJ 11/1/87; NYTBR 12/27/88)   **[791.43]**

3545 Harvey, Stephen. *Directed by Vincente Minnelli.* 1990, Harper & Row $29.95 (0-06-016263-5). A survey of the career of the American film director. "Essential for all film collections."—LJ (Rev: Choice 5/90; LJ 3/1/90; NYTBR 3/4/90)   **[791.43]**

3546   Haskell, Molly. *From Reverence to Rape: The Treatment of Women in the Movies.* **1987, Univ. of Chicago Pr. $39.95 (0-226-31884-2); paper $14.95 (0-226-31885-0).** A tracing of the depiction of women in motion pictures from the silent screen to the mid-1980s. (Rev: BL 4/15/74; CSM 5/1/74; LJ 3/1/74) **[791.43]**

3547   Haver, Ronald. *David O. Selznick's Hollywood.* **1980, Knopf $85.00 (0-394-42595-2).** An analysis of more than 50 films produced by Selznick with over 1,500 photographs. (Rev: BL 12/1/80; Choice 4/81; LJ 1/1/81) **[791.43]**

3548   Hepburn, Katharine. *Making of "The African Queen."* **1987, Knopf $15.95 (0-394-56272-0); NAL paper $9.95 (0-452-26145-7).** Memoirs by the motion picture actress of filming *The African Queen* with Bogart, Bacall, and Huston. (Rev: BL 10/1/87; NYTBR 9/13/87; Time 9/28/87) **[791.43]**

3549   Hepburn, Katharine. *Me: Stories of My Life.* **1991, McKay $25.00 (0-679-40051-6).** An illustrated autobiography of the motion picture actress. "Like Hepburn herself, definitely out of the ordinary."—BL (Rev: BL 10/1/91; NYTBR 9/29/91; Time 9/23/91) **[791.43]**

3550   Howard, Jean, and James Watters. *Jean Howard's Hollywood: A Photo Memoir.* **1990, Abrams $39.95 (0-8109-1190-6).** A portrayal of Hollywood and the motion picture industry during the 1940s and 1950s. (Rev: NYRB 12/21/89; NYTBR 12/3/89) **[791.43]**

3551   Insdorf, Annette. *Indelible Shadows: Film and the Holocaust.* **1990, Cambridge Univ. Pr. $24.50 (0-521-37279-8).** A study of the themes and styles of 80 films dealing with the Holocaust. "In the best tradition of film criticism."—PW (Rev: NYTBR 10/2/83; PW 5/6/83) **[791.43]**

3552   Jackson, Carlton. *Hattie: The Life of Hattie McDaniel.* **1989, Madison Books $18.95 (0-8191-7295-2).** A profile of actress Hattie McDaniel, who won an Oscar for her performance in *Gone with the Wind* and was also a notable singer and songwriter. (Rev: BL 10/1/89; LJ 9/15/89; NYTBR 10/15/89) **[791.43]**

3553   Jones, G. William. *Black Cinema Treasures: Lost and Found.* **1991, Univ. of North Texas Pr. $29.95 (0-929398-26-2).** An analysis of 22 films made by African-Americans between the 1920s and the 1950s that were discovered in 1983 in a Texas warehouse. (Rev: BL 7/91; LJ 7/91) **[791.43]**

3554   Kael, Pauline. *Hooked.* **1989, Dutton $24.95 (0-525-24705-X); paper $14.95 (0-525-48429-9).** A collection of film reviews by the *New Yorker* critic covering the years 1985 to 1988. (Rev: BL 9/1/88; LJ 2/15/89; NYTBR 3/19/89) **[791.43]**

3555   Kael, Pauline. *Movie Love: Complete Reviews, 1988–1991.* **1991, Dutton $24.95 (0-525-93313-1).** A collection of 80 reviews by the recently retired *New Yorker* film critic. (Rev: BL 8/91; LJ 8/91; NYTBR 10/13/91) **[791.43]**

3556   Kazan, Elia. *Elia Kazan: A Life.* **1989, Doubleday paper $12.95 (0-385-26103-9).** An autobiography of the film and theater director. "A triumph of compulsion, verve and the power of memory."—BL (Rev: BL 3/1/88; NYTBR 5/14/89; PW 2/24/89. Awards: BL, the 1980s) **[791.43]**

3557   Kendall, Elizabeth. *Runaway Bride: Hollywood Romantic Comedy of the 1930s.* **1990, Random $24.95 (0-394-51187-5).** A survey of the romantic comedy motion pictures of the 1930s including the works of Preston Sturges, Leo McCarey, George Stevens, and Frank Capra. (Rev: BL 9/15/90; NYTBR 11/4/90; PW 9/7/90) **[791.43]**

3558   Kerr, Walter. *The Silent Clowns.* **1990, Da Capo paper $18.95 (0-306-80387-9).** An examination of the comedy in the era of silent film with an emphasis on the works of Chaplin, Keaton, and Lloyd. "*The Silent Clowns* may just be the best book about silent screen comedy ever written."—LJ (Rev: Choice 4/76; LJ 11/15/75; NYTBR 11/23/75. Awards: ALA, 1975) **[791.43]**

3559   Kobal, John. *People Will Talk.* **1986, Knopf $25.00 (0-394-53660-6).** Over 40 interviews with motion picture actors and directors including Katharine Hepburn, Howard Hawks, and Joan Crawford. "An unusually appealing, informative volume."—PW (Rev: BL 1/15/86; LJ 1/86; PW 11/29/85) **[791.43]**

3560   Korda, Michael. *Charmed Lives: A Family Romance.* **1979, Random $15.00 (0-394-41954-5); Avon paper $3.95 (0-380-53017-1).** The author reminisces about his life and his filmmaking family. **[791.43]**

3561   Koszarski, Richard. *An Evening's Entertainment: The Age of the Silent Feature Picture, 1915–1928.* **1990, Macmillan $60.00 (0-684-18415-X).** This third volume in the History of American Cinema series traces the evolution of filmmaking in the late silent era. (Rev: Choice 7–8/91; NYTBR 9/1/91) **[791.43]**

3562   Kurosawa, Akira. *Something Like an Autobiography.* **1983, Random paper $10.95 (0-394-71439-3).** An autobiography of the Japanese filmmaker known for such motion pictures as *Rashomon*, *Yojimbo*, *Ran*, and *The Seven Samurai*. (Rev: Atl 7/82; BL 5/15/82; NYTBR 6/27/82) **[791.43]**

3563   Lax, Eric. *Woody Allen.* **1991, Knopf $24.00 (0-394-58349-3).** A biography of the American motion picture director known for such films as *Zelig*, *Crimes and Misdemeanors,* and *The Purple Rose of Cairo*. (Rev: BL 4/1/91; LJ 5/1/91; PW 3/29/91. Awards: BL, 1991) **[791.43]**

3564   Leaming, Barbara. *If This Was Happiness: A Biography of Rita Hayworth.* **1989, Viking $19.95 (0-670-81978-6).** A biography of the motion picture actress and former wife of Orson Welles. (Rev: LJ 9/1/89; NYTBR 11/19/89; Time 12/4/89) **[791.43]**

3565   Leaming, Barbara. *Orson Welles: A Biography.* **1985, Viking $19.95 (0-670-52895-1); Penguin paper $10.95 (0-14-012762-3).** The author paid frequent visits to Welles while writing this account of the filmmaker and actor's life and career. (REV: Choice 4/86; LJ 8/85; NYTBR 9/15/85) **[791.43]**

3566 Leff, Leonard J. *Hitchcock and Selznick: The Rich and Strange Collaboration of Alfred Hitchcock and David O. Selznick in Hollywood.* 1988, Grove-Weidenfeld paper $11.95 (1-55584-272-0). A study of the four films Hitchcock and Selznick collaborated on, and of the relationship between the two Hollywood legends. (REV: Choice 3/88; LJ 11/1/87; NYTBR 1/17/88) **[791.43]**

3567 Leff, Leonard J., and Jerold L. Simmons. *Dame in the Kimono: Hollywood, Censorship, and the Production Code from the 1920s to the 1960s.* 1989, Grove-Weidenfeld $22.50 (1-55584-224-0). A history of the Hays Office and its control over the censorship of Hollywood motion pictures from the 1920s to the 1960s. (REV: Atl 2/90; BL 1/1/90; NYTBR 1/28/90) **[791.43]**

3568 McGilligan, Patrick. *George Cukor: A Double Life.* 1991, St. Martin's $24.95 (0-312-05419-X). A biography of the American film director. "A highly readable, penetrating biography that's a must for film collections."—BL (REV: BL 11/15/91; PW 9/20/91) **[791.43]**

3569 MacLaine, Shirley. *Dancing in the Light.* 1986, Bantam $17.95 (0-553-05094-X); paper $4.95 (0-553-27557-7). The motion picture actress details her spiritual awakening and the evolution of her belief system. (REV: BL 9/15/85; LJ 11/1/85; PW 9/6/85) **[791.43]**

3570 McMurtry, Larry. *Film Flam: Essays on Hollywood.* 1988, Simon & Schuster paper $6.95 (0-671-63322-8). A collection of essays by the author of *The Last Picture Show* regarding Hollywood and the American film industry. (REV: BL 6/1/87; LJ 6/15/87; NYTBR 5/31/87) **[791.43]**

3571 Mamet, David. *On Directing Films.* 1991, Viking $18.95 (0-670-83033-X). An extended essay on the art of filmmaking by the American playwright and director of *House of Games.* (REV: BL 1/1/91; LJ 1/91) **[791.43]**

3572 Morley, Sheridan. *Elizabeth Taylor: A Celebration.* 1990, Viking $19.95 (1-85145-051-3). A biography of the motion picture actress and former wife of Richard Burton. "The most up-to-date and objective treatment . . . so far."—LJ (REV: LJ 12/89; PW 12/1/89) **[791.43]**

3573 Musser, Charles. *Emergence of Cinema: The American Screen to 1907.* 1990, Macmillan $60.00 (0-684-18413-3). This study of the American film industry from its beginnings to 1907 is the first volume of a projected ten-volume history of cinema in the United States. (REV: BL 3/1/91; Choice 6/91; NYTBR 9/1/91) **[791.43]**

3574 Neal, Patricia, and Richard Deneut. *As I Am.* 1989, Pocket paper $4.95 (0-671-67437-4). An autobiography of the motion picture and television actress. "Neal's honesty and strength infuse the book with life and raise it above the usual celebrity

autobiography."—LJ (REV: BL 3/15/88; LJ 5/1/88; PW 3/18/88) **[791.43]**

3575 Peters, Margot. *House of Barrymore.* 1990, Random $29.95 (0-394-55321-7). A biography of the family acting trio of Lionel, John, and Ethel Barrymore. (REV: LJ 10/1/90; NYTBR 11/25/90; Time 11/19/90) **[791.43]**

3576 Quirk, Lawrence J. *Fasten Your Seat Belts: The Passionate Life of Bette Davis.* 1990, Morrow $21.95 (0-688-08427-3); Dutton paper $5.95 (0-451-16950-6). A biography of the motion picture actress famous for her roles in such films as *Jezebel, The Little Foxes,* and *Whatever Happened to Baby Jane?* "The definitive Davis."—BL (REV: BL 1/1/90; LJ 2/1/90) **[791.43]**

3577 Rebello, Stephen. *Alfred Hitchcock and the Making of Psycho.* 1990, Dembner Books $24.95 (0-942637-14-3); HarperCollins paper $9.95 (0-06-097366-8). A study of the Hitchcock classic horror film adapted from the novel by Robert Bloch. (REV: BL 3/15/90; LJ 3/1/90) **[791.43]**

3578 Rebello, Stephen, and Richard Allen. *Reel Art: Great Posters from the Golden Age of the Silver Screen.* 1988, Abbeville $49.98 (0-89659-869-1). A study of the motion picture poster as art from the beginnings of film through the 1940s. (REV: LJ 1/89; NYTBR 12/11/88; Time 12/19/88) **[791.43]**

3579 Rhode, Eric. *History of the Cinema: From Its Origins to 1970.* 1985, Da Capo paper $13.95 (0-306-80233-3). Critical history of the origins, development, and history of film and filmmaking. (REV: Choice 10/76; TLS 3/12/76) **[791.43]**

3580 Roberts, Rachel. *No Bells on Sunday: The Rachel Roberts Journals.* Ed. by Alexander Walker. 1985, McGraw-Hill paper $6.95 (0-07-053126-9). Journals from the last three years of the English actress's life chronicling her slide toward suicide. (REV: BL 9/15/84; NYTBR 10/14/84; PW 7/20/84) **[791.43]**

3581 Robinson, David. *Chaplin: His Life and Art.* 1989, McGraw-Hill paper $14.95 (0-07-053182-X). Biography of Chaplin using his private papers and archives. "That a book can be exhaustive without also being exhausting is proven by Robinson's definitive account of the great silent film star."—BL (REV: BL 8/85; LJ 9/1/85; NYTBR 11/10/85. AWARDS: ALA, 1985) **[791.43]**

3582 Rosenblum, Ralph, and Robert Karen. *When the Shooting Stops . . . the Cutting Begins: A Film Editor's Story.* 1986, Da Capo paper $10.95 (0-306-80272-4). A survey of the history, art, and techniques of motion picture editing with personal anecdotes by the author. (REV: Choice 3/80; LJ 10/1/79; NYTBR 11/11/79) **[791.43]**

3583 Salamon, Julie. *Devil's Candy: The Bonfire of the Vanities Goes to Hollywood.* 1991, Houghton $24.95 (0-395-56996-6). The *Wall Street Journal* film critic's inside account of the making of the motion picture based on Tom Wolfe's *Bonfire of the Vanities.* (REV: LJ 11/15/91; PW 11/1/91) **[791.43]**

3584 Shipman, David. *Story of Cinema: A Complete Narrative History from the Beginnings to the Present.* 1986, St. Martin's paper $19.95 (0-312-76280-1). A survey history of film from its development in the late nineteenth century to the 1980s. (Rev: BL 10/15/84; LJ 11/1/84) **[791.43]**

3585 Spoto, Donald. *Dark Side of Genius: The Life of Alfred Hitchcock.* 1983, Little, Brown $24.95 (0-316-80723-0); Ballantine paper $4.95 (0-345-31462-X). A biography of the British master of motion picture suspense. "Answers the need for a definitive statement about the life and work of one of the world's best filmmakers."—BL (Rev: BL 3/1/83; NYTBR 3/6/83; Time 5/9/83) **[791.43]**

3586 Stein, Jean, and George Plimpton. *Edie: An American Biography.* 1989, Delacorte paper $10.95 (0-385-29791-2). A biography of the Andy Warhol film star who died at the age of 28 following a barbituate overdose. (Rev: BL 5/15/82; LJ 7/82; PW 5/14/82) **[791.43]**

3587 Steinem, Gloria, and George Barris. *Marilyn: Norma Jean.* 1988, NAL paper $4.95 (0-451-15596-3). An illustrated biography of the motion picture star Marilyn Monroe by the feminist writer and leader. (Rev: BL 12/1/86; LJ 2/1/87; NYTBR 12/21/86) **[791.43]**

3588 Sturges, Preston. *Preston Sturges.* 1990, Simon & Schuster $22.95 (0-671-67929-5). An autobiography of the American filmmaker known for such comedies as *The Miracle of Morgan's Creek* and *Sullivan's Travels.* "Unadulterated reading pleasure."—PW (Rev: BL 9/15/90; LJ 7/90; PW 8/3/90) **[791.43]**

3589 Temple Black, Shirley. *Child Star: An Autobiography.* 1988, McGraw-Hill $19.95 (0-07-005532-7); Warner paper $5.95 (0-446-35792-8). An autobiography of the child film star who later had a second career as a diplomat. (Rev: BL 9/15/88; Time 11/14/88; TLS 8/11/89) **[791.43]**

3590 Thomas, Bob. *Clown Prince of Hollywood: The Antic Life and Times of Jack L. Warner.* 1990, McGraw-Hill $19.95 (0-07-064259-1). A biography of the founder of the Warner Brothers motion picture studio. (Rev: LJ 5/15/90; NYTBR 7/15/90; PW 6/8/90) **[791.43]**

3591 Thomas, Frank, and Ollie Johnston. *Disney Animation: The Illusion of Life.* 1990, BDD Promotional Book $29.98 (0-7924-4085-4). An illustrated history of the development of animation at Disney Studios by two of the artists who were there from its beginnings. (Rev: Choice 3/82; CSM 1/20/82; LJ 12/15/81) **[791.43]**

3592 Truffaut, Francois. *Films in My Life.* 1985, Simon & Schuster paper $9.95 (0-671-24663-1). A collection of the French film director's writings on film dating from the 1950s to the 1970s. (Rev: BL 5/15/78; LJ 6/1/78; PW 5/29/78) **[791.43]**

3593 Van Gelder, Peter. *That's Hollywood: A Behind-the-Scenes Look at 60 of the Greatest Films of All Time.* 1990, HarperCollins $22.50 (0-06-055198-4); paper $10.95 (0-06-098512-6). Illus-trated accounts of the making of 60 famous motion pictures. (Rev: BL 10/15/90; LJ 10/1/90) **[791.43]**

3594 Williams, Linda. *Hard Core: Power, Pleasure, and the "Frenzy of the Visible."* 1990, Univ. of California Pr. $18.95 (0-520-06652-9); paper $12.95 (0-520-06653-7). A study of pornographic films and their depictions of sexual activity from the nineteenth century to the present. (Rev: Choice 9/90; LJ 10/15/89; New Rep 2/19/90) **[791.43]**

3595 Winters, Shelley. *Shelley: Also Known as Shirley.* 1981, Ballantine paper $3.50 (0-345-29506-4). Memoirs of the motion picture actress detailing her rise to stardom from her beginnings in a Brooklyn ghetto. (Rev: BL 6/1/80; LJ 5/15/80; NYTBR 6/8/80) **[791.43]**

3596 Wynn, Ned. *We Will Always Live in Beverly Hills: Growing Up Crazy in Hollywood.* 1990, Morrow $19.95 (0-688-08509-1). Memoirs by Keenan Wynn's son portraying life growing up in a Hollywood family and his encounters with such celebrities as Jane Fonda, Joan Crawford, Lana Turner, and Marlene Dietrich. (Rev: BL 11/1/90; LJ 11/1/90; PW 9/28/90) **[791.43]**

Radio

3597 King, Larry, and Peter Occhiogrosso. *Tell It to the King.* 1988, Putnam $16.95 (0-399-13244-9); Jove paper $4.95 (0-515-10022-6). Memoirs by the radio and television talk-show host regarding his career and personalities he has known. (Rev: BL 4/1/88; LJ 7/88; NYTBR 6/26/88) **[791.44]**

Television

3598 Arlen, Michael J. *View from Highway One: Essays about Television.* 1976, Farrar $8.95 (0-374-28371-0). Collection of critical essays, concerning the medium of television and its impact, that originally appeared in the *New Yorker.* (Rev: BL 11/1/76; NYTBR 10/10/76; Newsweek 12/27/76. Awards: ALA, 1976) **[791.45]**

3599 Buckley, William F., Jr. *On the Firing Line: The Public Life of Our Public Figures.* 1989, Random $22.50 (0-394-57568-7). A collection of interviews and segments of interviews from over 20 years of Buckley's "Firing Line" television show. (Rev: BL 3/1/89; LJ 4/15/89; Natl Rev 6/2/89) **[791.45]**

3600 Gitlin, Todd, ed. *Watching Television: A Pantheon Guide to Popular Culture.* 1986, Pantheon paper $11.95 (0-394-74651-1). A collection of seven essays regarding television and its reflection of American popular culture. (Rev: BL 12/1/86; Choice 6/87; NYTBR 2/8/87) **[791.45]**

3601 Hill, Douglas, and Jeff Weingrad. *Saturday Night: A Backstage History of "Saturday Night Live."* 1987, Random paper $8.95 (0-394-75053-5). A history of the first decade of the late-night NBC entertainment series. (Rev: LJ 3/15/86; NYTBR 3/2/86; Time 3/3/86) **[791.45]**

3602 Lichter, Linda. *Watching America: What Television Tells Us about Our Lives.* 1991, Prentice

Hall $9.95 (0-13-026824-0). An analysis of the results of a scientific study researching the content of American television programming and its effects on the viewer. (Rev: BL 5/15/91; PW 4/19/91) **[791.45]**

3603 Palmer, Edward L. *Television and America's Children: A Crisis of Neglect.* Ed. by George Gerbner and Martha Siefert. 1990, Oxford Univ. Pr. paper $8.95 (0-19-506321-X). A guide to television programming for children and the issues currently facing the industry. (Rev: Choice 4/89; CSM 10/14/88; LJ 9/15/88) **[791.45]**

3604 Winn, Marie. *Plug-in-Drug: Television, Children and the Family.* 1985, Penguin paper $7.95 (0-14-007698-0). Discussion of the detrimental effects of television viewing upon children. "A convincing, thoroughly researched work that reveals the depth of a critical problem and valuable methods for remedying the situation."—BL (Rev: BL 4/15/77; LJ 3/15/77; New Yorker 3/14/77. Awards: ALA, 1977) **[791.45]**

792 **Stage presentations**

3605 Adler, Stella. *Technique of Acting.* 1988, Ballantine $14.95 (0-553-05299-3). A survey of acting and its techniques by an actress and acting teacher who bases her approach on a Stanislavsky method. "Sure to become a classic."—LJ (Rev: BL 8/88; LJ 9/15/88) **[792]**

3606 Atkinson, Brooks. *Broadway 1900–1970.* 1985, Limelight paper $19.95 (0-87910-047-8). Reminiscences mixed with history of the Broadway theater scene in the first seven decades of this century by one of its top drama critics. (Rev: LJ 10/1/70; NYTBR 11/15/70; PW 8/24/70) **[792]**

3607 Brook, Peter. *Shifting Point: Theatre, Film, Opera, 1946–1987.* 1987, Harper & Row $22.50 (0-06-039073-5); paper $9.95 (0-06-091585-4). Essays regarding modern theater, film, and opera by the British director of *The Mahabharata.* "With its far-reaching perspective . . . this journal will reward even readers who are not familiar with the works discussed."—PW (Rev: BL 11/1/87; NYTBR 10/18/87; PW 9/18/87) **[792]**

3608 Brustein, Robert. *Reimagining American Theatre.* 1991, Hill & Wang $22.95 (0-8090-8057-5). A collection of essays from the *New Republic* discussing the state of American drama and theater in the 1980s and 1990s. (Rev: LJ 6/15/91; PW 6/7/91) **[792]**

3609 Burns, George. *Gracie: A Love Story.* 1988, Putnam $16.95 (0-399-13384-4); Penguin paper $7.95 (0-14-012656-2). Memoirs of the comedian's 40-year marriage and working relationship with Gracie Allen. (Rev: BL 9/15/88; LJ 11/15/88; NYTBR 11/27/88) **[792]**

3610 Fox, Ted. *Showtime at the Apollo.* 1983, Henry Holt paper $9.95 (0-03-060534-2). Illustrated entertainment history of the legendary Harlem theater. (Rev: Choice 1/84; LJ 9/1/83; NYTBR 1/8/84) **[792]**

3611 Henderson, Mary C. *Theatre in America: Two Hundred Years of Plays, Players and Productions.*

1986, Abrams $49.50 (0-8109-1084-5). A comprehensive history of theater in America over the past two centuries. (Rev: BL 2/15/87; Choice 2/87; LJ 1/87) **[792]**

3612 Houghton, Norris. *Entrances and Exits: A Life in and out of the Theatre.* 1991, Limelight $29.95 (0-87910-144-X). Memoirs of the author's 80 years in the American theater. "A candid and joyous celebration of a life well-lived."—BL (Rev: BL 3/1/91; LJ 2/1/91) **[792]**

3613 Olivier, Laurence. *On Acting.* 1987, Simon & Schuster paper $9.95 (0-671-64562-5). A reflection by the English actor regarding his greatest roles and the art of acting. (Rev: BL 11/15/86; LJ 11/15/86; NYTBR 11/16/86) **[792]**

Philosophy and theory

3614 Strasberg, Lee. *A Dream of Passion: The Development of the Method.* 1988, NAL paper $9.95 (0-452-26198-8). An account of method acting and how Strasberg redefined the theories of Stanislavsky as artistic director of New York's Actor's Studio. (Rev: LJ 10/15/87; New Rep 12/7/87; PW 8/28/87) **[792.01]**

Handbooks, techniques, procedures, apparatus, equipment, materials, miscellany

3615 Benedetti, Jean, ed. *Moscow Art Theatre Letters.* 1991, Routledge $29.95 (0-87030-084-8). A collection of letters by members of the Moscow Art Theatre concerning their experiences with the troupe and cofounder/director Konstantin Stanislavski. (Rev: LJ 11/15/91; PW 11/15/91) **[792.02]**

3616 Cronyn, Hume. *A Terrible Liar: A Memoir.* 1991, Morrow $23.00 (0-688-10080-5). Memoirs of the Canadian-born actor's career in theater and his marriage to actress Jessica Tandy. (Rev: NYTBR 9/15/91; PW 7/12/91) **[792.02]**

3617 Gold, Arthur, and Robert Fizdale. *Divine Sarah: A Life of Sarah Bernhardt.* 1991, Knopf $30.00 (0-394-52879-4). A biography of the late nineteenth- and early twentieth-century French actress. "An irresistibly good read."—BL (Rev: BL 9/15/91; LJ 8/91; NYTBR 9/22/91. Awards: BL, 1991) **[792.02]**

History

3618 Hagen, Uta. *A Challenge for the Actor.* 1991, Scribner $22.50 (0-684-19040-0). A historic survey of American theater with tips on acting written by a veteran of the stage. (Rev: BL 8/91; LJ 11/15/91) **[792.09]**

3619 Smith, Wendy. *Real Life Drama: The Group Theatre and America, 1931–1940.* 1990, Random $24.95 (0-394-57445-1). A history of the Group Theatre and its productions during the 1930s. "Required reading on the development of modern American theatre."—LJ (Rev: BL 10/1/90; LJ 11/1/90; PW 9/14/90. Awards: PW, 1990) **[792.09]**

Persons

3620 Auerbach, Nina. *Ellen Terry: Player in Her Time.* 1989, Norton paper $10.95 (0-393-30582-1). A biography of the nineteenth-century English actress examining the role of females in Victorian society. (Rev: Choice 11/87; LJ 6/15/87; PW 5/15/87) **[792.092]**

3621 Bragg, Melvyn. *Richard Burton: A Life.* 1989, Little, Brown $22.95 (0-316-10595-3); **Warner paper $5.95** (0-446-35938-6). A biography of the Welsh-born actor based on interviews with friends and family and including passages from his diaries. "The definitive treatment of one of the century's most gifted and wayward actors."—BL (Rev: BL 1/1/89; LJ 2/1/89; Time 2/20/89) **[792.092]**

3622 Brown, Jared. *Fabulous Lunts: A Biography of Alfred Lunt and Lynn Fontaine.* 1988, Macmillan paper $14.95 (0-689-70740-1). A dual biography of the theatrical couple. "A lively biography . . . successfully merges a documentary style with a winsome chattiness."—BL (Rev: BL 7/86; Choice 12/86; NYTBR 8/17/86. Awards: LJ, 1986) **[792.092]**

3623 Callow, Simon. *Charles Laughton: A Difficult Actor.* 1989, Grove-Weidenfeld paper $9.95 (0-8021-3169-7). A biography of the English actor. "Theatre biography of the first rank, written with elegance, wit, psychological probity and enthusiasm."—PW (Rev: LJ 4/15/88; New Yorker 7/25/88; PW 2/26/88. Awards: PW, 1988) **[792.092]**

3624 Gordon, Ruth. *My Side: The Autobiography of Ruth Gordon.* 1986, Donald I. Fine paper $9.95 (0-917657-81-0). Memoirs of the stage and motion picture actress regarding her career from 1915 to the mid-1970s. (Rev: BL 9/15/76; LJ 9/15/76; NYTBR 10/10/76) **[792.092]**

3625 Guinness, Alec. *Blessings in Disguise.* 1986, Knopf $17.95 (0-394-55237-7); **Warner paper $9.95** (0-446-38426-7). Memoirs of the British film and theater actor, with many anecdotes concerning others in his profession. "Sir Alec is in a class by himself, not only as an actor, but as a writer as well."—NYTBR (Rev: BL 2/15/86; LJ 3/15/86; NYTBR 4/6/86. Awards: LJ, 1986) **[792.092]**

3626 Hayes, Helen, and Katherine Hatch. *My Life in Three Acts.* 1990, Harcourt $19.95 (0-15-163695-8). Memoirs of the American actress's career on stage and in motion pictures. "Captures the history of American theatre by merely focusing on her own story."—NYTBR (Rev: BL 1/1/90; NYTBR 5/6/90; PW 2/16/90) **[792.092]**

3627 Hayward, Brooke. *Haywire.* 1981, Bantam paper $4.95 (0-553-27122-9). A Hollywood memoir by the daughter of Margaret Sullavan and Leland Hayward, and their family's problems. (Rev: BL 3/15/77; LJ 2/15/77; NYTBR 3/6/77) **[792.092]**

3628 Lewis, Robert. *Slings and Arrows: Theatre in My Life.* 1986, Scarborough $18.95 (0-8128-2965-4); paper $11.95 (0-8128-6237-6). A theater memoir by the Broadway director and acting teacher. "One of

the most penetrating works to be written about the theatre in several years."—PW (Rev: Choice 11/84; NYTBR 6/10/84; PW 4/6/84) **[792.092]**

3629 Prideaux, Tom. *Love or Nothing: The Life and Times of Ellen Terry.* 1988, Limelight paper $9.95 (0-87910-105-9). A biography of the celebrated English actress and close friend of George Bernard Shaw. (Rev: Choice 3/76; CSM 1/14/76; LJ 10/1/75) **[792.092]**

3630 Schneider, Alan. *Entrances: An American Director's Journey.* 1986, Viking $25.00 (0-670-80608-0); **Limelight paper $17.95** (0-87910-067-2). An autobiography of the American stage director focusing on his career in theater. (Rev: LJ 12/85; NYTBR 1/26/86; Time 1/20/86) **[792.092]**

3631 Weaver, William. *Duse: A Biography.* 1985, Harcourt paper $9.95 (0-15-626259-2). A biography of the nineteenth century Italian actress who was an international star and influenced the acting theories of Stanislavsky. (Rev: BL 9/1/84; Choice 3/85; LJ 9/1/84) **[792.092]**

Variety shows

3632 Benny, Jack, and Joan Benny. *Sunday Nights at Seven: The Jack Benny Story.* 1991, Warner paper $8.99 (0-446-39321-5). An autobiography of the American entertainer completed by his daughter after his death. (Rev: LJ 10/15/90; NYTBR 11/11/90; PW 9/28/90) **[792.7]**

3633 Burnett, Carol. *One More Time.* 1987, Avon paper $4.95 (0-380-70449-8). An autobiography of the American comedienne recounting her rise from poverty to stardom. "A rich moving memoir, worlds away from most movie-star biographies."—BL (Rev: BL 9/1/86; NYTBR 10/19/86; PW 9/12/86) **[792.7]**

3634 Rivers, Joan, and Richard Meryman. *Enter Talking.* 1986, Delacorte $17.95 (0-385-29440-9); **Dell paper $4.95** (0-440-12444-9). Memoirs of the comedienne's career in show business. (Rev: BL 4/1/86; LJ 5/15/86; Time 5/19/86) **[792.7]**

3635 Snyder, Robert W. *Voice of the City: Vaudeville and Popular Culture in New York, 1880–1930.* 1989, Oxford Univ. Pr. $19.95 (0-19-505285-4). The rise of vaudeville entertainment in late nineteenth- and early twentieth-century New York and its influence on popular culture. (Rev: LJ 11/1/89; NYTBR 3/14/90) **[792.7]**

3636 Stein, Charles W., ed. *American Vaudeville: As Seen by Its Contemporaries.* 1985, Da Capo paper $11.95 (0-306-80256-2). A collection of memoirs and essays on the history and development of American vaudeville theater. (Rev: Choice 2/85; LJ 9/15/84; NYTBR 11/11/84) **[792.7]**

Ballet and modern dance

3637 Bentley, Toni. *Winter Season: A Dancer's Journal.* 1984, Random paper $5.95 (0-394-72398-8). Memoirs of a dancer's season with the New York City Ballet. "It is hard to imagine a lover of ballet who would not enjoy this gracefully written little journal."—PW (Rᴇᴠ: CSM 10/8/82; NYTBR 8/29/82; PW 6/18/82)   **[792.8]**

3638   Buckle, Richard. *Diaghilev*. 1984, Macmillan paper $14.95 (0-689-70664-2). A biography of the Russian dance director and choreographer known for his work with his Les Ballet Russes company. (Rᴇᴠ: BL 11/15/79; LJ 10/1/79; Time 9/10/78)   **[792.8]**

3639   Danilova, Alexandra. *Choura: The Memoirs of Alexandra Danilova*. 1986, Knopf $20.00 (0-394-50539-5); Fromm International paper $11.95 (0-88064-103-7). An autobiography of the Russian ballerina exploring her dance career and her relationships with Diaghilev, Stravinsky, and Balanchine. (Rᴇᴠ: LJ 11/15/86; NYTBR 1/4/87; Newsweek 12/15/86)   **[792.8]**

3640   DeMille, Agnes. *Martha: The Life and Work of Martha Graham*. 1991, Random $30.00 (0-394-55643-7). A biography of the preeminent choreographer and influential figure in the history of modern dance. (Rᴇᴠ: BL 8/91; LJ 8/91; NYTBR 9/8/91. Aᴡᴀʀᴅs: LJ, 1991)   **[792.8]**

3641   DeMille, Agnes. *Portrait Gallery: Artists, Impresarios, Intimates*. 1990, Houghton $19.95 (0-395-52809-7). The American dancer and choreographer presents profiles of people who have influenced her life and art. (Rᴇᴠ: Atl 9/90; BL 7/90; LJ 6/15/90)   **[792.8]**

3642   Farrell, Suzanne, and Toni Bentley. *Holding On to the Air: An Autobiography*. 1990, Summit $19.95 (0-671-68222-9). The former New York City Ballet dancer's life and career. (Rᴇᴠ: BL 9/1/90; CSM 10/17/90; PW 7/27/90)   **[792.8]**

3643   Frank, Rusty E. *Tap! The Greatest Tap Dance Stars and Their Stories*. 1990, Morrow $34.95 (0-688-08949-6). The history of tap dancing and its greatest executioners in the first half of the twentieth century. "The definitive book."—Choice (Rᴇᴠ: Choice 3/91; LJ 11/15/90)   **[792.8]**

3644   Garcia-Marquez, Vincente. *Ballets Russes: Colonel de Basil's Ballets Russes de Monte Carlo, 1932–1952*. 1990, Knopf $50.00 (0-394-52875-1). An illustrated survey of the Ballets Russes de Monte Carlo dance company and its performances over its 20 years of existence. (Rᴇᴠ: BL 12/1/90; PW 10/12/90)   **[792.8]**

3645   Gordon, Suzanne. *Off Balance: The Real World of Ballet*. 1984, McGraw-Hill paper $7.95 (0-07-023770-0). A journalistic investigation into the world of ballet. "Should be required reading for any dancer or for any parent who is . . . encouraging a child to become a professional ballet dancer."—Choice (Rᴇᴠ: Choice 7–8/83; LJ 4/1/83; PW 3/25/83)   **[792.8]**

3646   Graham, Martha. *Blood Memory*. 1991, Doubleday $25.00 (0-385-26503-4). An autobiography of the late modern dancer and choreographer. "A remarkable final work from a singular artist."—BL (Rᴇᴠ: BL 8/91; LJ 8/91; NYTBR 9/8/91. Aᴡᴀʀᴅs: LJ, 1991)   **[792.8]**

3647   Hager, Bengt. *Swedish Ballet: Ballet Suedois*. 1990, Abrams $95.00 (0-8109-3803-0). An illustrated study of the innovative dance company that was based in Paris during the 1920s. "A must for all ballet enthusiasts."—Choice (Rᴇᴠ: BL 12/1/90; Choice 3/91; PW 12/7/90)   **[792.8]**

3648   Kirkland, Gelsey, and Greg Lawrence. *Dancing on My Grave: An Autobiography*. 1986, Doubleday $17.95 (0-385-19964-3); Jove paper $4.50 (0-515-09465-X). An autobiography of the ballerina known for her work with the New York City ballet and the American Ballet Theatre. "Rarely has a performing artist probed so searchingly and satisfyingly into the wellsprings of creativity."—PW (Rᴇᴠ: BL 10/1/86; NYTBR 10/19/86; PW 8/29/86)   **[792.8]**

3649   Kirkland, Gelsey, and Greg Lawrence. *Shape of Love*. 1989, Doubleday $19.95 (0-385-24918-7). The second volume of the ballerina's memoirs about her career in dance. (Rᴇᴠ: BL 9/1/90; LJ 9/1/90; PW 8/3/90)   **[792.8]**

3650   Morris, Michael. *Madam Valentino: The Many Lives of Natacha Rambova*. 1991, Abbeville $35.00 (1-55859-136-2). A biography of the dancer, writer, and spiritualist who became the second wife of silent screen legend Rudolph Valentino. (Rᴇᴠ: LJ 9/15/91; PW 8/2/91)   **[792.8]**

3651   Perlmutter, Donna. *Shadowplay: Anthony Tudor's Life in Dance*. 1991, Viking $24.95 (0-670-83937-X). A psychological examination of the life and works of the dancer and choreographer by the dance critic for the *Los Angeles Times*. (Rᴇᴠ: BL 5/15/91; LJ 6/15/91)   **[792.8]**

Choreography

3652   Mason, Francis. *I Remember Balanchine: Recollections of the Ballet Master by Those Who Knew Him*. 1991, Doubleday $25.00 (0-385-26610-3). Collected recollections of the American choreographer by 85 people who knew and worked with him. (Rᴇᴠ: LJ 6/15/91; PW 3/29/91)   **[792.82]**

793   Indoor games and amusements

Philosophy and theory

3653   Maguire, Jack. *Hopscotch, Hangman, Hot Potato and Ha Ha Ha: A Rulebook of Children's Games*. 1990, Prentice Hall paper $13.95 (0-13-631102-4). A rule book covering over 240 common children's games. (Rᴇᴠ: BL 8/90; LJ 9/1/90)   **[793.01]**

Social, folk, national dancing

3654   Blair, Fredrika. *Isadora: Portrait of the Artist as a Woman*. 1985, McGraw-Hill $24.95 (0-07-005598-X). A biography of the American modern dance pioneer. (Rᴇᴠ: BL 11/15/85; PW 11/1/85)   **[793.3]**

3655   Cunningham, Merce, and Jacqueline Lesschaeve. *Dancer and the Dance: Merce Cunningham in Conversation with Jacqueline Lesschaeve*. 1985, M. Boyars $27.50 (0-7145-2809-9). Interviews with the modern dance choreographer regarding his career and experiences with the art form. (REV: CSM 11/21/85; LJ 5/1/85; PW 3/22/89)   **[793.3]**

3656   Denby, Edwin. *Dance Writings.* **Ed. by Robert Cornfield and William Mackay. 1986, Knopf $40.00 (0-394-54416-1); paper $18.95 (0-394-74984-7).** Collected pieces of the critic's writings about dance with introductory essays regarding his life and work. (REV: Atl 9/87; Choice 6/87; LJ 2/1/87) **[793.3]**

3657   Haskins, Jim, and N. R. Mitgang. *Mr. Bojangles: The Biography of Bill Robinson.* **1988, Morrow $18.95 (0-688-07203-8).** A biography of the American tap dancer, vaudeville entertainer, and motion picture performer. (REV: BL 5/1/88; LJ 5/1/88; NYTBR 6/26/88)   **[793.3]**

3658   Jowitt, Deborah. *Time and the Dancing Image.* **1987, Morrow $22.95 (0-688-04910-9).** Essays on the history of dance, dance styles, and prominent dancers and choreographers by the dance critic for the *Village Voice.* "These obviously well-researched essays are extremely thoughtful and thought-provoking."—LJ (REV: BL 6/15/88; LJ 9/1/88; NYTBR 11/20/88)   **[793.3]**

3659   Kendall, Elizabeth. *Where She Danced: The Birth of American Art Dance.* **1984, Univ. of California Pr. paper $9.95 (0-520-05173-4).** The history and evolution of American dance in the late nineteenth and early twentieth centuries, with profiles of the careers of Isadora Duncan and Ruth St. Denis. (REV: Choice 11/79; Newsweek 7/16/79; PW 3/19/79. AWARDS: ALA, 1979)   **[793.3]**

3660   Long, Richard A. *Black Tradition in American Dance.* **1989, Rizzoli $27.50 (0-8478-1092-5).** An illustrated survey of the African-American contribution to twentieth-century dance. (REV: BL 1/1/90; LJ 1/90)   **[793.3]**

3661   Rose, Phyllis. *Jazz Cleopatra: Josephine Baker in Her Time.* **1989, Doubleday $22.50 (0-385-24891-1).** A biography of the African-American entertainer who achieved fame in Paris during the 1920s. (REV: LJ 8/89; New Rep 11/6/89; NYTBR 11/5/89)   **[793.3]**

3662   Siegel, Marcia B. *Days on Earth: The Dance of Doris Humphrey.* **1987, Yale Univ. Pr. $33.50 (0-300-03856-9).** A biography of the innovative modern dance choreographer. "The author has added an important chapter to dance history."—Choice (REV: Choice 7–8/88; CSM 3/21/88; LJ 11/1/87)   **[793.3]**

3663   Sorell, Walter. *Looking Back in Wonder: Diary of a Dance Critic.* **1986, Columbia Univ. Pr. $29.95 (0-231-06278-8).** Collected essays by the dance writer on dance and its relationship to other art forms. "Enjoyable and thought-provoking reading."—LJ (REV: Choice 2/87; LJ 7/86; PW 6/13/86)   **[793.3]**

3664   Stodelle, Ernestine. *Deep Song: The Dance Story of Martha Graham.* **1984, Schirmer $26.95 (0-02-872520-4).** A biography of the innovative modern dance choreographer. "Definitive . . . an enlightening portrait of one of America's most prestigious

and unpredictable artists."—Choice (REV: Choice 2/85; LJ 10/1/84; NYTBR 10/28/84)   **[793.3]**

3665   Taylor, Paul. *Private Domain: An Autobiography.* **1987, Knopf $22.95 (0-394-51683-4); North Point paper $12.95 (0-86547-322-6).** The life story of the former Martha Graham dancer who left to form his own company. "Unusually candid and witty."—LJ (REV: Choice 9/87; LJ 6/1/87; Time 5/11/87. AWARDS: LJ, 1987)   **[793.3]**

Magic and related activities

3666   Blackstone, Harry, Jr. *Blackstone Book of Magic and Illusion.* **1985, Newmarket $22.95 (0-937858-45-5).** A history of magic and illusion with instructions for performing feats of prestidigitation. (REV: BL 5/15/85; LJ 3/15/85; PW 3/29/85)   **[793.8]**

794   Indoor games of skill

3667   Peek, Stephen. *Game Plan: The Game Inventor's Handbook.* **1987, Betterway Pubs. paper $9.95 (0-932620-85-X).** A manual on the art of designing, producing, and marketing box and computer games. (REV: BL 1/15/88; LJ 1/88)   **[794]**

Chess

3668   Kasparov, Garry, and Donald Trelford. *Unlimited Challenge: The Autobiography of Garry Kasparov.* **1990, Grove-Weidenfeld $19.95 (0-8021-1103-3).** An autobiography of the Soviet world chess champion. (REV: LJ 11/1/90; PW 10/5/90)   **[794.1]**

795   Games of chance

Wheel and top games

3669   Bass, Thomas A. *Eudaemonic Pie.* **1986, Random paper $5.95 (0-394-74310-5).** How a group of Santa Cruz hackers applied computer technology in an attempt to beat the odds playing roulette in Las Vegas. "Completely captivating . . . this book will appeal to the rebel in everyone."—PW (REV: BL 6/1/85; NYTBR 5/19/85; PW 4/12/85)   **[795.2]**

Games based chiefly on skill

3670   Alvarez, A. *Biggest Game in Town.* **1985, Houghton paper $7.95 (0-395-38351-X).** An examination of Las Vegas and the gaming industry as reflected through the competition at the 1981 World Series of Poker. (REV: LJ 4/15/83; NYRB 6/2/83; NYTBR 5/8/83)   **[795.41]**

796   Athletic and outdoor sports and games

3671   Ashe, Arthur R. *A Hard Road to Glory: The History of the African-American Athlete.* **1988, Warner $100.90 (0-446-71006-7).** A three-volume history of African-American athletes from the seventeenth century to the present. (REV: CSM 12/28/88; LJ 11/15/88; NYTBR 12/4/88)   **[796]**

3672   Nelson, Mariah Burton. *Are We Winning Yet? How Women Are Changing Sports and Sports Are Changing Women.* **1991, Random $18.95 (0-394-57576-8).** A *Washington Post* columnist analyzes the status and role of female athletes in contemporary America. (Rev: BL 2/15/91; LJ 2/1/91; PW 2/8/91)   **[796]**

3673   Sheed, Wilfrid. *Baseball and Lesser Sports.* **1991, HarperCollins $19.95 (0-06-016531-6).** A collection of 36 essays on sports focusing on the game of baseball. "Informed and classy sportswriting."— BL (Rev: BL 4/15/91; LJ 6/1/91; PW 5/10/91)   **[796]**

3674   Vecsey, George. *A Year in the Sun: The Life and Times of a Sports Columnist.* **1989, Random $19.95 (0-8129-1678-6).** Memoirs of the *New York Times* columnist regarding his life covering the sports world. (Rev: BL 3/1/89; LJ 3/1/89; NYTBR 3/26/89)   **[796]**

Philosophy and theory

3675   Micheli, Lyle J., and Mark D. Jenkins. *Sportswise: An Essential Guide for Young Adult Athletes, Parents and Coaches.* **1990, Houghton $19.95 (0-395-51608-0); paper $9.95 (0-395-56408-5).** A guide to the safe enjoyment of competitive sports for young athletes. (Rev: BL 9/1/90; LJ 7/90)   **[796.01]**

Miscellany

3676   McKee, Steve. *Call of the Game.* **1987, McGraw-Hill $15.95 (0-07-045354-3).** An account of the author's experiences viewing a variety of American spectator sports. (Rev: BL 12/1/86; LJ 12/86; PW 10/17/86)   **[796.02]**

3677   Whittingham, Richard, ed. *Life in Sports: A Pictorial History of Sports from the Incomparable Archives of America's Greatest Picture Magazine.* **1988, Harper & Row paper $14.95 (0-06-091475-0).** A collection of 350 photographs detailing the history of sports coverage by *Life* magazine. "There is something in it for every sports fan."— NYTBR (Rev: BL 11/15/85; LJ 11/15/85; NYTBR 12/22/85)   **[796.02]**

Basketball

3678   Abdul-Jabbar, Kareem, and Mignon Mc-Carthy. *Kareem.* **1990, Random $18.95 (0-394-55927-4).** Professional basketball's all-time leading scorer reflects on his final season with the Los Angeles Lakers. (Rev: BL 2/1/90; LJ 3/15/90; NYTBR 3/25/90)   **[796.323]**

3679   Auerbach, Red, and Joe Fitzgerald. *On and Off the Court.* **1985, Macmillan $14.95 (0-02-504390-0).** The longtime Boston Celtics general manager and former coach presents his opinions on life and the game of basketball. (Rev: BL 11/1/85; LJ 11/1/85; PW 9/6/85)   **[796.323]**

3680   Barkley, Charles, and Roy S. Johnson. *Outrageous! The Fine Life and Flagrant Good Times of Basketball's Irresistible Force.* **1991, Simon & Schuster $19.50 (0-671-73799-6).** An autobiography of Charles Barkley, the outspoken power forward of the Philadelphia 76ers. (Rev: BL 11/15/91; PW 11/22/91)   **[796.323]**

3681   Bradley, Bill. *Life on the Run.* **1986, Bantam paper $3.95 (0-553-26152-5).** The former New York

Knicks forward talks about his career in professional basketball. "Irresistible not just to those close to professional basketball but to anyone interested in the experience of the professional athlete."—Newsweek (Rev: NYRB 5/27/76; NYTBR 5/2/76; Newsweek 5/10/76)   **[796.323]**

3682   Feinstein, John. *A Season Inside: One Year in College Basketball.* **1988, Random $18.95 (0-394-56891-5); Simon & Schuster paper $9.95 (0-671-68882-0).** The author of *A Season on the Brink* presents an overview of the 1987–1988 college basketball season focusing on dozens of teams from throughout the country. "A buoyant and entertaining tribute to college basketball."— NYTBR (Rev: BL 11/15/88; LJ 12/88; NYTBR 1/22/89)   **[796.323]**

3683   Feinstein, John. *A Season on the Brink: A Year with Bob Knight and the Indiana Hoosiers.* **1986, Macmillan $16.95 (0-02-537230-0); Simon & Schuster paper $9.95 (0-671-68882-0).** A portrait of Indiana University's basketball coach and team during the 1985–1986 season. (Rev: BL 11/15/86; LJ 11/1/86; NYTBR 2/8/87)   **[796.323]**

3684   Gandolfi, Giorgio, and Gerald S. Couzens. *Hoops! The Official National Basketball Players Association Guide to Playing Basketball.* **1986, McGraw-Hill paper $10.95 (0-07-013276-3).** Sixteen essays by NBA coaches on the fundamentals of the game of basketball. (Rev: BL 1/15/86; LJ 1/86)   **[796.323]**

3685   Halberstam, David. *Breaks of the Game.* **1983, Ballantine paper $4.95 (0-345-29625-7).** Professional basketball examined through the Portland Trail Blazers 1979–1980 season. "Arguably the most incisive look ever at pro basketball . . . the most significant sports book of the year."—BL (Rev: BL 10/1/81; CSM 12/30/81; New Rep 2/10/82. Awards: ALA, 1981)   **[796.323]**

3686   Johnson, Earvin, Jr., and Roy S. Johnson. *Magic's Touch: From Fast Break to Fundamentals with Basketball's Most Exciting Player.* **1989, Addison Wesley $17.95 (0-201-51794-9); paper $4.95 (0-201-55092-X).** Memoirs of the Los Angeles Lakers' point guard with his tips for better basketball play. (Rev: BL 9/15/89; LJ 10/1/89; PW 9/22/89)   **[796.323]**

3687   Levine, David L. *Life on the Rim: A Year in the Continental Basketball Association.* **1990, Macmillan $17.95 (0-02-570381-1).** An account of the author's experiences traveling with the Albany Patroons, a member of professional basketball's minor league. (Rev: BL 1/1/90; PW 12/8/89)   **[796.323]**

3688   Levine, Lee Daniel. *Bird: The Making of an American Sports Legend.* **1989, McGraw-Hill $17.95 (0-07-037477-5); Berkley paper $4.50 (0-425-11781-2).** A biography of the star basketball player for the Boston Celtics. "A lively contribution to sports literature."—NYTBR (Rev: BL 10/15/88; NYTBR 12/11/88)   **[796.323]**

3689   Peterson, Robert W. *Pro Basketball's Early Years: Cages to Jump Shots.* **1990, Oxford Univ. Pr. $22.95 (0-19-505310-9).** A history of the sport of basketball from its development by James Naismith in 1891 in Springfield, Massachusetts, to the mid-1950s. (REV: BL 10/1/90; LJ 9/1/90; PW 8/17/90) **[796.323]**

3690 Pluto, Terry. *Loose Balls: The Short, Wild Life of the American Basketball Association.* 1990, Simon & Schuster $21.95 (0-671-67390-4). An oral history of the American Basketball Association from its founding to its merger with the NBA. "A must read for hoop fans."—BL (REV: BL 10/1/90; LJ 9/15/90; Newsweek 12/10/90) **[796.323]**

3691 Ryan, Bob, and Terry Pluto. *Forty-eight Minutes: A Night in the Life of the NBA.* 1987, Macmillan $16.95 (0-02-597770-9); paper $9.95 (0-02-036050-9). An in-depth study of a professional basketball game between the Boston Celtics and the Cleveland Cavaliers with backgrounds of the teams and individuals involved in the contest. (REV: BL 12/15/87; LJ 12/87; NYTBR 3/13/88) **[796.323]**

3692 Shapiro, Leonard. *Big Man on Campus: John Thompson and the Georgetown Hoyas.* 1991, Henry Holt $19.95 (0-8050-1125-0). A biography of the Georgetown Hoyas basketball coach. "A sports book that, like its subject, stands above the crowd."—PW (REV: BL 1/15/91; LJ 2/1/91; PW 12/14/90) **[796.323]**

3693 Smith, Sam. *Jordan Rules.* 1991, Simon & Schuster $22.00 (0-671-74491-7). An account of the 1990–1991 Chicago Bulls championship season focusing on the team's star player Michael Jordan. "Meticulously reported and sparklingly written."—NYTBR (REV: BL 12/15/91; NYTBR 1/12/92) **[796.323]**

3694 Stauth, Cameron. *Franchise: Building a Winner with the World Champion Detroit Pistons, Basketball's Bad Boys.* 1990, Morrow $19.95 (0-688-09573-9). An examination of the development of the former world championship basketball team. "Brings fans as deep inside the NBA as they're likely to get without suiting up."—BL (REV: BL 4/15/90; LJ 5/15/90; PW 3/16/90) **[796.323]**

3695 Strom, Earl, and Blaine Johnson. *Calling the Shots: My Five Decades in the NBA.* 1990, Simon & Schuster $18.95 (0-671-66108-6). An autobiography of the former basketball official who spent 33 years refereeing games in the NBA. (REV: BL 12/1/90; LJ 12/90; NYTBR 1/13/91) **[796.323]**

3696 Valenti, John, and Ron Naclerio. *Swee' Pea and Other Playground Legends: Tales of Drugs, Violence and Basketball.* 1990, Michael Kesend $26.95 (0-935576-38-X); paper $13.95 (0-935576-39-8). A study of the life of Lloyd Daniels, a talented guard whose basketball career became derailed after involvement with crack cocaine. (REV: BL 12/1/90; LJ 12/90; NYTBR 12/23/90) **[796.323]**

3697 Wartenburg, Steve. *Winning Is an Attitude: A Season in the Life of John Chaney and the Temple Owls.* 1991, St. Martin's $18.95 (0-312-05538-2). An account of the 1989–1990 Temple Owls' basketball season. (REV: BL 12/15/90; LJ 12/90) **[796.323]**

Football

3698 Bissinger, H. G. *Friday Night Lights: A Town, a Team, and a Dream.* 1990, Addison Wesley $19.95 (0-201-19677-8). A portrait of high school football in the west Texas city of Odessa. (REV: CSM 9/10/90; LJ 8/90; PW 8/3/90) **[796.332]**

3699 Bradshaw, Terry, and Buddy Martin. *Looking Deep.* 1989, Contemporary $17.95 (0-8092-4266-4). An autobiography of the former Pittsburgh Steeler quarterback and member of the National Football League Hall of Fame. (REV: BL 9/15/89; NYTBR 11/19/89; PW 7/14/89) **[796.332]**

3700 Dickey, Glenn. *Just Win, Baby: Al Davis and His Raiders.* 1991, Harcourt $19.95 (0-15-146580-0). A biography of the controversial coach and owner of the Oakland/Los Angeles Raiders professional football team. (REV: BL 9/15/91; NYTBR 11/17/91) **[796.332]**

3701 Harris, David. *League: The Rise and Decline of the NFL.* 1987, Bantam paper $4.95 (0-553-26516-4). A history of the National Football League under the rule of Pete Rozelle from 1960 to the mid-1980s. (REV: BL 9/15/86; LJ 10/15/86; NYTBR 10/26/86. AWARDS: PW, 1986) **[796.332]**

3702 Izenberg, Jerry. *No Medals for Trying: A Week in the Life of a Pro Football Team.* 1990, Macmillan $18.95 (0-02-558215-1). A chronicle of a week with the New York Giants professional football team as it prepares for a confrontation with the Philadelphia Eagles. "A must-read for every pro football fan."—BL (REV: BL 9/15/90; NYTBR 10/7/90; PW 7/20/90) **[796.332]**

3703 Klecko, Joe, and Joe Fields. *Nose to Nose: Survival in the Trenches of the NFL.* 1989, Morrow $18.95 (0-688-05281-9). Memoirs of two professional football linemen regarding their careers playing for the New York Jets. (REV: BL 9/1/89; LJ 8/89; PW 7/21/89) **[796.332]**

3704 Leuthner, Stuart. *Iron Men: Bucko, Crazylegs and the Boys Recall the Golden Days of Professional Football.* 1988, Doubleday $18.95 (0-385-23977-7). An oral history of professional football from World War II to the first Super Bowl including interviews with Otto Graham, Crazylegs Hirsch, Pat Summerall, and Marion Motley. (REV: BL 9/15/88; LJ 12/88; PW 9/2/88) **[796.332]**

3705 Plimpton, George. *Paper Lion.* 1965, Holtzman Pr. $24.95 (0-941372-07-3); Harper & Row paper $8.95 (0-06-091540-4). Plimpton's story of his masquerade as a professional football quarterback for the Detroit Lions. "A vivid insight into the triumphs and tragedies, joys, sorrows, and daily monotonies that make up the life of the professional athlete."—PW (REV: BL 12/15/66; LJ 11/1/66; PW 10/10/66. AWARDS: NYTBR, 1966) **[796.332]**

3706 Telander, Rick. *Hundred Yard Lie: The Corruption of College Football and What We Can Do to Stop It.* 1989, Simon & Schuster $17.95 (0-671-68095-1); paper $8.95 (0-671-72788-5). An exposé of corruption within college football by a former Big

Ten player and *Sports Illustrated* writer. "An extraordinarily powerful statement by a knowledgeable insider."—BL (Rev: BL 10/15/89; PW 8/8/89) **[796.332]**

3707 **Walsh, Bill, and Glenn Dickey.** *Building a Champion: On Football and the Making of the 49ers.* 1990, St. Martin's $18.95 (0-312-04969-2). The former San Francisco 49ers coach discusses his career in football and the formation of the team that won Super Bowls in 1982, 1985, and 1989 under his direction. (Rev: BL 10/15/90; LJ 10/15/90; NYTBR 10/7/90) **[796.332]**

Tennis

3708 **Burwash, Peter, and John Tullins.** *Total Tennis.* 1989, Macmillan $22.50 (0-02-620401-0). Advice on methods of improving tennis skills and conditioning. (Rev: BL 9/1/89; LJ 9/15/89) **[796.342]**

3709 **Engelmann, Larry.** *Goddess and the American Girl: Suzanne Lenglen and Helen Wills.* 1988, Oxford Univ. Pr. $21.95 (0-19-504363-4). A look at the careers and personalities of two of women's tennis top stars of the 1930s and how they changed the game of tennis and the world's perception of female athletes. (Rev: Choice 11/88; LJ 4/1/88; NYTBR 6/12/88) **[796.342]**

3710 **Evans, Richard.** *Open Tennis: 1968–1988; the Players, the Politics, the Pressures, the Passions, and the Great Matches.* 1989, Greene $19.95 (0-8289-0720-X); paper $10.95 (0-8289-0721-8). The history of the development of modern tennis with profiles of its key figures and memorable moments. (Rev: BL 7/89; LJ 5/15/89; PW 4/21/89) **[796.342]**

3711 **Feinstein, John.** *Hard Courts: Real Life on the Professional Tennis Tours.* 1991, Random $22.50 (0-394-58333-7). An account of the author's experiences during a year traveling on the professional tennis circuit. (Rev: BL 8/91; CSM 8/23/91; NYTBR 8/25/91) **[796.342]**

3712 **Lloyd, Chris Evert, and John Lloyd.** *Lloyd on Lloyd.* 1986, Beaufort Books $14.95 (0-8253-0374-5). Memoirs of the professional tennis-playing couple regarding their careers in the game and their personal relationship. (Rev: BL 6/1/86; LJ 6/15/86) **[796.342]**

3713 **Marble, Alice, and Dale Leatherman.** *Courting Danger: My Adventures in World-Class Tennis, Golden-Age Hollywood, and High-Stakes Spying.* 1991, St. Martin's $19.95 (0-312-05389-X). An autobiography of the 1930s tennis star. "There is nary a dull moment in this fast-moving, glamourous tale."—PW (Rev: LJ 5/15/91; PW 4/12/91) **[796.342]**

3714 **Navratilova, Martina, and George Vecsey.** *Martina.* 1985, Knopf $16.95 (0-394-53640-1); Fawcett paper $4.95 (0-449-20982-2). A biography of the tennis star who defected to the United States at the age of 18 and dominated her sport in the 1980s. (Rev: BL 5/1/85; LJ 7/85; PW 5/17/85) **[796.342]**

Racquetball

3715 **Turner, Ed, and Marty Hogan.** *Skills and Strategies in Winning Racquetball.* 1987, Leisure Pr. paper $12.95 (0-88011-289-1). An introduction to the essential skills and techniques used in the sport of racquetball. (Rev: BL 12/1/87; Choice 6/88; LJ 12/87) **[796.343]**

Golf

3716 **Boswell, Thomas.** *Strokes of Genius.* 1989, Penguin paper $7.95 (0-14-011368-1). Collected essays regarding golf penned by the *Washington Post* sportswriter. "Required reading for anyone who follows professional golf."—BL (Rev: BL 4/15/87; CSM 7/27/87; LJ 4/15/87) **[796.352]**

3717 **Peper, George, Robin McMillan, and Jim Frank.** *Golf in America: The First One Hundred Years.* 1988, Abrams $39.95 (0-8109-1032-2). A history of the first century of golf in the United States with profiles of its greatest figures and most challenging courses. (Rev: LJ 11/15/88; PW 9/23/88) **[796.352]**

3718 **Player, Gary, and Desmond Tolhurst.** *Golf Begins at Fifty: Playing the Lifetime Game Better Than Ever.* 1988, Simon & Schuster $18.95 (0-671-63861-0); paper $12.95 (0-671-68319-5). A compilation of techniques and advice for the senior golfer. "A great find for avid golfers of all ages."—LJ (Rev: BL 6/15/88; LJ 6/15/88) **[796.352]**

3719 **Whitworth, Kathy, and Rhoda Glenn.** *Golf for Women.* 1990, St. Martin's $19.95 (0-312-04013-X). An illustrated guide to the fundamentals of golf for women by a top LPGA veteran. (Rev: BL 4/15/90; LJ 6/15/90) **[796.352]**

3720 **Wind, Herbert Warren.** *Following Through: Herbert Warren Wind on Golf.* 1986, Ticknor & Fields paper $10.95 (0-89919-483-4). Selections from two decades of the author's *New Yorker* golf columns. (Rev: BL 9/15/85; LJ 9/15/85; NYTBR 11/10/85) **[796.352]**

Baseball

3721 **Aaron, Henry, and Lonnie Wheeler.** *I Had a Hammer: The Hank Aaron Story.* 1991, HarperCollins $21.95 (0-06-016321-6). An autobiography of major league baseball's all-time home run king. "Beautifully written."—NYTBR (Rev: BL 2/1/91; NYTBR 4/1/91; PW 2/1/91) **[796.357]**

3722 **Alexander, Charles C.** *John McGraw.* 1988, Viking $19.95 (0-670-80730-3); Penguin paper $8.95 (0-14-009600-0). A biography of the New York Giants manager who led his baseball teams to ten National League pennants over the course of his 30-year career. (Rev: BL 4/1/88; LJ 3/15/88; PW 2/12/88) **[796.357]**

3723 **Alexander, Charles C.** *Ty Cobb: Baseball's Fierce Immortal.* 1984, Oxford Univ. Pr. $21.95 (0-19-503414-7). A study of the great Detroit Tiger outfielder and one of the five original inductees into baseball's Hall of Fame. (Rev: Choice 7–8/84; CSM 4/26/84; LJ 3/1/84) **[796.357]**

3724 Allen, Dick, and Tim Whitaker. *Crash! The Life and Times of Dick Allen.* 1989, Ticknor & Fields $17.95 (0-89919-657-8). An autobiography of the former professional baseball player. "Allen was (and is) one of modern sports' most interesting characters, and this insightful and endearing profile is long overdue."—BL (Rev: BL 10/1/89; NYRB 10/12/89; NYTBR 4/23/89) **[796.357]**

3725 Allen, Maury. *Roger Maris: A Man for All Seasons.* 1986, Donald I. Fine $16.95 (0-917657-94-2). A biography of the New York Yankees baseball player who broke Babe Ruth's single-season home-run record during the 1961 season. (Rev: BL 9/15/86; LJ 9/15/86; PW 8/8/86) **[796.357]**

3726 Angell, Roger. *Five Seasons: A Baseball Companion.* 1988, Simon & Schuster paper $8.95 (0-671-65692-9). A review of the baseball seasons from 1972 to 1976. "Not a dull paragraph in the book."—PW (Rev: LJ 4/1/77; NYTBR 5/15/77; PW 2/20/78) **[796.357]**

3727 Angell, Roger. *Late Innings.* 1983, Ballantine paper $4.50 (0-345-30936-7). Collection of essays about different aspects of our national pastime. "Angell was born to write about baseball."—NYRB (Rev: LJ 5/15/82; NYRB 9/23/82; Time 5/10/82. Awards: Time, 1982) **[796.357]**

3728 Angell, Roger. *Season Ticket: A Baseball Companion.* 1988, Houghton $18.95 (0-395-38165-7); Ballantine paper $4.95 (0-345-35814-7). A collection of Angell's *New Yorker* baseball columns covering the 1983–1987 seasons. (Rev: CSM 4/20/88; LJ 3/15/88; NYTBR 3/20/88) **[796.357]**

3729 Angell, Roger. *Summer Game.* 1986, Ballantine paper $3.95 (0-345-34192-9). A collection of essays spanning over a decade concerning the game of baseball. "Simply the most elegant, stylish and intelligent baseball writer in the country today."—LJ (Rev: LJ 4/15/72; NYRB 5/18/72; NYTBR 6/12/72) **[796.357]**

3730 Baylor, Don. *Don Baylor: Nothing but the Truth; a Baseball Life.* 1989, St. Martin's $18.95 (0-312-02906-3). An autobiography of the baseball veteran who spent 18 years in the major leagues with the Orioles, A's, Angels, Yankees, Red Sox, and Twins. (Rev: LJ 5/1/89; NYTBR 7/2/89; PW 3/3/89) **[796.357]**

3731 Bouton, Jim. *Ball Four: My Life and Hard Times Throwing the Knuckleball in the Big Leagues.* 1990, Macmillan $21.95 (0-02-513980-0); paper $12.95 (0-02-030665-2). One of the first "tell-all" sports confessionals. "The most intelligent and entertaining participant's account of the national pastime yet published."—New Yorker (Rev: LJ 7/70; NYTBR 7/26/70; New Yorker 7/25/70. Awards: Time, 1970) **[796.357]**

3732 Bruce, Janet. *Kansas City Monarchs: Champions of Black Baseball.* 1985, Univ. Pr. of Kansas $25.00 (0-7006-0273-9); paper $9.95 (0-7006-0343-3). A history and analysis of pre-World War II "Negro

League" baseball as exemplified by one of its most legendary teams. (Rev: Choice 3/86; LJ 9/1/85) **[796.357]**

3733 Carter, Gary, and John Hough, Jr. *Dream Season.* 1987, Harcourt $15.95 (0-15-126571-2). The former New York Mets catcher recounts the events of his life and his part in the 1986 World Champion baseball team. (Rev: BL 4/1/87; LJ 5/1/87; NYTBR 5/3/87) **[796.357]**

3734 Creamer, Robert. *Babe.* 1981, Holtzman Pr. $24.95 (0-941372-02-2). A profile of the New York Yankees slugger George Herman "Babe" Ruth. "Creamer's tone seems right-level but cheerful, without awe or cynicism, plainspoken and yet celebratory of a unique American figure."—NYTBR (Rev: LJ 6/15/74; NYTBR 10/13/74; Time 8/26/74) **[796.357]**

3735 Creamer, Robert. *Baseball in 1941.* 1991, Viking $19.95 (0-670-83374-6). An account of the events of the 1941 major league baseball season including DiMaggio's consecutive game hitting streak and Williams's .406 season. "The choice here for the season's best baseball book."—LJ (Rev: LJ 2/15/91; PW 4/5/91) **[796.357]**

3736 Creamer, Robert. *Stengel: His Life and Times.* 1990, Simon & Schuster paper $9.95 (0-671-70131-2). A biography of the former New York Yankees and New York Mets baseball manager. (Rev: CSM 10/12/84; LJ 2/15/84; NYTBR 3/25/84) **[796.357]**

3737 Cromartie, Warren, and Robert Whiting. *Slugging It Out in Japan: An American Leaguer in the Tokyo Outfield.* 1991, Kodansha $19.95 (4-7700-1423-6). Memoirs of the American-born outfielder's six seasons playing professional baseball for the Tokyo Giants. (Rev: BL 4/15/91; LJ 4/15/91) **[796.357]**

3738 Drysdale, Don, and Bob Verdi. *Once a Bum, Always a Dodger: My Life in Baseball.* 1990, St. Martin's $18.95 (0-312-03902-6). Memoirs of the former Brooklyn/Los Angeles Dodgers pitcher's career in professional baseball. (Rev: BL 1/1/90; LJ 2/1/90; PW 1/12/90) **[796.357]**

3739 Durso, Joseph. *Baseball and the American Dream.* 1986, Sporting News $16.95 (0-89204-220-6). A cultural history of baseball examining its impact on American society. (Rev: BL 8/86; LJ 6/1/86; NYTBR 7/20/86) **[796.357]**

3740 Falkner, David. *Nine Sides of the Diamond: Baseball's Great Glove Men on the Fine Art of Defense.* 1990, Random $18.95 (0-8129-1806-1). A study of baseball's greatest defensive players at each position and the skills and techniques that made them great. (Rev: BL 4/1/90; LJ 4/1/90; NYTBR 4/1/90) **[796.357]**

3741 Falkner, David. *Short Season: The Hard Work and High Times of Baseball in the Spring.* 1987, Penguin paper $6.95 (0-14-009850-X). A profile of professional baseball's annual rite of spring training. (Rev: BL 3/15/86; CSM 5/12/86; LJ 5/15/86)**[796.357]**

3742 Feller, Bob, and Bill Gilbert. *Now Pitching, Bob Feller: A Baseball Memoir.* 1990, Carol Publg.

Group $18.95 (1-55972-005-0); HarperCollins paper $8.95 (0-06-097373-0). An autobiography of the former Cleveland Indians pitcher dubbed "Rapid Robert" for his exceptional fastball. (REV: BL 4/1/90; LJ 2/15/90; NYTBR 4/1/90) **[796.357]**

3743   Frommer, Harvey. *New York City Baseball: The Last Golden Age, 1947–1957.* **1985, Macmillan paper $9.95 (0-689-70684-7).** A look at professional baseball in New York City in the decade prior to the relocation of the Brooklyn Dodgers and New York Giants to California. (REV: LJ 4/15/80; Natl Rev 5/29/81; NYTBR 6/15/80) **[796.357]**

3744   Gammons, Peter. *Beyond the Sixth Game.* **1986, Greene paper $6.95 (0-8289-0591-6).** A survey of major league baseball from 1975 to 1984 concentrating on the ups and downs of the Boston Red Sox. (REV: BL 3/15/85; CSM 4/25/85; LJ 3/15/85) **[796.357]**

3745   Goldstein, Warren Jay. *Playing for Keeps: A History of Early Baseball.* **1989, Cornell Univ. Pr. $21.95 (0-8014-1829-1).** A history of American baseball in the 1850s and 1860s. (REV: Choice 4/90; NYTBR 4/1/90) **[796.357]**

3746   Golenbock, Peter. *Bums: An Oral History of the Brooklyn Dodgers.* **1984, Putnam $17.95 (0-399-12846-8); Pocket paper $4.95 (0-671-55455-7).** An oral history of the Brooklyn Dodgers baseball team from the construction of Ebbets Field in 1912 to their relocation to Los Angeles. (REV: BL 9/15/84; LJ 9/15/84; NYTBR 12/30/84) **[796.357]**

3747   Golenbock, Peter. *Forever Boys: An Intimate Look at the Hidden Lives of Ex-Major League Ballplayers as They Played One More Time.* **1991, Carol Publg. Group $19.95 (1-55972-034-4).** A look at the initial season of the Senior Baseball League established for former professional baseball players over the age of 35. (REV: BL 12/15/90; LJ 12/90; PW 1/4/91) **[796.357]**

3748   Gregory, Robert. *Diz: Dizzy Dean and Baseball During the Great Depression.* **1991, Viking $22.00 (0-670-82141-1).** A biography of the St. Louis Cardinals star pitcher during the 1930s. (REV: BL 1/15/92; LJ 2/1/92; PW 11/29/91) **[796.357]**

3749   Halberstam, David. *Summer of '49.* **1989, Morrow $21.95 (0-688-06678-X); Avon paper $4.95 (0-380-71075-7).** An analysis of the 1949 American League baseball pennant race between the New York Yankees and the Boston Red Sox and how baseball was beginning to change into the modern game we know today. (REV: LJ 5/1/89; Newsweek 4/17/89; Time 5/22/89) **[796.357]**

3750   Hall, Donald. *Fathers Playing Catch with Sons: Essays on Sport (Mostly Baseball).* **1985, North Point paper $13.50 (0-86547-168-1).** Essays by the American poet regarding the appeal and enjoyment of baseball. (REV: BL 12/1/84; CSM 7/10/85; LJ 12/84) **[796.357]**

3751   Hanneman, David V. *Diamonds in the Rough: The Legend and Legacy of Tony Lucadello.* **1990, Eakin paper $12.95 (0-89015-666-2).** A portrait of the

life and career of former Philadelphia Phillies and Chicago Cubs baseball scout Tony Lucadello. (REV: BL 2/1/90; LJ 1/90) **[796.357]**

3752   Higgins, George V. *Progress of the Seasons: A Partisan's View of Forty Years of Baseball at Fenway Park.* **1989, Henry Holt $18.95 (0-8050-0913-2); Prentice Hall paper $8.95 (0-13-728304-0).** A look at 40 years of Boston Red Sox history as experienced by a lifetime fan, his father, and grandfather. (REV: Atl 5/89; LJ 4/15/89; NYTBR 4/23/89) **[796.357]**

3753   Houk, Ralph, and Robert Creamer. *Season of Glory: The Amazing Saga of the 1961 New York Yankees.* **1989, Pocket paper $4.50 (0-671-67411-0).** A chronicle of the legendary 1961 New York Yankees World Champion baseball team as narrated by their manager. (REV: BL 3/15/88; LJ 4/1/88; NYTBR 6/5/88) **[796.357]**

3754   Hynd, Noel. *Giants of the Polo Grounds: The Glorious Times of Baseball's New York Giants.* **1988, Doubleday $18.95 (0-385-23790-1).** An account of the New York Giants baseball team from their beginnings in the Polo Grounds in 1885 to their relocation to San Francisco in 1957. (REV: BL 4/15/88; NYTBR 6/5/88; PW 3/11/88) **[796.357]**

3755   Jackson, Bo, and Dick Schaap. *Bo Knows Bo: The Autobiography of a Ballplayer.* **1990, Doubleday $18.95 (0-385-41620-2).** An autobiography of the professional athlete known for his exploits with football's Los Angeles Raiders and baseball's Kansas City Royals. (REV: NYTBR 12/9/90; PW 10/5/90) **[796.357]**

3756   James, Bill, and Mary A. Wirth. *Bill James Historical Baseball Abstract.* **1985, Random $29.95 (0-394-53713-0).** A statistical and anecdotal analysis of the history of baseball by the author of *The Baseball Abstract.* (REV: LJ 1/86; NYTBR 12/8/85; Time 6/9/86) **[796.357]**

3757   Kahn, Roger. *Boys of Summer.* **1981, Holtzman Pr. $24.95 (0-941372-04-9); Harper & Row paper $9.95 (0-06-091416-5).** A history and tribute to the Brooklyn Dodgers baseball team of the 1950s tracing players' lives before, during, and after their stint with the team. (REV: LJ 2/15/72; Newsweek 3/13/72; PW 1/24/72) **[796.357]**

3758   Kahn, Roger. *Good Enough to Dream.* **1986, NAL paper $4.50 (0-451-15280-8).** An account of the author's ownership of a Utica, New York, minor league baseball team. "A glowing personal tribute to the magnetism of the game of baseball and a must for any sports collection."—BL (REV: BL 9/15/85; NYTBR 9/8/85) **[796.357]**

3759   Kahn, Roger. *Joe and Marilyn: A Memory of Love.* **1988, Avon paper $4.95 (0-380-70462-5).** The prominent baseball writer presents a study of the Joe DiMaggio-Marilyn Monroe marriage and relationship. (REV: BL 10/1/86; Natl Rev 1/30/87; NYTBR 11/9/86) **[796.357]**

3760   Kaplan, Jim. *Pine-Tarred and Feathered: A Year on the Baseball Beat.* **1985, Algonquin $15.95**

(0-912697-15-6). A baseball journalist's memoirs of his coverage of the 1983 season for *Sports Illustrated* magazine. (Rev: BL 3/15/85; CSM 7/10/85; LJ 4/1/85) **[796.357]**

3761 Kaplan, Jim. *Playing the Field: Why Defense Is the Most Fascinating Art in Major League Baseball.* **1987, Algonquin paper $13.95 (0-912697-36-9).** A look at the importance of defense to the game of baseball, with profiles of its greatest defensive players and memorable defensive moments. (Rev: BL 3/15/87; LJ 3/15/87; PW 2/20/87) **[796.357]**

3762 Koppett, Leonard. *New Thinking Fan's Guide to Baseball.* **1991, Simon & Schuster $22.95 (0-671-68330-6); paper $10.95 (0-671-73205-6).** A revised guide to the enjoyment and appreciation of the game of baseball. "A wonderful baseball book that cannot be praised too highly."—BL (Rev: BL 2/15/91; LJ 2/15/91; PW 2/15/91) **[796.357]**

3763 Krich, John. *El Beisbol: Travels Through the Pan-American Pastime.* **1989, Atlantic Monthly $18.95 (0-87113-303-2); Prentice Hall paper $8.95 (0-13-247990-7).** A look at the sport of baseball in the cultures of Puerto Rico, the Dominican Republic, Mexico, Nicaragua, and Venezuela. (Rev: LJ 5/1/89; PW 3/10/89) **[796.357]**

3764 Kuhn, Bowie. *Hardball: The Education of a Baseball Commissioner.* **1988, McGraw-Hill paper $5.95 (0-07-035598-3).** Memoirs of the baseball commissioner who held the position from 1969 to 1984. (Rev: LJ 5/1/87; New Rep 4/27/87; NYTBR 3/8/87) **[796.357]**

3765 Lamb, David. *Stolen Season: A Journey Through America and Baseball's Minor Leagues.* **1991, Random $20.00 (0-394-57608-X).** An account of the author's travels around the United States observing minor league baseball. "Should be read by anyone who has yet to savor the sounds and delights of a minor-league baseball game."—NYTBR (Rev: BL 3/1/91; LJ 2/15/91; NYTBR 4/7/91) **[796.357]**

3766 Luciano, Ron, and David Fisher. *Remembrance of Swings Past.* **1988, Bantam $17.95 (0-553-05262-4).** A third collection of memoirs and baseball anecdotes by the big league umpire. "Luciano's fans expect laughs, and he delivers."—BL (Rev: BL 5/15/88; LJ 6/1/88; NYTBR 5/15/88) **[796.357]**

3767 McCarthy, John P., Jr. *A Parent's Guide to Coaching Baseball.* **1989, Betterway paper $7.95 (1-55870-124-9).** A guide to teaching fundamental baseball skills for parents of little leaguers. (Rev: BL 11/15/89; LJ 1/90) **[796.357]**

3768 McIntosh, Ned. *Managing Little League Baseball.* **1985, Contemporary paper $9.95 (0-8092-5322-4).** A guide to effectively managing children's little league baseball. (Rev: BL 4/15/85; LJ 4/1/85) **[796.357]**

3769 Madden, Bill, and Moss Klein. *Damned Yankees: A No-Holds-Barred Account of Life with "Boss" Steinbrenner.* **1990, Warner $19.95 (0-446-**

51544-2). An account of the fate of the New York Yankees baseball team under the mismanagement of owner George Steinbrenner during the late 1970s and early 1980s. (Rev: NYTBR 4/1/90; Newsweek 4/16/90; PW 2/23/90) **[796.357]**

3770 Mantle, Mickey, and Herb Gluck. *The Mick.* **1987, Jove paper $3.95 (0-515-08599-5).** Memoirs of the former New York Yankee slugger's life and professional baseball career. (Rev: BL 6/1/85; LJ 7/85; Time 9/30/85) **[796.357]**

3771 Mantle, Mickey, and Phil Pepe. *My Favorite Summer, 1956.* **1991, Doubleday $18.95 (0-385-41261-4).** The former Yankee slugger recalls the 1956 major league baseball season. (Rev: BL 2/1/91; LJ 2/15/91; PW 2/1/91) **[796.357]**

3772 Miller, Marvin. *A Whole Different Ball Game: The Sport and Business of Baseball.* **1991, Carol Publg. Group $21.95 (1-55972-067-0).** A study of the business side of professional baseball as observed by the first executive director of the Major League Baseball Players Association. "A top sports book."—PW (Rev: BL 7/91; PW 5/24/91. Awards: BL, 1991) **[796.357]**

3773 Okrent, Daniel, and Steve Wuif. *Baseball Anecdotes.* **1989, Oxford Univ. Pr. $18.95 (0-19-504396-0).** A collection of famous and not-so-famous true baseball stories. (Rev: LJ 3/15/89; NYTBR 4/23/89; PW 2/17/89) **[796.357]**

3774 Pallone, Dave, and Alan Steinberg. *Behind the Mask: My Double Life in Baseball.* **1990, Viking $18.95 (0-670-83312-6).** Memoirs of a gay professional baseball umpire. (Rev: BL 5/1/90; LJ 7/90; NYTBR 7/22/90) **[796.357]**

3775 Peary, Danny, ed. *Cult Baseball Players: The Greats, the Flakes, the Weird and the Wonderful.* **1990, Simon & Schuster paper $10.95 (0-671-67172-3).** Selected pieces profiling the personalities and careers of some of baseball's great eccentrics and great players. (Rev: BL 1/1/90; LJ 1/12/90) **[796.357]**

3776 Reidenbaugh, Lowell. *Sporting News Selects Baseball's 25 Greatest Pennant Races.* **Ed. by Steve Zesch. 1988, Sporting News $19.95 (0-89204-280-X).** Accounts of the 25 most exciting baseball pennant races between the years 1904–1982. "Will lure any diamond fan worthy of the name."—PW (Rev: BL 12/1/87; LJ 10/1/87; PW 8/14/87) **[796.357]**

3777 Ritter, Lawrence S. *Glory of Their Times: The Story of the Early Days of Baseball Told by the Men Who Played It.* **1985, Random paper $7.95 (0-394-74106-4).** An oral history of American baseball prior to World War I based on interviews with 22 former players including Rube Marquand, Edd Roush, and Paul Waner. (Rev: BL 11/1/66; LJ 10/1/66; NYTBR 9/18/66) **[796.357]**

3778 Robinson, Frank, and Barry Stainback. *Extra Innings.* **1988, McGraw-Hill $16.95 (0-07-053183-8).** An autobiography of the baseball great focusing on reasons why so few African Americans hold positions of authority in the sport. "The most forthright sports volume in many years . . . certain to be talked about."—PW (REV: NYTBR 6/26/88; PW 4/22/88) **[796.357]**

3779   Robinson, Ray. *Home Run Heard 'Round the World: The Dramatic Story of the 1951 Giants-Dodgers Pennant Race.* **1991, HarperCollins $19.95 (0-06-016477-8).** An account of the dramatic 1951 National League pennant race decided by a ninth-inning home run in the third and final game of a playoff series. (REV: LJ 12/90; NYTBR 4/9/91) **[796.357]**

3780   Robinson, Ray. *Iron Horse: Lou Gehrig in His Time.* **1990, Norton $22.50 (0-393-02857-7).** A biography of the New York Yankees' first baseman who holds the professional baseball record for consecutive games played. (REV: BL 7/90; LJ 7/90; PW 6/15/90) **[796.357]**

3781   Rogosin, Donn. *Invisible Men: Life in Baseball's Negro Leagues.* **1985, Macmillan paper $9.95 (0-689-70687-1).** An illustrated history of African-American professional baseball in the United States and the Caribbean prior to Jackie Robinson's breaking of the sport's color barrier. (REV: BL 8/83; LJ 8/83; NYTBR 8/7/83) **[796.357]**

3782   Seidel, Michael. *Ted Williams: A Baseball Life.* **1991, Contemporary $19.95 (0-8092-4254-0).** A biography of the Boston Red Sox star of the 1940s and 1950s. "An accurate, evenhanded portrait."—LJ (REV: LJ 4/15/91; NYTBR 4/7/91) **[796.357]**

3783   Seymour, Harold. *Baseball: The People's Game.* **1990, Oxford Univ. Pr. $24.95 (0-19-503890-8); paper $12.95 (0-19-506907-2).** A history of nonprofessional baseball in the United States prior to the Second World War. (REV: Choice 10/90; LJ 7/90; NYRB 10/11/90) **[796.357]**

3784   Snider, Duke, and Bill Gilbert. *Duke of Flatbush.* **1988, Zebra $17.95 (0-8217-2469-X); paper $3.95 (0-8217-2698-6).** An autobiography of the former Brooklyn Dodger center fielder and member of baseball's Hall of Fame. (REV: NYTBR 7/17/88; PW 5/27/88) **[796.357]**

3785   Stout, Glenn, and Dick Johnson. *Ted Williams: A Portrait in Words and Pictures.* **1991, Walker $24.95 (0-8027-1140-5).** An illustrated tribute to the former Boston Red Sox slugger. (REV: LJ 5/1/91; NYTBR 4/7/91) **[796.357]**

3786   Sullivan, Neil J. *Minors: The Struggles and the Triumph of Baseball's Poor Relation from 1876 to the Present.* **1990, St. Martin's $19.95 (0-312-03864-X); paper $12.95 (0-312-05470-X).** The history and evolution of American minor league baseball. (REV: BL 3/1/90; LJ 3/1/90; NYTBR 6/24/90) **[796.357]**

3787   Talley, Rick. *Cubs of '69: Recollections of the Team That Should Have Been.* **1989, Contemporary $17.95 (0-8092-4501-9); paper $9.95 (0-8092-4156-0).** A look back at the Chicago Cubs baseball season of 1969 when they nearly won the National League pennant. "Even non-Cub fans will enjoy this lively, heartbreaking tale."—NYTBR (REV: BL 4/15/89; NYTBR 4/23/89) **[796.357]**

3788   Thorn, John, ed. *Armchair Book of Baseball.* **1985, Macmillan $19.95 (0-684-18462-6).** A collection of writings about baseball by over 60 contributors. "The ultimate baseball anthology."—LJ (REV: BL 11/1/85; LJ 10/15/85; Newsweek 11/25/85) **[796.357]**

3789   Thorn, John, and Bob Carroll. *Whole Baseball Catalog: The Ultimate Guide to the Baseball Marketplace.* **1990, Simon & Schuster paper $17.95 (0-671-68347-0).** An international compilation of baseball-related items. (REV: BL 3/1/90; LJ 2/15/90) **[796.357]**

3790   Tygiel, Jules. *Baseball's Great Experiment: Jackie Robinson and His Legacy.* **1983, Oxford Univ. Pr. $21.95 (0-19-503300-0); Random paper $9.95 (0-394-72593-X).** A history of the segregation and integration of African-American athletes into major league baseball from 1870 to 1959. (REV: Atl 8/83; LJ 7/83; Newsweek 8/15/83) **[796.357]**

3791   Whiting, Robert. *You Gotta Have Wa: When Two Cultures Collide on a Baseball Diamond.* **1989, Macmillan $17.95 (0-02-627661-5); Random paper $10.95 (0-679-72947-X).** A comparison of professional baseball in Japan and the United States. (REV: LJ 5/1/89; NYTBR 6/11/89; PW 4/14/89) **[796.357]**

3792   Will, George F. *Men at Work: The Craft of Baseball.* **1990, Macmillan $18.95 (0-02-628470-7); HarperCollins paper $9.95 (0-06-097372-2).** A study of the skills required in professional baseball by the political columnist. "A book for the serious baseball fan."—PW (REV: CSM 4/9/90; LJ 2/15/90; PW 2/23/90) **[796.357]**

3793   Wills, Maury, and Mike Celizic. *On the Run: The Never Dull and Often Shocking Life of Maury Wills.* **1991, Carroll & Graf $19.95 (0-88184-640-6).** An autobiography of the former Los Angeles Dodgers shortstop. "An irresistible read for the fan."—PW (REV: BL 4/15/91; PW 2/15/91) **[796.357]**

3794   Winegardner, Mark. *Prophet of the Sandlots: Journeys with a Major League Scout.* **1990, Atlantic Monthly $18.95 (0-87113-336-9); Prentice Hall paper $9.95 (0-13-726373-2).** Chronicle of the author's travels with a professional baseball scout in search of budding talent. (REV: BL 2/1/90; LJ 1/90; PW 12/8/89) **[796.357]**

3795   Winfield, Dave, and Tom Parker. *Winfield: A Player's Life.* **1988, Norton $16.95 (0-393-02467-9); Avon paper $4.50 (0-380-70709-8).** An autobiography of the baseball star covering his career up through his years as a New York Yankee. (REV: BL 4/15/88; LJ 4/15/88; NYTBR 4/24/88) **[796.357]**

3796   Zinsser, William. *Spring Training.* **1989, Harper & Row $16.95 (0-06-016059-4); Prentice Hall paper $8.95 (0-13-837899-1).** A look at the preseason training of the 1988 Pittsburgh Pirates baseball team in Bradenton, Florida. (REV: BL 4/1/89; LJ 4/15/89; NYTBR 4/23/89) **[796.357]**

Baseball—Miscellany

3797   Slocum, Frank. *Classic Baseball Cards: The Golden Years, 1886–1956.* **1987, Warner $79.95 (0-**

446-51392-X). An illustrated history of early baseball cards featuring over 9,000 actual-size reproductions. "The apotheosis of baseball book publishing."—NYTBR (Rev: BL 1/15/88; NYTBR 1/24/88)
[796.35702]

Running

3798   Baker, William J. *Jesse Owens: An American
Life.* 1986, Free Pr. $19.95 (0-02-901780-7); paper
$9.95 (0-02-901760-2). A biography of the African-
American athlete remembered for winning four
medals at the 1936 Berlin Olympic Games. (Rev:
Choice 1/87; CSM 8/29/86; LJ 6/1/86)   **[796.42]**

3799   Fixx, James F. *Complete Book of Running.*
1977, Random paper $18.95 (0-394-41159-5). The
physiology, practice, psychology, and health benefits of the sport of running. (Rev: Choice 4/78; LJ 10/1/
78; NYTBR 12/18/77)   **[796.42]**

3800   Harteis, Richard. *Marathon: A Story of Endur-
ance and Friendship.* 1989, Norton $18.95 (0-393-
02765-1). A memoir of the author's preparation to
run in the 1987 New York City Marathon and how
his friendship with poet and recent stroke victim
William Meredith helped give him inspiration.
(Rev: LJ 11/1/89; PW 9/15/89)   **[796.42]**

3801   Scott, Dave, and Liz Barrett. *Dave Scott's
Triathlon Training.* 1986, Simon & Schuster paper
$10.95 (0-671-60473-2). A nutrition and exercise
program for triathletes in training by a multi-
winner of the Ironman competition. (Rev: BL 12/1/
86; PW 7/18/86)   **[796.42]**

3802   Squires, Bill, and Raymond Krise. *Improving
Women's Running.* 1983, Greene paper $7.95 (0-
8289-0514-2). A handbook for women on methods of
improving running techniques and how to train for
competition. (Rev: BL 11/15/83; PW 7/22/83)   **[796.42]**

Outdoor life

3803   McManus, Patrick F. *Grasshopper Trap.* 1985,
Henry Holt $13.95 (0-03-000738-0); paper $6.95 (0-
8050-0111-5). A collection of 30 pieces regarding life
in the outdoors. "A writer who makes people laugh
out loud, hard."—NYTBR (Rev: BL 8/85; NYTBR 12/
15/85; PW 6/21/85)   **[796.5]**

Walking

3804   Fletcher, Colin. *Complete Walker III: The Joys
and Techniques of Hiking and Backpacking.* 1984,
Knopf $22.95 (0-394-51962-0); paper $16.95 (0-394-
72264-7). A handbook on hiking and backpacking
techniques and equipment. "The definitive manual
on the subject."—BL (Rev: BL 5/15/84; LJ 5/15/84;
NYTBR 6/3/84)   **[796.51]**

Mountaineering

3805   Blanchard, Smoke. *Walking Up and Down in
the World: Memories of a Mountain Rambler.*
1985, Sierra Club $15.95 (0-87156-827-6). A moun-
tain climber's recollections of his most notable
conquests. (Rev: LJ 1/85; PW 11/30/84)   **[796.522]**

3806   Bonington, Chris. *Mountaineer: Thirty Years
of Climbing on the World's Great Peaks.* 1990,
Sierra Club $29.95 (0-87156-618-4). The author re-
counts his experiences mountain climbing over a
period of four decades. (Rev: BL 5/1/90; PW 1/19/90)
[796.522]

3807   Curran, Jim. *K2: Triumph and Tragedy.* 1988,
Mountaineers $22.95 (0-89886-147-0); Houghton pa-
per$8.95 (0-395-48590-8). An account of the nine
expeditions that attempted to climb the world's
second highest mountain in 1986. "A gripping
story that belongs with the classics of moun-
taineering."—PW (Rev: LJ 2/15/88; NYTBR 4/30/89; PW
12/11/87)   **[796.522]**

3808   Gardiner, Steve. *Why I Climb: Personal Insights of Top Climbers; Robbins, Whittaker, Hill,
Sumner, Bonington, Lowe, and 23 Others.* 1990,
Stackpole paper $12.95 (0-8117-2321-6). Collected
portraits of nearly 30 notable twentieth-century
mountain climbers and their accomplishments.
(Rev: BL 5/1/90; LJ 5/1/90)   **[796.522]**

3809   Krakauer, Jon. *Eiger Dreams: Ventures
Among Men and Mountains.* 1990, Lyons & Burford $17.95 (1-55821-057-1). A collection of 12 essays
on mountain and rock climbing. "Thoughtful,
intelligent, and exciting work."—BL (Rev: BL 4/1/90;
NYTBR 6/10/90; PW 2/2/90)   **[796.522]**

3810   Sherwonit, Bill. *To the Top of Denali: Climbing Adventures on North America's Highest Peak.*
1990, Alaska Northwest paper $10.95 (0-88240-402-
4). Tales of the historic climbs of Alaska's Mt.
Denali from 1910 to the present. (Rev: BL 9/15/90; LJ
9/15/90)   **[796.522]**

Cycling and related activities

3811   Lemond, Greg, and Kent Gordis. *Greg
Lemond's Complete Book of Bicycling.* 1987, Putnam $22.95 (0-399-13229-5); paper $9.95 (0-399-51439-
2). A comprehensive look at the sport of bicycling
by the American Tour de France winner. "This is
the book for libraries needing one quality title on
bicycling."—BL (Rev: BL 10/1/87; LJ 7/87)   **[796.6]**

Automobile racing

3812   Henry, Alan. *Fifty Famous Motor Races.*
1988, Harper & Row $29.95 (0-85059-937-7). An
illustrated account of 50 of the greatest events in
automobile racing history. (Rev: BL 9/15/88; LJ 10/15/
88)   **[796.72]**

Boxing

3813   Anderson, Dave. *In the Corner: Great Boxing
Trainers Talk about Their Art.* 1991, Morrow
$20.00 (0-688-09446-5). Interviews with 12 boxing
trainers—including Angelo Dundee, Eddie Futch,
and Ray Arcel—about their craft, their relationships with the champions, and their most memorable bouts. "Ring fans will love this collection."—
PW (Rev: BL 4/1/91; LJ 4/1/91; PW 3/15/91)   **[796.83]**

3814   Berger, Phil. *Blood Season: Tyson and the
World of Boxing.* 1989, Morrow $18.95 (0-87795-962-

5). A biography of former heavyweight boxing champion Mike Tyson surveying the present state of the sport. "A valuable, clear-headed and much needed overview of the sport."—NYTBR (Rev: BL 7/89; LJ 6/15/89; NYTBR 8/20/89. Awards: BL, 1989) **[796.83]**

3815 Fried, Ronald K. *Corner Men: Great Boxing Trainers.* 1991, Four Walls Eight Windows $21.95 (0-941423-48-4). Collected profiles of boxing's greatest past and present trainers—including Jack Blackburn, the cornerman for Joe Louis, and the legendary Angelo Dundee, famous for assisting Muhammed Ali. (Rev: BL 4/1/91; LJ 4/1/91; NYTBR 5/12/91) **[796.83]**

3816 Hauser, Thomas. *Muhammed Ali: His Life and Times.* 1991, Simon & Schuster $24.95 (0-671-68892-8). A biography of the former world heavyweight boxing champion. "The first definitive biography."—NYTBR (Rev: BL 5/15/91; NYTBR 7/7/91) **[796.83]**

3817 Isenberg, Michael T. *John L. Sullivan and His America.* 1988, Univ. of Illinois Pr. $24.95 (0-252-01381-6). A portrait of the life and times of the nineteenth-century boxer generally recognized as the first world heavyweight champion. (Rev: Choice 6/88; LJ 3/15/88; TLS 7/15/88) **[796.83]**

3818 Liebling, A. J. *A Neutral Corner: Boxing Essays.* 1990, North Point $19.95 (0-86547-450-8). A collection of 15 essays culled from the *New Yorker* written during the 1950s and 1960s regarding the world of boxing. (Rev: BL 10/1/90; LJ 10/15/90; PW 8/31/90) **[796.83]**

3819 Oates, Joyce Carol. *On Boxing.* 1987, Doubleday $14.95 (0-385-23890-8); Zebra paper $3.95 (0-8217-2370-7). A survey of the sport of boxing by the author of *Them.* "A very good book . . . better than its subject."—NYTBR (Rev: LJ 1/87; NYTBR 3/15/87; Newsweek 3/9/87) **[796.83]**

3820 Oates, Joyce Carol, and Daniel Halpern, eds. *Reading the Fights: The Best Writing about the Most Controversial Sport.* 1988, Henry Holt $17.95 (0-8050-0510-2); Prentice Hall paper $9.95 (0-13-761149-3). Over 20 essays regarding the "sweet science" by such writers as Norman Mailer, George Plimpton, and A. J. Liebling. (Rev: LJ 2/1/88; PW 12/18/87) **[796.83]**

3821 Torres, Jose. *Fire and Fear: The Inside Story of Mike Tyson.* 1990, Warner paper $4.95 (0-446-21042-7). A profile of the heavyweight boxer and his life inside and outside the ring. (Rev: BL 7/89; NYTBR 7/30/89. Awards: BL, 1989) **[796.83]**

Ice hockey

3822 Dryden, Ken. *Game: A Thoughtful and Provocative Look at a Life in Hockey.* 1984, Penguin paper $6.95 (0-14-007412-0). Memoirs of the former Montreal Canadiens goalkeeper's career in professional ice hockey. (Rev: BL 11/15/83; LJ 11/15/83; PW 10/21/83) **[796.96]**

3823 Plimpton, George. *Open Net.* 1987, Penguin paper $6.95 (0-14-009709-0). An account of the author's preparation for a brief stint as a goaltender in an exhibition game for the Boston Bruins ice hockey team. (Rev: LJ 12/85; NYTBR 11/24/85; TLS 9/5/86) **[796.96]**

797 Aquatic and air sports

Boating

3824 Stapleton, Sid. *Stapleton's Powerboat Bible.* 1989, Morrow $22.95 (0-688-08448-6). A guide to the selection, purchase, and accessorizing of large power boats. (Rev: BL 10/15/89; LJ 11/1/89) **[797.1]**

Canoeing

3825 Kimber, Robert. *A Canoeist's Sketchbook.* 1991, Chelsea Green $21.95 (0-930031-50-4); paper $12.95 (0-930031-45-8). Essays on the author's experiences canoeing the American Northeast and eastern Canada. (Rev: BL 10/15/91; LJ 9/15/91) **[797.122]**

3826 Riviere, Bill. *Open Canoe.* 1985, Little, Brown paper $12.95 (0-316-74768-8). An illustrated introduction to the sport of canoeing. (Rev: BL 8/85; LJ 7/85) **[797.122]**

3827 Starkell, Don. *Paddle to the Amazon.* 1989, Prima $19.95 (0-914629-91-3). An account of the two-year, 12,000-mile canoe voyage made by the author and his sons from Winnipeg to Belem. (Rev: BL 7/89; LJ 7/89; PW 6/9/89) **[797.122]**

Sailboating

3828 Johnson, Peter. *Sail Magazine Book of Sailing.* 1989, Random $40.00 (0-394-57457-5). Illustrated history and guidebook to sailing from the seventeenth to the twentieth century. (Rev: BL 10/1/89; LJ 10/15/89) **[797.124]**

798 Equestrian sports and animal racing

Riding

3829 Gordon, Sally. *Rider's Handbook.* 1980, Putnam $19.95 (0-399-12556-6). An illustrated introduction to the styles and techniques of horseback riding. (Rev: BL 11/15/80; CSM 12/8/80) **[798.23]**

3830 Gordon-Watson, Mary. *Handbook of Riding.* 1982, Knopf $22.50 (0-394-52110-2). An instruction guide to the art of horseback riding by a former equestrian Olympic Gold Medalist. (Rev: BL 2/15/83; LJ 2/15/83) **[798.23]**

Horse racing

3831 Barich, Bill. *Laughing in the Hills.* 1981, Penguin paper $6.95 (0-14-005832-X). Memoirs of the author's experiences playing the horses and investigating the inner workings of a California racetrack. (Rev: BL 5/1/80; LJ 5/1/80; NYTBR 6/15/80) **[798.4]**

3832 Gifford, Barry. *A Day at the Races: The Education of a Racetracker.* 1988, Atlantic

Monthly $17.95 (0-87113-195-1). An inside view of the workings of a contemporary racetrack based on interviews conducted by the novelist. (REV: BL 5/1/88; LJ 5/15/88; PW 4/8/88)   **[798.4]**

3833 Stephens, Woody, and James Brough. *Guess I'm Lucky: Woody Stephens' Own Story.* **1987, Penguin paper $3.95 (0-14-010277-9).** An autobiography of the thoroughbred horse trainer whose career in horse racing spanned 40 years. (REV: LJ 11/15/85; PW 10/11/85)   **[798.4]**

799 Fishing, hunting, shooting

Fishing

3834 Camuto, Christopher. *Fly Fisherman's Blue Ridge.* **1990, Henry Holt $19.95 (0-8050-1466-7).** A journal detailing the author's fishing experiences in Virginia and the Carolinas. (REV: LJ 11/1/90; NYTBR 1/6/91; PW 9/28/90)   **[799.1]**

3835 Cole, John. *Tarpon Quest.* **1991, Lyons & Burford $16.95 (1-55821-097-0).** An account of the author's experiences fishing for tarpon off the Florida Keys. (REV: BL 3/15/91; NYTBR 6/9/91; PW 3/1/91)   **[799.1]**

3836 Fling, Paul N., and Donald L. Puterbaugh. *Fly-Fisherman's Primer.* **1985, Sterling paper $9.95 (0-8069-7890-2).** An introduction to the sport of fly-fishing. "This excellent introduction goes a long way toward making fly-fishing less daunting and more enjoyable."—BL (REV: BL 7/85; LJ 7/85) **[799.1]**

3837 Gierach, John. *Sex, Death and Fly-Fishing.* **1990, Simon & Schuster $19.95 (0-671-70738-8); paper $8.95 (0-671-68437-X).** Ruminations on various aspects of life and fly-fishing. "A treat for anglers and admirers of good writing."—BL (REV: BL 8/90; LJ 5/15/90)   **[799.1]**

3838 Gierach, John. *View from Rat Lake.* **1988, Simon & Schuster $17.95 (0-87108-743-X); paper $8.95 (0-671-67581-8).** Thirteen essays regarding fly fishing by the author of *Trout Bum.* "One of the wittiest and most articulate fishing writers."—LJ (REV: BL 3/1/88; LJ 2/1/88; PW 1/22/88)   **[799.1]**

3839 Gierach, John. *Where the Trout Are All as Long as Your Leg.* **1991, Lyons & Burford $15.95 (1-55821-098-9).** The author of *Sex, Death and Fly Fishing* discusses his favorite Colorado and Montana fishing spots. (REV: BL 2/1/91; LJ 2/15/91; NYTBR 6/9/91)   **[799.1]**

3840 Gingrich, Arnold. *Well-Tempered Angler.* **1987, NAL paper $8.95 (0-452-26008-6).** Musings on

the art and experience of fishing by the former *Esquire* editor. (REV: BL 12/1/65; LJ 9/15/65)   **[799.1]**

3841 Hersey, John. *Blues.* **1988, Random paper $6.95 (0-394-75702-5).** The American writer recounts the pleasures of fishing for, catching, and eating bluefish. (REV: Atl 7/87; NYTBR 5/31/87; Time 5/25/87)   **[799.1]**

3842 Lyons, Nick. *Confessions of a Fly-Fishing Addict.* **1989, Simon & Schuster paper $8.95 (0-671-67653-9).** A collection of nearly 50 of the author's columns from *Fly Fishing* magazine. (REV: BL 6/15/89; LJ 5/15/89; PW 5/5/89)   **[799.1]**

3843 Montgomery, M. R. *Way of the Trout: An Essay on Anglers, Wild Fish and Running Water.* **1991, Knopf $22.00 (0-394-58063-2).** A survey of tactics and strategies of fly fishing for trout intermingled with the author's personal reminiscences on the sport. "One of the most graceful and humane books on the subject in several years."— LJ (REV: BL 5/1/91; LJ 5/15/91)   **[799.1]**

3844 Paugh, Tom, ed. *Sports Afield Treasury of Fly Fishing.* **1989, Lyons & Burford $19.95 (1-55821-037-7).** An anthology of 52 essays from *Sports Afield* regarding fly fishing collected from the late 1800s to the present. (REV: BL 11/15/89; LJ 10/15/89) **[799.1]**

3845 Wetherell, W. D. *Upland Stream: Notes on the Fishing Passion.* **1991, Little, Brown $19.95 (0-316-93172-1).** Essays on fly fishing on the North American continent. "Will hit the soul of anyone who has spent any time in piscatorial pursuits."—BL (REV: BL 3/1/91; NYTBR 6/9/91; PW 2/15/91)   **[799.1]**

Hunting

3846 Kilgo, James. *Deep Enough for Ivorybills.* **1988, Algonquin $14.95 (0-912697-71-7); Doubleday paper $7.95 (0-385-26014-8).** An account of the author's hunting and fishing experiences and his enjoyment of nature and the outdoors. (REV: LJ 4/1/88; NYTBR 4/24/88; PW 3/11/88)   **[799.2]**

3847 Ortega y Gasset, Jose. *Meditations on Hunting.* **1986, Macmillan paper $9.95 (0-684-18630-6).** Reflections on hunting by the Spanish philosopher. (REV: Atl 7/72; New Yorker 7/22/72; PW 5/1/72)   **[799.2]**

3848 Walker, Tom. *Shadows on the Tundra: Alaskan Tales of Predator, Prey, and Man.* **1990, Stackpole $19.95 (0-8117-1724-0).** A guide to the wildlife of Alaska written by a guide with 25 years' experience. (REV: BL 1/15/90; LJ 12/89; PW 12/8/89)   **[799.2]**

800 LITERATURE AND RHETORIC

3849 Calvino, Italo. *Uses of Literature: Essays.* **1986, Harcourt $17.95 (0-15-193205-0); paper $8.95 (0-15-693250-4).** Collected essays of literary criticism and the applications of literature by the Italian writer. (Rev: BL 9/1/86; LJ 9/15/86; PW 9/19/86)　　**[800]**

801 Philosophy and theory

3850 Booth, Wayne C. *Company We Keep: An Ethics of Fiction.* **1988, Univ. of California Pr. $29.95 (0-520-06203-5).** An examination of the ways we find both positive and negative role models and behavioral patterns through fictional characters. (Rev: Choice 5/89; LJ 11/15/88; NYTBR 1/22/89)　　**[801]**

Criticism

3851 Poirier, Richard. *Renewal of Literature: Emersonian Reflections.* **1987, Random $19.95 (0-394-50140-3); Yale Univ. Pr. paper $10.95 (0-300-04086-5).** A tracing of the influence of Emerson and modernism upon subsequent writers. (Rev: BL 3/1/87; New Rep 4/27/87; PW 1/16/87)　　**[801.95]**

808 Rhetoric and collections of literature

3852 Barthes, Roland. *Lover's Discourse: Fragments.* **1978, Hill & Wang paper $8.95 (0-8090-1388-6).** A study of love and the language that surrounds it by the French semioticist. (Rev: CSM 1/10/79; LJ 8/78; Sat Rev 9/2/78)　　**[808]**

3853 Bradbury, Ray. *Zen in the Art of Writing.* **1990, J. Odell $18.95 (1-877741-02-7); paper $8.95 (1-877741-01-9).** Essays on the author's work and the creative process behind writing. (Rev: BL 1/1/90; LJ 4/1/90; PW 1/26/90)　　**[808]**

3854 Coles, Robert. *Call of Stories: Teaching and the Moral Imagination.* **1990, Houghton $18.95 (0-395-42935-8); paper $8.95 (0-395-52815-1).** The child psychiatrist explores the role and uses of fiction in the teaching of ethics and morality. (Rev: BL 1/15/89; LJ 3/1/89; NYTBR 2/26/89)　　**[808]**

3855 Edel, Leon. *Writing Lives: Principia Biographica.* **1984, Norton $15.95 (0-393-01882-2).** Ten essays regarding the art of writing biographies by the biographer of Willa Cather, Henry David Thoreau, and, most notably, Henry James. (Rev: BL 10/1/84; LJ 9/1/84; NYTBR 10/28/84)　　**[808]**

3856 Goldberg, Natalie. *Wild Mind: Living the Writer's Life.* **1990, Bantam $8.95 (0-553-34775-6).** The author's memoirs form the background for this guide to writing and developing writing skills. "An inspiring, inspired work."—BL (Rev: BL 10/1/90; LJ 10/1/90)　　**[808]**

3857 Heilbrun, Carolyn G. *Writing a Woman's Life.* **1988, Norton $14.95 (0-393-02601-9); Ballantine paper $6.95 (0-345-36256-X).** An examination of traditional and innovative methods of writing women's biographies and autobiographies. (Rev: LJ 10/15/88; NYTBR 1/8/89)　　**[808]**

3858 Higgins, George V. *On Writing: Advice for Those Who Write to Publish (Or Would Like To).* **1990, Henry Holt $19.95 (0-8050-1180-3).** A guide to developing marketable writing skills by the author of *The Friends of Eddie Coyle.* (Rev: Atl 7/90; BL 6/1/90; LJ 6/1/90. Awards: BL, 1990)　　**[808]**

3859 Jacobi, Peter. *Magazine Article: How to Think It, Plan It, Write It.* **1991, Writer's Digest $17.95 (0-89879-450-1).** A handbook for writers seeking publication in magazines. "An excellent how-to, guaranteed to satisfy requests from would-be authors."—BL (Rev: BL 2/1/91; LJ 2/15/91)　　**[808]**

3860 Kilpatrick, James J. *Writer's Art.* **1985, Andrews & McMeel paper $9.95 (0-8362-7925-5).** A primer on the art of writing properly and forcefully. (Rev: CSM 9/12/84; LJ 6/15/84; NYTBR 8/26/84)　　**[808]**

3861 Pachter, Marc, ed. *Telling Lives: The Biographer's Art.* **1981, Univ. of Pennsylvania Pr. paper $12.95 (0-8122-1118-9).** Essays by prominent biographers including Barbara Tuchman, Doris Kearns, and Justin Kaplan regarding their craft. (Rev: Choice 11/79; LJ 4/1/79; NYTBR 5/13/79)　　**[808]**

3862 Pitzer, Sara. *How to Write a Cookbook and Get It Published.* **1984, Writer's Digest $15.95 (0-89879-132-4).** Advice on the writing, publication, and marketing of cookbooks. (Rev: BL 6/15/84; LJ 6/1/84)　　**[808]**

3863 Steiner, George. *On Difficulty and Other Essays.* 1978, Oxford Univ. Pr. $21.95 (0-19-212208-8); paper $9.95 (0-19-52022-8). Essays regarding literature and language by the French-born economist and linguist. "A shrewd and essential collection that can be recommended without reservations."—BL (Rev: BL 1/1/79; Choice 5/79; CSM 4/6/79) **[808]**

3864 Williams, Joseph M. *Style: Toward Clarity and Grace.* 1990, Univ. of Chicago Pr. $17.95 (0-226-89914-4). A manual for writers on the development of style. (Rev: BL 11/1/90; LJ 11/15/90) **[808]**

Rhetoric of poetry

3865 Gibbons, Reginald, ed. *Poet's Work: 29 Poets on the Origins and Practice of Their Art.* 1989, Univ. of Chicago Pr. paper $12.95 (0-226-29054-9). An anthology of essays by 29 prominent modern poets regarding their work and the creative process. (Rev: BL 6/1/79; LJ 5/15/79; NYTBR 10/21/79) **[808.1]**

Rhetoric of fiction

3866 Gardner, John. *On Becoming a Novelist.* 1984, Harper & Row paper $8.95 (0-06-091126-3). Advice on the art of writing the novel and becoming a professional. "Superbly written, thoroughly original, eminently useful."—Choice (Rev: BL 5/15/83; Choice 11/83; LJ 4/15/83) **[808.3]**

3867 McCormack, Thomas. *Fiction Editor, the Novel and the Novelist.* 1988, St. Martin's $12.95 (0-312-02209-3). An editor's analysis of the role the editor plays in the creative process of the writing of fiction. (Rev: BL 2/15/89; LJ 3/1/89) **[808.3]**

3868 Nin, Anais. *Novel of the Future.* 1986, Ohio State Univ. Pr. paper $10.95 (0-8040-0879-5). A study of symbolism and the modern novel by the author of *The Diary of Anais Nin.* (Rev: CSM 1/14/69; LJ 11/15/68) **[808.3]**

Rhetoric of speech

3869 Cook, Jeff Scott. *Elements of Speechwriting and Public Speaking.* 1990, Macmillan $17.95 (0-02-527791-X). A guide to preparing and delivering effective public presentations. "A superior guide."—BL (Rev: BL 1/15/90; LJ 1/90) **[808.5]**

3870 Jamieson, Kathleen Hall. *Eloquence in an Electronic Age: The Transformation of Political Speech Making.* 1988, Oxford Univ. Pr. $24.95 (0-19-505539-X). An analysis of the history of American political speeches and public speaking focusing on changes brought about by technologies of the past 30 years. (Rev: Choice 1/89; CSM 8/10/88; NYTBR 10/30/88) **[808.5]**

Conversation

3871 Glass, Lillian. *Say It . . . Right: How to Talk in Any Social or Business Situation.* 1991, Putnam $18.95 (0-399-13588-X). A guide to improving interpersonal communications in a variety of situations. (Rev: BL 1/1/91; LJ 12/90) **[808.56]**

Collections of literary texts from more than one literature

3872 Fussell, Paul, ed. *Norton Book of Modern War.* 1990, Norton $24.95 (0-393-02909-3). A collection of twentieth-century writings on war. (Rev: BL 11/15/90; LJ 10/15/90) **[808.8]**

3873 Plimpton, George, ed. *Paris Review Anthology.* 1990, Norton $25.00 (0-393-02769-4). Selected fiction and poetry from nearly 30 years of the *Paris Review* magazine. (Rev: BL 3/15/90; LJ 3/1/90; PW 1/26/90) **[808.8]**

Collections of poetry

3874 Keenan, Deborah, and Roseann Lloyd, eds. *Looking for Home: Women Writing about Exile.* 1990, Milkweed Editions paper $11.95 (0-951943-45-X). A collection of women's poems concerning the experience of living in a foreign land. (Rev: BL 9/15/90; NYTBR 11/25/90; PW 8/17/90) **[808.81]**

809 Literary history and criticism

3875 Achebe, Chinua. *Hopes and Impediments: Selected Essays.* 1989, Doubleday $17.95 (0-385-24730-3); paper $9.95 (0-385-41479-X). Selected essays from a quarter-century of the Nigerian writer's career. (Rev: BL 10/15/89; NYTBR 11/12/89; TLS 9/23/88) **[809]**

3876 Auden, W. H. *Forewords and Afterwords.* 1973, Random $19.95 (0-394-483559-6); paper $12.95 (0-679-72485-0). A collection of literary criticism and short pieces by Auden, written between 1943 and 1972. (Rev: Choice 6/73; CSM 4/18/73; Newsweek 3/19/73) **[809]**

3877 Birkerts, Sven. *An Artificial Wilderness: Essays on 20th-Century Literature.* 1987, Morrow $20.95 (0-688-07113-9); Godine paper $14.95 (0-87923-807-0). Collected essays by the literary critic analyzing the work of major figures in contemporary world literature. (Rev: BL 10/15/87; LJ 10/15/87; NYTBR 11/8/87) **[809]**

3878 Dupee, F. W. *King of the Cats: And Other Remarks on Writers and Writing.* 1985, Univ. of Chicago Pr. $28.00 (0-226-17286-4); paper $12.50 (0-226-17287-2). Collected literary criticism on writers, their works, and the art of writing. (Rev: LJ 5/15/65; NYRB 8/5/65; NYTBR 6/27/85) **[809]**

3879 Gass, William H. *World Within the Word: Essays.* 1979, Godine paper $11.95 (0-87923-298-6). Collected essays of literary criticism and other topics by the writer and novelist. "He demonstrates a finer subtlety and as great a cogency as any critic now writing."—New Rep (Rev: CSM 7/24/78; LJ 5/1/78; New Rep 5/20/78) **[809]**

3880 Howe, Irving. *Celebrations and Attacks: Thirty Years of Literary and Cultural Commentary.* 1980, Harcourt paper $4.95 (0-15-616248-2). Collected essays of the American writer regarding twentieth-century culture and literature. (Rev: New Rep 6/2/79; NYRB 11/8/79; NYTBR 3/11/79) **[809]**

3881 Kakutani, Michiko. *Poet at the Piano: Portraits of Writers, Filmmakers and Performers at Work.* **1988, Random $18.95 (0-8129-1277-2); Bedrick paper $8.95 (0-87226-210-3).** Thirty-five interviews regarding the lives and works of such individuals as Milan Kundera, Joan Didion, Saul Bellow, and Steven Spielberg. (REV: BL 7/88; LJ 8/88; PW 5/20/88) **[809]**

3882 Levin, Harry. *Playboys and Killjoys: An Essay on the Theory and Practice of Comedy.* **1987, Oxford Univ. Pr. $21.95 (0-19-504856-3).** An analysis of comedy as a form of drama from the ancient Greeks to the twentieth century. (REV: Choice 6/87; LJ 11/15/86; NYTBR 3/8/87) **[809]**

3883 McCarthy, Mary. *Writing on the Wall and Other Literary Essays.* **1971, Harcourt paper $4.95 (0-15-698390-7).** A collection of 13 essays of literary criticism. "As waspish, fresh, engaging and occasionally as profound as ever."—LJ (REV: Choice 9/70; CSM 3/12/70; LJ 2/15/70) **[809]**

3884 Mallon, Thomas. *Book of One's Own: People and Their Diaries.* **1986, Penguin paper $7.95 (0-14-008665-X).** A study of diaries as a form of literature with over 100 examples from the past four centuries. (REV: Choice 3/85; NYTBR 3/31/85; New Yorker 1/21/85) **[809]**

3885 Milosz, Czeslaw. *Land of Ulro.* **1984, Farrar $17.95 (0-374-18323-6); paper $9.95 (0-374-51937-4).** The 1981 Nobel Prize winner for Literature discusses his intellectual development and the decline of European civilization over the past two centuries. (REV: BL 9/1/84; LJ 9/1/84; NYTBR 9/2/84) **[809]**

3886 Olsen, Tillie. *Silences.* **1984, Peter Smith $17.75 (0-8446-6091-4); Dell paper $9.95 (0-440-55011-4).** An exploration of the societal pressures writers, particularly women writers, face which make them unable to write or publish their works. (REV: Choice 12/78; LJ 8/78; NYTBR 7/30/78) **[809]**

3887 Ozick, Cynthia. *Metaphor and Memory: Essays.* **1989, Knopf $19.95 (0-394-56625-4).** Essays of literary criticism and remembrances mix in this collection by the author of *The Shawl.* (REV: BL 4/15/89; LJ 4/1/89; NYTBR 4/23/89) **[809]**

3888 Pritchett, V. S. *A Man of Letters: Selected Essays.* **1986, Random $19.95 (0-394-54982-1).** Fifty essays regarding English, American, and European literature from the seventeenth to twentieth centuries. (REV: BL 6/1/86; CSM 7/9/86; New Yorker 6/9/86) **[809]**

3889 Pritchett, V. S. *Myth Makers: Essays on European Novelists, Including Russian, Spanish and French.* **1979, Random $11.95 (0-394-50472-0).** Literary essays on various non-English or American writers including Tolstoy, Flaubert, Borges, and Garcia Marquez. (REV: BL 5/15/79; Choice 10/79; LJ 4/15/79. AWARDS: ALA, 1979) **[809]**

3890 Rosenfeld, Alvin H. *A Double Dying: Reflections on Holocaust Literature.* **1980, Indiana Univ. Pr. $27.50 (0-253-13337-8); paper $9.95 (0-253-20492-5).** A study of holocaust literature in the form of plays, memoirs, novels, diaries, and poetry examining the approach of writers to the subject. (REV: BL 7/15/80; Choice 9/80; LJ 3/15/80) **[809]**

3891 Russ, Joanna. *How to Suppress Women's Writing.* **1983, Univ. of Texas Pr. paper $7.95 (0-292-72445-4).** A study of past and present prejudice against women's literature by the noted science-fiction writer. (REV: Atl 11/83; Choice 1/84; LJ 11/15/83) **[809]**

3892 Sontag, Susan. *Against Interpretation: And Other Essays.* **1978, Hippocrene $20.50 (0-87052-352-X); Farrar paper $8.95 (0-374-52040-2).** A selection of 26 essays on a myriad of topics including film, literature, drama, and psychology. "A stimulating and avant-garde potpourri."—BL (REV: BL 3/1/66; LJ 2/1/66; Sat Rev 2/12/66. AWARDS: ALA, 1966) **[809]**

3893 Sontag, Susan. *Illness as Metaphor.* **1978, Farrar paper $5.95 (0-374-17443-1).** An extended essay comparing the psychological and social ramifications of disease as exemplified by tuberculosis in the nineteenth century and by cancer in our own. "A work of brilliance and conviction."—Choice (REV: Choice 12/78; LJ 6/1/78; New Rep 7/8/78. AWARDS: ALA, 1978) **[809]**

Critical appraisal of poetry

3894 Brodsky, Joseph. *Less Than One: Selected Essays.* **1986, Farrar $30.00 (0-374-18503-4); paper $12.95 (0-374-52055-0).** The first collection of essays by the exiled Russian poet to be published in the West. "Russian literature has not had a better ambassador to the West since Nabokov."—NYTBR (REV: CSM 3/28/86; NYTBR 7/13/86; PW 3/28/86. AWARDS: PW, 1986) **[809.1]**

3895 Eberhart, Richard. *Of Poetry and Poets.* **1979, Univ. of Illinois Pr. $24.95 (0-252-00630-5).** An analysis of twentieth-century verse and poets by the American Modernist writer. (REV: BL 5/1/79; LJ 3/15/79; NYTBR 7/8/79) **[809.1]**

3896 Hass, Robert. *Twentieth Century Pleasures: Prose on Poetry.* **1984, Ecco Pr. $17.95 (0-88001-045-2).** A collection of critical essays concerning poetry and poets of this century. "As a demonstration of the critic's craft, this collection is, both in substance and style, an exemplary volume."—BL (REV: BL 3/15/84; LJ 4/1/84; NYRB 11/7/85. AWARDS: LJ, 1984) **[809.1]**

3897 Lowell, Robert. *Collected Prose.* **1987, Farrar $25.00 (0-374-12625-9).** The prose writings of the noted American poet. "*Collected Prose*, full of inspired insights, reveals an electric and energetic mind."—Natl Rev (REV: Natl Rev 8/14/87; New Rep 3/30/87; NYTBR 7/12/87. AWARDS: LJ, 1987) **[809.1]**

3898 Roethke, Theodore. *On the Poet and His Craft: Selected Prose of Theodore Roethke.* **1965, Univ. of Washington Pr. paper $7.95 (0-295-74003-5).** Essays by the American poet on poetry—his own and that of others. "Perhaps all we shall ever learn from him about his attentions as a poet."—Choice

(Rev: Choice 10/65; CSM 9/16/65; Sat Rev 7/31/65. Awards: ALA, 1965)   **[809.1]**

Critical appraisal of drama

3899   **Brustein, Robert.** *Who Needs Theatre: Dramatic Opinions.* 1990, Atlantic Monthly paper $12.95 (0-87113-365-2). Essays on the American theater by the artistic director of the American Repertory Theatre. "A consummate volume . . . to be read and reread as the years go by."—BL (Rev: BL 10/1/87; LJ 9/15/87; NYTBR 9/20/87)   **[809.2]**

3900   **Kermode, Frank.** *Uses of Error: Selected Essays.* 1991, Harvard Univ. Pr. $24.95 (0-674-93152-1). Forty-four essays regarding aspects of literature by the English critic. (Rev: LJ 2/1/91; NYTBR 4/28/91)   **[809.2]**

3901   **Kerr, Walter.** *Tragedy and Comedy.* 1985, Da Capo paper $9.95 (0-306-80249-X). A look at the history and evolvement of the two primary forms of drama. "The most considerable volume of dramatic criticism and the principles that are behind it to be written by any modern dramatist in America."—LJ (Rev: BL 6/15/67; CSM 5/25/67; LJ 4/14/67. Awards: ALA, 1967)   **[809.2]**

Critical appraisal of fiction

3902   **Gass, William H.** *Fiction and the Figures of Life.* 1978, Godine paper $11.95 (0-87923-254-4). Essays of literary criticism about the art of writing. "A brilliant excursion into the essence of writing as a form of thought."—Choice (Rev: Choice 5/71; LJ 10/1/70; NYTBR 2/21/71)   **[809.3]**

3903   **Kundera, Milan.** *Art of the Novel.* 1987, Grove-Weidenfeld $17.95 (0-8021-0011-2); Harper & Row paper $7.95 (0-06-097204-1). The Czech author of *The Unbearable Lightness of Being* presents a collection of essays discussing novels, novelists, and the art of novel writing. (Rev: LJ 4/1/88; New Rep 3/21/88; NYTBR 4/13/88)   **[809.3]**

3904   **Lem, Stanislaw.** *Microworlds: Writings on Science Fiction and Fantasy.* 1986, Harcourt paper $5.95 (0-15-659443-9). A collection of essays highly critical of the literary quality of most contemporary science fiction. (Rev: Choice 6/85; LJ 2/1/85; NYTBR 3/24/85)   **[809.3]**

3905   **McCormack, Thomas.** *After Words: Novelists on Their Novels.* 1988, St. Martin's paper $9.95 (0-312-01382-5). Essays by authors of fiction on the writing process. Includes Truman Capote, Anthony Burgess, Norman Mailer, and Wright Morris. (Rev: LJ 1/1/69; NYTBR 3/2/69; Time 2/14/69)   **[809.3]**

3906   **Robbe-Grillet, Alain.** *For a New Novel: Essays on Fiction.* 1965, Ayer $17.00 (0-8369-1844-4); Northwestern Univ. Pr. paper $9.95 (0-8101-0821-6). A selection of literary criticism and theory by the French novelist. "A significant and challenging collection of essays."—LJ (Rev: Choice 6/66; LJ 3/1/66; NYTBR 4/3/66. Awards: NYTBR, 1966)   **[809.3]**

3907   **Roth, Philip.** *Reading Myself and Others.* 1975, Farrar $8.95 (0-374-24753-6); Penguin paper

$6.95 (0-14-007681-6). A series of essays and interviews by Roth assessing his work and creative processes in a volume also containing his views on other literary figures. (Rev: BL 6/1/75; LJ 5/15/75; PW 4/7/75)   **[809.3]**

3908   **Symons, Julian.** *Bloody Murder: From the Detective Story to the Crime Novel.* 1985, Viking $14.95 (0-670-80096-1); paper $6.95 (0-14-007263-2). A survey of the history and evolution of mystery, detective, and crime fiction. (Rev: BL 7/85; CSM 8/16/85; LJ 8/85)   **[809.3]**

3909   **West, Paul.** *Sheer Fiction.* 1987, McPherson $17.95 (0-914232-82-7). Literary essays and book reviews on twentieth-century literature by the author of *Rat Man of Paris.* (Rev: LJ 6/1/87; NYTBR 8/9/87; PW 3/13/87)   **[809.3]**

Critical appraisal of science fiction

3910   **Aldiss, Brian, and David Wingrove.** *Trillion Year Spree: The History of Science Fiction.* 1988, Avon paper $9.95 (0-380-70461-7). A history of science fiction from its beginnings through 1985 by a British master of the genre. (Rev: BL 11/15/86; LJ 11/15/86; TLS 10/31/86)   **[809.387]**

Critical appraisal of satire and humor

3911   **Redfern, Walter.** *Puns.* 1986, Basil Blackwell paper $12.95 (0-631-14909-0). A historical survey of puns and their linguistic uses. "A delightful book for anyone who loves language, literature or wordplay."—PW (Rev: CSM 4/10/85; NYTBR 2/17/85; PW 2/1/85)   **[809.7]**

810   AMERICAN LITERATURE IN ENGLISH

3912   **Baker, Houston A., Jr.** *Modernism and the Harlem Renaissance.* 1987, Univ. of Chicago Pr. $19.95 (0-226-03524-7). A tracing of modernist themes in the African-American literature of the early twentieth century. "A brilliant and important book."—PW (Rev: LJ 10/15/87; NYTBR 10/4/87; PW 8/28/87)   **[810]**

3913   **Cowley, Malcolm.** *Flower and the Leaf: A Contemporary Record of American Writing Since 1941.* Ed. by Donald W. Faulkner. 1986, Penguin paper $7.95 (0-14-007733-2). A collection of essays of literary criticism culled from the last four decades of Cowley's work. "The lucidity and economy of his prose . . . make even the oldest pieces seem fresh."—PW (Rev: CSM 5/1/85; LJ 12/84; PW 12/14/84)   **[810]**

3914   **Dardis, Tom.** *Some Time in the Sun: The Hollywood Years of F. Scott Fitzgerald, William Faulkner, Nathanael West, Adlous Huxley and James Agee.* 1989, Limelight paper $12.95 (0-87910-116-4). The Hollywood screenwriting careers of some of the top literary figures of our century. "Well worth reading for anyone interested in American literature, the economics of American authorship, or motion pictures."—Choice (Rev: Choice 12/76; NYTBR 8/8/76; PW 5/3/76)   **[810]**

3915 Donoghue, Denis. *Reading America: Essays on American Literature.* **1987, Knopf $22.95 (0-394-55939-8); Univ. of California Pr. paper $10.95 (0-520-06424-0).** Twenty-seven pieces by the Irish literary critic regarding American writers and their works. "The perfect book for those who want insight into American literature without pedantry."—LJ (Rev: LJ 9/15/87; NYTBR 9/27/87; PW 7/31/87)   **[810]**

3916 Epstein, Joseph. *Plausible Prejudices: Essays on American Writing.* **1985, Norton $17.95 (0-393-01918-7).** The editor of the *American Scholar* gives reasons for what he perceives as the general decline in quality of American literature in these essays on a variety of literary figures. (Rev: CSM 4/17/85; NYTBR 2/24/85; PW 1/11/85)   **[810]**

3917 Kazin, Alfred. *An American Procession: The Major American Writers from 1830 to 1930, the Crucial Century.* **1984, Knopf $18.95 (0-394-50378-3).** Survey of American literature from Emerson to Fitzgerald. "A refresher in the best sense: without any fundamental revision of our understanding of our classics, it vivaciously refreshes our awareness of them, and our gratitude for them."—New Yorker (Rev: NYTBR 5/13/84; New Yorker 6/18/84; Newsweek 5/21/84. Awards: LJ, 1984)   **[810]**

3918 Kazin, Alfred. *A Writer's America: Landscape in Literature.* **1988, Knopf $24.95 (0-394-57142-8).** An analysis of the role and impact of the American landscape and natural surroundings upon American writers and their works. (Rev: BL 9/15/88; LJ 10/1/88; NYTBR 10/23/88)   **[810]**

3919 Rubin, Louis D., Jr., ed. *History of Southern Literature.* **1986, Louisiana State Univ. Pr. paper $16.95 (0-8071-1643-2).** A collection of 70 essays by literary scholars tracing the history of the literature of the American South from 1607 to the present. "A must-buy for all literature collections."—BL (Rev: Choice 3/86; LJ 12/85; NYTBR 12/1/85)   **[810]**

3920 Wilson, R. Jackson. *Figures of Speech: American Writers and the Literary Marketplace from Benjamin Franklin to Emily Dickinson.* **1989, Knopf $24.95 (0-394-49696-5); Johns Hopkins paper $14.95 (0-8018-4003-1).** The development of writing as a profession in the United States is examined through the literary careers of Franklin, Emerson, Dickinson, William Lloyd Garrison, and Washington Irving. (Rev: BL 2/15/89; Choice 10/89; PW 12/23/88)   **[810]**

Miscellaneous writings

3921 Bell-Scott, Patricia, ed. *Double Stitch: Black Women Write about Mothers and Daughters.* **1991, Beacon $19.95 (0-8070-0910-5).** An anthology of writings by nearly 50 African-American women on the mother-daughter relationship. (Rev: BL 11/1/91; LJ 11/15/91)   **[810.8]**

3922 Bonner, Marita. *Frye Street and Environs: The Collected Works of Marita Bonner.* **Ed. by Joyce Flynn and Joyce Stricklin. 1989, Beacon paper $9.95 (0-8070-6309-6).** An anthology of writings by the African-American writer known for her

vivid depictions of Chicago ghetto life. (Rev: NYTBR 3/13/88; PW 12/4/87)   **[810.8]**

3923 Frost, Helen, ed. *Season of Dead Water: A Response in Prose and Poetry to the Oil Spill in Prince William Sound.* **1990, Breitenbush Books $19.95 (0-932576-82-6); paper $9.95 (0-932576-83-4).** A collection of 44 essays and poems about the environmental and personal impact of the 1989 *Exxon Valdez* oil spill. (Rev: BL 7/90; LJ 7/90)   **[810.8]**

3924 Sewell, Marilyn, ed. *Cries of the Spirit: A Celebration of Women's Spirituality.* **1991, Beacon $35.00 (0-8070-6812-8); paper $16.95 (0-8070-6813-6).** Collected verse by women regarding the religious and spiritual. "The best anthology available on contemporary women's poetry."—LJ (Rev: BL 12/15/90; LJ 2/1/91. Awards: LJ, 1991)   **[810.8]**

3925 Toth, Susan Allen, and John Coughlan, eds. *Reading Rooms.* **1991, Doubleday $25.00 (0-385-41291-6).** An anthology of writings by 67 authors on the impact of public libraries on their lives, including contributions by E. B. White, James Baldwin, Philip Roth, and Alfred Kazin. (Rev: BL 4/1/91; LJ 3/1/91; PW 2/22/91)   **[810.8]**

History and criticism

3926 Benstock, Shari. *Women of the Left Bank: Paris, 1900–1940.* **1986, Univ. of Texas Pr. $26.95 (0-292-79029-5); paper $12.95 (0-292-79040-6).** An analysis of the literature and experiences of women writers in Paris during the first four decades of the twentieth century. (Rev: Choice 4/87; LJ 11/15/86; PW 11/7/86)   **[810.9]**

3927 Cassady, Carolyn. *Off the Road: My Years with Cassady, Kerouac and Ginsberg.* **1990, Morrow $22.45 (0-688-08891-0).** Memoirs of the wife of Neal Cassady recalling her experiences with Beat generation figures Cassady, Jack Kerouac, and Allen Ginsberg. (Rev: BL 5/1/90; LJ 6/15/90; Time 7/30/90)   **[810.9]**

3928 Coltelli, Linda. *Winged Words: American Indian Writers Speak.* **1990, Univ. of Nebraska Pr. $22.50 (0-8032-1445-6).** Interviews with 11 Native American writers including Michael Dorris, Louise Erdrich, and M. Scott Momaday. (Rev: BL 8/90; LJ 8/90; PW 6/22/90)   **[810.9]**

3929 Cowley, Malcolm. *And I Worked at the Writer's Trade: Chapters of Literary History, 1918–1978.* **1979, Penguin paper $7.95 (0-14-005075-2).** A collection of essays spanning the career of one of the century's most important literary critics. (Rev: Choice 9/78; LJ 4/15/78; NYTBR 4/30/78. Awards: ALA, 1978; NBA, 1980)   **[810.9]**

3930 Cowley, Malcolm. *A Second Flowering: Works and Days of the Lost Generation.* **1980, Penguin paper $7.95 (0-14-005498-7).** A look at eight writers of the Lost Generation (Faulkner, Wolfe, Hemingway, Fitzgerald, Wilder, Cummings, Dos Passos, and Hart Crane) by one of the major literary critics of that era. (Rev: Choice 9/73; LJ 4/1/73; NYTBR 5/6/73. Awards: ALA, 1973)   **[810.9]**

3931   **Douglas, Ann.** *Feminization of American Culture.* **1988, Doubleday paper $11.95 (0-385-24241-7).** How the clergy and women of the nineteenth century in America combined to influence the thought of the century to come. "Provocative, thoughtful . . . a new and important insight into the cultural dilemmas of the 20th century."—LJ (REV: Atl 5/77; LJ 8/77; Time 5/30/77. AWARDS: Time, 1977) **[810.9]**

3932   **Evans, Mari, ed.** *Black Women Writers, 1950–1980: A Critical Evaluation.* **1984, Doubleday paper $13.95 (0-385-17125-0).** Critical essays about 15 post–World War II African-American women writers, and personal statements by them. (REV: BL 8/84; LJ 8/84; NYTBR 9/23/84) **[810.9]**

3933   **Fabre, Michel.** *From Harlem to Paris: Black American Writers in France, 1840-1980.* **1991, Univ. of Illinois Pr. $35.95 (0-252-01684-X).** An overview of the careers and social life of 60 African-American writers who relocated to France during the nineteenth and twentieth centuries. (REV: BL 11/1/91; PW 9/20/91) **[810.9]**

3934   **Hoffman, Daniel, ed.** *Harvard Guide to Contemporary American Writing.* **1979, Harvard Univ. Pr. $30.00 (0-674-37535-1); paper $14.95 (0-674-37537-8).** An overview of the prominent themes and trends in post-World War II American literature. "The best general survey available."—LJ (REV: BL 11/15/79; Choice 3/80; LJ 12/15/79) **[810.9]**

3935   **Huggins, Nathan.** *Harlem Renaissance.* **1971, Oxford Univ. Pr. paper $12.95 (0-19-501665-3).** A survey of the art, music, literature, and intellectual life in Harlem in the 1920s and Harlem's place in contemporary American culture. (REV: Choice 7–8/72; LJ 2/1/72; NYTBR 1/2/72) **[810.9]**

3936   **Kazin, Alfred.** *New York Jew.* **1978, Knopf $12.95 (0-394-49567-5).** The third volume of the influential literary critic's autobiography which spans from 1938 to the 1970s. "Mr. Kazin's latest memoir . . . should give pleasure to anybody interested in the literary history of our times."—NYTBR (REV: BL 4/15/78; LJ 4/1/78; NYTBR 5/7/78. AWARDS: ALA, 1978) **[810.9]**

3937   **Plimpton, George, ed.** *Writer's Chapbook: A Compendium of Fact, Opinion, Wit, and Advice from the 20th Century's Preeminent Writers.* **1989, Viking $19.95 (0-670-81565-9).** Selected commentaries from twentieth-century writers including Ezra Pound, Milan Kundera, Henry Miller, and W. H. Auden. (REV: BL 11/15/89; LJ 11/1/89; NYTBR 3/4/90) **[810.9]**

3938   **Reynolds, David S.** *Beneath the American Renaissance: The Subversive Imagination in the Age of Emerson and Melville.* **1988, Knopf $40.00 (0-394-54448-X); Harvard Univ. Pr. paper $14.95 (0-674-06565-4).** A study of the literature of the American Renaissance accenting its foundations in the popular culture of the day. (REV: BL 6/15/88; LJ 4/15/88; NYTBR 5/8/88) **[810.9]**

3939   **Ruas, Charles.** *Conversations with American Writers.* **1986, McGraw-Hill paper $7.95 (0-07-**054206-6).** A collection of 14 interviews with American authors, including Tennessee Williams, Robert Stone, Gore Vidal, and Truman Capote, taken from Ruas's New York radio show of the late 1970s. (REV: CSM 3/5/85; LJ 12/84; Time 12/24/84) **[810.9]**

3940   **Showalter, Elaine.** *Sister's Choice: Tradition and Change in American Women's Writing.* **1991, Oxford Univ. Pr. $21.95 (0-19-812383-3).** A collection of essays on literature by American women. "A good general-interest work."—BL (REV: BL 9/1/91; LJ 8/91) **[810.9]**

811   Poetry

3941   **Ackerman, Diane.** *Jaguar of Sweet Laughter: New and Selected Poems.* **1991, Random $18.00 (0-679-40214-4).** The fifth collection of poems by the author of *A Natural History of the Senses.* (REV: BL 4/1/91; LJ 5/1/91. AWARDS: BL, 1991) **[811]**

3942   **Adoff, Arnold, ed.** *Poetry of Black America: Anthology of the Twentieth Century.* **1973, Harper & Row $24.93 (0-06-020089-8).** A collection of poetry of over 140 African-American writers numbering over 600 poems. "By far the most extensive compilation of modern black poetry available."—LJ (REV: BL 7/1/73; Choice 11/73; LJ 7/73. AWARDS: ALA, 1973) **[811]**

3943   **Ai.** *Fate: New Poems.* **1991, Houghton $15.95 (0-395-55636-8); paper $8.95 (0-395-55637-6).** A collection of 16 lengthy poems by the author of *Sin.* (REV: BL 1/1/91; LJ 12/90; PW 12/21/90) **[811]**

3944   **Ammons, A. R.** *Collected Poems: 1951–1971.* **1972, Norton $17.50 (0-393-04241-3).** A retrospective from "a very important American poet."—LJ (REV: LJ 3/15/73; New Rep 12/2/72; NYTBR 11/19/72. AWARDS: ALA, 1972; NBA, 1973) **[811]**

3945   **Ansen, Alan.** *Contact Highs: Selected Poems, 1957–1987.* **1989, Dalkey Arch $19.95 (0-916583-44-9); paper $11.95 (0-916583-45-7).** Selections from 30 years of work by the Beat generation poet, who has lived in Greece for the past 20 years. "This may be one of the most significant poetry publications of the decade."—LJ (REV: BL 10/1/89; LJ 11/15/89; PW 10/20/89) **[811]**

3946   **Anzaldua, Gloria.** *Borderlands-La Frontera: The New Mestiza.* **1987, Spinsters/Aunt Lute paper $9.95 (0-933216-25-4).** In a mix of prose and poetry, the self-described Chicana lesbian-feminist looks at her Chicano heritage, the role of women in Hispanic culture and lesbians in a straight culture. "A powerful document that belongs in all collections with emphasis on Hispanic-American or feminist issues."—LJ (REV: Choice 4/88; LJ 9/1/87; PW 7/31/87. AWARDS: LJ, 1987) **[811]**

3947   **Ashbery, John.** *April Galleons.* **1987, Viking $15.95 (0-670-81958-1); Penguin paper $7.95 (0-14-058603-2).** A collection of pieces by the American poet and author of *Self-Portrait in a Convex Mirror.* "Ashbery's position as the Grand Old Man of American poetry seems secure."—TLS (REV: Choice 2/88; LJ 10/15/87; TLS 6/17/88) **[811]**

3948 Ashbery, John. *Flow Chart.* **1991, Knopf $20.00 (0-679-40201-2).** A modern epic poem by the American writer. "Ashbery at his most robust and determined."—LJ (Rᴇᴠ: LJ 5/1/91; PW 3/22/91) **[811]**

3949 Ashbery, John. *Selected Poems.* **1986, Penguin paper $11.95 (0-14-058553-2).** The author's selection of his finest work chosen from over three decades of poetry. "Essential . . . should be in all libraries."—BL (Rᴇᴠ: BL 3/15/86; CSM 12/31/85; LJ 1/86) **[811]**

3950 Ashbery, John. *Self-Portrait in a Convex Mirror.* **1976, Penguin paper $6.95 (0-14-042201-3).** A top collection by one of America's most influential poets. (Rᴇᴠ: Choice 10/75; NYTBR 8/2/75; TLS 7/25/75. Aᴡᴀʀᴅs: NBA, 1976; PP:Poetry, 1976) **[811]**

3951 Ashbery, John. *A Wave: Poems.* **1984, Viking $15.95 (0-670-75176-6).** A collection by the American poet. "Places Ashbery indisputably at the forefront of the ranks of English-speaking poets."—PW (Rᴇᴠ: LJ 5/15/84; Newsweek 7/16/84; PW 4/13/84) **[811]**

3952 Atwood, Margaret. *Selected Poems II: Poems Selected and New, 1976 to 1986.* **1987, Houghton paper $9.95 (0-395-45406-9).** A collection of poems culled from three of the Canadian author's previous works with 17 pieces new to this edition. (Rᴇᴠ: BL 11/1/87; LJ 11/1/87; NYTBR 4/3/88) **[811]**

3953 Berry, Wendell. *Collected Poems of Wendell Berry, 1957–1982.* **1985, North Point $16.50 (0-86547-189-4); paper $8.95 (0-86547-197-5).** A collection of eight works of poetry published over three decades. "A poet of rare compassion and grace, clarity and precision."—LJ (Rᴇᴠ: BL 4/1/85; LJ 4/15/85; NYTBR 11/24/85) **[811]**

3954 Berryman, John. *Collected Poems: 1937–1971.* **1989, Farrar $25.00 (0-374-12619-4).** Selections from over three decades and seven volumes of the author's poems. "A landmark volume central to the American poetry of this half-century."—BL (Rᴇᴠ: BL 10/15/89; LJ 11/1/89; NYTBR 10/8/89. Aᴡᴀʀᴅs: BL, 1989) **[811]**

3955 Berryman, John. *Dream Songs: His Toy, His Dream, His Rest.* **1969, Farrar $17.50 (0-374-14397-8); paper $12.95 (0-374-51670-7).** A collection of over 300 poems revolving around the life of an imaginary character named Henry. (Rᴇᴠ: LJ 10/15/68; NYTBR 11/3/68; PW 9/9/68. Aᴡᴀʀᴅs: ALA, 1968) **[811]**

3956 Berryman, John. *Henry's Fate and Other Poems, 1967–72.* **Ed. by John Haffenden. 1977, Farrar $7.95 (0-374-16950-0).** This second posthumously published collection continues the saga of his character Henry, which began in the author's *Dream Songs.* "Many of these poems . . . are as fine and moving as any Berryman ever wrote."—New Rep (Rᴇᴠ: Choice 9/77; New Rep 6/4/77; NYTBR 4/3/77. Aᴡᴀʀᴅs: ALA, 1977) **[811]**

3957 Bidart, Frank. *In the Western Night: Collected Poems, 1965–90.* **1991, Farrar $15.95 (0-374-17660-4).** Collected verse of the American poet. "Wild, rare stuff—as refreshing as it is absorbing."—BL (Rᴇᴠ: BL 5/15/90; LJ 5/1/90; New Rep 5/14/90) **[811]**

3958 Bishop, Elizabeth. *Geography III.* **1976, Farrar paper $6.95 (0-374-51440-2).** A collection of verse by the American poet who died in 1979. "The loudest complaint made about Elizabeth Bishop's poetry is that there is not more of it."—Time (Rᴇᴠ: BL 5/15/77; Newsweek 1/31/77; Time 3/21/77. Aᴡᴀʀᴅs: ALA, 1977) **[811]**

3959 Blackburn, Paul. *Collected Poems of Paul Blackburn.* **Ed. by Edith Jarolim. 1985, Persea $37.50 (0-89255-086-4).** An anthology of all of Blackburn's 523 published poems, along with others written before his death in 1971. Introduced by an analysis of his life and works by the editor. "An important, superb collection."—PW (Rᴇᴠ: LJ 10/1/85; NYTBR 11/10/85; PW 8/16/85) **[811]**

3960 Bly, Robert. *Loving a Woman in Two Worlds.* **1987, Harper & Row paper $6.95 (0-06-097083-9).** A collection of verse by the author of *Iron John* including the poems, "The Roots," "The Artist at Fifty," and "Shame." (Rᴇᴠ: NYTBR 10/13/85; PW 6/28/85) **[811]**

3961 Bly, Robert. *Selected Poems.* **1986, Harper & Row paper $9.95 (0-06-096048-5).** Poems selected from the first quarter-century of the writer's work. (Rᴇᴠ: BL 6/1/86; LJ 3/15/86; NYTBR 5/25/86) **[811]**

3962 Bly, Robert. *Sleepers Joining Hands.* **1985, Harper & Row paper $6.95 (0-06-090785-1).** A collection of verse by the American poet and author of the best seller *Iron John: A Book about Men.* "A rousing book, as anyone who has heard Bly read would expect . . . no library sampling current poetry should fail to get it."—LJ (Rᴇᴠ: LJ 10/1/72; NYTBR 2/18/73. Aᴡᴀʀᴅs: ALA, 1973) **[811]**

3963 Booth, Philip. *Relations: Selected Poems, 1950–1985.* **1986, Penguin paper $12.95 (0-14-058560-5).** Over 150 poems by the American writer. "An important collection by a poet who deserves to be better known."—LJ (Rᴇᴠ: Choice 10/86; LJ 6/1/86; NYTBR 12/14/86. Aᴡᴀʀᴅs: LJ, 1986) **[811]**

3964 Bronk, William. *Life Supports: New and Collected Poems.* **1981, North Point Pr. $20.00 (0-86547-039-1); paper $10.50 (0-86547-040-5).** Represents over three decades and contains over 400 poems from this American poet. (Rᴇᴠ: LJ 10/15/81; NYTBR 12/13/81. Aᴡᴀʀᴅs: NBA, 1982) **[811]**

3965 Bruchac, Joseph, ed. *Songs from This Earth on Turtle's Back: An Anthology of Poetry by American Indian Writers.* **1983, Greenfield Review Literary Center paper $9.95 (0-912678-58-5).** An anthology of contemporary poetry from authors representing 35 Native American tribes. (Rᴇᴠ: Choice 2/84; LJ 12/1/83; PW 9/23/83) **[811]**

3966 Carruth, Hayden. *Tell Me Again How the White Heron Rises and Flies Across the Nacreous River at Twilight Toward the Distant Islands.* **1989, New Directions paper $8.95 (0-8112-1104-5).** A collection of verse by the American poet and former poetry editor for *Harper's* magazine. "Not one poem in this amazing book deserves to go unread."—LJ (Rᴇᴠ: BL 9/1/89; LJ 9/15/89. Aᴡᴀʀᴅs: BL, 1989; BL, the 1980s) **[811]**

3967   Carver, Raymond. *A New Path to the Waterfall: Poems.* **1990, Atlantic Monthly $10.00 (0-87113-374-1).** Carver's last published collection of poetry written in the months just prior to his death. (Rev: LJ 5/15/89; PW 3/24/89. Awards: ALA, 1989; LJ, 1989)   **[811]**

3968   Carver, Raymond. *Ultramarine.* **1986, Random $14.95 (0-394-55379-9); paper $7.95 (0-394-75535-9).** The fifth collection of verse by the American poet and short story writer. (Rev: Choice 7–8/87; LJ 11/1/86; NYTBR 6/7/87)   **[811]**

3969   Casey, Michael. *Obscenities.* **1990, Ashod Pr. paper $6.50 (0-935102-25-6).** A collection of poems by a veteran about his experiences in Vietnam. "Casey has the best ear for soldiers' speech I have ever encountered."—Newsweek (Rev: LJ 7/72; NYTBR 5/14/72; Newsweek 6/12/72)   **[811]**

3970   Clampitt, Amy. *Archaic Figure: Poems.* **1987, Knopf $15.95 (0-394-55919-3); paper $8.95 (0-394-75090-X).** The third collection of poems by the author of *The Kingfisher* and *What the Light Was Like.* "A perdurable masterpiece of contemporary poetry."—PW (Rev: CSM 8/16/87; LJ 3/15/87; PW 2/20/87. Awards: PW, 1987)   **[811]**

3971   Clampitt, Amy. *Kingfisher.* **1983, Knopf $15.95 (0-394-52840-9); paper $14.95 (0-394-71251-X).** This collection was the debut offering of the American poet who later published *What the Light Was Like* and *Archaic Figure.* "It is hard to think of any poet who has written as well about the natural world as Amy Clampitt does."—NYTBR (Rev: LJ 1/15/83; NYRB 3/3/83; NYTBR 8/7/83. Awards: ALA, 1983; BL, the 1980s)   **[811]**

3972   Clampitt, Amy. *What the Light Was Like.* **1985, Knopf $14.95 (0-394-54318-1); paper $8.95 (0-394-72937-4).** The second collection by the American poet and author of *Kingsolver.* "A must for all poetry collections."—BL (Rev: BL 7/85; LJ 5/1/85; NYTBR 5/19/85)   **[811]**

3973   Clifton, Lucille. *Good Woman: Poems and a Memoir, 1969–1980.* **1987, BOA Editions $25.00 (0-918526-58-2); paper $12.00 (0-918526-59-0).** Collected poetry and autobiographical essays of the author. (Rev: CSM 2/5/88; NYTBR 2/19/89)   **[811]**

3974   Clifton, Lucille. *Next: New Poems.* **1987, BOA Editions $18.00 (0-918526-60-4); paper $9.00 (0-918526-61-2).** A collection of poems concerning death and personal loss. "Ms. Clifton's poetry is big enough to accommodate sorrow and madness and yet her vision emerges as overwhelmingly joyous and calm."—NYTBR (Rev: Choice 10/88; CSM 2/5/88; NYTBR 2/18/89)   **[811]**

3975   Corn, Alfred. *West Door: Poems.* **1988, Viking $17.95 (0-670-81956-5); Penguin paper $8.95 (0-14-058604-0).** The author's fifth collection of poetry. "His poems are delicious to the ear . . . they pace themselves gracefully, without a ripple of excess."—NYTBR (Rev: LJ 3/15/88; NYTBR 10/16/88; PW 11/27/87)   **[811]**

3976   Corso, Gregory. *Mindfield: New and Selected Poems.* **1989, Thunder's Mouth $24.95 (0-938410-85-7); paper $12.95 (0-938410-86-5).** Selected verse from the Beat generation poet covering his works from 1955 to 1989. "An important document in twentieth-century poetry."—BL (Rev: BL 12/1/89; Choice 2/90; LJ 10/15/89)   **[811]**

3977   Creely, Robert. *Collected Poems of Robert Creely, 1945–1975.* **1982, Univ. of California Pr. $35.00 (0-520-04243-3); paper $12.95 (0-520-04244-1).** Collected works of one of the poets of the Black Mountain School. "A major influence on contemporary poetics and new generations of writers."—CSM (Rev: Choice 7–8/83; CSM 5/13/83; LJ 3/1/83) **[811]**

3978   Creely, Robert. *Selected Poems.* **1991, Univ. of California Pr. $25.00 (0-520-06935-8).** A selection of 200 poems spanning the poet's career. (Rev: LJ 5/15/91; PW 5/3/91)   **[811]**

3979   Cullen, Countee. *My Soul's High Song: The Collected Writings of Countee Cullen, Voice of the Harlem Renaissance.* **1991, Doubleday $24.95 (0-385-41758-6); Anchor paper $14.95 (0-385-41295-9).** Collected prose and poetry writings by the African-American Harlem Renaissance figure. (Rev: BL 12/15/90; LJ 1/91; PW 11/30/90)   **[811]**

3980   Denby, Edwin. *Complete Poems.* **Ed. by Ron Padgett. 1986, Random $16.95 (0-394-54404-8).** The collected works of the late American poet. "The reader will be happily shocked to find a magical world, a *real* world transformed by one of the most imaginative poetic minds of the century."—BL (Rev: BL 8/86; NYTBR 11/2/86; PW 2/28/86. Awards: ALA, 1986)   **[811]**

3981   Dickey, James. *Buckdancer's Choice.* **1965, Univ. Presses of New England paper $9.95 (0-8195-1028-9).** A collection of verse by the Southern writer and author of the novels *Alnilam* and *Deliverance.* "This should be in all American poetry collections."—Choice (Rev: BL 12/1/65; Choice 10/66; NYTBR 2/6/66. Awards: NBA, 1966)   **[811]**

3982   Dickey, James. *Eagle's Mile.* **1990, Univ. Pr. of New England $20.00 (0-8195-2185-X); paper $9.95 (0-8195-1187-0).** A collection of verse by the American poet. "Takes readers on a soaring, swooping flight to the innermost reaches of consciousness."—PW (Rev: LJ 11/1/90; PW 10/19/90)   **[811]**

3983   Dickey, James. *Poems: 1957–1967.* **1967, Univ. Pr. of New England $20.00 (0-8195-3073-5); paper $12.95 (0-8195-6055-3).** Selections chosen by the author from four previously published works with several new poems. "A large collection that merits leisurely savoring."—BL (Rev: BL 6/1/67; Choice 10/67; LJ 4/1/67. Awards: ALA, 1967)   **[811]**

3984   Digges, Deborah. *Late in the Millennium.* **1989, Knopf $18.95 (0-394-58067-2).** The author's second published collection of poetry. (Rev: BL 2/15/90; LJ 11/1/89; PW 10/13/89. Awards: PW, 1989)   **[811]**

3985   Doolittle, Hilda. *Collected Poems, 1912–1944.* **Ed. by Louis L. Martz. 1986, New Directions $35.00 (0-8112-0876-1); paper $17.95 (0-8112-0971-7).**

Collected verse of the Modernist poet who wrote under the pen name "H. D." (Rev: Choice 4/84; LJ 10/15/83; TLS 4/27/84) **[811]**

3986 Dove, Rita. *Grace Notes.* 1989, Norton $16.95 (0-393-02719-8); paper $9.95 (0-393-30696-8). The fourth collection of poems by the 1987 Pulitzer Prize winner. "These poems should be read by anyone who loves poetry."—LJ (Rev: BL 9/15/89; LJ 12/89; PW 7/28/89) **[811]**

3987 Dove, Rita. *Thomas and Beulah.* 1985, Carnegie Mellon $14.95 (0-88748-045-4); paper $6.95 (0-88748-046-2). The life story of a couple told through poetry. (Rev: Choice 1/87; LJ 10/1/86; NYTBR 10/23/86. Awards: PP:Poetry, 1987) **[811]**

3988 Dunn, Stephen. *Between Angels.* 1990, Norton $15.95 (0-393-02691-4); paper $7.95 (0-393-30658-5). A collection of the poet's verse, including "Loveliness" and "About the Elk and the Coyotes That Killed Her Calf." "Right on target—as powerful as a sock to the jaw."—BL (Rev: BL 5/1/89; NYTBR 1/28/90; PW 3/3/89) **[811]**

3989 Dunn, Stephen. *Landscape at the End of the Century: Poems.* 1991, Norton $17.95 (0-393-02972-7). The eighth collection of verse by the American poet. (Rev: BL 4/15/91; LJ 3/15/91; PW 2/22/91) **[811]**

3990 Dunn, Stephen. *Local Time.* 1986, Morrow paper $6.95 (0-688-06296-2). The author's sixth collection of poems deals with interpersonal relationships and the difficulties people often have achieving closeness with each other. (Rev: LJ 3/1/86; NYRB 10/23/86; NYTBR 7/6/86) **[811]**

3991 Eberhart, Richard. *Collected Poems: 1930 to 1986.* 1988, Oxford Univ. Pr. $29.95 (0-19-504055-4). Eberhart won the NBA for his *Collected Poems: 1930–1976;* the cited volume contains another decade of his work. (Rev: BL 9/15/76; Choice 10/76; LJ 12/15/76. Awards: NBA, 1977) **[811]**

3992 Erdrich, Louise. *Baptism of Desire.* 1989, Harper & Row $16.95 (0-06-016213-9). A collection of poetry by the author of *Tracks* and *Love Medicine.* (Rev: Choice 7–8/90; LJ 12/89; PW 11/24/89) **[811]**

3993 Feldman, Irving. *All of Us Here.* 1986, Viking $17.95 (0-670-80026-0); Penguin paper $9.95 (0-14-058563-X). The seventh collection of poems by the American writer. "May well be Feldman's finest . . . a tour de force."—BL (Rev: BL 10/1/86; Choice 10/86; New Rep 7/14/86) **[811]**

3994 Forche, Carolyn. *Country Between Us.* 1982, Harper & Row paper $7.95 (0-06-090926-9). Poems recalling the author's experiences living in El Salvador in the late seventies. "An arresting and unforgettable voice."—Time (Rev: LJ 3/1/82; NYTBR 4/19/82; Time 3/15/82. Awards: ALA, 1982) **[811]**

3995 Gardner, John. *Jason and Medeia.* 1986, Random paper $6.95 (0-394-74060-2). The American writer's poetic interpretation of the Greek legend of Jason and the Golden Fleece. (Rev: Choice 11/73; LJ 4/15/73; Time 7/16/73) **[811]**

3996 Gilbert, Christopher. *Across the Mutual Landscape.* 1984, Graywolf paper $6.00 (0-915308-49-5). The first collection of poetry by a practicing psychotherapist. "An honest, substantial and very giving book."—PW (Rev: LJ 6/15/84; NYTBR 6/23/85; PW 4/27/84) **[811]**

3997 Gildner, Gary. *Blue Like the Heavens: New and Selected Poems.* 1984, Univ. of Pittsburgh Pr. paper $9.95 (0-8229-5358-7). Selections from four prior books dating back to the late sixties with new poems published for the first time in this collection. (Rev: BL 5/15/84; LJ 2/15/84) **[811]**

3998 Ginsberg, Allen. *Collected Poems: 1947 to 1980.* 1984, Harper & Row $27.50 (0-06-015341-5); paper $15.95 (0-06-091494-7). Nearly 40 years of Ginsberg's work collected in one volume. "An American publishing landmark and an immediate classic of international importance."—Choice (Rev: BL 12/1/84; Choice 4/85; LJ 12/84) **[811]**

3999 Ginsberg, Allen. *Fall of America: Poems of These States, 1965–1971.* 1972, City Lights paper $6.95 (0-87286-063-9). A collection of verse by the noted Beat poet and playwright. "Anyone who knows the poet only through *Howl* would do well to read this excellent collection."—LJ (Rev: Choice 6/73; LJ 6/1/73; NYTBR 4/15/73. Awards: NBA, 1974) **[811]**

4000 Gluck, Louise. *Ararat.* 1990, Ecco Pr. $17.95 (0-88001-247-1). The fifth collection of poetry by the author of *The Triumph of Achilles.* "No American poet writes better than Louise Gluck."—NYTBR (Rev: LJ 4/1/90; PW 2/16/90) **[811]**

4001 Gluck, Louise. *The Triumph of Achilles.* 1985, Ecco Pr. $13.50 (0-88001-081-9). This American poet's other works include *Firstborn, The Garden,* and *Descending Figure.* "Gluck is foremost among her generation of poets and no collection should be without all four of her full-length books."—LJ (Rev: LJ 9/15/85; NYRB 10/23/86; PW 7/26/85. Awards: LJ, 1985) **[811]**

4002 Greenberg, Alan. *Why We Live with Animals.* 1990, Coffee House paper $8.95 (0-918273-78-1). A collection by the American poet examining man's relationship to other animals. (Rev: BL 9/15/90; PW 7/27/90) **[811]**

4003 Haines, John. *News from the Glacier: Selected Poems, 1960–1980.* 1982, Univ. Pr. of New England $20.00 (0-8195-5064-7); paper $9.95 (0-8195-6072-3). A selection of poetry from the Alaskan writer representing his best work over a 20-year period. (Rev: LJ 7/82; NYTBR 10/31/82) **[811]**

4004 Hall, Donald. *Old and New Poems.* 1990, Ticknor & Fields $24.95 (0-89919-926-7); paper $12.95 (0-89919-954-2). Selected poems representing over 50 years of the career of the American writer. (Rev: BL 8/90; LJ 9/1/90; PW 6/29/90. Awards: LJ, 1990) **[811]**

4005 Hall, Donald. *One Day: A Poem in Three Parts.* 1988, Ticknor & Fields $16.95 (0-89919-817-1); paper $8.95 (0-89919-816-3). A poem examining the individual lives of three people and of life itself through their voices. (Rev: BL 9/1/88; PW 7/22/88. Awards: PW, 1988) **[811]**

4006 **Harris, Marie, and Kathleen Aguero, eds.** *An Ear to the Ground: An Anthology of Contemporary American Poetry.* 1989, Univ. of Georgia Pr. $30.00 (0-8203-1122-7); paper $14.95 (0-8203-1123-5). A collection of poetry by contemporary American minority writers. "If you purchase only one poetry anthology this year, make it this one."—BL (Rev: BL 6/1/89; PW 5/26/89. Awards: ALA, 1989; BL, 1989) **[811]**

4007 **Harrison, Jim.** *Selected and New Poems, 1961–1981.* 1982, Doubleday paper $8.95 (0-385-28945-6). Selected works of verse by the author of *Farmer* and *Warlock*. "One of the most unappreciated writers in America."—PW (Rev: LJ 6/15/82; NYTBR 12/12/82; PW 6/25/82) **[811]**

4008 **Hass, Robert.** *Field Guide.* 1973, Yale Univ. Pr. $14.95 (0-300-01650-6); paper $7.95 (0-300-01651-4). This author's debut collection contains many poems about his native San Francisco Bay area and includes "On the Coast Near Sausalito" and "Palo Alto: The Marshes." "A brilliant collection of lyrical statements about this poet's outer and inner lives . . . an important book, essential for every library."—Choice (Rev: Choice 12/73; LJ 5/15/73; PW 4/9/73. Awards: ALA, 1973) **[811]**

4009 **Hass, Robert.** *Human Wishes.* 1989, Ecco Pr. $17.95 (0-88001-211-0). The third collection of poetry by the author. "To read his poetry . . . gives one an almost visceral pleasure . . . a remarkable book."—NYTBR (Rev: LJ 8/89; NYTBR 11/12/89; PW 6/23/89) **[811]**

4010 **Hayden, Robert.** *Collected Poems.* Ed. by Frederick Glaysher. 1985, Liveright paper $8.95 (0-87140-138-X). Collected late work of the African-American poet. "An excellent compendium of the best poems by one of America's very best contemporary poets."—Choice (Rev: BL 7/85; Choice 1/86; LJ 6/1/85) **[811]**

4011 **Hecht, Anthony.** *Transparent Man.* 1990, Knopf $18.95 (0-394-58506-2). The fifth collection of verse by the American poet. (Rev: BL 5/15/90; LJ 6/15/90; NYTBR 7/22/90) **[811]**

4012 **Hirsch, Edward.** *Night Parade.* 1989, Knopf $18.95 (0-394-57720-5); paper $10.95 (0-679-72299-8). The third collection of verse by the American poet. "Few are able to encapsulate their histories as vividly or movingly."—LJ (Rev: BL 3/15/89; LJ 4/1/89; PW 2/24/89) **[811]**

4013 **Howard, Richard.** *Untitled Subjects.* 1983, Macmillan paper $6.95 (0-689-10136-8). A collection of poems about 15 figures from the Victorian Age. (Rev: LJ 10/15/69; NYTBR 4/12/70. Awards: PP:Poetry, 1970) **[811]**

4014 **Hugo, Richard.** *Making Certain It Goes On: The Collected Poems of Richard Hugo.* 1984, Norton $25.00 (0-393-01784-2). New and collected works of the American poet. "A substantial poet; his work belongs in every library."—BL (Rev: BL 3/15/84; CSM 8/3/84; NYTBR 2/26/84) **[811]**

4015 **Ignatow, David.** *New and Collected Poems, 1970–1985.* 1986, Univ. Pr. of New England paper $14.95 (0-8195-6174-6). New and collected works from the American poet. "Ignatow at the top of his form . . . he merits praise and honor for this beautiful book."—NYTBR (Rev: Choice 2/87; NYTBR 1/11/87; TLS 11/6/87) **[811]**

4016 **Ignatow, David.** *Shadowing the Ground.* 1991, Univ. Pr. of New England $20.00 (0-8195-2195-7). Reflections in verse on death and dying by the American poet. (Rev: BL 5/15/91; LJ 5/15/91; PW 5/3/91) **[811]**

4017 **Jacobsen, Josephine.** *Chinese Insomniacs: New Poems.* 1981, Univ. of Pennsylvania Pr. $20.95 (0-8122-7818-6); paper $10.95 (0-8122-1120-0). A "richly musical volume" of verse by the American poet.—LJ (Rev: LJ 10/1/81; NYTBR 4/19/82) **[811]**

4018 **Jarrell, Randall.** *Complete Poems.* 1969, Farrar $25.00 (0-374-12716-6); paper $12.95 (0-374-51305-8). This collection of Jarrell's poetry contains over 300 poems written during a 40-year period. "There are so many good things about Jarrell's poems and they are all here in this important volume."—Choice (Rev: Choice 10/69; LJ 2/15/69; NYTBR 2/2/69. Awards: ALA, 1969) **[811]**

4019 **Jeffers, Robinson.** *Collected Poetry of Robinson Jeffers: Vol. 1, 1920–1928.* Ed. by Tim Hunt. 1988, Stanford Univ. Pr. $60.00 (0-8047-1414-2). The first of four projected volumes of the collected works of the American poet known for his verse about California. (Rev: Choice 12/88; LJ 4/15/88) **[811]**

4020 **Johnson, Ronald.** *Book of the Green Man.* 1967, Norton $6.00 (0-393-04290-1). A poet from Kansas reflects on the year he spent living in England. "England should feel complimented, and poets will find inspiration in the sense of mystery and excitement."—Choice (Rev: Choice 4/68; LJ 2/1/67; Sat Rev 6/3/67. Awards: ALA, 1968) **[811]**

4021 **Kinnell, Galway.** *Past.* 1985, Houghton $13.95 (0-395-39385-X); paper $9.95 (0-395-39386-8). Kinnell's first offering since his *Selected Poems* won the Pulitzer Prize for Poetry in 1982 concerns the essence of time and its passing. "A major book by a major poet."—LJ (Rev: BL 11/15/85; LJ 11/15/85; PW 10/4/85. Awards: LJ, 1985) **[811]**

4022 **Kinnell, Galway.** *Selected Poems.* 1983, Houghton $12.50 (0-395-32045-3); paper $11.95 (0-395-32046-1). Selections from over 40 years of Kinnell's poetry. (Rev: LJ 5/15/82; NYTBR 9/19/82. Awards: NBA, 1983; PP:Poetry, 1983) **[811]**

4023 **Kinnell, Galway.** *When One Has Lived a Long Time Alone.* 1990, Knopf $18.95 (0-394-58856-8); paper $9.95 (0-679-73281-0). The tenth collection of verse by the Pulitzer Prize–winning poet. (Rev: LJ 10/15/90; PW 9/7/90) **[811]**

4024 **Kizer, Carolyn.** *Mermaids in the Basement: Poems for Women.* 1984, Copper Canyon $14.00 (0-914742-80-9); paper $7.00 (0-914742-81-7). A collection of new and previously published verse for women by the American poet. (REV: BL 11/1/84; Choice 4/85; LJ 10/1/84) **[811]**

4025 Kizer, Carolyn. *Nearness of You.* 1986, Copper Canyon $15.00 (0-914742-96-5); paper $10.00 (0-914742-97-3). A collection of poems about masculinity, men, and their relations with women. "This volume sums up and stands as testament to Kizer's gifts as an artist and as an extraordinary human being."—BL (REV: BL 2/15/87; LJ 11/1/86; NYTBR 3/22/87) **[811]**

4026 Kizer, Carolyn. *Yin: New Poems.* 1984, BOA Editions $18.00 (0-918526-44-2); paper $9.00 (0-918526-45-0). A collection by one of America's top feminist poets. (REV: BL 7/84; NYTBR 11/25/84. AWARDS: PP:Poetry, 1985) **[811]**

4027 Klein, Michael, ed. *Poets for Life: 76 Poets Respond to AIDS.* 1989, Crown $18.95 (0-517-57242-7). A collection of poetry about AIDS including works by Allen Ginsberg, Adrienne Rich, James Merrill, and Paul Monette. (REV: BL 6/15/89; LJ 6/1/89. AWARDS: ALA, 1989) **[811]**

4028 Kumin, Maxine. *Long Approach: Poems.* 1985, Viking $14.95 (0-670-80429-0); Penguin paper $7.95 (0-14-042342-7). An eighth collection of verse by the American poet. "Extraordinarily strong . . . another triumph from a poet who has become a national treasure."—BL (REV: BL 11/15/85; NYTBR 3/2/86; PW 8/23/85) **[811]**

4029 Kumin, Maxine. *Nurture: Poems.* 1989, Viking $17.95 (0-670-82438-0); Penguin paper $8.95 (0-14-058619-9). The ninth collection of poetry by the Pulitzer Prize-winning writer. "A masterful volume by one of our finest poets."—BL (REV: BL 2/1/89; LJ 3/1/89; NYTBR 11/5/89) **[811]**

4030 Kumin, Maxine. *Our Ground Time Here Will Be Brief.* 1982, Penguin paper $8.95 (0-14-042298-6). A selection of new and previously published verse representing 20 years of work by the American poet. (REV: BL 4/15/82; NYTBR 8/8/82; PW 4/2/82) **[811]**

4031 Kunitz, Stanley. *Poems of Stanley Kunitz: 1928 to 1978.* 1979, Little, Brown $19.95 (0-316-50711-3); paper $12.95 (0-316-50710-5). The American poet's collected work. "One can hardly fail to recommend this definitive statement of Kunitz's scope and range."—Choice (REV: BL 6/1/79; Choice 11/79; NYTBR 7/22/79. AWARDS: ALA, 1979) **[811]**

4032 Larsen, Wendy Wilder, and Thi Nga Tran. *Shallow Graves: Two Women and Vietnam.* 1986, Random $16.95 (0-394-54985-6). Poems reflecting on the Vietnam War experiences of an American teacher and a Vietnamese social worker. (REV: LJ 4/15/86; PW 3/7/86; Time 6/2/86) **[811]**

4033 Lee, Li-Young. *City in Which I Love You.* 1990, BOA Editions $18.00 (0-918526-82-5); paper $8.00 (0-918526-52-3). A collection of verse by the Indonesia-born poet, which was awarded the 1990 Lamont Poetry Selection. (REV: BL 10/1/90; LJ 9/1/90; PW 7/27/90. AWARDS: BL, 1990; PW, 1990) **[811]**

4034 Leithauser, Brad. *Hundreds of Fireflies.* 1982, Knopf paper $9.95 (0-394-74896-4). A collection of verse by the author of such novels as *Equal Distance* and *Hence.* "A poet whose talent is as entertaining as it is enlightening."—BL (REV: BL 1/15/82; New Rep 4/14/82; NYTBR 3/14/82) **[811]**

4035 Levertov, Denise. *Breathing the Water.* 1987, New Directions paper $6.95 (0-8112-1027-8). The fifteenth collection of poetry by the politically outspoken writer. "A marvelous gathering from one of our finest poets."—BL (REV: BL 8/87; LJ 5/1/87; PW 3/13/87) **[811]**

4036 Levine, Philip. *Ashes: Poems New and Old.* 1979, Macmillan paper $4.95 (0-689-10975-X). Selected verse from the American writer. "One of the indispensable poets."—Choice (REV: Choice 10/79; LJ 8/79; NYTBR 10/7/79. AWARDS: NBA, 1980) **[811]**

4037 Levine, Philip. *New Selected Poems.* 1991, Knopf $24.00 (0-679-40165-2). Verse drawn from the author's 1984 *Selected Poems* plus 15 more pieces. (REV: BL 5/15/91; LJ 6/15/91) **[811]**

4038 Levine, Philip. *What Work Is.* 1991, Knopf $19.00 (0-679-40166-0). A collection of verse by the poet examining physical labor and the life of the working-class. (REV: BL 5/15/91; LJ 5/1/91. AWARDS: ALA, 1992; LJ, 1991; NBA, 1991) **[811]**

4039 Logan, John. *Only the Dreamer Can Change the Dream: Selected Poems.* 1981, Ecco Pr. $14.95 (0-912946-77-6); paper $7.95 (0-912946-78-4). Selected verse from the American poet's first five books. (REV: BL 5/15/81; LJ 5/15/81; NYTBR 6/21/81) **[811]**

4040 Lowell, Robert. *Day by Day.* 1977, Farrar $12.95 (0-374-13525-8); paper $5.95 (0-374-51471-2). Lowell's last book of poetry published slightly before his death. "Vintage Lowell in the fullness of his powers."—CSM (REV: CSM 9/21/77; NYTBR 8/14/77; Newsweek 9/5/77. AWARDS: ALA, 1977; NYTBR, 1977) **[811]**

4041 Loy, Mina. *Last Lunar Baedeker: The Poems of Mina Loy.* 1982, Jargon Society $25.00 (0-912330-46-5). A collection of verse and other writings by the designer, actress, and poet who was regarded as one of the top Modernists of the 1920s. (REV: Choice 9/82; CSM 8/13/82; LJ 7/82) **[811]**

4042 Lux, Thomas. *Half Promised Land.* 1986, Houghton paper $6.95 (0-395-38256-4). Lux's fourth collection of poems, many of which deal with small-town life. "This is powerful poetry."—LJ (REV: Choice 11/86; LJ 5/15/86; NYTBR 4/19/87. AWARDS: LJ, 1986) **[811]**

4043 Lynch, Thomas. *Skating with Heather Grace.* 1987, Knopf paper $13.00 (0-394-74756-9). A debut collection by a Midwestern undertaker. "A remarkable first collection of verse heralding the arrival of an important poetic voice."—BL (REV: BL 3/15/88; LJ 3/1/87; NYTBR 10/4/87. AWARDS: ALA, 1987) **[811]**

4044 McGrath, Thomas. *Death Song.* 1991, Copper Canyon $17.00 (1-55659-036-9); paper $10.00 (1-55659-035-0). A posthumously published collection by the American poet. "One of our most important and distinctive poetic voices."—BL (Rev: BL 2/15/91; NYTBR 3/10/91; PW 1/18/91) **[811]**

4045 Matthews, William. *A Happy Childhood: Poems.* 1984, Little, Brown $12.95 (0-316-55073-6); paper $8.95 (0-316-55074-4). The sixth collection by the American poet. "No short review should attempt to discuss, let alone assess, the riches here."—BL (Rev: BL 5/15/84; LJ 4/15/84; NYTBR 7/1/84) **[811]**

4046 Meredith, William. *Partial Accounts: New and Selected Poems.* 1987, Knopf paper $10.95 (0-394-75191-4). Includes selections of Meredith's work spanning a 40-year period. (Rev: LJ 6/1/87; NYTBR 7/31/88. Awards: PP:Poetry, 1988) **[811]**

4047 Merrill, James. *Inner Room: Poems.* 1988, Knopf $16.95 (0-394-57248-3); paper $8.95 (0-679-72049-9). A collection of poetry by the author of *The Changing Light at Sandover.* "An enormously far-reaching reading experience."—PW (Rev: NYTBR 11/12/89; PW 10/21/89; TLS 12/2/88) **[811]**

4048 Merwin, W. S. *Rain in the Trees.* 1988, Knopf $16.95 (0-394-57039-1); paper $9.95 (0-394-75858-7). This collection focuses on the author's childhood, family life, and his feelings about love. "No surprises, just the same steady hand and vision we have come to expect from one of the giants of contemporary American poetry."—LJ (Rev: Choice 12/88; LJ 5/1/88; NYTBR 7/31/88) **[811]**

4049 Merwin, W. S. *Selected Poems.* 1988, Macmillan $22.95 (0-689-11970-4); paper $12.95 (0-689-70736-3). A selection of 100 poems chosen by the author to represent the best works from ten collections dating back to 1952. (Rev: BL 6/15/88; Choice 12/88; LJ 8/88) **[811]**

4050 Miles, Josephine. *Collected Poems, 1930–1983.* 1983, Univ. of Illinois Pr. $17.50 (0-252-01057-5). Collected works of the American poet including both previously published and unpublished works. "A fascinating record of our times and of a special temperament."—BL (Rev: BL 8/83; LJ 8/83; PW 6/10/83) **[811]**

4051 Moore, Marianne. *Complete Poems of Marianne Moore.* 1967, Viking $16.95 (0-670-23505-9); paper $8.95 (0-14-058601-6). The author's choice of her best 117 poems. "An excellent representation of Miss Moore's wit, her imagination and her skill at playing with words."—PW (Rev: LJ 10/15/67; NYTBR 11/26/67; PW 10/2/67. Awards: ALA, 1967) **[811]**

4052 Moss, Stanley. *Intelligence of Clouds.* 1989, Harcourt $13.95 (0-15-144850-7); paper $7.95 (0-15-644800-9). A collection of poems by the author of *Skull of Adam.* "A virtuoso performance by one of our country's best."—BL (Rev: BL 5/15/89; LJ 5/15/89; PW 4/7/89) **[811]**

4053 Mueller, Lisel. *Second Language: Poems.* 1986, Louisiana State Univ. Pr. paper $7.95 (0-8071-1337-9). A fourth collection of poetry by a former refugee from Nazi Germany who became a natural-

ized American citizen in 1945. (Rev: BL 1/1/87; LJ 9/15/86) **[811]**

4054 Nash, Ogden. *I Wouldn't Have Missed It: Selected Poems of Ogden Nash.* 1975, Little, Brown $19.95 (0-316-59830-5). A 400-poem chronologically arranged retrospective with an introduction by Archibald MacLeish. "Ogden Nash's sometimes wrenching rhymes and outrageous puns inspire imitations and incur the wrath of people who wish they could have thought of them first."—CSM (Rev: Choice 1/76; CSM 9/30/75; PW 7/7/75. Awards: ALA, 1975) **[811]**

4055 Nemerov, Howard. *Collected Poems of Howard Nemerov.* 1981, Univ. of Chicago Pr. paper $16.95 (0-226-57259-5). A retrospective of work by America's former poet laureate. (Rev: CSM 11/16/77; LJ 7/77; NYTBR 12/18/77. Awards: NBA, 1978; PP:Poetry, 1978) **[811]**

4056 Nemerov, Howard. *Inside the Onion.* 1984, Univ. of Chicago Pr. $9.95 (0-226-57244-7). Poems by the Pulitzer Prize winner and former American poet laureate. "A stunning collection."—LJ (Rev: BL 2/15/84; LJ 12/15/83) **[811]**

4057 Niatum, Duane, ed. *Harper's Anthology of Twentieth Century Native American Poetry.* 1988, Harper $24.95 (0-06-250665-X); paper $15.95 (0-06-250666-8). A collection of poems by 36 Native American writers. "Belongs in any collection that claims to represent the multiple voices of American literature today."—BL (Rev: BL 4/1/88; LJ 3/1/88. Awards: LJ, 1988) **[811]**

4058 Nye, Naomi S. *Hugging the Jukebox.* 1984, Breitenbush paper $6.95 (0-932576-23-0). A collection of poems depicting life in the American Southwest and Latin America. "The spirituality that characterizes the writings of Mark Strand and A. R. Ammons is present also in these lovely, durable poems."—LJ (Rev: BL 3/15/83; LJ 8/82. Awards: ALA, 1982) **[811]**

4059 Oates, Joyce Carol. *Time Traveler: Poems, 1983–1989.* 1989, Dutton $18.95 (0-525-24802-1); paper $9.95 (0-525-48505-8). A collection of 70 poems by the prolific author of *Them* and *The Goddess and Other Stories.* (Rev: BL 9/15/89; LJ 9/1/89; PW 7/28/89) **[811]**

4060 Olds, Sharon. *Dead and the Living.* 1984, Knopf paper $10.95 (0-394-71563-2). Olds's second collection of poetry is an examination of death and its effects on the living. (Rev: LJ 12/15/83; NYTBR 3/18/84; PW 11/11/83. Awards: ALA, 1984) **[811]**

4061 Olds, Sharon. *Gold Cell.* 1987, Knopf $16.95 (0-394-55699-2); paper $11.95 (0-394-74770-4). A collection of verse about motherhood and sexuality including the poems "Greed and Aggression" and "Summer Solstice, New York City." "That one poet can achieve such horror and yet such tenderness inside a single poem is astonishing."—PW (Rev: LJ 2/1/87; NYTBR 3/22/87; PW 1/23/87. Awards: ALA, 1987) **[811]**

4062 Oliver, Mary. *American Primitive.* 1983, Little, Brown $14.95 (0-316-65002-1); paper $7.95 (0-316-65004-8). A collection of verse celebrating nature and the American wilderness. "Never simply sweet, her poems gather insights from several sources and refine them to memorable art."—BL (Rev: BL 2/1/83; LJ 2/15/83; NYTBR 7/17/83. Awards: PP:Poetry, 1984) **[811]**

4063 Oliver, Mary. *Dream Work.* 1986, Atlantic Monthly $14.95 (0-87113-071-8); paper $8.95 (0-87113-069-6). A seventh poetry collection by the 1984 Pulitzer Prize winner. "A magical book."—BL (Rev: BL 9/1/86; Choice 11/86; LJ 6/1/86) **[811]**

4064 Olson, Charles. *Collected Poems of Charles Olson.* 1987, Univ. of California Pr. $45.00 (0-520-05764-3). This posthumous collection contains nearly all of Olson's output. "Perhaps the most important American postmodern poet."—LJ (Rev: Choice 3/88; LJ 1/88; TLS 8/30/88. Awards: LJ, 1987) **[811]**

4065 Perillo, Lucia Maria. *Dangerous Life.* 1989, Northeastern Univ. Pr. paper $8.95 (1-55553-059-1). A collection by the American poet, which won the Morse Poetry Prize for 1989. "Unique and refreshing . . . a poet worth watching."—Choice (Rev: BL 2/1/90; Choice 12/90) **[811]**

4066 Piercy, Marge. *Available Light.* 1988, Knopf paper $8.95 (0-394-75691-6). A collection of poems by the author of *Gone to Soldiers* regarding the physical and psychological effects of aging. (Rev: BL 4/1/88; LJ 5/15/88; PW 2/5/88) **[811]**

4067 Piercy, Marge. *Circles on the Water: Selected Poems of Marge Piercy.* 1982, Knopf paper $14.95 (0-394-70779-6). Collection of poems spanning over 20 years chosen by the author. "For anyone interested in what's been happening on the cutting edge during the past two decades, she's clearly essential reading."—NYTBR (Rev: BL 5/15/82; NYTBR 8/8/82; PW 4/9/82. Awards: ALA, 1982) **[811]**

4068 Piercy, Marge. *My Mother's Body.* 1985, Knopf $14.95 (0-394-54343-2); paper $9.95 (0-394-72945-5). This tenth collection of poems by the American writer examines her feelings regarding the death of her mother and the state of her marriage. (Rev: LJ 4/1/85; PW 3/8/85) **[811]**

4069 Pinsky, Robert. *History of My Heart.* 1985, Ecco Pr. paper $9.95 (0-88001-048-7). A collection of verse by the author of *An Explanation of America.* "A very good book by one of our very best young poets."—Choice (Rev: BL 3/15/84; Choice 9/84; LJ 3/15/84) **[811]**

4070 Plath, Sylvia. *Collected Poems.* 1981, Harper & Row paper $11.95 (0-06-090900-5). Edited by Ted Hughes, this is the most complete collection of Plath's poetry available. (Rev: LJ 11/1/81; NYTBR 11/22/81; TLS 2/12/82. Awards: ALA, 1981; PP:Poetry, 1982) **[811]**

4071 Poirier, Richard. *Robert Frost: The Work of Knowing.* 1990, Stanford Univ. Pr. $42.50 (0-8047-1741-9); paper $12.95 (0-8047-1742-7). Literary criticism that seeks to give Frost his rightful place in the American romantic tradition. "For the student seriously interested in Frost this book is indispensable."—Choice (Rev: BL 11/15/77; Choice 4/78; NYTBR 10/30/77. Awards: NYTBR, 1977) **[811]**

4072 Ponsot, Marie. *Green Dark.* 1988, Knopf $16.95 (0-394-57054-5). A collection of poems by the American author and translator. (Rev: BL 4/15/88; LJ 4/15/88) **[811]**

4073 Poulin, A. *Cave Dwellers.* 1991, Graywolf $18.95 (1-55597-139-3). The eighth collection by the American poet. "Clearly among the best poets of his generation . . . a must-buy."—BL (Rev: BL 2/15/91; LJ 2/15/91) **[811]**

4074 Rich, Adrienne. *An Atlas of the Difficult World: Poems, 1988–1991.* 1991, Norton $17.95 (0-393-03069-5). A collection of poems exploring life in the contemporary United States. "The title poem is worth the price of admission."—BL (Rev: BL 10/1/91; LJ 10/15/91. Awards: BL, 1991; LJ, 1991) **[811]**

4075 Rich, Adrienne. *Diving into the Wreck: Poems, 1971–1972.* 1973, Norton $10.95 (0-393-04370-3); paper $5.95 (0-393-04384-3). Poems exploring the issues of sex and sexuality. (Rev: Choice 10/73; LJ 5/15/73; NYRB 10/4/73. Awards: NBA, 1974) **[811]**

4076 Rich, Adrienne. *Dream of a Common Language: Poems, 1974–1977.* 1978, Norton paper $6.95 (0-393-04510-2). A collection by the American poet and author of the seminal feminist work *Of Woman Born: Motherhood as Experience and Institution.* "Adrienne Rich brings to her new work all the integrity, power and pure intelligence we have come to count on from her poetry."—LJ (Rev: LJ 3/1/78; New Rep 12/9/78; NYTBR 6/11/78. Awards: ALA, 1978) **[811]**

4077 Rich, Adrienne. *Fact of a Doorframe: Poems Selected and New, 1950–1984.* 1984, Norton $18.95 (0-393-01905-5); paper $10.95 (0-393-30204-0). Selected verse from over three decades of the American poet's work. (Rev: New Rep 1/7/85; NYTBR 1/20/85) **[811]**

4078 Rich, Adrienne. *Time's Power: Poems, 1985–1988.* 1989, Norton $15.95 (0-393-02677-9); paper $7.95 (0-393-30575-9). A fourteenth collection of poetry by the author of *Of Woman Born.* "A powerful volume as honest as it is comforting, as intensely personal as it is universal."—BL (Rev: BL 6/15/89; LJ 5/15/89; NYTBR 10/22/89) **[811]**

4079 Rich, Adrienne. *Your Native Land, Your Life: Poems.* 1986, Norton $14.95 (0-393-02318-4); paper $7.95 (0-393-30325-X). A collection of poems exploring the author's Jewish heritage and her life as a woman. "The best of Rich's books."—PW (Rev: LJ 4/15/86; NYTBR 1/18/87; PW 4/4/86. Awards: LJ, 1986) **[811]**

4080 Roethke, Theodore. *Collected Poems.* 1982, Univ. of Washington Pr. $19.95 (0-295-95973-8). A collection of all previously published works and 16 poems new to this volume. "A most important volume of American poetry . . . the whole body of work . . . is even more impressive and varied than one anticipated."—LJ (Rev: Choice 10/66; LJ 6/15/66; NYTBR 7/17/66. Awards: ALA, 1966) **[811]**

4081   Ryan, Michael. *God Hunger: Poems.* 1989, Viking $17.95 (0-670-82498-4); Penguin paper $9.95 (0-14-058620-2). The third collection of verse by the American poet. "A meticulous craftsman."—PW (REV: BL 6/15/89; LJ 6/15/89; PW 6/16/89) **[811]**

4082   Sarton, May. *Silence Now: New and Uncollected Earlier Poems.* 1988, Norton $14.95 (0-393-02651-5); paper $7.95 (0-393-30635-6). Poems regarding old age and the aging process by the American poet who wrote many of these pieces when she was in her mid-seventies. (REV: BL 10/15/88; LJ 11/1/88; PW 10/21/88) **[811]**

4083   Schnackenberg, Gjertrud. *Lamplit Answer.* 1986, Farrar $12.95 (0-374-51978-1). The second collection of poetry by the author of *Portraits and Elegies.* "Delightful . . . a book to savor."—BL (REV: BL 7/85; LJ 5/1/85; NYTBR 5/26/85) **[811]**

4084   Schultz, Philip. *Deep Within the Ravine.* 1984, Viking $14.95 (0-670-26609-4); Penguin paper $9.95 (0-14-042337-0). A second collection of verse by the American poet. (REV: BL 12/15/84; NYTBR 3/31/85; PW 9/7/84) **[811]**

4085   Schuyler, James. *Selected Poems.* 1988, Farrar $25.00 (0-374-25878-3); paper $12.95 (0-374-52166-2). Over 100 pieces selected from the life work of the American poet. "Schulyer has sought and often found sights, idioms and rhythms that are genuinely part of American cultural experience."—NYRB (REV: BL 6/15/88; LJ 6/15/88; NYRB 9/26/88)**[811]**

4086   Sexton, Anne. *Love Poems.* 1989, Houghton paper $9.95 (0-395-51760-5). Collected by a writer best remembered for her poems of intimacy and confession. "An excellent craftsman. Her poems read true to the ear."—LJ (REV: Choice 4/69; CSM 3/20/69; LJ 3/15/69. AWARDS: ALA, 1969) **[811]**

4087   Sexton, Anne. *Selected Poems of Anne Sexton.* Ed. by Diane W. Middlebrook and Diana H. George. 1988, Houghton $21.95 (0-395-44595-7); paper $11.95 (0-395-47782-4). Selections from the American poet's work. "Sexton is a groundbreaking, original poet who has earned a permanent place in American literature."—Choice (REV: BL 4/15/88; Choice 1/89; LJ 5/15/88) **[811]**

4088   Shapiro, Harvey. *Light Holds: Poems.* 1984, Univ. Pr. of New England $20.00 (0-8195-5097-3); paper $9.95 (0-8195-6096-0). The seventh collection of verse by the New York poet. "A marvelous evocation of city life."—LJ (REV: BL 7/84; LJ 2/15/84; NYTBR 4/1/84) **[811]**

4089   Shapiro, Harvey. *National Cold Storage Company: New and Selected Poems.* 1988, Univ. Pr. of New England $20.00 (0-8195-2152-3); paper $10.95 (0-8195-1153-6). A collection of poems by the former editor of the *New York Times Book Review.* "A monument to death, disappointment, and loss."—NYTBR (REV: LJ 10/1/88; NYTBR 12/11/88) **[811]**

4090   Simpson, Louis. *Best Hour of the Night.* 1983, Ticknor & Fields paper $6.95 (0-89919-204-1). A collection by the American poet and author of *At The End of the Open Road* and *Searching for the Ox.* (REV: LJ 11/15/83; NYTBR 1/29/84; PW 9/30/83) **[811]**

4091   Simpson, Louis. *Collected Poems.* 1988, Paragon $24.95 (1-55778-047-1); paper $12.95 (1-55778-411-6). Four decades of the American poet's work are represented in this collection chosen by the author. (REV: Choice 3/89; LJ 12/88; NYTBR 11/13/88) **[811]**

4092   Smith, William Jay. *Collected Poems, 1939–1989.* 1990, Macmillan $24.95 (0-684-19167-9). An anthology of the works of the American poet spanning over five decades. (REV: LJ 10/15/90; PW 10/12/90) **[811]**

4093   Snyder, Gary. *Turtle Island.* 1974, New Directions paper $5.95 (0-8112-0456-0). An ecological plea by one of America's top naturalist poets. (REV: BL 2/15/75; CSM 12/30/74; LJ 11/15/74. AWARDS: PP:Poetry, 1975) **[811]**

4094   Song, Cathy. *Picture Bride.* 1983, Yale Univ. Pr. paper $7.95 (0-300-02969-0). First collection from the Hawaiian-born poet. "A powerful collection, strongly rooted in nature."—LJ (REV: LJ 5/1/83; PW 4/1/83. AWARDS: ALA, 1983) **[811]**

4095   Soto, Gary. *Who Will Know Us?* 1990, Chronicle paper $8.95 (0-87701-673-9). Poems detailing the Mexican-American experience in California. "A poet of great appeal to general readers."—BL (REV: BL 8/90; LJ 9/1/90; PW 3/16/90. AWARDS: BL, 1990) **[811]**

4096   Stern, Gerald. *Paradise Poems.* 1984, Random $12.45 (0-394-53785-8). The fifth collection of verse by "one of our most musical poets."—LJ (REV: BL 2/1/85; LJ 8/84; NYTBR 11/11/84) **[811]**

4097   Strand, Mark. *Continuous Life.* 1991, Knopf $18.95 (0-394-58817-7). The first collection of verse published in more than a decade by the Poet Laureate of the United States. (REV: BL 2/1/91; LJ 11/1/90; NYTBR 3/24/91) **[811]**

4098   Strand, Mark. *Selected Poems.* 1990, Knopf paper $10.95 (0-679-73301-9). A collection of Strand's work from five previous books of poetry with some appearing for the first time in this volume. "He is one of the lucky writers whose control of memory increases with age."—NYTBR (REV: LJ 10/15/81; NYRB 10/8/81; NYTBR 1/18/81. AWARDS: ALA, 1980) **[811]**

4099   Swenson, May. *In Other Words: New Poems.* 1987, Knopf $16.95 (0-394-56175-9). A collection of verse by the critically acclaimed Utah-born poet who died in 1989. "A stylistic tour de force."—LJ (REV: LJ 9/15/87; New Rep 3/7/88; NYTBR 6/12/88. AWARDS: LJ, 1987) **[811]**

4100   Tate, James. *Reckoner.* 1986, Univ. Pr. of New England $20.00 (0-8195-5152-X); paper $9.95 (0-8195-6159-2). A collection of innovative poetry commenting on modern society. (REV: LJ 1/87; NYTBR 3/1/87) **[811]**

4101   Taylor, Henry. *Flying Change: Poems.* 1985, Louisiana State Univ. Pr. $13.95 (0-8071-1263-1);

paper $6.95 (0-8071-1264-X). A collection examining the many facets of rural life. (Rᴇᴠ: BL 3/15/86; LJ 12/85; NYTBR 5/4/86. Aᴡᴀʀᴅs: PP:Poetry, 1986) **[811]**

4102 Travisano, Thomas J. *Elizabeth Bishop: Her Artistic Development.* 1988, Univ. Pr. of Virginia $27.50 (0-8139-1159-1); paper $9.95 (0-8139-1226-1). An analysis of the evolution of the writing style of the American poet based on her letters, memoirs, and criticism. (Rᴇᴠ: Choice 11/88; LJ 6/1/88) **[811]**

4103 Updike, John. *Facing Nature: Poems.* Ed. by Judith Jores. 1985, Knopf $13.95 (0-394-54385-8). The fifth collection of poetry and light verse by the noted American writer. (Rᴇᴠ: LJ 2/15/85; Newsweek 8/26/85; NYTBR 4/28/85) **[811]**

4104 Van De Vanter, Lynda, and Joan A. Furey, eds. *Visions of War, Dreams of Peace: Writings of Women in the Vietnam War.* 1991, Warner paper $9.95 (0-446-39251-0). An anthology of verse written by American women who served in the Vietnam War. (Rᴇᴠ: BL 5/15/91; LJ 5/1/91) **[811]**

4105 Van Duyn, Mona. *Merciful Disguises: Published and Unpublished Poems.* 1973, Macmillan paper $9.95 (0-689-11294-7). Selections from over 40 years of the poet's work. "This volume shows beyond doubt that Mona Van Duyn is truly one of our important poets."—Choice (Rᴇᴠ: Choice 4/74; LJ 12/1/73; New Rep 10/6/73. Aᴡᴀʀᴅs: ALA, 1973) **[811]**

4106 Van Duyn, Mona. *Near Changes.* 1990, Knopf $18.95 (0-394-58444-9). A collection of verse from the American poet. "Quiet, contemplative, and reflective in a refreshingly straightforward way."—LJ (Rᴇᴠ: BL 3/15/90; LJ 3/15/90. Aᴡᴀʀᴅs: PP:Poetry, 1991) **[811]**

4107 Wagoner, David. *Through the Forest: Selected Poems, 1977–1987.* 1987, Atlantic Monthly $16.95 (0-87113-154-4); paper $7.95 (0-87113-153-6). A representative selection of the poet's finest work since *Collected Poems.* "Accessible, joyous poetry that belongs in every collection."—LJ (Rᴇᴠ: BL 8/87; LJ 8/87; PW 6/26/87) **[811]**

4108 Waldman, Anne, ed. *Out of This World: The Poetry Project at the St. Mark's Church-in-the-Bowery; An Anthology, 1966–1991.* 1991, Crown paper $20.00 (0-517-56681-8). An anthology of Poetry Project verse spanning four decades, includes selections from Creeley, Corso, and Guest. (Rᴇᴠ: BL 11/15/91; LJ 11/1/91; PW 11/15/91) **[811]**

4109 Walker, Alice. *Her Blue Body Everything We Know: Earthling Poems, 1965–1990, Complete.* 1991, Harcourt $22.95 (0-15-140040-7). Collected verse of the American poet over a 25-year period. "An important collection from a powerful poet."—BL (Rᴇᴠ: BL 4/15/91; LJ 4/15/91; PW 3/1/91) **[811]**

4110 Walker, Alice. *Horses Make a Landscape Look More Beautiful: Poems.* 1986, Harcourt $10.95 (0-15-142169-2); paper $3.95 (0-15-642173-9). The fourth collection of poetry by the author of *The Color Purple.* (Rᴇᴠ: LJ 10/15/84; NYTBR 4/7/85; PW 8/24/84) **[811]**

4111 Walker, Margaret. *This Is My Century: New and Collected Poems.* 1989, Univ. of Georgia Pr. $25.00 (0-8203-1134-0); paper $12.50 (0-8203-1135-9). Collected poetry by the African-American author of *Jubilee* and *Richard Wright: Daemonic Genius.* (Rᴇᴠ: BL 10/15/89; LJ 11/1/89) **[811]**

4112 Waring, Belle. *Refuge.* 1990, Univ. of Pittsburgh Pr. $16.95 (0-8229-3655-0); paper $8.95 (0-8229-5441-9). A collection of verse that won the 1990 Associate Writing Programs award for poetry. (Rᴇᴠ: BL 9/15/90; PW 8/31/90. Aᴡᴀʀᴅs: PW, 1990) **[811]**

4113 Warren, Robert Penn. *Chief Joseph of the Nez Perce.* 1983, Random $9.95 (0-394-53019-5); paper $7.95 (0-394-71356-7). A history in verse of the fate of Chief Joseph and the Nez Perce tribe in the nineteenth century as portrayed by the author of *All the King's Men.* (Rᴇᴠ: LJ 4/15/83; PW 3/4/83) **[811]**

4114 Warren, Robert Penn. *Now and Then: Poems, 1976 to 1978.* 1978, Random $11.95 (0-394-50164-0); paper $5.95 (0-394-73848-9). A selection by the former Poet Laureate of the United States. (Rᴇᴠ: Choice 12/78; LJ 8/78; New Rep 9/30/78. Aᴡᴀʀᴅs: ALA, 1978; PP:Poetry, 1979) **[811]**

4115 Wilbur, Richard. *New and Collected Poems.* 1988, Harcourt $27.95 (0-15-165206-6); paper $10.95 (0-15-665491-1). A collection encompassing Wilbur's six prior volumes of poetry and poems new to this work. (Rᴇᴠ: CSM 4/27/88; LJ 6/1/88; New Rep 5/16/88. Aᴡᴀʀᴅs: PP:Poetry, 1989) **[811]**

4116 Willard, Nancy. *Water Walker.* 1989, Knopf $18.95 (0-394-57208-4); paper $9.95 (0-679-72171-1). A poetry collection by the Newbery Award-winning children's writer. "A miraculous and wonderful book."—BL (Rᴇᴠ: BL 6/15/89; LJ 6/1/89; PW 5/12/89) **[811]**

4117 Williams, C. K. *Flesh and Blood.* 1988, Farrar paper $8.95 (0-374-52090-9). The fifth collection of poems by the author of *Tar* and *The Bacchae of Euripides.* "One of the most documentary and one of the most thoughtful poets working today."—NYTBR (Rᴇᴠ: LJ 5/1/87; NYTBR 8/23/87) **[811]**

4118 Williams, William Carlos. *Collected Poems of William Carlos Williams: 1909–1939.* Ed. by A. Walton Litz and Christopher MacGowan. 1986, New Directions $35.00 (0-8112-0999-7). First of two volumes of the collected poetry of William Carlos Williams. (Rᴇᴠ: Choice 4/87; LJ 10/1/86; NYTBR 1/4/87. Aᴡᴀʀᴅs: LJ, 1986) **[811]**

4119 Wormser, Brian. *Good Trembling.* 1985, Houghton $13.95 (0-317-14691-2); paper $4.95 (0-317-14692-0). A second collection by the American poet. "From first poem to last, Wormser's second book displays in subject and style an extraordinary talent."—BL (Rᴇᴠ: BL 4/1/85; PW 1/4/85) **[811]**

4120 Wright, Charles. *World of the Ten Thousand Things: Poems, 1980–1990.* 1991, Farrar $25.00 (0-374-29293-0). A collection of the American poet's work over the last decade. "An automatic and welcome purchase for any library."—Choice (Rᴇᴠ: Choice 2/91; NYTBR 2/14/91) **[811]**

4121 Wright, James. *Above the River: The Complete Poems.* 1990, Farrar $25.00 (0-374-12749-2). Collected verse by the Pulitzer Prize–winning poet. (Rev: BL 5/15/90; LJ 6/1/90; NYTBR 6/17/90. Awards: ALA, 1990) **[811]**

4122 Wright, James. *Collected Poems.* 1971, Univ. Presses of New England $25.00 (0-8195-4031-5); paper $14.95 (0-8195-6022-7). "Reading the *Collected Poems* of James Wright is like reading a history of the best contemporary American poetry."—Peter A. Stitt, NYTBR (Rev: LJ 2/15/71; New Rep 7/17/71; NYTBR 5/16/71. Awards: ALA, 1971; PP:Poetry, 1972) **[811]**

4123 Wright, James. *This Journey.* 1982, Random $10.50 (0-394-52365-2). A posthumously published collection of work by the Pulitzer Prize-winning poet. (Rev: BL 3/15/82; LJ 3/15/82; NYTBR 4/18/82) **[811]**

4124 Zweig, Paul. *Eternity's Woods.* 1985, Univ. Pr. of New England $20.00 (0-8195-5135-X); paper $9.95 (0-8195-6134-7). The third collection of poetry from Zweig, published just after his death at the age of 49. "A sad but noble testament to a life too soon completed."—BL (Rev: BL 8/85; LJ 3/1/85; NYTBR 5/16/85) **[811]**

Colonial period, 1607–1776

4125 Ostriker, Alicia S. *Stealing the Language: The Emergence of Women's Poetry in America.* 1987, Beacon paper $10.95 (0-8070-6303-7). A survey of American women's poetry from 1650 to the present, concentrating on the last 25 years. (Rev: BL 4/15/86; LJ 5/1/86; PW 3/21/86. Awards: LJ, 1986) **[811.1]**

1830–1861

4126 Kaplan, Justin. *Walt Whitman: A Life.* 1986, Simon & Schuster paper $12.95 (0-671-62257-9). Biography of the great nineteenth-century American poet. "Though long, his book makes lively reading, like a well-made novel, except that here facts are truly more fascinating than fiction."—BL (Rev: BL 10/15/80; NYTBR 11/9/80; Time 11/17/80. Awards: ALA, 1980; NYTBR, 1980; Time, 1980) **[811.3]**

1867–1900

4127 Sewall, Richard. *Life of Emily Dickinson.* 1974, Farrar paper $18.95 (0-374-51571-9). This exhaustive biography of Dickinson was described by the *New Yorker* as "fair-minded, reliable, of fine literary quality, and utterly engrossing." (Rev: LJ 11/1/74; New Rep 1/23/75; NYRB 1/23/75. Awards: ALA, 1975; NBA, 1975) **[811.4]**

4128 Wolff, Cynthia Griffin. *Emily Dickinson.* 1986, Knopf $25.00 (0-394-54418-8); Addison-Wesley paper $15.95 (0-201-16809-X). An extensive biography of the American poet. "Wolff's . . . in-depth portrait is as fascinating as it is well-written, and from it the Emily Dickinson who was both poet and woman . . . emerges clearly, vibrantly."—BL (Rev: BL 10/1/86; LJ 10/15/86; PW 1/9/87. Awards: PW, 1986) **[811.4]**

1900–

4129 Atlas, James. *Delmore Schwartz: The Life of an American Poet.* 1985, Harcourt paper $10.95 (0-15-625272-4). A biography of the man called by John Berryman "the most underrated poet in the twentieth century" based on interviews, autobiographical writings, and formerly unpublished manuscripts. "Reads with the pleasure of a good novel."—NYTBR (Rev: Choice 4/78; NYTBR 11/13/77; Newsweek 11/21/77. Awards: NYTBR, 1977) **[811.5]**

4130 Giovanni, Nikki. *Gemini: An Extended Autobiographical Statement on My First Twenty-Five Years of Being a Black Poet.* 1971, Macmillan $5.95 (0-672-51422-2); Penguin paper $4.95 (0-14-004264-4). A collection of autobiographical, critical, and political essays. "One of America's most brilliant, intense and militant black poets . . . she is vividly alive on every page."—Choice (Rev: BL 6/15/72; Choice 5/72; Time 1/17/72) **[811.5]**

4131 Rosenthal, M. L. *Our Life in Poetry: Selected Essays and Reviews.* 1991, Persea Books $47.50 (0-89255-149-6). Collected reviews from over four decades of writing by the American poet and critic. "A major book necessary for all collections."—LJ (Rev: LJ 5/1/91; PW 5/10/91) **[811.5]**

4132 Wolff, Geoffrey. *Black Sun: The Brief Transit and Violent Eclipse of Harry Crosby.* 1985, Random $8.95 (0-394-72472-0). A biography of the American poet, his hedonistic life, and shocking suicide. "A vividly drawn portrait of a man bent on self-destruction."—PW (Rev: LJ 8/76; Newsweek 9/6/76; PW 6/21/76) **[811.5]**

1900–1945

4133 Bates, Milton J. *Wallace Stevens: A Mythology of Self.* 1985, Univ. of California Pr. $32.50 (0-520-04909-8); paper $10.95 (0-520-05871-2). An examination of the life and work of the American poet. "A sophisticated, sensitive treatment of a complex, compelling subject."—BL (Rev: BL 8/85; CSM 9/4/85; LJ 8/85) **[811.52]**

4134 Brazeau, Peter. *Parts of a World: Wallace Stevens Remembered.* 1985, North Point $12.50 (0-86547-190-8). A biography of the American poet compiled from recollections of those who knew him. (Rev: Choice 4/84; LJ 11/1/83; NYTBR 11/20/83) **[811.52]**

4135 Burnshaw, Stanley. *Robert Frost Himself.* 1989, Braziller paper $12.95 (0-8076-1234-0). A biography of the American poet by his former editor, written in response to a caustic portrayal by former biographer Lawrence Thompson. (Rev: Atl 1/87; Choice 2/87; LJ 11/1/86) **[811.52]**

4136 Frank, Elizabeth. *Louise Bogan: A Portrait.* 1985, Knopf $24.95 (0-394-52484-5). Analysis of the life and work of one of the top American poets of our time. (Rev: Atl 2/85; LJ 11/15/84; NYTBR 3/3/85. Awards: PW, 1985; PP:Biography, 1985) **[811.52]**

4137 Hamalian, Linda. *A Life of Kenneth Rexroth.* 1991, Norton $25.00 (0-393-02944-1). A biography of the San Francisco Beat generation poet and writer. "Definitive, moving."—PW (REV: BL 2/15/91; LJ 4/1/91; PW 1/25/91) **[811.52]**

4138 Hamilton, Ian. *Robert Lowell: A Biography.* 1983, Random $19.95 (0-394-50965-X); paper $8.95 (0-394-71646-9). A biography of the American poet who was awarded the Pulitzer Prize in 1947 and 1974. "Hamilton brings to life the tortured man and poet."—Choice (REV: Atl 2/83; Choice 3/83; Newsweek 11/15/82. AWARDS: BL, the 1980s) **[811.52]**

4139 Laughlin, James. *Pound as Wuz: Essays and Lectures on Ezra Pound.* 1987, Graywolf $17.00 (1-55597-097-4); paper $9.50 (1-55597-098-2). Personal remembrances and literary essays regarding the life and work of Ezra Pound by his former publisher. (REV: Choice 5/88; CSM 9/30/87; PW 10/30/87) **[811.52]**

4140 Mariani, Paul. *William Carlos Williams: A New World Naked.* 1990, Norton paper $14.95 (0-393-30672-0). A massive biography of one of the century's most important American poets. (REV: LJ 10/1/81; New Rep 11/25/81; NYTBR 11/22/81. AWARDS: ALA, 1981) **[811.52]**

4141 Molesworth, Charles. *Marianne Moore: A Literary Life.* 1990, Macmillan $29.95 (0-689-11815-5). A literary biography of the American poet with criticism of her key works. (REV: BL 8/90; LJ 6/15/90; NYTBR 8/26/90) **[811.52]**

4142 Niven, Penelope. *Carl Sandburg.* 1991, Scribner $29.95 (0-684-19251-9). A biography of the life and work of the American poet and biographer of Lincoln. (REV: BL 5/1/91; LJ 7/91) **[811.52]**

4143 Pritchard, William H. *Randall Jarrell: A Literary Life.* 1989, Farrar $25.00 (0-374-24677-7). A study of the life and works of the American poet and literary critic. (REV: BL 2/1/90; NYTBR 5/6/90; PW 3/2/90) **[811.52]**

4144 Richardson, John. *Wallace Stevens: The Later Years, 1925–1955.* 1988, Morrow $27.95 (0-688-06860-X). The second and concluding volume of the author's biography of the American poet. "A rich and rewarding study."—BL (REV: BL 8/88; LJ 11/1/88; Natl Rev 12/9/88) **[811.52]**

4145 Sarton, May. *Sarton Selected.* Ed. by Bradford Dudley Dazil. 1991, Norton $22.95 (0-393-02968-9). An anthology of selected work from the American writer. (REV: LJ 5/15/91; PW 4/5/91) **[811.52]**

4146 Shapiro, Karl. *Reports of My Death: An Autobiography, Vol. 2.* 1990, Algonquin $22.95 (0-945575-28-9). The second volume of the American poet's autobiography. (REV: BL 4/1/90; LJ 4/15/90) **[811.52]**

4147 Shapiro, Karl. *The Younger Son: Poet, an Autobiography in Three Parts, Vol. 1.* 1988, Algonquin $17.95 (0-912697-86-5). The first volume of the poet's autobiography covers his childhood and adolescence in Maryland and Virginia. "One of the most intimate and notable accounts of one writer's

personal and poetic concerns."—BL (REV: BL 9/1/88; LJ 10/1/88; NYTBR 11/27/88) **[811.52]**

4148 Tytell, John. *Ezra Pound: The Solitary Volcano.* 1987, Doubleday paper $19.95 (0-385-19694-6). A biography of the American poet and literary figure. (REV: BL 8/87; LJ 9/15/87; PW 8/14/87) **[811.52]**

1945–

4149 Alexander, Paul. *This Rough Magic: A Biography of Sylvia Plath.* 1991, Viking $24.95 (0-670-81821-7). A biography of the poet who committed suicide at the age of 31. "The most objective portrayal yet."—PW (REV: BL 9/1/91; PW 8/16/91) **[811.54]**

4150 Clark, Tom. *Charles Olson: The Allegory of a Poet's Life.* 1991, Norton $27.95 (0-393-02958-1). A biography of the twentieth-century American poet. "Thorough and readable . . . highly recommended."—BL (REV: BL 4/15/91; LJ 3/15/91; PW 2/15/91) **[811.54]**

4151 Cowley, Malcolm. *Portable Malcolm Cowley.* 1990, Viking $21.95 (0-67082-721-5). Selected writings of the American literary critic and author of *Think Back on Us* and *Exile's Return.* (REV: LJ 6/1/90; New Rep 4/30/90) **[811.54]**

4152 Kalstone, David. *Becoming a Poet: Elizabeth Bishop with Marianne Moore and Robert Lowell.* 1989, Farrar $22.50 (0-374-10960-5). A study of the poetry of Elizabeth Bishop and of her friendships and artistic relationships with Lowell and Moore. "The most lucid and sympathetic readings of Bishop's verse that we yet possess."—LJ (REV: LJ 7/89; NYTBR 1/4/90) **[811.54]**

4153 Kent, George E. *A Life of Gwendolyn Brooks.* 1990, Univ. Pr. of Kentucky $25.00 (0-8131-1659-7). A biography of the African-American poet based on her private papers and interviews focusing on her career as a writer. (REV: BL 8/89; LJ 8/89; PW 7/21/89) **[811.54]**

4154 McClatchy, J. D. *White Paper: On Contemporary American Poetry.* 1990, Columbia Univ. Pr. $39.50 (0-231-06944-8); paper $14.50 (0-231-06945-6). Critical essays on American poets and their works since the 1950s. (REV: BL 5/15/89; LJ 5/15/89; NYTBR 7/9/89) **[811.54]**

4155 Mariani, Paul. *Dream Song: The Life of John Berryman.* Ed. by Maria Guarnaschelli. 1990, Morrow $29.95 (0-688-05026-3). A profile of the life and work of the Pulitzer Prize-winning American poet. (REV: BL 1/15/90; LJ 1/90; New Yorker 4/30/90) **[811.54]**

4156 Middlebrook, Diane Wood. *Anne Sexton: A Biography.* 1991, Houghton $24.95 (0-395-35362-9). A biography of the poet based in part on the records of her psychiatrist. "Absorbing, balanced . . . a tribute to the forcefulness of the poet's personality, to her work and to her biographer's unfailing craft."—PW (REV: BL 9/1/91; LJ 8/91; PW 7/5/91. AWARDS: LJ, 1991; PW, 1991) **[811.54]**

4157 Miles, Barry. *Ginsberg: A Biography.* 1989, Simon & Schuster $24.95 (0-06-097343-9); Harper & Row paper $10.95 (0-06-097343-9). A biography of the American poet based on the author's personal interviews with Ginsberg and access to his private papers. (REV: BL 8/89; NYTBR 10/1/89; TLS 3/9/90. AWARDS: BL, 1989) **[811.54]**

4158 Stevenson, Anne. *Bitter Fame: A Life of Sylvia Plath.* 1989, Houghton $19.95 (0-395-45374-7); paper $10.95 (0-395-53846-7). A biography of the American poet and author of *The Bell Jar.* "Arguably the best critical biography yet of the complex and controversial poet."—PW (REV: BL 8/89; NYTBR 8/27/89; PW 6/23/89. AWARDS: BL, 1989; PW, 1989) **[811.54]**

4159 Vendler, Helen. *Part of Nature, Part of Us: Modern American Poets.* 1980, Harvard Univ. Pr. $22.00 (0-674-65475-7). A collection of essays and reviews on modern and contemporary American poets and poetry. "The best poetry reviewer in America."—New Rep (REV: Choice 7–8/80; New Rep 3/23/80; NYTBR 3/29/80. AWARDS: ALA, 1980) **[811.54]**

4160 Zweig, Paul. *Departures: Memoirs.* 1986, Harper & Row $16.95 (0-06-015650-3); Penguin paper $6.95 (0-14-010527-1). Memoirs of the literary critic and poet regarding his life in Paris and his fight against an eventually fatal lymphatic cancer. (REV: BL 11/15/86; LJ 11/1/86; PW 10/24/86) **[811.54]**

812 Drama

4161 Fierstein, Harvey. *Safe Sex.* 1987, Macmillan $15.95 (0-689-11953-4). A collection of three one-act plays examining the psychological effects of AIDS by the author of *Torch Song Trilogy.* (REV: BL 12/1/87; LJ 1/88) **[812]**

4162 Fuller, Charles. *A Soldier's Play.* 1982, Hill & Wang paper $6.95 (0-374-52148-4). This play was later made into the critically acclaimed film, *A Soldier's Story.* (REV: BL 10/15/82; LJ 10/15/82. AWARDS: PP:Drama, 1982) **[812]**

4163 Mamet, David. *Glengarry Glenn Ross.* 1988, Grove paper $6.95 (0-394-62049-6). A play indicting the lack of mores in the American business world. (REV: BL 8/84; LJ 8/84. AWARDS: PP:Drama, 1984) **[812]**

4164 Norman, Marsha. *'Night, Mother.* 1983, Hill & Wang paper $6.95 (0-374-52138-7). This Pulitzer Prize–winning play was adapted into a major motion picture starring Anne Bancroft and Sissy Spacek. "Even in the silence of the printed page, Marsha Norman's riveting play resounds with unsettling power."—BL (REV: BL 9/1/83; LJ 9/1/83. AWARDS: PP:Drama, 1983) **[812]**

4165 Shepard, Sam. *Fool for Love and the Sad Lament of Pecos Bill on the Eve of Killing His Wife.* 1984, City Lights paper $6.95 (0-87286-150-3). Two plays by the American writer regarding life in the West. (REV: BL 4/1/84; LJ 4/1/84) **[812]**

4166 Wagner, Jane. *Search for Signs of Intelligent Life in the Universe.* 1986, Harper & Row $18.95

(0-06-015673-2); paper $9.95 (0-06-091431-9). A satirical theater piece written as a vehicle for Lily Tomlin. "A wonderfully comic and painful dose of truth straight from the heart."—LJ (REV: BL 10/15/86; LJ 12/86) **[812]**

4167 Wilkerson, Margaret B. *Nine Plays by Black Women.* 1986, NAL paper $5.95 (0-451-62820-9). A selection of nine plays authored by African-American women between 1950 and 1985. "Riveting, tragic, haunting . . . a must for every American drama collection."—BL (REV: BL 8/86; LJ 8/86) **[812]**

4168 Wilson, Lanford. *Hot L Baltimore.* 1973, Hill & Wang paper $6.95 (0-374-52165-4). A play about a seedy hotel and the characters that frequent it. "Provides excellent reading in the way that a first-rate short story does when one has only a small piece of time to invest."—New Rep (REV: Choice 3/74; New Rep 10/13/74. AWARDS: ALA, 1973) **[812]**

4169 Wilson, Lanford. *Talley's Folly.* 1980, Hill & Wang paper $5.95 (0-374-52157-3). A play by the American actor, director, and author of *Hot L Baltimore.* "A charming theatre piece whose strengths are retained on the printed page."—LJ (REV: BL 6/15/80; LJ 4/1/80. AWARDS: PP:Drama, 1980) **[812]**

4170 Zindel, Paul. *Effect of Gamma Rays on Man-in-the-Moon Marigolds.* 1971, Harper & Row $12.95 (0-06-026829-8); Bantam paper $3.95 (0-553-28028-7). Also chosen by the New York Drama Critics Circle as the Best American Play of the 1969–1970 season. (REV: BL 9/1/71; LJ 1/15/71. AWARDS: ALA, 1971; PP:Drama, 1971) **[812]**

1900–

4171 Hellman, Lillian. *Pentimento: A Book of Portraits.* 1974, NAL paper $4.50 (0-451-15442-8). Memoirs by the American playwright consisting of sketches of people she has known and their effect upon her own life. "Rarely do we get the opportunity to look so deeply into another's life."—LJ (REV: Choice 1/74; LJ 11/15/73; PW 7/16/73. AWARDS: ALA, 1973) **[812.5]**

4172 Sheaffer, Louis. *O'Neill: Son and Artist.* 1988, AMS Pr. $75.00 (0-404-20322-1). A biography of the American playwright covering the years from 1920 to his death in 1953. "The definitive biographical study of O'Neill . . . an indispensable work for anyone interested in American theater."—LJ (REV: CSM 12/19/73; LJ 9/1/73; NYTBR 11/25/73. AWARDS: PP:Biography, 1973) **[812.5]**

1900–1945

4173 Hellman, Lillian. *An Unfinished Woman: A Memoir.* 1969, Little, Brown $13.95 (0-316-35518-6). The first of three volumes of the dramatist's autobiography; they are available in one volume as *Three,* also published by Little, Brown. (REV: LJ 6/

15/69; NYTBR 6/29/69; Newsweek 6/30/69. AWARDS: ALA, 1969; NBA, 1970)   **[812.52]**

4174 Miller, Arthur. *Timebends: A Life*. 1987, Grove-Weidenfeld $24.95 (0-8021-0015-5); Harper & Row paper $10.95 (0-06-097178-9). Memoirs of the American playwright. "This beautifully written autobiography by the noted playwright draws us effortlessly into his life and times."—LJ (REV: LJ 10/15/87; New Yorker 12/14/87; Newsweek 11/16/87. AWARDS: ALA, 1987; LJ, 1987; PW, 1987)   **[812.52]**

4175 Rollyson, Carl. *Lillian Hellman: Her Legend and Her Legacy*. 1988, St. Martin's $24.95 (0-312-00049-9); paper $13.95 (0-312-03481-4). A biography of the outspoken American playwright and political activist. "The fullest and fairest account yet . . . a compulsively readable biography."—PW (REV: CSM 7/20/88; LJ 4/15/88; PW 3/25/88. AWARDS: BL, 1989)   **[812.52]**

4176 Wright, Williams. *Lillian Hellman: The Image, the Woman*. 1988, Ballantine paper $4.95 (0-345-34740-4). A portrait of the American playwright which often contradicts Hellman's autobiographical writings. "Literary biography as intriguing as it ever gets."—BL (REV: BL 11/15/86; CSM 3/9/87; New Rep 3/30/87)   **[812.52]**

1945–

4177 Spoto, Donald. *Kindness of Strangers: The Life of Tennessee Williams*. 1985, Little, Brown $19.95 (0-316-80781-8); Ballantine paper $4.95 (0-345-32618-0). A literary biography of the American playwright. "A thorough and moving consideration of the man and his art."—BL (REV: BL 2/15/85; Choice 7–8/85; LJ 3/1/85)   **[812.54]**

813 Fiction

4178 Brinkmeyer, Robert H., Jr. *Art and Vision of Flannery O'Connor*. 1990, Louisiana State Univ. Pr. $22.50 (0-8071-1492-8). A detailed look at six of the American writer's novels and short stories. "Indispensable to the subject."—LJ (REV: Choice 6/90; LJ 11/15/89)   **[813]**

4179 Brooks, Cleanth. *William Faulkner: First Encounters*. 1983, Yale Univ. Pr. $30.00 (0-300-02995-0); paper $11.95 (0-300-03399-0). An introduction to the works of William Faulkner for the beginning student and general reader. (REV: Choice 12/83; LJ 9/15/83; NYTBR 11/13/83)   **[813]**

4180 Fisher, Philip. *Hard Facts: Setting and Form in the American Novel*. 1985, Oxford Univ. Pr. $29.95 (0-19-503528-3); paper $9.95 (0-19-504131-3). A study and interpretation of four major American novels: James Fenimore Cooper's *Deerslayer;* Harriet Beecher Stowe's *Uncle Tom's Cabin;* and the Theodore Dreiser works *An American Tragedy* and *Sister Carrie*. (REV: Choice 5/85; LJ 4/15/85; TLS 11/22/85)   **[813]**

4181 Kazin, Alfred. *Bright Book of Life: American Novelists and Storytellers from Hemingway to Mailer*. 1980, Univ. of Notre Dame Pr. paper $9.95 (0-268-00664-4). Nine critical essays on pre- and

post-World War II writers, with a section on how the war influenced American literature. "There is no one reading or teaching contemporary literature who will want to miss glancing through this prismatic glass."—LJ (REV: Choice 9/73; LJ 4/15/73; NYTBR 5/20/73. AWARDS: ALA, 1973)   **[813]**

1861–1900

4182 Cott, Jonathan. *Wandering Ghost: The Odyssey of Lafcadio Hearn*. 1991, Knopf $24.95 (0-394-57192-5). A biography of the Irish-Greek-American writer known for his macabre stories and his portrayals of Japanese culture. (REV: BL 2/1/91; NYTBR 2/3/91; PW 12/21/90)   **[813.4]**

4183 Scharnhorst, Gary, and Jack Bales. *Lost Life of Horatio Alger*. 1985, Indiana Univ. Pr. $25.00 (0-253-14915-0). A biography of the nineteenth-century Unitarian minister and writer whose name became synonomous with rise from poverty to success. (REV: BL 4/1/85; Choice 3/86; TLS 10/18/85)   **[813.4]**

4184 Silverman, Kenneth. *Edgar A. Poe: Mournful and Never-Ending Remembrance*. 1991, Harper-Collins $25.00 (0-06-016715-7). A biography of the nineteenth-century storyteller, poet, and master of horror. (REV: LJ 10/15/91; PW 9/27/91)   **[813.4]**

4185 Toth, Emily. *Kate Chopin: A Life of the Author of "The Awakening."* 1990, Morrow $27.95 (0-688-09707-3). The biography of the late nineteenth-century American writer best known for her 1899 novel *The Awakening*. (REV: BL 10/1/90; LJ 10/15/90; NYTBR 12/30/90)   **[813.4]**

1900–

4186 Bawer, Bruce. *Diminishing Fictions: Essays on the Modern American Novel and Its Critics*. 1988, Graywolf $18.50 (1-55597-109-1). A criticism regarding the current state of American literature. "Top drawer criticism written as well as Bawer wishes most fiction were."—BL (REV: BL 6/1/88; LJ 6/15/88)   **[813.5]**

4187 Day, Douglas. *Malcolm Lowry: A Biography*. 1973, Oxford Univ. Pr. paper $9.95 (0-19-503523-2). A biography of the English author best known for *Under the Volcano*. (REV: New Rep 11/3/73; NYTBR 11/4/73; Time 10/29/73. AWARDS: NBA, 1974)   **[813.5]**

4188 Gayle, Addison. *Richard Wright: Ordeal of a Native Son*. 1983, Peter Smith $20.00 (0-8446-6000-0). A study of the life and work of the African-American writer and author of *Black Boy* and *Native Son*. (REV: BL 6/15/80; CSM 8/11/80; LJ 6/1/80)   **[813.5]**

4189 Gilman, Dorothy. *New Kind of Country*. 1985, Buccaneer $19.95 (0-89966-571-3); Fawcett paper $3.95 (0-449-21627-3). The writer known for her Mrs. Polifax series presents her thoughts about moving to a small fishing village in Nova Scotia. (REV: BL 9/1/78; LJ 9/1/78)   **[813.5]**

4190 Hemenway, Robert E. *Zora Neale Hurston: A Literary Biography*. 1977, Univ. of Illinois Pr. paper $10.95 (0-252-00807-3). A biography of the

African-American writer and member of the Harlem Renaissance movement. (Rev: Choice 4/78; New Rep 2/19/78; NYTBR 2/19/78)   **[813.5]**

4191 Hemingway, Gregory. *Papa: A Personal Memoir.* 1988, Paragon paper $8.95 (1-55778-068-4). Recollections of Ernest Hemingway by his youngest son. "One of the most affecting memoirs of recent years . . . one puts down the book in a kind of hush."—PW (Rev: LJ 8/76; NYTBR 5/30/76; PW 4/12/76)   **[813.5]**

4192 Himes, Chester. *Quality of Hurt—The Early Years: The Autobiography of Chester Himes.* 1990, Paragon paper $12.95 (1-55778-306-3). An autobiography of the novelist tracing his early life, his incarceration for armed robbery, his travels around the United States and Europe, and his eventual involvement in the literary world. (Rev: BL 7/15/72; New Yorker 3/18/72; PW 1/17/72)   **[813.5]**

4193 Howard, Maureen. *Facts of Life.* 1980, Penguin paper $6.95 (0-14-005500-2). An autobiography of the novelist. "A moving collection of reminiscences, dense but aerated with good humor."—CSM (Rev: Choice 1/79; CSM 11/22/78; NYTBR 11/12/78. Awards: NYTBR, 1978)   **[813.5]**

4194 Lewis, R. W. B. *Edith Wharton: A Biography.* 1985, Fromm International paper $12.95 (0-88064-020-0). A biography of the author of *The Age of Innocence* and *Ethan Frome.* "Not only a superb literary biography, but also a fascinating, detail-crammed evocation of life among the gifted, the affluent and the powerful between the Civil War and World War II."—LJ (Rev: LJ 8/75; Newsweek 9/22/75; Sat Rev 8/9/75. Awards: NYTBR, 1975; PP:Biography, 1976; Time, 1975)   **[813.5]**

4195 O'Connor, Flannery. *Habit of Being.* Ed. by Sally Fitzgerald. 1979, Farrar $30.00 (0-374-16769-9); paper $12.95 (0-374-52104-2). Selected letters of the American short story writer and novelist. (Rev: Choice 7–8/79; LJ 1/15/79; New Rep 3/10/79. Awards: ALA, 1979; NYTBR, 1979)   **[813.5]**

4196 West, Jessamyn. *Hide and Seek: A Continuing Journey.* 1987, Harcourt paper $8.95 (0-15-640150-9). A loosely collected memoir by the novelist written during a period of solitude at her Colorado home. "An insightful and humorous reflection on continuity and change in the American culture."—Choice (Rev: BL 6/1/73; Choice 9/73; PW 1/29/73) **[813.5]**

4197 Wolff, Geoffrey. *Duke of Deception: Memories of My Father.* 1990, Random paper $9.95 (0-679-72752-3). An autobiography detailing the author's relationship with his father. "First-rate . . . as lucid and complicated a story as a good novel."—NYTBR (Rev: BL 10/1/79; NYTBR 8/12/79; Sat Rev 9/29/79)   **[813.5]**

1900–1945

4198 Blotner, Joseph L. *Faulkner: A Biography.* 1991, Random paper $16.95 (0-679-73053-2). An updated, revised, and condensed version of the author's 1974 two-volume biography of Faulkner. (Rev: BL 4/1/84; Choice 9/84; LJ 4/15/84)   **[813.52]**

4199 Branden, Barbara. *Passion of Ayn Rand.* 1987, Doubleday paper $12.95 (0-385-24388-X). A biography of the twentieth-century writer and philosopher known for such novels as *Atlas Shrugged* and *The Fountainhead.* (Rev: Choice 12/86; LJ 6/15/86; PW 5/16/86)   **[813.52]**

4200 Cheever, Susan. *Home Before Dark.* 1985, Pocket paper $4.50 (0-671-60370-1). Remembrances of the writer John Cheever by his eldest daughter. "An intimate, deeply felt and often harrowing memoir."—NYTBR (Rev: BL 10/1/84; LJ 11/15/84; Newsweek 10/22/84. Awards: ALA, 1984; LJ, 1984; Time, 1984)   **[813.52]**

4201 Donald, David Herbert. *Look Homeward: A Life of Thomas Wolfe.* 1987, Little, Brown $24.95 (0-316-18952-9); Fawcett paper $12.95 (0-449-90286-2). The first biographer to have full access to Wolfe's private papers. (Rev: CSM 2/6/87; New Rep 3/23/87; Newsweek 2/2/87. Awards: ALA, 1987; LJ, 1987; PP:Biography, 1988)   **[813.52]**

4202 Donaldson, Scott. *John Cheever: A Biography.* 1988, Random $22.50 (0-394-54921-X); Delacorte paper $14.95 (0-385-29885-4). A study of the life and works of the American novelist and short story writer. (Rev: Atl 8/88; CSM 7/25/88; LJ 7/88)   **[813.52]**

4203 Drew, Bettina. *Nelson Algren: A Life on the Wild Side.* 1989, Putnam $24.95 (0-399-13422-0). A biography of the leftist writer of the 1930s and 1940s best known for such novels as *Man with the Golden Arm* and *A Walk on the Wild Side.* (Rev: LJ 10/15/89; NYTBR 11/26/89; PW 9/1/89)   **[813.52]**

4204 Elledge, Scott. *E. B. White: A Biography.* 1984, Norton $22.50 (0-393-01771-0). A biography of the American writer, essayist, and poet. (Rev: CSM 4/14/84; NYTBR 2/26/84; New Yorker 4/30/84)   **[813.52]**

4205 Fast, Howard. *Being Red.* 1990, Houghton $22.95 (0-395-55130-7). An autobiography of the American author highlighting his life and involvement in the Communist party. (Rev: BL 9/1/90; LJ 10/1/90; PW 1/4/91. Awards: PW, 1990)   **[813.52]**

4206 Fitzgerald, Zelda. *Collected Writings.* 1991, Scribner $24.95 (0-684-19297-7). Collected short stories, letters, a novel, a play, and miscellaneous writings by the wife of F. Scott Fitzgerald. (Rev: LJ 7/91; NYTBR 9/1/91)   **[813.52]**

4207 Griffin, Peter. *Along with Youth: Hemingway, the Early Years.* 1985, Oxford Univ. Pr. $19.95 (0-19-503680-8). The first of a projected three-volume biography traces Hemingway's life from his birth to age 22. "An illuminating book."—CSM (Rev: Choice 2/86; CSM 4/15/85; NYTBR 11/27/85)   **[813.52]**

4208 Herbst, Josephine. *Starched Blue Sky of Spain: And Other Memoirs.* 1991, HarperCollins $19.95 (0-06-016512-X). Four essays composed during the 1920s and 1930s dealing with the Spanish Civil War, the Soviet Union, and Nazi Germany. (Rev: NYTBR 8/25/91; PW 6/14/91)   **[813.52]**

4209 Hobson, Laura Z. *Laura Z: The Early Years and Years of Fulfillment.* 1987, Donald I. Fine

paper $12.95 (1-55611-057-X). An autobiography of the author of *Gentleman's Agreement*. "She knows the writer's life, and she writes it well."—NYTBR (REV: LJ 10/1/86; NYTBR 2/8/87)   **[813.52]**

4210 Hurston, Zora Neale. *Dust Tracks on a Road: An Autobiography*. **1984, Univ. of Illinois Pr. paper $8.95 (0-252-01047-7)**. An autobiography of the African-American author of *Their Eyes Were Watching God*. "One of the most significant American writers of this century."—TLS (REV: NYTBR 4/21/85; TLS 5/2/85)   **[813.52]**

4211 Johnson, Diane. *Dashiell Hammett: A Life*. **1987, Fawcett paper $8.95 (0-449-90223-4)**. An authorized biography of the mystery writer and husband of Lillian Hellman, emphasizing the last 30 years of his life. "Illuminates more of this intensely private man's character than any previous biographer."—PW (REV: NYTBR 10/16/83; Newsweek 10/17/83; PW 8/26/83)   **[813.52]**

4212 Karl, Frederick R. *William Faulkner: American Writer*. **1989, Grove-Weidenfeld $37.50 (1-55584-088-4)**. A massive biography of the American author of *As I Lay Dying* and *The Sound and the Fury*. "A monument to the critical biographer's art."—PW (REV: CSM 6/21/89; NYTBR 5/14/89; PW 3/3/89. AWARDS: PW, 1989)   **[813.52]**

4213 Kerman, Cynthia Earl, and Richard Eldridge. *Lives of Jean Toomer: A Hunger for Wholeness*. **1989, Louisiana State Univ. Pr. paper $12.95 (0-8071-1548-7)**. A biography of the African-American author of *Cane* and influential figure of the Harlem Renaissance. (REV: Choice 4/88; NYTBR 8/30/87)   **[813.52]**

4214 Kert, Bernice. *Hemingway Women*. **1986, Norton paper $11.95 (0-393-30270-9)**. A study of the lives and personalities of Hemingway's mother and wives and their influence upon his life and work. (REV: BL 6/15/83; LJ 5/15/83; PW 5/6/83)   **[813.52]**

4215 Langer, Elinor. *Josephine Herbst: The Story She Could Never Tell*. **1985, Warner paper $3.95 (0-446-32853-7)**. A biography of the American radical novelist and journalist of the 1920s and 1930s. (REV: Choice 12/84; LJ 7/84; NYTBR 8/5/84)   **[813.52]**

4216 Leider, Emily Wortis. *California's Daughter: Gertrude Atherton and Her Times*. **1991, Stanford $24.95 (0-8047-1820-2)**. A biography of the California writer. "A fascinating, worthwhile contribution to American literary history."—LJ (REV: BL 1/1/91; LJ 10/15/90; PW 1/25/91)   **[813.52]**

4217 Le Vot, Andre. *F. Scott Fitzgerald: A Biography*. **1984, Warner paper $9.95 (0-446-38065-2)**. A biography of the legendary writer by a professor of American literature at the Sorbonne. "Well-documented, stimulating and thorough, this excellent book will be invaluable to students and scholars alike."—LJ (REV: CSM 5/4/83; NYTBR 4/3/83; Sat Rev 6/83. AWARDS: ALA, 1983)   **[813.52]**

4218 Lingeman, Richard. *Theodore Dreiser, Vol. II: An American Journey, 1908–1945*. **1990, Putnam $39.95 (0-399-13520-0)**. The second and concluding

volume of the author's study of the life and work of the Indiana-born naturalist writer. (REV: BL 9/15/90; NYTBR 9/30/90; PW 8/3/90)   **[813.52]**

4219 Lynn, Kenneth S. *Hemingway: The Life and the Work*. **1987, Simon & Schuster $24.95 (0-671-49872-X); Fawcett paper $14.95 (0-449-90308-7)**. A biography of the American writer focusing on his personal life and its influence on his work. "A riveting, quite accessible account of a perennially popular writer."—BL (REV: BL 7/87; CSM 9/4/87; LJ 7/87)   **[813.52]**

4220 McKain, David. *Spellbound: Growing Up in God's Country*. **1988, Univ. of Georgia Pr. $18.95 (0-8203-1048-4); Simon & Schuster paper $8.95 (0-671-68621-6)**. Memoirs of small-town life in Pennsylvania during the 1940s and of the author's relationship with his parents. (REV: LJ 10/15/88; PW 9/2/88)   **[813.52]**

4221 Martin, Jay. *Nathanael West: The Art of His Life*. **1984, Carroll & Graf paper $8.95 (0-88184-030-0)**. A biography of the author of *Day of the Locust* and *Miss Lonelyhearts*. "Provides genuine insight into the personality, writing, and contributions of a complex, gifted man."—BL (REV: BL 10/1/70; NYTBR 7/12/70; Sat Rev 6/27/70)   **[813.52]**

4222 Oates, Stephen B. *William Faulkner: The Man and the Artist*. **1988, Harper paper $9.95 (0-06-091501-3)**. The life story of the American writer by the biographer of Lincoln, King, and John Brown. "Narrative biography at its best."—PW (REV: BL 5/15/87; LJ 6/1/87; PW 7/10/87)   **[813.52]**

4223 O'Brien, Sharon. *Willa Cather: The Emerging Voice*. **1986, Oxford Univ. Pr. $29.95 (0-19-504132-1); Fawcett paper $12.95 (0-449-90283-8)**. A literary biography covering the first 40 years of the life of the Nebraska writer. (REV: LJ 12/86; NYTBR 12/14/86; TLS 5/15/87)   **[813.52]**

4224 Prokosch, Frederic. *Voices: A Memoir*. **1983, Farrar $17.95 (0-374-28509-8); paper $8.95 (0-374-51857-2)**. The writer's memoirs of famous persons he has known. "A perfect string of a memoir . . . an elegant yet intimate literary record of the vanished presences of this century."—BL (REV: BL 3/15/83; NYRB 5/12/83; TLS 12/23/83)   **[813.52]**

4225 Pyron, Darden Asbury. *Southern Daughter: The Life of Margaret Mitchell*. **1991, Oxford Univ. Pr. $29.95 (0-19-505276-5)**. A biography of the Atlanta-born author of *Gone with the Wind*. "The definitive biography . . . utterly absorbing."—PW (REV: LJ 6/15/91; PW 8/2/91)   **[813.52]**

4226 Reynolds, Michael. *Hemingway: The Paris Years; A Writer's Life*. **1989, Basil Blackwell $24.95 (0-631-15352-7)**. A study of Hemingway's life in Paris in the 1920s. "Reynolds . . . with this volume firmly establishes himself as the leading Hemingway scholar."—LJ (REV: Choice 4/90; LJ 11/15/89; TLS 2/2/90. AWARDS: LJ, 1989)   **[813.52]**

4227 Swanberg, W. A. *Dreiser*. **1965, Macmillan $30.00 (0-684-14552-9)**. A biography of the turn-of-the-century social realist and author of *Sister*

Carrie and *An American Tragedy*. "Rich Americana that will summon up a nostalgia for the American literary past of the early 20th century."—LJ (Rev: Choice 7–8/65; LJ 3/15/65; NYTBR 6/3/65. Awards: ALA, 1965) **[813.52]**

4228 Walker, Margaret. *Richard Wright, Daemonic Genius: A Portrait of the Man, a Critical Look at His Work.* 1988, Warner $22.00 (0-446-71001-6). A biography of the author of *Native Son* and *Black Boy.* "This excellent flesh and blood portrait gets closer to the inner Wright than any previous volume."—PW (Rev: BL 11/15/87; LJ 11/1/87; PW 10/14/88. Awards: PW, 1988) **[813.52]**

4229 Welty, Eudora. *One Writer's Beginnings.* 1984, Harvard Univ. Pr. $10.00 (0-674-63925-1); Warner paper $3.95 (0-446-34301-3). Childhood reminiscences of the noted American author of such novels as *The Ponder Heart, The Optimist's Daughter,* and *The Robber Bridegroom.* "Her book will surely become a classic."—LJ (Rev: BL 2/15/84; LJ 2/15/84; NYTBR 2/19/84. Awards: ALA, 1984; LJ, 1984) **[813.52]**

4230 Woodress, James. *Willa Cather: A Literary Life.* 1987, Univ. of Nebraska Pr. $35.00 (0-8032-4734-6); paper $14.95 (0-8032-9708-4). A study of the life and work of the American author of *Death Comes for the Archbishop* and *My Antonia.* (Rev: Choice 6/88; LJ 2/1/88; NYTBR 10/11/87) **[813.52]**

4231 Wright, Richard. *American Hunger.* 1983, Harper & Row paper $8.95 (0-06-090991-9). The posthumously published sequel to the author's autobiographical *Black Boy.* "A poignant story of the growth of a great American writer."—BL (Rev: BL 5/15/77; LJ 5/1/77; Newsweek 5/30/77. Awards: ALA, 1977) **[813.52]**

1945–

4232 Agee, Joel. *Twelve Years: An American Boyhood in East Germany.* 1981, Farrar $14.95 (0-374-51715-0). Memoirs of the son of writer James Agee regarding his childhood in East Germany. (Rev: LJ 5/1/81; NYRB 7/16/81; Sat Rev 5/81) **[813.54]**

4233 Baker, Nicholson. *U and I: A True Story.* 1991, Random $18.00 (0-394-58994-7). The author of *Room Temperature* and *The Mezzanine* describes his infatuation with John Updike and his works. (Rev: BL 2/1/91; Newsweek 5/27/91; PW 3/8/91) **[813.54]**

4234 Boyd, Brian. *Vladimir Nabokov: The Russian Years.* 1990, Princeton Univ. Pr. $25.00 (0-691-06794-5). The first of a two-part biography of the Russian-American writer. "Essential for all libraries."—Choice (Rev: Choice 1/91; NYTBR 10/14/90; PW 8/10/90. Awards: NYTBR, 1990; PW, 1990; Time, 1990) **[813.54]**

4235 Bresee, Clyde. *Sea Island Yankee.* 1986, Algonquin $16.95 (0-912697-37-7). Memoirs of the author's youth on a small island off the coast of South Carolina. (Rev: LJ 5/15/86; NYTBR 6/1/86; PW 4/18/86) **[813.54]**

4236 Buffett, Jimmy. *Tales from Margaritaville: Fictional Facts and Factual Fictions.* 1989, Harcourt $16.95 (0-15-187983-4); Fawcett paper $9.95 (0-449-90542-X). A collection of essays and short stories written by the popular singer and songwriter concerning his travels, experiences, and life on Florida's Gulf Coast. (Rev: BL 9/15/89; NYTBR 11/26/89) **[813.54]**

4237 Burroughs, William S. *Queer.* 1985, Viking $14.95 (0-670-80833-4); Penguin paper $6.95 (0-14-008389-8). An autobiographical study of a month in the life of an addict in Latin America. "It helps us come to grips with the dark humor, violent energy and unsettling vision of this writer."—NYTBR (Rev: BL 10/1/85; LJ 10/1/85; NYTBR 11/3/85) **[813.54]**

4238 Carey, Gary. *Anita Loos: A Biography.* 1988, Knopf $24.95 (0-394-53127-2). A biography of the American novelist and playwright best known as the author of *Gentlemen Prefer Blondes.* "An enlightening and entertaining reading experience."—LJ (Rev: BL 10/1/88; LJ 11/1/88) **[813.54]**

4239 Charters, Ann. *Kerouac: A Biography.* 1987, St. Martin's paper $12.95 (0-312-00617-9). A biography of the author of *On the Road* with sidelights about other key members of the Beat generation. "Reveals not only Kerouac the man, but Kerouac the artist."—LJ (Rev: Choice 7–8/73; LJ 4/1/73; Time 4/2/73) **[813.54]**

4240 Clarke, Gerald. *Capote: A Biography.* 1986, Simon & Schuster $18.45 (0-671-22811-0); Ballantine paper $12.95 (0-345-36078-8). A biography of the American author of *In Cold Blood* and *Breakfast at Tiffany's.* "The liveliest and rowdiest literary biography in recent memory."—Time (Rev: NYTBR 6/12/88; PW 5/13/88; Time 5/30/88. Awards: PW, 1988; Time, 1988) **[813.54]**

4241 Crichton, Michael. *Travels.* 1988, Knopf $17.95 (0-394-56236-4); Ballantine paper $4.95 (0-345-35932-1). Memoirs of the author's travels in Mexico, Africa, Asia, and the South Pacific. (Rev: BL 4/15/88; LJ 6/15/88; NYTBR 6/26/88) **[813.54]**

4242 Dubus, Andre. *Broken Vessels.* 1991, Godine $19.95 (0-87923-885-2). Autobiographical essays by the American short story writer. "This magical volume contains some of the finest personal essays in recent memory."—PW (Rev: BL 6/1/91; LJ 7/91; PW 5/24/91. Awards: ALA, 1992; BL, 1991) **[813.54]**

4243 Exley, Frederick. *Pages from a Cold Island.* 1988, Random paper $6.95 (0-394-75977-X). Memoirs of Exley's experiences as a novelist coping with the success of his first novel and the failure of his second. "An exuberant meditation on the screwy complexities of success and failure . . . don't miss it."—LJ (Rev: LJ 5/15/75; NYTBR 4/20/75; Time 4/28/75) **[813.54]**

4244 Fraser, Sylvia. *My Father's House: A Memoir of Incest and of Healing.* 1988, Ticknor & Fields $17.95 (0-89919-779-5); Harper & Row paper $8.95 (0-06-097218-1). The Canadian novelist examines her childhood years as a victim of incest, a series of events she was unable to recall until her late forties. "Stunningly powerful."—LJ (Rev: BL 6/15/88; LJ 4/15/88; NYTBR 10/2/88) **[813.54]**

4245 Graham, Laurie. *Rebuilding the House.* 1990, Viking $17.95 (0-670-82891-2). A profile of the author's late husband and their eight-year marriage. (Rev: BL 6/15/90; NYTBR 7/8/90; PW 5/4/90) **[813.54]**

4246 Green, Michelle. *Dream at the End of the World: Paul Bowles and the Literary Renegades in Tangier.* 1991, HarperCollins $22.95 (0-06-016571-5). An account of the expatriate literary scene of Tangier, Morocco, of the 1950s and 1960s, which included such figures as Paul Bowles, Tennessee Williams, Allen Ginsberg, and William S. Burroughs. (Rev: BL 7/91; NYTBR 9/15/91) **[813.54]**

4247 Hamilton, Ian. *In Search of J. D. Salinger.* 1989, Random $17.95 (0-685-25524-7); paper $8.95 (0-679-72220-3). A revised biography of the elusive writer notable for a legal case in which Salinger sued the author to prevent publication of an initial version containing quotes from unpublished letters. (Rev: BL 5/15/88; Choice 2/89; LJ 7/88) **[813.54]**

4248 Heinlein, Robert A. *Grumbles from the Grave.* Ed. by Virginia Heinleina. 1989, Ballantine $19.95 (0-345-36246-2); paper $5.95 (0-345-36941-6). Posthumously published letters of the science fiction author as selected by his widow. (Rev: BL 12/15/89; LJ 1/90) **[813.54]**

4249 Hendin, Josephine. *Vulnerable People: A View of American Fiction Since 1945.* 1978, Oxford Univ. Pr. paper $7.95 (0-19-502620-9). Hendin analyzes the major themes in American literature from 1945 to 1975. "One of the most original and perceptive surveys of recent American fiction."—PW (Rev: BL 4/1/78; LJ 4/1/78; PW 4/17/78. Awards: ALA, 1978) **[813.54]**

4250 Hochschild, Adam. *Half the Way Home: A Memoir of Father and Son.* 1987, Penguin paper $6.95 (0-14-009610-8). The founder of *Mother Jones* describes his difficult relationship with his father. "An honest, sensitive, fascinating portrait of a father-son relationship . . . one of the most interesting books of the year."—LJ (Rev: BL 6/1/86; LJ 5/15/86; PW 5/2/86. Awards: ALA, 1986; LJ, 1986) **[813.54]**

4251 Kesey, Ken. *Demon Box.* 1986, Viking $18.95 (0-670-80912-8); Penguin paper $8.95 (0-14-008530-0). Autobiographical essays and stories from the author of *One Flew Over the Cuckoo's Nest.* (Rev: Choice 12/86; LJ 7/86; Time 9/8/86) **[813.54]**

4252 L'Engle, Madeleine. *Two-Part Invention: The Story of a Marriage.* 1988, Farrar $18.95 (0-374-28020-7); Harper & Row paper $8.95 (0-06-250501-7). An account of the author's 40-year marriage and her husband's struggle against cancer. "Surpasses her best work so far . . . a profound spiritual experience."—PW (Rev: BL 11/1/88; LJ 11/15/88; PW 10/14/88) **[813.54]**

4253 MacShane, Frank. *Into Eternity: The Life of James Jones, American Writer.* 1985, Houghton $18.95 (0-395-35355-6). A biography of the American writer known for such novels as *From Here to Eternity* and *The Thin Red Line.* (Rev: Choice 3/86; CSM 12/2/85; LJ 12/85) **[813.54]**

4254 Morgan, Ted. *Literary Outlaw: The Life and Times of William S. Burroughs.* 1988, Henry Holt $27.50 (0-8050-0901-9); Avon paper $12.95 (0-380-70882-5). An account of the life of the Beat writer known for such novels as *Wild Boys* and *Naked Lunch.* (Rev: Choice 3/89; LJ 10/15/88; NYTBR 11/13/88) **[813.54]**

4255 Morris, Wright. *Will's Boy: A Memoir.* 1982, Penguin paper $6.95 (0-14-006201-7). Recollections of the childhood and youth of the American novelist. (Rev: CSM 7/29/81; Newsweek 7/13/81; NYTBR 8/16/81) **[813.54]**

4256 Nicosia, Gerald. *Memory Babe: A Critical Biography of Jack Kerouac.* 1988, Penguin paper $9.95 (0-14-058016-6). A biography of the Beat writer of such novels as *On the Road* and *Satori in Paris.* "To call this book the definitive Kerouac biography is an understatement."—LJ (Rev: LJ 4/15/83; NYTBR 7/5/83) **[813.54]**

4257 Price, Reynolds. *Clear Pictures: First Loves, First Guides.* 1989, Macmillan $19.95 (0-689-12075-3); Ballantine paper $12.95 (0-345-36675-1). Memoirs of the North Carolina writer's youth and adolescence. "Remarkable . . . this lucid autobiography portrays a mind learning to trust and reach out to the world."—PW (Rev: LJ 5/15/89; NYTBR 6/4/89; PW 4/21/89) **[813.54]**

4258 Roberts, David. *Jean Stafford: A Biography.* 1988, Little, Brown $24.95 (0-316-74998-6); St. Martin's paper $14.95 (0-312-02934-9). A biography of the American writer and wife of Robert Lowell. "An accessible and sympathetic chronicle of a remarkable American woman."—LJ (Rev: Atl 9/88; BL 6/1/88; LJ 6/15/88) **[813.54]**

4259 Robinson, Jill. *Bed/Time/Story.* 1979, Fawcett paper $1.95 (0-449-24064-9). A confessional memoir of Robinson's descent into a world of casual sex and drug use, and how love helped her regain herself. "Robinson has seen it all, and tells it all, in this hard-hitting painfully honest book."—LJ (Rev: LJ 10/15/74; PW 9/2/74; NYTBR 10/27/74) **[813.54]**

4260 Rollyson, Carl. *Lives of Norman Mailer.* 1991, Paragon House $26.95 (1-55778-193-1). A critical biography discussing the life and works of the controversial writer. (Rev: BL 10/1/91; PW 9/6/91) **[813.54]**

4261 Roth, Philip. *The Facts: A Novelist's Autobiography.* 1988, Farrar $17.95 (0-374-15212-8); Penguin paper $7.95 (0-14-011405-X). The autobiography of the writer Philip Roth as told by his fictional alter ego Nathan Zuckerman. (Rev: NYRB 10/13/88; NYTBR 9/25/88; Time 9/19/88) **[813.54]**

4262 Roth, Philip. *Patrimony: A True Story.* 1991, Simon & Schuster $19.95 (0-671-70375-7). The American writer's tribute to his father and his influence upon his life and thought. (Rev: BL 12/1/90; LJ 1/91; NYTBR 1/6/91. Awards: ALA, 1992; PW, 1991; Time, 1991) **[813.54]**

4263 Sawyer-Laucanno, Christopher. *An Invisible Spectator: A Biography of Paul Bowles.* 1989,

Grove-Weidenfeld $24.95 (1-55584-116-3); Ecco Pr. paper $14.95 (0-88001-257-9). A biography of the American composer and author of *The Sheltering Sky*. (REV: Choice 10/89; LJ 4/15/89; NYTBR 8/6/89) **[813.54]**

4264   Silko, Leslie M. *Storyteller.* 1989, Arcade paper $12.95 (1-55970-005-X). The tales of the author's family and New Mexico tribal history provide a mix of nonfiction and folklore. (REV: LJ 5/1/81; NYTBR 5/24/81; PW 3/20/81) **[813.54]**

4265   Simpson, Robert. *Yesterday's Faces: A Study of Series Characters in the Early Pulp Magazines.* 1983, Bowling Green Univ. Pr. $20.95 (0-87972-217-7); paper $10.95 (0-89772-218-5). A study of key character figures in the pulp magazines from 1896–1957. (REV: BL 9/1/83; Choice 11/83) **[813.54]**

4266   Sutin, Lawrence. *Divine Invasions: A Life of Philip K. Dick.* 1991, Carol Publg. Group paper $12.95 (0-8065-1228-8). A biography of the influential American science fiction writer known for such novels as *The Man in the High Castle* and *Do Androids Dream of Electric Sheep?* (REV: BL 11/15/89; LJ 12/89; PW 10/20/89) **[813.54]**

4267   Theroux, Paul. *Sunrise with Seamonsters: Travels and Discoveries, 1964–1984.* 1986, Houghton paper $7.95 (0-395-41501-2). A collection of travel essays and criticism collected from a wide variety of sources. "For readers mainly familiar with Theroux's popular novels, this engaging selection of non-fiction will reveal his multifaceted talent."—BL (REV: BL 5/15/85; NYTBR 6/2/85; Newsweek 8/12/85. AWARDS: ALA, 1985) **[813.54]**

4268   Updike, John. *Self-Consciousness: Memoirs.* 1989, Knopf $19.95 (0-394-57222-X); Fawcett paper $5.95 (0-449-21821-X). Memoirs of the American author of *Witches of Eastwick* and *Rabbit Is Rich*. "This book is essential."—LJ (REV: LJ 2/15/89; Natl Rev 5/19/89; NYTBR 3/5/89. AWARDS: BL, 1989) **[813.54]**

4269   Wangerin, Walter, Jr. *Miz Lil and the Chronicles of Grace.* 1988, Harper & Row $14.95 (0-06-069267-7). Autobiographical stories tracing the author's life from childhood through adolescence and spiritual awakening. (REV: BL 12/1/88; LJ 2/1/89; NYTBR 1/8/89) **[813.54]**

4270   West, Jessamyn. *Woman Said Yes: Encounters with Life and Death.* 1986, Harcourt paper $6.95 (0-15-698290-0). Memoirs of illnesses that touched the author's life—her own illnesses and her sister Carmen's. (REV: LJ 3/15/76; NYTBR 5/2/76; Time 5/24/76) **[813.54]**

4271   Wolff, Tobias. *This Boy's Life: A Memoir.* 1989, Atlantic Monthly $18.95 (0-87113-248-6); Harper & Row paper $8.95 (0-06-097277-7). Memoirs of the American writer's childhood and adolescent years. "An unaffected and extraordinarily revealing work."—LJ (REV: CSM 2/16/89; LJ 1/89; NYTBR 1/15/89. AWARDS: BL, 1989; LJ, 1989) **[813.54]**

814   Essays

4272   Abbey, Edward. *One Life at a Time.* 1988, Henry Holt $17.95 (0-8050-0602-8); paper $7.95 (0-8050-0603-6). Collected essays by the outspoken conversationalist and author of *The Monkey-Wrench Gang* and *Desert Solitaire*. (REV: BL 1/15/88; LJ 2/1/88; NYTBR 2/28/88) **[814]**

4273   Baldwin, James. *Price of the Ticket: Collected Nonfiction, 1948–1985.* 1985, St. Martin's $29.95 (0-312-64306-3). Collected nonfiction pieces by the African-American writer spanning over 40 years and containing *Nobody Knows My Name, The Fire Next Time,* and *Notes of a Native Son*. (REV: CSM 12/6/85; New Rep 12/30/85; NYTBR 10/20/85) **[814]**

4274   Barth, John. *Friday Book: Essays and Other Nonfiction.* 1984, Putnam $17.95 (0-399-12997-9); paper $8.95 (0-399-51209-8). Collected miscellaneous nonfiction writings by the author of *Letters* and *Tidewater Tales*. (REV: BL 10/1/84; LJ 9/1/84; NYTBR 11/18/84) **[814]**

4275   Davenport, Guy. *Geography of the Imagination: 40 Essays.* 1981, North Point paper $13.95 (0-86547-001-4). Forty essays chosen from throughout the career of the American literary critic. (REV: LJ 5/1/81; Natl Rev 11/13/81; NYTBR 9/6/81) **[814]**

4276   Didion, Joan. *White Album.* 1990, Farrar paper $7.95 (0-374-52221-9). A collection of essays on various aspects of life in California during the 1960s and 1970s by the author of *Play It as It Lays* and *Salvador*. (REV: LJ 6/1/79; NYTBR 6/17/79; Time 8/20/79. AWARDS: NYTBR, 1979) **[814]**

4277   Dillard, Annie. *Writing Life.* 1989, Harper & Row $15.95 (0-06-016156-6). A collection of essays by the author of *Pilgrim at Tinker Creek* concerning the joys and frustrations of writing. "Self aware but never self-absorbed, these luminous meditations examine an extraordinary writing life."—PW (REV: BL 7/89; PW 7/14/89) **[814]**

4278   Ellison, Ralph. *Going to the Territory.* 1986, Random $19.95 (0-394-54050-6); paper $10.95 (0-394-75062-4). Collected essays by the author of *Invisible Man* regarding American writers and artists and their role in American society. (REV: Choice 11/86; New Rep 8/4/86; NYTBR 8/3/86) **[814]**

4279   Ephron, Delia. *Funny Sauce: Us, the Ex, the Ex's New Mate, the New Mate's Ex and the Kids.* 1986, Viking $14.95 (0-670-81240-4); NAL paper $3.95 (0-451-82180-7). Essays regarding relationships among extended family members. "Engaging . . . both funny and wise."—NYTBR (REV: BL 6/1/86; NYTBR 10/12/86; PW 9/12/86) **[814]**

4280   Frazier, Ian. *Nobody Better, Better Than Nobody.* 1987, Farrar $14.95 (0-374-22310-6); Penguin paper $6.95 (0-14-010-603-0). A collection of five journalistic pieces, originally appearing in the *New Yorker,* by the author of *Great Plains*. (REV: LJ 6/15/87; NYTBR 5/3/87; Time 5/25/87) **[814]**

4281   Galbraith, John Kenneth. *Annals of an Abiding Liberal.* Ed. by Andrea D. Williams. 1979,

Houghton $12.95 (0-395-27617-9). Thirty essays regarding economics and politics by the author of *The New Industrial State*. (REV: BL 9/1/79; NYTBR 9/30/79; Sat Rev 10/13/79) **[814]**

4282 Hoagland, Edward. *Courage of Turtles: Fifteen Essays by Edward Hoagland*. 1985, North Point paper $9.50 (0-86547-196-7). Collected essays on a wide range of subjects, including tugboats, taxidermy, the circus, and fatherhood. (REV: LJ 1/1/71; NYTBR 2/7/71; Newsweek 1/18/71) **[814]**

4283 Hoagland, Edward. *Heart's Desire: The Best of Edward Hoagland; Essays from Twenty Years*. 1988, Summit $22.95 (0-671-64985-X); paper $12.95 (0-671-66953-2). Thirty-five essays, some previously unpublished, collected from Hoagland's career. (REV: BL 9/1/88; LJ 9/15/88; NYTBR 4/30/89) **[814]**

4284 Hoagland, Edward. *Red Wolves and Black Bears*. 1976, Random $8.95 (0-394-40091-7); Penguin paper $7.95 (0-14-006686-1). A collection of essays on a wide variety of topics, many dealing with the theme of man's relationship to his natural surroundings. "One of our most truthful writers about nature . . . it's important to have an Edward Hoagland to tell us how things really are out there."—NYTBR (REV: LJ 5/5/76; NYTBR 6/13/76; PW 3/22/76) **[814]**

4285 Hoagland, Edward. *Tugman's Passage*. 1982, Random $12.50 (0-394-52268-0). A collection of essays and short pieces regarding man and nature. (REV: BL 2/15/82; LJ 3/15/82; NYTBR 3/21/82) **[814]**

4286 Hoagland, Edward. *Walking the Dead Diamond River*. 1985, North Point paper $10.00 (0-86547-208-4). Essays concentrating on the natural surroundings of the author's farm in Vermont and his home in New York City. "Polished, literate and probing essays on coping with life today, in which the details are superbly clear."—Choice (REV: Choice 9/73; NYTBR 3/25/73; Time 4/2/73. AWARDS: Time, 1973) **[814]**

4287 Lawrence, Kathleen Rockwell. *Boys I Didn't Kiss and Other Essays*. 1990, British American $17.95 (0-945167-34-2). Selected essays by the author of *Maud Gone* originally published in magazines or newspapers during the 1980s. (REV: LJ 10/1/90; PW 8/10/90) **[814]**

4288 Lopate, Phillip. *Against Joie de Vivre: Personal Essays*. 1989, Poseidon $18.95 (0-671-67679-2). A collection of essays by the author of *The Rug Merchant*. "A joy to read, and read again . . . these invigorating pieces breathe new life into the contemporary essay."—PW (REV: BL 6/1/89; LJ 5/15/89; PW 4/7/89) **[814]**

4289 McCarthy, Mary. *Occasional Prose: Essays*. 1985, Harcourt $17.95 (0-15-167810-3). Twenty-one essays by the outspoken writer regarding politics, literature, and gardening. (REV: CSM 6/27/85; LJ 4/1/85; NYTBR 5/5/85) **[814]**

4290 McPhee, John. *Pieces of the Frame*. 1975, Farrar $14.95 (0-374-23281-4); paper $9.95 (0-374-51498-4). McPhee on horse racing, scotch, Atlantic

City, Wimbledon, and gathering firewood—among other things. (REV: LJ 6/15/75; New Rep 7/5/75; NYTBR 6/22/75) **[814]**

4291 McPhee, John. *Table of Contents*. 1985, Farrar $15.95 (0-374-27241-7); paper $7.95 (0-374-52008-9). A collection of essays on aspects of nature and contemporary life. "His work is the standard by which most literary nonfiction is judged these days."—CSM (REV: CSM 12/3/85; Natl Rev 3/28/86; NYTBR 10/13/85) **[814]**

4292 Mamet, David. *Writing in Restaurants*. 1987, Penguin paper $6.95 (0-14-008981-0). Essays on theater and writing by the American playwright. (REV: Choice 4/87; NYTBR 12/14/86; PW 10/17/86) **[814]**

4293 Perrin, Noel. *First Person Rural: Essays of a Sometime Farmer*. 1990, Godine paper $9.95 (0-87923-833-X). Essays on country life and living by a former New Yorker who left his life there and bought a 100-acre farm in Vermont. (REV: CSM 8/23/78; NYTBR 7/23/78; Time 7/24/78) **[814]**

4294 Perrin, Noel. *Second Person Rural: More Essays of a Sometime Farmer*. 1980, Godine $13.95 (0-87923-341-9); Penguin paper $6.95 (0-14-005920-2). Essays regarding farm life and wisdom from the author of *First Person Rural*. (REV: BL 10/15/80; CSM 11/10/80; LJ 11/1/80) **[814]**

4295 Reed, Ishmael. *Writin' Is Fightin': Thirty-Seven Years of Boxing on Paper*. 1988, Macmillan $18.95 (0-689-11975-5). Collected essays of the African-American writer. "A consistently stimulating collection."—BL (REV: BL 7/88; LJ 7/88; PW 5/27/88. AWARDS: LJ, 1988) **[814]**

4296 Royster, Vincent. *Essential Royster: A Vincent Royster Reader*. Ed. by Edmund Fuller. 1985, Algonquin $18.95 (0-912697-19-9). Selected essays by the Pulitzer Prize-winning *Wall Street Journal* editor and columnist. (REV: CSM 5/8/85; LJ 6/15/85; PW 4/5/85) **[814]**

4297 Vidal, Gore. *At Home: Essays, 1983–1987*. 1988, Random $18.95 (0-394-57020-0); paper $9.95 (0-679-72528-8). A collection of 24 essays by the author of *Burr* on topics ranging from Henry James to Oliver North. "Vidal the essayist at the height of his powers."—PW (REV: BL 11/15/88; LJ 11/15/88; PW 9/30/88) **[814]**

4298 Vidal, Gore. *Matters of Fact and Fiction: Essays, 1973–1976*. 1977, Random $14.95 (0-394-41128-5). A collection of essays regarding literary criticism, politics, and American life. "A valuable contribution to current understanding of literature, government, society and self."—BL (REV: BL 3/1/77; LJ 3/1/77; NYTBR 4/17/77. AWARDS: ALA, 1977)**[814]**

4299 White, E. B. *Essays of E. B. White*. 1979, Harper & Row paper $9.95 (0-06-090662-6). A selection of essays from over four decades chosen by the author. "The collection epitomizes once again E. B. White's preeminence among modern essayists."—LJ (REV: LJ 7/77; NYTBR 9/25/77; Newsweek 10/3/77. AWARDS: ALA, 1977) **[814]**

1900–1945

4300   Flanner, Janet. *Darlinghissima: Letters to a Friend.* Ed. by Natalia Danesi Murray. **1986, Harcourt paper $10.95 (0-15-623937-X).** A collection of letters written to Murray between 1944 and 1975 by the former Paris correspondent for the *New Yorker.* (Rev: BL 9/15/85; LJ 10/1/85; PW 9/6/85) **[814.52]**

4301   Gellhorn, Martha. *View from the Ground.* **1988, Atlantic Monthly paper $9.95 (0-87113-212-5).** Selected essays from six decades of the journalist's writings. (Rev: BL 3/15/88; LJ 3/15/88; PW 2/19/88) **[814.52]**

4302   Howe, Irving. *Selected Writings, 1950–1990.* **1990, Harcourt $34.95 (0-15-180390-0).** A selection of four decades of essays from the American historian and social critic. (Rev: BL 10/15/90; LJ 8/90; PW 8/10/90) **[814.52]**

4303   Mencken, H. L. *Impossible H. L. Mencken: A Selection of His Best Newspaper Stories.* Ed. by Marion Elizabeth Rodgers. **1991, Doubleday $27.50 (0-385-26207-8).** A collection of newspaper stories by the twentieth-century journalist and social commentator ranging from 1904 to 1948 and including a foreword by Gore Vidal. (Rev: BL 10/15/91; LJ 9/1/91; PW 9/27/91) **[814.52]**

4304   White, E. B. *Writings from the New Yorker, 1925–1976.* **1990, HarperCollins $20.00 (0-06-016517-0).** Collected *New Yorker* columns spanning over 50 years by the author of *Charlotte's Web.* (Rev: BL 10/1/90; LJ 10/15/90) **[814.52]**

1945–

4305   Auchincloss, Louis. *Love Without Wings: Some Friendships in Literature and Politics.* **1991, Houghton $18.95 (0-395-55442-X).** A collection of essays examining the friendships of writers and political figures, including profiles of Henry James, Edith Wharton, Samuel Johnson, Henry Adams, and others. (Rev: Choice 9/91; NYTBR 2/10/91) **[814.54]**

4306   Baker, Russell. *There's a Country in My Cellar: The Best of Russell Baker.* **1990, Morrow $20.45 (0-688-09598-4).** One hundred fifty essays selected from nearly four decades of the author's *New York Times* columns. (Rev: BL 9/15/90; LJ 9/1/90; PW 8/3/90) **[814.54]**

4307   Barry, Dave. *Dave Barry's Greatest Hits.* **1988, Crown $16.95 (0-517-56944-2); Fawcett paper $8.95 (0-449-90406-7).** Collected humorous pieces by the Pulitzer Prize-winning columnist. "The funniest man in America."—NYTBR (Rev: BL 7/88; NYTBR 10/9/88; PW 5/27/88) **[814.54]**

4308   Burroughs, William S. *Adding Machine: Collected Essays.* **1986, Seaver Books $16.95 (0-8050-0000-3).** Collected essays by the author of *Naked Lunch.* (Rev: BL 5/1/86; LJ 6/1/86; PW 3/28/86) **[814.54]**

4309   Davies, Robertson. *Enthusiasms of Robertson Davies.* Ed. by Judith S. Grant. **1990, Viking $19.95 (0-670-82994-3).** Collected newspaper col-umns and book reviews by the Canadian writer. (Rev: BL 12/15/89; LJ 1/90; PW 1/12/90) **[814.54]**

4310   Ehrlich, Gretel. *Islands, the Universe, Home.* **1991, Viking $19.95 (0-670-82161-6).** Essays by the author of *The Solace of Open Spaces* on nature, her travels, and her recovery from an illness. (Rev: BL 9/1/91; PW 7/25/91) **[814.54]**

4311   Fiedler, Leslie. *Fiedler on the Roof: Essays.* **1991, Godine $19.95 (0-87923-859-3).** Twelve essays regarding Judaism and contemporary literature. "Gutsy, exciting, freewheeling."—PW (Rev: LJ 5/1/91; PW 3/22/91) **[814.54]**

4312   Goldbarth, Arthur. *A Sympathy of Souls: Essays.* **1990, Coffee House paper $9.95 (0-918273-77-3).** Eight essays from the American poet regarding life, literature, and popular culture. (Rev: BL 5/15/90; LJ 6/15/90; PW 5/4/90) **[814.54]**

4313   Gordon, Mary. *Good Boys and Dead Girls: And Other Essays.* **1991, Viking $19.95 (0-670-82567-0).** A collection of 28 book reviews and essays by the author of *Men and Angels.* (Rev: BL 3/1/91; LJ 2/15/91; PW 2/8/91) **[814.54]**

4314   Le Guin, Ursula K. *Dancing at the Edge of the World: Thoughts on Words, Women, Places.* **1989, Grove-Weidenfeld $19.95 (0-8021-1105-X); Harper & Row paper $8.95 (0-06-097289-0).** Collected essays and reviews regarding subjects from feminism to train travel by the science fiction writer. (Rev: BL 5/1/89; LJ 1/89; NYTBR 3/12/89) **[814.54]**

4315   Mairs, Nancy. *Plaintext: Deciphering a Woman's Life.* **1986, Univ. of Arizona Pr. $15.95 (0-8165-0892-5); Harper & Row paper $6.95 (0-06-097094-4).** Collected personal essays by the author on such topics as multiple sclerosis, suicide, and agoraphobia. (Rev: BL 1/1/86; NYTBR 4/27/86; PW 2/14/86) **[814.54]**

4316   Mamet, David. *Some Freaks.* **1989, Viking $16.95 (0-670-82933-1).** Collected essays of the American playwright regarding topics ranging from theater to anti-Semitism. (Rev: BL 9/15/89; LJ 10/15/89; NYTBR 12/17/89) **[814.54]**

4317   Merwin, W. S. *Unframed Originals: Recollections.* **1983, Macmillan $14.95 (0-689-11284-X).** Portraits of the poet's childhood and family. "An almost comic, often touching family portrait."—PW (Rev: BL 9/1/82; NYTBR 8/1/82; PW 5/14/82) **[814.54]**

4318   O'Rourke, P. J. *Republican Party Reptile: Essays and Outrages.* **1987, Atlantic Monthly paper $6.95 (0-87113-145-5).** Irreverent humorous essays regarding contemporary life and politics by the author of *Holidays in Hell.* (Rev: BL 4/1/87; LJ 6/15/87) **[814.54]**

4319   Rooney, Andy. *Word for Word.* **1987, Berkley paper $3.95 (0-425-10526-1).** Familiar essays by the columnist and "60 Minutes" regular. "A delightful compilation of timeless pieces that beg to be read and reread."—BL (Rev: BL 8/86; LJ 2/1/87; Time 11/3/86) **[814.54]**

4320 **Sanders, Scott Russell. *Paradise of Bombs.* 1987, Univ. of Georgia Pr. $14.95 (0-8203-0903-6); Simon & Schuster paper $6.95 (0-671-66093-4).** Autobiographical essays about childhood and the appreciation of nature. "Evocative and warmly humorous musings from a distinctive prose stylist."—BL (Rev: BL 3/1/87; LJ 4/1/87; NYTBR 5/24/87) **[814.54]**

4321 **Snyder, Gary. *Practice of the Wild.* 1990, North Point $22.95 (0-86547-453-2); paper $10.95 (0-86547-454-0).** Essays by the Pulitzer Prize–winning poet regarding nature and man's relationship to the wild. (Rev: BL 9/15/90; LJ 10/1/90; PW 8/17/90. Awards: BL, 1990; LJ, 1990) **[814.54]**

4322 **Trillin, Calvin. *American Stories.* 1991, Ticknor & Fields $19.95 (0-395-59367-0).** A collection of essays by the *New Yorker* contributor including writings about magicians Penn and Teller, ice cream magnates Ben and Jerry, and offbeat film critic Joe Bob Briggs. (Rev: BL 8/91; LJ 9/1/91) **[814.54]**

4323 **Updike, John. *Odd Jobs: Essays and Criticism.* 1991, Knopf $35.00 (0-679-40414-7).** Miscellaneous writings by the author of *The Coup.* "Whatever the topic, Updike never fails to offer a perspicacious comment and fresh observation."—PW (Rev: BL 10/1/91; LJ 9/1/91; PW 9/20/91. Awards: PW, 1991) **[814.54]**

4324 **Updike, John. *Picked Up Pieces.* 1989, Fawcett paper $4.50 (0-449-44781-2).** A collection of Updike's prose pieces, written between 1965 and 1975, on myriad subjects from literature to golf. (Rev: Choice 3/76; LJ 10/1/75; NYTBR 11/30/75) **[814.54]**

4325 **Vonnegut, Kurt, Jr. *Palm Sunday: An Autobiographical Collage.* 1984, Dell paper $4.95 (0-440-39606-1).** Collected autobiographical writings of the writer. "An invigorating tour of the novelist's activities, thoughts and fantasies."—BL (Rev: BL 2/1/81; LJ 2/15/81; Sat Rev 3/81) **[814.54]**

817 Satire and humor

4326 **Allen, Woody. *Side Effects.* 1980, Random $8.95 (0-394-51104-2); Ballantine paper $4.95 (0-345-34335-2).** A collection of 16 comic essays by the filmmaker and author of *Without Feathers.* (Rev: BL 11/1/80; LJ 10/1/80; PW 8/29/80) **[817]**

4327 **Allen, Woody. *Without Feathers.* 1986, Ballantine paper $4.95 (0-345-33697-6).** A series of humorous essays by the film director, writer, and actor. (Rev: BL 6/15/75; Newsweek 6/23/75; PW 3/31/75) **[817]**

4328 **Angell, Roger. *A Day in the Life of Roger Angell.* 1990, Penguin paper $7.95 (0-14-014407-2).** A series of humorous essays and parodies of literary figures that originally appeared in the *New Yorker.* (Rev: BL 2/1/71; LJ 10/1/70; PW 8/31/70) **[817]**

4329 **Blount, Roy, Jr. *Now Where Were We? Getting Back to Basic Truths That We Have Lost Sight of Through No Fault of My Own.* 1989, Random $17.95 (0-394-57419-2).** A collection of 50 humorous essays by the Georgia writer. "Blount at his

whimsical best."—BL (Rev: BL 3/15/89; NYTBR 4/2/89; PW 1/6/89) **[817]**

4330 **Lebowitz, Fran. *Metropolitan Life.* 1988, NAL paper $8.95 (0-452-26330-1).** A collection of humorous essays taken from the author's "Andy Warhol's Interview" column. (Rev: BL 3/1/78; NYTBR 3/26/78; PW 1/16/78) **[817]**

4331 **Perelman, S. J. *Baby It's Cold Outside.* 1987, Penguin paper $6.95 (0-14-008042-2).** A collection of over 30 pieces by the American humorist. (Rev: BL 9/1/70; NYTBR 8/30/70; PW 6/22/70) **[817]**

4332 **Perelman, S. J. *Vinegar Puss.* 1975, Amereon $16.95 (0-89190-421-2).** A collection of 22 of Perelman's magazine pieces, most of which deal with his life in London and his experiences while traveling. (Rev: LJ 3/1/75; New Rep 3/29/75; NYTBR 3/23/75) **[817]**

4333 **Pinkwater, Daniel. *Fish Whistle: Commentaries, Uncommentaries and Vulgar Excesses.* 1989, Addison Wesley $15.95 (0-201-51789-2); paper $7.95 (0-201-57000-9).** A collection of humorous pieces taken from the author's radio show segment broadcasts on National Public Radio. (Rev: BL 9/1/89; LJ 8/89; PW 7/14/89) **[817]**

4334 **Richler, Mordecai, ed. *Best of Modern Humor.* 1983, Knopf $30.00 (0-394-51531-5).** An anthology of post–World War II humor including contributions by S. J. Perelman, Woody Allen, Truman Capote, and Philip Roth. (Rev: LJ 11/15/83; PW 10/28/83; Time 11/7/83) **[817]**

4335 **Trillin, Calvin. *If You Can't Say Something Nice.* 1988, Penguin paper $7.95 (0-14-011483-1).** A collection of satirical essays regarding America and American life during the mid-1980s. (Rev: BL 9/1/87; LJ 9/15/87; NYTBR 11/8/87) **[817]**

4336 **Waters, John. *Crackpot: The Obsessions of John Waters.* 1987, Random paper $6.95 (0-394-75534-0).** Fifteen essays by the Baltimore-based film director. "Ferociously, loonily hilarious . . . incredibly good."—BL (Rev: BL 9/15/86; LJ 9/1/86; NYTBR 11/9/86) **[817]**

1945–

4337 **Novak, William, and Moshe Waldoks, eds. *Big Book of New American Humor: The Best Humor of the Past 25 Years from Woody Allen to Robin Williams.* 1990, Harper & Row paper $15.95 (0-06-096551-7).** An anthology of American humor from 1965 to 1990. (Rev: BL 10/15/90; LJ 10/1/90) **[817.54]**

818 Miscellaneous writings

4338 **Abbey, Edward. *Best of Edward Abbey.* 1988, Sierra Club paper $10.95 (0-87156-786-5).** Selections by the author of his finest fiction and nonfiction work from 1956 to 1984. (Rev: BL 10/15/84; LJ 9/1/84; NYTBR 12/16/84) **[818]**

4339 **Bishop, Elizabeth. *Collected Prose.* 1984, Farrar $17.50 (0-374-12628-3); paper $8.95 (0-374-51855-6).** A collection of 17 essays by the American writer best known for her poetry. "A genuine literary event."—BL (Rᴇᴠ: BL 2/1/84; Choice 4/84; LJ 2/15/84) **[818]**

4340   Capote, Truman. *A Capote Reader.* 1987, Random $25.00 (0-394-55647-X). A collection of writings by the author of *In Cold Blood.* "Few volumes . . . have been better designed to revive a great American author."—LJ (Rᴇᴠ: BL 11/15/87; LJ 10/1/87; NYRB 12/7/87) **[818]**

4341   Capote, Truman. *Dogs Bark: Public People and Private Places.* 1977, NAL paper $10.95 (0-452-25909-6). A collection of three decades of essays, primarily profiles on people he knew and places he had been. "Capote is an incomparable stylist . . . an almost impossible book to put down once you've started it."—NYTBR (Rᴇᴠ: Choice 1/74; New Rep 11/3/73; NYTBR 10/28/73) **[818]**

4342   Capote, Truman. *Music for Chameleons.* 1980, Random $11.95 (0-394-50826-2); NAL paper $4.95 (0-451-16180-7). A collection of fiction and nonfiction pieces by the author of *In Cold Blood.* (Rᴇᴠ: BL 7/1/80; New Rep 9/6/80; Sat Rev 7/80) **[818]**

4343   Cheever, John. *Journals of John Cheever.* 1991, Knopf $25.00 (0-394-57274-2). The collected private journals of the writer. (Rᴇᴠ: LJ 9/15/91; NYTBR 10/6/91. Awards: NYTBR, 1991; PW, 1991) **[818]**

4344   Davies, Robertson. *Papers of Samuel Marchbanks: Comprising "The Diary," "The Table Talk" and "A Garland of Miscellanea" by Samuel Marchbanks.* 1986, Viking $22.50 (0-670-81145-9); Penguin paper $9.95 (0-14-009771-6). Commentaries from a newspaper column the Canadian writer produced under the pseudonym Samuel Marchbanks. (Rᴇᴠ: BL 5/15/86; LJ 7/86; NYTBR 8/3/86) **[818]**

4345   Dunne, John Gregory. *Harp.* 1990, Simon & Schuster $19.95 (0-671-67236-3); paper $8.95 (0-671-72514-9). Memoirs of the author of *Red, White and Blue* and *True Confessions* penned soon after being informed by his physician that he was a prime candidate for a heart attack. (Rᴇᴠ: BL 7/89; NYTBR 9/10/89; Time 8/28/89) **[818]**

4346   Fisher, M. F. K. *As They Were.* 1983, Random paper $8.95 (0-394-71348-6). A series of essays constituting an informal autobiography by an author best known for her works on food. "*As They Were* . . . will take the gastronomic curse off Mrs. Fischer and convince a world quite ready to acclaim her as the doyenne of food writers that she deserves much higher literary status."—NYTBR (Rᴇᴠ: BL 4/15/82; NYTBR 6/6/82; Newsweek 6/14/82. Awards: ALA, 1982) **[818]**

4347   Hoffman, Daniel. *Poe Poe Poe Poe Poe Poe Poe.* 1990, Paragon paper $12.95 (1-55578-274-1). A study and personal reflection by the author on the works and life of Edgar Allan Poe. "An extremely resonant study-in-depth that makes compelling reading and exalts Poe's genius as few contemporary writers have done."—PW (Rᴇᴠ: LJ 3/15/72; NYTBR 2/13/72; PW 1/3/72) **[818]**

4348   Horgan, Paul. *Of America East and West: Selections from the Writings of Paul Horgan.* 1984, Farrar $25.50 (0-374-22428-5); paper $12.95 (0-374-51896-3). Selections from the works of the Southwest writer known for such books as *Far from Cibola* and *Great River: The Rio Grande in North American History.* (Rᴇᴠ: Choice 9/84; LJ 1/84; NYTBR 4/8/84) **[818]**

4349   Hurston, Zora Neale. *I Love Myself When I Am Laughing and Then Again When I Am Looking Mean and Impressive: A Zora Neale Hurston Reader.* Ed. by Alice Walker. 1979, Feminist Pr. $10.95 (0-912670-56-8); paper $9.95 (0-912670-66-5). An anthology of writings by the African-American author of *Their Eyes Were Watching God.* (Rᴇᴠ: Choice 6/80; LJ 11/15/79; NYTBR 12/30/79) **[818]**

4350   Le Seuer, Meridel. *Ripening: Selected Work, 1927–1980.* Ed. by Elaine Hedges. 1990, Feminist Pr. paper $10.95 (0-935312-41-2). Selected essays, fiction, and poetry by the leftist feminist writer. (Rᴇᴠ: Choice 6/82; LJ 4/15/82; NYTBR 4/19/82) **[818]**

4351   Moore, Marianne. *Complete Prose of Marianne Moore.* Ed. by Patricia G. Willis. 1986, Viking $24.95 (0-670-80451-7). Over 400 pieces of noted American poet Moore's prose spanning from 1907 to 1972. (Rᴇᴠ: Choice 4/87; New Rep 12/29/86. Awards: BL 9/1/86) **[818]**

4352   Percy, Walker. *Lost in the Cosmos: The Last Self-Help Book.* 1983, Farrar $14.95 (0-374-19165-4). A philosophical guide to the modern world by the author of *The Last Gentleman* and *The Moviegoer.* (Rᴇᴠ: BL 3/15/83; LJ 5/15/83; Newsweek 6/13/83) **[818]**

4353   Rich, Adrienne. *Blood, Bread and Poetry: Selected Prose, 1979–1985.* 1986, Norton $15.95 (0-393-02376-1); paper $7.95 (0-393-30397-7). Selected prose writings by the American feminist poet and author of *Of Women Born.* (Rᴇᴠ: BL 3/1/87; LJ 3/1/87; PW 12/5/86) **[818]**

4354   Saroyan, William. *Obituaries.* 1979, Creative Arts paper $15.00 (0-916870-17-0). Essays by the noted Armenian-American author regarding his thoughts and remembrances of those people listed in *Variety*'s annual obituary list for 1976. (Rᴇᴠ: BL 9/1/79; LJ 6/15/79; NYTBR 5/20/79) **[818]**

4355   Updike, John. *Assorted Prose.* 1965, Knopf $24.95 (0-394-41473-X). A selection of essays, reviews, and literary criticism chosen by Updike and written from 1955 to 1965. (Rᴇᴠ: NYTBR 6/13/65; Sat Rev 5/15/65; Time 5/21/65. Awards: NYTBR, 1965) **[818]**

4356   Walker, Alice. *In Search of Our Mother's Gardens: Womanist Prose.* 1983, Harcourt $16.95 (0-15-144525-7); paper $8.95 (0-15-644544-1). A collection of essays and letters concerning the author's life and literary influences. (Rᴇᴠ: BL 9/1/83; Choice 5/84; LJ 11/1/83) **[818]**

4357   Walker, Alice. *Living by the Word: Selected Writings, 1973–1987.* 1988, Harcourt $15.95 (0-15-152900-0); paper $8.95 (0-15-652865-7). A collection of essays regarding race, gender, and religion by the author of *The Color Purple*. (Rev: BL 3/1/88; LJ 5/1/88; NYTBR 6/5/88)   **[818]**

4358 Welty, Eudora. *Eye of the Story: Selected Essays and Reviews*. 1990, Random paper $8.95 (0-679-73004-4). Selections of nonfiction pieces written throughout her career. "This invigorating selection . . . constantly touches the place where literary critic and creative writer meet."—NYTBR (Rev: LJ 3/15/78; NYTBR 5/7/78; Sat Rev 4/29/78. Awards: NYTBR, 1978)   **[818]**

4359 Will, George F. *Morning After: American Successes and Excesses, 1981–1986*. 1986, Free Pr. $19.95 (0-02-934430-1); Macmillan paper $10.95 (0-02-055450-8). Collected essays regarding American politics and culture from the first half of the 1980s by the conservative newspaper and magazine columnist. (Rev: BL 11/1/86; CSM 10/8/86; Natl Rev 2/13/87)   **[818]**

1830–1861

4360 Harding, Walter. *Days of Henry Thoreau: A Biography*. 1983, Princeton Univ. Pr. $55.00 (0-691-06555-1); Dover paper $9.95 (0-486-24263-3). A biography of the American naturalist, philosopher, and writer. "Will undoubtedly be considered the definitive biography."—Choice (Rev: Choice 3/66; LJ 12/1/65; NYTBR 12/4/65. Awards: ALA, 1965)   **[818.3]**

1861–1900

4361 Kaplan, Justin. *Mr. Clemens and Mark Twain*. 1966, Simon & Schuster paper $10.95 (0-671-47071-X). A biography of Clemens from age 30 to his death. "Remarkable . . . undoubtedly . . . the portrait of Mark Twain for this generation."—Atl (Rev: Atl 8/66; LJ 6/1/66; NYTBR 7/3/66. Awards: ALA, 1966; NBA, 1967; NYTBR, 1966; PP:Biography, 1967)   **[818.4]**

4362 Lane, Ann J. *To Herland and Beyond: The Life and Work of Charlotte Perkins Gilman*. 1990, Pantheon $29.95 (0-394-50559-X); Dutton paper $12.95 (0-452-01080-2). A biography of the late nineteenth- and early twentieth-century feminist fiction writer. "An excellent meld of scholarship and fine writing."—BL (Rev: BL 3/15/90; NYTBR 7/15/90; PW 2/23/90)   **[818.4]**

4363 Sanborn, Margaret. *Mark Twain: The Bachelor Years*. 1990, Doubleday $24.95 (0-385-23702-2). A study of the early life and literary development of the American writer and social critic. (Rev: LJ 3/15/90; NYTBR 4/22/90; PW 3/2/90. Awards: PW, 1990)   **[818.4]**

1900–

4364 Bowles, Paul. *Without Stopping: An Autobiography*. 1985, Ecco Pr. paper $14.95 (0-88001-061-4). Memoirs of the early years of the American writer known for his short stories and the novel *The Sheltering Sky*. (Rev: BL 6/1/72; Choice 9/72; PW 1/17/72)   **[818.5]**

4365 Gelderman, Carol W. *Mary McCarthy: A Life*. 1988, St. Martin's $24.95 (0-312-00565-2); paper $12.95 (0-312-03482-2). An analysis of the life and work of the American writer. "A fine, intelligent

account of one of the century's most honorable women."—BL (Rev: BL 4/1/88; CSM 7/20/88; NYTBR 5/8/88)   **[818.5]**

4366 Gill, Brendan. *Here at the New Yorker*. 1987, Carroll & Graf paper $12.95 (0-88184-350-4). Remembrances of 40 years working at the *New Yorker*. "By far the best book on the subject . . . no one interested in American literature and culture since the 1920s should miss it."—Choice (Rev: Choice 5/75; LJ 2/1/75; NYTBR 2/6/75. Awards: ALA, 1975)   **[818.5]**

4367 McCarthy, Mary. *How I Grew*. 1988, Harcourt paper $8.95 (0-15-642185-2). Memoirs of the American writer of her youth and adolescence. "A genuine art work as original as any of her fiction."—NYTBR (Rev: LJ 4/15/87; NYRB 6/11/87; NYTBR 4/19/87)   **[818.5]**

4368 Ondaatje, Michael. *Collected Works of Billy the Kid*. 1984, Penguin paper $6.95 (0-14-007280-2). Biographical sketches in prose and poetry with accompanying photographs tell the life story of Billy the Kid. (Rev: BL 2/1/75; LJ 12/15/74; NYTBR 11/17/74)   **[818.5]**

4369 Sarton, May. *After the Stroke: A Journal*. 1988, Norton $16.95 (0-393-02533-0); paper $5.95 (0-393-30630-5). The firsthand mental and physical effects of stroke as described by the noted poet. "A moving example of courage in the face of adversity."—BL (Rev: BL 4/1/88; LJ 4/15/88; NYTBR 3/27/88)   **[818.5]**

4370 Sarton, May. *Plant Dreaming Deep*. 1984, Peter Smith $16.25 (0-8446-6094-9); Norton paper $4.95 (0-393-30108-7). Autobiographical sketches describing her home and life in New Hampshire. "Love is the genius of this small, but tender and often poignant, book by a woman of many insights."—NYTBR (Rev: CSM 4/4/68; LJ 12/15/67; NYTBR 2/4/68. Awards: ALA, 1968)   **[818.5]**

4371 Sarton, May. *A World of Light: Portraits and Celebrations*. 1976, Norton $17.95 (0-393-07506-0). Biographical portraits of friends and acquaintances of the author including sketches of Louise Bogan and Elizabeth Bowen. (Rev: Choice 12/76; LJ 9/1/76; NYTBR 10/3/76)   **[818.5]**

4372 Wilson, Edmund. *Twenties: From Notebooks and Diaries of the Period*. Ed. by Leon Edel. 1975, Farrar $15.00 (0-374-27963-2). An edited collection of Wilson's letters, notebooks, and diaries from the 1920s, sprinkled with the literary critic's anecdotes of his contemporaries. (Rev: BL 7/1/75; LJ 4/15/75; Newsweek 5/26/75)   **[818.5]**

1900–1945

4373 Bergreen, Laurence. *James Agee: A Life*. 1985, Penguin paper $8.95 (0-14-008064-3). A biography of the American screenwriter, poet, and novelist known for such works as *A Death in the Family* and *Let Us Now Praise Famous Men*. (Rev: Choice 11/84; LJ 6/15/84; NYTBR 7/8/84)   **[818.52]**

4374 Breslin, Jimmy. *Damon Runyon*. 1991, Ticknor & Fields $24.95 (0-89919-984-4). A biography of the Hearst journalist and short story writer by the writer of *The Gang That Couldn't Shoot Straight.* (Rev: BL 8/91; LJ 9/15/91; PW 8/9/91. Awards: BL, 1991) **[818.52]**

4375 Dahlberg, Edward. *Leafless American and Other Writings.* Ed. by Harold Billings. 1986, McPherson $20.00 (0-914232-83-5); paper $10.00 (0-914232-80-0). Collected essays, poetry, and book reviews by the author of *Bottom Dogs* and *Because I Was Flesh.* (Rev: LJ 6/15/67; NYTBR 3/5/67) **[818.52]**

4376 Dillon, Margaret. *A Little Original Sin: The Life and Work of Jane Bowles.* 1990, Doubleday paper $12.95 (0-385-41103-0). A literary biography of the American writer and her troubled life. "As full a view of this fascinating, tortured woman as we are likely to get."—Choice (Rev: Choice 11/81; LJ 6/1/81; PW 6/5/81) **[818.52]**

4377 Field, Andrew. *Djuna: The Formidable Miss Barnes.* 1985, Univ. of Texas Pr. paper $8.95 (0-292-71546-3). A biography of the American artist, playwright, and author of the novel *Nightwood.* (Rev: LJ 5/1/83; NYTBR 6/26/83; PW 4/22/83) **[818.52]**

4378 Frewin, Leslie Ronald. *Late Mrs. Dorothy Parker.* 1986, Macmillan $22.07 (0-02-541310-4). A biography of the American writer and critic. (Rev: BL 10/1/86; Choice 11/87; LJ 10/1/86) **[818.52]**

4379 Harrison, Gilbert A. *Enthusiast: A Life of Thornton Wilder.* 1986, Fromm International paper $12.95 (0-88064-053-7). A biography of the author of *Our Town* and *Bridge of San Luis Rey.* "A pleasure to read; a work both substantial and delightful."—BL (Rev: BL 10/15/83; LJ 10/15/83; NYTBR 11/6/83) **[818.52]**

4380 Mackinnon, Janice R., and Stephen R. Mackinnon. *Agnes Smedley: The Life and Times of an American Radical.* 1987, Univ. of California Pr. $29.95 (0-520-05966-2); paper $12.95 (0-520-06614-6). A biography of the American author and journalist who was banished from the United States for supporting the Chinese Communists in the 1930s and 1940s. (Rev: Choice 5/88; LJ 12/87; TLS 6/3/88) **[818.52]**

4381 Mencken, H. L. *Diary of H. L. Mencken.* Ed. by Charles Fecher. 1990, Knopf $30.00 (0-394-56877-X); Random paper $16.95 (0-679-73176-8). Diaries of the Baltimore-based social and literary critic written between 1930 and 1948. "Delightfully compulsive reading."—PW (Rev: BL 12/1/89; LJ 1/90; PW 12/1/89) **[818.52]**

4382 Rampersad, Arnold. *Life of Langston Hughes, Vol. I, 1902–1941: I, Too, Sing America.* 1986, Oxford Univ. Pr. $27.50 (0-19-504011-2); paper $9.95 (0-19-505426-1). The first volume of a two-volume biography of the black writer and key figure of the Harlem Renaissance. (Rev: BL 11/1/86; LJ 8/86; NYTBR 10/12/86. Awards: LJ, 1986; NYTBR, 1986) **[818.52]**

4383 Rampersad, Arnold. *Life of Langston Hughes, Vol. II, 1941–1967: I Dream a World.* 1989, Oxford Univ. Pr. paper $12.95 (0-19-506169-1). The second

and concluding volume of the author's biography of the African-American writer. "An absorbing critical biography that is also a deft social history of black America in the 20th century."—PW (Rev: LJ 9/15/88; NYTBR 10/9/88; PW 8/26/88) **[818.52]**

4384 Wescott, Glenway. *Continual Lessons: The Journals of Glenway Wescott, 1937–1955.* 1991, Farrar $25.00 (0-374-12889-8). Selected journals of the author of *The Grandmothers* concerning his life as a writer and homosexual. (Rev: BL 11/15/90; LJ 12/90; PW 11/16/90) **[818.52]**

4385 Wilson, Edmund. *Fifties: From Notebooks and Diaries of the Period.* Ed. by Leon Edel. 1986, Farrar $24.50 (0-374-52066-6). Selections from the notebooks and diaries of literary critic and writer Edmund Wilson. (Rev: LJ 9/1/86; NYTBR 8/31/86; PW 7/4/86) **[818.52]**

1945–

4386 Angelou, Maya. *All God's Children Need Traveling Shoes.* 1986, Random $15.95 (0-394-52143-9). This third volume of the author's memoirs concerns her travels and life in Ghana with her son. (Rev: LJ 3/15/86; NYTBR 5/11/86; PW 2/21/86) **[818.54]**

4387 Bowers, John. *In the Land of Nyx: Night and Its Inhabitants.* 1985, Carroll & Graf paper $7.95 (0-88164-163-3). A look at people who frequent the night for pleasure or work. "An uneven book—but its high spots are truly high."—New Yorker (Rev: LJ 5/1/84; NYTBR 4/8/84; New Yorker 4/16/84) **[818.54]**

4388 Brenner, David. *If God Wanted Us to Travel. . . .* 1990, Simon & Schuster $16.95 (0-671-70113-4); Pocket paper $8.95 (0-671-70114-2). A look at the lighter side of travel by the comedian and author of *Soft Pretzels with Mustard.* (Rev: BL 6/15/90; LJ 6/1/90) **[818.54]**

4389 Campbell, James. *Talking at the Gates: A Life of James Baldwin.* 1991, Viking $21.95 (0-670-82913-7). A biography of the author of *Go Tell It on the Mountain* and *The Fire Next Time.* "Marvelously illuminating."—PW (Rev: CSM 6/7/91; LJ 4/1/91; PW 3/1/91) **[818.54]**

4390 Cheuse, Alan. *Fall Out of Heaven: An Autobiographical Journey Across Russia.* $7.95, Atlantic Monthly paper 1989 (0-87113-300-8). Memoirs of the son of a Red Army pilot who traveled to Russia with his own son to see their family's ancestral home. (Rev: LJ 9/15/87; NYTBR 11/29/87; PW 7/10/87) **[818.54]**

4391 Conroy, Frank. *Stop-Time.* 1977, Penguin paper $7.95 (0-14-004446-9). Memoirs of a childhood and youth in New York and Florida. "One of the finest books about growing up I have ever read; the reader cannot help recognizing a part of himself in this book."—NYTBR (Rev: LJ 12/15/67; New Rep 11/11/67; NYTBR 11/12/67. Awards: NYTBR, 1967) **[818.54]**

4392 Cunningham, Laura. *Sleeping Arrangements.* 1989, Knopf $18.95 (0-394-56112-0). Memoirs of a New York childhood and of being reared by two bachelor uncles. (REV: BL 10/15/89; LJ 8/25/89; Newsweek 12/25/89) **[818.54]**

4393 Davis, Donald D. *Listening for the Crack of Dawn.* 1990, August House $17.95 (0-87483-153-9); paper $9.95 (0-87483-130-X). Memoirs of the author's youth in rural Appalachia. "Delightful . . . essential for regional collections."—LJ (REV: BL 10/1/90; LJ 10/15/90) **[818.54]**

4394 Dillard, Annie. *An American Childhood.* 1987, Harper & Row $17.95 (0-06-015805-0); paper $8.95 (0-06-091518-8). Memoirs of the Pittsburgh childhood of the author of *Pilgrim at Tinker Creek.* (REV: BL 8/87; LJ 9/1/87; NYTBR 9/27/87) **[818.54]**

4395 Grizzard, Lewis. *If I Ever Get Back to Georgia, I'm Gonna Nail My Feet to the Ground.* 1990, Random $17.95 (0-394-58725-1); Ballantine paper $5.99 (0-345-37270-0). The Georgia journalist writes about his experiences at the *Atlanta Journal, Chicago Sun-Times,* and *Atlanta Constitution.* (REV: BL 10/1/90; LJ 11/15/90; NYTBR 11/11/90) **[818.54]**

4396 Grumbach, Doris. *Coming into the End Zone: A Memoir.* 1991, Norton $19.95 (0-393-03009-1). A journal of the writer's reflections on life during her seventieth year. "A rare celebration of life."—PW (REV: BL 9/1/91; LJ 8/91; PW 7/5/91) **[818.54]**

4397 Hentoff, Nat. *Boston Boy: A Memoir.* 1987, Faber paper $7.95 (0-571-12951-X). The jazz critic and writer reflects on his Jewish childhood in the Boston of the 1930s and 1940s. "A delicious autobiography that ends far too soon."—BL (REV: BL 4/15/86; LJ 3/15/86; NYTBR 4/27/86) **[818.54]**

4398 Jones, Hettie. *How I Became Hettie Jones.* 1990, Dutton $18.95 (0-525-24840-4). Memoirs of the 1950s and 1960s written by the former wife of African-American writer LeRoi Jones (now Amiri Baraka). (REV: BL 1/15/90; NYTBR 3/11/90; PW 12/22/89) **[818.54]**

4399 Kazin, Alfred. *Starting Out in the Thirties.* 1989, Cornell Univ. Pr. paper $6.95 (0-8014-9562-8). Kazin's second volume of memoirs includes sketches of the major literary figures of the thirties. (REV: Choice 3/66; LJ 10/1/65; NYTBR 10/24/65. AWARDS: ALA, 1965; NYTBR, 1965) **[818.54]**

4400 Koller, Alice. *Stations of Solitude.* 1990, Morrow $19.95 (0-688-07940-7). Memoirs of the author's solitary life in her country home with her three dogs for company. (REV: BL 4/15/90; NYTBR 7/22/90) **[818.54]**

4401 Mewshaw, Michael. *Playing Away: Roman Holidays and Other Mediterranean Encounters.* 1990, Henry Holt paper $9.95 (0-8050-1225-7). Essays on life in Italy written by an American novelist who has lived in Rome for over a decade. (REV: BL 11/1/88; NYTBR 6/10/90) **[818.54]**

4402 Morrell, David. *Fireflies.* 1988, Dutton $16.95 (0-525-24680-0). A study of the death of the author's son from cancer told through a mixture of fiction and nonfiction. (REV: BL 9/1/88; LJ 10/1/88; PW 9/30/88) **[818.54]**

4403 Morris, Mary. *Wall to Wall: From Beijing to Berlin by Rail.* 1991, Doubleday $19.50 (0-385-41465-X). An account of the author's 1986 rail journey from China to Europe via the Soviet Union. (REV: BL 5/15/91; NYTBR 6/9/91; PW 5/10/91) **[818.54]**

4404 Nemerov, Howard. *Howard Nemerov Reader.* 1991, Univ. of Missouri Pr. $24.95 (0-8262-0776-6). Selected prose and poetry from over five decades by the former U.S. poet laureate. (REV: LJ 3/15/91; NYTBR 4/28/91; PW 2/22/91) **[818.54]**

4405 Niedecker, Lorine. *From This Condensery: The Complete Poems of Lorine Niedecker.* Ed. by Robert Bertholf. 1985, Jargon Society $30.00 (0-912330-57-0). The collected verse and prose of the American writer. "An item destined to increase in value to collections concentrating on American Literature and American Studies."—BL (REV: BL 3/15/86; Choice 6/86; NYTBR 1/26/86) **[818.54]**

4406 Ondaatje, Michael. *Running in the Family.* 1984, Penguin paper $6.95 (0-14-006966-6). Childhood memoirs of the Ceylonese-born author who emigrated to Canada at age 11. (REV: BL 10/1/82; LJ 11/15/82; New Yorker 12/28/82) **[818.54]**

4407 Oppenheimer, Judy. *Private Demons: The Life of Shirley Jackson.* 1988, Putnam $19.95 (0-395-13356-9); Fawcett paper $10.95 (0-449-90405-9). A biography of the American writer best known for her short stories. "A memorable closeup portrait."—New Yorker (REV: LJ 7/88; NYTBR 8/7/88; New Yorker 10/3/88) **[818.54]**

4408 Stein, Harry. *One of the Guys: The Wising Up of an American Man.* 1988, Simon & Schuster $17.95 (0-671-55704-1); Pocket paper $7.95 (0-671-68358-6). Essays by an *Esquire* columnist on maleness and masculinity in contemporary American society. (REV: BL 3/15/88; LJ 4/1/88; NYTBR 3/27/88) **[818.54]**

4409 Weatherby, W. J. *James Baldwin: Artist on Fire.* 1989, Donald I. Fine $19.95 (1-55611-126-6); Dell paper $5.95 (0-440-20573-5). A biography of the politically outspoken American writer and author of *The Fire Next Time* and *Go Tell It on the Mountain.* (REV: BL 4/15/89; LJ 5/1/89; PW 2/10/88) **[818.54]**

4410 Wolfe, Tom. *Purple Decades.* 1982, Farrar $17.50 (0-374-23927-4); Berkley paper $7.95 (0-425-06266-X). Twenty years of selected writings from the pen of Tom Wolfe. (REV: BL 10/1/82; NYTBR 10/10/82; PW 9/24/82) **[818.54]**

820 ENGLISH AND OLD ENGLISH LITERATURE

4411 Fussell, Paul. *The Great War and Modern Memory.* 1975, Oxford Univ. Pr. paper $9.95 (0-19-502171-1). A look at World War I, the literature which arose from it, and how the war changed our perceptions of the world. "Extraordinary and moving . . . a scrupulously argued and profoundly affecting account."—Time (REV: LJ 7/75; New Rep 10/

4/75; Time 10/20/75. Awards: NBA, 1976; Time, 1975; Time, the 1970s)   **[820]**

4412   Gilbert, Sandra M., and Susan Gubar. *Madwoman in the Attic: A Study of Women and the Literary Imagination in the 19th Century.* 1979, Yale Univ. Pr. paper $19.95 (0-300-02596-3). An analysis of nineteenth-century women writers and their works focusing on Jane Austen, Mary Shelley, Emily Dickinson, and the Brontës. (Rev: BL 12/15/79; Choice 1/80; NYTBR 12/9/79)   **[820]**

4413   Gray, Douglas, ed. *Oxford Book of Late Medieval Verse and Prose.* 1989, Oxford Univ. Pr. paper $12.95 (0-19-282245-4). An anthology of writings in the English language from the beginning of the fifteenth century to 1525. (Rev: LJ 1/86; TLS 12/27/85)   **[820]**

1837–1900

4414   Gilbert, Sandra M., and Susan Gubar, eds. *Norton Anthology of Literature by Women: The Tradition in English.* 1985, Norton $39.95 (0-393-01940-3); paper $28.95 (0-393-95391-2). A three-volume survey of literature by women in the English language from the Middle Ages to the present. (Rev: Atl 8/85; BL 4/15/85; LJ 4/15/85)   **[820.8]**

History and criticism

4415   Donoghue, Denis. *England, Their England: Commentaries on English Language and Literature.* 1988, Knopf $24.95 (0-394-56473-1). The third volume of the literary critic's series on the literature of English-speaking countries. (Rev: BL 9/15/88; LJ 10/15/88; NYTBR 12/25/88)   **[820.9]**

4416   Donoghue, Denis. *We Irish: On Irish Literature and Society.* 1988, Univ. of California Pr. $10.95 (0-520-06425-9). A study of Irish literature, culture, and "Irishness" by the distinguished critic. (Rev: Choice 3/87; CSM 10/3/86; LJ 9/15/86)   **[820.9]**

4417   Ellmann, Richard. *A Long the Riverrun: Selected Essays.* 1989, Knopf $21.95 (0-394-57768-X); Random paper $12.95 (0-679-72828-7). A collection of 20 essays regarding literature by the biographer of James Joyce and Oscar Wilde. (Rev: BL 3/1/89; LJ 2/15/89; NYTBR 3/19/89)   **[820.9]**

4418   Ford, Hugh. *Published in Paris: A Literary Chronicle of Paris in the 1920s and 1930s.* 1988, Macmillan paper $14.95 (0-02-032550-9). A study of the activities of writers and their publishers in Paris during the 1920s and 1930s. (Rev: BL 9/1/75; LJ 10/15/74; NYTBR 9/14/75)   **[820.9]**

4419   Gilbert, Sandra M., and Susan Gubar. *No Man's Land—The Place of the Woman Writer in the 20th Century, Vol. 1: The War of the Words.* 1988, Yale Univ. Pr. $27.50 (0-300-04005-9); paper $12.95 (0-300-04587-5). The first of a three-volume set by American feminist literary critics analyzing twentieth-century female writers, their work, and male writers' reactions to it. (Rev: Choice 4/88; LJ 11/15/87; NYTBR 2/7/88)   **[820.9]**

4420   Gilbert, Sandra M., and Susan Gubar. *No Man's Land—The Place of the Woman Writer in the 20th Century, Vol. 2: Sexchanges.* 1989, Yale Univ. Pr. $29.95 (0-300-04375-9). This second volume of a trilogy analyzing the role of the twentieth-century woman writer deals with gender and its impact upon literary output. "It will set the direction of feminist criticism for the next generation."—NYTBR (Rev: BL 2/15/89; LJ 3/1/89; NYTBR 2/19/89)   **[820.9]**

4421   Kenner, Hugh. *A Colder Eye: The Modern Irish Writers.* 1989, Johns Hopkins paper $12.95 (0-8018-3838-X). An appraisal of twentieth-century Irish literature focusing on the works of Joyce, Beckett, Synge, and Yeats. (Rev: BL 4/15/83; Choice 10/83; Natl Rev 7/22/83)   **[820.9]**

4422   Kenner, Hugh. *A Sinking Island: The Modern English Writers.* 1988, Knopf $22.95 (0-394-54254-1); Johns Hopkins paper $12.95 (0-8018-3837-1). A survey of the life and works of the major twentieth-century British writers including Conrad, Woolf, Eliot, and Lawrence. "For breadth and readability, few critics come close to Kenner."—LJ (Rev: BL 12/15/87; LJ 1/88; NYTBR 2/21/88)   **[820.9]**

4423   Kermode, Frank. *History and Value: The Clarendon Lectures and the Northcliffe Lectures.* 1989, Oxford Univ. Pr. paper $10.95 (0-19-812224-1). A study of political themes and issues in the literature of the 1930s. (Rev: BL 4/15/88; LJ 4/15/88; TLS 7/1/88)   **[820.9]**

4424   Lurie, Alison. *Don't Tell the Grown-Ups: Subversive Children's Literature.* 1990, Little, Brown $19.95 (0-316-53722-5). A study of subversive themes in children's literature during the nineteenth and twentieth centuries. (Rev: BL 3/15/90; LJ 2/15/90; NYTBR 3/11/90. Awards: BL, 1990)   **[820.9]**

4425   Pearson, John. *Sitwells: A Family's Biography.* 1980, Harcourt paper $7.95 (0-15-682-676-3). A collective biography of the literary family of Osbert, Edith, and Sachervell Sitwell. "Lively and authoritative . . . at one level the book engages the reader's serious interest; at another, that of literary gossip. It's tremendous fun."—LJ (Rev: LJ 3/1/79; NYTBR 4/15/79; PW 2/26/79. Awards: ALA, 1979) **[820.9]**

821   English poetry

4426   Archibald, Douglas. *Yeats.* 1983, Syracuse Univ. Pr. $25.00 (0-8156-2263-5); paper $12.95 (0-8156-2391-7). A biography of the Irish poet and dramatist who was awarded the Nobel Prize for Literature in 1923. (Rev: Choice 10/83; LJ 4/15/83; NYTBR 6/5/83)   **[821]**

4427   Auden, W. H. *Collected Poems.* 1991, Random paper $15.95 (0-679-73197-0). An anthology with revisions of the poetic work that Auden wished to preserve. "Delightful for any reader and invaluable for the scholar."—BL (Rev: BL 12/15/76; CSM 12/30/76; Newsweek 11/22/76. Awards: ALA, 1976)   **[821]**

4428   Baker, Russell, ed. *Norton Book of Light Verse.* 1986, Norton $17.95 (0-393-02366-4). A volume of light verse edited by the author of *Growing*

Up. "I found nearly everything I expected here, and much delightful stuff I didn't know existed."—Newsweek (Rᴇᴠ: CSM 11/26/86; LJ 11/15/86; Newsweek 12/15/86) **[821]**

4429 **Berke, Roberta.** *Bounds Out of Bounds: A Compass for Recent American and British Poetry.* **1981, Oxford Univ. Pr. $19.95 (0-19-502872-4).** "One of the best critiques of modern poetry to appear in many years, her book is a gem that will serve as a touchstone for poets, critics, and the general reader."—PW (Rᴇᴠ: Choice 9/81; LJ 4/1/81; PW 3/13/81. Aᴡᴀʀᴅs: ALA, 1981) **[821]**

4430 **Boland, Eavan.** *Outside History: Selected Poems, 1980–1990.* **1990, Norton $17.95 (0-393-02898-4).** The first collection of the Irish poet's verse to be published in the United States. (Rᴇᴠ: BL 1/1/91; NYTBR 4/21/91; PW 10/26/90) **[821]**

4431 **Crompton, Louis.** *Byron and Greek Love: Homophobia in 19th Century England.* **1985, Univ. of California Pr. $35.00 (0-520-05172-6); paper $12.95 (0-520-05732-5).** A work that attempts to give more understanding to the works of Byron by exploring attitudes toward homosexuality in the British society of his time. "An altogether original and excellent study which is a model of historical method."—LJ (Rᴇᴠ: Choice 7–8/85; LJ 2/1/85; New Rep 7/1/85. Aᴡᴀʀᴅs: PW, 1985) **[821]**

4432 **Ewart, Gavin.** *Gavin Ewart Show: Selected Poems, 1939–1985.* **1986, Bits Pr. $14.95 (0-933248-05-9); paper $8.95 (0-933248-06-7).** Selected works of the English poet. "A clever, lively, often extremely funny writer . . . his work is a display case of inventiveness and adaptation."—NYTBR (Rᴇᴠ: CSM 10/3/86; NYRB 1/29/87; NYTBR 8/17/86) **[821]**

4433 **Heaney, Seamus.** *Haw Lantern.* **1987, Farrar $12.95 (0-374-16837-7); paper $7.95 (0-374-52109-3).** A collection by the Irish poet. "There are more brilliant poets in Ireland today . . . but none uses more of the language more effectively."—CSM (Rᴇᴠ: CSM 10/28/87; New Rep 12/21/87; NYTBR 12/20/87) **[821]**

4434 **Heaney, Seamus.** *Seeing Things.* **1991, Farrar $18.95 (0-374-25776-0).** A collection of verse about the Irish writer's late father. (Rᴇᴠ: LJ 11/15/91; PW 11/1/91) **[821]**

4435 **Heaney, Seamus.** *Selected Poems, 1966–1987.* **1990, Farrar $20.00 (0-374-25868-6).** Selected verse from the Irish poet. "An ample selection of some of the best work by one of the finest contemporary poets."—LJ (Rᴇᴠ: BL 8/90; LJ 11/1/90; NYTBR 11/11/90) **[821]**

4436 **Heaney, Seamus.** *Station Island.* **1985, Farrar $11.95 (0-374-26978-5); paper $6.95 (0-374-51935-8).** "The best poet that Ireland has produced since Yeats."—Time "This may well be his best book."—LJ (Rᴇᴠ: LJ 12/84; NYTBR 3/10/85; Time 2/25/85. Aᴡᴀʀᴅs: ALA, 1985; LJ, 1985) **[821]**

4437 **Heaney, Seamus.** *Sweeney Astray.* **1984, Farrar $13.95 (0-374-27221-2); paper $7.95 (0-374-51894-7).** A retelling in verse of the Medieval Gaelic tale of King Sweeney by the acclaimed Irish poet. (Rᴇᴠ: LJ 5/1/84; NYTBR 5/27/84; Time 3/19/84) **[821]**

4438 **Hughes, Ted.** *Crow: From the Life and Songs of the Crow.* **1981, Harper & Row paper $7.95 (0-06-090905-6).** Eighty poems on the life of Crow from the creation to the apocalypse. "Reading 'Crow' is a profoundly disturbing experience . . . no mere book of verses, but a wild yet cunning wail of anguish and resilience."—NYTBR (Rᴇᴠ: LJ 7/71; NYTBR 4/18/71; Newsweek 4/12/71. Aᴡᴀʀᴅs: ALA, 1971) **[821]**

4439 **Hughes, Ted.** *New Selected Poems.* **1982, Harper & Row paper $13.95 (0-06-090925-0).** A collection of over 150 poems by the British poet from 1957 to the 1980s. "Contains some of the supreme poetry of the last two decades."—NYRB (Rᴇᴠ: LJ 2/15/82; NYRB 6/10/82; NYTBR 3/14/82) **[821]**

4440 **Hughes, Tom.** *Wolfwatching.* **1990, Farrar $14.95 (0-374-29199-3).** Poems by the Poet Laureate of England. "His new collection will no doubt cause more than one aspiring poet to cast their pens down in frustration and despair."—LJ (Rᴇᴠ: BL 11/15/90; LJ 12/90) **[821]**

4441 **Kennelly, Brendan.** *A Time for Voices: Selected Poems, 1960–1990.* **1990, Bloodaxe Books $30.00 (1-85224-096-2); paper $17.95 (1-85224-097-0).** Collected verse from three decades by the Irish poet. (Rᴇᴠ: BL 1/1/91; TLS 8/17/90) **[821]**

4442 **Larkin, Philip.** *Collected Poems.* **Ed. by Anthony Thwaite. 1989, Farrar $22.50 (0-374-12633-2).** A chronologically arranged selection of previously published and unpublished poems by the English poet. "Will ensure his hard-won niche in English poetry for decades to come."—BL (Rᴇᴠ: BL 4/1/89; New Yorker 7/17/89; TLS 10/14/88. Aᴡᴀʀᴅs: LJ, 1989)**[821]**

4443 **Pritchard, William H.** *Lives of the Modern Poets.* **1981, Oxford Univ. Pr. paper $8.95 (0-19-502989-5).** A study of the lives and works of nine key twentieth-century poets including William Carlos Williams, Ezra Pound, T. S. Eliot, and Hart Crane. (Rᴇᴠ: Choice 9/80; LJ 3/15/80; NYTBR 4/27/80) **[821]**

4444 **Rebsamen, Frederick, trans.** *Beowulf: A Verse Translation.* **1991, HarperCollins $18.95 (0-06-438437-3).** An updated translation by Frederick Rebsamen of the classic English poem. (Rᴇᴠ: BL 10/15/91; LJ 10/1/91) **[821]**

4445 **Smith, Stevie.** *Collected Poems.* **1983, New Directions paper $15.95 (0-8112-0882-6).** Collected works by the English poet illustrated with her drawings. "With this majesterial edition, the full recognition of the remarkable poetic achievement of Stevie Smith should be accelerated."—Choice (Rᴇᴠ: BL 6/15/76; Choice 7–8/76; LJ 6/1/76) **[821]**

4446 **Spender, Stephen.** *Collected Poems, 1928–1985.* **1986, Random $19.95 (0-394-54601-6); Oxford Univ. Pr. paper $12.95 (0-19-505210-2).** Selected and revised works by the English poet. "A portrait central to the literature of this century."—BL (Rᴇᴠ: BL 4/15/86; LJ 2/15/86; PW 12/6/85) **[821]**

4447 Walcott, Derek. *Arkansas Testament.* 1987, Farrar $14.95 (0-374-10582-0); paper $8.95 (0-374-52099-2). A collection of poems by the St. Lucian writer. "Walcott is honored by the language he writes in, and in turn he adds to that honor."—New Rep (Rev: LJ 10/15/87; New Rep 11/2/87; NYTBR 12/20/87) **[821]**

4448 Walcott, Derek. *Collected Poems: 1948 to 1984.* 1986, Farrar $25.00 (0-374-12626-7); paper $13.95 (0-374-52025-9). Selected works from the Caribbean writer's nine books of poetry. "The work of a supreme stylist whose concise imagery makes his world ours."—LJ (Rev: BL 4/15/86; LJ 2/15/86; NYTBR 2/2/86. Awards: LJ, 1986) **[821]**

4449 Walcott, Derek. *Fortunate Traveller.* 1982, Farrar $11.95 (0-374-15765-0); paper $8.95 (0-374-51744-4). Poetry depicting travels and places experienced by the Caribbean writer. (Rev: BL 1/1/82; LJ 12/15/81; New Rep 3/17/82) **[821]**

4450 Walcott, Derek. *Omeros.* 1989, Farrar $14.95 (0-374-22591-5). An epic poem about the life and adventures of Homer. (Rev: BL 11/15/90; NYTBR 10/7/90; PW 5/25/90. Awards: NYTBR, 1990) **[821]**

4451 Walcott, Derek. *Star-Apple Kingdom.* 1979, Farrar $7.95 (0-374-26974-2); paper $7.95 (0-374-51532-8). Poetry about the West Indies by the St. Lucian writer. "A beautiful and equivocal recounting of the freedom of the mind and . . . the conscience of the island man."—BL (Rev: BL 5/15/79; LJ 6/15/79; NYTBR 5/13/79. Awards: ALA, 1979) **[821]**

Early English period, 1066–1400

4452 Gardner, John. *Life and Times of Chaucer.* 1978, Random paper $9.95 (0-394-72500-X). The author was a professor of medieval literature as well as a noted novelist. "Scholars will dislike this book for its boisterous irreverence, occasional homely diction and purple passages, and unfashionable cheerfulness. General readers will like it—for the same reasons."—LJ (Rev: BL 3/15/77; CSM 4/23/77; LJ 4/15/77. Awards: ALA, 1977) **[821.1]**

4453 Howard, Donald Roy. *Chaucer: His Life, His Works, His World.* 1987, Dutton $29.95 (0-525-24400-X); Fawcett paper $12.95 (0-449-90341-9). A biography of the English medieval writer that was the synthesis of the former Stanford University professor's studies. "A fine synthesis of everything worth noting about Chaucer."—Choice (Rev: Atl 11/87; Choice 4/88; LJ 10/15/87. Awards: PW, 1987) **[821.1]**

Post-Elizabeth period, 1625–1702

4454 Greene, Graham. *Lord Rochester's Monkey: Being the Life of John Wilmot, Second Earl of Rochester.* 1989, Penguin paper $7.95 (0-14-010154-3). Originally written in 1934 but unpublished for 40 years, this is the life story of a seventeenth-century English poet noted for his scandalous public behavior. (Rev: BL 9/1/74; NYTBR 9/15/74; PW 8/5/74) **[821.4]**

4455 Winn, James Anderson. *John Dryden and His World.* 1987, Yale Univ. Pr. $37.50 (0-300-02994-2); paper $19.95 (0-300-04591-3). A study of the life and times of the English Restoration poet. "Few have captured Dryden's era so well."—LJ (Rev: Atl 11/87; Choice 2/88; LJ 8/87) **[821.4]**

Queen Anne period, 1702–1745

4456 Mack, Maynard. *Alexander Pope: A Life.* 1986, Norton $25.95 (0-393-02208-0). A biography of the eighteenth-century English poet with an analysis of his works. "Mack brings us both Pope and the age in a biography as entertaining as it is masterly."—PW (Rev: LJ 10/1/85; NYTBR 3/2/86; PW 12/6/85) **[821.5]**

1800–1837

4457 Gill, Stephen. *William Wordsworth: A Life.* 1989, Oxford Univ. Pr. $29.95 (0-19-812828-2). A biography of the English romantic poet. "Will appeal to anyone with an interest in Wordsworth."—LJ (Rev: LJ 4/1/89; NYTBR 6/11/89; PW 4/21/89) **[821.7]**

4458 Holmes, Richard. *Coleridge: Early Visions.* 1990, Viking $22.95 (0-670-80444-4). The first half of a biographical study of the English poet. "One wonders how the second volume of this work could be better than the first."—BL (Rev: Atl 6/90; BL 3/1/90; LJ 4/1/90) **[821.7]**

4459 Holmes, Richard. *Shelley: The Pursuit.* 1987, Penguin paper $12.95 (0-14-058037-9). The life story of the British lyric poet, Percy Bysshe Shelley. "A magnificent job of reassessment, a fresh and definitive portrait."—PW (Rev: BL 6/15/75; LJ 5/15/75; PW 3/24/75) **[821.7]**

Victorian period, 1837–1900

4460 Honan, Park. *Matthew Arnold: A Life.* 1983, Harvard Univ. Pr. paper $12.50 (0-674-55465-5). A biography of the English poet and writer. "Honan has written what will surely be recognized as the definitive biography."—LJ (Rev: BL 7/15/81; LJ 7/81; NYTBR 8/9/81) **[821.8]**

4461 Martin, Robert Bernard. *Gerard Manley Hopkins: A Very Private Life.* 1991, Putnam $29.95 (0-399-13610-X). A biography of the nineteenth-century English poet and Jesuit priest. "Superlative, often astonishing."—PW (Rev: BL 5/1/91; PW 5/3/91) **[821.8]**

4462 Martin, Robert Bernard. *Tennyson: The Unquiet Heart.* 1980, Oxford Univ. Pr. $39.95 (0-19-812072-9). A biography of the English poet focusing on his family, its background, and its influence upon his works. (Rev: CSM 12/10/80; LJ 11/15/80; NYTBR 12/14/80) **[821.8]**

1900–

4463 Bush, Ronald. *T. S. Eliot: A Study in Character and Style.* 1984, Oxford Univ. Pr. $29.95 (0-19-503376-0). A psychological profile of the poet and his work. "Penetrating . . . an outstanding work of criticism."—BL (Rev: Atl 4/84; BL 1/15/84; NYTBR 4/8/84) **[821.9]**

4464 Carpenter, Humphrey. *W. H. Auden: A Biography.* 1982, Houghton paper $10.95 (0-395-32439-4). A biography of the English poet focusing on his personal life. "With a flair for compelling and lively narrative and an eye for the perfect revealing detail, Carpenter has given us an engaging record of this complex personality."—LJ (Rev: BL 9/15/81; LJ 9/15/81; NYTBR 10/4/81. Awards: ALA, 1981) **[821.9]**

4465 Ferris, Paul. *Dylan Thomas: A Biography.* 1989, Paragon paper $12.95 (1-55778-215-6). A study of the life and works of the Welsh poet. "Perhaps the most personally revealing biography thus far, this resonant portrait makes vital connections between Thomas's life and art."—PW (Rev: BL 10/15/77; Choice 4/78; PW 11/13/78) **[821.9]**

4466 Gordon, Lyndall. *Eliot's New Life.* 1989, Farrar $9.95 (0-374-52205-7). The second and concluding volume of the author's biography of poet T. S. Eliot focusing on his personal life and its influence upon his work. (Rev: BL 11/15/88; LJ 9/1/88; Natl Rev 11/7/88) **[821.9]**

4467 Graves, Richard Perceval. *Robert Graves: The Years with Laura, 1926–1940.* 1990, Viking $24.95 (0-670-81327-3). This second volume of the author's biography of his uncle focuses on Robert Graves's relationship with poet Laura Riding. (Rev: LJ 12/1/90; NYTBR 11/11/90; TLS 8/3/90) **[821.9]**

4468 Jeffares, A. Norman. *W. B. Yeats: A New Biography.* 1989, Farrar $25.00 (0-374-28588-8). The author's second attempt at a biography of the Irish poet William Butler Yeats. "The best general introduction to Yeats's life currently available."—LJ (Rev: BL 12/15/89; LJ 12/89; TLS 3/10/89) **[821.9]**

4469 Logue, Christopher. *War Music: An Account of Books 16 to 19 in Homer's Iliad.* 1987, Farrar $12.95 (0-374-28648-5); paper $7.95 (0-374-52089-5). Logue's translation of a passage in Homer's epic tale. "As an introduction to the classics or as a modern poem, *War Music* knows few peers."—BL (Rev: BL 5/15/87; CSM 9/9/87) **[821.9]**

4470 Stallworthy, Jon. *Wilfred Owen: A Biography.* 1978, Oxford Univ. Pr. paper $4.95 (0-19-519774-7). An evaluation of the life and work of the British poet killed in the First World War. "Definitive, sympathetic yet unsentimental."—BL (Rev: BL 9/1/75; LJ 5/15/75; NYTBR 9/14/75) **[821.9]**

822 English drama

4471 Ndlovu, Duma, ed. *Woza Afrika! A Collection of South African Plays.* 1986, Braziller $16.95 (0-8076-1169-7); paper $8.95 (0-8076-1170-0). Six plays from South African playwrights regarding social injustice under the apartheid system. "A political and emotional bombshell."—LJ (Rev: BL 1/1/87; Choice 2/87; LJ 1/87) **[822]**

4472 Pinter, Harold. *Homecoming.* 1989, Grove-Weidenfeld paper $6.95 (0-8021-5105-1). A play regarding the return of an American professor with his new wife to his family in England. (Rev: BL 6/1/67; LJ 4/1/67; TLS 7/1/65. Awards: ALA, 1967) **[822]**

4473 Soyinka, Wole. *Ake: The Years of Childhood.* 1983, Random $14.95 (0-394-52807-7); paper $8.95 (0-394-72219-1). An autobiography of the Nigerian writer. "Unquestionably Africa's most versatile writer and arguably her finest . . . a classic of African autobiography."—NYTBR (Rev: Atl 9/82; LJ 8/82; NYTBR 10/10/82. Awards: ALA, 1982; NYTBR, 1982) **[822]**

4474 Stoppard, Tom. *Rosencrantz and Guildenstern Are Dead.* 1987, Grove-Weidenfeld paper $6.95 (0-8021-3033-X). A retelling of Shakespeare's *Hamlet* by the British playwright. (Rev: LJ 12/1/67; PW 11/13/67. Awards: ALA, 1967) **[822]**

4475 Tynan, Kathleen. *Life of Kenneth Tynan.* 1987, Morrow $22.95 (0-688-05080-8); paper $14.95 (0-688-08906-2). A revealing look at the British drama critic by his second wife. "An important biography of an important man of the theatre."—LJ (Rev: LJ 10/1/87; NYTBR 1/3/88; Time 12/7/87. Awards: Time, 1987) **[822]**

Elizabethan period, 1558–1625

4476 Frye, Northrop. *Northrop Frye on Shakespeare.* Ed. by Robert Sandler. 1988, Yale Univ. Pr. $8.95 (0-300-04208-6). Frye's criticism of ten Shakespearean plays. "A beautifully written work that will reward scholar and nonscholar."—LJ (Rev: BL 10/1/86; Choice 1/87; LJ 10/1/86. Awards: LJ, 1986)**[822.3]**

4477 Ornstein, Robert. *Shakespeare's Comedies: From Roman Farce to Romantic Mystery.* 1986, Univ. of Delaware Pr. $39.50 (0-87413-298-3). A study of the comedies of William Shakespeare. "This book will set a new standard for all later criticism."—Choice (Rev: Choice 3/87; LJ 10/15/86; TLS 4/10/87) **[822.3]**

William Shakespeare

4478 Levi, Peter. *Life and Times of William Shakespeare.* 1989, Henry Holt $29.95 (0-8050-1199-4). A biography of the bard by an Oxford University poetry professor. "One of the most knowledgeable, most readable books on the subject."—PW (Rev: BL 10/1/89; LJ 10/1/89; PW 8/18/89) **[822.33]**

4479 Taylor, Gary. *Reinventing Shakespeare: A Cultural History from the Restoration to the Present.* 1989, Grove-Weidenfeld $29.95 (1-55584-078-7); Oxford Univ. Pr. paper $12.95 (0-19-506679-0). A survey of four centuries of literary criticism of Shakespeare and his changing reputation. "A delightful, illuminating read."—LJ (Rev: Choice 1/90; LJ 6/15/89; New Rep 10/16/89) **[822.33]**

1900–

4480 Holroyd, Michael. *Bernard Shaw, Volume I: The Search for Love, 1856–1898.* 1988, Random $24.95 (0-394-52577-9); paper $15.95 (0-679-72505-9). The first volume of the author's biography of the Irish playwright and social critic. "There should be no need for another biography of George Bernard Shaw for perhaps a century, when the passing of time may require one."—NYTBR (Rev: LJ 10/1/88;

NYTBR 10/30/88; PW 8/19/88. Awards: LJ, 1988; NYTBR, 1988; PW, 1988) **[822.9]**

4481 Holroyd, Michael. *Bernard Shaw, Volume II: The Pursuit of Power, 1898–1914.* 1989, Random $24.95 (0-394-57553-9). The second volume of Holroyd's biography of George Bernard Shaw. "A genuinely great biography."—CSM (Rev: CSM 7/89; LJ 9/15/89; NYRB 12/21/89. Awards: LJ, 1989) **[822.9]**

4482 Holroyd, Michael. *Bernard Shaw, Volume III: The Lure of Fantasy, 1918–1950.* 1991, Random $30.00 (0-394-57554-7). This third and concluding volume of the author's biography of the Nobel Prize-winning writer covers the last 42 years of the Irishman's life. (Rev: BL 9/15/91; LJ 10/1/91; NYTBR 10/20/91) **[822.9]**

4483 Lahr, John. *Prick Up Your Ears: The Biography of Joe Orton.* 1986, Limelight paper $10.95 (0-87910-057-5). A biography of the English playwright based on his diaries. (Rev: BL 12/15/78; Newsweek 11/27/78; TLS 10/6/78) **[822.9]**

4484 O'Connor, Garry. *Sean O'Casey: A Life.* 1988, Macmillan $25.00 (0-689-11886-4). An authorized biography of the Irish playwright best known for *The Plough and the Stars* and *Juno and the Paycock.* (Rev: LJ 5/1/88; NYTBR 7/3/88; TLS 5/6/88) **[822.9]**

823 English fiction

4485 Auerbach, Nina. *Communities of Women: An Idea in Fiction.* 1978, Harvard Univ. Pr. $18.95 (0-674-15168-2); paper $8.95 (0-674-15169-0). A tracing of common themes in women's literature during the nineteenth and twentieth centuries. (Rev: Choice 4/79; LJ 8/78; PW 5/1/78) **[823]**

4486 Ellmann, Richard. *James Joyce.* 1982, Oxford Univ. Pr. $45.00 (0-19-503103-2); paper $18.95 (0-19-503381-7). A revised and updated edition of the author's acclaimed biography of the Irish writer. (Rev: BL 9/1/82; Newsweek 9/27/82; PW 6/25/82) **[823]**

4487 Frame, Janet. *Envoy from Mirror City: An Autobiography, Vol. 3.* 1985, Braziller $14.95 (0-8076-1124-7). An autobiography of the New Zealand writer describing her travels in Europe after receiving a literary grant. (Rev: LJ 9/15/85; NYTBR 10/6/85; TLS 1/10/86) **[823]**

4488 Mellor, Anne K. *Mary Shelley: Her Life, Her Fiction, Her Monsters.* 1988, Routledge $29.50 (0-415-02591-5); paper $14.95 (0-415-90147-2). A literary biography of the English author of *Frankenstein.* (Rev: BL 6/15/88; Choice 10/88; LJ 7/88) **[823]**

4489 Paton, Alan. *Journey Continued: An Autobiography.* 1988, Macmillan $22.50 (0-684-18946-1). The second volume of the autobiography of the South African author of *Cry, the Beloved Country* covers his life from 1948 to the late 1960s. (Rev: CSM 11/30/88; LJ 10/15/88; TLS 9/23/88) **[823]**

4490 Watt, Ian. *Conrad in the Nineteenth Century.* 1979, Univ. of California Pr. $35.00 (0-520-03683-2); paper $11.95 (0-520-04405-3). Combination of biography and literary criticism of Conrad to the year

1900. "A book that is nothing short of a masterpiece . . . one of the great critical works produced since the '50's."—NYTBR (Rev: Choice 7–8/80; LJ 1/15/80; NYTBR 3/9/80. Awards: ALA, 1980; NYTBR, 1980) **[823]**

1702–1745

4491 Backschneider, Paula R. *Daniel Defoe: His Life.* 1989, Johns Hopkins $29.95 (0-8018-3785-5). A biography of the English author of *Robinson Crusoe* and *Moll Flanders.* (Rev: Choice 2/90; LJ 10/15/89; NYTBR 1/14/90) **[823.5]**

4492 Battestin, Martin C., and Ruthe R. Battestin. *Henry Fielding: A Life.* 1990, Routledge $45.00 (0-415-01438-7). A biography of the eighteenth-century English author of such novels as *Joseph Andrews* and *Tom Jones.* "The definitive account of Fielding's life."—LJ (Rev: Choice 5/90; LJ 5/15/90; TLS 10/20/89) **[823.5]**

1800–1837

4493 Sunstein, Emily W. *Mary Shelley: Romance and Reality.* 1989, Little, Brown $24.95 (0-316-82246-9). A biography of the nineteenth-century English author. "The definitive biography of an important woman of letters."—LJ (Rev: Choice 5/89; LJ 1/89; NYTBR 2/12/89. Awards: LJ, 1989) **[823.7]**

1837–1900

4494 Ackroyd, Peter. *Dickens: Life and Times.* 1991, HarperCollins $35.00 (0-06-016602-9). The biographer of T. S. Eliot examines the life and era of the nineteenth-century English writer. (Rev: BL 12/1/90; NYTBR 1/13/91; PW 1/4/91. Awards: BL, 1991; PW, 1991) **[823.8]**

4495 Doyle, Arthur Conan. *Sherlock Holmes: The Published Apocrypha.* Ed. by Jack Tracy. 1980, Gaslight $18.95 (0-934468-24-9). A collection of seven Holmes pieces by Doyle, and four by other authors, using the famous detective character in plays and stories. (Rev: BL 11/1/80; LJ 2/1/81) **[823.8]**

4496 Fraser, Rebecca. *The Brontes: Charlotte Bronte and Her Family.* 1988, Crown $25.00 (0-517-56438-6); Fawcett paper $12.95 (0-449-90465-2). The life, works, and family of the nineteenth-century writer Charlotte Bronte are analyzed in this work by the daughter of historian Antonia Fraser. (Rev: BL 10/21/88; NYTBR 2/5/89; TLS 10/14/88) **[823.8]**

4497 Haight, Gordon S. *George Eliot: A Biography.* 1976, Oxford Univ. Pr. paper $8.95 (0-19-520085-3). A biography of the Victorian novelist known for such titles as *Adam Bede, Middlemarch,* and *Silas Marner.* "A full and satisfying account."—CSM (Rev: CSM 10/17/68; LJ 11/15/68; Newsweek 9/30/68) **[823.8]**

4498 Hall, N. John. *Trollope: A Biography.* 1991, Oxford Univ. Pr. $30.00 (0-19-812627-1). A biography of the nineteenth-century English writer known for such novels as *Barchester Towers* and *The Warden.* (Rev: BL 9/1/91; LJ 8/91; NYTBR 9/20/91) **[823.8]**

4499 Kaplan, Fred. *Dickens: A Biography.* 1988, Morrow $24.95 (0-688-04341-0); Avon paper $12.95 (0-380-70896-5). A biography of the nineteenth-century English novelist. "Marked by a winning mix of insight, narrative skill and shrewd judgment."—PW (REV: BL 10/1/88; LJ 9/1/88; PW 9/2/88. AWARDS: PW, 1988) **[823.8]**

4500 Millgate, Michael. *Thomas Hardy: A Biography.* 1985, Oxford Univ. Pr. paper $13.95 (0-19-281472-9). A detailed life story of the English writer known for such novels as *The Return of the Native, Jude the Obscure,* and *The Mayor of Casterbridge.* "What is sure to become the standard biography."—BL (REV: BL 3/15/82; Choice 9/82; CSM 7/30/82. AWARDS: ALA, 1982) **[823.8]**

4501 Skal, David J. *Hollywood Gothic: The Tangled Web of Dracula from Novel to Stage to Screen.* 1990, Norton $39.95 (0-393-02904-2); paper $15.95 (0-393-30805-7). A history of the adaptation of Bram Stoker's *Dracula* from novel to theater and film. (REV: BL 10/1/90; LJ 9/15/90; NYTBR 12/30/90) **[823.8]**

4502 Tomalin, Claire. *Invisible Woman: The Story of Nelly Ternan and Charles Dickens.* 1991, Knopf $25.00 (0-394-57999-3). A biography of the Victorian actress who was Charles Dickens' mistress during the last 13 years of his life. (REV: BL 3/15/91; New Rep 6/10/91; PW 2/1/91) **[823.8]**

4503 Wilson, Angus. *World of Charles Dickens.* 1985, Academy Chicago paper $12.95 (0-89733-172-9). A biography of Dickens and his time by the English novelist. "Extremely readable and entertaining."—Choice (REV: Choice 12/70; NYTBR 9/13/70; TLS 6/4/70) **[823.8]**

1900–

4504 Ambler, Eric. *Here Lies: An Autobiography.* 1986, Farrar $16.95 (0-374-16974-8); Mysterious paper $8.95 (0-89296-940-7). An autobiography of the writer known for his effective spy thrillers. "This account rings true and . . . will definitely engage his many fans."—BL (REV: Atl 11/86; BL 11/15/86; Newsweek 8/11/86) **[823.9]**

4505 Angier, Carole. *Jean Rhys: Life and Work.* 1991, Little, Brown $35.00 (0-316-04263-3). A literary biography of the British author of *Quartet* and *Wide Sargasso Sea.* (REV: BL 5/15/91; LJ 5/1/91; PW 4/19/91. AWARDS: BL, 1991) **[823.9]**

4506 Bedford, Sybille. *Aldous Huxley: A Biography.* 1985, Carroll & Graf paper $14.95 (0-88184-145-5). Detailed biography of the English writer and social critic. "The exemplary life study and critically important analysis is touched throughout with Bedford's thoughtful affection."—BL (REV: BL 2/1/75; LJ 12/1/74; Newsweek 12/9/74. AWARDS: ALA, 1974) **[823.9]**

4507 Burgess, Anthony. *You've Had Your Time: The Second Part of the Confessions.* 1991, Grove-Weidenfeld $23.50 (0-8021-1405-9). This second volume of the English writer's memoirs covers the years 1959 to 1982. (REV: LJ 5/15/91; NYTBR 4/28/91; PW 3/22/91) **[823.9]**

4508 Cash, Arthur H. *Laurence Sterne: The Later Years.* 1986, Routledge $60.00 (0-416-32930-6). The concluding volume of the eighteenth-century author of *Tristam Shandy.* "A model of scholarly achievement: well written, detailed and impassioned in its arguments . . . the definitive work on Sterne."—LJ (REV: Choice 3/87; LJ 12/86; NYTBR 1/13/87. AWARDS: LJ, 1987) **[823.9]**

4509 Christie, Agatha. *An Autobiography.* 1977, Boulevard $25.00 (0-396-07516-9). The mystery writer tells the story of her life. "Shows the struggles and complexities and contradictions that made this English lady the creator of the most cunningly deceptive plots of the half-century in which she reigned."—NYTBR (REV: Atl 12/77; LJ 11/15/77; NYTBR 11/13/77) **[823.9]**

4510 Dahl, Roald. *Boy: Tales of Childhood.* 1985, Farrar $12.95 (0-374-37374-4); Penguin paper $6.95 (0-14-008917-9). Childhood remembrances by the author of *James and the Giant Peach.* (REV: BL 2/1/85; NYTBR 1/20/85; TLS 11/30/84) **[823.9]**

4511 Dahl, Roald. *Going Solo.* 1986, Farrar $14.95 (0-374-16503-3); Penguin paper $6.95 (0-14-010306-6). The English novelist and children's writer recounts his experiences as a member of the Royal Air Force during the Second World War. (REV: BL 9/1/86; NYTBR 10/12/86; Time 11/3/86) **[823.9]**

4512 De-La-Noy, Michael. *Denton Welch: The Making of a Writer.* 1987, Penguin paper $7.95 (0-14-058009-3). A biography of the English short story writer and novelist who died at the age of 33. (REV: BL 4/1/85; Choice 5/85; PW 5/3/85) **[823.9]**

4513 Delbanco, Nicholas. *Group Portrait: Joseph Conrad, Stephen Crane, Ford Madox Ford, Henry James and H. G. Wells.* 1990, Carroll & Graf paper $9.95 (0-88184-584-1). An examination of the literary group consisting of Conrad, Crane, Ford, James, and Wells who lived close to one another in Sussex near the turn of the century. (REV: BL 4/15/82; CSM 7/21/82; PW 2/12/82) **[823.9]**

4514 De Salvo, Louise. *Virginia Woolf: The Impact of Childhood Sexual Abuse on Her Life and Work.* 1989, Beacon $22.95 (0-8070-6326-6); Ballantine paper $10.95 (0-345-36639-5). A study of the effects of forced incestuous sexual relations on the life and writings of Virginia Woolf. "A real contribution to the literature of women's lives truthfully described by women."—NYTBR (REV: BL 4/1/89; NYTBR 11/6/89; PW 3/10/89) **[823.9]**

4515 Everage, Dame Edna. *My Gorgeous Life: The Life, the Loves, the Legend.* 1992, Simon & Schuster $20.00 (0-671-70976-3). A fake biography of an outrageous celebrity penned by Australian comedian Barry Humphries. (REV: BL 12/15/91; LJ 1/92; PW 11/22/91) **[823.9]**

4516 Finney, Brian. *Christopher Isherwood: A Critical Biography.* 1979, Oxford Univ. Pr. $22.50 (0-19-520134-5). A life story of the British-born author of *Christopher and His Kind* and *Prater Violet.* (REV: BL 3/1/79; LJ 3/1/79; NYTBR 6/3/79) **[823.9]**

4517 Furbank, P. N. *E. M. Forster: A Life.* 1981, Harcourt paper $8.95 (0-15-62851-3). The life of the British author of *A Passage to India* and *Howard's End.* "This biography is not likely to be superseded for years to come."—NYTBR (Rev: LJ 9/15/78; NYTBR 11/12/78; PW 7/31/78. Awards: ALA, 1978; NYTBR, 1978) **[823.9]**

4518 Glendinning, Victoria. *Elizabeth Bowen.* 1986, Avon paper $3.50 (0-380-44354-6). The life and work of the Anglo-Irish novelist and short story writer. "A perfectly splendid biography."—LJ (Rev: LJ 1/15/78; NYTBR 1/15/78; Time 1/16/78) **[823.9]**

4519 Glendinning, Victoria. *Vita: A Biography of V. Sackville-West.* 1985, Morrow paper $9.95 (0-688-04111-6). The life of the British writer best remembered for her poetry, gardening books, and her relations with other members of the Bloomsbury Group. (Rev: BL 10/1/83; CSM 12/30/83; NYTBR 10/23/83) **[823.9]**

4520 Godden, Jon, and Rumer Godden. *Two Under the Indian Sun.* 1987, Morrow paper $8.95 (0-688-07422-7). A dual memoir of two sisters of their life in India from 1914 to 1919. "No one will be surprised at the beauty of this book—a collaboration of such note that it will be forever distinguished."—LJ (Rev: BL 7/15/66; LJ 5/1/66; NYTBR 6/12/66. Awards: ALA, 1966) **[823.9]**

4521 Godden, Rumer. *House with Four Rooms.* 1989, Morrow $18.95 (0-688-08629-2). The second volume of the author's memoirs of her life in Great Britain following her move from India. (Rev: BL 9/15/89; LJ 10/1/89; PW 9/1/89) **[823.9]**

4522 Godden, Rumer. *A Time to Dance, No Time to Weep: A Memoir.* 1987, Morrow $16.95 (0-688-072421-9). The first volume of the novelist's autobiography covering the years 1907–1946. "A delightful remembrance of a life well lived and well appreciated."—BL (Rev: BL 12/1/87; NYTBR 1/3/88; TLS 2/26/88) **[823.9]**

4523 Gordon, Lyndall. *Virginia Woolf: A Writer's Life.* 1985, Norton $17.95 (0-393-01891-1). A literary biography of the English author of *To the Lighthouse* and *Orlando.* "Few titles can match with this . . . when it comes to stylishness, insightfulness and readability."—LJ (Rev: Choice 5/85; LJ 2/15/85; NYTBR 2/10/85) **[823.9]**

4524 Hart, Anne. *Life and Times of Hercule Poirot.* 1990, Putnam $19.95 (0-399-13484-0); Berkley paper $8.95 (0-425-12274-3). A biography of the fictional detective drawn from the mystery novels of Agatha Christie. (Rev: BL 1/15/90; LJ 2/15/90) **[823.9]**

4525 Isherwood, Christopher. *Christopher and His Kind.* 1976, Farrar $18.95 (0-374-12330-6); paper $8.95 (0-374-52036-4). The English author's memoirs of his life in the 1930s beginning with his first visit to Berlin and ending with his arrival in the United States. (Rev: BL 12/1/76; LJ 12/1/76; NYTBR 11/28/76) **[823.9]**

4526 Isherwood, Christopher. *My Guru and His Disciples.* 1980, Farrar $12.95 (0-374-21702-5); paper $8.95 (0-374-52087-9). Memoirs of the British-born author of the *Berlin Stories* regarding his spiritual development and conversion to Hinduism. (Rev: BL 6/1/80; LJ 5/15/80; NYTBR 6/1/80) **[823.9]**

4527 Judd, Alan. *Ford Madox Ford.* 1991, Harvard Univ. Pr. $27.50 (0-674-30815-8). A biography of the English writer known for his novels *The Good Soldier* and the four-part *Parade's End.* (Rev: Choice 6/91; LJ 12/90; NYTBR 3/10/91) **[823.9]**

4528 Karl, Frederick R. *Joseph Conrad: The Three Lives.* 1979, Farrar $25.00 (0-374-18014-8); paper $14.95 (0-374-51547-8). A biography of the Polish-British author of *Lord Jim* and *Heart of Darkness.* (Rev: New Rep 2/3/79; Time 2/5/79; TLS 11/23/79) **[823.9]**

4529 Lawrence, D. H. *D. H. Lawrence's Manuscripts: The Correspondence of Frieda Lawrence, Jake Zeitlin and Others.* Ed. by Michael Squires. 1991, St. Martin's $35.00 (0-312-06109-9). A collection of letters from Lawrence to his wife and friends written during the 1920s and 1930s. (Rev: LJ 6/15/91; NYTBR 9/22/91) **[823.9]**

4530 Maddox, Brenda. *Nora: The Real Life of Molly Bloom.* 1988, Houghton $24.95 (0-395-36510-4); Fawcett paper $12.95 (0-449-90410-5). Biography of Nora, wife of James Joyce and inspiration for much of his work. "Maddox's biography can now be recommended as the first book to read about Joyce himself."—Newsweek (Rev: BL 6/1/88; LJ 6/15/88; Newsweek 6/20/88. Awards: ALA, 1988; PW, 1988) **[823.9]**

4531 Matthews, James F. *Voices: A Life of Frank O'Connor.* 1987, Macmillan paper $12.95 (0-689-70723-1). A biography of the Irish short story writer (1903–1966). "All readers will find the biography pleasant, informative, incisive reading."—Choice (Rev: Choice 10/83; New Rep 4/25/83; NYTBR 5/22/83) **[823.9]**

4532 Meyers, Jeffrey. *D. H. Lawrence: A Biography.* 1990, Knopf $24.95 (0-394-57244-0). A biography of the English author of *Sons and Lovers* and *The Rainbow.* "An excellent biography of a very complicated man."—Atl (Rev: Atl 8/90; BL 5/15/90; CSM 8/17/90. Awards: BL, 1990) **[823.9]**

4533 Meyers, Jeffrey. *Joseph Conrad: A Biography.* 1991, Scribner $27.50 (0-684-19230-6). A study of the life and work of the Polish-English writer by the biographer of Hemingway and Lawrence. (Rev: BL 3/1/91; LJ 2/15/91; PW 2/15/91) **[823.9]**

4534 Morgan, Janet. *Agatha Christie: A Biography.* 1985, Knopf $24.95 (0-394-52554-X). An authorized biography of the English mystery writer based on her private papers and interviews with friends and associates. (Rev: Choice 11/85; LJ 6/1/85; NYTBR 6/23/85) **[823.9]**

4535 Naipaul, V. S. *Finding the Center: Two Narratives.* 1985, Random paper $4.95 (0-394-74090-4). Two extended essays by the Trinidadian writer: one regarding his evolution as a writer—the other concerning his travels in the Ivory Coast. (Rev: BL 8/84; Newsweek 9/24/84; TLS 6/22/84) **[823.9]**

4536 Najder, Zdzislaw. *Joseph Conrad: A Chronicle.* 1983, Rutgers Univ. Pr. $45.00 (0-8135-0944-0). A biography of the Polish/English author of *Lord Jim* and *Nostromo.* "The fullest and perhaps the most clear-eyed biography of Conrad to date."—PW (REV: LJ 11/1/83; NYRB 3/1/84; PW 9/30/83) **[823.9]**

4537 Nolan, Christopher. *Under the Eye of the Clock: The Life Story of Christopher Nolan.* 1988, St. Martin's $16.95 (0-312-01266-7); Doubleday paper $7.95 (0-385-29713-0). An autobiography of an Irish writer and his struggle against cerebral palsy. (REV: LJ 2/1/88; NYTBR 3/13/88; TLS 7/31/87) **[823.9]**

4538 Pym, Barbara. *A Very Private Eye: An Autobiography in Diaries and Letters.* Ed. by Hazel Holt and Hilary Pym. 1985, Random paper $6.95 (0-394-73106-9). Collected diaries and letters of the English novelist. "One comes away . . . knowing Pym and loving her."—PW (REV: BL 6/1/84; LJ 6/1/84; PW 5/4/84) **[823.9]**

4539 Rose, Phyllis. *A Woman of Letters: A Life of Virginia Woolf.* 1978, Oxford Univ. Pr. $22.50 (0-19-502370-6); Harcourt paper $8.95 (0-15-698190-4). A biography of the English writer. "A total portrait . . . an exemplary melding of the literary Woolf with her private life."—BL (REV: BL 9/1/78; LJ 7/78; NYRB 12/21/78) **[823.9]**

4540 Shelden, Michael. *Orwell: The Authorized Biography.* 1991, HarperCollins $25.00 (0-06-016709-2). The authorized biography of the British author of *Coming Up for Air* written by an Indiana State English professor. (REV: BL 10/1/91; NYTBR 11/3/91) **[823.9]**

4541 Sherry, Norman. *Life of Graham Greene, Vol. 1: 1904 to 1939.* 1989, Viking $29.95 (0-670-81376-1); Penguin paper $15.95 (0-14-014450-1). The first volume of the biography of the British writer. "A massive and forceful biocritical opus of the formative years in the life of a major figure of world literature."—BL (REV: BL 4/1/89; PW 4/21/89; TLS 5/26/89. AWARDS: BL, 1989; BL, the 1980s; PW, 1989) **[823.9]**

4542 Spurling, Hilary. *Ivy: The Life of I. Compton-Burnett.* 1985, Columbia Univ. Pr. paper $16.50 (0-231-08383-1). A biography of the English novelist. "A compelling study of both English middle-class and intellectual life."—Choice (REV: Choice 4/85; LJ 2/1/85; Newsweek 12/24/84) **[823.9]**

4543 Spurling, Hilary. *Paul Scott: A Life.* 1991, Norton $24.95 (0-393-02938-7). A biography of the author of *The Raj Quartet.* "An impeccably researched and crafted biography."—LJ (REV: BL 3/15/91; LJ 3/1/91; PW 3/15/91) **[823.9]**

4544 Stannard, Martin. *Evelyn Waugh: The Early Years, 1903–1939.* 1987, Norton $24.95 (0-393-02450-4). The first of two volumes examining the British writer's life. "For the serious student of Waugh . . . a definitive biography."—NYTBR (REV: CSM 11/17/87; LJ 4/1/87; NYTBR 8/30/87. AWARDS: NYTBR, 1987) **[823.9]**

4545 Thomas, D. M., and Peter Knobler. *Memories and Hallucinations: A Memoir.* 1988, Viking $18.95 (0-670-82357-0); Penguin paper $8.95 (0-14-011546-3). Autobiographical writings by the author of *The White Hotel* discussing life and the creative process. (REV: LJ 10/1/88; TLS 7/1/88) **[823.9]**

4546 Tomalin, Claire. *Katherine Mansfield: A Secret Life.* 1988, Knopf $22.95 (0-394-56847-8); St. Martin's paper $13.95 (0-312-02937-3). A biography of the New Zealand-born short story writer who died at age 34. (REV: Choice 9/88; NYRB 3/17/88; NYTBR 5/15/88) **[823.9]**

4547 Wilson, A. N. *C. S. Lewis: A Biography.* 1990, Norton $22.50 (0-393-02813-5). A biography of the English fantasy writer and Christian apologist. (REV: NYTBR 2/18/90; Time 3/5/90; TLS 2/16/90. AWARDS: Time, 1990) **[823.9]**

4548 Woolf, Virginia. *A Passionate Apprentice: The Early Journals, 1897–1909.* Ed. by Mitchell A. Leaska. 1991, Harcourt $24.95 (0-15-171287-5). Journals of the English writer from her late teens and twenties. (REV: BL 12/15/90; NYTBR 2/17/91; PW 12/14/90) **[823.9]**

4549 Worthen, John. *D. H. Lawrence: The Early Years, 1885–1912.* 1991, Cambridge Univ. Pr. $35.00 (0-521-25419-1). This first volume of a planned three-piece biography traces the English writer from birth to the courtship of his future wife, Frieda Weekley. "A major event in modern literary studies."—LJ (REV: BL 9/15/91; LJ 7/91; NYTBR 9/22/91. AWARDS: BL, 1991; LJ, 1991) **[823.9]**

4550 Worthen, John. *D. H. Lawrence: A Literary Life.* 1989, St. Martin's $35.00 (0-312-03524-1). An examination of the life of D. H. Lawrence emphasizing his literary production and personal economic struggles. (REV: BL 11/1/89; Choice 4/90; LJ 11/1/90) **[823.9]**

824 English essays

4551 Bromvich, David. *Hazlitt: The Mind of a Critic.* 1985, Oxford Univ. Pr. paper $18.95 (0-19-503687-5). A literary biography of the life and works of the English essayist and literary critic. (REV: CSM 4/12/84; LJ 12/15/83; NYTBR 1/15/84) **[824]**

4552 Chatwin, Bruce. *What Am I Doing Here?* 1989, Viking $19.95 (0-670-82508-5); paper $9.95 (0-14-011577-3). A collection of essays and travelogues by the late British writer. (REV: BL 6/1/89; PW 6/23/89; TLS 6/16/89) **[824]**

4553 Gross, John, ed. *Oxford Book of Essays.* 1991, Oxford Univ. Pr. $30.00 (0-19-214185-6). An anthology of 114 essays spanning four centuries, including contributions by Bacon, Hazlitt, Thoreau, Wilde, Mencken, and Naipaul. (REV: BL 2/15/91; CSM 5/17/91; LJ 2/1/91) **[824]**

4554 Larkin, Philip. *Required Writing: Miscellaneous Pieces, 1955–1982.* 1984, Farrar $17.95 (0-374-24948-2); paper $9.95 (0-374-51840-8). Collected literary and autobiographical essays by the English poet. (REV: BL 5/15/84; LJ 6/15/84; NYTBR 8/12/84) **[824]**

4555 Woolf, Virginia. *Essays of Virginia Woolf, Vol. I: 1904–1912.* Ed. by Andrew McNeillie. 1987, Harcourt $19.95 (0-15-129055-5). The first volume of the essays of the English writer collected and published in chronological order. (REV: BL 2/15/87; LJ 3/1/87; TLS 12/12/86) **[824]**

4556 Woolf, Virginia. *Essays of Virginia Woolf, Vol. II: 1912–1918.* Ed. by Andrew McNeillie. 1988, Harcourt $22.95 (0-15-129056-3); paper $14.95 (0-15-629055-3). The second volume of the collected essays of the British writer. (REV: Choice 10/88; NYTBR 3/27/88; TLS 10/9/87) **[824]**

4557 Woolf, Virginia. *Essays of Virginia Woolf, Vol. III: 1919–1924.* Ed. by Andrew McNeillie. 1989, Harcourt $22.95 (0-15-129057-1). The third volume of the English writer's collected essays. "These excellently edited essays reconfirm her major importance."—LJ (REV: BL 3/15/89; LJ 5/1/89; NYTBR 4/23/89) **[824]**

1837–1900

4558 Kaplan, Fred. *Thomas Carlyle: A Biography.* 1983, Cornell Univ. Pr. $47.50 (0-8014-1508-X). A biography of the nineteenth-century British historian and essayist. (REV: Choice 3/84; LJ 11/15/83; NYTBR 1/8/84) **[824.8]**

1900–

4559 Smith, Joan. *Misogynies.* 1991, Fawcett $16.95 (0-449-90591-8). A collection of essays examining anti-female themes in modern society and culture. (REV: BL 12/1/90; LJ 12/90) **[824.9]**

827 English satire and humor

4560 Bradbury, Malcolm. *Unsent Letters: Irreverant Notes from a Literary Life.* 1988, Viking $16.95 (0-670-82070-9); Penguin paper $7.95 (0-14-010705-3). A collection of 18 letters the British writer would have liked to send, but didn't. "A joy for students, academics and writers."—LJ (REV: BL 7/88; LJ 6/15/88; Time 7/18/88) **[827]**

828 English miscellaneous writings

4561 Gordimer, Nadine. *Essential Gesture: Writing, Politics and Places.* 1988, Knopf $19.95 (0-394-57397-8); Penguin paper $9.95 (0-14-012212-5). A collection of pieces from the 1960s to the 1980s by the South African writer concerning politics and her profession in her native land. (REV: BL 10/1/88; LJ 10/15/88; PW 9/30/88) **[828]**

4562 Holmes, Richard. *Footsteps: Adventures of a Romantic Biographer.* 1987, Penguin paper $7.95 (0-14-008860-1). A collection of four biographical essays concerning episodes in the lives of four writers: Shelley, Wollstonecraft, Nerval, and Stevenson, and the methodology used to write the essays. "An extraordinarily lucid explanation of what goes on beyond simple research and recitation of facts in the presentation of quality biography."—BL (REV: BL 8/85; LJ 9/15/85; NYTBR 10/20/85. AWARDS: NYTBR, 1985) **[828]**

4563 Nolan, Christopher. *Dam-Burst of Dreams: The Writings of Christopher Nolan.* 1988, Ohio Univ. Pr. paper $9.95 (0-8214-0912-3). Collected prose and poetry by a British quadriplegic teenage writer who was unable to communicate until the age of 11. (REV: LJ 10/15/81; PW 8/14/81; TLS 6/18/82) **[828]**

4564 Orwell, George. *Collected Essays, Journalism and Letters.* Ed. by Sonia Orwell and Ian Angus. 1968, Harcourt $48.90 (0-15-118546-8). A three-volume set of collected essays, journalism, and letters of the English writer. (REV: New Rep 11/30/68; NYTBR 10/27/68; Newsweek 10/28/68. AWARDS: ALA, 1968; NYTBR, 1968) **[828]**

4565 Raban, Jonathan. *For Love and Money: A Writing Life, 1969–1989.* 1989, Harper & Row $22.50 (0-06-016166-3). Collected essays spanning 20 years in the writing career of the author of *Old Glory* and *Soft City.* (REV: LJ 9/1/89; NYTBR 10/1/89; TLS 12/11/87) **[828]**

4566 Smith, Stevie. *Me Again: Uncollected Writings of Stevie Smith.* 1982, Farrar $15.95 (0-374-20494-2). An anthology of the uncollected short stories, essays, poems, letters, reviews, and drawings of the English writer. (REV: LJ 6/1/82; NYTBR 5/15/82; Sat Rev 6/82) **[828]**

4567 Soyinka, Wole. *Isare: A Voyage Around Essay.* 1989, Random $18.95 (0-394-54077-8); paper $9.95 (0-679-73246-2). Memoirs by the Nigerian novelist regarding his youth, his family, and African cultural traditions. (REV: LJ 10/1/89; New Rep 12/11/89; NYTBR 11/12/89. AWARDS: BL, 1989) **[828]**

1702–1745

4568 Noakes, David. *Jonathan Swift, a Hypocrite Reversed: A Critical Biography.* 1986, Oxford Univ. Pr. $35.00 (0-19-812834-7). A portrait of the life and work of the author of *Gulliver's Travels.* "A definitive treatment for general readers."—BL (REV: BL 5/1/86; Choice 5/86; CSM 1/29/86) **[828.5]**

1745–1800

4569 Brady, Frank. *James Boswell: The Later Years, 1769–1795.* 1984, McGraw-Hill $24.95 (0-07-050558-6). The sequel to *James Boswell: The Early Years* by Frederick A. Pottle. "A monument to scholarship . . . does justice to a great writer by denying neither his flaws nor his considerable talents."—LJ (REV: Choice 1/85; LJ 11/1/84; NYTBR 1/13/85. AWARDS: LJ, 1984) **[828.6]**

4570 St. Clair, William. *Godwins and the Shelleys: The Biography of a Family.* 1989, Norton $32.50 (0-393-02783-X). A collective biography of the family of philosopher William Godwin, his wife Mary Wollstonecraft, their daughter Mary, and her husband Percy Shelley, and their other daughter, and her lover Lord Byron. "A model biography: flowingly written, impeccably researched, monumentally detailed."—BL (REV: BL 9/15/89; LJ 10/1/89; PW 9/8/89. AWARDS: PW, 1989) **[828.6]**

1837–1900

4571 Ellmann, Richard. *Oscar Wilde.* 1988, Knopf $24.95 (0-394-55484-1); **Random paper $11.95 (0-394-75984-2).** Biography of Wilde highly praised for its literary criticism of his works. (REV: LJ 12/87; Newsweek 2/15/88; TLS 10/2–8/87. AWARDS: ALA, 1988; LJ, 1988; PP:Biography, 1989) **[828.8]**

4572 Wilson, Angus. *Strange Ride of Rudyard Kipling.* 1979, Penguin paper $6.95 (0-14-005122-8). An exploration of Kipling's life and its relationship to his works. "The most complete and balanced picture of the man we are likely to get."—NYTBR (REV: CSM 4/12/78; LJ 11/15/77; NYTBR 3/12/78) **[828.8]**

1900–

4573 Amis, Kingsley. *Memoirs.* 1991, Summit $25.00 (0-671-74909-9). Memoirs of the British author of *Lucky Jim* and *Jake's Thing.* (REV: BL 9/1/91; NYTBR 9/8/91) **[828.9]**

4574 Barker, Dudley. *G. K. Chesterton.* 1975, Scarborough $5.95 (0-8128-1804-0). A biography of the English journalist, religious convert, and writer of the Father Brown mystery series. (REV: CSM 9/5/73; New Rep 9/8/73; NYTBR 8/19/73) **[828.9]**

4575 Bell, Quentin. *Virginia Woolf: A Biography.* 1974, Harcourt paper $14.95 (0-15-693580-5). Woolf's nephew presents the life story of his aunt, the English woman of letters, and member of the Bloomsbury Group. "A splendid example of the biographer's art."—Atl (REV: Atl 2/73; LJ 11/1/72; Time 11/20/72. AWARDS: ALA, 1972; Time, 1972) **[828.9]**

4576 Chaplin, Patrice. *Albany Park: An Autobiography.* 1987, Viking $16.95 (0-670-81243-9); Atlantic Monthly paper $8.95 (0-87113-257-5). Memoirs of the English novelist's travels in Spain as a teenager and her relationship with a man she met while hitchhiking along the Costa Brava. (REV: BL 3/15/87; LJ 4/1/87; TLS 6/6/86) **[828.9]**

4577 Greene, Graham. *Reflections.* 1991, Viking $19.95 (1-871061-19-9). An anthology of autobiographical pieces by the late British writer from the 1920s to the 1990s. (REV: LJ 5/15/91; PW 4/5/91; TLS 9/21/90) **[828.9]**

4578 Greene, Graham. *Ways of Escape.* 1981, Peter Smith $13.50 (0-8446-6289-5). The second volume of memoirs of the English writer recounting his adventures in Vietnam, Malaysia, South America, and Africa. (REV: CSM 2/9/81; LJ 2/15/81; PW 12/5/80) **[828.9]**

4579 Naipaul, Shiva. *Beyond the Dragon's Mouth.* 1986, Penguin paper $7.95 (0-14-008682-X). Collected essays on international travel and politics by the author of *Love and Death in a Hot Country.* (REV: LJ 2/15/85; New Rep 8/26/85; NYTBR 3/24/85) **[828.9]**

4580 Nicolson, Nigel. *Portrait of a Marriage.* 1973, Macmillan $10.00 (0-689-10574-6); paper $10.95 (0-689-70592-2). A study of Nicolson's parents, Harold Nicolson and Vita Sackville-West, prominent members of the Bloomsbury Group, and their unconventional marriage marked by homosexual affairs carried on by both of them. (REV: BL 1/1/74; Choice 1/74; LJ 10/15/73. AWARDS: ALA, 1973) **[828.9]**

4581 Orton, Joe. *Orton Diaries.* Ed. by John Lahr. 1987, Harper & Row $19.95 (0-06-015743-7); paper $8.95 (0-06-091498-X). A diary of the British playwright who was murdered by his homosexual lover in 1967. (REV: LJ 5/15/87; NYTBR 5/10/87; PW 3/20/87) **[828.9]**

4582 Thompson, E. P. *William Morris: Romantic to Revolutionary.* 1988, Stanford Univ. Pr. paper $19.95 (0-8047-1509-2). A biography of the British Victorian writer, artist, designer, and social thinker. (REV: Choice 10/77; LJ 8/77; NYTBR 5/15/77) **[828.9]**

4583 West, Rebecca. *Family Memories: An Autobiographical Journey.* 1988, Viking $19.95 (0-670-81354-2); Penguin paper $7.95 (0-14-009495-4). A posthumously published autobiography of the British novelist. "A luscious starting place for those who have the misfortune of being unfamiliar with her writing."—BL (REV: BL 3/15/88; LJ 2/15/88; TLS 11/20/87) **[828.9]**

4584 Woolf, Leonard. *Downhill All the Way: An Autobiography of the Years 1919–1939.* 1989, Harcourt paper $8.95 (0-15-626145-6). The fourth volume of Woolf's autobiography describes his relationship with his wife Virginia, the establishment of their publishing company Haworth Press, and remembrances of their many literary friends. (REV: BL 12/1/67; LJ 12/1/67; PW 10/16/67. AWARDS: ALA, 1967) **[828.9]**

4585 Woolf, Leonard. *Journey Not the Arrival Matters: An Autobiography of the Years 1939 to 1969.* 1989, Harcourt paper $8.95 (0-15-646523-X). The fifth and final volume of the author's autobiography. "Describes with wit and elegance and an understated emotion . . . the last journeys . . . of his remarkable life."—PW (REV: BL 6/1/70; CSM 3/26/70; PW 2/16/70) **[828.9]**

830 LITERATURE OF GERMANIC LANGUAGES

831 German poetry

4586 Celan, Paul. *Poems of Paul Celan.* 1989, Persea Books $24.95 (0-89255-140-2). The collected poems of the German writer presented in a bilingual edition. "Here is an artistry to cherish."—LJ (REV: LJ 5/1/89; New Rep 7/31/89; New Yorker 8/28/89) **[831]**

4587 Goethe, Johann Wolfgang von. *Goethe: Selected Poems.* Ed. by Christopher Middleton. 1988, Riverrun paper $17.95 (0-7145-4004-8). A bilingual introduction to the verse of Goethe. "As attractive and accessible as a reader can wish."—LJ (REV: BL 9/1/83; Choice 11/83; LJ 9/15/83) **[831]**

4588 Hermlin, Stephen. *Evening Light.* 1983, Fjord Pr. paper $6.95 (0-940242-03-6). The first work of the

East German poet to be translated into English. (Rev: NYTBR 9/18/83; PW 4/29/83) **[831]**

1750–1830

4589 Boyle, Nicholas. *Goethe: The Poet and the Age; Volume One; the Poetry of Desire (1749–1790).* 1991, Oxford Univ. Pr. $37.50 (0-19-815866-1). A biography of the eighteenth-century German writer. "Will become the definitive English work on Goethe."—LJ (Rev: Atl 4/91; LJ 1/91; TLS 5/10/91) **[831.6]**

1900–

4590 Prater, Donald. *A Ringing Glass: The Life of Rainer Marie Rilke.* 1986, Oxford Univ. Pr. $29.95 (0-19-815755-X). A biography of the German poet. (Rev: Choice 12/86; LJ 8/86; NYTBR 9/21/86) **[831.9]**

4591 Rilke, Rainer Marie. *Sonnets to Orpheus.* 1986, Simon & Schuster $13.95 (0-671-55708-4); paper $10.95 (0-671-61773-7). A new translation of the German poet's work. "The most readable Rilke in English to date."—Choice (Rev: BL 11/15/85; Choice 2/86; LJ 11/1/85) **[831.9]**

832 German drama

1900–

4592 Frisch, Max. *Montauk.* 1978, Harcourt paper $4.95 (0-15-661990-3). The Swiss novelist tells about his affair with an American woman and his relationships with other women in this self-analytical memoir. (Rev: Choice 10/76; LJ 5/15/76; New Yorker 5/24/76) **[832.9]**

4593 Lyon, James K. *Bertolt Brecht in America.* 1981, Princeton Univ. Pr. $49.50 (0-691-06443-1); paper $12.50 (0-691-01394-2). A study of German writer Bertolt Brecht, and his film and drama career, in the United States. "This study stands out for its readability, detail, unbiased view of its subject, and imaginative approach."—LJ (Rev: Choice 3/81; LJ 11/15/80; NYRB 2/5/81) **[832.9]**

833 German fiction

1900–

4594 Buber-Neumann, Margarete. *Milena: The Story of a Remarkable Friendship.* 1989, Schocken paper $8.95 (0-8052-0918-2). A biography of the Czech journalist who became Kafka's mistress and was eventually put to death for her anti-Nazi writings. (Rev: BL 4/15/88; LJ 4/15/88; NYTBR 6/21/88) **[833.9]**

4595 Canetti, Elias. *Torch in My Ear.* 1982, Farrar $16.50 (0-374-27847-4). An autobiography of the former winner of the Nobel Prize for Literature examining his years as a student in Germany and Austria. (Rev: CSM 9/10/82; LJ 8/82; NYRB 11/4/82) **[833.9]**

4596 Handke, Peter. *Afternoon of a Writer.* 1989, Farrar $14.95 (0-374-10207-4). This autobiographical essay on the life of a writer is the author's follow-up to his *The Weight of the World.* (Rev: LJ 9/1/89; New Yorker 12/25/89; PW 6/16/89) **[833.9]**

4597 Hayman, Ronald. *Brecht: A Biography.* 1983, Oxford Univ. Pr. $29.95 (0-19-520434-4). A biography of the German playwright and poet. "An extremely well-written, withering portrait."—BL (Rev: BL 1/1/84; LJ 10/1/83; NYTBR 11/27/83) **[833.9]**

4598 Hayman, Ronald. *Kafka: A Biography.* 1982, Oxford Univ. Pr. paper $8.95 (0-19-520411-5). A biography of the Czech writer. "Excellent . . . now becomes the standard work, popular as it may seem."—Choice (Rev: BL 1/15/82; Choice 5/82; LJ 3/15/82) **[833.9]**

4599 Jungk, Peter Stephan. *Franz Werfel: A Life in Prague, Vienna and Hollywood.* 1990, Grove-Weidenfeld $24.95 (0-8021-1097-5). A biography of the Czech author of *The Forty Days of Musa Dagh* and *The Song of Bernadette* tracing his life from his birth in Prague to his death in Los Angeles. (Rev: Atl 4/90; NYTBR 4/29/90; New Yorker 7/2/90) **[833.9]**

4600 Pawel, Ernst. *Nightmare of Reason: A Life of Franz Kafka.* 1984, Farrar $25.50 (0-374-22236-3); Random paper $7.95 (0-394-72948-X). Biography of the Czech author of *The Trial* and *Metamorphosis.* "Should be read by everyone who cares about Kafka."—New Yorker. (Rev: BL 5/15/84; New Yorker 6/18/84; Newsweek 6/18/84. Awards: ALA, 1984; LJ, 1984) **[833.9]**

4601 Wolf, Christa. *Cassandra: A Novel and Four Essays.* 1984, Farrar $17.95 (0-374-11956-2); paper $8.95 (0-374-51904-8). Four essays and a novel dealing with the ancient Greek Trojan War-era legend of Cassandra. (Rev: CSM 10/10/84; LJ 7/84; NYTBR 9/9/84) **[833.9]**

834 German essays

1900–

4602 Musil, Robert. *Posthumous Papers of a Living Author.* 1988, Eridanos Pr. $21.00 (0-941419-00-2); paper $12.00 (0-941419-01-0). A collection of satirical pieces written during the 1920s by the Austrian writer best known for his novel *The Man Without Qualities.* (Rev: CSM 3/9/88; LJ 3/15/88; NYTBR 4/10/88) **[834.9]**

838 German miscellaneous writings

4603 Scholem, Gershom. *Walter Benjamin: The Story of a Friendship.* 1981, JPS Phila $13.95 (0-8276-0197-2); paper $9.95 (0-8052-0870-4). Memoirs of the Jewish scholar regarding his relationship with philosopher Walter Benjamin. (Rev: Choice 7–8/82; LJ 12/15/81; NYTBR 5/16/82) **[838]**

1856–1900

4604 Livingstone, Angela. *Salome: Her Life and Work.* 1987, Moyer Bell paper $9.95 (0-918825-61-X). A biography of Lou Andreas-Salome, a writer and psycholanalyst who was acquainted with Freud, Nietzsche, Rilke, and Tolstoy. (Rev: BL 12/1/85; NYTBR 7/14/85; PW 5/17/85) **[838.8]**

1900–

4605   Handke, Peter. *Weight of the World*. 1984, Farrar $16.95 (0-374-28745-7); Macmillan paper $9.95 (0-02-051490-5). A diary by the Austrian novelist and playwright chronicling two years of his life in Paris. (REV: BL 6/1/84; Choice 11/84; New Rep 9/3/84)
[838.9]

839   Other Germanic literatures

Yiddish literature

4606   Aleichem, Sholem. *From the Fair: The Autobiography of Sholom Aleichem*. 1986, Penguin paper $7.95 (0-14-008830-X). Memoirs of the Russian-Jewish writer's youth in a small village at the turn of the century. "A beautiful introduction to Aleichem's life and writing."—BL (REV: BL 2/15/85; Choice 11/85; LJ 6/1/85)
[839.09]

4607   Grade, Chaim. *My Mother's Sabbath Days: A Memoir*. 1986, Knopf $19.95 (0-394-50980-3); Schocken paper $9.95 (0-8052-0839-9). Memoirs of the Lithuanian writer's childhood in the Jewish section of Vilna. (REV: Choice 5/87; LJ 11/1/86; NYTBR 11/16/86)
[839.09]

Afrikaans literature

4608   Breytenbach, Breyten. *End Papers: Essays, Letters, Articles of Faith, Workbook Notes*. 1986, Farrar $16.95 (0-374-14829-5); McGraw-Hill paper $8.95 (0-07-007677-4). Writings by the South African émigré about life in his former homeland. "A powerful and haunting collection . . . a potent political indictment."—BL (REV: BL 7/86; PW 6/13/86)
[839.36]

Swedish literature

4609   Lagercrantz, Olof. *August Strindberg*. 1984, Farrar $25.50 (0-374-10685-1); paper $12.95 (0-374-51941-2). A biography of the Swedish playwright and novelist known for such works as *Miss Julie* and *The Ghost Sonata*. (REV: Atl 2/85; Choice 3/85; New Yorker 5/27/85)
[839.7]

4610   Meyer, Michael A. *Strindberg: A Biography*. 1987, Oxford Univ. Pr. paper $14.95 (0-19-281995-X). A biography of the Swedish playwright known for *Miss Julie* and *Dance of Death*. "A full-scale literary biography of the highest caliber."—LJ (REV: Choice 1/86; LJ 9/1/85; TLS 10/25/85)
[839.7]

Danish and Norwegian literature

4611   Ferguson, Robert. *Enigma: The Life of Knut Hamsun*. 1987, Farrar $30.00 (0-374-14846-5); paper $14.95 (0-374-52093-3). A biography of the Norwegian Nobel Prize–winning author of *Hunger* and *Growth of the Soil*. (REV: Choice 11/87; LJ 5/15/87; NYTBR 6/7/87)
[839.8]

4612   Thurman, Judith. *Isak Dinesen: The Life of a Storyteller*. 1982, St. Martin's $19.95 (0-312-43737-4); paper $10.95 (0-312-43738-2). This biography, the result of seven years of research, made use of many formerly unavailable manuscripts. (REV: Choice 3/

83; LJ 10/15/82; Newsweek 11/27/82. AWARDS: ALA, 1982; NBA, 1983; NYTBR, 1982; Time, 1982)
[839.8]

840   LITERATURES OF ROMANCE LANGUAGES

4613   Harris, Frederick John. *Encounters with Darkness: French and German Writers on World War II*. 1983, Oxford Univ. Pr. $29.95 (0-19-503246-2); paper $8.95 (0-19-503580-1). An examination of the influences of World War II on postwar French and German literature. (REV: Choice 10/83; LJ 5/1/83; NYTBR 5/26/83)
[840]

843   French fiction

4614   Bugul, Ken. *Abandoned Baobab: The Autobiography of a Senegalese Woman*. 1991, Lawrence Hill Books $18.95 (1-55652-113-8); paper $9.95 (1-55652-114-6). The autobiography of a Senegalese woman describing her experiences living in France and Africa. "A beautiful, tragic book."—BL (REV: BL 12/15/91; PW 11/1/91)
[843]

4615   Vargas Llosa, Mario. *Perpetual Orgy: Flaubert and Madame Bovary*. 1986, Farrar $17.95 (0-374-23077-3); paper $8.95 (0-374-52062-3). An examination of the background, structure, literary techniques, and influence of Flaubert's *Madame Bovary* as seen by the Peruvian writer. (REV: Choice 7–8/87; LJ 1/87; Time 12/22/86)
[843]

1815–1848

4616   Maurois, Andre. *Prometheus: The Life of Balzac*. 1983, Carroll & Graf paper $11.95 (0-88184-023-8). The life story of the great French author of *Pere Goriot* and *Cousin Bette*. "An excellent biography, beautifully translated, filled with fascinating information about every phase of the life and work of the great genius that was Balzac."—Choice (REV: Choice 11/66; NYTBR 5/22/66; Sat Rev 7/9/66. AWARDS: ALA, 1966)
[843.7]

1900–

4617   Balakian, Anna. *Andre Breton: Magus of Surrealism*. 1971, Hawkshead Books $20.00 (0-19-501298-4). A study of the French writer associated with the schools of dada and surrealism. "Balakian's impressive integration of biography and critical analysis is erudite, lucid and illuminating . . . should stand as definitive."—LJ (REV: Choice 10/71; LJ 8/71; NYTBR 5/30/71)
[843.9]

4618   Bresler, Fenton. *Mystery of Georges Simenon*. 1985, Scarborough paper $9.95 (0-8128-6241-4). A biography of the prolific French mystery writer. "The best and fairest view we have of an extraordinary life."—NYTBR (REV: BL 10/15/83; NYTBR 10/30/83; PW 8/5/83)
[843.9]

4619   Lottman, Herbert. *Flaubert: A Biography*. 1989, Little, Brown $24.95 (0-316-53342-4); Fromm International paper $11.95 (0-88064-120-7). A portrait of the life and times of the nineteenth-century French author of such novels as *Madame Bovary* and *A Sentimental Education.* (Rev: BL 2/15/89; LJ 2/1/89; NYTBR 3/5/89) **[843.9]**

4620 **Murphy, Kenneth.** *Man's Fate, Man's Hope: The Life of Andre Malraux.* 1991, Grove-Weidenfeld $30.00 (0-8021-1033-9). A biography of the twentieth-century French writer and social activist. "This towering, vibrant biography is as kinetic and thought-provoking as its many-faceted subject."—PW (Rev: LJ 7/91; PW 6/14/91) **[843.9]**

4621 **Rabelais, Francois.** *Gargantua and Pantagruel.* Ed. by Burton Raffel. 1990, Norton $29.95 (0-393-02843-7). New translation of the sixteenth-century French classic. "A classic work, restored to its original complexity, humor, and gusto."—LJ (Rev: BL 8/90; LJ 8/90) **[843.9]**

4622 **Simenon, Georges.** *Intimate Memoirs.* 1984, Harcourt $22.95 (0-15-144892-2). An autobiography of the French mystery writer best known for the Maigret series. "A beautifully recaptured remembrance by an intense man."—BL (Rev: BL 4/15/84; LJ 6/15/84; Time 6/18/84) **[843.9]**

4623 **Vaillant, Janet G.** *Black, French, and African: A Life of Leópold Sédar Senghor.* 1990, Harvard Univ. Pr. $29.95 (0-674-07623-0). A biography of the African philosopher and writer who served as president of Senegal from 1960 to 1980. (Rev: LJ 7/90; NYRB 12/20/90; NYTBR 10/21/90) **[843.9]**

846 French letters

1600–1715

4624 **Mossiker, Frances.** *Madame de Sevigne: A Life and Letters.* 1985, Columbia Univ. Pr. paper $16.00 (0-231-06153-6). A biography of the seventeenth-century French noblewoman remembered for her letters, many of which are reproduced in this volume. (Rev: Atl 11/83; LJ 9/15/83; NYTBR 1/8/84) **[846.4]**

848 French miscellaneous writings

4625 **Alter, Robert, and Carol Cosman.** *A Lion for Love: A Critical Biography of Stendhal.* 1986, Harvard Univ. Pr. paper $9.95 (0-674-53575-8). A study of the life and work of the nineteenth-century French writer and author of *The Red and the Black.* (Rev: LJ 8/79; NYRB 9/27/79; NYTBR 10/7/79) **[848]**

4626 **Ayer, Alfred J.** *Voltaire.* 1986, Random $19.95 (0-394-54798-5). The British philosopher examines the life and ideas of the eighteenth-century French writer and comments on the relevance of his thought in the present day. (Rev: LJ 11/1/86; New Rep 3/2/87; NYTBR 11/2/86) **[848]**

4627 **Malraux, Andre.** *Lazarus.* 1978, Grove-Weidenfeld paper $2.95 (0-394-17068-7). Autobiographical writings examining the author's close encounters with death due to war and disease. (Rev: NYTBR 9/18/77; New Yorker 10/3/77; Sat Rev 8/20/77) **[848]**

1715–1789

4628 **Cranston, Maurice.** *Jean-Jacques: The Early Life and Work of Jean-Jacques Rousseau.* 1983, Norton $22.95 (0-393-01744-3). The first volume of a two-part biography of the eighteenth-century French philosopher and writer. "Highly original . . . a compellingly human portrait of an all too-human genius."—PW (Rev: Choice 9/83; LJ 5/15/83; PW 3/11/83) **[848.5]**

4629 **Cranston, Maurice.** *Noble Savage: Jean-Jacques Rousseau, 1754–1762.* 1991, Univ. of Chicago Pr. $32.50 (0-226-11863-0). The second of three volumes, this biography of the life of the French philosopher covers the years Rousseau wrote *Emile* and the *Social Contract.* (Rev: LJ 5/15/91; PW 4/5/91; TLS 3/1/91) **[848.5]**

1900–

4630 **Bair, Deidre.** *Simone de Beauvoir: A Biography.* 1990, Summit $24.95 (0-671-60681-6). A biography of the French philosopher, writer, and wife of Jean-Paul Sartre. "The most detailed account to date."—PW (Rev: BL 1/1/90; NYTBR 4/15/90; PW 2/2/90. Awards: BL, 1990; NYTBR, 1990) **[848.9]**

4631 **Cohen-Solal, Annie.** *Sartre: A Life.* 1987, Pantheon $24.95 (0-394-52525-6). A biography of the twentieth-century French existentialist philosopher and author of the novel *Nausea.* "Brings him to life in a startlingly touching way."—NYTBR (Rev: Choice 2/88; NYTBR 7/26/87; Newsweek 6/22/87) **[848.9]**

4632 **De Beauvoir, Simone.** *Adieux: A Farewell to Sartre.* 1985, Pantheon paper $8.95 (0-394-72898-X). Memoirs of the last ten years of the life of Jean-Paul Sartre containing a series of dialogues between the author and the philosopher. (Rev: BL 4/15/84; LJ 6/1/84; PW 3/16/84) **[848.9]**

4633 **Francis, Claude, and Fernande Gontier.** *Simone de Beauvoir: A Life . . . a Love Story.* 1987, St. Martin's $25.00 (0-312-00189-4); paper $12.95 (0-312-02324-3). A biography of the French writer focusing on her feminist thought and romantic life. (Rev: BL 6/1/87; Natl Rev 9/25/87; NYTBR 5/24/87) **[848.9]**

4634 **Gerassi, John.** *Jean-Paul Sartre: Hated Conscience of His Century; Vol. 1, Protestant or Protester.* 1989, Univ. of Chicago Pr. $19.95 (0-226-28797-1). This first volume of a study of the life of the French philosopher and writer covers the years from his birth to the end of World War II. "A brilliantly original biography."—PW (Rev: Choice 10/89; NYTBR 7/9/89; PW 4/28/89. Awards: PW, 1989) **[848.9]**

4635 **Hayman, Ronald.** *Sartre: A Life.* 1987, Simon & Schuster $19.95 (0-671-45942-2). An in-depth biography of the prominent French philosopher and writer. "The first definitive work on Sartre's life."—LJ (Rev: Choice 11/87; LJ 6/15/87; TLS 12/12/86. Awards: ALA, 1987) **[848.9]**

4636 **Lottman, Herbert.** *Colette: A Life.* 1991, Little, Brown $24.95 (0-316-53361-0). A biography of the

French author of *Cheri, The Vagabond,* and *Gigi.* (REV: BL 12/15/90; LJ 11/1/90)   **[848.9]**

4637   **Sarraute, Nathalie.** *Childhood: An Autobiography.* 1985, Braziller paper $8.95 (0-8076-1116-6). Memoirs of the French novelist regarding her youth spent between her estranged parents. (REV: Atl 4/84; CSM 8/2/84; NYTBR 4/1/84)   **[848.9]**

4638   **Steegmuller, Francis.** *Cocteau: A Biography.* 1986, Godine paper $15.95 (0-87923-606-X). Writing for the *New York Times,* Mark Schorer called this biography of the French artist, writer, and filmmaker "a model of the biographer's art." (REV: LJ 9/15/70; NYTBR 8/27/70; Sat Rev 9/19/70. AWARDS: ALA, 1970; NBA, 1971; NYTBR, 1970)   **[848.9]**

850   ITALIAN, ROMANIAN, RHAETO-ROMANIC

851   Italian poetry

4639   **Montale, Eugenio.** *The Storm and Other Things.* 1986, Norton paper $6.95 (0-393-30249-0). A collection of poetry by the Italian Nobel laureate. "His greatest book."—LJ (REV: Choice 6/86; LJ 2/15/86; NYTBR 2/23/86)   **[851]**

853   Italian fiction

4640   **Calvino, Italo.** *Six Memos for the Next Millennium.* 1988, Harvard Univ. Pr. $12.95 (0-674-81040-6). Six lectures regarding desirable qualities of literature that the Italian writer was scheduled to present at Harvard prior to his death. (REV: Choice 9/88; NYRB 9/29/88; NYTBR 3/20/88)   **[853]**

1814–1859

4641   **Ginzburg, Natalia.** *Manzoni Family.* 1989, Arcade paper $9.95 (1-55970-030-0). A biographical study of the nineteenth-century Italian writer Alessandro Manzoni and his family. (REV: Choice 3/88; LJ 11/1/87; TLS 8/28/87)   **[853.7]**

1900–

4642   **Levi, Primo.** *Mirror Maker: Stories and Essays.* 1989, Schocken $16.95 (0-8052-4076-4); paper $9.95 (0-8052-0989-1). A collection of poems, essays, and stories by the Italian author of *Other People's Trades.* (REV: BL 9/1/89; LJ 9/15/89; PW 7/28/89) **[853.9]**

854   Italian essays

4643   **Levi, Primo.** *Other People's Trades.* 1989, Simon & Schuster $18.95 (0-671-61149-6); paper $8.95 (0-671-70519-9). Over 40 essays by the Italian writer on a variety of subjects including chess, snakes, and word processing. (REV: LJ 3/15/89; NYTBR 5/7/89; Time 5/29/89)   **[854]**

4644   **Levi, Primo.** *Periodic Table.* 1986, Schocken paper $8.95 (0-8052-0811-9). Levi's memoirs of his youth in Mussolini's Italy and his career as a chemist before the war. "This beautifully crafted book . . . contains a wealth of wisdom about human relationships and values and the beauty of the

world."—NYTBR (REV: NYTBR 12/23/84; Newsweek 5/6/85; Time 1/28/85. AWARDS: NYTBR, 1985)   **[854]**

860   SPANISH AND PORTUGUESE LITERATURES

Persons

4645   **Byron, William.** *Cervantes: A Biography.* 1988, Paragon House paper $12.95 (1-55778-006-4). An analysis of the life and work of the sixteenth- and seventeenth-century Spanish writer and author of *Don Quixote.* (REV: Choice 3/79; LJ 9/15/78; NYTBR 4/8/78)   **[860.92]**

861   Spanish poetry

4646   **Borges, Jorge Luis.** *In Praise of Darkness.* 1974, Dutton paper $5.95 (0-525-03635-0). A bilingual selection of the great Argentine writer's poetry on such topics as his blindness, Israel, Buenos Aires, and James Joyce. (REV: Choice 10/74; NYRB 4/4/74; PW 1/21/74)   **[861]**

4647   **Huidobro, Vicente.** *Altazor: Or, A Voyage in a Parachute (1919), a Poem in VII Cantos.* 1988, Graywolf paper $8.50 (1-55597-106-7). A bilingual edition of the Chilean poet's epic work. "Belongs among the preeminent works of literary modernism . . . a vertiginous, exuberant, dazzling masterpiece."—BL (REV: BL 7/88; CSM 8/25/88; LJ 9/1/88)   **[861]**

4648   **Machado, Antonio.** *Times Alone: Selected Poems of Antonio Machado.* 1983, Univ. Pr. of New England $19.50 (0-8195-5087-6); paper $12.95 (0-8195-6081-2). Two hundred fifty selected works of verse spanning the career of the Spanish poet. "A standard . . . translation and scholarship of the highest caliber."—LJ (REV: Choice 12/82; LJ 10/1/82; TLS 2/18/83)   **[861]**

4649   **Neruda, Pablo.** *Heights of Macchu Picchu.* 1967, Farrar paper $8.95 (0-374-50648-5). A bilingual edition of a lengthy poem by the Chilean writer inspired by his visit to the Incan ruins. "Neruda . . . at the height of his poetic power."—Choice (REV: Choice 11/67; LJ 5/1/67; NYTBR 5/21/67. AWARDS: ALA, 1967)   **[861]**

4650   **Neruda, Pablo.** *Late and Posthumous Poems, 1968–1974.* Ed. by Ben Belitt. 1989, Grove-Weidenfeld $21.95 (0-8021-1078-9); paper $10.95 (0-8021-3145-X). A bilingual collection of poetry by the Chilean writer culled from nine of his books. (REV: BL 10/1/88; LJ 11/1/88; PW 9/30/88. AWARDS: PW, 1988)   **[861]**

4651   **Neruda, Pablo.** *Selected Odes of Pablo Neruda.* 1990, Univ. of California Pr. $40.00 (0-520-05944-1); paper $12.95 (0-520-07172-7). A bilingual selection of odes by the Chilean Nobel laureate. (REV: BL 2/15/91; TLS 6/28/91)   **[861]**

4652   **Paz, Octavio.** *Collected Poems, 1957–1987.* 1987, New Directions $37.50 (0-8112-1037-5). The most comprehensive collection of the recent work of the winner of the 1990 Nobel Prize for Literature. "This massive volume, offered in a bilingual format, represents a supreme achievement."—Choice (REV: Choice 6/88; CSM 12/23/87; LJ 10/15/87. AWARDS: LJ, 1987) **[861]**

4653 Paz, Octavio. *Other Voice: Essays in Modern Poetry.* 1991, Harcourt $16.95 (0-15-170449-X). A collection of essays on poetry by the 1990 Nobel Prize winner. (REV: BL 11/15/91; LJ 10/15/91) **[861]**

4654 Paz, Octavio. *Sor Juana: Or, the Traps of Faith.* 1988, Harvard Univ. Pr. $29.95 (0-674-82105-X); paper $12.95 (0-674-82106-8). A biography of the seventeenth-century Mexican writer and nun. "Daunting in its careful deliberation and revealing in its penetrating analysis."—BL (REV: BL 8/88; NYTBR 12/25/88; TLS 12/30/88) **[861]**

4655 Teitelboim, Volodia. *Neruda: An Intimate Biography.* 1991, Univ. of Texas Pr. $29.95 (0-292-75548-1). A biography of the Chilean poet written by a close personal friend who knew him for over four decades. (REV: LJ 11/1/91; PW 10/4/91) **[861]**

4656 Velez, Clemente Soto. *Blood That Keeps Singing: Selected Poems of Clemente Soto Velez.* 1991, Curbstone paper $9.95 (0-915306-78-6). A bilingual collection of verse from a veteran Puerto Rican writer. (REV: LJ 9/15/91; PW 8/30/91) **[861]**

863 Spanish fiction

1945–

4657 Goytisolo, Juan. *Forbidden Territory: The Memoirs of Juan Goytisolo, 1931–1956.* 1989, North Point $18.95 (0-86547-337-4). Memoirs of the Spanish writer and his life during the Spanish Civil War and under the dictatorship of Franco. (REV: LJ 11/15/88; NYTBR 2/12/89; TLS 5/19/89) **[863.64]**

4658 Goytisolo, Juan. *Realms of Strife: Memoirs, 1957–1982.* 1990, North Point $19.95 (0-86547-434-6). The second volume of the memoirs of the Spanish writer. "An important historical document and a moving personal testimony."—TLS (REV: BL 9/15/90; LJ 10/1/90; TLS 12/7/90) **[863.64]**

864 Spanish essays

4659 Fuentes, Carlos. *Myself with Others: Selected Essays.* 1988, Farrar $19.95 (0-374-21750-5). Literary essays by the Mexican writer discussing his work and that of fellow authors such as Garcia Marquez and Cervantes. (REV: LJ 4/15/88; NYTBR 7/17/88; New Yorker 5/16/88) **[864]**

4660 Paz, Octavio. *Alternating Current.* 1983, Seaver Books paper $7.95 (0-8050-0175-1). A collection of essays dealing with literature, art, and politics by the 1990 winner of the Nobel Prize for Literature. (REV: Atl 2/73; Choice 6/73; LJ 12/1/72) **[864]**

4661 Paz, Octavio. *Convergences: Essays on Art and Literature.* 1987, Harcourt $19.95 (0-15-122585-0). Essays by the Mexican Nobel Prize winner regarding language, literature, and culture. (REV: LJ 10/15/87; NYTBR 5/15/88; TLS 1/15/88) **[864]**

868 Spanish miscellaneous writings

4662 Cortazar, Julio. *Around the Day in Eighty Worlds.* 1986, North Point $22.50 (0-86547-203-3). A collection of miscellaneous pieces by the Argentine writer. "The best autobiography of Cortazar available in English."—Choice (REV: Choice 11/86; NYTBR 5/4/86) **[868]**

1910–1945

4663 Gibson, Ian. *Federico Garcia Lorca: A Life.* 1989, Pantheon $29.95 (0-394-50964-1); paper $15.95 (0-679-73157-1). A biography of the Spanish poet who was assassinated during the Spanish Civil War. "The definitive study."—BL (REV: BL 10/1/89; New Rep 1/1/90; NYTBR 10/8/89. AWARDS: LJ, 1989; NYTBR, 1989) **[868.62]**

880 HELLENIC LITERATURES; CLASSICAL GREEK

882 Classical Greek drama

4664 Kott, Jan. *Eating of the Gods: An Interpretation of Greek Tragedy.* 1987, Northwestern Univ. Pr. paper $14.95 (0-8101-0745-7). A study of the relationship between man and his gods in Ancient Greek tragedies. "Imaginative, scholarly and highly readable."—LJ (REV: Choice 9/73; LJ 6/1/73; NYTBR 7/19/73) **[882]**

883 Classical Greek epic poetry and fiction

Classical Greek epic poetry

4665 Homer. *Iliad.* 1990, Viking $35.00 (0-670-83510-2). A translation of the Greek classic by Robert Fagles. (REV: BL 8/90; LJ 8/90; NYTBR 10/7/90) **[883.01]**

4666 Homer. *Odyssey of Homer.* 1990, Univ. of California Pr. $35.00 (0-520-07021-6). A translation of the Greek epic poem by Allen Mandelbaum. "The most sophisticated English *Odyssey* yet seen."—New Rep (REV: BL 1/15/91; CSM 1/4/91; New Rep 4/8/91) **[883.01]**

889 Modern Greek

4667 Elytis, Odysseus. *Little Mariner.* 1988, Copper Canyon paper $9.00 (1-55659-014-8). A collection of poetry by the winner of the 1979 Nobel Prize for Literature. "Quite clearly Odysseus Elytis's most important work since he was awarded the Nobel Prize."—Choice (REV: Choice 2/89; PW 4/22/88. AWARDS: PW, 1988) **[889]**

4668 Ritsos, Yannis. *Exile and Return: Selected Poems, 1967–1974.* 1985, Ecco Pr. $17.50 (0-88001-017-7); paper $8.50 (0-88001-018-5). Selected works by the Greek poet written during his imprisonment and exile. "A stunning and powerful collection."—PW (REV: LJ 11/15/85; PW 10/4/85) **[889]**

1945–

4669 Kazantzakis, Nikos. *Report to Greco.* 1975, Simon & Schuster paper $12.95 (0-671-22027-6).

Memoirs of the Greek writer concerning his life, travels, and spirituality. "One of the most important books of the 20th century."—Choice (REV: Choice 9/65; LJ 7/65; NYTBR 8/15/65. AWARDS: ALA, 1965)
[889.34]

890   LITERATURES OF OTHER LANGUAGES

891   East Indo-European and Celtic

Modern Persian (Farsi)

4670 Khorsandi, Hadi. *Ayatollah and I: Iran's New Satire.* 1987, Readers International $14.95 (0-930523-36-9); paper $7.95 (0-930523-37-7). A political satire of current Iranian government and society presented by a former Iranian who now lives in London. (REV: LJ 12/87; PW 9/11/87. AWARDS: PW, 1987)
[891.55]

Russian literature

4671 Nabokov, Vladimir. *Lectures on Russian Literature.* Ed. by Frederick Bowers. 1982, Harcourt paper $11.95 (0-15-649591-0). Essays derived from lectures Nabokov gave for his literature classes at Cornell and Wellesley. "The lectures are very learned, very rich in critical insight, and often funny, but they are most extraordinary for the way Nabokov re-creates, in concrete sensuous detail, his experience in reading these Russian writers."—NYTBR (REV: CSM 1/20/82; NYTBR 10/25/81; Time 11/16/81. AWARDS: Time, 1981)
[891.7]

1800–1917

4672 De Courcel, Martine. *Tolstoy: The Ultimate Reconciliation.* 1988, Macmillan $27.50 (0-684-18569-5). A critical look at the life, works, and politics of the great Russian writer. "This marvelous biography . . . deserves to be read right along with *War and Peace* and *Anna Karenina*."—BL (REV: Choice 12/88; LJ 5/1/88; NYTBR 8/28/88)
[891.73]

4673 Dovlatov, Sergei. *Ours: A Russian Family Album.* 1989, Grove-Weidenfeld $15.95 (1-55584-281-X). A portrayal of four generations of the author's family under the Soviet system of government and of the author's life after his forced emigration to the United States. (REV: Atl 7/89; LJ 3/1/89; Newsweek 4/24/89)
[891.73]

4674 Frank, Joseph. *Dostoyevsky: The Seeds of Revolt, 1821–1849.* 1976, Princeton Univ. Pr. $45.00 (0-691-06260-9); paper $11.95 (0-691-01355-1). Volume 1 of Frank's life of Dostoyevsky covers his early years to his arrest for radicalism in 1849. "A colossal work: well documented, well written and well organized . . . a delight to read."—LJ (REV: Choice 2/77; LJ 9/1/76; NYTBR 11/21/76)
[891.73]

4675 Frank, Joseph. *Dostoyevsky: The Stir of Liberation, 1860–1865.* 1986, Princeton Univ. Pr. $45.00 (0-691-06652-3); paper $10.95 (0-691-01452-3). A study of the years following Dostoyevsky's forced exile to Siberia. "A work . . . that can hardly be

recommended too highly. Essential."—LJ (REV: Choice 1/87; CSM 9/5/86; LJ 3/15/87)
[891.73]

4676 Frank, Joseph. *Dostoyevsky: The Years of Ordeal, 1850–1859.* 1986, Princeton Univ. Pr. $35.00 (0-691-06576-4); paper $9.95 (0-691-01422-1). Volume 2 of a projected five-volume biography of the author of *Crime and Punishment* and *The Brothers Karamazov.* "Readers curious about how Dostoyevsky translated experience into ideas and then into art can welcome Frank as an indispensable guide."—Time (REV: LJ 11/15/83; NYRB 2/2/84; Time 1/30/84. AWARDS: Time, 1984)
[891.73]

4677 Kjetsaa, Geir. *Fyodor Dostoyevsky: A Writer's Life.* 1987, Viking $24.95 (0-670-81914-X); Fawcett paper $10.95 (0-449-90334-6). A biography of the nineteenth-century Russian writer drawing heavily on his notebooks, diaries, and letters. (REV: Choice 4/88; LJ 11/1/87; NYTBR 2/21/88)
[891.73]

4678 Pritchett, V. S. *Chekhov: A Spirit Set Free.* 1988, Random $17.95 (0-394-54650-4); paper $8.95 (0-679-72546-6). A literary biography of the Russian short story writer and playwright. "This wonderfully readable reappraisal will make readers want to turn to Chekhov's stories anew."—PW (REV: LJ 10/1/88; NYTBR 11/27/88; PW 8/4/88)
[891.73]

4679 Pritchett, V. S. *Gentle Barbarian: The Life and Work of Ivan Turgenev.* 1986, Ecco Pr. paper $9.50 (0-88001-120-3). A biography of the nineteenth-century Russian writer by the esteemed British literary critic. "As we read this book we realize we are in the presence of an artist in criticism, a virtuoso of lucid evocation and precise judgment."—NYTBR (REV: CSM 7/11/77; Sat Rev 5/14/77; NYTBR 5/22/77. AWARDS: NYTBR, 1977)
[891.73]

4680 Schapiro, Leonard. *Turgenev: His Life and Times.* 1982, Harvard Univ. Pr. paper $10.95 (0-674-91297-7). A biography of the nineteenth-century Russian playwright and novelist. (REV: Choice 7–8/79; LJ 3/15/79; NYTBR 3/4/79)
[891.73]

4681 Troyat, Henri. *Chekhov.* 1988, Fawcett paper $10.95 (0-449-90281-1). A biography of the Russian playwright by the biographer of Pushkin, Tolstoy, and Gogol. "The masterly English translation of this important biography is an essential acquisition."—LJ (REV: LJ 11/1/86; NYRB 12/4/86; Time 11/10/86. AWARDS: LJ, 1986)
[891.73]

4682 Wilson, A. N. *Tolstoy: A Biography.* 1988, Norton $25.00 (0-393-02585-3); Fawcett paper $14.95 (0-449-90449-0). A biography of the Russian writer penned by the British novelist. "The most human portrait of Tolstoy to date . . . a magnificent achievement."—PW (REV: LJ 8/88; PW 6/24/88; Time 8/15/88. AWARDS: Time, 1988)
[891.73]

1917–

4683 Akhmatova, Anna. *Complete Poems of Anna Akhmatova.* Ed. by Roberta Reeder and Ed Hogan. 1990, Zephyr $80.00 (0-939010-13-5). A two-volume bilingual collection of the work of the twentieth-century Russian poet. "A treasure for poetry lovers everywhere."—LJ (Rev: Choice 7–8/90; LJ 4/1/90; NYTBR 5/13/90. Awards: NYTBR, 1990)

[891.74]

4684 Aksyonov, Vassily. *In Search of Melancholy Baby: A Russian in America.* 1987, Random $15.95 (0-394-54364-5); paper $7.95 (0-394-75992-3). The Russian writer's reflections on American life and culture following his first five years of living in the United States. (Rev: BL 5/15/87; LJ 7/87; New Rep 9/7/87)

[891.74]

4685 Barnes, Christopher J. *Boris Pasternak: A Literary Biography, Vol. 1, 1890–1928.* 1989, Cambridge Univ. Pr. $69.50 (0-521-25957-6). The first volume of the author's biography and literary study of the Russian writer. "Will surely remain the authoritative life for many years."—TLS (Rev: NYTBR 9/2/90; TLS 2/9/90)

[891.74]

4686 Bethea, David M. *Khodasevich: His Life and Art.* 1983, Princeton Univ. Pr. $45.00 (0-691-06559-4); paper $14.50 (0-691-10179-5). A biography of the Russian writer who many rank among the top poets of the twentieth century. (Rev: Choice 5/84; LJ 9/15/83; NYTBR 11/27/83)

[891.74]

4687 Boyd, Brian. *Vladimir Nabokov: The American Years.* 1991, Princeton Univ. Pr. $35.00 (0-691-06797-X). The second and concluding volume of the author's biography of the Russian-born writer covering his years in the United States. "Definitive . . . Nabokov has found, at last, a biographer worthy of him."—NYTBR (Rev: BL 9/15/91; LJ 8/91; NYTBR 9/22/91. Awards: PW, 1991; Time, 1991) **[891.74]**

4688 Brodsky, Joseph. *A Part of Speech.* 1980, Farrar $15.95 (0-374-22987-2); paper $7.95 (0-374-51633-2). Collected verse regarding places and the mythological past by the Russian émigré poet. (Rev: CSM 8/11/80; LJ 7/80; NYRB 8/14/80)

[891.74]

4689 Brodsky, Joseph. *To Urania.* 1988, Farrar $14.95 (0-374-17253-6). Poems by the Nobel Prize–winning exiled Soviet poet. "Essential."—LJ (Rev: LJ 5/15/88; NYRB 11/24/88; NYTBR 11/27/88. Awards: LJ, 1988)

[891.74]

4690 Brown, Clarence. *Mandelstam.* 1978, Cambridge Univ. Pr. paper $14.95 (0-521-29347-2). A biographical and critical look at the life and work of the great Russian poet containing many examples of his poetry. "An excellent and most welcome introduction to the poet and a fine, knowing guide to his work."—NYTBR (Rev: BL 1/15/74; LJ 1/15/74; NYTBR 1/20/74)

[891.74]

4691 Brown, Clarence, ed. *Portable Twentieth Century Russian Reader.* 1985, Penguin paper $9.95 (0-14-015100-1). A survey of twentieth-century Russian literature from Chekhov to the 1980s. "A work of real excellence."—BL (Rev: BL 5/15/85; CSM 8/2/85; LJ 5/15/85)

[891.74]

4692 Chukovskaya, Lydia Korneevna. *To the Memory of Childhood.* 1988, Northwestern Univ. Pr. $24.95 (0-8101-0789-9); paper $9.95 (0-8101-0790-2). A Soviet dissident novelist's remembrances of her father, a Russian critic and children's author, and

his influence on her life and thought. (Rev: Choice 3/89; NYTBR 9/11/88; PW 6/17/88)

[891.74]

4693 Mandelstam, Nadezhda. *Hope Against Hope.* 1976, Macmillan paper $12.95 (0-689-70530-1). Memoirs of her husband, Osip Mandelstam, noted Russian poet, and his arrest, banishment, and death in a Stalinist concentration camp. "Any reader, even one for whom literature has no great significance, will be moved and grieved by this book."—Natl Rev (Rev: Choice 2/71; Natl Rev 12/29/70; NYTBR 10/18/70. Awards: ALA, 1970)

[891.74]

4694 Mandelstam, Osip. *Selected Poems of Osip Mandelstam.* 1984, Macmillan paper $9.95 (0-689-11425-7). Clarence Brown's translations of the Russian poet's work. "A sensitive and sensible selection of Mandelstam's poetry."—LJ (Rev: BL 6/15/74; LJ 12/15/73; NYTBR 1/20/74)

[891.74]

4695 Nabokov, Vladimir. *Speak, Memory: An Autobiography Revisited.* 1989, Random paper $9.95 (0-679-72339-0). Nabokov's early life: his ancestry; life before and after the Russian Revolution, which forced his family into exile in England; and his years in Western Europe. "The finest autobiography written in our time."—New Rep (Rev: Atl 1/67; New Rep 1/14/67; NYRB 11/3/66. Awards: ALA, 1967; NYTBR, 1967)

[891.74]

4696 Ratushinskaya, Irina. *Beyond the Limit: Poems.* 1987, Northwestern $22.95 (0-8101-0748-1); paper $10.95 (0-8101-0749-X). A collection of poems written in a Soviet labor camp while the poet was held as a political prisoner. "Even in translation, reading her poetry is a profound emotional experience."—NYTBR (Rev: Choice 10/87; LJ 6/1/87; NYTBR 6/28/87. Awards: LJ, 1987)

[891.74]

4697 Ratushinskaya, Irina. *Grey Is the Color of Hope.* 1988, Knopf $18.95 (0-394-57140-1); McKay paper $8.95 (0-679-72447-8). Memoirs of the author's three-and-a-half years spent in a Soviet forced labor camp. "Piercingly beautiful, gripping with its amazing stories of cruelty and survival."—PW (Rev: LJ 10/15/88; NYTBR 10/30/88; PW 8/26/88. Awards: LJ, 1988; PW, 1988)

[891.74]

4698 Ratushinskaya, Irina. *In the Beginning.* 1991, Knopf $23.00 (0-394-57141-X). Memoirs of the poet and author of *Grey Is the Color of Hope* describing her years of childhood and adolescence in the Soviet Union. (Rev: BL 3/1/91; LJ 3/1/91; PW 2/1/91)

[891.74]

4699 Tertz, Abram. *A Voice from the Chorus.* 1976, Farrar $10.00 (0-374-28500-4). Letters the author wrote to his wife while serving a sentence in Soviet forced-labor camps for publishing his works abroad. "A book that belongs to the modern classics in the literature of endurance."—LJ (Rev: LJ 6/15/76; NYRB 8/5/76; NYTBR 6/27/76)

[891.74]

4700 Tsvetaeva, Marina. *Selected Poems.* 1987, Dutton paper $12.95 (0-525-48283-0). Selected work from the twentieth-century Russian poet. "Her poetry is among the best of this century translated into English from any literature."—TLS (Rev: LJ 10/15/87; NYTBR 9/22/87; TLS 7/31/87)

[891.74]

4701   Voznesensky, Andrei. *An Arrow in the Wall: Selected Poetry and Prose.* Ed. by William Jay Smith and F. D. Reeve. 1988, Henry Holt paper $10.95 (0-8050-0784-9). Selected writings of the twentieth-century Soviet poet. "By far the best attempt so far made to bring a contemporary Russian poet into a Western context."—NYTBR (REV: LJ 2/1/87; NYRB 12/3/87; NYTBR 3/29/87. AWARDS: NYTBR, 1987)   **[891.74]**

4702   Yevtushenko, Yevgeny. *Collected Poems, 1952–1990.* 1990, Henry Holt $29.95 (0-8050-0696-6). Selected works from the career of the Soviet poet. "A vast hole remains on any shelf that does not hold this volume."—BL (REV: BL 11/15/90; LJ 12/90; PW 12/7/90)   **[891.74]**

Slavic literature

4703   Baranczak, Stanislaw. *Weight of the Body: Selected Poems.* 1990, Another Chicago $16.95 (0-929968-02-6); paper $8.95 (0-929968-01-8). A collection of verse by the Polish poet and Harvard professor. (REV: LJ 1/90; PW 11/24/89. AWARDS: PW, 1990)   **[891.8]**

4704   Baranczak, Stanislaw, and Clare Cavanaugh, eds. *Polish Poetry of the Last Two Decades of Communist Rule: Spoiling Cannibals' Fun.* 1991, Northwestern Univ. Pr. $39.95 (0-8101-0968-9); paper $14.95 (0-8101-0982-4). Poetry from 29 Polish writers written during the past two decades. (REV: BL 9/1/91; PW 8/30/91)   **[891.8]**

4705   Capek, Karel. *Toward the Radical Center: A Karel Capek Reader.* Ed. by Peter Kussi. 1990, Catbird Pr. $23.95 (0-945774-06-0); paper $13.95 (0-945774-07-9). A collection of writings by the Czechoslovakian author of *War with the Newts.* (REV: BL 2/15/90; LJ 6/1/90; NYTBR 3/25/90)   **[891.8]**

4706   Gombrowicz, Witold. *Diary 1957–1961, Vol. 2.* Ed. by Jan Kott. 1989, Northwestern Univ. Pr. $29.95 (0-8101-0716-3); paper $12.95 (0-8101-0717-1). The second volume of the diaries of the Polish writer who spent his later years in exile in Argentina. "A diary of extraordinary vitality and interest."—BL (REV: BL 7/89; Choice 3/90; PW 5/26/89. AWARDS: PW, 1989)   **[891.8]**

4707   Konwicki, Tadeusz. *New World Avenue and Vicinity.* 1991, Farrar $19.95 (0-374-22182-0). A collection of miscellaneous prose by the Polish author of *Bohin Manor.* (REV: BL 12/1/90; LJ 1/91; NYTBR 1/27/91)   **[891.8]**

4708   Kott, Jan, ed. *Four Decades of Polish Essays.* 1990, Northwestern Univ. Pr. $29.95 (0-8101-0862-3); paper $12.95 (0-8101-0863-1). Collected essays about politics and culture from Polish writers from the 1950s to the 1980s. (REV: BL 6/1/90; LJ 6/15/90; PW 4/27/90. AWARDS: PW, 1990)   **[891.8]**

4709   Milosz, Czeslaw. *Collected Poems, 1931–1987.* 1988, Ecco Pr. $39.95 (0-88001-173-4); paper $14.95 (0-88001-174-2). Collected poetry of the Polish Nobel laureate. "One of the most compelling and universally relevant voices of this century."—BL (REV: BL 4/15/88; LJ 4/15/88; NYTBR 6/19/88. AWARDS: BL, the 1980s; LJ, 1988)   **[891.8]**

4710   Milosz, Czeslaw. *Native Realm: A Search for Self-Definition.* 1981, Univ. of California Pr. paper $9.95 (0-520-04474-6). Autobiographical essays by the Nobel laureate detailing his life in Lithuania, Poland, and the United States. (REV: CSM 6/8/81; NYTBR 2/1/81; TLS 7/24/81)   **[891.8]**

4711   Seifert, Jaroslav. *Selected Poetry of Jaroslav Seifert.* 1987, Macmillan $9.95 (0-02-070760-6). Representative works of the Czech poet who received the 1984 Nobel Prize for Literature. (REV: LJ 8/86; PW 6/27/86)   **[891.8]**

892   Afro-Asiatic literature; Semitic

Hebrew literature

4712   Amichai, Yehuda. *Amen.* 1987, Milkweed paper $7.95 (0-915943-22-0). The third collection of the Israeli writer's poem to be translated into English. (REV: LJ 7/77; NYTBR 7/3/77; PW 5/9/77)   **[892.4]**

4713   Amichai, Yehuda. *Great Tranquility: Questions and Answers.* 1983, Harper & Row paper $7.95 (0-06-091085-2). A collection of verse by the esteemed Israeli poet. "In any language, Amichai is a major poet."—BL (REV: BL 8/83; LJ 9/1/83; NYTBR 11/13/83)   **[892.4]**

4714   Amichai, Yehuda. *Selected Poetry of Yehuda Amichai.* 1986, Harper & Row $29.95 (0-06-055001-5). A selection of the Israeli poet's best work from over 30 years. "As Israel's most popular poet, and one of the most gifted lyricists anywhere, Amichai belongs in every library."—BL (REV: BL 9/1/86; Choice 11/86; NYTBR 8/3/86)   **[892.4]**

4715   Pagis, Dan. *Variable Directions: The Selected Poetry.* 1989, North Point $21.95 (0-86547-383-8); paper $9.95 (0-86547-384-6). Selected works by the Israeli poet and Holocaust survivor. (REV: NYTBR 11/12/89; PW 5/12/89. AWARDS: PW, 1989)   **[892.4]**

4716   Singer, Isaac Bashevis. *In My Father's Court.* 1966, Farrar paper $5.95 (0-374-50592-6). Singer's remembrances of his childhood in Warsaw before World War I. "Well written and thoroughly enjoyable . . . gives the reader much insight into the author's other writing."—LJ (REV: BL 6/15/66; LJ 5/1/66; NYTBR 5/8/66. AWARDS: ALA, 1966; NYTBR, 1966)   **[892.4]**

895   Literatures of East and Southeast Asia

Chinese literature

4717   Barme, Geremie, and John Minsford. *Seeds of Fire: Chinese Voices of Conscience.* 1988, Hill & Wang $25.00 (0-8090-8521-6); Farrar paper $12.95 (0-374-52211-1). Selected writings of nearly 90 Chinese dissidents discussing life in China during the latter half of the 1980s. (REV: LJ 11/15/88; NYRB 3/16/89; NYTBR 4/2/89)   **[895.1]**

4718   Dao, Bei. *August Sleepwalker.* 1990, New Directions $16.95 (0-8112-1132-2); paper $8.95 (0-8112-1132-0). The first English translation of the contemporary Chinese poet's verse. (REV: LJ 5/15/90; NYTBR 8/12/90)   **[895.1]**

4719 Watson, Burton, ed. *Columbia Book of Chinese Poetry: From Early Times to the 13th Century.* 1984, Columbia Univ. Pr. $29.00 (0-231-05682-6). An anthology of early Chinese poetry containing over 420 poems by nearly 100 authors. (Rev: Choice 3/85; CSM 10/17/84; LJ 8/84)   **[895.1]**

Japanese literature

4720 Keene, Donald. *Dawn to the West: Japanese Literature in the Modern Era.* 1984, Holt $60.00 (0-03-062814-8). A critical survey of Japanese literature from the Meiji Restoration to the 1980s. (Rev: LJ 5/15/84; NYTBR 5/13/84; PW 2/3/84. Awards: LJ, 1984; NYTBR, 1984)   **[895.6]**

4721 Keene, Donald. *Pleasures of Japanese Literature.* 1988, Columbia Univ. Pr. $20.00 (0-231-06736-4). An introduction to the poetry, theater, and fiction of Japan by the author of *Dawn to the West.* (Rev: Choice 5/89; LJ 9/15/88; NYTBR 3/12/89)   **[895.6]**

4722 Sato, Hiroaki, and Burton Watson, eds. *From the Country of Eight Islands: An Anthology of Japanese Poetry.* 1986, Columbia Univ. Pr. paper $15.00 (0-231-06395-4). An English-language anthology of Japanese poetry from the eighth century to the present. "Not just a compilation of Japanese poems, but a primer for the study of the tradition itself . . . a landmark anthology."—PW (Rev: LJ 3/1/81; NYTBR 2/15/81; PW 12/12/80. Awards: ALA, 1981)   **[895.6]**

4723 Tanizaki, Junichiro. *Childhood Years.* 1988, Kodansha $17.95 (0-87011-863-3); paper $6.95 (0-87011-924-9). Childhood memories compiled by the Japanese writer. (Rev: NYRB 12/22/88; NYTBR 9/18/88)   **[895.6]**

4724 Yourcenar, Marguerite. *Mishima: A Vision of the Void.* 1986, Farrar $14.95 (0-374-21033-0); paper $7.95 (0-374-52061-5). A study of the life and thought of Japanese novelist Yukio Mishima. (Rev: Choice 3/87; LJ 11/1/86; TLS 3/27/87)   **[895.6]**

900 GEOGRAPHY AND HISTORY

901 Philosophy and theory

4725 Gay, Peter. *Freud for Historians.* **1985, Oxford Univ. Pr. $19.95 (0-19-503586-0).** An examination of the possible applications of the Freudian method to historical analysis. (Rev: Choice 2/86; LJ 8/85; NYTBR 9/8/85) **[901]**

4726 Lowenthal, David. *Past Is a Foreign Country.* **1986, Cambridge Univ. Pr. $32.50 (0-521-22415-2).** An illustrated study of man's relationship to the past. (Rev: Choice 9/86; LJ 5/1/86; PW 1/3/86) **[901]**

4727 Lukacs, John. *Historical Consciousness: Or the Remembered Past.* **1987, Schocken paper $13.95 (0-8052-0730-9).** An examination of man's consciousness of the past and its effects upon human lives and decision making. (Rev: Choice 12/68; LJ 7/68; Natl Rev 11/5/68) **[901]**

4728 McNeill, William H. *Rise of the West: A History of the Human Community.* **1970, Univ. of Chicago Pr. paper $14.95 (0-226-56144-5).** "The most stimulating and fascinating book that has ever set out to recount and explain the whole history of mankind."—NYTBR (Rev: CSM 8/8/63; NYTBR 10/6/63; Time 8/16/63. Awards: NBA, 1964) **[901]**

904 Collected accounts of events

4729 Friedrich, Otto. *End of the World: A History.* **1986, Fromm International paper $11.95 (0-88064-062-6).** An examination of different points in history when it was commonly believed that the world was close to an end from the Great Flood to the present. (Rev: Natl Rev 12/24/82; NYTBR 10/24/82; Time 10/11/82) **[904]**

4730 Keegan, John. *Face of Battle.* **1983, Penguin paper $6.95 (0-14-004897-9).** The history of combat conditions with emphasis on the battles of Agincourt, Waterloo, and the Somme by the noted military historian. "A remarkable, original, absorbing study."—New Yorker (Rev: NYTBR 11/7/76; New Yorker 11/15/76; Time 12/20/76. Awards: ALA, 1976) **[904]**

Events induced by human activities

4731 MacDonald, John. *Great Battlefields of the World.* **1988, Macmillan paper $24.95 (0-02-044464-8).** A study of 30 key military engagements from ancient times to the twentieth century enhanced by computer graphics illustrating reproductions of the battle sites. (Rev: BL 8/85; LJ 8/85; NYTBR 2/16/86) **[904.7]**

907 Education, research, related topics

Historical research

4732 Clive, John. *Not by Fact Alone: Essays on the Writing and Reading of History.* **1989, Knopf $27.50 (0-394-48953-5).** Essays regarding the writing of history by the historian who won a National Book Award in 1974 for his biography of Macauley. (Rev: LJ 4/15/89; NYTBR 3/11/90; TLS 2/2/90) **[907.2]**

4733 Fischer, David H. *Historian's Fallacies: Toward a Logic of Historical Thought.* **1970, Harper & Row paper $8.95 (0-06-131545-1).** An analysis of past fallacies of historians with a plea for the establishment of concrete standards of historiography. (Rev: Choice 6/70; LJ 5/15/70; New Yorker 4/11/70) **[907.2]**

4734 McNeill, William H. *Arnold J. Toynbee: A Life.* **1989, Oxford Univ. Pr. $24.95 (0-19-505863-1).** A biography of the British historian known for his multivolume *Study of History.* (Rev: LJ 4/15/89; NYRB 10/12/89; NYTBR 5/28/89) **[907.2]**

4735 Tuchman, Barbara W. *Practicing History: Selected Essays.* **1981, Knopf $16.50 (0-394-52086-6); Ballantine paper $8.95 (0-345-30363-6).** A series of essays concerning historiography and the art of writing history. "Reading this collection is comparable to enjoying a selection of effective short stories by an esteemed novelist."—BL (Rev: BL 6/15/81; LJ 8/81; NYTBR 9/27/81. Awards: ALA, 1981) **[907.2]**

909 World history

4736 Boorstin, Daniel J. *Discoverers: A History of Man's Search to Know His World and Himself.* **1983, Random $27.00 (0-394-40229-4); paper $12.95 (0-394-72625-1).** Man's quest for knowledge and the discoveries that followed, traced from antiquity to the twentieth century. "This remarkable work is the capstone of a remarkable historian's career."—LJ (Rev: LJ 11/15/83; NYTBR 11/27/83; Newsweek 11/23/83) **[909]**

4737 Carey, John, ed. *Eyewitness to History.* 1988, Harvard Univ. Pr. $24.95 (0-674-28750-9); Avon paper $10.95 (0-380-70895-7). A collection of 400 firsthand accounts of important historical events from ancient times to the twentieth century. (Rev: CSM 9/2/88; LJ 10/15/88; New Rep 10/24/88) **[909]**

4738 Chartier, Roger, ed. *History of Private Life, Vol. 3: Passions of the Renaissance.* 1989, Harvard Univ. Pr. $39.50 (0-674-39977-3). This third volume in a series examining daily life and customs in different eras looks at private culture during the Renaissance. (Rev: Choice 10/89; NYRB 11/9/89; NYTBR 4/16/89) **[909]**

4739 Connell, Evan S. *White Lantern.* 1989, North Point paper $9.95 (0-86547-364-1). Essays regarding human pluck and tenacity in the face of challenge by the author of *Mrs. Bridge*. (Rev: BL 6/15/80; LJ 6/15/80; NYTBR 7/20/80) **[909]**

4740 Darnton, Robert. *Kiss of Lamourette: Reflections on Cultural History.* 1989, Norton $19.95 (0-393-02753-8). A series of essays on cultural history and historiography. "This book should be essential reading for those who think that history must be either dull or irrelevant."—LJ (Rev: BL 11/1/89; Choice 5/90; LJ 11/15/89) **[909]**

4741 Duby, Georges, ed. *History of Private Life, Vol. 2: Revelations of the Medieval World.* 1988, Harvard Univ. Pr. $39.50 (0-674-39976-5). An analysis of the rise and development of the concepts of individualism and privacy during the Middle Ages. (Rev: BL 2/15/88; LJ 3/1/88; NYRB 3/17/88) **[909]**

4742 Eban, Abba. *Heritage: Civilization and the Jews.* 1986, Summit paper $16.95 (0-671-62881-X). An introduction to Jewish history by the Israeli statesman. (Rev: BL 9/1/84; LJ 11/1/84; PW 8/17/84) **[909]**

4743 Johnson, Paul. *A History of the Jews.* 1987, Harper & Row $24.95 (0-06-015698-8); paper $11.95 (0-06-091533-1). The 4,000-year recorded history of the Jewish people. "An excellent, non-scholarly history for general readers."—LJ (Rev: CSM 6/11/87; LJ 3/15/87; Time 5/11/87. Awards: LJ, 1987; Time, 1987) **[909]**

4744 Morris, Jan. *Among the Cities.* 1985, Oxford Univ. Pr. $21.95 (0-19-520489-1). Thirty-seven collected essays regarding cities of the world written between 1956 and 1984 by the noted travel writer. (Rev: BL 12/1/85; CSM 7/3/86) **[909]**

4745 Stavrianos, Leften S. *Lifelines from Our Past.* 1990, Pantheon $19.95 (0-394-56094-9). A critical study of the influence of man's past upon contemporary society and societal values. (Rev: BL 2/1/90; LJ 2/15/90) **[909]**

4746 Taplin, Oliver. *Greek Fire.* 1990, Macmillan $29.95 (0-689-12096-6). An illustrated study of the influence of ancient Greece upon the modern world. (Rev: LJ 7/90; Natl Rev 9/3/90; TLS 5/11/90) **[909]**

History with respect to racial, ethnic, national groups

4747 Arlen, Michael J. *Passage to Ararat.* Farrar $8.95 (0-374-22989-9). The author's search for his Armenian heritage. (Rev: NYTBR 8/7/85; Newsweek 8/18/75; Time 8/18/75. Awards: NBA, 1976; Time, 1975) **[909.04]**

4748 Yoors, Jan. *Gypsies.* 1987, Waveland Pr. paper $9.50 (0-88133-305-0). A firsthand account of Gypsy history and culture by a Belgian man who traveled around Eastern Europe for a decade with a Gypsy family. "Unsensational and unsentimental."—Atl (Rev: Atl 3/67; Choice 10/67; LJ 3/15/67. Awards: ALA, 1967) **[909.04]**

Ca. 500–1450/1500

4749 Armstrong, Karen. *Holy War: The Crusades and Their Impact on Today's World.* 1991, Doubleday $29.95 (0-385-24193-3). A survey of the history and legacy of the Christian Crusades of the Middle Ages. (Rev: BL 3/15/91; LJ 2/15/91) **[909.07]**

4750 Maalouf, Amin. *Crusades Through Arab Eyes.* 1985, Schocken $16.95 (0-8052-4004-7); paper $12.95 (0-8052-0898-4). A collection of accounts of the Christian crusades of the Middle Ages as recorded by Arab writers. (Rev: LJ 12/85; New Yorker 11/25/85) **[909.07]**

Modern history, 1450/1500–

4751 Braudel, Fernand. *The Mediterranean and the Mediterranean World in the Age of Philip II.* 1976, Harper & Row paper $26.90 (0-06-090566-2). A two-volume analysis of the social life and history of sixteenth-century Europe. "Probably the most significant historical work to appear since World War II."—NYTBR (Rev: Choice 6/74; NYTBR 5/18/75; New Yorker 4/1/74) **[909.08]**

4752 Braudel, Fernand. *Perspective of the World: Civilization and Capitalism, Vol. III.* 1984, Harper & Row $16.95 (0-06-091296-0). An economic history of the world from the fifteenth to eighteenth centuries focusing on Western Europe's rise to trade dominance. (Rev: BL 10/1/84; LJ 10/15/84; PW 8/17/84) **[909.08]**

4753 Braudel, Fernand. *Structures in Everyday Life: The Limits of the Possible.* 1985, Harper & Row paper $19.95 (0-06-091294-4). This is volume 1 of the renowned French historian's Civilization and Capitalism 15th–18th Century series analyzing the social and economic history of that era. (Rev: LJ 1/15/82; NYTBR 5/16/82; Sat Rev 2/82. Awards: ALA, 1982) **[909.08]**

4754 Braudel, Fernand. *Wheels of Commerce: Civilization and Capitalism 15th–18th Centuries.* 1983, Harper & Row $35.00 (0-06-015091-2). A study of national and international trade and commerce in the pre-industrial economy of the fifteenth through eighteenth centuries. (Rᴇᴠ: BL 3/1/83; New Yorker 7/18/83; NYTBR 7/10/83)   **[909.08]**

4755   Johnson, Paul. *Birth of the Modern: World Society, 1815–1830.* 1991, HarperCollins $35.00 (0-06-016574-X). A study of the political, social, and technological changes between 1815 and 1830. "Marvelously readable, vivid, immensely illuminating."—PW (Rᴇᴠ: BL 6/1/91; LJ 6/1/91; PW 5/3/91. Awards: BL, 1991; PW, 1991)   **[909.08]**

4756   Kennedy, Paul. *Rise and Fall of the Great Powers: Economic Change and Military Conflict from 1500 to 2000.* 1987, Random $24.95 (0-394-54674-1); paper $12.95 (0-679-72019-7). The history of the balance of power among nations over five centuries, focusing on the rise and fall of England, France, and Spain, and the rise of the United States in this century. (Rᴇᴠ: LJ 12/87; NYTBR 1/10/88; Time 2/15/88. Awards: LJ, 1988; NYTBR, 1988; Time, 1988)   **[909.08]**

4757   Tuchman, Barbara W. *March of Folly: From Troy to Vietnam.* 1984, Knopf $18.95 (0-394-52777-1); Ballantine paper $9.95 (0-345-30823-9). A study of four cases of historical folly by rulers or governments: the Trojan War; the pre-Reformation papacy; the American Revolution; and the American involvement in Vietnam. (Rᴇᴠ: BL 1/15/84; LJ 2/15/84; PW 1/27/84)   **[909.08]**

Areas, regions, places in general

4758   Fernea, Elizabeth Warnock, and Robert A. Fernea. *Arab World: Personal Encounters.* 1987, Doubleday paper $11.95 (0-385-23973-4). Two documentary filmmakers discuss the people they have met in the Arab world where they have worked for over four decades. (Rᴇᴠ: BL 5/1/85; LJ 5/15/85; PW 3/29/85)   **[909.09]**

4759   Hourani, Albert. *A History of the Arab Peoples.* 1991, Harvard Univ. Pr. $24.95 (0-674-39565-4). A history of the Arab world from pre-Islamic times to the present. (Rᴇᴠ: BL 3/1/91; LJ 1/91; Newsweek 2/18/91)   **[909.09]**

4760   Morris, James. *Farewell the Trumpets: The Decline of an Empire.* 1980, Harcourt paper $9.95 (0-15-630286-1). The third volume of Morris's trilogy about the rise and fall of the British Empire, covering the years 1897–1965. (Rᴇᴠ: BL 10/15/78; New Yorker 10/2/78; TLS 7/7/78)   **[909.09]**

18th century, 1700–1799

4761   Durant, Will, and Ariel Durant. *Rousseau and Revolution.* 1967, Simon & Schuster $32.95 (0-671-63058-X). The tenth and concluding volume of the Durants's epic, *Story of Civilization*, which covers from the beginning of written history to the French Revolution. (Rᴇᴠ: LJ 7/67; Sat Rev 9/23/67; Time 10/6/67. Awards: PP:NF, 1968)   **[909.7]**

1900–1999

4762   Beschloss, Michael R. *Crisis Years: Kennedy and Khrushchev, 1960–1963.* 1991, HarperCollins

$29.95 (0-06-016454-9). A study of Soviet-American relations during the Kennedy years. "An exciting and informative narrative that will appeal to a wide readership."—PW (Rᴇᴠ: BL 4/15/91; PW 4/19/91; Time 6/17/91)   **[909.82]**

4763   Caute, David. *Year of the Barricades: A Journey Through 1968.* 1988, Harper & Row paper $10.95 (0-06-091524-2). Social history of the New Left and its counterculture activities in Europe, the United States, and Latin America during the year 1968. (Rᴇᴠ: LJ 4/15/88; NYTBR 4/3/88; PW 12/18/87)   **[909.82]**

4764   Drucker, Peter F. *New Realities.* 1989, Harper & Row $19.95 (0-06-016129-9); paper $12.00 (0-06-091699-0). An overview of current and projected societal problems by a management expert. (Rᴇᴠ: CSM 6/29/89; LJ 6/1/89; NYTBR 6/18/89. Awards: BL, 1989)   **[909.82]**

4765   Eksteins, Modris. *Rites of Spring: The Great War and the Birth of the Modern Age.* 1990, Doubleday paper $12.95 (0-385-41202-9). An analysis of the ties between the rise of modernist culture and the cataclysmic events of the First World War. (Rᴇᴠ: Atl 3/89; LJ 2/15/89; Natl Rev 6/2/89)   **[909.82]**

4766   Green, Martin. *Von Rictofen Sisters: The Triumphant and Tragic Modes of Love.* 1988, Univ. of New Mexico Pr. paper $14.95 (0-8263-1038-9). The story of two sisters and their social circles—Else, who was Max Weber's mistress, and Frieda, who married D. H. Lawrence. (Rᴇᴠ: Choice 7–8/74; LJ 5/1/74; New Yorker 5/25/74)   **[909.82]**

4767   Hersh, Seymour. *Target Is Destroyed: What Really Happened to Flight 007 and What America Knew about It.* 1987, Random paper $4.95 (0-394-75527-8). An account of the destruction of a Korean Air Lines passenger jet by the Soviets in September 1983. "Dramatically broadens our knowledge of what did take place . . . Hersh's best book."—NYTBR (Rᴇᴠ: CSM 10/3/86; LJ 12/86; NYTBR 9/21/86. Awards: ALA, 1986; LJ, 1986)   **[909.82]**

4768   Hobsbawn, E. J. *Age of Empire, 1875–1914.* 1987, Pantheon $22.95 (0-394-56319-0). The concluding volume of the British historian's trilogy analyzing the nineteenth century. "Few, if any, present practitioners of the historian's craft can equal the astounding range and dazzling erudition of Mr. Hobsbawn's scholarship."—NYTBR (Rᴇᴠ: BL 2/15/88; LJ 2/15/88; TLS 2/12/88)   **[909.82]**

4769   Johnson, Paul. *Modern Times: The World from the Twenties to the Eighties.* 1985, Harper & Row paper $12.95 (0-06-091210-3). "There is a great deal of intellectual pleasure to be had from this distinguished and provocative work of history."—NYTBR (Rᴇᴠ: LJ 5/1/83; NYTBR 6/26/83; Time 6/6/83. Awards: BL, the 1980s; NYTBR, 1983; Time, 1983; Time, the 1980s)   **[909.82]**

4770   Kapuscinski, Ryszard. *Soccer War.* 1991, Knopf $20.00 (0-394-58413-9). Accounts of the Polish journalist's experiences reporting on 27 post-World War II wars and insurrections. "Journalism at its most incisive."—PW (Rev: BL 4/1/91; Newsweek 4/15/91; PW 3/1/91)   **[909.82]**

4771 Klingaman, William. *1919: The Year Our World Began.* 1987, St. Martin's $27.95 (0-317-59967-4); Harper & Row paper $12.95 (0-06-097251-3). A study of the social and political history of the year 1919. "A wonderful and exciting chronicle."—BL (Rev: BL 8/87; LJ 8/87; NYTBR 2/7/88)   **[909.82]**

4772 Kolakowski, Leszek. *Modernity on Endless Trial.* 1990, Univ. of Chicago Pr. $24.95 (0-226-45045-7). A collection of 24 essays written during the 1970s and 1980s on history and philosophy. (Rev: LJ 11/15/90; NYTBR 12/23/90; PW 10/26/90)   **[909.82]**

4773 Lifton, Robert Jay. *Future of Immortality: And Other Essays for a Nuclear Age.* 1987, Basic Books $21.95 (0-465-02597-8). Essays regarding the threat of nuclear destruction of the human race and its ramifications on the collective psyche. (Rev: BL 2/15/87; LJ 3/15/87; NYTBR 4/5/87)   **[909.82]**

4774 Mortimer, Edward. *World that FDR Built: Vision and Reality.* 1989, Macmillan $24.95 (0-684-18687-X). A study of FDR's policies during the meetings with Allied leaders at Yalta, Bretton Woods, and Dumbarton Oaks to plan for the future of the world at the end of World War II. (Rev: BL 2/1/89; LJ 2/15/89)   **[909.82]**

4775 O'Brien, Conor Cruise. *Passion and Cunning: Essays on Nationalism, Terrorism and Revolution.* 1989, Simon & Schuster paper $9.95 (0-671-68746-8). Essays by the Irish diplomat and writer concerning people and politics. (Rev: LJ 10/15/88; New Rep 9/12/88; NYTBR 11/6/88)   **[909.82]**

4776 Seldes, George. *Witness to a Century: Encounters with the Noted, the Notorious, and the Three SOB's.* 1988, Ballantine paper $12.95 (0-345-35329-3). Memoirs of the American newspaper reporter and writer regarding his experiences and acquaintances. (Rev: CSM 8/14/87; LJ 6/1/87; NYTBR 8/16/87)   **[909.82]**

4777 Szulc, Tad. *Then and Now: How the World Has Changed Since World War II.* 1990, Morrow $22.95 (0-688-07558-4). A survey of world political history since the Second World War. (Rev: BL 5/15/90; NYTBR 7/8/90; PW 5/25/90. Awards: PW, 1990)   **[909.82]**

4778 Wasserstein, Bernard. *Secret Lives of Trebitsch Lincoln.* 1988, Yale Univ. Pr. $30.00 (0-300-04076-8); paper $8.95 (0-14-011946-9). A biography of a Hungarian Jew who became a member of the British Parliament and performed Christian missionary work before becoming a Buddhist monk. "Surely the final word on a truly extraordinary career."—NYRB (Rev: LJ 9/15/88; NYRB 6/2/88; NYTBR 6/26/88)   **[909.82]**

910   GEOGRAPHY AND TRAVEL

4779 Berton, Pierre. *Arctic Grail: The Quest for the North West Passage and the North Pole, 1818–*

1909. 1988, Viking $24.95 (0-670-82491-7); Penguin paper $12.95 (0-14-011680-X). A Canadian scholar's review of nineteenth-century Arctic exploration. "By far the most lively and comprehensive history of 19th century polar exploration."—Choice (Rev: Atl 11/88; Choice 3/89; NYTBR 11/20/88. Awards: ALA, 1988)   **[910]**

4780 Hale, John R. *Renaissance Exploration.* 1972, Norton paper $6.95 (0-393-00635-2). The explorations and discoveries made during the era of the Renaissance. "A gem among many long and short books on the subject . . . a good buy and good reading for all."—LJ (Rev: LJ 7/72; New Yorker 7/15/72)   **[910]**

4781 Morris, Jan. *Destinations: Essays from Rolling Stone.* 1980, Oxford Univ. Pr. $21.95 (0-19-502708-6). A collection of ten travel essays originally appearing in *Rolling Stone* surveying such destinations as Panama, Cairo, and New York City. (Rev: CSM 6/9/80; LJ 5/15/80; NYTBR 4/27/80)   **[910]**

The earth (Physical geography)

4782 Bangs, Richard, and Christian Kallen. *Rivergods: Exploring the World's Great Wild Rivers.* 1985, Sierra Club paper $18.95 (0-87156-773-3). The authors recount their experiences rafting the wild rivers of the world. (Rev: BL 9/20/85; LJ 12/85; PW 9/20/85)   **[910.02]**

Miscellany

4783 Fussell, Paul. *Abroad: British Literary Traveling Between the Wars.* 1980, Oxford Univ. Pr. $22.95 (0-19-502767-1). A study of English writers and their travels between the First and Second World Wars, including Bertrand Russell, Lawrence Durrell, and Robert Graves. (Rev: LJ 8/80; NYTBR 8/31/80; Newsweek 9/22/80)   **[910.2]**

World travel guides

4784 Harris, Dale. *Help Yourself to Travel: A Consumer's Guide to Travel Planning.* 1989, World View CA paper $12.95 (0-929673-00-X). Advice for first-time foreign travelers regarding visa/passport regulations, customs tips, and frequently encountered situations. (Rev: BL 2/15/89; LJ 3/15/89)   **[910.202]**

4785 Malott, Gene, and Adele Malott. *Get Up and Go: A Guide for the Mature Traveler.* 1989, Gateway paper $10.95 (0-933469-06-3). A guide to planning, organizing, and enjoying travel, directed toward senior citizens. (Rev: BL 6/15/89; LJ 7/89)   **[910.202]**

Accounts of travel

4786 Barich, Bill. *Traveling Light.* 1985, Penguin paper $8.95 (0-14-007418-X). The author of *Laughing in the Hills* recounts his travels through Europe and the United States in a series of ten essays. (Rev: LJ 12/1/83; NYTBR 2/5/84; Time 2/6/84)   **[910.4]**

4787 Cahill, Tim. *A Wolverine Is Eating My Leg.* **1989, Random paper $8.95 (0-679-72026-X).** Collected travel writings by the author of *Jaguars Ripped My Flesh.* (REV: BL 2/15/89; LJ 2/15/89; NYTBR 5/14/89) **[910.4]**

4788 Fraser, Keith, ed. *Bad Trips.* **1991, Random paper $12.00 (0-679-72908-9).** A collection of essays by writers including Umberto Eco, Anita Desai, and Jonathan Raban describing the worst trips of their lives. (REV: LJ 6/15/91; NYTBR 6/9/91) **[910.4]**

4789 Joppien, Rudiger, and Bernard Smith. *Art of Captain Cook's Voyages.* **1988, Yale Univ. Pr. $140.00 (0-300-03450-4).** A two-volume illustrated documentation of the voyages of Captain Cook as recorded by the artists who accompanied him. (REV: Choice 12/85; LJ 10/15/85; NYTBR 8/11/85) **[910.4]**

4790 Morris, Jan. *Journeys.* **1985, Oxford Univ. Pr. $18.95 (0-19-503452-X); paper $8.95 (0-19-503606-9).** A collection of 14 travel essays. *Booklist* said, "After reading these descriptions, there is the feeling one has been to each locale—and what more could be asked of a travel writer?" (REV: BL 4/15/84; NYTBR 6/3/84; PW 4/13/84. AWARDS: BL, the 1980s) **[910.4]**

4791 Morrisby, Edwin. *Unpackaged Tours: World Travels off the Beaten Tracks.* **1988, Taplinger $17.95 (0-8008-7939-2).** The author combines his personal travel experiences with advice for others planning journeys to offbeat destinations. (REV: LJ 11/1/87; PW 2/19/88) **[910.4]**

4792 Newman, Steven M. *Worldwalk.* **1989, Morrow $19.95 (0-688-07762-5); Avon paper $5.95 (0-380-71150-8).** An account of an Ohio journalist's four-year walk around the world. (REV: NYTBR 6/11/89; PW 4/14/89) **[910.4]**

4793 Newsham, Brad. *All the Right Places: Traveling Light Through China, Japan and Russia.* **1989, Random $16.95 (0-394-57410-9); paper $9.95 (0-679-72713-2).** An account of a California backpacker's trip through China, Japan, and the Soviet Union. "A delight, not to be missed by libraries that collect travel literature."—BL (REV: BL 2/15/89; NYTBR 6/11/89; PW 2/3/89) **[910.4]**

4794 Palin, Michael. *Around the World in Eighty Days.* **1990, Parkwest $24.95 (0-563-20826-0).** An account of the English comedian's journey around the world using the transportation systems available in the nineteenth century. (REV: BL 8/90; LJ 9/15/90) **[910.4]**

4795 Pritchett, V. S. *At Home and Abroad: Travel Essays.* **1989, North Point $19.95 (0-86547-385-4).** Fourteen travel essays by the British novelist and literary critic regarding his experiences in Europe and the Americas. (REV: BL 3/1/89; CSM 7/10/89; NYTBR 6/11/89) **[910.4]**

4796 Roueche, Berton. *Sea to Shining Sea: People, Travel, Places.* **1987, Avon paper $4.50 (0-380-70265-7).** Selected travel essays by the French writer regarding his experiences in Europe and the United States. (REV: BL 1/15/86; LJ 1/86; NYTBR 1/26/86) **[910.4]**

4797 Schwartz, Brian M. *A World of Villages.* **1986, Crown $19.95 (0-517-55815-7).** An account of the author's six-year trek through the small settlements of Asia and Africa. (REV: LJ 5/15/86; NYTBR 9/21/86; PW 4/11/86) **[910.4]**

Ocean travel and seafaring adventures

4798 Buckley, Christopher. *Steaming to Bamboola: The World of a Tramp Freighter.* **1987, Penguin paper $6.95 (0-14-009922-0).** A recounting of the author's experiences on a tramp steamer crossing the Atlantic Ocean. (REV: Atl 5/82; CSM 7/7/82; Natl Rev 5/14/82) **[910.45]**

4799 Buckley, William F., Jr. *Airborne: A Sentimental Journey.* **1984, Little, Brown $19.95 (0-316-11438-3); paper $11.95 (0-316-11439-1).** The columnist's account of a sailing trip from Florida to Spain with his son. (REV: BL 9/20/76; CSM 12/17/76; Time 12/6/76) **[910.45]**

4800 Buckley, William F., Jr. *Atlantic High: A Celebration.* **1983, Little, Brown paper $10.95 (0-316-11440-5).** A chronicle of Buckley's sailing voyage across the Atlantic from the Virgin Islands to Spain. "Will delight anyone with a taste for sophisticated travel literature."—BL (REV: BL 8/82; NYTBR 9/5/82; Time 10/25/82) **[910.45]**

4801 Cogill, Burgess. *When God Was an Atheist Sailor: Memories of Childhood at Sea, 1902–1910.* **1990, Norton $17.95 (0-393-02716-3).** Memoirs of the author's first eight years of life aboard her father's ship. (REV: BL 12/1/89; PW 11/17/89. AWARDS: BL, 1990) **[910.45]**

4802 McPhee, John. *Looking for a Ship.* **1990, Farrar $18.95 (0-374-19077-1).** An account of the author's journey aboard a United States Merchant Marine ship from South Carolina through the Panama Canal and down the Pacific coast of South America. (REV: BL 7/90; LJ 8/90; PW 7/20/90) **[910.45]**

4803 Newby, Eric, ed. *A Book of Travelers' Tales.* **1987, Penguin paper $10.95 (0-14-009567-5).** Collected travel essays from early times to the present including pieces by Marco Polo, Samuel Johnson, Henry James, and Paul Theroux. (REV: BL 11/1/86; CSM 9/11/86; Time 7/28/86) **[910.45]**

4804 Robertson, Dougal. *Survive the Savage Sea.* **1984, Sheridan paper $13.95 (0-246-12509-8).** An account of the survival of Robertson and his family during 38 days stranded in the Pacific Ocean after their boat was sunk by killer whales. "A most compelling adventure story."—TLS (REV: BL 9/1/73; LJ 5/1/73; TLS 8/3/73) **[910.45]**

4805 Tomalin, Nicolas, and Ron Hall. *Strange Last Voyage of Donal Crowhurst.* **1979, Scarborough paper $7.95 (0-8128-6042-X).** The story of Crowhurst's fatal failed solo attempt to circumnavigate the globe in his trimaran based on his log entries and recorded tapes of the voyage. (REV: NYTBR 9/27/70; PW 7/6/70; TLS 8/21/70) **[910.45]**

4806 Whipple, A. B. C. *Challenge.* **1987, Morrow $19.95 (0-688-07112-0); paper $12.95 (0-688-08908-9).**

An account of a nineteenth-century American clipper ship's participation in a race around Cape Horn to California. (Rev: LJ 6/1/87; NYTBR 7/26/87)
[910.45]

Geography of and travel in areas, regions, places in general

4807   Buckley, William F., Jr. *Racing Through Paradise: A Pacific Passage.* **1988, Little, Brown paper $10.95 (0-316-11448-0).** An account of the author's 4,500-mile sailing voyage from Hawaii to New Guinea in 1985. (Rev: LJ 6/1/87; Natl Rev 7/31/87; NYTBR 5/31/87)
[910.91]

4808   Callahan, Steven. *Adrift: 76 Days Lost at Sea.* **1986, Houghton $15.95 (0-395-38206-8); Ballantine paper $4.95 (0-345-34083-3).** An account of the author's month-and-a-half of drifting on a rubber raft in the mid-Atlantic following the sinking of his boat off the Canary Islands. "Utterly captivating—a real page-turner."—BL (Rev: BL 1/1/86; LJ 12/85; NYTBR 1/12/86)
[910.91]

4809   Clarke, Thurston. *Equator: A Journey.* **1990, Avon paper $9.95 (0-380-70855-8).** The author recounts his experiences traveling around the earth along the equator over a three-year period. (Rev: BL 10/1/88; LJ 12/88; NYTBR 11/20/88)
[910.91]

4810   Millman, Lawrence. *Last Places: A Journey in the North.* **1990, Houghton $18.95 (0-395-43615-X).** An account of the author's journey from Scandinavia to Canada following a Viking trade route. (Rev: BL 1/1/90; LJ 1/90; NYTBR 6/10/90)
[910.91]

4811   Winchester, Simon. *Sun Never Sets: Travels to the Remaining Outposts of the British Empire.* **1988, Prentice Hall paper $8.95 (0-13-875881-6).** Accounts of the author's travels to remote islands of the world still held by Great Britain. "Warm, superbly written."—NYTBR (Rev: LJ 5/1/86; NYTBR 6/1/86; PW 3/14/86)
[910.91]

Geographers, travelers, explorers

4812   Heyerdahl, Thor, and Christopher Ralling. *Kon-Tiki Man: An Illustrated Biography of Thor Heyerdahl.* **1991, Chronicle $35.00 (0-8118-0026-1); paper $19.95 (0-8118-0069-5).** A biography of the anthropologist known for his explorations and theories regarding the travels of ancient man. "A stimulating chronicle of curiosity and wanderlust."—PW (Rev: BL 10/15/91; PW 9/6/91)
[910.92]

4813   Olds, Elizabeth Fagg. *Women of the Four Winds.* **1985, Houghton paper $9.95 (0-395-39584-4).** A collective biography of four members of the Society of Women Geographers who were pioneers in the fields of exploration and anthropology in the first decades of the twentieth century. (Rev: BL 10/1/85; LJ 9/1/85; PW 7/26/85)
[910.92]

4814   Rice, Edward. *Captain Sir Richard Francis Burton.* **1990, Macmillan $35.00 (0-684-19137-7); HarperCollins paper $15.00 (0-06-097394-3).** A biography of the legendary nineteenth-century British explorer of India, Africa, and the Arab world. (Rev: Atl 7/90; LJ 4/15/90; NYTBR 5/20/90)
[910.92]

912   Graphic representations of earth

4815   Wilford, John Noble. *Mapmakers.* **1981, Knopf $20.00 (0-394-46194-0); Random paper $13.95 (0-394-75303-8).** The history of cartography and its methods from earliest records to present-day mapping of other planets. "A thoroughly absorbing science and history, the work of an author who not only knows his subject but enjoys sharing it."—David McCullough, NYTBR (Rev: CSM 6/3/81; NYTBR 5/3/81; Newsweek 6/15/81. Awards: ALA, 1981)
[912]

914   Europe

4816   Enzensberger, Hans Magnus. *Europe, Europe: Forays into a Continent.* **1989, Pantheon $18.95 (0-394-55819-7).** The West German writer recounts his travels throughout Europe and discusses the future of the continent. (Rev: BL 4/15/89; NYRB 9/28/89; NYTBR 6/4/89)
[914]

Europe

4817   Brunhouse, Jay. *Adventuring on the Eurail Express.* **1989, Pelican paper $11.95 (0-88289-703-9).** A guide for Americans to train travel in Europe and Great Britain. "The next best thing to an actual trip."—BL (Rev: BL 3/15/89; LJ 4/15/89)
[914.04]

4818   Deutsch, Valerie, and Laura Sutherland. *Innocents Abroad: Traveling with Kids in Europe.* **1991, NAL paper $15.95 (0-452-26585-1).** A guide to European travel with children based on the authors' own experiences. (Rev: BL 2/1/91; LJ 1/91)
[914.04]

4819   Van Gelder, Lindsey, and Pamela Robin Brandt. *Are You Two . . . Together?* **1991, Random $18.00 (0-679-73599-2).** A guide to international travel for gay and lesbian couples. (Rev: BL 4/1/91; LJ 5/1/91)
[914.04]

British Isles

4820   Raban, Jonathan. *Coasting: A Private Journey.* **1988, Penguin paper $7.95 (0-14-010657-X).** An account of the author's solo voyage in a 30-foot ketch around the British Isles over a period of four years. (Rev: BL 2/15/87; LJ 3/1/87; NYTBR 2/1/87)
[914.1]

4821   Wright, Esmond. *American Guide to Britain.* **1987, Salem $24.95 (0-88162-268-0).** An illustrated travel guide and gazetteer for Americans touring Great Britain. (Rev: BL 4/1/87; LJ 5/1/87)
[914.1]

Scotland

4822   Crowl, Philip A. *Intelligent Traveler's Guide to Historic Scotland.* **1986, Congdon & Weed $35.00 (0-86553-158-7).** A travel guide to the historic sites of Scotland. (Rev: BL 7/86; LJ 7/86; NYTBR 6/1/86)
[914.11]

4823 Shenker, Israel. *In the Footsteps of Johnson and Boswell: A Modern Day Journey Through Scotland.* **1984, Oxford Univ. Pr. paper $7.95 (0-19-503470-8).** A retracing of the 1773 journey of Johnson and Boswell through Scotland discussing the changes of the past two centuries. (REV: CSM 6/11/82; LJ 4/15/82; NYTBR 3/21/82)　　**[914.11]**

England

4824 Blythe, Ronald. *Akenfield: Portrait of an English Village.* **1980, Pantheon paper $9.95 (0-394-73847-0).** A look at the changes taking place in the lives of the residents of a small village in East Anglia. "Amazingly successful in recording the life stories of villagers in their own words . . . fascinating in human interest and absorbing detail."—LJ (REV: Atl 9/69; LJ 9/1/69; NYTBR 9/21/69. AWARDS: ALA, 1969; NYTBR, 1969)　　**[914.2]**

4825 Jones, Christopher. *Great Palace: The Story of Parliament.* **1985, Parkwest $29.95 (0-88186-150-2).** An illustrated survey of the architectural development and legislative history of Britain's Parliament. (REV: BL 8/85; LJ 8/85)　　**[914.2]**

Central Europe

4826 Jones, Tristan. *Improbable Voyage: The Yacht Outward Leg into, Through and out of the Heart of Europe.* **1987, Morrow $18.95 (0-688-07243-7).** An account of the author's 2,300-mile sailing voyage from England to Turkey via the Rhine and Danube rivers. (REV: BL 5/1/87; LJ 5/1/87; NYTBR 5/31/87)　　**[914.3]**

France

4827 Ardagh, John. *Writer's France: A Regional Panorama.* **1990, Viking $29.95 (0-241-12351-8).** An overview of French literature examining the influence of the country's landscape on its writers. (REV: BL 4/15/90; LJ 4/15/90)　　**[914.4]**

4828 Brown, Michael. *South to Gascony.* **1990, Viking $24.95 (0-241-12694-0).** An introduction to the history, culture, and sights of the region of Southern France where the author makes his home. (REV: LJ 12/89; TLS 8/18/89)　　**[914.4]**

4829 Conran, Terence, Pierette Pompon Bailhache, and Maurice Croizard. *Terence Conran's France.* **1987, Little, Brown $34.95 (0-316-15327-3).** An illustrated tour of France and introduction to its culture by the British designer. (REV: BL 11/1/87; LJ 1/88)　　**[914.4]**

4830 Delbanco, Nicholas. *Running in Place: Scenes from the South of France.* **1990, Atlantic Monthly paper $9.95 (0-87113-362-8).** Memoirs of a series of visits over the course of 30 years to the South of France by the author and his family. (REV: BL 6/15/89; LJ 6/15/89; NYTBR 7/23/89)　　**[914.4]**

Italy

4831 Harrison, Barbara Grizzuti. *Italian Days.* **1989, Grove-Weidenfeld $21.95 (1-55584-311-5); Houghton paper $12.95 (0-395-55131-5).** The au-

thor's travels around Italy are intertwined with her search for her family's roots. "Such introspective ripeness is unusual in a travel book."—Newsweek (REV: Atl 8/89; NYTBR 9/10/89; Newsweek 8/14/89)　　**[914.5]**

Spain

4832 Michener, James A. *Iberia: Spanish Travels and Reflections.* **1968, Random $29.95 (0-394-42982-6); Fawcett paper $5.95 (0-317-69910-5).** Personal impressions of Spain and ten of its cities drawn from extensive travels. "Unfailingly interesting . . . he introduces us to civilization which is not quite identical with his own."—Atl (REV: Atl 5/68; BL 7/15/68; NYRB 12/19/68. AWARDS: ALA, 1968)　　**[914.6]**

Soviet Union

4833 Billington, James H. *Icon and the Axe: An Interpretive History of Russian Culture.* **1970, Random paper $16.95 (0-394-70846-6).** An introduction to Russian intellectual and cultural history. "The finest study of Russian culture produced by an American . . . an absolute must for all libraries."—Choice (REV: BL 9/1/66; Choice 11/66; LJ 5/1/66. AWARDS: ALA, 1966)　　**[914.7]**

4834 De Villiers, Mary. *Down the Volga: A Journey Through Mother Russia in a Time of Troubles.* **1992, Viking $22.00 (0-670-84353-9).** An account of the author's 1990 journey down the Volga River. (REV: BL 12/15/91; PW 11/8/91)　　**[914.7]**

4835 Grossfeld, Stan. *Whisper of Stars: A Siberian Journey.* **1988, Globe Pequot $24.95 (0-87106-679-3).** An illustrated account of the author's five-week visit to Siberia. (REV: BL 12/15/88; LJ 5/1/88; NYTBR 12/4/88)　　**[914.7]**

4836 Moorhouse, Geoffrey. *On the Other Side: A Journey Through Central Asia.* **1991, Henry Holt $21.95 (0-8050-1229-X).** An account of the author's seven-week trip through Soviet Central Asia sponsored by the National Geographic Society. (REV: BL 3/1/91; NYTBR 6/9/91; PW 2/22/91)　　**[914.7]**

4837 Thubron, Colin. *Where Nights Are Longest: Travels by Car Through Western Russia.* **1987, Atlantic Monthly paper $7.95 (0-87113-167-6).** The British writer recounts his experiences driving across European Russia, Georgia, and Armenia. (REV: LJ 5/1/84; NYRB 6/13/85; NYTBR 7/15/84)　　**[914.7]**

915 Asia

Asia

4838 Theroux, Paul. *Great Railway Bazaar: By Train Through Asia.* **1981, Ballantine paper $2.95 (0-345-30110-2).** Descriptions and tales from four months of traveling by train through Asia. "A voyage related with clarity, sensitivity and imagination."—BL (REV: BL 9/1/75; NYTBR 8/24/75; Newsweek 9/8/75. AWARDS: ALA, 1975; NYTBR, 1975)　　**[915.04]**

4839 Winchester, Simon. *Pacific Rising: The Emergence of a New World Culture.* **1991, Prentice Hall**

$22.95 (0-13-807793-2). An overview of the histories and cultures of the Pacific Rim nations by a *London Times* correspondent. "Delightful and informative."—PW (REV: BL 4/15/91; LJ 4/15/91; PW 2/22/91)   **[915.04]**

China

4840 Bangs, Richard, and Christian Kalley. *Riding the Dragon's Back: A River Journey on China's Yangtze.* 1989, Macmillan $29.95 (0-689-11932-1). An account of a 1987 American rafting expedition to explore China's Yangtze River. (REV: BL 9/15/89; LJ 8/89; PW 8/25/89)   **[915.1]**

4841 Bloodworth, Dennis. *Chinese Looking Glass.* 1980, Farrar $15.00 (0-374-12241-5); paper $8.95 (0-374-51493-3). A layman's introduction to the people, history, and culture of China. "An extremely readable, sophisticated, and, at times, quite amusing series of insights into the many facets of China."—Choice (REV: Choice 11/67; NYTBR 8/27/67; Newsweek 7/24/67. AWARDS: NYTBR, 1967)   **[915.1]**

4842 Bordewich, Fergus. *Cathay: A Journey in Search of Old China.* 1991, Prentice Hall $19.95 (0-13-202136-6). An account of the author's travels in search of remains of prerevolutionary culture in contemporary China. (REV: BL 1/15/91; PW 12/21/90)   **[915.1]**

4843 Kubota, Hiroji. *China.* 1985, Norton $75.00 (0-393-02243-9). A photographic essay of the People's Republic of China. (REV: BL 1/15/86; LJ 12/85; NYTBR 12/8/85)   **[915.1]**

4844 Power, Brian. *Ford of Heaven.* 1984, Kesend Pub. Ltd. $16.95 (0-935576-10-X). Memoirs by a writer of British-Irish ancestry of his childhood years in China. "A skillfully blended, true-life tale of personal and cultural awakening."—BL (REV: BL 12/15/84; LJ 1/85; NYTBR 1/27/85)   **[915.1]**

4845 Theroux, Paul. *Riding the Iron Rooster: By Train Through China.* 1988, Putnam $21.95 (0-399-13309-7); paper $4.95 (0-8041-0454-9). Theroux recounts his experiences during the year he spent traveling by train through China. "As in his previous works, he gives the reader much to relish and think about."—PW (REV: LJ 6/15/89; PW 4/8/88; Time 5/16/88)   **[915.1]**

4846 Thubron, Colin. *Behind the Wall: A Journey Through China.* 1988, Atlantic Monthly $18.95 (0-87113-242-7); Harper & Row paper $9.95 (0-06-097256-4). The author, who became fluent in Mandarin Chinese before his trip, recounts his experiences traveling in untouristed regions of China. (REV: LJ 10/15/88; NYTBR 11/27/88; TLS 9/11/87) **[915.1]**

4847 Wood, Frances. *A Companion to China.* 1990, St. Martin's $22.95 (0-312-04283-3). A travel guide to the People's Republic of China including surveys of its history and culture. (REV: LJ 4/1/90; NYTBR 6/10/90; TLS 4/26/89)   **[915.1]**

Japan

4848 Mura, David. *Turning Japanese: Memoirs of a Sansei.* 1991, Atlantic Monthly $19.95 (0-87113-431-4). Memoirs of a Japanese-American's experiences living in his ancestral homeland. "An eloquent account of a catharsis that illuminates both personal and societal aspects."—BL (REV: BL 2/1/91; LJ 2/1/91; NYTBR 3/31/91)   **[915.2]**

India

4849 Frater, Alexander. *Chasing the Monsoon.* 1991, Knopf $21.00 (0-394-58310-8). Accounts of the author's travels in India. "A brilliantly amusing book."—NYTBR (REV: LJ 4/1/91; NYTBR 4/21/91; Newsweek 6/3/91)   **[915.4]**

4850 Harvey, Andrew. *A Journey in Ladakh.* 1984, Houghton paper $8.95 (0-395-36670-4). A spiritual quest by the author to study Buddhist thought and philosophy in Kashmir. (REV: LJ 6/15/83; NYTBR 8/7/83; PW 5/20/83)   **[915.4]**

4851 Matthiessen, Peter. *Snow Leopard.* 1987, Penguin paper $8.95 (0-14-010266-3). Matthiessen's diary of an expedition to Nepal to observe the Himalayan blue sheep and search for the snow leopard. (REV: LJ 7/78; New Rep 9/23/78; NYTBR 8/3/78. AWARDS: ALA, 1978; NBA, 1979)   **[915.4]**

4852 Naipaul, V. S. *India: A Million Mutinies Now.* 1991, Viking $22.95 (0-670-83702-4). Reflections on the current state of his ancestral homeland by the Trinidad-born author of *Guerrillas* and *Among the Believers*. (REV: BL 12/1/90; NYTBR 12/30/90; Time 1/14/91. AWARDS: BL, 1991)   **[915.4]**

Pakistan

4853 Moorhouse, Geoffrey. *To the Frontier.* 1986, Harcourt paper $5.95 (0-15-690697-X). An account of the author's travels and experiences in Pakistan. (REV: LJ 2/15/85; NYTBR 6/16/85; Newsweek 6/3/85)   **[915.49]**

Middle East

4854 Glass, Charles. *Tribes with Flags: A Dangerous Passage Through the Chaos of the Middle East.* 1990, Atlantic Monthly $18.95 (0-87113-267-2). Memoirs of the former "ABC News" correspondent's travels in the Middle East, including the two months he spent as a hostage in Beirut. (REV: LJ 4/1/90; NYRB 7/19/90; PW 2/16/90)   **[915.6]**

4855 Hansen, Eric. *Motoring with Mohammed: Journeys to Yemen and the Red Sea.* 1991, Houghton $19.95 (0-395-48347-6). Memoirs of the author's experiences in Yemen following his rescue from a shipwreck off its coast. (REV: BL 2/1/91; LJ 2/1/91; NYTBR 2/24/91)   **[915.6]**

4856 Horwitz, Tony. *Baghdad Without a Map: And Other Misadventures in Arabia.* 1991, Dutton $18.95 (0-525-24960-5). The journalist recounts his travels and experiences reporting in the Middle East in the 1980s and early 1990s. (REV: BL 2/1/91; LJ 1/91; NYTBR 2/17/91)   **[915.6]**

Turkey

4857 Dodwell, Christina. *A Traveller on Horseback: In Eastern Turkey and Iran.* 1989, Walker $18.95 (0-8027-1078-6). An account of an Englishwoman's travels by horseback in Turkey, Iran, and Pakistan. "Armchair travel at its best."—BL (REV: BL 6/1/89; NYTBR 6/11/89; PW 2/17/89) **[915.61]**

4858 Settle, Mary Lee. *Turkish Reflections: A Biography of a Place.* 1991, Prentice Hall $19.95 (0-13-917675-6). Recollections of the author's travels in Turkey and her experiences among the Turkish people. (REV: BL 5/1/91; NYTBR 7/14/91; PW 4/19/91) **[915.61]**

Israel

4859 Bellow, Saul. *To Jerusalem and Back: A Personal Account.* 1985, Penguin paper $6.95 (0-14-0072373-X). Bellow's first work of nonfiction recounts an extended visit to Israel. "Few other writers have brought to the subject the exacting intelligence, the sense of style, and the presence that are Bellow's."—Atl (REV: Atl 12/76; New Rep 11/20/76; NYTBR 10/17/76. AWARDS: NYTBR, 1976) **[915.69]**

4860 Elon, Amos. *Israelis: Founders and Sons.* 1983, Penguin paper $8.95 (0-14-022476-9). The history of Zionism and the state of Israel by a second-generation Israeli. "Objective, well-balanced, sensitive, insightful . . . a substantial contribution to our understanding of Israel both past and present."—LJ (REV: BL 10/1/71; Choice 9/71; LJ 5/1/71. AWARDS: ALA, 1971) **[915.69]**

4861 Hasan, Sana. *Enemy in the Promised Land: An Egyptian Woman's Journey into Israel.* 1987, Pantheon $18.95 (0-394-52765-8); paper (0-8052-0853-4). An account of the three years the author, an Egyptian woman, spent living in Israel in the mid-1970s. (REV: BL 1/1/87; NYTBR 3/1/87) **[915.69]**

Indonesia

4862 Hansen, Eric. *Stranger in the Forest: On Foot Across Borneo.* 1989, Penguin paper $8.95 (0-14-011726-1). Hansen's 1,500-mile journey by foot across the interior of Borneo. "A first-rate adventure."—PW (REV: CSM 5/4/88; NYTBR 3/6/88; PW 12/25/87. AWARDS: ALA, 1988) **[915.98]**

4863 O'Hanlon, Redmond. *Into the Heart of Borneo.* 1985, Random $16.95 (0-394-54481-1); paper $7.95 (0-394-75540-5). An account of the British writer's two-month excursion into the interior of Borneo. (REV: NYRB 6/13/85; Time 4/8/85; TLS 11/30/84) **[915.98]**

916 Africa

4864 Bass, Thomas A. *Camping with the Prince: And Other Tales of Science in Africa.* 1990, Houghton $20.95 (0-395-41502-0); Penguin paper $9.95 (0-14-014870-1). Essays examining the efforts of contemporary scientists and their research in Africa. (REV: CSM 3/23/90; LJ 2/1/90; NYTBR 7/29/90) **[916]**

4865 Matthiessen, Peter. *African Silences.* 1991, Random $20.00 (0-679-40021-4). The author's observations of wildlife on two trips to Central and West Africa. (REV: LJ 6/15/91; PW 5/17/91) **[916]**

Egypt

4866 Pye-Smith, Charlie. *Other Nile.* 1986, Viking $18.95 (0-670-80204-2). Reflections on the author's travels through Egypt and the Sudan. (REV: BL 9/15/86; CSM 9/5/86; LJ 9/1/86) **[916.2]**

The Sudan

4867 Hoagland, Edward. *African Calliope: A Journey to the Sudan.* 1987, Penguin paper $7.95 (0-14-009543-8). Hoagland describes his travels in the Sudan, Africa's largest country, whose ethnic diversity has historically been the root of internal conflicts. (REV: BL 9/1/79; NYTBR 9/16/79; Sat Rev 9/15/79. AWARDS: ALA, 1979) **[916.24]**

Africa

4868 Chatwin, Bruce. *Viceroy of Ouidah.* 1988, Penguin paper $6.95 (0-14-011290-1). The tale of a Brazilian who fled his country to establish an African trading post and carried on an illicit slave trade during the nineteenth century. (REV: BL 9/15/80; LJ 11/1/80; PW 10/31/80) **[916.6]**

4869 Dodwell, Christina. *Travels with Pegasus: A Microlight Journey Across West Africa.* 1990, Walker $19.95 (0-8027-1125-1). An account of the author's journey by light plane through Niger, Cameroon, Nigeria, Chad, Mauritania, Mali, and Senegal. "A well-researched, entertaining and exciting book."—LJ (REV: LJ 10/1/90; PW 10/12/90) **[916.6]**

4870 Frank, Katherine. *Voyager Out: The Life of Mary Kingsley.* 1986, Houghton $18.95 (0-317-53370-3). A biography of the nineteenth-century African explorer and writer. (REV: Choice 2/87; LJ 9/15/86; NYTBR 11/30/86) **[916.6]**

4871 Moorhouse, Geoffrey. *Fearful Void: Across the Implacable Sahara a Man Goes in Search of Himself.* 1989, Crown paper $11.95 (0-517-57114-5). The author's story of his attempt to cross the Sahara, going from the Atlantic to the Nile. "The product of a keen observer and skilled writer, this account illumines little-traveled regions of both mind and planet."—LJ (REV: LJ 3/15/74; NYTBR 3/31/74; Newsweek 3/25/74. AWARDS: ALA, 1974) **[916.6]**

4872 Stevens, Stuart. *Malaria Dreams: An African Adventure.* 1989, Atlantic Monthly $18.95 (0-87113-278-8); paper $9.95 (0-87113-361-X). A chronicle of the author's three-month journey in a land rover from Central Africa to Europe. "Mr. Stevens has a wonderful eye for the curiosities of human behavior."—New Yorker (REV: BL 8/89; NYTBR 7/1/90; New Yorker 10/23/89) **[916.6]**

Africa south of the Sahara

4873 Alexander, Caroline. *One Dry Season: In the Footsteps of Mary Kingsley.* 1990, Knopf $18.95 (0-

394-57455-9); **Random** paper $9.95 (0-679-73189-X). The author retraces the African travels of Mary Kingsley, comparing the present-day region with Kingsley's writings of a century ago. (Rev: CSM 3/23/90; LJ 11/15/89; TLS 1/26/90) **[916.7]**

4874 Beard, Peter Hill. *End of the Game: The Last Word from Paradise.* 1988, Chronicle $40.00 (0-87701-521-X); paper $22.95 (0-87701-516-3). A study of the wildlife of Kenya, notable for its photographs taken over a four-year period by the author. "A first-rate piece of work which all Africanists, animal lovers and photo buffs will want to own."— NYTBR (Rev: BL 7/15/65; LJ 7/65; NYTBR 5/30/65. Awards: NYTBR, 1965) **[916.7]**

4875 McLynn, Frank. *Stanley: The Making of an African Explorer.* 1990, Scarborough $23.95 (0-8128-4008-9). A biography of the nineteenth-century British-American explorer. (Rev: LJ 11/1/90; NYTBR 12/30/90; TLS 10/20/89) **[916.7]**

4876 Naipaul, Shiva. *North of South: An African Journey.* 1980, Penguin paper $8.95 (0-14-004894-4). An account of the author's travels in Kenya, Tanzania, and Zambia examining the effects of colonialism in the area. (Rev: BL 4/15/79; Newsweek 5/21/79; PW 2/17/79) **[916.7]**

Zaire

4877 Hyland, Paul. *Black Heart: A Voyage into Central Africa.* 1990, Paragon House paper $10.95 (1-55778-323-3). An English poet's account of his voyage with his wife up the Zaire River, laced with accounts from historical figures who made the same trip. (Rev: BL 2/1/89; LJ 3/1/89; NYTBR 3/5/89) **[916.75]**

4878 Shoumatoff, Alex. *In Southern Light: Trekking Through Zaire and the Amazon.* 1990, Random paper $9.95 (0-679-73077-X). Account of the author's travels through the jungles of Brazil and Zaire. (Rev: BL 3/1/86; LJ 3/15/86; NYTBR 3/16/86) **[916.75]**

Central Africa

4879 Boyles, Denis. *Maneater's Motel and Other Stops on the Railway to Nowhere: An East African Traveler's Notebook.* 1991, Houghton $19.95 (0-395-58082-X). A chronicle of the author's railway journey through Kenya, Zanzibar, and Uganda. (Rev: BL 6/1/91; LJ 6/15/91; NYTBR 6/9/91) **[916.76]**

4880 Murphy, Dervla. *Cameroon with Egbert.* 1991, Overlook $21.95 (0-87951-415-9). A chronicle of the author's 1987 travels in the African nation of Cameroon with her teenage daughter and their packhorse. (Rev: LJ 3/1/91; PW 2/15/91) **[916.76]**

4881 Smith, Anthony. *Great Rift: Africa's Changing Valley.* 1989, Sterling $29.95 (0-8069-6907-5); paper $16.95 (0-8069-5814-6). The geology and ecology of the Great Rift Valley of Africa punctuated by the author's personal experiences while living there. (Rev: BL 3/1/89; LJ 12/89; PW 1/20/89) **[916.76]**

917 North America

4882 Cahill, Tim. *Road Fever: A High-Speed Travelogue.* 1991, Random $17.95 (0-394-57656-X). An account of a 23-day road trip from Tierra del Fuego to Prudhoe Bay undertaken by the author and a friend to set a world record. (Rev: BL 1/15/91; LJ 2/15/91; NYTBR 3/10/91) **[917]**

4883 Camus, Albert. *American Journals.* 1987, Paragon House $15.95 (0-913729-68-X). Journals of the French author's post-World War II trips to the United States, Canada, and South America. (Rev: CSM 8/7/87; NYTBR 8/16/87) **[917]**

4884 Meegan, George. *Longest Walk: An Odyssey of the Human Spirit.* 1989, Paragon House paper $12.95 (1-55778-230-X). An account of the author's seven year, nearly 20,000-mile walk from the tip of South America to the northernmost regions of Alaska. (Rev: LJ 1/88; PW 12/25/87) **[917]**

Canada

4885 Halsey, David, and Diana Landau. *Magnetic North: A Trek Across Canada.* 1990, Sierra Club $19.95 (0-87156-746-6); paper $12.00 (0-87156-566-8). A chronicle of a two-and-a-half-year journey by foot and canoe across Canada by a writer (Halsey) whose work had to be completed by another (Landau) following his death. (Rev: BL 10/15/90; NYTBR 12/2/90; PW 9/7/90) **[917.1]**

Mexico

4886 Ferguson, William M. *Mesoamerica's Ancient Cities.* 1990, Univ. Pr. of Colorado $45.00 (0-87081-173-8). A photographic guide to pre-Columbian ruins in Mexico and Central America. (Rev: BL 10/15/90; LJ 8/90) **[917.2]**

4887 Morris, Mary. *Nothing to Declare: Memoirs of a Woman Traveling Alone.* 1989, G. K. Hall $19.95 (0-8161-4730-2); Penguin paper $7.95 (0-14-009587-X). Memoirs of the author's experiences traveling, living, and working in Mexico and Central America. (Rev: LJ 4/1/88; NYTBR 5/1/88; Time 4/11/88) **[917.2]**

Central America

4888 Rushdie, Salman. *Jaguar's Smile: A Nicaraguan Journey.* 1987, Viking $12.95 (0-317-56603-2); Penguin paper $7.95 (0-14-010926-9). The author of *The Satanic Verses* reflects upon his 1986 visit to Nicaragua and the legacy of the Sandinista revolution. (Rev: BL 3/15/87; LJ 3/1/87; PW 1/23/87) **[917.28]**

Mexico

4889 Davis, Wade. *Serpent and the Rainbow: A Harvard Scientist Uncovers the Startling Truth about the Secret World of Haitian Voodoo and Zombies.* 1987, Warner paper $4.95 (0-446-34387-0). An eyewitness study of Haitian religious ceremonies and practices. (Rev: PW 11/22/85; Sat Rev 1/2/86; TLS 7/4/86) **[917.294]**

United States

4890 Angelou, Maya. *I Know Why the Caged Bird Sings.* 1970, Random $19.95 (0-394-42986-9); Bantam paper $3.95 (0-553-25615-7). Autobiographical account of the youth of an African American growing up in the South. "One of the best autobiographies of its kind that I have read."—LJ (REV: BL 6/15/70; LJ 3/15/70; Newsweek 3/2/70. AWARDS: ALA, 1970) **[917.3]**

4891 Boorstin, Daniel J. *Americans: The Democratic Experience.* 1973, Random $39.95 (0-394-48724-9); paper $10.95 (0-394-71011-8). The final volume analyzing the American character by the former librarian of Congress. (REV: CSM 6/27/73; LJ 7/73; NYTBR 7/29/73. AWARDS: ALA, 1973; PP:History, 1974) **[917.3]**

4892 Di Santo, Ronald L. *Guidebook to Zen and the Art of Motorcycle Maintenance.* 1990, Morrow $22.95 (0-688-08461-3); paper $12.45 (0-688-06069-2). An analysis and study guide to Robert Pirsig's 1974 book containing maps, letters, unpublished sections, book reviews, and an index. (REV: Choice 2/91; LJ 9/15/90; PW 8/17/90) **[917.3]**

4893 Heat-Moon, William Least. *Blue Highways: A Journey into America.* 1983, Little, Brown $18.95 (0-316-35395-7). An account of travels around the United States, driving through its rural "back roads." "Maybe twice a year I read a book I wish were even longer. This is one of them."—NYTBR (REV: LJ 11/1/82; NYTBR 2/6/83; Time 1/24/83. AWARDS: ALA, 1983; Time, 1983) **[917.3]**

4894 Hobson, Archie, ed. *Remembering America: A Sampler of the WPA American Guide Series.* 1985, Columbia Univ. Pr. $27.50 (0-231-06050-5); Macmillan paper $11.95 (0-02-033280-7). Selections from the Federal Writers Project guides to the American states produced under the auspices of the WPA during the 1930s. (REV: BL 11/1/85; CSM 6/14/85; NYTBR 6/2/85) **[917.3]**

4895 Kammen, Michael. *People of Paradox: An Inquiry Concerning the Origins of American Civilization.* 1980, Oxford Univ. Pr. paper $9.95 (0-19-502803-1). An analysis of the often contradictory nature of American culture, its history, and origins. (REV: Choice 2/73; LJ 8/72; NYTBR 10/1/72. AWARDS: PP:History, 1973) **[917.3]**

4896 Kerr, Jean P., Oliver Jensen, and Murray Belsky, eds. *American Album.* Houghton paper $19.95 (0-828-13075-2). A collection of over 300 nineteenth-century American photographs selected by the editors of *American Heritage.* "More than a documentary of American photography . . . an unusually vivid record of the life of the anonymous multitudes."—NYTBR (REV: NYTBR 9/8/68; New Yorker 11/30/68; Newsweek 10/14/68. AWARDS: ALA, 1968) **[917.3]**

4897 Kuralt, Charles. *A Life on the Road.* 1990, Putnam $19.95 (0-399-13488-3). Memoirs of the CBS journalist's life and career. (REV: BL 9/15/90; LJ 10/1/90; NYTBR 10/28/90) **[917.3]**

4898 Parfit, Michael. *Chasing the Glory: Travels Across America.* 1989, Macmillan paper $8.95 (0-02-035680-3). The author of *South Light* recounts his airborne journey around the United States tracing the route Lindbergh flew following his return from Paris in 1927. (REV: BL 10/1/88; NYTBR 1/1/89; PW 8/26/88) **[917.3]**

4899 Pindell, Terry. *Making Tracks: An American Rail Odyssey.* 1990, Grove-Weidenfeld $24.95 (0-8021-1279-X). An account of the author's train travels through the United States covering all of Amtrak's routes. (REV: BL 7/90; LJ 6/15/90; NYTBR 9/9/90) **[917.3]**

4900 Pirsig, Robert M. *Zen and the Art of Motorcycle Maintenance: An Inquiry into Values.* 1974, Morrow $22.95 (0-688-00230-7); Bantam paper $5.95 (0-553-27747-2). A cross-country motorcycle trip becomes the basis for a philosophical discussion between father and son. "Extraordinary . . . the piercing clarity of feeling between father and son lifts the book to majesty."—Newsweek (REV: LJ 5/1/74; Newsweek 4/29/74; Time 4/15/74. AWARDS: ALA, 1974; Time, 1974; Time, the 1970s) **[917.3]**

4901 Tomkins, Calvin. *Living Well Is the Best Revenge.* 1982, Dutton paper $6.95 (0-525-48249-0). A dual biography of Sara and Gerald Murphy, American expatriates who lived in Paris during the 1920s and cultivated friendships with the Fitzgeralds, Hemingway, Stravinsky, Picasso, and Dos Passos, among others. (REV: LJ 9/15/71; NYTBR 7/18/71; Time 7/19/71. AWARDS: Time, 1971) **[917.3]**

4902 Wall, Joseph F. *Andrew Carnegie.* 1989, Univ. of Pittsburgh Pr. $49.95 (0-8229-3828-6); paper $19.95 (0-8229-5904-6). A biography of the nineteenth-century Scottish-born American entrepreneur and philanthropist. "A masterly study . . . a definitive biography."—PW (REV: LJ 11/15/70; NYTBR 10/11/70; PW 7/20/70) **[917.3]**

Northeastern United States

4903 Conot, Robert. *American Odyssey.* 1986, Wayne State Univ. Pr. paper $16.95 (0-8143-1806-1). The history of Detroit from its founding to an examination of its social and economic problems of the 1960s and 1970s, including race relations, the state of the automobile industry, and profiles of the prominent citizens of the city. (REV: Choice 11/74; LJ 7/74; NYTBR 6/30/74) **[917.4]**

4904 Durham, Michael S., and Michael Melford. *Mid-Atlantic States: New York, New Jersey, Pennsylvania.* 1989, Stewart, Tabori & Chang $24.95 (1-55670-060-1); paper $17.95 (1-55670-050-4). This illustrated guide to the historic sites of the Mid-Atlantic states is part of a Smithsonian series covering the United States. (REV: BL 4/1/89; LJ 3/1/89) **[917.4]**

4905 Wiencek, Henry. *Southern New England: Massachusetts, Connecticut, Rhode Island.* 1989, Stewart, Tabori & Chang $24.95 (0-55670-059-8); paper $17.95 (0-55670-051-2). A Smithsonian guide to the historic sites of the southern New England states. (REV: BL 4/1/89; LJ 3/1/89) **[917.4]**

4906 Wiencek, Henry. *Virginia and the Capital Region: Washington, D.C., Virginia, Maryland,*

Delaware. 1989, Stewart, Tabori & Chang $24.95 (1-55670-058-X); paper $17.95 (1-55670-048-2). Part of a Smithsonian series detailing the points of historic interest in different regions of the country. (Rev: BL 4/1/89; LJ 3/1/89) **[917.4]**

New York

4907 Wilson, Edmund. *Upstate: Records and Recollections of Northern New York.* 1990, Syracuse Univ. Pr. paper $15.95 (0-374-27963-2). A journal kept at the literary critic's summer home with reflections on his life, the region, and his writings. "The book achieves an astonishing novelistic force and narrative momentum . . . far more moving and substantial than would seem possible from its apparently casual diary form."—NYTBR (Rev: LJ 6/15/71; NYTBR 8/29/71; Newsweek 8/30/71. Awards: ALA, 1971; NYTBR, 1971) **[917.47]**

Southeastern United States (South Atlantic states)

4908 Ellis, Jerry. *Walking the Trail: One Man's Journey Along the Trail of Tears.* 1991, Delacorte $19.00 (0-385-30448-X). An account of the author's trip following the route taken by the Cherokee tribe on its forced relocation from Alabama to Oklahoma in 1838. (Rev: BL 11/1/91; LJ 9/15/91) **[917.5]**

4909 Murray, Albert. *South to a Very Old Place.* 1991, Random paper $9.00 (0-679-73695-6). Memoirs of the author about his life and the essence of the American South. (Rev: BL 4/15/72; NYTBR 6/4/72; PW 11/15/71) **[917.5]**

Virginia

4910 Peters, James Edwards. *Arlington National Cemetery: Shrine to America's Heroes.* 1988, Woodbine $16.95 (0-933149-23-9); paper $12.95 (0-933149-04-2). The history of the United States' national cemetery in Virginia with profiles of some of the notable persons laid to rest there. (Rev: BL 12/1/86; LJ 3/1/87) **[917.55]**

North Carolina

4911 Bailey, Anthony. *Outer Banks.* 1989, Farrar $18.95 (0-374-22835-3); paper $8.95 (0-374-52228-6). The author's experiences on the Outer Banks of North Carolina before, during, and after Hurricane Gloria struck the coastline. "To read his travel books . . . is to share the experience of being there."—BL (Rev: BL 5/1/89; LJ 5/1/89; PW 5/12/89) **[917.56]**

South Carolina

4912 Carawan, Guy, and Candie Carawan, eds. *Ain't You Got a Right to the Tree of Life? The People of Johns Island, South Carolina—Their Faces, Their Words, and Their Songs.* 1989, Univ. of Georgia Pr. $29.95 (0-8203-1132-4). The life of the people of Johns Island, a primarily rural community composed of the descendents of plantation slaves and largely removed from modern American life. (Rev: Choice 4/68; LJ 5/15/67; NYTBR 6/11/67. Awards: ALA, 1967) **[917.57]**

Florida

4913 Williams, Joy. *Florida Keys: A History and Guide.* 1988, Random paper $9.95 (0-679-72176-2). A history and tourist guide to the Florida Keys by a resident of Key West. (Rev: BL 6/1/87; LJ 4/1/87) **[917.59]**

Alabama

4914 Shaw, Nate. *All God's Dangers: The Life of Nate Shaw.* Ed. by Theodore Rosengarten. 1989, Random $12.95 (0-679-72761-2). The autobiography of an illiterate Alabama farmer who told his life story to Rosengarten. (Rev: New Rep 10/12/74; New Yorker 11/18/74; Time 11/18/74. Awards: ALA, 1974; NBA, 1975; NYTBR, 1974) **[917.61]**

Western United States

4915 Conover, Ted. *Whiteout: Lost in Aspen.* 1991, Random $20.00 (0-394-57469-9). A chronicle of the author's experiences living among the elite in Aspen, Colorado, tracing his encounters with the likes of John Denver, Don Johnson, Melanie Griffith, Hunter S. Thompson, and Jack Nicholson. (Rev: BL 12/15/91; PW 11/1/91) **[917.8]**

4916 Frazier, Ian. *Great Plains.* 1989, Farrar $17.95 (0-374-21723-8); Penguin paper $9.95 (0-14-013170-1). A compendium of folklore, geography, and history concerning the American Great Plains based on the author's extensive travels and research. (Rev: CSM 7/11/89; New Rep 8/7/89; PW 1/27/89. Awards: PW, 1989) **[917.8]**

4917 Heat-Moon, William Least. *PrairyErth (A Deep Map).* 1991, Houghton $24.95 (0-395-48602-5). A detailed portrait of Chase County, Kansas, by the author of *Blue Highways.* "A feat of sustained watchfulness, concentration, passion, and spiritual vigor."—BL (Rev: BL 8/91; LJ 10/1/91; NYTBR 10/27/91. Awards: BL, 1991; LJ, 1991) **[917.8]**

4918 Lavender, David. *Way to the Western Sea: Lewis and Clark Across the Continent.* 1988, Harper & Row $22.95 (0-06-015982-0); Doubleday paper $12.95 (0-385-41155-3). A re-creation of Lewis and Clark's exploratory expedition across the North American continent. (Rev: Choice 5/89; LJ 12/88; NYTBR 2/19/89) **[917.8]**

4919 Pern, Stephen. *Great Divide: A Walk Through America Along the Continental Divide.* 1988, Viking $17.95 (0-670-82100-4); Penguin paper $7.95 (0-14-009593-4). An Englishman's description of his seven-month walk from Mexico to Canada along the Continental Divide. (Rev: LJ 6/15/88; NYTBR 6/5/88; TLS 1/22/88) **[917.8]**

Great Basin and Pacific Slope Region of the United States

4920 Berger, Bruce. *Telling Distance: Conversations with the American Desert.* 1990, Breitenbush Books $19.95 (0-932576-74-5). Fifty essays extolling the life and human enjoyment of the Southwestern deserts. "Belongs on the shelf with all great desert literature."—BL (Rev: BL 7/90; CSM 10/1/90; NYTBR 9/2/90. Awards: BL, 1990) **[917.9]**

4921   Casey, Robert L. *Journey to the High Southwest: A Traveler's Guide.* 1988, Globe Pequot paper $17.95 (0-87106-659-9). A guide to travel and sightseeing in the Four Corners region. (REV: BL 3/15/85; LJ 3/15/85)   **[917.9]**

4922   Lavender, David. *River Runners of the Grand Canyon.* 1985, Univ. of Arizona Pr. $9.95 (0-8165-0940-9). Biographical portraits of people who have ridden the dangerous waters of the Colorado River through the Grand Canyon. (REV: BL 9/1/85; LJ 9/1/85; PW 7/19/85)   **[917.9]**

Nevada

4923   Thompson, Hunter S. *Fear and Loathing in Las Vegas: A Savage Journey to the Heart of the American Dream.* 1989, Random paper $8.95 (0-679-72419-2). The Gonzo journalist's experiences in Las Vegas—missing the car race he was sent to cover, heading halfway back to Los Angeles, and returning to attend a top-level drug conference. "The funniest piece of American prose since 'Naked Lunch.' "—NYTBR (REV: LJ 8/72; NYTBR 7/23/72; TLS 11/3/72)   **[917.93]**

Oregon

4924   Stafford, Kim R. *Having Everything Right: Essays of Place.* 1986, Confluence Pr. $14.95 (0-917652-60-6); Penguin paper $6.95 (0-14-010254-X). Collected essays regarding different aspects of the life, culture, and history of Oregon. (REV: BL 8/86; LJ 7/86; NYTBR 8/3/86)   **[917.95]**

4925   Sullivan, William L. *Listening for Coyote: A Walk Across Oregon's Wilderness.* 1988, Morrow $17.95 (0-688-07880-X); Henry Holt paper $10.95 (0-8050-1250-8). A journal recording the events of the author's 65-day, 1,300-mile journey across the wilds of Oregon. (REV: LJ 10/1/88; NYTBR 12/4/88; PW 7/8/88)   **[917.95]**

918   South America

4926   Chatwin, Bruce. *In Patagonia.* 1988, Penguin paper $7.95 (0-14-011291-X). An account of the author's travels around southern Argentina. "Mr. Chatwin makes a splendid guide because he is learned, humorous and observant, he writes extremely well, and he is resoutely blind to the commonplace. His book may well prove a classic in its field."—Atl (REV: Atl 8/78; NYTBR 7/16/78; New Yorker 10/9/78. AWARDS: ALA, 1978; NYTBR, 1978)   **[918]**

4927   Kane, Joe. *Running the Amazon.* 1989, Knopf $19.95 (0-394-55331-4); Random paper $9.95 (0-679-72902-X). An account of the voyage of the first people to paddle the Amazon River from its origins in the Peruvian Andes to the Atlantic Ocean. (REV: LJ 5/15/89; NYTBR 7/30/89; PW 4/21/89)   **[918]**

4928   Read, Piers Paul. *Alive: The Story of the Andes Survivors.* 1979, Avon paper $4.95 (0-380-00321-X). The story of a Uruguayan rugby team whose plane crashed in the Andes and how some members of the group were able to survive for 70 days before their rescue. (REV: LJ 9/15/74; NYTBR 4/7/74; Newsweek 4/22/74)   **[918]**

4929   Theroux, Paul. *Old Patagonian Express: By Train Through the Americas.* 1989, Houghton paper $9.95 (0-395-52105-X). The author's experiences traveling by train from Boston south to Argentina. "Theroux is one of the best of today's travel writers, and this book will help to maintain his reputation."—LJ (REV: LJ 9/1/79; New Rep 9/22/79; NYTBR 8/26/79)   **[918]**

South America

4930   Shukman, Henry. *Sons of the Moon.* 1990, Macmillan $17.95 (0-684-19204-7). Accounts of the author's travels in Argentina, Bolivia, and Peru in search of pre-Incan cultures. (REV: BL 4/1/90; LJ 3/15/90)   **[918.04]**

Brazil

4931   Allen, Benedict. *Who Goes Out in the Midday Sun? An Englishman's Trek Through the Amazon Jungle.* 1986, Viking $18.95 (0-670-81032-0). An account of the author's overland and river journey from the Orinoco River to the Amazon. "An incredible odyssey, strikingly relived."—BL (REV: BL 5/1/86; LJ 5/15/86; TLS 8/2/85)   **[918.1]**

4932   McIntyre, Loren. *Amazonia.* 1991, Sierra Club $40.00 (0-87156-641-9). A photo-essay on the Amazon region by a former *National Geographic* reporter who has lived in South America for five decades. (REV: LJ 10/1/91; PW 8/2/91)   **[918.1]**

4933   Ricciardi, Mirella. *Vanishing Amazon.* 1991, Abrams $49.50 (0-8109-3915-0). A photo-essay with 220 pictures of three tribes in the wilds of the Amazon rain forest. (REV: LJ 11/1/91; PW 10/11/91. AWARDS: LJ, 1991)   **[918.1]**

4934   Thomsen, Moritz. *Saddest Pleasure: A Journey on Two Rivers.* 1990, Graywolf paper $9.00 (1-55597-124-5). An account of the author's experiences traveling in the jungles of South America. (REV: LJ 3/1/90; NYTBR 6/10/90; PW 2/16/90. AWARDS: PW, 1990)   **[918.1]**

Ecuador

4935   Kling, Kevin, and Nadia Christensen. *Ecuador: Island of the Andes.* 1988, Thames & Hudson $40.00 (0-500-01440-X). A photographic study of the culture and scenery of the South American nation. (REV: LJ 8/88; NYTBR 6/5/88; PW 3/11/88)   **[918.6]**

919   Other areas

Pacific Ocean

4936   Withey, Lynne. *Voyages of Discovery: Captain Cook and the Exploration of the Pacific.* 1987, Morrow $19.95 (0-688-0515-4); Univ. of California Pr. paper $12.95 (0-520-06564-6). An account of the three voyages to the Pacific undertaken by the eighteenth-century English explorer James Cook. (Rev: BL 9/15/87; Choice 6/88; NYTBR 5/1/88) **[919.04]**

New Zealand

4937 Shadbolt, Maurice, and Brian Brake. *Reader's Digest Guide to New Zealand.* 1988, Reader's Digest $39.95 (0-86438-037-2). An illustrated travel guide to New Zealand by one of the nation's most prominent novelists. (Rev: BL 12/15/88; LJ 11/15/88) **[919.31]**

Australia

4938 Chatwin, Bruce. *Songlines.* 1987, Viking $18.95 (0-670-80605-6); Penguin paper $8.95 (0-14-009429-6). A retelling of Australian aborigine myths and legends by the British author of *In Patagonia.* (Rev: BL 7/87; Time 8/24/87; TLS 9/4/87) **[919.4]**

4939 Finkelstein, Dave, and Jack London. *Greater Nowheres: A Journey Through the Australian Bush.* 1990, Simon & Schuster paper $9.95 (0-671-68485-X). An account of the authors' experiences on an eight-month trip through the Australian outback. (Rev: BL 7/88; LJ 6/15/88) **[919.4]**

Tasmania

4940 Conrad, Peter. *Behind the Mountain: Return to Tasmania.* 1989, Poseidon $18.95 (0-671-67373-4); Simon & Schuster paper $9.95 (0-671-70573-3). An account of the author's return to his birthplace and childhood home after two decades abroad. "Extraordinarily interesting reading."—TLS (Rev: LJ 2/15/89; NYTBR 4/9/89; TLS 10/21/89) **[919.46]**

South Pacific

4941 Varawa, Joana McIntyre. *Changes in Latitude: An Uncommon Anthropology.* 1989, Atlantic Monthly $19.95 (0-87113-319-9); Harper & Row paper $8.95 (0-06-097319-6). A California anthropologist's account of her marriage to a Fiji Islander half her age. (Rev: NYTBR 9/3/89; Newsweek 7/17/89; PW 3/31/89) **[919.6]**

Arctic regions

4942 Abramson, Howard S. *Hero in Disgrace: The Life of Arctic Explorer Frederick A. Cook.* 1991, Paragon House $21.95 (1-55778-322-5). A biography of the early twentieth-century Arctic explorer who may have reached the North Pole before Peary. (Rev: BL 5/15/91; PW 4/19/91) **[919.8]**

4943 Bockstoce, John. *Arctic Passages: A Unique Small-Boat Voyage Through the Great Northern Waterway.* 1991, Morrow $22.95 (0-688-08839-2). An account of the author's seafaring voyages in the Arctic undertaken over a period of 20 years. (Rev: BL 2/15/91; LJ 3/1/91; PW 2/8/91) **[919.8]**

4944 Haines, John. *The Stars, the Snow, the Fire: 25 Years in the Northern Wilderness.* 1989, Graywolf $16.00 (1-55597-117-2). A collection of the author's essays about life in the interior of Alaska. "Peerless . . . an invaluable addition to American

literature."—BL (Rev: BL 5/15/89; LJ 6/1/89; NYTBR 12/10/89) **[919.8]**

4945 Herbert, Wally. *Noose of Laurels: Peary, Cook, and the Race to the North Pole.* 1989, Macmillan $22.50 (0-689-12034-6); paper $12.95 (0-385-41355-6). An account of Robert Peary's attempts to reach the North Pole based on newly released personal records of the explorer. "A valuable addition to Arctic history, and a gripping adventure story."—PW (Rev: LJ 6/15/89; PW 5/19/89; Time 7/31/89) **[919.8]**

4946 Hildebrand, John. *Reading the River: A Voyage Down the Yukon.* 1988, Houghton $17.95 (0-395-42480-1). A description of the author's three-month, 2,000-mile journey by canoe down the Yukon River. "A finely written account of coming to terms with one's self."—LJ (Rev: BL 5/15/88; LJ 7/88; PW 5/27/88) **[919.8]**

4947 Modzelewski, Michael. *Inside Passage: Living with Killer Whales, Bald Eagles, and Kwakiutl Indians.* 1991, HarperCollins $19.95 (0-06-016533-2). A chronicle of the author's year-and-a-half among the wildlife and peoples of a British Columbian island. (Rev: BL 3/15/91; PW 3/1/91) **[919.8]**

4948 Oxenhorn, Harvey. *Tuning the Rig: A Journey to the Arctic.* 1990, Harper & Row $22.95 (0-06-016351-8). A journal of the author's experiences aboard a North Atlantic ocean research vessel. "A captivating travel-adventure story."—PW (Rev: LJ 4/1/90; NYTBR 4/22/90; PW 3/30/90) **[919.8]**

Antarctica

4949 Halle, Louis J. *Sea and the Ice: A Naturalist in Antarctica.* 1989, Cornell Univ. Pr. paper $12.95 (0-8014-9575-X). An ornithologist's view of the natural history and history of Antarctica based on a trip aboard a U.S. Coast Guard ice breaker. (Rev: Atl 10/73; BL 12/15/73; PW 4/9/73) **[919.89]**

4950 Huntford, Roland. *Shackleton.* 1987, Fawcett paper $12.95 (0-449-90269-2). A biography of the British explorer who failed in his efforts to reach the South Pole. "Readers interested in polar exploration will find this book hard to put down."—PW (Rev: LJ 1/86; Newsweek 1/13/86; PW 12/13/85) **[919.89]**

4951 Monteuch, Colin. *Wild Ice: Antarctic Journeys.* 1990, Smithsonian Inst. $29.95 (0-87474-395-8). An illustrated record of four naturalist photographers' trips to Antarctica. (Rev: BL 11/15/90; LJ 11/15/90) **[919.89]**

4952 Parfit, Michael. *South Light: A Journey to the Last Continent.* 1989, Macmillan paper $8.95 (0-02-023620-4). A description of the author's four-month trip to Antarctica. "This is the best of travel writing, combining exhilarating adventure with intellectual discovery."—LJ (Rev: BL 1/1/86; LJ 1/86; NYTBR 3/9/86. Awards: ALA, 1986) **[919.89]**

4953 Pyne, Stephen J. *The Ice: A Journey to Antarctica.* 1986, Univ. of Iowa Pr. $39.50 (0-87745-152-4); paper $4.95 (0-345-34845-1). The result of the author's three-month excursion to the least known of the earth's continents. "More about ice than you knew you wanted to know, yet sheer compelling significance holds attention page by page."—Ruth Kirk, NYTBR (REV: Choice 3/87; LJ 11/15/86; NYTBR 1/11/87. AWARDS: NYTBR, 1987) **[919.89]**

Extraterrestrial worlds

4954 Jastrow, Robert. *Journey to the Stars: Space Exploration—Tomorrow and Beyond.* 1989, Bantam $18.95 (0-553-05386-8); paper $9.95 (0-553-34909-0). A look at the future of space exploration and man's search for extraterrestrial life forms. (REV: BL 8/89; LJ 9/15/89; NYTBR 11/19/89) **[919.9]**

4955 Murray, Bruce C. *Journey into Space: The First 30 Years of Space Exploration.* 1989, Norton $19.95 (0-393-02675-2); paper $14.95 (0-393-30703-4). A history of the first three decades of space exploration as recounted by the former head of California's Jet Propulsion Laboratory. (REV: BL 6/15/89; CSM 8/22/89; LJ 7/89) **[919.9]**

4956 Oberg, James E., and Alcestis R. Oberg. *Pioneering Space: Living on the Next Threshold.* 1986, McGraw-Hill $16.95 (0-07-048034-6); paper $4.95 (0-07-048039-7). An exploration of human life in space based on accounts of Soviet cosmonauts and American astronauts. (REV: BL 1/1/86; Choice 4/86; PW 12/6/85) **[919.9]**

920 BIOGRAPHY, GENEALOGY, INSIGNIA

4957 Anthony, Carolyn, ed. *Family Portraits: Remembrances by Twenty Distinguished Writers.* 1989, Doubleday $18.95 (0-385-26415-1). Twenty contemporary writers reflect on the influence of their families upon their lives and work. (REV: LJ 11/1/89; NYTBR 11/19/89) **[920]**

4958 Berlin, Isaiah. *Personal Impressions.* Ed. by Henry Hardy. 1988, Peter Smith $16.25 (0-8446-6297-6); Penguin paper $7.95 (0-14-006313-7). Fourteen essays regarding friends and acquaintances of the author, including Franklin D. Roosevelt, Winston Churchill, and Felix Frankfurter. (REV: BL 12/1/80; New Rep 1/31/81; Sat Rev 1/81) **[920]**

4959 Goodwin, Doris Kearns. *Fitzgeralds and the Kennedys.* 1988, St. Martin's paper $5.95 (0-312-90933-0). A look at both sides of the Kennedy family up until the inauguration of John Fitzgerald Kennedy. "The richest history yet of two much-chronicled families."—LJ (REV: LJ 2/15/87; New Rep 3/16/87; NYTBR 4/23/87. AWARDS: ALA, 1987) **[920]**

4960 Hersey, John. *Life Sketches.* 1991, Random paper $10.95 (0-679-73196-2). A collection of essays by the author of *Hiroshima* concerning people he has known, including sketches of Sinclair Lewis, Harry Truman, Lillian Hellman, and Erskine Caldwell. (REV: BL 2/15/89; LJ 4/1/89; NYTBR 5/7/89) **[920]**

4961 Isaacson, Walter, and Evan Thomas. *Wise Men: Six Friends and the World They Made; Acheson, Bohlen, Harriman, Kennan, Lovett, McCoy.* 1988, Simon & Schuster paper $14.95 (0-671-65712-7). A collective biography of six American statesmen who shaped U.S. foreign policy following World War II. (REV: New Rep 2/19/87; NYTBR 11/2/86; PW 8/29/86) **[920]**

4962 Monroe, Sylvester, and Peter Goldman. *Brothers: A Story of Courage and Survival Against the Odds of Today's Society.* 1988, Morrow $18.95 (0-688-07622-X); Ballantine paper $4.95 (0-345-36156-3). Monroe, a *Newsweek* reporter, visits the housing project of his youth and traces the lives of a dozen of his childhood friends. "An impassioned overview of growing up poor, black and male in America."—BL (REV: BL 6/1/88; LJ 8/88; NYTBR 8/28/88) **[920]**

4963 Ward, Geoffrey C. *American Originals: The Private Worlds of Some Singular Men and Women.* 1991, HarperCollins $22.95 (0-06-016694-0). A collection of 40 profiles of American men and women by the author of *The Civil War*, including sketches of Alger Hiss, Jack Dempsey, and Lillian Hellman. (REV: BL 9/1/91; LJ 9/1/91) **[920]**

4964 Whittemore, Reed. *Whole Lives: Shapers of Modern Biography.* 1989, Johns Hopkins $19.95 (0-8018-3817-7). Life stories of the great modern biographers intertwined with commentary concerning the art of biography. "Essential reading for anyone interested in biography as a genre."—LJ (REV: BL 10/15/89; Choice 3/90; LJ 11/15/89) **[920]**

Women

4965 Barker-Benfield, G. J., and Catherine Clinton. *Portraits of American Women: From Settlement to the Present.* 1991, St. Martin's $35.00 (0-312-05789-8). Biographical portraits of 25 notable American women from the seventeenth century to the present, including profiles of Eleanor Roosevelt, Pochahontes, Betty Friedan, and Mary Todd Lincoln. (REV: BL 4/15/91; LJ 5/1/91) **[920.72]**

4966 Coman, Carolyn. *Body and Soul: Ten American Women.* 1988, Hill & Co. $27.50 (0-940595-13-3); paper $14.95 (0-940595-16-8). The lives of ten American women are presented through words and photographs. "As great, thoughtful and haunting Americana as Agee and Evans' *Let Us Now Praise Famous Men*."—BL (REV: BL 4/1/88; PW 3/11/88) **[920.72]**

4967 Culley, Margo, ed. *A Day at a Time: The Diary Literature of American Women from 1764 to the Present.* 1985, Feminist Pr. $29.95 (0-935312-50-1); paper $12.95 (0-935512-51-X). An anthology of excerpts from the diaries of 29 American women. "A delightful treasure trove for those interested in the variety of women's experiences in the United States."—PW (REV: LJ 2/15/86; NYTBR 3/16/86; PW 11/15/85. AWARDS: PW, 1985) **[920.72]**

4968 Fraser, Antonia. *Warrior Queens.* 1989, Knopf $22.95 (0-394-54939-2); Random paper $12.95 (0-679-72816-3). A history of the military leadership of female heads of state during wartime from Cleopatra to Margaret Thatcher. (REV: LJ 3/1/89; New Yorker 4/24/89; TLS 11/11/88) **[920.72]**

4969 Ione, Carole. *Pride of Family: Four Generations of American Women of Color.* 1991, Summit $19.95 (0-671-54453-5). A chronicle of four generations of an African-American family, including excerpts from the diary of the author's great-grandmother. (REV: BL 8/91; LJ 8/91) **[920.72]**

929 Genealogy, names, insignia

4970 Egerton, John. *Generations: An American Family.* 1983, Univ. Pr. of Kentucky $9.00 (0-8131-1482-9). The history of the Ledford family of Kentucky as related by Burnam and Addie Ledford, and one hundred members of their immediate family. "A rich contribution to the Americana treasury."—PW (REV: LJ 8/83; NYTBR 11/6/83; PW 7/1/83. AWARDS: ALA, 1983) **[929]**

Family histories

4971 Critchfield, Richard. *Those Days: An American Album.* 1987, Dell paper $8.95 (0-317-59955-0). The author's family history from 1880 to 1940 in North Dakota traced from personal recollections and written records. (REV: BL 5/15/86; LJ 3/1/86; NYTBR 3/23/86. AWARDS: ALA, 1986) **[929.2]**

4972 Haley, Alex. *Roots: The Saga of an American Family.* 1976, Doubleday $21.95 (0-385-03787-2); Dell paper $5.95 (0-440-17464-3). Haley traces his family history through seven generations to West Africa and his ancestors' abduction into American slavery. "Poignant family history at its best . . . a superb book."—LJ (REV: LJ 10/15/76; NYTBR 9/26/76; Newsweek 10/18/76. AWARDS: ALA, 1976; NYTBR, 1976) **[929.2]**

4973 Lewis, R. W. B. *Jameses: A Family Narrative.* 1991, Farrar $35.00 (0-374-17861-5). A history of the remarkable family that produced writer Henry and philosopher William from the family's arrival from Ireland in 1789 to the twentieth century. (REV: BL 6/15/91; LJ 8/91; NYTBR 10/10/91. AWARDS: ALA, 1992; BL, 1991; LJ, 1991) **[929.2]**

4974 Maxwell, William. *Ancestors.* 1985, Godine paper $9.95 (0-87923-574-8). Maxwell traces his family history back to Scotland in this work, but concentrates on an examination of his living relations in the Midwest, and particularly in his hometown of Lincoln, Illinois. (REV: CSM 7/1/71; LJ 6/1/71; NYTBR 8/8/71) **[929.2]**

4975 Montgomery, M. R. *Saying Goodbye: A Memoir of Two Fathers.* 1989, Knopf $18.95 (0-394-57333-1). Memoirs of the author's relationships with his father and father-in-law. "A thoughtful blend of history and personal reminiscence."—BL (REV: BL 5/15/89; LJ 4/1/89; NYTBR 6/4/89) **[929.2]**

4976 Morgenthau, Henry III. *Mostly Morgenthaus: A Family History.* 1991, Ticknor & Fields $24.95 (0-89919-976-3). A history of the Morgenthau family from its arrival in the United States from Germany in 1866 to the present. (REV: LJ 6/15/91; NYTBR 9/8/91; PW 6/17/91) **[929.2]**

4977 Nagel, Paul C. *Descent from Glory: Four Generations of the John Adams Family.* 1983, Oxford Univ. Pr. $29.95 (0-19-503172-5); paper $12.95 (0-19-503445-7). A biography of the John and Abigail Adams family and the generations that followed. "May well be the model for family studies for years to come."—LJ (REV: Choice 6/83; LJ 12/1/82; NYTBR 2/20/83) **[929.2]**

4978 Strouse, Jean. *Alice James: A Biography.* 1984, Houghton paper $8.95 (0-395-36147-8). A biography of the younger sister of William and Henry James, known primarily for the diary of her last three years. "An important book for those interested in women's history, in literary biography and for those who want to gain insight into the inner workings of human beings."—CSM (REV: BL 11/15/80; CSM 4/1/80; LJ 11/1/80. AWARDS: ALA, 1980) **[929.2]**

4979 Tifft, Susan E., and Alex S. Jones. *Patriarch: The Rise and Fall of the Bingham Dynasty.* 1991, Summit $24.95 (0-671-63167-5). A study of the Kentucky family whose newspaper empire collapsed due to family infighting. "The definitive examination of a contemporary American tragedy."—BL (REV: BL 5/1/91; PW 2/8/91; Time 4/29/91) **[929.2]**

4980 Yardley, Jonathan. *Our Kind of People: The Story of an American Family.* 1989, Grove-Weidenfeld $21.95 (1-55584-174-0). A study of the author's parents, their values, and their relationship through 50 years of marriage. "An engaging, heart-warming story that brings readers closer to understanding a vanished time."—BL (REV: BL 2/1/89; LJ 2/1/89; NYTBR 3/19/89) **[929.2]**

Genealogical sources

4981 Redford, Dorothy S., and Michael D'Orso. *Somerset Homecoming: Discovering a Lost Heritage.* 1988, Doubleday $18.95 (0-385-24245-X); paper $9.95 (0-385-24246-8). The author's research into her personal genealogy and how her efforts led to a mass reunion of over 2,000 relatives of former slaves at a North Carolina plantation. (REV: Atl 11/88; BL 8/88; LJ 10/1/88) **[929.3]**

Royal houses, peerage, gentry, orders of knighthood

4982 Gies, Frances. *Knight in History.* 1987, Harper & Row paper $9.95 (0-06-091413-0). A historical survey of knights and knighthood with profiles of prominent individuals. (REV: LJ 10/15/84; Natl Rev 11/29/85; NYTBR 12/9/84) **[929.7]**

930 HISTORY OF ANCIENT WORLD

Archaeology

4983 Throckmorton, Peter. *Sea Remembers: Shipwrecks and Archaeology.* 1987, Grove-Weidenfeld $29.95 (1-55584-093-0). Essays regarding the discoveries made and techniques used by maritime archaeologists. "As beautiful as it is informative."—LJ (REV: Atl 2/88; BL 2/1/88; LJ 1/88) **[930.1]**

World history in 1st century A. D.

4984 **Klingaman, William.** *First Century: Emperors, Gods and Everyman.* 1990, HarperCollins $24.95 (0-06-016447-6). A survey of the history of the first century in the Middle East, China, and Europe. (REV: BL 10/1/90; LJ 10/1/90; PW 8/17/90) **[930.5]**

932 Egypt

4985 **Drower, Margaret S.** *Flinders Petrie: A Life in Archaeology.* 1985, David & Charles $65.00 (0-575-03667-2). A biography of the British archaeologist known for his work in Egypt and Palestine. (REV: Choice 4/86; LJ 12/85; TLS 9/20/85) **[932]**

4986 **Hornung, Erik.** *Valley of the Kings: Horizon and Enlightenment.* 1990, Timken $50.00 (0-943221-07-2). An illustrated survey of the tombs of Thebes and their treasures. (REV: BL 10/1/90; Choice 2/91; LJ 9/15/90) **[932]**

4987 **James, T. G. H.** *Pharoah's People: Scenes from Life in Imperial Egypt.* 1986, Univ. of Chicago Pr. $20.00 (0-226-39193-0); paper $12.95 (0-226-39194-9). A study of daily life in Egypt from 1550 to 1000 B.C. by the keeper of Egyptian antiquities for the British Museum. (REV: Choice 1/85; LJ 7/84; TLS 9/28/84) **[932]**

4988 **Mertz, Barbara.** *Red Land, Black Land: Daily Life in Ancient Egypt.* 1990, Bedrick paper $14.95 (0-87226-222-7). A study of the customs and culture of the ancient Egyptians by the author of *Temples, Tombs, and Hieroglyphs.* (REV: BL 9/1/66; LJ 12/15/66; PW 10/16/67) **[932]**

4989 **Romer, John.** *Ancient Lives: Daily Life in the Egypt of the Pharoahs.* 1990, Henry Holt paper $12.95 (0-8050-1244-3). An illustrated survey of the life and culture of ancient Egypt. (REV: Choice 3/85; NYTBR 2/17/85; TLS 3/1/85) **[932]**

Earliest history to 332 B. C.

4990 **Reeves, Nicholas.** *Complete Tutankhamen: The King, the Tomb, the Royal Treasure.* 1990, Thames & Hudson $24.95 (0-500-05058-9). An account of the contents of the tomb of the Egyptian boy king discovered in 1922 by Howard Carter. (REV: BL 1/1/91; LJ 1/91) **[932.01]**

Hellenistic, Roman, Byzantine periods, 332 B. C.-640 A. D.

4991 **Hughes-Hallett, Lucy.** *Cleopatra: Histories, Dreams and Distortions.* 1990, Harper & Row $27.50 (0-06-016216-3). A study of the portrayal of the ancient Egyptian Queen Cleopatra VII throughout history. "A fascinating and humorous work, and one that is more than worth the effort of absorbing."—TLS (REV: BL 4/1/90; NYTBR 6/10/90; TLS 2/23/90) **[932.02]**

933 Palestine

4992 **Grant, Michael.** *History of Ancient Israel.* 1984, Macmillan paper $14.95 (0-684-18084-7). The history of ancient Israel from the rise of civilization to the sacking of Jerusalem in 70 A.D. (REV: BL 6/1/84; LJ 6/1/84; NYTBR 8/12/84) **[933]**

936 Europe north and west of Italy

British Isles to 410

4993 **Hawkins, Gerald S., and John B. White.** *Stonehenge Decoded.* 1988, Hippocrene $18.95 (0-88029-147-8); Dell paper $4.50 (0-385-28974-X). A look at the history, legends, and the authors' theories concerning the mysterious English archaeological site of Stonehenge. "Fascinating reading."—PW (REV: BL 12/15/65; Choice 2/66; PW 10/3/66. AWARDS: ALA, 1965) **[936.1]**

Celtic regions to 486

4994 **Roy, James C.** *The Road Wet, the Wind Close: Celtic Ireland.* 1988, Dufour paper $16.95 (0-8023-1283-7). An examination of early Irish and Celtic culture from 7000 B.C. to A.D. 1169 written for the general reader. (REV: BL 11/1/86; Choice 1/87) **[936.4]**

938 Greece

4995 **Boardman, John, Jasper Griffin, and Oswyn Murray, eds.** *Oxford History of the Classical World: Greece and the Hellenistic World.* 1988, Oxford Univ. Pr. paper $18.95 (0-19-282165-2). A history of Ancient Greece presented in a series of essays by noted Classical scholars. "Popular history at its best."—NYTBR (REV: Choice 1/87; CSM 11/19/86; NYTBR 10/5/86) **[938]**

4996 **Boardman, John, Jasper Griffin, and Oswyn Murray, eds.** *Oxford History of the Classical World: The Roman World.* 1988, Oxford Univ. Pr. paper $18.95 (0-19-282166-0). A survey of the history and culture of Ancient Rome. "Consistently superior in quality of perception and explanation."—BL (REV: BL 1/1/87; CSM 11/19/86; NYTBR 10/5/86) **[938]**

4997 **Garland, Robert.** *Greek Way of Life: From Conception to Old Age.* 1989, Cornell Univ. Pr. $45.00 (0-8014-2335-X). A portrayal of daily life and living conditions in Ancient Greece by the author of *Greek Way of Death.* (REV: BL 11/1/89; LJ 11/15/89; TLS 5/11/90) **[938]**

4998 **Grant, Michael.** *Visible Past: Greek and Roman History from Archaelogy.* 1990, Macmillan $27.50 (0-684-19124-5). A study of 50 ancient archaelogical sites and the historical information we have gained from them. (REV: BL 12/1/90; LJ 11/15/90) **[938]**

4999 **Green, Peter.** *Alexander of Macedon.* 1991, Univ. of California Pr. $34.95 (0-520-07165-4). This biography of the fourth-century B.C. military leader is a condensed version of the author's 1974 work. "A marvelous read."—NYTBR (REV: LJ 9/15/91; NYTBR 9/22/91) **[938]**

Period of Athenian supremacy, 479–431 B. C.

5000 **Kagan, Donald.** *Pericles of Athens and the Birth of Democracy.* 1990, Free Pr. $22.50 (0-02-

916825-2). The Yale professor's account of the origins and development of democracy in ancient Athens. (Rev: LJ 11/15/90; Natl Rev 12/3/90; New Rep 1/28/91)   **[938.04]**

939   Other parts of ancient world

5001   Moscati, Sabatino, ed. *Phoenicians.* 1989, Abbeville $125.00 (0-89659-892-6). An illustrated survey of the history and cultural legacy of the Phoenicians. "Here for the first time Phoenician civilization can be understood in its entirety."—LJ (Rev: LJ 3/15/89; NYTBR 6/4/89; TLS 3/3/89)   **[939]**

5002   Saggs, H. W. *Civilization Before Greece and Rome.* 1989, Yale Univ. Pr. $29.95 (0-300-04440-2). A study of the civilizations and contributions of the Ancient Near East including the Babylonian, Egyptian, Sumerian, and Hittite societies. "An accurate and lively picture of an area typically neglected by Western educators."—LJ (Rev: Choice 6/89; LJ 3/15/89)   **[939]**

940   GENERAL HISTORY OF EUROPE

Education, research, related topics

5003   Hughes, H. Stuart. *Gentleman Rebel: The Memoirs of H. Stuart Hughes.* 1990, Houghton $24.95 (0-395-56316-X). An autobiography of the American historian describing his experiences as an intelligence officer, diplomat, and political activist. (Rev: BL 11/1/90; LJ 11/1/90; PW 9/28/90)   **[940.07]**

1453–

5004   Hobsbawn, E. J. *Age of Capital: 1848 to 1875.* 1984, NAL paper $3.95 (0-452-00696-1). The British Marxist historian examines the rise of capitalism in the world following the European revolutions of 1848. (Rev: Choice 10/76; NYTBR 5/9/76; PW 1/27/76)   **[940.2]**

Period of French Revolution and Napoleon I, 1789–1815

5005   Howarth, David, and Stephen Howarth. *Lord Nelson: The Immortal Memory.* 1989, Viking $24.95 (0-670-81729-5); Penguin paper $9.95 (0-14-010146-2). A biography of the English naval commander who was killed in battle during the victorious engagement off Cape Trafalgar. (Rev: CSM 3/24/89; LJ 2/1/89; NYTBR 3/26/89)   **[940.27]**

World War I

5006   Schneider, Dorothy, and Carl J. Schneider. *Into the Breach: American Women Overseas in World War I.* 1991, Viking $24.95 (0-670-83936-1). A study of the journalistic and relief efforts of American women in Europe during World War I. (Rev: LJ 6/15/91; PW 5/24/91)   **[940.3]**

5007   Tuchman, Barbara W. *Proud Tower: A Portrait of the World Before the War, 1890–1914.* 1966, Macmillan $21.95 (0-02-620300-6); Bantam paper $6.95 (0-553-25602-5). A profile of Western European society in the years prior to World War I. "As remarkable a work as *The Guns of August,* this is an essential purchase."—LJ (Rev: BL 11/15/65; LJ 12/1/65; Sat Rev 1/15/66. Awards: ALA, 1966)   **[940.3]**

World War I—Military history

5008   Farwell, Byron. *The Great War in Africa, 1914–1918.* 1987, Norton $18.95 (0-393-02369-9). A military history of the campaigns of World War I in the European colonies of Africa. (Rev: BL 11/15/86; LJ 12/86; PW 11/14/86)   **[940.4]**

5009   Ley, Ronald. *Whisper of Espionage: Wolfgang Kohler and the Apes of Tenerife.* 1990, Avery $19.95 (0-89529-432-X). A biography of the German scientist and spy noted for his studies of ape behavior conducted on the Canary Islands. (Rev: BL 1/1/90; Choice 6/90)   **[940.4]**

5010   Massie, Robert K. *Dreadnought: Britain, Germany and the Coming of the Great War.* 1991, Random $35.00 (0-394-52833-6). An analysis of the tensions between Britain and Germany from the turn of the century to the outbreak of World War I. "Massie makes history not merely palatable but scrumptious."—BL (Rev: BL 9/15/91; PW 9/27/91. Awards: BL, 1991)   **[940.4]**

5011   Wilson, Jeremy. *Lawrence of Arabia: The Authorized Biography of T. E. Lawrence.* 1991, Atheneum $35.00 (0-689-11934-8). A biography of the British guerrilla leader of the Arab revolt against the Turks based on his private papers and recently released British government documents. (Rev: BL 6/1/90; NYTBR 6/10/90; PW 3/23/90. Awards: NYTBR, 1990)   **[940.4]**

1918–

5012   Large, David Clay. *Between Two Fires: Europe's Path in the 1930s.* 1990, Norton $22.50 (0-393-02751-1). A study of eight key events in Europe during the 1930s. (Rev: Choice 5/90; NYTBR 2/25/90; PW 11/24/89)   **[940.5]**

World War II

5013   Appleman-Jurman, Alicia. *Alicia: My Story.* 1988, Bantam $18.95 (0-553-05317-5). An autobiography of a woman who survived the Holocaust as a girl and later emigrated first to Palestine and later to the United States. (Rev: BL 9/1/88; NYTBR 1/1/89; PW 10/7/88)   **[940.53]**

5014   Arad, Yitzhak, ed. *Pictorial History of the Holocaust.* 1990, Macmillan $75.00 (0-02-897011-X). Photographic history of the Holocaust. "The definitive collection of Holocaust photographs."—Choice (Rev: BL 12/15/90; Choice 2/91)   **[940.53]**

5015   Bar-On, Dan. *Legacy of Silence: Encounters with Children of the Third Reich.* 1989, Harvard Univ. Pr. $25.00 (0-674-52185-4). Interviews with 13 children of Nazi parents form the basis of this work examining their lives and psychological states. (Rev: BL 9/15/89; LJ 9/1/89)   **[940.53]**

5016 Bauman, Janina. *Winter in the Morning: A Young Girl's Life in the Warsaw Ghetto and Beyond, 1939–1945.* **1986, Free Pr. $18.95** (0-02-902530-3). An account of the survival of a Jewish girl, her mother, and her sister in Poland during World War II. (Rev: BL 6/1/86; LJ 3/1/86; NYTBR 4/6/86) **[940.53]**

5017 Bles, Mark. *A Child at War: The True Story of a Young Belgian Resistance Fighter.* **1991, Mercury House $20.95** (1-56279-004-8). The story of a Belgian teenager who joined the Resistance and survived World War II. "Reads like the wildest fiction . . . an incredible memoir of survival."—BL (Rev: BL 3/1/91; LJ 3/1/91) **[940.53]**

5018 Botting, Douglas. *From the Ruins of the Reich: Germany, 1945–1949.* **1985, Crown $17.95** (0-577-55865-3); **NAL paper $10.95** (0-452-00816-6). A study of postwar Germany and its attempt to recover from the social and physical devastation of World War II. (Rev: BL 12/15/85; LJ 11/1/85) **[940.53]**

5019 Camus, Albert. *Between Hell and Reason: Essays from the Resistance Newspaper Combat, 1944–1947.* **1991, Wesleyan Univ. Pr. $35.00** (0-8195-5188-0); **paper $14.95** (0-8195-5189-9). A collection of political editorials by the French writer taken from the journal *Combat*, which he edited during the mid to late 1940s. (Rev: BL 9/15/91; LJ 9/15/91) **[940.53]**

5020 Collier, Richard. *Fighting Words: The War Correspondents of World War Two.* **1990, St. Martin's $17.95** (0-312-03828-3). A study of the lives and work of the American and British journalists and photographers who covered World War II. (Rev: BL 3/15/90; LJ 2/1/90; PW 2/2/90) **[940.53]**

5021 David, Kati. *A Child's War: World War II Through the Eyes of Children.* **1989, Four Walls Eight Windows $17.95** (0-941423-24-7). Memoirs of 15 people who were between the ages of five and ten during World War II recounting their remembrances of the conflict. (Rev: BL 5/1/87; LJ 5/1/89) **[940.53]**

5022 Dawidowicz, Lucy S. *From That Place and Time: A Memoir, 1938–1947.* **1989, Norton $21.95** (0-393-02674-4). The historian and author of *War Against the Jews* recounts her personal experiences during World War II and the Holocaust with the aid of 100 letters she wrote to Jewish friends and relatives in Lithuania from her New York home. (Rev: BL 5/1/89; LJ 5/15/89; PW 3/24/89) **[940.53]**

5023 Dawidowicz, Lucy S. *War Against the Jews, 1933–1945.* **1986, Free Pr. $22.95** (0-02-908030-4); **Bantam paper $10.95** (0-553-34302-5). The history of the Holocaust in Nazi Germany and Poland. "Summarizes in human (and inhuman) terms as well as any single book can the ghastly scope of the tragedy."—PW (Rev: Choice 11/75; NYTBR 4/20/75; PW 3/3/75. Awards: ALA, 1975; NYTBR, 1975) **[940.53]**

5024 Djilas, Milovan. *Wartime.* **1980, Harcourt paper $7.95** (0-15-694712-9). The memoirs of the former vice president of Yugoslavia, who was deposed and imprisoned by the Tito regime. "Djilas makes the

nightmare he lived through as vivid as if it were the reader's."—New Yorker (Rev: LJ 5/15/77; New Yorker 8/22/77; Newsweek 7/25/77. Awards: ALA, 1977) **[940.53]**

5025 Douglas, Roy. *World War, 1939–1945: The Cartoonist's Version.* **1990, Routledge $29.95** (0-415-03049-8). Political cartoons selected from World War II Axis and Allied nations. "A powerful lesson in social history."—LJ (Rev: Choice 6/90; LJ 5/15/90) **[940.53]**

5026 Dower, John W. *War Without Mercy: Race and Power in the Pacific War.* **1987, Pantheon paper $11.95** (0-394-75172-8). An investigation into how concepts of race influenced the fighting on both Japanese and American sides on the Pacific conflict. (Rev: LJ 4/1/86; New Rep 8/4/86; PW 3/28/86) **[940.53]**

5027 Dubosq, Genevieve. *My Longest Night.* **1986, Seaver Books paper $9.95** (0-8050-0150-6). Memories of D-Day and its aftermath by a French girl who lived in a small town in Normandy during the invasion. (Rev: BL 6/15/81; CSM 5/11/81; PW 3/6/81) **[940.53]**

5028 Dwork, Deborah. *Children with a Star: Jewish Youth in Nazi Europe.* **1991, Yale Univ. Pr. $25.00** (0-300-05054-2). An examination of the fate of Jewish children in Nazi-occupied Europe. "Adds a poignant new dimension to Holocaust studies."—PW (Rev: BL 3/1/91; LJ 2/15/91; PW 2/1/91) **[940.53]**

5029 Edmonds, Robin. *Big Three: Churchill, Roosevelt, and Stalin in Peace and War.* **1991, Norton $24.95** (0-393-02889-5). A study of the summit meetings between Allied leaders during World War II. "An important historical work."—LJ (Rev: BL 3/1/91; LJ 2/15/91; PW 1/25/91) **[940.53]**

5030 Eisenhower, David. *Eisenhower: At War, 1943–1945.* **1986, Random $29.95** (0-394-41237-0). Eisenhower's grandson examines the general's role and strategies as supreme Allied commander for the invasion of Europe. "Exhaustively detailed and thoroughly researched, this volume throws new light on most of the subjects covered."—BL (Rev: BL 7/86; Choice 2/87; Time 9/15/86. Awards: Time, 1986) **[940.53]**

5031 Epstein, Helen. *Children of the Holocaust: Conversations with Sons and Daughters of Survivors.* **1988, Penguin paper $7.95** (0-14-011284-7). The author presents her research on the psychology of the children of Holocaust survivors. "Eminently successful in indicating how individuals and families have coped with their own unique Holocaust experience."—Choice (Rev: Choice 9/79; LJ 5/15/79; Newsweek 5/14/79. Awards: ALA, 1979) **[940.53]**

5032 Feis, Herbert. *Between War and Peace: The Potsdam Conference.* **1983, Greenwood $48.50** (0-313-24219-4). Reprint of the 1960 title detailing the last major conference of the Allies in World War II. (Rev: CSM 8/23/60; NYTBR 8/21/60; Sat Rev 10/1/60. Awards: PP:History, 1961) **[940.53]**

5033 Figes, Eva. *Little Eden: A Child at War.* 1987, Persea Books $14.95 (0-89255-121-6). Memoirs of the author's childhood in England as a Jewish refugee whose family fled from Nazi Germany. "Her crystal-clear prose and gimlet insights render this a compelling journey through time."—PW (Rev: LJ 6/15/87; NYTBR 8/16/87; PW 6/5/87)   **[940.53]**

5034 Fleming, Gerald. *Hitler and the Final Solution.* 1984, Univ. of California Pr. paper $9.95 (0-520-06022-9). An examination of Hitler's role in the Holocaust based on documents and interviews. (Rev: Choice 6/85; NYTBR 1/6/85; PW 10/15/84) **[940.53]**

5035 Frank, Anne. *Diary of Anne Frank: The Critical Edition.* 1989, Doubleday $35.00 (0-385-24013-6). The complete English language version of Anne Frank's diary is complemented by historical essays regarding the Holocaust, the fate of Frank's family, and the story of how the journal was saved and published. (Rev: BL 5/15/89; LJ 6/1/89; NYTBR 7/2/89)   **[940.53]**

5036 Gies, Miep, and Alison Leslie Gold. *Anne Frank Remembered: The Story of the Woman Who Helped to Hide the Frank Family.* 1988, Simon & Schuster paper $7.95 (0-671-66234-1). Memoirs of the woman who hid Anne Frank and her family from the Nazis and saved Frank's journal for later publication. (Rev: BL 4/1/87; LJ 5/15/87; NYTBR 5/10/87)   **[940.53]**

5037 Gilbert, Martin. *Holocaust: The History of the Jews of Europe During the Second World War.* 1986, Henry Holt $24.95 (0-03-062416-9); paper $12.95 (0-8050-0348-7). A chronicle of the Holocaust from 1933 to 1945 containing many firsthand accounts of the events. (Rev: CSM 3/26/86; LJ 2/1/86; PW 12/13/85)   **[940.53]**

5038 Gilbert, Martin. *Second World War: A Complete History.* 1989, Henry Holt $29.95 (0-8050-0534-X). A summary of the Second World War by the biographer of Churchill, weaving personal anecdotes and human interest details into the larger diplomatic conflicts. (Rev: LJ 11/1/89; NYTBR 11/26/89; TLS 9/1/89. Awards: LJ, 1989)   **[940.53]**

5039 Gottfryd, Bernard. *Anton the Dove Fancier and Other Tales of the Holocaust.* 1990, Simon & Schuster paper $7.95 (0-671-69137-6). Memoirs of the author's family and others he knew who perished in Poland under the Nazi persecutions. "A meaningful, earnest addition to Holocaust literature."—PW (Rev: BL 6/1/90; LJ 7/90; PW 7/6/90)   **[940.53]**

5040 Herzstein, Robert E. *Roosevelt and Hitler: Prelude to War.* 1989, Paragon House $24.95 (1-55778-021-8). An examination of World War II regarding the conflict as a personal ideological clash between Roosevelt and Hitler. "An important and fascinating work."—LJ (Rev: BL 11/15/89; LJ 11/1/89; PW 10/13/89)   **[940.53]**

5041 Josephs, Jeremy. *Swastika Over Paris.* 1989, Arcade $19.95 (1-55970-036-X). A profile of the Paris Jewish community under Nazi occupation as told

through the story of two individuals. (Rev: BL 10/1/89; LJ 9/15/89; PW 8/18/89)   **[940.53]**

5042 Keegan, John. *Second World War.* 1990, Viking $29.95 (0-670-82359-7); Penguin paper $14.95 (0-14-011341-X). The British military historian presents a single-volume history of the Second World War. "Keegan . . . displays in his writing the richness and readability of style that have rightly earned him a huge following."—BL (Rev: BL 10/1/89; LJ 11/1/89; Newsweek 1/29/90. Awards: BL, 1989)**[940.53]**

5043 Ketchum, Richard. *Borrowed Years, 1938–1941: America on the Way to War.* 1989, Random $29.95 (0-394-56011-6). A chronicle of U.S. history and popular culture from the Munich Conference to the bombing of Pearl Harbor. "An enticing piece of reporting."—BL (Rev: BL 10/1/89; LJ 10/1/89; NYTBR 2/11/90)   **[940.53]**

5044 Klingaman, William. *1941: Our Lives in a Year on the Edge.* 1988, Harper & Row $24.95 (0-06-015948-0); paper $10.95 (0-06-091619-2). A look at the social history, culture, and events of the pivotal year 1941. (Rev: Choice 3/89; CSM 1/20/89; LJ 10/1/88)   **[940.53]**

5045 Langer, Lawrence L. *Holocaust Testimonies: The Ruins of Memory.* 1991, Yale Univ. Pr. $25.00 (0-300-04966-8). A study of the testimonies of Holocaust survivors preserved on video at Yale University. "Essential reading for anyone interested in Holocaust studies."—LJ (Rev: BL 2/1/91; LJ 2/1/91; PW 2/8/91. Awards: NYTBR, 1991)   **[940.53]**

5046 Lanzmann, Claude. *Shoah: An Oral History of the Holocaust.* 1987, Pantheon $11.95 (0-394-55142-7); paper $6.95 (0-394-74329-6). A complete text with still photos from the 9½-hour film documenting the Holocaust. "A significant and terrifyingly moving work."—BL (Rev: BL 1/1/86; LJ 11/15/85)   **[940.53]**

5047 Leckie, Robert. *Delivered from Evil: The Saga of World War II.* 1987, Harper & Row $29.95 (0-06-015812-3); paper $12.95 (0-06-091535-8). A single-volume history of the Second World War. "A first-class popular history of the war, lively, entertaining, emotionally gripping and continuously informative."—PW (Rev: BL 10/1/87; LJ 9/1/87; PW 9/4/87)   **[940.53]**

5048 Levi, Primo. *Moments of Reprieve.* 1986, Summit $14.95 (0-671-60535-6); Penguin paper $6.95 (0-14-009370-2). The life stories of 15 people Levi met at Auschwitz. (Rev: BL 2/1/86; New Rep 7/28/86; PW 12/20/85)   **[940.53]**

5049 Levi, Primo. *Survival in Auschwitz: And, the Reawakening; Two Memoirs.* 1988, Macmillan paper $4.95 (0-02-034310-8). Memoirs of the author's experiences in the Auschwitz death camp and its effects on his life and thought. (Rev: New Rep 7/28/86; PW 12/20/85)   **[940.53]**

5050 Lewin, Abraham. *A Cup of Tears: A Diary of the Warsaw Ghetto.* Ed. by Antony Polonsky. 1988, Basil Blackwell $19.95 (0-631-16215-1). A diary recording daily life in the Warsaw ghetto during the Second World War. (REV: LJ 2/1/89; Choice 10/89; TLS 2/24/89) **[940.53]**

5051 McPherson, Malcolm C. *Blood of His Servants.* **1986, Berkley $3.95 (0-425-08647-X).** An account of the search, capture, trial, and imprisonment of a Nazi war criminal tracked by the son of a family he murdered. "A book that cannot be put aside until its 300-odd pages are read."—NYTBR (REV: LJ 2/15/84; NYTBR 4/29/84; PW 3/2/84) **[940.53]**

5052 Marrus, Michael R. *Holocaust in History.* **1987, Univ. Pr. of New England $25.00 (0-87451-425-8); NAL paper $9.95 (0-452-00953-7).** A study of literature dealing with the Holocaust and attempting to place it in history. (REV: BL 9/15/87; Choice 4/88; LJ 10/1/87) **[940.53]**

5053 Mayer, Arno J. *Why Did the Heavens Not Darken? The Final Solution in History.* **1988, Pantheon $27.95 (0-394-57154-1).** The evolution of Nazi thought and policy regarding the fate of the Jews and how the "final solution" came to be carried out against them. (REV: BL 3/15/89; NYTBR 2/19/89; PW 11/18/88) **[940.53]**

5054 Mee, Charles L., Jr. *Meeting at Potsdam.* **1974, M. Evans $10.95 (0-87131-167-4).** An account of the last major conference of World War II between the Allies that helped shape the postwar world. "An appealing examination of the characters and issues . . . an achievement of popular history of the first order."—LJ (REV: LJ 2/1/75; Newsweek 3/24/75; Sat Rev 3/8/75. AWARDS: ALA, 1975) **[940.53]**

5055 Miller, Judith. *One by One, by One: Facing the Holocaust.* **1990, Simon & Schuster $21.95 (0-671-64472-6).** A comparative study of the portrayal of the Holocaust in several European nations and the United States. (REV: BL 4/1/90; LJ 4/15/90; NYTBR 4/29/90) **[940.53]**

5056 Morgan, Ted. *An Uncertain Hour: The French, the Germans, the Jews and the City of Lyon, 1940–1945.* **1990, Morrow $21.95 (0-87795-989-7).** An examination of the 1987 trial of Klaus Barbie and of the relationship between the French and Germans in Lyon during World War II. (REV: BL 11/15/89; LJ 12/89; NYTBR 12/31/89) **[940.53]**

5057 Morhange-Bégué, Claude. *Chamberet: Recollections from an Ordinary Childhood.* **1987, Marlboro Pr. $14.95 (0-910395-25-X); paper $9.00 (0-910395-26-8).** Recollections of a French girl whose mother was sent to Auschwitz for Resistance activities but survived and was later reunited with her daughter. (REV: LJ 1/88; NYTBR 1/24/88) **[940.53]**

5058 Nir, Yehuda. *Lost Childhood: A Memoir.* **1989, Harcourt $19.95 (0-15-158862-7).** Memoirs of the author's childhood in Nazi-occupied Poland and how he and two family members were able to survive the anti-Jewish persecution. (REV: BL 9/1/89; LJ 9/1/89; NYTBR 12/31/89) **[940.53]**

5059 Origo, Iris. *War in Val D'Orcia: An Italian War Diary, 1943–1944.* **1984, Godine $14.95 (0-87923-500-4); paper $8.95 (0-87923-476-8).** World War II memoirs of an Italian woman who harbored refugees from German and Italian forces on her Tuscan farm. (REV: Choice 7–8/84; LJ 4/15/84; NYTBR 7/1/84) **[940.53]**

5060 Overy, Richard, and Andrew Wheatcroft. *Road to War: Origins of World War II.* **1990, Random $24.95 (0-394-58260-8).** An analysis of the causes of World War II by two English historians. "A concise, highly readable account."—PW (REV: BL 5/1/90; LJ 5/1/90; PW 3/9/90) **[940.53]**

5061 Read, Anthony, and David Fisher. *Deadly Embrace: Hitler, Stalin and the Nazi-Soviet Pact, 1939–1941.* **1988, Norton $25.00 (0-393-02528-4); paper $12.95 (0-393-30651-8).** An examination of the German-Soviet Non-Aggression Pact of 1939. (REV: Choice 2/89; LJ 10/15/88; NYRB 3/30/89) **[940.53]**

5062 Roiphe, Anne. *A Season for Healing: Reflections on the Holocaust.* **1988, Summit $17.95 (0-671-66753-X).** An essay examining how the Jewish reaction to the Holocaust has affected Jewish postwar relations throughout the world. (REV: BL 9/15/88; PW 9/2/88. AWARDS: PW, 1988) **[940.53]**

5063 Rosenberg, David, ed. *Testimony: Contemporary Writers Make the Holocaust Personal.* **1989, Random $24.95 (0-8129-1817-7).** Twenty-seven writers examine the impact of the Holocaust upon their lives. (REV: BL 11/1/89; LJ 12/89; NYTBR 1/28/90) **[940.53]**

5064 Shatyn, Bruno. *A Private War: Surviving in Poland on False Papers, 1941–1945.* **1985, Wayne State Univ. Pr. $32.50 (0-8143-1775-8).** An autobiography of a Polish Jewish youth who created false identification papers for himself and his relatives and survived the Holocaust. (REV: Choice 9/85; LJ 5/1/85) **[940.53]**

5065 Sherwin, Martin J. *A World Destroyed: Hiroshima and the Origins of the Arms Race.* **1987, Random paper $11.95 (0-394-75204-X).** A look at the relationship between politicians and scientists during and after the development of the atomic bomb, and how crucial government decisions led to its proliferation after World War II. (REV: Choice 3/76; LJ 9/1/75; NYTBR 12/21/75) **[940.53]**

5066 Simmons, Thomas E. *Escape from Archangel: An American Merchant Seaman at War.* **1990, Univ. Pr. of Mississippi $17.95 (0-87805-461-8).** An account of an American merchant seaman who was taken captive by Soviet authorities and sent to a forced labor camp during World War II. (REV: BL 11/15/90; LJ 11/1/90; PW 10/5/90) **[940.53]**

5067 Smith, Gene. *Dark Summer: An Intimate History of the Events That Led to World War II.* **1989, Macmillan paper $9.95 (0-02-037390-2).** An overview of the events of the summer of 1939 when the world was on the verge of the outbreak of World War II. (REV: BL 11/1/87; LJ 11/15/87; PW 10/30/87) **[940.53]**

5068 Smith, Graham. *When Jim Crow Met John Bull: Black American Soldiers in World War II in Britain.* **1987, St. Martin's $24.95 (0-312-01596-8).** A study of relations between the British and the

100,000 African-American soldiers who served there during World War II. (Rev: LJ 2/1/88; NYTBR 3/6/88; TLS 2/12/88) **[940.53]**

5069 Spiegelman, Art. *Maus: A Survivor's Tale.* **1986, Pantheon paper $9.95 (0-394-74723-2).** The first volume of a two-part comic strip detailing the experiences of the author's father during the Holocaust. "A stunning addition to Holocaust literature."—BL (Rev: BL 9/1/86; New Rep 6/22/87; Newsweek 9/22/86) **[940.53]**

5070 Spiegelman, Art. *Maus: A Survivor's Tale II and Hence My Troubles Began.* **1991, Pantheon $18.00 (0-394-55655-0).** A cartoon biography tracing the author's father's experiences at Auschwitz and as a Holocaust survivor. (Rev: BL 10/15/91; NYTBR 11/3/91. Awards: NYTBR, 1991; PW, 1991; PP: Special award, 1992) **[940.53]**

5071 Stone, I. F. *War Years, 1939–1945.* **1988, Little, Brown $18.95 (0-316-81771-6).** A collection of the author's columns for the *Nation* on World War II. "These pieces meld into a vivid newsreel that throws light on the 1940s—and the 80s."—PW (Rev: Choice 5/89; LJ 9/15/88; PW 7/1/88) **[940.53]**

5072 Sutherland, Christine. *Monica.* **1990, Farrar $21.95 (0-374-21215-5).** An account of the life of Monica Massy-Beresford, an active member of the Danish resistance against Nazi occupation. (Rev: BL 6/1/90; LJ 6/15/90; NYTBR 8/12/90) **[940.53]**

5073 Szwajger, Adina Blady. *I Remember Nothing More: The Warsaw Children's Hospital and the Jewish Resistance.* **1991, Pantheon $20.00 (0-679-40034-6).** Memoirs of a pediatrician who worked in the Warsaw ghetto under the Nazi occupation. "In the literature of the Holocaust, this journal is among the most memorable, haunting, and elegantly crafted."—PW (Rev: LJ 2/1/91; NYTBR 4/7/91; PW 1/11/91) **[940.53]**

5074 Tec, Nechama. *Dry Tears: The Story of a Lost Childhood.* **1984, Oxford Univ. Pr. paper $8.95 (0-19-503500-3).** The survival of a Jewish family in Poland during World War II as recounted by the author, who was eight at the time of the Nazi occupation. (Rev: LJ 5/1/82; PW 2/12/82) **[940.53]**

5075 Tec, Nechama. *When Light Pierced the Darkness: Christian Rescue of Jews in Nazi-Occupied Poland.* **1987, Oxford Univ. Pr. paper $8.95 (0-19-505194-7).** An account of a Jewish girl who was able to survive Nazi persecution due to the efforts of a Christian family that sheltered her for the duration of the war. (Rev: Choice 10/86; CSM 4/16/86; LJ 1/86) **[940.53]**

5076 Toland, John. *Last 100 Days.* **1966, Bantam paper $10.95 (0-553-34208-8).** A comprehensive look at the last three months of World War II in Europe. "Continually compelling . . . essential reading for anyone interested in the most terrible war in history."—Newsweek (Rev: Choice 9/66; NYTBR 2/13/66; Newsweek 3/7/66. Awards: ALA, 1966; NYTBR, 1966) **[940.53]**

5077 Toland, John. *Rising Sun: The Decline and Fall of the Japanese Empire, 1936–1945.* **1982, Bantam paper $6.95 (0-553-26435-4).** "Popular history in the best sense of the term."—NYTBR (Rev: Choice 3/71; CSM 12/18/70; NYTBR 11/29/70. Awards: PP:NF, 1971) **[940.53]**

5078 Tory, Avraham. *Surviving the Holocaust: The Kovno Ghetto Diary.* **Ed. by Martin Gilbert. 1990, Harvard Univ. Pr. $34.95 (0-674-85810-7).** A journal recording daily life in a Lithuanian Jewish ghetto under Nazi occupation. (Rev: BL 11/1/90; Choice 9/90; LJ 6/1/90) **[940.53]**

5079 Watt, Donald Cameron. *How War Came: The Immediate Origins of the Second World War.* **1989, Pantheon $29.95 (0-394-57916-X); paper $16.95 (0-679-73093-1).** A detailed look at the 11 months between the Munich Conference and the outbreak of World War II. (Rev: NYRB 10/12/89; NYTBR 9/3/89; New Yorker 10/23/89. Awards: NYTBR, 1989) **[940.53]**

5080 Weinstein, Frida Scheps. *A Hidden Childhood: A Jewish Girl's Sanctuary in a French Convent, 1942–1945.* **1986, Hill & Wang paper $6.95 (0-8090-1529-3).** An autobiography of a Jewish girl's life within a French country convent where she was sheltered from persecution during World War II. (Rev: BL 5/1/85; LJ 5/15/85; NYTBR 9/30/85) **[940.53]**

5081 Wicks, Ben. *No Time to Wave Goodbye.* **1989, St. Martin's $15.95 (0-312-03407-5).** An account of the mass evacuations of children from London during World War II based on the author's personal experience and the recollections of others who lived through the events. (Rev: BL 9/1/89; LJ 9/1/89; TLS 12/23/88) **[940.53]**

5082 Wiesenthal, Simon. *Justice Not Vengeance: Recollections.* **1990, Grove-Weidenfeld $21.95 (1-55584-341-7).** Memoirs of the Holocaust survivor who has devoted his life to tracking down Nazi war criminals. (Rev: BL 1/15/90; LJ 2/1/90; PW 1/5/90) **[940.53]**

5083 Wilhelm, Maria de Blasio. *Other Italy: Italian Resistance in World War II.* **1988, Norton $18.95 (0-393-02568-3).** A history of the Italian resistance during World War II against both the Nazi occupation and the Fascist government. (Rev: Choice 9/1/88; LJ 9/1/88; PW 7/8/88) **[940.53]**

5084 Wyman, David S. *Abandonment of the Jews: America and the Holocaust, 1941–1945.* **1984, Pantheon $19.95 (0-394-42813-7); paper $12.95 (0-394-74077-7).** America's lack of response to the plight of the Jews during World War II. "For the informed lay reader, this is the best available survey of the subject."—LJ (Rev: Choice 4/85; LJ 10/1/84; NYTBR 12/16/84. Awards: NYTBR, 1985; PW, 1985) **[940.53]**

5085 Yahil, Leni. *Holocaust: The Fate of European Jewry, 1932–1945.* **1990, Oxford Univ. Pr. $35.00 (0-19-504522-X).** A history of the Holocaust in Europe as perceived by an Israeli scholar. "The most comprehensive one-volume work available."—LJ

(REV: BL 10/1/90; LJ 10/1/90; NYTBR 11/4/90. AWARDS: LJ, 1990)   **[940.53]**

5086 Zuccotti, Susan. *Italians and the Holocaust: Persecution, Rescue and Survival*. 1987, Basic Books $19.95 (0-465-03622-8). A study of the effects of the Holocaust on Italian Jews revealing how and why their survival rate was much higher than that of other occupied European nations. (REV: Atl 7/87; Choice 9/87; LJ 2/15/87)   **[940.53]**

World War II—Military history

5087 Abzug, Robert H. *Inside the Vicious Heart: Americans and the Liberation of Nazi Concentration Camps*. 1985, Oxford Univ. Pr. $24.95 (0-19-503597-6); paper $9.95 (0-19-504236-0). An account of the psychological reactions of American soldiers who discovered and liberated the Nazi death camps at the end of World War II. (REV: Choice 9/85; LJ 5/15/85)   **[940.54]**

5088 Ambrose, Stephen E. *Pegasus Bridge: June 6, 1944*. 1988, Simon & Schuster paper $7.95 (0-671-67156-1). An account of the British capture of two bridges vital to the Allied cause in the opening hours of D-Day. (REV: BL 4/1/85; LJ 3/1/85; NYTBR 4/28/85)   **[940.54]**

5089 Anderson, Clarence E., and Joseph P. Hamelin. *To Fly and Fight: Memoirs of a Triple Ace*. 1990, St. Martin's $19.95 (0-312-05171-9). Memoirs of a former Air Force test pilot and veteran of bombing runs in World War II and Vietnam. (REV: BL 11/1/90; LJ 10/15/90; PW 10/12/90)   **[940.54]**

5090 Arad, Yitzhak. *Belzec, Sobibor, Treblinka: The Operation Reinhard Death Camps*. 1987, Indiana Univ. Pr. $29.95 (0-253-34293-7). A history of the Nazi death camps of Belzec, Sobibor, and Treblinka in occupied Poland. (REV: Choice 10/87; LJ 5/15/87; NYTBR 6/28/87)   **[940.54]**

5091 Armor, John C., Peter Wright, and Ansel Adams. *Manzanar*. 1988, Random $27.50 (0-8129-1727-8). A photographic essay by Ansel Adams is complemented by the authors' writings about life in the California internment camp for Japanese Americans. (REV: BL 11/1/88; LJ 11/1/88; NYTBR 2/12/89)   **[940.54]**

5092 Barnett, Correlli. *Engage the Enemy More Closely: The Royal Navy in the Second World War*. 1991, Norton $35.00 (0-393-02918-2). A study of the activities and operations of the British Royal Navy during World War II. (REV: BL 6/1/91; LJ 5/15/91; PW 4/26/91. AWARDS: BL, 1991)   **[940.54]**

5093 Berube, Allan. *Coming Out Under Fire: The History of Gay Men and Women in World War II*. 1990, Free Pr. $22.95 (0-02-903100-1); Dutton paper $10.95 (0-452-26598-3). A study of homosexuals who served in American armed forces during World War II. (REV: LJ 3/1/90; NYTBR 4/8/90; PW 2/2/90)   **[940.54]**

5094 Boas, Jacob. *Boulevard des Miseres: The Story of Transit Camp Westerbork*. 1985, Shoe String $22.50 (0-208-01977-4). A portrait of the workings of a Nazi concentration camp in Holland that served as a way station for Jews before their deportation to the death camps. (REV: BL 4/15/85; LJ 7/85; NYTBR 10/20/85)   **[940.54]**

5095 Bradley, Omar, and Clay Blair. *A General's Life: An Autobiography*. 1989, TAB $19.95 (0-8306-3312-X); Simon & Schuster paper $15.95 (0-671-41024-5). The World War II and Korean War general's autobiography completed after his death in 1981 by Blair, who had worked closely with him on the project. (REV: Choice 7–8/83; CSM 4/27/83; LJ 2/1/83)   **[940.54]**

5096 Breuer, William B. *Operation Torch: The Allied Gamble to Invade North Africa*. 1988, St. Martin's paper $3.95 (0-312-90125-9). An account of the 1942 Allied invasion of North Africa. (REV: BL 2/15/86; LJ 2/1/86; PW 2/14/86)   **[940.54]**

5097 Breuer, William B. *Retaking the Philippines: America's Return to Corregidor and Bataan, July 1944–March 1945*. 1987, St. Martin's paper $3.95 (0-312-90788-5). A military and political history of General MacArthur's reconquest of the Philippines. (REV: BL 11/15/86; LJ 11/15/86; PW 10/31/86)   **[940.54]**

5098 Casey, William J. *Secret War Against Hitler*. 1988, Regnery Gateway $19.95 (0-89526-563-X); Berkley paper $4.50 (0-425-11615-8). An account of American World War II intelligence activities as recalled by the former CIA director. (REV: BL 5/15/88; LJ 4/15/88; NYTBR 9/25/88)   **[940.54]**

5099 Charles, H. Robert. *Last Man Out*. Ed. by Melissa Roberts. 1988, Eakin $16.95 (0-89015-647-6). An account of the building of the Burma Road during World War II by the Japanese by a former prisoner of war involved in its construction. (REV: LJ 5/15/88; NYTBR 9/19/88)   **[940.54]**

5100 Clare, George. *Last Waltz in Vienna: The Rise and Destruction of a Family, 1842–1942*. 1981, Henry Holt paper $9.95 (0-8050-1039-4). A biography of the author's family from the mid-nineteenth century to its dissolution during the Holocaust. (REV: LJ 3/15/82; NYTBR 3/28/82; TLS 3/26/82) **[940.54]**

5101 D'Este, Carlo. *Bitter Victory: The Battle for Sicily, 1943*. 1988, Dutton $27.50 (0-525-24471-9). A study of the 1943 campaign for the control of Sicily. "A major contribution to World War II history."—BL (REV: BL 8/88; NYTBR 11/27/88; TLS 9/16/88)   **[940.54]**

5102 Durand, Arthur A. *Stalag Luft III: The Secret Story*. 1988, Louisiana State Univ. Pr. $29.95 (0-8071-1352-2); Simon & Schuster paper $10.95 (0-671-68298-9). A history of the German World War II prisoner of war camp. (REV: BL 5/1/88; Choice 12/88; PW 5/6/88)   **[940.54]**

5103 Ellis, John. *Brute Force: Allied Strategy and Tactics in the Second World War*. 1990, Viking $29.95 (0-670-80773-7). A critical view of World War II Allied strategy contending that the war could have ended sooner using different tactics. (REV: BL 10/1/90; LJ 9/15/90; PW 8/24/90)   **[940.54]**

5104 Felsen, Milt. *Anti-Warrior: A Memoir.* 1989, Univ. of Iowa Pr. $24.95 (0-87745-222-9); paper $9.95 (0-87745-241-5). Memoirs of an American veteran who served in the Abraham Lincoln Brigade during the Spanish Civil War and was held as a prisoner of war in Germany during the Second World War. (REV: LJ 3/15/89; PW 2/17/89) **[940.54]**

5105 Frank, Richard B. *Guadalcanal.* 1990, Random $34.95 (0-394-58875-4). An account of the six-month land and sea battle between American and Japanese forces for control of the strategic Solomon Island. "Highly readable . . . first-rate military history."—PW (REV: BL 10/1/90; LJ 9/15/90; PW 10/19/90) **[940.54]**

5106 Fussell, Paul. *Wartime: Understanding and Behavior in the Second World War.* 1989, Oxford Univ. Pr. $19.95 (0-19-503797-9); paper $9.95 (0-19-506577-8). A study of the lives and mental state of American and British soldiers of World War II. "This brilliant, engaging cultural history quietly subverts our whitewashed collective memory of the war."—PW (REV: New Rep 11/13/89; Newsweek 9/4/89; PW 7/14/89) **[940.54]**

5107 Gesensway, Deborah, and Mindy Roseman. *Beyond Words: Images from America's Concentration Camps.* 1987, Cornell Univ. Pr. $29.95 (0-8014-1919-0); paper $18.95 (0-8014-9522-9). Recollections and art works of Japanese-Americans who were interned in U.S. concentration camps. (REV: Choice 10/87; LJ 5/1/87; NYTBR 7/19/87) **[940.54]**

5108 Green, Anne Bosanko. *One Woman's War: Letters Home from the Women's Army Corps, 1944–46.* 1989, Minnesota Historical Society $22.50 (0-87351-246-4). Selected letters from a Women's Army Corps member written to her family about her World War II experiences. (REV: BL 12/1/89; LJ 12/89) **[940.54]**

5109 Hammel, Eric. *Guadalcanal: Starvation Island.* 1987, Crown $24.95 (0-517-56417-3). An analysis of the 1942 struggle between the Japanese and American armed forces for the control of the island of Guadalcanal. "The most comprehensive popular account to date."—PW (REV: BL 2/15/87; LJ 2/15/87; PW 1/30/87) **[940.54]**

5110 Hapgood, David, and David Richardson. *Monte Cassino.* 1987, Berkley paper $3.95 (0-425-08480-9). An account of the destruction of the Benedictine abbey of Monte Cassino by American armed forces in 1944. "There are many works on the battle but none finer than this . . . popular history at its best."—LJ (REV: BL 3/15/84; LJ 3/1/84; NYTBR 3/25/84. AWARDS: LJ, 1984) **[940.54]**

5111 Hastings, Max. *Overlord: D-Day and the Battle for Normandy.* 1985, Simon & Schuster paper $10.95 (0-671-55435-2). An examination of the Allied and Nazi ground forces involved in D-Day and ensuing battles for position in Normandy. (REV: NYTBR 6/24/84; New Yorker 6/18/84; TLS 6/8/84) **[940.54]**

5112 Hastings, Max, and George Stevens, Jr. *Victory over Europe: D-Day to V-E Day.* 1985, Little, Brown $25.00 (0-316-81334-6). Hastings's historical account of the last days of World War II in Europe, accompanied by still pictures from a documentary film shot by Stevens, an American director. (REV: BL 6/15/85; PW 4/12/85; TLS 5/17/85) **[940.54]**

5113 Hillesum, Etty. *An Interrupted Life: The Diaries of Etty Hillesum, 1941–1943.* 1983, Pantheon $13.95 (0-394-53217-1); Pocket paper $4.95 (0-671-66655-X). A diary of a Dutch Jewish woman who lived under the German occupation before being sent to her death in Auschwitz. (REV: LJ 12/15/83; New Rep 3/26/84; NYTBR 1/29/84) **[940.54]**

5114 Hoyt, Edwin P. *Japan's War: The Great Pacific Conflict, 1853–1952.* 1986, McGraw-Hill $19.95 (0-07-030612-5); Da Capo paper $14.95 (0-306-80348-8). A history of Japan's relations with the United States told from the Japanese perspective and concentrating on World War II and the American occupation following the war. (REV: BL 1/15/86; LJ 3/15/86; NYTBR 4/6/86) **[940.54]**

5115 Hoyt, Edwin P. *To the Marianas: War in the Central Pacific.* 1983, Avon paper $3.95 (0-380-65839-9). A military history of the war in the Pacific theater in 1944. (REV: BL 2/1/81; LJ 2/15/81; PW 10/31/80) **[940.54]**

5116 Huberband, Shimon. *Kiddush Hashem: Jewish Religious and Cultural Life in Poland during the Holocaust.* 1988, KTAV $35.00 (0-88125-118-6); $19.95 paper (0-88125-121-6). A Polish Orthodox rabbi's description of Jewish religious life under Nazi rule up to the point of his death in Treblinka in 1942. (REV: Choice 10/88; LJ 9/1/87; NYTBR 1/17/88) **[940.54]**

5117 Hynes, Samuel. *Flights of Passage: Recollections of a World War II Aviator.* 1988, Naval Institute Pr. $16.95 (0-87021-215-X); Pocket paper $4.50 (0-671-67410-2). Memoirs of a Marine lieutenant's training and service in the Pacific theater of World War II as a bomber pilot. (REV: LJ 5/1/88; Natl Rev 6/24/88; Time 3/7/88) **[940.54]**

5118 Keegan, John. *Six Armies in Normandy: From D-Day to the Liberation of Paris.* 1983, Penguin paper $8.95 (0-14-005293-3). The story of D-Day, the Battle of Normandy, and the drive to Paris told in terms of the six armies that took part in the conflict—American, British, Canadian, Polish, French, and German. "A must for even occasional readers of military history."—BL (REV: BL 4/1/82; Choice 11/82; NYTBR 8/15/82. AWARDS: ALA, 1982) **[940.54]**

5119 Koger, Fred. *Countdown! Thirty-Five Missions Over Germany.* 1990, Algonquin $18.95 (0-945575-17-3). An account of the author's 35 missions flown over Germany during World War II as a B-17 bomber pilot. (REV: LJ 9/15/90; PW 8/31/90) **[940.54]**

5120 Kurzman, Dan. *Day of the Bomb: Countdown to Hiroshima.* 1987, McGraw-Hill paper $5.95 (0-07-035688-2). Studies of the events leading up to the atomic bombing of Hiroshima and its effects upon the people involved. (REV: BL 10/1/85; PW 10/25/85) **[940.54]**

5121   Kurzman, Dan. *Final Voyage: The Sinking of the USS Indianapolis.* 1990, Atheneum $19.95 (0-689-12007-9). A study of the 1945 sinking of an American cruiser by the Japanese near the close of World War II. (Rev: Choice 12/90; LJ 5/15/90; NYTBR 8/12/90)   **[940.54]**

5122   La Forte, Robert S., and Ronald E. Marcello, eds. *Remembering Pearl Harbor: Eyewitness Accounts by U.S. Military Men and Women.* 1991, Scholarly Research $24.95 (0-8420-2371-2). Selections from over 350 interviewees who witnessed the Japanese bombing of Pearl Harbor on December 7, 1941. (Rev: BL 12/1/90; LJ 11/1/90; PW 12/14/90)   **[940.54]**

5123   Larrabee, Eric. *Commander in Chief: Franklin Delano Roosevelt, His Lieutenants and Their War.* 1987, Harper & Row $25.00 (0-06-039050-6); Simon & Schuster paper $12.95 (0-671-66382-8). A study of the relationship between FDR and his military commanders. "A delight to read, the book is as fluently written as it is sophisticated."—LJ (Rev: BL 3/1/87; LJ 5/1/87; NYTBR 8/16/87)   **[940.54]**

5124   Layton, Edwin T., and Roger Pineau. *"And I Was There": Pearl Harbor and Midway—Breaking the Secrets.* 1985, Morrow $19.95 (0-688-04883-8); paper $12.95 (0-688-06968-1). Memoirs of a former rear admiral and naval intelligence officer regarding the Japanese attack on Pearl Harbor and the American victory at the Battle of Midway. (Rev: BL 12/1/85; LJ 2/1/86; New Yorker 4/14/86)   **[940.54]**

5125   Levi, Primo. *Drowned and the Saved.* 1988, Summit $17.95 (0-671-63280-9); Random paper $8.95 (0-679-72186-X). The Italian writer's final work, completed shortly before his suicide, contains his remembrances of and meditations upon the Holocaust. (Rev: New Rep 3/21/88; NYTBR 1/10/88; Time 12/28/87)   **[940.54]**

5126   Lewis, Norman. *Naples '44.* 1985, Pantheon paper $7.95 (0-394-72300-7). The author kept this diary while serving in Naples with the British Field Security Police. "If for some reason I were limited to owning no more than ten books on World War II, Lewis's would be one of them."—Ted Morgan, Sat Rev (Rev: NYTBR 3/18/79; Newsweek 4/2/79; Sat Rev 7/7/79. Awards: ALA, 1979)   **[940.54]**

5127   Liddell-Hart, B. H. *History of the Second World War.* 1980, Putnam paper $15.95 (0-399-50445-1). Liddell-Hart's final work; a product of 20 years of research. "A military study of incomparable importance . . . the best military study of the war and a must for any library."—Choice (Rev: Choice 6/71; LJ 4/15/71; PW 2/1/71. Awards: ALA, 1971)   **[940.54]**

5128   Lifton, Betty Jean. *A Place Called Hiroshima.* 1985, Kodansha $24.95 (0-87011-649-5). An illustrated study of the city of Hiroshima and its recovery after the dropping of the atomic bomb. (Rev: BL 10/1/85; LJ 7/85; PW 6/21/85)   **[940.54]**

5129   Loftus, John. *Belarus Secret: The Nazi Connection in America.* 1982, Knopf $18.95 (0-394-52292-3); Paragon House paper $12.95 (1-55778-138-

9). An account of the sheltering of Nazi criminals in the United States following World War II in exchange for anti-Soviet intelligence. (Rev: Choice 4/83; CSM 2/2/83; LJ 12/15/82)   **[940.54]**

5130   Lukacs, John. *Duel 10 May–31 July 1940: The Eighty-Day Struggle Between Churchill and Hitler.* 1991, Ticknor & Fields $19.95 (0-89919-967-4). An examination of the personal ideological and political struggle between Churchill and Hitler and their nations in the summer of 1940. (Rev: BL 12/15/90; LJ 12/90; NYTBR 3/3/91)   **[940.54]**

5131   Manchester, William. *Goodbye, Darkness: A Memoir of the Pacific War.* 1980, Little, Brown $17.95 (0-316-54501-5); Dell paper $5.95 (0-440-32907-8). The author of *The Death of a President* discusses his personal experiences as a U.S. Marine sergeant in the South Pacific during World War II. "The most probing and searing account of combat in World War II."—Natl Rev (Rev: CSM, 9/10/80; LJ 9/1/80; Natl Rev 11/14/80. Awards: ALA, 1980; BL, the 1980s)   **[940.54]**

5132   Mendenhall, Corwin. *Submarine Diary.* 1990, Algonquin $18.95 (0-945575-34-3). A diary of a submarine officer detailing his experiences during World War II in the Pacific theater. (Rev: BL 12/15/90; LJ 12/90; PW 12/7/90)   **[940.54]**

5133   Montyn, Jan, and Dirk Ayelt Kooiman. *Lamb to Slaughter.* 1986, Carroll & Graf paper $8.95 (0-88184-207-9). Memoirs of a Dutch youth's experiences in the German navy during World War II. (Rev: BL 2/1/85; LJ 2/1/85)   **[940.54]**

5134   Mowat, Farley. *And No Birds Sang.* 1980, Little, Brown $14.95 (0-316-58695-1); Bantam paper $3.95 (0-7704-2237-3). The Canadian writer's remembrances of his service in World War II in southern Italy and Sicily. (Rev: CSM 4/14/80; LJ 1/15/80; NYTBR 2/24/80)   **[940.54]**

5135   Muirhead, John. *Those Who Fall.* 1986, Random $18.95 (0-394-54983-X); Pocket paper $4.50 (0-671-64944-2). Memoirs of a B-17 bomber pilot who flew missions over Italy, Germany, and Rumania prior to his being shot down and captured in Bulgaria. "One of the finest World War II reminiscences to be published in recent years."—BL (Rev: BL 1/1/87; LJ 1/87; NYTBR 2/15/87)   **[940.54]**

5136   Pergrin, David E., and Eric Hammel. *First Across the Rhine: The Story of the 291st Engineer Combat Battalion.* 1989, Macmillan $21.95 (0-689-12033-8); Ivy Books paper $4.95 (0-8041-0615-0). The history of the 291st Engineer Combat Battalion and its heroic campaigns during World War II. (Rev: BL 5/15/89; LJ 6/1/89; PW 5/5/89)   **[940.54]**

5137   Phibbs, Brendan. *Other Side of Time: A Combat Surgeon in World War II.* 1989, Pocket paper $4.50 (0-671-66574-X). Memoirs of a surgeon's experiences serving in the European theater of the Second World War. "One of the finest memoirs, medical or military, of recent note."—BL (Rev: BL 5/15/87; LJ 5/15/87; PW 4/17/87)   **[940.54]**

5138 Pogue, Forrest C. *George C. Marshall: Statesman, 1945–1959.* 1987, Viking $29.95 (0-670-81042-8); Penguin paper $12.95 (0-14-011909-4). The fourth and concluding volume of the author's study of the American general and statesman's life, focusing on his post-World War II career. (Rev: Atl 6/87; LJ 6/15/87; NYTBR 6/28/87) **[940.54]**

5139 Posner, Gerald L., and John Ware. *Mengele: The Complete Story.* 1987, Dell paper $4.95 (0-440-15579-7). An account of the infamous Nazi doctor and his years as a fugitive from the end of World War II to his 1979 death in Brazil. (Rev: BL 5/1/86; LJ 6/1/86; NYRB 5/28/87) **[940.54]**

5140 Potter, E. B. *Bull Halsey: A Biography.* 1985, Naval Institute Pr. $24.95 (0-87021-146-3). A biography of the American Admiral William Halsey noted for his successful naval campaigns in the Pacific during World War II. (Rev: BL 10/15/85; Choice 3/86; LJ 11/1/85) **[940.54]**

5141 Prange, Gordon W. *At Dawn We Slept: The Untold Story of Pearl Harbor.* 1982, Penguin paper $14.95 (0-14-006455-9). An examination of the Japanese bombing of Pearl Harbor by a historian who spent nearly four decades researching the event. (Rev: BL 10/1/81; New Rep 12/30/81; TLS 6/4/82) **[940.54]**

5142 Prange, Gordon W. *December 7, 1941: The Day the Japanese Attacked Pearl Harbor.* 1988, McGraw-Hill $22.95 (0-07-050682-5); Warner paper $14.95 (0-446-38997-8). A chronological presentation of the events surrounding the bombing of Pearl Harbor based on eyewitness accounts by the author of *At Dawn We Slept.* (Rev: BL 10/15/87; Choice 5/88; LJ 10/15/87) **[940.54]**

5143 Ramsey, Edwin Price, and Stephen J. Rivele. *Lieutenant Ramsey's War.* 1990, Knightsbridge $19.95 (1-877961-58-2). An autobiography of a former World War II guerrilla leader in the Philippines who stayed to fight after the bulk of Allied forces evacuated. (Rev: LJ 10/15/90; PW 9/28/90) **[940.54]**

5144 Ross, Bill D. *Iwo Jima: Legacy of Valor.* 1986, Random paper $10.95 (0-394-74288-5). An account of the fierce month-long battle between Japanese and American troops for control of the strategic island of Iwo Jima. (Rev: LJ 3/5/85; NYTBR 4/21/85; Newsweek 3/25/85) **[940.54]**

5145 Sajer, Guy. *Forgotten Soldier.* 1988, Nautical and Aviation $19.95 (0-933852-82-7); Pergamon paper $15.95 (0-08-037437-9). Remembrances of a German soldier's experiences fighting in the Wehrmacht during World War II. "Few memoirs can compare with this work in range of feeling, depths of self-analysis, or vivid recounting of combat."—LJ (Rev: Atl 2/71; LJ 12/15/70; Time 1/25/71. Awards: ALA, 1971) **[940.54]**

5146 Salisbury, Harrison E. *900 Days: The Siege of Leningrad.* 1985, DaCapo paper $15.95 (0-306-80253-8). The siege of Leningrad by the German army from 1941 to 1944. "His book is certainly the most detailed account of the siege written in a Western language, and also the most moving."—NYRB (Rev: LJ 2/15/69; NYRB 4/10/69; Newsweek 1/27/69. Awards: ALA, 1969) **[940.54]**

5147 Selden, Kyoto, and Mark Selden, eds. *Atomic Bomb: Voices from Hiroshima and Nagasaki.* 1989, M. E. Sharpe $29.95 (0-87332-556-7); paper $14.95 (0-87332-773-X). Collected writings and photographs detailing the stories of individuals who survived the bombings of Hiroshima and Nagasaki. (Rev: BL 10/15/89; LJ 9/15/89) **[940.54]**

5148 Sheehan, Susan. *A Missing Plane.* 1986, Putnam $18.95 (0-399-13183-3); Berkley paper $3.50 (0-425-10553-9). An account of the 1982 recovery of an American bomber in New Guinea that had been missing since the Second World War. (Rev: BL 10/15/86; LJ 11/15/86; NYTBR 10/19/86) **[940.54]**

5149 Spector, Ronald H. *Eagle Against the Sun: The American War with Japan.* 1984, Free Pr. $24.95 (0-02-930360-5). A study of the American-Japanese conflict in World War II by a military history scholar. "The best one-volume account of the war in the Pacific to date."—LJ (Rev: Choice 3/85; LJ 11/1/84; NYTBR 12/16/84. Awards: LJ, 1984) **[940.54]**

5150 Stevenson, William. *Man Called Intrepid: The Secret War.* 1982, Ballantine paper $4.95 (0-345-31023-3). The wartime activities of Sir William Stephenson, a Canadian who coordinated British intelligence actions against the Axis from New York. (Rev: BL 5/1/76; NYTBR 2/29/76; PW 1/12/76) **[940.54]**

5151 Thomas, Gordon, and Max Morgan-Witts. *Ruin from the Air: The Atomic Mission to Hiroshima.* 1990, Scarborough paper $14.95 (0-8128-8509-0). An updated and expanded version of the authors' *Enola Gay,* detailing the mission to drop the atomic bomb on the Japanese city of Hiroshima during World War II. (Rev: BL 9/1/90; LJ 8/90) **[940.54]**

5152 Van der Vat, Dan. *Pacific Campaign: World War II; the U.S.-Japanese Naval War, 1941–1945.* 1991, Simon & Schuster $28.00 (0-671-73899-2). An analysis of the naval war between Japan and the United States in the Pacific during World War II. "A valuable addition to all military collections."—BL (Rev: BL 12/1/91; PW 11/15/91) **[940.54]**

5153 Vassiltchikov, Marie. *Berlin Diaries, 1940–1945.* 1987, Knopf $19.95 (0-394-55624-0); Random paper $8.95 (0-394-75777-7). A diary of a Russian emigré who lived in Berlin during World War II and was involved in the failed assassination attempt on Hitler in July 1944. (Rev: LJ 2/15/87; Natl Rev 3/27/87; NYRB 4/9/87) **[940.54]**

5154 Waterford, Helen. *Commitment to the Dead: One Woman's Journey Toward Understanding.* 1987, Random paper $9.95 (0-939650-62-2). Memoirs of a German Jewish woman who survived Auschwitz, but lost her friends and family in the death camp. (Rev: BL 10/1/87; Choice 4/88; LJ 11/15/87) **[940.54]**

5155 Watt, George. *Comet Connection: Escape from Hitler's Europe.* 1990, Univ. Pr. of Kentucky $21.00 (0-8131-1720-8). An account of an American pilot's escape to freedom through Belgium, France, and Spain after his plane was downed in 1943. (REV: BL 6/15/90; LJ 5/15/90; PW 6/8/90) **[940.54]**

5156 Weintraub, Stanley. *Long Day's Journey into War: December 7, 1941.* 1991, Dutton $26.95 (0-525-93344-1). A study of the social and political climate of the world on the day Pearl Harbor was bombed. "Without question one of the best and most important Second World War-oriented books to emerge in the past ten years."—BL (REV: BL 9/15/91; LJ 7/91; NYTBR 9/1/91. AWARDS: LJ, 1991; PW, 1991) **[940.54]**

5157 Whiting, Charles. *Battle of Hurtgen Forest: The Untold Story of a Disastrous Campaign.* 1988, Crown $18.95 (0-517-56675-3). An account of the controversial six-month battle for the control of Hurtgen Forest in which American troops suffered 30,000 casualties. (REV: LJ 2/1/89; PW 3/3/89) **[940.54]**

5158 Willmott, H. P. *Great Crusade: A New Complete History of the Second World War.* 1990, Free Pr. $24.95 (0-02-934715-7). A single-volume history of the Second World War. "His concision is remarkable; his commentary illuminating."—Natl Rev (REV: LJ 10/15/90; Natl Rev 12/17/90) **[940.54]**

5159 Winston, Keith. *V . . . Mail: Letters of a World War II Combat Medic.* Ed. by Sarah Winston. 1985, Algonquin $14.95 (0-912697-28-8). Letters from a World War II combat medic to his wife detailing his training and service in the European theater. (REV: BL 11/1/85; LJ 9/15/85; NYTBR 10/6/85) **[940.54]**

1945–

5160 Kramer, Jane. *Europeans.* 1988, Farrar $22.95 (0-374-14939-9); Penguin paper $10.95 (0-14-012808-5). A collection of 30 essays originally published in the *New Yorker* regarding various aspects of European life, culture, and politics. (REV: BL 9/15/88; LJ 11/15/88; NYTBR 12/25/88) **[940.55]**

5161 Lewis, Flora. *Europe: A Tapestry of Nations.* 1988, Simon & Schuster paper $10.95 (0-671-66829-3). A survey of the history and culture of 25 European countries by a *New York Times* correspondent. (REV: BL 10/15/87; LJ 12/87; PW 10/9/87) **[940.55]**

941 British Isles

5162 Girouard, Mark. *Return to Camelot: Chivalry and the English Gentleman.* 1981, Yale Univ. Pr. $45.00 (0-300-02739-7); paper $15.95 (0-300-03473-3). A study of nineteenth-century English manners tracing their origins to the medieval code of chivalry. (REV: NYRB 11/19/81; NYTBR 10/19/81; Newsweek 10/12/81) **[941]**

5163 Gissing, Vera. *Pearls of Childhood.* 1989, St. Martin's $16.95 (0-312-02963-2). Memoirs of the author's childhood during and after World War II. (REV: BL 5/15/89; LJ 6/1/89) **[941]**

5164 Hibbert, Christopher. *English: A Social History, 1066–1945.* 1987, Norton $39.95 (0-393-02371-0). A study of English social life and customs from the time of William the Conqueror to the end of the Second World War. (REV: Choice 9/87; LJ 5/15/87; NYTBR 4/12/87) **[941]**

Norman period, 1066–1154

5165 Wood, Michael. *Domesday: A Search for the Roots of England.* 1988, Facts on File $24.95 (0-8160-1832-4). An examination of the Domesday Book, a census of England conducted in 1066, with reproductions from the original manuscripts. (REV: LJ 6/1/88; PW 3/4/88) **[941.02]**

Tudor period, 1485–1603

5166 Fraser, Antonia. *Mary, Queen of Scots.* 1984, Dell paper $6.95 (0-440-35476-5). A biography of the Scottish queen beheaded by Elizabeth I in 1587. "Full of interesting detail . . . rich in human interest."—NYTBR (REV: LJ 12/15/69; NYTBR 11/23/69; Time 10/17/69. AWARDS: ALA, 1969) **[941.05]**

1714–1837

5167 Ayling, Stanley. *Edmund Burke: His Life and Opinions.* 1988, St. Martin's $19.95 (0-312-02686-2). A biography of the eighteenth-century Irish/English political theorist that draws heavily upon Burke's personal papers. (REV: BL 1/1/89; LJ 2/15/89; TLS 12/16/88) **[941.07]**

5168 Cruickshank, Dan, and Neil Burton. *Life in the Georgian City.* 1990, Viking $35.00 (0-670-81266-8). A portrait of everyday life in eighteenth-century London. (REV: NYTBR 12/2/90; TLS 5/11/90) **[941.07]**

5169 Erickson, Carolly. *Bonnie Prince Charles: A Biography.* 1989, Morrow $19.95 (0-688-06087-0); paper $12.95 (0-688-10006-6). A biography of the eighteenth-century British prince whose efforts to restore the Stuart line to the monarchy failed. (REV: BL 12/1/88; LJ 12/88; NYTBR 1/8/89) **[941.07]**

5170 Erickson, Carolly. *Our Tempestuous Day: A History of Regency England.* 1987, Morrow paper $8.95 (0-688-07292-5). A study of the Regency period of early nineteenth-century England by the historian known for her series of Tudor biographies. (REV: Choice 7–8/86; LJ 1/86; NYTBR 6/29/86) **[941.07]**

5171 Fraser, Flora. *Emma, Lady Hamilton.* 1988, Paragon House paper $10.95 (1-55778-008-0). A biography of the blacksmith's daughter who married Lord Hamilton, was the mistress of Admiral Nelson, and the subject of portraits by Romney. "This highly readable work becomes the standard life."—LJ (REV: LJ 4/1/87; PW 2/27/87; TLS 12/5/86) **[941.07]**

1837–

5172 Bradford, Sarah. *Disraeli.* 1983, Scarborough $19.95 (0-8128-2399-2); paper $12.95 (0-8128-6251-1). A life of the nineteenth-century British prime minister. "Reliable and well written . . . the best work on Disraeli for the general reader."—TLS (REV: LJ 3/15/83; NYTBR 7/10/83; TLS 1/28/83) **[941.08]**

5173 **Cannadine, David.** *Pleasures of the Past.* **1989, Norton $19.95 (0-393-02756-2).** Collected book reviews on British history written during the 1980s. "Beautiful pieces of prose, recommended for anyone with a historical bent."—BL (REV: BL 10/1/89; LJ 10/15/89; NYTBR 11/19/89) **[941.08]**

5174 **Chesshyre, Robert.** *Return of a Native Reporter.* **1988, Viking $18.95 (0-670-81734-1).** A caustic look at England in the latter half of the 1980s by a former correspondent of the *London Observer* who returned to his homeland after working for four years in the United States. (REV: BL 6/15/88; NYTBR 8/28/88; TLS 11/27/87) **[941.08]**

5175 **Clive, John.** *Macaulay: The Shaping of the Historian.* **1987, Harvard Univ. Pr. $14.95 (0-674-54005-0).** A thorough examination of the first 38 years of the English historian's life. (REV: Atl 4/73; NYTBR 4/1/73; Newsweek 8/6/73. AWARDS: ALA, 1973; NBA, 1974; NYTBR, 1973; Time, 1973) **[941.08]**

5176 **Colville, John.** *Fringes of Power: 10 Downing Street Diaries, 1939–1955.* **1987, Norton paper $12.95 (0-393-30411-6).** Diaries of the private secretary to Prime Ministers Churchill and Attlee. "One of the most interesting and readable of the major diaries of World War II and its aftermath."—PW (REV: NYTBR 11/24/85; Newsweek 11/25/85; PW 10/11/85) **[941.08]**

5177 **Critchfield, Richard.** *An American Looks at Britain.* **1990, Doubleday $21.95 (0-385-24456-8).** A study of contemporary British society and culture and its decline during the twentieth century. (REV: BL 5/15/90; NYTBR 7/15/90; PW 4/27/90) **[941.08]**

5178 **Ewart-Biggs, Jane.** *Pay, Pack and Follow: Memoirs.* **1986, Academy Chicago $16.95 (0-89733-186-9); paper $8.95 (0-89733-206-7).** Memoirs of the wife of a British diplomat describing their experiences in Algeria, Belgium, France, and Ireland. (REV: LJ 4/15/86; TLS 5/31/85) **[941.08]**

5179 **Gilbert, Martin.** *Winston S. Churchill, 1945–1965, Vol. VIII: Never Despair.* **1988, Houghton $40.00 (0-395-41918-2).** The eighth and concluding volume of Churchill's official biography. "A lively, stimulating biographical statement worthy of its complicated, consequential subject."—BL (REV: BL 9/15/88; LJ 11/1/88; NYTBR 10/23/88) **[941.08]**

5180 **Girouard, Mark.** *English Town: A History of Urban Life.* **1990, Yale Univ. Pr. $39.95 (0-300-04635-9).** An illustrated history of the rise, development, and organization of English towns and cities. (REV: BL 9/1/90; CSM 8/22/90; TLS 5/11/90) **[941.08]**

5181 **Heald, Tom.** *Philip: A Portrait of the Duke of Edinburgh.* **1991, Morrow $23.00 (0-688-10199-2).** The official biography of the British prince, written with the cooperation of Buckingham Palace to commemorate the duke's seventieth birthday. (REV: BL 10/15/91; LJ 10/1/91) **[941.08]**

5182 **Healey, Denis.** *Time of My Life.* **1990, Norton $29.95 (0-393-02875-5).** An autobiography of the British Labor party figure and former defense minister. "Literate, entertaining, and revealing."—New Yorker (REV: NYTBR 9/23/90; New Yorker 12/3/90; PW 8/17/90) **[941.08]**

5183 **Himmelfarb, Gertrude.** *Marriage and Morals Among the Victorians and Other Essays.* **1987, Random paper $9.95 (0-394-75290-2).** A collection of essays regarding influential English thinkers of the nineteenth century and their impact upon society and morality. (REV: BL 4/1/86; NYTBR 3/23/86; TLS 7/25/86) **[941.08]**

5184 **Hoare, Philip.** *Serious Pleasures: The Life of Stephen Tennant.* **1991, Viking $29.95 (0-241-12416-6).** A biography of the English writer and artist known for his wit and eccentricities. (REV: LJ 12/90; NYTBR 2/3/91; PW 11/30/90) **[941.08]**

5185 **Horne, Alistair.** *Harold Macmillan: 1894–1986.* **1989, Viking $52.45 (0-670-80502-5).** A two-volume biography of the former British prime minister. "Essential for modern British history collections."—LJ (REV: LJ 2/1/89; NYTBR 4/5/89; TLS 10/14/88. AWARDS: NYTBR, 1989) **[941.08]**

5186 **James, Robert Rhodes.** *Anthony Eden: A Biography.* **1987, McGraw-Hill $22.95 (0-07-032285-6).** A biography of the British statesman and former prime minister based on Eden's private papers. (REV: BL 7/87; LJ 7/87; TLS 10/31/86) **[941.08]**

5187 **Jenkins, Peter.** *Mrs. Thatcher's Revolution: The Ending of the Socialist Era.* **1988, Harvard Univ. Pr. $25.00 (0-674-58832-0); paper $12.95 (0-674-58833-9).** A chronicle of the social and political changes that took place in Great Britain under the direction of former Prime Minister Thatcher. (REV: BL 9/15/88; NYTBR 10/2/88; TLS 2/19/88) **[941.08]**

5188 **Longford, Elizabeth.** *Pebbled Shore: The Memoirs of Elizabeth Longford.* **1986, Knopf $19.95 (0-394-53764-5).** Memoirs of the British biographer and mother of Antonia Fraser and Thomas Pakenham. (REV: LJ 11/1/86; NYTBR 10/26/86; TLS 8/29/86) **[941.08]**

5189 **Mack, John E.** *A Prince of Our Disorder: The Life of T. E. Lawrence.* **1978, Little, Brown paper $14.95 (0-316-54229-6).** A psychological biography of Lawrence by the former head of the Harvard Medical School Department of Psychology. (REV: CSM 5/5/76; LJ 4/1/76; NYTBR 3/21/76. AWARDS: PP:Biography, 1977) **[941.08]**

5190 **Manchester, William.** *Last Lion: Biography of Winston Churchill, 1932–1940.* **1988, Little, Brown $24.95 (0-316-54512-0); Dell paper $13.95 (0-440-50047-8).** The second installment of a projected three-part biography. "The best Churchill biography for the plain readers of this generation."—Newsweek (REV: NYTBR 11/27/88; Newsweek 12/12/88; Time 10/31/88. AWARDS: Time, the 1980s) **[941.08]**

5191 **Manchester, William.** *Last Lion: Visions of Glory, 1874–1932.* **1983, Little, Brown $25.00 (0-316-54503-1); Dell paper $13.95 (0-440-54681-8).** The first volume of Manchester's biography of Winston

Churchill spans the years from Churchill's birth to his break with the Conservative Party in 1932. "There are more insightful books about Churchill and more carefully written ones, but none is better reading."—LJ (Rev: LJ 5/1/83; Natl Rev 7/8/83; Time 5/9/83. Awards: Time, 1983)   **[941.08]**

5192 Parker, John. *Prince Philip: His Secret Life.* **1991, St. Martin's $19.95 (0-312-06444-6).** A biography and genealogy of Britain's Prince Philip published to coincide with his seventieth birthday. (Rev: BL 10/15/91; LJ 10/1/91)   **[941.08]**

5193 Pearson, John. *Selling of the Royal Family: The Mystique of the British Monarchy.* **1987, Jove paper $4.50 (0-515-09276-2).** A study of the media presentation of the British royal family from the time of Queen Victoria to the present. (Rev: BL 5/15/86; LJ 6/1/86; PW 4/11/86)   **[941.08]**

5194 Stansky, Peter. *Gladstone: A Progress in Politics.* **1981, Norton paper $8.95 (0-393-00037-0).** A biography of the British prime minister who served four terms in the nineteenth century and was the political rival of Disraeli. (Rev: BL 5/15/79; Choice 11/79; PW 4/16/79)   **[941.08]**

5195 Thompson, Dorothy. *Queen Victoria: The Woman, the Monarchy and the People.* **1990, Random $18.95 (0-394-53709-2).** A biography of the queen who ruled Great Britain from 1837 to 1901. (Rev: BL 8/90; LJ 8/90)   **[941.08]**

5196 Westall, Robert. *Children of the Blitz: Memories of Wartime Childhood.* **1988, Penguin paper $11.95 (0-14-007404-X).** Collected memoirs of English children who survived the air raids on their nation in World War II. (Rev: BL 2/15/86; LJ 3/1/86; PW 11/29/85)   **[941.08]**

5197 Wilson, A. N. *Eminent Victorians.* **1990, Norton $25.00 (0-563-20719-1).** Essays by the British writer on key figures of the Victorian period, including profiles of Prince Albert, Charlotte Brontë, and William Gladstone. (Rev: Choice 1/91; CSM 8/1/90; LJ 6/1/90)   **[941.08]**

5198 Wilson, Trevor. *Myriad Faces of War: Britain and the Great War, 1914–1918.* **1986, Basil Blackwell $49.95 (0-7456-0093-X); paper $19.95 (0-7456-0645-8).** An assessment of the social and historical effects of the First World War on Great Britain. (Rev: LJ 11/15/86; NYTBR 1/25/87; TLS 5/15/87) **[941.08]**

5199 Young, Hugo. *Iron Lady: A Biography of Margaret Thatcher.* **1989, Farrar $25.00 (0-374-22651-2).** A biography of the former English prime minister. "A model political biography . . . indispensable to understanding Mrs. Thatcher."—NYTBR (Rev: LJ 9/1/89; NYTBR 11/12/89; PW 8/11/89)   **[941.08]**

5200 Ziegler, Philip. *King Edward VIII: A Biography.* **1991, Knopf $24.95 (0-394-57730-2).** A biography of the English king who abdicated the throne to marry an American in 1936. "The best and now most definitive biography."—LJ (Rev: BL 11/15/90; LJ 1/91; NYTBR 2/10/91)   **[941.08]**

5201 Ziegler, Philip. *Mountbatten.* **1985, Knopf $24.95 (0-394-52098-X).** The official biography of the British admiral who was the last viceroy of India. "A remarkably lively and human portrait."—Time (Rev: Choice 9/85; LJ 5/1/85; Time 5/13/85. Awards: LJ, 1985; Time, 1985)   **[941.08]**

Ireland—History

5202 Belfrage, Sally. *Living with War: A Belfast Year.* **1988, Penguin paper $8.95 (0-14-011292-8).** An American writer's account of the year she spent in Belfast interviewing the residents of Northern Ireland. (Rev: LJ 8/87; New Yorker 11/16/87; PW 8/7/87)   **[941.5]**

5203 Dillon, Eilis. *Inside Ireland.* **1984, Beaufort Books $17.95 (0-340-26342-3).** An overview of Ireland and its recent history by one of its most noted writers. (Rev: BL 3/15/84; LJ 3/15/84; PW 2/10/84)   **[941.5]**

5204 Donleavy, J. P. *A Singular Country.* **1990, Norton $18.95 (0-393-02760-0).** The author of *The Ginger Man* presents a portrait of contemporary Ireland and the Irish people. (Rev: BL 4/1/90; New Yorker 7/16/90; PW 4/6/90. Awards: BL, 1990)   **[941.5]**

5205 Foster, R. F. *Modern Ireland, 1600–1972.* **1989, Allen Lane $35.00 (0-7139-9010-4); Penguin paper $15.95 (0-14-012510-8).** An overview of Irish history from the beginning of the seventeenth century to the 1970s focusing on the rise of Irish nationalism and the development of Ireland as a nation. (Rev: BL 3/1/89; NYTBR 6/4/89; PW 1/27/89)   **[941.5]**

5206 Robinson, Tim. *Stones of Aran: Pilgrimage.* **1989, Viking $18.95 (0-670-82485-2); paper $8.95 (0-14-011565-X).** A descriptive and historical portrait of a group of islands off Ireland's southwest coast. "A gem-like addition to the travel genre."—PW (Rev: NYTBR 12/3/89; PW 6/9/89; TLS 6/9/89)   **[941.5]**

5207 Tall, Deborah. *Island of the White Cow: Memories of an Irish Island.* **1986, Macmillan $14.95 (0-689-11650-0); paper $8.95 (0-689-70722-3).** An account of the author's experiences living on a largely unpopulated island off the west coast of Ireland for five years. (Rev: BL 1/1/86; LJ 1/86; PW 12/6/85)   **[941.5]**

Ulster   Northern Ireland

5208 Donoghue, Denis. *Warrenpoint.* **1990, Knopf $19.45 (0-394-53966-4).** Memoirs of the literary critic's career and life as a Catholic in Northern Ireland. (Rev: BL 10/15/90; LJ 8/90; NYTBR 10/14/90)   **[941.6]**

Republic of Ireland—History

5209 Williams, Niall, and Christine Breen. *O Come Ye Back to Ireland: Our First Year in County Clare.* **1987, Soho Pr. $16.95 (0-939149-07-9); paper $8.95 (0-939149-22-2).** A story of a couple who left New York's publishing world to settle on a farm in Ireland. (Rev: LJ 10/15/87; NYTBR 1/17/88; PW 8/28/87)   **[941.7]**

5210 **Williams, Niall, and Christine Breen.** *When Summer's in the Meadow.* **1989, Soho Pr. $17.95 (0-939149-23-0).** The sequel to the authors' *O Come Ye Back to Ireland* describing their lives on an Irish farm after relocating from New York. (REV: BL 3/15/89; CSM 6/8/89; LJ 2/15/89) **[941.7]**

942　England and Wales

Early history to 1066

5211 **Ashe, Geoffrey.** *Discovery of King Arthur.* **1987, Henry Holt paper $9.95 (0-8050-0115-8).** A study of the truth behind the Arthurian legends as seen by a British historian. (REV: Atl 3/85; BL 2/15/85; LJ 3/15/85) **[942.01]**

Period of Houses of Lancaster and York, 1399–1485

5212 **Ross, Charles.** *Richard III.* **1982, Univ. of California Pr. $30.00 (0-520-04589-0); paper $9.95 (0-520-05075-4).** A biography of the legendary king of England examining the legacy of his 26-month long reign. (REV: BL 3/1/82; LJ 12/15/81; TLS 1/22/82) **[942.04]**

Tudor period, 1485–1603

5213 **Erickson, Carolly.** *Bloody Mary.* **1985, St. Martin's paper $10.95 (0-312-08508-7).** A biography of Henry VIII's eldest daughter who unsuccessfully attempted to restore Catholicism to England. "A very effective and readable presentation of Mary's side of the story . . . superior storytelling."—LJ (REV: Choice 5/78; LJ 2/15/78; NYTBR 1/15/78. AWARDS: ALA, 1978) **[942.05]**

5214 **Erickson, Carolly.** *Mistress Anne: The Exceptional Life of Anne Boleyn.* **1985, Summit paper $10.95 (0-671-60651-4).** A biography of the second wife of Henry VIII by the author of *The First Elizabeth* and *Bloody Mary.* (REV: BL 4/1/84; LJ 5/1/84; NYTBR 7/8/84) **[942.05]**

5215 **Loades, David.** *Mary Tudor: A Life.* **1989, Basil Blackwell $29.95 (0-631-15453-1).** A biography of the eldest daughter of Henry VIII who ruled England as Mary I. "This full, well-rounded biography provides the best treatment of Mary yet."—LJ (REV: Choice 7/90; LJ 1/90) **[942.05]**

5216 **Marius, Richard.** *Thomas More: A Biography.* **1985, Random paper $12.95 (0-394-74146-3).** A biography of the sixteenth-century English statesman, author, and martyr. "Marius is well-qualified to write the first full-length biography of More's life, his times and his writings . . . a beautiful book."—Choice (REV: Choice 2/85; LJ 9/1/84; NYTBR 1/6/85. AWARDS: LJ, 1984) **[942.05]**

5217 **Ridley, Jasper.** *Elizabeth I: The Shrewdness of Virtue.* **1988, Viking $24.95 (0-670-81526-8); Penguin paper $11.95 (0-88064-110-X).** A biography of Queen Elizabeth I of England examining the effects of her 45-year reign upon English society. "No Tudor buff will want to miss it."—LJ (REV: BL 12/15/87; Choice 6/88; LJ 1/88) **[942.05]**

5218 **Ridley, Jasper.** *Henry VIII.* **1985, Viking $24.95 (0-670-80699-4); Fromm International paper $12.95 (0-88064-066-9).** A study of the life and rule of the sixteenth-century English Tudor king. (REV: BL 6/15/85; LJ 7/85; NYTBR 8/11/85) **[942.05]**

5219 **Ridley, Jasper.** *Tudor Age.* **1990, Overlook $29.95 (0-87951-405-1).** A political and social history of sixteenth-century England under the Tudor dynasty. (REV: BL 11/1/90; LJ 9/15/90) **[942.05]**

5220 **Scarisbrick, J. J.** *Henry VIII.* **1968, Univ. of California Pr. paper $9.95 (0-520-01130-9).** A biography of the Tudor king who established the Reformation in England. "By far the best biography of Henry VIII yet written."—NYTBR (REV: Choice 11/68; LJ 8/68; NYTBR 7/7/68. AWARDS: ALA, 1968) **[942.05]**

5221 **Sugden, John.** *Sir Francis Drake.* **1991, Henry Holt $29.95 (0-8050-1489-6).** The biography of the sixteenth-century English explorer and pirate. "Long-overdue . . . no armchair admiral will want to miss this one."—PW (REV: BL 4/1/91; LJ 2/1/91; PW 2/1/91) **[942.05]**

Stuart and Commonwealth periods, 1603–1714

5222 **Fraser, Antonia.** *Cromwell: The Lord Protector.* **1986, Donald I. Fine paper $11.95 (0-917657-90-X).** The life and times of the Puritan leader of the English civil war. "A literary and historical work of major importance."—LJ (REV: BL 12/15/73; LJ 11/15/73; TLS 7/20/73. AWARDS: ALA, 1973) **[942.06]**

1837–

5223 **Blake, Robert.** *Disraeli.* **1987, Carroll & Graf paper $14.50 (0-88184-296-6).** Biography of the nineteenth-century British statesman, prime minister, and novelist. "An important portrait illuminating not only the man but the period."—BL (REV: BL 3/1/67; LJ 2/1/67; NYTBR 3/5/67. AWARDS: NYTBR, 1967) **[942.08]**

5224 **Farwell, Byron.** *Queen Victoria's Little Wars.* **1985, Norton $9.95 (0-393-30235-0).** A study of the over 200 wars and military skirmishes involving the armies of the British Empire during the reign of Queen Victoria. (REV: LJ 8/72; NYRB 11/30/72; PW 11/20/72) **[942.08]**

5225 **Sykes, Christopher.** *Nancy: The Life of Lady Astor.* **1984, Academy Chicago paper $4.95 (0-89733-098-6).** The life story of Virginia-born Nancy Langhorne, who married Lord Astor and became the first female member of the British Parliament. "A warm, perceptive portrait of one of the 20th century's truly great women."—LJ (REV: BL 3/15/73; LJ 9/15/72; NYTBR 11/26/72) **[942.08]**

5226 **Woodham-Smith, Cecil.** *Queen Victoria: From Her Birth to the Death of the Prince Consort.* **1986, Donald I. Fine paper $9.95 (0-917657-95-0).** A biography of the British queen tracing her life from 1819 to 1861. "She has achieved the first responsibility and joy of a biographer—breathed life into her subject, given her total credibility and placed her inviolably in the fabric of her time."—PW (REV: LJ 11/1/72;

New Yorker 12/9/72; PW 9/25/72. Awards: ALA, 1972)
[942.08]

Wales

5227 Morris, Jan. *Matter of Wales: Epic Views of a Small Country.* **1986, Oxford Univ. Pr. paper $10.95 (0-19-504221-2).** The noted travel writer presents her thoughts about the culture and sights of her native Wales. (Rev: CSM 3/1/85; LJ 4/1/85; TLS 3/1/85)
[942.9]

943 Central Europe; Germany

5228 Brinton, William M., and Alan Rinzler, eds. *Without Force or Lies: Voices from the Revolution of Central Europe in 1989–1990.* **1990, Mercury House $15.95 (0-916515-78-8); paper $10.95 (0-916515-92-3).** Collected writings and documents tracing key events in the history of Central and Eastern Europe in 1989–1990. (Rev: BL 11/1/90; LJ 8/90; PW 9/14/90)
[943]

Germany—History, 1705–1790

5229 Asprey, Robert B. *Frederick the Great: The Magnificent Enigma.* **1988, Ticknor & Fields paper $12.95 (0-89919-840-6).** A biography of the eighteenth-century Prussian leader who distinguished himself in the military campaigns of the Seven Years' War and the War of the Austrian Succession. (Rev: BL 9/15/86; Choice 3/87; LJ 10/15/86)
[943.05]

Germany—History, 1866–

5230 Astor, Gerald. *"Last" Nazi: The Life and Times of Dr. Joseph Mengele.* **1985, Donald I. Fine $18.95 (0-917657-46-2).** A biography of the Nazi death camp doctor who fled to South America following the end of World War II. (Rev: BL 10/15/85; LJ 11/1/85; PW 9/27/85)
[943.08]

5231 Böll, Heinrich. *What's to Become of the Boy?* **1985, Penguin paper $5.95 (0-14-008321-9).** Memoirs of the German writer regarding his childhood and adolescent years during the Third Reich. (Rev: Choice 3/85; Newsweek 10/15/84; NYTBR 10/7/84)
[943.08]

5232 Breitman, Richard. *Architect of Genocide: Himmler and the Final Solution.* **1991, Knopf $23.00 (0-394-56841-9).** The biography of the Nazi SS leader who developed and implemented plans for "the Final Solution." "An exceptional piece of work."—BL (Rev: BL 4/15/91; LJ 4/15/91; PW 4/5/91)
[943.08]

5233 Charman, Terry. *German Home Front, 1939–1945.* **1989, Philosophical Library $35.00 (0-8022-2568-3).** An illustrated history of the German citizenry during World War II. (Rev: BL 12/15/89; LJ 1/90)
[943.08]

5234 Craig, Gordon A. *Germans.* **1982, Putnam $15.95 (0-399-12436-5); NAL paper $9.95 (0-452-00897-2).** A history of Germany and German culture in the nineteenth and twentieth centuries. (Rev: BL 12/1/81; New Rep 2/24/82; NYTBR 3/14/82)
[943.08]

5235 Craig, Gordon A. *Germany: 1866 to 1945.* **1978, Oxford Univ. Pr. paper $17.95 (0-19-502724-8).** A survey of modern German history from the Seven Weeks' War to the end of World War II. "Likely to become a classic . . . belongs in every library."—Choice (Rev: Choice 2/79; NYTBR 1/21/79; New Yorker 9/11/78)
[943.08]

5236 Crankshaw, Edward. *Bismarck.* **1983, Penguin paper $10.95 (0-14-006344-7).** A biography of the nineteenth-century German chancellor and statesman examining his personal life and personality. (Rev: NYRB 11/19/81; PW 12/17/82; Sat Rev 11/81)
[943.08]

5237 Engelmann, Bernt. *In Hitler's Germany: Everyday Life in the Third Reich.* **1986, Pantheon $21.95 (0-394-52449-7).** A study of day-to-day life in Nazi Germany based on interviews with citizens who lived under Hitler's rule. (Rev: LJ 1/87; NYTBR 3/8/87)
[943.08]

5238 Fest, Joachim C. *Face of the Third Reich: Portraits of the Nazi Leadership.* **1977, Pantheon paper $7.96 (0-394-73407-6).** Biographies of the key members of the Nazi leadership, their relationship to each other, and an analysis of the bureaucracy of the Third Reich. (Rev: LJ 6/1/70; NYTBR 5/24/70; TLS 3/19/70)
[943.08]

5239 Fest, Joachim C. *Hitler.* **1975, Random paper $16.95 (0-394-72023-7).** A German scholar's interpretation of the life of the Nazi leader. "What gives this monumental biography its authority is the careful coordination of historical details and character analysis."—Atl (Rev: Atl 5/74; LJ 7/74; Time 5/6/74)
[943.08]

5240 Flood, Charles Bracelen. *Hitler: The Path to Power.* **1989, Houghton $24.95 (0-395-35312-2).** A study of Hitler's rise to power between the end of the First World War and his release from prison after serving time for his role in the Beer Hall Putsch. (Rev: BL 3/1/89; LJ 3/15/89; NYTBR 4/16/89. Awards: BL, 1989)
[943.08]

5241 Grass, Günter. *Two States, One Nation? Against the Unenlightened Clamoring for a Reunified Germany.* **1990, Harcourt $18.95 (0-15-192270-5).** Essays by the German writer opposing the reunification of East and West Germany. (Rev: LJ 9/15/90; PW 9/7/90)
[943.08]

5242 Harris, Robert. *Selling Hitler: The Extraordinary Story of the Con Job of the Century—The Faking of the Hitler Diaries.* **1986, Pantheon $18.95 (0-394-55336-5).** An examination of the 1983 forgery and publication of the alleged diaries of Adolf Hitler. (Rev: BL 4/1/86; LJ 5/15/86; NYTBR 4/13/86)
[943.08]

5243 Hohne, Heinz. *Order of the Death's Head: The Story of Hitler's SS.* **1986, Ballantine paper $6.95 (0-345-34504-5).** An examination of the history and organization of the Schutzstaffel, Hitler's elite police corps under the leadership of Himmler. "One of the best documented and most authoritative works on the Nazi era that has ever been published in English."—Choice (REV: Choice 6/70; LJ 4/15/70; NYTBR 4/15/70) **[943.08]**

5244 Kruger, Horst. *A Crack in the Wall: Growing up Under Hitler.* **$8.95, Fromm International paper 1986 (0-88064-052-9).** Memoirs of a German journalist's childhood under the Third Reich. (REV: BL 6/15/82; LJ 6/1/82; PW 4/16/82) **[943.08]**

5245 Lewin, Ronald. *Hitler's Mistakes.* **1987, Morrow paper $6.95 (0-688-07289-5).** An examination of the strategic and tactical errors made by the German leader in his conduct of the war against the Allied forces. (REV: BL 1/15/86; Choice 7–8/86; LJ 1/86) **[943.08]**

5246 Mann, Golo. *Reminiscences and Reflections: A Youth in Germany.* **1990, Norton $25.00 (0-393-02871-2).** Memoirs of the son of writer Thomas Mann describing his life in Germany during the 1920s and early 1930s. "An unusual and engrossing blend of private and public history."—CSM (REV: BL 9/1/90; CSM 11/27/90; NYTBR 9/16/90) **[943.08]**

5247 Marsh, David. *Germans: The Pivotal Nation.* **1990, St. Martin's $22.95 (0-312-05095-X).** A study of the reunited Germany and its role in the world community. (REV: BL 10/15/90; LJ 9/15/90; NYTBR 11/11/90) **[943.08]**

5248 Muller, Ingo. *Hitler's Justice: The Courts of the Third Reich.* **1991, Harvard Univ. Pr. $29.95 (0-674-40418-1).** A study of the role and actions of lawyers and judges in the justice system of Hitler's Germany. (REV: LJ 12/90; NYTBR 4/28/91) **[943.08]**

5249 Posner, Gerald L. *Hitler's Children: Sons and Daughters of Leaders of the Third Reich Talk about Themselves.* **1991, Random $20.50 (0-394-58299-3).** Profiles of the lives of children of Third Reich leaders, including the sons and daughters of Hermann Goering, Josef Mengele, and Rudolf Hess. (REV: BL 1/1/91; LJ 2/15/91; PW 3/15/91) **[943.08]**

5250 Reichel, Sabine. *What Did You Do in the War, Daddy? Growing Up German.* **1989, Hill & Wang $19.95 (0-8090-9685-4).** The author's memoirs of her childhood in postwar Germany, reconciling her country's recent past. (REV: BL 2/15/89; LJ 4/1/89; NYTBR 6/25/89) **[943.08]**

5251 Schmidt, Helmut. *Men and Powers: A Political Memoir.* **1990, Random $24.95 (0-394-56994-6).** Memoirs of the former West German chancellor regarding world leaders he has known. (REV: BL 1/1/90; LJ 2/15/90; NYTBR 4/8/90) **[943.08]**

5252 Schneider, Peter. *German Comedy: Scenes of Life after the Wall.* **1991, Farrar $19.95 (0-374-10201-5).** A study of the ramifications of a reunited Germany by the author of *The Wall Jumper*. (REV: LJ 10/1/91; NYTBR 10/6/91; PW 8/31/91) **[943.08]**

5253 Shales, Amity. *Germany: The Empire Within.* **1991, Farrar $19.95 (0-374-25605-5).** Profiles of German citizens provide the backdrop for analysis of the newly reunited German state. (REV: LJ 2/15/91; Natl Rev 4/29/91; PW 12/14/90) **[943.08]**

5254 Sichovsky, Peter. *Born Guilty: Children of Nazi Families.* **1988, Basic Books $17.95 (0-465-00742-2).** An examination of the lives and minds of children and grandchildren of Nazis involved in the Holocaust. (REV: BL 1/1/88; LJ 1/88; NYTBR 3/20/88) **[943.08]**

5255 Speer, Albert. *Inside the Third Reich.* **1981, Macmillan paper $10.95 (0-02-037500-X).** While serving his prison sentence as a war criminal, Hitler's former architect and confidant compiled these memoirs of his years serving Nazi Germany. "Probably the most important source of personal information on Hitler that we are likely to see."—NYTBR (REV: LJ 7/70; NYTBR 8/23/70; Time 9/7/70. AWARDS: ALA, 1970; NYTBR, 1970; Time, 1970) **[943.08]**

5256 Speer, Albert. *Spandau: The Secret Diaries.* **1981, Pocket paper $3.95 (0-671-42447-5).** Diaries kept during the 20 years Speer spent in Spandau Prison serving his sentence for war crimes. "May surpass his first book *Inside the Third Reich* as a genuine historical source and human document."—LJ (REV: LJ 3/15/76; Natl Rev 5/28/76; NYRB 3/18/76) **[943.08]**

5257 Stern, Fritz. *Gold and Iron: Bismarck, Bleishroder and the Building of the German Empire.* **1979, Random paper $14.95 (0-394-74034-3).** How the relationship between Bismarck, the nineteenth-century German diplomat, and Bleishroder, a Jewish financier, laid the foundation for the modern German state. (REV: Choice 5/77; New Rep 2/26/77; NYTBR 2/27/77) **[943.08]**

5258 Toland, John. *Adolf Hitler.* **1986, Ballantine paper $12.95 (0-345-33848-0).** An exhaustive biography of the Nazi leader based on over 250 interviews. "Toland has seemingly made future biographies of Hitler per se superfluous."—Choice (REV: Choice 12/76; LJ 8/76; NYTBR 9/26/76. AWARDS: ALA, 1976) **[943.08]**

5259 Turner, Henry A. *German Big Business and the Rise of Hitler.* **1985, Oxford Univ. Pr. $35.00 (0-19-503492-9).** A study of the relationship between German business and Nazi leaders from the fall of the Weimar Republic to the accession of Hitler to power. (REV: Choice 5/85; LJ 2/1/85; New Rep 1/21/85) **[943.08]**

Northeastern Germany—History

5260 Andreas-Friedrich, Ruth. *Battleground Berlin: Diaries, 1945–1948.* **1990, Paragon House $18.95 (1-55778-191-5).** Remembrances of life in Berlin under Russian occupation forces following the end of World War II. (REV: BL 8/90; LJ 9/1/90; PW 8/3/90) **[943.1]**

5261 Borneman, John. *After the Wall: East Meets West in the New Berlin.* **1991, Basic Books $19.95 (0-465-00083-5).** A study of life in Berlin following the dismantling of the wall based on conversations with the city's residents. (REV: BL 1/15/91; LJ 2/15/91; PW 1/4/91) **[943.1]**

5262 Clare, George. *Before the Wall: Berlin Days, 1946–1948.* **1990, Dutton $18.95 (0-525-24896-X).**

Memoirs of a former Austrian who served in the British army occupation forces in Berlin following World War II. (Rev: BL 9/15/90; LJ 10/1/90; PW 8/10/90) **[943.1]**

5263 Darnton, Robert. *Berlin Journal, 1989–1990.* **1991, Norton $22.95 (0-393-02970-0).** A chronicle of life in Berlin before, during, and after the collapse of the wall as witnessed by the author of *The Kiss of Lamourette.* (Rev: BL 6/1/91; LJ 5/1/91; NYTBR 7/14/91) **[943.1]**

5264 Tusa, Ann, and John Tusa. *Berlin Airlift.* **1988, Macmillan $24.95 (0-689-11513-X).** A recounting of the 1948 Allied airlift to maintain control of West Berlin. "Impeccably wrought and exciting to read."—BL (Rev: BL 1/15/89; LJ 2/1/89; TLS 11/11/88) **[943.1]**

5265 Wyden, Peter. *Wall: The Berlin Story.* **1989, Simon & Schuster $27.50 (0-671-55510-3).** The history of the Berlin Wall and the effect the division of the city had on its inhabitants. "As entertaining as it is revealing."—BL (Rev: BL 10/1/89; LJ 11/15/89; PW 10/6/89) **[943.1]**

Austria and Liechtenstein—History

5266 Brook, Stephen. *Vanished Empire.* **1990, Morrow $21.95 (0-688-09212-8).** A look at the contemporary cities of Vienna, Budapest, and Prague by the author of *Honkytonk Gelato.* (Rev: BL 2/1/90; LJ 1/90; PW 12/15/89) **[943.6]**

5267 Hamann, Brigitte. *Reluctant Empress: A Biography of Elisabeth of Austria.* **1986, Knopf $25.00 (0-394-53717-3).** A portrait of the wife of Emperor Franz Joseph I of Austria, drawing heavily on Elisabeth's own letters and poetry. (Rev: LJ 10/15/86; NYTBR 2/8/87; PW 9/26/86. Awards: PW, 1986) **[943.6]**

5268 Herzstein, Robert E. *Waldheim: The Missing Years.* **1989, Paragon House paper $12.95 (1-55778-221-0).** An investigation into the World War II activities of Austrian President Kurt Waldheim. (Rev: Choice 7–8/88; LJ 6/15/88; NYTBR 5/27/88) **[943.6]**

5269 Hofmann, Paul. *Viennese: Splendor, Twilight and Exile.* **1988, Doubleday $22.50 (0-385-23974-2); paper $10.95 (0-385-23975-0).** A cultural and societal history of the city of Vienna as described by a former resident. "The most comprehensive, informative and lively introduction to the city currently available."—NYTBR (Rev: BL 11/1/88; LJ 10/15/88; NYTBR 10/30/88) **[943.6]**

5270 Morton, Frederic. *Thunder at Twilight: Vienna 1913–1914.* **1989, Macmillan $22.50 (0-684-19143-1).** A study of the culture and personalities that made up Vienna just prior to the outbreak of World War I. "A work of astonishing literary energy and historical insight."—PW (Rev: Atl 12/89; LJ 11/1/89; PW 10/13/89. Awards: PW, 1989) **[943.6]**

5271 Schorske, Carl E. *Fin-de-Siecle Vienna: Politics and Culture.* **1980, Random paper $16.95 (0-394-74478-0).** "This is a highly important book for all collections of European intellectual history."—LJ

(Rev: Choice 6/80; LJ 12/1/79; Newsweek 1/14/80. Awards: PP:NF, 1981; Time, 1980) **[943.6]**

5272 Seward, Desmond. *Metternich: The First Emperor.* **1991, Viking $22.95 (0-670-82600-6).** A biography of the nineteenth-century Austrian diplomat. (Rev: BL 11/15/91; LJ 10/15/91) **[943.6]**

Czechoslovakia—History

5273 Hampl, Patricia. *A Romantic Education.* **1983, Houghton paper $9.95 (0-395-34638-X).** Hampl describes her family and heritage, and how her trip to Prague helped her feel more in touch with her ancestors. (Rev: BL 1/15/81; LJ 2/1/81; PW 1/23/81. Awards: ALA, 1981) **[943.7]**

5274 Havel, Vaclev. *Disturbing the Peace: A Conversation with Karel Hvizdala.* **1990, Knopf $19.95 (0-394-58441-4).** An interview between an exiled Czech journalist and the literary figure who became the Czechoslovakian president. (Rev: BL 5/15/90; CSM 7/26/90; LJ 6/15/90. Awards: LJ, 1990) **[943.7]**

5275 Kovaly, Heda Margolius. *Under a Cruel Star: A Life in Prague, 1941–1968.* **1989, Penguin paper $8.95 (0-14-012643-0).** A Czech Jew recalls her family's persecution under the Nazis and the Communist regime of Czechoslovakia. (Rev: CSM 3/13/87; LJ 1/87; PW 10/10/86) **[943.7]**

Poland—History

5276 Adelson, Alan, and Robert Lapides, eds. *Lodz Ghetto: Personal Narratives from a Community Under Siege.* **1989, Viking paper $29.95 (0-670-82983-8).** A written testimony left behind by those who lived in Lodz during the Nazi liquidation. (Rev: BL 11/1/89; LJ 10/1/89; NYRB 9/28/89. Awards: LJ, 1989) **[943.8]**

5277 Davies, Norman. *Heart of Europe: A Short History of Poland.* **1986, Oxford Univ. Pr. paper $10.95 (0-19-285152-7).** A concise history of Poland presented in reverse chronological order. "The best history of Poland available in English."—Choice (Rev: Choice 2/85; CSM 7/3/86; NYTBR 12/23/84) **[943.8]**

5278 Dobroszycki, Lucian, ed. *Chronicle of the Lodz Ghetto, 1941–1944.* **1984, Yale Univ. Pr. $50.00 (0-300-03208-0); paper $21.95 (0-300-03924-7).** Life in a Jewish ghetto in German-occupied Poland, recorded on a day-to-day basis, and edited by a survivor who lived there. "One of the most remarkable Holocaust publications of recent years."—LJ (Rev: LJ 8/84; NYRB 9/27/84; NYTBR 8/19/84. Awards: ALA, 1984; LJ, 1984) **[943.8]**

5279 Kaufman, Michael T. *Mad Dreams, Saving Graces: Poland, a Nation in Conspiracy.* **1989, Random $19.95 (0-394-55486-8).** An analysis of social changes in Poland in the 1980s by a former *New York Times* Warsaw correspondent. (Rev: CSM 10/2/89; New Rep 7/17/89; NYTBR 6/18/89) **[943.8]**

5280 Michnik, Adam. *Letters from Prison and Other Essays.* **1986, Univ. of California Pr. $30.00 (0-520-05371-0); paper $10.95 (0-520-06175-6).** Letters written from prison by the Polish political and

labor leader who helped found the Solidarity union. (REV: CSM 12/11/86; LJ 10/1/86; PW 8/15/86)
[943.8]

5281 Toranska, Teresa. *Them: Stalin's Polish Puppets.* 1988, Harper & Row paper $9.95 (0-06-091493-9). An account of the effects of the Stalinist purges in Poland as told by five former Polish Communist party members. (REV: LJ 3/1/87; NYTBR 3/17/87; PW 2/6/87)
[943.8]

Hungary—History

5282 Fenyvesi, Charles. *When the World Was Whole: A Family Album.* 1990, Viking $19.95 (0-670-83180-8). Memoirs of the author's youth in Hungary and of the life of his ancestors. "A lyrical memoir filled with long-cherished stories and dreams."—BL (REV: BL 9/15/90; LJ 7/90; PW 7/6/90. AWARDS: BL, 1990)
[943.9]

944 France and Monaco

5283 Darnton, Robert. *Great Cat Massacre and Other Episodes in French Cultural History.* 1985, Random paper $8.95 (0-394-7297-7). Six essays regarding eighteenth-century French history and culture. (REV: LJ 12/1/83; New Rep 4/16/84; NYTBR 2/12/84)
[944]

5284 Fink, Carole. *Marc Bloch: A Life in History.* 1989, Cambridge Univ. Pr. $29.95 (0-521-37300-X). A biography of the French historian who was involved in the French Resistance prior to his capture and murder by the Gestapo. (REV: LJ 8/89; NYRB 4/26/90; NYTBR 10/1/89)
[944]

5285 Goldberg, Michael. *Namesake.* 1982, Yale Univ. Pr. $25.00 (0-300-02790-7); paper $9.95 (0-300-04049-0). An account of the author's search to reclaim his Jewish past, which took him to La Paz to interview Klaus Barbie and to Uganda, where he was involved in the Entebbe hijacking and raid. (REV: LJ 8/82; NYTBR 9/5/82; PW 7/2/82)
[944]

5286 Herbert, Zbigniew. *Barbarian in the Garden.* 1986, Harcourt paper $7.95. A collection of essays on the history and culture of ten small towns in France and Italy as penned by a Polish poet. (REV: Choice 1/86; CSM 7/3/86; LJ 9/1/85)
[944]

5287 Ladurie, Emmanuel Le Roy. *Carnival in Romans.* 1979, Braziller paper $8.95 (0-8076-0991-9). A study of sixteenth-century French society and values based on a Mardi Gras celebration that turned violent in the city of Romans. (REV: LJ 11/1/79; NYTBR 11/8/79; PW 10/8/79)
[944]

5288 Ladurie, Emmanuel Le Roy. *Montaillou: The Promised Land of Error.* 1979, Random paper $8.95 (0-394-72964-1). An attempt to reconstruct the society and daily life of a medieval French village. "He never allows method to eclipse the humanity with which he deals . . . an intellectually exciting book and a moving one as well."—Newsweek (REV: CSM 9/20/78; NYRB 10/12/78; Newsweek 8/14/78. AWARDS: ALA, 1978)
[944]

5289 Mayle, Peter. *Toujours Provence.* 1991, Knopf $20.00 (0-679-40254-5). The second volume of the author's experiences living in the south of France. "Pure enchantment . . . the next best thing to being in the Midi."—PW (REV: LJ 5/1/91; PW 5/10/91)
[944]

5290 Mayle, Peter. *A Year in Provence.* 1990, Knopf $19.95 (0-394-57230-0). An account of the author's move to southern France and the people and customs he encountered there. "A Francophile's delight."—LJ (REV: CSM 7/31/90; LJ 4/1/90; TLS 8/4/89. AWARDS: LJ, 1990)
[944]

5291 Tuchman, Barbara W. *A Distant Mirror: The Calamitous Fourteenth Century.* 1978, Knopf $45.00 (0-394-40026-1); Ballantine paper $12.95 (0-345-34957-1). The history of the fourteenth century as reflected in the life of a French feudal lord. (REV: Atl 10/78; LJ 9/1/78; Time 9/18/78. AWARDS: ALA, 1978; NBA, 1980; Time, 1978)
[944]

5292 Weber, Eugen. *My France: Politics, Culture, Myth.* 1991, Harvard Univ. Pr. $24.95 (0-674-59575-0). An introduction to French culture laced with autobiographical pieces by the Romanian-born writer. "A model of historical research."—LJ (REV: LJ 1/91; NYTBR 2/27/91)
[944]

France—History, 1589–1789

5293 Bernier, Olivier. *Louis XIV: A Royal Life.* 1987, Doubleday $19.95 (0-385-19785-3). A biography of the seventeenth-century French monarch by the author of *Secrets of Marie Antoinette.* (REV: BL 11/1/87; LJ 11/1/87; NYTBR 1/31/88)
[944.03]

5294 Ladurie, Emmanuel Le Roy. *Jasmin's Witch: A Case of Possession in 17th Century France.* 1987, Braziller $17.95 (0-8076-0991-9). An examination of witchcraft and witch trials in seventeenth-century France by the renowned French historian. (REV: LJ 8/87; PW 6/26/87)
[944.03]

France—History, 1789–1804

5295 Bernier, Olivier. *Words of Fire, Deeds of Blood: The Mob, the Monarchy and the French Revolution.* 1989, Little, Brown $21.95 (0-316-09206-1); Doubleday paper $12.95 (0-385-41333-5). An account of the French Revolution focusing on the collapse of the monarchy of Louis XVI. (REV: BL 6/15/89; NYTBR 7/9/89; PW 3/24/89)
[944.04]

5296 Blanc, Olivier. *Last Letters: Prisons and Prisoners of the French Revolution.* 1987, Farrar $22.50 (0-374-18386-4); paper $9.95 (0-374-52188-3). A collection of 150 letters written by persons imprisoned and condemned to die during the French Revolution. (REV: Choice 12/87; LJ 9/1/87; PW 6/19/87)
[944.04]

5297 Bosher, J. F. *French Revolution.* 1989, Norton paper $9.95 (0-393-95997-X). A study of the causes, events, and consequences of the French Revolution. "Nicely written, well organized and thoroughly researched."—Choice (REV: Choice 3/89; LJ 10/15/88; New Rep 7/31/89)
[944.04]

5298 Hibbert, Christopher. *Days of the French Revolution: The Day-to-Day Story of the Revolution.* 1981, Morrow paper $12.95 (0-688-00746-5). The British historian recounts the events from the beginning of the French Revolution in 1789 to the rise of Napoleon. (Rev: BL 9/15/80; LJ 10/1/80; NYTBR 11/12/80)   **[944.04]**

5299 Manceron, Claude. *Blood of the Bastille: Age of the French Revolution, 1787–1789.* 1990, Simon & Schuster $29.95 (0-671-67848-5); paper $14.95 (0-671-73293-5). A study of the events leading up to the 1789 storming of the Bastille and the outbreak of the French Revolution. (Rev: BL 12/15/89; PW 11/24/89)   **[944.04]**

5300 Schama, Simon. *Citizens: A Chronicle of the French Revolution.* 1989, Knopf $29.95 (0-394-55948-7); Random paper $16.95 (0-679-72610-1). An analysis of the events of the French Revolution by an English scholar who currently lives in the United States. "As no other recent historian of the Revolution, Schama brings back to life the excitement—and harrowing terror—of an epochal human event."—Newsweek (Rev: New Rep 4/17/89; NYTBR 3/19/89; Newsweek 4/3/89. Awards: BL, 1989; NYTBR, 1989; Time, the 1980s)   **[944.04]**

5301 Walter, Jakob. *Diary of a Napoleonic Foot Soldier.* Ed. by Marc Raeff. 1991, Doubleday $20.00 (0-385-41696-2). A diary kept by a German foot soldier during the 1812 march on Russia. (Rev: BL 8/91; PW 7/12/91)   **[944.04]**

France—History, 1815–1848

5302 Weber, Eugen. *France: Fin-de-Siecle.* 1986, Harvard Univ. Pr. $22.50 (0-674-31812-9). A study of the social history of late nineteenth-century France. "Thoughtful, provocative and delightful in its literacy."—Choice (Rev: BL 9/1/86; LJ 9/1/86; PW 8/8/86)   **[944.06]**

France—History, 1848–1870

5303 Jardin, Andre. *Tocqueville: A Biography.* 1988, Farrar $34.50 (0-374-27836-9); paper $14.95 (0-374-52190-5). A biography of the French politician and writer remembered for his observations of the United States in his book *Democracy in America.* (Rev: New Rep 12/5/88; New Yorker 11/14/88; Time 1/6/89)   **[944.07]**

France—History, 1870–

5304 Aron, Raymond. *Memoirs: Fifty Years of Political Reflection.* 1990, Holmes & Meier $45.00 (0-8419-1113-4). Memoirs of the French journalist, author, and university professor. (Rev: Choice 10/90; LJ 1/90; New Rep 4/16/90)   **[944.08]**

5305 Bernstein, Richard. *Fragile Glory: A Portrait of France and the French.* 1990, Knopf $25.00 (0-394-58340-X); Dutton paper $10.95 (0-452-26678-5). A study of France and contemporary French society by a former *New York Times* Paris bureau chief. (Rev: BL 9/15/90; LJ 9/1/90; NYTBR 10/7/90)   **[944.08]**

5306 Carles, Emilie, and Robert Destanque. *A Life of Her Own: A Countrywoman in 20th-Century France.* 1991, Rutgers Univ. Pr. $19.95 (0-8135-1641-2). Memoirs of a teacher and activist portraying life in rural France during this century. (Rev: Choice 10/91; NYTBR 6/2/91; PW 2/15/91. Awards: ALA, 1992)   **[944.08]**

5307 Cook, Don. *Charles de Gaulle: A Biography.* 1984, Putnam paper $22.95 (0-399-12858-1). A biography of the French political leader who played key roles in World War II and the French-Algerian conflict. (Rev: LJ 12/1/83; NYTBR 1/22/84; Time 3/5/84)   **[944.08]**

5308 Cronin, Vincent. *Paris on the Eve: 1900–1914.* 1991, St. Martin's $24.95 (0-312-04876-9). A social, cultural, and intellectual history of Paris in the years preceding the outbreak of World War I. (Rev: BL 4/15/91; LJ 3/15/91; PW 3/8/91)   **[944.08]**

5309 Duras, Marguerite. *War: A Memoir.* 1987, Pantheon paper $6.95 (0-394-75039-X). The French writer remembers France during the war in four autobiographical pieces and two fictionalized accounts. "No recent memoir has evoked the 1940s in France so eloquently."—Time (Rev: LJ 7/86; NYTBR 5/4/86; Time 4/28/86. Awards: ALA, 1986; LJ, 1986)   **[944.08]**

5310 Gold, Arthur, and Robert Fizdale. *Misia: The Life of Misia Sert.* 1980, Knopf $16.95 (0-394-48710-9). A biography of the Polish-French model and patron of the arts who was a key figure in the turn-of-the-century literary and artistic world in Paris. (Rev: LJ 1/15/80; NYTBR 2/10/80; Newsweek 3/3/80)   **[944.08]**

5311 Hallie, Philip P. *Lest Innocent Blood Be Shed: The Story of the Village of Le Chambon and How Goodness Happened There.* 1980, Harper & Row paper $8.95 (0-16-132051-X). An account of the French Resistance in the city of Le Chambon and how the lives of Jewish refugees were saved through the community's efforts. (Rev: BL 3/1/79; NYTBR 4/15/79; PW 2/19/79)   **[944.08]**

5312 Lacouture, Jean. *De Gaulle: The Rebel, 1890–1944.* 1990, Norton $29.95 (0-393-02699-X). The first of a two-volume biography of the French military and political leader. (Rev: BL 11/1/90; LJ 11/15/90; PW 9/28/90. Awards: LJ, 1990; PW, 1990)   **[944.08]**

5313 Smith, Bonnie G. *Confessions of a Concierge: Madame Lucie's History of Twentieth Century France.* 1985, Yale Univ. Pr. $22.50 (0-300-03316-8); paper $7.95 (0-300-04038-5). Memoirs of a French concierge melded with the author's observations combine to provide this portrait of the lives of working-class women in France during the twentieth century. (Rev: Atl 9/85; LJ 12/85; TLS 1/17/86)   **[944.08]**

5314 Wiser, William. *Crazy Years: Paris in the Twenties.* 1990, Thames & Hudson paper $12.95 (0-500-27589-0). An illustrated social and cultural history of Paris during the 1920s. (Rev: BL 11/1/83; CSM 12/2/83; NYTBR 10/30/83)   **[944.08]**

Monaco

5315   Spada, James. *Grace: The Secret Lives of a Princess.* 1987, Doubleday $17.95 (0-385-19299-1); Dell paper $4.95 (0-440-20107-1). A biography of the motion picture actress who became Princess Grace of Monaco. "This well-researched, fascinating account will be in heavy demand."—LJ (Rev: BL 4/1/87; LJ 5/1/87; PW 3/6/87)   **[944.949]**

945   Italian Peninsula and adjacent islands

Italy—History, 1122–1300

5316   Simon, Kate. *A Renaissance Tapestry: The Gonzaga of Mantua.* 1989, Harper & Row paper $8.95 (0-06-091558-7). The author of *Bronx Primitive* explores the world of the Italian Renaissance city-state of Mantua and its cultural legacy. (Rev: BL 1/1/88; LJ 2/15/88; New Yorker 4/11/88)   **[945.04]**

Italy—History, 1300–1494

5317   Hibbert, Christopher. *House of Medici: Its Rise and Fall.* 1980, Morrow paper $12.95 (0-688-05339-4). The story of the family of bankers and merchants that controlled Renaissance Florence. "An exceptionally sound and well written popular history . . . does justice to a colorful family and epoch without indulging in sensationalism."—Choice (Rev: Choice 5/75; LJ 3/1/75; TLS 1/24/75. Awards: ALA, 1975)   **[945.05]**

Italy—History, 1494–1527

5318   Cloulas, Ivan. *Borgias.* 1989, Watts $24.95 (0-531-15101-8). A biography of the Spanish family that contained two popes and numerous political leaders. "A balanced narrative likely to become the standard work."—LJ (Rev: Choice 10/89; LJ 4/15/89; PW 3/17/89)   **[945.06]**

Italy—History, 1796–1900

5319   Mack Smith, Denis. *Cavour: A Biography.* 1985, Knopf $18.95 (0-394-53885-4). A biography of the Italian diplomat who played a crucial role in the unification of Italy. "The wealth of evidence and clarity of judgement that Mack Smith has shown in his earlier works are everywhere evident here."—Choice (Rev: Choice 12/85; CSM 6/21/85; NYTBR 9/1/85)   **[945.08]**

Italy, History, 1900–

5320   Mack Smith, Denis. *Mussolini: A Biography.* 1982, Knopf $20.00 (0-394-50694-4); Random paper $12.95 (0-394-71658-2). A biography of the fascist leader who ruled Italy from 1922 to 1943. "A remarkable political biography."—LJ (Rev: LJ 5/15/82; New Yorker 8/30/82; TLS 4/9/82)   **[945.09]**

5321   Murray, William. *Last Italian: Portrait of a People.* 1991, Prentice Hall $19.95 (0-13-508227-7). A portrait of contemporary Italy and the Italian people as seen by a *New Yorker* correspondent. (Rev: LJ 5/15/91; NYTBR 7/14/91; PW 4/12/91)   **[945.09]**

5322   Segre, Dan Vittorio. *Memoirs of a Fortunate Jew.* 1988, Dell paper $4.95 (0-440-20188-8). Memoirs of the author's youth in Mussolini's Italy and how he fled to Palestine at age 16 to escape his native country following the enactment of anti-Jewish legislation. (Rev: BL 2/15/87; LJ 3/15/87; NYTBR 3/29/87)   **[945.09]**

5323   Simeti, Mary T. *On Persephone's Island: A Sicilian Journal.* 1986, Knopf $18.95 (0-394-54988-0); North Point paper $11.95 (0-86547-282-3). A journal of a year in Sicily by a former American who lives in Palermo with her Sicilian husband. "A very engaging book that dispels one-sided notions about Sicily."—LJ (Rev: Atl 5/86; LJ 3/15/86; PW 3/7/86)   **[945.09]**

5324   Stille, Alexander. *Benevolence and Betrayal: Five Italian Jewish Families Under Fascism.* 1991, Summit $25.00 (0-671-67152-9). An American journalist's study of the fates of five Jewish Italian families during the 1930s and 1940s. (Rev: LJ 11/15/91; NYTBR 1/12/92)   **[945.09]**

Venice—History

5325   Norwich, John J. *A History of Venice.* 1989, Random paper $14.95 (0-679-72197-5). A political history of the Italian city and Republic from the fifth to the eighteenth centuries. (Rev: LJ 3/1/82; NYTBR 5/30/82; TLS 6/11/82)   **[945.31]**

Rome—History

5326   Hibbert, Christopher. *Rome: The Biography of a City.* 1985, Norton $25.00 (0-393-01984-5); Penguin paper $14.95 (0-14-007078-8). An illustrated history of the Italian city from Etruscan times to the twentieth century. (Rev: BL 6/15/85; LJ 6/15/85; TLS 7/12/85)   **[945.63]**

946   Iberian Peninsula and adjacent islands

5327   Lewis, Norman. *Voices of the Old Sea.* 1986, Penguin paper $5.95 (0-14-007780-4). An account of the destructive effects of tourism on the life and culture of a small Spanish fishing village. (Rev: Atl 7/85; LJ 4/1/85; TLS 1/4/85)   **[946]**

Spain—History, 711–1479

5328   Fletcher, Richard. *Quest for El Cid.* 1990, Knopf $24.95 (0-394-57447-8); Oxford Univ. Pr. paper $8.95 (0-19-506955-2). A biography of the eleventh-century Castilian hero that attempts to separate the legend from the truth. (Rev: BL 3/15/90; LJ 3/1/90; TLS 10/6/89)   **[946.02]**

Spain—History, 1516–1700

5329   Howarth, David. *Voyage of the Armada: The Spanish Story.* 1982, Penguin paper $8.95 (0-14-006315-3). A history of the development and destruction of the sixteenth-century Spanish fleet. (Rev: Atl 11/81; NYTBR 9/27/81; TLS 12/18/81)   **[946.04]**

Spain—History, 1598–1808

5330   Brown, Jonathan, and John Huxtable Elliot. *A Palace for a King: The Buen Retiro and the Court* *of Philip IV.* 1980, Yale Univ. Pr. $55.00 (0-300-02507-6); paper $17.95 (0-300-03621-3). A study of the design, construction, and social life of the seventeenth-century palace of King Philip IV. "A marvelously graceful synthesis of art and politics."—BL (REV: BL 12/15/80; Choice 3/81; LJ 10/15/80) **[946.05]**

Spain—History, 1931–

5331 Fraser, Ronald. *Blood of Spain: An Oral History of the Spanish Civil War.* 1986, Pantheon paper $12.95 (0-394-73854-3). An oral history of the Spanish Civil War based on over 300 interviews. (REV: BL 5/1/79; LJ 5/1/79; NYTBR 6/17/79)　　**[946.08]**

5332 Frerck, Robert, and Alastair Reid. *Eternal Spain: The Spanish Rural Landscape.* 1991, Abrams $75.00 (0-8109-3252-0). An essay accompanied by photographs depicting and exploring the essence of the Spanish landscape. (REV: BL 10/15/91; PW 10/4/91)　　**[946.08]**

5333 Payne, Stanley G. *Franco Regime, 1936–1975.* 1987, Univ. of Wisconsin Pr. $30.00 (0-299-11070-2). A study of the political and social history of the Franco dictatorship in Spain and its influence upon the contemporary nation. (REV: LJ 10/1/87; NYRB 2/4/88; NYTBR 12/27/87)　　**[946.08]**

5334 Tisa, John. *Recalling the Good Fight: An Autobiography of the Spanish Civil War.* 1985, Greenwood Pr. $39.95 (0-89789-078-7); paper $16.95 (0-89789-079-5). Memoirs of the author's experiences as a soldier and journalist during the Spanish Civil War. (REV: LJ 10/1/85; PW 10/25/85)　　**[946.08]**

5335 Yglesias, Jose. *Franco Years.* 1977, Macmillan $10.00 (0-672-52352-3). The author's interviews with Spanish citizens in 1975–1976 concerning life under the Franco dictatorship are collected and analyzed in this work. (REV: BL 12/15/77; LJ 12/1/77; PW 8/22/77)　　**[946.08]**

947　Eastern Europe; Soviet Union

5336 Bobrick, Benson. *Fearful Majesty: The Life and Reign of Ivan the Terrible.* 1987, Putnam $22.95 (0-399-13256-2); Paragon House paper $12.95 (1-55778-226-1). A biography of the infamous sixteenth-century ruler who became the first czar of Russia. (REV: LJ 8/87; NYTBR 11/8/87)　　**[947]**

5337 De Madariaga, Isabel. *Russia in the Age of Catherine the Great.* 1982, Yale Univ. Pr. $60.00 (0-300-02515-7); paper $18.95 (0-300-02843-1). A study of the life and times of the German-born Russian empress who expanded the boundaries of her nation and infused her court with European ideas and culture. (REV: CSM 5/20/81; LJ 2/15/81; NYTBR 4/19/81)　　**[947]**

5338 Ignatieff, Michael. *Russian Album.* 1987, Viking $18.95 (0-670-81057-6); Penguin paper $7.95 (0-14-008808-3). The author traces his Russian family tree to 1815. "A vivid, fascinating account by a gifted writer."—NYTBR (REV: BL 8/87; LJ 7/87; NYTBR 8/23/87)　　**[947]**

5339 Massie, Suzanne. *Pavlovsk: The Life of a Palace.* 1990, Little, Brown $29.95 (0-316-54970-3). An illustrated history of the eighteenth-century Leningrad palace. "Handsomely produced and highly readable."—CSM (REV: BL 9/15/90; CSM 12/7/90; LJ 8/90)　　**[947]**

5340 Raeff, Marc. *Understanding Imperial Russia: State and Society in the Old Regime.* 1984, Columbia Univ. Pr. $27.00 (0-231-05842-X); paper $13.00 (0-231-05843-8). A survey of the political and social history of Russia from the reign of Peter the Great to the end of the nineteenth century. (REV: Choice 2/85; LJ 8/84; NYTBR 1/20/85)　　**[947]**

5341 Troyat, Henri. *Catherine the Great.* 1984, Berkley paper $4.95 (0-425-07981-3). A biography of Catherine II of Russia, the empress who expanded Russian borders and was a great champion of European culture. "Recommended without hesitation for general readers."—LJ (REV: BL 6/15/80; LJ 11/1/80; Sat Rev 11/80. AWARDS: ALA, 1980)　　**[947]**

5342 Vishniac, Roman. *A Vanished World.* 1983, Farrar $65.00 (0-374-28247-1); paper $19.95 (0-374-52023-2). Nearly 200 photographs documenting Jewish life in Poland during the latter half of the 1930s. (REV: Choice 2/84; LJ 12/15/83; New Rep 12/19/83)　　**[947]**

Soviet Union—History, 1796–1855

5343 Crankshaw, Edward. *Shadow of the Winter Palace: Russia's Drift to Revolution, 1825–1917.* 1978, Penguin paper $8.95 (0-14-004622-4). A history of the era from the Decembrist uprising to the Russian Revolution. "Provides exciting reading for the layman and new historical perspectives for the specialist."—PW (REV: BL 10/15/76; NYTBR 9/5/76; PW 6/14/76)　　**[947.07]**

Soviet Union—History, 1855–

5344 Binyon, Michael. *Life in Russia.* 1985, Berkley paper $4.50 (0-425-98188-5). Collected impressions of Russian society and life by a former *London Times* correspondent. (REV: BL 2/15/84; LJ 5/1/84; Newsweek 3/12/84)　　**[947.08]**

5345 Clark, Ronald W. *Lenin.* 1987, Harper & Row $27.95 (0-06-015802-6); paper $10.95 (0-06-091698-2). A biography of the Russian revolutionary leader and theoretician. "Should become a standard."—LJ (REV: BL 11/15/88; LJ 12/88; PW 9/23/88)　　**[947.08]**

5346 Cohen, Stephen F., and Katrina Van Den Heuvel. *Voices of Glasnost: Interviews with Gorbachev's Reformers.* 1989, Norton $19.95 (0-393-02625-6); paper $12.95 (0-393-30735-2). Interviews with 14 Soviet leaders discussing internal reforms and the possible future direction of their nation. (REV: BL 10/1/89; LJ 11/1/89; NYTBR 11/26/89)　　**[947.08]**

5347 Conquest, Robert. *Harvest of Sorrow: Soviet Collectivization and the Terror-Famine.* 1987, Oxford Univ. Pr. paper $9.95 (0-19-505180-7). The history of Stalin's collectivization designed to eliminate private farms and the famine that followed and claimed over ten million lives in the late 1920s and early 1930s. (Rev: BL 9/15/86; Choice 2/87; NYTBR 10/26/86) **[947.08]**

5348 **Conquest, Robert.** *Stalin: Breaker of Nations.* **1991, Viking $25.00 (0-670-84089-0).** A biography of the Soviet leader based on newly available sources by the author of *The Great Terror: A Reassessment.* (Rev: BL 10/1/91; PW 9/13/91) **[947.08]**

5349 **Conquest, Robert.** *Stalin and the Kirov Murder.* **1990, Oxford Univ. Pr. paper $7.95 (0-19-506337-6).** A study of the 1934 assassination of Leningrad politician Sergei Kirov and of the role Stalin played in the murder. (Rev: Natl Rev 11/25/88; NYTBR 1/25/89) **[947.08]**

5350 **Conquest, Robert.** *Tyrants and Typewriters: Communiques from the Struggle for Truth.* **1989, Lexington Books $19.95 (0-669-21222-9).** Collected essays from over three decades by the historian analyzing the life and legacy of Joseph Stalin. (Rev: BL 1/15/90; Choice 5/90; TLS 10/5/90. Awards: BL, 1989) **[947.08]**

5351 **Cullen, Robert.** *Twilight of Empire: Inside the Crumbling Soviet Bloc.* **1991, Atlantic Monthly $21.95 (0-87113-472-1).** A *Newsweek* reporter's analysis of recent changes in the Soviet Union and Eastern Europe. (Rev: BL 10/1/91; LJ 10/1/91) **[947.08]**

5352 **Daniels, Robert V.** *Red October: Bolshevik Revolution of 1917.* **1984, Beacon paper $11.95 (0-8070-5645-6).** An account of the events surrounding the October 1917 Bolshevik Revolution. (Rev: Choice 3/68; LJ 9/15/67; NYTBR 11/26/67) **[947.08]**

5353 **Daniloff, Nicholas.** *Two Lives, One Russia.* **1988, Houghton $19.95 (0-395-44601-5); Avon paper $4.95 (0-380-70841-8).** An account by the American journalist of his abduction by the KGB in Moscow in 1986. (Rev: BL 9/15/88; Natl Rev 11/7/88; NYTBR 10/16/88) **[947.08]**

5354 **De Jonge, Alex.** *Stalin and the Shaping of the Soviet Union.* **1986, Morrow $19.95 (0-688-04730-0); paper $12.95 (0-688-07291-7).** A portrait of the former Soviet leader analyzing his role in the development of the USSR. (Rev: CSM 3/28/86; LJ 2/15/86; NYTBR 4/27/86) **[947.08]**

5355 **Doder, Dusko.** *Shadows and Whispers: Power Politics Inside the Kremlin from Brezhnev to Gorbachev.* **1986, Random $19.95 (0-394-54998-8); Penguin paper $7.95 (0-14-010526-3).** A study of the changing Soviet leadership in the 1980s by the former Moscow bureau chief of the *Washington Post.* (Rev: Choice 3/87; LJ 1/87; NYRB 5/28/87) **[947.08]**

5356 **Doder, Dusko, and Louise Branson.** *Gorbachev: Heretic in the Kremlin.* **1990, Viking $24.95 (0-670-82472-0).** A study of the life and political agenda of the former Soviet leader. "If you read only one book about Gorbachev, let it be this one."—BL (Rev: BL 4/15/90; LJ 6/1/90; NYTBR 6/17/90) **[947.08]**

5357 **Garton Ash, Timothy.** *Magic Lantern: The Revolution of '89 Witnessed in Warsaw, Buda-* *pest, Berlin, and Prague.* **1990, Random $17.95 (0-394-58884-3).** Accounts of the changes witnessed in Eastern Europe by the author in 1989. (Rev: Choice 2/91; CSM 7/19/90; NYTBR 7/22/90) **[947.08]**

5358 **Gurevich, David.** *From Lenin to Lennon: A Memoir of Russia in the Sixties.* **1991, Harcourt $21.95 (0-15-149825-3).** Memoirs of Soviet life and culture during the 1960s by an émigré who relocated to the United States in 1975. (Rev: BL 4/15/91; LJ 4/15/91; PW 3/8/91) **[947.08]**

5359 **Heller, Mikhail, and Aleksandr Nekrich.** *Utopia in Power: The History of the Soviet Union from 1917 to the Present.* **1988, Summit paper $14.95 (0-671-64535-8).** A history of the Soviet Union concentrating on the rule of the Communist party and resistance against it. "Marvelous . . . an immensely powerful and rewarding book."—NYTBR (Rev: BL 8/86; LJ 9/1/86; NYTBR 9/21/86) **[947.08]**

5360 **Hosking, Geoffrey.** *Awakening of the Soviet Union.* **1990, Harvard Univ. Pr. $19.95 (0-674-05550-0).** An analysis of recent reforms initiated in the Soviet Union and of that nation's possible future direction. (Rev: LJ 11/15/89; NYTBR 4/8/90; TLS 3/16/90) **[947.08]**

5361 **Kaiser, Robert G.** *Russia: The People and the Power.* **1984, Pocket paper $5.95 (0-671-50324-3).** An examination of the lives and attitudes of average Soviet citizens by the former *Washington Post* reporter. (Rev: Choice 6/76; CSM 2/10/76; LJ 1/15/76) **[947.08]**

5362 **Kaiser, Robert G.** *Why Gorbachev Happened: His Triumphs and His Failure.* **1991, Simon & Schuster $24.95 (0-671-73692-2).** A study of the former Soviet president, his reforms, and his place in his nation's history. (Rev: BL 5/15/91; LJ 5/15/91; PW 3/22/91) **[947.08]**

5363 **Khrushchev, Sergei.** *Khrushchev on Khrushchev.* **1990, Little, Brown $19.95 (0-316-49194-2).** The son of the former Soviet leader examines his father's life and legacy. (Rev: BL 4/15/90; LJ 5/1/90; PW 4/13/90) **[947.08]**

5364 **Laqueur, Walter.** *Long Road to Freedom: Russia and Glasnost.* **1989, Macmillan $21.95 (0-684-19030-3); paper $9.95 (0-02-034090-7).** An analysis of the reforms taking place in the Soviet Union. "A major contribution."—LJ (Rev: LJ 4/1/89; Natl Rev 6/2/89; NYTBR 5/28/89) **[947.08]**

5365 **Laqueur, Walter.** *Stalin: The Glasnost Revelations.* **1990, Macmillan $24.95 (0-684-19203-9).** An examination of Stalin and his legacy in the Soviet Union based on recently disclosed documents. (Rev: LJ 10/15/90; Natl Rev 12/3/90; NYTBR 11/18/90) **[947.08]**

5366 **Lee, Andrea.** *Russian Journal.* **1981, Random $13.50 (0-394-51891-8); paper $5.95 (0-394-71127-0).** A recounting of the author's experiences living in Moscow and Leningrad as part of an exchange program. "A splendid evocation of existence in the USSR."—BL (Rev: BL 9/15/81; New Rep 2/24/82; Newsweek 10/19/81) **[947.08]**

5367 Lincoln, W. Bruce. *Passage Through Armageddon: The Russians in War and Revolution, 1914–1918*. 1987, Simon & Schuster paper $14.95 (0-671-64560-9). A history of Russia from the beginning of the First World War through the Revolution and its immediate aftermath. (Rev: BL 9/1/86; Choice 1/87; LJ 9/15/86) **[947.08]**

5368 Lincoln, W. Bruce. *Red Victory: A History of the Russian Civil War*. 1990, Simon & Schuster $24.95 (0-671-63166-7); paper $14.95 (0-671-73286-2). The third and concluding volume of the author's survey of the events and aftermath of the Russian Revolution. (Rev: LJ 2/15/90; NYTBR 2/25/90; TLS 4/6/90) **[947.08]**

5369 Markovna, Nina. *Nina's Journey: A Memoir of Stalin's Russia and the Second World War*. 1989, Regnery Gateway $21.95 (0-89526-550-8). Memoirs of the author's childhood in the Soviet Union during the Second World War. (Rev: BL 11/15/89; LJ 12/89; NYTBR 2/11/90. Awards: BL, 1989) **[947.08]**

5370 Massie, Robert K. *Nicholas and Alexandra*. 1967, Macmillan $29.95 (0-689-10177-5); Dell paper $6.95 (0-440-36358-6). The story of the last of the Romanov czars and the coming of the Russian Revolution. "What makes Massie's book stand out is the brilliance and seeming ease with which he re-creates a whole era."—PW (Rev: BL 9/1/67; LJ 7/67; PW 6/12/67. Awards: ALA, 1967) **[947.08]**

5371 Medvedev, Roy. *Let History Judge: The Origins and Consequences of Stalinism*. 1989, Columbia Univ. Pr. $57.50 (0-231-06350-4); paper $19.50 (0-231-06351-2). An expanded and revised edition of the author's 1972 work based on newly recovered sources regarding the career of Joseph Stalin and the effects his policies of terror had on Soviet and world history. (Rev: LJ 6/1/89; New Rep 9/18/89; NYTBR 6/4/89) **[947.08]**

5372 Medvedev, Zhores A. *Gorbachev*. 1986, Norton $15.95 (0-393-02038-7). A biography of the former Soviet leader analyzing his role in shaping the future of the USSR (Rev: BL 5/1/86; LJ 7/86; NYTBR 7/20/86) **[947.08]**

5373 Nudel, Ida. *Hand in the Darkness: The Autobiography of a Refusenik*. 1990, Warner $22.95 (0-446-51445-4); paper $13.99 (0-446-39325-8). A Russian Jew describes her 16-year effort to emigrate from the Soviet Union and reunite with her family in Israel. (Rev: BL 11/1/90; LJ 11/1/90; PW 10/5/90)**[947.08]**

5374 Pipes, Richard. *History of the Russian Revolution*. 1990, Random $39.50 (0-394-50241-8). A history of the Russian Revolution from the final years of the nineteenth century to the Bolshevik triumph in October 1917. "The serious general reader will gain vast information painlessly and even pleasurably."—BL (Rev: BL 9/1/90; LJ 11/1/90; PW 8/17/90. Awards: LJ, 1990; PW, 1990) **[947.08]**

5375 Pond, Elizabeth. *From the Yaroslavsky Station: Russia Perceived*. 1987, Universe paper $12.95 (0-87663-536-2). The author's reflections on, and analysis of, the Soviet Union following a journey on the Trans-Siberian Express. "A deep-

reaching portrait of many layers of Soviet civilization that goes far beyond mere travel writing."—CSM (Rev: CSM 11/9/81; LJ 10/1/81; NYTBR 11/29/81. Awards: ALA, 1981) **[947.08]**

5376 Salisbury, Harrison E. *Black Night, White Snow: Russia's Revolutions, 1905–1917*. 1981, DaCapo paper $14.95 (0-306-80154-X). An examination of the forces, causes, and personalities that led to the Russian Revolution. "The first book that one should read on its subject."—Newsweek (Rev: Choice 5/78; NYTBR 1/29/78; Newsweek 2/13/78. Awards: ALA, 1978) **[947.08]**

5377 Schapiro, Leonard. *Russian Revolutions of 1917: The Origins of Modern Communism*. 1986, Basic Books paper $12.95 (0-465-07156-2). An assessment of how Lenin led the Bolsheviks to success during the 1917 revolution in Russia. (Rev: LJ 5/15/84; NYTBR 9/23/84; PW 4/6/84) **[947.08]**

5378 Schapiro, Leonard. *Russian Studies*. Ed. by Ellen Dahrendorf. 1987, Viking $24.95 (0-670-81281-1); Penguin paper $9.95 (0-14-009376-1). Writings about Soviet history and the leaders of the Russian Revolution. (Rev: LJ 11/15/86; NYTBR 2/22/87; TLS 3/20/87) **[947.08]**

5379 Schecter, Jerrold, and Leona Schecter. *Back in the U.S.S.R.: An American Family Returns to Moscow*. 1989, Macmillan $24.95 (0-684-18996-8). A sequel to the authors' *An American Family in Moscow* describing their visit to the Soviet Union of the mid-1980s. "This rich book will profit anyone interested in contemporary Soviet history."—BL (Rev: BL 1/1/89; LJ 2/1/89; NYTBR 2/12/89) **[947.08]**

5380 Sheehy, Gail. *Gorbachev: The Man Who Changed the World*. 1990, HarperCollins $22.95 (0-06-016547-2). A biography of the former Soviet leader by the author of *Passages* and *Pathfinders*. (Rev: BL 1/1/91; LJ 12/90; Natl Rev 2/11/91) **[947.08]**

5381 Shevardnadze, Edward. *Future Belongs to Freedom*. 1991, Free Pr. $22.95 (0-02-928617-4). A discussion by the former Soviet foreign minister of the recent past and future of his country. (Rev: LJ 10/15/91; PW 9/13/91) **[947.08]**

5382 Shipler, David K. *Russia: Broken Idols, Solemn Dreams*. 1989, Random $22.50 (0-8129-1788-X); Penguin paper $8.95 (0-14-012271-0). The former *New York Times* Moscow correspondent and author of *Arab and Jew* recounts his experiences living and working in the Soviet Union in the late 1970s. (Rev: CSM 3/28/84; NYTBR 11/20/83; PW 9/28/84) **[947.08]**

5383 Shoumatoff, Alex. *Russian Blood*. 1989, Random paper $12.95 (0-679-72578-4). A tracing of the author's heritage and his family's role in Russian history. "Vivid, urbane, accessible, and immensely informative."—BL (Rev: BL 5/15/82; LJ 4/15/82; PW 4/9/82) **[947.08]**

5384 Smith, Hedrick. *New Russians*. 1990, Random $24.95 (0-394-58190-3). A study of contemporary Soviet society and the effects of recent political reforms upon the people and nation as seen by the author of *The Russians.* (Rev: BL 12/1/90; LJ 12/90; PW 11/2/90) **[947.08]**

5385 Smith, Hedrick. *Russians.* 1983, Random $24.95 (0-8129-1086-9); Ballantine paper $5.95 (0-345-31746-7). The former *New York Times* Moscow bureau chief describes his impressions of the Russian people and life in Russia. "This book is marvelous at suggesting what it means to be a citizen of the U.S.S.R."—Natl Rev (Rev: LJ 9/15/76; Natl Rev 2/20/76; NYTBR 1/25/76. Awards: ALA, 1976) **[947.08]**

5386 Taubman, William, and Jane A. Taubman. *Moscow Spring: January to June 1988.* 1989, Summit $18.95 (0-671-67731-4); Simon & Schuster paper $9.95 (0-671-70058-8). The authors recount changes they witnessed taking place in Soviet society during the first six months of 1988. "A fascinating book about a topic of vast importance."—LJ (Rev: LJ 3/15/89; NYTBR 4/23/89; Newsweek 6/26/89) **[947.08]**

5387 Tucker, Robert C. *Stalin in Power: The Revolution from Above, 1928–1941.* 1990, Norton $29.95 (0-393-02881-X). A study of the first years of Stalin's reign over the Soviet Union. (Rev: BL 10/15/90; LJ 11/15/90; PW 9/14/90) **[947.08]**

5388 Ulam, Adam B. *Stalin: The Man and His Era.* 1989, Beacon paper $16.95 (0-8070-7005-X). A biography of the Soviet dictator who took command of his nation after the death of Lenin. "Altogether splendid."—Newsweek (Rev: CSM 11/21/73; New Rep 7/20/74; Newsweek 11/26/73) **[947.08]**

5389 Volkogonov, Dmitri. *Stalin: Triumph and Tragedy.* 1991, Grove-Weidenfeld $29.95 (0-8021-1165-3). A biography of the Soviet leader based on newly released documents. "The most candid and fullest reappraisal of Stalin to date."—PW (Rev: BL 8/91; PW 7/19/91) **[947.08]**

5390 Yeltsin, Boris. *Against the Grain: An Autobiography.* 1990, Summit $19.95 (0-671-70055-3). An autobiography of the Russian political leader and chief rival of Mikhail Gorbachev. (Rev: BL 6/1/90; NYTBR 3/25/90; Time 3/19/90) **[947.08]**

5391 Yevtushenko, Yevgeny. *Fatal Half Measures: The Culture of Democracy in the Soviet Union.* 1991, Little, Brown $21.95 (0-316-96883-8). Collected essays and writings of the Soviet poet about his nation and its recent reforms. "Astonishingly rich."—PW (Rev: BL 4/15/91; LJ 2/15/91; PW 1/11/91) **[947.08]**

949 Other parts of Europe

Netherlands (Holland)—History

5392 Schama, Simon. *Embarrassment of Riches: An Interpretation of Dutch Culture in the Golden Age.* 1987, Knopf $39.95 (0-394-51075-5); Univ. of California Pr. paper $16.95 (0-520-06147-0). A look at eighteenth-century Dutch culture—its abundance and its achievements. (Rev: LJ 5/15/87; NYTBR 7/5/87; New Yorker 9/14/87. Awards: NYTBR, 1987) **[949.2]**

Greece—History

5393 Gage, Nicholas. *Eleni.* 1983, Random $19.95 (0-394-52093-9); Ballantine paper $5.95 (0-345-32494-3). A former reporter for the *New York Times* tells the story of the execution of his mother during the Greek Civil War and his search for the truth about her death. (Rev: CSM 6/8/83; New Rep 5/16/83; Time 4/25/83. Awards: ALA, 1983; BL, the 1980s) **[949.5]**

5394 Gage, Nicholas. *A Place for Us: Eleni's Family in America.* 1989, Houghton $19.95 (0-395-45517-0). This sequel to *Eleni* describes the author's fleeing to America with his three sisters to escape the Greek Civil War and begin a new life. (Rev: BL 9/15/89; LJ 11/15/89; Time 10/16/89. Awards: BL, 1989; LJ, 1989) **[949.5]**

5395 Norwich, John J. *Byzantium: The Early Centuries.* 1989, Knopf $29.95 (0-394-53778-5). This first of a three-volume history of the Byzantine Empire covers the years 274–800. "The most comprehensive survey for the general reader."—LJ (Rev: BL 3/15/89; CSM 12/1/89; LJ 3/1/89. Awards: LJ, 1989) **[949.5]**

Balkan Peninsula—History

5396 Magris, Claudio. *Danube.* 1989, Farrar $22.95 (0-374-13465-0). An introduction to the Danube River and the cultures of the countries that it flows through. "A multidisciplinary essay of enthralling character and stylistic distinction."—BL (Rev: BL 7/89; LJ 9/15/89; TLS 8/18/89) **[949.6]**

Romania—History

5397 Codrescu, Andrei. *A Hole in the Flag: A Romanian Exile's Story of Return and Revolution.* 1991, Morrow $21.00 (0-688-08805-8). An account of the National Public Radio announcer's return to his native land to observe the revolution that toppled the Ceausescus. (Rev: LJ 6/15/91; PW 5/10/91. Awards: LJ, 1991) **[949.8]**

5398 Florescu, Radu R., and Raymond T. McNally. *Dracula, Prince of Many Faces: His Life and His Times.* 1989, Little, Brown $19.95 (0-316-28655-9); paper $10.95 (0-316-28656-7). A biography of the fifteenth-century Romanian prince who was the basis for the legends of Count Dracula. (Rev: BL 10/1/89; LJ 9/15/89) **[949.8]**

950 GENERAL HISTORY OF ASIA; FAR EAST

5399 Iyer, Pico. *Video Night in Kathmandu: And Other Reports from the Not-So-Far East.* 1988, Knopf $19.95 (0-394-55027-7); Random paper $10.95 (0-679-72216-5). An account of the influence of American popular culture in Asia based on the author's travels through ten Far Eastern countries. (Rev: BL 4/1/88; LJ 4/1/88; PW 2/26/88) **[950]**

Study and history

5400 Said, Edward W. *Orientalism.* 1979, Random paper $10.95 (0-394-74067-X). A study of the Western idea of the East and its influence upon history and cultural developments. (Rev: BL 9/15/78; LJ 11/1/78; NYTBR 2/18/79)   **[950.07]**

Period of Mongol and Tatar empires, 1162–1480

5401   Rossabi, Morris. *Khubilai Khan: His Life and Times.* **1988, Univ. of California Pr. $25.00 (0-520-05913-1).** A portrait of the life and times of the thirteenth-century Mongol ruler. "This excellent biography will undoubtedly become and remain the standard . . . for years to come."—Choice (Rev: Choice 1/89; LJ 4/15/88; NYTBR 9/11/88)   **[950.2]**

951   China and adjacent areas

5402   Ching, Frank. *Ancestors: Nine Hundred Years in the Life of a Chinese Family.* **1988, Morrow $22.95 (0-688-04461-1); Ballantine paper $12.95 (0-449-90353-2).** Thirty-three generations of the author's family traced back to the eleventh century. "Brings to life the last nine centuries of Chinese history and culture as almost no other work in the English language has done."—NYTBR (Rev: LJ 3/1/88; NYTBR 4/3/88; PW 1/29/88)   **[951]**

5403   Fairbank, John King. *Great Chinese Revolution: 1800 to 1985.* **1986, Harper & Row $20.95 (0-06-039057-3); paper $7.50 (0-06-039076-0).** A survey of modern Chinese history by one of the leading experts on the subject. "Gathers together a lifetime of scholarship . . . will be widely read for decades."—LJ (Rev: LJ 9/1/86; NYTBR 10/19/86; TLS 1/9/87. Awards: LJ, 1986)   **[951]**

5404   Li, Kwei. *Golden Lilies.* **1990, Viking $17.95 (0-670-83438-6).** A translation of letters written in the late nineteenth and early twentieth centuries by a Chinese woman to her husband and mother-in-law. (Rev: BL 10/1/90; LJ 10/15/90)   **[951]**

5405   Pan, Lynn. *Sons of the Yellow Emperor: A History of the Chinese Diaspora.* **1990, Little, Brown $22.95 (0-316-69010-4).** An examination of Chinese immigrants and the communities they founded throughout the world. (Rev: BL 9/15/90; LJ 10/1/90; PW 8/17/90. Awards: BL, 1990)   **[951]**

5406   Spence, Jonathan. *Death of Woman Wang.* **1979, Penguin paper $6.95 (0-14-005121-X).** A look at the society of seventeenth-century rural China as personified by a peasant woman who was murdered by her husband. (Rev: BL 7/1/78; CSM 9/14/78; New Rep 6/3/78)   **[951]**

5407   Spence, Jonathan. *Gate of Heavenly Peace: The Chinese and Their Revolution, 1895–1980.* **1982, Random paper $10.95 (0-14-006279-3).** "One of the most important and readable works in the field of Asian history . . . there is no other work to match this in sweep, vivacity and humanity."—LJ (Rev: LJ 9/15/81; NYTBR 10/18/81; Newsweek 11/9/81. Awards: ALA, 1981; NYTBR, 1981)   **[951]**

5408   Trevor-Roper, Hugh. *Hermit of Peking: The Hidden Life of Sir Edmund Backhouse.* **1986, Fromm International paper $10.95 (0-88064-063-4).** The life of a British scholar of China whose works have been proven to be fabrications. "A classic of

its kind . . . an absolute corker."—NYTBR (Rev: BL 4/15/77; New Rep 6/4/77; NYTBR 4/24/77)   **[951]**

5409   Van Slyke, Lyman. *Yangtze: Nature, History, and the River.* **1988, Addison Wesley $14.95 (0-201-08894-0).** A look at the Yangtze River in China and the history of civilization upon its shores. (Rev: LJ 6/15/88; PW 5/20/88)   **[951]**

5410   Waldron, Arthur. *Great Wall of China: From History to Myth.* **1990, Cambridge Univ. Pr. $39.50 (0-521-36518-X).** A historical survey of the myths and truths surrounding China's Great Wall. (Rev: LJ 7/90; PW 6/15/90)   **[951]**

China—History, 1644–1912

5411   Spence, Jonathan. *Search for Modern China.* **1990, Norton $29.95 (0-393-02708-2).** A survey of Chinese political history and trends over the past four centuries. (Rev: LJ 4/15/90; NYTBR 5/13/90; PW 3/16/90. Awards: LJ, 1990; NYTBR, 1990; PW, 1990)   **[951.03]**

5412   Warner, Marina. *Dragon Empress: Life and Times of Tz'u-Hsi, 1835–1908, Empress Dowager of China.* **1986, Macmillan paper $9.95 (0-689-70714-2).** A study of the last decades of the Ch'ing Dynasty as portrayed through the life of the Empress Dowager Tz'u-Hsi. (Rev: BL 1/15/73; LJ 12/15/72; TLS 1/5/73)   **[951.03]**

China—History, 1912–1949

5413   Cochran, Sherman, Andrew C. K. Hsieh, and Janis Cochran. *One Day in China: May 21, 1936.* **1985, Yale Univ. Pr. $35.00 (0-300-02834-2); paper $12.95 (0-300-03400-8).** A collection of over 400 essays on China during the mid-1930s, originally published in Chinese in 1936. (Rev: Choice 9/83; LJ 4/15/83; NYTBR 6/19/83)   **[951.04]**

5414   Salisbury, Harrison E. *Long March: The Untold Story.* **1985, Harper & Row $22.95 (0-06-039044-1); McGraw-Hill paper $7.95 (0-07-054471-9).** In 1984, Salisbury retraced the path of the Long March, a 6,000-mile trek made by Mao and his followers in 1934, and interviewed the surviving participants to reconstruct the events for this book. (Rev: Choice 2/86; LJ 9/1/85; NYTBR 9/29/85)   **[951.04]**

China—History, 1949–

5415   Bennett, Gordon A., and Ronald N. Montaperto. *Red Guard: The Political Biography of Dai Hsiao-Ai.* **1971, Peter Smith $12.00 (0-8446-4710-1).** The story of the Cultural Revolution in China as experienced by a student activist and former Red Guard member who defected to Hong Kong. (Rev: Choice 12/71; NYTBR 6/20/71; Time 3/1/71)   **[951.05]**

5416   Bonavia, David. *Chinese.* **1989, Penguin paper $7.95 (0-14-010479-8).** A survey of contemporary Chinese society and culture by the former *Time* Beijing correspondent. "An excellent, highly readable overview."—BL (Rev: BL 11/15/80; LJ 10/15/80; NYTBR 11/23/80)   **[951.05]**

5417   Butterfield, Fox. *China: Alive in the Bitter Sea*. 1982, Times Books $24.95 (0-8129-0927-5); Bantam paper $12.95 (0-553-34219-3). A report on post-Mao Chinese culture by the correspondent who opened the *New York Times* Peking bureau in 1979. (Rev: CSM 6/9/82; NYRB 5/27/82; Sat Rev 5/82. Awards: NBA, 1983)   **[951.05]**

5418   Byron, John, and Robert Pack. *Claws of the Dragon: Kang Sheng—the Evil Genius Behind Mao—and His Legacy of Terror in People's China*. 1991, Simon & Schuster $27.95 (0-671-69537-1). A biography of the former Chinese Communist party security chief and political ally of Jiang Qing. (Rev: BL 11/15/91; PW 12/13/91)   **[951.05]**

5419   Cheng, Nien. *Life and Death in Shanghai*. 1987, Grove-Weidenfeld $19.95 (0-8021-1205-6); Penguin paper $9.95 (0-14-010870-X). A woman's story of her unjust detention for seven years as a Chinese political prisoner. "Her intelligence, independent spirit and determination shine through in this revealing memoir of the Cultural Revolution."—LJ (Rev: CSM 6/22/87; LJ 7/87; NYTBR 5/31/87. Awards: LJ, 1987; NYTBR, 1987)   **[951.05]**

5420   Clayre, Alasdair. *Heart of the Dragon*. 1986, Houghton paper $14.95 (0-395-41837-2). An illustrated survey of Chinese culture and history written as a companion piece to the PBS television series. (Rev: BL 5/15/85; LJ 5/1/85; PW 4/5/85)   **[951.05]**

5421   Frolic, B. Michael. *Mao's People: Sixteen Portraits of Life in Revolutionary China*. 1980, Harvard Univ. Pr. $20.00 (0-674-54846-9); paper $8.95 (0-674-54845-0). Interviews with 16 former Chinese citizens about the history and social trends of China since the Revolution. (Rev: LJ 7/80; New Rep 5/31/80; NYTBR 5/18/80)   **[951.05]**

5422   Garside, Roger. *Coming Alive: China after Mao*. 1981, McGraw-Hill $12.95 (0-07-022914-7). The changes in Chinese government and society after the death of Mao are analyzed in this work by a former secretary for the British Embassy in Beijing. (Rev: Choice 7–8/81; LJ 3/1/81; NYTBR 4/12/81. Awards: ALA, 1981)   **[951.05]**

5423   Liang, Heng, and Judith Shapiro. *After the Nightmare: A Survivor of the Cultural Revolution Reports on China Today*. 1986, Knopf $16.95 (0-394-55153-2). The authors of *Son of the Revolution* recall their return trip to China and present their opinions regarding China's future. (Rev: LJ 6/15/86; Natl Rev 7/18/86; NYTBR 6/22/86)   **[951.05]**

5424   Liang, Heng, and Judith Shapiro. *Son of the Revolution*. 1984, Random paper $8.95 (0-394-72274-4). An autobiography of a former member of the Red Guards and his experience during the Chinese Cultural Revolution. "Essential reading for anyone seeking something more than a surface understanding of today's China."—CSM (Rev: CMS 4/23/83; NYRB 3/12/83; NYTBR 2/13/83)   **[951.05]**

5425   Lizhi, Fang. *Bringing Down the Great Wall: Writing on Science, Culture and Democracy in China*. 1991, Knopf $19.95 (0-394-58842-8). Collected essays and speeches by the author, a Chinese physicist and educator. (Rev: BL 1/15/91; LJ 1/91; PW 1/25/91)   **[951.05]**

5426   Lord, Bette Bao. *Legacies: A Chinese Memoir*. 1990, Knopf $19.95 (0-394-58325-6). Memoirs of the author's experiences in China during the turbulent year of 1989. (Rev: LJ 4/1/90; NYTBR 4/15/90; Time 3/12/90. Awards: ALA, 1990; Time, 1990)   **[951.05]**

5427   Luo, Zi-ping. *A Generation Lost: China Under the Cultural Revolution*. 1989, Henry Holt $19.95 (0-8050-0957-4). A scientist's story of her family's travails under the Chinese Cultural Revolution. "A tragic family drama that mirrors the dislocation of a generation."—PW (Rev: LJ 1/90; NYTBR 3/11/90; PW 12/8/89)   **[951.05]**

5428   Mahoney, Rosemary. *Early Arrival of Dreams: A Year in China*. 1990, Ballantine $18.95 (0-449-90552-7). Memoirs of the author's year teaching English in China directly preceding the Tiananmen Square massacre. (Rev: BL 9/15/90; LJ 9/15/90; NYTBR 10/28/90)   **[951.05]**

5429   Morath, Inge, and Arthur Miller. *Chinese Encounters*. 1979, Farrar $25.00 (0-374-12208-3). The noted playwright and his wife record their impressions of Chinese society based on their travels and interviews with Chinese citizens. (Rev: BL 12/15/79; LJ 1/1/80; NYTBR 10/14/79)   **[951.05]**

5430   Nathan, Andrew J. *China's Crisis: Dilemmas of Reform and Prospects for Democracy*. 1990, Columbia Univ. Pr. $24.50 (0-231-07284-8). The Chinese reform movement of the late 1980s and its influences on official political, economic, and social policies. (Rev: Choice 10/90; LJ 5/1/90)   **[951.05]**

5431   Salisbury, Harrison E. *New Emperors: China in the Era of Mao and Deng*. 1992, Little, Brown $24.95 (0-316-80920-1). An analysis of the life and legacies of Chinese leaders Mao Zedong and Deng Xiaoping. "Salisbury's crowning achievement . . . deserves to become a classic."—PW (Rev: BL 12/1/91; LJ 2/1/92; PW 12/20/91)   **[951.05]**

5432   Salzmann, Mark. *Iron and Silk: In Which a Young American Encounters Swordsmen, Bureaucrats and Other Citizens of Contemporary China*. 1986, Random $17.95 (0-394-55156-7); paper $6.95 (0-679-72634-9). An American recounts his experiences during the two years he spent teaching and studying in China's Hunan province. (Rev: LJ 2/1/87; NYTBR 2/1/87; Time 3/2/87)   **[951.05]**

5433   Schell, Orville. *Discos and Democracy: China in the Throes of Reform*. 1988, Pantheon $19.95 (0-394-56829-X); Doubleday paper $9.95 (0-385-26187-X). A study of Chinese societal changes in the 1980s based on the author's year in China and his continued scholarship regarding the world's most populous nation. (Rev: LJ 5/15/88; NYTBR 6/19/88; PW 4/29/88)   **[951.05]**

5434   Schell, Orville. *To Get Rich Is Glorious: China in the Eighties*. 1986, NAL paper $3.95 (0-451-62437-8). A look at the spread of capitalism and private enterprise through China. "Schell has written about China extensively and with the utmost taste for years, and this striking account of a country in transition continues that tradition."—BL (Rev: BL 2/15/85; LJ 2/15/85; Newsweek 3/11/85. Awards: ALA, 1985) **[951.05]**

5435 Seagrave, Sterling. *Soong Dynasty.* 1986, Harper & Row paper $10.95 (0-06-091318-5). An account of the Soong family and their influence on modern China. Their family members included T. V. Soong and two daughters who married Sun Yat-Sen and Chiang Kai-Shek. (Rev: BL 3/1/85; NYTBR 3/17/85; PW 1/25/85. Awards: ALA, 1985; PW, 1985) **[951.05]**

5436 Smedley, Agnes. *Portraits of Chinese Women in Revolution.* Ed. by Jan MacKinnon and Steve MacKinnon. 1976, Feminist Pr. paper $10.95 (0-912670-44-4). Eighteen profiles of Chinese women based on interviews the American correspondent conducted during the 1920s and 1930s. (Rev: BL 3/1/77; Choice 7–8/77. Awards: ALA, 1976) **[951.05]**

5437 Terrill, Ross. *Madame Mao: The White-Boned Demon.* 1985, Bantam paper $11.95 (0-553-34189-8). A biography of the Chinese actress who became the wife of Mao Zedong and was a key member of the Gang of Four. (Rev: BL 2/15/84; LJ 2/1/84; Newsweek 2/20/84) **[951.05]**

5438 Thurston, Anne F. *Enemies of the People: The Ordeal of the Intellectuals in China's Great Cultural Revolution.* 1988, Harvard Univ. Pr. paper $12.50 (0-674-25375-2). A study of the effects of the Chinese Cultural Revolution of the mid-1960s on intellectuals and intellectual life in China based on interviews with 50 individuals who survived the upheaval. (Rev: Choice 10/87; LJ 2/1/87; NYTBR 2/22/87) **[951.05]**

5439 Tong, Shen, and Marianne Yen. *Almost a Revolution.* 1990, Houghton $19.95 (0-395-54693-1). A memoir of a Chinese student leader in the 1989 democracy movement regarding the events leading up to the Tiananmen Square massacre. "No one who cares about modern China should miss this document."—PW (Rev: BL 11/1/90; LJ 11/1/90; PW 9/28/90) **[951.05]**

5440 Woodruff, John. *China in Search of Its Future: Years of Great Reform, 1982–87.* 1989, Univ. of Washington Pr. $19.95 (0-295-96803-6). A study of China and its social reforms in the 1980s under the rule of Deng Xiaoping by a former Beijing correspondent for the *Baltimore Sun.* (Rev: BL 9/1/89; LJ 4/15/89; NYTBR 6/4/89) **[951.05]**

5441 Yi, Mu, and Mark V. Thompson. *Crisis at Tiananmen: Students, Press and Reform in China.* 1989, China Books paper $12.95 (0-8351-2290-5). Documents and journalistic accounts tracing the events leading to the 1989 Tiananmen Square massacre. (Rev: BL 2/1/90; LJ 2/1/90) **[951.05]**

Beijing—History

5442 Human Rights in China Staff. *Children of the Dragon: The Story of Tiananmen Square.* 1990, Macmillan paper $22.50 (0-02-033520-2). A chronicle of the events surrounding the 1989 student massa-

cre in Beijing's Tiananmen Square. (Rev: BL 6/1/90; LJ 6/1/90; PW 6/22/90) **[951.1]**

5443 Morrison, Hedda. *A Photographer in Old Peking.* 1986, Oxford Univ. Pr. $29.95 (0-19-584056-9). Over 200 photographs of Beijing in the 1930s and 1940s taken by a German photographer. (Rev: BL 12/1/86; Choice 1/87; LJ 11/15/86) **[951.1]**

Shanghai—History

5444 Sergeant, Harriet. *Shanghai: Collision Point of Cultures, 1918/1939.* 1991, Crown $25.00 (0-517-57025-4). A survey of the social, political, and cultural history of Shanghai between the wars. (Rev: BL 4/1/91; TLS 2/15/91) **[951.13]**

Hong Kong—History

5445 Morris, Jan. *Hong Kong.* 1988, Random $22.50 (0-394-55097-8); paper $8.95 (0-679-72486-9). The British travel writer's reflections upon the city of Hong Kong at the brink of its takeover by the People's Republic of China. (Rev: CSM 3/30/89; NYTBR 1/29/89; Time 1/6/89) **[951.25]**

Tibet—History

5446 Avedon, John F. *In Exile from the Land of the Snows.* 1985, Random paper $10.95 (0-394-74071-8). The history and culture of Tibet based on the author's interviews with the exiled Dalai Lama and focusing on its postrevolutionary control by Communist China. (Rev: BL 4/15/84; CSM 7/30/84; NYTBR 6/24/84. Awards: ALA, 1984) **[951.5]**

5447 Gyatso, Tenzin, and Galen Rowell. *My Tibet.* 1990, Univ. of California Pr. $35.00 (0-520-07109-3). A collection of photographs of Tibet taken by Galen Rowell with accompanying text by Dalai Lama. "Mr. Rowell has caught the natural beauty of that nation as no other photographer has done before."—NYTBR (Rev: BL 11/15/90; LJ 9/15/90; NYTBR 9/30/90) **[951.5]**

Korea—History

5448 Alexander, Bevin. *Korea: The First War We Lost.* 1986, Hippocrene Books $24.95 (0-87052-135-7). A military history of the Korean conflict. (Rev: BL 6/1/86; LJ 6/15/86; NYTBR 8/3/86) **[951.9]**

5449 Appleman, Roy Edgar. *East of Chosin: Entrapment and Breakout in Korea, 1950.* 1987, Texas A & M Univ. Pr. $28.50 (0-89096-283-9). An account of a marine division that was surrounded and decimated by Chinese troops in late 1950. (Rev: NYTBR 4/19/87; PW 3/13/87) **[951.9]**

5450 Berry, Henry. *Hey, Mac, Where Ya Been? Living Memories of the U.S. Marines in the Korean War.* 1988, St. Martin's $22.95 (0-312-017772-3); paper $4.95 (0-312-91605-1). Oral history of the Korean War taken from interviews with 60 marine veterans of the conflict. (Rev: BL 5/15/88; LJ 6/1/88; PW 5/13/88) **[951.9]**

5451 Hastings, Max. *Korean War.* 1988, Simon & Schuster paper $10.95 (0-671-66834-X). A survey history of the military and political events of the Korean War. (Rev: LJ 12/87; NYTBR 11/29/87; TLS 12/11/87) **[951.9]**

5452   Knox, Donald, and Alfred Coppel. *Korean War: Uncertain Victory, Vol. 2.* **1988, Harcourt $29.95 (0-15-147289-0).** The second volume of an oral history of the Korean War that covers the years from 1951 to 1953. (Rev: BL 5/1/88; LJ 5/1/88; New Rep 5/2/88) **[951.9]**

5453   Stephens, Michael Gregory. *Lost in Seoul and Other Discoveries on the Korean Peninsula.* **1990, Random $18.95 (0-394-57482-6).** An account of the author's experiences in South Korea visiting his wife's family. "A useful and insightful introduction to the people of Korea."—LJ (Rev: CSM 4/5/90; LJ 2/15/90; NYTBR 2/25/90) **[951.9]**

5454   Stokesbury, James L. *A Short History of the Korean War.* **1988, Morrow $18.95 (0-688-06377-2); paper $8.95 (0-688-09513-5).** A compact history of the Korean War from the North Korean attack of 1950 to the Panmunjan negotiations following the cease-fire. (Rev: BL 9/1/88; Choice 12/88; LJ 9/1/88) **[951.9]**

5455   Toland, John. *In Mortal Combat: Korea, 1950–1953.* **1991, Morrow $25.00 (0-688-10079-1).** An overview history of the Korean War by the author of *The Rising Sun.* "Panoramic, gripping and to a remarkable degree, original in its insights."—NYTBR (Rev: BL 10/1/91; LJ 9/1/91; NYTBR 10/13/91) **[951.9]**

5456   Whelan, Richard. *Drawing the Line: The Korean War, 1950–1953.* **1990, Little, Brown $24.95 (0-316-93403-8).** A political history of the Korean War by the biographer of Robert Capa. (Rev: BL 3/15/90; LJ 3/15/90; NYTBR 5/6/90) **[951.9]**

952   Japan

5457   Barthes, Roland. *Empire of Signs.* **1982, Hill & Wang paper $6.95 (0-8090-1502-1).** An examination of Japanese culture and society by the French writer. "One of Barthes's most accessible books . . . an enlightening experience."—PW (Rev: BL 11/15/82; LJ 10/15/82; PW 9/24/82) **[952]**

5458   Booth, Alan. *Roads to Sata: A 2000-Mile Walk Through Japan.* **1987, Penguin paper $6.95 (0-14-009566-7).** Accounts of the author's experiences during a walk between the northern and southern extremes of the island nation. (Rev: LJ 10/1/86; PW 10/24/86; TLS 6/6/86) **[952]**

5459   Morley, John David. *Pictures from the Water Trade: Adventures of a Westerner in Japan.* **1986, Harper & Row paper $7.95 (0-06-097041-3).** A student's excursion into the bars, cabarets, and nightlife of Japan. "Travel literature at its best."—NYTBR (Rev: NYTBR, 6/2/85; Time 8/19/85; TLS 1/3/86. Awards: Time, 1985) **[952]**

5460   Morris, Ivan. *Nobility of Failure: Tragic Heroes in the History of Japan.* **1988, Farrar paper $14.95 (0-374-52120-4).** The lives of tragic figures in Japanese history are examined, particularly those

who committed suicide rather than face ignoble defeat. (Rev: Choice 2/76; New Rep 12/20/75; PW 6/16/75) **[952]**

5461   Morris-Suzuki, Tessa. *Showa: An Inside History of Hirohito's Japan.* **1985, Schocken $18.95 (0-8052-3944-8).** Profiles the lives of three individuals—a business manager, a potter, and a writer—who grew up during the reign of the Emperor Hirohito. (Rev: LJ 2/15/85; PW 2/1/85; TLS 1/11/85) **[952]**

5462   Popham, Peter. *Tokyo: The City at the End of the World.* **1985, Kodansha $15.95 (0-87011-726-2).** The culture, design, and recent history of Japan's largest city. (Rev: BL 12/15/85; LJ 1/86; New Yorker 12/30/85) **[952]**

5463   Reischauer, Edwin O. *Japanese Today: Change and Continuity.* **1988, Belknap Pr. $25.00 (0-674-47181-4); Harvard Univ. Pr. paper $12.50 (0-674-47182-2).** A revised and updated version of the author's 1977 *The Japanese.* "An excellent survey for undergraduates and general readers."—LJ (Rev: CSM 2/24/88; LJ 1/88; PW 2/12/88) **[952]**

5464   Seidensticker, Edward. *Low City, High City, Tokyo from Edo to the Earthquake: How the Shogun's Ancient Capital Became a Great Modern City, 1867–1923.* **1985, Creative Arts paper $13.95 (0-916870-88-X).** A cultural history tracing the development of Tokyo in the late nineteenth and early twentieth centuries. (Rev: LJ 4/15/83; NYTBR 9/11/83; TLS 11/25/83) **[952]**

5465   Seidensticker, Edward. *Tokyo Rising: The City Since the Great Earthquake.* **1990, Knopf $24.95 (0-394-54360-2).** A study of the city of Tokyo from the 1923 earthquake to the present. (Rev: LJ 4/15/90; NYRB 6/28/90; NYTBR 4/1/90) **[952]**

5466   Totman, Conrad. *Japan Before Perry: A Short History.* **1981, Univ. of California Pr. paper $11.95 (0-520-04134-8).** The history of Japan from prehistoric cultures to 1853, the year of Perry's arrival. "A well-written and balanced introduction that should be acquired by public and undergraduate libraries."—LJ (Rev: Choice 11/81; LJ 8/81. Awards: ALA, 1981) **[952]**

History, 1185–1868

5467   McClellan, Edwin. *Woman in the Crested Kimono: The Life of Shibue Io and Her Family Drawn from Mori Ogai's "Shibue Cushai."* **1985, Yale Univ. Pr. $27.50 (0-300-03484-9); paper $10.95 (0-300-04618-9).** A biography of a nineteenth-century Japanese woman who was the wife of a samurai. Based on a biography of her family by Japanese writer Mori Ogai. (Rev: BL 9/1/85; LJ 9/1/85; NYTBR 9/15/85) **[952.02]**

5468   Wiley, Peter Booth, and Korogi Ichiro. *Yankees in the Land of the Gods: Commodore Perry and the Opening of Japan.* **1990, Viking $24.95 (0-670-81507-1).** An account of the 1853 American mission to Japan and its effects upon United States and Japanese relations and trade in the Pacific. (Rev: BL 12/15/90; LJ 10/15/90; PW 10/19/90) **[952.02]**

History, 1868–1945

5469 Behr, Edward. *Hirohito: Behind the Myth.* 1989, Random $22.50 (0-394-58702-9); paper $14.95 (0-679-73171-7). A biography of the Japanese emperor concentrating on his role before and during the Second World War. "A stirring biography certain to arouse considerable debate."—BL (Rev: BL 9/15/89; LJ 1/90; PW 9/1/89)   **[952.03]**

History, 1945–

5470 Christopher, Robert C. *Japanese Mind: The Goliath Explained.* 1984, Ballantine paper $7.95 (0-317-07487-3). A look at the values and society of the Japanese particularly in their applications to trade and business. "A superb overview of contemporary Japanese society . . . intelligent and thought-provoking."—LJ (Rev: Choice 10/83; LJ 4/15/83; Newsweek 8/8/83)   **[952.04]**

5471 Field, Norma. *In the Realm of a Dying Emperor.* 1991, Pantheon $22.00 (0-679-40504-6). A biography analyzing the life, legacy, and reputation of Japan's former emperor Hirohito. (Rev: LJ 9/1/91; NYRB 12/5/91)   **[952.04]**

5472 Iyer, Pico. *Lady and the Monk: Four Seasons in Kyoto.* 1991, Knopf $22.00 (0-679-40308-6). The author of *Video Nights in Katmandu* recounts his experiences during the year he spent living in Japan. "Told with a remarkable ear for dialogue and an uncanny sensitivity to people and places."—BL (Rev: BL 9/1/91; LJ 9/1/91; NYTBR 9/29/91)   **[952.04]**

5473 Tasker, Peter. *The Japanese: Portrait of a Nation.* 1989, NAL paper $9.95 (0-452-00983-9). An introduction to the history, culture, and contemporary society of Japan by a British writer. (Rev: BL 4/15/88; LJ 6/1/88; TLS 4/29/88)   **[952.04]**

5474 Wolferen, Karel Van. *Enigma of Japanese Power: People and Politics in a Stateless Nation.* 1989, Knopf $24.95 (0-394-57796-5). An analysis of the Japanese economy and society and how mutually held misconceptions threaten Japan's relationship with the West. (Rev: BL 4/1/89; NYRB 7/20/89; NYTBR 5/14/89)   **[952.04]**

953 Arabian Peninsula and adjacent areas

5475 Lacey, Robert. *Kingdom.* 1983, Avon paper $5.95 (0-380-61762-5). The history of Saudi Arabia in this century interwoven with personal accounts by the author. "Lacey's fluent account comes alive like few other studies of the contemporary Arab world."—BL (Rev: BL 1/15/82; LJ 4/1/82; PW 1/8/82. Awards: ALA, 1982)   **[953]**

1926–

5476 Theroux, Peter. *Sandstorms: Days and Nights in Arabia.* 1990, Norton $18.95 (0-393-02841-0). Memoirs of the author's experiences as a teacher and journalist in Egypt and Saudi Arabia. (Rev: BL 5/15/90; CSM 8/27/90; NYTBR 6/24/90)   **[953.05]**

954 South Asia; India

5477 Naipaul, V. S. *India: A Wounded Civilization.* 1977, Random paper $6.95 (0-394-72463-1). The noted writer from Trinidad made several extended trips to India, the land of his ancestors. These are his perceptions of that country. "This is an indispensable book for anyone who wants seriously to come to grips with the experience of that tortured land."—NYTBR (Rev: LJ 7/77; NYTBR 6/12/77; Newsweek 6/6/77. Awards: ALA, 1977; NYTBR, 1977)   **[954]**

5478 Wolpert, Stanley. *India.* 1991, Univ. of California Pr. $24.95 (0-520-07217-0). A survey of over 4,000 years of Indian history and culture. "If one were to read a single book about India in a lifetime, this should be it."—LJ (Rev: BL 4/1/91; LJ 3/1/91)   **[954]**

India—History, 1785–1947

5479 Allen, Charles, and Sharada Dwivedi. *Lives of the Indian Princes.* 1985, Crown $24.95 (0-517-55689-8). Studies of the lives of the princes who ruled the 565 autonomous states within India while the nation was under British sovereignty. (Rev: BL 5/1/85; LJ 5/1/85; TLS 8/2/85)   **[954.03]**

5480 Hibbert, Christopher. *Great Mutiny: India 1857.* 1980, Penguin paper $7.95 (0-14-004752-2). A study of the 1857 Sepoy Mutiny in which Indian troops, serving under British rule, rose up against the British in a failed insurrection. (Rev: BL 11/1/78; New Rep 11/11/78; Newsweek 10/23/78)   **[954.03]**

5481 Mason, Philip. *Men Who Ruled India.* 1985, Norton $27.50 (0-393-01946-2). A social and political history of India and its rulers from the beginning of the seventeenth century to its partition. (Rev: LJ 7/85; PW 4/19/85)   **[954.03]**

5482 Trevelyan, Raleigh. *Golden Oriole: A Two-Hundred-Year History of an English Family in India.* 1987, Viking $24.95 (0-670-81184-X); Simon & Schuster paper $12.95 (0-671-66977-X). A study of British rule and its influence in India as reflected through the history of the author's family on the subcontinent. (Rev: CSM 10/8/87; NYTBR 11/22/87; TLS 6/5/87)   **[954.03]**

India—History, 1947–1971

5483 Collins, Larry, and Dominique Lapierre. *Freedom at Midnight.* 1976, Avon paper $5.95 (0-380-00693-6). The story of the end of the British Empire in India and the creation of independent India and Pakistan are told in this work by the authors of *O Jerusalem.* (Rev: LJ 9/15/75; NYTBR 10/26/75; PW 8/18/75)   **[954.04]**

5484 Gupte, Pranay. *Mother India: A Political Biography of Indira Gandhi.* 1992, Scribner $24.95 (0-684-19296-9). A critical appraisal of the life and political career of the former Indian prime minister. (Rev: BL 1/1/92; PW 11/13/91)   **[954.04]**

5485 Malhotra, Inder. *Indira Gandhi: A Personal and Political Biography.* 1991, Northeastern Univ. Pr. $29.95 (1-55553-095-8). A portrayal of the former Indian leader by a longtime friend and journalist.

"A superb, balanced, riveting portrait."—PW (Rev: LJ 3/15/91; PW 2/15/91)   **[954.04]**

India—History, 1971–

5486   Grass, Gunter. *Show Your Tongue.* 1989, Harcourt $34.95 (0-15-182090-2); paper $19.95 (0-15-682330-6). An account of the German writer's experiences living with his wife in Calcutta. (Rev: BL 5/15/89; NYTBR 5/12/89; PW 4/21/89)   **[954.05]**

Calcutta—History

5487   Lapierre, Dominique. *City of Joy.* 1986, Warner paper $4.95 (0-446-32386-1). A look inside one of Calcutta's most notorious slums with portraits of some of the people who live and work there. (Rev: LJ 11/1/85; NYRB 5/29/86; NYTBR 11/3/85. Awards: ALA, 1985)   **[954.14]**

Pakistan—History

5488   Bhutto, Benazir. *Daughter of Destiny: An Autobiography.* 1989, Simon & Schuster $21.95 (0-671-66983-4); paper $9.95 (0-671-69603-3). Benazir Bhutto's account of her life as the daughter of former Pakistani leader Zulkifar Al Bhutto and of her rise to the post of prime minister. (Rev: NYRB 3/2/89; PW 2/10/89; TLS 12/23/89)   **[954.9]**

955   Iran

5489   Arjomand, Said Amir. *Turban for the Crown: The Islamic Revolution in Iran.* 1988, Oxford Univ. Pr. $30.00 (0-19-504257-3); paper $9.95 (0-19-504258-1). The history and analysis of the roots and causes of the 1979 Iranian Revolution. (Rev: BL 6/15/88; Choice 1/89; NYTBR 7/31/88)   **[955]**

5490   Bakhash, Shaul. *Reign of the Ayatollahs: Iran and the Islamic Revolution.* 1990, Basic Books paper $11.95 (0-465-06890-1). An appraisal of the events leading to, during, and following the Iranian Revolution by a journalist who witnessed the uprising. (Rev: Choice 3/85; LJ 9/15/84; NYTBR 10/21/84)   **[955]**

5491   Kapuscinski, Ryszard. *Shah of Shahs.* 1985, Harcourt $12.95 (0-15-181483-X); Random paper $7.95 (0-394-74074-2). A Polish journalist's view of the rise and fall of the shah of Iran. "An extraordinary account by a keenly observant journalist."—BL (Rev: BL 3/1/85; LJ 3/15/85; NYTBR 4/7/85. Awards: ALA, 1985)   **[955]**

5492   Kennedy, Moorehead. *Ayatollah in the Cathedral: Reflections of a Hostage.* 1986, Hill & Wang $17.95 (0-8090-2765-8). The former diplomat recounts his experiences as a hostage in the 1979 Iranian takeover of the American Embassy in Tehran. (Rev: Choice 12/86; LJ 7/86; PW 6/13/86)   **[955]**

5493   Mottahedeh, Roy. *Mantle of the Prophet: Religion and Politics in Iran.* 1986, Pantheon paper $11.95 (0-394-74865-4). A history of modern Iranian politics, education, and religious training centered on the life and scholarship of a mullah. (Rev: Choice 1/86; CSM 10/4/85; NYRB 1/30/86)   **[955]**

5494   Sick, Gary. *All Fall Down: America's Tragic Encounter with Iran.* 1986, Penguin paper $8.95 (0-14-008837-7). The inside story of the Iranian Revolution and hostage crisis by a former Carter administration National Security Council member. "Sick's book is wise, even profound."—New Rep (Rev: New Rep 7/8/85; NYTBR 6/16/85; PW 4/12/85. Awards: NYTBR, 1985)   **[955]**

5495   Wright, Robin. *In the Name of God: The Khomeini Decade, 1979–1989.* 1989, Simon & Schuster $19.95 (0-671-67235-5). A survey of the cultural changes in Iran from the 1979 Revolution to the death of the Ayatollah Khomeini. "The best account of Khomeini's Iran to date."—NYTBR (Rev: BL 10/1/89; LJ 10/15/89; NYTBR 11/26/89)   **[955]**

1906–

5496   Christopher, Warren. *American Hostages in Iran: The Conduct of a Crisis.* 1986, Yale Univ. Pr. paper $14.95 (0-300-03584-5). An account of negotiations between the United States and Iran for the release of American hostages as recounted by the former Carter administration deputy secretary of state. (Rev: Choice 9/85; LJ 5/1/85; NYTBR 7/14/85)   **[955.05]**

956   Middle East (Near East)

5497   Carter, Jimmy. *Blood of Abraham: Insights into the Middle East.* 1985, Houghton $15.95 (0-395-37722-6); paper $7.95 (0-395-41498-9). An examination of the past, present, and future of the Middle East by the former president. (Rev: LJ 5/1/85; NYTBR 4/28/85; PW 3/22/85)   **[956]**

5498   Friedman, Thomas L. *From Beirut to Jerusalem.* 1989, Farrar $19.95 (0-374-15894-0); Doubleday paper $12.95 (0-385-41372-6). The *New York Times'* Pulitzer Prize-winning reporter's views of his ten years in Israel and Lebanon. "A masterful blend of reportage and poetic detail."—LJ (Rev: LJ 7/89; Newsweek 7/24/89; Time 7/10/89. Awards: BL, 1989; LJ, 1989; NBA, 1989; NYTBR, 1989)   **[956]**

5499   Fromkin, David. *A Peace to End All Peace: Creating the Modern Middle East, 1914–1922.* 1989, Henry Holt $39.95 (0-8050-0857-8). An exploration of the collapse of the Ottoman Empire, and the creation of the modern Middle East. "This outstanding book puts most pieces of the Middle East puzzle into place in a way that no one volume has done before."—NYTBR (Rev: BL 8/89; NYTBR 8/27/89; New Yorker 12/11/89. Awards: BL, 1989; NYTBR, 1989)   **[956]**

5500   Halabi, Rafik. *West Bank Story: An Israeli Arab's View of Both Sides of a Tangled Conflict.* 1985, Harcourt paper $7.95 (0-15-695724-8). An examination of the past, present, and future of the Israeli-occupied West Bank as seen by an Israeli Druse Arab. (Rev: BL 2/1/82; LJ 2/1/82; PW 1/1/82)   **[956]**

5501   Herzog, Chaim. *Arab-Israeli Wars: War and Peace in the Middle East, from the War of Independence Through Lebanon.* 1983, Random paper $12.95 (0-394-71746-5). An overview of armed conflict between Arabs and Israelis, including the

1948 War of Independence, the 1956 Sinai Campaign, the 1967 Six Day War, the 1973 Yom Kippur War, and the Israeli involvement in Lebanon. (REV: LJ 9/1/82; PW 7/2/82; TLS 11/19/82) **[956]**

5502 Wallach, John, and Janet Wallach. *Still Small Voices: The Real Heroes of the Arab-Israeli Conflict.* **1989, Harcourt $18.95 (0-15-184970-6); Carol Publg. Group paper $9.95 (0-8065-1171-0).** Portraits of a dozen Arabs and Jews living in the Israeli-occupied territories of the West Bank and the Gaza Strip. (REV: BL 3/1/89; LJ 3/15/89; NYTBR 7/9/89) **[956]**

Middle East—History, 1945–1980

5503 Kunstel, Marcia, and Joseph Albright. *Their Promised Land: Arab and Jew in History's Cauldron.* **1990, Crown $19.95 (0-517-57231-1).** An analysis of the lives of Palestinian Arabs and Israeli Jews who live in a small valley near Jerusalem. (REV: BL 9/1/90; LJ 9/1/90; PW 9/28/90) **[956.04]**

5504 Said, Edward W., and Christopher Hitchens, eds. *Blaming the Victims: Spurious Scholarship and the Palestinian Question.* **1988, Routledge $50.00 (0-86091-175-6); paper $14.95 (0-86091-887-4).** A series of essays presenting a case for the establishment of a Palestinian nation and highly critical of the United States' anti-Palestinian stance from 1948 to the present. (REV: BL 1/15/88; LJ 1/88; PW 12/18/87) **[956.04]**

5505 Wright, Robin. *Sacred Rage: The Wrath of Militant Islam.* **1986, Simon & Schuster paper $8.95 (0-671-62811-9).** An exploration of the historical roots and causes of terrorism toward Western nations in the Middle East. (REV: BL 10/1/85; CSM 10/25/85; PW 9/13/85) **[956.04]**

Middle East—History, 1980–

5506 Dickey, Christopher. *Expats: Travels in Arabia, from Tripoli to Teheran.* **1990, Atlantic Monthly $18.95 (0-87113-337-7).** Accounts of the European and American workers and expatriates the author encountered during his travels in the Arab world. (REV: BL 7/90; LJ 6/15/90; TLS 9/7/90) **[956.05]**

Iraq—History

5507 Al Khalil, Samir. *Republic of Fear: The Politics of Modern Iraq.* **1989, Univ. of California Pr. $25.00 (0-520-06442-9).** The history of modern Iraq and its political leadership since the ascension of the Ba'th party to power in 1968. (REV: Choice 10/89; LJ 4/1/89) **[956.7]**

5508 Karsh, Efraim, and Inari Rautsi. *Saddam Hussein: A Political Biography.* **1991, Free Pr. $22.95 (0-02-917063-X).** A study of the life and times of the Iraqi leader. (REV: LJ 5/15/91; NYTBR 5/5/91) **[956.7]**

5509 Miller, Judith, and Laurie Mylroie. *Saddam Hussein and the Crisis in the Gulf.* **1990, Random paper $5.95 (0-8129-1921-1).** An analysis of Hussein's rise to power in Iraq and his quest for regional dominance. (REV: BL 12/15/90; LJ 1/91; NYTBR 11/11/90) **[956.7]**

5510 Sciolino, Elaine. *Outlaw State: Saddam Hussein's Quest for Power and the Gulf Crisis.* **1991, Wiley $22.95 (0-471-54299-7).** An analysis of the recent history of Iraq and its foreign relations by a longtime *New York Times* journalist. (REV: BL 7/91; LJ 7/91) **[956.7]**

Syria—History

5511 Ma'oz, Moshe. *Assad: The Sphinx of Damascus.* **1990, Grove-Weidenfeld paper $9.95 (1-55584-433-2).** A biography of Syrian President Hafiz al-Assad analyzing his nation's current and future role in the Middle East. (REV: Choice 1/89; LJ 9/15/88; NYTBR 1/1/89) **[956.91]**

5512 Seale, Patrick. *Asad of Syria: The Struggle for the Middle East.* **1989, Univ. of California Pr. $25.00 (0-520-06667-7); paper $14.95 (0-520-06976-5).** A biography of the Syrian President Hafiz al-Assad surveying the role of Syria in the contemporary Middle East. (REV: Choice 10/89; LJ 4/1/89; PW 3/17/89) **[956.91]**

Lebanon—History

5513 Ajami, Fouad, and Eli Reed. *Beirut: City of Regrets.* **1988, Norton $34.95 (0-393-02490-3); paper $19.95 (0-393-30507-4).** Photographs and text detailing the destruction of the city of Beirut during the early 1980s. (REV: LJ 7/88; NYTBR 7/17/88; PW 6/17/88) **[956.92]**

5514 Fisk, Robert. *Pity the Nation: Lebanon at War.* **1990, Macmillan $24.95 (0-689-12105-9).** A study of Lebanon's recent history and diplomatic relations by a former *London Times* correspondent. "Should be read by everyone interested in the Middle East."—PW (REV: BL 11/15/90; LJ 1/91; PW 10/26/90) **[956.92]**

5515 Khalidi, Rashid. *Under Siege: P.L.O. Decisionmaking during the 1982 War.* **1985, Columbia Univ. Pr. $30.00 (0-231-06186-2); paper $12.50 (0-231-06187-0).** Accounts of PLO political action and diplomatic maneuvering during the 1982 Lebanese war. (REV: Choice 5/86; NYTBR 12/15/85; PW 11/8/85) **[956.92]**

5516 Mackey, Sandra. *Lebanon: The Death of a Nation.* **1989, Congdon & Weed $22.95 (0-86553-204-4).** A survey of the history of Lebanon, the often conflicting cultures that make up the nation, and the problems it faces in the present and future. (REV: BL 7/89; LJ 7/89; NYTBR 7/23/89) **[956.92]**

5517 Makdisi, Jean Said. *Beirut Fragments: A War Memoir.* **1990, Persea Books $17.95 (0-89255-150-X).** Memoirs of the author's life in war-torn Beirut since 1972 when she moved there with her Lebanese husband. (REV: LJ 9/1/90; NYTBR 9/16/90; PW 7/27/90) **[956.92]**

5518 Petran, Tabitha. *Struggle over Lebanon.* **1987, Monthly Review $27.50 (0-85345-651-8); paper $14.00 (0-85345-652-6).** The social and political history of Lebanon since the sixteenth century tracing the roots of the present-day conflict. (REV: Choice 1/88; LJ 5/15/87)   **[956.92]**

Israel—History

5519   Avineri, Shlomo. *Making of Modern Zionism: The Intellectual Origins of the Jewish State.* 1984, Basic Books paper $11.95 (0-465-04331-3). A history of the development of Zionist thought in the nineteenth and twentieth centuries. (REV: Choice 1/82; New Rep 10/21/81; NYTBR 11/8/81)   **[956.94]**

5520   Avishai, Bernard. *Tragedy of Zionism: Revolution and Democracy in the Land of Israel.* 1985, Farrar $19.95 (0-374-27863-6); paper $8.95 (0-374-52044-5). An examination of the theory of Zionism and its reality as practiced in contemporary Israel. (REV: CSM 11/4/85; LJ 9/15/85; Natl Rev 11/29/85)   **[956.94]**

5521   Chafets, Ze'ev. *Heroes and Hustlers, Hard Hats and Holymen: Inside the New Israel.* 1987, Morrow paper $7.95 (0-688-07294-1). A survey of contemporary Israeli society by the American-born former director of Israel's Government Press Office. (REV: BL 6/1/86; LJ 4/15/86; NYTBR 4/13/86)   **[956.94]**

5522   Collins, Larry, and Dominique Lapierre. *O Jerusalem!* 1988, Simon & Schuster paper $10.95 (0-671-66241-4). The 1947–1948 battle for the city of Jerusalem between Arabs and Jews. "A spellbinding, heartbreaking, marvellously readable nonstop thriller."—Choice (REV: Choice 3/73; CSM 5/17/72; NYTBR 5/14/72)   **[956.94]**

5523   Dan, Uri, and Yossi Harel. *To the Promised Land: The Birth of Israel.* 1988, Doubleday $24.95 (0-385-24597-1). An illustrated history of the events that led to the creation of Israel in 1948. (REV: BL 4/1/88; LJ 3/1/88)   **[956.94]**

5524   Dayan, Yael. *My Father, His Daughter.* 1985, Farrar $17.95 (0-374-21695-9). The author remembers her father, the legendary Israeli military commander and politician. "Not only a fascinating memoir, but an intimate and fascinating history of Israel."—LJ (REV: BL 10/15/85; LJ 10/1/85; NYTBR 11/3/85)   **[956.94]**

5525   Elon, Amos. *Herzl.* 1985, Schocken paper $12.95 (0-8052-0790-2). A biography of Theodor Herzl, the Austrian journalist, generally regarded as the father of modern Zionism. "Essential reading for an understanding of the Middle East."—LJ (REV: Choice 6/75; LJ 6/15/75; New Rep 2/8/75)   **[956.94]**

5526   Elon, Amos. *Jerusalem: City of Mirrors.* 1989, Little, Brown $19.95 (0-316-23388-9). A study of Jerusalem's past, present, and future as seen by the noted Israeli journalist. (REV: BL 8/89; LJ 9/1/89; NYTBR 10/1/89)   **[956.94]**

5527   Friedlander, Saul. *When Memory Comes.* 1980, Avon paper $3.50 (0-380-50807-9). Memoirs of an Israeli historian who escaped the Holocaust and fled to Palestine to fight for the state of Israel. (REV: BL 7/15/79; NYRB 10/25/79; NYTBR 7/15/79)   **[956.94]**

5528   Gorkin, Michael. *Days of Honey, Days of Onion: The Story of a Palestinian Family in Israel.* 1991, Beacon $24.95 (0-8070-6902-7). The story of a Palestinian family living in Israel from 1949 to the present. "An intimate, revealing, unbiased probe . . . a valuable and engaging report."—PW (REV: BL 10/15/91; LJ 9/15/91; PW 7/12/91)   **[956.94]**

5529   Grossman, David. *Yellow Wind.* 1988, Farrar $17.95 (0-374-29345-7). The Israeli journalist and novelist reports on his experiences touring the West Bank in a book highly critical of his country's policies and actions there. (REV: LJ 4/15/88; NYTBR 3/6/88; Newsweek 3/14/88. AWARDS: LJ, 1988)   **[956.94]**

5530   Halkin, Hillel. *Letters to an American Jewish Friend: A Zionist's Polemic.* 1977, Jewish Publication Soc. paper $8.95 (0-8276-0207-3). A series of letters from an American-born Israeli to an American friend arguing that the only place for a Jew to live is Israel. (REV: BL 11/1/77; New Rep 1/14/78; PW 5/16/77)   **[956.94]**

5531   Harkabi, Yehoshafat. *Israel's Fateful Hour.* 1988, Harper & Row $22.50 (0-06-016039-X); paper $10.95 (0-06-091613-3). The Hebrew University of Jerusalem professor argues that a negotiated settlement to form a Palestinian state would be in the best national interest of Israel. (REV: BL 11/1/88; Choice 3/89; NYTBR 11/20/89)   **[956.94]**

5532   Laqueur, Walter. *History of Zionism.* 1989, Schocken paper $16.95 (0-8052-0899-2). The history of Zionism over the past three centuries from its European roots to the establishment of the state of Israel. "Sympathetic but fairly well-balanced in its viewpoint . . . the best single volume for the general reader."—LJ (REV: LJ 8/72; NYTBR 11/12/72; Newsweek 10/16/72)   **[956.94]**

5533   Meir, Golda. *My Life.* 1976, Dell paper $1.95 (0-440-15656-4). An autobiography of the former Israeli prime minister from her youth in Russia to the Yom Kippur War. (REV: NYTBR 11/30/75; Newsweek 11/3/75; PW 9/22/75)   **[956.94]**

5534   O'Brien, Conor Cruise. *Siege: The Saga of Israel and Zionism.* 1987, Simon & Schuster paper $12.95 (0-671-63310-4). A history of Zionism, the state of Israel, and its relations with its surrounding nations. "An informed and balanced account of the long and seemingly endless tragedy of Middle East politics."—Time (REV: CSM 3/12/86; LJ 3/15/86; Time 4/21/86. AWARDS: LJ, 1986; Time, 1986)   **[956.94]**

5535   Oz, Amos. *In the Land of Israel.* 1984, Random paper $7.95 (0-394-72728-2). Essays by the noted novelist originally written for a series of newspaper articles regarding aspects of life in contemporary Israel. (REV: Atl 12/83; LJ 11/15/83; NYTBR 11/6/83)   **[956.94]**

5536   Perlmutter, Amos. *Life and Times of Menachem Begin.* 1987, Doubleday $21.95 (0-385-18926-5). A political biography of the former Israeli prime minister. "A biography done with deep understanding, a portrayal that is both authoritative and convincing."—NYTBR (Rev: CSM 6/26/87; New Rep 6/8/87; NYTBR 6/21/87) **[956.94]**

5537 Reinharz, Jehuda. *Chaim Weizmann: The Making of a Zionist Leader.* **1985, Oxford Univ. Pr. $35.00 (0-19-503446-5).** This first volume of a projected two-volume biography of Israel's first president covers his life to the outbreak of World War I. "As this book shows, he personified Jewish history."—NYTBR (Rev: Choice 9/85; LJ 4/1/85; NYTBR 6/30/85) **[956.94]**

5538 Rose, Norman. *Chaim Weizmann: A Biography.* **1986, Viking $24.95 (0-670-80469-X).** A biographical study of Israel's first president. (Rev: CSM 12/30/86; LJ 11/1/86; NYTBR 11/23/86) **[956.94]**

5539 Safran, Nadav. *Israel: The Embattled Ally.* **1978, Harvard Univ. Pr. $33.00 (0-674-46881-3); paper $14.50 (0-674-46882-1).** The history of Israel and its relationship with the United States. "Intelligent, readable and packed with information . . . a model of impartiality."—PW (Rev: Choice 7–8/78; NYTBR 3/12/78; PW 12/26/78) **[956.94]**

5540 Said, Edward W. *Question of Palestine.* **1980, Random paper $7.95 (0-394-74527-2).** An examination of the history and current plight of the Palestinian people and their search for a homeland. (Rev: LJ 11/15/79; NYRB 6/12/80; NYTBR 1/20/80) **[956.94]**

5541 Schiff, Ze'ev, and Ya'ari Ehud. *Intifada: The Palestinian Uprising—Israel's Third Front.* **1990, Simon & Schuster $22.95 (0-671-67530-3); paper $10.95 (0-671-73291-9).** Two Israeli journalists' views of the Palestinian uprising and its effects upon their nation. (Rev: BL 2/1/90; Natl Rev 5/28/90; PW 1/12/90) **[956.94]**

5542 Sharon, Ariel, and David Chanoff. *Warrior: The Autobiography of Ariel Sharon.* **1989, Simon & Schuster $24.95 (0-671-60555-0); paper $14.95 (0-671-70593-8).** An autobiography of the controversial Israeli military commander and government minister. "Engrossing . . . this major work reveals much about high-level policy making in Israel."—PW (Rev: LJ 9/1/89; NYTBR 9/3/89; PW 7/21/89) **[956.94]**

5543 Teveth, Shabtai. *Ben-Gurion: The Burning Ground, 1886–1948.* **1988, Houghton paper $12.95 (0-395-48358-1).** A biography of the Zionist leader and first prime minister of Israel. (Rev: Choice 11/87; LJ 7/87; NYTBR 6/21/87) **[956.94]**

5544 Turki, Fawaz. *Soul in Exile: Lives of a Palestinian Revolutionary.* **1987, Monthly Review $26.00 (0-85345-746-8); paper $10.00 (0-85345-747-6).** The autobiography of an exiled Palestinian presenting a personal view of his people's lack of a homeland and government. "An extraordinarily vivid and poignant illustration of the Palestinian condition, past and present."—BL (Rev: BL 3/15/88; LJ 4/15/88) **[956.94]**

5545 Wallach, Janet, and John Wallach. *Arafat: In the Eyes of the Beholder.* **1990, Carol Publg. Group $21.95 (0-8184-0533-3).** A biography of the PLO

leader based on interviews with Arafat, his family, and acquaintants. (Rev: BL 7/90; LJ 9/1/90; PW 9/7/90) **[956.94]**

5546 Wolf, Aaron. *A Purity of Arms: An American in the Israeli Army.* **1989, Doubleday $19.95 (0-385-26036-9).** The story of an American who emigrated to Israel and spent two years of service in the Israeli army. (Rev: BL 11/1/89; LJ 11/15/89; PW 10/13/89) **[956.94]**

958 Central Asia

Afghanistan—History

5547 Bonner, Arthur. *Among the Afghans.* **1987, Duke $29.95 (0-8223-0783-9).** Personal experiences of the *New York Times* correspondent highlight this survey of recent Afghan history. (Rev: BL 11/1/87; LJ 11/1/87; NYTBR 11/8/87) **[958.1]**

5548 Borovik, Artyom. *Hidden War: A Russian Journalist's Account of the Soviet War in Afghanistan.* **1991, Atlantic Monthly $19.95 (0-87113-283-4).** A Soviet journalist recounts his experiences during a month spent with his nation's troops during the Afghanistan war. (Rev: BL 11/1/90; NYTBR 1/13/91; PW 11/23/90) **[958.1]**

5549 Kaplan, Robert D. *Soldiers of God: With the Mujahidin in Afghanistan.* **1990, Houghton $19.95 (0-395-52132-7).** A journalist's account of his experiences with rebel forces in Afghanistan. "One of the most moving and emotional works to be written in this decade."—LJ (Rev: LJ 12/89; New Yorker 2/19/90; PW 12/89) **[958.1]**

5550 Waller, John H. *Beyond the Khyber Pass: The Road to British Disaster in the First Afghan War.* **1990, Random $24.95 (0-394-56934-2).** An account of the British defeat in the 1839–1842 Afghan War. "One of the best nonfiction books of the year."—BL (Rev: BL 6/1/90; LJ 6/1/90) **[958.1]**

Soviet Central Asia

5551 Leighton, Ralph. *Tuva or Bust! Richard Feynman's Last Journey.* **1991, Norton $19.95 (0-393-02953-0).** A tale of the efforts of physicist Richard Feynman to visit a remote region of the Soviet Union. "A tale of adventure, heartbreak and rare friendship."—PW (Rev: LJ 3/1/91; PW 2/22/91) **[958.4]**

959 Southeast Asia

5552 Chanda, Nayan. *Brother Enemy: The War after the War.* **1986, Harcourt $24.95 (0-15-114420-6); Macmillan paper $12.95 (0-02-049361-4).** A study of armed conflicts in Vietnam and Cambodia following the American withdrawal from Southeast Asia in 1975. (Rev: CSM 12/28/86; LJ 12/86; NYTBR 12/28/86) **[959]**

Cambodia—History

5553 Becker, Elizabeth. *When the War Was Over: The Voices of Cambodia's Revolution and Its People.* **1986, Simon & Schuster $19.95 (0-317-**

53639-7). A history of the Cambodian genocide during the late 1970s under the rule of the Khmer Rouge. (Rev: CSM 11/17/86; Natl Rev 2/27/87; PW 8/15/87)   **[959.6]**

5554   Criddle, Joan D., and Teeda Butt Man. *To Destroy You Is No Loss: The Odyssey of a Cambodian Family.* 1989, Doubleday paper $9.95 (0-385-26628-6). The story of a Cambodian family's experiences under the rule of the Pol Pot regime and the family's eventual emigration to the United States. "A poignant testimony to the human will to survive."—PW (Rev: LJ 7/87; NYTBR 8/2/87; PW 6/5/87)   **[959.6]**

5555   Freeman, Michael, and Roger Warner. *Angkor: The Hidden Glories.* 1990, David Larkin Books $45.00 (0-395-53757-6). An illustrated survey of the twelfth-century ruins of Angkor in present-day Cambodia. (Rev: BL 10/1/90; LJ 9/15/90)   **[959.6]**

5556   Ngor, Haing S., and Roger Warner. *Haing Ngor: A Cambodian Odyssey.* 1989, Warner paper $12.95 (0-446-38990-0). Real life experiences under the Pol Pot regime by the actor who played Dith Pran in *The Killing Fields*. (Rev: BL 2/15/88; LJ 2/1/88; NYTBR 2/21/88)   **[959.6]**

5557   Sheehy, Gail. *Spirit of Survival.* 1987, Bantam paper $4.95 (0-553-26573-3). The author of *Passages* tells the story of a Cambodian girl she adopted whose family members were victims of the Pol Pot regime. "An intensely personal narrative that almost belies the subject's universal significance."—BL (Rev: BL 4/15/86; LJ 6/1/86; PW 4/4/86)   **[959.6]**

5558   Szymusiak, Molyda. *Stones Cry Out: A Cambodian Childhood, 1975–1980.* 1986, Hill & Wang $17.95 (0-8090-8844-4). An account of a Cambodian girl's five-year struggle to survive and escape the Pol Pot regime. (Rev: NYTBR 10/5/86; Newsweek 7/28/86; PW 5/2/86)   **[959.6]**

Vietnam—History

5559   Alvarez, Everett, Jr., and Anthony S. Pitch. *Chained Eagle.* 1989, Donald I. Fine $18.95 (1-55611-167-3). Memoirs of the first American prisoner of war taken during the Vietnam War, and his eight years of captivity. (Rev: BL 11/1/89; LJ 11/1/89; Natl Rev 3/19/90)   **[959.7]**

5560   Balaban, John. *Remembering Heaven's Face: A Moral Witness in Vietnam.* 1991, Poseidon $19.95 (0-671-69065-5). Memoirs of the author's humanitarian service in Vietnam as a conscientious objector. (Rev: BL 6/15/91; LJ 5/15/91; PW 5/10/91)   **[959.7]**

5561   Baritz, Loren. *Backfire: American Culture and the Vietnam War.* 1986, Ballantine paper $3.95 (0-345-33121-4). A look at American cultural values and how they influenced decisions of involvement and prosecution of the war in Vietnam. (Rev: BL 1/15/85; Choice 6/85; CSM 3/29/85)   **[959.7]**

5562   Beesley, Stanley W. *Vietnam: The Heartland Remembers.* 1987, Univ. of Oklahoma Pr. $18.95

(0-8061-2062-2); paper $7.95 (0-8061-2162-9). An oral history of over 30 Oklahoma veterans and their wives or widows regarding their lives during and after the Vietnam War. (Rev: BL 8/87; LJ 7/87; PW 7/17/87)   **[959.7]**

5563   Boettcher, Thomas D. *Vietnam: The Valor and the Sorrow; from the Homefront to the Front Lines in Words and Pictures.* 1985, Little, Brown paper $16.95 (0-316-10081-1). A history of French and American involvement in Vietnam. "Readers searching for a comprehensive, evenhanded account of our longest war need look no further than this excellent volume."—NYTBR (Rev: BL 7/85; LJ 6/15/85; NYTBR 6/2/85)   **[959.7]**

5564   Brace, Ernest C. *Code to Keep: Prisoner in Vietnam.* 1988, State Mutual $48.00 (0-7090-3560-8); St. Martin's paper $4.95 (0-312-91501-2). An autobiography of a civilian held as a prisoner of war in Vietnam following his capture in Laos in 1965. (Rev: BL 11/1/88; LJ 1/88; PW 12/25/87)   **[959.7]**

5565   Broughton, Jack. *Going Downtown: The War Against Hanoi and Washington.* 1988, Crown $18.95 (0-517-56738-5); Pocket paper $4.95 (0-671-67862-0). An indictment of American management of the air war in Vietnam by a veteran pilot who served in both the Vietnamese and Korean conflicts. (Rev: LJ 9/1/88; PW 7/8/88)   **[959.7]**

5566   Broyles, William, Jr. *Brothers in Arms: A Journey from War to Peace.* 1987, Avon paper $4.50 (0-380-70355-6). The story of a U.S. Marine lieutenant who returned to Vietnam 15 years after combat. "Few books capture the essence of the Vietnam War and its aftermath so vividly as this one."—PW (Rev: LJ 6/1/86; Newsweek 6/15/86; PW 4/25/86. Awards: LJ, 1986)   **[959.7]**

5567   Butler, David. *Fall of Saigon: Scenes from the Sudden End of a Long War.* Dell paper $4.95 (0-440-12431-X). The last two months of the Vietnam War and the final collapse of South Vietnam based on the author's experiences and interviews with U.S. and South Vietnamese military personnel. (Rev: BL 4/15/85; Choice 9/86; CSM 7/15/85)   **[959.7]**

5568   Caputo, Philip. *A Rumor of War.* 1987, Ballantine paper $5.95 (0-345-33122-2). Recollections of a marine officer's tour of duty in Vietnam. "When his book is closed, no explanation of the chasm between veteran and civilian is necessary; it has been amply demonstrated."—BL (Rev: BL 5/15/77; NYTBR 5/29/77; New Yorker 6/13/77. Awards: ALA, 1977)   **[959.7]**

5569   Chinnery, Philip D. *Life on the Line: Stories of Vietnam Air Combat.* 1988, St. Martin's $17.95 (0-312-02599-8); paper $4.95 (0-312-92010-5). An oral history of 36 combat pilots who served in the Vietnam War, by a British journalist. (Rev: BL 2/15/89; PW 1/20/89; LJ 2/15/89)   **[959.7]**

5570   Christian, David, and William Hoffer. *Victor Six: The Saga of America's Youngest, Most Decorated Officer in Vietnam.* 1990, McGraw-Hill $19.95 (0-07-010856-0). Memoirs of a former army reconnaissance leader's experiences in Vietnam and following the war. (REV: BL 9/1/90; LJ 8/90; PW 7/6/90)   **[959.7]**

5571 De Forest, Orrin M., and David Chanoff. *Slow Burn: The Rise and Bitter Fall of American Intelligence in Vietnam.* **1990, Simon & Schuster $19.95 (0-671-69258-5).** A former CIA officer who served in Vietnam examines the gathering and use of American intelligence during the war. (REV: BL 4/15/90; NYTBR 4/22/90; PW 3/16/90)   **[959.7]**

5572 Donovan, David. *Once a Warrior King.* **1986, Ballantine paper $4.95 (0-345-33316-0).** A former United States Army lieutenant recounts his experiences as a trainer and advisor of South Vietnamese troops in the Mekong Delta. "One of the best books to come out of the Vietnam experience."—BL (REV: BL 6/1/85; LJ 6/1/85; NYTBR 6/30/85)   **[959.7]**

5573 Fall, Bernard. *Last Reflections on a War.* **1987, Schocken paper $8.95 (0-8052-0329-X).** A posthumously published collection of essays on the Vietnam War selected by the author's widow. (REV: BL 5/1/68; Newsweek 11/20/67; PW 11/13/67)   **[959.7]**

5574 Glasser, Ronald J. *365 Days.* **1971, Braziller paper $7.95 (0-8076-0995-1).** An account by a former military doctor in Japan who treated American servicemen wounded in Vietnam. "It is inconceivable that anyone could read his book without being overwhelmed by its searing descriptions of . . . shattered soldiers."—PW (REV: Atl 10/71; LJ 7/71; PW 7/5/71. AWARDS: ALA, 1971; Time, 1971)   **[959.7]**

5575 Grant, Zalin. *Facing the Phoenix: The Political Defeat of the United States in Vietnam.* **1991, Norton $22.50 (0-393-02925-5).** A study of American efforts to combat leftist political organization in South Vietnamese communities. (REV: BL 1/15/91; LJ 1/91; NYTBR 2/3/91)   **[959.7]**

5576 Grant, Zalin. *Over the Beach: The Air War in Vietnam.* **1986, Norton $18.95 (0-393-02332-X).** An account of the combat exploits of a naval air squadron during the Vietnam War. (REV: BL 10/1/86; LJ 11/1/86; NYTBR 1/11/87)   **[959.7]**

5577 Greene, Bob. *Homecoming: When the Soldiers Returned from Vietnam.* **1989, Putnam $17.95 (0-399-13386-0); Ballantine paper $4.95 (0-345-36408-2).** Collected letters written to the newspaper columnist by Vietnam veterans describing their return to the U.S. after service. (REV: BL 11/15/88; LJ 1/89; NYTBR 1/22/89)   **[959.7]**

5578 Hayslip, Le Ly, and Jay Wurts. *When Heaven and Earth Changed Places: A Vietnamese Woman's Journey from War to Peace.* **1989, Doubleday $18.95 (0-385-24758-3); NAL paper $9.95 (0-452-26417-0).** A Vietnamese woman's story of her youth during the Vietnam War, her marriage to an American, and her emigration to the United States. (REV: CSM 8/3/89; LJ 5/15/89; NYTBR 6/25/89)   **[959.7]**

5579 Herr, Michael. *Dispatches.* **1978, Avon paper $4.50 (0-380-01976-0).** Herr, *Esquire* correspondent in Vietnam in 1967–1968, recounts his war experiences. "Nothing else has come so close to conveying how different the Vietnam War was from any

other we have fought . . . the best book to have been written about Vietnam."—NYTBR (REV: NYTBR 11/20/77; Newsweek 11/14/77; Time 11/7/77. AWARDS: ALA, 1977; NYTBR, 1977; Time, 1977; Time, the 1970s)   **[959.7]**

5580 Isaacs, Arnold. *Without Honor: Defeat in Vietnam and Cambodia.* **1983, Johns Hopkins $35.00.** The conclusion of the Vietnam War—the signing of the Paris Peace Agreements, the war's expansion into Cambodia, and the withdrawal of American troops. "A definitive, beautifully written work."—Choice (REV: Choice 12/83; LJ 10/1/83; Newsweek 10/3/83. AWARDS: ALA, 1983)   **[959.7]**

5581 Kahin, George McTurnan. *Intervention: How America Became Involved in Vietnam.* **1987, Doubleday paper $14.95 (0-385-24099-6).** A study of America's increasing involvement in Vietnam from the end of World War II to the mid-1960s. (REV: Choice 10/86; LJ 4/1/86; NYTBR 8/10/86)   **[959.7]**

5582 Kane, Rod. *Veteran's Day: A Vietnam Memoir.* **1990, Crown $18.95 (0-517-56905-1).** Memoirs of a combat medic who served in Vietnam and the physical and psychological problems he faced following the war. (REV: LJ 11/15/89; PW 12/8/89; Newsweek 2/5/90)   **[959.7]**

5583 Karnow, Stanley. *Vietnam: A History.* **1984, Penguin paper $12.95 (0-14-007324-8).** A survey history of French and American involvement in Vietnam that was the basis for the PBS television series. (REV: BL 9/1/83; NYTBR 10/16/83; PW 8/19/83)   **[959.7]**

5584 Kovic, Ron. *Born on the Fourth of July.* **1989, Pocket paper $4.50 (0-671-68149-4).** Kovic describes his war experiences, his gradual disillusionment, and his eventual joining of the Vietnam Veterans Against the War. The basis for the 1989 motion picture. "The most personal and honest testament published thus far by anyone who fought in the Vietnam War."—NYTBR (REV: Atl 9/76; NYTBR 8/15/76; Newsweek 9/20/76. AWARDS: ALA, 1976; NYTBR, 1976)   **[959.7]**

5585 Lopes, Sal. *Wall: Images and Offerings from the Vietnam Veterans Memorial.* **1987, Collins SF $19.95 (0-00-217974-1).** Fifteen photographers capture moments at Washington's Vietnam Veterans Memorial. "Extremely powerful . . . almost overwhelming."—LJ (REV: BL 11/15/87; LJ 11/15/87)**[959.7]**

5586 Lunn, Hugh. *Vietnam: A Reporter's War.* **1987, Scarborough $18.95 (0-8128-3088-1); Univ. of Queensland Pr. paper $10.95 (0-7022-2018-3).** Memoirs of an Australian war correspondent's experiences in Vietnam in 1967 and 1968. (REV: LJ 4/1/86; PW 2/14/86)   **[959.7]**

5587 Mangold, Tom, and John Penycate. *Tunnels of Cu Chi.* **1987, Berkley paper $4.50 (0-425-08951-7).** A profile of the Vietcong underground tunnel system surrounding Saigon and how the guerrillas used it to gain advantage against American troops during the Vietnam War. (REV: BL 5/15/85; LJ 5/15/85; NYTBR 6/23/85)   **[959.7]**

5588 **Mason, Patience H. C.** *Recovering from the War: A Woman's Guide to Helping Your Vietnam Vet, Your Family and Yourself.* 1990, Viking $22.95 (0-670-81587-X); Penguin paper $9.95 (0-14-009912-3). A guide to the diagnosis and treatment of Post-Traumatic Stress Disorder for wives of Vietnam veterans. (Rev: BL 1/1/90; LJ 1/90; PW 12/22/89) **[959.7]**

5589 **Maurer, Harry.** *Strange Ground: An Oral History of Americans in Vietnam, 1945–1975.* 1989, Henry Holt $29.45 (0-8050-0919-1); Avon paper $12.95 (0-380-70931-7). Collected firsthand accounts by Americans of their experiences in Vietnam from the end of World War II through the Vietnam War. "The most gut-wrenching, heartrending account to date."—PW (Rev: BL 12/15/88; LJ 12/88; PW 11/25/88) **[959.7]**

5590 **New York Vietnam Veterans Memorial Commission.** *Dear America: Letters Home from Vietnam.* Ed. by Bernard Edelman. 1985, Norton $13.95 (0-393-01998-5); Pocket paper $4.95 (0-671-69178-3). People responding to a request by the commission submitted items to be included in a New York memorial to Vietnam veterans. Of the letters submitted, over 200 were selected for inclusion in this volume. (Rev: LJ 6/1/85; PW 4/5/85. Awards: LJ, 1985; PW, 1985) **[959.7]**

5591 **Nguyen, Tien Hung, and Jerrold Schecter.** *Palace File: The Remarkable Story of the Secret Letters from Nixon and Ford to the President of South Vietnam and the American Promises That Were Never Kept.* 1989, Harper & Row paper $10.95 (0-06-091572-2). Thirty-one previously unpublished letters from American presidents to South Vietnamese President Thieu provide the background for this exposé of American duplicity toward our ally. (Rev: LJ 11/1/86; New Rep 3/9/87; NYTBR 1/18/87) **[959.7]**

5592 **Nixon, Richard M.** *No More Vietnams.* 1986, Avon paper $4.50 (0-380-70119-7). The former president reflects on the Vietnam War and its legacy. (Rev: BL 3/1/85; LJ 4/1/85; Natl Rev 5/3/85) **[959.7]**

5593 **Norman, Geoffrey.** *Bouncing Back: How a Heroic Band of POWs Survived Vietnam.* 1990, Houghton $19.95 (0-395-45186-8). A study of how American POWs taken captive during the Vietnam War were able to psychologically survive and recover from their experiences. (Rev: BL 9/1/90; LJ 8/90; PW 6/29/90) **[959.7]**

5594 **Norman, Michael.** *These Good Men: Friendships Forged from War.* 1990, Crown $17.95 (0-517-55984-6); Pocket paper $4.95 (0-671-73173-4). The author recounts his search to find and reunite 11 surviving members of a U.S. Marine combat unit. (Rev: BL 11/1/89; LJ 11/15/89; NYTBR 1/14/90) **[959.7]**

5595 **Novak, Marian Faye.** *Lonely Girls with Burning Eyes: A Wife Recalls Her Husband's Journey Home from Vietnam.* 1991, Little, Brown $19.95 (0-316-61323-1). A U.S. Marine's wife describes her family's experiences surrounding the Vietnam War and its aftermath. (Rev: BL 1/15/91; LJ 1/91; PW 11/23/90) **[959.7]**

5596 **Oberdorfer, Don.** *Tet!* 1984, DaCapo paper $11.95 (0-306-80210-4). An examination of the planning, execution, and consequences of the communist Vietnamese New Year's offensive in 1968, generally considered the turning point of the Vietnam War. "A superior study of the interaction of war, politics and world opinion."—PW (Rev: Choice 3/72; NYTBR 10/17/71; PW 7/12/71) **[959.7]**

5597 **O'Brien, Tim.** *If I Die in a Combat Zone.* 1989, Doubleday paper $8.95 (0-385-29774-2). O'Brien recounts his experiences as an infantryman in Vietnam. "Brilliantly and quietly evokes the foot soldier's daily life . . . a beautiful, painful book."—NYTBR (Rev: New Rep 5/12/73; NYTBR 7/1/73; New Yorker 7/16/73) **[959.7]**

5598 **Page, Tim.** *Page after Page.* 1990, Macmillan $19.95 (0-689-12088-5). Memoirs of an American free-lance photographer's career and experiences in Vietnam and Asia during the 1960s. (Rev: BL 9/15/89; LJ 9/15/89; PW 8/11/89) **[959.7]**

5599 **Palmer, Laura.** *Shrapnel in the Heart: Letters and Remembrances from the Vietnam Memorial.* 1987, Random $17.95 (0-394-56027-2); paper $7.95. A collection of letters and other items left at the Vietnam Veterans Memorial, and interviews with the family members who left them. "A heartbreaking reminder of the consequence of war."—LJ (Rev: 0-394-75988-5; Atl 3/88; BL 11/15/87; LJ 12/87. Awards: LJ, 1987) **[959.7]**

5600 **Prados, John, and Ray W. Stubbe.** *Valley of Decision: The Siege of Khe Sahn.* 1991, Houghton $29.95 (0-395-55003-3). A military history of the battle between North Vietnamese and American forces for one of the most heavily contested sites of the Vietnam War. (Rev: BL 11/15/91; PW 9/23/91) **[959.7]**

5601 **Puller, Lewis B., Jr.** *Fortunate Son.* 1991, Grove-Weidenfeld $21.95 (0-8021-1218-8). An autobiography chronicling the Vietnam War experiences of the son of World War II marine hero "Chesty" Puller. (Rev: LJ 6/1/91; PW 4/26/91. Awards: PP: Biography, 1992) **[959.7]**

5602 **Roy, Jules.** *Battle of Dienbienphu.* 1984, Carroll & Graf paper $10.95 (0-88184-034-3). The conclusive battle in 1954 between the French and Vietnamese armies is examined by a former French Army officer who served in Indochina. (Rev: Choice 9/65; LJ 2/1/65; NYTBR 3/7/65. Awards: ALA, 1965; NYTBR, 1965) **[959.7]**

5603 **Sack, John.** *M.* 1990, Avon paper $3.95 (0-380-69866-8). Experiences of the army's first Advanced Infantry Training Brigade M Company from basic training to combat in Vietnam. (Rev: BL 4/15/67; NYTBR 5/14/67; Time 11/17/67. Awards: ALA, 1967) **[959.7]**

5604 **Safer, Morley.** *Flashbacks: On Returning to Vietnam.* 1990, Random $18.95 (0-394-58374-4). The CBS journalist compares his 1989 visit to Vietnam with his experiences as a correspondent during the war. (Rev: LJ 4/15/90; NYTBR 4/15/90; Time 4/30/90) **[959.7]**

5605 Santoli, Al. *Everything We Had: An Oral History of the Vietnam War.* **Ballantine paper $3.95 (0-345-32279-7).** The author, a Vietnam veteran, interviewed 33 others who served in Vietnam. "One of the most powerful documents to come out of the Vietnam War."—Ron Kovic (REV: LJ 4/15/81; Newsweek 5/4/81; Time 4/20/81. AWARDS: ALA, 1981)   **[959.7]**

5606 Schell, Jonathan. *Real War: Classic Reporting on the Vietnam War.* **1988, Pantheon $7.95 (0-394-75550-2).** This volume contains reprints of *The Village of Ben Suc* and *The Military Half: An Account of Destruction in Quang Ngai and Quang Tin*, two of Schell's accounts of the war in Vietnam. (REV: BL 1/15/88; NYTBR 2/28/88)   **[959.7]**

5607 Scruggs, Jan C., and Joel L. Swerdlow. *To Heal a Nation: The Vietnam Veterans Memorial.* **1988, Harper & Row paper $10.95 (0-06-091354-1).** A history of the Vietnam Veterans Memorial from its conception to completion. (REV: BL 5/15/85; LJ 6/1/85; PW 4/5/85)   **[959.7]**

5608 Sevy, Grace, ed. *American Experience in Vietnam.* **1989, Univ. of Oklahoma Pr. $24.95 (0-8061-2211-0).** An anthology of writings concerning America's involvement in Vietnam. (REV: BL 10/1/89; LJ 10/1/89)   **[959.7]**

5609 Shawcross, William. *Sideshow: Kissinger, Nixon and the Destruction of Cambodia.* **1987, Simon & Schuster paper $13.95 (0-671-64103-4).** Based on over 300 interviews and formerly undisclosed documents, Shawcross argues that the expansion of the Vietnam War into Cambodia by the American government led to the destruction of that nation and its eventual takeover by the Khmer Rouge. (REV: LJ 4/15/79; NYRB 6/28/79; NYTBR 4/22/79. AWARDS: ALA, 1979; NYTBR, 1979)   **[959.7]**

5610 Terry, Wallace. *Bloods: An Oral History of the Vietnam War by Black Veterans.* **1985, Ballantine paper $5.95 (0-345-31197-3).** A former *Time* correspondent in Vietnam interviews 20 black veterans. "It will stand as a vivid testimonial to the sacrifices of blacks for the American war effort."—Choice (REV: Choice 12/84; LJ 9/15/84; Time 8/20/84. AWARDS: ALA, 1984; Time, 1984)   **[959.7]**

5611 Todd, Oliver. *Cruel April: 1975—The Fall of Saigon.* **1990, Norton $24.95 (0-393-02787-2).** A French journalist's account of the fall of Saigon and his disillusionment with the government of North Vietnam. (REV: BL 9/1/90; LJ 8/90)   **[959.7]**

5612 Truong, Nhu Tang, David Chanoff, and Doan Van Toai. *A Vietcong Memoir.* **1986, Random paper $10.95 (0-394-74309-1).** The personal narrative of an ex-Viet Cong describing his career as a revolutionary, his eventual disillusionment with the Vietnamese government, and his flight from Vietnam with the boat people. (REV: BL 4/15/85; LJ 6/1/85; NYTBR 5/26/85)   **[959.7]**

5613 Vu, Tran Tri. *Lost Years: My 1,632 Days in Vietnamese Relocation Camps.* **1989, IEAS paper $15.00 (1-55729-006-7).** The author's account of the

five years he spent in North Vietnamese prisons. (REV: LJ 9/15/89; PW 6/9/89)   **[959.7]**

5614 Walker, Keith. *A Piece of My Heart: The Stories of 26 American Women Who Served in Vietnam.* **1987, Ballantine paper $4.95 (0-345-33997-5).** The oral histories of nurses, WACs, Red Cross aides, and a disc jockey who served in the Vietnam War. (REV: LJ 2/1/86; NYTBR 5/25/86)   **[959.7]**

5615 Willenson, Kim. *Bad War: An Oral History of the Vietnam Conflict.* **1988, NAL paper $8.95 (0-452-26063-9).** An oral history of the Vietnam War including interviews with Joan Baez, Eugene McCarthy, Alexander Haig, and J. William Fulbright. (REV: BL 6/15/87; LJ 9/1/87; PW 5/15/87)   **[959.7]**

5616 Williams, William Appleman, ed. *America in Vietnam: A Documentary History.* **1985, Doubleday $19.95 (0-385-19752-7); paper $10.95 (0-385-19201-0).** A history of America's involvement in Vietnam based on official documents. (REV: BL 2/1/85; LJ 1/85)   **[959.7]**

5617 Wintle, Justin. *Romancing Vietnam: Inside the Boat Country.* **1991, Pantheon $25.00 (0-679-40621-2).** A portrait of life in contemporary Vietnam based on the author's three-month visit during 1989 and 1990. (REV: BL 11/15/91; LJ 1/92; PW 10/18/91)   **[959.7]**

Indonesia

5618 Barley, Nigel. *Not a Hazardous Sport.* **1989, Henry Holt $19.95 (0-8050-0960-4).** An anthropologist recounts his experiences among Torajar tribesmen on a remote Indonesian island. (REV: BL 7/89; LJ 4/15/89; TLS 3/31/89)   **[959.8]**

Philippines—History

5619 Johnson, Bryan. *Four Days of Courage: The Untold Story of the People Who Brought Marcos Down.* **1987, Free Pr. $19.95 (0-317-58077-9).** A firsthand account of the 1986 Philippine Revolution that overthrew Ferdinand Marcos and replaced him with the government of Corazon Aquino. (REV: BL 6/1/87; LJ 6/1/87; NYTBR 6/14/87)   **[959.9]**

5620 Jones, Gregg R. *Red Revolution: Inside the Philippine Guerrilla Movement.* **1989, Westview $26.95 (0-8133-0644-2).** A newspaper correspondent's account of the underground Communist guerrilla movement in the Philippines and its fight against the Marcos and Aquino governments. (REV: Atl 9/89; LJ 9/1/89; NYTBR 9/10/89)   **[959.9]**

5621 Karnow, Stanley. *In Our Image: America's Empire in the Philippines.* **1989, Random $24.95 (0-394-54975-9); Ballantine paper $14.95 (0-345-32816-7).** An analysis of American involvement in the Philippines following the conclusion of the Spanish-American War by the author of *Vietnam: A History*. (REV: BL 3/1/89; LJ 4/1/89; NYTBR 4/2/89. AWARDS: PP: History, 1990)   **[959.9]**

5622 Kessler, Richard J. *Rebellion and Repression in the Philippines.* **1989, Yale Univ. Pr. $25.00 (0-**

300-04406-2). An examination of the roots and present state of the leftist rebellion in the Philippines. "A supremely authoritative book."—CSM (Rev: CSM 3/8/90; LJ 9/1/89; PW 7/28/89) **[959.9]**

5623 Miller, Stuart C. *Benevolent Assimilation: The American Conquest of the Philippines, 1899–1903.* 1982, Yale Univ. Pr. $37.50 (0-300-02697-8); paper $14.95 (0-300-03081-9). An account of the American rule of the Philippine Islands following the Spanish-American War. (Rev: Choice 1/83; LJ 10/15/82; NYTBR 11/21/82) **[959.9]**

960 GENERAL HISTORY OF AFRICA

5624 Boyles, Denis. *African Lives: White Lies, Tropical Truth, Darkest Gossip and Rumblings of Rumor.* 1988, Grove-Weidenfeld $18.95 (1-55584-034-5); Ballantine paper $8.95 (0-345-35666-7). An anecdotal history of white explorers of the African continent and their exploits. (Rev: LJ 9/1/88; NYTBR 12/25/88; PW 7/8/88) **[960]**

5625 Mazrui, Ali A. *Africans: A Triple Heritage.* 1987, Little, Brown paper $17.95 (0-316-55201-1). An introduction to the history, culture, and current problems of the African continent. (Rev: LJ 1/87; NYTBR 11/16/86; PW 8/14/87) **[960]**

5626 Pakenham, Thomas. *Scramble for Africa: 1876–1912.* 1991, Random $32.00 (0-394-51576-5). A study of European colonial adventures in Africa during the late nineteenth and early twentieth centuries by the author of *The Boer War.* (Rev: BL 11/15/91; NYTBR 12/8/91; PW 11/1/91) **[960]**

5627 Ungar, Sanford J. *Africa: The People and Politics of an Emerging Continent.* 1989, Simon & Schuster paper $14.95 (0-671-67565-6). An overview of the African continent with a detailed look at the nations of Kenya, Liberia, Nigeria, and South Africa. (Rev: BL 8/85; LJ 9/15/85; NYTBR 9/1/85) **[960]**

5628 Whitaker, Jennifer. *How Can Africa Survive?* 1988, Harper & Row $19.95 (0-06-039089-1); Council on Foreign Relations paper $12.95 (0-87609-054-4). An examination of Africa's current problems and likely future by a senior analyst for the Council on Foreign Relations. (Rev: BL 5/15/88; LJ 9/15/88; NYTBR 7/24/88) **[960]**

961 Tunisia and Libya

Libya—History

5629 Harris, Lillian Craig. *Libya: Qadhafi's Revolution and the Modern State.* 1986, Westview $33.00 (0-8133-0075-4). A study of the Libyan nation under the rule of Moammar Qadhafi. (Rev: Choice 2/87; LJ 10/15/86) **[961.2]**

962 Egypt and Sudan

5630 Lewis, David Levering. *Race to Fashoda: European Colonialism and African Resistance in the Scramble for Africa.* 1989, Grove-Weidenfeld paper $11.95 (1-55584-278-X). A study of the events surrounding the 1898 Fashoda Crisis in the Sudan. (Rev: Choice 7–8/88; NYTBR 2/28/88; TLS 4/22/88) **[962]**

Egypt—History, 1922–

5631 Sadat, Anwar. *In Search of Identity: An Autobiography.* 1979, Harper & Row paper $9.95 (0-06-132071-4). An autobiography of the former Egyptian president. "Must reading . . . for all those who want to know something about Egypt, the Arab-Israeli conflict and a central figure in the Middle East."—Choice (Rev: Choice 11/78; CSM 4/26/78; PW 4/3/78) **[962.05]**

963 Ethiopia

5632 Kapuscinski, Ryszard. *Emperor: Downfall of an Autocrat.* 1989, Random paper $7.95 (0-679-72203-3). An account of the 1974 overthrow of Emperor Haile Selassie of Ethiopia as seen by the Polish journalist. (Rev: LJ 12/15/82; NYRB 8/18/83; Newsweek 4/11/83) **[963]**

965 Algeria

5633 Horne, Alistair. *A Savage War of Peace: Algeria, 1954–1962.* 1987, Penguin paper $8.95 (0-14-010191-8). The Algerian struggle for independence from France. "A brilliant work of synthesis . . . objective, balanced, sympathetic to both sides, without, however, losing its sense of injustice."—Choice (Rev: Choice 9/78; CSM 5/24/78; NYTBR 3/18/78. Awards: NYTBR, 1978) **[965]**

5634 Porch, Douglas. *Conquest of the Sahara.* 1986, Fromm International paper $11.95 (0-88064-061-8). The author of *Conquest of Morocco* examines the nineteenth-century French occupation of Tunisia and Algeria. (Rev: Choice 4/85; LJ 11/1/84; Newsweek 1/28/85) **[965]**

Algeria—History, 1830–1962

5635 Kobak, Annette. *Isabelle: The Life of Isabelle Eberhardt.* 1989, Knopf $22.95 (0-394-57691-8); Random paper $10.95 (0-679-72821-X). A biography of a nineteenth-century Swiss-born woman who converted to Islam, traveled the Arab world disguised as an Arab boy, and whose writings made her a celebrity in Europe prior to her accidental death at age 27. (Rev: LJ 4/15/89; NYTBR 4/23/89; TLS 6/10/88) **[965.03]**

966 West Africa and offshore islands

5636 Packer, George. *Village of Waiting.* 1988, Random paper $8.95 (0-394-75754-8). The author recounts his experiences working as a teacher for the Peace Corps in the West African nation of Togo. (Rev: Atl 9/88; CSM 11/8/88; LJ 10/1/88) **[966]**

967 Central Africa and offshore islands

5637 Harden, Blaine. *Africa: Dispatches from a Fragile Continent.* 1990, Norton $22.50 (0-393-02882-8). Accounts of the author's experiences traveling through Sub-Saharan Africa. (Rev: BL 10/1/90; LJ 9/15/90; PW 8/17/90) **[967]**

5638 Lamb, David. *Africans.* 1983, Random $17.95 (0-394-51887-X); paper $8.95 (0-394-75308-9). A survey of contemporary sub-Saharan Africa by a former *Los Angeles Times* correspondent. "Essential reading for an understanding of modern-day Africa."— NYTBR (Rev: CSM 3/11/83; LJ 3/1/83; NYTBR 2/6/83. Awards: ALA, 1983) **[967]**

5639 Shoumatoff, Alex. *African Madness.* 1988, Knopf $18.95 (0-394-56914-8); Random paper $9.95 (0-679-72545-8). The author's four trips to Africa for the *New Yorker* to investigate the Bokassa regime, the murder of Dian Fossey, AIDS, and the ecology of Madagascar. (Rev: BL 11/15/88; PW 9/23/88; Time 11/21/88) **[967]**

Angola—History

5640 Kapuscinski, Ryszard. *Another Day of Life.* 1987, Harcourt $14.95 (0-15-107563-8). The Polish journalist's firsthand account of the Angolan civil war of the mid-1970s. (Rev: Atl 5/87; BL 2/1/87; NYTBR 2/15/87) **[967.3]**

Zaire—History

5641 Tidwell, Mike. *Ponds of Kalambayi: An African Sojourn.* 1990, Lyons & Burford $19.95 (1-55821-078-4). An account of the author's two years in Zaire teaching fish farming techniques as a member of the Peace Corps. (Rev: LJ 8/90; PW 8/10/90) **[967.51]**

Kenya—History

5642 Bentsen, Cheryl. *Maasai Days.* 1989, Summit $19.95 (0-671-66035-7). The author recounts her experiences among the Masai people of Kenya. "An interesting, well-crafted, if not heartening book."— BL (Rev: BL 9/1/89; LJ 8/89; NYTBR 10/8/89. Awards: ALA, 1989) **[967.62]**

5643 Gallmann, Kuki. *I Dreamed of Africa.* 1991, Viking $22.95 (0-670-83612-5). Memoirs of an Italian-born writer's experiences living in Kenya with her family. (Rev: BL 4/1/91; NYTBR 6/2/91; PW 3/8/91) **[967.62]**

5644 Huxley, Elspeth. *Out in the Midday Sun: My Kenya.* 1987, Viking $18.95 (0-670-81183-1); Penguin paper $6.95 (0-14-009256-0). A sequel to the author's *Flame Trees of Thika* about her life in Kenya. (Rev: LJ 2/1/87; NYTBR 3/22/87; TLS 1/31/86) **[967.62]**

968 Southern Africa

5645 Clark, June Vendall. *Starlings Laughing: A Memoir of Africa.* 1991, Morrow $23.00 (0-688-10540-8). An autobiography of the author's experiences growing up in Rhodesia and Botswana. (Rev: BL 4/1/91; LJ 4/15/91; PW 3/15/91) **[968]**

5646 Gordimer, Nadine, and David Goldblatt. *Lifetimes Under Apartheid.* 1986, Knopf $30.00 (0-317-47546-0). Excerpts from Gordimer's fiction are interspersed with Goldblatt's photographs in this work detailing the abuses of South Africa's apartheid system. (Rev: BL 2/1/87; LJ 3/1/87) **[968]**

5647 Morris, Donald R. *Washing of the Spears: The Rise and Fall of the Zulu Nation.* 1986, Simon & Schuster paper $14.95 (0-671-62822-4). The history of the Zulu tribe, which conquered much of South Africa in the nineteenth century before its defeat by the British army. "Vivid and accurate, enthusiastic yet detached, and blessedly free from moral indignation for or against either side."—NYTBR (Rev: Atl 10/65; Natl Rev 10/5/65; NYTBR 7/4/65. Awards: ALA, 1965) **[968]**

5648 Sparks, Allister. *Mind of South Africa.* 1990, Knopf $24.95 (0-394-58108-3). The history and present state of race relations in South Africa as seen by a Johannesburg journalist. (Rev: BL 2/1/90; LJ 3/15/90; NYTBR 6/14/90. Awards: LJ, 1990) **[968]**

5649 Thompson, Leonard. *History of South Africa.* 1990, Yale Univ. Pr. $29.95 (0-300-04815-7). A history of South Africa from its first settlement to the present. (Rev: BL 6/1/90; LJ 5/15/90; NYTBR 7/15/90) **[968]**

South Africa—History, 1814–1910

5650 Rotberg, Robert I. *Founder: Cecil Rhodes and the Enigma of Power.* 1988, Oxford Univ. Pr. $35.00 (0-19-504968-3); paper $16.95 (0-19-506668-5). A biography of the diamond magnate and South African political leader. "The last word on the man."—BL (Rev: Atl 12/88; Choice 5/89; NYTBR 1/1/89) **[968.04]**

South African (Second Anglo-Boer) War—1899–1902

5651 Pakenham, Thomas. *Boer War.* 1979, Random $29.95 (0-394-42742-4). A survey of the Boer War (1899–1902) between British and Dutch settlers in South Africa, often regarded as a turning point in the history of the British Empire. "Without question, the best study yet of the Boer War."—LJ (Rev: Choice 4/80; LJ 11/1/79; NYTBR 11/18/79. Awards: NYTBR, 1979) **[968.048]**

South Africa—History, 1961–

5652 Boetie, Dugmore. *Familiarity Is the Kingdom of the Lost.* 1989, Four Walls Eight Windows paper $6.95 (0-941423-20-4). An autobiography tracing the author's life under South Africa's apartheid system. (Rev: BL 4/15/70; LJ 12/15/69; TLS 7/24/69) **[968.06]**

5653 Davis, Stephen M. *Apartheid's Rebels: Inside South Africa's Hidden War.* 1987, Yale Univ. Pr. $27.50 (0-300-03991-3); paper $9.95 (0-300-03992-1). A profile of the African National Congress and other South African groups seeking political reform. (Rev: Choice 2/88; LJ 10/1/87; NYTBR 11/15/87) **[968.06]**

5654 Heard, Anthony Hazlitt. *Cape of Storms: A Personal History of the Crisis in South Africa.* 1990, Univ. of Arkansas Pr. $21.95 (1-55728-167-X); paper $11.95 (1-55728-168-8). A journalist's account of his experiences reporting under the South African government. (Rev: LJ 9/15/90; NYTBR 12/9/90) **[968.06]**

5655 Leach, Graham. *South Africa: No Easy Path to Peace.* 1987, Routledge paper $8.95 (0-413-15330-4). An analysis of recent reforms made by the South African government with speculations about the country's future direction. (REV: BL 6/15/86; LJ 7/86; TLS 8/15/86) **[968.06]**

5656 Malan, Rian. *My Traitor's Heart: A South African Exile Returns to Face His Country, His Tribe and His Conscience.* 1990, Atlantic Monthly $19.95 (0-87113-229-X); Random paper $10.95 (0-679-73215-2). Memoirs of an Afrikaner who left his native South Africa to avoid military service and later returned to reflect upon his nation and his life. (REV: CSM 2/23/90; LJ 12/89; Newsweek 1/22/90. AWARDS: ALA, 1990) **[968.06]**

5657 Mandela, Winnie. *Part of My Soul Went with Him.* Ed. by Anne Benjamin and Mary Benson. 1985, Norton $14.95 (0-393-02215-3); paper $5.95 (0-393-30290-3). An autobiography based on interviews with Winnie Mandela and her correspondence with her imprisoned husband, Nelson Mandela, the South African anti-apartheid leader. (REV: BL 2/1/86; Choice 7–8/86; LJ 11/15/85. AWARDS: PW, 1985) **[968.06]**

5658 Mathabane, Mark. *Kaffir Boy: The True Story of a Black Youth's Coming of Age in Apartheid South Africa.* 1986, Macmillan $19.95 (0-02-581800-7); NAL paper $8.95 (0-452-25943-6). An autobiography detailing the author's childhood and adolescent years living under South Africa's apartheid system. (REV: Choice 10/86; CSM 5/2/86; LJ 4/15/86) **[968.06]**

5659 Mattera, Don. *Sophiatown: Coming of Age in South Africa.* 1989, Beacon $15.95 (0-8070-0206-2). An autobiography of the South African political activist regarding his early life in a Johannesburg ghetto. (REV: LJ 2/15/89; NYTBR 5/14/89; TLS 6/24/88) **[968.06]**

5660 Meer, Fatima. *Higher Than Hope: The Biography of Nelson Mandela.* 1991, HarperCollins paper $10.95 (0-06-092066-1). A biography of the African National Congress leader who was recently released from imprisonment in South Africa. (REV: BL 3/15/90; Choice 9/90; NYRB 9/27/90) **[968.06]**

5661 Modisane, Bloke. *Blame Me on History.* 1990, Simon & Schuster paper $9.95 (0-671-70067-7). Memoirs of a black South African actor's life under the apartheid system. (REV: BL 6/1/90; LJ 3/15/90; PW 5/25/90) **[968.06]**

5662 Turnley, David C., and Alan Cowell. *Why Are They Weeping? South Africans Under Apartheid.* 1988, Stewart, Tabori & Chang $35.00 (1-55670-044-X); paper $19.95 (1-55670-054-7). Documentary photographs by Turnley and an essay by Cowell are used to present a record of contemporary life under apartheid in South Africa. (REV: BL 1/1/89; LJ 2/1/89; NYTBR 1/1/89) **[968.06]**

Botswana, Lesotho, Swaziland, Namibia

5663 Shostak, Marjorie. *Nisa: The Life and Words of a Kung Woman.* 1981, Harvard Univ. Pr. $28.00 (0-674-62485-8); Random paper $8.95 (0-394-71126-2). A series of 15 interviews with a Kung woman forms the basis for this study detailing life among a hunter-gatherer group in the Kalahari Desert. (REV: LJ 12/15/81; NYRB 12/17/81; PW 9/25/81) **[968.8]**

970   GENERAL HISTORY OF NORTH AMERICA

5664 Burch, Ernest S., Jr., and Werner Forman. *Eskimos.* 1988, Univ. of Oklahoma Pr. $24.95 (0-8061-2126-2). An illustrated introduction to Eskimo life and culture. "An exceptionally alluring primer on the subject."—BL (REV: BL 9/1/88; LJ 9/1/88) **[970]**

5665 Deloria, Vine, Jr. *Custer Died for Your Sins: An Indian Manifesto.* 1988, Univ. of Oklahoma Pr. paper $9.95 (0-8061-2129-7). This study of the Native American in contemporary society was a key document in the American Indian movement of the 1970s. (REV: LJ 10/15/69; Newsweek 10/13/69; Time 10/10/69) **[970]**

5666 Jonaitis, Aldona. *From the Land of the Totem Poles: The Northwest Coast Indian Art Collection at the American Museum of Natural History.* 1988, Univ. of Washington Pr. $40.00 (0-295-96572-X). An illustrated history of the Northwest Coast Indian art collection at the American Museum of Natural History, the most extensive of its type in the world. (REV: Choice 9/88; CSM 7/1/88; LJ 7/88) **[970]**

5667 Malaurie, Jean. *Last Kings of Thule: With the Polar Eskimos, as They Face Their Destiny.* 1985, Univ. of Chicago Pr. paper $17.50 (0-226-50284-8). The author's account of his life among and studies of the Eskimos. "A poignant, endlessly informative valedictory that relives a great Arctic adventure in the tradition of Peary, Cook and Rasmussen."—Time (REV: LJ 9/15/82; PW 6/18/82; Time 10/25/82. AWARDS: Time, 1982) **[970]**

5668 Matthiessen, Peter. *Indian Country.* 1991, Penguin paper $9.95 (0-14-013023-3). An account of a dozen Native American tribes and their struggle against the United States government to regain their ancestral lands. (REV: LJ 3/1/84; NYTBR 7/29/84; PW 2/10/84) **[970]**

5669 Momaday, N. Scott. *Names: A Memoir.* 1987, Univ. of Arizona Pr. paper $9.95 (0-8165-1046-6). An autobiographical essay by the Native American writer regarding his life and philosophy as a member of the Kiowa tribe. (REV: Choice 5/77; LJ 1/15/77; NYTBR 3/6/77) **[970]**

5670 Weatherford, Jack. *Indian Givers: How the Indians of America Transformed the World.* 1988, Crown $17.95 (0-517-56969-8); Fawcett paper $8.95 (0-449-90496-2). An examination of the contributions of Native Americans to world culture and how discoveries made in the New World changed the Old. (REV: BL 10/15/88; LJ 11/1/88; PW 9/2/88) **[970]**

Early history to 1599

5671 Dor Ner, Zvi. *Columbus and the Age of Discovery.* 1991, Morrow $40.00 (0-688-08545-8). An illustrated accompaniment to the PBS series tracing the voyages and legacy of Columbus. (Rᴇᴠ: BL 10/15/91; LJ 8/91)   **[970.01]**

5672   Fernandez-Armesto, Felipe. *Columbus*. 1991, Oxford Univ. Pr. $21.95 (0-19-215898-8). A biography of the explorer and "discoverer" of the Americas. (Rᴇᴠ: BL 10/15/91; LJ 8/91)   **[970.01]**

5673   Granzotto, Gianni. *Christopher Columbus*. 1988, Univ. of Oklahoma Pr. paper $10.95 (0-8061-2100-9). A portrait of the fifteenth-century explorer by an Italian scholar. (Rᴇᴠ: BL 10/1/85; LJ 10/15/85; PW 8/30/85)   **[970.01]**

5674   Morison, Samuel Eliot. *European Discovery of America: The Southern Voyages, A.D. 1492–1616*. 1974, Oxford Univ. Pr $35.00 (0-19-501823-0). A sequel to Morison's *Northern Voyages, A.D. 500–1600*. "The classic account of the exploration and discovery of the Western world."—Choice (Rᴇᴠ: Choice 2/75; CSM 10/9/74; NYTBR 10/13/74. Aᴡᴀʀᴅs: ALA, 1974)   **[970.01]**

5675   Sale, Kirkpatrick. *Conquest of Paradise: Christopher Columbus and the Columbian Legacy*. 1990, Knopf $24.45 (0-394-57429-X). An examination of the life of Christopher Columbus and the myths that surround him. "Merits a place on all libraries' shelves."—LJ (Rᴇᴠ: BL 10/15/90; LJ 10/15/90; PW 9/7/90)   **[970.01]**

5676   Wilford, John Noble. *Mysterious History of Columbus: An Exploration of the Man, the Myth, the Legacy*. 1991, Knopf $24.00 (0-679-40476-7). A biography of the fifteenth-century explorer examining his legacy and history's view of his exploits. (Rᴇᴠ: BL 9/1/91; LJ 10/15/91; PW 8/2/91)   **[970.01]**

Specific native peoples

5677   Josephy, Alvin M., Jr. *Nez Perce Indians and the Opening of the Northwest*. 1979, Univ. of Nebraska Pr. $15.95 (0-8032-2555-5); paper $14.95 (0-8032-75551-X). The history of the Nez Perce tribe and its contact with white settlers from befriending of Lewis and Clark to its betrayal by and combat with U.S. government troops. (Rᴇᴠ: Choice 3/66; LJ 11/15/65; Time 11/19/65. Aᴡᴀʀᴅs: ALA, 1965)   **[970.3]**

5678   Scully, Vincent. *Pueblo: Mountain, Village, Dance*. 1989, Univ. of Chicago Pr. $60.00 (0-226-74392-6); paper $19.95 (0-226-74393-4). The culture of the Pueblo Indians of Arizona and New Mexico as conveyed by their art, architecture, ceremonies, and surroundings. (Rᴇᴠ: Choice 3/76; NYRB 10/16/75; TLS 1/23/76. Aᴡᴀʀᴅs: ALA, 1975)   **[970.3]**

5679   Weltfish, Gene. *Lost Universe: Pawnee Life and Culture*. 1977, Univ. of Nebraska Pr. $35.00 (0-8032-0934-7); paper $10.95 (0-8032-5871-2). A re-creation of Pawnee Indian life and culture of the 1860s as it existed in Missouri and Nebraska. "Sympathetic, scholarly and well written, giving the reader the feel of Pawnee life."—Choice (Rᴇᴠ: BL 4/15/65; Choice 7–8/65; LJ 2/15/65. Aᴡᴀʀᴅs: ALA, 1965)   **[970.3]**

Native peoples in specific places in North America

5680   Brown, Dee. *Bury My Heart at Wounded Knee: An Indian History of the American West*. 1971, Holt $24.95 (0-8050-1045-9). The history of the American West from 1860 to 1890, as seen and described by Native Americans. (Rᴇᴠ: Choice 6/71; NYTBR 3/7/71; New Yorker 2/13/71. Aᴡᴀʀᴅs: ALA, 1971; Time, 1971)   **[970.4]**

Government relations with North American native people

5681   Josephy, Alvin M., Jr. *Red Power: The American Indians' Fight for Freedom*. 1985, Univ. of Nebraska Pr. paper $7.50 (0-8032-7563-3). The history of the American-Indian civil rights movement of the 1960s. "An essential handbook for anyone concerned with the never ending struggle of Native Americans to obtain freedoms that other Americans have long taken for granted."—Dee Brown (Rᴇᴠ: CSM 9/16/71; LJ 6/1/71; NYTBR 8/29/71)   **[970.5]**

971   Canada

5682   Hoffman, Eva. *Lost in Translation: A Life in a New Language*. 1989, Dutton $18.95 (0-525-24601-0); paper $7.95 (0-14-012773-9). Experiences of a woman who emigrated from Poland to Canada as a teenager. "Hoffman makes one feel intensely the pain of an abrupt rupture with one's culture and native language."—LJ (Rᴇᴠ: BL 1/15/89; LJ 1/89; NYTBR 1/15/89)   **[971]**

5683   Macfarlane, David. *Come from Away: Memory, War, and the Search for a Family's Past*. 1991, Poseidon $20.00 (0-671-74705-3). Memoirs of the author's life in Newfoundland mixed with glimpses of the Canadian province's history and culture. (Rᴇᴠ: BL 9/1/91; LJ 9/15/91; PW 7/19/91. Aᴡᴀʀᴅs: BL, 1991)   **[971]**

5684   Malcolm, Andrew H. *Canadians*. 1985, Random $17.95 (0-8129-1158-X); Bantam paper $9.95 (0-553-34262-2). A detailed look at our northern neighbors—their history, geography, culture, regional differences, and their relationship with the United States. (Rᴇᴠ: BL 12/15/84; LJ 2/1/85; NYTBR 3/10/85)   **[971]**

5685   Richler, Mordecai. *Home Sweet Home: My Canadian Album*. 1984, Knopf $16.95 (0-394-53756-4); Penguin paper $6.95 (0-14-007639-5). A collection of essays by the Canadian writer regarding his homeland. (Rᴇᴠ: BL 5/1/84; NYTBR 6/3/84; PW 3/23/84)   **[971]**

History—Prairie provinces

5686   Newman, Peter C. *Caesars of the Wilderness: The Story of the Hudson's Bay Company*. 1988, Penguin paper $8.95 (0-14-011456-4). An account of the development of the Hudson's Bay Company and its influence upon Canadian history. (Rᴇᴠ: Choice 5/88; LJ 12/87; NYTBR 12/20/87)   **[971.2]**

5687   Newman, Peter C. *Company of Adventurers: The Story of Hudson's Bay Company*. 1987, Penguin paper $9.95 (0-14-010139-X). A history of the British trading company whose commercial dealings played a significant role in the development and colonization of the Canadian frontier. (Rev: Choice 4/86; LJ 12/85; NYTBR 12/15/85)   **[971.2]**

972 Middle America; Mexico

5688 Kurlansky, Mark. *A Continent of Islands: Searching for the Caribbean Destiny.* 1991, Addison Wesley $22.95 (0-201-52396-5). An overview of the cultures and histories of the Caribbean nations. "Highly recommended for all collections."—LJ (Rev: LJ 1/92; PW 11/29/91)   **[972]**

5689 Schele, Linda, and David Freidel. *A Forest of Kings: The Untold Story of the Maya.* 1990, Morrow $29.95 (0-688-07456-1). An illustrated survey of classical Mayan culture and history based on recently deciphered hieroglyphs. (Rev: BL 10/1/90; LJ 8/90; PW 8/31/90)   **[972]**

5690 Wright, Ronald. *Time Among the Maya: Travels in Belize, Guatemala, and Mexico.* 1989, Grove-Weidenfeld $22.95 (1-55584-291-7). An account of the author's travels to prehistoric Mayan ruins in Mexico and Central America. (Rev: LJ 2/15/89; New Yorker 7/3/89; PW 2/10/89)   **[972]**

Mexico—History, 1867–

5691 Knight, Alan. *Mexican Revolution.* 1986, Cambridge Univ. Pr. $109.00 (0-521-24475-7); Univ. of Nebraska Pr. paper $30.00 (0-8032-7770-9). A two-volume historic survey of the Mexican Revolution. (Rev: Choice 11/86; LJ 6/15/86; TLS 5/29/86)   **[972.08]**

5692 Reavis, Dick J. *Conversations with Moctezuma: Ancient Shadows over Modern Life in Mexico.* 1990, Morrow $19.45 (0-688-07999-7). An overview of Mexican history and tradition and how its legacy influences the modern-day nation. (Rev: BL 2/1/90; LJ 1/90; NYTBR 2/25/90)   **[972.08]**

5693 Riding, Alan. *Distant Neighbors: A Portrait of the Mexicans.* 1984, Knopf $18.95 (0-394-50005-9); Random paper $8.95 (0-679-72441-9). An analysis of the history, culture, and present economic and political state of our neighbor to the south by a longtime *New York Times* correspondent. "No better book exists to convey an understanding of Mexico than this."—LJ (Rev: Atl 2/85; CSM 4/11/85; LJ 1/85. Awards: LJ, 1985)   **[972.08]**

Central America—History

5694 Chace, James. *Endless War: How We Got Involved in Central America and What Can Be Done.* 1984, Random paper $4.95 (0-394-72779-7). A survey of American involvement in Latin American countries over the past 150 years. (Rev: Choice 2/85; LJ 10/15/84; NYTBR 10/7/84)   **[972.8]**

5695 Krauss, Clifford. *Inside Central America: Its People, Politics, and History.* 1991, Summit $19.95 (0-671-66400-X). A survey of the history and culture of the Central American nations. (Rev: BL 3/1/91; LJ 3/1/91; PW 2/22/91)   **[972.8]**

5696 Marnham, Patrick. *So Far from God: A Journey to Central America.* 1986, Penguin paper $6.95 (0-14-008556-4). A British reporter's travels in Mexico and Central America. "This is not a reference book; it is a journey. It puts the reader on the bus, at the altar or in the bar and lets him see for himself."—NYTBR (Rev: LJ 8/85; New Rep 2/10/86; NYTBR 8/25/85)   **[972.8]**

Guatemala—History

5697 Anderson, Marilyn, and Jonathan Garlock. *Granddaughters of Corn: Portraits of Guatemalan Women.* 1988, Curbstone $35.00 (0-915306-64-6); paper $19.95 (0-915306-60-3). A study of the Guatemalan political repression as told through first-hand accounts of Indian women of that nation. (Rev: BL 10/15/88; LJ 11/15/88)   **[972.81]**

5698 Maslow, Jonathan. *Bird of Life, Bird of Death: A Naturalist's Journey Through a Land of Political Turmoil.* 1987, Dell paper $6.95 (0-440-50708-1). Maslow's quest to find and photograph the quetzal bird leads him into the political strife of Guatemala. "An especially revealing and troubling account of his travel and opinions."—BL (Rev: BL 5/1/86; LJ 3/1/86; PW 1/10/86. Awards: ALA, 1986)   **[972.81]**

Nicaragua—History

5699 Christian, Shirley. *Nicaragua: Revolution in the Family.* 1986, Random paper $8.95 (0-394-74457-8). A detailed look at the Sandinista revolution from the fall of Somoza to late 1984. (Rev: LJ 9/15/85; Natl Rev 6/28/85; NYTBR 7/28/85)   **[972.85]**

5700 Cruz, Arturo. *Memoirs of a Counter-Revolutionary: Life with the Contras, the Sandinistas and the CIA.* 1989, Doubleday $19.95 (0-385-24879-2). Memoirs of a former Sandinista who broke with the Nicaraguan government in 1982 and later joined Contra forces. (Rev: BL 9/15/89; LJ 9/1/89)   **[972.85]**

5701 Davis, Peter. *Where Is Nicaragua?* 1988, Simon & Schuster paper $8.95 (0-671-65720-8). The maker of the film "Hearts and Minds" recounts his visits to Nicaragua, and his interviews with Nicaraguan citizens and political leaders. "A cogent, thoroughly integrated portrait of Nicaragua's history, culture, politics, personalities and contemporary ambience."—LJ (Rev: Choice 9/87; LJ 4/15/87; NYTBR 4/12/87. Awards: LJ, 1987)   **[972.85]**

5702 Dillon, Sam. *Commandos: The CIA and Nicaragua's Contra Rebels.* 1991, Henry Holt $27.50 (0-8050-1475-6). A Miami journalist's analysis of Nicaragua's Contra rebels, their war against the Sandinista government, and the CIA's activities during the conflict. (Rev: NYTBR 9/29/91; PW 8/23/91)   **[972.85]**

5703 Kinzer, Stephen. *Blood of Brothers: Life and War in Nicaragua.* 1991, Putnam $24.95 (0-399-13594-4). A study of the Sandinista government of Nicaragua during the 1980s and of U.S. government efforts to overthrow it. "Without doubt the best contemporary history of the Sandinista decade to appear."—NYTBR (Rev: LJ 3/15/91; NYTBR 4/7/91; PW 2/15/91. Awards: LJ, 1991)   **[972.85]**

Panama—History

5704 **Buckley, Kevin.** *Panama: The Whole Story.* **1991, Simon & Schuster $19.95 (0-671-72794-0).** An account of the American involvement in Panama from 1985 through the aftermath of the 1989 invasion. "Reads like a spy thriller . . . a gripping account."—PW (REV: LJ 6/1/91; NYRB 6/13/91; PW 5/3/91) **[972.87]**

5705 **Dinges, John.** *Our Man in Panama: How General Noriega Used the United States and Made Millions in Drugs and Arms.* **1990, Random $21.95 (0-394-54910-4).** A study of Manuel Noriega's illegal activities and his relationship with the United States government. (REV: BL 3/1/90; New Rep 5/28/90; NYTBR 2/18/90) **[972.87]**

5706 **Kempe, Frederick.** *Divorcing the Dictator: America's Bungled Affair with Noriega.* **1990, Putnam $22.95 (0-399-13517-0).** An account of the role of the United States in the rise and fall of Panamanian strongman Manuel Noriega. (REV: BL 3/15/90; NYTBR 2/18/90; New Yorker 5/21/90. AWARDS: BL, 1990) **[972.87]**

5707 **Koster, R. M., and Guillermo Sanchez Borbon.** *In the Time of the Tyrants: Panama, 1968–1990.* **1990, Norton $22.95 (0-393-02696-5).** A study of internal Panamanian politics and U.S.-Panama relations from 1968 to the beginning of the 1990s. (REV: BL 10/15/90; LJ 10/1/90; PW 8/31/90) **[972.87]**

5708 **McCullough, David.** *Path Between the Seas: The Creation of the Panama Canal, 1870–1914.* **1978, Simon & Schuster paper $13.95 (0-671-24409-4).** The story of the building of the Panama Canal from the failed attempt by the French to its completion by the Americans. (REV: Choice 10/77; LJ 5/15/77; Sat Rev 6/11/77. AWARDS: ALA, 1977; NBA, 1978; NYTBR, 1977) **[972.87]**

Cuba—History

5709 **Brugioni, Dino A.** *Eyeball to Eyeball: The Inside Story of the Cuban Missile Crisis.* **1992, Random $35.00 (0-679-40523-2).** An American aerial reconnaissance expert details the events surrounding the 1962 Cuban missile crisis. "A solid, gripping detailed chronicle."—PW (REV: LJ 11/15/91; PW 11/29/91) **[972.91]**

5710 **Geyer, Georgia Anne.** *Guerrilla Prince: The Real Story of the Rise and Fall of Fidel Castro.* **1991, Little, Brown $19.95 (0-316-30893-5).** A biography of the Cuban revolutionary and political leader. (REV: BL 12/1/90; LJ 1/91; PW 12/14/90) **[972.91]**

5711 **Lunt, Lawrence K.** *Leave Me My Spirit.* **1991, Affiliated Writers of America $19.95 (0-918080-58-4).** Memoirs of a former CIA spy who spent 14 years in Cuban prisons. "A testament to the admirable, unwavering human spirit."—LJ (REV: LJ 5/1/91; NYTBR 1/27/91) **[972.91]**

5712 **Szulc, Tad.** *Fidel: A Critical Portrait.* **1987, Avon paper $5.95 (0-380-69956-7).** A monumental study of the Cuban leader concentrating on his

formative years. "This biography is certain to become one of the standard references on its subject."—Choice (REV: BL 10/15/86; Choice 3/87; LJ 1/87. AWARDS: ALA, 1986) **[972.91]**

5713 **Timerman, Jacobo.** *Cuba: A Journey.* **1990, Knopf $18.95 (0-394-53910-9).** An account of life under the Castro regime as viewed by the Argentine journalist and author of *Prisoner Without a Name: Cell Without a Number.* (REV: BL 9/15/90; NYTBR 10/21/90; Time 10/15/90. AWARDS: BL, 1990) **[972.91]**

5714 **Wyden, Peter.** *Bay of Pigs: The Untold Story.* **1980, Simon & Schuster paper $12.95 (0-671-25413-8).** An account of the failed U.S. attempts to spark an anti-Castro revolution in Cuba in the early 1960s. "A masterful reconstruction."—PW (REV: BL 7/1/79; LJ 5/1/79; PW 4/16/79) **[972.91]**

Haiti—History

5715 **Gold, Herbert.** *Best Nightmare on Earth: A Life in Haiti.* **1991, Prentice Hall $19.95 (0-13-372327-5).** Memoirs of the author's experiences over 40 years as a student, tourist, and journalist in Haiti. (REV: BL 1/15/91; TLS 6/28/91) **[972.94]**

Trinidad—History

5716 **Naipaul, V. S.** *Loss of El Dorado.* **1984, Random paper $5.95 (0-394-72124-1).** The myth of El Dorado and its effects upon the history of the author's native home, the island of Trinidad. "Mr. Naipaul has not only given us a lesson in history, he has shown us how it is best written."—NYTBR (REV: Atl 5/70; NYTBR 5/24/70; Time 5/25/70. AWARDS: Time, 1970) **[972.983]**

973 United States

5717 **Anthony, Carl Sferrazza.** *First Ladies: The Saga of the Presidents' Wives and Their Power, 1961–1990.* **1991, Morrow $29.95 (0-688-10562-9).** This second volume of the author's history of U.S. first ladies and their influence covers the presidents' wives from Jacqueline Kennedy to Barbara Bush. (REV: LJ 4/1/91; PW 3/6/91) **[973]**

5718 **Anthony, Carl Sferrazza.** *First Ladies, Vol. 1: A History of America's First Ladies and the Power Behind the Presidency.* **1990, Greenwillow $24.95 (0-688-07704-8).** A history of the first ladies of the United States and their influence, from Martha Washington to Jacqueline Kennedy. (REV: LJ 8/90; PW 7/13/90) **[973]**

5719 **Barber, John David.** *Presidential Character: Predicting Character in the White House.* **1985, Prentice Hall paper $32.80 (0-13-698986-1).** A psychological study of American presidents categorizing them into four major types of characters, and arguing that presidential performance is predictable based on their type. "Well-documented and thought-provoking."—BL (REV: BL 11/15/72; Choice 12/72; LJ 7/72) **[973]**

5720 Barry, Dave. *Dave Barry Slept Here: A Sort of History of the United States.* 1989, Fawcett paper $15.95 (0-394-56541-X). A comic survey history of the United States by the syndicated columnist. (REV: LJ 5/15/89; NYTBR 6/18/89; PW 4/21/89) **[973]**

5721 Brogan, Hugh. *Longman History of the United States.* 1986, Morrow $24.50 (0-688-06467-1); Penguin paper $7.95 (0-14-022527-7). A history of the United States as interpreted by a British scholar. (REV: CSM 6/2/86; LJ 7/86; TLS 5/24/85) **[973]**

5722 Burns, James MacGregor. *Vineyard of Liberty: The American Experiment.* 1982, Knopf $22.95 (0-394-50546-8); Random paper $15.95 (0-394-71629-9). The first volume of Burns's survey of American history covering the years from the ratification of the Constitution to the Emancipation Proclamation. "A superbly written general history."—LJ (REV: CSM 2/12/82; LJ 12/15/81; NYRB 2/18/82) **[973]**

5723 Commager, Henry Steele. *Empire of Reason: How Europe Imagined and America Realized the Enlightenment.* 1984, Peter Smith $17.25 (0-8446-6088-4); Oxford Univ. Pr. paper $9.95 (0-19-503062-1). The history of Enlightenment thought in Europe and how the theories became manifested in the creation of the United States. (REV: Choice 11/77; LJ 4/15/77; Sat Rev 5/14/77) **[973]**

5724 Fischer, David H. *Albion's Seed: Four British Folkways in America.* 1989, Oxford Univ. Pr. $39.95 (0-19-503794-4). How four separate subcultures of seventeenth- and eighteenth-century Great Britain colonized America and developed into distinct subcultures here. (REV: LJ 9/15/89; New Rep 10/30/89; NYRB 2/1/90) **[973]**

5725 Franklin, John Hope. *Race and History: Selected Essays.* 1990, Louisiana Univ. Pr. $29.95 (0-8071-1547-9). Selected essays regarding twentieth-century African-American history and culture. (REV: New Rep 4/30/90; NYTBR 6/3/90; PW 12/22/89) **[973]**

5726 Jones, Howard Mumford. *O Strange New World: American Culture; the Formative Years.* 1982, Greenwood Pr. $48.50 (0-313-23494-9). Jones traces the development of American culture and its divergence from European culture. (REV: CSM 10/8/64; New Yorker 9/12/64; Sat Rev 9/12/64. AWARDS: PP:NF, 1965) **[973]**

5727 Jordan, Winthrop D. *White over Black: American Attitudes Toward the Negro, 1550–1812.* 1968, Univ. of North Carolina Pr. $39.95 (0-8078-1055-X); Norton paper $13.95 (0-393-00841-X). A study of American racial attitudes from the sixteenth to early nineteenth centuries. "The most informed and impressive pronouncement on the subject."—C. Vann Woodward in NYTBR (REV: BL 6/1/68; Choice 4/68; NYTBR 3/31/68. AWARDS: NBA, 1969) **[973]**

5728 Kammen, Michael. *Mystic Chords of Memory: The Transformation of Tradition in American Culture.* 1991, Knopf $40.00 (0-394-57769-8). The author of *A Machine That Would Go of Itself* examines the evolution of themes common in American culture throughout history. (REV: BL 10/15/91; LJ 9/15/91) **[973]**

5729 Lemann, Nicholas. *Promised Land: The Great Black Migration and How It Changed America.* 1991, Knopf $24.95 (0-394-56004-3). A study of the postdepression migration of over five million African Americans from the Deep South to the North and West and its consequences for American society. (REV: BL 3/1/91; NYTBR 2/24/91; Time 3/11/91. AWARDS: ALA, 1992; Time, 1991) **[973]**

5730 McFarland, Gerald. *Scattered People: An American Family Moves West.* 1985, Pantheon $17.95 (0-394-53841-2). The author traces the history of U.S. settlement of the West through his own family's relocations from Massachusetts to the Midwest before settling in California. (REV: BL 8/85; Choice 2/86; LJ 9/15/85) **[973]**

5731 Meinig, D. W. *Shaping of America: A Geographical Perspective on 500 Years of History, Atlantic America, 1492–1800.* 1988, Yale Univ. Pr. $19.95 (0-300-03882-8). A study of the geographic factors that influenced the settlement and development of the Atlantic coast of North America. (REV: Choice 12/86; LJ 8/86; NYTBR 8/17/86) **[973]**

5732 Millett, Allan Reed, and Peter Maslowski. *For the Common Defense: A Military History of the United States, 1607–1983.* 1984, Free Pr. $24.95 (0-02-921580-3). The history of the American military in times of war and peace over the past four centuries. (REV: LJ 11/1/84; New Rep 2/11/85; NYTBR 2/3/85) **[973]**

5733 Morris, Richard Brandon. *Witnesses at the Creation: Hamilton, Madison, Jay and the Constitution.* 1986, NAL paper $9.95 (0-452-25867-7). An analysis of the roles Alexander Hamilton, James Madison, and John Jay played in the formation of the United States Constitution. (REV: BL 1/1/86; Choice 2/86; LJ 9/1/85) **[973]**

5734 Murray, Pauli. *Song in a Weary Throat: An American Pilgrimage.* 1987, Harper & Row $24.95 (0-06-015704-6). An autobiography of the woman who was one of the first female ordained Episcopal priests—her life as a teacher, activist, lawyer, poet, and writer. (REV: Choice 10/87; CSM 4/9/87; LJ 3/1/87. AWARDS: LJ, 1987) **[973]**

5735 Orlean, Susan. *Saturday Night.* 1990, Knopf $19.95 (0-394-57336-6). An analysis of the traditional American search for entertainment on Saturday nights. (REV: CSM 6/11/90; LJ 3/15/90; PW 3/23/90) **[973]**

5736 Schlesinger, Arthur M., Jr. *Cycles of American History.* 1986, Houghton $22.95 (0-395-37887-7). Essays examining the cyclical nature of politics in the history of the United States. (REV: CSM 12/3/86; LJ 11/1/86; NYRB 11/6/86) **[973]**

5737 Schlesinger, Arthur M., Jr. *Disuniting of America.* 1991, Norton $14.95 (0-393-03380-5). An analysis by the liberal historian of the impact of multiculturalism upon American academia. (REV: BL 1/1/92; PW 12/13/91) **[973]**

5738 **Slotkin, Richard.** *Fatal Environment: The Myth of the Frontier in the Age of Industrialization, 1800–1890.* 1986, Univ. Pr. of New England paper $19.95 (0-8195-6183-5). An analysis of the myth of the American frontier and its influence upon the development of the United States in the nineteenth century. (REV: BL 4/1/85; Choice 9/85; LJ 4/15/85) **[973]**

5739 **Smith, Richard Norton, and Timothy Walch, eds.** *Farewell to the Chief: Former Presidents in American Public Life.* 1990, High Plains $22.50 (0-9623333-2-8); paper $9.50 (0-9623333-3-6). Profiles of the careers and activities of U.S. presidents following their terms in office. (REV: BL 8/90; LJ 8/90) **[973]**

5740 **Sterling, Dorothy, ed.** *We Are Your Sisters: Black Women in the 19th Century.* 1985, Norton paper $13.95 (0-393-30252-0). A history of African-American women in the U.S. during the nineteenth century based on interviews and primary sources. (REV: BL 9/1/83; CSM 6/26/84; LJ 12/1/83) **[973]**

5741 **Takaki, Ronald.** *Strangers from a Different Shore: A History of Asian Americans.* 1989, Little, Brown $24.95 (0-316-83109-3); Penguin paper $11.95 (0-14-013885-4). The history of Asian immigration to the United States and the lives and communities they established in America. "The best volume yet published on the subject."—NYTBR (REV: CSM 9/18/89; LJ 7/89; NYTBR 8/27/89. AWARDS: ALA, 1989) **[973]**

5742 **Tindall, George Brown.** *America: A Narrative History.* 1988, Norton $25.95 (0-393-95680-6). A two-volume survey of American history from pre-Columbian times to the Reagan administration. (REV: BL 2/15/84; LJ 2/15/84) **[973]**

5743 **Wilkinson, Alec.** *Riverkeeper.* 1991, Knopf $20.00 (0-394-57313-7). Profiles of three Americans who earn their livelihoods on the nation's oceans and waterways. (REV: BL 7/91; LJ 8/91; PW 5/31/91) **[973]**

5744 **Zaslowsky, Dyan.** *These American Lands: Parks, Wilderness, and the Public Lands.* 1986, Holt $19.95 (0-03-006184-9). A look at American public lands and the governmental agencies that oversee their use and conservation. (REV: BL 9/1/88; LJ 9/1/86; NYTBR 1/11/87) **[973]**

History—Racial, ethnic, national groups

5745 **Campbell, Bebe Moore.** *Sweet Summer: Growing Up with and Without My Dad.* 1989, Putnam $18.95 (0-399-13415-8). Memoirs of the author's relationship with and changing perceptions of her father and of life in North Carolina during the civil rights movement. (REV: BL 6/1/89; LJ 4/1/89; PW 3/31/89. AWARDS: BL, 1989) **[973.04]**

5746 **Comer, James P.** *Maggie's American Dream: The Life and Times of a Black Family.* 1988, NAL $18.95 (0-453-00588-8); Dutton paper $8.95 (0-452-26318-2). A story of a black middle-class family as told through the words of the author's mother, Maggie, and the author's memoirs of his family and education. (REV: BL 11/15/88; CSM 12/9/88; LJ 11/1/88) **[973.04]**

5747 **Cone, James H.** *Martin and Malcolm and America: A Dream or a Nightmare.* 1990, Orbis Books $22.95 (0-88344-721-5). A comparative study of the lives and ideas of civil rights leaders Malcolm X and Martin Luther King, Jr. "A landmark analysis."—NYTBR (REV: Choice 6/91; NYTBR 3/17/91) **[973.04]**

5748 **Davis, Marilyn P.** *Mexican Voices, American Dreams: An Oral History of Mexican Immigration to the United States.* 1990, Seaver Books $24.95 (0-8050-1216-8). An oral history of 90 Mexicans and Mexican Americans examining their perceptions of the United States and their lives as Americans. (REV: BL 11/1/90; LJ 9/15/90; PW 8/24/90) **[973.04]**

5749 **Dershowitz, Alan M.** *Chutzpah.* 1991, Little, Brown $22.95 (0-316-18137-4). An analysis of contemporary American Jews and Judaism by the outspoken attorney. (REV: LJ 6/1/91; PW 4/12/91) **[973.04]**

5750 **Forman, James.** *Making of Black Revolutionaries.* 1985, Open Hand paper $16.95 (0-940880-10-5). A revised edition of the memoirs of the author's role in the civil rights movement as executive secretary of the Student Nonviolent Coordinating Committee. (REV: NYTBR 7/14/85; PW 8/9/85) **[973.04]**

5751 **Franklin, John Hope.** *George Washington Williams: A Biography.* 1985, Univ. of Chicago Pr. $24.95 (0-226-26083-6). A biography of the nineteenth-century pastor, politician, and historian. "Splendid . . . one of the most exciting biographies recently published."—Choice (REV: BL 10/15/85; Choice 3/86; LJ 10/15/85) **[973.04]**

5752 **Gatewood, Willard B.** *Aristocrats of Color: The Black Elite, 1880–1920.* 1990, Indiana Univ. Pr. $39.95 (0-253-32552-8). A social and political history of the African-American upper class around the turn of the century. (REV: BL 10/1/90; LJ 7/90; PW 10/19/90) **[973.04]**

5753 **Harding, Vincent.** *Hope and History: Why We Must Share the Story of the Movement.* 1990, Orbis paper $9.95 (0-88344-664-2). The influence and significance of the 1960s civil rights movement on America in the 1990s. (REV: BL 12/1/90; NYTBR 2/24/91) **[973.04]**

5754 **Kingston, Maxine Hong.** *China Men.* 1980, Knopf $22.95 (0-394-42463-8); Random paper $9.95 (0-679-72328-5). The men of the author's family as well as other male Chinese Americans are profiled. (REV: CSM 8/11/80; LJ 6/15/80; NYTBR 6/15/80. AWARDS: ALA, 1980; BL, the 1980s; NBA, 1981; NYTBR, 1980; Time, 1980) **[973.04]**

5755 **Njeri, Itabari.** *Every Good-Bye Ain't Gone: Family Portraits and Personal Escapades.* 1990, Random $17.95 (0-8129-1805-3); paper $9.95 (0-679-73242-X). Memoirs of the author's childhood and family life in New York during the 1950s. (REV: Atl 3/90; BL 1/1/90; NYTBR 2/4/90) **[973.04]**

5756 **Reedy, George E.** *From the Ward to the White House: The Irish in American Politics.* 1991, Macmillan $22.95 (0-684-18977-1). A historical overview of the role of the Irish and their descendants in American politics. (Rev: BL 1/15/91; LJ 2/1/91; PW 1/25/91) **[973.04]**

5757 Simons, Howard. *Jewish Times: Voices of the American Jewish Experience.* **1988, Houghton $22.95 (0-395-44680-5); Doubleday paper $12.95 (0-385-26697-9).** Over 225 interviews form the basis for this oral history of the Jewish experience in twentieth-century America. (Rev: BL 9/15/88; LJ 10/15/88; PW 8/19/88) **[973.04]**

5758 Sowell, Thomas. *Ethnic America: A History.* **1983, Basic Books paper $10.95 (0-465-02075-5).** A study of nine ethnic groups and their economic development after emigration to America. (Rev: BL 10/1/81; New Rep 10/14/81; PW 5/29/81) **[973.04]**

Education, research, related topics

5759 Fitzgerald, Frances. *America Revised: History Schoolbooks in the Twentieth Century.* **1980, Random paper $3.95 (0-394-74439-X).** A survey of the changing presentation of American history in secondary school textbooks. (Rev: BL 10/1/79; LJ 9/1/79; Newsweek 10/15/79) **[973.07]**

History and description with respect to kinds of persons

5760 Vanderbilt, Arthur T. *Fortune's Children: The Fall of the House of Vanderbilt.* **1989, Morrow $24.95 (0-688-07279-8).** A family portrait of the Vanderbilts spanning four generations and tracing the rise and fall of their wealth and influence. (Rev: BL 7/89; LJ 7/89; PW 7/7/89) **[973.08]**

History, Early history to 1607

5761 Morison, Samuel Eliot. *European Discovery of America: The Northern Voyages, A.D. 500–1600.* **1971, Oxford Univ. Pr. $35.00 (0-19-501377-8).** Survey of the history of the exploration of North America by Europeans. "A tour de force . . . his success is finally not so much historiographic as literary."—NYTBR (Rev: NYTBR 4/18/71; Newsweek 4/17/71; Time 4/19/71. Awards: ALA, 1971; NYTBR, 1971; Time, 1971) **[973.1]**

History, 1607–1775

5762 Bailyn, Bernard. *Peopling of British North America: An Introduction.* **1986, Knopf $19.95 (0-394-55392-6); Random paper $5.95 (0-394-75779-3).** This introduction to the author's *Voyages to the West* provides a survey history of transatlantic migration to North America from Great Britain. (Rev: BL 7/86; Choice 4/87; NYTBR 8/17/86) **[973.2]**

5763 Burns, James MacGregor. *Workshop of Democracy: The American Experiment from the Emancipation Proclamation to the Eve of the New Deal.* **1985, Knopf $30.00 (0-394-51275-8); Random paper $12.95 (0-394-74320-2).** A survey of American history from the Civil War to the Great Depression. "Popular history at its best."—LJ (Rev: Choice 1/86; CSM 9/24/85; LJ 8/85) **[973.2]**

5764 Jennings, Francis. *Empire of Fortune: Crowns, Colonies and Tribes in the Seven Years'*

War in America. **1988, Norton $27.50 (0-393-02537-3); paper $10.95 (0-393-30640-2).** A revisionist history of the French and Indian wars of 1754 to 1763. (Rev: LJ 3/15/88; NYTBR 5/15/88; PW 1/29/88) **[973.2]**

History—Periods of Revolution and Confederation, 1775–1789

5765 Bailyn, Bernard. *Ideological Origins of the American Revolution.* **1967, Harvard Univ. Pr. $21.00 (0-674-44300-4); paper $9.95 (0-674-44301-2).** Traces the European origins of the ideas that led to the revolution. (Rev: Choice 12/67; LJ 4/15/67; NYTBR 6/25/67. Awards: PP:History, 1968) **[973.3]**

5766 Bailyn, Bernard. *Ordeal of Thomas Hutchinson.* **1974, Harvard Univ. Pr. $27.00 (0-674-64160-4); paper $10.95 (0-674-64161-2).** A biography of the last royal governor of Massachusetts, a look at the American Revolution from a Loyalist view. (Rev: CSM 4/17/74; New Rep 5/4/74; NYRB 3/21/74. Awards: ALA, 1974; NBA, 1975) **[973.3]**

5767 Birnbaum, Louis D. *Red Dawn at Lexington: "If They Mean to Have a War, Let It Begin Here."* **1986, Houghton $18.95 (0-395-38814-7).** An account of the events surrounding the opening battles of the American Revolution. "First-rate . . . a pleasure to read."—PW (Rev: BL 4/15/86; LJ 5/1/86; PW 2/28/86) **[973.3]**

5768 Bowen, Catherine D. *Miracle at Philadelphia: The Story of the Constitutional Convention, May to September 1787.* **1986, Little, Brown $18.95 (0-316-10378-0); paper $8.95 (0-316-10398-5).** A day-by-day account of the Constitutional Convention with detailed portraits of the personalities involved. "Mrs. Bowen brings freshness and vitality to a familiar subject."—BL (Rev: BL 12/15/66; CSM 12/1/66; LJ 10/1/66. Awards: ALA, 1966) **[973.3]**

5769 Bowen, Catherine D. *Most Dangerous Man in America: Scenes from the Life of Benjamin Franklin.* **1986, Little, Brown $8.95 (0-316-10379-9).** Interpretations of key events in the life of the eighteenth-century American statesman and inventor. (Rev: Choice 2/75; LJ 11/1/74; New Rep 11/2/74) **[973.3]**

5770 Buel, Joy Day, and Richard Buel, Jr. *Way of Duty: A Woman and Her Family in Revolutionary America.* **1984, Norton $19.95 (0-393-01767-2).** A biography, based on the family papers, of an eighteenth-century American minister's daughter who married a revolutionary officer. (Rev: Choice 9/84; NYTBR 2/5/84; PW 11/25/83) **[973.3]**

5771 Dull, Jonathan R. *A Diplomatic History of the American Revolution.* **1985, Yale Univ. Pr. $25.00 (0-300-03419-9); paper $9.95 (0-300-03886-0).** A history of diplomatic relations between the American colonies and Europe during the American Revolution. (Rev: BL 10/15/85; Choice 6/86; LJ 11/1/85) **[973.3]**

5772 Flexner, James T. *George Washington in the American Revolution, 1775–1783.* **1968, Little, Brown $25.00 (0-316-28595-1).** An account of Washington's years as commander in chief of the colonial army. "Although this splendidly written history is the second volume of an intended three-volume biography of George Washington, it stands alone as an effective and important history of the American Revolution."—Choice (Rev: Choice 7/68; LJ 2/15/68; NYTBR 3/31/68. Awards: ALA, 1968) **[973.3]**

5773 Maier, Pauline. *From Resistance to Revolution: Colonial Radicals and the Development of American Opposition to Britain, 1765–1776.* **1973, Random paper $9.95 (0-394-71937-9).** The roots, rise, and development of anti-British thought in the era just prior to the revolutionary war. "A well written, important and original contribution to the intellectual history of the American Revolution."—Choice (Rev: Choice 10/72; LJ 7/72; NYTBR 5/21/72) **[973.3]**

5774 Middlekauff, Robert. *Glorious Cause: The American Revolution, 1763–1789.* **1985, Oxford Univ. Pr. $39.95 (0-19-502921-6); paper $14.95 (0-19-503575-5).** A survey of events central to the American Revolution from the 1763 Treaty of Paris to the Constitutional Convention. (Rev: BL 5/1/82; LJ 3/15/82; New Rep 10/25/82) **[973.3]**

5775 Morris, Richard Brandon. *Forging of the Nation, 1781–1789.* **1987, Harper & Row $22.95 (0-06-015733-X); paper $8.95 (0-06-091424-6).** An examination of the events leading up to the writing of the U.S. Constitution and the replacement of the Articles of Confederation. (Rev: Choice 10/87; LJ 4/15/87; NYTBR 6/14/87) **[973.3]**

5776 Morris, Richard Brandon. *Peacemakers: The Great Powers and American Independence.* **1983, Northeastern Univ. Pr. $37.50 (0-930350-35-9).** The international diplomacy that led to the Treaty of Paris that ended the American revolutionary war. "Easily surpasses all previous accounts."—Choice (Rev: Choice 1/66; LJ 10/1/65; NYTBR 11/14/65. Awards: ALA, 1965; NYTBR, 1965) **[973.3]**

5777 Nelson, Paul David. *Anthony Wayne: Soldier of the Early Republic.* **1985, Indiana Univ. Pr. $29.95 (0-253-30751-1).** A biography of the American general known for his campaigns against the British during the American Revolution and his later battles against Native Americans. (Rev: BL 1/1/86; Choice 3/86; LJ 9/15/85) **[973.3]**

5778 Randall, Willard Sterne. *Benedict Arnold: Patriot and Traitor.* **1990, Morrow $27.45 (1-55710-034-9).** A revisionist biography of the American revolutionary war general. (Rev: BL 7/90; NYTBR 8/26/90; PW 6/29/90) **[973.3]**

5779 Smith, Page. *A New Age Now Begins: A People's History of the American Revolution.* **1989, Penguin paper $31.90 (0-14-095354-X).** A two-volume history of the American Revolution. "Everything a general history should be . . . he recaptures the spirit of '76 as well as anyone who lives in our century can hope to."—Choice (Rev: Choice 9/76; CSM 3/23/76; NYTBR 2/22/76) **[973.3]**

5780 Wills, Garry. *Inventing America: Jefferson's Declaration of Independence.* **1979, Random paper $7.95 (0-394-72735-5).** "There is no better account . . . of the fears, divisions, loyalties and priorities of the men who dominated the Continental Congress. This book is also one of the best studies of Jefferson yet to appear."—NYTBR (Rev: NYRB 8/17/78; NYTBR 7/2/78; Newsweek 7/17/78. Awards: ALA, 1978; NYTBR, 1978) **[973.3]**

5781 Wright, Esmond. *Franklin of Philadelphia.* **1986, Harvard Univ. Pr. $27.95 (0-674-31809-9); paper $12.95 (0-674-31810-2).** A biography of the eighteenth-century American statesman, writer, and scientist. "Authoritative, readable . . . will delight anyone interested in Franklin."—PW (Rev: CSM 4/23/86; LJ 3/15/86; PW 3/14/86) **[973.3]**

5782 Zobel, Hiller. *Boston Massacre.* **1971, Norton paper $9.95 (0-393-00606-9).** An account of the events leading up to the Boston Massacre, the event itself, and its repercussions. "A definitive reappraisal of a much misunderstood episode in pre-Revolutionary War history."—BL (Rev: BL 7/15/70; Choice 6/70; LJ 12/15/70) **[973.3]**

History, 1775–1789

5783 Alden, John R. *George Washington: A Biography.* **1984, Louisiana State Univ. Pr. $24.95 (0-8071-1153-8); Dell paper $5.95 (0-440-32836-5).** A biography of the American revolutionary leader and first president of the United States. "The best single-volume biography of Washington ever written."—LJ (Rev: Choice 1/85; LJ 5/1/84; NYTBR 8/5/84) **[973.4]**

5784 Brodie, Fawn. *Thomas Jefferson: An Intimate History.* **1975, Bantam paper $5.95 (0-553-27335-3).** The personality and personal life of Jefferson is explored in this psychological biography. "A compelling compassionate case history of the inner Jefferson."—LJ (Rev: BL 4/15/74; LJ 4/15/74; NYTBR 4/7/74) **[973.4]**

5785 Ferling, John E. *First of Men: A Life of George Washington.* **1988, Univ. of Tennessee Pr. $44.95 (0-87049-562-3); paper $22.50 (0-87049-628-X).** A biography of the first president of the United States. "Well-documented, gracefully written, and engaging history—clearly the most informative one-volume study."—Choice (Rev: Choice 3/89; LJ 8/88; PW 6/10/88) **[973.4]**

5786 Flexner, James T. *George Washington: Anguish and Farewell, 1793–1799.* **1972, Little, Brown $25.00 (0-316-28602-8).** The fourth and concluding volume of the series covers Washington's second term as president, his years out of office, and his death. "This, with the earlier volumes may be the definitive personal biography of Washington."—LJ (Rev: LJ 2/1/73; NYTBR 11/19/72; Newsweek 11/20/72) **[973.4]**

5787 Flexner, James T. *George Washington and the New Nation, 1783–1793.* **1970, Little, Brown $25.00 (0-316-28600-1).** This third volume of Flexner's biography of Washington covers his five years of retirement at Mount Vernon and his subsequent election and first term as president. (Rev: LJ 9/15/70; NYTBR 10/25/70; Sat Rev 11/21/70) **[973.4]**

5788 Flexner, James T. *Young Hamilton: A Biography.* **1978, Little, Brown $19.95 (0-316-28594-3).** The first 26 years in the life of Alexander Hamilton as seen by the noted biographer of Washington. "The insights offered, with the expected impeccable scholarship and graceful style, are fascinating . . . a brilliant portrait."—PW (Rev: LJ 5/1/78; Newsweek 3/20/78; PW 1/16/78) **[973.4]**

5789 **Hawke, David Freeman.** *Benjamin Rush: Revolutionary Gadfly.* **1971, Irvington $24.50 (0-672-51599-7).** A biography (to 1789) of the revolutionary war doctor who helped spur Pennsylvania to join the union, signed the Declaration of Independence, and urged social and educational reform. (Rev: Choice 1/72; LJ 8/71; NYTBR 1/2/72) **[973.4]**

5790 **Levin, Phyllis Lee.** *Abigail Adams: A Biography.* **1987, St. Martin's $24.95 (0-312-00007-3); Ballantine paper $10.95 (0-345-35473-7).** A biography of the wife of the second president of the United States and mother of the sixth. (Rev: Choice 10/87; CSM 6/10/87; NYTBR 6/7/87) **[973.4]**

5791 **McDonald, Forrest.** *Alexander Hamilton: A Biography.* **1982, Norton paper $10.95 (0-393-30048-X).** A biography of the first secretary of the treasury of the United States and key contributor to the *Federalist Papers.* (Rev: Choice 2/80; LJ 8/79; NYTBR 9/23/79) **[973.4]**

5792 **McLaughlin, Jack.** *Jefferson and Monticello: The Biography of a Builder.* **1988, Henry Holt $29.95 (0-8050-0482-3).** An investigation into Jefferson, Monticello, and the nearly six decades he spent on its design and construction. (Rev: BL 4/1/88; LJ 4/15/88; NYTBR 7/31/88. Awards: LJ, 1988) **[973.4]**

5793 **Nagel, Paul C.** *Adams Women: Abigail and Louisa Adams, Their Sisters and Daughters.* **1987, Oxford Univ. Pr. $24.95 (0-19-503874-6).** A study of the female figures of the Adams family by the author of *Descent from Glory,* which focused on John Adams and John Quincy Adams. (Rev: BL 9/15/87; LJ 8/87; NYTBR 10/25/87) **[973.4]**

5794 **Schwartz, Barry.** *George Washington: The Making of an American Symbol.* **1987, Free Pr. $22.50 (0-02-928141-5); Cornell Univ. Pr. paper $12.95 (0-8014-9747-7).** A history of the reputation and mythical status of the first American president. (Rev: Choice 11/87; LJ 9/1/87; NYTBR 9/13/87) **[973.4]**

5795 **Withey, Lynne.** *Dearest Friend: A Life of Abigail Adams.* **1982, Free Pr. $17.95 (0-02-934760-2); paper $9.95 (0-02-934770-X).** A biography of the wife of President John Adams based on her letters and journals. (Rev: Choice 12/81; LJ 9/15/81; NYTBR 9/20/81) **[973.4]**

History, Administration of Thomas Jefferson, 1801–1809

5796 **Cunningham, Noble E., Jr.** *In Pursuit of Reason: The Life of Thomas Jefferson.* **1987, Louisiana State Univ. Pr. $24.95 (0-8071-1375-1); Ballantine paper $10.95 (0-345-35380-3).** An appraisal of the life of the third president of the United States. (Rev: Choice 11/87; LJ 5/1/87; NYTBR 6/14/87) **[973.46]**

5797 **Malone, Dumas.** *Jefferson and His Time: Jefferson the President, Second Term 1805–1809.* **1975, Little, Brown $27.50 (0-316-54465-5); paper $12.95 (0-316-54464-7).** Volume five of a massive biography of our third president examines his second term. "A brilliant, living, breathing account of Jefferson placed in his historical setting."—PW (Rev: LJ 5/1/74; Natl Rev 5/10/74; PW 2/14/74) **[973.46]**

5798 **Malone, Dumas.** *Jefferson and His Time: The Sage of Monticello.* **1982, Little, Brown $27.50 (0-316-54463-9).** The sixth and final volume of Malone's biography of Jefferson covers his years following the presidency to his death. "Malone is . . . unquestionably Jefferson's finest biographer."—LJ (Rev: Atl 8/81; LJ 6/15/81; New Rep 8/1/81. Awards: ALA, 1981) **[973.46]**

History, 1809–1845

5799 **Bartlett, Irving H.** *Daniel Webster.* **1981, Norton paper $8.95 (0-393-00996-3).** A biography of the nineteenth-century American lawyer, statesman, and orator. (Rev: Choice 11/78; LJ 4/15/78; NYTBR 7/23/78) **[973.5]**

5800 **Berton, Pierre.** *Invasion of Canada: 1812–1813.* **1988, Penguin paper $4.95 (0-14-010855-6).** An account of the invasion of British Canada by American troops during the War of 1812. (Rev: BL 11/15/80; LJ 9/15/80; PW 9/26/80) **[973.5]**

5801 **Elting, John.** *Amateurs to Arms: A Military History of the War of 1812–1815.* **1991, Algonquin $24.95 (0-945575-08-4).** An overview of the military history and key battles of the War of 1812. "Essential for any public or academic library."—LJ (Rev: BL 10/1/91; LJ 8/91) **[973.5]**

5802 **Hickey, Donald R.** *War of 1812: A Forgotten Conflict.* **1989, Univ. of Illinois Pr. $32.50 (0-252-01613-0); paper $14.95 (0-252-06059-8).** A summary of the events and consequences of the War of 1812. (Rev: BL 11/15/89; Choice 5/90) **[973.5]**

5803 **Kennedy, Roger G.** *Greek Revival America.* **1989, Stewart, Tabori & Chang $85.00 (1-55670-094-6); AIA paper $49.95 (1-558350-42-X).** An illustrated survey of the architecture and social history of the United States during the first half of the nineteenth century. (Rev: BL 10/15/89; LJ 10/15/89; NYTBR 12/3/89) **[973.5]**

5804 **McCoy, Drew R.** *Last of the Fathers: James Madison and the Republican Legacy.* **1989, Cambridge Univ. Pr. $29.95 (0-521-36407-8).** An examination of Madison's life following his retirement from the White House. (Rev: BL 3/15/89; Choice 10/89; LJ 4/15/89) **[973.5]**

5805 **Niven, John.** *Martin Van Buren: The Romantic Age of American Politics.* **1983, Oxford Univ. Pr. $45.00 (0-19-503238-1).** A portrait of the life and times of the eighth president of the United States. "Will probably become the standard Van Buren biography."—Choice (Rev: Choice 10/83; LJ 5/1/83; PW 5/13/83) **[973.5]**

5806 Peterson, Merrill D. *Great Triumvirate: Webster, Clay, and Calhoun.* 1988, Oxford Univ. Pr. paper $12.95 (0-19-505686-8). A study of the lives and careers of three prominent U.S. senators in the first half of the nineteenth century. (Rev: BL 7/87; New Rep 11/9/87; NYTBR 11/8/87)   **[973.5]**

5807 Preston, Dickson J. *Young Frederick Douglass: The Maryland Years.* 1985, Johns Hopkins paper $9.95 (0-8018-2739-6). An examination of the family history and first 20 years in the life of the nineteenth-century writer, statesman, and abolitionist. (Rev: Choice 3/81; LJ 11/15/80)   **[973.5]**

5808 Remini, Robert V. *Andrew Johnson and the Course of American Democracy, 1833–1845.* 1984, Harper & Row $27.95 (0-06-015279-6). This third volume of Jackson's life by Remini covers his second term as president until his death. (Rev: Choice 10/84; LJ 5/1/84; NYTBR 10/28/84. Awards: NBA, 1984)   **[973.5]**

5809 Remini, Robert V. *Henry Clay: Statesman for the Union.* 1991, Norton $35.00 (0-393-03004-0). The noted biographer of Andrew Jackson examines the life and legacy of the nineteenth-century American diplomat and politician. (Rev: LJ 8/91; NYTBR 10/27/91; PW 8/16/91)   **[973.5]**

5810 Watson, Harry C. *Liberty and Power: The Politics of Jacksonian America.* 1990, Farrar $22.95 (0-8090-6546-0); paper $9.95 (0-374-52196-4). A study of the political, social, and economic issues facing the United States during the Jacksonian era. (Rev: BL 1/15/90; Choice 6/90; LJ 1/90)   **[973.5]**

History, 1845–1861

5811 Chalfant, William Y. *Cheyennes and Horse Soldiers: The 1857 Expedition and the Battle of Solomon's Ford.* 1989, Univ. of Oklahoma Pr. $24.95 (0-8061-2194-7). An examination of the expedition and events leading up to the first armed battle between the Cheyenne Indians and the United States Army. (Rev: BL 8/89; Choice 3/90; NYTBR 9/24/89)   **[973.6]**

5812 Eisenhower, John S. D. *So Far from God: The U.S. War with Mexico, 1846–48.* 1989, Random $24.95 (0-394-56051-5); Doubleday paper $12.95 (0-385-41214-2). The history of the politics and military conflicts of the Mexican-American War by the son of the former president and retired army general. (Rev: CSM 5/23/89; LJ 4/15/89; NYTBR 4/2/89. Awards: BL, 1989)   **[973.6]**

5813 Freehling, William W. *Road to Disunion: Secessionists at Bay, 1776–1854.* 1990, Oxford Univ. Pr. $30.00 (0-19-505814-3). A history of the events that led to the secession of the American South from independence to the Kansas-Nebraska Act. (Rev: Choice 1/91; LJ 8/90; NYTBR 9/30/90. Awards: LJ, 1990)   **[973.6]**

5814 Herr, Pamela. *Jessie Benton Fremont: American Woman of the 19th Century.* 1987, Watts $24.95 (0-531-15011-9); Univ. of Oklahoma Pr. paper $14.95 (0-8061-2159-9). A biography of the daughter of U.S. Senator Thomas Hart Benton and wife of explorer/politician John C. Fremont. "An earnest and detailed biography of a remarkable 19th century American woman."—BL   **[973.6]**

5815 Jacobs, Harriet A. *Incidents in the Life of a Slave Girl: Written by Herself.* Ed. by Jean F. Yellin. 1987, Harvard Univ. Pr. $37.50 (0-674-44745-X); paper $9.95 (0-674-44746-8). A narrative by an African-American slave whose authorship was established 120 years after its composition. (Rev: Choice 12/87; NYTBR 11/22/87; TLS 12/4/87)   **[973.6]**

5816 Oates, Stephen B. *To Purge This Land with Blood: A Biography of John Brown.* 1984, Univ. of Massachusetts Pr. paper $14.95 (0-87023-458-7). A psychological portrait of the leader of the raid on Harper's Ferry. "Deserves to be the standard biography of John Brown for years to come."—Choice (Rev: Choice 12/70; LJ 7/70; Newsweek 7/6/70)   **[973.6]**

5817 Potter, David M. *Impending Crisis: 1848 to 1861.* 1976, Harper & Row paper $12.95 (0-06-131929-5). This survey, which looks at the years leading to the Civil War, was deemed "magnificent" by *Newsweek*. (Rev: Choice 7–8/76; LJ 3/15/76; Newsweek 3/8/76. Awards: PP:NF, 1977)   **[973.6]**

History, 1861–1865

5818 Bowers, John. *Stonewall Jackson: Portrait of a Soldier.* 1989, Morrow $19.95 (0-688-05747-0). A biography of the Confederate general who was mistakenly killed by his own troops following the battle of Chancellorsville. (Rev: BL 5/15/89; LJ 5/15/89; NYRB 10/12/89)   **[973.7]**

5819 Brandt, Nat. *Man Who Tried to Burn New York.* 1986, Syracuse Univ. Pr. $24.95 (0-8156-0207-3); paper $11.95 (0-8156-0227-8). The history of a plot by Confederates to set New York afire in retaliation for Sherman's March. "A masterpiece of popular history."—LJ (Rev: Choice 1/87; LJ 8/86; PW 6/27/86)   **[973.7]**

5820 Chesnut, Mary. *Mary Chesnut's Civil War.* Ed. by C. Vann Woodward. 1981, Yale Univ. Pr. $45.00 (0-300-02459-2); paper $16.95 (0-300-02979-0). This Civil War diary by a Confederate woman is one of the most revealing personal documents of the war. (Rev: CSM 3/9/81; LJ 3/1/81; TLS 11/6/81. Awards: PP:History, 1982)   **[973.7]**

5821 Connelly, Thomas L. *Marble Man: Robert E. Lee and His Image in American Society.* 1977, LSU Pr. paper $9.95 (0-8071-0474-4). A revisionist study of Lee's reputation following his death that seeks to replace Lee, the myth, with Lee, the man. "An excellent reappraisal."—LJ (Rev: Choice 11/77; LJ 6/1/77; PW 4/4/77)   **[973.7]**

5822 Davis, Burke. *Long Surrender.* 1985, Random $19.95 (0-394-52083-1); paper $9.95 (0-679-72409-5). A study of the last days of the Confederacy focusing on the capture of Jefferson Davis and the events leading to Lee's surrender at Appomattox. (Rev: BL 4/15/85; LJ 3/15/85; Natl Rev 10/18/85)   **[973.7]**

5823 Evans, Eli N. *Judah P. Benjamin: The Jewish Confederate.* 1988, Free Pr. $24.95 (0-02-90880-1); paper $12.95 (0-02-909911-0). A biography of the U.S. senator who served as a member of the Confederate Cabinet following secession. (REV: Choice 5/88; LJ 12/87; NYTBR 4/14/88) **[973.7]**

5824 Foote, Shelby. *Civil War: A Narrative.* 1974, Random $114.95 (0-394-49517-9); paper $65.85 (0-394-74913-8). A three-volume chronicle of the American Civil War. (REV: Atl 12/74; New Rep 11/30/74; Time 1/6/75. AWARDS: Time, 1975) **[973.7]**

5825 Frassanito, William A. *Gettysburg: A Journey in Time.* 1976, Macmillan paper $17.95 (0-684-14696-7). The story of the Battle of Gettysburg is told through narrative and all extant photographs of the conflict. "An intoxicating transport back in time."—BL (REV: BL 7/1/75; Choice 9/75; LJ 6/15/75. AWARDS: ALA, 1975) **[973.7]**

5826 Glatthaar, Joseph T. *Forged in Battle: The Civil War Alliance of Black Soldiers and White Officers.* 1989, Free Pr. $24.95 (0-02-911815-8); Dutton paper $12.95 (0-452-01068-3). An examination of the relationship between black soldiers and their white officers during the American Civil War. (REV: LJ 10/1/89; NYRB 4/12/90; NYTBR 1/14/90) **[973.7]**

5827 Gooding, James Henry. *On the Altar of Freedom: A Black Soldier's Civil War Letters from the Front.* Ed. by Virginia Matzke Adams. 1991, Univ. of Massachusetts Pr. $21.95 (0-870-23745-4). Collected letters written by an African-American Union soldier detailing his experiences during the Civil War. (REV: LJ 10/1/91; NYTBR 11/17/91) **[973.7]**

5828 Holzer, Harold. *Lincoln Image: Abraham Lincoln and the Popular Print.* 1984, Macmillan $35.00 (0-684-18072-3). A collection of over 100 photographs, prints, and drawings depicting Abraham Lincoln and his changing historical image. (REV: Choice 5/84; CSM 3/13/84; LJ 3/15/84) **[973.7]**

5829 Josephy, Alvin M., Jr. *Civil War in the American West.* 1991, Knopf $27.50 (0-394-56482-0). A historic survey of the battles of the American Civil War that were fought west of the Mississippi River. (REV: BL 11/1/91; LJ 11/1/91) **[973.7]**

5830 Lincoln, Abraham. *Lincoln on Democracy: An Anthology.* Ed. by Mario M. Cuomo and Harold Holzer. 1990, HarperCollins $24.95 (0-06-039126-X). Collected writings of Abraham Lincoln on democracy. (REV: BL 10/15/90; LJ 10/15/90) **[973.7]**

5831 Linderman, Gerald F. *Embattled Courage: The Experience of Combat in the American Civil War.* 1987, Free Pr. $22.50 (0-02-919760-0); paper $11.95 (0-02-919761-9). A study of the effects of the Civil War on the values and morals of the American soldier and the nation. (REV: Choice 9/87; NYTBR 7/5/87; PW 3/13/87) **[973.7]**

5832 McFeely, William S. *Frederick Douglass.* 1991, Norton $24.95 (0-393-02823-2). A biography of the nineteenth-century African-American social critic, abolitionist, and reformer. "The most penetrating study yet of any black person . . . an extraordinary book."—LJ (REV: BL 12/1/90; LJ 2/1/91; NYTBR 2/17/91) **[973.7]**

5833 McPherson, James M. *Abraham Lincoln and the Second American Revolution.* 1991, Oxford Univ. Pr. $19.95 (0-19-505542-X). Seven essays analyzing Lincoln's role in the changes in American society during the Civil War. (REV: BL 12/1/90; NYTBR 1/20/91; PW 12/7/90) **[973.7]**

5834 Mitchell, Reid. *Civil War Soldiers: Their Expectations and Their Experiences.* 1988, Viking $19.95 (0-670-81742-2); Simon & Schuster paper $8.95 (0-671-68641-0). A look at the opinions, psychological state, and physical environment of the soldiers who fought in the American Civil War. (REV: BL 8/88; Choice 1/89; LJ 9/15/88) **[973.7]**

5835 Myers, Robert Manson. *Children of Pride: A True Story of Georgia and the Civil War.* 1987, Yale Univ. Pr. paper $15.95 (0-300-04053-9). A collection of 14 years of letters to and from the family of the Reverend Charles Jones of Georgia from 1854 to 1868. "An incredibly real picture of life, mores, customs and opinions of the Old South."—LJ (REV: LJ 6/15/72; New Rep 5/13/72; Newsweek 4/24/72. AWARDS: ALA, 1972; NBA, 1973; NYTBR, 1972; Time, 1972) **[973.7]**

5836 Nolan, Alan T. *Lee Considered: General Robert E. Lee and Civil War History.* 1991, Univ. of North Carolina Pr. $22.95 (0-8078-1956-5). A revisionist study of the life and legend of Confederate military leader Robert E. Lee. (REV: BL 4/15/91; LJ 4/15/91; NYTBR 7/7/91) **[973.7]**

5837 Oates, Stephen B. *Abraham Lincoln: The Man Behind the Myths.* 1985, NAL paper $7.95 (0-452-00939-1). A comparison between the mythological Lincoln and the reality of the man by the author of *With Malice Toward None.* (REV: BL 1/15/84; CSM 5/25/84; LJ 3/15/84) **[973.7]**

5838 Paludan, Phillip Shaw. *A People's Contest: The Union and Civil War, 1861–1865.* 1988, Harper & Row $27.95 (0-06-015903-0); paper $9.95 (0-06-091607-9). An analysis of the economic and social impact of the Civil War upon the North. (REV: BL 10/15/88; Choice 5/89; NYTBR 1/25/89) **[973.7]**

5839 Royster, Charles. *Destructive War: William Tecumseh Sherman, Stonewall Jackson and the Americans.* 1991, Knopf $30.00 (0-394-52485-3). A comparative analysis of the personalities and military activities of Generals Sherman and Jackson during the Civil War. (REV: BL 10/1/91; NYTBR 11/3/91; PW 8/30/91) **[973.7]**

5840 Sears, Stephen W. *George B. McClellan: The Young Napoleon.* 1988, Ticknor & Fields $24.95 (0-89919-264-5). A biography of the controversial Union Civil War general. "An exemplary biography written with style and a sense of history."—BL (REV: BL 8/88; LJ 11/1/88; NYTBR 10/30/88) **[973.7]**

5841 Sears, Stephen W. *Landscape Turned Red: The Battle of Antietam.* 1983, Ticknor & Fields $18.95 (0-89919-172-X); Warner paper $6.95 (0-446-35503-8). An account of the clash between the armies of Lee and McClellan that became the

bloodiest single-day battle of the American Civil War. (Rev: BL 6/1/83; LJ 5/15/83; Newsweek 7/18/83)
[973.7]

5842 Trudeau, Noah Andre. *Bloody Roads South: The Wilderness to Cold Harbor, May–June 1864.* 1989, Little, Brown $19.95 (0-316-85326-7). An examination of Grant's victorious campaign against Lee's armies in Virginia during May and June of 1864. (Rev: BL 9/1/89; LJ 8/89; PW 7/28/89)   **[973.7]**

5843 Turner, Justin G., and Linda L. Turner. *Mary Todd Lincoln: Her Life and Letters.* 1987, Fromm International paper $12.95 (0-88064-073-1). A biographical study of the wife of Abraham Lincoln based on her correspondence. "The most comprehensive portrait . . . thus far chronicled."—PW (Rev: LJ 9/1/72; NYTBR 9/24/72; PW 7/10/72)   **[973.7]**

5844 Ward, Geoffrey C. *Civil War: An Illustrated History.* 1990, Knopf $50.00 (0-394-56285-2). This illustrated history of the American Civil War was designed to accompany the acclaimed PBS television series. (Rev: BL 8/90; LJ 9/1/90; NYTBR 9/9/90. Awards: BL, 1990; LJ, 1990)   **[973.7]**

5845 Wert, Jeffry D. *Mosby's Rangers.* 1990, Simon & Schuster $22.95 (0-671-67360-2). A study of a Confederate guerrilla organization of 200 individuals and their exploits during the American Civil War. "Well-researched, objectively written, this is a first-class history."—PW (Rev: BL 10/1/90; LJ 10/15/90; PW 9/7/90)   **[973.7]**

5846 Wheeler, Richard. *Sword over Richmond: An Eyewitness History of McClellan's Peninsula Campaign.* 1989, Crown $6.98 (0-517-68021-1). An account of the failed 1862 campaign by McClellan to capture the Confederate capital based on the letters and journals of soldiers involved in the quest. (Rev: Choice 7–8/86; LJ 4/1/86; NYTBR 4/27/86)   **[973.7]**

5847 Wilkinson, Warren. *Mother, May You Never See the Sights I Have Seen: The 57th Massachusetts Veteran Volunteers in the Army of the Potomac, 1864–1865.* 1990, HarperCollins $30.00 (0-06-016257-0); Morrow paper $15.00 (0-688-10871-7). The story of the Union's 57th Massachusetts regiment based on the writings of the soldiers who served in that unit. (Rev: Choice 7–8/90; NYTBR 5/13/90; PW 2/23/90)   **[973.7]**

5848 Woodworth, Steven E. *Jefferson Davis and His Generals: The Failure of the Confederate Command in the West.* 1990, Univ. Pr. of Kansas $25.00 (0-7006-0461-8). A study of the Confederate military and its leadership on the western front during the American Civil War. (Rev: BL 7/90; Choice 11/90; LJ 7/90)   **[973.7]**

History, 1865–1901

5849 Foner, Eric. *Reconstruction: America's Unfinished Revolution, 1863–1877.* 1988, Harper & Row $29.95 (0-06-015851-4); paper $14.95 (0-06-015851-4). The history of the Reconstruction era from the Emancipation Proclamation to the election of Rutherford B. Hayes as president. "A

masterful work by the preeminent historian of the era."—LJ (Rev: LJ 4/1/88; New Rep 8/1/88; NYRB 5/12/88. Awards: LJ, 1988)   **[973.8]**

5850 Hoehling, A. A. *After the Guns Fell Silent: A Post-Appomattox Narrative, April 1865–March 1866.* 1990, Madison Books $24.95 (0-8191-7805-5). A study of the immediate effects of the American Civil War based on writings of the period. (Rev: BL 9/15/90; LJ 9/15/90)   **[973.8]**

5851 Litwack, Leon F. *Been in the Storm So Long: The Aftermath of Slavery.* 1980, Random paper $15.95 (0-394-74398-9). A study of the transition of nineteenth century black Americans from slavery to freedom. "Belongs on that short shelf on indispensable works of Southern history."—David Herbert Donald (Rev: LJ 5/1/79; New Rep 6/9/79; NYTBR 6/10/79. Awards: ALA, 1979; NBA, 1981; PP:History, 1980)   **[973.8]**

5852 O'Toole, Patricia. *Five of Hearts: An Intimate Portrait of Henry Adams and His Friends, 1880–1918.* 1990, Crown $25.00 (0-517-56350-9). A study of the life, times, and social circle of American historian Henry Adams at the turn of the century. (Rev: Choice 12/90; NYTBR 8/12/90; PW 3/2/90)   **[973.8]**

5853 Sandoz, Mari. *Battle of the Little Bighorn.* n.d, Amereon $15.95 (0-89190-879-X); Univ. of Nebraska Pr. paper $5.95 (0-8032-9100-0). An account of the battle between Custer's forces and the Sioux Indians. "The best account of the battle ever written."—NYTBR (Rev: BL 9/1/66; LJ 5/15/66; NYTBR 7/3/66. Awards: ALA, 1966)   **[973.8]**

5854 Schlereth, Thomas J. *Victorian America: Transformations in Everyday Life, 1876–1915.* 1991, HarperCollins $25.00 (0-06-016218-X). An analysis of social life and its changes in the United States from 1876 to the outbreak of the First World War. (Rev: BL 7/91; NYTBR 12/15/91)   **[973.8]**

5855 Smith, Page. *Rise of Industrial America: A People's History of Post-Reconstruction America.* 1984, McGraw-Hill $29.95 (0-07-058572-5); Penguin paper $15.95 (0-14-012262-1). This survey of American history from 1879–1906 is the sixth volume of Smith's *People's History of the United States.* (Rev: BL 3/15/84; LJ 2/15/84; NYTBR 3/11/84)   **[973.8]**

5856 Trefousse, Hans. *Andrew Johnson: A Biography.* 1989, Norton $25.00 (0-393-02673-6). A biography of the seventeenth president of the United States. "The most exhaustive, scrupulous and meticulously documented treatment of Andrew Johnson's life and career that has yet appeared."—NYRB (Rev: Choice 1/90; LJ 8/89; NYRB 5/17/90)   **[973.8]**

History, Administration of Ulysses Simpson Grant, 1869–1877

5857 Ambrose, Stephen E. *Crazy Horse and Custer: The Parallel Lives of Two American Warriors.* 1986, NAL paper $12.95 (0-452-00934-0). A dual biography of General George A. Custer and the Sioux leader Crazy Horse by the author of *Eisenhower* and *Nixon.* (Rev: BL 10/15/75; LJ 12/15/75; PW 9/1/75)   **[973.82]**

5858 Utley, Robert M. *Cavalier in Buckskin: George Armstrong Custer and the Western Military Frontier.* 1988, Univ. of Oklahoma Pr. $21.95 (0-8061-2150-5). A psychological biography of General Custer focusing on the events leading up to the Battle of Little Big Horn. "An immensely readable popular history and a definitive statement on its subject."—BL (Rev: BL 10/15/88; PW 8/19/88) **[973.82]**

History, 1901–

5859 Ball, George W. *The Past Has Another Pattern: Memoirs.* 1983, Norton paper $9.95 (0-393-30142-7). Memoirs of the former American diplomat who served in the Kennedy and Johnson administrations. (Rev: CSM 7/14/82; LJ 5/15/82; NYTBR 5/2/82) **[973.9]**

5860 Clifford, Clark, and Richard Holbroke. *Counsel to the President: A Memoir.* 1991, Random $25.00 (0-394-56995-4). Memoirs of the American statesman's service under Presidents Truman and Johnson. (Rev: LJ 5/15/91; PW 5/3/91; Time 5/27/91) **[973.9]**

5861 Coates, James. *Armed and Dangerous: The Rise of the Survivalist Right.* 1987, Hill & Wang $17.95 (0-8090-2742-9); Farrar paper (0-374-52125-5). An account of the rise and development of American racist right-wing groups. "An important contribution to the history of our time."—PW (Rev: BL 10/1/87; NYTBR 11/29/87; PW 9/4/87) **[973.9]**

5862 Coffey, Thomas M. *Iron Eagle: The Turbulent Life of Curtis LeMay.* 1986, Crown $18.95 (0-517-55188-8); Avon paper $4.95 (0-380-70480-3). A biography of the American Air Force general noted for his innovative World War II bombing techniques and his role in the Berlin airlift. (Rev: BL 6/1/86; LJ 5/30/86; NYTBR 10/5/86) **[973.9]**

5863 Davis, John H. *Kennedys: Dynasty and Disaster, 1848 to 1983.* 1984, McGraw $24.95 (0-07-015860-6); paper $5.95 (0-07-015862-2). A history of the Kennedy family in the United States from its arrival from Ireland in 1848. (Rev: BL 5/1/84; Natl Rev 11/2/84; NYTBR 7/15/84) **[973.9]**

5864 Diggins, John Patrick. *Proud Decades: America in War and Peace, 1941–1960.* 1988, Norton $19.95 (0-393-02548-9); paper $11.95 (0-393-95656-3). A survey of American history, culture, and society from Pearl Harbor to Kennedy's election as president. (Rev: BL 9/15/88; LJ 10/1/88; NYTBR 10/9/88) **[973.9]**

5865 Donovan, Hedley. *Roosevelt to Reagan: A Reporter's Encounters with Nine Presidents.* 1987, Harper & Row paper $8.95 (0-06-039067-0). Memoirs of the *Washington Post* and *Time* journalist who reported on presidents from Roosevelt to Reagan. (Rev: BL 5/15/85; LJ 5/15/85; NYTBR 6/9/85) **[973.9]**

5866 Gubernick, Lisa Rebecca. *Squandered Fortune: The Life and Times of Huntington Hartford.* 1991, Putnam $24.95 (0-399-13572-3). The rise and fall of the life and fortune of the A & P heir. (Rev: NYTBR 2/3/91; PW 11/23/90) **[973.9]**

5867 Jacoby, Russell. *Last Intellectuals: American Culture in the Age of Academe.* 1987, Basic Books $18.95 (0-465-03812-3); Farrar paper $9.95 (0-374-52175-1). The author argues that nonacademic-based intellectuals in America are a dying breed, much to the detriment of contemporary American culture. (Rev: Atl 10/87; BL 10/1/87; LJ 9/1/87) **[973.9]**

5868 Keith, Slim, and Annette Tapert. *Slim: Memories of a Rich and Imperfect Life.* 1990, Simon & Schuster $22.95 (0-671-63164-0). Memoirs of the California social figure who married director Howard Hawks and knew such luminaries as Ernest Hemingway, Truman Capote, and Clark Gable. (Rev: BL 8/90; PW 5/25/90) **[973.9]**

5869 Marling, Karal Ann. *George Washington Slept Here: Colonial Revivals and American Culture, 1876–1986.* 1988, Harvard Univ. Pr. $39.95 (0-674-34951-2). A look at the symbolic use of the portrait of the first president and other colonial figures in American popular culture. (Rev: Choice 4/89; LJ 1/89; NYTBR 11/6/88) **[973.9]**

5870 Mead, Walter Russell. *Mortal Splendor: The American Empire in Transition.* 1988, Houghton paper $9.95 (0-395-46809-4). An analysis of American foreign policy and relations since the end of the Vietnam War. (Rev: BL 4/15/87; Choice 10/87; NYTBR 5/17/87) **[973.9]**

5871 Miller, Donald L. *Lewis Mumford: A Life.* 1989, Grove-Weidenfeld $24.95 (1-55584-244-5). A biography of the author and social critic Lewis Mumford. "Will undoubtedly become the standard work on Mumford's life."—BL (Rev: Atl 7/89; BL 7/89; LJ 6/1/89) **[973.9]**

5872 Milosz, Czeslaw. *Visions of San Francisco Bay.* 1982, Farrar $14.95 (0-374-28488-1); paper $9.95 (0-374-51763-0). A collection of 32 essays by the Nobel laureate describing his life in California and contrasting it with his former life in Poland. (Rev: BL 8/82; LJ 1/1/83; NYTBR 10/17/82) **[973.9]**

5873 Rudnick, Lois Palken. *Mabel Dodge Luhan: New Woman, New Worlds.* 1987, Univ. of New Mexico Pr. paper $14.95 (0-8263-0995-X). A biography of the American writer and patron of the arts known for her involvement in the Taos, New Mexico, art community. (Rev: Choice 3/85; NYTBR 1/6/85; PW 10/12/84) **[973.9]**

5874 Terkel, Studs. *American Dreams: Lost and Found.* 1980, Pantheon $14.95 (0-394-50793-2); paper $4.95 (0-345-32993-7). Interviews with 100 Americans on their ambitions, their expectations of life, and what the American dream means to them. "Who touches the book of *American Dreams* touches not one but one hundred men and women and, by implication, millions more."—Time (Rev: LJ 11/1/80; Newsweek 10/13/80; Time 9/29/80. Awards: Time, 1980) **[973.9]**

5875 Vanden Heuvel, Katrina, ed. *Nation, 1865–1990: Selections from the Independent Magazine of Politics and Culture.* 1990, Thunder's Mouth $21.95 (1-560250-01-1); paper $14.95 (1-56025-023-2).

Selected writings from 125 years of *The Nation.* (Rev: BL 10/15/90; LJ 11/1/90; PW 10/12/89)   **[973.9]**

History, 1901–1953

5876 Acheson, Dean. *Present at the Creation: My Years in the State Department.* **1987, Norton $29.95 (0-393-07448-X).** A reprint of the memoirs of Truman's secretary of state. (Rev: Natl Rev 12/30/69; NYTBR 10/12/69; Newsweek 10/13/69. Awards: ALA, 1969; NYTBR, 1969; PP:History, 1970)   **[973.91]**

5877 Beschloss, Michael R. *Eisenhower: A Centennial Life.* **1990, Harper & Row $29.95 (0-06-016418-2).** An illustrated biography celebrating the one-hundredth anniversary of the birth of the American president and World War II military leader. (Rev: BL 9/1/90; LJ 9/15/90)   **[973.91]**

5878 Beschloss, Michael R. *Kennedy and Roosevelt: The Uneasy Alliance.* **1987, Harper & Row paper $8.95 (0-06-097095-2).** An examination of the relationship between U.S. Ambassador to England Joseph Kennedy and President Roosevelt in the years directly preceding the outbreak of the Second World War. (Rev: LJ 4/1/80; New Rep 5/26/80; NYTBR 6/22/80)   **[973.91]**

5879 Blum, John Morton. *V Was for Victory: Politics and American Culture During World War II.* **1977, Harcourt paper $10.95 (0-15-693628-3).** How World War II affected the life, politics, economic structure, and social attitudes of America. (Rev: LJ 4/15/76; Newsweek 6/7/76; PW 3/29/76)   **[973.91]**

5880 Boyer, Paul S. *By the Bomb's Early Light: American Thought and Culture at the Dawn of the Atomic Age.* **1986, Pantheon $11.95 (0-394-52878-6); paper $10.36 (0-394-74767-4).** A study of American thought on the atomic bomb from 1945 to 1950. (Rev: Choice 3/86; LJ 11/1/85; Newsweek 11/25/85)   **[973.91]**

5881 Brinkley, Alan. *Voices of Protest: Huey Long, Father Coughlin and the Great Depression.* **1983, Random paper $9.95 (0-394-71628-0).** A look at the leaders of two populist movements of the 1930s, and the movements' influence and history. (Rev: Choice 9/82; New Rep 7/12/82; NYRB 9/23/82. Awards: NBA, 1983)   **[973.91]**

5882 Caro, Robert A. *Means of Ascent: The Years of Lyndon Johnson.* **1990, Knopf $24.95 (0-394-52835-2).** This second volume of the author's biography of Lyndon B. Johnson traces his political career from 1941 to his election to Congress in 1948. (Rev: BL 3/15/90; CSM 3/23/90; Time 3/5/90. Awards: Time, 1990)   **[973.91]**

5883 Caro, Robert A. *Path to Power: The Years of Lyndon B. Johnson, Vol. 1.* **1982, Knopf $29.95 (0-394-49973-5); Random paper $16.95 (0-679-72945-3).** Volume 1 of Caro's massive treatment of LBJ covers the years 1908–1941. "A masterful narrative on a grand scale . . . by far the most significant Johnson book to appear."—LJ (Rev: Choice 4/83; CSM 12/3/82; LJ 12/15/82. Awards: ALA, 1982)   **[973.91]**

5884 Casdorph, Paul D. *Let the Good Times Roll: Life at Home in America During World War II.* **1989, Paragon House $21.95 (1-55778-164-8).** A look at life in the United States during the Second World War. "Very well-written and provocative . . . popular history at its best."—LJ (Rev: BL 10/1/89; LJ 10/15/89)   **[973.91]**

5885 Cooper, John Milton, Jr. *Warrior and the Priest: Woodrow Wilson and Theodore Roosevelt.* **1985, Harvard Univ. Pr. paper $9.95 (0-674-94751-7).** A dual biography comparing the lives and personalities of Presidents Wilson and Roosevelt. "Clear, well-written and brilliantly organized . . . comparative biography at its best."—Choice (Rev: Choice 4/84; LJ 10/1/83; NYTBR 11/20/83)   **[973.91]**

5886 Davis, Kenneth S. *FDR: The New Deal Years, 1933–1937.* **1986, Random $29.95 (0-394-52753-4).** The third volume in a four-piece biography studies Roosevelt's first term as president and the introduction of the New Deal. (Rev: BL 9/1/86; LJ 9/15/86; NYTBR 9/28/86. Awards: NYTBR, 1986)   **[973.91]**

5887 Davis, Kenneth S. *FDR: The New York Years, 1928–1933.* **1985, Random $19.95 (0-394-51671-0).** Volume two of Davis's biography of FDR examines his term as governor of New York and his first campaign for president. (Rev: Choice 3/86; New Rep 3/17/86; NYTBR 1/19/86. Awards: NYTBR, 1986)   **[973.91]**

5888 Donovan, Robert J. *Conflict and Crisis: The Presidency of Harry S. Truman, 1945–1948.* **1979, Norton paper $11.95 (0-393-00924-6).** The first of two volumes about the Truman presidency by a former White House correspondent covers his first term. "Donovan's inside knowledge of the interpersonal forces at work behind the public decisions adds a touch of spice to contemporary history."—PW (Rev: CSM 12/13/77; LJ 11/1/77; PW 11/1/77)   **[973.91]**

5889 Donovan, Robert J. *Tumultuous Years: The Presidency of Harry S. Truman, 1949–1952.* **1984, Norton paper $9.95 (0-393-30164-8).** A survey of Truman's second term including the Korean War, the clash with MacArthur, the development of the hydrogen bomb, and McCarthyism. "The most comprehensive reading of Truman's second term . . . a must reading for all students of the postwar period."—Choice (Rev: Choice 2/83; LJ 8/82; NYTBR 10/3/82. Awards: NYTBR, 1982)   **[973.91]**

5890 Felsenthal, Carol. *Alice Roosevelt Longworth.* **1988, Putnam $21.95 (0-399-13258-9); St. Martin's paper $13.95 (0-312-02536-X).** A biography of the eldest daughter of Theodore Roosevelt, who lived to age 96 and was a prominent figure in Washington social circles throughout her life. (Rev: BL 3/1/88; LJ 2/15/88; NYTBR 3/13/88)   **[973.91]**

5891 Harris, Mark Jonathan, ed. *Homefront: America During World War II.* **1984, Putnam $17.95 (0-399-12899-9).** Collected interviews with Americans who lived in the U.S. during the Second World War. "A wealth of recollections and an insightful yet sobering look at the still-felt personal effects of the war."—BL (Rev: BL 3/1/84; LJ 2/15/84; NYTBR 2/26/84)   **[973.91]**

5892 Heckscher, August. *Woodrow Wilson.* 1991, Scribner $35.00 (0-684-19312-4). A biography of the former American president based on recently published collected papers. (Rev: LJ 9/15/91; PW 8/16/91) **[973.91]**

5893 Hodgson, Godfrey. *Colonel: The Life and Wars of Henry Stimson, 1867–1950.* 1990, Knopf $24.95 (0-394-57441-9). A biography of the American secretary of war and secretary of state who served under administrations from Taft to Truman. (Rev: Atl 11/90; CSM 1/15/91; NYTBR 10/21/90) **[973.91]**

5894 Karl, Barry D. *Uneasy State: The United States from 1915 to 1945.* 1984, Univ. of Chicago Pr. $22.50 (0-226-43519-3). An analysis of American political history from 1915 to 1945 by a University of Chicago history professor. (Rev: Choice 6/84; LJ 12/15/83; NYTBR 10/7/84) **[973.91]**

5895 Kemp, Giles, and Edward Claflin. *Dale Carnegie: The Man Who Influenced Millions.* 1989, St. Martin's $15.95 (0-312-02896-2). A biography of the influential author of *How to Win Friends and Influence People.* (Rev: BL 7/89; LJ 6/15/89; PW 6/16/89) **[973.91]**

5896 Klingaman, William. *1929: The Year of the Great Crash.* 1989, Harper & Row $22.50 (0-06-016081-0). A chronological history of the year 1929 and the beginnings of the Great Depression by the author of *1919* and *1941.* (Rev: BL 6/15/89; LJ 7/89; NYTBR 10/29/89) **[973.91]**

5897 Lash, Joseph P. *Dealers and Dreamers: A New Look at the New Deal.* 1988, Doubleday $24.95 (0-385-18716-5). The author of *Eleanor and Franklin* looks at the personalities and policies of the New Deal. "Few writers compose history as fluidly and as warmly personalized."—BL (Rev: BL 4/15/88; Choice 11/88; PW 5/6/88) **[973.91]**

5898 Lash, Joseph P. *Eleanor: The Years Alone.* 1972, Norton $14.95 (0-393-07361-0); NAL paper $10.95 (0-452-00771-2). Eleanor Roosevelt's years following the death of FDR, including her activism in social causes and her service as a delegate to the United Nations. "The author's understanding of the movements she supported is as rich as his understanding of the remarkable human being he celebrates."—New Yorker (Rev: LJ 9/15/72; New Yorker 8/19/72; Time 8/7/72. Awards: ALA, 1972) **[973.91]**

5899 Lash, Joseph P. *Eleanor and Franklin: The Story of Their Relationship Based on Eleanor Roosevelt's Private Papers.* 1971, Norton $15.95 (0-393-07459-4); NAL paper $5.95 (0-451-14076-1). The first in a series of works by Lash examining the life of Eleanor Roosevelt. (Rev: LJ 9/15/71; New Rep 10/16/71; Newsweek 10/18/71. Awards: ALA, 1971; NBA, 1972; NYTBR, 1971; PP:Biography, 1972; Time, 1971) **[973.91]**

5900 McCullough, David. *Mornings on Horseback.* 1982, Simon & Schuster paper $13.95 (0-671-44754-8). A look at the family background and early life of Theodore Roosevelt. (Rev: LJ 5/15/81; NYTBR 7/26/81; Time 7/20/81. Awards: ALA, 1981; NBA, 1982) **[973.91]**

5901 McElvaine, Robert S., ed. *Down and Out in the Great Depression: Letters from the Forgotten Man.* 1983, Univ. of North Carolina Pr. paper $9.95 (0-8078-4099-8). A selection of 173 letters written by American citizens to government officials, primarily the Roosevelts, during the Great Depression. "A good book for any student of the period, capturing people's moods well."—LJ (Rev: LJ 2/15/83; NYTBR 2/6/83; New Yorker 3/14/83. Awards: ALA, 1983) **[973.91]**

5902 McElvaine, Robert S. *Great Depression: America, 1929–1941.* 1985, Random paper $10.95 (0-8129-6343-1). An overview of the causes and effects of the Great Depression in the United States. "It would be hard to find a fairer or more balanced account of how the American people and their leaders learned to grapple with their greatest economic crisis."—NYTBR (Rev: BL 1/1/84; LJ 12/1/83; NYTBR 1/22/84) **[973.91]**

5903 McJimsey, George. *Harry Hopkins: Ally of the Poor and Defender of Democracy.* 1987, Harvard Univ. Pr. $25.00 (0-674-37287-5). A biography of the former head of the Works Progress Administration and one of FDR's key advisors. (Rev: Choice 9/87; LJ 4/15/87; NYTBR 7/12/87) **[973.91]**

5904 Marquis, Alice Goldfarb. *Hopes and Ashes: The Birth of Modern Times, 1929–1939.* 1986, Free Pr. $22.50 (0-02-920250-7). A study of the spread and development of culture and cultural activities in the United States during the 1930s. (Rev: Choice 5/87; LJ 12/86; NYTBR 12/28/86) **[973.91]**

5905 Miller, Merle. *Plain Speaking: An Oral Biography of Harry S. Truman.* 1986, Berkley paper $4.95 (0-425-09499-5). An oral history of the thirty-third president based on conversations with him and those who knew him. "An important contribution to the literature of our times."—PW (Rev: CSM 1/23/74; Newsweek 2/4/74; PW 8/26/74. Awards: ALA, 1974) **[973.91]**

5906 Morgan, Ted. *FDR: A Biography.* 1986, Simon & Schuster paper $13.95 (0-671-62812-7). A portrait of the former president by the biographer of Maugham and Churchill. "An excellent account: well-researched, expertly organized, adeptly written."—BL (Rev: BL 10/15/85; Choice 2/86; NYTBR 10/13/85) **[973.91]**

5907 Morris, Roger. *Richard Milhous Nixon: The Rise of an American Politician.* 1989, Henry Holt $27.50 (0-8050-1121-8). This first of a proposed three-volume biography of Nixon covers the years from his birth to the 1952 "Checkers" speech. (Rev: BL 10/1/89; NYTBR 11/12/89; Time 11/6/89) **[973.91]**

5908 Pells, Richard H. *Liberal Mind in a Conservative Age.* 1989, Univ. Pr. of New England paper $19.95 (0-8195-6225-4). A profile of American intellectual life and thought during the 1940s and 1950s. (Rev: BL 1/15/85; Choice 6/85; LJ 12/84) **[973.91]**

5909 Perrett, Geoffrey. *Days of Sadness, Years of Triumph: The American People, 1939–1945.* 1985, Univ. of Wisconsin Pr. paper $13.95 (0-299-10394-3). A look at the social changes that took place in America during the years of World War II.

"Rich-textured, upbeat . . . an impressive, enspiriting American cavalcade."—PW (Rᴇᴠ: LJ 3/15/73; NYRB 4/5/73; PW 1/22/73. Aᴡᴀʀᴅs: ALA, 1973) **[973.91]**

5910 Sheed, Wilfrid. *Clare Boothe Luce.* **1984, Berkley paper $7.95 (0-425-05978-2).** A biography of the American stateswoman and wife of Time-Life founder Henry Luce. (Rᴇᴠ: New Rep 3/3/82; NYRB 4/1/82; Time 2/22/82) **[973.91]**

5911 Simon, Rita, ed. *As We Saw the Thirties: Essays on Social and Political Movements of a Decade.* **1967, Univ. of Illinois Pr. paper $9.95 (0-252-74533-7).** A collection of a series of lectures by leaders of social movements of the 1930s given at the University of Illinois in the mid-1960s. (Rᴇᴠ: Atl 6/67; BL 11/1/67; LJ 6/15/67. Aᴡᴀʀᴅs: ALA, 1967) **[973.91]**

5912 Smith, Richard Norton. *Thomas E. Dewey and His Times.* **1982, Simon & Schuster $22.50 (0-317-12800-0).** A biography of the former Republican governor of New York and failed presidential candidate. "Will remain the standard biography for some time."—BL (Rᴇᴠ: BL 6/1/82; Choice 11/82; NYTBR 8/22/82) **[973.91]**

5913 Smith, Richard Norton. *An Uncommon Man: The Triumph of Herbert Hoover.* **1990, High Plains paper $14.50 (0-9623333-1-X).** A biography of the former president stressing the years after his term in office as a social activist and elder statesman. (Rᴇᴠ: BL 6/15/84; Choice 12/84; NYTBR 9/2/84) **[973.91]**

5914 Stott, William. *Documentary Expression and Thirties America.* **1986, Univ. of Chicago Pr. paper $12.95 (0-226-77559-3).** A study of the rise of documentary style in the United States during the 1930s analyzing the works of Walker Evans, James Agee, and Margaret Bourke-White among others. (Rᴇᴠ: BL 4/15/74; Choice 4/74; NYTBR 1/20/74) **[973.91]**

5915 Terkel, Studs. *Hard Times: An Oral History of the Great Depression in America.* **1986, Pantheon paper $8.95 (0-394-74691-0).** The Great Depression as seen through the words of over 160 Americans who lived through it. "A social document of immense interest."—BL (Rᴇᴠ: BL 7/1/70; LJ 4/15/70; NYTBR 4/19/70. Aᴡᴀʀᴅs: ALA, 1970) **[973.91]**

5916 Truman, Harry S. *Letters Home.* **Ed. by Monte M. Poen. 1984, Putnam $16.95 (0-399-12866-2).** A collection of the former president's letters, diaries, and remembrances. (Rᴇᴠ: BL 2/1/84; LJ 2/1/84; PW 1/27/84) **[973.91]**

5917 Truman, Margaret. *Bess W. Truman.* **1987, Jove paper $4.50 (0-515-08973-7).** A biography of the former first lady by her daughter. "A fascinating, intimate study . . . the most revealing view of the personal side of the Truman relationship now available."—Choice (Rᴇᴠ: BL 3/1/86; Choice 9/86; PW 2/28/86) **[973.91]**

5918 Truman, Margaret. *Harry S. Truman.* **1984, Morrow paper $10.95 (0-688-03924-3).** A biography of President Truman by his daughter. "Probably the closest, clearest and most engaging view of Truman's private life and personality that we will

ever have."—LJ (Rᴇᴠ: BL 2/1/73; CSM 1/3/73; LJ 2/15/73. Aᴡᴀʀᴅs: ALA, 1973) **[973.91]**

5919 Ward, Geoffrey C. *First Class Temperament: The Emergence of Franklin D. Roosevelt.* **1989, Harper & Row $27.95 (0-06-016066-7); paper $12.95 (0-06-092026-2).** The second volume of the author's biography of the former president. "A fascinating, well-balanced scholarly treatment . . . a significant contribution to the understanding of FDR."—LJ (Rᴇᴠ: BL 7/89; LJ 7/89; NYTBR 8/20/89) **[973.91]**

5920 Watkins, T. H. *Righteous Pilgrim: The Life and Times of Harold Ickes, 1874–1952.* **1989, Henry Holt $29.95 (0-8050-0917-5).** A biography of the American statesman who served as secretary of the interior under Roosevelt and Truman. (Rᴇᴠ: BL 9/15/90; LJ 9/1/90; PW 7/20/90. Aᴡᴀʀᴅs: LJ, 1990; PW, 1990) **[973.91]**

History, 1953–

5921 Ambrose, Stephen E. *Eisenhower: The President.* **1985, Simon & Schuster paper $14.95 (0-671-60565-8).** The second and concluding volume of the author's biography of Eisenhower assesses his years as president of the United States. (Rᴇᴠ: Choice 2/85; New Rep 10/22/84; NYTBR 9/9/84) **[973.92]**

5922 Ambrose, Stephen E. *Nixon: The Education of a Politician, 1913–1962.* **1988, Simon & Schuster paper $10.95 (0-671-65722-4).** "Distinguished by its unusual objectivity . . . this wonderfully detailed synthesis of the presidential years is unsurpassed."—LJ (Rᴇᴠ: CSM 5/7/87; LJ 5/1/87; NYTBR 4/26/87. Aᴡᴀʀᴅs: LJ, 1987; Time, 1987) **[973.92]**

5923 Ambrose, Stephen E. *Nixon: Ruin and Recovery, 1973–1990.* **1991, Simon & Schuster $27.50 (0-671-69188-0).** This third and concluding volume of the author's biography of Nixon covers the years from his resignation from the presidency to 1990. "Highly recommended for those seeking to fathom the Nixon enigma."—PW (Rᴇᴠ: BL 9/15/91; LJ 10/15/91; PW 9/20/91. Aᴡᴀʀᴅs: BL, 1991) **[973.92]**

5924 Ambrose, Stephen E. *Nixon: The Triumph of a Politician, 1962–1972.* **1989, Simon & Schuster $24.95 (0-671-52837-8).** The second volume of the author's biography of Richard M. Nixon covers the years following his defeat in the 1962 California gubernatorial race to his reelection as president in 1972. (Rᴇᴠ: LJ 11/1/89; Natl Rev 11/24/89; NYTBR 11/12/89) **[973.92]**

5925 Anderson, Martin. *Revolution.* **1988, Harcourt $19.95 (0-15-177087-5).** An account of the early years of the Reagan administration by the former assistant to the president for policy development. (Rᴇᴠ: LJ 6/15/88; Natl Rev 9/16/88; NYTBR 5/15/88) **[973.92]**

5926 Arnold, Eve. *In America.* **1983, Knopf $35.00 (0-394-52235-4).** A photographic essay documenting contemporary American life by the author of *In China.* "Arnold's stunning book provides a deep and revealing cross section of American culture."—BL (Rᴇᴠ: BL 2/1/84; Choice 4/84; LJ 2/1/84) **[973.92]**

5927 Belin, David W. *Final Disclosure: The Full Truth about the Assassination of President Kennedy.* **1988, Macmillan $19.95 (0-684-18976-3).** An analysis of the theories surrounding the Kennedy assassination that concludes that Oswald acted alone in the killing. (REV: BL 9/15/88; LJ 12/88; PW 9/16/88) **[973.92]**

5928 Beschloss, Michael R. *Mayday: Eisenhower, Khruschev and the U-2 Affair.* **1987, Harper & Row paper $8.95 (0-06-091407-6).** An account of the American spy plane shot down over the Soviet Union in 1960 and the consequences of the event. "A revealing examination of one of the most mystifying and repercussive episodes in Cold War history."—BL (REV: BL 2/1/86; CSM 5/1/86; TLS 12/5/86. AWARDS: ALA, 1986) **[973.92]**

5929 Bloom, Allen. *Closing of the American Mind: Education and the Crisis of Reason.* **1988, Simon & Schuster paper $8.95 (0-671-65715-1).** Bloom's controversial analysis of the current state of higher education. "This volume brims with ideas, all of which demand our attention."—BL (REV: BL 4/15/87; Choice 9/87; Natl Rev 4/24/87. AWARDS: BL, the 1980s) **[973.92]**

5930 Blount, Roy, Jr. *Crackers.* **1988, Ballantine paper $3.95 (0-345-00868-5).** An examination of the life and culture of the American South by the Georgia writer. (REV: LJ 9/1/80; New Rep 9/27/80; NYTBR 9/28/80) **[973.92]**

5931 Blount, Roy, Jr. *Not Exactly What I Had in Mind.* **1985, Atlantic Monthly $14.95 (0-87113-031-9); Penguin paper $6.95 (0-14-009328-1).** A series of humorous essays on life in the 1980s. "Consistently funny fare."—BL (REV: BL 10/1/85; LJ 10/15/85; NYTBR 11/17/85) **[973.92]**

5932 Branch, Taylor. *Parting the Waters: America in the King Years, 1954–1963.* **1988, Simon & Schuster $24.95 (0-671-46097-8); paper $14.95 (0-671-68742-5).** The first volume of a planned two-part history of Martin Luther King, Jr., and the civil rights movement. (REV: LJ 1/89; NYTBR 11/27/88; Newsweek 11/28/88. AWARDS: LJ, 1988; NYTBR, 1988; PP:History, 1988; Time, 1988; Time, the 1980s) **[973.92]**

5933 Burns, James MacGregor. *Crosswinds of Freedom: The American Experiment, Vol. III.* **1989, Knopf $35.00 (0-394-51276-6).** This concluding third volume of Burns's history of the United States covers the years of the New Deal to the present. (REV: BL 4/1/89; LJ 4/1/89; NYTBR 5/14/89. AWARDS: BL, 1989) **[973.92]**

5934 Califano, Joseph A., Jr. *Triumph and Tragedy of Lyndon Johnson: The White House Years.* **1991, Simon & Schuster $25.00 (0-671-66489-1).** Memoirs of Lyndon Johnson by his former domestic adviser. "An intimate, balanced and basically sympathetic portrait."—PW (REV: BL 10/15/91; LJ 10/1/91; PW 8/23/91) **[973.92]**

5935 Campbell, Will D. *Forty Acres and a Goat: A Memoir.* **1986, Peachtree $14.95 (0-931948-97-5); paper $8.95 (0-06-061301-7).** The author of *Brother to a Dragonfly* recounts his involvement in the civil rights movement of the 1950s and 1960s. (REV: LJ 10/15/86; NYTBR 11/16/86; PW 8/29/86) **[973.92]**

5936 Cannon, Lou. *President Reagan: The Role of a Lifetime.* **1991, Simon & Schuster $24.95 (0-671-54294-X).** A biography of the former American president. "Essential reading for anyone who wants to understand the star of politics in the 1980's."—Time (REV: LJ 4/15/91; NYRB 6/13/91; Time 4/15/91) **[973.92]**

5937 Carter, Jimmy. *Keeping Faith: Memoirs of a President.* **1983, Bantam paper $12.95 (0-553-34571-0).** Memoirs of the former president's years in office. (REV: LJ 12/15/82; NYRB 12/16/82; PW 10/29/82) **[973.92]**

5938 Carter, Paul Allen. *Another Part of the Fifties.* **1983, Columbia Univ. Pr. $30.00 (0-231-05222-7).** An overview of the social, political, and intellectual climate of the 1950s in the United States. (REV: BL 7/83; Choice 2/84; LJ 7/83) **[973.92]**

5939 Carter, Rosalynn. *First Lady from Plains.* **1988, Fawcett paper $3.95 (0-449-44529-1).** Memoirs of the former first lady regarding the Carter years in office. (REV: CSM 5/10/84; NYTBR 4/15/84; Newsweek 5/7/84) **[973.92]**

5940 Chancellor, John. *Peril and Promise: A Commentary on America.* **1990, Harper & Row $16.95 (0-06-016336-4).** The longtime "NBC News" commentator presents his program for American political reform. (REV: BL 3/15/90; CSM 6/18/90; PW 4/6/90) **[973.92]**

5941 Collier, Peter, and David Horowitz. *Kennedys: An American Dream.* **1985, Warner paper $4.95 (0-446-32702-6).** A study of the Kennedy family from its roots in Ireland to the present generation. (REV: LJ 9/15/84; New Rep 8/27/84; NYTBR 6/17/84) **[973.92]**

5942 Cooke, Alistair. *America Observed: From the 1940s to the 1980s.* **1988, Knopf $19.95 (0-394-57342-0).** A collection of 58 pieces, most of which were written for the *Manchester Guardian*, regarding America and Americans. (REV: BL 11/15/88; LJ 11/15/88; Natl Rev 2/24/89) **[973.92]**

5943 Dallek, Robert. *Lone Star Rising: Lyndon B. Johnson and His Times, 1908–1960.* **1991, Oxford Univ. Pr. $30.00 (0-19-505435-0).** First of a two-volume biography of the former president by a UCLA professor. "The most lucid and level headed look at this great and contrary figure we are likely to have for a long time."—Newsweek (REV: LJ 6/1/91; NYTBR 7/21/91; Newsweek 7/22/91. AWARDS: LJ, 1991) **[973.92]**

5944 Davidson, Sara. *Loose Change.* **1984, Pocket paper $4.50 (0-671-50434-7).** A look at the 1960s and after in the lives of the author and two of her female college friends. "Absorbing and moving . . . a vivid, memorable book."—PW (REV: BL 7/1/77; LJ 5/15/77; PW 4/11/77) **[973.92]**

5945 DeBenedetti, Charles. *An American Ordeal: The Antiwar Movement of the Vietnam Era.* **1990, Syracuse Univ. Pr. $49.50 (0-8156-0244-8); paper $16.95 (0-8156-0245-6).** A history of the development of the American antiwar movement during the 1950s, 1960s, and 1970s. "A definitive social, cultural, and historical analysis of the cycle of protest during the Vietnam War era."—BL (Rev: BL 5/15/90; LJ 4/1/90; NYTBR 6/17/90)   **[973.92]**

5946 Dickstein, Morris. *Gates of Eden: American Culture in the Sixties.* **1989, Penguin paper $8.95** (0-14-011617-6). The thoughts that led to the 1960s traced through literary antecedents. "A stimulating overview of the painful birth of a new sensibility among a new generation."—PW (Rev: NYTBR 3/13/77; Newsweek 3/28/77; PW 12/27/76. Awards: NYTBR, 1977)   **[973.92]**

5947 Draper, Theodore. *A Very Thin Line: The Iran-Contra Affair.* **1991, Hill & Wang $27.95** (0-8090-9613-7). An examination of the Iran-Contra affair. "The fullest and most authoritative account to date."—PW (Rev: LJ 6/1/91; NYRB 6/13/91; PW 4/26/91)   **[973.92]**

5948 Dugger, Ronnie. *Politician: The Life and Times of Lyndon B. Johnson.* **1982, Norton $18.95** (0-393-01598-X). A biography of Johnson's life up to his selection as Senate majority leader by a longtime Texas journalist. (Rev: BL 3/1/82; NYTBR 5/9/82; PW 3/5/82)   **[973.92]**

5949 Ehrenreich, Barbara. *Worst Years of Our Lives: Irreverent Notes from a Decade of Greed.* **1990, Pantheon $18.95** (0-394-57847-3). Collected essays on the 1980s by the author of *Re-making Love: the Feminization of Sex.* (Rev: BL 5/15/90; LJ 4/15/90; NYTBR 5/20/90)   **[973.92]**

5950 Epstein, Joseph. *Familiar Territory: Observations on American Life.* **1979, Oxford Univ. Pr. $22.95** (0-19-502604-7). A collection of essays regarding American culture by the editor and columnist of the *American Scholar.* (Rev: LJ 9/1/79; New Rep 11/10/79; NYTBR 11/4/79)   **[973.92]**

5951 Fallows, James. *More Like Us: An American Plan for American Recovery.* **1989, Houghton $18.95** (0-395-49857-0); paper **$8.95** (0-395-52810-0). The author of *National Defense* argues in his second book that America needs to rediscover its values and exploit its own distinctive national characteristics to successfully compete in today's world economy. (Rev: CSM 5/12/89; LJ 3/30/89; NYTBR 3/26/89)   **[973.92]**

5952 Gitlin, Todd. *The Sixties: The Years of Hope, Days of Rage.* **1987, Bantam $19.95** (0-553-05233-0); paper **$14.95** (0-553-34601-6). A former SDS president presents his view of the events of the 1960s. "A triumph of lucidly written popular history."—PW (Rev: CSM 1/8/88; NYTBR 11/8/87; PW 10/2/87. Awards: PW, 1987)   **[973.92]**

5953 Goldwater, Barry, and Jack Casserly. *Goldwater.* **1988, Doubleday $21.95** (0-385-23947-5). An autobiography of the former U.S. senator from Arizona. "As appealing as any contemporary politician's apologia is ever likely to be."—BL (Rev: BL 8/88; LJ 10/15/88; NYTBR 10/16/88)   **[973.92]**

5954 Goodwin, Richard N. *Remembering America: A Voice from the Sixties.* **1988, Little, Brown $19.95** (0-316-32024-2); **Harper & Row paper $10.95** (0-06-097241-6). Memoirs of political life in the 1960s by a high-level member of the Kennedy and Johnson administrations. (Rev: BL 9/1/88; CSM 9/14/88; NYTBR 9/4/88. Awards: ALA, 1988)   **[973.92]**

5955 Greene, Bob. *Be True to Your School: A Diary of 1964.* **1987, Macmillan $18.95** (0-689-11612-8); **Ballantine paper $3.95** (0-345-35394-3). A diary recounting the author's 1964 year in high school. "A poignant, funny, charming memoir."—PW (Rev: LJ 4/15/87; PW 2/27/87)   **[973.92]**

5956 Halberstam, David. *Best and the Brightest.* **1983, Penguin paper $10.95** (0-14-006983-6). A study of the men who formed the U.S. government of the Kennedy and Johnson administrations, and how their decisions entangled America in the Vietnam War. "An immense study and a major perspective on American involvement in Vietnam."—PW (Rev: LJ 11/1/72; PW 10/9/72; Time 11/27/72. Awards: ALA, 1972; Time, 1972)   **[973.92]**

5957 Hamilton, Charles V. *Adam Clayton Powell, Jr.: The Political Biography of an American Dilemma.* **1991, Atheneum $24.95** (0-689-12062-1). A Columbia University professor's biography of the U.S. congressman remembered for his flamboyant personality and civil rights activities. (Rev: LJ 7/91; NYTBR 10/20/91; PW 7/5/91. Awards: LJ, 1991)   **[973.92]**

5958 Hertsgaard, Mark. *On Bended Knee: The Press and the Reagan Presidency.* **1988, Farrar $22.50** (0-374-25197-5); **Schocken paper $11.95** (0-8052-0960-3). A study of the relationship between the Reagan administration and the press. (Rev: BL 9/15/88; LJ 11/1/88; PW 7/22/88)   **[973.92]**

5959 Hinckley, Jack, and Jo Ann Hinckley. *Breaking Points.* **1985, Berkley paper $3.95** (0-425-08784-0). Reflections of the parents of the failed presidential assassin on their son's life and how his actions affected theirs. (Rev: BL 5/1/85; LJ 5/15/85; PW 5/3/85)   **[973.92]**

5960 Hodgson, Godfrey. *America in Our Time: From World War II to Nixon . . . What Happened and Why.* **1978, Random paper $10.96** (0-394-72517-4). A history of postwar America through the Nixon years as analyzed by a British journalist. "The best account of the 1960s available."—Choice (Rev: BL 1/15/77; Choice 3/77; LJ 12/1/76)   **[973.92]**

5961 Hurt, Henry. *Reasonable Doubt: An Investigation into the Assassination of John F. Kennedy.* **1987, Henry Holt paper $12.95** (0-8050-0360-6). An examination of the Kennedy assassination, the investigations that followed it, and the theories surrounding the event. (Rev: BL 11/15/85; LJ 3/1/86; NYTBR 2/23/86)   **[973.92]**

5962 Johnson, Haynes. *Sleepwalking Through History: America in the Reagan Years.* **1991, Norton $24.95** (0-393-02937-9). A study of the United States under the leadership of President Reagan written by a *Washington Post* reporter. "A stunning indictment."—PW (Rev: BL 2/1/91; LJ 2/1/91; PW 12/21/90) **[973.92]**

5963   Kennedy, Robert F. *Thirteen Days: A Memoir of the Cuban Missile Crisis.* 1969, NAL paper $4.95 (0-451-62794-6). The former attorney general's memoirs of the Cuban missile crisis in 1962. (Rev: CSM 2/6/69; LJ 2/1/69; NYTBR 1/19/69) **[973.92]**

5964   Kuralt, Charles. *On the Road with Charles Kuralt.* 1985, Putnam $15.95 (0-399-13087-X); Fawcett paper $5.95 (0-449-13067-3). Essays reflecting on American life and culture based on the author's travels throughout the United States. (Rev: BL 7/85; LJ 9/15/85; PW 7/12/85) **[973.92]**

5965   Kutler, Stanley I. *Wars of Watergate: The Last Crisis of Richard Nixon.* 1990, Knopf $24.95 (0-394-56234-8). A study of the history and legacy of the Watergate crisis of 1972–1974. (Rev: BL 6/15/90; CSM 6/6/90; LJ 4/15/90) **[973.92]**

5966   Lapham, Lewis H. *Imperial Masquerade.* 1990, Grove-Weidenfeld $21.95 (1-55584-449-9). A collection of 70 essays on life and culture in the 1980s. (Rev: BL 2/1/90; LJ 11/15/89) **[973.92]**

5967   Lasch, Christopher. *Culture of Narcissism: American Life in an Age of Diminishing Expectations.* 1979, Warner paper $4.95 (0-446-32104-4). A gloomy look at American culture and values in the 1970s. (Rev: Choice 5/79; LJ 11/15/78; Newsweek 1/22/79. Awards: ALA, 1979; NBA, 1980; NYTBR, 1979) **[973.92]**

5968   Lekachman, Robert. *Visions and Nightmares: America after Reagan.* 1986, Macmillan $19.95 (0-02-572031-9); paper $9.95 (0-02-073710-6). A forecast of post-Reagan American society. "A very stimulating look with great insight."—Choice (Rev: Choice 4/88; NYTBR 3/14/87; PW 2/13/87) **[973.92]**

5969   Lukas, J. Anthony. *Nightmare: The Underside of the Nixon Years.* 1988, Penguin paper $10.95 (0-14-011279-4). A study of the scandals of the Nixon Administrations. "Lukas's account is by far the best in encompassing in one book all those unsavory, illegal, and just barely legal activities embraced by the term 'Watergate.' "—Choice (Rev: Choice 6/76; LJ 12/15/75; Newsweek 2/9/76. Awards: ALA, 1976) **[973.92]**

5970   McKeever, Porter. *Adlai Stevenson: His Life and Legacy.* 1989, Morrow $24.95 (0-688-06661-5). A biography of the man who served as governor of Illinois, unsuccessfully ran as the Democratic candidate for president, and served as American ambassador to the United Nations for the Kennedy administration. (Rev: BL 6/15/89; NYTBR 7/16/89; PW 5/12/89) **[973.92]**

5971   Mayer, Jane, and Doyle McManus. *Landslide: The Unmaking of the President, 1984–1988.* 1988, Houghton $21.95 (0-395-45185-X). A look at the increasing internal problems of the Reagan administration's second term following the revelations of the Iran-Contra affair. (Rev: BL 12/1/88; CSM 10/19/88; NYTBR 10/9/88) **[973.92]**

5972   Melanson, Philip H. *Robert F. Kennedy Assassination: New Revelations on the Conspiracy and Cover-Up.* 1991, Shalpolsky $19.95 (1-56171-036-9). An investigative report of the 1968 assassination of Robert Kennedy offering alternative theories to the conclusion that Sirhan Sirhan acted alone. (Rev: BL 9/1/91; LJ 10/1/91) **[973.92]**

5973   Morris, Willie. *North Toward Home.* 1967, Yoknapatawpha $17.95 (0-916242-15-3); paper $11.95 (0-916242-16-1). An autobiography divided into three sections: the author's youth in Mississippi, his education in Texas, and the move to a new home in New York. "Mr. Morris is a compassionate observer of life, with a reporter's desire for honesty."—LJ (Rev: BL 2/1/68; LJ 9/15/67; PW 10/2/67. Awards: ALA, 1967) **[973.92]**

5974   Morrison, Joan, and Robert K. Morrison. *From Camelot to Kent State: The Sixties Experience in the Words of Those Who Lived It.* 1987, Random $12.95 (0-8129-1715-4). An oral history documenting key events and movements of the 1960s. (Rev: BL 11/1/87; LJ 11/1/87; NYTBR 2/21/88) **[973.92]**

5975   Morrow, Lance. *Fishing in the Tiber.* 1989, Henry Holt paper $12.95 (0-8050-1181-1). A collection of pieces written for *Time* magazine on aspects of American politics and cultural life. "A veritable feast, entertaining and thought-provoking."—LJ (Rev: BL 6/1/88; LJ 9/1/88; PW 5/27/88) **[973.92]**

5976   Moyers, Bill. *A World of Ideas.* 1989, Doubleday $39.95 (0-385-26278-7); paper $25.00 (0-385-26346-5). A collection of over 40 interviews conducted by the author with public figures regarding the current state of America and its future. (Rev: BL 4/1/89; LJ 4/15/89; NYTBR 6/4/89) **[973.92]**

5977   Murray, Charles. *Losing Ground: American Social Policy, 1950–1980.* 1986, Basic Books paper $13.95 (0-465-04232-5). A study of post-World War II American social policies and practices. (Rev: LJ 10/1/84; Natl Rev 12/14/84) **[973.92]**

5978   Newfield, Jack. *Robert Kennedy: A Memoir.* 1988, NAL paper $8.95 (0-452-26064-7). A reporter's memoirs of the former attorney general and U.S. senator. (Rev: Atl 7/69; LJ 7/69; NYTBR 7/6/69) **[973.92]**

5979   Newman, Edwin. *I Must Say: Edwin Newman on English, the News, and Other Matters.* 1988, Warner $18.95 (0-446-51423-3); paper $9.95 (0-446-39099-2). A collection of 150 of the journalist's columns on various topics of national culture and general interest. (Rev: BL 11/1/88; LJ 11/15/88; PW 10/7/88) **[973.92]**

5980   Nixon, Richard M. *In the Arena: A Memoir of Victory, Defeat and Renewal.* 1990, Simon & Schuster $21.95 (0-671-70096-0). Memoirs of the former president examining the Watergate scandal, his resignation, and his post-White House years. (Rev: BL 5/1/90; New Rep 10/1/90; NYTBR 4/29/90) **[973.92]**

**5981   Nixon, Richard M. *RN: Memoirs of Richard Nixon.* 1990, Simon & Schuster paper $17.95 (0-

671-70741-8). Memoirs of the former president focusing on the foreign policy of his administration. (REV: Choice 12/78; CSM 6/21/78; NYTBR 6/11/78) **[973.92]**

5982 Noonan, Peggy. *What I Saw at the Revolution: A Political Life in the Reagan Era.* 1990, Random $19.95 (0-394-56495-2); Ivy Books paper $5.95 (0-8041-0760-2). An account of the Reagan years by his former speechwriter. (REV: BL 1/1/90; Natl Rev 2/19/90; Time 2/19/90. AWARDS: Time, 1990) **[973.92]**

5983 Nye, Joseph S., Jr. *Bound to Lead: The Changing Nature of American Power.* 1990, Basic Books $19.95 (0-465-00743-0). A study of the current state of American power and its proper applications. (REV: LJ 3/15/90; NYRB 6/28/90; NYTBR 4/15/90) **[973.92]**

5984 Oakley, J. Ronald. *God's Country: America in the Fifties.* 1986, Dembner Books $24.95 (0-934878-70-6). A survey of the political and cultural history of the United States in the 1950s. (REV: BL 5/1/86; Choice 12/86; LJ 5/1/86) **[973.92]**

5985 O'Brien, Geoffrey. *Dream Time: Chapters from the Sixties.* 1988, Viking $15.95 (0-670-81844-5); Penguin paper $7.95 (0-14-010362-7). A collection of 13 essays portraying aspects of the social and political life of the 1960s. (REV: BL 6/15/88; NYTBR 9/11/88; PW 4/29/88) **[973.92]**

5986 Oshinsky, David M. *A Conspiracy So Immense: The World of Joe McCarthy.* 1985, Free Pr. $19.95 (0-02-923490-5); paper $10.95 (0-02-923760-2). A social history of the McCarthy era and its background. "The best balanced biography to date."—Choice (REV: Choice 10/83; LJ 4/15/83; NYTBR 6/5/83) **[973.92]**

5987 Parmet, Herbert S. *Richard Nixon and His America.* 1990, Little, Brown $24.95 (0-316-69232-8). A biography of the former president written with access to Nixon's private papers. (REV: LJ 12/89; NYTBR 1/7/90; PW 11/10/89) **[973.92]**

5988 Peirce, Neal R., and Jerry Hagstrom. *Book of America: Inside Fifty States Today.* 1983, Norton $27.50 (0-393-01639-0). An overview of the 50 states covering their culture, history, and demographic make-ups. "Intelligent, candid, lively, literate and wholly readable."—PW (REV: BL 6/1/83; LJ 6/1/83; PW 5/6/83) **[973.92]**

5989 Raban, Jonathan. *Hunting Mister Heartbreak: A Discovery of America.* 1991, Thorndike Pr. $25.00 (0-06-018209-1). Accounts of the British writer's travels in America including visits to Washington State, Alabama, Florida, and New York. (REV: LJ 4/15/91; PW 3/15/91; Time 5/13/91) **[973.92]**

5990 Regan, Donald T. *For the Record: From Wall Street to Washington.* 1988, Harcourt $21.95 (0-15-163966-3); St. Martin's paper $4.95 (0-312-91518-7). Memoirs of the former U.S. secretary of the treasury and presidential chief of staff regarding his service during the Reagan administration. (REV: BL 6/1/88; CSM 8/8/88; LJ 8/88) **[973.92]**

5991 Reich, Robert B. *Tales of a New America.* 1987, Random $19.95 (0-8129-1624-7); paper $8.95 (0-394-75706-8). An analysis of America's current standing and influence in international affairs and politics. (REV: Natl Rev 4/24/87; NYTBR 3/22/87; PW 2/4/87) **[973.92]**

5992 Reston, James. *Lone Star: The Life of John Connally.* 1989, Harper & Row $25.00 (0-06-016196-5). An examination of the life and career of the former governor of Texas, Nixon administration cabinet member, and presidential candidate. (REV: LJ 10/1/89; NYTBR 11/26/89; PW 10/6/89) **[973.92]**

5993 Rusk, Dean, and Richard Rusk. *As I Saw It.* 1990, Norton $29.95 (0-393-02650-7). An autobiography of the former secretary of state as told to his son, focusing on his role in the formation of American policy during the Vietnam War. (REV: LJ 6/1/90; NYTBR 7/1/90; Time 7/30/90) **[973.92]**

5994 Schell, Jonathan. *Observing the Nixon Years.* 1989, Pantheon $19.95 (0-394-57495-8); Random paper $9.95 (0-679-72951-5). One hundred journalistic pieces from the *New Yorker* regarding the Nixon and Ford administrations during the Vietnam War and the Watergate crisis. (REV: BL 3/1/89; LJ 4/1/89; NYTBR 4/9/89) **[973.92]**

5995 Schieffer, Bob, and Gary P. Gates. *Acting President.* 1989, Dutton $18.95 (0-525-24752-1); paper $9.95 (0-525-48579-1). An examination of the Reagan presidency and the influence of his aides and advisors. (REV: BL 7/89; Choice 2/90; LJ 9/1/89) **[973.92]**

5996 Schlesinger, Arthur M., Jr. *Robert Kennedy and His Times.* 1978, Houghton $19.95 (0-395-24897-3); Ballantine paper $5.95 (0-345-32547-8). An intimate portrait of RFK by a close friend of the Kennedy family. (REV: Atl 10/78; LJ 8/78; Time 9/4/78. AWARDS: ALA, 1978; NBA, 1979) **[973.92]**

5997 Schlosstein, Steven. *End of the American Century.* 1989, Congdon & Weed $22.95 (0-86553-201-0); Contemporary paper $13.95 (0-86553-217-6). A comparative study of the present and future economic and political status of the Pacific Rim nations and the United States. (REV: LJ 12/89; NYRB 3/1/90; NYTBR 2/18/90) **[973.92]**

5998 Sorenson, Theodore C. *Kennedy.* 1988, Harper & Row paper $10.95 (0-06-091530-7). A biography of JFK by his former speechwriter and assistant. "A historically important and warmly human document that . . . evokes the vivid personality of the subject."—BL (REV: BL 11/1/65; CSM 10/7/65; LJ 10/15/65. AWARDS: ALA, 1965) **[973.92]**

5999 Stern, Jane, and Michael Stern. *Sixties People.* 1990, Knopf $24.95 (0-394-57050-2). An exploration of the essence of the 1960s by the authors of *The Encyclopedia of Bad Taste.* (REV: BL 1/1/90; LJ 1/90; PW 1/5/90) **[973.92]**

6000 Taylor, John. *Circus of Ambition: The Culture of Wealth and Power in the Eighties.* 1989, Warner $19.95 (0-446-51484-5); paper $12.95 (0-446-39157-3). A study of the American societal drive for wealth and power during the Reagan years. (Rev: BL 10/1/89; LJ 8/89; NYTBR 10/29/89) **[973.92]**

6001 Terkel, Studs. *Great Divide: Second Thoughts on the American Dream.* 1988, Pantheon $18.95 (0-394-57053-7); Avon paper $4.95 (0-380-70854-X). In this follow-up oral history to his *American Dreams: Lost and Found,* Terkel interviews Americans on how the 1980s have affected their hopes and aspirations. (Rev: BL 8/88; LJ 10/1/88; PW 8/5/88) **[973.92]**

6002 Thompson, Hunter S. *Generation of Swine: Tales of Shame and Degradation in the Eighties, Gonzo Papers, Vol. II.* 1988, Summit $18.95 (0-671-66147-7); Random paper $8.95 (0-679-72237-8). Selected commentaries on the 1980s culled from the author's *San Francisco Examiner* column. (Rev: BL 5/15/88; NYTBR 8/14/88) **[973.92]**

6003 Thompson, Hunter S. *Songs of the Doomed: More Notes on the Death of the American Dream.* 1990, Summit $21.95 (0-685-39068-3); Pocket paper $9.00 (0-671-74326-0). A collection of writings spanning the journalistic career of the author of *Fear and Loathing in Las Vegas.* (Rev: BL 11/1/90; NYTBR 11/25/90) **[973.92]**

6004 Trillin, Calvin. *With All Disrespect: More Uncivil Liberties.* 1986, Penguin paper $6.95 (0-14-008819-9). A collection of Trillin's irreverent columns for *The Nation* on contemporary life in America. (Rev: LJ 5/1/85; Natl Rev 7/26/85; NYTBR 4/14/85) **[973.92]**

6005 Viorst, Milton. *Fire in the Streets: America in the 1960s.* 1981, Simon & Schuster paper $14.95 (0-671-42814-4). A study of the causes and manifestations of social disorder and discontent in the 1960s. "A thorough, balanced and readable recreation of a turbulent era."—PW (Rev: BL 1/15/80; LJ 12/1/79; Sat Rev 1/19/80) **[973.92]**

6006 Weller, Jack E. *Yesterday's People: Life in Contemporary Appalachia.* 1965, Univ. Pr. of Kentucky paper $7.00 (0-8131-0109-3). A Presbyterian minister tells of his 13 years living and working among the people of Appalachia. "A minor classic."—Choice (Rev: BL 1/15/66; Choice 4/66; LJ 12/15/65. Awards: ALA, 1965) **[973.92]**

6007 Wicker, Tom. *One of Us: Richard Nixon and the American Dream.* 1991, Random $24.95 (0-394-55066-8). A portrait of the former president analyzing his place in American society and the national psyche. "A definitive interpretation of Nixon and his culture."—LJ (Rev: BL 12/15/90; LJ 2/1/91; NYTBR 3/10/91) **[973.92]**

6008 Will, George F. *Suddenly: The American Idea Abroad and at Home, 1986–1990.* 1990, Free Pr. $22.50 (0-02-934435-2). A collection of nearly 200 essays from the political columnist. (Rev: BL 10/1/90; LJ 11/1/90; NYTBR 12/23/90) **[973.92]**

6009 Wills, Garry. *Nixon Agonistes: The Crisis of the Self-Made Man.* 1970, Cherokee $29.95 (0-385-18286-4). A look at Richard Nixon, his role in American intellectual history, and the nation that

elected him president. "A very skillfully organized report on critical aspects of modern society, discoursing philosophically on morals, economics, intellectuals and liberalism."—CSM (Rev: Choice 2/71; CSM 12/5/70; Time 11/2/70. Awards: Time, 1970; Time, the 1970s) **[973.92]**

6010 Wills, Garry. *Reagan's America: With a New Chapter on the Legacy of the Reagan Era.* 1988, Penguin paper $10.95 (0-14-010557-3). An investigation into the political career of Ronald Reagan, the societal changes that have taken place in recent America, and how Reagan himself reflects the values of current American society. (Rev: BL 12/1/86; LJ 2/1/87; Time 1/26/87) **[973.92]**

6011 Wolfe, Tom. *Kandy Kolored Tangerine-Flake Streamline Baby.* 1987, Farrar $19.95 (0-374-18064-4); paper $7.95 (0-374-50468-7). Wolfe's first book contains 28 essays on various aspects of popular culture. "A vivid, audacious, alert and individual view of our times."—Choice (Rev: Choice 9/65; LJ 6/1/65; NYTBR 6/27/65. Awards: NYTBR, 1965) **[973.92]**

6012 Woodward, Bob, and Carl Bernstein. *Final Days.* 1989, Simon & Schuster paper $8.95 (0-671-69087-6). An inside view of the last year and a half of the Nixon presidency. "Its contribution to our understanding of the aftermath of the events broadly labeled 'Watergate' is immense."—LJ (Rev: BL 5/15/76; Choice 7–8/76; LJ 6/15/76) **[973.92]**

6013 Wright, Lawrence. *In the New World: Growing Up with America, 1960–1984.* 1987, Knopf $18.95 (0-394-54282-7); Random paper $8.95 (0-394-75964-8). Memoirs of the author's experiences growing up in the 1960s and 1970s. "An important book."—LJ (Rev: BL 12/15/87; LJ 1/88; NYTBR 2/7/88) **[973.92]**

974 Northeastern United States

6014 Cronon, William. *Changes in the Land: Indians, Colonists and the Ecology of New England.* 1983, Hill & Wang paper $7.95 (0-8090-0158-6). An account of the environmental changes caused by Native Americans and later by colonists in New England. "A story that is fresh, ingenious, compelling and altogether important."—NYTBR (Rev: LJ 6/1/83; Newsweek 9/19/83; NYTBR 5/20/84) **[974]**

6015 Piersen, William D. *Black Yankees: The Development of an Afro-American Subculture in 18th Century New England.* 1988, Univ. of Massachusetts Pr. $25.00 (0-87023-586-9); $12.95 paper (0-87023-587-7). A study of the African-American subculture that developed in several communities in eighteenth-century Massachusetts, Connecticut, and Rhode Island. (Rev: Choice 9/88; LJ 2/1/88) **[974]**

History—Colonial period, 1620–1776

6016 Demos, John Putnam. *Entertaining Satan: Witchcraft and the Culture of Early New England.* 1982, Oxford Univ. Pr. $35.00 (0-19-503131-8); paper $12.95 (0-12-503378-7). A study of the belief in witchcraft and its persecution in seventeenth-century New England. (Rev: Choice 4/83; LJ 9/1/82; NYTBR 9/19/82) **[974.02]**

United States—History—Maine

6017 Smith, Robert. *My Life in the North Woods.* **1986, Atlantic Monthly $17.95 (0-87113-074-2).** Memoirs of the author's life in a Maine logging camp during the depression. (Rev: LJ 9/15/86; PW 7/18/86) **[974.1]**

6018 Ulrich, Laurel Thatcher. *Midwife's Tale: The Life of Martha Ballard Based on Her Diary, 1785–1812.* **1990, Knopf $24.95 (0-394-56844-3).** A biography of a Maine midwife based on her diaries and notebooks. (Rev: BL 3/1/90; CSM 4/24/90; NYTBR 3/4/90. Awards: PP:History, 1991) **[974.1]**

United States—History—New Hampshire

6019 Kumin, Maxine. *In Deep: Country Essays.* **1987, Viking $16.95 (0-670-81431-8); Beacon paper $8.95 (0-8070-6323-1).** Essays by the Pulitzer Prize-winning poet regarding farm life and country living. (Rev: BL 6/15/87; LJ 9/1/87; NYTBR 8/30/87) **[974.2]**

United States—History—Massachusetts

6020 Green, Martin. *Mount Vernon Street Warrens: A Boston Story, 1860–1910.* **1990, Macmillan $24.95 (0-684-19109-1).** A portrait of the family that made a fortune in papermaking and played a key role in the social and cultural development of Boston in the late nineteenth and early twentieth centuries. (Rev: BL 2/15/90; NYTBR 6/3/90; PW 2/2/90) **[974.4]**

6021 Kenney, Charles, and Robert L. Turner. *Dukakis: An American Odyssey.* **1989, Houghton paper $7.95 (0-395-49282-3).** A biography of the former Massachusetts governor and failed 1988 Democratic presidential candidate. (Rev: CSM 3/4/88; LJ 4/15/88; NYTBR 5/1/88) **[974.4]**

6022 Schama, Simon. *Dead Certainties (Unwarranted Speculations).* **1991, Knopf $21.00 (0-679-40213-6).** Studies of the deaths of James Wolfe, British commander during the Seven Years' War, and George Parkman, Harvard professor and uncle of historian Francis Parkman, who is the link between these two unrelated tales. (Rev: BL 5/1/91; LJ 4/15/91; PW 4/5/91. Awards: PW, 1991) **[974.4]**

United States—History—Connecticut

6023 Powers, Ron. *Far from Home: The Life and Loss of Two American Towns.* **1991, Random $22.00 (0-394-57034-0).** A history of the rise and decline of the American cities of Cairo, Illinois, and Kent, Connecticut. (Rev: BL 3/15/91; LJ 4/15/91; PW 4/12/91. Awards: LJ, 1991) **[974.6]**

United States—History—New York

6024 Anderson, Jervis. *This Was Harlem: A Cultural Portrait, 1900–1950.* **1983, Farrar paper $14.95 (0-374-51757-6).** A look at the social and cultural life of Harlem in the first half of the twentieth century. "An engaging, popular and informative history."— Choice (Rev: BL 2/15/82; Choice 10/82; CSM 6/16/82. Awards: ALA, 1982) **[974.7]**

6025 Auchincloss, Louis. *Vanderbilt Era: Profiles of a Gilded Age.* **1989, Macmillan $19.95 (0-684-19112-1).** A social history of upper-class New York in the late nineteenth and early twentieth centuries. (Rev: Atl 9/89; PW 4/14/89; Time 5/15/89) **[974.7]**

6026 Bookbinder, Bernie. *City of the World: New York and Its People.* **1989, Abrams $39.95 (0-8109-1383-6).** An illustrated history of New York City from the mid-nineteenth century to the present. (Rev: LJ 3/1/90; PW 12/1/89) **[974.7]**

6027 Brown, Claude. *Manchild in the Promised Land.* **1965, Macmillan $15.95 (0-02-517320-0); NAL paper $4.95 (0-451-15741-9).** Reflections on a childhood in the slums of Harlem. "A mature autobiography of the coming of age of one hidden human being, whose experience and generation are absolutely critical to any future history of the American people."—NYTBR (Rev: Choice 12/65; NYTBR 8/22/65; Newsweek 8/16/65. Awards: ALA, 1965; NYTBR, 1965) **[974.7]**

6028 Buckley, Gail Lumet. *The Hornes: An American Family.* **1986, Knopf $18.95 (0-394-51306-1); NAL paper $4.95 (0-451-15671-4).** The daughter of Lena Horne traces the Horne family history from the Civil War to the present. (Rev: Choice 11/86; LJ 7/86; NYTBR 7/6/86) **[974.7]**

6029 Champlin, Charles. *Back There Where the Past Was: A Small-Town Boyhood.* **1989, Syracuse Univ. Pr. $18.95 (0-8156-0235-9).** The film critic's memoirs of his childhood and adolescence in Hammondsport, New York. (Rev: BL 5/15/89; LJ 4/1/89; NYTBR 9/17/89) **[974.7]**

6030 Charyn, Jerome. *Metropolis: New York as Myth, Marketplace and Magical Land.* **1987, Avon paper $8.95 (0-380-70401-3).** A combination memoir and tribute to New York City, examining many of the people and individuals that make up the modern day metropolis. (Rev: BL 7/86; NYTBR 7/27/86; PW 6/6/86. Awards: ALA, 1986) **[974.7]**

6031 Dunlap, David W. *On Broadway: A Journey Uptown Over Time.* **1990, Rizzoli $65.00 (0-8478-1181-6).** A photographic tour and history of one of Manhattan's most famous streets. "Arresting and authoritative."—NYTBR (Rev: LJ 2/1/91; NYTBR 11/2/90) **[974.7]**

6032 Gornick, Vivian. *Fierce Attachments: A Memoir.* **1987, Farrar $15.95 (0-374-15485-6); Simon & Schuster paper $7.95 (0-671-65757-7).** A memoir of growing up in a Jewish tenement in New York, focusing on the author's stormy relationship with her mother. "A fine unflinchingly, honest book."—NYTBR (Rev: BL 8/87; NYTBR 4/26/87; PW 3/13/87. Awards: ALA, 1987) **[974.7]**

6033 Kessner, Thomas. *Fiorello H. La Guardia and the Making of Modern New York.* **1989, McGraw-Hill $24.95 (0-07-03244-X).** A biography of the three-term mayor of New York (1934–1945), whose service was noted for its social concern and reforms. (Rev: CSM 10/18/89; LJ 10/1/89; NYTBR 10/15/89. Awards: LJ, 1989) **[974.7]**

6034 Kisseloff, Jeff. *You Must Remember This: An Oral History of Manhattan from the 1890s to World War II.* 1989, Harcourt $24.95 (0-15-187988-5); Schocken paper $14.95 (0-8052-0979-4). An oral history of Manhattan's past as remembered by over 130 New Yorkers. (Rev: LJ 6/1/89; NYTBR 7/9/89; Newsweek 5/1/89) **[974.7]**

6035 Klinkenborg, Verlyn. *Last Fine Time.* 1991, Knopf $19.95 (0-394-57195-9). A history of a Buffalo, New York, bar and the Polish-American family who ran it from the 1920s to 1970. "This book deserves a wide readership."—LJ (Rev: BL 12/1/90; LJ 12/90; NYTBR 1/20/91. Awards: ALA, 1992; BL, 1991) **[974.7]**

6036 Knowler, Donald. *Falconer of Central Park.* 1984, Karz-Cohl $14.95 (0-943828-62-7); Bantam paper $8.95 (0-553-34205-3). A chronicle of a year of bird and nature watching in New York's Central Park. (Rev: LJ 5/15/84; NYTBR 8/5/84; PW 4/13/84) **[974.7]**

6037 Koch, Edward I. *Politics.* 1986, Warner paper $4.50 (0-446-32300-4). Reflections on the political life and the political process by the former mayor of New York. (Rev: LJ 4/1/86; NYTBR 12/22/85) **[974.7]**

6038 Koch, Edward I., and Leland T. Jones. *All the Best: Letters from a Feisty Mayor.* 1990, Simon & Schuster $19.95 (0-671-69365-4). Selected letters from the former mayor of New York responding to events during his 12-year term. (Rev: CSM 5/7/90; LJ 4/15/90; Natl Rev 6/11/90) **[974.7]**

6039 McElvaine, Robert S. *Mario Cuomo: A Biography.* 1988, Macmillan $19.95 (0-684-18970-4). A biography of the governor of New York by the author of *The Great Depression.* (Rev: Atl 3/88; Choice 11/88; PW 4/15/88) **[974.7]**

6040 Morris, Jan. *Manhattan '45.* 1987, Oxford Univ. Pr. $21.95 (0-19-503870-3); paper $9.95 (0-19-506664-2). A re-creation of the social and cultural climate of Manhattan in the mid-1940s by the Welsh travel writer. (Rev: LJ 4/1/87; NYTBR 4/19/87; Time 4/20/87) **[974.7]**

6041 O'Connor, John C., and Edward I. Koch. *His Eminence and Hizzoner: A Candid Exchange.* 1989, Avon paper $4.95 (0-380-70715-2). A discussion of viewpoints between the former mayor of New York and the Roman Catholic archbishop. (Rev: BL 4/15/89; NYTBR 3/26/89) **[974.7]**

6042 Oppersdorff, Mathias, and Alice Wolf Gilborn. *Adirondack Faces.* 1991, Syracuse Univ. Pr. $34.95 (0-8156-0260-X). A collection of 53 portraits of local residents from the holdings of the Adirondack Museum. "An appealing piece of Americana."—PW (Rev: LJ 9/1/91; PW 5/17/91) **[974.7]**

6043 Rivera, Edward. *Family Installments: Memories of Growing Up Hispanic.* 1983, Penguin paper $8.95 (0-14-006726-4). Memoirs of the author's family's relocation from Puerto Rico to New York City. (Rev: BL 10/1/82; LJ 9/1/82; PW 6/18/82) **[974.7]**

6044 Simon, Kate. *Bronx Primitive: Portraits in a Childhood.* 1983, Harper & Row paper $8.95 (0-06-091067-4). Simon's memoirs of growing up in an immigrant neighborhood in the Bronx following World War I. "Candid and unsentimental, her narrative is an unsparing slice of life."—PW (Rev: NYTBR 5/23/82; PW 4/2/82; Time 4/19/82. Awards: NYTBR, 1982; Time, 1982) **[974.7]**

6045 Simon, Kate. *Etchings in an Hourglass.* 1990, HarperCollins $19.95 (0-06-016219-8). This third and concluding volume of the author's memoirs examines her years as an adult. "Eloquent testimony of a bold, creative and examined life, fully lived."—BL (Rev: BL 7/90; LJ 6/15/90; NYTBR 8/19/90) **[974.7]**

6046 Simon, Kate. *A Wider World: Portraits in an Adolescence.* 1987, Harper & Row paper $6.95 (0-06-091379-7). These memoirs of Simon's teenage years during the Great Depression are a sequel to her *Bronx Primitive.* (Rev: LJ 2/15/86; Newsweek 5/12/76; Time 2/24/86. Awards: Time, 1986) **[974.7]**

6047 Sukenick, Ronald. *Down and In: Life in the Underground.* 1987, Morrow $17.95 (0-688-06589-9); Macmillan paper $10.95 (0-02-008731-4). Memoirs of life in the artistic underground of Greenwich Village during the 1950s and 1960s. (Rev: Choice 1/88; NYTBR 11/1/87) **[974.7]**

United States—History—Pennsylvania

6048 Boyette, Michael. *Let It Burn! The Philadelphia Tragedy.* 1989, Contemporary $18.95 (0-8092-4543-4). The history of the MOVE organization, an African-American radical group whose Philadelphia headquarters was destroyed in a police bombing that led to a fire that consumed an additional 60 homes. (Rev: BL 7/89; LJ 7/89; PW 5/12/89) **[974.8]**

6049 McCullough, David. *Johnstown Flood.* 1987, Peter Smith $16.25 (0-8446-6292-5); Simon & Schuster paper $9.95 (0-671-20714-8). An account of the 1889 flood that killed upwards of 2,000 people in Pennsylvania. "A first-rate example of the documentary method."—New Yorker (Rev: LJ 2/15/68; New Yorker 5/11/68; PW 1/15/68) **[974.8]**

6050 Wallace, Anthony F. *Rockdale: The Growth of an American Village in the Early Industrial Revolution.* 1980, Norton paper $12.95 (0-393-00991-2). A chronicle of the growth and changes in a small Pennsylvania manufacturing town in the nineteenth century. (Rev: CSM 8/16/78; LJ 5/15/78; New Rep 8/19/78) **[974.8]**

975 Southeastern United States

6051 Oakes, James. *Slavery and Freedom: An Interpretation of the Old South.* 1990, Knopf $22.95 (0-394-53677-0). A study of slavery and its legacy in the American South. (Rev: BL 3/1/90; LJ 3/1/90; PW 1/19/90) **[975]**

6052 Woodward, C. Vann. *Thinking Back: The Perils of Writing History.* 1986, Louisiana State Univ. Pr. $14.95 (0-8071-1304-2). An analysis of the southern historian's career reflecting on historiographical methods and their application to his work. (REV: Choice 7–8/86; LJ 4/1/86; NYRB 3/13/86)

[975]

1865–

6053 Naipaul, V. S. *A Turn in the South.* 1989, Knopf $18.95 (0-394-56477-4); Random paper $9.95 (0-679-72488-5). The Trinidad-born writer reflects upon his experiences traveling in the American South. (REV: LJ 3/1/89; Natl Rev 2/24/89; NYTBR 2/5/89)

[975.04]

United States—History—Maryland

6054 Thomas, Ella Gertrude Clanton. *Secret Eye: The Journal of Ella Gertrude Clanton Thomas.* Ed. by Virginia I. Burr. 1990, Univ. of North Carolina Pr. $34.95 (0-8078-1897-6); paper $12.95 (0-8078-4273-7). A journal of a nineteenth-century Georgia socialite tracing the changes in southern culture brought on by the Civil War and Reconstruction. (REV: LJ 2/15/90; PW 1/26/90)   **[975.2]**

United States—History—Washington, D. C.

6055 Brinkley, David. *Washington Goes to War.* 1988, Knopf $18.95 (0-394-51025-9); paper $4.95 (0-345-35979-8). An account of the nation's capital during the Second World War. "Exceptionally well written and enriched with wry wit."—LJ (REV: CSM 4/13/88; LJ 4/1/88; NYTBR 5/8/88. AWARDS: LJ, 1988)

[975.3]

6056 Parker, Robert, and Richard Rushke. *Capitol Hill in Black and White.* 1989, Jove paper $3.95 (0-515-10189-3). Washington memoirs of a former assistant to Lyndon Johnson and a headwaiter of the Senate dining room. (REV: LJ 5/1/86; PW 4/4/86)

[975.3]

6057 Seale, William. *President's House: A History.* 1987, Abrams $39.95 (0-8109-1490-5). A two-volume social history of the White House from its construction to the beginning of the Eisenhower administration. (REV: BL 4/1/87; Choice 5/87; LJ 2/15/87)   **[975.3]**

United States—History—Virginia

6058 Dabney, Virginia Bell. *Once There Was a Farm: A Country Childhood Remembered.* 1990, Random $17.95 (0-394-58211-X); Ballantine paper $8.95 (0-345-36502-X). Memories of the author's early life on a Virginia farm. (REV: BL 4/15/90; LJ 4/1/90; NYTBR 4/1/90)   **[975.5]**

6059 Edds, Margaret. *Claiming the Dream: The Victorious Campaign of Douglas Wilder of Virginia.* 1990, Algonquin $17.95 (0-912697-85-7). A study of the successful political campaign of the nation's first African-American governor. (REV: Choice 2/91; LJ 5/15/90)   **[975.5]**

6060 Horton, Tom. *Bay Country: Reflections of a Chesapeake Dweller.* 1987, Johns Hopkins $16.95 (0-8018-3525-9); Ticknor & Fields paper $7.95 (0-89919-837-6). A look at the natural environment of the Chesapeake Bay area and how the human presence has affected the flora and fauna of the

region. (REV: BL 10/15/87; LJ 11/15/87; NYTBR 11/8/87. AWARDS: LJ, 1987)   **[975.5]**

6061 Isaac, Rhys. *Transformation of Virginia, 1740–1790.* 1982, Univ. of North Carolina Pr. $34.95 (0-8078-1489-X); Norton paper $12.95 (0-393-95693-8). Study of the development of the society of eighteenth-century Virginia. "It must be the starting point for all further work on the subject."—TLS (REV: LJ 4/15/82; NYRB 1/20/83; TLS 2/25/83. AWARDS: PP:History, 1983)   **[975.5]**

6062 King, Florence. *Confessions of a Failed Southern Lady.* 1986, Bantam paper $3.95 (0-553-25356-5). Memoirs of a southern woman. "A thought-provoking and incredibly funny account of growing up Southern and female."—BL (REV: BL 1/1/85; LJ 12/84; NYTBR 2/10/85)   **[975.5]**

6063 Langhorne, Elizabeth. *Monticello: A Family Story.* 1987, Algonquin $21.95 (0-912697-58-X). A study of Thomas Jefferson's family and social life at his Virginia estate. (REV: Choice 11/87; LJ 5/15/87)   **[975.5]**

6064 Noel Hume, Ivor. *Martin's Hundred: The Discovery of a Lost Colonial Virginia Settlement.* 1982, Knopf $25.00 (0-394-50728-2); Dell paper $9.95 (0-385-29281-3). An archaeologist's story of the discovery of an early seventeenth-century colonial settlement. "Balances scholarship and popular reporting . . . an exceptionally handsome book."—Newsweek (REV: BL 3/1/82; LJ 3/15/82; Newsweek 7/5/82. AWARDS: ALA, 1982)   **[975.5]**

United States—History—South Carolina

6065 Fields, Mamie Garvin, and Karen E. Fields. *Lemon Swamp and Other Places: A Carolina Memoir.* 1985, Free Pr. $21.95 (0-02-910160-3); paper $9.95 (0-02-910550-1). Memoirs of an African-American woman's life in Charleston, S. C., from her birth in 1888 to the 1980s. (REV: BL 3/1/84; CSM 12/2/83; LJ 11/15/83)   **[975.7]**

6066 Hammond, James H. *Secret and Sacred: The Diaries of James Henry Hammond, a Southern Slaveholder.* Ed. by Carol K. Bleser. 1989, Oxford Univ. Pr. paper $9.95 (0-19-506163-2). The edited diaries of a former U.S. senator from South Carolina who was a plantation slave owner. "Among the most intriguing, revealing, and infuriating personal accounts to come out of the South."—LJ (REV: Choice 3/89; LJ 10/15/88; PW 6/24/88)   **[975.7]**

6067 Joyner, Charles. *Down by the Riverside: A South Carolina Slave Community.* 1984, Univ. of Illinois Pr. $24.95 (0-252-01058-2); paper $9.95 (0-252-01305-0). A re-creation and history of slave life on a South Carolina plantation from the slaves' arrival from Africa to their eventual freedom. (REV: BL 7/84; Choice 2/85; LJ 6/1/84)   **[975.7]**

6068 Rosengarten, Theodore. *Tombee: Portrait of a Cotton Planter.* Ed. by Susan W. Walker. 1988, McGraw-Hill paper $12.95 (0-07-053821-2). A study of a southern slaveholder and cotton plantation owner, Thomas Chaplin. The book is divided into two sections: the first, a biography, and the second, a 15-year daily journal kept by Chaplin himself. (REV: CSM 8/4/86; LJ 7/86; PW 6/6/86. AWARDS: ALA, 1986)

[975.7]

United States—History—Georgia

6069 Buck, Polly Stone. *Blessed Town: Oxford, Georgia, at the Turn of the Century.* 1986, Algonquin $14.95 (0-912697-38-5). Memories of small-town southern life during the first decade of the twentieth century. (REV: BL 9/1/86; LJ 11/1/86; PW 7/18/86)

[975.8]

United States—History—Florida

6070 Allman, T. D. *Miami: City of the Future.* 1988, Atlantic Monthly $22.50 (0-87113-102-1); paper $5.95 (0-87113-227-3). A historical and contemporary portrait of Florida's largest and most cosmopolitan city. (REV: BL 3/15/87; LJ 4/1/87; NYTBR 5/10/87)

[975.9]

6071 Didion, Joan. *Miami.* 1988, Pocket paper $7.95 (0-671-66820-X). An examination of Miami as a melting pot for Latin cultures, concentrating on the impact Cuban exiles have made on the city. (REV: Choice 3/88; CSM 11/12/87; LJ 10/1/87)

[975.9]

6072 Rieff, David. *Going to Miami: Exiles, Tourists and Refugees in the New America.* 1988, Penguin paper $7.95 (0-14-011091-7). A profile of the Florida city and the changes it has undergone in recent decades due to increased immigration from Latin nations. (REV: BL 8/87; Natl Rev 11/20/87; NYTBR 8/23/87)

[975.9]

United States—History—Alabama

6073 Brooks, Sara. *You May Plow Here: The Narrative of Sara Brooks.* Ed. by Thordis Simonsen. 1986, Norton $12.95 (0-393-02257-9); Simon & Schuster paper $6.95 (0-671-63848-3). An account of the life of an African-American domestic worker from her childhood in the Deep South through her 30 years of employment in the North. (REV: BL 1/15/86; LJ 1/86; NYTBR 3/9/86)

[976.1]

United States—History—Mississippi

6074 Cagin, Seth, and Philip Dray. *We Are Not Afraid: The Story of Goodman, Schwerner, and Chaney and the Civil Rights Campaign for Mississippi.* 1989, Bantam paper $5.95 (0-553-28269-7). An account of the murder of three civil rights workers in Mississippi in 1964. "Riveting . . . surely one of the best books on the civil rights movement."—PW (REV: Choice 10/88; LJ 5/1/88; PW 3/11/88. AWARDS: ALA, 1988; LJ, 1988; PW, 1988)

[976.2]

6075 Taulbert, Clifton. *Once Upon a Time When We Were Colored.* 1989, Council Oak Books $16.95 (0-933031-19-X). Memoirs of childhood and adolescence growing up in an African-American family in Mississippi during the 1950s. (REV: LJ 7/89; NYTBR 2/18/90; PW 5/12/89)

[976.2]

United States—History—Louisiana

6076 Kurtz, Michael L., and Morgan D. Peoples. *Earl K. Long: The Saga of Uncle Earl and Louisiana Politics.* 1990, Louisiana State Univ. Pr. $24.95 (0-8071-1577-0). A biography of the former Louisiana governor and U.S. congressman. (REV: Choice 7–8/90; LJ 3/1/90; NYRB 2/14/91)

[976.3]

United States—History—Texas

6077 Brook, Stephen. *Honkytonk Gelato: Travels Through Texas.* 1988, Paragon House paper $8.95 (1-55778-005-6). A British writer's accounts of his travels and experiences in the Lone Star State. (REV: BL 9/15/85; LJ 9/15/85; NYTBR 9/29/85)

[976.4]

6078 Ivins, Molly. *Molly Ivins Can't Say That, Can She?* 1991, Random $23.00 (0-679-40445-7). A collection of previously published pieces by the *Dallas Times-Herald* columnist. (REV: LJ 9/1/91; NYTBR 10/20/91)

[976.4]

6079 Kramer, Jane. *Last Cowboy.* 1988, Farrar paper $6.95 (0-374-52118-2). A look at the contemporary American cowboy. (REV: LJ 2/1/78; NYTBR 2/22/78; Time 1/23/78. AWARDS: NBA, 1981)

[976.4]

6080 Long, Jeff. *Duel of Eagles: The Mexican and United States Fight for the Alamo.* 1990, Morrow $22.45 (0-688-07252-6). An account of the 1835–36 war for the independence of Texas. (REV: BL 7/90; LJ 7/90; PW 6/29/90)

[976.4]

United States—History—Arkansas

6081 Abbott, Shirley. *Bookmaker's Daughter: A Memory Unbound.* 1991, Ticknor & Fields $19.95 (0-89919-518-0). Memoirs of the author's childhood as the daughter of an Arkansas bookmaker. (REV: BL 5/1/91; PW 5/24/91)

[976.7]

6082 Middleton, Harry. *Earth Is Enough: Growing Up in a World of Trout and Old Men.* 1989, Simon & Schuster $18.95 (0-671-67459-5); paper $8.95 (0-671-70700-0). Memoirs of the author's childhood with his grandfather and great uncle on their farm in the Ozarks. (REV: BL 7/89; LJ 7/89; NYTBR 7/30/89. AWARDS: BL, 1989)

[976.7]

United States—History—Tennessee

6083 Middleton, Harry. *On the Spine of Time: An Angler's Love of the Smokies.* 1991, Simon & Schuster $18.95 (0-671-69141-4). Memoirs of the author's fishing experiences in the Great Smoky Mountains. (REV: BL 2/15/91; LJ 2/15/91; PW 1/18/91)

[976.8]

United States—History—Kentucky

6084 Brenner, Marie. *House of Dreams: The Bingham Family of Louisville.* 1988, Random $19.95 (0-394-55831-6); Avon paper $4.95 (0-380-70727-6). A collective biography of the Louisville, Kentucky, newspaper owners and their family. (REV: NYRB 4/28/88; NYTBR 3/27/88; Time 4/4/88)

[976.9]

6085 Merrill, Boynton, Jr. *Jefferson's Nephews: A Frontier Tragedy.* 1987, Univ. Pr. of Kentucky paper $17.00 (0-8131-0173-5). The story of a murder committed by two of Thomas Jefferson's nephews in Kentucky in 1911. "A first-rate piece of social history . . . offers the reader a real treat."—Choice (Rev: Choice 5/77; New Rep 3/12/77; Newsweek 1/10/77) **[976.9]**

6086 Reid, B. L. *First Acts: A Memoir.* 1988, Univ. of Georgia Pr. $16.95 (0-8203-1015-8). An account of the author's life growing up in a southern family during the Great Depression and World War II. (Rev: LJ 8/88; NYTBR 12/18/88; PW 6/24/88) **[976.9]**

977 North central United States

6087 Gilbert, Bill. *God Gave Us This Country: Tekamthi and the First American Civil War.* 1989, Macmillan $22.50 (0-689-11632-2). A history of the conflict between American settlers and soldiers and Northwest Ordinance tribes under the leadership of Tecumseh. (Rev: BL 5/15/89; NYTBR 8/6/89; PW 5/5/89) **[977]**

United States—History—Ohio

6088 Kline, David. *Great Possessions: An Amish Farmer's Journal.* 1990, North Point $16.95 (0-86547-405-2). Essays celebrating the Amish way of life and farming. (Rev: BL 4/15/90; LJ 3/1/90; NYTBR 5/6/90) **[977.1]**

United States—History—Indiana

6089 Hoppe, David, ed. *Where We Live: Essays about Indiana.* 1989, Indiana Univ. Pr. $22.50 (0-253-32801-2); paper $7.95 (0-253-20540-9). A collection of a dozen essays on Indiana by different writers. (Rev: BL 8/89; LJ 8/89) **[977.2]**

United States—History—Illinois

6090 Farber, David. *Chicago '68.* 1988, Univ. of Chicago Pr. $19.95 (0-226-23800-8). A recounting of the events of the tumultuous year 1968 in Chicago focusing on the violence that surrounded the August Democratic National Convention. (Rev: CSM 6/3/88; LJ 2/1/88; NYTBR 4/3/88) **[977.3]**

6091 Royko, Mike. *Boss: Richard J. Daley of Chicago.* 1988, NAL paper $8.95 (0-452-26167-8). A revealing look at the former mayor of Chicago and his political machine. "An occasion for celebration . . . the revelations are, in telling detail, astonishing."—Studs Terkel, NYTBR (Rev: BL 6/15/71; LJ 6/1/71; PW 1/18/71) **[977.3]**

United States—History—Michigan

6092 Moskowitz, Faye. *A Leak in the Heart: Tales from a Woman's Life.* 1987, Godine $13.95 (0-87923-551-9); paper $8.95 (0-87923-659-0). Autobiographical pieces describing the author's childhood and adolescence in an Orthodox Jewish family in Michigan. (Rev: BL 5/1/85; LJ 5/1/85; PW 3/29/85) **[977.4]**

United States—History—Iowa

6093 Harnack, Curtis. *We Have All Gone Away.* 1988, Iowa State Univ. Pr. paper $5.95 (0-8138-1903-2). Reminiscences of a farm youth in Iowa during the Great Depression. "A country plum of a book, written with genuine affection and vivid recall."—PW (Rev: LJ 4/15/73; NYTBR 4/15/73; PW 1/8/73) **[977.7]**

6094 Toth, Susan Allen. *Blooming: A Small-Town Girlhood.* 1985, Ballantine paper $3.95 (0-345-32123-5). Memoirs of the author's childhood growing up in Ames, Iowa, during the 1950s. (Rev: BL 5/1/81; NYTBR 5/24/81; PW 4/3/81) **[977.7]**

United States—History—Missouri

6095 Powers, Ron. *White Town Drowsing.* 1987, Penguin paper $7.95 (0-14-010409-7). Memoirs about Hannibal, Missouri, comparing the city as it was in the author's youth with the present-day community. (Rev: BL 12/1/86; LJ 11/1/86; NYTBR 11/30/86) **[977.8]**

978 Western United States

6096 Baker, Will. *Mountain Blood.* 1986, Univ. of Georgia Pr. $14.95 (0-8203-0819-6). Seven essays and folktales taken from the mountainous regions of the American West. "Well-written, humorous and insightful."—LJ (Rev: BL 2/15/86; LJ 2/15/86; PW 1/31/86. Awards: ALA, 1986) **[978]**

6097 Barsness, Larry. *Heads, Hides and Horns: The Compleat Buffalo Book.* 1985, Texas Christian Univ. paper $19.50 (0-87565-017-1). An illustrated history of the American bison and its exploitation by the settlers of the West. (Rev: BL 5/1/86; Choice 6/86; LJ 6/15/86) **[978]**

6098 Bowden, Charles. *Desierto: Memories of the Future.* 1991, Norton $18.95 (0-393-02935-2). A study of corruption, greed, and drug-running in the southern Arizona and northern Mexico deserts. (Rev: BL 5/15/91; PW 4/19/91) **[978]**

6099 Broder, Patricia Janis. *Shadows on Glass: The Indian World of Ben Wittick.* 1990, Rowman & Littlefield $39.95 (0-8476-7631-5). A collection of over 200 photographs of the peoples of the American Southwest taken by nineteenth-century photographer Ben Wittick. (Rev: BL 1/15/91; NYTBR 6/2/91) **[978]**

6100 Goetzmann, William H. *Exploration and Empire: The Explorer and the Scientist in the Winning of the American West.* 1978, Norton paper $14.95 (0-393-00881-9). A study of the expression and development of the American West during the nineteenth century. "A major contribution to the field of cultural and intellectual history."—Choice (Rev: Choice 11/66; LJ 4/1/66; NYTBR 8/21/66. Awards: PP:History, 1967) **[978]**

6101 Limerick, Patricia Nelson. *Legacy of Conquest: The Unbroken Past of the American West.* 1987, Norton $17.95 (0-393-02390-7). A study contrasting the historical myth and reality of the

American West. (REV: BL 6/15/87; Choice 12/87; PW 5/22/87) **[978]**

6102 Slatta, Richard W. *Cowboys of the Americas.* 1990, Yale Univ. Pr. $35.00 (0-300-04529-8). A history of the myth and reality of the cowboy and cowboy life in North and South America. (REV: BL 8/90; Choice 2/91; LJ 9/1/90) **[978]**

6103 Smith, Sherry L. *View from Officers' Row: Army Perceptions of Western Indians.* 1990, Univ. of Arizona Pr. $24.95 (0-8165-1018-0). A study of the U.S. frontier Army's concepts of Native Americans and their cultures. (REV: Choice 7–8/90; LJ 2/15/90) **[978]**

1800–1899

6104 Paul, Rodman W. *Far West and the Great Plains in Transition, 1859–1900.* 1988, Harper & Row $24.95 (0-06-015836-0); paper $9.95 (0-06-091448-3). A history of the settlement and development of the American West in the latter half of the nineteenth century. (REV: Choice 10/88; LJ 2/15/88; NYTBR 6/19/88) **[978.02]**

United States—History—Kansas

6105 Goodrich, Thomas. *Bloody Dawn: The Story of the Lawrence Massacre.* 1991, Kent State Univ. Pr. $26.00 (0-87338-442-3). An account of the 1863 massacre of the citizenry of Lawrence, Kansas, by Confederate troops during the Civil War. (REV: BL 12/1/91; LJ 11/1/91) **[978.1]**

6106 Parker, Tony. *Bird, Kansas.* 1989, Knopf $19.95 (0-394-57794-9). An oral history by a British journalist compiled from interviews with residents of a small town in Kansas. (REV: BL 6/15/89; LJ 6/15/89; Time 7/31/89) **[978.1]**

6107 Stratton, Joanna. *Pioneer Women: Voices from the Kansas Frontier.* 1982, Simon & Schuster $11.95 (0-671-44748-3). The author's great-grandmother collected the diaries and memoirs of 800 women settlers of Kansas. Fifty years later their stories were found and became the basis for this work. (REV: Choice 6/81; CSM 4/15/81; LJ 3/1/81. AWARDS: ALA, 1981) **[978.1]**

United States—History—South Dakota

6108 Crow Dog, Mary, and Richard Erdoes. *Lakota Woman.* 1990, Grove-Weidenfeld $17.95 (0-8021-1101-7). The autobiography of a Sioux woman describing her life on a South Dakota Indian reservation. (REV: Atl 5/90; BL 3/1/90; NYTBR 7/1/90) **[978.3]**

United States—History—North Dakota

6109 Low, Ann Marie. *Dust Bowl Diary.* 1984, Univ. of Nebraska Pr. $20.00 (0-8032-2864-3); paper $7.95 (0-8032-7913-2). A picture of North Dakota during the Great Depression through the diary, letters, and remembrances of the author. "Captures the essence of the dust bowl experience."—Choice (REV: Choice 4/85; LJ 12/84; NYTBR 3/31/85. AWARDS: LJ, 1984) **[978.4]**

United States—History—Wyoming

6110 Ehrlich, Gretel. *Solace of Open Spaces.* 1986, Penguin paper $6.95 (0-14-008113-5). The American poet's reflections upon the inner peace and inspiration she felt after moving from the East Coast to Wyoming. (REV: LJ 11/11/85; Natl Rev 7/4/86; NYTBR 12/1/85) **[978.7]**

United States—History—New Mexico

6111 DeBuys, William, and Alex Harris. *River of Traps: A Village Life.* 1990, Univ. of New Mexico Pr. $19.95 (0-8263-1182-2). An account of the authors' lives on a northern New Mexico farm and of the friendship they developed with an elderly neighbor. (REV: NYTBR 9/23/90; PW 8/3/90) **[978.9]**

6112 Frazier, Kendrick. *People of Chaco: A Canyon and Its Culture.* 1988, Norton paper $11.95 (0-393-30496-5). An overview of the culture of Chaco Canyon, New Mexico, one of the most highly developed prehistoric peoples of the Americas. (REV: Choice 4/87; LJ 10/15/86) **[978.9]**

979 Great Basin and Pacific Slope States

6113 Keegan, Marcia K. *Enduring Culture: A Century of Photography of the Southwest Indians.* 1991, Clear Light Pubs. $29.95 (0-940666-11-1). A collection of nineteenth- and early twentieth-century photographs of Native Americans juxtaposed with portraits taken by the author over the past 25 years. (REV: LJ 4/15/91; NYTBR 6/2/91) **[979]**

6114 Miller, Tom. *On the Border: Portraits of America's Southwestern Frontier.* 1985, Univ. of Arizona Pr. paper $9.95 (0-8165-0943-3). A study of the U.S.-Mexican border and the people who live near it based on the author's travels along the border from Texas to California. (REV: BL 6/1/81; LJ 6/15/81; NYTBR 7/12/81) **[979]**

6115 Tisdale, Sallie. *Stepping Westward: The Long Search for Home in the Pacific Northwest.* 1991, Henry Holt $19.95 (0-8050-1353-9). A survey of the history and natural world of the Pacific Northwest as written by a native of Oregon. "A loving, literate work."—LJ (REV: BL 9/15/91; LJ 9/1/91) **[979]**

1800–1899

6116 Batman, Richard. *James Pattie's West: The Dream and the Reality.* 1986, Univ. of Oklahoma Pr. paper $13.95 (0-8061-1977-2). A biography of a Missouri trader who headed west to trap furs in the 1830s and recorded his experiences and impressions in a series of journals. (REV: NYTBR 5/11/86; PW 2/21/86) **[979.02]**

United States—History—Arizona

6117 Watkins, Ronald J. *High Crimes and Misdemeanors: The Terms and Trials of Former Governor Evan Mecham.* 1990, Morrow $19.95 (0-688-09051-6). An account of the events surrounding the 1988 impeachment of Arizona Governor Evan Mecham. (REV: BL 4/1/90; LJ 4/1/90; PW 4/13/90) **[979.1]**

United States—History—Utah

6118 Martin, Russell. *A Story That Stands Like a Dam: Glen Canyon and the Struggle for the Soul of the West.* **1989, Henry Holt $24.95 (0-8050-0822-5).** An account of the conception and construction of the still controversial Glen Canyon Dam project. (Rev: BL 11/1/89; LJ 10/15/89; PW 10/13/89) **[979.2]**

United States—History—California

6119 Conaway, James. *Napa: The Story of an American Eden.* **1990, Houghton $24.95 (0-395-46880-9).** An overview of the Northern California wine region and the winemakers who have developed it into one of the world's finest producers of wine. (Rev: BL 9/15/90; LJ 9/15/90; NYTBR 10/21/90) **[979.4]**

6120 Friedrich, Otto. *City of Nets: A Portrait of Hollywood in the 1940's.* **1986, Harper & Row $25.00 (0-06-015626-0); paper $10.95 (0-06-091439-4).** A social history of Hollywood in the 1940s including portraits of the writers, musicians, gangsters, and movie people who made up the community in that era. "One of the best books ever written about Hollywood."—PW (Rev: LJ 11/1/86; Newsweek 11/17/86; PW 9/19/86. Awards: PW, 1986) **[979.4]**

6121 Holliday, J. S. *World Rushed In: The California Gold Rush Experience; an Eyewitness Account of a Nation Heading West.* **1983, Simon & Schuster paper $14.95 (0-671-25538-X).** The California Gold Rush is reflected through the diary and letters of William Swain, a prospector who spent two years looking for gold. "Other books will provide more facts and figures, but no other recent title will give a better idea of the day-to-day concerns of the forty-niners or their outlook on life."—LJ (Rev: BL 12/15/81; Choice 4/82; LJ 11/15/81. Awards: ALA, 1982) **[979.4]**

6122 Kahrl, William L. *Water and Power: The Conflict over Los Angeles' Water Supply in the Owens Valley.* **1982, Univ. of California Pr. $27.50 (0-520-04431-2); paper $13.95 (0-520-05068-1).** A history of Los Angeles' efforts to obtain water from the Owens River Valley. (Rev: Choice 10/82; LJ 7/82; NYRB 10/21/82) **[979.4]**

6123 Kingston, Maxine Hong. *Woman Warrior: Memoirs of a Girlhood Among Ghosts.* **1977, Random paper $4.95 (0-394-72392-9).** Memoir of a Chinese-American woman growing up in California, and her relationship with her ancestral past. "Thousands of books have bubbled up out of that American melting pot. This should be one of those that will be remembered."—Time (Rev: NYTBR 11/7/76; Newsweek 10/11/76; Time 12/6/76. Awards: ALA, 1976; NYTBR, 1976; Time, 1976; Time, the 1970s) **[979.4]**

6124 Myerhoff, Barbara. *Number Our Days.* **1980, Simon & Schuster paper $10.95 (0-671-25430-8).** A study of the lives and culture of Jewish emigrés from Eastern Europe who formed a community in and around Venice, California. (Rev: Choice 9/79; NYTBR 4/1/79; PW 1/1/79) **[979.4]**

6125 Rice, Clyde. *A Heaven in the Eye.* **1990, Breitenbush Books paper $10.95 (0-932576-84-2).** Memoirs of the author's life in the Pacific Northwest and Northern California during the 1920s and 1930s. "This unique book will hold the attention of readers everywhere."—BL (Rev: BL 8/84; LJ 8/84; PW 6/15/84) **[979.4]**

6126 Rice, Clyde. *Nordi's Gift.* **1990, Breitenbush Books $21.95 (0-932576-77-X).** This second volume of the author's autobiography traces the years from 1934 to 1955 and is the sequel to *A Heaven in the Eye.* (Rev: BL 1/1/91; NYTBR 11/25/90) **[979.4]**

6127 Rorabaugh, W. J. *Berkeley at War: The 1960's.* **1989, Oxford Univ. Pr. $24.95 (0-19-505877-1).** An account of the social and political turmoil surrounding the University of California Berkeley campus from the beginnings of the free speech movement in 1964 to the 1969 People's Park demonstrations. (Rev: BL 6/1/89; Choice 11/89; LJ 4/15/89) **[979.4]**

6128 Shilts, Randy. *Mayor of Castro Street: The Life and Times of Harvey Milk.* **1988, St. Martin's paper $10.95 (0-312-01900-9).** A biography of the gay San Francisco politician who was assassinated with Mayor George Moscone in 1978. "Essential for gay collections and an excellent addition for public libraries."—LJ (Rev: BL 2/15/82; LJ 2/1/82; PW 1/15/82) **[979.4]**

6129 Soto, Gary. *Living Up the Street: Narrative Recollections.* **1985, Strawberry Hill paper $7.95 (0-89407-064-9).** The poet's memoirs of growing up in a Mexican-American family in Fresno, California. (Rev: BL 8/85; LJ 9/1/85) **[979.4]**

6130 Starr, Kevin. *Americans and the California Dream, 1850–1915.* **1973, Oxford Univ. Pr. $25.00 (0-19-501644-0); paper $14.95 (0-19-504233-6).** The history of the settlement of California in the latter half of the nineteenth century and of the ideas and individuals that spurred its rapid growth. (Rev: Choice 10/73; New Yorker 8/6/73; Time 12/24/73. Awards: Time, 1973) **[979.4]**

6131 Starr, Kevin. *Inventing the Dream: California Through the Progressive Era.* **1985, Oxford Univ. Pr. $24.95 (0-19-503489-9).** Starr's second volume on the history and culture of California covers the years 1850 to 1920 and concentrates on the phenomenal growth of the southern half of the state. "Posterity is not going to forget this book."—NYTBR (Rev: Choice 9/85; NYTBR 2/24/85; Newsweek 5/27/85) **[979.4]**

6132 Starr, Kevin. *Material Dreams: Southern California Through the 1920s.* **1990, Oxford Univ. Pr. $24.95 (0-19-504487-8).** This third volume of the author's history of California concentrates on the growth and development of Southern California in the first part of the twentieth century. (Rev: Atl 3/90; CSM 6/12/90; LJ 12/89) **[979.4]**

United States—History—Oregon

6133 Egan, Timothy. *Good Rain: Across Time and Terrain in the Pacific Northwest.* **1990, Knopf**

$19.95 (0-394-57724-8). Accounts of the author's travels in Washington, Oregon, and British Columbia. "An excellent and timely portrait."—CSM (Rev: CSM 9/10/90; LJ 7/90; NYTBR 7/29/90)   **[979.5]**

United States—History—Washington

6134   Espy, Willard R. *Oysterville: Roads to Grandpa's Village.* **1985, Crown paper $11.95** (0-517-54913-1). Espy traces his family history to the seventeenth century and looks at his hometown, Oysterville, Washington. "Sly humor and wonderfully vivid detail enrich this heartwarming family saga."—PW (Rev: CSM 6/15/77; LJ 5/15/77; PW 2/28/77. Awards: ALA, 1977)   **[979.7]**

United States—History—Alaska

6135   Haines, John. *Stories We Listened To.* **1986, Bench Pr. paper $8.00** (0-930769-01-5). A short collection of essays regarding life on the Alaskan frontier. "He has the eye of an Audubon and the style of a Thoreau."—NYTBR (Rev: BL 3/15/87; NYTBR 3/29/87)   **[979.8]**

6136   Hatfield, Fred. *North of the Sun: A Memoir of the Alaskan Wilderness.* **1990, Carol Publg. Group $16.95** (1-55972-043-3). Memoirs of the author's hunting, fishing, and living experiences in the wilds of Alaska. (Rev: BL 10/15/90; LJ 10/1/90; PW 9/28/90)   **[979.8]**

6137   Kusz, Natalie. *Road Song.* **1990, Farrar $18.95** (0-374-25121-5). An account of the author's childhood in Alaska with her family. "This beautifully written memoir is a testament to the importance of family, honesty, courage and hope."—LJ (Rev: BL 10/15/90; LJ 10/1/90; PW 8/24/90)   **[979.8]**

6138   Leo, Richard. *Edges of the Earth: A Family's Alaskan Odyssey.* **1991, Henry Holt $19.95** (0-8050-1575-2). An account by a New Yorker who left the city to resettle with his girlfriend in the Alaskan wilderness. "Leo's absorbing story is filled with adventure as well as emotion."—PW (Rev: BL 8/91; PW 8/6/91)   **[979.8]**

6139   McPhee, John. *Coming into the Country.* **1977, Farrar $19.95** (0-374-12645-3); **Bantam paper $4.95** (0-553-25527-4). Accounts of travels in the Alaskan wilderness and the people who live there. "McPhee has acted as the antenna in a far-off place that few will see. He has brought back a wholly satisfying voyage of spirit and mind."—Time. (Rev: Atl 1/78; NYTBR 11/27/77; Time 12/5/77. Awards: ALA, 1977; NYTBR, 1977; Time, 1977)   **[979.8]**

6140   Scott, Alasdair. *Tracks Across Alaska: A Dog Sled Journey.* **1990, Atlantic Monthly $19.95** (0-87113-389-X). The author's account of his 800-mile dog sled trek through Alaska. (Rev: BL 9/15/90; LJ 9/1/90; NYTBR 9/9/90)   **[979.8]**

980   GENERAL HISTORY OF SOUTH AMERICA

6141   Galeano, Eduardo H. *Memory of Fire: Genesis, Vol. I.* **1987, Pantheon paper $11.95** (0-394-74730-5). An account of the early history of Latin America before and after Columbus. (Rev: Choice 1/86; CSM 3/7/86; LJ 10/1/85)   **[980]**

6142   Rosenberg, Tina. *Children of Cain: Violence and the Violent in Latin America.* **1991, Morrow $25.00** (0-688-08465-6). A study of recent political violence in Latin America, including profiles of the current Peruvian rebellion, the Colombian drug wars, and recent military terrorism in Argentina. (Rev: LJ 8/91; NYTBR 9/8/91; PW 7/5/91)   **[980]**

981   Brazil

6143   Hemming, John. *Amazon Frontier: The Defeat of the Brazilian Indians.* **1987, Harvard Univ. Pr. $29.95** (0-674-01725-0). A history of relations and interactions between European immigrants and native Brazilian peoples from the eighteenth to twentieth centuries. (Rev: Choice 5/88; NYTBR 1/31/88; TLS 10/16/87)   **[981]**

6144   Popescu, Petru. *Amazon Beaming.* **1991, Viking $25.00** (0-670-82997-8). A chronicle of the exploits of a *National Geographic* researcher in South America seeking the source of the Amazon and of his experiences among the Mayoruna Indian tribe. "An extraordinary, gripping tale."—PW (Rev: BL 8/91; LJ 8/91; PW 7/5/91)   **[981]**

6145   Smith, Anthony. *Explorers of the Amazon.* **1990, Viking $21.95** (0-670-81310-9). A history of Amazon exploration from the seventeenth century to the twentieth. (Rev: BL 1/1/90; LJ 11/15/89; PW 11/24/89)   **[981]**

982   Argentina

6146   Crassweller, Robert O. *Perón and the Enigmas of Argentina.* **1988, Norton paper $12.95** (0-393-30543-0). A portrait of the former Argentine president. "Biography-as-history in the best sense of the term . . . the best single-volume history of 20th century Argentina."—NYTBR (Rev: Choice 6/87; LJ 1/87; NYTBR 1/18/87)   **[982]**

6147   Crawley, Eduardo. *A House Divided: Argentina, 1880–1980.* **1984, St. Martin's $35.00** (0-312-39254-0). A survey of Argentine history from 1880 through the Falklands/Malvinas War. (Rev: Choice 4/85; LJ 2/1/85; TLS 8/2/85)   **[982]**

983   Chile

6148   Constable, Pamela, and Arturo Valenzuela. *A Nation of Enemies: Chile Under Pinochet.* **1991, Norton $24.95** (0-393-03011-3). A chronicle of the political career and social impact of the Chilean dictator Pinochet from 1973 to 1989 based on interviews with citizens who lived under his rule. (Rev: LJ 8/91; NYTBR 10/20/91; PW 7/25/91. Awards: BL, 1991)   **[983]**

6149   Davis, Nathaniel. *Last Two Years of Salvador Allende.* **1985, Cornell Univ. Pr. $28.50** (0-8014-1791-0). A study of the political career and assassination of the Chilean president as seen by the U.S. ambassador to Chile during that era. (Rev: Choice 9/85; LJ 4/1/85; NYTBR 6/30/85)   **[983]**

6150 Garcia Marquez, Gabriel. *Clandestine in Chile: The Adventures of Miguel Littin.* 1987, Henry Holt $13.95 (0-8050-0322-3). The Colombian writer tells the story of a Chilean filmmaker's efforts to expose the excesses of the Pinochet regime. "The best reportage available about conditions in Chile today."—PW (Rev: BL 5/15/87; CSM 9/4/87; PW 5/15/87)　**[983]**

6151 Meiselas, Susan, ed. *Chile: From Within, 1973–1988.* 1990, Norton $39.95 (0-393-02817-8); paper $19.95 (0-393-30653-4). A collection of photographs by 16 Chileans documenting life under the dictatorship of General Pinochet. "An extraordinary visual memoir."—NYTBR (Rev: BL 3/15/91; LJ 4/1/91; NYTBR 2/24/91)　**[983]**

6152 Politzer, Patricia. *Fear in Chile: Lives Under Pinochet.* 1989, Pantheon $19.95 (0-394-56476-6). Fourteen interviews with Chileans detailing the climate of fear and uncertainty under the regime of General Pinochet. (Rev: BL 11/1/89; LJ 11/1/89; NYTBR 12/10/89)　**[983]**

6153 Timerman, Jacobo. *Chile: Death in the South.* 1987, Knopf $15.95 (0-394-53838-2); Random paper $6.95 (0-679-72012-X). A study of repression and human rights violations practiced under the dictatorship of Chile's General Augusto Pinochet. (Rev: Choice 7–8/88; LJ 1/88; NYTBR 1/10/88)　**[983]**

985 Peru

6154 Bode, Barbara. *No Bells to Toll: Destruction and Creation in the Andes.* 1989, Macmillan $27.50 (0-684-19065-6); Paragon House paper $14.95 (1-55778-389-6). A study of the 1970 Peruvian earthquake and avalanche and its effects upon the people of the region that was devastated. (Rev: BL 6/15/89; NYTBR 8/13/89; PW 6/2/89)　**[985]**

6155 Hemming, John. *Conquest of the Incas.* 1973, Harcourt paper $17.95 (0-15-622300-7). The history of the collapse of the Incan empire from its first contact with the Spanish in 1527 to the death of the last Inca king in 1610. (Rev: LJ 10/15/70; NYRB 11/5/70; TLS 12/18/70)　**[985]**

6156 Morrison, Tony, and Gerald S. Hawkins. *Mystery of the Nasca Lines.* 1987, Antique Collectors' Club $29.50 (1-869901-06-1). The authors present their research and theories regarding the mysterious figures on the Nasca plain of Peru depicting animals and strange designs. "Expertly written, superbly illustrated, riveting."—PW (Rev: LJ 4/15/79; NYTBR 4/22/79; PW 3/5/79)　**[985]**

986 Colombia and Ecuador

6157 Lourie, Peter. *Sweat of the Sun, Tears of the Moon: A Chronicle of an Incan Treasure.* 1991, Macmillan $19.95 (0-689-12111-3). A chronicle of the author's search for a hidden Incan treasure in the Ecuadoran Andes. (Rev: BL 3/1/91; NYTBR 6/9/91; PW 2/1/91)　**[986]**

Ecuador

6158 Miller, Tom. *Panama Hat Trail: A Journey to South America.* 1988, Random paper $6.95 (0-394-75774-2). An overview of the Panama hat industry in Ecuador from straw harvesting to the marketplace. (Rev: CSM 9/16/86; LJ 7/86; PW 6/6/86)　**[986.6]**

987 Venezuela

6159 Good, Kenneth, and David Chanoff. *Into the Heart: One Man's Pursuit of Love and Knowledge among the Yanomama.* 1991, Simon & Schuster $21.95 (0-671-72874-1). An account of the author's experiences living and working among the Yanomama Indian tribe of South America. (Rev: BL 12/15/90; LJ 1/15/91; PW 11/16/90)　**[987]**

Uruguay

6160 Weschler, Lawrence. *A Miracle, a Universe: Settling Accounts with Torturers.* 1990, Pantheon $22.95 (0-394-58207-1). An account of the use of torture by the military regimes of Uruguay and Brazil against political enemies during the 1960s and 1970s. (Rev: BL 4/1/90; LJ 3/15/90; NYTBR 4/15/90)　**[989.5]**

990　GENERAL HISTORY OF OTHER AREAS

994　Australia

6161 Colebrook, Joan. *House of Trees: Memoirs of an Australian Childhood.* 1987, Farrar $18.95 (0-374-17310-9); Penguin paper $7.95 (0-14-011482-3). Memoirs of the author's childhood in northern Australia during the 1920s. (Rev: LJ 11/1/87; NYTBR 1/17/88; PW 10/23/87)　**[994]**

6162 Hughes, Robert. *Fatal Shore: The Epic of Australia's Founding.* 1986, Knopf $24.95 (0-394-50668-5); Random paper $12.95 (0-394-75366-6). The history of the development of Australia, written by the author of *The Shock of the New.* "Mr. Hughes tells a story that has epic range and the fascination of a great adventure."—NYTBR (Rev: Atl 1/87; LJ 11/1/86; Time 2/2/87. Awards: BL, the 1980s; LJ, 1987; NYTBR, 1987; Time, 1987)　**[994]**

6163 Morgan, Sally. *My Place: An Aborigine's Stubborn Quest for Her Truth, Heritage and Origins.* 1988, Henry Holt $19.95 (0-8050-0911-6); Arcade paper $9.95 (1-55970-054-8). An autobiography of an Australian aborigine detailing her search for her roots and for the culture of her people. (Rev: LJ 10/1/88; NYTBR 2/19/89; TLS 1/1/88)　**[994]**

6164 Terrill, Ross. *Australians.* 1988, Simon & Schuster paper $8.95 (0-671-66239-2). A survey of the people, land, history, and culture of Australia by the Melbourne-born author of *The White Boned Demon.* (Rev: Atl 9/87; BL 9/1/87; LJ 8/87)　**[994]**

996　Other parts of Pacific　　Polynesia

6165 Irvine, Lucy. *Castaway: A Story of Survival.* 1985, Dell paper $4.50 (0-440-11069-6). An account of the author's year on a remote South Pacific island with a gentleman she met through a London newspaper advertisement. (REV: BL 3/1/84; LJ 4/1/84; NYTBR 4/8/84)   **[996]**

South Central Pacific

6166   Howarth, David. *Tahiti: A Paradise Lost.* 1985, Penguin paper $7.95 (0-14-008095-3). A history of the European presence in Tahiti from 1767 to the present. (REV: BL 11/1/83; LJ 12/1/83; NYTBR 1/22/84)
[996.2]

997   Atlantic Ocean islands

6167   Hastings, Max, and Simon Jenkins. *Battle for the Falklands.* 1984, Norton paper $10.95 (0-393-30198-2). An examination of the war between Great Britain and Argentina over control of the Falkland/Malvina Islands. "No future history of the war will

be written without reference to this superb account."—PW (REV: Newsweek 7/4/83; PW 4/29/83; Time 8/8/83)   **[997]**

998   Arctic islands and Antarctica

6168   Counter, S. Allen. *North Pole Legacy: Black, White and Eskimo.* 1991, Univ. of Massachusetts Pr. $24.95 (0-87023-736-5). An account of the author's search for living relatives of Arctic explorers Matthew A. Henson and Robert E. Peary. (REV: BL 5/15/91; LJ 5/1/91; NYTBR 6/30/91)   **[998]**

6169   Guttridge, Leonard F. *Icebound: The Jeannette Expedition's Quest for the North Pole.* 1986, Naval Institute Pr. $24.95 (0-87021-330-X); Paragon House paper $9.95 (0-913729-99-X). An account of an 1870 expedition to the North Pole that ended in disaster. (REV: Choice 1/87; LJ 6/1/86; NYTBR 8/10/86)
[998]

PART TWO

FICTION

BIOGRAPHICAL FICTION

6170 Ackroyd, Peter. *Chatterton*. 1987, Grove-Weidenfeld $17.95 (0-8021-0041-4); paper $8.95 (0-345-35822-8). A contemporary literary researcher studying the life of eighteenth-century English poet Thomas Chatterton forms the basis for this sweeping novel that covers events in three centuries. "Skillful, engaging, thought-provoking."—LJ (Rev: LJ 1/88; New Rep 2/22/88; Time 1/18/88)

6171 Alexander, Lynne. *Safe Houses*. 1987, Dell paper $4.50 (0-440-17640-9). A fictionalized account dramatizing Raoul Wallenberg's activities to save and house World War II refugees. (Rev: LJ 10/15/85; NYTBR 12/22/85; TLS 7/5/85)

6172 Ballard, J. G. *Kindness of Women*. 1991, Farrar $19.95 (0-374-18110-1). A sequel to *Empire of the Sun* recording the fictionalized life of the author during the three decades following World War II. "A piercingly honest, vibrant record of a very contemporary life."—PW (Rev: BL 8/91; LJ 9/1/91; PW 7/25/91)

6173 Booth, Martin. *Dreaming of Samarkand*. 1990, Morrow $19.95 (0-688-09529-1). A fictionalized account of the life of James E. Flecker, poet, playwright, novelist, politician, and friend of T. E. Lawrence. (Rev: LJ 4/15/90; NYTBR 7/1/90; PW 3/9/90)

6174 Buechner, Frederick. *Brendan*. 1988, Harper & Row paper $8.95 (0-06-061178-2). A history of the life and times of St. Brendan the Navigator, set in Ireland in the fifth and sixth centuries. (Rev: BL 5/15/87; LJ 6/1/87; PW 4/10/87)

6175 Buechner, Frederick. *Godric*. 1983, Harper & Row paper $8.95 (0-06-061162-6). A tale of the life of the twelfth-century English saint. (Rev: LJ 1/15/81; NYTBR 11/23/80; Newsweek 11/10/80)

6176 Bukowski, Charles. *Hollywood*. 1989, Black Sparrow $20.00 (0-87685-764-0); paper $11.00 (0-87685-763-2). An autobiographical novel regarding the filming of the motion picture *Barfly*. (Rev: LJ 5/15/89; NYTBR 6/11/89; TLS 8/11/89)

6177 Burroughs, William S. *Last Words of Dutch Schultz: A Fiction in the Form of a Film Script*. 1987, Seaver paper $4.95 (0-8050-0179-4). An illustrated screenplay concerning the life of Prohibition Era gangster Dutch Schultz. (Rev: Choice 4/76; LJ 6/1/75; NYTBR 6/22/75)

6178 Chase-Riboud, Barbara. *Sally Hemings*. 1980, Avon paper $4.95 (0-380-48686-5). An account of the life of Thomas Jefferson's black mistress and mother of five of his children. (Rev: LJ 6/15/79; New Rep 7/7/79; PW 4/23/79)

6179 Cheuse, Alan. *The Light Possessed*. 1990, Gibbs Smith $19.95 (0-87905-363-1); HarperCollins paper $9.95 (0-06-097411-7). A fictionalized account of the life of American artist Georgia O'Keeffe. (Rev: BL 9/1/90; Choice 2/91; PW 8/31/90)

6180 Childress, Mark. *Tender*. 1990, Crown $19.95 (0-517-57603-1). A fictionalized account of the life of Elvis Presley. "A realistic, moving account of the early days of rock 'n' roll."—LJ (Rev: BL 9/15/90; LJ 9/1/90; PW 7/20/90)

6181 Colegate, Isabel. *Deceits of Time*. 1988, Viking $17.95 (0-670-82400-3); Penguin paper $7.95 (0-14-012768-2). A fictionalized account of the life of Neil Campion, a former British flying ace in World War I who turned to politics after the war. (Rev: BL 10/15/88; New Yorker 1/23/89; PW 9/16/88)

6182 DeLillo, Don. *Libra*. 1988, Viking $19.95 (0-670-82317-1); Penguin paper $4.95 (0-451-82210-2). A fictional life of Lee Harvey Oswald and how he became involved in the assassination of President Kennedy. "The richest novel so far by Don DeLillo."—NYTBR (Rev: NYRB 7/24/88; NYTBR 7/24/88; PW 7/1/88. Awards: ALA, 1988; NYTBR, 1988; PW, 1988))

6183 Duras, Marguerite. *The Lover*. 1987, Simon & Schuster $14.95 (0-671-64105-0); Harper & Row paper $8.95 (0-06-097040-5). The fictionalized memoirs of the author's life in French Indochina prior to World War II. "A small masterpiece."—LJ (Rev: BL 6/1/85; LJ 6/1/85; NYBR 6/27/85. Awards: ALA, 1985))

6184 Epstein, Leslie. *King of the Jews*. 1989, Summit paper $8.95 (0-671-69003-5). A fictionalized account of the life of Mordechai Chaim Rumkowski who attempted to govern the Jewish ghetto of Lodz, Poland, under Nazi occupation. (Rev: BL 2/

15/79; NYTBR 2/15/79; PW 12/11/78. Awards: ALA, 1979; NYTBR, 1979))

6185   Ernaux, Annie. *A Woman's Story.* 1991, Four Walls Eight Windows $15.95 (0-941423-51-4). A fictionalized account of the author's mother's struggle with Alzheimer's disease. (Rev: BL 4/15/91; LJ 4/1/91; PW 3/8/91)

6186   Figes, Eva. *Light.* 1984, Ballantine paper $3.50 (0-345-31898-6). A fictionalized portrait of the last years of French artist Claude Monet. (Rev: LJ 11/15/83; NYTBR 10/16/83; PW 8/26/83)

6187   Garrett, George. *Death of the Fox.* 1985, Morrow paper $11.95 (0-688-03464-0). A portrait of the last hours of Sir Walter Raleigh with flashbacks to key moments in the life of the Renaissance man. (Rev: NYTBR 9/26/71; Newsweek 9/20/71; Sat Rev 10/29/71. Awards: ALA, 1971))

6188   Gould, Lois. *La Presidenta.* 1989, Farrar paper $8.95 (0-374-52180-8). A fictionalized account of the life of Argentine political figure Eva Peron. (Rev: LJ 5/15/81; PW 3/27/81)

6189   Griffiths, Paul. *Myself and Marco Polo.* 1990, Random $17.95 (0-394-58296-9). A fictionalized account of the life and times of the thirteenth-century Italian explorer as related by his cell-mate while imprisoned in a Genoese jail. (Rev: BL 2/15/90; LJ 3/1/90; PW 1/12/90)

6190   Hagerfors, Lennart. *Whales in Lake Tanganyika.* 1989, Grove-Weidenfeld $16.95 (0-8021-1095-9). A fictionalized account of explorer Henry Stanley's expedition to find missing missionary David Livingstone. (Rev: Choice 2/90; LJ 4/1/89; Newsweek 5/8/89)

6191   Hansen, Brooks, and Nick Davis. *Boone.* 1990, Summit $19.95 (0-671-68108-7). A fictionalized account of the life of British entertainer Eton Arthur Boone. (Rev: BL 6/15/90; NYTBR 8/5/90)

6192   Herr, Michael. *Walter Winchell.* 1990, Knopf $18.95 (0-394-58372-8). A fictionalized account of the life of the American journalist by the author of the Vietnam classic *Dispatches.* (Rev: BL 3/1/90; NYTBR 5/20/90; Newsweek 4/23/90)

6193   Kanturkova, Eva. *My Companions in the Bleak House.* 1987, Overlook $19.95 (0-87951-289-X). An autobiographical novel focusing on the author's political imprisonment in a Prague prison. (Rev: LJ 11/15/87; NYTBR 12/13/87; PW 10/2/87)

6194   Kennedy, William P. *Legs.* 1983, Penguin paper $7.95 (0-14-006484-2). A fictional biography of Jack "Legs" Diamond, an Albany lawyer who turned to bootlegging during the Prohibition years. (Rev: BL 5/1/75; New Rep 5/24/75; Newsweek 6/23/75)

6195   Kim, Richard E. *Lost Names: Scenes from a Boyhood in Japanese-Occupied Korea.* 1988, Universe $14.95 (0-87663-678-4). A fictionalized portrait of the author's youth during the 1930s and 1940s in Korea under Japanese occupation. (Rev: BL 10/1/70; LJ 6/15/70; Sat Rev 8/22/70)

6196   Kundera, Milan. *Book of Laughter and Forgetting.* 1987, Penguin paper $7.95 (0-14-009693-0). An autobiographical novel tracing the author's life in Czechoslovakia and the events that led to his departure in 1975. (Rev: New Rep 12/20/80; NYTBR 11/30/80; Newsweek 11/24/80)

6197   Lawrence, D. H. *Mr. Noon.* 1984, Cambridge Univ. Pr. $24.95 (0-521-25251-2); Penguin paper $8.95 (0-14-008341-3). An unfinished autobiographical novel Lawrence worked on during the 1920s concerning his European travels and the beginnings of his relationship with his future wife, Frieda. (Rev: Choice 3/85; New Rep 12/10/84; NYTBR 12/16/84)

6198   Leffland, Ella. *The Knight, Death and the Devil.* 1990, Morrow $22.95 (0-688-05836-1). A fictional biography of Nazi second-in-command and World War I hero Hermann Goering. (Rev: BL 12/1/89; LJ 2/1/90; PW 12/1/89)

6199   Mailer, Norman. *Executioner's Song.* 1979, Little, Brown $25.00 (0-316-54417-5). A fictional re-creation of the life, murder trial, and execution of Gary Gilmore. (Rev: New Rep 10/27/79; NYTBR 10/7/79; Newsweek 10/1/79. Awards: ALA, 1980; NYTBR, 1979; PP:Fiction, 1980))

6200   Malouf, David. *An Imaginary Life.* 1985, Brazilier paper $6.95 (0-8076-1114-X). A fictitious re-creation of the life of the first-century Roman poet Ovid after he was sentenced to exile in the East by the Emperor Augustus. (Rev: LJ 3/1/78; NYTBR 4/23/78; PW 1/30/78)

6201   Miller, Henry. *Crazy Cock.* 1991, Grove-Weidenfeld $18.95 (0-8021-1412-1). The first publication of an early autobiographical novel by Miller written between 1928 and 1930. (Rev: BL 9/1/91; LJ 9/15/91)

6202   Mullins, Edwin. *Master Painter.* 1989, Doubleday $19.95 (0-385-24371-5). A fictional reconstruction of the life of fifteenth-century Flemish painter Jan van Eyck. (Rev: LJ 4/1/89; PW 2/10/89)

6203   Nevin, David. *Dream West.* 1984, Putnam $17.95 (0-399-12742-9). A fictional account of the life of the nineteenth-century American explorer, soldier, and politician John C. Fremont. (Rev: BL 1/1/84; LJ 12/1/83; PW 11/25/83)

6204   Parini, Jay. *Last Station: A Novel of Tolstoy's Last Year.* 1990, Henry Holt $21.95 (0-8050-1176-5). A fictional study of the turbulent last year of the life of the Russian writer. "An unexpectedly successful and subtle masterpiece."—TLS (Rev: BL 7/90; CSM 8/10/90; TLS 12/28/90)

6205   Renault, Mary. *Praise Singer.* 1988, Random paper $6.95 (0-394-75102-7). The life of the poet Simonides is the basis for this portrait of sixth-century B.C. Greece before it was threatened by the armies of Persia. (Rev: CSM 3/21/79; LJ 10/1/78; TLS 11/23/79)

6206 Roa Bastos, Augusto. *I, The Supreme.* **1986, Knopf $18.95 (0-394-53535-9); Random paper $10.95 (0-394-75264-3).** The Paraguayan novelist's tale of the early ninteenth-century dictator José Gaspar Rodríguez de Francia as told by the ruler from his deathbed. (REV: BL 4/15/86; LJ 4/1/86; NYTBR 4/6/86)

6207 Salisbury, Harrison E. *Gates of Hell.* **1987, Da Capo paper $12.95 (0-306-80309-7).** A fictionalized account of the life of Aleksandr Solzhenitsyn from his experiences in World War II to his imprisonment for antiregime writings. (REV: BL 11/15/75; LJ 10/1/75)

6208 Scott, Joanna. *Arrogance.* **1990, Simon & Schuster $18.45 (0-671-69547-9).** A fictionalized account of the life of Austrian expressionist artist Egon Shiele, set in Vienna in the years prior to World War I. "A dazzling, disturbing collage of a novel."—LJ (REV: BL 7/90; LJ 7/90; NYTBR 8/19/90)

6209 Stone, Irving. *Origin: A Biographical Novel of Charles Darwin.* **1980, Doubleday $14.95 (0-385-12064-8); NAL paper $5.95 (0-451-16810-0).** A fictional biography of Darwin beginning with his selection to be a crew member of the *Beagle.* "A fascinating life, a welcome book."—LJ (REV: LJ 8/80; NYTBR 9/14/80; PW 6/13/80)

6210 Styron, William. *Confessions of Nat Turner.* **1967, Random $24.95 (0-394-42099-3); Bantam paper $4.95 (0-553-26916-X).** A fictional account of the life of the man who led a slave revolt in Virginia during the early 1830s. (REV: LJ 10/1/67; NYRB 10/26/67; Sat Rev 10/7/67. AWARDS: ALA, 1967; NYTBR, 1967; PP:Fiction, 1967))

6211 Tertz, Abram. *Goodnight!* **1989, Viking $22.95 (0-670-80165-8).** An account of Soviet writer Andrei Sinyavsky's childhood and young adulthood and his arrest, trial, and imprisonment for shipping his novels to the West for publication. (REV: BL 9/15/89; NYTBR 12/17/89; Time 12/25/89)

6212 Vidal, Gore. *Burr.* **1988, Ballantine paper $4.95 (0-345-00884-7).** A biographical portrait of the life and times of the former vice-president who was indicted for his participation in the duel that killed Alexander Hamilton. (REV: LJ 11/1/73; Newsweek 11/5/73; Time 11/5/73. AWARDS: ALA, 1973; Time, 1973))

6213 West, Rebecca. *Sunflower.* **1987, Viking $18.95 (0-670-81386-9); Penguin paper $7.95 (0-14-009497-0).** An uncompleted novel by West based on her love for British newspaper magnate Lord Beaverbrook and her affair with H. G. Wells. "A fascinating psychological portrait of female anxiety."—LJ (REV: BL 10/15/86; CSM 2/12/87; LJ 12/86)

6214 West, Rebecca. *This Real Night.* **1986, Penguin paper $6.95 (0-14-008684-6).** A posthumously published autobiographical work about the author's youth. "A fascinating glimpse into a superb stylist's workshop."—LJ (REV: LJ 3/1/85; PW 1/25/85; Time 3/15/85)

6215 Williams, John. *Augustus.* **1979, Penguin paper $6.95 (0-14-005127-9).** A fictional retelling of the life of the Roman Emperor Augustus told through the journals and writings of his friends and family. (REV: LJ 9/1/72; New Yorker 11/25/72; PW 9/18/72. AWARDS: NBA, 1973))

6216 Yourcenar, Marguerite. *Abyss.* **1976, Farrar $15.00 (0-374-10040-3); paper $12.95 (0-374-51666-9).** A fictional portrait of the life and times of the sixteenth-century philosopher Zeno. (REV: Choice 9/76; LJ 9/15/76; Newsweek 6/28/76)

6217 Zeldis, Chayym. *Brothers: A Novel of Supreme Seduction.* **1986, Shapolsky paper $8.95 (0-933503-60-1).** A fictional retelling of the life of Christ as told by his brother. (REV: BL 7/1/76; NYTBR 5/16/76)

6218 Zhang, Xianliang. *Getting Used to Dying.* **1991, HarperCollins $19.95 (0-06-016521-9).** An autobiography of the author's experiences under oppressive Communist Chinese regimes. (REV: BL 12/1/90; LJ 12/90; PW 11/16/90)

DETECTIVE AND MYSTERY FICTION

6219 Abella, Alex. *Killing of the Saints.* 1991, Crown $20.00 (0-517-58509-X). A debut novel chronicling a series of crimes in the Cuban-American community of Los Angeles. (REV: BL 9/1/91; NYTBR 9/29/91; PW 7/19/91)

6220 Adler, Warren. *American Quartet.* 1986, Lynx Books paper $3.95 (1-55802-368-2). A Washington, D.C., policewoman investigates a series of murders with possible ties to a planned political assassination. (REV: LJ 4/1/82; NYTBR 10/17/82)

6221 Aird, Catherine. *Last Respects.* 1986, Bantam paper $2.95 (0-553-25811-7). A pair of detectives investigate the apparent murder of a man found floating dead in a river. (REV: PW 7/30/82; TLS 10/29/82)

6222 Ambler, Eric. *Siege of the Villa Lipp.* 1983, Amereon $19.95 (0-89190-465-4). An Anglo-Argentine tax-loophole expert and extortionist is pursued by a Dutch investigator. "Naturally first-class . . . totally gripping."—LJ (REV: BL 9/15/77; LJ 5/1/77; Time 6/6/77)

6223 Ashford, Jeffrey. *A Crime Remembered.* 1988, St. Martin's $14.95 (0-312-02181-X). An investigation into a contemporary British murder case that seems to have connections with an accidental death that occurred during the Second World War. (REV: BL 9/1/88; PW 7/8/88)

6224 Auster, Paul. *City of Glass.* 1985, Sun & Moon $13.95 (0-940650-52-5); Penguin paper $5.95 (0-14-009731-7). A mystery writer allows himself to be perceived as a real-life detective in this first volume of the author's New York trilogy. (REV: NYTBR 11/3/85; New Yorker 12/30/85; PW 9/20/85)

6225 Auster, Paul. *Ghosts.* 1986, Sun & Moon $12.95 (0-940650-70-3); Penguin paper $5.95 (0-14-009735-X). This second installment of the author's New York trilogy concerns the intertwining lives of two private detectives. "A richly-developed, thought provoking work."—BL (REV: BL 6/15/86; New Yorker 8/18/86; PW 5/16/86)

6226 Babson, Marian. *Murder, Murder, Little Star.* 1988, Bantam paper $3.50 (0-553-27430-8). The cast of a motion picture plots to kill an obnoxious child actress. (REV: BL 3/15/80; LJ 1/1/80; PW 1/11/80)

6227 Babson, Marian. *Twelve Deaths of Christmas.* 1987, Dell paper $3.25 (0-440-19183-1). A London killer stalks the city streets in the days before Christmas. (REV: BL 10/15/80; PW 10/17/80)

6228 Ball, John. *Van: A Tale of Terror.* 1989, St. Martin's $18.95 (0-312-02667-6). A fictional recreation of a series of true murders committed in Southern California, written by the author of *In the Heat of the Night.* (REV: BL 3/1/89; PW 1/6/89)

6229 Barnard, Robert. *At Death's Door.* 1988, Macmillan $15.95 (0-684-19001-X); Dell paper $3.95 (0-440-20448-8). A young English woman is murdered while researching a tell-all biography about her famous actress mother. (REV: BL 9/1/88; LJ 10/1/88; PW 9/2/88)

6230 Barnard, Robert. *Case of the Missing Brontë.* 1986, Dell paper $3.50 (0-440-11108-0). The tale of a murder connected to a handwritten manuscript that may be a lost novel of Emily Brontë's. (REV: BL 6/15/83; NYTBR 11/13/83; PW 6/3/83)

6231 Barnard, Robert. *Cherry Blossom Corpse.* 1988, Dell paper $3.50 (0-440-20178-0). A Scotland Yard detective assists Norwegian police in the investigation of a murder while vacationing in that country. (REV: BL 6/15/87; PW 6/12/87; Time 8/17/87)

6232 Barnard, Robert. *A City of Strangers.* 1990, Macmillan $17.95 (0-684-19192-X). The arson murder of a despicable Yorkshire family follows its announcement of plans to move to a middle-class neighborhood. "As good an example as any of the humorous murder novel at its unpretentious best."—NYTBR (REV: BL 6/15/90; CSM 11/30/90; NYTBR 10/14/90)

6233 Barnard, Robert. *Death and the Chaste Apprentice.* 1989, Macmillan $17.95 (0-684-19002-8). A theatrical performance at an English pub is brought to an abrupt conclusion by the stabbing death of the bar owner. (REV: BL 6/15/89; PW 7/14/89; TLS 12/28/89)

6234 Barnard, Robert. *Death and the Princess.* 1985, Dell paper $3.50 (0-440-12153-1). Scotland Yard superintendent Perry Trethowan is called upon to serve as bodyguard for a princess in England's royal family. (Rev: BL 10/1/82; PW 8/13/82; TLS 7/2/82)

6235 Barnard, Robert. *Death by Sheer Torture.* 1985, Dell paper $3.50 (0-440-11976-6). A detective seeks clues to the death of his father, whose corpse was found strapped to a do-it-yourself torture machine. "A sheer delight."—BL (Rev: BL 3/15/82; LJ 3/1/82; Newsweek 3/22/82)

6236 Barnard, Robert. *Death in a Cold Climate.* 1986, Dell paper $3.50 (0-440-11829-8). Inspector Fergamo searches for clues concerning the death of an Englishman found buried in ice in northern Norway. (Rev: PW 1/30/81; TLS 4/18/80)

6237 Barnard, Robert. *Death of a Literary Widow.* 1981, Dell paper $3.50 (0-440-11821-2). This murder mystery set in a small English town involves an American researcher. "Tops of its kind."—NYTBR (Rev: LJ 12/15/80; NYTBR 1/4/81)

6238 Barnard, Robert. *Death of a Perfect Mother.* 1982, Dell paper $3.50 (0-440-12030-6). A chronicle of the last week in the life of a domineering mother whose children plot her murder. "Will send both chills and chortles through your system."—BL (Rev: BL 9/15/81; Newsweek 10/19/81; PW 7/10/81)

6239 Barnard, Robert. *Death of a Salesperson: And Other Untimely Exits.* 1989, Macmillan $16.95 (0-684-19088-5). A collection of 16 short mysteries by the British writer. "The perfect book to have at hand when time does not permit reading of a full-length mystery."—BL (Rev: BL 12/15/89; LJ 1/90; PW 11/17/89)

6240 Barnard, Robert. *Fête Fatale.* 1985, Macmillan $13.95 (0-684-18469-9); Dell paper $3.95 (0-440-12652-5). An amateur sleuth tracks the killer of a man slain at an annual church festival in a small English town. (Rev: BL 9/15/85; NYTBR 12/22/85; PW 10/4/85)

6241 Barnard, Robert. *A Little Local Murder.* 1989, Dell paper $3.95 (0-440-14882-0). The first American printing of a 1976 British novel about jealousy and murder in a small village about to be the focus of an international radio broadcast. (Rev: BL 3/15/83; LJ 4/1/83; PW 2/11/83)

6242 Barnard, Robert. *Out of the Blackout.* 1985, Macmillan $12.95 (0-684-18282-3); Dell paper $3.95 (0-440-16761-2). A boy who believes himself an orphan discovers clues that may lead to the whereabouts of his living parents. "Wonderful, Dickensian . . . a brilliantly written novel."—BL (Rev: BL 5/1/85; LJ 6/1/85; PW 4/26/85)

6243 Barnard, Robert. *Political Suicide.* 1986, Macmillan $13.95 (0-684-18625-X); Dell paper $3.95 (0-440-16946-1). The death of a British Parliament member finds Scotland Yard detectives investigating his political rivals as suspects in the case. (Rev: BL 2/1/86; New Yorker 7/14/86; PW 2/17/86)

6244 Barnard, Robert. *A Scandal in Belgravia.* 1991, Macmillan $17.95 (0-684-19322-1). A British cabinet minister turns sleuth following his retirement to investigate the murder of a former colleague. "Great stuff."—LJ (Rev: BL 8/91; LJ 7/91; PW 6/7/91)

6245 Barnard, Robert. *School for Murder.* 1985, Dell paper $3.50 (0-440-17605-0). The murder of an abusive schoolboy in an English prep school spurs an investigation. (Rev: CSM 4/12/84; LJ 3/1/84; NYTBR 3/25/84)

6246 Barnard, Robert. *Skeleton in the Grass.* 1988, Macmillan $15.95 (0-684-18948-8); Dell paper $43.95 (0-440-20327-9). This novel by the popular British mystery writer involves an investigation into the persecution of an English pacifist falsely accused of the murder of a child during the 1930s. "Superior work from a talented writer."—LJ (Rev: BL 3/1/88; LJ 5/1/88; TLS 7/22/88)

6247 Barnes, Linda. *Coyote.* 1990, Delacorte $17.95 (0-385-30012-3). A private investigator's search for an immigrant's working papers uncovers a series of murders of Salvadoran women. (Rev: BL 9/1/90; LJ 10/1/90)

6248 Barnes, Linda. *Snake Tattoo.* 1989, St. Martin's $17.95 (0-312-02643-9); Ballantine paper $3.95 (0-449-21759-0). A female private investigator seeks the whereabouts of a teenage runaway who turned to prostitution. (Rev: BL 2/1/89; LJ 2/1/89; PW 1/6/89)

6249 Barnes, Linda. *A Trouble of Fools.* 1988, Fawcett paper $3.50 (0-449-21640-3). A female Boston private eye searches for a woman's missing brother and uncovers possible connections to the IRA. (Rev: BL 11/1/87; PW 11/6/87)

6250 Barth, Richard. *Blood Doesn't Tell.* 1989, St. Martin's $15.95 (0-312-02547-5); Fawcett paper $3.95 (0-449-21797-3). An amateur detective in his 70s discovers a baby-selling scheme after he attempts to adopt a son. (Rev: BL 3/1/89; PW 2/10/89)

6251 Barth, Richard. *Condo Kill.* 1985, Macmillan $13.95 (0-684-18474-5). A landlord-tenant disagreement over a potential development project leads to murder. (Rev: BL 11/15/85; PW 10/4/85)

6252 Baxt, George. *Tallulah Bankhead Murder Case.* 1988, International Polygonics paper $5.75 (0-930330-89-7). A HUAC informer is found shot to death in this mystery set in the early 1950s and featuring many Hollywood celebrities as characters. (Rev: BL 11/15/87; PW 10/16/87; Time 2/1/88)

6253 Bayer, William. *Blind Side.* 1989, Random $18.95 (0-394-57257-2); NAL paper $4.95 (0-451-16664-7). A journalist/photographer searches for a missing model whose roommate has been murdered. (Rev: BL 4/15/89; PW 4/7/89)

6254 Bayer, William. *Pattern Crimes.* 1988, NAL paper $4.95 (0-451-15281-6). A Jerusalem detective investigating a series of murders unveils a terrorist plot to destroy the Dome of the Rock. (Rev: BL 3/15/87; LJ 4/1/87; PW 3/6/87)

6255 Bayer, William. *Peregrine.* **1988, Ballantine paper $3.50 (0-345-00755-7).** A New York newscaster becomes involved with a man who trains falcons to kill following the capture on film of a bird attacking a young girl at Rockefeller Center. (REV: BL 10/15/81; PW 7/17/81. AWARDS: Edgar, 1981)

6256 Bayer, William. *Switch.* **1984, Simon & Schuster $13.95 (0-317-05158-X); NAL paper $4.95 (0-451-15356-1).** A New York police detective searches for clues to the murders of two women whose heads were severed and found with the other's torso. "An excellent police procedural, well written and perfectly paced."—LJ (REV: BL 6/15/84; LJ 6/1/84; PW 5/4/84)

6257 Beaton, M. C. *Death of a Gossip.* **1988, Ivy Books paper $2.95 (0-8041-0226-0).** The death of a gossip columnist at a Scottish fishing school is investigated by Detective Macbeth. (REV: BL 3/1/85; PW 2/15/85)

6258 Beaton, M. C. *Death of a Hussy.* **1990, St. Martin's $14.95 (0-312-05071-2).** A mystery set in the Scottish Highlands about an investigation into the death of a woman with four suitors seeking her hand in marriage. (REV: BL 11/1/90; NYTBR 12/30/90; PW 10/19/90)

6259 Beaton, M. C. *Death of a Perfect Wife.* **1989, St. Martin's $15.95 (0-312-03322-2).** A Scottish detective investigates the murder of a woman leading an anti-smoking and health food campaign. (REV: BL 11/15/89; NYTBR 12/10/89; PW 10/29/89)

6260 Beck, K. K. *Body in the Volvo.* **1987, Walker $16.95 (0-8027-5685-9); Ivy paper $3.50 (0-8041-0371-2).** A Seattle auto repairman discovers his boss's body in the trunk of a Volvo. (REV: LJ 11/1/87; NYTBR 12/6/87)

6261 Beinhart, Larry. *No One Rides for Free.* **1987, Avon paper $3.95 (0-380-70283-5).** This debut novel concerns a New York attorney's testimony to the Securities Exchange Commission about a financial scandal to avoid serving a jail sentence. "A superior crime novel."—LJ (REV: BL 1/15/86; LJ 2/1/86; PW 12/6/85)

6262 Bellak, George. *Third Friday.* **1988, Morrow $18.95 (0-688-04399-2).** A businessman investigates the falling death of his partner, deemed a suicide by law enforcement authorities. (REV: BL 3/15/88; LJ 3/1/88)

6263 Belsky, Dick. *One for the Money.* **1986, Academy Chicago paper $4.95 (0-89733-221-0).** A New York sleuth/reporter investigates the circumstances surrounding the death of an aspiring actress. (REV: BL 9/15/85; CMS 10/22/85)

6264 Blain, W. Edward. *Passion Play.* **1990, Putnam $19.95 (0-399-13528-6).** A series of murders takes place at an exclusive Virginia boarding school while students prepare for a Shakespeare production. (REV: BL 2/15/90; LJ 3/1/90; PW 2/9/90)

6265 Bloch, Robert. *Night of the Ripper.* **1986, Tor paper $3.50 (0-8125-0070-9).** A fictional reassessment of the crimes of Jack the Ripper as told by the author of *Psycho.* (REV: BL 10/1/84; PW 7/27/84)

6266 Block, Lawrence. *Burglar in the Closet.* **1986, Pocket paper $3.50 (0-671-61704-4).** A burglar happens upon a murder while robbing a New York apartment and hides in the closet to escape detection. "A good time is guaranteed."—NYTBR (REV: BL 7/15/78; LJ 8/78; NYTBR 11/19/78)

6267 Block, Lawrence. *Burglar Who Liked to Quote Kipling.* **1986, Pocket paper $3.50 (0-671-61831-8).** Burglar Bernie Rhodenbarr is arrested in connection with a murder he stumbled upon while trying to steal a rare book. (REV: BL 10/15/79; NYTBR 11/4/79; PW 8/6/79)

6268 Block, Lawrence. *Burglar Who Painted Like Mondrian.* **1986, Pocket paper $3.50 (0-671-49581-X).** Burglar Bernie Rhodenbarr becomes involved in a murder while committing a burglary to raise ransom money to free his girlfriend's cat. (REV: LJ 9/1/83; New Yorker 1/2/84; PW 7/1/83)

6269 Block, Lawrence. *Eight Million Ways to Die.* **1989, Jove paper $3.95 (0-515-08090-X).** Private investigator Matthew Scudder searches for a prostitute's killer in the streets of New York. "An interesting and even superior book."—NYTBR (REV: BL 9/15/82; NYTBR 8/22/82; PW 6/25/82)

6270 Block, Lawrence. *Out on the Cutting Edge.* **1989, Morrow $17.95 (0-688-09069-9); Avon paper $4.95 (0-380-70993-7).** Detective Scudder investigates the case of a missing actress and the apparent suicide of an acquaintance. (REV: BL 9/1/89; NYTBR 10/15/89; PW 8/18/89)

6271 Block, Lawrence. *Stab in the Dark.* **1989, Jove paper $3.50 (0-515-09885-X).** A New York detective forced into retirement takes on the case of a young woman who was murdered nearly a decade before. (REV: NYTBR 11/29/81; PW 8/14/81)

6272 Block, Lawrence. *A Ticket to the Boneyard.* **1990, Morrow $18.95 (0-688-09070-2).** Matt Scudder becomes involved in the investigation of a series of murders of New York women. "As near perfect as a private eye thriller can get."—PW (REV: BL 8/90; PW 7/6/90)

6273 Block, Lawrence. *When the Sacred Ginmill Closes.* **1990, Jove paper $3.95 (0-515-10278-4).** Alcoholic private investigator Matt Scudder investigates the murder of a New York salesman's wife in this tale by the author of *Eight Million Ways to Die.* (REV: BL 3/1/86; LJ 4/1/86; PW 2/28/86)

6274 Bond, Michael. *Monsieur Pamplemousse.* **1986, Fawcett paper $2.95 (0-449-20956-3).** The author of the Paddington Bear children's book presents the first in a series of detective stories featuring a retired French sleuth turned gourmet. "A wonderfully wacky whodunit."—BL (REV: BL 3/15/85; PW 2/8/85)

6275 Bond, Michael. *Monsieur Pamplemousse Aloft.* **1989, Fawcett $14.95 (0-449-90455-5).** A former Parisian police inspector turned gourmet becomes embroiled in a mystery in a small French seaside resort housing a diplomatic conference between French and English officials. (Rev: BL 9/15/89; PW 7/28/89)

6276 Bond, Michael. *Monsieur Pamplemousse and the Secret Mission*. 1987, Fawcett paper $3.95 (0-449-21128-2). Gourmet sleuth Pamplemousse and his bloodhound assistant investigate a hotel whose food is said to produce rampant sexual desire following consumption. "A deliciously racy caper."—BL (Rev: BL 2/1/86; LJ 2/1/86; PW 12/20/85)

6277 Borthwick, J. S. *Student Body*. 1987, St. Martin's paper $3.50 (0-312-90738-9). The story of the investigation into the death of a graduate student found encased in an artwork at a Maine college. (Rev: BL 10/1/86; LJ 10/1/86; PW 8/22/86)

6278 Bottoms, David. *Easter Weekend*. 1990, Houghton $17.95 (0-395-51528-9). A kidnapping plot in Macon, Georgia, leads to murder in this author's second novel. (Rev: BL 2/1/90; LJ 2/1/90; PW 12/22/89)

6279 Boyer, Rick. *Billingsgate Shoal*. 1982, Houghton $11.95 (0-395-32041-0); Ivy Books paper $3.95 (0-8041-0551-0). A Massachusetts dentist torn by guilt over an accidental drowning is plagued by a series of strange incidents once he begins investigating the tragedy. (Rev: LJ 5/1/82; NYTBR 10/3/82; PW 3/12/82. Awards: Edgar, 1982))

6280 Boyer, Rick. *Daisy Ducks*. 1988, Ivy Books paper $3.50 (0-8041-0293-7). A Boston dentist and his friends seek to regain a fortune hidden in Hong Kong by a group of Vietnam commandos. (Rev: BL 8/86; LJ 7/86; PW 7/4/86)

6281 Boyer, Rick. *Gone to Earth*. 1990, Fawcett $16.95 (0-440-90556-X). Oral surgeon/sleuth Doc Adams is pursued by tough characters after investigating the deaths of four bikers. (Rev: BL 8/90; NYTBR 9/30/90; PW 7/27/90)

6282 Boyle, Thomas. *Brooklyn Three*. 1991, Viking $18.95 (0-670-83019-4). The third volume in the author's trilogy of police procedurals featuring detective Francis De Sales. (Rev: BL 5/15/91; NYTBR 7/7/91)

6283 Boyle, Thomas. *Only the Dead Know Brooklyn*. 1985, Godine $15.95 (0-87923-565-9); Penguin paper $3.50 (0-14-009257-9). Brooklyn investigators search for an abducted university professor held by a radical group demanding educational reforms. (Rev: LJ 7/85; PW 6/14/85)

6284 Bradbury, Ray. *Death Is a Lonely Business*. 1985, Knopf $15.95 (0-394-54702-0); Bantam paper $3.95 (0-553-26447-8). This mystery, concerning the investigation into a series of 1950s Venice Beach murders, was Bradbury's first nonscience fiction novel in a quarter-century. (Rev: BL 9/1/85; LJ 10/1/85; PW 8/23/85)

6285 Brautigan, Richard. *Dreaming of Babylon: A Private-Eye Novel 1942*. 1978, Dell paper $4.95 (0-385-28221-4). A San Francisco private-eye investigates the disappearance of a body from the city morgue. "A masterful comedy mixed with pathos."—BL (Rev: BL 11/15/77; LJ 8/77; PW 6/20/77)

6286 Breen, Jon L. *Triple Crown*. 1986, Walker $13.95 (0-8027-5627-1). A radio announcer investigates a series of threatening letters that lead to a murder during horse racing's triple crown. (Rev: BL 2/15/86; LJ 1/86)

6287 Brent, Madeleine. *Golden Urchin*. 1987, Fawcett paper $3.95 (0-449-21389-7). An English girl brought up by Australian aborigines escapes from the tribe only to find herself being trailed by a man who seeks to kill her. (Rev: BL 2/15/87; CSM 3/6/87; PW 12/19/86)

6288 Brett, Simon. *Dead Giveaway*. 1987, Dell paper $3.50 (0-440-11914-6). The murder of the master of ceremonies of a television quiz show occurs while actor/detective Charles Paris is on the set. (Rev: BL 1/1/86; PW 1/10/86; TLS 9/19/86)

6289 Brett, Simon. *Dead Romantic*. 1988, Dell paper $3.50 (0-440-20043-1). The story of a love triangle that leads to the murder of one of the participants. "A dazzlingly tricky mystery, sure to fool the sharpest clue trackers."—PW (Rev: BL 4/1/86; PW 5/2/86; Time 7/7/86)

6290 Brett, Simon. *Mrs. Presumed Dead*. 1989, Macmillan $17.95 (0-684-18851-1); Dell paper $3.95 (0-440-20552-2). Sleuth Melita Pargeter searches to find the former owner of her suburban home. "Delivers solid mystery, deft characterization and delightful entertainment."—PW (Rev: BL 2/15/89; LJ 4/1/89; PW 3/24/89)

6291 Brett, Simon. *A Nice Class of Corpse*. 1990, Dell paper $3.95 (0-440-20113-6). An investigation follows the robbery of an English woman who fell to her death from her hotel room. (Rev: Atl 2/87; LJ 1/87; NYTBR 3/8/87)

6292 Brett, Simon. *A Series of Murders*. 1989, Macmillan $16.95 (0-684-19096-6). Actor/detective Charles Paris investigates the murder of a cast member of the television series in which he plays a sleuth. (Rev: BL 9/1/89; NYTBR 10/8/89; PW 9/1/89)

6293 Brett, Simon. *A Shock to the System*. 1985, Macmillan $13.95 (0-684-18351-X); Dell paper $3.50 (0-440-18200-X). A corporate officer turns to a life of crime to advance his career. (Rev: BL 4/1/85; PW 3/29/85; TLS 2/15/85)

6294 Brett, Simon. *Tickled to Death and Other Stories of Crime and Suspense*. 1985, Macmillan $13.95 (0-684-18486-9); Dell paper $3.50 (0-440-18541-6). A collection of a dozen mystery stories by the veteran novelist known for his works featuring sleuth/actor Charles Paris. (Rev: BL 9/15/85; PW 7/26/85; Time 11/4/85)

6295 Brett, Simon. *What Bloody Man Is That?* 1989, Dell paper $3.50 (0-440-20344-9). Charles Paris takes multiple roles in a theater production of *Macbeth* in which one of the key players is murdered. "One of the better books in a popular series."—NYTBR (Rev: BL 8/87; NYTBR 10/11/87; TLS 9/18/87)

6296　Browne, Gerald A. *Green Ice.* **1984, Berkley paper $3.95 (0-425-10917-8).** A New Yorker flies to Colombia and steals a shipment of emeralds to bring back to the United States. (Rev: BL 5/15/78; LJ 5/1/78; PW 4/3/78)

6297　Browne, Gerald A. *Stone 588.* **1987, Berkley paper $4.95 (0-425-09884-2).** A precious-stone dealer attempts to retrieve a stolen crystal that has mystical healing capabilities. (Rev: BL 1/1/86; PW 1/17/86)

6298　Browne, Howard. *Scotch on the Rocks.* **1991, St. Martin's $14.95 (0-312-05509-9).** A poor farming family attempts to turn its discovery of a cache of scotch into large sums of money in this tale set during the Prohibition Era. (Rev: BL 1/15/91; PW 1/4/91)

6299　Buchanan, Edna. *Nobody Lives Forever.* **1990, Random $17.95 (0-394-57551-2).** This police procedural about tracking a south Florida serial killer with multiple personalities is the debut novel of a former *Miami Herald* crime reporter. (Rev: LJ 2/1/90; NYTBR 3/18/90; PW 1/5/90)

6300　Bugliosi, Vincent T., and William Stadiem. *Lullaby and Good Night.* **1987, NAL $17.95 (0-453-00570-5); paper $4.95 (0-451-15708-7).** A story based on the 1920s case of a New York woman framed on prostitution charges by her husband after her attempted escape with their child. (Rev: NYTBR 1/24/88; PW 10/7/88)

6301　Burke, James Lee. *Black Cherry Blues.* **1989, Little, Brown $17.95 (0-316-11699-8).** A Dave Robicheaux novel regarding his chase of two murderous thugs who threatened the life of his adopted daughter. (Rev: BL 6/15/89; Newsweek 10/2/89; PW 7/7/89. Awards: Edgar, 1990))

6302　Burke, James Lee. *Heaven's Prisoners.* **1989, Pocket paper $3.95 (0-671-67629-6).** A former New Orleans detective who witnessed a plane crash becomes involved in the investigation of a drug-smuggling ring following false reports of the incident in the media. (Rev: BL 2/15/88; LJ 4/1/88; PW 3/25/88)

6303　Burke, James Lee. *A Morning for Flamingos.* **1990, Little, Brown $18.95 (0-316-11721-8).** An attempt on his life leads Cajun detective Dave Robicheaux to a job working undercover for the Drug Enforcement Administration in New Orleans. (Rev: BL 8/90; New Yorker 1/28/91; PW 8/24/90)

6304　Burke, James Lee. *Neon Rain.* **1988, Pocket paper $3.95 (0-671-65217-6).** A Louisiana homicide detective on a bayou fishing trip finds a body that leads to a search for a drug-running and illicit arms-sale ring. (Rev: BL 1/15/87; LJ 3/1/87; PW 2/13/87)

6305　Burley, W. J. *Wycliffe and the Quiet Virgin.* **1988, Avon paper $2.95 (0-380-70510-9).** Inspector Wycliffe searches for the man who killed a local

woman and abducted his daughter during their Christmas vacation. (Rev: BL 10/15/86; TLS 6/27/86)

6306　Burns, Rex. *Avenging Angel.* **1984, Penguin paper $4.95 (0-14-007104-0).** The clues surrounding a series of Colorado murders whose victims are left holding drawings of an angel lead a detective to investigate a Mormon sect. (Rev: BL 2/15/83; LJ 2/1/83; PW 1/14/83)

6307　Burns, Rex. *Ground Money.* **1986, Viking $15.95 (0-670-80904-7); Penguin paper $3.95 (0-14-008515-7).** Denver detectives investigate the murder of a rodeo rider. "Burns has never written better, and he has never had a better story to tell."—New Yorker (Rev: BL 6/15/86; LJ 6/1/86; New Yorker 6/16/86)

6308　Burns, Rex. *Killing Zone.* **1988, Viking $17.95 (0-670-81955-7); Penguin paper $3.95 (0-14-010532-8).** The investigation into the murder of a Denver politician reveals a history of corruption and adultery. (Rev: BL 3/15/88; PW 3/18/88)

6309　Burns, Rex. *Suicide Season.* **1987, Viking $16.95 (0-670-81540-3).** An investigation into a Denver espionage case leads to a trail of murder and suicide. (Rev: BL 6/1/87; LJ 6/1/87; PW 4/24/87)

6310　Butler, Gwendoline. *Coffin and the Paper Man.* **1991, St. Martin's $16.95 (0-312-05835-7).** This English police procedural traces the investigation of a young man's death in London's docklands. (Rev: BL 6/15/91; PW 5/24/91)

6311　Campbell, Robert. *Alice in La-La Land.* **1988, Pocket paper $3.95 (0-671-66931-1).** Los Angeles private investigator Whistler is hired to protect a television star's self-destructive wife. (Rev: BL 11/1/87; LJ 11/1/87; PW 9/25/87)

6312　Campbell, Robert. *Cat's Meow.* **1988, NAL $16.95 (0-453-00615-9).** A Chicago priest is found murdered in his church amid the remnants of a cult ritual. (Rev: BL 9/1/88; LJ 10/1/88; PW 9/2/88)

6313　Campbell, Robert. *Gift Horse's Mouth.* **1990, Pocket $17.95 (0-671-67586-9).** A detective enters a congressional race in a search for the murderer of the secretary of a Democratic party leader. (Rev: BL 9/15/90; NYTBR 12/23/90; PW 10/12/90)

6314　Campbell, Robert. *In La-La Land We Trust.* **1986, Mysterious $15.95 (0-89296-170-8).** Investigator Whistler witnesses a car crash at Hollywood and Vine that reveals a mysterious body without a head. (Rev: NYTBR 12/28/86; PW 10/23/87)

6315　Campbell, Robert. *Juice.* **1989, Poseidon $18.95 (0-671-66624-X); Pocket paper $4.95 (0-671-67454-4).** A small-time horseplayer in Los Angeles is plagued by organized crime loan collectors. (Rev: BL 2/1/89; NYTBR 5/28/89; PW 2/3/89)

6316　Campbell, Robert. *Junkyard Dog.* **1986, NAL paper $3.95 (0-451-15899-7).** The investigation of a murder at a Chicago abortion clinic leads a detective to organized crime figures. (Rev: BL 7/86; NYTBR 9/14/86; PW 5/23/86)

6317 Campbell, Robert. *Nibbled to Death by Ducks.* **1989, Pocket $17.95 (0-671-67585-0).** A man investigates the drowning of a friend at a rest home in this story by the author of *Junkyard Dog.* (REV: BL 10/15/89; PW 9/29/89)

6318 Campbell, Robert. *The Six Hundred Pound Gorilla.* **1987, NAL paper $3.50 (0-451-15390-1).** A Chicago detective investigates the murders of two men found in a gay bathhouse frequented by a gorilla. "An expert piece of work in which wacky humor and high seriousness are palatably mixed."—NYTBR (REV: BL 1/15/87; NYTBR 5/3/87; PW 1/9/87)

6319 Candy, Edward. *Words for Murder Perhaps.* **1984, Ballantine paper $2.75 (0-345-31952-4).** An English professor is suspected in a series of murders in which poems are left at the scene of the crime. "A classic mystery."—NYTBR (REV: BL 2/1/84; LJ 1/84; NYTBR 3/4/84)

6320 Cannell, Dorothy. *Thin Woman.* **1985, Penguin paper $4.50 (0-14-007947-5).** A woman inherits her wealthy uncle's castle under the condition that she fulfill a list of rigorous requirements. (REV: BL 6/1/84; LJ 7/84; PW 5/4/84)

6321 Caudwell, Sarah. *Sirens Sang of Murder.* **1989, Delacorte $16.95 (0-385-29784-X).** A tax attorney becomes romantically involved with a woman targeted for murder in this story by the author of *The Shortest Way to Hades.* (REV: BL 10/1/89; PW 9/22/89; TLS 9/1/89)

6322 Caudwell, Sarah. *Thus Was Adonis Murdered.* **1982, Penguin paper $3.95 (0-14-006310-2).** English friends attempt to prove through a series of the accused's letters that a friend held in a Venice jail was innocent of a murder. (REV: PW 10/23/81; TLS 4/17/81)

6323 Caunitz, William J. *Black Sand.* **1989, Crown $18.95 (0-517-57226-5).** A Greek policeman joins forces with a New York team searching for stolen antiquities in Manhattan. (REV: BL 12/15/88; NYTBR 4/2/89)

6324 Caunitz, William J. *Suspects.* **1986, Crown $17.95 (0-517-55864-5); Bantam paper $4.95 (0-553-26705-1).** The murder of a Brooklyn policeman and shopkeeper are investigated in this procedural by NYPD Lieutenant Anthony Scanlon. (REV: BL 8/86; NYTBR 9/7/86; PW 6/20/86)

6325 Chandler, Raymond, and Robert B. Parker. *Poodle Springs.* **1989, Putnam $18.95 (0-399-13482-4).** This novel featuring detective Philip Marlowe was left unfinished at Chandler's death and was finished by Robert B. Parker. (REV: Atl 10/89; BL 6/15/89; LJ 7/89)

6326 Chehak, Susan Taylor. *Story of Annie D.* **1989, Houghton $17.95 (0-395-51013-9); Fawcett paper $4.95 (0-449-21885-6).** This debut novel concerns a small-town Nebraska widow who becomes involved in the investigation of the murders of three young women. "Absolutely stunning."—NYTBR (REV: BL 4/15/89; NYTBR 7/9/89; PW 3/31/89)

6327 Chesbro, George C. *Bone.* **1989, Mysterious $17.95 (0-89296-292-5).** An amnesiac homeless man attempts to prove his innocence of a series of murders of street people. (REV: BL 3/1/89; PW 1/27/89)

6328 Christie, Agatha. *Curtain.* **1985, Pocket paper $3.95 (0-671-54717-8).** A posthumously published novel chronicling the events surrounding the death of detective Hercule Poirot. "Will be prized for years to come."—LJ (REV: LJ 8/75; Newsweek 10/6/75; TLS 9/26/75)

6329 Christie, Agatha. *Sleeping Murder.* **1979, Amereon $17.95 (0-88411-387-6); Bantam paper $3.50 (0-553-25678-5).** A posthumously published Christie novel chronicling the final case of Miss Marple and her investigation in an 18-year-old murder case involving a woman strangled by a man with monkey paws. (REV: BL 10/15/76; NYTBR 9/19/76; Time 9/20/76)

6330 Clark, Mary Higgins. *Weep No More, My Lady.* **1988, Dell paper $4.95 (0-440-20098-9).** An investigation follows the death of a noted actress at a posh California health spa. (REV: BL 5/1/87; CSM 8/19/87; NYTBR 6/28/87)

6331 Cleary, Jon. *Dragons at the Party.* **1988, Morrow $17.95 (0-688-07487-1).** A botched assassination attempt on a politician spurs a Sydney detective to investigate. (REV: BL 1/15/88; PW 11/20/87)

6332 Cleary, Jon. *Now and Then, Amen.* **1989, Morrow $18.95 (0-688-08390-0).** An Australian writer's story of the investigation of the murder of a nun whose body was found outside a brothel. (REV: BL 2/15/89; LJ 2/1/89; PW 12/16/88)

6333 Cody, Liza. *Head Case.* **1990, Bantam paper $3.95 (0-553-27645-X).** A British detective searches for a missing teenage girl who is the prime suspect in a murder. (REV: BL 5/1/86; CSM 8/6/86; PW 5/16/86)

6334 Cody, Liza. *Under Contract.* **1990, Bantam paper $3.95 (0-553-28345-6).** A London detective is hired to provide security for a group of depraved rock musicians. (REV: LJ 6/1/87; NYTBR 8/2/87; PW 4/24/87)

6335 Cohan, Tony. *Canary.* **1981, Acrobat Books $13.95 (0-385-17086-6).** The eyewitness to the murder of a female singer is hampered by a police cover-up in this novel detailing practices in the music business. (REV: LJ 7/81; NYTBR 8/2/81; PW 5/1/81)

6336 Colbert, James. *Profit and Sheen.* **1988, Jove paper $3.95 (0-515-09910-4).** A former cop joins forces with a cocaine dealer but is forced to turn himself in to the Drug Enforcement Administration following a murder. (REV: BL 9/1/86; New Yorker 10/13/86; PW 7/18/86)

6337 Collins, Max Allan. *Midnight Haul.* **1990, Knightsbridge paper $4.95 (1-877961-71-X).** A series of mysterious suicides in a New Jersey community leads a journalist to investigate local toxic waste sites. (REV: BL 12/1/86; LJ 11/15/86; NYTBR 2/8/87)

6338   **Collins, Max Allan.** *True Detective.* **1983, St. Martin's $14.95 (0-312-82051-8).** A Chicago private detective searches for a woman's missing brother in this novel set during the 1930s and includes Eliot Ness, Al Capone, and Franklin D. Roosevelt as characters. (REV: BL 1/15/84; LJ 1/84; PW 11/18/83)

6339   **Collins, Michael.** *Castrato.* **1989, Donald I. Fine $17.95 (1-55611-113-4).** A private investigator tries to locate a missing mercenary and suspected drug-runner in a case set in Santa Barbara, California. (REV: BL 3/1/89; LJ 3/1/89; PW 1/20/89)

6340   **Collins, Michael.** *Minnesota Strip.* **1987, Donald I. Fine $17.95 (1-55611-032-4); Harlequin Books paper $3.95 (0-373-97093-5).** One-armed detective Dan Fortune investigates the murder of a child prostitute in Manhattan. (REV: BL 7/87; LJ 7/87; PW 5/29/87)

6341   **Constantine, K. C.** *Always a Body to Trade.* **1983, Godine $13.95 (0-87923-458-X).** Police Chief Martin Balzic's investigation is threatened by the actions of a new mayor. (REV: NYTBR 4/21/85; TLS 10/11/85)

6342   **Constantine, K. C.** *Joey's Case.* **1988, Mysterious $15.95 (0-89296-347-6); paper $4.50 (0-445-40786-7).** Police Chief Martin Balzic investigates the shooting death of the son of a small-town Pennsylvania coal miner. (REV: PW 3/4/88; TLS 12/9/88)

6343   **Constantine, K. C.** *Man Who Liked Slow Tomatoes.* **1982, Godine $13.95 (0-87923-407-5).** A small-town police chief searches for the murderer of a local tomato farmer. "An intelligent, compassionate and moving book, as well as top-notch entertainment."—PW (REV: BL 12/1/81; CSM 7/28/82; PW 12/11/81)

6344   **Constantine, K. C.** *Man Who Liked to Look at Himself.* **1982, Godine $13.95 (0-87923-407-5).** Police Chief Martin Balzic's murder investigation is complicated by a state police officer in this story of a dismemberment killing set in Pennsylvania. (REV: NYTBR 12/23/73; PW 10/29/73)

6345   **Constantine, K. C.** *Rocksburg Railroad Murders.* **1988, Godine paper $3.95 (0-87923-662-0).** Police Chief Martin Balzic investigates the murder of a former schoolmate in this mystery set in Rocksburg, Pennsylvania. (REV: NYTBR 2/11/73; PW 1/1/73)

6346   **Constantine, K. C.** *Upon Some Midnights Clear.* **1985, Godine $15.95 (0-87923-570-5); Penguin paper $3.50 (0-14-009404-0).** Rocksburg, Pennsylvania, Police Chief Martin Balzic investigates a series of crimes on the eve of the Christmas season in this seventh installment of the series. (REV: BL 9/15/85; PW 8/9/85)

6347   **Cook, Thomas H.** *The City When It Rains.* **1990, Putnam $19.95 (0-399-13555-3).** A crime photographer becomes convinced that the alleged suicide of a Manhattan woman was, in fact, a murder. "First-rate crime noir and much more."—LJ (REV: BL 12/15/90; LJ 1/91; PW 12/14/90)

6348   **Cook, Thomas H.** *Flesh and Blood.* **1989, Putnam $17.95 (0-399-13409-3).** A New York private investigator tracking the murderer of an elderly woman traces the woman's family history. (REV: BL 1/1/89; LJ 1/89; PW 10/21/88)

6349   **Cook, Thomas H.** *Sacrificial Ground.* **1988, Putnam $16.95 (0-399-13339-9); Warner paper $4.95 (0-446-35220-9).** An Atlanta policeman searches for the killer of a pregnant teenager. (REV: BL 3/1/88; LJ 3/1/88; PW 1/15/88)

6350   **Cook, Thomas H.** *Streets of Fire.* **1989, Putnam $18.95 (0-399-13490-5).** A story of the murder of an African-American girl in 1963 Alabama and its ramifications. (REV: BL 6/1/89; LJ 8/89; PW 7/7/89)

6351   **Cornwell, Patricia Daniels.** *Body of Evidence.* **1991, Scribner $18.95 (0-684-19240-3).** The death of a romance writer is investigated by medical examiner Dr. Kay Scarpatta for forensic details that may provide clues to the identity of the murderer. (REV: BL 10/1/90; LJ 1/91; PW 12/7/90)

6352   **Cornwell, Patricia Daniels.** *Post-Mortem.* **1990, Macmillan $16.95 (0-684-19141-5).** A Virginia medical examiner looks for clues to the identity of a serial killer/rapist in this debut novel by a former police reporter. (REV: BL 1/15/90; NYTBR 1/7/90)

6353   **Crosby, John.** *Party of the Year.* **1979, Scarborough $9.95 (0-8128-2606-X).** A New York bodyguard is hired to protect the life of an Italian contessa. "His most consistent, brilliantly observed book."—NYTBR (REV: BL 7/15/79; LJ 6/1/79; NYTBR 7/29/79)

6354   **Cross, Amanda.** *Death in a Tenured Position.* **1986, Ballantine paper $4.95 (0-345-34041-8).** A mystery concerning the poisoning death of Harvard's only female English professor. (REV: BL 4/15/81; LJ 4/1/81; PW 2/13/81)

6355   **Cross, Amanda.** *The James Joyce Murder.* **1987, Ballantine paper $3.95 (0-345-34686-6).** Professor Fansler supervises a literary project in the Berkshires and becomes involved in the investigation of a murder. (REV: LJ 5/1/67; PW 1/9/67; TLS 6/29/67)

6356   **Cross, Amanda.** *Poetic Justice.* **1979, Avon paper $3.50 (0-380-44222-1).** A mystery intertwined with studies of English poet W. H. Auden by the author of *The James Joyce Murder.* (REV: BL 7/1/70; LJ 4/1/70; NYTBR 6/21/70)

6357   **Cross, Amanda.** *Question of Max.* **1987, Ballantine paper $3.95 (0-345-35489-3).** A case involving a graduate student studying the work of a late novelist whose body was found near the writer's summer home. (REV: BL 10/15/76; CSM 9/15/76; PW 6/21/76)

6358   **Cross, Amanda.** *Theban Mysteries.* **1979, Avon paper $3.50 (0-380-45021-6).** A mystery set in a New York girls school engaged in the study of the works of Sophocles. (REV: LJ 9/1/71; PW 7/5/71; TLS 4/28/71)

6359   **Cross, Amanda.** *A Trap for Fools.* **1989, Dutton $16.95 (0-525-24754-8); Ballantine paper $4.95**

(0-345-35947-X). Sleuth/professor Kate Fansler seeks the killer of a colleague at New York University. (Rev: BL 4/15/89; Newsweek 4/10/89; PW 2/3/89)

6360   Crumley, James. *Dancing Bear.* **1984, Random paper $6.95 (0-394-72576-X).** A private investigator who is hired to trail a couple becomes the target of hit men in this novel set in Montana and Washington. (Rev: BL 4/15/83; LJ 4/1/83; PW 2/18/83)

6361   Crumley, James. *Wrong Case.* **1985, Random paper $7.95 (0-394-73558-7).** An alcoholic private investigator finds a trail of underworld murders during his search for a client's missing brother. (Rev: BL 7/15/75; LJ 6/1/75; Newsweek 6/23/75)

6362   Curtis, Jack. *Glory.* **1988, Dutton $18.95 (0-525-24668-1); NAL paper $4.50 (0-451-40133-6).** A series of brutal murders are investigated by a policeman. "A first-rate thriller and an excellent choice for pleasure reading."—LJ (Rev: BL 5/15/88; LJ 9/1/88; PW 6/10/88)

6363   Daley, Robert. *Hands of a Stranger.* **1986, NAL paper $4.95 (0-451-16376-1).** A chronicle of the investigation into the rape of a police officer's wife in a Manhattan hotel, by the author of *Prince of the City.* "A sensitive and powerful story."—LJ (Rev: BL 8/85; LJ 8/85; PW 6/28/85)

6364   Daley, Robert. *Man with a Gun.* **1988, Simon & Schuster $18.95 (0-671-61883-0); Pocket paper $4.95 (0-671-67320-3).** The story of a New York deputy police commissioner and his dealings with the press and city politicians. (Rev: BL 1/1/88; New Yorker 5/16/88; PW 12/25/87)

6365   Daniel, Mark. *Unbridled.* **1990, Ticknor & Fields $17.95 (0-89919-922-4).** This author's first novel tells the story of a steeplechase jockey hired by criminals to throw a key race. "A most promising debut."—BL (Rev: BL 1/15/90; NYTBR 2/4/90; PW 11/24/89)

6366   Davis, Dorothy Salisbury. *Habit of Fear.* **1987, Macmillan $17.95 (0-684-18887-2); Harlequin Books paper $3.50 (0-373-26031-8).** A woman recovering from rape and facing the breakup of her marriage travels to Ireland to find the whereabouts of her long-lost father. (Rev: BL 11/15/87; LJ 11/1/87; PW 10/23/87)

6367   Davis, Lindsey. *Shadows in Bronze.* **1991, Crown $19.00 (0-517-57612-0).** A historical mystery set in Rome during the first-century reign of the Emperor Vespasian. (Rev: LJ 3/15/91; PW 2/1/91)

6368   Davis, Lindsey. *Silver Pigs.* **1989, Crown $18.95 (0-517-57363-6).** Detective Falco searches for clues to a series of murders in this novel set in first-century Rome under the reign of the Emperor Vespasian. (Rev: BL 8/89; LJ 9/1/89; TLS 11/17/89)

6369   De Andrea, William L. *Killed in the Ratings.* **1986, Harcourt paper $4.95 (0-15-647050-0).** The story of murder and blackmail set in the competitive world of corporate television. (Rev: BL 4/15/78; LJ 5/1/78; NYTBR 4/2/78)

6370   De Andrea, William L. *Killed on the Rocks.* **1990, Mysterious $17.95 (0-89296-210-0).** Investigator Matt Cobb searches for clues surrounding the murder of a billionaire killed during negotiations for a takeover bid. (Rev: BL 10/15/90; LJ 10/1/90)

6371   Dexter, Colin. *Dead of Jericho.* **1988, Bantam paper $3.95 (0-553-27237-3).** Inspector Morse searches for clues to the hanging death of a pregnant Englishwoman. (Rev: BL 12/15/81; TLS 6/5/81)

6372   Dexter, Colin. *Last Seen Wearing.* **1989, Bantam paper $3.95 (0-553-28003-1).** Inspector Morse searches for the person responsible for the murder of an Oxford teacher and the disappearance of one of her students. (Rev: LJ 7/76; TLS 4/23/76)

6373   Dexter, Colin. *Secret of Annexe Three.* **1988, Bantam paper $3.95 (0-553-27549-6).** Inspector Morse investigates a murder committed on New Year's Eve at an Oxford hotel. (Rev: BL 9/15/87; PW 10/23/87; TLS 4/17/87)

6374   Dexter, Colin. *Service of All the Dead.* **1988, Bantam paper $3.95 (0-553-27239-X).** Inspector Morse searches for the murderer of an English churchwarden who was stabbed to death in his vestry. (Rev: BL 3/15/80; TLS 3/7/80)

6375   Dexter, Colin. *Silent World of Nicholas Quinn.* **1988, Bantam paper $3.95 (0-553-27238-1).** Inspector Morse investigates the murder of a low-level British official. "A classic whodunit in the best British tradition."—PW (Rev: BL 11/15/77; LJ 11/1/77; PW 9/19/77)

6376   Dibdin, Michael. *Vendetta.* **1991, Doubleday $18.50 (0-385-42120-6).** A Venetian inspector becomes the target of Sardinian criminals following his investigation into the murder of an Italian financier. (Rev: BL 11/15/91; PW 9/27/91)

6377   Dickinson, Peter. *Hindsight.* **1984, Pantheon paper $3.95 (0-394-72603-0).** A biographer's research into a writer's life leads a friend to reexamine the circumstances of a teacher's death four decades before. (Rev: BL 11/1/83; PW 9/9/83)

6378   Dickinson, Peter. *Lively Dead.* **1982, Pantheon paper $2.95 (0-394-73317-7).** Two bodies pickled in alcohol are found in an English home in this mystery by the author of *Sleep and His Brother.* (Rev: BL 9/15/75; NYTBR 11/2/75; PW 6/2/75)

6379   Dickinson, Peter. *Old English Peep Show.* **1984, Random paper $3.95 (0-394-76202-2).** Inspector Pibble looks into circumstances surrounding an apparent suicide at a British historical theme park called "Old England." (Rev: CSM 4/17/69; LJ 3/1/69; NYTBR 4/13/69)

6380   Dickinson, Peter. *Skeleton-in-Waiting.* **1989, Pantheon $16.95 (0-394-58002-8).** This novel deals with crimes and scandals surrounding fictitious members of the British royal family. (Rev: BL 11/15/89; LJ 12/89; PW 11/3/89)

6381   Dickinson, Peter. *Sleep and His Brother.* **1986, Pantheon paper $3.95 (0-394-74452-7).** Inspector

Pibble becomes involved in a case involving children who suffer from a mysterious rare disease. (Rev: BL 7/15/71; LJ 4/1/71; New Yorker 6/12/71)

6382 **Doherty, P. C.** *Death of a King.* **1987, Bantam paper $2.95 (0-553-26333-1).** A fourteenth-century English clerk investigates the death of King Edward II. "Beautifully written and thoroughly researched."—PW (Rev: BL 12/15/85; PW 11/15/85)

6383 **Doolittle, Jerome.** *Body Scissors.* **1990, Pocket $17.95 (0-671-70752-3).** A security check on an ambitious politician reveals clues pointing toward a role in the murder of his daughter. (Rev: BL 10/15/90; LJ 9/1/90; PW 9/28/90)

6384 **Douglas, Carole Nelson.** *Good Night, Mr. Holmes.* **1991, Tor $18.95 (0-312-93210-3).** The story of an amateur female sleuth greatly admired by Sherlock Holmes. (Rev: BL 10/15/90; NYTBR 12/16/90; PW 9/28/90)

6385 **Downey, Timothy.** *A Splendid Executioner.* **1988, Ivy paper $2.95 (0-8041-0217-1).** A killer stalks victims from a journalist's list of the worst people of New York City. (Rev: BL 1/1/87; NYTBR 3/29/87)

6386 **Drummond, John Keith.** *'Tis the Season to Be Dying: A Mathilda Worthing Mystery.* **1988, St. Martin's $16.95 (0-312-01901-7).** A mystery set in California regarding the poisoning murder of a wealthy family patriarch. (Rev: LJ 6/1/88; PW 5/6/88)

6387 **Dunlap, Susan.** *A Dinner to Die For.* **1990, Dell paper $3.50 (0-440-20495-X).** A Berkeley setting provides the backdrop for an investigation into the poisoning murder of a cafe owner at his elite restaurant. (Rev: BL 10/15/87; LJ 11/1/87; PW 10/23/87)

6388 **Dunne, Dominick.** *An Inconvenient Woman.* **1990, Crown $19.95 (0-517-58024-1).** A Los Angeles journalist investigates the possible cover-up of a murder originally ruled a suicide in this novel by the author of *The Two Mrs. Grenvilles.* (Rev: NYTBR 6/10/90; PW 5/4/90; Time 7/2/90)

6389 **Dunne, John Gregory.** *True Confessions.* **1988, Pocket paper $4.50 (0-671-65874-3).** Recollections of a Los Angeles policeman regarding his work on a brutal mutilation murder case that shook the city in the 1940s. (Rev: BL 1/15/78; LJ 12/1/77; Natl Rev 12/9/77)

6390 **Early, Jack.** *Donato and Daughter.* **1989, NAL paper $4.95 (0-451-40122-0).** The NYPD searches for a nun killer in a story told from the viewpoints of both the investigators and the murderer. (Rev: BL 3/15/88; PW 1/15/88)

6391 **Eco, Umberto.** *Name of the Rose.* **1983, Harcourt $24.95 (0-15-144647-4); Warner paper $5.95 (0-446-35720-0).** A series of murders in a fourteenth-century Avignon monastery leads to an investigation by an English monk. (Rev: BL 5/15/83; LJ 4/1/83; NYTBR 6/5/83. Awards: NYTBR, 1983))

6392 **Ehle, John.** *Widow's Trial.* **1989, Harper & Row $17.95 (0-06-016154-X); paper $8.95 (0-06-092010-6).** A story of the trial of a North Carolina woman who murdered her husband. (Rev: LJ 9/15/89; NYTBR 10/15/89; PW 8/11/89)

6393 **Elkins, Aaron J.** *Curses!* **1989, Mysterious $15.95 (0-89296-263-1); paper $3.95 (0-445-40864-2).** An anthropologist uncovers signs of an ancient Mayan curse while on a dig in the Yucatan. "A well written effort . . . perfect for an evening's entertainment."—LJ (Rev: LJ 2/1/89; NYTBR 4/2/89; PW 1/6/89)

6394 **Elkins, Aaron J.** *Dark Place.* **1986, Warner paper $2.95 (0-445-20041-3).** An anthropologist attempts to solve the murders of three hikers in Washington State whose bones were found in a rain forest. (Rev: BL 9/1/83; PW 7/29/83)

6395 **Ellin, Stanley.** *Dark Fantastic.* **1983, Mysterious $13.95 (0-89296-059-0); Berkley paper $3.50 (0-425-08081-1).** A private investigator attempts to foil a plot by a terminally ill professor to blow up the apartment building where they live. "Deftly plotted, populated with vivid characters and masterfully and sinisterly executed."—BL (Rev: BL 6/1/83; Newsweek 7/11/83; PW 5/27/83)

6396 **Ellin, Stanley.** *Mirror, Mirror on the Wall.* **1979, Buccaneer $12.95 (0-89966-083-5).** A New York man who finds a dead body in his apartment confesses the sins of his life in this psychological mystery. (Rev: BL 12/1/72; LJ 10/1/72; Time 9/18/72)

6397 **Ellroy, James.** *Black Dahlia.* **1987, Mysterious $16.95 (0-89296-206-2); paper $4.95 (0-445-40525-2).** A fictional re-creation of the infamous, unsolved Black Dahlia murder set in 1947 Los Angeles. (Rev: BL 9/15/87; CSM 10/2/87; LJ 10/1/87)

6398 **Ellroy, James.** *L.A. Confidential.* **1990, Mysterious $19.95 (0-89296-293-3).** A sweeping portrait of the Los Angeles crime world of the late 1940s by the author of *Black Dahlia.* (Rev: NYTBR 7/15/90; PW 4/13/90. Awards: BL, 1990)

6399 **Ellroy, James.** *Suicide Hill.* **1986, Mysterious $15.95 (0-89296-235-6); Warner paper $4.95 (0-445-40852-9).** The Los Angeles Police Department and FBI join forces in the investigation of a series of Los Angeles bank robberies in this novel by the author of *L.A. Confidential.* (Rev: BL 4/15/86; PW 3/7/86)

6400 **Emerson, Earl W.** *Black Hearts and Slow Dancing.* **1988, Morrow $17.95 (0-688-07533-9); Penguin paper $3.95 (0-14-011732-6).** A Seattle-area fireman is appointed temporary chief of police and conducts an investigation into the death of a former firefighter. "An expert, readable job with a likeable hero."—NYTBR (Rev: BL 1/15/88; LJ 2/1/88; NYTBR 3/6/88)

6401 **Estleman, Loren D.** *Downriver.* **1988, Houghton $15.95 (0-395-41073-8); Fawcett paper $3.95 (0-449-21623-3).** An Amos Walker novel set in Detroit about the private eye's efforts to recover money for an ex-con just released from prison. "Estleman is one of the major current practitioners of the tough-guy private eye novel, and he is at his best here."—NYTBR (Rev: BL 1/15/88; NYTBR 3/6/88; Time 2/1/88)

6402 Estleman, Loren D. *Midnight Man.* 1987, Fawcett paper $3.50 (0-449-21135-5). Detroit private investigator Amos Walker tracks three members of a military group who shot and killed a pair of police officers. (REV: LJ 7/82; NYTBR 8/22/82; PW 6/11/82)

6403 Estleman, Loren D. *Motor City Blues.* 1986, Fawcett paper $3.50 (0-449-21133-9). Detroit private investigator Amos Walker's search for a gangster's girlfriend leads him to a series of pornographic pictures and a seedy bordello. "Expertly written."—NYTBR (REV: LJ 7/80; NYTBR 10/26/80; PW 6/20/80)

6404 Estleman, Loren D. *Silent Thunder.* 1990, Fawcett paper $4.95 (0-449-21854-6). A Detroit murder victim is found to have a huge arsenal in his home in this case investigated by Amos Walker. (REV: BL 4/15/89; NYTBR 4/16/89)

6405 Ferrigno, Robert. *Horse Latitudes.* 1990, Morrow $18.95 (0-688-09060-5). This first novel by a California journalist details the search of a former drug dealer for his ex-wife after a murder is committed at her home. "A perfect escape into quirky, sunny, sexy postmodern suspense."—PW (REV: BL 1/1/90; PW 1/5/90; Time 3/26/90)

6406 Fielding, Joy. *Deep End.* 1987, NAL paper $4.50 (0-451-14802-9). A series of family and personal problems test a woman's sanity and are followed by threatening telephone calls that put her over the edge. (REV: BL 3/15/86; LJ 3/1/86; PW 1/24/86)

6407 Flynn, Don. *Murder Isn't Enough.* 1989, Jove paper $3.95 (0-515-10151-6). This debut novel concerns a court journalist who finds a trail of corruption when he investigates the allegedly accidental death of his predecessor. (REV: BL 8/83; NYTBR 11/13/83)

6408 Flynn, Don. *Ordinary Murder.* 1987, Walker $16.95 (0-8027-5687-5); Jove paper $3.50 (0-515-10283-0). A New York journalist investigates the possible murder of the son of an acquaintance. (REV: BL 12/1/87; NYTBR 1/31/88)

6409 Fonseca, Rubem. *Bufo and Spallanzani.* 1990, Dutton $18.95 (0-525-24872-2). A novelist/private investigator accused of murder examines charges of insurance fraud by members of his office. (REV: BL 7/90; PW 6/22/90)

6410 Fonseca, Rubem. *High Art.* 1987, Carroll & Graf paper $7.95 (0-88184-343-1). A Brazilian attorney seeking clues to a series of murders of prostitutes finds himself on the trail of a mysterious videotape at the center of the crimes. (REV: BL 7/86; LJ 8/86; NYTBR 9/7/86)

6411 Francis, Dick. *Banker.* 1986, Fawcett paper $5.95 (0-449-21199-1). The story of an investigation into a case of an expensive stud horse whose offspring are born deformed following its purchase by a horse breeder. "A furiously paced, stunningly constructed tale."—BL (REV: BL 12/1/82; CSM 4/20/82; TLS 12/10/82)

6412 Francis, Dick. *Bolt.* 1988, Fawcett paper $4.95 (0-449-21239-4). A jockey searches for the killer of two horses owned by a French businessman. (REV: LJ 3/1/87; PW 1/30/87; Time 4/27/87)

6413 Francis, Dick. *Bonecrack.* 1990, Pocket paper $4.50 (0-671-70467-2). An organized crime figure forces a track to give his son the best horses to ride in a series of important races. (REV: BL 7/15/72; LJ 7/72; TLS 12/31/71)

6414 Francis, Dick. *Break In.* 1986, Putnam $17.95 (0-399-13121-3); Fawcett paper $5.95 (0-449-20755-2). A jockey investigates a series of damaging rumors appearing in print regarding practices of his horse-trainer sister and her husband. (REV: BL 1/15/86; LJ 3/1/86; PW 1/24/86)

6415 Francis, Dick. *The Edge.* 1989, Putnam $18.95 (0-399-13414-X); Fawcett paper $5.95 (0-449-21719-1). A mystery set on board a trans-Canadian train involving members of the English and Canadian horse-racing world. (REV: Atl 3/89; BL 11/15/88; PW 12/9/88)

6416 Francis, Dick. *Forfeit.* 1987, Fawcett paper $4.95 (0-449-21272-6). A horse-racing writer is blackmailed to fix a race by organized crime figures who threaten the life of his wife. (REV: Atl 3/69; LJ 3/1/69; NYTBR 3/16/69. AWARDS: Edgar, 1969)

6417 Francis, Dick. *High Stakes.* 1990, Pocket paper $4.50 (0-671-70468-0). A British inventor develops an elaborate scheme to regain money from a crooked trainer and bookmaker who he believes fixed horse races and bilked him out of money. (REV: BL 5/15/76; New Rep 7/26/76; TLS 10/31/75)

6418 Francis, Dick. *Hot Money.* 1988, Putnam $17.95 (0-399-13349-6); Fawcett paper $4.95 (0-449-21240-8). A jockey searches to find out who killed his father's fifth wife and who is trying to kill his father. (REV: BL 1/15/88; LJ 4/1/88; NYTBR 5/1/88)

6419 Francis, Dick. *Longshot.* 1990, Putnam $19.95 (0-399-13581-2). A writer commissioned to write a horse trainer's biography becomes involved in the investigation of a racetrack murder. (REV: BL 9/1/90; CSM 12/17/90; PW 8/24/90)

6420 Francis, Dick. *Odds Against.* 1987, Fawcett paper $5.95 (0-449-21269-6). A crippled former jockey seeks answers to the decline of a once respectable racetrack. (REV: NYTBR 4/3/66; PW 1/31/66; TLS 11/11/65)

6421 Francis, Dick. *Proof.* 1985, Putnam $16.95 (0-399-13036-5); Fawcett paper $4.95 (0-449-20754-4). A jockey searches for liquor distributors who are marketing inferior scotches and wines under high-priced labels. (REV: BL 12/1/84; NYTBR 3/24/85; TLS 3/29/85)

6422 Francis, Dick. *Reflex.* 1986, Fawcett paper $4.95 (0-449-21173-8). The story of a jockey who finds evidence of a blackmailing scheme following the death of a track photographer. (REV: BL 2/15/81; LJ 4/1/81; Newsweek 4/6/81)

6423 Francis, Dick. *Smokescreen.* 1990, Pocket paper $4.50 (0-671-70470-2). An English motion picture actor travels to South Africa to determine why a friend's horses often falter at the ends of races. (Rev: LJ 3/1/73; PW 11/27/72; TLS 12/1/72)

6424 Francis, Dick. *Whip Hand.* 1987, Fawcett paper $5.95 (0-449-21274-2). A former jockey investigates a series of deaths involving the horses of a trainer. (Rev: BL 4/15/80; LJ 6/1/80; TLS 3/7/80. Awards: Edgar, 1980)

6425 Fraser, Antonia. *Cavalier Case.* 1991, Bantam $17.95 (0-553-07126-2). Sleuth Jemima Shore is commissioned to produce a television series exploring haunted English homes in this mystery by the noted biographer and historian. (Rev: BL 11/1/90; PW 11/23/90; TLS 6/29/90)

6426 Fraser, Antonia. *Jemima Shore's First Case and Other Stories.* 1987, Norton $14.95 (0-393-02453-9); Bantam paper $3.95 (0-553-28073-2). A collection of 13 mystery stories including four featuring the exploits of the author's character Jemima Shore. (Rev: BL 4/15/87; PW 4/24/87)

6427 Fraser, Antonia. *Oxford Blood.* 1989, Bantam paper $3.95 (0-553-28070-8). Jemima Shore investigates an attempted murder that takes place while she is filming a television program about Oxford. (Rev: NYTBR 10/13/85; PW 8/9/85; TLS 11/22/85)

6428 Fraser, Antonia. *Quiet as a Nun.* 1982, Norton paper $3.95 (0-393-30120-6). Jemima Shore investigates the apparent starvation death of a wealthy nun in a convent school. (Rev: BL 11/1/77; NYTBR 9/4/77; TLS 5/27/77)

6429 Fraser, Antonia. *Your Royal Hostage.* 1989, Bantam paper $3.95 (0-553-28019-8). Jemima Shore investigates an animal rights group responsible for the kidnapping of a member of the British royal family. (Rev: BL 12/15/87; CSM 3/23/88; LJ 1/88)

6430 Freeling, Nicholas. *King of the Rainy Country.* 1975, Penguin paper $3.95 (0-14-002853-6). Inspector Van der Valk seeks a missing tycoon wanted for information he may have regarding a crime. (Rev: NYTBR 11/27/66; PW 10/24/66; TLS 1/20/66. Awards: Edgar, 1966)

6431 Freeling, Nicholas. *Those in Peril.* 1991, Mysterious $18.95 (0-89296-412-X); paper $4.99 (0-446-40089-0). French police commissioner Henri Castang resorts to unorthodox measures to capture a professor suspected of sexual misconduct. (Rev: BL 1/1/91; NYTBR 2/10/91; PW 12/7/90)

6432 Friedman, Kinky. *A Case of Lone Star.* 1988, Berkley paper $3.50 (0-425-11185-7). Real-life country musician Friedman spins a tale of a murderer stalking musicians at New York's Lone Star Cafe. (Rev: BL 8/87; NYTBR 10/11/87; PW 7/10/87)

6433 Friedman, Kinky. *Frequent Flyer.* 1989, Morrow $16.95 (0-688-08166-5); Berkley paper $4.50 (0-425-12345-6). Investigator Friedman searches for the whereabouts of a friend when he discovers that the body in the casket at the friend's funeral is

someone else's. (Rev: BL 8/89; LJ 7/89; NYTBR 10/15/89)

6434 Friedman, Kinky. *Musical Chairs.* 1991, Morrow $18.95 (0-688-09148-2). Real-life musician Friedman investigates a fictional series of murders of his band members in this novel set in the New York music world. (Rev: BL 3/1/91; LJ 3/1/91; PW 1/11/91)

6435 Fyfield, Frances. *Not That Kind of Place.* 1990, Simon & Schuster $17.95 (0-671-67666-0). A detective and his prosecutor wife find themselves on different sides of a muder case in this story set in an English village. (Rev: LJ 3/1/90; NYTBR 6/3/90; PW 3/16/90)

6436 Fyfield, Frances. *A Question of Guilt.* 1990, Pocket $17.95 (0-671-67664-4). An attorney's debut mystery about the murder of a solicitor's wife. (Rev: NYTBR 8/27/89; PW 6/9/89)

6437 Gardner, John E. *Return of Moriarty.* 1981, Berkley paper $3.50 (0-425-05093-9). This late Victorian mystery pitting Sherlock Holmes and his archrival Moriarty is based on speculation that Holmes and Moriarty survived death in the Alps. (Rev: BL 1/1/75; LJ 11/1/74; PW 9/6/74)

6438 Garfield, Brian. *Necessity.* 1984, St. Martin's $13.95 (0-312-56258-6). A woman seeks to regain her child from her husband after she discovers her husband's role in a mafia drug-smuggling scheme. (Rev: BL 5/15/84; LJ 4/15/84; PW 3/30/84)

6439 Gash, Joe. *Newspaper Murders.* 1987, Warner paper $3.95 (0-446-34290-4). The death of a newspaper reporter is falsely blamed on a religious cult while detectives search for the real killer. (Rev: BL 9/15/85; PW 8/30/85)

6440 Gash, Jonathan. *Firefly Gadroon.* 1985, Penguin paper $3.95 (0-14-008007-4). British antique dealer/sleuth Lovejoy seeks clues to a murder surrounding a silver forgery/smuggling ring in the eighth volume of the series. (Rev: BL 9/1/84; NYTBR 11/4/84)

6441 Gash, Jonathan. *Gold by Gemini.* 1988, NAL paper $3.95 (0-451-82185-8). Antique dealer/sleuth Lovejoy gets involved with unsavory characters following a trip to the Isle of Man to examine a cache of Roman coins. (Rev: BL 7/15/79; LJ 9/1/79; NYTBR 8/19/79)

6442 Gash, Jonathan. *Grail Tree.* 1979, Amereon $16.95 (0-88411-559-3); NAL paper $3.95 (0-451-82186-6). An antique dealer asked to authenticate the Holy Grail becomes involved in an investigation following his client's death in a bombing. (Rev: BL 5/15/80; LJ 6/1/80; PW 4/25/80)

6443 Gash, Jonathan. *Jade Woman.* 1988, St. Martin's $17.95 (0-312-02224-7); Penguin paper $4.50 (0-14-012280-X). Lovejoy attempts to take over an antique business in Hong Kong and becomes involved with a criminal triad. "Best in the series so far."—PW (Rev: BL 12/15/88; LJ 2/1/89; PW 12/16/88)

6444 Gash, Jonathan. *Judas Pair*. 1988, Penguin paper $3.95 (0-14-010528-X). An antique dealer tries to trace the owner of a pair of rare dueling pistols used as murder weapons. (REV: BL 2/15/78; PW 10/17/77; TLS 12/16/77)

6445 Gash, Jonathan. *Moonspender*. 1988, Penguin paper $4.50 (0-14-010646-4). Antique expert Lovejoy is hounded by organized crime figures who force him to appear on a television quiz show. "Marvelously satisfying . . . storytelling at its very best."—LJ (REV: BL 2/15/87; LJ 2/1/87; PW 1/30/87)

6446 Gash, Jonathan. *Pearlhanger*. 1986, Penguin paper $3.95 (0-14-008468-1). British antique dealer/sleuth Lovejoy investigates the whereabouts of a legendary pearl linked to a series of murders. (REV: BL 3/15/85; NYTBR 6/23/85; PW 4/5/85)

6447 Gash, Jonathan. *Spend Game*. 1982, Penguin paper $3.95 (0-14-006190-8). Lovejoy searches for a mysterious railway pass that may provide clues to a murder of a colleague. (REV: BL 5/1/81; PW 4/3/81; TLS 7/18/80)

6448 Gash, Jonathan. *Tartan Sell*. 1987, Penguin paper $3.95 (0-14-009745-7). British antique dealer/sleuth Lovejoy becomes involved in a Scottish group responsible for the making of fake antiques in this novel by the author of *Moonspender*. (REV: BL 4/15/86; NYTBR 7/6/86; PW 3/28/86)

6449 Gash, Jonathan. *Vatican Rip*. 1983, Penguin paper $3.95 (0-14-006431-1). British antique dealer/sleuth Lovejoy becomes involved in a plot to heist furniture from the Vatican in this fifth segment of the series. (REV: BL 12/15/81; LJ 1/1/82; NYTBR 2/21/82)

6450 George, Elizabeth. *A Great Deliverance*. 1988, Bantam $16.95 (0-553-05244-6). An investigation into the case of a young girl accused of patricide in rural England. (REV: BL 6/15/88; PW 4/22/88)

6451 George, Elizabeth. *A Suitable Vengeance*. 1991, Bantam $19.00 (0-553-07407-5). A Scotland Yard detective searches for clues to the murders of several of his friends and acquaintances in this mystery by an English writer. (REV: BL 4/15/91; PW 4/12/91)

6452 Gilbert, Michael. *Long Journey Home*. 1986, Penguin paper $3.95 (0-14-008384-7). A former English businessman leaves his New Zealand-bound plane in Rome to investigate his former Italian company and is pursued throughout Europe by organized crime figures. (REV: BL 7/85; New Yorker 5/20/85; TLS 11/29/85)

6453 Gill, B. M. *Time and Time Again*. 1990, Macmillan $16.95 (0-684-19174-1). A businesswoman and political activist remains friends with her former cellmates following her release from prison for her part in a melee surrounding a political rally. (REV: BL 3/1/90; NYTBR 3/18/90; PW 1/12/90)

6454 Gill, Bartholomew. *Death of a Joyce Scholar*. 1989, Morrow $18.95 (0-688-08713-2). A Dublin policeman investigates the murder of a Trinity College scholar who specializes in the study of the works of Joyce. "Profoundly clever."—NYTBR (REV: BL 5/1/89; NYTBR 6/18/89; PW 4/21/89. AWARDS: BL, 1989)

6455 Gill, Bartholomew. *McGarr and the Legacy of a Woman Scorned*. 1987, Penguin paper $3.50 (0-14-009609-4). Inspector McGarr examines the circumstances surrounding the murder of a spinster in a small Irish town. (REV: BL 3/15/86; PW 2/28/86)

6456 Gilman, Dorothy. *Mrs. Polifax on the China Station*. 1985, State Mutual $24.95 (0-7090-1333-7); Fawcett paper $3.95 (0-449-20840-0). Mrs. Polifax enters China on the trail of an engineer and finds herself meeting a series of government officials and intelligence agents. (REV: BL 8/83; LJ 9/1/83)

6457 Gilman, Dorothy. *Nun in the Closet*. 1986, Fawcett paper $3.95 (0-449-21167-3). An order of nuns discovers that its inherited dwelling contains money stashed in secret places. "Delicate fun and excellent of its kind."—LJ (REV: BL 3/1/75; LJ 2/1/75; PW 1/19/76)

6458 Gilman, Dorothy. *Tightrope Walker*. 1986, Ballantine paper $4.95 (0-449-21177-0). A young female detective and her boyfriend search for a murderer in this novel by the writer known for her Mrs. Polifax series. (REV: BL 7/15/79; LJ 5/1/79; PW 4/16/79)

6459 Gordon, Alison. *Dead Pull Hitter*. 1989, St. Martin's $15.95 (0-312-03319-2). A mystery involving the murders of two star players of a Toronto baseball team. (REV: NYTBR 10/22/89; PW 7/7/89)

6460 Gores, Joe. *Come Morning*. 1986, Mysterious $15.95 (0-89296-243-7). Following his release from prison, an ex-convict is tracked by criminals and insurance investigators for his knowledge of the whereabout of stolen diamonds. (REV: LJ 3/1/86; PW 2/7/86; Time 4/14/86)

6461 Gosling, Paula. *Wynchford Murders*. 1988, Harlequin Books paper $3.50 (0-373-26009-1). A detective searches for the brutal killer of women in his small English hometown. (REV: BL 1/1/87; LJ 1/87)

6462 Gould, Heywood. *Double Bang*. 1989, Pocket paper $4.50 (0-671-67835-3). A New York detective searches for the hired killer who shot and killed his partner. (REV: BL 3/1/88; LJ 3/1/88; PW 1/15/88)

6463 Grafton, Sue. *A Is for Alibi*. 1987, Bantam paper $4.50 (0-553-27991-2). Kinsey Millhone searches for clues surrounding an eight-year-old murder case of a woman falsely accused of poisoning her husband in the debut volume of this popular series. (REV: BL 4/1/82; Newsweek 6/7/82; PW 3/12/82)

6464 Grafton, Sue. *B Is for Burglar*. 1985, Holt $14.95 (0-03-001889-7); Bantam paper $4.50 (0-553-28034-1). This second Kinsey Millhone mystery, set in the mythical city of Santa Theresa, involves her search for a missing Florida woman. (REV: BL 5/15/85; PW 4/5/85)

6465 Grafton, Sue. *C Is for Corpse.* 1986, Holt $14.95 (0-03-001888-9); Bantam paper $4.50 (0-553-28036-8). Kinsey Millhone begins to investigate the attempted murder of a client who is killed soon after Millhone begins work on the case. (Rev: BL 3/1/86; LJ 4/1/86; PW 3/14/86)

6466 Grafton, Sue. *D Is for Deadbeat.* 1987, Henry Holt $15.95 (0-8050-0248-0); Bantam paper $4.50 (0-553-27163-8). The drowning of a man convicted of a drunk-driving homicide is suspected by Kinsey Millhone to be murder. "A must purchase for crime collections."—BL (Rev: BL 4/1/87; LJ 5/1/87; PW 3/27/87)

6467 Grafton, Sue. *E Is for Evidence.* 1988, Henry Holt $15.95 (0-8050-0459-9); Bantam paper $4.50 (0-553-27955-6). Private investigator Kinsey Millhone attempts to exonerate herself from charges that she received funds from a falsified insurance claim. (Rev: BL 3/1/88; CSM 8/30/88; Newsweek 7/18/88)

6468 Grafton, Sue. *F Is for Fugitive.* 1989, Henry Holt $15.94 (0-8050-0460-2); Bantam paper $4.50 (0-553-28478-9). Millhone investigates the murder of a pregnant young woman that took place in a California beach town nearly two decades in the past. (Rev: NYTBR 11/21/89; PW 3/17/89)

6469 Grafton, Sue. *G Is for Gumshoe.* 1990, Henry Holt $16.95 (0-8050-0461-0). Private investigator Kinsey Millhone tries to avoid a hit man's efforts to kill her. (Rev: BL 3/15/90; Newsweek 5/14/90; PW 3/30/90)

6470 Graham, Caroline. *Death of a Hollow Man.* 1990, Morrow $17.95 (0-688-09116-4). An actor slain with a fake prop during a production of *Amadeus* in front of a full theater spurs an investigation by Inspector Tom Barnaby. "Don't miss this."—LJ (Rev: BL 1/15/90; LJ 1/90; PW 11/3/89)

6471 Graham, Caroline. *Killings at Badger's Drift.* 1989, Avon paper $3.50 (0-380-70563-X). A police team investigates a series of poisoning deaths in a quaint English village. (Rev: BL 12/1/87; LJ 1/88; PW 11/13/87)

6472 Granger, Bill. *El Murders.* 1989, Warner paper $4.95 (0-446-35209-8). The murder of a man—witnessed by a policeman—outside Chicago's elevated railway spurs investigative action into a series of crimes in the city. (Rev: BL 6/1/87; LJ 7/87; PW 5/15/87)

6473 Gray, A. W. *Bino.* 1989, NAL paper $3.95 (0-451-40129-8). This debut novel set in Texas concerns a lawyer searching for the murderers of one of his clients. "An unusually absorbing, convincing, well-written piece of work."—NYTBR (Rev: BL 2/15/88; NYTBR 3/27/88; PW 12/18/87)

6474 Green, Kate. *Shattered Moon.* 1986, Dell paper $3.95 (0-440-17593-3). A Los Angeles psychic tarot reader gets involved in an investigation into murders that appear to be connected to cards in the deck. (Rev: BL 1/1/86; PW 11/29/85)

6475 Greenleaf, Stephen. *Book Case.* 1991, Morrow $19.95 (0-688-07669-6). A private investigator searches for details surrounding a sex scandal about to be revealed in the pages of a small-press publication. (Rev: NYTBR 2/10/91; PW 11/2/90)

6476 Greenleaf, Stephen. *Fatal Obsession.* 1985, Ballantine paper $2.95 (0-345-33287-3). A California investigator returns to his Iowa hometown to settle a family estate and becomes involved in the investigation of the hanging death of his nephew. (Rev: BL 4/15/83; CSM 6/1/84; Time 7/14/83)

6477 Greenwood, John. *Mosley by Moonlight.* 1985, Walker $12.95 (0-8027-5606-9); Bantam paper $2.95 (0-553-25630-0). An English police procedural concerning a man whose second wife has disappeared in circumstances similar to those of his first wife's disappearance. "All the proper pleasures of detective fiction are here."—TLS (Rev: BL 1/15/85; LJ 2/1/85; TLS 10/26/84)

6478 Greenwood, L. B. *Sherlock Holmes and the Case of the Raleigh Legacy.* 1987, St. Martin's paper $2.95 (0-312-90843-1). Sherlock Holmes investigates a mysterious note left to a descendant of Sir Walter Raleigh in this novel, which attempts to re-create the Doyle character. (Rev: BL 11/15/86; New Yorker 1/19/87)

6479 Grimes, Martha. *Anodyne Necklace.* 1983, Little, Brown $15.95 (0-316-32882-0); Dell paper $4.50 (0-440-10280-4). A detective and a former lord search for the murderer of a woman in an English village in this story that won the Nero Wolfe Award for best mystery of 1983. (Rev: BL 6/1/83; LJ 6/1/83; PW 5/6/83)

6480 Grimes, Martha. *Dirty Duck.* 1984, Little, Brown $14.95 (0-316-32883-9); Dell paper $4.50 (0-440-12050-0). A murderer tracks members of an American tour group sightseeing in England and leaves verse as clues following his crimes. "A masterful example of Grimes's ingenuity."—PW (Rev: BL 4/15/84; LJ 4/1/84; PW 2/24/84)

6481 Grimes, Martha. *Five Bells and Bladebone.* 1987, Little, Brown $15.95 (0-316-32889-8); Dell paper $4.50 (0-440-20133-0). Scotland Yard investigator Richard Jury seeks clues to the murders of two lovers in separate English cities. (Rev: BL 7/87; NYTBR 9/13/87; Time 8/17/87)

6482 Grimes, Martha. *Help the Poor Struggler.* 1985, Little, Brown $15.95 (0-316-32884-7); Dell paper $4.50 (0-440-13584-2). The murder of three children in a west England town leads a detective to investigate a 20-year-old case with similarities. (Rev: BL 4/15/85; LJ 5/1/85; PW 3/15/85)

6483 Grimes, Martha. *I Am the Only Running Footman.* 1986, Little, Brown $15.95 (0-316-32887-1); Dell paper $4.50 (0-440-13924-4). Scotland Yard detectives investigate a pair of connected murders, one of which occurred outside a pub named "I Am the Only Running Footman." (Rev: BL 11/15/86; CSM 2/6/87; PW 10/10/86)

6484 Grimes, Martha. *Jerusalem Inn.* 1984, Little, Brown $15.95 (0-316-32879-0); Dell paper $4.50 (0-440-14181-8). Sleuth Richard Jury seeks to locate the living relations of an acquaintance who was murdered. "A virtuoso performance."—LJ (REV: BL 11/15/84; LJ 11/1/84)

6485 Grimes, Martha. *Man with a Load of Mischief.* 1981, Little, Brown $15.95 (0-316-32880-4); Dell paper $4.50 (0-440-15327-1). A British police inspector attempts to solve a series of murders where the victims' bodies are placed in or near village pubs. (REV: LJ 9/1/81; PW 7/17/81)

6486 Grimes, Martha. *Old Silent.* 1989, Little, Brown $18.95 (0-316-32318-7). An investigator who witnesses a woman murder her husband searches for the motives behind the shooting. (REV: BL 6/15/89; NYTBR 9/24/89; PW 6/23/89)

6487 Hall, James W. *Bones of Coral.* 1991, McKay $19.50 (0-679-40017-6). A pair of Miami lovers investigate a conspiracy connected to the deaths of both their fathers two decades in the past. (REV: BL 3/15/91; LJ 3/1/91; PW 2/1/91)

6488 Hall, James W. *Under Cover of Daylight.* 1987, Norton $16.95 (0-393-02484-9). A Florida man searches for the killer of his foster mother, whose body was found on a boat off the Keys with evidence of marijuana aboard. "A great first novel."—LJ (REV: LJ 9/1/87; Newsweek 12/7/87; PW 8/28/87)

6489 Hall, Robert Lee. *Ben Franklin and a Case of Christmas Murder.* 1991, St. Martin's $17.95 (0-312-05383-5). Benjamin Franklin investigates the death of a friend in this mystery set in eighteenth-century London. (REV: BL 1/15/91; PW 11/30/90)

6490 Hammett, Dashiell. *Continental Op.* 1989, Random paper $7.95 (0-679-72258-0). A collection of seven stories originally published in pulp magazines during the 1920s and 1930s by the author of *The Maltese Falcon.* (REV: Atl 2/75; BL 12/15/74; PW 12/15/74)

6491 Hammond, Gerald. *Whose Dog Are You?* 1991, St. Martin's $15.95 (0-312-05536-6). A Scottish writer's story of a sleuth's investigation into a murder with a possible connection to a stray spaniel. (REV: BL 4/15/91; PW 3/8/91)

6492 Hansen, Joseph. *Backtrack.* 1982, Countryman $12.95 (0-914378-96-1); Penguin paper $3.95 (0-14-006782-5). A teenage boy attempts to solve the mystery of his father's death in this non-Brandstetter tale by Hansen. (REV: BL 11/1/82; LJ 11/1/82; NYTBR 1/16/83)

6493 Hansen, Joseph. *The Boy Who Was Buried This Morning.* 1990, Viking $16.95 (0-670-83324-X). Dave Brandstetter becomes involved with a Los Angeles neo-Nazi group while investigating the murder of a young man. "A worthy addition to classic Southern California detective stories."—PW (REV: BL 3/1/90; LJ 5/1/90; PW 4/6/90)

6494 Hansen, Joseph. *Death Claims.* 1980, Henry Holt paper $3.95 (0-8050-0622-2). Dave Brandstetter investigates the murder of a southern Californian drug addict. (REV: NYTBR 1/21/73; New Yorker 3/17/73)

6495 Hansen, Joseph. *Early Graves.* 1988, Mysterious paper $3.95 (0-445-40735-2). A Los Angeles serial killer preys on AIDS victims. "Not the first novel to deal with the impact of AIDS . . . but it will probably rank with the best."—Time (REV: BL 2/1/88; PW 10/23/87; Time 2/1/88)

6496 Hansen, Joseph. *Gravedigger.* 1985, Henry Holt paper $4.95 (0-8050-0196-4). Dave Brandstetter searches for a missing girl who survived a religious cult massacre in this sixth segment of the series. (REV: BL 3/1/82; LJ 4/1/82; Newsweek 6/7/82)

6497 Hansen, Joseph. *Little Dog Laughed.* 1987, Henry Holt paper $4.95 (0-8050-0627-3). Dave Brandstetter investigates the murder of a journalist just prior to his exposé on corruption in a Latin American government. (REV: BL 10/15/86; NYTBR 1/18/87; Time 12/22/86)

6498 Hansen, Joseph. *The Man Everybody Was Afraid Of.* 1981, Henry Holt paper $3.95 (0-8050-0723-7). An officer's murder falsely pinned on a gay rights activist in a small California town spurs the investigation by Dave Brandstetter. (REV: BL 9/15/78; LJ 9/1/78)

6499 Hansen, Joseph. *Nightwork.* 1985, Henry Holt paper $3.95 (0-8050-1055-6). Dave Brandstetter investigates allegations of truckers transporting illegal substances in this seventh novel in the series. (REV: BL 6/15/84; NYTBR 4/8/84; PW 1/27/84)

6500 Hansen, Joseph. *Obedience.* 1988, Mysterious $16.95 (0-89296-296-8). Dave Brandstetter investigates possible connections between the murders of Vietnamese businessmen and a California drug-smuggling ring. (REV: BL 11/1/88; LJ 10/1/88; PW 11/4/88)

6501 Hansen, Joseph. *Steps Going Down.* 1985, Countryman $14.95 (0-88150-054-2); Penguin paper $3.50 (0-14-008810-5). A Dave Brandstetter story involving a male prostitute who entices his young lover to commit a series of crimes leading up to a murder. (REV: BL 10/15/85; PW 9/13/85; Time 11/4/85)

6502 Hansen, Joseph. *Troublemaker.* 1981, Henry Holt paper $3.95 (0-8050-0812-8). Insurance investigator Dave Brandstetter looks into the murder of a gay bar owner. "A skillful piece of work in the West Coast private-eye tradition."—NYTBR (REV: LJ 8/75; NYTBR 12/28/75; PW 7/28/75)

6503 Harrison, Colin. *Break and Enter.* 1990, Crown $17.95 (0-517-57281-8). A district attorney assigned to a murder case involving a local politician finds evidence of a citywide cover-up of the crime. (REV: BL 2/1/90; LJ 3/1/90; PW 3/30/90)

6504 Harrison, Ray. *Harvest of Death.* 1988, St. Martin's $16.95 (0-312-02218-2); Berkley paper $3.95 (0-425-11979-3). A police officer investigates a series of murders in a small English village in which his cousin is the prime suspect. (Rev: BL 12/1/88; PW 10/28/88)

6505　Hart, Roy. *A Fox in the Night.* **1988, St. Martin's $15.95 (0-312-02212-3).** A British detective searches for a killer responsible for the drowning death of a rich woman. "A finely honed step-by-step police procedural with loving attention to detail."—LJ (Rev: BL 11/1/88; LJ 11/1/88; PW 10/7/88)

6506　Harvey, John. *Cutting Edge.* **1991, Henry Holt $16.95 (0-8050-1264-8).** A British policeman investigates a series of three stabbings at a local hospital. (Rev: BL 6/15/91; PW 5/10/91)

6507　Harvey, John. *Rough Treatment.* **1990, Henry Holt $17.95 (0-8050-0983-3).** English detective Charles Resnick investigates a case involving a television director found storing large quantities of cocaine in his home. (Rev: BL 6/15/90; LJ 6/1/90; PW 5/25/90)

6508　Havill, Steven F. *Heartshot.* **1991, St. Martin's $16.95 (0-312-05442-4).** An angry sheriff investigates drug trafficking in a small New Mexico town following a car crash that takes the lives of three local teenagers. (Rev: BL 3/1/91; PW 2/1/91)

6509　Haymon, S. T. *Death of a God.* **1987, St. Martin's $14.95 (0-312-00119-3); Bantam paper $3.95 (0-553-27266-7).** An investigation into the crucifixion death of a British rock singer. "An unusually rich, sensitive piece of work in the finest British tradition."—NYTBR (Rev: BL 3/15/87; NYTBR 4/26/87)

6510　Haymon, S. T. *A Very Particular Murder.* **1989, St. Martin's $16.95 (0-312-02998-5).** An investigation follows the poisoning murder of a Nobel Prize–winning physicist at an international meeting of scientists held in London. (Rev: BL 8/89; NYTBR 8/27/89)

6511　Healy, Jeremiah. *Yesterday's News.* **1989, Harper & Row $16.95 (0-06-015922-7); Simon & Schuster paper $4.50 (0-671-69584-3).** A cover-up of a murder by local media and police is uncovered by a Boston private investigator. "An excellent hard-boiled thriller with a memorable conclusion."—BL (Rev: BL 8/89; NYTBR 8/13/89; PW 6/16/89)

6512　Heffernan, William. *Ritual.* **1989, NAL $18.95 (0-453-00618-3); paper $4.95 (0-451-16397-4).** A New York policeman investigates a series of murders committed in the ritualistic style of the ancient Toltecs. "The suspense is excruciating . . . should keep readers in a state of frenzy until the last page."—PW (Rev: BL 3/1/89; PW 2/3/89)

6513　Hiassen, Carl. *Double Whammy.* **1988, Putnam $16.95 (0-399-13297-X); Warner paper $4.95 (0-446-35276-4).** A news photographer seeks clues to a series of deaths in this Florida tale of bass fishing and murder. (Rev: LJ 1/88; NYTBR 3/6/88; PW 11/20/87)

6514　Hiassen, Carl. *Native Tongue.* **1991, Knopf $21.00 (0-394-58796-0).** A Florida journalist investigates a plan to develop a tourist resort on one of the Keys in this novel by the author of *Skintight.* "A

rowdy, rollicking cartoon strip of a novel."—NYTBR (Rev: BL 8/91; NYTBR 10/20/91; PW 7/12/91)

6515　Hiassen, Carl. *Skintight.* **1989, Putnam $18.95 (0-399-13489-1).** A tough Vietnam veteran, now a Florida investigator, looks into the disappearance of a college student who just had plastic surgery. (Rev: BL 6/1/89; NYTBR 10/15/89; PW 6/23/89)

6516　Hiassen, Carl. *Tourist Season.* **1986, Putnam $15.95 (0-399-13145-0); Warner paper $3.95 (0-446-34345-5).** A detective investigates a plot to drive tourists out of Florida to save the state for future generations. (Rev: NYTBR 2/15/87; PW 1/16/87)

6517　Higgins, George V. *Outlaws.* **1988, Zebra paper $4.50 (0-8217-2472-X).** Boston police track a group of former 1960s radicals responsible for a series of armored-car robberies. (Rev: BL 6/15/87; PW 7/10/87; Time 9/14/87)

6518　Hill, Reginald. *Bones and Silence.* **1990, Delacorte $17.95 (0-385-30130-8).** Inspector Dalziel witnesses a murder, but his account seems to differ from the known facts surrounding the case. "A complex, challenging and diverting novel from one of the most cogent of detective writers."—TLS (Rev: BL 8/90; LJ 7/90; TLS 8/17/90)

6519　Hill, Reginald. *Child's Play.* **1987, Macmillan $13.95 (0-02-551590-X); Warner paper $3.95 (0-446-34533-4).** Dalziel and Pascoe investigate a couple of supposedly unrelated murders that follow the announcement that a dead Yorkshire woman's estate will pass to a long-missing son. "One of the better books in the series."—NYTBR (Rev: NYTBR 3/15/87; PW 12/19/86; TLS 10/30/87)

6520　Hill, Reginald. *Deadheads: A Murder Mystery.* **1984, Macmillan $12.95 (0-02-551560-8); NAL paper $3.95 (0-451-15895-4).** Inspector Pascoe investigates a series of seemingly accidental deaths in a Yorkshire town with the same individual as the beneficiary. (Rev: BL 6/1/84; CSM 10/5/84; NYTBR 6/24/84)

6521　Hill, Reginald. *Exit Lines.* **1986, NAL paper $3.50 (0-451-14252-7).** Yorkshire detectives Dalziel and Pascoe search for clues to a series of murders occurring on the same night, one of which implicates Dalziel as a prime suspect. (Rev: BL 5/15/85; LJ 5/1/85; PW 3/29/85)

6522　Hill, Reginald. *A Killing Kindness.* **1989, International Polygonics paper $5.95 (1-55882-003-5).** Detectives Dalziel and Pascoe investigate a series of English murders where the killer leaves flowers and a quote from Hamlet at the crime sites. (Rev: NYTBR 4/5/81; PW 2/27/81; TLS 12/26/80)

6523　Hill, Reginald. *A Pinch of Snuff.* **1990, Dell paper $3.95 (0-440-16912-7).** Detectives Pascoe and Dalziel investigate the death of an English pornographer whose murder is suspected to be connected to a snuff film. (Rev: BL 1/15/79; LJ 1/1/79)

6524　Hill, Reginald. *Ruling Passion.* **1990, Dell paper $3.95 (0-440-16889-9).** A Yorkshire detective investigates the murders of four of his former

Oxford classmates. "An English murder mystery of the finest quality."—New Yorker (REV: BL 10/15/77; PW 7/11/77; TLS 4/13/73)

6525   Hillerman, Tony. *Blessing Way.* **1990, Armchair Detective $18.95 (0-922890-09-9); Harper & Row paper $4.95 (0-06-100001-9).** Lieutenant Joe Leaphorn investigates a murder allegedly committed by a manifestation of a Navajo god. "A first novel of unusual competence and pleasure."—TLS (REV: BL 5/1/70; LJ 5/15/70; TLS 12/25/70)

6526   Hillerman, Tony. *Coyote Waits.* **1990, Harper & Row $19.95 (0-06-016370-4).** Navajo tribal police officers Chee and Leaphorn investigate a series of murders on the reservation. "Hillerman is a mystery writer extraordinaire, and in *Coyote Waits,* he's at his best."—CSM (REV: BL 5/15/90; CSM 7/11/90; NYTBR 6/24/90)

6527   Hillerman, Tony. *Dance Hall of the Dead.* **1989, Harper & Row paper $4.95 (0-06-100002-7).** The story of the investigation into the murder of a Zuni ritual dancer told by the author of *A Thief of Time.* (REV: BL 10/15/73; LJ 10/1/73; PW 8/27/73. AWARDS: Edgar, 1973)

6528   Hillerman, Tony. *Dark Wind.* **1989, Harper & Row paper $4.95 (0-06-100003-5).** Navajo tribal policeman Jim Chee investigates the whereabouts of a shipment of cocaine missing from the wreckage of a plane. (REV: CSM 5/5/82; LJ 3/1/82; New Rep 9/20/82)

6529   Hillerman, Tony. *Ghostway.* **1986, Avon paper $4.95 (0-380-70024-7).** Detective Jim Chee searches for a missing Navajo man and his daughter and for clues to a recent murder. (REV: BL 1/1/85; LJ 2/1/85; PW 11/30/84)

6530   Hillerman, Tony. *Listening Woman.* **1990, Harper & Row paper $4.95 (0-06-100029-9).** Joe Leaphorn investigates the deaths of a pair of Navajo women in this story by the author of *Dance Hall of the Dead.* (REV: BL 6/15/78; LJ 5/1/78; PW 3/13/78)

6531   Hillerman, Tony. *People of Darkness.* **1988, Harper & Row paper $4.95 (0-06-080950-7).** Jim Chee investigates a mysterious Navajo religious cult with possible ties to a murder in this novel by the author of *A Thief of Time.* (REV: NYTBR 1/4/81; New Yorker 12/29/80)

6532   Hillerman, Tony. *Skinwalkers.* **1987, Harper & Row $19.95 (0-06-015695-3); paper $4.95 (0-06-080893-4).** Leaphorn and Chee team up to investigate the murders of four Navajos in this mystery novel by the author of *A Thief of Time.* (REV: BL 11/15/86; LJ 1/87; New Yorker 2/2/87)

6533   Hillerman, Tony. *Talking God.* **1989, Harper & Row $17.95 (0-06-016118-3).** Leaphorn and Chee investigate a mysterious man who donated a pair of skeletons to the Smithsonian that were stolen from a Navajo reservation. (REV: BL 5/1/89; NYTBR 6/18/89; Time 6/19/89)

6534   Hillerman, Tony. *Thief of Time.* **1988, Harper & Row $15.45 (0-06-015938-3); paper $4.95 (0-06-100004-3).** A mystery involving the murder of an anthropologist and the thievery of prehistoric relics from her research site. (REV: BL 5/15/88; Newsweek 7/18/88; Time 7/4/88)

6535   Hjortsberg, William. *Falling Angel.* **1986, Warner paper $3.95 (0-446-31432-3).** A New York private investigator searches for a popular singer who escaped from a private psychiatric clinic in this novel that mixes elements of the detective and occult genres. (REV: NYTBR 2/4/79; Newsweek 10/9/78; PW 9/18/78)

6536   Holland, Isabelle. *Bump in the Night.* **1988, Doubleday $16.95 (0-385-23891-6); Fawcett paper $3.95 (0-449-21770-1).** A New York police detective's search for a missing eight-year-old leads him into the world of child prostitution. (REV: BL 11/15/88; LJ 11/1/88)

6537   Holland, Isabelle. *A Fatal Advent.* **1989, Doubleday $16.95 (0-385-24815-6).** A reverend turns sleuth following a murder committed on the stairway leading to his parish house. (REV: BL 10/15/89; PW 10/6/89)

6538   Hornig, Doug. *Dark Side.* **1986, Mysterious $15.95 (0-89296-168-6).** A private investigator is hired by an alarm company to look into the death of a man whose widow is suing for damages over a faulty alarm. (REV: BL 10/15/86; NYTBR 11/30/86; PW 8/29/86)

6539   Innes, Michael. *Death at the Chase.* **1986, Penguin paper $3.95 (0-14-003243-6).** A Scotland Yard detective becomes embroiled in a mystery after being hit by a stone while accidentally trespassing on a man's property. (REV: BL 5/1/70; NYTBR 3/15/70)

6540   Isaacs, Susan. *Magic Hour.* **1991, HarperCollins $21.95 (0-06-016573-1).** The murder of a motion picture executive in his Long Island home leads Detective Steve Brady to investigate the many potential suspects in the crime. (REV: BL 11/15/90; NYTBR 1/20/91; PW 11/30/90)

6541   Izzi, Eugene. *Prime Roll.* **1990, Bantam paper $3.95 (0-553-28376-6).** The story of a gambler who becomes involved in an organized crime plot to murder a labor union leader. (REV: BL 3/15/90; PW 2/9/90)

6542   Jackson, Jon A. *Grootka.* **1990, Countryman $19.95 (0-88150-179-4).** A series of three Detroit murders puts retired cop Grootka on the trail of a young computer-whiz psychopath. "Mr. Jackson stands right up there with the best of the urban crime chroniclers."—NYTBR (REV: BL 9/1/90; CSM 12/17/90; NYTBR 11/25/90)

6543   Jahn, Michael. *Night Rituals.* **1982, Norton $12.95 (0-393-01630-7).** Several New York murder sites are found to contain evidence of North American Indian ritual ceremonies. (REV: BL 10/15/82; LJ 10/1/82; PW 9/3/82)

6544 James, P. D. *Black Tower*. 1987, Warner paper $3.95 (0-446-34824-4). Scotland Yard detective Dalgliesh investigates a series of unexplained deaths at the English nursing home where he is recovering from an illness. (REV: BL 9/15/75; LJ 7/75; PW 8/18/75)

6545 James, P. D. *Death of an Expert Witness*. 1988, Warner paper $4.95 (0-446-31472-5). Detective Adam Dalgleish investigates the murder of a medical examiner. (REV: LJ 11/1/77; New Yorker 3/6/78; Time 4/17/78)

6546 James, P. D. *Devices and Desires*. 1990, Knopf $19.95 (0-394-58070-2). Detective Adam Dalgleish tracks a serial killer preying on the women of a small English community. (REV: BL 11/1/89; LJ 12/89; NYTBR 1/28/90)

6547 James, P. D. *Shroud for a Nightingale*. 1988, Warner paper $4.95 (0-446-31303-3). A series of murders of student nurses at a British hospital is investigated by detective Dalgleish. (REV: BL 1/1/72; NYTBR 1/16/72; TLS 10/22/71)

6548 James, P. D. *Skull Beneath the Skin*. 1988, Warner paper $4.95 (0-446-35372-8). An actress is found murdered on a small island off the English coast after receiving a series of threatening messages. (REV: LJ 7/82; Newsweek 9/13/82; PW 7/2/82)

6549 James, P. D. *A Taste for Death*. 1986, Knopf $18.95 (0-394-55583-X); Warner paper $4.95 (0-446-32352-7). The deaths of two citizens in a small London church lead Inspector Dalgliesh to investigate a suspected cover-up of the crime. (REV: BL 8/86; CSM 10/31/86; TLS 6/27/86. AWARDS: BL, the 1980s)

6550 James, P. D. *Unnatural Causes*. 1988, Warner paper $4.95 (0-446-31219-3). Detective Dalgleish investigates the mysterious mutilation murder of an English writer. (REV: PW 8/14/67; TLS 5/18/67)

6551 James, P. D. *An Unsuitable Job for a Woman*. 1987, Warner paper $3.95 (0-446-34832-5). A female Cambridge detective investigates the apparent suicide of her partner in this tale by the author of *Devices and Desires*. (REV: LJ 4/1/73; NYTBR 4/22/73; PW 1/29/73)

6552 Johnson, Paul. *Killing the Blues*. 1987, St. Martin's $16.95 (0-312-01054-0). A 1960s holdout seeks clues to the murder of a woman in his small New York hometown. (REV: BL 11/1/87; LJ 11/1/87; PW 10/23/87)

6553 Jones, Cleo. *Case of the Fragmented Woman*. 1986, St. Martin's $15.95 (0-312-12328-0); Harlequin paper $3.50 (0-373-26004-0). The story of an investigation into the murder of a television actress whose body parts appear in a series of unusual situations. (REV: BL 11/1/86; PW 11/7/86)

6554 Kakonis, Tom. *Criss Cross*. 1989, St. Martin's $18.95 (0-312-03728-7). An ex-convict and his friends plan the Christmas Eve robbery of a Grand Rapids convenience store. (REV: BL 1/1/90; CSM 12/17/90; PW 11/10/89)

6555 Kakonis, Tom. *Double Down*. 1991, Dutton $19.95 (0-525-93326-3). A pair of professional gamblers attempt to raise $300,000 in two weeks to pay their debts to organized crime figures. "This may be the best crime novel to appear in the first half of 1991."—BL (REV: BL 7/91; PW 5/31/91)

6556 Kakonis, Tom. *Michigan Roll*. 1988, St. Martin's $16.95 (0-312-02252-2); paper $3.95 (0-312-91684-1). A first novel involving an ex-felon and former English professor turned cardsharp. "A shimmering debut."—BL (REV: BL 9/15/88; LJ 10/15/88; PW 7/22/88)

6557 Kallen, Lucille. *C. B. Greenfield: A Little Madness*. 1987, Ballantine paper $3.50 (0-345-31119-1). This fifth C. B. Greenfield novel finds the New England newspaper owner plagued by love and a murder. (REV: BL 3/1/86; LJ 3/1/86; PW 1/31/86)

6558 Kallen, Lucille. *C. B. Greenfield: No Lady in the House*. 1984, Ballantine paper $3.95 (0-345-32396-3). This third C. B. Greenfield novel has the Connecticut newspaper owner investigating a series of local burglaries and real estate scams. (REV: BL 2/15/82; PW 12/18/81)

6559 Kallen, Lucille. *C. B. Greenfield: The Tanglewood Murder*. 1985, Ballantine paper $3.95 (0-345-33143-5). A newspaper editor seeks clues to the death of a concert violinist who died at a Berkshires concert. (REV: BL 9/1/80; LJ 10/1/80; PW 8/1/80)

6560 Kaminsky, Stuart M. *Bullet for a Star*. 1985, Mysterious paper $3.95 (0-89296-147-3). A 1940s Hollywood tale of blackmail involving Errol Flynn, Edward G. Robinson, and Peter Lorre as characters. (REV: BL 10/15/77; NYTBR 8/21/77; PW 6/13/77)

6561 Kaminsky, Stuart M. *A Cold Red Sunrise*. 1988, Macmillan $16.95 (0-684-18905-4); Ivy Books paper $3.50 (0-8041-0428-X). Inspector Rostnikov investigates the death of a dissident's daughter in Siberia in this fifth segment of the series. (REV: BL 11/15/88; Time 4/3/89. AWARDS: Edgar, 1989)

6562 Kaminsky, Stuart M. *Down for the Count*. 1990, Warner paper $4.50 (0-445-40908-8). A mystery involving heavyweight boxing great Joe Louis as the suspect in a brutal murder. (REV: BL 3/15/85; PW 2/1/85)

6563 Kaminsky, Stuart M. *Murder on the Yellow Brick Road*. 1979, Penguin paper $3.95 (0-14-005124-4). Judy Garland finds a murdered munchkin on the set of *The Wizard of Oz* and hires a private eye to find the killer. (REV: NYTBR 4/23/78; PW 2/20/78)

6564 Kaminsky, Stuart M. *Rostnikov's Vacation*. 1991, Scribner $19.95 (0-684-19022-2). Inspector Rostnikov becomes involved in a murder investigation while vacationing in Yalta. (REV: BL 9/15/91; LJ 10/1/91)

6565 Katzenbach, John. *In the Heat of the Summer*. 1987, Ballantine paper $3.95 (0-345-34404-9). A Miami newspaper journalist receives a series of calls from a killer following each murder the man commits. (REV: LJ 4/1/82; PW 3/26/82; Time 7/5/82)

6566   Katzenbach, John. *Traveler.* **1988, Ballantine paper $4.95 (0-345-34709-9).** A police detective investigates the rape and murder of her niece by a serial killer. "An intense carefully sustained exercise in psychological terror."—BL (REV: BL 1/1/87; NYTBR 3/15/87)

6567   Keating, H. R. F. *Bats Fly Up for Inspector Ghote.* **1984, Academy Chicago paper $4.95 (0-89733-120-6).** Inspector Ghote is transferred to another department of the Bombay police to investigate charges of internal corruption. (REV: LJ 9/1/74; NYTBR 10/20/74; TLS 7/19/74)

6568   Keating, H. R. F. *Body in the Billiard Room.* **1987, Viking $15.95 (0-670-81744-9); Penguin paper $3.95 (0-14-010171-3).** Inspector Ghote searches for a murderer at the former hill station of Ootacamund. (REV: BL 9/15/87; PW 9/25/87; Time 2/1/88)

6569   Keating, H. R. F. *Filmi, Filmi, Inspector Ghote.* **1985, Academy Chicago paper $4.95 (0-89733-138-9).** Inspector Ghote becomes an actor in an Indian film to investigate the murder of a motion picture star. (REV: BL 5/15/77; LJ 4/1/77; PW 2/21/77)

6570   Keating, H. R. F. *Inspector Ghote Draws a Line.* **1985, Academy Chicago paper $4.95 (0-89733-135-7).** Inspector Ghote looks into a series of terrorist notes threatening the life of a small-town judge. (REV: BL 4/15/79; LJ 5/1/79; PW 3/5/79)

6571   Keating, H. R. F. *Inspector Ghote Hunts the Peacock.* **1985, Academy Chicago paper $4.95 (0-89733-179-6).** The Indian inspector's first trip to England to deliver a paper at an international convention, and his investigation into the whereabouts of a missing relative. (REV: LJ 10/1/68; NYTBR 8/25/68; PW 7/1/68)

6572   Keating, H. R. F. *Inspector Ghote Trusts the Heart.* **1983, Academy Chicago paper $4.95 (0-89733-083-8).** Inspector Ghote trails a swindler throughout India by train. (REV: LJ 9/1/72; NYTBR 7/16/72; TLS 12/31/71)

6573   Keating, H. R. F. *Under a Monsoon Cloud.* **1986, Viking $15.95 (0-670-80367-7).** Inspector Ghote is placed on trial for his role in the cover-up in a Bombay murder. (REV: BL 9/1/86; LJ 9/1/86; PW 7/25/86)

6574   Kellerman, Jonathan. *Butcher's Theatre.* **1988, Bantam $19.95 (0-553-05251-9); paper $4.95 (0-553-27510-0).** A Jewish police inspector in Jerusalem searches for the murderer of young Arab girls. "A stunning work."—LJ (REV: BL 1/1/88; LJ 3/1/88; PW 1/15/88)

6575   Kellerman, Jonathan. *Over the Edge.* **1987, Macmillan $17.95 (0-689-11635-7); NAL paper $4.95** (0-451-15219-0). A psychological study of a psychotic arrested in connection with a series of murders of gay men in Los Angeles. "Truly outstanding."—LJ (REV: BL 4/1/87; LJ 4/1/87; PW 2/27/87)

6576   Kellerman, Jonathan. *Silent Partner.* **1989, Bantam $18.95 (0-553-05370-1); paper $5.95 (0-553-28592-0).** A California child psychologist/detective seeks clues to the motive behind the suicide of a former lover. (REV: BL 6/1/89; PW 8/25/89)

6577   Kellerman, Jonathan. *Time Bomb.* **1990, Bantam $19.95 (0-553-05796-0).** A detective, a school, and a child psychologist investigate a sniper shooting at an elementary school. "A marvelous read."—NYTBR (REV: BL 7/90; NYTBR 10/14/90; PW 8/31/90)

6578   Kellerman, Jonathan. *When the Bough Breaks.* **1986, NAL paper $4.95 (0-451-15874-1).** The debut novel by a child psychologist set in Los Angeles about a group of sexual deviants running a foster home. (REV: BL 3/15/85; LJ 3/1/85; PW 1/25/85)

6579   Kelly, Mary Anne. *Park Lane South, Queens.* **1990, St. Martin's $16.95 (0-312-03907-7).** Three sisters search for a child killer when a body is found near their New York home. (REV: BL 2/15/90; LJ 2/1/90; PW 1/19/90)

6580   Kemelman, Harry. *One Fine Day the Rabbi Bought a Cross.* **1987, Morrow $15.95 (0-688-05631-8); Fawcett paper $3.95 (0-449-20687-4).** Rabbi Small investigates a possible PLO conspiracy surrounding the murder of an American professor in Jerusalem. (REV: BL 2/1/87; PW 1/30/87)

6581   Kemelman, Harry. *Saturday the Rabbi Went Hungry.* **1987, Fawcett paper $3.50 (0-449-21392-7).** Rabbi Small buries a suicide victim in a Jewish cemetery and is forced to prove his suspicion that the man was murdered. (REV: LJ 9/1/66; NYTBR 7/24/66; Time 9/30/66)

6582   Kemelman, Harry. *Someday the Rabbi Will Leave.* **1986, Fawcett paper $3.95 (0-449-20945-8).** Rabbi Small assists the local police with the investigation into a fatal hit-and-run automobile accident. (REV: BL 1/15/85; PW 1/18/75; TLS 12/27/85)

6583   Kemelman, Harry. *Sunday the Rabbi Stayed Home.* **1985, Fawcett paper $3.50 (0-449-21000-6).** Rabbi Small visits a Massachusetts college and becomes involved in the investigation of the death of a student found in a beach house. "Detective fiction at its most telling as social commentary."—NYTBR (REV: CSM 3/27/69; LJ 3/15/69; NYTBR 3/2/69)

6584   Kemelman, Harry. *Tuesday the Rabbi Saw Red.* **1986, Fawcett paper $3.50 (0-449-21321-8).** Rabbi Small takes a position teaching Jewish philosophy at a New England college and becomes involved in the investigation into the bombing death of a colleague. (REV: BL 2/1/74; CSM 1/16/74; NYTBR 3/3/74)

6585 Kemelman, Harry. *Wednesday the Rabbi Got Wet.* **1986, Fawcett paper $3.50 (0-449-21328-5).** Rabbi Small takes the case of a pharmacist's son who allegedly caused the death of a man by improperly filling a prescription. (REV: BL 10/15/76; NYTBR 9/12/76; PW 7/12/76)

6586 Kent, Bill. *Under the Boardwalk.* **1990, Windsor paper $4.50 (1-55817-347-1).** This debut novel features an honest cop fighting internal corruption and street crime in Atlantic City. (REV: BL 11/15/88; NYTBR 12/11/88; PW 11/1/88)

6587 Kienzle, William X. *Eminence.* **1990, Ballantine paper $4.95 (0-345-35395-1).** The attempted murder of a newspaper journalist brings detective/priest Father Koesler into the investigation of the crime. (REV: BL 3/15/89; PW 2/3/89)

6588 Kienzle, William X. *Rosary Murders.* **1989, Ballantine paper $4.95 (0-345-35668-3).** A former priest's tale of the investigation of a series of Detroit murders of priests and nuns left holding a rosary in their hands. (REV: LJ 5/1/79; PW 2/5/79)

6589 Kiker, Douglas. *Death at the Cut.* **1988, Random $15.95 (0-394-56952-0); Ballantine paper $3.95 (0-345-35993-3).** A journalist covering a senator's political campaign discovers the corpse of a drowned woman with connections to the candidate. (REV: NYTBR 8/14/88; New Yorker 8/8/88; PW 4/1/88)

6590 Kiker, Douglas. *Murder on Clam Pond.* **1988, Ballantine paper $3.50 (0-345-34095-7).** A chronicle of the murder of an elderly Cape Cod woman and the investigation into her death. (REV: BL 11/15/86; PW 10/10/86; Time 12/22/86)

6591 Klein, Zachary W. *Still Among the Living.* **1990, Harper & Row $18.95 (0-06-016411-5).** A drug-taking, alcoholic Boston sleuth investigates a series of crimes including a New Jersey wife-beating case. "Gritty and fast-moving."—PW (REV: BL 8/90; NYTBR 8/26/90; PW 6/15/90)

6592 Klein, Zachary W. *Two Way Toll.* **1991, HarperCollins $19.95 (0-06-016420-4).** Boston private investigator Matt Jacob investigates a death that takes him back to the slum of his childhood. "A taut, compelling story."—PW (REV: BL 10/1/91; PW 9/13/91)

6593 Koenig, Joseph. *Floater.* **1986, Mysterious $16.95 (0-89296-173-2).** The search for an ex-convict who seduces and then murders wealthy Florida women. "A splendid procedural expressed in sharp, economical yet sensitive prose."—NYTBR (REV: BL 11/1/86; NYTBR 2/22/87)

6594 Koenig, Joseph. *Little Odessa.* **1988, Viking $17.95 (0-670-81954-9); Ballantine paper $3.95 (0-345-36061-3).** A Russian-born stripper is accused of an assault in this novel set in the area of Brooklyn known as Little Odessa. (REV: NYTBR 6/26/88; PW 2/12/88)

6595 Koenig, Joseph. *Smuggler's Notch.* **1989, Viking $17.95 (0-670-82341-4).** A Vermont sheriff pursues a psychopath terrorizing his community. (REV: BL 12/15/88; NYTBR 2/5/89)

6596 Langley, Bob. *Churchill Diamonds.* **1986, Walker $15.95 (0-8027-0934-6).** The robbery of over 180 diamonds leads investigators to examine the history of the jewels. (REV: BL 12/15/86; PW 11/7/86)

6597 Langton, Jane. *Emily Dickinson Is Dead.* **1984, St. Martin's $13.95 (0-312-24434-7); Penguin paper $4.50 (0-14-007771-5).** A murder and arson plague a literary conference devoted to the study of the works of Emily Dickinson. (REV: BL 6/1/84; LJ 5/1/84; PW 3/23/84)

6598 Langton, Jane. *Good and Dead.* **1986, St. Martin's $15.95 (0-312-33865-1); Penguin paper $3.95 (0-14-012687-2).** A series of murders plagues a church congregation in a small New England village. (REV: New Yorker 2/9/87; PW 9/19/86)

6599 Lathen, Emma. *Something in the Air.* **1988, Simon & Schuster $16.95 (0-671-66599-5); Pocket paper $3.95 (0-671-68356-X).** This mystery, set in Boston, concerns an investigation into the murder of an airline executive. (REV: NYTBR 10/9/88; PW 9/9/88)

6600 Leonard, Elmore. *La Brava.* **1984, Avon paper $3.95 (0-380-69237-6).** A former Secret Service agent becomes the target of a scam in Miami following his romantic involvement with a motion picture actress. (REV: CSM 11/4/83; Newsweek 11/14/83; PW 10/7/83. AWARDS: Edgar, 1983)

6601 Leonard, Elmore. *Cat Chaser.* **1983, Avon paper $3.95 (0-380-64642-0).** Thugs trail a former Marine hotel owner who becomes involved with the ex-wife of a Dominican general. (REV: LJ 7/82; New Yorker 7/12/82; PW 5/7/82)

6602 Leonard, Elmore. *City Primeval: High Noon in Detroit.* **1982, Avon paper $3.95 (0-380-56952-3).** A Hispanic cop searches for a judge's killer in this Detroit tale of murder and blackmail by the author of *Stick*. (REV: BL 12/1/80; LJ 12/1/80; PW 8/22/80)

6603 Leonard, Elmore. *Freaky Deaky.* **1988, Morrow $18.95 (0-87795-975-7); Warner paper $5.95 (0-446-35039-7).** A Detroit police officer investigates the bombing murders of former radicals in this novel by the author of *Glitz*. (REV: BL 2/15/88; LJ 4/1/88; Time 5/16/88)

6604 Leonard, Elmore. *Get Shorty.* **1990, Delacorte $21.95 (0-385-30150-2).** A Miami organized crime loan shark seeking to collect debts becomes involved in the motion picture business. "Leonard's best book in years, and he isn't even coming off a slump."—BL (REV: BL 6/1/90; PW 6/15/90; Time 8/13/90)

6605 Leonard, Elmore. *Glitz.* **1983, Morrow $14.95 (0-87795-632-4); Warner paper $4.95 (0-446-34343-9).** A Miami cop is sent to Puerto Rico to recover from a gunshot wound and becomes romantically involved with a prostitute in this novel set in San Juan and Atlantic City. (REV: LJ 2/1/85; New Yorker 2/18/85; Newsweek 2/4/85)

6606 Leonard, Elmore. *Killshot.* 1989, Morrow $18.95 (1-557-10041-1); Warner paper $5.95 (0-446-35041-9). Two criminals seek to track down and murder people who witnessed a failed extortion attempt. "Crime fiction doesn't get any better . . . a bravura performance."—PW (Rev: BL 2/15/89; Newsweek 4/10/89; PW 2/10/89)

6607 Leonard, Elmore. *Split Images.* 1983, Avon paper $3.95 (0-380-63107-5). A Detroit killer and a former police officer track a police officer's girl friend in this novel by the author of *Freaky Deaky.* (Rev: LJ 2/1/82; NYTBR 4/18/82; Newsweek 3/22/82)

6608 Leonard, Elmore. *Stick.* 1984, Avon paper $3.95 (0-380-67652-4). An ex-convict just released from prison finds himself running with a group of high rollers. "Sharply written, and as shapely as a sonata . . . a fine book."—New Yorker (Rev: LJ 2/1/83; New Yorker 3/7/83; Newsweek 7/11/83; BL, the 1980s)

6609 Lescroart, John T. *Dead Irish.* 1990, Donald I. Fine $18.95 (1-55611-159-2). A former San Francisco policeman searches for clues to the events surrounding a friend's suicide. (Rev: BL 1/15/90; LJ 1/90; PW 10/27/89)

6610 Lescroart, John T. *Son of Holmes.* 1986, Donald I. Fine $15.95 (0-917657-64-0); Dorchester paper $3.25 (0-8439-2461-6). Research reveals that the son of Sherlock Holmes may be none other than the gourmand sleuth Nero Wolfe. (Rev: BL 4/15/86; PW 2/21/86)

6611 Leuci, Bob. *Captain Butterfly.* 1987, Freundlich $16.95 (0-317-58348-4). A female officer investigates stories of police using torture to coerce confessions. "As good as they come: nervy, smooth and dead-on convincing."—NYTBR (Rev: BL 4/15/89; PW 5/12/89)

6612 Leuci, Bob. *Doyle's Disciples.* 1984, Freudlich $14.95 (0-88191-006-6). A detective's investigation of a series of Harlem police murders uncovers a decade-long trail of corruption. (Rev: LJ 8/84; NYTBR 1/6/85; PW 7/6/84)

6613 Levine, Paul J. *To Speak for the Dead.* 1990, Bantam $17.95 (0-553-05747-2). A physician framed for murder by an acquaintance searches for the real criminal to clear his name. (Rev: BL 8/90; LJ 7/90; PW 6/22/90)

6614 Lewin, Elsa. *I, Anna.* 1985, Mysterious $15.95 (0-89296-118-X). An investigator becomes emotionally involved in the case of a divorcée who killed a man following a sexual assault. (Rev: BL 4/1/85; LJ 4/1/85)

6615 Lieberman, Herbert H. *Nightbloom.* 1984, Putnam $16.95 (0-399-12904-9). A New York detective searches for a murderer who tosses heavy objects off tall buildings onto unsuspecting pedestrians. (Rev: LJ 5/1/84; PW 2/24/84)

6616 Lindsey, David L. *In the Lake of the Moon.* 1990, Bantam paper $4.95 (0-553-28344-8). A homicide detective searches for the source of a series of photographs that show his father in an unflatter-ing light. "Thriller writing of the first order."—BL (Rev: BL 3/15/88; LJ 5/1/88; NYTBR 7/17/88)

6617 Lindsey, David L. *Mercy.* 1990, Doubleday $19.95 (0-385-24813-X). The story of an investigation into a series of brutal murders of lesbians in Houston, Texas. (Rev: BL 3/1/90; PW 3/23/90)

6618 Lindsey, David L. *Spiral.* 1988, Pocket paper $4.50 (0-671-64666-4). A Mexican gang chases corrupt former government officials through Texas. "Top-notch mystery fare."—BL (Rev: BL 10/15/86; LJ 10/1/86; PW 9/12/86)

6619 Llewellyn, Caroline. *Lady of the Labyrinth.* 1990, Scribner $19.95 (0-684-18920-8). A yacht owner seeks clues to the identities of men attempting to sabotage his boating business. (Rev: BL 3/1/90; LJ 2/15/90; PW 2/2/90)

6620 Llewellyn, Sam. *Dead Reckoning.* 1989, Simon & Schuster paper $3.50 (0-671-64659-1). A British mystery about the sabotage of the rudders of racing yachts. (Rev: BL 3/15/88; NYTBR 5/22/88; PW 2/12/88)

6621 Llewellyn, Sam. *Death Roll.* 1990, Summit $17.95 (0-671-67045-X). An Australian sailor practicing for the America's Cup challenge trails criminals over the high seas after finding evidence of misdoings at his boat yard. (Rev: BL 4/1/90; PW 2/2/90; TLS 7/21/89)

6622 Lochte, Dick. *Sleeping Dog.* 1986, Warner paper $3.95 (0-446-32661-5). A Los Angeles detective becomes involved in the search for a teenager's missing dog. (Rev: NYTBR 11/17/85; PW 10/4/85)

6623 Lovesey, Peter. *Abracadaver.* 1989, Harper & Row paper $4.50 (0-06-081000-9). A detective in Victorian London investigates a series of musicians' murders. "Pleasant reading, even charming reading."—NYTBR (Rev: LJ 12/1/72; NYTBR 10/15/72; TLS 7/7/72)

6624 Lovesey, Peter. *Bertie and the Seven Bodies.* 1990, Mysterious $16.95 (0-89296-399-9). A murder mystery set on an English estate in 1890 involving the deaths of several members of a dinner party. "In the best tradition of blithe detection."—TLS (Rev: BL 1/15/90; PW 12/1/89; TLS 6/1/90)

6625 Lovesey, Peter. *Bertie and the Tinman.* 1988, Mysterious $15.95 (0-89296-196-1). The Prince of Wales sets out to solve the case of a famous jockey who committed suicide in this novel set in 1886. (Rev: NYTBR 3/27/88; Time 2/1/88; TLS 12/25/87)

6626 Lovesey, Peter. *Detective Wore Silk Drawers.* 1989, Harper & Row paper $4.50 (0-06-080999-X). A decapitated body found in the Thames leads detectives into the world of banned sporting contests. (Rev: LJ 8/71; NYTBR 8/8/71/; PW 7/5/71)

6627 Lovesey, Peter. *Last Detective.* 1991, Doubleday $18.50 (0-385-42114-1). A British detective searches for the killer of a former soap opera star in this novel set in Bath. (Rev: BL 9/1/91; NYTBR 10/20/91; PW 8/18/91. Awards: BL, 1991)

6628   Lovesey, Peter. *Mad Hatter's Holiday.* **1990, Borgo Pr. $19.95 (0-8095-9022-0); Harper & Row paper $4.50 (0-06-081022-X).** A Victorian mystery set in a fashionable British beach resort. (REV: PW 7/2/73; TLS 6/15/73)

6629   Lovesey, Peter. *On the Edge.* **1990, Mysterious $16.95 (0-89296-363-8).** Two friends hatch a plot to murder each other's husbands. (REV: BL 2/15/89; NYTBR 3/12/89; PW 1/6/89)

6630   Lovesey, Peter. *Rough Cider.* **1987, Mysterious $15.95 (0-89296-194-5); Warner paper $3.95 (0-445-40545-7).** A young American woman confronts her university professor, who testified in the wartime murder trial of her father. (REV: NYTBR 7/12/87; PW 4/17/87)

6631   Lovesey, Peter. *Swing, Swing Together.* **1990, Borgo Pr. $19.95 (0-8095-9023-9); Harper & Row paper $4.50 (0-06-081023-8).** Cribb and Thackeray investigate a mystery set in Victorian England that coincides with London's search for Jack the Ripper. (REV: LJ 10/1/76; NYTBR 9/26/76)

6632   Lutz, John. *Blood Fire.* **1990, Henry Holt $17.95 (0-8050-0969-8).** A Florida private investigator becomes involved in a case involving a murderous drug dealer. (REV: BL 11/1/90; PW 12/7/90)

6633   Lutz, John. *Diamond Eyes.* **1990, St. Martin's $15.95 (0-312-05074-7).** The story of a private investigator's search for the airplane bomber that killed his client. (REV: BL 11/90; PW 10/5/90)

6634   Lutz, John. *Flame.* **1989, Henry Holt $17.95 (0-8050-0968-X).** Florida detective Fred Carver investigates the bombing of a boat and its potential ties to drug-running activities. (REV: BL 12/15/89; TLS 8/24/90)

6635   Lutz, John. *Kiss.* **1988, Henry Holt $17.95 (0-8050-0412-2); Avon paper $3.95 (0-380-70934-1).** A private detective investigates a series of suspicious, medically related deaths in a Florida retirement home. (REV: BL 6/1/88; LJ 9/1/88; PW 7/22/88)

6636   Lutz, John. *Scorcher.* **1988, Avon paper $3.95 (0-380-70526-5).** An Orlando, Florida, private investigator searches for the blow-torch killer of his son and others. (REV: BL 10/15/87; LJ 9/1/87; PW 9/4/87)

6637   Lutz, John. *Time Exposure.* **1989, St. Martin's $16.95 (0-312-02990-X).** A private investigator searches for missing St. Louis officials who are suspects in an embezzlement scheme. (REV: BL 7/89; PW 6/16/89)

6638   Lutz, John. *Tropical Heat.* **1987, Avon paper $3.95 (0-380-70309-2).** A Florida private eye investigates the death of a woman's lover that local police ruled a suicide. (REV: BL 6/1/86; LJ 6/1/86; PW 5/23/86)

6639   Lyons, Arthur. *Other People's Money.* **1989, Mysterious $17.95 (0-89296-218-6); paper $4.95 (0-445-40903-7).** A case involving missing museum artifacts, a pair of murders, and illicit dealings by a museum director to purchase items for his personal collection. (REV: BL 6/15/89; NYTBR 7/30/89; PW 5/19/89)

6640   McBain, Ed. *Another Part of the City.* **1986, Mysterious $15.95 (0-89296-153-8).** NYPD detective Bryan Riorden searches for the killer of a Little Italy restaurant owner. (REV: New Yorker 8/4/86; PW 3/7/86)

6641   McBain, Ed. *Cinderella.* **1987, Mysterious paper $4.50 (0-445-40898-7).** A Florida detective is murdered while investigating two cases in this novel by the author known for his 87th Precinct series. "The action keeps up until the final sentence."—Time (REV: BL 2/15/86; LJ 4/1/86; Time 7/7/86)

6642   McBain, Ed. *Downtown.* **1991, Morrow $20.00 (0-688-08736-1).** A Florida man is framed for a New York murder in this story by the author of *Cinderella.* "Funny, hilarious, entertaining and a great deal of fun to read."—NYTBR (REV: NYTBR 9/8/91; PW 7/5/91)

6643   McBain, Ed. *Eight Black Horses.* **1986, Avon paper $3.95 (0-380-70029-8).** Police detectives seek a villain dubbed "The Deaf Man" in this 87th Precinct novel. (REV: BL 5/15/85; PW 6/14/85; Time 11/4/85)

6644   McBain, Ed. *Goldilocks.* **1988, Windsor paper $3.95 (1-55817-108-8).** Details concerning a physician's private life are uncovered during the investigation of the murder of his wife and daughters. (REV: BL 3/15/78; PW 11/28/77; TLS 7/21/78)

6645   McBain, Ed. *House That Jack Built.* **1989, Mysterious paper $3.95 (0-445-40623-2).** A defense attorney defends a man accused of murdering his AIDS-afflicted brother at his Florida home. (REV: BL 7/88; PW 5/20/88)

6646   McBain, Ed. *Poison.* **1988, Avon paper $3.95 (0-380-70030-1).** An 87th Precinct novel involving the investigation of a team of detectives into a nicotine poisoning murder. (REV: BL 1/1/87; CSM 4/3/87; PW 1/16/87)

6647   McBain, Ed. *Puss in Boots.* **1988, Warner paper $3.95 (0-445-40621-6).** An investigation into a murder leads an attorney into the pornographic underworld. (REV: BL 5/15/87; PW 5/22/87)

6648   McBain, Ed. *Tricks.* **1989, Avon paper $3.95 (0-380-70383-1).** This 87th Precinct novel follows an investigation into the Halloween murders of New York liquor store employees. (REV: NYTBR 1/8/89; PW 11/18/88)

6649   McBain, Ed. *Vespers: A Novel of the 87th Precinct.* **1990, Morrow $18.95 (0-87795-987-0).** An 87th Precinct novel about the murder of a Roman Catholic priest by a Satanic cult. (REV: NYTBR 1/7/90; PW 11/10/89)

6650   McBain, Ed. *Widows.* **1991, Morrow $19.00 (0-688-10219-0).** An 87th Precinct novel detailing the investigation into the murder of a lawyer and his wife. (REV: BL 12/1/90; PW 12/7/90)

6651 McCall, Dan. *Triphammer*. 1990, Atlantic Monthly $18.95 (0-87113-333-4). A Cornell University professor's novel portraying the daily life and personal feelings of an Ithaca policeman. (Rev: BL 1/1/90; LJ 11/15/89; NYTBR 2/4/90)

6652 McCammon, Robert R. *Boy's Life*. 1991, Pocket $21.95 (0-671-74226-4). A teenage boy looks for details about the death of a car crash victim in a small town in Alabama in 1964. (Rev: BL 5/15/91; LJ 7/91; PW 5/31/91)

6653 McClure, James. *Artful Egg*. 1986, Pantheon paper $5.95 (0-394-72126-8). The murder of a controversial South African writer is investigated by Lieutenant Kramer and his Bantu aide. (Rev: BL 3/1/85; NYTBR 6/9/85; PW 2/1/85)

6654 McClure, James. *Gooseberry, Fool*. 1983, Pantheon paper $2.95 (0-394-71059-2). The Christmastime murder of a young South African man is investigated by Lieutenant Kramer and his Bantu sergeant assistant. "A fascinating book, not to be missed."—LJ (Rev: LJ 7/74; NYTBR 9/1/74; PW 4/22/73)

6655 McClure, James. *Song Dog*. 1991, Mysterious $17.95 (0-89296-274-7). A prequel to the author's series featuring South African detectives Kramer and Zondi that explains how the pair met. (Rev: BL 8/91; LJ 7/91; PW 6/21/91)

6656 McClure, James. *Steam Pig*. 1982, Pantheon paper $2.95 (0-394-71021-5). A pair of South African detectives, one white, one Bantu, investigate the murder of a piano teacher. "Truly tough, brutal, unfair, and quite impossible to put down."—LJ (Rev: LJ 11/1/72; NYTBR 10/22/72; PW 7/31/72)

6657 McClure, James. *Sunday Hangman*. 1985, Pantheon paper $2.95 (0-394-72992-7). Lieutenant Kramer investigates a series of hanging deaths of criminals in this South African mystery. (Rev: BL 1/15/78; NYTBR 1/8/78)

6658 McCrumb, Sharyn. *If Ever I Return, Pretty Peggy-O*. 1990, Macmillan $17.95 (0-684-19104-0). A small Tennessee town is racked by a murder and a series of threats the week a 1966 class reunion is scheduled. (Rev: BL 4/15/90; NYTBR 5/20/90; PW 2/23/90)

6659 McCrumb, Sharyn. *Missing Susan*. 1991, Ballantine $17.00 (0-345-36575-5). Forensic anthropologist Elizabeth MacPherson becomes involved in the investigation of a murder following a bus tour of England's most infamous crime scenes. (Rev: BL 9/1/91; NYTBR 9/15/91)

6660 McCrumb, Sharyn. *Windsor Knot*. 1990, Ballantine $16.95 (0-345-36583-6). On the eve of her wedding forensic anthropologist Elizabeth MacPherson investigates the death of a neighbor's spouse. (Rev: BL 9/1/90; NYTBR 10/14/90; PW 7/27/90)

6661 McDonald, Gregory. *Confess, Fletch*. 1976, Avon paper $3.95 (0-380-00814-9). Fletch marries and becomes embroiled in art theft, kidnapping, and a murder in this mystery set in Italy and Boston. (Rev: NYTBR 12/19/76; PW 9/13/76)

6662 McDonald, Gregory. *Fletch*. 1976, Avon paper $3.95 (0-380-00645-6). A California journalist slips into a scheme involving drugs and a faked murder following a chance encounter with a person on the street. "Entertaining reading all the way through."—NYTBR (Rev: BL 3/15/75; LJ 2/1/75; NYTBR 2/16/75)

6663 McDonald, Gregory. *Fletch, Too*. 1987, Warner paper $3.95 (0-446-34614-4). While on his honeymoon Fletch witnesses a murder at an airport in Kenya. (Rev: BL 9/15/86; NYTBR 11/9/86; PW 8/8/86)

6664 McDonald, Gregory. *Fletch Won*. 1985, Warner $14.95 (0-446-51325-3); paper $4.50 (0-446-34095-2). Fletch recalls his first case as a reporter investigating the murder of an attorney. (Rev: BL 7/85; CSM 10/22/85; Time 11/4/85)

6665 McDonald, Gregory. *Flynn's In*. 1984, Mysterious $15.95 (0-89296-085-X). Detective/reporter Fletch solves a series of murders committed among the members of an elite club of financiers. "Ideal under-the-beach-umbrella reading."—Time (Rev: BL 6/15/84; PW 4/6/84; Time 7/9/84)

6666 MacDonald, John D. *Cinnamon Skin*. 1986, Fawcett paper $4.95 (0-449-12873-3). Travis McGee seeks the criminal who planted a fatal bomb aboard a boat. (Rev: BL 5/1/82; Natl Rev 1/21/83; PW 4/23/82)

6667 MacDonald, John D. *Empty Copper Sea*. 1980, Amereon $16.95 (0-89190-778-5). Travis McGee sets out to save a sailor's reputation in this seventeenth installment in the Florida-based series. (Rev: BL 9/15/78; New Yorker 11/6/78; PW 7/10/78)

6668 MacDonald, John D. *Good Old Stuff: 13 Early Stories*. 1985, Fawcett paper $4.95 (0-449-12952-7). A collection of 13 short stories published in pulp magazines by MacDonald in the 1940s and 1950s. (Rev: BL 9/15/82; LJ 11/1/82; PW 9/3/82)

6669 MacDonald, John D. *Green Ripper*. 1979, Amereon $16.95 (0-89190-779-3). Travis McGee seeks revenge on a group of terrorists responsible for the death of his girl friend. (Rev: BL 9/15/79; PW 7/30/79; Time 10/15/79. Awards: NBA, 1980)

6670 MacDonald, John D. *Lonely Silver Rain*. 1985, Knopf $15.95 (0-394-53899-4); Fawcett paper $4.95 (0-449-12509-2). Travis McGee becomes involved in fighting drug traffickers in Florida and Mexico after finding three bodies aboard a formerly missing yacht. (Rev: BL 12/15/84; LJ 3/1/85; PW 1/18/85)

6671 McDonald, Ross. *Blue Hammer*. 1979, Amereon $18.95 (0-89190-095-0); Bantam paper $3.95 (0-553-27548-8). A Lew Archer novel about the efforts of a California family to recover a stolen painting. (Rev: Atl 7/76; BL 6/15/76; PW 5/3/76)

6672 McGinley, Patrick. *Bogmail*. 1982, Penguin paper $4.95 (0-14-006195-9). A man who believes he has committed a perfect murder receives a series of blackmail letters in this novel set in Ireland. (Rev: BL 5/15/81; Newsweek 7/27/81; Time 8/17/81)

6673   **McIlvanney, William.** *Papers of Tony Veitch.* **1984, Pantheon paper $2.95 (0-394-73486-6).** Police Inspector Laidlaw investigates the poisoning of a Glasgow vagrant found with a list of names and addresses in his hand. (Rev: BL 5/15/83; New Yorker 6/6/83; PW 4/8/83)

6674   **McInerny, Ralph.** *Basket Case.* **1988, St. Martin's paper $3.50 (0-312-91157-2).** After finding an abandoned baby on a doorstep, Father Dowling investigates the murder of the baby's father. (Rev: BL 10/1/87; PW 10/2/87)

6675   **McInerny, Ralph.** *Body and Soil.* **1989, Macmillan $17.95 (0-689-12036-2).** The author known for his Father Dowling series tells the story of a small-town Indiana lawyer's investigation of the murder of a man during divorce proceedings. (Rev: BL 5/1/89; LJ 5/1/89; PW 3/31/89)

6676   **MacKinnon, Colin.** *Finding Hoseyn.* **1988, Penguin paper $4.50 (0-14-010453-4).** An investigation into the death of an Israeli engineer leads an American journalist to track down his terrorist killer. (Rev: CSM 9/23/86; LJ 2/1/86; PW 11/29/85)

6677   **MacLeod, Charlotte.** *Corpse in Oozak's Pond.* **1987, Mysterious $15.95 (0-89296-188-0); paper $3.95 (0-445-40683-6).** A series of contemporary Massachusetts college murders are found to bear startling resemblances to a group of turn-of-the-century crimes. (Rev: BL 4/15/87; PW 3/20/87; TLS 1/30/87)

6678   **MacLeod, Charlotte.** *Family Vault.* **1980, Avon paper $3.50 (0-380-49080-3).** The corpse of a nightclub dancer is discovered in a family crypt in Boston. (Rev: BL 4/15/79; TLS 6/6/80)

6679   **McQuillan, Karin.** *Deadly Safari.* **1990, St. Martin's $17.95 (0-312-03808-9).** The deaths of members of a company shooting television commercials in Kenya spur an investigation by local authorities. (Rev: BL 1/1/90; NYTBR 4/8/90; PW 12/8/89)

6680   **Mailer, Norman.** *Tough Guys Don't Dance.* **1984, Random $16.95 (0-394-53786-6); Ballantine paper $3.95 (0-345-32321-1).** A Provincetown writer wakes up after a drinking binge to discover evidence of a murder in his automobile and home. (Rev: BL 7/84; PW 6/29/84; Time 8/6/84. Awards: Time, 1984)

6681   **Malone, Michael.** *Time's Witness.* **1989, Little, Brown $19.95 (0-316-54480-9).** A Vietnam veteran, now a North Carolina police chief, uncovers a trail of political corruption surrounding the case of a young man scheduled to be executed for killing a policeman. (Rev: BL 3/15/89; NYTBR 4/23/89; PW 3/10/89)

6682   **Malone, Michael.** *Uncivil Seasons.* **1988, Pocket paper $3.95 (0-671-65838-7).** A pair of mismatched North Carolina detectives seek to unravel a mystery involving an aristocratic family in this novel by the author of *Handling Sin.* "A first-rate page turner."—BL (Rev: BL 10/15/83; LJ 10/1/83; NYTBR 11/13/83)

6683   **Marsh, Ngaio.** *Light Thickens.* **1987, Jove paper $3.50 (0-515-07359-8).** A posthumously published novel about an omen of danger plaguing a British acting troupe's production of Macbeth. (Rev: BL 9/1/82; LJ 10/1/82; PW 8/13/82)

6684   **Marsh, Ngaio.** *Photo Finish.* **1987, Jove paper $3.50 (0-515-07505-1).** A mystery written by the author when in her 80s involving the murder of an opera star in New Zealand. "Vintage Marsh . . . a book that should make all readers happy."—NYTBR (Rev: NYTBR 1/18/81; PW 8/28/81)

6685   **Marshall, William.** *Faces in the Crowd.* **1991, Mysterious $19.95 (0-89296-367-0).** A search for a missing prostitute reveals a complex conspiracy in this late nineteenth-century New York mystery. (Rev: BL 7/91; PW 7/5/91)

6686   **Marshall, William.** *New York Detective.* **1989, Mysterious $17.95 (0-89296-366-2); paper $4.95 (0-445-40921-5).** A story set in late nineteenth-century New York about police efforts to find the killer stalking members of a Civil War platoon. (Rev: BL 11/15/89; NYTBR 12/10/89)

6687   **Marston, Edward.** *Merry Devils.* **1989, St. Martin's $16.95 (0-312-02970-5).** A series of mysterious events and a death plague an Elizabethan theater group. (Rev: BL 12/15/89; LJ 1/90; PW 11/24/89)

6688   **Martin, Lee.** *Mensa Murders.* **1990, St. Martin's $15.95 (0-312-05126-3).** A Fort Worth detective investigates a series of murders of members of an organization for people with extremely high IQs. (Rev: BL 12/1/90; PW 11/2/90)

6689   **Matera, Lia.** *Good Fight.* **1990, Simon & Schuster $17.95 (0-671-68561-9).** A lawyer defending a suspect in an FBI murder finds herself the subject of government investigations. (Rev: BL 1/1/90; PW 11/17/89)

6690   **Matera, Lia.** *Prior Convictions.* **1991, Simon & Schuster $17.95 (0-671-68560-0).** An ex-lawyer is charged in a federal fraud case in this novel set in San Francisco during the 1960s. "Matera again demonstrates that she is one of today's best mystery writers."—PW (Rev: NYTBR 3/24/91; PW 2/1/91)

6691   **Matheson, Don.** *Stray Cat.* **1987, Summit $15.95 (0-671-64112-3); Pocket paper $3.50 (0-671-66508-1).** A Boston detective becomes romantically involved with a prostitute trying to set him up in a scam. (Rev: NYTBR 9/13/87; PW 7/31/87)

6692   **Mathis, Edward.** *Out of the Shadows.* **1990, Macmillan $17.95 (0-684-19038-9).** A detective searching for a missing inheritor finds a trail that leads to the world of pornography and possibly murder. (Rev: BL 7/90; LJ 7/90; PW 6/22/90)

6693   **Matsumoto, Seicho.** *Inspector Imanishi Investigates.* **1989, Soho Pr. $18.95 (0-939149-28-1).** A translation of a 1961 work by Japan's top mystery writer about an investigation into the death of an unknown man found on Tokyo train tracks. (Rev: BL 9/1/89; NYTBR 10/15/89; PW 7/14/89)

6694 Melville, James. *A Sort of Samurai.* 1985, Fawcett paper $2.95 (0-449-20821-4). The investigation into the death of a German businessman in Japan reveals a series of past illicit activities. (REV: LJ 3/1/82; PW 3/5/82; TLS 10/2/81)

6695 Millar, Margaret. *Ask for Me Tomorrow.* 1985, International Polygonics paper $4.95 (0-930330-15-3). A Mexican-American lawyer searches for the missing husband of a woman in this novel set in Southern California and Mexico. (REV: BL 1/15/77; LJ 11/1/76; PW 8/16/76)

6696 Millar, Margaret. *Beyond This Point Are Monsters.* 1985, International Polygonics paper $4.95 (0-530330-31-5). A study of a court case revolving around the disappearance and alleged death of a California ranch hand. (REV: BL 12/15/70; LJ 10/1/70; PW 7/6/70)

6697 Millar, Margaret. *Murder of Miranda.* 1980, Amereon $17.95 (0-89190-156-6); International Polygonics paper $4.95 (0-930330-95-1). A lawyer searches for the whereabouts of a missing Palm Springs widow. (REV: NYTBR 4/29/79; TLS 2/22/80)

6698 Millar, Margaret. *Spider Webs.* 1988, International Polygonics paper $5.95 (0-930330-76-5). A posthumously published novel about the investigation and trial involving a murder committed aboard a Californian's yacht. "A brilliantly paced novel with a powerhouse ending."—BL (REV: BL 9/1/86; LJ 9/1/86; PW 7/25/86)

6699 Moore, Barbara. *Wolf Whispered Death.* 1988, Dell paper $3.50 (0-440-20117-9). An investigation into the death of a man killed by a large caninelike beast on the Navajo reservation. (REV: BL 3/15/86; NYTBR 5/11/86)

6700 Morice, Anne. *Murder Post-Dated.* 1986, Bantam paper $2.95 (0-553-25652-1). A female detective investigates the strange series of coincidences surrounding a woman's disappearance. "Morice at her ingenious best."—BL (REV: BL 2/15/84; LJ 3/1/84; PW 1/6/84)

6701 Mortimer, John. *Rumpole a la Carte.* 1991, Viking $18.95 (0-670-83284-7). Six stories concerning the experiences of Judge Horace Rumpole in the English legal system. (REV: BL 11/15/90; CSM 3/1/91; PW 10/26/90)

6702 Mosley, Walter. *Devil in a Blue Dress.* 1990, Norton $18.95 (0-393-02854-2). An African-American detective trails a killer responsible for a series of murders in Los Angeles in this debut novel set during the 1940s. "A strong novel, with a skillful understanding of the genre and a lively talent for invention."—New Yorker (REV: BL 6/15/90; LJ 6/1/90; New Yorker 9/17/90)

6703 Mosley, Walter. *A Red Death.* 1991, Norton $18.95 (0-393-02998-0). A Los Angeles detective turns government spy in exchange for leniency from the IRS in this novel set during the 1950s. (REV: BL 6/15/91; LJ 6/1/91; PW 5/17/91)

6704 Moyes, Patricia. *Night Ferry to Death.* 1985, Henry Holt $13.95 (0-03-004477-4); paper $3.95 (0-8050-0116-6). Superintendent Tibbett and his wife investigate a death aboard a ferry while returning from a vacation. (REV: BL 10/15/85; TLS 6/20/86)

6705 Moyes, Patricia. *A Six-Letter Word for Death.* 1983, Henry Holt paper $3.95 (0-8050-0244-8). A crossword puzzle sent to a police chief seems to contain clues pointing to the identity of a murderer. (REV: BL 5/15/83; LJ 6/1/83; PW 4/29/83)

6706 Muller, Marcia. *Cavalier in White.* 1988, Harlequin Books paper $3.50 (0-373-26008-3). Two detectives search for a stolen Frans Hals artwork in California. (REV: BL 5/15/86; LJ 6/1/86; PW 5/16/86)

6707 Muller, Marcia. *Games to Keep the Dark Away.* 1984, St. Martin's $10.95 (0-312-31620-8). This fourth volume in the Sharon McCone series finds the private investigator on the trail of a missing Bay Area woman. (REV: BL 2/15/84; NYTBR 4/15/84; PW 12/16/83)

6708 Muller, Marcia. *Legend of the Slain Soldiers.* 1985, Walker $13.95 (0-8027-5617-4). A historian is murdered while researching a book that would tell the truth about the deaths of depression-era Chicano farm workers. (REV: BL 8/85; PW 6/21/85)

6709 Muller, Marcia. *Shape of Dread.* 1989, Mysterious $16.95 (0-89296-271-2); paper $4.95 (0-445-40916-9). Private investigator Sharon McCone investigates the murder of a San Francisco stand-up comic that took place two years before and for which a possibly innocent man was convicted. (REV: BL 10/15/89; NYTBR 12/24/89; PW 10/31/89)

6710 Muller, Marcia. *There's Nothing to Be Afraid Of.* 1990, Mysterious paper $4.95 (0-445-40901-0). A series of crimes and murders plagues the Vietnamese residents of a San Francisco hotel. (REV: BL 8/85; LJ 9/1/85; PW 7/12/85)

6711 Muller, Marcia. *There's Something in a Sunday.* 1989, Mysterious $15.95 (0-89296-270-4). A San Francisco private investigator hired to protect a client searches for her killer following her murder. (REV: BL 2/15/89; NYTBR 3/12/89; PW 1/6/89)

6712 Muller, Marcia. *Trophies and Dead Things.* 1990, Mysterious $16.95 (0-89296-417-0); paper $4.99 (0-89296-418-9). A Sharon McCone mystery involving a search for the connections between four beneficiaries named in a murdered man's will. (REV: BL 9/1/90; NYTBR 11/4/90; PW 9/7/90)

6713 Muller, Marcia, and Bill Pronzini. *Beyond the Grave.* 1986, Walker $15.95 (0-8027-5651-4). A California art museum director becomes obsessed with a search for missing art treasures detailed in a late nineteenth-century letter. (REV: LJ 9/1/86; PW 9/12/86)

6714 Murphy, Dallas. *Lover Man.* 1988, Pocket paper $3.95 (0-671-66188-4). A mystery novel about an investigation into the murder of a New York policeman's girl friend. "A first novel of unusual skill."—NYTBR (REV: BL 7/87; NYTBR 9/13/87; PW 6/15/87)

6715 Murray, William. *Getaway Blues.* **1990, Bantam $17.95 (0-553-07029-0).** The description of a horseplayer's season at the Santa Anita racetrack working as a chauffeur for a man contemplating suicide. (Rev: BL 8/90; NYTBR 8/26/90; PW 7/13/90)

6716 Murray, William. *King of the Nightcap.* **1989, Bantam $16.95 (0-553-05392-2); paper $4.50 (0-553-28426-6).** A magician and horse racing aficionado tracks down the man who absconded with his winning ticket from a California racetrack. (Rev: BL 8/89; New Yorker 9/25/89; PW 6/2/89)

6717 Nabb, Magdalen. *The Marshal and the Madwoman.* **1989, Penguin paper $3.95 (0-14-011881-0).** Marshal Guarnaccia investigates the suicide of a Venice woman who apparently left no family behind. "This superb novel rises far above the staples of the genre."—PW (Rev: BL 11/1/88; NYTBR 1/22/89; PW 10/21/88)

6718 Nabb, Magdalen. *The Marshal and the Murderer.* **1988, Penguin paper $3.95 (0-14-010678-2).** The death of a Swiss potter leads a Florence detective to uncover the secrets of a former Nazi collaborator. "A superbly crafted thriller."—BL (Rev: BL 12/15/87; PW 11/20/87)

6719 Nabb, Magdalen. *The Marshal's Own Case.* **1990, Macmillan $17.95 (0-684-19201-2).** Marshal Guarnaccia explores the Italian underworld while investigating the murder of a transsexual prostitute. (Rev: BL 6/15/90; LJ 6/1/90; PW 6/8/90)

6720 Nava, Michael. *Goldenboy.* **1988, Alyson $14.95 (1-55583-141-9).** An attorney defends a gay man on murder charges in this novel that critically examines the current state of justice for homosexuals in the United States. (Rev: BL 2/1/88; LJ 3/1/88; PW 1/22/88)

6721 Oates, Joyce Carol. *Mysteries of Winterthurn.* **1985, Berkley paper $4.50 (0-425-08022-6).** Three mysteries about the failed cases of a detective in the Adirondacks near the end of the nineteenth century. (Rev: CSM 2/11/84; LJ 1/84; PW 12/23/83)

6722 O'Connell, Jack. *Box Nine.* **1992, Mysterious $17.95 (0-89296-472-3).** This debut novel has a pair of Massachusetts detectives searching for the makers and distributors of a drug that causes homicidal behavior. "A definite discovery."—PW (Rev: BL 11/15/91; PW 11/15/91)

6723 Olden, Marc. *Gaijin.* **1987, Jove paper $3.95 (0-515-09194-4).** Two former World War II rivals face off again in a story of organized crime set in Japan. (Rev: BL 6/1/86; PW 5/9/86)

6724 Oliver, Anthony. *Cover-Up.* **1987, Doubleday $12.95 (0-385-25361-5); Fawcett paper $3.50 (0-449-21466-4).** An investigation into the murder of an English art dealer starts the search for a valuable missing piece of art. (Rev: BL 5/1/87; LJ 5/1/87)

6725 Oliver, Anthony. *Pew Group.* **1985, Fawcett paper $2.95 (0-449-20594-0).** This debut mystery concerns the search by a widow and a police officer for a valuable stolen piece of pottery. (Rev: BL 4/1/81; LJ 4/1/81; PW 2/6/81)

6726 Olmstead, Robert. *Trail of Heart's Blood Wherever We Go.* **1990, Random $19.95 (0-394-57539-3).** A series of murders takes the lives of residents of a small New Hampshire town in this novel by the author of *Soft Water.* (Rev: BL 6/1/90; New Yorker 10/1/90; PW 4/13/90)

6727 Oster, Jerry. *Internal Affairs.* **1990, Bantam $16.95 (0-553-05729-4).** A New York Police Department Internal Affairs officer investigates the murder of a police commissioner who was also a childhood friend. (Rev: BL 1/15/90; NYTBR 2/4/90; PW 12/22/89)

6728 Oster, Jerry. *Sweet Justice.* **1986, Ace paper $3.95 (0-441-79126-3).** Two New York City police officers search for a killer who is murdering members of one of the officer's Vietnam War platoon. (Rev: LJ 2/1/85; New Yorker 7/15/85; PW 11/30/84)

6729 Papazoglou, Orania. *Death's Savage Passion.* **1987, Penguin paper $3.50 (0-14-009967-0).** Sleuth Patience McKenna searches for clues to the murder of a New York publisher. (Rev: LJ 7/86; PW 6/13/86)

6730 Paretsky, Sara. *Bitter Medicine.* **1987, Morrow $17.95 (0-688-06448-5); Ballantine paper $4.95 (0-345-34722-6).** A series of unexplained deaths in a Chicago hospital are investigated by private investigator V. I. Warshawski. (Rev: LJ 5/1/87; Newsweek 7/13/87; TLS 11/13/87)

6731 Paretsky, Sara. *Blood Shot.* **1988, Delacorte $17.95 (0-440-50035-4); Dell paper $4.50 (0-440-20420-8).** Private eye V. I. Warshawski returns home to South Chicago to investigate a series of crimes at a chemical plant. "Her best and boldest to date."—NYTBR (Rev: BL 7/88; NYTBR 10/9/88; PW 7/22/88)

6732 Paretsky, Sara. *Burn Marks.* **1990, Delacorte $17.95 (0-385-29892-7).** This sixth novel featuring V. I. Warshawsky finds the private eye investigating the murder of a friend of her down-and-out aunt. (Rev: BL 1/15/90; NYTBR 6/17/90; PW 1/26/90)

6733 Paretsky, Sara. *Deadlock.* **1984, Ballantine paper $3.95 (0-345-31954-0).** Private investigator V. I. Warshawsky seeks clues to the death of her hockey star cousin. (Rev: BL 3/1/84; LJ 2/1/84; PW 12/23/83)

6734 Paretsky, Sara. *Indemnity Only.* **1985, Ballantine paper $4.95 (0-345-33634-8).** This novel, which introduced private eye V. I. Warshawsky, finds the sleuth on the trail of a banker's missing son. (Rev: LJ 2/1/82; PW 12/4/81)

6735 Parker, Robert B. *Catskill Eagle.* **1986, Dell paper $4.95 (0-440-11132-3).** Spenser attempts to rescue his former girlfriend from her current lover's gun-running father. (Rev: CSM 7/3/85; LJ 6/1/85; Time 7/1/85)

6736 Parker, Robert B. *Ceremony.* **1987, Dell paper $4.50 (0-440-10933-0).** Spenser looks for clues to the disappearance of a runaway teen in the pornography underworld. (REV: BL 12/15/81; LJ 3/1/82; Newsweek 6/7/82)

6737 Parker, Robert B. *Early Autumn*. 1987, Dell paper $4.95 (0-440-12214-7). Spenser, hired to find a runaway boy by his parents, learns of their emotional abuse of him and blackmails them to leave the boy alone. (REV: CSM 5/11/81; LJ 1/1/81; PW 12/19/80)

6738 Parker, Robert B. *God Save the Child*. 1987, Dell paper $4.95 (0-440-12899-4). Spenser searches for a missing Boston teenager held for ransom in this second novel of the series. (REV: NYTBR 12/15/74; PW 9/23/74)

6739 Parker, Robert B. *Godwulf Manuscript*. 1987, Dell paper $4.50 (0-440-12961-3). Spenser searches for a missing fourteenth-century manuscript stolen from a university library. (REV: PW 11/19/73; TLS 8/30/73)

6740 Parker, Robert B. *Judas Goat*. 1979, Amereon $15.95 (0-89190-371-2); Dell paper $4.50 (0-440-14196-6). Detective Spenser searches for the people responsible for the murder of the family of a London businessman in a restaurant bombing. (REV: BL 6/15/78; PW 6/26/78; Time 11/20/78)

6741 Parker, Robert B. *Looking for Rachel Wallace*. 1987, Dell paper $4.95 (0-440-15316-6). Private investigator Spenser searches for the kidnappers of a lesbian writer who hired him as her bodyguard. (REV: BL 3/15/80; LJ 2/1/80; PW 2/1/80)

6742 Parker, Robert B. *Mortal Stakes*. 1987, Dell paper $4.95 (0-440-15758-7). Spenser discovers an underground pornography/blackmail ring while investigating the fixing of Boston Red Sox baseball games. (REV: BL 1/15/76; LJ 10/1/75; PW 9/8/75)

6743 Parker, Robert B. *Pale Kings and Princes*. 1988, Simon & Schuster $14.95 (0-671-66073-X); Dell paper $4.50 (0-440-200004-0). Spenser investigates police involvement in a drug/murder scheme in Wheaton, Massachusetts. (REV: BL 3/15/87; CSM 6/6/87; Time 7/27/87)

6744 Parker, Robert B. *Playmates*. 1989, Putnam $17.95 (0-399-13425-5); Berkley paper $4.95 (0-425-12001-5). Spenser investigates a college basketball team's illegal fixing of games and uncovers the illiteracy of one of the team's star players. (REV: BL 2/1/89; LJ 4/1/89; NYTBR 4/23/89)

6745 Parker, Robert B. *Promised Land*. 1987, Dell paper $4.95 (0-440-17197-0). Spenser searches for a missing Boston wife who is plagued by loan sharks in this fourth volume of the series. (REV: BL 11/15/76; New Rep 10/16/76; PW 7/26/76)

6746 Parker, Robert B. *Stardust*. 1990, Putnam $18.95 (0-399-13537-5). Spenser is hired to protect a television star whose life has been threatened. (REV: CSM 12/17/90; NYTBR 7/8/90; PW 5/4/90)

6747 Parker, Robert B. *Valediction*. 1986, Dell paper $4.95 (0-440-19246-3). A depressed Spenser

fights a drug-dealing religious cult following his breakup with his girlfriend. (REV: BL 2/1/84; LJ 3/1/84; PW 2/24/84)

6748 Parker, Robert B. *Widening Gyre*. 1984, Dell paper $4.95 (0-440-19535-7). Spenser investigates the origins of a videotape showing a congressional candidate's wife engaged in sexual acts. (REV: BL 2/1/83; LJ 4/1/83; PW 2/4/83)

6749 Parker, T. Jefferson. *Laguna Heat*. 1987, St. Martin's paper $4.50 (0-312-90995-0). A Laguna Beach detective investigates a series of murders linked by a 35-year-old journal that may contain clues to the identity of his mother's killer. (REV: BL 8/85; LJ 9/1/85; PW 6/28/85)

6750 Parrish, Frank. *Fly in the Cobweb*. 1988, Harper & Row paper $3.95 (0-06-080901-9). A burglar goes into hiding after he witnesses a murder during the commission of a robbery. "A masterpiece of its kind."—BL (REV: BL 1/1/86; LJ 1/86; TLS 4/23/86)

6751 Paul, Barbara. *Prima Donna at Large*. 1985, St. Martin's $15.95 (0-312-64414-0). The story of an investigation into the fatal poisoning of an operatic baritone's throat spray set at New York's Metropolitan Opera House in the 1910s. (REV: BL 9/1/85; LJ 9/1/85; PW 7/5/85)

6752 Pearce, Michael. *Mamur Zapt and the Return of the Carpet*. 1991, Doubleday $14.95 (0-385-41520-6). Egyptian and English authorities clash following an attempted assassination in 1908 Cairo. "An outstandingly well-wrought and satisfying mystery."—PW (REV: NYTBR 12/23/90; PW 9/21/90; TLS 8/26/88)

6753 Pearson, Ridley. *Undercurrents*. 1989, St. Martin's paper $4.95 (0-312-91485-7). A Seattle police investigator leads his team on the search for a brutal serial killer. "Exceptional . . . vivid, compulsively readable."—BL (REV: BL 3/15/88; PW 3/18/88)

6754 Perry, Anne. *Bethlehem Road*. 1990, St. Martin's $17.95 (0-312-04266-3). A police inspector investigates a series of murders of British politicians in this novel set in 1888. "A sterling performance and a collection must."—LJ (REV: LJ 6/1/90; NYTBR 8/5/90)

6755 Perry, Anne. *Death in the Devil's Acre*. 1989, Fawcett paper $3.95 (0-449-44776-6). While investigating a murder, a nineteenth-century English inspector finds his wife and sister involved in the London world of prostitution. (REV: BL 10/1/85; LJ 10/1/85)

6756 Perry, Anne. *Face of a Stranger*. 1990, Fawcett $17.95 (0-449-90530-6). A London police detective suffering from acute amnesia is put in charge of an investigation into the murder of a Crimean War veteran in this novel set in Victorian England. (REV: LJ 10/1/90; NYTBR 11/18/90; PW 9/14/90)

6757 Perry, Anne. *Silence in Hanover Close*. 1988, St. Martin's $17.95 (0-312-01824-X); Fawcett paper $3.95 (0-449-21686-1). A Victorian novel about an English police inspector wrongly accused of a prostitute's murder. "Superb, memorable reading."—LJ (REV: LJ 7/88; PW 6/17/88)

6758 Perry, Thomas. *Metzger's Dog.* **1984, Ace paper $3.50 (0-441-52867-8).** A gang involved in a series of university thefts steals some confidential CIA papers from a professor's office. "A very funny, sharply written book that should not be missed."—NYTBR (REV: NYTBR 10/30/83; New Yorker 11/4/83)

6759 Peters, Ellis. *Confession of Brother Haluin.* **1989, Mysterious $15.95 (0-89296-349-2); $3.95 paper (0-445-40855-3).** Brother Cadfael accompanies a fellow monk on his journey of penance for a sin committed during his youth. (REV: BL 2/1/89; PW 1/6/89; TLS 7/22/88)

6760 Peters, Ellis. *Dead Man's Ransom.* **1986, Fawcett paper $4.95 (0-449-20819-2).** A medieval mystery featuring Brother Cadfael and his search for the killer of a local sheriff. (REV: BL 3/15/85; LJ 3/1/85; PW 2/8/85)

6761 Peters, Ellis. *Leper of St. Giles.* **1985, Fawcett paper $4.95 (0-449-20541-X).** The case of a man murdered just prior to his wedding to a wealthy heiress spurs Brother Cadfael to investigate in this mystery set in the twelfth century. (REV: LJ 6/1/82; PW 3/19/82; TLS 10/16/81)

6762 Peters, Ellis. *Monk's Hood.* **1986, Fawcett paper $3.95 (0-449-20699-8).** Twelfth-century Benedictine monk Brother Cadfael investigates a poisoning death that results in an estate left to the church but implicates a fellow monk in the murder. (REV: BL 5/1/81; CSM 7/15/81; PW 4/10/81)

6763 Peters, Ellis. *A Morbid Taste for Bones.* **1985, Fawcett paper $4.95 (0-449-20700-5).** The battle over a Welsh saint's bones leads to a murder and a subsequent investigation by Brother Cadfael. (REV: BL 3/1/79; TLS 10/21/77)

6764 Peters, Ellis. *A Rare Benedictine.* **1989, Mysterious $19.95 (0-89296-397-2).** A collection of three stories tracing Brother Cadfael's development as a sleuth. (REV: BL 1/1/90; NYTBR 12/24/89)

6765 Peters, Ellis. *Raven in the Foregate.* **1987, Fawcett paper $3.95 (0-449-21225-4).** Brother Cadfael investigates the murder of a priest found floating in a pond on Christmas Day, 1141. (REV: LJ 11/1/86; PW 9/12/86; TLS 10/3/86)

6766 Pickard, Nancy. *Bum Steer.* **1990, Pocket $16.95 (0-671-68040-4).** A Kansas cattle baron who suddenly bequeaths his ranch to a civic foundation on the condition that his family's entry be barred is found murdered. (REV: BL 1/1/90; LJ 1/90; PW 1/12/90)

6767 Pickard, Nancy. *Dead Crazy.* **1988, Macmillan $16.95 (0-684-18761-2); Pocket paper $3.95 (0-671-70267-X).** Amateur detective Jenny Cain investigates two murders that follow her charity's efforts to purchase a local church as a facility to care for the mentally ill. (REV: BL 9/15/88; PW 7/29/88)

6768 Pickard, Nancy. *I.O.U.* **1991, Pocket $17.95 (0-671-68041-2).** Amateur detective Jenny Cain investigates the roots of her recently deceased mother's mental illness. (REV: BL 2/15/91; PW 2/15/91)

6769 Pickard, Nancy. *Marriage Is Murder.* **1987, Macmillan $14.95 (0-684-18760-4).** A New England town experiences a series of murders of husbands who are wife abusers. (REV: BL 9/15/87; PW 8/14/87)

6770 Pileggi, Nicholas. *Blye, Private Eye.* **1987, Pocket paper $3.95 (0-671-63117-9).** A chronicle of the adventures of a New York private investigator working on a series of cases. "A virtual primer on detection."—NYTBR (REV: LJ 2/1/77; NYTBR 2/27/77; Time 3/28/77)

6771 Pronzini, Bill. *Bones.* **1985, St. Martin's $12.95 (0-312-08769-1).** The nameless detective investigates the three-decade-old mysterious death of the father of a mystery writer he admires. (REV: BL 6/1/85; LJ 7/85; PW 5/3/85)

6772 Pronzini, Bill. *Shackles.* **1988, St. Martin's $16.95 (0-312-01818-5); Dell paper $3.95 (0-440-20523-9).** Following his escape from kidnappers, the nameless detective tries to hunt down his abductors. (REV: BL 6/1/88; PW 5/20/88)

6773 Pyle, A. M. *Trouble Making Toys.* **1985, Walker $13.95 (0-8027-5610-7).** The investigation into the death of a toy company executive reveals another company's efforts to steal trade secrets. (REV: BL 6/15/85; LJ 7/85; PW 6/7/85)

6774 Radley, Sheila. *Chief Inspector's Daughter.* **1988, Bantam paper $3.50 (0-553-26942-9).** An English chief inspector investigates the murder of his daughter's boss. (REV: BL 1/15/81; PW 11/28/80)

6775 Radley, Sheila. *Fate Worse Than Death.* **1987, Bantam paper $3.50 (0-553-26538-5).** The story of an investigation by a Suffolk policeman into the murder of a woman just prior to her wedding day. (REV: BL 3/15/86; CSM 9/19/86; PW 2/7/86)

6776 Radley, Sheila. *This Way Out.* **1989, Macmillan $16.95 (0-684-19125-3).** In this ghoulish tale, two men meet during a traffic jam and eventually plot to kill one man's mother-in-law and the other man's father-in-law. (REV: BL 10/1/89; PW 9/22/89)

6777 Radley, Sheila. *Who Saw Him Die?* **1988, Macmillan $14.95 (0-684-18883-X); Bantam paper $3.50 (0-553-27607-7).** Detective Quantrill investigates the murders of a local alcoholic and a newcomer in a small English town. (REV: CSM 3/23/88; PW 2/12/88)

6778 Randisi, Robert J., ed. *Mean Streets: The Second Private Eye Writers of America Anthology.* **1990, Mysterious $18.95 (0-89296-265-8).** A collection of 12 short mystery stories by writers including John Lutz, Sue Grafton, Bill Pronzini, and Stuart Kaminsky. (REV: BL 10/1/86; LJ 11/1/86)

6779 Ray, Robert J. *Hit Man Cometh.* **1989, Dell paper $3.95 (0-440-20466-6).** A California policeman chases a hit man who made a failed attempt to assassinate a clergyman with political aspirations. (Rev: BL 2/1/88; LJ 2/1/88; PW 12/18/87)

6780   Reed, Ishmael. *Last Days of Louisiana Red.* **1989, Macmillan paper $8.95 (0-689-70731-2).** A satiric mystery thriller set in Berkeley during the 1960s concerning the bitter rivalry between two southern food companies. (Rev: BL 12/1/74; Choice 3/75; CSM 3/75)

6781   Reed, Ishmael. *Mumbo Jumbo.* **1989, Macmillan paper $9.95 (0-689-70730-4).** A detective novel set in the 1920s featuring two African-American investigators on the trail of a jazz-inspired dance craze known as the Jes Grew. (Rev: BL 9/15/72; LJ 10/1/72; Time 8/14/72)

6782   Reeves, Robert N. *Doubting Thomas.* **1984, Crown $12.95 (0-517-55616-2).** An English professor becomes implicated in a murder that was committed at a horse racetrack. (Rev: BL 2/1/85; CSM 4/16/85; LJ 2/1/85)

6783   Reeves, Robert N. *Peeping Thomas.* **1990, Crown $18.95 (0-517-57024-6).** A Boston University professor investigates the bombing of an adult bookstore that took the life of an anti-pornography protester. (Rev: BL 10/1/90; LJ 9/1/90; PW 8/17/90)

6784   Rendell, Ruth. *Bridesmaid.* **1989, Mysterious $17.95 (0-89296-388-3); Warner paper $4.95 (0-445-40912-6).** A couple who meet at a wedding plan to commit murders to prove their love to each other. (Rev: BL 5/1/89; LJ 6/1/89)

6785   Rendell, Ruth. *A Judgment in Stone.* **1978, Amereon $15.95 (0-89190-888-9); Bantam paper $2.95 (0-553-26285-8).** An English family of four is murdered by an enraged maid in this novel by the author of *Speaker of Mandarin.* "One of Ruth Rendell's best."—NYTBR (Rev: BL 4/15/78; LJ 1/1/78; NYTBR 2/26/78)

6786   Rendell, Ruth. *Lake of Darkness.* **1981, Bantam paper $2.95 (0-553-26398-6).** A psychotic killer stalks a London lottery winner in this novel by the author of *The Veiled One.* (Rev: BL 9/1/80; NYTBR 11/9/80; PW 6/13/80)

6787   Rendell, Ruth. *Live Flesh: A Novel of Suspense.* **1986, Pantheon $15.95 (0-394-55544-1).** A criminal who shot and paralyzed a policeman wants to develop a friendship with the officer following his release from prison. (Rev: BL 8/86; CSM 10/24/86; PW 7/11/86)

6788   Rendell, Ruth. *Murder Being Once Done.* **1983, Amereon $15.95 (0-89190-372-0).** A police procedural concerning the investigation into the death of a woman killed at a London mausoleum. (Rev: LJ 2/1/73; NYTBR 12/10/72)

6789   Rendell, Ruth. *Shake Hands Forever.* **1986, Bantam paper $3.50 (0-553-25970-9).** A police procedural investigating the death of an English woman whose body was discovered by her mother-in-law. (Rev: BL 10/15/75; NYTBR 11/23/75; PW 6/23/75)

6790   Rendell, Ruth. *Speaker of Mandarin.* **1984, Ballantine paper $4.95 (0-345-30274-5).** Inspector Wexford investigates the deaths of a group of British citizens on a tour of China. (Rev: NYTBR 1/29/84; PW 8/12/83)

6791   Rendell, Ruth. *Tree of Hands.* **1986, Ballantine paper $3.50 (0-345-31200-7).** A psychological thriller concerning the visit by an insane mother to her daughter that begins a series of events that culminates in an abduction and a murder. "One of the author's finest."—BL (Rev: BL 1/1/85; LJ 3/1/85; PW 1/4/85)

6792   Rendell, Ruth. *An Unkindness of Ravens.* **1986, Ballantine paper $3.95 (0-345-32746-2).** A militant feminist organization is suspected in a series of English murders investigated by Inspector Wexford. (Rev: BL 7/85; LJ 9/1/85; PW 7/5/85)

6793   Rendell, Ruth. *Veiled One.* **1988, Pantheon $17.95 (0-394-57206-8); Ballantine paper $4.95 (0-345-35994-1).** Inspector Wexford investigates the garrotting death of a middle-class woman by looking into the lives and habits of her suburban neighbors. (Rev: BL 6/1/88; New Yorker 10/3/88; Time 8/8/88)

6794   Robinson, Leah Ruth. *Blood Run.* **1988, NAL $17.95 (0-453-00611-6); paper $4.50 (0-451-40143-3).** This first novel by a medical technician concerns the investigation into the apparent suicide of a surgeon on a hospital staff. (Rev: BL 9/1/88; PW 7/29/88)

6795   Robinson, Peter. *A Deadicated Man.* **1991, Scribner $17.95 (0-684-19265-9).** An investigation into the murder of an archaeologist in a small English village. (Rev: BL 8/91; PW 6/14/91)

6796   Roosevelt, Elliott. *Hyde Park Murder.* **1986, Avon paper $3.95 (0-380-70058-1).** Eleanor Roosevelt serves as the reconciliator of a romance in this story that features Joseph Kennedy, Sam Rayburn, and Fiorello La Guardia as characters. (Rev: BL 5/15/85; LJ 7/85; PW 5/31/85)

6797   Roosevelt, Elliott. *Murder in the Oval Office.* **1989, St. Martin's $17.95 (0-312-02259-X); Avon paper $4.50 (0-380-70528-1).** Eleanor Roosevelt investigates the murder of a southern congressman slain at the White House. (Rev: BL 12/15/88; PW 1/27/89)

6798   Rosenberg, Robert. *Crimes of the City.* **1991, Simon & Schuster $18.95 (0-671-70222-X).** A Jerusalem investigator seeks clues to the stabbing murders of three nuns. "A superior thriller . . . very well written, sensitive and beautifully plotted."—NYTBR (Rev: NYTBR 3/31/91; PW 12/21/90)

6799   Ross, Jonathan. *Daphne Dead and Done For.* **1991, St. Martin's $15.95 (0-312-05408-4).** A former policeman's novel about a detective's investigation into a classified advertisement that may provide clues to a woman's murder. (Rev: BL 2/1/91; PW 2/15/91)

6800 Roubaud, Jacques. *Hortense Is Abducted.* **1989, Dalkey Arch. $19.95 (0-916583-38-4).** Fantastic mystery novel by a French writer about a sleuth investigating the murder of a dog. (Rev: BL 6/15/89; LJ 6/15/89; NYTBR 8/13/89)

6801 Ruell, Patrick. *Dream of Darkness.* **1991, Countryman $17.95 (0-88150-178-6).** A teenager's recurring nightmares lead her to search for the truth concerning the lives of her parents in Uganda. (Rev: BL 12/1/90; LJ 1/91; PW 12/21/90)

6802 Russell, Alan. *No Sign of Murder.* **1990, Walker $17.95 (0-8027-5767-7).** A San Francisco detective searches for a missing deaf teenage model in this author's debut novel. (Rev: BL 10/15/ 90; NYTBR 11/1/90)

6803 Sanders, Lawrence. *Fourth Deadly Sin.* **1985, Putnam $17.95 (0-399-13062-4); Berkley paper $4.95 (0-425-09078-7).** New York detectives investigate the hammering death of a psychiatrist. (Rev: BL 3/15/85; NYTBR 7/28/85; PW 6/28/85)

6804 Sauter, Eric. *Skeletons.* **1990, Dutton $18.95 (0-525-24874-8).** A Philadelphia policeman searches for the man who killed his girlfriend. (Rev: BL 5/15/ 90; LJ 5/1/90; PW 4/27/90)

6805 Scherfig, Hans. *Stolen Spring.* **1986, Fjord $15.95 (0-940242-20-6); paper $7.95 (0-940242-00-1).** The translation of a Danish novel originally published in the 1930s about the murder of a teacher at a Copenhagen prep school. "His best novel . . . a masterful blend of suspense and satire."—NYTBR (Rev: NYTBR 3/15/87; PW 4/11/86. Awards: PW, 1986)

6806 Schopen, Bernard. *Desert Look.* **1990, Mysterious $17.95 (0-89296-354-9).** A Nevada private eye tries to find facts relating to his mother's death in the desert three decades before. (Rev: BL 5/15/90; NYTBR 6/24/90; PW 4/20/90)

6807 Schulman, Sarah. *After Delores.* **1988, Dutton $16.95 (0-525-24641-X); NAL paper $7.95 (0-452-26228-3).** A lesbian amateur detective tracks the killer of a New Jersey go-go dancer and personal friend. (Rev: BL 5/1/88; NYTBR 5/15/88; PW 3/11/88)

6808 Shagan, Steve. *Vendetta.* **1987, Bantam paper $4.50 (0-553-26733-7).** An investigation of a series of murders of adult film stars in Los Angeles uncovers the world of drug dealing and pornography. (Rev: BL 5/15/86; LJ 7/86)

6809 Sherwood, John. *A Botanist at Bay.* **1986, Ballantine paper $2.95 (0-345-33023-4).** A woman joins in the search for a missing botanist in New Zealand following her arrival in that country to care for her expectant daughter. (Rev: BL 9/15/85; PW 7/12/85; TLS 8/2/85)

6810 Simenon, Georges. *Maigret Bides His Time.* **1986, Harcourt paper $3.95 (0-15-655151-9).** Maigret cracks a 20-year-old jewel robbery ring in this work written during the 1960s. (Rev: BL 4/15/85; New Yorker 7/1/85; PW 3/8/85)

6811 Simenon, Georges. *Maigret on the Riviera.* **1988, Harcourt $14.95 (0-15-155149-9); paper $5.95 (0-15-655158-6).** Maigret searches for the killer of a financier on the French Riviera in this novel originally published in 1940. "Simenon at his best."—BL (Rev: BL 4/1/88; LJ 5/1/88; PW 3/11/88)

6812 Simon, Roger L. *Straight Man.* **1986, Random $15.95 (0-394-55837-5); Warner paper $3.95 (0-446-34389-7).** A Los Angeles detective investigates the murder of the straight man of a famous comedy team. (Rev: BL 10/15/86; NYTBR 11/9/86; PW 8/29/86)

6813 Simpson, Dorothy. *Dead on Arrival.* **1989, Bantam paper $3.95 (0-553-27000-1).** Two investigators search for clues to a motive in the case of the murder of an identical twin. (Rev: BL 12/1/86; LJ 1/87)

6814 Simpson, Dorothy. *Element of Doubt.* **1989, Bantam paper $3.95 (0-553-28175-5).** Detective Luke Thanet investigates the death of a promiscuous young woman in a small English town. "A sublime mystery by one of the best purveyors of the genre."—BL (Rev: BL 3/15/88; PW 1/29/88)

6815 Simpson, Dorothy. *Night She Died.* **1985, Bantam paper $3.50 (0-553-27772-3).** An English police officer searches for the killer of a young woman in this procedural by the author of *Element of Doubt.* (Rev: BL 5/1/81; LJ 5/1/81; PW 5/1/81)

6816 Sjowall, Maj, and Per Wahloo. *Abominable Man.* **1979, Amereon $16.95 (0-89190-378-X).** Detective Martin Beck investigates the murder of a Stockholm policeman in his hospital bed. (Rev: LJ 11/1/72; PW 8/14/72; Sat Rev 10/28/72)

6817 Sjowall, Maj, and Per Wahloo. *Copkiller: The Story of a Crime.* **1975, Amereon $18.95 (0-89190-377-1).** Swedish policeman Martin Beck searches for a missing woman and the killer of a cop in two interrelated cases. (Rev: BL 7/15/75; PW 3/3/75; TLS 9/ 26/75)

6818 Sjowall, Maj, and Per Wahloo. *Fire Engine That Disappeared.* **1977, Random paper $4.95 (0-394-72340-6).** Swedish detectives investigate the explosion of a Stockholm apartment house and the fire department's delayed response to the incident. (Rev: BL 3/15/71; NYTBR 1/31/71; PW 11/23/70)

6819 Sjowall, Maj, and Per Wahloo. *Laughing Policeman.* **1977, Random paper $4.95 (0-394-72341-4).** Detectives investigate the mass murder of passengers aboard a Swedish bus. (Rev: BL 4/15/70; NYTBR 3/8/70; TLS 2/26/71. Awards: Edgar, 1970)

6820 Sjowall, Maj, and Per Wahloo. *Locked Room: The Story of a Crime.* **1980, Random paper $4.95 (0-394-74274-5).** Martin Beck investigates the murder of a Stockholm blackmailer in this novel by the Swedish husband-wife mystery writing team. (Rev: BL 12/15/73; LJ 8/73; TLS 9/6/74)

6821 Sjowall, Maj, and Per Wahloo. *Terrorists.* **1977, Random paper $4.95 (0-394-72452-6).** This, the final installment of the Swedish authors' Martin Beck novels, concerns the attempted assassination of an American politician in Sweden. (Rev: BL 11/15/ 76; LJ 11/1/76; TLS 5/26/77)

6822　**Skvorecky, Josef.** *Mournful Demeanour of Lieutenant Borukva: Detective Tales.* 1987, Norton $15.95 (0-393-02470-9). Twelve detective stories written by the Czech author of *Engineer of Human Souls* during the 1960s. (Rev: BL 9/1/87; Choice 1/88; LJ 8/87)

6823　**Smith, Janet L.** *Sea of Troubles.* 1990, Borgo Pr. $22.95 (0-8095-4208-0); Perseverance Pr. paper $8.95 (0-960-26769-7). A Seattle lawyer uncovers a kidnapping/murder plot while vacationing in the San Juan Islands. "An author to watch."—LJ (Rev: LJ 4/1/90; NYTBR 4/29/90; PW 3/23/90)

6824　**Smith, Joan.** *A Masculine Ending.* 1988, Macmillan $15.95 (0-684-18938-0); Fawcett paper $3.95 (0-449-21688-8). A feminist amateur sleuth investigates the possible connection between a death in Paris and the slaying of an Oxford professor. (Rev: NYTBR 6/19/88; PW 2/26/88)

6825　**Smith, Julie.** *Axeman's Jazz.* 1991, St. Martin's $19.95 (0-312-06295-8). A female New Orleans homicide detective searches for a serial killer. (Rev: BL 9/15/91; NYTBR 9/29/91; PW 7/12/91)

6826　**Smith, Julie.** *New Orleans Mourning.* 1990, St. Martin's $17.95 (0-312-03892-5). A story of the shooting death of a Mardi Gras king and its investigation, as told by a former *New Orleans Times-Picayune* reporter. (Rev: BL 3/1/90; NYTBR 3/4/ 90; PW 1/19/90. Awards: Edgar, 1991)

6827　**Smith, Martin Cruz.** *Polar Star.* 1989, Random $19.95 (0-394-57819-8). The sequel to *Gorky Park*, detailing the further adventures of Detective Renko aboard a Bering Sea fishing vessel. (Rev: NYTBR 7/16/89; Time 7/3/89; TLS 12/8/89)

6828　**Smith, Mitchell.** *Daydreams.* 1987, McGraw-Hill $17.95 (0-07-059082-6); NAL paper $4.95 (0-451-40089-5). The murder of a prostitute covered up by the government and the New York Police Department to prevent a political scandal is uncovered by an investigative team. (Rev: BL 8/87; LJ 7/87; PW 6/12/ 87)

6829　**Smith, Rosamond.** *Nemesis.* 1990, Dutton $18.95 (0-525-24881-1). A composer is mysteriously murdered following his rape of one of his students in this novel written under Joyce Carol Oates' penname. (Rev: BL 6/1/90; LJ 7/90; PW 6/8/90)

6830　**Solomita, Stephen.** *Force of Nature.* 1989, Putnam $18.95 (0-399-13491-3); Avon paper $4.95 (0-380-70949-X). A police detective nearing retirement trains his replacement while tracking a murderous drug dealer. (Rev: LJ 9/1/89; NYTBR 10/8/89; PW 8/18/ 89)

6831　**Solomita, Stephen.** *A Twist of the Knife.* 1988, Putnam $17.95 (0-399-13401-8); Avon paper $4.95 (0-380-70997-X). A veteran New York detective searching for the killer of his girl friend investigates the activities of a feminist terrorist group. (Rev: BL 10/1/ 88; LJ 10/1/88; PW 8/26/88)

6832　**Spikol, Art.** *Physalia Incident.* 1988, Viking $16.95 (0-670-81222-6); Penguin paper $3.95 (0-14-009325-7). A reporter investigates a diver's death by a poisonous jellyfish in the Caribbean. (Rev: BL 3/1/ 88; LJ 2/1/88; PW 1/22/88)

6833　**Stacey, Susannah.** *Body of Opinion: A Superintendent Bone Mystery.* 1990, Simon & Schuster $17.95 (0-671-69170-8). Superintendent Bone searches for the killer of a transvestite shot at a rock and roll party. (Rev: LJ 2/1/90; NYTBR 2/18/90; PW 12/8/89)

6834　**Stevenson, Richard.** *Ice Blues.* 1987, Penguin paper $3.95 (0-14-009403-2). A gay Albany private investigator finds a corpse in his car trunk to open this novel by the author of *Third Man Out*. (Rev: BL 2/15/86; LJ 3/1/86; PW 1/17/86)

6835　**Stewart, Edward.** *Privileged Lives.* 1988, Delacorte $18.95 (0-385-29652-5); Dell paper $4.95 (0-440-20230-2). An heiress revives from a coma to learn that her husband was tried and acquitted of the attempted murder that rendered her unconscious. (Rev: BL 4/1/88; NYTBR 7/24/88; PW 4/1/88)

6836　**Stout, David.** *Carolina Skeletons.* 1988, Mysterious $16.95 (0-89296-264-X). The story of an African-American man searching for the truth surrounding the execution of an uncle for murder during the 1940s. (Rev: BL 5/1/88; NYTBR 7/31/88; PW 4/15/88)

6837　**Stout, David.** *Night of the Ice Storm.* 1991, Mysterious $19.95 (0-89296-415-4). An investigation into the bludgeoning murder of a priest during an upstate New York blizzard 20 years before is detailed by the author of *Carolina Skeletons*. (Rev: BL 3/1/91; NYTBR 4/14/91; PW 3/8/91)

6838　**Stroud, Carsten.** *Sniper's Mom.* 1990, Bantam $18.95 (0-553-07004-5). A New York policeman who specializes in shooting hostage-takers becomes the scapegoat in the shooting deaths of two cops. (Rev: BL 9/1/90; LJ 10/1/90; PW 8/10/90)

6839　**Symons, Julian.** *A Criminal Comedy.* 1987, Penguin paper $3.50 (0-14-009621-3). Jealousy between two partners running a travel agency leads to murder during a tour of Venice. "His best mystery ever . . . a zestful work of a master still challenging his craft."—Time (Rev: BL 12/1/85; LJ 1/ 86; Time 2/24/86)

6840　**Symons, Julian.** *Death's Darkest Face.* 1990, Viking $16.95 (0-670-83286-3). A man seeks the answers to a mysterious murder he witnessed as a young child. (Rev: BL 9/15/90; PW 8/31/90; TLS 5/25/90)

6841　**Symons, Julian.** *Kentish Manor Murders.* 1988, Viking $15.95 (0-670-82142-X); Penguin paper $3.95 (0-14-010872-6). An English detective searches for a missing undiscovered Sherlock Holmes story. "A smart, sophisticated, verbally rich, and expertly planned novel."—BL (Rev: BL 6/1/88; PW 6/10/88; TLS 11/4/88)

6842　**Symons, Julian.** *Players and the Game.* 1984, Penguin paper $3.95 (0-14-003808-6). A horror film buff turns to a life of crime in this story roughly based on the infamous Moors murder case. (Rev: LJ 11/1/72; NYTBR 10/22/72; PW 7/10/72)

6843 **Symons, Julian.** *Three-Pipe Problem.* **1989, Penguin paper $4.95 (0-14-010903-X).** A contemporary actor playing the role of Sherlock Holmes becomes involved in the investigation of a murder involving a martial arts expert. (Rev: NYTBR 7/20/75; PW 3/3/75; TLS 2/21/75)

6844 **Taibo, Paco I., II.** *Shadow of the Shadow.* **1991, Viking $18.95 (0-670-83177-8).** A portrait of four friends who become entangled in a series of murders in 1920s Mexico City. (Rev: LJ 6/1/91; PW 5/17/91)

6845 **Tanenbaum, Robert K.** *Depraved Indifference.* **1989, NAL $18.95 (0-453-00679-5).** A New York lawyer investigates the cover-up of a case concerning a policeman killed by a Croatian terrorist bomb. (Rev: NYTBR 11/26/89; PW 7/14/89)

6846 **Tanenbaum, Robert K.** *Immoral Certainty.* **1991, Dutton $18.95 (0-525-24941-9).** The story of the investigation into a series of New York murders as written by a former homicide cop. (Rev: BL 11/15/90; LJ 11/15/90; PW 10/26/90)

6847 **Tapply, William G.** *Dead Meat.* **1988, Ballantine paper $3.50 (0-345-34730-7).** A lawyer investigates a series of murders at a Maine lodge that is the center of controversy between white residents and Native Americans. (Rev: BL 3/15/87; NYTBR 6/21/87; PW 1/30/87)

6848 **Tapply, William G.** *Dead Winter.* **1989, Delacorte $16.95 (0-385-29711-4).** A Boston lawyer enters a case to find a murderer and clear the name of a friend accused of the crime. (Rev: BL 4/15/89; LJ 5/1/89; PW 3/24/89)

6849 **Tapply, William G.** *Dutch Blue Error.* **1985, Ballantine paper $2.95 (0-345-32341-6).** A private detective investigates a series of murders of stamp collectors and the forgeries of philatelic collectibles. (Rev: BL 12/15/84; LJ 1/85; PW 10/26/84)

6850 **Taylor, Andrew.** *Our Father's Lies.* **1986, Penguin paper $3.50 (0-14-008838-5).** An English family refuses to accept that their father committed suicide and launches an investigation into his death. (Rev: BL 11/1/85; CSM 12/5/85; TLS 11/29/85)

6851 **Thomas, Donald.** *Ripper's Apprentice.* **1989, St. Martin's $16.95 (0-312-03420-2).** A Victorian tale of a poisoner who preyed on ladies of the evening. "A necessary acquisition."—LJ (Rev: BL 9/1/89; LJ 9/1/89)

6852 **Thomas, Ross.** *Briarpatch.* **1988, Penguin paper $3.95 (0-14-010581-6).** A government agency investigates the car bomb murder of a policewoman. (Rev: BL 10/15/84; Newsweek 11/19/84; PW 9/28/84. Awards: Edgar, 1984)

6853 **Thomas, Ross.** *Fourth Durango.* **1989, Mysterious $18.95 (0-89296-213-5); paper $4.95 (0-445-40915-0).** The mayor, police chief, and a group of

detectives search for a killer stalking a small California community. (Rev: BL 6/15/89; NYTBR 9/24/89; PW 6/23/89)

6854 **Thompson, Gene.** *A Cup of Death.* **1987, Random $16.95 (0-394-56140-6); Ballantine paper $3.50 (0-345-35881-3).** A San Francisco lawyer defends a young man charged with the murder of one of his friends. "A near-perfect addition to the genre."—PW (Rev: NYTBR 4/10/88; PW 11/6/87)

6855 **Thompson, Gene.** *Murder Mystery.* **1985, Ballantine paper $3.95 (0-345-32446-3).** A lawyer's investigation of a San Francisco murder leads him to a stolen copy of a painting by Raphael. (Rev: LJ 10/1/80; NYTBR 1/18/81; New Yorker 3/2/81)

6856 **Thorp, Roderick.** *Rainbow Drive.* **1987, Ivy Books paper $4.95 (0-8041-0170-1).** Homicide detective Mike Gallagher investigates a series of five Hollywood murders in this novel by the author of *The Detective.* (Rev: BL 10/1/86; NYTBR 11/30/86)

6857 **Trigoboff, Joseph.** *Bone Orchard.* **1990, Walker $18.95 (0-8027-5758-8); NAL paper $4.50 (0-451-17014-8).** New York detective Adam Yablonsky investigates the murder of a male stripper and prostitute, which may have connections to members of the U.N. diplomatic corps. "A disturbing and involving tale."—PW (Rev: NYTBR 6/3/90; PW 3/2/90)

6858 **Truman, Margaret.** *Murder at the Kennedy Center.* **1989, Random $17.95 (0-394-57602-0); paper $5.95 (0-449-21208-4).** A presidential campaign worker is murdered backstage at the Kennedy Center and the candidate's son and wife are implicated. (Rev: BL 6/1/89; PW 6/9/89)

6859 **Truman, Margaret.** *Murder on Capitol Hill.* **1988, Warner paper $4.95 (0-446-31518-4).** The death of a U.S. senator spurs an investigation by a special Senate subcommittee. "A convincing portrait of Washington as well as good mystery writing."—LJ (Rev: BL 7/1/81; LJ 8/81)

6860 **Uhnak, Dorothy.** *False Witness.* **1986, Fawcett paper $3.95 (0-449-21097-9).** A model who is brutally disfigured in a violent attack accuses her surgeon of the crime when she awakens following an operation. (Rev: BL 6/1/81; LJ 7/81. Awards: PW 6/5/81)

6861 **Vachss, Andrew.** *Blossom.* **1990, Knopf $17.95 (0-394-58523-2).** This fifth Burke novel by a New York attorney features the private investigator on the trail of a sniper responsible for a series of lover's lane shootings in Indiana. (Rev: BL 5/15/90; PW 5/4/90)

6862 **Vachss, Andrew.** *Blue Belle.* **1988, Knopf $15.95 (0-394-57228-9); NAL paper $4.95 (0-451-16290-0).** Burke searches for a drive-by shooter preying on New York prostitutes in Vachss' third novel in the series. "Certifies Vachss as a first-rate writer on crime."—LJ (Rev: BL 9/1/88; LJ 10/1/88; PW 7/29/88)

6863 **Vachss, Andrew.** *Flood.* **1985, Donald I. Fine $17.95 (0-917657-43-8); Pocket paper $4.50 (0-671-61905-5).** Private investigator Burke searches for a crazed Vietnam veteran responsible for a series of rapes and murders of preteen girls. (REV: BL 9/15/85; LJ 9/1/85; PW 8/2/85)

6864 Vachss, Andrew. *Strega.* **1987, Knopf $18.95 (0-394-55937-1); NAL paper $4.50 (0-451-15179-8).** Ex-convict/private investigator Burke takes on a child pornography ring in this novel by the author of *Blossom.* (REV: BL 3/15/87; LJ 4/15/87; NYTBR 5/31/87)

6865 Valin, Jonathan. *Day of Wrath.* **1983, Avon paper $3.50 (0-380-63917-3).** Cincinnati Detective Stoner looks for a runaway teenager. (REV: BL 7/82; PW 4/2/82)

6866 Valin, Jonathan. *Dead Letter.* **1983, Avon paper $3.50 (0-380-61366-2).** Harry Stoner searches for missing confidential government secrets and a former Green Beret in this third novel in the Cincinnati-based series. (REV: BL 9/15/81; PW 8/7/81)

6867 Valin, Jonathan. *Extenuating Circumstances.* **1989, Delacorte $15.95 (0-385-29683-5); Dell paper $3.95 (0-440-20630-8).** A detective investigates the death of a politician at the hands of two male prostitutes. (REV: BL 2/1/89; PW 1/13/89; Time 4/3/89)

6868 Valin, Jonathan. *Final Notice.* **1984, Avon paper $3.50 (0-380-57983-X).** Detective Harry Stoner searches for a murderer who leaves clues in books held at the Cincinnati Public Library. (REV: BL 9/15/80; NYTBR 1/25/81; PW 9/19/80)

6869 Valin, Jonathan. *Fire Lake.* **1989, Dell paper $3.50 (0-440-20145-4).** A Cincinnati detective searches for an old friend who has attempted suicide. (REV: BL 9/1/87; LJ 9/1/87; PW 7/17/87)

6870 Valin, Jonathan. *Life's Work.* **1987, Dell paper $3.50 (0-440-14790-5).** The search for a missing professional football player leads a detective to a trail of grisly murders. (REV: BL 8/86; LJ 9/1/86; PW 7/11/86)

6871 Valin, Jonathan. *Lime Pit.* **1983, Avon paper $3.50 (0-380-55442-9).** A Cincinnati private investigator's search for a missing teenager leads him to a forced child-pornography ring. (REV: BL 5/1/80; LJ 3/1/80; PW 2/22/80)

6872 Van de Wetering, Janwillem. *Blond Baboon.* **1987, Ballantine paper $2.95 (0-345-34497-9).** The accidental death of the daughter of a former cabaret singer is proved to be murder. (REV: BL 4/15/78; PW 1/16/78; Time 4/17/78)

6873 Van de Wetering, Janwillem. *Hard Rain.* **1988, Ballantine paper $3.95 (0-345-33964-9).** Amsterdam homicide detectives search for clues in a series of murders connected to the world of Dutch finance. "One of the best in an outstanding series."—LJ (REV: BL 11/15/86; LJ 11/1/86; PW 9/26/86)

6874 Vine, Barbara. *A Dark-Adapted Eye.* **1987, Bantam paper (0-553-26498-2).** This first novel written by Ruth Rendell under the Vine pen name records a woman's descriptions of a murder she witnessed as a child 40 years earlier. (REV: BL 6/1/86; PW 5/30/86; Time 4/18/86. AWARDS: Edgar, 1986)

6875 Vine, Barbara. *Gallowglass.* **1990, Crown $18.95 (0-517-57744-5).** A pair of male lovers are enticed to take part in a kidnapping plot. "Gripping from the first word to the absolutely unpredictable close."—PW (REV: LJ 5/15/90; PW 3/9/90; Time 7/2/90)

6876 Walker, Walter. *A Dime to Dance By.* **1985, Penguin paper $3.95 (0-14-007347-7).** A Boston attorney's investigation into a police shooting of a burglar uncovers corruption in city politics. (REV: BL 6/1/83; LJ 6/1/83; PW 4/15/83)

6877 Walker, Walter. *Immediate Prospect of Being Hanged.* **1989, Viking $17.95 (0-670-82247-7); NAL paper $4.50 (0-451-40207-3).** A Massachusetts attorney discloses disturbing secrets about influential local figures while investigating the strangling death of a young woman. (REV: BL 5/1/89; LJ 3/1/89; PW 1/27/89)

6878 Walker, Walter. *Rules of the Knife Fight.* **1986, Harper & Row $17.95 (0-06-015646-5).** A Boston teenager forced to marry his pregnant girlfriend is found murdered in California in this story told by a series of characters involved in the case. (REV: BL 9/15/86; LJ 10/1/86; PW 8/22/86)

6879 Wallace, Robert. *To Catch a Forger.* **1989, St. Martin's $14.95 (0-312-03443-1).** An Australian writer's story of an art dealer's investigation into forgeries of the works of Degas. (REV: LJ 9/1/89; PW 7/14/89)

6880 Wambaugh, Joseph. *Delta Star.* **1984, Bantam paper $4.95 (0-553-26217-3).** Los Angeles cops investigate a plot to award the Nobel Prize to an undeserving scientist and a pair of mysterious deaths that could be murders. "Blue-collar fiction at its best."—Newsweek (REV: LJ 2/15/83; Newsweek 5/2/83; PW 1/7/83)

6881 Wambaugh, Joseph. *Glitter Dome.* **1981, Bantam paper $4.95 (0-553-26302-1).** Two cops are led into the Los Angeles underworld while investigating the murder of a film executive. (REV: BL 4/1/81; LJ 5/1/81; Time 6/8/81)

6882 Wambaugh, Joseph. *The Golden Orange.* **1990, Morrow $18.95 (0-688-09408-2).** A story of love and deception between a divorcée and a retired Orange County, California, policeman. "Virtually sure to be hailed as Wambaugh's best."—PW (REV: Choice 10/90; NYTBR 5/6/90; PW 3/23/90)

6883 Wambaugh, Joseph. *Secrets of Harry Bright.* **1986, Bantam paper $4.95 (0-553-26021-9).** Los Angeles detectives are hired to find the murderer of a Palm Springs millionaire's son. (REV: BL 9/1/85; Time 10/28/85)

6884 Ward, Donald. *Death Takes the Stage.* **1988, St. Martin's $15.95 (0-312-02128-3); paper $7.95 (0-312-03474-1).** Debut murder mystery set in the theater world of Los Angeles. "Have a ball. A fresh new talent has arrived."—NYTBR (REV: NYTBR 8/28/88; PW 6/3/88)

6885 Weesner, Theodore. *True Detective.* 1988, Avon paper $4.50 (0-380-70499-4). A New Hampshire detective pursues a university student who abducted and killed a young boy. (Rev: BL 3/1/87; PW 1/16/87. Awards: ALA, 1987)

6886 Weinman, Irving. *Tailor's Dummy.* 1987, Fawcett paper $3.95 (0-449-21201-7). A New York detective and an art dealer's wife team up to solve the murder of her husband in this debut novel. (Rev: BL 2/1/86; LJ 2/1/86; PW 12/20/85)

6887 West, Pamela. *Yours Truly, Jack the Ripper.* 1989, Dell paper $3.50 (0-440-20259-0). A speculative investigation into the identity of the infamous nineteenth-century Whitechapel killer points toward a person of great fame as the prime suspect. "An outstanding work."—LJ (Rev: LJ 10/1/87; PW 10/16/87)

6888 West, Paul. *Women of Whitechapel: And Jack the Ripper.* 1991, Random $22.00 (0-394-58733-2). The author of *Rat Man of Paris* traces the lives of the victims of Jack the Ripper prior to their deaths. "A true literary achievement."—BL (Rev: BL 3/15/91; NYTBR 5/12/89; PW 2/15/91)

6889 Westlake, Donald E. *Bank Shot.* 1987, Mysterious paper $4.95 (0-445-40883-9). Criminals plot to rob a bank temporarily housed in a trailer in this novel with characters introduced in the author's *Hot Rock.* (Rev: BL 7/15/72; NYTBR 4/16/72; PW 1/24/72)

6890 Westlake, Donald E. *Good Behavior.* 1988, Tor paper $3.95 (0-8125-1060-7). A thief hiding in a convent makes a deal with the nuns to attempt to rescue a sister abducted by her father. (Rev: BL 5/15/86; NYTBR 6/22/86; PW 3/21/86)

6891 Westlake, Donald E. *Help! I Am Being Held Prisoner.* 1989, Mysterious paper $4.50 (0-445-40344-6). A neophyte felon learns of an interior tunnel system from prison through which convicts plan to rob the banks of a neighboring city. (Rev: LJ 6/1/74; NYTBR 7/14/74; PW 3/18/74)

6892 Westlake, Donald E. *High Adventure.* 1985, Mysterious $15.95 (0-89296-123-6); Warner paper $3.95 (0-8125-1056-9). A drug runner and art forger falsifies the discovery of a Mayan temple on his Belize estate. (Rev: BL 4/1/85; LJ 6/11/85; PW 4/19/85)

6893 Westlake, Donald E. *Hot Rock.* 1987, Mysterious paper $3.95 (0-445-40608-9). This fast-paced novel details a plot to steal a priceless African emerald from a New York museum. (Rev: BL 9/1/70; LJ 6/1/70; PW 3/16/70)

6894 Westlake, Donald E. *Jimmy the Kid.* 1989, Mysterious paper $3.95 (0-445-40747-6). The story of a preteen genius kidnapped and held for ransom on an abandoned farm. (Rev: BL 9/15/74; NYTBR 11/17/74; PW 9/16/74)

6895 Westlake, Donald E. *Kahawa.* 1984, Tor paper $3.95 (0-8125-1050-X). A group of Westerners and Africans plot to hijack a coffee train in this novel set in Kenya and Uganda. (Rev: BL 12/15/81; LJ 2/15/82; PW 1/15/82)

6896 Westlake, Donald E. *Trust Me on This.* 1988, Mysterious $16.95 (0-89296-176-7); Warner paper $4.50 (0-445-40807-3). A murder victim's body found near a tabloid newspaper's offices stirs little interest due to the victim's lack of notoriety. (Rev: BL 5/1/88; PW 4/8/88; Time 8/8/88)

6897 White, Teri. *Max Trueblood and the Jersey Desperado.* 1987, Mysterious $15.95 (0-89296-253-4). A hired killer meets his assigned target and becomes friends with him. (Rev: LJ 4/1/87; PW 3/13/87)

6898 Wilcox, James. *Miss Undine's Living Room.* 1988, Harper & Row paper $6.95 (0-06-091502-1). This third novel by Wilcox concerns the mysterious death of a Tula Springs man who was pushed from a two-story window while caring for an ailing elderly man. (Rev: BL 9/1/87; New Yorker 11/16/87; PW 6/26/87)

6899 Wilhelm, Kate. *Death Qualified: A Mystery of Chaos.* 1991, St. Martin's $22.95 (0-312-05853-5). At the request of her father, a lawyer comes out of retirement to take the case of an Oregon woman who allegedly murdered her husband. "This dark, chilling tale is the work of a master."—BL (Rev: BL 5/1/91; LJ 6/15/91; PW 5/24/91)

6900 Willeford, Charles. *Miami Blues.* 1985, Ballantine paper $3.95 (0-345-32016-6). A psychopath on the run steals a Miami police officer's badge and gun. "Truly an entertainment to relish."—New Yorker (Rev: NYTBR 9/2/84; New Yorker 4/23/84; PW 12/2/83)

6901 Willeford, Charles. *Sideswipe.* 1988, Ballantine paper $3.95 (0-345-34947-4). A retired Miami homicide detective living on a small Florida island tracks a gang responsible for the armed robbery of a local supermarket. (Rev: CSM 4/3/87; LJ 2/1/87; TLS 7/1/88)

6902 Willeford, Charles. *Way We Die Now.* 1988, Random $15.95 (0-394-56525-8); Ballantine paper $3.95 (0-345-35332-3). A Miami detective takes an undercover assignment to search for a group of Haitian migrant workers missing in the swamps of the Everglades. (Rev: BL 4/15/88; PW 3/11/88; Time 8/8/88)

6903 Wilson, Gahan. *Eddy Deco's Last Caper.* 1987, Random paper $14.95 (0-8129-1671-9). Illustrated hard-boiled mystery by the noted cartoonist. (Rev: BL 1/1/88; PW 11/13/87)

6904 Wiltse, David. *Home Again.* 1987, Avon paper $3.95 (0-380-70392-0). A former FBI agent-turned-lawyer becomes involved in the search for the murderer of a childhood friend in Nebraska. (Rev: BL 6/15/86; NYTBR 9/14/86; PW 5/2/86)

6905 Wiltse, David. *Prayer for the Dead.* 1991, Putnam $19.95 (0-399-13687-X). An FBI agent investigates a serial killer responsible for the deaths of 15 men in a Connecticut town. (Rev: BL 6/15/91; PW 5/17/91)

6906 Wolfe, Gene. *Pandora by Holly Hollander.* 1990, St. Martin's $17.95 (0-312-85010-7). A teenage girl solves the murder of her uncle by using the clues derived from a Pandora's box. (Rev: BL 11/15/90; LJ 11/15/90; PW 10/26/90)

6907 Wolfe, Susan. *Last Billable Hour.* 1989, St. Martin's $15.95 (0-312-02566-1); Ivy paper $3.95 (0-8041-0540-5). A California lawyer aids a police investigation into the murder of another attorney in his firm. (Rev: BL 3/1/89; LJ 3/1/89; PW 1/20/89)

6908 Womack, Steven. *Murphy's Fault.* 1990, St. Martin's $17.95 (0-312-03896-8). The debut novel set in New Orleans concerns a journalist's efforts to uncover a shady real estate deal that involves local bankers, politicians, and attorneys. "A vigorous and well written addition to the genre."—PW (Rev: NYTBR 3/4/90; PW 12/8/89)

6909 Womack, Steven. *Smash Cut.* 1991, St. Martin's $18.95 (0-312-06467-5). A New Orleans investigator tackles a murder and political corruption in this sequel to the 1990 *Murphy's Fault.* (Rev: BL 9/15/91; LJ 10/1/91)

6910 Wood, Ted. *Corkscrew.* 1989, Harlequin paper $3.50 (0-373-26024-5). A Canadian policeman in a resort town investigates possible ties between the death of a young boy and a recently arrived motorcycle gang. (Rev: BL 11/15/87; LJ 11/1/87; PW 10/23/87)

6911 Wood, Ted. *Dead in the Water.* 1984, Bantam paper $2.95 (0-7704-2006-0). A policeman retires from urban work to become the sole law enforcement agent at a small Canadian tourist resort. (Rev: BL 10/1/83; LJ 9/1/83; PW 7/15/83)

6912 Wood, Ted. *Fool's Gold.* 1988, Harlequin paper $3.50 (0-373-26019-9). A Canadian police chief investigates a series of murders that follows the discovery of gold in his small town. (Rev: LJ 3/1/86; NYTBR 6/22/86; PW 1/24/86)

6913 Woods, Sara. *Most Deadly Hate.* 1987, Avon paper $3.50 (0-380-70477-3). A child custody investigation turns to homicide after the mother is found strangled. (Rev: BL 2/15/86; PW 1/24/86)

6914 Woods, Sara. *Nor Live So Long.* 1988, Avon paper $3.50 (0-380-70478-1). A barrister investigates a series of murders of women in an English village. "Ranks among the best of Woods's popular series."—PW (Rev: BL 7/86; PW 6/6/86)

6915 Woods, Sara. *Put Out the Light.* 1985, St. Martin's $13.95 (0-312-65702-1); Avon paper $3.50 (0-380-70476-5). An acting troupe suffers through a series of strange incidents that culminate in an actress's murder. (Rev: BL 11/15/85; PW 10/25/85)

6916 Woods, Stuart. *Chiefs.* 1981, Norton $14.95 (0-393-01461-4); Avon paper $4.95 (0-380-70347-5). A story tracking a series of murders of young black men over a period of four decades in a small Georgia town. (Rev: BL 4/15/81; LJ 5/1/81; PW 4/3/81)

6917 Wright, Eric. *A Sensitive Case.* 1990, Macmillan $17.95 (0-684-19132-6). A Toronto detective investigates the murder of a massage therapist who had many influential clients among her customers. (Rev: BL 4/1/90; LJ 4/1/90; PW 2/9/90)

6918 Wright, Jim. *Last Frame.* 1990, Carroll & Graf $16.95 (0-88184-569-8). A photographer in possession of compromising photographs finds himself pursued by a group of would-be blackmailers. (Rev: BL 8/90; LJ 7/90; PW 6/8/90)

6919 Wright, L. R. *Fall from Grace.* 1991, Viking $18.95 (0-670-83130-1). A Canadian Mountie in British Columbia investigates the drowning death of a young man. (Rev: BL 10/15/91; PW 9/6/91)

6920 Wright, L. R. *The Suspect.* 1985, Viking $15.95 (0-670-80596-3); Penguin paper $3.95 (0-14-010477-1). A British Columbian detective seeks the reason an elderly widower killed his brother-in-law. (Rev: BL 5/1/85; LJ 6/1/85; PW 4/12/85. Awards: Edgar, 1985)

6921 Yaffe, James. *Nice Murder for Mom.* 1988, St. Martin's $15.95 (0-312-02260-3); paper $3.50 (0-373-26044-X). A New York detective who moved to Colorado in search of a more peaceful life finds himself involved in the investigation of the murder of a local college professor. (Rev: LJ 11/1/88; PW 10/7/88)

6922 Yorke, Margaret. *A Small Deceit.* 1991, Viking $18.95 (0-670-83977-9). The psychological portrait of a man guilty of rape and murder following his release from prison. (Rev: BL 8/91; PW 7/5/91)

6923 Zahara, Irene, ed. *Second Womansleuth Anthology: Contemporary Mystery Stories by Women.* 1989, Crossing Pr. $20.95 (0-89594-368-0); paper $7.95 (0-89594-367-0). A collection of stories by female writers featuring women sleuths. "Consistently superb . . . do not miss this one."—LJ (Rev: BL 9/15/89; LJ 10/1/89)

FABLES

6924 **Agnon, S. Y. *In the Heart of the Seas: A Story of a Journey to the Land of Israel*. 1987, Schocken paper $6.95 (0-8052-0647-7).** A fable regarding the journey of a group of European Jews to Israel and the fantastic event that occurs along the way. (Rev: BL 6/15/67; LJ 5/15/67; PW 1/9/67)

6925 **Barthelme, Donald. *Dead Father*. 1986, Penguin paper $6.95 (0-14-008667-6).** An army of 19 people cart the corpse of a gigantic father to his burial site. (Rev: Atl 12/75; NYTBR 11/9/75; PW 9/29/75. Awards: NYTBR, 1975)

6926 **Fuller, John. *Flying to Nowhere*. 1984, Brazilier $10.95 (0-8076-1087-9).** A Welsh religious pilgrimage becomes the center for an abbot's experimentation to locate the site of the soul in the human body. (Rev: LJ 3/15/84; NYTBR 3/4/84; PW 12/9/83)

6927 **O'Faolain, Sean. *And Again?* 1989, Carol Publg. Group $16.95 (1-55972-003-4).** A man makes a deal with God to live his life over in reverse to avoid death. "A novel of amazing originality and inventiveness."—NYTBR (Rev: LJ 9/1/89; NYTBR 9/17/89; PW 7/21/89)

6928 **Ustinov, Peter. *Old Man and Mr. Smith: A Fable*. 1991, Little, Brown $19.95 (1-55970-134-X).** God and Satan meet to examine contemporary human society on a tour of earth. (Rev: LJ 5/15/91; PW 4/19/91)

6929 **Welzenbach, Michael. *Conversations with a Clown*. 1991, Atlantic Monthly $18.95 (0-87113-395-4).** The story of the life of a 500-year-old clown who was the subject of portraits of famous artists over the centuries. (Rev: BL 11/15/90; LJ 12/90; PW 10/19/90)

6930 **Willard, Nancy. *Things Invisible to See*. 1984, Knopf $19.95 (0-394-54058-1); Bantam paper $3.95 (0-553-27652-2).** This debut novel concerns a man who challenges Death to a baseball game after accidentally paralyzing a woman with a thrown ball. (Rev: BL 12/1/84; LJ 12/84; PW 11/2/84. Awards: LJ, 1985)

FANTASTIC FICTION

6931   Abe, Kobo. *Ark Sakura.* **1988, Knopf $18.95 (0-394-55836-7); Random paper $8.95 (0-679-72161-4).** A Japanese "Noah" gathers people inside a mountain in the hopes of surviving nuclear destruction and rebuilding society after the holocaust. (REV: BL 4/1/88; LJ 4/1/88; New Yorker 5/9/88)

6932   Adams, Richard. *Maia.* **1989, NAL paper $6.95 (0-451-14035-4).** The tale of the exploits of two heroic slave women of the Belkan empire, as told by the author of *Watership Down.* (REV: LJ 1/85; PW 11/2/84)

6933   Adams, Richard. *Watership Down.* **1974, Macmillan $29.95 (0-02-700030-3); Avon paper $5.50 (0-380-00293-0).** The adventures of a group of rabbits searching for a new home in rural England after being displaced following the destruction of their warren. (REV: BL 4/1/74; Newsweek 3/18/74; TLS 12/8/74. AWARDS: ALA, 1974; NYTBR, 1974)

6934   Aldiss, Brian. *Frankenstein Unbound.* **1990, Warner paper $4.95 (0-446-36036-8).** A twenty-first-century man travels back in time to early nineteenth-century Switzerland and encounters Frankenstein, George Byron, and Mary Shelley. (REV: BL 7/15/74; LJ 8/74; Time 8/5/74)

6935   Aldiss, Brian. *Malacia Tapestry.* **1990, Harper & Row paper $3.95 (0-06-100063-9).** The story of the life of an actor in a medieval fantasy world resembling Renaissance Italy and illustrated by the works of Tiepolo. (REV: BL 7/1/77; LJ 6/1/77; TLS 7/23/76)

6936   Amis, Kingsley. *Alteration.* **1988, Carroll & Graf paper $3.95 (0-88184-432-2).** A story set in contemporary England under Roman Catholicism about a young boy who must choose whether or not to be castrated in order to serve his faith in a choir. (REV: BL 1/1/77; PW 11/22/76; Time 1/3/77)

6937   Anthony, Piers. *Crewel Lye: A Caustic Yarn.* **1987, Ballantine paper $4.95 (0-345-34599-1).** A tale of friendship between a magical princess and ghosts in the kingdom of Xanth. (REV: BL 12/1/84; LJ 2/15/85; PW 11/30/84)

6938   Appel, Allen. *Time after Time.* **1985, Carroll & Graf $17.95 (0-88184-182-X); Dell paper $6.95 (0-440-59116-3).** A historian with the ability to transport himself through time travels to the Russian Revolution to discover secrets concerning his father. (REV: BL 10/1/85; NYTBR 1/26/86; PW 9/27/85)

6939   Appel, Allen. *Twice Upon a Time.* **1990, Dell paper $4.95 (0-440-20576-X).** The sequel to *Time after Time,* about the adventures of a historian and his lover who time-travel from the 1980s to the year 1876. (REV: BL 4/15/88; LJ 4/1/88; PW 2/19/88)

6940   Atwood, Margaret. *The Handmaid's Tale.* **1986, Houghton $16.95 (0-395-40425-8); Fawcett paper $5.95 (0-449-44829-0).** A futuristic tale of an antifemale distopian United States renamed the Republic of Gilead. (REV: Choice 5/86; NYTBR 2/9/86; Time 2/10/86. AWARDS: ALA, 1986; NYTBR, 1986; PW, 1986; Time, 1986)

6941   Auster, Paul. *In the Country of Last Things.* **1987, Viking $15.95 (0-670-81445-8); Penguin paper $6.95 (0-14-009705-8).** A portrait of an unnamed major city following economic and social collapse as told through the letters of a young woman trapped amid the chaos. (REV: Choice 9/87; LJ 1/87; PW 2/6/87)

6942   Ball, Margaret. *The Shadow Gate.* **1991, Baen paper $4.95 (0-671-72032-5).** A Texan finds herself transported to a magical world resembling medieval France following a neurological research experiment. (REV: BL 1/1/91; PW 12/14/90)

6943   Ballard, J. G. *High Rise.* **1988, Carroll & Graf paper $3.50 (0-88184-400-4).** Vignettes of life in a huge London apartment complex populated by upper- and middle-class tenants. (REV: BL 6/1/77; LJ 5/15/77; PW 1/31/77)

6944   Barthelme, Donald. *The King.* **1990, Harper & Row $14.95 (0-06-016195-7).** King Arthur and the Knights of the Round Table are transported through time to the twentieth century to do battle with Hitler's forces in this story by the author of *The Dead Father.* (REV: BL 3/1/90; New Yorker 7/9/90; PW 3/23/90)

6945   Beagle, Peter S. *Folk of the Air.* **1987, Ballantine paper $4.50 (0-345-34699-8).** The story of a contemporary San Francisco acting troupe that accidently conjures up a group of medieval warriors. (Rev: NYTBR 1/18/87; PW 12/12/86)

6946   Beagle, Peter S. *Last Unicorn.* **1987, Ballantine paper $3.95 (0-345-35367-6).** The last unicorn on earth roams the planet in search of other members of her species. (Rev: BL 3/15/68; LJ 5/15/68; PW 1/8/68. Awards: ALA, 1968)

6947   Bear, Greg. *Eon.* **1986, Bluejay $16.95 (0-312-94144-7); Tor paper $4.95 (0-8125-0566-2).** A time-altering asteroid from the future affects the fates of those people on earth who have contact with it. "A spellbinding, atmospheric work."—BL (Rev: BL 7/85; CSM 1/3/86; LJ 9/15/85)

6948   Bear, Greg. *Eternity.* **1988, Warner $16.95 (0-446-51402-0); paper $3.95 (0-445-20547-4).** The sequel to the author's *Eon,* examining civilization on an alternate version of earth while the original planet undergoes reconstruction following nuclear war. (Rev: LJ 10/15/88; PW 9/2/88)

6949   Bear, Greg. *Queen of Angels.* **1990, Warner $19.95 (0-446-51400-4).** Investigators ponder the motives behind the murder of a poet by a group of his followers in this novel set in twenty-first-century Los Angeles. (Rev: BL 6/1/90; LJ 6/15/90; NYTBR 9/2/90)

6950   Berger, Thomas. *Arthur Rex: A Legendary Novel.* **1990, Little, Brown paper $10.95 (0-316-09158-8).** The story of King Arthur and the Knights of the Round Table imbued with late twentieth-century mores. "A most rewarding book."—Choice (Rev: BL 10/1/78; Choice 12/78; LJ 11/1/78)

6951   Berman, Mitch. *Time Capsule.* **1987, Putnam $18.95 (0-399-13197-3).** This author's debut novel concerns the journeys of a jazz musician seeking other humans following his survival of a nuclear holocaust. (Rev: NYTBR 3/22/87; PW 12/26/86)

6952   Bester, Alfred. *Golem 100.* **1981, Pocket paper $2.95 (0-671-82047-8).** The story of three individuals on a futuristic American East Coast in search of a homicidal beast known as the Golem. (Rev: BL 6/1/80; NYTBR 9/14/80; PW 3/7/80)

6953   Bishop, Michael. *Blooded on Arachne.* **1982, Arkham $13.95 (0-87054-093-9).** Eleven stories and two poems written during the 1970s including "Rogue Tomato," "Spacemen and the Gypsies," and "Cathadonian Odyssey." (Rev: BL 2/15/82; LJ 1/15/82; PW 12/4/81)

6954   Bishop, Michael. *No Enemy But Time.* **1989, Bantam paper $4.95 (0-553-28187-9).** An anthropologist time-travels to an Africa populated by early hominids. (Rev: BL 7/82; LJ 4/15/82; PW 3/19/82. Awards: Nebula, 1983)

6955   Bishop, Michael. *Unicorn Mountain.* **1988, Morrow $18.45 (0-87795-953-6); Bantam paper $4.95 (0-553-27904-1).** A Colorado rancher joins forces with a Native American friend to try to save the world's last remaining herd of unicorns. (Rev: BL 6/1/88; LJ 5/15/88; PW 4/29/88)

6956   Blaylock, James P. *Homonculus.* **1986, Ace paper $2.95 (0-441-34258-2).** A tale of scientific discovery set in Victorian England revolving around a process designed to revive the dead. (Rev: BL 3/1/86; PW 2/14/86)

6957   Bosse, Malcolm. *Mister Touch.* **1991, Ticknor & Fields $21.95 (0-89919-965-8).** Survivors of a worldwide plague leave New York to rebuild civilization in Arizona. (Rev: BL 4/1/91; LJ 3/1/91; PW 2/22/91)

6958   Bradley, Marion Zimmer. *House between the Worlds.* **1984, Ballantine paper $4.95 (0-345-31646-0).** A comatose man under the influence of brain-enhancing drugs explores the spiritual world. (Rev: BL 6/1/80; LJ 5/15/80; PW 2/8/80)

6959   Bradley, Marion Zimmer. *Mists of Avalon.* **1987, Ballantine paper $12.95 (0-345-35049-9).** The story of King Arthur as told by the women who knew him. "Vastly ambitious and stunningly successful."—PW (Rev: BL 11/15/82; LJ 12/15/82; PW 12/15/82)

6960   Bradley, Marion Zimmer, ed. *Sword and Sorceress II: An Anthology of Heroic Fantasy.* **1986, DAW paper $3.95 (0-88677-360-1).** A collection of 12 fantasy stories featuring female heroes selected by the author of *The Mists of Avalon.* (Rev: BL 7/85; LJ 5/15/85)

6961   Bradley, Marion Zimmer, Julian May, and Andre Norton. *Black Trillium.* **1990, Doubleday $18.95 (0-385-26185-3).** The compilation work of three authors regarding a future kingdom ruled by triplet daughters. (Rev: BL 6/15/80; LJ 8/90)

6962   Brin, David. *Postman.* **1986, Bantam paper $3.95 (0-553-25704-8).** An extended version of an earlier Brin short story about postnuclear holocaust America and a man in a postman's uniform struggling to survive. (Rev: BL 9/15/85; LJ 10/15/85; PW 9/6/85)

6963   Brin, David. *Practice Effect.* **1985, Bantam paper $3.95 (0-553-26981-X).** A scientist on a planet in a parallel universe discovers that items are perfected by use rather than worn out. (Rev: BL 6/1/84; LJ 3/15/84; PW 2/24/84)

6964   Brinkley, William. *Last Ship.* **1988, Viking $19.95 (0-670-80981-0); Ballantine paper $9.95 (0-345-35982-8).** A futuristic tale of an American ship that survives a worldwide nuclear holocaust and roams the seas in search of a safe harbor to rebuild civilization. (Rev: LJ 2/1/88; NYTBR 5/22/88; Time 2/29/88)

6965   Butler, Octavia. *Imago.* **1989, Warner $19.95 (0-446-51472-1); paper $4.95 (0-445-20977-1).** Aliens assist humans in survival following nuclear holocaust and mate to form a new type of being. (Rev: BL 5/1/89; PW 4/14/89)

6966   Butler, Octavia. *Wild Seed.* **1988, Warner paper $3.95 (0-445-20537-7).** A tale of two Africans, one 3,600 years old and the other 300, who have discovered life-extension techniques and move to eighteenth-century America. (Rev: BL 9/1/80; PW 6/20/80)

6967 Card, Orson Scott. *Prentice Alvin.* **1989, Tor $17.95 (0-312-93141-7).** A nineteenth-century tale of magic revolving around an American secular preacher whose powers have destined him for a showdown with evil. (Rev: BL 12/1/88; LJ 2/15/89; PW 12/23/88)

6968 Card, Orson Scott. *Wyrms.* **1987, Morrow $16.95 (0-87795-894-7); Tor paper $3.95 (0-8125-3357-7).** The story of a young woman in a biologically manipulated future world who, prophecy has decreed, will either save or destroy society. (Rev: BL 8/87; NYTBR 10/18/87; PW 5/29/87)

6969 Carkeet, David. *I Been There Before.* **1987, Penguin paper $6.95 (0-14-009422-9).** Samuel Clemens is resurrected in the mid-1980s and returns to visit some of his old haunts, bringing formerly undiscovered writings from his past. (Rev: BL 10/15/85; PW 8/23/85; Time 12/2/85)

6970 Carter, Angela. *Heroes and Villains.* **1988, Penguin paper $6.95 (0-14-005652-1).** A futuristic novel where man has evolved into several different genera following a nuclear holocaust. (Rev: LJ 11/1/70; PW 7/6/70; TLS 11/20/69)

6971 Cherryh, C. J. *Cherenvog.* **1990, Ballantine $18.95 (0-345-35954-2).** A sequel to *Rusalka*, about a trio of forest inhabitants whose lives are threatened by a force of evil invading the woods. (Rev: BL 10/15/90; LJ 10/15/90; PW 9/7/90)

6972 Cherryh, C. J. *Rusalka.* **1989, Ballantine $18.95 (0-345-35953-4).** Two young men forced to flee their community find themselves in a forest filled with magical beings and supernatural powers. (Rev: BL 9/1/89; LJ 9/15/89; PW 9/8/89)

6973 Cook, Glen. *Tower of Fear.* **1989, St. Martin's $16.95 (0-312-93193-X).** A tale of a society attempting to free itself from the grip of their conquerers. (Rev: BL 9/15/89; LJ 9/15/89; PW 9/8/89)

6974 Coover, Robert. *Whatever Happened to Gloomy Gus of the Chicago Bears?* **1989, Macmillan $7.95 (0-02-042781-6).** A speculative novel portraying the football career of a Richard Nixon who chose sports over politics. "A hugely entertaining novel."—TLS (Rev: LJ 10/1/87; NYTBR 9/27/87; TLS 7/1/88)

6975 Crichton, Michael. *Jurassic Park.* **1990, Knopf $19.45 (0-394-58816-9).** The cloning of dinosaurs on a Costa Rican island leads to the development of a huge theme park to show off the beasts. "His best by far since *The Andromeda Strain*."—Time (Rev: BL 10/1/90; CSM 11/21/90; Time 11/12/90)

6976 Crowley, John. *Aegypt.* **1987, Bantam $17.95 (0-553-05194-6); paper $8.95 (0-553-34592-3).** The mystical story of a history professor who finds a series of supernatural fables he has read to be true. "A breathtaking fantasy, compellingly told."—BL (Rev: BL 2/1/87; LJ 3/15/87; PW 2/20/87)

6977 Crowley, John. *Novelty.* **1989, Doubleday $18.95 (0-385-26171-3); paper $6.95 (0-385-26347-3).** A collection of four stories with fantastic themes by the author of *Aegypt*, including "The Nightingale Sings at Night." (Rev: NYTBR 5/21/89; PW 4/14/89)

6978 Cullen, Brian. *What Niall Saw: The Unabridged Testimony of a Seven-Year-Old.* **1986, St. Martin's $11.95 (0-312-86613-5).** The diary of a seven-year-old Irish boy detailing the effects of nuclear holocaust upon Dublin. (Rev: BL 9/1/86; PW 8/29/86)

6979 De Lint, Charles. *Drink Down the Moon.* **1990, Ace paper $3.95 (0-441-16861-2).** A Canadian musician befriends the last of the world's fairies. "Amply displays DeLint's innate charm and compelling storytelling."—LJ (Rev: BL 5/15/90; LJ 6/15/90)

6980 De Lint, Charles. *Little Country.* **1991, Morrow $22.95 (0-688-10366-9).** A young girl becomes transported to a land of magic following her discovery of a book hidden by her grandfather. (Rev: BL 1/15/91; LJ 2/15/91)

6981 Dickson, Gordon R. *Dragon Knight.* **1990, St. Martin's $19.95 (0-312-93129-8).** A fantastic tale of a twentieth-century Englishman and his wife who are transported to medieval England where they fight evil powers and sorcerers. (Rev: LJ 11/15/90; PW 10/5/90)

6982 Eddings, David. *Diamond Throne.* **1989, Ballantine $18.95 (0-345-35691-8); paper $5.95 (0-345-36769-3).** Four persons journey throughout their world in search of the cure for a mysterious disease plaguing their nation's queen. (Rev: BL 3/15/89; LJ 4/15/89; PW 3/24/89)

6983 Eddings, David. *Ruby Knight.* **1990, Ballantine $19.95 (0-345-37043-0).** Servants of the Queen of Elehia search for the antidote to a poison she has been given by her nation's religious leader. "A thoroughly enjoyable fantasy/adventure."—PW (Rev: BL 11/1/90; LJ 12/90; PW 11/30/90)

6984 Ende, Michael. *Momo.* **1986, Penguin paper $6.95 (0-14-007916-5).** An illustrated tale by the German author of *Neverending Story* detailing the life of a young woman in a society where time is controlled and disseminated. (Rev: BL 1/1/85; LJ 1/85; PW 12/21/85)

6985 Ende, Michael. *Neverending Story.* **1984, Penguin paper $8.95 (0-14-007431-7).** A German novelist's story of a child who becomes the protagonist of a fantasy book he is reading and gets trapped in a make-believe world. (Rev: BL 11/15/83; Newsweek 11/14/83; PW 8/19/83)

6986 Engel, Alan. *Variant.* **1989, Donald I. Fine $17.95 (1-55611-114-2).** Two boys genetically engineered to become superhuman soldiers escape from the Soviet Union to France. (Rev: LJ 1/89; NYTBR 3/19/89)

6987 Feist, Raymond E. *Silverthorn.* **1986, Bantam paper $3.95 (0-553-25928-8).** A group of four battle an enemy who is able to command evil spirits from beyond the grave. (REV: BL 7/85; LJ 6/15/85)

6988 Feist, Raymond E., and Janny Wurts. *Servant of the Empire.* 1990, Doubleday $19.95 (0-385-24718-4). The story of a country's ruler torn between her duty to her nation and her love for an enemy slave. (REV: BL 10/15/90; LJ 10/15/90; PW 8/10/90)

6989 Foster, Alan Dean. *Cyber Way.* 1990, Ace paper $4.50 (0-441-13245-6). The destruction of a Navajo work of art pits powers of native mysticism against modern technology. (REV: BL 5/1/90; LJ 5/15/90; PW 4/20/90)

6990 Gabaldon, Diana. *Outlander.* 1991, Delacorte $20.00 (0-385-30230-4). A wartime nurse is magically transported to eighteenth-century Scotland in this tale of love and witchcraft. "Escape fiction at its best."—BL (REV: BL 7/91; LJ 7/91)

6991 Gardner, John. *Grendel.* 1989, Random paper $7.95 (0-679-72311-0). The first-hand account of the exploits of Grendel the monster, based on the medieval story of Beowulf. (REV: CSM 9/9/71; LJ 9/1/71; Time 9/20/71. AWARDS: ALA, 1971; Time, 1971)

6992 Gerrold, David. *Man Who Folded Himself.* 1976, Amereon $16.95 (0-88411-191-1). A time-travel fantasy regarding the life of a man who became two different people following transportation to another era. (REV: BL 5/1/73; PW 12/11/72)

6993 Goldstein, Lisa. *Dream Years.* 1989, Bantam paper $3.95 (0-553-27657-3). French writers and artists of the 1920s are transported in time to take part in the student rebellions of 1968 Paris. (REV: BL 8/85; LJ 8/85; PW 7/5/85)

6994 Grahn, Judy. *Mundane's World.* 1988, Crossing Pr. $26.95 (0-89594-317-4); paper $10.95 (0-89594-316-6). The tale of the coming-of-age of five girls in a prehistoric society dominated by women. (REV: LJ 11/15/88; PW 9/9/88)

6995 Haldeman, Joe. *Worlds Apart: A Novel of the Future.* 1983, Viking $14.95 (0-685-06795-5). A postapocalyptic tale of a woman living in a satellite while her husband tries to survive on a ravaged earth. (REV: BL 9/15/83; LJ 9/15/83; PW 8/19/83)

6996 Hambly, Barbara. *Silicon Mage.* 1988, Ballantine paper $3.95 (0-345-33763-8). A computer scientist uses a computer to attack an evil sorcerer in another dimension. (REV: BL 4/15/88; LJ 4/15/88; PW 2/26/88)

6997 Hand, Elizabeth. *Wintering.* 1990, Bantam paper $4.95 (0-553-28772-9). A portrait of life in Washington, D.C., following a nuclear holocaust in a society fragmented into warring groups. "A visionary masterpiece."—LJ (REV: BL 10/1/90; LJ 9/15/90; NYTBR 12/9/90)

6998 Harness, Charles L. *Krono.* 1989, Avon paper $3.50 (0-380-70701-2). An overpopulated earth in the future uses time travel to colonize the past and relieve overcrowding. (REV: LJ 11/15/88; PW 9/16/88)

6999 Harrison, Harry. *Technicolor Time Machine.* 1985, Tor paper $2.95 (0-8125-3970-2). The story of a Hollywood motion-picture crew that uses a time machine to travel to the eleventh century to film a Viking epic. (REV: PW 7/3/67; TLS 5/30/68)

7000 Hernon, Peter. *Earthly Remains.* 1989, Carol Publg. Group $18.95 (1-55972-010-7). The remains of John the Baptist and Jesus Christ are found in a cave near the site where the Dead Sea Scrolls are located. (REV: BL 11/15/89; LJ 10/1/89; PW 9/15/89)

7001 Hill, Carol. *Eleven Million Mile High Dancer.* 1986, Penguin paper $6.95 (0-14-008694-3). The story of a female astronaut and physicist who saves the earth from certain destruction. (REV: NYTBR 3/31/85; PW 1/4/85)

7002 Hjortsberg, William. *Grey Matters.* 1971, Ultramarine $20.00 (0-671-20976-0). A portrait of a future world ruled by human brains without bodies. (REV: LJ 7/71; NYTBR 10/31/71; Newsweek 11/29/71)

7003 Hoban, Russell. *Riddley Walker.* 1990, Simon & Schuster paper $8.95 (0-671-70127-4). A portrait of English civilization struggling to rebuild itself after nuclear destruction. (REV: BL 5/15/81; Newsweek 6/29/81; Time 6/22/81. AWARDS: Time, 1981)

7004 Hogan, James P. *Proteus Operation.* 1986, Bantam paper $4.95 (0-553-25698-X). In a world under Nazi domination, English and American scientists develop a time machine to go back in history and undo German victory. (REV: BL 11/15/85; LJ 10/15/85; PW 9/20/85)

7005 Holdstock, Robert. *Lavondyss: Journey to an Unknown Region.* 1989, Morrow $18.95 (0-688-09185-7). A Neolithic-era girl enters a mystical forest filled with magic in search of her missing older brother. (REV: BL 8/89; LJ 8/89; PW 7/7/89)

7006 Holdstock, Robert. *Mythago Wood.* 1986, Berkley paper $2.95 (0-425-08785-9). Two young boys explore a forest near their family home and encounter fantastical beings. (REV: BL 11/15/85; LJ 11/15/85; PW 10/4/85)

7007 Huff, Tanya. *Gate of Darkness, Circle of Light.* 1989, DAW paper $3.95 (0-88677-386-5). A group of social outcasts join forces to fight evil in the futuristic city of Toronto. (REV: BL 11/1/89; LJ 11/15/89)

7008 Jacobson, Mark. *Gojiro.* 1991, Atlantic Monthly $19.95 (0-87113-396-2). A human and a giant lizard become good friends based on their common experiences as survivors of atomic explosions. (REV: BL 3/15/91; LJ 2/15/91; PW 2/1/91)

7009 James, Dakota. *Milwaukee, the Beautiful.* 1986, Donald I. Fine $16.95 (0-917657-15-2). A portrait of Milwaukee as a twenty-first-century ecological utopia threatened by an outside world facing famine and starvation. (REV: LJ 4/15/86; PW 3/14/86)

7010 Johnson, Denis. *Fiskadero.* **1985, Knopf $14.95 (0-394-53839-0).** A portrait of the Florida Keys six decades after nuclear war, populated by a variety of tribes and mutated humans. "Johnson . . . confirms his exceptional talent with this remarkable novel."—PW (Rev: BL 4/15/85; Newsweek 7/8/85; PW 3/15/85)

7011 Kabakov, Alexander. *No Return.* **1990, Morrow $14.95 (0-688-09978-5).** A futuristic novella portraying life in the Soviet Union following the collapse of perestroika. (Rev: BL 9/1/90; LJ 10/1/90; PW 8/3/90)

7012 Kay, Guy Gavriel. *Tigana.* **1990, Viking $22.95 (0-670-83333-9).** A small group of citizens attempt to maintain personal freedoms during a worldwide struggle for power between rival sorcerers. (Rev: BL 6/1/90; LJ 8/90; PW 6/22/90)

7013 King, Stephen. *Eyes of the Dragon.* **1987, Viking $18.95 (0-670-81458-X); NAL paper $4.95 (0-451-16658-2).** A medieval tale of a wizard with supernatural forces who frames and unjustly imprisons a prince for the murder of a king. (Rev: LJ 12/86; NYTBR 2/22/87; PW 12/5/86)

7014 King, Stephen. *Waste Lands.* **1992, NAL paper $14.95 (0-452-26740-4).** This third volume of the Dark Tower series portrays the adventures of Ronald the Gunfighter and two companions in their quest for the Dark Tower. (Rev: BL 10/15/91; PW 11/8/91. Awards: BL, 1991)

7015 Kushner, Ellen. *Thomas the Rhymer.* **1990, Morrow $18.45 (1-557-10046-2).** A tale of a medieval minstrel on a seven-year journey away from the human world. (Rev: BL 3/15/90; LJ 3/15/90; PW 2/16/90)

7016 Lafferty, R. A. *Not to Mention Camels.* **1976, Ultramarine $20.00 (0-672-52178-4).** A man who dies a series of deaths awakens in parallel worlds with the same personality. "A delightful panache of prose and imagination."—BL (Rev: BL 9/1/76; NYTBR 10/3/76; PW 4/19/76)

7017 Lawhead, Stephen R. *Taliesin.* **1987, Good News paper $10.95 (0-89107-407-4).** Former students on the continent of Atlantis find the British Isles following the sinking of their homeland. (Rev: BL 9/1/87; LJ 8/87)

7018 Lee, Tanith. *A Heroine of the World.* **1989, DAW paper $4.50 (0-88677-362-8).** A young woman captured by a warring tribe lives with them for a period of time before escaping to freedom. (Rev: BL 8/89; LJ 8/89; PW 7/21/89)

7019 Le Guin, Ursula K. *Always Coming Home.* **1987, Bantam paper $4.95 (0-553-26280-7).** An illustrated story of a futuristic postholocaust civilization in the United States. (Rev: BL 8/85; LJ 9/15/85; Newsweek 11/18/85)

7020 Le Guin, Ursula K. *Farthest Shore.* **1972, Macmillan $16.95 (0-689-30054-9); Bantam paper $3.95 (0-553-26847-3).** This third installment of the Earthsea series concerns the efforts of a young man to learn the secrets of wizardry in order to help save a dying planet. (Rev: BL 11/1/72; LJ 10/15/72; TLS 4/6/73)

7021 Le Guin, Ursula K. *Lathe of Heaven.* **1982, Bentley $14.00 (0-8376-0464-8); Avon paper $3.50 (0-380-01320-7).** A portrait of a twenty-first-century man whose apocalyptic dreams come true. (Rev: LJ 11/1/71; Natl Rev 2/4/72; PW 10/4/71)

7022 Le Guin, Ursula K. *Tehanu: The Last Book of Earthsea.* **1990, Macmillan $15.95 (0-689-31595-3).** This fourth and concluding book of the Earthsea tetralogy chronicles the life of Tenar, a woman who alternates between periods of great powers and no powers. (Rev: NYTBR 5/20/90; New Yorker 7/23/90; PW 1/19/90)

7023 Le Guin, Ursula K. *Wind's Twelve Quarters.* **1987, Harper & Row paper $6.95 (0-06-091434-3).** A collection of 17 stories from the 1960s and 1970s with introductory essays by the author. (Rev: BL 1/1/76; LJ 10/15/75; TLS 7/30/75)

7024 MacAvoy, R. A. *Book of Kells.* **1989, Bantam paper $3.50 (0-553-25260-7).** Twentieth-century time-travelers visit tenth-century Ireland ruled by Norsemen. (Rev: BL 10/1/85; LJ 8/85; PW 7/5/85)

7025 MacAvoy, R. A. *Damiano's Lute.* **1984, Bantam paper $2.95 (0-553-25977-6).** A wizard doomed to die an early death roams medieval Europe in search of experiences. "This book cannot be too highly recommended."—BL (Rev: BL 7/84; LJ 5/15/84)

7026 MacAvoy, R. A. *Grey Horse.* **1987, Bantam paper $3.95 (0-553-26557-1).** A fairy arrives in an Irish village to court a woman he loves. (Rev: BL 7/87; LJ 4/15/87)

7027 MacAvoy, R. A. *King of the Dead.* **1991, Morrow $19.00 (0-688-09600-X).** The sequel to *Lens of the World* concerning the adventures of an optician devoted to preventing a disastrous war on a neighboring planet. (Rev: BL 11/1/91; PW 10/4/91)

7028 MacAvoy, R. A. *Lens of the World.* **1990, Morrow $18.95 (0-688-09484-8).** The fictional memoirs of the life of an orphan servant of the King of Vestinglon, set in an alternative world much like our own. (Rev: BL 5/1/90; LJ 5/15/90; PW 4/20/90)

7029 MacAvoy, R. A. *Twisting the Rope.* **1986, Bantam paper $3.50 (0-553-26026-X).** An ancient man known as the "Black Dragon" courts a contemporary California woman who is in a musical group and becomes involved in a murder investigation following the slaying of the group's piper. (Rev: BL 12/1/86; CSM 6/5/87; LJ 10/15/86)

7030 McCaffrey, Anne. *All the Weyrs of Pern.* **1991, Ballantine $20.00 (0-345-36892-4).** The Dragonriders devise a computer to combat the threat of Thread that imperils their world in this addition to the Pern series. (Rev: BL 10/1/91; LJ 11/15/91)

7031 McCaffrey, Anne. *Crystal Singer.* **1985, Ballantine paper $4.95 (0-345-32786-1).** A story of a gifted singer who assists a group of miners searching for crystal on the planet Ballybarn. (REV: BL 7/82; LJ 8/82; PW 6/25/82)

7032 McCaffrey, Anne. *Dragonsdawn*. 1989, Ballantine paper $4.95 (0-345-36286-1). A comet threatens life on the planet Pern in this sixth installment in the author's Dragonriders of Pern series. (REV: BL 9/1/88; LJ 10/15/88; PW 9/16/88)

7033 McCaffrey, Anne. *Pegasus in Flight*. 1990, Ballantine $19.95 (0-345-36896-7). Earth people with special psychic powers are chosen to settle extraterrestrial worlds. (REV: BL 11/1/90; LJ 12/90; PW 10/12/90)

7034 McCaffrey, Anne. *White Dragon*. 1986, Ballantine paper $3.95 (0-345-34167-8). An adventurer on dragonback explores the mysteries of the planet Pern. (REV: BL 9/1/78; LJ 6/1/78; PW 4/24/78)

7035 McElroy, Joseph. *Plus*. 1987, Carroll & Graf paper $8.95 (0-88184-289-3). A terminally ill engineer agrees to have his brain placed in orbit as a communication link between space and earth. (REV: NYTBR 3/20/77; PW 12/6/75)

7036 McIntyre, Vonda. *Dreamsnake*. 1986, Dell paper $3.95 (0-440-11729-1). A magic healer, whose sorcery depends on a serpent, searches for a replacement after her original snake is killed. (REV: LJ 4/15/78; NYTBR 6/25/78; PW 4/3/78. AWARDS: Hugo, 1979; Nebula, 1979)

7037 McQuinn, Donald E. *Warrior*. 1990, Ballantine paper $8.95 (0-345-36504-6). In this tale by the author of the 1983 novel *Targets*, a tribal man seeks to reestablish civilization following a nuclear holocaust. (REV: BL 11/1/90; LJ 10/15/90)

7038 May, Julian. *Adversary*. 1984, Houghton $16.95 (0-395-34410-7); Ballantine paper $4.95. Rival factions of human races attempt to escape domination by a group of aliens. (REV: BL 3/1/84; LJ 4/15/84; PW 3/9/84)

7039 May, Julian. *Golden Torc*. 1985, Ballantine paper $4.95 (0-345-32419-6). Humans in the twenty-second century find themselves transported back in time to the Pliocene era. (REV: BL 3/1/82; LJ 2/15/82; PW 12/11/81)

7040 May, Julian. *Newborn King*. 1983, Houghton $16.95 (0-395-32211-1); Ballantine paper $4.95 (0-345-34749-8). A story of a power struggle between a European king, his allies, and rebel forces in exile in North America set in Pliocene times. (REV: BL 3/1/83; LJ 2/15/83; PW 12/24/82)

7041 Moffett, Judith. *Ragged World*. 1991, St. Martin's $18.95 (0-312-05499-8). An alien being arrives from space to help earth solve social and environmental problems. (REV: BL 2/15/91; NYTBR 6/9/91)

7042 Mooney, Ted. *Easy Travel to Other Planets*. 1981, Farrar $11.95 (0-374-14633-0); Ballantine paper (0-345-00867-7). A woman falls in love with a dolphin as nuclear war threatens the world. "A wonderful first novel by a masterful new novelist."—PW (REV: LJ 9/15/81; Newsweek 10/19/81; PW 7/31/81. AWARDS: ALA, 1981)

7043 Moorcock, Michael. *An Alien Heat*. 1987, Ace paper $2.95 (0-441-13660-5). A futuristic immortal travels back in time to the nineteenth century and returns to his own time with an increased understanding of the human condition. (REV: LJ 2/15/73; PW 1/22/73)

7044 Morrow, James. *Only Begotten Daughter*. 1990, Morrow $19.95 (0-688-05284-3). The story of the birth, death, and resurrection of the daughter of God in New Jersey during the 1970s. (REV: LJ 2/15/90; NYTBR 3/18/90; PW 12/15/89)

7045 Morrow, James. *This Is the Way the World Ends*. 1989, Ace paper $3.95 (0-441-80711-9). Six survivors of World War III are placed on trial for war crimes after a nuclear holocaust destroys most of life on earth. (REV: BL 4/1/86; PW 4/25/86)

7046 Murakami, Haruki. *Hard-Boiled Wonderland and the End of the World*. 1991, Kodansha $21.95 (4-7700-1544-5). A Tokyo secret agent has his brain implanted with an intelligence device that begins to overwhelm his mind with images that supplant reality. "Murakami's ingenuity and inventiveness cannot fail to intoxicate; this is a bravura performance."—PW (REV: BL 9/1/91; LJ 9/1/91; PW 8/2/91. AWARDS: BL, 1991)

7047 Murphy, Pat. *The City, Not Long After*. 1989, Doubleday $17.95 (0-385-24925-X); Bantam paper $4.50 (0-553-28370-7). A portrait of the city of San Francisco a decade after a global plague wipes out the rest of the world. (REV: BL 3/15/89; LJ 3/15/89; PW 2/3/89)

7048 Murphy, Pat. *Falling Woman*. 1986, Tor $14.95 (0-312-93230-8). An archaeologist able to communicate with Mayan spirits leads his daughter in re-creation of ancient rituals. (REV: BL 9/1/86; LJ 10/15/86; PW 9/26/86. AWARDS: Nebula, 1988)

7049 Newman, Sharon. *Guinevere Evermore*. 1986, St. Martin's paper $6.95 (0-312-35324-3). A retelling of the Arthurian legend and the relations between Guinevere, King Arthur, Lancelot, and the breakup of the Round Table. (REV: BL 6/1/85; LJ 4/15/85; PW 3/29/85)

7050 Park, Paul. *Sugar Rain*. 1989, Morrow $19.95 (1-557-10025-2); Avon paper $3.95 (0-380-71179-6). A Starbridge Chronicles story about life on an earth controlled by an oppressive theocracy. (REV: LJ 5/15/89; NYTBR 8/20/89; PW 4/14/89)

7051 Perry, Elaine. *Another Present Era*. 1990, Farrar $18.95 (0-374-10528-6). A speculative portrait of a contemporary world where communications with aliens takes place while the planet is threatened with impending ecological disaster. (REV: BL 6/1/90; LJ 7/90. AWARDS: BL, 1990)

7052 Pohl, Frederik. *Coming of the Quantum Cats*. 1986, Bantam paper $3.95 (0-553-25286-2). A fantasy story exploring travel between a series of parallel universes existing at the same given moment of time during the 1980s. (REV: LJ 4/15/86; PW 3/28/86; TLS 7/31/87)

7053   Roberts, Keith. *Kiteworld.* **1988, Ace paper $3.50** (0-441-44851-8). Interconnected stories portraying a postnuclear-holocaust England ruled by a rigid theocracy. (REV: BL 5/15/86; LJ 6/15/86; PW 4/25/86)

7054   Robinson, Kim Stanley. *Gold Coast.* **1988, Tor $18.95** (0-312-93050-X). A futuristic vision of California's Orange County in the mid-twenty-first century, as told through the lives of a poet and his family. (REV: BL 2/15/88; NYTBR 4/24/88; PW 1/8/88)

7055   Robinson, Kim Stanley. *Icehenge.* **1990, Tor paper $3.95** (0-8125-0267-1). Earth's historians search for clues regarding a Martian revolt that took place over three centuries in the past. (REV: BL 12/15/84; PW 8/24/84)

7056   Robinson, Kim Stanley. *Memory of Whiteness.* **1986, Tor paper $3.50** (0-8125-5235-0). An expansion of a 1977 novella concerning the travels and adventures of a group of interstellar musicians touring the universe. (REV: BL 9/15/85; CSM 9/18/86; LJ 9/15/85)

7057   Robinson, Kim Stanley. *Planet on the Table.* **1986, Tor $14.95** (0-312-93595-1); **paper $3.50** (0-8125-5237-7). A collection of eight short fantasy tales from the 1970s and 1980s, including Hugo and Nebula award nominees, by the author of *The Memory of Whiteness.* (REV: BL 5/1/86; NYTBR 9/21/86; PW 6/13/86)

7058   Robinson, Kim Stanley. *Wild Shore.* **1984, Ace paper $3.50** (0-441-88874-4). A portrait of life in the United States six decades after nuclear war. (REV: BL 4/15/84; PW 1/27/84)

7059   Ryman, Geoff. *Child Garden: Or, a Low Comedy.* **1990, St. Martin's $19.95** (0-312-05002-X). A futuristic study of the life of a young girl living in an overpopulated London during the twenty-first century. (REV: BL 10/15/90; LJ 10/15/90; PW 8/24/90)

7060   Salmonson, Jessica A., ed. *What Did Miss Darrington See? An Anthology of Feminist Supernatural Fiction.* **1989, Feminist Pr. $29.95** (1-55861-005-7); **paper $10.95** (1-55861-006-5). A collection of 24 international supernatural short stories by women. (REV: BL 9/1/89; PW 7/14/89. AWARDS: PW, 1989)

7061   Scarborough, Elizabeth Ann. *Healer's War.* **1988, Doubleday $17.95** (0-385-24828-8); **Bantam paper $4.50** (0-553-28252-2). A fantastic tale of magic and combat set during the Vietnam War written by a former military nurse. (REV: BL 11/1/88; PW 9/16/88. AWARDS: Nebula, 1990)

7062   Schenck, Hilbert. *Chronosequence.* **1988, St. Martin's $17.95** (0-312-93079-8). A diary purchased at an auction describing unusual occurrences on Nantucket Island leads a female astronomer to take to the seas to solve its mysteries. (REV: BL 7/88; LJ 6/15/88; PW 6/3/88)

7063   Scliar, Moacyr. *Max and the Cats.* **1990, Ballantine paper $7.95** (0-345-36707-3). A Nazi refugee finds himself haunted by the appearance of cats that mysteriously preface important events in

his life. (REV: BL 5/15/90; LJ 5/1/90; PW 4/13/90. AWARDS: PW, 1990)

7064   Silverberg, Robert. *Lord Valentine's Castle.* **1981, Bantam paper $4.50** (0-553-25097-3). An amnesiac juggler joins a traveling performance group in hopes that he can discover his true identity. (REV: BL 4/1/80; PW 3/21/80; TLS 11/7/80)

7065   Silverberg, Robert. *Tom O'Bedlam.* **1985, Donald I. Fine $16.95** (0-917657-31-4); **Warner paper $3.95** (0-446-34002-2). Postnuclear-holocaust Californians create a religion based on the recurring dreams of many members of society. (REV: LJ 8/85; PW 6/7/85)

7066   Simak, Clifford. *Visitors.* **1988, Ballantine paper $2.95** (0-345-00761-1). Box-shaped aliens invade earth via Minnesota and begin eating the world's forests. "One of the most engaging novels of alien invasion ever written."—LJ (REV: BL 4/1/80; LJ 12/15/79; PW 9/2/80)

7067   Slonczewski, Joan. *A Door into Ocean.* **1986, Ultramarine $20.00** (0-87795-763-0); **Avon paper $3.95** (0-380-70150-2). A portrait of life on two planets, one based on war and competition, the other on cooperation. (REV: BL 12/15/85; LJ 12/85; PW 1/13/86)

7068   Smith, Basil A. *Scallion Stone.* **1980, Whispers $12.00** (0-918372-07-0). A collection of five English fantasy stories unpublished during the author's lifetime. (REV: BL 12/15/80; PW 9/5/80)

7069   Spinrad, Norman. *Little Heroes.* **1988, Bantam paper $4.95** (0-553-27033-8). A futuristic view of artificially created rock and roll stars set in the America of the near future. (REV: BL 7/87; LJ 6/15/87; NYTBR 10/8/87)

7070   Sterling, Bruce. *Artificial Kid.* **1981, Ace paper $2.95** (0-441-03095-5). A portrait of the life of a great street fighter in a futuristic ultra-violent society. (REV: BL 7/15/80; PW 5/9/80)

7071   Stewart, Mary. *Wicked Day.* **1984, Fawcett paper $4.95** (0-449-20519-3). The story of Merlin the magician as told by his archenemy Mordred. (REV: BL 9/1/83; LJ 9/15/83; NYTBR 1/1/84)

7072   Streiber, Whitley, and James W. Kunetka. *Nature's End: The Consequences of the 20th Century.* **1987, Warner paper $4.95** (0-446-34355-2). An India-based group in the twenty-first century plots to kill one-third of the earth's population in order to alleviate an overpopulation crisis. (REV: BL 4/15/86; LJ 4/15/86; PW 3/7/86)

7073   Sturgeon, Theodore. *Godbody.* **1986, Donald I. Fine $14.95** (0-917657-61-6); **NAL paper $3.95** (0-451-16304-4). A self-proclaimed messiah appears in a small town and is murdered, but leaves behind a group of believers to carry on and spread his message. (REV: BL 3/15/86; LJ 3/15/86; PW 2/21/86)

7074   Tarr, Judith. *Alamut.* **1989, Doubleday $19.95** (0-385-24720-6). An elf travels to the medieval Middle East to confront the forces of Saladin and the

Assassins. "An excellent story, with superb historical scholarship and sound plotting."—BL (REV: BL 1/1/90; LJ 12/89)

7075 Tepper, Sheri S. *Beauty.* 1991, Doubleday $20.00 (0-385-41939-2); paper $12.00 (0-385-41940-6). A fantasy that includes Cinderella, Snow White, and the Seven Dwarfs as characters traces the life of a princess. "A beautiful book from one of the genre's best writers."—PW (REV: BL 7/91; PW 7/12/91)

7076 Tepper, Sheri S. *Grass.* 1989, Doubleday $18.95 (0-385-26012-2); Bantam paper $4.95 (0-553-28565-3). A pair of humans flee earth for the planet of Grass following a worldwide epidemic. (REV: BL 9/1/89; LJ 9/15/89; PW 8/11/89)

7077 Tiptree, James, Jr. *Brightness Falls from the Air.* 1985, Tor $14.95 (0-312-93097-6). The story of life on a planet where birdlike creatures produce a substance that causes euphoria in human beings. (REV: BL 2/1/85; LJ 2/15/85; NYTBR 6/16/85)

7078 Tolkien, J. R. R. *Silmarillion.* 1977, Houghton $10.95 (0-395-25730-1); Ballantine paper $4.95 (0-345-32581-8). A precursor to the author's *Lord of the Rings*, portraying the creation and development of the society of Middle-Earth. (REV: BL 9/15/77; LJ 8/77; NYTBR 10/23/77)

7079 Turner, George. *Drowning Terrors.* 1988, Morrow $18.95 (1-55710-038-1). A portrait of twenty-first-century Melbourne society threatened by rising oceanic levels. (REV: BL 9/1/88; Choice 2/89; LJ 9/15/88)

7080 Vance, Jack. *Augmented Agent and Other Stories.* 1986, Underwood-Miller $20.00 (0-88733-020-7); Ace paper $3.50 (0-441-03610-4). Eight previously uncollected early stories by the veteran science fiction/fantasy writer. (REV: BL 4/15/86; LJ 4/15/86; PW 3/28/86)

7081 Vinge, Joan. *Snow Queen.* 1989, Warner paper $4.95 (0-445-20529-6). The story of the clone of a nation's ruler controlled by an overseeing computer. (REV: BL 5/1/80; PW 2/8/80. AWARDS: Hugo, 1981)

7082 Vinge, Joan. *Summer Queen.* 1991, Warner $21.95 (0-446-51397-0). This story of the early years of a teenage queen's reign over her planet is the third in a series that began with *Snow Queen* and *World's End*. (REV: BL 9/1/91; LJ 9/15/91)

7083 Vonnegut, Kurt, Jr. *Galapagos.* 1986, Dell paper $5.95 (0-440-12779-3). A portrait of life in a deevolutionized human society in the Galapagos, set a million years in the future. (REV: BL 9/1/85; NYRB 12/19/85; TLS 11/8/85)

7084 Wangerin, Walter, Jr. *Book of Sorrows.* 1985, Harper & Row $15.45 (0-06-250929-2); paper $8.95 (0-06-250936-5). The sequel to *Book of the Dun Cow* concerning the fight of a group of animals against evil and death. (REV: BL 6/15/85; LJ 6/15/85; NYTBR 8/11/85. AWARDS: LJ, 1985)

7085 Wangerin, Walter, Jr. *Book of the Dun Cow.* 1978, Harper & Row $12.95 (0-06-026346-6); paper

$8.95 (0-06-250937-3). A fantasy based on an Irish legend regarding the uprisings of animals against a rival rooster/spirit and the source of ultimate evil and its armies. (REV: BL 2/15/79; Choice 7–8/79; PW 6/5/78. AWARDS: NBA, 1980)

7086 Watson, Ian. *Chekhov's Journey.* 1989, Carroll & Graf $16.95 (0-88184-523-X). A tale of a Russian actor playing Chekhov on the stage who is transported into the body and mind of the writer. (REV: BL 10/15/89; LJ 11/15/89)

7087 Wilhelm, Kate. *Cambio Bay.* 1990, St. Martin's $17.95 (0-312-03800-3). Two women fleeing from murderers take refuge in a home filled with supernatural powers. (REV: BL 2/15/90; LJ 3/15/90; PW 2/16/90)

7088 Wilhelm, Kate. *Children of the Wind.* 1989, St. Martin's $16.95 (0-312-03303-6). Five novellas including "The Blue Ladies," "A Brother to Dragons, a Companion of Owls," and "The Girl Who Fell into the Sky." (REV: BL 9/15/89; LJ 10/15/89; PW 9/22/89)

7089 Williams, Tad. *Dragonbone Chair.* 1988, DAW $19.95 (0-8099-0003-3); paper $5.95 (0-88677-384-9). A boy with knowledge of magic attempts to save civilization from excesses of the evil king. (REV: BL 8/88; LJ 9/15/88; PW 8/19/88)

7090 Williams, Tad. *Tailchaser's Song.* 1986, DAW paper $4.95 (0-88677-374-1). A cat society fights an evil feline god who threatens the existence of all cats. (REV: BL 10/15/85; LJ 11/15/85; PW 9/27/85)

7091 Willis, Connie. *Lincoln's Dreams.* 1987, Bantam $15.95 (0-553-05197-0); paper $3.95 (0-553-27025-7). A woman has the dreams of Robert E. Lee as she relives and fights the Civil War. (REV: BL 3/15/87; LJ 4/15/87; PW 4/31/87)

7092 Wilson, F. Paul. *Dydeetown World.* 1979, Baen paper $3.50 (0-671-69828-1). A story of crime and detection set in the underworld of a huge futuristic city. (REV: BL 7/89; PW 6/16/89)

7093 Wilson, Robert Charles. *The Divide.* 1990, Doubleday $19.95 (0-385-24947-0); paper $8.95 (0-385-26655-3). The story of a man whose personality splits and deteriorates following a series of hormone experiments conducted by the CIA. "A literate thriller, a superbly crafted novel of character."—NYTBR (REV: LJ 12/89; NYTBR 2/11/90; PW 12/8/89)

7094 Wingrove, David. *Chung Kuo: The Middle Kingdom.* 1990, Delacorte $22.95 (0-385-29873-0). The portrait of an overpopulated world dominated by China two centuries in the future. (REV: BL 11/15/89; LJ 12/89; NYTBR 3/4/90)

7095 Wittig, Monique. *Les Guerilleres.* 1985, Beacon paper $8.95 (0-8070-6301-0). This French novel depicts a future world where packs of women attack cities ruled by men. (REV: Newsweek 10/25/71; PW 8/9/71)

7096 Wolfe, Gene. *Castleview.* 1990, Tor $19.95 (0-312-85008-5). A small community in Illinois is plagued by a series of mysterious accidents after the image of a huge castle appears in the sky. (Rev: BL 1/1/90; LJ 3/15/90)

7097   Wolfe, Gene. *Citadel of the Autarch.* **1983, Ultramarine $29.95 (0-671-45251-7); Pocket paper $3.50 (0-671-49666-2).** The fourth and concluding volume of the Book of the New Sun series chronicling the further adventures of Severian the torturer. (Rev: LJ 12/15/82; NYTBR 5/22/83)

7098   Wolfe, Gene. *Claw of the Conciliator.* **1983, Pocket paper $2.95 (0-671-47425-1).** The further adventures of the banished torturer Severian on the planet Urth under a dying sun. (Rev: BL 2/1/81; PW 1/30/81. Awards: Nebula, 1982)

7099   Wolfe, Gene. *Free Live Free.* **1984, Mark Ziesing $45.00 (0-9612970-1-8); Tor paper $3.95 (0-8125-5813-8).** Four persons are led by various means to a doomed house in this story by the author of the Book of the New Sun series. "Mature, literate work from an excellent writer."—LJ (Rev: BL 10/1/85; LJ 11/15/85; PW 9/27/85)

7100   Wolfe, Gene. *Shadow of the Torturer.* **1984, Pocket paper $3.50 (0-671-54066-1).** A torturer in a futuristic world is cast out following lenient treatment of a client he loves. (Rev: BL 7/1/80; PW 3/7/80)

7101   Wolfe, Gene. *Soldier of Arete.* **1989, St. Martin's $17.95 (0-312-93185-9).** An ancient Greek soldier suffers from an illness that impairs his memory but enables him to communicate with the Gods. (Rev: BL 8/89; LJ 10/15/89; PW 9/8/89)

7102   Wolfe, Gene. *Soldier of the Mist.* **1987, Tor paper $3.95 (0-8125-5815-4).** A historical fantasy about an ancient Roman soldier who can communicate with the Gods and his accounts of the Persian Wars. (Rev: BL 6/15/86; LJ 11/15/86; PW 9/19/86)

7103   Wolfe, Gene. *Sword of the Lictor.* **1983, Pocket paper $3.50 (0-671-49945-9).** The third volume of the Book of the New Sun series portraying the former torturer Severian as the warden of a prison. (Rev: LJ 1/15/82; PW 11/13/81)

7104   Wolfe, Gene. *Urth of the New Sun.* **1987, Tor $17.95 (0-312-93033-X).** A resident of Urth travels to visit the masters of the universe in order to gain a new sun to save his planet. (Rev: BL 9/1/87; LJ 10/15/87; PW 10/16/87)

7105   Woolley, Persia. *Queen of the Summer Stars.* **1990, Simon & Schuster $19.95 (0-671-62201-3).** An examination of the marriage of King Arthur to Queen Guinevere and her relationship to the knight Lancelot. (Rev: BL 5/1/90; LJ 6/1/90; PW 4/20/90)

7106   Wrede, Patricia A. *Mairelon the Magician.* **1991, Tor $17.95 (0-312-85041-7).** An account of a woman's adventures as a magician's apprentice in early eighteenth-century England. "Will charm readers of both Regency romances and fantasies."—PW (Rev: BL 5/15/91; LJ 5/15/91; PW 4/19/91)

7107   Wu, William F. *Hong on the Range.* **1989, Walker $17.95 (0-8027-6862-8).** A futuristic vision of an American West populated by cyborgs. (Rev: BL 5/15/89; PW 2/24/89)

7108   Zelazny, Roger. *Blood of Amber.* **1987, Avon paper $3.95 (0-380-89636-2).** The seventh volume of the author's Amber series chronicles the adventures of a swordfighter named Merlin Corey and his battles against a series of antagonistic enemies. (Rev: BL 9/15/86; LJ 9/15/86; PW 7/25/86)

7109   Zelazny, Roger. *Knight of Shadows.* **1990, Avon paper $3.95 (0-380-75501-7).** Magician Merlin is forced to choose between two rival courts in this segment of the author's Amber series. (Rev: BL 10/15/89; LJ 10/15/89)

GENERAL FICTION

7110 Abbey, Edward. *Black Sun*. 1990, Borgo Pr. **$24.95 (0-8095-4064-9); Capra Pr. paper $9.95 (0-88496-319-5).** The story of the affair between a young woman and a recently divorced forest fire watcher, as told by the author of *Desert Solitaire*. (REV: BL 8/1/71; LJ 4/15/71; NYTBR 6/13/71)

7111 Abbey, Edward. *Fool's Progress: An Honest Novel*. 1988, Henry Holt **$19.95 (0-8050-0921-3); Avon paper $9.95 (0-380-70856-6).** An Arizona man faced with hard times pays a visit to his brother's West Virginia farm in this story by the author of *Desert Solitaire*. "A powerful, almost hauntingly beautiful novel."—LJ (REV: BL 8/88; LJ 11/1/88; Time 11/28/88)

7112 Abbey, Edward. *Hayduke Lives!* 1990, Little, Brown **$18.95 (0-316-00411-1).** The posthumously published sequel to the author's classic *The Monkey Wrench Gang* about an environmentalist group's re-formation to battle developers taking over a canyon in the American Southwest. (REV: BL 11/15/89; LJ 12/89; NYTBR 2/4/90)

7113 Abbey, Edward. *The Monkey-Wrench Gang*. 1985, Dream Garden **$17.95 (0-942688-18-X); Avon paper $4.95 (0-380-00741-X).** Four environmentalists sabotage a developer's projects in Northern Arizona and Southern Utah in this novel by the author of *Desert Solitaire*. (REV: BL 10/15/75; Newsweek 1/5/76; PW 7/7/75)

7114 Abbott, Margot. *The Last Innocent Hour*. 1991, St. Martin's **$22.95 (0-312-06377-6).** This debut novel concerns an American woman assigned to duty in postwar Germany who is plagued by her Nazi contacts during the 1930s. (REV: BL 8/91; LJ 9/15/91; PW 8/2/91)

7115 Abe, Kobo. *Ruined Map*. 1981, Putnam paper **$5.95 (0-399-50470-2).** The story of a Japanese detective's search for the missing husband of a client. Written by the author of *The Face of Another*. (REV: Atl 7/69; CSM 8/14/69; LJ 5/1/69)

7116 Abish, Walter. *How German Is It*. 1980, New Directions **$14.95 (0-8112-0775-7); paper $8.95 (0-8112-0776-5).** This portrait of postwar Germany as depicted through the lives of two brothers and their friends was awarded the first PEN/Faulkner Award. (REV: LJ 9/1/80; Natl Rev 5/29/81; Newsweek 5/4/81)

7117 Ableman, Paul. *I Hear Voices*. 1990, Mc-Pherson **$18.00 (0-929701-05-4); paper $10.00 (0-929701-04-6).** This novel, originally published in France during the 1960s, explores the thought processes of a schizophrenic confined to a mental institution. (REV: BL 8/90; LJ 7/90; NYTBR 11/25/90)

7118 Achebe, Chinua. *Anthills of the Savannah*. 1988, Doubleday **$16.95 (0-385-01664-6).** Two school friends opposed to a corrupt dictatorship in Central Africa are hunted by supporters of the regime. (REV: BL 2/15/88; Choice 6/88; PW 12/18/87)

7119 Achebe, Chinua. *Arrow of God*. 1989, Doubleday paper **$7.95 (0-385-01480-5).** The story of the chief of a Nigerian Ibo tribe who sends one of his sons off to a Christian mission school. (REV: BL 3/15/68; LJ 2/1/68; PW 10/2/67)

7120 Achebe, Chinua. *Man of the People*. 1989, Doubleday paper **$6.95 (0-385-08616-4).** The Nigerian writer examines political corruption in his native land. (REV: BL 10/15/66; Time 8/19/66; TLS 2/3/66)

7121 Ackroyd, Peter. *First Light*. 1989, Grove-Weidenfeld **$19.95 (0-8021-1161-0).** Odd characters flock to a newly discovered Neolithic English archaeological site. "Establishes his reputation as a leading voice in British letters."—LJ (REV: BL 8/89; LJ 7/89; PW 7/28/89)

7122 Adams, Alice. *Families and Survivors*. 1984, Penguin paper **$6.95 (0-14-007375-2).** A series of vignettes ranging from the beginning of World War II to the 1970s tell the story of a Southern girl's life before and after her move to California. (REV: CSM 2/20/75; New Yorker 2/10/75; Newsweek 2/3/75)

7123 Adams, Alice. *Listening to Billie*. 1984, Penguin paper **$6.95 (0-14-007376-0).** The story of the relationship between a single mother and her daughter by the author of *Families and Survivors*. "A treasure, with not a word to spare."—LJ (REV: BL 12/15/77; LJ 1/1/78; New Rep 2/4/78)

7124 **Adams, Alice.** *Second Chance.* **1988, Knopf $18.95 (0-394-56824-9); Fawcett paper $4.95 (0-449-14612-X).** A character study of a group of elderly friends in the 1960s in Northern California facing aging and death together. (REV: BL 2/15/88; LJ 4/1/88; NYTBR 5/1/88)

7125 **Adams, Alice.** *Superior Women.* **1984, Knopf $16.95 (0-394-53632-0); Fawcett paper $3.95 (0-449-20746-3).** A chronicle of the lives of five female friends who met at Radcliffe from the 1940s to the early 1980s. (REV: LJ 9/15/84; NYTBR 9/23/84; PW 6/22/84)

7126 **Adams, Richard.** *Plague Dogs.* **1986, Fawcett paper $4.95 (0-449-21182-7).** The story of two laboratory research dogs who escape a medical facility carrying a plague. (REV: Atl 4/78; LJ 4/1/78; New Yorker 3/20/78)

7127 **Adler, Renata.** *Pitch Dark.* **1983, Knopf $12.95 (0-394-50374-0).** This novel chronicles the travels of a woman following the breakup of her affair with a married man. (REV: BL 11/15/83; LJ 12/15/83; Time 12/5/83. AWARDS: Time, 1983)

7128 **Agee, Jonis.** *Sweet Eyes.* **1991, Crown $18.95 (0-517-57515-9).** An exploration of the friendship between a young woman and the lone African-American man in the small Iowa town in which they live. (REV: BL 1/1/91; LJ 1/91; NYTBR 3/3/91)

7129 **Agnon, S. Y.** *A Simple Story.* **1987, Schocken $14.95 (0-8052-3999-5); paper $8.95 (0-8052-0820-8).** This story, originally written in Hebrew in 1935, concerns life in the Jewish ghetto of a small Polish town near the turn of the century. (REV: BL 12/15/85; NYTBR 12/22/85; New Yorker 3/3/86)

7130 **Aguilera-Malta, Demetrio.** *Babelandia.* **1985, Humana $19.95 (0-89603-065-2).** An Ecuadorian writer's portrait of life under a Latin American dictatorship as told through a series of vignettes of black humor. (REV: Choice 10/85; LJ 5/15/85)

7131 **Aitmatov, Chingiz.** *Day Lasts More Than a Hundred Years.* **1983, Indiana Univ. Pr. $30.00 (0-253-11595-7); paper $12.50 (0-253-20482-8).** A study of one day in the life of a Kazakh man set in the near future when the United States and Russia are on the brink of a momentous accord. (REV: BL 2/15/84; Choice 2/84; New Yorker 4/23/84)

7132 **Aksyonov, Vassily.** *The Burn.* **1984, Random $18.95 (0-394-52492-6).** A portrait of the Soviet intelligentsia during the 1960s by a writer who was forced to leave the Soviet Union following the book's publication in the West. (REV: LJ 9/15/84; Newsweek 11/26/84; TLS 11/2/84)

7133 **Aksyonov, Vassily.** *Quest for an Island.* **1987, PAJ Pubs. $17.95 (1-55554-020-1).** A collection of four short stories and two works of drama written between the late 1960s and the 1980s by the Soviet emigré author of *Say Cheese!* (REV: BL 1/1/88; Choice 6/88; NYTBR 1/24/88)

7134 **Aksyonov, Vassily.** *Say Cheese!* **1989, Random $19.95 (0-394-54363-7).** In this satire a controversial Russian photographer is tailed by government agents after he privately publishes a collection of his work. (REV: BL 8/89; New Rep 9/18/89; PW 6/16/89)

7135 **Alberts, Laurie.** *Tempting Fate.* **1988, Washington Square Pr. paper $6.95 (0-671-66049-7).** An independent young woman in search of self moves to Alaska and becomes friends with a group of Tlingit Indians. "This novel has an immediacy that keeps the reader absorbed from beginning to end."—BL (REV: BL 4/15/87; LJ 4/15/87; PW 3/20/87)

7136 **Alegria, Claribel.** *Luisa in Realityland.* **1987, Curbstone $17.95 (0-915306-70-0); paper $9.95 (0-915306-69-7).** A collection of short fiction, poems, and retold fables by the Salvadoran writer portraying Central American life and culture. (REV: Choice 1/88; CSM 3/31/88; NYTBR 9/18/88)

7137 **Aleichem, Sholem.** *The Bloody Hoax.* **1992, Indiana Univ. Pr. $29.95 (0-253-30401-6).** The first English translation of a novel portraying Jewish life in a large Russian city prior to World War I. (REV: LJ 11/15/91; PW 11/8/91)

7138 **Allen, Charlotte Vale.** *Illusions.* **1989, Ivy Books $4.50 (0-8041-0190-6).** The chance meeting between a woman and a man on an airplane leads from possible romance to sexual assault. (REV: BL 5/15/87; LJ 5/1/87; PW 4/5/87)

7139 **Allende, Isabel.** *Eva Luna.* **1988, Knopf $18.95 (0-394-57253-4); Bantam paper $4.95 (0-553-28058-9).** This magical realist tale of the life of a South American woman paints a microcosm of the twentieth century on that continent. (REV: LJ 10/15/88; PW 8/19/88; TLS 4/7/89. AWARDS: ALA, 1988; LJ, 1988)

7140 **Allende, Isabel.** *House of the Spirits.* **1985, Knopf $17.95 (0-394-53097-9); Bantam paper $5.95 (0-553-25865-6).** This debut novel by the Chilean writer traces the life of the Trueba family during the twentieth century. "Magda Bogin's excellent translation . . . makes the reading of this novel an unforgettable experience."—CSM (REV: CSM 6/7/85; NYTBR 7/18/85; Sat Rev 5/85. AWARDS: ALA, 1985; BL, the 1980s)

7141 **Allende, Isabel.** *Of Love and Shadows.* **1987, Knopf $17.95 (0-394-54962-7); Bantam paper $5.95 (0-553-27360-4).** An account of political terrorism in an unspecified South American nation and the efforts of two reporters to expose the government's excesses. (REV: CSM 5/27/87; LJ 5/1/87; NYTBR 7/12/87)

7142 **Alther, Lisa.** *Kinflicks.* **1977, NAL paper $4.95 (0-451-15685-4).** A woman in her late 20s separated from her husband returns to her Tennessee hometown to care for her ailing mother. (REV: LJ 3/1/76. AWARDS: New Yorker 3/29/76; PW 1/26/76; ALA, 1976)

7143 **Alther, Lisa.** *Original Sins.* **1985, NAL paper $4.95 (0-451-13966-6).** A novel by the author of *Kinflicks* tracing the lives of five small-town Tennessee children growing up during the 1960s and 1970s. (REV: BL 2/15/81; LJ 3/15/81; Time 4/27/81)

7144 **Alvarez, Julia.** *How the Garcia Girls Lost Their Accents.* **1991, Algonquin $16.95 (0-945575-57-**

2). Fifteen interrelated stories chronicling the assimilation of four Dominican sisters into American society. "A gifted, evocative storyteller of promise."—LJ (REV: LJ 5/1/91; PW 4/5/91. AWARDS: ALA, 1992; LJ, 1991)

7145 Amado, Jorge. *Dona Flor and Her Two Husbands*. 1988, Avon paper $7.95 (0-380-75469-X). The story of a Bahia, Brazil, woman who remarries following the death of her first husband during Carnival. (REV: Choice 3/70; CSM 12/18/69; LJ 7/69)

7146 Amado, Jorge. *Shepherds of the Night*. 1988, Avon paper $7.95 (0-380-75471-4). Three stories set in Brazil that portray the lives of the denizens of the Bahian waterfront. (REV: BL 3/1/67; LJ 1/15/67; Newsweek 1/30/67. AWARDS: ALA, 1967)

7147 Amado, Jorge. *Showdown*. 1989, Bantam paper$8.95 (0-553-34666-0). A tale of two Brazilian plantation owners who raise private armies to settle a dispute. (REV: LJ 2/1/88; NYTBR 2/7/88; Time 2/15/88)

7148 Amado, Jorge. *Tent of Miracles*. 1988, Avon paper $7.95 (0-380-75472-X). This novel traces the events of the previous century where a Brazilian man's local folklore book was destroyed by authorities prior to its publication. (REV: LJ 7/71; NYTBR 10/24/71; Sat Rev 8/28/71. AWARDS: ALA, 1971)

7149 Amado, Jorge. *Two Deaths of Quincas Wateryell: A Tall Tale*. 1988, Avon paper $5.95 (0-380-75476-2). The body of a man who left his family to pursue a life of pleasure is treated to a final fling by his friends when his corpse is returned to his hometown. (REV: LJ 12/15/65; Sat Rev 1/8/66. AWARDS: NYTBR, 1965)

7150 Amiel, Joseph. *Birthright*. 1985, Macmillan $17.95 (0-689-11508-3); Fawcett paper $4.50 (0-449-12872-5). The portrait of a family of Western European financiers whose internecine rivalries force a daughter to move to New York. (REV: BL 3/15/85; LJ 3/15/85; PW 2/1/85)

7151 Amiel, Joseph. *Deeds*. 1988, Fawcett paper $4.95 (0-449-14527-0). An account of the rise and fall of a New York real-estate financier and of his arranged marriage with the daughter of his father's business colleague. (REV: BL 12/1/87; LJ 2/1/88; PW 12/4/87)

7152 Amis, Kingsley. *Difficulties with Girls: A Novel*. 1989, Summit $18.95 (0-671-67582-6). The study of an English couple during the late 1960s and the effects on their marriage of the husband's obsession with women. (REV: Natl Rev 5/19/89; Time 4/24/89; TLS 9/23/88)

7153 Amis, Kingsley. *Folks Who Live on the Hill*. 1990, Summit $18.95 (0-671-70816-3). A portrait by the author of *Lord Jim* of a divorced man living with his widowed sister in a London suburb. (REV: CSM 8/8/90; LJ 7/90; Time 6/4/90)

7154 Amis, Kingsley. *Girl, 20*. 1989, Summit $8.95 (0-671-67120-0). An account of the affair between an English musician in his 50s and a young teenage girl. "First-rate Amis, a wonderfully funny novel."—Newsweek (REV: BL 2/15/72; NYTBR 1/16/72; Newsweek 3/6/72)

7155 Amis, Kingsley. *Jake's Thing*. 1980, Penguin paper $5.95 (0-14-005096-5). A tale of an Oxford professor and his relationships with women that examines the ties between sexuality and love. (REV: Choice 11/79; LJ 4/1/79; NYRB 5/17/79)

7156 Amis, Kingsley. *Stanley and the Women*. 1988, Harper & Row paper $6.95 (0-06-097145-2). A study of the relationships between a British newspaper ad man, his wife, ex-wife, mother-in-law, and psychiatrist. (REV: Atl 11/85; Time 9/30/85; TLS 5/25/84)

7157 Amis, Martin. *London Fields*. 1990, Crown $19.95 (0-517-57718-6). Amis's sixth novel portrays London on the brink of collapse at the end of the twentieth century. "A stunning achievement."—CSM (REV: CSM 4/11/90; NYTBR 3/4/90; PW 1/5/90. AWARDS: NYTBR, 1990; PW, 1990)

7158 Amis, Martin. *Money: A Suicide Note*. 1986, Penguin paper $8.95 (0-14-008891-1). A portrait of the self-destructive life of television director John Self, by the British author of *London Fields*. (REV: New Rep 5/6/85; Newsweek 3/25/85; Time 3/11/85. AWARDS: Time, 1985)

7159 Amis, Martin. *Rachel Papers*. 1988, Crown paper $8.95 (0-517-56777-6). Amis's first novel concerns a young Englishman's plans to seduce a young woman named Rachel Seth-Smith. (REV: BL 6/15/74; LJ 3/1/74; TLS 11/16/73)

7160 Amis, Martin. *Success*. 1987, Crown $15.95 (0-517-56649-4). Amis's third novel, portraying the fictional memoirs of two misogynist men, was originally published in England in 1978. (REV: BL 8/87; LJ 9/1/87; PW 7/10/87)

7161 Amis, Martin. *Time's Arrow*. 1991, Crown $18.00 (0-517-58515-4). The story of a German American who lives his life backwards from the 1980s through the Holocaust and before. (REV: BL 8/91; LJ 8/91; NYTBR 11/17/91)

7162 Anderson, Jessica. *Tirra Lirra by the River*. 1984, Penguin paper $6.95 (0-14-006945-3). An elderly woman returns from Britain to her native Australia and tells stories of her life from her sickbed. (REV: LJ 12/1/83; Newsweek 1/23/84; PW 3/4/83)

7163 Ang, Li. *Butcher's Wife*. 1990, Beacon paper $9.95 (0-8070-8323-2). This fictional retelling of the Shanghai murder of an abusive husband by his wife was originally published in Taiwan in 1983. (REV: BL 10/15/86; LJ 12/86; PW 10/10/86)

7164 Appelfeld, Aharon. *For Every Sin*. 1989, Grove-Weidenfeld $15.95 (1-55584-318-2). The observations and reflections of a Holocaust survivor on his walk from the death camp to his home. (REV: LJ 4/15/89; NYTBR 5/21/89; TLS 9/1/89)

7165 Appelfeld, Aharon. *The Healer*. 1990, Grove-Weidenfeld $16.95 (0-8021-1223-4). A Jewish man visits a traditional healer when his ailing daughter fails to respond to modern medicine. "A small but disturbing masterpiece."—BL (REV: BL 5/15/90; LJ 6/1/90; PW 4/13/90)

7166   Appelfeld, Aharon. *Immortal Barfuss.* **1989, Harper & Row paper $7.95 (0-06-097201-6).** A portrait of the life of a death camp survivor who remains silent about his experiences until he meets a fellow victim of the Holocaust. (REV: BL 1/1/88; LJ 1/88; NYTBR 2/28/88)

7167   Apple, Max. *Propheteers.* **1987, Harper & Row paper $7.95 (0-06-096158-9).** A satire concerning the actions of two citizens who dared to oppose the construction of Walt Disney World. (REV: NYTBR 3/15/87; Newsweek 2/23/87; Time 2/23/87)

7168   Apple, Max. *Zip: A Novel of the Left and Right.* **1986, Warner paper $3.50 (0-446-34179-7).** A Detroit junkman discovers a talented Puerto Rican boxer working in his yard. (REV: LJ 7/78; New Rep 6/24/78; Newsweek 7/10/78)

7169   Archer, Jeffrey. *Kane and Abel.* **1985, Fawcett paper $4.95 (0-449-21018-9).** This novel covers six decades in the lives of two men born on the same day: one, a successful American financier; the other, a son of a Polish peasant. (REV: LJ 3/15/80; PW 1/18/80)

7170   Arenas, Reinaldo. *Farewell to the Sea.* **1985, Viking $18.95 (0-670-52960-5); Penguin paper $7.95 (0-14-006636-5).** A portrait of life under the regime of Castro as depicted by a Cuban writer in exile. (REV: BL 9/15/85; PW 9/20/85; Sat Rev 11/85)

7171   Arensberg, Ann. *Group Sex: A Romantic Comedy.* **1986, Knopf $15.95 (0-394-55310-1); Pocket paper $5.95 (0-671-64362-2).** The story of the romance between a New York editor and a theater director by the author of the ABA-winning *Sister Wolf.* (REV: NYTBR 10/5/86; PW 7/18/86)

7172   Arensberg, Ann. *Sister Wolf.* **1987, Washington Square Pr. paper $5.95 (0-671-64507-2).** The first novel by Arensberg regarding a Hungarian emigré who sets up a roving shelter for wolves on her New England farm. (REV: BL 10/15/80; Newsweek 10/20/80; PW 8/29/80. AWARDS: NBA, 1981)

7173   Argueta, Manlio. *One Day of Life.* **1991, Random paper $9.95 (0-679-73243-8).** A portrait of the waking hours of the life of a Salvadorean peasant woman torn between her loyalties to the Roman Catholic church and her government. (REV: LJ 9/1/83; NYTBR 10/2/83; PW 7/15/83)

7174   Ariyoshi, Sawako. *The Twilight Years.* **1988, Kodansha paper $5.95 (0-87011-852-8).** A Japanese family cares for a widowed grandfather. (REV: BL 1/15/85; NYTBR 1/20/85; PW 9/14/84)

7175   Arnold, Emily. *Life Drawing.* **1986, Delacorte $15.95 (0-385-29437-9); Dell paper $4.95 (0-440-20025-3).** An actress and artist move among the New York art world during the 1950s and early 1960s. (REV: BL 3/1/86; NYTBR 3/30/86)

7176   Arnold, Janis. *Daughters of Memory.* **1991, Algonquin $16.95 (0-945575-68-8).** Two Texas sisters—one who moved away, one who stayed on the farm—tell the stories of their lives in alternating voices. (REV: BL 9/1/91; LJ 8/91)

7177   Arnold, Jean. *Scissor Man.* **1991, Doubleday $18.95 (0-385-41508-7).** The lives of a doctor and his wife are disrupted following the arrival of the woman's twin on their remote Latin American island. "An unforgettable, beautifully articulated tale."—BL (REV: BL 3/1/91; LJ 1/91; NYTBR 2/10/91)

7178   Arrabal, Fernando. *Tower Struck by Lightning.* **1988, Viking $16.95 (0-670-81346-X).** A Spanish playwright chronicles a world championship chess match between an American and a Russian in Paris. (REV: Choice 11/88; LJ 6/15/88; PW 5/20/88)

7179   Arthur, Elizabeth. *Bad Guys.* **1986, Knopf $16.95 (0-394-55442-6).** An Alaskan juvenile detention camp noted for its innovative reforms is invaded by a terrorist group. (REV: BL 11/1/86; LJ 10/1/86; PW 9/5/86)

7180   Ascher, Carol. *The Flood.* **1987, Crossing Pr. $22.95 (0-89594-227-5); paper $8.95 (0-89594-256-9).** A young Kansas girl whose parents survived the Holocaust is exposed to anti-Semitism in this novel set during the 1950s. (REV: BL 4/15/87; LJ 5/15/87; PW 3/6/87)

7181   Astley, Thea. *Beachmasters.* **1988, Penguin paper $6.95 (0-14-010946-3).** An Australian writer's story of a small South Pacific island's revolt against colonial powers. "A work of considerable power and distinction."—LJ (REV: LJ 4/1/86; NYTBR 6/22/86; TLS 11/15/85)

7182   Astley, Thea. *Reaching Tin River.* **1990, Putnam $19.95 (0-399-13532-4).** A novel depicting a young Australian girl's coming of age in a boarding home and in her mother's hostel for wayward travelers. (REV: LJ 4/1/90; NYTBR 4/22/90; PW 1/26/90)

7183   Astley, Thea. *Two by Astley: A Kindness Cup—The Acolyte.* **1988, Putnam $18.95 (0-399-13363-1).** Two short novels originally published in Australia during the 1970s. "A writer of astonishing gifts."—PW (REV: LJ 5/15/88; NYTBR 7/31/88; PW 4/1/88)

7184   Attoe, David. *Lion at the Door.* **1989, Little, Brown $17.95 (0-316-05800-9).** A study of the life of the daughter of an abusive English miner, from her childhood in the 1940s through adulthood in the 1970s. (REV: BL 2/1/89; LJ 3/1/89; PW 2/10/89)

7185   Atwood, Margaret. *Bodily Harm.* **1982, Ultramarine $20.00 (0-671-44153-1); Bantam paper $4.95 (0-553-27455-4).** A Canadian journalist vacationing in the Caribbean becomes involved in an island revolution. (REV: BL 1/15/82; LJ 2/15/82; NYTBR 3/21/82)

7186   Atwood, Margaret. *Cat's Eye.* **1989, Doubleday $18.95 (0-385-26007-5); Bantam paper $5.95 (0-553-28247-6).** The story of a painter's return to her native Toronto and her reflections on how the people she knew there shaped her life. (Rev: BL 12/15/88; LJ 2/1/89; Time 2/6/89. Awards: ALA, 1989; BL, the 1980s; LJ, 1989)

7187   Atwood, Margaret. *Lady Oracle.* **1987, Fawcett paper $5.95 (0-449-21376-5).** A study of the lingering effects of obesity and past trauma in the life of a female novelist. "A high point in fiction about women."—LJ (Rev: Choice 2/77; LJ 9/1/76; Newsweek 10/4/76)

7188   Atwood, Margaret. *Life Before Man.* **1987, Fawcett paper $4.95 (0-449-21377-3).** A woman recovering from a friend's suicide witnesses her husband and a coworker drifting toward an affair. (Rev: LJ 1/15/80; Newsweek 2/18/80; Time 2/25/80. Awards: ALA, 1980)

7189   Atwood, Margaret. *Surfacing.* **1987, Fawcett paper $4.95 (0-449-21375-7).** A woman searches a forest in Quebec for her father following his disappearance from his cabin. (Rev: BL 5/1/73; NYTBR 3/4/73; PW 1/29/73)

7190   Auchincloss, Louis. *Diary of a Yuppie.* **1987, St. Martin's paper $3.95 (0-317-62209-9).** A journal of a New York lawyer tracing the rise of his business success and the collapse of his marriage. (Rev: LJ 7/86; NYTBR 8/31/86; Newsweek 9/15/86)

7191   Auchincloss, Louis. *Golden Calves.* **1990, St. Martin's paper $3.95 (0-312-91487-3).** A portrait of the rivalry between a curator and the director of a Manhattan art museum that seeks to expand its collection by acquiring the estate of an elderly collector. (Rev: BL 4/1/88; CSM 5/20/88; PW 3/18/88)

7192   Auchincloss, Louis. *Honorable Men.* **1986, McGraw-Hill paper $4.95 (0-07-002434-0).** A chronicle of the marriage and divorce of a wealthy Connecticut lawyer and the daughter of a formerly prestigious New York family. (Rev: LJ 9/15/85; NYRB 12/19/85; NYTBR 10/13/85)

7193   Auchincloss, Louis. *House of the Prophet.* **1980, Houghton $10.95 (0-395-29084-8).** A character study of a lawyer told through the recollections of his friends and acquaintances. (Rev: Atl 5/80; CSM 5/7/80; LJ 3/1/80)

7194   Auster, Paul. *Locked Room.* **1987, Sun & Moon $13.95 (0-317-54163-3); Penguin paper $6.95 (0-14-009736-8).** A narrator details his search for a friend who disappeared and left his family behind. "Page-turning fiction that is rich and compelling."—PW (Rev: BL 1/1/87; PW 12/19/86; TLS 12/11/87)

7195   Auster, Paul. *Moon Palace.* **1989, Viking $18.95 (0-670-82509-3); Penguin paper $7.95 (0-14-011585-4).** A young man chronicles the life of an aging invalid in this story by the author of *In the Country of Lost Things.* (Rev: BL 1/15/89; NYTBR 3/19/89; TLS 4/28/89)

7196   Auster, Paul. *The Music of Chance.* **1990, Viking $18.95 (0-670-83535-8).** A man who receives a small fortune leaves his family to travel around the United States with a rambling gambler. (Rev: BL 9/1/90; LJ 9/1/90; NYRB 1/17/91)

7197   Austin, Doris Jean. *After the Garden.* **1987, NAL $17.95 (0-453-00538-1); paper $8.95 (0-452-26079-5).** A coming-of-age story of an African-American New Jersey woman from the beginning of World War II through the early 1960s. (Rev: LJ 7/87; NYTBR 8/16/87)

7198   Bache, Ellyn. *Safe Passage.* **1988, Crown $16.95 (0-517-56807-1).** A chronicle of a family's efforts to determine whether their son survived the 1983 terrorist bombing of U.S. Marine barracks in Lebanon. (Rev: BL 6/1/88; LJ 9/1/88; PW 6/24/88)

7199   Bachmann, Ingeborg. *Malina.* **1990, Holmes & Meier $29.95 (0-8419-1192-4).** An Australian writer's exploration of a love triangle that ends in the murder of one of its members. (Rev: Choice 5/91; LJ 10/1/90; NYTBR 2/10/91)

7200   Baker, Nicholson. *The Mezzanine.* **1988, Grove-Weidenfeld $15.95 (1-55584-258-5); Random paper $7.95 (0-679-72576-8).** A catalog of the thoughts of a man buying shoelaces during his lunch hour. (Rev: Atl 12/88; LJ 11/1/88; NYTBR 2/5/89)

7201   Baker, Nicholson. *Room Temperature.* **1990, Grove-Weidenfeld $16.95 (0-8021-1224-2).** The second novel by Baker regarding a young man's narration of events surrounding his care for a baby girl dubbed "The Bug." "A small masterpiece by an extraordinarily gifted young writer."—PW (Rev: BL 2/1/90; LJ 3/15/90; PW 2/9/90. Awards: LJ, 1990)

7202   Baker, Nicholson. *Vox.* **1992, Random $15.00 (0-394-58995-5).** The fictional record of an explicit telephone conversation between a man and a woman, as depicted by the author of *The Mezzanine.* (Rev: BL 11/15/91; LJ 11/15/91)

7203   Balaban, John. *Coming Down Again.* **1989, Simon & Schuster paper $8.95 (0-671-67537-0).** A poet's novel about two Americans arrested in Burma on charges of drug possession and their efforts to escape. (Rev: BL 6/1/85; New Yorker 8/26/85)

7204   Baldwin, James. *Just Above My Head.* **1990, Dell paper $5.95 (0-440-14777-8).** A man recounts the details of the life and death of his younger brother and his career as a singer and preacher in Harlem during the 1950s and 1960s. (Rev: CSM 9/26/79; New Yorker 11/26/79)

7205   Ballantyne, Sheila. *Imaginary Crimes.* **1983, Penguin paper $7.95 (0-14-006540-7).** The fictional memoirs of a Seattle girl who raises her younger sister after the death of their mother. (Rev: BL 2/15/82; LJ 2/15/82; Newsweek 2/22/82. Awards: ALA, 1982)

7206   Ballard, J. G. *Day of Creation.* **1988, Farrar $17.95 (0-374-13527-4); Macmillan paper $7.95 (0-02-041514-1).** The story of a Western doctor who discovers a river in Saharan Africa and hopes to use its water to improve the lives of local inhabitants. (Rev: PW 2/19/88; Time 4/25/88; TLS 9/11/87)

7207   Bambara, Toni C. *Salt Eaters.* **1981, Random paper $5.95 (0-394-75050-0).** This first novel by the noted short-story writer concerns the personal relations between two African-American women in

Georgia during the late 1970s. (Rev: LJ 4/1/80; New Yorker 5/5/80; PW 2/8/80)

7208 Banks, Iain M. *Canal Dreams.* **1991, Doubleday $19.00 (0-385-41814-0).** A futuristic story of a woman seeking revenge against a terrorist for the death of her lover. (Rev: BL 8/91; LJ 8/91)

7209 Banks, Russell. *Affliction.* **1989, Harper & Row $18.95 (0-06-016142-6); paper $8.95 (0-06-092007-6).** A study of two New Hampshire brothers and the descent of the elder into violence and madness. (Rev: BL 8/89; LJ 8/89; New Rep 9/11/89)

7210 Banks, Russell. *Continental Drift.* **1986, Ballantine paper $4.95 (0-345-33021-8).** A New Hampshire repairman becomes involved in drug-running and illegal immigration schemes after he moves in with his brother in Florida. (Rev: Atl 2/85; LJ 4/15/85; PW 1/11/85. Awards: ALA, 1985; LJ, 1985; PW, 1985)

7211 Banks, Russell. *Sweet Hereafter.* **1991, Harper-Collins $20.00 (0-06-016703-3).** A novel by the author of *Continental Drift* tracing the effects of a tragic school bus accident upon a New York community. (Rev: NYTBR 9/15/91; PW 6/14/91. Awards: ALA, 1992; PW, 1991)

7212 Banville, John. *Book of Evidence.* **1990, Macmillan $17.95 (0-684-19180-6).** A murderer tells the story of his life and his crime from his jail cell. "It is difficult to imagine a reader who would not find *Book of Evidence* both terrifying and moving."—PW (Rev: BL 3/15/90; LJ 3/1/90; PW 2/9/90)

7213 Banville, John. *Newton Letter.* **1987, Godine $12.95 (0-87923-638-8); paper $9.95 (0-87923-771-6).** A historian and biographer seeks to set the record straight regarding an important letter written by scientist Isaac Newton to the philosopher John Locke. (Rev: BL 6/15/87; NYTBR 7/19/87; New Yorker 4/27/87)

7214 Barfoot, Joan. *Duet for Three.* **1987, Beaufort Books $15.95 (0-8253-0393-1); Avon paper $3.95 (0-380-70375-0).** The story of the reconciliation of an elderly mother and daughter brought about through the efforts of a granddaughter. "A book of uncommon depth."—BL (Rev: BL 12/1/86; LJ 12/86; PW 10/30/87. Awards: ALA, 1987)

7215 Barker, Pat. *Blow Your House Down.* **1984, Putnam $13.95 (0-399-13011-X).** Barker's second novel traces the effects of a series of murders of English prostitutes upon the psyches of community members. (Rev: LJ 9/1/84; NYTBR 10/21/84; PW 7/6/84)

7216 Barker, Pat. *Century's Daughter.* **1986, Putnam $18.95 (0-399-13174-4).** An elderly English woman tries to decide whether to enter a convalescent home in this novel set during the mid-1980s. (Rev: NYTBR 12/21/86; PW 8/28/87)

7217 Barker, Pat. *Union Street.* **1984, Ballantine paper $4.95 (0-345-31501-4).** A portrait of working-class life in England as reflected through the lives of seven women. "Powerful . . . a novel of unex-

pected joy."—LJ (Rev: LJ 9/1/83; NYTBR 10/2/83; PW 7/22/83)

7218 Barnes, Julian. *Flaubert's Parrot.* **1990, Random paper $8.95 (0-679-73136-9).** A retired physician obsessed with the nineteenth-century French writer searches for the present location of Flaubert's stuffed parrot. (Rev: LJ 4/1/85; NYRB 4/25/85; PW 12/21/84. Awards: NYTBR, 1985)

7219 Barnes, Julian. *A History of the World in 10½ Chapters.* **1989, Knopf $18.95 (0-394-58061-3); Random paper $9.95 (0-679-73137-7).** Stories detailing historical incidents of the world ranging in time from Noah to the twentieth century. (Rev: BL 9/1/89; NYTBR 10/1/89; TLS 6/30/89. Awards: NYTBR, 1989)

7220 Barnes, Julian. *Staring at the Sun.* **1987, Knopf $15.95 (0-394-55821-9); Harper & Row paper $7.95 (0-06-097148-7).** A chronicle of the events of the century-long life of an English woman prone to wild flights of fantasy. (Rev: LJ 4/1/87; NYTBR 4/12/87; Time 7/27/87. Awards: NYTBR, 1987)

7221 Barnes, Julian. *Talking It Over.* **1991, Knopf $22.00 (0-679-40525-9).** Three English friends reflect on their experiences and interrelations in this novel by the author of *Flaubert's Parrot*. (Rev: BL 9/1/91; NYTBR 10/1/91; PW 8/2/91)

7222 Barnhardt, Wilton. *Emma, Who Saved My Life.* **1989, St. Martin's $19.95 (0-312-02911-X); paper $4.95 (0-312-92183-7).** An Illinois graduate moves to New York to share an apartment with an aspiring artist and poet in this novel set during the 1960s and 1970s. (Rev: BL 4/1/89; LJ 6/1/89; PW 4/7/89)

7223 Barrett, Andrea. *Lucid Stars.* **1988, Dell paper $7.95 (0-440-55000-9).** A chronicle of 20 years in the life of a New England woman and her immediate family tracing her courtship, marriage, and divorce. (Rev: BL 9/1/88; LJ 10/1/88; TLS 5/12/89)

7224 Barry, Lynda. *Good Times Are Killing Me.* **1988, Real Comet paper $16.95 (0-941104-22-2).** An illustrated 70-page novel told through the voice of a 12-year-old that chronicles the deterioration of her friendship with a girl of another race. (Rev: BL 10/1/88; New Yorker 3/6/89; PW 10/21/88)

7225 Barth, John. *Chimera.* **1985, Fawcett paper $4.95 (0-449-21113-4).** This experimental novel by the author of *The Sot-Weed Factor* is based on three mythological tales of Ancient Greece and Persia. (Rev: Choice 12/72; Natl Rev 10/13/72; Newsweek 1/1/73. Awards: NBA, 1973)

7226 Barth, John. *Giles Goat Boy: Or, the Revised New Syllabus.* **1987, Doubleday paper $9.95 (0-385-24086-4).** A young man who is raised on a goat farm enters a university divided into two rival colleges. (Rev: Choice 10/66; Newsweek 11/15/66; Time 8/5/66. Awards: ALA, 1966)

7227 Barth, John. *Last Voyage of Somebody the Sailor.* **1991, Little, Brown $22.95 (0-316-08251-1).** A Maryland man becomes trapped in the Baghdad of *One Thousand and One Nights* and is called upon to tell a story of life in America. (Rev: BL 11/1/90; LJ 12/90; PW 12/21/90)

7228 Barth, John. *Tidewater Tales.* 1987, Putnam $24.95 (0-399-13247-3); Fawcett paper $12.95 (0-449-90293-5). This sequel to *Sabbatical* concerns two weeks in the lives of a couple aboard a boat in Chesapeake Bay. "Probably the only piece of experimental fiction that can double as summer beach reading."—LJ (Rev: LJ 6/15/87; New Rep 8/10/87; NYTBR 6/28/87)

7229 Barthelme, Donald. *Paradise.* 1987, Penguin paper $6.95 (0-14-010358-9). Three young female models move in with a married architect following his relocation to New York. (Rev: BL 12/15/86; LJ 11/15/86; Newsweek 11/3/86)

7230 Barthelme, Frederick. *Natural Selection.* 1990, Viking $18.95 (0-670-83113-1); paper $8.95 (0-14-012889-1). A Houston suburban family is split up when the disaffected father decides to move to another house in this novel by the author of *Two Against One.* (Rev: BL 7/90; NYTBR 8/19/90)

7231 Barthelme, Frederick. *Second Marriage.* 1985, Penguin paper $6.95 (0-14-008274-3). A story set in the American South during the early 1980s about a man whose first and second wives come to live in the same house with him. (Rev: BL 12/1/84; LJ 9/15/84; PW 8/3/84)

7232 Barthelme, Frederick. *Tracer.* 1986, Penguin paper $4.95 (0-14-008969-1). The author of *Chroma* tells the story of a man who becomes romantically involved with his sister-in-law while going through divorce proceedings with his wife. (Rev: BL 8/85; NYTBR 9/28/86; TLS 3/21/86)

7233 Barthelme, Frederick. *Two Against One.* 1988, Grove-Weidenfeld $17.95 (1-55584-214-3); Macmillan paper $7.95 (0-02-030445-5). A wife leaves her middle-aged husband only to return to their home with her lover. (Rev: BL 9/15/88; NYTBR 11/13/89; TLS 9/15/89)

7234 Bassani, Giorgio. *The Heron.* 1986, Harcourt paper $5.95 (0-15-640085-5). Remembrances of a Jew who survived the Nazi occupation and its effects on his life and thought. (Rev: BL 5/15/70; LJ 3/15/70; NYTBR 4/12/70)

7235 Bates, H. E. *My Uncle Silas.* 1984, Graywolf paper $7.00 (0-915308-63-0). A collection of stories told to a nephew about his 90-year-old uncle comprise this novel originally published in 1939. (Rev: BL 11/1/84; PW 9/28/84; TLS 12/28/84)

7236 Battle, Lois. *Past Is Another Country.* 1990, Viking $19.95 (0-670-82576-X). A portrait of life within a failing western Australian convent by the author of *War Brides.* (Rev: BL 6/1/90; NYTBR 8/19/90)

7237 Battle, Lois. *Southern Women.* 1985, St. Martin's paper $3.95 (0-312-90328-6). This story of three generations of women in a Georgian family focuses on the exploits of a romance writer who moves to New York to make it in the literary world. (Rev: BL 3/15/84; LJ 5/1/84; PW 3/23/84)

7238 Bauer, Douglas. *Dexterity.* 1989, Simon & Schuster $18.95 (0-671-64997-3); Fawcett paper $4.95 (0-449-21864-3). This author's first novel concerns an upstate New York woman who leaves her

husband and the effects of her action on both their lives. (Rev: Atl 5/89; NYTBR 5/7/89; PW 2/10/89)

7239 Bausch, Richard. *Mr. Field's Daughter.* 1990, Macmillan paper $8.95 (0-02-028145-5). A Minnesota banker searches for his recently eloped daughter. "Reveals an author of rare and penetrating gifts working at the height of his powers."—NYTBR (Rev: BL 5/1/89; NYTBR 8/27/89; PW 3/17/89. Awards: ALA, 1989; PW, 1989)

7240 Bawden, Nina. *Family Money.* 1991, St. Martin's $17.95 (0-312-06351-2). A chronicle of the deterioration of an English widow's relationship with her family after she is involved in an assault that affects her memory and behavior. (Rev: BL 11/1/91; LJ 11/15/91)

7241 Baxter, Charles. *First Light.* 1987, Viking $17.95 (0-670-81701-5); Penguin paper $6.95 (0-14-010091-1). An examination of a strained family visit over the Fourth of July holiday told in reverse chronological order. (Rev: BL 9/1/87; Choice 12/87; Time 9/14/87)

7242 Beachy, Stephen. *Whistling Song.* 1991, Norton $19.95 (0-393-02964-6). A chronicle of the road travels across America of a teenager who escapes from an orphanage following the deaths of his parents. (Rev: LJ 7/91; NYTBR 9/8/91)

7243 Beattie, Ann. *Chilly Scenes of Winter.* 1991, Random paper $9.95 (0-679-73234-9). Beattie's debut novel is set in Washington, D.C., and concerns a young man's love for a married woman. "The funniest novel of unhappy yearning that one could imagine . . . a delight."—NYTBR (Rev: CSM 9/29/76; NYTBR 8/15/76; New Yorker 11/29/76)

7244 Beattie, Ann. *Falling in Place.* 1987, Warner paper $4.95 (0-446-31454-4). Beattie's second novel is set in New York during the late 1970s and concerns the affair between a 40-year-old married man and a woman in her mid-20s who tries to escape her circle of college friends. (Rev: BL 5/1/80; NYTBR 5/11/80; Time 5/12/80. Awards: NYTBR, 1980)

7245 Beattie, Ann. *Love Always.* 1986, Random paper $7.95 (0-394-74418-7). A Vermont advice columnist whose love life is in disarray receives a visit from her television actress niece. (Rev: BL 5/1/85; LJ 7/85; Time 7/1/85)

7246 Beattie, Ann. *Picturing Will.* 1989, Random $18.95 (0-394-56987-3). A Virginia photographer moves to New York to marry an artist who introduces her and her son to the underside of Manhattan life. "Beattie's best novel."—Newsweek (Rev: BL 12/1/89; Newsweek 1/22/90; PW 12/1/89)

7247 Beauman, Sally. *Dark Angel.* 1990, Bantam $19.95 (0-553-05762-6). This romantic novel by the author of the best-seller *Destiny* traces the fate of an English family from 1910 to the mid-1980s. (Rev: BL 6/1/90; LJ 9/1/90; PW 6/29/90)

7248 Beauman, Sally. *Destiny.* 1988, Bantam paper $4.95 (0-553-27018-4). This best-selling debut romance features the ups and downs of a love between a French jewelry magnate and a young Alabama woman. (Rev: BL 3/15/87; NYTBR 4/12/87)

7249 Becker, Jurek. *Bronstein's Children.* **1988, Harcourt $19.95 (0-15-114350-1).** A teenage German Jew catches his father and two friends beating a former Nazi guard at a cottage on the family property. (REV: BL 10/15/88; LJ 12/88; PW 9/16/88)

7250 Becker, Jurek. *Sleepless Days.* **1986, Harcourt paper $5.95 (0-15-682765-4).** An East German schoolteacher is kept under observation by his government for his professed stance against totalitarianism. (REV: BL 10/1/79; NYTBR 9/16/79; TLS 12/14/79)

7251 Beckett, Samuel. *Company.* **1980, Grove-Weidenfeld $8.95 (0-8021-5128-0).** A man lying on his back recalls moments from his past in this short novella by the French-Irish writer. (REV: LJ 11/15/80; NYTBR 11/2/80; TLS 6/27/80)

7252 Beckett, Samuel. *Lost Ones.* **1972, Grove-Weidenfeld $10.00 (0-394-48276-X); paper $8.95 (0-8021-3092-5).** In a universe contained in a small cylinder, its inhabitants are doomed to climbing ladders in search of an escape from the container. (REV: BL 1/15/73; LJ 1/1/73; TLS 8/11/72)

7253 Beckett, Samuel. *Mercier and Camier.* **1975, Grove-Weidenfeld $10.00 (0-8021-1196-3); paper $6.95 (0-8021-5136-1).** This novel, originally written in French in 1946, concerns the adventures of two men on an aimless quest and contains many elements similar to the author's classic play *Waiting for Godot.* (REV: BL 6/15/75; LJ 5/15/75; TLS 12/13/74)

7254 Beer, Ralph. *Blind Corral.* **1987, Penguin paper $6.95 (0-14-010265-5).** A young man discharged from military service following an injury returns to his Montana home to visit his father and grandfather. (REV: BL 5/1/86; LJ 6/15/86; New Yorker 7/7/86. AWARDS: LJ, 1986)

7255 Bell, Christine. *Perez Family.* **1990, Norton $19.95 (0-393-02798-8).** The adventures of a Cuban political prisoner striving to be reunited with his family in Miami. "A rollicking story full of surprises; quite out of the ordinary."—LJ (REV: BL 7/90; LJ 7/90; PW 6/29/90. AWARDS: ALA, 1990)

7256 Bell, Christine. *The Saint.* **1985, Pineapple Pr. $9.95 (0-910923-21-3); Pocket paper $6.95 (0-671-63847-5).** The story of a New Yorker's life living on a Latin American hacienda with her husband and his family. (REV: NYTBR 11/17/85; PW 9/27/85)

7257 Bell, Madison Smartt. *Doctor Sleep.* **1991, Harcourt $19.95 (0-15-126100-8).** An insomniac London hypnotist takes on a series of cases, including a young man who wants the doctor to cure him of heroin addiction. (REV: BL 11/15/90; LJ 11/1/90; NYTBR 1/6/91)

7258 Bell, Madison Smartt. *Soldier's Joy.* **1989, Ticknor & Fields $19.95 (0-89919-836-8); Penguin paper $8.95 (0-14-013359-3).** Two Vietnam veterans readjust to civilian life in Tennessee. "A poetic and haunting novel—written with great clarity, purpose and love."—BL (REV: BL 5/15/89; LJ 5/15/89; PW 4/21/89)

7259 Bell, Madison Smartt. *Straight Cut.* **1987, Penguin paper $3.95 (0-14-010471-2).** A film editor and his wife are embroiled in an international drug deal in this third novel by the author of *Waiting for the End of the World.* (REV: NYTBR 10/12/86; PW 7/4/86)

7260 Bell, Madison Smartt. *Waiting for the End of the World.* **1986, Penguin paper $6.95 (0-14-009330-3).** A former artist organizes a terrorist group whose aim is to detonate an atomic weapon in Times Square. (REV: BL 8/85; New Yorker 11/11/85; PW 6/28/85)

7261 Bell, Madison Smartt. *Year of Silence.* **1989, Penguin paper $6.95 (0-14-011533-1).** An examination of the effects of a woman's suicide upon her friends, family, and acquaintances. (REV: Choice 4/88; LJ 12/87; NYTBR 11/15/87)

7262 Bellow, Saul. *Bellarosa Connection.* **1989, Penguin paper $6.95 (0-14-012686-4).** A retired widower tells the story of how his father's nephew came to the United States fleeing European fascism during the 1930s. (REV: LJ 10/1/89; Time 10/2/89; TLS 10/27/89)

7263 Bellow, Saul. *The Dean's December.* **1985, Penguin paper $4.50 (0-14-007269-1).** A Chicago university professor pays a visit to his dying mother in Rumania and reflects upon his life and career in the United States. (REV: BL 12/1/81; NYTBR 1/10/82; Time 1/18/82)

7264 Bellow, Saul. *Herzog.* **1984, Penguin paper $6.95 (0-14-007270-5).** A middle-aged Jewish college professor and writer reflects on his life in this work by the author of *Dangling Man.* (REV: LJ 9/1/64; New Rep 9/19/64; Newsweek 9/21/64. AWARDS: NBA, 1965)

7265 Bellow, Saul. *Humboldt's Gift.* **1984, Penguin paper $8.95 (0-14-007271-3).** A playwright and historian muses on the death of a poet friend in this novel based in part on the life of Delmore Schwartz. (REV: Choice 11/75; NYTBR 9/18/75; Time 8/25/75. AWARDS: ALA, 1975; NYTBR, 1975; PP:Fiction, 1976; Time, 1975; Time, the 1970s)

7266 Bellow, Saul. *More Die of Heartbreak.* **1987, Morrow $17.95 (0-688-06935-5); Dell paper $4.95 (0-440-20110-1).** A character study examining the relationship between a Russian literature professor and his botanist uncle. (REV: NYTBR 5/24/87; PW 5/8/87; Time 6/15/87. AWARDS: NYTBR, 1987; PW, 1987; Time, 1987)

7267 Bellow, Saul. *Mr. Sammler's Planet.* **1984, Penguin paper $8.95 (0-14-007317-5).** An account of the life of a Holocaust survivor living in New York City. (REV: BL 4/1/70; New Rep 2/7/70; Time 2/9/70. AWARDS: ALA, 1970; NBA, 1971; Time, 1970)

7268 Bellow, Saul. *A Theft.* **1989, Penguin paper $6.95 (0-14-011969-8).** A novella concerning the theft of an emerald ring from an Indiana woman who relocated to New York. (REV: New Yorker 5/1/89; Newsweek 3/20/89; Time 3/6/89)

7269 Benedict, Elizabeth. *Beginner's Book of Dreams.* 1988, Knopf $18.95 (0-394-55157-5); Bantam paper $8.95 (0-553-34703-9). The coming of age of a New York girl with an alcoholic mother and an absent father during the late 1960s. (REV: BL 4/1/88; LJ 5/1/88; PW 2/12/88)

7270 Benedict, Elizabeth. *Slow Dancing.* 1990, Bantam paper $7.95 (0-553-34811-6). This debut novel chronicles a decade of friendship between two college friends. (REV: BL 2/15/85; LJ 3/15/85; NYTBR 3/3/85)

7271 Benedict, Helen. *A World Like This.* 1990, Dutton $17.95 (0-525-24831-5). A study of the relationship between a young woman recently paroled from a juvenile detention facility and the older sister she moves in with. (REV: BL 1/1/90; LJ 12/89; NYTBR 4/8/90)

7272 Benet, Juan. *Return to Region.* 1985, Columbia Univ. Pr. $24.00 (0-231-05456-4). A story by a Spanish writer, and translated by Gregory Rabassa, describing a region in the Pyrenees from which travelers never return. "Brilliant . . . a lovely, sad book."—NYTBR (REV: Choice 11/85; NYTBR 9/15/85)

7273 Berger, John. *G.* 1980, Pantheon paper $10.95 (0-394-73967-1). This story of the amorous escapades of a half-Italian lover in Europe was awarded the Booker Prize. (REV: BL 11/1/72; NYTBR 9/10/72; Newsweek 9/11/72)

7274 Berger, Thomas. *Being Invisible.* 1987, Little, Brown $16.95 (0-316-09158-8); Penguin paper $6.95 (0-14-010871-8). A writer gains the power to become invisible in this novel by the author of *Little Big Man.* (REV: BL 3/15/87; NYTBR 4/12/87; TLS 7/22/88)

7275 Berger, Thomas. *Changing the Past.* 1989, Little, Brown $18.95 (0-316-09149-9). An editor receives the ability to change his past, and following a series of experiments with alternate careers, returns to his present-day life. (REV: LJ 8/89; Time 9/11/89; TLS 4/27/90)

7276 Berger, Thomas. *The Feud.* 1983, Delacorte $14.95 (0-385-29221-X). The story of an escalating feud between two small-town American families. (REV: BL 2/1/83; New Rep 5/23/83; PW 3/18/83)

7277 Berger, Thomas. *Houseguest.* 1988, Little, Brown $16.95 (0-316-09163-4); Penguin paper $7.95 (0-14-012004-1). The story of a family and their increasingly threatening house guest. (REV: BL 3/15/88; LJ 3/1/88; Time 4/11/88)

7278 Berger, Thomas. *Neighbors.* 1980, Delacorte paper $9.95 (0-385-28745-3). The story of two wild neighbors who move into middle-class suburbia. (REV: LJ 3/15/80; NYTBR 4/6/80; Time 4/7/80. AWARDS: Time, 1980)

7279 Berger, Thomas. *Reinhart's Women.* 1989, Little, Brown $8.95 (0-316-11601-7). This fourth volume in the Carlo Reinhart series traces the impact of women on Reinhart's life. (REV: BL 7/1/81; LJ 9/1/81; Time 10/21/81)

7280 Berger, Thomas. *Vital Parts.* 1990, Little, Brown paper $9.95 (0-316-09225-8). The third novel in the author's Reinhart series portrays the character as a middle-aged man obsessed with cryonics. (REV: BL 9/1/70; Choice 9/70; Newsweek 4/20/70)

7281 Bergland, Martha. *A Farm Under a Lake.* 1989, Graywolf $17.95 (1-55597-119-9). A husband and wife who were born and raised on neighboring midwestern farms search for an existence comparable to the life they had as youths. (REV: BL 6/15/89; NYTBR 7/9/89; PW 4/28/89)

7282 Bergman, Deborah. *River of Glass.* 1990, Putnam $19.95 (0-399-13533-2). This tragic life story of a French girl was originally written in French in 1937. (REV: BL 4/15/90; LJ 3/15/90; PW 2/2/90)

7283 Bernays, Anne. *Growing Up Rich.* 1986, Macmillan paper $6.95 (0-684-18648-9). A portrait of the lives of two teenagers who become the wards of a Boston professor following the deaths of their parents in an airplane crash. "Endlessly fascinating."—NYTBR (REV: BL 12/1/75; CSM 9/17/75; NYTBR 10/5/75)

7284 Bernays, Anne. *Professor Romeo.* 1989, Grove-Weidenfeld $18.95 (1-55584-218-6). A Harvard psychology professor's love life with his students creates a scandal in this novel by the author of *Growing Up Rich.* "Vivid . . . a work of sharp irony."—NYTBR (REV: NYTBR 7/23/89; PW 5/12/89)

7285 Bernhard, Thomas. *Concrete.* 1986, Univ. of Chicago Pr. paper $10.95 (0-226-04398-3). A narrator tells the story of his efforts to produce a monumental work of research into the life of the composer Mendelssohn. (REV: BL 5/15/84; New Yorker 2/4/85; TLS 9/28/84)

7286 Bernhard, Thomas. *The Loser.* 1991, Knopf $19.00 (0-394-57239-4). The musings by the late Austrian writer concerning his fictitious relationship with Canadian pianist Glenn Gould. (REV: BL 9/1/91; LJ 8/91; PW 7/5/91)

7287 Bernhard, Thomas. *Wittgenstein's Nephew: A Friendship.* 1989, Knopf $17.95 (0-394-56376-X); Univ. of Chicago Pr. paper $8.95 (0-226-04392-4). The study of the relationship between a writer and a nephew of the Austrian philosopher in a mental ward of a hospital. (REV: BL 12/1/88; LJ 4/1/89; TLS 8/28/87)

7288 Bernhard, Thomas. *Woodcutters.* 1988, Knopf $15.95 (0-394-55152-X); Univ. of Chicago Pr. paper $10.95 (0-226-04396-7). The Austrian novelist's story of a man who, during a Vienna dinner party thrown in honor of an actor, recounts the events of his last two decades. (REV: LJ 2/1/88; NYTBR 2/14/88; PW 12/18/87)

7289 Bernlef, J. *Out of Mind.* 1989, Godine $16.95 (0-87923-734-1). A Dutch writer's story of a man afflicted with Alzheimer's disease telling the tale of his life and his mental decline. (REV: NYTBR 9/17/89; PW 6/2/89)

7290 Berry, Wendell. *Memory of Old Jack.* **1975, Harcourt paper $6.95 (0-15-658670-3).** Remembrances and reflections of a Kentucky man in his 90s. (REV: LJ 1/15/74; NYTBR 3/31/74; PW 12/31/73. AWARDS: ALA, 1974)

7291 Berry, Wendell. *Remembering.* **1988, North Point $14.95 (0-86547-330-7); paper $7.95 (0-86547-331-5).** A journalist reflects upon his life in the small Kentucky town where he grew up. (REV: BL 11/15/88; PW 9/16/88)

7292 Billington, Rachel. *Loving Attitudes.* **1988, Morrow $15.95 (0-688-07574-6).** A London married couple receive an unexpected visit from the woman's illegitimate daughter after a 20-year separation. (REV: BL 7/88; NYTBR 8/7/88)

7293 Binchy, Maeve. *Circle of Friends.* **1991, Delacorte $19.95 (0-385-30149-9).** An examination of the friendships between three college-age young women in Dublin. (REV: BL 11/1/90; LJ 12/90; NYTBR 12/30/90)

7294 Binchy, Maeve. *Echoes.* **1989, Dell paper $4.95 (0-440-12209-0).** A story of life in an Irish coastal tourist community set during the 1950s and 1960s by the author of *Firefly Summer.* "A topnotch tearjerker."—BL (REV: BL 11/1/85; LJ 12/85; PW 11/1/85)

7295 Binchy, Maeve. *Firefly Summer.* **1988, Delacorte $19.95 (0-440-50017-6); Dell paper $4.95 (0-440-20149-4).** An Irish-American returns to the country of his ancestry to construct a large hotel in rural Ireland in this novel by the author of *Light a Penny Candle.* (REV: BL 9/1/88; NYTBR 9/18/88; PW 7/15/88)

7296 Binchy, Maeve. *Light a Penny Candle.* **1989, Dell paper $5.95 (0-440-14795-6).** An English woman develops a friendship with an Irish family in this debut novel by Binchy. (REV: BL 2/15/83; LJ 2/15/83; PW 1/28/83)

7297 Binchy, Maeve. *Silver Wedding.* **1989, Delacorte $17.95 (0-385-29826-9).** A chronicle of the events and profiles of the personalities involved in a twenty-fifth wedding anniversary celebration of an Anglo-Irish London couple. (REV: BL 9/15/89; NYTBR 9/10/89; PW 7/28/89)

7298 Bird, Sarah. *Boyfriend School.* **1989, Doubleday $16.95 (0-385-24694-3); Pocket paper $3.95 (0-671-68454-X).** A journalist covering a convention of romance writers makes new friends who are determined to find her a suitable mate. (REV: BL 3/1/89; LJ 3/15/89)

7299 Birmingham, Stephen. *Auerbach Will.* **1985, Berkley paper $4.50 (0-425-10020-0).** The aging matron of a wealthy Jewish merchandising family recounts her life and examines the possible future of the family fortune in this novel by the author of *Our Crowd.* (REV: BL 8/83; LJ 8/83; PW 6/24/83)

7300 Bitov, Andrei. *Pushkin House.* **1987, Farrar $22.50 (0-374-23934-7); McKay paper $13.95 (0-679-73009-5).** The fictional biography of a Russian man killed in a duel at the age of 30. "This dazzling book expands our view of the possibilities of the contem-porary novel."—LJ (REV: Choice 3/88; LJ 11/1/87; TLS 7/22/88)

7301 Blackwood, Caroline. *Corrigan.* **1986, Penguin paper $6.95 (0-14-007732-4).** A woman's involvement with a handicapped man leads to strained relations with her daughter. (REV: LJ 5/1/85; NYTBR 7/14/85; TLS 10/19/84)

7302 Blair, Sydney. *Buffalo.* **1991, Viking $18.95 (0-670-83554-4).** This debut novel chronicles the adjustment of a Virginia Vietnam veteran to rural life after his return from the war. (REV: LJ 2/1/91; PW 1/11/91)

7303 Blakeslee, Mermer. *Same Blood.* **1989, Houghton $16.95 (0-395-48601-7); Ivy paper $3.95 (0-8041-0573-1).** A woman tries to come to grips with the death of her three-year-old son in this novel set in the Catskills. (REV: BL 12/15/88; NYTBR 6/4/89; PW 11/14/88)

7304 Bloom, Harry. *Transvaal Episode.* **1981, Second Chance $16.95 (0-933256-24-8); paper $8.95 (0-933256-25-6).** This novel, originally published in 1956 in South Africa, chronicles the escalation of a shooting incident into a race riot. (REV: BL 1/1/82; Choice 3/83; PW 1/14/83)

7305 Boissard, Janine. *Christmas Lessons.* **1984, Little, Brown $15.95 (0-316-10097-8).** A French family gathering at Christmas provides four sisters the opportunity to discuss their adult lives and problems. (REV: BL 9/15/84; LJ 9/15/84; PW 7/27/84)

7306 Böll, Heinrich. *And Never Said a Word.* **1979, McGraw-Hill paper $5.95 (0-07-006421-0).** A portrait of a strained marriage set in the aftermath of World War II in Germany. (REV: LJ 5/1/78; New Yorker 8/7/78; PW 4/3/78)

7307 Böll, Heinrich. *The Clown.* **Peter Smith $16.25 (0-8446-6202-X); McGraw-Hill paper $6.95 (0-07-006430-X).** An examination of a single night's events in the life of a 27-year-old clown. (REV: BL 3/1/65; CSM 2/11/65; NYTBR 1/24/65. AWARDS: ALA, 1965)

7308 Böll, Heinrich. *Group Portrait with Lady.* **1976, Avon paper $4.95 (0-380-00020-2).** A portrait of a German woman's life as told through the voices of her friends, family, and acquaintances. (REV: BL 7/1/73; NYTBR 5/6/73; PW 3/19/73. AWARDS: ALA, 1973)

7309 Böll, Heinrich. *Lost Honor of Katharina Blum: Or, How Violence Develops and Where It Can Lead.* **1976, McGraw-Hill paper $6.95 (0-07-006429-6).** A German maid brings her wanted criminal lover to a family's home in this novel by the author of *Group Portrait with Lady.* (REV: Choice 10/75; LJ 4/15/75; New Rep 4/26/75)

7310 Böll, Heinrich. *Women in a River Landscape: A Novel in Dialogues and Soliloquies.* **1988, Knopf $18.95 (0-394-56375-1).** An analysis of contemporary Germany and the German people as told through the conversations of its citizens in this novel by the Nobel laureate. (REV: BL 6/15/88; LJ 7/88; NYTBR 7/24/88)

7311 Bosse, Malcolm. *Fire in Heaven.* **1987, Bantam paper $4.95 (0-553-26203-3).** This sequel to *The Warlord* depicts the lives of an American man and his Russian wife during the turmoil of the aftermath of World War II in China and Southeast Asia. (Rev: BL 1/15/86; PW 1/3/86)

7312 Boswell, Robert. *Crooked Hearts.* **1987, Knopf $17.95 (0-394-55706-9); Dell paper $9.95 (0-440-50260-8).** The story of a Yuma, Arizona, family of six by the author of the short-story collection *Dancing in the Movies.* "An insightful, nicely turned, amazingly agile piece of work."—NYTBR (Rev: BL 5/15/87; NYTBR 7/5/87; New Yorker 8/17/87)

7313 Boswell, Robert. *Geography of Desire.* **1989, Knopf $18.95 (0-394-57690-X).** A fictional chronicle of the life and loves of an American expatriate running a Central American hotel. (Rev: BL 9/1/89; LJ 8/89)

7314 Bourjaily, Vince. *Old Soldier.* **1990, Donald I. Fine $18.95 (1-55611-198-3).** A former army sergeant on a fishing trip in Maine learns that his brother has contracted the AIDS virus. "A moving and exceptionally well-written novel."—NYTBR (Rev: BL 9/1/90; NYTBR 10/28/90)

7315 Bowen, Elizabeth. *Eva Trout: Or, Changing Scenes.* **1987, Penguin paper $6.95 (0-14-008542-4).** A chronicle of eight years of a British woman's life in France, Great Britain, and the United States. (Rev: CSM 10/24/68; PW 9/2/68; Time 11/1/68. Awards: ALA, 1968)

7316 Bowen, John. *The Girls: A Story of Village Life.* **1987, Atlantic Monthly $16.95 (0-87113-137-4); NAL paper $7.95 (0-452-26077-9).** A story of the friendship of two young women in an English village, one of whom bears a child out of wedlock. (Rev: NYTBR 4/26/87; PW 2/27/87)

7317 Bowering, Marilyn. *To All Appearances a Lady.* **1990, Viking $18.95 (0-670-83340-1).** A Canadian poet's story of a man who becomes filled with the spirit of his mother following her funeral, tracing her life back to her birth in Hong Kong. (Rev: BL 4/15/90; LJ 5/1/90; PW 4/13/90)

7318 Boyd, Blanche McCrary. *Revolution of Little Girls.* **1991, Knopf $19.00 (0-679-40090-7).** A coming-of-age story set in South Carolina during the 1950s and 1960s focusing on a young girl's experimentation with drugs, alcohol, and sex. (Rev: BL 4/15/91; PW 3/15/91)

7319 Boyd, William. *A Good Man in Africa.* **1983, Penguin paper $7.95 (0-14-005887-7).** The chronicle of a British diplomat's experiences in Nigeria, written by an author of English descent who was born and raised in Africa. (Rev: LJ 5/1/82; PW 2/26/82; TLS 1/30/81)

7320 Boyd, William. *New Confessions.* **1988, Morrow $19.95 (0-688-07761-7); Penguin paper $8.95 (0-14-010699-5).** A fictional account of the life of a Scottish film director working on a motion picture epic based on *The Confessions of Jean-Jacques Rousseau.* (Rev: LJ 6/1/88; Time 5/30/88; TLS 9/25/87)

7321 Boyd, William. *Stars and Bars.* **1986, Penguin paper $6.95 (0-14-008889-X).** A British art expert tries to immerse himself in American society while on a business assignment in New York. (Rev: BL 5/1/85; LJ 4/15/85; New Rep 7/8/85)

7322 Boylan, Clare. *Black Baby.* **1989, Doubleday $18.95 (0-385-26101-2).** A portrait of the friendship between an aging Dublin spinster and a young black woman. (Rev: BL 11/15/89; LJ 11/1/89; PW 9/22/89)

7323 Boyle, T. Coraghessan. *Budding Prospects.* **1985, Penguin paper $6.95 (0-14-008151-8).** Boyle's second novel concerns a group of California businessmen growing marijuana during the early 1980s. (Rev: BL 4/15/84; LJ 4/15/84; NYTBR 7/1/84)

7324 Boyle, T. Coraghessan. *East Is East.* **1990, Viking $19.95 (0-670-83220-0); Penguin paper $8.95 (0-14-013167-1).** A Japanese sailor jumps ship off the coast of the southeastern United States and attempts to evade the pursuit of American officials. "This irresistible novel is T. Coraghessan Boyle's best yet."—Gail Godwin, NYTBR (Rev: BL 6/1/90; NYTBR 9/9/90; PW 3/30/90. Awards: ALA, 1990; PW, 1990)

7325 Bradbury, Malcolm. *Cuts.* **1988, Penguin paper $5.95 (0-14-010846-7).** A novella set during the 1980s focusing on the exploits of a writer working for a struggling British television company. (Rev: New Rep 12/14/87; PW 9/11/87; TLS 6/12/87)

7326 Bradfield, Scott. *History of Luminous Motion.* **1989, Knopf $17.95 (0-394-57875-9); Random paper $8.95 (0-679-72943-7).** The story of an eight-year-old psychopath and his cross-country travels with his mother. "A penetrating, frightening symbolic look at the state of childhood in America."—NYTBR (Rev: BL 7/89; NYTBR 9/24/89; TLS 12/8/89)

7327 Bradford, Barbara Taylor. *Hold the Dream.* **1985, Doubleday $17.95 (0-385-18128-0).** The sequel to the author's *A Woman of Substance* regarding the transfer of the Harte empire from Emma to her grandchildren. (Rev: BL 4/15/85; LJ 7/85; PW 3/29/85)

7328 Bradford, Barbara Taylor. *To Be the Best.* **1988, Doubleday $19.95 (0-385-24579-3); Bantam paper $5.95 (0-553-27953-X).** This third and final volume of a trilogy that began with *A Woman of Substance* and *Hold the Dream* traces the lives of the descendants of merchandising magnate Emma Harte. (Rev: BL 5/15/88; NYTBR 7/31/88)

7329 Bradford, Barbara Taylor. *A Woman of Substance.* **1984, Doubleday $19.95 (0-385-12050-8); Bantam paper $5.95 (0-553-27790-1).** A millionaire in her 70s seeks revenge after learning of a plot by her children to usurp her financial dynasty. (Rev: BL 7/15/79; LJ 7/79; PW 4/2/79)

7330 Bradford, Richard. *Red Sky at Morning.* **1986, Harper & Row paper $8.95 (0-06-091361-4).** The story of a youth's coming of age in New Mexico after his father's departure to serve in World War II. (Rev: BL 9/1/68; LJ 4/15/68; PW 3/11/68)

7331 Bradley, David. *Chaneysville Incident.* **1990, Harper & Row paper $9.95 (0-06-091681-8).** An African-American historian's search for the truth about the lives and deaths of his father and grandfather. (REV: CSM 5/20/81; LJ 5/15/81; NYTBR 4/19/81. AWARDS: NYTBR, 1981)

7332 Bradley, David. *South Street.* **1988, Peter Smith $16.25 (0-8446-6323-9); Macmillan paper $6.95 (0-684-18674-8).** A portrayal of life in a South Philadelphia ghetto. "An impressive first novel pulsing with vitality."—BL (REV: BL 12/15/75; Choice 12/75; LJ 10/15/75)

7333 Bradley, John Ed. *Tupelo Nights.* **1988, Atlantic Monthly $17.95 (0-87113-175-7); Penguin paper $6.95 (0-14-011899-3).** A college football star returns to his Southern hometown in an attempt to reestablish ties with friends and family. (REV: BL 3/1/88; PW 2/19/88; TLS 11/25/88)

7334 Bram, Christopher. *In Memory of Angel Clare.* **1989, Donald I. Fine $17.95 (1-55611-138-X); NAL paper $9.95 (0-452-26434-0).** A group of gay friends debate the best way to console and comfort a young man following the death of his older lover. (REV: BL 6/15/89; PW 5/19/89)

7335 Bram, Christopher. *Surprising Myself.* **1988, Henry Holt paper $8.95 (0-8050-0669-9).** A gay man compares his personal relationship with another man with his sister's marriage. (REV: BL 5/1/87; LJ 4/1/87; PW 4/17/87)

7336 Brandon, Jay. *Fade the Heat.* **1990, Pocket $18.95 (0-671-70260-2).** An attorney tells the story of the political intrigue surrounding the court case of the son of a Texas district attorney who was accused of rape. (REV: BL 5/1/90; LJ 5/15/90; PW 6/8/90)

7337 Braudy, Susan. *What the Movies Made Me Do.* **1985, Knopf $15.95 (0-394-53246-5); McGraw-Hill paper $4.95 (0-317-56919-8).** An examination of the personal and social life of a New York film executive working on a film about the life of Christ. "Virtually impossible to put down."—PW (REV: BL 9/15/85; LJ 9/1/85; PW 7/19/85)

7338 Braverman, Kate. *Lithium for Medea.* **1989, Penguin paper $7.95 (0-14-012641-4).** This debut novel traces the life of a drug addict in Los Angeles among a family of manic-depressives with a father hospitalized for terminal cancer. (REV: LJ 3/1/79; NYTBR 8/5/79; PW 2/12/79)

7339 Braverman, Kate. *Palm Latitudes.* **1988, Simon & Schuster $18.95 (0-671-64547-0); Penguin paper $8.95 (0-14-012640-6).** A story detailing the lives of three Mexican-American women set in the barrio of East Los Angeles. (REV: LJ 6/1/88; PW 4/29/88)

7340 Breytenbach, Breyten. *Memory of Snow and of Dust.* **1989, Farrar $22.95 (0-374-20766-6).** A pair of expatriate Africans living in Paris are separated following the return of one to his South African homeland, where he is imprisoned for political activities. (REV: BL 7/89; NYTBR 10/22/89)

7341 Brink, Andre. *A Dry White Season.* **1984, Penguin paper $8.95 (0-14-006890-2).** A schoolteacher investigates the circumstances surrounding the death of a black South African teenager. (REV: CSM 3/10/80; LJ 2/15/80; NYTBR 3/23/80)

7342 Brink, Andre. *Rumors of Rain.* **1984, Penguin paper $6.95 (0-14-006891-0).** An internal portrait of an Afrikaner tycoon trying to maintain his fortune and beliefs in a crumbling South Africa. (REV: LJ 1/1/79; New Rep 10/21/78; Newsweek 10/9/78)

7343 Briskin, Jacqueline. *Dreams Are Not Enough.* **1987, Berkley paper $4.50 (0-425-10179-7).** A story tracing three decades in the life of a film star. "Near impossible to stop reading . . . the story is relentless."—LJ (REV: BL 12/1/86; LJ 2/1/87)

7344 Briskin, Jacqueline. *Too Much Too Soon.* **1985, Putnam $17.95 (0-399-13071-3).** A portrait of three English sisters taken under the wing of their rich California uncle. (REV: BL 5/1/85; LJ 7/85; PW 6/21/85)

7345 Brodkey, Harold. *Runaway Soul.* **1991, Farrar $30.00 (0-374-25286-6).** This 800-page novel by the author of *Stories in an Almost Classical Mode* traces the life of an adopted young man growing up in a St. Louis home. (REV: BL 9/15/91; LJ 11/1/91. AWARDS: PW, 1991)

7346 Brodsky, Michael. *Dyad.* **1989, Four Walls Eight Windows $23.95 (0-941423-30-1); paper $11.95 (0-941423-31-X).** A story of the relationship between a dying father and his bohemian son. (REV: Choice 7–8/90; LJ 11/15/89; NYTBR 12/24/89)

7347 Brodsky, Michael. *Xman.* **1987, Four Walls Eight Windows $21.95 (0-941423-01-8); paper $11.95 (0-941423-02-6).** An experimental novel portraying the bleak daily life of an Everyman, set in New York. (REV: LJ 9/15/87; NYTBR 11/15/87; PW 9/11/87)

7348 Brookfield, Amanda. *A Cast of Smiles.* **1991, St. Martin's $15.95 (0-312-05399-1).** A fictional examination of the lives of a group of socially active contemporary Londoners. "An insightful, engaging second novel. . . highly recommended."—LJ (REV: BL 2/15/91; LJ 2/15/91)

7349 Brookner, Anita. *Brief Lives.* **1991, Random $20.00 (0-394-58548-8).** The memoirs of an English woman concerning her marriage and adultery with a married man. (REV: BL 1/15/91; LJ 3/15/91; NYTBR 7/21/91)

7350 Brookner, Anita. *Debut.* **1990, Random paper $8.95 (0-679-72712-4).** The author's debut novel concerns a middle-aged English professor reflecting upon her life's experiences with love and men. "A precise and haunting little performance."—NYTBR (REV: LJ 3/1/81; NYTBR 3/29/81; PW 1/30/81)

7351 Brookner, Anita. *Family and Friends.* **1986, Pocket paper $6.95 (0-671-62575-6).** A Jewish European family flees fascism during the 1930s to establish themselves in London. (REV: BL 7/85; LJ 10/1/85; NYRB 12/5/85)

7352 Brookner, Anita. *A Friend from England.* 1988, Pantheon $15.95 (0-394-56387-5); Harper & Row paper $6.95 (0-06-097202-5). A story tracing the development of friendship between a London bookstore owner and her friends' daughter. (REV: BL 1/15/88; LJ 3/1/88; TLS 8/21/87)

7353 Brookner, Anita. *Hotel du Lac.* 1986, Dutton paper $7.95 (0-525-48497-3). This tale of a British woman in hiding at a Swiss hotel following a personal scandal won the 1984 Booker Prize for best English novel. "An immensely satisfying novel by a civilized writer."—PW (REV: BL 1/15/85; LJ 2/15/85; PW 1/4/85. AWARDS: PW, 1985)

7354 Brookner, Anita. *Latecomers.* 1989, Pantheon $16.95 (0-394-57172-X); paper $8.95 (0-679-72668-3). An examination of the lifelong friendship of two European refugees who fled to England to escape persecution. "At the peak of her form . . . a quiet little masterpiece."—PW (REV: CSM 5/10/89; NYTBR 4/2/89; PW 2/24/89)

7355 Brookner, Anita. *Look at Me.* 1983, Pantheon $11.95 (0-394-52944-8); Dutton paper $7.95 (0-525-48156-7). A socially reclusive London librarian befriends a couple but returns to her former life-style following a failed romance. "A stunning character study."—LJ (REV: CSM 10/19/83; LJ 4/1/83; NYTBR 5/22/83)

7356 Brookner, Anita. *Misalliance.* 1987, Pantheon $14.95 (0-394-55340-3); Harper & Row paper $6.95 (0-06-097134-7). The chronicle of a woman's recovery after her husband leaves her for a younger woman. (REV: CSM 6/18/87; LJ 5/1/87; NYTBR 3/29/87)

7357 Broughton, T. Alan. *Winter's Journey.* 1981, Fawcett paper $2.95 (0-449-24369-9). An American mother and her son discover new lives and new loves in Rome in this novel set during the 1950s. (REV: Atl 2/80; NYTBR 1/20/80; New Yorker 2/25/80)

7358 Brown, James. *Final Performance.* 1988, Morrow $18.95 (0-688-06842-1). A story tracing the lives of two California brothers, one engaged in a motion picture career, the other a petty criminal. (REV: BL 2/1/88; LJ 2/1/88; PW 12/11/87)

7359 Brown, Larry. *Joe.* 1991, Algonquin $19.95 (0-945575-61-0). This story of the lives of poor Mississippi laborers focuses on a man who works for a lumber company that employs a destitute young man. "With this powerful, immensely affecting novel Brown comes into his own as a writer of stature."—PW (REV: BL 8/91; LJ 8/91; PW 7/19/91. AWARDS: ALA, 1992; BL, 1991; PW, 1991)

7360 Brown, Rita Mae. *Bingo.* 1989, Bantam paper $4.95 (0-553-28220-4). A pair of elderly sisters compete for the affections of a recently arrived gentleman in this novel with characters first introduced in the author's *Six of One.* (REV: BL 8/88; LJ 10/15/88; PW 9/9/88)

7361 Brown, Rita Mae. *Six of One.* 1983, Bantam paper $4.95 (0-553-27887-8). A study of the lifelong rivalry between two Pennsylvania sisters from childhood to adulthood. (REV: BL 7/15/78; CSM 11/22/78; LJ 9/1/78)

7362 Brown, Rosellen. *Autobiography of My Mother.* 1981, Ballantine paper $2.95 (0-345-28738-X). A study of the relationship between a mother and daughter with radically different philosophies and values. (REV: Atl, 7/76; NYTBR 6/20/76; Newsweek 6/14/76. AWARDS: ALA, 1976)

7363 Brown, Rosellen. *Civil Wars.* 1984, Knopf $16.95 (0-394-53478-6); Penguin paper $6.95 (0-14-007783-9). The story of two white former civil rights workers whose Mississippi neighborhood has become predominantly African American over the years. (REV: BL 3/1/84; CSM 8/15/85; LJ 4/15/84. AWARDS: ALA, 1984)

7364 Browne, Gerald A. *Hot Siberian.* 1989, Morrow $19.95 (0-87795-965-X); Avon paper $4.95 (0-380-70332-7). This story about the precious-gem trade concerns the illegal smuggling of diamonds from the Soviet Union to England. (REV: BL 11/15/88; NYTBR 2/12/89; PW 12/2/88)

7365 Browne, Gerald A. *19 Purchase Street.* 1986, Berkley paper $4.95 (0-425-09138-4). A group composed of American intelligentsia wrestles control of organized crime from the mob and runs it in its own style. (REV: LJ 10/1/82; PW 7/16/82)

7366 Brownmiller, Susan. *Waverly Place.* 1989, Grove-Weidenfeld $18.95 (0-8021-1090-8); NAL paper $4.95 (0451-16324-9). A fictional account of the 1987 New York child abuse murder case of Lisa Steinberg as related by friends and acquaintances of the family. (REV: BL 12/1/88; LJ 2/15/89)

7367 Bryers, Paul. *Coming First.* 1988, Atlantic Monthly paper $7.95 (0-87113-224-9). A fictional analysis of contemporary sex roles and sexuality as viewed through the life of a British television director. (REV: BL 5/1/88; PW 3/18/88; TLS 7/17/87)

7368 Buchanan, Cynthia. *Maiden.* 1987, Dell paper $4.95 (0-440-35174-X). The story of the life and adventures of a 30-year-old virgin who moves into a swinging singles apartment in Los Angeles. "A brilliant, hysterically funny book."—LJ (REV: BL 3/1/72; LJ 11/1/71; Time 2/7/72)

7369 Buckley, Christopher. *Wet Work.* 1991, Knopf $19.95 (0-394-57193-2). A tale of a grandfather's rage and search for revenge following his grandson's death from a drug overdose written by the author of *The White House Mess.* (REV: BL 1/15/91; LJ 2/15/91; NYTBR 2/27/91)

7370 Buckley, Christopher. *The White House Mess.* 1986, Knopf $16.95 (0-394-54940-6); Penguin paper $4.50 (0-14-009793-7). The fictional memoirs of a member of a Democratic administration following the Reagan presidency as written by a former speechwriter for George Bush. (REV: CSM 4/7/86; Natl Rev 5/9/86; NYTBR 3/16/86)

7371 Buechner, Frederick. *Final Beast.* 1982, Harper & Row $13.45 (0-06-061159-6). A portrait of the life and teachings of a Pentecostal reverend leading his congregation. "A well written, fast moving, deeply probing novel."—Choice (Rev: BL 2/15/65; Choice 7–8/65; LJ 12/15/64. Awards: ALA, 1965)

7372 **Buechner, Frederick.** *Love Feast.* **1984, Harper & Row paper $3.95 (0-06-061167-7).** A New Jersey evangelical preacher throws a Thanksgiving party for his congregation at his home. (Rev: BL 11/1/74; Choice 2/75; PW 7/15/74)

7373 **Buechner, Frederick.** *Open Heart.* **1984, Harper & Row paper $3.95 (0-06-061166-9).** This sequel to *Lion Country* portrays a Texas Christian preacher challenging death and waiting for the arrival of a Messiah. (Rev: BL 7/15/72; Choice 12/72; Natl Rev 6/23/72)

7374 **Buechner, Frederick.** *Treasure Hunt.* **1984, Harper & Row paper $3.95 (0-06-061168-5).** This sequel to *Lion Country, Open Heart,* and *Love Feast* tracks the legacy of minister Leo Bebb after his death as chronicled by his followers. (Rev: BL 7/1/77; LJ 6/15/77; NYTBR 10/30/77)

7375 **Bufalino, Gesualdo.** *Plague-Sower.* **1988, Eridanos Pr. $22.00 (0-941419-12-6); paper $13.00 (0-941419-13-4).** This American debut of a Sicilian writer chronicles the life of a World War II survivor living in an Italian tuberculosis sanitorium. (Rev: Choice 5/89; PW 9/26/88. Awards: PW, 1988)

7376 **Bulgakov, Mikhail.** *Master and Margarita.* **1987, Grove-Weidenfeld paper $7.95 (0-8021-3011-9).** A portrait of the lives of Soviet artists and writers during the 1920s. "A masterpiece. There is no doubt about it."—LJ (Rev: LJ 10/15/67; NYTBR 10/22/67; Newsweek 10/23/67. Awards: ALA, 1967; NYTBR, 1967)

7377 **Burgess, Anthony.** *Any Old Iron.* **1989, Random $19.95 (0-394-57484-2).** A chronicle of the effects of war on several generations of a twentieth-century Welsh family by the author of *A Clockwork Orange.* (Rev: Atl 3/89; LJ 2/1/89; PW 12/9/88)

7378 **Burgess, Anthony.** *Earthly Powers.* **1980, Macmillan $16.95 (0-686-85722-4).** A study of the relationship between an elderly gay English writer and a Roman Catholic cardinal as the writer composes an account of a miracle that happened to a friend. (Rev: LJ 12/15/80; Newsweek 11/24/80; TLS 10/24/80)

7379 **Burgess, Anthony.** *Pianoplayers.* **1987, Simon & Schuster paper $4.95 (0-671-63792-4).** Memoirs of a young English woman regarding her father's life as a piano player and her own experiences as the mistress of a school for men to improve their sexual performance. "First-rate satiric humor from a literary virtuoso."—BL (Rev: BL 8/86; Time 11/17/86; TLS 8/29/86)

7380 **Burke, Martyn.** *Ivory Joe.* **1991, Bantam $19.95 (0-553-07182-3).** A Canadian novelist's story of a nine-year-old girl's experiences on the road with her mother's rhythm and blues band. (Rev: BL 1/15/91; PW 12/14/90)

7381 **Burke, Phyllis.** *Atomic Candy.* **1989, Atlantic Monthly $17.95 (0-87113-374-5); paper $9.95 (0-87113-364-4).** The life of the daughter of a Boston politician serves as the basis for this examination of American political life during the 1960s and 1970s. (Rev: LJ 4/1/89; TLS 4/6/90)

7382 **Burroughs, William S.** *Western Lands.* **1987, Viking $18.95 (0-670-81352-4); Penguin paper $7.95 (0-14-009456-3).** This third volume in the author's trilogy, which includes *Cities of the Red Night* and *The Place of Dead Roads,* concerns man's struggle to reach paradise. "A remarkable achievement."—PW (Rev: LJ 11/1/87; NYTBR 1/3/88; PW 10/30/87)

7383 **Burton, Gabrielle.** *Heartbreak Hotel.* **1988, Penguin paper $6.95 (0-14-010819-X).** The story of seven women recovering at a rest home in Buffalo, New York. "Will have readers laughing and sighing with bittersweet recognition."—BL (Rev: BL 10/1/86; LJ 10/15/86; TLS 9/18/87)

7384 **Busch, Frederick.** *Closing Arguments.* **1991, Ticknor & Fields $19.95 (0-395-58968-1).** A portrait of the relationship between a lawyer and his client, containing flashbacks to the attorney's experiences in the jungles of Vietnam. (Rev: BL 6/1/91; LJ 7/91; NYTBR 8/18/91)

7385 **Busch, Frederick.** *Sometimes I Live in the Country.* **1986, Godine $15.95 (0-87923-622-1).** A Brooklyn-born boy and his ex-policeman father encounter the Ku Klux Klan in their new upstate New York neighborhood. (Rev: BL 5/1/86; LJ 5/1/86; PW 4/4/86)

7386 **Busch, Niven.** *Titan Game.* **1989, Random $17.95 (0-394-57537-7).** A sophisticated tank developed at a California research plant goes out of control and begins a killing spree. "Reads well and moves like a bullet."—NYTBR (Rev: NYTBR 11/26/89; PW 9/8/89)

7387 **Bushell, Agnes.** *Local Deities.* **1990, Curbstone paper $11.95 (0-915306-82-4).** A study of the effects of a couple's radical activities upon the lives of their children. "A book rich in character and incident, blessed with a noble theme."—LJ (Rev: BL 12/15/89; LJ 12/89)

7388 **Buttenweiser, Paul.** *Their Pride and Joy.* **1988, Dell paper $8.95 (0-440-50073-7).** This second novel by a psychoanalyst traces the lives of a troubled New York Jewish family during the early 1960s. (Rev: LJ 9/15/87; PW 7/10/87)

7389 **Byatt, A. S.** *Possession: A Romance.* **1990, Random $22.95 (0-394-58623-9).** The story of two contemporary scholars attempting to find proof of a romantic relationship between two Victorian-era poets. (Rev: NYTBR 10/21/90; PW 8/24/90; Time 11/15/90. Awards: ALA, 1990; NYTBR, 1990; PW, 1990; Time, 1990)

7390 **Cabrera Infante, G.** *Infante's Inferno.* **1985, Avon paper $4.95 (0-380-69965-6).** A pun-filled work tracing the sexual exploits of a Havana man during the 1940s. (Rev: BL 4/1/84; LJ 5/1/84; NYTBR 5/6/84)

7391 **Cain, George.** *Blueschild Baby.* **1987, Ecco Pr. paper $7.50 (0-88001-133-5).** This debut novel depicts the life of a drug addict in Harlem. "The most important work of fiction by an Afro-American since *Native Son*."—NYTBR (Rev: LJ 12/15/70; NYTBR 1/17/71)

7392 Calvino, Italo. *Castle of Crossed Destinies*. 1979, Harcourt paper $7.95 (0-15-615455-2). An illustrated tale of a group of mute characters lost in a forest who tell the stories of their lives through a series of tarot cards. (Rev: BL 1/15/77; LJ 2/1/77; Newsweek 2/14/77)

7393 Calvino, Italo. *If on a Winter's Night a Traveler*. 1982, Harcourt paper $7.95 (0-15-645380-0). A novel consisting of fragments of the beginnings of ten works of fiction connected by a narrator seeking to find the rest of the missing books. (Rev: BL 2/15/81; LJ 4/1/81; Time 5/25/81)

7394 Calvino, Italo. *Mr. Palomar*. 1985, Harcourt $12.95 (0-15-162835-1); paper $5.95 (0-15-662780-9). Twenty-seven episodes chronicle the observations of an astronomer in this novel by the Italian author of *Invisible Cities*. (Rev: LJ 9/15/85; NYTBR 9/29/85; Newsweek 10/21/85. Awards: LJ, 1985; NYTBR, 1985)

7395 Cameron, Carey. *Daddy Boy*. 1989, Algonquin $15.95 (0-912697-84-9). The story of the relationship between an oil millionaire and his youngest daughter set in Hollywood during the 1960s. (Rev: NYTBR 6/18/89; PW 1/27/89)

7396 Cameron, Peter. *Leap Year*. 1989, Harper & Row $18.95 (0-06-016252-X). This satirical look at the everyday lives of New Yorkers in the late 1980s is the first novel by the author of the short-story collection *One Way or Another*. (Rev: LJ 3/1/90; NYTBR 2/25/90; PW 12/22/89)

7397 Camp, John. *Empress File*. 1991, Henry Holt $18.95 (0-8050-1545-0). The sequel to *Fool's Run* is about the efforts of Kidd, an artist/computer whiz/tough guy, to expose political corruption in a small Mississippi town. "A fast-moving, stylish delight, with dialogue that crackles."—PW (Rev: BL 3/15/91; LJ 3/15/91; PW 2/15/91)

7398 Camp, John. *Fool's Run*. 1989, Henry Holt $14.95 (0-8050-0990-6); NAL paper $4.95 (0-451-16712-0). A thriller about a computer hacker employed by an entrepreneur to tamper with the files of a business rival. (Rev: BL 7/89; NYTBR 10/15/89; PW 7/21/89)

7399 Canin, Ethan. *Blue River*. 1991, Houghton $19.95 (0-395-49854-6). A Wisconsin doctor recalls his early life with the older brother that raised him in this novel by the author of *Emperor of the Air*. (Rev: BL 8/91; NYTBR 10/20/91)

7400 Cantor, Jay. *Krazy Kat: A Novel in Five Panels*. 1987, Knopf $16.95 (0-394-55025-0); Macmillan paper $7.95 (0-02-042081-1). A fictionalized adult version updating the adventures of the comic strip character that ran in American newspapers from 1913 to 1944. (Rev: LJ 1/88; Newsweek 2/29/88; PW 12/11/87)

7401 Capote, Truman. *Answered Prayers: The Unfinished Novel*. 1987, Random $16.95 (0-394-55645-3); NAL paper $8.95 (0-452-26137-6).** Capote's long-unfinished novel detailing the intimate lives of many prominent figures in his social and literary circles. (Rev: LJ 10/1/87; New Yorker 9/21/87; Time 9/7/87)

7402 Caraganis, Lynn. *Cousin It*. 1991, Ticknor & Fields $19.95 (0-89919-945-3). A coming-of-age novel set in 1958 chronicling the life of an orphan raised by her cousins in San Jose. (Rev: BL 1/15/91; New Yorker 4/22/91)

7403 Carey, Peter. *Bliss*. 1986, Harper & Row paper $8.95 (0-06-091355-X). A man who comes out of a coma following a heart attack has a series of family secrets revealed to him that confirm his belief that he has died and gone to Hell. "Entertainment with considerable bite."—LJ (Rev: BL 1/1/82; LJ 2/15/82; Newsweek 4/19/82)

7404 Carey, Peter. *Illywhacker*. 1986, Harper & Row paper $9.95 (0-06-091331-2). A 139-year-old man tells the story of his life in Australia in this novel by the author of *Bliss*. (Rev: BL 7/85; NYTBR 11/17/85; PW 5/31/85)

7405 Carkeet, David. *Full Catastrophe*. 1990, Simon & Schuster $18.95 (0-671-64319-3). A bachelor linguist enters an American household to save a failing marriage. (Rev: BL 2/15/90; LJ 1/90; PW 12/1/89)

7406 Carmello, Charles. *La Mattanza: The Sicilian Madness*. 1986, Freundlich $17.95 (0-88191-040-6). A story of organized crime regarding a mafia son preparing to take over the helm of his family's affairs. (Rev: BL 12/15/86; LJ 12/86)

7407 Carr, Robyn. *Mind Tryst*. 1991, St. Martin's $19.95 (0-312-07034-9). A woman trying to escape her past life in Southern California encounters resistance after moving to a small Colorado town. "Will strike a chord with single women everywhere."—BL (Rev: BL 1/15/92; LJ 1/92; PW 12/13/91)

7408 Carson, Michael. *Brothers in Arms*. 1988, Pantheon $16.95 (0-394-57213-0); NAL paper $8.95 (0-452-26309-3). An English boy seeks to escape the torments of his youth by joining a monastery. (Rev: BL 9/1/88; New Yorker 11/28/88; PW 8/15/88)

7409 Carter, Michelle. *On Other Days While Going Home*. 1987, Morrow $15.95 (0-688-07074-4); Penguin paper $6.95 (0-14-010972-2). A chronicle of a teenage orphan's wandering search for fulfillment on the highways of America. "Appealing, original and stylistically deft."—BL (Rev: BL 6/15/87; NYTBR 11/15/87)

7410 Cartier, Xam. *Muse-Echo Blues*. 1991, Harmony $18.00 (0-517-57793-3). A friendship between a composer and a jazz musician provides a portrait of African-American cultural life during the 1940s. (Rev: BL 4/1/91; LJ 4/15/91; PW 3/22/91. Awards: BL, 1991)

7411 Casey, John. *Spartina*. 1989, Knopf $18.95 (0-394-50098-9); Avon paper $8.95 (0-380-71104-4). The story of a Rhode Island fisherman who constructs a boat and becomes self-employed. (Rev: LJ 6/1/89;

NYTBR 6/25/89; PW 4/21/89. Awards: ALA, 1989; NBA, 1989; PW, 1989)

7412   Casey, John. *Testimony and Demeanor.* **1990, Avon paper $8.95 (0-380-71239-3).** A collection of four novellas including "Connaissance des Arts," "Mandarin in a Farther Field," "A More Complete Cross-Section," and the title story. (Rev: LJ 7/79; New Rep 5/19/79; Time 7/9/79)

7413   Castedo, Elena. *Paradise.* **1990, Grove-Weidenfeld $19.95 (1-55584-279-8); Warner paper $10.99 (0-446-39345-2).** This Chilean writer's debut novel portrays the life of a Spanish family living in exile in South America to escape the excesses of the Franco regime. (Rev: LJ 2/15/90; NYTBR 4/1/90; PW 12/22/89)

7414   Caudle, Neil. *Voices from Home.* **1989, Putnam $19.95 (0-399-13421-2).** A Southern teenage girl moves in with her wild father after her mother leaves with her new husband for Chicago. "An accomplished first novel, full of compassion and wit and marvelous language."—NYTBR (Rev: BL 7/89; LJ 7/89; PW 6/9/89)

7415   Chabon, Michael. *Mysteries of Pittsburgh.* **1988, Morrow $16.95 (0-688-07632-7); Harper & Row paper $7.95 (0-06-097212-2).** A college student gains exposure to the Pittsburgh underworld and explores his sexuality during his summer break. (Rev: NYTBR 4/3/88; New Yorker 12/19/88; PW 2/12/88)

7416   Chace, Susan. *Intimacy.* **1988, Random $14.95 (0-394-57030-8); NAL paper $7.95 (0-452-26375-1).** A New York journalist in her late 30s tries to come to grips with the emotional pain of her childhood. (Rev: BL 1/15/89; PW 12/23/88)

7417   Chafets, Ze'ev. *Inherit the Mob.* **1991, Random $19.00 (0-679-40263-2).** A journalist finds he has inherited a family fortune tied to organized crime. (Rev: BL 6/15/91; NYTBR 8/25/91)

7418   Chapin, Kim. *Dogwood Afternoons.* **1985, Farrar $13.95 (0-374-14316-1).** A Southern race car driver recalls his life on his last day prior to a fatal accident. (Rev: LJ 7/85; PW 6/14/85)

7419   Chappell, Fred. *Brighten the Corner Where You Are.* **1989, St. Martin's $15.95 (0-312-03297-8); paper $8.95 (0-312-05057-7).** A North Carolina teacher is called before his school board to explain his teachings on evolution in this novel set just after World War II. "Old-fashioned in the best sense of the word . . . a warm, engaging story."—BL (Rev: BL 9/1/89; LJ 8/89; PW 7/14/89)

7420   Chappell, Fred. *I Am One of You Forever.* **1987, Louisiana State Univ. Pr. paper $6.95 (0-8071-1410-3).** A fictional memoir recording life on a North Carolina farm during the 1940s. (Rev: BL 4/15/85; LJ 5/15/85; PW 3/15/85)

7421   Charyn, Jerome. *War Cries Over Avenue C.* **1985, Donald I. Fine $17.95 (0-917657-30-6).** A story chronicling the life of a former Vietnam nurse on the streets of New York's Lower East Side. (Rev: LJ 7/85; NYTBR 6/16/85; PW 3/29/85)

7422   Chase, Joan. *During the Reign of the Queen of Persia.* **1984, Ballantine paper $3.95 (0-345-31525-1).** Two sets of cousins tell stories of three generations of a family in this novel set in Ohio during the 1950s. "A marvelous novel."—LJ (Rev: LJ 6/15/83; NYTBR 6/12/83; Time 7/18/83. Awards: ALA, 1983; NYTBR, 1983)

7423   Chase, Joan. *Evening Wolves.* **1989, Farrar $19.95 (0-374-15003-6); Ballantine paper $4.95 (0-345-36285-3).** The author's second novel portrays a dysfunctional family carrying on after the death of the mother. "A magnificently involving, imaginative and memorable novel."—PW (Rev: BL 3/1/89; NYTBR 5/28/89; PW 3/3/89)

7424   Chatwin, Bruce. *On the Black Hill.* **1983, Viking $14.75 (0-670-52492-1); Penguin paper $7.95 (0-14-006896-1).** English twins who have lived a reclusive life on a farm are treated to a liberating airplane flight on their eightieth birthday. (Rev: LJ 11/1/82; NYRB 1/20/83; NYTBR 1/2/83. Awards: ALA, 1983)

7425   Chatwin, Bruce. *Utz.* **1989, Viking $16.95 (0-670-82497-6); Penguin paper $7.95 (0-14-011576-5).** A novella concerning the life of a porcelain collector under a repressive Czech regime and the fate of his priceless collection following his death. (Rev: Atl 2/89; Newsweek 1/30/89; TLS 9/23/88)

7426   Cheek, Mavis. *Parlor Games.* **1989, Simon & Schuster $18.95 (0-671-68309-8).** The events of a woman's fortieth birthday turn her life upside down in this satirical novel set in a fashionable London suburb. "A delicious, wickedly funny book."—LJ (Rev: BL 10/15/89; LJ 10/15/89; PW 8/25/89)

7427   Cheever, John. *Bullet Park.* **1987, Ballantine paper $3.95 (0-345-35006-5).** Suburban violence erupts in New York between the Hammer and Nailles families. "A remarkably convincing fantasy."—TLS (Rev: CSM 5/1/69; Newsweek 4/28/69; TLS 10/30/69)

7428   Cheever, John. *Falconer.* **1977, Knopf $13.95 (0-394-41071-8); Ballantine paper $3.95 (0-345-33145-1).** The study of the life of a drug-addicted professor serving time in prison for the murder of his brother. (Rev: LJ 2/1/77; NYTBR 3/8/77; Time 2/28/77. Awards: NYTBR, 1977; Time, 1977)

7429   Cheever, John. *Oh What a Paradise It Seems.* **1986, Ballantine paper $3.95 (0-345-33832-4).** An elderly man fights to restore a local pond to its formerly unpolluted state. "Cheever at his best."—LJ (Rev: BL 12/15/81; LJ 2/1/82; New Yorker 4/5/82)

7430   Chehak, Susan Taylor. *Harmony.* **1990, Houghton $18.95 (0-89919-941-0).** Studies of the lives of two women friends in a small Iowa town, one trapped in an abusive marriage, the other formerly married to a convicted murderer. "Compelling, well-crafted . . . beautifully written."—LJ (Rev: LJ 9/15/90; NYTBR 12/9/90; PW 8/24/90)

7431 Cheong, Fiona. *Scent of the Gods.* **1991,** **Norton $19.95 (0-393-03024-5).** This debut novel concerns a Chinese family's life in Singapore during the 1960s. "A story exquisitely poised between the specific and the mythic, delicately narrated and profoundly resonant."—PW (REV: BL 9/15/91; PW 8/9/91)

7432 Chernoff, Maxine. *Plain Grief.* **1991, Summit $19.00 (0-671-72463-0).** This debut novel explores the tensions within a Chicago family that surface over a Thanksgiving holiday. (REV: BL 8/91; LJ 7/91; NYTBR 9/22/91)

7433 Chesney, Marion. *Finessing Clarissa.* **1989, St. Martin's $14.95 (0-312-03341-9); paper $3.95 (0-312-92283-3).** The fourth installment in the author's School for Manners series concerns a London charm school designed to make young ladies more marriageable by improving their manners and looks. (REV: BL 10/15/89; PW 10/6/89)

7434 Cheuse, Alan. *Grandmother's Club.* **1988, Penguin paper $6.95 (0-14-010484-4).** The story focuses on tales of a New York grandmother and her son, a rabbi. (REV: BL 10/1/86; Choice 1/87; PW 8/22/86)

7435 Childress, Mark. *V for Victor.* **1988, Knopf $18.95 (0-345-56871-0); Ballantine paper $3.95 (0-345-35427-3).** A teenage boy is sent to care for his ailing grandmother in Alabama during the years of World War II. (REV: BL 11/15/88; CSM 5/22/89; NYTBR 2/19/89)

7436 Chin, Frank. *Donald Duk.* **1991, Coffee House paper $9.95 (0-918273-83-8).** A portrait of the life of a Chinese-American boy in San Francisco who is forced to reassess his ethnic background and history on the eve of his twelfth Chinese New Year. (REV: LJ 2/15/91; NYTBR 3/31/91; PW 2/8/91)

7437 Chute, Carolyn. *Beans of Egypt, Maine.* **1986, Warner paper $4.95 (0-446-30010-1).** A series of vignettes portraying life in the Bean family set in a small Maine lumber town. "Fiction at its most involving, resonant and clear."—PW (REV: NYTBR 1/13/85; Newsweek 2/25/85; PW 11/16/84. AWARDS: ALA, 1985)

7438 Chute, Carolyn. *Letourneau's Used Auto Parts.* **1988, Ticknor & Fields $16.95 (0-89919-500-8); Harper & Row paper $7.95 (0-06-097225-4).** The story of the owner of an automobile salvage lot set in the author's fictional community of Egypt, Maine. (REV: BL 4/15/88; New Rep 7/11/88; PW 4/29/88)

7439 Cisneros, Sandra. *House on Mango Street.* **1991, Random paper $9.00 (0-679-73477-5).** This depiction of life in a Chicago Hispanic ghetto by the author of *Woman Hollering Creek and Other Stories* was originally published in 1984. "Ms. Cisneros has compressed great force into this small, brilliant work."—Atl (REV: Atl 6/91; BL 10/15/84)

7440 Clancy, Tom. *Hunt for Red October.* **1984, Naval Institute Pr. $18.95 (0-87021-285-0); Berkley paper $5.95 (0-425-12027-9).** The story of an advanced Soviet submarine making its way toward American waters to defect while under pursuit by Russian forces. (REV: BL 11/1/84; LJ 10/15/84; PW 8/17/84)

7441 Clancy, Tom. *Patriot Games.* **1987, Putnam $19.95 (0-399-13241-4); Berkley paper $5.95 (0-425-10972-0).** A plot to kidnap members of the British royal family is thwarted by Jack Ryan, a character introduced in the author's *Hunt for Red October.* (REV: BL 6/1/87; LJ 8/87; PW 6/5/87)

7442 Clark, Mary Higgins. *Stillwatch.* **1986, Dell paper $4.95 (0-440-18305-7).** A young woman is chased by unknown assailants following her return to the Washington, D.C., home where her parents were murdered when she was a child. (REV: BL 10/1/84; NYTBR 12/9/84)

7443 Clark, Mary Higgins. *A Stranger Is Watching.* **1980, Dell paper $4.95 (0-440-18127-5).** A lunatic with a murder record kidnaps a pair of innocent citizens. (REV: BL 3/15/78; PW 12/26/77)

7444 Clarke, Arthur C. *Ghost from the Grand Banks.* **1990, Bantam $19.95 (0-553-07222-6).** Groups of rescue teams attempt to raise the *Titanic* by the centennial of its sinking. (REV: BL 10/15/90; LJ 11/15/90; PW 10/5/90)

7445 Clavell, James. *Noble House: A Novel of Contemporary Hong Kong.* **1981, Delacorte $22.95 (0-385-28737-2); Dell paper $5.95 (0-440-16484-2).** An eventful week in the life of a Hong Kong trading firm as described by the author of *Tai-Pan.* (REV: CSM 6/24/81; NYTBR 5/3/81; Time 7/6/81)

7446 Clavell, James. *Whirlwind.* **1986, Morrow $22.95 (0-688-06663-1); Avon paper $5.95 (0-380-70312-2).** The story of a British helicopter company involved in the turmoil of the Iranian Revolution. (REV: BL 10/1/86; LJ 11/1/86; PW 9/12/86)

7447 Clewlow, Carol. *Keeping the Faith.* **1990, Poseidon $16.95 (0-671-67117-0).** A portrayal of life within a fundamentalist Christian sect by a British writer. "An exquisitely wrought novel."—NYTBR (REV: BL 2/1/90; NYTBR 3/11/90; PW 12/15/89)

7448 Cliff, Michelle. *No Telephone to Heaven.* **1988, Dutton $17.95 (0-525-24508-1); paper $7.95 (0-525-48370-5).** A Jamaican-born woman raised and educated in the United States and England returns to her homeland in order to rediscover herself and her past. "A strong, confident, poetic work."—BL (REV: BL 6/15/87; LJ 7/87; PW 6/5/87)

7449 Clifford, Francis. *Amigo, Amigo.* **1985, Academy Chicago paper $4.95 (0-89733-136-2).** A former Nazi leader hiding incognito as a rural dentist in Latin America is pursued by an English journalist. (REV: New Yorker 12/31/73; PW 7/16/73; TLS 10/26/73)

7450 Coe, Christopher. *I Look Divine.* **1988, Random paper $5.95 (0-394-75995-8).** A portrait of the life and early death of a narcissistic man, recounted by his brother. (REV: BL 9/15/87; NYTBR 8/30/87; PW 8/21/87)

7451   Coetzee, J. M. *Age of Iron.* **1990, Random $18.95 (0-394-58859-2).** A chronicle of the last days of a South African woman dying of cancer in her Cape Town home, surrounded by a servant and an alcoholic she befriended. "A brilliant, chilling look at the spiritual costs of apartheid."—LJ (Rev: BL 6/1/90; LJ 8/90; NYRB 11/8/90. Awards: ALA, 1990; BL, 1990; LJ, 1990)

7452   Coetzee, J. M. *Foe.* **1987, Viking $15.95 (0-670-81398-2); Penguin paper $6.95 (0-14-009623-X).** An updated revision of the story of Robinson Crusoe detailing the adventures of an English castaway and her life with Friday. (Rev: BL 12/15/86; LJ 12/86; New Rep 3/9/87)

7453   Coetzee, J. M. *Life and Times of Michael K.* **1985, Penguin paper $6.95 (0-14-007448-1).** The study of the life of a lower-class South African gardener persecuted by the military in a futuristic vision of that nation under civil war. (Rev: CSM 12/12/83; NYRB 2/2/84; NYTBR 12/11/83. Awards: ALA, 1984; NYTBR, 1984)

7454   Coetzee, J. M. *Waiting for the Barbarians.* **1982, Penguin paper $6.95 (0-14-006110-X).** A reluctant administrator oversees a frontier colonial settlement in this novel by the South African writer. (Rev: BL 3/1/82; CSM 6/11/82; NYTBR 4/18/82. Awards: BL, the 1980s; NYTBR, 1982)

7455   Cohen, Arthur A. *In the Days of Simon Stern.* **1987, Univ. of Chicago Pr. paper $10.95 (0-226-11254-3).** A portrait of the life of the son of Polish Jewish immigrants in New York. (Rev: BL 7/15/73; Newsweek 6/11/73; Time 7/9/73)

7456   Cohen, Richard. *Say You Want Me.* **1988, Soho Pr. $17.95 (0-939149-12-5).** An artist working at home has an affair with a young woman while his wife works to support the family. "A haunting and beautifully written novel."—PW (Rev: LJ 8/88; NYTBR 8/28/88; PW 5/13/88)

7457   Colegate, Isabel. *Glimpse of Sion's Glory and Other Stories.* **1986, Penguin paper $5.95 (0-14-008374-X).** A collection of three novellas by the author of *The Shooting Party* including "Distant Cousins," "The Girl Who Had Lived Among Artists," and the title story. (Rev: BL 10/1/85; LJ 10/15/85; NYTBR 11/17/85)

7458   Collins, Larry, and Dominique LaPierre. *Fifth Horseman.* **1981, Avon paper $4.95 (0-380-54734-1).** An atomic bomb smuggled into New York is threatened to be detonated by Libyan terrorists unless Israel evacuates the occupied territories. (Rev: BL 7/15/80; LJ 8/80; NYTBR 8/17/80)

7459   Collins, Merle. *Angel.* **1988, Seal Pr. paper $8.95 (0-931188-64-4).** A Caribbean poet's portrait of life on the island of Grenada in the early 1980s as seen through the lives of a woman and her daughter. (Rev: LJ 10/1/88; PW 7/22/88)

7460   Colwin, Laurie. *Another Marvelous Thing.* **1986, Knopf $13.95 (0-394-55128-1); Penguin paper $5.95 (0-14-009854-2).** Eight interconnected stories tracing the history of a New York financier's affair with a married woman. (Rev: BL 2/15/86; TLS 2/27/87)

7461   Colwin, Laurie. *Family Happiness.* **1990, Harper & Row paper $7.95 (0-06-097272-6).** The daughter of a wealthy New York family reexamines her life following an affair with an artist. "A powerful novel that demands to be read."—BL (Rev: BL 8/82; LJ 8/82; Newsweek 9/27/82)

7462   Colwin, Laurie. *Goodbye Without Leaving.* **1990, Poseidon $18.95 (0-671-70706-X).** A story of the life of a back-up singer for a soul music group before, during, and after her experience with the band. (Rev: BL 4/15/90; LJ 5/1/90; PW 3/9/90)

7463   Condon, Richard. *Prizzi's Family.* **1987, Jove paper $4.50 (0-515-09106-5).** A prequel to the Prizzi series tracing the life of hit man Charley Partanna. (Rev: BL 7/86; PW 8/15/86; Time 9/22/86)

7464   Condon, Richard. *Prizzi's Glory.* **1988, Dutton $17.95 (0-525-24689-4); NAL paper $4.95 (0-451-16468-7).** This third novel in the Prizzi trilogy concerns the efforts of the organized crime family to enter legitimate business. "There is no more accomplished or entertaining satirist working today."—New Yorker (Rev: BL 8/88; LJ 10/1/88; New Yorker 12/26/88)

7465   Condon, Richard. *Prizzi's Honor.* **1983, Berkley paper $3.95 (0-425-09507-X).** Love and deception mix in this tale of two mob enforcers who fall in love. (Rev: LJ 3/15/82; NYTBR 4/18/82; TLS 6/11/82)

7466   Condon, Richard. *Winter Kills.* **1975, Dell paper $2.25 (0-440-16007-3).** The story of a fictional assassination of an American president in Philadelphia in 1960 and the uncovering of a plot by the president's father to commit the deed. (Rev: BL 7/15/74; NYTBR 5/26/74; PW 3/18/74)

7467   Connell, Evan S. *The Connoisseur.* **1987, North Point paper (0-86547-245-9).** The story of a New York antique collector whose purchase of a pre-Columbian figurine changes his life and becomes an obsession. (Rev: LJ 8/74; PW 6/10/74; Time 9/2/74. Awards: Time, 1974)

7468   Connell, Evan S. *Mr. Bridge.* **1981, North Point paper $9.95 (0-86547-056-1).** A portrait of the lives of a middle-aged Kansas married couple. (Rev: Choice 9/69; CSM 5/22/69; Time 6/20/69)

7469   Conroy, Pat. *Lords of Discipline.* **1980, Old NY Book Shop $13.95 (0-317-43154-4); Bantam paper $5.95 (0-553-27136-9).** A tale of prejudice and torture set at a South Carolina military academy. (Rev: BL 9/15/80; LJ 10/1/80; Sat Rev 10/80)

7470   Conroy, Pat. *Prince of Tides.* **1986, Houghton $19.95 (0-395-35300-9); Bantam paper $5.95 (0-553-26888-0).** A suicide attempt by a Southern-born poet living in New York causes her brother to visit to help sort out her past and present life. (Rev: BL 7/86; LJ 10/15/86; Time 10/13/86)

7471   Cook, Robin. *Coma.* **1977, NAL paper $4.95 (0-451-15953-5).** A young nurse's life is threatened when she investigates a series of mysterious comas that overtake patients at a Boston hospital. "A page turner not to be missed."—LJ (Rev: BL 5/15/77; LJ 5/15/77; PW 2/7/77)

7472 Cook, Robin. *Mindbend.* **1985, Putnam $15.95 (0-399-12966-9); NAL paper $4.95 (0-451-14108-3).** A pharamaceutical company brainwashes doctors into prescribing their toxic products in this novel by the author of *Coma.* (Rev: BL 2/15/85; PW 1/25/85)

7473 Cooke, Elizabeth. *Complicity.* **1988, Little, Brown $16.95 (0-316-15507-1).** A New England mother and her daughter present different views of their lives and family relationships in this debut novel. (Rev: BL 11/1/87; NYTBR 2/28/88; PW 12/4/87)

7474 Coonts, Stephen. *Under Siege.* **1990, Pocket $19.95 (0-671-72229-8).** The city of Washington, D.C., and the U.S. government come under attack by a group of murderous Colombian drug cartel terrorists. "Escape reading at its best."—NYTBR (Rev: BL 10/1/90; NYTBR 11/18/90; PW 8/24/90)

7475 Cooper, Rand Richards. *The Last to Go: A Family Chronicle.* **1988, Harcourt $16.95 (0-15-148430-9); Avon paper $7.95 (0-380-70862-0).** Interrelated stories chronicle the rise and fall of a marriage and its effects on the family's children. "A first-rate piece of work."—PW (Rev: BL 10/1/88; New Yorker 3/23/89; PW 8/26/88)

7476 Coover, Robert. *Gerald's Party.* **1987, NAL paper $8.95 (0-452-25878-2).** A chronicle of the events of a single bizarre evening dinner party by the author of *The Origin of the Brunists.* (Rev: LJ 2/1/86; New Rep 3/24/86; NYTBR 12/29/85)

7477 Coover, Robert. *Origin of the Brunists.* **1989, Norton paper $10.95 (0-393-30600-3).** Coover's first novel tracks the development and spread of a religious cult from its origins in a Pennsylvania mining town. (Rev: PW 11/6/67; TLS 4/27/67)

7478 Coover, Robert. *Pinocchio in Venice.* **1991, Simon & Schuster $19.95 (0-671-64471-8).** The author of *Gerald's Party* chronicles the further adventures of Pinocchio. "Coover is at his best in this wildly comic fable."—LJ (Rev: BL 4/15/91; LJ 1/91; NYTBR 1/27/91)

7479 Coover, Robert. *Spanking the Maid.* **1982, Grove-Weidenfeld $14.95 (0-8021-5152-3).** An examination of the sexual relationship between a man and his maid that centers on a spanking and roles of dominance and submission. "Very nearly flawless."—NYTBR (Rev: BL 6/15/82; LJ 8/82; NYTBR 6/27/82)

7480 Coppel, Alfred. *Show Me a Hero.* **1987, Harcourt $16.95 (0-15-182080-5); Ivy Books paper $3.95 (0-8041-0232-5).** Private citizens arrange a hostage-rescue mission in Libya by using a Tunisian filming project as their cover. (Rev: BL 2/15/87; LJ 5/1/87; PW 2/20/87)

7481 Corman, Avery. *Fifty.* **1988, Ivy paper $3.95 (0-8041-0300-3).** A divorced sportswriter turns 50 and suffers from a midlife crisis in this novel by the

author of *Kramer vs. Kramer.* "A delightful study of the pitfalls of aging, marriage, and modern family life."—BL (Rev: BL 8/87; LJ 7/87; Time 9/7/87)

7482 Corman, Avery. *Kramer vs. Kramer.* **1988, Ivy Books paper $4.95 (0-8041-0360-7).** A failing marriage leads to a child custody battle over a couple's four-year-old son. (Rev: BL 9/15/77; LJ 8/77; PW 6/20/77)

7483 Cornwell, Bernard. *Killer's Wake.* **1989, Putnam $19.95 (0-399-13458-1); Harper & Row paper $4.95 (0-06-100046-9).** An English heir's life is put in danger following the theft of a Van Gogh painting. (Rev: BL 8/89; PW 6/16/89)

7484 Cortazar, Julio. *A Certain Lucas.* **1984, Knopf $12.95 (0-394-50723-1).** A three-part novel chronicling the life and thoughts of an Argentine writer living in exile in France. "A wonderfully whimsical and technically dazzling performance."—BL (Rev: BL 5/15/84; LJ 5/15/84; New Yorker 6/18/84)

7485 Cortazar, Julio. *Hopscotch.* **1987, Pantheon paper $8.95 (0-394-75284-8).** An experimental novel by the Argentine writer set in Paris and Buenos Aires. (Rev: Choice 7–8/67; New Rep 4/23/66; TLS 3/9/67)

7486 Coughlin, T. Glen. *Hero of New York.* **1987, St. Martin's $3.95 (0-312-90730-3).** The portrayal of a policeman facing trial on brutality charges and how the proceedings affect his family and personal life. "A beautiful first novel."—LJ (Rev: BL 2/15/86; LJ 2/1/86; New Yorker 9/29/86)

7487 Coulter, Hope Norman. *Dry Bones.* **1990, August House $17.95 (0-87483-152-0).** A fictional study of the effects of the discovery of a fossil upon the citizenry of a small Arkansas town. (Rev: BL 10/1/90; LJ 8/90; PW 8/10/90)

7488 Courtenay, Bruce. *Power of One.* **1989, Random $18.95 (0-394-57520-2); Ballantine paper $5.95 (0-345-35992-5).** An Australian writer who was born in South Africa traces the life of a child in that country during the years of World War II. (Rev: CSM 6/1/89; LJ 5/1/89; NYTBR 7/2/89)

7489 Covington, Vicki. *Gathering Home.* **1988, Simon & Schuster $17.95 (0-671-66055-1); Penguin paper $7.95 (0-14-012709-7).** This story of an adopted Alabama teenager's acceptance of her birth and adoptive parents is the author's first novel. (Rev: LJ 11/15/88; PW 7/29/88)

7490 Cravens, Gwyneth. *Gates of Paradise.* **1990, Ticknor & Fields $18.95 (0-89919-981-X).** A study of one day in the failing marriage between a female minister and her art-historian husband. (Rev: BL 11/1/90; LJ 10/15/90)

7491 Cravens, Gwyneth. *Heart's Desire.* **1986, Knopf $16.95 (0-394-55245-8).** A chronicle of changes in the lives of seven Southwest family members over the course of a year in the late 1960s. (Rev: BL 5/1/86; LJ 5/15/86; PW 3/21/86)

7492 Crews, Harry. *Body.* **1990, Simon & Schuster $18.95 (0-671-69576-2).** A young Georgia woman prepares for a national bodybuilding contest in this novel by the author of *The Knockout Artist*. (REV: BL 7/90; Choice 12/90; PW 6/29/90)

7493 Crone, Moira. *A Period of Confinement.* **1986, Putnam $18.95 (0-399-13136-1).** A first novel tracing the circumstances that lead a Baltimore artist to leave her infant for a career in New York. (REV: LJ 7/86; NYTBR 8/31/86; PW 6/13/86)

7494 Cronley, Jay. *Walking Papers.* **1988, Random $16.95 (0-394-56947-4); Ballantine paper $3.95 (0-345-34807-9).** A novelist rearranges his life following a financially devastating divorce settlement. (REV: BL 8/88; LJ 8/88)

7495 Cunningham, Michael. *A Home at the End of the World.* **1990, Farrar $16.95 (0-374-17250-1).** A story tracing the friendship of a group of Cleveland boys from the 1960s to the 1980s and how their lives are touched by the AIDS epidemic. (REV: BL 11/1/90; LJ 10/15/90; PW 8/17/90. AWARDS: BL, 1990; PW, 1990)

7496 Currie, Ellen. *Available Light.* **1987, Pocket paper $6.95 (0-317-56210-X).** This writer's first novel chronicles the fantastic events that occur when a gambling man leaves his lover. (REV: LJ 3/1/86; Newsweek 3/3/86; PW 12/20/85. AWARDS: PW, 1986)

7497 Cussler, Clive. *Treasure.* **1988, Simon & Schuster $18.95 (0-671-62613-2); Pocket paper $5.95 (0-671-70465-2).** Dirk Pitt searches for the missing treasures of the Library of Alexandria off the coast of Greenland while simultaneously attempting to prevent the invasion of the United States by a foreign nation. (REV: BL 3/15/88; NYTBR 5/29/88)

7498 Daley, Robert. *A Faint Cold Fear.* **1990, Little, Brown $17.95 (0-316-17184-0).** A New York policeman and a journalist team up to fight drug traffickers in Bogotá. "A well-written, true-to-life account of drug wars fought not by stock characters but by real people."—LJ (REV: LJ 9/15/90; NYTBR 10/14/90; PW 8/10/90)

7499 Dann, Patty. *Mermaids.* **1986, Ticknor & Fields $13.95 (0-89919-471-0); NAL paper $3.95 (0-451-16925-5).** The story of the relationship between a fanatically religious teenage girl and her promiscuous mother. (REV: BL 9/1/86; New Yorker 1/19/87; PW 8/1/86)

7500 Davidsen, Leif. *Sardine Deception.* **1986, Fjord Pr. paper $6.95 (0-940242-15-X).** A Danish journalist investigates the death of his wife in a Basque terrorist attack in Spain. (REV: NYTBR 5/4/86; PW 3/14/86. AWARDS: PW, 1986)

7501 Davidson, Robyn. *Ancestors.* **1989, Simon & Schuster $19.95 (0-671-68062-5).** A portrait of the life of an orphaned girl growing up in Australia by the author of the nonfiction title *Tracks*. (REV: NYTBR 11/12/89; TLS 8/25/89)

7502 Davies, Robertson. *Fifth Business.* **1977, Penguin paper $4.95 (0-14-004387-X).** A schoolteacher in a small Canadian village obsessed with a woman who barely knows him is the center of one of many interconnected stories in this novel by the author of *The Rebel Angels*. "Elegant entertainment, soundly original, a really good novel."—New Yorker (REV: BL 2/1/71; CSM 12/31/70; New Yorker 12/26/70)

7503 Davies, Robertson. *Lyre of Orpheus.* **1989, Viking $19.95 (0-670-82416-4); Penguin paper $8.95 (0-14-011433-5).** The completion of an unfinished opera by Hoffman leads to a reenactment of the Arthurian legend by contemporary people in this novel by the Canadian writer. (REV: BL 12/15/88; NYTBR 1/8/89; Time 12/26/88. AWARDS: BL, 1989)

7504 Davies, Robertson. *The Manticore.* **1977, Penguin paper $5.95 (0-14-004388-9).** Following the death of his father, a Canadian magician undergoes psychoanalysis in Switzerland to sort out his life, in this novel containing characters from the author's *Fifth Business*. (REV: LJ 11/1/72; PW 9/25/72; Time 12/11/72)

7505 Davies, Robertson. *Murther and Walking Spirits.* **1991, Viking $21.95 (0-670-84189-7).** A Canadian newspaper editor discovers secrets of his life and of his ancestors following his murder by his wife's lover. (REV: LJ 10/1/91; NYTBR 11/17/91; PW 9/6/91)

7506 Davies, Robertson. *Rebel Angels.* **1983, Penguin paper $8.95 (0-14-006271-8).** A Renaissance manuscript disappears from a Canadian university. (REV: BL 10/15/81; LJ 1/1/82; TLS 3/26/82)

7507 Davies, Robertson. *What's Bred in the Bone.* **1986, Penguin paper $8.95 (0-14-009711-2).** Details of the life of a Canadian art expert and forger are revealed in this novel told by three trustees of the man's estate following his death. (REV: LJ 11/15/85; New Yorker 1/27/86; Newsweek 12/2/85)

7508 Davies, Robertson. *World of Wonders.* **1977, Penguin paper $6.95 (0-14-004389-6).** This third volume of the Deptford trilogy concerns the adventures of a Canadian magician filming a motion picture in Switzerland. "A novel of stunning verbal energy and intelligence."—NYTBR (REV: NYTBR 4/25/76; PW 2/23/76; Time 5/17/76. AWARDS: ALA, 1976)

7509 Davis, Kathryn. *Labrador.* **1988, Farrar $17.95 (0-374-18251-5); Doubleday paper $8.95 (0-385-26515-8).** A story of the relationship between two New Hampshire sisters set during the 1960s, as told by the younger sibling. (REV: BL 7/88; NYTBR 8/14/88; PW 6/3/88)

7510 Davis, Thulani. *1959.* **1991, Grove-Weidenfeld $18.95 (0-8021-1230-7).** A debut novel chronicling the experiences of a 12-year-old boy in Virginia during the rise of the civil rights movement. (REV: BL 1/1/92; PW 12/6/91)

7511 Davis-Gardner, Angela. *Forms of Shelter.* **1991, Ticknor & Fields $19.95 (0-395-59312-3).** A coming-of-age novel concerning the life of a young Southern woman growing up fatherless. (REV: BL 8/91; LJ 9/1/91; PW 8/2/91)

7512 De Bernieres, Louis. *War of Don Emmanuel's Nether Parts.* **1991, Morrow $20.00 (0-688-11129-7).**

A novel in which citizens of a Latin American town beset by military and political corruption flee to establish a utopian community in the jungle. (Rev: LJ 1/92; PW 12/6/91)

7513 De Haven, Tom. *Sunburn Lake: A Trilogy.* 1988, Viking $18.95 (0-670-80930-6); Penguin paper $7.95 (0-14-008549-1). Three interconnected stories set in New Jersey ranging in time from the 1930s to the twenty-first century, written by the author of *Funny Papers.* (Rev: BL 8/88; NYTBR 9/4/88; PW 6/10/88)

7514 Delattre, Pierre. *Walking on Air.* 1987, Graywolf paper $8.00 (0-915308-95-9). A story of the travels of a circus whose seven acts include a woman who walks on air as the finale. (Rev: BL 6/1/80; LJ 5/15/80; TLS 12/12/80)

7515 Del Guidice, Daniele. *Lines of Light.* 1988, Harcourt $19.95 (0-15-152420-3). A portrait of a friendship between a physicist and a writer that develops at a scientific research facility near Geneva. "A stimulating, peculiarly entertaining and, at times, moving work of art."—NYTBR (Rev: NYTBR 6/26/88; PW 4/22/88)

7516 DeLillo, Don. *Mao II.* 1991, Viking $19.95 (0-670-83904-3). A reclusive writer in a self-imposed exile plans a dramatic career comeback with the help of a photographer friend. "Reconfirms DeLillo's status as a modern master."—PW (Rev: BL 2/15/91; PW 4/12/91; Time 6/10/91. Awards: Time, 1991)

7517 DeLillo, Don. *The Names.* 1989, Random paper $10.95 (0-679-72295-5). The story of an American expatriate businessman living in Athens and growing rich off his Third World investments. (Rev: BL 9/1/82; LJ 10/1/82; Time 11/8/82. Awards: ALA, 1982)

7518 DeLillo, Don. *Players.* 1989, Random paper $7.95 (0-679-72293-9). A New York couple in their 30s become involved with a terrorist ring centered in Queens. (Rev: BL 11/1/77; LJ 8/77; PW 6/6/77)

7519 DeLillo, Don. *Ratner's Star.* 1989, Random paper $8.95 (0-679-72292-0). A Nobel Prize–winning teenage mathematician receives a message from extraterrestrial beings essential to the future survival of life on earth. (Rev: BL 10/1/76; NYTBR 6/20/76; PW 4/12/76)

7520 DeLillo, Don. *Running Dog.* 1989, Random paper $7.95 (0-679-72294-7). A magazine writer investigates the romantic life and art dealings of a U.S. senator in this novel by the author of *Libra.* (Rev: BL 9/15/78; LJ 8/78; Sat Rev 9/16/78)

7521 DeLillo, Don. *White Noise.* 1985, Viking $16.95 (0-670-80373-1). A professor of Hitler Studies at a Midwestern university narrates the events surrounding a local toxic waste accident. (Rev: LJ 2/1/85; NYTBR 1/13/85; PW 11/1/84. Awards: ALA, 1985; BL, the 1980s; LJ, 1985; NBA, 1985; PW, 1985)

7522 DeLynn, Jane. *Real Estate.* 1989, Ballantine paper $3.95 (0-345-35978-X). A satire of the lives of New Yorkers and their concerns with the local real estate market set during the 1980s by the author of *In Thrall.* (Rev: BL 3/15/88; PW 1/8/88)

7523 Demetz, Hana. *Journey from Prague Street.* 1990, St. Martin's $16.95 (0-312-03852-6). A portrait of the life of a Czechoslovakian Holocaust survivor following World War II. (Rev: LJ 4/1/90; NYTBR 7/1/90; PW 2/9/90)

7524 Desai, Anita. *Clear Light of Day.* 1989, Penguin paper $6.95 (0-14-010859-9). A study of the lives of two Hindu sisters before, during, and after the partition of India. (Rev: CSM 1/28/81; NYTBR 11/23/80; TLS 9/5/80. Awards: ALA, 1980)

7525 Desai, Anita. *Fire on the Mountain.* 1985, South Asia Books $7.50 (0-8364-1455-1); Penguin paper (0-14-005347-6). An Indian woman is forced to care for her great-granddaughter at her mountain retreat following the girl's mother's mental illness. (Rev: BL 10/1/77; LJ 11/15/77; New Yorker 11/14/77)

7526 Desai, Anita. *In Custody.* 1989, Penguin paper $7.95 (0-14-010868-8). An account of a disastrous interview by an Indian academic with a poet who writes verse in an obscure language. (Rev: New Rep 3/18/85; PW 1/4/85; TLS 10/19/84)

7527 Desnoes, Edmundo. *Memories of Underdevelopment and Inconsolable Memories.* 1990, Rutgers Univ. Pr. $37.00 (0-8135-1536-X); paper $14.00 (0-8135-1537-8). A journal recording the experiences of a Cuban writer in the late 1950s and early 1960s. "Subjectively posed social commentary executed with extraordinary compassion."—BL (Rev: BL 9/1/67; New Rep 7/8/67; NYTBR 6/11/67. Awards: NYTBR, 1967)

7528 Devon, Gary. *Lost.* 1986, Knopf $17.95 (0-394-53836-6); Warner paper $4.95 (0-446-34489-3). The tale of a psychopathic 11-year-old who terrorizes his family and community. "If you like your suspense fast-paced and tilted to the macabre, *Lost* will deliver."—NYTBR (Rev: BL 7/86; LJ 10/15/86; NYTBR 12/14/86)

7529 DeVries, Peter. *Consenting Adults, or the Duchess Will Be Furious.* 1981, Penguin paper $5.95 (0-14-005833-8). The chronicle of the social and sexual adventures of Ted Peachum on his road to becoming a soap opera star. (Rev: BL 7/1/80; Newsweek 9/1/80; PW 6/13/80)

7530 DeVries, Peter. *Madder Music.* 1982, Penguin paper $5.95 (0-14-006133-9). A man with psychiatric problems assumes the identity of Groucho Marx in this novel by the author of *The Prick of Noon.* (Rev: BL 9/15/77; LJ 10/1/77; New Yorker 11/28/77)

7531 DeVries, Peter. *Peckham's Marbles.* 1987, McGraw-Hill paper $4.95 (0-07-016650-1). A comic tale of a commercially unsuccessful writer's search to locate all the readers of his lone novel. (Rev: Atl 11/86; LJ 10/1/86; NYTBR 11/2/86)

7532 DeVries, Peter. *Prick of Noon.* 1986, Penguin paper $5.95 (0-14-008685-4). An Arkansas pornography king seeks to gain social respectability. (Rev: BL 3/15/85; PW 3/15/85; Time 4/22/85)

7533 DeVries, Peter. *Sauce for the Goose.* 1982, Penguin paper $4.95 (0-14-006281-5). In this novel by the author of *Consenting Adults,* a young Terre

Haute woman seeks to expose practices of sexual harassment at a major magazine (REV: New Yorker 10/19/81; Newsweek 10/5/81; Time 9/21/81)

7534 DeVries, Peter. *Slouching Towards Kalamazoo.* **1983, Little, Brown $13.95 (0-316-18172-2); Penguin paper $6.95 (0-14-007070-2).** The story of a North Dakota schoolteacher who moves to Kalamazoo to bear the child of one of her students. (REV: BL 3/15/83; PW 6/3/83; TLS 8/26/83)

7535 Dew, Robb Forman. *Dale Loves Sophie to Death.* **1982, Penguin paper $6.95 (0-14-006183-5).** A married couple that regularly spend summers apart are brought together by their son's illness in this debut novel. (REV: BL 5/15/81; Newsweek 5/4/81; PW 3/16/81. AWARDS: NBA, 1982)

7536 Dexter, Pete. *Brotherly Love.* **1991, Random $22.00 (0-394-58573-2).** A story spanning 25 years in the lives of a family of Irish laborers with mob ties, by the author of *Paris Trout.* (REV: LJ 10/1/91; NYTBR 10/13/91; PW 8/2/91. AWARDS: PW, 1991)

7537 Dexter, Pete. *Paris Trout.* **1988, Random $17.95 (0-394-56370-0); Penguin paper $7.95 (0-14-012206-0).** A story set in the 1950s concerning a Southern businessman who murders a black woman and receives a light punishment for the crime. (REV: NYTBR 7/24/88; Newsweek 9/26/88; PW 5/13/88. AWARDS: ALA, 1988; NBA, 1988; PW, 1988)

7538 Dibdin, Michael. *Dirty Tricks.* **1991, Summit $18.00 (0-671-69545-2).** A story of the ruthless rise of an ESL teacher during the Thatcher years. "A wickedly funny tour de force."—PW (REV: BL 9/15/91; NYTBR 10/6/91; PW 8/2/91. AWARDS: BL, 1991)

7539 Dibdin, Michael. *Tryst.* **1990, Summit paper $17.95 (0-671-69543-6).** A British psychiatrist becomes involved with an emotionally disturbed young man. (REV: BL 12/15/89; LJ 12/89; PW 11/3/89)

7540 Dick, Philip K. *Broken Bubble.* **1988, Morrow $16.95 (1-55710-012-8).** A novel written by a science fiction writer during the 1950s about the lives of four Californians. "A fascinating, totally believable account of life in the age of anxiety."—PW (REV: BL 6/1/88; LJ 6/15/88; PW 5/27/88)

7541 Dickey, James. *Alnilam.* **1987, Doubleday $19.95 (0-385-06549-3); Windsor paper $4.95 (1-55817-086-3).** A blind carnival owner seeks the truth surrounding the death of his son in an air force accident. (REV: BL 4/1/87; LJ 6/1/87; Time 6/29/87)

7542 Dickey, James. *Deliverance.* **1986, Dell paper $3.95 (0-440-31868-8).** The story of three friends on a fishing trip in the dangerous back woods of Georgia. (REV: BL 5/1/70; New Yorker 5/2/70; PW 2/9/70. AWARDS: ALA, 1970)

7543 Dickinson, Charles. *Rumor Has It.* **1991, Morrow $18.95 (0-688-10225-5).** A chronicle of the last days of a Chicago tabloid paper as recounted by a news editor for the publication. "Provides top-notch entertainment with a deep emotional pitch."—BL (REV: BL 12/1/90; LJ 11/15/90; NYTBR 1/20/91)

7544 Dickinson, Charles. *Waltz in Marathon.* **1984, NAL paper $6.95 (0-452-25593-7).** This debut novel portrays the life of an aging wealthy loan shark in Marathon, Michigan. (REV: CSM 12/2/83; PW 8/26/83)

7545 Dickinson, Charles. *Widows' Adventures.* **1989, Morrow $18.45 (0-688-08924-0); Avon paper $8.95 (0-380-70847-7).** A chronicle of the adventures of two elderly widowed sisters on a road trip from Chicago to Los Angeles to visit relations. (REV: BL 8/1/89; LJ 8/89; PW 8/4/89)

7546 Dickinson, Peter. *Perfect Gallows.* **1987, Pantheon $16.95 (0-394-56311-5); International Polygonics paper $8.95 (1-55882-004-3).** A portrait of an aspiring English actor on the eve of the Allied invasion of Europe during World War II. (REV: BL 1/1/88; PW 11/27/87; Time 2/1/88)

7547 Dickinson, Peter. *Tefuga.* **1987, Pantheon paper $4.95 (0-394-71581-7).** A journalist travels to Africa to film a documentary about the lives of his parents who were minor British diplomatic figures involved in an international controversy. (REV: BL 3/15/86; LJ 3/1/86; NYTBR 4/20/86)

7548 Didion, Joan. *Democracy.* **1985, Pocket paper $3.95 (0-671-54633-3).** A study of the effects of a presidential campaign upon the candidate's wife. (REV: Atl 5/84; LJ 4/15/84; Newsweek 4/16/84)

7549 Didion, Joan. *Play It as It Lays.* **1990, Farrar paper $7.95 (0-374-52171-9).** A chronicle of the events leading to the nervous breakdown of a Southern California woman. (REV: BL 9/15/70; LJ 7/70; Time 8/10/70. AWARDS: ALA, 1970; Time 1970)

7550 Diehl, Margaret. *Me and You.* **1990, Soho Pr. $18.95 (0-939149-13-1).** A California artist struggling with alcohol problems moves to New York in hopes of changing her life. "Well written, thought-provoking and powerful."—LJ (REV: BL 1/1/90; LJ 2/1/90; PW 1/19/90)

7551 Dixon, Melvin. *Vanishing Rooms.* **1991, Dutton $18.95 (0-525-24965-6).** The effects of the violent death of a gay New York man upon the man's lover, a female friend of his, and a teenager involved in the gang that committed the murder. "Powerful—rich in psychological insight."—LJ (REV: LJ 1/91; PW 1/18/91)

7552 Dixon, Stephen. *Frog.* **1991, British American $29.00 (0-945167-43-1); paper $17.00 (0-945167-41-5).** A 769-page fictional portrait of the life and family of writer Howard Tetch. (REV: LJ 1/92; NYTBR 11/17/91)

7553 Djerassi, Carl. *Cantor's Dilemma.* **1989, Doubleday $18.95 (0-385-26183-7).** Controversy surrounds the scientific research techniques of a biological research team following their reception of a Nobel Prize. (REV: BL 9/1/89; LJ 8/89; PW 8/18/89)

7554 Dobyns, Stephen. *After Shocks/Near Escapes.* **1991, Viking $19.95 (0-670-83914-0).** A fictional study of the effects of the 1960 earthquake upon a Chilean family. (REV: BL 5/1/91; LJ 4/15/91; PW 4/12/91)

7555 Dobyns, Stephen. *A Boat Off the Coast.* 1987, Viking $16.95 (0-670-81668-X); Penguin paper $3.95 (0-14-010047-4). Two childhood friends in Maine hatch a scheme to alleviate their financial woes by obtaining a boat load of cocaine. "The writing is hard, the pace taut, the characters fully dimensional."—BL (Rev: BL 11/1/87; LJ 10/1/87; PW 10/2/87)

7556 Dobyns, Stephen. *Two Deaths of Señora Puccini.* 1988, Viking $17.95 (0-670-81980-8); Penguin paper $7.95 (0-14-010567-0). A group of friends at a dinner party hear the story of a doctor's relationship with his lover. "As spellbinding and resonant as an unsettling dream."—PW (Rev: BL 6/1/88; LJ 5/15/88; PW 4/22/88)

7557 Doctorow, E. L. *Book of Daniel.* 1971, Random $14.95 (0-394-43271-8); Fawcett paper $4.50 (0-449-21430-3). The eldest son of a Jewish couple executed for allegedly passing on atomic secrets to the Soviet Union reflects upon his parents' lives. (Rev: LJ 6/15/71; New Rep 6/25/71; Newsweek 6/7/71. Awards: ALA, 1971; Time, 1971)

7558 Dodge, Jim. *Stone Junction: An Alchemical Potboiler.* 1990, Atlantic Monthly $19.95 (0-87113-331-8). This coming-of-age novel traces the adventures of a child and his teenage mother and their involvement with a mysterious organization. "A rollicking, frequently surprising adventure-cum-fairy tale."—NYTBR (Rev: BL 3/15/90; NYTBR 2/4/90; PW 11/24/89)

7559 Doerr, Harriet. *Stones for Ibarra.* 1985, Penguin paper $6.95 (0-14-011218-9). The story of a California couple who leave their American home to reopen a family copper mine in Mexico. "This first novel is eloquent, poignant, insightful, and never sentimental."—BL (Rev: BL 11/1/83; PW 11/4/83; TLS 5/24/85. Awards: NBA, 1984)

7560 Doig, Ivan. *Ride with Me, Mariah Montana.* 1990, Macmillan $18.95 (0-689-12019-2). This third and concluding volume of the author's Montana trilogy chronicles the travels of a family across the state in a recreational vehicle. (Rev: BL 9/15/90; LJ 9/15/90; PW 7/20/90)

7561 Donald, Anabel. *Smile, Honey.* 1988, Mercury House $19.95 (0-916515-59-1); paper $8.95 (0-916515-88-5). A story of a former British child star who makes a living by exploiting her past fame. (Rev: NYTBR 10/8/89; PW 8/25/89)

7562 Donleavy, J. P. *Destinies of Darcy Dancer, Gentleman.* 1990, Atlantic Monthly paper $9.95 (0-87113-289-3). The amorous adventures of a young Irish horseman growing up without his parents on a large country estate. "An irresistible novel."—New Yorker (Rev: BL 10/1/77; Choice 2/78; New Yorker 12/19/77)

7563 Donleavy, J. P. *Leila: Further Adventures in the Life and Destinies of Darcy Dancer, Gentleman.* 1990, Atlantic Monthly $9.95 (0-87113-288-5). This sequel to *Destinies of Darcy Dancer, Gentleman* traces the title character's further adventures on

his Irish estate in the years following World War II. (Rev: LJ 9/15/83; NYTBR 10/30/83; PW 8/12/83)

7564 Donoso, Jose. *Curfew.* 1988, Grove-Weidenfeld $18.95 (1-55584-166-X). Life under the oppressive Pinochet regime is portrayed by the Chilean author of *The Obscene Bird of Night.* (Rev: BL 5/1/88; Choice 10/88; NYTBR 5/9/88)

7565 Donoso, Jose. *Obscene Bird of Night.* 1979, Godine paper $10.95 (0-87923-191-2). An surrealistic novel by the Chilean writer concerning villagers living out the exploits of a local legend. (Rev: CSM 6/27/73; LJ 5/1/73; NYTBR 6/17/73)

7566 Dorfman, Ariel. *Last Song of Manuel Sandero.* 1987, Viking $18.95 (0-670-80214-X); Penguin paper $7.95 (0-14-008896-2). Fetuses refuse to be born and organize a protest against a Latin American nation suffering from political repression. (Rev: Choice 10/87; NYTBR 2/15/87; PW 12/12/86)

7567 Dorris, Michael. *A Yellow Raft in Blue Water.* 1987, Henry Holt $16.95 (0-8050-0045-3); Warner paper $8.95 (0-446-38787-8). The story of three generations of Native-American women dealing with life on and off the reservation. (Rev: BL 3/1/87; LJ 5/1/87; NYTBR 6/7/87. Awards: ALA, 1987)

7568 Dorris, Michael, and Louise Erdrich. *Crown of Columbus.* 1991, HarperCollins $21.95 (0-06-016079-9). Two college professors work on research projects concerning Columbus's voyage and legacy in this collaborative novel by a husband/wife team. "A sure-fire winner on all levels."—LJ (Rev: BL 2/15/91; LJ 3/15/91; PW 3/1/91)

7569 Douglas, Ellen. *Can't Quit You Baby.* 1989, Penguin paper $7.95 (0-14-012102-1). A chronicle of the relations between a white woman and her black maid in the American South during the 1960s and 1970s. "Confirms Douglas as one of our most important writers."—PW (Rev: BL 5/15/88; LJ 6/15/88; PW 5/13/88)

7570 Dovlatov, Sergei. *A Foreign Woman.* 1991, Grove-Weidenfeld $17.95 (0-8021-1342-7). A chronicle of the life of a Soviet woman who emigrates from the Soviet Union to New York. "A funny, sad, and tender novel."—BL (Rev: BL 8/91; NYTBR 9/1/91)

7571 Dovlatov, Sergei. *The Suitcase.* 1990, Grove-Weidenfeld $16.95 (0-8021-1246-3). A novel by a Soviet emigré living in the United States in which the narrator recalls how he acquired each clothing article in his suitcase. (Rev: Choice 12/90; PW 4/13/90; NYTBR 9/2/90)

7572 Dovlatov, Sergei. *The Zone: A Prison Camp Guard's Story.* 1985, Knopf $14.95 (0-394-53522-7). A fictional portrait of life in a Soviet forced-labor camp as told by one of the prison guards. (Rev: BL 10/15/85; LJ 10/15/85; PW 8/16/85)

7573 Doyle, Roddy. *The Commitments.* 1989, Random paper $6.95 (0-679-72174-6). An Irish novelist's story of a Dublin soul music group. (Rev: NYTBR 7/23/89; PW 6/2/89)

7574 Drabble, Margaret. *Ice Age.* 1985, NAL paper $9.95 (0-452-26351-4). Studies of the lives of a dozen English people undergoing psychological or emotional stress set during the mid-1970s. (REV: CSM 12/21/77; LJ 9/1/77; NYTBR 10/9/77)

7575 Drabble, Margaret. *Middle Ground.* 1989, Ivy Books paper $4.95 (0-8041-0362-3). A London journalist approaching middle age returns to her hometown to trace the paths of the lives of her contemporaries. (REV: LJ 8/80; NYTBR 9/7/80; PW 7/25/80. AWARDS: ALA, 1980)

7576 Drabble, Margaret. *Millstone.* 1989, NAL paper $7.95 (0-452-26126-0). The story of an unmarried English scholar in her 20s who chooses to bear her lover's child without his knowledge. (REV: BL 6/1/66; PW 4/25/66; TLS 9/23/65)

7577 Drabble, Margaret. *A Natural Curiosity.* 1989, Viking $19.95 (0-670-82837-8); Penguin paper $8.95 (0-14-012228-1). This sequel to *The Radiant Way* traces the lives of three female friends in the latter half of the 1980s. (REV: LJ 7/89; Time 9/4/89; TLS 9/29/89. AWARDS: BL, 1989)

7578 Drabble, Margaret. *Needle's Eye.* 1989, Ivy Books paper $4.95 (0-8041-0364-X). The story of a custody fight between an idealistic woman and her rich ex-husband over the couple's three children. (REV: LJ 6/1/72; NYTBR 6/12/72; PW 5/8/72)

7579 Drabble, Margaret. *The Radiant Way.* 1989, Ivy Books paper $4.95 (0-8041-0365-8). An exploration of the lives and friendships of three English women during the first half of the 1980s. (REV: New Yorker 11/16/87; Time 11/16/87; TLS 5/1/87)

7580 Drabble, Margaret. *Realms of Gold.* 1989, Ivy Books paper $4.95 (0-8041-0363-1). A chronicle of the events surrounding the separation and reunion of a middle-aged English couple. (REV: Choice 4/76; LJ 10/1/75; Newsweek 11/17/75. AWARDS: ALA, 1975)

7581 Drabble, Margaret. *Waterfall.* 1986, NAL paper $8.95 (0-452-26192-9). A story of the love affair between a recently separated English woman and the husband of her cousin. (REV: Choice 3/70; LJ 9/1/69; TLS 5/22/69)

7582 Duberstein, Larry. *Marriage Hearse.* 1987, Permanent Pr. $17.95 (0-932966-76-4); Dell paper $4.50 (0-440-20195-0). The first part of a trilogy about a middle-aged writer contemplating leaving his wife and family for a younger woman. (REV: BL 5/15/87; NYTBR 5/10/87; PW 3/13/87)

7583 Dubus, Andre. *The Last Worthless Evening: Four Novellas and Two Short Stories.* 1986, Godine $15.95 (0-87923-642-6); Crown paper $8.95 (0-517-56625-2). A collection of four novellas and two short stories, including "Rose" and "Dressed Like Summer Leaves." "The majesty of these pieces remains long after the reader closes the book."—PW (REV: BL 12/1/86; PW 10/17/86; Time 11/10/86. AWARDS: ALA, 1986)

7584 Dubus, Andre. *Voices from the Moon.* 1985, Crown paper $6.95 (0-517-55846-7). A short novel by the noted short story writer regarding a father's love and engagement to his son's former wife. (REV: BL 9/15/84; LJ 10/1/84; PW 7/13/84)

7585 Dukore, Margaret Mitchell. *Bloom.* 1987, Dell paper $4.95 (0-440-30632-9). A woman from an entertainment industry family searches for her personal identity in Hollywood and Hawaii. (REV: BL 9/1/85; LJ 10/1/85; PW 8/23/85)

7586 Duncan, Robert Lipscomb. *In the Enemy Camp.* 1985, Delacorte $15.95 (0-385-29388-7). Terrorists attempt to take over Indonesia's petroleum industry in this thriller set in contemporary Southeast Asia. (REV: BL 6/1/85; LJ 6/1/85; PW 4/26/85)

7587 Dunn, Katherine. *Geek Love.* 1989, Knopf $18.95 (0-394-56902-4); Warner paper $9.95 (0-446-39130-1). The tale of a family of freaks purposely created for exhibition by their carnival-owner parents. "A brilliant, suspenseful, heartbreaking tour de force."—PW (REV: BL 3/15/89; LJ 3/15/89; PW 1/13/89. AWARDS: PW, 1989)

7588 Dunne, Dominick. *People Like Us.* 1988, Crown $19.95 (0-517-58024-1); Bantam paper $5.95 (0-553-25891-5). A portrait of society life in Manhattan during the 1980s leading to a climatic ball, by the author of *The Two Mrs. Grenvilles.* (REV: BL 6/15/88; NYTBR 7/10/88; PW 5/13/88)

7589 Dunne, Dominick. *Two Mrs. Grenvilles.* 1985, Crown $14.95 (0-517-55713-4); Bantam paper $5.95 (0-553-25891-5). This story of the son of a wealthy family accidentally shot to death by his wife was based on the 1955 Woodward murder case. (REV: BL 6/1/85; LJ 7/85; PW 5/17/85)

7590 Dunne, John Gregory. *Dutch Shea, Jr.* 1983, Pocket paper $3.95 (0-671-46170-2). A portrait of the life of a divorced embezzling Irish defense attorney in Hartford whose daughter has been blown up in an IRA terrorist attack in London. (REV: BL 2/15/82; LJ 4/1/82; Time 3/29/82)

7591 Dunne, John Gregory. *Red, White and Blue.* 1988, St. Martin's paper $4.95 (0-312-90965-9). A portrait of America from the 1960s to the 1980s is depicted through the life of a journalist with family political connections and a wife with leftist sympathies. "An insightfully provocative slice of Americana."—BL (REV: BL 1/15/87; PW 1/30/87; TLS 10/16/87)

7592 Duranti, Francesca. *Happy Ending.* 1991, Random $17.95 (0-394-57548-2). An Italian novelist portrays the intricate sex lives of a Tuscan family. (REV: LJ 1/91; NYTBR 2/24/91; PW 12/7/90)

7593 Duras, Marguerite. *Blue Eyes, Black Hair.* 1988, Pantheon $13.95 (0-394-56320-4); Random paper $6.95 (0-679-72280-7). The tale of the meeting of two French bisexual lovers and their reasons for mutual attraction. (REV: BL 2/15/88; LJ 3/1/88; PW 1/22/88)

7594 Duras, Marguerite. *Emily L.* 1989, Pantheon $15.95 (0-394-57233-5); paper $7.95 (0-679-72901-1). A story of a French woman in a failing affair plagued by an unfinished poem from her youth. "A volume that confirms Duras's reputation as a master."— PW (REV: BL 4/15/89; NYTBR 5/28/89; PW 2/24/89)

7595 Durrenmatt, Friedrich. *Assignment: On Observing the Observer of the Observers.* **1988, Random $14.95 (0-394-56010-8); paper $7.95 (0-679-72233-5).** A psychiatrist hires a filmmaker to trace the steps of his murdered wife by using her journal to uncover the mysteries behind her death. (REV: CSM 6/3/88; LJ 4/15/88; NYTBR 6/12/88)

7596 Eberstadt, Fernanda. *Isaac and His Devils.* **1991, Knopf $22.00 (0-394-58496-1).** A fictional study tracing the coming of age of a New England mathematical genius. "A rich novel, full of promise for the author's future."—LJ (REV: BL 4/1/91; LJ 3/15/91; PW 2/15/91)

7597 Eco, Umberto. *Foucault's Pendulum.* **1989, Harcourt $22.95 (0-15-132765-3).** An Italian historian researching the history of the medieval Knights Templar discovers a long-hidden plan designed to release supernatural powers to rule the world. "Even more intricate and absorbing than . . . *The Name of the Rose.*"—Time (REV: BL 9/15/89; NYTBR 10/15/89; PW 9/8/89. AWARDS: BL, 1989; NYTBR, 1989; PW, 1989)

7598 Edgerton, Clyde. *Floatplane Notebooks.* **1988, Algonquin $16.95 (0-945575-00-9); Ballantine paper $4.95 (0-345-35984-4).** A chronicle of the annual meetings of a Southern family over the course of 15 years by the author of *Walking Across Egypt.* (REV: BL 9/1/88; LJ 10/1/88; PW 7/1/88. AWARDS: PW, 1988)

7599 Edgerton, Clyde. *Killer Diller.* **1991, Algonquin $17.95 (0-945575-53-X).** Twenty-four-year-old Wesley Benfield, a mischievous delinquent introduced in the author's *Walking Across Egypt,* deals with life at a halfway house in North Carolina. (REV: BL 2/1/91; LJ 2/1/91; PW 12/21/90)

7600 Edgerton, Clyde. *Raney.* **1985, Algonquin $12.95 (0-912697-17-2); Bantam paper $4.95 (0-345-32982-1).** A humorous tale chronicling the first two years of marriage between a conservative North Carolinian and a liberal Georgian. (REV: BL 2/1/85; LJ 4/1/85; PW 1/4/85)

7601 Edgerton, Clyde. *Walking Across Egypt.* **1987, Algonquin $14.95 (0-912697-51-2); Ballantine paper $4.95 (0-345-34649-1).** A portrait of a friendship between a Southern grandmother and a younger man. (REV: BL 3/15/87; LJ 3/15/87; PW 2/6/87)

7602 Edmonds, Walter D. *South African Quirt.* **1985, Little, Brown $14.95 (0-316-21153-2).** A portrait of the struggle of wills between an abusive father and his preteen son. "A pleasure to read."— LJ (REV: BL 3/1/85; LJ 3/15/85; Newsweek 5/13/85)

7603 Edwards-Yearwood, Grace. *In the Shadow of the Peacock.* **1988, McGraw-Hill $17.95 (0-07-019037-2); Ivy Books paper $3.95 (0-8041-0419-0).** A portrait of the lives of three women in Harlem from the 1940s to the 1960s centering on the social life of the neighborhood bar dubbed "The Peacock." (REV: CSM 6/17/88; NYTBR 5/22/88; PW 1/8/88)

7604 Ehrlichman, John. *China Card.* **1987, Warner paper $4.50 (0-446-34577-6).** The former Nixon aide tells a fictional story of a China expert's secret negotiations prior to Kissinger's historic trip. (REV: BL 5/15/86; LJ 7/86)

7605 Eisenstadt, Jill. *From Rockaway.* **1987, Knopf $15.95 (0-394-55970-3); Random paper $6.95 (0-394-75761-0).** The story of the lives of four Irish-American teens after high school in Rockaway, New York, set in the early 1980s. (REV: BL 9/1/87; LJ 9/15/87; PW 8/7/87)

7606 Eliade, Mircea. *Youth Without Youth: And Other Novellas.* **1988, Ohio State Univ. Pr. $18.95 (0-8142-0457-0).** Three surrealistic novellas by the Rumanian writer and religious scholar written during the 1970s. Includes "The Cape," "Nineteen Roses," and the title story. (REV: BL 6/15/88; LJ 7/88; NYTBR 3/5/88)

7607 Elkin, Stanley. *Living End.* **1985, Dutton paper $7.95 (0-525-48158-3).** A murdered Minneapolis shopkeeper is sent to hell after his death. "Will surely be celebrated as a minor classic."—TLS (REV: BL 7/1/79; LJ 5/1/79; TLS 1/18/80)

7608 Elkin, Stanley. *The MacGuffin.* **1991, Simon & Schuster $19.95 (0-671-67324-6).** A street commissioner of an unnamed American city convinces himself that there is a conspiracy underway to remove him from office in this novel by the author of *The Living End.* (REV: BL 1/1/91; LJ 2/1/91; PW 1/16/91)

7609 Elkin, Stanley. *Rabbi of Lud.* **1987, Macmillan $17.95 (0-684-18902-X); paper $8.95 (0-684-19013-3).** A portrait of the life of a New Jersey rabbi and his congregation by the author of *The MacGuffin.* (REV: BL 9/15/87; PW 9/11/87)

7610 Ellis, Bret Easton. *Less Than Zero.* **1987, Penguin paper $3.95 (0-14-010927-7).** A debut novel portraying the empty and decadent lives of a group of Southern California friends on Christmas break from college. (REV: Newsweek 7/8/85; PW 4/12/85; Sat Rev 7–8/85)

7611 Ellison, Emily. *Picture Makers.* **1990, Morrow $18.95 (0-688-09581-X).** The story of an artist and his family set in Georgia and South Carolina from 1967 to 1988. (REV: BL 6/15/90; LJ 6/1/90; NYTBR 10/14/90)

7612 Elman, Richard. *Tar Beach.* **1991, Sun & Moon $12.95 (1-55713-117-1).** A chronicle of an uneventful day in the life of a Jewish boy in Brooklyn set in the year 1947. (REV: NYTBR 12/15/91; PW 11/29/91)

7613 Emecheta, Buchi. *Double Yoke.* **1983, Braziller paper $6.95 (0-8076-1128-X).** A young African woman is forced to choose between her boyfriend and her academic career in this novel by an African-born writer who lives in London. (REV: LJ 8/83; New Yorker 4/23/84; PW 7/1/83)

7614 Emecheta, Buchi. *Family.* **1990, Braziller $17.95 (0-8076-1245-6); paper $8.95 (0-8076-1250-2).** A

Jamaican girl, in search of a better life, makes her way to London to join her parents who left her with her grandmother on a Caribbean island. "A fine addition to any library."—LJ (Rev: BL 2/1/90; LJ 3/1/90; NYTBR 4/29/90)

7615   Enchi, Fumiko. *Masks*. 1983, Random paper $7.95 (0-394-72218-3). A Japanese woman serves as a medium for ancestral spirits in this novel originally published in Japan in 1959. (Rev: BL 5/15/83; LJ 4/15/83; PW 3/4/83)

7616   Endo, Shusaku. *Scandal*. 1988, Dufour $28.00 (0-7206-0682-9); Random paper $8.95 (0-679-72355-2). A writer attempts to clear his name of scandalous activities performed by a double in this novel by the author of *The Samurai*. (Rev: New Yorker 3/6/89; PW 6/10/88; TLS 4/29/88)

7617   Engel, Monroe. *Fish*. 1985, Univ. of Chicago Pr. paper $6.95 (0-226-20835-4). A Boston man in a midlife crisis seeks escape from his personal responsibilities following his divorce and the death of his father. (Rev: BL 11/1/81; LJ 10/15/81; PW 7/31/81)

7618   Ephron, Nora. *Heartburn*. 1985, Pocket paper $3.95 (0-671-60316-7). The fictional memoirs of a cookbook writer focusing on the events that led her two marriages to failure. (Rev: BL 3/15/83; NYTBR 4/24/83; Time 4/11/83)

7619   Erdrich, Louise. *Beet Queen*. 1986, Henry Holt $16.95 (0-8050-0058-5); Bantam paper $8.95 (0-553-34723-3). A chronicle of four decades in the lives of three North Dakota orphans by the author of *Love Medicine* and *Tracks*. (Rev: LJ 8/86; NYTBR 8/31/86; PW 7/4/86. Awards: ALA, 1986; LJ, 1986; PW, 1986)

7620   Erdrich, Louise. *Love Medicine*. 1985, Bantam paper $8.95 (0-553-34423-4). The story of the lives of two families of Chippewa Indians traced over five decades. (Rev: BL 9/1/84; NYTBR 12/23/84; TLS 2/22/85. Awards: ALA, 1984; BL, the 1980s; NYTBR, 1985)

7621   Erdrich, Louise. *Tracks*. 1988, Henry Holt $18.95 (0-8050-0895-0); Harper & Row paper $8.95 (0-06-097245-9). The story of a band of Chippewa Indians struggling against internal and external forces to save their land and culture. (Rev: Choice 12/88; LJ 9/1/88; PW 7/22/88. Awards: ALA, 1988; LJ, 1988; PW, 1988)

7622   Erickson, Steve. *Tours of the Black Clock*. 1989, Poseidon $18.95 (0-671-64921-3). A mythical narrative examining the nature of evil in the world and Hitler's place in history. (Rev: BL 1/1/89; PW 11/11/88; TLS 7/28/89)

7623   Estaver, Paul. *His Third, Her Second*. 1989, Soho Pr. $17.95 (0-939149-25-7). A chronicle of the life of a Washington, D.C., family. "A thoroughly engaging first novel with an enormous range."—NYTBR (Rev: NYTBR 4/2/89; PW 2/24/89)

7624   Exley, Frederick. *Last Notes from Home*. 1988, Random $18.95 (0-394-40519-6); paper $8.95 (0-679-72456-7). This concluding volume in the trilogy that began with *A Fan's Notes* and *Pages from a*

Cold Island concerns the fictionalized Fred Exley's relationship with his dying older brother. (Rev: BL 9/1/88; Time 10/24/88)

7625   Fast, Howard. *Confession of Joe Cullen*. 1989, Houghton $18.95 (0-395-50936-X); Dell paper $5.95 (0-440-20669-3). A man's confession concerning the death of a Honduran priest leads to a drug- and arms-running scheme involving Contras and government officials. (Rev: BL 6/15/89; LJ 5/15/89)

7626   Fast, Howard. *The Outsider*. 1985, Dell paper $3.95 (0-440-16778-7). This story of a man who becomes a rabbi in a small Connecticut town traces his life from the end of World War II through the 1960s. "A thoughtful, at times touching story."—NYTBR (Rev: BL 6/1/84; LJ 6/15/84; NYTBR 9/23/84)

7627   Feinberg, David. *Eighty-Sixed*. 1989, Viking $18.95 (0-670-82315-5); Penguin paper $7.95 (0-14-011252-9). A portrait of the gay community's reaction to the AIDS epidemic focusing on one man's life during the 1970s and 1980s. "A harrowing first-person account."—NYTBR (Rev: BL 12/15/88; LJ 11/1/88; NYTBR 2/26/89)

7628   Feinberg, David. *Spontaneous Combustion*. 1991, Viking $19.95 (0-670-83813-6). A collection of interconnected stories about the life of a gay man who has tested HIV-positive. "Perhaps the best sustained work of gay male humor ever published."—BL (Rev: BL 9/15/91; NYTBR 11/17/91)

7629   Ferrell, Anderson. *Where She Was*. 1985, Knopf $13.95 (0-394-53521-9); Pocket paper $6.95 (0-671-62438-5). The portrait of a couple's life on a North Carolina tobacco farm. "At its best this book has the power to transport us to a world that resonates with mystery."—NYTBR (Rev: BL 10/15/85; Newsweek 11/11/85; NYTBR 11/24/85)

7630   Fields, Jeff. *Cry of Angels*. 1979, Ballantine paper $2.95 (0-345-28204-3). A portrayal of the life of a Georgia teenage orphan living in a convalescent hospital with his great aunt. "A novel to touch the soul and cheer the heart."—LJ (Rev: BL 7/15/74; CSM 6/5/74; LJ 6/1/74)

7631   Figes, Eva. *Ghosts*. 1988, Pantheon $16.95 (0-394-57159-2). The author of *Nelly's Version* chronicles a year in the life of an aging woman filled with reflections on the people she has known. (Rev: BL 8/88; NYTBR 9/25/88; TLS 6/3/88)

7632   Figes, Eva. *Waking*. 1983, Pantheon paper $7.95 (0-394-72227-2). A novel consisting of seven chapters, each portraying a key event in the life of the narrator. "A sorrowful and often beautifully written work that raises painful questions about women's place in the family and society."—TLS (Rev: BL 4/1/82; LJ 4/15/82; TLS 1/23/81)

7633   Finney, Ernest J. *Winterchill*. 1989, Morrow $16.95 (0-688-08305-6). The story of the fate of a group of California plum farmers tracing their lives from the 1950s to the 1980s. "Those who enjoy John Steinbeck and William Faulkner will find much pleasure in Finney's novel."—LJ (Rev: LJ 2/15/89; PW 12/9/88)

7634 Fisher, Carrie. *Postcards from the Edge.* **1990, Pocket paper $4.95 (0-671-72473-8).** The story of a Hollywood motion picture actress in a substance abuse rehabilitation clinic with other members of her profession. (Rev: BL 6/15/87; LJ 8/87; Time 8/24/87)

7635 Fitzgerald, Penelope. *Innocence.* **1987, Henry Holt $16.95 (0-8050-0373-8); Carroll & Graf paper $7.95 (0-88184-537-X).** A novel set in Italy during the 1950s about a young English woman who moves in with an artistocratic Florentine family. (Rev: BL 3/1/87; NYTBR 5/10/87; PW 3/6/87)

7636 Fitzgerald, Penelope. *Offshore.* **1987, Henry Holt $15.95 (0-8050-0561-7); Carroll & Graf paper $7.95 (0-88184-476-4).** This study of the lives of a group of people living on barges in the Thames was awarded Britain's prestigious Booker Prize. (Rev: BL 10/1/87; New Yorker 1/11/88; PW 7/17/87)

7637 Flanagan, Mary. *Trust.* **1989, Random paper $8.95 (0-679-72281-5).** The story of a couple's custody battle for their daughter and of a trust fund set up by the child's mother. (Rev: BL 4/15/88; NYTBR 5/8/88; PW 2/26/88)

7638 Flynt, Candace. *Mother Love.* **1987, Farrar $18.95 (0-374-21374-7); NAL paper $7.95 (0-452-26076-0).** A story of three North Carolina sisters and their relationship with their mother. "A delightful novel, a work of enormous beauty and psychological insight."—NYTBR (Rev: BL 5/1/87; LJ 5/1/87; NYTBR 6/28/87)

7639 Ford, Elaine. *Monkey Bay.* **1989, Viking $17.95 (0-670-82752-2); Penguin paper $7.95 (0-14-012057-2).** A Maine woman living with an irresponsible boyfriend finds her life disrupted when her 22-year-old daughter returns from California to live with her. (Rev: BL 6/1/89; NYTBR 8/6/89; PW 6/9/89)

7640 Ford, Richard. *Sportswriter.* **1986, Random paper $6.95 (0-394-74325-3).** A portrait of a sportswriter left on his own following his divorce and the death of his eldest son. "One of the best writers of his generation."—Newsweek (Rev: Newsweek 4/7/86; PW 2/21/86; Time 3/24/86)

7641 Ford, Richard. *Ultimate Good Luck.* **1987, Random paper $5.95 (0-394-75089-6).** An American Vietnam veteran travels to Mexico in an effort to release his girlfriend's brother held in an Oaxacan jail on drug charges. (Rev: NYTBR 5/31/81; Newsweek 5/11/81; PW 3/13/81)

7642 Ford, Richard. *Wildlife.* **1990, Atlantic Monthly $18.95 (0-87113-348-2).** A teenager watches his family fall apart in this novel set in Great Falls, Montana, in the early 1960s. (Rev: BL 6/1/90; LJ 6/1/90; Time 6/4/90)

7643 Forsyth, Frederick. *Day of the Jackal.* **1982, Bantam paper $5.95 (0-553-26630-6).** Internal French security forces plot to assassinate Charles de Gaulle using a hit man known as the Jackal.

(Rev: LJ 9/1/71; New Yorker 8/28/71; TLS 7/2/71. Awards: Edgar, 1971)

7644 Forsyth, Frederick. *Negotiator.* **1989, Bantam $19.95 (0-553-05361-2).** A group of United States and Soviet conspirators plot to kidnap the son of the president to delay the passage of a treaty that would limit both nations' ambitions to gain power in the Middle East. (Rev: BL 3/15/89; Newsweek 4/24/89)

7645 Fowles, John. *The Magus.* **1978, Little, Brown $19.95 (0-316-29092-0); Dell paper $5.95 (0-440-35162-6).** This second novel by the English author concerns the experiences of a British teacher in Greece. (Rev: BL 2/1/66; Choice 9/66; NYTBR 1/9/66. Awards: NYTBR, 1966)

7646 Fowles, John. *Mantissa.* **1982, Little, Brown $16.95 (0-316-28980-9); NAL paper $7.95 (0-452-25429-9).** The fictional analysis of a writer's creative processes and sexual obsessions by the author of *Daniel Martin.* (Rev: Atl 11/82; BL 7/82; New Yorker 9/13/82)

7647 Fox, Paula. *God of Nightmares.* **1990, North Point $18.95 (0-86547-432-X).** A young woman moves from her New York home to the New Orleans French Quarter following the death of her father in this novel set during the early 1940s. (Rev: BL 3/1/90; NYTBR 7/8/90; PW 2/2/90)

7648 Fox, Paula. *A Servant's Tale.* **1984, North Point $16.50 (0-86547-164-9); Penguin paper $6.95 (0-14-008386-3).** A Caribbean-born maid in her late 40s leaves her New York job to return to her home island. (Rev: BL 9/1/84; LJ 9/1/84; PW 6/29/84)

7649 Fox, Paula. *Widow's Children.* **1986, North Point paper $9.95 (0-86547-251-3).** The account of a bon voyage party with five persons in attendance. "The most elegant exploration I have read of the chaos of modern life."—New Rep (Rev: BL 9/15/76; CSM 10/22/76; New Rep 1/15/77)

7650 Frame, Janet. *Living in the Maniototo.* **1979, Brazilier $8.95 (0-8076-0926-9); paper $4.95 (0-8076-0958-7).** The story of a New Zealand writer who inherits a California home while in the process of writing a novel. (Rev: New Yorker 9/17/79; PW 6/18/79; Time 8/6/79)

7651 Frame, Ronald. *Sandmouth.* **1988, Knopf $19.95 (0-394-56357-3).** A depiction of life in an English coastal community in a novel containing dozens of characters. (Rev: BL 1/1/88; LJ 1/88; PW 11/27/87)

7652 Francisco, Patricia Weaver. *Cold Feet.* **1988, Simon & Schuster $18.95 (0-671-63165-9).** A former draft-dodger returns to the United States from Canada to find his friends and family changed. (Rev: BL 11/15/88; LJ 11/15/88)

7653 Franks, Lucinda. *Wild Apples.* **1991, Random $20.00 (0-394-57578-4).** This journalist's first novel portrays the lives of a pair of sisters left to tend their family's New York apple farm after the death of their mother. (Rev: LJ 6/1/91; PW 6/28/91)

7654 **Franzen, Jonathan.** *Strong Motion.* 1992, Farrar $21.95 (0-374-27105-4). This second novel by the author of *The Twenty-Seventh City* concerns the love relationship of a seismologist as Boston is struck by a series of mysterious earthquakes. (REV: BL 12/1/91; LJ 11/15/91)

7655 **Franzen, Jonathan.** *Twenty-Seventh City.* 1988, Farrar $19.95 (0-374-27972-1); Avon paper $8.95 (0-380-70840-X). An Indian woman with terrorist sympathies is selected to head the St. Louis Police Department in this author's debut novel. (REV: BL 9/1/88; LJ 11/1/88; New Yorker 12/19/88)

7656 **Frayn, Michael.** *The Trick of It.* 1990, Viking $17.95 (0-670-82985-4). A college professor tells the story of his relationship with his famous writer wife through a series of letters to a friend. "As wickedly funny as it is intelligent and perceptive . . . a reader's delight."—PW (REV: BL 2/15/90; NYTBR 3/18/90; PW 1/5/90)

7657 **Freed, Lynn.** *Home Ground.* 1987, Penguin paper $7.95 (0-14-008948-9). A chronicle of the experiences of a Jewish girl growing up in South Africa during the 1950s. (REV: BL 8/86; LJ 8/86; TLS 5/9/86)

7658 **Freeman, Judith.** *Chinchilla Farm.* 1989, Norton $19.95 (0-393-02722-8); Random paper $9.95 (0-679-73052-4). After her husband leaves her, a Utah woman heads for Los Angeles and ends up living in the ghetto. "A beautifully written, quietly humorous, affecting realistic novel that captures the feel of the West."—CSM (REV: BL 9/15/89; CSM 6/1/90; NYTBR 12/17/89)

7659 **Fremlin, Celia.** *Possession.* 1985, Academy Chicago paper $4.95 (0-89733-169-9). The story of an English woman's obsession with a young man slated to be her son-in-law. (REV: NYTBR 10/19/69; TLS 7/3/69. AWARDS: ALA, 1992)

7660 **French, Marilyn.** *Her Mother's Daughter.* 1988, Ballantine paper $5.95 (0-345-35362-5). This novel chronicles four generations of New York women and their relations with their mothers and daughters by the author of *The Women's Room.* (REV: BL 7/87; LJ 10/15/87; PW 9/11/87)

7661 **French, Marilyn.** *The Women's Room.* 1988, Ballantine paper $5.95 (0-345-35361-7). The chronicle of a middle-aged woman's awakening to social injustice toward females in contemporary society. (REV: NYTBR 10/16/77; PW 8/29/77. AWARDS: ALA, 1977)

7662 **Frisch, Max.** *Bluebeard.* 1984, Harcourt paper $3.95 (0-15-613198-6). The self-examination of a doctor accused and acquitted of murdering his former wife. "A stylistically superb, chilling portrait of human guilt and its destructive powers."—PW (REV: LJ 6/1/83; NYTBR 7/10/83; PW 6/10/83)

7663 **Frisch, Max.** *Man in the Holocene.* 1981, Harcourt paper $4.95 (0-15-656952-3). A Swiss widower reads a series of books and ponders the meaning of human existence. "Profound, courageous and stoic in response, this book will no doubt be considered a masterpiece."—CSM (REV: CSM 8/20/80; LJ 8/80; PW 5/9/80)

7664 **Frucht, Abby.** *Snap.* 1988, Ticknor & Fields $17.95 (0-89919-501-6). The debut novel by a winner of the Iowa Short Fiction Award chronicling the lives and misunderstandings of two contemporary married couples. (REV: NYTBR 4/24/88; PW 12/18/87)

7665 **Fuentes, Carlos.** *Christopher Unborn.* 1989, Farrar $22.95 (0-374-12334-9); Random paper $12.95 (0-679-73222-5). The story told by a fetus waiting to be born into a Mexico fraught with environmental and political problems. (REV: LJ 10/1/89; NYTBR 8/20/89; TLS 12/15/89. AWARDS: LJ, 1989)

7666 **Fuentes, Carlos.** *Distant Relations.* 1982, Farrar $11.95 (0-374-14082-0); paper $8.95 (0-374-51813-0). A Parisian nobleman journeys to Latin America to solve mysteries surrounding his youth and ancestry. (REV: BL 3/15/82; LJ 3/15/82; PW 2/19/82)

7667 **Fugard, Athol.** *Tsotsi.* 1983, Penguin paper $5.95 (0-14-006272-6). A novel by the South African playwright regarding a petty thief who finds meaning in his life after adopting an abandoned baby. (REV: LJ 4/1/81; NYTBR 2/1/81; TLS 5/2/80)

7668 **Fust, Milan.** *Story of My Wife: The Reminiscences of Captain Storr.* 1987, PAJ $18.95 (1-55554-018-X); Random paper $8.95 (0-679-72217-3). Fictional memoirs of a Dutch sea captain recalling his life with his French wife. First published in Hungary in 1957 and containing a preface by George Konrad. (REV: NYTBR 3/6/88; PW 11/20/87)

7669 **Gaddis, William.** *Carpenter's Gothic.* 1985, Viking $16.95 (0-670-69793-1); Penguin paper $6.95 (0-14-008993-4). An abusive Vietnam veteran attempts to parlay his wife's inheritance into a fortune in this novel by the author of *The Recognitions.* (REV: LJ 7/85; NYTBR 7/7/85; PW 5/24/85. AWARDS: PW, 1985)

7670 **Gaines, Ernest J.** *A Gathering of Old Men.* 1983, Knopf $17.95 (0-394-51468-8); Random paper $4.95 (0-394-72591-3). The murder of a Cajun sharecropper leads 17 African-American men and one white woman to plead guilty to the crime. (REV: CSM 12/2/83; LJ 8/83; NYTBR 10/30/83)

7671 **Gaite, Carmen Martin.** *Back Room.* 1983, Columbia Univ. Pr. $24.50 (0-231-05458-0). A Spanish novelist's portrait of a girl's life under the Franco regime as recounted to an interviewer. (REV: Choice 5/84; LJ 12/1/83; PW 10/14/83)

7672 **Gaitskill, Mary.** *Two Girls, Fat and Thin.* 1991, Poseidon $18.95 (0-671-68540-6). Two women brought together by their interest in a a religious cult become friends and share secrets of their mental and physical abuse as children. (REV: BL 2/15/91; LJ 2/1/91; NYTBR 2/17/91)

7673 **Galbraith, John Kenneth.** *A Tenured Professor.* 1990, Houghton $19.95 (0-395-47100-1). A tale of a Harvard professor whose economic theories lead his family to vast riches. (REV: Atl 3/90; BL 11/15/89; LJ 1/90)

7674　Galgut, Damon. *A Sinless Season.* **1985, Penguin paper $5.95 (0-14-007077-X).** A South African writer's portrait of the lives of three young men held in a juvenile detention facility. (REV: BL 4/1/85; NYTBR 3/31/85; PW 3/1/85)

7675　Ganesan, Indira. *The Journey.* **1990, Knopf $18.95 (0-394-56838-9).** An Indian emigré family returns to its native island off the coast of India for a funeral after living for a decade in the United States. "A lyrical and spell-casting debut."—BL (REV: BL 5/15/90; LJ 5/15/90; New Yorker 9/17/90)

7676　Garcia Marquez, Gabriel. *Autumn of the Patriarch.* **1977, Avon paper $4.95 (0-380-01774-1).** A portrait of the reign of a despotic Latin American ruler told in reverse chronological order by the Colombian novelist. (REV: LJ 11/15/76; NYTBR 10/31/76; Time 11/1/76. AWARDS: ALA, 1976; NYTBR, 1976; Time, 1976)

7677　Garcia Marquez, Gabriel. *Chronicle of a Death Foretold.* **1983, Knopf $18.95 (0-394-53074-8); Ballantine paper $5.95 (0-345-31002-0).** Garcia Marquez re-creates the events leading to a murder as retold three decades after the death. "A fine introduction to the 1982 Nobel Prize winner."—LJ (REV: BL 3/1/83; LJ 4/1/83; NYBR 4/14/83. AWARDS: ALA, 1983; NYTBR, 1983; Time, 1983)

7678　Garcia Marquez, Gabriel. *Collected Novellas.* **1990, HarperCollins $22.95 (0-06-016384-4).** This collection includes the formerly published novellas "Leaf Storm," "No One Writes to the Colonel," and "Chronicle of a Death Foretold." (REV: BL 9/15/90; LJ 9/15/90)

7679　Garcia Marquez, Gabriel. *In Evil Hour.* **1980, Avon paper $4.95 (0-380-52167-9).** A novel written during the 1950s by the Colombian Nobel laureate about the residents of a small Latin American town whose sins are broadcast by a person who posts notes detailing their most intimate exploits. (REV: LJ 10/15/79; NYTBR 11/11/79; PW 7/30/79)

7680　Garcia Marquez, Gabriel. *One Hundred Years of Solitude.* **1970, Harper & Row $28.00 (0-06-011418-5); Avon paper $4.95 (0-380-01503-X).** The story of the Buendia family and their role in the history of the city of Macondo. (REV: LJ 2/15/70; Sat Rev 3/7/70; Time 3/16/70. AWARDS: ALA, 1970; Time, 1970; Time, the 1970s)

7681　Gardiner, John Rolfe. *In the Heart of the Whole World.* **1988, Knopf $17.95 (0-394-56901-6).** A Virginia secondary schoolteacher becomes obsessed with one of his young female students. (REV: LJ 10/1/88; NYTBR 10/2/88; PW 8/26/88)

7682　Gardner, John. *Micklesson's Ghosts.* **1989, Random paper $9.95 (0-679-72308-0).** A New York professor in his 50s and in the midst of a divorce moves to rural Pennsylvania where he becomes obsessed with a local teenage girl. (REV: LJ 5/15/82; PW 4/9/82; TLS 10/22/82)

7683　Gardner, John. *October Light.* **1989, Random paper $8.95 (0-679-72133-9).** A crazed Vermont farmer imprisons his sister in an attic where she reads a paperback novel incorporated into this story. (REV: Choice 3/77; NYTBR 12/26/76; Time 12/20/76. AWARDS: ALA, 1976; NYTBR, 1976; Time, 1976)

7684　Gardner, John. *Sunlight Dialogues.* **1987, Random paper $6.95 (0-394-74394-6).** A depiction of the efforts of a small-town upstate New York police chief to capture a murderous criminal dubbed the Sunlight Man. (REV: BL 2/15/73; LJ 9/1/72; Time 1/1/73. AWARDS: ALA, 1972; Time, 1972)

7685　Gardner, Martin. *Flight of Peter Fromm.* **1989, Farrar paper $8.95 (0-374-52187-5).** An account of the spiritual development of divinity school teacher Peter Fromm. (REV: BL 3/1/74; LJ 9/15/73; NYTBR 12/23/73)

7686　Garfield, Brian. *Death Wish.* **1990, Bantam paper $3.95 (0-553-28326-X).** This tale of a New Yorker who becomes a vigilante following the murder of his wife was the basis of the popular Charles Bronson film. (REV: BL 12/1/72; NYTBR 10/8/72)

7687　Garnett, Henrietta. *Family Skeletons.* **1987, Knopf $15.95 (0-317-58075-2).** This author's debut novel details the life of an orphan raised by her uncle in a remote part of Ireland. (REV: BL 3/15/87; LJ 3/1/87)

7688　Gaskin, Catherine. *Ambassador's Woman.* **1990, Avon paper $4.95 (0-380-70174-X).** A story tracing several decades of friendship between a wealthy American woman and an upper-class English woman of limited fortune. (REV: BL 3/15/86; LJ 3/1/86; NYTBR 5/18/86)

7689　Gebler, Carlo. *Eleventh Summer.* **1985, Dutton $13.95 (0-525-24331-3).** A study of the effects of a mother's suicide upon a preteen boy who is forced to live with his grandparents following the incident. (REV: BL 9/15/85; PW 8/9/85)

7690　Gebler, Carlo. *Work and Play.* **1988, St. Martin's $12.95 (0-312-01847-9); Simon & Schuster paper $7.95 (0-671-68417-5).** A Dublin-born college dropout returns to London to continue a bohemian way of life after being left out of his late father's will. (REV: BL 4/15/88; PW 3/4/88; TLS 7/3/87)

7691　Gee, Maggie. *Christopher and Alexandra.* **1991, Ticknor & Fields $19.95 (0-395-60484-2).** A story of two middle-aged lovers who give up their former lives and families to travel together. "An engrossing story well told."—LJ (REV: BL 2/1/92; LJ 1/92; PW 12/13/91)

7692　Gess, Denise. *Red Whiskey Blues.* **1989, Crown $17.95 (0-517-55990-0).** A New Jersey widow recovering from the death of her husband falls in love with a divorced playwright. (REV: BL 2/15/89; LJ 3/1/89; PW 12/23/88)

7693　Ghose, Zulfikar. *A Different World.* **1985, Overlook $22.50 (0-87951-982-7).** The story of twentieth-century Brazilian politics concerning a man torn between his allegiance to an oppressive government and a band of guerrilla warriors bent on revolution. (REV: LJ 4/1/85; PW 12/7/84)

7694 Ghosh, Amitav. *Circle of Reason.* **1986, Viking $17.95 (0-670-80984-5); Penguin paper $8.95 (0-670-82633-2).** An Indian artist falsely accused of terrorist activities is chased from the subcontinent through the Arab world in this writer's debut novel. (REV: BL 6/1/86; Choice 3/87; PW 5/9/86)

7695 Ghosh, Amitav. *Shadow Lines.* **1989, Viking $17.95 (0-670-82633-2); Penguin paper $7.95 (0-14-011835-7).** A Bengali boy tells the story of his life in prepartition India and of his family's relations with English friends. (REV: LJ 5/1/89; New Rep 8/7/89; PW 4/7/89)

7696 Gibbons, Kaye. *Ellen Foster.* **1987, Algonquin $11.95 (0-912697-52-0); Random paper $8.95 (0-679-72866-X).** A Southern preteen girl is forced to live with her drunken father following the death of her mother. (REV: BL 9/1/87; LJ 4/15/87; New Rep 2/29/88)

7697 Gifford, Barry. *Sailor's Holiday: The Wild Life of Sailor and Lula.* **1991, Random $19.00 (0-394-40149-0).** This sequel to the author's *Wild at Heart* chronicles the further adventures of Sailor and Lula. (REV: BL 3/15/91; LJ 3/1/91; PW 2/1/91)

7698 Gifford, Barry. *Wild at Heart: The Story of Sailor and Lula.* **1990, Grove-Weidenfeld $17.95 (0-8021-1181-5).** A chronicle of the flight of an ex-convict and his girlfriend, whose mother has hired a private detective to track them down. (REV: BL 2/15/90; New Yorker 6/4/90; PW 1/12/90. AWARDS: BL, 1990)

7699 Gilchrist, Ellen. *Anna Papers.* **1988, Little, Brown $16.95 (0-316-31316-5).** The journals of a noted writer are found by her sister after her suicide in this novel by the author of the short story collection *Victory Over Japan.* (REV: LJ 11/1/88; PW 8/12/88)

7700 Gilchrist, Ellen. *I Cannot Get You Close Enough.* **1990, Little, Brown $17.95 (0-316-31313-6).** This collection of three novellas portrays the lives of members of a North Carolina family. "A thoroughly engaging work."—LJ (REV: BL 8/90; LJ 9/15/90; PW 8/17/90)

7701 Gill, John. *The Tenant.* **1985, Academy Chicago $14.95 (0-89733-142-7); paper $3.95 (0-89733-141-5).** The story of an English couple who film the wife's sexual encounters with tenants who rent their cottage until the husband loses his mind. "An amazingly polished first novel."—LJ (REV: BL 5/1/85; LJ 6/1/85)

7702 Giniger, Henry. *Reasons of the Heart.* **1987, Watts $16.95 (0-531-15047-X).** A debut novel portraying the friendship of an elderly ex-schoolteacher and a young drug dealer formed on the streets of Manhattan. (REV: LJ 3/1/87; NYTBR 4/19/87; PW 3/13/87)

7703 Ginzburg, Natalia. *City and the House.* **1987, Seaver $16.95 (0-8050-0392-4); Arcade paper $8.95 (1-55970-029-7).** Letters between family members in Italy and New Jersey chronicle their lives over a period of three years. (REV: BL 4/1/87; LJ 4/1/87; PW 4/17/87)

7704 Ginzburg, Natalia. *Family and Borghesia.* **1988, Henry Holt $15.95 (0-8050-0856-X).** Two novellas concerning death by the author of *Valentino and Sagittarius.* "Only confirms her position as one of Italy's best and most idiosyncratic writers."—NYTBR (REV: BL 10/15/88; NYTBR 1/1/89; PW 9/16/88)

7705 Ginzburg, Natalia. *Road to the City.* **1990, Arcade $16.95 (1-55970-052-1).** Two novellas describing the experiences of country people visiting Italian cities. (REV: LJ 3/1/90; New Yorker 7/16/90; PW 2/16/90)

7706 Ginzburg, Natalia. *Valentino and Sagittarius.* **1988, Henry Holt $17.95 (0-8050-0683-4).** Two novellas set after World War II dealing with the relationships of Italian daughters and their mothers. (REV: BL 2/15/88; LJ 3/1/88; PW 2/26/88)

7707 Ginzburg, Natalia. *Voices in the Evening.* **1989, Arcade $16.95 (1-55970-016-5).** This novel written in 1961 portrays the fortunes of a northern Italian businessman and his family during and after World War II. (REV: LJ 9/15/89; New Yorker 10/23/89; PW 8/25/89)

7708 Glaister, Lesley. *Honor Thy Father.* **1991, Macmillan $18.95 (0-689-12129-6).** In this debut novel, an elderly woman recounts the history of her family's troubles stemming from the actions of her father. (REV: BL 4/15/91; PW 3/22/91)

7709 Glasscock, Sarah. *Anna L. M. N. O.* **1988, Random $17.95 (0-394-55930-4).** This debut novel chronicles the life of a small-town West Texas hairdresser. "A powerful and affecting novel with complex, well-drawn characters."—LJ (REV: BL 11/15/88; LJ 11/15/88; PW 9/9/88)

7710 Glendinning, Victoria. *Grown-Ups.* **1989, Knopf $18.95 (0-394-57947-X).** The acclaimed British biographer's first novel examines the life of a despicable English writer and television host. (REV: LJ 12/89; NYTBR 1/7/90; PW 11/10/89)

7711 Glynn, Thomas. *The Building.* **1985, Knopf $18.95 (0-394-54582-6).** A portrait of a deteriorating Brooklyn slum building and its tenants. (REV: LJ 1/86; Time 12/30/85)

7712 Glynn, Thomas. *Watching the Body Burn.* **1989, Knopf $18.95 (0-394-57176-2).** A chronicle of the unpredictable life of a child with an alcoholic father in the years following World War II. (REV: Choice 6/89; LJ 12/88; PW 11/4/88)

7713 Godden, Rumer. *Peacock Spring.* **1986, Penguin paper $3.95 (0-14-032005-9).** An English diplomat brings his two daughters to India in order to live openly with their tutor. (REV: BL 1/1/76; Newsweek 4/12/76; Time 4/19/76)

7714 Godey, John. *Taking of Pelham One, Two, Three.* **1973, Amereon $19.95 (0-88411-649-2).** A New York City subway car is hijacked by four men who hold it for ransom pending payment of cash by the city's mayor. (REV: BL 5/1/73; LJ 3/1/73; NYTBR 3/4/73)

7715 Godwin, Gail. *Father Melancholy's Daughter.* **1991, Morrow $21.95 (0-688-06531-7).** An examination of the relationship between a Virginia minister and his daughter from her childhood to adolescence. "A sure success: essential for fiction collections."—LJ (Rev: BL 12/15/90; LJ 2/1/91; Time 3/25/91)

7716 Godwin, Gail. *Finishing School.* **1985, Viking $16.95 (0-670-31494-3); Avon paper $4.95 (0-380-69869-2).** The reflections of a woman concerning her teenage relationship with an older woman that shaped her early life. (Rev: New Rep 2/25/85; PW 11/23/84; Time 2/11/85. Awards: PW, 1985; Time, 1985)

7717 Godwin, Gail. *Glass People.* **1986, Penguin paper $6.95 (0-14-008222-0).** A disaffected California attorney reexamines her life during a visit to her mother's forest cabin. (Rev: BL 11/15/72; LJ 8/72; Sat Rev 10/28/72)

7718 Godwin, Gail. *A Mother and Two Daughters.* **1983, Avon paper $4.95 (0-380-61598-3).** A man's death causes his wife and two daughters to rearrange their lives in this novel set in North Carolina. (Rev: LJ 11/15/81; PW 12/4/81; Time 1/25/82)

7719 Godwin, Gail. *Odd Woman.* **1985, Penguin paper $7.95 (0-14-008221-2).** A portrait of the life of a North Carolina woman in the midst of an affair with a married New York art history professor. (Rev: CSM 11/20/74; NYTBR 10/20/74; PW 8/26/74. Awards: ALA, 1974)

7720 Godwin, Gail. *A Southern Family.* **1987, Morrow $18.95 (0-688-06530-9); Avon paper $4.95 (0-380-70313-0).** An exploration of the effects of a suicide on the members of a Southern family. (Rev: CSM 8/31/87; LJ 9/1/87; PW 8/14/87. Awards: LJ, 1987; PW, 1987)

7721 Godwin, Gail. *Violet Clay.* **1988, Penguin paper $6.95 (0-14-008220-4).** A New York sketch artist who relocated from South Carolina examines the direction of her life and career following the loss of her job. (Rev: LJ 5/15/78; NYTBR 5/21/78; PW 3/27/78)

7722 Gold, Herbert. *Dreaming.* **1988, Donald I. Fine $17.95 (1-55611-071-5); Dell paper $4.95 (0-440-20430-5).** A portrait of life in San Francisco during the 1980s focusing on a California salesman entertaining a Soviet journalist at a local restaurant. (Rev: BL 3/1/88; NYTBR 3/27/88)

7723 Gold, Herbert. *A Girl of Forty.* **1986, Donald I. Fine $16.95 (0-917657-63-2); Dell paper $4.95 (0-440-20431-3).** A Berkeley son takes revenge on his father for an extramarital affair. "May stand hereafter as *the* definitive California novel . . . a zinger."—PW (Rev: PW 6/6/86; Time 9/1/86)

7724 Golding, William. *Darkness Visible.* **1985, Harcourt paper $8.95 (0-15-623931-0).** A chronicle of the life of a man disfigured as a child by burns suffered during the blitz in World War II. "A novel of the greatest interest, one that is here to stay."—TLS (Rev: Atl 11/79; LJ 10/1/79; TLS 11/23/79)

7725 Golding, William. *Paper Men.* **1985, Harcourt paper $5.95 (0-15-670800-0).** A would-be biographer chases a drunken writer across Europe and causes havoc in the writer's personal life. (Rev: Atl 4/84; LJ 3/15/84; NYTBR 4/16/84)

7726 Golding, William. *The Pyramid.* **1968, Harcourt paper $3.95 (0-15-674703-0).** An examination of the English class systems as traced through three decades of life in a small village. (Rev: BL 9/1/67; LJ 8/67; TLS 6/1/67. Awards: ALA, 1967)

7727 Goldstein, Rebecca. *Dark Sister.* **1991, Viking $19.95 (0-670-83556-0).** A novelist works on a piece of fiction in the style of Henry James that tells the story of her relationship with her own sister. "A sinuous, demanding and brilliantly inventive performance."—BL (Rev: BL 6/1/91; LJ 6/1/91; PW 5/10/91)

7728 Goldstein, Rebecca. *Late-Summer Passion of a Woman of Mind.* **1989, Farrar $18.95 (0-374-18406-2); Random paper $8.95 (0-679-72823-6).** A German-American philosophy professor examines her past and her father's role in the German war machine during World War II. (Rev: BL 2/1/89; LJ 2/15/89)

7729 Goldstein, Rebecca. *Mind-Body Problem.* **1985, Dell paper $4.95 (0-440-35651-2).** This debut novel depicts the relationship of a graduate philosophy student and her mathematical-genius husband. (Rev: LJ 10/15/83; NYTBR 9/25/83; Newsweek 10/10/83)

7730 Gordimer, Nadine. *Burger's Daughter.* **1980, Penguin paper $8.95 (0-14-005593-2).** The daughter of a South African political figure flees to Europe in search of a new life following her father's death. (Rev: LJ 7/79; PW 7/2/79; Sat Rev 9/29/79)

7731 Gordimer, Nadine. *A Guest of Honor.* **1983, Penguin paper $6.95 (0-14-003696-2).** A fictional account of the visit of a British colonel to the inauguration of the president of a newly independent colony state in Africa. (Rev: CSM 11/5/70; LJ 11/1/70; NYTBR 11/1/70)

7732 Gordimer, Nadine. *July's People.* **1982, Penguin paper $5.95 (0-14-006140-1).** A white family turns to a former servant for help in this novel depicting a revolution in South Africa set in the near future. (Rev: NYTBR 6/7/81; PW 4/17/81; Time 6/8/81. Awards: ALA, 1981)

7733 Gordimer, Nadine. *Late Bourgeois World.* **1983, Penguin paper $5.95 (0-14-005614-9).** A chronicle of a day in the life of a Johannesburg divorcée who reflects on her experiences following her ex-husband's suicide. (Rev: BL 6/15/66; LJ 6/1/66; PW 5/2/66)

7734 Gordimer, Nadine. *My Son's Story.* **1990, Farrar $19.95 (0-374-21751-3).** A South African colored father has an affair with a white activist, which changes his relations with his wife and children. (Rev: BL 9/15/90; LJ 11/1/90; Time 10/29/90. Awards: BL, 1990; LJ, 1990; NYTBR, 1990; PW, 1990; Time, 1990)

7735 Gordimer, Nadine. *A Sport of Nature.* **1987, Knopf $18.95 (0-394-54802-7); Penguin paper $7.95**

(0-14-008470-3). A tale of a white woman caught up in the struggle for black freedom in South Africa. "Lays bare the inequities of apartheid."—LJ (Rev: LJ 4/15/87; NYTBR 5/3/87; Time 4/6/87. Awards: LJ, 1987; Time, 1987)

7736 Gordon, Mary. *Company of Women.* **1981, Random $12.95 (0-394-50508-5); paper $4.95 (0-345-32972-4).** A study of the interrelationships of five women who meet on weekly religious retreats. (Rev: NYTBR 2/15/81; Newsweek 2/16/81; Sat Rev 2/81)

7737 Gordon, Mary. *Final Payments.* **1986, Ballantine paper $4.95 (0-345-32973-2).** This first novel of Gordon's concerns a young woman who devotes her life to the care of her invalid father and his influence upon her even after his death. (Rev: LJ 3/15/78; NYTBR 4/16/78; Sat Rev 3/4/78. Awards: ALA, 1978; NYTBR 4/16/78)

7738 Gordon, Mary. *Men and Angels.* **1986, Ballantine paper $4.50 (0-345-32925-2).** A married couple's academic pursuits on two continents leave their two children in the care of a hired helper. (Rev: BL 2/1/85; LJ 3/15/85; Newsweek 4/1/85. Awards: ALA, 1985)

7739 Gordon, Mary. *The Other Side.* **1989, Viking $19.95 (0-670-82566-2); Penguin paper $9.95 (0-14-014408-0).** The life of an Irish-American family set in Ireland and the United States by the author of *Men and Angels.* (Rev: BL 7/89; PW 8/4/89; TLS 1/26/90. Awards: ALA, 1989; PW, 1989)

7740 Goudge, Eileen. *Garden of Lies.* **1989, Viking $19.95 (0-670-82458-5); NAL paper $5.95 (0-451-16291-9).** A story of two New York women who were switched at birth in the maternity ward and grew up to fall in love with the same man. (Rev: NYTBR 7/1/90; PW 6/22/90)

7741 Gould, Lois. *A Sea-Change.* **1988, Farrar paper $6.95 (0-374-52085-2).** The story of the life of a young model coming to terms with a rape. Written by the author of *Such Good Friends.* (Rev: BL 9/1/76; NYTBR 9/19/76; PW 6/28/76)

7742 Goytisolo, Juan. *Landscapes after the Battle.* **1987, Seaver $17.95 (0-8050-0393-2).** Short portraits of life in the mean streets of Paris as depicted by the Spanish writer. (Rev: Choice 11/87; LJ 4/15/87; PW 4/24/87)

7743 Grass, Günter. *The Flounder.* **1978, Harcourt $12.00 (0-15-131486-1); paper $11.95 (0-15-631935-7).** A chronicle of the past lives of a narrator known as the Flounder tracing his relations with women from the Stone Age to the twentieth century. "As rich, challenging and inventive as anything he's written."—PW (Rev: NYTBR 11/12/78; PW 9/18/78; Time 10/23/78. Awards: NYTBR, 1978; Time, 1978)

7744 Grass, Günter. *Headbirths: Or, the Germans Are Dying Out.* **1990, Harcourt paper $8.95 (0-15-63999-5).** A pair of German schoolteachers reflect on their nation and its recent history in this fictional commentary by the author of *The Flounder.* (Rev: BL 2/15/82; LJ 3/15/82; TLS 4/23/82)

7745 Grass, Günter. *Local Anaesthetic.* **1989, Harcourt paper $9.95 (0-15-652940-8).** An account of the relations between a German teacher and his two students, one of whom plans to set himself afire to protest the Vietnam War. (Rev: BL 5/1/70; CSM 4/9/70; Time 4/13/70. Awards: Time, 1970)

7746 Grass, Günter. *The Rat.* **1987, Harcourt $17.95 (0-15-175920-0); paper $9.95 (0-15-675830-X).** This portrait of a future earth dominated by rats marks the return of character Oscar Mazerath, first introduced in the author's classic *The Tin Drum.* "Wildly entertaining as well as thought provoking."—LJ (Rev: BL 5/15/87; LJ 7/87; PW 5/22/87)

7747 Grau, Shirley Ann. *Keepers of the House.* **1985, Avon paper $4.50 (0-380-70047-6).** A portrait of three generations of a Mississippi family by the author of *The House on Coliseum Street.* (Rev: LJ 3/1/64; NYTBR 3/22/64; Sat Rev 3/21/64. Awards: PP:Fiction, 1965)

7748 Graves, Ralph. *August People.* **1986, Zebra paper $3.95 (0-8217-1863-0).** A story of the conflict between an aging American professor and a daughter-in-law who challenges his rule over his family. (Rev: BL 5/15/85; LJ 6/1/85; Time 7/15/85)

7749 Gray, Alasdair. *1982 Janine.* **1985, Penguin paper $6.95 (0-14-007110-5).** A chronicle of a night of sexual fantasies of a traveling worker in his Glasgow hotel room. (Rev: CSM 10/5/84; New Rep 11/12/84; NYTBR 10/28/84)

7750 Gray, Francine du Plessix. *Lovers and Tyrants.* **1988, Norton paper $7.95 (0-393-30547-3).** A French journalist recounts her experiences living in France and the United States in this novel by the author of *World Without End.* (Rev: BL 10/1/76; CSM 12/8/76; Newsweek 10/11/76)

7751 Greenberg, Joanne. *Of Such Small Differences.* **1988, Henry Holt $18.95 (0-8050-0902-7); NAL paper $4.50 (0-451-16419-9).** The adult life of a blind and deaf poet and his relationship with an actress he falls in love with. (Rev: BL 6/15/88; NYTBR 10/30/88; PW 7/15/88. Awards: ALA, 1988)

7752 Greenberg, Joanne. *Simple Gifts.* **1987, Henry Holt paper $7.95 (0-8050-0540-4).** A Colorado ranching family turns their home and property into a tourist attraction following the advice of a government agent. (Rev: BL 6/1/86; LJ 8/86; PW 6/27/86)

7753 Greene, Graham. *Captain and the Enemy.* **1988, Viking $17.95 (0-670-82405-4); Penguin paper $7.95 (0-14-012418-7).** A chronicle of the adventures of a preteen boy abducted by a man known as the Captain, who leads him on operations in London and Central America. (Rev: BL 7/88; NYTBR 10/23/88; Time 10/31/88)

7754 Greene, Graham. *Comedians.* **1966, Viking $14.95 (0-670-23208-4); Penguin paper $4.95 (0-14-002766-1).** Life in Haiti under the regime of "Papa Doc" Duvalier as depicted by the author of *The Power and the Glory.* (Rev: Choice 3/66; LJ 1/15/66; TLS 1/27/66. Awards: NYTBR, 1966)

7755 Greene, Graham. *Dr. Fischer of Geneva: Or the Bomb Party.* 1982, Viking $20.00 (0-670-27522-0). A tale of a wealthy eccentric who throws parties and forces his friends to perform feats of daring or unusual acts in order to receive gifts and his continued friendship. (Rev: LJ 5/15/80; Newsweek 5/19/80; TLS 3/28/80)

7756 Greene, Graham. *Honorary Consul.* 1983, Viking $20.95 (0-670-37832-0); Pocket paper $3.95 (0-671-63249-3). A British consul is kidnapped in a remote section of Argentina. (Rev: LJ 8/73; Newsweek 9/17/73; Time 9/17/73. Awards: Time, 1973)

7757 Greene, Graham. *Monsignor Quixote.* 1982, Simon & Schuster $12.95 (0-671-45818-3); Pocket paper $3.95 (0-317-47470-7). A retelling of the Cervantes classic set in contemporary Spain. (Rev: BL 8/82; LJ 9/1/82; PW 7/16/82)

7758 Greene, Graham. *Travels with My Aunt.* 1977, Penguin paper $4.95 (0-14-003221-5). A bank manager meets his aunt at his mother's funeral and embarks on a series of intercontinental adventures with her. (Rev: BL 4/1/70; Choice 9/70; Time 1/19/70)

7759 Greenfeld, Josh. *Return of Mr. Hollywood.* 1989, Carroll & Graf paper $8.95 (0-88184-486-1). A novel by the author of *A Child Called Noah* concerning a film director's return to his Brooklyn home. (Rev: LJ 5/15/84; Newsweek 8/13/84; Time 5/7/84)

7760 Greer, Ben. *Loss of Heaven.* 1988, Doubleday $19.95 (0-385-23616-6). A portrayal of the lives of four brothers raised by their grandmother in North Carolina during the 1960s. "A fascinating story from a wonderful writer."—LJ (Rev: BL 10/15/88; LJ 11/1/88)

7761 Gregory, Stephen. *The Cormorant.* 1988, St. Martin's $13.95 (0-312-01753-7); paper $3.50 (0-312-91314-1). A nephew appointed to take care of his dead uncle's cormorant finds that the bird harbors evil spirits. (Rev: LJ 4/15/88; NYTBR 7/24/88; PW 4/1/88)

7762 Grenville, Kate. *Lilian's Story.* 1986, Viking $16.95 (0-670-80929-2); Penguin paper $6.95 (0-14-008547-5). This portrait of the life of an obese woman was this Australian writer's first novel. "A work of considerable power and beauty."—NYTBR (Rev: BL 8/86; NYTBR 9/7/86; PW 6/13/86)

7763 Griffith, Patricia Browning. *World Around Midnight.* 1991, Putnam $22.95 (0-399-13590-1). A young woman returns to the small Texas town of her childhood to settle her father's estate and finds herself running the community newspaper while embroiled in a series of family crises. (Rev: BL 12/15/90; LJ 1/91; PW 1/25/91. Awards: ALA, 1992)

7764 Grossman, David. *See Under: Love.* 1989, Farrar $22.95 (0-374-25731-0); Washington Square Pr. paper $9.95 (0-671-70112-6). An Israeli writer's portrait of the young son of Holocaust survivors and how his parents' memories affected him. "An incredibly original and imaginative novel by one of Israel's truly gifted young writers."—LJ (Rev: LJ 2/1/89; NYRB 9/28/89; PW 2/17/90. Awards: LJ, 1989; PW, 1989)

7765 Grossman, David. *Smile of the Lamb.* 1991, Farrar $19.95 (0-374-26639-5). This novel, written before the author's acclaimed *See Under: Love,* concerns the lives of four individuals living in Israeli-occupied territory. "A bold work of great range and vision by one of Israel's finest writers."—BL (Rev: BL 12/1/90; LJ 1/91; PW 10/26/90)

7766 Grossman, Judith. *Her Own Terms.* 1987, Soho Pr. $16.95 (0-939149-11-7); Ivy Books paper $3.95 (0-8041-0394-1). This debut novel depicts the life of a middle-class English woman educated at Oxford during the 1950s and 1960s. (Rev: LJ 1/88; NYTBR 1/24/88; PW 11/13/87)

7767 Grumley, Michael. *Life Drawing.* 1991, Grove-Weidenfeld $17.95 (0-8021-1438-5). A coming-of-age novel regarding the development of the sexuality of a gay man. Written by an author who died of AIDS in 1988. (Rev: BL 8/91; LJ 9/1/91)

7768 Grunwald, Lisa. *Summer.* 1987, Warner paper $3.95 (0-446-34377-3). A college student learns of her mother's terminal illness and plots to cause a plane crash that will take the lives of both of her parents. (Rev: BL 12/1/85; LJ 1/86; PW 5/22/87)

7769 Grunwald, Lisa. *Theory of Everything.* 1991, Knopf $20.00 (0-394-58149-0). A physicist on the brink of a unified field theory finds himself on the verge of a nervous breakdown due to personal problems. (Rev: BL 3/1/91; PW 2/1/91; Time 4/15/91)

7770 Guest, Judith. *Ordinary People.* 1986, Ballantine paper $5.95 (0-345-3305-8). An upper-middle-class Illinois teenager attempts suicide and is treated for mental illness following a fatal boating accident that took the life of his brother. (Rev: BL 7/15/76; LJ 5/1/76; Time 7/19/76. Awards: ALA, 1976)

7771 Gurewich, David. *Travels with Dubinsky and Clive.* 1987, Viking $16.95 (0-670-81621-3). This Russian-born writer's debut work tracks the adventures of two Soviet Jews who emigrate to the United States. "A very entertaining novel."—BL (Rev: BL 6/1/87; LJ 6/15/87; PW 5/22/87)

7772 Gurney, A. R., Jr. *Snow Ball.* 1986, Carroll & Graf paper $4.50 (0-88184-214-1). The story of tension between WASPs and Buffalo, New York, ethnics on the eve of a gala thrown by the city to celebrate the revival of its downtown area. (Rev: BL 12/1/84; LJ 12/84)

7773 Gustafsson, Lars. *Tennis Players.* 1983, New Directions $13.00 (0-8112-0861-3); paper $6.25 (0-8112-0862-1). A foreign professor's year teaching at a Texas university. (Rev: BL 3/15/83; LJ 4/15/83; PW 2/11/83)

7774 Guy, David. *Autobiography of My Body.* 1991, Dutton $19.95 (0-525-24974-5). A chronicle of the sexual confessions of a journalist who enters a series of erotic adventures following the collapse of his marriage. (Rev: BL 11/90; LJ 12/90)

7775 Guy, David. *Second Brother.* 1986, NAL paper $6.95 (0-452-25887-1). The story of the life of a teenager growing up in Pittsburgh during the

1960s in the shadow of a talented older brother. (REV: LJ 9/1/85; NYTBR 11/3/85; PW 7/12/85)

7776   Guy, Rosa. *My Love, My Love: Or, the Peasant Girl.* **1985, Holt $12.95 (0-03-000507-8).** A story of the relationship between a Caribbean peasant girl and the wealthy landowner she falls in love with. "A haunting allegory that touches the heart."—BL (REV: BL 9/15/85; LJ 10/15/85; PW 8/30/85)

7777   Haddad, Carolyn. *A Mother's Secret.* **1988, Harcourt $19.95 (0-15-162666-9); Ivy Books paper $4.50 (0-8041-0403-4).** The story of a Jewish child, adopted in wartime, who is reunited with her birth mother in Israel four decades after the war. (REV: BL 3/1/88; LJ 3/15/88; PW 1/22/88)

7778   Hagedorn, Jessica. *Dogeaters.* **1990, Random $19.95   (0-394-57498-2).** This Philippines-born writer's debut novel tells of a schoolgirl growing up in Manila during the Marcos regime. "Exceptionally well written and emotionally wrenching."—LJ (REV: BL 3/1/90; LJ 4/1/90; PW 2/9/90. AWARDS: PW, 1990)

7779   Hailey, Elizabeth Forsyth. *A Woman of Independent Means.* **1978, Viking $17.95 (0-670-77795-1); Avon paper $4.50 (0-380-42390-1).** A portrait of the life of an independent Texas woman born at the turn of the century. (REV: CSM 6/14/78; NYTBR 5/28/78; PW 3/20/78)

7780   Hale, Robert. *Elm at the Edge of the Earth.* **1990, Norton $19.95 (0-393-02861-5).** This debut novel chronicles the life of a child forced to live with his aunt and uncle following the severe illness of his mother. (REV: BL 6/15/90; PW 5/25/90)

7781   Haley, Susan Charlotte. *Getting Married in Buffalo Jump.* **1987, Dutton $17.95 (0-525-24528-6).** A college-educated woman in a small Canadian farming town plans to marry a Soviet emigré farmhand. (REV: LJ 7/87; NYTBR 8/16/87)

7782   Hamill, Pete. *Loving Women: A Novel of the Fifties.* **1989, Random $19.95 (0-394-57528-8); Windsor paper $5.50 (1-55817-385-4).** A New Yorker recalls his love life in the 1950s in this novel set in New York and Florida. (REV: BL 2/15/89; PW 2/17/89)

7783   Hamilton, William. *Lap of Luxury.* **1990, Atlantic Monthly $17.95 (0-87113-246-X); paper $8.95 (0-87113-342-3).** A New York artist/art historian marries into the family of a society heiress. (REV: BL 10/15/88; LJ 11/15/88; PW 9/9/88)

7784   Hamilton-Paterson, James. *That Time in Malomba.* **1990, Soho Pr. $18.95 (0-939149-42-7).** An examination of relationships and misunderstandings between Westerners and natives in an unnamed Third World country. (REV: BL 8/90; New Yorker 11/12/90; PW 7/6/90)

7785   Handke, Peter. *Across.* **1986, Farrar $14.95 (0-374-10054-3); Macmillan paper $6.95 (0-02-051540-5).** The story of an Austrian teacher who murders a man he sees painting a swastika on a tree. "It confirms Mr. Handke's stature as one of the most original and provocative of contemporary writers."—NYTBR (REV: Choice 2/87; NYTBR 7/27/86; PW 4/25/86)

7786   Handke, Peter. *Repetition.* **1988, Farrar $18.95 (0-374-24934-2); Macmillan paper $8.95 (0-02-020762-X).** A young Austrian man leaves his city to search for a missing brother and to return to the Slovenia of his ancestors. "A complex, thoughtful, and poignant book."—CSM (REV: BL 5/15/88; CSM 7/8/88; PW 4/29/88)

7787   Handke, Peter. *Slow Homecoming.* **1985, Farrar $16.95 (0-374-26635-2); Macmillan paper $8.95 (0-02-051530-8).** A collection of three interrelated stories by an Austrian playwright and novelist. "Postmodernism in its most exciting and challenging form."—Choice (REV: Choice 9/85; LJ 6/15/85; PW 4/19/85)

7788   Hannah, Barry. *Geronimo Rex.* **1987, Penguin paper $7.95 (0-14-010514-X).** The debut novel by the author of *Ray,* portraying the coming of age of a young man in the contemporary American South. "A stunning piece of entertainment."—NYTBR (REV: BL 2/15/72; NYTBR 5/14/72; Time 4/17/72)

7789   Hannah, Barry. *Hey Jack!* **1988, Penguin paper $6.95 (0-14-011185-9).** A Mississippi writer spins a tale about himself and the university town where he lives in this novel by the author of *Geronimo Rex.* (REV: BL 9/1/87; PW 7/17/87)

7790   Hannah, Barry. *Ray.* **1987, Penguin paper $5.95 (0-14-010515-8).** A chronicle of the adventures of a rapscallion of an Alabama doctor by the author of *Airships.* (REV: BL 9/15/80; Newsweek 12/15/80; Time 1/12/81)

7791   Hannah, Barry. *Tennis Handsome.* **1987, Macmillan paper $4.95 (0-684-18811-2).** A story by the author of *Airships* tracing the intertwined lives of a handsome tennis star and a former Vietnam POW from Mississippi. (REV: BL 3/15/83; LJ 3/1/83; Time 7/4/83)

7792   Hansen, Ron. *Mariette in Ecstasy.* **1991, HarperCollins $20.00 (0-06-018214-8).** A story of the spiritual life of a young woman who enters a New York convent at the age of 19. (REV: NYTBR 10/22/91; PW 8/23/91)

7793   Hanson, Dick. *The Incursion.* **1988, Avon paper $3.95 (0-380-70554-0).** A series of computer mishaps throws the defense, transportation, and communications systems of the United States into chaos. "A superior writer with a pronounced streak of poetry."—NYTBR (REV: LJ 4/15/87; NYTBR 7/12/87; PW 3/6/87)

7794   Hardwick, Elizabeth. *Sleepless Nights.* **1990, Random paper $8.95 (0-679-72426-5).** A series of vignettes and reminiscences during sleepless nights tell the life story of a Kentucky woman who moved to New York in search of a new life. (REV: CSM 6/13/79; LJ 4/15/79; NYTBR 4/29/79. AWARDS: NYTBR, 1979)

7795   Harrigan, Stephen. *Aransas.* **1986, Pacesetter Pr. paper $8.95 (0-87719-057-7).** A Texas Gulf Coast dolphin trainer falls in love with a conservationist and they plot together to set a group of dolphins free. (REV: BL 3/15/80; LJ 3/1/80; Newsweek 4/21/80)

7796 Harrington, William. *Virus.* **1991, Morrow $17.45 (0-688-09064-8).** A computer expert creates a series of viruses to disrupt American transportation and communication systems, and becomes embroiled in a Colombian drug cartel scheme. "A surefire hit."—LJ (REV: BL 12/15/90; LJ 12/90; PW 11/16/90)

7797 Harris, Marilyn. *Hatter Fox.* **1973, Random $12.95 (0-394-48514-9); Ballantine paper $3.95 (0-345-33157-5).** The story of the relationship between a mentally ill Native American and a doctor who attempts to free her from an institution. (REV: BL 11/1/73; CSM 8/22/73; Newsweek 9/17/73)

7798 Harris, Marilyn. *Lost and Found.* **1991, Crown $20.00 (0-517-58333-X).** A chronicle of a young woman's life with a series of foster parents following her accidental separation from her original adopted family. (REV: BL 6/1/91; LJ 7/91)

7799 Harris, Mark. *Speed.* **1990, Donald I. Fine $19.95 (1-55611-180-0).** A young boy growing up in New York after World War II narrates the story of his stuttering brother. (REV: BL 6/15/90; LJ 8/90; PW 6/29/90. AWARDS: BL, 1990)

7800 Harris, Thomas. *Black Sunday.* **1990, Dell paper $5.95 (0-440-20614-6).** A terrorist threatens to disrupt the Super Bowl in New Orleans with explosives supplied by Palestinians. (REV: LJ 4/1/75; PW 2/2/76)

7801 Harris, Thomas. *Red Dragon.* **1981, Putnam $13.95 (0-399-12442-X); Dell paper $5.95 (0-440-20615-4).** This story of an FBI agent called out of retirement to track down a serial killer was the basis of the motion picture *Manhunter.* (REV: LJ 11/1/81; NYTBR 11/9/81; Sat Rev 11/81)

7802 Harris, Thomas. *Silence of the Lambs.* **1988, St. Martin's $18.95 (0-312-02282-4); paper $5.95 (0-312-91543-8).** An FBI agent elicits aid from a convicted cannibalistic serial killer to help capture a serial murderer currently on the loose. (REV: BL 6/1/88; LJ 9/15/88; PW 6/10/88)

7803 Harrison, Carey. *Richard's Feet.* **1990, Henry Holt $22.95 (0-8050-1404-7).** This debut novel, set just after World War II, is about an Englishman who changes his identity to live in Germany following his discovery of a murder. (REV: BL 11/15/90; LJ 9/15/90; PW 8/10/90)

7804 Harrison, Claire. *Somebody's Baby.* **1989, Doubleday $17.95 (0-385-26087-3); NAL paper $3.95 (0-451-16533-0).** The pregnancy of a 15-year-old girl throws a family into turmoil. (REV: NYTBR 7/9/89; PW 5/5/89)

7805 Harrison, Jim. *Dalva.* **1989, Pocket paper $7.95 (0-671-67817-5).** An account of a Nebraska woman's search for the whereabouts of her illegitimate child. "A compelling novel, essential for

fiction collections."—LJ (REV: CSM 6/13/88; LJ 4/1/88; PW 1/29/88)

7806 Harrison, Jim. *Legends of the Fall.* **1989, Dell paper $8.95 (0-440-55015-7).** A collection of three interrelated stories of betrayal and revenge by the author of *Warlock* and *Farmer.* (REV: NYTBR 6/17/79; Newsweek 7/9/79; PW 3/19/79)

7807 Harrison, Jim. *Warlock.* **1988, Dell paper $8.95 (0-440-55019-X).** A Michigan doctor employs a man to observe the lives of his former wife and derelict son in Florida. "There are pleasures of all sorts to be had . . . in this stylish entertainment."—NYTBR (REV: BL 7/15/81; LJ 10/1/81; NYTBR 11/22/81)

7808 Harrison, Jim. *Woman Lit by Fireflies.* **1990, Houghton $19.95 (0-395-48884-2); Pocket paper $8.00 (0-671-74452-6).** A collection of three novellas concerning moral choices and the past. Includes "Brown Dog," "Sunset Limited," and the title story. (REV: BL 4/1/90; LJ 6/1/90; NYTBR 9/16/90)

7809 Hart, Martin. *Bearers of Bad Tidings: A Story of Father and Son.* **1987, Schocken $13.95 (0-8052-8176-2).** A Dutch novel examining the relationship between a gravedigger father and his son, who finds out that he has less than a year to live. (REV: LJ 8/85; PW 6/21/85)

7810 Hassler, Jon. *Grand Opening.* **1987, Morrow $17.95 (0-688-06649-6); Ballantine paper $3.95 (0-345-35016-2).** A Catholic family is confronted by prejudice when it moves to a Minnesota Lutheran town and opens a business. (REV: LJ 6/15/87; NYTBR 6/7/87; PW 4/17/87)

7811 Hassler, Jon. *Love Hunter.* **1988, Ballantine paper $3.95 (0-345-35017-0).** A hunting trip is arranged by two friends to stage an accidental shooting to put a man suffering from multiple sclerosis out of his misery. (REV: BL 9/1/81; LJ 5/15/81; PW 5/8/81)

7812 Hassler, Jon. *North of Hope.* **1990, Ballantine $19.95 (0-345-36910-6).** A Roman Catholic priest discovers romantic love following his reassignment to his childhood parish. (REV: BL 9/1/90; LJ 8/90; PW 8/10/90)

7813 Hauser, Thomas. *Hawthorne Group.* **1991, Tor $18.95 (0-312-85161-8).** An actress becomes involved with a mysterious company that deals in murder and the trade of nuclear weapons. "Few writers currently in action would be able to match the mounting tension of *The Hawthorne Group.*"—NYTBR (REV: BL 4/15/91; NYTBR 5/6/91)

7814 Hawkes, John. *Blood Oranges.* **1972, New Directions paper $8.95 (0-8112-0061-2).** A story by the author of *Second Skin* concerning two couples exploring their sexuality in an unnamed Mediterranean country. (REV: NYTBR 9/19/71; TLS 10/15/71)

7815 Hawkes, John. *Death, Sleep and the Traveler.* **1974, New Directions $6.95 (0-8112-0522-3).** This story chronicles two love triangles that lead to death and murder. Written by the author of *The

Lime Twig. (REV: BL 5/1/74; Choice 7–8/74; New Rep 4/20/74)

7816 Hawkes, John. *Humors of Blood and Skin: A John Hawkes Reader.* **1984, New Directions paper $12.95 (0-8112-0907-5).** A collection of four short stories and ten sections of novels by the author of *The Lime Twig* and *Second Skin.* (REV: NYTBR 11/25/84; PW 8/10/84)

7817 Hawkes, John. *Travesty.* **1976, New Directions paper $5.95 (0-8112-0640-8).** An automobile driver plans an accident designed to kill himself, his daughter, and her husband on a European road. (REV: LJ 3/15/76; New Rep 5/8/76; New Yorker 4/19/76)

7818 Hawkes, John. *Virginie: Her Two Lives.* **1983, Carroll & Graf paper $7.95 (0-88184-054-8).** A story chronicling the lives of a twentieth-century French girl who is the reincarnation of an eighteenth-century young woman. (REV: BL 4/15/82; NYTBR 6/27/82; PW 4/16/82)

7819 Hawkes, John. *Whistlejacket.* **1988, Grove-Weidenfeld $17.95 (1-55584-049-3); Macmillan paper $7.95 (0-02-043581-6).** A novel chronicling the events leading to the death of a man who was kicked to death by his horse. (REV: NYTBR 8/17/88; PW 6/3/88)

7820 Hazzard, Shirley. *Bay of Noon.* **1988, Penguin paper $6.95 (0-14-010450-X).** A woman recalls the events of her youth in Naples in the years following World War II. (REV: BL 5/15/70; Choice 7–8/70; NYTBR 4/5/70)

7821 Hazzard, Shirley. *Transit of Venus.* **1990, Penguin paper $8.95 (0-14-010747-9).** A chronicle of the lives of two orphaned Australian sisters in England and the United States over the course of three decades. "A strong, deep, poetic, vibrant novel."—PW (REV: BL 4/1/80; PW 12/10/79; Time 7/14/80)

7822 Head, Bessie. *A Question of Power.* **1974, Heinemann paper $7.00 (0-435-90720-4).** The story of an English-African woman who leaves her native South Africa to take a teaching position in Botswana. "Representative of the best in contemporary African fiction."—LJ (REV: Choice 7–8/74; LJ 3/15/74; PW 2/11/74. AWARDS: ALA, 1992)

7823 Hearon, Shelby. *Five Hundred Scorpions.* **1987, Macmillan $18.95 (0-689-11584-9).** A man abandons his career and family to join an all-female anthropological team conducting research in Mexico. (REV: BL 4/1/87; NYTBR 5/10/87; PW 2/27/87)

7824 Hearon, Shelby. *Owning Jolene.* **1988, Knopf $17.95 (0-394-57175-4).** A Texas girl shuttled between her separated parents and relatives becomes the subject of a series of portraits by an artist. (REV: BL 11/15/88; NYTBR 1/22/89; New Yorker 3/27/89)

7825 Hebert, Ernest. *A Little More Than Kin.* **1982, Ultramarine $20.00 (0-89366-139-2).** This portrait of a small-town New Hampshire family is the sequel to the author's *The Dogs of March.* (REV: BL 8/82; LJ 7/82; PW 6/4/82)

7826 Hebert, Ernest. *Live Free or Die.* **1990, Viking $19.95 (0-670-83133-6).** A story about life in a small New Hampshire town focusing on the fate of two young lovers and the local environment. (REV: LJ 11/1/90; NYTBR 12/30/90; PW 9/2/90)

7827 Hegi, Ursula. *Floating in My Mother's Palm.* **1990, Poseidon $17.95 (0-671-68947-9).** A fictional study of the German people during the 1950s trying to come to terms with their recent past. (REV: BL 3/15/90; LJ 3/1/90; PW 1/5/90)

7828 Hein, Christopher. *Distant Lover.* **1989, Pantheon $16.95 (0-394-56634-3); paper $8.95 (0-679-72898-8).** This novel by an East German writer revolves around a female physician in Berlin and her relationship with an architect. (REV: LJ 4/1/89; NYTBR 5/7/89)

7829 Heinemann, Larry. *Paco's Story.* **1986, Farrar $15.95 (0-374-22847-7); paper $7.95 (0-14-012761-5).** A Vietnam veteran recently released from a mental institution takes a job in a Texas restaurant and tries to readjust to life. (REV: LJ 12/86; NYTBR 11/8/87; PW 9/25/87. AWARDS: NBA, 1987)

7830 Heller, Joseph. *Good as Gold.* **1989, Dell paper $5.95 (0-440-20440-2).** The story of a Jewish professor and writer's experiences following his election to a government cabinet post. (REV: BL 3/1/79; LJ 3/15/79; New Rep 3/10/79)

7831 Heller, Joseph. *Something Happened.* **1989, Dell paper $5.95 (0-440-20441-0).** A suburban businessman examines his life and finds that despite his apparent successes, he feels unfulfilled. (REV: NYTBR 10/6/74; Newsweek 10/14/74; PW 8/19/74. AWARDS: ALA, 1974; NYTBR, 1974)

7832 Heller, Steve. *Automotive History of Lucky Kellerman.* **1989, Doubleday paper $7.95 (0-385-26351-1).** This debut novel concerns an ailing Missouri man who leads a reclusive life to achieve his dream of restoring a 1932 Ford. (REV: NYTBR 11/1/87; PW 8/21/87)

7833 Helprin, Mark. *A Soldier of the Great War.* **1991, Harcourt $24.95 (0-15-183600-0).** An Italian veteran and professor in his 70s tells the story of his life to a teenager who accompanies him on a long walk from Rome to a hill town. "A gripping, poignant and universally relevant moral fable."—PW (REV: CSM 6/3/91; LJ 4/15/91; PW 3/8/91. AWARDS: LJ, 1991; PW, 1991)

7834 Helwig, David. *Of Desire.* **1991, Viking $19.95 (0-670-82592-1).** A story of a family's reaction to a father's disappearance. "Demonstrates Helwig's grasp of character and the nuances of psychological insight."—PW (REV: BL 12/1/90; PW 11/30/90)

7835 Hemingway, Ernest. *Garden of Eden.* **1987, Macmillan $18.95 (0-684-18693-4); paper $8.95 (0-684-71795-9).** A posthumously published story of a love triangle between a writer and two women on the French Riviera. (REV: Natl Rev 5/23/86; Newsweek 5/19/86; Time 5/26/86)

7836 Hemingway, Ernest. *Islands in the Stream.* **1980, Macmillan $40.00 (0-684-16499-X); paper $12.95 (0-684-14642-8).** A posthumously published autobiographical novel regarding the narrator's fishing and drinking adventures in Cuba and Bimini. "As likable and heartbreaking a book as Ernest Hemingway ever wrote."—CSM (Rev: Choice 4/71; CSM 10/8/70; NYTBR 10/4/70)

7837 Herley, Richard. *Penal Colony.* **1988, Morrow $18.95 (0-688-06622-4); Ballantine paper $3.95 (0-345-35875-9).** A falsely accused man is sentenced to an island penal colony without borders or rules. (Rev: LJ 2/15/88; PW 12/18/87)

7838 Herman, Michelle. *Missing.* **1990, Ohio State Univ. Pr. $15.95 (0-8142-0503-8).** An elderly Jewish grandmother searches for a misplaced box of beads. (Rev: BL 4/15/90; LJ 5/1/90; PW 2/9/90)

7839 Herrick, Amy. *At the Sign of the Naked Waiter.* **1991, HarperCollins $20.00 (0-06-016534-0).** A debut novel that traces the real and fantasy lives of a modern woman from youth to adulthood. (Rev: BL 2/1/92; LJ 1/92; PW 11/29/91)

7840 Herring, Robert. *McCampbell's War.* **1986, Viking $16.95 (0-670-80501-7).** A man fights against developers who threaten his Tennessee cabin and the burial sites of his family. (Rev: BL 3/15/86; LJ 5/15/86; PW 3/21/86)

7841 Herron, Carolivia. *Thereafter Johnnie.* **1991, Random $18.95 (0-394-57644-6).** This debut novel portrays the life of a teenage African-American girl in Washington, D.C., left on her own following the suicide of her mother. (Rev: LJ 5/1/91; NYTBR 6/23/91; PW 3/1/91)

7842 Higgins, George V. *A Choice of Enemies.* **1985, Carroll & Graf paper $3.50 (0-88184-121-8).** A Massachusetts Speaker of the House fights for his political life in this novel by the author of *The Friends of Eddie Coyle.* (Rev: Atl 2/84; BL 10/1/83; CSM 3/1/84)

7843 Higgins, George V. *The Friends of Eddie Coyle.* **1987, Penguin paper $3.95 (0-14-010232-9).** The story of the lives of Boston gangsters, focusing on the portrayal of Eddie Coyle, a small-time hood and gunrunner. (Rev: NYTBR 2/6/72; Newsweek 2/7/72; Time 2/21/72)

7844 Higgins, George V. *Trust.* **1989, Henry Holt $18.95 (0-8050-0955-8).** A car salesman attempts to destroy evidence of a sex scandal. (Rev: BL 9/15/89; NYTBR 1/21/90; TLS 12/28/89. Awards: BL, 1989)

7845 Higgins, George V. *Victories.* **1991, Henry Holt $19.95 (0-8050-1219-2).** A former Red Sox baseball star runs for Congress in Vermont in the late 1960s. (Rev: BL 10/15/90; LJ 11/1/90; PW 10/5/90)

7846 Highsmith, Patricia. *Edith's Diary.* **1989, Atlantic Monthly paper $8.95 (0-87113-296-6).** This novel traces two decades in the lives of a leftist couple who move from New York to rural Pennsylvania. "A masterpiece . . . much more frightening,

and more extraordinary than Highsmith's other books."—TLS (Rev: BL 9/15/77; PW 4/1/77; TLS 5/20/77)

7847 Highsmith, Patricia. *Found in the Street.* **1989, Atlantic Monthly $16.95 (0-87113-208-7); paper $8.95 (0-87113-326-1).** An aspiring model moves to New York's Greenwich Village and befriends two men in this novel by the English master of the psychological suspense story. (Rev: BL 10/1/87; NYTBR 11/1/87; New Yorker 1/4/88)

7848 Highsmith, Patricia. *Those Who Walk Away.* **1988, Atlantic Monthly paper $7.95 (0-87113-259-1).** A suspense novel regarding a woman's father tracking her husband, whom he blames for the suicide of his daughter. (Rev: NYTBR 4/30/67; PW 1/23/67)

7849 Hijuelos, Oscar. *The Mambo Kings Play Songs of Love.* **1989, Farrar $18.95 (0-374-20135-0); Harper & Row paper $9.95 (0-06-097327-7).** A story of a Cuban music group's efforts to achieve fame and wealth in the United States during the mid-1950s. (Rev: BL 8/89; Newsweek 8/21/89; PW 6/2/89. Awards: BL, 1989; PP:Fiction, 1990; PW, 1989)

7850 Hijuelos, Oscar. *Our House in the Last World.* **1983, Persea Books $18.95 (0-89255-069-4); Pocket paper $3.95 (0-671-50785-0).** This first novel by the author of *The Mambo Kings Play Songs of Love* traces the life of a Cuban family in New York from the early 1940s through the mid-1970s. (Rev: BL 9/15/83; LJ 6/1/83; PW 4/15/83)

7851 Hill, Niki. *Death Grows on You.* **1991, Michael Joseph $18.95 (0-7181-3351-X).** A witness to an IRA bombing in Belfast is forced to hide her family from terrorists. (Rev: BL 1/15/91; LJ 12/90; PW 11/30/90)

7852 Hill, Rebecca. *Among Birches.* **1987, Penguin paper $6.95 (0-14-009852-6).** The story of a two-decade-long Minnesota marriage on the brink of collapse due to infidelities. (Rev: BL 3/15/86; LJ 4/1/86; PW 1/24/86)

7853 Hlasko, Marek. *Killing the Second Dog.* **1990, Cane Hill paper $8.95 (0-943433-04-5).** A Polish writer traces the lives of two emigrants to Israel who turn to hustling after they fail to find jobs. (Rev: NYTBR 6/17/90; PW 1/19/90. Awards: PW, 1990)

7854 Hoagland, Edward. *Seven Rivers West.* **1986, Summit $18.95 (0-671-60753-7); Penguin paper $6.95 (0-14-010276-0).** The adventures of two friends in the mountains of the western United States and Canada by the author of the essay collection *The Courage of Turtles.* (Rev: BL 7/86; LJ 8/86; PW 8/1/86)

7855 Hoban, Russell. *Medusa Frequency.* **1987, Atlantic Monthly $16.95 (0-87113-165-X); paper $8.95 (0-87113-368-7).** The author of *Turtle Diary* tells of a struggling English writer's efforts to write a futuristic novel entitled "Third Novel." (Rev: BL 10/1/87; PW 9/18/87; TLS 9/4/87)

7856 Hoban, Russell. *Turtle Diary.* **1986, Pocket paper $3.95 (0-671-61833-4).** Two Britons plan to free giant turtles from the London Zoo. "Well-written, funny, poignant, and convincing."—LJ (Rev: BL 2/1/ 76; LJ 4/1/76; PW 12/15/75)

7857 Hobbie, Douglas. *Boomfell.* **1991, Henry Holt $19.95 (0-8050-1534-5).** A Boston schoolteacher/ writer reunites with a friend after a period of separation that causes him to reassess the direction of his life. (Rev: LJ 6/1/91; PW 4/19/91)

7858 Hoffman, Alice. *At Risk.* **1988, Putnam $17.95 (0-399-13367-4); Berkley paper $4.95 (0-425-11738-3).** A chronicle of the reactions of the citizenry of a New England town to the news that a sixth-grade girl contracted AIDS through a blood transfusion. "With simple, affecting prose Hoffman . . . brings the AIDS crisis home to us all."—LJ (Rev: LJ 7/88; NYTBR 7/17/88; Newsweek 8/1/99. Awards: LJ, 1988)

7859 Hoffman, Alice. *The Drowning Season.* **1983, NAL paper $7.95 (0-452-26302-6).** A novel tracing three generations of a family from Russia to New York, by the author of *Illumination Night.* (Rev: NYTBR 7/15/79; Newsweek 8/20/79; PW 4/23/79. Awards: ALA, 1979)

7860 Hoffman, Alice. *Fortune's Daughter.* **1985, Putnam $15.95 (0-399-13056-X); Fawcett paper $3.95 (0-449-44545-3).** A depiction of the effects of a past and present pregnancy upon a pair of female friends. (Rev: LJ 4/1/85; NYTBR 3/24/85; PW 2/1/85)

7861 Hoffman, Alice. *Illumination Night.* **1987, Putnam $18.95 (0-399-13282-1); Fawcett paper $3.95 (0-449-21594-6).** The story of six people attending an annual celebration at Martha's Vineyard by the author of *Fortune's Daughter.* "A marvelous novel."—New Yorker (Rev: BL 7/87; New Yorker 9/28/ 87; PW 6/19/87. Awards: ALA, 1987; PW, 1987)

7862 Hoffman, Alice. *Seventh Heaven.* **1990, Putnam $18.95 (0-399-13535-9).** A divorced woman is persecuted by her new Long Island neighbors in this novel set during the 1950s. "Confirms her place as one of the best writers of her generation."—Newsweek (Rev: BL 4/1/90; Newsweek 8/20/90; Time 8/6/90. Awards: ALA, 1990; BL, 1990)

7863 Hofmann, Gert. *Spectacle at the Tower.* **1984, Fromm International $14.95 (0-88064-013-8); paper $8.95 (0-88064-114-2).** A German writer's story of an entertainment spectacle performed for tourists in Southern Italy involving the deaths of children. (Rev: Choice 9/84; LJ 5/1/84; PW 2/17/84)

7864 Hollinghurst, Alan. *Swimming-Pool Library.* **1988, Random $16.95 (0-394-57025-1); paper $8.95 (0-679-72256-4).** A portrait of gay life in London prior to the outbreak of AIDS. "Few novels in recent years have been better written, and none I know of has been more intelligent."—TLS (Rev: LJ 9/1/88; PW 7/29/88; TLS 2/19/88)

7865 Holt, Victoria. *Snare of Serpents.* **1990, Doubleday $19.95 (0-385-41385-8).** A young Scottish woman's life is thrown into chaos when she is accused of the murder of her father's new wife. (Rev: BL 7/90; PW 6/29/90)

7866 Hope, Christopher. *Hottentot Room.* **1987, Farrar $16.95 (0-374-17284-6).** An account of a London-based club for South African expatriates. (Rev: LJ 5/1/87; NYTBR 7/19/87; TLS 9/19/86)

7867 Horgan, Paul. *Thin Mountain Air.* **1977, Farrar $8.95 (0-374-27466-5).** A chronicle of the life of a young man in New Mexico following his family's relocation from New York because of his father's tuberculosis. (Rev: BL 9/15/77; Choice 12/77; TLS 7/14/ 78)

7868 Horgan, Paul. *Whitewater.* **1987, Univ. of Texas Pr. paper $10.95 (0-292-79038-4).** A story tracing the adventures of three teenagers in a small west Texas town. (Rev: CSM 10/1/70; LJ 8/70; Sat Rev 10/3/70)

7869 Hospital, Janette Turner. *Charades.* **1990, Bantam paper $5.95 (0-553-28505-X).** A young Australian woman searches for her father and the truth about her background during a journey that takes her to England, Canada, and the United States. (Rev: BL 1/1/89; NYTBR 3/12/89. Awards: BL, 1989)

7870 Howard, Clark. *Hard City.* **1990, Dutton $21.95 (0-525-24857-9).** A youth escapes from a series of foster homes and a drug-addicted mother to hit the tough streets of Chicago. (Rev: LJ 3/1/90; NYTBR 8/26/90)

7871 Howard, Maureen. *Before My Time.* **1980, Penguin paper $6.95 (0-14-005503-7).** The story of a middle-age writer consumed with ennui. (Rev: Atl 3/ 75; LJ 10/15/74; Time 1/27/75)

7872 Howatch, Susan. *Glamorous Powers.* **1988, Knopf $18.95 (0-394-57145-2); Fawcett paper $5.95 (0-449-21728-0).** This sequel to *Glittering Images* chronicles the relationship between an Anglican monk who left his order and his former head abbot. (Rev: BL 10/1/88; NYTBR 1/29/89; PW 9/2/88)

7873 Howatch, Susan. *Glittering Images.* **1988, Fawcett paper $4.95 (0-449-21436-2).** A bishop accused of misdoings is investigated by a British theologian at the request of his archbishop. "An ambitious and lifelike work of uncommon depth."—BL (Rev: BL 9/1/87; LJ 9/15/87; PW 8/21/87)

7874 Howatch, Susan. *Sins of the Fathers.* **1985, Fawcett paper $4.95 (0-449-20798-6).** This sequel to *The Rich Are Different* chronicles the fortunes of the Van Zales family from the end of World War II to the 1960s. (Rev: BL 5/15/80; LJ 5/15/80; PW 5/16/80)

7875 Howatch, Susan. *Ultimate Prizes.* **1989, Knopf $18.95 (0-394-58064-8); Fawcett paper $5.95 (0-449-21811-2).** A sequel to the author's *Glamorous Powers* chronicling an archdeacon's romantic involvement with a young society girl and a family death that challenges his faith. (Rev: BL 8/89; PW 8/ 18/89)

7876 Howatch, Susan. *Wheel of Fortune.* **1985, Fawcett paper $5.95 (0-449-20624-6).** The chronicle of five generations of a Welsh family on their private estate spanning the years from 1913 to the 1960s. (REV: BL 5/1/84; LJ 6/1/84; PW 4/20/84)

7877 Hrabel, Bohumil. *Too Loud a Solitude*. 1991, Harcourt $17.95 (0-15-190491-X). Reflections on life by a Czech man who has been working in a recycling plant for over three decades. (REV: LJ 9/15/ 90; New Yorker 10/22/90; PW 7/27/90)

7878 Hudson, Helen. *Criminal Trespass*. 1985, Put- nam $16.95 (0-399-13055-1). A portrait of African-American life and race relations in a small Alabama town during the 1940s. (REV: BL 4/15/85; LJ 4/ 15/85; PW 2/15/85)

7879 Hughes, David. *Pork Butcher*. 1988, New Amsterdam paper $9.95 (0-941533-49-2). A former member of a Nazi-occupying force faced with a terminal illness returns to France to confess his part in a wartime atrocity. (REV: LJ 6/1/85; NYTBR 5/ 19/85; TLS 11/29/85)

7880 Hulme, Keri. *Bone People*. 1985, Louisiana State Univ. Pr. $19.95 (0-8071-1284-4); Penguin paper $8.95 (0-14-008922-5). This Pegasus Prize–winning novel studies the relations between two Maori adults and a child of European ancestry washed ashore following a shipwreck off the New Zealand coast. (REV: BL 10/15/85; Choice 2/86; LJ 11/1/ 85)

7881 Humphreys, Josephine. *Fireman's Fair*. 1991, Viking $19.95 (0-670-83907-8). A South Carolina lawyer gives up his profession to seek personal fulfillment following a disastrous hurricane that struck Charleston. (REV: LJ 4/1/91; PW 3/1/91; Time 5/ 27/91)

7882 Humphreys, Josephine. *Rich in Love*. 1987, Viking $16.95 (0-670-81810-0); Penguin paper $7.95 (0-14-010283-3). A study of the effects of a parental divorce and a sister's marriage upon a Southern teenager. (REV: LJ 8/87; New Rep 10/19/87; PW 7/10/87. AWARDS: PW, 1987)

7883 Hunnicutt, Ellen. *Suite for Calliope*. 1987, Walker $17.95 (0-8027-0965-6); Dell paper $7.95 (0-440-50088-5). A small-town Indiana teenager flees her family and hooks up with a traveling circus. (REV: LJ 7/87; PW 5/22/87)

7884 Hunter, Stephen. *Day Before Midnight*. 1990, Bantam paper $4.95 (0-553-28235-2). A military special forces team attempts to stop terrorists who plan to launch a nuclear missile against the Soviet Union. (REV: BL 11/15/88; NYTBR 4/23/89; PW 11/11/88)

7885 Husted, Darrell. *A Perfect Family*. 1988, Brit- ish American $16.95 (0-945167-02-4). An analysis of the events that led up to a college student's murder of his entire family. (REV: BL 9/15/88; LJ 10/15/88)

7886 Hyde, Elizabeth. *Her Native Colors*. 1989, Dell paper $7.95 (0-440-55014-9). Two childhood friends reunite following a long period of separation prior to a wedding. (REV: BL 5/15/86; LJ 4/15/86; PW 3/14/86)

7887 Hyman, Tom. *Riches and Honor*. 1985, Vi- king $17.95 (0-670-80508-4); Bantam paper $4.50 (0-553-26141-X). A former Nazi posing as a Jew is awarded the post of ambassador to Israel and becomes involved in a plot to free his MIA son trapped in Vietnam. (REV: BL 8/85; LJ 8/85)

7888 Hynes, James. *Wild Colonial Boy*. 1990, Mac- millan $18.95 (0-689-12089-3). A fictional account of American-Irish supporters of the IRA in Northern Ireland. (REV: BL 4/15/90; LJ 3/15/90; PW 2/9/90)

7889 Ibarguengoitia, Jorge. *Two Crimes*. 1984, Go- dine $13.95 (0-87923-520-9); Avon paper $3.95 (0-380-89616-8). A Mexican writer's tale of a petty criminal seeking to escape from a small town to Mexico City. "Delightful to read."—LJ (REV: BL 8/84; LJ 7/84; PW 6/ 15/84)

7890 Ingalls, Rachel. *Binstead's Safari*. 1988, Si- mon & Schuster paper $6.95 (0-671-65955-3). A professor on an African expedition to research legends associated with lions finds his love for his wife rekindled on the trip. (REV: BL 2/1/88; NYTBR 4/ 17/88; Time 4/11/88)

7891 Ingalls, Rachel. *End of Tragedy*. 1989, Simon & Schuster $16.95 (0-671-66037-3); paper $7.95 (0-671-69600-9). Four novellas by an American writer who lives in England including "Friends in the Country," "An Artist's Life," "In the Act," and the title story. (REV: NYTBR 5/9/89; Newsweek 2/13/89; Time 2/20/89)

7892 Ingalls, Rachel. *I See a Long Journey*. 1987, Simon & Schuster paper $6.95 (0-671-63999-4). A collection of three novellas—"On Ice," "Blessed Art Thou," and the title story. "Ms. Ingalls is an original. She is right up there with the masters of the novella."—NYTBR (REV: BL 9/15/86; NYTBR 8/31/ 86; PW 7/25/86)

7893 Ingalls, Rachel. *Mrs. Caliban*. 1983, Harvard Common $12.95 (0-87645-112-1); Dell paper $6.95 (0-440-50003-6). This short novel by the author of *I See a Long Journey* was selected by the British Book Marketing Council as one of the 20 best American novels published since World War II. (REV: Choice 2/ 87; NYTBR 12/28/86)

7894 Ingalls, Rachel. *Pearlkillers*. 1988, Simon & Schuster paper $6.95 (0-671-66240-6). This collection of four novellas by the author of *Mrs. Caliban* includes "This Time Lucky," "People to People," "The Treasure," and "Captain Hendrik's Story." (REV: BL 8/87; LJ 8/87; TLS 5/9/86)

7895 Inman, Robert. *Home Fires Burning*. 1987, Little, Brown $17.95 (0-316-41892-7); Ballantine paper $4.95 (0-345-35076-6). This author's debut novel portrays the life of a Southern small-town newspaper editor during the years of World War II. "An emotionally gripping, captivating novel."—BL (REV: BL 1/15/87; PW 11/28/86)

7896 Inman, Robert. *Old Dogs and Children*. 1991, Little, Brown $19.95 (0-316-41897-8). An aging matron in a small Southern town reflects on the

changes and lessons of 70 years of life. (REV: BL 1/1/
91; LJ 12/90; PW 11/30/90)

7897   Innes, Hammond. *High Stand.* **1988, McGraw-
Hill paper $4.95 (0-07-031738-0).** This environmental
thriller depicts the search for an abducted Canadian timber businessman. (REV: BL 9/15/86; LJ 9/1/86;
PW 8/8/86)

7898   Irving, Clifford. *Trial.* **1990, Simon & Schuster $18.95 (0-671-66422-0).** A Houston defense attor-
ney attempts to salvage his reputation by returning to practice after serving a jail sentence for
perjury. "Most readers will want to read this at one
sitting."—LJ (REV: LJ 9/1/90; NYTBR 11/18/90; PW 8/10/
90)

7899   Irving, John. *Cider House Rules.* **1985, Morrow $18.95 (0-688-03036-X); Bantam paper $5.95 (0-
553-25800-1).** The story of a Maine doctor who runs
an orphanage where he performs abortions for
women on the side. (REV: LJ 6/1/85; NYTBR 5/26/85;
Time 6/3/85. AWARDS: Time, 1985)

7900   Irving, John. *A Prayer for Owen Meany.* **1989,
Morrow $19.95 (0-688-07708-0); Ballantine paper
$5.95 (0-345-36179-2).** A story tracing the lives of two
friends from childhood to adulthood and detailing
how the life of one inspired the other to become a
Christian. (REV: BL 3/1/89; CSM 4/19/89; Time 4/3/89.
AWARDS: ALA, 1989)

7901   Irving, John. *Water Method Man.* **1990, Ballantine paper $4.95 (0-345-36742-1).** This second novel
by the author of *The Cider House Rules* chronicles
the life of a man born with a urinary tract defect.
(REV: LJ 6/15/72; NYTBR 9/10/72; PW 4/3/72)

7902   Irwin, Robert. *Limits of Vision.* **1986, Viking
$12.95 (0-670-80797-4); Penguin paper $4.95 (0-14-
008886-5).** The portrait of a woman obsessed with
cleanliness. "An astonishing work of imagination
and erudition."—PW (REV: BL 7/86; NYTBR 8/24/86;
PW 6/13/87; TLS 4/25/86)

7903   Isaacs, Susan. *Almost Paradise.* **1985, Ballantine paper $5.95 (0-345-31677-0).** A chronicle of the
rise and fall of a couple's marriage and fortune.
(REV: LJ 2/1/84; NYTBR 2/12/84)

7904   Isaacs, Susan. *Compromising Positions.*
1985, Jove paper $4.95 (0-515-09302-5). A bored New
York housewife seeks to alleviate her ennui by
helping track the killer of a local dentist. (REV: BL 6/
15/78; PW 1/23/78; TLS 11/3/78)

7905   Isherwood, Christopher. *Meeting by the River.*
1988, Farrar paper $7.95 (0-374-52076-3). An English-
man who travels to India to study religion and
become a monk is confronted by his brother on the
eve of his vows. (REV: New Rep 4/15/67; NYTBR 6/25/67;
PW 2/13/67)

7906   Ishiguro, Kazuo. *An Artist of the Floating
World.* **1989, Random paper $8.95 (0-679-72266-1).**
An artist's reflections upon his past and present
form the basis for this look at Japanese society
before and after World War II. (REV: LJ 5/15/86; PW 3/
28/86; TLS 2/14/86. AWARDS: ALA, 1986)

7907   Ishiguro, Kazuo. *A Pale View of Hills.* **1990,
Random paper $8.95 (0-679-72267-X).** A first novel
concerning a Japanese woman living in England
who receives a visit from a daughter who survived
the atomic bombing of Nagasaki. (REV: BL 4/15/82;
NYTBR 5/9/82; TLS 2/19/82. AWARDS: ALA, 1982)

7908   Ishiguro, Kazuo. *Remains of the Day.* **1989,
Knopf $18.95 (0-394-57343-9); Random paper $9.95
(0-679-73172-5).** An English butler reflects upon his
life and his three decades of service for his lord.
(REV: BL 10/15/89; NYTBR 10/8/89; PW 8/11/89. AWARDS:
ALA, 1989; BL, 1989; NYTBR, 1989; PW, 1989)

7909   Islas, Arturo. *Migrant Souls.* **1990, Morrow
$16.95 (0-688-07410-3).** A profile of Mexican-
American families struggling for identity while
living on the border of Texas and Mexico. (REV: BL 2/
1/90; LJ 2/1/90; PW 12/8/89)

7910   Jacobson, Harold. *Coming from Behind.* **1985,
Academy Chicago paper $6.95 (0-89733-155-9).** A
story of the life of an English literature professor
employed at an institution of higher learning
whose standards do not meet his own. (REV: NYTBR
1/15/84; PW 10/21/83)

7911   Jaffe, Rona. *After the Reunion.* **1986, Dell
paper $5.99 (0-440-10047-X).** The sequel to the
author's *Class Reunion* tracing the further lives of
four female Radcliffe graduates as their twenty-
fifth-year reunion approaches. (REV: BL 7/85; LJ 8/85;
PW 6/28/85)

7912   Jaffe, Rona. *Class Reunion.* **1986, Dell paper
$4.95 (0-440-11288-5).** A chronicle of the twentieth
anniversary class reunion of four Radcliffe College
sorority friends who attended school together
during the 1950s. (REV: NYTBR 7/8/79; Time 7/2/79)

7913   James, P. D. *Innocent Blood.* **1988, Warner
paper $4.95 (0-446-31177-4).** A young English woman
searches to find the truth about her birth parents
after reaching adulthood. "Establishes Miss James
as a first-rate writer without any qualifying genre
tag."—Newsweek (REV: BL 5/1/80; Newsweek 5/12/80;
PW 3/7/80)

7914   Janowitz, Tama. *American Dad.* **1987, Crown
paper $7.95 (0-517-56573-0).** A young man's account
of his relationships with his psychiatrist father and
poet mother. Written by the author of *A Cannibal in
Manhattan.* (REV: BL 4/15/81; LJ 3/15/81)

7915   Janowitz, Tama. *A Cannibal in Manhattan.*
**1987, Crown $17.95 (0-517-56624-9); Washington
Square Pr. paper $7.95 (0-671-66598-7).** A former
tribal chief and cannibal marries a New York
heiress who introduces him to the social life of
Manhattan. (REV: BL 9/1/87; LJ 10/15/87; Time 10/19/87)

7916   Jelinek, Elfriede. *Wonderful, Wonderful
Times.* **1990, Consort Book Sales paper $13.95 (1-
852421-68-1).** A portrait of the depraved life-styles of
an Austrian family in the aftermath of World War
II. (REV: PW 11/23/90; TLS 11/2/90. AWARDS: PW, 1990)

7917   Jen, Gish. *Typical American.* **1991, Houghton
$19.95 (0-395-54689-3).** A fictional story of Chinese-

American immigrants who struggle to make it in the United States after they flee the 1949 Communist takeover of China. (Rev: BL 3/1/91; NYTBR 3/31/91; PW 1/18/91)

7918 Jenks, Tom. *Our Happiness.* **1990, Bantam $19.95 (0-553-07016-X); paper $8.95 (0-553-34854-X).** An examination of the family life and personal pain of a man who accidentally murdered a man a decade earlier. (Rev: BL 5/15/90; LJ 5/15/90)

7919 Jersild, P. C. *Children's Island.* **1986, Univ. of Nebraska Pr. $25.95 (0-8032-2569-5); paper $11.50 (0-8032-7567-6).** A ten-year-old child roams the streets of Stockholm after escaping from the care of his parents in this novel by a Swedish writer. (Rev: LJ 12/86; NYTBR 12/21/86)

7920 Jersild, P. C. *House of Babel.* **1987, Univ. of Nebraska Pr. $25.95 (0-8032-2570-9); paper $13.95 (0-8032-7568-4).** A Swedish writer's indictment of the medical profession takes the form of a novel concerning the treatment of an elderly heart patient in a Stockholm hospital. (Rev: LJ 2/1/88; PW 11/27/87)

7921 Jhabvala, Ruth Prawer. *Heat and Dust.* **1988, Peter Smith $15.50 (0-8446-6335-2); Simon & Schuster paper $7.95 (0-671-64657-5).** A study of the effects of the British legacy in India as told through the lives of two women. (Rev: LJ 1/15/76; NYTBR 4/4/76; TLS 11/7/75. Awards: ALA, 1976; NYTBR, 1976)

7922 Jhabvala, Ruth Prawer. *Three Continents.* **1987, Morrow $18.95 (0-688-07184-8); Simon & Schuster paper $7.95 (0-671-66362-3).** Two Americans become involved with a mystical religious sect in this tenth novel by the author of *Out of India*. (Rev: BL 8/87; NYTBR 8/23/87; Newsweek 8/24/87)

7923 Jhabvala, Ruth Prawer. *Travelers.* **1987, Simon & Schuster paper $7.95 (0-671-64378-9).** Two English travelers recount their experiences exploring the Indian subcontinent. "A novel full of excellent characterizations and evocative moods."—LJ (Rev: BL 9/1/73; Choice 10/73; LJ 8/73. Awards: ALA, 1973)

7924 Jia, Pingwa. *Turbulence.* **1991, Louisiana State Univ. Pr. $22.95 (0-8071-1687-4).** This 1991 Pegasus Prize winner concerns the lives of Chinese peasants adjusting to a free-market economy during the 1980s. (Rev: LJ 8/91; PW 8/30/91)

7925 Johnson, Charles. *Faith and the Good Thing.* **1987, Macmillan paper $9.95 (0-689-70720-7).** The story of a Georgia woman's search for satisfaction and meaning in life. Written by the author of *Middle Passage*. (Rev: Choice 2/75; NYTBR 1/12/75)

7926 Johnson, Denis. *Angels.* **1989, Random paper $7.95 (0-394-75987-7).** Johnson's first novel concerns the adventures of two California drifters who meet on a bus bound for Pittsburgh. (Rev: LJ 8/83; Newsweek 10/2/83; PW 7/22/83)

7927 Johnson, Denis. *Stars at Noon.* **1986, Knopf $15.95 (0-394-53840-4); paper $5.95 (0-394-75427-1).** Johnson's second novel chronicles the lives of an American woman and an English businessman trapped in a chaotic Managua during the mid-1980s. (Rev: BL 9/1/86; NYTBR 9/28/86)

7928 Johnson, Diane. *Health and Happiness.* **1990, Knopf $19.95 (0-394-58717-0).** A fictional portrait of life at a San Francisco hospital written by the author of *Persian Nights*. (Rev: BL 8/90; LJ 9/15/90)

7929 Johnson, Diane. *Persian Nights.* **1987, Knopf $17.95 (0-394-55804-9); Fawcett paper $4.50 (0-449-21514-8).** A tale of an American archaeologist in Iran just prior to the collapse of the Shah's government. (Rev: BL 3/15/87; LJ 3/15/87; NYTBR 4/23/87)

7930 Johnson, Uwe. *Anniversaries.* **1975, Harcourt $10.00 (0-15-107561-1).** An East German woman defects to the United States and keeps a journal regarding her new life in New York. "A distinguished and marvelous book."—LJ (Rev: LJ 1/15/75; NYTBR 2/23/75; Sat Rev 2/23/75)

7931 Jolley, Elizabeth. *Cabin Fever.* **1991, HarperCollins $19.95 (0-06-016622-3).** This sequel to *My Father's Moon* traces the thoughts of an English nurse as she reflects on her recent past and on an affair with a married man that left her pregnant. (Rev: BL 7/91; LJ 7/91; NYTBR 7/7/91)

7932 Jolley, Elizabeth. *Foxybaby.* **1986, Penguin paper $5.95 (0-14-008380-4).** The story of a group of aging society matrons at a mind/body improvement program, by the author of *The Well*. (Rev: BL 9/1/85; LJ 10/1/85; NYTBR 11/24/85)

7933 Jolley, Elizabeth. *Milk and Honey.* **1986, Persea Books paper $8.95 (0-89255-103-8).** A novel in the form of a monologue chronicling the thoughts of a former cellist turned salesman following a tragic accident that left him unable to play the cello. (Rev: BL 5/15/86; LJ 5/15/86; PW 4/11/86)

7934 Jolley, Elizabeth. *Miss Peabody's Inheritance.* **1985, Penguin paper $6.95 (0-14-007743-X).** A woman's correspondence with an Australian writer leads to her involvement with his novel-in-progress. (Rev: BL 10/1/84; LJ 11/1/84; PW 9/14/84)

7935 Jolley, Elizabeth. *Mr. Scobie's Riddle.* **1984, Penguin paper $6.95 (0-14-007490-2).** A portrait of life in an ineptly run Australian nursing home by the author of *Miss Peabody's Inheritance*. (Rev: BL 10/1/84; LJ 11/1/84; PW 9/28/84)

7936 Jolley, Elizabeth. *My Father's Moon.* **1989, Harper & Row $15.95 (0-06-016062-4); paper $8.95 (0-06-091659-1).** A student nurse raised in a lower-class English family recounts her experiences at a military hospital following World War II. (Rev: BL 4/15/89; PW 2/24/89; TLS 7/28/89)

7937 Jolley, Elizabeth. *Newspaper of Claremont Street.* **1987, Viking $14.95 (0-670-80946-2); Penguin paper $6.95 (0-14-008582-3).** An Australian cleaning woman tells the personal stories of the residents of a suburban street. (Rev: BL 11/15/87; LJ 1/88; Time 12/7/87)

7938 Jolley, Elizabeth. *Palomino*. 1987, Persea Books $15.95 (0-89255-116-X). Two Australian women develop a friendship and live together on a farm in this novel by the author of *Milk and Honey*. (REV: LJ 5/15/87; New Yorker 9/14/87; PW 5/1/87)

7939 Jolley, Elizabeth. *Sugar Mother*. 1988, Harper & Row $16.95 (0-06-015940-5); paper $7.95 (0-06-091588-9). An Australian professor falls in love with his neighbor's daughter while his wife practices medicine overseas. (REV: LJ 6/1/88; PW 5/6/88; TLS 3/3/89)

7940 Jolley, Elizabeth. *The Well*. 1986, Viking $14.95 (0-670-81103-3); Penguin paper $6.95 (0-14-008901-2). An orphaned Australian girl living on a farm has her life transformed following a tragic accident that leaves a man dead. "Jolley at her best."—BL (REV: BL 11/1/86; New Rep 2/23/87; PW 9/26/86)

7941 Jones, Gayl. *Corregidora*. 1986, Beacon paper $8.95 (0-8070-6315-0). A study of the spiritual emptiness in the historical past and personal present of an African-American woman. (REV: LJ 8/75; New Rep 6/28/75; Time 6/16/75)

7942 Jones, Gayl. *Eva's Man*. 1987, Beacon paper $7.95 (0-8070-6319-3). The story of the tragic life of a woman imprisoned for the murder of her lover in a hotel room five years earlier. (REV: BL 4/15/76; LJ 3/15/76; Newsweek 4/12/76)

7943 Jones, Kaylie. *A Soldier's Daughter Never Cries*. 1990, Bantam $19.95 (0-553-07017-7); paper $7.95 (0-553-34930-9). Written by the daughter of writer James Jones, this is the story of expatriate Americans living in Paris who adopt a French child. (REV: BL 6/1/90; LJ 6/1/90; PW 6/8/90)

7944 Jones, Louis B. *Ordinary Money*. 1990, Viking $18.95 (0-670-82856-4). Two middle-aged former childhood friends become involved in a counterfeiting scheme. (REV: BL 12/1/89; LJ 12/89; PW 10/27/89)

7945 Jones, Madison. *A Cry of Absence*. 1989, Louisiana State Univ. Pr. paper $9.95 (0-8071-1579-7). A Tennessee town is torn by racial tensions following the murder of an African-American man by two local white men. (REV: LJ 5/15/71; New Rep 6/26/71)

7946 Jones, Peter. *Delivery*. 1990, Crown $18.95 (0-517-57780-1). A terrorist group hijacks seven nuclear bombs being transported to New Mexico and threatens to detonate them at sites scattered throughout the United States. (REV: LJ 11/1/90; PW 11/2/90)

7947 Jones, R. S. *Force of Gravity*. 1991, Viking $19.95 (0-670-83591-9). A first novel chronicling the life of a man drifting toward insanity. "An astonishing debut."—PW (REV: BL 5/1/91; PW 4/5/91)

7948 Jones, Robert F. *Blood Tide*. 1990, Atlantic Monthly $18.95 (0-87113-317-2). A group of Americans seeking to reclaim a stolen boat becomes embroiled in warfare against Filipino drug traffickers. (REV: BL 3/15/90; LJ 2/1/90; PW 1/26/90)

7949 Jong, Erica. *How to Save Your Own Life*. 1977, Holt $8.95 (0-03-017726-X); NAL paper $4.95 (0-451-15948-9). This sequel to *Fear of Flying* chronicles the further adventures of Isadora Wing. "A joyous, exhilarating, miraculous novelistic flight."—LJ (REV: BL 2/1/77; LJ 1/15/77; PW 1/17/77)

7950 Jong, Erica. *Parachutes and Kisses*. 1985, NAL paper $4.95 (0-451-13877-5). This chronicle of the amorous exploits of Isadora Wing in her late 30s continues the series that began with *Fear of Flying* and *How to Save Your Own Life*. (REV: BL 8/84; LJ 10/1/84; PW 8/10/84)

7951 Jonsson, Reidar. *My Life as a Dog*. 1990, Farrar $17.95 (0-374-35108-2). A teenage Swedish boy comes to terms with the death of his mother in this novel that was adapted into an internationally acclaimed motion picture. (REV: BL 6/15/90; PW 4/27/90; TLS 10/13/89)

7952 Joyce, William. *First Born of an Ass*. 1989, Watermark paper $10.50 (0-922820-04-X). A weak young Pennsylvania man develops substantial muscle after answering a Charles Atlas mail-order advertisement. (REV: BL 2/1/90; LJ 12/89)

7953 Just, Ward. *American Ambassador*. 1987, Houghton $17.95 (0-395-42694-4). An American diplomat's son becomes a member of a radical West German terrorist group. (REV: BL 3/1/87; LJ 3/1/87; PW 1/16/87)

7954 Just, Ward. *Jack Gance*. 1989, Houghton $17.95 (0-395-49337-4); Ivy Books paper $4.95 (0-8041-0571-5). The rise of a politician through the Chicago machine to the U.S. Congress. (REV: CSM 1/89; LJ 1/89; NYTBR 1/1/89)

7955 Just, Ward. *The Translator*. 1991, Houghton $21.95 (0-395-57168-5). A portrait of the marriage of a German translator and an American woman living in Paris. (REV: BL 8/91; NYTBR 10/27/91. AWARDS: BL, 1991)

7956 Kadare, Ismail. *Chronicle in Stone*. 1987, New Amsterdam Books $19.95 (0-941533-00-X); paper $10.95 (0-941533-50-6). An Albanian writer portrays a young boy's coming of age during World War II. (REV: NYTBR 1/24/88; PW 2/24/89; TLS 7/3/87)

7957 Kalb, Marvin, and Ted Koppel. *In the National Interest*. 1980, Fawcett paper $1.75 (0-449-23743-5). A pair of television news journalists tell the story of the international crisis that follows the kidnapping of the wife of a U.S. cabinet member during a tour of the Middle East. (REV: BL 11/15/77; NYTBR 11/13/77)

7958 Kaplan, Johana. *O My America!* 1981, Avon paper $3.50 (0-380-56515-3). A daughter discovers details about the life and activities of her leftist father by interviewing his friends and acquaintances. (REV: LJ 1/15/80; NYTBR 1/13/80; Sat Rev 3/15/80)

7959 Karbo, Karen. *Diamond Lane*. 1991, Putnam $21.95 (0-399-13597-9). A documentary filmmaker returns from an extended stay in Africa to enter the

Hollywood motion picture world. "Savvy, surprising, and funny."—BL (Rev: BL 4/1/91; PW 3/15/91)

7960 Karbo, Karen. *Trespassers Welcome Here.* **1989, Putnam $17.95 (0-399-13437-9).** This first novel by the author concerns the interactions of a group of Soviet immigrants with Americans at a Southern California university. (Rev: NYTBR 5/21/89; PW 2/10/89; TLS 5/25/90)

7961 Kauffman, Janet. *Collaborators.* **1986, Knopf $13.95 (0-394-55080-3); Penguin paper $5.95 (0-14-009342-7).** A study of the relationship between a mother and her pre-teen daughter living on a Pennsylvania Mennonite farm. (Rev: LJ 5/15/86; NYTBR 4/20/86)

7962 Kawabata, Yasunari. *Beauty and Sadness.* **1981, Putnam paper $9.95 (0-399-50529-6).** A Japanese writer takes a trip to visit his former mistress in this novel that was the last the author wrote before his 1972 suicide. (Rev: Atl 3/75; Choice 9/75; PW 1/13/75)

7963 Kawabata, Yasunari. *The Lake.* **1980, Kodansha paper $5.95 (0-87011-365-8).** A novel written during the 1950s by the Japanese Nobel Prize winner regarding the scandal that arises following a high school teacher's affair with one of his students. (Rev: BL 10/15/74; CSM 8/21/74; PW 4/22/74)

7964 Kawabata, Yasunari. *Master of Go.* **1981, Putnam paper $7.95 (0-399-50528-8).** This story chronicling the events of a 1938 go championship in Japan was originally written by the Nobel laureate during the mid-1950s and translated into English by Edward Seidensticker for this edition. (Rev: BL 11/15/72; LJ 9/15/72; Time 10/9/72)

7965 Kawabata, Yasunari. *Old Capital.* **1987, North Point $15.95 (0-86547-278-5); paper $8.95 (0-86547-411-7).** This first English translation of a 1962 novel set in Kyoto concerns the life of a girl abandoned as a baby on the doorstep of a kimono dealer. (Rev: Choice 11/87; LJ 5/1/87; PW 5/22/87)

7966 Kawabata, Yasunari. *Sound of the Mountain.* **1981, Putnam paper $5.95 (0-399-50527-X).** An exploration of the life of a family elder who becomes involved in the personal problems of his children. (Rev: NYTBR 6/14/70; Newsweek 6/1/70; Sat Rev 6/6/70)

7967 Keeble, John. *Broken Ground.* **1989, Harper & Row paper $8.95 (0-06-091523-4).** A story of a Vietnam veteran in charge of a mysterious construction project for an Oregon government prison. "An eerie vision of great intensity."—NYTBR (Rev: NYTBR 3/6/88; New Yorker 2/22/88; PW 9/25/87)

7968 Kees, Weldon. *Fall Quarter.* **1990, Story Line $18.95 (0-934257-43-4).** This previously unpublished story written during the 1930s is about a midwestern writer turned professor and is the only known novel by the author. (Rev: BL 9/1/90; NYTBR 11/25/90; PW 7/13/90)

7969 Keillor, Garrison. *Lake Wobegon Days.* **1985, Viking $17.95 (0-670-80514-9); Penguin paper $8.95** (0-14-013161-2). Vignettes of life in the fictional town of Lake Wobegon, Minnesota, as introduced on the author's "Prairie Home Companion" radio show. (Rev: LJ 11/1/85; PW 7/26/85; Time 9/2/85. Awards: PW, 1985)

7970 Kemal, Yashar. *They Burn the Thistles.* **1982, Writers & Readers paper $4.95 (0-906-49536-9).** This tale of the struggle by the peasants of a small village against their greedy landlords is the Turkish writer's sequel to *Memed, My Hawk.* (Rev: BL 6/1/77; NYTBR 7/10/77; PW 2/21/77)

7971 Keneally, Thomas. *Flying Hero Class.* **1991, Warner $19.95 (0-446-51582-5).** An account of the fate of a hijacked plane whose passengers include a group of Aborigine performers. (Rev: BL 2/15/91; LJ 3/15/91; PW 2/15/91)

7972 Kennedy, Raymond. *Lulu Incognito.* **1988, Random paper $7.95 (0-394-75641-X).** A story of a young woman with a minor clerk job who becomes the personal secretary of a wealthy Massachusetts woman. (Rev: BL 2/15/88; LJ 3/1/88; PW 1/8/88)

7973 Kennedy, William P. *Ironweed.* **1988, Penguin paper $4.50 (0-14-008103-8).** This portrayal of low-down life in Albany, New York, is part of the author's Albany cycle that includes *Legs* and *Billy Phelan's Greatest Game.* (Rev: New Rep 2/14/83; NYTBR 1/23/83; Time 1/24/83. Awards: ALA, 1983; NYTBR, 1983; PP:Fiction, 1984; Time, 1983)

7974 Kennedy, William P. *Toy Soldiers.* **1988, St. Martin's $19.95 (0-312-01478-3).** A thriller concerning the PLO terrorist takeover of an exclusive American boys school in Italy. (Rev: BL 6/15/88; LJ 6/15/88; PW 4/29/88)

7975 Kenney, Susan. *In Another Country.* **1985, Penguin paper $6.95 (0-14-007407-4).** Six interconnected stories regarding a woman's adjustment to the death of her father, the terminal illness of her husband, the insanity of her mother, and the accidental death of her dog at her own hands. (Rev: CSM 8/3/84; NYTBR 8/5/84; Time 6/11/84. Awards: ALA, 1984)

7976 Kenney, Susan. *Sailing.* **1988, Viking $18.95 (0-670-81229-3); Penguin paper $8.95 (0-14-009333-8).** This sequel to *In Another Country* concerns the lives of an artist and professor couple in a small Maine town. (Rev: BL 2/1/88; LJ 3/15/88; PW 2/5/88)

7977 Keyes, Daniel. *Flowers for Algernon.* **1966, Harcourt $17.95 (0-15-131510-8); Bantam paper $3.50 (0-553-25665-3).** A journal of a mentally retarded adult who becomes a temporary genius following brain surgery. "A gripping and touching insight into the world of the mentally deficient."—BL (Rev: BL 6/1/66; PW 2/28/66; TLS 7/21/66. Awards: Nebula, 1967; NYTBR, 1966)

7978 Kiefer, Warren. *Perpignan Exchange.* **1990, Donald I. Fine $18.95 (1-55611-227-0).** A fugitive from Egyptian authorities becomes involved in an airplane hijacking. (Rev: BL 12/1/90; LJ 11/1/90; PW 10/19/90)

7979 Kiely, Benedict. *Nothing Happens in Carmincross.* 1985, Godine $16.95 (0-87923-585-3); paper$8.95 (0-87923-725-2). An Irish American visits Northern Ireland to attend the wedding of his niece. "Will surely be a classic of Irish and world literature."—LJ (REV: BL 11/1/85; LJ 11/1/85; NYRB 5/8/86)

7980 Killens, John Oliver. *Cotillion: Or One Good Bull Is Half the Herd.* 1988, Ballantine paper $3.95 (0-345-352164-9). The story of a young African-American writer trying to compose a definitive black comedy. (REV: Atl 2/71; LJ 12/1/70; Sat Rev 3/6/71)

7981 Kincaid, Jamaica. *Annie John.* 1985, Farrar $18.95 (0-374-10521-9); NAL paper $6.95 (0-452-26016-7). A study of the life of a teenage girl on the West Indian island of Antigua. (REV: LJ 4/1/85; NYTBR 4/7/85; TLS 11/29/85. AWARDS: ALA, 1985; LJ, 1985)

7982 Kincaid, Jamaica. *Lucy.* 1990, Farrar $16.95 (0-374-19434-3). The study of the life of a teenage West Indian immigrant who takes a job as a live-in maid in New York. "A novel no one should miss."—LJ (REV: BL 10/1/90; CSM 11/26/90; LJ 11/1/90. AWARDS: BL, 1990; PW, 1990)

7983 King, Stephen. *Bachman Books.* 1986, NAL paper $5.95 (0-451-14736-7). A collection of four early novels written by King under the pen name of Richard Bachman including *Running Man, Long Walk, Road Work,* and *Rage.* (REV: BL 10/1/85; PW 9/6/85)

7984 King, Stephen. *Misery.* 1987, Viking $18.95 (0-670-81364-8); NAL paper $5.95 (0-451-15355-3). A romance novelist is terrorized by a fan who rescues him from an automobile accident after he reveals the plot of his latest book to her. (REV: LJ 5/1/87; NYTBR 5/31/87; PW 5/1/87)

7985 King, Stephen. *The Shining.* 1990, Doubleday $21.95 (0-385-12167-9); NAL paper $4.95 (0-451-16091-6). A family is terrorized during a winter spent overseeing a hotel in this novel by the author of *Salem's Lot.* (REV: BL 3/1/77; LJ 2/1/77)

7986 King, Stephen. *The Stand.* 1978, Doubleday $18.95 (0-385-12168-7); NAL paper $5.95 (0-451-16095-9). A group of survivors escape a deadly epidemic spread from a laboratory where scientists were doing research into germ warfare. (REV: BL 12/1/78; LJ 11/15/78; New Yorker 1/15/79)

7987 King, Tabitha. *Pearl.* 1988, NAL $18.95 (0-453-00626-4); paper $4.95 (0-451-16262-5). An African-American woman becomes romantically involved with two men following a move to Maine. "An unforgettable reading experience."—LJ (REV: LJ 11/15/88; PW 9/9/88)

7988 King, Tabitha. *The Trap.* 1985, Macmillan $15.95 (0-02-563140-3); NAL paper $4.95 (0-451-16030-4). A family visits their summer home only to find a group of criminals living there. "A gripping story with an electrifying climax."—LJ (REV: BL 4/1/85; LJ 4/1/85; PW 2/15/85)

7989 King, Thomas. *Medicine River.* 1990, Viking $18.95 (0-670-82962-5). A portrait of life on an Alberta Blackfoot reservation. "An astonishingly good first novel."—LJ (REV: BL 10/1/90; LJ 8/90; PW 8/10/90)

7990 Kingsolver, Barbara. *Animal Dreams.* 1990, Harper & Row $19.95 (0-06-016350-X). A woman returns to her Arizona home to care for her ailing father and finds herself facing a mining company that threatens the quality of the local environment. (REV: BL 8/90; LJ 8/90; PW 6/22/90. AWARDS: ALA, 1990; LJ, 1990; PW, 1990)

7991 Kingsolver, Barbara. *Bean Trees.* 1988, Harper & Row $16.95 (0-06-015863-8); paper $8.95 (0-06-091554-4). A woman who leaves her Kentucky home to search for a new life in the West finds herself working in a Tucson tire repair shop that serves as a way station for Central American refugees. (REV: BL 3/1/88; CSM 4/22/88; NYTBR 4/10/88)

7992 Kingston, Maxine Hong. *Tripmaster Monkey: His Fake Book.* 1989, Knopf $19.95 (0-394-56831-1); Random paper $9.95 (0-679-72789-2). A recent Berkeley graduate stages a street performance to celebrate Chinese-American culture in this story set in the late 1960s. (REV: BL 2/15/89; LJ 4/1/89; New Rep 4/17/89)

7993 Klass, Perri. *Other Women's Children.* 1990, Random $19.95 (0-394-58699-9). A portrait of the life and career of a female pediatrician by the author of *Recombinations.* (REV: Newsweek 10/22/90; PW 7/20/90)

7994 Klass, Perri. *Recombinations.* 1985, Putnam $17.95 (0-399-13090-X). A Manhattan genetic researcher has an affair with a coworker in this novel by the author of *I Am Having an Adventure.* (REV: LJ 10/1/85; Newsweek 11/11/85; PW 8/16/85)

7995 Klavan, Andrew. *Don't Say a Word.* 1991, Pocket paper $19.95 (0-671-74008-3). The life of a New York psychiatrist is threatened by the actions of two of his patients. "Guaranteed to keep the reader's heart pounding right up to the last page."—LJ (REV: BL 4/15/91; LJ 4/1/91; PW 3/29/91)

7996 Klein, Norma. *That's My Baby.* 1988, Viking $16.95 (0-670-81730-9); Fawcett paper $3.95 (0-449-70356-8). A young playwright incorporates the experiences of two love affairs into a work of drama. (REV: BL 5/15/88; LJ 6/1/88; PW 5/13/88)

7997 Klima, Ivan. *Love and Garbage.* 1991, Knopf $20.00 (0-394-5876-9). A Czech writer wanders the streets of Prague with friends and reflects upon his nation and society. (REV: LJ 5/1/91; PW 3/22/91)

7998 Klima, Ivan. *My First Loves.* 1988, Harper & Row $14.95 (0-06-015866-2); Norton paper $7.95 (0-393-30601-1). A Czech writer traces the life of a boy from his World War II childhood to adulthood in a series of four connected stories. (REV: NYTBR 2/21/88; PW 12/14/87; TLS 1/23/87)

7999 Knowles, John. *Peace Breaks Out.* 1982, Bantam paper $3.95 (0-553-27574-7). The author's sequel to *A Separate Peace* portrays life in a New Hampshire boys boarding school in the years following World War II. (REV: BL 12/15/80; LJ 1/15/81; NYTBR 3/22/81)

8000 Koch, Stephen. *Bachelor's Bride.* **1986, M. Boyars $18.95 (0-7145-2856-0).** A fictionalized portrait of the New York art world in the early 1960s. "A shrewd, engrossing insider's view."—PW (REV: BL 7/86; PW 6/6/86; TLS 10/3/86)

8001 Kociancich, Vlady. *Last Days of William Shakespeare.* **1991, Morrow $20.00 (0-688-10432-0).** An Argentine story of government corruption involving a national theater group that has staged Hamlet for over 70 years. (REV: LJ 4/15/91; PW 3/15/91)

8002 Konecky, Edith. *A Place at the Table.* **1989, Random $16.95 (0-394-57522-9).** A story of the relationship between a New York writer suffering from cancer and a friend on the brink of madness. (REV: LJ 4/1/89; NYTBR 6/4/89; PW 3/10/89)

8003 Konrad, George. *The Case Worker.* **1987, Penguin paper $6.95 (0-14-009946-8).** This first novel by the Hungarian writer, which revolves around the experiences of a Budapest social worker, is based on the author's decade of work in that profession. (REV: Choice 9/74; LJ 2/1/74; New Yorker 3/11/74. AWARDS: ALA, 1974)

8004 Konrad, George. *City Builder.* **1987, Penguin paper $6.95 (0-14-009947-6).** A Hungarian architect recounts his recent family history in this novel by the author of *The Case Worker.* (REV: BL 10/1/77; Newsweek 2/6/78; Time 11/28/77)

8005 Konrad, George. *The Loser.* **1982, Harcourt paper $7.95 (0-15-653584-X).** The Hungarian writer portrays the odyssey of a countryman who experienced the Second World War, the Holocaust, and the domination by the Soviet Union. (REV: LJ 9/15/82; NYTBR 9/26/82; Time 1/17/83)

8006 Konwicki, Tadeusz. *A Minor Apocalypse.* **1983, Farrar $16.95 (0-374-20928-6).** The story of a Polish writer who plans to set himself afire in front of Communist Party headquarters to protest Soviet domination. (REV: LJ 6/1/83; New Yorker 1/2/84; PW 6/10/83)

8007 Konwicki, Tadeusz. *Moonrise, Moonset.* **1987, Farrar $19.95 (0-374-21241-4).** A collection of journals by the Polish writer regarding the state of his native land in the early 1980s. (REV: BL 8/87; LJ 8/87; PW 6/26/87)

8008 Konwicki, Tadeusz. *Polish Complex.* **1982, Farrar $12.95 (0-374-23548-1).** A group of Polish citizens reflect on the history of their nation in the aftermath of World War II. (REV: LJ 3/15/82; NYRB 3/4/82; NYTBR 1/10/82)

8009 Koontz, Dean R. *Bad Place.* **1990, Putnam $19.95 (0-399-13498-0).** A man suffering from amnesia is pursued by his siblings seeking revenge for the alleged murder of their mother. (REV: LJ 12/89; NYTBR 2/18/90; PW 11/24/89)

8010 Koontz, Dean R. *Strangers.* **1986, Putnam $17.95 (0-399-13143-4); Berkley paper $4.95 (0-425-09217-8).** Six strangers who once spent a night in the same Nevada motel have bizarre recurring nightmares and begin receiving odd messages through the mail that eventually reunite them. (REV: BL 3/1/86; LJ 4/15/86; NYTBR 6/15/86)

8011 Kornblatt, Joyce Reiser. *White Water.* **1987, Dell paper $3.95 (0-440-39324-8).** This debut novel chronicles the lives of five members of an American family. (REV: BL 5/15/85; NYTBR 7/7/85)

8012 Kosinski, Jerzy. *Being There.* **1985, Bantam paper $4.50 (0-553-27930-0).** A gardener whose only prior exposure to the world is television becomes regarded as a social and business prophet. (REV: LJ 4/1/71; Sat Rev 4/24/71; Time 4/26/71)

8013 Kosinski, Jerzy. *Blind Date.* **1989, Arcade paper $8.95 (1-55970-003-3).** A chronicle of the political and amorous adventures of an East European immigrant businessman in New York. (REV: BL 10/15/77; Choice 2/78; Newsweek 11/21/77)

8014 Kosinski, Jerzy. *Passion Play.* **1989, Arcade paper $8.95 (1-55970-023-8).** A chronicle of the travels and sexual exploits of a polo player, as depicted by the author of *Cockpit.* (REV: Newsweek 9/10/79; PW 7/23/79; TLS 4/25/80)

8015 Kosinski, Jerzy. *Pinball.* **1989, Arcade paper $8.95 (1-55970-004-1).** A struggling musician is employed by a woman to find the whereabouts and identity of a mysterious, popular rock star. (REV: BL 1/1/82; LJ 2/15/82; Time 3/22/82)

8016 Kosinski, Jerzy. *Steps.* **1988, Random paper $5.95 (0-394-75716-5).** A novel by the author of *The Painted Bird* about the romantic and political adventures of an exile in Europe and America. (REV: Choice 2/69; Newsweek 10/21/68; TLS 8/5/69. AWARDS: NBA, 1969)

8017 Kotzwinkle, William. *Fan Man.* **1987, Dutton paper $7.95 (0-525-48307-1).** A chronicle of the events of several days and nights in the life of an eccentric neurotic living on New York's Lower East Side. (REV: New Rep 3/2/74; NYTBR 2/10/74; TLS 11/22/74)

8018 Kotzwinkle, William. *Midnight Examiner.* **1989, Houghton $17.95 (0-395-49859-7).** A tabloid magazine editor tries to save a friend from the grasp of a New York mobster. (REV: BL 3/15/89; LJ 4/1/89; Newsweek 5/8/89)

8019 Kramer, Kathryn. *A Handbook for Visitors from Outer Space.* **1985, Random paper $5.95 (0-394-72989-7).** This debut novel set in New England in the near future chronicles details in the lives of an American family. "Nobody who loves novels should miss it."—CSM (REV: BL 6/15/84; CSM 9/5/84; NYTBR 8/5/84)

8020 Krantz, Judith. *I'll Take Manhattan.* **1986, Crown $18.95 (0-517-56110-7); Bantam paper $5.95 (0-553-26407-9).** A tale of family infighting among a Manhattan publishing dynasty. "Will keep readers turning pages late into the night."—LJ (Rev: LJ 5/15/86; PW 3/14/86; Time 4/28/86)

8021 Kundera, Milan. *Farewell Party.* **1987, Penguin paper $7.95 (0-14-009694-9).** A pregnant nurse attempts to slap a jazz musician with a paternity suit in this novel set at a Czech spa. (Rev: BL 11/15/76; Choice 12/76; NYTBR 9/5/76)

8022 Kundera, Milan. *Immortality.* **1991, Grove-Weidenfeld $21.95 (0-8021-1111-4).** Two sisters fight for the affections of a man in Paris in this novel, which includes ruminations by Kundera on death, immortality, and recent European culture and history. (Rev: NYTBR 4/28/91; PW 3/29/91; Time 5/13/91. Awards: BL, 1991; Time, 1991)

8023 Kundera, Milan. *The Joke.* **1987, Penguin paper $7.95 (0-14-009692-2).** A new translation of the Czech writer's first novel regarding the life and fate of a young man who sends a humorous postcard interpreted as critical of the Party line. (Rev: LJ 11/1/82; New Rep 2/14/83; New Yorker 2/21/83)

8024 Kundera, Milan. *Life Is Elsewhere.* **1986, Penguin paper $8.95 (0-14-006470-2).** A chronicle of the political life of a Czech poet who joins the Communist party following World War II. "First-rate fiction."—LJ (Rev: LJ 8/74; Newsweek 7/29/74; Time 8/5/74)

8025 Kundera, Milan. *Unbearable Lightness of Being.* **1984, Harper & Row $19.95 (0-06-015258-3); paper $9.95 (0-06-091465-3).** Profiles of the lives of four people in post-1968 Czechoslovakia by the author of *The Joke.* (Rev: LJ 5/1/84; NYTBR 4/29/84; Time 4/16/84. Awards: LJ, 1984; NYTBR, 1984; Time, 1984; Time, the 1980s)

8026 Kupfer, Fern. *Surviving the Seasons.* **1989, Dell $18.95 (0-440-50115-6).** This author's first novel tells the story of a Florida widow and widower who comfort each other after the deaths of their spouses. (Rev: BL 9/15/87; LJ 8/87; NYTBR 11/1/87)

8027 Kurzweil, Allen. *A Case of Curiosities.* **1992, Harcourt $19.95 (0-15-115793-6).** A man purchases a box that contains the remnants of an eighteenth-century Frenchman's life, which becomes an object of devotion and obsession. "As moving as it is fresh and exciting."—BL (Rev: BL 10/15/91; LJ 11/1/91)

8028 Laidlaw, Brett. *Three Nights in the Heart of the Earth.* **1989, NAL paper $7.95 (0-452-26220-8).** The psychological portrait of an English professor on the brink of a mental breakdown trapped with his family in a three-day Minnesota blizzard. (Rev: BL 1/15/88; LJ 1/88; PW 12/4/87)

8029 Lamott, Anne. *All New People.* **1989, North Point $16.95 (0-86547-394-3).** A woman under hypnosis relives the crucial episodes of her life after her return to her northern California hometown. "A novel of rare sensitivity and emotional power."—PW (Rev: BL 10/1/89; LJ 8/89; PW 8/4/89)

8030 Lamott, Anne. *Hard Laughter.* **1987, North Point paper $8.95 (0-86547-280-7).** A debut novel chronicling the reactions of a California family to

their father's treatment for a brain tumor. (Rev: LJ 10/15/80; NYTBR 10/12/80)

8031 L'Amour, Louis. *Last of the Breed.* **1987, Bantam paper $4.95 (0-553-28042-2).** A story of a Native American U.S. Army officer captured by the Soviets who escapes from prison to survive as a fugitive in the Siberian winter. (Rev: LJ 7/6/86; NYTBR 7/6/86; Time 8/4/86)

8032 Lane, Linda, and Nancy Lee Andrews. *Malibu 90625.* **1990, Morrow $8.95 (0-688-08038-3).** A surprise visit by the mistress of a famous Hollywood director sends his career and family life into a tailspin. (Rev: BL 6/1/90; LJ 5/15/90; PW 5/25/90)

8033 Langford, Cameron. *Winter of the Fisher.* **1985, Norton paper $5.95 (0-393-30283-0).** A fictional account of a year in the life of a marten. "An exciting story . . . a delightful book."—LJ (Rev: LJ 3/1/71; NYTBR 5/2/71; New Yorker 6/26/71)

8034 Lansbury, Carol. *Grotto.* **1989, Knopf $19.95 (0-394-57438-9).** An illegitimate Sicilian girl obsessed with myths flees to Australia in search of love and adventure. (Rev: BL 4/15/89; NYTBR 5/21/89; PW 3/3/89)

8035 Lansbury, Carol. *Ringarra.* **1987, Ivy Books paper $3.95 (0-8041-0119-1).** An American woman engaged to an Australian man becomes obsessed with an arrogant, loathsome sheep rancher in this story by the author of *Grotto.* (Rev: NYTBR 3/23/86; PW 1/10/86)

8036 Larsen, Eric. *An American Memory.* **1988, Algonquin $12.95 (0-912697-68-7); Doubleday paper $7.95 (0-385-26255-8).** This debut novel chronicles three generations of a Minnesota farming family of Scandinavian ancestry. (Rev: NYTBR 5/29/88; PW 2/19/88)

8037 Lassalle, Caroline. *Breaking the Rules.* **1987, Viking $16.95 (0-670-81522-5); Penguin paper $6.95 (0-14-008979-9).** A writer working on Cyprus composes a biography of five women with interconnected lives. (Rev: BL 12/15/86; CSM 2/26/87; PW 10/31/86)

8038 Law-Yone, Wendy. *Coffin Tree.* **1988, Beacon paper $8.95 (0-8070-8301-1).** A woman is forced to flee her native Burma and emigrates to New York with her brother. (Rev: Atl 6/83; BL 4/15/83; PW 3/4/83)

8039 Lawrence, Kathleen Rockwell. *Maud Gone.* **1987, NAL paper $4.50 (0-451-40180-8).** A woman leaves her husband on the eve of their child's birth following her discovery of a series of infidelities. (Rev: BL 7/85; LJ 7/86; NYTBR 9/21/86)

8040 Leavitt, David. *Equal Affections.* **1989, Grove-Weidenfeld $18.95 (1-55584-202-X); Harper & Row paper $8.95 (0-06-097287-4).** A portrait of a mother's illness and death and its effects upon her four children and husband. "A compassionate, moving work."—LJ (Rev: BL 11/1/88; LJ 1/89; TLS 6/19/89)

8041 Leavitt, David. *Lost Language of Cranes.* **1986, Knopf $17.95 (0-394-53873-0); Bantam paper**

$8.95 (0-553-34665-X). A gay New York writer reveals his homosexuality to his father in this novel by the author of the short-story collection *Family Dancing.* (REV: LJ 9/15/86; NYTBR 10/5/86)

8042 Le Compte, Jane. *Moon Passage.* **1989, Harper & Row $16.95 (0-06-016120-5); paper $8.95 (0-06-091690-7).** A study of the relationship between a 45-year-old California woman and the 20-year-old who claims to be in love with her husband. (REV: LJ 5/1/89; NYTBR 6/25/89)

8043 Lee, Gus. *China Boy.* **1991, Dutton $19.95 (0-525-24994-X).** A portrait of Chinese-American life in San Francisco following World War II. (REV: LJ 4/1/91; PW 3/22/91; Time 6/3/91)

8044 Lehrer, Jim. *Crown Oklahoma.* **1989, Putnam $18.95 (0-399-13434-4).** The PBS newsman's sequel to *Kick the Can* about the scandal that arises after Oklahoma is declared a center for organized crime on a network news broadcast. (REV: BL 5/1/89; LJ 4/15/89; PW 3/17/89)

8045 Lehrer, Jim. *Kick the Can.* **1988, Putnam $17.95 (0-399-13350-X); Ballantine paper $3.95 (0-345-36024-9).** A chronicle set during the 1950s about the adventures of two teenage petty hoodlums in Texas, Kansas, and Oklahoma. (REV: BL 5/15/88; LJ 4/15/88; NYTBR 5/29/88)

8046 Leithauser, Brad. *Equal Distance.* **1984, Knopf $17.95 (0-394-53971-0); NAL paper $7.95 (0-452-25820-0).** This debut novel by a poet traces the lives of three Americans living in Japan. (REV: BL 12/1/84; LJ 12/84; Newsweek 3/25/85)

8047 Leithauser, Brad. *Hence.* **1989, Knopf $18.95 (0-394-57311-0); Penguin paper $8.95 (0-14-012854-9).** A story of a Boston chess match between a 21-year-old champion and a computer, set in the near future. (REV: BL 1/15/89; NYTBR 3/30/89)

8048 Lelchuk, Alan. *Brooklyn Boy.* **1989, McGraw-Hill $19.95 (0-07-037163-6).** The fictionalized memoirs of a Brooklyn boy chronicling his experiences growing up during the 1950s and 1960s. (REV: BL 10/15/89; LJ 10/15/89)

8049 Lemann, Nancy. *Lives of the Saints.* **1986, NAL paper $7.95 (0-452-25886-3).** This debut novel set in New Orleans chronicles the life of a young man following the death of his younger brother. (REV: LJ 6/15/85; New Rep 6/24/85; NYRB 6/27/85)

8050 Lentin, Ronit. *Night Train to Mother.* **1990, Cleis Pr. $24.95 (0-939416-32-8); paper $9.95 (0-939416-33-6).** A Jewish woman returns to her mother's ancestral home in Rumania during World War II in search of her mother's past. (REV: BL 3/15/90; LJ 4/1/90)

8051 Lenz, Siegfried. *Heritage.* **1981, Hill & Wang paper $8.95 (0-8090-1512-9).** An elderly European man tells the story of the destruction of his community's local museum and its effects on the town and its citzenry. (REV: BL 5/15/81; NYTBR 7/19/81; PW 4/17/81)

8052 Leonard, Elmore. *Bandits.* **1988, Warner paper $4.95 (0-446-30130-2).** A crew of bandits plot to steal millions of dollars from a Nicaraguan in the United States who is raising money for Contra activities. (REV: NYTBR 1/4/87; Newsweek 1/5/87; Time 1/12/87)

8053 Lerman, Rhoda. *God's Ear.* **1988, Henry Holt $19.95 (0-8050-0413-0).** A Hasidic rabbi who becomes a New York life insurance salesman finds himself challenged by the deathbed wishes of his father. (REV: NYTBR 7/2/89; PW 3/3/89)

8054 Lesley, Craig. *River Song.* **1989, Houghton $18.95 (0-395-43083-6); Dell paper $8.95 (0-440-50311-6).** A Native American rodeo rider is reunited with his son after a long separation in this sequel to the author's *Winterkill.* (REV: BL 5/1/89; LJ 5/15/89; PW 4/14/89)

8055 Lesley, Craig. *Winterkill.* **1986, Dell paper $5.95 (0-440-39589-5).** A debut novel portraying the life of the son of a Nez Perce holy man. (REV: BL 4/15/84; LJ 5/1/84; PW 4/6/84)

8056 Lessing, Doris. *Briefing for a Descent into Hell.* **1981, Knopf paper $5.95 (0-394-74662-7).** A first-hand tale of madness as told through the eyes of a former college professor interned in a psychiatric hospital. (REV: LJ 2/15/71; NYRB 5/6/71; Time 3/8/71)

8057 Lessing, Doris. *Fifth Child.* **1988, Knopf $16.95 (0-394-57105-3); Random paper $6.95 (0-679-72182-7).** A London couple's fifth child terrorizes his parents and siblings before being committed to an institution. (REV: LJ 3/15/88; PW 1/29/88; Time 3/14/88. AWARDS: ALA, 1988)

8058 Lessing, Doris. *Good Terrorist.* **1986, Random paper $5.95 (0-394-74629-5).** A study of the lives and motives of a group of London-based terrorists. (REV: NYRB 12/19/85; PW 7/5/85; TLS 9/13/85. AWARDS: PW, 1985)

8059 Lessing, Doris. *Memoirs of a Survivor.* **1988, Random paper $6.95 (0-394-75759-9).** A portrait of English society in chaos, set in the near future, following the disintegration of social mores. (REV: BL 9/1/75; PW 4/28/75; Time 6/16/75. AWARDS: Time, 1975)

8060 Lessing, Doris. *Summer Before the Dark.* **1983, Random paper $6.95 (0-394-71095-9).** A London woman travels through Europe on a voyage of self-discovery while her husband pursues scholarly research in the United States. (REV: LJ 3/15/73; Newsweek 5/4/73; Time 5/21/73. AWARDS: NYTBR, 1973; Time, 1973)

8061 Lester, Julius. *Do Lord Remember Me.* **1985, Holt $13.95 (0-03-071534-2).** A Mississippi preacher reviews his experiences on the last day of his life on earth. "A rich and moving reading experience."—BL (REV: BL 12/15/84; NYTBR 2/17/85; PW 11/2/84. AWARDS: ALA, 1985)

8062 Levi, Primo. *Monkey's Wrench.* **1987, Penguin paper $7.95 (0-14-010357-0).** A novel in the form of a monologue recording the international adventures of a professional heavy-equipment rigger. "A model of interplay between storytellers and listeners."—Time (REV: BL 10/1/86; LJ 10/15/86; Time 11/17/86)

8063 **Levin, Ira.** *Boys from Brazil.* **1976, Random $8.95 (0-394-40267-7).** Dr. Mengele clones Nazis in Brazil and plots a series of assassinations in the United States and Europe in a plan to resurrect the Reich. (REV: BL 2/15/76; LJ 4/15/76; New Yorker 3/8/76)

8064 **Levin, Jenifer.** *Shimoni's Lover.* **1987, Harcourt $18.95 (0-15-181990-4).** A story tracing the lives of the four sons of a legendary Israeli military leader. (REV: LJ 9/15/87; NYTBR 11/29/87; PW 7/24/87)

8065 **Levin, Michael.** *Socratic Method.* **1988, Ivy Books paper $3.95 (0-8041-0376-3).** A portrait of a New York law school and the efforts of a young law professor to attain tenure. "An energetic, intelligently motivated and often extremely funny book."—NYTBR (REV: LJ 11/1/87; NYTBR 12/27/87; PW 10/16/87)

8066 **Levinson, Deidre.** *Modus Vivendi.* **1985, Penguin paper $6.95 (0-14-008097-X).** An English professor moves to New York to continue her academic career at the expense of her family and personal life. (REV: LJ 7/84; NYTBR 9/2/84; PW 6/8/84)

8067 **Lezama Lima, Jose.** *Paradiso.* **1988, Univ. of Texas Pr. paper $12.95 (0-292-76507-X).** This Cuban novelist's work, originally published in Spanish in 1966 and translated by Gregory Rabassa, concerns a young man's search to know his father. (REV: BL 9/1/74; Choice 7–8/74; LJ 4/1/74)

8068 **L'Heureux, John.** *An Honorable Profession.* **1991, Viking $19.95 (0-670-82919-6).** A high school teacher is blamed by a Boston man for the suicide of his son. (REV: BL 11/15/90; NYTBR 1/27/91; PW 11/9/90)

8069 **L'Heureux, John.** *A Woman Run Mad.* **1988, Viking $17.95 (0-670-81752-X); Avon paper $3.95 (0-380-70686-5).** A psychosexual thriller about a married man and his relationship with a glamorous woman hiding a dark secret. (REV: BL 11/15/87; NYTBR 1/31/88; PW 11/13/87)

8070 **Liddy, G. Gordon.** *Monkey Handlers.* **1990, St. Martin's $19.95 (0-312-05127-1).** Former Navy SEAL Michael Stone is called on to save investigators in trouble after discovering a laboratory engaged in shocking animal experiments. (REV: NYTBR 10/14/90; PW 8/3/90)

8071 **Limonov, Edward.** *Memoir of a Russian Punk.* **1990, Grove-Weidenfeld $18.95 (0-8021-1026-6).** An account of the life of a teenage alcoholic thief in Kharkov during the 1950s. (REV: BL 11/15/90; LJ 11/1/90; PW 10/12/90)

8072 **Lipman, Eleanor.** *Then She Found Me.* **1990, Pocket $18.95 (0-671-68614-3).** A Boston talk-show host seeks out her birth daughter following the death of the girl's adoptive parents. (REV: BL 4/15/90; LJ 3/15/90; PW 2/9/90)

8073 **Lish, Gordon.** *Peru.* **1987, Macmillan paper $8.95 (0-684-18764-7).** A late-night newscast evokes

memories in the narrator of how he killed another child when he was six years old. (REV: NYTBR 2/2/86; New Yorker 3/10/86; PW 12/6/85)

8074 **Lispector, Clarice.** *Passion According to G. H.* **1988, Univ. of Minnesota Pr. $19.95 (0-8166-1711-2); paper $8.95 (0-8166-1712-0).** A Brazilian writer probes the thoughts of a woman at home by herself in this neoexistentialist novel. (REV: LJ 10/15/88; NYTBR 1/8/89; PW 8/19/88)

8075 **Lively, Penelope.** *According to Mark.* **1989, Harper & Row paper $7.95 (0-06-097199-1).** A biographer searches for the truth about the life of an English literary figure of the 1920s. (REV: BL 11/15/85; LJ 11/15/85; NYTBR 1/5/86)

8076 **Lively, Penelope.** *City of the Mind.* **1991, HarperCollins $19.95 (0-06-016666-5).** A recently divorced London architect reminisces about his life as he roams the city. By the author of *Moon Tiger.* (REV: BL 6/15/91; LJ 8/91; NYTBR 9/1/91. AWARDS: BL, 1991)

8077 **Lively, Penelope.** *Moon Tiger.* **1988, Grove-Weidenfeld $15.95 (0-8021-1027-4); Harper & Row paper $7.95 (0-06-097200-9).** This story of the remembrances of a terminally ill historian captured the Booker Prize. "Provocative and memorable, the book is a significant achievement."—PW (REV: BL 4/15/88; LJ 3/15/88; PW 2/12/88)

8078 **Lively, Penelope.** *Passing On.* **1990, Grove-Weidenfeld $16.95 (0-8021-1155-6).** A study of the lives of a spinster librarian and her single brother following the death of their mother. "Lively's great talent as a writer of adult fiction is confirmed."—LJ (REV: BL 2/1/90; LJ 3/1/90; TLS 4/7/89. AWARDS: ALA, 1990)

8079 **Lively, Penelope.** *Road to Litchfield.* **1990, Grove-Weidenfeld $17.95 (0-8021-1134-3).** The first American publication of the British author's debut novel regarding a woman who comes to know her father during his illness. (REV: BL 12/15/90; LJ 1/91; PW 11/23/90)

8080 **Livesey, Margot.** *Homework.* **1990, Viking $18.95 (0-670-83000-3).** A woman finds that her daughter is trying to sabotage her new love relationship following the family's relocation from London to Edinburgh. (REV: BL 2/1/90; LJ 12/89; NYTBR 5/6/90)

8081 **Llewellyn, Caroline.** *Masks of Rome.* **1988, Macmillan $16.95 (0-684-18921-6); Ivy Books paper $3.95 (0-8041-0375-5).** An American art expert discovers that a valuable artwork owned by an Italian family is a forgery. (REV: BL 7/88; LJ 7/88; PW 5/27/88)

8082 **Lo, Stephen C.** *Incorporation of Eric Chung.* **1989, Algonquin $14.95 (0-945575-18-1).** A fictional chronicle of a Chinese immigrant's adaptation to American culture. (REV: BL 9/15/89; LJ 10/15/89; PW 8/18/89)

8083 **Lodge, David.** *Changing Places.* **1979, Penguin paper $5.95 (0-14-004656-9).** A novel set in 1969 concerning two university professors, one American, one English, who exchange teaching posts. (REV: PW 8/13/79; TLS 2/14/75)

8084 Lodge, David. *Nice Work*. 1989, Viking $18.95 (0-670-82806-8); Penguin paper $7.95 (0-14-013396-8). An account of an unlikely friendship between a literature teacher at an English university and a factory manager. "Stylishly written and eminently readable."—CSM (REV: CSM 3/8/89; Newsweek 8/7/89; PW 6/2/89. AWARDS: PW, 1989)

8085 Lodge, David. *Small World: An Academic Romance*. 1989, Warner paper $4.95 (0-446-35999-8). The chronicle of a teacher on a worldwide chase after a graduate student and of a group of academics competing for a prestigious chair. "The funniest and nastiest novel of academic satire since *Lucky Jim*."—Newsweek (REV: LJ 3/15/85; Newsweek 6/3/85; PW 1/18/85. AWARDS: PW, 1985)

8086 Lodge, David. *Souls and Bodies*. 1990, Penguin paper $7.95 (0-14-013018-7). A character study of a group of university students tracing their lives to middle-age and examining the role Roman Catholicism played in their lives and thought. (REV: LJ 12/15/81; New Rep 4/7/82; NYTBR 1/31/82)

8087 Lopate, Phillip. *Confessions of Summer*. 1979, Sun & Moon $10.00 (0-385-12619-0). A chronicle of the development of a New York social worker's love affair with his best friend's girl over a period of three years. (REV: BL 7/15/79; LJ 5/15/79)

8088 Lopate, Phillip. *Rug Merchant*. 1987, Viking $16.95 (0-670-81434-2); Penguin paper $6.95 (0-14-009676-0). A Persian immigrant's life as a rug merchant in New York, depicted by the author of *Bachelorhood*. (REV: BL 1/15/87; CSM 5/20/87; PW 1/23/87. AWARDS: ALA, 1987)

8089 Lord, Shirley. *One of My Very Best Friends*. 1985, Crown $16.95 (0-517-55711-8); Berkley paper $3.95 (0-425-09702-1). A story spanning two-and-a-half decades chronicling the relationship between two English women whose friendship becomes a bitter rivalry. (REV: NYTBR 10/27/85; PW 8/9/85)

8090 Lott, Bret. *Jewel*. 1991, Pocket $20.00 (0-671-74038-5). The story of a Mississippi woman's relationship with her Down's syndrome daughter, as told by the author of *A Dream of Old Leaves*. (REV: LJ 9/15/91; PW 8/23/91)

8091 Lott, Bret. *Man Who Owned Vermont*. 1987, Viking $16.95 (0-670-81582-9). A portrait of the life of a Massachusetts salesman during and following the collapse of his marriage. "An uncommonly good first effort."—BL (REV: BL 5/15/87; LJ 6/1/87; Time 7/27/87)

8092 Lott, Bret. *A Stranger's House*. 1988, Viking $17.95 (0-670-82246-9); Pocket paper $7.95 (0-671-68328-4). This second novel by the author of *The Man Who Owned Vermont* details four months in the life of a Massachusetts woman unable to bear a child. (REV: BL 6/15/88; LJ 9/1/88)

8093 Lourie, Richard. *First Loyalty*. 1985, Harcourt $17.95 (0-15-131287-7); Dell paper $3.95 (0-440-12572-

3). A thriller that involves the efforts of a Soviet scientist to smuggle a mind-expanding drug to the Western world. (REV: CSM 8/2/85; LJ 7/85; NYTBR 8/4/85)

8094 Lourie, Richard. *Zero Gravity*. 1987, Harcourt $16.95 (0-15-199984-8); Dell paper $4.50 (0-440-20191-8). A satirical account of a failed joint project by the United States and the Soviet Union to land two poets on the moon. (REV: BL 9/1/87; LJ 9/1/87)

8095 Louvish, Simon. *Therapy of Avram Blok*. 1985, Scarborough $16.95 (0-8128-3062-8). A work of black humor concerning the exploits of a Jewish man who dies at Auschwitz but whose spirit is reborn only to see Jerusalem destroyed by an atomic bomb. "Wildly entertaining fiction by a creative and gifted writer."—BL (REV: BL 9/1/85; LJ 12/85; PW 7/26/85)

8096 Lowry, Beverly. *Breaking Gentle*. 1988, Viking $17.95 (0-670-82245-0). A Texas couple confront the thievery and drug abuse of their teenage daughter in this novel by the author of *The Perfect Sonya*. (REV: BL 7/88; NYTBR 8/14/88)

8097 Lowry, Beverly. *The Perfect Sonya*. 1987, Viking $16.95 (0-670-81413-X); Penguin paper $6.95 (0-14-009654-X). A New York actress comes to terms with the death of her father. (REV: BL 5/15/87; NYTBR 7/26/87)

8098 Ludlum, Robert. *Holcroft Covenant*. 1984, Bantam paper $5.95 (0-553-26019-7). A secret fund allegedly to be dispersed to Holocaust survivors and their families is revealed to be part of a plan to rebuild the Reich. (REV: BL 4/15/78; LJ 4/1/78)

8099 Ludlum, Robert. *Icarus Agenda*. 1988, Random $19.95 (0-394-54397-1); Bantam paper $5.95 (0-553-27800-2). A U.S. congressman goes undercover to assist the CIA in a hostage situation in the Middle East, then returns to take on an international arms dealer. (REV: BL 1/1/88; LJ 2/15/88)

8100 Lurie, Alison. *Foreign Affairs*. 1984, Random $15.95 (0-394-54076-X); Avon paper $7.95 (0-380-70990-2). Two American researchers become involved in affairs while in England on sabbatical. "A wry wonderful book that should have a wide audience."—LJ (REV: BL 8/84; LJ 8/84; Time 10/15/84. AWARDS: ALA, 1984; LJ, 1984; PP:Fiction, 1985)

8101 Lurie, Alison. *Imaginary Friends*. 1986, Avon paper $4.50 (0-380-70073-5). A group of New Yorkers believe they are communicating with extraterrestrial beings. (REV: BL 10/15/67; LJ 8/67; TLS 7/6/67)

8102 Lurie, Alison. *Nowhere City*. 1986, Avon paper $4.50 (0-380-70070-0). A historian and his wife try to adjust to living in Los Angeles after relocating from New York in this novel by the author of *Foreign Affairs*. (REV: LJ 1/15/66; Newsweek 1/10/66; PW 7/3/67)

8103 Lurie, Alison. *The Truth about Lorin Jones*. 1988, Little, Brown $18.95 (0-316-53720-9); Avon paper $7.95 (0-380-70807-8). A would-be biographer attempts to chronicle the life of an American artist she helped make famous by a posthumous retrospective of her work. (Rev: NYTBR 9/4/88; PW 7/8/88; TLS 7/8/88)

8104 Lurie, Alison. *War Between the Tates.* **1974, Random $16.95 (0-394-46201-7).** The marriage between a New York college professor and his wife becomes strained following his affair with a younger woman. (Rev: BL 9/15/74; LJ 8/74; New Rep 8/10/74)

8105 Lynn, Jonathan, and Anthony Jay. *Complete Yes Minister: The Diaries of a Cabinet Minister by the Right Hon. James Hacker M.P.* **1987, Salem $19.95 (0-88162-272-9); Harper & Row paper $10.95 (0-06-097165-7).** The fictional diary of a British civil servant under the Thatcher cabinet, which was the basis for a BBC series. (Rev: BL 9/1/87; CSM 12/28/87; PW 4/17/87)

8106 Maas, Peter. *Father and Son.* **1989, Simon & Schuster $18.95 (0-671-63172-1); Harper & Row paper $5.50 (0-06-100020-5).** The relationship between an Irish-American father and son becomes strained when the son becomes involved in a gun-running scheme in support of the IRA. (Rev: BL 3/1/89; LJ 2/15/89; PW 1/6/89)

8107 McAlmon, Robert. *Village: As It Happened Through a Fifteen Year Period.* **1990, Univ. of New Mexico Pr. paper $14.95 (0-8263-1200-4).** The first American edition of the Lost Generation figure's 1924 novel regarding life in small-town Nebraska. (Rev: NYTBR 7/22/90; PW 1/4/91. Awards: PW, 1990)

8108 McCaig, Donald. *Nop's Trials.* **1984, Crown $14.95 (0-517-55189-6).** An examination of the effects of a collie's abduction on the dog and its owner. (Rev: Atl 5/84; CSM 6/5/84; LJ 4/1/84)

8109 McCall, Dan. *Jack the Bear.* **1981, Fawcett paper $1.95 (0-449-70009-7).** A teenage narrator tells the story of his life with an irresponsible father and a three-year-old brother. (Rev: CSM 4/17/74; LJ 4/1/74; PW 2/11/74)

8110 McCandless, Anthony. *Burke Foundation.* **1986, Scarborough $15.95 (0-8128-3038-5).** A man searches for details surrounding the World War II battle death of his father. (Rev: LJ 9/15/85; PW 7/19/85)

8111 McCarthy, Mary. *Birds of America.* **1971, Harcourt $11.95 (0-15-112770-0).** A chronicle of the adventures of an American teenage boy studying in Paris. "An enormously enjoyable, intelligent, civilized novel."—TLS (Rev: CSM 6/10/71; NYTBR 5/16/71; TLS 9/17/71)

8112 McCarthy, Mary. *Cannibals and Missionaries.* **1979, Harcourt $10.95 (0-15-115387-6).** Terrorists hijack a plane bound for Teheran to the Netherlands and hold it for ransom for political demands. (Rev: BL 9/15/79; NYTBR 9/20/79; PW 8/13/79)

8113 McClanahan, Ed. *Natural Man.* **1983, Farrar $11.50 (0-374-21969-9); Penguin paper $5.95 (0-14-007042-7).** A small-town Kentucky tale set in the 1940s of a 15-year-old boy determined to lose his virginity by his next birthday. (Rev: BL 4/15/83; Newsweek 5/23/83; PW 1/28/83)

8114 McCloy, Kristin. *Velocity.* **1988, Random $16.95 (0-394-57022-7); Pocket paper $7.95 (0-671-68920-7).** In this author's first novel, a woman in her 20s spends a summer with her father following her mother's death and has a secret affair with a wild biker. (Rev: BL 9/1/88; PW 8/5/88. Awards: LJ 11/1/88)

8115 McCorkle, Jill. *Ferris Beach.* **1990, Algonquin $18.95 (0-945575-39-4).** A coming-of-age novel set in the Deep South tracing the life of a young girl through high school. "McCorkle keeps getting better . . . clearly an impressive improvement in her craft."—BL (Rev: BL 9/1/90; LJ 9/15/90; PW 8/3/90)

8116 McCorkle, Jill. *July 7th.* **1984, Algonquin $17.95 (0-912697-12-1).** This author's second novel tells of the false accusation of an African-American man of the murder of a North Carolina convenience store clerk. (Rev: BL 9/15/84; NYTBR 10/7/84; PW 7/27/84)

8117 McCorkle, Jill. *Tending to Virginia.* **1987, Algonquin $15.95 (0-912697-65-2); Fawcett paper $4.95 (0-449-21624-1).** Three generations of a North Carolina woman's family converge at her grandmother's home to support her during her pregnancy. (Rev: BL 9/15/87; LJ 9/1/87; PW 8/14/87)

8118 McCormick, Ann Du Mais. *Northern Exposure.* **1989, St. Martin's $16.95 (0-312-03899-2).** A woman reestablishes ties to former friends and lovers following her divorce. "Poignant, delightful . . . highly recommended for the thirty-something generation."—LJ (Rev: BL 12/15/89; LJ 1/90; PW 11/17/89)

8119 McCormmach, Russell. *Night Thoughts of a Classical Physicist.* **1982, Harvard Univ. Pr. $20.00 (0-674-62460-2).** A German theoretical physicist reflects on his work and discoveries made in the field during the years surrounding the First World War. (Rev: LJ 2/1/82; NYRB 4/29/82; Time 3/1/82)

8120 McCoy, Maureen. *Summertime.* **1988, Pocket paper $6.95 (0-671-62188-2).** Three generations of Iowa women react to the illness of a family member stricken with leukemia. (Rev: BL 4/1/87; LJ 4/15/87; PW 2/20/87)

8121 McCullough, Colleen. *An Indecent Obsession.* **1981, Harper & Row $14.95 (0-06-014920-5); Avon paper $4.95 (0-380-60376-4).** An account of life in an Australian military mental hospital at the conclusion of World War II. (Rev: LJ 8/81; NYTBR 10/25/81; PW 9/4/81)

8122 McDermott, Alice. *A Bigamist's Daughter.* **1988, HarperCollins paper $7.95 (0-06-097142-8).** A debut novel regarding a young woman who reveals family secrets to an aspiring writer with whom she has fallen in love. (Rev: BL 2/15/82; NYTBR 2/21/82; Newsweek 3/22/82)

8123 McDermott, Alice. *That Night.* **1987, Farrar $14.95 (0-374-27361-8); Harper & Row paper $6.95 (0-06-097141-X).** A chronicle of the legacy of a fight among a group of Long Island men during the early 1960s. "This stunning set piece is remarkable for its psychological acuity and artful prose."—BL

(Rev: BL 3/15/87; PW 2/13/87; Time 7/27/87. Awards: PW, 1987)

8124 McDonald, Gregory. *A World Too Wide.* **1987, Hilland $17.95 (0-940595-07-9).** A portrait of the reunion of family and friends at a Tennessee farm for a wedding by the author of the Fletch detective series. (Rev: BL 10/1/87; LJ 10/1/87)

8125 McElroy, Joseph. *The Letter Left to Me.* **1988, Knopf $16.95 (0-394-57196-7); Carroll & Graf paper $6.95 (0-88184-536-1).** A teenage boy receives a letter left by his late father to be opened after his death in this novel by the author of *Women and Men.* (Rev: BL 10/15/88; NYTBR 10/9/88)

8126 McElroy, Joseph. *Lookout Cartridge.* **1985, Carroll & Graf paper $9.95 (0-88184-147-1).** A chronicle of the efforts of a filmmaker to find and restore a motion picture. "*Lookout Cartridge* is the rarest kind of achievement."—NYTBR (Rev: CSM 4/30/75; LJ 2/1/75; NYTBR 2/2/75)

8127 McElroy, Joseph. *Women and Men.* **1987, Knopf $27.50 (0-394-50344-9).** A huge novel by the author of *Lookout Cartridge* portraying the lives of two individuals who live in a New York apartment building. (Rev: BL 2/15/87; LJ 2/15/87; NYTBR 4/12/87)

8128 McEwan, Ian. *Cement Garden.* **1988, Penguin paper $6.95 (0-14-011282-0).** Four English children conceal the deaths of their parents from their community and explore a life of depravity. (Rev: PW 9/4/78; Sat Rev 10/14/78; TLS 9/29/78)

8129 McEwan, Ian. *The Child in Time.* **1988, Penguin paper $7.95 (0-14-011246-4).** A writer's three-year-old daughter disappears while the two are shopping at a supermarket. "A beautifully rendered, very disturbing read."—PW (Rev: BL 9/1/87; PW 8/7/87; Time 9/21/87. Awards: Time, 1987)

8130 McFarland, Dennis. *Music Room.* **1990, Houghton $19.95 (0-395-54417-3).** A brother searching for reasons behind his sibling's suicide comes across a series of family secrets. (Rev: LJ 4/1/90; PW 2/16/90; TLS 8/31/90. Awards: PW, 1990)

8131 McGahern, John. *Amongst Women.* **1990, Viking $17.95 (0-670-81182-3).** A study of a domineering father—a former Irish Republican Army member—and his family. Set in Ireland after World War II. "A most satisfying addition to a very distinguished body of work."—LJ (Rev: BL 7/90; LJ 8/90; TLS 5/18/90. Awards: BL, 1990)

8132 McGahern, John. *The Pornographer.* **1983, Penguin paper $6.95 (0-14-006489-3).** An Irish bachelor writer of soft-porn literature for magazines becomes romantically involved with a woman in her late 30s. (Rev: LJ 12/15/79; Newsweek 11/5/79; TLS 1/11/80)

8133 McGarrity, Mark. *White Rush/Green Fire.* **1991, Morrow $20.00 (0-688-08658-6).** A thriller written under the pen name of Bartholomew Gill about six friends who are pursued by Colombian drug lords after their discovery of a failed drug deal. (Rev: BL 9/1/91; LJ 8/91; PW 7/12/91)

8134 McGrath, Patrick. *The Grotesque.* **1989, Poseidon $17.95 (0-671-66509-X).** A paleontologist recounts the events that led to the murder of his daughter's fiance in this novel by the author of *Blood and Water and Other Tales.* (Rev: NYTBR 5/28/89; PW 3/31/89; TLS 12/29/89)

8135 McGrath, Patrick. *Spider.* **1990, Poseidon $18.95 (0-671-66510-3); Random paper $10.00 (0-679-73630-1).** A schizophrenic records the events of his childhood and his present in a journal following his return to the neighborhood of his youth and the site of his mother's murder. (Rev: BL 7/90; LJ 8/90; PW 8/3/90)

8136 McGuane, Thomas. *Bushwhacked Piano.* **1984, Random paper $8.95 (0-394-72642-1).** An account of a rebellious young man's adventures on a cross-country motorcycle trip by the author of *Something to Be Desired.* (Rev: BL 6/1/71; New Yorker 9/11/71)

8137 McGuane, Thomas. *Keep the Change.* **1989, Houghton $18.95 (0-395-48887-7); Random paper $9.95 (0-679-73033-8).** An artist leaves his girlfriend and Florida home to relocate to his late father's Montana cattle ranch. (Rev: CSM 10/16/89; NYTBR 9/24/89; PW 10/12/90)

8138 McGuane, Thomas. *Ninety-Two in the Shade.* **1973, Farrar $8.95 (0-374-22259-2); Penguin paper $6.95 (0-14-009907-7).** A character study of the lives of three rival Key West fishing guides. (Rev: NYTBR 7/29/73; Newsweek 7/23/73; Time 8/6/73. Awards: ALA, 1973; Time, 1973)

8139 McGuane, Thomas. *Nobody's Angel.* **1982, Random $14.50 (0-394-52264-8); paper $6.95 (0-394-70565-3).** An army tank captain retires from the service to live on his family's Montana ranch. (Rev: Natl Rev 6/11/82; NYTBR 3/7/82)

8140 McGuane, Thomas. *Something to Be Desired.* **1985, Random paper $6.95 (0-394-73156-5).** A Montana man leaves his family to reunite with a former lover who has turned to a life of crime. (Rev: BL 10/15/84; LJ 11/1/84; NYTBR 12/16/84)

8141 Machlis, Joseph. *Stefan in Love.* **1991, Norton $19.95 (0-393-03005-9).** The story of a Hungarian man who abandons his family to move to America with a younger woman when he finds his affair with her is about to be disclosed. "A warm, thoughtful, well-written book."—BL (Rev: BL 8/91; LJ 7/91; PW 7/5/91)

8142 McIlroy, Kevin. *Fifth Station.* **1988, Algonquin $12.95 (0-912697-76-8); Macmillan paper $6.95 (0-02-034622-0).** Two brothers move to New Mexico following the death of their younger brother in a steel mill accident. (Rev: BL 3/1/88; PW 2/19/88)

8143 McInerny, Jay. *Bright Lights, Big City.* **1984, Random paper $5.95 (0-394-72641-3).** The author's first novel depicts New York fast-lane living during the 1980s. (Rev: LJ 10/1/84; New Rep 12/3/84; NYTBR 11/25/84)

8144 McMillan, Terry. *Disappearing Acts.* **1989, Viking $18.95 (0-670-82461-5).** A chronicle of the rise and fall of a love affair told in alternating chapters by the man and the woman involved, by the author of *Mama.* (REV: BL 6/1/89; New Yorker 11/13/89; PW 6/16/89)

8145 McMillan, Terry. *Mama.* **1989, Pocket paper $7.95 (0-671-70362-5).** A chronicle of a Detroit African-American family from the 1960s to the 1980s. (REV: BL 1/1/87; New Yorker 3/16/87; PW 11/28/86)

8146 McMurtry, Larry. *All My Friends Are Going to Be Strangers.* **1989, Simon & Schuster paper $7.95 (0-671-68103-6).** A young Texas writer moves to California and sells the movie rights to his first novel. (REV: BL 5/15/72; New Rep 4/1/72; Time 4/3/72. AWARDS: Time, 1972)

8147 McMurtry, Larry. *Cadillac Jack.* **1987, Simon & Schuster paper $7.95 (0-671-63720-7).** The portrait of a former radio cowboy and his amorous adventures among the women of Washington, D.C. (REV: BL 9/1/82; LJ 10/1/72; PW 7/30/82)

8148 McMurtry, Larry. *Desert Rose.* **1987, Simon & Schuster paper $7.95 (0-671-63721-5).** A story of a Las Vegas stripper trying to make a living for herself and her daughter in the Nevada desert. (REV: BL 8/83; LJ 9/1/83; PW 6/24/83)

8149 McMurtry, Larry. *Some Can Whistle.* **1989, Simon & Schuster $19.95 (0-671-64267-7); paper $5.95 (0-671-72213-1).** In this sequel to *All My Friends Are Going to Be Strangers,* a wealthy sit-com writer rescues his long-lost daughter from a bad life in Houston. (REV: BL 9/15/89; New Yorker 12/4/89; PW 9/8/89)

8150 McMurtry, Larry. *Somebody's Darling.* **1987, Simon & Schuster paper $6.95 (0-317-56596-6).** A story by the author of *The Desert Rose* chronicling the life of a female director in Hollywood. (REV: BL 10/15/78; PW 9/18/78; Time 11/13/78)

8151 McMurtry, Larry. *Texasville.* **1990, Simon & Schuster paper $5.95 (0-671-72474-6).** The further adventures of the residents of the town of Thalia, Texas, first introduced in the author's *The Last Picture Show.* (REV: LJ 4/1/87; NYTBR 4/19/87; New Yorker 6/15/87)

8152 McNamee, Thomas. *A Story of Deep Delight.* **1990, Viking $19.95 (0-670-81896-8).** A fictional chronicle of three generations of a Chickasaw Indian family set in and around Memphis during the nineteenth and twentieth centuries. (REV: BL 9/15/90; LJ 10/1/90; PW 8/3/90)

8153 McNamer, Deidre. *Rima in the Weeds.* **1991, HarperCollins $19.95 (0-06-016523-5).** A first novel regarding a family's move from Chicago to a small town in Montana during the 1960s. (REV: BL 1/15/91; LJ 1/91; NYTBR 2/17/91)

8154 McPherson, William. *To the Sargasso Sea.* **1987, Simon & Schuster $18.95 (0-671-55207-4); Pocket paper $7.95 (0-671-66030-6).** This sequel to the author's *Testing the Current* traces the protago-nist's life as a playwright during the 1940s. "A well-crafted meditative tale."—BL (REV: BL 6/15/87; PW 4/17/87; Time 7/27/87)

8155 McWilliam, Candia. *A Little Stranger.* **1989, Doubleday $15.95 (0-385-26309-0); Ballantine paper $3.95 (0-345-36552-6).** A story of a slightly outrageous English nanny and the four-year-old only child of an aristocratic family she cares for. (REV: BL 7/89; LJ 7/89; TLS 1/27/89)

8156 Madden, David. *Pleasure Dome.* **1979, Macmillan $10.00 (0-672-52533-4).** An aspiring teenage writer immerses himself in literature and literary symbols to escape the empty life led by his Southern family. (REV: BL 9/15/79; NYTBR 11/11/79; PW 8/13/79)

8157 Madden, David. *Suicide's Wife.* **1978, Macmillan $8.95 (0-672-52492-9).** A woman is left to care for three children following the suicide of her poet husband. "A definitive portrait of depression . . . masterly."—Time (REV: BL 11/1/78; Newsweek 10/9/78; Time 10/30/78. AWARDS: ALA, 1978)

8158 Mahfouz, Naguib. *Autumn Quail.* **1990, Doubleday $16.95 (0-385-26453-4); paper $7.95 (0-385-26454-2).** This portrait of the life of an Egyptian civil servant during the 1952 revolution was originally published in Arabic in 1962. (REV: BL 11/15/90; LJ 8/90; NYTBR 8/26/90)

8159 Mahfouz, Naguib. *The Beggar.* **1990, Doubleday $17.95 (0-385-26455-0); paper $7.95 (0-385-26456-9).** This novel originally published in Arabic in 1965 concerns an Egyptian lawyer who abandons his career and family life to search for personal fulfillment. (REV: BL 11/15/90; LJ 8/90; PW 7/13/90)

8160 Mahfouz, Naguib. *Beginning and the End.* **1989, Doubleday $19.95 (0-385-26457-7); paper $9.95 (0-385-26458-5).** This novel about an upper middle-class family living in poverty in Cairo during World War II was originally published in Arabic in 1949. (REV: BL 10/1/89; NYTBR 12/10/89)

8161 Mahfouz, Naguib. *Respected Sir.* **1990, Doubleday $17.95 (0-385-26479-8); paper $7.95 (0-385-26480-1).** A chronicle of an Egyptian clerk's rise in the government bureaucracy by the 1988 Nobel Prize winner. (REV: BL 11/15/90; LJ 8/90; PW 7/13/90. AWARDS: PW, 1990)

8162 Mahfouz, Naguib. *Thief and the Dogs.* **1989, Doubleday $16.95 (0-385-26461-5); paper $7.95 (0-385-26462-3).** This novel set in Egypt during the early 1950s is about an ex-convict who seeks revenge on his jailers. Originally published in Arabic in 1961. (REV: BL 10/1/89; LJ 10/1/89; PW 9/8/89)

8163 Mahfouz, Naguib. *Wedding Song.* **1989, Doubleday $16.95 (0-385-26463-1); paper $7.95 (0-385-26464-X).** Four members of an acting troupe present different versions of the same events in this novel by the Egyptian Nobel laureate. (REV: BL 10/1/89; LJ 10/1/89; PW 9/8/89. AWARDS: PW, 1989)

8164 Mailer, Norman. *An American Dream.* **1987, Henry Holt paper $8.95 (0-8050-0349-5).** A former congressman and friend of John F. Kennedy becomes involved in the murders of two women. (REV: BL 5/15/65; Choice 7–8/65; Time 3/19/65. AWARDS: NYTBR, 1965)

8165 Mailer, Norman. *Why Are We in Vietnam?* **1982**, Holt paper $5.95 (0-03-059977-6). In this novel by the author of *Ancient Evenings*, a teenage Texan boy recounts the events of an Alaskan hunting trip undertaken with his father. (REV: NYTBR 9/25/67; Newsweek 9/18/67; Sat Rev 9/16/67. AWARDS: NYTBR, 1967)

8166 Maitland, Sara. *Three Times Table.* **1991**, Henry Holt $18.95 (0-8050-1576-0). A character study of a grandmother, mother, and daughter living together in a London home. "Genuinely intriguing, clever enough to prompt rereading and rich enough to reward the effort."—NYTBR (REV: BL 3/15/91; LJ 3/15/91; NYTBR 4/21/91)

8167 Major, Clarence. *My Amputations.* **1986**, Fiction Collect. $15.95 (0-914590-96-0). A felon writer kidnaps a writer who, he claims, stole his idea for a novel. (REV: BL 8/86; Choice 12/86; LJ 7/86)

8168 Major, Clarence. *Painted Turtle: Woman with Guitar.* **1988**, Sun & Moon $14.95 (1-55713-002-7). A story of the life of a Zuñi folksinger and her travels across the United States. (REV: BL 7/88; Choice 3/89; NYTBR 10/30/88)

8169 Malamud, Bernard. *Dubin's Lives.* **1979**, Farrar $10.00 (0-374-14414-1). A married biographer suffering from writer's block enters into an affair with a younger woman. "A moving, compelling and deeply personal novel."—LJ (REV: BL 3/1/79; LJ 1/15/79; Newsweek 2/12/79. AWARDS: ALA, 1979)

8170 Malamud, Bernard. *God's Grace.* **1982**, Farrar $13.50 (0-374-16465-7); Avon paper $3.95 (0-380-64519-X). The story of the second Great Flood and the lone human survivor who lives, only due to an oversight by God. (REV: LJ 7/82; Newsweek 9/6/82; PW 6/25/82)

8171 Malamud, Bernard. *Tenants.* **1988**, Farrar paper $8.95 (0-374-52102-6). A Jewish writer and an African-American tenant live in conflict in a New York apartment building. (REV: BL 11/1/71; LJ 10/15/71; PW 8/23/71)

8172 Malone, Michael. *Foolscap.* **1991**, Little, Brown $21.95 (0-316-54527-9). In this novel by the author of *Handling Sin*, an American professor chases a friend to England after the friend steals a play he has written. (REV: LJ 10/1/91; PW 8/9/91)

8173 Malone, Michael. *Handling Sin.* **1986**, Little, Brown $17.95 (0-316-54455-8); Simon & Schuster paper $5.95 (0-671-70961-5). A North Carolina man and a friend travel to New Orleans to fulfill the conditions set by the man's father to collect an inheritance. (REV: BL 4/1/86; CSM 3/26/86; PW 3/7/86. AWARDS: ALA, 1986; PW, 1986)

8174 Marek, Richard. *Works of Genius.* **1987**, Macmillan $17.95 (0-689-11889-9). The portrait of a great writer abusive to his friends, family, and business associates, written by an E.P. Dutton executive. "A compelling and terrifying story."—BL (REV: BL 6/15/87; LJ 7/87; PW 5/8/87)

8175 Markson, David. *Springer's Promise.* **1990**, Dalkey Arch. paper $9.95 (0-916583-57-0). A New York writer chronicles the events of a recent love affair in his latest novel. (REV: LJ 5/1/77; NYTBR 8/7/77)

8176 Markson, David. *Wittgenstein's Mistress.* **1988**, Dalkey Arch $20.00 (0-916583-25-2). The journal of a woman who believes she is the last living human on earth. (REV: BL 5/15/88; NYTBR 5/22/88; PW 4/1/88)

8177 Markus, Julia. *Friends Along the Way.* **1987**, Dell paper $4.95 (0-440-32761-X). In this novel by the author of *Uncle*, an American woman troubled by her marriage and career finds friendship during an extended visit to Rome. (REV: BL 8/85; Newsweek 9/2/85; PW 6/7/85)

8178 Marlowe, Katherine. *Heart's Desires.* **1991**, Donald I. Fine $19.95 (1-55611-226-2). A debut novel about a woman's efforts to recover from the murder of her mother and brother. (REV: BL 1/15/91; LJ 1/91)

8179 Marsh, Fabienne. *Long Distances.* **1989**, Pocket paper $6.95 (0-671-67400-5). A series of letters between a scholarly man in England and his filmmaker wife in the United States details their relationship and their marriage. "A surprisingly accomplished and unusual effort for a first-time author."—BL (REV: BL 2/15/88; NYTBR 3/13/88; PW 1/8/88)

8180 Marsh, Fabienne. *Moralist of the Alphabet Streets.* **1991**, Algonquin $15.95 (0-945575-47-5). A teenage leukemia victim in remission spends a summer with his grandmother at her beach home. (REV: BL 2/15/91; LJ 3/1/91)

8181 Marshall, Paule. *Daughters.* **1991**, Atheneum $19.95 (0-689-12139-3). A portrait of the life of a Caribbean woman transplanted to New York City. "A carefully considered, graceful and lingeringly ponderable tale."—BL (REV: BL 7/91; PW 7/19/91. AWARDS: BL, 1991)

8182 Marshall, Paule. *Praisesong for the Widow.* **1984**, Dutton paper $8.95 (0-525-48303-9). An African-American woman debarks from a cruise ship on the Caribbean island of Grenada to search for her ancestral roots. (REV: BL 12/1/82; LJ 1/1/83; TLS 9/16/82)

8183 Martin, David. *Final Harbor.* **1985**, Carroll & Graf paper $4.95 (0-88184-215-X). The story of a group of religious fanatics and con artists who meet at a Virginia revival during the 1960s. (REV: BL 9/1/84; NYTBR 10/7/84; PW 6/29/84)

8184 Martin, Russell. *Beautiful Islands.* **1988**, Linden Pr. $17.95 (0-671-64662-1); Fawcett paper $3.95 (0-449-21736-1). A Colorado astronaut suffers depression and disillusionment about his life and role in America's space program following the *Challenger* disaster. (REV: LJ 4/1/88; PW 2/26/88)

8185 Martin, Valerie. *A Recent Martyr.* **1987, Houghton $16.95 (0-395-43613-3); Random paper $7.95 (0-679-72158-4).** In a plague-ridden New Orleans of the near future, a nurse engages in an affair during the epidemic. (REV: PW 7/14/89; TLS 10/28/88)

8186 Martorell, Joanot, and Marti J. De Galba. *Tirant Lo Blanc.* **1984, Schocken $21.95 (0-8052-3852-2); Warner paper $4.95 (0-446-32584-8).** The first English translation of a fifteenth-century Catalan classic about the exploits of a French knight, notable for its portrayal of women. (REV: CSM 8/3/84; NYTBR 7/15/84; PW 5/4/84)

8187 Maso, Carole. *Ghost Dance.* **1986, North Point $16.95 (0-86547-239-4).** A young woman analyzes the tragic events that led to the destruction of her family in this debut novel. (REV: BL 5/1/86; LJ 7/86; PW 4/25/86)

8188 Mason, Anita. *The Racket.* **1991, Dutton $19.95 (0-525-93351-4).** A history teacher provides a safe haven for her fugitive cousin in this novel set in Brazil. "Superb suspense spiked with a sinuous, understated wit and a shrewd intellect."—BL (REV: BL 8/91; LJ 9/15/91)

8189 Mason, Bobbie Ann. *In Country.* **1985, Harper & Row $19.95 (0-06-015469-1); paper $8.95 (0-06-091350-9).** A teenage girl whose father was killed in the Vietnam War finds his diary recording his combat experiences. (REV: BL 8/85; LJ 10/1/85; PW 7/19/85. AWARDS: BL, the 1980s; LJ, 1985; PW, 1985)

8190 Mason, Bobbie Ann. *Spence and Lila.* **1988, Harper & Row $12.95 (0-06-015911-1); paper $7.95 (0-06-091559-5).** A short novel by the author of *In Country* about a married couple facing the severe illness of the wife. (REV: BL 4/15/88; CSM 7/15/88; Time 7/4/88)

8191 Mason, Robert. *Weapon.* **1989, Putnam $18.95 (0-399-13447-6); Berkley paper $4.50 (1-55773-309-0).** This first novel by the author of *Chickenhawk* is about the development and disappearance of a robot designed to be a killing machine. "Very well written. Put it at the top of your list."—NYTBR (REV: BL 3/15/89; NYTBR 5/7/89; PW 2/24/89)

8192 Mathews, Harry. *Cigarettes.* **1988, Macmillan paper $8.95 (0-02-013971-3).** An account of the lives of 14 characters prominent in the New York art scene of the 1960s. (REV: BL 10/1/87; LJ 10/15/87; PW 9/4/87)

8193 Mathias, Bernard. *Caretakers.* **1988, Viking $17.95 (0-670-82127-6); Penguin paper $7.95 (0-14-010839-4).** A story about Holocaust survivors and their son after they flee Romania for a new life in France. (REV: Choice 2/89; LJ 4/15/88; PW 5/20/88)

8194 Matthiessen, Peter. *At Play in the Fields of the Lord.* **1987, Random paper $8.95 (0-394-75083-7).** Four missionaries are sent to the Amazon jungle to convert members of the Niaruna tribe to Christian-

ity. (REV: LJ 10/1/65; NYTBR 11/7/65; Time 11/19/65. AWARDS: ALA, 1965)

8195 Matthiessen, Peter. *Far Tortuga.* **1988, Random paper $10.95 (0-394-75667-3).** A story of the wreck of a turtle-fishing ship off the coast of Central America and the efforts of its crew to survive. (REV: LJ 4/15/75; NYTBR 5/25/75; Time 5/26/75. AWARDS: ALA, 1975; NYTBR, 1975; Time, 1975)

8196 Maupin, Armistead. *Sure of You.* **1989, Harper & Row $18.95 (0-06-016164-7); paper $10.95 (0-06-096404-9).** The sixth and final installment of the author's Tales of the City chronicling gay life in San Francisco during the 1970s and 1980s. (REV: LJ 9/15/89; Newsweek 10/30/89; TLS 3/9/90)

8197 Memmi, Albert. *Scorpion.* **1975, O'Hara $9.95 (0-87955-908-X); paper $7.95 (0-87955-906-3).** A Tunisian doctor tries to piece together his missing brother's journal. (REV: Choice 11/71; LJ 9/1/71; PW 4/12/71)

8198 Meriwether, Louise. *Daddy Was a Number Runner.* **1986, Feminist Pr. paper $8.95 (0-935312-57-9).** A portrait of the life of a young African-American girl growing up on the mean streets of Harlem. (REV: LJ 2/15/70; NYTBR 6/28/70; PW 1/19/70. AWARDS: ALA, 1970)

8199 Merkin, Daphne. *Enchantment.* **1986, Harcourt $16.95 (0-15-128791-0).** A young woman's life in a Jewish immigrant family during the 1950s is depicted in this story. (REV: LJ 8/86; PW 7/18/86)

8200 Metcalf, John. *Adult Entertainment.* **1990, St. Martin's $15.95 (0-312-03790-2).** A collection by a British-Canadian writer of three short stories and the novellas "Polly Ongle" and "Travelling Northward." "A first-rate collection."—PW (REV: BL 11/15/89; LJ 1/90; PW 11/10/89)

8201 Metzger, Deena. *What Dinah Thought.* **1989, Viking $19.95 (0-670-82750-9).** A Jewish-American filmmaker falls in love with a Palestinian while filming in Jerusalem. (REV: BL 9/1/89; LJ 8/89; PW 8/11/89)

8202 Michael, Sami. *Refuge.* **1988, JPS Phila. $19.95 (0-8276-0308-8).** An Israeli writer's portrait of a Communist Jewish group and their activities during the Yom Kippur War. (REV: LJ 11/1/88; PW 9/23/88)

8203 Michaels, Leonard. *Men's Club.* **1981, Farrar $10.95 (0-374-20782-8).** Seven men meet regularly to discuss their lives and their experiences with women. (REV: BL 3/15/81; NYTBR 4/12/81; Time 4/27/81)

8204 Michener, James A. *The Drifters.* **1971, Random $29.95 (0-394-46200-9).** The story of six young people from different nations who meet on the Costa Brava and travel through Europe and North Africa together. (REV: LJ 4/1/71; PW 4/5/71)

8205 Michener, James A. *Legacy.* **1988, Fawcett paper $4.95 (0-449-21641-1).** An Iran-Contra scandal figure examines his family history and his conscience to determine the direction of his testimony before the Senate. (REV: BL 8/87; LJ 9/15/87; PW 9/4/87)

8206 Michener, James A. *Space.* **1985, Random $14.95 (0-394-55041-2).** Michener's retelling of the events and personalities responsible for the success of the American space program in the post-World War II era. (REV: BL 8/82; LJ 9/1/82; Natl Rev 5/27/83)

8207 Mickle, Shelley Fraser. *Queen of October.* **1989, Algonquin $15.95 (0-945575-21-1).** The story of a teenage girl living with her grandparents in Arkansas during court proceedings regarding her custody. "A finely crafted, moving novel from a writer to remember."—BL (REV: BL 9/15/89; LJ 10/15/89; PW 8/25/89)

8208 Miller, Hugh. *Home Ground.* **1991, St. Martin's $18.95 (0-312-05099-2).** A Welsh nurse in her 40s returns to her hometown to care for an ill, aging estate owner. (REV: BL 12/15/90; LJ 12/90; PW 11/9/90)

8209 Miller, Sue. *Family Pictures.* **1990, Harper & Row $19.95 (0-06-016397-6).** A study of an autistic child's effects upon a family of eight chronicled over five decades. "A big, wonderful, deeply absorbing novel."—Newsweek (REV: BL 2/15/90; Newsweek 4/30/90; PW 2/23/90. AWARDS: ALA, 1990; PW, 1990)

8210 Miller, Sue. *The Good Mother.* **1987, Dell paper $4.95 (0-440-12938-9).** The story of a divorcee whose sexual awakening through an affair leads to a court case that robs her of the custody of her child. (REV: CSM 4/30/86; LJ 5/15/86; PW 3/14/86. AWARDS: PW, 1986)

8211 Millhauser, Steven. *Edwin Mullhouse: The Life and Death of an American Writer, 1943–1954.* **1985, Penguin paper $6.95 (0-14-007782-0).** The biography of a ficticious American writer who died before reaching adolescence. (REV: BL 11/15/72; New Rep 9/16/72; Time 9/25/72. AWARDS: Time, 1972)

8212 Millhauser, Steven. *Portrait of a Romantic.* **1977, Pocket paper $6.95 (0-317-56014-X).** This second novel by the author concerns a man in his late 20s reflecting on his years of adolescence. (REV: Choice 1/78; LJ 8/77; NYTBR 10/2/77)

8213 Minot, Susan. *Monkeys.* **1987, Pocket paper $6.95 (0-671-70361-7).** An episodic novel that traces the lives of a Boston family with seven children over the course of a decade and a half. (REV: BL 5/1/86; New Rep 6/23/86; Time 6/9/86)

8214 Mishima, Yukio. *Forbidden Colors.* **1981, Putnam paper $8.95 (0-399-50490-7).** This novel, originally published in Japan in 1953, concerns the relationship between a beautiful, narcissistic gay boy and an aging writer. (REV: LJ 3/15/68; PW 2/5/68; Time 5/24/68)

8215 Mishima, Yukio. *Runaway Horses.* **1990, Random paper $10.95 (0-679-72240-8).** The second volume of the Sea of Tranquility series, featuring the leader of a right-wing rebellion who plans the assassination of Japanese business leaders. (REV: BL 9/1/73; LJ 5/1/73; PW 4/2/73)

8216 Mishima, Yukio. *Temple of Dawn.* **1973, Knopf $13.95 (0-394-46614-4); Random paper $10.95 (0-679-72242-4).** This third volume in the Sea of Fertility series covers the years 1940–1956 and the visits of a Japanese lawyer to India and Thailand. (REV: Choice 2/74; LJ 8/73; Time 10/15/73)

8217 Mishima, Yukio. *Thirst for Love.* **1981, Putnam paper $7.95 (0-399-50494-X).** This novel, first published in Japan in 1950, concerns the doomed relationship between a widow and her young servant. (REV: LJ 9/1/69; TLS 7/2/70)

8218 Mitgang, Herbert. *Get These Men Out of the Hot Sun.* **1987, Donald I. Fine paper $7.95 (1-55611-029-4).** A satirical work regarding a 1976 presidential race between Spiro Agnew and Hubert Humphrey that portrays a number of the era's political figures. (REV: BL 5/15/72; LJ 4/1/72; NYTBR 3/26/72)

8219 Mo, Timothy. *Sour Sweet.* **1985, Random paper $9.95 (0-394-73680-X).** A Chinese family running a restaurant in London becomes involved with a triad responsible for heroin trafficking. (REV: LJ 5/1/85; PW 2/8/85. AWARDS: ALA, 1985)

8220 Modarressi, Taghi. *Pilgrim's Rules of Etiquette.* **1989, Doubleday $18.95 (0-385-23879-7).** This Persian writer's second novel concerns the effects upon a former teacher of the death of one of his students during the Iran-Iraq war. (REV: BL 8/89; New Rep 12/4/89; PW 7/7/89)

8221 Mojtabai, A. G. *Ordinary Time.* **1989, Doubleday $17.95 (0-385-26416-X).** A story of the faith of three residents of a small Texas town. (REV: BL 9/1/89; NYTBR 9/24/89; PW 8/4/89. AWARDS: BL, 1989)

8222 Momaday, N. Scott. *Ancient Child.* **1989, Doubleday $18.95 (0-385-27972-8); HarperCollins paper $8.95 (0-06-097345-5).** In this novel by the author of *House Made of Dawn*, a San Francisco painter is drawn into a mystic relationship with an Oklahoma Native American woman. (REV: BL 9/1/89; LJ 8/89)

8223 Momaday, N. Scott. *House Made of Dawn.* **1989, Harper & Row paper $7.95 (0-06-091633-8).** A debut novel by the author telling the story of a Kiowa Indian who chooses to assume the life-style of his grandfather. (REV: LJ 6/15/68; NYTBR 6/9/68; PW 4/1/68. AWARDS: PP:Fiction, 1969)

8224 Monette, Paul. *Afterlife.* **1990, Crown $18.95 (0-517-57339-3).** A group of three HIV-positive men commiserate after the deaths of their lovers in this novel by the author of the nonfiction *Borrowed Time*. (REV: BL 2/1/90; LJ 3/1/90; PW 2/9/90)

8225 Monette, Paul. *Halfway Home.* **1991, Crown $20.00 (0-517-58329-1).** The portrait of a California AIDS victim examining his relationship with his family. (REV: BL 4/1/91; PW 3/8/91; Time 5/6/91)

8226 Montecino, Marcel. *Big Time.* **1990, Morrow $19.95 (0-688-09374-4).** A popular singer flees from organized crime figures seeking to collect an outstanding debt. (REV: LJ 8/90; NYTBR 9/9/90)

8227 Mooney, Ted. *Traffic and Laughter.* **1990, Random $19.95 (0-394-58478-3).** This second novel by the author of *Easy Travel to Other Planets* concerns a Los Angeles disc jockey who travels to South Africa on a diplomatic mission. "A work of high art—intelligent, sophisticated and funny, a truly original book."—NYTBR (Rev: New Rep 12/10/90; NYTBR 12/16/90; PW 8/24/90)

8228 Moorcock, Michael. *Mother London.* **1989, Crown $18.95 (0-517-57183-8); Harper & Row paper $8.95 (0-06-097309-9).** A history of the lives of three English psychiatric patients in London from the beginnings of World War II to the administration of Thatcher. (Rev: LJ 2/15/89; PW 12/23/88)

8229 Moore, Brian. *Catholics.* **1986, Dutton paper $6.95 (0-525-48206-7).** An account of Irish monks in a small abbey performing Latin masses, considered to be acts of heresy by the Church. "A masterpiece of satire."—LJ (Rev: BL 7/15/73; LJ 3/1/73; TLS 11/10/72. Awards: ALA, 1973)

8230 Moore, Brian. *Color of Blood.* **1988, Dutton paper $7.95 (0-525-48422-1).** A portrait of a Roman Catholic cardinal torn between loyalty to a popular democratic rebellion and the socialist totalitarian government currently in power. (Rev: NYRB 12/17/87; NYTBR 9/27/87; TLS 10/2/87)

8231 Moore, Brian. *Great Victorian Collection.* **1985, Dutton paper $7.95 (0-525-48178-8).** A Canadian historian dreams of Victorian artifacts, which miraculously appear in the parking lot of his California hotel. (Rev: BL 7/1/75; New Yorker 8/4/75; PW 4/28/75)

8232 Moore, Brian. *I Am Mary Dunne.* **1985, Dutton paper $7.95 (0-525-48179-6).** The chronicle of one day in the life of a New York woman reflecting on the men in her past and on her present life. (Rev: LJ 6/15/88; New Yorker 6/29/88; PW 4/22/68)

8233 Moore, Brian. *Lies of Silence.* **1990, Doubleday $19.95 (0-385-41385-8).** A hotel owner in Northern Ireland becomes involved in an Irish Republican Army terrorist plot in this novel by the author of *Cold Heaven.* (Rev: BL 8/90; CSM 9/24/90; PW 6/22/90)

8234 Moore, Brian. *Mangan Inheritance.* **1979, Farrar $10.95 (0-374-20194-3).** A writer who inherits his wife's fortune travels to Ireland in search of a famous literary ancestor. "A psychological puzzle revealed with awesome dexterity."—BL (Rev: BL 10/15/79; LJ 10/1/79; Newsweek 10/15/79)

8235 Moore, Brian. *Temptation of Eileen Hughes.* **1981, Farrar $11.95 (0-374-27285-9).** A young Irish woman is befriended by the wealthy family of her employer and accompanies them on a week-long trip to London. (Rev: BL 5/1/81; LJ 5/15/81; PW 5/8/81)

8236 Moore, Lorrie. *Anagrams.* **1986, Knopf $15.95 (0-394-55294-6); Penguin paper $6.95 (0-14-010328-7).** A character study of a multifaceted woman in her 30s portrayed through a series of literary puzzles, by the author of *Self-Help.* (Rev: BL 10/1/86; LJ 10/1/86; PW 8/15/86)

8237 Moore, Susanna. *My Old Sweetheart.* **1990, Penguin paper $6.95 (0-14-006783-3).** A debut novel portraying the coming of age of a preteen girl in Hawaii burdened by caring for her drug-addicted mother. "A novel of great beauty and strength . . . an auspicious debut."—PW (Rev: LJ 10/15/82; Newsweek 11/8/82; PW 8/6/82)

8238 Moore, Susanna. *Whiteness of Bones.* **1989, Doubleday $17.95 (0-385-26646-4); Penguin paper $7.95 (0-14-013020-9).** A young woman moves from Hawaii to New York on a voyage of self-discovery in this second novel by the author of *My Old Sweetheart.* (Rev: BL 12/1/88; NYRB 4/27/89; PW 12/23/88)

8239 Morante, Elsa. *History.* **1984, Random paper $10.95 (0-394-72496-8).** A portrait of Italy during and directly following World War II as told through the story of one Italian family. (Rev: BL 4/1/77; LJ 4/15/77; PW 3/7/77. Awards: ALA, 1977)

8240 Moravia, Alberto. *Time of Desecration.* **1980, Farrar $12.95 (0-374-27781-8).** A beautiful Roman woman recounts her life and sexual adventures in the form of an interview in this novel by the Italian writer. "A shocking, brilliant, and brooding study."—BL (Rev: BL 5/15/80; LJ 6/15/80; New Rep 6/21/80)

8241 Moravia, Alberto. *Voyeur.* **1987, Farrar $18.95 (0-374-28544-6).** An Italian professor becomes obsessed with a black woman living in a Roman apartment. (Rev: BL 5/15/87; LJ 5/15/87; PW 2/27/87)

8242 Morgan, Seth. *Homeboy.* **1990, Random $19.95 (0-394-57577-6).** This debut novel by an ex-convict depicts life on the mean streets of San Francisco. (Rev: BL 3/1/90; LJ 3/15/90; Time 5/21/90)

8243 Morris, Jan. *Last Letters from Hav.* **1989, Random paper $6.95 (0-394-75564-2).** The noted travel writer creates a fictional Mediterranean nation and describes its history and culture. "A delightful, spirited performance."—Newsweek (Rev: BL 5/1/85; Newsweek 5/27/85; Time 7/1/85)

8244 Morris, Mary. *Waiting Room.* **1989, Doubleday $17.95 (0-385-26169-1); Penguin paper $8.95 (0-14-013344-5).** A train trip to visit her brother in a drug rehabilitation center provides the narrator time to reflect on her family's history. (Rev: BL 5/15/89; NYTBR 7/2/89; TLS 4/27/90)

8245 Morris, Mary McGarry. *A Dangerous Woman.* **1991, Viking $19.95 (0-670-83699-0).** This second novel by the author of *Vanished* explores the psychological and social problems of a 32-year-old Vermont woman following a group sexual assault. (Rev: BL 10/15/90; NYTBR 1/13/91; Time 1/28/91. Awards: ALA, 1992; LJ, 1991; PW, 1991; Time, 1991)

8246 Morris, Mary McGarry. *Vanished.* **1988, Viking $16.95 (0-670-82216-7); Pocket paper $6.95 (0-671-67943-0).** A man who leaves his family for a younger woman kidnaps a child and begins a five-year sojourn around the United States. (Rev: BL 5/1/88; LJ 5/1/88; TLS 5/12/89)

8247   Morris, Wright. *Fire Sermon.* 1979, Univ. of Nebraska Pr. paper $3.50 (0-8032-8104-8). The story of an elderly man and his great-nephew who pick up a pair of hitchhikers on their way to a funeral. (Rev: BL 10/15/71; LJ 8/71; Time 10/18/71. Awards: ALA, 1971; Time, 1971)

8248   Morris, Wright. *Fork River Space Project.* 1981, Univ. of Nebraska Pr. paper $5.95 (0-8032-8112-9). A story set in a small Kansas ghost town regarding a group waiting for the arrival of a UFO. (Rev: Choice 1/78; LJ 9/1/77; NYTBR 9/25/77)

8249   Morris, Wright. *A Life.* 1980, Univ. of Nebraska Pr. paper $3.95 (0-8032-8106-4). This sequel to *Fire Sermon* chronicles the journeys of an old man to places important in his personal past. (Rev: Atl 9/73; LJ 9/15/73; Time 9/24/73)

8250   Morris, Wright. *Plains Song: For Female Voices.* 1990, Godine paper $10.95 (0-87923-835-6). A tracing of three generations of a Plains family. (Rev: CSM 1/14/80; New Rep 2/9/80; NYTBR 12/30/79. Awards: ALA, 1980; NBA, 1981)

8251   Morrison, Toni. *Bluest Eye.* 1984, Pocket paper $3.95 (0-671-53146-8). Morrison's first novel concerns the childhood years of an African-American girl growing up in Ohio during the 1940s. (Rev: BL 8/24/70; Choice 10/71; NYTBR 11/1/70)

8252   Morrison, Toni. *Sula.* 1973, Knopf $22.95 (0-394-48044-9); NAL paper $7.95 (0-452-26349-2). The story of the life of an African-American woman and her return to her Ohio hometown a decade after she ran away from it. (Rev: LJ 8/73; NYTBR 12/30/73; Newsweek 1/7/74)

8253   Morrison, Toni. *Tar Baby.* 1981, Knopf $22.50 (0-394-42329-1); NAL paper $7.95 (0-452-26012-4). In this novel by the author of *Song of Solomon*, a Philadelphia couple's life is disrupted by the arrival of an American fugitive at their Caribbean retirement home. (Rev: CSM 4/13/81; New Rep 3/21/81; NYTBR 3/29/81)

8254   Mortimer, John. *Paradise Postponed.* 1986, Penguin paper $7.95 (0-14-009864-X). An English clergyman's will leaves his fortune to a politician, which causes his family to take the case to court to prove his insanity. (Rev: BL 2/15/86; NYTBR 3/30/86; TLS 11/15/85)

8255   Mortimer, John. *Summer's Lease.* 1988, Viking $19.95 (0-670-81984-0); Penguin paper $7.95 (0-14-010573-5). A study of life in a small Italian city populated by a large contingent of English travelers and expatriates. (Rev: LJ 7/88; NYTBR 7/31/88; PW 5/13/88)

8256   Mortimer, John. *Titmuss Regained.* 1990, Viking $19.95 (0-670-82333-3). This sequel to *Paradise Postponed* traces the further adventures of a minor cabinet member of the Thatcher government. "Mortimer at his best: moving, funny, literate and profound."—PW (Rev: BL 2/15/90; NYTBR 4/29/90; PW 2/2/90)

8257   Mortman, Doris. *Rightfully Mine.* 1989, Bantam $18.95 (0-553-05376-0); paper $5.95 (0-553-28416-9). An Ohio woman becomes a New York antique expert after her husband deserts her and gets involved in the investigation of smuggled fake antique furniture. (Rev: BL 5/15/89; NYTBR 8/13/89; PW 6/2/89)

8258   Mosher, Howard Frank. *A Stranger in the Kingdom.* 1989, Doubleday $18.95 (0-385-24400-2). An African-American Presbyterian minister is accused of a young woman's murder in this novel set in Vermont during the early 1950s. (Rev: BL 9/1/89; NYTBR 10/29/89; PW 8/4/89)

8259   Moskowitz, Bette Ann. *Leaving Barney.* 1988, Henry Holt $17.95 (0-8050-0536-6). The accidental death of a Bronx woman's husband leaves her to sort out her life and organize a support group for widows. (Rev: BL 4/15/88; LJ 4/1/88; PW 3/18/88)

8260   Mosley, Nicholas. *The Accident.* 1985, Dalkey Arch. $20.00 (0-916583-10-4); paper $7.95 (0-916583-11-2). The tale of an Oxford professor's romantic relationships with two of his female students and their effects on his life and marriage. (Rev: LJ 5/1/66; PW 2/21/66; TLS 1/14/65)

8261   Mosley, Nicholas. *Impossible Object.* 1985, Dalkey Arch $20.00 (0-916583-08-2); paper $7.95 (0-916583-09-0). A portrait of two people having an extramarital affair and the stories of those whose lives it affects. (Rev: CSM 2/6/69; LJ 3/1/69; Sat Rev 1/25/69)

8262   Mosley, Nicholas. *Judith.* 1991, Dalkey Arch. $19.95 (0-916583-69-4). This epistolary novel tracing the life of a contemporary woman was written by the author of *Hopeful Monsters*. (Rev: BL 3/1/91; LJ 2/1/91)

8263   Mrabet, Mohammed. *Love with a Few Hairs.* 1975, City Lights paper $6.95 (0-87286-192-9). A Moroccan writer's story of a young man's efforts to win the love of a young woman by using witchcraft. (Rev: Choice 10/68; NYTBR 9/8/68; PW 2/12/68)

8264   Mudimbe, V. Y. *Before the Birth of the Moon.* 1989, Simon & Schuster $18.95 (0-671-67566-4); paper $7.95 (0-671-66840-4). A story of political intrigue involving the relationship between a ruler and a prostitute in Zaire during the 1960s. "Mudimbe . . . is a fascinating and important writer by almost any standard."—NYTBR (Rev: NYTBR 4/30/89; PW 11/4/88)

8265   Mukherjee, Bharati. *Jasmine.* 1989, Grove-Weidenfeld $18.95 (0-8021-1032-0). An Indian immigrant traces her life in the United States from her arrival in Florida to her present-day life in Iowa. (Rev: BL 7/89; PW 7/7/89; TLS 4/27/90. Awards: BL, 1989; PW, 1989)

8266   Mulisch, Harry. *Last Call.* 1989, Viking $18.95 (0-670-82549-2). The reflections of a man born into a family of entertainers who never achieved personal success in the business. "A virtuoso performance . . . clearly earns Mulisch and Dutch fiction a wider audience."—LJ (Rev: BL 2/1/89; LJ 1/89; New Yorker 7/24/89. Awards: BL, 1989)

8267 Munro, Alice. *Lives of Girls and Women.* **1989, NAL paper $7.95 (0-452-25975-4).** This first novel from the Canadian writer details the life of a girl in a small town from youth to the brink of adulthood. (REV: BL 3/1/73; LJ 1/1/73; New Yorker 1/6/73)

8268 Murakami, Haruki. *A Wild Sheep Chase.* **1989, Kodansha $19.95 (0-87011-905-2); NAL paper $8.95 (0-452-26516-9).** This novel originally published in Japanese in 1982 is about a businessman's efforts to track down a mutant sheep believed to be on the island of Hokkaido. (REV: BL 9/15/89; Choice 5/90; PW 8/25/89)

8269 Murdoch, Iris. *Accidental Man.* **1988, Penguin paper $7.95 (0-14-003611-3).** A study of the life of an American scholar living in England to avoid the Vietnam War draft. (REV: Choice 4/72; PW 11/29/71; Time 2/7/72)

8270 Murdoch, Iris. *Black Prince.* **1983, Penguin paper $8.95 (0-14-003934-1).** A retired taxman sets out to create a great novel and falls in love with the young daughter of his best friend. (REV: Choice 9/73; Newsweek 6/18/83; Time 6/18/73. AWARDS: ALA, 1973; Time, 1973)

8271 Murdoch, Iris. *Book and the Brotherhood.* **1988, Viking $19.95 (0-670-81912-3); Penguin paper $8.95 (0-14-101470-4).** A portrait of an aging group of college classmates who pledged to financially assist a colleague in order that he could write a book. (REV: LJ 12/87; NYRB 3/31/88; NYTBR 1/31/88)

8272 Murdoch, Iris. *Bruno's Dream.* **1976, Penguin paper $4.95 (0-14-003176-6).** A dying Englishman in his 80s receives a series of visits from his relatives. "No bleaker, more perceptive portrait of senility can ever have been written."—Time (REV: LJ 12/15/68; Newsweek 1/20/69; Time 2/21/69. AWARDS: ALA, 1969)

8273 Murdoch, Iris. *A Fairly Honourable Defeat.* **1979, Penguin paper $5.95 (0-14-003332-7).** The story of two couples, one gay and one heterosexual, and the efforts of a jealous friend to disrupt both relationships. (REV: LJ 12/15/69; NYTBR 2/8/70; Time 3/9/70)

8274 Murdoch, Iris. *Good Apprentice.* **1987, Penguin paper $7.95 (0-14-009815-1).** An Englishman responsible for the accidental death of a friend devotes his life to repentance in search of forgiveness. (REV: LJ 12/85; NYTBR 1/12/86; Time 1/6/86)

8275 Murdoch, Iris. *Henry and Cato.* **1977, Penguin paper $6.95 (0-14-004569-4).** In this novel by the author of *A Word Child*, two childhood friends separated as youths are reunited in adulthood. (REV: Choice 4/77; PW 8/22/77; TLS 9/24/76)

8276 Murdoch, Iris. *Message to the Planet.* **1990, Viking $22.95 (0-670-82999-4).** The English writer's twenty-fourth novel concerns the relationships between a philosopher, his historian student, and a painter. "Her most challenging work yet."—LJ (REV: BL 11/1/89; LJ 12/89; PW 12/15/89)

8277 Murdoch, Iris. *Nuns and Soldiers.* **1982, Penguin paper $6.95 (0-14-006143-6).** A novel tracing the effects of a man's death on his widow and family, by the English author of *Under the Net*. (REV: CSM 2/9/81; LJ 11/15/80; Sat Rev 1/81)

8278 Murdoch, Iris. *The Philosopher's Pupil.* **1984, Penguin paper $7.95 (0-14-007614-X).** An aging philosopher visits an English spa town to make arrangements for the future life of his recently orphaned granddaughter. (REV: LJ 6/1/83; NYTBR 7/17/83; Time 6/27/83. AWARDS: ALA, 1983)

8279 Murdoch, Iris. *Sacred and Profane Love Machine.* **1984, Penguin paper $5.95 (0-14-004111-7).** In this novel by the author of *The Sea, the Sea*, a married middle-aged psychologist with a mistress is forced to choose between two women. (REV: Choice 3/75; LJ 8/74; TLS 3/22/74)

8280 Murdoch, Iris. *The Sea, the Sea.* **1980, Penguin paper $6.95 (0-14-005199-6).** A director attempting to write his memoirs following his retirement receives a series of visits from his former lovers. "An elegant psychological comedy of manners."—BL (REV: BL 10/1/78; LJ 9/1/78; TLS 8/25/78. AWARDS: ALA, 1978)

8281 Murdoch, Iris. *A Word Child.* **1987, Penguin paper $6.95 (0-14-008153-4).** A civil servant narrates the story of his involvement in two accidental deaths and their effects on his life. (REV: BL 9/15/75; NYTBR 8/24/75; TLS 4/18/75)

8282 Murphy, Gloria. *Down Will Come Baby.* **1991, Donald I. Fine $18.95 (1-55611-196-7).** A young girl living in Boston following the dissolution of her parents' marriage is befriended by a neighbor with questionable motives. (REV: BL 1/15/91; LJ 1/91)

8283 Murray, Albert. *Spyglass Tree.* **1991, Pantheon $20.00 (0-394-58887-8).** A fictional re-creation of the author's college years at Tuskeegee University during the 1940s. "Brilliant—in every sense of the word."—BL (REV: BL 11/1/91; Newsweek 12/9/91)

8284 Muske-Dukes, Carol. *Dear Digby.* **1989, Viking $16.95 (0-670-82506-9).** An advice columnist for a feminist publication gets fed up with her post and begins writing haughty replies to letters. "A novel full of sharp insights and surprising images."—NYTBR (REV: LJ 3/15/89; NYTBR 4/16/89; PW 2/3/89)

8285 Nabokov, Vladimir. *Ada or Ardor: A Family Chronicle.* **1990, Random paper $12.95 (0-679-72522-9).** A love affair between the title character and the story's narrator is revealed to be incestuous in this novel detailing the marriages of two sisters. (REV: LJ 6/1/69; Newsweek 5/5/69; TLS 10/2/69. AWARDS: ALA, 1969)

8286 Nabokov, Vladimir. *Despair.* **1989, Random paper $7.95 (0-679-72343-9).** The author's English translation of an early Russian work concerning an apparent madman's plot to kill a vagrant who he believes has a face identical to his. (REV: LJ 5/15/66; Newsweek 5/16/66; PW 5/9/66. AWARDS: NYTBR, 1966)

8287 Nabokov, Vladimir. *King, Queen, Knave.* **1989, Random paper $8.95 (0-679-72340-4).** A novel originally written in Russian by Nabokov at the age of 28 regarding a young man seduced by his aunt who enters into a plot with her to murder his uncle. (Rev: LJ 5/1/68; PW 3/11/68; Time 5/17/68)

8288 Nabokov, Vladimir. *Look at the Harlequins!* **1990, Random paper $9.95 (0-679-72728-0).** A Russian novelist living in Switzerland recalls his life with four wives over five decades in this story by the author of *Lolita.* (Rev: LJ 10/15/74; Newsweek 10/7/74; PW 9/2/74. Awards: Time, 1974; Time, the 1970s)

8289 Nabokov, Vladimir. *Transparent Things.* **1989, Random paper $6.95 (0-679-72541-5).** A novel depicting eight years in the life of an American publisher staying at a hotel he and his late wife once frequented. (Rev: LJ 9/1/72; PW 9/4/72; Time 12/11/72. Awards: Time, 1972)

8290 Naipaul, V. S. *A Bend in the River.* **1989, Random paper $7.95 (0-679-72202-5).** An Arab merchant moves to the interior of Africa to conduct business in a country plagued by political instability. (Rev: Choice 10/79; LJ 5/15/79; NYTBR 5/13/79. Awards: NYTBR, 1979)

8291 Naipaul, V. S. *Enigma of Arrival.* **1987, Knopf $17.95 (0-394-50971-4); Random paper $6.95 (0-394-75760-2).** A fictional study of life in a small English town as seen through the eyes of a Trinidad-born writer. (Rev: CSM 4/15/87; LJ 3/1/87; NYTBR 3/22/87)

8292 Naipaul, V. S. *Guerrillas.* **1980, Random paper $5.95 (0-394-74492-6).** A portrait of life on a multicultural Caribbean island during civil unrest. "A challenging novel—absorbing, complex and disturbing."—Newsweek (Rev: LJ 10/1/75; NYTBR 11/18/75; Newsweek 12/1/75. Awards: NYTBR, 1975)

8293 Naipaul, V. S. *Mimic Men.* **1985, Random paper $5.95 (0-394-73232-4).** The memoirs of a former Caribbean political leader reflecting on his life from his exile in London. (Rev: LJ 9/15/67; PW 7/10/67; TLS 4/27/67)

8294 Narayan, R. K. *Talkative Man.* **1987, Viking $15.95 (0-670-81341-9); Penguin paper $5.95 (0-14-010134-9).** The story of the effects of the visit of a researcher upon the citizenry of Malgudi. (Rev: BL 4/1/87; NYTBR 3/29/87; TLS 10/3/86)

8295 Narayan, R. K. *World of Nagaraj.* **1990, Viking $18.95 (0-670-83132-8).** A portrayal of the lives of residents in the Indian town of Malgudi, focusing on the exploits of the Sanskrit scholar Nagaraj. (Rev: BL 3/15/90; LJ 6/1/90; PW 3/30/90)

8296 Nathan, Robert Stuart. *White Tiger.* **1988, Warner paper $4.95 (0-446-35206-3).** A police officer's investigation into a friend's death unearths corruption at the highest levels of Chinese government. (Rev: BL 7/87; NYTBR 9/6/87)

8297 Naumoff, Lawrence. *Night of the Weeping Women.* **1988, Atlantic Monthly $16.95 (0-87113-187-0); Ivy Books paper $3.95 (0-8041-0488-3).** This author's debut novel concerns the deterioration of a North Carolina marriage over a Thanksgiving holiday. (Rev: BL 6/15/88; LJ 6/15/88; PW 5/13/88)

8298 Naylor, Gloria. *Linden Hills.* **1986, Penguin paper $7.95 (0-14-008829-6).** Two young boys search for the secrets of a man who founded an exclusive community for wealthy African Americans known as Linden Hills. (Rev: CSM 3/1/85; LJ 4/15/85; NYTBR 3/3/85)

8299 Naylor, Gloria. *Women of Brewster Place: A Novel in Seven Stories.* **1989, NAL paper $3.95 (0-451-82202-1).** Portraits of the lives of seven African-American women living on a single street of an urban American city. (Rev: BL 6/1/82; LJ 6/15/82; NYTBR 8/22/82. Awards: NBA, 1983)

8300 Newman, Charles. *Promisekeeper.* **1971, Ultramarine $20.00 (0-671-20822-5).** A novel with an experimental form that explores the rise and fall of a doomed love affair. (Rev: LJ 6/1/71; NYTBR 8/1/71)

8301 Newman, Charles. *White Jazz.* **1984, Ultramarine paper $7.95 (0-385-18863-3).** The portrait of a week in the life of a man who feels stifled by contemporary society and technology. "A demonstration of the philosophy and talents of an extremely intelligent writer."—NYTBR (Rev: LJ 1/84; NYTBR 1/15/84; PW 12/9/83)

8302 Nichols, John. *Milagro Beanfield War.* **1987, Ballantine paper $4.95 (0-345-34446-4).** A conflict in a small Mexican-American community in northern New Mexico pits the residents of the town against the powers of the state in a battle for local water rights. (Rev: Choice 1/75; LJ 9/1/74; PW 7/22/74)

8303 Nichols, John. *Wizard of Loneliness.* **1987, Norton paper $7.95 (0-393-30473-6).** A coming-of-age story concerning a ten-year-old boy raised by his grandfather near the end of World War II. (Rev: BL 5/1/66; PW 1/17/66)

8304 Nielsen, Alfred. *Summer of the Paymaster.* **1990, Norton $19.95 (0-393-02888-7).** A friend awaits the return of a marine from Vietnam in this novel set in 1968 on Staten Island. (Rev: LJ 10/15/90; NYTBR 11/18/90; PW 8/17/90)

8305 Norman, Howard. *Northern Lights.* **1988, Pocket paper $6.95 (0-671-65877-8).** A Canadian man raised in a remote northern village reflects on his childhood friendship with a young Native American boy. (Rev: Atl 6/87; NYTBR 4/12/87; PW 2/13/87. Awards: PW, 1987)

8306 Nossack, Hans Erich. *Wait for November.* **1982, Fromm International $14.95 (0-88064-004-9).** This novel, originally published in Germany in 1955, traces the life of a young woman who leaves her family to live with an obsessive writer. (Rev: LJ 7/82; NYTBR 7/18/82)

8307 Nova, Craig. *Good Son.* **1989, Doubleday paper $8.95 (0-385-29717-3).** The portrait of a relationship between a demanding father and his World War II veteran son. (Rev: BL 7/82; LJ 7/82; NYTBR 10/3/82)

8308 Nova, Craig. *Tornado Alley.* 1989, Delacorte $18.95 (0-385-29710-6). Intertwined stories of several characters living in small, desolate towns in Pennsylvania and California. (Rev: BL 5/15/89; PW 3/17/89)

8309 Nunn, Kem. *Unassigned Territory.* 1988, Dell paper $7.95 (0-440-50009-5). A tale of a religious cult in the California desert during the 1960s by the author of *Tapping the Source.* (Rev: BL 7/87; New Yorker 8/31/87; PW 5/15/87)

8310 Oakley, Ann. *Men's Room.* 1989, Macmillan $18.95 (0-689-12050-8); Ivy Books paper $4.95 (0-8041-0647-9). A single woman carries on a decade-long affair with a married man. "Anyone who wonders what women *really* want should read it."—BL (Rev: BL 3/15/89; LJ 3/1/89; PW 2/3/89)

8311 Oates, Joyce Carol. *American Appetites.* 1989, Dutton $18.95 (0-525-24725-4); Harper & Row paper $8.95 (0-06-097278-5). A couple's marriage is threatened by an escalating conflict that develops over the course of a single evening. "Oates is here working at the very top of her form."—Time (Rev: LJ 12/88; PW 11/4/88; Time 1/9/89)

8312 Oates, Joyce Carol. *Expensive People.* 1990, Ontario Rev. paper $9.95 (0-86538-069-4). A story of the events surrounding the killing of a mother by her child. (Rev: LJ 10/15/68; NYRB 1/2/69; PW 8/12/68)

8313 Oates, Joyce Carol. *I Lock the Room Upon Myself.* 1990, Ecco Pr. $17.95 (0-88001-260-9). A young woman born late in the nineteenth century in upstate New York is inspired by a painting by Fernand Khnopff. "Essential to the Oates canon."—LJ (Rev: LJ 10/15/90; NYTBR 11/11/90; New Yorker 1/7/91)

8314 Oates, Joyce Carol. *Marya: A Life.* 1986, Dutton $16.95 (0-525-24374-7); Berkley paper $3.95 (0-425-10688-8). An account of the first three decades of life of an orphaned woman who became a professor and critic. (Rev: LJ 3/15/86; NYTBR 3/2/86; Newsweek 3/24/86)

8315 Oates, Joyce Carol. *Rise of Life on Earth.* 1991, New Directions $16.95 (0-8112-1171-1). A formerly abused 11-year-old foster child seeks revenge on the world through a string of murders. (Rev: BL 4/15/91; New Yorker 5/13/91; PW 3/15/91)

8316 Oates, Joyce Carol. *Solstice.* 1986, Berkley paper $3.95 (0-425-09204-6). The story of the development of a friendship between two women in rural Pennsylvania. (Rev: LJ 11/15/84; Newsweek 1/21/85; PW 11/16/84)

8317 Oates, Joyce Carol. *Son of the Morning.* 1979, Fawcett paper $2.75 (0-449-24073-8). A chronicle of the career of a Pentecostal child evangelist from youth to adulthood. "Oates at the passionate and compassionate peak of her powers."—BL (Rev: BL 7/15/78; Choice 1/79; LJ 8/78)

8318 Oates, Joyce Carol. *Them.* 1984, Fawcett paper $5.95 (0-449-20692-0). The story of a family living in poverty in a Detroit ghetto, tracing their lives from the Depression to the inner-city riots of the 1960s. (Rev: NYTBR 9/28/69; PW 9/7/70; Time 10/10/69. Awards: ALA, 1969; NBA, 1970)

8319 Oates, Joyce Carol. *You Must Remember This.* 1987, Dutton $19.95 (0-525-24545-6); Harper & Row paper $8.95 (0-06-097169-X). A portrait of a love affair between an uncle and his niece set in New York during the 1950s. "A well-developed novel that will rank among her best."—LJ (Rev: BL 6/1/87; LJ 7/87; NYTBR 8/16/87)

8320 O'Brien, Dan. *In the Center of the Nation.* 1991, Atlantic Monthly $21.95 (0-87113-441-1). A rivalry develops between a group of South Dakota cattle ranchers and a local bank president who is attempting to purchase local land for mineral rights. (Rev: LJ 5/15/91; NYTBR 8/18/91; PW 4/12/91)

8321 O'Brien, Dan. *Spirit of the Hills.* 1988, Crown $17.95 (0-517-56727-X); Pocket paper $6.95 (0-671-67609-1). A tale of South Dakota ranchers searching for a wolf threatening their livestock intertwined with the story of a man seeking his brother's killer. "An exciting, absorbing and extremely well-written book."—NYTBR (Rev: NYTBR 4/3/88; PW 2/12/88)

8322 O'Brien, Edna. *Country Girls Trilogy: An Epilogue.* 1986, Farrar $18.95 (0-374-13027-2); NAL paper $9.95 (0-452-26182-1). Three novels written by the Irish author during the 1960s—*The Country Girls, The Lonely Girl,* and *Girls in Their Married Bliss.* (Rev: BL 5/1/86; NYTBR 5/11/86)

8323 O'Brien, Edna. *High Road.* 1988, Farrar $18.95 (0-374-29273-6); NAL paper $8.95 (0-452-26306-9). A story of the friendship that develops between two women who meet on a Mediterranean resort island. (Rev: BL 11/15/88; NYTBR 11/20/88; Time 11/21/88)

8324 O'Brien, Tim. *Nuclear Age.* 1989, Doubleday paper $8.95 (0-385-29775-0). The story of four decades in the life of a man plagued by visions of the impending nuclear destruction of the world. (Rev: BL 8/85; PW 8/9/85; TLS 3/28/86)

8325 O'Connor, Sheila. *Tokens of Grace: A Novel of Stories.* 1990, Milkweed Ed. paper $9.95 (0-915943-47-6). A debut novel set in 1968 about a ten-year-old girl suddenly entrusted with the care of her two younger sisters. (Rev: BL 8/90; NYTBR 8/5/90)

8326 O'Grady, Timothy. *Motherland.* 1990, Henry Holt $19.95 (0-8050-1230-3). This debut novel concerns the search of an Irish writer for his missing mother with assistance from a medieval family journal. (Rev: LJ 2/15/90; PW 1/12/90; TLS 3/24/89)

8327 O'Hehir, Diana. *I Wish This War Were Over.* 1989, Pocket paper $6.95 (0-671-67873-6). A young woman sets out on a journey to rescue her mother from a disastrous affair with a married man in this novel set during the early 1940s. (Rev: CSM 3/1/85; LJ 2/15/84; PW 1/6/84)

8328 Olmstead, Robert. *Soft Water.* 1988, Random paper $6.95 (0-394-75752-1). This debut novel is about a self-sufficient man from Maine who is forced to track the gun-running killers of his brother. (Rev: BL 3/15/88; LJ 3/15/88; PW 2/5/88)

8329 Olshan, Joseph. *A Warmer Season.* **1987, McGraw-Hill $15.95 (0-07-083641-8); Ballantine paper $3.95 (0-318-33438-0).** This author's second novel portrays the relations of Italian and Jewish youngsters in an East Coast city. "A novel about teenagers of compelling interest to adults."—NYTBR (Rev: BL 5/15/87; NYTBR 8/16/87; PW 5/1/87)

8330 Olshan, Joseph. *Waterline.* **1989, Doubleday $18.95 (0-385-26505-0).** A seven-year-old boy witnesses an accidental drowning and is haunted by feelings of guilt. (Rev: BL 9/15/89; LJ 9/15/89; NYTBR 11/5/89)

8331 Onetti, Juan Carlos. *Body Snatcher.* **1991, Pantheon $22.00 (0-679-40178-4).** Battle between a bordello and the citizenry of a small Uruguayan town. "Powerful . . . a significant contribution to the art of Latin American fiction."—LJ (Rev: LJ 5/1/91; PW 3/29/91)

8332 Ortese, Anna Maria. *The Iguana.* **1987, McPherson $14.95 (0-914232-87-8).** A novel originally published in Italian in 1965 chronicling the adventures of an aristocrat who sails to an island inhabited by three brothers and their servant. (Rev: Choice 3/88; LJ 10/1/87; NYTBR 11/22/87)

8333 Osborn, Karen. *Patchwork.* **1991, Harcourt $19.95 (0-15-171292-1).** Three South Carolina sisters spin tales of their family's history from the Depression to the 1980s. (Rev: LJ 5/1/91; NYTBR 8/25/91; PW 5/10/91)

8334 Otto, Whitney. *How to Make an American Quilt.* **1991, Villard $18.00 (0-679-40070-2).** The lives of nine women in a central California quilting club are portrayed in this author's debut work of fiction. "Remarkable . . . an affirmation of the strength and power of individual lives."—NYTBR (Rev: BL 1/15/91; NYTBR 3/24/91; PW 2/8/91)

8335 Oz, Amos. *Black Box.* **1988, Harcourt $19.95 (0-15-112888-X); Random paper $8.95 (0-679-72185-1).** A series of letters from four family members traces the group's dissolution over the years. (Rev: CSM 6/15/88; LJ 4/15/88; TLS 6/24/88)

8336 Oz, Amos. *Elsewhere, Perhaps.* **1985, Harcourt paper $9.95 (0-15-628475-8).** A study of the lives of four families living on an Israeli kibbutz prior to the outbreak of the 1967 war. (Rev: BL 2/1/74; NYTBR 11/18/73; TLS 2/22/74)

8337 Oz, Amos. *A Perfect Peace.* **1985, Harcourt $16.95 (0-15-171696-X).** An Israeli novelist's story of two kibbutz members before and after the Six Day War. (Rev: BL 5/15/85; LJ 6/15/85; NYTBR 6/2/85)

8338 Oz, Amos. *To Know a Woman.* **1991, Harcourt $19.95 (0-15-190499-5).** A retired Israeli spy reflects on his marriage and married life following the death of his wife. (Rev: BL 1/15/91; LJ 2/1/91; NYTBR 2/27/91)

8339 Oz, Amos. *Unto Death: Crusade and Late Love.* **1978, Harcourt paper $3.95 (0-15-693170-2).** Two illustrated novellas depicting examples of anti-Semitism in medieval and modern times. "Haunting and truly unforgettable."—LJ (Rev: BL 11/15/75; LJ 10/1/75; New Rep 11/29/75)

8340 Ozick, Cynthia. *Cannibal Galaxy.* **1984, Dutton paper $7.95 (0-525-48133-8).** A Holocaust refugee and former astronomer becomes a teacher of Western and Jewish culture at a Midwestern elementary school. (Rev: CSM 11/4/83; LJ 8/83; Time 9/5/83)

8341 Ozick, Cynthia. *Messiah of Stockholm.* **1987, Knopf $15.95 (0-394-54701-2); Random paper $5.95 (0-394-75690-0).** A Swedish journalist's search for the truth about his father and his father's writings. (Rev: BL 3/1/87; LJ 3/1/87; NYTBR 3/22/87. Awards: BL, the 1980s; LJ, 1987)

8342 Ozick, Cynthia. *The Shawl.* **1989, Knopf $12.95 (0-394-57976-3); Random paper $7.95 (0-679-72926-7).** Two interconnected stories with the same protagonist separated by 30 years. Consists of the novella "Rosa" and the title story. (Rev: BL 9/1/89; NYTBR 9/10/89; PPW 7/28/89. Awards: ALA, 1989; BL, 1989; NYTBR, 1989; PW, 1989)

8343 Pagnol, Marcel. *Jean de Florette and Manon of the Spring.* **1988, North Point paper $14.95 (0-86547-312-9).** These two French novels concerning peasant life were the subjects of popular films during the late 1980s. (Rev: BL 2/15/88; LJ 3/1/88; PW 1/29/88)

8344 Palliser, Charles. *Sensationist.* **1991, Ballantine $15.00 (0-345-36958-0).** This second novel by the author of *The Quincunx* tells the story of a destructive love affair between an artist and a hedonist prone to experiment with sex and drugs. (Rev: BL 4/15/91; LJ 5/1/91)

8345 Palmer, William. *Good Republic.* **1991, Viking $19.95 (0-670-83571-4).** This debut novel concerns the return of a man to his native Baltic republic following years of exile in Great Britain. (Rev: BL 3/1/91; LJ 2/15/91; PW 2/22/91)

8346 Paral, Vladimir. *Catapult: A Timetable of Rail, Sea and Air Ways to Paradise.* **1989, Catbird Pr. $15.95 (0-945774-04-4).** This portrayal of Czech life prior to the 1968 Soviet invasion as told by a chemical engineer is the author's first work translated into English. (Rev: LJ 4/15/89; NYTBR 6/18/89; PW 2/17/89)

8347 Parent, Gail. *A Sign of the Eighties.* **1988, Jove paper $4.50 (0-515-09711-X).** The search by a New York feminist in her 30s for a perfect husband. "Funny and fast paced from start to finish."—BL (Rev: BL 5/1/87; LJ 6/15/87; PW 4/10/87)

8348 Parkin, Frank. *Krippendorf's Tribe.* **1988, Dell paper $4.95 (0-440-20182-9).** An English anthropologist invents the existence of an Amazonian tribe and falsifies research in order to receive grant monies. "An ingenious performance."—Time (Rev: LJ 2/1/86; NYTBR 3/2/86; Time 2/17/86)

8349   Parkin, Frank. *Mind and Body Shop.* **1988, Dell paper $4.95 (0-440-20183-7).** A British professor opens classroom sessions in a whorehouse in this second novel by the author of *Krippendorf's Tribe.* (REV: LJ 8/87; NYTBR 8/16/87; PW 6/12/87)

8350   Parks, Tim. *Goodness.* **1991, Grove-Weidenfeld $17.95 (0-8021-1390-7).** A missionary's son considers euthanasia to put an end to the suffering of his severely deformed child. "A writer of stunning talent."—BL (REV: BL 10/1/91; LJ 9/15/91; PW 7/25/91)

8351   Parks, Tim. *Loving Roger.* **1987, Grove-Weidenfeld $15.95 (0-8021-0016-3); Penguin paper $6.95 (0-14-011359-9).** A London woman narrates the story of how she came to kill her lover. (REV: LJ 10/1/87; PW 10/16/87)

8352   Parris, P. B. *Waltzing in the Attic.* **1990, Doubleday $18.95 (0-385-41272-X).** A young Nebraska woman chronicles the continuing cycle of abuse in her family. (REV: BL 8/90; LJ 7/90; PW 6/15/90)

8353   Paton, Alan. *Ah, But Your Land Is Beautiful.* **1983, Macmillan $10.95 (0-684-17830-3).** A look at life in South Africa during the 1950s when the rigidity of the apartheid system was setting in. (REV: NYTBR 4/19/82; Newsweek 3/15/82; PW 1/15/82)

8354   Patrick, Vincent. *Family Business.* **1990, Pocket paper $4.50 (0-671-68671-2).** Three criminals plot a bank heist in this novel by the author of *The Pope of Greenwich Village.* (REV: BL 10/15/85; LJ 11/1/85; PW 9/20/85)

8355   Pavic, Milorad. *Landscape Painted with Tea.* **1990, Knopf $19.95 (0-394-58217-9).** A chronicle of a series of dream lives by the Yugoslavian author of *The Dictionary of the Khazars.* (REV: BL 9/1/90; NYTBR 12/16/90)

8356   Pearson, T. R. *Gospel Hour.* **1991, Morrow $19.95 (0-688-09480-5).** An account of a Southern man revived from apparent death who becomes a gospel preacher after his recovery. "His tallest and most hilarious tale so far."—NYTBR (REV: BL 1/15/91; LJ 2/15/91; NYTBR 4/7/91)

8357   Pearson, T. R. *Last of How It Was.* **1988, Ballantine paper $4.95 (0-345-35640-3).** Members of a North Carolina family recount a series of events in their town, including a search for a stolen car that led to murder. (REV: NYTBR 11/1/87; PW 7/17/87)

8358   Pearson, T. R. *Off for the Sweet Hereafter.* **1987, Ballantine paper $4.50 (0-345-34369-7).** This second novel by the author of *A Short History of a Small Place* traces the exploits of a pair of criminals around the state of North Carolina. (REV: BL 6/15/86; LJ 6/1/86; NYTBR 6/15/86)

8359   Pearson, T. R. *A Short History of a Small Place.* **1986, Ballantine paper $4.95 (0-345-34369-7).** In this debut novel, the narrator tells the stories of strange characters and events in a small North Carolina town. "An original and wonderful novel; an auspicious debut."—PW (REV: BL 10/1/85; NYTBR 7/85; PW 5/10/85)

8360   Pei, Lowry. *Family Resemblances.* **1988, Random paper $6.95 (0-394-65528-6).** This debut novel is a coming-of-age story about a teenager who spends an eventful summer with her unmarried aunt. (REV: BL 6/15/86; LJ 4/15/86; NYTBR 4/20/86)

8361   Pelletier, Cathie. *Once Upon a Time on the Banks.* **1989, Viking $19.95 (0-670-82776-2).** A planned wedding of a Maine woman to a French Canadian Catholic creates family tension in this novel set during the late 1960s. (REV: BL 9/1/89; LJ 8/89; PW 8/18/89)

8362   Percy, Walker. *Lancelot.* **1977, Farrar $8.95 (0-374-18313-9); Ivy Books paper $3.95 (0-8041-0380-1).** In this novel by the author of *The Moviegoer*, a man explores the essence of good and evil after learning of his wife's infidelities. (REV: CSM 3/2/77; LJ 3/1/77; New Rep 2/5/77. AWARDS: ALA, 1977)

8363   Percy, Walker. *Last Gentleman.* **1966, Farrar $17.95 (0-364-18372-4); paper $9.95 (0-374-50916-6).** A Southern man befriends a family and makes a pilgrimage with them to their home to bring their son there to die. (REV: BL 9/1/66; NYTBR 6/26/66; Time 6/17/66. AWARDS: NYTBR, 1966)

8364   Percy, Walker. *Love in the Ruins.* **1971, Farrar $22.95 (0-374-19302-9).** A story regarding American political party rivalries set in the near future. "Imaginative, high-spirited and superlatively well-written."—PW (REV: BL 7/1/71; PW 3/28/71; Time 5/17/71. AWARDS: ALA, 1971; Time, 1971)

8365   Percy, Walker. *Second Coming.* **1980, Farrar $12.95 (0-374-25674-8); Ivy Books paper $4.95 (0-8041-0542-1).** In this sequel to *The Last Gentleman*, Williston Bibb Barrett contemplates dropping out of society but meets an escapee from a mental hospital who changes his mind. (REV: BL 6/15/80; CSM 8/20/80; New Rep 7/5/80. AWARDS: ALA, 1980)

8366   Percy, Walker. *Thanatos Syndrome.* **1987, Farrar $17.95 (0-374-27354-5); Ivy Books paper $4.95 (0-8041-0220-1).** A psychiatrist searches for the cause of strange behavior by the citizenry of a small Louisiana town. (REV: Atl 4/87; Natl Rev 5/22/87; Time 3/30/87)

8367   Perec, George. *Life: A User's Manual.* **1988, Godine $24.95 (0-87923-700-7); paper $14.95 (0-87923-751-1).** A fictional inventory of the contents of a Paris apartment house at a precise moment in time. "A classic of contemporary fiction."—PW (REV: BL 11/15/87; New Rep 2/8/88; PW 10/9/87)

8368   Perec, George. *W: Or the Memory of Childhood.* **1988, Godine $16.95 (0-87923-756-2).** Two intertwined stories told in alternate chapters examine the author's childhood and the society of a fictional European nation. (REV: BL 11/15/88; Choice 7–8/89; LJ 11/15/88)

8369   Perriam, Wendy. *Devils, for a Change.* **1990, St. Martin's $19.95 (0-312-04300-7).** A former nun adjusts to post-convent living in contemporary London. (REV: LJ 4/1/90; PW 3/9/90)

8370   Perry, Richard. *Montgomery's Children.* 1985, NAL paper $7.95 (0-452-25674-7). The story of an African-American family in a small New York town and the effects of modernization on the community from 1948 to 1980. (Rev: BL 11/15/83; LJ 12/1/83; PW 10/28/83)

8371   Perry, Thomas. *Butcher's Boy.* 1984, Ace paper $3.95 (0-441-08955-0). A hit man finds both the U.S. government and organized crime figures after him following arrangements made for the assassination of a senator. "A notable piece of entertainment."—New Yorker (Rev: LJ 8/82; New Yorker 9/20/82; PW 4/2/82)

8372   Perutz, Kathrin. *Writing for Love and Money.* 1991, Univ. of Arkansas Pr. $17.95 (1-55728-211-0). The fictionalized memoirs of an academic writer who has turned to ghostwriting popular novels of questionable literary merit. (Rev: BL 7/91; PW 8/9/91)

8373   Pesetsky, Bette. *Midnight Sweets.* 1989, Ivy Books paper $5.95 (0-8041-0533-2). The story of a twice-divorced woman with five children who strives to turn her cookie recipes into financial success. (Rev: BL 11/1/88; NYTBR 11/13/88; PW 9/2/88)

8374   Peters, Elizabeth. *Naked Once More.* 1989, Warner $17.95 (0-446-51482-9); paper $4.95 (0-446-36032-5). An author commissioned to write the sequel to a novel by a deceased writer is plagued by the friends and family of the late author. (Rev: BL 7/89; PW 7/14/89. Awards: BL, 1989)

8375   Petesch, Natalie L. M. *Duncan's Colony.* 1982, Ohio Univ. Pr. $21.95 (0-8040-0401-3). A group of survivalists form a colony in the American Southwest designed to survive a nuclear holocaust. (Rev: LJ 6/1/82; TLS 10/15/82)

8376   Petievich, Gerald. *Shakedown.* 1989, Pocket paper $4.50 (0-671-67964-3). An FBI agent seeks witnesses willing to testify against Las Vegas organized crime figures. "Put this book high on your list. It is as good as they come."—NYTBR (Rev: BL 4/1/88; NYTBR 6/26/88; PW 12/11/87)

8377   Petrakis, Harry M. *Ghost of the Sun.* 1990, St. Martin's $18.95 (0-312-04319-8). This sequel to the author's 1966 novel, *A Dream of Kings,* concerns the further adventures of a Greek-American man in Chicago. "A most satisfying novel that can be read independently of its predecessor."—LJ (Rev: BL 5/15/90; LJ 5/15/90; PW 5/4/90)

8378   Phillips, Caryl. *Final Passage.* 1990, Penguin paper $7.95 (0-14-012796-8). A West Indian couple leave their Caribbean home to search for a better life in London in this novel by the author of *Higher Ground.* (Rev: BL 1/1/90; LJ 1/90; NYTBR 4/29/90)

8379   Phillips, Caryl. *Higher Ground: A Novel in Three Parts.* 1989, Viking $17.95 (0-670-82620-0); Penguin paper $7.95 (0-14-011806-3). A collection of three novellas about racial exploitation, ranging in setting from the eighteenth to the twentieth centuries. (Rev: BL 8/89; LJ 8/89; PW 6/23/89)

8380   Phillips, Jayne Anne. *Machine Dreams.* 1985, Pocket paper $3.95 (0-671-53290-1). A chronicle of family history told by four West Virginians tracing the group from the 1930s to the Vietnam War. (Rev: BL 6/15/84; NYTBR 7/1/84; Time 7/16/84. Awards: ALA, 1984; BL, the 1980s; NYTBR, 1985)

8381   Piercy, Marge. *Braided Lives.* 1982, Ultramarine $20.00 (0-671-43834-4); Fawcett paper $4.95 (0-449-21300-5). Portrayal of the life of a politically active feminist writer from her teenage years to age 40. (Rev: LJ 1/1/82; NYTBR 2/7/82; PW 12/11/81)

8382   Piercy, Marge. *Dance the Eagle to Sleep.* 1982, Fawcett paper $3.95 (0-449-20114-7). A profile of four characters involved in a radical group known as "The Indians." (Rev: Newsweek 11/23/70; PW 8/31/70; Time 10/26/70. Awards: ALA, 1970)

8383   Piercy, Marge. *Fly Away Home.* 1988, Fawcett paper $4.95 (0-449-44527-5). An Italian-American cookbook writer in her 40s suspects that her husband is carrying on an affair with another woman. "Piercy's most accessible novel, and therefore, her most politically powerful."—CSM (Rev: BL 1/1/84; CSM 5/4/84; LJ 3/15/84)

8384   Piercy, Marge. *Small Changes.* 1985, Fawcett paper $4.95 (0-449-21083-9). The story of two American women trapped in dead-end marriages during the 1960s, by the author of *Vida.* "An extraordinary performance."—LJ (Rev: BL 2/15/74; LJ 8/73; PW 6/18/73)

8385   Piercy, Marge. *Summer People.* 1989, Summit $19.95 (0-671-67856-6); Fawcett paper $5.95 (0-449-21842-2). The story of the breakup of an 11-year ménage à trois between a Massachusetts married couple and a fashion designer. (Rev: BL 3/15/89; PW 4/7/89)

8386   Piercy, Marge. *Vida.* 1981, Ultramarine $20.00 (0-671-40110-6); Fawcett paper $4.95 (0-449-20850-8). A chronicle of the life of a revolutionary wanted in connection with a bombing. "A powerful novel, written with insight, wit and remorseless energy."—TLS (Rev: LJ 1/15/80; NYTBR 2/24/80; TLS 3/7/80)

8387   Pilcher, Rosamunde. *Shell Seekers.* 1987, St. Martin's $19.95 (0-312-01058-3); Dell paper $5.95 (0-440-20204-3). An English grandmother returns to her family home after suffering a heart attack in this novel set during World War II. "A deeply satisfying story, written with love and confidence."—NYTBR (Rev: BL 12/1/87; LJ 1/88; NYTBR 2/7/88)

8388   Pinter, Harold. *Dwarfs.* 1990, Grove-Weidenfeld $17.95 (0-8021-1385-0). This unpublished 1950s novel by the playwright consists almost entirely of theatrical dialog among a group of three English dwarfs. (Rev: LJ 10/15/90; PW 8/31/90)

8389   Pirsig, Robert M. *Lila: An Inquiry into Morals.* 1991, Bantam $22.50 (0-553-07737-6). A fictional study of morality by the author of *Zen and the Art of Motorcycle Maintenance* depicting the adventures of the novel's narrator aboard a sailboat with a wise woman. (REV: BL 9/15/91; NYTBR 10/13/91; PW 8/16/91. AWARDS: BL, 1991)

8390 Plain, Belva. *Evergreen.* **1979, Delacorte $19.95 (0-385-28299-0); Dell paper $5.95 (0-440-13278-9).** The story of a Jewish woman and her family following her immigration from Poland to New York as a teenager. "Will be treasured and reread for years to come."—LJ (REV: BL 7/1/78; LJ 5/15/78; PW 3/13/78)

8391 Plante, David. *The Accident.* **1991, Ticknor & Fields $18.95 (0-395-56925-7).** The experiences of an American atheist who goes to Belgium to study at a prominent Catholic university. (REV: LJ 3/15/91; PW 3/8/91)

8392 Plante, David. *The Catholic.* **1981, Macmillan $9.95 (0-689-11189-4).** A tale of gay sexual obsession set in Boston during the 1960s, by the author of *The Family* and *The Country*. (REV: BL 2/1/86; PW 1/24/86)

8393 Plante, David. *The Country.* **1981, Macmillan $9.95 (0-689-11189-4).** The depiction of a family reunion outside Providence, Rhode Island, following a funeral. (REV: BL 10/1/81; New Rep 10/7/81; NYRB 11/19/81. AWARDS: ALA, 1981)

8394 Plath, Sylvia. *Bell Jar.* **1983, Bantam paper $4.95 (0-553-27835-5).** A posthumously published novel by the American poet about the short and painful career of a New York magazine editor sinking toward a mental breakdown. (REV: LJ 10/1/71; PW 3/1/71; Time 6/21/71)

8395 Pohl, Frederik. *Chernobyl.* **1987, Bantam $18.95 (0-553-05210-1); paper $4.50 (0-553-27193-8).** The noted science fiction writer's fictional recreation of the 1986 Soviet nuclear disaster at Chernobyl. (REV: LJ 8/87; PW 7/17/87)

8396 Polite, Carlene Hatcher. *Flagellants.* **1988, Beacon paper $7.95 (0-8070-6321-5).** Exploration of the lives of two African-Americans who move from the South to Greenwich Village, as told through a series of dialogues. (REV: New Rep 6/24/67; PW 4/17/67)

8397 Popham, Melinda Worth. *Skywater.* **1990, Graywolf $17.95 (1-55597-127-X).** A group of coyotes wander the American West in search of uncontaminated water following the pollution of their former supply by humans. (REV: BL 4/15/90; PW 3/23/90. AWARDS: ALA, 1990)

8398 Popovac, Gwynn. *Wet Paint.* **1987, Ballantine paper $3.95 (0-345-34739-0).** A debut novel chronicling the coming of age of a young female artist in Los Angeles during the early 1960s. (REV: BL 11/15/86; LJ 11/15/86)

8399 Porter, Connie. *All-Bright Court.* **1991, Houghton $19.95 (0-395-53271-X).** This debut novel portrays the life of an African-American family that migrated from the South to Buffalo in search of work in the steel mills. (REV: BL 7/91; LJ 6/15/91; New Yorker 9/9/91. AWARDS: ALA, 1992)

8400 Portis, Charles. *Gringos.* **1991, Simon & Schuster $18.95 (0-671-72457-6).** The story of a group of American expatriates living in Mexico and attempting to commune with the spirits of the ancient Mayans. (REV: BL 1/15/91; LJ 1/91; NYTBR 1/20/91)

8401 Portis, Charles. *Masters of Atlantis.* **1985, Knopf $15.95 (0-394-54683-0); McGraw-Hill paper $6.95 (0-07-050503-9).** The chronicle of six decades of a secret society by the author of *True Grit*. (REV: BL 10/1/85; New Yorker 11/25/85; Newsweek 9/30/85)

8402 Potok, Chaim. *Book of Lights.* **1981, Knopf $19.95 (0-394-52031-9); Fawcett paper $4.95 (0-449-24569-1).** A Jewish orphan in a seminary seeks answers in the mystic teachings of the Kabbalah. "Luminous, majestic, knowing, and very moving fiction."—BL (REV: BL 7/1/81; LJ 9/1/81; Time 10/19/81)

8403 Potok, Chaim. *Gift of Asher Lev.* **1990, Knopf $19.95 (0-394-57212-2).** This third volume of the Asher Lev series depicts the artist's return to his home city of Brooklyn following a period of exile in France. (REV: BL 2/1/90; LJ 3/15/90; TLS 11/2/90)

8404 Potok, Chaim. *My Name Is Asher Lev.* **1972, Knopf $22.95 (0-394-46137-1); Fawcett paper $4.95 (0-449-20714-5).** A chronicle of the early life of an artist raised in a traditional Hasidic Brooklyn home. (REV: BL 6/15/72; LJ 4/15/72; NYTBR 4/16/72)

8405 Potok, Chaim. *The Promise.* **1969, Knopf $22.95 (0-394-44163-X); Fawcett paper $4.95 (0-449-20910-5).** This sequel to the author's *The Chosen* concerns the efforts of a rabbi and a psychologist to help the schizophrenic teenage child of a friend. (REV: LJ 4/15/69; NYTBR 9/14/69; PW 6/15/70)

8406 Powell, Anthony. *The Fisher King.* **1986, Norton $15.95 (0-393-02363-X); paper $7.95 (0-393-30502-3).** A chronicle of the voyage of a educational cruise around Great Britain featuring a photographer nicknamed "the Fisher King." (REV: BL 9/15/86; New Yorker 10/20/86; PW 8/1/86)

8407 Powell, Anthony. *Hearing Secret Harmonies.* **1986, Warner paper $8.95 (0-445-20146-0).** The final volume of 12 of A Dance to the Music of Time series, bringing the novel to its conclusion in the 1970s. (REV: BL 3/15/76; NYTBR 4/11/76; PW 2/16/76. AWARDS: NYTBR, 1976)

8408 Powell, Padgett. *Edisto.* **1984, Farrar $11.95 (0-374-14651-9); 1985 paper $5.95 (0-03-003184-2).** A depiction of the life of a 12-year-old boy growing up on the South Carolina shore. "A work of extraordinary skill . . . few books afford such entertaining reading."—LJ (REV: LJ 3/15/84; Newsweek 4/16/84; Time 4/2/84. AWARDS: ALA, 1984; Time, 1984)

8409 Powell, Padgett. *A Woman Named Drown.* **1987, Farrar $14.95 (0-374-29204-3); Henry Holt paper $7.95 (0-8050-0750-4).** A Tennessee graduate student is dumped by his girlfriend via a letter from Europe in this second novel by the author of *Edisto*. "A potent, funny, one-of-a-kind sort of book."—NYTBR (REV: LJ 5/1/87; NYTBR 6/7/87; Time 5/18/87)

8410 **Powers, J. F.** *Wheat That Springeth Green.* **1988, Knopf $18.95 (0-394-49609-4); Pocket paper $8.95 (0-671-68221-0).** A study of the daily lives of a group of Minnesota Roman Catholic priests by the author of *Morte d'Urban.* (REV: BL 7/88; PW 8/29/88; Time 8/29/88. AWARDS: ALA, 1988; BL, the 1980s; PW, 1988)

8411 **Powers, John R.** *Junk-Drawer Corner-Store Front-Porch Blues.* **1992, Dutton $19.00 (0-525-93405-7).** A Los Angeles writer facing middle age reassesses his life following the hospitalization of his mother. (REV: BL 1/1/92; LJ 1/92; PW 11/15/91)

8412 **Powers, Richard.** *Gold Bug Variations.* **1991, Morrow $23.00 (0-688-09891-6).** A chronicle of the descent of a promising research scientist from a challenging post to a minor job. "The decade is not likely to bring another novel half as challenging or original."—PW (REV: LJ 6/15/91; NYTBR 8/25/91; PW 6/14/91. AWARDS: PW, 1991; Time, 1991)

8413 **Powers, Richard.** *Prisoner's Dilemma.* **1988, Morrow $19.95 (0-688-07350-6); Macmillan paper $9.95 (0-02-036055-X).** A terminally ill father with mysterious symptoms analyzes his relationship with his wife and four children. (REV: LJ 2/15/88; New Rep 4/25/88; PW 2/19/88)

8414 **Powers, Richard.** *Three Farmers on Their Way to a Dance.* **1985, Morrow $17.95 (0-688-04201-5); McGraw-Hill paper $4.95 (0-07-050608-6).** A pair of Americans search for clues to the identities of three German farmers depicted in an August Sander photograph. "An unusually expansive and thought-provoking novel."—BL (REV: BL 8/85; LJ 9/15/85)

8415 **Poyer, David.** *Gulf.* **1990, St. Martin's $19.95 (0-312-05096-8).** A depiction of a naval war in the Persian Gulf between Iran and the United States during the last days of the Reagan administration. "A sure-fire winner."—LJ (REV: LJ 8/90; NYTBR 9/23/90; PW 8/3/90)

8416 **Price, Reynolds.** *Foreseeable Future.* **1991, Atheneum $21.95 (0-689-12110-5).** A collection of three novellas by the author of *The Tongues of Angels,* including "Back Before Day," "Fare to the Moon," and the title story. (REV: BL 3/1/91; LJ 4/1/91; PW 3/15/91)

8417 **Price, Reynolds.** *Good Hearts.* **1989, Ballantine paper $4.95 (0-345-35707-8).** The sequel to the author's 1962 novel *A Long and Happy Life* detailing events in the protagonists' lives and marriage over nearly three decades. (REV: LJ 4/15/88; New Rep 7/4/88; NYTBR 5/8/88)

8418 **Price, Reynolds.** *Kate Vaiden.* **1987, Ballantine paper $4.95 (0-345-34358-1).** A North Carolina woman reflects on her life and the murder/suicide of her parents. (REV: BL 5/15/86; CSM 6/25/86; LJ 6/1/86. AWARDS: ALA, 1986; BL, the 1980s; LJ, 1986; PW, 1986)

8419 **Price, Reynolds.** *Love and Work.* **1987, Ballantine paper $3.50 (0-345-34995-4).** The study of a writer's efforts to come to terms with the death of his parents. (REV: PW 3/25/68; TLS 12/5/68)

8420 **Price, Reynolds.** *Source of Light.* **1988, Ballantine paper $4.95 (0-345-34993-8).** A portrait of the lives of a North Carolina father and son set during the mid-1950s. (REV: BL 2/15/81; LJ 3/1/81; NYTBR 4/26/81)

8421 **Price, Reynolds.** *Tongues of Angels.* **1990, Macmillan $18.95 (0-689-12093-1).** The reflections of an artist concerning a childhood friendship during summer camp over three decades before. (REV: BL 2/15/90; NYTBR 5/13/90; Time 5/14/90. AWARDS: BL, 1990)

8422 **Price, Richard.** *Bloodbrothers.* **1985, Penguin paper $6.95 (0-14-008345-6).** A New York teenager is forced to choose between staying with his family or taking a rewarding job following his graduation from high school. (REV: Atl 5/76; BL 2/1/76; LJ 2/15/76. AWARDS: ALA, 1976)

8423 **Price, Richard.** *The Breaks.* **1984, Penguin paper $6.95 (0-14-007037-0).** A character study of a recent college graduate in search of fulfillment. (REV: NYRB 3/31/83; NYTBR 2/13/83; Sat Rev 3/83)

8424 **Price, Richard.** *Ladies' Man.* **1985, Penguin paper $6.95 (0-14-008346-4).** A New York salesman looks for love in Manhattan after his girlfriend walks out on him. (REV: BL 9/1/78; LJ 8/78; Sat Rev 9/30/78)

8425 **Prince, Peter.** *Good Father.* **1985, Carroll & Graf $13.95 (0-88184-113-7).** The friendship of two men recently separated from their wives and sons spurs on one of the men to begin a custody battle to regain his child. (REV: NYTBR 4/7/85; PW 12/7/84; TLS 11/4/83)

8426 **Pringle, Terry.** *Preacher's Boy.* **1988, Algonquin $15.95 (0-912697-77-6); Ballantine paper $4.95 (0-345-36045-1).** The study of the relationships between a small-town Texas Baptist preacher, his son, and his son's aspiring rock-star girlfriend. (REV: BL 3/15/88; LJ 5/1/88; PW 2/5/88)

8427 **Prose, Francine.** *Bigfoot Dreams.* **1987, Penguin paper $6.95 (0-14-009837-2).** A writer for a sensationalist tabloid becomes dismayed when one of his fantastic stories comes true. (REV: BL 4/1/86; LJ 4/1/86; PW 2/28/86)

8428 **Puig, Manuel.** *Betrayed by Rita Hayworth.* **1987, Dutton paper $7.95 (0-525-48285-7).** The story of an Argentine family obsessed by old American motion pictures. (REV: BL 10/15/71; Newsweek 10/25/71; PW 7/19/71. AWARDS: ALA, 1971)

8429 **Puig, Manuel.** *Heartbreak Tango: A Serial.* **1987, Dutton paper $7.95 (0-525-48288-1).** A young man's romantic exploits are recounted by the women of a small Argentine town following his death. "No recommendation is too high for this novel."—LJ (REV: BL 12/15/73; LJ 10/15/73; NYTBR 10/15/73. AWARDS: ALA, 1973)

8430 **Puig, Manuel.** *Kiss of the Spider Woman.* **1985, Random paper $6.95 (0-394-74475-6).** A love relationship between two men in a Buenos Aires jail cell punctuated by one of the men's retelling of plots of old motion pictures. (REV: BL 4/1/79; LJ 5/15/79; PW 2/12/79. AWARDS: ALA, 1979)

8431 **Puig, Manuel.** *Tropical Night Falling.* **1991, Simon & Schuster $18.50 (0-671-67996-1).** This final work by the late Argentine novelist traces the lives of two Buenos Aires sisters following their relocation to Brazil. (REV: BL 9/1/91; PW 8/23/91)

8432 **Purdy, James.** *Mourners Below.* **1984, Dutour $26.00 (0-7206-0621-7).** In this novel by the author of *Malcolm*, the deaths of two elder brothers haunt the life of a surviving sibling. (REV: New Rep 7/18/81; NYTBR 7/26/81; PW 4/17/81)

8433 **Puzo, Mario.** *The Sicilian.* **1985, Bantam paper $5.95 (0-553-25282-8).** A portrayal of the Sicilian Mafia in the years following World War II. (REV: Natl Rev 4/5/85; NYTBR 12/9/84; Newsweek 11/26/84)

8434 **Pym, Barbara.** *An Academic Question.* **1987, NAL paper $7.95 (0-452-25996-7).** A posthumously published work regarding the choice of an English woman between her husband's career and her own fulfillment. (REV: NYTBR 9/7/86; Newsweek 11/10/86; PW 7/11/86)

8435 **Pym, Barbara.** *Excellent Women.* **1988, Dutton paper $7.95 (0-525-48377-2).** A single English woman in her 30s comes to discover her self-worth in her relations with others in this novel, originally published in Great Britain in 1952. (REV: BL 10/15/78; CSM 11/8/78; TLS 9/30/77)

8436 **Pym, Barbara.** *A Few Green Leaves.* **1989, Dutton paper $8.95 (0-525-48511-2).** A chronicle of the lives of an anthropologist and a clergyman in a small English village, by the author of *Excellent Women*. (REV: BL 9/15/80; NYTBR 2/1/81; TLS 7/18/80)

8437 **Pym, Barbara.** *A Glass of Blessings.* **1989, Dutton paper $8.95 (0-525-48512-0).** This novel, portraying the life of a married couple living at the home of the wife's mother, was originally published in England in 1958. (REV: BL 4/1/80; LJ 6/15/80; Newsweek 4/14/80. AWARDS: ALA, 1980)

8438 **Pym, Barbara.** *Jane and Prudence.* **1987, Harper & Row paper $6.95 (0-06-097101-0).** This novel, originally published in Great Britain in 1953, concerns the friendship of a young woman with her former literature tutor. (REV: BL 10/1/81; LJ 11/1/81; New Yorker 11/2/81)

8439 **Pym, Barbara.** *Less than Angels.* **1970, Dutton paper $8.95 (0-525-48571-6).** A posthumously published reprint of a 1950s novel that details the lives and observations of a pair of London-based anthropologists. (REV: BL 1/1/81; Newsweek 1/19/81; PW 12/5/80)

8440 **Pym, Barbara.** *Quartet in Autumn.* **1988, Dutton paper $7.95 (0-525-48379-9).** A portrait of four clerks in an office who are facing the ends of their working lives. (REV: LJ 10/15/78; Newsweek 10/28/78; TLS 9/30/77)

8441 **Pym, Barbara.** *Sweet Dove Died.* **1988, Dutton paper $7.95 (0-525-48380-2).** A woman in her 40s meets a widower but rejects his love in favor of his 24-year-old nephew. "A little masterpiece."—PW (REV: LJ 3/15/79; Newsweek 4/16/79; PW 3/12/79)

8442 **Pym, Barbara.** *An Unsuitable Attachment.* **1986, Harper & Row paper $7.95 (0-06-097055-3).** This novel, written in 1963 and originally rejected for publication, concerns an aging librarian engaged in a May-December romance. (REV: BL 4/15/82; NYTBR 6/20/82; PW 4/2/82)

8443 **Pynchon, Thomas.** *Crying of Lot 49.* **1986, Harper & Row paper $7.95 (0-06-091307-X).** Pynchon's second novel concerns a California housewife chosen to be the executor of the estate of a former lover. (REV: LJ 3/15/66; NYTBR 5/1/66; Newsweek 5/2/66. AWARDS: NYTBR, 1966)

8444 **Pynchon, Thomas.** *Vineland.* **1990, Little, Brown $19.95 (0-316-72444-0).** Pynchon's first novel since *Gravity's Rainbow* is an analysis of contemporary American culture and the legacy of its recent past, set in northern California in 1984. (REV: BL 1/15/90; LJ 2/1/90; Time 1/15/90. AWARDS: BL, 1990; LJ, 1990; Time, 1990)

8445 **Quindlen, Anna.** *Object Lessons.* **1991, Random $19.00 (0-394-56965-2).** This portrait of a preteen girl set during the 1960s in New York is the essayist's first novel. "Intelligent, highly entertaining and laced with acute perceptions about the nature of day-to-day family life."—NYTBR (REV: BL 1/15/91; NYTBR 4/14/91; PW 2/1/91)

8446 **Raban, Jonathan.** *Foreign Land.* **1985, Viking $16.95 (0-670-80767-2); Penguin paper $6.95 (0-14-008266-2).** A tale of the return to England of a man who lived most of his life in Africa only to find that his native land, friends, and family are far different than his memories of them. (REV: LJ 10/1/85; NYTBR 11/3/85; Time 11/11/85)

8447 **Raskin, Barbara.** *Current Affairs.* **1990, Random $19.95 (0-394-57994-1).** A journalist's discovery of a secret document sheds new light on the truth behind the Iran-Contra affair. (REV: BL 6/15/90; LJ 8/90)

8448 **Rathbone, Julian.** *Greenfinger.* **1987, Viking $16.95 (0-670-81588-8); Penguin paper $3.95 (0-14-009913-1).** American big business makes a cooperative effort to destroy a superior strain of corn developed in Costa Rica. "Will remind readers of vintage Graham Greene."—PW (REV: LJ 7/87; New Yorker 10/19/87; PW 5/22/87)

8449 **Read, Piers Paul.** *A Season in the West.* **1989, Random $16.95 (0-394-57530-X).** A writer, a Czech defector in London, becomes romantically involved with his translator in this novel by the author of *Alive!* (REV: BL 4/15/89; PW 3/10/89; TLS 9/9/88)

8450 **Rebeta-Burditt, Joyce.** *Cracker Factory.* **1986, Bantam paper $3.95 (0-553-26228-9).** The story of an alcoholic mother forced by mental illness to live in a Cleveland institution and of her efforts to recover from madness. (REV: BL 1/1/77; LJ 1/15/77; PW 1/3/77)

8451   Rechy, John. *Bodies and Souls*. 1983, Carroll & Graf $17.95 (0-88184-003-3); paper $8.95 (0-88184-004-1). This story chronicling the adventures of three teenage runaways in the streets of Los Angeles is written by the author of *City of Night*. (REV: LJ 7/83; NYTBR 7/10/83)

8452   Rechy, John. *Marilyn's Daughter*. 1988, Carroll & Graf $18.95 (0-88184-272-9). The story of the daughter of Marilyn Monroe and Robert Kennedy and her search to determine the identities of her parents. (REV: BL 7/88; Choice 10/88; NYTBR 11/6/88)

8453   Reed, Ishmael. *Reckless Eyeballing*. 1986, St. Martin's $12.95 (0-312-66580-6); Macmillan paper $7.95 (0-689-70728-6). A satirical story concerning an African-American playwright's efforts to get his play produced on Broadway. "Engaging, disturbing and really funny."—Choice (REV: BL 3/1/86; Choice 10/86; PW 1/24/86)

8454   Reed, Ishmael. *Terrible Threes*. 1989, Macmillan $16.95 (0-689-11893-7). This follow-up to the author's *Terrible Twos* is a satirical look at American politics in the near future. (REV: BL 3/1/89; NYTBR 5/7/89; PW 1/20/89)

8455   Reed, Ishmael. *Terrible Twos*. 1988, Macmillan paper $8.95 (0-689-70727-4). This satire regarding American politics and society is set in the near future under an administration headed by a male model. (REV: BL 5/1/82; NYTBR 7/18/82; PW 5/7/82)

8456   Reich, Tova. *Master of the Return*. 1988, Harcourt $19.95 (0-15-157880-X). A portrait of a group of Hasidic Jewish penitents and their lives in contemporary Jerusalem. (REV: BL 4/1/88; NYTBR 5/29/88; PW 2/26/88)

8457   Reidinger, Paul. *Best Man*. 1989, Alyson paper $7.95 (1-55583-149-4). A study of the complications arising from the breakup of a San Francisco *ménage à trois* between friends. (REV: BL 10/1/86; LJ 11/1/86)

8458   Reiss, Bob. *Divine Assassin*. 1987, Berkley paper $3.95 (0-425-09721-8). A former Middle East hostage seeking revenge for the death of a friend sets off to assassinate Libyan leader Moammar Quadafi. "A mind-jarring thriller."—BL (REV: BL 5/15/85; LJ 6/1/85)

8459   Reveley, Edith. *In Good Faith*. 1985, Overlook $15.95 (0-87951-992-4). An English couple living and working in Rome are entrusted with the temporary care and supervision of a friend's teenage daughter. (REV: BL 8/85; LJ 7/85; PW 5/17/85)

8460   Reynolds, Clay. *The Vigil*. 1988, Southern Methodist Univ. Pr. paper $8.95 (0-87074-269-8). A debut novel about a woman who remains in a small Texas town following the disappearance of her teenage daughter there. (REV: LJ 1/86; NYTBR 2/16/86)

8461   Rhys, Jean. *Quartet*. 1990, Carroll & Graf paper $7.95 (0-88184-538-8). A reprint of the English author's first novel originally published in 1928 concerning a young woman living in Paris who turns to a French couple following her husband's imprisonment. (REV: CSM 5/20/71; LJ 8/71; PW 2/15/71)

8462   Ribeiro, Joao Ubaldo. *Sergeant Getulio*. 1984, Avon paper $2.95 (0-380-67082-8). A Brazilian writer's first-person story of a brutal Latin American military man hired to capture a political rival. (REV: Atl 2/78; LJ 1/15/78; Newsweek 1/30/78)

8463   Ricci, Nino. *Book of Saints*. 1991, Knopf $19.00 (0-679-40118-0). A story set in 1960 Italy about a seven-year-old boy's discovery of some secrets of his parents. (REV: BL 4/15/91; LJ 5/1/91; PW 3/1/91)

8464   Rice, Luanne. *Secrets of Paris*. 1991, Viking $19.95 (0-670-82773-8). An American couple's marriage falters in Paris after the husband has an affair with his co-worker. (REV: LJ 4/15/91; PW 4/19/91)

8465   Richler, Mordecai. *Joshua Then and Now*. 1985, Bantam paper $4.95 (0-7704-2035-4). The memoirs of a Montreal man raised in a Jewish ghetto and his life as a journalist. (REV: LJ 5/15/80; Time 6/16/80; TLS 9/26/80. AWARDS: Time, 1980)

8466   Ritz, David. *Family Blood*. 1991, Donald I. Fine $19.95 (1-55611-176-2). A fictionalized account of criminal activities within the music industry during the 1940s. "A hurricane of a novel."—LJ (REV: BL 1/1/91; LJ 1/91; PW 1/11/91)

8467   Rivabella, Omar. *Requiem for a Woman's Soul*. 1987, Penguin paper $4.95 (0-14-009773-2). An Argentine writer's story of the abduction and torture of a young woman and of the Catholic priest who receives a copy of her journal. (REV: CSM 8/1/86; PW 3/21/86; TLS 2/27/87. AWARDS: ALA, 1986)

8468   Rivers, Caryl. *Girls Forever Brave and True*. 1987, Pocket paper $3.95 (0-671-62694-9). A pair of high school friends introduced in the author's *Virgins* reunite as adults in the politically charged climate of Washington, D.C., during the late 1960s. (REV: NYTBR 6/29/86; TLS 9/5/86)

8469   Robbins, Tom. *Another Roadside Attraction*. 1990, Bantam paper $8.95 (0-553-34948-1). A story by the author of *Still Life with Woodpecker* chronicling the journey of the body of Christ after the Second Coming. (REV: BL 9/15/71; Natl Rev 6/26/71)

8470   Robbins, Tom. *Even Cowgirls Get the Blues*. 1990, Bantam paper $8.95 (0-553-34949-X). The adventures of a young female hitchhiker who uses her oversized thumbs to great advantage. (REV: BL 5/15/76; LJ 6/15/76)

8471   Robbins, Tom. *Jitterbug Perfume*. 1985, Bantam $15.95 (0-553-05068-0); paper $8.95 (0-553-34898-1). This series of vignettes is set in New Orleans and revolves around the theme of death and eternal life, as written by the author of *Still Life with Woodpecker*. (REV: LJ 1/85; NYTBR 12/9/84; PW 10/12/84)

8472   Robbins, Tom. *Still Life with Woodpecker.* **1990, Bantam paper $8.95 (0-553-34897-3).** A story of the relationship between a young woman and an anarchist revolutionary bomber. "A novel which will cause the reader both to think and to smile a good deal."—TLS (Rev: BL 9/1/80; PW 7/25/80; TLS 10/31/80)

8473   Robertson, Don. *Ideal, Genuine Man.* **1988, Putnam $25.00 (0-399-19993-4); NAL paper $4.50 (0-451-15801-6).** An elderly couple in Pasadena, Texas, face the woman's death from cancer. Includes an introduction by Stephen King. (Rev: BL 5/1/88; PW 9/4/87)

8474   Robertson, Don. *Praise the Human Season.* **1983, Ballantine paper $3.95 (0-345-29528-5).** The journal of a cross-country drive taken by an ailing couple in their 70s. (Rev: BL 7/15/74; LJ 7/74; PW 5/20/74)

8475   Robertson, Mary E. *Family Life.* **1987, Macmillan $18.95 (0-689-11890-2); Penguin paper $8.95 (0-14-011285-5).** The breakup of a family over a summer due to infidelities by the father, an anthropologist. (Rev: LJ 8/87; New Yorker 10/12/87; PW 6/12/87)

8476   Robertson, Mary E. *What I Have to Tell You.* **1989, Doubleday $17.95 (0-385-26232-9).** A Virginia woman engages in a nationwide search for her missing truck-driver husband. (Rev: BL 9/15/89; LJ 9/15/89)

8477   Robinson, Marilynne. *Housekeeping.* **1981, Farrar $15.95 (0-374-17313-3); Bantam paper $7.95 (0-553-34663-6).** An eccentric aunt comes to the Washington home of two young girls to care for them following the deaths of their mother and grandmother. (Rev: BL 11/15/80; NYTBR 2/8/81; Time 2/2/81. Awards: NYTBR, 1981)

8478   Robison, Mary. *Oh!* **1987, Godine paper $8.95 (0-87923-675-2).** The chronicle of several weeks in the life of an eccentric Cleveland family. (Rev: LJ 6/1/81; New Rep 9/9/81; NYTBR 8/23/81)

8479   Robison, Mary. *Subtraction.* **1991, Knopf $19.95 (0-394-53943-5).** A poet searches for her runaway husband in Houston and the South in this novel by the author of *Oh!* (Rev: BL 1/15/91; PW 12/21/90)

8480   Rochlin, Doris. *In the Spanish Ballroom.* **1991, Doubleday $19.95 (0-385-26564-6).** A study of the personal relationships between members of a troubled American family. "A tight, well-constructed and balanced novel."—NYTBR (Rev: LJ 1/91; NYTBR 1/27/91; PW 11/2/90)

8481   Rockland, Michael Aaron. *A Bliss Case.* **1989, Coffee House paper $9.95 (0-918273-55-2).** This debut novel concerns an English professor who quits his job to move to India and join a religious commune. (Rev: LJ 9/1/89; NYTBR 10/15/89; PW 7/28/89)

8482   Rogan, Barbara. *Cafe Nevo.* **1987, Macmillan $19.95 (0-689-11840-6); NAL paper $7.95 (0-452-26141-4).** A study of the artistic and literary life within a Tel Aviv cafe. (Rev: BL 6/1/87; LJ 6/1/87; PW 5/1/87)

8483   Rogers, Thomas. *Confession of a Child of the Century, by Samuel Heather.* **1972, Ultramarine $20.00 (0-671-21266-4).** Memoirs of an Episcopal bishop's son who becomes a prisoner of war, a defector to China, and a political expert for the CIA. (Rev: BL 9/1/72; NYTBR 6/12/72; Time 6/10/72. Awards: ALA, 1972)

8484   Roiphe, Anne. *Lovingkindness.* **1987, Summit $18.95 (0-671-64079-8); Warner paper $4.95 (0-446-35274-8).** A New York feminist learns that her daughter has joined an Orthodox religious community in Jerusalem in this novel by the author of *Up the Sandbox.* (Rev: BL 8/87; PW 6/19/87; TLS 5/6/88)

8485   Roiphe, Anne. *Torch Song.* **1976, Farrar $8.95 (0-374-27848-2).** The study of a rebel writer as described by his girlfriend and, later, wife. (Rev: BL 2/15/77; LJ 12/1/76; TLS 3/25/77)

8486   Rose, Daniel Asa. *Flipping for It.* **1987, St. Martin's $14.95 (0-312-00124-X); paper $7.95 (0-312-02211-5).** A debut novel chronicling an American couple's divorce and child custody fight. (Rev: NYTBR 2/22/87; New Yorker 4/27/87; PW 2/6/87)

8487   Rossner, Judith. *August.* **1989, Warner paper $5.95 (0-446-35224-1).** A study of a self-destructive teenage girl's relationships with her psychoanalyst, her mother, and her mother's lesbian lover. (Rev: BL 6/15/83; NYTBR 7/24/83; Newsweek 8/1/83)

8488   Rossner, Judith. *His Little Women.* **1990, Summit $19.95 (0-671-64858-6).** A woman reestablishes ties and love with her estranged first husband four years after he walked out on her. (Rev: BL 1/15/90; NYTBR 4/22/90)

8489   Roszak, Theodore. *Flicker.* **1991, Summit $19.95 (0-671-72831-8).** A fictional story of the influence of motion pictures upon a man's life, actions, and psyche. "The perfect film buff's novel."—BL (Rev: BL 4/15/91; NYTBR 6/30/91)

8490   Roth, Joseph. *Hotel Savoy, Fallmerayer the Stationmaster, the Bust of the Emperor.* **1986, Overlook $16.95 (0-87951-211-3).** The first English translation of a novel and two short stories originally published in Germany during the 1920s and 1930s by a writer who committed suicide in Paris in 1939. (Rev: BL 12/15/86; New Yorker 11/23/87; TLS 1/16/87)

8491   Roth, Philip. *Anatomy Lesson.* **1983, Farrar $14.95 (0-374-10491-3); Fawcett paper $3.95 (0-449-20614-9).** This third volume in Roth's Zuckerman series finds the writer suffering from an undetermined illness. (Rev: LJ 11/1/83; New Yorker 11/7/83; Time 11/7/83. Awards: NYTBR, 1983; Time, 1983)

8492   Roth, Philip. *The Breast.* **1989, Farrar $19.95 (0-374-11651-2); Penguin paper $5.95 (0-14-007679-4).** A former literature professor is turned into a huge female breast in this novel by the author of *Goodbye, Columbus.* (Rev: BL 2/15/73; NYTBR 9/17/72; Time 9/25/72)

8493 Roth, Philip. *Counterlife.* **1987, Farrar $18.95 (0-374-13026-4); paper $7.95 (0-14-012421-7).** The fifth and concluding volume of the Zuckerman series tracing the writer's last years and death. (Rev: LJ 2/15/87; PW 11/20/87; Time 1/4/88. Awards: LJ, 1987; NYTBR, 1987; PW, 1987; Time, 1987)

8494 Roth, Philip. *Ghost Writer.* **1979, Farrar $8.95 (0-374-16189-5); Fawcett paper $4.95 (0-449-20209-4).** The first of the Zuckerman series, portraying the young writer on a visit to the home of an established Jewish literary figure. (Rev: BL 9/1/79; NYTBR 9/2/79; Time 9/3/79. Awards: ALA, 1979; NYTBR, 1979)

8495 Roth, Philip. *My Life as a Man.* **1985, Penguin paper $5.95 (0-14-007680-8).** Fictionalized accounts of a writer's life are juxtaposed with the events as they really happened. "A virtuoso performance."—BL (Rev: BL 7/1/74; Newsweek 6/3/74; PW 4/8/74)

8496 Roth, Philip. *Portnoy's Complaint.* **1969, Random $15.00 (0-394-44198-2); Fawcett paper $4.95 (0-449-20291-7).** A Jewish lawyer undergoing psychoanalysis reveals the history of his sexual life and fantasies. (Rev: LJ 2/15/69; Newsweek 2/24/69; Time 2/21/69. Awards: ALA, 1969)

8497 Roth, Philip. *Professor of Desire.* **1977, Farrar $8.95 (0-374-23756-5); Penguin paper $6.95 (0-14-007677-8).** A man torn between his physical and intellectual desires tells of his self-examination and of his worldwide sexual encounters. (Rev: LJ 9/15/77; New Yorker 10/31/77; Time 9/26/77. Awards: Time, 1977)

8498 Roth, Philip. *When She Was Good.* **1967, Random $10.95 (0-394-45187-2); Penguin paper $5.95 (0-14-007676-X).** A novel chronicling three generations of a Midwestern family and focusing on the personal life of a young woman and the collapse of her marriage. (Rev: NYTBR 6/11/67; TLS 12/21/67. Awards: NYTBR, 1967)

8499 Roth, Philip. *Zuckerman Bound: A Trilogy and Epilogue.* **1985, Farrar $22.50 (0-374-29943-9); paper $9.95 (0-374-51899-8).** A collection of Roth's Zuckerman series comprised of *The Ghost Writer*, *Zuckerman Unbound*, and *The Anatomy Lesson*, with a previously unpublished epilogue by the author. (Rev: BL 5/1/85; NYTBR 5/19/85; Newsweek 6/24/85. Awards: Time, the 1980s)

8500 Roziner, Felix. *A Certain Finkelmeyer.* **1991, Norton $19.95 (0-393-02962-X).** The fictional account of a Jewish poet's life as told by a Russian emigré writer who lives in the United States. "Roziner . . . should earn a wide audience with this powerful, poignant tale."—PW (Rev: BL 3/15/91; LJ 4/1/91; PW 3/1/91. Awards: BL, 1991)

8501 Rubens, Bernice. *Mr. Wakefield's Crusade.* **1985, Delacorte $15.95 (0-385-29417-4).** A chronicle of the events that led a self-described failure to take part in a murder investigation. (Rev: BL 10/15/85; LJ 11/1/85; PW 9/20/85)

8502 Rudnick, Paul. *I'll Take It.* **1989, Knopf $18.95 (0-394-57917-8); Ballantine paper $4.95 (0-345-36225-X).** A story of three aging sisters who are compulsive shoppers. "Great fun . . . an amusing, warmhearted book."—NYTBR (Rev: BL 5/1/89; NYTBR 6/11/89; PW 4/7/89)

8503 Rush, Norman. *Mating.* **1991, Knopf $23.00 (0-394-54472-2).** A female anthropologist tells the story of her relationship with a man who oversees a society of dispossessed African women in Botswana. (Rev: BL 7/91; NYTBR 9/22/91. Awards: BL, 1991; NBA, 1991; NYTBR, 1991; PW, 1991; Time, 1991)

8504 Rushdie, Salman. *Midnight's Children.* **1981, Knopf $22.50 (0-394-51470-X); paper $5.95 (0-380-58099-3).** The life story of an Indian child born on the day his nation gained independence from Britain. (Rev: New Rep 5/23/81; NYTBR 4/19/91; Newsweek 4/20/81. Awards: NYTBR, 1981)

8505 Rushdie, Salman. *Satanic Verses.* **1989, Viking $19.95 (0-670-82537-9).** The story of the fates of two men from India who survive an airplane bombing and are thrust into the world of modern London. (Rev: BL 11/1/88; NYTBR 1/29/89; Time 2/13/89. Awards: BL, 1989; NYTBR, 1989)

8506 Rushdie, Salman. *Shame.* **1983, Knopf $19.95 (0-394-53408-5); Random paper $9.95 (0-679-72204-1).** The second novel by the author of *Midnight's Children* chronicles the political and romantic exploits of a man in modern Pakistan. (Rev: BL 9/15/83; NYTBR 11/13/83; Time 11/14/83. Awards: ALA, 1983)

8507 Rushforth, Peter. *Kindergarten.* **1989, Godine paper $9.95 (0-87923-701-5).** Three English sons react to the death of their mother in a terrorist attack. (Rev: Choice 11/80; LJ 6/1/80; NYTBR 8/17/80)

8508 Russell, Paul. *Boys of Life.* **1991, Dutton $18.95 (0-525-93327-1).** The fictional memoirs of a jailed former film star recounting his experiences making a series of violent gay films as a young man. "It is, to date, the great American novel of gay male experience."—BL (Rev: BL 7/91; PW 5/31/91. Awards: BL, 1991)

8509 Russell, Paul. *Salt Point.* **1990, Dutton $18.95 (0-525-24832-3); paper $8.95 (0-452-26592-4).** This debut novel by the author of *The Boys of Life* depicts a love triangle between friends in Poughkeepsie, New York. (Rev: BL 2/15/90; NYTBR 5/6/90; PW 1/12/90)

8510 Russo, Richard. *Mohawk.* **1989, Random paper $8.95 (0-679-72577-6).** This debut novel portrays life in a small upstate New York town struggling through poor economic times during the mid-1960s. (Rev: BL 9/15/86; PW 8/8/86)

8511 Russo, Richard. *Risk Pool.* **1988, Random $19.95 (0-394-56527-4); paper $8.95 (0-679-72334-X).** A man returns to the small New York community of his youth and chronicles the changes in this second novel by the author of *Mohawk*. (Rev: LJ 11/15/88; New Yorker 2/6/89; PW 9/16/88. Awards: PW, 1988)

8512 Ryan, Charles. *Capricorn Quadrant.* **1990, NAL $18.95 (0-453-00737-6).** A sophisticated Russian bomber begins an attack on the United States following a computer mishap. (Rev: LJ 6/1/90; NYTBR 9/16/90)

8513 Sager, Carole Bayer. *Extravagant Gestures.* 1987, Ace paper $3.95 (0-441-22372-9). A songwriter's novel regarding the reconciliation between a mother and daughter during the mother's terminal illness. (Rev: BL 9/1/85; LJ 9/1/85; PW 7/26/85)

8514 Saint, H. F. *Memoirs of an Invisible Man.* 1988, Dell paper $4.95 (0-440-20122-5). An account of a stock trader's life as an invisible man following a chemical mishap. (Rev: BL 3/1/87; CSM 5/29/87; Time 4/27/87)

8515 Saiter, Susan Sullivan. *Cheerleaders Can't Afford to Be Nice.* 1990, Donald I. Fine $18.95 (1-55611-181-9). A daughter chronicles the workings of her dysfunctional Midwestern family in this debut novel. (Rev: BL 9/15/90; LJ 12/90; PW 10/26/90)

8516 Salzmann, Mark. *Laughing Sutra.* 1991, Random $18.95 (0-394-57009-X). This first novel by the author of *Iron and Silk* concerns a Buddhist's search for the key to immortality. (Rev: BL 12/1/90; NYTBR 1/27/91; PW 10/2/90)

8517 Sanchez, Thomas. *Mile Zero.* 1989, Knopf $19.95 (0-394-57859-7); Random paper $10.95 (0-679-73260-8). An alcoholic ex-radical becomes involved in a search for a killer in this novel set in Key West by the author of *Rabbit Boss.* (Rev: BL 10/1/89; NYTBR 10/1/89; PW 8/4/89. Awards: PW, 1989)

8518 Sanchez, Thomas. *Rabbit Boss.* 1989, Random paper $8.95 (0-679-72671-7). Four generations of a group of Washo Native Americans living near Lake Tahoe are depicted in this novel written by the author of *Mile Zero.* "A remarkable achievement."—TLS (Rev: LJ 5/1/73; PW 4/2/73; TLS 3/1/74)

8519 Sanders, Dori. *Clover.* 1990, Algonquin $13.95 (0-945575-26-2). A young African-American girl is forced to live with her white stepmother following the death of her father. (Rev: BL 3/1/90; LJ 3/1/90; PW 1/19/90)

8520 Sanders, Lawrence. *Timothy's Game.* 1988, Putnam $18.95 (0-399-13368-2); Berkley paper $5.50 (0-425-11641-7). A collection of three novellas featuring the adventures of a Wall Street financial investigator first introduced in the author's *Timothy Files.* (Rev: BL 5/15/88; NYTBR 7/31/88; PW 6/17/88)

8521 Sandlin, Tim. *Western Swing.* 1989, Ivy Books paper $3.95 (0-8041-0466-2). A story of the marriage between a Wyoming western novelist and his country-western singer wife. (Rev: BL 3/1/88; LJ 4/1/88; PW 2/26/88)

8522 Santiago, Danny. *Famous All Over Town.* 1984, NAL paper $8.95 (0-452-25974-6). A study of the life of a Mexican-American teenager in an East Los Angeles barrio. (Rev: LJ 3/15/83; NYTBR 4/24/83; PW 1/21/85)

8523 Sarraute, Nathalie. *You Don't Love Yourself.* 1990, Braziller paper $17.95 (0-8076-1254-5). A monologue on self-loathing in the form of a novel by the French writer and author of *Tropisms.* (Rev: LJ 11/15/90; NYTBR 11/18/90)

8524 Sarton, May. *Crucial Conversations.* 1980, Norton paper $3.95 (0-393-00986-6). A letter written by a 50-year-old American woman expresses her desire to leave a nearly three-decade-old marriage. (Rev: BL 7/1/75; LJ 6/15/75; PW 3/31/75)

8525 Sarton, May. *Education of Harriet Hatfield.* 1989, Norton $18.95 (0-393-02695-7); paper $5.95 (0-393-30665-8). A woman who opens a feminist bookstore in a Boston suburb finds herself the target of local gossip. (Rev: BL 5/15/89; LJ 6/1/89; TLS 3/9/90)

8526 Sarton, May. *A Reckoning.* 1978, Norton $11.95 (0-393-08828-6). The portrait of a terminally ill book editor suffering through the last months of her life. "Packed with insights, warmth, courage, compassion, and love."—CSM (Rev: Atl 12/78; CSM 2/12/79; LJ 9/1/78. Awards: ALA, 1978)

8527 Saul, John Ralston. *Paradise Eater.* 1989, McGraw-Hill $17.95 (0-07-054865-X); Fawcett paper $3.95 (0-449-21790-6). A story set in the Bangkok underworld about the efforts of a Canadian journalist to flee from unknown killers. (Rev: BL 10/15/83; LJ 11/1/88; PW 8/19/88)

8528 Savage, Georgia. *Home Tibet.* 1991, Graywolf $18.95 (1-55597-144-X). An Australian novelist's story of a teenage girl who seeks refuge in a boardinghouse following her rape by her father. "Vividly written and occasionally quite moving."—NYTBR (Rev: LJ 4/1/91; NYTBR 6/16/91; PW 2/22/91. Awards: LJ, 1991)

8529 Savic, Sally. *Elysian Fields.* 1988, Macmillan $14.95 (0-684-18854-6). An Ohio woman searches for her missing musician husband on the streets of New Orleans. (Rev: BL 6/15/88; LJ 8/88; PW 6/3/88)

8530 Sayers, Valerie. *Due East.* 1987, Doubleday paper $15.95 (0-385-23673-5). In this debut novel by a Southern writer, a motherless pregnant teenager whose boyfriend died of a drug overdose assumes responsibility for her baby. (Rev: LJ 2/15/87; NYTBR 3/8/87; PW 1/30/87)

8531 Sayers, Valerie. *How I Got Him Back: Or, Under the Cold Moon's Shine.* 1989, Doubleday $17.95 (0-385-24376-6). This second novel by the author of *Due East* concerns the efforts of two South Carolina women to win their husbands back from other women. (Rev: NYTBR 1/29/89; PW 11/11/88)

8532 Sayers, Valerie. *Who Do You Love?* 1991, Doubleday $18.95 (0-385-41085-9). A portrait of a South Carolina family awaiting a marriage on the eve of the assassination of John F. Kennedy. (Rev: BL 2/1/91; LJ 1/91; PW 1/4/91)

8533 Sayles, John. *Los Gusanos.* 1991, HarperCollins $22.95 (0-06-016653-3). A group of exiled Cuban Americans in Miami form an assault force to launch an attack to regain their homeland. "An exciting, instructive and highly readable novel."—LJ (Rev: BL 3/15/91; LJ 4/15/91; PW 4/12/91. Awards: BL, 1991)

8534 Sayles, John. *Union Dues.* 1985, Little, Brown paper $7.95 (0-316-72234-8). A group of West Virginia mine workers fight against union exploitation during the late 1960s. (Rev: BL 9/15/77; LJ 9/1/77; PW 5/2/77)

8535 **Schaeffer, Susan Fromberg.** *Anya.* **1976, Avon paper $4.95 (0-380-00573-5).** A portrayal of three decades in the life of a Polish-Jewish woman who survived the Holocaust and relocated to the United States following the end of the war. (Rev: BL 10/1/74; NYTBR 10/20/74; PW 7/29/74)

8536 **Schaeffer, Susan Fromberg.** *Injured Party.* **1987, St. Martin's paper $3.95 (0-312-90624-2).** A married woman suffering from an illness meets the terminally ill former fiancé she has not seen for over two decades. (Rev: BL 8/86; LJ 9/15/86; PW 8/1/86)

8537 **Schine, Cathleen.** *To the Birdhouse.* **1990, Farrar $16.95 (0-374-27828-8).** A daughter attempts to separate her mother from an odious boyfriend. (Rev: LJ 5/15/90; New Yorker 6/4/90; PW 2/23/90)

8538 **Schmidt, Heidi J.** *Rose Thieves.* **1990, Harcourt $18.95 (0-15-179013-2).** A series of connected stories trace the lives of a New England couple and their four children over three decades. "Delightful. . . a very fine book for a general audience."—LJ (Rev: BL 10/15/90; LJ 9/15/90; PW 7/27/90)

8539 **Schneider, Nina.** *The Woman Who Lived in a Prologue.* **1985, Avon paper $3.95 (0-380-59881-7).** A 73-year-old Jewish-American woman traces her own life and the lives of the four generations that followed her. (Rev: CSM 3/10/81; LJ 11/15/79; Newsweek 2/4/80)

8540 **Schneider, Peter.** *Wall Jumper.* **1985, Pantheon paper $8.95 (0-394-72882-3).** A German author's portrait of the lives of Berlin citizens living on both sides of the Wall. (Rev: BL 2/1/84; LJ 4/1/84; PW 11/16/83)

8541 **Schor, Sandra.** *Great Letter E.* **1990, North Point $18.95 (0-86547-397-8).** In this author's debut novel, a New York optometrist obsessed with the ideas of Spinoza fails to notice his personal world collapsing around him. (Rev: LJ 11/1/89; NYTBR 2/25/90; PW 12/8/89)

8542 **Schulman, Helen.** *Out of Time.* **1991, Atheneum $19.95 (0-689-12122-9).** A study of the effects of a son's death on the structure and dynamics of his family. (Rev: LJ 6/15/91; PW 5/24/91)

8543 **Schwartz, Lynne Sharon.** *Disturbances in the Field.* **1985, Bantam paper $8.95 (0-553-34377-7).** A mother attempts to readjust to life following an automobile accident that takes the lives of two of her children. (Rev: BL 7/83; LJ 8/83; PW 7/22/83)

8544 **Schwartz, Lynne Sharon.** *Leaving Brooklyn.* **1989, Houghton $15.95 (0-395-51091-0); Penguin paper $7.95 (0-14-013197-3).** A story of a Brooklyn girl's sexual awakening at the hands of her optometrist set during the 1950s. (Rev: LJ 4/15/89; NYTBR 4/30/89)

8545 **Schwartz, Lynne Sharon.** *Rough Strife.* **1985, Harper & Row paper $8.95 (0-06-091282-0).** A story

tracing two decades of the relationship of a middle-aged East Coast couple who met in Italy. (Rev: LJ 6/15/80; New Rep 6/14/80; Time 6/30/80)

8546 **Scliar, Moacyr.** *Strange Nation of Rafael Mendes.* **1988, Crown $19.95 (0-517-56776-8); Ballantine paper $4.95 (0-345-34861-3).** A Brazilian novelist's tale of a Jewish man blackmailed into losing his business. (Rev: BL 11/1/88; LJ 1/88; PW 11/6/87)

8547 **Scofield, Sandra.** *Beyond Deserving.* **1991, Permanent Pr. $21.95 (1-87794-607-9).** A portrait of the lives and relationships between the families of twin brothers living in Oregon. (Rev: NYTBR 10/13/91; PW 7/25/91)

8548 **Scott, Paul.** *Day of the Scorpion.* **1979, Avon paper $4.95 (0-380-40923-2).** This second volume of the author's Raj Quartet concerns Indian society in the last years of British rule. (Rev: LJ 10/15/68; PW 8/19/68; TLS 9/12/68)

8549 **Scott, Paul.** *Division of the Spoils.* **1979, Avon paper $4.50 (0-380-45054-2).** The fourth and concluding novel of The Raj Quartet takes place in India just prior to its partition. (Rev: LJ 9/15/75; NYTBR 10/12/75; TLS 5/23/75. Awards: ALA, 1975)

8550 **Scott, Paul.** *Jewel in the Crown.* **1979, Avon paper $4.50 (0-380-40410-9).** This examination of the relations between the English and Indians set in pre-partition times is the first volume of the author's Raj Quartet. "A rich and moving story."—BL (Rev: BL 7/15/66; LJ 10/1/66; New Yorker 7/2/66. Awards: ALA, 1966)

8551 **Scott, Paul.** *Staying On.* **1979, Avon paper $3.50 (0-380-46045-9).** The portrait of an elderly British couple living out their lives in a fading Indian hill station. (Rev: BL 9/1/77; NYTBR 8/21/77; Newsweek 8/8/77. Awards: ALA, 1977; NYTBR, 1977)

8552 **Scott, Paul.** *Towers of Silence.* **1979, Avon paper $4.50 (0-380-44198-5).** This third volume of the author's Raj Quartet details the arrest and trial of a group of Indians for the gang rape of a young English woman. (Rev: BL 6/15/72; Time 3/27/72; TLS 10/8/71)

8553 **See, Carolyn.** *Golden Days.* **1987, McGraw-Hill $15.95 (0-07-056120-6); Fawcett paper $3.95 (0-449-21437-0).** A portrait of the lives of several Los Angeles women before a nuclear holocaust destroys the city. (Rev: BL 10/1/86; NYTBR 11/30/86; PW 8/15/86. Awards: PW, 1986)

8554 **See, Carolyn.** *Making History.* **1991, Houghton $19.95 (0-395-59221-6).** Members of a Southern California family examine their lives following a traffic accident. Written by the author of *Golden Days.* (Rev: BL 9/1/91; NYTBR 9/15/91. Awards: PW, 1991)

8555 **See, Carolyn.** *Rhine Maidens.* **1989, Fawcett paper $3.95 (0-449-21709-4).** This story of the tenuous relationship between a California woman and her daughter is told in alternating voices. (Rev: LJ 10/15/81; Newsweek 10/15/81; PW 8/7/81)

8556 Selby, Hubert, Jr. *Requiem for a Dream.* **1988, Thunder's Mouth paper $9.95 (0-938410-56-3).** A portrait of four drug-addicted New Yorkers depicted by the author of *Last Exit to Brooklyn.* (REV: LJ 10/15/78; NYTBR 11/19/78; Newsweek 9/25/78)

8557 Sennett, Richard. *Frog Who Dared to Croak.* **1982, Farrar $11.95 (0-374-15884-3).** The chronicle of the life of a Hungarian Communist party member who spoke out against the system following the 1958 revolt. "A novel that demands—and rewards—close reading."—BL (REV: BL 6/1/82; LJ 6/1/82; PW 4/23/82)

8558 Serote, Mongane Wally. *To Every Birth Its Blood.* **1989, Thunder's Mouth $19.95 (0-938410-71-7); paper $10.95 (0-938410-70-9).** A South African poet tells the story of a journalist imprisoned for his investigation into government treatment of blacks in his nation. (REV: BL 3/15/89; LJ 4/1/89)

8559 Seth, Vikram. *Golden Gate.* **1987, Random paper $5.95 (0-394-75013-2).** This portrait in verse of the lives of a group of San Francisco yuppies during the 1980s was written by an Indian-born writer. (REV: New Rep 4/21/86; Newsweek 4/14/86; PW 2/21/86)

8560 Seton, Cynthia Propper. *A Private Life.* **1984, Norton paper $4.95 (0-393-30187-7).** A magazine editor's trip to France to interview his famous aunt leads him to revelations about his family. (REV: BL 12/15/81; LJ 4/1/82; PW 3/5/82)

8561 Settle, Mary Lee. *Charley Bland.* **1989, Farrar $17.95 (0-374-12078-1).** A West Virginia writer flees to Paris and has a destructive affair with a man she has adored from afar. (REV: BL 5/15/89; LJ 6/15/89; PW 6/23/89. AWARDS: PW, 1989)

8562 Settle, Mary Lee. *Killing Ground.* **1988, Macmillan paper $9.95 (0-684-18849-X).** The fifth and final volume of the Beulah Quintet, concerning a woman's return to her West Virginia hometown after an 18-year absence. (REV: LJ 7/82; New Rep 4/15/82; PW 4/30/82)

8563 Sexton, Linda. *Points of Light.* **1988, Little, Brown $16.95 (0-316-78200-9); Avon paper $4.50 (0-380-70684-9).** A study of the effects of the death of a baby girl on her mother and family. (REV: LJ 12/87; NYTBR 1/24/88; PW 11/6/87. AWARDS: ALA, 1988)

8564 Sexton, Linda. *Private Acts.* **1991, Little, Brown $19.95 (0-316-78203-3).** A fictional portrait of the public and private lives of New York bankers during the mid-1980s. (REV: BL 2/15/91; PW 1/25/91)

8565 Seymour, Gerald. *Field of Blood.* **1986, Ace paper $3.95 (0-441-23422-4).** The story of an IRA assassin turned informer and his relationship to a British army officer as he prepares to testify against fellow Irishmen. (REV: LJ 8/85; PW 7/5/85)

8566 Shabtai, Yaakov. *Past Continuous.* **1985, JPS Phila. $16.95 (0-8276-0239-1); Schocken paper $11.95 (0-8052-0868-2).** This account of nine months in the lives of three Tel Aviv men was originally

published in Israel in 1977. (REV: New Rep 5/27/85; NYRB 10/10/85; NYTBR 4/21/85)

8567 Shabtai, Yaakov. *Past Perfect.* **1987, Viking $18.95 (0-670-81308-7).** The late Israeli writer's sequel to *Past Continuous* continues to chronicle the life of a structural engineer in Tel Aviv. (REV: BL 8/87; Choice 3/88; PW 6/26/87)

8568 Shaginian, Marietta. *Mass-Mend: Yankees in Petrograd.* **1991, Ardis $35.00 (0-88233-971-0).** A novel written in Moscow during the 1920s and set in an imaginary New York portrays the lives of American workers. (REV: NYTBR 8/18/91; TLS 9/13/91)

8569 Shahan, Nathan. *Rosendorf Quartet.* **1991, Grove-Weidenfeld $18.95 (0-8021-1234-X).** A chronicle of the lives of four Jewish musicians in Germany and Israel. "There's never a wrong note in this unusually fine novel."—BL (REV: BL 8/91; LJ 8/91)

8570 Shainberg, Lawrence. *Memories of Amnesia.* **1988, British American $16.95 (0-945167-00-8); Ivy Books paper $3.95 (0-8041-0539-1).** A neurosurgeon attempts to diagnose and treat his own brain disorders. (REV: BL 9/15/88; New Yorker 1/23/89; PW 7/15/88)

8571 Shammas, Anton. *Arabesques.* **1988, Harper & Row $16.95 (0-06-015744-5); paper $8.95 (0-06-091583-8).** This Israeli Arab writer's novel traces the lives of the members of a Palestinian family. (REV: Choice 10/88; NYTBR 4/17/88; PW 3/18/88. AWARDS: NYTBR, 1988)

8572 Shange, Ntozake. *Betsey Brown.* **1985, St. Martin's $12.95 (0-312-07727-0); paper $8.95 (0-312-07728-9).** An examination of the effects of court-ordered school busing on an African-American family, set in St. Louis in 1959. "A memorable, quietly powerful book."—PW (REV: BL 3/1/85; NYTBR 5/12/85; PW 3/22/85)

8573 Sharp, Paula. *Woman Who Was Not All There.* **1988, Harper & Row $17.95 (0-06-015989-8); paper $8.95 (0-06-091602-8).** A chronicle of a decade in the lives of an English nurse and her four children. (REV: LJ 9/1/88; New Yorker 10/24/88; PW 7/1/88)

8574 Shaw, Irwin. *Bread Upon the Waters.* **1983, Dell paper $5.95 (0-440-10844-6).** A millionaire becomes involved with a middle-class New York family after their teenage daughter saves him from a mugging. (REV: NYTBR 8/23/81; PW 7/3/81)

8575 Shaw, Irwin. *Rich Man, Poor Man.* **1971, Dell paper $4.95 (0-440-17424-4).** This saga of a German-American family from World War II through the 1960s is set in New York, Texas, and Hollywood. (REV: NYTBR 10/4/70; New Yorker 3/13/71; PW 7/13/70)

8576 Sheed, Wilfrid. *Boys of Winter.* **1987, Knopf $17.95 (0-317-58854-0); McGraw-Hill paper $5.95 (0-07-056497-3).** A satire regarding a writer's colony in the Hamptons as narrated by a venomous publisher. (REV: BL 8/87; NYTBR 8/2/87; PW 6/19/87)

8577   Sheed, Wilfrid. *Max Jamison.* **1970, Farrar $6.50 (0-374-20476-4).** Sheed's novel consists of a monologue of a New York film and drama critic concerning his life and career. (REV: BL 6/15/70; Newsweek 5/4/70; Time 5/11/70. AWARDS: Time, 1970)

8578   Sheed, Wilfrid. *Office Politics.* **1989, I. R. Dee paper $9.95 (0-929587-09-X).** A fictional look behind the scenes at a literary magazine. (REV: BL 9/1/66; NYTBR 9/11/66; Sat Rev 9/17/66. AWARDS: NYTBR, 1966)

8579   Shields, Carol. *Swann.* **1989, Viking $17.95 (0-670-82822-X); Penguin paper $7.95 (0-14-013429-8).** The story of four scholars who meet at a symposium to study and discuss the works of a fictitious poet. (REV: Atl 8/89; BL 5/15/89; PW 5/12/89)

8580   Shields, David. *Dead Languages.* **1989, Knopf $18.95 (0-394-57388-9); Harper & Row paper $8.95 (0-06-097291-2).** A stuttering boy narrates the story of his life and his speech therapy during his college years. "An original, entertaining, and beautifully styled work of fiction."—BL (REV: BL 4/1/89; LJ 4/1/89; PW 3/10/89)

8581   Shreve, Anita. *Eden Close.* **1989, Harcourt $17.95 (0-15-127582-3).** Two childhood friends reunite in this debut novel 15 years after a brutal crime changed one of their lives forever. (REV: LJ 8/89; NYTBR 9/3/89; PW 7/7/89)

8582   Shreve, Anita. *Strange Fits of Passion.* **1991, Harcourt $19.95 (0-15-185760-1).** A journalist gives the daughter of an abused woman who murdered her husband the notes she used to write a book about the case. (REV: BL 2/15/91; New Yorker 6/10/91; PW 1/25/91)

8583   Shreve, Susan Richards. *Daughter of the New World.* **1992, Doubleday $20.00 (0-385-26976-7).** A fictional chronicle of the family life and reflections of a great-grandmother from the 1890s to 1989. (REV: BL 11/1/91; LJ 1/92; PW 11/29/91)

8584   Shriver, Lionel. *Bleeding Heart.* **1990, Farrar $19.95 (0-374-11432-3).** The story of the relationship between an American woman and an IRA terrorist in Belfast. (REV: BL 9/1/90; LJ 9/1/90; PW 7/20/90)

8585   Shulman, Alix Kates. *In Every Woman's Life.* **1987, Knopf $17.95 (0-394-55724-7); Ballantine paper $3.95 (0-345-35412-5).** An exploration of the personal secrets of members of an American family by the author of *Memoirs of an Ex-Prom Queen.* (REV: BL 6/15/87; NYTBR 5/31/87)

8586   Shulman, Alix Kates. *Memoirs of an Ex-Prom Queen.* **1985, Academy Chicago paper $8.95 (0-98733-173-7).** An aging former prom queen whose self-worth has always been based on her physical beauty searches for her identity. "Should appeal to virtually every woman."—PW (REV: BL 6/15/72; LJ 2/15/72; Newsweek 5/1/72)

8587   Shulman, Alix Kates. *On the Stroll.* **1987, Academy Chicago paper $8.95 (0-89733-243-1).** Portraits of the lives of a bag lady, a prostitute, and a teenage runaway who frequent a New York bus station. (REV: LJ 8/81; NYTBR 9/27/81; PW 7/31/81)

8588   Siddons, Anne Rivers. *Heartbreak Hotel.* **1984, Ballantine paper $4.95 (0-345-31953-2).** A portrait of the life of a young woman at an Alabama university during the early 1950s. (REV: LJ 10/1/76; NYTBR 9/12/76; PW 7/19/76)

8589   Siddons, Anne Rivers. *Homeplace.* **1987, Harper $17.95 (0-06-015758-5); Ballantine paper $4.95 (0-345-35457-5).** A Manhattan journalist returns to his Southern hometown and rekindles past family connections severed two decades before. (REV: BL 3/1/87; LJ 4/1/87; PW 5/1/87)

8590   Siddons, Anne Rivers. *Peachtree Road.* **1988, Harper & Row $18.95 (0-06-015799-2); Ballantine paper $5.95 (0-345-36272-1).** A chronicle of four decades in the life of an aristocratic Atlanta family. (REV: BL 7/88; PW 8/5/88)

8591   Sidhwa, Bapsi. *Cracking India.* **1991, Milkweed Editions $18.95 (0-915943-51-4).** A fictionalized account of the 1947 partition of India, as recorded by a polio victim. (REV: BL 9/15/91; NYTBR 10/6/91; PW 7/25/91)

8592   Simmons, Charles. *Wrinkles.* **1978, Farrar $8.95 (0-374-29333-3); Penguin paper $6.95 (0-14-011419-X).** A series of vignettes traces the life of a minor writer as death approaches. (REV: LJ 9/15/78; NYTBR 11/12/78; Time 10/30/78. AWARDS: NYTBR, 1978)

8593   Simpson, Mona. *Anywhere but Here.* **1986, Knopf $18.95 (0-394-55283-0); Random paper $9.95 (0-394-75559-6).** A Wisconsin woman and her daughter leave their home for a new beginning in California. "An achievement that lands her in the front ranks of our best younger novelists."—LJ (REV: LJ 3/15/87; Newsweek 2/2/87; TLS 6/26/87. AWARDS: ALA, 1987)

8594   Sinclair, Clive. *Cosmetic Effects.* **1990, Viking $18.95 (0-670-83341-X).** A film producer unwittingly becomes involved in a terrorist plot to blow up an airplane. (REV: BL 5/15/90; PW 3/30/90)

8595   Singer, Isaac Bashevis. *Enemies: A Love Story.* **1987, Farrar paper $8.95 (0-374-51522-0).** The chronicle of a Holocaust survivor's life with three wives in New York in the years following World War II. (REV: BL 10/1/72; LJ 6/1/72; Newsweek 6/26/72. AWARDS: ALA, 1972)

8596   Singer, Isaac Bashevis. *Penitent.* **1983, Farrar $13.95 (0-374-23064-1); Fawcett paper $3.95 (0-449-20612-2).** An American penitent fed up with materialistic gain travels to Israel in search of spiritual fulfillment. (REV: BL 8/83; PW 8/5/83; TLS 3/23/84)

8597   Singer, Isaac Bashevis. *Scum.* **1991, Farrar $19.95 (0-374-25511-3).** An Argentine Jew returns to his native Poland and becomes involved in the lifestyle of the underworld following the death of his son. (REV: BL 12/1/90; LJ 1/91; NYTBR 3/24/91)

8598   Skvorecky, Josef. *Bass Saxophone.* **1985, Pocket paper $5.95 (0-671-55681-9).** Two novellas connected by the theme of jazz, including an introductory essay on the importance of the music form in Czechoslovakia under German and Soviet occupation. (REV: BL 1/1/79; LJ 12/15/78; Newsweek 1/22/79)

8599 Skvorecky, Josef. *Engineer of Human Souls.* **1984, Knopf $17.95 (0-394-50500-X).** A Czech writer and teacher who fled to Canada following the Soviet invasion reflects on his past and current lives. "A marvelous exploration of the human condition."—BL (REV: BL 10/1/84; NYRB 9/27/84; PW 5/18/84)

8600 Skvorecky, Josef. *Miracle Game.* **1991, Knopf $22.95 (0-394-57220-3).** A Czechoslovakian man's quest to discover the mystery of a miraculous statue in a village church forms the basis for this novel set in the years prior to the 1968 Soviet invasion. (REV: BL 1/15/91; LJ 2/1/91; NYTBR 2/10/91)

8601 Slaughter, Carolyn. *The Banquet.* **1987, Penguin paper $4.95 (0-14-006662-4).** The story of an Englishman who becomes obsessed with a sales clerk at a large London department store. (REV: LJ 5/15/84; NYTBR 7/15/84)

8602 Slaughter, Carolyn. *A Perfect Woman.* **1987, Penguin paper $4.95 (0-14-006663-2).** The story of a family torn apart by a father's extramarital affair. "*A Perfect Woman* has a satisfying bite and the sweet tag of just desserts."—NYTBR (REV: BL 1/15/85; NYTBR 4/21/85; PW 12/21/84)

8603 Slavitt, David. *Salazar Blinks.* **1988, Macmillan $16.95 (0-689-12030-3); paper $7.95 (0-02-045211-X).** A story of the last days of the reign of Portuguese dictator Antonio Salazar as told by a journalist censored under his rule. (REV: BL 10/15/88; LJ 11/1/88; NYTBR 2/26/89)

8604 Small, David. *Alone.* **1991, Norton $19.95 (0-393-02991-3).** An alcoholic novelist traces his life's failures and tragedies and reassesses his philosophy of living. "An emotionally authentic, brooding and voracious work."—BL (REV: BL 5/15/91; LJ 6/1/91; PW 4/26/91)

8605 Smiley, Jane. *Ordinary Love and Good Will.* **1989, Knopf $17.95 (0-394-57772-8).** Two novellas examining child-parent relationships by the author of *The Greenlanders.* "Remarkable work. Smiley is a genuine, first-rate talent."—LJ (REV: BL 10/1/89; LJ 9/15/89; PW 9/1/89. AWARDS: PW, 1989)

8606 Smiley, Jane. *A Thousand Acres.* **1991, Knopf $23.00 (0-394-57773-6).** A story of three daughters who inherit their father's Iowa farm, by the author of *Ordinary Love and Good Will.* "Her best yet . . . a story of stunning insight and impact."—PW (REV: LJ 10/1/91; PW 8/23/91. AWARDS: PW, 1991; PP:Fiction, 1992)

8607 Smith, Charlie. *Crystal River.* **1991, Simon & Schuster $20.00 (0-671-70530-X).** A collection of three novellas set in the Florida Panhandle. (REV: BL 8/91; PW 6/14/91)

8608 Smith, Charlie. *Lives of the Dead.* **1990, Simon & Schuster $19.95 (0-671-70531-8); Pocket paper $9.00 (0-671-74713-4).** In this story by the author of *Shine Hawk,* a motion picture director becomes consumed by images of a movie-in-progress regarding the exploits of a serial killer. (REV: BL 7/90; NYTBR 9/23/90; PW 7/27/90)

8609 Smith, Charlie. *Shine Hawk.* **1988, British American $17.95 (0-945167-01-6); Pocket paper $7.95 (0-671-68498-1).** In this novel set in Georgia, three friends undertake a journey to bury a brother of one of the men. (REV: BL 9/15/88; LJ 10/1/88; PW 7/22/88)

8610 Smith, Lee. *Black Mountain Breakdown.* **1986, Ballantine paper $4.50 (0-345-33849-9).** A study of the blooming of an adolescent Virginia girl's sexuality following her father's death. (REV: BL 3/15/81; NYTBR 3/29/81; PW 12/12/80)

8611 Smith, Lee. *Fair and Tender Ladies.* **1988, Putnam $17.95 (0-399-13382-8); Ballantine paper $4.95 (0-345-36208-X).** A series of letters traces the life of an Appalachian woman from her youth to middle age. "Smith's best work yet."—LJ (REV: CSM 11/25/88; LJ 9/15/88; PW 7/8/88. AWARDS: ALA, 1988; PW, 1988)

8612 Smith, Lee. *Family Linen.* **1985, Putnam $15.95 (0-399-13080-2); Ballantine paper $4.95 (0-345-33642-9).** Details surrounding the death of the father of a Southern woman are revealed to her while under hypnosis. (REV: BL 12/1/85; LJ 8/85; PW 7/5/85)

8613 Smith, Lee. *Fancy Strut.* **1987, Ballantine paper $4.50 (0-345-34025-6).** An account of the celebration commemorating the 150th anniversary of the founding of a small Alabama town. (REV: LJ 11/15/73; NYTBR 10/7/73; PW 8/20/73)

8614 Smith, Lee. *Oral History.* **1984, Ballantine paper $4.95 (0-345-31607-X).** The story of a Southern college girl who returns to her Virginia hometown to compile an oral history of her family. (REV: BL 3/1/83; NYTBR 7/10/83; PW 5/13/83)

8615 Smith, Martin Cruz. *Nightwing.* **1982, Jove paper $3.95 (0-515-08502-2).** A Navajo deputy and a scientist join forces to stop a plague spread by vampire bats. (REV: BL 11/1/77; PW 7/25/77; Time 4/17/78)

8616 Smith, Martin Cruz. *Stallion Gate.* **1986, Random $17.95 (0-394-53006-3); Ballantine paper $4.95 (0-345-31079-9).** A Native American army sergeant tries to find evidence of spying on a top-secret atom bomb project. (REV: NYTBR 5/4/86; PW 3/14/86; Time 5/12/86)

8617 Smith, Mary-Ann Tirone. *Book of Phoebe.* **1986, Dell paper $5.95 (0-440-50742-1).** A coming-of-age story of a teenager who flees her New York home to bear a child in secret in Paris. "A very special literary debut."—BL (REV: Atl 8/85; BL 5/15/85; PW 4/26/85)

8618 Smith, Peter J. *Make-Believe Balloons.* **1989, Atlantic Monthly $18.95 (0-87113-318-0); paper $9.95 (0-87113-367-9).** A promising New York artist runs away with a young Texas woman in this author's second novel. "Wrenchingly funny."—NYTBR (Rev: BL 7/89; NYTBR 7/2/89)

8619 Smith, Rita Pratt. *In the Forest at Midnight.* **1989, Donald I. Fine $18.95 (1-55611-131-2).** This debut novel is about a British woman's sexual coming of age in India during the 1940s. (Rev: BL 5/15/89; LJ 4/1/89; PW 3/24/89)

8620 Smith, Rosamond. *Lives of the Twins.* **Avon paper $3.95 (0-380-70656-3).** A woman has an affair with her psychotherapist and his identical twin in this story written under Joyce Carol Oates's pseudonym. (Rev: NYTBR 2/12/89; PW 12/2/88)

8621 Smoodin, Roberta. *White Horse Cafe.* **1988, Penguin paper $6.95 (0-14-009838-0).** A story of two Mexican-American restaurant owners in California who become involved in a jewelry smuggling scheme. (Rev: BL 3/15/88; LJ 4/1/88)

8622 Solzhenitsyn, Aleksandr. *Cancer Ward.* **1984, Random $16.95 (0-394-60499-7).** A portrait of life in a six-bed Soviet ward for the treatment of cancer patients. (Rev: PW 10/7/68; Sat Rev 11/9/68; TLS 9/19/68)

8623 Solzhenitsyn, Aleksandr. *First Circle.* **1990, Borgo Pr. $29.95 (0-8095-9000-X); Harper & Row paper $14.95 (0-06-091683-4).** An inside look at the workings of a Soviet scientific research station composed of political prisoners in the late 1940s. (Rev: LJ 10/15/68; NYRB 12/9/68; PW 8/12/68)

8624 Somers, Jane. *Diary of a Good Neighbor.* **1983, Knopf $12.95 (0-394-52970-7).** An account of the life of an English magazine editor who befriends and cares for an elderly neighbor woman. (Rev: LJ 4/1/83; PW 3/4/83)

8625 Sommer, Scott. *Hazzard's Head.* **1985, Pocket $14.95 (0-671-55678-9); paper $5.95 (0-671-62894-1).** A New York writer with multiple personalities narrates the conflicts between the 13 persons housed within his body. "Shrewd, funny, daring and unexpectedly moving."—NYTBR (Rev: BL 9/15/85; NYTBR 10/27/85)

8626 Sorrentino, Gilbert. *Blue Pastoral.* **1983, North Point $18.00 (0-86547-095-2).** The chronicle of a family's travels around America in search of the perfect musical phrase. (Rev: LJ 4/1/83; NYTBR 6/19/83; PW 4/1/83)

8627 Sorrentino, Gilbert. *Odd Number.* **1985, North Point $16.50 (0-86547-212-2).** A questioner's examination of a witness reveals the inner workings of the criminal underworld in this experimental novel. (Rev: BL 10/15/85; LJ 10/1/85)

8628 Sorrentino, Gilbert. *Under the Shadow.* **1991, Dalkey Arch. $19.95 (0-916583-84-8).** A collection of 59 intertwined vignettes by the author of *Mulligan Stew.* "Arguably his best book to date . . . an intellectual page-turner."—PW (Rev: BL 11/15/91; PW 9/6/91)

8629 Southerland, Ellease. *Let the Lion Eat Straw.* **1980, NAL paper $3.50 (0-451-14675-1).** A six-year-old African-American girl is transplanted from her North Carolina foster home to live with her birth mother in Brooklyn. (Rev: BL 5/15/79; LJ 4/1/79; NYTBR 6/3/79)

8630 Spanidou, Irini. *God's Snake.* **1986, Norton $15.95 (0-393-02320-6); Penguin paper $6.95 (0-14-010360-0).** A first novel concerning the fantasy life of the daughter of a military man, set during the Greek civil war. "A remarkable debut."—Newsweek (Rev: LJ 8/86; Newsweek 11/10/86; PW 7/11/86)

8631 Spark, Muriel. *Abbess of Crewe.* **1984, Putnam paper $6.95 (0-399-50952-6).** The story of a scandal at an English convent and the efforts of nuns to bug and wiretap the building in order to document the misdoings of one of the sisters. (Rev: BL 10/15/74; Choice 3/75; Newsweek 11/11/74)

8632 Spark, Muriel. *Driver's Seat.* **1984, Putnam paper $6.95 (0-399-50928-3).** A woman in her 30s in search of love and adventure meets a young man wanted in a brutal stabbing case. (Rev: Choice 9/71; Newsweek 11/30/70; Time 10/26/70)

8633 Spark, Muriel. *A Far Cry from Kensington.* **1988, Houghton $17.95 (0-395-47694-1); Avon paper $7.95 (0-380-70786-1).** A London widow and editor reflects on the English literary life of the 1950s. (Rev: Atl 8/88; LJ 7/88; Time 7/4/88. Awards: ALA, 1988)

8634 Spark, Muriel. *Loitering with Intent.* **1990, Avon paper $7.95 (0-380-70935-X).** Memoirs of an English author writing a novel based on several characters currently writing their memoirs. (Rev: LJ 5/15/81; New Yorker 6/8/81; Time 7/6/81)

8635 Spark, Muriel. *Only Problem.* **1984, Putnam $14.95 (0-399-12987-1); paper $7.95 (0-399-51126-1).** A story of the life of a Canadian man who deserts his wife to devote his time to the study of the Book of Job on a French estate. (Rev: BL 3/15/84; New Yorker 7/23/84; TLS 9/7/84)

8636 Spark, Muriel. *Symposium.* **1990, Houghton $18.95 (0-395-51101-1).** The lives and secrets of ten upper-class Britons are revealed during the course of a dinner party. (Rev: BL 10/15/90; PW 10/26/90; TLS 9/21/90. Awards: Time, 1990)

8637 Spark, Muriel. *Territorial Rights.* **1984, Putnam paper $6.95 (0-399-50930-5).** A young English male ex-prostitute travels to Venice to be near a Bulgarian woman he has become obsessed with. "Beautifully put together and effortlessly entertaining."—NYTBR (Rev: BL 5/1/79; LJ 4/15/79; NYTBR 5/20/79)

8638 Spencer, Elizabeth. *Salt Line.* **1985, Penguin paper $6.95 (0-14-007665-4).** This portrait of the Mississippi coastline following the destruction of Hurricane Camille is set during the early 1970s. (Rev: LJ 1/84; NYTBR 1/29/84; PW 11/18/83)

8639 Spencer, Scott. *Waking the Dead.* **1986, Knopf $17.95 (0-394-54356-4).** A lawyer-politician's girlfriend is killed in a terrorist bombing in Minnesota. (Rev: BL 3/15/86; NYTBR 5/18/86; PW 4/11/86)

8640 Steel, Danielle. *Family Album.* 1985, Delacorte $19.95 (0-385-29392-5); Dell paper $5.95. A movie star and an army officer who met during World War II are the subject of this story, which traces their lives through the 1960s. "Engrossing reading."—LJ (REV: BL 1/1/85; CSM 3/21/85; LJ 3/1/85)

8641 Steel, Danielle. *Secrets.* 1985, Delacorte $19.95 (0-385-29418-2); Dell paper $5.95 (0-440-17648-4). A chronicle of the romantic and sexual adventures of six members of a television soap opera cast. (REV: BL 9/15/85; LJ 10/15/85)

8642 Steel, Danielle. *Star.* 1989, Delacorte $19.95 (0-440-50072-9); Dell paper $5.95 (0-440-20557-3). A portrait of the life and intrigue surrounding a San Francisco family in the years following World War II. "The vintage Steel fans thirst for."—NYTBR (REV: BL 12/15/88; PW 12/23/88; NYTBR 3/26/89)

8643 Stegner, Wallace. *All the Little Live Things.* 1979, Univ. of Nebraska Pr. $25.95 (0-8032-4110-0); paper $7.95 (0-8032-9109-4). A New York editor retires to California following the suicide of his son. (REV: BL 9/1/67; Choice 3/68; LJ 10/1/67. AWARDS: ALA, 1967)

8644 Stegner, Wallace. *Angle of Repose.* 1985, Fawcett paper $4.95 (0-449-20988-1). An ailing writer analyzes his marriage and that of his grandparents after his wife leaves him. (REV: BL 6/1/71; LJ 4/1/71; PW 2/15/71. AWARDS: PP:Fiction, 1972)

8645 Stegner, Wallace. *Crossing to Safety.* 1987, Random $18.95 (0-394-56200-3); Penguin paper $8.95 (0-14-011249-9). A story tracing the lives of two Vermont couples from the 1930s through the 1970s. "A wonderfully rich, warm, and affecting book."—LJ (REV: BL 9/1/87; LJ 10/1/87; PW 7/31/87. AWARDS: ALA, 1987; PW, 1987)

8646 Stegner, Wallace. *Recapitulation.* 1986, Univ. of Nebraska Pr. paper $7.95 (0-8032-9165-5). A visit to the narrator's childhood home in Utah brings back memories of his youth. (REV: BL 3/15/79; CSM 2/12/79; NYTBR 2/24/79)

8647 Stegner, Wallace. *Spectator Bird.* 1979, Univ. of Nebraska Pr. paper $5.95 (0-8032-9107-8). An elderly man reflects on his visit to his ancestral home in Denmark made two decades in the past. (REV: Atl 6/76; BL 4/15/76; Time 7/12/76. AWARDS: NBA, 1977)

8648 Steinke, Darcy. *Up Through the Water.* 1989, Doubleday $16.95 (0-385-24687-0). A North Carolina woman in love with two men receives a summer-long visit from her teenage son at her island home. (REV: BL 5/15/89; NYTBR 7/2/89)

8649 Stephens, Jack. *Triangulation.* 1989, Crown $18.95 (0-517-57539-6). A novel portraying the lives of a group of Baltimore citizens whose paths are destined to be intertwined. (REV: LJ 11/15/89; PW 10/6/89)

8650 Stern, Richard. *A Father's Words.* 1990, Univ. of Chicago Pr. paper $9.95 (0-226-77322-1). A middle-class father is disappointed with his eldest son's life and unsure about his own future. (REV: BL 4/1/86; New Yorker 8/18/86; Newsweek 3/24/86)

8651 Stewart, Jean. *Body's Memory.* 1989, St. Martin's $16.95 (0-312-02875-X). A portrayal of a 30-year-old woman's struggle against cancer and her readjustment to her inability to walk following the removal of a tumor. (REV: LJ 6/1/89; PW 4/28/89)

8652 Stewart, Michael. *Blindsight.* 1990, St. Martin's paper $3.95 (0-312-92264-7). A father facing blindness counts on the cooperation of his psychopathic son to obtain an operation that could restore his sight. (REV: LJ 2/15/88; PW 2/5/88)

8653 Stone, Robert. *Children of Light.* 1986, Knopf $17.95 (0-394-52573-6). Tales of drugs and debauchery in Hollywood from the pen of the author of *A Hall of Mirrors.* (REV: NYTBR 3/16/86; PW 1/24/86; Time 3/10/86. AWARDS: ALA, 1986; PW, 1986)

8654 Stone, Robert. *Dog Soldiers.* 1987, Penguin paper $8.95 (0-14-009835-6). An American correspondent in Vietnam becomes involved in smuggling drugs between Southeast Asia and California. (REV: LJ 12/15/74; NYTBR 11/3/74; Time 11/11/74. AWARDS: ALA, 1974; NBA, 1975; NYTBR, 1974; Time, 1974)

8655 Stone, Robert. *A Flag for Sunrise.* 1981, Knopf $15.95 (0-394-40757-1). An anthropologist is enlisted by the CIA to investigate the political actions of a religious organization in a Central American country. (REV: NYTBR 10/18/81; Newsweek 10/26/81; Time 10/26/81. AWARDS: NYTBR, 1981; Time, 1981)

8656 Stone, Robert. *A Hall of Mirrors.* 1987, Penguin paper $7.95 (0-14-009834-8). An account of a group of unsavory characters in New Orleans during the 1960s and their involvement in a political rally that turned violent. (REV: LJ 8/67; NYTBR 9/24/67; Sat Rev 8/19/67. AWARDS: NYTBR, 1967)

8657 Straight, Susan. *Aquaboogie: A Novel in Stories.* 1990, Milkweed paper $9.95 (0-91594-359-X). This novel, which won the Milkweed National Fiction Prize, portrays several months in the lives of residents of a Los Angeles-area ghetto. (REV: NYTBR 11/8/90; PW 1/4/91. AWARDS: PW, 1990)

8658 Straub, Peter. *Koko.* 1988, Dutton $19.95 (0-525-24660-6); NAL paper $5.95 (0-451-16214-5). A group of Vietnam veterans searches for a Southeast Asian killer the veterans believe was a member of their platoon. "His most gripping, most hallucinogenic thriller to date."—PW (REV: NYTBR 10/9/88; PW 8/12/88)

8659 Streiber, Whitley. *Billy.* 1990, Putnam $19.95 (0-399-13584-7). The abduction of an adolescent boy by a 44-year-old man leads to a cross-country chase by the boy's family and law enforcement agents. (REV: BL 6/1/90; NYTBR 8/19/90. AWARDS: BL, 1990)

8660 Stuart, Alexander. *War Zone.* 1989, Doubleday $16.95 (0-385-24953-5); Bantam paper $8.95 (0-553-34878-7). This debut novel portrays the shattering effects of father-daughter incest on an English family. (Rev: BL 3/15/89; NYTBR 6/4/89; PW 1/27/89)

8661 Styron, William. *Sophie's Choice.* 1979, Random $29.95 (0-394-46109-6); Bantam paper $4.95 (0-553-25960-1). A Southern writer, who lives in the same New York apartment complex as a Holocaust survivor, seeks to write a book about her experiences and discovers the horrible secret she has kept hidden for years. (Rev: BL 5/1/79; LJ 6/1/79; Time 6/11/79. Awards: NBA, 1980)

8662 Sukenick, Ronald. *Out.* 1973, Ohio Univ. Pr. $12.95 (0-8040-0630-X). The chronicle of a narrator's journey from the Lower East Side to California. "Sukenick is not only an uncommonly talented writer, but a sensitive and powerful one."—NYTBR (Rev: BL 9/15/73; LJ 5/15/73; NYTBR 10/21/73)

8663 Suskind, Patrick. *Pigeon.* 1988, Knopf $14.95 (0-394-56315-8); Pocket paper $5.95 (0-671-66770-X). A war orphan bank guard creates an antiseptic lifestyle to shelter himself from the world, which is shattered one day by the appearance of a pigeon in his apartment. (Rev: Atl 7/88; BL 6/1/88; NYTBR 6/26/88)

8664 Swift, Edward. *Christopher Park Regulars.* 1989, British American $17.95 (0-945167-16-4). Portraits of 12 eccentrics who frequent a small Manhattan park. "A rare and startling treasure."—NYTBR (Rev: BL 6/15/89; NYTBR 8/20/89; PW 4/21/89)

8665 Swift, Graham. *Out of This World.* 1988, Poseidon Pr. $16.95 (0-671-65827-1); Pocket paper $7.95 (0-671-65828-X). The story of the bitter relationship between a photographer and his daughter, told in alternating chapters and voices. (Rev: BL 9/15/88; NYTBR 9/11/88; TLS 3/11/88)

8666 Swift, Graham. *Sweet-Shop Owner.* 1985, Pocket paper $7.95 (0-671-54611-2). This first novel by the English author of *Shuttlecock* portrays the last day in the life of a man yearning to see his daughter one last time. (Rev: BL 5/15/85; LJ 5/15/85; PW 4/26/85)

8667 Tallent, Elizabeth. *Museum Pieces.* 1985, Knopf $14.95 (0-394-53928-1); Holt paper $7.95 (0-03-008003-7). This author's first novel is set in Santa Fe and concerns the life and interrelations between an archaeologist, his daughter, and his estranged wife. (Rev: BL 3/1/85; LJ 5/1/85; PW 2/1/85)

8668 Tan, Amy. *Joy Luck Club.* 1989, Putnam $18.95 (0-399-13420-4); Ivy Books paper $5.95 (0-8041-0630-4). The story of a group of Chinese-American women who meet to play mah-jongg and tell stories of their past and present lives. "A wonderful book!"—LJ (Rev: BL 3/1/89; LJ 2/15/89; PW 12/23/88. Awards: ALA, 1989; BL, 1989; LJ, 1989; PW, 1989)

8669 Tan, Amy. *Kitchen God's Wife.* 1991, Putnam $21.95 (0-399-13578-2). A Chinese-American mother tells her daughter details of her life in China. (Rev: BL 4/15/91; LJ 6/1/91; Time 6/3/91. Awards: ALA, 1992; BL, 1991; PW, 1991)

8670 Tanizaki, Junichiro. *Naomi.* 1985, Knopf $15.95 (0-394-53663-0). A novel originally written in Japanese during the 1920s concerning the doomed love between a 28-year-old man and a teenager. (Rev: BL 10/1/85; LJ 10/1/85; TLS 4/4/86)

8671 Tannen, Mary. *Second Sight.* 1987, Knopf $16.95 (0-394-56204-8); Ivy Books paper $3.95 (0-8041-0389-5). This debut novel traces the lives of a dozen characters in an industrial New Jersey city. (Rev: BL 1/15/88; New Yorker 4/25/87; PW 11/20/87)

8672 Taylor, Elizabeth. *Wedding Group.* 1985, Penguin paper $6.95 (0-14-016114-7). A study of the relations between a British newlywed couple and an overly assertive mother-in-law. "Sheer delight."—LJ (Rev: BL 4/15/68; LJ 2/1/68; PW 1/29/68)

8673 Taylor, Peter. *A Summons to Memphis.* 1986, Knopf $15.95 (0-394-41062-9); Ballantine paper $4.95 (0-345-34660-2). A tale of a New Yorker's return to his native Tennessee to help solve a family crisis. "A rich, subtly nuanced novella by a master of the craft."—PW (Rev: NYRB 9/25/86; PW 8/1/86; Time 9/29/86. Awards: ALA, 1986; PW, 1986; PP:Fiction, 1986; Time, 1986)

8674 Texier, Catherine. *Panic Blood.* 1990, Viking $18.95 (0-670-83231-6). A woman attempts to save her daughter from the custody claims of the father, a former lover who never helped raise his child. (Rev: NYTBR 4/15/90; PW 2/2/90)

8675 Tharu, Susie, and K. Lalita, eds. *Women Writing in India, 600 B.C. to the Present: Vol. 1, 600 B.C. to the Early Twentieth Century.* 1991, Feminist Pr. $49.95 (1-55861-026-X); paper $24.95 (1-55861-027-8). The first volume of a projected two-volume anthology of writings by Indian women. (Rev: BL 1/1/91; LJ 5/15/91)

8676 Theroux, Alexander. *An Adultery.* 1988, Macmillan paper $8.95 (0-02-008821-3). This story of an affair between a terminally ill, married art gallery worker on the verge of divorce and a painter is set in New England. By the author of *Darconville's Cat.* (Rev: BL 10/15/87; LJ 10/15/87; Natl Rev 2/19/88)

8677 Theroux, Paul. *Chicago Loop.* 1991, Random $19.00 (0-679-40188-1). The story of a Chicago businessman living a double life and whose sexual obsessions lead to murder. (Rev: LJ 4/1/91; NYTBR 3/17/91; Time 3/25/91)

8678 Theroux, Paul. *Family Arsenal.* 1976, Houghton $8.95 (0-395-24400-5). A disenchanted former Vietnam consul becomes involved in a London family's terrorist activities. (Rev: LJ 9/1/76; NYTBR 7/11/76; Time 8/2/76. Awards: Time, 1976)

8679 Theroux, Paul. *Half Moon Street.* 1986, Pocket paper $5.95 (0-671-60289-6). Two novellas—one that deals with an American woman drawn to prostitution in London, the other with a twin who has identity problems following his brother's death. (Rev: BL 9/1/84; Newsweek 10/22/84; PW 8/24/84)

8680 Theroux, Paul. *Mosquito Coast.* 1983, Avon paper $4.95 (0-380-61945-8). The adventures of a

Massachusetts family that leaves American life and culture behind to start anew in the jungles of Honduras. (REV: New Rep 2/24/82; NYRB 4/15/82; Sat Rev 2/82)

8681 **Theroux, Paul.** *My Secret History.* **1989, Putnam $21.95 (0-399-13424-7); Ivy Books paper $5.95 (0-8041-0514-6).** The chronicle of a Boston-born writer's travels in Europe, Asia, and Africa. "The most consistently entertaining of the author's more than two dozen books."—Time (REV: PW 5/22/89; Time 5/22/89; TLS 7/7/89)

8682 **Theroux, Paul.** *Picture Palace.* **1978, Houghton $9.95 (0-395-26475-8); Pocket paper $4.95 (0-671-63844-0).** A 70-year-old Massachusetts photographer prepares for a retrospective of her work and reexamines the events of her life and career. (REV: BL 5/1/78; CSM 6/28/76; PW 5/1/78. AWARDS: ALA, 1978)

8683 **Thomas, D. M.** *Lying Together.* **1990, Viking $17.95 (0-670-83218-9).** This fourth novel of the author's Russian Quartet finds a group of characters from the first three novels arguing about the authorship and credit of those volumes. (REV: BL 5/15/90; PW 8/16/90)

8684 **Thomas, D. M.** *White Hotel.* **1981, Pocket paper $4.95 (0-671-66148-5).** A fictional patient of Sigmund Freud undergoes psychoanalysis to determine causes of mysterious body pains. (REV: LJ 2/1/81; NYTBR 3/15/81; Time 3/16/81. AWARDS: NYTBR, 1981; Time, 1981)

8685 **Thomas, Maria.** *Antonia Saw the Oryx First.* **1987, Soho Pr. $17.95 (0-939149-02-8); paper $8.95 (0-939149-20-6).** A white woman working in a Tanzanian hospital befriends local blacks after her lover leaves her to return to his African wife. (REV: LJ 5/15/87; NYTBR 6/7/87; PW 6/7/87)

8686 **Thomas, Rosie.** *Bad Girls, Good Women.* **1990, Bantam paper $5.95 (0-533-28394-4).** Two teenage girls leave their suburban homes to live in London during the mid-1950s. (REV: LJ 4/1/89; NYTBR 5/7/89; PW 2/24/89)

8687 **Thomas, Rosie.** *Strangers.* **1988, Pocket paper $4.50 (0-671-66704-1).** A London housewife has an affair with a man after they survive a terrorist bombing together. "A spellbinding contemporary novel."—LJ (REV: LJ 7/87; NYTBR 7/12/87; PW 5/1/87)

8688 **Thomas, Rosie.** *A Woman of Our Times.* **1990, Bantam $19.95 (0-553-05795-2).** A woman gives up her failing marriage to achieve her own financial success. (REV: BL 8/90; LJ 9/15/90; PW 8/17/90)

8689 **Thomas, Ross.** *Out on the Rim.* **1987, Mysterious $17.95 (0-89296-212-7); paper $4.95 (0-445-40693-3).** A group of Americans sent to the Philippines to bribe a guerrilla leader to retire makes plans to abscond with the bribe money. (REV: New Yorker 12/7/87; Newsweek 10/19/87; Time 9/28/87)

8690 **Thomsen, Rupert.** *Dreams of Leaving.* **1988, Macmillan $19.95 (0-689-11957-7).** A debut novel regarding the efforts of a London man raised in foster homes to locate his true parents. (REV: BL 3/1/88; LJ 4/15/88; PW 2/26/88)

8691 **Thon, Melanie Rae.** *Meteors in August.* **1990, Random $18.95 (0-394-57664-0).** This debut novel traces a young woman's coming of age in a small Montana community. "A pleasure to read."—LJ (REV: BL 9/1/90; LJ 8/90; PW 7/6/90)

8692 **Thornton, Lawrence.** *Imagining Argentina.* **1987, Doubleday $16.95 (0-385-24027-9); Bantam paper $8.95 (0-553-34579-6).** A portrait of life in Argentina during the repressive military regime of the late 1970s and early 1980s as told through the eyes of a man who has the ability to envision the fates of those taken political prisoners. (REV: LJ 10/1/87; NYTBR 9/20/87; PW 7/31/87. AWARDS: ALA, 1987; PW, 1987)

8693 **Thurm, Marian.** *Walking Distance.* **1988, Penguin paper $6.95 (0-14-101756-8).** This debut novel chronicles the relationship between a young New York mother and a man dying of cancer. (REV: LJ 4/1/87; New Yorker 6/1/87; PW 2/27/87)

8694 **Toibin, Colm.** *The South.* **1991, Viking $18.95 (0-670-83870-5).** A debut novel by an Irish writer regarding a woman's life with a Spanish anarchist in Spain and Ireland. "An exceedingly well-crafted novel . . . a rich and remarkable debut."—PW (REV: LJ 7/91; NYTBR 9/15/91; PW 7/5/91)

8695 **Toland, John.** *Occupation.* **1987, Doubleday $19.95 (0-385-19819-1); Tor paper $4.95 (0-8125-8902-5).** This sequel to *Gods of War* by a Pulitzer Prize–winning historian traces the fates of two families in Japan under American occupation following World War II. (REV: BL 10/15/87; PW 9/11/87)

8696 **Tolkin, Michael.** *The Player.* **1988, Atlantic Monthly $17.95 (0-87113-228-1); Random paper $7.95 (0-679-72254-8).** A motion picture executive carries on with his life after he brutally strangles a screenwriter in a parking lot. (REV: NYTBR 7/24/88; New Yorker 12/19/88; PW 4/29/88)

8697 **Toole, John Kennedy.** *Confederacy of Dunces.* **1980, Louisiana State Univ. Pr. $18.95 (0-8071-0657-7); Grove-Weidenfeld paper $9.95 (0-8021-3020-8).** This story of a 30-year-old man and his relationship with his mother is set in a seedy section of New Orleans. (REV: BL 6/1/80; New Rep 7/19/80; Newsweek 5/26/80. AWARDS: BL, the 1980s; PP:Fiction, 1981)

8698 **Toole, John Kennedy.** *Neon Bible.* **1989, Grove-Weidenfeld $15.95 (0-8021-1108-4); paper $9.95 (0-8021-3207-3).** An unfinished novel written by the Pulitzer Prize winner at the age of 16 concerning a boy's life in the post-World War II South. "An astonishing accomplishment for an adolescent . . . it deserves a wide audience."—LJ (REV: BL 2/1/89; LJ 4/1/89; TLS 3/30/89)

8699 **Toussaint, Jean-Philippe.** *The Bathroom.* **1990, Dutton paper $7.95 (0-525-48538-4).** A chronicle of a Frenchman's periodic escapes to the solitude of his bathroom. (REV: NYTBR 4/29/90; PW 2/2/90. AWARDS: PW, 1990)

8700 Trevor, William. *Children of Dynmouth.* **1977, Viking paper $11.95 (0-670-21665-8).** The adventures of a young fatherless teenager who meddles in the lives of the citizens of an Irish seaside town. "The work of a master storyteller."—New Yorker (REV: BL 3/1/77; New Yorker 6/27/77; PW 1/17/77)

8701 Trevor, William. *Mrs. Eckdorf in O'Neill's Hotel.* **1985, Penguin paper $6.95 (0-14-006014-6).** A portrait of a crumbling Dublin hotel run by an elderly deaf woman for her relations and the city's orphans. (REV: NYTBR 1/25/70; Time 1/26/70)

8702 Trevor, William. *Two Lives.* **1991, Viking $21.95 (0-670-83933-7).** A collection of two novellas by the Irish writer, including "My House in Umbria" and "Reading Turgenev." "These are haunting, sensitive and richly imagined stories."—BL (REV: BL 6/1/91; NYTBR 9/8/91. AWARDS: NYTBR, 1991; PW, 1991)

8703 Trott, Susan. *Sightings.* **1988, Harper & Row paper $6.95 (0-06-097158-4).** A story of a California teenager sent to Paris to escape from family turmoil, and the lover she meets there. "A splendid entertainment."—NYTBR (REV: LJ 6/15/87; NYTBR 8/9/87; PW 5/8/87)

8704 Tulloch, Lee. *Fabulous Nobodies: A Novel about a Girl Who's in Love with Her Clothes.* **1989, Morrow $17.95 (0-688-07552-5); Harper & Row paper $7.95 (0-06-097318-8).** A satirical story of a 20-year-old New Yorker's adventures in the ultrahip East Village during the mid-1980s. "Ms. Tulloch's voice is sharp, affectionate, and hilarious."—NYTBR (REV: BL 3/15/89; NYTBR 6/11/89; PW 2/17/89)

8705 Turow, Scott. *Burden of Proof.* **1990, Farrar $22.95 (0-374-11734-9).** Attorney Sandy Stern, first introduced in *Presumed Innocent*, attempts to find the reasons behind his wife's suicide and to come to terms with life without her. (REV: BL 4/15/90; LJ 6/1/90; Time 6/1/90. AWARDS: Time, 1990)

8706 Turow, Scott. *Presumed Innocent.* **1987, Farrar $18.95 (0-374-23713-1); Warner paper $4.95 (0-446-35098-2).** A first novel detailing a murder case and the personal involvement of the prosecuting attorney in the crime. (REV: LJ 6/1/87; NYTBR 6/28/87; PW 5/22/87. AWARDS: PW, 1987)

8707 Ty-Casper, Linda. *Awaiting Trespass: A Passion.* **1985, Readers International $14.95 (0-930523-11-3); paper $7.95 (0-930523-12-1).** A Philippine writer's portrait of a wealthy family's life under the Marcos regime. (REV: BL 12/1/85; LJ 10/15/85; PW 8/30/85)

8708 Tyler, Anne. *Accidental Tourist.* **1985, Knopf $18.95 (0-394-54689-X); Berkley paper $4.95 (0-425-11423-6).** A Baltimore travel guide writer is faced with a failing marriage following the death of his son. (REV: LJ 9/15/85; NYTBR 9/8/85; Time 9/16/85. AWARDS: ALA, 1985; LJ, 1985; PW, 1985; Time, 1985; Time, the 1980s)

8709 Tyler, Anne. *Breathing Lessons.* **1988, Knopf $18.95 (0-394-57234-3); Berkley paper $5.50 (0-425-11774-X).** A journey to a funeral spurs reflections on life and love by a Baltimore married couple. (REV: Newsweek 9/26/88; PW 7/1/88; Time 9/5/88. AWARDS: ALA, 1988; PW, 1988; PP:Fiction, 1989; Time, 1988)

8710 Tyler, Anne. *Celestial Navigation.* **1985, Berkley paper $4.50 (0-425-09840-0).** The story of an agoraphobic Baltimore artist and his life with a young woman who moves into his boarding home. (REV: BL 7/1/74; NYTBR 4/28/74; PW 12/10/73)

8711 Tyler, Anne. *Clock Winder.* **1987, Berkley paper $4.50 (0-425-09902-4).** A young woman takes a job as a handyperson for a Baltimore widow and is confronted with the bizarre behavior of her three mentally unstable sons. (REV: BL 7/1/77; LJ 3/15/72; New Rep 5/13/72)

8712 Tyler, Anne. *Dinner at the Homesick Restaurant.* **1982, Knopf $22.95 (0-394-52381-4); Berkley paper $4.95 (0-425-09868-0).** A Baltimore family reminisces about the desertion of their father while reunited at the deathbed of their mother. (REV: BL 12/15/81; NYTBR 3/14/82; Time, 4/15/82. AWARDS: ALA, 1982; BL, the 1980s; NYTBR, 1982; Time, 1982)

8713 Tyler, Anne. *Earthly Possessions.* **1985, Berkley paper $4.50 (0-425-10167-3).** A small-town woman planning an escape from her family is abducted and taken hostage by a fugitive bank robber. (REV: BL 5/1/77; New Rep 5/28/77; PW 3/14/77)

8714 Tyler, Anne. *Morgan's Passing.* **1980, Knopf $13.95 (0-394-50958-7); Berkley paper $4.50 (0-425-09872-9).** A chronicle of the varied life of a Baltimore man with seven children, by the author of *Saint Maybe.* (REV: BL 3/1/80; LJ 3/15/80; Newsweek 3/24/80)

8715 Tyler, Anne. *Saint Maybe.* **1991, Knopf $22.00 (0-679-40361-2).** A young man indirectly responsible for his brother's suicide seeks atonement over the next two decades. (REV: BL 6/1/91; NYTBR 8/25/91; PW 6/14/91. AWARDS: PW, 1991)

8716 Tyler, Anne. *Searching for Caleb.* **1987, Berkley paper $4.50 (0-425-09876-1).** The story of family's 60-year search for a missing runaway relative. (REV: LJ 12/15/75; NYTBR 1/18/76; Sat Rev 3/6/76. AWARDS: ALA, 1976)

8717 Tyler, Anne. *A Slipping-Down Life.* **1989, Berkley paper $4.50 (0-425-10362-5).** The story of a North Carolina girl obsessed with a local rock music star. (REV: BL 6/15/70; LJ 3/15/70; NYTBR 3/15/70)

8718 Ucko, Barbara. *Scarlett Greene.* **1986, St. Martin's $18.95 (0-312-00184-3).** The story of a high school senior who moves to Wisconsin to attend college and escape her Southern hometown. (REV: LJ 4/1/87; PW 1/9/77)

8719 Unger, Douglas. *Leaving the Land.* **1988, Ballantine paper $3.50 (0-345-00753-0).** A story chronicling three decades in the life of a Midwestern farming family who had been driven out of existence by agribusiness. (REV: Atl 3/84; Newsweek 12/17/84; Time 2/20/84. AWARDS: ALA, 1984; LJ, 1984)

8720 Updike, John. *Bech.* 1970, Knopf $13.95 (0-394-41638-4); Random paper $5.95 (0-394-74590-4). Seven interrelated stories concerning the life of a Jewish writer in his 40s who fears his best days may be behind him. "Crisp, touching, wry and perceptive."—BL (REV: BL 9/1/70; NYTBR 6/21/70; Time 6/22/70. AWARDS: NYTBR, 1970; Time, 1970)

8721 Updike, John. *Bech Is Back.* 1982, Knopf $13.95 (0-394-52806-9); Fawcett paper $2.95 (0-449-20277-1). Connected stories tracing events in the life of a Jewish-American novelist that began in the 1970 *Bech: A Book*. (REV: NYRB 11/18/82; NYTBR 10/17/82; Time 10/18/82. AWARDS: ALA, 1982; NYTBR, 1982; Time, 1982)

8722 Updike, John. *The Coup.* 1978, Knopf $24.95 (0-394-50268-X); Fawcett paper $4.50 (0-449-24259-5). A story of life and politics in the fictional African nation of Kush as narrated by its president-in-exile. (REV: LJ 10/15/78; NYTBR 12/10/78; Time 12/18/78. AWARDS: ALA, 1979; NYTBR, 1978; Time, 1978)

8723 Updike, John. *Marry Me: A Romance.* 1976, Knopf $22.95 (0-394-40856-X); Fawcett paper $3.95 (0-449-20361-1). Members of two married Connecticut couples engage in an extramarital affair. "A dazzling performance, cleverly and beautifully written."—LJ (REV: BL 10/1/76; LJ 10/15/76; Newsweek 11/8/76. AWARDS: ALA, 1976)

8724 Updike, John. *A Month of Sundays.* 1975, Knopf $16.95 (0-394-49551-9); Fawcett paper $3.95 (0-449-20795-1). The journal of a clergyman sentenced to a month in a rehabilitation home, revealing his personal life and sexual history. "Updike's most playful, most cerebral, most self-regarding novel."—Newsweek (REV: BL 4/1/75; LJ 2/1/75; Newsweek 3/3/75)

8725 Updike, John. *Of the Farm.* 1965, Knopf $17.95 (0-394-43898-1); Fawcett paper $3.95 (0-449-21451-6). The account of a three-day visit by a family to the Pennsylvania farm where the protagonist was raised. (REV: BL 12/1/65; LJ 12/1/65; NYTBR 11/14/65. AWARDS: ALA, 1965)

8726 Updike, John. *Rabbit at Rest.* 1990, Knopf $21.45 (0-394-58815-0). The fourth and final volume of the Rabbit Angstrom series, chronicling his last year of life. "Completes the most authoritative and most magical portrait yet written of the past four decades of American life."—Time (REV: BL 9/1/90; NYTBR 9/30/90; Time 10/15/90. AWARDS: BL, 1990; LJ, 1990; NYTBR, 1990; PP:Fiction, 1991; PW, 1990; Time, 1990)

8727 Updike, John. *Rabbit Is Rich.* 1981, Knopf $22.50 (0-394-52087-4); Fawcett paper $5.95 (0-449-24548-9). The third volume of the Rabbit Angstrom saga tracing his life during the 1970s. (REV: BL 6/1/81; NYTBR 9/27/81; Time 10/5/81. AWARDS: ALA, 1981; BL, the 1980s; NBA, 1982; NYTBR, 1981; PP:Fiction, 1982; Time, the 1980s)

8728 Updike, John. *Rabbit Redux.* 1971, Knopf $19.95 (0-394-47273-X); Fawcett paper $5.95 (0-449-20934-2). The second volume of the saga of Rabbit Angstrom and his family, set at the end of the

1960s. (REV: BL 1/15/72; LJ 11/1/71; Time 11/15/71. AWARDS: NYTBR, 1971; Time, 1971)

8729 Updike, John. *Roger's Version.* 1986, Knopf $17.95 (0-394-55435-3); Fawcett paper $4.95 (0-449-21288-2). The story of a divinity professor who believes the existence of God can be scientifically proven by use of a computer. "A typically witty and erudite performance."—Time (REV: NYTBR 8/31/86; Newsweek 9/8/86; Time 8/25/86. AWARDS: NYTBR, 1986; Time, 1986)

8730 Updike, John. *S.* 1988, Knopf $17.95 (0-394-56835-4); Fawcett paper $4.95 (0-449-21652-7). The story of a woman who leaves her family to join an Arizona commune and becomes involved with a religious cult leader. (REV: LJ 4/15/88; Natl Rev 5/13/88; Time 2/29/88. AWARDS: Time, 1988)

8731 Updike, John. *Witches of Eastwick.* 1984, Knopf $19.95 (0-394-53760-2). The story of three modern-day Rhode Island witches who acquired psychic powers following separation from their husbands and find themselves confronting the devil at his New England estate. (REV: LJ 5/1/84; NYTBR 5/13/84; Time 5/7/84. AWARDS: Time, 1984)

8732 Uris, Leon. *Mitla Pass.* 1988, Doubleday $19.95 (0-385-18792-0); Bantam paper $5.95 (0-553-28280-8). A chronicle of the sojourns of a writer and his family from Russia to America to Israel by the author of *Trinity* and *Exodus*. (REV: BL 9/15/88; LJ 11/1/88; NYTBR 1/1/89)

8733 Uris, Leon. *QBVII.* 1972, Bantam paper $4.95 (0-553-25957-1). The story of the trial that follows a writer's accusation of atrocities committed by a Polish surgeon during World War II. (REV: LJ 12/1/70; PW 10/5/70)

8734 Vandenburgh, Jane. *Failure to Zigzag.* 1990, Avon paper $8.95 (0-380-71019-6). The story of a young Southern California girl forced to live with her grandparents after her mother is placed in a mental institution. "Splendid . . . a writer of great daring and skill to match."—Newsweek (REV: BL 3/1/89; Newsweek 4/3/89; PW 1/6/89)

8735 Van der Haeghe, Guy. *My Present Age.* 1985, Ticknor & Fields $15.95 (0-89919-384-6). A Canadian writer's debut work concerns a former department store employee's search for his former wife and his efforts to compose his first novel. (REV: BL 8/85; PW 6/28/85; TLS 8/22/86)

8736 Vargas Llosa, Mario. *Aunt Julia and the Scriptwriter.* 1982, Farrar $17.50 (0-374-10691-6); Avon paper $9.95 (0-380-70046-8). The story of the courtship between a young radio newswriter and his aunt. (REV: CSM 9/10/82; NYTBR 8/1/82; Time 8/9/82. AWARDS: ALA, 1982; NYTBR, 1982; Time, 1982; Time, the 1980s)

8737 Vargas Llosa, Mario. *Conversation in the Cathedral.* 1984, Farrar paper $12.95 (0-374-51815-7). A Gregory Rabassa translation of the Peruvian writer's story of corruption among his nation's leaders during the 1950s. (REV: BL 1/15/75; Choice 6/75; LJ 11/15/74)

8738 Vargas Llosa, Mario. *In Praise of the Stepmother.* 1990, Farrar $18.95 (0-374-17583-7). A chronicle of the intermingled erotic lives of a 40-year-old woman, her new husband, and his prepubescent son from a previous marriage. "Reflects an artistry of sophistication . . . almost infinite. An unreservedly brilliant work."—PW (REV: BL 8/90; New Yorker 10/1/90; PW 8/10/90)

8739 Vargas Llosa, Mario. *Real Life of Alejandro Matya.* 1986, Farrar $16.95 (0-374-24776-5); Random paper $8.95 (0-679-72478-8). A novelist searches to uncover details regarding the life of a former classmate who participated in a failed revolution three decades earlier. (REV: BL 12/15/85; LJ 1/86; Time 3/10/86)

8740 Vargas Llosa, Mario. *Storyteller.* 1989, Farrar $17.95 (0-374-27085-6). The story of a man who recognizes a portrait of a storyteller, intertwined with tales of the storyteller himself. (REV: BL 9/1/89; Choice 4/90; LJ 9/15/89. AWARDS: BL, 1989)

8741 Vargas Llosa, Mario. *Who Killed Palomino Molero?* 1988, Macmillan paper $6.95 (0-02-022570-9). Two Peruvian detectives attempt to solve a three-decade-old murder case involving the torture of an air force soldier. "An absorbing, multidimensional tale."—BL (REV: BL 5/15/87; LJ 6/1/87; NYTBR 5/31/87)

8742 Vassilikos, Vassilis. *Z.* 1985, Pantheon paper $3.95 (0-394-72990-0). A fictional account of a Greek political assassination set in the early 1960s, which was made into a motion picture of the same name. (REV: LJ 12/1/68; NYTBR 11/17/68; PW 9/9/68)

8743 Vaughn, Elizabeth Dewberry. *Many Things Have Happened Since He Died and Here Are the Highlights.* 1990, Doubleday $17.95 (0-385-26500-X). The memoirs of a wife-abuse victim attempting to gain control of her life following a series of personal tragedies. (REV: BL 2/15/90; LJ 2/15/90; PW 1/26/90)

8744 Vesaas, Tarjei. *Birds.* 1985, Dufour $23.00 (0-7206-0701-9). An orphaned Norwegian girl cares for her helpless brother whose only joy seems to derive from contact with birds. (REV: CSM 2/11/70; LJ 7/69; NYTBR 9/14/69. AWARDS: ALA, 1969)

8745 Vetter, Craig. *Striking It Rich.* 1991, Morrow $18.00 (0-688-10609-9). The experiences of a man who leaves his family to take part in a Wyoming oil boom. (REV: BL 6/15/91; LJ 7/91; PW 6/7/91)

8746 Vidal, Gore. *Kalki.* 1978, Random $14.95 (0-394-42053-5); Ballantine paper $4.95 (0-345-27873-9). A Vietnam veteran becomes the center of an American religious cult after he convinces people he is the reincarnated form of a Hindu god. (REV: BL 4/1/78; Newsweek 4/10/78; PW 2/20/78)

8747 Vine, Barbara. *House of Stairs.* 33.95, NAL paper 1990 (0-451-40211-1). An English woman rekindles her acquaintance with a woman who has just been released from prison in this novel written under Ruth Rendell's pen name. (REV: BL 4/15/89; NYTBR 6/11/89; PW 6/22/90)

8748 Vizinczey, Stephen. *In Praise of Older Women: The Amorous Recollections of Andras Vajda.* 1986, Atlantic Monthly $12.95 (0-87113-083-1). The story of a Hungarian student's love affairs in Italy and Eastern Europe. "A delightful, charming, richly ironic book."—LJ (REV: LJ 3/15/66; PW 2/21/66. AWARDS: NYTBR, 1966)

8749 Vogan, Sara. *In Shelly's Leg.* 1985, Graywolf paper $7.50 (0-915308-67-3). This debut novel concerns the rivalry between two women for the affections of a musician at a bar in Montana. (REV: BL 4/1/81; LJ 2/15/81; Time 7/6/81)

8750 Voinovich, Vladimir. *Fur Hat.* 1989, Harcourt $17.95 (0-15-139100-9). A story of a veteran Soviet writer who receives a poor quality hat from his union symbolizing his relative worth. (REV: BL 10/15/89; LJ 10/1/89; NYBR 3/15/90)

8751 Vonnegut, Kurt, Jr. *Bluebeard.* 1988, Dell paper $4.95 (0-440-20196-9). An artist character introduced in the author's *Breakfast of Champions* narrates this story of how he came to write his memoirs. (REV: BL 8/87; LJ 1/88; PW 9/25/87)

8752 Vonnegut, Kurt, Jr. *Breakfast of Champions: Or, Goodbye Blue Monday!* 1975, Dell paper $4.95 (0-440-13148-0). Vonnegut reintroduces his science fiction writer character, Kilgore Trout, in this story chronicling the descent of Midwestern car dealer Dwayne Hoover toward madness. (REV: BL 4/15/73; NYTBR 5/13/73; TLS 7/20/73)

8753 Vonnegut, Kurt, Jr. *Deadeye Dick.* 1985, Dell paper $3.95 (0-440-11765-8). A 50-year-old hotel owner living in Haiti reflects on his life and how he accidently destroyed a town with a neutron bomb. (REV: CSM 12/3/82; LJ 10/1/82; Natl Rev 12/10/82)

8754 Vonnegut, Kurt, Jr. *Hocus Pocus: Or, What's the Hurry, Son?* 1990, Putnam $19.95 (0-399-13524-3). A portrait of the United States in the near future as seen by a man awaiting trial for his role in a prison escape attempt. "Vonnegut at his fanciful and playful best."—PW (REV: PW 7/6/90; TLS 10/26/90)

8755 Vonnegut, Kurt, Jr. *Jailbird.* 1983, Dell paper $7.95 (0-385-29280-5). A study of the life of a low-level Watergate criminal following his release from prison. (REV: BL 10/1/79; LJ 10/15/79; Newsweek 10/1/79. AWARDS: ALA, 1979)

8756 Vonnegut, Kurt, Jr. *Slapstick: Or Lonesome No More.* 1977, Dell paper $4.95 (0-440-18009-0). A renaming scheme developed by a future president to create unity causes fragmentation of the nation. "One of Vonnegut's best."—LJ (REV: BL 10/1/76; LJ 10/1/76; New Rep 9/25/76)

8757 Von Rezzori, Gregor. *Death of My Brother Abel.* 1985, Viking $19.95 (0-670-26227-7). A Rumanian-born writer narrates a monologue portraying life in Europe in the aftermath of World War II. "An unparalleled fictional portrait of modern Europe."—LJ (REV: CSM 10/4/85; LJ 8/85; PW 7/12/85)

8758 Voznesenskaya, Julia. *Women's Decameron.* 1986, Atlantic Monthly $18.95 (0-87113-101-3); paper $9.95 (0-8050-0601-X). A collection of ten days of stories told by ten women in a Soviet maternity ward, patterned after the classic medieval work by Boccaccio. (REV: LJ 10/1/86; NYTBR 10/26/86; TLS 3/14/86)

8759 Wakefield, Dan. *Going All the Way.* 1989, Dutton paper $8.95 (0-525-48472-8). The story of the friendship between a Korean war veteran and a former high school athlete, set in the mid-1950s in Indianapolis. (REV: NYTBR 8/9/70; Newsweek 7/27/70; TLS 2/19/71)

8760 Wakefield, Dan. *Starting Over.* 1973, Delacorte paper $7.95 (0-440-08256-0). A recently divorced public relations man changes his career and remarries in this story by the author of *Going All The Way.* (REV: LJ 5/1/73; Newsweek 7/9/73; Time 7/16/73)

8761 Walker, Alice. *Color Purple.* 1982, Harcourt $14.95 (0-15-119153-0). The story of the lives of two sisters separated for three decades, as told through their letters to each other. (REV: LJ 6/1/82; NYRB 8/12/82; NYTBR 7/25/82. AWARDS: BL, the 1980s; NBA, 1983; PP:Fiction, 1983)

8762 Walker, Alice. *Meridian.* 1976, Harcourt $14.95 (0-15-159265-9). The life of an African-American girl growing up in the South forms the basis for this sweeping portrayal of the civil rights movement. (REV: LJ 5/1/76; Newsweek 5/31/76; PW 3/29/76)

8763 Walker, Alice. *Temple of My Familiar.* 1989, Harcourt $19.95 (0-15-188533-8); Pocket paper $5.95 (0-671-68399-3). A series of characters from around the world tell their life stories to form a collage portrait of the African-American experience. (REV: LJ 3/15/89; NYTBR 4/30/89; Time 5/1/89)

8764 Walser, Martin. *Swan Villa.* 1982, Holt $14.95 (0-03-059372-7). The story of a real-estate broker who fails in his efforts to purchase a key estate. "Modern German fiction at its best."—PW (REV: BL 7/82; Newsweek 10/25/82; PW 6/25/82)

8765 Wambaugh, Joseph. *Blue Knight.* 1973, Dell paper $4.95 (0-440-10607-9). Wambaugh's second novel portrays the life of a Los Angeles street cop near the end of his career. (REV: BL 7/15/72; LJ 1/15/72; PW 1/3/72)

8766 Wambaugh, Joseph. *New Centurions.* 1972, Dell paper $4.95 (0-440-16417-6). Wambaugh's first novel traces the lives of three Los Angeles policemen from the early 1960s to the outbreak of the Watts riots. (REV: BL 3/1/71; LJ 4/1/71; PW 12/13/71)

8767 Wang, Anyi. *Baotown.* 1989, Norton $17.95 (0-393-02711-2). A fictional portrait of life in rural China, as depicted through the lives of the residents of a small community. (REV: BL 10/15/89; LJ 9/15/89; PW 8/18/89)

8768 Ward, Robert. *Red Baker.* 1986, Pocket paper $5.95 (0-671-61747-8). A study of the life of a veteran

steel-mill worker who loses his job. "Cannot fail to touch anyone who has ever been a part of blue-collar America."—LJ (REV: BL 4/15/85; LJ 5/1/85; PW 2/22/85)

8769 Warner, Marina. *Lost Father.* 1989, Simon & Schuster $18.95 (0-671-67455-2). A novel in the form of a young woman's memoirs about her parents and grandparents in southern Italy. (REV: LJ 4/15/89; PW 3/10/89; TLS 9/16/88)

8770 Warren, Robert Penn. *A Place to Come To.* 1977, Random $12.95 (0-394-41064-5). The chronicle of the rise of a poor Alabama boy to scholarly pursuits and academic honors. "An altogether masterful performance."—LJ (REV: BL 2/15/77; Choice 6/77; LJ 2/1/77)

8771 Wassmo, Herbjorg. *House with the Blind Glass Windows.* 1987, Seal Press-Feminist $16.95 (0-931188-51-2); paper $9.95 (0-931188-50-4). A story of a stepfather who sexually abuses and torments his wife's daughter set in post-World War II Norway. "A deeply moving novel."—NYTBR (REV: LJ 11/15/87; PW 9/11/87)

8772 Weale, Anne. *All My Worldly Goods.* 1989, St. Martin's $22.95 (0-312-03965-4). A saga of an American orphan who marries into an English family. "Essential for public libraries."—LJ (REV: BL 1/15/90; LJ 1/90)

8773 Weaver, Gordon. *World Quite Round: Two Stories and a Novella.* 1986, Louisiana State Univ. Pr. $15.95 (0-8071-1291-7); paper $9.95 (0-8071-1326-3). A collection of three fiction pieces exploring art and its relation to life: the novella "The Interpreter" and the short stories "The Parts of Sleep" and "Ah Art, Ah Life." (REV: Choice 10/86; LJ 5/15/86; PW 4/25/86)

8774 Weaver, Will. *Red Earth, White Earth.* 1987, Simon & Schuster paper $4.50 (0-671-61988-8). A novel set during the 1950s detailing the rivalry between Native Americans and European descendants over Minnesota lands. (REV: BL 9/1/86; LJ 10/15/86; PW 8/15/86)

8775 Weber, Janice. *Secret Life of Eva Hathaway.* 1985, Donald I. Fine $16.95 (0-917657-32-2). A composer, dissatisfied with her marriage, enters into an affair with an opera singer. "Brilliant . . . has one laughing out loud from start to finish."—LJ (REV: LJ 9/1/85; PW 6/21/85)

8776 Weeks-Pearson, Tony. *Dodo.* 1986, Viking $14.95 (0-948681-00-4). An English schoolteacher searches for a living example of the presumedly extinct dodo bird. (REV: LJ 11/15/86; TLS 5/23/86)

8777 Weir, John. *Irreversible Decline of Eddie Socket.* 1989, Harper & Row $17.95 (0-06-016162-0). The picaresque tale of a young man who contracts AIDS and travels across Europe and the United States in search of himself. (REV: BL 9/15/89; LJ 10/1/89. AWARDS: BL, 1989)

8778 Weisman, John. *Blood Cries.* 1987, Viking $17.95 (0-670-81381-8). An American reporter finds evidence of wrongdoings by the Israeli government while on assignment in Jerusalem. "A startling portrait of politics in modern Israel."—BL (Rev: BL 5/15/87; LJ 4/15/87; PW 4/3/87)

8779   **Welch, James.** *Indian Lawyer.* **1990, Norton $18.95 (0-393-02896-8).** A Blackfoot lawyer in Helena, Montana, becomes the target of a blackmail smear scheme in this novel by the author of *Fool's Crow.* (Rev: BL 10/15/90; NYTBR 11/25/90; PW 8/10/90)

8780   **Welch, James.** *Winter in the Blood.* **1986, Penguin paper $5.95 (0-14-008644-7).** A debut novel concerning the life of a Native American living on a Montana reservation with his mother and grandmother. (Rev: LJ 12/1/74; Newsweek 11/11/74; PW 9/30/74)

8781   **Weldon, Fay.** *Cloning of Joanna May.* **1990, Viking $18.95 (0-670-83090-9).** Following her husband's death, a woman discovers that he had four of her eggs cloned and begins a search for her doubles. (Rev: BL 11/15/89; NYTBR 3/25/90; PW 1/19/90)

8782   **Weldon, Fay.** *Darcy's Utopia.* **1991, Viking $18.95 (0-670-83645-1).** A pair of journalists interview a famous social theorist concerning her plans for an ideal society. "Ambitious, provocative and unremittingly entertaining."—PW (Rev: BL 12/1/90; LJ 1/91; PW 1/18/91)

8783   **Weldon, Fay.** *Heart of the Country.* **1988, Viking $17.95 (0-670-81875-5); Penguin paper $7.95 (0-14-010397-X).** A comic novel regarding a mother's attempts to cope with the disappearance of her husband with his secretary. (Rev: NYTBR 12/11/88; New Yorker 12/26/88; TLS 2/13/87)

8784   **Weldon, Fay.** *Hearts and Lives of Men.* **1988, Viking $18.95 (0-317-66204-X); Dell paper $4.95 (0-440-20322-8).** A study of the unhappy marriage of a London art dealer and artist set during the 1960s and 1970s. "Superior feminist beach reading."—Time (Rev: BL 12/15/87; LJ 1/88; Time 4/11/88)

8785   **Weldon, Fay.** *Leader of the Band.* **1989, Viking $18.95 (0-670-82440-2).** An astronomer leaves her attorney husband for a jazz musician. (Rev: BL 6/1/89; LJ 5/15/89; PW 4/28/89)

8786   **Weldon, Fay.** *Letters to Alice: On First Reading Jane Austen.* **1990, Carroll & Graf paper $6.95 (0-88184-599-X).** A series of letters from an aunt to her teenage niece discussing the virtues of literature and in particular the works of Jane Austen. "Highly entertaining and not just for Austen fans."—LJ (Rev: BL 6/1/85; LJ 6/1/85; NYTBR 6/30/85)

8787   **Weldon, Fay.** *Life and Loves of a She-Devil.* **1985, Ballantine paper $4.95 (0-345-32375-0).** A woman who loses her husband to a romance novelist seeks revenge on the two of them in this novel by the author of *Praxis.* (Rev: BL 9/1/84; LJ 11/1/84; NYTBR 9/30/84)

8788   **Weldon, Fay.** *Life Force.* **1992, Viking $21.00 (0-670-84146-3).** The life of a noted British lover by the author of *Darcy's Utopia.* (Rev: BL 11/15/91; PW 11/29/91)

8789   **Weldon, Fay.** *Puffball.* **1990, Penguin paper $6.95 (0-14-013118-3).** A woman's dreams of a perfect marriage and country home are shattered. (Rev: BL 7/15/80; LJ 9/1/90; PW 7/4/80)

8790   **Weldon, Fay.** *Shrapnel Academy.* **1987, Viking $15.95 (0-670-81482-2); Penguin paper $6.95 (0-14-009746-5).** A dinner party at a military academy serves as the setting for this criticism of militaristic thinking. (Rev: BL 2/15/87; LJ 3/1/87; TLS 7/1/87. Awards: ALA, 1987)

8791   **Wells, Dee.** *Jane.* **1987, Harper & Row paper $7.95 (0-06-097078-2).** A female American newspaper critic living in England has three lovers and becomes pregnant by one of them. (Rev: Choice 5/74; PW 12/9/74; TLS 10/26/83)

8792   **Welt, Elly.** *Berlin Wild.* **1986, Viking $17.95 (0-670-80925-X).** A Jewish scientist reviews her feelings of guilt after surviving the Holocaust by working in a Berlin research facility. (Rev: NYTBR 3/27/88; PW 11/13/87)

8793   **Welty, Eudora.** *Losing Battles.* **1970, Random $13.95 (0-394-43421-8); paper $8.95 (0-679-72882-1).** An account of a Mississippi family reunion in celebration of a grandmother's ninetieth birthday. (Rev: Atl 4/70; NYTBR 4/12/70; Time 5/4/70. Awards: ALA, 1970; NYTBR, 1970; Time, 1970)

8794   **Welty, Eudora.** *Optimist's Daughter.* **1972, Random $13.95 (0-394-48017-1); paper $5.95 (0-394-72667-7).** An examination of a Mississippi family's dynamics as told through the memories of a young woman. (Rev: Atl 6/72; LJ 6/1/72; Time 9/5/72. Awards: ALA, 1972; PP:Fiction, 1972; Time, 1972)

8795   **Wesley, Mary.** *Harnessing Peacocks.* **1990, Penguin paper $7.95 (0-14-012393-8).** A young single mother supporting her son through prostitution in a small Cornish town encounters a stranger who seems to know her. (Rev: BL 4/1/86; LJ 4/1/86; PW 3/14/86)

8796   **Wesley, Mary.** *Not That Sort of Girl.* **1988, Viking $17.95 (0-670-82121-7); Penguin paper $6.95 (0-14-010826-2).** An elderly widow considers marriage to a French lover she has had amorous liaisons with over the years. (Rev: BL 4/15/88; NYTBR 6/12/88; PW 3/18/88)

8797   **Wesley, Mary.** *A Sensible Life.* **1990, Viking $18.95 (0-670-83338-X).** The chronicle of the life of an upper-class English woman from the 1920s through the 1960s. (Rev: BL 6/15/90; LJ 5/15/90; TLS 3/16/90)

8798   **West, Michael Lee.** *Crazy Ladies.* **1990, Longstreet $18.95 (0-929264-38-X); Ivy Books paper $4.99 (0-8041-0829-3).** A story of the reunion of three generations of women in the small town of Crystal Falls, Tennessee. (Rev: BL 9/1/90; NYTBR 10/21/90; PW 7/13/90)

8799   **West, Paul.** *I'm Expecting to Live Quite Soon.* **1970, Ultramarine $20.00 (0-06-014553-6).** In this novel by the author of *Rat Man of Paris,* an English woman explores her sexuality while her husband is serving time in jail for an accidental murder. "Lives at once by the grace of the extraordinary gifts of its author."—NYTBR (REV: LJ 4/15/70; NYTBR 5/3/70; PW 2/23/70)

8800 West, Paul. *Place in Flowers Where Pollen Rests.* **1988, Doubleday $19.95 (0-385-24565-3); Macmillan paper $9.95 (0-02-038260-X).** An examination of a Hopi Indian's life, from his youth on a reservation to the Vietnam War and eventual involvement in the adult film world. (REV: BL 9/1/88; LJ 9/15/88; PW 7/29/88)

8801 West, Paul. *Rat Man of Paris.* **1987, Macmillan paper $6.95 (0-02-026250-7).** A story of a man who flashes rats at Parisians and tourists and is plagued by memories of Nazi atrocities in the French village where he grew up. (REV: NYTBR 2/16/86; New Yorker 3/24/86; PW 1/17/86)

8802 West, Rebecca. *Cousin Rosamund.* **1987, Penguin paper $6.95 (0-14-010130-6).** A novel left unfinished at the author's death that would have been the final volume of the series that began with the publication of *The Fountain Overflows* in 1957. (REV: BL 2/1/86; LJ 4/1/86; PW 3/21/86)

8803 Wharton, William. *Dad.* **1982, Avon paper $4.95 (0-380-58594-4).** An examination of the effects of the illness of a mother and father upon their son and grandson. (REV: NYRB 8/13/81; Newsweek 6/1/81; Time 6/1/81)

8804 Wharton, William. *Last Lovers.* **1991, Farrar $18.95 (0-374-18389-9).** A study of the development of a friendship between an American painter and an elderly blind woman in Paris. (REV: BL 3/15/91; LJ 4/15/91; PW 3/22/91)

8805 Wharton, William. *Tidings.* **1987, Henry Holt $17.95 (0-8050-0532-3); McGraw-Hill paper $9.95 (0-07-069504-0).** A Christmas gathering reunites a family of six Americans in rural France in this novel by the author of *Dad.* (REV: BL 9/15/87; LJ 9/15/87; TLS 4/8/88)

8806 Wheeler, Charles. *Snakewalk.* **1989, Crown $16.95 (0-517-57205-2).** A young man blinded in a boating accident attends a special school for the blind in this debut novel. (REV: BL 5/15/89; LJ 6/1/89; PW 5/5/89)

8807 White, Edmund. *Beautiful Room Is Empty.* **1988, Knopf $17.95 (0-394-56444-8); Ballantine paper $4.95 (0-345-35151-7).** This sequel to *A Boy's Own Story* traces a gay man's personal life from his college years through his late 20s. (REV: LJ 3/1/88; PW 1/22/88; Time 4/11/88)

8808 White, Edmund. *A Boy's Own Story.* **1983, NAL paper $8.95 (0-452-26352-2).** A first-person story of the life of a gay American boy's childhood and adolescence. (REV: LJ 9/1/82; NYTBR 10/10/82; PW 8/6/82)

8809 White, Edmund. *Caracole.* **1986, NAL paper $7.95 (0-452-25881-2).** A story chronicling the heterosexual exploits of a group of urban city dwellers,

by the author of *States of Desire: Travels in Gay America.* (REV: LJ 9/15/85; NYTBR 9/15/85; TLS 3/14/86)

8810 White, Patrick. *Memoirs of Many in One.* **1988, Viking $15.95 (0-670-81320-6).** The fictitious remembrances and fantasies of an elderly woman, as described by the Australian Nobel laureate. (REV: LJ 9/1/86; NYTBR 10/26/86; PW 8/15/86)

8811 Whitney, Phyllis A. *Domino.* **1983, Fawcett paper $3.50 (0-449-20418-9).** A young woman's return to a Colorado ghost town may reveal the details surrounding the death of her father. (REV: BL 10/15/79; PW 8/6/79)

8812 Whitney, Phyllis A. *Poinciana.* **1984, Fawcett paper $4.95 (0-449-20439-1).** A young woman marries a 60-year-old financier and moves into his Palm Beach mansion following the mysterious death of her first husband. (REV: BL 9/1/80; LJ 10/15/80; PW 8/15/80)

8813 Whitney, Phyllis A. *Silversword.* **1987, Doubleday $15.95 (0-385-23666-2); Fawcett paper $4.50 (0-449-21278-5).** A Hawaiian-born woman finds the mother she believed dead to be alive and mentally ill. (REV: BL 11/1/86; LJ 12/86)

8814 Whitney, Phyllis A. *Spindrift.* **1981, Fawcett paper $3.95 (0-449-22746-4).** A young woman searches for clues from relatives to explain the mysterious circumstances surrounding the death of her father. (REV: BL 5/15/75; PW 1/27/75)

8815 Wideman, John Edgar. *A Glance Away.* **1975, Chatham Bookseller $7.95 (0-911680-50-9); Holt paper $6.95 (0-03-005602-0).** Wideman's first novel concerns a recovering Pittsburgh drug addict's efforts to regain control over his life. (REV: BL 1/1/68; LJ 7/67; PW 6/19/67)

8816 Wideman, John Edgar. *Philadelphia Fire.* **1990, Henry Holt $18.95 (0-8050-1266-4).** An African-American writer returns to his native Philadelphia to write a book about the 1985 MOVE incident and rekindles ties to his family and the city. (REV: BL 8/90; NYTBR 9/30/90; Time 10/1/90. AWARDS: BL, 1990; Time, 1990)

8817 Wideman, John Edgar. *Reuben.* **1988, Penguin paper $7.95 (0-14-010595-6).** An attorney moves into a Pittsburgh ghetto to offer legal advice to residents from his trailer. (REV: BL 9/1/87; LJ 11/1/87; PW 9/11/87)

8818 Wideman, John Edgar. *Sent for You Yesterday.* **1983, Avon paper $3.50 (0-380-82644-5).** The chronicle of several generations of an African-American family in Pittsburgh, written by the author of *Brothers and Keepers.* (REV: BL 6/1/83; NYTBR 5/15/83; PW 2/25/83. AWARDS: ALA, 1983)

8819 Wiesel, Elie. *A Beggar in Jerusalem.* **1989, Schocken paper $8.95 (0-8052-0897-6).** A group of beggars congregate near the Wailing Wall in Jerusalem to tell stories of the Jewish people following the recapture of the Wall during the Six-Day War. (REV: BL 4/15/70; NYRB 5/7/70; PW 12/14/70. AWARDS: ALA, 1970)

8820 **Wiesel, Elie.** *Fifth Son.* **1989, Warner paper $4.95 (0-446-35930-0).** The American son of a Holocaust survivor travels to Germany after finding out details of his father's life within the death camps. (Rev: BL 2/15/85; LJ 5/1/85; NYTBR 3/24/85)

8821 **Wiesel, Elie.** *Testament.* **1981, Summit $13.95 (0-671-44833-1); Bantam paper $3.95 (0-553-20810-1).** The memoirs of a Russian-Jewish poet killed in the Stalinist purges, as told by a young man who memorized a smuggled manuscript before emigrating to Israel. "Wiesel at his best."—LJ (Rev: BL 2/1/81; LJ 3/1/81; Natl Rev 6/12/81)

8822 **Wiesel, Elie.** *Twilight.* **1988, Summit $17.95 (0-671-64407-6); Warner paper $9.95 (0-446-39066-6).** A group of Jews in a New York mental hospital examine the legacy of the Holocaust and discuss history's treatment of their people. (Rev: BL 6/15/88; LJ 6/1/88; NYRB 8/18/88)

8823 **Wiggins, Marianne.** *John Dollar.* **1989, Harper & Row $17.95 (0-06-016070-5); paper $8.95 (0-06-091655-9).** A young English widow meets a sea captain after accepting a teaching job in Burma. "Mesmerizing . . . one of those literary milestones readers will recognize and treasure."—PW (Rev: CSM 3/20/89; New Rep 3/27/89; PW 11/18/88)

8824 **Wilcox, James.** *Modern Baptists.* **1990, Harper & Row paper $8.95 (0-06-091985-X).** The author's first novel portrays everyday life in Tula Springs, Louisiana. "A wonderfully funny explosion of comedy that is solidly based . . . on a serious understanding of life."—New Yorker (Rev: LJ 6/1/83; New Yorker 7/18/83; PW 4/29/83)

8825 **Wilcox, James.** *North Gladiola.* **1986, Harper & Row paper $5.95 (0-06-091345-2).** This author's follow-up to the novel *Modern Baptists* chronicles the further adventures of the citizenry of Tula Springs, Louisiana. (Rev: LJ 4/1/85; Newsweek 6/10/85; PW 4/12/85)

8826 **Wilcox, James.** *Sort of Rich.* **1989, Harper & Row $17.95 (0-06-016099-3); paper $8.95 (0-06-091707-5).** A widower marries a younger woman, who finds they have little in common after moving into his Louisiana home. "An exceedingly well-crafted tale."—Time (Rev: BL 4/15/89; PW 3/17/89; Time 6/19/89)

8827 **Wilder, Thornton.** *Eighth Day.* **1987, Carroll & Graf paper $4.95 (0-88184-339-3).** A study of the effects of an Illinois murder on two families living in a small town. (Rev: BL 5/15/67; LJ 4/1/67; PW 1/23/67. Awards: ALA, 1967; NBA, 1967; NYTBR, 1967)

8828 **Willeford, Charles.** *Burnt Orange Heresy.* **1990, Random $7.95 (0-679-73252-7); Creative Arts paper $3.95 (0-679-73252-7).** The story of an art critic's meeting with a legendary artist who has shown only one painting in his seven-decade-long career. (Rev: BL 10/15/71; LJ 8/71; New Yorker 11/6/71)

8829 **Williams, John A.** *Click Song.* **1987, Thunder's Mouth paper $10.95 (0-938410-43-1).** The story of an African-American writer who is attempting to balance his personal life and career and fight racial prejudice in the literary world. (Rev: BL 1/1/82; LJ 2/15/82; Sat Rev 4/82)

8830 **Williams, John A.** *The Man Who Cried I Am.* **1985, Thunder's Mouth paper $10.95 (0-938410-24-5).** A chronicle of the life of an African-American writer from the 1930s through the 1960s. "An important document of its time."—LJ (Rev: BL 12/15/67; LJ 9/15/67; NYTBR 10/29/67. Awards: NYTBR, 1967)

8831 **Williams, Joy.** *State of Grace.* **1990, Random paper $8.95 (0-679-72619-5).** A father obsessed with his daughter's life-style and morality follows her throughout the United States. (Rev: Choice 11/73; NYTBR 4/22/73; PW 2/19/73)

8832 **Williams, Philip Lee.** *All the Western Stars.* **1988, Peachtree $15.95 (0-934601-47-X); Ballantine paper $3.95 (0-345-35869-4).** Two retired friends run away from a convalescent home to become fugitives in the West. "An extraordinarily winning tale."—PW (Rev: BL 4/15/88; LJ 5/1/88; PW 4/1/88)

8833 **Williams, Thomas.** *Moon Pinnace.* **1988, Doubleday paper $8.95 (0-385-24247-6).** A college-educated New Hampshire boy flees from the love of the girl next door to travel to California on his motorcycle in this novel set in the aftermath of World War II. (Rev: NYTBR 8/17/86; PW 5/30/86. Awards: PW, 1986)

8834 **Williams, Thomas.** *Whipple's Castle.* **1988, Doubleday paper $9.95 (0-385-24249-2).** A portrait of a group of youngsters growing up during the 1940s in a small industrial New Hampshire community. (Rev: LJ 3/15/69; NYTBR 2/26/69; PW 2/16/70)

8835 **Willis, Ted.** *Green Leaves of Summer: The Second Season of Rosie Carr.* **1989, St. Martin's $17.95 (0-312-03354-0).** A working London widow becomes politically active in this novel set in the aftermath of World War II. "This heartwarming saga . . . is essential for all popular fiction collections."—LJ (Rev: BL 8/89; LJ 8/89; PW 6/16/89)

8836 **Wilson, A. N.** *Bottle in the Smoke.* **1990, Viking $18.95 (0-670-83221-9).** This sequel to *Incline Our Hearts*, set in bohemian 1950s London, traces Julian Ramsey's attempts at writing and acting. (Rev: BL 8/90; NYTBR 8/26/90; PW 6/8/90)

8837 **Wilson, A. N.** *Incline Our Hearts.* **1989, Viking $17.95 (0-670-82358-9); Penguin paper $7.95 (0-14-011337-1).** A chronicle of the childhood years of an English boy raised by his aunt and uncle by the noted biographer and novelist. "Delightfully written . . . as enchanting as it is intelligent."—NYTBR (Rev: BL 2/1/89; LJ 12/88; NYTBR 2/26/89)

8838 **Wing, Avra.** *Angie, I Says.* **1991, Warner $16.95 (0-446-51580-9).** A pregnant New York woman is forced to choose between her boyfriend and a charming Manhattan lawyer in this debut novel. (Rev: BL 8/91; NYTBR 9/15/91; PW 6/28/91)

8839 **Winterson, Jeanette.** *Oranges Are Not the Only Fruit.* **1987, Atlantic Monthly paper $6.95 (0-87113-163-3).** A British writer's debut novel concerning a teenage girl at odds with the religious beliefs of her parents. (Rev: LJ 10/15/87; NYTBR 11/8/87)

8840　**Wiser, William.** *Circle Tour.* **1988, Macmillan $19.95 (0-689-11928-3).** A novel whose narrator assumes the identity of a late poet and travels through Florida and Ireland in a descent into madness. "Vastly entertaining."—NYTBR (Rev: BL 3/15/88; LJ 5/1/88; NYTBR 3/27/88)

8841　**Woiwode, Larry.** *Born Brothers.* **1988, Farrar $19.95 (0-374-11553-2); Penguin paper $8.95 (0-14-012185-4).** A chronicle of the relations between two North Dakotan brothers originally introduced in the author's *Beyond the Bedroom Wall.* (Rev: BL 5/15/88; NYTBR 8/14/88; PW 6/10/88)

8842　**Woiwode, Larry.** *What I'm Going to Do, I Think.* **1969, Farrar $5.95 (0-374-28792-9).** The story of a newlywed couple's marriage and of the husband's plot to kill his wife. (Rev: LJ 4/1/69; NYTBR 5/4/69; PW 3/30/70. Awards: ALA, 1969)

8843　**Wolf, Christa.** *Accident: A Day's News.* **1989, Farrar $15.95 (0-374-10046-2).** A chronicle of the events of one day in a woman's life at the time of the nuclear accident at Chernobyl. (Rev: BL 6/1/89; CSM 4/27/89; NYTBR 4/23/89. Awards: BL, 1989)

8844　**Wolfe, Thomas.** *Good Child's River.* **1991, Univ. of North Carolina Pr. $21.95 (0-8078-2002-4).** An unfinished novel by the author of *Look Homeward, Angel* re-creates the relationship of Wolfe with theater designer Aline Bernstein. (Rev: BL 10/15/91; LJ 9/15/91; PW 8/30/91)

8845　**Wolfe, Tom.** *Bonfire of the Vanities.* **1987, Farrar $19.95 (0-374-11534-6); Bantam paper $5.95 (0-553-27597-6).** A Wall Street broker's life is changed following an accidental death in this novel portraying life in New York in the early 1980s. "Not just Wolfe's most successful book to date but one of the most impressive novels of the decade."—LJ (Rev: LJ 11/15/87; NYTBR 11/1/87; Time 11/9/87. Awards: LJ, 1987; NYTBR, 1987; PW, 1987; Time, 1987; Time, the 1980s)

8846　**Wolff, Geoffrey.** *Final Club.* **1990, Knopf $19.95 (0-394-57820-1).** A novel tracing a young man's experiences at Princeton and beyond set during the late 1950s and 1960s. "An unforgettable picture of a privileged time and place."—PW (Rev: NYTBR 9/16/90; PW 7/20/90)

8847　**Wolff, Geoffrey.** *Providence.* **1986, Viking $16.95 (0-670-80461-4).** An account of the events that follow a middle-class family's targeting by a group of young sociopaths. (Rev: NYTBR 2/16/86; PW 11/22/85; Time 7/7/86)

8848　**Wolitzer, Hilma.** *In the Flesh.* **1989, Ivy Books paper $3.95 (0-8041-0508-1).** A New York woman in her late 50s faces the departure of her husband following a long, apparently happy marriage. (Rev: BL 9/15/77; LJ 9/15/77; PW 7/11/77)

8849　**Wolitzer, Hilma.** *In the Palomar Arms.* **1983, Farrar $14.95 (0-374-17656-6); Ivy Books paper $3.95 (0-8041-0511-1).** A young woman whose life is

on hold while she waits for the divorce of her lover reexamines her life after beginning a job at a California convalescent home. (Rev: BL 4/15/83; LJ 6/15/83; PW 4/15/83)

8850　**Wolitzer, Hilma.** *Silver.* **1988, Farrar $18.95 (0-374-26422-8); Ivy Books paper $4.95 (0-8041-0485-9).** The continuing story of a dissatisfied married New York couple originally introduced in the author's *In the Flesh.* (Rev: BL 5/15/88; PW 6/3/88; Time 7/4/88)

8851　**Wolitzer, Meg.** *This Is Your Life.* **1988, Crown $17.95 (0-517-56929-9); Penguin paper $7.95 (0-14-012430-6).** An overweight New York mother makes a career as a stand-up comic poking fun at her fatness. (Rev: BL 10/15/88; NYTBR 12/11/88; PW 8/26/88)

8852　**Wood, Barbara.** *Vital Signs.* **1986, NAL paper $4.95 (0-451-16499-7).** The story of three female doctors, tracing their education, training, and careers. "Entertainment fiction at its best."—BL (Rev: BL 2/1/85; LJ 2/15/85; PW 12/21/84)

8853　**Woods, Stuart.** *Under the Lake.* **1988, Avon paper $4.50 (0-380-70519-2).** A reporter investigates rumors of drugs and murder surrounding a small-town Georgia sheriff. (Rev: BL 4/1/87; LJ 6/1/87; PW 4/3/87)

8854　**Woodworth, Kate.** *Racing into the Dark.* **1989, Dutton $18.95 (0-525-24766-1); Ivy Books paper $3.95 (0-8041-0584-7).** A first novel examining the development of insanity in a young woman and its effects upon her family. "An emotionally gripping story."—BL (Rev: BL 4/1/89; LJ 4/1/89; PW 3/17/89)

8855　**Wouk, Herman.** *Inside, Outside.* **1985, Little, Brown $19.95 (0-316-95504-3); Avon paper $4.95 (0-380-70100-6).** The fictional memoirs of a Jewish attorney in the Nixon White House who served as an assistant during the Watergate crisis. (Rev: BL 2/15/85; LJ 3/15/85; Natl Rev 6/14/85)

8856　**Wright, Sarah E.** *This Child's Gonna Live.* **1986, Feminist Pr. paper $9.95 (0-935312-67-6).** A story of the lives of an African-American woman and her four children in a Maryland ghetto. (Rev: LJ 5/15/69; NYTBR 6/29/69)

8857　**Wright, Stephen.** *M31: A Family Romance.* **1988, Crown $17.95 (0-517-56869-1); Ballantine paper $3.95 (0-345-36180-6).** A story, by the author of *Meditations in Green,* about an odd American family of seven obsessed with flying saucers. (Rev: BL 6/15/88; LJ 8/88; NYTBR 7/17/88)

8858　**Yamashita, Karen Tei.** *Through the Arc of the Rain Forest.* **1990, Coffee House paper $9.95 (0-918273-82-X).** This first novel portrays an international cast responsible for the destruction of a segment of the Amazon rain forest. (Rev: BL 8/90; LJ 9/1/90; PW 7/20/90. Awards: BL, 1990)

8859　**Yates, Richard.** *Cold Spring Harbor.* **1986, Delacorte $16.95 (0-385-29502-2).** A story of the social life of Americans on the homefront set during the summer of 1942 on Long Island. (Rev: BL 9/1/86; LJ 9/1/86; Newsweek 9/1/86)

8860 **Yates, Richard. *Easter Parade*. 1989, Random paper $8.95 (0-679-72230-0).** An examination of the lives of two sisters from childhood to middle age. (REV: Atl 10/76; LJ 9/15/76; NYTBR 9/19/76. AWARDS: ALA, 1976; NYTBR, 1976)

8861 **Yates, Richard. *A Good School*. 1979, Dell paper $8.95 (0-440-03246-6).** The study of life in a Connecticut boarding school just prior to the outbreak of World War II. (REV: LJ 9/1/78; NYTBR 11/12/78; New Yorker 9/4/78)

8862 **Yates, Richard. *Young Hearts Crying*. 1984, Delacorte $16.95 (0-385-29269-4).** A chronicle of the rise and fall of an American marriage traced over three decades, by the author of *Revolutionary Road*. (REV: BL 8/84; LJ 9/15/84; PW 8/10/84)

8863 **Yehoshua, A. B. *Five Seasons*. 1989, Doubleday $19.95 (0-385-23130-X); Dutton paper $9.95 (0-525-48555-4).** A chronicle of the first year of a widower's life following the death of his wife after a seven-year battle against cancer. (REV: BL 1/1/89; LJ 12/88; New Rep 2/27/89. AWARDS: ALA, 1989)

8864 **Yehoshua, A. B. *The Lover*. 1985, Dutton paper $10.95 (0-525-48400-0).** A man who is in Israel to take care of his ailing grandmother befriends a family and becomes the lover of a married woman. (REV: LJ 11/1/78; NYRB 12/21/78; NYTBR 11/19/78)

8865 **Yevtushenko, Yevgeny. *Wild Berries*. 1989, Henry Holt paper $12.95 (0-8050-1178-1).** This first novel by the Russian poet depicts modern life in Siberia through a series of vignettes. (REV: BL 6/15/84; Choice 11/84; LJ 9/1/84)

8866 **Yglesias, Rafael. *The Murderer Next Door*. 1990, Crown $19.95 (0-517-58010-1); Ballantine paper $5.99 (0-345-36428-7).** A fictionalized account of a 1987 case in which a man awaiting trial for the murder of his wife received custody of their child. "A disturbing and quite powerful novel."—NYTBR (REV: LJ 8/90; NYTBR 10/14/90; PW 7/6/90)

8867 **Yglesias, Rafael. *Only Children*. 1988, Morrow $19.95 (0-688-07219-4); Ballantine paper $4.95 (0-345-36031-1).** A chronicle of five years in the lives of two sets of New York parents. (REV: LJ 5/1/88; NYTBR 7/17/88; PW 4/1/88)

8868 **Young, Al. *Seduction by Light*. 1988, Dell paper $7.95 (0-440-55003-3).** The life of an African-American maid in Santa Monica who gets a job working for a Hollywood producer. "Brilliant, funny and sweet."—NYTBR (REV: BL 1/1/89; LJ 11/15/88; NYTBR 2/5/89)

8869 **Yount, John. *Toots in Solitude*. 1983, St. Martin's $13.95 (0-312-80904-2); paper $5.95 (0-312-80905-0).** The story of a Korean War veteran who withdraws from society to live in a treehouse. "A tale written with zest and read with pleasure."—NYTBR (REV: LJ 1/84; NYTBR 1/29/84; Newsweek 2/20/84; PW 12/2/83)

8870 **Yourcenar, Marguerite. *Two Lives and a Dream*. 1987, Farrar $16.95 (0-374-28019-3).** Contains three novellas, "An Obscure Man," "A Lovely Morning," and "Anna, soror . . . ," by the first female member of the Academie Française. (REV: BL 4/15/87; LJ 4/1/87; PW 2/27/87)

8871 **Zellerbach, Merla. *Rittenhouse Square*. 1989, Random $18.95 (0-394-57668-3).** A Philadelphia woman gains success in business at the expense of her personal life. (REV: LJ 2/15/90; NYTBR 3/18/90; PW 12/22/89)

8872 **Zhang, Xianliang. *Half of Man Is Woman*. 1988, Norton $17.95 (0-393-02586-1).** A chronicle of the life of a poet who spent two decades in prison on false charges raised during the Cultural Revolution. (REV: BL 8/88; LJ 9/1/88; NYRB 11/10/88)

8873 **Zinik, Zinovy. *Mushroom Picker*. 1988, St. Martin's $16.95 (0-312-02616-1).** The first novel translated into English of a Russian emigré writer concerns the social life of Moscow. (REV: BL 12/15/88; NYTBR 2/19/89; TLS 1/8/88)

8874 **Zion, Sidney. *Markers*. 1990, Donald I. Fine $19.95 (0-917657-08-X).** The fictional portrait of the friendly rivalry between a journalist and a lawyer, which includes Joe Kennedy, Robert Kennedy, and LBJ among its characters. (REV: Natl Rev 6/11/90; NYTBR 5/20/90; PW 3/9/90)

8875 Ackroyd, Peter. *Hawksmoor.* 1987, Harper & Row paper $8.95 (0-06-091390-8). A police investigator trying to solve a series of murders in twentieth-century London searches for clues in an eighteenth-century case with striking similarities. (REV: NYTBR 1/19/86; PW 11/22/85; Time 2/24/86)

8876 Agnon, S. Y. *Shira.* 1989, Schocken $24.95 (0-8052-4043-8). The story of the affair between a married German-Jewish Hebrew University émigré professor and a nurse, set in Palestine during the 1930s. (REV: BL 9/1/89; LJ 9/15/89; NYRB 3/29/90)

8877 Aleichem, Sholem. *In the Storm.* 1984, Putnam $15.95 (0-399-12922-7). The first English translation of the 1907 novel portraying life in Kiev during the failed 1905 revolution. (REV: BL 2/1/84; LJ 3/1/84; PW 1/27/84)

8878 Altieri, Daniel, and Eleanor Cooney. *Court of the Lions.* 1989, Morrow $19.95 (0-87795-902-1). A novel set during eighth-century China regarding the struggle of the T'ang dynasty to maintain rule. (REV: BL 12/1/88; LJ 11/15/88; PW 11/11/88)

8879 Appelfeld, Aharon. *Age of Wonders.* 1989, Godine paper $11.95 (0-87923-798-8). Recollections of Jewish life in pre–World War II Austria as told by an Israeli visiting the city of his childhood. "A deeply moving novel."—LJ (REV: CSM 4/7/82; LJ 12/15/81; Newsweek 12/14/81)

8880 Appelfeld, Aharon. *Badenheim 1939.* 1980, Godine $14.95 (0-87923-342-7); paper $9.95 (0-87923-799-6). A study of life in a popular Austrian-Jewish resort town prior to the outbreak of World War II. (REV: BL 11/1/80; NYRB 2/5/81; PW 10/17/80)

8881 Appelfeld, Aharon. *The Retreat.* 1985, Penguin paper $5.95 (0-14-007660-3). An actress retires to a Jewish-owned resort outside Vienna in the years just prior to the outbreak of World War II. (REV: BL 3/15/84; LJ 3/1/84; Time 5/28/84)

8882 Aridjis, Homero. *1492: The Life and Times of Juan Cabezon of Castile.* 1991, Summit $19.95 (0-671-64499-8). A portrait of the life of a Jewish man facing exile and the Inquisition during fifteenth-century Spain. (REV: BL 6/15/91; NYTBR 6/16/91)

8883 Astley, Thea. *It's Raining in Mango: Pictures from a Family Album.* 1988, Penguin paper $6.95 (0-14-011403-3). A chronicle of four generations of an Australian family from its arrival on the continent during the nineteenth century through the twentieth century. (REV: BL 10/15/87; PW 9/4/87)

8884 Astor, Brooke. *Last Blossom in the Plum Tree.* 1988, St. Martin's paper $3.95 (0-312-90545-9). Two elderly widows find romance in the late 1920s in New York. (REV: NYTBR 6/29/86; Time 7/28/86)

8885 Auchincloss, Louis. *Watchfires.* 1982, Houghton $13.95 (0-395-31546-8). A portrait of the crumbling and resurrection of the marriage of a nineteenth-century New York lawyer. (REV: BL 2/1/82; NYTBR 5/2/82; PW 3/15/82)

8886 Auel, Jean M. *Clan of the Cave Bear.* 1980, Crown $18.95 (0-517-54202-1); Bantam paper $5.95 (0-553-25042-6). This portrayal of the life of a Cro-Magnon woman adopted by a group of Neanderthals is the first of the author's Earth's Children series. (REV: BL 7/15/80; NYTBR 8/31/80; PW 7/18/80)

8887 Auel, Jean M. *Mammoth Hunters.* 1985, Crown $19.95 (0-517-55627-8); Bantam paper $4.95 (0-553-26096-0). This third volume in the author's Earth's Children series chronicles the adventures of protagonist Ayla among a tribe of mammoth hunters. (REV: LJ 1/86; Newsweek 11/18/85; Time 12/9/85)

8888 Auel, Jean M. *Valley of Horses.* 1982, Crown $18.95 (0-517-54489-X); Bantam paper $5.50 (0-553-28092-9). This sequel to *Clan of the Cave Bear* tells of a young woman's effort to reunite with Cro-Magnon people following her expulsion from a Neanderthal tribe. (REV: BL 8/82; LJ 9/15/82; NYTBR 9/26/82)

8889 Bailey, Anthony. *Major Andre.* 1987, Farrar $15.95 (0-374-19917-5). A British-American envoy tells the story of Benedict Arnold's offer to surrender West Point to the British in 1780. (REV: BL 7/87; PW 5/29/87; Time 7/27/87)

8890 Bassani, Giorgio. *Behind the Door.* 1976, Harcourt paper $3.95 (0-15-611685-5). A portrayal of the friendship of a group of adolescent Italian boys in Ferrara during the early 1930s. (Rev: BL 10/15/72; LJ 8/72; NYTBR 10/1/72)

8891 **Bassani, Giorgio.** *Garden of the Finzi-Continis.* 1977, Harcourt paper $6.95 (0-15-634570-6). A chronicle of the life of an Italian-Jewish family during the 1920s and 1930s amid a rising tide of social intolerance toward Jews. (Rev: BL 7/15/65; LJ 6/15/65; Time 8/6/65. Awards: ALA, 1966)

8892 **Beckett, Mary.** *Give Them Stones.* 1988, Morrow $14.95 (0-688-07562-2); paper $6.95 (0-06-097213-0). This story of a woman's life in Belfast encompasses the conflicts between Northern Irish Catholics and Protestants during the 1930s and 1940s. (Rev: LJ 2/15/88; NYTBR 6/12/88; PW 1/8/88)

8893 **Benet, Juan.** *A Mediation.* 1983, Persea Books paper $8.95 (0-89255-065-1). A portrait of life during the Spanish Civil War translated by Gregory Rabassa and originally written in 1969. (Rev: Choice 9/82; CSM 7/9/82; LJ 5/1/82)

8894 **Benitez-Rojo, Antonio.** *Sea of Lentils.* 1990, Univ. of Massachusetts Pr. $22.95 (0-87023-723-3). Four tales by a Cuban writer analyzing the effects of European colonization on the Americas. "Convincing and compelling."—NYTBR (Rev: LJ 8/90; NYTBR 12/16/90; PW 8/31/90)

8895 **Benson, E. F.** *Make Way for Lucia.* 1988, Harper & Row paper $16.95 (0-06-091508-0). A collection of the author's seven Queen Lucia novels originally published during the 1920s and 1930s portraying the life of an English matron. (Rev: BL 7/1/77; LJ 5/15/77; PW 4/4/77)

8896 **Berberova, Nina.** *Tattered Cloak: And Other Novels.* 1991, Knopf $21.00 (0-679-40281-0). Six novellas portraying the lives of Russians who fled to Europe following the 1917 Revolution. (Rev: BL 5/1/91; LJ 5/1/91; PW 4/19/91)

8897 **Berger, Thomas.** *Sneaky People.* 1990, Little, Brown paper $9.95 (0-316-09222-3). In this story set during the 1930s, a man plans the murder of his wife so that he may marry a young prostitute. By the author of *The Houseguest.* (Rev: BL 6/15/75; LJ 8/75; PW 3/10/75)

8898 **Bermant, Chaim.** *The Patriarch.* 1982, Ace paper $3.25 (0-441-65366-9). A Russian Jew emigrates to Scotland during the late nineteenth century in this novel that traces his life through the end of World War II. (Rev: LJ 5/1/81; NYTBR 8/2/81; PW 3/20/81)

8899 **Bernhard, Virginia.** *A Durable Fire.* 1990, Morrow $27.45 (0-688-08900-3). A fictional account of the settling of the first permanent American colony in Jamestown, Virginia. (Rev: BL 2/1/90; LJ 3/1/90; PW 1/12/90)

8900 **Bienek, Horst.** *First Polka.* 1984, Fjord Pr. $15.95 (0-940242-08-7); paper $7.95 (0-940242-07-9). A portrait of life on the Polish-German border in the days prior to the Nazi invasion of 1939. "A powerful, rich book."—NYRB (Rev: NYRB 4/26/84; PW 1/27/84)

8901 **Bosse, Malcolm.** *Warlord.* 1984, Bantam paper $4.95 (0-553-26523-7). A portrait of China in 1927 on the brink of civil war between the forces of Chiang Kai-shek and Mao Zedong. "As richly textured as a tapestry."—Time (Rev: LJ 5/15/83; PW 3/4/83; Time 7/4/83)

8902 **Boyd, William.** *Ice-Cream War: A Tale of the Empire.* 1984, Penguin paper $7.95 (0-14-006571-7). Boyd's second novel chronicles the experiences of two English brothers serving in East Africa during World War I. "A thoroughly satisfying book that should please the most discriminating reader."—LJ (Rev: LJ 4/15/83; NYTBR 2/27/83; PW 1/28/83)

8903 **Boyle, T. Coraghessan.** *Water Music.* 1983, Penguin paper $8.95 (0-14-006550-4). A chronicle of the African explorations of the eighteenth-century adventurer Mungo Park and his efforts to map the Niger River. "A very funny and well-written literary work."—BL (Rev: BL 10/15/81; LJ 11/15/81; PW 10/9/81)

8904 **Boyle, T. Coraghessan.** *World's End.* 1987, Viking $19.95 (0-670-81489-X); Penguin paper $9.95 (0-14-02993-9). This third novel by the author traces the life of a Dutch-American man and his ancestors over a period of three centuries. (Rev: LJ 9/1/87; PW 8/28/87; TLS 8/26/88. Awards: PW, 1987)

8905 **Bradshaw, Gillian.** *Imperial Purple.* 1988, Houghton $18.95 (0-395-43635-4). A Roman woman becomes involved in a plot to overthrow Emperor Theodosius II in this novel set in the fifth century. (Rev: BL 11/1/88; LJ 11/15/88; PW 10/7/88)

8906 **Breslin, Jimmy.** *Table Money.* 1987, Penguin paper $4.95 (0-14-010046-6). A multigenerational tale of an Irish-American New York family from the mid-nineteenth century to the 1980s. (Rev: NYTBR 5/18/86; Newsweek 5/26/86; Time 5/5/86)

8907 **Brink, Andre.** *A Chain of Voices.* 1983, Penguin paper $6.95 (0-14-006538-5). A story of a nineteenth-century South African slave revolt led by a tortured servant. (Rev: BL 5/15/82; LJ 5/1/82; PW 4/2/82)

8908 **Brown, Mary.** *Playing the Jack.* 1986, McGraw-Hill paper $4.95 (0-07-008295-2). An eighteenth-century English orphan adopted by a traveling acting troupe is eventually forced to work in a London whorehouse. (Rev: LJ 4/1/85; PW 2/15/85)

8909 **Brown, Rita Mae.** *High Hearts.* 1987, Bantam paper $4.95 (0-553-27888-6). A Southern woman poses as a man to join her husband in battle with the forces of the Confederacy. (Rev: BL 3/15/86; LJ 5/1/86; PW 3/28/86)

8910 **Brown, Rita Mae.** *Southern Discomfort.* 1983, Bantam paper $4.50 (0-553-23108-1). This portrait of life in Montgomery, Alabama, in the years following World War I, focuses on the love affair between a white woman in her late 20s and a black teenager. (Rev: BL 12/1/81; LJ 2/1/82; PW 1/29/82)

8911 Buch, Hans Christoph. *Wedding at Port-au-Prince.* **1986, Harcourt $17.95 (0-15-195598-0).** This German novel depicts two nineteenth-century examples of European intrusion into the political affairs of Haiti. (REV: LJ 10/15/86; PW 9/5/86; TLS 8/28/87)

8912 Buechner, Frederick. *Wizard's Tide.* **1990, HarperCollins $13.95 (0-06-061160-X).** A story of a family's financial collapse during the depression as witnessed by an 11-year-old boy. "This charming book is nostalgic without being sentimental."—LJ (REV: BL 5/15/90; LJ 6/1/90; PW 5/4/90)

8913 Buloff, Joseph. *From the Old Marketplace.* **1990, Harvard Univ. Pr. $19.95 (0-674-32503-6).** A portrait of life in turn-of-the-century Lithuania. (REV: CSM 2/21/91; LJ 11/1/90; NYTBR 3/3/91)

8914 Burgess, Anthony. *Kingdom of the Wicked.* **1986, Pocket paper $4.95 (0-671-62527-6).** A portrait of Roman society in the first century A.D. and the spread of Christianity throughout the empire. (REV: Atl 12/85; BL 7/85; PW 8/30/85)

8915 Burns, Olive Ann. *Cold Sassy Tree.* **1984, Ticknor & Fields $17.95 (0-89919-309-9); Dell paper $9.95 (0-440-51442-8).** A first novel regarding family relations and social life in small-town Georgia at the dawn of the twentieth century. (REV: CSM 12/7/84; LJ 10/15/84; Natl Rev 4/5/85)

8916 Burroughs, William S. *Cities of the Red Night: A Boy's Book.* **1982, Holt paper $6.95 (0-03-061521-6).** An account of a boy's adventures aboard a pirate ship in eighteenth-century Madagascar, written by the author of *Naked Lunch.* (REV: BL 11/15/80; LJ 11/15/80; TLS 3/27/81)

8917 Bykov, Vasil. *Sign of Misfortune.* **1990, Allerton Pr. $19.95 (0-89864-049-0).** A Byelorussian writer's portrait of a family's hard times under the reign of Stalin and the Nazi occupation. "A timely and valuable contribution to the knowledge of the U.S.S.R."—LJ (REV: BL 4/1/90; LJ 3/1/90; PW 2/23/90)

8918 Calvino, Italo. *Invisible Cities.* **1978, Harcourt paper $5.95 (0-15-645380-0).** A series of fictional conversations between Kublai Khan and Marco Polo regarding the traits of fabled cities. (REV: LJ 9/1/74; New Rep 12/28/74; New Yorker 2/24/75. AWARDS: ALA, 1974)

8919 Camon, Ferdinando. *Fifth Estate.* **1987, Marlboro Pr. $16.95 (0-910395-29-2); paper $9.95 (0-910395-30-6).** This novel set during the 1930s portrays an Italian city girl's six-month visit with a peasant family. Includes a preface by film director Pier Paolo Pasolini. (REV: LJ 5/15/88; NYTBR 1/24/88; PW 2/12/88)

8920 Carey, Peter. *Oscar and Lucinda.* **1988, Harper & Row $18.95 (0-06-015908-1); paper $8.95 (0-06-091592-7).** The story of two English settlers in nineteenth-century Australia who are determined to build a church in the outback. (REV: NYTBR 5/29/88; PW 4/29/88; Time 6/13/88. AWARDS: Time, 1988)

8921 Chesney, Marion. *Rake's Progress.* **1987, St. Martin's $12.95 (0-312-00674-8).** A Regency novel that reveals the exploits of members of an upper-class English household in the early nineteenth century. (REV: BL 8/87; LJ 7/87; PW 6/26/87)

8922 Chesney, Marion. *Refining Felicity: Being the First Volume of the Schools for Manners.* **1988, St. Martin's $14.95 (0-312-02288-3).** A group of nineteenth-century English spinsters open a charm school to make young women more marriageable. (REV: BL 10/15/88; LJ 11/15/88; PW 9/23/88)

8923 Childress, Mark. *A World Made of Fire.* **1984, Knopf $14.95 (0-394-53634-7).** This debut novel is set in the Deep South during the early 1900s and portrays the life of a widow after five of her seven children are killed in a fire at their home. (REV: BL 10/1/84; LJ 10/15/84; PW 8/17/84)

8924 Clavell, James. *Shogun: A Novel of Japan.* **1983, Delacorte $21.95 (0-385-29224-4); Dell paper $5.95 (0-440-17800-2).** A novel detailing the experiences of a seventeenth-century English sailor in Japan at the side of a rising ruler embroiled in a struggle for power. (REV: BL 9/1/75; LJ 7/75; NYTBR 6/22/75)

8925 Cohen, Robert. *Organ Builder.* **1989, Harper & Row paper $8.95 (0-06-091616-8).** A debut novel about the attorney son of a nuclear physicist and his recollections about the development of the atomic bomb at Los Alamos. (REV: BL 6/1/88; LJ 6/15/88; NYTBR 9/25/88)

8926 Colgate, Isabel. *Shooting Party.* **1982, Avon paper $3.50 (0-380-59543-5).** A group of English hunters meet on a large estate for a three-day sporting spree on the eve of the outbreak of World War I. (REV: BL 4/1/81; PW 4/24/81; Time 7/6/81)

8927 Conde, Maryse. *Children of Segu.* **1989, Viking $18.95 (0-670-82981-1).** The Guadeloupian author presents the story of the struggle of the African nation of Mali for independence from French occupying forces in the nineteenth century. (REV: BL 10/15/89; PW 9/15/89)

8928 Condon, Richard. *A Trembling Upon Rome.* **1983, Putnam $18.95 (0-399-12834-4).** A portrait of intrigue set in fifteenth-century Rome as financiers attempt to control the Vatican and its riches. (REV: BL 7/83; NYTBR 9/4/83; TLS 8/3/84)

8929 Cookson, Catherine. *Bannaman Legacy.* **1989, Summit paper $8.95 (0-671-68250-4).** In this novel set in the late nineteenth century, a young Englishman tries to prove the innocence of his father following the theft of money from a mill. (REV: LJ 5/15/85; PW 3/22/85)

8930 Cookson, Catherine. *Harrogate Secret.* **1990, Simon & Schuster paper $8.95 (0-671-70520-2).** The story of a young Victorian Englishman's rise out of poverty. (REV: BL 4/1/88; LJ 6/1/88; PW 4/15/88)

8931 Cornwell, Bernard. *Sharpe's Waterloo: Richard Sharpe and the Waterloo Campaign, 15 June to 18 June 1815.* **1990, Viking $18.95 (0-670-80868-**

7). The eleventh novel in the series tracing the career of an English soldier during the Napoleonic Wars. (Rev: BL 5/1/90; PW 4/27/90. Awards: BL, 1990)

8932 Crace, Jim. *Gift of Stones.* **1989, Macmillan $16.95 (0-684-19070-2); paper $7.95 (0-02-031160-5).** Flint workers of the Stone Age are visited by ships bringing new technology that threatens to change their way of life. "This is writing at the highest level of poetic accomplishment, a book that demands more than one delighted reading."—PW (Rev: LJ 4/1/89; PW 2/10/89; TLS 9/2/88)

8933 Crichton, Michael. *Great Train Robbery.* **1987, Dell paper $4.95 (0-440-13099-9).** A fictional recreation of the infamous nineteenth-century train robbery of gold bullion. (Rev: BL 7/15/75; CSM 6/11/75; NYTBR 6/22/75)

8934 De Haven, Tom. *Funny Papers.* **1986, Penguin paper $6.95 (0-14-008680-1).** This story of a late-nineteenth-century street urchin and a newspaper reporter whose lives come together is set in the streets of New York. (Rev: New Yorker 3/18/85; PW 11/30/84; Sat Rev 3/85)

8935 Deighton, Len. *Winter.* **1987, Knopf $19.95 (0-394-55177-X); Ballantine paper $4.95 (0-345-35931-3).** A tale of a Berlin family from the turn of the century to the end of the Third Reich as told through the lives of two brothers. (Rev: LJ 1/88; PW 11/13/87; Time 12/28/87)

8936 Delderfield, R. F. *Give Us This Day.* **1987, Pocket paper $4.95 (0-671-63545-X).** This third volume of the saga of the Swann family traces their lives from the end of the Victorian Age to the beginning of World War I. (Rev: LJ 9/15/73; NYTBR 11/18/73; PW 10/8/73)

8937 Delderfield, R. F. *God Is an Englishman.* **1986, Pocket paper $4.95 (0-671-62722-8).** A novel set in nineteenth-century India and England tracing the exploits of a family of traveling salesmen. (Rev: BL 9/1/70; LJ 9/1/70; NYTBR 9/13/70)

8938 Dell, George F. *Earth Abideth.* **1986, Ohio State Univ. Pr. $14.95 (0-8142-0411-2).** A previously unpublished story written in 1938 depicting the life of an Ohio farming family in the late nineteenth and early twentieth centuries. (Rev: BL 10/1/86; LJ 9/15/86; PW 7/25/86)

8939 DeMarinis, Rick. *Year of the Zinc Penny.* **1989, Norton $17.95 (0-393-02758-9); Harper & Row paper $7.95 (0-06-097339-0).** A preteen boy narrates the story of his reunion with his mother following a three-year separation in this novel set in 1943 Los Angeles. (Rev: Choice 1/90; LJ 7/89; PW 8/11/89)

8940 De Rosa, Peter. *Rebels: The Irish Uprising of 1916.* **1991, Doubleday $25.00 (0-385-26752-5).** A fictionalized account of the events surrounding the 1916 Easter uprising in Ireland. "An accessible, fast-moving treatment ideal for the public library audience."—BL (Rev: BL 2/15/91; LJ 2/1/91; PW 1/18/91)

8941 Desai, Anita. *Baumgartner's Bombay.* **1989, Knopf $18.95 (0-394-57229-7); Penguin paper $7.95 (0-14-013176-0).** The story of a German Jew who flees to India to escape Nazi persecution. (Rev: BL 3/15/89; LJ 3/15/89; NYTBR 4/9/89. Awards: ALA, 1989; BL, 1989)

8942 Dickinson, Peter. *A Summer in the Twenties.* **1987, Pantheon paper $4.95 (0-394-75186-8).** A study of English social life between the wars. "As absorbingly readable, as well-written, as entertaining as anything Peter Dickinson has written."—TLS (Rev: BL 7/1/81; PW 5/15/81; TLS 5/1/81)

8943 Döblin, Alfred. *A People Betrayed: November 1918, a German Revolution.* **1983, Fromm International $10.95 (0-88064-007-3).** A fictional study of Berlin society following the conclusion of World War I by the German author of *Berlin Alexanderplatz.* (Rev: LJ 3/1/83; NYTBR 8/17/83; PW 1/21/83)

8944 Doctorow, E. L. *Billy Bathgate.* **1989, Random $19.95 (0-394-52529-9); Harper & Row paper $5.95 (0-06-100007-8).** A portrayal of the New York gangster world of the 1930s as related through the words of a 15-year-old boy. "Immensely affecting."—PW (Rev: NYTBR 2/26/89; PW 1/6/89; Time 2/27/89. Awards: BL, 1989; NYTBR, 1989; PW, 1989; Time, the 1980s)

8945 Doctorow, E. L. *Loon Lake.* **1988, Fawcett paper $4.95 (0-449-21603-9).** A depression-era drifting New Jersey man following a young woman finds himself invited into a millionaire's Adirondack estate. (Rev: NYTBR 9/28/80; PW 8/8/80; Time 9/22/80. Awards: NYTBR, 1980; Time, 1980)

8946 Doctorow, E. L. *Ragtime.* **1975, Random $21.95 (0-394-46901-1); Fawcett paper $4.95 (0-449-21428-1).** A mix of fictional narrative with early twentieth-century historical figures by the author of *Loon Lake.* (Rev: NYRB 8/7/75; NYTBR 7/6/75; Time 7/14/75. Awards: ALA, 1975; NYTBR, 1975; Time, 1975; Time, the 1970s)

8947 Doctorow, E. L. *World's Fair.* **1986, Fawcett paper $4.95 (0-449-21237-8).** The story of the first nine years of life of a Bronx child in the 1930s as narrated by the youth and several family members. (Rev: BL 9/15/85; LJ 10/15/85; PW 9/13/85. Awards: ALA, 1985; LJ, 1985; NBA, 1985; PW, 1985)

8948 Doig, Ivan. *English Creek.* **1985, Penguin paper $7.95 (0-14-008442-8).** A man remembers his life as a teenager on his family's Montana ranch during the late 1930s. (Rev: BL 10/15/84; CSM 12/24/84; New Yorker 1/12/85)

8949 Doig, Ivan. *Sea Runners.* **1983, Penguin paper $8.95 (0-14-006780-9).** A group of indentured servants escape from a fur-trading company and try to reach the Pacific Northwest from Alaska. "A winning combination of Northwest history, muscular prose, and raw adventure."—BL (Rev: BL 9/1/82; LJ 9/1/82; PW 7/9/82)

8950 Doxey, William. *Cousins to the Kudzu.* **1985, Louisiana State Univ. Pr. $18.95 (0-8071-1225-9).** Small-town life in Georgia during the 1930s as portrayed through a series of vignettes depicting the lives of a community's citizens. (Rev: BL 4/15/85; LJ 5/15/85)

8951   Drury, Allen. *Return to Thebes.* **1978, Dell paper $1.95 (0-440-17296-9).** A study of fourteenth-century B.C. Egypt concerning the lives of Akhenaten and Nefertiti and the passing of the throne to Akhenaten's brother Tutankhamen. (REV: BL 2/1/77; LJ 2/15/77)

8952   Ducornet, Rikki. *Entering Fire.* **1987, City Lights paper $6.95 (0-317-60498-8).** A French botanist's son becomes obsessed with the Fascist cause in this novel set prior to the outbreak of World War II. (REV: NYTBR 6/10/87; PW 3/20/87)

8953   Duggan, William. *Great Thirst.* **1985, Delacorte $16.95 (0-385-29387-9); Dell paper $4.95 (0-440-33171-4).** The story of six generations of the BaNave tribe that settled in the Kalahari and confronted both severe living conditions and the threat of colonialism. "A rich epic of Africa's struggles."—NYTBR (REV: BL 9/15/85; LJ 10/1/85; NYTBR 11/17/85)

8954   Dunnett, Dorothy. *Niccolo Rising.* **1986, Knopf $18.95 (0-394-53107-8); Dell paper $4.95 (0-440-20072-5).** A portrait of the daily business life of fifteenth-century Flanders and its trading rivalry with France and Italy. (REV: BL 9/15/86; LJ 9/1/86; NYTBR 10/19/86)

8955   Dunnett, Dorothy. *Race of Scorpions.* **1990, Knopf $19.95 (0-394-57107-X).** A fifteenth-century traveling Dutch businessman becomes embroiled in conflicts between the Italian city-states. (REV: BL 2/1/90; CSM 12/24/90; PW 3/2/90)

8956   Dunnett, Dorothy. *Spring of the Rain.* **1988, Knopf $19.95 (0-394-56437-5); paper $4.95 (0-440-20355-4).** This sequel to the author's *Niccolo Rising* is set in fifteenth-century Italy and concerns a trading expedition to the Far East. (REV: BL 6/1/88; PW 6/10/88)

8957   Dunphy, Jack. *Murderous McLaughlins.* **1988, McGraw-Hill $16.95 (0-07-018316-3).** The life of an Irish-American immigrant woman living in south Philadelphia at the turn of the century and her relationship with her grandson. (REV: BL 5/1/88; LJ 5/15/88; PW 4/1/88)

8958   Edwards, G. B. *Book of Ebenezer Le Page.* **1987, Moyer Bell Ltd. paper $8.95 (0-317-60708-1).** The fictionalized memoirs of the author's life on the island of Guernsey from the early 1900s to the 1960s. (REV: CSM 3/25/81; Sat Rev 3/81; TLS 3/27/81)

8959   Ehle, John. *Winter People.* **1988, Harper & Row paper $4.95 (0-06-080939-6).** The lives of an Appalachian family are changed when a drifter comes to live with them in this novel set during the depression. (REV: BL 2/15/82; LJ 3/15/82; PW 1/15/82)

8960   Elegant, Robert S. *Dynasty.* **1984, Fawcett paper $4.95 (0-449-20603-3).** The story of the financial dynasty of a Hong Kong businessman from Victorian times to the takeover of China by the Communists. "An outstanding historical novel which is both entertaining and informative."—LJ (REV: CSM 10/12/77; LJ 8/77; PW 5/23/77)

8961   Elegant, Robert S. *Manchu.* **1982, Fawcett paper $4.95 (0-449-24445-8).** An English Jesuit narrates his role in the seventeenth-century fall of the Ming dynasty in China. "Fiction that both entertains and instructs."—LJ (REV: BL 9/1/80; LJ 9/15/80; PW 8/22/90)

8962   Elliott, Sumner Locke. *Waiting for Childhood.* **1988, Harper & Row paper $7.95 (0-06-091506-4).** A family of seven carries on after the parents' death in this novel set during the 1910s in Australia. (REV: LJ 9/1/87; New Yorker 10/19/87; PW 7/10/87)

8963   Emery, John. *Sky People.* **1988, Soho $18.95 (0-939149-10-9).** A German man and his colleagues seek gold in the mountains of New Guinea in this novel set during the 1930s. (REV: BL 4/1/88; NYTBR 4/24/88; PW 2/12/88)

8964   Endo, Shusaku. *The Samurai.* **1982, Harper & Row $12.95 (0-06-859852-1); Random paper $9.95 (0-394-72726-6).** A group of seventeenth-century samurai are sent from Japan to establish trade and communications with Roman Catholic missionaries in Latin America and Europe. (REV: BL 11/1/82; LJ 10/1/82; TLS 5/21/82)

8965   Endo, Shusaku. *Wonderful Fool.* **1983, Harper & Row $13.95 (0-06-859853-X).** This fictional recounting of the experiences of a French vagabond in sixteenth-century Japan was originally published in that country in 1959. (REV: LJ 11/1/83; PW 9/9/83; Sat Rev 12/83)

8966   Epstein, Leslie. *Pinto and Sons.* **1990, Houghton $19.95 (0-395-54704-0).** The story of a Hungarian immigrant who leaves his Boston medical career to join the California Gold Rush and befriends a group of Modoc Indians. (REV: BL 11/15/90; LJ 10/1/90; PW 9/7/90)

8967   Epstein, Seymour. *A Special Destiny.* **1986, Donald I. Fine $17.95 (0-917657-84-5).** A story of a Brooklyn boy's career as a playwright and salesman in the days prior to the outbreak of World War II. (REV: LJ 7/86; PW 5/23/86)

8968   Farrell, J. G. *Siege of Krisnapur.* **1985, Carroll & Graf paper $4.95 (0-88184-195-1).** A fictional account of the Sepoy mutiny of 1857 against British sovereignty in India. (REV: LJ 8/74; Time 9/30/74; TLS 9/21/73)

8969   Farrell, J. G. *Troubles.* **1986, Carroll & Graf paper $4.95 (0-88184-269-9).** A fictional retelling of the series of events in Ireland during the 1910s known as the Troubles. (REV: LJ 9/15/71; New Yorker 9/25/71; TLS 1/22/71)

8970   Figes, Eva. *Nelly's Version.* **1988, Pantheon paper $8.95 (0-679-72035-9).** A servant character drawn from *Wuthering Heights* analyzes her life with a new outlook following an attack of amnesia. (REV: BL 8/88; LJ 10/1/88; PW 7/22/88)

8971   Figes, Eva. *Seven Ages.* **1986, Pantheon $14.95 (0-394-55540-6).** Studies of the lives of seven British women from the Middle Ages to the twentieth century. (Rev: Atl 2/87; LJ 12/85; NYTBR 2/22/87)

8972   Findley, Timothy. *Not Wanted on the Voyage.* **1985, Doubleday $17.95 (0-385-29415-8); Dell paper $4.95 (0-440-36499-X).** A fictional portrait of Noah preparing the Ark for the Great Flood. (Rev: BL 10/1/85; NYTBR 11/10/85; TLS 11/1/85)

8973   Fitzgerald, Penelope. *Beginning of Spring.* **1989, Henry Holt $18.95 (0-8050-0981-7); Carroll & Graf paper $8.95 (0-88184-598-1).** A story set in Moscow in the years prior to the outbreak of World War I chronicling the breakup of an English family. (Rev: NYTBR 5/7/89; PW 2/17/88; TLS 9/23/88)

8974   Flagg, Fannie. *Fried Green Tomatoes at the Whistle Stop Cafe.* **1987, Random $17.95 (0-394-56152-X); McGraw-Hill paper $5.95 (0-07-021257-0).** The story of a unique friendship between two women who run a cafe in a small Alabama town during the depression. (Rev: BL 9/1/87; NYTBR 10/18/87; PW 8/28/87)

8975   Flanagan, Thomas. *Tenants of Time.* **1988, Dutton $22.95 (0-525-24619-3); Warner paper $5.95 (0-446-35342-6).** A tale of Ireland's struggle for independence in the first half of the nineteenth century. "Historical fiction at its best."—PW (Rev: NYTBR 1/3/88; PW 11/6/87; Time 1/11/88. Awards: NYTBR, 1988; PW, 1988; Time, 1988)

8976   Flanagan, Thomas. *Year of the French.* **1989, Henry Holt paper $12.95 (0-8050-1020-3).** A wartime novel set in 1798 with the forces of Great Britain threatening to invade Ireland and of the French–Irish alliance awaiting the invasion. "An exceptionally fine book that will be read, enjoyed and remembered."—LJ (Rev: LJ 5/1/79; Newsweek 5/14/79; PW 5/19/79)

8977   Fleming, Thomas. *Spoils of War.* **1985, Putnam $18.95 (0-399-12968-5); Avon paper $4.50 (0-380-70065-4).** A fictional portrait of the United States from the end of the Civil War to the dawn of the twentieth century. (Rev: BL 2/15/85; PW 1/11/85)

8978   Follett, Ken. *Pillar of the Earth.* **1989, Morrow $22.95 (0-688-04659-2); NAL paper $5.95 (0-451-16689-2).** The power struggle for the crown following the death of King Henry I in twelfth-century England. (Rev: BL 6/15/89; LJ 7/89; PW 6/22/90)

8979   Forbath, Peter. *Last Hero.* **1988, Simon & Schuster $21.95 (0-671-24285-7); Warner paper $12.95 (0-446-39179-4).** The story of British explorer Henry M. Stanley's efforts to rescue the Emin Pasha from Khartoum in 1887. (Rev: BL 8/88; LJ 10/15/88; PW 8/26/88)

8980   Forrest, Leon. *Two Wings to Veil My Face.* **1988, Another Chicago Pr. paper $8.95 (0-9614644-4-5).** A chronicle of the life of a 91-year-old African-American woman as recorded by her grandson, spanning from the 1860s to the 1950s. (Rev: NYTBR 2/26/84; PW 1/6/84)

8981   Forster, Margaret. *Lady's Maid: A Novel of the Nineteenth Century.* **1991, Doubleday $19.95 (0-**385-41792-6).** An exploration of the relationship between a house servant and the writing couple of Elizabeth Barrett and Robert Browning. (Rev: BL 2/15/91; LJ 1/91; PW 1/11/91)

8982   Fowles, John. *French Lieutenant's Woman.* **1969, Little, Brown $24.95 (0-316-29099-8); NAL paper $4.95 (0-451-16375-3).** A love triangle set in Victorian times between a scientist and two women, by the author of *A Maggot.* (Rev: CSM 11/13/69; NYTBR 11/9/69; Time 11/7/69. Awards: ALA, 1969)

8983   Fowles, John. *A Maggot.* **1985, Little, Brown $19.95 (0-316-28994-9); NAL paper $4.50 (0-451-14476-7).** A story set in eighteenth-century England chronicling the adventures of five people traveling by horseback in the country. (Rev: BL 7/85; CSM 10/8/85; Time 9/9/85)

8984   Fraser, George MacDonald. *Flashman and the Dragon.* **1986, Knopf $16.95 (0-394-55357-8); NAL paper $8.95 (0-452-26191-0).** Memoirs of a British envoy during the nineteenth-century Taiping Rebellion in China. (Rev: BL 3/1/86; Newsweek 5/5/86; PW 3/7/86)

8985   Fraser, George MacDonald. *Pyrates.* **1984, Knopf $16.95 (0-394-53837-4); NAL paper $8.95 (0-452-25764-6).** An account of a sea captain's efforts to recover a stolen crown from a group of renegade pirates. (Rev: Atl 9/84; LJ 7/84; NYTBR 10/21/84)

8986   Fuentes, Carlos. *Campaign.* **1991, Farrar $22.95 (0-374-11828-0).** A portrait of the life of an Argentine rebel set during the 1820s rebellions of Latin American nations against Spanish rule. (Rev: LJ 9/1/91; NYTBR 10/6/91; PW 8/2/91)

8987   Fuentes, Carlos. *Old Gringo.* **1985, Farrar $14.95 (0-374-22578-8); paper $7.95 (0-06-097258-0).** A speculative investigation into the circumstances surrounding the mysterious disappearance of American writer Ambrose Bierce in Mexico in 1913. (Rev: Atl 12/85; BL 11/1/85; LJ 11/1/85)

8988   Fuentes, Carlos. *Terra Nostra.* **1976, Farrar paper $14.95 (0-374-51750-9).** A sweeping portrait of Spain and its colonies from the medieval era to the eighteenth century with flashbacks to the past. "Significant achievements in fiction happen infrequently: this is one."—PW (Rev: Choice 4/77; NYTBR 11/7/76; PW 8/2/76. Awards: ALA, 1976)

8989   Gaines, Ernest J. *Autobiography of Miss Jane Pittman.* **1982, Bantam paper $3.95 (0-553-26357-9).** Recollections of a century-old former slave tracing the events of her life from the Civil War to the civil rights movement. (Rev: LJ 3/1/71; Sat Rev 5/1/71. Awards: ALA, 1971; Time, 1971)

8990   Garcia Marquez, Gabriel. *The General in His Labyrinth.* **1990, Knopf $19.95 (0-394-58258-6).** A novel tracing the final years of the Latin American liberator Simon Bolivar. (Rev: BL 7/90; Newsweek 10/8/90; Time 9/17/90. Awards: BL, 1990; Time, 1990)

8991   Gardner, John. *Wreckage of Agathon.* **1985, Dutton paper $8.95 (0-525-48180-X).** A story of the life of a rebellious youth of ancient Greece written by the author of *Grendel*. (REV: BL 1/1/71; Newsweek 9/21/70; Time 11/9/70)

8992 Garrett, George. *Entered from the Sun.* **1990, Doubleday $21.95 (0-385-19095-6).** Two men become immersed in the world of Elizabethan theater while investigating the death of sixteenth-century playwright Christopher Marlowe. (REV: BL 9/1/90; LJ 9/1/90; PW 7/6/90)

8993 George, Margaret. *Autobiography of Henry VIII: With Notes by His Fool, Will Somers.* **1986, St. Martin's $19.95 (0-312-06145-5); Ballantine paper $10.95 (0-345-34275-5).** A debut novel presenting the fictionalized memoirs of the sixteenth-century English king as discovered by his court jester. (REV: BL 7/86; LJ 9/15/86)

8994 Giardina, Denise. *Storming Heaven.* **1987, Norton $16.95 (0-393-02440-7); Ivy Books paper $3.95 (0-8041-0297-X).** The story of early twentieth-century efforts to organize coal miners in West Virginia. "As fast-paced and completely readable as a thriller."—PW (REV: BL 6/15/87; LJ 7/87; PW 5/15/87)

8995 Gibbons, Kaye. *A Cure for Dreams.* **1991, Algonquin $14.95 (0-945575-33-5).** A woman recounts the events of her mother's life during the depression in the American South. (REV: LJ 2/15/91; NYTBR 5/12/91; PW 1/25/91)

8996 Gidley, Charles. *Armada.* **1988, Viking $19.95 (0-670-81807-0).** A study of the defeat of the Spanish Armada in the sixteenth century focusing on the exploits of a disgruntled Spanish sailor who became a spy for the English. (REV: BL 1/1/88; LJ 1/88; PW 12/11/87)

8997 Goddard, Robert. *In Pale Batallions.* **1988, Poseidon $18.95 (0-671-64945-0); Pocket paper $4.95 (0-671-64946-9).** A chronicle of three generations of life on an English estate before, during, and after World War I. "Enthralling to the final pages."—LJ (REV: BL 9/15/88; LJ 11/1/88; PW 8/12/88)

8998 Goddard, Robert. *Painting the Darkness.* **1989, Simon & Schuster $19.95 (0-671-64947-7).** A missing man who is presumed dead reappears to claim an inheritance in nineteenth-century London. (REV: BL 8/89; LJ 9/1/89; PW 7/28/89)

8999 Golding, William. *Close Quarters.* **1987, Farrar $16.95 (0-374-12510-4).** The Nobel Laureate's sequel to *Rites of Passage* details the continuing adventures of passengers aboard a ship on its way to Australia in the early nineteenth century. (REV: BL 3/1/87; LJ 4/15/87; Time 6/8/87)

9000 Golding, William. *Fire Down Below.* **1989, Farrar $17.95 (0-374-25381-1).** The concluding volume of a trilogy that includes *Rites of Passage* and *Close Quarters* about the voyage of an English ship to Australia in the nineteenth century. "The best sea fiction we've had since Conrad."—LJ (REV: BL 12/1/88; LJ 1/89; TLS 3/17/89)

9001 Golding, William. *Rites of Passage.* **1980, Farrar $14.95 (0-374-25086-3).** An account of a

nineteenth-century voyage by ship from England to Australia focusing on the experiences of a clergyman and a politician. (REV: LJ 10/1/80; NYTBR 11/2/80; TLS 10/17/80)

9002 Grade, Chaim. *Rabbis and Wives.* **1987, Schocken paper $8.95 (0-8052-0840-2).** Three novellas portraying life in Lithuania between the World Wars. "A near-must for the literature collection."—BL (REV: BL 12/15/82; LJ 12/15/82; PW 10/1/82)

9003 Grass, Günter. *Dog Years.* **1989, Harcourt paper $12.95 (0-15-626112-X).** This third volume of the author's Danzig trilogy traces the lives of two boys—one Jewish, one gentile—in the years between World Wars I and II. (REV: BL 4/1/65; CSM 5/27/65; LJ 3/1/65. AWARDS: NYTBR, 1965)

9004 Grass, Günter. *Meeting at Telgte.* **1981, Harcourt $9.95 (0-15-158588-1); paper $8.95 (0-15-658575-8).** A fictional account of the meeting of German writers in Telgte near the end of the Thirty Years War to discuss the future course of German literature. (REV: CSM 5/11/81; PW 3/27/81; Time 5/18/81)

9005 Gregory, Philippa. *Favored Child.* **1990, Pocket paper $5.95 (0-671-67911-2).** A tale set in eighteenth-century England regarding the restoration of a faded estate to its prior glory. (REV: BL 7/89; LJ 7/89; PW 5/12/89)

9006 Grenville, Kate. *Joan Makes History.* **1988, British American $17.95 (0-945167-09-1).** Interwoven stories of 11 fictional female characters named Joan who played a part in historical events from the eighteenth century to the present day. (REV: LJ 11/15/88; NYTBR 12/18/88; New Yorker 3/27/89)

9007 Grumbach, Doris. *The Ladies.* **1985, Fawcett paper $3.50 (0-449-20818-4).** A story based on a true event concerning the eighteenth-century elopement of two young Irish women. "Beautiful, witty, touching."—TLS (REV: BL 10/1/84; PW 7/27/84; TLS 7/12/85)

9008 Gurganus, Allan. *Oldest Living Confederate Widow Tells All.* **1989, Knopf $21.95 (0-394-54537-0).** A 99-year-old widow of a Confederate soldier tells the story of her life and of the American South as she witnessed it. (REV: LJ 5/1/89; New Rep 10/30/89; PW 6/23/89. AWARDS: LJ, 1989; PW, 1989)

9009 Haasse, Hella S. *In a Dark Wood Wandering: A Novel of the Middle Ages.* **1989, Academy Chicago $22.95 (0-89733-336-5).** A historical novel centering on the life of French king Charles VI's nephew, poet Charles d'Orleans, during the Hundred Years' War. "Four-star historical fiction."—BL (REV: BL 8/89; LJ 9/1/89; NYTBR 12/17/89. AWARDS: BL, 1989)

9010 Haasse, Hella S. *Scarlet City: A Novel of 16th Century Italy.* **1990, Academy Chicago $22.95 (0-89733-349-7).** A portrait of political intrigue during sixteenth-century Italy between papal and resurrectional forces. "A brilliant picture of an uncertain age."—LJ (REV: BL 9/15/90; LJ 8/90)

9011 **Hall, Rodney.** *Captivity Captive.* **1988, Farrar $15.95 (0-374-11889-2); Simon & Schuster paper $7.95 (0-671-677441-2).** A novel that speculates a solution to the unsolved nineteenth-century murders of three children in Australia. "Should confirm Hall's reputation as a writer of exceptional talent."—PW (REV: LJ 1/88; NYTBR 2/14/88; PW 12/4/87)

9012 **Hall, Rodney.** *Second Bridegroom.* **1991, Farrar $19.95 (0-374-25668-3).** A story of the life of a nineteenth-century English convict sent to Australia who lives with aborigines following his escape from prison. (REV: LJ 7/91; NYTBR 9/1/91)

9013 **Halter, Marek.** *Book of Abraham.* **1987, Dell paper $4.95 (0-440-10841-1).** A history of a Jewish family and of the Jewish people from the first century A.D. to the Holocaust. (REV: BL 2/15/86; NYTBR 4/6/86; Time 5/5/86)

9014 **Hamilton-Paterson, James.** *Gerontius.* **1991, Soho Pr. $19.95 (0-939149-48-6).** This 1989 Whitbread Prize–winning novel tells the story of English composer Edward Elgar's voyage on the Amazon during the 1920s. "A literate, intelligent and entertaining work."—PW (REV: CSM 5/16/91; LJ 4/1/91; PW 1/25/91)

9015 **Hanlon, Emily.** *Petersburg.* **1988, Putnam $19.95 (0-399-13374-7); Ivy Books paper $4.95 (0-8041-0484-0).** The story of the lives and roles of four people during the 1905 St. Petersburg Revolution. (REV: LJ 8/88; PW 7/15/88)

9016 **Hareven, Shulamith.** *Miracle Hater.* **1988, North Point paper $8.95 (0-86547-329-3).** The story of a Jewish man freed from slavery by Moses who decides to live a life of solitude because he believes that the lawgiver's miracles will bring only pain and sorrow to his people. (REV: BL 3/15/88; LJ 3/15/88; PW 2/5/88. AWARDS: PW, 1988)

9017 **Harrison, Sue.** *Mother Earth Father Sky.* **1990, Doubleday $19.95 (0-385-41159-6).** A novel set in the year 7056 B.C. tracing the lives of a teenage girl and her baby brother, the sole survivors of a vicious massacre. (REV: BL 4/15/90; LJ 5/1/90; NYTBR 6/17/90)

9018 **Heller, Joseph.** *God Knows.* **1984, Knopf $19.95 (0-394-52919-7); Dell paper $5.95 (0-440-20438-0).** Fictional recollections of King David on his life and his relationship with God. (REV: NYTBR 9/23/84; PW 8/3/84; Time 9/2/84)

9019 **Heller, Joseph.** *Picture This.* **1988, Putnam $19.95 (0-399-13355-0); Ballantine paper $4.95 (0-345-35886-4).** A fictional study of the Rembrandt painting "Aristotle Contemplating the Bust of Homer" that shifts in time from seventeenth-century Europe to the era of the Greek writer. (REV: LJ 9/1/88; PW 7/1/88)

9020 **Helprin, Mark.** *Winter's Tale.* **1983, Harcourt $14.95 (0-15-197203-6); Pocket paper $4.95 (0-671-62118-1).** A portrait of New York in the twentieth century as told by an immigrant with supernatural powers who lives, dies, and is reborn in the city.

(REV: BL 8/83; CSM 9/2/83; LJ 8/83. AWARDS: ALA, 1983; BL, the 1980s)

9021 **Hersey, John.** *Antonietta.* **1991, Knopf $21.00 (0-679-40194-6).** A novel concerning the adventures of a Stradivarius violin from its construction in 1699, tracing the instrument's use by a series of famous composers over the centuries. (REV: BL 3/15/91; LJ 5/15/91; PW 3/29/91)

9022 **Hersey, John.** *The Call.* **1986, Penguin paper $8.95 (0-14-008695-1).** An account of the life of a Christian missionary in China. (REV: New Rep 5/13/85; NYRB 5/30/85; NYTBR 5/12/85)

9023 **Hofmann, Gert.** *Parable of the Blind.* **1986, Fromm International $14.95 (0-88064-051-0); paper $7.95 (0-88064-113-4).** A speculative account of the events surrounding the Breughel painting "Parable of the Blind." (REV: LJ 2/15/86; NYRB 8/14/86; NYTBR 1/26/86)

9024 **Hogan, Linda.** *Mean Spirit.* **1990, Atheneum $19.95 (0-689-12101-6).** A portrait of two Osage families in Oklahoma during the 1920s struggling to maintain Native American traditions in the twentieth century. "Makes a lasting impression."—BL (REV: BL 10/1/90; LJ 11/1/90; PW 8/3/90)

9025 **Holland, Cecelia.** *Bear Flag.* **1990, Houghton $19.95 (0-395-48886-9).** A historical novel about California and its rise to statehood following its revolt against Mexico in the mid-nineteenth century. (REV: BL 6/15/90; LJ 6/15/90; PW 4/13/90)

9026 **Holland, Cecelia.** *Pillar of the Sky.* **1985, Knopf $17.95 (0-394-53538-3).** This tale concerning an ancient English tribe proposes a solution to the mysteries of Stonehenge. (REV: BL 4/1/85; LJ 6/1/85; PW 4/19/85)

9027 **Holmes, Marjorie.** *Three from Galilee: The Young Man from Nazareth.* **1986, Bantam paper $3.50 (0-553-26166-5).** A speculative tale of the life of Christ from adolescence to the beginning of his ministry. (REV: BL 8/85; PW 6/28/85)

9028 **Holt, Victoria.** *House of a Thousand Lanterns.* **1974, Doubleday $9.95 (0-385-00817-1).** A story set in Victorian England and Hong Kong regarding the import/export business of a pair of families dealing in Chinese artworks. (REV: NYTBR 10/13/74; PW 5/13/74)

9029 **Holt, Victoria.** *India Fan.* **1988, Doubleday $18.95 (0-385-24600-5); Fawcett paper $4.95 (0-449-21697-7).** A story set during the Victorian era depicting the life of a woman who accompanies a friend and her husband to live in India. (REV: BL 8/88; LJ 8/88; NYTBR 11/6/88)

9030 **Houston, James A.** *White Dawn: An Eskimo Saga.* **1989, Harcourt paper $6.95 (0-15-696256-X).** A fictional retelling of an 1896 incident where three men were taken into a tribe of Eskimos following an Arctic shipwreck. (REV: LJ 4/1/71; NYTBR 5/16/71; Time 5/10/71. AWARDS: ALA, 1971)

9031 Howatch, Susan. *The Rich Are Different.* **1985, Fawcett paper $4.95 (0-449-20770-6).** Five characters narrate this family saga of New York financiers in this story set during the 1920s and 1930s. (REV: BL 5/1/77; LJ 3/1/77)

9032 Hrabel, Bohumil. *I Served the King of England.* **1989, Harcourt $17.95 (0-15-145745-X).** The story of Czech politics from the 1920s to the 1950s as told through the life of a waiter. By the author of *Closely Watched Trains.* (REV: LJ 4/1/89; PW 1/20/89; TLS 5/12/89)

9033 Humphrey, William. *No Resting Place.* **1989, Delacorte $18.95 (0-385-29729-7); Doubleday paper $10.95 (0-385-30079-4).** Historical fiction re-creating the early nineteenth-century forced relocation of the Cherokee nation from Georgia to Tennessee to Texas. "A beautiful story, highly recommended."— LJ (REV: LJ 5/15/89; NYTBR 6/25/89; Time 6/19/89)

9034 Ibbotson, Eva. *Madensky Square.* **1988, St. Martin's $16.95 (0-312-02246-8).** A diary of one year in the life of a dressmaker set in pre-World War I Vienna. (REV: NYTBR 1/15/89; PW 9/2/88)

9035 Jakes, John. *Heaven and Hell.* **1987, Harcourt $19.95 (0-15-131075-0); Dell paper $5.95 (0-440-20170-5).** A novel tracing the fortunes of two American families—one Northern, one Southern—in the years following the American Civil War. (REV: BL 9/15/87; LJ 11/15/87; PW 9/18/87)

9036 Jakes, John. *North and South.* **1982, Harcourt $24.95 (0-15-166998-8); Dell paper $5.95 (0-440-16205-X).** A study of two American families—one Northern, one Southern—from the 1840s to the outbreak of the Civil War. "This is historical novel writing at its best."—LJ (REV: BL 1/15/82; CSM 4/17/82; LJ 2/15/82)

9037 Jenkins, Dan. *Fast Copy.* **1988, Simon & Schuster $19.95 (0-671-60206-3); paper $5.95 (0-312-91767-8).** A newspaper tries to expose a robbery ring led by a Texas Ranger in this story set in a small town during the 1930s. (REV: BL 9/15/88; NYTBR 11/13/88; PW 9/30/88)

9038 Jennings, Gary. *Aztec.* **1981, Avon paper $4.95 (0-380-55889-0).** The story of the Aztec empire and its fall as related by a man who survived the Spanish conquest. (REV: Atl 1/81; LJ 10/15/80; NYTBR 12/14/81)

9039 Johnson, Charles. *Middle Passage.* **1990, Macmillan $17.95 (0-689-11968-2).** A recently freed slave, fleeing from a marriage prospect, accidentally stows aboard an illegal and maniacally run slave ship on its way to Africa in 1830. (REV: Choice, 1/91; LJ 5/1/90; PW 4/6/90. AWARDS: LJ, 1990; NBA, 1990; PW, 1990)

9040 Jones, Douglas C. *Come Winter.* **1989, Henry Holt $19.95 (0-8050-0944-2).** The life of a family in a small west Arkansas town from the end of the Civil War to the end of the nineteenth century. (REV: BL 9/15/89; LJ 9/1/89; PW 8/11/89)

9041 Jones, Douglas C. *Remember Santiago.* **1988, Henry Holt $19.95 (0-8050-0776-8).** A tale of the Spanish-American War, tracing the adventures of a group of Americans who served in the conflict. (REV: BL 10/15/88; PW 9/2/88)

9042 Jones, Rod. *Julia Paradise.* **1989, Penguin paper $6.95 (0-14-010077-6).** An Australian novelist's tale of Westerners in China during the 1920s focuses on the relationship between a missionary's daughter and her psychoanalyst. "There are no flaws in this tour de force, which on a second reading maintains its mesmerizing effect."— Newsweek (REV: Newsweek 12/7/87; PW 7/24/87; TLS 2/26/88)

9043 Jong, Erica. *Fanny: Being the True Adventures of Fanny Hackabout-Jones.* **1981, NAL paper $4.95 (0-451-15890-3).** The fictional memoirs of the eighteenth-century London prostitute Fanny Hill. (REV: LJ 7/80; NYTBR 8/17/80; PW 6/20/80)

9044 Jong, Erica. *Serenissima: A Novel of Venice.* **1988, Dell paper $4.95 (0-440-20104-7).** A contemporary actress transported in time to the sixteenth century to perform *The Merchant of Venice* opposite Shakespeare falls in love with the Bard himself. (REV: LJ 4/15/87; TLS 9/18/87)

9045 Kaye, M. M. *Far Pavilions.* **1978, St. Martin's. $12.95 (0-312-28259-1); Bantam paper $4.95 (0-553-22797-1).** A story of life in nineteenth-century India as seen by a British orphan raised as a servant in a rajah's palace. (REV: LJ 11/1/78; NYTBR 11/2/78; New Yorker 10/9/78)

9046 Keillor, Garrison. *WLT: A Radio Romance.* **1991, Viking $19.95 (0-670-81857-7).** The story of a pair of Minnesota brothers who founded a radio station during the 1920s and their careers prior to the rise of television. (REV: BL 9/15/91; PW 8/23/91. AWARDS: BL, 1991)

9047 Keneally, Thomas. *Chant of Jimmy Blacksmith.* **1983, Penguin paper $6.95 (0-14-006973-9).** A fictional study of a series of nineteenth-century Australian ax murders of colonists committed by an Aborigine. (REV: BL 10/1/72; PW 7/3/72; Time 8/28/72)

9048 Keneally, Thomas. *Playmaker.* **1988, Harper & Row paper $8.95 (0-06-097189-4).** The story of the performance of an eighteenth-century English play by actors recruited from an Australian penal colony to celebrate the birthday of the king. (REV: BL 9/15/87; LJ 9/15/87; PW 8/7/87)

9049 Kennedy, William P. *Billy Phelan's Greatest Game.* **1983, Penguin paper $7.95 (0-14-006340-4).** A gambler leads the search for a kidnapped politician's son in this novel set in Albany during the 1930s. "Hard to resist."—Atl (REV: Atl 6/78; PW 3/13/78; Sat Rev 4/29/78)

9050 Kennedy, William P. *Quinn's Book.* **1989, Penguin paper $8.95 (0-14-007737-5).** A journalist's memoirs of his youth in Albany, New York, during the middle of the nineteenth century. "An important work of fiction."—LJ (REV: LJ 4/1/88; NYTBR 5/22/88; Time 3/16/88. AWARDS: LJ, 1988)

9051 Kinstler, Clysta. *Moon Under Her Feet.* **1989, Harper & Row $17.95 (0-06-250466-5).** This alternate feminist history of the life of Christ finds him the husband of Mary Magdalene and father of her child. (REV: NYTBR 7/9/89; PW 5/5/89)

9052 Konwicki, Tadeusz. *Bohin Manor.* **1990, Farrar $18.95 (0-374-11523-0).** The life of a nineteenth-century Lithuanian woman who marries a neighbor out of fear of becoming a spinster. "An exquisite and insightful fable."—BL (REV: BL 6/1/90; LJ 6/15/90; NYBR 7/19/90)

9053 Kubicki, Jan. *Breaker Boys.* **1987, Atlantic Monthly $17.95 (0-87113-112-9).** A story of turn-of-the-century labor organizer Mother Jones and her efforts to gain better working conditions for Pennsylvania miners. (REV: LJ 2/1/87; PW 12/5/86)

9054 Kunstler, James Howard. *An Embarrassment of Riches.* **1988, Tor paper $3.95 (0-8125-8498-8).** A chronicle of the adventures and experiences of a botanist sent by Thomas Jefferson to explore the American wilderness. (REV: BL 5/15/85; 6/1/85; PW 4/19/85)

9055 Kurten, Bjorn. *Dance of the Tiger: A Novel of the Ice Age.* **1980, Pantheon $10.95 (0-394-51267-7).** A paleontologist's tale of warring Scandinavian Neanderthal and Cro-Magnon groups with an introduction by Stephen Jay Gould. (REV: LJ 1/1/81; NYTBR 10/26/80; PW 8/15/80)

9056 Kurten, Bjorn. *Singletusk: A Novel of the Ice Age.* **1986, Pantheon $14.95 (0-394-55352-7).** This sequel to the author's *Dance of the Tiger* presents a paleontologist's speculative view of the relations between Cro-Magnon and Neanderthal man. (REV: BL 8/86; LJ 7/86; PW 6/20/86)

9057 Larsen, Jeanne. *Silk Road: A Novel of Eighth-Century China.* **1989, Henry Holt $19.95 (0-8050-0958-2); Fawcett paper $9.95 (0-449-90523-3).** The debut novel by a Chinese literature scholar about the life of a slave girl in eighth-century China. (REV: LJ 5/1/89; NYTBR 9/10/89; PW 5/26/89)

9058 Lauterstein, Ingeborg. *Water Castle.* **1981, Houghton $12.95 (0-395-29471-1).** This debut novel portrays the life of a wealthy Austrian family during the late 1930s. (REV: BL 1/15/81; LJ 3/15/81; NYTBR 1/25/81)

9059 Levi, Jean. *Chinese Emperor.* **1987, Harcourt $18.95 (0-15-117649-3); Random paper $8.95 (0-394-75996-6).** A fictionalized history of China in the third century B.C. focusing on the rise and fall of the Qin Dynasty. (REV: BL 10/15/87; NYTBR 10/4/87; PW 9/11/87)

9060 Levi, Primo. *If Not Now, When?* **1986, Penguin paper $8.95 (0-14-008497-4).** The story of an Eastern European group of Jews struggling to survive in a forest against Nazi oppression, who use their dreams of an independent Israel for inspiration. (REV: Choice 10/85; Newsweek 5/6/85; PW 2/22/85. AWARDS: PW, 1985)

9061 Lincoln, C. Eric. *The Avenue, Clayton City.* **1988, Morrow $17.95 (0-688-07702-1); Ballantine paper $3.95 (0-345-36034-6).** The story of race rela-

tions among working-class citizens in a small Southern town during the 1930s. (REV: BL 2/15/88; CSM 6/16/88; LJ 3/1/88)

9062 Lindgren, Torgny. *Bathsheba.* **1989, Harper & Row $17.95 (0-06-015963-4).** A Swedish writer retells the story of David and Bathsheba in this novel originally written in 1984. (REV: LJ 5/15/89; PW 3/17/89; TLS 7/14/89)

9063 Littell, Robert. *Revolutionist.* **1988, Bantam $18.95 (0-553-05260-8).** The story of a Russian-American who participates in the Revolution and becomes a confidant of Josef Stalin. (REV: BL 2/1/88; LJ 5/1/88; PW 4/22/88)

9064 Llywelyn, Morgan. *Druids.* **1990, Morrow $20.00 (0-688-08819-8).** A fictional re-creation of the first-century wars between Celtic and Roman forces in Gaul. (REV: BL 12/1/90; LJ 1/91; PW 12/21/90)

9065 Loy, Rosetta. *Dust Roads of Monferrato.* **1991, Knopf $20.00 (0-394-58849-5).** A novel tracing the history of an Italian family beginning in the later years of the eighteenth century. (REV: BL 3/1/91; PW 2/8/91; TLS 11/9/90)

9066 Lurie, Alison. *Only Children.* **1990, Avon paper $7.95 (0-380-70875-2).** A study of the events of a depression-era Independence Day weekend in the Catskills during the stay of two couples and their children at a schoolmaster's farm. "A funny, enchanting novel."—CSM (REV: CSM 5/14/79; PW 3/12/79; Time 6/11/79)

9067 Maalouf, Amin. *Leo Africanus.* **1989, Norton $17.95 (0-393-02630-2).** A story set during the fourteenth and fifteenth centuries regarding a Moorish man's life in exile in Europe and North Africa following his expulsion from Spain. (REV: CSM 7/24/89; LJ 1/89; PW 10/21/88)

9068 McCarry, Charles. *Bride of the Wilderness.* **1989, NAL paper $4.95 (0-451-15958-6).** A novel set in the eighteenth century depicting the adventures of an English colonist who travels to New England to claim an inheritance and there begins a romance with a French soldier. (REV: BL 6/15/88; NYTBR 4/23/89; PW 6/3/88)

9069 McCullough, Colleen. *First Man in Rome.* **1990, Morrow $22.95 (0-688-09368-X).** The story of the life of a Roman politician who serves as consul for six terms just prior to the fall of the Republic. "McCullough's massive work will mesmerize motivated readers."—BL (REV: BL 8/90; LJ 9/15/90; Time 10/15/90)

9070 MacDonald, Malcolm. *A Notorious Woman.* **1989, St. Martin's $22.95 (0-312-02623-4).** The story of a young Victorian English woman who becomes impregnated by her lover, and unknowingly travels to America carrying his child. "Splendid historical fiction from a master of the genre."—BL (REV: BL 3/1/89; LJ 2/15/89; PW 1/13/89)

9071 Mackin, Jeanne. *Frenchwoman.* **1989, St. Martin's $18.95 (0-312-03346-X).** The story of a seamstress set in late eighteenth- and early nineteenth-century France and America. "Well written and entirely believable."—LJ (Rev: BL 11/1/89; LJ 12/89; PW 10/13/89)

9072 McMahon, Thomas. *Loving Little Egypt.* **1987, Viking $16.95 (0-670-81228-5); Penguin paper $6.95 (0-14-009331-1).** A visually impaired scientist invents a special communication system for the blind in this novel set during the 1920s. "An intriguing and enjoyable romp."—LJ (Rev: LJ 2/1/87; PW 12/12/86. Awards: ALA, 1987)

9073 McMahon, Thomas. *McKay's Bees.* **1986, Avon paper $2.75 (0-380-53579-3).** As the outbreak of the American Civil War threatens, a group of Bostonians move to the Kansas frontier to raise bees. (Rev: BL 9/1/79; CSM 8/15/79; Time 10/8/79)

9074 McMahon, Thomas. *Principles of American Nuclear Chemistry.* **1981, Avon paper $2.95 (0-380-54122-X).** The story of the development of the atomic bomb in Los Alamos, New Mexico, as narrated by a physicist's sons. (Rev: BL 10/1/70; PW 5/18/70; Time 8/24/70)

9075 McPherson, William. *Testing the Current.* **1987, Pocket paper $6.95 (0-671-64404-1).** A chronicle of the observations of an American youth during the Great Depression. (Rev: New Rep 4/30/84; NYTBR 3/18/84; Newsweek 5/14/84)

9076 Mahfouz, Naguib. *Palace of Desire.* **1991, Doubleday $22.95 (0-385-26467-4).** This second volume of the author's Cairo Trilogy is set during the 1920s and portrays a middle-aged man reentering society following a self-imposed period of penance. (Rev: BL 12/1/90; LJ 1/91; NYTBR 1/20/91)

9077 Mahfouz, Naguib. *Palace Walk.* **1990, Doubleday $22.95 (0-385-26465-8).** This study of an Egyptian merchant's family during the early 1940s is the first volume of the author's Cairo Trilogy. (Rev: BL 11/15/89; LJ 12/89; NYTBR 2/4/90. Awards: ALA, 1990)

9078 Mailer, Norman. *Ancient Evenings.* **1983, Little, Brown $19.95 (0-316-54410-8); Warner paper $5.95 (0-446-35769-3).** A portrayal of daily life in ancient Egypt as told through the four reincarnations of Menenhetet. (Rev: BL 3/1/83; LJ 4/1/83; Newsweek 4/18/83)

9079 Malamud, Bernard. *The Fixer.* **1989, Pocket paper $4.95 (0-671-69851-6).** A fictional retelling of the historical trial of a Russian Jew accused of the murder of a child in 1911. (Rev: BL 10/15/66; CSM 9/8/66; NYTBR 9/4/66. Awards: ALA, 1966; NBA, 1967; NYTBR, 1966; PP:Fiction, 1967)

9080 Marius, Richard. *The Coming of Rain.* **1991, Rutledge Hill paper $12.95 (1-55853-142-4).** A debut novel portraying the lives of the inhabitants of a Tennessee community in the aftermath of the Civil War. (Rev: Choice 5/70; LJ 9/1/69)

9081 Marks, Peter. *Skullduggery.* **1987, Carroll & Graf $17.95 (0-88184-319-9).** A fictional account of the 1912 anthropology scandal involving Piltdown man and its resolution four decades later. (Rev: BL 8/87; PW 6/26/87)

9082 Markus, Julia. *Uncle.* **1987, Dell paper $3.95 (0-440-39187-3).** A portrait of a Jewish family in New Jersey during the depression that focuses on the lives of a young woman and her uncle. "Brilliant . . . a novel that should renew faith in the vitality of contemporary fiction."—Choice (Rev: Choice 3/79; CSM 3/79; LJ 9/15/78)

9083 Martin, Valerie. *Mary Reilly.* **1990, Doubleday $18.95 (0-385-24968-3).** A diary recording the experiences of a servant who lived in the same house as the legendary Dr. Jekyll. (Rev: BL 12/1/89; NYTBR 2/4/90; PW 12/8/89. Awards: BL, 1990)

9084 Martinez, Tomas Eloy. *Perón Novel.* **1988, Pantheon $19.95 (0-394-55838-3); Random paper $10.95 (0-679-72279-3).** A historical novel recounting the events leading to the return of Juan Perón from exile in Spain to his native Argentina. (Rev: BL 3/15/88; CSM 5/6/88; LJ 4/15/88)

9085 Mattiessen, Peter. *Killing Mister Watson.* **1990, Random $21.95 (0-394-55400-0).** A study of the life and murder of a legendary Florida gunman. "An important and provocative book."—LJ (Rev: BL 4/15/90; LJ 6/1/90; NYTBR 6/24/90)

9086 Mehta, Gita. *Raj.* **1989, Simon & Schuster $19.95 (0-671-43248-6).** A chronicle of life in a small Indian principality from the end of the reign of Queen Victoria to the mid-twentieth century. (Rev: BL 3/1/89; NYRB 5/18/89; NYTBR 4/9/89)

9087 Michener, James A. *Alaska.* **1988, Random $22.50 (0-394-55154-0); Fawcett paper $6.95 (0-449-21726-4).** A fictionalized history of Alaska from its early geological development to the twentieth century. (Rev: BL 5/15/88; CSM 7/27/88)

9088 Michener, James A. *Caribbean.* **1989, Random $22.95 (0-394-56561-4).** A fictional history of the Caribbean from prehistoric times to the twentieth century by the author of *Texas* and *Space.* (Rev: BL 9/1/89; PW 9/29/89)

9089 Michener, James A. *Centennial.* **1974, Random $35.00 (0-394-47970-X); Fawcett paper $5.95 (0-449-44522-4).** The story of a Colorado town named Centennial, tracing its history from prehistoric times to the 1970s. "A fascinating blend of history and fiction."—PW (Rev: CSM 9/25/74; LJ 9/1/74; PW 7/8/74)

9090 Michener, James A. *Chesapeake.* **1978, Random $39.95 (0-394-50079-2); Fawcett paper $5.95 (0-449-21158-4).** A history of the Chesapeake Bay region from the sixteenth to the twentieth century as reflected through the lives of four families. (Rev: BL 7/15/78; CSM 9/18/78; LJ 7/78)

9091 Michener, James A. *Covenant.* **1981, Random $17.95 (0-394-50505-0); Fawcett paper $5.95 (0-449-44523-2).** A fictionalized history of South Africa from prehistoric times to the present. (Rev: BL 9/1/80; CSM 11/10/80; PW 10/3/80)

9092 Michener, James A. *Journey.* **1989, Random $16.95 (0-394-57826-0).** A tale of a failed nineteenth-century British expedition to the gold fields of the Yukon. (Rev: BL 4/1/89; PW 5/12/89)

9093 **Michener, James A.** *Poland.* **1983, Random $17.95 (0-394-53189-2); Fawcett paper $6.95 (0-449-20587-8).** A survey of Polish history as told through the lives of three families from the thirteenth to the twentieth century. (Rev: CSM 9/14/83; LJ 9/1/83; Natl Rev 11/11/83)

9094 **Michener, James A.** *Texas.* **1986, Univ. of Texas Pr. $125.00 (0-292-78071-0); Fawcett paper $6.95 (0-449-21092-8).** A fictional treatment of the history of Texas as reported by a special governor's committee appointed to investigate the state's past. (Rev: BL 9/15/85; LJ 10/15/85; Newsweek 9/23/85)

9095 **Milosz, Czeslaw.** *Issa Valley.* **1981, Farrar $13.95 (0-374-17798-8); paper $9.95 (0-374-51695-2).** A young boy presents his account of the events that led to the independence of Lithuania following the conclusion of the First World War. (Rev: LJ 8/81; PW 4/17/81; TLS 7/24/81)

9096 **Mishima, Yukio.** *Spring Snow.* **1990, Random paper $10.95 (0-679-72241-6).** The first volume of the author's Sea of Fertility series about an early twentieth-century love affair between a young man and the fiancée of a prince. "A rare and beautiful novel."—PW (Rev: BL 9/1/72; CSM 6/14/72; PW 5/22/72)

9097 **Moravia, Alberto.** *1934.* **1983, Farrar $14.50 (0-374-22254-1).** In this novel by the author of *Time of Desecration*, an Italian scholar considers suicide as the world falls into fascism. "A deep, disturbing, lovely and very remarkable book."—BL (Rev: BL 12/1/82; LJ 3/1/83; Time 5/30/83)

9098 **Morrison, Toni.** *Beloved.* **1987, Knopf $18.95 (0-394-53597-9); NAL paper $9.95 (0-452-26446-4).** A portrait of the lives of former slaves in Reconstruction-era Ohio. (Rev: BL 7/87; LJ 9/1/87; NYTBR 9/13/87. Awards: ALA, 1987; BL, the 1980s; LJ, 1987; NYTBR, 1987; PP:Fiction, 1988; PW, 1987)

9099 **Morrison, Toni.** *Song of Solomon.* **1977, Knopf $22.50 (0-394-49784-8); NAL paper $8.95 (0-452-26011-6).** This story of a Michigan African-American family traces the life of a son from his birth during the depression in a tale of discovery of his family's past and of his self. (Rev: LJ 9/1/77; NYTBR 9/11/77; Time 9/12/77. Awards: ALA, 1977; NYTBR, 1977; Time, 1977)

9100 **Mosley, Nicholas.** *Hopeful Monsters.* **1991, Dalkey Arch. $21.95 (0-916583-85-6).** This overview of twentieth-century science and philosophy, as told through the life and letters of a physicist and his wife, contains fictional portraits of Brecht, Einstein, and Wittgenstein. (Rev: LJ 8/91; PW 9/20/91. Awards: LJ, 1991)

9101 **Munif, Abdelrahman.** *Cities of Salt.* **1989, Random paper $12.95 (0-394-75526-X).** A study of the effects of oil on a fictional Arab emirate during the 1920s. (Rev: CSM 9/2/88; LJ 3/15/88; TLS 3/3/89)

9102 **Munif, Abdelrahman.** *The Trench.* **1991, Pantheon $25.00 (0-394-57672-1).** The second volume of the Jordanian writer's Cities of Salt trilogy portraying the life of a doctor's family in a small Persian Gulf city during the 1930s. (Rev: BL 11/1/91; NYTBR 11/3/91)

9103 **Murray, Albert.** *Train Whistle Guitar.* **1989, Northeastern Univ. Pr. paper $10.95 (1-55553-051-6).** A portrait of the lives of two young black men growing up in rural Alabama during the 1920s. (Rev: Choice 7–8/74; CSM 4/10/74; LJ 8/74)

9104 **Naylor, Gloria.** *Mama Day.* **1988, Ticknor & Fields $17.95 (0-89919-716-7); Random paper $9.95 (0-679-72181-9).** A tale of African-American life on a South Carolina island over the past three centuries. "Funny and entertaining, evocative and powerful."—TLS (Rev: BL 12/15/87; PW 12/18/87; TLS 6/3/88. Awards: ALA, 1988)

9105 **Neville, Katherine.** *The Eight.* **1990, Ballantine paper $5.95 (0-345-36623-9).** A story of the efforts of a series of individuals throughout history to solve a puzzling code contained in a medieval chess set. (Rev: BL 2/15/89; LJ 3/1/89; PW 11/4/88)

9106 **New, Christopher.** *Shanghai.* **1986, Bantam paper $4.50 (0-553-25781-1).** This story of a British customs agent in Shanghai traces the history of the city from the early twentieth century to the Japanese occupation. (Rev: BL 5/1/85; LJ 6/1/85)

9107 **Nissenson, Hugh.** *Tree of Life.* **1985, Harper & Row $15.95 (0-06-015143-9).** A journal of a widower minister raising a family on an early nineteenth-century Ohio farm. (Rev: BL 10/1/85; PW 8/16/85; Time 10/21/85. Awards: PW, 1985; Time, 1985)

9108 **Norman, Hilary.** *Chateau Ella.* **1988, Dell $19.95 (0-440-50018-4); paper $4.95 (0-440-20040-7).** The story of a Hungarian Jewish woman and her family spanning from World War I Europe to contemporary New York. "A well told, absorbing tale."—LJ (Rev: BL 10/15/88; LJ 10/15/88; PW 8/26/88)

9109 **Oates, Joyce Carol.** *Bellefleur.* **1990, Dutton paper $11.95 (0-525-48567-8).** This novel by the author of *Them* traces the family history of French aristocrats living in New York over six generations. (Rev: CSM 9/8/80; LJ 7/80; Time 8/25/80)

9110 **O'Brian, Patrick.** *Letter of Marque.* **1990, Norton $18.95 (0-393-02874-7).** The captain of a private vessel is given permission by the British navy to attack English enemies at sea in this early nineteenth-century tale. (Rev: LJ 8/90; PW 7/6/90)

9111 **O'Faolain, Julia.** *No Country for Young Men.* **1986, Carroll & Graf $19.50 (0-88184-297-4).** An Irish nun forced to leave her convent and an Irish American who returns to the home of his ancestors form the basis for this look at Irish history from the 1920s to the 1980s. (Rev: BL 12/1/86; LJ 1/87; New Yorker 3/16/86)

9112 **Ondaatje, Michael.** *In the Skin of a Lion.* **1987, Knopf $16.95 (0-394-56363-8); Penguin paper $7.95 (0-14-011309-6).** A portrait of life in underclass Toronto during the 1920s and 1930s. "Does for Toronto what Joyce did for Dublin . . . a powerful and revelatory accomplishment."—TLS (Rev: LJ 9/1/87; PW 7/31/87; TLS 9/4/87. Awards: LJ, 1987)

9113 Ouologuem, Yambo. *Bound to Violence.* 1971, Heinemann paper $8.00 (0-435-90099-4). A writer from Mali traces the history of a fictional African nation from the early thirteenth century to the aftermath of World War II. (REV: BL 9/1/71; NYTBR 3/7/71; Time 3/15/71. AWARDS: ALA, 1971; NYTBR, 1971; Time, 1971)

9114 Palliser, Charles. *Quincunx.* 1990, Ballantine $25.00 (0-345-35463-5). This revival of a Victorian novel is set in early nineteenth-century England and explores the search of a fatherless boy for his self-identity. (REV: LJ 12/89; NYTBR 3/4/90; Time 1/29/90. AWARDS: Time, 1990)

9115 Pamuk, Orhan. *White Castle.* 1991, Braziller $17.50 (0-8076-1264-2). A Turkish novelist's story of a seventeenth-century Italian slave captured by Turks and forcibly brought to Istanbul. (REV: CSM 4/12/91; PW 2/22/91; TLS 10/12/90)

9116 Parini, Jay. *Patch Boys.* 1988, Henry Holt paper $8.95 (0-8050-0770-9). A depiction of the life of Italian-American teenagers in a Pennsylvania mining town during the summer of 1925. (REV: BL 10/1/86; LJ 11/1/86; PW 9/5/86)

9117 Pavic, Milorad. *Dictionary of the Khazars: A Lexicon Novel in 100,000 Words.* 1988, Knopf $19.95 (0-318-33404-6); Random paper $9.95 (0-679-72461-3). A Yugoslavian novel, which is available in both "male" and "female" editions, tracing the history of the fictional seventh-century tribe of the Khazars. (REV: BL 10/15/88; LJ 11/15/88; NYTBR 11/20/88. AWARDS: NYTBR, 1988)

9118 Peck, Robert Norton. *Hallapoosa.* 1988, Walker $16.95 (0-8027-1016-6). Set in depression-era Florida, this is the story of two youngsters who are sent to live with their uncle following the deaths of their parents. (REV: LJ 5/15/88; PW 4/1/88)

9119 Penman, Sharon K. *Falls the Shadow.* 1988, Henry Holt $19.95 (0-8050-0300-2); Ballantine paper $10.95 (0-345-36033-8). A historically based story of a thirteenth-century earl who sought to limit the powers of English king Henry III. "Thoroughly engrossing."—PW (REV: BL 3/15/88; LJ 7/88; PW 4/8/88)

9120 Penman, Sharon K. *Sunne in Splendour.* 1990, Ballantine paper $12.95 (0-345-36313-2). A portrait of fifteenth-century England during the Wars of the Roses with portrayals of kings Richard III and Henry VII. "A historical novel of the first rank."—PW (REV: BL 8/82; LJ 9/1/82; NYTBR 12/19/82)

9121 Perutz, Leo. *By Night Under the Stone Bridge.* 1990, Arcade $18.95 (1-55970-055-6). A tale of the late sixteenth-century war between Austria and Bohemia as viewed by a Czech-Austrian writer. (REV: Atl 6/90; LJ 3/1/90; NYTBR 5/27/90)

9122 Phillips, Caryl. *Cambridge.* 1991, Knopf $19.95 (0-679-40532-1). A portrait of Caribbean slave life during the nineteenth century, as told through the voices of an African man and a young English woman. (REV: BL 1/1/92; LJ 2/1/92; PW 12/13/91)

9123 Pilpel, Robert H. *Between Eternities.* 1985, Harcourt $19.95 (0-15-111928-7). Life in second-century Rome as revealed through the fictional memoirs of Lucius the Swift, friend of Marcus Aurelius. (REV: LJ 10/15/85; PW 9/27/85)

9124 Potok, Chaim. *Davita's Harp.* 1985, Knopf $16.95 (0-394-54290-8); Fawcett paper $4.95 (0-449-20775-7). A story of a depression-era Jewish-American couple who embrace Communism and the effects their political beliefs have upon their daughter. (REV: BL 12/15/84; NYTBR 3/31/85; PW 1/4/85)

9125 Potok, Chaim. *In the Beginning.* 1986, Fawcett paper $4.95 (0-449-20911-3). An Orthodox Jewish son of Polish immigrants studies doctrinal teachings in the Bronx during the 1930s in his quest to become a theologian. (REV: LJ 10/15/75; New Yorker 11/17/75; Time 11/3/75)

9126 Price, Reynolds. *Surface of Earth.* 1989, Ballantine paper $4.95 (0-345-34994-6). A story chronicling three generations of two Southern families from 1903 to 1944. (REV: BL 9/15/75; New Yorker 10/13/75; PW 5/26/75)

9127 Pym, Barbara. *Crampton Hodnet.* 1986, NAL paper $8.95 (0-452-25816-2). This study of two couples in Oxford during the 1930s was written in 1939 by Pym at the age of 16. (REV: BL 4/1/85; CSM 6/7/85; Time 6/24/85)

9128 Ransmayr, Christopher. *Last World: A Novel with an Ovidian Repertory.* 1990, Grove-Weidenfeld $18.95 (0-8021-1167-X). An admirer of the Roman poet Ovid visits him at his place of exile on the Black Sea. (REV: BL 2/15/90; NYTBR 5/27/90; PW 2/2/90. AWARDS: BL, 1990)

9129 Rattray, Everett T. *Adventures of Jeremiah Dimon: A Novel of Old East Hampton.* 1985, Pushcart Pr. $17.95 (0-916366-34-0). A nineteenth-century New York teenager runs away to the Caribbean on a voyage of discovery and returns later to his home in the Hamptons. (REV: LJ 8/85; PW 6/14/85)

9130 Reed, Ishmael. *Flight to Canada.* 1989, Macmillan paper $8.95 (0-689-70733-9). A story of a slave who escapes to freedom in Canada during the American Civil War. (REV: BL 9/15/76; LJ 8/76; Sat Rev 10/2/76)

9131 Renault, Mary. *Mask of Apollo.* 1988, Random paper $6.95 (0-394-75105-1). The adventures of an actor in Ancient Greece. (REV: BL 10/15/66; LJ 9/1/66; Sat Rev 10/1/66)

9132 Renault, Mary. *Persian Boy.* 1972, Pantheon $15.95 (0-394-48191-7); Random paper $6.95 (0-394-75101-9). Alexander the Great's personal eunuch traces the life of the conquerer from his mid-twenties to his death. (REV: Atl 12/72; LJ 10/15/72; Sat Rev 12/9/72)

9133 Rhys, Jean. *Good Morning, Midnight.* 1986, Norton $7.95 (0-393-30394-2). This story, chronicling the lives of a group of expatriates living in Paris during the 1930s, was first published in England in

1939. "A classic, as alive today as when it was written."—NYTBR (Rev: New Rep 7/4/70; NYTBR 3/22/70; PW 1/26/70)

9134 Rice, Anne. *Cry to Heaven.* **1988, Windsor paper $4.95 (1-55817-105-3).** An eighteenth-century Italian tale tracing the life of a young man castrated as a teenager to increase his vocal capabilities. (Rev: BL 6/15/82; LJ 8/82; PW 6/18/82)

9135 Rice, Anne. *Feast of All Saints.* **1986, Ballantine paper $5.95 (0-345-33453-1).** A portrait of antebellum New Orleans society and its intricate racially based class system. "A fascinating glimpse into a little known and intriguing segment of American history."—LJ (Rev: BL 1/15/80; LJ 1/15/80; PW 11/26/79)

9136 Richler, Mordecai. *Solomon Gursky Was Here.* **1990, Knopf $19.95 (0-394-53995-8).** A novel tracing the exploits of the unwitting explorer Ephraim Gursky and his offspring from the early nineteenth century through the 1980s. "His best novel yet. Essential."—LJ (Rev: BL 2/15/90; LJ 4/1/90; Time 5/14/90. Awards: PW, 1990)

9137 Riley, Judith Merkle. *A Vision of Light.* **1989, Delacorte $19.95 (0-440-50109-1).** A tale of a fourteenth-century English midwife and doctor as recorded by a monk. (Rev: BL 11/1/88; LJ 1/89; PW 11/18/88)

9138 Robson, Lucia St. Clair. *Tokaido Road: A Novel of Feudal Japan.* **1991, Ballantine $19.95 (0-345-37026-0).** A historical novel set in eighteenth-century Japan depicting the efforts of a young woman to avenge the forced suicide of her father. (Rev: BL 4/1/91; LJ 2/15/91)

9139 Roesch, E. P. *Ashana.* **1990, Random $19.95 (0-394-56963-6).** A tale of an eighteenth-century Alaskan woman abducted by Russian fur traders. (Rev: BL 8/90; LJ 6/90; PW 7/13/90)

9140 Rooke, Leon. *Shakespeare's Dog.* **1986, Ecco Pr. paper $8.50 (0-88001-093-2).** A story of the lives of Shakespeare and Anne Hathaway as witnessed and narrated by their dog. "A delightfully vivid portrait, coursing with life."—LJ (Rev: BL 6/1/83; LJ 5/1/83; PW 3/11/83)

9141 Rossner, Judith. *Emmeline.* **1984, Pocket paper $3.95 (0-671-52785-1).** A nineteenth-century American teenage farm girl is forced to leave home to work in a factory. "Rossner has never been better: a stunning, haunting book."—LJ (Rev: LJ 9/1/80; Newsweek 9/29/80; PW 7/25/80)

9142 Roth, Joseph. *Emperor's Tomb.* **1984, Overlook $22.50 (0-87951-985-1).** The first English translation of the Austrian novelist's work concerning that nation's history from the collapse of the Austro-Hungarian Empire to the 1938 Anschluss. (Rev: LJ 10/1/84; PW 8/17/84)

9143 Rutherford, Edward. *Sarum: The Novel of England.* **1990, Outlet Book $5.99 (0-517-03389-5).** A fictional tracing of the history of Salisbury, England, from prehistoric times through the twentieth century. (Rev: CSM 10/2/87; LJ 9/15/87; NYTBR 9/13/87)

9144 Rybakov, Anatoli. *Children of the Arbat.* **1988, Little, Brown $19.95 (0-316-76372-1); Dell paper $4.95 (0-440-20353-8).** A study of the lives of several young Moscow citizens during the Stalinist purges of the 1930s. (Rev: Atl 6/88; New Rep 5/23/88; Time 6/6/88)

9145 Safire, William. *Freedom.* **1987, Doubleday $24.95 (0-385-15903-X); Avon paper $5.95 (0-380-70584-2).** An examination of Lincoln's first year and a half in office with 100 pages discussing the historical basis for the novel. "One of the very few truly significant Civil War novels."—LJ (Rev: CSM 9/4/87; LJ 8/87; PW 7/10/87)

9146 Santmyer, Helen Hooven. *"... And Ladies of the Club."* **1988, Putnam $19.95 (0-399-12965-0); Berkley paper $7.95 (0-425-10243-2).** This story, about a group of Ohio women who form a literary club, traces their lives from 1868 to 1932. (Rev: BL 4/15/84; LJ 5/15/84; Natl Rev 10/5/84)

9147 Saramago, Jose. *Baltasar and Bimunda.* **1987, Harcourt $17.95 (0-15-110555-3).** A Portuguese writer's story of an eighteenth-century scheme to construct a flying machine. (Rev: NYTBR 11/1/87; PW 10/9/87; TLS 3/18/88)

9148 Savage, Thomas. *Corner of Rife and Pacific.* **1988, Morrow $16.95 (0-688-07092-2); Penguin paper $7.95 (0-14-013279-1).** An early twentieth-century Montana ranching community is portrayed through the life of one of the town's founders and his family. (Rev: BL 7/88; LJ 8/88; PW 5/20/88. Awards: PW, 1988)

9149 Schaeffer, Susan Fromberg. *Madness of a Seduced Woman.* **1984, Bantam paper $5.50 (0-553-24112-5).** The story of an early twentieth-century woman who finds that her lover is engaged to another and whose rage leads her to murder him. (Rev: LJ 3/15/83; NYTBR 5/22/83; PW 2/25/83)

9150 Sennett, Richard. *Palais-Royal.* **1986, Knopf $17.95 (0-394-54538-9).** Letters between the two sons of a London architect provide a portrait of life in England and France during the 1830s and 1840s. (Rev: BL 12/15/86; LJ 12/86; PW 11/7/86)

9151 Settle, Mary Lee. *Scapegoat.* **1980, Random $11.95 (0-394-50477-1); Macmillan paper $9.95 (0-684-18848-1).** A coal miner's strike goes awry in West Virginia in this novel set in 1912 by the author of *Blood Tie.* (Rev: BL 9/1/80; LJ 9/15/80; PW 8/15/90)

9152 Seymour, Arabella. *A Passion in the Blood.* **1986, Warner paper $3.50 (0-446-30153-1).** The story of a nineteenth-century woman who inherits a fortune and enters the male-dominated world of horse breeding and racing. (Rev: LJ 10/1/85; PW 8/23/85)

9153 Shaara, Michael. *The Killer Angels: A Novel about the Four Days at Gettysburg.* **1974, McKay $19.95 (0-679-50466-4); Ballantine paper $5.95 (0-345-34810-9).** A fictional re-creation of the Battle of

Gettysburg based on the historical record. (REV: LJ 9/1/74; NYTBR 10/20/74; PW 7/8/74. AWARDS: PP:Fiction, 1975)

9154   Shadbolt, Maurice. *Season of the Jew.* **1989, Godine paper $10.95 (0-87923-753-8).** A fictional account of a nineteenth-century Maori uprising in New Zealand. "A vital, moving, richly detailed sharing of feelings about humanity and inhumanity."—BL (REV: BL 5/1/87; Choice 10/87; LJ 5/15/87)

9155   Sher, Anthony. *Middlepost.* **1989, Knopf $19.95 (0-394-57436-2).** A Yiddish-speaking Lithuanian Jew is forced to leave his country and emigrates to South Africa in this novel set at the beginning of the twentieth century. (REV: BL 4/15/89; LJ 4/1/89; TLS 9/30/88)

9156   Shreve, Susan Richards. *A Country of Strangers.* **1990, Doubleday paper $8.95 (0-385-26775-4).** A novel set in the early 1940s examining race relations in Virginia on an estate formerly run by sharecroppers. (REV: BL 1/1/89; LJ 1/89; TLS 11/24/89)

9157   Sienkiewicz, Henryk. *With Fire and Sword.* **1991, Hippocrene $24.95 (0-87052-974-9).** The first English-language translation of the initial volume of the Polish author's trilogy depicting life in that nation in the seventeenth century. "Will take its place beside such works as *The Iliad* as one of the great pieces of epic literature."—LJ (REV: BL 5/1/91; LJ 3/15/91; PW 3/22/91)

9158   Silber, Joan. *In the City.* **1987, Viking $16.95 (0-670-81479-2); Penguin paper $6.95 (0-14-009742-2).** A character study of a New Jersey woman who leaves her parents and becomes immersed in the art and literary world of Greenwich Village during the 1920s. (REV: CSM 4/10/87; LJ 2/1/87; PW 1/23/87)

9159   Silman, Roberta. *Beginning the World Again.* **1990, Viking $19.95 (0-670-83062-3).** The development of the atomic bomb as told by the wives of physicists working on the project. (REV: BL 10/1/90; LJ 10/1/90)

9160   Singer, Isaac Bashevis. *King of the Fields.* **1988, Farrar $18.95 (0-374-18128-4); NAL paper $8.95 (0-452-26312-4).** A portrait of prehistoric Poland tracing the development of a hunter-gatherer society to an agriculturally based economy. (REV: BL 6/1/88; LJ 7/88; Time 10/31/88)

9161   Singer, Isaac Bashevis. *Manor.* **1987, Farrar paper $12.95 (0-374-52080-1).** A study of a nineteenth-century Polish family by the author of *Scum.* (REV: NYRB 10/26/67; NYTBR 11/5/67; Time 10/20/67. AWARDS: NYTBR, 1967)

9162   Singer, Isaac Bashevis. *Shosha.* **1978, Farrar $8.95 (0-374-26336-1); paper $8.95 (0-374-52142-5).** The story of a young man's search for a lost love set in Warsaw during the 1930s. (REV: Newsweek 7/23/78; PW 5/15/78; Time 7/3/78. AWARDS: Time, 1978; Time, the 1970s)

9163   Smiley, Jane. *Greenlanders.* **1988, Knopf $19.95 (0-394-55120-6); Ivy Books paper $4.95 (0-8041-0453-0).** An epic story of a fourteenth-century Scandinavian community in Greenland and its efforts to survive and colonize the island. (REV: BL 3/1/88; CSM 9/7/88; PW 3/25/88)

9164   Soister, Helena. *Prophecies.* **1990, Bantam $18.95 (0-553-05878-9).** Two widows from England discover magic and evil during a visit to Belgium in a historical mystery set in the sixteenth century. (REV: BL 7/90; LJ 6/15/90)

9165   Solzhenitsyn, Aleksandr. *August 1914.* **1989, Farrar $40.00 (0-374-10683-5); paper $19.95 (0-374-51999-4).** The story of a disastrous attack by Russian troops on East Prussia during the opening months of World War I. (REV: LJ 10/15/72; Newsweek 9/18/72; Time 9/25/72. AWARDS: ALA, 1972; Time, 1972)

9166   Sorrentino, Gilbert. *Aberration of Starlight.* **1980, Random $9.95 (0-394-51189-1).** The chronicle of a New Jersey family on vacation during the 1930s. "One of our best writers at the top of his form."—LJ (REV: LJ 10/15/80; New Rep 8/30/80; NYTBR 8/10/80)

9167   Souza, Marcio. *Emperor of the Amazon.* **1980, Avon paper $2.95 (0-380-76270-4).** The fictionalized memoirs of a man who witnessed the events surrounding an 1899 attempted revolution in Brazil at the height of the rubber boom. (REV: LJ 9/15/80; NYTBR 10/19/80; New Yorker 9/29/80)

9168   Stadler, Matthew. *Landscape: Memory.* **1990, Macmillan $19.95 (0-684-19185-7).** A young man comes of age in San Francisco in the years following the 1906 earthquake and fire. "An unusual and impressive debut."—NYTBR (REV: NYTBR 1/6/91; PW 7/13/90)

9169   Stewart, Fred Mustard. *Ellis Island.* **1984, NAL paper $3.95 (0-451-12671-8).** A novel tracing the lives of five immigrants from different parts of Europe who sail together on a ship to the United States in 1907. (REV: BL 11/15/82; NYTBR 3/6/83; PW 12/3/82)

9170   Storm, Hyemeyohsts. *Seven Arrows.* **1985, Ballantine paper $14.95 (0-345-32901-5).** An illustrated story of the efforts of Plains Indians to resist Caucasian settlers from usurping their lands. (REV: BL 1/1/73; LJ 7/72; PW 5/1/72. AWARDS: ALA, 1972)

9171   Süskind, Patrick. *Perfume: The Story of a Murderer.* **1986, Knopf $16.95 (0-394-55084-6); Pocket paper $4.50 (0-671-64370-3).** The story of an eighteenth-century French child born with no scent and how the deformity leads him to a life of crime. (REV: LJ 10/15/86; NYTBR 9/21/86; Time 10/20/86)

9172   Suyin, Han. *The Enchantress.* **1985, Bantam $16.95 (0-553-05071-0).** The story of twins' journeys through eighteenth-century China and Thailand following the burning of their parents as witches in France. (REV: BL 11/1/84; LJ 3/15/85; PW 11/23/84)

9173   Tannahill, Ruth. *World, the Flesh and the Devil.* **1987, Crown $17.95 (0-517-56227-8); Ivy Books paper $4.95 (0-8041-0227-9).** A portrait of fifteenth-century Scotland on the brink of civil war during the reign of James I. "In every respect this is a marvelous story, told by a master storyteller."—PW (REV: LJ 5/15/87; PW 1/9/87)

9174   Tax, Meredith. *Union Square*. 1988, Morrow $18.75 (0-688-05069-7); Avon paper $4.95 (0-380-70906-6). The life of a Jewish family in New York during the 1920s and 1930s. (REV: NYTBR 1/1/89; PW 8/12/88)

9175   Thomas, Elizabeth Marshall. *Reindeer Moon*. 1987, Houghton $17.95 (0-395-42112-8); Pocket paper $4.50 (0-671-64886-1). An anthropologist's first novel portraying the life of a young girl in a Siberian hunter-gatherer group 20 millennia in the past. (REV: NYTBR 3/22/87; New Yorker 3/30/87; PW 12/5/86. AWARDS: PW, 1987)

9176   Thomas, Rosie. *White Dove*. 1986, Viking $18.95 (0-670-80013-9); Bantam paper $4.95 (0-553-26457-5). An English woman becomes involved in leftist causes and falls in love with a Spanish Civil War volunteer. (REV: BL 5/1/86; LJ 5/15/86; PW 4/18/86)

9177   Toer, Pramoedya Ananta. *This Earth of Mankind*. 1991, Morrow $23.00 (0-688-09373-6). The Indonesian author of *The Fugitive* tells the story of a young man's love for a prostitute, which brings him into conflict with authorities at the turn of the century. (REV: LJ 9/1/91; PW 8/16/91)

9178   Tremain, Rose. *Restoration: A Novel of 17th Century England*. 1990, Viking $19.95 (0-670-83109-3). A portrait of the life of a minor assistant to the English king Charles II. (REV: LJ 2/1/90; PW 2/2/90; TLS 9/29/89. AWARDS: PW, 1990)

9179   Trevor, William. *Fools of Fortune*. 1984, Penguin paper $6.95 (0-14-006982-8). The life of an Irish Protestant boy whose father and sisters were killed in a raid by English troops in the years following World War I. (REV: BL 7/83; LJ 9/1/83; Time 10/10/83)

9180   Trevor, William. *Silence in the Garden*. 1988, Viking $17.95 (0-670-82404-6); Penguin paper $7.95 (0-14-012712-7). A chronicle of an Irish family living on an island off County Cork during the 1930s. (REV: BL 7/88; PW 7/8/88; TLS 6/10/88)

9181   Tryon, Thomas. *Wings of the Morning*. 1990, Knopf $22.95 (0-394-52389-X). The first in a series by the author portraying life in early nineteenth-century Connecticut. "Unalloyed pleasure for fans of this genre."—PW (REV: BL 8/90; LJ 9/1/90; PW 7/27/90)

9182   Urquhart, Jane. *Whirlpool*. 1989, Godine $17.95 (0-87923-806-2). A nineteenth-century Niagara Falls setting provides the backdrop for this story of a poet's obsession with a young married woman he sees reading the works of Robert Browning. (REV: BL 2/15/90; LJ 4/15/90; PW 12/15/89)

9183   Vargas Llosa, Mario. *War of the End of the World*. 1984, Farrar $18.95 (0-374-28651-5); Avon paper $9.95 (0-380-69987-7). The Peruvian writer tells the story of a Brazilian rebellion at the beginning of the twentieth century. (REV: Choice 12/

84; New Rep 10/8/84; NYTBR 8/12/84. AWARDS: NYTBR, 1984)

9184   Vernon, John. *Peter Doyle*. 1991, Random $22.00 (0-394-58249-7). A tale of the nineteenth-century travels of the thumb and penis of Napoleon after his death. (REV: BL 1/15/91; LJ 3/15/91)

9185   Veryan, Patricia. *Dedicated Villain*. 1989, St. Martin's $19.95 (0-312-02570-X); Fawcett paper $3.95 (0-449-21800-7). The story of love and a hunt for treasure set in mid-eighteenth-century Flanders and England. (REV: BL 3/15/89; LJ 3/1/89; PW 2/17/89)

9186   Vidal, Gore. *Creation*. 1986, Ballantine paper $5.95 (0-345-34020-5). A portrait of Athens and Greece in the fifth century B.C. as told by a Persian emissary. (REV: BL 2/15/81; New Rep 4/25/81; PW 2/20/81)

9187   Vidal, Gore. *1876*. 1976, Random $19.95 (0-394-49750-3); Ballantine paper $4.95 (0-345-00886-3). Aaron Burr's bastard son returns to the United States from a European journalistic and political career in hope of receiving a diplomatic post under the Tilden presidency. (REV: BL 3/1/76; PW 1/19/76; Time 3/1/76. AWARDS: ALA, 1976; Time, 1976)

9188   Vidal, Gore. *Empire*. 1988, Ballantine paper $4.95 (0-345-35472-9). The fifth novel in Vidal's series that traces the course of American history from 1890 to 1910 and the rise of the United States to a world power. (REV: BL 5/15/87; LJ 7/87; Newsweek 6/15/87)

9189   Vidal, Gore. *Lincoln*. 1984, Random $19.95 (0-394-52895-6); Ballantine paper $4.95 (0-345-00885-5). A fictional re-creation of the years of Abraham Lincoln's presidency. (REV: CSM 7/25/84; LJ 6/1/84; NYRB 7/19/84)

9190   Vollmann, William T. *Ice Shirt*. 1990, Viking $19.95 (0-670-83239-1). This chronicle of the adventures of a Viking family in North America from 200 to 1000 is the first of a projected seven-novel series. (REV: LJ 10/1/90; NYTBR 10/14/90)

9191   Von Rezzori, Gregor. *Memoirs of an Anti-Semite*. 1991, Random paper $10.95 (0-679-73182-2). Five interconnected stories tracing the narrator's life in Rumania in the 1920s to Rome in the 1970s. "Brilliant, haunting, complex . . . truly compelling reading."—LJ (REV: BL 4/15/81; LJ 6/5/81; Time 9/14/81)

9192   Walker, Margaret. *Jubilee*. 1984, Bantam paper $5.50 (0-553-27383-3). A novel about the Civil War and its aftermath as told through the life of a former slave. (REV: CSM 9/29/66; NYTBR 9/25/86; Sat Rev 9/24/66)

9193   Ward, Andrew. *Blood Seed: A Novel of India*. 1985, Viking $17.95 (0-670-58934-9). An eight-year-old boy undertakes a journey to reach the home of his mother in this novel set in nineteenth-century India. (REV: LJ 9/1/85; NYTBR 12/22/85)

9194   Watkins, Paul. *In the Blue Light of African Dreams*. 1990, Houghton $18.95 (0-395-55136-6). An

American serving in the French Foreign Legion in Morocco plans to win the prize offered for the first Europe–United States flight. (REV: LJ 8/90; New Yorker 10/9/90; PW 7/6/90)

9195 Wendorf, Patricia. *Double Wedding Ring.* 1990, Viking $19.95 (0-241-12742-4). The story of the settlement of English immigrant farmers in the United States during the middle of the nineteenth century. "Those who enjoy historical fiction will savor this marvelous novel."—LJ (REV: LJ 9/15/90; PW 8/3/90)

9196 West, Jessamyn. *Massacre at Fall Creek.* 1976, Peter Smith $17.75 (0-8446-6274-7); Harcourt paper $6.95 (0-15-657681-3). A re-creation of a nineteenth-century incident in which a group of Indiana settlers were hung for their part in the massacre of a group of Native Americans. (REV: BL 5/1/75; LJ 4/15/75; NYTBR 4/27/75)

9197 West, Jessamyn. *State of Stony Lonesome.* 1984, Harcourt $12.95 (0-15-184903-X). This story of a California family and a young girl's coming of age is set during the early 1920s. (REV: BL 1/15/85; LJ 11/15/84; PW 9/7/84)

9198 West, Paul. *Lord Byron's Doctor.* 1989, Doubleday $19.95 (0-385-26129-2). The fictitious diary of poet Lord Byron's doctor detailing his experiences traveling through Europe with Byron and the Shelleys. "A powerful book."—NYTBR (REV: BL 9/15/89; NYTBR 9/3/89; Time 9/11/89)

9199 Wharton, William. *Pride.* 1987, Dell paper $4.95 (0-440-37118-X). A portrait of the life of a New Jersey depression-era family focusing on the labor activities of the father. (REV: BL 9/1/85; LJ 9/15/85; TLS 4/18/86)

9200 Wheatcroft, John. *Catherine, Her Book.* 1987, Associated Univ. Presses $17.95 (0-8453-4742-X). A fictionalized eighteenth-century journal chronicling the events witnessed by a woman on the estate of Wuthering Heights. (REV: BL 3/15/84; NYTBR 2/19/84)

9201 White, Patrick. *A Fringe of Leaves.* 1984, Penguin paper $8.95 (0-14-004409-4). A nineteenth-century woman taken captive by aborigines following a shipwreck plans her escape to freedom. (REV: Choice 4/77; LJ 12/1/76; PW 11/21/77)

9202 Wiesel, Elie. *The Oath.* 1986, Schocken paper $8.95 (0-8052-0808-9). An elderly man tells the story of a Russian pogrom against Jews and methods the Jewish people used to fight back. (REV: BL 1/15/74; LJ 1/1/74; NYTBR 11/18/73)

9203 Wilder, Thornton. *Theophilus North.* 1988, Carroll & Graf paper $4.95 (0-88184-382-2). The adventures of a former teacher in Newport, Rhode Island, during the 1920s. "Compulsively readable in the best Wilder tradition."—BL (REV: BL 9/15/73; Choice 2/74; New Yorker 10/29/73)

9204 Williams, Sherley Anne. *Dessa Rose: A Riveting Story of the South during Slavery.* 1986, Morrow $15.95 (0-688-05113-8); Berkley paper $3.95

(0-425-10337-4). The story of the ante-bellum American South focusing on the institution of slavery and its effects upon both blacks and whites. (REV: LJ 6/15/86; NYTBR 8/3/86; PW 5/30/86)

9205 Wilson, A. N. *Gentlemen in England: A Vision.* 1986, Viking $17.95 (0-670-80971-3); Penguin paper $6.95 (0-14-008721-4). A novel set in Victorian England portraying the personal lives of a geologist and his family, written by the biographer of Tolstoy. (REV: CSM 3/19/86; Time 3/17/86; TLS 9/6/85)

9206 Winterson, Jeanette. *The Passion.* 1988, Atlantic Monthly $16.95 (0-87113-183-8); Random paper $8.95 (0-679-72437-0). A French soldier during the Napoleonic Wars falls in love with a woman in Moscow and flees with her to Venice. (REV: NYTBR 8/7/88; PW 4/1/88; TLS 6/26/87)

9207 Winthrop, Elizabeth. *In My Mother's House.* 1988, Doubleday $19.95 (0-385-17121-8); NAL paper $4.95 (0-451-16657-4). This debut novel chronicles the life of a New York family plagued by tragedy from the late nineteenth century through the latter half of the twentieth. (REV: LJ 6/15/88; NYTBR 8/7/88; PW 5/6/88)

9208 Woiwode, Larry. *Beyond the Bedroom Wall: A Family Album.* 1975, Farrar $17.95 (0-374-11237-1); Penguin paper $8.95 (0-14-012186-2). A history of several generations of North Dakota's Neumiller family. (REV: NYTBR 9/28/75; Sat Rev 9/6/75; Time 9/29/75. AWARDS: ALA, 1975)

9209 Wolf, Christa. *No Place on Earth.* 1982, Farrar $11.95 (0-374-22298-3); paper $7.95 (0-374-51775-4). A profile of a nineteenth-century meeting of German literary figures. (REV: LJ 9/1/82; NYTBR 10/10/82; PW 6/25/82)

9210 Wolf, Joan. *Daughter of the Red Deer.* 1991, Dutton $19.95 (0-525-93379-4). A fictional study of the life of a prehistoric Cro-Magnon tribe living in the Pyrenees. (REV: BL 10/15/91; LJ 9/15/91)

9211 Wood, Barbara. *Green City in the Sun.* 1988, Random $19.95 (0-394-55966-5); Fawcett paper $4.95 (0-449-14595-6). A chronicle of three generations of British settlers in Kenya throughout the twentieth century. "A warm immensely appealing historic epic."—BL (REV: BL 2/1/88; PW 3/4/88)

9212 Woodman, Richard. *Bomb Vessel.* 1986, Walker $15.95 (0-8027-0886-2). A study of Royal Navy politics in the early nineteenth century under the command of Lord Nelson. (REV: LJ 2/15/86; PW 1/17/86)

9213 Woodman, Richard. *Private Revenge.* 1990, St. Martin's $16.95 (0-312-04405-4). The adventures of an early nineteenth-century British ship captain sailing the seas between India and China. (REV: LJ 6/1/90; PW 5/25/90)

9214 Worboys, Anne. *Aurora Rose.* 1989, NAL paper $4.95 (0-451-16211-0). A story set in the nineteenth century regarding the affair between an English lord and his maid who are immigrating to

New Zealand along with the lord's wife. (REV: LJ 5/15/88; PW 4/8/88)

9215 Yourcenar, Marguerite. *Fires.* **1981, Farrar $12.95 (0-374-15500-3); paper $8.95 (0-374-51748-7).** A collection of nine historical prose poems originally written in French in 1935. (REV: LJ 6/1/81; NYTBR 10/4/81; PW 5/1/81)

9216 Zaroulis, Nancy. *Massachusetts.* **1991, Fawcett $19.95 (0-449-90586-1).** A novel surveying the history of Massachusetts over four centuries as told through the life of a family who arrived on the *Mayflower.* (REV: BL 2/15/91; LJ 1/91; PW 2/8/91)

HUMOROUS FICTION

9217 Berger, Thomas. *Who Is Teddy Villanova?* **1978, Dell paper $3.95 (0-385-29149-3).** A comic spoof of detective stories involving an inept New York-based private eye. "Intelligent, witty, rude and extremely funny."—TLS (Rev: LJ 5/1/77; NYTBR 3/20/77; TLS 12/16/77)

9218 Blount, Roy, Jr. *First Hubby.* **1990, Random $18.95 (0-394-57420-6).** A portrait of the husband of the first female president of the United States. (Rev: LJ 6/15/90; NYTBR 6/10/90; Time 6/25/90)

9219 DeVries, Peter. *Forever Panting.* **1982, Penguin paper $5.95 (0-14-006188-6).** An actor becomes sexually attracted to his wife's stepmother. "An extremely funny book. . . . New readers could well start here."—TLS (Rev: BL 7/1/73; PW 3/12/73; TLS 8/10/73)

9220 Eisenstadt, Jill. *Kiss Out.* **1991, Random $19.95 (0-394-58230-6).** A comic story centering on a family musical group and the lead singer's rich fiancée in this second novel by the author of *From Rockaway.* (Rev: BL 1/1/91; LJ 3/15/91; NYTBR 3/17/91)

9221 Frazier, Ian. *Dating Your Mom.* **1986, Farrar $11.95 (0-374-13508-8); Penguin paper $5.95 (0-14-009678-7).** Twenty-five short humorous pieces by a *New Yorker* staff writer and author of *Great Plains.* (Rev: BL 1/15/86; NYTBR 1/5/86; Time 3/3/86)

9222 Harrington, Donald. *Cockroaches of Stay More.* **1989, Harcourt $19.95 (0-15-118270-1); Random paper $9.95 (0-679-72808-2).** A depiction of the social life and activities of a cockroach city in the Ozarks. "A consistently amusing and clever tale."—BL (Rev: BL 3/1/89; NYTBR 4/23/89; PW 1/13/89)

9223 Lefcourt, Peter. *The Deal.* **1991, Random $19.00 (0-679-40152-0).** Satire by a screenwriter about a Hollywood treatment of a play regarding the nineteenth-century English politicians Disraeli and Gladstone. "A laugh-out-loud, thoroughly enjoyable novel."—PW (Rev: BL 3/1/91; LJ 4/1/91; PW 2/22/91)

9224 Robbins, Tom. *Skinny Legs and All.* **1990, Bantam $19.95 (0-553-05775-8).** An American religious fanatic and his followers plot to bring on Armageddon and the return of Christ by destroying a Muslim holy place in Jerusalem. "Robbins at his best."—LJ (Rev: BL 1/15/90; LJ 3/1/90; PW 2/16/90)

LOVE STORIES

9225 Adams, Alice. *Rich Rewards.* 1990, Fawcett paper $4.95 (0-449-14652-9). A divorcée reunites with a former French lover following the dissolution of her marriage. "A finely crafted work by a talented writer."—LJ (Rev: BL 7/15/80; LJ 8/80; PW 7/18/80)

9226 Andersdatter, Karla. *Doorway.* 1990, Plain View Pr. $17.95 (0-911051-50-3). The story of a love triangle set in Northern California. "Heartfelt and thoroughly engrossing."—BL (Rev: BL 10/1/90; LJ 10/1/90)

9227 Baldwin, James. *If Beale Street Could Talk.* 1986, Dell paper $4.95 (0-440-34060-8). A story of the love between a young African-American couple and the efforts of their families to free the man from jail. (Rev: BL 7/1/74; NYTBR 5/19/74; PW 3/25/74)

9228 Barlow, Linda. *Leaves of Fortune.* 1988, Doubleday $18.95 (0-385-23385-X); Dell paper $4.95 (0-440-20471-2). A portrait of a long-established Boston tea magnate family centering on the love between two cousins. (Rev: BL 8/88; LJ 10/1/88; NYTBR 9/25/88)

9229 Billington, Rachel. *Theo and Matilda.* 1991, HarperCollins $21.95 (0-06-016483-2). Intertwined love stories tracing the romance of an English couple set in four different historical periods. "Lavishly entertaining."—PW (Rev: BL 5/15/91; PW 4/26/91)

9230 Bosworth, Sheila. *Almost Innocent.* 1986, Penguin paper $6.95 (0-14-008443-6). This debut novel set in New Orleans examines the love between the narrator's parents. (Rev: BL 12/15/84; LJ 11/1/84; NYTBR 12/30/84)

9231 Bracewell, Michael. *Divine Concepts of Physical Beauty.* 1990, Knopf $18.95 (0-394-58383-3). Three English women vie for the love and affection of a single man. (Rev: BL 5/1/90; PW 3/23/90; TLS 10/27/89)

9232 Brookner, Anita. *Lewis Percy.* 1990, Pantheon $18.95 (0-394-58446-5). The love and marriage of a reclusive young man and a shy library assistant are torn apart by the attentions of an actress. "A standout even among the author's critically acclaimed oeuvre."—PW (Rev: BL 1/15/90; CSM 4/26/90; PW 1/12/90)

9233 Brookner, Anita. *Providence.* 1984, Pantheon $13.95 (0-394-52945-6); Dutton paper $7.95 (0-525-48157-5). The story of a love affair between two academics at a university by the author of *Look At Me.* (Rev: BL 2/1/84; CSM 3/15/84; LJ 1/84)

9234 Busch, Frederick. *Harry and Catherine.* 1990, Knopf $18.95 (0-394-57425-7). Two middle-aged men fight for the affections of a recently divorced woman. (Rev: LJ 3/1/90; NYTBR 3/11/90; PW 1/26/90)

9235 Casey, John. *An American Romance.* 1990, Avon paper $9.95 (0-380-71240-7). This debut novel chronicles the development of love between two young people and their experiences in Iowa and Hollywood together. (Rev: Natl Rev 8/19/77; NYTBR 4/24/77; Newsweek 4/25/77)

9236 Colwin, Laurie. *Happy All the Time.* 1985, Penguin paper $7.95 (0-14-007687-5). Two cousins and best friends fall in love with and marry different types of women. (Rev: Atl 10/78; LJ 9/15/78; Newsweek 10/9/78)

9237 Ferlinghetti, Lawrence. *Love in the Days of Rage.* 1988, Dutton $15.95 (0-525-24881-9); paper $6.95 (0-525-48541-4). A love story by the American poet looking at the relationship between an American artist and French banker who become involved in the Paris student protests of 1968. (Rev: BL 9/15/88; LJ 10/1/88)

9238 Fowles, John. *Daniel Martin.* 1977, Little, Brown $19.95 (0-316-28959-0); NAL paper $4.50 (0-451-12210-0). A film writer reunites with a former friend whose wife was his true love in his younger years. "Clearly in the line of the finest English novels."—Choice (Rev: BL 9/15/77; Choice 12/77; Time 9/12/77. Awards: Time, 1977)

9239 French, Marilyn. *Bleeding Heart.* 1988, Ballantine paper $4.95 (0-345-00866-9). A tale of a divorced professor and an executive with a disabled wife who fall in love. (Rev: BL 3/15/80; NYTBR 3/16/80; PW 1/18/80)

9240 Garcia Marquez, Gabriel. *Love in the Time of Cholera.* 1988, Knopf $18.95 (0-394-56161-9). The story of the relationship between a widow and a long-lost friend who reenters her life. "This shining and heartbreaking novel may be one of the greatest love stories ever told."—NYTBR (REV: LJ 3/15/88; NYTBR 4/10/88; Time 3/28/88. AWARDS: ALA, 1988; BL, the 1980s; LJ, 1988; NYTBR, 1988; PW, 1988; Time, 1988; Time, the 1980s)

9241 Gardner, John. *Nickel Mountain: A Pastoral Novel*. 1989, Random paper $8.95 (0-394-74393-8). A study of a Catskill restaurant owner whose life was changed by the love of a younger woman. (REV: Atl 2/74; NYTBR 12/9/73; Time 12/31/73)

9242 Gibbons, Kaye. *A Virtuous Woman*. 1989, Algonquin $13.95 (0-945575-09-2); Random paper $8.95 (0-679-72844-9). A series of flashbacks detail the course of a 25-year marriage as told by a widower following the death of his wife. "A subtle, evocative, and romantic novel."—BL (REV: BL 4/1/89; NYTBR 4/30/89; TLS 9/15/89)

9243 Grumbach, Doris. *Chamber Music*. 1980, Fawcett paper $2.50 (0-449-24721-4). A 90-year-old woman reviews her life, love, and marriage to a composer who died of syphilis as a young man. (REV: New Rep 3/10/79; Newsweek 3/19/79; PW 1/15/79)

9244 Hazzard, Shirley. *Evening of the Holiday*. 1988, Penguin paper $6.95 (0-14-010451-8). A story of the relationship between a young British girl and an older man in rural Italy. (REV: BL 2/1/66; NYTBR 1/9/66; Time 1/14/66)

9245 Johnson, Joyce. *In the Night Cafe*. 1989, Dutton $17.95 (0-525-24741-6). The story of a doomed love and marriage between Joanna, the book's narrator, and Tom, an artist, provides the basis for this novel set in the early 1960s New York art world. (REV: LJ 3/1/89; NYTBR 4/30/89; PW 1/27/89)

9246 Kraft, Eric. *Herb 'n' Lorna: A Love Story*. 1988, Crown $17.95 (0-517-55941-2); Dutton paper $8.95 (0-525-48513-9). A fictionalized portrait of the lives and love of the author's grandparents. "A charmer."—LJ (REV: BL 3/15/88; LJ 4/1/88; PW 2/26/88)

9247 McCullough, Colleen. *Thorn Birds*. 1977, Harper & Row $19.95 (0-06-012956-5); Avon paper $3.95 (0-380-01817-9). An Australian saga spanning from World War II to the late 1960s regarding the love between the Irish priest and a young woman. (REV: BL 5/1/77; LJ 5/1/77; Newsweek 4/25/77)

9248 Murdoch, Iris. *Nice and the Good*. 1978, Penguin paper $6.95 (0-14-003034-4). An examination of the positive and negative power of love as manifested in the lives of the colleagues of a British civil servant following his suicide. (REV: Choice 4/68; LJ 12/15/67; Time 1/5/68)

9249 Nabokov, Vladimir. *Mary*. 1989, Random paper $6.95 (0-679-72620-9). Nabokov's first novel, originally written in Russian in 1925, concerns the love of the narrator for a woman he remembers while housed in a German boarding home. (REV: NYTBR 10/25/70; Newsweek 11/16/70; PW 8/3/70)

9250 Narayan, R. K. *Painter of Signs*. 1983, Penguin paper $5.95 (0-14-006259-9). A Malgudi novel about the relationship of a sign painter and the younger woman he falls in love with. (REV: NYTBR 6/20/76; New Yorker 7/5/76; Newsweek 7/4/76)

9251 Nichols, John. *Sterile Cuckoo*. 1987, Norton paper $7.95 (0-393-30472-8). This debut novel chronicles the rise and fall of love between two college students. (REV: LJ 3/1/65; NYTBR 1/17/65)

9252 Oates, Joyce Carol. *Because It Is Bitter and Because It Is My Heart*. 1990, Dutton $19.95 (0-525-24860-9). An unconsummated love between a young white girl and a young black man set in New York during the 1950s. (REV: BL 2/1/90; LJ 4/1/90; PW 2/23/90. AWARDS: PW, 1990)

9253 Pintauro, Joseph. *Cold Hands*. 1986, NAL paper $7.95 (0-452-25885-5). A story tracing the development of love between two gay men from childhood to adulthood. "Deceptively simple, hauntingly beautiful."—NYTBR (REV: BL 1/1/80; NYTBR 12/2/79)

9254 Priestley, J. B. *Found, Lost, Found*. 1977, Scarborough $8.95 (0-8128-2164-5). A love story chronicling the relationship between an alcoholic and a playwright who sets the condition that he must give up drinking for their love to continue. (REV: BL 3/1/77; LJ 4/1/77; PW 1/3/77)

9255 Rivers, Caryl. *Intimate Enemies*. 1987, Dutton $17.95 (0-525-24611-8); Pocket paper $3.95 (0-671-66548-0). The story of a former political activist's love relationship with an angry Vietnam veteran. (REV: BL 11/15/87; LJ 12/87; PW 10/23/87)

9256 Roth, Philip. *Deception*. 1990, Simon & Schuster $18.95 (0-671-70374-9). The depiction of the lives and relationship between an American writer and his English lover told entirely in dialogue. (REV: BL 2/15/90; New Rep 4/30/90; NYTBR 3/11/90)

9257 Savan, Glenn. *White Palace*. 1987, Bantam paper $8.95 (0-553-34419-6). A young St. Louis widower finds love with an older woman in this novel that was adapted for a motion picture starring Susan Sarandon and James Spader. (REV: BL 7/87; NYTBR 9/13/87; PW 5/8/87)

9258 Settle, Mary Lee. *Celebration*. 1986, Farrar $17.95 (0-374-12005-6). An American anthropologist and a Scottish geologist meet and fall in love at London's British Museum. (REV: BL 7/86; Newsweek 11/10/86; PW 8/22/86. AWARDS: PW, 1986)

9259 Spencer, Scott. *Endless Love*. 1979, Knopf $19.95 (0-394-50605-7); Ballantine paper $4.95 (0-345-35624-1). The story of a love-obsessed young man who destroys his girlfriend's family's home following a parentally imposed ban on seeing his girlfriend. "Compellingly readable . . . a virtuoso performance."—LJ (REV: BL 10/15/79; LJ 9/1/79; NYTBR 9/23/79. AWARDS: ALA, 1979)

9260 Tung, Chieh-Yuan. *Master Tung's Western Chamber Romance: A Chinese Chantefable*. 1983, Books on Demand paper $66.80 (0-685-16303-2). The English translation of a twelfth-century Chinese narrative ballad concerning the love between a scholar and a politician's daughter. (Rᴇᴠ: Choice 12/76; TLS 4/1/77. Aᴡᴀʀᴅs: NBA, 1977)

9261 **Wesley, Mary.** *Second Fiddle.* **1989, Viking $18.95 (0-670-82693-6); Penguin paper $7.95 (0-14-011947-7).** The love between a 45-year-old English woman and a man more than two decades younger. (Rᴇᴠ: BL 6/15/89; NYTBR 7/30/89; PW 5/12/89)

9262 **Wright, L. R.** *Love in the Temperate Zone.* **1988, Viking $17.95 (0-670-81173-4).** A Canadian woman falls in love with a musician after finding out about her husband's string of infidelities. (Rᴇᴠ: BL 12/15/87; LJ 1/88; NYTBR 1/17/88)

OCCULT FICTION

9263 Adams, Richard. *Girl in a Swing.* **1989, NAL paper $4.95 (0-451-15437-1).** An art dealer with extrasensory perception falls in love with a German woman who has parapsychic powers. (REV: Choice 9/80; LJ 4/1/80; NYRB 5/29/80)

9264 Aickman, Robert. *Wine-Dark Sea: A Collection.* **1988, Morrow $18.95 (1-557-10035-7).** Eleven previously uncollected short stories with elements of horror by a late British author. "A remarkable collection by an author who deserves to be better known."—PW (REV: BL 10/15/88; LJ 10/15/88; PW 8/19/88)

9265 Amis, Kingsley. *Green Man.* **1986, Academy Chicago paper $5.95 (0-89733-220-2).** The alcoholic proprietor of an English inn encounters the spirit of a seventeenth-century murderer who once lived on the premises. (REV: BL 11/15/70; Natl Rev 8/25/70; PW 6/8/70)

9266 Ansa, Tina McElroy. *Baby of the Family.* **1989, Harcourt $18.95 (0-15-110431-X).** A debut novel about a Georgia child born with the ability to communicate with ghosts. "Ansa tells a good quirky story, and she tells it with humor, grace and great respect for the power of the particular."—NYTBR (REV: BL 11/1/89; NYTBR 11/26/89; PW 9/8/89)

9267 Anthony, Piers. *Shade of the Tree.* **1987, Tor paper $3.95 (0-8125-3103-5).** A series of mysterious deaths haunt a Florida family in this creepy story by the veteran science fiction/fantasy writer. (REV: BL 3/15/86; LJ 4/15/86)

9268 Barker, Clive. *Cabal: The Nightbreed.* **1988, Poseidon $18.95 (0-671-62688-4); Pocket paper $4.50 (0-671-68514-7).** A collection consisting of the title novella and four short stories by the British horror writer. "They demonstrate why the gleefully gory Mr. Barker is at the top of his genre."—NYTBR (REV: BL 9/15/88; NYTBR 12/18/88; PW 8/26/88)

9269 Barker, Clive. *Clive Barker's Books of Blood, Vols. I–III.* **1987, Berkley paper $8.95 (0-425-10356-0).** The collected gruesome horror tales from the British author of *The Damnation Game.* (REV: BL 12/15/86; PW 5/2/86. AWARDS: PW, 1986)

9270 Barker, Clive. *Damnation Game.* **1987, Putnam $18.95 (0-399-13278-3); Berkley paper $4.95 (1-55773-113-6).** Barker's first novel focuses on a group of Londoners with paranormal powers, including a man able to resurrect the dead. (REV: LJ 5/15/87; PW 4/24/87)

9271 Barker, Clive. *Great and Secret Show: The First Book of the Art.* **1990, Harper & Row $19.95 (0-06-016276-7).** A man begins to lose his mind when the secret of the meaning of life is revealed to him. "Amazingly believable and compulsively readable."—LJ (REV: LJ 1/90; NYTBR 2/11/90; Time 3/19/90)

9272 Blatty, William Peter. *The Exorcist.* **1984, Bantam paper $4.50 (0-553-27010-9).** A child who becomes possessed by the Devil is the target of an exorcism by two Jesuit priests in this novel, which was the basis for the popular motion picture of the same name. (REV: NYTBR 6/6/71; Newsweek 5/10/71)

9273 Campbell, Ramsey. *Ancient Images.* **1989, Macmillan $18.95 (0-684-19081-8); Tor paper $4.95 (0-8125-0263-9).** An investigation of murder leads to the discovery of an unreleased horror movie made five decades before. (REV: BL 5/15/89; LJ 5/15/89; PW 4/28/89)

9274 Campbell, Ramsey. *Incarnate.* **1984, Tor paper $3.95 (0-8125-1650-8).** Five victims of a medical dream experiment gone awry seek to find the source of power controlling their lives. "A masterful horror tale."—BL (REV: BL 8/83; PW 8/26/83)

9275 Cox, Michael, and R. A. Gilbert, eds. *Oxford Book of English Ghost Stories.* **1989, Oxford Univ. Pr. paper $9.95 (0-19-282666-2).** An anthology of 42 ghost stories from the 1820s to the 1980s, including contributions by Sir Walter Scott, H. G. Wells, and Bram Stoker. (REV: BL 3/1/87; TLS 11/21/86)

9276 Coyne, John. *Fury.* **1989, Warner $18.95 (0-446-51420-9); paper $4.95 (0-446-36030-9).** A woman's past lives take over her present in horrifying ways following a visit to a channeler. (REV: LJ 8/89; PW 8/18/89)

9277 Cramer, Kathryn, and Peter D. Paultz, eds. *Architecture of Fear.* **1989, Avon paper $3.95 (0-**

380-70553-2). An anthology of 14 horror stories by contemporary authors including Ramsey Campbell, Dean Koontz, and Joyce Carol Oates. (REV: BL 10/15/87; LJ 10/15/87; PW 9/18/87)

9278   Danvers, Dennis. *Wilderness.* **1991, Poseidon $18.95 (0-671-72827-X).** The experiences of a woman who turns into a werewolf during a full moon. "Utterly seductive and fulfilling."—BL (REV: BL 4/1/91; LJ 3/15/91; PW 3/1/91)

9279   Datlow, Ellen, ed. *Blood Is Not Enough.* **1990, Berkley paper $3.95 (0-425-12178-X).** A collection of 15 stories and two poems about vampires, including works by Tanith Lee, Dan Simmons, and Gahan Wilson. (REV: BL 1/15/89; PW 11/11/88)

9280   Etchison, Dennis, ed. *Cutting Edge.* **1987, St. Martin's paper $3.95 (0-312-90772-9).** A collection of horror stories by writers including Clive Barker, Peter Straub, Joe Haldeman, and Ramsey Campbell. "An exciting and satisfying collection that could well mark a turning point for the genre."—LJ (REV: LJ 10/1/86; PW 8/29/86)

9281   Farris, John. *Son of the Endless Night.* **1986, Tor paper $4.50 (0-8125-8266-7).** A tale of a satanic cult that imprisons family members with evil spirits and leads them to commit murder. "One of the better supernatural novels."—LJ (REV: BL 2/1/85; LJ 2/15/85; PW 12/21/84)

9282   Feist, Raymond E. *Faerie Tale.* **1988, Doubleday $17.95 (0-385-23623-9); Bantam paper $4.95 (0-553-27783-9).** An evil forest spirit terrorizes a family in rural New York. (REV: BL 12/15/87; CSM 2/9/88; LJ 3/1/88)

9283   Gaiman, Neil. *Good Omens: The Nice and Accurate Prophecies of Agnes Nutter, Witch.* **1990, Workman $18.95 (0-89480-853-2).** An Antichrist born in England sets off forces that threaten to end the world while a small group struggles to prevent the impending disaster. (REV: BL 9/15/90; LJ 9/15/90; PW 7/20/90)

9284   Gale, Patrick. *Facing the Tank.* **1989, Dutton $17.95 (0-525-24737-8).** A small English village noted for unusual occurrences becomes the focus of an American scholar searching for the paranormal. (REV: BL 3/1/89; LJ 4/15/89; PW 2/3/89)

9285   Geary, Patricia. *Living in Ether.* **1987, Bantam paper $3.50 (0-553-26329-3).** A first novel regarding a single Hollywood spiritualist and her relations with her clients and family. (REV: BL 4/15/82; LJ 4/1/82; PW 2/19/82)

9286   Grant, Charles L. *Pet.* **1987, Tor paper $3.95 (0-8125-1848-9).** A child calls a stallion to life from a work of art to save him from a murderer, but the horse goes on a rampage of its own. (REV: BL 5/15/86; PW 5/9/86)

9287   Hawkes, Judith. *Julian's House.* **1989, Ticknor & Fields $18.95 (0-89919-906-2).** Stories of a haunted Massachusetts home told by a series of residents forced to vacate the premises. (REV: LJ 10/15/89; NYTBR 12/10/89)

9288   Herbert, James. *Moon.* **1986, Crown $14.95 (0-517-56278-2); NAL paper $4.50 (0-451-40056-9).** A British psychic is plagued by visions of ghastly murders that become true. (REV: LJ 9/15/86; NYTBR 11/16/86)

9289   Hill, Susan. *Woman in Black: A Ghost Story.* **1986, Godine $15.95 (0-87923-576-4).** An illustrated English ghost story about a village haunted by a dead woman's restless spirit. (REV: BL 8/86; PW 6/6/86)

9290   King, Stephen. *Carrie.* **1990, Doubleday $18.95 (0-385-08695-4); NAL paper $3.95 (0-451-15744-3).** An alienated teenager uses her telekinetic powers for a terrible retaliation against her cruel peers. (REV: NYTBR 5/26/74; PW 2/25/74)

9291   King, Stephen. *Christine.* **1983, Viking $22.95 (0-670-22026-4); NAL paper $4.95 (0-451-16044-4).** The evil spirit of a former owner inhabits a teenager's Plymouth automobile. "A prize in the King tradition."—LJ (REV: BL 2/1/83; LJ 3/1/83; PW 2/25/83)

9292   King, Stephen. *Cujo.* **1981, Viking $22.95 (0-670-45193-2); NAL paper $4.95 (0-451-16135-1).** A rabid Saint Bernard terrorizes a Maine family and town. "A biting novel of gut-twisting terror and suspense."—PW (REV: BL 5/15/81; LJ 7/81; PW 7/17/81)

9293   King, Stephen. *Dark Half.* **1989, Viking $21.95 (0-670-82982-X).** A writer becomes plagued by an undeveloped twin lodged inside his brain in this story by the modern horror master. (REV: BL 8/89; CSM 1/22/90; PW 9/1/89)

9294   King, Stephen. *Different Seasons.* **1982, Viking $22.95 (0-670-27266-3); NAL paper $5.95 (0-451-16753-8).** A collection of four short novels, including "Rita Hayworth and Shawshank Deception," "The Apt Pupil," and "The Body and the Breathing Method." (REV: NYTBR 8/29/82; PW 6/18/82)

9295   King, Stephen. *Firestarter.* **1980, Viking $22.95 (0-670-31541-9); NAL paper $4.50 (0-451-15031-7).** Government agents tracking a couple who were subjects of drug experiments are plagued by a child with psychic ability to set objects afire. (REV: BL 6/15/80; LJ 8/80; PW 7/25/80)

9296   King, Stephen. *Night Shift: Excursions into Horror.* **1990, Doubleday $19.95 (0-385-12991-2); NAL paper $4.95 (0-451-16045-2).** A collection of 20 horrific short stories by the author of *Salem's Lot.* (REV: BL 3/15/78; PW 11/28/77)

9297   King, Stephen. *Pet Sematary.* **1983, Doubleday $19.95 (0-385-18244-9); NAL paper $4.95 (0-451-15775-3).** A Maine doctor unleashes unforeseen evil forces after making a pact with Death. "The most frightening book he has ever written."—PW (REV: LJ 10/15/83; NYTBR 11/6/83; PW 9/23/83)

9298   King, Stephen. *Skeleton Crew.* **1985, Putnam $18.95 (0-399-13039-X); NAL paper $4.95 (0-451-14293-4).** A collection of 20 stories and two poems by the author of *The Shining,* including tales in the horror, science fiction, and fantasy genres. "A

showcase for his enormous talent and range."—LJ
(Rev: LJ 5/1/85; PW 4/19/85; Time 7/1/85)

9299 Klein, T. E. D. *Ceremonies.* **1984, Viking
$16.95 (0-670-20982-1); Bantam paper $4.95 (0-553-
26175-4).** An elderly man manipulates younger
people to commit evil acts in a New Jersey town.
"A spellbinding tale that readers won't want to put
down."—BL (Rev: BL 6/15/84; PW 4/20/84)

9300 Klein, T. E. D. *Dark Gods: Four Tales.* **1985,
Viking $16.95 (0-670-80590-4); Bantam paper $3.95
(0-553-25801-X).** Four stories of people whose lives
are affected by supernatural forces. "Klein writes
with a care and literacy rarely found in modern
horror tales."—PW (Rev: BL 7/85; LJ 7/85; PW 5/24/85)

9301 Koontz, Dean R. *Midnight.* **1989, Putnam
$19.95 (0-399-13390-9); Berkley paper $4.95 (0-425-
11870-3).** A computer experiment gone awry turns
the people of a California town into murderers.
"Good page-turning fiction designed to keep a
reader up well after midnight."—NYTBR (Rev: LJ
12/88; NYTBR 3/26/88; PW 11/4/88)

9302 Kotzwinkle, William. *The Exile.* **1988, Dutton
paper $7.95 (0-525-48378-0).** A modern-day motion
picture actor finds himself believing he is a refugee
from Nazi forces in World War II Berlin. "A
psychological tour de force."—BL (Rev: BL 5/15/87;
NYTBR 5/10/87; PW 4/3/87)

9303 Lee, Tanith. *Book of the Damned: The Secret
Books of Paradys-I.* **1990, Overlook $19.95 (0-
87951-408-6).** Three novellas with horror and fantasy elements set in a French town over a period of
centuries. (Rev: BL 11/15/90; LJ 11/15/90; PW 10/26/90)

9304 Levin, Ira. *Rosemary's Baby.* **1979, Dell paper
$2.25 (0-440-17541-0).** A New York family moves into
an exclusive apartment complex that the wife
comes to believe is inhabited by witches who want
to possess her baby. (Rev: BL 5/15/67; LJ 4/15/67; PW 1/
30/67. Awards: NYTBR, 1967)

9305 Levin, Ira. *Stepford Wives.* **1979, Dell paper
$2.25 (0-440-18294-8).** In this novel by the author of
Rosemary's Baby, the women of a small New
England town are replaced by robots who cater to
their husbands' whims. (Rev: BL 12/1/72; NYTBR 10/
15/72; TLS 11/24/72)

9306 Lichtenberg, Jacqueline. *Those of My Blood.*
1988, St. Martin's $19.95 (0-312-02298-0). The fate of
earth's vampires and their ancestral planetary
home is at stake as human exploration threatens
their existence. (Rev: BL 12/1/88; LJ 11/15/88; PW 10/14/
88)

9307 Lovecraft, H. P. *Dunwich Horror and Others.*
1985, Arkham $17.95 (0-87054-037-8). A collection of
the original versions of 16 horror stories published
by the English writer in magazines during the
1920s and 1930s. (Rev: BL 4/1/85; NYTBR 5/19/85; PW
3/8/85)

9308 McCormack, Eric. *Paradise Motel.* **1989, Viking $17.95 (0-670-82425-9); Penguin paper $7.95 (0-
14-011451-3).** A narrator's dying grandfather tells

him the stories of four brutally victimized children, but when the narrator embarks on a search
to find the youths he only encounters more stories
of evil. (Rev: BL 9/1/89; NYTBR 11/26/89; PW 7/21/89)

9309 McGrath, Patrick. *Blood and Water: And
Other Tales.* **1989, Ballantine paper $3.95 (0-345-
35585-7).** A collection of 13 creepy stories by the
English-born author of *The Grotesque.* (Rev: NYTBR
3/6/88; PW 12/25/87)

9310 Michaels, Barbara. *Ammie, Come Home.*
1989, Berkley paper $3.95 (0-425-09949-0). A group
of eighteenth-century ghosts work deeds through
twentieth-century people in this novel set in
Washington, D.C. (Rev: LJ 11/15/68; NYTBR 12/15/68;
PW 8/26/68)

9311 Norman, Marsha. *Fortune Teller.* **1987, Random $18.95 (0-394-55500-7); Bantam paper $4.50 (0-
553-27284-5).** A psychic sees into the future and
witnesses events surrounding her daughter, which
she cannot stop from happening. (Rev: BL 3/1/87; LJ
4/15/87; PW 3/6/87)

9312 Oates, Joyce Carol. *Night-Side: 18 Tales.* **1980,
Fawcett paper $2.50 (0-449-24206-4).** A collection of
18 macabre tales by the American writer, includ-
ing "Famine Country," "Fatal Women," and "The
Snowstorm." (Rev: LJ 10/15/77; New Rep 11/26/77;
NYTBR 10/23/77)

9313 Perucho, Joan. *Natural History.* **1988, Knopf
$17.95 (0-394-57058-8); Ballantine paper $4.95 (0-
345-36560-7).** This first English translation of a
three-decade-old novel concerns a thirteenth-century vampire's adventures in twentieth-century
Catalonia. (Rev: BL 1/15/90; LJ 2/15/89; TLS 2/16/90.
Awards: BL, 1989)

9314 Prose, Francine. *Hungry Hearts.* **1983, Pantheon $12.95 (0-394-52767-4).** A possessing spirit
haunts the cast of a Jewish acting troupe on its
travels in North and South America. (Rev: NYTBR 3/
6/83; New Yorker 3/7/83; PW 12/24/82)

9315 Ptacek, Kathryn, ed. *Women of Darkness.*
1989, Tor paper $3.95 (0-8125-2443-8). An anthology
of 20 contemporary horror stories written by
women. (Rev: BL 12/15/88; LJ 12/88; PW 10/7/88)

9316 Rice, Anne. *Interview with the Vampire.* **1986,
Ballantine paper $5.95 (0-345-33766-2).** A debut
novel regarding the memoirs of a two-century-old
vampire. (Rev: BL 6/15/76; LJ 5/1/76; PW 3/8/76)

9317 Rice, Anne. *Queen of the Damned: The Third
Book of the Vampire Chronicles.* **1988, Knopf
$18.95 (0-394-55823-5); Ballantine paper $5.95 (0-
345-35152-5).** This third segment in Rice's Chronicles of the Vampires concerns a plot by a vampire
leader to eliminate most men on earth. "Rice is
doing for the vampire genre what Dashiell Hammett did for that of the private detective."—LJ
(Rev: LJ 10/1/88; PW 8/12/88)

9318 Rice, Anne. *Vampire Lestat.* **1985, Knopf
$24.95 (0-394-53443-3); Ballantine paper $5.95 (0-
345-31386-0).** This second volume of the author's

Chronicles of the Vampires details the life of a vampire rock star. "Outclasses most contemporary horror fiction and is a novel to be savored."—LJ (Rev: BL 9/1/85; LJ 10/1/85; NYTBR 10/27/85)

9319   Rice, Anne. *Witching Hour.* **1990, Knopf $22.45 (0-394-58786-3).** The history of a family of witches over five centuries written by the author of *The Vampire Lestat.* (Rev: BL 9/15/90; LJ 10/15/90; Newsweek 11/5/90)

9320   Saul, John Ralston. *Creature.* **1989, Bantam $12.95 (0-553-05354-X); paper $4.95 (0-553-28411-8).** A small town in Colorado becomes the site of a hormone experiment that causes murderous behaviors by members of the local high school football team. (Rev: BL 2/15/89; LJ 4/1/89)

9321   Shepard, Lucius. *Green Eyes.* **1984, Ace paper $2.95 (0-441-30274-2).** Futuristic biological developments make temporary revival of the dead possible. (Rev: BL 5/15/84; PW 3/30/84)

9322   Simmons, Dan. *Summer of Night.* **1990, Putnam $22.95 (0-399-13573-1).** A group of schoolchildren search for a monster that killed a classmate. "An oustandingly eerie and truly horrifying tale."—PW (Rev: BL 12/1/90; PW 12/14/90)

9323   Straub, Peter. *Floating Dragon.* **1985, Berkley paper $5.50 (0-425-09725-0).** A Connecticut town is struck by a series of gruesome murders following the release of a gas from a chemical research facility. "Vastly entertaining."—NYTBR (Rev: NYTBR 3/6/83; PW 11/12/82; TLS 3/11/83)

9324   Straub, Peter. *Ghost Story.* **1981, Pocket paper $3.95 (0-671-44198-1).** The ghost of an actress killed five decades before tracks down an elderly group of men. (Rev: LJ 4/15/79; Newsweek 4/8/79; PW 2/12/79)

9325   Wilson, F. Paul. *Keep.* **1986, Jove paper $3.95 (0-515-08875-7).** A supernatural force terrorizes a Rumanian fort during World War II. (Rev: BL 7/1/81; PW 6/5/81)

9326   Wright, T. M. *School.* **1990, St. Martin's $17.95 (0-312-85042-5).** A family's occupation of an abandoned school stirs frightening memories of the death of their son. (Rev: BL 8/90; LJ 7/90)

9327   Yarbro, Chelsea Quinn. *Candle for D'Artagnan.* **1989, St. Martin's $22.95 (0-312-93202-2).** A tale of a French vampire in the seventeenth century and her relationships with kings, royal advisors, and the Three Musketeers. (Rev: BL 10/15/89; PW 10/6/89)

9328   Yarbro, Chelsea Quinn. *Flame in Byzantium.* **1987, Tor $17.95 (0-312-93026-7).** A sixth-century Roman vampire flees to Byzantium following war and finds herself the target of persecution. (Rev: LJ 9/1/87; Pw 9/16/87)

SCIENCE FICTION

9329 **Adams, Douglas.** *Dirk Gently's Holistic Detective Agency.* **1989, Pocket paper $4.95 (0-671-69267-4).** This novel by the author of *The Hitchhiker's Guide to the Galaxy* chronicles the exploits of an interstellar private detective who makes use of science to solve mysteries. (REV: BL 7/87; NYTBR 5/8/88; Time 9/7/87)

9330 **Adams, Douglas.** *Hitchhiker's Guide to the Galaxy.* **1990, Pocket paper $4.95 (0-671-70159-2).** An alien friend saves Arthur Dent from earth's destruction and presents Dent with a travel guide to the universe. "Hilarious and irrepressibly clever."—LJ (REV: LJ 9/15/80; NYTBR 1/25/81; PW 7/18/80)

9331 **Adams, Douglas.** *Long Dark Tea-Time of the Soul.* **1989, Simon & Schuster $17.95 (0-671-62583-7); Pocket paper $4.95 (0-671-69404-9).** Science fiction detective Dirk Gently is called upon to investigate events surrounding a mysterious London explosion involving the god Thor. (REV: BL 1/15/89; PW 1/13/89)

9332 **Adams, Douglas.** *Restaurant at the End of the Universe.* **1982, Crown $12.95 (0-517-54535-7).** A portrait of the social scene at a chic outer-space restaurant by the author of *The Hitchhiker's Guide to the Galaxy.* "One of the best pieces of SF humor available."—LJ (REV: LJ 2/15/82; NYTBR 10/24/82)

9333 **Adams, Douglas.** *So Long and Thanks for All the Fish.* **1988, Pocket paper $4.50 (0-671-66493-X).** Space traveler Arthur Dent returns to earth following an eight-year-long voyage he undertook after he believed the planet to have been destroyed. (REV: BL 12/15/84; Time 3/11/85)

9334 **Aldiss, Brian.** *Helliconia Spring.* **1984, Berkley paper $3.95 (0-425-08895-2).** The first volume of the author's series chronicling the development of life on a planet much like earth. (REV: NYTBR 2/26/84; PW 10/14/83)

9335 **Aldiss, Brian.** *Helliconia Summer.* **1986, Ace paper $3.95 (0-425-08650-X).** This sequel to *Helliconia Spring* depicts evolution on a planet where seasons last for decades. (REV: BL 9/15/83; LJ 11/15/83; PW 9/30/83)

9336 **Aldiss, Brian.** *Helliconia Winter.* **1987, Berkley paper $3.95 (0-425-08994-0).** The third and concluding volume of the Helliconia series regarding a planet sinking into an ice age. "Undoubtedly the grandest work of its author."—BL (REV: BL 3/1/85; LJ 4/15/85; PW 3/22/85)

9337 **Aldiss, Brian.** *Last Orders.* **1989, Carroll & Graf $17.95 (0-88184-458-6).** A collection of 14 futuristic stories written during the 1970s concerning the fate of the earth and civilizations on distant planets. (REV: LJ 4/15/89; NYTBR 5/21/89; PW 3/10/89)

9338 **Allen, Roger MacBridge.** *Torch of Honor.* **1986, Baen paper $3.50 (0-671-65607-4).** A soldier from earth with a super weapon infiltrates the planet under siege by Fascist space troops. (REV: BL 4/15/85; PW 1/11/85)

9339 **Anderson, Poul.** *Boat of a Million Years.* **1989, Tor $19.95 (0-312-93199-9).** A group of interconnected stories and novellas about a series of men from different points in history who are unable to die natural deaths. (REV: BL 9/15/89; LJ 11/15/89; PW 10/16/89)

9340 **Anthony, Piers.** *And Eternity.* **1990, Morrow $15.45 (0-688-08688-8).** The sequel to Anthony's *For Love of Evil* and the concluding volume of his Incarnations of Immortality series. (REV: LJ 12/89; PW 11/3/89)

9341 **Anthony, Piers.** *Anthonology.* **1986, Tor paper $3.50 (0-8125-3114-0).** A collection of 21 science fiction short stories with commentaries by the author. (REV: BL 3/1/85; LJ 3/15/85)

9342 **Apostolou, John L., and Martin Greenberg, eds.** *Best Japanese Science Fiction Stories.* **1989, Dembner Books $16.95 (0-942637-06-2); paper $9.95 (0-942637-28-3).** A collection of 13 science fiction short stories translated from the Japanese over the past two decades. (REV: BL 2/15/89; NYTBR 4/9/89)

9343 **Asimov, Isaac.** *Fantastic Voyage.* **1986, Houghton $16.95 (0-395-07352-9); Bantam paper $4.50 (0-553-27572-0).** Five miniaturized people in a submarine inside an important scientist's body are sent to destroy a life-threatening blood clot. (REV: LJ 5/1/66; PW 1/17/66; Sat Rev 3/26/66)

9344 Asimov, Isaac. *Fantastic Voyage II: Destination Brain.* **1987, Doubleday $18.95 (0-385-23926-2); Bantam paper $4.95 (0-553-27327-2).** A kidnapped American is miniaturized and injected into the body of a comatose Soviet physicist in hopes of recovering secrets stored in the scientist's brain. (REV: CSM 1/27/88; LJ 9/15/87; PW 8/7/87)

9345 Asimov, Isaac. *Foundation and Earth.* **1986, Doubleday $16.95 (0-385-23312-4); Ballantine paper $4.95 (0-345-33996-7).** A councilman of a foundation designed to plot the future of the universe scraps five-century-long plans and takes an interplanetary tour to observe the state of other civilizations. (REV: CSM 11/13/86; LJ 10/15/86)

9346 Asimov, Isaac. *Foundation's Edge.* **1982, Doubleday $14.95 (0-385-17725-9); Ballantine paper $4.95 (0-345-30898-0).** An organism holds the key to the control of human destiny in this sequel to the Foundation trilogy. (REV: BL 9/15/82; LJ 10/15/82; NYTBR 12/19/82. AWARDS: Hugo, 1983)

9347 Asimov, Isaac. *Nemesis.* **1989, Doubleday $18.95 (0-385-24792-3).** A star discovered closer to the earth than Alpha Centauri is colonized but threatens the planet when it begins moving toward it. (REV: BL 8/89; LJ 8/89)

9348 Asimov, Isaac. *Prelude to Foundation.* **1988, Doubleday $18.95 (0-385-23313-2); Bantam paper $4.95 (0-553-27839-8).** Asimov returns to the first installment of the Foundation series to portray the life of the scientist who developed "psychohistory." (REV: BL 4/1/88; LJ 5/15/88; PW 4/22/88)

9349 Asimov, Isaac. *Robots and Empire.* **1986, Ballantine paper $4.50 (0-345-32894-9).** Two robots assist humans in their efforts to colonize the universe in this novel featuring characters first introduced in *The Robots of Dawn.* (REV: LJ 9/15/85; NYTBR 10/20/85; PW 8/2/85)

9350 Asimov, Isaac. *Robots of Dawn.* **1984, Ballantine paper $4.95 (0-345-31571-5).** A human-looking robot attempts to save earth from interplanetary threats. (REV: BL 9/15/83; PW 9/2/83)

9351 Asimov, Isaac, and Robert Silverberg. *Nightfall.* **1990, Doubleday $19.95 (0-385-26341-4).** An expanded version of a 1941 Asimov short story considering the effects of an eclipse upon the society of a distant planet that has never known darkness. (REV: BL 10/1/90; LJ 10/15/90)

9352 Attansio, A. A. *Last Legends of Earth.* **1989, Doubleday $18.95 (0-385-26392-9); paper $8.95 (0-385-26393-7).** Alien races embattled billions of years in the future use humans as pawns in war. (REV: BL 9/1/89; LJ 9/15/89; PW 8/4/89)

9353 Ballard, J. G. *Crystal World.* **1988, Farrar paper $7.95 (0-374-52096-8).** The story of a world threatened by the crystallization of the planet's rain forests, written by the author of *Empire of the Sun.* (REV: Choice 9/66; LJ 5/1/66; NYTBR 5/15/66)

9354 Ballard, J. G. *Memories of the Space Age.* **1988, Arkham $16.95 (0-87054-157-9).** Eight short stories written over three decades regarding the future of human exploration of space. (REV: PW 11/4/88; TLS 1/13/89)

9355 Banks, Iain M. *Player of Games.* **1989, St. Martin's $16.95 (0-312-02630-7).** A game master leaves home to play the universe's most challenging game, Azad, the outcome of which could have far-reaching consequences for civilization. (REV: LJ 2/15/89; PW 12/9/88)

9356 Bear, Greg. *Blood Music.* **1986, Ace paper $2.95 (0-441-06796-4).** An expanded version of a pseudonymous novella regarding a scientist's development of cognitive thinking chips that can be injected into humans. "Solidifies his position as a writer of remarkable talent and fresh vision."—LJ (REV: BL 2/1/85; LJ 3/15/85; PW 3/15/85)

9357 Bear, Greg. *Forge of God.* **1987, Tor $17.95 (0-312-93021-6).** Aliens with unstoppable powers plan an invasion of earth. (REV: BL 8/87; LJ 9/15/87; PW 8/21/87)

9358 Benford, Gregory. *Across the Sea of Suns.* **1984, Ultramarine $20.00 (0-671-44668-1); Bantam paper $4.50 (0-553-28211-5).** Scientists discover an apparent plan to destroy planets capable of sustaining organic life. (REV: LJ 2/15/84; PW 12/2/83)

9359 Benford, Gregory. *Against Infinity.* **1983, Ultramarine $20.00 (0-671-46491-4).** Mysterious forces of unknown origin endanger the lives of human settlers on one of Jupiter's moons. (REV: BL 5/1/83; LJ 4/15/83; PW 2/18/83)

9360 Benford, Gregory. *Great Sky River.* **1988, Bantam paper $4.95 (0-553-27318-3).** A story of humans fleeing a race of intelligent metal beings taking over the earth. (REV: BL 10/15/87; CSM 2/9/88; LJ 12/87. AWARDS: BL, the 1980s)

9361 Benford, Gregory. *In the Ocean of Night.* **1987, Bantam paper $3.95 (0-553-26578-4).** In this novel by the author of *Great Sky River,* a future rebel astronaut becomes indispensable to America's space program. (REV: BL 4/1/78; LJ 1/15/78; PW 8/22/77)

9362 Benford, Gregory. *Tides of Light.* **1989, Bantam $17.95 (0-553-05322-1).** Human survivors battle hostile alien groups that threaten their existence in this sequel to *Great Sky River.* (REV: BL 11/15/88; LJ 2/15/89; NYTBR 4/9/89)

9363 Benford, Gregory. *Timescape.* **1983, Pocket paper $3.95 (0-671-50632-3).** Scientists from the future communicate with a physicist in the past to warn him of the dangers of environmental pollution in this novel set in the years 1998 and 1962. (REV: NYTBR 6/28/81; PW 6/5/81; TLS 12/5/80)

9364 Benford, Gregory, and David Brin. *Heart of the Comet.* **1986, Bantam paper $4.50 (0-553-25839-7).** A group of colonists from earth attempt to populate Halley's Comet and ride it on a seven-decade-long voyage around the sun. (REV: BL 1/15/86; CSM 5/16/86; LJ 2/15/86)

9365   Bishop, Michael. *Secret Ascension.* **1987, Tor $16.95 (0-312-93031-3).** The spirit of science fiction writer Philip K. Dick appears during an imaginary fourth term of President Nixon in 1982. (REV: BL 10/15/87; LJ 11/15/87; PW 10/9/87)

9366   Bishop, Michael. *Stolen Faces.* **1977, Ultramarine $20.00 (0-06-010362-0).** As punishment for an insubordinance charge, an officer is sent to the planet Texcatl to oversee a society of lepers schooled in the rites of the Aztecs. (REV: BL 6/1/77; LJ 4/15/77; TLS 1/27/78)

9367   Bonanno, Margaret Wender. *The Others.* **1990, St. Martin's $19.95 (0-312-05140-9).** A story of the struggle between two species—one intellectually advanced, one primitive—for control of the planet. (REV: BL 10/15/90; LJ 9/15/90; PW 9/7/90)

9368   Bova, Ben. *Colony.* **1988, Tor paper $3.95 (0-8125-3245-7).** A novel set in the near future regarding the establishment of a space colony populated by test-tube perfect humans seeking to escape a polluted earth. (REV: BL 10/1/78; PW 5/29/78)

9369   Bova, Ben. *Millennium.* **1976, Random $8.95 (0-394-49421-0).** A futuristic depiction of war between Soviet and American forces halted by the cooperative actions of both countries' lunar troops. (REV: LJ 4/1/76; PW 2/9/76)

9370   Bova, Ben. *Voyagers.* **1989, Tor paper $4.95 (0-8125-0076-8).** United States and Soviet forces cooperate when the planet is threatened by the approach of an alien craft from Jupiter. (REV: BL 9/15/81; PW 6/26/81)

9371   Bradbury, Ray. *Toynbee Convector.* **1988, Knopf $17.95 (0-394-54703-9); Bantam paper $3.95 (0-553-27957-2).** A collection of 23 science fiction stories including "One for His Lordship, and One for the Road!" and "Trapdoor." (REV: BL 5/1/88; LJ 6/15/88; Time 6/27/88)

9372   Brin, David. *Earth.* **1990, Bantam $19.95 (0-553-05778-2).** Ecological disasters and the discovery of a black hole within the interior of the earth spell potential doom for the planet. (REV: BL 4/1/90; LJ 4/15/90)

9373   Brin, David. *Startide Rising.* **1984, Bantam paper $4.95 (0-553-27418-X).** A spaceship crew consisting of dolphins and humans crash-lands on a planet filled with toxic water. (REV: BL 1/1/84; LJ 8/83; PW 8/12/83. AWARDS: Hugo, 1984; Nebula, 1984)

9374   Brin, David. *Uplift War.* **1987, Phantasia Pr. $22.00 (0-932096-44-1); Bantam paper $4.50 (0-553-25121-X).** Humans enlist the forces of other animals to save earth from invading aliens. "A necessary acquisition for nearly any sf collection."—BL (REV: BL 9/1/87; LJ 6/15/87. AWARDS: Hugo, 1988)

9375   Brooke-Rose, Christine. *Xorandor.* **1988, Avon paper $2.95 (0-380-70407-2).** A pair of English twins communicate with a mysterious rock by means of computer language. "Her most accessible work to date."—TLS (REV: BL 6/15/86; NYTBR 8/3/86; TLS 7/11/86)

9376   Brunner, John. *A Maze of Stars.* **1991, Ballantine $18.00 (0-345-36541-0).** An interplanetary spaceship is sent on an endless voyage to observe 600 human colonies placed throughout space. (REV: BL 5/15/91; LJ 6/15/91; NYTBR 7/14/91. AWARDS: BL, 1991)

9377   Brunner, John. *Sheep Look Up.* **1981, Ballantine paper $3.50 (0-685-00691-3).** A portrait of life in a twenty-first-century Denver on the brink of total ecological collapse. (REV: BL 11/1/72; LJ 8/72; Natl Rev 10/13/72)

9378   Brunner, John. *Shockwave Rider.* **1984, Bantam paper $3.95 (0-345-32431-5).** A portrait of a utopian world where people are bred and genetically designed for specific societal purposes. (REV: BL 6/1/75; LJ 2/1/75)

9379   Budrys, Algis. *Michaelmas.* **1986, Warner paper $3.50 (0-445-20316-1).** A human society dominated by a journalist with a master computer is threatened by the reappearance of a dead astronaut. (REV: BL 7/1/77; LJ 8/77; Newsweek 5/23/77)

9380   Burroughs, William S. *Ticket That Exploded.* **1967, Grove-Weidenfeld $7.95 (0-8021-5150-7).** An experimental science fiction novel by the author of *Naked Lunch* mixing elements of a story about an alien invasion with Burroughs's "cut-up" techniques. (REV: LJ 6/1/67; NYTBR 6/18/67)

9381   Butler, Jack. *Nightshade.* **1989, Atlantic Monthly $18.95 (0-87113-315-6).** A novel set on Mars featuring a human hero and 350 vampires written by the author of *Jujitsu for Christ.* "Tremendous lighthearted fun."—NYTBR (REV: NYTBR 9/3/89; New Yorker 11/13/89)

9382   Cadigan, Pat. *Patterns.* **1989, Ursus Imprints $19.95 (0-942861-07-X).** A collection of 14 science fiction/fantasy stories written during the 1980s. (REV: BL 10/15/89; LJ 10/15/89)

9383   Calvino, Italo. *Cosmicomics.* **1976, Harcourt paper $5.95 (0-15-622600-6).** Twelve short stories regarding the creation of the universe as witnessed by a character named Qfwfq. (REV: LJ 11/15/68; NYTBR 8/25/68; PW 6/3/68)

9384   Card, Orson Scott. *Ender's Game.* **1985, Tor $13.95 (0-312-93028-1); paper $3.95 (0-317-57062-5).** A child sent to a space military academy devotes his life to preparing for future wars. "Card at the height of his very considerable powers."—BL (REV: BL 12/1/84; CSM 9/18/86; LJ 2/15/85. AWARDS: Hugo, 1986; Nebula, 1986)

9385   Card, Orson Scott. *Red Prophet.* **1987, Tor $17.95 (0-312-93043-7).** The story of an alternative world in which a young man attempts to prevent a war between colonists and Native Americans. (REV: BL 12/15/87; LJ 2/15/88)

9386   Card, Orson Scott. *Seventh Son.* **1987, St. Martin's $17.95 (0-312-93019-4).** An eighteenth-century alternative world provides the setting for a seventh son with magical powers on the run from forces of evil. "A tribute to the art of storytelling."—LJ (REV: BL 5/1/87; LJ 6/15/87; PW 6/5/87)

9387 **Card, Orson Scott.** *Speaker for the Dead.* **1986, Tor $15.95 (0-312-93738-5); paper $3.95 (0-8125-3257-0).** The sequel to *Ender's Game* portraying the role of Ender Wiggins in a war between colonists and aliens. (Rev: BL 12/15/85; LJ 2/15/86; PW 1/24/86. Awards: Hugo, 1987; Nebula, 1987)

9388 **Card, Orson Scott.** *Treason.* **1988, St. Martin's $18.95 (0-312-02304-9); paper $4.95.** A rewritten version of the author's 1979 novel formerly titled *A Planet Called Treason.* "Exemplifies Card's talent for creating disturbingly compelling, beautifully written stories."—LJ (Rev: BL 10/15/88; LJ 10/15/88; PW 9/16/88)

9389 **Card, Orson Scott.** *Xenocide.* **1991, Tor $21.95 (0-312-85056-5).** In the sequel to *Speaker for the Dead,* a deadly virus threatens to disrupt life and society on the planet Lusitania. "A priority purchase."—LJ (Rev: BL 5/15/91; LJ 5/15/91)

9390 **Chalker, Jack L.** *Midnight at the Well of Souls.* **1985, Tor paper $3.95 (0-345-32445-5).** Four humans visit the planet Well World where people transform into other creatures. (Rev: BL 11/1/77; LJ 7/77; PW 6/6/77)

9391 **Cherryh, C. J.** *Cyteen.* **1988, Warner $18.95 (0-446-51428-4).** The murder of a genetic engineer haunts his scientist double. "Cherryh's talent for intense, literate storytelling maintains interest throughout this long, complex novel."—LJ (Rev: BL 3/15/88; LJ 5/15/88; PW 4/22/88. Awards: Hugo, 1989)

9392 **Cherryh, C. J.** *Rimrunners.* **1989, Warner $19.95 (0-446-51514-0); paper $4.95 (0-445-20979-8).** A marine becomes separated from her spaceship and is forced to reveal personal and military secrets when captured by a pirate vessel. (Rev: BL 4/15/89; LJ 5/15/89; PW 4/28/89)

9393 **Clarke, Arthur C.** *Imperial Earth.* **1987, Ballantine paper $3.95 (0-345-35250-5).** A twenty-third-century scientist makes a trip from Titan to represent his nation at an interstellar conference on earth. "Will hold any reader's attention long into the night."—BL (Rev: BL 2/1/76; LJ 1/15/76; NYTBR 1/8/76)

9394 **Clarke, Arthur C.** *Songs of Distant Earth.* **1987, Ballantine paper $4.95 (0-345-32240-1).** Refugees fleeing an earth destroyed by a worldwide disaster land on an oceanic planet filled with human colonists. (Rev: LJ 4/15/86; NYTBR 5/11/86; TLS 10/31/86)

9395 **Clarke, Arthur C.** *2001: A Space Odyssey.* **1968, NAL paper $3.95 (0-451-15580-7).** A book based on the film of the same title concerning a space mission in the near future directed by an intelligent computer named HAL. (Rev: LJ 8/68; New Yorker 9/21/68)

9396 **Clarke, Arthur C.** *2010: Odyssey Two.* **1987, Ballantine paper $3.95 (0-345-00661-5).** A joint Soviet–American mission is sent to trace the path of the *Discovery* and examine a mysterious black monolith. (Rev: BL 9/1/82; CSM 12/3/82; LJ 11/15/82)

9397 **Clarke, Arthur C.** *2061: Odyssey Three.* **1989, Ballantine paper $4.95 (0-345-35879-1).** The sequel to the author's *2010: Odyssey Two,* detailing missions to Halley's comet and Jupiter's moon Europa. (Rev: BL 11/1/87; LJ 12/87; PW 11/27/87)

9398 **Cowper, Richard.** *Clone.* **1979, Pocket paper $1.75 (0-671-82543-7).** A portrayal of life on earth in the late twenty-first century, when rapidly evolving apes demand equal rights with humans. (Rev: PW 8/6/72; TLS 2/2/73)

9399 **Crichton, Michael.** *Andromeda Strain.* **1969, Knopf $18.95 (0-394-41525-6); Dell paper $4.50 (0-440-10199-9).** An American satellite returns to earth with a deadly virus that kills most of the residents of an Arizona town. (Rev: CSM 6/26/69; LJ 6/15/69; Newsweek 5/26/69)

9400 **Crichton, Michael.** *Sphere.* **1987, Knopf $17.95 (0-394-56110-4); Ballantine paper $5.95 (0-345-35314-5).** A scientist investigates a spaceship located on the floor of the Pacific Ocean. (Rev: BL 5/15/87; Newsweek 7/20/87; Time 6/22/87)

9401 **Crichton, Michael.** *Terminal Man.* **1988, Ballantine paper $4.95 (0-345-35462-1).** Computer-controlled electrodes are planted into the brain of a dangerous psychopath in an attempted cure. (Rev: Atl 5/72; LJ 3/15/72; PW 2/28/72)

9402 **Delany, Samuel R.** *Dhalgren.* **1983, Bantam paper $4.95 (0-553-25391-3).** A story of the life of a poet and rebel youth leader in a future America following an unnamed disaster. (Rev: BL 6/1/75; LJ 3/15/75; NYTBR 2/16/75)

9403 **Delany, Samuel R.** *Stars in My Pocket Like Grains of Sand.* **1984, Bantam $16.95 (0-553-05053-2).** A story portraying life in a future universe with over 6,000 known inhabited worlds, written by the author of *Dhalgren.* (Rev: BL 11/1/84; LJ 11/15/84; PW 11/9/84)

9404 **Dick, Philip K.** *Radio Free Albemuth.* **1985, Ultramarine $15.00 (0-89366-172-4); Avon paper $3.50 (0-380-70288-6).** A portrayal of a fascist United States set in the near future by the author of *Flow My Tears, the Policeman Said.* (Rev: BL 12/1/85; LJ 12/85)

9405 **Dickson, Gordon R.** *Forever Man.* **1986, Ace $16.95 (0-441-24712-1); paper $3.50 (0-441-24713-X).** A fighter pilot seeks to find information about aliens engaged in a battle against humans. (Rev: BL 9/1/86; PW 8/15/86)

9406 **Dickson, Gordon R.** *Way of the Pilgrim.* **1987, Ace $16.95 (0-441-87486-X); paper $4.50 (0-441-87487-8).** The subjugation of earth's citizenry by alien giants leads to resistance and revolt. (Rev: BL 9/1/87; LJ 5/15/87; PW 3/27/87)

9407 **Disch, Thomas M.** *On Wings of Song.* **1979, Ultramarine $20.00 (0-312-58466-0); Carroll & Graf paper $3.95 (0-88184-443-8).** A novel set in a near-future America following the development of a device that allows individuals to fly at will. (REV: PW 6/11/79; TLS 12/7/79)

9408 Disch, Thomas M. *Three Thirty-Four.* 1987, Carroll & Graf paper $3.95 (0-88184-340-7). Interconnected tales concerning the lives of a group of people in one urban dwelling, set during the 2300s. (REV: NYTBR 9/8/74; PW 1/7/74)

9409 Engh, M. J. *Arslan.* 1987, Morrow $17.95 (0-87795-884-X); Tor paper $3.95 (0-8125-3676-2). This novel, first published in paperback in 1976, concerns a conquering Asian warlord bent on the earth's destruction. (REV: BL 5/1/87; NYTBR 3/28/76; PW 4/10/87)

9410 Farmer, Philip José. *Dayworld.* 1986, Berkley paper $3.50 (0-425-08474-4). A portrait of a futuristic world that is so overcrowded that people are allowed to live outside in a state of suspended animation for one day a week. (REV: BL 11/15/84; LJ 2/15/85; PW 1/4/85)

9411 Farmer, Philip José. *Fabulous Riverboat.* 1985, Berkley paper $3.50 (0-425-09958-X). The story of a planet populated by all the people who ever lived on earth and the efforts of Mark Twain to discover the world's secrets. (REV: BL 4/1/72; PW 11/15/71)

9412 Farmer, Philip José. *Magic Labyrinth.* 1984, Berkley paper $3.50 (0-425-09550-9). The fourth and final volume of the Riverworld series features a confrontation between Samuel Clemens and King John in a story that also features Hermann Goering, Tom Mix, and Sir Richard Burton as characters. (REV: BL 7/15/80; PW 5/9/80; Time 7/28/80)

9413 Forward, Robert L. *Dragon's Egg.* 1983, Ballantine paper $3.95 (0-345-31666-5). A portrait of life on a collapsed neutron star under forces of extreme gravity. (REV: BL 7/1/80; LJ 4/15/80; PW 3/14/80)

9414 Forward, Robert L. *Starquake.* 1986, Ballantine paper $3.95 (0-345-31233-3). Scientists observing a neutron star establish communications with the body's inhabitants. (REV: BL 10/15/85; LJ 10/15/85)

9415 Gibson, William. *Count Zero.* 1986, Ultramarine $15.95 (0-89366-170-8); Ace paper $3.95 (0-441-11773-2). A portrait of a future world where technology runs rampant, by the author of *Neuromancer.* (REV: LJ 3/15/86; TLS 6/20/86)

9416 Gibson, William. *Mona Lisa Overdrive.* 1988, Bantam $17.95 (0-553-05250-0); paper $4.95 (0-553-28174-7). A story of a teenage hooker living in a futuristic highly technological society, by the author of *Neuromancer.* "The undisputed champion of cyberpunk."—NYTBR (REV: BL 7/88; LJ 10/15/88; NYTBR 12/11/88)

9417 Gibson, William. *Neuromancer.* 1984, Ace paper $3.95 (0-441-56959-5). Cyberpunk novel portraying the adventures of a computer hacker in the twenty-first century. (REV: NYTBR 11/24/85; TLS 12/7/84. AWARDS: Hugo, 1985; Nebula, 1985)

9418 Haldeman, Joe. *The Forever War.* 1985, Ballantine paper $3.50 (0-345-32489-7). A portrait of the life of a human infantryman and his experiences during a 700-year-long war between earth and the planet Aldebaran. (REV: BL 6/1/75; NYTBR 3/23/75. AWARDS: Hugo, 1976; Nebula, 1976)

9419 Haldeman, Joe. *Mindbridge.* 1976, Ultramarine $20.00 (0-89366-143-0). An alien creature enables some humans to have telepathic powers in this story set in the middle of the twenty-first century. (REV: BL 10/1/76; LJ 9/15/76; NYTBR 2/24/77)

9420 Harrison, Harry. *West of Eden.* 1985, Bantam paper $4.95 (0-553-26551-2). Dinosaurs that evolved further rather than becoming extinct fight humans in a war for control of the earth. (REV: BL 6/1/84; LJ 8/84; PW 6/15/84)

9421 Heinlein, Robert A. *Cat Who Walks Through Walls: A Comedy of Manners.* 1988, Ace paper $4.95 (0-441-09499-6). A man who discovers his wife is an alien is sent on a mission to destroy an omnipotent computer in this story set some time in the near future. (REV: BL 8/85; LJ 11/15/85; NYTBR 12/22/85)

9422 Heinlein, Robert A. *Job: A Comedy of Justice.* 1985, Ballantine paper $4.95 (0-345-31650-9). A reverend finds himself transported to a parallel universe where he is transformed into an international businessman. (REV: BL 8/84; CSM 12/10/84; NYTBR 11/11/84)

9423 Heinlein, Robert A. *The Moon Is a Harsh Mistress.* 1989, Trafalgar $22.95 (0-450-50280-5); Ace paper $3.95 (0-441-53699-9). The story of a twenty-first-century prison revolt at a lunar penal institution. (REV: LJ 6/15/66; Natl Rev 12/13/66; PW 5/23/66. AWARDS: Hugo, 1967)

9424 Heinlein, Robert A. *Past Through Tomorrow.* 1988, Ace paper $5.50 (0-441-65304-9). A collection of 21 stories ranging in time from the late 1930s to early 1960s including the novel-length "Methuselah's Children." (REV: BL 7/1/67; LJ 4/15/67)

9425 Heinlein, Robert A. *Time Enough for Love: The Lives of Lazarus Long.* 1986, Berkley paper $4.95 (0-425-10224-6). The memoirs of a 2,000-year-old man chronicled by the author of *Stranger in a Strange Land.* (REV: BL 11/1/73; LJ 9/15/73; NYTBR 9/23/73)

9426 Herbert, Frank. *Chapterhouse: Dune.* 1985, Putnam $17.95 (0-399-13027-6); Berkley paper $7.95 (0-425-09214-3). This sixth volume of the Dune series concerns the efforts of The Sisterhood to save the universe from its warring factions. (REV: BL 3/1/85; LJ 3/15/85; NYTBR 6/16/85)

9427 Herbert, Frank. *Children of Dune.* 1987, Ace paper $4.95 (0-441-10402-9). This third volume in the Dune series following *Dune* and *Dune Messiah* concerns life on a waterless planet. "An unqualified success."—NYTBR (REV: LJ 6/1/76; NYTBR 8/1/76; PW 3/8/76)

9428 Herbert, Frank. *Dosadi Experiment.* **1984, Berkley paper $3.95 (0-425-10244-0).** In this novel by the author of *Dune*, humans compete for survival with froglike creatures on the planet Dosadi. (REV: BL 9/1/77; LJ 10/1/77; PW 7/4/77)

9429 Herbert, Frank. *God Emperor of Dune.* **1986, Berkley paper $7.95 (0-425-06128-0).** The fourth in the Dune series, set three-and-one-half millenia after the first three titles, portrays the metamorphosis of an aging ruler into a huge worm. "The best since *Dune* itself."—PW (REV: BL 4/1/81; NYTBR 5/17/81; PW 3/27/81)

9430 Herbert, Frank. *Heretics of Dune.* **1984, Putnam $16.95 (0-399-12898-0); Berkley paper $4.50 (0-425-08732-8).** This fifth installment in the Dune series traces life on two planets, as reflected through the eyes of two children. (REV: LJ 3/15/84; NYTBR 6/10/84; PW 2/10/84)

9431 Herbert, Frank. *White Plague.* **1987, Ace paper $4.95 (0-441-88569-1).** A mad biologist seeks revenge by introducing a deadly plague into Ireland following a terrorist bombing that kills his family. (REV: BL 7/82; PW 7/9/82; Time 11/15/82)

9432 Hogan, James P. *Code of the Lifemaker.* **1984, Ballantine paper $3.95 (0-345-30549-3).** An alien robot society on Titan is threatened by earth humans bent on the moon's economic exploitation. (REV: BL 7/83; LJ 6/15/83; PW 5/13/83)

9433 Hogan, James P. *Genesis Machine.* **1987, Ballantine paper $2.95 (0-345-34756-0).** A tale of the discovery of a unified field theory that helps save the earth and makes interstellar travel feasible. (REV: BL 4/1/78; PW 4/3/78)

9434 Jeter, K. W. *Farewell Horizontal.* **1989, St. Martin's $16.95 (0-312-02574-2); NAL paper $3.95 (0-451-16278-1).** A portrait of an artist's creative life in a self-contained floating world. (REV: BL 1/15/89; LJ 2/15/89; PW 12/2/88)

9435 Kessel, John. *Good News from Outer Space.* **1989, St. Martin's $18.95 (0-312-93178-6); Tor paper $4.95 (0-8125-0905-6).** The story of a group of religious fanatics awaiting the millennium and of a reporter who finds evidence that aliens are on their way to visit the earth. (REV: LJ 9/15/89; PW 8/11/89)

9436 Kilworth, Garry. *Theatre of Timesmiths.* **1986, Warner paper $3.50 (0-445-20116-9).** The futuristic story of a post-nuclear holocaust England threatened by encroaching walls of ice. (REV: PW 6/21/85; TLS 5/18/84)

9437 Kress, Nancy. *Alien Light.* **1988, Morrow $18.95 (0-87795-940-4); Avon paper $3.50 (0-380-70706-3).** Humans colonize an alien planet, while their warlike, competitive behavior is observed by a cooperative, peaceful society. (REV: BL 12/15/87; LJ 12/87; PW 12/25/87)

9438 Kress, Nancy. *Brain Rose.* **1990, Morrow $22.95 (0-688-09452-X).** Brain surgery allows people to relive their past lives in this novel set in the third decade of the twenty-first century. (REV: BL 12/1/89; LJ 12/89)

9439 Lee, Tanith. *Dreams of Dark and Lights: The Great Short Fiction of Tanith Lee.* **1986, Arkham $21.95 (0-87054-153-6).** A collection of 23 science fiction, fantasy, and horror stories. "A must for Lee fans, and a good introduction for those new to her work."—PW (REV: BL 8/86; PW 7/4/86)

9440 Lee, Tanith. *Silver Metal Lover.* **1985, Crown paper $6.95 (0-517-55853-X).** A teenager falls in love with a robot in a doomed relationship. (REV: BL 6/1/82; PW 3/19/82)

9441 Le Guin, Ursula K. *The Dispossessed: An Ambiguous Utopia.* **1976, Avon paper $3.95 (0-380-00382-1).** A portrait of two planets revolving around the same star with differing social systems. (REV: CSM 6/26/74; Time 8/5/74; TLS 6/20/75. AWARDS: Hugo, 1975; Nebula, 1975)

9442 Le Guin, Ursula K. *Left Hand of Darkness.* **1983, Ace paper $3.95 (0-441-47812-3).** A portrait of life and society on a sexually ambiguous planet where gender is defined for only a short period of time each year. (REV: LJ 6/15/70; TLS 1/8/70. AWARDS: Hugo, 1970; Nebula, 1970)

9443 Le Guin, Ursula K. *The Word for World Is Forest.* **1978, Ace paper $3.50 (0-441-90915-9).** This portrait of the lost Edenic forest world of the Athsheans serves as an allegory for the societies of Southeast Asia. (REV: BL 6/1/76; TLS 7/8/77)

9444 Lem, Stanislaw. *Eden.* **1989, Harcourt $19.95 (0-15-127580-7).** A story originally published in Poland in 1959 concerning a spaceship's crash on an alien planet and the efforts of its six crew members to communicate with the world's inhabitants. (REV: BL 9/15/89; LJ 8/89; TLS 2/9/90. AWARDS: BL, 1989)

9445 Lem, Stanislaw. *Fiasco.* **1987, Harcourt $17.95 (0-15-130640-0); paper $6.95 (0-15-630630-1).** Space explorers encounter a ghost planet with signs of technology but no apparent life forms. (REV: BL 5/15/87; PW 4/10/87; Time 6/1/87)

9446 Lem, Stanislaw. *Futurological Congress.* **1985, Harcourt paper $5.95 (0-15-634040-2).** A man attends a Costa Rican-hosted conference in the future where human behavior and thought are controlled by mind-altering drugs placed in the air and water. (REV: BL 2/1/75; Choice 4/75; LJ 11/15/74)

9447 Lem, Stanislaw. *Imaginary Magnitude.* **1985, Harcourt paper $7.95 (0-15-644180-2).** A collection of prefaces to five imaginary futuristic works of literature and science. "Head and shoulders above most science fiction."—BL (REV: BL 8/84; NYTBR 9/2/84; PW 6/15/84)

9448 Lem, Stanislaw. *Memoirs of a Space Traveler: Further Reminiscences of Ijon Tichy.* **1983, Harcourt paper $5.95 (0-15-658635-5).** A collection of nine stories regarding the internal and interstellar voyages of space traveler Ijon Tichy. (REV: LJ 1/15/82; NYTBR 9/19/82; TLS 3/19/82)

9449 Lessing, Doris. *Documents Relating to the Sentimental Agents in the Volyen Empire.* 1983, Random $12.95 (0-394-52968-5); paper $4.95 (0-394-72386-4). An agent of the Canopean Empire records his experiences in documents and journals. "The most approachable of Lessing's Canopean fare."— CSM (Rev: CSM 6/22/83; LJ 3/1/83; NYTBR 4/3/83)

9450 Lessing, Doris. *Making of the Representative for Planet Eight.* 1988, Random paper $6.95 (0-679-72015-4). The story of a planet sunk into the ice age by the tilting of its axis and the efforts of its inhabitants to survive the disaster. (Rev: BL 12/15/81; LJ 2/1/82; TLS 4/2/82)

9451 Lessing, Doris. *Marriages Between Zones Three, Four and Five.* 1980, Knopf $13.95 (0-394-50914-5); Random paper $8.95 (0-394-79478-2). A series of marriages between interplanetary societal groups are undertaken to form alliances between them. "Lessing at her best: imaginative, persuasive, probing."—Choice (Rev: Choice 11/80; LJ 4/1/80; Time 4/21/80)

9452 Lichtenberg, Jacqueline. *Dreamspy.* 1989, St. Martin's $19.95 (0-312-03327-3). Two rival groups, one alien and one human, fight for control of interstellar travel systems. (Rev: BL 11/15/89; LJ 11/15/89; PW 10/27/89)

9453 Lynn, Elizabeth A. *Sardonyx Net.* 1985, Berkley paper $3.50 (0-425-08635-6). The story of a society where slaves are controlled by a drug whose reserve supplies are rapidly diminishing. (Rev: BL 2/15/82; PW 11/13/81)

9454 MacDonald, Ian. *Desolation Road.* 1988, Bantam paper $3.95 (0-553-27057-5). A community of misfits on Mars becomes the center of resistance to an authoritative oppressive government. (Rev: LJ 2/15/88; PW 1/22/88)

9455 McIntyre, Vonda. *Transition.* 1991, Bantam paper $4.95 (0-553-28850-4). A confrontation between space explorers and residents of the Tau Ceti planets. "McIntyre at her best."—LJ (Rev: BL 1/1/91; LJ 12/90)

9456 McKillip, Patricia. *Fool's Run.* 1988, Warner paper $4.95 (0-445-20518-0). A mass murderer visited in outer planetary prison by her sister sets off a series of psychic disturbances throughout the universe. (Rev: BL 5/15/87; CSM 6/5/87; LJ 4/15/87)

9457 Malzburg, Barry N. *Beyond Apollo.* 1989, Carroll & Graf paper $3.50 (0-88184-551-5). Mysterious circumstances surround the death of the captain of humankind's first trip to the planet Venus. (Rev: NYTBR 4/14/74; TLS 8/23/74)

9458 Martin, George R. R. *Dying of the Light.* 1990, Baen paper $3.50 (0-671-69861-3). The protagonist journeys to a planet in search of a long-lost love after receiving a jewel with a compelling message. (Rev: BL 1/1/78; LJ 10/15/77)

9459 Martin, George R. R. *Sandkings.* 1986, Pocket paper $2.95 (0-671-42663-X). Seven pieces of short

fiction combining elements of science fiction and horror. (Rev: BL 12/15/81; LJ 12/15/81; PW 11/6/81)

9460 May, Julian. *Intervention.* 1987, Houghton $18.95 (0-395-43782-2); Ballantine paper $4.95 (0-345-35523-7). A fictional account of the arms race from the end of World War II through the twenty-first century that enlists the aid of psychic aliens to help humans solve problems. "A superb piece of speculative fiction."—LJ (Rev: BL 8/87; LJ 8/87)

9461 Milan, Victor. *Cybernetic Samurai.* 1986, Ace paper $3.50 (0-441-13234-0). A Japanese-produced artificially intelligent robot is endowed with the moral code of the samurai. (Rev: BL 8/85; LJ 8/85; PW 6/21/85)

9462 Milan, Victor. *Cybernetic Shogun.* 1990, Morrow $19.45 (1-557-10003-9). The sequel to *Cybernetic Samurai* concerning the rivalry for power between the offsprings of an artificially intelligent computer. (Rev: BL 3/1/90; LJ 2/15/90; PW 1/19/90)

9463 Moffett, Judith. *Pennterra.* 1988, Harlequin Books paper $3.95 (0-373-30305-X). A utopian planet receives visits from humans who threaten its ecology and a long-established settlement from earth. (Rev: BL 9/15/87; LJ 9/15/87; PW 9/25/87)

9464 Niven, Larry. *Integral Trees.* 1985, Ballantine paper $4.95 (0-345-32065-4). A thick ball of gas surrounding a distant planet is able to sustain the lives of its human colonists. "This superbly blended combination of hard sf and human adventure deserves a wide readership."—LJ (Rev: BL 2/1/84; LJ 3/15/84; PW 1/20/84)

9465 Niven, Larry. *Long Arm of Gil Hamilton.* 1986, Ballantine paper $3.50 (0-345-34238-0). Three novellas cataloging the exploits of futuristic detective Gil Hamilton. (Rev: BL 6/1/76; PW 1/12/76)

9466 Niven, Larry. *World Out of Time.* 1986, Ballantine paper $3.95 (0-345-33696-8). A space traveler on a long voyage returns to earth to find its climate and societies radically changed. "Will challenge the most sophisticated readers."—BL (Rev: BL 9/1/76; LJ 9/1/76; PW 8/23/76)

9467 Niven, Larry, and Jerry Pournelle. *Footfall.* 1986, Ballantine paper $4.95 (0-345-32344-0). Aliens with pachydermic features take over the earth and begin a war with humans over the planet. "Thought provoking and exciting . . . highly recommended."—LJ (Rev: BL 4/15/85; LJ 5/15/85; NYTBR 9/8/85)

9468 Niven, Larry, and Jerry Pournelle. *Lucifer's Hammer.* 1985, Fawcett paper $4.95 (0-449-20813-3). Human society waits apprehensively while a comet ventures closer and closer to the earth. "One of the most ambitious disaster novels to date."— NYTBR (Rev: BL 7/1/77; LJ 7/77; NYTBR 11/13/77)

9469 Niven, Larry, and Jerry Pournelle. *Oath of Fealty.* 1984, Pocket paper $3.95 (0-671-53227-8). A portrait of life in a futuristic enclosed city situated near Los Angeles. "Well-told, fast moving and consistently interesting."—BL (REV: BL 9/15/81; LJ 10/15/81; PW 9/18/81)

9470 Piercy, Marge. *He, She and It.* **1991, Knopf $22.00 (0-679-40408-2).** Two linked stories set in the twenty-first and sixteenth centuries weaving a tale of life after nuclear holocaust and the persecution of Jews in a Prague ghetto. (REV: BL 9/1/91; LJ 9/1/91; PW 8/23/91)

9471 Piercy, Marge. *Woman on the Edge of Time.* **1985, Fawcett paper $4.95 (0-449-21082-0).** A Mexican-American woman unsatisfied with life uses psychic powers to see the alternative life she could have led in the twenty-first century. (REV: BL 7/15/76; Choice 10/76; NYTBR 6/20/76)

9472 Platt, Charles. *Silicon Man.* **1991, Bantam paper $4.50 (0-553-28950-0).** An FBI agent investigating a deadly new weapon is kidnapped by its designer to be used in a test to transfer the contents of a human brain to a computer. (REV: BL 2/15/91; NYTBR 4/21/91)

9473 Pohl, Frederik. *Gateway.* **1987, Ballantine paper $4.95 (0-345-34690-4).** An asteroid formerly inhabited by aliens is discovered and researched by astronauts who study the remnants of a lost generation. (REV: BL 4/1/77; LJ 3/1/77; TLS 1/27/78. AWARDS: Hugo, 1978; Nebula, 1978)

9474 Pohl, Frederik. *Homegoing.* **1990, Ballantine paper $4.95 (0-345-36550-X).** The experiences of a human living among the marsupial-like Hakh'hli. (REV: BL 2/1/89; LJ 3/15/89; PW 2/10/89)

9475 Pohl, Frederik. *Midas World.* **1984, Tor paper $2.95 (0-8125-4925-2).** A prologue and six stories portraying a futuristic society overwhelmed by an overabundance of goods and resources. (REV: BL 9/1/83; LJ 6/15/83; PW 6/17/83)

9476 Pohl, Frederik. *Narabedla Ltd.* **1989, Ballantine paper $4.95 (0-345-36026-5).** The trail of a series of mysterious deaths of entertainers leads to an organization called Narabedla Ltd. (REV: BL 2/15/88; LJ 3/15/88; PW 2/19/88)

9477 Pohl, Frederik. *World at the End of Time.* **1990, Ballantine $17.95 (0-345-33976-2).** Frozen and reanimated humans face destruction of the planet by warfare after being in a state of suspended animation for thousands of years. (REV: BL 5/15/90; LJ 6/15/90)

9478 Poyer, D. C. *Stepfather Bank.* **1988, St. Martin's paper $3.50 (0-312-91045-2).** A portrait of the life of a twenty-first-century poet who is the last remaining free spirit in an otherwise sterile society. (REV: BL 8/87; LJ 8/87; PW 7/3/87)

9479 Preuss, Paul. *Human Error.* **1987, Tor paper $3.95 (0-8125-4987-2).** Laboratory-created intelligence chips designed to increase human brain capacity have varying results when tested on human subjects. (REV: BL 11/15/85; PW 10/4/85)

9480 Preuss, Paul. *Starfire.* **1988, Tor $17.95 (0-312-93056-9).** A former astronaut leads a perilous mission to asteroids to obtain minerals. (REV: BL 4/15/88; LJ 3/15/88)

9481 Resnick, Mike. *Ivory: A Legend of Past and Future.* **1988, Tor $17.95 (0-312-93093-3); paper $4.95 (0-8125-0042-3).** Twelve stories tracing seven millennia from the nineteenth century in Africa to a space search for the last of the Masai tribe. (REV: LJ 9/15/88; PW 7/29/88)

9482 Robinson, Kim Stanley. *Pacific Edge.* **1990, St. Martin's $18.95 (0-312-85097-2).** A futuristic vision of Orange County, California, as a twenty-first-century ecological utopia. (REV: BL 11/1/90; NYTBR 12/9/90; PW 10/12/90)

9483 Scott, Melissa. *Five-Twelfths of Heaven.* **1990, Simon & Schuster paper $3.95 (0-671-69883-4).** A young woman escapes from an oppressive government dominating a known universe and makes her way via spaceship to the mysterious planet earth. (REV: BL 6/1/85; LJ 3/15/85)

9484 Sheffield, Charles. *Sight of Proteus.* **1988, Ballantine paper $3.95 (0-345-34433-2).** A first novel regarding two scientists who have developed techniques to change the human body into other forms. (REV: BL 1/1/79; LJ 1/1/79)

9485 Silverberg, Robert. *At Winter's End.* **1989, Warner $4.95 (0-446-35397-3).** Six tribes living in caves fight for survival on earth following a new ice age. (REV: CSM 7/1/88; LJ 4/15/88; PW 3/11/88)

9486 Silverberg, Robert. *Beyond the Safe Zone: Collected Short Fiction of Robert Silverberg.* **1986, Donald I. Fine $18.95 (0-917657-60-8); Warner paper $3.95 (0-446-30173-6).** A collection of 27 science fiction short stories and novellas by the prolific writer. (REV: BL 3/1/86; PW 3/27/86)

9487 Silverberg, Robert. *Born with the Dead.* **1988, Tor paper $2.95 (0-8125-5952-5).** Three novellas exploring the fate of men's souls after death, including "Going," "Thomas the Proclaimer," and the title story. (REV: NYTBR 8/24/75; PW 3/14/75; TLS 8/8/75)

9488 Silverberg, Robert. *New Springtime.* **1990, Warner $19.95 (0-446-51442-X).** A war between the evolutionary descendants of insects and primates follows the retreat of an ice age in a story set in the far distant future. (REV: BL 4/1/90; LJ 4/15/90)

9489 Silverberg, Robert. *Star of Gypsies.* **1986, Donald I. Fine $18.95 (0-917657-92-6); Warner paper $5.95 (0-445-20618-7).** The story of an interstellar gypsy empire and its rivalry with human colonists set in the distant future and covering 3,000 years. (REV: BL 8/86; LJ 9/15/86; PW 8/1/86)

9490 Silverberg, Robert. *Tower of Glass.* **1987, Warner $3.95 (0-446-34509-1).** A futuristic novel about a twenty-third-century society where androids outnumber humans. (REV: LJ 12/1/70; PW 8/24/70)

9491 Simmons, Dan. *Fall of Hyperion.* **1990, Doubleday $18.95 (0-385-24950-0); paper $8.95 (0-385-**

26747-9). This sequel to the author's *Hyperion* chronicles the struggles of seven earth colonists against artificially intelligent beings on the planet. (REV: BL 3/1/90; LJ 3/15/90; PW 2/9/90. AWARDS: BL, 1990)

9492 Sladek, John. *Muller-Fokker Effect.* **1973, Pocket paper $0.95 (0-671-77622-3).** Computer tapes with human personality traits influence the actions of a future U.S. government. (REV: LJ 1/1/72; NYTBR 11/14/71; PW 10/18/71)

9493 Spinrad, Norman. *Child of Fortune.* **1986, Bantam paper $4.50 (0-553-25690-4).** The story of a young woman seeking a purpose in life and her adventures on an interplanetary voyage. (REV: BL 6/15/85; NYTBR 9/8/85)

9494 Spinrad, Norman. *Russian Spring.* **1991, Bantam $20.00 (0-553-07586-1).** An American engineer moves to the Soviet Union to become involved in its program of space exploration and development. "Intelligent, detailed, well constructed, and emotionally compelling."—BL (REV: BL 9/1/91; LJ 8/91)

9495 Spinrad, Norman. *Void Captain's Tale.* **1983, Ultramarine $20.00 (0-671-43483-7).** A study of life aboard a spaceship guided by a lovestruck captain, traveling through a section of the universe known as the Void, written by the author of *Russian Spring.* "An impressive and important work."—PW (REV: NYTBR 5/22/83; PW 11/5/82)

9496 Steele, Allen M. *Clarke County, Space.* **1990, Berkley paper $3.95 (0-441-11044-4).** Life on the world's first space colony is disrupted when it accepts a refugee fleeing from earth. (REV: BL 12/1/90; LJ 12/90)

9497 Sterling, Bruce. *Islands in the Net.* **1989, Ace paper $4.50 (0-441-37423-9).** A computer-dominated earth in the near future where individuals try to cope with rampant technologies. (REV: BL 6/1/88; LJ 6/15/88; PW 5/20/88)

9498 Sterling, Bruce, ed. *Mirrorshades: The Cyberpunk Anthology.* **1986, Morrow $16.95 (0-87795-868-8).** A collection of 12 cyberpunk stories from the early 1980s, including contributions by Greg Bear, William Gibson, Rudy Rucker, and Pat Cadigan. (REV: BL 12/15/86; LJ 12/86; NYTBR 1/18/87)

9499 Strugatsky, Arkady, and Boris Strugatsky. *Time Wanderers.* **1988, St. Martin's paper $2.95 (0-312-91020-7).** A futuristic story of earth under the domination of the time-traveling Wanderers written by the Soviet sibling science fiction team. (REV: BL 4/1/87; LJ 4/15/87)

9500 Tepper, Sheri S. *Raising the Stones.* **1990, Doubleday $19.95 (0-385-41510-9).** A stuggle for dominance between rival societies on a far distant solar system. (REV: LJ 8/90; PW 7/13/90)

9501 Theroux, Paul. *O-Zone.* **1987, Ivy Books paper $4.95 (0-8041-0151-5).** A portrait of the United States 75 years in the future where segments of the Midwest contaminated by nuclear waste are beginning to be reexplored and resettled. (REV: BL 6/1/86; PW 7/25/86; Time 9/1/86)

9502 Tiptree, James, Jr. *Out of the Everywhere and Other Extraordinary Visions.* **1981, Ballantine paper $2.75 (0-345-28485-2).** A collection of ten short stories with science fiction themes including the title story, "Beaver Tears," and "The Screwfly Solution." "Sf at its very best."—LJ (REV: BL 3/1/82; LJ 12/15/81; PW 11/13/81)

9503 Tiptree, James, Jr. *Starry Rift.* **1986, Tor $14.95 (0-312-93744-X).** A collection of three stories dealing with future space exploration, including "Collision," "The Only Neat Thing to Do," and "Good Night, Sweethearts." (REV: BL 5/1/86; LJ 6/15/86; PW 5/30/86)

9504 Turner, George. *Brain Child.* **1991, Morrow $20.00 (0-688-10595-5).** An Australian writer's story of that nation in the next century when it is ruled by genetically engineered superhumans. (REV: BL 5/1/91; LJ 4/15/91; PW 4/19/91)

9505 Varley, John. *Persistence of Vision.* **1984, Berkley paper $2.95 (0-425-07300-9).** Nine stories of life in the future and human adaptations to changes in technology. "The best single-author sf collection in years."—LJ (REV: BL 7/1/78; LJ 6/15/78; PW 5/22/78)

9506 Vinge, Vernon. *Peace War.* **1984, Ultramarine $20.00 (0-317-58849-4); Baen paper $3.50 (0-671-55965-6).** Three individuals from the past attempt to overthrow an oppressive government running a futuristic world. (REV: BL 9/1/84; LJ 9/15/84)

9507 Watson, Ian. *Embedding.* **1990, Carroll & Graf paper $3.95 (0-88184-554-X).** Watson's debut novel chronicles the efforts of a linguist seeking the origins of human language through a series of experiments involving infants and children. (REV: BL 9/1/75; Choice 10/75; TLS 11/9/75)

9508 Watson, Ian. *Flies of Memory.* **1991, Carroll & Graf $18.95 (0-88184-782-8).** A chronicle of the world's reaction to the visit of aliens and their trip to Rome. "One of the most ambitious and rewarding science fiction novels of the year."—PW (REV: BL 11/15/91; PW 11/8/91)

9509 Wilhelm, Kate. *Huysman's Pets.* **1986, Bluejay $15.95 (0-312-94219-2); Ace paper $3.50 (0-441-35441-6).** A writer attempts to save the world's children from a mad scientist's attempts to misuse his breakthrough research. (REV: BL 1/1/86; LJ 2/15/86; PW 1/3/86)

9510 Williams, Walter John. *Voice of the Whirlwind.* **1987, Tor $16.95 (0-312-93013-5).** A clone of a combat hero searches for reasons behind the hero's death. "One of the most exciting—and readable—writers of new wave sf."—LJ (REV: BL 5/1/87; LJ 5/15/87; PW 4/3/87)

9511 Willis, Connie. *Fire Watch.* **1986, Bantam paper $3.50 (0-553-26045-6).** A collection of a novella and 11 science fiction stories, which includes two Nebula Award winners. (REV: BL 2/15/85; LJ 2/15/85; PW 1/18/85)

9512 Zahn, Timothy. *A Coming of Age.* **1984, Bluejay $14.95 (0-312-94058-0); Baen paper $3.50 (0-671-65578-7).** The story of a scientist's efforts to determine why children on the planet have telepathic and telekinetic powers that they lose upon reaching puberty. (REV: BL 2/1/85; PW 12/14/84)

9513 Zelazny, Roger. *Doors of His Face, the Lamps of His Mouth and Other Stories.* **1987, Avon paper $3.50 (0-380-01146-8).** Fifteen science fiction tales from the 1960s including the Nebula Award–winning title story. (REV: LJ 6/1/71; PW 5/3/71)

9514 Zelazny, Roger. *Doorways in the Sand.* **1976, Ultramarine $20.00 (0-89366-140-6); Avon paper $2.95 (0-380-00949-8).** A story regarding future interplanetary commerce and trade between earth and other societies. (REV: BL 4/1/76; LJ 3/15/76; NYTBR 5/23/76)

9515 Zelazny, Roger. *Eye of Cat.* **1982, Ultramarine $20.00 (0-671-25519-3).** An alien seeks the last surviving Navajo in order to help him save the earth from a predator threatening world destruction. (REV: LJ 10/15/82; NYTBR 12/19/82)

9516 Zelazny, Roger. *Frost and Fire: Fantasy and Science Fiction Stories.* **1989, Morrow $16.95 (0-688-08942-9); Avon paper $3.50 (0-380-75775-3).** Short stories by the veteran science fiction writer including the Hugo-winning "Permafrost." "A solid contribution to SF literature."—LJ (REV: BL 7/89; LJ 6/15/89)

9517 Zelazny, Roger. *Trumps of Doom.* **1986, Avon paper $3.50 (0-380-89635-4).** A twentieth-century adopted earthling makes a voyage to his ancestral home planet Amber to clear up mysteries haunting his life. (REV: BL 5/15/85; LJ 5/15/85; PW 4/12/85)

9518 Zembrowski, George. *Omega Point Trilogy.* **1983, Ace paper $2.75 (0-441-62381-6).** A civil war between humans and a genetically altered race leaves the earth in a state of exhaustion. (REV: BL 1/15/84; PW 10/14/83)

9519 Zindell, David. *Neverness.* **1988, Donald I. Fine $18.95 (0-917657-97-7); Bantam paper $4.95 (0-553-27903-3).** A space pilot receives a history-changing message from a godlike force from beyond the universe. (REV: BL 2/15/88; LJ 3/15/88)

SHORT STORIES

9520 Abe, Kobo. *Beyond the Curve.* 1991, Kodansha $18.95 (4-7700-1465-1). A collection of surrealist short stories by the author of *The Face of Another.* "Confirms his reputation as one of Japan's most significant modern writers."—PW (Rev: BL 3/15/91; NYTBR 3/17/91; PW 2/22/91)

9521 Achebe, Chinua. *Girls at War and Other Stories.* 1986, Fawcett paper $3.50 (0-449-30046-3). Twelve stories regarding aspects of contemporary life in Nigeria and the lingering effects of colonialism in West Africa. (Rev: BL 5/1/73; LJ 5/1/73; New Yorker 4/14/73)

9522 Achebe, Chinua, and C. L. Innes, eds. *African Short Stories.* 1985, Heinemann paper $7.50. A selection of short stories collected from a variety of African regions and written between the 1930s and 1980s. (Rev: LJ 2/15/85; NYTBR 8/11/85; PW 1/11/86)

9523 Adams, Alice. *After You're Gone.* 1989, Knopf $18.95 (0-394-57926-7). A collection of 14 stories about women in California and Maryland by the author of *Rich Rewards.* (Rev: BL 7/89; LJ 8/89; PW 7/14/89)

9524 Adams, Alice. *Beautiful Girl.* 1987, Fawcett paper $3.95 (0-449-21412-5). Sixteen stories of love in human relationships. (Rev: LJ 12/15/78; NYTBR 1/14/79; Newsweek 1/8/79. Awards: ALA, 1979)

9525 Adams, Alice. *Return Trips.* 1985, Knopf $14.95 (0-394-53633-9); Fawcett paper $3.95 (0-449-20953-9). A collection of 15 stories by the author of *Beautiful Girl.* "Nobody writes better about falling in love than Alice Adams."—NYTBR (Rev: BL 7/85; CSM 10/6/85; NYTBR 9/1/85)

9526 Adler, John Morel. *Hunt Out of the Thicket.* 1990, Algonquin $14.95 (0-945575-06-8). A collection of ten stories regarding hunting and fishing in the Deep South. (Rev: BL 9/1/90; LJ 8/90; PW 7/6/90)

9527 Alden, Paulette Bates. *Feeding the Eagles.* 1988, Graywolf $16.00 (1-55597-111-3); paper $8.00 (1-55597-116-4). A debut collection of 11 short stories chronicling the life of an ex-Southerner who moves to Minnesota with her attorney husband. (Rev: NYTBR 10/16/88; PW 8/5/88)

9528 Aleichem, Sholem. *Tevye the Dairyman and the Railroad Stories.* 1988, Schocken paper $10.95 (0-8052-0905-0). Nearly 30 stories detailing Jewish life in Russia and Eastern Europe in the late nineteenth and early twentieth centuries. (Rev: Choice 12/87; LJ 7/87; NYTBR 1/24/88)

9529 Allen, Paula Gunn, ed. *Spider Woman's Granddaughters: Traditional Tales and Contemporary Writing by Native American Women.* 1989, Beacon $19.95 (0-8070-8100-0); Fawcett paper $11.95 (0-449-90508-X). Twenty-four traditional and contemporary short stories and tales by female Native-American writers. "A treasure for scholars and general readers alike."—LJ (Rev: LJ 8/89; NYTBR 5/14/89; PW 4/14/89)

9530 Allende, Isabel. *Stories of Eva Luna.* 1991, Macmillan $18.95 (0-689-12102-4). A collection of 23 short stories told by the protagonist of Allende's third book, *Eva Luna.* (Rev: BL 10/15/90; LJ 12/90; PW 11/16/90)

9531 Ambler, Eric. *Waiting for Orders: The Complete Short Stories of Eric Ambler.* 1991, Mysterious $18.95 (0-89296-241-0). A collection of six mystery stories and two suspense stories written by the English master during the years 1939 and 1940. (Rev: BL 2/1/91; PW 1/4/91)

9532 Amis, Martin. *Einstein's Monsters.* 1987, Crown $12.95 (0-517-56520-X); Random paper $8.95 (0-679-72996-8). Five short stories exploring aspects of the threat of a nuclear holocaust. (Rev: LJ 6/1/87; Time 6/22/87; TLS 5/1/87)

9533 Anderman, Janusz. *Poland under Black Light.* 1985, Readers International $12.50 (0-930523-13-X). Thirty short stories portraying life in Poland under martial law during the early 1980s. (Rev: BL 12/1/85; Choice 4/86; LJ 1/86)

9534 Anderson, Jessica. *Stories from the Warm Zone and Sydney Stories.* 1987, Viking $15.95 (0-670-81626-4); Penguin paper $6.95 (0-14-009708-2). A collection of seven short stories and a novella by the Australian writer and author of *Tirra Lirra by the River.* "All the stories are unforgettable."—PW (Rev: NYTBR 11/29/87; PW 10/2/87; TLS 2/26/88)

9535 Antler, Joyce, ed. *America and I: Short Stories by American Jewish Women Writers.* **1990, Beacon $19.95 (0-8070-3604-8).** Twenty-three stories by twentieth-century American Jewish women writers including Rebecca Goldstein, Cynthia Ozick, and Edna Ferber. (Rev: BL 7/90; LJ 7/90)

9536 Apple, Max. *Free Agents.* **1985, Harper & Row paper $6.95 (0-06-091140-9).** Twenty short stories by the author of *Zip* including "Bridging," "Walt and Will," and "Carbo-Loading." (Rev: BL 4/15/84; LJ 5/1/84; PW 3/30/84)

9537 Apple, Max. *Oranging of America and Other Stories.* **1987, Penguin paper $5.95 (0-14-010310-4).** Ten satirical short stories concerning such targets as Archie Moore, Immanuel Velikovsky, Fidel Castro, and Gerald Ford. (Rev: LJ 10/15/76; Newsweek 12/6/76; PW 11/21/77)

9538 Astley, Thea. *Hunting the Wild Pineapple.* **1991, Putnam $19.95 (0-399-13561-8).** Works of short fiction by an Australian writer set in Queensland, including "The Curate Breaker" and "Ladies Need Only Apply." (Rev: BL 1/15/91; LJ 1/91; NYTBR 12/23/90)

9539 Atwood, Margaret. *Bluebeard's Egg and Other Stories.* **1987, Fawcett paper $4.95 (0-449-21417-6).** This second collection of short stories by the Canadian writer includes "The Salt Garden," "Scarlet Ibis," "The Sunrise," and "Hurricane Hazel." (Rev: BL 9/15/86; Choice 6/87; LJ 11/15/86)

9540 Atwood, Margaret. *Wilderness Tips.* **1991, Doubleday $20.00 (0-385-42106-0).** A collection of ten pieces of short fiction by the author of *Cat's Eye,* including the stories "The Bog Man" and "Hairball." (Rev: LJ 11/1/91; PW 10/4/91)

9541 Auchincloss, Louis. *Fellow Passengers: A Novel in Portraits.* **1989, Houghton $18.95 (0-395-49853-8).** A collection of ten biographical sketches linked by a common narrator. "A remarkable book."—TLS (Rev: BL 3/15/89; PW 1/20/89; TLS 8/24/90)

9542 Auchincloss, Louis. *Partners.* **1990, St. Martin's paper $4.50 (0-312-92006-7).** Interconnected stories portraying the decline of a long-established Wall Street law firm, by the author of *The Rector of Justin.* (Rev: LJ 12/15/73; NYTBR 2/24/74; Time 2/4/74)

9543 Auchincloss, Louis. *Skinny Island: More Tales of Manhattan.* **1988, St. Martin's paper $3.95 (0-317-67200-2).** Twelve short stories set in New York from the nineteenth century to the present. "Elegant fiction."—NYTBR (Rev: NYTBR 5/24/87; PW 4/3/87; Time 5/11/87)

9544 Bachmann, Ingeborg. *Thirtieth Year.* **1987, Holmes & Meier $19.95 (0-8419-1068-5).** A collection of seven short stories by an Austrian writer originally published in that country in 1961. (Rev: Choice 2/88; NYTBR 11/29/87)

9545 Bainbridge, Beryl. *Mum and Mr. Armitage.* **1987, McGraw-Hill paper $7.95 (0-07-003264-5).** A collection of 12 stories including "Clap Hands, Here Comes Charlie" and "Beggars Would Ride."

"Faultlessly crafted . . . every story in this collection is a gem."—PW (Rev: BL 8/87; LJ 8/87; PW 6/12/87)

9546 Ballard, J. G. *War Fever.* **1991, Farrar $18.95 (0-374-28645-0).** Fourteen short stories from the 1970s, 1980s, and 1990s concerning the contemporary world and its near future as described by the noted science fiction writer. (Rev: LJ 4/15/91; PW 2/15/91; Time 3/25/91)

9547 Bambara, Toni C. *Gorilla, My Love.* **1981, Random paper $4.95 (0-394-75049-7).** A collection of 16 stories predominantly concerning the lives of African-American children. "Fresh, funny, insightful and moving."—LJ (Rev: BL 12/1/72; LJ 9/1/72; NYTBR 10/15/72)

9548 Bambara, Toni C. *Sea Birds Are Still Alive: Collected Stories.* **1982, Random paper $6.95 (0-394-71176-9).** Ten short stories portraying aspects of the African-American experience by the author of *Gorilla, My Love.* (Rev: LJ 6/1/77; Newsweek 5/2/77; PW 1/3/77)

9549 Barnett, Allen. *The Body and Its Dangers and Other Stories.* **1990, St. Martin's $15.95 (0-312-04272-8).** This debut collection of six short stories explores the relationship between human sexuality and mortality and features several stories about AIDS. (Rev: BL 7/90; NYTBR 7/15/90; PW 6/22/90)

9550 Barth, John. *Lost in the Funhouse: Fiction for Print, Type, Lone Voice.* **1988, Doubleday paper $8.95 (0-385-24087-2).** Fourteen short experimental pieces regarding the life of the author and the art of writing. (Rev: LJ 9/15/68; Newsweek 9/30/68; Time 9/27/68)

9551 Barthelme, Donald. *Forty Stories.* **1989, Penguin paper $7.95 (0-14-011245-6).** A collection of 40 short stories not included in the 1981 *Sixty Stories.* (Rev: BL 9/1/87; PW 8/14/87; TLS 5/13/88)

9552 Barthelme, Donald. *Great Days.* **1979, Farrar $7.95 (0-374-16628-5); Pocket paper $2.50 (0-671-83673-0).** Sixteen pieces by the author of *The Dead Father* including "Belief," "The Crisis," and "The King of Jazz." (Rev: LJ 1/1/79; Choice 5/79; Newsweek 2/5/79)

9553 Barthelme, Donald. *Success.* **1980, Pocket paper $2.95 (0-671-83204-2).** A collection of 16 stories by the American writer, including "The Sandman," "Florence Green," and "The Party." (Rev: BL 1/1/73; Choice 3/73; Newsweek 11/6/72. Awards: ALA, 1972)

9554 Barthelme, Frederick. *Chroma.* **1988, Penguin paper $6.95 (0-14-010753-7).** A collection of 15 short stories by the author of *Two Against One,* including "Magic Castle" and "Trick Scenery." (Rev: LJ 5/1/87; PW 3/6/87)

9555 Barthelme, Frederick. *Moon Deluxe.* **1984, Penguin paper $6.95 (0-14-007130-X).** This first collection of short fiction by the author of *Tracer* contains 17 stories, including "Shopgirls" and "Raincheck." "As solid as Cheever at his best."—LJ (Rev: BL 8/83; LJ 9/15/83; NYTBR 7/31/83)

9556 **Bass, Rick.** *The Watch.* **1989, Norton $16.95 (0-393-02623-X); Pocket paper $6.95 (0-671-69222-X).** A debut collection of stories set in the South and Montana by a geologist/writer. (REV: LJ 12/88; Newsweek 1/9/89; Time 2/20/89)

9557 **Bates, H. E.** *Elephant's Nest in a Rhubarb Tree and Other Stories.* **1989, New Directions $17.95 (0-8112-1087-1); paper $9.95 (0-8112-1088-X).** A collection of 20 stories from the 50-year career of the English writer, who died in 1974. (REV: BL 4/15/89; NYTBR 6/11/89; PW 3/10/89. AWARDS: PW, 1989)

9558 **Bates, H. E.** *A Month by the Lake and Other Stories.* **1987, New Directions $17.95 (0-8112-1035-9); paper $8.95 (0-8112-1036-7).** A posthumous collection of 17 short stories by the British writer. (REV: BL 9/1/87; PW 8/7/87. AWARDS: PW, 1987)

9559 **Bausch, Richard.** *Fireman's Wife and Other Stories.* **1990, Simon & Schuster $18.45 (0-671-66137-X).** Ten short stories by the author of *Mr. Field's Daughter,* including "Consolation" and "Letter to the Lady of the House." (REV: BL 7/90; LJ 7/90; PW 6/8/90)

9560 **Baxter, Charles.** *A Relative Stranger.* **1990, Norton $17.95 (0-393-02867-4).** This collection of 13 stories by the author of *First Light* includes "The Old Fascist in Retirement," about the last days of poet Ezra Pound. (REV: BL 9/1/90; LJ 8/90; PW 7/20/90. AWARDS: BL, 1990)

9561 **Baxter, Charles.** *Through the Safety Net.* **1986, Penguin paper $6.95 (0-14-008995-0).** A collection of 11 stories by an American writer. "Baxter's stories are intelligent, original, gracefully written, always moving, frequently funny and—that rarest of compliments—wise."—NYTBR (REV: BL 7/85; Choice 12/85; NYTBR 8/25/85)

9562 **Beattie, Ann.** *The Burning House.* **1987, Ballantine paper $3.95 (0-345-35182-7).** A collection of 16 short stories by the author of *Chilly Scenes of Winter,* including "Waiting," "Learning to Fall," "Running Dreams," and the title story. (REV: BL 10/15/82; CSM 2/9/83; NYTBR 9/26/82. AWARDS: NYTBR, 1982)

9563 **Beattie, Ann.** *Distortions.* **1991, Random paper $9.95 (0-679-73235-7).** The debut short story collection by the author including "The Lifeguard," "Fancy Flights," "Victor Blue," and "Wolf Dreams." (REV: BL 9/15/76; CSM 9/29/76; PW 5/31/76)

9564 **Beattie, Ann.** *Secrets and Surprises.* **1985, Warner paper $3.95 (0-446-31381-5).** This second collection of short stories by the author includes "A Vintage Thunderbird" and "Distant Music." (REV: Choice 4/79; CSM 1/31/79; Newsweek 1/22/79)

9565 **Beattie, Ann.** *What Was Mine: And Other Stories.* **1991, Random $20.00 (0-394-40077-X).** Twelve short stories portraying the lives of middle-class Americans by the author of *Falling in Place.* (REV: BL 1/15/91; LJ 4/15/91; PW 3/15/91)

9566 **Beattie, Ann.** *Where You'll Find Me: And Other Stories.* **1987, Macmillan paper $7.95 (0-02-016560-9).** A collection of 15 short stories set on the East Coast by the author of *Love Always.* (REV: CSM 11/10/86; LJ 10/1/86; TLS 8/14/87)

9567 **Bell, Madison Smartt.** *Barking Man and Other Stories.* **1990, Ticknor & Fields $18.85 (0-89919-835-X).** A collection of short stories by the author of *Soldier's Joy.* "Sure to add to the author's growing reputation."—LJ (REV: BL 3/1/90; LJ 3/15/90; PW 2/23/90)

9568 **Bell, Madison Smartt.** *Zero db: And Other Stories.* **1988, Penguin paper $6.95 (0-14-010629-4).** Eleven stories ranging in setting from the slums of Hoboken, New Jersey, to the battlefield of Little Big Horn written by the author of *Doctor Sleep.* (REV: BL 1/15/87; LJ 2/1/87; PW 12/12/86)

9569 **Bellow, Saul.** *Him with His Foot in His Mouth and Other Stories.* **1985, Pocket paper $4.50 (0-671-55247-3).** Five short stories including "Silver Dish," "Zetland: By a Character Witness," "Cousins," "What Kind of Day Did You Have?" and the title piece. "The best possible introduction to Bellow's tumultuous world."—Time (REV: LJ 6/15/84; NYTBR 5/20/84; Time 5/14/84. AWARDS: LJ, 1984; NYTBR, 1984; Time, 1984; Time, the 1980s)

9570 **Bellow, Saul.** *Mosby's Memoirs and Other Stories.* **1984, Penguin paper $5.95 (0-14-007318-3).** Six short stories from the 1950s and 1960s including "The Gonzaga Manuscripts," "Looking for Mr. Green," and "Leaving the Yellow House." (REV: LJ 10/15/68; PW 8/19/68; Time 11/8/68)

9571 **Benedict, Pinckney.** *Town Smokes.* **1987, Ontario Rev. paper $9.95 (0-86538-058-9).** Nine stories set in the South by an author who was 23 at the time this book was written. "Libraries, large and small . . . cannot afford to pass up this phenomenal debut collection."—Choice (REV: BL 5/15/87; Choice 12/87; LJ 5/15/87)

9572 **Berger, John.** *Once in Europa.* **1987, Pantheon $14.95 (0-394-53992-3); paper $8.95 (0-394-75164-7).** This collection of short stories portraying the lives of peasants in the French Alps is the sequel to the author's *Pig Earth.* (REV: BL 2/1/87; LJ 3/1/87; PW 2/6/87)

9573 **Berger, John.** *Pig Earth.* **1988, Pantheon paper $8.95 (0-394-75739-4).** Short stories depicting life in a French peasant town, by the author of *G.* (REV: LJ 9/15/80; New Rep 9/20/80; PW 6/27/80)

9574 **Berriault, Gina.** *The Infinite Passion of Expectation.* **1982, North Point paper $12.50 (0-86547-082-0).** A collection of 25 stories set in the San Francisco Bay Area, including "Death of a Lesser Man," "The Bystander," and "The Search for J. Kruper." (REV: BL 11/1/82; LJ 11/15/82; PW 9/24/82)

9575 **Berry, Wendell.** *Wild Birds: Six Stories of the Port William Membership.* **1989, North Point paper $8.95 (0-86547-217-3).** A collection revolving around the residents of the small Kentucky town of Port William. (REV: LJ 2/15/86; NYTBR 4/13/86; TLS 6/26/87)

9576 Bissoondath, Neil. *Digging Up the Mountains.* **1988, Penguin paper $6.95 (0-14-008935-7).** Fourteen stories by the Canadian author about life in the colonial Third World and his birthplace of Trinidad. (REV: BL 7/86; Choice 12/86; PW 8/20/86)

9577 Bissoondath, Neil. *On the Eve of Uncertain Tomorrows.* **1991, Clarkson N. Potter $18.95 (0-7475-0718-X).** Short stories portraying the lives of immigrants in Canada by the author of *A Casual Brutality.* (REV: NYTBR 5/26/91; TLS 11/23/91)

9578 Bly, Carol. *Backbone.* **1985, Milkweed Editions $12.95 (0-915943-05-0); paper $7.95 (0-915943-36-0).** An illustrated collection of five stories set in Minnesota, including "The Last of the Gold Star Mothers" and "The Dignity of Life." (REV: BL 4/1/85; NYTBR 1/27/85)

9579 Bly, Carol. *Tomcat's Wife and Other Stories.* **1991, HarperCollins $19.95 (0-06-016504-9).** The second collection of short stories by the author contains eight tales set in contemporary Minneapolis-St. Paul. "Joyce's 'Dubliners' comes to mind sometimes, reading these stories."—NYTBR (REV: NYTBR 3/31/91; PW 2/22/91. AWARDS: ALA, 1992)

9580 Blythe, Ronald. *Visitors: The Stories of Ronald Blythe.* **1985, Harcourt $16.95 (0-15-193912-8).** A collection of 20 stories written from the 1950s through the 1970s by the British author of *Akenfield.* (REV: BL 12/15/85; NYTBR 12/8/85; PW 10/25/85)

9581 Böll, Heinrich. *Casualty.* **1987, Farrar $16.95 (0-374-11967-8); Norton paper $7.95 (0-393-30599-6).** Twenty-two stories depicting life in Germany during and in the aftermath of World War II. "Rich, stunning tales told by a master."—PW (REV: Choice 9/87; LJ 5/1/87; PW 3/27/87)

9582 Böll, Heinrich. *Stories of Heinrich Böll.* **1986, Knopf $25.00 (0-394-51405-X); McGraw-Hill paper $9.95 (0-07-006422-9).** Sixty-seven pieces ranging from short stories to novellas by the German Nobel laureate. (REV: BL 2/1/86; Choice 9/86; PW 1/3/86)

9583 Bombal, Maria Luisa. *New Islands and Other Stories.* **1988, Cornell Univ. Pr. paper $6.95 (0-8014-9538-5).** Five stories by a Chilean writer concerning women and love written during the 1930s and 1940s and containing a preface by Jorge Luis Borges. (REV: BL 8/82; CSM 10/25/83; PW 6/11/82)

9584 Bonnie, Fred. *Too Hot, and Other Maine Stories.* **1987, Dog Ear paper $9.95 (0-937966-22-3).** A collection of short fiction concerning the exploits of young people in Maine written by a former native of the state. (REV: BL 8/87; PW 7/3/87)

9585 Borges, Jorge Luis. *The Aleph and Other Stories, 1933 to 1969.* **1979, Dutton paper $8.95 (0-525-47539-7).** A compilation of 20 short stories and an autobiographical essay by the Argentine master. "An excellent introduction to his work."—LJ (REV: CSM 11/13/70; LJ 1/1/71; NYTBR 12/13/70)

9586 Borges, Jorge Luis. *Book of Sand.* **1979, Dutton paper $5.95 (0-525-47540-0).** A collection of 13 stories by the Argentine writer. "Marvelous, thought-provoking reading . . . a major literary event."—PW (REV: Choice 1/78; NYTBR 10/16/77; PW 8/15/77)

9587 Boswell, Robert. *Dancing in the Movies.* **1986, Univ. of Iowa Pr. $14.95 (0-87745-134-6).** Six short stories by the 1985 winner of the Iowa School of Letters Award for Short Fiction. (REV: Choice 10/86; LJ 1/86; PW 11/8/85)

9588 Bowen, Elizabeth. *Collected Stories of Elizabeth Bowen.* **1981, Knopf $25.00 (0-394-51666-4).** A complete collection of the Anglo-Irish writer's 79 short stories published over four decades. (REV: CSM 3/9/81; NYTBR 2/8/81; PW 12/19/80. AWARDS: ALA, 1981)

9589 Bowles, Paul. *Collected Stories of Paul Bowles, 1939–1976.* **1983, Black Sparrow $20.00 (0-87685-397-1); paper $15.00 (0-87685-396-3).** Thirty-nine stories collected from over four decades including "The Time of Friendship," "The Circular Valley," "Pages from Cold Point," and "At Paso Rojo." (REV: BL 11/1/79; LJ 10/1/79; NYTBR 9/30/79)

9590 Bowles, Paul. *A Distant Episode: The Selected Stories.* **1989, Ecco Pr. paper $11.95 (0-88001-204-8).** A selection of 24 stories spanning four decades of the work of the author of *The Sheltering Sky.* "Proves beyond doubt Bowles' originality and right to literary legend."—PW (REV: BL 1/15/89; LJ 12/88; PW 12/16/88. AWARDS: BL, 1989)

9591 Boyd, William. *On the Yankee Station.* **1985, Penguin paper $4.95 (0-14-006087-1).** Fifteen short stories by the author of *An Ice Cream War* set in the United States, Europe, Africa, and Vietnam. (REV: NYTBR 8/5/84; Newsweek 1/14/85; Time 7/30/84)

9592 Boyle, T. Coraghessan. *Descent of Man and Other Stories.* **1980, McGraw-Hill paper $4.95 (0-07-006956-5).** Seventeen short stories by the author of *Budding Prospects* including "Bloodfall," "Green Hell," and "We Are Norsemen." (REV: BL 2/15/79; LJ 1/15/79; PW 1/8/79)

9593 Boyle, T. Coraghessan. *Greasy Lake and Other Stories.* **1986, Penguin paper $7.95 (0-14-007781-2).** A collection of stories by the author of *Water Music,* including "Stones in My Passway, Hellhound on My Trail." "Boyle proves himself in this second story collection truly a master of the genre."—PW (REV: BL 4/1/85; LJ 5/15/85; PW 3/15/85)

9594 Boyle, T. Coraghessan. *If the River Was Whiskey.* **1989, Viking $17.95 (0-670-82690-1).** A collection of 16 stories including "Modern Love," "Sorry Fugu," and the title tale. (REV: BL 5/15/89; LJ 3/15/89; NYTBR 5/14/89. AWARDS: ALA, 1989; BL, 1989; NYTBR, 1989)

9595 Bradbury, Ray. *Stories of Ray Bradbury.* **1980, Knopf $29.95 (0-394-51335-5).** A collection of 100 short stories with an introduction by the author. (REV: BL 9/1/80; LJ 9/15/80; Time 10/13/80)

9596   **Bradley, Jane.** *Power Lines: And Other Stories.* **1989, Univ. of Arkansas Pr. $17.95 (1-55728-110-6); paper $8.95 (1-55728-111-4).** This debut collection of short stories by a teacher and playwright is set in the American South and includes "Noises" and "Mistletoe." (REV: BL 9/1/89; LJ 9/15/89; PW 7/28/89)

9597   **Brautigan, Richard.** *Revenge of the Lawn: Stories, 1962–1970.* **1980, Pocket paper $2.95 (0-671-41852-1).** Collected short stories from the 1960s by the author of *Trout Fishing in America.* (REV: LJ 10/15/71; NYTBR 1/16/72; Sat Rev 12/4/71)

9598   **Braverman, Kate.** *Squandering the Blue.* **1990, Ballantine $17.95 (0-449-90551-9).** Twelve short stories about women in Los Angeles and Hawaii form this author's debut fiction collection. (REV: BL 9/1/90; LJ 9/1/90; NYTBR 12/16/90)

9599   **Breton, Marcela, ed.** *Hot and Cool: Jazz Short Stories.* **1990, NAL paper $9.95 (0-452-26389-1).** A collection of 19 stories from 1930 to 1987 about jazz and jazz musicians, including tales by Peter DeVries, Amiri Baraka, Julio Cortazar, and James Baldwin. (REV: BL 6/1/90; LJ 4/1/90; New Yorker 6/18/90)

9600   **Broch, Hermann.** *The Guiltless.* **1987, North Point paper $12.50 (0-86547-305-6).** A collection of 11 stories by an Austrian writer portraying life in Germany from 1913 to 1933. (REV: BL 6/1/74; LJ 5/1/74; PW 11/19/73)

9601   **Brodkey, Harold.** *Stories in an Almost Classical Mode.* **1988, Knopf $24.95 (0-394-50699-5); Random paper $12.95 (0-679-724-31-1).** Eighteen short stories and novellas published over a quarter of a century including "The Shooting Range," "Angel," and "Largely an Oral History of My Mother." (REV: BL 9/1/88; Choice 3/89; PW 7/29/88. AWARDS: NYTBR, 1988)

9602   **Brooks, Jeremy.** *Doing the Voices.* **1986, Viking $14.95 (0-948681-01-2).** A collection of four stories by the English writer best known for his 1960 novel *Jampot Smith.* (REV: LJ 12/86; TLS 6/6/86)

9603   **Brown, Larry.** *Big Bad Love.* **1990, Algonquin $17.95 (0-945575-46-7); Random paper $10.00 (0-679-73491-0).** A collection of short fiction by the author of *Dirty Work,* including "Falling Out of Love," "Discipline," "Waiting for the Ladies," and "92 Days." (REV: BL 9/15/90; NYTBR 9/2/90; PW 7/27/90)

9604   **Brown, Larry.** *Facing the Music.* **1988, Algonquin $12.95 (0-912697-91-1).** Ten short stories about men in the contemporary South. (REV: LJ 9/15/88; PW 7/8/88)

9605   **Brown, Mary Ward.** *Tongues of Flame.* **1987, Pocket paper $5.95 (0-671-64157-3).** A debut collection of 11 tales reflecting the changing contemporary American South by an Alabama writer. (REV: BL 7/86; LJ 7/86; NYTBR 8/24/86)

9606   **Burgess, Anthony.** *Devil's Mode.* **1989, Random $18.95 (0-394-57670-5).** Burgess's first short fiction collection contains nine tales of historical and geographical interest. "Marvels of experiment and imagination."—PW (REV: BL 9/15/89; PW 9/22/89; TLS 12/15/89)

9607   **Burke, James Lee.** *The Convict and Other Stories.* **1990, Little, Brown paper $7.95 (0-316-11699-8).** A collection of nine stories set in Louisiana and Texas by a Southern American writer. (REV: BL 11/15/85; Choice 3/86; LJ 11/1/85)

9608   **Busch, Frederick.** *Absent Friends.* **1989, Knopf $18.95 (0-394-57426-5).** A collection of 14 stories about separation, including "Dog Song" and "Name the Name." (REV: LJ 4/1/89; NYTBR 5/7/89; PW 3/24/89)

9609   **Busch, Frederick.** *Too Late American Boyhood Blues.* **1984, Godine $15.95 (0-87923-511-X).** A collection of ten stories depicting the lives of contemporary American men, including "Making Change" and "The New Honesty." "A splendid collection."—LJ (REV: BL 7/84; LJ 7/84; PW 6/8/84)

9610   **Buzzati, Dino.** *Siren: A Selection of Dino Buzzati.* **1984, North Point paper $10.50 (0-86547-159-2).** A collection of 12 short stories plus the novella "Barnabo of the Mountains" by the Italian writer. (REV: LJ 10/1/84; NYTBR 10/28/84)

9611   **Calvino, Italo.** *Difficult Loves.* **1985, Harcourt paper $6.95 (0-15-626055-7).** A collection of 28 stories written during the 1940s and 1950s by the author of *Invisible Cities.* (REV: LJ 10/1/84; NYRB 12/6/84; Newsweek 10/8/84. AWARDS: LJ, 1984)

9612   **Calvino, Italo.** *Marcovaldo: Or, the Seasons in the City.* **1983, Harcourt paper $3.95 (0-15-657204-4).** Twenty stories set in a northern Italian city tracing the life of a laborer over four seasons. (REV: CSM 1/11/84; LJ 2/15/84; New Yorker 9/10/84)

9613   **Calvino, Italo.** *Under the Jaguar Sun.* **1988, Harcourt $12.95 (0-15-192820-7); paper $7.95 (0-15-692794-2).** Three stories of a proposed set of five—uncompleted at the time of Calvino's death—regarding the senses of smell, taste, and hearing. "Exquisite fare from one of Italy's masters."—PW (REV: BL 9/1/88; LJ 9/15/88; New Rep 10/17/88)

9614   **Cameron, Peter.** *One Way or Another.* **1987, Harper & Row paper $5.95 (0-06-091421-1).** Fourteen stories regarding young people in their teens and twenties. "Cameron is one of the best writers about middle-class youth since Salinger."—BL (REV: BL 5/15/86; LJ 7/86; PW 4/11/86)

9615   **Canin, Ethan.** *Emperor of the Air.* **1988, Houghton $15.95 (0-395-42976-5); paper $7.95 (0-06-097208-4).** This debut collection of short fiction by a California writer contains nine stories including "American Beauty" and "Star Food." "An engrossing achievement."—LJ (REV: LJ 2/1/88; NYTBR 2/14/88; PW 12/25/87)

9616   **Caponegro, Mary.** *Star Cafe and Other Stories.* **1990, Macmillan $17.95 (0-684-19113-X).** This debut collection includes three short stories and the novella "Sebastian." "Eclectic and impressive."—NYTBR (REV: BL 5/15/90; NYTBR 9/16/90)

9617 Card, Orson Scott. *Maps in a Mirror: The Short Fiction of Orson Scott Card.* **1990, Tor $19.95 (0-312-85047-6).** A collection of 46 short pieces of science fiction and horror by the author of *Ender's Game.* "An important volume."—LJ (Rev: BL 9/15/90; LJ 11/15/90; PW 8/17/90)

9618 Carey, Josephine. *Good Gossip.* **1992, Random $18.00 (0-394-57638-1).** This collection of 11 short stories related by a single narrator marks the debut of this New York writer. (Rev: BL 12/15/91; PW 11/22/91)

9619 Carter, Angela. *Saints and Strangers.* **1986, Viking $13.95 (0-670-81139-4); Penguin paper $5.95 (0-14-008973-X).** Eight short stories, including a fictional retelling of the Lizzie Borden case, a reexamination of Peter and the Wolf, and a tale looking at the relationship between Tamerlane and his wife. (Rev: BL 8/86; New Rep 9/7/86; NYTBR 9/7/86. Awards: ALA, 1986; NYTBR, 1986)

9620 Carver, Ann, and Cheng Sung-Sheng, eds. *Bamboo Shoots after the Rain: Contemporary Stories by Women Writers of Taiwan.* **1991, Feminist Pr. $35.00 (1-55861-017-0); paper $14.95 (1-55861-018-9).** An anthology of short stories by female Taiwanese writers. (Rev: BL 1/1/91; PW 12/21/90)

9621 Carver, Raymond. *Cathedral.* **1989, Random paper $8.95 (0-679-72369-2).** Twelve short stories by the American writer and poet. (Rev: NYRB 11/24/83; NYTBR 9/11/83; Newsweek 9/5/83. Awards: ALA, 1983; NYTBR, 1983)

9622 Carver, Raymond. *What We Talk about When We Talk about Love.* **1981, Knopf $16.50 (0-394-51684-2); Random paper $8.95 (0-679-72305-6).** A collection of 17 stories, including "Why Don't You Dance?" and "So Much Water So Close to Home." (Rev: BL 4/1/81; Newsweek 4/27/81; PW 3/6/81. Awards: ALA, 1981; BL, the 1980s)

9623 Carver, Raymond. *Where I'm Calling From: New and Selected Stories.* **1988, Atlantic Monthly $19.95 (0-87113-216-8); Random paper $8.95 (0-679-72231-9).** Thirty-seven new and selected short stories. (Rev: CSM 7/28/88; NYTBR 5/15/88; PW 3/25/88. Awards: ALA, 1988; NYTBR, 1988; PW, 1988)

9624 Chabon, Michael. *A Model World and Other Stories.* **1991, Morrow $18.95 (0-688-09553-4).** A collection of 11 pieces of short fiction by the author of *The Mysteries of Pittsburgh.* "Should help cement Chabon's status as one of the best of America's young fiction writers."—LJ (Rev: BL 1/15/91; LJ 2/15/91; NYTBR 5/26/91)

9625 Cheever, John. *Stories of John Cheever.* **1978, Knopf $29.95 (0-394-50087-3); Ballantine paper $6.95 (0-345-33567-8).** A collection of 61 stories by Cheever including "The World of Apples," "The Country Husband," and "The Enormous Radio." (Rev: LJ 9/15/78; NYTBR 12/3/78; Time 10/16/78. Awards: ALA, 1978; NYTBR, 1978; PP:Fiction, 1979; Time, 1978; Time, the 1970s)

9626 Chen, Jo-Hsi. *Execution of Mayor Yin and Other Stories from the Great Proletarian Cultural Revolution.* **1978, Indiana Univ. Pr. paper $8.95 (0-253-20231-0).** Eight stories of life under the Cultural Revolution by a Taiwan-born woman who lived in the People's Republic of China during the 1960s and 1970s. (Rev: LJ 5/15/78; PW 4/3/78; TLS 6/9/78. Awards: ALA, 1978)

9627 Cisneros, Sandra. *Woman Hollering Creek and Other Stories.* **1991, Random $18.00 (0-394-57654-3).** The Mexican-American writer's second collection of stories includes "Eyes of Zapata" and "Never Marry a Mexican." "Not only a gifted writer but an absolutely essential one."—NYTBR (Rev: BL 4/15/91; NYTBR 5/26/91; Newsweek 6/3/91. Awards: BL, 1991; LJ, 1991)

9628 Clark, Mary Higgins. *Anastasia Syndrome: And Other Stories.* **1989, Simon & Schuster $19.95 (0-671-67367-X).** This first collection of the author's short fiction contains four stories and a novella about a woman who claims she is the missing daughter of Czar Nicholas. (Rev: BL 11/1/89; NYTBR 12/3/89; PW 9/29/89)

9629 Clifford, Sigerson. *Red-Haired Woman: And Other Stories.* **1990, Dufour paper $9.95 (0-85342-882-4).** A posthumously published collection of short stories by an Irish playwright set in his native country. (Rev: BL 3/15/90; NYTBR 7/8/90)

9630 Collins, Linda. *Going to See the Leaves.* **1986, Viking $15.95 (0-670-80881-4).** A debut collection of eight short stories about the acceptance of middle age. "A wonderful collection."—PW (Rev: BL 3/1/86; NYTBR 3/9/86; PW 1/24/86)

9631 Colwin, Laurie. *Lone Pilgrim.* **1990, Harper-Collins paper $7.95 (0-06-097270-X).** This second collection of the author's short fiction contains the stories "An Old-Fashioned Story" and "The Achieve of, the Mastery of the Thing." (Rev: LJ 2/15/81; Time 3/9/81; TLS 8/7/81)

9632 Connelly, John. *Man's Work.* **1987, Algonquin $14.95 (0-912697-55-5); Penguin paper $7.95 (0-14-010677-4).** A debut collection of ten short stories about the lives of middle-class Americans. "A writer worth our attention."—NYTBR (Rev: BL 6/15/87; NYTBR 3/22/87; PW 1/16/87)

9633 Conroy, Frank. *Midair.* **1986, Penguin paper $5.95 (0-14-008984-5).** Eight stories by the author of *Stop-Time,* including "Mysterious Case of R," "The Sense of Meeting," and "Roses." (Rev: BL 9/15/85; LJ 10/1/85; New Rep 11/18/85)

9634 Cooper, J. California. *A Piece of Mine.* **1984, Wild Trees Pr. paper $7.95 (0-931125-06-6).** Twelve short stories portraying the lives of contemporary African-American women. (Rev: Choice 5/85; LJ 12/84; PW 11/2/84)

9635 Coover, Robert. *A Night at the Movies: Or, You Must Remember This.* **1988, Macmillan paper $7.95 (0-02-019120-0).** A collection of short stories retelling and reinterpreting themes of American motion pictures by the author of *Gerald's Party.* (Rev: BL 1/15/87; Choice 5/87; Newsweek 1/5/87)

9636   Coover, Robert. *Pricksongs and Descants.* 1970, NAL paper $8.95 (0-452-26360-3). Twenty-one short fictional pieces including "The Hat Act," "The Magic Poker," "The Baby Sitter," and "In a Train Station." (REV: LJ 9/15/69; Newsweek 12/1/69; Sat Rev 10/25/69)

9637   Cortazar, Julio. *All Fires the Fire and Other Stories.* 1988, Pantheon paper $7.95 (0-394-75358-5). Eight stories by the Argentine author of *Hopscotch.* "Superbly crafted and thought-provoking."—BL (REV: BL 11/1/73; LJ 7/73; NYTBR 9/9/73)

9638   Cortazar, Julio. *We Love Glenda So Much and Other Tales.* 1984, Random paper $11.95 (0-394-72297-3). A collection of ten stories by the Argentine writer, including "Story with Spiders," "Clone," and "Stories I Tell Myself." (REV: BL 3/1/83; LJ 4/15/83; PW 1/21/85)

9639   Coward, Noel. *Collected Stories of Noel Coward.* 1986, Dutton paper $11.95 (0-525-48210-5). Twenty short stories collected from four previously published works representing four decades of the author's tales. (REV: BL 2/1/84; LJ 1/84; TLS 3/25/83)

9640   Crace, Jim. *Continent.* 1988, Harper & Row paper $6.95 (0-06-091477-7). Seven short stories concerning the impact of the West upon the Third World. (REV: LJ 3/1/87; NYTBR 6/28/87; TLS 10/3/86)

9641   Currey, Richard. *Wars of Heaven.* 1990, Houghton $18.95 (0-395-50227-6); Penguin paper $9.00 (0-679-73465-1). A collection of six short stories and a novella set in rural West Virginia during the 1930s. "Powerful . . . richly rewarding."—BL (REV: BL 2/15/90; LJ 2/15/90; PW 12/22/89)

9642   Dahl, Roald. *Ah, Sweet Mystery of Life.* 1990, Knopf $18.95 (0-394-58265-9). Seven short stories written during the 1940s by the author of the children's classics *James and the Giant Peach* and *Charlie and the Chocolate Factory.* "A literary event."—LJ (REV: BL 3/15/90; LJ 4/15/90; PW 3/16/90)

9643   Davenport, Guy. *Da Vinci's Bicycle.* 1979, Johns Hopkins paper $7.95 (0-8018-2220-3). Ten short pieces containing fictional accounts of the lives of ten historical personages, including Richard Nixon, Leonardo da Vinci, and Gertrude Stein. (REV: NYTBR 6/17/79; PW 4/9/79)

9644   Davenport, Guy. *Ecologues: Short Stories by Guy Davenport.* 1981, North Point paper $11.00 (0-86547-030-8). A collection of eight stories by the literary critic and English professor. (REV: BL 6/1/81; Choice 2/82; LJ 5/15/81)

9645   Dazai, Osamu. *Self Portraits.* 1991, Kodansha $18.95 (0-87011-779-3). Twenty autobiographical stories by the Japanese author of *The Setting Sun.* (REV: BL 1/15/91; NYTBR 3/3/91; PW 12/14/90)

9646   DeMarinis, Rick. *Coming Triumph of the Free World.* 1988, Viking $16.95 (0-670-81982-4). A collection of 14 short stories by the author of *The Year of the Zinc Penny.* (REV: BL 6/1/88; NYTBR 10/30/88; PW 5/20/88)

9647   DeMarinis, Rick. *Voice of America.* 1991, Norton $18.95 (0-393-02967-0). Fifteen stories about the United States and American culture in the years following World War II. (REV: NYTBR 6/30/91; PW 3/29/91)

9648   Desai, Anita. *Games at Twilight.* 1983, Penguin paper $7.95 (0-14-005348-4). A collection of 11 stories set in India by the author of *In Custody.* (REV: BL 5/1/80; LJ 5/15/80; PW 4/4/80)

9649   De Salvo, Louise, ed. *Territories of the Voice.* 1989, Beacon $19.95 (0-8070-8320-8). A collection of 27 short stories by Irish women writers. "A rich sampler of feminist Irish fiction."—BL (REV: BL 12/15/89; LJ 1/90)

9650   Dickinson, Charles. *With or Without: And Other Stories.* 1987, Knopf $15.95 (0-394-55492-2); Macmillan paper $7.95 (0-02-019560-5). A collection of ten short stories about small-town white American men by the author of *Waltz in Marathon.* (REV: NYTBR 6/21/87; PW 3/20/87)

9651   Dilworth, Sharon. *Long White.* 1988, Univ. of Iowa Pr. $17.95 (0-87745-216-4); Norton paper $7.95 (0-393-30647-X). This collection of short stories set on Michigan's Upper Peninsula won the 1988 Iowa Short Fiction Award. (REV: BL 10/15/88; PW 9/20/88)

9652   Doctorow, E. L. *Lives of the Poets: Six Stories and a Novella.* 1984, Random $14.95 (0-394-52530-2). Six interrelated stories and the title novella by the author of *Ragtime.* (REV: CSM 1/4/85; LJ 11/15/84; NYTBR 11/11/84. AWARDS: ALA, 1984; LJ, 1984; NYTBR, 1984)

9653   Dodd, Susan M. *Hell-Bent Men and Their Cities.* 1990, Viking $17.95 (0-670-82606-5). A collection of 15 short stories including "Don't Get Around Much Anymore" and "Undeniably Sweet-Talk." (REV: BL 12/15/89; LJ 12/89; PW 11/3/89)

9654   Dorrie, Doris. *Love, Pain and the Whole Damn Thing.* 1989, Knopf $16.95 (0-394-57799-X). Four stories by the German film director, including "Money," "Paradise," "Men," and "Straight to the Heart." (REV: LJ 5/15/89; NYTBR 9/10/89; TLS 12/22/89)

9655   Drew, Eileen. *Blue Taxis: Stories about Africa.* 1989, Milkweed paper $9.95 (0-915943-41-7). A collection of nine stories about the lives of expatriate Americans in Africa. "Genuinely inspired prose."—BL (REV: BL 11/1/89; NYTBR 2/25/90)

9656   Dubus, Andre. *Selected Stories.* 1988, Godine $22.50 (0-87923-736-8); Random paper $10.95 (0-679-72533-4). A collection of 23 selected stories from the 1970s and 1980s by the noted Massachusetts storyteller. (REV: BL 9/15/88; LJ 1/89; PW 9/23/88. AWARDS: ALA, 1988)

9657   Dubus, Andre. *The Times Are Never So Bad.* 1983, Godine $14.95 (0-87923-459-8); paper $8.95 (0-87923-641-8). A collection of eight short stories and the novella "The Pretty Girl." (REV: LJ 7/83; NYTBR 6/26/83; Newsweek 7/18/83. AWARDS: ALA, 1983)

9658 Dubus, Andre III. *Cage Keeper and Other Stories.* **1989, Dutton $17.95 (0-525-24691-6); NAL paper $7.95 (0-452-26371-9).** A collection of short stories, several of which are set in prisons, by the son of writer Andre Dubus. "Reveals a talent that may one day make him equal to his father in narrative mastery."—LJ (Rev: BL 2/1/89; LJ 1/89; PW 10/21/89)

9659 Dufresne, John. *Way That Water Enters Stone.* **1991, Norton $18.95 (0-393-02924-7).** A collection of short stories set in New England that won the PEN fiction award. (Rev: BL 3/15/91; NYTBR 4/21/91; PW 1/11/91)

9660 Dumas, Henry. *Goodbye, Sweetwater: New and Selected Stories.* **1988, Thunder's Mouth $19.95 (0-938410-59-8); paper $10.95 (0-938410-58-X).** Collected and previously unpublished short stories by an African-American writer who was killed in a 1968 accident. (Rev: Choice 9/88; NYTBR 6/26/88; PW 4/22/88. Awards: PW, 1988)

9661 Dunlop, Lane, ed. *A Late Chrysanthemum.* **1986, North Point $16.50 (0-86547-229-7); paper $9.95 (0-86547-230-0).** Lane Dunlop's translations of 21 stories from seven twentieth-century Japanese writers including Kawabata, Naoya, Osamu, and Abe. "A sterling collection."—BL (Rev: BL 6/15/86; Choice 11/86; NYTBR 8/10/86)

9662 Durban, Pam. *All Set about with Fever Trees and Other Stories.* **1985, Godine $15.95 (0-87923-569-1).** A debut collection of seven stories concerning women in the American South. "Extraordinary and mesmerizing."—NYTBR (Rev: BL 8/85; Choice 2/86; NYTBR 10/13/85)

9663 Dybek, Stuart. *Childhood and Other Neighborhoods.* **1986, Ecco Pr. paper $8.50 (0-88001-106-8).** A collection of 11 stories regarding the coming of age of youngsters in Chicago during the 1950s and 1960s. (Rev: Atl 2/80; LJ 11/15/79; NYTBR 2/24/80)

9664 Ehrlich, Gretel. *Drinking Dry Clouds: Stories from Wyoming.* **1991, Capra Pr. paper $9.95 (0-88496-315-2).** Fourteen short stories by the author of *Heart Mountain* set in Wyoming during and after World War II. (Rev: LJ 6/15/91; NYTBR 5/26/91; PW 4/19/91)

9665 Eisenberg, Deborah. *Transactions in a Foreign Currency.* **1986, Knopf $15.95 (0-394-54598-2); Penguin paper $6.95 (0-14-009855-0).** Seven stories concerning the empty lives of some contemporary urban American women. (Rev: BL 3/15/86; NYTBR 3/9/86; PW 2/7/86)

9666 Eldridge, Marian. *Woman at the Window.* **1989, Univ. of Queensland Pr. paper $12.95 (0-7022-2200-3).** Sixteen short stories by an Australian writer set in Australia including "Capital Gains" and "Settle Down Country." (Rev: BL 4/15/90; LJ 6/1/90; NYTBR 4/29/90)

9667 Endo, Shusaku. *Stained Glass Elegies: Stories by Shusaku Endo.* **1984, Dufour $26.00 (0-7206-0629-2).** Eleven short stories regarding Christianity in Japan by the author of *The Samurai.* (Rev: LJ 5/1/85; Natl Rev 3/28/86; NYTBR 7/21/85)

9668 Eprile, Tony. *Temporary Sojourner and Other South African Stories.* **1989, Simon & Schuster paper $8.95 (0-671-64596-X).** A collection of autobiographical stories by a South African writer now living in the United States. (Rev: NYTBR 8/20/89; PW 6/23/89)

9669 Epstein, Joseph. *Goldin Boys.* **1991, Norton $19.95 (0-393-03022-9).** This collection is the first work of fiction by the noted *American Scholar* editor and essayist. (Rev: BL 9/15/91; LJ 10/1/91; NYTBR 11/3/91)

9670 Falco, Edward. *Plato at Scratch Daniels and Other Stories.* **1990, Univ. of Arkansas Pr. $18.95 (1-55728-156-4); paper $9.95 (1-55728-157-2).** A collection of 12 short stories previously published in American magazines including "This World That World" and "Peace, Brother." (Rev: BL 6/15/90; LJ 8/90)

9671 Findley, Thomas. *Stones.* **1990, Delacorte paper $9.95 (0-385-300002-6).** Nine Toronto stories set in and around a mental institution. "Powerful, well-honed stories."—LJ (Rev: BL 2/15/90; LJ 2/1/90; PW 12/22/89)

9672 Fink, Ida. *A Scrap of Time and Other Stories.* **1987, Pantheon $15.95 (0-394-55806-5); Schocken paper $6.95 (0-8052-0869-0).** A collection of 23 short stories concerning the Holocaust by an Israeli writer who survived in Poland during World War II. "Here is some of the finest fiction to come out of the Holocaust."—BL (Rev: BL 6/1/87; LJ 8/87; PW 5/29/87. Awards: ALA, 1987)

9673 Finney, Ernest J. *Birds Landing.* **1986, Univ. of Illinois Pr. $11.95 (0-252-0311-5).** Eight short stories depicting desolate lives in middle-class America. (Rev: BL 7/86; PW 6/6/86)

9674 Firbank, Ronald. *Complete Short Stories.* **1990, Dalkey Arch. $19.95 (0-916583-60-0); paper $9.95 (0-916583-61-9).** A collection of 11 short stories and assorted poems composed by the English writer between 1903 and 1908. (Rev: BL 10/1/90; PW 7/13/90)

9675 Fisher, M. F. K. *Sister Age.* **1983, Knopf $12.95 (0-394-53066-7); Random paper $8.95 (0-394-72385-6).** Sixteen short stories by the noted culinary writer regarding the aging process. (Rev: LJ 5/15/83; New Rep 6/6/83; NYTBR 5/29/83)

9676 Floyd, Patty Lou. *Silver De Soto.* **1987, Country Oak $14.95 (0-933031-03-3); Pocket paper $5.95 (0-671-66939-7).** This debut collection of short stories details the life of a young woman growing up in Oklahoma during the depression. "An unforgettable journey into adulthood."—NYTBR (Rev: NYTBR 1/10/88; 10/28/88)

9677 Ford, Richard. *Rock Springs.* **1988, Random paper $6.95 (0-394-75700-9).** Ten short stories set in Montana by the author of *The Sportswriter.* (Rev: BL 9/1/87; NYTBR 9/20/87; Time 11/16/87)

9678 Fowles, John. *Ebony Tower.* **1974, Little, Brown $19.95 (0-316-29093-9); NAL paper $4.50 (0-451-15691-9).** Five stories by the author of *A Maggot,* including a translation of a twelfth-century love story from the French original. (REV: LJ 10/1/74; Newsweek 11/25/74; Time 12/2/74. AWARDS: Time, 1974)

9679 Franzen, Bill. *Hearing from Wayne: And Other Stories.* **1988, Knopf $15.95 (0-394-55501-5); Harper & Row paper $7.95 (0-06-09732-7).** A collection of 18 short stories with American midwestern male narrators. (REV: BL 4/1/88; NYTBR 4/10/88; PW 2/26/88)

9680 Freeman, David. *A Hollywood Education: Tales of Movie Dreams and Easy Money.* **1987, Dell paper $6.95 (0-440-53738-X).** A series of short stories detailing life as a writer in Hollywood. "One of the most enjoyable books in this overwrought genre."—LJ (REV: BL 6/15/86; LJ 7/86; PW 5/16/86)

9681 Fuentes, Carlos. *Burnt Water.* **1986, Farrar $7.95 (0-374-51988-9).** An anthology of 11 of the author's short stories collected from works previously published in Spanish. (REV: BL 11/1/80; LJ 10/1/80; PW 8/8/80)

9682 Fuentes, Carlos. *Constancia, and Other Stories for Virgins.* **1990, Farrar $17.95 (0-374-12886-3).** Selected short stories by the Mexican writer including "The Prisoner of Las Lomas" and "Viva Mi Fama." "Superlative short fiction by one of the greatest living masters of the Spanish language."—LJ (REV: BL 3/1/90; LJ 4/15/90; NYTBR 4/8/90)

9683 Gaitskill, Mary. *Bad Behavior.* **1989, Random paper $7.95 (0-679-72327-7).** A debut collection of nine short stories. "A vital and gifted new writer, one whose work has an unusual importance at this time."—NYTBR (REV: LJ 6/1/88; NYTBR 8/21/88; New Yorker 10/10/88)

9684 Gallagher, Tess. *Lover of Horses: And Other Stories.* **1987, Harper & Row paper $7.95 (0-06-091435-1).** A collection of 12 stories by a poet dealing with the American working class. "Rewarding reading from a gifted writer."—PW (REV: LJ 8/86; NYTBR 9/28/86; PW 7/18/86)

9685 Gallant, Mavis. *Home Truths: Selected Canadian Stories.* **1985, Random $17.95 (0-394-53198-1); Dell paper $4.50 (0-440-33659-7).** Sixteen stories set in Canada during the 1930s and 1940s. "Not to be missed by any library that wants the best of modern fiction."—LJ (REV: BL 4/1/85; LJ 5/1/85; NYTBR 5/5/85)

9686 Gallant, Mavis. *In Transit.* **1989, Random $17.95 (0-394-57575-X).** Twenty short stories from the 1950s and 1960s that originally appeared in the *New Yorker.* "One of the great story writers of our time . . . it is tempting to pronounce this volume perfect."—PW (REV: BL 3/15/89; LJ 4/1/89; PW 2/24/89)

9687 Gallant, Mavis. *Overhead in a Balloon: Twelve Stories of Paris.* **1987, Random $16.95 (0-394-54511-7); Norton paper $7.95 (0-393-30546-5).** Twelve stories by the Canadian writer set in Paris and largely drawn from the pages of the *New Yorker.* (REV: BL 4/1/87; LJ 3/15/87; PW 2/6/87)

9688 Gallant, Mavis. *Pegnitz Junction.* **1984, Graywolf paper $6.00 (0-915308-60-6).** Five short stories and a novella portraying life in Germany and France in the aftermath of World War II. "A memorable collection."—TLS (REV: Choice 9/73; PW 3/12/73; TLS 3/15/74)

9689 Garcia Marquez, Gabriel. *Collected Stories.* **1985, Harper & Row paper $8.95 (0-06-091306-1).** Twenty-six stories from the author's collections *No One Writes to the Colonel, Innocent Erendira,* and *Leaf Storm.* (REV: BL 9/1/84; Choice 3/85; Time 12/31/84)

9690 Gardner, John. *Art of Living: And Other Stories.* **1989, Random paper $8.95 (0-679-72350-1).** Ten short stories that explore the relationship between art and life written by the author of *October Light.* (REV: BL 3/1/81; Choice 9/81; LJ 7/81)

9691 Gardner, John. *King's Indian: Stories and Tales.* **1989, Random paper $8.95 (0-679-72193-2).** Nine short allegorical stories by the author of *Nickel Mountain* including "Tales of Queen Louisa," "The Midnight Reader," and the title piece. (REV: LJ 10/15/74; NYTBR 12/15/74; Time 12/30/74)

9692 Gass, William H. *In the Heart of the Heart of the Country and Other Stories.* **1981, Godine paper $10.95 (0-87923-374-5).** A collection of two novellas and three short stories by the author of *Omensetter's Luck.* (REV: BL 1/1/68; LJ 1/15/68; Newsweek 4/1/68)

9693 Gerber, Merrill Joan. *Honeymoon.* **1985, Univ. of Illinois Pr. $11.95 (0-252-01205-4).** This collection of stories by an American writer is set in New York and Los Angeles. (REV: LJ 9/15/85; NYTBR 12/15/85)

9694 Gessel, Van C., and Tomone Matsumoto, eds. *Showa Anthology: Modern Japanese Short Stories.* **1986, Kodansha $18.95 (0-87011-739-4).** An anthology of stories by 20 writers tracing the development of the modern Japanese short story from the 1920s to the 1980s. (REV: CSM 10/26/89; NYTBR 9/10/89)

9695 Gilchrist, Ellen. *Drunk with Love: A Book of Stories.* **1986, Little, Brown $15.95 (0-316-31311-4).** A collection of 13 stories including "The Annunciation" and "The Emancipator." (REV: BL 9/1/86; PW 7/18/86)

9696 Gilchrist, Ellen. *Light Can Be Both Wave and Particle: A Book of Stories.* **1989, Little, Brown $17.95 (0-316-31318-1); paper $8.95 (0-316-31312-2).** A collection of 11 short stories by the author of *Victory over Japan.* (REV: BL 7/89; LJ 8/89; NYTBR 10/22/89)

9697 Gilchrist, Ellen. *Victory over Japan: A Book of Stories.* **1985, Little, Brown $15.95 (0-316-31303-3); paper $7.95 (0-316-31307-6).** A collection of 14 stories by a Mississippi writer including the tales "Music," "Rhoda," and "Looking over Jordan." (REV: BL 11/1/84; Newsweek 2/18/85; PW 7/27/84. AWARDS: ALA, 1984; NBA, 1984)

9698 Gingher, Marianne. *Teen Angel and Other Stories of Young Love.* **1988, Macmillan $17.95 (0-689-11967-4); Ballantine paper $3.95 (0-345-35783-3).** A collection of six stories concerning the coming of age of adolescents. (REV: BL 6/1/88; NYTBR 9/4/88; PW 4/29/88)

9699 Glancy, Diane. *Trigger Dance.* **1991, Fiction Collection $18.95 (0-932571-35-X); paper $8.95 (0-932511-35-X).** A collection of short stories concerning the lives of Native Americans by an author of Cherokee descent. (REV: LJ 12/90; NYTBR 2/3/91)

9700 Godwin, Gail. *Mr. Bedford and the Muses.* **1984, Avon paper $4.95 (0-380-69377-1).** The title novella and five short stories including "A Father's Pleasure" and "The Angry Year" by the author of *A Mother and Two Daughters.* "A masterful collection."—LJ (REV: BL 5/15/83; CSM 9/2/83; LJ 8/83)

9701 Goodman, Allegra. *Total Immersion.* **1989, Harper & Row $16.95 (0-06-015998-7).** A collection of 11 stories about the lives of Orthodox Jews in contemporary society. (REV: LJ 5/15/89; PW 3/24/89)

9702 Gordimer, Nadine. *Crimes of Conscience.* **1991, Heinemann paper $8.95 (0-435-90668-2).** A collection of 11 short stories—ten previously published and one unpublished—from the 1980s by the Nobel Prize winner. "An excellent introduction to some of the author's best work."—BL (REV: BL 5/1/91; NYTBR 6/2/91)

9703 Gordimer, Nadine. *Jump and Other Stories.* **1991, Farrar $19.95 (0-374-18055-5).** A collection of short fiction by the South African Nobel laureate including "Home," "Safe Houses," and "The Moment the Gun Went Off." (REV: BL 7/91; LJ 8/91; NYTBR 9/29/91. AWARDS: PW, 1991)

9704 Gordimer, Nadine. *Selected Stories.* **1983, Penguin paper $6.95 (0-14-006737-X).** Over 30 stories selected from over three decades of work by the Nobel laureate. (REV: BL 3/15/76; LJ 4/1/76; Newsweek 4/19/76)

9705 Gordimer, Nadine. *Soldier's Embrace.* **1982, Penguin paper $6.95 (0-14-005925-3).** Twelve stories portraying life in contemporary South Africa. "Illuminating, brilliant. Gordimer is in top form."—PW (REV: BL 6/15/80; LJ 9/1/80; PW 6/27/80)

9706 Gordimer, Nadine. *Something Out There.* **1986, Penguin paper $6.95 (0-14-007711-1).** A novella and nine stories with largely South African settings focusing on the social and political life of its citizenry. (REV: NYTBR 7/29/84; PW 4/20/84; TLS 3/30/84)

9707 Gordon, Caroline. *Collected Stories of Caroline Gordon.* **1990, Louisiana State Univ. Pr. paper $16.95 (0-8071-1630-0).** A complete set of the author's 22 stories set largely in Kentucky and Tennessee and written during the 1940s and 1950s. (REV: BL 3/1/81; Choice 9/81; NYTBR 4/19/81)

9708 Gordon, Mary. *Temporary Shelter.* **1988, Ballantine paper $3.95 (0-345-35193-2).** A collection of 18 short stories by the author of *Final Payments.*

(REV: BL 1/15/87; Time 4/20/87; TLS 7/17/87. AWARDS: ALA, 1987)

9709 Goyen, William. *Had I a Hundred Mouths: New and Selected Stories, 1947–1983.* **1985, Crown $15.95 (0-517-55764-9); Persea Books paper $9.95 (0-89255-110-0).** A collection of 21 stories by a Texas writer who died in 1983. Contains an introduction by Joyce Carol Oates assessing his work. (REV: BL 6/1/85; CSM 9/16/85; PW 4/5/85)

9710 Greenberg, Joanne. *High Crimes and Misdemeanors.* **1981, Avon paper $2.95 (0-380-55657-X).** This collection of ten stories portraying the lives of Jews in the American West and Midwest is written by the author of *I Never Promised You a Rose Garden.* (REV: BL 3/1/80; LJ 12/15/79; NYTBR 2/3/80)

9711 Greene, Graham. *Collected Stories.* **1973, Viking $16.95 (0-670-22911-3); Penguin paper $7.95 (0-14-008070-8).** Forty short stories culled from the author's collections *May We Borrow Your Husband?*, *A Sense of Reality*, and *21 Stories*, plus three previously unpublished works. (REV: BL 12/1/73; NYTBR 9/9/73; TLS 10/20/72)

9712 Grenville, Kate. *Bearded Ladies.* **1985, Univ. of Queensland Pr. paper $11.95 (0-7022-1716-6).** A collection of 13 short stories regarding Australian women who deviate from socially accepted norms. (REV: BL 3/1/85; PW 11/23/84; TLS 10/18/85)

9713 Gummerman, Jay. *We Find Ourselves in Moontown.* **1989, Knopf $16.95 (0-394-57459-1); Random paper $8.95 (0-679-72430-3).** A collection of ten stories depicting hard life in the American West. (REV: BL 4/15/89; PW 3/10/89; TLS 7/21/89)

9714 Gurganus, Allan. *White People.* **1991, Knopf $21.95 (0-394-58841-X).** A collection of ten stories and two novellas by the author of *Oldest Living Confederate Widow Tells All.* "A collection to be savored and reread while we wait for more."—PW (REV: BL 11/15/90; NYTBR 2/3/91; PW 11/23/90. AWARDS: LJ, 1991)

9715 Guterson, David. *The Country Ahead of Us, the Country Behind.* **1989, Harper & Row $16.95 (0-06-016097-7).** A debut collection of short fiction set in the Pacific Northwest. "A fine collection."—LJ (REV: BL 6/15/89; LJ 7/89; PW 5/26/89)

9716 Hall, Donald. *The Ideal Bakery.* **1987, North Point $14.95 (0-86547-273-4); Harper & Row paper $6.95 (0-06-097166-5).** A collection of 12 stories written by the American poet over the course of a quarter-century. "This book of stories is brilliant."—NYTBR (REV: BL 5/15/87; LJ 6/15/87; NYTBR 8/2/87)

9717 Halpern, Daniel, ed. *Art of the Tale: An International Anthology of Short Stories, 1945–1985.* **1986, Viking $24.95 (0-670-80592-0); Penguin paper $12.95 (0-14-007949-1).** A collection of the best international short stories from a four-decade period, including works by such masters of the form as Calvino, Greene, Pritchett, and Borges. (REV: BL 9/15/86; TLS 3/27/87)

9718 Hannah, Barry. *Airships.* 1985, Random paper $5.95 (0-394-72913-7). A collection of 20 short stories by the author of *Ray* and *Geronimo Rex.* (REV: LJ 5/15/78; NYTBR 4/23/78; Time 5/15/78)

9719 Hannah, Barry. *Captain Maximus: Short Stories and a Screen Treatment.* 1985, Knopf $11.95 (0-394-54458-7); Penguin paper $5.95 (0-14-008811-3). A collection of seven short stories and the screenplay "Power and Light" written by the author of *Airships.* (REV: LJ 5/15/85; NYTBR 6/9/85; Sat Rev 5/85)

9720 Hansen, Ron. *Nebraska.* 1989, Atlantic Monthly $16.95 (0-87113-252-4). Eleven stories by the author of *Desperadoes* including "Can I Just Sit Here For a While?" "Belongs in the best tradition of American literature."—PW (REV: NYTBR 2/19/89; PW 11/25/88)

9721 Harazelet, Ehud. *What Is It Then Between Us?* 1988, Macmillan $15.95 (0-684-18919-4); paper $7.95 (0-02-051750-5). A debut collection of short fiction by an Israeli-American writer including "What Everyone Wants" and "No Word for Mercy." (REV: LJ 6/1/88; NYTBR 8/7/88)

9722 Hartley, L. P. *Complete Short Stories of L. P. Hartley.* 1986, Beaufort Books $24.95 (0-8253-0353-2). A complete collection of 51 short stories by the twentieth-century English writer. (REV: BL 10/1/86; NYTBR 12/14/86; PW 9/26/86)

9723 Hauptman, William. *Good Rockin' Tonight.* 1988, Bantam paper $7.95 (0-553-34557-5). Nine stories set in Texas, including the title story about a man who finds his redemption through the death of Elvis. (REV: BL 8/88; LJ 11/1/88; PW 9/2/88)

9724 Helprin, Mark. *Ellis Island and Other Stories.* 1984, Dell paper $4.95 (0-440-32204-9). Ten stories and the title novella by the author of *Winter's Tale.* "The entire collection is a virtuoso performance."—PW (REV: BL 12/15/80; CSM 4/13/81; PW 11/21/80)

9725 Hempel, Amy. *At the Gates of the Animal Kingdom.* 1990, Knopf $17.95 (0-394-57174-6). A collection of 16 short stories by the author of *Reasons to Live.* (REV: LJ 4/15/90; NYTBR 3/11/90; Newsweek 4/2/90)

9726 Henley, Patricia. *Friday Night at Silver Star.* 1986, Graywolf paper $7.50 (0-915308-84-3). A debut collection of eight stories set in the Pacific Northwest, which won the Montana Arts Council First Book Award. (REV: BL 5/15/86; NYTBR 7/6/86; PW 4/25/86. AWARDS: ALA, 1986)

9727 Henson, Robert. *Transports and Disgraces.* 1980, Univ. of Illinois Pr. $11.95 (0-252-00840-5); paper $8.95 (0-252-00841-3). A collection of five short stories concerning historical events and personalities, from the biblical Joshua to the nineteenth-century murderess Lizzie Borden. (REV: BL 12/15/80; LJ 11/1/80; PW 10/17/80)

9728 Hersey, John. *Fling and Other Stories.* 1990, Knopf $19.95 (0-394-58338-8). A first collection of short fiction by the veteran American author of *Hiroshima* and *A Bell for Adano.* (REV: BL 2/15/90; LJ 3/15/90; PW 2/16/90)

9729 Hillis, Rick. *Limbo River.* 1990, Univ. of Pittsburgh Pr. $17.95 (0-8229-3653-4). A collection of short stories set in Canada that was awarded the 1990 Drue Heinz Prize. "Each story in this collection is a beautifully cut jewel, original and very entertaining."—LJ (REV: BL 9/1/90; LJ 8/90; PW 6/29/90)

9730 Himes, Chester. *Collected Stories of Chester Himes.* 1991, Thunder's Mouth $24.95 (1-56025-020-8); paper $12.95 (1-56025-021-6). A collection of 60 stories written over a period of six decades by the author of *Cotton Comes to Harlem.* (REV: BL 5/1/91; LJ 5/15/91; PW 4/5/91)

9731 Homes, A. M. *Safety of Objects.* 1990, Norton $17.95 (0-393-02884-4); Random paper $9.00 (0-679-73629-8). A collection of ten stories exploring the dark side of suburbia. "Strong stuff from a writer bound to attract attention."—BL (REV: BL 7/90; NYTBR 9/2/90; PW 6/8/90)

9732 Hood, Mary. *And Venus Is Blue.* 1986, Ticknor & Fields $15.95 (0-89919-431-1); Pocket paper $5.95 (0-671-63669-3). A collection of short fiction including the stories "Moths," "Finding the Chain," and "Desire Call of the Wild Hen." (REV: NYTBR 8/17/86; PW 6/20/86)

9733 Hospital, Janette Turner. *Dislocations.* 1988, Louisiana State Univ. Pr. $16.95 (0-8071-1508-8). A collection of 17 stories set in Australia, Canada, and India, including "Port After Port, the Same Baggage" and "You Gave Me Hyacinths." (REV: BL 9/15/88; LJ 9/15/88; PW 7/8/88. AWARDS: LJ, 1988)

9734 Houston, Pam. *Cowboys Are My Weakness.* 1992, Norton $19.95 (0-393-03077-6). Twelve stories chronicling the adventures and misadventures of women and cowboys. (REV: BL 12/1/91; LJ 11/15/91; PW 10/25/91)

9735 Huddle, David. *Only the Little Bone.* 1988, Godine paper $9.95 (0-87923-774-0). Six autobiographical short stories and a novella set in small-town Virginia. "Lovingly wrought, these are classic pieces."—BL (REV: BL 6/15/86; Choice 12/86; PW 5/9/86)

9736 Huggan, Isabel. *Elizabeth Stories.* 1987, Viking $15.95 (0-670-81303-6); Penguin paper $6.95 (0-14-010199-3). Eight related stories tracing a young woman's development through childhood and adolescence. "An engaging collection, beautifully written and highly recommended."—LJ (REV: BL 4/1/87; LJ 4/1/87; PW 4/3/87)

9737 Humphrey, William. *Collected Stories of William Humphrey.* 1986, Dell paper $4.95 (0-440-31338-4). A collection by an American writer of 22 stories set in Oklahoma and Texas. (REV: BL 7/85; LJ 7/85; PW 5/24/85)

9738 Hunnicutt, Ellen. *In the Music Library.* 1987, Univ. of Pittsburgh Pr. $17.95 (0-8229-3567-8); Ecco Pr. paper $8.95 (0-88001-210-2). A collection of ten short stories by the author of *Suite for Calliope,* which was awarded the Drue Heinz Literature Prize. (REV: LJ 9/1/87; NYTBR 10/11/87; PW 8/21/87)

9739 **Jacobsen, Josephine.** *On the Island: New and Selected Stories.* **1989, Ontario Rev. $18.95 (0-86538-067-8).** A compilation of 20 new and previously published stories by the American writer and poet. "A find collection that demands much and gives much in return."—Choice (REV: BL 6/15/89; Choice 10/89; LJ 5/15/89)

9740 **Jason, Kathrine, ed.** *Name and Tears and Other Stories: Forty Years of Italian Fiction.* **1990, Graywolf $17.95 (1-55797-132-6).** Thirty-one stories by 26 Italian writers including Umberto Eco, Dino Buzzati, Natalia Ginzburg, Alberto Moravia, and Italo Calvino. (REV: Choice 12/90; PW 6/15/90)

9741 **Jhabvala, Ruth Prawer.** *Out of India.* **1987, Simon & Schuster paper $7.95 (0-671-64221-9).** A selection of 15 of the author's stories set in India culled from previously published collections. (REV: NYTBR 5/25/86; Time 5/12/86; TLS 4/24/87. AWARDS: ALA, 1986; NYTBR, 1986)

9742 **Johnson, Charles.** *Sorcerer's Apprentice: Tales and Conjurations.* **1987, Penguin paper $5.95 (0-14-009865-8).** The first collection of short fictional pieces by the author of *Middle Passage.* "A magnificent collection."—LJ (REV: Choice 6/86; LJ 2/15/86; PW 12/13/85)

9743 **Johnson, Willis.** *The Girl Who Would Be Russian and Other Stories.* **1986, Harcourt $15.95 (0-15-135691-2).** A collection of seven short stories portraying a group of Russian immigrants adjusting to life in New England. (REV: BL 3/15/86; LJ 3/1/86; New Yorker 4/7/86)

9744 **Jolley, Elizabeth.** *Stories.* **1988, Viking $17.95 (0-670-82113-6); Penguin paper $7.95 (0-14-008581-5).** A collection of 21 stories from two previously published volumes by the Australian writer. (REV: BL 3/1/88; LJ 4/15/88; PW 2/19/88)

9745 **Jolley, Elizabeth.** *Woman in a Lampshade.* **1986, Penguin paper $6.95 (0-14-008418-5).** A collection of short stories by the Australian author of *The Well* and *Foxybaby.* (REV: BL 11/1/86; NYTBR 11/16/86; PW 8/8/86)

9746 **Just, Ward.** *Congressman Who Loved Flaubert and Other Washington Stories.* **1990, Carroll & Graf paper $8.95 (0-88184-587-6).** Nine stories concerning the political and social life of Washington, D.C. (REV: BL 9/15/73; NYTBR 8/26/73; PW 5/21/73)

9747 **Just, Ward.** *Twenty-one Selected Stories.* **1990, Houghton $22.95 (0-395-53756-8).** Twenty-one stories from the 1970s and 1980s including "About Boston" and "The Congressman Who Loved Flaubert." "These stories will add to Just's literary stature."—PW (REV: BL 5/15/90; CSM 6/27/90; PW 3/30/90. AWARDS: BL, 1990)

9748 **Kali for Women Staff.** *Truth Tales: Contemporary Stories by Women Writers of India.* **1990, Feminist Pr. $29.95 (1-55861-011-1); paper $9.95 (1-**

55861-012-X**).** Seven recent stories by female Indian writers translated from seven major languages of the subcontinent. (REV: BL 7/90; PW 10/12/90. AWARDS: PW, 1990)

9749 **Kalpakian, Linda.** *Dark Continent and Other Stories.* **1989, Viking $17.95 (0-670-82531-X).** Six stories set in California and Idaho by the author of *Fair Augusto and Other Stories.* (REV: BL 9/1/89; LJ 8/89; PW 8/4/89)

9750 **Kalpakian, Linda.** *Fair Augusto and Other Stories.* **1986, Graywolf paper $8.00 (0-915308-90-8).** A debut collection of short stories by an Armenian-American writer. "Surprisingly powerful."—BL (REV: BL 1/15/87; LJ 2/1/87)

9751 **Kaplan, David Michael.** *Comfort.* **1988, Penguin paper $6.95 (0-14-009624-8).** A debut collection of 12 stories exploring human relationships. "Writing of powerful insight and beauty, a talented first collection."—LJ (REV: BL 1/15/87; LJ 1/87; PW 12/26/86)

9752 **Kauffman, Janet.** *Obscene Gestures for Women.* **1989, Knopf $16.95 (0-394-57411-7); Random paper $8.95 (0-679-73055-9).** A collection of 15 short short stories by the author of *Places in the World a Woman Could Walk.* (REV: BL 9/1/89; 9/1/89; NYTBR 9/24/89)

9753 **Kauffman, Janet.** *Places in the World a Woman Could Walk.* **1985, Penguin paper $5.95 (0-14-007664-6).** A collection of 12 short stories set in Michigan and Ohio including "At Odds," "How Many Boys," and "The Mechanics of Good Times." (REV: CSM 2/9/84; LJ 11/15/83; PW 11/11/83. AWARDS: LJ, 1984)

9754 **Kawabata, Yasunari.** *Palm-of-the-Hand Stories.* **1988, North Point $19.95 (0-86547-325-0); paper $9.95 (0-86547-412-5).** Seventy short stories by the Nobel Prize–winning Japanese writer representing five decades of his work. (REV: BL 8/88; LJ 8/88; PW 6/3/88)

9755 **Kees, Weldon.** *The Ceremony and Other Stories.* **1984, Graywolf paper $6.00 (0-915308-53-3).** A selection of 14 stories by the American poet collected from magazines and written during the 1930s, 1940s, and 1950s. "Amazingly fresh . . . could have been as easily written this year as almost half a century ago."—Choice (REV: BL 6/15/84; Choice 11/84; PW 5/11/84)

9756 **Keillor, Garrison.** *Happy to Be Here.* **1990, Penguin paper $8.95 (0-14-013182-5).** Twenty-nine stories by the former host of National Public Radio's "Prairie Home Companion." (REV: LJ 1/15/82; NYTBR 2/28/82; Time 2/1/82)

9757 **Keillor, Garrison.** *Leaving Home: A Collection of Lake Wobegon Stories.* **1987, Viking $18.95 (0-670-81976-X); NAL paper $4.95 (0-451-82197-1).** Thirty-six stories from the author's "Prairie Home Companion" radio show. (REV: BL 8/87; LJ 10/1/87; Newsweek 10/5/87)

9758 **Keillor, Garrison.** *We Are Still Married: Stories and Letters.* **1989, Viking $18.95 (0-670-82647-**

2); **Penguin paper $8.95 (0-14-013156-6).** Ten poems and 57 stories taken primarily from the pages of the *New Yorker* by the former radio storyteller. (REV: BL 2/1/89; NYTBR 4/9/89; Time 5/15/89)

9759 Kelman, James. *Greyhound for Breakfast.* 1988, Farrar $15.95 (0-374-16687-0). A collection of 47 stories and prose poems about street life in the author's native Glasgow. (REV: BL 2/1/88; NYTBR 3/20/88; PW 12/25/87)

9760 Kiely, Benedict. *A Letter to Peachtree: And Nine Other Stories.* 1988, Godine $17.95 (0-87923-727-9). A collection of ten short stories by the Irish writer. "As lyrical a fiction writer as any working in the English language today."—BL (REV: BL 5/1/88; LJ 5/15/88; NYTBR 8/21/88)

9761 Kiely, Benedict. *State of Ireland: A Novella and Seventeen Short Stories.* 1980, Godine $16.95 (0-87923-320-6). Seventeen stories and the novella "Proxopera" studying the lives of Catholics in Northern Ireland. (REV: BL 10/1/80; New Rep 11/29/80; NYTBR 11/16/80. AWARDS: ALA, 1980)

9762 Kingsolver, Barbara. *Homeland: And Other Stories.* 1989, Harper & Row $16.95 (0-06-016112-4); paper $8.95 (0-06-091701-6). A collection of 12 short stories by the author of *Animal Dreams* and *The Bean Trees*. (REV: BL 5/15/89; LJ 5/15/89; PW 4/7/89. AWARDS: ALA, 1989)

9763 Kinsella, W. P. *Dance Me Outside: More Tales from the Ermineskin Reserve.* 1986, Godine $14.95 (0-87923-583-7). Seventeen stories about the Native Americans living on an Alberta reservation. (REV: BL 5/15/86; CSM 5/28/86; LJ 7/86)

9764 Kirn, Walter. *My Hard Bargain.* 1990, Random $18.95 (0-394-58303-5). A debut collection of 13 stories about the lives of Mormons and Midwestern farmers. (REV: CSM 12/7/90; LJ 9/1/90; New Yorker 12/24/90)

9765 Klass, Perri. *I Am Having an Adventure.* 1986, Putnam $17.95 (0-399-13146-9); NAL paper $8.95 (0-452-25931-2). A collection of 21 short stories by the author of *Recombinations*. (REV: LJ 8/86; NYTBR 7/13/86)

9766 Klima, Ivan. *My Merry Mornings: Stories from Prague.* 1985, Readers International $14.95 (0-930523-04-0); paper $7.95 (0-930523-05-9). Seven stories formerly banned in Czechoslovakia portraying life in that nation following the 1968 Soviet invasion. (REV: CSM 8/2/85; LJ 5/1/85; PW 3/15/85)

9767 Koger, Lisa. *Farlanburg Stories.* 1990, Norton $17.95 (0-393-02856-9). This author's debut collection of ten short stories is set in a fictional Southern town. "If this first effort is any indication, there is little doubt that Koger will become one of the prominent voices of Southern fiction."—LJ (REV: BL 7/90; LJ 6/15/90; NYTBR 8/19/90)

9768 Krist, Gary. *Garden State.* 1988, Harcourt $16.95 (0-15-134292-X); Random paper $7.95 (0-679-72515-6). A collection of eight humorous stories depicting life in suburban New Jersey. (REV: BL 10/1/88; NYTBR 11/6/88)

9769 La Chapelle, Mary. *House of Heroes and Other Stories.* 1988, Crown $18.95 (0-517-56782-2); Random paper $8.95 (0-679-72457-5). This debut collection of ten short stories portrays the lives of individuals living in America's Great Lakes region. (REV: BL 8/88; LJ 8/88; PW 6/10/88)

9770 La Puma, Salvatore. *Boys of Bensonhurst.* 1987, Univ. of Georgia Pr. $15.95 (0-8203-0891-9). This debut collection of short stories portrays the lives of Brooklyn teenagers growing up in the early 1940s. (REV: LJ 2/1/87; NYTBR 3/29/87; PW 12/19/86)

9771 Lasdun, James. *Delirium Eclipse and Other Stories.* 1987, Norton paper $7.95 (0-393-30503-1). Nine stories by an English writer with surprise as the theme, including "England's Finest," "Dead Labor," and the title story. (REV: BL 5/1/86; LJ 6/15/86; PW 6/6/86)

9772 Lauber, Lynn. *White Girls.* 1990, Norton $17.95 (0-393-02717-1). Seventeen interconnected stories tracing the preteen and adolescent years of a Union, Ohio, girl who has an affair with a young black man. (REV: BL 1/15/90; LJ 2/15/90; PW 11/24/89)

9773 Laughlin, James. *Random Stories.* 1990, Moyer Bell $18.95 (1-55921-029-X). Twelve short stories written during the 1930s by the founder of New Directions publishing house. It contains a foreword to the collection by Octavio Paz. (REV: LJ 12/90; PW 10/5/90)

9774 Leavitt, David. *Family Dancing.* 1984, Knopf $13.95 (0-394-53872-2); Warner paper $4.95 (0-446-32845-6). This debut collection of nine stories by the author was published when he was 23 years of age. (REV: LJ 8/84; New Rep 12/24/84; Newsweek 1/14/85)

9775 Leavitt, David. *A Place I've Never Been.* 1990, Viking $18.95 (0-670-82196-9). A collection of ten short stories including "Gravity," "I See London, I See France," and "Chips at Home." "Both entertaining and profoundly moving."—LJ (REV: BL 9/15/90; LJ 8/90; PW 7/13/90. AWARDS: LJ, 1990)

9776 Leedom-Ackerman, Joanne. *No Marble Angels.* 1985, Texas Center for Writers $13.95 (0-916092-10-0); Saybrook paper $7.95 (0-933071-12-4). A collection of nine short stories dealing with the theme of separation, including "The Tutor," "The Beginning of Violence," and "History Lesson." (REV: CSM 1/3/86; NYTBR 11/3/85)

9777 Leffland, Ella. *Last Courtesies, and Other Stories.* 1985, Graywolf paper $8.50 (0-915308-71-1). A collection of short stories by the California-born author of *Mrs. Munck.* (REV: BL 9/15/80; LJ 8/80; NYTBR 10/5/80)

9778 Le Guin, Ursula K. *Orsinian Tales.* 1976, Ultramarine $20.00 (0-06-012561-6); Harper & Row paper $6.95 (0-06-091433-5). Eleven short stories set in an imaginary Central European country, ranging in time from the twelfth century to the 1960s. (REV: Choice 3/77; LJ 10/1/76; PW 7/26/76)

9779 Lesser, Ellen. *Shoplifter's Apprentice.* **1988, Simon & Schuster $17.95 (0-671-64882-9); Pocket paper $7.95 (0-671-69318-2).** A collection of short stories by the author of *The Other Woman* including "Madame Bartova's School of Ballet." (Rev: NYTBR 6/4/89; PW 3/24/89)

9780 Lessing, Doris. *Stories.* **1980, Random paper $12.95 (0-394-74249-4).** Collected stories from the author's *Habit of Loving, Temptation of Jack Orken,* and *A Men and Two Women,* plus a novella previously unpublished in the United States. (Rev: LJ 5/15/78; NYTBR 6/4/78; Newsweek 5/22/78. Awards: NYTBR, 1978)

9781 Levi, Primo. *Sixth Day and Other Stories.* **1990, Simon & Schuster $18.95 (0-671-67617-5).** A collection of short stories by the author of *If Not Now, When?* including "Psychophant" and "His Own Blacksmith." (Rev: BL 4/15/90; CSM 8/16/90; LJ 6/15/90)

9782 L'Heureux, John. *Comedians.* **1990, Viking $17.95 (0-670-82918-8).** A collection of 11 short stories and a novella by the author of *A Woman Run Mad.* (Rev: NYTBR 2/18/90; PW 12/1/89)

9783 Liben, Meyer. *Justice Hunger.* **1986, Schocken paper $8.95 (0-8052-0804-6).** A collection of ten stories set during the Great Depression concerning the lives of leftist New Yorkers. (Rev: Choice 4/68; LJ 2/15/67; New Rep 3/18/67)

9784 Lind, Jakov. *Soul of Wood and Other Stories.* **1986, Farrar paper $6.95 (0-8090-1526-9).** A novella and six stories by the Jewish-Austrian writer concerned with the fate of European Jews in the twentieth century. (Rev: BL 3/1/65; LJ 3/1/65; NYTBR 1/24/65. Awards: ALA, 1965)

9785 Lindgren, Torgny. *Merab's Beauty and Other Stories.* **1990, Harper & Row $17.95 (0-06-016229-5).** Fourteen tales of nineteenth-century Sweden by the author of *Bathsheba.* (Rev: BL 2/15/90; LJ 1/90; PW 12/22/89)

9786 Lipman, Eleanor. *Into Love and Out Again.* **1987, Viking $15.95 (0-670-81193-9); Pocket paper $6.95 (0-671-65676-7).** A collection of 16 stories of love, marriage, and human relations set in a New England town. (Rev: LJ 2/15/87; NYTBR 4/26/87)

9787 Lively, Penelope. *Pack of Cards: Stories, 1978–1986.* **1989, Grove-Weidenfeld $19.95 (0-8021-1156-4); Harper & Row paper $8.95 (0-06-097315-3).** A collection of 34 stories by the author of *Moon Tiger.* "Confirms Lively's place as one of Britain's most imaginative and important contemporary writers."—LJ (Rev: LJ 4/1/89; NYTBR 5/21/89; PW 2/3/89)

9788 Loader, Jayne. *Wild America.* **1989, Grove-Weidenfeld $17.95 (0-8021-1106-8); Ivy Books paper $4.95 (0-8041-0644-4).** A debut collection of short fiction including "I Was a Hollywood Sex Slave by Carrie Jo Starkweather." (Rev: BL 4/15/89; NYTBR 5/14/89)

9789 Lombreglia, Ralph. *Men under Water.* **1990, Doubleday $17.95 (0-385-26335-X).** The debut collection of nine short stories by this American writer. "Deft and biting entertainment."—PW (Rev: LJ 3/15/90; NYTBR 4/15/90; PW 1/26/90)

9790 Long, David. *Flood of '64.* **1987, Ecco Pr. $16.95 (0-88001-127-0).** Ten short stories by a Montana writer portraying life in that state. (Rev: LJ 3/15/87; NYTBR 7/15/87; PW 1/16/87)

9791 Lott, Bret. *A Dream of Old Leaves.* **1989, Viking $16.95 (0-670-82807-6).** A collection of 15 short stories by the author of *The Man Who Owned Vermont.* (Rev: BL 8/89; LJ 6/1/89; NYTBR 9/10/89)

9792 Louie, David Wong. *Pangs of Love.* **1991, Knopf $19.00 (0-394-58957-2).** The debut set of 11 short stories by a Long Island writer. "A strong new voice in the growing chorus of Chinese-American literature."—BL (Rev: BL 5/15/91; LJ 6/1/91; PW 5/10/91)

9793 Lowell, Susan. *Ganado Red.* **1988, Milkweed paper $9.95 (0-915943-26-3).** A collection of eight stories and the title novella that traces the history of a Navajo rug from its design and construction through a series of owners. (Rev: NYTBR 10/2/88; PW 4/29/88. Awards: PW, 1988)

9794 Lucas, Russell. *Evenings at Mongili's and Other Stories.* **1991, Summit $18.95 (0-671-72746-X).** A debut collection by an Indian-born English writer containing short stories set in Bombay during the 1940s and 1950s. (Rev: BL 12/1/90; NYTBR 1/27/91; PW 11/16/90. Awards: ALA, 1992)

9795 Lustig, Arnost. *Diamonds of the Night.* **1986, Northwestern Univ. Pr. $29.95 (0-8101-0705-8); paper $15.95 (0-8101-0706-6).** A collection of stories by a Czech Holocaust survivor portraying the lives of children in the Nazi death camps. (Rev: BL 10/1/86; NYTBR 11/2/86)

9796 McCullers, Carson. *Collected Stories.* **1987, Houghton $18.95 (0-395-44179-X); paper $10.95 (0-395-44243-5).** A collection of all 21 of McCullers's short stories plus her short novels *Member of the Wedding* and *Ballad of the Sad Cafe.* (Rev: BL 6/1/87; LJ 8/87)

9797 McEwan, Ian. *In Between the Sheets, and Other Stories.* **1990, Penguin paper $6.95 (0-14-011281-2).** A collection of seven short stories by the English writer, which includes "Dead as They Come," "Pornography," and "Reflections of a Kept Ape." (Rev: LJ 9/1/79; PW 6/25/79)

9798 McGahern, John. *High Ground.* **1987, Viking $15.95 (0-670-81181-5).** Ten short stories written by the author of *The Pornographer* and set in his native Ireland. (Rev: BL 12/15/86; LJ 12/86; NYTBR 2/8/87)

9799 McGuane, Thomas. *To Skin a Cat.* **1987, Random paper $5.95 (0-394-75521-9).** This debut collection of short fiction by the author contains 13 stories set in Montana. (Rev: BL 10/1/86; PW 8/29/86; TLS 8/14/87)

9800 MacLaverty, Bernard. *A Time to Dance and Other Stories.* 1985, Braziller paper $5.95 (0-8076-1135-2). A collection of ten short stories set in Scotland and Ireland, including "Phonefun Limited," "No Joke," and "The Beginnings of a Sin." (REV: LJ 11/15/82; PW 7/23/82; TLS 5/14/82)

9801 MacLeod, Alistair. *Lost Salt Gift of Blood: New and Selected Stories.* 1988, Ontario Rev. paper $10.95 (0-86538-063-5). A collection of 11 stories set in Eastern Canada portraying the lives of Scottish immigrants. (REV: BL 6/15/88; LJ 6/15/88; PW 4/29/88. AWARDS: PW, 1988)

9802 McPherson, James A. *Elbow Room.* 1987, Macmillan paper $6.95 (0-684-18822-8). This second collection of short fiction by the author contains 12 stories, including "Why I Like Country Music" and "The Story of a Scar." (REV: LJ 8/77; NYTBR 9/25/77; PW 7/25/77. AWARDS: PP: Fiction, 1978)

9803 Malamud, Bernard. *The People: And Other Uncollected Stories.* 1989, Farrar $18.95 (0-374-23067-6). A collection of 14 stories and one unfinished novel by the author of *The Fixer.* "An excellent overview of his career . . . a must-have volume."—PW (REV: NYTBR 11/19/89; PW 9/22/89; Time 11/20/89)

9804 Malamud, Bernard. *Stories of Bernard Malamud.* 1983, Farrar $17.95 (0-374-27037-6); NAL paper $8.95 (0-452-25911-8). Twenty-five stories selected by Malamud from the output of his writing career. "The master storyteller at his best."—LJ (REV: BL 9/15/83; LJ 12/1/83; PW 9/23/83. AWARDS: ALA, 1983; BL, the 1980s)

9805 Markham, Beryl. *Splendid Outcast: Beryl Markham's African Stories.* 1987, North Point $14.95 (0-86547-301-3); Dell paper $7.50 (0-440-50030-3). A collection of eight stories about African life by the aviatrix and author of *West with the Night.* (REV: BL 9/1/87; NYTBR 8/23/87; PW 8/28/87)

9806 Martin, Valerie. *Consolation of Nature and Other Stories.* 1988, Houghton $16.95 (0-395-46788-8); Random paper $6.95 (0-679-72159-2). This debut collection of ten pieces of short fiction includes "Death Goes to a Party" and "Elegy for Dead Animals." (REV: BL 1/15/88; PW 12/11/87)

9807 Martin, Wendy, ed. *We Are the Stories We Tell: The Best Short Stories by North American Women since 1945.* 1990, Pantheon $29.95 (0-394-58179-2); paper $9.95 (0-679-72881-3). Twenty-four post-World War II stories including works by Alice Munro, Margaret Atwood, Eudora Welty, and Anne Tyler. (REV: BL 4/15/90; LJ 5/15/90; PW 3/23/90)

9808 Maruya, Saiichi. *Rain in the Wind.* 1990, Kodansha $17.95 (0-87011-940-0). A collection of three short stories and a novella originally written in Japanese and translated by Donald Keene. (REV: BL 3/1/90; LJ 5/15/90; NYTBR 7/29/90)

9809 Mason, Bobbie Ann. *Love Life.* 1989, Harper & Row $17.95 (0-06-016042-X); paper $8.95 (0-06-091668-0). Fifteen stories by the author of *In Country* set in her native Kentucky and Tennessee. (REV: BL 1/1/89; LJ 3/15/89; NYTBR 3/12/89)

9810 Mason, Bobbie Ann. *Shiloh and Other Stories.* 1990, Harper & Row paper $8.95 (0-06-091068-2). A collection of short stories set in western Kentucky by the author of *In Country.* (REV: New Rep 11/1/82; Newsweek 11/15/82; Time 1/3/83. AWARDS: ALA, 1982; Time, 1983)

9811 Masters, Olga. *A Long Time Dying.* 1989, Norton $18.95 (0-391-02688-4). Seventeen short stories set in New South Wales during the 1930s concerning the lives of rural farmers. (REV: BL 5/15/89; LJ 4/15/89; PW 2/24/89)

9812 Matthews, Jack. *Dirty Tricks.* 1990, Johns Hopkins $26.00 (0-8018-4054-6); paper $10.95 (0-8018-4056-6). A collection of stories dealing with death including "Funeral Plots" and "The Farthest Reach of Candy Nights." (REV: LJ 10/15/90; PW 8/17/90)

9813 Matthiessen, Peter. *On the River Styx and Other Stories.* 1989, Random $17.95 (0-394-55399-3). Ten short stories selected from four decades of work by the author of *Far Tortuga.* (REV: BL 3/1/89; NYTBR 5/14/89; TLS 9/22/89)

9814 Maxwell, William. *Billie Dyer and Other Stories.* 1992, Knopf $18.00 (0-679-40832-0). A collection of seven stories by the octagenarian author portraying the Illinois of his youth. (REV: BL 11/15/91; PW 11/8/91)

9815 Meinke, Peter. *Piano Tuner.* 1986, Univ. of Georgia Pr. $15.95 (0-8203-0844-7). A collection of fourteen stories, some taking place in the United States and others examining the exploits of Americans abroad. "Storytelling at its best."—LJ (REV: BL 5/1/86; LJ 5/15/86; PW 5/16/86)

9816 Menaker, Daniel. *The Old Left and Other Stories.* 1987, Knopf $15.95 (0-394-54678-4); Penguin paper $5.95 (0-14-010852-1). Short stories regarding the relationship of an aging radical and his schoolteacher nephew. "A realistic, moving, often amusing collection."—BL (REV: BL 4/15/87; LJ 4/15/87; PW 3/13/87. AWARDS: ALA, 1987)

9817 Michaels, Leonard. *I Would Have Saved Them If I Could.* 1975, Farrar $8.95 (0374-17411-3); paper $6.95 (0-374-51713-4). A collection of short stories by the American author of *The Men's Club.* "An important literary event."—NYTBR (REV: Atl 10/75; BL 11/1/75; NYTBR 8/4/75. AWARDS: NYTBR, 1975)

9818 Miller, Sue. *Inventing the Abbotts and Other Stories.* 1987, Harper & Row $15.95 (0-06-015755-0); Dell paper $8.95 (0-440-54070-4). A collection of short stories by the author of *The Good Mother.* "Wholly engrossing."—BL (REV: BL 4/15/87; LJ 5/1/87; NYTBR 5/24/87)

9819 Millhauser, Steven. *Barnum Museum.* 1990, Poseidon $18.95 (0-671-68640-2). A collection of ten short stories including "The Sepia Postcard," "The Invention of Robert Herendeen," and the title story. (REV: BL 6/15/90; LJ 6/1/90; Time 7/2/90)

9820 **Millhauser, Steven.** *In the Penny Arcade.* **1985, Knopf $14.95 (0-394-54660-1); Pocket paper $5.95 (0-317-55999-0).** Seven short stories by the author of *Edwin Mulhouse.* "Millhauser continues to prove himself one of our very best writers and stylists."—LJ (REV: Choice 7–8/86; LJ 1/86; NYTBR 1/19/86)

9821 **Mishima, Yukio.** *Acts of Worship.* **1989, Kodansha $17.95 (0-87011-937-0).** A collection of seven short stories translated from the Japanese into English for the first time. "Truly representative of the writer at his best."—BL (REV: BL 11/1/89; Choice 4/90; LJ 11/15/89)

9822 **Mitsios, Helen, ed.** *New Japanese Voices: The Best Contemporary Fiction from Japan.* **1990, Atlantic Monthly $18.95 (0-87113-426-8).** An anthology of 12 stories by contemporary Japanese writers including an introduction by Jay McInerny. "Should firmly resolve debates about the vitality of Japanese fiction."—PW (REV: NYTBR 2/17/91; PW 12/21/90)

9823 **Moore, Lorrie.** *Like Life.* **1990, Knopf $18.95 (0-394-58101-6).** Eight short stories including "You're Ugly, Too," "Emergency. Love. Emergency.," and the title story. (REV: CSM 8/2/90; NYTBR 5/20/90; PW 2/23/90. AWARDS: PW, 1990)

9824 **Moore, Lorrie.** *Self-Help.* **1986, NAL paper $7.95 (0-452-25821-9).** Nine stories concerning young women, including "The Kid's Guide to Divorce" and "What Is Seized." (REV: BL 3/15/85; LJ 3/15/85; TLS 11/8/85)

9825 **Morazzoni, Marta.** *Girl in a Turban.* **1988, Knopf $16.95 (0-394-56115-5).** This debut collection of short fiction by an Italian writer contains five stories including one about the death of Mozart. "A writer of exceptional talent."—PW (REV: BL 9/1/88; LJ 9/1/88; PW 7/15/88)

9826 **Mordden, Ethan.** *Everybody Loves You: Further Adventures in Gay Manhattan.* **1988, St. Martin's $16.95 (0-312-02201-8); paper $8.95 (0-312-03334-6).** A fictional portrait of gay male life in New York told through a series of short vignettes. (REV: LJ 10/1/88; PW 7/15/88)

9827 **Morris, Mary.** *Bus of Dreams.* **1986, Viking paper $7.95 (0-14-008971-3).** A collection of 15 stories by the author of *Nothing to Declare.* "A collection to be savored for its fine writing and emotional resonance."—PW (REV: BL 6/1/85; LJ 6/1/85; PW 4/12/85)

9828 **Morris, Wright.** *Collected Stories, 1948–1986.* **1986, Harper & Row $17.95 (0-06-015639-2); Godine paper $10.95 (0-87923-752-X).** A collection of 26 short stories, 14 formerly uncollected, by the Nebraska author of *The Field of Vision.* (REV: NYTBR 12/14/86; Time 12/1/86)

9829 **Moyer, Kermit.** *Tumbling.* **1988, Univ. of Illinois Pr. $11.95 (0-252-01525-8).** A debut collection of seven stories about children's perceptions of the world and their relations with adults. (REV: NYTBR 8/28/88; PW 6/24/88)

9830 **Mukherjee, Bharati.** *Middleman and Other Stories.* **1989, Fawcett paper $3.95 (0-449-21718-3).** A collection of short stories depicting immigrant life in the United States. (REV: BL 9/1/88; LJ 6/1/88; PW 5/6/88. AWARDS: ALA, 1988; PW, 1988)

9831 **Mungoshi, Charles.** *Setting Sun and the Rolling World: Selected Stories.* **1989, Beacon paper $8.95 (0-8070-8321-6).** A collection of 17 short stories written over two decades by a writer from Zimbabwe examining life in his country. (REV: BL 9/15/89; LJ 9/15/89; PW 8/4/89)

9832 **Munro, Alice.** *Beggar Maid: Stories of Flo and Rose.* **1984, Penguin paper $6.95 (0-14-006011-1).** Ten interrelated short stories that trace the life of a woman from childhood to marriage to a successful career. (REV: LJ 10/1/79; New Rep 10/13/79; Sat Rev 10/13/79)

9833 **Munro, Alice.** *Friend of My Youth.* **1990, Knopf $18.95 (0-394-58442-2).** Ten stories set in southern Ontario by the Canadian writer. (REV: NYTBR 3/18/90; PW 1/19/90; Time 7/2/90. AWARDS: ALA, 1990; NYTBR, 1990; PW, 1990; Time, 1990)

9834 **Munro, Alice.** *Moons of Jupiter.* **1983, Knopf $13.95 (0-394-52952-9); Penguin paper (0-14-006547-4).** Eleven stories by the author of *The Beggar Maid,* including "Prue," "Dulse," and "Mrs. Cross and Mrs. Kidd." (REV: BL 2/15/83; LJ 2/15/83; NYTBR 3/20/83. AWARDS: NYTBR, 1983)

9835 **Munro, Alice.** *The Progress of Love.* **1986, Knopf $16.95 (0-394-55272-4); Penguin paper $6.95 (0-14-009879-8).** A collection of short stories by the Canadian writer examining family dynamics. "Excellent reading."—LJ (REV: LJ 9/15/86; NYTBR 9/14/86; PW 7/4/86. AWARDS: LJ, 1986; NYTBR, 1986; PW, 1986)

9836 **Naoya, Shiga.** *Paper Door: And Other Stories.* **1987, North Point $14.95 (0-86547-260-2); paper $8.95 (0-86547-419-2).** A collection of 17 short stories by the Japanese writer dating from the turn of the twentieth century. (REV: BL 3/15/87; LJ 2/15/87; NYTBR 4/5/87)

9837 **Narayan, R. K.** *Malgudi Days.* **1985, Penguin paper $6.95 (0-14-006910-0).** Thirty-two stories portraying life in the author's fictional Indian town of Malgudi. "Distinguished writing; rewarding reading."—BL (REV: BL 2/1/82; NYTBR 3/7/82; PW 1/22/82)

9838 **Narayan, R. K.** *Under the Banyan Tree and Other Stories.* **1985, Viking $16.95 (0-670-80452-5); Penguin paper $6.95 (0-14-008012-0).** Twenty-eight stories portraying life in rural India set in the author's fictional community of Malgudi. (REV: LJ 7/85; Newsweek 8/26/85; Time 8/12/85)

9839 **Nin, Anais.** *Delta of Venus.* **1990, Pocket paper $4.95 (0-671-68015-3).** Fifteen short pieces of erotica Nin was commissioned to write during the 1940s. "Full-bodied, feminist erotica—a fine post-humous addition to Nin's literary legacy."—LJ (Rev: LJ 5/1/77; NYTBR 7/10/77; PW 4/11/77)

9840 Nissenson, Hugh. *Elephant and My Jewish Problem: Short Stories and Journals, 1957–1987.* **1988, Harper & Row $18.95 (0-06-015985-5); paper $8.95 (0-06-091624-9).** A collection of previously published short stories and unpublished journals regarding the Eichmann and Barbie trials. (Rev: BL 10/15/88; NYTBR 12/11/88; PW 9/16/88)

9841 Nordan, Lewis. *All-Girl Football Team.* **1986, Louisiana State Univ. Pr. $15.95 (0-8071-1341-7); Random paper $5.95 (0-394-75701-7).** A collection of nine stories set in the Mississippi Delta region connected by use of the same narrator. "A collection to savor and treasure."—PW (Rev: BL 10/1/86; NYTBR 11/30/86; PW 9/5/86)

9842 Nordan, Lewis. *Music of the Swamp.* **1991, Algonquin $15.95 (0-945575-76-9).** A collection of ten interrelated stories about a boy growing up in the Mississippi Delta during the 1950s. Written by the author of *The All-Girl Football Team.* (Rev: LJ 8/91; PW 6/28/91. Awards: ALA, 1992)

9843 Norris, Leslie. *Girl from Cardigan.* **1988, Gibbs Smith $15.95 (0-87905-296-1); paper $8.95 (0-87905-337-2).** A collection of 16 pieces of short fiction by the Welsh poet and writer. (Rev: NYTBR 5/22/88; PW 2/26/88)

9844 Oates, Joyce Carol. *Assignation.* **1988, Ecco Pr. $16.95 (0-88001-200-5); Harper & Row paper $7.95 (0-06-097246-7).** A collection of 44 short pieces regarding the turmoils of love and romance. "These stories reveal a master of the form writing at her efficient, full-tilt best."—PW (Rev: BL 9/1/88; PW 7/22/88)

9845 Oates, Joyce Carol. *Heat and Other Stories.* **1991, Dutton $21.95 (0-525-93330-1).** A gathering of 25 stories by the author of *American Appetites.* "Oates continues to thrill her admirers, annoy her detractors, and woo new readers."—BL (Rev: BL 6/1/91; LJ 7/91; NYTBR 8/4/91)

9846 Oates, Joyce Carol. *Raven's Wing.* **1987, Dutton paper $8.95 (0-525-48333-0).** A collection of 16 stories by the author of *Them,* including "Surf City" and "Golden Gloves." "A dazzling collection . . . a searing, faultless performance."—LJ (Rev: LJ 10/15/86; NYTBR 10/5/86)

9847 O'Brien, Dan. *Eminent Domain.* **1987, Univ. of Iowa Pr. $13.95 (0-87745-170-2); Crown paper $7.95 (0-517-57550-7).** A collection of ten short stories by a South Dakota biologist who was awarded the 1986 Iowa Short Fiction Award. (Rev: BL 8/87; LJ 4/15/87; PW 3/13/87)

9848 O'Brien, Edna. *A Fanatic Heart: Selected Stories of Edna O'Brien.* **1984, Farrar $17.95 (0-374-15342-6); NAL paper $9.95 (0-452-26116-3).** A collection of 29 selected stories by the Irish writer, including "The Connor Girls," "My Mother's Mother," and "A Scandalous Woman." (Rev: BL 11/15/84; NYTBR 11/18/84; PW 10/12/84)

9849 O'Brien, Edna. *Lantern Slides.* **1990, Farrar $18.95 (0-374-18332-5).** Twelve short stories concerning love by the Irish writer including "The Widow," "Long Distance," and "Dramas." (Rev: LJ 6/1/90; PW 5/4/90; TLS 6/8/90)

9850 O'Connor, Flannery. *Complete Stories.* **1971, Farrar $35.00 (0-374-12752-2); paper $9.95 (0-374-51536-0).** Thirty-one pieces including the contents of O'Connor's two previously published story collections. (Rev: BL 1/15/72; LJ 1/1/72. Awards: NBA, 1972)

9851 O'Connor, Frank. *Collected Stories.* **1981, Knopf $20.00 (0-394-51602-8); Random paper $12.95 (0-394-71048-7).** Sixty-seven selected stories by the Irish writer. (Rev: LJ 7/81; NYTBR 9/20/81; Newsweek 9/7/81. Awards: ALA, 1981)

9852 Oe, Kenzaburo, ed. *Crazy Iris and Other Stories of the Atomic Aftermath.* **1985, Grove-Weidenfeld $22.50 (0-394-54944-9).** Nine stories by Japanese writers regarding aspects of the atomic bombings of Hiroshima and Nagasaki. (Rev: LJ 9/15/85; NYTBR 9/8/85; TLS 10/26/84)

9853 O'Faolain, Sean. *Collected Stories of Sean O'Faolain.* **1983, Little, Brown $29.95 (0-316-63294-5).** A collection of 90 short stories covering over 1,300 pages penned by the Irish writer. (Rev: CSM 10/12/83; LJ 10/1/83; NYTBR 10/30/83)

9854 Okri, Ben. *Stars of the New Curfew.* **1989, Viking $17.95 (0-670-82520-4); Penguin paper $7.95 (0-14-011602-8).** Short stories set in West Africa that examine aspects of that continent's culture and social structure. (Rev: BL 5/15/89; PW 5/19/89; Time 6/19/89)

9855 Ozick, Cynthia. *Levitation: Five Fictions.* **1983, Dutton paper $7.95 (0-525-48442-6).** A collection of stories by the author of *The Shawl,* including "From a Refugee's Notebook," "Shots," and the title story. (Rev: LJ 1/1/81; Newsweek 2/15/82; TLS 4/23/82)

9856 Ozick, Cynthia. *Pagan Rabbi and Other Stories.* **1983, Dutton paper $6.95 (0-525-48026-9).** A collection of short stories by the author of *The Shawl.* "Will delight and challenge the discriminating reader of fiction."—LJ (Rev: LJ 2/15/71; Newsweek 5/10/71; PW 2/15/71)

9857 Paley, Grace. *Enormous Changes at the Last Minute.* **1974, Farrar paper $6.95 (0-374-51524-7).** A collection of 15 stories concerning life in New York, including "Samuel," "Distance," and "An Interest in Life." (Rev: BL 5/1/74; Choice 5/74; Newsweek 3/11/74)

9858 Paley, Grace. *Later the Same Day.* **1985, Farrar $13.95 (0-374-18409-7); Penguin paper $6.95 (0-14-008641-2).** Short stories of life in New York by the author of *Little Disturbances of Man.* (Rev: LJ 4/1/85; New Rep 4/29/85; PW 2/8/85. Awards: LJ, 1985; PW, 1985)

9859 Pancake, Breece D'J. *Stories of Breece D'J Pancake.* **1983, Little, Brown $15.95 (0-316-69012-0); Henry Holt paper $6.95 (0-8050-0720-2).** Twelve stories by a West Virginia author who took his own life at the age of 27. (REV: BL 12/1/82; LJ 12/1/82; PW 12/3/82. AWARDS: ALA, 1983)

9860 Penner, Jonathan. *Private Parties.* **1983, Univ. of Pittsburgh Pr. $17.95 (0-8229-3448-4).** This collection of 14 short stories that won the Drue Heinz Prize includes "Uncle Hersh" and "Frankenstein Meets the Ant People." "An astonishing debut."—CSM (REV: BL 9/1/83; CSM 1/11/84; PW 8/19/83)

9861 Phillips, Jayne Anne. *Black Tickets.* **1989, Dell paper $8.95 (0-440-55022-X).** Twenty-seven short stories regarding love and male–female relations by the author of *Machine Dreams*. (REV: BL 10/1/79; Newsweek 10/22/79; PW 7/16/79)

9862 Phillips, Jayne Anne. *Fast Lanes.* **1988, Pocket paper $5.95 (0-671-64014-3).** Seven short stories by the author of *Black Tickets* and *Machine Dreams*. (REV: BL 2/1/87; LJ 3/15/87; NYTBR 5/3/87)

9863 Pilcher, Rosamunde. *Blue Bedroom and Other Stories.* **1990, St. Martin's paper $3.95 (0-312-92312-0).** Thirteen stories concerning aspects of domestic life written by the author of *The Shell Seekers*. (REV: BL 6/1/85; LJ 7/85; PW 6/14/85)

9864 Porter, Katherine Anne. *Collected Stories of Katherine Anne Porter.* **1979, Harcourt paper $9.95 (0-15-618876-7).** A compilation of 27 stories by the American writer including "Holiday," "The Leaning Tower," and "Pale Horse, Pale Rider." (REV: BL 11/1/65; LJ 10/1/66; New Rep 9/4/65. AWARDS: NBA, 1965; PP:Fiction, 1966)

9865 Powell, Padgett. *Typical.* **1991, Farrar $19.00 (0-374-28022-3).** A collection of 23 short stories by the author of *Edisto*, including "Flood," "The Winnowing of Mrs. Schuping," and "Wayne's Fate." (REV: BL 6/15/91; LJ 7/91; NYTBR 7/21/91)

9866 Pritchard, Melissa. *Spirit Seizures.* **1987, Univ. of Georgia Pr. $15.95 (0-8203-0959-1); Macmillan paper $8.95 (0-02-036070-3).** This debut collection of 17 stories by the author was a Flannery O'Connor Award winner. (REV: BL 11/15/87; NYTBR 11/22/87; PW 10/16/87)

9867 Pritchett, V. S. *A Careless Widow and Other Stories.* **1989, Random $16.95 (0-394-57612-8).** Five stories by the veteran British writer, including "Cocky Olly," "A Trip to the Seaside," and the title story. (REV: BL 9/15/89; CSM 9/1/87; PW 7/28/89)

9868 Pritchett, V. S. *Collected Stories.* **1982, Random paper $20.00 (0-394-52417-9).** Twenty-nine stories collected from five decades by the English writer. (REV: BL 2/15/82; PW 4/9/82; Sat Rev 5/82)

9869 Pritchett, V. S. *Complete Collected Stories.* **1991, Random $35.00 (0-679-40215-2).** A collection of 82 short stories by the English writer. "As a body of work, Pritchett's stories can stand comparison with any others written in this century."—PW (REV: BL 2/1/91; NYTBR 3/24/91; PW 2/22/91. AWARDS: NYTBR, 1991)

9870 Pritchett, V. S. *More Collected Stories.* **1983, Random $17.95 (0-394-53128-0); paper $8.95 (0-394-72584-0).** Twenty-four short stories selected from seven previously published volumes. "A strong sampling of Pritchett's mastery."—BL (REV: BL 7/83; CSM 10/20/83; PW 7/8/83)

9871 Prose, Francine. *Women and Children First.* **1988, Pantheon $16.95 (0-394-56573-8); Ivy Books paper $3.95 (0-8041-0415-8).** A collection of short fiction pieces by the author of the novels *Bigfoot Dreams* and *Household Saints*. (REV: BL 3/1/88; LJ 3/1/88; PW 1/15/88)

9872 Proulx, E. Annie. *Heart Songs: And Other Stories.* **1990, Harper & Row paper $7.95 (0-06-097279-3).** Eleven short stories set in rural Vermont portraying the joys and rigors of the farming life. (REV: BL 10/1/88; LJ 11/1/88; PW 8/19/88)

9873 Pym, Barbara. *Civil to Strangers: And Other Writings.* **1989, NAL paper $8.95 (0-452-26138-4).** A collection of previously unpublished fiction by the English writer. (REV: LJ 11/15/87; NYTBR 1/17/88; TLS 12/25/87)

9874 Pynchon, Thomas. *Slow Learner: Early Stories.* **1985, Little, Brown $14.95 (0-316-72442-4); paper $8.95 (0-316-72443-2).** Five of Pynchon's early short stories from the late 1950s and early 1960s formerly uncollected in book form and prefaced by an autobiographical essay from the author. (REV: Choice 9/84; NYTBR 4/15/84; Time 4/23/84)

9875 Quammen, David. *Blood Line: Stories of Fathers and Sons.* **1988, Graywolf paper $8.00 (1-55597-100-8).** A collection of three stories involving father—son relationships by the author of *Natural Acts* and *The Flight of the Iguana*. "Powerful, thought-provoking, masterly crafted work."—LJ (REV: BL 1/1/88; LJ 3/1/88; PW 12/4/87)

9876 Raphael, Lev. *Dancing on Tisha B'Av.* **1990, St. Martin's $15.95 (0-312-04862-9).** A collection of 19 stories regarding aspects of Judaism and/or homosexuality. "Each story is a spellbinding delight."—BL (REV: BL 11/1/90; LJ 11/1/90)

9877 Rendell, Ruth. *New Girl Friend and Other Stories of Suspense.* **1987, Ballantine paper $3.95 (0-345-32879-5).** A collection of 11 mystery, horror, and fantastic stories by the veteran British writer, including the Edgar-winning title story. (REV: BL 2/15/86; CSM 4/25/86; Time 5/5/86)

9878 Rhys, Jean. *Collected Short Stories.* **1987, Norton $19.95 (0-393-02375-3).** A collection of short stories by the English writer set in the Caribbean, England, and France. (REV: BL 10/1/86; LJ 11/15/86)

9879 Rive, Richard. *Advance, Retreat: Selected Short Stories.* **1989, St. Martin's $16.95 (0-312-03689-2).** A selection from three decades of work by a South African writer murdered at his Cape Town home in 1989. "This human, sharply observant collection of stories shows . . . a voice that lingers long after one has read the stories."—NYTBR (Rev: BL 12/15/89; LJ 12/89; NYTBR 1/7/90)

9880 Robinson, Roxana. *A Glimpse of Scarlet: And Other Stories.* 1991, HarperCollins $18.95 (0-06-016331-3). A collection of 12 short stories by the biographer of Georgia O'Keeffe. "These gemlike stories may be her finest work."—BL (Rev: BL 5/15/91; NYTBR 6/30/91; PW 4/5/91)

9881 Robison, Mary. *Amateur's Guide to the Night.* 1989, Godine paper $9.95 (0-87923-802-X). A collection of 13 minimalist stories, including "Look at Me Go," "Yours," and the title story. (Rev: CSM 1/11/84; NYTBR 11/27/83; PW 9/30/83)

9882 Robison, Mary. *Believe Them.* 1988, Knopf $15.95 (0-394-53942-7); Macmillan paper $7.95 (0-02-036380-X). A collection of 11 short stories with eccentric but engaging characters in slice-of-life vignettes. (Rev: NYTBR 7/31/88; New Yorker 12/19/88; PW 4/15/88)

9883 Robison, Mary. *Days: Twenty Stories.* 1986, Godine paper $8.95 (0-87923-605-1). A collection of short stories by the author of *Oh!* "A first collection to be read and re-read with attention."—LJ (Rev: BL 7/1/79; LJ 5/15/79; PW 4/16/79)

9884 Rothschild, Michael. *Wondermonger.* 1990, Viking $17.95 (0-670-83326-6). A collection of nine stories by an American artist and writer dating back to the early 1970s. (Rev: BL 5/15/90; NYTBR 9/16/90; PW 4/27/90)

9885 Runyon, Damon. *Romance in the Roaring Forties and Other Stories.* 1986, Morrow paper $9.95 (0-688-06148-6). Twenty stories representing the best of Runyon selected from formerly published collections and literary magazines. (Rev: BL 1/15/86; LJ 1/86)

9886 Rush, Norman. *Whites.* 1987, Macmillan paper $6.95 (0-02-023841-X). Six stories set in Botswana portraying relations between native Africans and white colonists. (Rev: BL 2/15/86; NYTBR 3/23/86; Newsweek 6/2/86. Awards: ALA, 1986; NYTBR, 1986)

9887 Ruta, Suzanne. *Stalin in the Bronx: And Other Stories.* 1987, Grove-Weidenfeld $16.95 (0-8021-0018-X). A debut collection of short fiction including "The Shoe Clerk" and "In Fionna's Country." (Rev: NYTBR 11/29/87; PW 10/9/87)

9888 Saiki, Jessica. *Once, a Lotus Garden and Other Stories.* 1987, New Rivers paper $7.95 (0-89823-087-X). This illustrated debut collection of 20 stories portrays the lives of Japanese living in Hawaii prior to the outbreak of World War II. (Rev: NYTBR 7/5/87; PW 3/6/87. Awards: PW, 1987)

9889 Salter, James. *Dusk and Other Stories.* 1989, North Point $14.95 (0-86547-277-7); paper $7.95 (0-86547-389-7). A collection of 11 stories including "Twenty Minutes," "Foreign Shores," and "American Express." (Rev: NYTBR 4/16/89; TLS 5/25/90)

9890 Sams, Ferrol. *Widow's Mite and Other Stories.* 1987, Peachtree $14.95 (0-934601-26-7); Pen-guin paper $6.95 (0-14-011250-2). A physician/writer's collection of eight stories detailing aspects of life in small-town Georgia. (Rev: BL 12/15/87; LJ 12/87; NYTBR 12/13/87)

9891 Saroyan, William. *My Name Is Saroyan: A Collection.* Ed. by James H. Tashijian. 1983, Putnam $22.50 (0-698-11229-6); Harcourt paper $8.95 (0-15-662333-1). Ninety-seven short stories, five poems, and four plays by the author of *The Human Comedy* collected from Armenian publications of the 1930s and 1940s. (Rev: BL 6/1/83; NYTBR 8/21/83; PW 6/10/83)

9892 Schinto, Jeanne. *Shadow Bands.* 1988, Ontario Rev. paper $9.95 (0-86538-065-1). A debut collection of 12 stories including "The Motorcycle Riders." (Rev: LJ 12/88; PW 9/30/88)

9893 Schulberg, Budd. *Love, Action, Laughter and Other Sad Tales.* 1990, Random $17.95 (0-394-57619-5). A collection of 16 short stories from the 1930s to the 1980s by the author of *What Makes Sammy Run?* (Rev: LJ 12/89; NYTBR 2/4/90)

9894 Schwartz, Jonathan. *The Man Who Knew Cary Grant: Stories.* 1988, Random $16.95 (0-394-56967-9); NAL paper $8.95 (0-452-26310-7). Interconnected stories tracing the life of the only son of a well-known composer. (Rev: LJ 11/1/88; NYTBR 10/23/88; Newsweek 11/7/88)

9895 Schwartz, Lynne Sharon. *Acquainted with the Night: And Other Stories.* 1985, Harper & Row $8.95 (0-06-091297-9). A collection of 16 short stories by the author of *Disturbances in the Field*, including "The Age of Analysis" and the title story. (Rev: BL 6/1/84; LJ 7/84; PW 6/1/84)

9896 Schwartz, Lynne Sharon. *Melting Pot: And Other Subversive Stories.* 1989, Penguin paper $7.95 (0-14-011381-9). A collection of 11 stories including "Killing the Bees" and "The Infidel" by the author of the novel *Rough Strife.* (Rev: Choice 2/88; LJ 10/15/87; PW 7/31/87)

9897 Schwartz, Steven. *Lives of the Fathers.* 1991, Univ. of Illinois Pr. $16.95 (0-252-01815-X). A collection of ten stories that won the Illinois Short Fiction Award, including the tales "Summer of Love" and "Legacy." (Rev: BL 7/91; PW 8/30/91)

9898 Selby, Hubert, Jr. *Song of the Silent Snow.* 1986, M. Boyars $16.95 (0-7145-2840-4); Grove-Weidenfeld paper $6.95 (0-8021-3008-9). A collection of 15 short stories by the author of *Last Exit to Brooklyn.* (Rev: BL 5/15/86; LJ 5/15/86; TLS 9/5/86)

9899 Selzer, Richard. *Imagine a Woman: And Other Stories.* 1990, Random $18.95 (0-394-58535-6). A collection of six short stories on aspects of health and medicine by the surgeon/author of *Mortal Lessons.* (Rev: BL 11/15/90; LJ 12/90; PW 9/28/90)

9900 Sexson, Linda. *Margaret of the Imperfections.* 1989, Persea $16.95 (0-89255-131-3); paper $9.95 (0-89255-147-X). A debut collection of ten short stories by a Montana writer, including "Hope Chest,"

"Foxglove," and the title story. (REV: LJ 9/15/88; NYTBR 10/23/88; PW 6/17/88)

9901   Shacochis, Bob. *Easy in the Islands.* **1984, Crown $13.95 (0-517-55549-2); Penguin paper $7.95 (0-14-008301-4).** This debut collection of nine stories set in the Caribbean was awarded *Playboy*'s prize for best new fiction. (REV: BL 12/1/84; LJ 2/1/85. AWARDS: NBA, 1985)

9902   Shacochis, Bob. *Next New World.* **1989, Crown $16.95 (0-517-57067-X); Penguin paper $7.95 (0-14-012105-6).** A collection of eight short stories by the Pennsylvania-born American writer. (REV: LJ 12/88; NYTBR 2/19/89; Time 1/16/89)

9903   Shalamov, Varlam. *Graphite.* **1981, Norton $14.95 (0-393-01476-2).** Thirty stories concerning the lives and fates of political prisoners held in Soviet forced-labor camps based on the author's own experiences. (REV: BL 10/1/81; LJ 12/1/81; PW 8/21/81)

9904   Shalamov, Varlam. *Kolyma Tales.* **1982, Norton paper $5.95 (0-393-00077-X).** Twenty-four stories based on the author's experiences as a prisoner in a Soviet labor camp. (REV: LJ 3/1/80; NYRB 8/14/80; NYTBR 5/4/80)

9905   Shapard, Robert, and James Thomas, eds. *Sudden Fiction: American Short-Short Stories.* **1986, Gibbs-Smith paper $10.95 (0-87905-265-1).** A collection of 70 stories no longer than five pages in length from 40 authors including Bernard Malamud, Raymond Carver, John Updike, John Cheever, and Grace Paley. (REV: BL 10/1/86; LJ 11/1/86; NYTBR 11/23/86)

9906   Shaw, Irwin. *Short Stories: Five Decades.* **1983, Dell paper $7.95 (0-440-34075-6).** A collection of 63 stories chosen by the author to represent his work of five decades. (REV: BL 10/1/78; LJ 12/15/78; Time 11/6/78)

9907   Singer, Isaac Bashevis. *Collected Stories of Isaac Bashevis Singer.* **1982, Farrar $19.95 (0-374-12631-3); paper $12.95 (0-374-51788-6).** A collection of 47 stories selected by the Nobel Laureate. (REV: CSM 4/9/82; PW 1/8/82; Time 4/5/82. AWARDS: ALA, 1982; Time, 1982; Time, the 1980s)

9908   Singer, Isaac Bashevis. *A Crown of Feathers and Other Stories.* **1974, Farrar paper $7.95 (0-374-51624-3).** Twenty-four stories from the 1970s regarding the lives of Polish Jews both in pre-World War II Europe and the postwar United States. (REV: BL 12/15/73; New Rep 11/3/73; Newsweek 11/12/73. AWARDS: NBA, 1974)

9909   Singer, Isaac Bashevis. *Death of Methuselah and Other Stories.* **1988, Farrar $17.95 (0-374-13563-0); paper $8.95 (0-452-26215-1).** Twenty stories set in times varying from the Biblical era to the twentieth century including "The Jew from Babylon" and "A Peephole in the Gate." (REV: BL 2/1/88; LJ 3/15/88; NYTBR 4/17/88)

9910   Singer, Isaac Bashevis. *The Image and Other Stories.* **1985, Farrar $16.95 (0-374-17465-2); paper $8.95 (0-374-52079-8).** Twenty-two stories set in

Warsaw, New York, by the Nobel Prize-winning author. "This marvelous collection will draw consistent admiration from readers of fine literature."—BL (REV: BL 5/1/85; NYTBR 6/30/85; PW 5/10/85)

9911   Smiley, Jane. *Age of Grief.* **1987, Knopf $15.95 (0-394-55848-0); Ivy Books paper $3.95 (0-8041-0368-2).** A collection of five short stories and the title novella concerning baby boomers in middle age. "The stories are fine; the novella is splendid."—NYTBR (REV: BL 9/15/87; LJ 8/87; NYTBR 9/6/87)

9912   Smith, Ken. *Decoys and Other Stories.* **1985, Confluence Pr. $12.95 (0-917652-53-3).** A collection of short stories by the American writer portraying ranching life and postwar life of military veterans. "An emotionally powerful collection."—LJ (REV: BL 3/15/86; LJ 12/85)

9913   Smith, Lee. *Cakewalk.* **1986, Ballantine paper $3.95 (0-345-33950-9).** Fourteen stories including two O. Henry Award winners concerning the lives of Southern women. "Quite simply excellent writing."—BL (REV: BL 11/1/81; LJ 10/15/81; PW 8/14/81)

9914   Smith, Lee. *Me and My Baby View the Eclipse.* **1990, Putnam $18.95 (0-399-13507-3).** A collection of short stories set in the American South by the author of *Cakewalk.* (REV: BL 2/1/90; NYTBR 2/11/90; PW 12/22/89. AWARDS: ALA, 1990)

9915   Sontag, Susan. *I, Etcetera.* **1978, Farrar $8.95 (0-374-17402-4); paper $8.95 (0-374-52074-7).** Eight experimental stories from the 1960s and 1970s from the author of *Death Kit.* (REV: BL 10/1/78; LJ 9/15/78; NYTBR 11/26/78)

9916   Spark, Muriel. *Stories of Muriel Spark.* **1986, NAL paper $8.95 (0-452-25880-4).** Twenty-seven short stories by the author of *Memento Mori* including "The Gentile Jewesses," "The First Year of My Life," and "The Black Madonna." (REV: LJ 10/1/85; Newsweek 9/16/85; PW 8/16/85)

9917   Spencer, Elizabeth. *Jack of Diamonds and Other Stories.* **1988, Viking $15.95 (0-670-82261-2); Penguin paper $6.95 (0-14-012252-4).** A collection of five stories by a Mississippi-born writer set in the South, New York, and Quebec. "A great pleasure, not to be missed."—LJ (REV: BL 6/15/88; LJ 7/88; Time 8/15/88)

9918   Spencer, Elizabeth. *Stories of Elizabeth Spencer.* **1983, Penguin paper $9.95 (0-14-006436-2).** A collection of 33 stories from the 1940s to the 1970s penned by the Mississippi writer. (REV: BL 2/15/81; LJ 3/1/81; NYTBR 3/1/81. AWARDS: ALA, 1981)

9919   Spilman, Richard. *Hot Fudge.* **1990, Simon & Schuster $17.95 (0-671-68544-9).** A collection of six stories portraying the lives of average Midwestern Americans. "A moving and impressive collection."—NYTBR (REV: NYTBR 7/29/90; PW 2/16/90)

9920   Stafford, Jean. *Collected Stories.* 1969, Farrar $17.50 (0-374-12632-1). A collection of 30 short stories including "Cops and Robbers," "The Hope Chest," and "Children Are Bored on Sunday." (REV: Choice 9/69; CSM 3/13/69; Newsweek 3/3/69. AWARDS: PP:Fiction, 1970)

9921   Stegner, Wallace. *Collected Stories of Wallace Stegner.* 1990, Random $21.95 (0-394-58409-0). A collection of 30 stories by the author of *Spectator Bird.* "Certain to be definitive for all libraries and all readers."—Choice (REV: BL 1/15/90; Choice 10/90; PW 1/26/90. AWARDS: ALA, 1990; BL, 1990; PW, 1990)

9922   Stern, Daniel. *Twice Told Tales.* 1989, British American Pr. $17.95 (0-945167-13-X); Norton paper $8.95 (0-393-30723-9). Six stories adapted from other writers' works including tales taken from Henry James, E. M. Forster, and Ernest Hemingway. (REV: BL 5/15/89; LJ 6/15/89; PW 5/5/89)

9923   Stern, Richard. *Noble Rot: Stories, 1949–1988.* 1989, Grove-Weidenfeld $22.95 (0-8021-1056-8). A collection of 32 short stories culled from four decades of literary magazines and previously published collections. (REV: BL 12/1/88; PW 12/2/88)

9924   Stern, Steve. *Lazar Malkin Enters Heaven.* 1987, Viking $16.95 (0-670-81379-6); Penguin paper $6.95 (0-15-010948-X). Nine tall tales about Jewish-American life including "Shimmele Fly-By-Night" and "The Ghost and Saul Bozoff." (REV: BL 2/15/87; LJ 1/87; PW 12/12/86)

9925   Straub, Peter. *Houses Without Doors.* 1990, Dutton $19.95 (0-525-24924-9); paper $5.99 (0-451-17082-2). A collection of 13 stories and short pieces by the author of *Koko,* including "A Short Guide to the City" and "Mrs. God." "Reveals Straub at his spellbinding best."—PW (REV: BL 1/15/91; NYTBR 10/30/90; PW 10/5/90)

9926   Swift, Graham. *Learning to Swim and Other Stories.* 1986, Pocket paper $6.95 (0-671-61834-2). Eleven stories originally published in British magazines by the author of *Shuttlecock.* (REV: BL 4/15/85; LJ 5/15/85; Newsweek 6/24/85)

9927   Tabucchi, Antonio. *Letter from Casablanca.* 1986, New Directions $17.95 (0-8112-0985-7); paper $7.95 (0-8112-0986-5). A collection of eight short stories, including "Heavenly Bliss," "Voices," "The Little Gatsby," and the title story. (REV: Choice 11/86; PW 5/16/86. AWARDS: PW, 1986)

9928   Tallent, Elizabeth. *In Constant Flight.* 1987, Henry Holt paper $6.95 (0-8050-0109-3). A collection of 11 short stories by the author of *Museum Pieces,* including "Asteroids," "Comings and Goings," and "Ice." (REV: PW 3/4/83; Sat Rev 6/83)

9929   Tallent, Elizabeth. *Time with Children.* 1987, Knopf $15.95 (0-394-55783-2); Macmillan paper $7.95 (0-02-045540-2). A collection of 13 stories examining American family life by the author of the novel *Museum Pieces.* "A standout collection."—PW (REV: BL 10/15/87; PW 9/4/87; TLS 7/8/88)

9930   Tamer, Zakaria. *Tigers on the Tenth Day and Other Stories.* 1985, Salem $12.95 (0-7043-2465-2). A collection of 24 stories and parables by a Syrian writer, including "The Water's Crime" and "The Stale Loaf." (REV: BL 9/1/85; Choice 5/86; NYTBR 9/22/85)

9931   Taylor, Peter. *Collected Stories of Peter Taylor.* 1986, Penguin paper $9.95 (0-14-008361-8). Twenty-nine stories by the author of *A Summons to Memphis* including "Je Suis Perdu," "Dean of Men," and "First Heat." (REV: LJ 11/1/69; NYTBR 10/19/69; Newsweek 10/20/69. AWARDS: NYTBR, 1969)

9932   Taylor, Peter. *In the Miro District and Other Stories.* 1983, Carroll & Graf $7.95 (0-88184-005-X); paper $3.95 (0-88184-347-4). Eight short stories including "The Captain's Son," "The Throughway," and "The Hand of Emmagene." "Reinforces the claims of his many readers that he is, indeed, the finest living writer of the genre."—Choice (REV: Choice 10/77; PW 2/7/77; Sat Rev 5/14/77. AWARDS: ALA, 1977)

9933   Taylor, Peter. *The Old Forest and Other Stories.* 1986, Ballantine paper $4.95 (0-345-32778-0). A collection of 14 stories set in the cities of the American South by the author of *A Summons to Memphis.* (REV: NYTBR 2/17/85; PW 12/21/85; Time 2/4/85. AWARDS: NYTBR, 1985; PW, 1985)

9934   Theroux, Paul. *Consul's File.* 1984, Pocket paper $3.50 (0-671-49825-8). Twenty interrelated short stories set in a Malaysian village tracking the experiences of an American consul during his two-year assignment. (REV: BL 7/1/77; LJ 8/77; New Rep 9/10/77. AWARDS: ALA, 1977)

9935   Thomas, Maria. *African Visas: A Novella and Stories.* 1991, Soho $19.95 (0-939149-54-0). A posthumously published novella and six stories set in Africa by the author of *Antonia Saw the Oryx First.* "Funny, poignant, wise, incisive, sexy and enlightening."—NYTBR (REV: BL 9/15/91; NYTBR 9/22/91; PW 7/5/91)

9936   Thomas, Maria. *Come to Africa and Save Your Marriage and Other Stories.* 1987, Soho Pr. $14.95 (0-939149-06-0); paper $6.95 (0-939149-21-4). Fourteen stories set in East Africa, the author's home for more than a decade. "A collection of enormous emotional impact."—PW (REV: Choice 1/88; PW 7/24/87)

9937   Thompson, Sandra. *Close-ups.* 1984, Univ. of Georgia Pr. $15.95 (0-8203-0683-5). This collection of 12 stories won the Flannery O'Connor Short Fiction Award. (REV: BL 4/15/84; LJ 12/15/83; PW 11/11/83)

9938   Thon, Melanie Rae. *Girls in the Grass.* 1991, Random $18.00 (0-394-57663-2). A collection of 11 short stories by the author of *Meteors in August.* "An unusually rich and varied collection."—BL (REV: BL 6/1/91; LJ 4/15/91; NYTBR 7/14/91)

9939   Thurm, Marian. *Floating.* 1988, Penguin paper $6.95 (0-14-011072-0). A collection of stories set in New England, New York, and Florida by the author of *These Things Happen.* "An enriching addition for most fiction collections."—LJ (REV: LJ 2/1/84; NYTBR 3/4/84; PW 12/2/83)

9940 Thurm, Marian. *These Things Happen.* 1990, Pocket paper $5.95 (0-671-68329-2). This second collection of short fiction by the author of *Walking Distance* contains ten stories. (REV: BL 9/1/88; NYTBR 10/27/88; PW 8/26/88)

9941 Tilghman, Christopher. *In a Father's Place.* 1990, Farrar $18.95 (0-374-17558-6). The debut collection of short fiction by an American writer including "On the Rivershore" and "Hole in the Day." "A very readable and maturely realized collection."—LJ (REV: BL 4/15/90; LJ 5/15/90; NYTBR 5/6/90. AWARDS: ALA, 1990)

9942 Tolstaya, Tatyana. *On the Golden Porch.* 1989, Knopf $17.95 (0-394-57798-1); Random paper $8.95 (0-394-72483-0). Thirteen stories by the great grand-niece of Leo Tolstoy set in contemporary Moscow and St. Petersburg. (REV: LJ 5/1/89; NYRB 6/1/89; NYTBR 4/30/89)

9943 Tournier, Michel. *The Fetishist.* 1985, NAL paper $6.95 (0-452-25755-7). A collection of 14 stories by the French author of *The Ogre* regarding aspects of human sexuality. (REV: BL 1/1/85; NYRB 11/8/84; NYTBR 9/9/84)

9944 Traven, B. *Night Visitor, and Other Stories.* 1987, Schocken paper $5.95 (0-8052-8167-3). Ten short stories examining the Indians of Mexico and their cultural legacy by the author of *The Treasure of the Sierra Madre.* (REV: BL 6/15/66; Choice 7/66; LJ 5/1/66. AWARDS: ALA, 1966)

9945 Trevor, William. *Family Sins and Other Stories.* 1990, Viking $18.95 (0-670-83257-X). A collection of 12 short stories by the Irish writer set mainly in his native land during the 1940s. "In this collection, one of the great short story writers of our age holds his own, turning out gem after gem."—PW (REV: BL 4/1/90; PW 3/9/90; TLS 1/26/90)

9946 Trevor, William. *News from Ireland: And Other Stories.* 1986, Viking $16.95 (0-670-81069-X); Penguin paper $6.95 (0-14-008857-1). Twelve short stories set in Ireland, England, and Italy by the author of *Fools of Fortune.* "Will enhance any general fiction collection."—LJ (REV: BL 4/1/86; NYTBR 6/8/86; PW 3/28/86)

9947 Tsushima, Yuko. *Shooting Gallery and Other Stories.* 1988, Pantheon paper $7.95 (0-394-75743-2). Eight stories concerning the lives of modern Japanese women written by the daughter of novelist Osamu Dazai. (REV: LJ 4/1/88; PW 2/26/88; TLS 4/28/89)

9948 Ueda, Makoto, ed. *Mother of Dreams and Other Short Stories: Portrayals of Women in Modern Japanese Fiction.* 1986, Kodansha $19.95 (0-87011-775-0). A collection of short stories depicting modern Japanese women by such authors as Fumiko Enchi, Kobo Abe, and Yasunari Kawabata. (REV: Choice 1/87; NYTBR 12/28/86; PW 9/26/86)

9949 Updike, David. *Out on the Marsh.* 1988, Godine $16.95 (0-87923-728-7); NAL paper $7.95 (0-452-26219-4). A collection of 15 stories about adolescence by the son of writer John Updike. (REV: BL 8/1/88; PW 4/22/88; TLS 7/21/89)

9950 Updike, John. *Museums and Women and Other Stories.* 1972, Knopf $15.00 (0-394-48173-9); Random paper $8.95 (0-394-74762-3). A collection of 29 stories including five of the author's popular Maples stories. (REV: LJ 8/72; PW 8/28/72; Time 10/16/72)

9951 Updike, John. *Music School and Other Stories.* 1966, Knopf $22.95 (0-394-43727-6); Random paper $6.95 (0-394-74510-8). A collection of 20 stories most of which appeared originally in the *New Yorker.* (REV: BL 10/15/66; LJ 9/15/66; Time 9/23/66)

9952 Updike, John. *Problems, and Other Stories.* 1979, Knopf $19.95 (0-394-50705-3); Fawcett paper $4.50 (0-449-21103-7). A collection of stories from the *New Yorker* and other magazines by the author of *Rabbit Redux.* (REV: CSM 11/7/79; NYRB 11/8/79; Newsweek 10/29/79. AWARDS: ALA, 1979)

9953 Updike, John. *Too Far to Go: The Maples Stories.* 1982, Fawcett paper $4.95 (0-449-20016-7). Seventeen stories that trace the decline of a marriage over a period of two decades. (REV: BL 3/1/79; LJ 3/1/79; NYTBR 4/8/79. AWARDS: NYTBR, 1979)

9954 Updike, John. *Trust Me.* 1987, Knopf $17.95 (0-394-55833-2); Fawcett paper $5.95 (0-449-21498-2). A collection of 22 short stories by the author of *The Coup.* "Updike at his best."—BL (REV: BL 3/1/87; NYTBR 4/26/87; Time 5/4/87)

9955 Vargas Llosa, Mario. *Cubs and Other Stories.* 1989, Farrar $6.95 (0-374-52194-8). A collection containing a novella and six short stories written during the 1950s by the Peruvian author of *The Time of the Hero.* (REV: BL 10/1/79; LJ 10/1/79; PW 7/2/79)

9956 Vaughn, Stephanie. *Sweet Talk.* 1990, Random $16.95 (0-394-57605-5). This first collection of the author's short fiction contains ten stories. "Superb . . . perfectly modulated prose."—BL (REV: BL 1/1/90; NYTBR 2/4/90)

9957 Velie, Alan R., ed. *Lightning Within: An Anthology of Contemporary American Indian Fiction.* 1991, Univ. of Nebraska Pr. $19.95 (0-8032-4659-5). An anthology of nine stories by contemporary Native-American writers including selections by M. Scott Momaday, James Welch, Michael Dorris, and Louise Erdrich. (REV: BL 5/15/91; LJ 4/15/91; PW 3/15/91)

9958 Verlaine, M. J. *A Bad Man Is Easy to Find.* 1989, St. Martin's $15.95 (0-312-02920-9). A collection of intertwined stories on life in New York including "New York Women" and "The Nude Scene." (REV: BL 8/89; LJ 5/15/89; PW 6/9/89)

9959 Vogan, Sara. *Scenes from the Homefront.* 1987, Univ. of Illinois Pr. $11.95 (0-252-01430-8); Bantam paper $7.95 (0-553-34751-9). Eleven stories previously published in literary magazines by the author of *In Shelly's Leg*. "Displays a stunning range of voice."—PW (REV: BL 7/87; PW 8/14/87)

9960 Voinovich, Vladimir. *In Plain Russian*. 1979, Farrar $11.95 (0-374-17580-2). Nine short stories by the Russian writer from the 1960s and 1970s portraying the society and history of his native country. (REV: BL 7/15/79; LJ 7/79; NYTBR 10/7/79)

9961 Volk, Patricia. *All It Takes*. 1990, Macmillan $17.95 (0-689-12061-3); Random paper $8.95 (0-679-73044-3). Fifteen stories examining aspects of love by the author of *White Light* including "The Miami Dolphins" and "Mystery Salad." (REV: BL 12/15/89; LJ 12/89; PW 11/10/89)

9962 Vollmann, William T. *Rainbow Stories*. 1989, Macmillan $19.95 (0-689-11961-5). A collection of 13 intertwined stories set in San Francisco's Haight-Ashbury district. (REV: BL 6/15/89; LJ 6/15/89)

9963 Vonnegut, Kurt, Jr. *Welcome to the Monkey House*. 1970, Dell paper $4.95 (0-440-19478-4). A collection of short pieces written during the 1960s by the author of *Mother Night*. (REV: CSM 12/5/68; PW 6/3/68; Time 8/30/68)

9964 Walker, Alice. *You Can't Keep a Good Woman Down*. 1982, Harcourt $5.95 (0-15-699778-9). A collection of 13 stories by the author of *The Color Purple*, including "Porn," "Coming Apart," and "The Abortion." (REV: BL 4/1/81; LJ 4/15/81; PW 3/20/81)

9965 Wallace, David Foster. *Girl with Curious Hair*. 1989, Norton $17.95 (0-393-02757-0). A collection of short fiction including stories about LBJ, punk rock, a McDonald's reunion, and David Letterman. "A challenging high-voltage collection."—BL (REV: BL 8/89; LJ 8/89; NYTBR 11/5/89)

9966 Walser, Robert. *Masquerade: And Other Stories*. 1982, Farrar $16.00 (0-374-25901-1). A collection of 64 short stories by the German-Swiss writer from the 1910s and 1920s. (REV: BL 5/1/90; LJ 6/15/90; PW 3/23/90. AWARDS: PW, 1990)

9967 Walser, Robert. *Selected Stories*. 1982, Farrar $16.00 (0-374-25901-1); paper $8.95 (0-374-52054-2). Collected pieces composed by a German-Swiss writer between 1907 and 1929 prior to his institutionalization in a sanitarium. (REV: BL 8/82; LJ 9/1/82; NYTBR 10/24/82)

9968 Weaver, Will. *A Gravestone Made of Wheat and Other Stories*. 1989, Simon & Schuster $16.95 (0-671-67097-2); Graywolf paper $8.95 (1-55597-125-3). Twelve stories about midwesterners by the author of *Red Earth, White Earth*. (REV: LJ 2/15/89; NYTBR 3/12/89; PW 11/25/89)

9969 Weldon, Fay. *Polaris and Other Stories*. 1989, Penguin paper $6.95 (0-14-009747-3). A collection of 12 stories by the English author of *Darcy's Utopia*. (REV: BL 6/1/89; LJ 5/15/89; NYTBR 6/4/89)

9970 Welty, Eudora. *Collected Stories of Eudora Welty*. 1980, Harcourt $29.95 (0-15-118994-3); paper $11.95 (0-15-618921-6). A collection of Welty's four previously published short story volumes with two new stories and an introduction by the author. (REV: BL 9/15/80; NYTBR 11/2/80; Time 11/3/80. AWARDS: ALA, 1980; BL, the 1980s; NYTBR, 1980; Time, 1980)

9971 West, Jessamyn. *Collected Stories of Jessamyn West*. 1986, Harcourt $17.95 (0-15-119010-0); paper $10.95 (0-15-618979-8). Thirty-six short stories by the Indian-born author of *Massacre at Fall Creek*. (REV: BL 11/15/86; LJ 12/86; PW 9/26/86)

9972 Wideman, John Edgar. *Fever*. 1989, Henry Holt $16.95 (0-8050-1184-6); Penguin paper $7.95 (0-14-014347-5). A collection of 12 short stories by the author of *Brothers and Keepers* and *Philadelphia Fire*. "An estimable addition to Wideman's oeuvre."—BL (REV: BL 11/1/89; LJ 11/1/89; NYTBR 12/10/89)

9973 Wiggins, Marianne. *Bet They'll Miss Us When We're Gone*. 1991, HarperCollins $19.95 (0-06-016139-6). A collection of 13 stories by the author of *John Dollar*. (REV: LJ 6/1/91; PW 5/3/91)

9974 Wiggins, Marianne. *Herself in Love: And Other Stories*. 1987, Viking $16.95 (0-670-81552-7); Penguin paper $6.95 (0-14-011227-8). This first collection of short fiction by the author contains 13 stories, including "Gandy Dancing" and "Riding Up Front with Carl and Marl." (REV: CSM 8/5/87; LJ 7/87; NYTBR 10/18/87)

9975 Wilbur, Ellen. *Wind and Birds and Human Voices and Other Stories*. 1984, S. Wright $15.00 (0-913773-11-5). This debut collection of ten short stories by an American writer contains the title story, which concerns the life of a gifted musical genius trapped for three decades in a mental hospital. (REV: LJ 5/15/84; NYTBR 10/14/84)

9976 Williams, Joy. *Escapes*. 1990, Atlantic Monthly $18.95 (0-87113-332-6). This second collection of short fiction by the Florida writer includes "Rot," "The Little Winter," and "Lu-Lu." (REV: BL 12/1/89; NYTBR 1/21/90; PW 11/3/89)

9977 Williams, Joy. *Taking Care*. 1985, Random paper $5.95 (0-394-72912-9). A collection of short fiction by the Florida-based author of the novel *State of Grace*. (REV: BL 4/1/82; NYTBR 2/14/82)

9978 Williams, Tennessee. *Collected Stories*. 1985, New Directions $19.95 (0-8112-0952-0); Ballantine paper $5.95 (0-345-33587-2). Collected short stories by the American playwright with a foreword by Gore Vidal. (REV: Choice 3/86; LJ 10/15/85; PW 9/6/85. AWARDS: PW, 1985)

9979 Wilson, Leigh Ann. *Wind*. 1989, Morrow $17.95 (0-688-08111-8); NAL paper $8.95 (0-452-26383-2). A collection of six short stories depicting the lives of alienated teenagers in upstate New York. (REV: BL 2/1/89; LJ 2/1/89; PW 11/18/88)

9980 Wilson, Robley, Jr. *Terrible Kisses*. 1989, Simon & Schuster $17.95 (0-671-67919-8). Fourteen short stories by an American author set in the United States and Europe, including "Praises" and "Payment in Kind." (REV: CSM 7/18/89; LJ 6/15/89; TLS 2/9/90. AWARDS: ALA, 1989)

9981 Wilson, William S. *Why I Don't Write Like Franz Kafka.* 1984, Ecco Pr. paper $7.50 (0-88001-070-3). A collection of short stories by an American writer. "Extraordinary . . . a demanding, exhilarating work."—NYTBR (REV: BL 6/15/78; NYTBR 1/1/78)

9982 Woiwode, Larry. *Neumiller Stories.* 1989, Farrar $17.95 (0-374-22061-1). A collection of 13 stories by the North Dakota writer from the 1960s and 1970s and including characters from the novel *Beyond the Bedroom Wall.* (REV: NYTBR 12/17/89; PW 11/10/89)

9983 Wolff, Tobias. *Back in the World.* 1985, Houghton $15.95 (0-395-35416-1); Bantam paper $7.95 (0-553-34325-4). This second collection of short fiction by the author contains ten stories, including "Desert Breakdown, 1968" and "The Missing Person." (REV: LJ 10/15/85; NYTBR 10/20/85; PW 8/30/85)

9984 Wolff, Tobias. *Barracks Thief and Selected Stories.* 1984, Ecco Pr. $12.50 (0-88001-035-5); Bantam paper $7.95 (0-553-34675-X). The PEN/Faulkner Award–winning title novella is paired with six stories selected from Wolff's collection *In the Garden of the North American Martyrs.* (REV: NYTBR 6/2/85; Newsweek 4/7/86)

9985 Wolff, Tobias. *In the Garden of the North American Martyrs: A Collection of Short Stories.* 1990, Ecco Pr. $14.95 (0-912946-82-2); paper $8.95 (0-88001-245-5). A debut collection of short stories by an upstate New York writer, including "An Episode in the Life of Professor Brooke" and "Face to Face." (REV: Choice 1/82; LJ 10/1/81; PW 8/28/81)

9986 Woolf, Virginia. *Complete Shorter Fiction of Virginia Woolf.* Ed. by Susan Dick. 1986, Harcourt paper $8.95 (0-15-621250-1). A collection of 45 published and previously unpublished short stories by the English writer. (REV: LJ 2/1/86; NYTBR 1/19/86; TLS 12/27/85)

9987 Wyndham, Francis. *Mrs. Henderson.* 1986, Moyer Bell $14.95 (0-918825-49-0); paper $6.95 (0-918825-60-1). A novella and four stories portraying people faced with unusual situations by the author of *Out of War.* "This quirky collection makes me marvel and laugh out loud."—PW (REV: BL 11/15/86; PW 10/17/86)

9988 Yarbrough, Steve. *Family Men.* 1990, Louisiana State Univ. Pr. $18.95 (0-8071-1619-X). Eleven short stories concerning small-town family life in Mississippi. "Regional in setting, but universal in appeal."—LJ (REV: LJ 9/15/90; PW 8/3/90)

9989 Yates, Richard. *Liars in Love.* 1981, Dell paper $9.95 (0-318-36002-0). Seven stories of unrequited love written by the author of *The Easter Parade.* "These stories are so exquisite, so stunningly crafted . . . they take your breath away." —PW (REV: Atl 11/81; LJ 11/15/81; PW 9/11/81)

9990 Yehoshua, A. B. *Continuing Silence of a Poet: The Collected Stories of A. B. Yehoshua.* 1991, Penguin paper $9.95 (0-14-014844-2). A collection of short stories by the Israeli author of *Five Seasons.* (REV: NYTBR 5/26/91; TLS 8/26/88)

9991 Yourcenar, Marguerite. *Oriental Tales.* 1985, Farrar $12.95 (0-374-22728-4); paper $7.95 (0-374-51997-8). The first English translation of ten short stories originally published in France in 1938. (REV: LJ 9/15/85; NYTBR 9/22/85; TLS 11/8/85)

9992 Zalygin, Sergei, ed. *New Soviet Fiction: Sixteen Short Stories.* 1989, Abbeville $24.95 (0-89659-881-0). A collection of 16 stories from Soviet writers written during the 1980s. "Splendid . . . essential for all fiction collections."—LJ (REV: LJ 6/15/89; New Rep 10/2/89)

9993 Zoline, Pamela. *Heat Death of the Universe and Other Stories.* 1988, McPherson $20.00 (0-914232-89-4); paper $10.00 (0-914232-88-6). A collection of five stories from a Colorado writer spanning over 20 years. (REV: BL 3/15/88; Choice 12/88; PW 3/11/88)

SPORTS STORIES

9994 Beckham, Barry. *Runner Mack.* **1984, Howard Univ. Pr. paper $6.95 (0-88258-116-3).** An account of a prospective baseball player waiting for a chance to play professional ball prior to his drafting by the Army. (REV: BL 9/15/72; LJ 8/72; PW 7/17/72)

9995 Charyn, Jerome. *Seventh Babe.* **1984, Avon paper $2.95 (0-380-51540-7).** A baseball tale chronicling the exploits of a renegade third baseman with the Red Sox and the Negro Leagues during the 1920s. (REV: LJ 5/15/79; NYTBR 5/6/79; PW 3/26/79)

9996 Coover, Robert. *Universal Baseball Association Inc., J. Henry Waugh, Prop.* **1971, NAL paper $8.95 (0-452-26030-2).** The story of a fantasy dice baseball league and its players created in the mind of an accountant. "A fine baseball novel, the best I can remember."—NYTBR (REV: LJ 6/15/68; NYTBR 7/7/68; PW 4/15/68)

9997 Crews, Harry. *Knockout Artist.* **1989, Harper & Row paper $7.95 (0-06-091574-9).** Story about a former boxer in New Orleans who has the ability to knock himself out and his life with a group of entertainers with unusual talents. (REV: BL 4/1/88; LJ 4/15/88; PW 2/26/88)

9998 DeLillo, Don. *End Zone.* **1986, Penguin paper $8.95 (0-14-008568-8).** A study of West Texas college football depicted by the author of *Libra* and *White Noise.* (REV: BL 7/1/72; NYTBR 4/9/72; New Yorker 5/6/72)

9999 Exley, Frederick. *A Fan's Notes: A Fictional Memoir.* **1988, Random paper $7.95 (0-679-72076-6).** A chronicle of the life of the writer son of a noted athlete and his football obsession that centers on the career of New York Giants running back Frank Gifford. (REV: LJ 9/15/68; NYTBR 10/6/68; Time 10/25/68)

10000 Fante, John. *1933 Was a Bad Year.* **1985, Black Sparrow $20.00 (0-87685-656-3); paper $8.50 (0-87685-655-5).** A Colorado bricklayer seeks escape from his father's profession and dreams of becoming a professional baseball player. (REV: BL 2/1/86; New Yorker 6/2/86; TLS 3/20/87)

10001 Gaines, Charles. *Stay Hungry.* **1985, Ballantine paper $3.50 (0-345-31966-4).** The story of the rise and fall of a Birmingham, Alabama, bodybuilder.

"A subtle and strange book . . . written with freshness and style: an unusual achievement."—TLS (REV: LJ 10/15/72; PW 6/12/72; TLS 6/15/73. AWARDS: ALA, 1972)

10002 Gardner, Leonard. *Fat City.* **1986, Random paper $6.95 (0-394-74316-4).** A portrait of the lives of two California boxers trying to make a living in the lower level of the sport. (REV: LJ 9/1/69; NYTBR 8/31/69; PW 8/31/70)

10003 Gent, Peter. *North Dallas after Forty.* **1989, Random $19.95 (0-394-55426-4).** This sequel to *North Dallas Forty* chronicles the post-retirement careers of football players introduced in that novel. (REV: BL 10/15/89; LJ 12/89)

10004 Gent, Peter. *North Dallas Forty.* **1984, Ballantine paper $4.95 (0-345-31670-3).** A story by a former professional football player regarding a fictional lineman's life with the Dallas Cowboys. (REV: NYTBR 10/28/73; Newsweek 9/24/73; PW 7/2/73)

10005 Gethers, Peter. *Getting Blue.* **1987, Delacorte $16.95 (0-385-29523-5); Dell paper $8.95 (0-440-50185-7).** Story of a professional baseball player who makes a key play in the World Series following a lackluster career in the majors. (REV: LJ 4/1/87; NYTBR 4/26/87; PW 1/23/87)

10006 Gorman, Edward. *Blood Game.* **1989, Evans $14.95 (0-87131-596-3).** A nineteenth-century tale of a former bounty hunter who becomes involved with an unsavory boxing promoter. (REV: BL 11/1/89; LJ 11/1/89)

10007 Hallberg, William. *Rub of the Green.* **1988, Doubleday $17.95 (0-385-24568-8); Bantam paper $8.95 (0-553-34734-9).** A debut novel chronicling the life of a golfer from his youth to a prison term. "A story to be enjoyed by nongolfers and savored by those who love the game."—NYTBR (REV: BL 6/15/88; LJ 7/88; NYTBR 11/13/88)

10008 Harris, Mark. *It Seemed Like Forever.* **1989, Univ. of Nebraska Pr. paper $9.50 (0-8032-7244-8).** A story by the author of *Bang the Drum Slowly* chronicling the events leading up to the release of pitcher Henry Wiggen at age 39 from professional baseball. (REV: LJ 10/1/79; NYTBR 9/30/79)

10009 **Hough, John, Jr.** *Conduct of the Game.* **1986, Harcourt $14.95 (0-15-121625-8); Warner paper $3.95 (0-446-34555-5).** A chronicle of an umpire's rise from the minor leagues to the majors in the 1950s and 1960s. (REV: CSM 5/8/86; LJ 7/86; PW 3/14/86)

10010 **Jenkins, Dan.** *Semi-Tough.* **1972, Macmillan $14.95 (0-689-10518-5); NAL paper $3.95 (0-451-13793-0).** A fictional account of a New York Giants football team preparing to face the New York Jets in the Super Bowl. (REV: LJ 10/15/72; NYTBR 9/17/72; PW 7/3/72)

10011 **Jenkins, Dan.** *You Gotta Play Hurt.* **1991, Simon & Schuster $22.95 (0-671-68332-2).** A portrait of the life of a Texas sports columnist by the author of *Semi-Tough.* (REV: LJ 9/15/91; PW 8/9/91)

10012 **Kinsella, W. P.** *Further Adventures of Slugger McBatt.* **1988, Houghton $16.95 (0-395-47592-9).** A collection of baseball stories by the author of *Shoeless Joe* including the tales "K-Mart" and "Reports Concerning the Death of the Seattle Albatross Are Somewhat Exaggerated." (REV: BL 5/15/88; LJ 6/1/88; PW 4/8/88)

10013 **Kinsella, W. P.** *Shoeless Joe.* **1987, Ballantine paper $4.95 (0-345-34256-9).** This author's first novel was the basis of the popular motion picture *Field of Dreams* and concerns an Iowa man's efforts to build a baseball field on his farm so Joe Jackson and members of the infamous 1919 Black Sox can play the game again. "The most imaginative and original baseball novel since *The Natural.*"—PW (REV: BL 3/15/82; Newsweek 8/23/82; PW 2/26/82)

10014 **Plimpton, George.** *Curious Case of Sidd Finch.* **1987, Macmillan $14.95 (0-02-597650-8); Berkley paper $3.95 (1-55773-064-4).** A tale of a Buddhist monk who develops the world's fastest baseball pitch. "Written with flair, high spirits and consummate craft."—BL (REV: BL 5/15/87; NYTBR 7/5/87; Time 6/8/87)

10015 **Quarrington, Paul.** *King Leary.* **1988, Doubleday $16.95 (0-385-25138-6).** A Canadian ice hockey legend relives the key moments of his life in this novel by a Toronto-based writer. (REV: NYTBR 5/1/88; PW 2/5/88)

10016 **Roth, Philip.** *Great American Novel.* **1985, Penguin paper $5.95 (0-14-007678-6).** A portrait of a fictional baseball team during World War II whose exploits were erased from history when the league they played in was dissolved following scandal. (REV: BL 9/1/73; LJ 5/1/73; TLS 9/21/73)

10017 **Sayles, John.** *Pride of the Bimbos.* **1987, Macmillan paper $8.95 (0-684-18872-4).** A chronicle of the exploits of a five-man carnival baseball team based in Brooklyn playing on a circuit in Florida and Georgia. (REV: BL 9/15/75; LJ 7/75; Time 7/7/75)

10018 **Stein, Harry.** *Hoopla.* **1986, St. Martin's paper $7.95 (0-312-38983-3).** A fictional re-creation of the 1919 Black Sox scandal as told by a Chicago infielder. "Earns a place among the splendid novels about sports."—NYTBR (REV: BL 9/15/83; CSM 4/5/84; NYTBR 1/15/84)

SPY STORIES

10019 Aaron, David. *Agent of Influence.* **1989, Putnam $19.95 (0-399-13378-X); Avon paper $4.95 (0-380-71005-6).** An attorney representing a French client attempting to purchase an American media conglomerate discovers that the man is a KGB agent. (REV: NYTBR 5/28/89; PW 10/28/88; Time 2/27/89)

10020 Aaron, David. *State Scarlet.* **1988, Pocket paper $4.50 (0-671-65090-4).** American intelligence agents attempt to thwart terrorists who threaten the United States with nuclear weapons unless it pulls its troops out of Europe. "A political thriller on a par with the best of the genre."—LJ (REV: BL 3/1/87; LJ 3/15/87; PW 2/13/87)

10021 Aleshovsky, Yuz. *The Hand: Or, the Confession of an Executioner.* **1990, Farrar $22.95 (0-374-16770-2).** A KGB agent searches for those who murdered his family, an event he witnessed as a child. (REV: BL 2/15/90; LJ 4/1/90; PW 2/2/90)

10022 Allen, Thomas B., and Norman Polmar. *Ship of Gold.* **1988, St. Martin's paper $3.95 (0-312-91123-8).** The CIA investigates the murder of an American submarine officer who accidentally sank a Japanese ship that had been granted safe passage during World War II. (REV: LJ 4/1/87; NYTBR 6/7/87; PW 2/13/87)

10023 Ambler, Eric. *Care of Time.* **1981, Farrar $11.95 (0-374-11897-3); Berkley paper $2.95 (0-425-08894-4).** A ghostwriter hired to write a book on terrorism becomes a CIA dupe in a plot to gain access to a psychopathic Arab leader. (REV: BL 7/1/81; Newsweek 8/31/81; TLS 6/5/81)

10024 Ambler, Eric. *Intercom Conspiracy.* **1986, Farrar paper $3.95 (0-324-51968-4).** Two intelligence agents from smaller NATO countries plot to blackmail Soviets and Americans by leaking state secrets. (REV: CSM 10/2/69; LJ 9/1/69)

10025 Anthony, Evelyn. *Albatross.* **1983, Putnam $14.95 (0-399-12773-9).** The story of a woman's search to discover the identity of a mole in British intelligence who helped assassinate her husband. (REV: BL 3/15/83; CSM 10/7/83; LJ 4/15/83)

10026 Anthony, Evelyn. *Company of Saints.* **1984, Putnam $15.95 (0-399-12895-6); Jove paper $3.95 (0-515-08360-7).** The first female head of British intelligence seeks to foil a plot by a group of Soviet terrorists. (REV: BL 3/1/84; LJ 6/15/84; PW 6/1/84)

10027 Archer, Jeffrey. *A Matter of Honor.* **1987, Pocket paper $4.95 (0-671-64159-X).** A former British officer receives letters from his father regarding the location of a Nazi treasure that both the CIA and KGB want. (REV: BL 6/15/86; LJ 8/86; NYTBR 7/27/86)

10028 Bagley, Desmond. *Enemy.* **1979, Fawcett paper $1.95 (0-449-23906-3).** A spy's search for the criminal who threw acid in his girlfriend's face leads him to London and Stockholm. "Solid, well-constructed, supremely professional."—TLS (REV: BL 4/15/78; PW 1/9/78; TLS 10/21/77)

10029 Bagley, Michael. *Plutonium Factor.* **1987, Schocken $13.95 (0-8052-8227-0).** A British intelligence agent searches for the man who hijacked a planeload of plutonium in order to build a nuclear weapon for blackmail purposes. (REV: LJ 9/15/85; PW 7/19/85)

10030 Benchley, Peter. *Q Clearance.* **1987, Berkley paper $4.50 (0-441-69400-4).** A former journalist turned presidential political advisor is duped by a Soviet spy network. (REV: BL 5/15/86; LJ 7/86; NYTBR 7/29/86)

10031 Boyer, Rick. *Moscow Metal.* **1987, Houghton $15.95 (0-395-42737-1); Ivy Books paper $3.50 (0-8041-0292-9).** A series of poisoning murders and abductions potentially masterminded by KGB agents in Massachusetts bring FBI and CIA investigators to a New England town. (REV: BL 6/15/87; LJ 6/1/87)

10032 Brinkley, Joel. *Circus Master's Mission.* **1989, Random $18.95 (0-394-57570-9).** A Pulitzer Prize–winning journalist's novel set in the mid-1980s about a CIA plot to embroil the United States in an all-out war to topple Nicaragua's Sandinista regime. (REV: LJ 7/89; NYTBR 7/2/89; PW 6/9/89)

10033 Brown, Dale. *Day of the Cheetah.* **1989, Donald I. Fine $18.95 (1-55611-121-5); Berkley paper $5.50 (0-425-12043-0).** The prototype of an advanced

American fighter is stolen by the Soviet KGB in this story set in the near future. (REV: BL 5/15/89; LJ 6/15/89)

10034 Buckley, William F., Jr. *High Jinx.* **1987, Dell paper $4.95 (0-440-13957-0).** Covert operations by Western intelligence to overthrow a Soviet-backed Albanian regime fail due to treasonous leaks by British and American sources. (REV: BL 2/15/86; LJ 3/15/86; Natl Rev 5/23/86)

10035 Buckley, William F., Jr. *Mongoose R.I.P.: A Blackford Oakes Novel.* **1989, Dell paper $4.50 (0-440-20231-0).** A fictional account of the attempted assassination of Castro and the counterplot to assassinate President Kennedy. (REV: CSM 1/8/88; Natl Rev 1/22/88; NYTBR 1/24/88)

10036 Buckley, William F., Jr. *See You Later Alligator.* **1986, Dell paper $3.95 (0-440-17682-4).** CIA agent Blackford Oakes visits Havana during the 1962 Cuban missile crisis for a meeting with Fidel Castro and Che Guevara. (REV: BL 2/15/85; Natl Rev 3/8/85; PW 1/18/85)

10037 Buckley, William F., Jr. *Stained Glass.* **1982, Avon paper $3.95 (0-380-54791-0).** In this novel set during the 1950s, intelligence agent Blackie Oakes attempts to quash a plan to reunify East and West Germany. (REV: Choice 1/79; NYTBR 4/1/79; PW 2/12/79. AWARDS: NBA, 1980)

10038 Buckley, William F., Jr. *Story of Henri Tod.* **1989, Dell paper $4.50 (0-440-18327-8).** CIA agent Blackford Oakes tries to determine Soviet intentions following the 1961 construction of the Berlin Wall. "Flawless entertainment."—LJ (REV: CSM 2/24/84; LJ 3/1/84; PW 11/25/83)

10039 Burgess, Anthony. *Tremor of Intent.* **1977, Norton paper $6.95 (0-393-00416-3).** The efforts of an English spy to recapture a scientist who defected to the U.S.S.R. (REV: LJ 11/1/66; PW 9/26/66; Time 10/14/66. AWARDS: NYTBR, 1966)

10040 Carroll, James. *Firebird.* **1989, Dutton $18.95 (0-525-24726-2); NAL paper $5.95 (0-451-16289-7).** An FBI agent seeks the mole responsible for leaking American atomic secrets during the late 1940s. (REV: BL 12/15/88; CSM 3/24/89; PW 12/16/88)

10041 Clancy, Tom. *Cardinal of the Kremlin.* **1988, Putnam $19.95 (0-399-13345-3); Berkley paper $5.95 (0-425-11684-0).** A CIA advisor discovers secret Soviet space war advances during arms control talks meant to halt their progress. (REV: CSM 7/5/88; LJ 7/88; Time 7/25/88)

10042 Clancy, Tom. *Clear and Present Danger.* **1989, Putnam $21.95 (0-399-13440-9); Berkley paper $5.95 (0-425-12212-3).** The CIA plots the rescue of U.S. military forces involved in covert operations against a Colombian drug cartel. (REV: Newsweek 8/21/89; PW 7/14/89; Time 8/21/89)

10043 Clancy, Tom. *Sum of All Fears.* **1991, Putnam $24.95 (0-399-13615-0).** A fictional analysis of the threat of nuclear proliferation and terrorism in the Middle East penned by the best-selling author of

Red Storm Rising. (REV: BL 6/15/91; NYTBR 7/28/91; PW 6/14/91)

10044 Cohen, Arthur A. *A Hero in His Time.* **1987, Univ. of Chicago Pr. paper $9.95 (0-226-11252-7).** A minor Russian poet attending an international conference in New York is called upon to deliver a ciphered message in poem to a KGB agent. (REV: LJ 2/15/76; NYTBR 1/25/76; Time 1/5/76)

10045 Collins, Larry. *Fall from Grace.* **1990, NAL paper $5.95 (0-451-16572-1).** A fictionalized study of a massive English disinformation campaign conducted against Nazi intelligence forces. (REV: BL 8/85; PW 5/10/85; Time 7/1/85)

10046 Coltrane, James. *Talon: A Novel of Suspense.* **1978, Macmillan $8.95 (0-672-52391-4).** A CIA interpreter of satellite photographs suspects a plot after observing a suspicious cloud cover over Tibet. (REV: LJ 2/1/78; NYTBR 2/26/78; New Yorker 3/27/78)

10047 Cook, Bob. *Paper Chase.* **1990, St. Martin's $14.95 (0-312-04400-3).** Four former British intelligence agents find themselves pursued by the CIA following their writing of fictitious memoirs. (REV: LJ 4/15/90; NYTBR 4/15/90; PW 3/9/90)

10048 Cornford, Philip. *Catalyst.* **1991, Bantam $19.50 (0-553-07122-X).** A KGB agent works in tandem with a CIA operative to track down assassins responsible for the deaths of American and Soviet cold war figures. (REV: BL 7/91; NYTBR 8/18/91; PW 6/14/91)

10049 Crisp, N. J. *Ninth Circle.* **1987, Viking $16.95 (0-670-81321-4); Windsor paper $3.95 (1-55817-305-6).** A woman searches for clues concerning her husband's death while working for the CIA in West Germany. (REV: BL 8/88; LJ 7/88; PW 9/24/88)

10050 Crosby, John. *Men in Arms.* **1983, Scarborough House $14.95 (0-8128-2885-2); paper $3.50 (0-8128-8086-2).** A former CIA agent turned medieval history professor attempts to rescue his daughter from her involvement in an arms trafficking scheme. (REV: LJ 5/1/83; New Yorker 7/25/83; PW 3/25/83)

10051 Cullen, Robert. *Soviet Sources.* **1990, Atlantic Monthly $19.95 (0-87113-358-X).** An American journalist becomes involved in a Soviet KGB plot to fabricate a story of the Russian leader's illness. (REV: LJ 5/1/90; PW 4/13/90; Time 7/2/90)

10052 Deighton, Len. *Berlin Game.* **1989, Ballantine paper $4.95 (0-345-01071-X).** A British intelligence agent tries to uncover the identity of a Soviet double agent and rescue a special agent trapped in East Germany. (REV: LJ 12/1/83; NYTBR 1/8/84; PW 11/4/83)

10053 Deighton, Len. *London Match.* **1985, Knopf $17.95 (0-394-54937-6); Ballantine paper $4.95 (0-345-01073-6).** The concluding volume of the author's Game/Set/Match trilogy, concerning the efforts of British intelligence agent Samson to clear his name following his wife's defection to the Soviet Union. (REV: CSM 4/9/86; LJ 12/85; Time 1/13/86)

10054 Deighton, Len. *Mexico Set.* 1985, Knopf $16.95 (0-394-53525-1); Ballantine paper $4.95 (0-345-01072-8). This second volume of the author's Game/Set/Match trilogy finds British intelligence agent Samson and his boss trailing a KGB agent in Mexico City. (Rev: CSM 3/1/85; LJ 1/85; PW 12/14/84)

10055 Deighton, Len. *Spy Line.* 1989, Knopf $18.95 (0-394-55179-6). This thrilling sequel to *Spy Hook* begins with British intelligence agent Samson a fugitive in Berlin because he is accused of spying for the Soviets. (Rev: BL 10/1/89; NYTBR 12/17/89; PW 10/6/89)

10056 Deighton, Len. *Spy Story.* 1985, Ballantine paper $4.95 (0-345-31569-3). A British intelligence agent becomes involved in London war games involving United States and British commanders. (Rev: CSM 9/11/74; LJ 9/1/74; PW 8/5/74)

10057 Deighton, Len. *XPD.* 1983, Ballantine paper $4.95 (0-345-31337-2). Intelligence agents attempt to keep secret the transcripts of a 1940 meeting in Belgium between Hitler and Churchill. (Rev: LJ 4/1/81; PW 3/13/81; Time 4/27/81)

10058 De Mille, Nelson. *Charm School.* 1989, Warner paper $4.95 (0-446-35320-5). An investigation of the fate of an American soldier missing in action in Vietnam who was sighted by an American tourist in the Soviet Union leads to a CIA mission to rescue a group of Americans trapped in an espionage training camp. (Rev: BL 3/15/88; LJ 5/1/88; PW 3/18/88)

10059 Easterman, Daniel. *Brotherhood of the Tomb.* 1990, Doubleday $19.95 (0-385-24178-X). A CIA agent is commissioned to protect the pope following a discovery in Israel that could rock the foundations of the Church. (Rev: BL 7/90; NYTBR 8/19/90; PW 6/22/90)

10060 Follett, Ken. *Eye of the Needle.* 1978, Morrow $17.95 (0-87795-186-1); NAL paper $4.95 (0-451-16348-6). A German spy in World War II seeks to escape pursuit of British intelligence agents in order to reveal Allied plans for D-Day. (Rev: BL 7/15/78; New Yorker 8/21/78; PW 5/28/78. Awards: Poe, 1978)

10061 Follett, Ken. *Key to Rebecca.* 1980, Morrow $12.95 (0-688-13734-8); NAL paper $4.95 (0-451-15510-6). English intelligence attempts to find the identity of a Nazi spy in World War II Cairo. (Rev: BL 9/1/80; LJ 9/15/80; Time 9/29/80)

10062 Follett, Ken. *Lie Down with Lions.* 1986, Morrow $18.95 (0-688-05891-4); NAL paper $4.95 (0-451-14642-5). A French woman and a CIA agent attempt to avoid capture by the KGB while escaping from Afghanistan. (Rev: BL 12/15/85; LJ 2/1/86; NYTBR 1/26/86)

10063 Follett, Ken. *Triple.* 1979, Morrow $18.95 (0-87795-223-X); NAL paper $5.95 (0-451-16354-0). Israelis hijack a ship filled with uranium in order to construct nuclear weapons in a tale involving the intelligence forces of three nations. (Rev: BL 2/15/80; Time 11/5/79)

10064 Forbes, Bryan. *Endless Game.* 1987, NAL paper $4.95 (0-451-40205-7). The trail of clues to the murder of a former British intelligence agent in a nursing home leads an investigating spy to Moscow. (Rev: BL 11/15/85; CSM 4/9/86; PW 11/8/85)

10065 Forsyth, Frederick. *Fourth Protocol.* 1984, Viking $17.95 (0-670-32637-2); Bantam paper $5.95 (0-553-25113-9). Russian spies attempt to fix English elections and break up the NATO alliance. (Rev: BL 7/84; CSM 9/7/84; PW 6/22/84)

10066 Francis, Clare. *Wolf Winter.* 1988, Morrow $19.95 (0-688-06376-4); Avon paper $4.95 (0-380-70689-X). An investigation into the deaths of two NATO spies on the Soviet-Norwegian border in a story set during the early 1960s. "Immensely satisfying."—NYTBR (Rev: LJ 12/87; NYTBR 3/20/88; PW 11/13/87)

10067 Freemantle, Brian. *Betrayals.* 1989, Tor $18.95 (0-312-93138-7). An American woman discovers her boyfriend is a CIA spy following his abduction by Lebanese terrorists. (Rev: BL 1/15/89; PW 12/16/88)

10068 Freemantle, Brian. *Blind Run.* 1986, Bantam paper $3.95 (0-553-26503-2). A British intelligence agent seeks to protect a KGB mole who is his Moscow connection. (Rev: BL 6/15/86; New Yorker 7/21/86; PW 6/13/86)

10069 Freemantle, Brian. *Run Around.* 1989, Bantam $16.95 (0-553-05307-8); paper $4.95 (0-553-28407-X). A spy attempts to thwart a terrorist attack on world leaders at an international peace conference in Switzerland. (Rev: BL 3/15/89; NYTBR 6/25/89; PW 3/17/89)

10070 Gardner, John E. *Garden of Weapons.* 1981, McGraw-Hill $11.95 (0-07-022851-5); Mysterious paper $4.50 (0-89296-097-3). A British agent in contact with East German spies becomes alarmed that his contacts may be compromised following the defection of a Russian officer. (Rev: BL 2/15/81; LJ 3/1/81; PW 1/23/81)

10071 Gardner, John E. *License Renewed.* 1990, Berkley paper $4.50 (0-425-12463-0). Bond attempts to stop a mad scientist from destroying the world's nuclear power plants. (Rev: BL 5/15/81; CSM 7/15/81; Time 7/6/81)

10072 Gardner, John E. *No Deals, Mr. Bond.* 1988, Berkley paper $4.50 (1-55773-020-2). Superspy James Bond is sent on a mission to protect British undercover agents from a team of Soviet assassins. "One that absolutely shouldn't be missed."—LJ (Rev: BL 2/1/87; LJ 4/15/87; PW 3/6/87)

10073 Gardner, John E. *Secret Generations.* 1985, Putnam $17.95 (0-399-13037-3); Berkley paper $4.50 (0-441-75760-X). A chronicle of a British family's involvement in the Secret Service in the years prior to and including the First World War. (Rev: BL 10/15/85; CSM 12/5/85; PW 10/4/85)

10074 Garfield, Brian. *Hopscotch.* 1976, Fawcett paper $1.75 (0-449-22747-2). A legendary retired spy, who is writing explicit memoirs regarding his career in espionage, is tracked by both Soviet and American intelligence to keep him from revealing state secrets. (REV: NYTBR 6/8/75; PW 1/27/75. AWARDS: Edgar, 1975)

10075 Goldman, William. *Marathon Man.* 1974, Amereon $17.95 (0-88411-653-0); Dell paper $4.95 (0-440-15502-9). A New York college student is mistaken for a secret agent and becomes the target of a sadistic, former Nazi spy. (REV: LJ 9/15/74; PW 9/2/74)

10076 Granger, Bill. *Zurich Numbers.* 1984, Crown $14.95 (0-517-55446-1); Pocket paper $3.95 (0-671-55399-2). An American journalist and her spy lover flee from Soviet and American agents following their disclosure of an illicit Eastern European slave market. (REV: BL 7/84; LJ 9/1/84; PW 7/6/84)

10077 Greene, Graham. *Human Factor.* 1988, Pocket paper $4.50 (0-318-33014-8). The tale of a South African forced to flee his country who resettles in Great Britain and becomes a double agent for the Soviet Union. "Greene at his most riveting."—PW (REV: BL 3/15/78; NYTBR 2/26/78; PW 1/16/78. AWARDS: ALA, 1978)

10078 Gross, Martin. *Red President.* 1988, Berkley paper $4.50 (1-55773-136-5). A KGB-supported U.S. senator is elected president of the United States. (REV: BL 1/1/87; LJ 2/1/87)

10079 Hall, Adam. *Quiller.* 1985, Jove paper $4.50 (0-515-08415-8). A spy seeks to determine the truth about the attack on an American submarine by Soviet forces. (REV: BL 1/1/86; PW 10/25/85)

10080 Hall, Adam. *Quiller Memorandum.* 1986, Jove paper $3.50 (0-515-08503-0). While searching for the whereabouts of World War II war criminals, a British agent stumbles across a dangerous plot threatening the political stability of the world. (REV: NYTBR 3/28/65; Sat Rev 4/24/65. AWARDS: Edgar, 1965)

10081 Hallahan, William. *Catch Me: Kill Me.* 1974, Macmillan $6.95 (0-672-52311-6). The whereabouts of a Soviet Jewish poet kidnapped from Grand Central Station are traced by a CIA agent. (REV: PW 1/17/77; Time 4/17/78; TLS 10/27/78. AWARDS: Edgar, 1977)

10082 Higgins, Jack. *Confessional.* 1986, NAL paper $4.95 (0-451-16536-5). A KGB assassin from Northern Ireland is believed by British intelligence to be stalking the pope on his visit to England. "Tense . . . riveting . . . what a thriller should be."—NYTBR (REV: BL 6/15/85; LJ 6/1/85; NYTBR 7/21/85)

10083 Hill, Reginald. *Spy's Wife.* 1990, Warner paper $4.95 (0-446-35985-8). An Englishwoman tries to readjust to life following the defection of her husband from British intelligence to the East. (REV: LJ 10/1/80; PW 7/4/80; TLS 4/18/80)

10084 Hone, Joseph. *Oxford Gambit.* 1988, Macmillan paper $4.95 (0-02-033281-5). British intelligence searches for the identity of a Russian mole planted in their secret service. "Hone brings considerable honor to the Graham Greene tradition of writing espionage novels."—NYTBR (REV: BL 10/1/80; NYTBR 11/16/80; New Yorker 1/5/81)

10085 Howard, Hampton. *Friends, Russians and Countrymen.* 1989, St. Martin's paper $3.95 (0-312-91667-1). CIA agents attempt to find the identity of a Paris government agent who is leaking secrets to the Soviets. "Confirms the emergence of a strong contender for top honors in spy writing."—LJ (REV: BL 3/1/88; LJ 3/15/88; PW 1/15/88)

10086 Howlett, John. *Murder of a Moderate Man.* 1986, St. Martin's $15.95 (0-312-00055-3); Harlequin Books paper $3.95 (0-373-97083-8). Western intelligence tries to stop an Arab team out to murder an Iranian dissident in London. "British espionage at its best."—NYTBR (REV: NYTBR 2/22/87; PW 11/28/86)

10087 Hoyt, Richard. *Head of State.* 1986, Tor paper $3.95 (0-8125-0489-5). A Russian poet, assisted by a CIA agent, plots to exchange the stolen head of Lenin for emigration of Jews to Israel. (REV: BL 10/1/85; LJ 9/15/85)

10088 Hoyt, Richard. *Siege.* 1987, Tor $16.95 (0-312-93017-8); paper $4.95 (0-8125-0029-6). The seizure of Gibraltar by terrorists puts the CIA into action to reclaim it in this satire of espionage novels. (REV: LJ 7/87; PW 6/12/87)

10089 Hoyt, Richard. *Trotsky's Run.* 1983, Tor paper $3.50 (0-523-48079-2). Kim Philby attempts to reveal that a candidate for the U.S. presidency is a KGB agent who believes himself to be Leon Trotsky. "A superbly written stunner."—NYTBR (REV: NYTBR 8/7/83; PW 7/1/83)

10090 Hugo, Richard. *Last Judgment.* 1987, Scarborough $16.95 (0-8128-3044-X); Windsor paper $4.50 (1-55817-114-2). A spy story featuring a British counterterrorist agent seeking a stolen da Vinci painting and tracking a mysterious weapon appropriated from Nazi vaults. (REV: NYTBR 4/19/87; PW 3/7/86)

10091 Hunter, Stephen. *Spanish Gambit.* 1985, Crown $15.95 (0-517-55731-2); Ace paper $3.95 (0-441-77776-7). A British agent seeks to prove that a former childhood friend is working as a Russian spy. (REV: BL 7/85; LJ 8/85; PW 5/31/85)

10092 Hyde, Anthony. *Red Fox.* 1986, Ballantine paper $4.95 (0-345-32839-6). A former journalist seeks his girlfriend's missing father and his fortune and becomes mixed up in a KGB plot to obtain the money. (REV: BL 6/15/85; PW 7/12/85; TLS 12/27/85)

10093 Hyman, Tom. *Prussian Blue.* 1991, Viking $19.95 (0-670-82996-X). A journalist attempts to locate intelligence documents that may be damaging to the U.S. government. (REV: BL 3/15/91; LJ 2/15/91; PW 2/8/91)

10094 Ignatius, David. *Agents of Innocence.* 1988, Avon paper $4.50 (0-380-70593-1). The story of CIA Middle East covert activities in the 1960s and 1970s regarding the infiltration of a Palestinian terrorist group. "A spy novel of formidable power."—LJ (REV: CSM 10/21/87; LJ 9/15/87; PW 7/24/87)

10095 Isaacs, Susan. *Shining Through.* **1988, Harper & Row $18.95 (0-06-015979-0); Ballantine paper $5.95 (0-345-35803-1).** A lawyer's secretary becomes involved in a secret spy mission in Berlin during World War II. "A truly compulsive read."—PW (REV: BL 7/88; NYTBR 9/11/88; PW 6/3/88)

10096 Ison, Graham. *Confirm or Deny.* **1989, St. Martin's $17.95 (0-312-03803-8).** Two botched operations in Eastern Europe blamed on security leaks provoke a search for a mole in British intelligence. (REV: LJ 1/90; NYTBR 2/25/90; PW 11/17/89)

10097 Kaminsky, Stuart M. *A Fire Red Rain.* **1988, Ivy Books paper $3.50 (0-8041-0279-1).** A Moscow KGB inspector searches for the murderer of Russian circus performers. (REV: BL 5/15/87; New Yorker 10/12/87; PW 4/17/87)

10098 Kaminsky, Stuart M. *Man Who Walked Like a Bear.* **1990, Macmillan $16.95 (0-684-19023-0).** A Russian inspector tries to escape capture by KGB agents. (REV: BL 4/15/90; PW 4/13/90)

10099 Kaplan, Andrew. *War of the Raven.* **1990, Simon & Schuster $19.95 (0-671-70758-2).** A tale of espionage involving an American spy's efforts to obtain Nazi secrets in pre-World War II Argentina. "Smashing, sexy, and unforgettable."—PW (REV: BL 8/90; LJ 8/90; PW 6/29/90)

10100 Koontz, Dean R. *Watchers.* **1987, Putnam $17.95 (0-399-13263-5); Berkley paper $4.95 (0-425-10746-9).** KGB agents stalk a dog with human level intelligence that escaped from a genetic research lab. (REV: BL 1/1/87; LJ 3/1/87; PW 12/19/86)

10101 Kosinski, Jerzy. *Cockpit.* **1989, Arcade paper $8.95 (1-55970-022-X).** A chronicle of the exploits of an exiled spy, as recounted by the author of *Steps.* (REV: BL 9/1/75; Choice 3/76; LJ 6/15/75)

10102 Langley, Bob. *Autumn Tiger.* **1986, Walker $15.95 (0-8027-0884-6).** A CIA agent is sent to Paris to find the identity of an East German agent who wants to defect to the West. (REV: BL 7/86; PW 5/23/86)

10103 Le Carre, John. *Honourable Schoolboy.* **1977, Knopf $24.95 (0-394-41645-7); Bantam paper $4.95 (0-553-25197-X).** British intelligence agent George Smiley tracks the identity of a high-level Russian mole stationed in China. "The ultimate espionage novel."—PW (REV: Newsweek 9/26/77; PW 7/18/77; TLS 9/9/77. AWARDS: Time, 1977)

10104 Le Carre, John. *Little Drummer Girl.* **1983, Knopf $24.95 (0-394-53015-2); Bantam paper $5.95 (0-553-26757-4).** The story of a British female spy who infiltrates a Palestinian terrorist organization with the help of Israeli intelligence. (REV: BL 1/1/83; LJ 2/1/83; PW 12/17/82)

10105 Le Carre, John. *A Perfect Spy.* **1986, Knopf $18.95 (0-394-55141-9); Bantam paper $5.95 (0-553-26456-7).** A British double agent goes into temporary hiding to write following the death of his

father and is pursued by intelligence men who fear he may have defected to the East. (REV: LJ 4/1/86; NYTBR 4/13/86; Time 4/28/86. AWARDS: NYTBR, 1986; Time, 1986)

10106 Le Carre, John. *Russia House.* **1989, Knopf $19.95 (0-394-57789-2); Bantam paper $5.95 (0-553-28534-3).** British intelligence receives a document portraying the ineptness of the Soviet military, and dispatches an agent to Moscow to find the author of the document to determine its validity. (REV: BL 5/1/89; CSM 6/13/89; Time 5/29/89. AWARDS: BL, 1989)

10107 Le Carre, John. *Secret Pilgrim.* **1991, Knopf $21.95 (0-394-58842-8).** Reflections of a British intelligence agent on his three decades of service and his current post as instructor at a spy training school. (REV: BL 12/1/90; PW 11/16/90; Time 1/14/91)

10108 Le Carre, John. *Smiley's People.* **1979, Knopf $12.95 (0-394-50843-2); Bantam paper $5.95 (0-553-26487-7).** Smiley searches for the murderer of an Estonian emigré who was killed while attempting to deliver a message concerning Smiley's KGB arch-rival Karla. "The ultimate espionage novel."—PW (REV: BL 2/15/80; Newsweek 12/24/79; PW 10/10/80. AWARDS: BL, The 1980s)

10109 Le Carre, John. *Tinker, Tailor, Soldier, Spy.* **1974, Knopf $17.95 (0-394-49219-6); Bantam paper $5.95 (0-553-26778-7).** George Smiley searches for clues to the identity of a Russian mole within the top ranks of British intelligence. (REV: BL 7/15/74; NYTBR 6/30/74; PW 4/8/74)

10110 Lee, Stan. *Dunn's Conundrum.* **1985, Warner paper $3.95 (0-446-34133-9).** A counterespionage agent discovers a plot to destroy the Soviet army in this debut novel. (REV: LJ 12/84; PW 1/4/85)

10111 Lee, Stan. *God Project.* **1990, Grove-Weidenfeld $19.95 (0-8021-1128-9).** The CIA undertakes a confidential research project without the knowledge of the American government. (REV: BL 1/90; NYTBR 1/14/90)

10112 Littell, Robert. *Amateur.* **1990, Bantam paper $4.95 (0-553-28390-1).** A CIA code breaker attempts to track down and kill terrorists responsible for the death of his girlfriend. "A topnotch book by a literate master of the craft."—LJ (REV: BL 3/15/81; LJ 5/1/81; PW 3/13/81)

10113 Littell, Robert. *Sisters.* **1990, Bantam paper $4.95 (0-553-25831-1).** In this novel set in 1963, two CIA agents employ a scam to control a KGB operative working in New York. "As slick a thriller as they come."—NYTBR (REV: LJ 2/1/86; NYTBR 2/2/86)

10114 Ludlum, Robert. *Aquitaine Progression.* **1984, Random $17.95 (0-394-53674-6); Bantam paper$5.95 (0-553-26256-4).** An American agent attempts to thwart the plans of a neo-fascist military group to take over the Western world. "Ludlum at his best."—BL (REV: BL 1/15/84; LJ 2/15/84; PW 1/6/84)

10115 **Ludlum, Robert.** *Bourne Identity.* **1984, Bantam paper $5.95 (0-553-26011-1).** Jason Bourne loses his memory following a gunshot wound and finds clues to his identity in a Swiss bank vault. (REV: LJ 4/15/80; PW 2/8/80; Time 4/14/80)

10116 **Ludlum, Robert.** *Bourne Supremacy.* **1986, Random $19.95 (0-394-54396-3); Bantam paper $5.95 (0-553-26322-6).** A man posing as Jason Bourne attempts takeover of Hong Kong by a series of political assassinations and is tracked by the real Bourne. (REV: BL 2/1/86; LJ 3/15/86; Time 3/10/86)

10117 **Ludlum, Robert.** *Parsifal Mosaic.* **1982, Random $15.95 (0-394-52111-0); Bantam paper $5.95 (0-553-25270-4).** In this thriller by the author of *The Icarus Agenda,* an intelligence agent orders the death of his traitor spy girlfriend but sights her alive on the streets of Rome. (REV: BL 2/1/82; PW 1/29/82)

10118 **McEwan, Ian.** *The Innocent.* **1990, Doubleday $18.95 (0-385-41370-X).** A novel based on the efforts of British and American spies to gain access to Russian communications in East Berlin during the mid-1950s. (REV: BL 6/1/90; NYTBR 6/3/90; Newsweek 6/4/90)

10119 **Mailer, Norman.** *Harlot's Ghost.* **1991, Random $30.00 (0-394-58832-0).** A sweeping novel of 1,300-plus pages portraying the activities of American intelligence following World War II as told from the viewpoint of the CIA. (REV: BL 9/1/91; LJ 9/1/91; NYTBR 9/29/91. AWARDS: BL, 1991; PW, 1991)

10120 **Markstein, George.** *Soul Hunters.* **1987, Franklin Watts $15.95 (0-531-15033-X); Windsor paper $3.95 (1-55817-062-6).** A British agent suspects that a series of seemingly unrelated incidents are part of a complex scheme to catapult the Western world into war. "Jam-packed with some of the most frighteningly believable and refreshingly entertaining characters in print."—LJ (REV: BL 2/15/87; LJ 6/15/87; PW 2/27/87)

10121 **Morris, M. E.** *Sword of the Shaheen.* **1990, Presidio Pr. $18.95 (0-89141-328-6).** Soviets and Americans join forces to combat an Arab terrorist group after the group uses Russian nuclear weapons to destroy an American ship and threaten the city of San Antonio. (REV: LJ 12/89; NYTBR 1/14/90)

10122 **O'Neill, Frank.** *Roman Circus.* **1990, Simon & Schuster $19.95 (0-671-68336-5).** An Italian-American intelligence agent is sent to Italy to investigate the terrorist murder of an American general. "It is to most books of its genre what a Henry James novel is to a Horatio Alger story."—NYTBR (REV: LJ 1/90; NYTBR 1/14/90)

10123 **Pentecost, Hugh.** *Nightmare Time.* **1988, Simon & Schuster paper $3.50 (0-317-70123-1).** An air force major involved in a secret SDI program is kidnapped by spies in New York. (REV: BL 5/15/86; PW 5/16/86)

10124 **Pickering, Paul.** *Blue Gate of Babylon.* **1989, Random $18.95 (0-394-57637-3).** A British spy is sent to Berlin during the early 1960s in order to run a brothel and track down a Nazi war criminal. "A terrific novel by a terrific writer."—BL (REV: BL 11/1/89; NYTBR 12/17/89; PW 9/29/89)

10125 **Proffitt, Nicholas.** *Embassy House.* **1986, Bantam $16.95 (0-553-05128-8); paper $4.50 (0-553-26134-7).** A depiction of CIA assassinations and tortures carried out in Southeast Asia during the Vietnam War era. (REV: BL 4/1/86; LJ 4/15/86; PW 4/18/86)

10126 **Quammen, David.** *Soul of Viktor Tronko.* **1987, Doubleday $17.95 (0-385-19596-6); Dell paper $4.50 (0-440-20177-2).** The writer's CIA friend is found murdered following his transmission of a message regarding the two-decade-old defection of a Russian spy. "A stylish must for devotees of the genre."—PW (REV: BL 6/15/87; LJ 7/87; PW 5/8/87)

10127 **Royce, Kenneth.** *Third Arm.* **1983, Carroll & Graf paper $3.50 (0-88184-051-3).** A British intelligence agent collaborates with an international terrorist group working in London. (REV: NYTBR 6/8/80; PW 2/29/80)

10128 **Sebastian, Tim.** *Saviour's Gate.* **1991, Delacorte $19.95 (0-385-29881-1).** A British spy uncovers a plot by a Soviet leader to defect to the United States. (REV: BL 5/15/91; LJ 5/15/91; PW 3/29/91)

10129 **Seymour, Gerald.** *Harry's Game.* **1987, Berkley paper $3.50 (0-425-10511-3).** A British spy hunts down the IRA murderer of an English politician in Northern Ireland. (REV: CSM 10/9/75; New Yorker 11/17/75; PW 8/4/75)

10130 **Seymour, Gerald.** *Running Target.* **1990, Morrow $19.95 (0-688-05201-0); HarperCollins paper $4.95 (0-06-100143-0).** A British intelligence agent goes to Iran to track down a drug dealer responsible for the death of a cabinet minister's daughter. "Seymour delivers the goods in this tense and involving tale."—BL (REV: BL 12/1/89; NYTBR 3/11/90; PW 12/8/89)

10131 **Smith, Martin Cruz.** *Gorky Park.* **1981, Random $13.95 (0-394-51748-2); Ballantine paper $5.95 (0-345-29834-9).** New York and Moscow police attempt to find the murderer who left three mutilated bodies in Gorky Park in Moscow. (REV: CSM 4/13/81; LJ 4/1/81; TLS 6/5/81)

10132 **Swift, Graham.** *Shuttlecock.* **1985, Pocket paper $7.95 (0-671-54612-0).** A filing clerk finds evidence of his father's misdoings as a spy during World War II. (REV: BL 4/15/85; LJ 5/15/85; Newsweek 6/24/85)

10133 **Thomas, Craig.** *Lion's Run.* **1986, Bantam paper $4.50 (0-553-25824-9).** A tale of a series of frames and counterframes between high-level KGB and British intelligence agents. (REV: BL 9/15/85; LJ 11/15/85; PW 10/11/85)

10134 **Thomas, Craig.** *Wildcat.* **1989, Putnam $19.95 (0-399-13412-3); Jove paper $4.95 (0-515-10186-9).** A thriller involving two spies—one English, one East German—who plot and counterplot against each other over four decades. (Rev: BL 12/1/88; PW 12/2/88)

10135   Thomas, D. M. *Sphinx.* **1987, Viking $17.95 (0-670-81415-6); Pocket paper $4.95 (0-671-64158-1).** A British journalist falls in love with a young Russian woman who he suspects may be a KGB operative. (Rev: LJ 12/86; NYTBR 1/18/87; TLS 6/27/86)

10136   Thomas, Ross. *Mordida Man.* **1988, Berkley paper $3.95 (0-425-11098-2).** A group of Libyan terrorists kidnaps the brother of the President of the United States and holds him hostage to exchange for a terrorist they believe to be in the hands of the CIA. (Rev: BL 3/15/81; LJ 6/15/81; PW 1/16/81)

10137   Thomas, Ross. *Twilight at Mac's Place.* **1990, Mysterious $19.95 (0-89296-214-3).** The attendees of a former CIA agent's funeral become the targets of a plot to murder them all. "Thomas is at his best here . . . a sophisticated, winning performance."—BL (Rev: BL 9/15/90; NYTBR 10/21/90; PW 9/14/90)

10138   Trenhaile, John. *Gates of Exquisite Views.* **1989, NAL paper $4.95 (0-451-16140-8).** Intelligence agents from several countries attempt to gain access to a robot designed to fly war planes. "Neatly paced suspense from a master of the genre."—BL (Rev: BL 11/1/87; PW 11/20/87)

10139   Trenhaile, John. *Man Called Kyril.* **1986, Jove paper $3.50 (0-515-07633-3).** KGB agents seek the identity of a British informant in Moscow. (Rev: BL 3/15/83; LJ 4/15/83; PW 2/4/83)

10140   Trevanian. *Eiger Sanction.* **1984, Ballantine paper $4.95 (0-345-31737-8).** This novel concerning a professional assassin set in the Swiss Alps was the basis for a motion picture that starred Clint Eastwood. (Rev: BL 1/1/73; LJ 12/1/72; PW 7/10/72)

10141   Truman, Margaret. *Murder in the CIA.* **1987, Random $17.95 (0-394-55795-6); Fawcett paper $4.95 (0-449-21275-0).** A CIA agent tries to find the motive behind the murder of a colleague at London's Heathrow Airport. (Rev: BL 9/15/87; LJ 11/1/87; PW 10/9/87)

10142   Vonnegut, Kurt, Jr. *Mother Night.* **1979, Delacorte paper $12.95 (0-440-05851-1).** The confessions of an American war criminal convicted of aiding and abetting the Nazi cause through radio broadcasts that were in reality coded intelligence messages. (Rev: Choice 9/66; LJ 6/1/66; PW 2/21/66)

10143   Walser, Martin. *No Man's Land.* **1989, Henry Holt $18.95 (0-8050-0667-2).** A West German born in East Germany becomes a spy for NATO. "A curious and powerful novel by one of West Germany's finest novelists."—NYTBR (Rev: BL 1/1/89; Choice 11/89; NYTBR 1/22/89)

10144   Woods, Stuart. *Deep Lie.* **1987, Avon paper $4.95 (0-380-70266-5).** A CIA agent finds evidence of an impending Soviet invasion of Sweden. "One of the very best spy thrillers this reviewer has seen."—LJ (Rev: BL 12/15/85; LJ 2/1/86; NYTBR 3/16/86)

10145 Amos, James. *The Memorial: A Novel of the Vietnam War.* **1989, Crown $19.95 (0-517-56971-X); Avon paper $3.95 (0-380-71195-8).** A tale of a Marine company during the Vietnam War and its efforts to cut Vietcong supply lines, as told by a member of the group who reminisces after a visit to the Vietnam War Memorial. (REV: BL 6/1/89; LJ 6/15/89)

10146 Andersch, Alfred. *Winterspelt: A Novel about the Last Days of World War II.* **1980, Dufour $30.00 (0-7206-0550-4).** A story of life in Belgium at the site of a fierce battle between German and American troops during the late stages of World War II. "No summary can do justice to the depth and scope of this ambitious novel."—NYTBR (REV: BL 7/15/78; LJ 6/15/78; NYTBR 7/30/78)

10147 Argo, Ronald. *Year of the Monkey.* **1989, Simon & Schuster $19.95 (0-671-66360-7).** A journalist employed by the CIA uses connections to probe illicit activities during the Vietnam War. (REV: BL 6/15/89; LJ 6/15/89; PW 5/12/89)

10148 Asscher-Pinkhof, Clara. *Star Children.* **1987, Wayne State Univ. Pr. $29.95 (0-8143-1846-0).** A fictionalized account of the author's experiences as a teacher who stayed with children in the Nazi death camps and escaped to Palestine in a trade for German prisoners. "This powerful document is worthy to stand beside Anne Frank's diary."—LJ (REV: Choice 6/87; LJ 12/86)

10149 Badanes, Jerome. *Final Opus of Leon Solomon.* **1989, Knopf $18.95 (0-394-57221-1); Simon & Schuster paper $8.95 (0-671-70303-X).** A Holocaust survivor considering suicide decides to chronicle the events of his life on paper before committing the act. (REV: BL 12/15/88; LJ 12/88; New Yorker 4/3/89)

10150 Ballard, J. G. *Empire of the Sun.* **1987, Pocket paper $4.50 (0-671-64877-2).** A boy's story of World War II in Shanghai under Japanese occupation based on Ballard's own childhood experiences. (REV: LJ 11/1/84; NYTBR 11/11/84; PW 8/24/84)

10151 Becker, Jurek. *Jakob the Liar.* **1990, Schocken $19.95 (0-8052-4097-7).** The residents of a Nazi-occupied Jewish ghetto in 1943 are given hope by false stories trumpeting the impending arrival of Soviet troops. (REV: LJ 5/15/90; TLS 8/3/90)

10152 Begley, Louis. *Wartime Lies.* **1991, Knopf $19.00 (0-679-40016-8).** A portrait of two Holocaust survivors under the Nazi occupation of Warsaw. "A moving addition to Holocaust literature and one well recommended."—LJ (REV: LJ 5/1/91; PW 3/22/91; Time 5/27/91. AWARDS: LJ, 1991; NYTBR, 1991; PW, 1991)

10153 Berent, Mark. *Rolling Thunder.* **1989, Putnam $19.95 (0-399-13439-5); Jove paper $4.95 (0-515-10190-7).** A Vietnam veteran's novel describing the missions by U.S. Air Force pilots in support of ground forces. "An unusually arresting book about the early days of Vietnam."—NYTBR (REV: NYTBR 9/17/89; PW 3/24/89)

10154 Bienek, Horst. *Time Without Bells.* **1988, Macmillan $19.95 (0-689-11930-5).** A German writer's portrait of Poland under Nazi occupation focusing on the events of Good Friday 1943 when German troops removed church bells to melt down to make armaments. (REV: BL 12/15/87; Choice 7–8/88; LJ 1/88)

10155 Bodey, Donald. *F. N. G.* **1985, Viking $15.95 (0-670-80724-9); Ballantine paper $3.95 (0-345-33945-2).** A portrait of a year in the life of an American infantryman in Vietnam. "Fiction so vivid it could easily be mistaken for an actual historical account."—BL (REV: BL 10/15/85; LJ 11/15/85)

10156 Böll, Heinrich. *A Soldier's Legacy.* **1986, Penguin paper $6.95 (0-14-008320-0).** A short novel investigating the circumstances surrounding the suspicious death of a German officer during World War II. (REV: LJ 6/1/85; New Rep 10/21/85; NYTBR 6/23/85)

10157 Bond, Larry. *Red Phoenix.* **1990, Warner paper $5.95 (0-446-35968-8).** North Korea invades South Korea setting off a military confrontation involving the United States. "Wonderfully entertaining . . . deserves to be the best seller it is."—NYTBR (REV: BL 4/1/89; NYTBR 7/16/89; PW 3/31/89)

10158 Borden, G. F. *Easter Day, 1941.* **1987, Morrow $16.95 (0-688-06538-4).** An Allied tank crew is trapped behind Nazi lines following the North African desert battle against Rommel. "Exciting blood-and-guts action."—BL (REV: BL 3/15/87; LJ 3/15/87; PW 1/30/87)

10159 **Borowski, Tadeusz.** *This Way for the Gas, Ladies and Gentlemen.* **1976, Penguin paper $6.95 (0-14-004114-1).** This collection of 12 short stories by a Polish writer who committed suicide at the age of 27, deals with the author's experiences at Auschwitz. (REV: New Rep 4/10/76; NYTBR 2/29/76)

10160 **Brandys, Kazimierz.** *Rondo.* **1989, Farrar $19.95 (0-374-25200-9).** The son of a Polish general recounts his activities in Nazi-occupied Poland and the aftermath of World War II under Russian dominance. "Impossible to forget."—LJ (REV: LJ 9/15/89; New Rep 10/9/89; NYTBR 11/19/89)

10161 **Briskin, Mae.** *Tree Still Stands.* **1991, Norton $17.95 (0-393-02894-1).** During World War II a Polish-Jewish girl and her family flee through Europe to escape Nazi persecution. (REV: BL 1/15/91; LJ 12/90; PW 11/23/90)

10162 **Britton, Christopher.** *Paybacks.* **1985, Donald I. Fine $16.95 (0-917657-20-9); Warner paper $3.95 (0-445-20216-5).** The cover-up of death at a U.S. Marine training camp leads to a courtroom trial near the end of the Vietnam War. (REV: BL 4/15/85; LJ 5/15/85; PW 4/5/85)

10163 **Brown, Larry.** *Dirty Work.* **1989, Algonquin $16.95 (0-945575-20-3); Random paper $9.95 (0-679-73049-4).** Two disabled Mississippi men confined to a veteran's hospital discuss their lives and experiences during and after the Vietnam War. (REV: BL 8/89; LJ 7/89; PW 6/9/89. AWARDS: LJ, 1989)

10164 **Buchheim, Lothart-Gunther.** *The Boat.* **1988, Dell paper $4.95 (0-440-20063-6).** A former German U-boat commander's novel of life aboard a submarine in the North Atlantic during World War II. (REV: LJ 5/15/75; New Rep 5/24/75; PW 4/7/75)

10165 **Bulgakov, Mikhail.** *White Guard.* **1987, Academy Chicago paper $8.95 (0-89733-246-6).** A novel portraying the life of a Kiev family during the Russian Civil War in 1918 and 1919. (REV: Choice 10/71; LJ 9/1/71; Newsweek 6/21/71)

10166 **Burland, Brian.** *A Fall from Aloft.* **1987, Norton paper $6.95 (0-393-30346-2).** A teenage boy is sent from Bermuda to England to continue his studies via a commercial ship during the height of the German U-boat threat in World War II. (REV: BL 2/1/70; Sat Rev 1/10/70)

10167 **Camon, Ferdinando.** *Life Everlasting.* **1987, Marlboro Pr. $17.95 (0-910395-31-4); paper $10.95 (0-910395-32-2).** A story detailing the lives of a group of Italian peasant soldiers near the end of World War II. (REV: LJ 5/15/88; Newsweek 1/24/88; PW 2/12/88)

10168 **Caputo, Philip.** *Horn of Africa.* **1980, Holt $12.95 (0-03-042136-5); Dell paper $4.95 (0-440-33675-9).** This writer's first novel concerns the efforts of three Westerners to smuggle weaponry to rebel forces fighting Ethiopians in Eritrea. (REV: BL 9/1/80; LJ 12/15/80; PW 8/22/80)

10169 **Caputo, Philip.** *Indian Country.* **1988, Bantam paper $4.95 (0-553-27029-X).** A portrait of the family life of an emotionally shattered Vietnam

veteran living on Michigan's Upper Peninsula. (REV: NYTBR 5/17/87; PW 3/6/87)

10170 **Celine, Louis-Ferdinand.** *Castle to Castle.* **1987, Carroll & Graf paper $8.95 (0-88184-360-1).** The first English translation of the 1957 French work portraying the life of a Nazi collaborator in a detention camp near the end of World War II. (REV: LJ 11/15/68; Sat Rev 2/1/69; Time 2/28/69)

10171 **Clancy, Tom.** *Red Storm Rising.* **1986, Putnam $19.95 (0-399-13149-3); Berkley paper $5.95 (0-425-10107-X).** The Soviet Union invades Western Europe as a diversionary tactic to gain control of the petroleum resources of the Persian Gulf. (REV: CSM 7/31/86; NYTBR 7/27/86; Time 8/11/86)

10172 **Coulonges, Henri.** *Farewell, Dresden.* **1989, Simon & Schuster $18.95 (0-671-61779-6).** Story of the final days of World War II in Dresden and Czechoslovakia as told by a 12-year-old girl. "Its images are unforgettable."—CSM (REV: BL 12/15/88; CSM 4/5/89; PW 12/16/88)

10173 **Crichton, Robert.** *Secret of Santa Vittoria.* **1986, Carroll & Graf paper $3.95 (0-88184-267-2).** The story of the efforts of the citizenry of an Italian town during World War II to hide its precious wine supply from approaching Nazi troops. (REV: BL 12/15/66; NYTBR 8/28/66; Newsweek 8/29/66. AWARDS: ALA, 1966; NYTBR, 1966)

10174 **Currey, Richard.** *First Light.* **1989, Penguin paper $6.95 (0-14-011945-0).** A medical veteran's first novel concerns the effects of the Vietnam War on a young soldier from Kentucky. (REV: BL 4/1/88; LJ 5/15/88; PW 3/18/88)

10175 **Davis, George.** *Coming Home.* **1984, Howard Univ. Pr. paper $6.95 (0-88258-118-X).** A look at the lives of three U.S. Army pilots stationed in Thailand during the Vietnam War. (REV: BL 4/15/72; Choice 9/72; NYTBR 1/9/72)

10176 **Deighton, Len.** *Goodbye, Mickey Mouse.* **1983, Ballantine paper $4.95 (0-345-31146-9).** The tale of a group of American fighter pilots flying bombing missions over Nazi Germany from bases in England. (REV: BL 9/1/72; NYTBR 11/14/82; PW 9/10/82)

10177 **Deighton, Len.** *SS-GB: Nazi-Occupied Britain, 1941.* **1984, Ballantine paper $4.95 (0-345-31809-9).** A speculative novel regarding the consequences of the Nazi occupation of Britain in 1941 if Hitler had not attacked the Soviet Union and opened up an Eastern front. (REV: BL 2/15/79; Newsweek 2/19/79; PW 1/1/79)

10178 **Delibes, Miguel.** *Stuff of Heroes.* **1990, Random $21.95 (0-394-57746-9).** An examination of the splintering of a family during the Spanish Civil War. "An important novel by a modern master."—LJ (REV: BL 9/15/90; LJ 9/1/90; PW 7/6/90)

10179 **Del Vecchio, John M.** *For the Sake of All Living Things.* **1990, Bantam $19.95 (0-553-05742-1).** A fictional examination of the events surrounding the Khmer Rouge genocide in Cambodia during the late 1970s by the author of *The Thirteenth Valley*. (Rev: NYTBR 2/18/90; PW 1/12/90)

10180 Del Vecchio, John M. *Thirteenth Valley.* **1984, Bantam paper $5.95 (0-553-26020-0).** A portrait of the experiences of three American men on combat assignments late in the Vietnam War. "One of the finest novels to come out of the Vietnam War."— PW (Rev: LJ 9/15/82; Newsweek 7/26/82; PW 6/4/82. Awards: ALA, 1982)

10181 De Mille, Nelson. *Word of Honor.* **1987, Warner paper $4.50 (0-446-30158-2).** A veteran is placed on trial for war atrocities committed 15 years earlier while he was serving in Vietnam. (Rev: BL 10/1/85; LJ 4/1/85; PW 10/4/85)

10182 Doane, Michael. *Surprise of Burning.* **1990, Ballantine paper $4.95 (0-345-35899-6).** A child born during a bombing attack in World War II London becomes a war photographer in this novel set in Algeria and Vietnam. "As sophisticated and achieved an exercise in point of view and narrative consciousness as anything in recent years."—TLS (Rev: BL 3/15/88; PW 2/12/88; TLS 1/13/89)

10183 Donnelly, Frances. *Shake Down the Stars.* **1989, St. Martin's $18.95 (0-312-01819-3); paper $5.95 (0-312-91729-5).** A story tracing the effects of World War II on three young English women from the same village. "Impossible to put down."—PW (Rev: BL 12/15/88; LJ 2/1/89; PW 1/6/89)

10184 Dorfman, Ariel. *Widows.* **1989, Penguin paper $7.95 (0-14-011659-1).** A Chilean-exile writer's tale, set in occupied Greece during World War II, concerning a series of men's deaths and the reactions of their widows. (Rev: Choice 10/83; LJ 6/1/83; PW 4/1/83)

10185 Ehrlich, Gretel. *Heart Mountain.* **1988, Viking $18.95 (0-670-82160-8); Penguin paper $8.95 (0-14-010906-4).** A tale of a Japanese-American internment camp in Wyoming during World War II and of a small town located near the detention facility. "An eloquent evocation of a shameful episode in American history."—BL (Rev: BL 10/15/88; LJ 10/1/88; PW 8/12/88)

10186 Ely, Scott. *Starlight.* **1988, Warner paper $4.50 (0-446-34911-9).** A mystical debut novel portraying the lives of members of a combat unit in Vietnam. (Rev: LJ 4/15/87; NYTBR 4/19/87; PW 2/20/87)

10187 Fleming, Thomas. *Time and Tide.* **1989, Bantam paper $4.95 (0-553-27456-2).** A story of life aboard the American World War II carrier *Jefferson City* in the South Pacific whose crew was accused of fleeing a naval battle against the Japanese. (Rev: BL 7/87; LJ 8/87; PW 7/24/87)

10188 Forsyth, Frederick. *Dogs of War.* **1982, Bantam paper $5.95 (0-553-26846-5).** The coup d'état in an unnamed African country is engineered by a British entrepreneur seeking control of the nation's natural resources. (Rev: BL 7/15/74; LJ 8/74; PW 5/27/74)

10189 Gracq, Julien. *Opposing Shore.* **1987, Columbia Univ. Pr. $25.00 (0-231-05788-1).** A story of a three-decade-long war between Mediterranean nations originally published in France during the early 1950s. (Rev: BL 6/15/86; LJ 8/86; PW 5/16/86)

10190 Greene, Graham. *Tenth Man.* **1986, Pocket paper $3.95 (0-671-61171-2).** The first publication of a novel written in 1944 portraying life in a French town under Nazi occupation during World War II. "Among the best produced by this 20th century master."—PW (Rev: LJ 3/15/85; PW 2/15/85; Time 3/11/85)

10191 Haldeman, Joe. *War Year.* **1984, Avon paper $2.95 (0-380-67975-2).** A diary chronicling the experiences of an American teenage combat soldier in Vietnam. (Rev: BL 9/15/72; NYTBR 5/21/72)

10192 Hartog, Jan de. *Captain.* **1988, Nautical & Aviation $19.95 (0-933852-83-5).** A portrayal of the life of a World War II Dutch tugboat captain. (Rev: Atl 12/66; BL 2/15/67; Newsweek 12/12/66. Awards: ALA, 1967; NYTBR, 1966)

10193 Heinemann, Larry. *Close Quarters.* **1986, Penguin paper $6.95 (0-14-008578-5).** A story of the experiences of an American combat soldier in Vietnam from his arrival in 1967 to his return to the United States following the Tet offensive. (Rev: BL 9/1/77; LJ 6/1/77; PW 3/7/77)

10194 Hendricks, G. C. *Second War.* **1990, Viking $17.95 (0-670-83018-6).** An American pilot shot down over Vietnam behind enemy lines suffers a nervous breakdown on the way home to the United States. "Will complement any war fiction collection."—LJ (Rev: BL 4/1/90; LJ 2/1/90; PW 2/9/90)

10195 Herrick, William. *Hermanos!* **1983, Second Chance $16.95 (0-933256-38-8); paper $10.95 (0-933256-42-6).** A portrait of volunteer soldiers who fought with Republican Army forces during the Spanish Civil War as members of the Abraham Lincoln Brigade. (Rev: LJ 9/1/69; NYTBR 10/26/69)

10196 Hickey, James. *Chrysanthemum in the Snow: The Novel of the Korean War.* **1990, Crown $19.95 (0-517-57402-0).** An examination of the lives and actions of a group of American soldiers during the Korean War. (Rev: LJ 8/90; PW 4/20/90)

10197 Higgins, Jack. *Cold Harbour.* **1990, Simon & Schuster $19.95 (0-671-68425-6).** A group of Englishmen masquerade as Nazis to infiltrate spies from a Cornish town onto the Continent in this novel by the author of *The Eagle Has Landed*. (Rev: BL 1/1/90; NYTBR 3/4/90)

10198 Higgins, Jack. *Eagle Has Flown.* **1991, Simon & Schuster $21.95 (0-671-72458-4).** This sequel to *The Eagle Has Landed* concerns a plot to free a German officer from captivity in England. "The master of the World War II thriller . . . at the top of his form."—PW (Rev: BL 3/1/91; NYTBR 3/31/91; PW 1/25/91)

10199 Higgins, Jack. *The Eagle Has Landed.* **1989, Pocket paper $4.95 (0-671-66529-4).** The fictional story of an unsuccessful Nazi attempt to kidnap Winston Churchill in 1943. (Rev: CSM 6/23/75; LJ 5/15/75; PW 4/14/75)

10200 Ibuse, Masuji. *Black Rain.* **1980, Kodansha paper $6.95 (0-87011-364-X).** A portrait of the life of a man who survived the bombing of Hiroshima as told through his journal recording the event and its aftermath. (Rev: Choice 2/70; LJ 10/1/69. Awards: ALA, 1969)

10201 Jakes, John. *Love and War.* **1984, Harcourt $19.95 (0-15-154496-4); Dell paper $5.95 (0-440-15016-7).** This sequel to *North and South* portrays the lives of one Union family and one Confederate family during the American Civil War. (Rev: NYTBR 11/4/84; PW 9/28/84)

10202 Jenks, Tom, ed. *Soldiers and Civilians: Americans at War and Home.* **1986, Bantam $16.95 (0-553-05180-6); paper $8.95 (0-553-34312-2).** A collection of short war stories, mostly set in Vietnam, by authors including Don DeLillo, John Sayles, and Bobbie Ann Mason. (Rev: BL 12/1/86; PW 9/26/86)

10203 Jones, Douglas C. *Barefoot Brigade.* **1989, Tor paper $4.95 (0-8125-8459-7).** The story of an Arkansas family that joins the Confederate Army and fights in a series of key Civil War battles. (Rev: BL 7/82; LJ 9/1/82; PW 7/23/82)

10204 Jones, Douglas C. *Elkhorn Tavern.* **1989, Tor paper $4.95 (0-8125-8457-0).** Arkansas homesteaders fight in a Civil War battle that threatens to destroy their community. (Rev: BL 10/1/80; LJ 9/1/80; NYTBR 11/6/80)

10205 Karmel, Ilona. *An Estate of Memory.* **1986, Feminist Pr. paper $11.95 (0-935312-64-1).** Four Jewish women trapped in a Nazi concentration camp in Poland plot to smuggle a child to safety. (Rev: Choice 1/70; LJ 4/15/69; NYTBR 9/2/69)

10206 Keneally, Thomas. *A Family Madness.* **1987, Viking paper $6.95 (0-14-009796-1).** The tale of a Belorussian family that assists Nazis in Holocaust-related activities in hopes that German victory will bring their people an independent homeland. (Rev: LJ 4/1/86; Time 3/31/86; TLS 10/18/85)

10207 Keneally, Thomas. *Gossip from the Forest.* **1985, Harcourt paper $6.95 (0-15-636469-7).** A novel examining the meeting between German and British representatives to discuss the terms of an armistice to conclude World War I. (Rev: LJ 4/15/76; Newsweek 4/19/76; TLS 9/19/75)

10208 Keneally, Thomas. *Schindler's List.* **1983, Penguin paper $8.95 (0-14-006784-1).** A fictional portrait of a real-life Polish factory owner who saved the lives of thousands of Jews from certain death by offering them employment and refuge. (Rev: LJ 10/1/82; Newsweek 1/10/83; PW 8/20/82. Awards: NYTBR, 1982)

10209 Keneally, Thomas. *To Asmara.* **1989, Warner $18.95 (0-446-51542-6); paper $10.95 (0-446-39171-9).** The story of an Australian journalist reporting on the fight for independence by Eritrean rebel troops against Ethiopian forces. (Rev: BL 9/1/89; NYTBR 10/1/89; PW 8/25/89)

10210 King, Benjamin. *A Bullet for Stonewall.* **1990, Pelican $17.95 (0-88289-768-3).** A speculative historical novel revolving around a Union plot to assassinate Confederate general Stonewall Jackson. (Rev: BL 5/1/90; LJ 6/1/90)

10211 Kis, Danilo. *Hourglass.* **1990, Farrar $19.95 (0-374-17287-0).** An examination of the life of a Jewish railway clerk during World War II as told through a series of interlocking stories. (Rev: BL 7/90; LJ 7/90; NYTBR 10/7/90. Awards: BL, 1990)

10212 Kogawa, Joy. *Obasan.* **1982, Godine paper $10.95 (0-87923-491-1).** A tale of Japanese-Canadian girls' experiences in a forced relocation camp during the Second World War. (Rev: LJ 5/1/82; NYTBR 9/5/82; PW 4/2/82. Awards: ALA, 1982)

10213 Kosinski, Jerzy. *Painted Bird.* **1983, Random $6.95 (0-394-60433-4); Bantam paper $4.95 (0-553-26520-2).** A unique story of a Christian Polish child's experiences surviving the Nazi occupation that is told without one word of dialog. (Rev: BL 1/1/66; LJ 10/1/65; PW 9/12/66. Awards: NYTBR, 1965)

10214 Leffland, Ella. *Rumors of Peace.* **1985, Harper & Row paper $8.95 (0-06-091301-0).** A young woman grows up in California during World War II. (Rev: CSM 8/13/79; LJ 7/79; NYTBR 7/22/79)

10215 Lenz, Siegfried. *German Lesson.* **1986, New Directions paper $10.95 (0-8112-0982-2).** A portrait of life in northern Germany near the end of World War II. (Rev: LJ 12/1/71; Newsweek 4/10/72; Sat Rev 3/18/72)

10216 Lustig, Arnost. *Indecent Dreams.* **1988, Northwestern Univ. Pr. $17.95 (0-8101-0773-2); paper $9.95 (0-8101-0909-3).** Three novellas portraying Jewish life under European occupation by Nazi forces. (Rev: BL 5/15/88; LJ 6/15/88; PW 5/13/88)

10217 McCutchan, Philip. *Last Farewell.* **1991, St. Martin's $17.95 (0-312-05458-0).** A story set during World War I tracing the voyage of a doomed passenger ship from New York to Great Britain. (Rev: BL 2/15/91; LJ 2/1/91; PW 1/18/91)

10218 MacDonald, Roger. *1915.* **1989, Univ. of Queensland Pr. paper $12.95 (0-7022-2134-1).** A tale of the experiences of two Australian friends sent to fight in the disastrous Battle of Gallipoli. (Rev: LJ 2/1/80; Newsweek 3/17/80; PW 12/10/79)

10219 MacLean, Alistair. *Force Ten from Navarone.* **1984, Fawcett paper $2.95 (0-449-20574-6).** A story of a World War II mission to rescue Allied hostages and destroy a vital communication bridge in Yugoslavia. (Rev: BL 11/15/68; PW 9/23/68)

10220 MacLean, Alistair. *San Andreas.* **1986, Fawcett paper $4.50 (0-449-20970-9).** A British hospital ship en route from Canada to Scotland is menaced by German submarines during World War II. (Rev: BL 9/1/85; LJ 11/1/85; PW 8/16/85)

10221   Malouf, David. *Great World.* **1991, Pantheon $21.95 (0-679-40176-8).** A story of the relationship between two men who meet in a Japanese prisoner-of-war camp during World War II as told by an Australian writer. "The writing is powerful, engaging, dynamic. This should not be missed."— LJ (Rev: LJ 3/1/91; PW 1/25/91; TLS 4/6/90. Awards: LJ, 1991)

10222   Maspero, Francis. *Cat's Grin.* **1989, New Amsterdam paper $9.95 (0-941533-33-6).** A study of a teenager's life in France following the deportation of his parents to Nazi death camps. (Rev: LJ 5/1/86; New Yorker 11/24/86; PW 3/14/86)

10223   Metz, Don. *Catamount Bridge.* **1989, Harper & Row paper $6.95 (0-06-091570-6).** This debut novel set during the 1960s portrays a Vermont family torn apart by opposing views on the Vietnam War. "A novel to relish and rejoice in."—New Yorker (Rev: LJ 1/88; New Yorker 3/21/88; PW 12/4/87)

10224   Miller, Rex. *Profane Men: A Novel of Vietnam.* **1989, NAL paper $4.50 (0-451-40169-7).** American soldiers working on a covert intelligence project become assassination targets of the U.S. military. (Rev: BL 7/89; PW 6/16/89. Awards: BL, 1989)

10225   Milosz, Czeslaw. *Seizure of Power.* **1982, Farrar $14.95 (0-374-25788-4); paper $6.95 (0-374-51697-9).** This portrait of 1944 Warsaw caught between Russian and German armies was the Nobel laureate's first work of fiction. (Rev: CSM 9/10/82; Newsweek 10/4/82)

10226   Mulisch, Harry. *The Assault.* **1985, Pantheon paper $6.95 (0-394-54245-2).** A Dutch author's account of a young man's search to find the truth about the deaths of three family members at the hands of the Nazis near the end of the World War II. (Rev: CSM 7/16/85; NYRB 12/5/85; Newsweek 7/8/85)

10227   O'Brien, Tim. *Going after Cacciato.* **1989, Doubleday paper $9.95 (0-385-28349-0).** A member of a Vietnam platoon decides to desert and walk to Paris as the rest of the group searches for a missing comrade. (Rev: CSM 3/9/78; NYTBR 2/12/78; TLS 11/17/78. Awards: ALA, 1978; NBA, 1979)

10228   O'Brien, Tim. *Things They Carried: A Work of Fiction.* **1990, Houghton $18.95 (0-395-51598-X).** Twenty-two stories examining the lives and psyches of a platoon of Vietnam soldiers in 1970. (Rev: BL 3/15/90; NYTBR 3/11/90; PW 1/26/90. Awards: ALA, 1990; BL, 1990; NYTBR, 1990; PW, 1990)

10229   Oda, Makoto. *The Bomb.* **1990, Kodansha $18.95 (0-87011-981-8).** The development and detonation of the atomic bomb that destroyed Hiroshima as told through the lives of several people in Japan and the American Southwest. (Rev: NYTBR 8/12/90; PW 6/22/90)

10230   Peters, Ralph. *Red Army.* **1989, Pocket $18.95 (0-671-67668-7).** A portrait of a futuristic victorious war by Russian forces over NATO, as detailed from a Soviet point of view. "A very engaging read."— Newsweek (Rev: LJ 4/1/89; Newsweek 5/22/89; PW 3/10/89)

10231   Piercy, Marge. *Gone to Soldiers.* **1988, Fawcett paper $5.95 (0-449-21557-1).** A story set during World War II that traces the war's effects on the lives of a dozen characters. (Rev: CSM 5/29/87; LJ 4/1/87; PW 3/20/87)

10232   Pynchon, Thomas. *Gravity's Rainbow.* **1987, Penguin paper $12.95 (0-14-010661-8).** A portrait of life in London near the end of World War II as the city awaits the arrival and detonation of a German V-2 rocket. (Rev: LJ 3/1/74; NYTBR 3/11/73; Time 3/5/73. Awards: ALA, 1973; NBA, 1974; NYTBR, 1973; Time, 1973; Time, the 1970s)

10233   Read, Piers Paul. *Free Frenchman.* **1987, Random $19.95 (0-394-55887-1); Ivy paper $4.95 (0-8041-0253-8).** The experiences of a French Catholic before and during the Nazi occupation of France. "At once a fine adventure story and a telling historical portrait."—BL (Rev: BL 2/1/87; Choice 7–8/87; LJ 3/15/87)

10234   Robinson, Derek. *War Story.* **1988, Knopf $18.95 (0-394-56389-1).** The story of a World War I British fighter pilot and his training and preparation for air battle in France. "An excellent novel."— LJ (Rev: BL 4/15/88; LJ 4/1/88; PW 2/12/88)

10235   Rudner, Lawrence. *The Magic We Do Here.* **1988, Houghton $16.95 (0-395-45034-9).** This American writer's debut novel tells the story of a Polish Jewish boy's life and his efforts to escape persecution by the Nazis. (Rev: NYTBR 8/7/88; PW 4/8/88)

10236   Schaeffer, Susan Fromberg. *Buffalo Afternoon.* **1989, Knopf $19.95 (0-394-57178-9); Ivy Books paper $5.95 (0-8041-0580-4).** The story of a young Italian-American's life before, during, and after Vietnam. "One of the best treatments of the Vietnam War to date."—NYTBR (Rev: LJ 4/1/89; NYTBR 5/21/89; PW 3/10/89. Awards: ALA, 1989; LJ, 1989; PW, 1989)

10237   Schmidt, Arno. *Scenes from the Life of a Faun: A Short Novel.* **1983, M. Boyars $13.95 (0-7145-2762-9); $8.95 paper (0-7145-2763-7).** A German writer's portrayal of the life of a civil servant during World War II. "An excellent introduction to his work."—TLS (Rev: LJ 12/1/83; NYTBR 5/8/83; TLS 4/8/83)

10238   Shah, Idries. *Kara Kush.* **1986, Scarborough $17.95 (0-8128-3098-9).** A fictionalized account by an Afghan writer tracing the activities of a guerrilla leader during the war with the Soviet Union. (Rev: Atl 7/86; LJ 5/15/86; PW 4/11/86)

10239   Shepard, Jim. *Paper Doll.* **1986, Knopf $15.95 (0-394-55519-8).** An account of a group of American bomber pilots stationed in England during World War II awaiting their first air raid on Nazi Germany. (Rev: LJ 11/15/86; NYRB 12/18/86; NYTBR 11/9/86)

10240   Spencer, Elizabeth. *Night Travellers.* **1991, Viking $19.95 (0-670-83915-9).** A portrait of the lives of a group of Vietnam War protesters in the United States and Canada during the 1960s. "So moving it will make your heart ache."—PW (Rev: BL 5/1/91; LJ 6/15/91; PW 5/24/91)

10241 Szczypiorski, Andrzej. *Beautiful Mrs. Seidenman.* **1990, Grove-Weidenfeld $18.95 (0-8021-1140-8); Random paper $9.95 (0-679-73214-4).** A fictional account of the life of a blond, blue-eyed Jewish woman in World War II Warsaw. (Rev: Choice 6/90; NYTBR 2/18/90; TLS 8/3/90)

10242 Toer, Pramoedya Ananta. *The Fugitive.* **1990, Morrow $16.95 (0-688-08698-5).** This story of the occupation of Indonesia by the Japanese during World War II was first published in 1950 and is the author's first work to be translated into English. "An important and vital writer . . . his work has finally been brought to the attention of American readers."—NYTBR (Rev: BL 1/12/90; LJ 3/1/90; NYTBR 5/20/90)

10243 Toland, John. *Gods of War.* **1985, Doubleday $17.95 (0-385-18007-1); Tor paper $4.95 (0-8125-8900-9).** A portrait of two families, one Japanese and one American, from the beginnings of war in the Pacific Theater to the atomic bombings of Hiroshima and Nagasaki. "Compelling as information and impressive as performance."—NYTBR (Rev: LJ 4/1/85; NYTBR 4/21/85; PW 1/25/85)

10244 Tournier, Michel. *Ogre.* **1984, Pantheon paper $10.95 (0-394-72407-0).** A deformed Frenchman's efforts to save children from Nazi persecution during World War II. (Rev: BL 11/1/72; LJ 7/72; PW 6/12/72)

10245 Voinovich, Ivan. *Life and Extraordinary Adventures of Private Ivan Chonkin.* **1976, Farrar paper $9.75 (0-374-51752-5).** A satirical work regarding the adventures of a Soviet private in 1941 prior to and during the Nazi invasion. (Rev: BL 1/15/77; NYTBR 1/23/77; PW 12/13/76)

10246 Vonnegut, Kurt, Jr. *Slaughterhouse Five: Or, the Children's Crusade.* **1969, Smith $15.50 (0-8446-6366-2); Dell paper $5.95 (0-440-18029-5).** A fictionalized account of the Allied bombing of Dresden as experienced by an American POW and based on Vonnegut's own childhood experiences. (Rev: LJ 3/1/69; NYTBR 4/6/69; Time 4/11/69. Awards: ALA, 1969; NYTBR, 1969)

10247 Watkins, Paul. *Night over Day over Night.* **1988, Knopf $17.95 (0-394-57047-2); Avon paper $7.95 (0-380-70737-3).** The story of a German teenager who joins Hitler's SS in 1944 and experiences combat near the end of the Nazi war effort. "Must be ranked among the best in the genre."—New Yorker (Rev: BL 3/15/88; New Yorker 8/8/88; PW 2/12/88)

10248 Weil, Jiri. *Life with a Star.* **1989, Farrar $18.95 (0-374-18737-1).** This novel, written during the 1940s, portrays Prague and the persecution of Czech Jews under Nazi occupation and is based on the author's own experiences. (Rev: New Rep 9/4/89; NYTBR 6/18/89; New Yorker 10/2/89)

10249 Weil, Jiri. *Mendelssohn Is on the Roof.* **1991, Farrar $23.95 (0-374-20810-7).** This novel, originally published in Czech in 1960, concerns life in Czechoslovakia during the Nazi occupation and focuses on the plight of the Jews in that nation. (Rev: BL 4/15/91; LJ 2/15/91)

10250 Wesley, Mary. *Camomile Lawn.* **1990, Penguin paper $7.95 (0-14-102392-X).** A chronicle of the effects of the events surrounding World War II on seven English cousins and two Austrian-Jewish refugees. (Rev: BL 4/1/84; LJ 6/1/84; PW 3/16/84)

10251 West, Paul. *Very Rich Hours of Count Von Stauffenberg.* **1989, Overlook $22.50 (0-87951-368-3).** This fictional account of the failed 1944 plot to assassinate Hitler centers on the role of organizer Claus Von Stauffenberg. (Rev: BL 7/15/80; LJ 8/80; PW 6/6/80)

10252 Wetherell, W. D. *Chekhov's Sister.* **1990, Little, Brown $17.95 (0-316-93162-4).** An account of the life of the sister of Chekhov living in his Yalta home during World War II. (Rev: LJ 2/15/90; NYTBR 3/25/90; PW 1/26/90)

10253 Wharton, William. *Birdy.* **1980, Avon paper $4.95 (0-380-47282-1).** A first novel regarding the visit of a young man to his childhood friend in an army psychiatric hospital. (Rev: New Rep 2/10/79; Newsweek 1/8/79; Sat Rev 2/3/79. Awards: NBA, 1980)

10254 Wharton, William. *A Midnight Clear.* **1983, Ballantine paper $3.95 (0-345-31291-0).** A tale of the fate of a World War II squadron whose members were selected for their high intelligence. (Rev: BL 6/15/82; LJ 9/1/82; PW 6/25/82)

10255 Wicker, Tom. *Unto This Hour.* **1985, Berkley paper $4.95 (0-425-07583-4).** A fictional re-creation of the American Civil War conflict remembered as the Second Battle of Bull Run. "Comes about as close as fiction can to conveying the actual horror, chaos and excitement of war."—PW (Rev: BL 11/1/83; LJ 1/84; PW 12/9/83)

10256 Wiesel, Elie. *Gates of the Forest.* **1989, Schocken paper $8.95 (0-8052-0896-8).** The study of a fugitive Jewish youth in World War II and his search for identity. "Broodingly haunting."—BL (Rev: BL 7/1/66; NYTBR 6/12/66; Sat Rev 5/28/66)

10257 Wiley, Richard. *Soldiers in Hiding.* **1986, Atlantic Monthly $14.95 (0-87113-046-7).** The story of a Japanese-American man forced to join the Japanese army when traveling in that nation at the outbreak of World War II. "A masterful, emotionally searing drama."—BL (Rev: BL 2/15/86; CSM 4/23/86; PW 12/20/85)

10258 Williams, John A. *Captain Blackman.* **1988, Thunder's Mouth paper $10.95 (0-938410-68-7).** A presentation of the history of the African-American soldier in American wars, as told through the flashbacks and dreams of a Vietnam combatant. (Rev: BL 9/1/72; Choice 12/72; PW 2/28/72)

10259 Wouk, Herman. *War and Remembrance.* **1978, Little, Brown $19.95 (0-316-95501-9); Simon & Schuster paper $5.95 (0-671-67288-6).** This sequel to *Winds of War* traces the lives of the Henry family from Pearl Harbor to the end of World War II. (Rᴇᴠ: CSM 10/23/78; NYTBR 11/12/78; Newsweek 10/9/78)

10260　**Wouk, Herman.** *Winds of War.* **1971, Little, Brown $24.95 (0-316-95500-0); Pocket paper $5.95 (0-671-67287-8).** A story of the family of an American naval attaché in the years prior to the United States' entry into World War II. (Rᴇᴠ: BL 2/15/72; LJ 11/1/71; PW 9/20/71)

10261　**Wright, Stephen.** *Meditations in Green: A Novel of Vietnam.* **1983, Macmillan $14.95 (0-684-18010-3); paper $8.95 (0-684-18973-9).** A chronicle of the experiences of a military intelligence officer serving in Vietnam who interprets aerial photographs to determine the location of enemy troops. "An important—and disturbing—contribution to the literature of the war."—CSM (Rᴇᴠ: BL 10/1/83; CSM 11/4/83; PW 8/12/83. Aᴡᴀʀᴅs: ALA, 1983)

WESTERN STORIES

10262 Brautigan, Richard. *Hawkline Monster: A Gothic Western.* 1981, Pocket paper $2.95 (0-671-43786-0). A turn-of-the-century Oregon tale regarding two women who seduce two gunmen in the hope of subduing a local monster. (Rev: LJ 8/74; NYTBR 9/8/74; Newsweek 9/9/74)

10263 Brown, Dee. *Creek Mary's Blood.* 1981, Pocket paper $4.95 (0-317-56791-8). A novel tracing several generations of a Creek Indian family from the seventeenth century to the Battle of Little Big Horn. (Rev: BL 2/15/80; LJ 3/1/80; PW 2/8/80)

10264 Charyn, Jerome. *Darlin' Bill.* 1985, Donald I. Fine paper $8.95 (0-917657-40-3). The adventures of a woman traveling around the Old West who meets and falls in love with Wild Bill Hickok. "A comic historical novel offering an exceptionally wide range of pleasures."—NYTBR (Rev: LJ 11/1/80; NYTBR 12/7/80; PW 10/3/80)

10265 Dexter, Pete. *Deadwood.* 1986, Random $17.95 (0-394-53669-X); Viking paper $4.95 (0-14-009910-7). A chronicle of the adventures of Wild Bill Hickok and Calamity Jane in Deadwood, South Dakota. (Rev: LJ 4/1/86; NYTBR 4/20/86; Time 6/2/86)

10266 Dodd, Susan M. *Mamaw.* 1988, Grossman $18.95 (0-670-82180-2); Ballantine paper $3.95 (0-345-36297-7). A fictional story of the life of the woman who was the mother of outlaws Frank and Jesse James. (Rev: BL 8/88; New Yorker 11/28/88; PW 7/1/88)

10267 Doig, Ivan. *Dancing at the Rascal Fair.* 1987, Macmillan $18.95 (0-689-11764-7); Harper & Row paper $8.95 (0-06-097181-9). Nineteenth-century Scottish immigrants attempt to establish a sheep ranch in Montana. (Rev: BL 7/87; LJ 9/15/87; PW 7/31/87)

10268 Estleman, Loren D. *Bloody Season.* 1988, Bantam $15.95 (0-553-05231-4); paper $3.95 (0-553-27494-5). A fictional retelling of the events surrounding the 1881 shootout at the O.K. Corral in Tombstone, Arizona. (Rev: BL 11/15/87; LJ 1/88; PW 11/6/87)

10269 Flynn, Robert. *North to Yesterday.* 1985, Texas Christian Univ. $16.95 (0-87565-014-7); paper $9.95 (0-87565-015-5). Following the death of his wife, a man takes his son on a Texas longhorn cattle drive. (Rev: BL 7/1/67; LJ 7/67; PW 4/3/67. Awards: NYTBR, 1967)

10270 Fowler, Karen Joy. *Sarah Canary.* 1991, Henry Holt $21.95 (0-8050-1753-4). This debut work of fiction tells the story of a Chinese laborer working in the Pacific Northwest in the latter half of the nineteenth century. "An extraordinarily strong first novel."—NYTBR (Rev: NYTBR 11/10/91; PW 8/23/91)

10271 Gloss, Molly. *Jump Off Creek.* 1989, Houghton $16.95 (0-395-51086-4). The story of a woman who leaves the East following the death of her husband to homestead and settle in nineteenth-century Oregon. (Rev: BL 9/1/89; LJ 7/89; PW 7/21/89)

10272 Gorman, Edward, ed. *Westeryear: Stories about the West, Past and Present.* 1988, Evans $14.95 (0-87131-553-X). A collection of 23 stories of the American West, including works by Elmore Leonard, Max Brand, O. Henry, and Harlan Ellison. (Rev: BL 10/15/88; PW 9/30/88)

10273 Gorman, Edward. *What the Dead Men Say.* 1990, Evans $15.95 (0-87131-614-5). A Western story of a man and his nephew in search of revenge against the three men who murdered his daughter. (Rev: BL 8/90; LJ 7/90)

10274 Hall, Oakley. *Bad Lands.* 1988, Bantam paper $4.50 (0-553-27265-9). A portrait of the rivalry between cattlemen and a newly arrived Scottish immigrant, set in South Dakota during the 1880s. (Rev: LJ 6/15/78; Newsweek 6/5/78; PW 4/10/78)

10275 Hansen, Ron. *Assassination of Jesse James by the Coward Robert Ford.* 1990, Norton paper $8.95 (0-393-30679-8). A portrait of the last days of the legendary outlaw and the aftermath of his death. (Rev: CSM 12/28/83; Newsweek 11/14/83; PW 9/9/83)

10276 Hansen, Ron. *Desperadoes.* 1990, Norton paper $8.95 (0-393-30680-1). The reminiscences of one of the outlaw Dalton brothers regarding life in the Old West. (Rev: NYTBR 6/3/79; New Yorker 6/25/79; Newsweek 4/9/79)

10277 Jones, Douglas C. *Search for Temperance Moon.* **1991, Henry Holt $22.50 (0-8050-1387-3).** A United States Marshal enlists the assistance of an Arkansas madam in solving a murder outside his jurisdiction. (REV: BL 4/15/91; LJ 5/1/91; PW 4/26/91)

10278 Jones, Douglas C. *Season of the Yellow Leaf.* **1987, Tor paper $3.95 (0-8125-8450-3).** A young girl kidnapped by Comanches during the 1830s is raised by members of the Indian tribe. (REV: BL 9/15/83; LJ 10/1/83; PW 8/19/83)

10279 L'Amour, Louis. *Jubal Sackett.* **1986, Bantam paper $4.95 (0-553-27739-1).** The North Dakota writer's tale of an adventurer's experiences in the American West during the seventeenth century. (REV: BL 5/1/85; LJ 6/1/85; NYTBR 6/2/85)

10280 L'Amour, Louis. *Lonesome Gods.* **1984, Bantam paper $4.95 (0-553-27518-6).** In this story set in the nineteenth century, a boy is abandoned to die in the California desert but lives to seek revenge against his enemies in later life. (REV: BL 2/15/83; LJ 4/1/83; PW 2/18/83)

10281 McCarthy, Cormac. *Blood Meridian: Or the Evening Redness in the West.* **1986, Ecco Pr. paper $9.50 (0-88001-092-4).** A teenager joins a group of criminals on their rampage across the Old West. (REV: BL 3/1/85; LJ 3/1/85; PW 1/18/85. AWARDS: BL, the 1980s)

10282 McMurtry, Larry. *Anything for Billy.* **1988, Simon & Schuster $18.95 (0-671-64269-5); paper $5.50 (0-671-67091-3).** Recollections of Billy the Kid as told by an Eastern journalist. (REV: BL 9/1/88; NYTBR 10/16/88; PW 8/19/88)

10283 McMurtry, Larry. *Buffalo Girls.* **1990, Simon & Schuster $19.95 (0-671-68518-X).** A fictional re-creation of the Old West through the later life of Calamity Jane. (REV: LJ 10/1/90; NYTBR 10/7/90; TLS 2/15/91)

10284 McMurtry, Larry. *Lonesome Dove.* **1985, Simon & Schuster $21.95 (0-671-50420-7).** A tale of two gunfighters who steal a herd of Mexican cattle and drive them from Texas to Montana. (REV: BL 5/15/85; Newsweek 6/3/85; Time 6/10/85. AWARDS: ALA, 1985; BL, the 1980s; PP:Fiction, 1986)

10285 Matthews, Greg. *Heart of the Country.* **1988, Zebra paper $4.50 (0-8217-2299-9).** A tale of the American West concerning a half-Native American, half-Caucasian man's search for meaning in a changing land. (REV: CSM 6/9/86; LJ 4/15/86; NYTBR 5/4/86)

10286 Meschery, Joanne. *A Gentleman's Guide to the Frontier.* **1990, Simon & Schuster $19.95 (0-671-46369-1).** Two contemporary travelers' journeys across the American West spur family memories and stories from the nineteenth century. (REV: BL 4/1/90; LJ 1/90; NYTBR 6/24/90)

10287 Portis, Charles. *True Grit.* **1969, NAL paper $3.95 (0-451-16022-3).** The search by a 14-year-old girl in Indian territory for her father's killer. (REV: BL 9/1/68; LJ 5/1/68; PW 4/1/68)

10288 Proctor, George W. *Walks Without a Soul.* **1990, Doubleday $14.95 (0-385-24470-3).** A Texas slave, whose wife is captured by Comanches, escapes to freedom to live among Native Americans when he accompanies ranchers in an attempt to regain their property. (REV: BL 8/90; LJ 6/15/90)

10289 Schofield, Susan Clark. *Refugio, They Named You Wrong.* **1991, Algonquin $17.95 (0-945575-60-2).** A portrait of the life of a nineteenth-century Texas man on the run for the murder of his brother. (REV: BL 4/15/91; LJ 3/15/91; PW 1/25/91)

10290 Svee, Gary D. *Sanctuary.* **1990, Walker $18.95 (0-8027-4113-4).** The story of a nineteenth-century itinerant preacher's arrival in a small Montana town. (REV: BL 12/15/90; LJ 11/15/90)

10291 Swarthout, Gordon. *Old Colts.* **1985, Donald I. Fine $15.95 (0-917657-18-7); paper $6.95 (0-917657-70-5).** An aging Bat Masterson and Wyatt Earp plan a bank heist in Dodge City. "A dandy entertainment."—LJ (REV: BL 5/15/85; LJ 6/1/85)

10292 Thomson, David. *Silver Light.* **1990, Knopf $19.95 (0-394-55622-4).** A historical examination of some fictional and real personalities of the American West, as told through a series of time shifts, flashbacks, and personal reminiscences. (REV: BL 3/1/90; LJ 2/15/90; NYTBR 4/1/90)

10293 Welch, James. *Fools Crow.* **1986, Viking $18.95 (0-670-81121-1); Penguin paper $8.95 (0-14-008937-3).** The story of a group of Blackfoot Indians struggling to survive and retain their homeland during the nineteenth century. (REV: Choice 4/87; LJ 10/15/86; NYTBR 11/2/86. AWARDS: LJ, 1986)

AUTHOR INDEX

Authors are arranged alphabetically by last name. Authors' and joint authors' names are followed by book titles—which are also arranged alphabetically—and the text entry number.

Aaron, David. *Agent of Influence,* 10019
  State Scarlet, 10020
Aaron, Henry. *I Had a Hammer,* 3721
Abbey, Edward. *Best of Edward Abbey,* 4338
  Black Sun, 7110
  Fool's Progress, 7111
  Hayduke Lives! 7112
  The Monkey-Wrench Gang, 7113
  One Life at a Time, 4272
Abbott, Jack Henry. *In the Belly of the Beast,* 1741
Abbott, Margot. *The Last Innocent Hour,* 7114
Abbott, Shirley. *Bookmaker's Daughter,* 6081
Abbott, Sidney. *Sappho Was a Right-On Woman,* 725
Abdul-Jabbar, Kareem. *Kareem,* 3678
Abe, Keishi, ed. *Jazz Giants,* 3402
Abe, Kobo. *Ark Sakura,* 6931
  Beyond the Curve, 9520
  Ruined Map, 7115
Abegglen, James C. *Kaisha,* 2931
Abell, Sam. *Stay This Moment,* 3334
Abella, Alex. *Killing of the Saints,* 6219
Abernathy, Ralph D. *And the Walls Came Tumbling Down,* 856
Abish, Walter. *How German Is It,* 7116
Ableman, Paul. *I Hear Voices,* 7117
Abourezk, James G. *Advise and Dissent,* 998
Abrahams, Roger D., ed. *African Folktales,* 1878
  Afro-American Folktales, 1879
Abram, Norma (jt. author). *This Old House Guide to Building and Remodeling Materials,* 2866
Abrams, Richard S. *Will It Hurt the Baby?* 2515
Abramson, Howard S. *Hero in Disgrace,* 4942
Abramson, Jeffrey B. *Electronic Commonwealth,* 880
Abramson, Louis (jt. author). *Thin Kids,* 2323
Aburdene, Patricia (jt. author). *Megatrends 2000,* 674
Abzug, Robert H. *Inside the Vicious Heart,* 5087
Achebe, Chinua. *Anthills of the Savannah,* 7118
  Arrow of God, 7119
  Girls at War and Other Stories, 9521
  Hopes and Impediments, 3875
  Man of the People, 7120
Achebe, Chinua, ed. *African Short Stories,* 9522
Acheson, Dean. *Present at the Creation,* 5876
Achterberg, Jeanne. *Woman as Healer,* 2280
Ackerley, J. R. *My Father and Myself,* 703
Ackerman, Diane. *Jaguar of Sweet Laughter,* 3941
  Moon by Whale Light, 2183
  A Natural History of the Senses, 2296
Ackroyd, Peter. *Chatterton,* 6170
  Dickens, 4494

  First Light, 7121
  Hawksmoor, 8875
Adams, Alice. *After You're Gone,* 9523
  Beautiful Girl, 9524
  Families and Survivors, 7122
  Listening to Billie, 7123
  Return Trips, 9525
  Rich Rewards, 9225
  Second Chance, 7124
  Superior Women, 7125
Adams, Ansel. *Ansel Adams,* 3294
  Examples, 3295
Adams, Ansel (jt. author). *Manzanar,* 5091
Adams, Carol J. *Sexual Politics of Meat,* 263
Adams, Douglas. *Dirk Gently's Holistic Detective Agency,* 9329
  Hitchhiker's Guide to the Galaxy, 9330
  Last Chance to See, 2198
  Long Dark Tea-Time of the Soul, 9331
  Restaurant at the End of the Universe, 9332
  So Long and Thanks for All the Fish, 9333
Adams, James Ring. *Big Fix,* 1068
Adams, Randall. *Adams v. Texas,* 1253
Adams, Richard. *Girl in a Swing,* 9263
  Maia, 6932
  Plague Dogs, 7126
  Watership Down, 6933
Adams, Steven. *The Impressionists,* 3215
Adato, Michelle. *Safety Second,* 1545
Adcock, Dan (jt. author). *Your Child at Play,* 217
Adelson, Alan, ed. *Lodz Ghetto,* 5276
Adler, Bill. *Bill Adler's Chance of a Lifetime,* 2925
Adler, John Morel. *Hunt Out of the Thicket,* 9526
Adler, Margot. *Drawing Down the Moon,* 136
Adler, Mortimer J. *Guidebook to Learning,* 1
  Reforming Education, 1772
Adler, Renata. *Pitch Dark,* 7127
  Reckless Disregard, 1254
Adler, Richard. *You Gotta Have Heart,* 3481
Adler, Stella. *Technique of Acting,* 3605
Adler, Warren. *American Quartet,* 6220
Adoff, Arnold, ed. *Poetry of Black America,* 3942
Ady, Ronald W. *Investment Evaluator,* 1074
Africa News Staff. *Africa News Cookbook,* 2752
Agee, Joel. *Twelve Years,* 4232
Agee, Jonis. *Sweet Eyes,* 7128
Agee, Philip. *On the Run,* 918
Agnon, S. Y. *In the Heart of the Seas,* 6924
  Shira, 8876
  A Simple Story, 7129

Entries 1–6169 are nonfiction; entries 6170–10293 are fiction

Aguero, Kathleen (jt. author). *An Ear to the Ground*, 4006

Aguilera-Malta, Demetrio. *Babelandia*, 7130

Ahlstrom, Sydney E. *Religious History of the American People*, 292

Ai. *Fate*, 3943

Aickman, Robert. *Wine-Dark Sea*, 9264

Aidells, Bruce. *Hot Links and Country Flavors*, 2834

Aird, Catherine. *Last Respects*, 6221

Aisenberg, Nadya. *Women of Academe*, 1808

Aitchison, Stewart. *A Wilderness Called Grand Canyon*, 1959

Aitmatov, Chingiz. *Day Lasts More Than a Hundred Years*, 7131

Ajami, Fouad. *Beirut*, 5513
  Vanished Imam, 410

Akhmatova, Anna. *Complete Poems of Anna Akhmatova*, 4683

Aksyonov, Vassily. *The Burn*, 7132
  In Search of Melancholy Baby, 4684
  Quest for an Island, 7133
  Say Cheese! 7134

Alberts, Laurie. *Tempting Fate*, 7135

Albright, Joseph (jt. author). *Their Promised Land*, 5503

Alcock, John. *Sonoran Desert Summer*, 2129

Alden, John R. *George Washington*, 5783

Alden, Paulette Bates. *Feeding the Eagles*, 9527

Aldiss, Brian. *Frankenstein Unbound*, 6934
  Helliconia Spring, 9334
  Helliconia Summer, 9335
  Helliconia Winter, 9336
  Last Orders, 9337
  Malacia Tapestry, 6935
  Trillion Year Spree, 3910

Aldrin, Buzz. *Men from Earth*, 2568

Alegria, Claribel. *Luisa in Realityland*, 7136

Aleichem, Sholem. *The Bloody Hoax*, 7137
  From the Fair, 4606
  In the Storm, 8877
  Tevye the Dairyman and the Railroad Stories, 9528

Aleshovsky, Yuz. *The Hand*, 10021

Alexander, Ann (jt. author). *Your Child*, 2900

Alexander, Bevin. *Korea*, 5448

Alexander, Caroline. *One Dry Season*, 4873

Alexander, Charles C. *John McGraw*, 3722
  Ty Cobb, 3723

Alexander, Lynne. *Safe Houses*, 6171

Alexander, Paul. *This Rough Magic*, 4149

Alexander, Shana. *Nutcracker*, 1672

Alexander, Terry Pink. *Make Room for Twins*, 2514

Al Khalil, Samir. *Republic of Fear*, 5507

Allard, William Albert. *Photographic Essay*, 3287

Allegre, Claude. *Behavior of the Earth*, 2075

Allen, Benedict. *Who Goes Out in the Midday Sun?* 4931

Allen, Charles. *Lives of the Indian Princes*, 5479

Allen, Charlotte Vale. *Illusions*, 7138

Allen, Dick. *Crash!* 3724

Allen, Joseph P. *Entering Space*, 2569

Allen, Maury. *Roger Maris*, 3725

Allen, Michael Patrick. *Founding Fortunes*, 1008

Allen, Paula Gunn, ed. *Spider Woman's Granddaughters*, 9529

Allen, Richard (jt. author). *Reel Art*, 3578

Allen, Robert G. *Nothing Down*, 1086

Allen, Roger MacBridge. *Torch of Honor*, 9338

Allen, Thomas B. *Guardian of the Wild*, 1111
  Ship of Gold, 10022

War Games, 1367

Allen, Thomas P. (jt. author). *Rickover*, 1381

Allen, Woody. *Side Effects*, 4326
  Without Feathers, 4327

Allende, Isabel. *Eva Luna*, 7139
  House of the Spirits, 7140
  Of Love and Shadows, 7141
  Stories of Eva Luna, 9530

Allman, T. D. *Miami*, 6070

Allman, William F. *Apprentices of Wonder*, 2301

Alpert, Hollis. *Life and Times of Porgy and Bess*, 3467

Alter, Robert. *A Lion for Love*, 4625

Alter, Robert, ed. *Literary Guide to the Bible*, 295

Alther, Lisa. *Kinflicks*, 7142
  Original Sins, 7143

Altieri, Daniel. *Court of the Lions*, 8878

Altman, Lawrence K. *Who Goes First?* 2533

Alvarez, A. *Biggest Game in Town*, 3670
  Offshore, 2539
  Savage God, 264

Alvarez, Everett, Jr. *Chained Eagle*, 5559

Alvarez, Julia. *How the Garcia Girls Lost Their Accents*, 7144

Alvarez, Luis W. *Alvarez*, 2037

Alverson, Marianne. *Under African Sun*, 658

Amado, Jorge. *Dona Flor and Her Two Husbands*, 7145
  Shepherds of the Night, 7146
  Showdown, 7147
  Tent of Miracles, 7148
  Two Deaths of Quincas Wateryell, 7149

Ambler, Eric. *Care of Time*, 10023
  Here Lies, 4504
  Intercom Conspiracy, 10024
  Siege of the Villa Lipp, 6222
  Waiting for Orders, 9531

Ambrose, Stephen E. *Crazy Horse and Custer*, 5857
  Eisenhower, 5921
  Nixon: The Education of a Politician, 5922
  Nixon: Ruin and Recovery, 5923
  Nixon: The Triumph of a Politician, 5924
  Pegasus Bridge, 5088

American Academy of Pediatrics. *Caring for Your Baby and Young Child*, 2882

American Forestry Association Staff, ed. *Shading Our Cities*, 3089

Ames, Louise Bates. *Your Ten-to-Fourteen-Year-Old*, 220

Amichai, Yehuda. *Amen*, 4712
  Great Tranquility, 4713
  Selected Poetry of Yehuda Amichai, 4714

Amiel, Joseph. *Birthright*, 7150
  Deeds, 7151

Amis, Kingsley. *Alteration*, 6936
  Difficulties with Girls, 7152
  Folks Who Live on the Hill, 7153
  Girl, 20, 7154
  Green Man, 9265
  Jake's Thing, 7155
  Memoirs, 4573
  Stanley and the Women, 7156

Amis, Martin. *Einstein's Monsters*, 9532
  London Fields, 7157
  Money, 7158
  Rachel Papers, 7159
  Success, 7160
  Time's Arrow, 7161

Ammons, A. R. *Collected Poems*, 3944

Amos, James. *The Memorial*, 10145

Entries 1–6169 are nonfiction; entries 6170–10293 are fiction

Entries 1–6169 are nonfiction; entries 6170–10293 are fiction

Ashton, Dore, ed. *Twentieth-Century Artists on Art*, 3013

Ashworth, William. *Late, Great Lakes*, 1605

Asimov, Isaac. *Exploding Suns*, 2024
  Fantastic Voyage, 9343
  Fantastic Voyage II, 9344
  Foundation and Earth, 9345
  Foundation's Edge, 9346
  Nemesis, 9347
  Nightfall, 9351
  Prelude to Foundation, 9348
  Relativity of Wrong, 1990
  Robots and Empire, 9349
  Robots of Dawn, 9350

Aslet, Clive. *Last Country Houses*, 3131

Aslett, Don. *Stain Buster's Bible*, 2879

Asman, David, ed. *Wall Street Journal on Management*, 2940

Asprey, Robert B. *Frederick the Great*, 5229

Asscher-Pinkhof, Clara. *Star Children*, 10148

Astley, Thea. *Beachmasters*, 7181
  Hunting the Wild Pineapple, 9538
  It's Raining in Mango, 8883
  Reaching Tin River, 7182
  Two by Astley, 7183

Astor, Brooke. *Last Blossom in the Plum Tree*, 8884

Astor, Gerald. *"Last" Nazi*, 5230

Astrachan, Anthony. *How Men Feel*, 547

Atkinson, Brooks. *Broadway 1900–1970*, 3606

Atkinson, Rick. *Long Grey Line*, 1326

Atlas, James. *Delmore Schwartz*, 4129

Attansio, A. A. *Last Legends of Earth*, 9352

Attenborough, David. *First Eden*, 1946
  Living Planet, 2109

Attoe, David. *Lion at the Door*, 7184

Atwood, Margaret. *Bluebeard's Egg and Other Stories*, 9539
  Bodily Harm, 7185
  Cat's Eye, 7186
  The Handmaid's Tale, 6940
  Lady Oracle, 7187
  Life Before Man, 7188
  Selected Poems II, 3952
  Surfacing, 7189
  Wilderness Tips, 9540

Aubrey, Charles A. *Team Work*, 2933

Auchincloss, Louis. *Diary of a Yuppie*, 7190
  Fellow Passengers, 9541
  Golden Calves, 7191
  Honorable Men, 7192
  House of the Prophet, 7193
  Love Without Wings, 4305
  Partners, 9542
  Skinny Island, 9543
  Vanderbilt Era, 6025
  Watchfires, 8885

Auden, W. H. *Collected Poems*, 4427
  Forewords and Afterwords, 3876

Auel, Jean M. *Clan of the Cave Bear*, 8886
  Mammoth Hunters, 8887
  Valley of Horses, 8888

Auerbach, Nina. *Communities of Women*, 4485
  Ellen Terry, 3620

Auerbach, Paul S. *Medicine for the Outdoors*, 2369

Auerbach, Red. *On and Off the Court*, 3679

Auletta, Ken. *Greed and Glory on Wall Street*, 1095
  Three Blind Mice, 1837
  Underclass, 1529

Aunapu, Greg (jt. author). *Ringmaster*, 3511

Auster, Paul. *City of Glass*, 6224
  Ghosts, 6225
  In the Country of Last Things, 6941
  Locked Room, 7194
  Moon Palace, 7195
  The Music of Chance, 7196

Austin, Doris Jean. *After the Garden*, 7197

Austin, James (jt. author). *How to Find Help for a Troubled Kid*, 1520

Austin, Nancy K. (jt. author). *A Passion for Excellence*, 2950

Avedon, John F. *In Exile from the Land of the Snows*, 5446

Aveni, Anthony. *Empires of Time*, 2029

Avineri, Shlomo. *Making of Modern Zionism*, 5519

Avins, Mimi (jt. author). *Angela Lansbury's Positive Moves*, 2339

Avis, Warren. *Take a Chance to Be First*, 2910

Avishai, Bernard. *Tragedy of Zionism*, 5520

Axcell, Claudia. *Simple Foods for the Pack*, 2688

Axelrod, Alan. *Art of the Golden West*, 3079

Ayer, Alfred J. *Thomas Paine*, 799
  Voltaire, 4626

Ayling, Stanley. *Edmund Burke*, 5167

Azbel, Mark Ya. *Refusenik*, 847

Babson, Marian. *Murder, Murder, Little Star*, 6226
  Twelve Deaths of Christmas, 6227

Bacall, Lauren. *Lauren Bacall by Myself*, 3514

Bach, Steven. *Final Cut*, 3515

Bache, Ellyn. *Safe Passage*, 7198

Bachmann, Ingeborg. *Malina*, 7199
  Thirtieth Year, 9544

Backschneider, Paula R. *Daniel Defoe*, 4491

Badanes, Jerome. *Final Opus of Leon Solomon*, 10149

Baden, Michael. *Unnatural Death*, 2349

Baetjer, Katherine (jt. author). *Canaletto*, 3266

Baez, Joan. *And a Voice to Sing With*, 3380

Bagdikian, Ben H. *Media Monopoly*, 464

Baggett, Nancy. *International Chocolate Cookbook*, 2816

Bagley, Desmond. *Enemy*, 10028

Bagley, Michael. *Plutonium Factor*, 10029

Bagley, T. H. (jt. author). *KGB*, 1324

Baida, Peter. *Poor Richard's Legacy*, 261

Bailey, Anthony. *Major Andre*, 8889
  Outer Banks, 4911

Bailey, George. *Galileo's Children*, 1199

Bailey, Janet. *Keeping Food Fresh*, 2687

Bailey, Lee. *Lee Bailey's Southern Food and Plantation Houses*, 2755

Bailhache, Pierette Pompon (jt. author). *Terence Conran's France*, 4829

Bailly, Jean-Christophe. *Duchamp*, 3032

Bailyn, Bernard. *Ideological Origins of the American Revolution*, 5765
  Ordeal of Thomas Hutchinson, 5766
  Peopling of British North America, 5762
  Voyagers to the West, 523

Bainbridge, Beryl. *Mum and Mr. Armitage*, 9545

Bair, Deirdre. *Simone de Beauvoir*, 4630

Baker, Houston A., Jr. *Modernism and the Harlem Renaissance*, 3912

Baker, Kenneth. *Minimalism*, 3072

Baker, Nicholson. *The Mezzanine*, 7200
  Room Temperature, 7201
  U and I, 4233

Entries 1–6169 are nonfiction; entries 6170–10293 are fiction

Entries 1–6169 are nonfiction; entries 6170–10293 are fiction

Entries 1–6169 are nonfiction; entries 6170–10293 are fiction

Entries 1–6169 are nonfiction; entries 6170–10293 are fiction

Entries 1–6169 are nonfiction; entries 6170–10293 are fiction

Entries 1–6169 are nonfiction; entries 6170–10293 are fiction

Entries 1–6169 are nonfiction; entries 6170–10293 are fiction

Entries 1–6169 are nonfiction; entries 6170–10293 are fiction

Entries 1–6169 are nonfiction; entries 6170–10293 are fiction

Entries 1–6169 are nonfiction; entries 6170–10293 are fiction

Entries 1–6169 are nonfiction; entries 6170–10293 are fiction

Entries 1–6169 are nonfiction; entries 6170–10293 are fiction

Entries 1–6169 are nonfiction; entries 6170–10293 are fiction

Entries 1–6169 are nonfiction; entries 6170–10293 are fiction

Entries 1–6169 are nonfiction; entries 6170–10293 are fiction

Crease, Robert P. *Second Creation*, 2061
Creasy, Rosalind. *Cooking from the Garden*, 2589
  Earthly Delights, 2590
Creely, Robert. *Collected Poems of Robert Creely, 1945–1975*, 3977
  Selected Poems, 3978
Creese, Walter L. *Crowning of the American Landscape*, 3083
Crespo, Michael. *Watercolor Day by Day*, 3204
Crewdson, John. *By Silence Betrayed*, 1509
Crews, Harry. *Body*, 7492
  Knockout Artist, 9997
Crichton, Michael. *Andromeda Strain*, 9399
  Great Train Robbery, 8933
  Jurassic Park, 6975
  Sphere, 9400
  Terminal Man, 9401
  Travels, 4241
Crichton, Robert. *Secret of Santa Vittoria*, 10173
Criddle, Joan D. *To Destroy You Is No Loss*, 5554
Crisp, N. J. *Ninth Circle*, 10049
Critchfield, Richard. *An American Looks at Britain*, 5177
  Those Days, 4971
  Villages, 785
Critchley, T. A. (jt. author). *Maul and the Pear Tree*, 1694
Croizard, Maurice (jt. author). *Terence Conran's France*, 4829
Cromartie, Warren. *Slugging It Out in Japan*, 3737
Crompton, Louis. *Byron and Greek Love*, 4431
Crone, Moira. *A Period of Confinement*, 7493
Cronin, Vincent. *Paris on the Eve*, 5308
Cronley, Jay. *Walking Papers*, 7494
Cronon, William. *Changes in the Land*, 6014
Cronyn, Hume. *A Terrible Liar*, 3616
Crosby, David. *Long Time Gone*, 3435
Crosby, Faye J. *Juggling*, 560
Crosby, John. *Men in Arms*, 10050
  Party of the Year, 6353
Cross, Amanda. *Death in a Tenured Position*, 6354
  The James Joyce Murder, 6355
  Poetic Justice, 6356
  Question of Max, 6357
  Theban Mysteries, 6358
  A Trap for Fools, 6359
Crouch, Stanley. *Notes of a Hanging Judge*, 631
Crouch, Tom D. *Bishop's Boys*, 2558
Crow Dog, Mary. *Lakota Woman*, 6108
Crowl, Philip A. *Intelligent Traveler's Guide to Historic Scotland*, 4822
Crowley, John. *Aegypt*, 6976
  Novelty, 6977
Crowley, Patricia. *Not My Child*, 1510
Cruickshank, Dan. *Life in the Georgian City*, 5168
Crumley, James. *Dancing Bear*, 6360
  Wrong Case, 6361
Cruse, Harold. *Plural but Equal*, 646
Cruz, Arturo. *Memoirs of a Counter-Revolutionary*, 5700
Csikzentmihaly, Mihaly. *Flow*, 195
Culhane, John. *American Circus*, 3512
Cullen, Brian. *What Niall Saw*, 6978
Cullen, Countee. *My Soul's High Song*, 3979
Cullen, Robert. *Soviet Sources*, 10051
  Twilight of Empire, 5351
Culler, Jonathan. *Roland Barthes*, 1896
Culley, Margo, ed. *A Day at a Time*, 4967
Cunningham, Ann Marie (jt. author). *Ryan White*, 1456
Cunningham, Laura. *Sleeping Arrangements*, 4392

Cunningham, Marion. *Fannie Farmer Baking Book*, 2840
  Fannie Farmer Cookbook, 2705
Cunningham, Merce. *Dancer and the Dance*, 3655
Cunningham, Michael. *A Home at the End of the World*, 7495
Cunningham, Noble E., Jr. *In Pursuit of Reason*, 5796
Curb, Rosemary, ed. *Lesbian Nuns*, 320
Curnonsky, pseud. *Larousse Traditional French Cooking*, 2768
Curran, Jim. *K2*, 3807
Currey, Richard. *First Light*, 10174
  Wars of Heaven, 9641
Currie, Ellen. *Available Light*, 7496
Currie, Elliot. *Confronting Crime*, 1740
Curry, Hayden, and Denis Clifford. *Legal Guide for Lesbian and Gay Couples*, 728
Curtis, Jack. *Glory*, 6362
Curtis, William J. R. *Le Corbusier*, 3091
Cussler, Clive. *Treasure*, 7497
Cvancara, Alan M. *Sleuthing Fossils*, 2084

Dabney, Virginia Bell. *Once There Was a Farm*, 6058
Dadie, Bernard Binlin. *Black Cloth*, 1886
Dahl, Linda. *Stormy Weather*, 3408
Dahl, Roald. *Ah, Sweet Mystery of Life*, 9642
  Boy, 4510
  Going Solo, 4511
Dahl, Robert A. *Democracy and Its Critics*, 825
Dahlberg, Edward. *Leafless American and Other Writings*, 4375
Dahlby, Tracy (jt. author). *M.D.*, 2283
Dalai Lama. *Freedom in Exile*, 387
Dalby, Lisa C. *Geisha*, 706
Daley, Robert. *A Faint Cold Fear*, 7498
  Hands of a Stranger, 6363
  Man with a Gun, 6364
  Prince of the City, 1569
Dallek, Robert. *American Style of Foreign Policy*, 963
  Lone Star Rising, 5943
Dallin, Alexander. *Black Box*, 909
Dally, Ann. *Inventing Motherhood*, 741
Dalrymple, Helen (jt. author). *Advertising in America*, 2961
Daly, Herman E. *For the Common Good*, 1009
Daly, Mary. *Beyond God the Father*, 433
  Pure Lust, 561
  Webster's First New Intergalactic Wickedary of the English Language, 562
Damerell, Reginald G. *Education's Smoking Gun*, 1770
Damrosch, Barbara. *Garden Primer*, 2591
Dan, Uri. *To the Promised Land*, 5523
Dana, Nancy. *Successful Breastfeeding*, 2902
Dana, Nancy (jt. author). *Dr. Mom*, 2894
Dance, Stanley. *World of Count Basie*, 3409
Daniel, Mark. *Unbridled*, 6365
Daniels, Robert V. *Red October*, 5352
Daniloff, Nicholas. *Two Lives, One Russia*, 5353
Danilova, Alexandra. *Choura*, 3639
Dann, Patty. *Mermaids*, 7499
Dannen, Fredrick. *Hit Men*, 1154
Danto, Arthur C. *Connections to the World*, 116
  Encounters and Reflections, 3015
Danvers, Dennis. *Wilderness*, 9278
Dao, Bei. *August Sleepwalker*, 4718
Dardis, Tom. *Some Time in the Sun*, 3914
Darling, David. *Deep Time*, 2005
Darlington, David. *Angels' Visits*, 2673

Entries 1–6169 are nonfiction; entries 6170–10293 are fiction

Entries 1–6169 are nonfiction; entries 6170–10293 are fiction

Entries 1–6169 are nonfiction; entries 6170–10293 are fiction

Entries 1–6169 are nonfiction; entries 6170–10293 are fiction

Waterfall, 7581
Draper, Robert. *Rolling Stone Magazine*, 29
Draper, Theodore. *A Present of Things Past*, 966
   A Very Thin Line, 5947
Dray, Philip (jt. author). *We Are Not Afraid*, 6074
Drew, Bettina. *Nelson Algren*, 4203
Drew, David. *Kurt Weill*, 3360
Drew, Eileen. *Blue Taxis*, 9655
Drew, Elizabeth. *Election Journal*, 883
Drewal, Henry. *Yoruba*, 3138
Drosnin, Michael. *Citizen Hughes*, 1172
Drower, Margaret S. *Flinders Petrie*, 4985
Drucker, Peter F. *Frontiers of Management*, 2922
   Innovation and Entrepreneurship, 2943
   Managing in Turbulent Times, 2923
   Managing the Nonprofit Organization, 2928
   New Realities, 4764
Drummond, John Keith. *'Tis the Season to Be Dying*,
   6386
Drury, Allen. *Return to Thebes*, 8951
Drury, Bob (jt. author). *Incident at Howard Beach*, 1693
Druyan, Ann (jt. author). *Comet*, 2022
Dryden, Ken. *Game*, 3822
Drysdale, Don. *Once a Bum, Always a Dodger*, 3738
D'Souza, Dinesh. *Illiberal Education*, 1762
Dubal, David. *Reflections from the Keyboard*, 3492
Duberman, Martin. *Black Mountain*, 1816
   Cures, 551
   Mother Earth, 1132
   Paul Robeson, 3506
Duberman, Martin, ed. *Hidden from History*, 729
Duberstein, Larry. *Marriage Hearse*, 7582
Dubinsky, Rostislav. *Stormy Applause*, 3496
Dublin, Max. *Futurehype*, 495
Dubofsky, Melvyn. *Big Bill Haywood*, 1045
Dubos, Rene. *Wooing of Earth*, 509
Dubos, Rene (jt. author). *Only One Earth*, 430
Dubosq, Genevieve. *My Longest Night*, 5027
DuBrin, Andrew J. *Winning Office Politics*, 2911
Dubus, Andre. *Broken Vessels*, 4242
   The Last Worthless Evening, 7583
   Selected Stories, 9656
   The Times Are Never So Bad, 9657
   Voices from the Moon, 7584
Dubus, Andre, III. *Cage Keeper and Other Stories*, 9658
Duby, Georges. *Age of the Cathedrals*, 3036
Duby, Georges, ed. *History of Private Life, Vol. 2*, 4741
Ducornet, Rikki. *Entering Fire*, 8952
Duff, Susan. *Post-Pregnancy Diet*, 2324
Duffy, Brian (jt. author). *Fall of Pan Am 103*, 1559
Dufresne, John. *Way That Water Enters Stone*, 9659
Duggan, William. *Great Thirst*, 8953
Dugger, Ronnie. *Politician*, 5948
Duke, Dennis. *America's Glorious Quilts*, 3182
Dukore, Margaret Mitchell. *Bloom*, 7585
Dull, Jonathan R. *A Diplomatic History of the American
   Revolution*, 5771
Dumas, Henry. *Goodbye, Sweetwater*, 9660
Duncan, Dayton. *Grass Roots*, 878
Duncan, Robert Lipscomb. *In the Enemy Camp*, 7586
Dunlap, David W. *On Broadway*, 6031
Dunlap, Helen Duff (jt. author). *Why Johnny Can't Con-
   centrate*, 186
Dunlap, Susan. *A Dinner to Die For*, 6387
Dunlap, Thomas R. *Saving America's Wildlife*, 2657
Dunlop, Lane, ed. *A Late Chrysanthemum*, 9661
Dunn, Katherine. *Geek Love*, 7587

Dunn, Stephen. *Between Angels*, 3988
   Landscape at the End of the Century, 3989
   Local Time, 3990
Dunne, Dominick. *An Inconvenient Woman*, 6388
   People Like Us, 7588
   Two Mrs. Grenvilles, 7589
Dunne, Gerald T. *Hugo Black and the Judicial Revolu-
   tion*, 1289
Dunne, John Gregory. *Dutch Shea, Jr.*, 7590
   Harp, 4345
   Red, White and Blue, 7591
   True Confessions, 6389
Dunnett, Dorothy. *Niccolo Rising*, 8954
   Race of Scorpions, 8955
   Spring of the Rain, 8956
Dunning, Joan. *Loon*, 2216
Dunphy, Jack. *Murderous McLaughlins*, 8957
Dupee, F. W. *King of the Cats*, 3878
DuPont, Diana C. (jt. author). *Photography*, 3335
Dupree, Nathalie. *New Southern Cooking*, 2773
Durand, Arthur A. *Stalag Luft III*, 5102
Durant, Ariel (jt. author). *Rousseau and Revolution*,
   4761
Durant, Will. *Rousseau and Revolution*, 4761
Duranti, Francesca. *Happy Ending*, 7592
Duras, Marguerite. *Blue Eyes, Black Hair*, 7593
   Emily L, 7594
   The Lover, 6183
   War, 5309
Durban, Pam. *All Set about with Fever Trees and Other
   Stories*, 9662
Durgnat, Raymond. *King Vidor, American*, 3533
Durham, Frank. *Frame of the Universe*, 2006
Durham, Michael S. *Mid-Atlantic States*, 4904
   Powerful Days, 848
Durrell, Gerald. *Amateur Naturalist*, 2110
Durrell, Lee (jt. author). *Amateur Naturalist*, 2110
Durrenmatt, Friedrich. *Assignment*, 7595
Durso, Joseph. *Baseball and the American Dream*, 3739
Dwivedi, Sharada (jt. author). *Lives of the Indian
   Princes*, 5479
Dwork, Deborah. *Children with a Star*, 5028
Dworkin, Andrea. *Intercourse*, 709
   Letters from a War Zone, 594
Dworkin, Ronald M. *Law's Empire*, 1215
   A Matter of Principle, 1216
Dwyer, John M. *Body at War*, 2374
Dybek, Stuart. *Childhood and Other Neighborhoods*,
   9663
Dychtwald, Ken. *Age Wave*, 541
Dylan, Bob. *Lyrics*, 3438
Dyson, Freeman J. *Infinite in All Directions*, 1936
   Weapons and Hope, 910

Earley, Pete. *Family of Spies*, 925
   Hot House, 1743
Early, Jack. *Donato and Daughter*, 6390
Easterlin, Richard. *Birth and Fortune*, 520
Easterman, Daniel. *Brotherhood of the Tomb*, 10059
Easton, Robert (jt. author). *Native American Architec-
   ture*, 3112
Eaton, Jan. *Encyclopedia of Sewing Techniques*, 2868
Eban, Abba. *Heritage*, 4742
Eberhart, Richard. *Collected Poems*, 3991
   Of Poetry and Poets, 3895
Eberstadt, Fernanda. *Isaac and His Devils*, 7596
Ebert, Roger. *A Kiss Is Still a Kiss*, 3534

Entries 1–6169 are nonfiction; entries 6170–10293 are fiction

Entries 1–6169 are nonfiction; entries 6170–10293 are fiction

Ende, Michael. *Momo*, 6984
  Neverending Story, 6985
Endo, Shusaku. *The Samurai*, 8964
  Scandal, 7616
  Stained Glass Elegies, 9667
  Wonderful Fool, 8965
Engel, Alan. *Variant*, 6986
Engel, Monroe. *Fish*, 7617
Engelmann, Bernt. *In Hitler's Germany*, 5237
Engelmann, Larry. *Goddess and the American Girl*, 3709
Engh, M. J. *Arslan*, 9409
English, T. J. *Westies*, 1642
Enright, D. J., ed. *Oxford Book of Death*, 112
Enzensberger, Hans Magnus. *Europe, Europe*, 4816
Ephron, Delia. *Funny Sauce*, 4279
Ephron, Nora. *Heartburn*, 7618
Eprile, Tony. *Temporary Sojourner and Other South African Stories*, 9668
Epstein, Edward Jay. *Agency of Fear*, 1594
Epstein, Helen. *Children of the Holocaust*, 5031
Epstein, Joseph. *Ambition*, 463
  Familiar Territory, 5950
  Goldin Boys, 9669
  A Line Out for a Walk, 102
  Partial Payments, 103
  Plausible Prejudices, 3916
Epstein, Leslie. *King of the Jews*, 6184
  Pinto and Sons, 8966
Epstein, Seymour. *A Special Destiny*, 8967
Erdoes, Richard, ed. *American Indian Myths and Legends*, 1888
Erdoes, Richard (jt. author). *Lakota Woman*, 6108
Erdrich, Louise. *Baptism of Desire*, 3992
  Beet Queen, 7619
  Love Medicine, 7620
  Tracks, 7621
Erdrich, Louise (jt. author). *Crown of Columbus*, 7568
Erffa, Helmut Von. *Paintings of Benjamin West*, 3226
Erickson, Carolly. *Bloody Mary*, 5213
  Bonnie Prince Charles, 5169
  Mistress Anne, 5214
  Our Tempestuous Day, 5170
Erickson, Steve. *Tours of the Black Clock*, 7622
Erikson, Erik H. *Gandhi's Truth*, 250
Ernaux, Annie. *A Woman's Story*, 6185
Escott, Colin. *Good Rockin' Tonight*, 3440
Esperti, Robert A. *Loving Trust*, 1277
Esposito, John L. *Islam*, 408
Esposito, Mary Ann. *Ciao Italia*, 2774
Espy, Willard R. *Oysterville*, 6134
Estaver, Paul. *His Third, Her Second*, 7623
Estleman, Loren D. *Bloody Season*, 10268
  Downriver, 6401
  Midnight Man, 6402
  Motor City Blues, 6403
  Silent Thunder, 6404
Etchison, Dennis, ed. *Cutting Edge*, 9280
Ettinger, Elzbieta. *Rosa Luxemburg*, 1130
Evans, Eli N. *Judah P. Benjamin*, 5823
Evans, Howard Ensign. *Pleasures of Entomology*, 2204
Evans, Mari, ed. *Black Women Writers, 1950–1980*, 3932
Evans, Michelle. *Fearless Cooking for Crowds*, 2851
Evans, Peter. *Ari*, 1851
Evans, Richard. *Open Tennis*, 3710
Evans, Sara M. *Born for Liberty*, 565
Evans, Walker (jt. author). *Walker Evans*, 3338
Everage, Dame Edna. *My Gorgeous Life*, 4515

Everett, Melissa. *Breaking Ranks*, 926
Evers, Christoper. *Old House Doctor*, 2860
Ewart, Gavin. *Gavin Ewart Show*, 4432
Ewart-Biggs, Jane. *Pay, Pack and Follow*, 5178
Ewen, Stuart. *All Consuming Images*, 693
Ewing, David W. *Inside the Harvard Business School*, 2908
Ewing, Russ (jt. author). *Buried Dreams*, 1677
Exley, Frederick. *A Fan's Notes*, 9999
  Last Notes from Home, 7624
  Pages from a Cold Island, 4243
Eyman, Scott. *Mary Pickford*, 3536

Fabre, Michel. *From Harlem to Paris*, 3933
Fackenheim, Emil L. *What Is Judaism?* 395
Faderman, Lillian. *Surpassing the Love of Men*, 711
Fadiman, Clifton, ed. *Living Philosophies*, 129
Fairbank, John King. *Great Chinese Revolution*, 5403
Fairley, John. *Arthur C. Clarke's World of Strange Powers*, 139
Falco, Edward. *Plato at Scratch Daniels and Other Stories*, 9670
Falk, Candace A. *Love, Anarchy and Emma Goldman*, 1133
Falkner, David. *Nine Sides of the Diamond*, 3740
  Short Season, 3741
Fall, Bernard. *Last Reflections on a War*, 5573
Fallis, Greg. *How to Be Your Own Detective*, 1570
Fallows, James. *More Like Us*, 5951
  National Defense, 1335
Faludi, Susan. *Backlash*, 595
Fante, John. *1933 Was a Bad Year*, 10000
Farber, David. *Chicago '68*, 6090
Farber, Stephen. *Outrageous Conduct*, 1258
Farmer, James. *Lay Bare the Heart*, 859
Farmer, Philip José. *Dayworld*, 9410
  Fabulous Riverboat, 9411
  Magic Labyrinth, 9412
Farquhar, John W. *Last Puff*, 2345
Farrell, J. G. *Siege of Krisnapur*, 8968
  Troubles, 8969
Farrell, Suzanne. *Holding On to the Air*, 3642
Farris, John. *Son of the Endless Night*, 9281
Farwell, Byron. *Eminent Victorian Soldiers*, 1336
  The Great War in Africa, 1914–1918, 5008
  Queen Victoria's Little Wars, 5224
Fassett, Kaffe. *Glorious Knits*, 3179
Fast, Howard. *Being Red*, 4205
  Confession of Joe Cullen, 7625
  The Outsider, 7626
Faux, Marian. *Roe vs. Wade*, 1259
Favier, Jean. *World of Chartres*, 3124
Fay, Francesca C. *Childbearing after 35*, 2506
Fayer, Steve (jt. author). *Voices of Freedom*, 849
Featherstone, Joseph. *Schools Where Children Learn*, 1792
Feazel, Charles T. *Grizzly Years*, 2236
Fehrenbacher, Don E. *Dred Scott Case*, 1271
Feiden, Karyn. *Hope and Help for Chronic Fatigue Syndrome*, 2427
Fein, Leonard. *Where Are We?* 620
Feinberg, David. *Eighty-Sixed*, 7627
  Spontaneous Combustion, 7628
Feinstein, John. *Hard Courts*, 3711
  A Season Inside, 3682
  A Season on the Brink, 3683
Feis, Herbert. *Between War and Peace*, 5032

Entries 1–6169 are nonfiction; entries 6170–10293 are fiction

Entries 1–6169 are nonfiction; entries 6170–10293 are fiction

Entries 1–6169 are nonfiction; entries 6170–10293 are fiction

Entries 1–6169 are nonfiction; entries 6170–10293 are fiction

Entries 1–6169 are nonfiction; entries 6170–10293 are fiction

Entries 1–6169 are nonfiction; entries 6170–10293 are fiction

Entries 1–6169 are nonfiction; entries 6170–10293 are fiction

Entries 1–6169 are nonfiction; entries 6170–10293 are fiction

Entries 1–6169 are nonfiction; entries 6170–10293 are fiction

Entries 1–6169 are nonfiction; entries 6170–10293 are fiction

Entries 1–6169 are nonfiction; entries 6170–10293 are fiction

Entries 1–6169 are nonfiction; entries 6170–10293 are fiction

Hebert, Ernest. *A Little More Than Kin*, 7825
  Live Free or Die, 7826
Hecht, Ann. *Art of the Loom*, 3176
Hecht, Anthony. *Transparent Man*, 4011
Hecht, Helen. *Simple Pleasures*, 2715
Hecht, Susanna. *Fate of the Forest*, 2136
Heckscher, August. *Woodrow Wilson*, 5892
Hederman, Angela (jt. author). *A Tuscan in My Kitchen*, 2790
Heffernan, William. *Ritual*, 6512
Hegi, Ursula. *Floating in My Mother's Palm*, 7827
Heilbroner, David. *Rough Justice*, 1269
Heilbroner, Robert L. *Marxism*, 1126
  Nature and Logic of Capitalism, 1012
Heilbrun, Carolyn G. *Writing a Woman's Life*, 3857
Heilman, Grant. *Farm*, 2583
Hein, Christopher. *Distant Lover*, 7828
Heinemann, Larry. *Close Quarters*, 10193
  Paco's Story, 7829
Heinlein, Robert A. *Cat Who Walks Through Walls*, 9421
  Grumbles from the Grave, 4248
  Job, 9422
  The Moon Is a Harsh Mistress, 9423
  Past Through Tomorrow, 9424
  Time Enough for Love, 9425
Heinrich, Bernd. *Bumblebee Economics*, 2207
  In a Patch of Fireweed, 2113
  Ravens in Winter, 2222
Heisenberg, Werner. *Physics and Beyond*, 2066
Helfand, William H. (jt. author). *Pharmacy*, 1407
Heller, Joseph. *God Knows*, 9018
  Good as Gold, 7830
  No Laughing Matter, 2412
  Picture This, 9019
  Something Happened, 7831
Heller, Mikhail. *Utopia in Power*, 5359
Heller, Robert. *Decision Makers*, 1190
Heller, Steve. *Automotive History of Lucky Kellerman*, 7832
Hellerstein, David. *Battles of Life and Death*, 2271
Hellman, Lillian. *Pentimento*, 4171
  An Unfinished Woman, 4173
Helprin, Mark. *Ellis Island and Other Stories*, 9724
  A Soldier of the Great War, 7833
  Winter's Tale, 9020
Helwig, David. *Of Desire*, 7834
Helyar, John (jt. author). *Barbarians at the Gate*, 1192
Hemenway, Robert E. *Zora Neale Hurston*, 4190
Hemingway, Ernest. *Dangerous Summer*, 3510
  Garden of Eden, 7835
  Islands in the Stream, 7836
Hemingway, Gregory. *Papa*, 4191
Hemming, John. *Amazon Frontier*, 6143
  Conquest of the Incas, 6155
Hemming, Robert (jt. author). *Tales of the Iron Road*, 617
Hemming, Roy. *Discovering Great Music*, 3352
Hempel, Amy. *At the Gates of the Animal Kingdom*, 9725
Hemphill, Paul. *Me and the Boy*, 746
Henderson, Bill, ed. *Rotten Reviews*, 23
Henderson, Mary C. *Theatre in America*, 3611
Hendin, Herbert. *Age of Sensation*, 221
  Suicide in America, 1459
Hendin, Josephine. *Vulnerable People*, 4249
Hendricks, G. C. *Second War*, 10194
Hendrickson, Robert. *American Talk*, 1908
Henley, Patricia. *Friday Night at Silver Star*, 9726

Hennessee, Judith A. (jt. author). *Unnatural Death*, 2349
Hennessey, James J. *American Catholics*, 360
Henry, Alan. *Fifty Famous Motor Races*, 3812
Henry, Jules. *Pathways to Madness*, 2429
Hensel, Bruce. *Smart Medicine*, 2308
Hensley, Tim (jt. author). *Steam, Steel and Stars*, 1848
Henson, Robert. *Transports and Disgraces*, 9727
Hentoff, Nat. *Boston Boy*, 4397
Hepburn, Katharine. *Making of "The African Queen,"* 3548
  Me, 3549
Herbert, Frank. *Chapterhouse*, 9426
  Children of Dune, 9427
  Dosadi Experiment, 9428
  God Emperor of Dune, 9429
  Heretics of Dune, 9430
  White Plague, 9431
Herbert, James. *Moon*, 9288
Herbert, John. *Inside Christie's*, 1822
Herbert, Robert L. *Impressionism*, 3247
Herbert, Wally. *Noose of Laurels*, 4945
Herbert, Zbigniew. *Barbarian in the Garden*, 5286
Herbst, Josephine. *Starched Blue Sky of Spain*, 4208
Herken, Gregg. *Counsels of War*, 1338
Herley, Richard. *Penal Colony*, 7837
Herman, Michelle. *Missing*, 7838
Herman, Stephen P. *Parent vs. Parent*, 1279
Herman, Woody. *Woodchopper's Ball*, 3416
Hermlin, Stephen. *Evening Light*, 4588
Hernandez, Gilbert. *Reticent Heart*, 3151
Hernandez, Jaime. *Lost Women and Other Stories*, 3152
Hernon, Peter. *Earthly Remains*, 7000
Herr, Michael. *Dispatches*, 5579
  Walter Winchell, 6192
Herr, Pamela. *Jessie Benton Fremont*, 5814
Herrera, Hayden. *Frida*, 3274
  Frida Kahlo, 3275
Herrero, Stephen. *Bear Attacks*, 2335
Herrick, Amy. *At the Sign of the Naked Waiter*, 7839
Herrick, William. *Hermanos!* 10195
Herring, Robert. *McCampbell's War*, 7840
Herriot, James. *James Herriot's Dog Stories*, 2639
Herrnstein, Richard J. (jt. author). *Crime and Human Nature*, 1736
Herron, Carolivia. *Thereafter Johnnie*, 7841
Hersey, John. *Antonietta*, 9021
  Blues, 3841
  The Call, 9022
  Fling and Other Stories, 9728
  Life Sketches, 4960
Hersh, Reuben (jt. author). *Descartes' Dream*, 1981
  Mathematical Experience, 1982
Hersh, Seymour. *Price of Power*, 973
  Target Is Destroyed, 4767
Hertsgaard, Mark. *On Bended Knee*, 5958
Hertz, Sue. *Caught in the Crossfire*, 1602
Hertzberg, Arthur. *Jews in America*, 623
Herzlich, Claudine. *Illness and Self in Society*, 694
Herzog, Chaim. *Arab-Israeli Wars*, 5501
Herzstein, Robert E. *Roosevelt and Hitler*, 5040
  Waldheim, 5268
Hesburgh, Theodore M. *God, Country, Notre Dame*, 1811
Hess, Alan. *Googie*, 3121
Hess, John L. *Taste of America*, 2667
Hess, Karen (jt. author). *Taste of America*, 2667
Hession, Charles H. *John Maynard Keynes*, 1013
Hetzer, Linda. *Fancy Folds*, 2852

Entries 1–6169 are nonfiction; entries 6170–10293 are fiction

Entries 1–6169 are nonfiction; entries 6170–10293 are fiction

Entries 1–6169 are nonfiction; entries 6170–10293 are fiction

Entries 1–6169 are nonfiction; entries 6170–10293 are fiction

Entries 1–6169 are nonfiction; entries 6170–10293 are fiction

Entries 1–6169 are nonfiction; entries 6170–10293 are fiction

Entries 1–6169 are nonfiction; entries 6170–10293 are fiction

Entries 1–6169 are nonfiction; entries 6170–10293 are fiction

Entries 1–6169 are nonfiction; entries 6170–10293 are fiction

Entries 1–6169 are nonfiction; entries 6170–10293 are fiction

Entries 1–6169 are nonfiction; entries 6170–10293 are fiction

Entries 1–6169 are nonfiction; entries 6170–10293 are fiction

Entries 1–6169 are nonfiction; entries 6170–10293 are fiction

Entries 1–6169 are nonfiction; entries 6170–10293 are fiction

Entries 1–6169 are nonfiction; entries 6170–10293 are fiction

Entries 1–6169 are nonfiction; entries 6170–10293 are fiction

Entries 1–6169 are nonfiction; entries 6170–10293 are fiction

Entries 1–6169 are nonfiction; entries 6170–10293 are fiction

Entries 1–6169 are nonfiction; entries 6170–10293 are fiction

Snow Leopard, 4851
Mattiessen, Peter. *Killing Mister Watson*, 9085
Matusow, Allen J. *Unraveling of America*, 807
Maupin, Armistead. *Sure of You*, 8196
Maurer, Charles (jt. author). *World of the Newborn*, 213
Maurer, Daphne. *World of the Newborn*, 213
Maurer, Harry. *Strange Ground*, 5589
Mauries, Patrick. *Fornasetti*, 3171
Maurois, Andre. *Prometheus*, 4616
Maxwell, William. *Ancestors*, 4974
   Billie Dyer and Other Stories, 9814
May, Ernest R. (jt. author). *Thinking in Time*, 1309
May, Julian. *Adversary*, 7038
   Golden Torc, 7039
   Intervention, 9460
   Newborn King, 7040
May, Julian (jt. author). *Black Trillium*, 6961
May, Rollo. *Power and Innocence*, 504
Mayer, Arno J. *Why Did the Heavens Not Darken?* 5053
Mayer, Jane. *Landslide*, 5971
Mayer, Jean. *Dr. Jean Mayer's Diet and Nutrition Guide*, 2321
Mayer, Martin. *Greatest-Ever Bank Robbery*, 1070
   Markets, 1091
   The Met, 3475
Mayer, Musa. *Night Studio*, 3232
Mayle, Peter. *Toujours Provence*, 5289
   A Year in Provence, 5290
Maynard, Joyce. *Domestic Affairs*, 750
Mazrui, Ali A. *Africans*, 5625
Mead, Margaret. *Blackberry Winter*, 425
Mead, Walter Russell. *Mortal Splendor*, 5870
Medawar, Jean. *Very Dedicated Preference*, 2376
Medawar, P. B. *Threat and the Glory*, 1937
Medawar, Peter. *Limits of Science*, 1938
Medvedev, Grigori. *Truth about Chernobyl*, 1562
Medvedev, Roy. *Let History Judge*, 5371
Medvedev, Zhores A. *Gorbachev*, 5372
   Legacy of Chernobyl, 1563
   Soviet Science, 1954
Mee, Charles L., Jr. *Meeting at Potsdam*, 5054
Meegan, George. *Longest Walk*, 4884
Meer, Fatima. *Higher Than Hope*, 5660
Meeropol, Michael (jt. author). *We Are Your Sons*, 1655
Meeropol, Robert. *We Are Your Sons*, 1655
Mehta, Gita. *Raj*, 9086
Mehta, Ved. *Ledge Between the Streams*, 1488
   Stolen Light, 1489
   Vedi, 1490
Meinig, D. W. *Shaping of America*, 5731
Meinke, Peter. *Piano Tuner*, 9815
Meir, Golda. *My Life*, 5533
Meisel, Louis K. *Richard Estes*, 3233
Meiselas, Susan, ed. *Chile*, 6151
Melanson, Philip H. *Robert F. Kennedy Assassination*, 5972
Melford, Michael (jt. author). *Mid-Atlantic States*, 4904
Melina, Lois Ruskai. *Raising Adoptive Children*, 2891
Mellon, James, ed. *Bullwhip Days*, 903
   Face of Lincoln, 3344
Mellor, Anne K. *Mary Shelley*, 4488
Melman, Yossi. *Master Terrorist*, 505
Melman, Yossi (jt. author). *Every Spy a Prince*, 939
Meltzer, Milton. *Dorothea Lange*, 3304
Melville, James. *A Sort of Samurai*, 6694
Memmi, Albert. *Scorpion*, 8197
Menaker, Daniel. *The Old Left and Other Stories*, 9816

Mencken, H. L. *Diary of H. L. Mencken*, 4381
   Impossible H. L. Mencken, 4303
Mendenhall, Corwin. *Submarine Diary*, 5132
Meredith, William. *Partial Accounts*, 4046
Merilees, William J. *Attracting Backyard Wildlife*, 2658
Meriwether, Louise. *Daddy Was a Number Runner*, 8198
Merkin, Daphne. *Enchantment*, 8199
Merot, Alain. *Nicholas Poussin*, 3252
Merrill, Boynton, Jr. *Jefferson's Nephews*, 6085
Merrill, James. *Inner Room*, 4047
Merser, Cheryl. *"Grown-Ups,"* 540
Mertz, Barbara. *Red Land, Black Land*, 4988
Merwin, W. S. *Rain in the Trees*, 4048
   Selected Poems, 4049
   Unframed Originals, 4317
Meryman, Richard (jt. author). *Enter Talking*, 3634
Meschery, Joanne. *A Gentleman's Guide to the Frontier*, 10286
Metcalf, John. *Adult Entertainment*, 8200
Metz, Don. *Catamount Bridge*, 10223
Metz, Ella (jt. author). *Original Salt-Free Diet Cookbook*, 2703
Metzger, Deena. *What Dinah Thought*, 8201
Mewshaw, Michael. *Playing Away*, 4401
Meyer, John A. *Lung Cancer Chronicles*, 2481
Meyer, Michael A. *Strindberg*, 4610
Meyer, Michael R. *Alexander Complex*, 1143
Meyer, Peter. *Death of Innocence*, 1712
Meyer, Peter (jt. author). *Dark Obsession*, 1524
Meyerowitz, Joshua. *No Sense of Place*, 469
Meyers, Jeffrey. *D. H. Lawrence*, 4532
   Joseph Conrad, 4533
Michael, Sami. *Refuge*, 8202
Michaels, Barbara. *Ammie, Come Home*, 9310
Michaels, Leonard. *I Would Have Saved Them If I Could*, 9817
   Men's Club, 8203
Michaels, Leonard, ed. *State of the Language*, 1901
Micheli, Lyle J. *Sportswise*, 3675
Michener, James A. *Alaska*, 9087
   Caribbean, 9088
   Centennial, 9089
   Chesapeake, 9090
   Covenant, 9091
   The Drifters, 8204
   Iberia, 4832
   Journey, 9092
   Legacy, 8205
   Poland, 9093
   Space, 8206
   Texas, 9094
Michnik, Adam. *Letters from Prison and Other Essays*, 5280
Mickle, Shelley Fraser. *Queen of October*, 8207
Middlebrook, Diane Wood. *Anne Sexton*, 4156
Middlekauff, Robert. *Glorious Cause*, 5774
Middleton, Harry. *Earth Is Enough*, 6082
   On the Spine of Time, 6083
Milan, Victor. *Cybernetic Samurai*, 9461
   Cybernetic Shogun, 9462
Milani, Myrna M. *Invisible Leash*, 2641
Milbank, Caroline Rennolds. *New York Fashion*, 1862
Miles, Barry. *Ginsberg*, 4157
Miles, Hugh. *Kingdom of the Ice Bear*, 1970
Miles, Josephine. *Collected Poems, 1930–1983*, 4050
Miles, Rosalind. *Women's History of the World*, 581
Millar, Margaret. *Ask for Me Tomorrow*, 6695

Entries 1–6169 are nonfiction; entries 6170–10293 are fiction

Entries 1–6169 are nonfiction; entries 6170–10293 are fiction

Entries 1–6169 are nonfiction; entries 6170–10293 are fiction

Moss, Cynthia. *Elephant Memories*, 2233
  Portraits in the Wild, 2224
Moss, Michael. *Palace Coup*, 1099
Moss, Ralph W. *Free Radical*, 2128
Moss, Robert A. *Why Johnny Can't Concentrate*, 186
Moss, Roger W. *American Country House*, 3133
Moss, Stanley. *Intelligence of Clouds*, 4052
Mosse, George L. *Nationalism and Sexuality*, 719
Mosser, Monique, ed. *Architecture of Western Gardens*, 3087
Mossiker, Frances. *Madame de Sevigne*, 4624
Mott, Lawrie. *Pesticide Alert*, 1555
Mott, Michael. *Seven Mountains of Thomas Merton*, 342
Mottahedeh, Roy. *Mantle of the Prophet*, 5493
Mowat, Farley. *And No Birds Sang*, 5134
  Sea of Slaughter, 2120
  Woman in the Mists, 2255
Moyer, Kermit. *Tumbling*, 9829
Moyers, Bill. *A World of Ideas*, 5976
Moyers, Bill (jt. author). *Global Dumping Ground*, 1561
Moyes, Patricia. *Night Ferry to Death*, 6704
  A Six-Letter Word for Death, 6705
Moynihan, Daniel Patrick. *Family and Nation*, 1531
  On the Law of Nations, 984
Mozeson, I. E. (jt. author). *Place I Call Home*, 1526
Mrabet, Mohammed. *Love with a Few Hairs*, 8263
Mrkvicka, Edward F., Jr. *The Bank Book*, 1063
Mudimbe, V. Y. *Before the Birth of the Moon*, 8264
Mueller, John. *Retreat from Doomsday*, 1344
Mueller, L. Ann. *Recovering*, 2441
Mueller, Lisel. *Second Language*, 4053
Muggeridge, Malcolm. *Chronicles of Wasted Time*, 75
Muirhead, John. *Those Who Fall*, 5135
Mukherjee, Bharati. *Jasmine*, 8265
  Middleman and Other Stories, 9830
Mulisch, Harry. *The Assault*, 10226
  Last Call, 8266
Muller, Ingo. *Hitler's Justice*, 5248
Muller, Marcia. *Beyond the Grave*, 6713
  Cavalier in White, 6706
  Games to Keep the Dark Away, 6707
  Legend of the Slain Soldiers, 6708
  Shape of Dread, 6709
  There's Nothing to Be Afraid Of, 6710
  There's Something in a Sunday, 6711
  Trophies and Dead Things, 6712
Muller, Richard. *Nemesis—The Death Star*, 2086
Mullins, Edwin. *Master Painter*, 6202
Mulvagh, Jane. *Vogue History of 20th Century Fashion*, 1863
Mumford, Lewis. *Myth of the Machine*, 2263
Mundl, Kurt (jt. author). *On Life and Living*, 2188
Mungoshi, Charles. *Setting Sun and the Rolling World*, 9831
Munif, Abdelrahman. *Cities of Salt*, 9101
  The Trench, 9102
Munro, Alice. *Beggar Maid*, 9832
  Friend of My Youth, 9833
  Lives of Girls and Women, 8267
  Moons of Jupiter, 9834
  The Progress of Love, 9835
Munro, Eleanor. *Memoir of a Modernist's Daughter*, 3050
  On Glory Roads, 370
  Originals, 3076
Munro, Eleanor, ed. *Wedding Readings*, 113
Muolo, Paulo (jt. author). *Inside Job*, 1071

Mura, David. *Turning Japanese*, 4848
Murakami, Haruki. *Hard-Boiled Wonderland and the End of the World*, 7046
  A Wild Sheep Chase, 8268
Murano, Vincent. *Cop Hunter*, 1575
Murcia, Andy. *Man to Man*, 2483
Murdoch, Iris. *Accidental Man*, 8269
  Black Prince, 8270
  Book and the Brotherhood, 8271
  Bruno's Dream, 8272
  A Fairly Honourable Defeat, 8273
  Good Apprentice, 8274
  Henry and Cato, 8275
  Message to the Planet, 8276
  Nice and the Good, 9248
  Nuns and Soldiers, 8277
  The Philosopher's Pupil, 8278
  Sacred and Profane Love Machine, 8279
  The Sea, the Sea, 8280
  A Word Child, 8281
Murphy, Bruce Allen. *Brandeis-Frankfurter Connection*, 1292
  Fortas, 1293
Murphy, Dallas. *Lover Man*, 6714
Murphy, Dervla. *Cameroon with Egbert*, 4880
Murphy, Gloria. *Down Will Come Baby*, 8282
Murphy, Kenneth. *Man's Fate, Man's Hope*, 4620
Murphy, Pat. *The City, Not Long After*, 7047
  Falling Woman, 7048
Murphy, William M. *Prodigal Father*, 3242
Murray, Alan S. (jt. author). *Showdown at Gucci Gulch*, 1243
Murray, Albert. *South to a Very Old Place*, 4909
  Spyglass Tree, 8283
  Train Whistle Guitar, 9103
Murray, Albert (jt. author). *Good Morning Blues*, 3404
Murray, Bruce C. *Journey into Space*, 4955
Murray, Charles. *Apollo*, 2575
  Losing Ground, 5977
Murray, Edmund P. (jt. author). *My Bridge to America*, 1176
Murray, Janet Horowitz. *Strong-Minded Women*, 583
Murray, John A., ed. *Republic of Rivers*, 1963
Murray, K. M. Elizabeth. *Caught in the Web of Words*, 1906
Murray, Oswyn (jt. author). *Oxford History of the Classical World: Greece and the Hellenistic World*, 4995
  Oxford History of the Classical World: The Roman World, 4996
Murray, Pauli. *Song in a Weary Throat*, 5734
Murray, William. *Getaway Blues*, 6715
  King of the Nightcap, 6716
  Last Italian, 5321
Musheno, Elizabeth. *Fast and Easy Home Decorating*, 2867
Musicant, Ivan. *Banana Wars*, 985
Musil, Robert. *Posthumous Papers of a Living Author*, 4602
Muske-Dukes, Carol. *Dear Digby*, 8284
Musser, Charles. *Emergence of Cinema*, 3573
Musto, David. *American Disease*, 1473
Mydans, Carl. *Carl Mydans*, 3305
Myerhoff, Barbara. *Number Our Days*, 6124
Myers, Robert Manson. *Children of Pride*, 5835
Mylroie, Laurie (jt. author). *Saddam Hussein and the Crisis in the Gulf*, 5509
Myrdal, Jan. *Report from a Chinese Village*, 779

Entries 1–6169 are nonfiction; entries 6170–10293 are fiction

Entries 1–6169 are nonfiction; entries 6170–10293 are fiction

Entries 1–6169 are nonfiction; entries 6170–10293 are fiction

Entries 1–6169 are nonfiction; entries 6170–10293 are fiction

Palin, Michael. *Around the World in Eighty Days*, 4794

Palliser, Charles. *Quincunx*, 9114
  Sensationist, 8344

Pallister, David. *South Africa, Inc*, 1182

Pallone, Dave. *Behind the Mask*, 3774

Palmer, Christopher. *Composer in Hollywood*, 3379

Palmer, Edward L. *Television and America's Children*, 3603

Palmer, Laura. *Shrapnel in the Heart*, 5599

Palmer, Laura (jt. author). *In the Absence of Angels*, 1448

Palmer, Robert. *Deep Blues*, 3396

Palmer, William. *Good Republic*, 8345

Paludan, Phillip Shaw. *A People's Contest*, 5838

Palumbo, Ron (jt. author). *Abbott and Costello in Hollywood*, 3537

Pamuk, Orhan. *White Castle*, 9115

Pan, Lynn. *Sons of the Yellow Emperor*, 5405

Pancake, Breece D'J. *Stories of Breece D'J Pancake*, 9859

Pangle, Thomas L. *Spirit of Modern Republicanism*, 808

Pannor, Reuben (jt. author). *Lethal Secrets*, 2346

Panos, Louis G. (jt. author). *Edward Teller*, 2039

Pantano, James A. *Living with Angina*, 2385

Papadakis, Andreas (jt. author). *Post-Modern Design*, 3169

Papazoglou, Orania. *Death's Savage Passion*, 6729

Paper, Lewis J. *Empire*, 1835

Paral, Vladimir. *Catapult*, 8346

Parent, Gail. *A Sign of the Eighties*, 8347

Parenti, Michael J. *Inventing Reality*, 38

Paret, Peter, ed. *Makers of Modern Strategy from Machiavelli to the Nuclear Age*, 1348

Paretsky, Sara. *Bitter Medicine*, 6730
  Blood Shot, 6731
  Burn Marks, 6732
  Deadlock, 6733
  Indemnity Only, 6734

Parfit, Michael. *Chasing the Glory*, 4898
  South Light, 4952

Parini, Jay. *Last Station*, 6204
  Patch Boys, 9116

Park, Edwards. *Treasures of the Smithsonian*, 31

Park, Paul. *Sugar Rain*, 7050

Parker, Beulah. *A Mingled Yarn*, 2419

Parker, John. *Prince Philip*, 5192

Parker, Peter. *Ackerley*, 76

Parker, Robert. *Capitol Hill in Black and White*, 6056

Parker, Robert B. *Catskill Eagle*, 6735
  Ceremony, 6736
  Early Autumn, 6737
  God Save the Child, 6738
  Godwulf Manuscript, 6739
  Judas Goat, 6740
  Looking for Rachel Wallace, 6741
  Mortal Stakes, 6742
  Pale Kings and Princes, 6743
  Playmates, 6744
  Promised Land, 6745
  Stardust, 6746
  Valediction, 6747
  Widening Gyre, 6748

Parker, Robert B. (jt. author). *Poodle Springs*, 6325

Parker, Robert M., Jr. *Wines of the Rhone Valley and Provence*, 2675

Parker, T. Jefferson. *Laguna Heat*, 6749

Parker, Tom (jt. author). *Winfield*, 3795

Parker, Tony. *Bird, Kansas*, 6106

Parkin, Frank. *Krippendorf's Tribe*, 8348
  Mind and Body Shop, 8349

Parks, Gordon. *Choice of Weapons*, 3306
  Voices in the Mirror, 3307

Parks, Tim. *Goodness*, 8350
  Loving Roger, 8351

Parmet, Herbert S. *Richard Nixon and His America*, 5987

Parris, P. B. *Waltzing in the Attic*, 8352

Parrish, Frank. *Fly in the Cobweb*, 6750

Parry, Francis Fox. *Three-War Marine*, 1387

Parry, Linda. *William Morris Textiles*, 3195

Parson, Mary Jean. *Managing the One-Person Business*, 2926

Pasternak, Alexander. *A Vanished Present*, 3103

Patai, Daphne, ed. *Brazilian Women Speak*, 584

Patai, Raphael. *Arab Mind*, 426
  Seed of Abraham, 643

Paterson, Allen. *Herbs in the Garden*, 2601

Patner, Andrew. *I. F. Stone*, 77

Paton, Alan. *Ah, But Your Land Is Beautiful*, 8353
  Journey Continued, 4489
  Toward the Mountain, 1780

Patout, Alex. *Patout's Cajun Home Cooking*, 2797

Patrick, Vincent. *Family Business*, 8354

Patterson, Orlando. *Freedom Volume One*, 696
  Slavery and Social Death, 676

Patterson, Suzy (jt. author). *Food and Friends*, 2689

Patton, Paul (jt. author). *Voyager*, 2564

Patton, Phil. *Open Road*, 1855

Paugh, Tom, ed. *Sports Afield Treasury of Fly Fishing*, 3844

Paul, Barbara. *Prima Donna at Large*, 6751

Paul, Jim. *Catapult*, 2543

Paul, Rodman W. *Far West and the Great Plains in Transition, 1859–1900*, 6104

Paulos, John A. *Beyond Numeracy*, 1978
  Innumeracy, 1979

Paulson, Dennis, ed. *Voices of Survival in the Nuclear Age*, 1357

Paultz, Peter D. (jt. author). *Architecture of Fear*, 9277

Pavic, Milorad. *Dictionary of the Khazars*, 9117
  Landscape Painted with Tea, 8355

Pawel, Ernst. *Labyrinth of Exile*, 810
  Nightmare of Reason, 4600

Pawlowski, Gareth L. *How They Became the Beatles*, 3453

Payer, Lynn. *Medicine and Culture*, 1423

Payne, Stanley G. *Franco Regime, 1936–1975*, 5333

Paz, Octavio. *Alternating Current*, 4660
  Collected Poems, 1957–1987, 4652
  Convergences, 4661
  Monkey Grammarian, 1895
  Other Voice, 4653
  Sor Juana, 4654

Peace, Judy B. *Boy Child Is Dying*, 811

Peacock, Doug. *Grizzly Years*, 2240

Peacock, John. *Chronicle of Western Fashion*, 1864

Pearce, Michael. *Mamur Zapt and the Return of the Carpet*, 6752

Pearsall, Paul. *Super Marital Sex*, 2347

Pearson, David. *Natural House Book*, 2865

Pearson, John. *Selling of the Royal Family*, 5193
  Sitwells, 4425

Pearson, Nathan W., Jr. *Goin' to Kansas City*, 3419

Pearson, Ridley. *Undercurrents*, 6753

Pearson, T. R. *Gospel Hour*, 8356

Entries 1–6169 are nonfiction; entries 6170–10293 are fiction

Entries 1–6169 are nonfiction; entries 6170–10293 are fiction

Entries 1–6169 are nonfiction; entries 6170–10293 are fiction

Entries 1–6169 are nonfiction; entries 6170–10293 are fiction

Quindlen, Anna. *Object Lessons*, 8445
Quinn, Susan. *A Mind of Her Own*, 158
Quirk, Lawrence J. *Fasten Your Seat Belts*, 3576

Raban, Jonathan. *Coasting*, 4820
  For Love and Money, 4565
  Foreign Land, 8446
  Hunting Mister Heartbreak, 5989
Rabelais, Francois. *Gargantua and Pantagruel*, 4621
Rachels, James. *Created from Animals*, 248
Rachlin, Harvey. *Making of a Cop*, 1576
Radetsky, Peter. *Invisible Invaders*, 2368
Radley, Sheila. *Chief Inspector's Daughter*, 6774
  Fate Worse Than Death, 6775
  This Way Out, 6776
  Who Saw Him Die? 6777
Radner, Gilda. *It's Always Something*, 2480
Raeff, Marc. *Understanding Imperial Russia*, 5340
Raffan, Richard. *Turning Wood with Richard Raffan*, 2538
Rainer, J. Kenyon. *First Do No Harm*, 2491
Raines, Barbara (jt. author). *A Tuscan in My Kitchen*, 2790
Raines, Howell. *My Soul Is Rested*, 864
Ralling, Christopher (jt. author). *Kon-Tiki Man*, 4812
Rampersad, Arnold. *Life of Langston Hughes, Vol. I, 1902–1941*, 4382
  Life of Langston Hughes, Vol. II, 1941–1967, 4383
Ramsey, Edwin Price. *Lieutenant Ramsey's War*, 5143
Rand, Paul. *Paul Rand*, 3282
Randall, Willard Sterne. *Benedict Arnold*, 5778
Randisi, Robert J., ed. *Mean Streets*, 6778
Ranke-Heinemann, Uta. *Eunuchs for the Kingdom of Heaven*, 312
Ransmayr, Christopher. *Last World*, 9128
Ransohoff, Rita M. *Venus after 40*, 720
Raphael, Lev. *Dancing on Tisha B'Av*, 9876
Raphael, Ray. *Men from the Boys*, 550
Rapoport, Judith L. *Boy Who Couldn't Stop Washing*, 2430
Rapoport, Louis. *Redemption Song*, 1533
Rapp, Joel. *Mr. Mother Earth's Most Rewarding Houseplants*, 2621
Raskin, Barbara. *Current Affairs*, 8447
Rasponi, Lanfranco. *Last Prima Donnas*, 3476
Rathbone, Julian. *Greenfinger*, 8448
Rattray, Everett T. *Adventures of Jeremiah Dimon*, 9129
Ratushinskaya, Irina. *Beyond the Limit*, 4696
  Grey Is the Color of Hope, 4697
  In the Beginning, 4698
Raup, David M. *Nemesis Affair*, 2087
Rautsi, Inari (jt. author). *Saddam Hussein*, 5508
Ravitch, Diane. *Schools We Deserve*, 1758
  Troubled Crusade, 1759
Raviv, Dan. *Every Spy a Prince*, 939
Rawlence, Christopher. *Missing Reel*, 3317
Rawls, John. *A Theory of Justice*, 1224
Ray, Robert J. *Hit Man Cometh*, 6779
Raymo, Chet. *Virgin and the Mousetrap*, 1940
Rayner, Lynn (jt. author). *Best Medicine*, 2306
Razina, Tatyana. *Folk Art in the Soviet Union*, 3063
Read, Anthony. *Deadly Embrace*, 5061
Read, Kenneth E. *Return to the High Valley*, 686
Read, Piers Paul. *Alive*, 4928
  Free Frenchman, 10233
  A Season in the West, 8449

Read, William J. (jt. author). *Role-Sharing Marriage*, 757
Rearden, Steven L. (jt. author). *From Hiroshima to Glasnost*, 986
Reaves, John. *How to Find Help for a Troubled Kid*, 1520
Reavis, Dick J. *Conversations with Moctezuma*, 5692
Rebello, Stephen. *Alfred Hitchcock and the Making of Psycho*, 3577
  Reel Art, 3578
Rebeta-Burditt, Joyce. *Cracker Factory*, 8450
Rebsamen, Frederick, trans. *Beowulf*, 4444
Rechy, John. *Bodies and Souls*, 8451
  Marilyn's Daughter, 8452
Redfern, Ron. *Making of a Continent*, 2082
Redfern, Walter. *Puns*, 3911
Redford, Dorothy S. *Somerset Homecoming*, 4981
Redondi, Pietro. *Galileo*, 323
Reed, Billy (jt. author). *Thoroughbred*, 2632
Reed, Eli (jt. author). *Beirut*, 5513
Reed, Ishmael. *Flight to Canada*, 9130
  Last Days of Louisiana Red, 6780
  Mumbo Jumbo, 6781
  Reckless Eyeballing, 8453
  Terrible Threes, 8454
  Terrible Twos, 8455
  Writin' Is Fightin', 4295
Reedy, George E. *From the Ward to the White House*, 5756
  U.S. Senate, 1002
Reedy, Jerry (jt. author). *God, Country, Notre Dame*, 1811
Reese, Thomas J. *Archbishop*, 327
Reeves, Hubert. *Atoms of Silence*, 2015
Reeves, Nicholas. *Complete Tutankhamen*, 4990
Reeves, Robert N. *Doubting Thomas*, 6782
  Peeping Thomas, 6783
Regan, Donald T. *For the Record*, 5990
Regan, Tom. *Case for Animal Rights*, 271
Regis, Ed. *Great Mambo Chicken and the Transhuman Condition*, 1924
Regis, Edward. *Who Got Einstein's Office?* 2
Register, Cheri. *Are Those Kids Yours?* 1521
Rehnquist, William. *Supreme Court*, 1296
Reich, Nancy B. *Clara Schumann*, 3495
Reich, Robert B. *Next American Frontier*, 827
  Resurgent Liberal, 1209
  Tales of a New America, 5991
  Work of Nations, 1016
Reich, Tova. *Master of the Return*, 8456
Reichel, Sabine. *What Did You Do in the War, Daddy?* 5250
Reid, Alastair (jt. author). *Eternal Spain*, 5332
Reid, B. L. *First Acts*, 6086
Reidelbach, Maria. *Completely Mad*, 3156
Reidenbaugh, Lowell. *Sporting News Selects Baseball's 25 Greatest Pennant Races*, 3776
Reidinger, Paul. *Best Man*, 8457
Reimers, David M. *Still the Golden Door*, 896
Reinharz, Jehuda. *Chaim Weizmann*, 5537
Reinhold, Toni (jt. author). *Untamed*, 3513
Reinisch, June M. *Kinsey Institute New Report on Sex*, 2348
Reischauer, Edwin O. *Japanese Today*, 5463
Reisner, Marc. *Cadillac Desert*, 1109
  Game Wars, 1583
Reiss, Bob. *Divine Assassin*, 8458
Rejnis, Ruth (jt. author). *All America's Real Estate Book*, 2853

Entries 1–6169 are nonfiction; entries 6170–10293 are fiction

Entries 1–6169 are nonfiction; entries 6170–10293 are fiction

Entries 1–6169 are nonfiction; entries 6170–10293 are fiction

Entries 1–6169 are nonfiction; entries 6170–10293 are fiction

Entries 1–6169 are nonfiction; entries 6170–10293 are fiction

Entries 1–6169 are nonfiction; entries 6170–10293 are fiction

Entries 1–6169 are nonfiction; entries 6170–10293 are fiction

Entries 1–6169 are nonfiction; entries 6170–10293 are fiction

Entries 1–6169 are nonfiction; entries 6170–10293 are fiction

Entries 1–6169 are nonfiction; entries 6170–10293 are fiction

Entries 1–6169 are nonfiction; entries 6170–10293 are fiction

Entries 1–6169 are nonfiction; entries 6170–10293 are fiction

Entries 1–6169 are nonfiction; entries 6170–10293 are fiction

Entries 1–6169 are nonfiction; entries 6170–10293 are fiction

Entries 1–6169 are nonfiction; entries 6170–10293 are fiction

Entries 1–6169 are nonfiction; entries 6170–10293 are fiction

Entries 1–6169 are nonfiction; entries 6170–10293 are fiction

Entries 1–6169 are nonfiction; entries 6170–10293 are fiction

Entries 1–6169 are nonfiction; entries 6170–10293 are fiction

Entries 1–6169 are nonfiction; entries 6170–10293 are fiction

Entries 1–6169 are nonfiction; entries 6170–10293 are fiction

Entries 1–6169 are nonfiction; entries 6170–10293 are fiction

Entries 1–6169 are nonfiction; entries 6170–10293 are fiction

Entries 1–6169 are nonfiction; entries 6170–10293 are fiction

TITLE INDEX

References are to entry numbers, not page numbers.

Entries 1–6169 are nonfiction; entries 6170–10293 are fiction

Entries 1–6169 are nonfiction; entries 6170–10293 are fiction

Entries 1–6169 are nonfiction; entries 6170–10293 are fiction

Entries 1–6169 are nonfiction; entries 6170–10293 are fiction

Entries 1–6169 are nonfiction; entries 6170–10293 are fiction

Entries 1–6169 are nonfiction; entries 6170–10293 are fiction

Entries 1–6169 are nonfiction; entries 6170–10293 are fiction

Entries 1–6169 are nonfiction; entries 6170–10293 are fiction

Entries 1–6169 are nonfiction; entries 6170–10293 are fiction

Entries 1–6169 are nonfiction; entries 6170–10293 are fiction

Entries 1–6169 are nonfiction; entries 6170–10293 are fiction

Entries 1–6169 are nonfiction; entries 6170–10293 are fiction

Entries 1–6169 are nonfiction; entries 6170–10293 are fiction

Entries 1–6169 are nonfiction; entries 6170–10293 are fiction

Entries 1–6169 are nonfiction; entries 6170–10293 are fiction

Entries 1–6169 are nonfiction; entries 6170–10293 are fiction

Entries 1–6169 are nonfiction; entries 6170–10293 are fiction

Entries 1–6169 are nonfiction; entries 6170–10293 are fiction

Entries 1–6169 are nonfiction; entries 6170–10293 are fiction

Entries 1–6169 are nonfiction; entries 6170–10293 are fiction

Entries 1–6169 are nonfiction; entries 6170–10293 are fiction

Duke of Deception: Memories of My Father, 4197

Duke of Flatbush, 3784

Duke University Medical Center Book of Diet and Fitness, 2328

Duncan's Colony, 8375

Dungeon Master: The Disappearance of James Dallas Egbert III, 1511

Dunn's Conundrum, 10110

Dunwich Horror and Others, 9307

A Durable Fire, 8899

During the Reign of the Queen of Persia, 7422

Duse: A Biography, 3631

Dusk and Other Stories, 9889

Dust Bowl Diary, 6109

Dust Roads of Monferrato, 9065

Dust Tracks on a Road: An Autobiography, 4210

Dutch Blue Error, 6849

Dutch Shea, Jr., 7590

Dwarfs, 8388

Dyad, 7346

Dydeetown World, 7092

Dying of the Light, 9458

Dylan Thomas: A Biography, 4465

Dynasty, 8960

E. B. White: A Biography, 4204

E Is for Evidence, 6467

E. M. Forster: A Life, 4517

Eagle: The History of American Airlines, 1852

Eagle Against the Sun: The American War with Japan, 5149

Eagle and the Lion: The Tragedy of American-Iranian Relations, 956

Eagle Has Flown, 10198

The Eagle Has Landed, 10199

Eagle on the Street: Based on the Pulitzer Prize-Winning Account of the SEC's Battle with Wall Street, 1255

Eagle's Mile, 3982

An Ear to the Ground: An Anthology of Contemporary American Poetry, 4006

Earl K. Long: The Saga of Uncle Earl and Louisiana Politics, 6076

Earliest Relationship: Parents, Infants and the Drama of Early Attachment, 761

Early American Gardens: "For Meate or Medicine," 2598

Early Arrival of Dreams: A Year in China, 5428

Early Autumn, 6737

Early Graves, 6495

Early Jazz: Its Roots and Musical Development, 3421

Early Man and the Cosmos: Explorations in Astroarchaeology, 1994

Early Reagan: The Rise to Power, 3535

Earth, 9372

Earth Abideth, 8938

Earth Is Enough: Growing Up in a World of Trout and Old Men, 6082

Earthly Delights, 2590

Earthly Possessions, 8713

Earthly Powers, 7378

Earthly Remains, 7000

Earthright, 1614

East Is East, 7324

East of Chosin: Entrapment and Breakout in Korea, 1950, 5449

Easter Day, 1941, 10158

Easter Parade, 8860

Easter Weekend, 6278

Easy in the Islands, 9901

Easy Travel to Other Planets, 7042

Eat for Health: Fast and Simple Ways of Eliminating Diseases Without Medical Assistance, 2320

Eat Right, Eat Well: The Italian Way, 2776

Eating of the Gods: An Interpretation of Greek Tragedy, 4664

Ebony Tower, 9678

Echoes, 7294

Echoes in the Darkness, 1726

Echoes of Revolt: The Masses, 1911–1917, 1123

Eclipse: A Nightmare, 1487

Ecologues: Short Stories by Guy Davenport, 9644

Economic Emergence of Women, 591

Economics in Perspective: A Critical History, 1005

Economics of Chaos: On Revitalizing the American Economy, 1207

Economics of Politics and Race: An International Perspective, 638

Ecuador: Island of the Andes, 4935

Ed School Follies: The Miseducation of America's Teachers, 1779

Eddy Deco's Last Caper, 6903

Eden, 9444

Eden Close, 8581

Eden Express, 2466

Edgar A. Poe: Mournful and Never-Ending Remembrance, 4184

The Edge, 6415

Edge City: Life on the New Frontier, 786

Edges of Science: Crossing the Boundary from Physics to Metaphysics, 2033

Edges of the Earth: A Family's Alaskan Odyssey, 6138

Edie: An American Biography, 3586

Edisto, 8408

Edith Wharton: A Biography, 4194

Edith's Diary, 7846

Edmund Burke: His Life and Opinions, 5167

Educating for Character: How Our Schools Can Teach Respect and Responsibility, 1760

Education of Harriet Hatfield, 8525

Education of the Senses: Victoria to Freud, 714

Educational Renaissance: Our Schools at the Turn of the 21st Century, 1773

Education's Smoking Gun: How Teachers' Colleges Have Destroyed Education in America, 1770

Edward Teller: Giant of the Golden Age of Physics, 2039

Edwin Mullhouse: The Life and Death of an American Writer, 1943–1954, 8211

Edwin Pope Collection, 50

Effect of Gamma Rays on Man-in-the-Moon Marigolds, 4170

Eggs: Nature's Perfect Package, 2189

Eichmann in My Hands, 1653

Eiger Dreams: Ventures Among Men and Mountains, 3809

Eiger Sanction, 10140

The Eight, 9105

Eight Black Horses, 6643

Eight Million Ways to Die, 6269

1876, 9187

Eighth Day, 8827

Eighth Day of Creation: Makers of the Revolution in Biology, 2144

Eighty-Sixed, 7627

Eileen Yin-Fei Lo's New Cantonese Cooking: Classic and Innovative Recipes from China's Haute Cuisine, 2814

Einstein: The Life and Times, 2040

Einstein in America: The Scientist's Conscience in the Age of Hitler and Hiroshima, 2047

Einstein's Monsters, 9532

Eisenhower: At War, 1943–1945, 5030

Eisenhower: A Centennial Life, 5877

Eisenhower: The President, 5921

Elbow Room, 9802

Elder Care: Choosing and Financing Long-Term Care, 1439

Eleanor: The Years Alone, 5898

Eleanor and Franklin: The Story of Their Relationship Based on Eleanor Roosevelt's Private Papers, 5899

Election Journal: The Political Events of 1987–1988, 883

Election of 1988: Reports and Interpretations, 889

Electric Kool-Aid Acid Test, 427

Electrifying America: Social Meanings of a New Technology, 1880–1940, 2534

Electronic Commonwealth: The Impact of New Media Technologies on Democratic Politics, 880

Element of Doubt, 6814

Elements of Speechwriting and Public Speaking, 3869

Eleni, 5393

Entries 1–6169 are nonfiction; entries 6170–10293 are fiction

Entries 1–6169 are nonfiction; entries 6170–10293 are fiction

Entries 1–6169 are nonfiction; entries 6170–10293 are fiction

Entries 1–6169 are nonfiction; entries 6170–10293 are fiction

Entries 1–6169 are nonfiction; entries 6170–10293 are fiction

Entries 1–6169 are nonfiction; entries 6170–10293 are fiction

Entries 1–6169 are nonfiction; entries 6170–10293 are fiction

Entries 1–6169 are nonfiction; entries 6170–10293 are fiction

Entries 1–6169 are nonfiction; entries 6170–10293 are fiction

Entries 1–6169 are nonfiction; entries 6170–10293 are fiction

Entries 1–6169 are nonfiction; entries 6170–10293 are fiction

Entries 1–6169 are nonfiction; entries 6170–10293 are fiction

Entries 1–6169 are nonfiction; entries 6170–10293 are fiction

Entries 1–6169 are nonfiction; entries 6170–10293 are fiction

Entries 1–6169 are nonfiction; entries 6170–10293 are fiction

Entries 1–6169 are nonfiction; entries 6170–10293 are fiction

Entries 1–6169 are nonfiction; entries 6170–10293 are fiction

Entries 1–6169 are nonfiction; entries 6170–10293 are fiction

Entries 1–6169 are nonfiction; entries 6170–10293 are fiction

Entries 1–6169 are nonfiction; entries 6170–10293 are fiction

Entries 1–6169 are nonfiction; entries 6170–10293 are fiction

Entries 1–6169 are nonfiction; entries 6170–10293 are fiction

Entries 1–6169 are nonfiction; entries 6170–10293 are fiction

Entries 1–6169 are nonfiction; entries 6170–10293 are fiction

Entries 1–6169 are nonfiction; entries 6170–10293 are fiction

Entries 1–6169 are nonfiction; entries 6170–10293 are fiction

Entries 1–6169 are nonfiction; entries 6170–10293 are fiction

Entries 1–6169 are nonfiction; entries 6170–10293 are fiction

Entries 1–6169 are nonfiction; entries 6170–10293 are fiction

Entries 1–6169 are nonfiction; entries 6170–10293 are fiction

Entries 1–6169 are nonfiction; entries 6170–10293 are fiction

cally Sound Home Environment, 2865

Natural Man, 8113

Natural Obsessions: The Search for the Oncogene, 2476

Natural Selection, 7230

Nature and Culture: American Landscape and Painting, 3209

Nature and Logic of Capitalism, 1012

Nature of Australia: A Portrait of the Island Continent, 1967

Nature of Love, Vol. 3: The Modern World, 131

Nature of Reality: The Universe after Einstein, 2053

The Nature of the Child, 210

Nature of Time, 121

Nature's End: The Consequences of the 20th Century, 7072

Nazis in Skokie: Freedom, Community, and the First Amendment, 833

Ndebele: The Art of an African Tribe, 3007

Near Changes, 4106

Nearness of You, 4025

Nebraska, 9720

Necessity, 6438

Needle's Eye, 7578

Needs of Strangers, 1388

Negotiator, 7644

Neighbors, 7278

Nelly's Version, 8970

Nelson Algren: A Life on the Wild Side, 4203

Nelson Mandela: The Man and His Movement, 831

Nemesis (Asimov), 9347

Nemesis (Smith), 6829

Nemesis Affair: A Story of the Death of Dinosaurs and the Ways of Science, 2087

Nemesis—The Death Star: The Story of a Scientific Revolution, 2086

Neon Bible, 8698

Neon Rain, 6304

Neruda: An Intimate Biography, 4655

Net of Magic: Wonders and Deceptions in India, 137

Neumiller Stories, 9982

Neuro: Life on the Front Lines of Brain Surgery and Neurological Medicine, 2418

Neuromancer, 9417

A Neutral Corner: Boxing Essays, 3818

Never Be Tired Again, 2336

Never Too Thin: A History of American Women's Obsession with Weight Loss, 586

Never Too Young to Die: The Death of Len Bias, 1467

Neverending Story, 6985

Neverness, 9519

New Age: Notes of a Fringe-Watcher, 134

A New Age Now Begins: A People's History of the American Revolution, 5779

New American Grandparent: A Place in the Family, a Life Apart, 738

New American Poverty, 618

New Americans: An Oral History; Immigrants and Refugees in the U.S. Today, 897

New and Collected Poems (Wilbur), 4115

New and Collected Poems, 1970–1985 (Ignatow), 4015

New Basics Cookbook, 2736

New Centurions, 8766

New Comics Anthology, 3147

New Complete Book of Pasta: An Italian Cookbook, 2846

New Confessions, 7320

New Corporate Strategy, 2939

New Dinosaurs: An Alternative Evolution, 2090

New Emperors: China in the Era of Mao and Deng, 5431

New Girl Friend and Other Stories of Suspense, 9877

New House Book, 2859

New Industrial State, 1014

New Islands and Other Stories, 9583

New Japanese Voices: The Best Contemporary Fiction from Japan, 9822

New Kind of Country, 4189

New Laurel's Kitchen: A Handbook for Vegetarian Cookery and Nutrition, 2683

New Medically Based No-Nonsense Beauty Book, 2870

New Money Masters: Winning Investment Strategies of Soros-Lynch-Steinhardt-Rogers-Neff-Waryer-Michaelis-Carret, 1084

New Orleans Jazz Fest: A Pictorial History, 3425

New Orleans Mourning, 6826

New Our Bodies, Ourselves, 2305

New Painting: Impressionism, 1874–1886, 3253

A New Path to the Waterfall: Poems, 3967

New Politics of Inequality, 1205

New Realities, 4764

New Russians, 5384

New Selected Poems (Hughes), 4439

New Selected Poems (Levine), 4037

New Shostakovich, 3367

New Southern Cooking, 2773

New Southwestern Cooking, 2772

New Soviet Fiction: Sixteen Short Stories, 9992

New Springtime, 9488

New Thinking Fan's Guide to Baseball, 3762

New West Coast Cuisine, 2680

New World Avenue and Vicinity, 4707

New World Guide to Beer, 2679

New World Visions of Household Gods and Sacred Places: American Art and the Metropolitan Museum, 1650–1914, 3077

New York City Baseball: The Last Golden Age, 1947–1957, 3743

New York Detective, 6686

New York Fashion: The Evolution of American Style, 1862

New York Jew, 3936

New York 1913: The Armory Show and the Paterson Strike Pageant, 3018

New York 1930: Architecture and Urbanism Between Two World Wars, 3114

New York Times Book of Personal Finance, 1054

New York Times Book of Science Literacy: What Everyone Needs to Know from Newton to Knuckleball, 1915

New York Times Cook Book: The Classic Gourmet Cookbook for the Home Kitchen with Hundreds of New Recipes, 2766

New York Times More Sixty-Minute Gourmet, 2708

New York Unbound: The City and the Politics of the Future, 1397

Newborn King, 7040

News from Ireland: And Other Stories, 9946

News from the Glacier: Selected Poems, 1960–1980, 4003

Newspaper Murders, 6439

Newspaper of Claremont Street, 7937

Newton Letter, 7213

Newton's Madness: Further Tales of Clinical Neurology, 2414

Next: New Poems, 3974

Next American Frontier, 827

Next Century, 496

Next Left: The History of a Future, 1206

Next New World, 9902

Next 100 Years: Shaping the Fate of Our Living Earth, 516

Nez Perce Indians and the Opening of the Northwest, 5677

Nibbled to Death by Ducks, 6317

Nicaragua: Revolution in the Family, 5699

Niccolo Rising, 8954

Nice and the Good, 9248

A Nice Class of Corpse, 6291

Nice Murder for Mom, 6921

Nice Work, 8084

Nicholas and Alexandra, 5370

Nicholas Poussin, 3252

Nicholas Roerich: The Life and Art of a Russian Master, 3268

Entries 1–6169 are nonfiction; entries 6170–10293 are fiction

Nickel Mountain: A Pastoral Novel, 9241

Nietzsche: Life as Literature, 286

A Night at the Movies: Or, You Must Remember This, 9635

Night Ferry to Death, 6704

Night Life: Nature from Dusk to Dawn, 2197

Night Lights: Bedtime Stories for Parents in the Dark, 2899

'Night, Mother, 4164

Night of the Ice Storm, 6837

Night of the Ripper, 6265

Night of the Weeping Women, 8297

Night over Day over Night, 10247

Night Parade, 4012

Night Rituals, 6543

Night She Died, 6815

Night Shift: Excursions into Horror, 9296

Night-Side: 18 Tales, 9312

Night Studio: A Memoir of Philip Guston by His Daughter, 3232

Night Thoughts of a Classical Physicist, 8119

Night Train to Mother, 8050

Night Travellers, 10240

Night Visitor, and Other Stories, 9944

Nightbloom, 6615

Nightfall, 9351

Nightmare: The Underside of the Nixon Years, 5969

Nightmare of Reason: A Life of Franz Kafka, 4600

Nightmare Time, 10123

The Nightmare Years, 1930–1940: Twentieth Century Journey—A Memoir of a Life and the Times, Volume 2, 86

Nightshade, 9381

Nightwing, 8615

Nightwork, 6499

Nina's Journey: A Memoir of Stalin's Russia and the Second World War, 5369

Nine-Headed Dragon River: Zen Journals, 1969–1982, 389

900 Days: The Siege of Leningrad, 5146

Nine Plays by Black Women, 4167

Nine Sides of the Diamond: Baseball's Great Glove Men on the Fine Art of Defense, 3740

1982 Janine, 7749

1915, 10218

1959, 7510

1941: Our Lives in a Year on the Edge, 5044

1919: The Year Our World Began, 4771

1999: The Global Challenges We Face in the Next Decade, 987

1934, 9097

1933 Was a Bad Year, 10000

1929: The Year of the Great Crash, 5896

19 Purchase Street, 7365

19th Century Art, 3010

19th Century Sculpture, 3140

Ninety-nine Gnats, Nits, and Nibblers, 2203

Ninety-Two in the Shade, 8138

Ninth Circle, 10049

Nisa: The Life and Words of a Kung Woman, 5663

Nixon: The Education of a Politician, 1913–1962, 5922

Nixon: Ruin and Recovery, 1973–1990, 5923

Nixon: The Triumph of a Politician, 1962–1972, 5924

Nixon Agonistes: The Crisis of the Self-Made Man, 6009

No Apologies: A Survival Guide and Handbook for the Disabled Written by the Real Authorities, 2875

No Bells on Sunday: The Rachel Roberts Journals, 3580

No Bells to Toll: Destruction and Creation in the Andes, 6154

No Country for Young Men, 9111

No Deals, Mr. Bond, 10072

No Direction Home: The Life and Music of Bob Dylan, 3457

No Enemy But Time, 6954

No-Hysterectomy Option: Your Body—Your Choice, 2498

No Idle Hands: The Social History of American Knitting, 3180

No Laughing Matter, 2412

No Less a Woman: Ten Women Shatter the Myths about Breast Cancer, 1417

No Man's Land, 10143

No Man's Land—The Place of the Woman Writer in the 20th Century, Vol. 1: The War of the Words, 4419

No Man's Land—The Place of the Woman Writer in the 20th Century, Vol. 2: Sexchanges, 4420

No Marble Angels, 9776

No Medals for Trying: A Week in the Life of a Pro Football Team, 3702

No Milk Today: How to Live with Lactose Intolerance, 2394

No More Heroes: Madness and Psychiatry in War, 2428

No More Sleepless Nights: The Complete Program for Ending Insomnia, 2425

No More Vietnams, 5592

No Neutral Ground, 1231

No One Rides for Free, 6261

No Place on Earth, 9209

No Resting Place, 9033

No Return, 7011

No Sense of Place: The Impact of Electronic Media on Social Behavior, 469

No Sign of Murder, 6802

No Telephone to Heaven, 7448

No Time to Wave Goodbye, 5081

No Turning Back: Two Nuns' Battle with the Vatican Over Women's Right to Choose, 345

Nobel Dreams: Power, Deceit, and the Ultimate Experiment, 2055

Nobility of Failure: Tragic Heroes in the History of Japan, 5460

Noble Horse, 2633

Noble House: A Novel of Contemporary Hong Kong, 7445

Noble Rot: Stories, 1949–1988, 9923

Noble Savage: Jean-Jacques Rousseau, 1754–1762, 4629

Nobody Better, Better Than Nobody, 4280

Nobody Lives Forever, 6299

Nobody's Angel, 8139

Nolo's Simple Will Book, 1275

None of the Above: Behind the Myth of Scholastic Aptitude, 1782

Noose of Laurels: Peary, Cook, and the Race to the North Pole, 4945

Nop's Trials, 8108

Nor Live So Long, 6914

Nora: The Real Life of Molly Bloom, 4530

Nordi's Gift, 6126

North and South, 9036

North Dallas after Forty, 10003

North Dallas Forty, 10004

North Gladiola, 8825

North of Hope, 7812

North of South: An African Journey, 4876

North of the Sun: A Memoir of the Alaskan Wilderness, 6136

North Pole Legacy: Black, White and Eskimo, 6168

North to Yesterday, 10269

North Toward Home, 5973

Northern Exposure, 8118

Northern Lights, 8305

Northrop Frye on Shakespeare, 4476

Norton Anthology of Literature by Women: The Tradition in English, 4414

Norton Book of Light Verse, 4428

Norton Book of Modern War, 3872

Norton Book of Nature Writing, 1948

Nose to Nose: Survival in the Trenches of the NFL, 3703

Not a Hazardous Sport, 5618

Not by Fact Alone: Essays on the Writing and Reading of History, 4732

A Not Entirely Benign Procedure: Four Years as a Medical Student, 2272

Not Exactly What I Had in Mind, 5931

Not My Child: A Mother Confronts Her Child's Sexual Abuse, 1510

Not That Kind of Place, 6435

Not That Sort of Girl, 8796

Entries 1–6169 are nonfiction; entries 6170–10293 are fiction

Entries 1–6169 are nonfiction; entries 6170–10293 are fiction

Entries 1–6169 are nonfiction; entries 6170–10293 are fiction

tiveness in Architecture and Design, 3134

An Orphan in History: One Man's Triumphant Search for His Roots, 664

Orphans: Real and Imaginary, 1525

Orsinian Tales, 9778

Orson Welles: A Biography, 3565

Orton Diaries, 4581

Orwell: The Authorized Biography, 4540

Oscar and Lucinda, 8920

Oscar Wilde, 4571

Other Italy: Italian Resistance in World War II, 5083

Other Nile, 4866

Other Nuremberg: The Untold Story of the Tokyo War Crimes Trials, 1225

Other People's Money, 6639

Other People's Trades, 4643

The Other Side, 7739

Other Side of Time: A Combat Surgeon in World War II, 5137

Other Voice: Essays in Modern Poetry, 4653

Other Women's Children, 7993

The Others, 9367

Otherworld Journeys: Accounts of Near-Death Experiences in Medieval and Modern Times, 143

Our Common Lands: Defending the National Parks, 1280

Our Father's Lies, 6850

Our Ground Time Here Will Be Brief, 4030

Our Happiness, 7918

Our House in the Last World, 7850

Our Kind of People: The Story of an American Family, 4980

Our Life in Poetry: Selected Essays and Reviews, 4131

Our Man in Panama: How General Noriega Used the United States and Made Millions in Drugs and Arms, 5705

Our Tempestuous Day: A History of Regency England, 5170

Ours: A Russian Family Album, 4673

Ourselves Growing Older: Women Aging with Knowledge and Power, 564

Out, 8662

Out in the Midday Sun: My Kenya, 5644

Out of Control, 961

Out of India, 9741

Out of Mind, 7289

Out of Step: An Unquiet Life in the 20th Century, 280

Out of the Blackout, 6242

Out of the Cold: New Thinking for American Foreign and Defense Policy for the 20th Century, 982

Out of the Everywhere and Other Extraordinary Visions, 9502

Out of the Shadows, 6692

Out of This World, 8665

Out of This World: The Poetry Project at the St. Mark's Church-in-the-Bowery; An Anthology, 1966–1991, 4108

Out of Time, 8542

Out on the Cutting Edge, 6270

Out on the Marsh, 9949

Out on the Rim, 8689

Out There: The Government's Secret Quest for Extraterrestrials, 4

Outcats: Jazz Composers, Instrumentalists, and Singers, 3411

Outer Banks, 4911

Outlander, 6990

Outlands: Journeys to the Outer Edges of Cape Cod, 1957

Outlaw State: Saddam Hussein's Quest for Power and the Gulf Crisis, 5510

Outlaws, 6517

Outrageous! The Fine Life and Flagrant Good Times of Basketball's Irresistible Force, 3680

Outrageous Acts and Everyday Rebellions, 610

Outrageous Conduct: Art, Ego and the Twilight Zone Case, 1258

Outside History: Selected Poems, 1980–1990, 4430

The Outsider, 7626

Over the Beach: The Air War in Vietnam, 5576

Over the Edge, 6575

Overcoming Bladder Disorders, 2399

Overdrawn: The Collapse of American Savings, 1072

Overhead in a Balloon: Twelve Stories of Paris, 9687

Overlay: Contemporary Art and the Art of Prehistory, 2985

Overlord: D-Day and the Battle for Normandy, 5111

Overworked American: The Unexpected Decline of Leisure, 697

Owning Jolene, 7824

Oxford and Cambridge, 1814

Oxford Blood, 6427

Oxford Book of Death, 112

Oxford Book of English Ghost Stories, 9275

Oxford Book of Essays, 4553

Oxford Book of Late Medieval Verse and Prose, 4413

Oxford Book of Prayer, 383

Oxford Gambit, 10084

Oxford History of the Classical World: Greece and the Hellenistic World, 4995

Oxford History of the Classical World: The Roman World, 4996

Oxford Illustrated History of Christianity, 338

Oysters of Locmariaquer, 2651

Oysterville: Roads to Grandpa's Village, 6134

Ozone Crisis: The Fifteen Year Evolution of a Sudden Global Emergency, 1617

Pablo Picasso: A Retrospective, 3259

Pacific Campaign: World War II; the U.S.-Japanese Naval War, 1941–1945, 5152

Pacific Edge, 9482

Pacific Rising: The Emergence of a New World Culture, 4839

Pack of Cards: Stories, 1978–1986, 9787

Packaging Your Home for Profit: How to Sell Your House or Condo for More Money in Less Time, 1100

Paco's Story, 7829

Paddle to the Amazon, 3827

Pagan Rabbi and Other Stories, 9856

Pagans and Christians, 339

Page after Page, 5598

Pages from a Cold Island, 4243

Painted Bird, 10213

Painted Turtle: Woman with Guitar, 8168

Painted Word, 3220

Painter of Signs, 9250

Painting the Darkness, 8998

Paintings in the Hermitage, 3201

Paintings in the Musee d'Orsay, 3219

Paintings of Benjamin West, 3226

Palace Coup: The Inside Story of Hotel Magnates Harry and Leona Helmsley, 1099

Palace File: The Remarkable Story of the Secret Letters from Nixon and Ford to the President of South Vietnam and the American Promises That Were Never Kept, 5591

A Palace for a King: The Buen Retiro and the Court of Philip IV, 5330

Palace of Desire, 9076

Palace Walk, 9077

Palais-Royal, 9150

Pale Kings and Princes, 6743

A Pale View of Hills, 7907

Palm Latitudes, 7339

Palm-of-the-Hand Stories, 9754

Palm Sunday: An Autobiographical Collage, 4325

Palomino, 7938

Panama: The Whole Story, 5704

Panama Hat Trail: A Journey to South America, 6158

Panda's Thumb: More Reflections in Natural History, 2164

Pandora by Holly Hollander, 6906

Pangs of Love, 9792

Panic Blood, 8674

Entries 1–6169 are nonfiction; entries 6170–10293 are fiction

Entries 1–6169 are nonfiction; entries 6170–10293 are fiction

Entries 1–6169 are nonfiction; entries 6170–10293 are fiction

Entries 1–6169 are nonfiction; entries 6170–10293 are fiction

Entries 1–6169 are nonfiction; entries 6170–10293 are fiction

Entries 1–6169 are nonfiction; entries 6170–10293 are fiction

Entries 1–6169 are nonfiction; entries 6170–10293 are fiction

Entries 1–6169 are nonfiction; entries 6170–10293 are fiction

Entries 1–6169 are nonfiction; entries 6170–10293 are fiction

Entries 1–6169 are nonfiction; entries 6170–10293 are fiction

Entries 1–6169 are nonfiction; entries 6170–10293 are fiction

Entries 1–6169 are nonfiction; entries 6170–10293 are fiction

A Six-Letter Word for Death, 6705
Six Memos for the Next Millennium, 4640
Six of One, 7361
Sixth Day and Other Stories, 9781
The Sixties: The Years of Hope, Days of Rage, 5952
Sixties People, 5999
Skating with Heather Grace, 4043
Skeleton Crew, 9298
Skeleton in the Grass, 6246
Skeleton-in-Waiting, 6380
Skeletons, 6804
Sketches from a Life, 948
Skills and Strategies in Winning Racquetball, 3715
Skinny Island: More Tales of Manhattan, 9543
Skinny Legs and All, 9224
Skintight, 6515
Skinwalkers, 6532
Skull Beneath the Skin, 6548
Skullduggery, 9081
Sky Juice and Flying Fish: Traditional Caribbean Cooking, 2779
Sky People, 8963
Sky's the Limit: A Century of Chicago Skyscrapers, 3093
Sky's the Limit: A Defense of the Earth, 3346
Skyscraper, 3119
Skyscraper: The Making of a Building, 2971
Skywater, 8397
Slapstick: Or Lonesome No More, 8756
Slaughterhouse Five: Or, the Children's Crusade, 10246
Slave Culture: Nationalist Theory and the Foundations of Black America, 653
Slavery and Freedom, 651
Slavery and Freedom: An Interpretation of the Old South, 6051
Slavery and Human Progress, 665
Slavery and Social Death: A Comparative Study, 676
Slavery in the 20th Century, 677
Slaves Without Masters: The Free Negro in the Antebellum South, 451
Sleep and His Brother, 6381
Sleep Management Plan, 2343
Sleepers Joining Hands, 3962
Sleeping Arrangements, 4392
Sleeping Dog, 6622
Sleeping Murder, 6329
Sleepless Days, 7250
Sleepless Nights, 7794
Sleepwalking Through History: America in the Reagan Years, 5962
Sleuthing Fossils: The Art of Investigating Past Life, 2084
Slim: Memories of a Rich and Imperfect Life, 5868

Slings and Arrows: Theatre in My Life, 3628
A Slipping-Down Life, 8717
Slouching Towards Kalamazoo, 7534
Slow Burn: The Rise and Bitter Fall of American Intelligence in Vietnam, 5571
Slow Dancing, 7270
Slow Homecoming, 7787
Slow Learner: Early Stories, 9874
Slugging It Out in Japan: An American Leaguer in the Tokyo Outfield, 3737
Small Business Handbook, 2921
Small Changes, 8384
Small Craft Advisory: A Book about the Building of a Boat, 2546
A Small Deceit, 6922
Small Endearments: 19th Century Quilts for Children, 3183
A Small Farm in Maine, 2585
Small Victories: The Real World of a Teacher, Her Students and Their High School, 1801
Small World: An Academic Romance, 8085
Smart Cookies Don't Crumble: A Modern Women's Guide to Living and Loving Her Own Life, 568
Smart Medicine: How to Get the Most Out of Your Checkup and Stay Healthy, 2308
Smart Schools, Smart Kids: Why Do Some Schools Work? 1776
Smash Cut, 6909
Smile, Honey, 7561
Smile of the Lamb, 7765
Smiley's People, 10108
Smokescreen, 6423
Smuggler's Notch, 6595
Snake Tattoo, 6248
Snakewalk, 8806
Snap, 7664
Snare of Serpents, 7865
Sneaky People, 8897
Sniper's Mom, 6838
Snow Ball, 7772
Snow Leopard, 4851
Snow Queen, 7081
So Far from God: A Journey to Central America, 5696
So Far from God: The U.S. War with Mexico, 1846–48, 5812
So Little Time: Essays on Gay Life, 552
So Long and Thanks for All the Fish, 9333
Soccer War, 4770
Social Brain: Discovering the Networks of the Mind, 2288
A Social History of Madness: The World Through the Eyes of the Insane, 1461
Socialism: Past and Future, 1121
Socialism and America, 1122
Society of Mind, 179

Sociobiology: The New Synthesis, 2193
Socrates: Ironist and Moral Philosopher, 275
Socratic Method, 8065
Soft Water, 8328
Soho Walls: Beyond Graffiti, 3207
Solace of Open Spaces, 6110
Soldier of Arete, 7101
A Soldier of the Great War, 7833
Soldier of the Mist, 7102
Soldiers: A History of Men in Battle, 1340
Soldiers and Civilians: Americans at War and Home, 10202
A Soldier's Daughter Never Cries, 7943
Soldier's Embrace, 9705
Soldiers in Hiding, 10257
Soldier's Joy, 7258
A Soldier's Legacy, 10156
Soldiers of God: With the Mujahidin in Afghanistan, 5549
A Soldier's Play, 4162
Solidarity Forever: An Oral History of the I. W. W., 1042
Solitude: A Return to the Self, 237
Solo Parenting: Your Essential Guide, 212
Solomon Gursky Was Here, 9136
Solstice, 8316
Some Can Whistle, 8149
Some Freaks, 4316
Some Just Clap Their Hands: Raising a Handicapped Child, 2890
Some Time in the Sun: The Hollywood Years of F. Scott Fitzgerald, William Faulkner, Nathanael West, Adlous Huxley and James Agee, 3914
Some Women, 3345
Somebody's Baby, 7804
Somebody's Darling, 8150
Someday, 269
Someday the Rabbi Will Leave, 6582
Someone Was Here: Profiles in the AIDS Epidemic, 1457
Somerset Homecoming: Discovering a Lost Heritage, 4981
Something Happened, 7831
Something in the Air, 6599
Something Like an Autobiography, 3562
Something Out There, 9706
Something to Be Desired, 8140
Sometimes I Live in the Country, 7385
Somoza Falling: A Case Study in the Making of U.S. Foreign Policy, 980
Son of Holmes, 6610
Son of the Endless Night, 9281
Son of the Morning, 8317
Son of the Morning Star: Custer and the Little Bighorn, 1368
Son of the Revolution, 5424

Entries 1–6169 are nonfiction; entries 6170–10293 are fiction

Entries 1–6169 are nonfiction; entries 6170–10293 are fiction

Entries 1–6169 are nonfiction; entries 6170–10293 are fiction

Entries 1–6169 are nonfiction; entries 6170–10293 are fiction

Entries 1–6169 are nonfiction; entries 6170–10293 are fiction

Entries 1–6169 are nonfiction; entries 6170–10293 are fiction

Entries 1–6169 are nonfiction; entries 6170–10293 are fiction

Entries 1–6169 are nonfiction; entries 6170–10293 are fiction

Entries 1–6169 are nonfiction; entries 6170–10293 are fiction

Entries 1–6169 are nonfiction; entries 6170–10293 are fiction

Entries 1–6169 are nonfiction; entries 6170–10293 are fiction

Entries 1–6169 are nonfiction; entries 6170–10293 are fiction

Entries 1–6169 are nonfiction; entries 6170–10293 are fiction

Entries 1–6169 are nonfiction; entries 6170–10293 are fiction

Entries 1–6169 are nonfiction; entries 6170–10293 are fiction

Entries 1–6169 are nonfiction; entries 6170–10293 are fiction

SUBJECT INDEX

All references are to entry numbers, not page numbers. An (F) following an entry number signifies a work of fiction.

U.S. stateswoman, 5910
of women, writing methods, 3857
women's rights crusaders, 590, 845
women writers, 51, 4127, 4128, 4136, 4141, 4149, 4156, 4185
writers, 4182–4184, 4198, 4201–4204, 4207, 4211–4213, 4215–4219, 4221–4223, 4225–4228, 4234, 4238–4240, 4247, 4253, 4256, 4258, 4260, 4263, 4266, 4354, 4360–4363, 4373, 4374, 4381, 4382, 4389, 4452–4468, 4486, 4488, 4490–4494, 4496–4500, 4502, 4503, 5184, 8211(F)
Zionist founder, 810
Biologist, autobiography, 2113
Biology, 2109–2118
book reviews, 2112
essays, 2115–2118
ethics of, 235
in information theory, 9
television series on, 2109
Biotechnology
business history, 1165
effects of, 257, 486
university-corporation ties in, 1157
Bird, Larry, biography, 3688
Birds
behavior, 2209, 2212
exotic, 2213, 2214
extinct, 2221
fantasy fiction, 7077(F)
illustrated history, 2210
in New England, 2222
ocean, 2215, 2217, 2218
rehabilitation, 2659, 2660
Birdwatching, 2211, 2213
in Central Park (New York), 6036
history, 2210
Birth control method, (Dalkon Shield I.U.D.), 1179
Birth parents, stories, 8629(F), 8690(F)
Bishop, Elizabeth, literary criticism on works of, 4102, 4152
Bismarck, Otto von, biography, 5236
Black, Hugo
civil liberties and, 1300
Supreme Court career, 1289
Black, Shirley Temple, biography, 3589
Black bears, dangers posed by, 2335
Black Dahlia murder, fictional re-creation, 6397(F)
Black English dialect, history and usage, 1769, 1907
Blackfoot Indians
stories, 7989(F), 8779(F)
western story, 10293(F)
Black holes, 2009, 2050
science fiction, 9372(F)
Black Madonna, 380

Blackmail
mysteries, 6369(F), 6416(F), 6422(F), 6560(F), 6602(F), 6672(F), 6737(F), 6742(F), 6820(F), 6918(F)
stories, 8546(F), 8779(F)
Black Mountain College, history, 1816
Black Mountain School, poetry of, 3977, 3978
Bladder disorders, care and treat-ment, 2399, 2400
Blindness
in children, 1477
from mugging incident, 1487
Blind person(s)
biography, 1785
communication system for, 9072(F)
memoirs, 1487–1490
stories, 7541(F), 7751(F), 8804(F)
Blizzard(s)
family chronicle, 8028(F)
March 1988 (in U.S.), 2077
mystery, 6837(F)
Böll, Heinrich, memoirs, 5231
Bloch, Marc, biography, 5284
Blood clot, science fiction, 9343(F)
Blood transfusions, AIDS from, 1448, 1456, 7858(F)
Bloomsbury Group, biographies, 4519, 4523, 4539, 4575, 4580
Blue-collar groups, 450, 1034, 8768(F)
Bluefish, fishing for, 3841
Blues music, 3392–3398
recordings, 3397
Blunt, Anthony, biography, 936
Boarding schools, leader prepara-tion at, 1803
Boat dwellers, 7228(F)
Boating, 3824, 3825. See also Sailing
Boats
design and buiding, 2546
mysteries, 6666(F), 6704(F)
upgrading of, 2545
Boccioni, Umberto, exhibition cata-log, 3006
Bodybuilding
memoirs, 2879
stories, 7952(F), 10001(F)
by women, 7492(F)
Body care, 2869
Body language, psychology, 180
Boer War (1899–1902), 5651
Boetie, Dugmore, autobiography, 5651
Bogan, Louise, biography, 4136
Bohemia, war with Austria in 16th century, 9121(F)
Bohemian life, story, 7690(F)
Boleyn, Anne, biography, 5214
Bolivia, search for pre-Incan culture in, 4930
Bolshevik Revolution. See under So-viet Union
Bombay, mysteries, 6567(F)–6573(F)

Bombs. See also Atomic bomb
on airplanes, 8505(F)
mysteries, 6633(F), 6634(F), 6666(F), 6740(F), 6783(F), 6845(F), 6852(F)
Bonner, Elena, memoirs, 1636
Bonney, William H. See Billy the Kid
Bonnie Prince Charlie. See Stuart, Charles Edward
biography, 5169
Bon voyage party, 7649(F)
Bookmaker, memoirs, 6081
Books
for children (guide), 25, 26
mystery, 6868(F)
Bookshop owner, biography, 60
Boone, Eton Arthur, fictional por-trait, 6191(F)
Boorn-Colvin murder case, 1707
Bootlegger, fictional biography, 6194(F)
Borden, Lizzie, trial, 1704
Borgia family, collective biography, 5318
Bork, Robert, defeat for Supreme Court, 1285, 1286
Borneo, travel in, 4862, 4863
Borofsky, Jonathan, exhibition cata-log, 2992
Boston, mysteries, 6592(F), 6599(F), 6661(F), 6678(F), 6691(F), 6738(F), 6848(F), 6878(F)
Boston Massacre, events leading to, 5782
Boston Red Sox, fans' memoirs, 3752
Boston Strangler, 1686
Boston University, mystery, 6783(F)
Boswell, James, biography, 4569
Botanist
Jefferson-appointed, 9054(F)
mystery, 6809(F)
Botany, 2171–2180
economic, 2174
essays, 2612
illustrations, 2175, 2178
introduction to, 2172, 2177
for layperson, 2172, 2177
Botswana, teacher's chronicle, 7822(F)
Bourke-White, Margaret, biography, 3298
Bouton, Jim, autobiography, 3731
Bowen, Elizabeth, biography, 4518
Bowles, Jane, biography, 4376
Bowles, Paul
autobiography, 4364
biography, 4263
Boxing
African-Americans in, 3814, 3816, 3821
biographies, 3814, 3816, 3817, 3821
essays, 3818, 3820
mystery, 6562(F)
stories, 7168(F), 9997(F), 10002(F), 10006(F)

Mines, in Appalachia, labor disputes at, 1048

Mine workers, fight against exploitation, 8534(F)

Miniaturized persons, science fiction, 9343(F), 9344(F)

Minimalist art, 3072

Minimalist short stories, 9881(F)

Mining community, in Pennsylvania, 791

Minkow, Barry, fraud perpetrated by, 1640

Minnesota
  fantasy fiction, 7066(F)
  farm life, 784
  Native American rivalry with white residents, 8774(F)
  short stories, 9527(F), 9579(F), 9756(F)–9758(F)
  stories, 7969(F), 9046(F)

Minolta, president's biography, 1176

Minorities
  preferential policies for, 1037
  in United States. See under individual minorities

Miro, Joan, personal recollections about, 3034

Miscarriages, causes and avoidance, 2520, 2521

Mishima, Yukio, biography, 4724

Misogynists, 7160(F)

Misogyny, as literary theme, 4559

Missile crisis, in Cuba (1962), 5709
  Robert Kennedy memoirs, 5963

Missing persons, search for, 7194(F)

Missionaries
  in Amazon jungle, 8194(F)
  in China, 332, 333, 9022(F), 9042(F)
  history of, 331
  in Pacific and South America, 330

Mississippi
  African-American family memoirs, 6075
  short stories, 9841(F), 9842(F), 9988(F)
  stories, 7359(F), 7747(F), 7789(F), 8794(F)

Mississippi River, wildlife, 2137

Missouri
  Pawnee Indians, 5679
  small-town memoirs, 6094

Mitchell, Margaret, biography, 4225

Models. See Fashion models

Modern art
  Armory Show introduction of (1913), 3018
  development and meaning, 3030, 3220
  essays, 3026
  Panza collection, 3021
  surveys, 3047, 3220

Modern dance
  autobiography, 3646
  biographies, 3640, 3655, 3662, 3664, 3665

history, 3659

Modern history, 4755, 4761–4778

Modernist culture, World War I and, 4765

Modernist poetry, 3985, 4041

Modigliani, Amedeo, biography, 3052

Modoc Indians, historical novel, 8966(F)

Mohammed, biography, 409

Molecular psychology, of human behavior, 167

Moles (spies), 10025(F), 10040(F), 10068(F), 10084(F), 10096(F), 10103(F), 10109(F)

Momaday, N. Scott, autobiography, 5669

Monaco, Princess Grace of, biography, 5315

Monaghan, Thomas, biography, 1180

Monastery, stories, 6391(F), 7408(F)

Monet, Claude
  artistic techniques, 3250
  fictional portrait, 6186(F)
  series paintings, 3262

Monette, Paul, AIDS memoirs, 1451

Money
  guide to raising, for business start-up, 2925
  status in America related to, 619

Mongolfier brothers, dual biography, 2559

Monkeys, in scientific research, 8070(F)

Monks
  mysteries, 6759(F)–6765(F)
  stories, 7872(F), 7905(F), 8229(F)

Monroe, Marilyn
  biography, 3587
  marriage with Joe DiMaggio, 3759
  in story plot, 8452(F)

Monroe, Sylvester, housing project memoirs, 4962

Monster story, 9322(F)

Montana
  coming-of-age story, 8691(F)
  dinosaur fossils, 2091
  family chronicles, 7254(F), 7560(F), 7642(F), 8153(F), 8948(F)
  fly-fishing in, 3839
  mystery, 6360(F)
  Native American chronicles, 8779(F), 8780(F)
  ranching community chronicle, 9148(F)
  short stories, 9556(F), 9677(F), 9790(F), 9799(F), 9900(F)
  stories, 8137(F), 8139(F), 8140(F), 8153(F), 8749(F), 8948(F), 9148(F)
  western stories, 10263(F), 10267(F), 10284(F), 10290(F)

Monte Cassino, World War II battle for, 5110

Montefiore Hospital, effects on surrounding community, 1433

Montgomery, M. R., father-son memoirs, 4975

Monticello
  design and construction, 5792
  family and social life at, 6063

Moon
  science fiction, 9423(F), 9432(F)
  space flights to, 2575

Moonshine, beverage control officer's story on, 1670

Moore, Charles, civil rights photography of, 848

Moore, Marianne, biography, 4141

Moors murder case, mystery about, 6842(F)

Moors (people), historical novel, 9067(F)

Moral choices, novellas on, 7806(F)

Morality
  in children, 205, 2881
  Christian, 311, 312
  fictional study, 8389(F)
  role of fiction in teaching of, 3854
  in Victorian period, 5183

Moral philosophy. See Ethics

Morals, in America, 660

More, Thomas, biography, 5216

Morgan, Julia, life and works, 3099

Morgan banking dynasty, family history, 1060

Morgenthau family, history, 4976

Morisot, Berthe, biography, 3248

Mormon Church, murder and forgery scandal of, 1705, 1713

Mormonism
  biographies, 365, 366
  history of, 367
  mystery, 6306(F)
  short stories, 9764(F)

Morrell, David, memoirs of son's death, 4402

Morris, Mary, China rail journey memoirs, 4403

Morris, William, biography, 4582

Morris, Willie, autobiography, 5973

Morris, Wright, childhood memoirs, 4235

Morris textiles, 3195

Moscow
  historical novel, 8973(F)
  social life, 8873(F)

Moscow Art Theatre, letters by members, 3615

Moses, fictional chronicle of, 9016(F)

Mother(s)
  custody and protection laws affecting, 1273
  divorce effects on, 770
  Japanese, son's memoirs, 573
  murder of children by, 1683, 8312(F)
  of pregnant teenagers, 1527
  stories about, 8478(F), 8507(F), 8543(F), 8563(F)